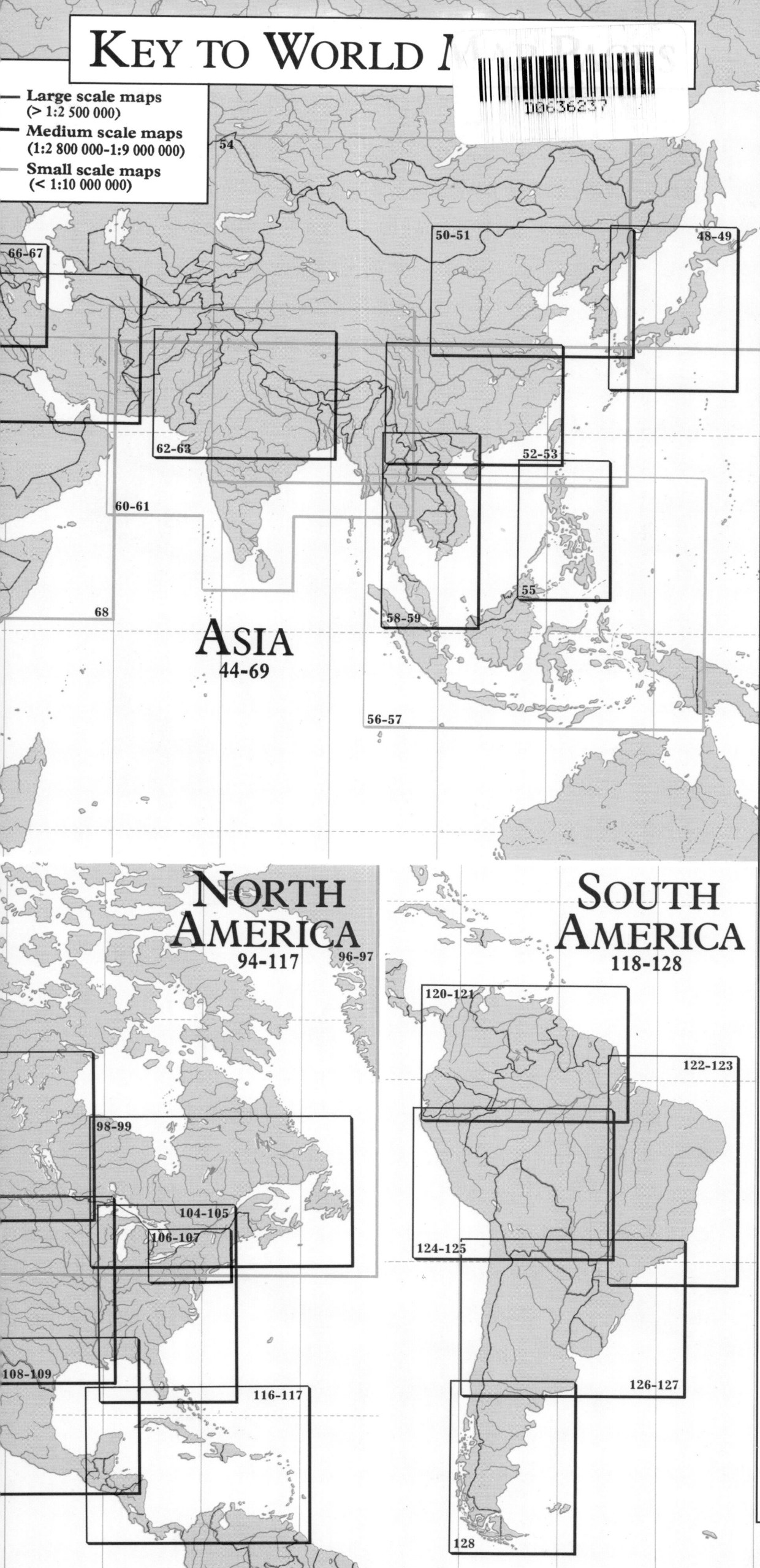

KEY TO WORLD MAPS

- ▬ **Large scale maps**
  (> 1:2 500 000)
- ▬ **Medium scale maps**
  (1:2 800 000–1:9 000 000)
- ▬ **Small scale maps**
  (< 1:10 000 000)

10636237

54

66–67

50–51   48–49

62–63   52–53

60–61

68   55

ASIA
44-69

58–59

56–57

NORTH   SOUTH
AMERICA   AMERICA
94-117 96–97 118-128

120–121

98–99   122–123

104–105

106–107   124–125

108–109

116–117   126–127

128

COUNTRY INDEX

Afghanistan	60	Laos	58
Albania	38–39	Latvia	40
Algeria	74–75	Lebanon	69
Angola	80–81	Lesotho	85
Argentina	126, 128	Liberia	78
Armenia	67	Libya	73
Australia	88–91	Lithuania	40
Austria	19, 20–21	Luxembourg	17
Azerbaijan	67		
		Macedonia	38–39
Bahamas	116–117	Madagascar	85
Bangladesh	61	Malawi	83
Barbados	117	Malaysia	55–56
Belgium	17	Mali	78–79
Belize	116	Malta	37
Belorussia	40	Mauritania	78
Benin	79	Mauritius	71
Bhutan	61	Mexico	114–115
Bolivia	124–125	Moldavia	42
Bosnia-		Mongolia	54
Herzegovina	21	Morocco	74
Botswana	84–85	Mozambique	83
Brazil	120–127		
Brunei	55	Namibia	84
Bulgaria	38–39	Nepal	63
Burkina Faso	78–79	Netherlands	16–17
Burma	61	New Zealand	87
Burundi	82	Nicaragua	116
		Niger	79
Cambodia	58–59	Nigeria	79
Cameroon	82	Northern Ireland	15
Canada	96–101	Norway	8–9
Central African			
Republic	82	Oman	68
Chad	73		
Chile	126, 128	Pakistan	62
China	50–54	Panama	116
Colombia	120	Papua New Guinea	86
Congo	82	Paraguay	126–127
Costa Rica	116	Peru	124
Croatia	21	Philippines	55
Cuba	116–117	Poland	20
Cyprus	37	Portugal	30–31
Czech Republic	20–21	Puerto Rico	117
Denmark	11	Qatar	65
Djibouti	68		
Dominican Republic	117	Romania	38
		Russia	40–45
Ecuador	120	Rwanda	82
Egypt	76		
El Salvador	116	Saudi Arabia	68
England	12–13	Scotland	14
Equatorial Guinea	82	Senegal	78
Estonia	40	Sierra Leone	78
Ethiopia	68, 77	Singapore	59
		Slovak Republic	20–21
Fiji	87	Slovenia	33
Finland	8–9	Somali Republic	68
France	24–27	South Africa	84–85
French Guiana	121	Spain	28–31
		Sri Lanka	60
Gabon	80	Sudan	77
Gambia	78	Surinam	121
Georgia	43	Swaziland	85
Germany	18–19	Sweden	8–9
Ghana	78–79	Switzerland	22–23
Greece	39	Syria	67
Greenland	4		
Guatemala	116	Taiwan	53
Guinea	78	Tajikistan	44
Guinea-Bissau	78	Tanzania	82–83
Guyana	121	Thailand	58–59
		Togo	79
Haiti	117	Trinidad and	
Honduras	116	Tobago	117
Hong Kong	53	Tunisia	75
Hungary	21	Turkey	66–67
		Turkmenistan	44
Iceland	8		
India	60–63	Uganda	82
Indonesia	56–57	Ukraine	42
Iran	64–65	United Arab Emirates	65
Iraq	64–65	United Kingdom	12–15
Irish Republic	15	USA	102–113
Israel	69	Uruguay	126–127
Italy	32–35	Uzbekistan	44
Ivory Coast	78		
		Venezuela	120–121
Jamaica	116	Vietnam	58–59
Japan	48–49		
Jordan	69	Wales	12–13
Kazakhstan	44	Yemen	68
Kenya	82	Yugoslavia	38–39
Kirghizia	44		
Korea, North	51	Zaïre	80–81
Korea, South	51	Zambia	83
Kuwait	64–65	Zimbabwe	83

PHILIP'S

GREAT WORLD ATLAS

PHILIP'S

GREAT WORLD ATLAS

First published in Great Britain in 1993
by George Philip Limited,
an imprint of Reed Consumer Books Limited,
Michelin House, 81 Fulham Road, London SW3 6RB,
and Auckland, Melbourne, Singapore and Toronto

Cartography by Philip's

Copyright © 1993 Reed International Books Limited

ISBN 0-540-05743-6

A CIP catalogue record for this book is available from
the British Library

Printed in Italy

PHILIP'S WORLD MAPS

The reference maps which form the main body of this atlas have been prepared in accordance with the highest standards of international cartography to provide an accurate and detailed representation of the earth. The scales and projections used have been carefully chosen to give balanced coverage of the world, while emphasizing the most densely populated and economically significant regions. A hallmark of Philip's mapping is the use of hill shading and relief colouring to create a graphic impression of landforms: this makes the maps exceptionally easy to read. However, knowledge of the key features employed in the construction and presentation of the maps will enable the reader to derive the fullest benefit from the atlas.

Map sequence

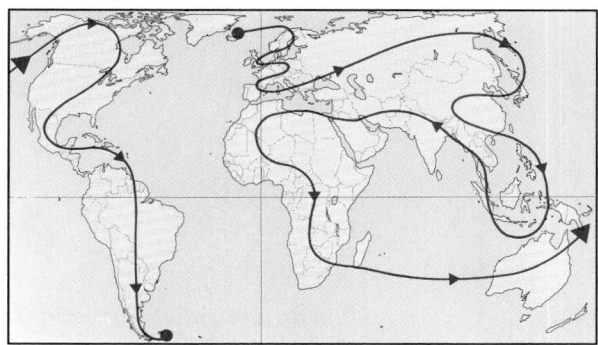

The atlas covers the earth continent by continent: first Europe; then its land neighbour Asia (mapped north before south, in a clockwise sequence), then Africa, Australia and Oceania, North America and South America. This is the classic arrangement adopted by most cartographers since the 16th century. For each continent, there are maps at a variety of scales. First, physical relief and political maps of the whole continent. Then a series of larger-scale maps of the regions within the continent, each followed, where required, by still larger-scale maps of the most important or densely populated areas. The governing principle is that by turning the pages of the atlas, the reader moves steadily from north to south through each continent, with each map overlapping its neighbours. A key map showing this sequence, and the area covered by each map, can be found on the endpapers of the atlas.

Map presentation

With very few exceptions (eg for the Arctic and Antarctic), the maps are drawn with north at the top, regardless of whether they are presented upright or sideways on the page. In the borders will be found the map title; a locator diagram showing the area covered and the page numbers for maps of adjacent areas; the scale; the projection used; the degrees of latitude and longitude; and the letters and figures used in the index for locating place names and geographical features. Physical relief maps also have a height reference panel identifying the colours used for each layer of contouring.

Map symbols

Each map contains a vast amount of detail which can only be conveyed clearly and accurately by the use of symbols. Points and circles of varying sizes locate and identify the relative importance of towns and cities; different styles of type are employed for administrative, geographical and regional place names. A variety of pictorial symbols denote landscape features such as glaciers, marshes and reefs, and man-made structures including roads, railways, airports, canals and dams. International borders are shown by red lines. Where neighbouring countries are in dispute, for example in the Middle East, the maps show the *de facto* boundary between nations, regardless of the legal or historical situation. The symbols are explained on the first page of the World Maps section of the atlas.

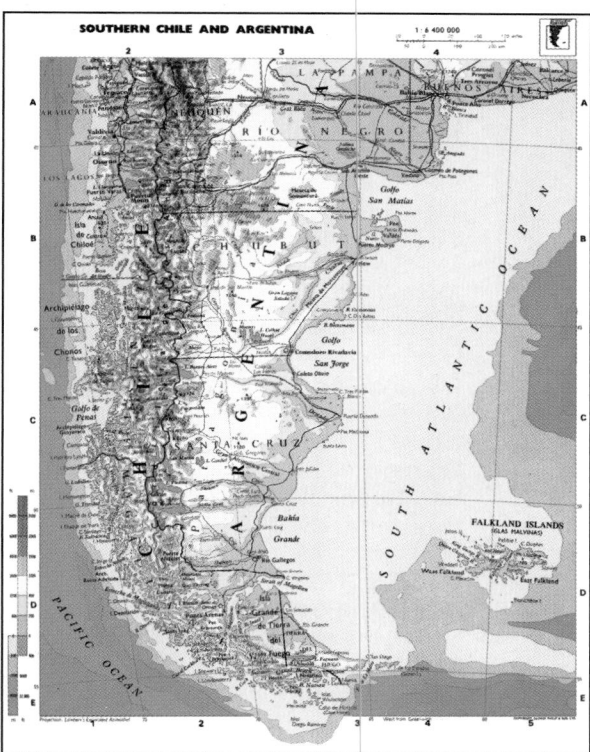

Map scales

1: 16 000 000
1 inch = 252 statute miles

The scale of each map is given in the numerical form known as the 'representative fraction'. The first figure is always one, signifying one unit of distance on the map; the second figure, usually in millions, is the number by which the map unit must be multiplied to give the equivalent distance on the earth's surface. Calculations can easily be made in centimetres and kilometres, by dividing the earth units figure by 100 000 (ie deleting the last five 0s). Thus 1:1 000 000 means 1 cm = 10 km. The calculation for inches and miles is more laborious, but 1 000 000 divided by 63 360 (the number of inches in a mile) shows that 1:1 000 000 means approximately 1 inch = 16 miles. The table below provides distance equivalents for scales down to 1:50 000 000.

LARGE SCALE		
1: 1 000 000	1 cm = 10 km	1 inch = 16 miles
1: 2 500 000	1 cm = 25 km	1 inch = 39.5 miles
1: 5 000 000	1 cm = 50 km	1 inch = 79 miles
1: 6 000 000	1 cm = 60 km	1 inch = 95 miles
1: 8 000 000	1 cm = 80 km	1 inch = 126 miles
1: 10 000 000	1 cm = 100 km	1 inch = 158 miles
1: 15 000 000	1 cm = 150 km	1 inch = 237 miles
1: 20 000 000	1 cm = 200 km	1 inch = 316 miles
1: 50 000 000	1 cm = 500 km	1 inch = 790 miles
SMALL SCALE		

Measuring distances

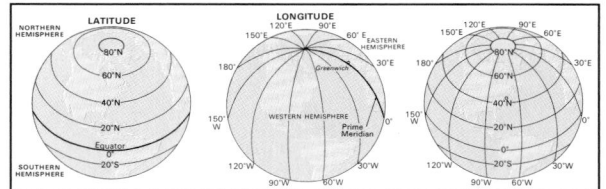

Although each map is accompanied by a scale bar, distances cannot always be measured with confidence because of the distortions involved in portraying the curved surface of the earth on a flat page. As a general rule, the larger the map scale (ie the lower the number of earth units in the representative fraction), the more accurate and reliable will be the distance measured. On small-scale maps such as those of the world and of entire continents, measurement may only be accurate along the 'standard parallels', or central axes, and should not be attempted without considering the map projection.

Map projections

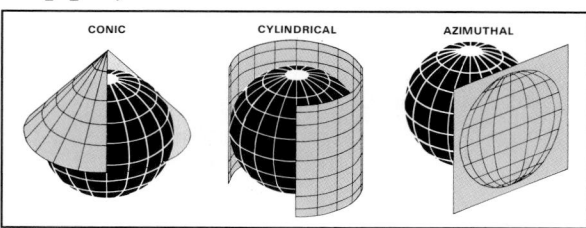

Unlike a globe, no flat map can give a true scale representation of the world in terms of area, shape and position of every region. Each of the numerous systems that have been devised for projecting the curved surface of the earth on to a flat page involves the sacrifice of accuracy in one or more of these elements. The variations in shape and position of landmasses such as Alaska, Greenland and Australia, for example, can be quite dramatic when different projections are compared.

For this atlas, the guiding principle has been to select projections that involve the least distortion of size and distance. The projection used for each map is noted in the border. Most fall into one of three categories - conic, cylindrical or azimuthal - whose basic concepts are shown above. Each involves plotting the forms of the earth's surface on a grid of latitude and longitude lines, which may be shown as parallels, curves or radiating spokes.

Latitude and longitude

Accurate positioning of individual points on the earth's surface is made possible by reference to the geometrical system of latitude and longitude. Latitude *parallels* are drawn west-east around the earth and numbered by degrees north and south of the Equator, which is designated 0° of latitude. Longitude *meridians* are drawn north-south and numbered by degrees east and west of the *prime meridian,* 0° of longitude, which passes through Greenwich in England. By referring to these co-ordinates and their sub-divisions of minutes (1/60th of a degree) and seconds (1/60th of a minute), any place on earth can be located to within a few hundred yards. Latitude and longitude are indicated by blue lines on the maps; they are straight or curved according to the projection employed. Reference to these lines is the easiest way of determining the relative positions of places on different maps, and for plotting compass directions.

Name forms

For ease of reference, both English and local name forms appear in the atlas. Oceans, seas and countries are shown in English throughout the atlas; country names may be abbreviated to their commonly accepted form (eg Germany, not Federal Republic of Germany). Conventional English forms are also used for place names on the smaller-scale maps of the continents. However, local name forms are used on all large-scale and regional maps, with the English form given in brackets only for important cities - the large-scale map of European Russia thus shows Moskva (Moscow). For countries which do not use a Roman script, place names have been transcribed according to the systems adopted by the British and US Geographic Names Authorities. For China, the Pin Yin system has been used, with some more widely known forms appearing in brackets, as with Beijing (Peking). Both English and local names appear in the index, the English form being cross-referenced to the local form.

CONTENTS

WORLD STATISTICS

Countries x
Cities xi
Distances xii
Climate xiii
Physical Dimensions xiv-xv

INTRODUCTION TO WORLD GEOGRAPHY

The Universe 2-3
The Solar System 4-5

THE EARTH
Time and Motion 6-7
Geology 8-9
Oceans 10-11
Atmosphere 12-13
Climate 14-15
Water 16-17
Landscape 18-19
Environment 20-21

PEOPLE
Demography 22-23
Cities 24-25
The Human Family 26-27
Conflict and Cooperation 28-29

PRODUCTION
Agriculture 30-31
Energy 32-33
Minerals 34-35
Manufacturing 36-37
Trade 38-39

QUALITY OF LIFE
Wealth 40-41
Standards 42-43
Health 44-45
Environment 46-47

WORLD MAPS

1-128

THE WORLD

Map Symbols
1

The World: Political 1:64 000 000
2-3

Arctic Ocean 1:28 000 000
Greenland
4

Antarctica 1:28 000 000
5

EUROPE

Europe: Physical 1:16 000 000
6

Europe: Political 1:16 000 000
7

Scandinavia and the Baltic Lands 1:4 000 000
Norway, Sweden, *Finland*, Iceland
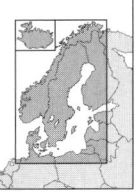
8-9

Denmark and Southern Sweden 1:2 000 000
Denmark, *Norway, Sweden*

10-11

England and Wales 1:1 600 000
Isle of Man, Channel Islands

12-13

Scotland 1:1 600 000

14

Ireland 1:1 600 000
Irish Republic, Northern Ireland

15

NOTE
The titles to the World Maps list the main countries, states and provinces covered by each map. A name given in *italics* indicates that only part of the country is shown on the map.

Netherlands, Belgium and Luxembourg 1:1 000 000

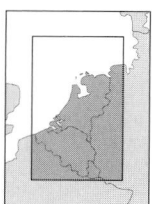

16-17

Germany 1:2 000 000

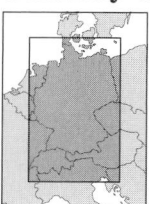

18-19

Middle Europe 1:2 800 000
Austria, Czech Republic, Slovak Republic, Hungary, Poland, Bosnia-Herzegovina, Croatia, Slovenia, Yugoslavia

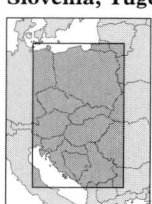

20-21

Switzerland 1:800 000
Liechtenstein

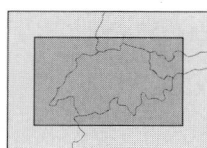

22-23

Northern France 1:2 000 000

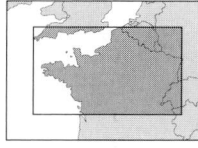

24-25

Southern France 1:2 000 000
Corsica, Monaco

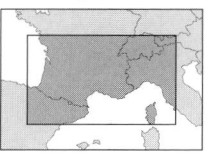

26-27

Eastern Spain 1:2 000 000
Andorra

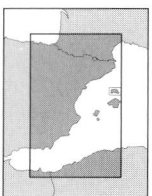

28-29

Western Spain and Portugal 1:2 000 000

30-31

Northern Italy, Slovenia and Croatia
1:2 000 000
San Marino, Slovenia, *Croatia*

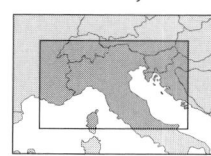

32-33

Southern Italy 1:2 000 000
Sardinia, Sicily

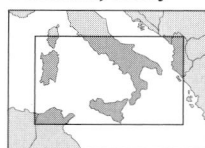

34-35

Balearics, Canaries and Madeira 1:800 000 / 1:1 040 000
Mallorca, Menorca, Ibiza, Tenerife

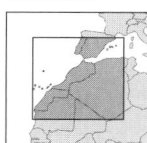

36

Malta, Crete, Corfu, Rhodes and Cyprus
1:800 000 / 1:1 600 000

37

The Balkans 1:2 800 000
Yugoslavia, Romania, Bulgaria, Greece, Albania, Macedonia

38-39

Western Russia, Belorussia and the Baltic States 1:4 000 000
Russia, Estonia, Latvia, Lithuania, Belorussia, *Ukraine*

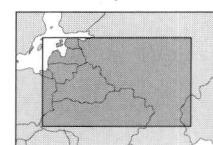

40-41

Ukraine, Moldavia and the Caucasus 1:4 000 000
Russia, Ukraine, Georgia, *Armenia, Azerbaijan,* Moldavia

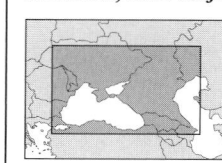

42-43

ASIA

Russia and Central Asia
1:16 000 000
Russia, Kazakhstan, Turkmenistan, Uzbekistan

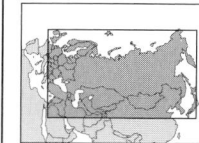

44-45

Asia: Physical
1:40 000 000

46

Asia: Political
1:40 000 000

47

Japan 1:4 000 000
Ryukyu Islands

48-49

Northern China and Korea
1:4 800 000
North Korea, South Korea

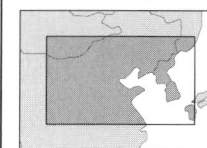

50-51

Southern China 1:4 800 000
Hong Kong, Taiwan, Macau

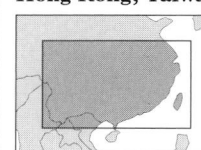

52-53

China 1:16 000 000
Mongolia

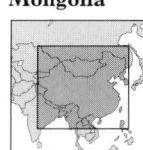

54

Philippines 1:6 000 000

55

Indonesia 1:10 000 000
Malaysia, Singapore, Brunei

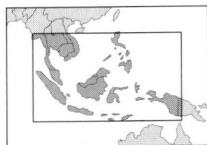

56-57

Mainland South-East Asia
1:4 800 000
Thailand, Vietnam, Cambodia,
Laos

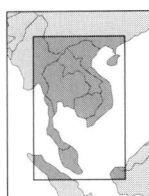

58-59

South Asia 1:8 000 000
India, Pakistan, Bangladesh,
Burma, Sri Lanka, Afghanistan

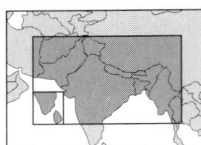

60-61

The Indo-Gangetic Plain
1:4 800 000
India, *Pakistan*, Nepal, Kashmir

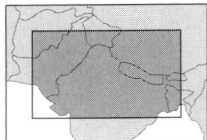

62-63

The Middle East 1:5 600 000
Iran, Iraq, *Saudi Arabia*, United
Arab Emirates, Kuwait, Qatar

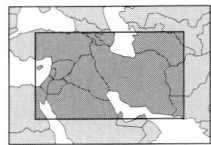

64-65

Turkey 1:4 000 000
Syria

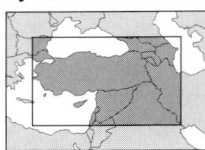

66-67

**Arabia and the Horn of
Africa** 1:12 000 000
Saudi Arabia, Oman, Yemen,
Somalia, Ethiopia, Eritrea,
Djibouti

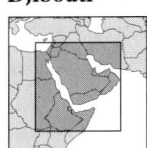

68

The Near East 1:2 000 000
Israel, Lebanon, *Jordan*

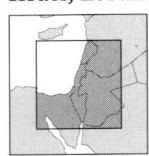

69

AFRICA

Africa: Physical
1:32 000 000
70

Africa: Political
1:32 000 000
71

Northern Africa 1:12 000 000
Libya, Chad, Niger

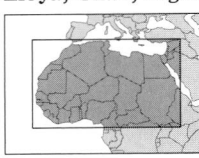

72-73

North-West Africa
1:6 400 000
Algeria, Morocco, Tunisia,
Mauritania, Niger, Mali

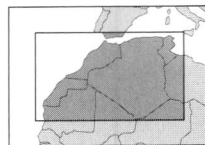

74-75

The Nile Valley 1:6 400 000
Egypt, Sudan, Eritrea, *Ethiopia*
The Nile Delta 1:3 200 000

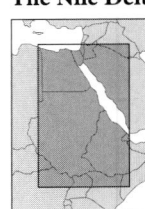

76-77

West Africa 1:6 400 000
Nigeria, Ivory Coast, Ghana,
Senegal, Guinea, Burkina Faso

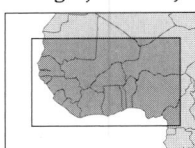

78-79

**Central and Southern
Africa** 1:12 000 000
Zaïre, Angola, Cameroon, Congo,
Gabon, Central African Republic

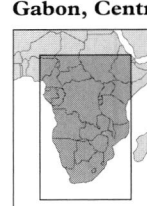

80-81

East Africa 1:6 400 000
Kenya, Tanzania, Zambia,
Uganda, Malawi

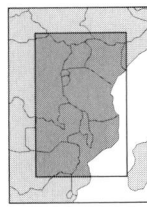

82-83

Southern Africa 1:6 400 000
South Africa, Zimbabwe,
Madagascar, *Mozambique*,
Botswana, Namibia

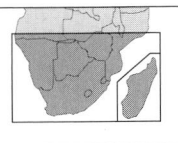

84-85

AUSTRALIA AND OCEANIA

Australia and Oceania: Physical and Political
1:32 000 000
86

New Zealand 1:4 800 000
Fiji, Tonga, Samoa

87

Western Australia
1:6 400 000
Northern Territory

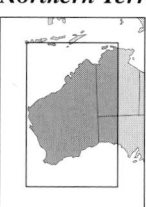

88-89

Eastern Australia 1:6 400 000
New South Wales, Queensland, Victoria, *South Australia*,
Tasmania

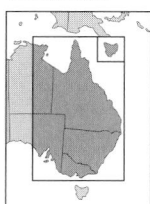

90-91

Pacific Ocean 1:43 200 000
Kiribati, Vanuatu, New Caledonia, Tuvalu, Micronesia, French Polynesia
92-93

NORTH AMERICA

North America: Physical
1:28 000 000
94

North America: Political
1:28 000 000
95

Canada 1:12 000 000
Northwest Territories, Yukon
Alaska 1:24 000 000

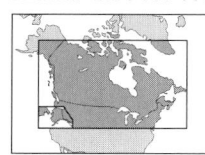

96-97

Eastern Canada 1:5 600 000
Quebec, *Ontario*, **Newfoundland**

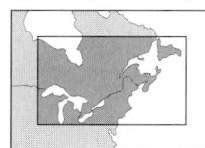

98-99

Western Canada 1:5 600 000
British Columbia, Alberta, Saskatchewan, Manitoba

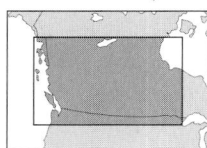

100-101

United States 1:9 600 000
Hawaii 1:8 000 000

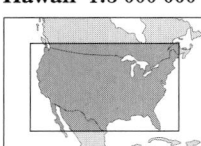

102-103

Eastern United States
1:4 800 000

104-105

North-Eastern United States 1:2 000 000
New York, New England, *Pennsylvania*

106-107

Middle United States
1:4 800 000

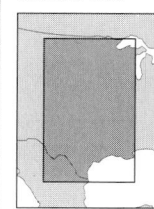

108-109

Western United States
1:4 800 000

110-111

Central and Southern California and Washington 1:2 000 000

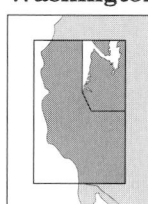

112-113

Mexico 1:6 400 000

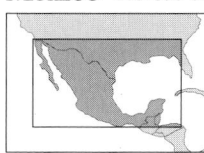

114-115

Central America and the West Indies 1:6 400 000
Guatemala, Nicaragua, Cuba, Jamaica, Panama, Haiti

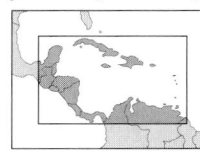

116-117

SOUTH AMERICA

South America: Physical
1:24 000 000
118

South America: Political
1:24 000 000
119

South America – North-West 1:6 400 000
Colombia, Venezuela, *Brazil*,
Ecuador, Guyana

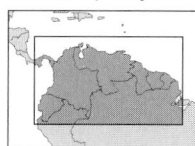

120-121

Eastern Brazil 1:6 400 000

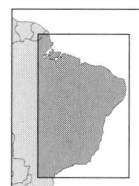

122-123

South America – West
1:6 400 000
Peru, *Brazil*, **Bolivia**

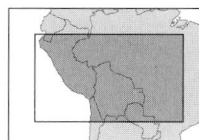

124-125

Central South America
1:6 400 000
Argentina, *Chile*, *Brazil*,
Paraguay, Uruguay

126-127

Southern Chile and Argentina 1:6 400 000

128

INDEX TO WORLD MAPS

129-224

World Statistics: Countries

This alphabetical list includes all the countries and territories of the world. If a territory is not completely independent, then the country it is associated with is named. The area figures give the total area of land, inland water and ice. Units for areas and populations are thousands. The annual income is the Gross National Product per capita in US dollars. The figures are the latest available, usually 1991.

Country/Territory	Area km² *Thousands*	Area miles² *Thousands*	Population *Thousands*	Capital	Annual Income US $
Adélie Land (Fr.)	432	167	0.03	-	-
Afghanistan	652	252	16,433	Kabul	450
Albania	28.8	11.1	3,250	Tirana	1,000
Algeria	2,382	920	24,960	Algiers	2,020
American Samoa (US)	0.20	0.08	39	Pago Pago	6,000
Amsterdam Is. (Fr.)	0.05	0.02	0.03	-	-
Andorra	0.45	0.17	52	Andorra-la-Vella	-
Angola	1,247	481	10,020	Luanda	620
Anguilla (UK)	0.09	0.04	8	The Valley	-
Antigua & Barbuda	0.44	0.17	77	St John's	4,770
Argentina	2,767	1,068	32,322	Buenos Aires	2,780
Armenia	29.8	11.5	3,416	Yerevan	2,150
Aruba (Neths.)	0.19	0.07	60	Oranjestad	6,000
Ascension Is. (UK)	0.09	0.03	1.5	Georgetown	-
Australia	7,687	2,968	17,086	Canberra	16,590
Australian Antarctic Territory	6,120	2,363	0	-	-
Austria	83.9	32.4	7,712	Vienna	20,380
Azerbaijan	86.6	33.4	7,451	Baku	1,670
Azores (Port.)	2.2	0.87	260	Ponta Delgada	-
Bahamas	13.9	5.4	253	Nassau	11,720
Bahrain	0.68	0.26	503	Manama	6,910
Bangladesh	144	56	115,594	Dacca	220
Barbados	0.43	0.17	255	Bridgetown	6,630
Belau (US)	0.46	0.18	15	Koror	-
Belgium	30.5	11.8	9,845	Brussels	19,300
Belize	23	8.9	188	Belmopan	2,050
Belorussia	207.6	80.1	10,374	Minsk	3,110
Benin	113	43	4,736	Porto-Novo	380
Bermuda (UK)	0.05	0.02	61	Hamilton	25,000
Bhutan	47	18.1	1,517	Thimphu	180
Bolivia	1,099	424	7,400	La Paz/Sucre	650
Bosnia-Herzegovina	51.2	19.8	4,364	Sarajevo	-
Botswana	582	225	1,291	Gaborone	2,590
Bouvet Is. (Nor.)	0.05	0.02	0.02	-	-
Brazil	8,512	3,286	153,322	Brasilia	2,920
British Antarctic Terr. (UK)	1,709	660	0.3	Stanley	-
British Indian Ocean Terr. (UK)	0.08	0.03	3	-	-
Brunei	5.8	2.2	266	Bandar Seri Begawan	6,000
Bulgaria	111	43	9,011	Sofia	1,840
Burkina Faso	274	106	9,001	Ouagadougou	350
Burma (Myanmar)	677	261	41,675	Rangoon	500
Burundi	27.8	10.7	5,438	Bujumbura	210
Cambodia	181	70	8,246	Phnom Penh	200
Cameroon	475	184	11,834	Yaoundé	940
Canada	9,976	3,852	26,522	Ottawa	21,260
Canary Is. (Spain)	7.3	2.8	1,700	Las Palmas/Santa Cruz	-
Cape Verde Is.	4	1.6	370	Praia	750
Cayman Is. (UK)	0.26	0.10	27	Georgetown	-
Central African Republic	623	241	3,039	Bangui	390
Chad	1,284	496	5,679	Ndjamena	220
Chatham Is. (NZ)	0.96	0.37	0.05	Waitangi	-
Chile	757	292	13,386	Santiago	2,160
China	9,597	3,705	1,139,060	Beijing (Peking)	370
Christmas Is. (Aus.)	0.14	0.05	2.3	The Settlement	-
Cocos (Keeling) Is. (Aus.)	0.01	0.005	0.70	-	-
Colombia	1,139	440	32,987	Bogotá	1,280
Comoros	2.2	0.86	551	Moroni	500
Congo	342	132	2,271	Brazzaville	1,120
Cook Is. (NZ)	0.24	0.09	18	Avarua	900
Costa Rica	51.1	19.7	2,994	San José	1,930
Croatia	56.5	21.8	4,784	Zagreb	-
Crozet Is. (Fr.)	0.51	0.19	35	-	-
Cuba	111	43	10,609	Havana	3,000
Cyprus	9.3	3.6	702	Nicosia	8,640
Czech Republic	78.9	30.4	10,299	Prague	2,370
Denmark	43.1	16.6	5,140	Copenhagen	23,660
Djibouti	23.2	9	409	Djibouti	1,000
Dominica	0.75	0.29	83	Roseau	2,440
Dominican Republic	48.7	18.8	7,170	Santo Domingo	950
Ecuador	284	109	10,782	Quito	1,020
Egypt	1,001	387	53,153	Cairo	620
El Salvador	21	8.1	5,252	San Salvador	1,070
Equatorial Guinea	28.1	10.8	348	Malabo	330
Estonia	44.7	17.3	1,600	Tallinn	3,830
* Ethiopia	1,222	472	50,974	Addis Ababa	120
Falkland Is. (UK)	12.2	4.7	2	Stanley	-
Faroe Is. (Den.)	1.4	0.54	47	Tórshavn	23,660
Fiji	18.3	7.1	765	Suva	1,830
Finland	338	131	4,986	Helsinki	24,400
France	552	213	56,440	Paris	20,600
French Guiana (Fr.)	90	34.7	99	Cayenne	2,500
French Polynesia (Fr.)	4	1.5	206	Papeete	6,000
Gabon	268	103	1,172	Libreville	3,780
Gambia, The	11.3	4.4	861	Banjul	360
Georgia	69.7	26.9	5,571	Tbilisi	1,640
Germany	357	138	79,479	Berlin	17,000
Ghana	239	92	15,028	Accra	400
Gibraltar (UK)	0.007	0.003	31	-	4,000
Greece	132	51	10,269	Athens	6,230
Greenland (Den.)	2,176	840	57	Godthåb	6,000
Grenada	0.34	0.13	85	St George's	2,180
Guadeloupe (Fr.)	1.7	0.66	344	Basse-Terre	7,000
Guam (US)	0.55	0.21	119	Agana	6,000
Guatemala	109	42	9,197	Guatemala City	930
Guinea	246	95	5,756	Conakry	450
Guinea-Bissau	36.1	13.9	965	Bissau	190
Guyana	215	83	796	Georgetown	290
Haiti	27.8	10.7	6,486	Port-au-Prince	370
Honduras	112	43	5,105	Tegucigalpa	570
Hong Kong (UK)	1.1	0.40	5,801	-	13,200
Hungary	93	35.9	10,344	Budapest	2,690
Iceland	103	40	255	Reykjavik	22,580
India	3,288	1,269	843,931	Delhi	330
Indonesia	1,905	735	179,300	Jakarta	610
Iran	1,648	636	58,031	Tehran	2,320
Iraq	438	169	18,920	Baghdad	2,000
Ireland	70.3	27.1	3,523	Dublin	10,780
Israel	27	10.3	4,659	Jerusalem	11,330
Italy	301	116	57,663	Rome	18,580
Ivory Coast	322	125	11,998	Abidjan	690
Jamaica	11	4.2	2,420	Kingston	1,380
Jan Mayen Is. (Nor.)	0.38	0.15	0.06	-	-
Japan	378	146	123,537	Tokyo	26,920
Johnston Is. (US)	0.002	0.0009	0.30	-	-
Jordan	89.2	34.4	4,009	Amman	1,120
Kazakhstan	2,717	1,049	17,104	Alma Ata	2,470
Kenya	580	224	24,032	Nairobi	340
Kerguelen Is. (Fr.)	7.2	2.8	0	-	-
Kermadec Is. (NZ)	0.03	0.01	0	-	-
Kirghizia	198.5	76.6	4,568	Bishkek	1,550
Kiribati	0.72	0.28	66	Tarawa	750
Korea, North	121	47	21,773	Pyongyang	900
Korea, South	99	38.2	43,302	Seoul	6,340
Kuwait	17.8	6.9	2,143	Kuwait City	16,380
Laos	237	91	4,139	Vientiane	230
Latvia	63.1	24.4	2,700	Riga	3,410
Lebanon	10.4	4	2,701	Beirut	2,000

Country/Territory	Area km² *Thousands*	Area miles² *Thousands*	Population *Thousands*	Capital	Annual Income US $
Lesotho	30.4	11.7	1,774	Maseru	580
Liberia	111	43	2,607	Monrovia	500
Libya	1,760	679	4,545	Tripoli	5,800
Liechtenstein	0.16	0.06	29	Vaduz	33,000
Lithuania	65.2	25.2	3,751	Vilnius	2,710
Luxembourg	2.6	1	384	Luxembourg	31,080
Macau (Port.)	0.02	0.006	479	-	2,000
Macedonia	25.3	9.8	2,174	Skopje	-
Madagascar	587	227	11,197	Antananarivo	210
Madeira (Port.)	0.81	0.31	280	Funchal	-
Malawi	118	46	8,556	Lilongwe	230
Malaysia	330	127	17,861	Kuala Lumpur	2,490
Maldives	0.30	0.12	215	Malé	460
Mali	1,240	479	8,156	Bamako	280
Malta	0.32	0.12	354	Valletta	6,850
Mariana Is. (US)	0.48	0.18	22	Saipan	-
Marshall Is.	0.18	0.07	42	Dalap-Uliga-Darrit	-
Martinique (Fr.)	1.1	0.42	341	Fort-de-France	4,000
Mauritania	1,025	396	2,050	Nouakchott	510
Mauritius	1.9	0.72	1,075	Port Louis	2,420
Mayotte (Fr.)	0.37	0.14	84	Mamoundzou	-
Mexico	1,958	756	86,154	Mexico City	2,870
Micronesia, Fed. States	0.70	0.27	103	Palikir	-
Midway Is. (US)	0.005	0.002	0.45	-	-
Moldavia	33.7	13	4,458	Kishinev	2,170
Monaco	0.002	0.0001	29	-	20,000
Mongolia	1,567	605	2,190	Ulan Bator	400
Montserrat (UK)	0.10	0.04	13	Plymouth	-
Morocco	447	172	25,061	Rabat	1,030
Mozambique	802	309	15,656	Maputo	70
Namibia	824	318	1,781	Windhoek	1,120
Nauru	0.02	0.008	10	Domaneab	-
Nepal	141	54	18,916	Katmandu	180
Netherlands	41.9	16.2	15,019	Amsterdam	18,560
Neths. Antilles (Neths.)	0.99	0.38	189	Willemstad	6,000
New Caledonia (Fr.)	19	7.3	168	Nouméa	4,000
New Zealand	269	104	3,429	Wellington	12,140
Nicaragua	130	50	3,871	Managua	340
Niger	1,267	489	7,732	Niamey	300
Nigeria	924	357	108,542	Lagos/Abuja	290
Niue (NZ)	0.26	0.10	3	Alofi	-
Norfolk Is. (Aus.)	0.03	0.01	2	Kingston	-
Norway	324	125	4,242	Oslo	24,160
Oman	212	82	1,502	Muscat	5,220
Pakistan	796	307	112,050	Islamabad	400
Panama	77.1	29.8	2,418	Panama City	2,180
Papua New Guinea	463	179	3,699	Port Moresby	820
Paraguay	407	157	4,277	Asunción	1,210
Peru	1,285	496	22,332	Lima	1,020
Peter 1st Is. (Nor.)	0.18	0.07	0	-	-
Philippines	300	116	61,480	Manila	740
Pitcairn Is. (UK)	0.03	0.01	0.06	Adamstown	-
Poland	313	121	38,180	Warsaw	1,830
Portugal	92.4	35.7	10,525	Lisbon	5,620
Puerto Rico (US)	8.9	3.4	3,599	San Juan	6,330
Qatar	11	4.2	368	Doha	15,860
Queen Maud Land (Nor.)	2,800	1,081	0	-	-
Réunion (Fr.)	2.5	0.97	599	St-Denis	4,000
Romania	238	92	23,200	Bucharest	1,340
Ross Dependency (NZ)	435	168	0	-	-
Russia	17,075	6,592	149,527	Moscow	3,220
Rwanda	26.3	10.2	7,181	Kigali	260
St Christopher/Nevis	0.36	0.14	44	Basseterre	3,960
St Helena (UK)	0.12	0.05	7	Jamestown	-
St Lucia	0.62	0.24	151	Castries	2,500
St Paul Is. (Fr.)	0.007	0.003	0	-	-
St Pierre & Miquelon (Fr.)	0.24	0.09	7	St-Pierre	-
St Vincent/Grenadines	0.39	0.15	116	Kingstown	1,730
San Marino	0.06	0.02	24	San Marino	-
São Tomé & Príncipe	0.96	0.37	121	São Tomé	350
Saudi Arabia	2,150	830	14,870	Riyadh	7,070
Senegal	197	76	7,327	Dakar	720
Seychelles	0.46	0.18	67	Victoria	5,110
Sierra Leone	71.7	27.7	4,151	Freetown	210
Singapore	0.62	0.24	3,003	Singapore	12,890
Slovak Republic	49	18.9	5,269	Bratislava	1,650
Slovenia	20.3	7.8	1,963	Ljubljana	-
Solomon Is.	28.9	11.2	321	Honiara	560
Somalia	638	246	7,497	Mogadishu	150
South Africa	1,221	471	35,282	Pretoria	2,530
South Georgia (UK)	3.8	1.4	0.05	-	-
South Sandwich Is. (UK)	0.38	0.15	0	-	-
Spain	505	195	38,959	Madrid	12,460
Sri Lanka	65.6	25.3	16,993	Colombo	500
Sudan	2,506	967	25,204	Khartoum	400
Surinam	163	63	422	Paramaribo	3,610
Svalbard (Nor.)	62.9	24.3	4	Longyearbyen	-
Swaziland	17.4	6.7	768	Mbabane	1,060
Sweden	450	174	8,618	Stockholm	25,490
Switzerland	41.3	15.9	6,712	Bern	33,510
Syria	185	71	12,116	Damascus	1,110
Taiwan	36	13.9	20,300	Taipei	6,600
Tajikistan	143.1	55.2	5,680	Dushanbe	1,050
Tanzania	945	365	25,635	Dar es Salaam	100
Thailand	513	198	57,196	Bangkok	1,580
Togo	56.8	21.9	3,531	Lomé	410
Tokelau (NZ)	0.01	0.005	2	Nukunonu	-
Tonga	0.75	0.29	95	Nuku'alofa	1,100
Trinidad & Tobago	5.1	2	1,227	Port of Spain	3,620
Tristan da Cunha (UK)	0.11	0.04	0.33	Edinburgh	-
Tunisia	164	63	8,180	Tunis	1,510
Turkey	779	301	57,326	Ankara	1,820
Turkmenistan	488.1	188.5	3,838	Ashkhabad	1,700
Turks & Caicos Is. (UK)	0.43	0.17	10	Grand Turk	-
Tuvalu	0.03	0.01	10	Funafuti	600
Uganda	236	91	18,795	Kampala	160
Ukraine	603.7	233.1	51,940	Kiev	2,340
United Arab Emirates	83.6	32.3	1,589	Abu Dhabi	19,860
United Kingdom	243.3	94	54,889	London	16,750
United States	9,373	3,619	249,975	Washington	22,560
Uruguay	177	68	3,094	Montevideo	2,860
Uzbekistan	447.4	172.7	21,627	Tashkent	1,350
Vanuatu	12.2	4.7	147	Port Vila	1,120
Vatican City	0.0004	0.0002	1	-	-
Venezuela	912	352	19,735	Caracas	2,610
Vietnam	332	127	66,200	Hanoi	300
Virgin Is. (UK)	0.15	0.06	13	Road Town	-
Virgin Is. (US)	0.34	0.13	117	Charlotte Amalie	12,000
Wake Is.	0.008	0.003	0.30	-	-
Wallis & Futuna Is. (Fr.)	0.20	0.08	18	Mata-Utu	-
Western Sahara	266	103	179	El Aaiún	-
Western Samoa	2.8	1.1	164	Apia	930
Yemen	528	204	11,282	Sana	540
Yugoslavia	102.3	39.5	10,642	Belgrade	2,940
Zaire	2,345	906	35,562	Kinshasa	230
Zambia	753	291	8,073	Lusaka	420
Zimbabwe	391	151	9,369	Harare	620

** Eritrea formally declared full independence from Ethiopia on 24th May 1993*

WORLD STATISTICS: CITIES

This list shows the principal cities with more than 500,000 inhabitants (for China only cities with more than 1 million are included). The figures are taken from the most recent census or estimate available, and as far as possible are the population of the metropolitan area, e.g. greater New York, Mexico or London. All the figures are in thousands. The top 20 world cities are indicated with their rank in brackets following the name.

Afghanistan
Kabul 1,127
Algeria
Algiers 1,722
Oran 664
Angola
Luanda 1,200
Argentina
Buenos Aires [8] 10,728
Cordoba 1,055
Rosario 1,016
Mendoza 668
La Plata 611
San Miguel de Tucumán 571
Armenia
Yerevan 1,199
Australia
Sydney 3,531
Melbourne 2,965
Brisbane 1,215
Perth 1,083
Adelaide 1,013
Austria
Vienna 1,483
Azerbaijan
Baku 1,757
Bangladesh
Dacca 4,770
Chittagong 1,840
Khulna 860
Rajshahi 430
Belgium
Brussels 970
Antwerp 500
Belorussia
Minsk 1,589
Gomel 500
Bolivia
La Paz 993
Brazil
São Paulo [3] 16,832
Rio de Janeiro [7] 11,141
Belo Horizonte 3,446
Recife 2,945
Pôrto Alegre 2,924
Salvador 2,362
Fortaleza 2,169
Curitiba 1,926
Brasilia 1,557
Nova Iguaçu 1,325
Belem 1,296
Santos 1,200
Goiâna 928
Campinas 845
Manaus 834
São Gonçalo 731
Guarulhos 718
Duque de Caxias 666
Santo Andre 637
Osasco 594
São Bernado do Campo 566
São Luis 564
Natal 512
Bulgaria
Sofia 1,129
Burma (Myanmar)
Rangoon 2,459
Mandalay 533
Cambodia
Phnom Penh 500
Cameroon
Douala 1,030
Yaoundé 654
Central African Rep.
Bangui 597
Chad
Ndjamena 512
Canada
Toronto 3,427
Montréal 2,921
Vancouver 1,381
Ottawa-Hull 819
Edmonton 785
Calgary 671
Winnipeg 623
Québec 603
Hamilton 557

Chile
Santiago 4,858
China
Shanghai [5] 12,320
Beijing (Peking) [10] 9,750
Tianjin 5,459
Shenyang 4,285
Wuhan 3,493
Guangzhou 3,359
Chongqing 2,832
Harbin 2,668
Chengdu 2,642
Xi'an 2,387
Zibo 2,329
Nanjing 2,290
Nanchang 2,289
Lupanshui 2,247
Taiyuan 1,929
Changchun 1,908
Dalian 1,682
Zhaozhuang 1,612
Zhengzhou 1,610
Kunming 1,516
Jinan 1,464
Tangshan 1,410
Guiyang 1,403
Lanzhou 1,391
Linyi 1,385
Pingxiang 1,305
Qiqihar 1,301
Anshan 1,298
Qingdao 1,273
Xintao 1,272
Hangzhou 1,271
Fushun 1,270
Yangcheng 1,265
Yulin 1,255
Dongguang 1,230
Chao'an 1,227
Xiaogan 1,219
Fuzhou 1,205
Suining 1,195
Changsha 1,193
Shijiazhuang 1,187
Jilin 1,169
Xintai 1,167
Puyang 1,125
Baotou 1,119
Bozhou 1,112
Zhongshan 1,073
Luoyang 1,063
Laiwu 1,054
Leshan 1,039
Urumchi 1,038
Ningbo 1,033
Datong 1,020
Huainan 1,019
Heze 1,017
Handan 1,014
Linhai 1,012
Macheng 1,010
Changshu 1,004
Colombia
Bogotá 4,185
Medellin 1,506
Cali 1,397
Barranquilla 920
Cartagena 560
Congo
Brazzaville 596
Croatia
Zagreb 1,175
Cuba
Havana 2,059
Czech Republic
Prague 1,215
Denmark
Copenhagen 1,339
Dominican Rep.
Santo Domingo 1,313
Ecuador
Guayaquil 1,301
Quito 1,110
Egypt
Cairo [18] 6,325
Alexandria 2,893
El Giza 1,858
Shubra el Kheima 711
El Salvador
San Salvador 973

Ethiopia
Addis Ababa 1,686
Finland
Helsinki 987
France
Paris [13] 8,510
Lyons 1,170
Marseilles 1,080
Lille 935
Bordeaux 628
Toulouse 523
Georgia
Tbilisi 1,194
Germany
Berlin 3,301
Hamburg 1,594
Munich 1,189
Cologne 928
Essen 623
Frankfurt 619
Dortmund 584
Düsseldorf 563
Stuttgart 552
Leipzig 545
Bremen 533
Duisburg 525
Dresden 518
Hanover 500
Ghana
Accra 965
Greece
Athens 3,027
Thessalonika 872
Guatemala
Guatemala 2,000
Guinea
Conakry 705
Haiti
Port-au-Prince 1,144
Honduras
Tegucigalpa 605
Hong Kong
Kowloon 2,302
Hong Kong 1,176
Tsuen Wan 690
Hungary
Budapest 2,115
India
Calcutta [11] 9,194
Bombay [14] 8,243
Delhi 5,729
Madras 4,289
Bangalore 2,922
Ahmadabad 2,548
Hyderabad 2,546
Poona 1,686
Kanpur 1,639
Nagpur 1,302
Jaipur 1,015
Lucknow 1,008
Coimbatore 920
Patna 919
Surat 914
Madurai 908
Indore 829
Varanasi 797
Jabalpur 757
Agra 747
Vadodara 744
Cochin 686
Dhanbad 678
Bhopal 671
Jamshedpur 670
Allahabad 650
Ulhasnagar 649
Tiruchchirappalli 610
Ludhiana 606
Srinagar 606
Vishakhapatnam 604
Amritsar 595
Gwalior 556
Calicut 546
Vijayawada 543
Meerut 537
Dharwad 527
Trivandrum 520
Salem 519
Solapur 515
Jodhpur 506
Ranchi 503

Indonesia
Jakarta [16] 7,348
Surabaya 2,224
Medan 1,806
Bandung 1,567
Semarang 1,026
Palembang 787
Ujung Pandang 709
Malang 512
Iran
Tehran [20] 6,043
Mashhad 1,464
Esfahan 987
Tabriz 971
Shiraz 848
Ahvaz 580
Bakhtaran 561
Qom 543
Iraq
Baghdad 4,649
Basra 617
Mosul 571
Ireland
Dublin 921
Italy
Rome 2,817
Milan 1,464
Naples 1,203
Turin 1,012
Palermo 731
Genoa 715
Ivory Coast
Abidjan 1,850
Bouaké 640
Jamaica
Kingston 525
Japan
Tokyo [6] 11,829
Yokohama 2,993
Osaka 2,636
Nagoya 2,116
Sapporo 1,543
Kyoto 1,479
Kobe 1,411
Fukuoka 1,160
Kawasaki 1,089
Kitakyushu 1,056
Hiroshima 1,044
Sakai 818
Chiba 789
Sendai 700
Okayama 572
Kumamoto 556
Kagoshima 531
Higashiosaka 523
Hamamatsu 514
Amagasaki 509
Funabashi 507
Jordan
Amman 1,160
Irbid 680
Kazakhstan
Alma Ata 1,108
Karaganda 614
Astrakhan 509
Kenya
Nairobi 1,429
Mombasa 500
Kirghizia
Bishkek 616
Korea, North
Pyongyang 2,639
Hamhung 775
Chongjin 754
Chinnampo 691
Sinuiju 500
Korea, South
Seoul [9] 10,513
Pusan 3,754
Taegu 2,206
Inchon 1,604
Kwangju 1,165
Taejon 866
Ulsan 551
Latvia
Riga 915
Lebanon
Beirut 702
Libya
Tripoli 980

Benghazi 650
Lithuania
Vilnius 582
Macedonia
Skopje 505
Madagascar
Antananarivo 703
Malaysia
Kuala Lumpur 1,103
Mali
Bamako 646
Mauritania
Nouakchott 500
Mexico
Mexico City [1] 18,748
Guadalajara 2,587
Monterrey 2,335
Puebla 1,218
León 947
Torreón 730
San Luis Potosi 602
Ciudad Juárez 596
Mérida 580
Culiacán Rosales 560
Mexicali 511
Moldavia
Kishinev 565
Mongolia
Ulan Bator 500
Morocco
Casablanca 2,158
Rabat-Salé 893
Fès 548
Mozambique
Maputo 1,070
Netherlands
Rotterdam 1,040
Amsterdam 1,038
The Hague 684
Utrecht 526
New Zealand
Auckland 885
Nicaragua
Managua 682
Nigeria
Lagos 1,097
Ibadan 1,060
Ogbomosho 527
Norway
Oslo 643
Pakistan
Karachi 5,208
Lahore 2,953
Faisalabad 1,104
Rawalpindi 795
Hyderabad 752
Multan 722
Gujranwala 659
Peshawar 556
Panama
Panama City 625
Paraguay
Asunción 708
Peru
Lima-Callao 4,605
Arequipa 592
Philippines
Manila 1,728
Quezon City 1,326
Cebu 552
Caloocan 525
Poland
Warsaw 1,671
Lodz 852
Krakow 744
Wroclaw 640
Poznan 586
Portugal
Lisbon 1,612
Oporto 1,315
Puerto Rico
San Juan 1,816
Romania
Bucharest 2,014
Russia
Moscow [12] 8,967
St Petersburg 5,020
Nizhniy Novgorod 1,438
Novosibirsk 1,436
Yekaterinburg 1,367

Samara 1,257
Chelyabinsk 1,179
Omsk 1,148
Kazan 1,094
Perm 1,091
Ufa 1,083
Rostov 1,020
Volgograd 999
Krasnoyarsk 912
Saratov 905
Voronezh 887
Vladivostok 648
Izhevsk 635
Yaroslavl 633
Togliatti 630
Irkutsk 626
Simbirsk 625
Krasnodar 620
Barnaul 602
Khaborovsk 601
Novokuznetsk 600
Orenburg 547
Penza 543
Tula 540
Kemerovo 520
Ryazan 515
Tomsk 502
Naberezhniye-Chelni 501
Saudi Arabia
Riyadh 2,000
Jedda 1,400
Mecca 618
Medina 500
Senegal
Dakar 1,382
Singapore
Singapore 2,680
Somali Republic
Mogadishu 1,000
South Africa
Cape Town 1,912
Johannesburg 1,726
East Rand 1,038
Durban 982
Pretoria 823
Port Elizabeth 652
West Rand 647
Vereeniging 540
Spain
Madrid 3,123
Barcelona 1,694
Valencia 739
Seville 668
Zaragoza 596
Malaga 595
Sri Lanka
Colombo 1,412
Sudan
Omdurman 600
Khartoum 510
Sweden
Stockholm 1,471
Gothenburg 720
Malmö 500
Switzerland
Zurich 839
Syria
Damascus 1,361
Aleppo 1,308
Taiwan
Taipei 2,680
Kaohsiung 1,343
Taichung 715
Tainan 657
Panchiao 506
Tajikistan
Dushanbe 595
Tanzania
Dar es Salaam 1,100
Thailand
Bangkok 5,609
Tunisia
Tunis 774
Turkey
Istanbul 5,495
Ankara 2,252
Izmir 1,490
Adana 776
Bursa 614

Uganda
Kampala 500
Ukraine
Kiev 2,587
Kharkov 1,611
Dnepropetrovsk 1,179
Odessa 1,115
Donetsk 1,110
Zaporozhye 884
Lvov 790
Krivoy Rog 713
Mariupol 529
Lugansk 509
Nikolayev 503
United Kingdom
London [17] 6,378
Manchester 1,669
Birmingham 1,400
Liverpool 1,060
Glasgow 730
Newcastle 617
Uruguay
Montevideo 1,248
United States
New York [2] 18,087
Los Angeles [4] 14,532
Chicago [15] 8,066
San Francisco [19] 6,253
Philadelphia 5,899
Detroit 4,665
Boston 4,172
Washington 3,924
Dallas 3,885
Houston 3,711
Miami 3,193
Atlanta 2,834
Cleveland 2,760
Seattle 2,559
San Diego 2,498
Minneapolis-SP. 2,464
St Louis 2,444
Baltimore 2,382
Pittsburgh 2,243
Phoenix 2,122
Tampa 2,068
Denver 1,858
Cincinnati 1,729
Kansas City 1,575
Milwaukee 1,572
Portland 1,414
Sacramento 1,385
Norfolk 1,380
Columbus 1,344
San Antonio 1,323
New Orleans 1,307
Indianapolis 1,237
Buffalo 1,176
Providence 1,118
Charlotte 1,112
Hartford 1,108
Salt Lake City 1,065
San Jose 712
Memphis 653
Jacksonville 610
Uzbekistan
Tashkent 2,073
Venezuela
Caracas 3,247
Maracaibo 1,295
Valencia 1,135
Maracay 857
Barquisimeto 718
Vietnam
Ho Chi Minh 3,900
Hanoi 3,100
Haiphong 1,279
Da Nang 500
Yemen
San'a 500
Yugoslavia
Belgrade 1,470
Zaïre
Kinshasa 2,654
Lubumbashi 543
Zambia
Lusaka 900
Zimbabwe
Harare 681
Bulawayo 500

WORLD STATISTICS: DISTANCES

The table shows air distances in miles and kilometres between thirty major cities. Known as 'Great Circle' distances, these measure the shortest routes between the cities, which aircraft use where possible. The maps show the world centred on six individual cities, and illustrate, for example, why direct flights from Japan to northern America and Europe are across the Arctic regions, and Singapore is on the direct line route from Europe to Australia. The maps have been constructed on an Azimuthal Equidistant projection, on which all distances measured through the centre point are true to scale. The circular lines are drawn at 5,000, 10,000 and 15,000 km from the central city.

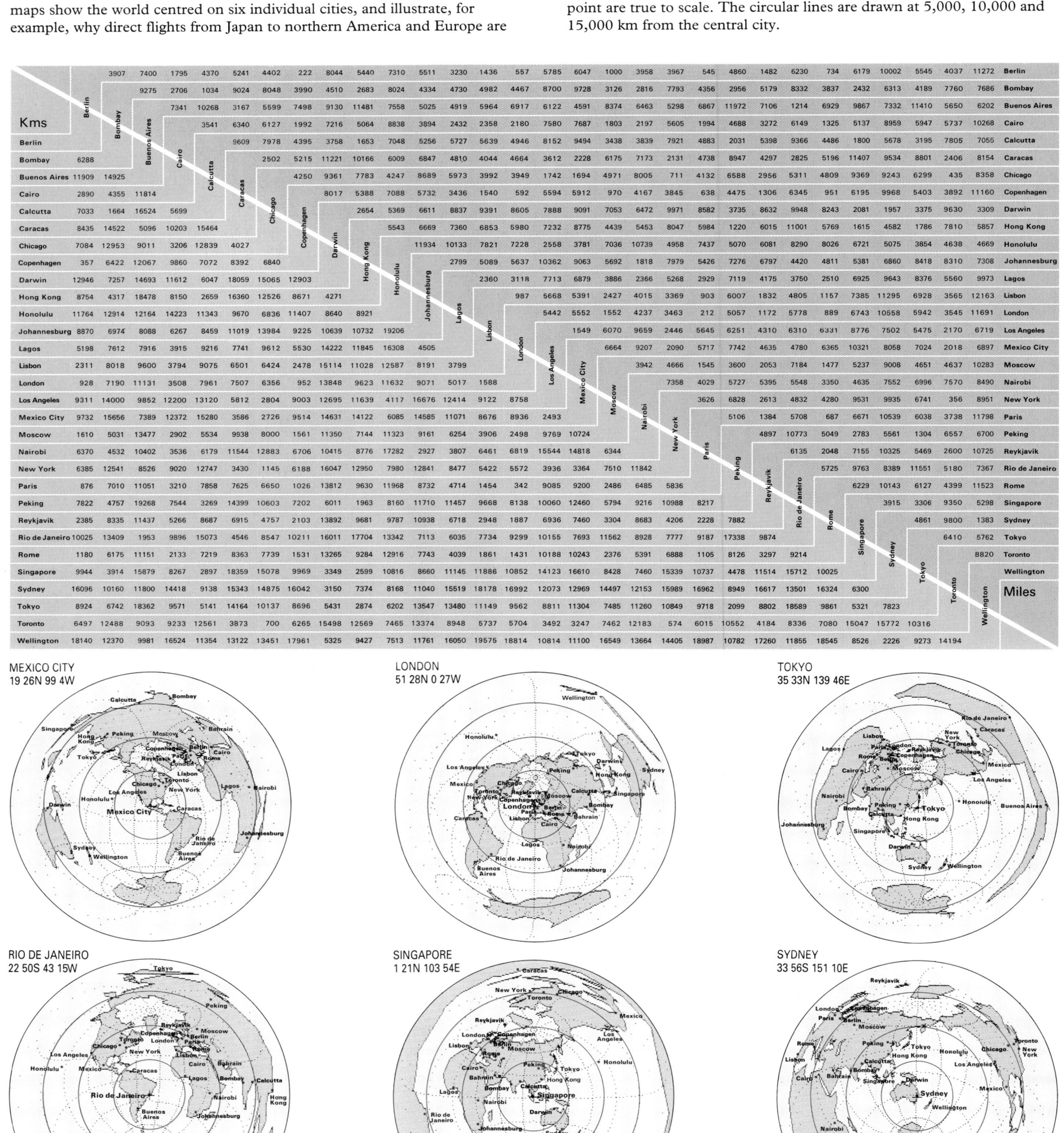

MEXICO CITY
19 26N 99 4W

LONDON
51 28N 0 27W

TOKYO
35 33N 139 46E

RIO DE JANEIRO
22 50S 43 15W

SINGAPORE
1 21N 103 54E

SYDNEY
33 56S 151 10E

World Statistics: Climate

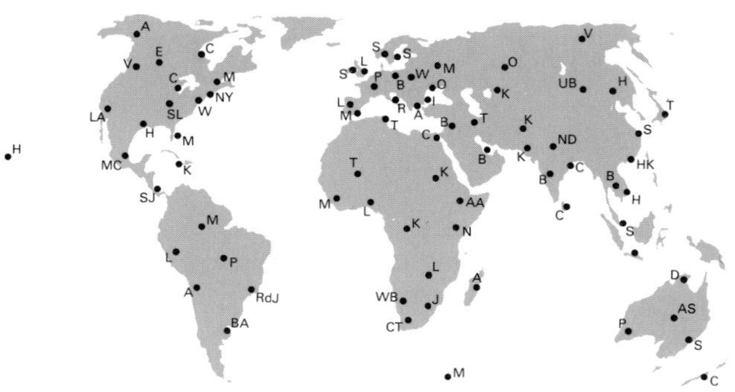

Rainfall and temperature figures are provided for more than 70 cities around the world. As climate is affected by altitude, the height of each city is shown in metres beneath its name. For each month, the figures in red show average temperature in degrees Celsius or centigrade, and in blue the total rainfall or snow in millimetres; the average annual temperature and total annual rainfall are at the end of the rows.

EUROPE

	Jan.	Feb.	Mar.	Apr.	May	June	July	Aug.	Sept.	Oct.	Nov.	Dec.	Year
Athens, Greece	62	37	37	23	23	14	6	7	15	51	56	71	402
107 m	10	10	12	16	20	25	28	28	24	20	15	11	18
Berlin, Germany	46	40	33	42	49	65	73	69	48	49	46	43	603
55 m	-1	0	4	9	14	17	19	18	15	9	5	1	9
Istanbul, Turkey	109	92	72	46	38	34	34	30	58	81	103	119	816
114 m	5	6	7	11	16	20	23	23	20	16	12	8	14
Lisbon, Portugal	111	76	109	54	44	16	3	4	33	62	93	103	708
77 m	11	12	14	16	17	20	22	23	21	18	14	12	17
London, UK	54	40	37	37	46	45	57	59	49	57	64	48	593
5 m	4	5	7	9	12	16	18	17	15	11	8	5	11
Málaga, Spain	61	51	62	46	26	5	1	3	29	64	64	62	474
33 m	12	13	16	17	19	29	25	26	23	20	16	13	18
Moscow, Russia	39	38	36	37	53	58	88	71	58	45	47	54	624
156 m	-13	-10	-4	6	13	16	18	17	12	6	-1	-7	4
Odessa, Ukraine	57	62	30	21	34	34	42	37	37	13	35	71	473
64 m	-3	-1	2	9	15	20	22	22	18	12	9	1	10
Paris, France	56	46	35	42	57	54	59	64	55	50	51	50	619
75 m	3	4	8	11	15	18	20	19	17	12	7	4	12
Rome, Italy	71	62	57	51	46	37	15	21	63	99	129	93	744
17 m	8	9	11	14	18	22	25	25	22	17	13	10	16
Shannon, Irish Republic	94	67	56	53	61	57	77	79	86	86	96	117	929
2 m	5	5	7	9	12	14	16	16	14	11	8	6	10
Stockholm, Sweden	43	30	25	31	34	45	61	76	60	48	53	48	554
44 m	-3	-3	-1	5	10	15	18	17	12	7	3	0	7

ASIA

	Jan.	Feb.	Mar.	Apr.	May	June	July	Aug.	Sept.	Oct.	Nov.	Dec.	Year
Bahrain	8	18	13	8	<3	0	0	0	0	0	18	18	81
5 m	17	18	21	25	29	32	33	34	31	28	24	19	26
Bangkok, Thailand	8	20	36	58	198	160	160	175	305	206	66	5	1,397
2 m	26	28	29	30	29	29	28	28	28	28	26	25	28
Beirut, Lebanon	191	158	94	53	18	3	<3	<3	5	51	132	185	892
34 m	14	14	16	18	22	24	27	28	26	24	19	16	21
Bombay, India	3	3	3	<3	18	485	617	340	264	64	13	3	1,809
11 m	24	24	26	28	30	29	27	27	27	28	27	26	27
Calcutta, India	10	31	36	43	140	297	325	328	252	114	20	5	1,600
6 m	20	22	27	30	30	30	29	29	29	28	23	19	26
Colombo, Sri Lanka	89	69	147	231	371	224	135	109	160	348	315	147	2,365
7 m	26	26	27	28	28	27	27	27	27	27	26	26	27
Harbin, China	6	5	10	23	43	94	112	104	46	33	8	5	488
160 m	-18	-15	-5	6	13	19	22	21	14	4	-6	-16	3
Ho Chi Minh, Vietnam	15	3	13	43	221	330	315	269	335	269	114	56	1,984
9 m	26	27	29	30	29	28	28	28	27	27	27	26	28
Hong Kong	33	46	74	137	292	394	381	361	257	114	43	31	2,162
33 m	16	15	18	22	26	28	28	28	27	25	21	18	23
Jakarta, Indonesia	300	300	211	147	114	97	64	43	66	112	142	203	1,798
8 m	26	26	27	27	27	27	27	27	27	27	27	26	27
Kabul, Afghanistan	31	36	94	102	20	5	3	3	<3	15	20	10	338
1,815 m	-3	-1	6	13	18	22	25	24	20	14	7	3	12
Karachi, Pakistan	13	10	8	3	3	18	81	41	13	<3	3	5	196
4 m	19	20	24	28	30	31	30	29	28	28	24	20	26
Kazalinsk, Kazakhstan	10	10	13	13	15	5	5	8	8	10	13	15	125
63 m	-12	-11	-3	6	18	23	25	23	16	8	-1	-7	7
New Delhi, India	23	18	13	8	13	74	180	172	117	10	3	10	640
218 m	14	17	23	28	33	34	31	30	29	26	20	15	25
Omsk, Russia	15	8	8	13	31	51	51	51	28	25	18	20	318
85 m	-22	-19	-12	-1	10	16	18	16	10	1	-11	-18	-1
Shanghai, China	48	58	84	94	94	180	147	142	130	71	51	36	1,135
7 m	4	5	9	14	20	24	28	28	23	19	12	7	16
Singapore	252	173	193	188	173	173	170	196	178	208	254	257	2,413
10 m	26	27	28	28	28	28	28	27	27	27	27	27	27
Tehran, Iran	46	38	46	36	13	3	3	3	3	8	20	31	246
1,220 m	2	5	9	16	21	26	30	29	25	18	12	6	17
Tokyo, Japan	48	74	107	135	147	165	142	152	234	208	97	56	1,565
6 m	3	4	7	13	17	21	25	26	23	17	11	6	14
Ulan Bator, Mongolia	<3	<3	3	5	10	28	76	51	23	5	5	3	208
1,325 m	-26	-21	-13	-1	6	14	16	14	8	-1	-13	-22	-3
Verkhoyansk, Russia	5	5	3	5	8	23	28	25	13	8	8	5	134
100 m	-50	-45	-32	-15	0	12	14	9	2	-15	-38	-48	-17

AFRICA

	Jan.	Feb.	Mar.	Apr.	May	June	July	Aug.	Sept.	Oct.	Nov.	Dec.	Year
Addis Ababa, Ethiopia	<3	3	25	135	213	201	206	239	102	28	<3	0	1,151
2,450 m	19	20	20	20	19	18	18	19	21	22	21	20	20
Antananarivo, Madagas.	300	279	178	53	18	8	8	10	18	61	135	287	1,356
1,372 m	21	21	21	19	18	15	14	15	17	19	21	21	19
Cairo, Egypt	5	5	5	3	3	<3	0	0	<3	<3	3	5	28
116 m	13	15	18	21	25	28	28	28	26	24	20	15	22
Cape Town, South Africa	15	8	18	48	79	84	89	66	43	31	18	10	508
17 m	21	21	20	17	14	13	12	13	14	16	18	19	17
Johannesburg, S. Africa	114	109	89	38	25	8	8	8	23	56	107	125	709
1,665 m	20	20	18	16	13	10	11	13	16	18	19	20	16
Khartoum, Sudan	<3	<3	<3	<3	3	8	53	71	18	5	<3	0	158
390 m	24	25	28	31	33	34	32	31	32	32	28	25	29
Kinshasa, Zaïre	135	145	196	196	158	8	3	3	31	119	221	142	1,354
325 m	26	26	27	27	26	24	23	24	25	26	26	26	25
Lagos, Nigeria	28	46	102	150	269	460	279	64	140	206	69	25	1,836
3 m	27	28	29	28	28	26	26	25	26	26	28	28	27
Lusaka, Zambia	231	191	142	18	3	<3	<3	0	<3	10	91	150	836
1,277 m	21	22	21	21	19	16	16	18	22	24	23	22	21
Monrovia, Liberia	31	56	97	216	516	973	996	373	744	772	236	130	5,138
23 m	26	26	27	27	26	25	24	25	25	25	26	26	26
Nairobi, Kenya	38	64	125	211	158	46	15	23	31	53	109	86	958
1,820 m	19	19	19	19	18	16	16	16	18	19	18	18	18
Timbuktu, Mali	<3	<3	3	<3	5	23	79	81	38	3	<3	<3	231
301 m	22	24	28	32	34	35	32	30	32	31	28	23	29
Tunis, Tunisia	64	51	41	36	18	8	3	8	33	51	48	61	419
66 m	10	11	13	16	19	23	26	27	25	20	16	11	18
Walvis Bay, South Africa	<3	5	8	3	3	<3	<3	3	<3	<3	<3	<3	23
7 m	19	19	19	18	17	16	15	14	14	15	17	18	18

AUSTRALIA, NEW ZEALAND AND ANTARCTICA

	Jan.	Feb.	Mar.	Apr.	May	June	July	Aug.	Sept.	Oct.	Nov.	Dec.	Year
Alice Springs, Australia	43	33	28	10	15	13	8	8	8	18	31	38	252
579 m	29	28	25	20	15	12	12	14	18	23	26	28	21
Christchurch, N. Zealand	56	43	48	48	66	66	69	48	46	43	48	56	638
10 m	16	16	14	12	9	6	6	7	9	12	14	16	11
Darwin, Australia	386	312	254	97	15	3	<3	3	13	51	119	239	1,491
30 m	29	29	29	29	28	26	25	26	28	29	30	29	28
Mawson, Antarctica	11	30	20	10	44	180	4	40	3	20	0	0	362
14 m	0	-5	-10	-14	-15	-16	-18	-18	-19	-13	-5	-1	-11
Perth, Australia	8	10	20	43	130	180	170	149	86	56	20	13	881
60 m	23	23	22	19	16	14	13	13	15	16	19	22	18
Sydney, Australia	89	102	127	135	127	117	117	76	73	71	73	73	1,181
42 m	22	22	21	18	15	13	12	13	15	18	19	21	17

NORTH AMERICA

	Jan.	Feb.	Mar.	Apr.	May	June	July	Aug.	Sept.	Oct.	Nov.	Dec.	Year
Anchorage, Alaska, USA	20	18	15	10	13	18	41	66	66	56	25	23	371
40 m	-11	-8	-5	2	7	12	14	13	9	2	-5	-11	2
Chicago, Ill., USA	51	51	66	71	86	89	84	81	79	66	61	51	836
251 m	-4	-3	2	9	14	20	23	22	19	12	5	-1	10
Churchill, Man., Canada	15	13	18	23	32	44	46	58	51	43	39	21	402
13 m	-28	-26	-20	-10	-2	6	12	11	5	-2	-12	-22	-7
Edmonton, Alta., Canada	25	19	19	22	43	77	89	78	39	17	16	25	466
676 m	-15	-10	-5	4	11	15	17	16	11	6	-4	-10	3
Honolulu, Hawaii, USA	104	66	79	48	25	18	23	28	36	48	64	104	643
12 m	23	18	19	20	22	24	25	26	26	24	22	19	22
Houston, Tex., USA	89	76	84	91	119	117	99	99	104	94	89	109	1,171
12 m	12	13	17	21	24	27	28	29	26	22	16	12	21
Kingston, Jamaica	23	15	23	31	102	89	38	91	99	180	74	36	800
34 m	25	25	25	26	26	28	28	28	27	27	26	26	26
Los Angeles, Calif., USA	79	76	71	25	10	3	<3	<3	5	15	31	66	381
95 m	13	14	14	16	17	19	21	22	21	18	16	14	17
Mexico City, Mexico	13	5	10	20	53	119	170	152	130	51	18	8	747
2,309 m	12	13	16	18	19	19	17	18	18	16	14	13	16
Miami, Fla., USA	71	53	64	81	173	178	155	160	203	234	71	51	1,516
8 m	20	20	22	23	25	27	28	28	27	25	22	21	24
Montréal, Que., Canada	72	65	74	74	66	82	90	92	88	76	81	87	946
57 m	-10	-9	-3	6	13	18	21	20	15	9	2	-7	6
New York, N.Y., USA	94	97	91	81	81	84	107	109	86	89	76	91	1,092
96 m	-1	-1	3	10	16	20	23	23	21	15	7	2	11
St Louis, Mo., USA	58	64	89	97	114	114	89	86	81	74	71	64	1,001
173 m	0	1	7	13	19	24	26	26	22	15	8	2	14
San José, Costa Rica	15	5	20	46	229	241	211	241	305	300	145	41	1,798
1,146 m	19	19	21	21	22	21	21	21	21	20	20	19	20
Vancouver, B.C., Canada	154	115	101	60	52	45	32	41	67	114	150	182	1,113
14 m	3	5	6	9	12	15	17	17	14	10	6	4	10
Washington, D.C., USA	86	76	91	84	94	99	112	109	94	74	66	79	1,064
22 m	1	2	7	12	18	23	25	24	20	14	8	3	13

SOUTH AMERICA

	Jan.	Feb.	Mar.	Apr.	May	June	July	Aug.	Sept.	Oct.	Nov.	Dec.	Year
Antofagasta, Chile	0	0	0	<3	<3	3	5	3	<3	3	<3	0	13
94 m	21	21	20	18	16	15	14	14	15	16	18	19	17
Buenos Aires, Argentina	79	71	109	89	76	61	56	61	79	86	84	99	950
27 m	23	23	21	17	13	9	10	11	13	15	19	22	16
Lima, Peru	3	<3	<3	<3	5	5	8	8	8	3	3	<3	41
120 m	23	24	24	22	19	17	17	16	17	18	19	21	20
Manaus, Brazil	249	231	262	221	170	84	58	38	46	107	142	203	1,811
44 m	28	28	28	27	28	28	28	28	29	29	29	28	28
Paraná, Brazil	287	236	239	102	13	<3	3	5	28	127	231	310	1,582
260 m	23	23	23	23	23	21	21	22	24	24	24	23	23
Rio de Janeiro, Brazil	125	122	130	107	79	53	41	43	66	79	104	137	1,082
61 m	26	26	25	24	22	21	21	21	21	22	23	25	23

WORLD STATISTICS: PHYSICAL DIMENSIONS

Each topic list is divided into continents and within a continent the items are listed in order of size. The order of the continents is as in the atlas, Europe through to South America. Certain lists down to this mark > are complete; below they are selective. The world top ten are shown in square brackets; in the case of mountains this has not been done because the world top 30 are all in Asia. The figures are rounded as appropriate.

WORLD, CONTINENTS, OCEANS

	km²	miles²	%
The World	509,450,000	196,672,000	-
Land	149,450,000	57,688,000	29.3
Water	360,000,000	138,984,000	70.7
Asia	44,500,000	17,177,000	29.8
Africa	30,302,000	11,697,000	20.3
North America	24,241,000	9,357,000	16.2
South America	17,793,000	6,868,000	11.9
Antarctica	14,100,000	5,443,000	9.4
Europe	9,957,000	3,843,000	6.7
Australia & Oceania	8,557,000	3,303,000	5.7
Pacific Ocean	179,679,000	69,356,000	49.9
Atlantic Ocean	92,373,000	35,657,000	25.7
Indian Ocean	73,917,000	28,532,000	20.5
Arctic Ocean	14,090,000	5,439,000	3.9

SEAS

Pacific	km²	miles²
South China Sea	2,318,000	895,000
Bering Sea	2,268,000	875,000
Sea of Okhotsk	1,528,000	590,000
East China & Yellow	1,249,000	482,000
Sea of Japan	1,008,000	389,000
Gulf of California	162,000	62,500
Bass Strait	75,000	29,000

Atlantic	km²	miles²
Caribbean Sea	2,766,000	1,068,000
Mediterranean Sea	2,516,000	971,000
Gulf of Mexico	1,543,000	596,000
Hudson Bay	1,232,000	476,000
North Sea	575,000	223,000
Black Sea	452,000	174,000
Baltic Sea	397,000	153,000
Gulf of St Lawrence	238,000	92,000

Indian	km²	miles²
Red Sea	438,000	169,000
The Gulf	239,000	92,000

MOUNTAINS

Europe		m	ft
Mont Blanc	France/Italy	4,807	15,771
Monte Rosa	Italy/Switzerland	4,634	15,203
Dom	Switzerland	4,545	14,911
Weisshorn	Switzerland	4,505	14,780
Matterhorn/Cervino	Italy/Switzerland	4,478	14,691
Mt Maudit	France/Italy	4,465	14,649
Finsteraarhorn	Switzerland	4,275	14,025
Aletschhorn	Switzerland	4,182	13,720
Jungfrau	Switzerland	4,158	13,642
Barre des Ecrins	France	4,103	13,461
Gran Paradiso	Italy	4,061	13,323
Piz Bernina	Italy/Switzerland	4,052	13,294
Ortles	Italy	3,899	12,792
Monte Viso	Italy	3,841	12,602
Grossglockner	Austria	3,797	12,457
Wildspitze	Austria	3,774	12,382
Weisskügel	Austria/Italy	3,736	12,257
Dammastock	Switzerland	3,640	11,942
Tödi	Switzerland	3,623	11,886
Presanella	Italy	3,556	11,667
Monte Adamello	Italy	3,554	11,660
Mulhacén	Spain	3,478	11,411
Pico de Aneto	Spain	3,404	11,168
Marmolada	Italy	3,342	10,964
Etna	Italy	3,340	10,958
> Musala	Bulgaria	2,925	9,596
Olympus	Greece	2,917	9,570
Gerlachovka	Slovak Republic	2,655	8,711
Galdhöpiggen	Norway	2,469	8,100
Pietrosul	Romania	2,305	7,562
Hvannadalshnúkur	Iceland	2,119	6,952
Narodnaya	Russia	1,894	6,214
Ben Nevis	UK	1,343	4,406

Asia		m	ft
Everest	China/Nepal	8,848	29,029
Godwin Austen (K2)	China/Kashmir	8,611	28,251
Kanchenjunga	India/Nepal	8,598	28,208
Lhotse	China/Nepal	8,516	27,939
Makalu	China/Nepal	8,481	27,824
Cho Oyu	China/Nepal	8,201	26,906
Dhaulagiri	Nepal	8,172	26,811
Manaslu	Nepal	8,156	26,758
Nanga Parbat	Kashmir	8,126	26,660
Annapurna	Nepal	8,078	26,502
Gasherbrum	China/Kashmir	8,068	26,469
Broad Peak	India	8,051	26,414
Gosainthan	China	8,012	26,286
Disteghil Sar	Kashmir	7,885	25,869
Nuptse	Nepal	7,879	25,849
Masherbrum	Kashmir	7,826	25,676
Nanda Devi	India	7,817	25,646
Rakaposhi	Kashmir	7,788	25,551
Kamet	India	7,756	25,446
Namcha Barwa	China	7,756	25,446
Gurla Mandhata	China	7,728	25,354
Muztag	China	7,723	25,338
Kongur Shan	China	7,719	25,324
Tirich Mir	Pakistan	7,690	25,229
Saser	Kashmir	7,672	25,170
> Pik Kommunizma	Tajikistan	7,495	24,590
Aling Gangri	China	7,315	23,999
Elbrus	Russia	5,633	18,481
Demavand	Iran	5,604	18,386
Ararat	Turkey	5,165	16,945
Gunong Kinabalu	Malaysia (Borneo)	4,101	13,455
Yu Shan	Taiwan	3,997	13,113
Fuji-san	Japan	3,776	12,388
Rinjani	Indonesia	3,726	12,224
Mt Rajang	Philippines	3,364	11,037
Pidurutalagala	Sri Lanka	2,524	8,281

Africa		m	ft
Kilimanjaro	Tanzania	5,895	19,340
Mt Kenya	Kenya	5,199	17,057
Ruwenzori	Uganda/Zaïre	5,109	16,762
Ras Dashan	Ethiopia	4,620	15,157
Meru	Tanzania	4,565	14,977
Karisimbi	Rwanda/Zaïre	4,507	14,787
Mt Elgon	Kenya/Uganda	4,321	14,176
Batu	Ethiopia	4,307	14,130
Gughe	Ethiopia	4,200	13,779
Toubkal	Morocco	4,165	13,665
Irhil Mgoun	Morocco	4,071	13,356
Mt Cameroon	Cameroon	4,070	13,353
Teide	Spain (Tenerife)	3,718	12,198
Thabana Ntlenyana	Lesotho	3,482	11,424
> Emi Kussi	Chad	3,415	11,204
Mt aux Sources	Lesotho/S. Africa	3,282	10,768
Mt Piton	Réunion	3,069	10,069

Oceania		m	ft
Puncak Jaya	Indonesia	5,029	16,499
Puncak Mandala	Indonesia	4,760	15,617
Puncak Trikora	Indonesia	4,750	15,584
Mt Wilhelm	Papua New Guinea	4,508	14,790
> Mauna Kea	USA (Hawaii)	4,208	13,806
Mauna Loa	USA (Hawaii)	4,169	13,678
Mt Cook	New Zealand	3,753	12,313
Mt Balbi	Solomon Is.	2,743	8,999
Orohena	Tahiti	2,241	7,352
Mt Kosciusko	Australia	2,230	7,316

North America		m	ft
Mt McKinley	USA (Alaska)	6,194	20,321
Mt Logan	Canada	6,050	19,849
Citlaltepetl	Mexico	5,700	18,701
Mt St Elias	USA/Canada	5,489	18,008
Popocatepetl	Mexico	5,452	17,887
Mt Foraker	USA (Alaska)	5,304	17,401
Ixtaccihuatl	Mexico	5,286	17,342
Lucania	USA (Alaska)	5,226	17,145
Mt Steele	Canada	5,011	16,440
Mt Bona	USA (Alaska)	5,005	16,420
Mt Blackburn	USA (Alaska)	4,996	16,391
Mt Sanford	USA (Alaska)	4,949	16,237
Mt Wood	Canada	4,848	15,905
Nevado de Toluca	Mexico	4,670	15,321
Mt Fairweather	USA (Alaska)	4,663	15,298
Mt Whitney	USA	4,418	14,495
Mt Elbert	USA	4,399	14,432
Mt Harvard	USA	4,395	14,419
Mt Rainier	USA	4,392	14,409
Blanca Peak	USA	4,364	14,317
Long's Peak	USA	4,345	14,255
Nevado de Colima	Mexico	4,339	14,235
Mt Shasta	USA	4,317	14,163
Tajumulco	Guatemala	4,217	13,835
> Gannett Peak	USA	4,202	13,786
Mt Waddington	Canada	3,994	13,104
Mt Robson	Canada	3,954	12,972
Chirripó Grande	Costa Rica	3,837	12,589
Loma Tinta	Haiti	3,175	10,417

South America		m	ft
Aconcagua	Argentina	6,960	22,834
Illimani	Bolivia	6,882	22,578
Bonete	Argentina	6,872	22,546
Ojos del Salado	Argentina/Chile	6,863	22,516
Tupungato	Argentina/Chile	6,800	22,309
Pissis	Argentina	6,779	22,241
Mercedario	Argentina/Chile	6,770	22,211
Huascaran	Peru	6,768	22,204
Llullaillaco	Argentina/Chile	6,723	22,057
Nudo de Cachi	Argentina	6,720	22,047
Yerupaja	Peru	6,632	21,758
N. de Tres Cruces	Argentina/Chile	6,620	21,719
Incahuasi	Argentina/Chile	6,601	21,657
Ancohuma	Bolivia	6,550	21,489
Sajama	Bolivia	6,520	21,391
Coropuna	Peru	6,425	21,079
Ausangate	Peru	6,384	20,945
Cerro del Toro	Argentina	6,380	20,932
Ampato	Peru	6,310	20,702
Chimborasso	Ecuador	6,267	20,561
> Cotopaxi	Ecuador	5,897	19,347
Cayambe	Ecuador	5,796	19,016
S. Nev. de S. Marta	Colombia	5,775	18,947
Pico Bolivar	Venezuela	5,007	16,427

Antarctica		m	ft
Vinson Massif		4,897	16,066
Mt Kirkpatrick		4,528	14,855
Mt Markham		4,349	14,268

OCEAN DEPTHS

Atlantic Ocean	m	ft	
Puerto Rico (Milwaukee) Deep	9,200	30,183	[7]
Cayman Trench	7,680	25,197	[10]
Gulf of Mexico	5,203	17,070	
Mediterranean Sea	5,121	16,801	
Black Sea	2,211	7,254	
North Sea	310	1,017	
Baltic Sea	294	965	
Hudson Bay	111	364	

Indian Ocean	m	ft
Java Trench	7,450	24,442
Red Sea	2,266	7,434
Persian Gulf	73	239

Pacific Ocean	m	ft	
Mariana Trench	11,022	36,161	[1]
Tonga Trench	10,822	35,505	[2]
Japan Trench	10,554	34,626	[3]
Kuril Trench	10,542	34,586	[4]
Mindanao Trench	10,497	34,439	[5]
Kermadec Trench	10,047	32,962	[6]
Peru-Chile Trench	8,050	26,410	[8]
Aleutian Trench	7,822	25,662	[9]
Middle American Trench	6,662	21,857	

Arctic Ocean	m	ft
Molloy Deep	5,608	18,399

LAND LOWS

		m	ft
Caspian Sea	Europe	-28	-92
Dead Sea	Asia	-400	-1,312
Lake Assal	Africa	-156	-512
Lake Eyre North	Oceania	-16	-52
Death Valley	N. America	-86	-282
Valdés Peninsula	S. America	-40	-131

RIVERS

Europe

		km	miles
Volga	Caspian Sea	3,700	2,300
Danube	Black Sea	2,850	1,770
Ural	Caspian Sea	2,535	1,574
Dnieper	Volga	2,285	1,420
Kama	Volga	2,030	1,260
Don	Volga	1,990	1,240
Petchora	Arctic Ocean	1,790	1,110
Oka	Volga	1,480	920
Belaya	Kama	1,420	880
Dniester	Black Sea	1,400	870
Vyatka	Kama	1,370	850
Rhine	North Sea	1,320	820
N. Dvina	Arctic Ocean	1,290	800
Desna	Dnieper	1,190	740
Elbe	North Sea	1,145	710
Vistula	Baltic Sea	1,090	675
Loire	Atlantic Ocean	1,020	635
W. Dvina	Baltic Sea	1,019	633

Asia

		km	miles
Yangtze	Pacific Ocean	6,380	3,960 [3]
Yenisey-Angara	Arctic Ocean	5,550	3,445 [5]
Ob-Irtysh	Arctic Ocean	5,410	3,360 [6]
Hwang Ho	Pacific Ocean	4,840	3,005 [7]
Amur	Pacific Ocean	4,510	2,800 [9]
Mekong	Pacific Ocean	4,500	2,795 [10]
Lena	Arctic Ocean	4,400	2,730
Irtysh	Ob	4,250	2,640
Yenisey	Arctic Ocean	4,090	2,540
Ob	Arctic Ocean	3,680	2,285
Indus	Indian Ocean	3,100	1,925
Brahmaputra	Indian Ocean	2,900	1,800
Syr Darya	Aral Sea	2,860	1,775
Salween	Indian Ocean	2,800	1,740
Euphrates	Indian Ocean	2,700	1,675
Vilyuy	Lena	2,650	1,645
Kolyma	Arctic Ocean	2,600	1,615
Amu Darya	Aral Sea	2,540	1,575
Ural	Caspian Sea	2,535	1,575
Ganges	Indian Ocean	2,510	1,560
Si Kiang	Pacific Ocean	2,100	1,305
Irrawaddy	Indian Ocean	2,010	1,250
Tarim-Yarkand	Lop Nor	2,000	1,240
Tigris	Indian Ocean	1,900	1,180
Angara	Yenisey	1,830	1,135
Godavari	Indian Ocean	1,470	915
Sutlej	Indian Ocean	1,450	900
Yamuna	Indian Ocean	1,400	870

Africa

		km	miles
Nile	Mediterranean	6,670	4,140 [1]
Zaïre/Congo	Atlantic Ocean	4,670	2,900 [8]
Niger	Atlantic Ocean	4,180	2,595
Zambezi	Indian Ocean	2,740	1,700
Oubangi/Uele	Zaïre	2,250	1,400
Kasai	Zaïre	1,950	1,210
Shaballe	Indian Ocean	1,930	1,200
Orange	Atlantic Ocean	1,860	1,155
Cubango	Okavango Swamps	1,800	1,120
Limpopo	Indian Ocean	1,600	995
Senegal	Atlantic Ocean	1,600	995
Volta	Atlantic Ocean	1,500	930
Benue	Niger	1,350	840

Australia

		km	miles
Murray-Darling	Indian Ocean	3,720	2,310
Darling	Murray	3,070	1,905
Murray	Indian Ocean	2,575	1,600
Murrumbidgee	Murray	1,690	1,050

North America

		km	miles
Mississippi-Missouri	Gulf of Mexico	6,020	3,740 [4]
Mackenzie	Arctic Ocean	4,240	2,630
Mississippi	Gulf of Mexico	3,780	2,350
Missouri	Mississippi	3,725	2,310
Yukon	Pacific Ocean	3,185	1,980
Rio Grande	Gulf of Mexico	3,030	1,880
Arkansas	Mississippi	2,340	1,450
Colorado	Pacific Ocean	2,330	1,445
Red	Mississippi	2,040	1,270
Columbia	Pacific Ocean	1,950	1,210
Saskatchewan	Lake Winnipeg	1,940	1,205
Snake	Columbia	1,670	1,040
Churchill	Hudson Bay	1,600	990
Ohio	Mississippi	1,580	980
Brazos	Gulf of Mexico	1,400	870
St Lawrence	Atlantic Ocean	1,170	730

South America

		km	miles
Amazon	Atlantic Ocean	6,430	3,990 [2]
Paraná-Plate	Atlantic Ocean	4,000	2,480
Purus	Amazon	3,350	2,080
Madeira	Amazon	3,200	1,990
São Francisco	Atlantic Ocean	2,900	1,800
Paraná	Plate	2,800	1,740
Tocantins	Atlantic Ocean	2,640	1,640
Paraguay	Paraná	2,550	1,580
Orinoco	Atlantic Ocean	2,500	1,550
Pilcomayo	Paraná	2,500	1,550
Araguaia	Tocantins	2,250	1,400
Juruá	Amazon	2,000	1,240
Xingu	Amazon	1,980	1,230
Ucayali	Amazon	1,900	1,180
Marañón	Amazon	1,600	990
Uruguay	Plate	1,600	990
Magdalena	Caribbean Sea	1,540	960

LAKES

Europe

		km²	miles²
Lake Ladoga	Russia	18,400	7,100
Lake Onega	Russia	9,700	3,700
Saimaa system	Finland	8,000	3,100
Vänern	Sweden	5,500	2,100
Rybinsk Res.	Russia	4,700	1,800

Asia

		km²	miles²
Caspian Sea	Asia	371,000	143,000 [1]
Aral Sea	Kazakh./Uzbek.	36,000	13,900 [6]
Lake Baykal	Russia	31,500	12,200 [9]
Tonlé Sap	Cambodia	20,000	7,700
Lake Balkhash	Kazakhstan	18,500	7,100
Dongting Hu	China	12,000	4,600
Issyk Kul	Kirghizia	6,200	2,400
Lake Urmia	Iran	5,900	2,300
Koko Nur	China	5,700	2,200
Poyang Hu	China	5,000	1,900
Lake Khanka	China/Russia	4,400	1,700
Lake Van	Turkey	3,500	1,400
Ubsa Nur	China	3,400	1,300

Africa

		km²	miles²
Lake Victoria	E. Africa	68,000	26,000 [3]
Lake Tanganyika	C. Africa	33,000	13,000 [7]
Lake Malawi/Nyasa	E. Africa	29,000	11,000 [10]
Lake Chad	C. Africa	25,000	9,700
Lake Turkana	Ethiopia/Kenya	8,500	3,300
Lake Volta	Ghana	8,500	3,300
Lake Bangweulu	Zambia	8,000	3,100
Lake Rukwa	Tanzania	7,000	2,700
Lake Mai-Ndombe	Zaïre	6,500	2,500
Lake Kariba	Zambia/Zimbabwe	5,300	2,000
Lake Mobutu	Uganda/Zaïre	5,300	2,000
Lake Nasser	Egypt/Sudan	5,200	2,000
Lake Mweru	Zambia/Zaïre	4,900	1,900
Lake Cabora Bassa	South Africa	4,500	1,700
Lake Kyoga	Uganda	4,400	1,700
Lake Tana	Ethiopia	3,630	1,400
Lake Kivu	Rwanda/Zaïre	2,650	1,000
Lake Edward	Uganda/Zaïre	2,200	850

Australia

		km²	miles²
Lake Eyre	Australia	9,000	3,500
Lake Torrens	Australia	5,800	2,200
Lake Gairdner	Australia	4,800	1,900

North America

		km²	miles²
Lake Superior	Canada/USA	82,200	31,700 [2]
Lake Huron	Canada/USA	59,600	23,000 [4]
Lake Michigan	USA	58,000	22,400 [5]
Great Bear Lake	Canada	31,500	12,200 [8]
Great Slave Lake	Canada	28,700	11,100
Lake Erie	Canada/USA	25,700	9,900
Lake Winnipeg	Canada	24,400	9,400
Lake Ontario	Canada/USA	19,500	7,500
Lake Nicaragua	Nicaragua	8,200	3,200
Lake Athabasca	Canada	8,000	3,100
Smallwood Res.	Canada	6,530	2,520
Reindeer Lake	Canada	6,400	2,500
Lake Winnipegosis	Canada	5,400	2,100
Nettilling Lake	Canada	5,500	2,100
Lake Nipigon	Canada	4,850	1,900
Lake Manitoba	Canada	4,700	1,800

South America

		km²	miles²
Lake Titicaca	Bolivia/Peru	8,200	3,200
Lake Poopo	Peru	2,800	1,100

ISLANDS

Europe

		km²	miles²
Great Britain	UK	229,880	88,700 [8]
Iceland	Atlantic Ocean	103,000	39,800
Ireland	Ireland/UK	84,400	32,600
Novaya Zemlya (N.)	Russia	48,200	18,600
W. Spitzbergen	Norway	39,000	15,100
Novaya Zemlya (S.)	Russia	33,200	12,800
Sicily	Italy	25,500	9,800
Sardinia	Italy	24,000	9,300
N. E. Spitzbergen	Norway	15,000	5,600
Corsica	France	8,700	3,400
Crete	Greece	8,350	3,200
Zealand	Denmark	6,850	2,600

Asia

		km²	miles²
Borneo	S. E. Asia	737,000	284,000 [3]
Sumatra	Indonesia	425,000	164,000 [6]
Honshu	Japan	230,000	88,800 [7]
Celebes	Indonesia	189,000	73,000
Java	Indonesia	126,700	48,900
Luzon	Philippines	104,700	40,400
Mindanao	Philippines	95,000	36,700
Hokkaido	Japan	78,400	30,300
Sakhalin	Russia	76,400	29,500
Sri Lanka	Indian Ocean	65,600	25,300
Taiwan	Pacific Ocean	36,000	13,900
Kyushu	Japan	35,700	13,800
Hainan	China	34,000	13,100
Timor	Indonesia	33,600	13,000
Shikoku	Japan	18,800	7,300
Halmahera	Indonesia	18,000	6,900
Ceram	Indonesia	17,150	6,600
Sumbawa	Indonesia	15,450	6,000
Flores	Indonesia	15,200	5,900
Samar	Philippines	13,100	5,100
Negros	Philippines	12,700	4,900
Bangka	Indonesia	12,000	4,600
Palawan	Philippines	12,000	4,600
Panay	Philippines	11,500	4,400
Sumba	Indonesia	11,100	4,300
Mindoro	Philippines	9,750	3,800
Buru	Indonesia	9,500	3,700
Bali	Indonesia	5,600	2,200
Cyprus	Mediterranean	3,570	1,400
Wrangel Is.	Russia	2,800	1,000

Africa

		km²	miles²
Madagascar	Indian Ocean	587,000	226,600 [4]
Socotra	Indian Ocean	3,600	1,400
Réunion	Indian Ocean	2,500	965
Tenerife	Atlantic Ocean	2,350	900
Mauritius	Indian Ocean	1,865	720

Oceania

		km²	miles²
New Guinea	Indon./Pap. NG	780,000	301,080 [2]
New Zealand (S.)	New Zealand	150,500	58,100
New Zealand (N.)	New Zealand	114,400	44,200
Tasmania	Australia	67,800	26,200
New Britain	Papua NG	37,800	14,600
New Caledonia	Pacific Ocean	16,100	6,200
Viti Levu	Fiji	10,500	4,100
Hawaii	Pacific Ocean	10,450	4,000
Bougainville	Papua NG	9,600	3,700
Guadalcanal	Solomon Is.	6,500	2,500
Vanua Levu	Fiji	5,550	2,100
New Ireland	Papua NG	3,200	1,200

North America

		km²	miles²
Greenland	Greenland	2,175,600	839,800 [1]
Baffin Is.	Canada	508,000	196,100 [5]
Victoria Is.	Canada	212,200	81,900 [9]
Ellesmere Is.	Canada	212,000	81,800 [10]
Cuba	Cuba	114,500	44,200
Newfoundland	Canada	96,000	37,100
Hispaniola	Atlantic Ocean	76,200	29,400
Banks Is.	Canada	67,000	25,900
Devon Is.	Canada	54,500	21,000
Melville Is.	Canada	42,400	16,400
Vancouver Is.	Canada	32,150	12,400
Somerset Is.	Canada	24,300	9,400
Jamaica	Caribbean Sea	11,400	4,400
Puerto Rico	Atlantic Ocean	8,900	3,400
Cape Breton Is.	Canada	4,000	1,500

South America

		km²	miles²
Tierra del Fuego	Argentina/Chile	47,000	18,100
Falkland Is. (E.)	Atlantic Ocean	6,800	2,600
South Georgia	Atlantic Ocean	4,200	1,600
Galapagos (Isabela)	Pacific Ocean	2,250	870

XV

INTRODUCTION TO WORLD GEOGRAPHY

The Universe 2,
The Solar System 4,
The Earth: Time and Motion 6, Geology 8, Oceans 10, Atmosphere 12,
Climate 14, Water 16, Landscape 18, Environment 20,
People: Demography 22, Cities 24, The Human Family 26,
Conflict and Cooperation 28,
Production: Agriculture 30, Energy 32, Minerals 34,
Manufacturing 36, Trade 38,
Quality of Life: Wealth 40, Standards 42, Health 44, Environment 46

THE UNIVERSE

4: ORBITS OF THE PLANETS

PLANETARY DATA

About 15 billion years ago, time and space began with the most colossal explosion in cosmic history: the 'Big Bang' that initiated the universe. According to current theory, in the first millionth of a second of its existence it expanded from a dimensionless point of infinite mass and density into a fireball about 30 billion kilometres across; and it has been expanding ever since.

It took almost a million years for the primal fireball to cool enough for atoms to form. They were mostly hydrogen, still the most abundant material in the universe. But the new matter was not evenly distributed around the young universe, and a few billion years later atoms in relatively dense regions began to cling together under the influence of gravity, forming distinct masses of gas separated by vast expanses of empty space. These first proto-galaxies, to begin with, were dark places: the universe had cooled. But gravitational attraction continued its work, condensing matter into coherent lumps inside the galactic gas clouds. About three billion years later, some of these masses had contracted so much that internal pressure produced the high temperatures necessary to bring about nuclear fusion: the first stars were born.

There were several generations of stars, each feeding on the wreckage of its extinct predecessors as well as the original galactic gas swirls. With each new generation, progressively larger atoms were forged in stellar furnaces and the galaxy's range of elements, once restricted to hydrogen, grew larger. About ten billion years after the Big Bang, a star formed on the outskirts of our galaxy with enough matter left over to create a retinue of planets. Some 4.7 billion years after that, a few planetary atoms had evolved into structures of complex molecules that lived, breathed and eventually pointed telescopes at the sky.

They found that their Sun is just one of more than 100 billion stars in the home galaxy alone. Our galaxy, in turn, forms part of a local group of 25 or so similar structures, some much larger than our own; there are at least 100 million other galaxies in the universe as a whole. The most distant ever observed, a highly energetic galactic core known only as Quasar PKS 2000-330, lies about 15 billion light-years away.

LIFE OF A STAR

For most of its existence, a star produces energy by the nuclear fusion of hydrogen into helium at its core. The duration of this hydrogen-burning period – known as the main sequence – depends on the star's mass; the greater the mass, the higher the core temperatures and the sooner the star's supply of hydrogen is exhausted. Dim, dwarf stars consume their hydrogen slowly, eking it out over a thousand billion years or more. The Sun, like other stars of its mass, should spend about 10 billion years on the main sequence; since it was formed less than five billion years ago, it still has half its life left.

Once all a star's core hydrogen has been fused into helium, nuclear activity moves outward into layers of unconsumed hydrogen. For a time, energy production sharply increases: the star grows hotter and expands enormously, turning into a so-called red giant. Its energy output will increase a thousandfold, and it will swell to a hundred times its present diameter.

After a few hundred million years, helium in the core will become sufficiently compressed to initiate a new cycle of nuclear fusion: from helium to carbon. The star will contract somewhat, before beginning its last expansion, in the Sun's case engulfing the Earth and perhaps Mars. In this bloated condition, the Sun's outer layers will break off into space, leaving a tiny inner core, mainly of carbon, that shrinks progressively under the force of its own gravity: dwarf stars can attain a density more than 10,000 times that of normal matter, with crushing surface gravities to match. Gradually, the nuclear fires will die down, and the Sun will reach its terminal stage: a black dwarf, emitting insignificant amounts of energy.

However, stars more massive than the Sun may undergo another transformation. The additional mass allows gravitational collapse to continue indefinitely: eventually, all the star's remaining matter shrinks to a point, and its density approaches infinity – a state that will not permit even sub-atomic structures to survive.

The star has become a black hole: an anomalous 'singularity' in the fabric of space and time. Although vast coruscations of radiation will be emitted by any matter falling into its grasp, the singularity itself has an escape velocity that exceeds the speed of light, and nothing can ever be released from it. Within the boundaries of the black hole, the laws of physics are suspended, but no physicist can ever observe the extraordinary events that may occur.

THE END OF THE UNIVERSE

The likely fate of the universe is disputed. One theory (top) dictates that the expansion begun at the time of the Big Bang will continue 'indefinitely', with ageing galaxies moving farther and farther apart in an immense, dark graveyard. Alternately, (bottom) gravity may overcome the expansion. Galaxies will fall back together until everything is again concentrated at a single point, followed by a new Big Bang and a new expansion, in an endlessly repeated cycle. The first theory is supported by the amount of visible matter in the universe; the second assumes there is enough dark material to bring about the gravitational collapse.

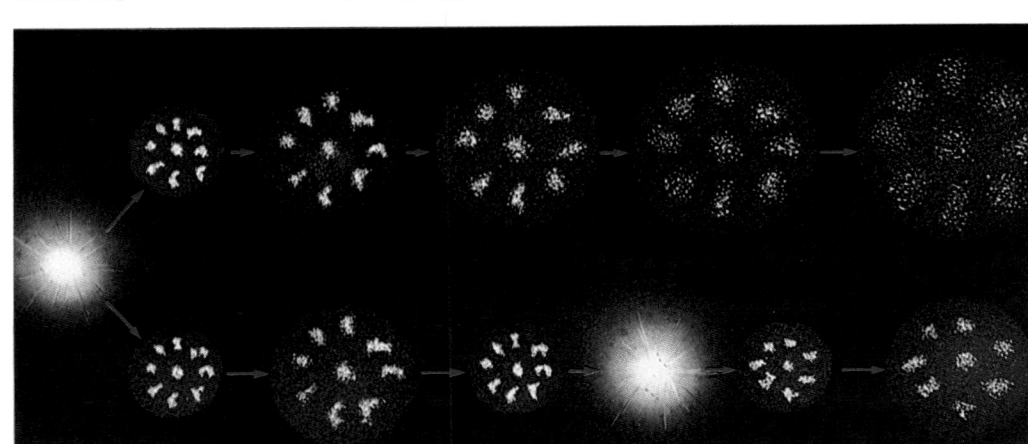

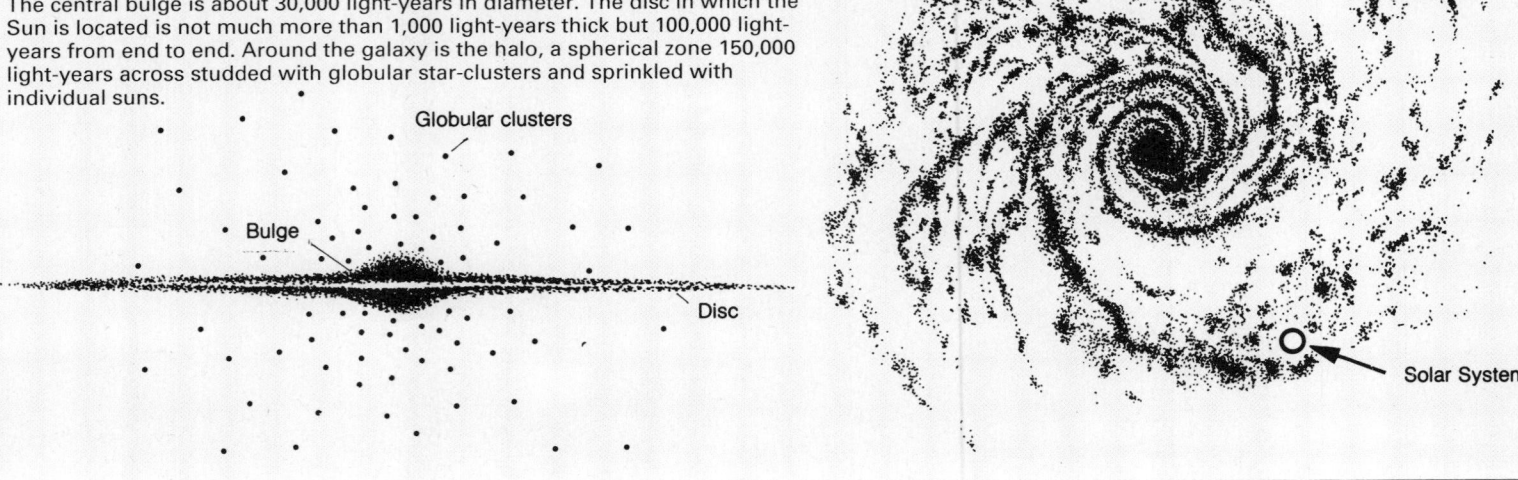

GALACTIC STRUCTURES

The universe's 100 million galaxies show clear structural patterns, originally classified by the American astronomer Edwin Hubble in 1925. Spiral galaxies like our own (top row) have a central, almost spherical bulge and a surrounding disc composed of spiral arms. Barred spirals (bottom row) have a central bar of stars across the nucleus, with spiral arms trailing from the ends of the bar. Elliptical galaxies (far left) have a uniform appearance, ranging from a flattened disc to a near sphere. So-called SO galaxies (left row, right) have a central bulge, but no spiral arms. A few have no discernible structure at all. Galaxies also vary enormously in size, from dwarfs only 2,000 light-years across to great assemblies of stars 80 or more times larger.

THE HOME GALAXY

The Sun and its planets are located in one of the spiral arms, a little less than 30,000 light-years from the galactic centre and orbiting around it in a period of more than 200 million years. The centre is invisible from the Earth, masked by vast, light-absorbing clouds of interstellar dust. The galaxy is probably around 12 billion years old and, like other spiral galaxies, has three distinct regions. The central bulge is about 30,000 light-years in diameter. The disc in which the Sun is located is not much more than 1,000 light-years thick but 100,000 light-years from end to end. Around the galaxy is the halo, a spherical zone 150,000 light-years across studded with globular star-clusters and sprinkled with individual suns.

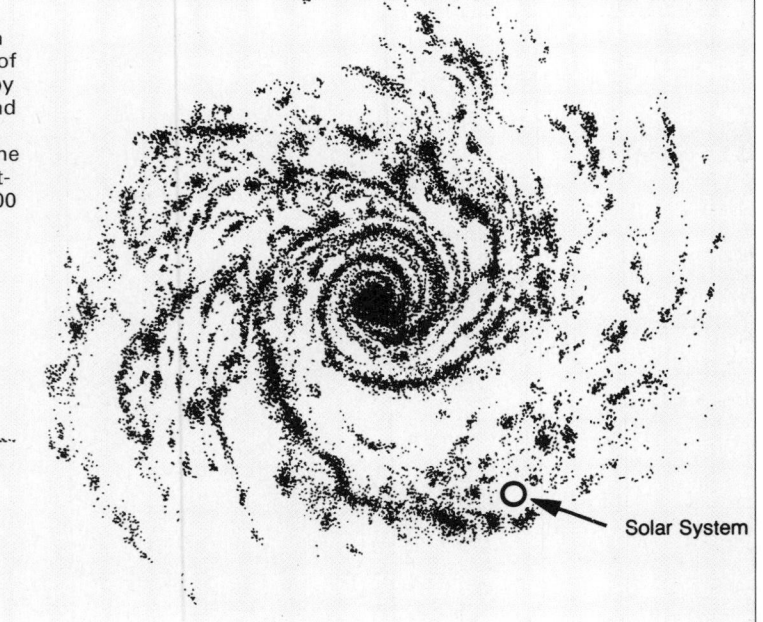

Globular clusters

Bulge

Disc

Solar System

Star charts are drawn as projections of a vast, hollow sphere with the observer in the middle. Each circle below represents one hemisphere, centred on the north and south celestial poles respectively – projections of the Earth's poles in the heavens. At the present era, the north pole is marked by the star Polaris; the south pole has no such convenient reference point. The rectangular map shows the stars immediately above and below the celestial equator.

Astronomical coordinates are normally given in terms of 'Right Ascension' for longitude and 'Declination' for latitude or altitude. Since the stars appear to rotate around the Earth once every 24 hours, Right Ascension is measured eastward – anti-clockwise – in hours and minutes. One hour is equivalent to 15 angular degrees; zero on the scale is the point at which the Sun crosses the celestial equator at the spring equinox, known to astronomers as the First Point in Aries. Unlike the Sun, stars always rise and set at the same point on the horizon. Declination measures (in degrees) a star's angular distance above or below the celestial equator.

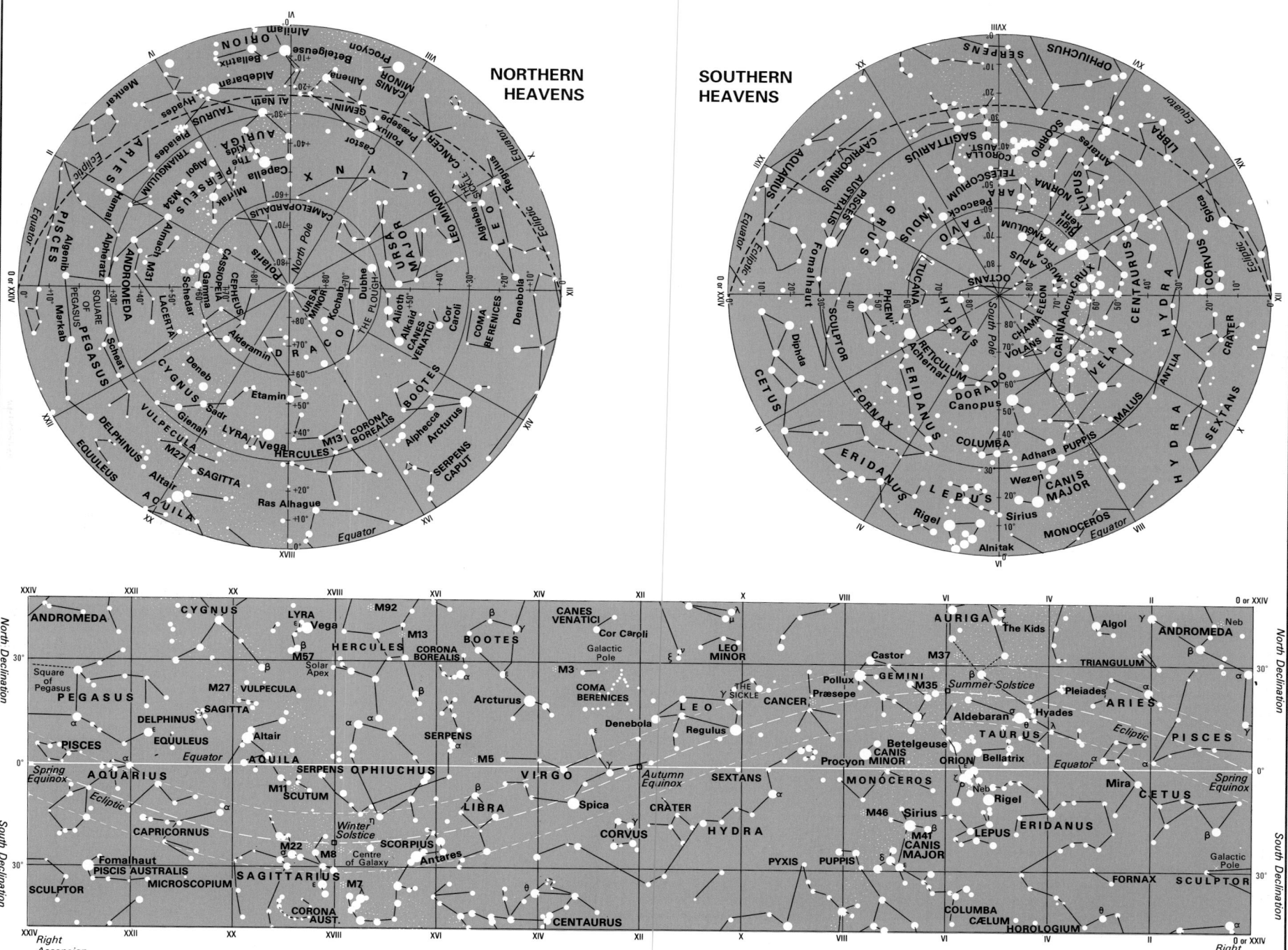

NORTHERN HEAVENS

SOUTHERN HEAVENS

THE CONSTELLATIONS

The constellations and their English names

Andromeda	Andromeda
Antila	Air Pump
Apus	Bird of Paradise
Aquarius	Water-carrier
Aquila	Eagle
Ara	Altar
Aries	Ram
Auriga	Charioteer
Boötes	Herdsman
Caelum	Chisel
Camelopardalis	Giraffe
Cancer	Crab
Canes Venatici	Hunting Dogs
Canis Major	Great Dog
Canis Minor	Little Dog
Capricornus	Goat
Carina	Keel
Cassiopeia	Cassiopeia
Centaurus	Centaur
Cepheus	Cepheus
Cetus	Whale
Chamaeleon	Chameleon
Circinus	Compasses
Columba	Dove
Coma Berenices	Berenice's Hair
Corona Australis	Southern Crown
Corona Borealis	Northern Crown
Corvus	Crow
Crater	Cup
Crux	Southern Cross
Cygnus	Swan
Delphinus	Dolphin
Dorado	Swordfish
Draco	Dragon
Equuleus	Little Horse
Eridanus	Eridanus
Fornax	Furnace
Gemini	Twins
Grus	Crane
Hercules	Hercules
Horologium	Clock
Hydra	Water Snake
Hydrus	Sea Serpent
Indus	Indian
Lacerta	Lizard
Leo	Lion
Leo Minor	Little Lion
Lepus	Hare
Libra	Scales
Lupus	Wolf
Lynx	Lynx
Lyra	Harp
Mensa	Table
Microscopium	Microscope
Monoceros	Unicorn
Musca	Fly
Norma	Level
Octans	Octant
Ophiuchus	Serpent Bearer
Orion	Orion
Pavo	Peacock
Pegasus	Winged Horse
Perseus	Perseus
Phoenix	Phoenix
Pictor	Easel
Pisces	Fishes
Piscis Austrinus	Southern Fish
Puppis	Ship's Stern
Pyxis	Mariner's Compass
Reticulum	Net
Sagitta	Arrow
Sagittarius	Archer
Scorpius	Scorpion
Sculptor	Sculptor
Scutum	Shield
Serpens	Serpent
Sextans	Sextant
Taurus	Bull
Telescopium	Telescope
Triangulum	Triangle
Triangulum Australe	Southern Triangle
Tucana	Toucan
Ursa Major	Great Bear
Ursa Minor	Little Bear
Vela	Sails
Virgo	Virgin
Volans	Flying Fish
Vulpecula	Fox

THE NEAREST STARS

The 20 nearest stars, excluding the Sun, with their distance from Earth in light-years*

Proxima Centauri	4.3
Alpha Centauri A	4.3
Alpha Centauri B	4.3
Barnard's Star	6.0
Wolf 359	8.1
Lal 21185	8.2
Sirius A	8.7
Sirius B	8.7
UV Ceti A	9.0
UV Citi B	9.0
Ross 154	9.3
Ross 248	10.3
Epsilon Eridani	10.8
L 789-6	11.1
Ross 128	11.1
61 Cygni A	11.2
61 Cygni B	11.2
Procyon A	11.3
Procyon B	11.3
Epsilon Indi	11.4

Many of the nearest stars, like Alpha Centauri A and B, are doubles, orbiting about the common centre of gravity and to all intents and purposes equidistant from Earth. Many of them are dim objects, with no name other than the designation given by the astronomers who investigated them. However, they include Sirius, the brightest star in the sky, and Procyon, the seventh brightest. Both are far larger than the Sun: of the nearest stars only Epsilon Eridani is similar in size and luminosity.

* A light-year equals approx. 9,500,000,000,000 kilometres

THE SOLAR SYSTEM

2: THE HOME GALAXY

6: THE SEASONS
   DAY & NIGHT

7: THE MOON

Lying 27,000 light years from the centre of one of billions of galaxies that comprise the observable universe, our solar system contains nine planets and their moons, innumerable asteroids and comets and a miscellany of dust and gas, all tethered by the immense gravitational field of the Sun, the middling-sized star whose thermonuclear furnaces provide them all with heat and light. The solar system was probably formed about 4.6 billion years ago, when a spinning cloud of gas, mostly hydrogen but seeded with other, heavier elements, condensed enough to ignite a nuclear reaction and create a star. The Sun still accounts for almost 99.9% of the system's total mass; one planet, Jupiter, contains most of the remainder.

By composition as well as distance, the planetary array divides quite neatly in two: an inner system of four small, solid planets, including the Earth, and an outer system, from Jupiter to Neptune, of four huge gas giants. Between the two groups lies a scattering of asteroids, perhaps as many as 40,000; possibly the remains of a planet destroyed by some unexplained catastrophe, they are more likely to be debris left over from the solar system's formation, prevented by the gravity of massive Jupiter from coalescing into a larger body. The ninth planet, Pluto, seems to be a world of the inner system type: small, rocky and something of an anomaly.

By the 1990s, the solar system also included some newer anomalies: several thousand spacecraft. Most were in orbit around the Earth, but some had probed far and wide around the system. The information beamed back by these robotic investigators has transformed our knowledge of our celestial environment.

Much of the early history of science is the story of people trying to make sense of the errant points of light that were all they knew of the planets. Now, men have themselves stood on the Earth's Moon; probes have landed on Mars and Venus and orbiting radars have mapped far distant landscapes with astonishing accuracy. In the 1980s, the US Voyagers skimmed all four major planets of the outer system, bringing new revelations with each close approach. Only Pluto, inscrutably distant in an orbit that takes it 50 times the Earth's distance from the Sun, remains unvisited by our messengers.

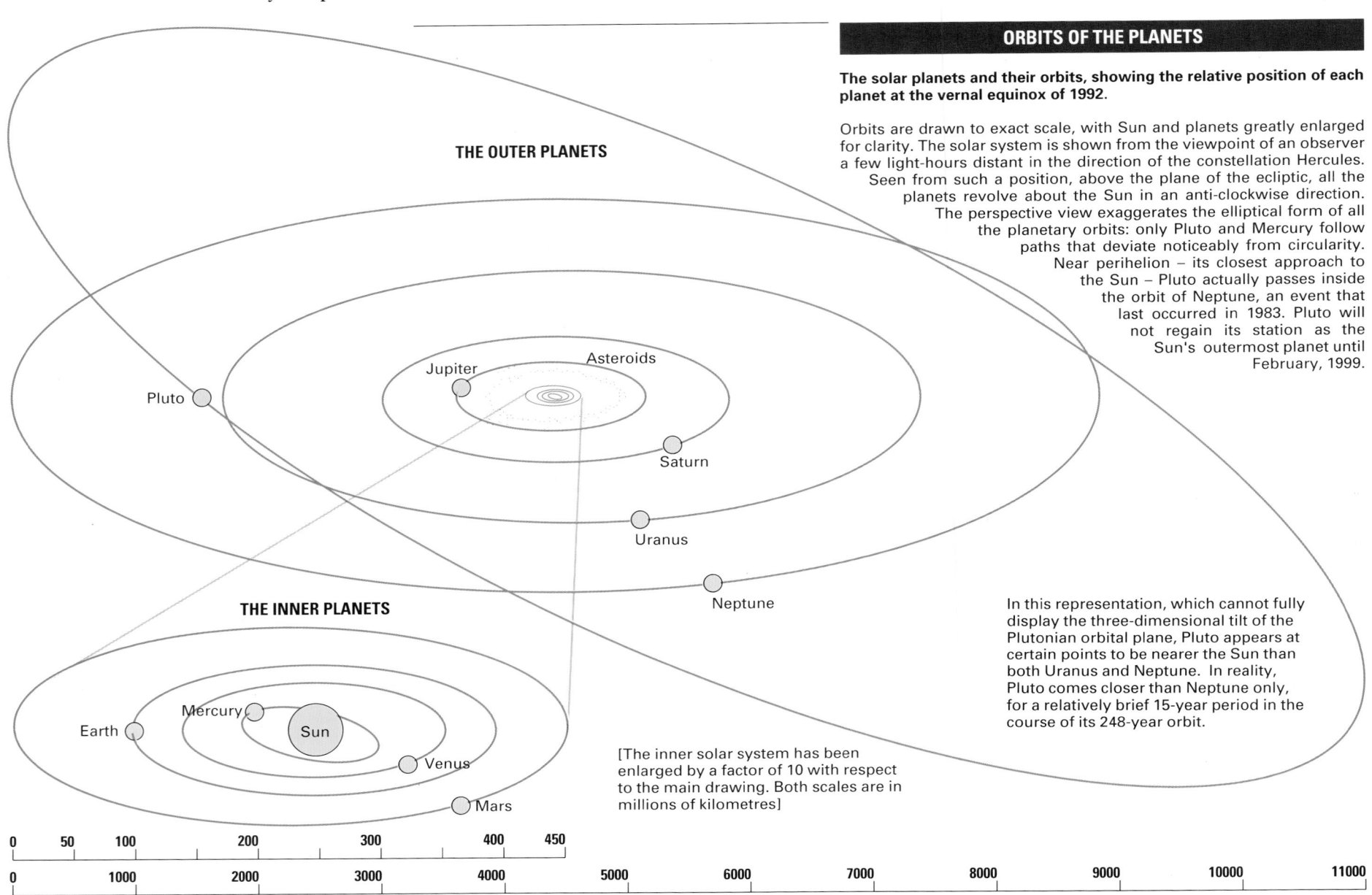

ORBITS OF THE PLANETS

The solar planets and their orbits, showing the relative position of each planet at the vernal equinox of 1992.

Orbits are drawn to exact scale, with Sun and planets greatly enlarged for clarity. The solar system is shown from the viewpoint of an observer a few light-hours distant in the direction of the constellation Hercules. Seen from such a position, above the plane of the ecliptic, all the planets revolve about the Sun in an anti-clockwise direction. The perspective view exaggerates the elliptical form of all the planetary orbits: only Pluto and Mercury follow paths that deviate noticeably from circularity. Near perihelion – its closest approach to the Sun – Pluto actually passes inside the orbit of Neptune, an event that last occurred in 1983. Pluto will not regain its station as the Sun's outermost planet until February, 1999.

In this representation, which cannot fully display the three-dimensional tilt of the Plutonian orbital plane, Pluto appears at certain points to be nearer the Sun than both Uranus and Neptune. In reality, Pluto comes closer than Neptune only, for a relatively brief 15-year period in the course of its 248-year orbit.

THE OUTER PLANETS

Pluto · Jupiter · Asteroids · Saturn · Uranus · Neptune

THE INNER PLANETS

Earth · Mercury · Sun · Venus · Mars

[The inner solar system has been enlarged by a factor of 10 with respect to the main drawing. Both scales are in millions of kilometres]

| 0 | 50 | 100 | 200 | 300 | 400 | 450 |
| 0 | 1000 | 2000 | 3000 | 4000 | 5000 | 6000 | 7000 | 8000 | 9000 | 10000 | 11000 |

PLANETARY DATA

	Mean distance from Sun (million km)	Mass (Earth = 1)	Period of orbit (Earth years)	Period of rotation (Earth days)	Equatorial diameter (km)	Average density (water = 1)	Surface gravity (Earth = 1)	Escape velocity (km/sec)	Number of known satellites
Sun	-	332,946	-	25.38	1,392,000	1.41	27.9	617.5	-
Mercury	58.3	0.06	0.241	58.67	4,878	5.5	0.38	4.27	0
Venus	107.7	0.8	0.615	243	12,104	5.25	0.90	10.36	0
Earth	149.6	1.0	1.00	0.99	12,756	5.52	1.00	11.18	1
Mars	227.3	0.1	1.88	1.02	6,794	3.94	0.38	5.03	2
Jupiter	777.9	317.8	11.86	0.41	142,800	1.33	2.64	60.22	16
Saturn	1,427.1	95.2	29.63	0.42	120,000	0.706	1.16	36.25	17
Uranus	2,872.3	14.5	83.97	0.45	52,000	1.70	1.11	22.4	15
Neptune	4,502.7	17.2	164.8	0.67	48,400	1.77	1.21	23.9	8
Pluto	5,894.2	0.002	248.63	6.38	3,000	5.50	0.47	5.1	1

Planetary days are given in sidereal time -- that is, with respect to the stars rather than the Sun. Most of the information in the table was confirmed by spacecraft and often obtained from photographs and other data transmitted back to the Earth. In the case of Pluto, however, only earthbound observations have been made, and no spacecraft can hope to encounter it until well into the table. Given the planet's small size and great distance, figures for its diameter and rotation period cannot be definitive.

Since Pluto does not appear to be massive enough to account for the perturbations in the orbits of Uranus and Neptune that led to its 1930 discovery, it is quite possible that a tenth and even more distant planet may exist. Once Pluto's own 248-year orbit has been observed for long enough, further discrepancies may give a clue as to any tenth planet's whereabouts. Even so, distance alone would make it very difficult to locate, especially since telescopes powerful enough to find it are normally engaged in galactic study.

THE PLANETS

Mercury is the closest planet to the Sun and hence the fastest-moving. It has no significant atmosphere and a cratered, wrinkled surface very similar to that of Earth's moon.

Venus has much the same physical dimensions as Earth. However, its carbon dioxide atmosphere is 90 times as dense, accounting for a runaway greenhouse effect that makes the Venusian surface, at 475°C, the hottest of all the planets. Radar mapping shows relatively level land with volcanic regions whose sulphurous discharges explain the sulphuric acid rains reported by soft-landing space probes before they succumbed to Venus's fierce climate.

Earth seen from space is easily the most beautiful of the inner planets; it is also, and more objectively, the largest, as well the only home of known life. Living things are the main reason why the Earth is able to retain a substantial proportion of corrosive and highly reactive oxygen in its atmosphere, a state of affairs that contradicts the laws of chemical equilibrium; the oxygen in turn supports the life that constantly regenerates it.

Mars was once considered the likeliest of the other planets to share Earth's cargo of life: seasonal expansion of dark patches strongly suggested vegetation and the planet's apparent icecaps indicated the vital presence of water. But close inspection by spacecraft brought disappointment: chemical reactions account for the seeming vegetation, the icecaps are mainly frozen carbon dioxide and whatever oxygen the planet once possessed is now locked up in the iron-bearing rock that covers its cratered surface and gives it its characteristic red hue.

Jupiter masses almost three times as much as all the other planets together; had it scooped up a little more matter during its formation, it might have evolved into a small companion star for the Sun. The planet is mostly gas, under intense pressure in the lower atmosphere above a core of fiercely compressed hydogen and helium. The upper layers form strikingly-coloured rotating belts, the outward sign of the intense storms created by Jupiter's rapid diurnal rotation. Close approaches by spacecraft have shown an orbiting ring system, and discovered several previously unknown moons: Jupiter has at least 16.

Saturn is structurally similar to Jupiter, rotating fast enough to produce an obvious bulge at its equator. Ever since the invention of the telescope, however, Saturn's rings have been the feature that has attracted most observers. Voyager probes in 1980 and 1981 sent back detailed pictures that showed them to be composed of thousands of separate ringlets, each in turn made up of tiny icy particles, interacting in a complex dance that may serve as a model for the study of galactic and even larger structures.

Uranus was unknown to the ancients: although it is faintly visible to the naked eye, it was not discovered until 1781. Its composition is broadly similar to Jupiter and Saturn, though its distance from the Sun ensures an even colder surface temperature. Observations in 1977 suggested the presence of a faint ring system, amply confirmed when Voyager 2 swung past the planet in 1986.

Neptune is always more than four billion kilometres from Earth, and despite its diameter of almost 50,000 km it can only be seen by telescope. Its 1846 discovery was the result of mathematical predictions by astronomers seeking to explain irregularities in the orbit of Uranus, but until Voyager 2 closed with the planet in 1989 little was known of it. Like Uranus, it has a ring system; Voyager's photographs revealed a total of eight moons.

Pluto is the most mysterious of the solar planets, if only because even the most powerful telescopes can scarcely resolve it from a point of light to a disc. It was discovered as recently as 1930, like Neptune as the result of perturbations in the orbits of the two then outermost planets. Its small size as well as its eccentric and highly tilted orbit have led to suggestions that it is a former satellite of Neptune, somehow liberated from its primary. In 1978 Pluto was found to have a moon of its own, Charon, apparently half the size of Pluto itself.

Mean distance from Sun in million kilometres

Mercury	58.3
Venus	107.7
Earth	149.6
Mars	227.9
Jupiter	777.9
Saturn	1,427.1
Uranus	2,872.3
Neptune	4,502.7
Pluto	5,894.2

THE EARTH: TIME & MOTION

4:	ORBITS OF THE PLANETS
11:	OCEAN CURRENTS
12:	CIRCULATION OF THE AIR

The basic unit of time measurement is the day, one rotation of the Earth on its axis. The subdivision of the day into hours, minutes and seconds is arbitrary and simply for our convenience. Our present calendar is based on the solar year of 365.24 days, the time taken by the Earth to orbit the Sun. As the Earth rotates from west to east, the Sun appears to rise in the east and set in the west. When the Sun is setting in Shanghai, on the opposite side of the world New York is just emerging into sunlight. Noon, when the sun is directly overhead, is coincident at all places on the same meridian, with shadows pointing directly toward the poles.

Calendars based on the movements of the Sun and Moon have been used since ancient times. The Julian Calendar, with its leap year, introduced by Julius Caesar, fixed the average length of the year at 365.25 days, which was about 11 minutes too long (the Earth completes its orbit in 365 days, 5 hours, 48 minutes and 46 seconds of mean solar time). The cumulative error was rectified by the Gregorian Calendar, introduced by Pope Gregory XIII in 1582, when he decreed that the day following October 4 was October 15, and that century years do not count as leap years unless divisible by 400. England did not adopt the reformed calendar until 1752, when it found itself 11 days behind the continent.

Britain imposed the Gregorian Calendar on all its possessions, including the American colonies. All dates preceding September 2 were marked O.S., for Old Style.

EARTH DATA

Maximum distance from the Sun (Aphelion): 152,007,016 km.
Minimum distance from Sun (Perihelion): 147,000,830 km.
Obliquity of the ecliptic: 23° 27' 08".
Length of year - solar tropical (equinox to equinox): 365.24 days
Length of year - sidereal (fixed star to fixed star): 365.26 days
Length of day - mean solar day: 24h, 03m, 56s.
Length of day - mean sidereal day: 23h, 56m, 04s.

Superficial area: 510,000,000 sq. km.
Land surface: 149,000,000 sq. km. (29.2%)
Water surface: 361,000,000 sq. km. (70.8%)
Equatorial circumference: 40,077 km.
Polar circumference: 40,009 km.
Equatorial diameter: 12,756.8 km.
Polar diameter: 12,713.8 km.
Equatorial radius: 6,378.4 km.
Polar radius: 6,356.9 km.
Volume of the Earth: 1,083,230 x 10^6 cu. km.
Mass of the Earth: 5.9 x 10^{21} tonnes

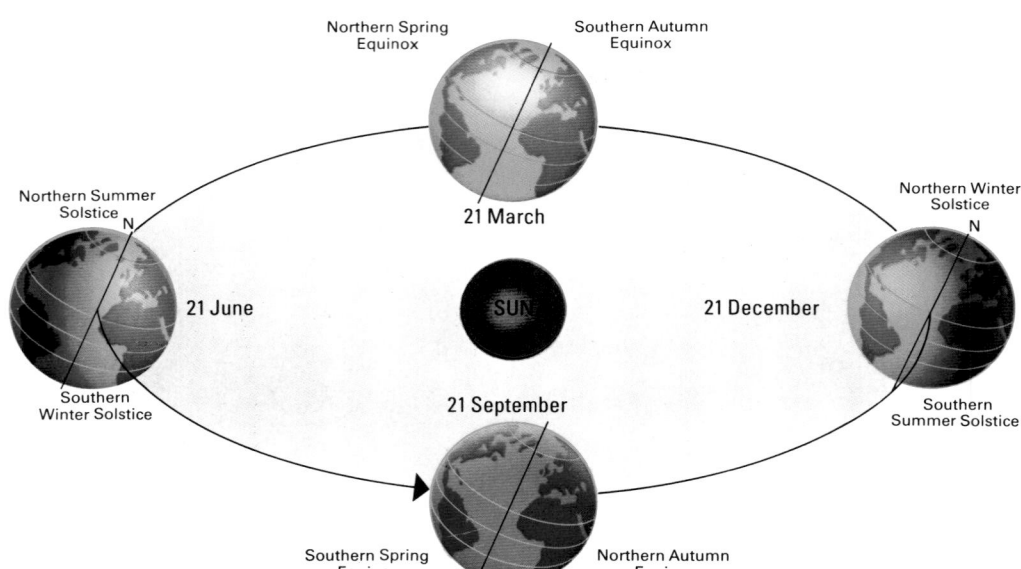

THE SEASONS

The Earth revolves around the Sun once a year in an 'anti-clockwise' direction, tilted at a constant angle 66½°. In June, the northern hemisphere is tilted towards the Sun: as a result it receives more hours of sunshine in a day and therefore has its warmest season, summer. By December, the Earth has rotated halfway round the Sun so that the southern hemisphere that is tilted towards the Sun has its summer; the hemisphere that is tilted away from the Sun has winter. On 21 June the Sun is directly overhead at the Tropic of Cancer (23½° N), and this is midsummer in the northern hemisphere. Midsummer in the southern hemisphere occurs on 21 December, when the Sun is overhead at the Tropic of Capricorn (23½° S).

DAY & NIGHT

The Sun appears to rise in the east, reach its highest point at noon, and then set in the west, to be followed by night. In reality it is not the Sun that is moving but the Earth revolving from west to east.

At the summer solstice in the northern hemisphere (21 June), the Arctic has total daylight and the Antarctic total darkness. The opposite occurs at the winter solstice (21 December). At the equator, the length of day and night are almost equal all year.

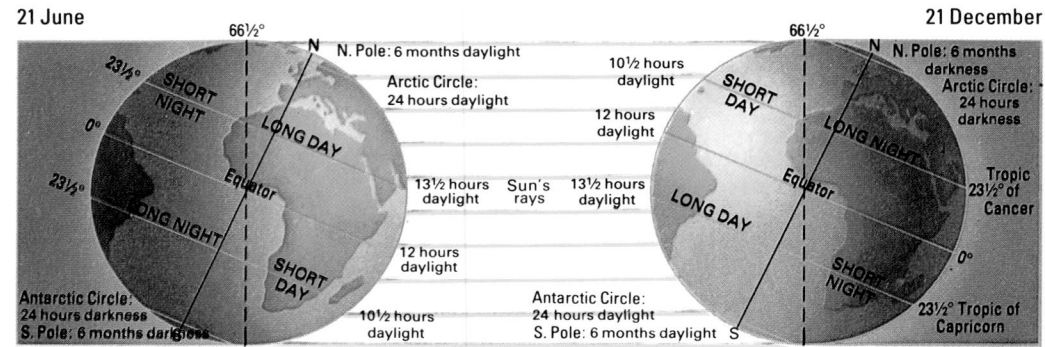

THE SUN'S PATH

The diagrams on the left illustrate the apparent path of the Sun at (A) the equator, (B) in mid-latitude (45°), (C) at the Arctic Circle (66½°) and (D) at the North Pole, where there are six months of continuous daylight and six months of continuous night.

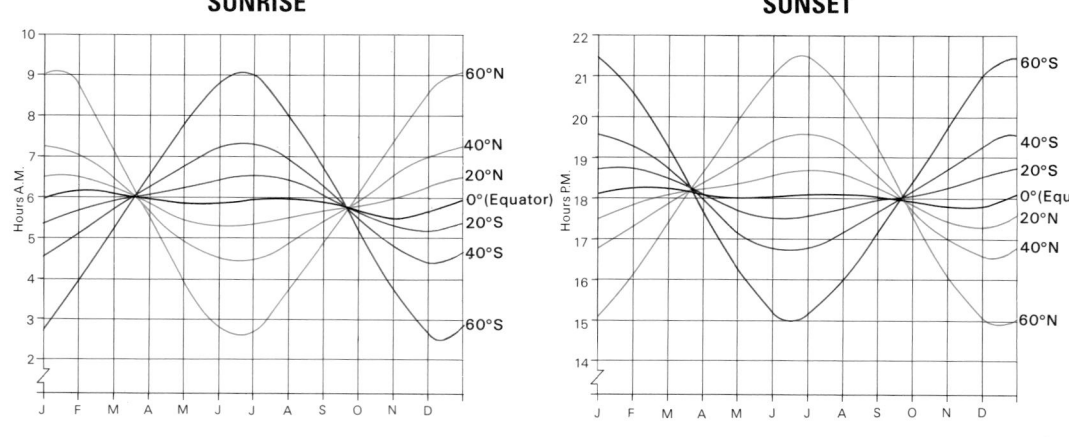

MEASUREMENTS OF TIME

Astronomers distinguish between solar time and sidereal time. Solar time derives from the period taken by the Earth to rotate on its axis: one rotation defines a solar day. But the speed of the Earth along its orbit around the Sun is not constant. The length of day - or 'apparent solar day' - as defined by the apparent successive transits of the Sun - is irregular because the Earth must complete more than one rotation before the Sun returns to the same meridian. The constant sidereal day is defined as the interval between two successive apparent transits of a star, or the first point of Aries, across the same meridian. If the Sun is at the equinox and overhead at a meridian one day, then the next day it will be to the east by approximately 1°. Thus the Sun will not cross the meridian until four minutes after the sidereal noon.

From the diagrams on the right it is possible to discover the time of sunrise or sunset on a given date and for latitudes between 60°N and 60°S.

SUNRISE

SUNSET

PHASES OF THE MOON

New moon	Crescent moon	Half moon, first quarter	Gibbous moon	Full moon	Waning moon	Half moon, third quarter	Old moon

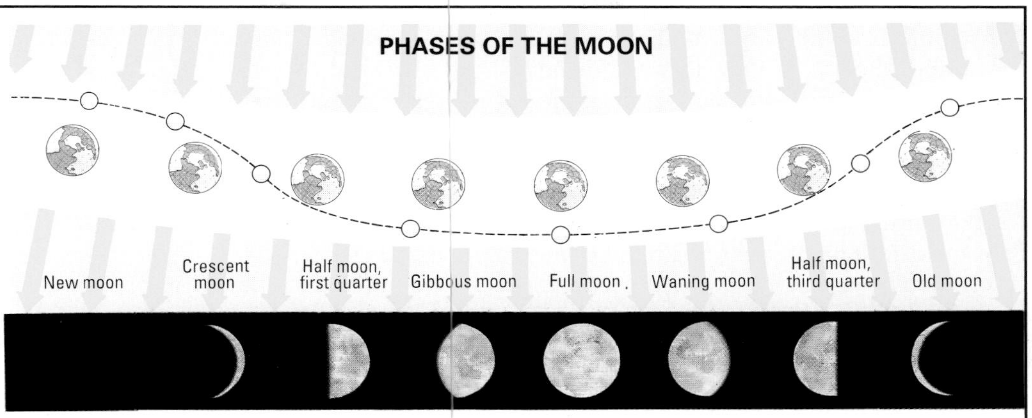

The Moon rotates more slowly than the Earth, making one complete turn on its axis in just over 27 days. Since this corresponds to its period of revolution around the Earth, the Moon always presents the same hemisphere or face to us, and we never see 'the dark side'. The interval between one full Moon and the next (and between new Moons) is about 29½ days - a lunar month. The apparent changes in the shape of the Moon are caused by its changing position in relation to the Earth; like the planets, it produces no light of its own and shines only by reflecting the rays of the Sun.

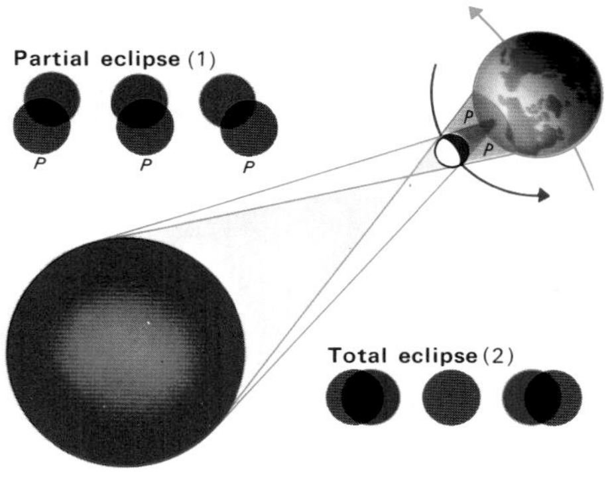

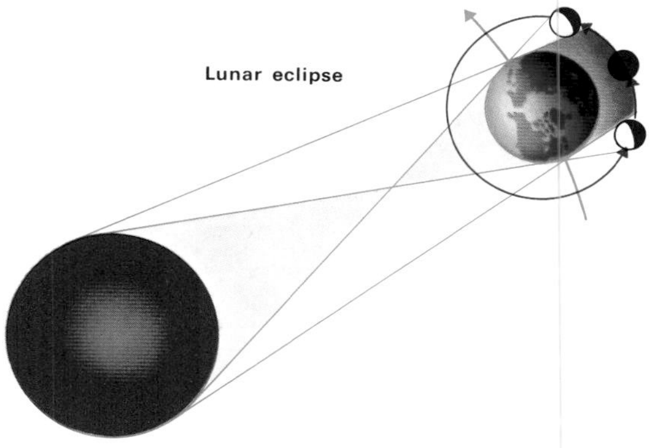

Partial eclipse (1)

Total eclipse (2)

Lunar eclipse

ECLIPSES

When the Moon passes between the Sun and the Earth it causes a partial eclipse of the Sun (1) if the Earth passes through the Moon's outer shadow (P), or a total eclipse (2) if the inner cone shadow crosses the Earth's surface. In a lunar eclipse, the Earth's shadow crosses the Moon and, again, provides either a partial or total eclipse. Eclipses of the Sun and the Moon do not occur every month because of the 5° difference between the plane of the Moon's orbit and the plane in which the Earth moves. In the 1990s only 14 lunar eclipses are possible, for example, seven partial and seven total; each is visible only from certain, and variable, parts of the world. The same period witnesses 13 solar eclipses - six partial (or annular) and seven total.

TIDES

The daily rise and fall of the ocean's tides are the result of the gravitational pull of the Moon and that of the Sun, though the effect of the latter is only 46.6% as strong as that of the Moon. This effect is greatest on the hemisphere facing the Moon and causes a tidal 'bulge'. When lunar and solar forces pull together, with Sun, Earth and Moon in line (near new and full Moons), higher 'spring tides' (and lower low tides) occur; when lunar and solar forces are least coincidental with the Sun and Moon at an angle (near the Moon's first and third quarters), 'neap tides' occur, which have a small tidal range.

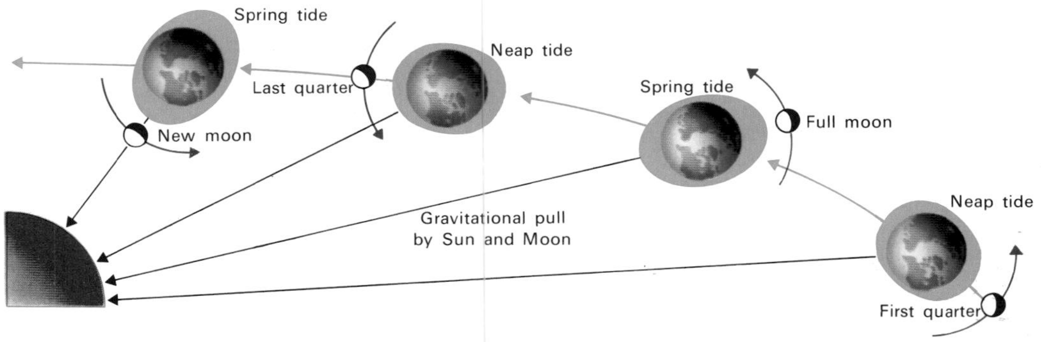

Spring tide · Neap tide · Last quarter · New moon · Spring tide · Full moon · Neap tide · First quarter · Gravitational pull by Sun and Moon

MOON DATA

Distance from Earth: The Moon orbits at a mean distance of 384,199.1 km, at an average speed of 3,683 km/h in relation to the Earth.

Size & mass: The average diameter of the Moon is 3,475.1 km. It is 400 times smaller than the Sun but is about 400 times closer to the Earth, so we see them as the same size. The Moon has a mass of 7.348×10^{19} tonnes, with a density 3.344 times that of water.

Visibility: Only 59% of the Moon's surface is directly visible from Earth. Reflected light takes 1.25 seconds to reach Earth - compared to 8 minutes 27.3 seconds for light from the Sun.

Temperature: With the Sun overhead the temperature on the lunar equator can reach 117.2°C [243°F]. At night it can sink to -162.7°C [-261°F].

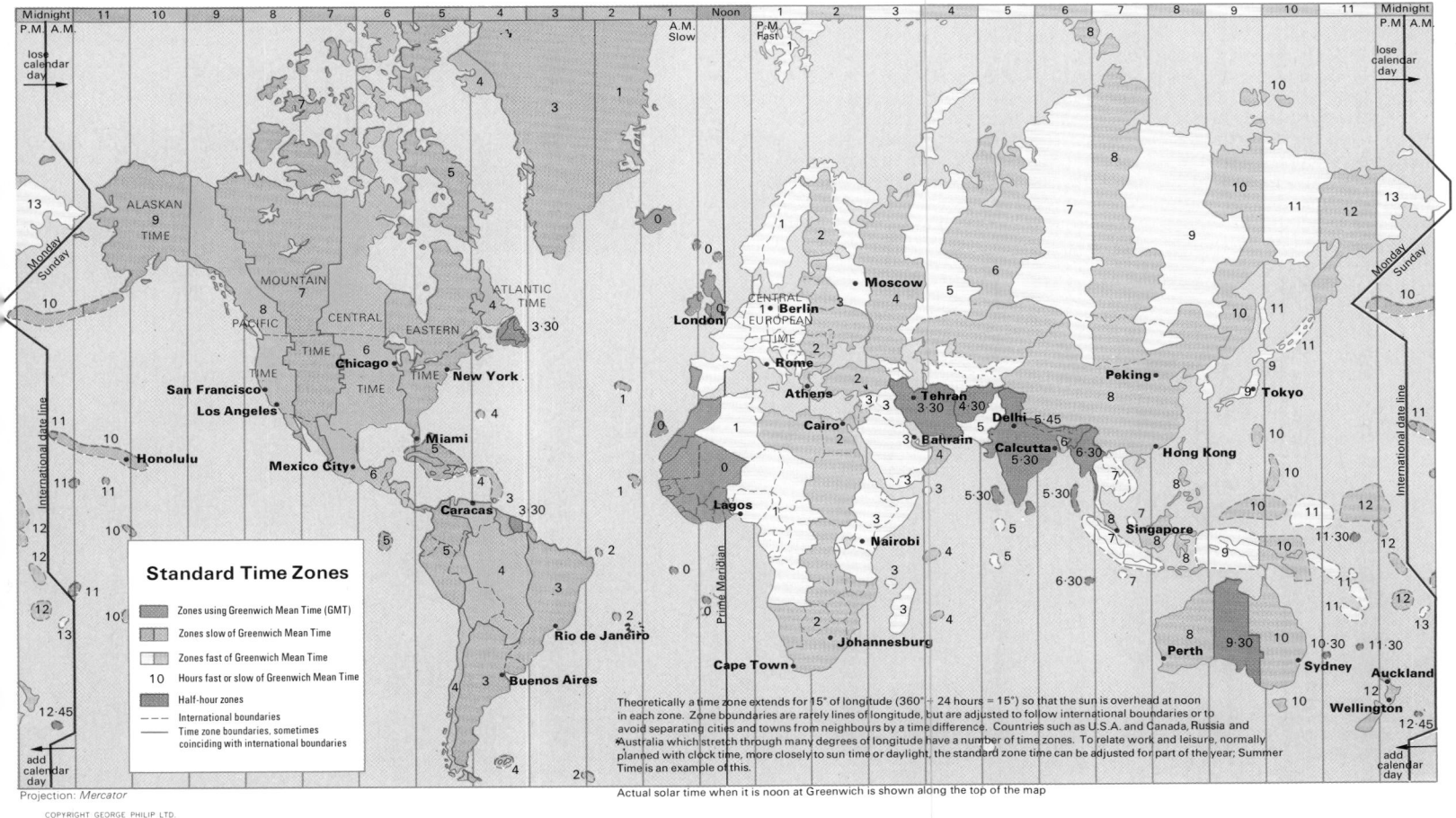

TIME ZONES

The Earth rotates through 360° in 24 hours, and therefore it moves 15° every hour. The world is divided into 24 standard time zones, each centred on lines of longitude at 15° intervals, so that every country falls within one or more agreed zones. The Greenwich meridian, based on the location of the Royal Observatory in London, lies at the centre of the first zone. All places to the west of Greenwich are one hour behind for every 15° of longitude; places to the east are ahead by one hour for every 15°.

When it is 12 noon at the Greenwich meridian, 180° east it is midnight of the same day – while 180° west the day is only just beginning. To overcome this the International Date Line was established, approximately following the 180° meridian. Thus if you travelled eastwards from Japan (140° East) to Samoa (170° West) you would pass from Sunday night into Sunday morning.

Standard Time Zones

- Zones using Greenwich Mean Time (GMT)
- Zones slow of Greenwich Mean Time
- Zones fast of Greenwich Mean Time
- 10 Hours fast or slow of Greenwich Mean Time
- Half-hour zones
- International boundaries
- Time zone boundaries, sometimes coinciding with international boundaries

Theoretically a time zone extends for 15° of longitude (360° ÷ 24 hours = 15°) so that the sun is overhead at noon in each zone. Zone boundaries are rarely lines of longitude, but are adjusted to follow international boundaries or to avoid separating cities and towns from neighbours by a time difference. Countries such as U.S.A. and Canada, Russia and Australia which stretch through many degrees of longitude have a number of time zones. To relate work and leisure, normally planned with clock time, more closely to sun time or daylight, the standard zone time can be adjusted for part of the year; Summer Time is an example of this.

Actual solar time when it is noon at Greenwich is shown along the top of the map

Projection: *Mercator*

COPYRIGHT GEORGE PHILIP LTD.

THE EARTH: GEOLOGY

18: THE SPREADING EARTH
    TYPES OF ROCK
    MOUNTAIN BUILDING

19: MOULDING THE LAND

21: THE CARBON CYCLE

34: MINERALS

The origin of the Earth is still open to conjecture, although the most widely accepted theory is that it was formed from a solar cloud consisting mainly of hydrogen 4,600 million years ago. The cloud condensed, forming the planets. The lighter elements floated to the surface of the Earth, where they cooled to form a crust; the inner material remained hot and molten. The first rocks were formed over 3,500 million years ago, but the Earth's surface has since been constantly altered.

The crust consists of a brittle, low-density material varying from 5 to 50 kilometres deep beneath the continents, consisting predominately of silica and aluminum: hence its name, 'sial'. Below the sial is a basaltic layer known as 'sima', comprising mainly silica and magnesium. The crust accounts for only 1.5 per cent of the Earth's volume.

Immediately below the crust the mantle begins, with a distinct change in density and chemical properties. The rock is rich in iron and magnesium silicates, and temperatures reach 1,600°C. The rigid upper mantle extends down to a depth of about 1,000 kilometres, below which is a more viscous lower mantle about 1,900 kilometres thick.

The outer core, measuring about 2,310 kilometres thick, consists of molten iron and nickel at 2,100°C to 5,000°C, possibly separated from the less dense mantle by an oxidized shell. About 5,000 kilometres below the surface is a liquid transition zone, below which is the solid inner core, a sphere of about 2,700 kilometres diameter where rock is three times as dense as in the crust. The temperature at the centre of the Earth is probably about 5,000°C.

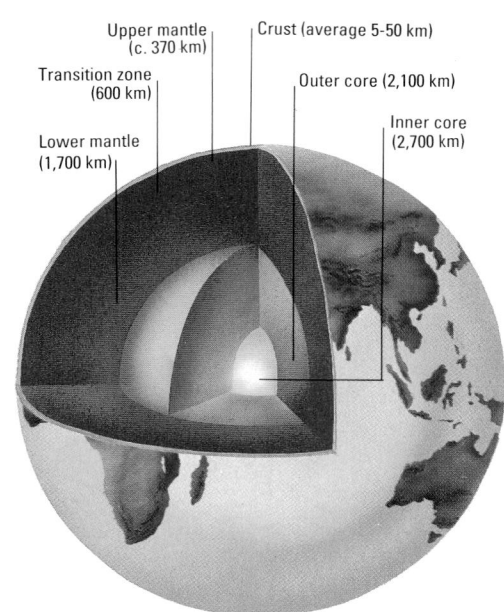

Upper mantle (c. 370 km)
Crust (average 5-50 km)
Transition zone (600 km)
Outer core (2,100 km)
Lower mantle (1,700 km)
Inner core (2,700 km)

The complementary, almost jigsaw-puzzle fit of the Atlantic coasts led to Alfred Wegener's proposition of continental drift in Germany (1915). His theory suggested that an ancient super-continent, which he called Pangaea, incorporating all the Earth's land masses, gradually split up to form the continents we know today. By 180 million years ago Pangaea had divided into two major groups and the southern part, Gondwanaland, had itself begun to break up with India and Antarctica-Australia becoming isolated. By 135 million years ago the widening of the splits in the North Atlantic and Indian Oceans persisted, a South Atlantic gap had appeared and India continued to move 'north' towards Asia. By 65 million years ago South America had completely split from Africa.
To form today's pattern India 'collided' with Asia (crumpling up sediments to form the Himalayas); South America rotated and moved west to connect with North America; Australia separated from Antarctica and moved north; and the familiar gap developed between Greenland and Europe.

CONTINENTAL DRIFT

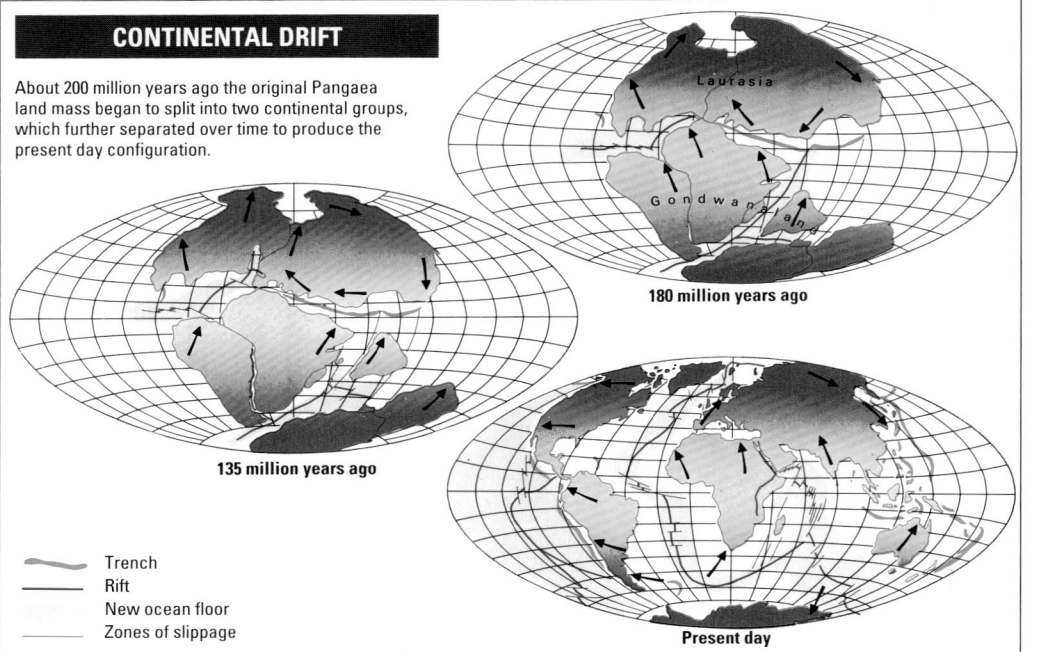

About 200 million years ago the original Pangaea land mass began to split into two continental groups, which further separated over time to produce the present day configuration.

Laurasia

Gondwanaland

180 million years ago

135 million years ago

Present day

～～ Trench
── Rift
── New ocean floor
── Zones of slippage

PLATE TECTONICS

The original debate about the drift theory of Wegener and others formed a long prelude to a more radical idea: plate tectonics. The discovery that the continents are carried along on the top of slowly-moving crustal plates (which float on heavier liquid material – the lower mantle – much as icebergs do on water) provided the mechanism for the drift theories to work. The plates converge and diverge along margins marked by seismic and volcanic activity. Plates diverge from mid-ocean ridges where molten lava pushes up and forces the plates apart at a rate of up to 40 mm a year; converging plates form either a trench (where the oceanic plates sink below the lighter continental rock) or mountain ranges (where two continents collide).

The debate about plate tectonics is not over, however. In addition to abiding questions such as what force actually moves the plates (massive convection currents in the Earth's interior is the most popular explanation), and why many volcanoes and earthquakes occur in mid-plate (such as Hawaii and central China), evidence began to emerge in the early 1990s that, with more sophisticated equipment and models, the whole theory might be in doubt.

EARTHQUAKES

Earthquake magnitude is usually rated according to either the Richter or the Modified Mercalli scale, both devised by seismologists in the 1930s. The Richter scale measures absolute earthquake power with mathematical precision: each step upwards represents a ten-fold increase in shockwave amplitude. Theoretically, there is no upper limit, but the largest earthquakes measured have been rated at between 8.8 and 8.9. The 12–point Mercalli scale, based on observed effects, is often more meaningful, ranging from I (earthquakes noticed only by seismographs) to XII (total destruction); intermediate points include V (people awakened at night; unstable objects overturned), VII (collapse of ordinary buildings; chimneys and monuments fall); and IX (conspicuous cracks in ground; serious damage to reservoirs).

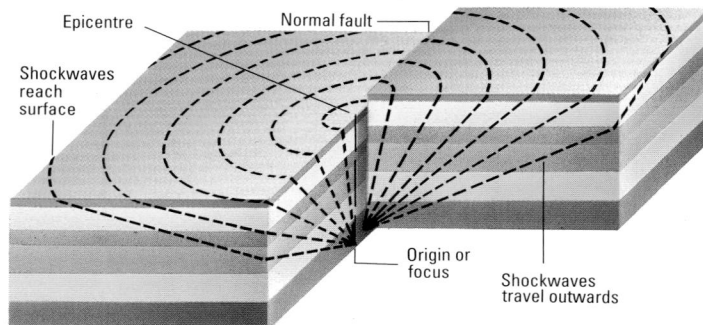

Epicentre
Normal fault
Shockwaves reach surface
Origin or focus
Shockwaves travel outwards

NOTABLE EARTHQUAKES SINCE 1900

Year	Location	Mag.	Deaths
1906	San Francisco, USA	8.3	503
1906	Valparaiso, Chile	8.6	22,000
1908	Messina, Italy	7.5	83,000
1915	Avezzano, Italy	7.5	30,000
1920	Gansu, China	8.6	180,000
1923	Yokohama, Japan	8.3	143,000
1927	Nan Shan, China	8.3	200,000
1932	Gansu, China	7.6	70,000
1934	Bihar, India/Nepal	8.4	10,700
1935	Quetta, India*	7.5	60,000
1939	Chillan, Chile	8.3	28,000
1939	Erzincan, Turkey	7.9	30,000
1960	Agadir, Morocco	5.8	12,000
1962	Khorasan, Iran	7.1	12,230
1963	Skopje, Yugoslavia	6.0	1,000
1964	Anchorage, Alaska	8.4	131
1968	N. E. Iran	7.4	12,000
1970	N. Peru	7.7	66,794
1972	Managua, Nicaragua	6.2	5,000
1974	N. Pakistan	6.3	5,200
1976	Guatemala	7.5	22,778
1976	Tangshan, China	8.2	650,000
1978	Tabas, Iran	7.7	25,000
1980	El Asnam, Algeria	7.3	20,000
1980	S. Italy	7.2	4,800
1985	Mexico City, Mexico	8.1	4,200
1988	N.W. Armenia	6.8	55,000
1990	N. Iran	7.7	36,000

The highest magnitude recorded on the Richter scale is 8.9, in Japan on 2 March 1933 (2,990 deaths). The most devastating quake ever was at Shaanxi (Shensi), central China, on 24 January 1566, when an estimated 830,000 people were killed.

* now Pakistan

DISTRIBUTION

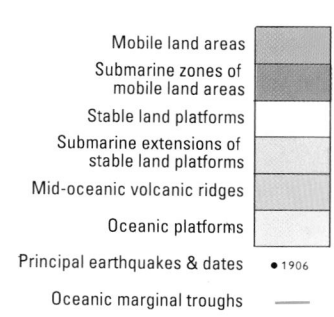

Mobile land areas
Submarine zones of mobile land areas
Stable land platforms
Submarine extensions of stable land platforms
Mid-oceanic volcanic ridges
Oceanic platforms
Principal earthquakes & dates • 1906
Oceanic marginal troughs ──

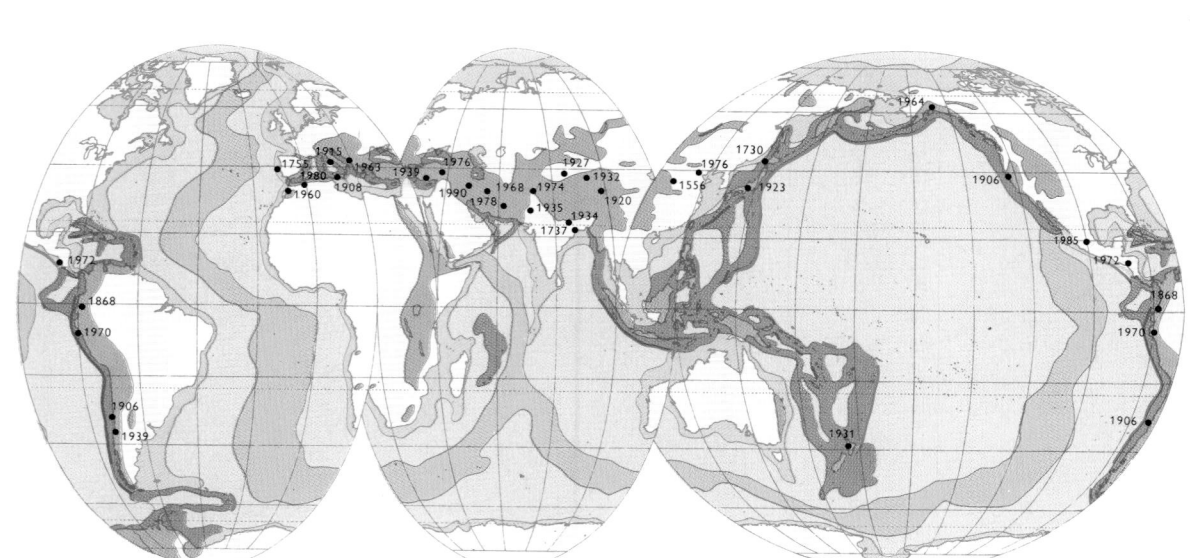

Earthquakes are a series of rapid vibrations originating from the the slipping or faulting of parts of the Earth's crust when stresses within build to breaking point, and usually occur at depths between 8 and 30 kilometres.

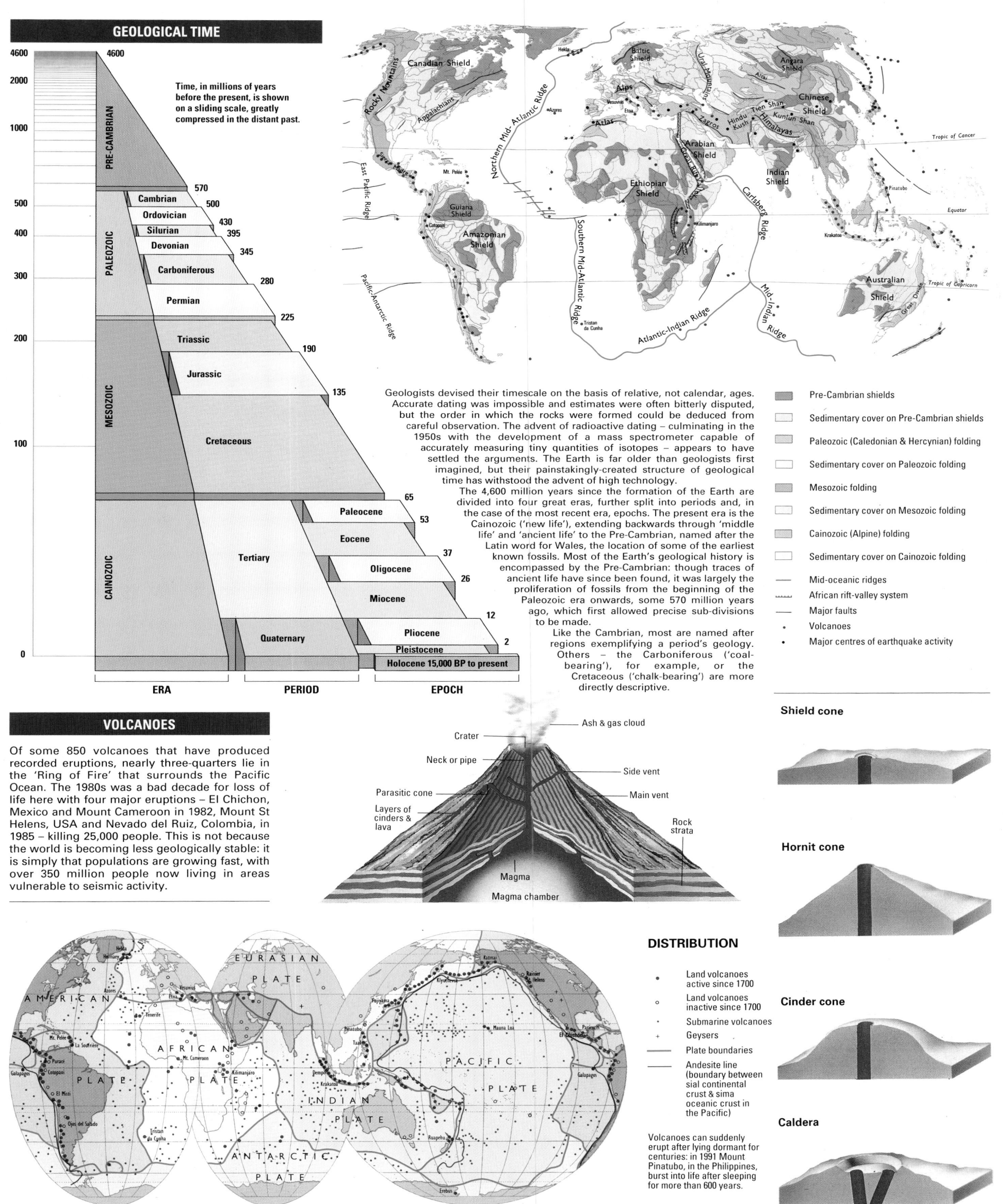

GEOLOGICAL TIME

4600
4600

Time, in millions of years before the present, is shown on a sliding scale, greatly compressed in the distant past.

PRE-CAMBRIAN		
PALEOZOIC	Cambrian	570
	Ordovician	500
	Silurian	430
	Devonian	395
	Carboniferous	345
	Permian	280
MESOZOIC	Triassic	225
	Jurassic	190
	Cretaceous	135
CAINOZOIC	Tertiary	Paleocene 65
		Eocene 53
		Oligocene 37
		Miocene 26
	Quaternary	Pliocene 12
		Pleistocene 2
		Holocene 15,000 BP to present

ERA **PERIOD** **EPOCH**

Geologists devised their timescale on the basis of relative, not calendar, ages. Accurate dating was impossible and estimates were often bitterly disputed, but the order in which the rocks were formed could be deduced from careful observation. The advent of radioactive dating – culminating in the 1950s with the development of a mass spectrometer capable of accurately measuring tiny quantities of isotopes – appears to have settled the arguments. The Earth is far older than geologists first imagined, but their painstakingly-created structure of geological time has withstood the advent of high technology.

The 4,600 million years since the formation of the Earth are divided into four great eras, further split into periods and, in the case of the most recent era, epochs. The present era is the Cainozoic ('new life'), extending backwards through 'middle life' and 'ancient life' to the Pre-Cambrian, named after the Latin word for Wales, the location of some of the earliest known fossils. Most of the Earth's geological history is encompassed by the Pre-Cambrian: though traces of ancient life have since been found, it was largely the proliferation of fossils from the beginning of the Paleozoic era onwards, some 570 million years ago, which first allowed precise sub-divisions to be made.

Like the Cambrian, most are named after regions exemplifying a period's geology. Others – the Carboniferous ('coal-bearing'), for example, or the Cretaceous ('chalk-bearing') are more directly descriptive.

- ▨ Pre-Cambrian shields
- ▢ Sedimentary cover on Pre-Cambrian shields
- ▨ Paleozoic (Caledonian & Hercynian) folding
- ▢ Sedimentary cover on Paleozoic folding
- ▨ Mesozoic folding
- ▢ Sedimentary cover on Mesozoic folding
- ▨ Cainozoic (Alpine) folding
- ▢ Sedimentary cover on Cainozoic folding
- — Mid-oceanic ridges
- ⌇ African rift-valley system
- — Major faults
- • Volcanoes
- ● Major centres of earthquake activity

VOLCANOES

Of some 850 volcanoes that have produced recorded eruptions, nearly three-quarters lie in the 'Ring of Fire' that surrounds the Pacific Ocean. The 1980s was a bad decade for loss of life here with four major eruptions – El Chichon, Mexico and Mount Cameroon in 1982, Mount St Helens, USA and Nevado del Ruiz, Colombia, in 1985 – killing 25,000 people. This is not because the world is becoming less geologically stable: it is simply that populations are growing fast, with over 350 million people now living in areas vulnerable to seismic activity.

Crater — Ash & gas cloud
Neck or pipe
Parasitic cone — Side vent
— Main vent
Layers of cinders & lava
Rock strata
Magma
Magma chamber

DISTRIBUTION

- • Land volcanoes active since 1700
- ○ Land volcanoes inactive since 1700
- + Submarine volcanoes
- + Geysers
- — Plate boundaries
- — Andesite line (boundary between sial continental crust & sima oceanic crust in the Pacific)

Volcanoes can suddenly erupt after lying dormant for centuries: in 1991 Mount Pinatubo, in the Philippines, burst into life after sleeping for more than 600 years.

Shield cone

Hornit cone

Cinder cone

Caldera

THE EARTH: OCEANS

7:	TIDES
16:	HYDROLOGICAL CYCLE WATER DISTRIBUTION
17:	WATERSHEDS
18:	THE SPREADING EARTH
39:	SHIPPING
47:	WATER POLLUTION

The Earth is a misnamed planet: almost 71% of its total surface area – 360,059,000 square kilometres – is covered by its oceans and seas. This great cloak of liquid water gives the planet its characteristic blue appearance from space, and is one of two obvious differences between the Earth and its near-neighbours in space, Mars and Venus. The other difference is the presence of life, and the two are closely linked.

In a strict geographical sense, the Earth has only three oceans: the Atlantic, the Pacific and the Indian. Sub-divided vertically instead of horizontally, however, there are many more. The most active is the sunlit upper layer, home of most sea-life and the vital interface between air and water. In this surface zone, huge energies are exchanged between the oceans and the atmosphere above; it is also a kind of membrane through which the ocean breathes, absorbing enormous quantities of carbon dioxide and partially exchanging them for oxygen, largely through the phytoplankton, tiny plants that photosynthesize solar energy and provide the food base for all other marine life.

As depth increases, light and colour fade away, the longer wavelengths dying first. At 50 metres, the ocean is a world of green and blue and violet; at 100 metres, only blue remains; by 200 metres, there is only a dim twilight. The temperature falls away with the light until some time before 1,000 metres – the precise depth varies – there occurs a temperature change almost as abrupt as the transition between air and water far above.

Below this thermocline, at a near-stable 3°C, the waters are forever unmoved by the winds of the upper world and are stirred only by the slow action of deep ocean currents. The pressure is crushing, touching 1,000 atmospheres in the deepest trenches: a force of one tonne bearing down on every square centimetre.

Yet even here the oceans support life, and not only the handful of strange, deep-sea creatures that find a living in the near-empty abyss. The deep ocean serves as a gigantic storehouse both for heat and for assorted atmospheric chemicals, regulating and balancing the proportions of various trace compounds and elements and ensuring a large measure of stability for both the climate and the ecology that depend on it.

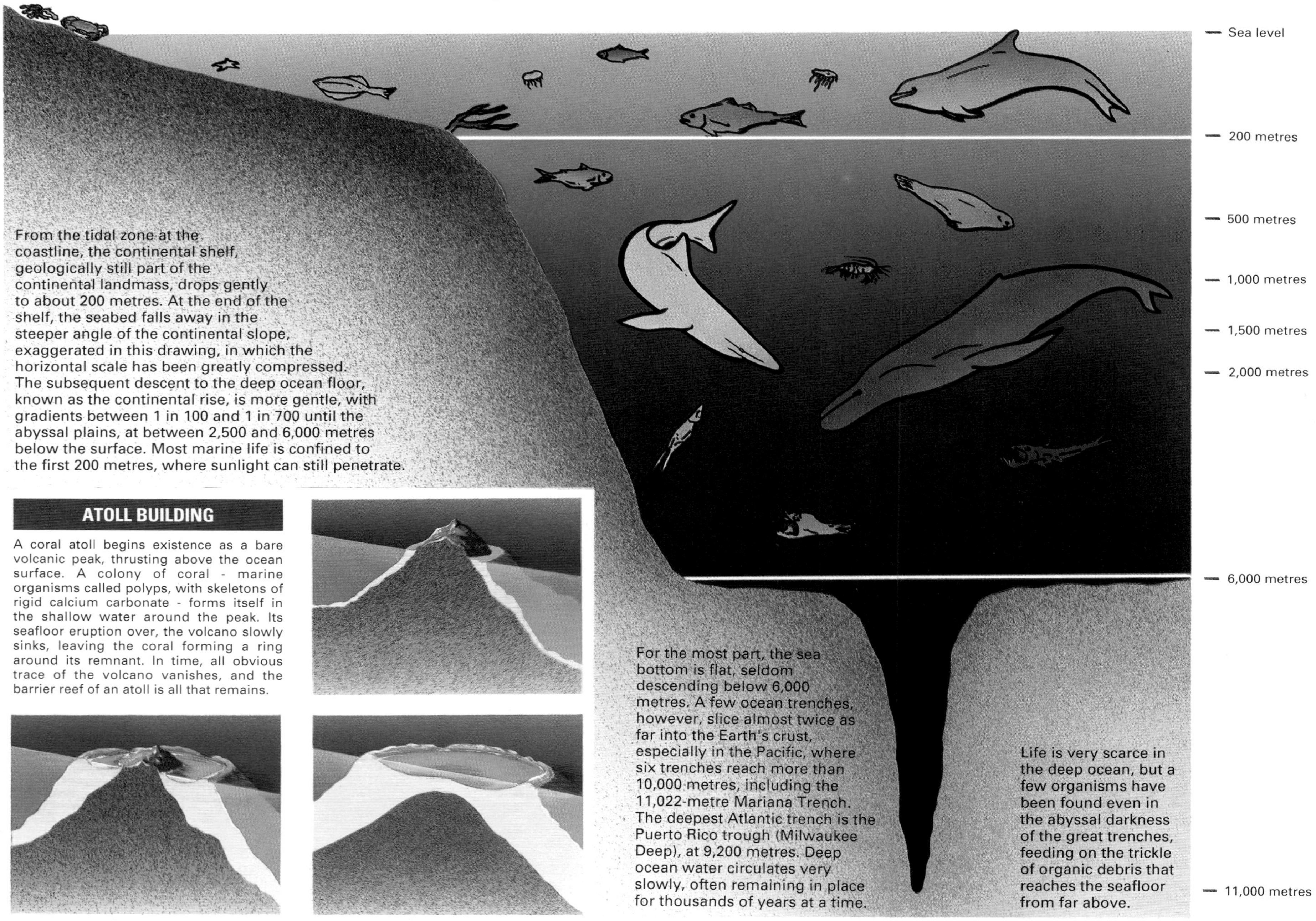

From the tidal zone at the coastline, the continental shelf, geologically still part of the continental landmass, drops gently to about 200 metres. At the end of the shelf, the seabed falls away in the steeper angle of the continental slope, exaggerated in this drawing, in which the horizontal scale has been greatly compressed. The subsequent descent to the deep ocean floor, known as the continental rise, is more gentle, with gradients between 1 in 100 and 1 in 700 until the abyssal plains, at between 2,500 and 6,000 metres below the surface. Most marine life is confined to the first 200 metres, where sunlight can still penetrate.

— Sea level
— 200 metres
— 500 metres
— 1,000 metres
— 1,500 metres
— 2,000 metres
— 6,000 metres
— 11,000 metres

ATOLL BUILDING

A coral atoll begins existence as a bare volcanic peak, thrusting above the ocean surface. A colony of coral - marine organisms called polyps, with skeletons of rigid calcium carbonate - forms itself in the shallow water around the peak. Its seafloor eruption over, the volcano slowly sinks, leaving the coral forming a ring around its remnant. In time, all obvious trace of the volcano vanishes, and the barrier reef of an atoll is all that remains.

For the most part, the sea bottom is flat, seldom descending below 6,000 metres. A few ocean trenches, however, slice almost twice as far into the Earth's crust, especially in the Pacific, where six trenches reach more than 10,000 metres, including the 11,022-metre Mariana Trench. The deepest Atlantic trench is the Puerto Rico trough (Milwaukee Deep), at 9,200 metres. Deep ocean water circulates very slowly, often remaining in place for thousands of years at a time.

Life is very scarce in the deep ocean, but a few organisms have been found even in the abyssal darkness of the great trenches, feeding on the trickle of organic debris that reaches the seafloor from far above.

PROFILE OF AN OCEAN

The deep ocean floor is no more uniform than the surface of the continents, although it was not until the development of effective sonar equipment that it was possible to examine submarine contours in detail. The Atlantic (right) and the Pacific show similar patterns. Off-shore comes the continental shelf, sliding downwards to the continental slope and the steeper continental rise, after which the seabed rolls onward into the abyssal plains. In the wide Pacific, these are interrupted by gently-rising abyssal hills; in both oceans, the plains extend all the way to the mid-oceanic ridges, where the upwelling of new crustal material is constantly forcing the oceans wider. Volcanic activity is responsible for the formation of seamounts and tablemounts or guyots, their flat-topped equivalents. In this cross-section, only the Azores are high enough to break the surface and become islands.

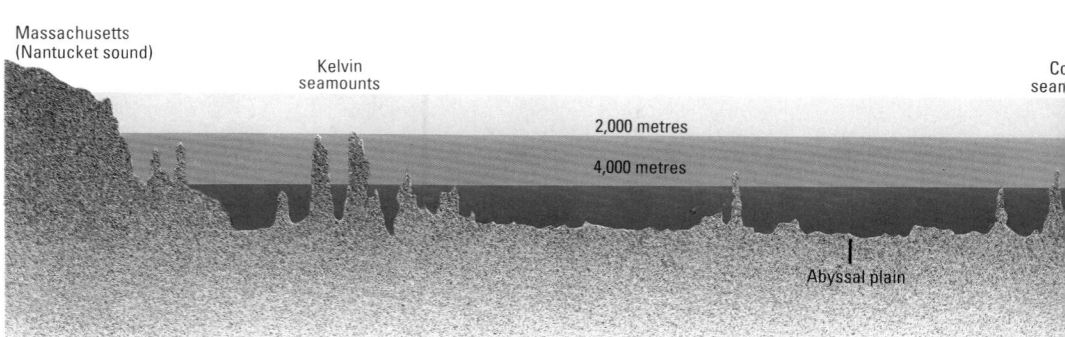

Massachusetts (Nantucket sound)

Kelvin seamounts

Co seam

2,000 metres

4,000 metres

Abyssal plain

OCEAN CURRENTS

NORTH

Arctic

Atlantic Ocean

SOUTH

Antarctic

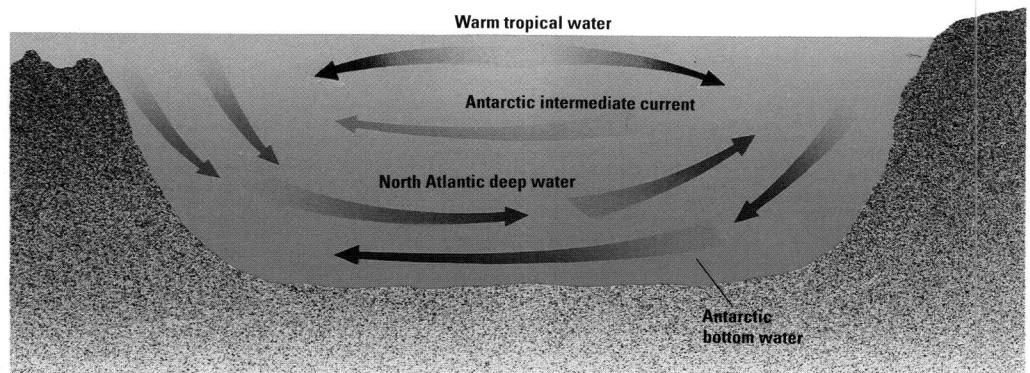

Warm tropical water

Antarctic intermediate current

North Atlantic deep water

Antarctic bottom water

Moving immense quantities of energy as well as billions of tonnes of water every hour, the ocean currents are a vital part of the great heat engine that drives the Earth's climate. They themselves are produced by a twofold mechanism. At the surface, winds push huge masses of water before them; in the deep ocean, below an abrupt temperature gradient that separates the churning surface waters from the still depths, density variations cause slow vertical movements.

The pattern of circulation of the great surface currents is determined by the displacement known as the Coriolis effect. As the Earth turns beneath a moving object - whether it is a tennis ball or a vast mass of water - it appears to be deflected to one side. The deflection is most obvious near the equator, where the Earth's surface is spinning eastward at 1700 km/h; currents moving poleward are curved clockwise in the northern hemisphere and anti-clockwise in the southern.

The result is a system of spinning circles known as gyres. The Coriolis effect piles up water on the left of each gyre, creating a narrow, fast-moving stream that is matched by a slower, broader returning current on the right. North and south of the equator, the fastest currents are located in the west and in the east respectively. In each case, warm water moves from the equator and cold water returns to it. Cold currents often bring an upwelling of nutrients with them, supporting the world's most economically important fisheries.

Depending on the prevailing winds, some currents on or near the equator may reverse their direction in the course of the year - a seasonal variation on which Asian monsoon rains depend, and whose occasional failure can bring disaster to millions of people.

CURRENTS & TEMPERATURES

(Northern Hemisphere: winter)

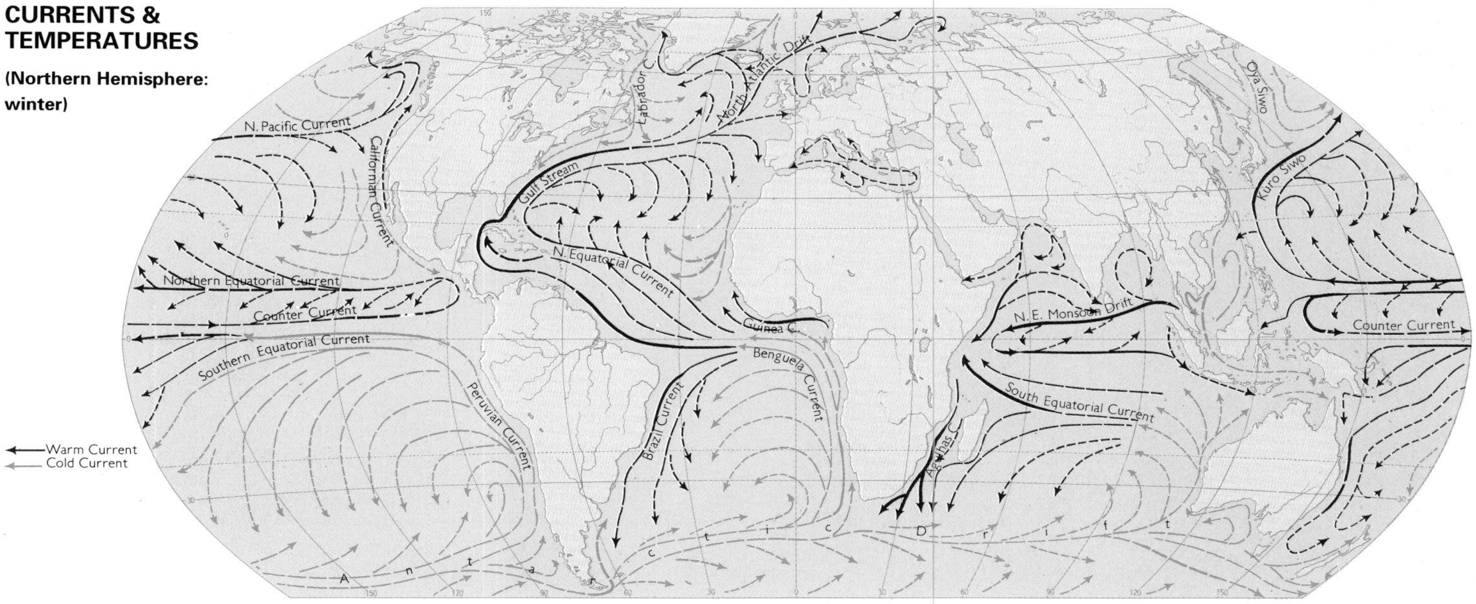

→ Warm Current
→ Cold Current

CURRENTS & TEMPERATURES

(Northern Hemisphere: summer)

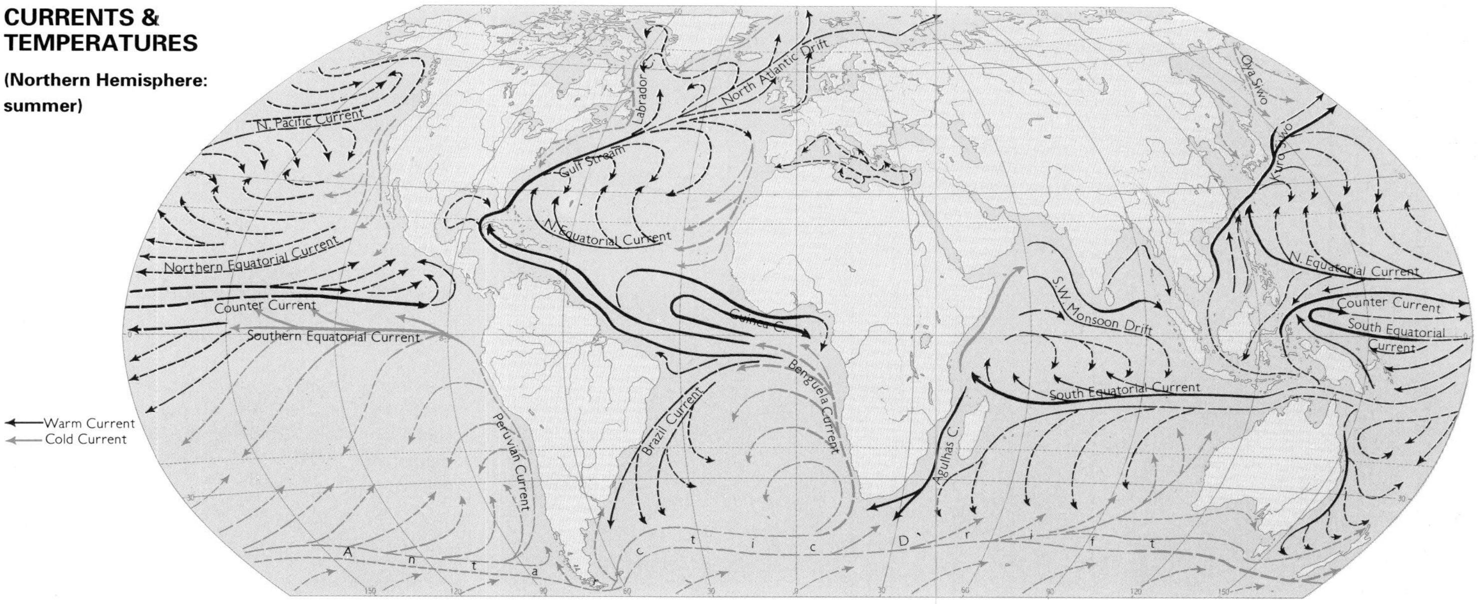

→ Warm Current
→ Cold Current

SEAWATER

The chemical composition of the sea, in grams per tonne of seawater, excluding the elements of water itself

Chlorine	19400
Sodium	10800
Magnesium	1290
Sulphur	904
Calcium	411
Potassium	392
Bromine	67
Strontium	8.1
Boron	4.5
Fluorine	1.3
Lithium	0.17
Rubidium	0.12
Phosphorus	0.09
Iodine	0.06
Barium	0.02
Arsenic	0.003
Cesium	0.0003

Seawater also contains virtually every other element, although the quantities involved are too small for reliable measurement. In natural conditions, its composition is broadly consistent across the world's seas and oceans; but especially in coastal areas, variations, sometimes substantial, may be caused by the presence of industrial waste and sewage sludge.

Mid-Atlantic ridge — Atlantic seamount — Azores — Josephine seamounts — Gettysburg seamounts — Gibraltar

THE EARTH: ATMOSPHERE

11:	OCEAN CURRENTS
15:	BEAUFORT WIND SCALE
21:	SOLAR ENERGY GREENHOUSE EFFECT
46:	GREENHOUSE POWER
47:	ACID RAIN

Extending from the surface far into space, the atmosphere is a meteor shield, a radiation deflector, a thermal blanket and a source of chemical energy for the Earth's diverse inhabitants. Five-sixths of its mass is found in the first 15 kilometres, the troposphere, no thicker in relative terms than the skin of an onion. Clouds, cyclonic winds, precipitation and virtually all the phenomena we call weather occur in this narrow layer. Above, a thin layer of ozone blocks ultra-violet radiation. Beyond 100 kilometres, atmospheric density is lower than most laboratory vacuums, yet these tenuous outer reaches, composed largely of hydrogen and helium, trap cosmic debris and incoming high-energy particles alike.

CIRCULATION OF THE AIR

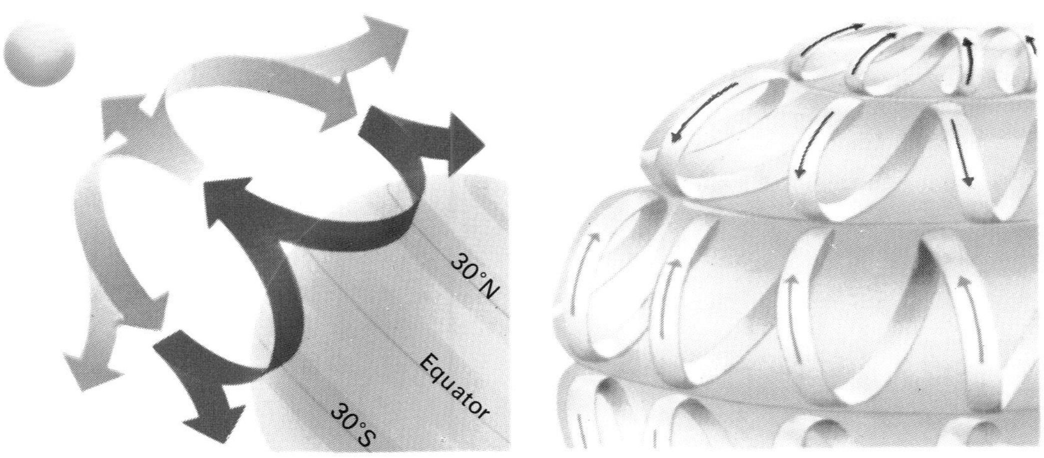

30°N

Equator

30°S

STRUCTURE OF ATMOSPHERE

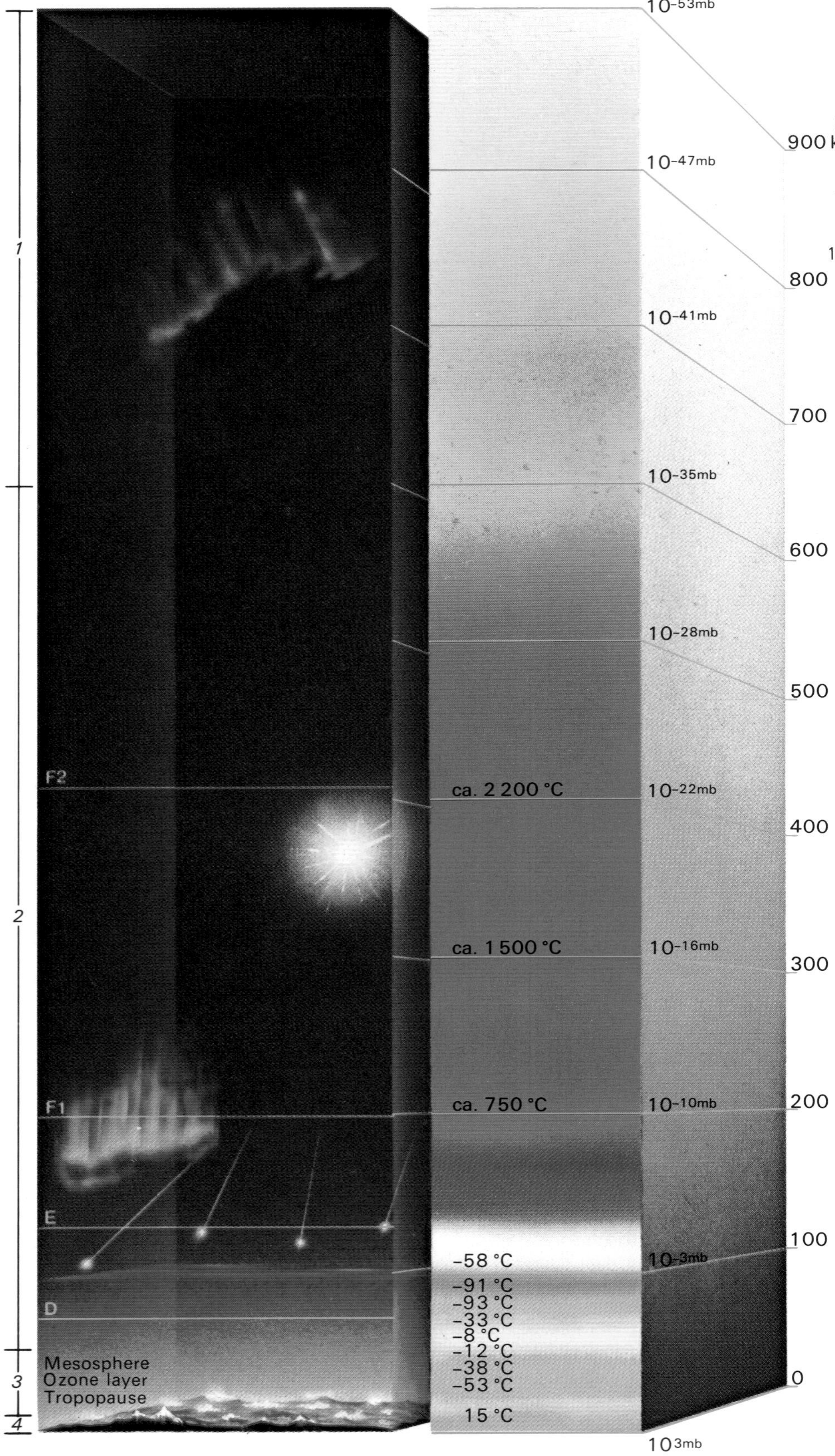

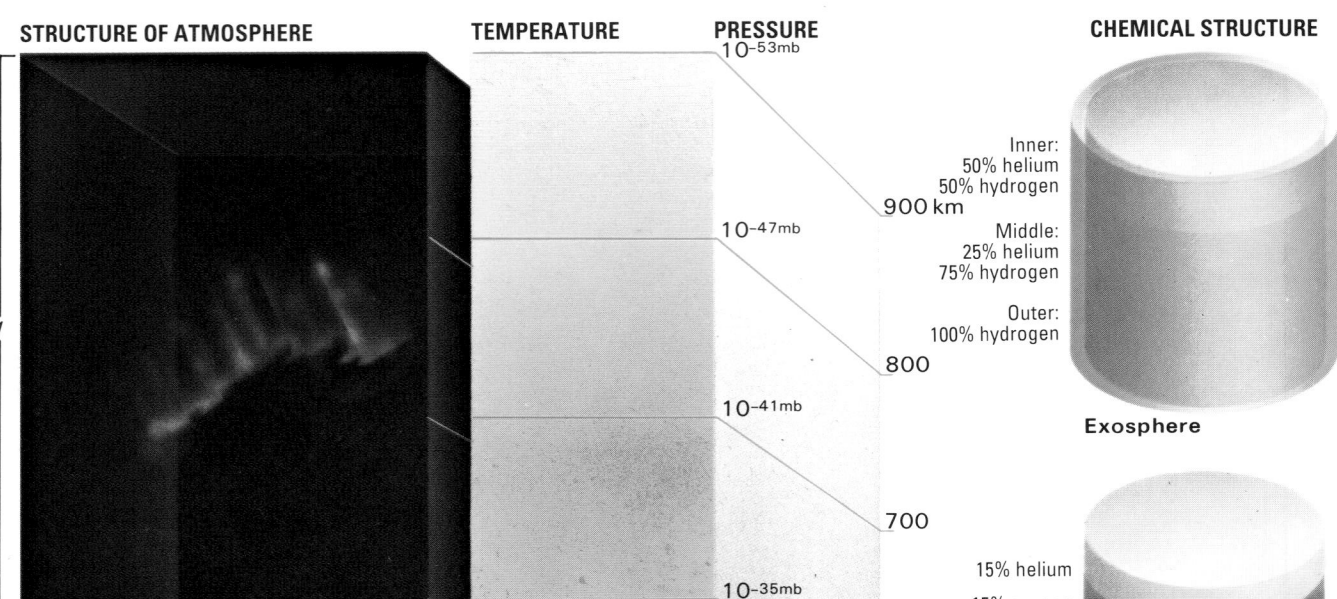

F2

F1

E

D

Mesosphere
Ozone layer
Troposphere

1

2

3

4

TEMPERATURE

ca. 2 200 °C

ca. 1 500 °C

ca. 750 °C

−58 °C
−91 °C
−93 °C
−33 °C
−8 °C
−12 °C
−38 °C
−53 °C

15 °C

PRESSURE

10^{-53}mb

10^{-47}mb

10^{-41}mb

10^{-35}mb

10^{-28}mb

10^{-22}mb

10^{-16}mb

10^{-10}mb

10^{-3}mb

10^{3}mb

900 km

800

700

600

500

400

300

200

100

0

CHEMICAL STRUCTURE

Inner:
50% helium
50% hydrogen

Middle:
25% helium
75% hydrogen

Outer:
100% hydrogen

Exosphere

15% helium

15% oxygen & atomic oxygen

70% nitrogen

Ionosphere

1% ozone
1% argon

18% oxygen

80% nitrogen

Stratosphere

1% argon

21% oxygen

78% nitrogen

Troposphere

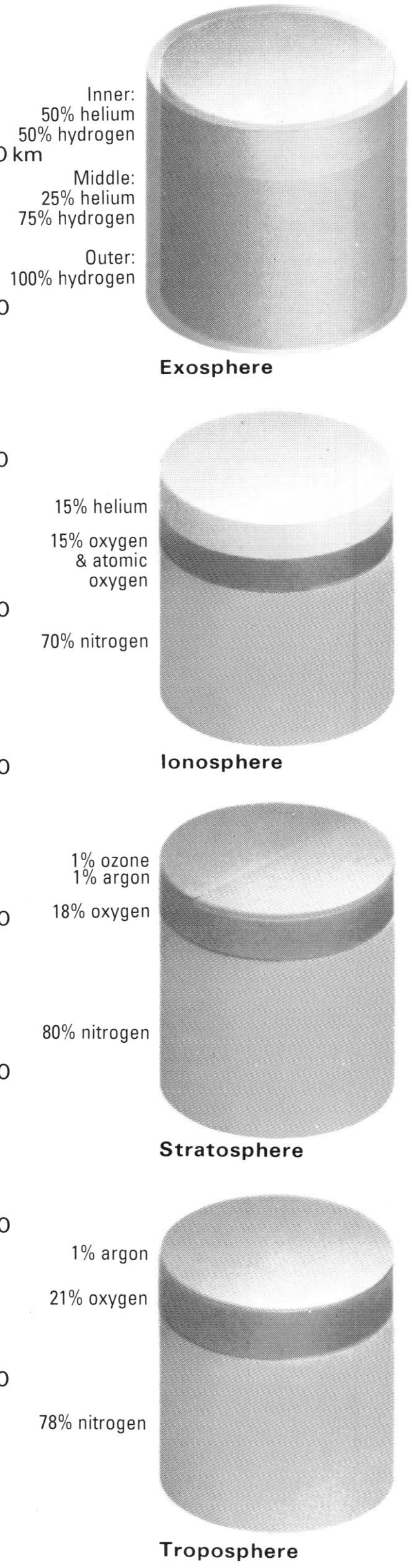

Exosphere
The atmosphere's upper layer has no clear outer boundary, merging imperceptibly with interplanetary space. Its lower boundary, at an altitude of approximately 600 kilometres, is almost equally vague. The exosphere is mainly composed of hydrogen and helium in changing proportions, with a small quantity of atomic oxygen up to 600 kilometres. Helium vanishes with increasing altitude, and above 2,400 kilometres the exosphere is almost entirely hydrogen.

Ionosphere
Gas molecules in the ionosphere, mainly helium, oxygen and nitrogen, are electrically charged - ionized - by the Sun's radiation. Within the ionosphere's range of 50 to 600 kilometres in altitude, they group themselves into four layers, known conventionally as D, E, F1 and F2, all of which can reflect radio waves of differing frequencies. The high energy of ionospheric gas gives it a notional temperature of more than 2,000°C, although its density is negligible. The auroras - *aurora borealis* and its southern counterpart, *aurora australis* - occur in the ionosphere when charged particles from the Sun interact with the Earth's magnetic fields, at their strongest near the poles.

Stratosphere
Separated at its upper and lower limits by the distinct thresholds of the stratopause and the tropopause, the stratosphere is a remarkably stable layer between 50 kilometres and about 15 kilometres. Its temperature rises from -55°C at its lower extent to approximately O°C near the stratopause, where a thin layer of ozone absorbs ultra-violet radiation. "Mother-of-pearl" or nacreous cloud occurs at about 25 kilometres' altitude. Stratospheric air contains enough ozone to make it poisonous, although it is in any case far too rarified to breathe.

Troposphere
The narrowest of all the atmospheric layers, the troposphere extends up to 15 kilometres at the equator but only 8 kilometres at the poles. Since this thin region contains about 85% of the atmosphere's total mass and almost all of its water vapour, it is also the realm of the Earth's weather. Temperatures fall steadily with increasing height by about 1°C for every 100 metres above sea level.

Heated by the relatively high surface temperatures near the Earth's equator, air expands and rises to create a belt of low pressure. Moving northward towards the poles, it gradually cools, sinking once more and producing high pressure belts at about latitudes 30° North and South. Water vapour carried with the air falls as rain, releasing vast quantities of energy as well as liquid water when it condenses.

The high and low pressure belts are both areas of comparative calm, but between them, blowing from high to low pressure areas, are the prevailing winds. The atmospheric circulatory system is enormously complicated by the Coriolis effect brought about by the spinning Earth: winds are deflected to the right in the northern hemisphere and to the left in the southern, giving rise to the typically cyclonic pattern of swirling clouds carried by the moving masses of air.

Although clouds appear in an almost infinite variety of shapes and sizes, there are recognizable features that form the basis of a classification first put forward by Luke Howard, a London chemist, in 1803 and later modified by the World Meteorological Organization. The system derives from the altitude of clouds and whether they form hairlike filaments ('cirrus'), heaps or piles ('cumulus') or layers ('stratus'). Each characteristic carries some kind of message – not always a clear one – to forecasters about the weather to come.

CLASSIFICATION OF CLOUDS

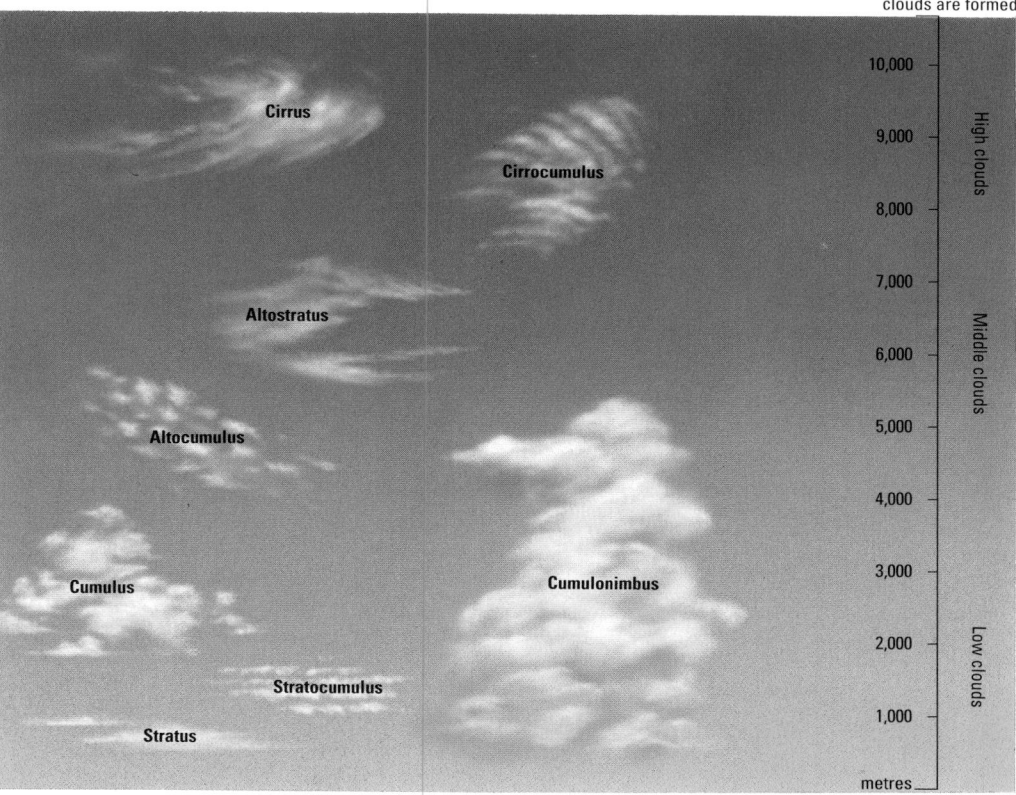

Altitude at which clouds are formed

Clouds form when damp, usually rising, air is cooled. Thus they form when a wind rises to cross hills or mountains; when a mass of air rises over, or is pushed up by, another mass of denser air; or when local heating of the ground causes convection currents. The types of clouds are classified according to altitude as high, middle, or low. The high ones, composed of ice crystals, are cirrus, cirrostratus and cirrocumulus. The middle clouds are altostratus, a grey or bluish striated, fibrous, or uniform sheet producing light drizzle, and altocumulus, a thicker and fluffier version of cirrocumulus. The low clouds include nimbostratus, a dark grey layer that brings almost continuous rain or snow; cumulus, a detached 'heap' – brilliant white in sunlight but dark and flat at the base; and stratus, which forms dull, overcast skies at low altitudes. Cumulonimbus, associated with storms and rains, heavy and dense with flat base and a high, fluffy outline, can be tall enough to occupy middle as well as low altitudes.

PRESSURE & WINDS

January

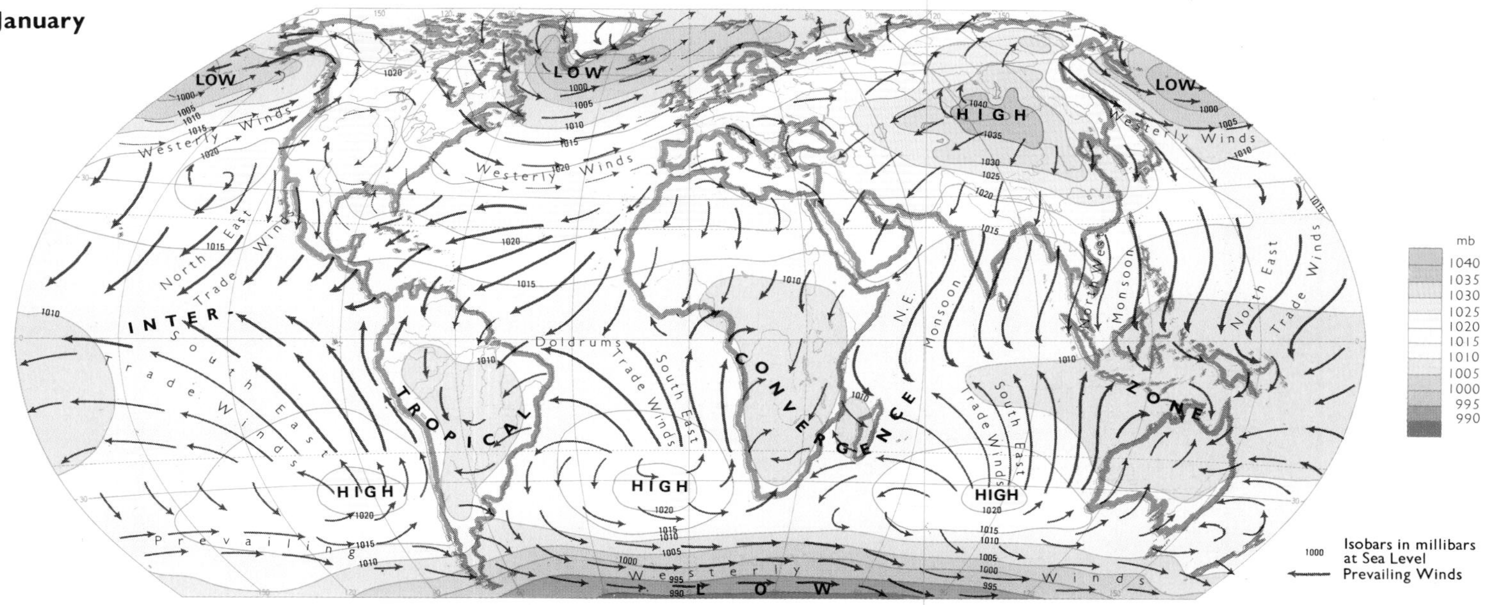

July

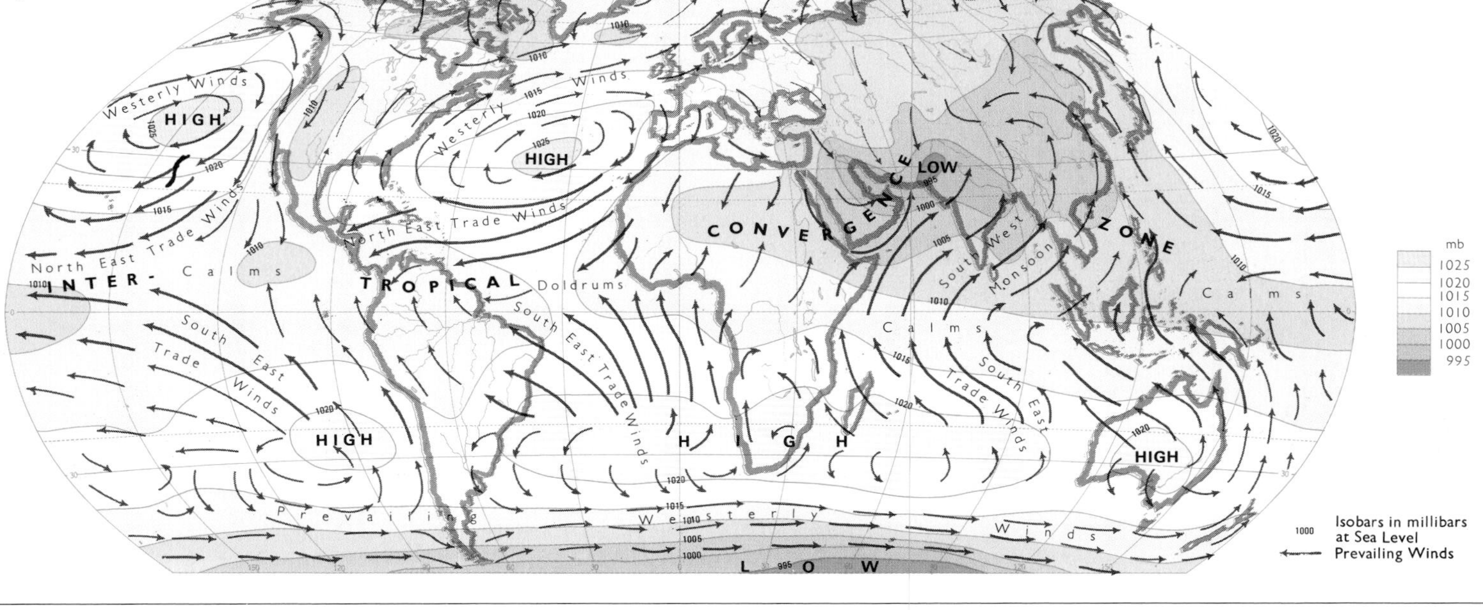

CLIMATE RECORDS

Pressure & Winds

Highest barometric pressure: Agata, Siberia, USSR, 1,083.8 mb [32 in] at altitude 262 m [862 ft], 31 Dec. 1968.

Lowest barometric pressure: Typhoon Tip, 480 km [300 mls] west of Guam, Pacific Ocean, 870 mb [25.69 in], 12 Oct. 1979.

Highest recorded windspeed: Mt Washington, New Hampshire, USA 371 kph [231 mph], 12 Apr. 1934. This is three times as strong as hurricane force on the Beaufort Scale.

Windiest place: Commonwealth Bay, George V Coast, Antarctica, where gales frequently reach over 320 kph [200 mph].

Worst recorded storm: Bangladesh (then East Pakistan) cyclone*, 13 Nov. 1970 – over 300,000 dead or missing. The 1991 cyclone, Bangladesh's and the world's second worst in terms of loss of life, killed an estimated 138,000.

Worst recorded tornado: Missouri/Illinois/Indiana, USA, 18 Mar. 1925 – 792 deaths. The tornado was only 275 m (300 yds) wide.

* Tropical cyclones are known as hurricanes in Central and North America and as typhoons in the Far East

THE EARTH: CLIMATE

11:	OCEAN CURRENTS
12:	CIRCULATION OF THE AIR
13:	CLASSIFICATION OF CLOUDS PRESSURE & WINDS
16:	HYDROLOGICAL CYCLE
17:	NATURAL VEGETATION
21:	GREENHOUSE EFFECT
30:	LAND USE
46:	GLOBAL WARMING

Climate is weather in the long term: the seasonal pattern of hot and cold, wet and dry, averaged over time. At the simplest level, it is caused by the uneven heating of the Earth. Surplus heat at the equator passes towards the poles, levelling out the energy differential. Its passage is marked by a ceaseless churning of the atmosphere and the oceans, further agitated by the the Earth's diurnal spin and the motion it imparts to moving air and water. The heat's means of transport – by winds and ocean currents, by the continual evaporation and recondensation of water molecules – is the weather itself.

There are four basic types of climate, each open to considerable sub-division: tropical, desert, temperate and polar. But although latitude is obviously a critical factor, it is not the only determinant. The differential heating of land and sea, the funnelling and interruption of winds and ocean currents by landmasses and mountain ranges, and the transpiration of vegetation: all combine to add complexity. New York, Naples and the Gobi Desert share almost the same latitude, for example, but their climates are very different. And although the sheer intricacy of the weather system often defies day-to-day prediction in these or any other places – despite the satellites and number-crunching supercomputers with which present-day meteorologists are equipped – their climatic patterns retain a year-on-year stability.

They are not indefinitely stable, however. The planet regularly passes through long, cool periods of around 100,000 years: these are the ice ages, probably caused by recurring long-term oscillations in the Earth's orbital path and fluctuations in the Sun's energy output. In the present era, the Earth is nearest to the Sun in the middle of the northern hemisphere's winter; 11,000 years ago, at the end of the last ice age, the northern winter fell with the Sun at its most distant.

Left to its own devices, the climate even now should be drifting towards another glacial period. But global warming caused by increasing carbon dioxide levels in the atmosphere, largely the result of 20th-century fuel-burning and deforestation, may well precipitate change far faster than the great, slow cycles of the solar system.

CLIMATE REGIONS

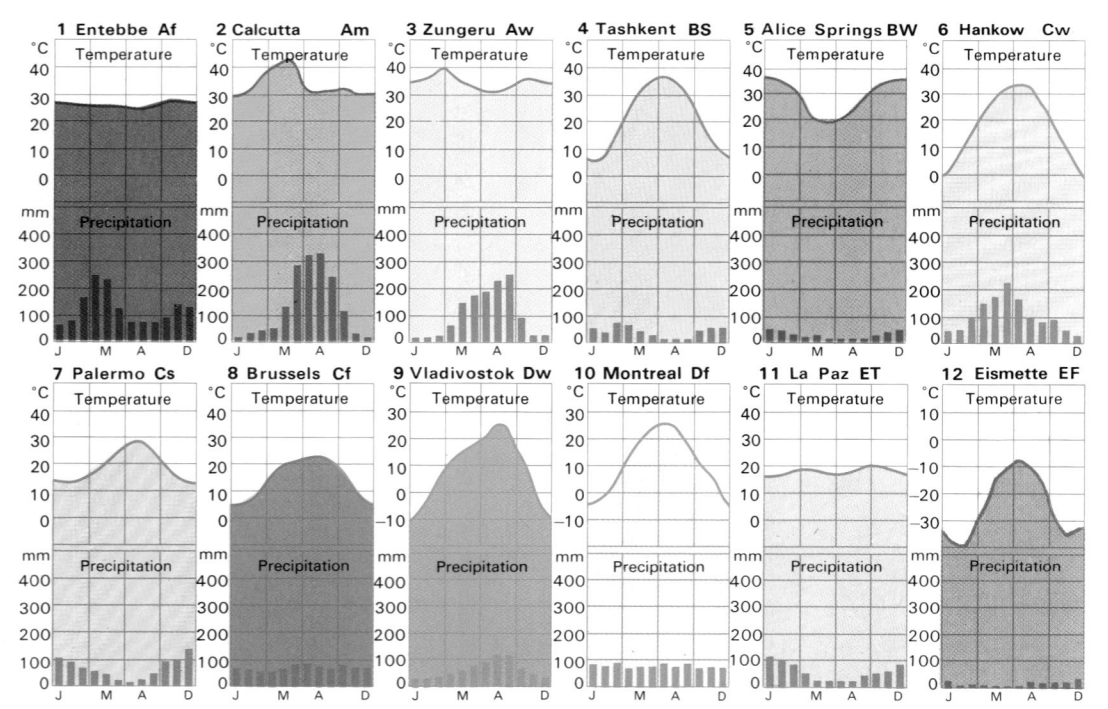

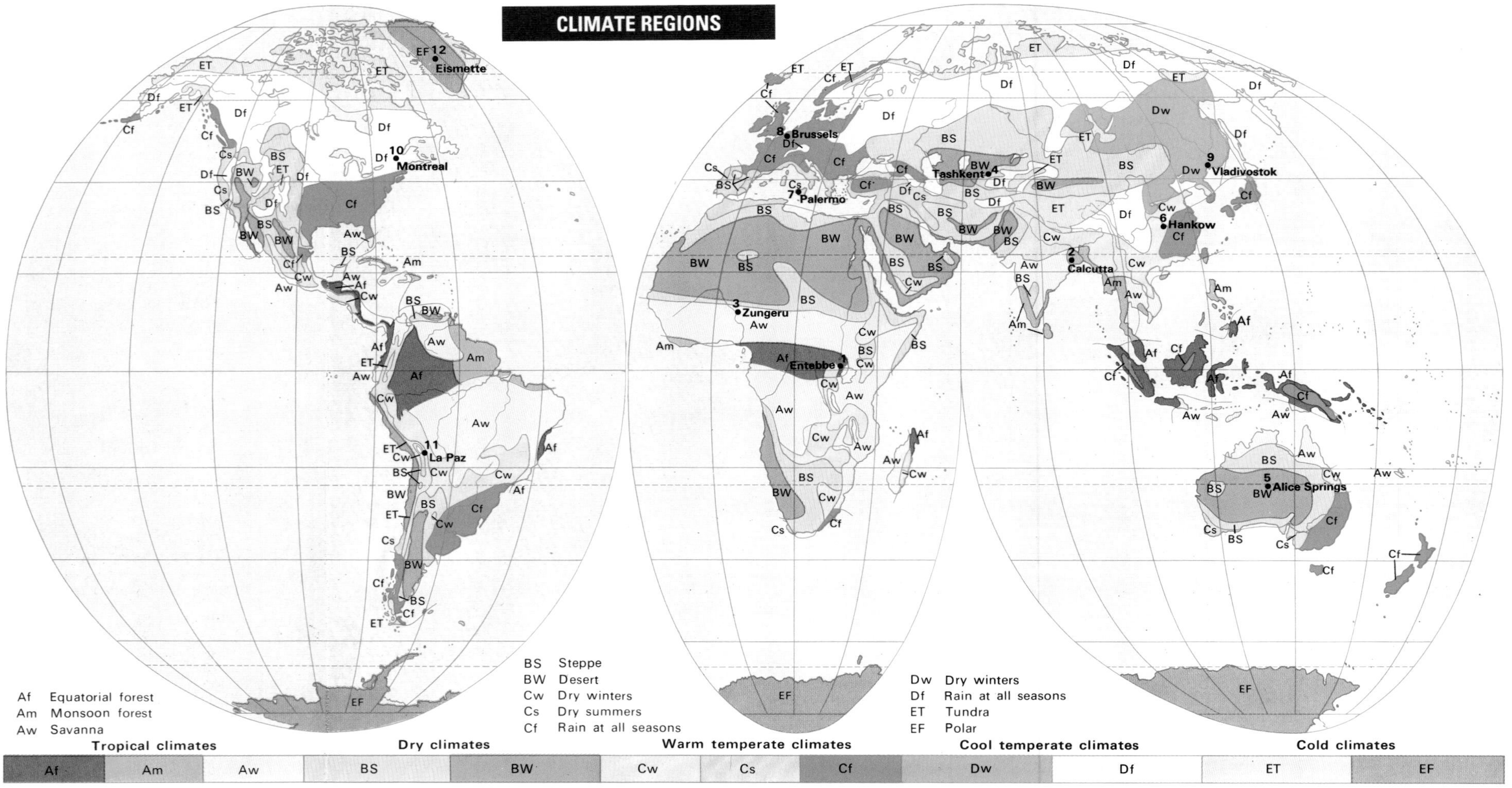

Af Equatorial forest
Am Monsoon forest
Aw Savanna

BS Steppe
BW Desert
Cw Dry winters
Cs Dry summers
Cf Rain at all seasons

Dw Dry winters
Df Rain at all seasons
ET Tundra
EF Polar

Af	Am	Aw	BS	BW	Cw	Cs	Cf	Dw	Df	ET	EF
Tropical climates			Dry climates		Warm temperate climates			Cool temperate climates			Cold climates

Climate graphs: 1 Entebbe Af, 2 Calcutta Am, 3 Zungeru Aw, 4 Tashkent BS, 5 Alice Springs BW, 6 Hankow Cw, 7 Palermo Cs, 8 Brussels Cf, 9 Vladivostok Dw, 10 Montreal Df, 11 La Paz ET, 12 Eismette EF (each showing Temperature °C and Precipitation mm, months J M A D)

CLIMATE & WEATHER TERMS

Absolute humidity: amount of water vapour contained in a given volume of air.
Cloud cover: amount of cloud in the sky; measured in oktas (from 1 - 8), with 0 clear, & 8 total cover.
Condensation: the conversion of water vapour, moisture in the air into liquid.
Cyclone: violent storm resulting from counter clockwise rotation of winds in the northern hemisphere & clockwise in the southern: called hurricane in N. America, typhoon in the Far East.
Depression: approximately circular area of low pressure.
Dew: water droplets condensed out of the air after the ground has cooled at night.
Dew point: temperature at which air becomes saturated (reaches a relative humidity of 100%) at a constant pressure.
Drizzle: precipitation where drops are less than 0.5 mm (0.02 in) in diameter.
Evaporation: conversion of water from liquid into vapour, or moisture in the air.
Frost: dew that has frozen when the air temperature falls below freezing point.
Hail: frozen rain; small balls of ice, often falling during thunder storms.
Hoar frost: formed on objects when the dew point is below freezing point.
Humidity: amount of moisture in the air.
Isobar: cartographic line connecting places of equal atmospheric pressure.
Isotherm: cartographic line connecting places of equal temperature.
Lightning: massive electrical discharge released in thunderstorm from cloud to cloud or cloud to ground, the result of the tip becoming positively charged & the bottom negatively charged.
Precipitation: measurable rain, snow, sleet or hail.
Prevailing wind: most common direction of wind at a given location.
Rain: precipitation of liquid particles with diameter larger than 0.5 mm (0.02 in).
Relative humidity: amount of water vapour contained in a given volume of air at a given temperature.
Sleet: translucent or transparent ice-pellets (partially melted snow).
Snow: formed when water vapour condenses below freezing point.
Thunder: sound produced by the rapid expansion of air heated by lightning.
Tidal wave: giant ocean wave generated by earthquakes (tsunami) or cyclonic winds.
Tornado: severe funnel-shaped storm that twists as hot air spins vertically (waterspout at sea).
Whirlwind: rapidly rotating column of air, only a few metres across made visible by dust.

WINDCHILL FACTOR

In sub-zero weather, even moderate winds significantly reduce effective temperatures. The chart below shows the windchill effect across a range of speeds. Figures in the pink zone are not dangerous to well-clad people; in the blue zone, the risk of serious frostbite is acute.

	Wind speed (km/h)				
	16	32	48	64	80
0°C	-8	-14	-17	-19	-20
-5°C	-14	-21	-25	-27	-28
-10°C	-20	-28	-33	-35	-36
-15°C	-26	-36	-40	-43	-44
-20°C	-32	-42	-48	-51	-52
-25°C	-38	-49	-56	-59	-60
-30°C	-44	-57	-63	-66	-68
-35°C	-51	-64	-72	-74	-76
-40°C	-57	-71	-78	-82	-84
-45°C	-63	-78	-86	-90	-92
-50°C	-69	-85	-94	-98	-100

BEAUFORT WIND SCALE

Named for the 19th-century British naval officer who devised it, the Beaufort Scale assesses wind speed according to its effects. It was originally designed as an aid for sailors, but has since been adapted for use on land.

Scale	Wind speed kph	mph	Effect
0	0-1	0-1	**Calm** Smoke rises vertically
1	1-5	1-3	**Light air** Wind direction shown only by smoke drift
2	6-11	4-7	**Light breeze** Wind felt on face; leaves rustle; vanes moved by wind
3	12-19	8-12	**Gentle breeze** Leaves and small twigs in constant motion; wind extend small flag
4	20-28	13-18	**Moderate** Raises dust and loose paper; small branches move
5	29-38	19-24	**Fresh** Small trees in leaf sway; crested wavelets on inland waters
6	39-49	25-31	**Strong** Large branches move; difficult to use umbrellas; overhead wires whistle
7	50-61	32-38	**Near gale** Whole trees in motion; difficult to walk against wind
8	62-74	39-46	**Gale** Twigs break from trees; walking very difficult
9	75-88	47-54	**Strong gale** Slight structural damage
10	89-102	55-63	**Storm** Trees uprooted; serious structural damage
11	103-117	64-72	**Violent Storm** Widespread damage
12	118+	73+	**Hurricane**

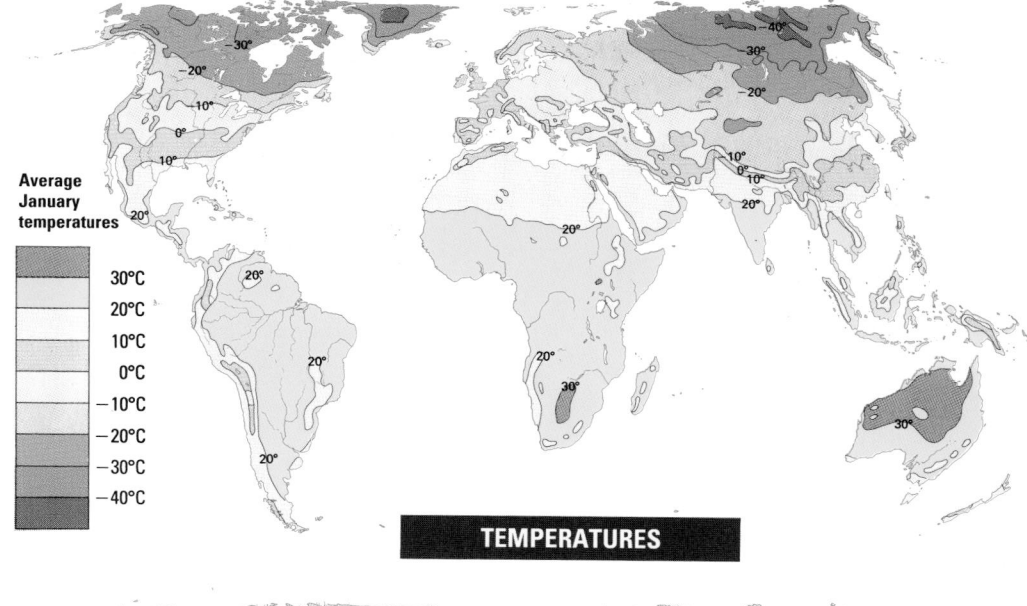

Average January temperatures

30°C
20°C
10°C
0°C
-10°C
-20°C
-30°C
-40°C

TEMPERATURES

Average July temperatures

30°C
20°C
10°C
0°C
-10°C

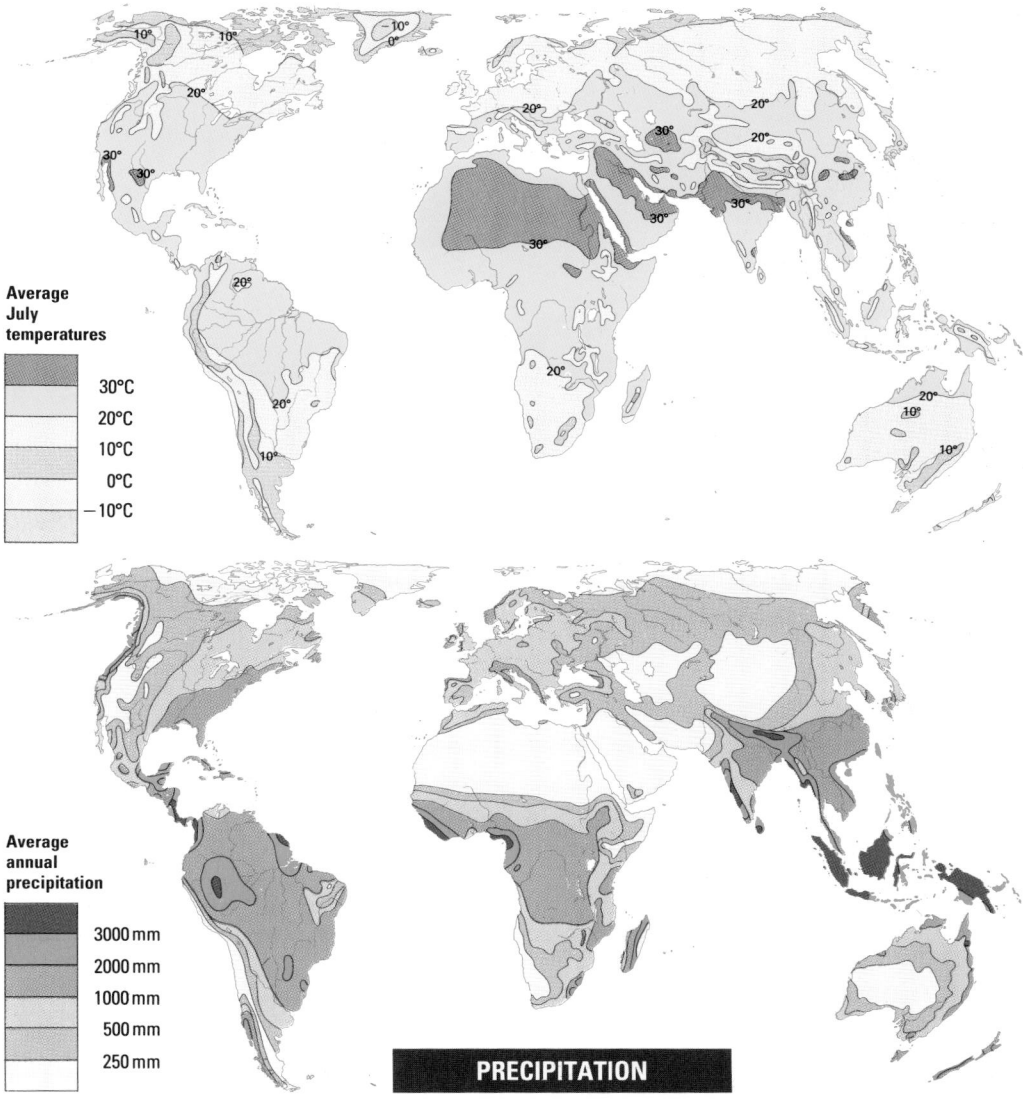

Average annual precipitation

3000 mm
2000 mm
1000 mm
500 mm
250 mm

PRECIPITATION

CLIMATE RECORDS

Temperature

Highest recorded temperature: Al Aziziyah, Libya, 58°C [136.4°F], 13 Sep. 1922.

Highest mean annual temperature: Dallol, Ethiopia, 34.4°C [94°F], 1960-66.

Longest heatwave: Marble Bar, W. Australia, 162 days over 38°C [100°F], 23 Oct. 1923 - 7 Apr. 1924.

Lowest recorded temperature (outside poles): Verkhoyansk, Siberia, USSR -68°C [-90°F], 6 Feb. 1933. Verkhoyansk also registered the greatest annual range of temperature: - 70°C to 37°C [-94°F to 98°F].

Lowest mean annual temperature: Polus Nedostupnosti, Pole of Cold, Antarctica, -57.8°C [-72°F].

Precipitation

Driest place: Arica, N. Chile, 0.8mm [0.03 in] per year (60-year average).

Longest drought: Calama, N. Chile: no recorded rainfall in 400 years to 1971.

Wettest place (average): Tututendo, Colombia: mean annual rainfall 11,770 mm [463.4 in].

Wettest place (12 months): Cherrapunji, Meghalaya, N.E. India, 26,470 mm [1,040 in], Aug. 1860 to Aug. 1861. Cherrapunji also holds the record for rainfall in one month: 930 mm [37 in] July 1861.

Wettest place (24 hours): Cilaos, Réunion, Indian Ocean, 1,870 mm [73.6 in], 15-16 Mar. 1952.

Heaviest hailstones: Gopalganj, Bangladesh, up to 1.02 kg [2.25 lb], 14 Apr. 1986 (killed 92 people).

Heaviest snowfall (continuous): Bessans, Savoie, France, 1730 mm [68 in] in 19 hours, 5-6 Apr. 1969.

Heaviest snowfall (season/year): Paradise Ranger Station, Mt Rainier, Washington, USA, 31,102 mm [1,224.5 in], 19 Feb. 1971 to 18 Feb. 1972.

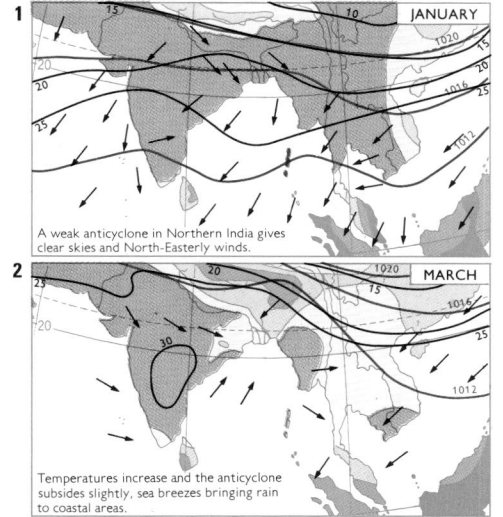

1 JANUARY

A weak anticyclone in Northern India gives clear skies and North-Easterly winds.

2 MARCH

Temperatures increase and the anticyclone subsides slightly, sea breezes bringing rain to coastal areas.

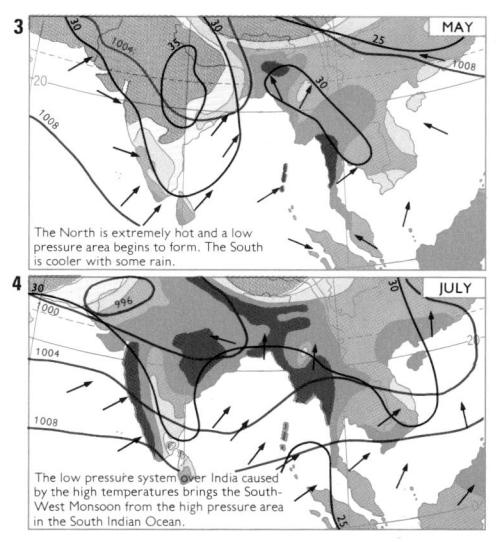

3 MAY

The North is extremely hot and a low pressure area begins to form. The South is cooler with some rain.

4 JULY

The low pressure system over India caused by the high temperatures brings the South-West Monsoon from the high pressure area in the South Indian Ocean.

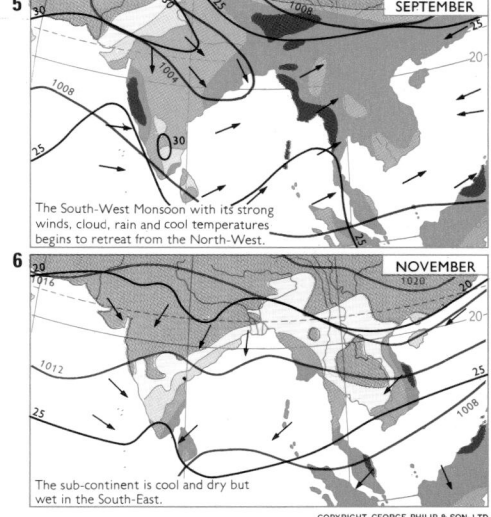

5 SEPTEMBER

The South-West Monsoon with its strong winds, cloud, rain and cool temperatures begins to retreat from the North-West.

6 NOVEMBER

The sub-continent is cool and dry but wet in the South-East.

COPYRIGHT. GEORGE PHILIP & SON. LTD.

THE MONSOON

While it is crucial to the agriculture of South Asia, the monsoon that follows the dry months is unpredictable - in duration as well as intensity. A season of very heavy rainfall, causing disastrous floods, can be succeeded by years of low precipitation, leading to serious drought.

Monthly rainfall

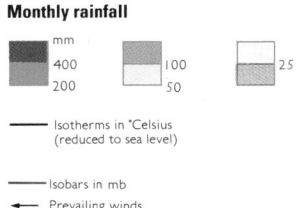

mm
400
200
100
50
25

Isotherms in °Celsius (reduced to sea level)

Isobars in mb

Prevailing winds

THE EARTH: WATER

14: TYPES OF PRECIPITATION

15: RAINFALL
    THE MONSOON
    CLIMATE RECORDS

19: SHAPING FORCES:
    RIVERS & GLACIERS

Fresh water is essential to all terrestrial life, from the humblest bacterium to the most advanced technological society. Yet freshwater resources form a minute fraction of the Earth's 1.41 billion cubic kilometres of water: most human needs must be met from the 2,000 cubic kilometres circulating in rivers at any one time. Agriculture accounts for huge quantities: without large-scale irrigation, most of the world's people would starve. And since fresh water is just as essential for most industrial processes – smelting a tonne of nickel, for example, requires about 4,000 tonnes of water – the combination of growing population and advancing industry has put water supplies under strain.

Fortunately water is seldom used up: the planet's hydrological cycle circulates it with benign efficiency, at least on a global scale. More locally, though, human activity can cause severe shortages: water for industry and agriculture is being withdrawn from many river basins and underground aquifers faster than natural recirculation can replace it.

THE HYDROLOGICAL CYCLE

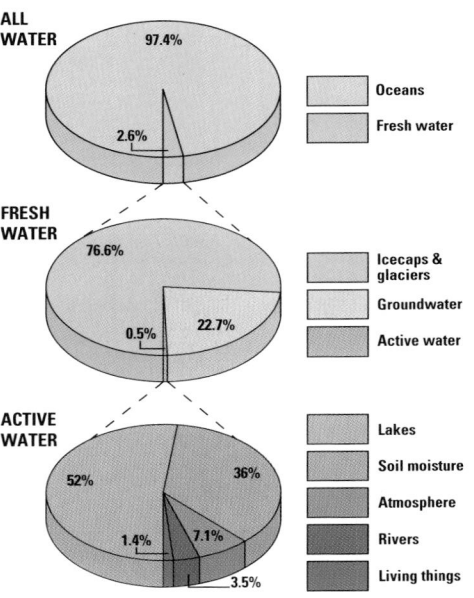

Precipitation on land

Precipitation on ocean

Evaporation from vegetation

Evaporation from soil

Evaporation from lakes & ponds

Evaporation from vegetation & streams

Evaporation from oceans

Intercepted by vegetation

Groundwater to soil

Groundwater to lakes & streams

Groundwater to vegetation

Groundwater to oceans

WATER DISTRIBUTION

The distribution of planetary water, by percentage. Oceans and icecaps together account for more than 99% of the total; the breakdown of the remainder is estimated.

ALL WATER — 97.4%, 2.6%
- Oceans
- Fresh water

FRESH WATER — 76.6%, 0.5%, 22.7%
- Icecaps & glaciers
- Groundwater
- Active water

ACTIVE WATER — 52%, 36%, 1.4%, 7.1%, 3.5%
- Lakes
- Soil moisture
- Atmosphere
- Rivers
- Living things

Almost all the world's water is 3,000 million years old, and all of it cycles endlessly through the hydrosphere, though at different rates. Water vapour circulates over days, even hours, deep ocean water circulates over millenia and ice-cap water remains solid for millions of years.

Water vapour is constantly drawn into the air from the Earth's rivers, lakes, seas and plant transpiration. In the atmosphere, it circulates around the planet, transporting energy as well as water itself. When the vapour cools it falls as rain or snow, and returns to the surface to evaporate once more. The whole cycle is driven by the Sun.

WATER RUNOFF

Annual freshwater runoff by continent in cubic kilometres

- Asia
- North America
- South America
- Australasia
- Europe
- Africa

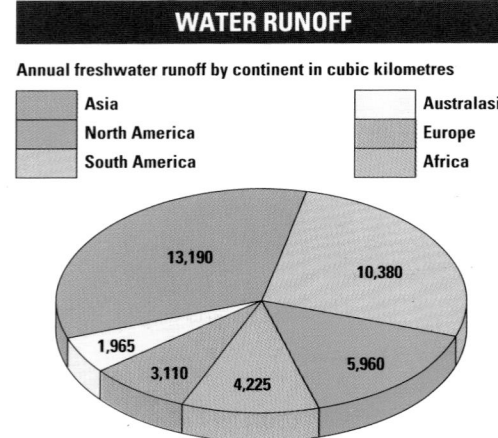

13,190 — 10,380 — 1,965 — 3,110 — 4,225 — 5,960

WATER UTILIZATION

The percentage breakdown of water usage by sector, selected countries (1980s)

Domestic | Industrial | Agriculture

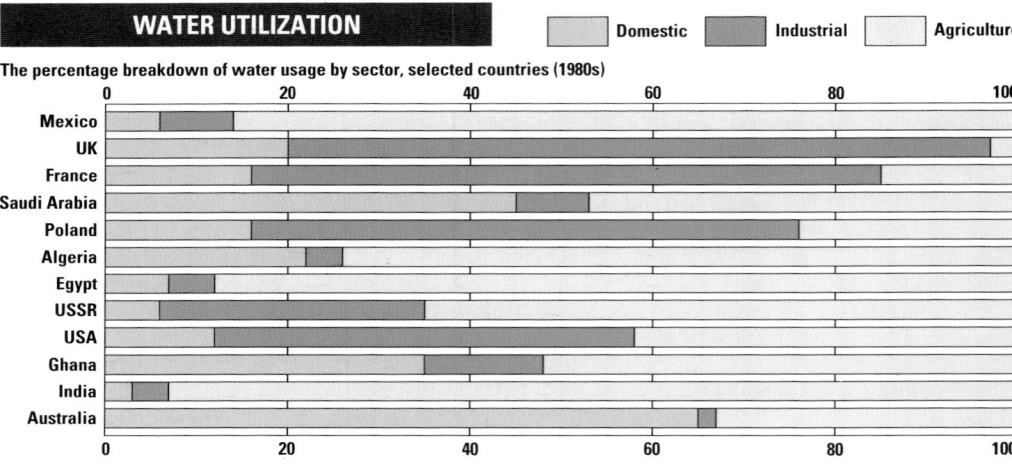

Mexico
UK
France
Saudi Arabia
Poland
Algeria
Egypt
USSR
USA
Ghana
India
Australia

0   20   40   60   80   100

WATER SUPPLY

Percentage of total population with access to safe drinking water (latest available year, 1980s)

- Over 90%
- 75 - 90%
- 60 - 75%
- 45 - 60%
- 30 - 45%
- Under 30%

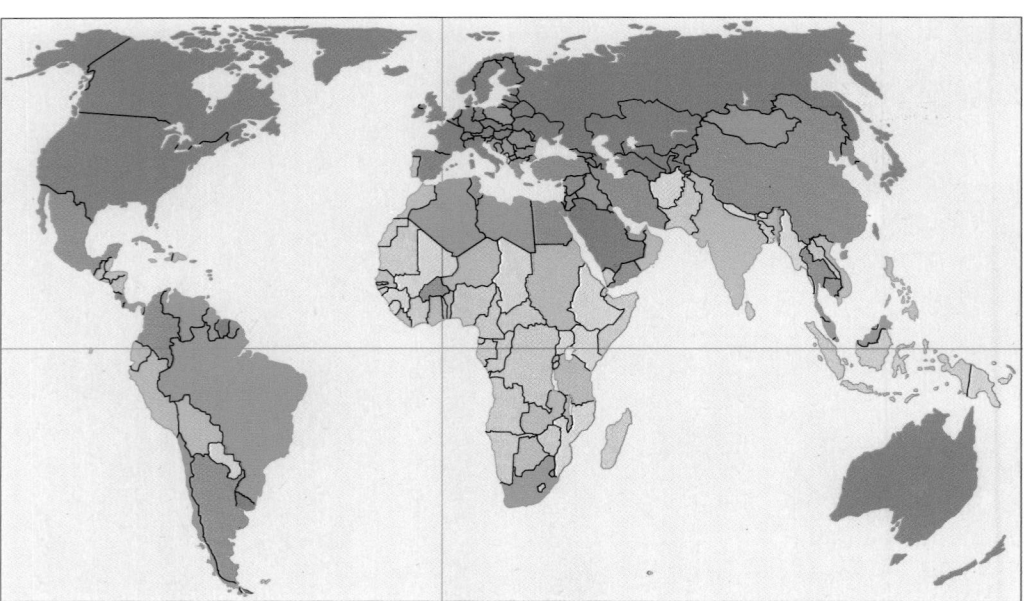

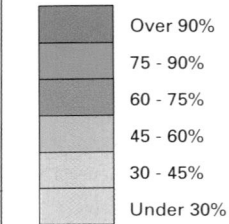

Least well provided countries (rural areas only):

Country	%	Country	%
Paraguay	8%	Guinea	15%
Mozambique	12%	Mauritania	17%
Uganda	12%	Malawi	17%
Angola	15%	Morocco	17%

WATERSHEDS

The world's major rivers; those named are the longest, led by the Nile and the Amazon

WHERE THE RIVERS RUN
Pacific Ocean
Indian Ocean
Arctic Ocean
Atlantic Ocean
Caribbean Sea
Mediterranean Sea
Inland basins
ARCTIC OCEAN
Yukon
Mackenzie
Peace
Nelson
Columbia
Missouri
St. Lawrence
Colorado
Rio Grande
Mississippi
ATLANTIC
OCEAN
Caribbean Sea
Orinoco
PACIFIC
OCEAN
Negro
Amazon
Japurá
Tocantins
Madeira
São Francisco
Ucayali
Paraguay
Paraná
Yenisey
Ob
Lena
Irtysh
Angara
Amur
Rhine
Volga
Syr Darya
Danube
Mediterranean Sea
Tigris
Amu Darya
Hwang Ho
Nile
Euphrates
Yangtze-Kiang
Brahmaputra
Ganges
Si-Kiang
Indus
Irrawaddy
Arabian Sea
Bay of Bengal
Salween
White Nile
Mekong
Volta
Niger
INDIAN
OCEAN
Zaïre
Zambezi
Orange
Darling
Murray

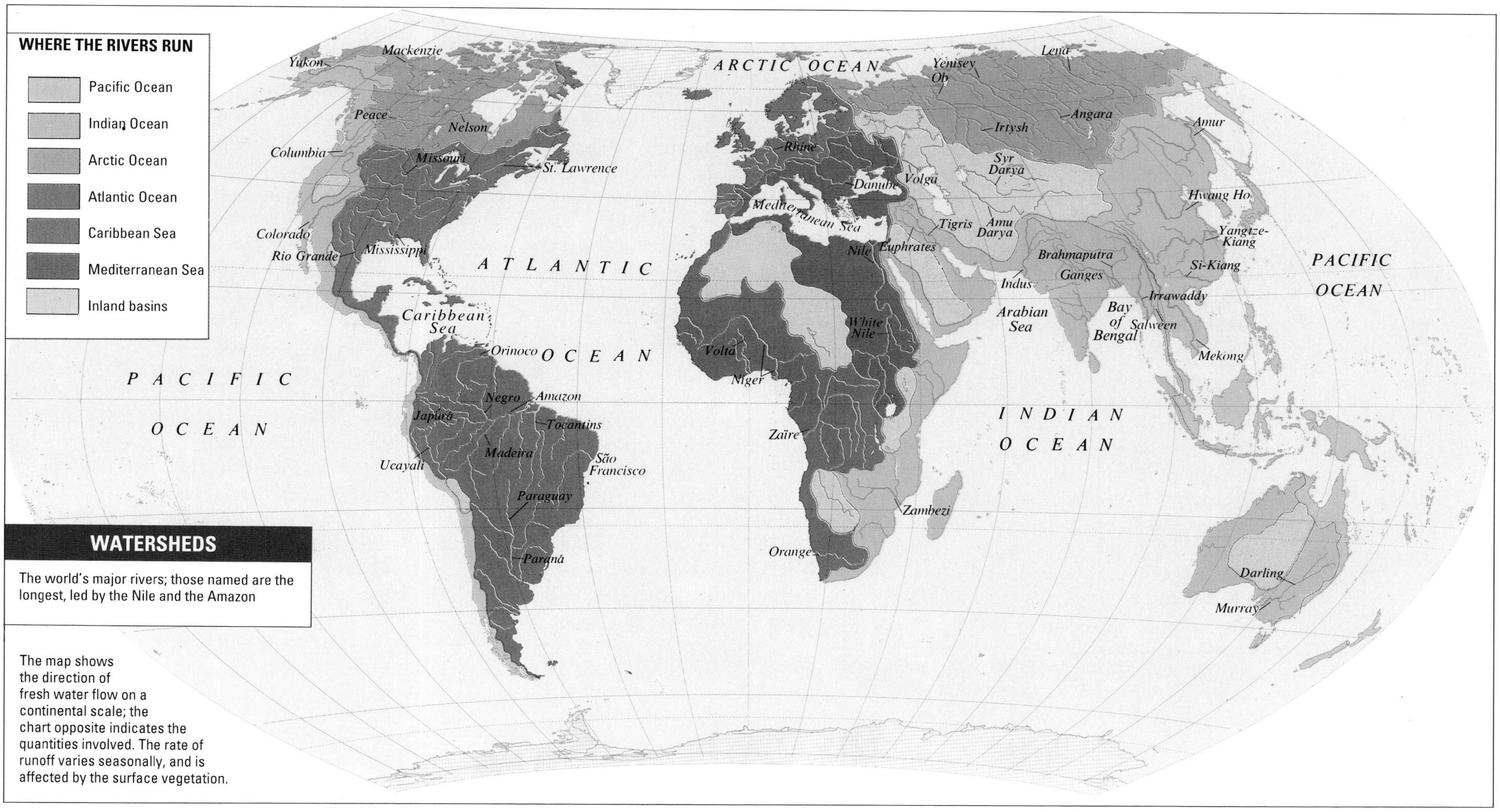

The map shows the direction of fresh water flow on a continental scale; the chart opposite indicates the quantities involved. The rate of runoff varies seasonally, and is affected by the surface vegetation.

LAND USE BY CONTINENT

Forest
Permanent pasture & rough grazing
Permanent crops & plantations
Arable
Non-productive
NORTH AMERICA
32.2%
37.6%
17.3%
12.6%
0.3%
EUROPE
33.4%
19.3%
26.8%
17.5%
3%
ASIA
20.2%
37.8%
25%
1.2%
16%
SOUTH AMERICA
13.4%
6.6%
1.5%
51.8%
26.7%
AFRICA
23.2%
44%
26.6%
0.6%
5.6%
AUSTRALIA
23.5%
18.5%
5.7%
0.1%
52.2%

The proportion of productive land has reached its upper limit in Europe, and in Asia more than 80% of potential cropland is already under cultivation. Elsewhere, any increase is often matched by corresponding losses due to desertification and erosion; projections for 2025 show a decline in cropland per capita for all continents, most notably in Africa.

NATURAL VEGETATION

Regional variation in vegetation

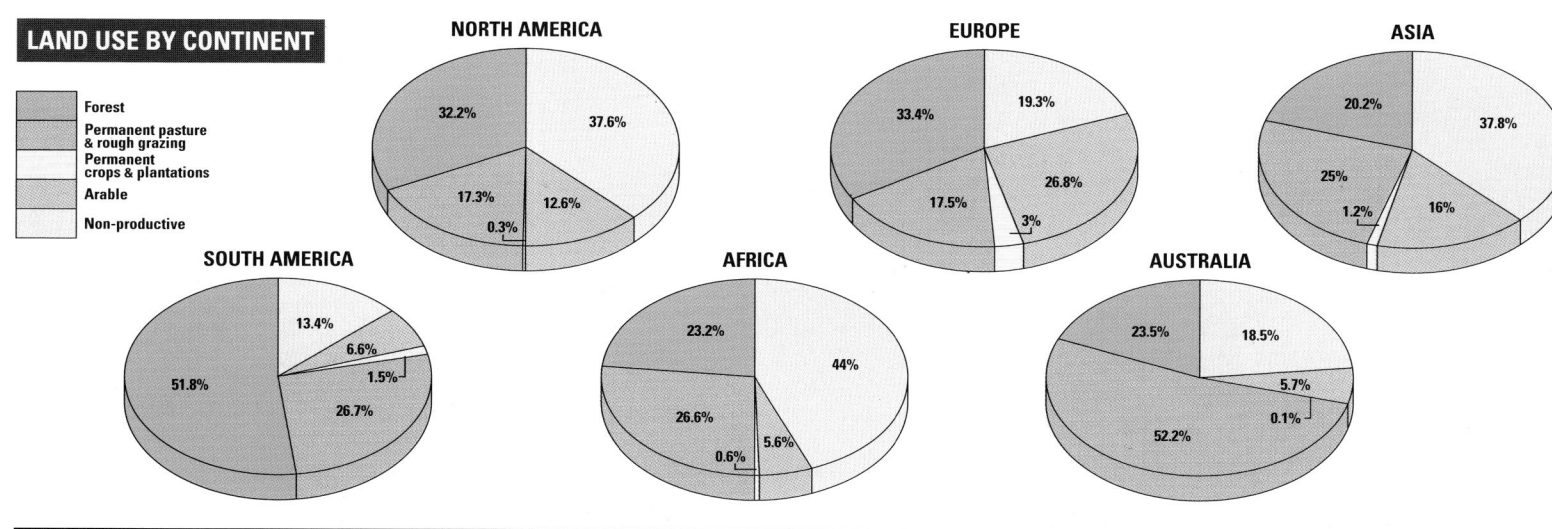

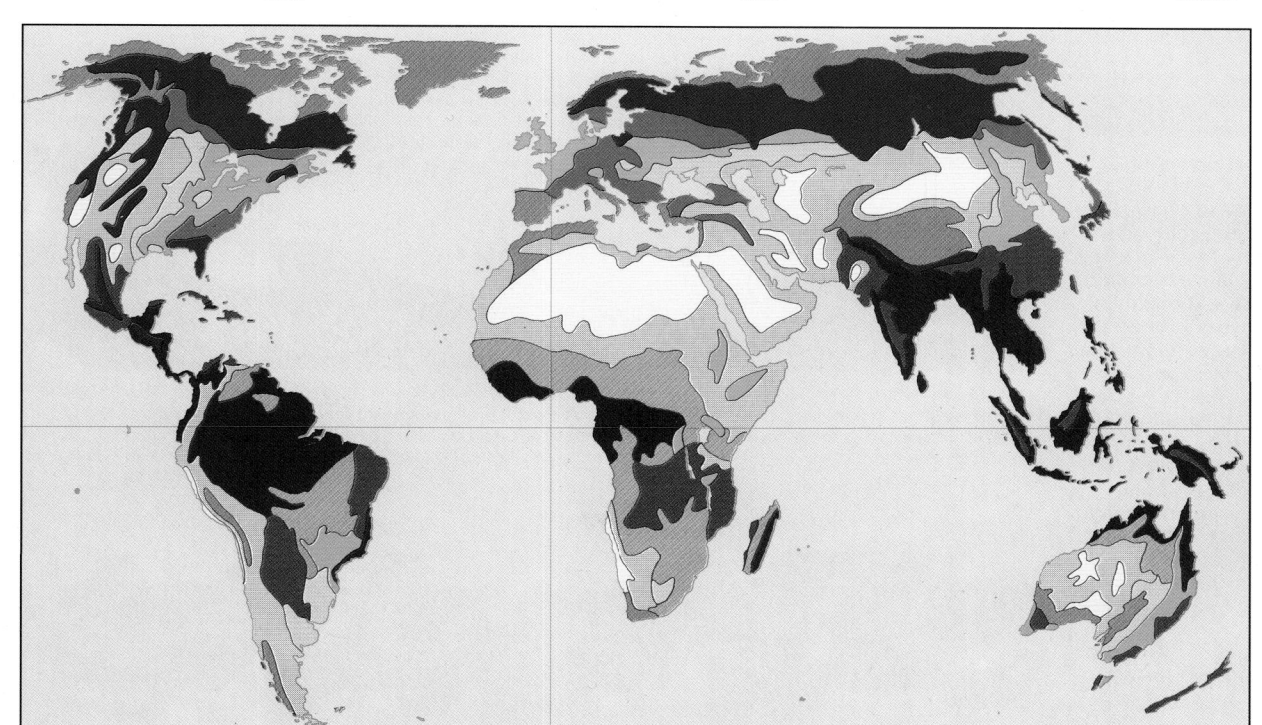

Tundra & mountain vegetation
Needleleaf evergreen forest
Mixed needleleaf evergreen & broadleaf deciduous trees
Broadleaf deciduous woodland
Mid-latitude grassland
Evergreen broadleaf & deciduous trees & shrubs
Semi-desert scrub
Desert
Tropical grassland (savanna)
Tropical broadleaf rainforest & monsoon forest
Sub-tropical broadleaf & needleleaf forest

The map illustrates the natural climax vegetation of a region, as dictated by its climate and topography. In most cases, human agricultural activity has drastically altered the vegetation pattern. Western Europe, for example, lost most of its broadleaf forest many centuries ago, and irrigation has turned some natural semi-desert into productive land.

THE EARTH: LANDSCAPE

8:	THE EARTH'S STRUCTURE
	PLATE TECTONICS
9:	GEOLOGICAL TIME
	VOLCANOES
10:	OCEANS
16:	HYDROLOGICAL CYCLE
34:	STRUCTURAL REGIONS

Above and below the surface of the oceans, the features of the Earth's crust are constantly changing. The phenomenal forces generated by convection currents in the molten core of our planet carry the vast segments or 'plates' of the crust across the globe in an endless cycle of creation and destruction. New crust emerges along the central depths of the oceans, where molten magma flows from the margins of neighbouring plates to form the massive mid-ocean ridges. The sea floor spreads, and where ocean plates meet continental plates, they dip back into the earth's core to melt once again into magma.

Less dense, the continental plates 'float' among the oceans, drifting into and apart from each other at a rate which is almost imperceptibly slow. A continent may travel little more than 25 millimetres per year – in an average lifetime, Europe will move no more than a man's height – yet in the vast span of geological time, this process throws up giant mountain ranges and opens massive rifts in the land's surface.

The world's greatest mountain ranges have been formed in this way – the Himalayas by the collision of the Indo-Australian and Eurasian plates, the Andes by the meeting of the Nazca and South American plates. The Himalayas are a classic example of 'fold mountains', formed by the crumpling of the Earth's surface where two land masses have been driven together. The coastal range of the Andes, by contrast, was formed by the upsurge of molten volcanic rock created by the friction of the continent 'overriding' the ocean plate.

Destruction of the landscape, however, begins as soon as it is formed. Wind, water, ice and sea, the main agents of erosion, mount a constant assault that even the hardest rocks cannot withstand. Mountain peaks may dwindle by as little as a few millimetres each year, but if they are not uplifted by further movements of the crust they will eventually be reduced to rubble. Water is the most powerful destroyer – it has been estimated that 100 billion tonnes of rock is washed into the oceans every year.

When water freezes, its volume increases by about nine per cent, and no rock is strong enough to resist this pressure. Where water has penetrated tiny fissures or seeped into softer rock, a severe freeze followed by a thaw may result in rockfalls or earth-slides, creating major destruction in a few minutes. Over much longer periods, acidity in rainwater breaks down the chemical composition of porous rocks like limestone, eating away the rock to form deep caves and tunnels. Chemical decomposition also occurs in riverbeds and glacier valleys, hastening the process of mechanical erosion.

Rivers and glaciers, like the sea itself, generate much of their effect through abrasion – pounding the landscape with the debris they carry with them. But as well as destroying they also create new landscapes, many of them spectacular : vast deltas, as at the mouth of the Mississippi or the Nile; cliffs, rock arches and stacks, as on the south coast of Australia; and the fjords cut by long-melted glaciers in British Columbia, Norway and New Zealand.

The vast ridges that divide the Earth's crust beneath each of the world's major oceans mark the boundaries between tectonic plates which are moving very gradually in opposite directions. As the plates shift apart, molten magma rises from the Earth's core to seal the rift and the sea floor slowly spreads towards the continental landmasses. The rate of sea floor spreading has been calculated by magnetic analysis of the rock – at about 40 mm [1.5 in] a year in the North Atlantic. Near the ocean shore, underwater volcanoes mark the line where the continental rise begins. As the plates meet, much of the denser ocean crust dips beneath the continental plate and is melted back into the magma.

THE SPREADING EARTH

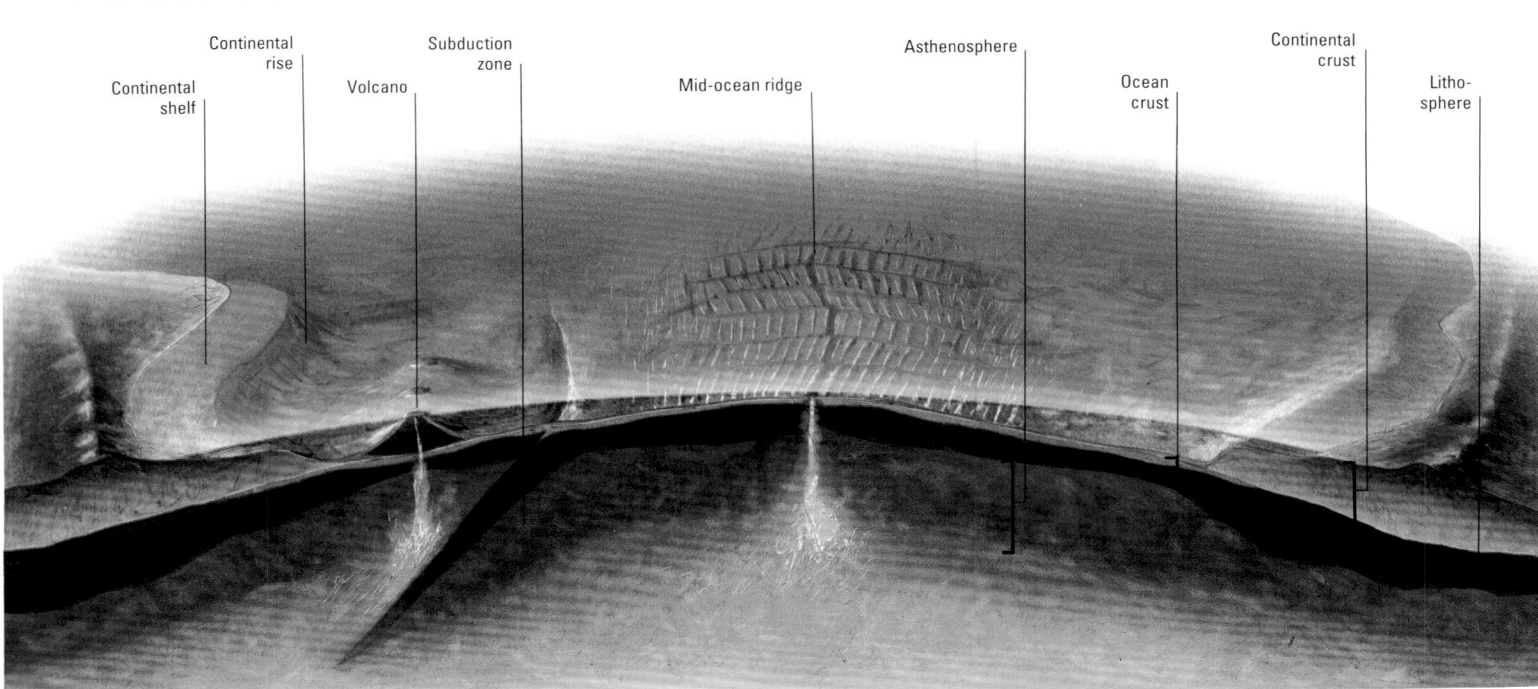

Continental shelf · Continental rise · Volcano · Subduction zone · Mid-ocean ridge · Asthenosphere · Ocean crust · Continental crust · Lithosphere

TYPES OF ROCK

Rocks are divided into three types, according to the way in which they are formed:

Igneous rocks, including granite and basalt, are formed by the cooling of magma from within the Earth's crust.

Metamorphic rocks, such as slate, marble and quartzite, are formed below the Earth's surface by the compression or baking of existing rocks.

Sedimentary rocks, like sandstone and limestone, are formed on the surface of the Earth from the remains of living organisms and eroded fragments of older rocks.

MOUNTAIN BUILDING

Mountains are formed when pressures on the Earth's crust caused by continental drift become so intense that the surface buckles or cracks. This happens most dramatically where two tectonic plates collide : the Rockies, Andes, Alps, Urals and Himalayas resulted from such impacts. These are all known as fold mountains, because they were formed by the compression of the rocks, forcing the surface to bend and fold like a crumpled rug.

The other main building process is when the crust fractures to create faults, allowing rock to be forced upwards in large blocks; or when the pressure of magma within the crust forces the surface to bulge into a dome, or erupts to form a volcano. Large mountain ranges may reveal a combination of those features; the Alps, for example, have been compressed so violently that the folds are fragmented by numerous faults and intrusions of molten rock.

Over millions of years, even the greatest mountain ranges can be reduced by erosion to a landscape known as a peneplain.

Types of fold: Geographers give different names to the degrees of fold that result from continuing pressure on the rock strata. A simple fold may be symmetric, with even slopes on either side, but as the pressure builds up, one slope becomes steeper and the fold becomes asymmetric. Later, the ridge or 'anticline' at the top of the fold may slide over the lower ground or 'syncline' to form a recumbent fold. Eventually, the rock strata may break under the pressure to form an overthrust and finally a nappe fold.

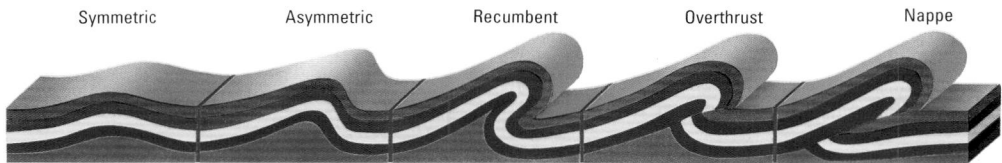

Symmetric · Asymmetric · Recumbent · Overthrust · Nappe

Types of fault: Faults are classified by the direction in which the blocks of rock have moved. A normal fault results when a vertical movement causes the surface to break apart; compression causes a reverse fault. Sideways movement causes shearing, known as a strike-slip fault. When the rock breaks in two places, the central block may be pushed up in a horst fault, or sink in a graben fault.

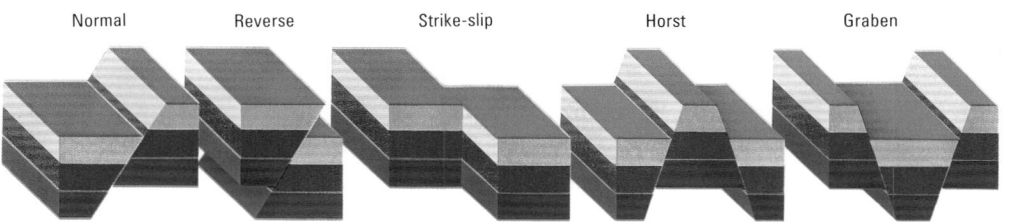

Normal · Reverse · Strike-slip · Horst · Graben

MOULDING THE LAND

While hidden forces of extraordinary power are moving the continents from below the Earth's crust, the more familiar elements of wind and water; heat and cold combine to sculpt the surface of the landscape. Erosion by weathering is seen in desert regions, where rocks degrade imperceptibly into sand through the effects of changing temperatures and strong winds.

The power of water is fiercer still. Coastlines change faster than most landscape features, both by erosion and by the build-up of sand and pebbles carried by the sea. In severe storms, giant waves pound the shoreline with rocks and boulders, and frequently destroy concrete coastal defences; but even in quieter conditions, the sea steadily erodes cliffs and headlands and creates new land in the form of sand-dunes, spits and salt-marshes.

Rivers, too, are incessantly at work shaping the landscape on their way to join the sea. In highland regions, where the flow is rapid, they cut deep gorges and V-shaped valleys. As they reach more gentle slopes, rivers release some of the debris they have carried downstream, broadening out and raising levees along their banks by depositing mud and sand. In the lowland plains, they may drift into meanders, depositing more sediment and even building deltas when they finally approach the sea.

Ice has created some of the world's dramatic landscapes. As glaciers move slowly downhill, they scrape away rock from the mountains and valley sides, creating spectacular landscape features.

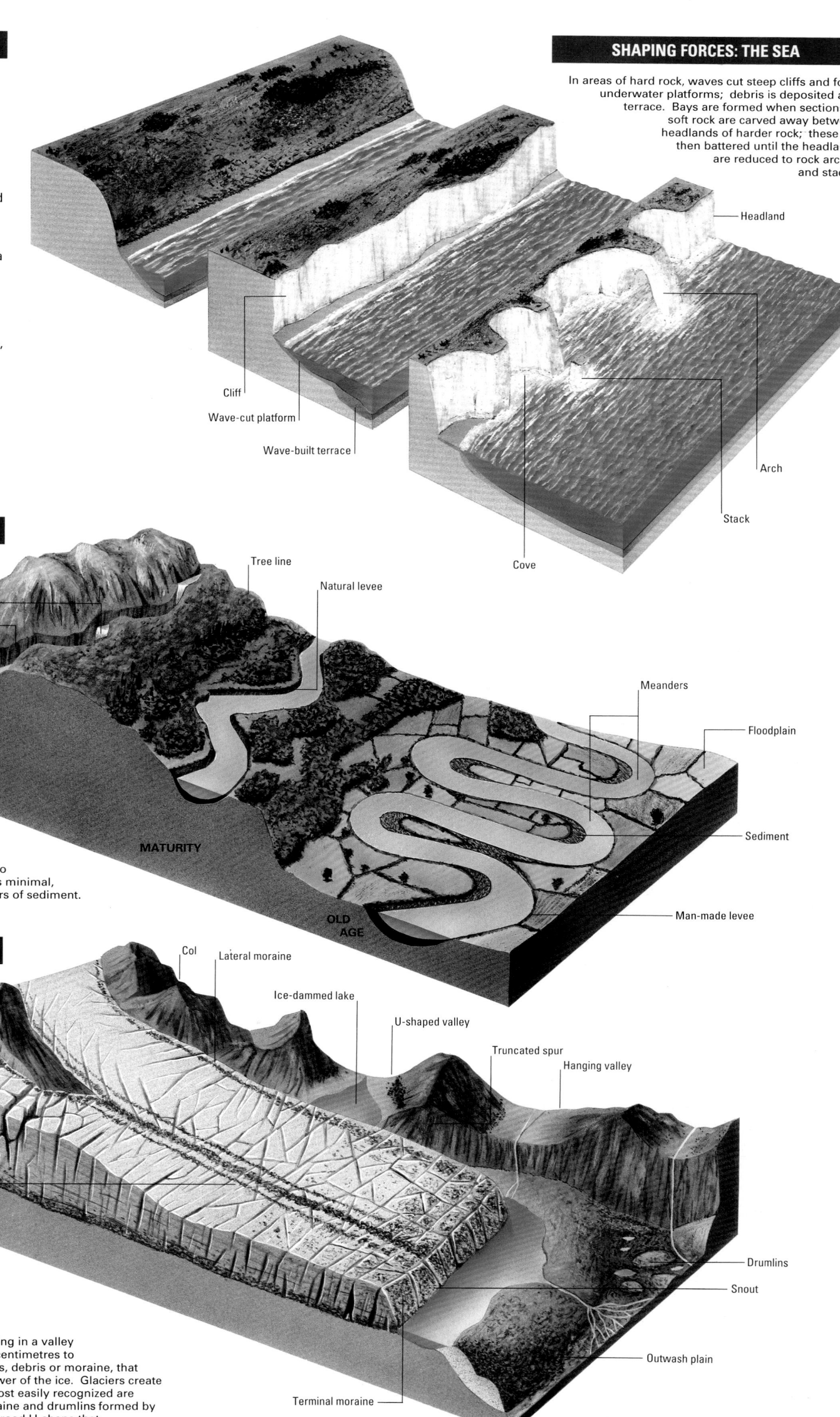

SHAPING FORCES: THE SEA

In areas of hard rock, waves cut steep cliffs and form underwater platforms; debris is deposited as a terrace. Bays are formed when sections of soft rock are carved away between headlands of harder rock; these are then battered until the headlands are reduced to rock arches and stacks.

Headland

Cliff

Wave-cut platform

Wave-built terrace

Arch

Stack

Cove

SHAPING FORCES: RIVERS

Waterfall

Gorge

V-shaped valley

Tree line

Natural levee

Meanders

Floodplain

YOUTH

MATURITY

Sediment

Man-made levee

OLD AGE

Rivers shape the landscape according to the speed of their flow. In their youthful, upland stage they erode soft rocks quickly, cutting steep narrow valleys and tumbling in waterfalls over harder rock. As they mature they deposit some debris and erode outwards to widen the valley. In their old age, where the gradient is minimal, they meander across wide plains, depositing deep layers of sediment.

SHAPING FORCES: GLACIERS

Arête

Col

Lateral moraine

Ice-dammed lake

U-shaped valley

Truncated spur

Hanging valley

Crevasse

Medial moraine

Drumlins

Snout

Outwash plain

Terminal moraine

Glaciers are formed from compressed snow accumulating in a valley head or cirque. They move downhill at a rate of a few centimetres to several metres per day, eroding large quantities of rocks, debris or moraine, that is caught up by the glacier and adds to the abrasive power of the ice. Glaciers create numerous distinctive landscape features: among the most easily recognized are hanging valleys, cut by tributary glaciers; terminal moraine and drumlins formed by rock debris deposited when a glacier retreats; and the broad U-shape that distinguishes a glacial valley from one cut by a river.

19

THE EARTH: ENVIRONMENT

10:	OCEANS
12:	ATMOSPHERE
17:	NATURAL VEGETATION
46:	CARBON DIOXIDE GREENHOUSE POWER GLOBAL WARMING
47:	ACID RAIN DESERTIFICATION DEFORESTATION WATER POLLUTION

Unique among the planets, the Earth has been the home of living creatures for most of its existence. Precisely how these improbable assemblies of self-replicating chemicals ever began remains a matter of conjecture, but the planet and its passengers have matured together for a very long time. Over three billion years, life has not only adapted to its environment: it has also slowly changed that environment to suit itself.

The planet and its biosphere – the entirety of its living things – function like a single organism. The British scientist James Lovelock, who first stated this 'Gaia hypothesis' in the 1970s, went further: the planet, he declared, actually was a living organism, equipped on a colossal scale with the same sort of stability-seeking mechanisms used by lesser lifeforms like bacteria and humans to keep themselves running at optimum efficiency.

Lovelock's theory was inspired by a study of the Earth's atmosphere, whose constituents he noted are very far from the state of chemical equilibrium observed elsewhere in the solar system. The atmosphere has contained a substantial amount of free oxygen for the last two billion years; yet without constant renewal, the oxygen molecules would soon be locked permanently in oxides. The nitrogen, too, would find chemical stability, probably in nitrates (accounting for some of the oxygen). Without living plants and algae to remove it, carbon dioxide would steadily increase from its present-day 0.03%; in a few million years, it would form a thick blanket similar to the atmosphere of lifeless Venus, where surface temperatures reach 475°C.

It is not enough, however, for the biosphere simply to produce oxygen. While falling concentrations would be first uncomfortable and ultimately fatal for most contemporary life, at levels above the current 21% even moist vegetation is highly inflammable, and a massive conflagration becomes almost inevitable – a violent form of negative feedback to set the atmosphere on the path back to sterile equilibrium.

Fortunately, the biosphere has evolved over eons into a subtle and complex control system, sensing changes and reacting to them quickly but gently, tending always to maintain the balance it has achieved.

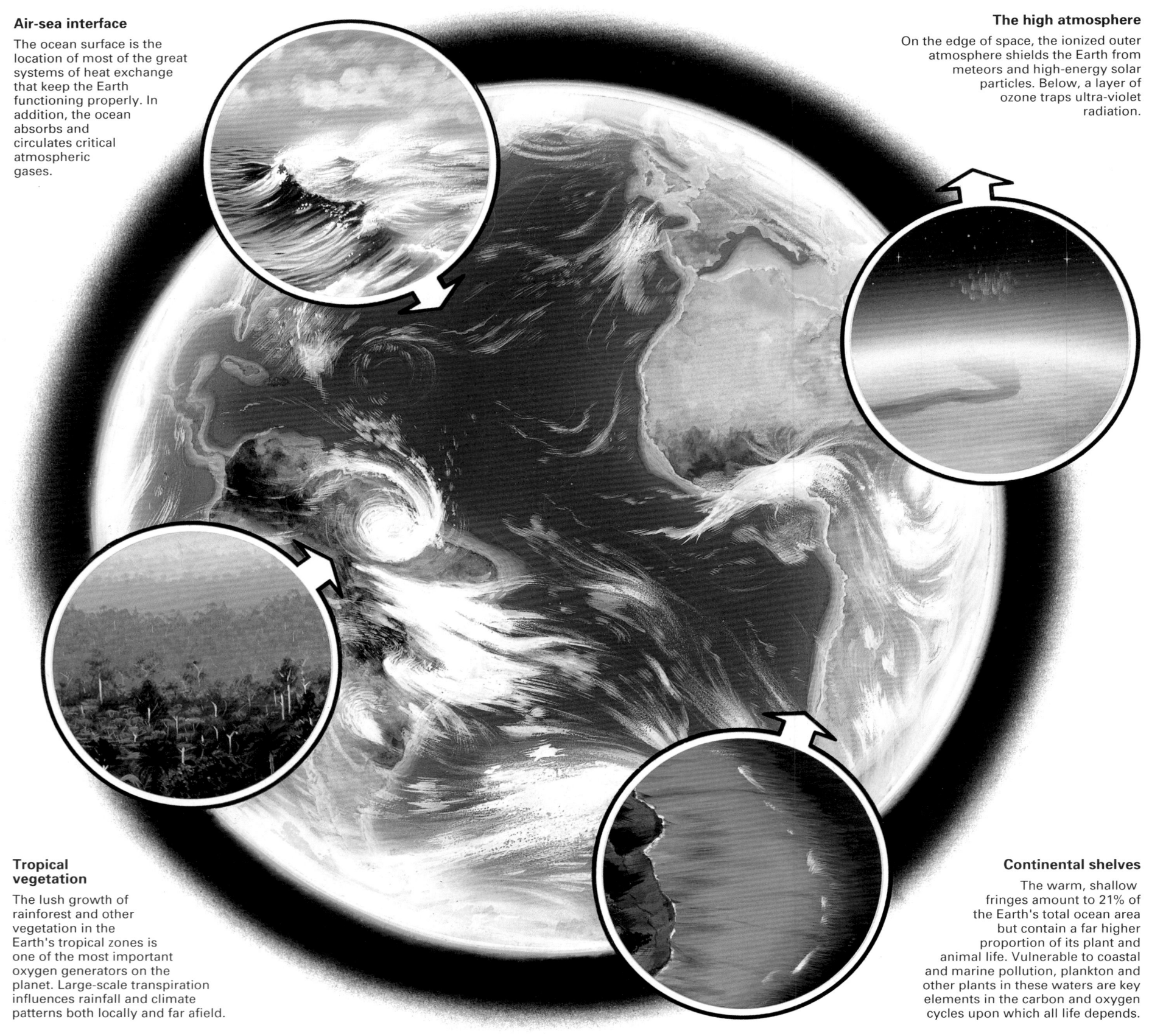

Air-sea interface

The ocean surface is the location of most of the great systems of heat exchange that keep the Earth functioning properly. In addition, the ocean absorbs and circulates critical atmospheric gases.

The high atmosphere

On the edge of space, the ionized outer atmosphere shields the Earth from meteors and high-energy solar particles. Below, a layer of ozone traps ultra-violet radiation.

Tropical vegetation

The lush growth of rainforest and other vegetation in the Earth's tropical zones is one of the most important oxygen generators on the planet. Large-scale transpiration influences rainfall and climate patterns both locally and far afield.

Continental shelves

The warm, shallow fringes amount to 21% of the Earth's total ocean area but contain a far higher proportion of its plant and animal life. Vulnerable to coastal and marine pollution, plankton and other plants in these waters are key elements in the carbon and oxygen cycles upon which all life depends.

20

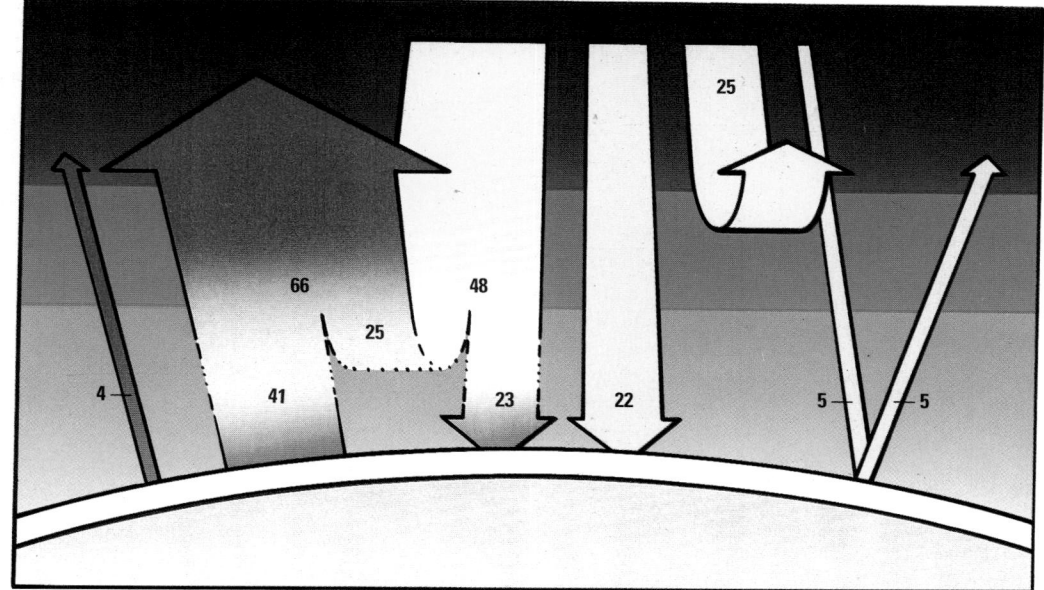

THE EARTH'S ENERGY BALANCE

Apart from a modest quantity of internal heat from its molten core, the Earth receives all its energy from the Sun. If the planet is to remain at a constant temperature, it must re-radiate exactly as much as it receives. Even a minute surplus would lead to a warmer Earth, a deficit to a cooler one; because the planetary energy budget is constantly audited by the laws of physics, which do not permit juggling, it must balance with absolute precision. The temperature at which thermal equilibrium is reached depends on a multitude of interconnected factors. Two of the most important are the relative brightness of the Earth – its index of reflectivity, called the albedo – and the heat-trapping capacity of the atmosphere – the celebrated 'greenhouse effect'.

Because the Sun is very hot, most of its energy arrives in the form of relatively short-wave radiation: the shorter the waves, the more energy they carry. Some of the incoming energy is reflected straight back into space, exactly as it arrived; some is absorbed by the atmosphere on its way towards the surface; some is absorbed by the earth itself. Absorbed energy heats the Earth and its atmosphere alike. But since its temperature is very much lower than that of the Sun, outgoing energy is emitted at much longer infra-red wavelengths. Some of the outgoing radiation escapes directly into outer space; some of it is reabsorbed by the atmosphere. Atmospheric energy eventually finds its way back into space, too, after a complex series of interactions. These include the air movements we call the weather and, almost incidentally, the maintenance of life on Earth.

This diagram does not attempt to illustrate the actual mechanisms of heat exchange, but gives a reasonable account (in percentages) of what happens to 100 energy 'units'. Short-wave radiation is shown in yellow, long-wave in red.

THE CARBON CYCLE

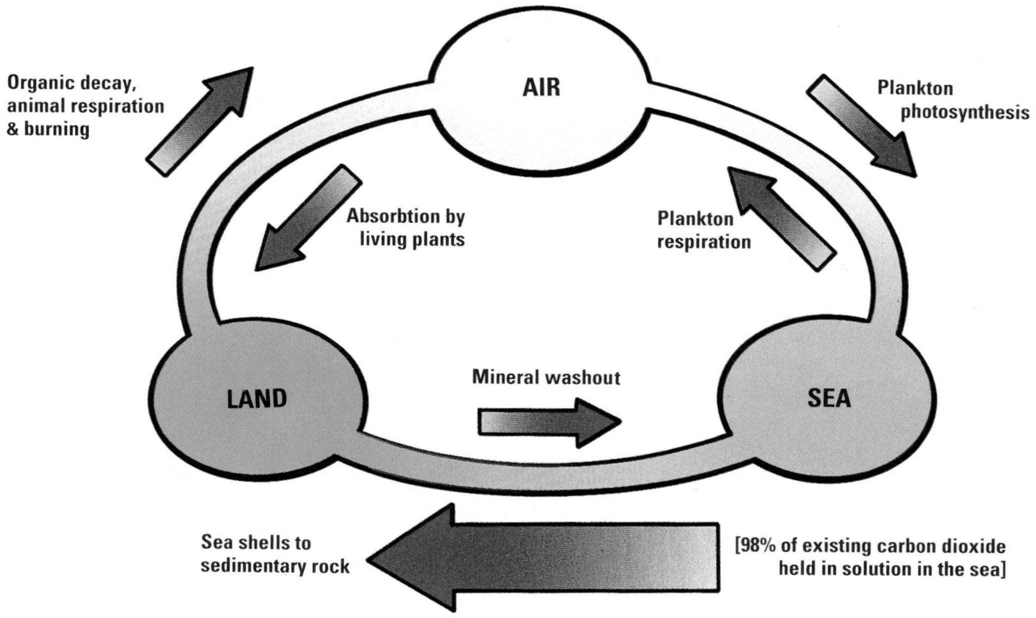

Most of the constituents of the atmosphere are kept in constant balance by complex cycles in which life plays an essential and indeed a dominant part. The control of carbon dioxide, which left to its own devices would be the dominant atmospheric gas, is possibly the most important, although since all the Earth's biological and geophysical cycles interact and interlock, it is hard to separate them even in theory and quite impossible in practice.

The Earth has a huge supply of carbon, only a small quantity of which is in the form of carbon dioxide. Of that, around 98% is dissolved in the sea; the fraction circulating in the air amounts to only 340 parts per million of the atmosphere, where its capacity as a greenhouse gas is the key regulator of the planetary temperature. In turn, life regulates the regulator, keeping carbon dioxide concentrations below danger level.

If all life were to vanish tomorrow from the Earth, the atmosphere would begin the process of change immediately, although it might take several million years to achieve a new, inorganic stability. First, the oxygen content would begin to fall away; with no more assistance than a little solar radiation, a few electrical storms and its own high chemical potential, oxygen would steadily combine with atmospheric nitrogen and volcanic outgassing. In doing so, it would yield sufficient acid to react with carbonaceous rocks such as limestone, releasing carbon dioxide. Once carbon dioxide levels exceeded about 1%, its greenhouse power would increase disproportionately. Rising temperatures – well above the boiling point of water would speed chemical reactions; in time, the Earth's atmosphere would consist of little more than carbon dioxide and superheated water vapour.

Living things, however, circulate carbon. They do so first by simply existing: after all, the carbon atom is the basic building block of living matter. During life, plants absorb atmospheric carbon dioxide, incorporating the carbon itself into their structure – leaves and trunks in the case of land plants, shells

in the case of plankton and the tiny creatures that feed on it. The oxygen thereby freed is added to the atmosphere, at least for a time. Most plant carbon is returned to circulation when the plants die and decay, combining once more with the oxygen released during life. However, a small proportion – about one part in 1000 – is removed almost permanently, buried beneath mud on land, at sea sinking as dead matter to the ocean floor. In time, it is slowly compressed into sedimentary rocks such as limestone and chalk.

But in the evolution of the Earth, nothing is quite permanent. On an even longer timescale, the planet's crustal movements force new rock upward in mid-ocean ridges. Limestone deposits are

moved, and sea levels change; ancient limestone is exposed to weathering, and a little of its carbon is released to be fixed in turn by the current generation of plants.

The carbon cycle has continued quietly for an immensely long time, and without gross disturbance there is no reason why it would not continue almost indefinitely in the future. However, human beings have found a way to release fixed carbon at a rate far faster than existing global systems can recirculate it. Oil and coal deposits represent the work of millions of years of carbon accumulation; but it has taken only a few human generations of high-energy scavenging to endanger the entire complex regulatory cycle.

Diagram labels:

Organic decay, animal respiration & burning

AIR

Plankton photosynthesis

Absorbtion by living plants

Plankton respiration

LAND

Mineral washout

SEA

Sea shells to sedimentary rock

[98% of existing carbon dioxide held in solution in the sea]

THE GREENHOUSE EFFECT

Constituting barely 0.03% of the atmosphere, carbon dioxide has a hugely disproportionate effect on the Earth's climate and even its habitability. Like the glass panes in a greenhouse, it is transparent to most incoming short-wave radiation, which passes freely to heat the planet beneath. But when the warmed earth re-transmits that energy, in the form of longer-wave infra-red radiation, the carbon dioxide functions as an opaque shield, so that the planetary surface (like the interior of a greenhouse) stays relatively hot.

Recent increases in CO_2 levels are causing alarm: global warming associated with a runaway greenhouse effect could bring disaster. But a serious reduction would be just as damaging, with surface temperatures falling dramatically; during the last ice age, for example, the carbon dioxide concentration was around 180 parts per million, and a total absence of the gas would likely leave the planet a ball of ice, or at best frozen tundra.

The diagram shows incoming sunlight as yellow; high-energy ultra-violet (blue) is trapped by the ozone layer while outgoing heat from the warmed Earth (red) is partially retained by carbon dioxide.

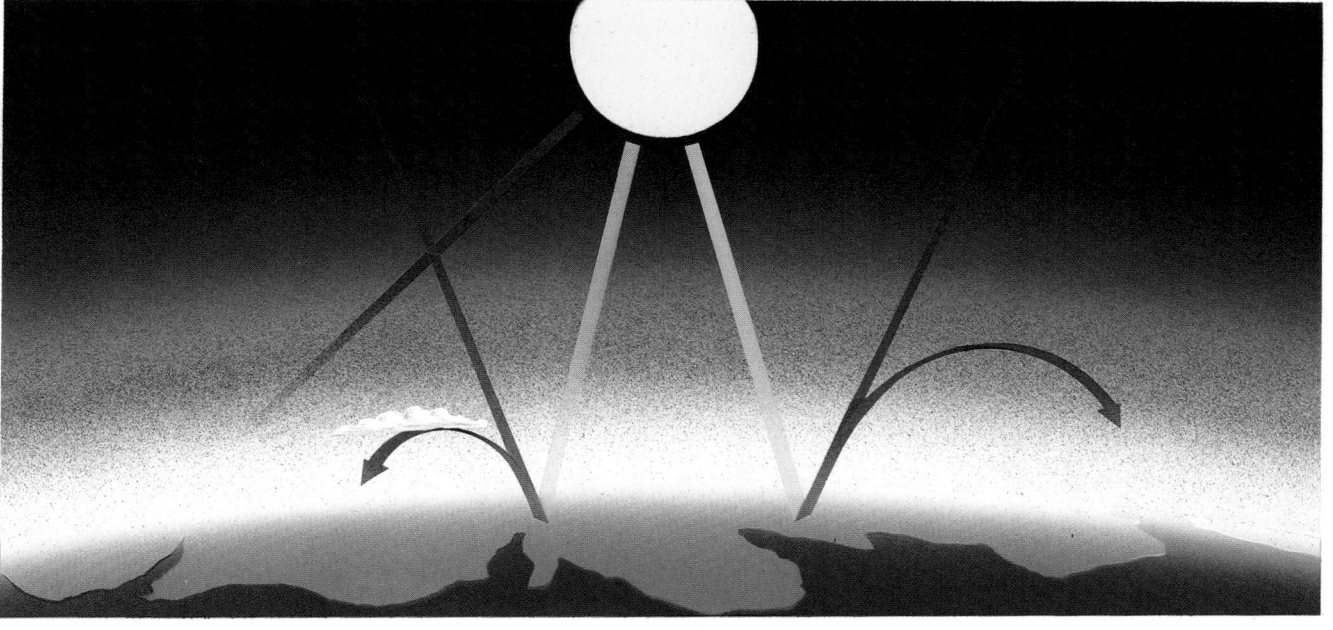

PEOPLE: DEMOGRAPHY

24:	URBANIZATION OF THE EARTH URBAN POPULATION
25:	LARGEST CITIES
31:	FOOD & POPULATION
40:	WEALTH & POPULATION
46:	HUMAN EXPANSION

As the 20th century draws to its close, the Earth's population increases by nearly 10,000 every hour – enough to fill a new major city every week. The growth is almost entirely confined to the developing world, which accounted for 67% of total population in 1950 and is set to reach 84% by 2025. In developed countries, populations are almost static, and in some places, such as Germany, are actually falling. In fact, there is a clear correlation between wealth and low fertility: as incomes rise, reproduction rates drop.

The decline is already apparent. With the exception of Africa, the actual rates of increase are falling nearly everywhere. The structure of populations, however, ensures that human numbers will continue to rise even as fertility diminishes. Developed nations, like the UK, have an even spread across ages, and usually a growing proportion of elderly people: the over-75s often outnumber the under-5s, and women of child-bearing age form only a modest part of the total. Developing nations fall into a pattern somewhere between that of Kenya and Brazil: the great majority of their people are in the younger age groups, about to enter their most fertile years. In time, even Kenya's population profile should resemble the developed model, but the transition will come about only after a few more generations' growth.

It remains to be seen whether the planet will tolerate the population growth that seems inevitable before stability is reached. More people consume more resources, increasing the strain on an already troubled environment. However, more people should mean a greater supply of human ingenuity – the only commodity likely to resolve the crisis .

LARGEST NATIONS

The world's most populous nations, in millions (1989)

1.	China	1120
2.	India	812
3.	USA	250
4.	Indonesia	179
5.	Brazil	147
6.	Russia	147
7.	Japan	123
8.	Nigeria	109
9.	Pakistan	109
10.	Bangladesh	107
11.	Mexico	84
12.	Germany	79
13.	Vietnam	66
14.	Philippines	60
15.	Italy	58
16.	UK	57
17.	Turkey	57
18.	France	56
19.	Thailand	55
20.	Iran	55
21.	Egypt	53
22.	Ukraine	52
23.	Ethiopia	51
24.	S. Korea	43
25.	Burma	41

CROWDED NATIONS

Population per square kilometre (1989), exc. nations of less than one million

1.	Hong Kong	5826.2
2.	Singapore	4401.6
3.	Bangladesh	795.4
4.	Mauritius	577.3
5.	Taiwan	554.2
6.	Netherlands	439.0
7.	S. Korea	432.3
8.	Puerto Rico	412.9
9.	Belgium	328.5
10.	Japan	327.0
11.	Lebanon	283.2
12.	Rwanda	280.1
13.	India	273.1
14.	Sri Lanka	259.6
15.	El Salvador	251.3
16.	Trinidad & Tobago	246.2
17.	UK	236.8
18.	Germany	224.9
19.	Israel	224.6
20.	Jamaica	219.3

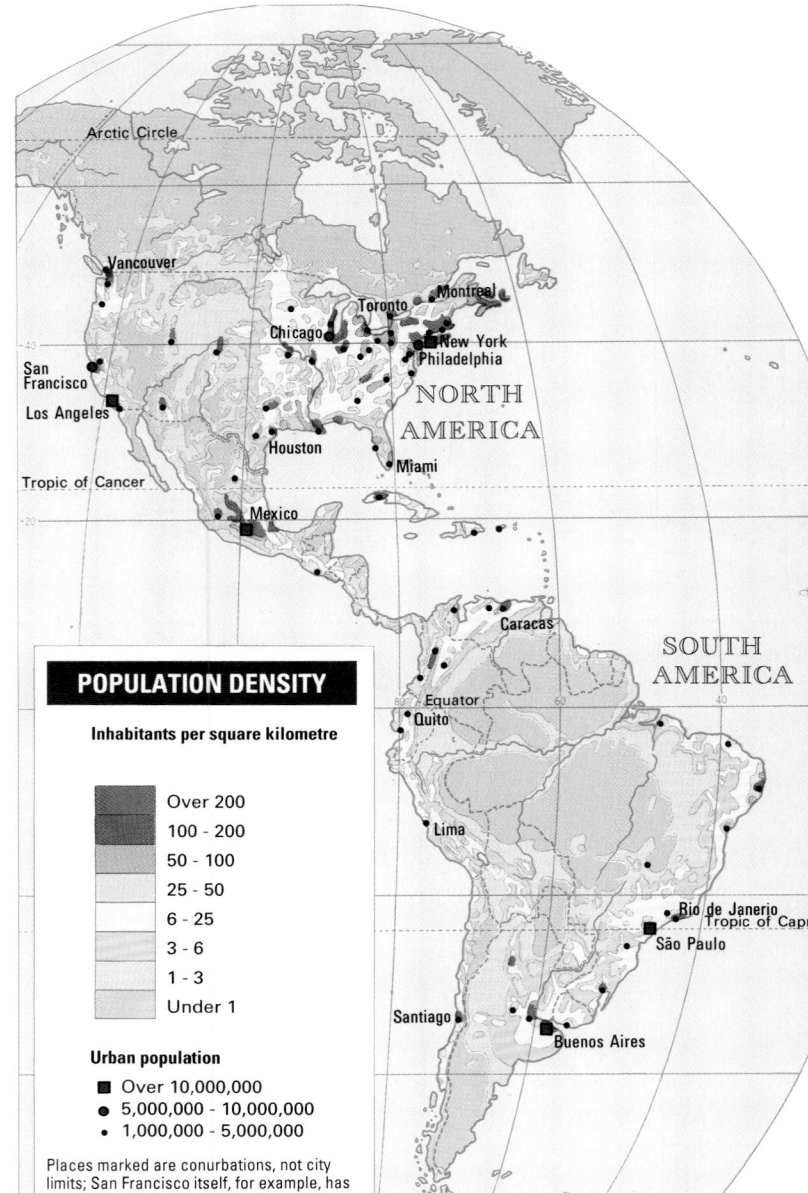

POPULATION DENSITY

Inhabitants per square kilometre

- Over 200
- 100 - 200
- 50 - 100
- 25 - 50
- 6 - 25
- 3 - 6
- 1 - 3
- Under 1

Urban population

- ■ Over 10,000,000
- ● 5,000,000 - 10,000,000
- • 1,000,000 - 5,000,000

Places marked are conurbations, not city limits; San Francisco itself, for example, has an official population of less than a million.

Projection : Mollweide's Interrupted Homolographic

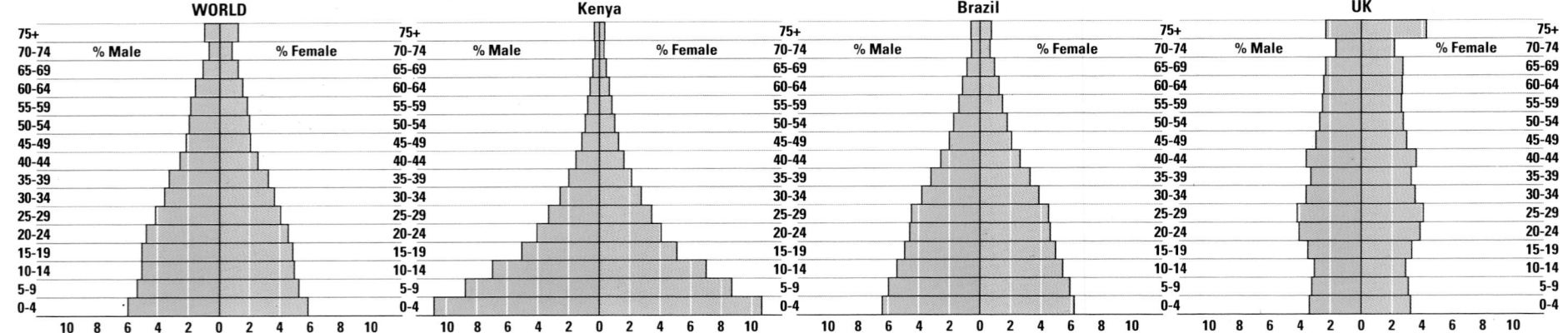

WORLD   Kenya   Brazil   UK

RATES OF GROWTH

Apparently small rates of population growth lead to dramatic increases over two or three generations. The table below translates annual percentage growth into the number of years required to double a population.

% change	Doubling time
0.5	139.0
1.0	69.7
1.5	46.6
2.0	35.0
2.5	28.1
3.0	23.4
3.5	20.1
4.0	17.7

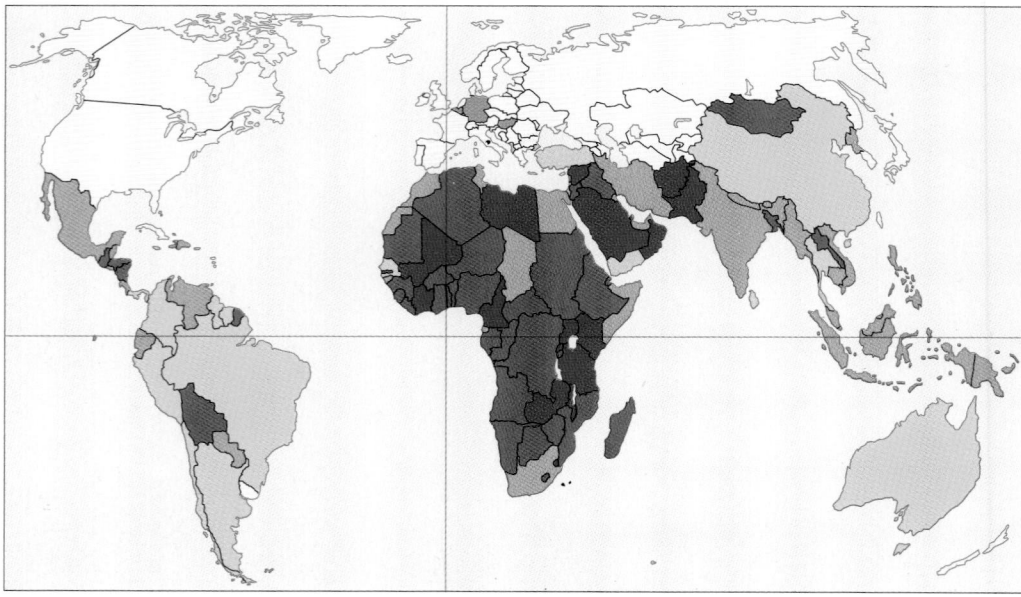

POPULATION CHANGE

Estimated percentage change in total population, between 1990 and 2000

- Over 40% gain
- 30 - 40% gain
- 20 - 30% gain
- 10 - 20% gain
- 0 - 10% gain
- No change or population loss

Top 5 countries		Bottom 5 countries	
Afghanistan	+60%	Hungary	-0.2%
Mali	+56%	Singapore	-0.2%
Tanzania	+55%	Grenada	-2.4%
Ivory Coast	+47%	Tonga	-3.2%
Saudi Arabia	+46%	Germany	-3.2%

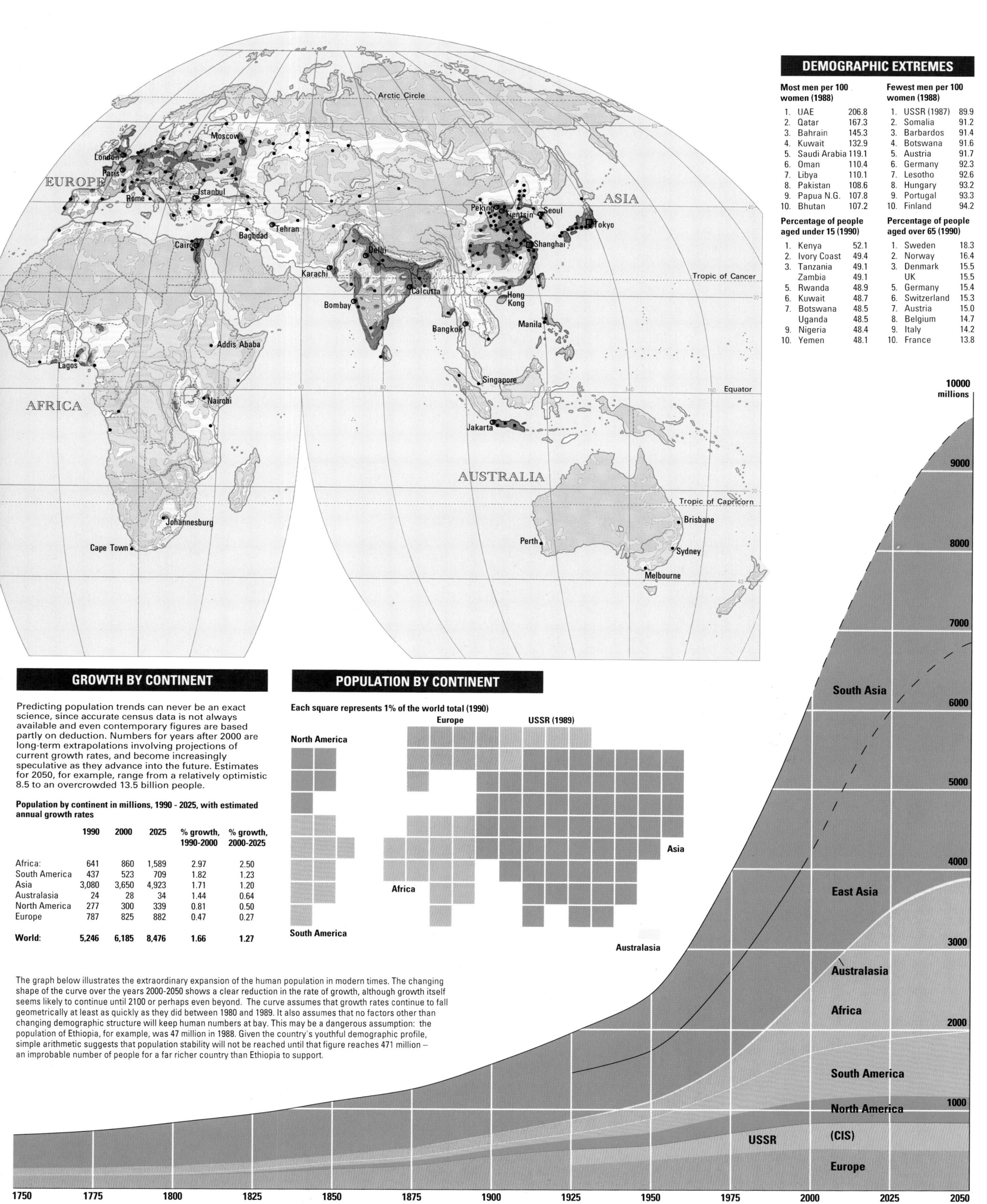

Arctic Circle

EUROPE
London
Paris
Moscow
Rome
Istanbul
ASIA
Tehran
Baghdad
Cairo
Peking
Tientsin
Seoul
Tokyo
Delhi
Shanghai
Karachi
Tropic of Cancer
Calcutta
Bombay
Hong Kong
Bangkok
Manila
Lagos
AFRICA
Addis Ababa
Nairobi
Singapore
Equator
Jakarta
AUSTRALIA
Johannesburg
Tropic of Capricorn
Brisbane
Cape Town
Perth
Sydney
Melbourne

DEMOGRAPHIC EXTREMES

Most men per 100 women (1988)		Fewest men per 100 women (1988)	
1. UAE	206.8	1. USSR (1987)	89.9
2. Qatar	167.3	2. Somalia	91.2
3. Bahrain	145.3	3. Barbardos	91.4
4. Kuwait	132.9	4. Botswana	91.6
5. Saudi Arabia	119.1	5. Austria	91.7
6. Oman	110.4	6. Germany	92.3
7. Libya	110.1	7. Lesotho	92.6
8. Pakistan	108.6	8. Hungary	93.2
9. Papua N.G.	107.8	9. Portugal	93.3
10. Bhutan	107.2	10. Finland	94.2

Percentage of people aged under 15 (1990)		Percentage of people aged over 65 (1990)	
1. Kenya	52.1	1. Sweden	18.3
2. Ivory Coast	49.4	2. Norway	16.4
3. Tanzania	49.1	3. Denmark	15.5
Zambia	49.1	UK	15.5
5. Rwanda	48.9	5. Germany	15.4
6. Kuwait	48.7	6. Switzerland	15.3
7. Botswana	48.5	7. Austria	15.0
Uganda	48.5	8. Belgium	14.7
9. Nigeria	48.4	9. Italy	14.2
10. Yemen	48.1	10. France	13.8

GROWTH BY CONTINENT

Predicting population trends can never be an exact science, since accurate census data is not always available and even contemporary figures are based partly on deduction. Numbers for years after 2000 are long-term extrapolations involving projections of current growth rates, and become increasingly speculative as they advance into the future. Estimates for 2050, for example, range from a relatively optimistic 8.5 to an overcrowded 13.5 billion people.

Population by continent in millions, 1990 - 2025, with estimated annual growth rates

	1990	2000	2025	% growth, 1990-2000	% growth, 2000-2025
Africa:	641	860	1,589	2.97	2.50
South America	437	523	709	1.82	1.23
Asia	3,080	3,650	4,923	1.71	1.20
Australasia	24	28	34	1.44	0.64
North America	277	300	339	0.81	0.50
Europe	787	825	882	0.47	0.27
World:	5,246	6,185	8,476	1.66	1.27

POPULATION BY CONTINENT

Each square represents 1% of the world total (1990)

North America
Europe
USSR (1989)
Asia
Africa
South America
Australasia

The graph below illustrates the extraordinary expansion of the human population in modern times. The changing shape of the curve over the years 2000-2050 shows a clear reduction in the rate of growth, although growth itself seems likely to continue until 2100 or perhaps even beyond. The curve assumes that growth rates continue to fall geometrically at least as quickly as they did between 1980 and 1989. It also assumes that no factors other than changing demographic structure will keep human numbers at bay. This may be a dangerous assumption: the population of Ethiopia, for example, was 47 million in 1988. Given the country's youthful demographic profile, simple arithmetic suggests that population stability will not be reached until that figure reaches 471 million — an improbable number of people for a far richer country than Ethiopia to support.

10000 millions
9000
8000
7000
South Asia
6000
5000
East Asia
4000
Australasia
3000
Africa
2000
South America
North America
1000
USSR
(CIS)
Europe

1750 1775 1800 1825 1850 1875 1900 1925 1950 1975 2000 2025 2050

PEOPLE: CITIES

16:	WATER SUPPLY
22:	POPULATION DENSITY
39:	THE GREAT PORTS

In 1750, barely three humans in every hundred lived in a city; by 2000, more than half of a vastly greater world population will find a home in some kind of urban area. In 1850, only London and Paris had more than a million inhabitants; by 2000, at least 24 cities will each contain over ten million people. The increase is concentrated in the Third World, if only because levels of urbanization in most developed countries - more than 90% in the UK and Belgium, and almost 75% in the USA, despite that country's great open spaces - have already reached practical limits.

Such large-scale concentration is relatively new to the human race. Although city life has always attracted country-dwellers in search of trade, employment or simply human contact, until modern times they paid a high price. Crowding and poor sanitation ensured high death rates, and until about 1850, most cities needed a steady flow of incomers simply to maintain their populations: there were 600,000 more deaths than births in 18th-century London, for example, and some other large cities showed an even worse imbalance.

With improved public health, cities could grow from their own human resources, and large-scale urban living became a commonplace in the developed world. Since about 1950, the pattern has been global. Like their counterparts in 19th-century Europe and the USA, the great new cities are driven into rapid growth by a kind of push-pull mechanism. The push is generated by agricultural overcrowding: only so many people can live from a single plot of land, and population pressure drives many into towns; The pull comes from the possibilities of economic improvement, an irresistible lure to the world's rural hopefuls.

Such improvement is not always obvious: the typical Third World city, with millions of people living (often illegally) in shanty towns and many thousands existing homelessly on the ill-made streets, does not present a great image of prosperity. Yet modern shanty towns are healthier than industrializing Pittsburgh or Manchester in the last century, and these human ant-hills teem with industry as well as squalor: throughout the world, above-average rates of urbanization have gone hand-in-hand with above-average economic growth. Surveys consistently demonstrate that Third World city-dwellers are generally better off than their rural counterparts, whose poverty is less concentrated but often more desperate. This only serves to increase the attraction of the city for the rural poor.

However, the sheer speed of the urbanization process threatens to overwhelm the limited abilities of city authorities to provide even rudimentary services and administration. The 24 million people expected to live in Mexico City by 2000, for example, would swamp a more efficient local government than Mexico can provide. Improvements are often swallowed up by the relentless rise in urban population: although safe drinking water should reach 75% of Third World city-dwellers by the end of the century - a considerable achievement - population growth will add 100 million to the list of those without it.

THE URBANIZATION OF THE EARTH

City-building, 1850-2000; each white spot represents a city of at least one million inhabitants.

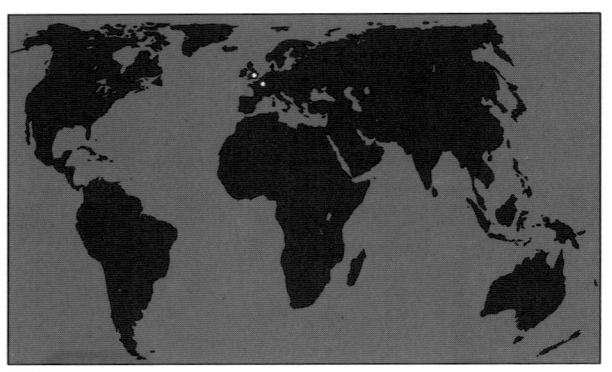

1850

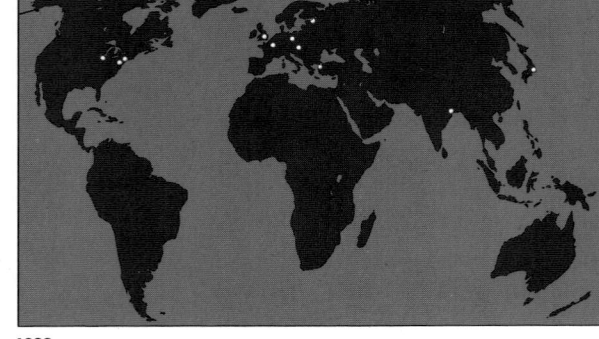

1900

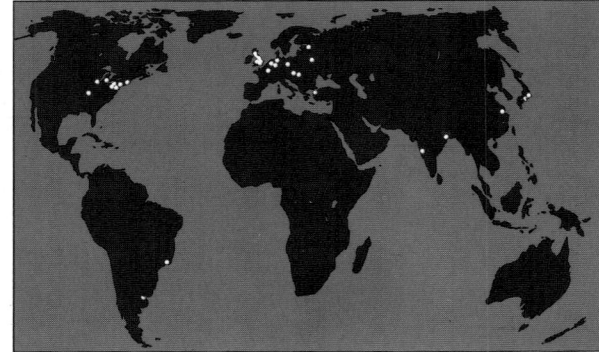

1925

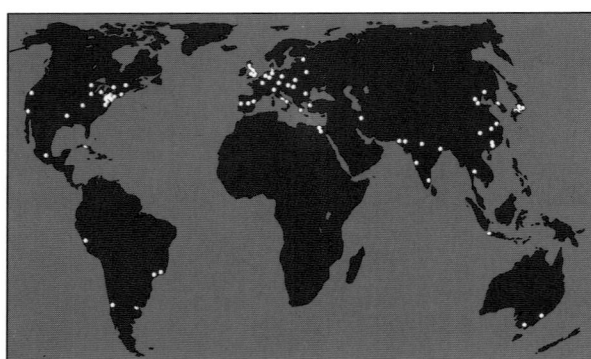

1950

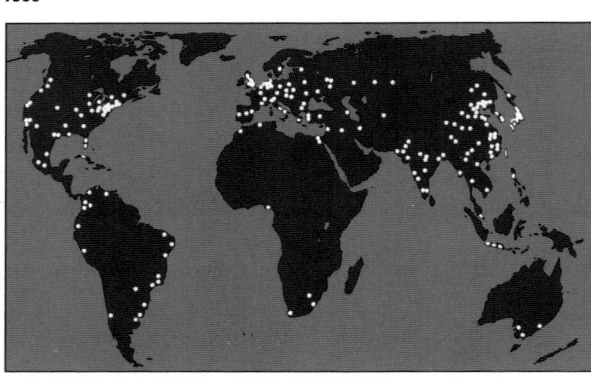

1975

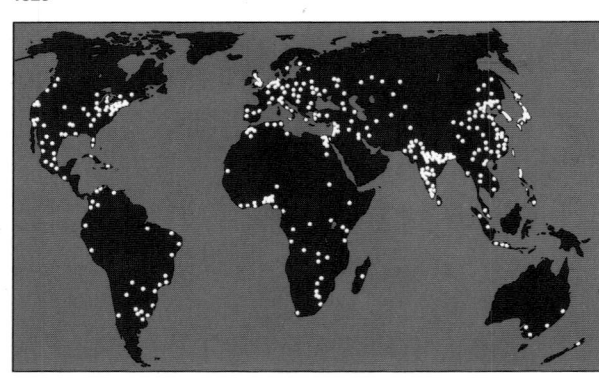

2000

URBAN POPULATION

Percentage of total population living in towns & cities (1990)

- Over 80%
- 60 - 80%
- 40 - 60%
- 20 - 40%
- Under 20%

Most urbanized		Least urbanized	
Singapore	100%	Nepal	10%
Belgium	97%	Burkina Faso	9%
Kuwait	96%	Rwanda	8%
Hong Kong	93%	Burundi	7%
UK	93%	Bhutan	5%

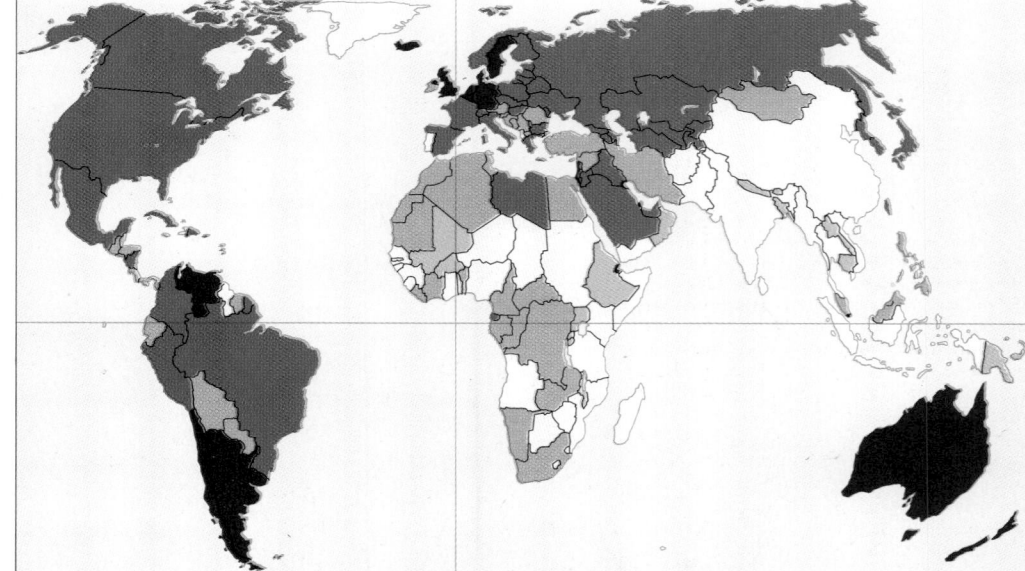

Projection: Modified Hammer Equal Area   * Statistics for each of the new republics of the former U.S.S.R. and Yugoslavia are not yet available. The map shows the statistics for the entire U.S.S.R. and Yugoslavia.

EXPANDING CITIES

The growth of the world's largest cities, 1950-2000. Intermediate rings indicate relative size in 1970 & 1985.

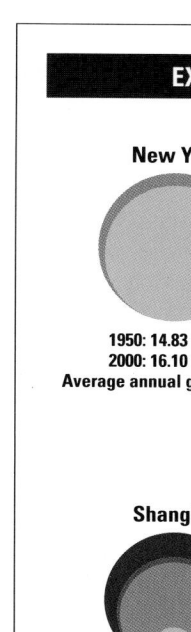

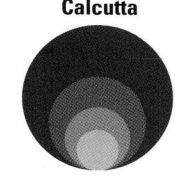

New York
1950: 14.83 million
2000: 16.10 million
Average annual growth: 0.16%

London
1950: 8.35 million
2000: 10.79 million
Average annual growth: 0.51%

Tokyo
1950: 6.25 million
2000: 21.32 million
Average annual growth: 2.5%

Buenos Aires
1950: 5.25 million
2000: 13.05 million
Average annual growth: 1.8%

Calcutta
1950: 4.45 million
2000: 15.94 million
Average annual growth: 2.6%

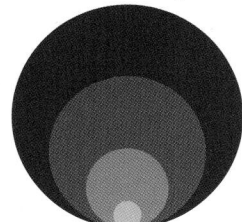

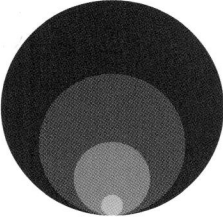
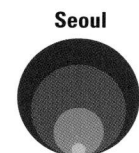

Shanghai
1950: 4.3 million
2000: 14.69 million
Average annual growth: 2.5%

Mexico City
1950: 2.97 million
2000: 24.44 million
Average annual growth: 4.3%

Rio de Janeiro
1950: 2.94 million
2000: 13.0 million
Average annual growth: 3.0%

São Paulo
1950: 2.28 million
2000: 23.6 million
Average annual growth: 4.8%

Seoul
1950: 1.45 million
2000: 12.97 million
Average annual growth: 4.5%

Each set of circles illustrates a city's size in 1950, 1970, 1985 and 2000. In most cases, expansion has been steady and, often, explosive. New York and London, however, went through patches of negative growth during the period. In New York, the world's largest city in 1950, population reached a peak around 1970. London shrank slightly between 1970 and 1985 before resuming a very modest rate of increase. In both cases, the divergence from world trends can be explained in part by counting methods: each is at the centre of a great agglomeration, and definitions of where 'city limits' lie may vary over time. But their relative decline also matches a pattern often seen in mature cities in the developed world, where urbanization, already at a very high level, has reached a plateau.

CITIES IN DANGER

As the 1980s advanced, most industrial countries, alarmed by acid rain and urban smog, took significant steps to limit air pollution. These controls, however, are expensive to install and difficult to enforce, and clean air remains a luxury most developed as well as developing cities must live without.

Those taking part in the United Nations' Global Environment Monitoring System (right) frequently show dangerous levels of pollutants ranging from soot to sulphur dioxide and photo-chemical smog; air in the majority of cities without such sampling equipment is likely to be at least as bad.

URBAN AIR POLLUTION

The world's most polluted cities: number of days each year when sulphur dioxide levels exceeded the WHO threshold of 150 micrograms per cubic metre (averaged over 4 to 15 years, 1970s - 1980s)

Sulphur dioxide is the main pollutant associated with industrial cities. According to the World Health Organization, more than seven days in a year above 150 µg per cubic metre bring a serious risk of respiratory disease: at least 600 million people live in urban areas where SO_2 concentrations regularly reach damaging levels.

- Manila, Philippines
- Calcutta, India
- Milan, Italy
- Zagreb, Yugoslavia
- Guangzhou, China
- Madrid, Spain
- Peking (Beijing), China
- Xian, China
- Seoul, South Korea
- Tehran, Iran
- Shenyang, China

120   90   60   30

INFORMAL CITIZENS

Proportion of population living in squatter settlements, selected cities in the developing world (1980s)

Urbanization in most Third World countries has been coming about far faster than local governments can provide services and accommodation for the new city-dwellers. Many – in some cities, most – find their homes in improvised squatter settlements, often unconnected to power, water and sanitation networks. Yet despite their ramshackle housing and marginal legality, these communities are often the most dynamic part of a city economy. They are also growing in size; and given the squatters' reluctance to be counted by tax-demanding authorities, the percentages shown here are likely to be underestimates.

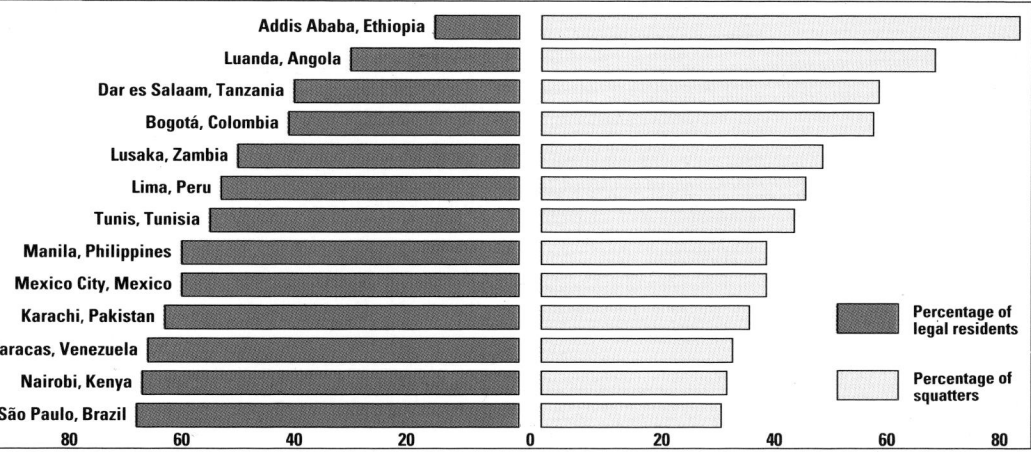

- Addis Ababa, Ethiopia
- Luanda, Angola
- Dar es Salaam, Tanzania
- Bogotá, Colombia
- Lusaka, Zambia
- Lima, Peru
- Tunis, Tunisia
- Manila, Philippines
- Mexico City, Mexico
- Karachi, Pakistan
- Caracas, Venezuela
- Nairobi, Kenya
- São Paulo, Brazil

80 60 40 20 0 20 40 60 80

■ Percentage of legal residents
□ Percentage of squatters

LARGEST CITIES

The world's most populous cities, in millions of inhabitants, based on estimates for the year 2000*

1.	Mexico City	24.4
2.	São Paulo	23.6
3.	Tokyo-Yokohama	21.3
4.	New York	16.1
5.	Calcutta	15.9
6.	Bombay	15.4
7.	Shanghai	14.7
8.	Tehran	13.7
9.	Jakarta	13.2
10.	Buenos Aires	13.1
11.	Rio de Janeiro	13.0
12.	Seoul	13.0
13.	Delhi	12.8
14.	Lagos	12.4
15.	Cairo-Giza	11.8
16.	Karachi	11.6
17.	Manila-Quezon	11.5
18.	Peking (Beijing)	11.5
19.	Dhaka	11.3
20.	Osaka-Kobe	11.2
21.	Los Angeles	10.9
22.	London	10.8
23.	Bangkok	10.3
24.	Moscow	10.1
25.	Tientsin (Tianjin)	10.0
26.	Lima-Callao	8.8
27.	Paris	8.8
28.	Milan	8.7
29.	Madras	7.8
30.	Baghdad	7.7
31.	Chicago	7.0
32.	Bogotá	6.9
33.	Hong Kong	6.1
34.	St Petersburg	5.8
35.	Pusan	5.8
36.	Santiago	5.6
37.	Shenyang	5.5
38.	Madrid	5.4
39.	Naples	4.5
40.	Philadelphia	4.3

[City populations are based on urban agglomerations rather than legal city limits. In some cases, such as Tokyo-Yokohama and Cairo-Giza, where two adjacent cities have merged into one concentration, they have been regarded as a single unit]

* For list of largest cities in 1990, see page XI

URBAN ADVANTAGES

Despite overcrowding and poor housing, living standards in the developing world's cities are almost invariably better than in the surrounding countryside. Resources - financial, material and administrative - are concentrated in the towns, which are usually also the centres of political activity and pressure. Governments - frequently unstable, and rarely established on a solid democratic base - are usually more responsive to urban discontent than rural misery. In many countries, especially in Africa, food prices are often kept artificially low, appeasing underemployed urban masses at the expense of agricultural development. The imbalance encourages further cityward migration, helping to account for the astonishing rate of post-1950 urbanization and putting great strain on the ability of many nations to provide even modest improvements for their people.

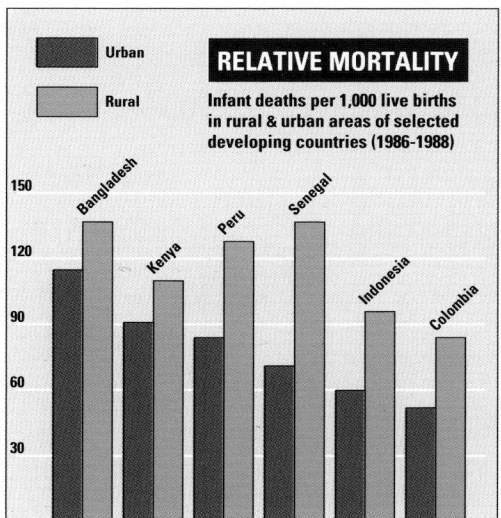

RELATIVE MORTALITY

■ Urban
■ Rural

Infant deaths per 1,000 live births in rural & urban areas of selected developing countries (1986-1988)

150 120 90 60 30

Bangladesh, Kenya, Peru, Senegal, Indonesia, Colombia

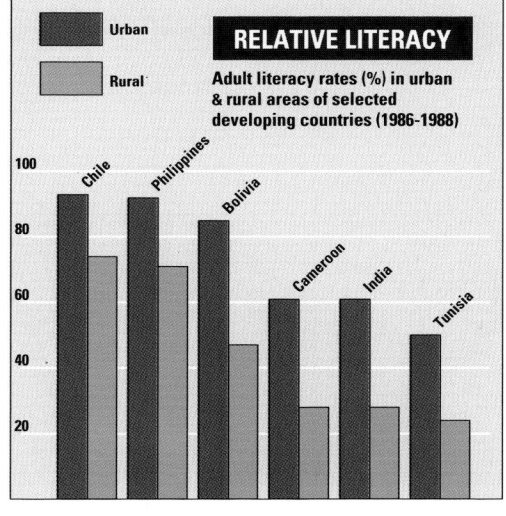

RELATIVE LITERACY

■ Urban
■ Rural

Adult literacy rates (%) in urban & rural areas of selected developing countries (1986-1988)

100 80 60 40 20

Chile, Philippines, Bolivia, Cameroon, India, Tunisia

PEOPLE: THE HUMAN FAMILY

22: POPULATION DENSITY

28: THE WORLD'S REFUGEES
WAR SINCE 1945

29: UNITED NATIONS
INTERNATIONAL ORGANIZATIONS

46: THE HISTORY OF HUMAN EXPANSION

Strictly speaking, all human beings belong to a single race: *Homo sapiens* has no sub-species. But although all humans are inter-fertile, anthropologists and geneticists distinguish three main racial types, whose differences reflect not so much evolutionary origin as long periods of separation.

Racial affinities are not always obvious. The Caucasoid group stems from Europe, North Africa and India, but still includes Australian aboriginals within its broad type; Mongoloid peoples comprise American Indians and Eskimos as well as most Chinese, central Asians and Malays; Negroids are mostly of African origin, but also include the Papuan peoples of New Guinea.

Migration in modern times has mingled racial groups to an unprecedented extent, and most nations now have some degree of racially mixed population.

Language is almost the definition of a particular human culture; the world has well over 5,000, most of them with only a few hundred thousand speakers. In one important sense, all languages are equal: although different vocabularies and linguistic structures greatly influence patterns of thought, all true human languages can carry virtually unlimited information. But even if there is no theoretical difference in the communicative power of English and one of the 500 or more tribal languages of Papua New Guinea, for example, an English speaker has access to very much more of the global culture than a Papuan who knows no other tongue.

Like language, religion encourages the internal cohesion of a single human group at the expense of creating gulfs of incomprehension between different groups. All religions satisfy a deep-seated human need, assigning men and women to a comprehensible place in what most of them still consider a divinely ordered world. But religion is also a means by which a culture can assert its individuality: the startling rise of Islam in the late 20th century is partly a response by large sections of the developing world to the secular, Western-inspired world order from which many non-Western peoples feel excluded. Like uncounted millions of human beings before them, they find in their religion not only a personal faith but a powerful group identity.

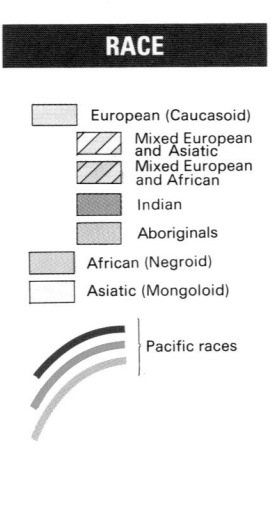

RACE

- European (Caucasoid)
- Mixed European and Asiatic
- Mixed European and African
- Indian
- Aboriginals
- African (Negroid)
- Asiatic (Mongoloid)
- Pacific races

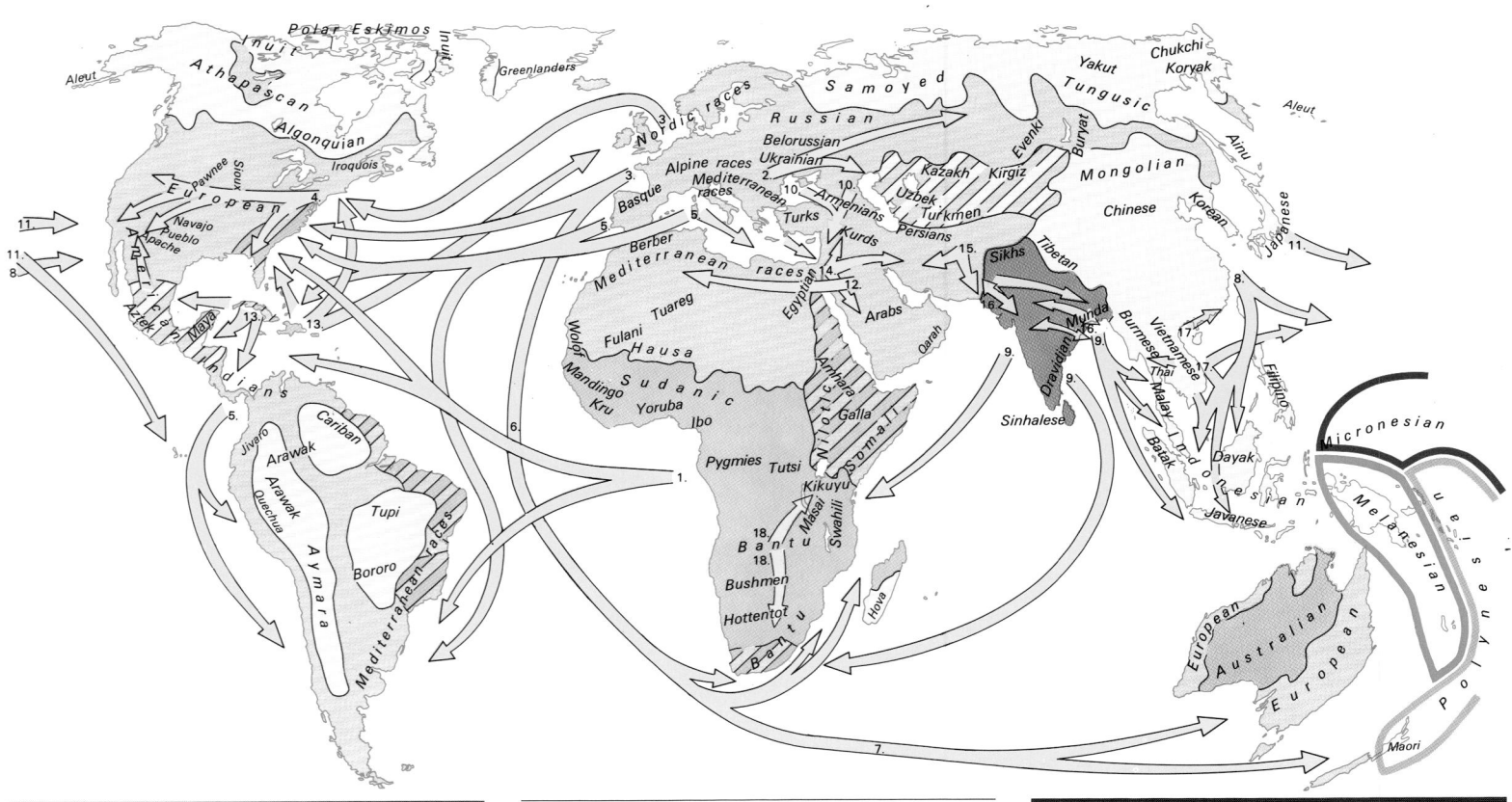

MOVEMENTS OF POPULATION

1. Africa to America (slaves), c. 1500-1860
2. Western Russia to Siberia, c. 1850-1950
3. W., E. & N. Europe to N. America, c. 1850-1900
4. From East Coast N. America, c. 1860-1960
5. Southern Europe to America, c. 1880-1920
6. Europe to S., E. & Central Africa, c. 1880-1950
7. Europe to Australia & N. Zealand, c. 1840-1950
8. China to S-E Asia & N. America, c. 1900-1950
9. India to Africa & South-East Asia, c. 1860-1910

Major migrations of peoples since 600 AD

10. European & N. American Jews to Israel, 1948-
11. Japan to N. & S. America, c. 1870-1910
12. Arabs to North Africa, 7th-9th centuries
13. C. America to N. America & Europe, c. 1950-1970
14. Migration in the Middle East, c. 1950-
15. Refugees from Afghanistan, 1979-
16. Migration in India, 1946-
17. Migration in & from South-East Asia, c. 1960-
18. Spread of the Bantu peoples, c. 1700-1900

BUILDING THE USA

U.S. Immigration 1820-1990

'Give me your tired, your poor/Your huddled masses yearning to breathe free....'

So starts Emma Lazarus's poem *The New Colossus*, inscribed on the Statue of Liberty. For decades the USA was the magnet that attracted millions of immigrants, notably from Central and Eastern Europe, the flow peaking in the early years of this century.

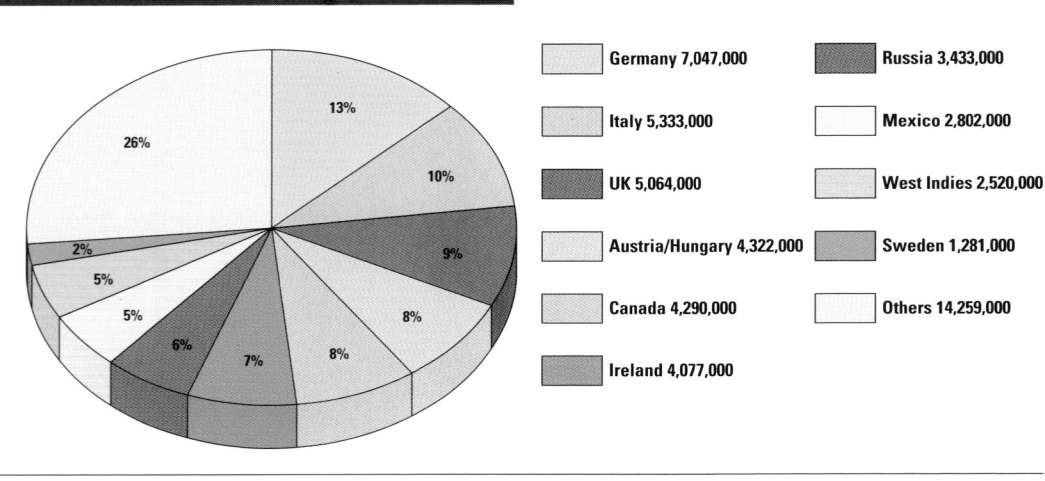

- Germany 7,047,000
- Italy 5,333,000
- UK 5,064,000
- Austria/Hungary 4,322,000
- Canada 4,290,000
- Ireland 4,077,000
- Russia 3,433,000
- Mexico 2,802,000
- West Indies 2,520,000
- Sweden 1,281,000
- Others 14,259,000

MIGRATION

The movement of migrants in thousands (1985-1990)

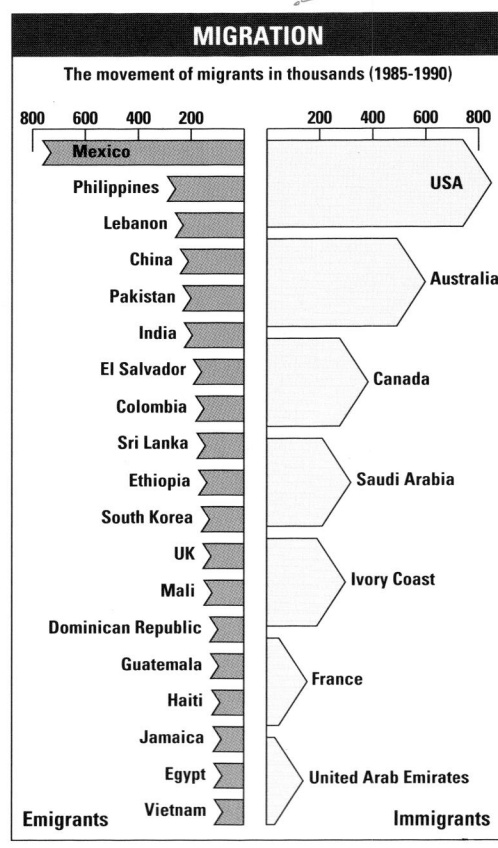

Emigrants: Mexico, Philippines, Lebanon, China, Pakistan, India, El Salvador, Colombia, Sri Lanka, Ethiopia, South Korea, UK, Mali, Dominican Republic, Guatemala, Haiti, Jamaica, Egypt, Vietnam

Immigrants: USA, Australia, Canada, Saudi Arabia, Ivory Coast, France, United Arab Emirates

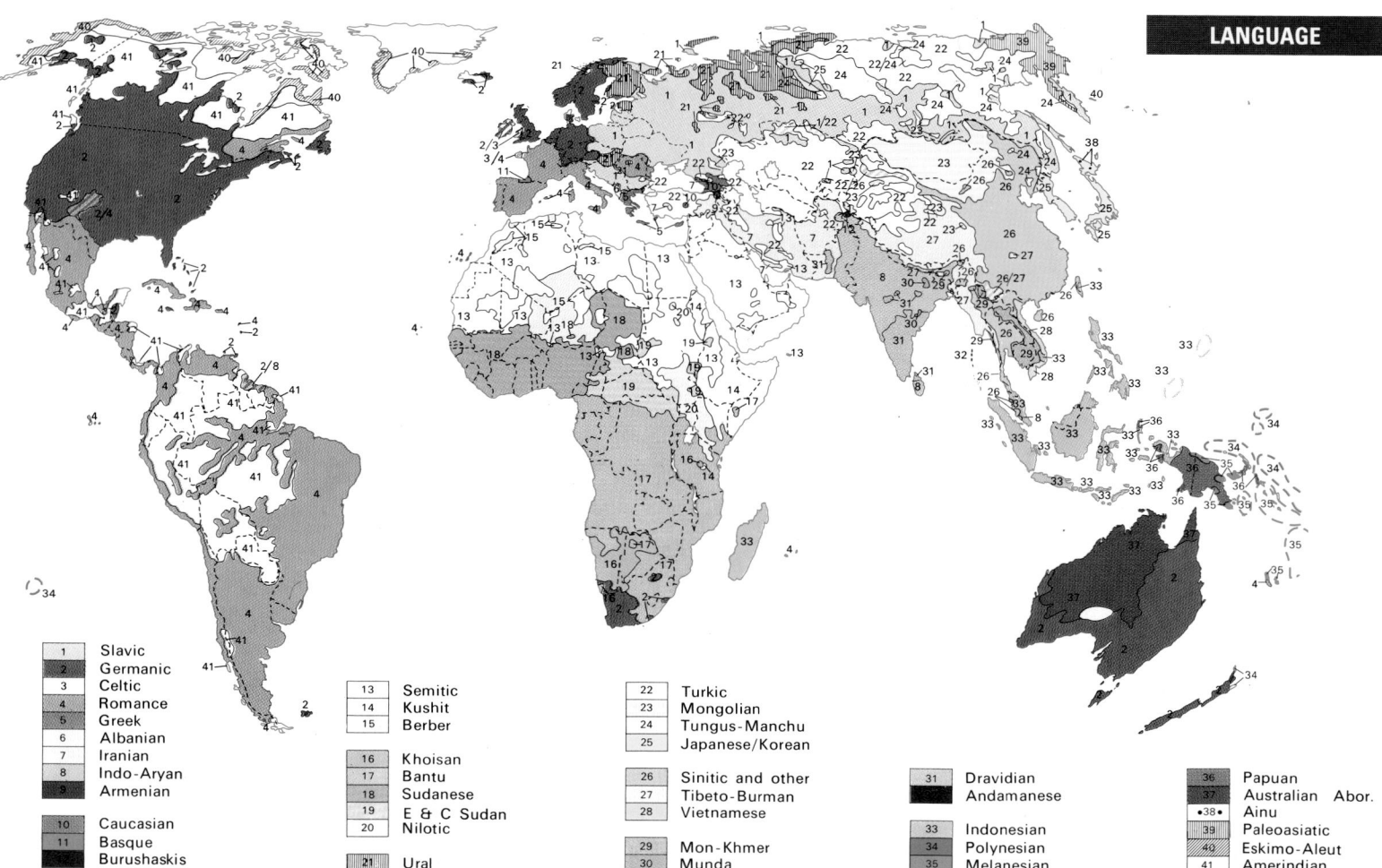

OFFICIAL LANGUAGES

Language	Total population	World %
English	1400m	27.0%
Chinese	1070m	19.1%
Hindi	700m	13.5%
Spanish	280m	5.4%
Russian	270m	5.2%
French	220m	4.2%
Arabic	170m	3.3%
Portuguese	160m	3.0%
Malay	160m	3.0%
Bengali	150m	2.9%
Japanese	120m	2.3%

1	Slavic
2	Germanic
3	Celtic
4	Romance
5	Greek
6	Albanian
7	Iranian
8	Indo-Aryan
9	Armenian

10	Caucasian
11	Basque
	Burushaskis

13	Semitic
14	Kushit
15	Berber

16	Khoisan
17	Bantu
18	Sudanese
19	E & C Sudan
20	Nilotic

21	Ural

22	Turkic
23	Mongolian
24	Tungus-Manchu
25	Japanese/Korean

26	Sinitic and other
27	Tibeto-Burman
28	Vietnamese

29	Mon-Khmer
30	Munda

31	Dravidian
	Andamanese

33	Indonesian
34	Polynesian
35	Melanesian

36	Papuan
37	Australian Abor.
•38•	Ainu
39	Paleoasiatic
40	Eskimo-Aleut
41	Amerindian

Languages form a kind of tree of development, splitting from a few ancient proto-tongues into branches that have grown apart and further divided with the passage of time. English and Hindi, for example, both belong to the great Indo-European family, although the relationship is only apparent after much analysis and comparison with non-Indo-European languages such as Chinese or Arabic; Hindi is part of the Indo-Aryan subgroup; English is a member of Indo-European's Germanic branch; French, another Indo-European tongue, traces its descent through the Latin, or Romance, branch. A few languages – Basque is one example – have no apparent links with any other, living or dead. Most modern languages, of course, have acquired enormous quantities of vocabulary from each other.

MOTHER TONGUES

Native speakers of the major languages, in millions (1989)

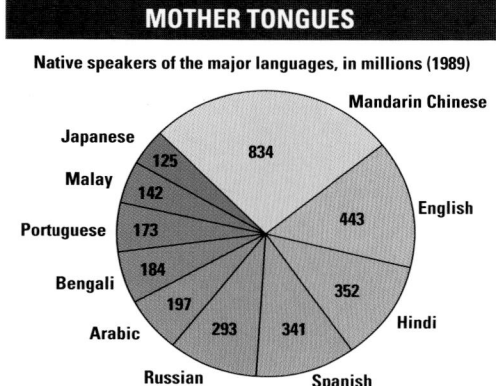

- Mandarin Chinese 834
- English 443
- Hindi 352
- Spanish 341
- Russian 293
- Arabic 197
- Bengali 184
- Portuguese 173
- Malay 142
- Japanese 125

Religions are not as easily mapped as the physical contours of landscape. Divisions are often blurred and frequently overlapping: most nations include people of many different faiths – or no faith at all. Some religions, like Islam and Christianity, have proselytes worldwide; others, like Hinduism and Confucianism, are restricted to a particular area, though modern migrations have taken some Indians and Chinese very far from their cultural origins. It is also difficult to show the degree to which religion exercises control over daily life: Christian Western Europe, for example, is nowadays far less dominated by its religion than are the Islamic nations of the Middle East. Similarly, figures for the major faiths' adherents make no distinction between nominal believers enrolled at birth and those for whom religion is a vital part of existence.

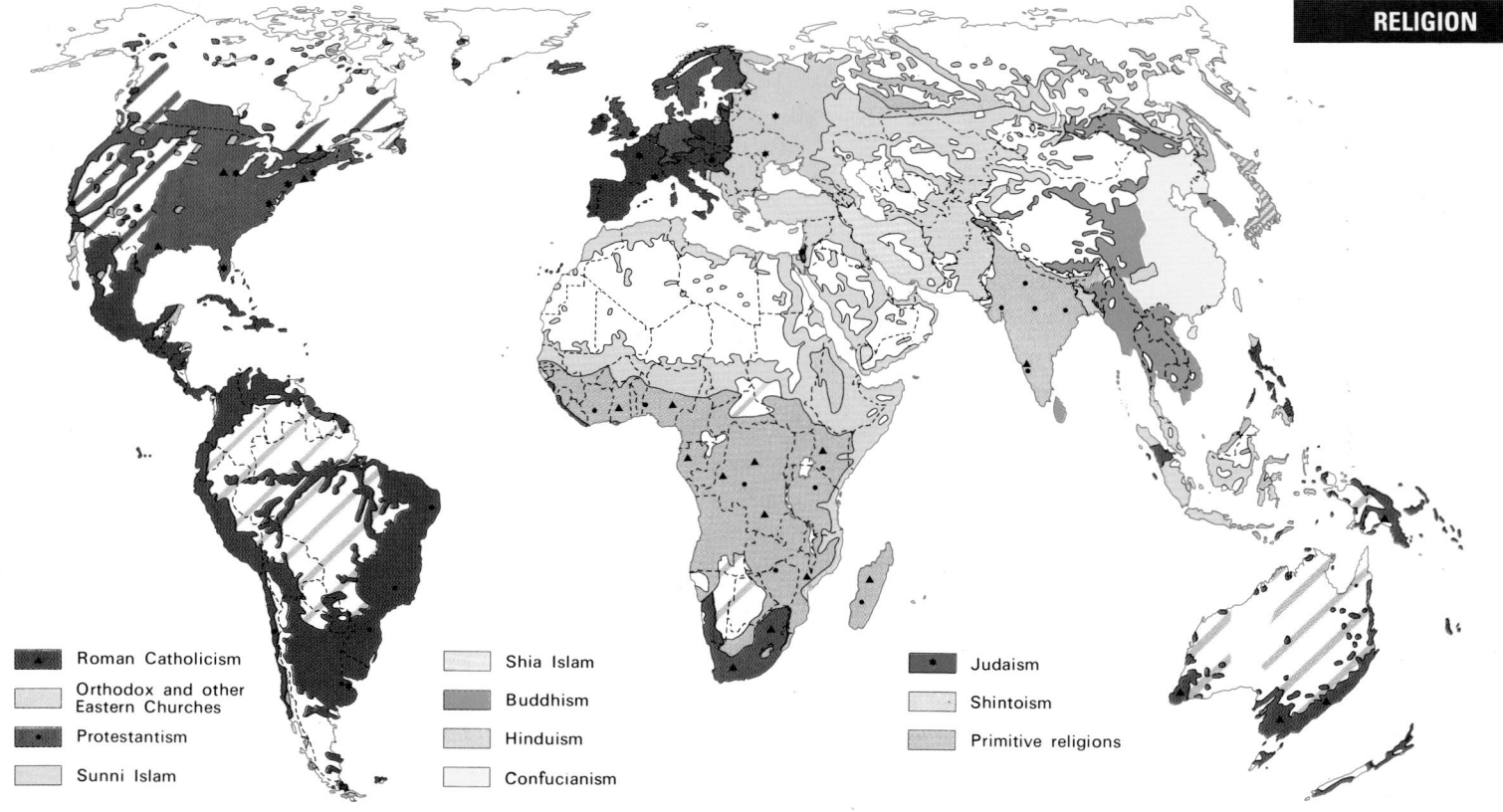

RELIGIOUS ADHERENTS

Christian	1667m
Roman Catholic	952m
Protestant	337m
Orthodox	162m
Anglican	70m
Other Christian	148m
Muslim	881m
Sunni	841m
Shia	40m
Hindu	663m
Buddhist	312m
Chinese folk	172m
Tribal	92m
Jewish	18m
Sikhs	17m

- Roman Catholicism
- Orthodox and other Eastern Churches
- Protestantism
- Sunni Islam
- Shia Islam
- Buddhism
- Hinduism
- Confucianism
- Judaism
- Shintoism
- Primitive religions

PEOPLE: CONFLICT & COOPERATION

26: RACE
    MIGRATION

27: RELIGION

46: HUMAN EXPANSION

Humans are social animals, rarely functioning well except in groups. Evolution has made them so: hunter-gatherers in cooperative bands were far more effective than animals that prowled alone. Agriculture, the building of cities and industrialization are all developments that depended on human cooperative ability – and in turn increased the need for it.

Unfortunately, human groups do not always cooperate so well with other human groups, and friction between them sometimes leads to cooperatively organized violence. War is itself a very human activity, with no real equivalent in any other species. Always murderous, it is sometimes purposeful and may even be very effective. The colonization of the Americas and Australia, for example, was in effect the waging of aggressive war by well-armed Europeans against indigenous peoples incapable of offering a serious defence.

More often, war achieves little but death and ruin. However, the great 20th-century wars appear to have cured the notoriously aggressive Europeans of their previous bad habits, although at the cost of between 50 and 100 million dead. The relative peace in the postwar developed world is at least partly due to the nuclear weapons with which rival powers have armed themselves – weapons so powerful that their use would leave a scarcely habitable planet with no meaningful distinction between victor and vanquished.

Yet warfare remains endemic: the second half of the 20th century was one of the bloodiest periods in history, and death by organized violence remains unhappily common. The map below attempts to show the serious conflicts that have scarred the Earth since 1945. Most are civil wars in poor countries, rather than international conflicts between rich ones; some of them are still unresolved, while others, like apparently extinct volcanoes, may erupt again at intervals, adding to the world's miserable population of refugees.

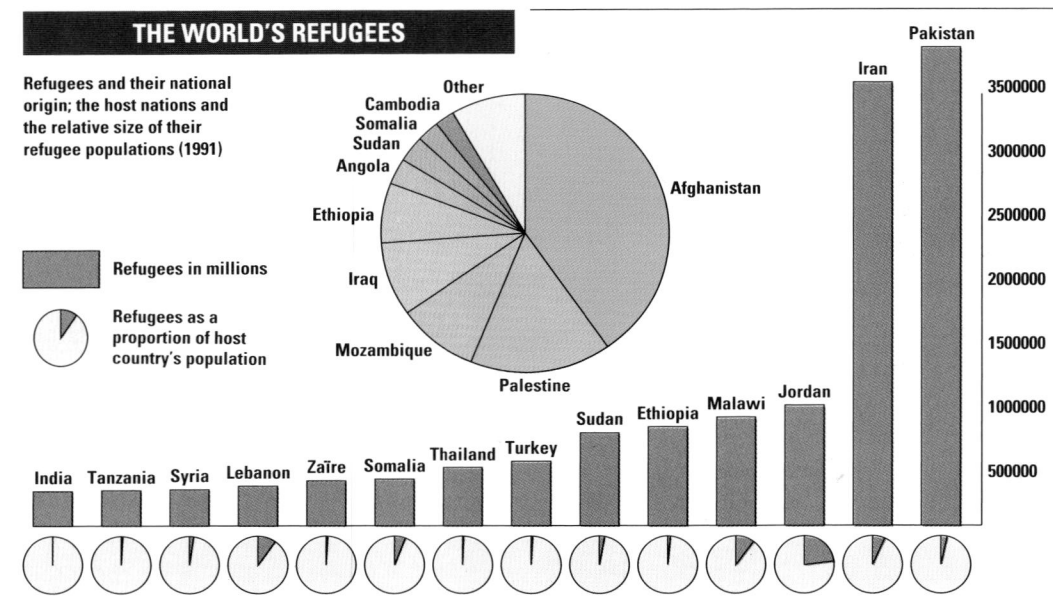

THE WORLD'S REFUGEES

Refugees and their national origin; the host nations and the relative size of their refugee populations (1991)

■ Refugees in millions

◔ Refugees as a proportion of host country's population

Pie chart origins: Other, Cambodia, Somalia, Sudan, Angola, Ethiopia, Iraq, Mozambique, Palestine, Afghanistan

Bar chart destinations: India, Tanzania, Syria, Lebanon, Zaïre, Somalia, Thailand, Turkey, Sudan, Ethiopia, Malawi, Jordan, Iran, Pakistan

Bar scale: 500000, 1000000, 1500000, 2000000, 2500000, 3000000, 3500000

The pie-chart shows the origins of the world's refugees, the bar-chart their destinations. According to the United Nations High Commissioner for Refugees in 1990, there were almost 15 million of them, a number that continued to increase and was almost certain to be amplified during the decade. Some have fled from climatic change, some from economic disaster and others from political persecution; the great majority are the victims of war.
All but a few who make it overseas seek asylum in neighbouring countries, which are often the least equipped to deal with them and where they are rarely welcome. Lacking any rights or power, they frequently become an embarrassment and a burden to their reluctant hosts.
Usually, the best any refugee can hope for is rudimentary food and shelter in temporary camps that all to often become semi-permanent, with little prospect of assimilation by host populations: many Palestinians, for example, have been forced to live in camps since 1948.

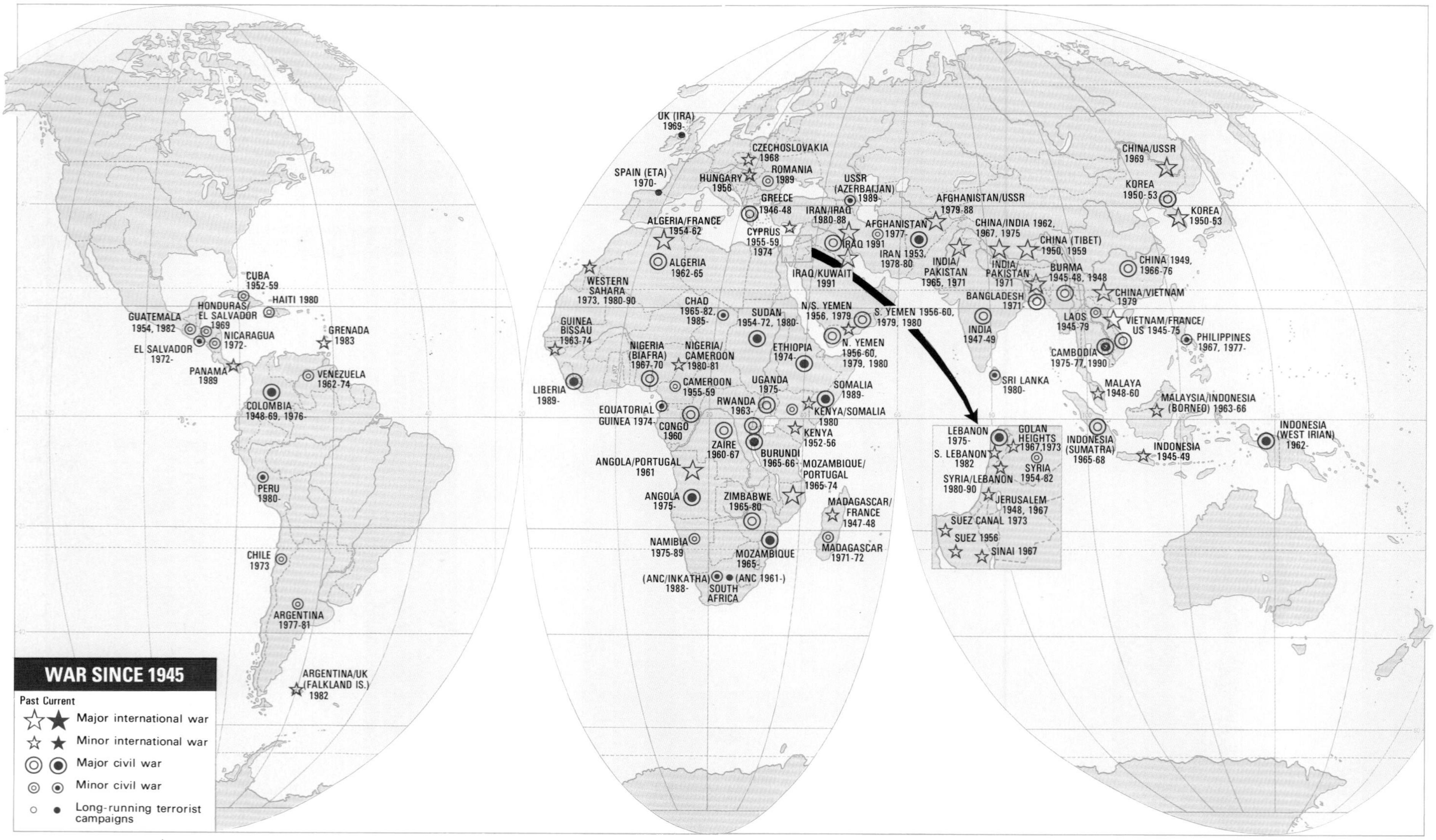

WAR SINCE 1945

Past	Current	
☆	★	Major international war
☆	★	Minor international war
◎	◉	Major civil war
⊙	⊙	Minor civil war
○	●	Long-running terrorist campaigns

COPYRIGHT GEORGE PHILIP LTD.

UNITED NATIONS

The United Nations Organization was born as World War II drew to its conclusion. Six years of strife had strengthened the world's desire for peace, but an effective international organization was needed to help achieve it. That body would replace the League of Nations which, since its inception in 1920, had signally failed to curb the aggression of at least some of its member nations. At the United Nations Conference on International Organization held in San Francisco, the United Nations Charter was drawn up. Ratified by the Security Council and signed by 51 nations, it came into effect on 24 October 1945.

The Charter set out the aims of the organization: to maintain peace and security, and develop friendly relations between nations; to achieve international cooperation in solving economic, social, cultural and humanitarian problems; to promote respect for human rights and fundamental freedoms; and to harmonize the activities of nations in order to achieve these common goals.

By 1992, the UN had expanded to more than 160 member countries; it is the largest international political organization, employing 23,000 people worldwide; its headquarters in New York accounts for 7,000 staff and it also has major offices in Rome, Geneva and Vienna.

The United Nations has six principal organs:

The General Assembly
The forum at which member nations discuss moral and political issues affecting world development, peace and security meets annually in September, under a newly-elected President whose tenure lasts one year. Any member can bring business to the agenda, and each member nation has one vote. Decisions are made by simple majority, save for matters of very great importance, when a two-thirds majority is required. While the General Assembly has no powers of enforcement, its recommendations to member nations are regarded as persuasive and it is empowered to instruct UN organs or agencies to implement its decisions.

The Security Council
A legislative and executive body, the Security Council is the primary instrument for establishing and maintaining international peace by attempting to settle disputes between nations. It has the power to dispatch UN forces to stop aggression, and member nations undertake to make armed forces, assistance and facilities available as required. The Security Council has ten temporary members elected by the General Assembly for two-year terms, and five permanent members - China, France, Russia, UK and USA. On questions of substance, the vote of each of the permanent members is required within the necessary nine-vote majority.

The Economic and Social Council
By far the largest United Nations executive, the Council operates as a conduit between the General Assembly and the many United Nations agencies it instructs to implement Assembly decisions, and whose work it coordinates. The Council also sets up commissions to examine economic conditions, collects data and issues studies and reports, and may make recommendations to the Assembly. The Council's overall aim is to help the peoples of the world with education, health and human rights. It has 54 member countries, elected by the General Assembly to three-year terms.

The Secretariat
This is the staff of the United Nations, and its task is to administer the policies and programmes of the UN and its organs, and assist and advise the Head of the Secretariat, the Secretary-General – a full-time, non-political, appointment made by the General Assembly.

The Trusteeship Council
The Council administers trust territories with the aim of promoting their advancement. Only one remains - the Trust Territory of the Pacific Is. (Palau), administered by the USA.

The International Court of Justice (the World Court)
The World Court is the judicial organ of the United Nations. It deals only with United Nations disputes and all members are subject to its jurisdiction, which includes both cases submitted to it by member nations and matters especially provided for in the Charter or in treaties. The Court's decisions are only binding in respect of a particular dispute; failure to heed a judgement may involve recourse to the Security Council. There are 15 judges, elected for nine-year terms by the General Assembly and the Security Council. The Court sits in The Hague.

United Nations agencies and programmes, and inter-governmental agencies coordinated by the UN, contribute to harmonious world development. Social and humanitarian operations include:

United Nations Development Programme (UNDP): plans and funds projects to help developing countries make better use of resources. Voluntary pledges of $1.3 billion were made for 1990, to fund almost 7,000 projects in 152 countries.

United Nations International Childrens' Fund (UNICEF): created at the General Assembly's first session in 1945 to help children in the aftermath of World War II, it now provides basic healthcare and aid worldwide. Voluntarily funded, three-quarters of its income is derived from government donations.

United Nations Fund for Population Activities (UNFPA): promotes awareness of population issues and family planning, providing appropriate assistance.

Food & Agriculture Organization (FAO): aims to raise living standards and nutrition levels in rural areas by improving food production and distribution.

United Nations Educational, Scientific & Cultural Organization (UNESCO): promotes international cooperation through broader and better education.

World Health Organization (WHO): promotes and provides for better health care, public and environmental health and medical research.

Membership: There are 13 independent states who are not members of the UN – Andorra, Kiribati, Liechtenstein, N. Korea, S. Korea, Monaco, Nauru, San Marino, Switzerland, Taiwan, Tonga, Tuvalu and Vatican City. By 1992, the successor states of the former USSR had either joined or were planning to join. There were 51 members in 1945. Official languages are Chinese, English, French, Russian, Spanish and (a recent addition) Arabic.

Funding: The UN budget for 1988-1989 was US $ 1,788,746,000. Contributions are assessed by members' ability to pay, with the maximum 25% of the total, the minimum 0.01%. Contributions for 1988-1989 were: USA 25%, Japan 11.38%, USSR 9.99%, W. Germany 8.08%, France 6.25%, UK 4.86%, Italy 3.99%, Canada 3.09%, Spain 1.95%, Netherlands 1.65% (others 23.75%).

Peacekeeping: The UN has been involved in 18 peacekeeping operations worldwide since 1945, five of which (Afghanistan/Pakistan, Iran/Iraq, Angola, Namibia and Honduras) were initiated in 1988-1989. In June 1991 UN personnel totalling over 11,000 were working in eight separate areas.

NATO: North Atlantic Treaty Organization (formed 1949). It continues after 1991 despite the winding up of the Warsaw Pact.
OAU: Organization of African Unity (1963). Its 52 members represent over 90% of Africa's population.
ASEAN: Association of South-East Asian Nations (1967).
OAS: Organization of American States (1949). It aims to promote social and economic cooperation between developed countries of North America and developing nations of Latin America.
LAIA: Latin American Integration Association (1980).
OECD: Organization for Economic Cooperation and Development (1961). The 24 major Western free-market economies plus Yugoslavia as associate member. 'G7' is its 'inner group' of USA, Canada, Japan, UK, Germany, Italy and France.
COMMONWEALTH: The Commonwealth of Nations evolved from the British Empire; it comprises 18 nations recognizing the British monarch as head of state and 32 with their own heads of state.
OPEC: Organization of Petroleum Exporting Countries (1960). It controls about three-quarters of the world's oil supply.

EC: European Community (1957). The original 'Common Market' now aims to integrate economies, coordinate social developments and bring about political union. Members of what is now the world's biggest market share agricultural and industrial policies and tariffs on trade. Over 60 ACP nations are affiliated under the Lomé Convention of 1975.

United Nations agencies are involved in many aspects of international trade, safety and security:
General Agreement on Tariffs and Trade (GATT): sponsors international trade negotiations and advocates a common code of conduct.
International Maritime Organization (IMO): promotes unity amongst merchant shipping, especially in regard to safety, marine pollution and standardization.
International Labour Organization (ILO): seeks to improve labour conditions and promote productive employment to raise living standards.
World Meteorological Organization (WMO): promotes cooperation in weather observation, reporting and forecasting.
World Intellectual Property Organization (WIPO): seeks to protect intellectual property such as artistic copyright, scientific patents and trademarks.
Disarmament Commission: considers and makes recommendations to the General Assembly on disarmament issues.
International Atomic Energy Agency (IAEA): fosters development of peaceful uses for nuclear energy, establishes safety standards and monitors the destruction of nuclear material designed for military use.

The World Bank comprises three United Nations agencies:
International Monetary Fund (IMF): cultivates international monetary cooperation and expansion of trade.
International Bank for Reconstruction & Development (IBRD): provides funds and technical assistance to developing countries.
International Finance Corporation (IFC): Encourages the growth of productive private enterprise in less developed countries.

OECD: Organization for Economic Cooperation and Development (1961). The 24 major Western free-market economies plus Yugoslavia as an associate member. 'G7' is its 'inner group' of USA, Canada, Japan, UK, Germany, Italy and France.
COMMONWEALTH: The Commonwealth of Nations evolved from the British Empire; it comprises 18 nations recognizing the British monarch as head of state and 32 nations with their own heads of state.
OPEC: Organization of Petroleum Exporting Countries (1960). It controls three-quarters of the world's oil supply.

PRODUCTION: AGRICULTURE

14: CLIMATE REGIONS

15: TEMPERATURE & PRECIPITATION

16: WATER UTILIZATION

17: NATURAL VEGETATION LAND USE BY CONTINENT

36: DIVISION OF EMPLOYMENT

46: HUMAN EXPANSION

The invention of agriculture transformed human existence more than any other development, though it may not have seemed much of an improvement to its first practitioners. Primitive farming required brutally hard work, and it tied men and women to a patch of land, highly vulnerable to local weather patterns and to predators, especially human predators – drawbacks still apparent in much of the world today. It is difficult to imagine early humans being interested in such an existence while there were still animals around to hunt and wild seeds and berries to gather. Probably the spur was population pressure, with consequent overhunting and scarcity.

Despite its difficulties, the new life-style had a few overwhelming advantages. It supported far larger populations, eventually including substantial cities, with all the varied cultural and economic activities they allowed. Later still, it furnished the surpluses that allowed industrialization, another enormous step in human development.

Machines relieved many farmers of their burden of endless toil, and made it possible for relatively small numbers to provide food for more than five billion people.

Then as now, the whole business of farming involves the creation of a severely simplified ecology, under the tutelage and for the benefit of the farmer. Natural plant life is divided into crops, to be protected and nurtured, and weeds, the rest, to be destroyed. From the earliest days, crops were selectively bred to increase their food yield, usually at the expense of their ability to survive, which became the farmer's responsibility; 20th-century plant geneticists have carried the technique to highly productive extremes. Due mainly to new varieties of rice and wheat, world grain production has increased by 70% since 1965, more than doubling in the developing countries, although such high yields demand equally high consumption of fertilizers and pesticides to maintain them. Mechanized farmers in North America and Europe

continue to turn out huge surpluses, although not without environmental costs.

Where production is inadequate, the reasons are as likely to be political as agricultural. Africa, the only continent where food production per capita is actually falling, suffers acutely from economic mis - management, as well as from the perennial problems of war and banditry. Dismal harvests in the USSR, despite its excellent farmland, helped bring about the collapse of the Soviet system.

There are other limits to progress. Increasing population puts relentless pressure on farmers not only to maintain high yields but also to increase them. Most of the world's potential cropland is already under the plough. The over-working of marginal land is one of the prime causes of desertification; new farmlands burned out of former rainforests are seldom fertile for long. Human numbers may yet outrun the land's ability to feed them, as they did almost 10,000 years ago.

SELF-SUFFICIENCY IN FOOD

Balance of trade in food products as a percentage of total trade in food products (1988)

- Over 50% surplus
- 10 - 50% surplus
- 10% either side
- 10 - 50% deficit
- Over 50% deficit

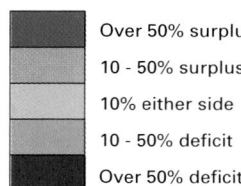

Most self-sufficient		Least self-sufficient	
Uganda	93%	Algeria	-97%
Argentina	92%	Saudi Arabia	-95%
Burma	86%	Czechoslovakia	-92%
Chile	82%	Venezuela	-92%
Iceland	82%	Gabon	-88%
Uruguay	82%	Oman	-88%
Kenya	80%	Syria	-88%
New Zealand	80%	Egypt	-86%
Costa Rica	79%	Japan	-85%

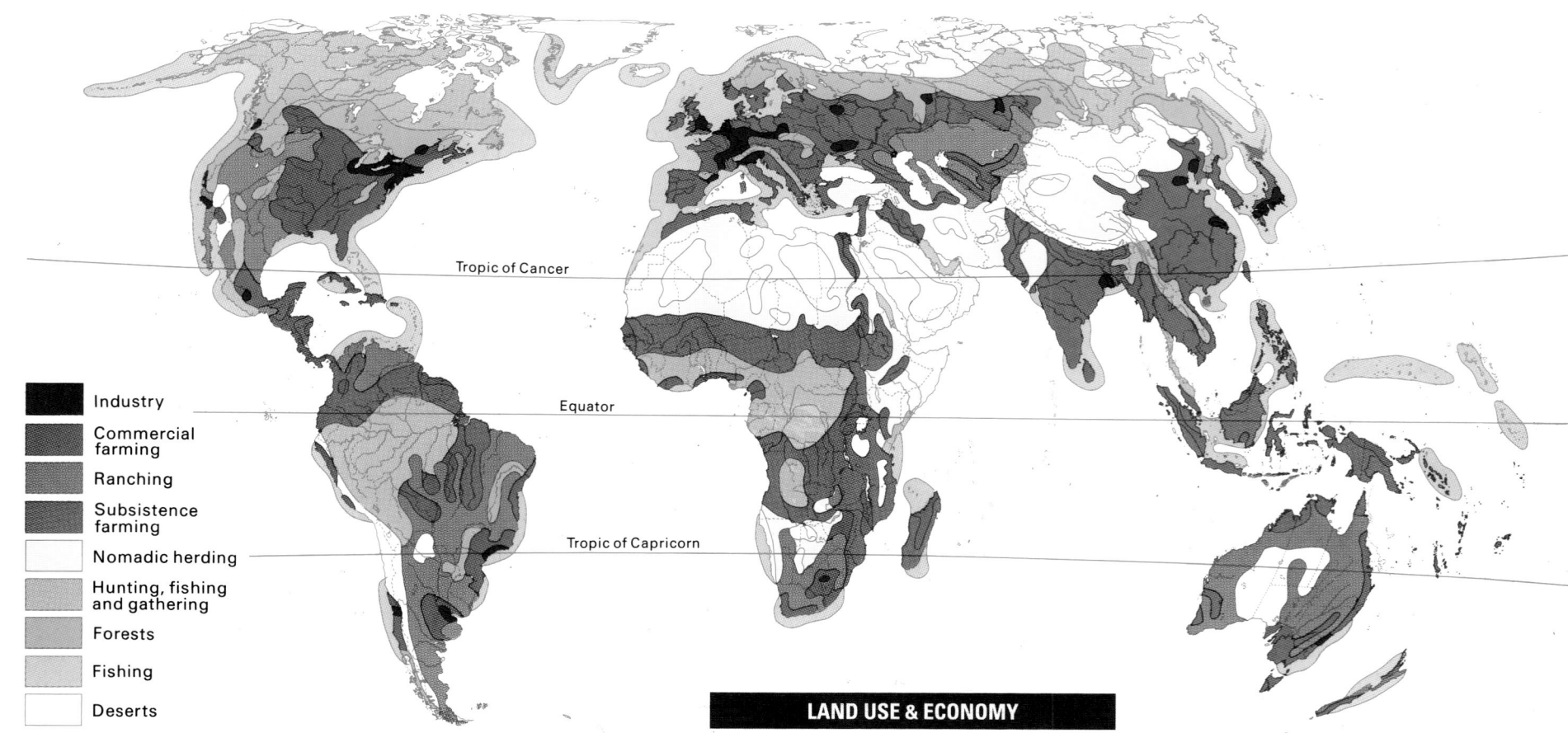

Tropic of Cancer

Equator

Tropic of Capricorn

- Industry
- Commercial farming
- Ranching
- Subsistence farming
- Nomadic herding
- Hunting, fishing and gathering
- Forests
- Fishing
- Deserts

LAND USE & ECONOMY

STAPLE CROPS

Cereals are grasses with starchy, edible seeds; every important civilization has depended on them as a source of food. The major cereal grains contain about 10% protein and 75% carbohydrate; grain is easy to store, handle and transport, and contributes more than any other group of foods to the energy and protein content of human diet. If all the cereals were consumed directly by man, there would be no shortage of food in the world, but a considerable proportion of the total output is used as animal feed.

Starchy tuber crops or root crops, represented here by potatoes and cassava, are second in importance only to cereals as staple foods; easily cultivated, they provide high yields for little effort and store well – potatoes for up to six months, cassava for up to a year in the ground. Protein content is low (2% or less), and starch content high; some minerals and vitamins are present, but populations that rely heavily on these crops may suffer from malnutrition.

Separate figures for Russia, Ukraine and the other successors of the defunct USSR are not yet available

Wheat: Grown in a range of climates, with most varieties - including the highest-quality bread wheats - requiring temperate conditions. Mainly used in baking, it is also used for pasta and breakfast cereals.

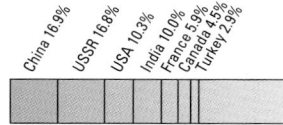

World total (1989): 538,056,000 tonnes

Maize: Originating in the New World and still an important human food in Africa and Latin America, in the developed world it is processed into breakfast cereals, oil, starches and adhesives. It is also used for animal feed.

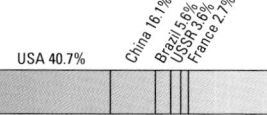

World total (1989): 470,318,000 tonnes

Oats: Most widely used to feed livestock, but eaten by humans as oatmeal or porridge. Oats have a beneficial effect on the cardio-vascular system, and human consumption is likely to increase.

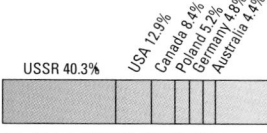

World total (1989): 42,197,000 tonnes

Millet: The name covers a number of small grained cereals, members of the grass family with a short growing season. Used to produce flour and meal, animal feed and fermented to make beer, especially in Africa.

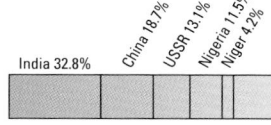

World total (1989): 30,512,000 tonnes

Cassava: A tropical shrub that needs high rainfall (over 1000 mm annually) and a 10 - 30 month growing season to produce its large, edible tubers. Used as flour by humans, as cattle feed and in industrial starches.

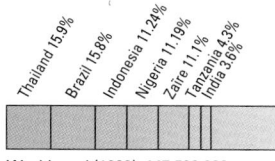

World total (1989): 147,500,000 tonnes

Rice: Thrives on the high humidity and temperatures of the Far East, where it is the traditional staple food of half the human race. Usually grown standing in water, rice responds well to continuous cultivation, with three or four crops annually.

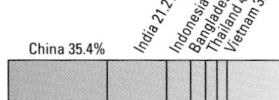

World total (1989): 506,291,000 tonnes

Barley: Primarily used as animal feed, but widely eaten by humans in Africa and Asia. Elsewhere, malted barley furnishes beer and spirits. Able to withstand the dry heat of sub-arid tropics, its growing season is only 80 days.

World total (1989): 168,964,000 tonnes

Rye: Hardy and tolerant of poor and sandy soils, it is an important foodstuff and animal feed in Central and Eastern Europe and the USSR. Rye produces a dark, heavy bread as well as alcoholic drinks.

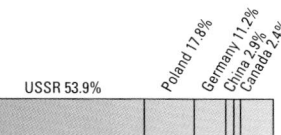

World total (1989): 34,893,000 tonnes

Potatoes: The most important of the edible tubers, potatoes grow in well-watered, temperate areas. Weight for weight less nutritious than grain, they are a human staple as well as an important animal feed.

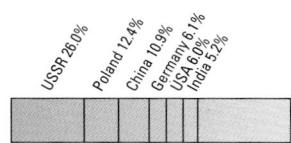

World total (1989): 276,740,000 tonnes

Soya: Beans from soya bushes are very high - 30-40% - in protein. Most are processed into oil and proprietary protein foods. Consumption since 1950 has tripled, mainly due to the health-conscious developed world.

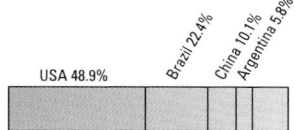

World total (1989): 107,350,000 tonnes

IMPORTANCE OF AGRICULTURE

Percentage of the total population dependent on agriculture (1990)

- Over 75% dependent
- 50 - 75% dependent
- 25 - 50% dependent
- 10 - 25% dependent
- Under 10% dependent

Top 5 countries		Bottom 5 countries	
Nepal	92%	UK	2.0%
Rwanda	91%	Belgium	1.8%
Burundi	91%	Bahrain	1.7%
Bhutan	91%	Hong Kong	1.2%
Niger	87%	Singapore	1.0%

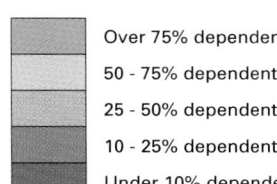

FOOD & POPULATION

Comparison of food production and population by continent (1989). The left column indicates percentage shares of total world food production; the right shows population in proportion.

	FOOD	POPULATION
Australasia	1.2%	0.4%
Europe	27.6%	15.5%
Asia	44.5%	58.3%
S. America	6.5%	6.7%
N. America	13.8%	7.1%
Africa	6.7%	12.0%

ANIMAL PRODUCTS

Separate figures for Russia, Ukraine and the other successors of the defunct USSR are not yet available

Traditionally, food animals subsisted on land unsuitable for cultivation, supporting agricultural production with their fertilizing dung. But free-ranging animals grow slowly and yield less meat than those more intensively reared; the demands of urban markets in the developed world have encouraged the growth of factory-like production methods. A large proportion of staple crops, especially cereals, are fed to animals, an inefficient way to produce protein but one likely to continue as long as people value meat and dairy products in their diet.

Cheese: Least perishable of all dairy products, cheese is milk fermented with selected bacterial strains to produce a foodstuff with a potentially immense range of flavours and textures. The vast majority of cheeses are made from cow's milk, although sheep and goat cheeses are highly prized.

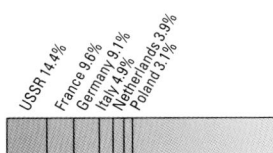

World total (1989): 14,475,276 tonnes

Lamb & Mutton: Sheep are the least demanding of domestic animals. Although unsuited to intensive rearing, they can thrive on marginal pastureland incapable of supporting beef cattle on a commercial scale. Sheep are raised as much for their valuable wool as for the meat that they provide, with Australia the world leader.

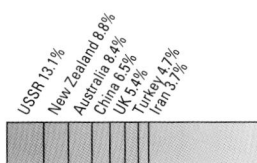

World total (1989): 6,473,000 tonnes

Beef & Veal: Most beef and veal is reared for home markets, and the top five producers are also the biggest consumers. The USA produces nearly a quarter of the world's beef and eats even more. Australia, with its small domestic market, is by far the largest exporter.

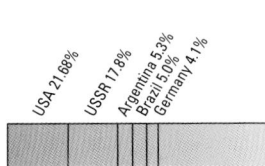

World total (1989): 49,436,000 tonnes

SUGARS

Sugar cane: Confined to tropical regions, cane sugar accounts for the bulk of international trade in the commodity. Most is produced as a foodstuff, but some countries, notably Brazil and South Africa, distil sugar cane and use the resulting ethyl alcohol to make motor fuels.

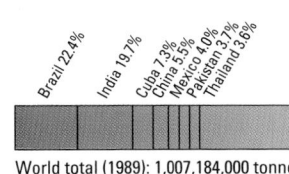

World total (1989): 1,007,184,000 tonnes

Milk: Many human groups, including most Asians, find raw milk indigestible after infancy, and it is often only the starting point for other dairy products such as butter, cheese and yoghurt. Most world milk production comes from cows, but sheep's milk and goats' milk are also important.

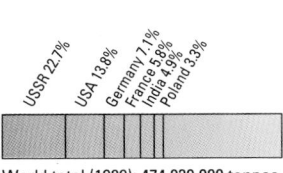

World total (1989): 474,020,000 tonnes

Butter: A traditional source of vitamin A as well as calories, butter has lost much popularity in the developed world for health reasons, although it remains a valuable food. Most butter from India, the world's second-largest producer, is clarified into ghee, which has religious as well as nutritional importance.

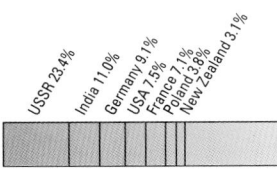

World total (1989): 7,611,826 tonnes

Pork: Although pork is forbidden to many millions, notably Muslims, on religious grounds, more is produced than any other meat in the world, mainly because it is the cheapest. It accounts for about 90% of China's meat output, although per capita meat consumption is relatively low.

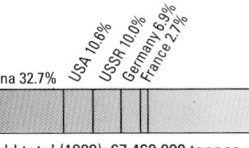

World total (1989): 67,460,000 tonnes

Fish: Commercial fishing requires large shoals of fish, often of only one species, within easy reach of markets. Although the great majority are caught wild in the sea, fish-farming of both marine and freshwater species is assuming increasing importance, especially as natural stocks become depleted.

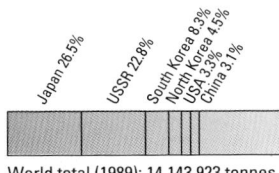

World total (1989): 14,143,923 tonnes

Sugar beet: A temperate crop closely related to the humble beetroot, sugar beet's yield after processing is indistinguishable from cane sugar. Sugar beet is steadily replacing sugar cane imports in Europe, to the detriment of the developing countries that rely on it as a major cash crop.

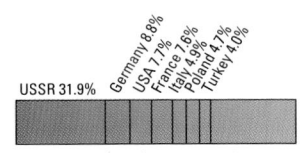

World total (1989): 305,882,000 tonnes

31

PRODUCTION: ENERGY

39: WORLD SHIPPING

46: CARBON DIOXIDE
    GREENHOUSE POWER
    CO₂ PRODUCERS
    GLOBAL WARMING

47: MARINE POLLUTION

We live in a high-energy civilization. While vast discrepancies exist between rich and poor – a North American consumes 13 times as much energy as a Chinese, for example – even developing nations have more power at their disposal than was imaginable a century ago. Abundant energy supplies keep us warm or cool, fuel our industries and our transport systems, even feed us: high-intensity agriculture, with its fertilizers, pesticides and machinery, is heavily energy-dependent.

Unfortunately, most of the world's energy comes from fossil fuels: coal, oil and gas deposits laid down over many millions of years. These are the Earth's capital, not its income, and we are consuming that capital at an alarming rate. New discoveries have persistently extended the known reserves: in 1989, the reserves-to-production ratio for oil assured over 45 years' supply, an improvement of almost a decade on the 1970 situation. But despite the effort and ingenuity of prospectors, stocks are clearly limited. They are also very unequally distributed, with the Middle East accounting for most oil reserves, and the CIS, especially Russia, possessing an even higher proportion of the world's natural gas. Coal reserves are more evenly shared, and also more plentiful: coal will outlast oil and gas by a very wide margin.

It is possible to reduce energy demand by improving efficiency: most industrial nations have dramatically increased output since the 1970s without a matching rise in energy consumption. But as fossil stocks continue to diminish, renewable energy sources – solar, wave and wind power, as well as more conventional hydroelectricity – must take on steadily greater importance.

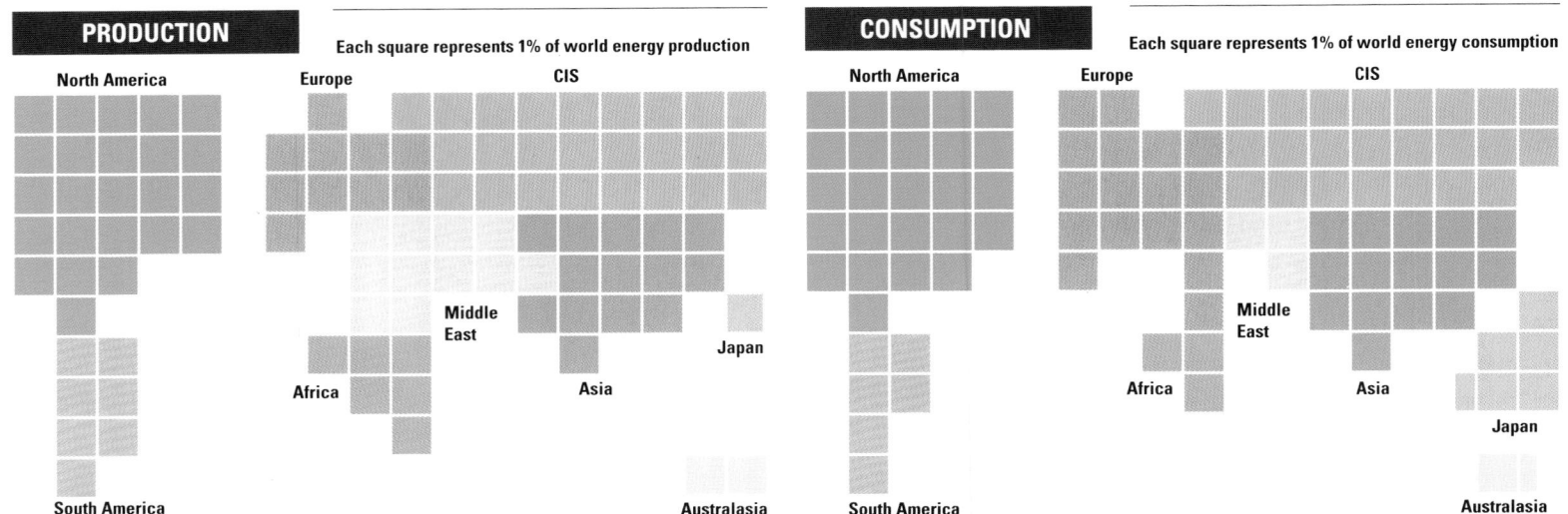

PRODUCTION

Each square represents 1% of world energy production

North America Europe CIS

Middle East Japan

Africa Asia

South America Australasia

CONSUMPTION

Each square represents 1% of world energy consumption

North America Europe CIS

Middle East Japan

Africa Asia

South America Australasia

CONVERSIONS

For historical reasons, oil is still traded in barrels. The weight and volume equivalents shown below are all based on average density 'Arabian light' crude oil, and should be considered approximate.

The energy equivalents given for a tonne of oil are also somewhat imprecise: oil and coal of different qualities will have varying energy contents, a fact usually reflected in their price on world markets.

1 barrel:

    0.136 tonnes
    159 litres
    35 Imperial gallons
    42 US gallons

1 tonne:

    7.33 barrels
    1185 litres
    256 Imperial gallons
    261 US gallons

1 tonne oil:

    1.5 tonnes hard coal
    3.0 tonnes lignite
    12,000 kWh

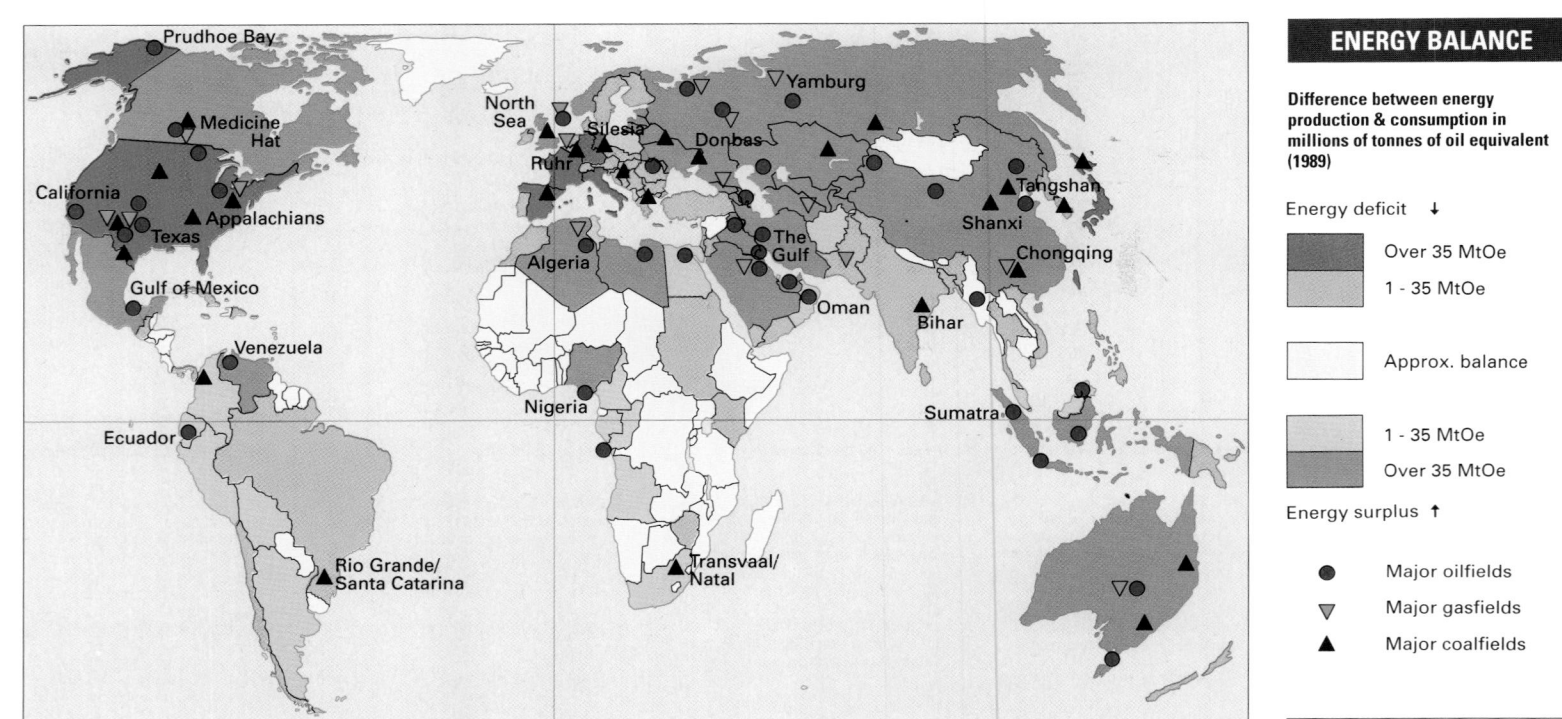

ENERGY BALANCE

Difference between energy production & consumption in millions of tonnes of oil equivalent (1989)

Energy deficit ↓

(dark)	Over 35 MtOe
(medium)	1 - 35 MtOe
(white)	Approx. balance
(light)	1 - 35 MtOe
(dark)	Over 35 MtOe

Energy surplus ↑

● Major oilfields
▽ Major gasfields
▲ Major coalfields

Map labels: Prudhoe Bay, Medicine Hat, California, Texas, Appalachians, Gulf of Mexico, Venezuela, Ecuador, Rio Grande/Santa Catarina, North Sea, Silesia, Ruhr, Donbas, Yamburg, Algeria, The Gulf, Oman, Nigeria, Bihar, Sumatra, Tangshan, Shanxi, Chongqing, Transvaal/Natal

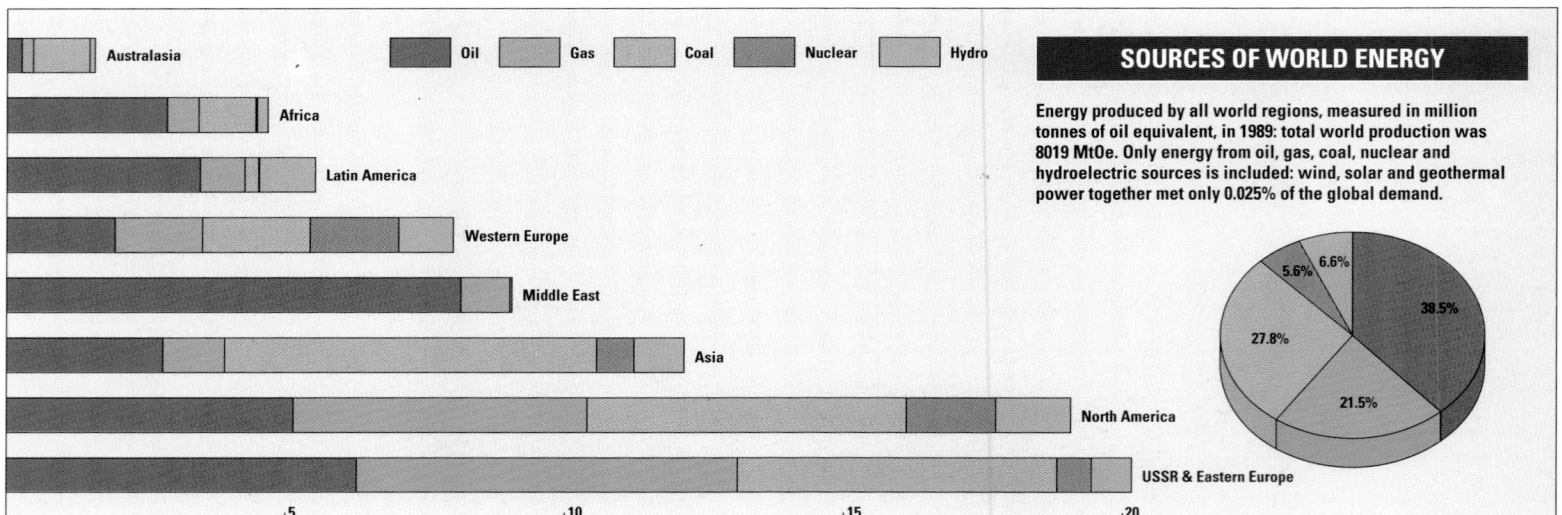

Australasia | Oil | Gas | Coal | Nuclear | Hydro
Africa
Latin America
Western Europe
Middle East
Asia
North America
USSR & Eastern Europe

5   10   15   20

SOURCES OF WORLD ENERGY

Energy produced by all world regions, measured in million tonnes of oil equivalent, in 1989: total world production was 8019 MtOe. Only energy from oil, gas, coal, nuclear and hydroelectric sources is included: wind, solar and geothermal power together met only 0.025% of the global demand.

Pie chart: 38.5%, 21.5%, 27.8%, 5.6%, 6.6%

FOSSIL FUEL RESERVES

Known world reserves in years as a multiple of annual production, 1970, 1980 and 1989

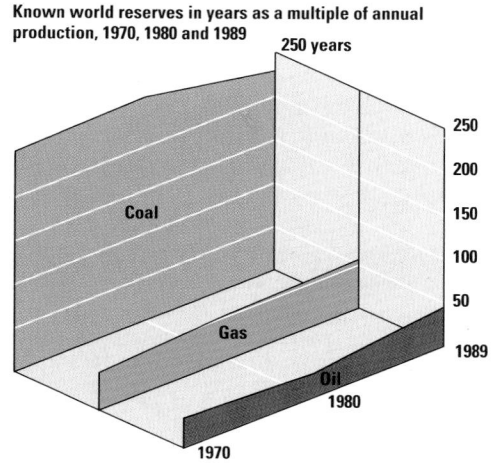

ENERGY AND OUTPUT

Tonnes of oil equivalent consumed to produce US $1000 of GDP, four industrial nations (1973-89)

Intensity of energy use is a rough indicator of efficiency: the 1973-4 oil crisis caused a dramatic improvement in each of the countries illustrated, though the USA remains relatively profligate. Exactly comparable figures for communist economies are not available, but estimates suggest that for equivalent production, the USSR and China use between two and four times as much energy as the USA.

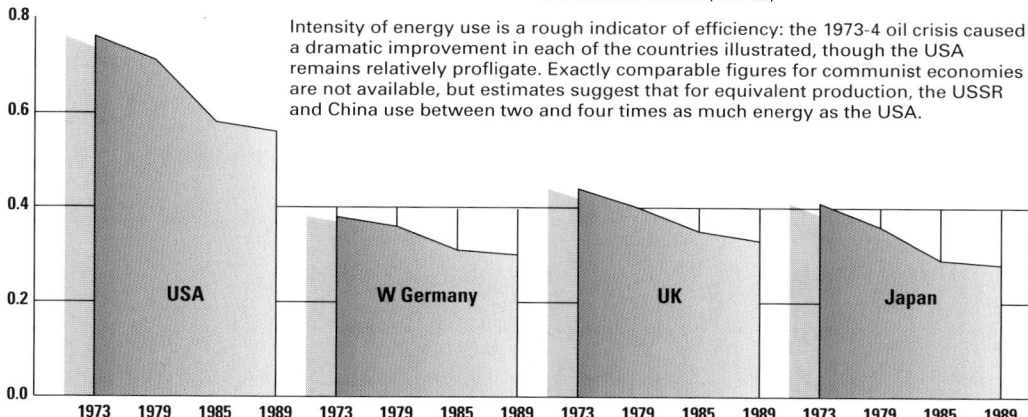

COAL RESERVES

World coal reserves by region & country, thousand million tonnes (1988)

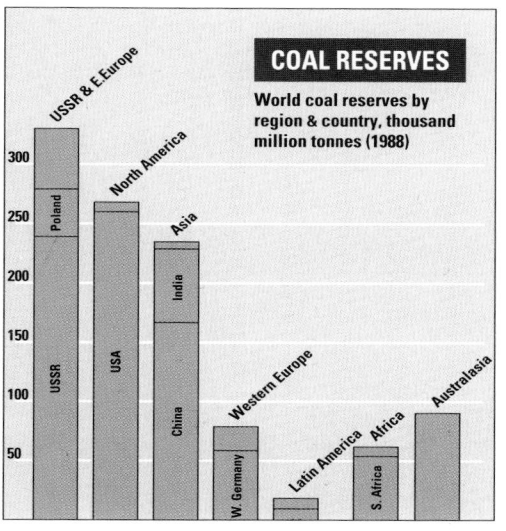

GAS RESERVES

World natural gas reserves by region & country, thousand million tonnes (1988)

Ca: Canada
In: Indonesia
Ma: Malaysia
AD: Abu Dhabi
SA: Saudi Arabia
Qa: Qatar
Iq: Iraq
No: Norway
Ne: Netherlands
Ve: Venezuela
Mx: Mexico
Al: Algeria
Ni: Nigeria

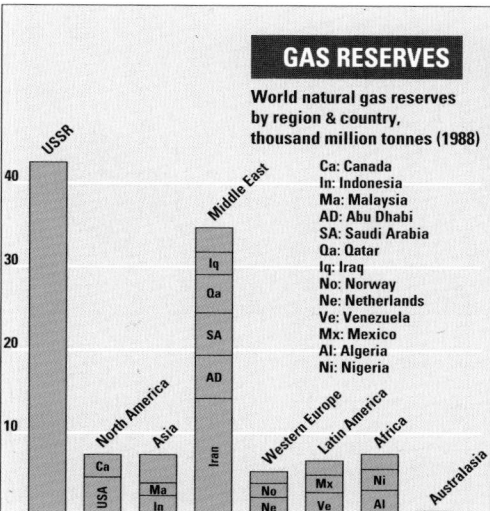

OIL RESERVES

World oil reserves by region & country, thousand million tonnes (1988)

AD: Abu Dhabi
Ve: Venezuela
Mx: Mexico

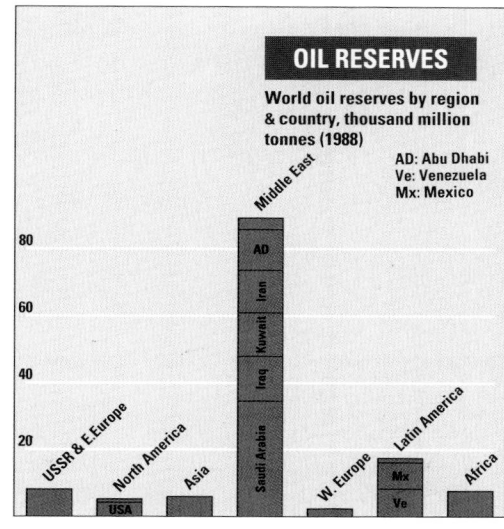

OIL MOVEMENTS

Major world movements of oil in millions of tonnes (1989)

Middle East to Western Europe	195.5
Middle East to Japan	150.0
Middle East to Asia (exc. Japan and China)	127.5
Latin America to USA	126.1
Middle East to USA	94.1
USSR to Western Europe	78.1
North Africa to Western Europe	93.5
West Africa to Western Europe	39.6
West Africa to USA	59.8
Canada to USA	45.0
South-East Asia to Japan	42.2
Latin America to Western Europe	28.7
Western Europe to USA	28.7
Middle East to Latin America	20.5

Total world movements: 1577 million tonnes

Only inter-regional movements in excess of 20 million tonnes are shown. Other Middle Eastern oil shipments throughout the world totalled 47.4 million tonnes; miscellaneous USSR oil exports amounted to 88.8 million tonnes.

FUEL EXPORTS

Fuels as a percentage of total value of all exports (1986)

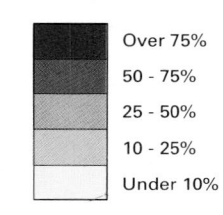

Over 75%
50 - 75%
25 - 50%
10 - 25%
Under 10%

Direction of trade

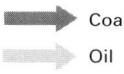

Coal
Oil

Arrows show the major trade direction of selected fuels, & are proportional to export value

NUCLEAR POWER

Percentage of electricity generated by nuclear power stations, leading nations (1988)

1.	France	70%	11. W. Germany	34%
2.	Belgium	66%	12. Japan	28%
3.	Hungary	49%	13. Czechoslovakia	27%
4.	South Korea	47%	14. UK	18%
5.	Sweden	46%	15. USA	17%
6.	Taiwan	41%	16. Canada	16%
7.	Switzerland	37%	17. Argentina	12%
8.	Finland	36%	18. USSR	11%
9.	Spain	36%	19. Yugoslavia	6%
10.	Bulgaria	36%	20. Netherlands	5%

The decade 1980-1990 was a bad time for the nuclear power industry. Major projects regularly ran vastly over-budget, and fears of long-term environmental damage were heavily reinforced by the 1986 Soviet disaster at Chernobyl. Although the number of reactors in service continued to increase throughout the period, orders for new plant shrank dramatically, and most countries cut back on their nuclear programmes.

HYDROELECTRICITY

Percentage of electricity generated by hydroelectrical power stations, leading nations (1988)

1.	Paraguay	99.9%	11. Laos	95.5%
2.	Zambia	99.6%	12. Nepal	95.2%
3.	Norway	99.5%	13. Iceland	94.0%
4.	Congo	99.1%	14. Uruguay	93.0%
5.	Costa Rica	98.3%	15. Brazil	91.7%
6.	Uganda	98.3%	16. Albania	87.2%
7.	Rwanda	97.7%	17. Fiji	81.4%
8.	Malawi	97.6%	18. Ecuador	80.7%
9.	Zaïre	97.4%	19. C. African Rep.	80.4%
10.	Cameroon	97.2%	20. Sri Lanka	80.4%

Countries heavily reliant on hydroelectricity are usually small and non-industrial: a high proportion of hydroelectric power more often reflects a modest energy budget than vast hydroelectric resources. The USA, for instance, produces only 8% of power requirements from hydroelectricity; yet that 8% amounts to more than three times the hydro-power generated by all of Africa.

ALTERNATIVE ENERGY SOURCES

Solar: Each year the sun bestows upon the Earth almost a million times as much energy as is locked up in all the planet's oil reserves, but only an insignificant fraction is trapped and used commercially. In some experimental installations, mirrors focus the sun's rays on to boilers, whose steam generates electricity by spinning turbines. Solar cells turn the sunlight into electricity directly, and although efficiencies are still low, advancing technology offers some prospect of using the sun as the main world electricity source by 2100.
Wind: Caused by uneven heating of the Earth, winds are themselves a form of solar energy. Windmills have been used for centuries to turn wind power into mechanical work; recent models, often arranged in banks on gust-swept high ground, usually generate electricity.
Tidal: The energy from tides is potentially enormous, although only a few installations have been built to exploit it. In theory at least, waves and currents could also provide almost unimaginable power, and the thermal differences in the ocean depths are another huge well of potential energy. But work on extracting it is still in the experimental stage.
Geothermal: The Earth's temperature rises by 1°C for every 30 metres' descent, with much steeper temperature gradients in geologically active areas. El Salvador, for example, produces 39% of its electricity from geothermal power stations. More than 130 are operating worldwide.
Biomass: The oldest of human fuels ranges from animal dung, still burned in cooking fires in much of North Africa and elsewhere, to sugar cane plantations feeding high-technology distilleries to produce ethanol for motor vehicle engines. In Brazil and South Africa, plant ethanol provides up to 25% of motor fuel. Throughout the developing world most biomass energy comes from firewood: although accurate figures are impossible to obtain, it may yield as much as 10% of the world's total energy consumption.

PRODUCTION: MINERALS

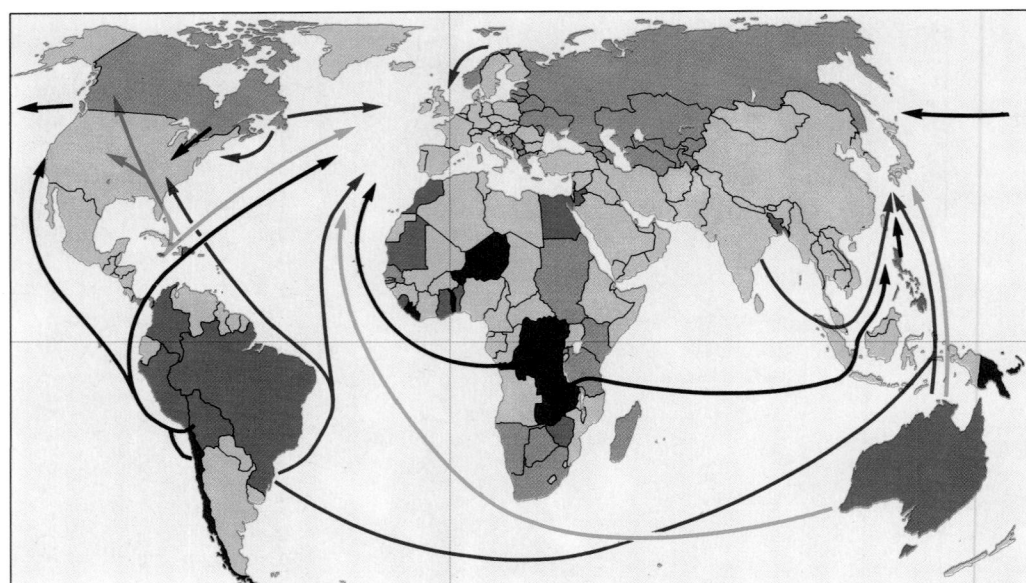

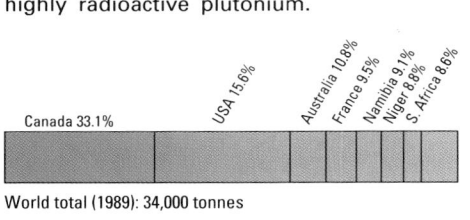

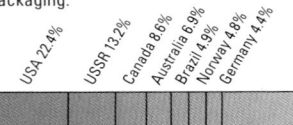

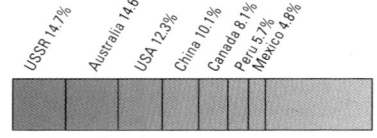

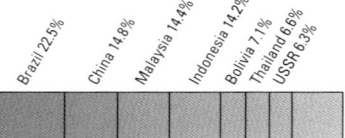

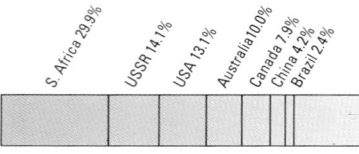

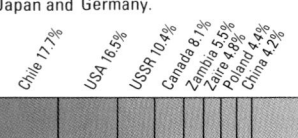

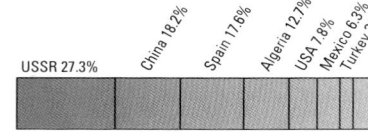

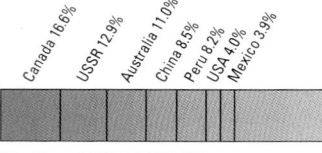

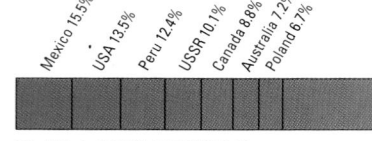

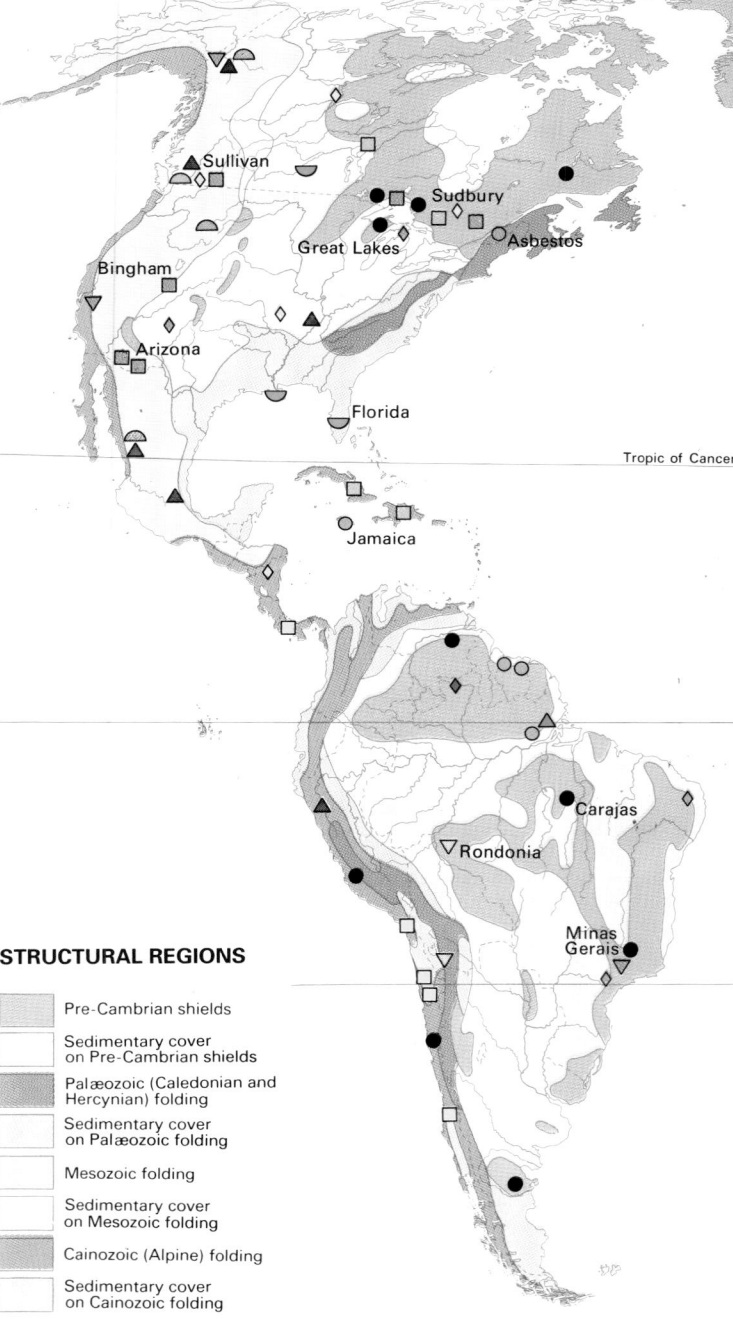

19: GEOLOGY

37: PATTERNS OF PRODUCTION

39: WORLD SHIPPING

Even during the Stone Age, when humans often settled near the outcrops of flint on which their technology depended, mineral resources have attracted human exploiters. Their descendants have learned how to make use of almost every known element. These elements can be found, in one form or another, somewhere in the Earth's bountiful crust. Iron remains the most important, but modern industrial civilization has a voracious appetite for virtually all of them.

Mineral deposits once dictated the site of new industries; today, most industrial countries are heavily dependent on imports for many of their key materials. Most mining, and much refining of raw ores, is done in developing countries, where labour is cheap.

The main map below shows the richest sources of the most important minerals at present; some reserves – lead and mercury, for example – are running very low. The map takes no account of undersea deposits, most of which are considered inaccessible. Growing shortages, though, may encourage submarine mining: plans have already been made to recover the nodules of manganese found widely scattered on ocean floors.

MINERAL EXPORTS

Minerals & metals as a percentage of total exports (1986)

Over 50%

10 - 50%

5 - 10%

Under 5%

Direction of trade

Copper
Iron
Bauxite
(Aluminium)

URANIUM

In its pure state, uranium is an immensely heavy, white metal; but although spent uranium is employed as projectiles in anti-missile cannon, where its mass ensures a lethal punch, its main use is as a fuel in nuclear reactors, and in nuclear weaponry. Uranium is very scarce: the main source is the rare ore pitchblende, which itself contains only 0.2% uranium oxide. Only a minute fraction of that is the radioactive U^{235} isotope, though so-called breeder reactors can transmute the more common U^{238} into highly radioactive plutonium.

Canada 33.1% | USA 15.6% | Australia 10.8% | France 9.5% | Namibia 9.1% | Niger 8.8% | S. Africa 8.6%

World total (1989): 34,000 tonnes

METALS

Separate figures for Russia, Ukraine and the other successors of the defunct USSR are not as yet available

Aluminium: Produced mainly from its oxide, bauxite, which yields 25% of its weight in aluminium. The cost of refining and production is often too high for producer-countries to bear, so bauxite is largely exported. Lightweight and corrosion resistant, aluminium alloys are widely used in aircraft, vehicles, cans and packaging.

USA 22.4% | USSR 13.2% | Canada 8.6% | Australia 6.9% | Brazil 4.9% | Norway 4.8% | Germany 4.4%

World total (1989): 18,000,000 tonnes *

Copper: Derived from low-yielding sulphide ores, copper is an important export for several developing countries. An excellent conductor of heat and electricity, it forms part of most electrical items, and is used in the manufacture of brass and bronze. Major importers include Japan and Germany.

Chile 17.7% | USA 16.5% | USSR 10.4% | Canada 8.1% | Zambia 5.5% | Zaire 4.4% | Poland 4.4% | China 4.2%

World total (1989): 9,100,000 tonnes *

Lead: A soft metal, obtained mainly from galena (lead sulphide), which occurs in veins associated with iron, zinc and silver sulphides. Its use in vehicle batteries accounts for the USA's prime consumer status; lead is also made into sheeting and piping. Its use as an additive to paints and petrol is decreasing.

USSR 14.7% | Australia 14.6% | USA 12.3% | China 10.1% | Canada 8.1% | Peru 5.7% | Mexico 4.9%

World total (1989): 3,400,000 tonnes *

Mercury: The only metal that is liquid at normal temperatures, most is derived from its sulphide, cinnabar, found only in small quantities in volcanic areas. Apart from its value in thermometers and other instruments, most mercury production is used in anti-fungal and anti-fouling preparations, and to make detonators.

USSR 27.3% | China 18.2% | Spain 17.6% | Algeria 12.7% | USA 7.8% | Mexico 6.3% | Turkey 3.7%

World total (1989): 5,500,000 kilograms *

DIAMOND

Most diamond is found in kimberlite, or 'blue ground', a basic peridotite rock; erosion may wash the diamond from its kimberlite matrix and deposit it with sand or gravel on river beds. Only a small proportion of the world's diamond, the most flawless, is cut into gemstones - 'diamonds'; most is used in industry, where the material's remarkable hardness and abrasion resistance finds a use in cutting tools, drills and dies, as well as in styluses. Australia, not among the top 12 producers at the beginning of the 1980s, had by 1986 become world leader and by 1989 was the source of 37.5% of world production. The other main producers were Zaïre (18.9%), Botswana (16.3%), the then USSR (11.8%) and South Africa (9.7%). Between them, these five nations accounted for over 94% of the world total of 96,600,000 carats - at 0.2 grams per carat, almost one tonne.

Tin: Soft, pliable and non-toxic, used to coat 'tin' (tin-plated steel) cans, in the manufacture of foils and in alloys. The principal tin-bearing mineral is cassiterite (SnO_2), found in ore formed from molten rock. Producers and refiners were hit by a price collapse in 1991.

Brazil 22.5% | China 14.8% | Malaysia 14.4% | Indonesia 14.2% | Bolivia 7.1% | Thailand 6.6% | USSR 6.3%

World total (1989): 223,000 tonnes *

Zinc: Often found in association with lead ores, zinc is highly resistant to corrosion, and about 40% of the refined metal is used to plate sheet steel, particularly vehicle bodies – a process known as galvanizing. Zinc is also used in dry batteries, paints and dyes.

Canada 16.6% | USSR 12.9% | Australia 11.0% | China 8.5% | Peru 8.2% | USA 4.0% | Mexico 3.9%

World total (1989): 7,300,000 tonnes *

Gold: Regarded for centuries as the most valuable metal in the world and used to make coins, gold is still recognized as the monetary standard. A soft metal, it is alloyed to make jewellery; the electronics industry values its corrosion resistance and conductivity.

S. Africa 28.9% | USSR 14.1% | USA 13.1% | Australia 10.0% | Canada 7.9% | China 4.7% | Brazil 2.4%

World total (1989): 2,026,000 kilograms *

Silver: Most silver comes from ores mined and processed for other metals (including lead and copper). Pure or alloyed with harder metals, it is used for jewellery and ornaments. Industrial use includes dentistry, electronics, photography and as a chemical catalyst.

Mexico 15.5% | USA 13.5% | Peru 12.4% | USSR 10.1% | Canada 8.8% | Australia 7.2% | Poland 6.7%

World total (1989): 14,896,000 kilograms *

* Figures for aluminium are for refined metal, all other figures refer to ore production.

STRUCTURAL REGIONS

Pre-Cambrian shields

Sedimentary cover on Pre-Cambrian shields

Palæozoic (Caledonian and Hercynian) folding

Sedimentary cover on Palæozoic folding

Mesozoic folding

Sedimentary cover on Mesozoic folding

Cainozoic (Alpine) folding

Sedimentary cover on Cainozoic folding

IRON & FERRO-ALLOYS

Ever since the art of high-temperature smelting was discovered, some time in the second millennium BC, iron has been by far the most important metal known to man. The earliest iron ploughs transformed primitive agriculture and led to the first human population explosion, while iron weapons - or the lack of them - ensured the rise or fall of entire cultures.

Widely distributed around the world, iron ores usually contain 25-60% iron; blast furnaces process the raw product into pig-iron, which is then alloyed with carbon and other minerals to produce steels of various qualities. From the time of the Industrial Revolution steel has been almost literally the backbone of modern civilization, the prime structural material on which all else is built.

Iron-smelting usually developed close to sources of ore and, later, to the coalfields that fueled the furnaces. Today, most ore comes from a few richly-endowed locations where large-scale mining is possible. Iron and steel plants are generally built at coastal sites so that giant ore carriers, which account for a sizeable proportion of the world's merchant fleet, can easily discharge their cargoes.

World production of pig iron and ferro-alloys (1988). All countries with an annual output of more than one million tonnes are shown

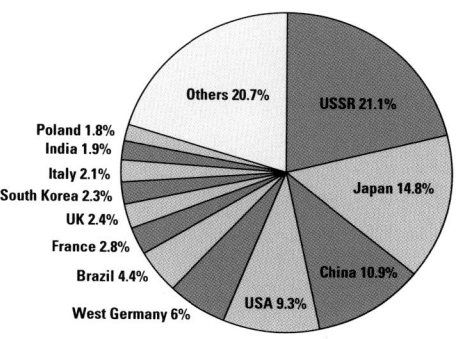

USSR 21.1%
Japan 14.8%
China 10.9%
USA 9.3%
West Germany 6%
Brazil 4.4%
France 2.8%
UK 2.4%
South Korea 2.3%
Italy 2.1%
India 1.9%
Poland 1.8%
Others 20.7%

Total world production: 545 million tonnes

Development of world production of pig iron and ferro-alloys (1945-1988) in million tonnes

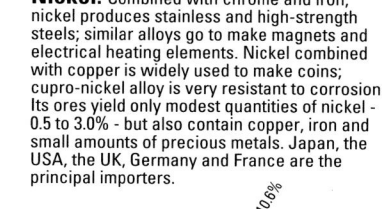

1945, 1950, 1955, 1960, 1965, 1970, 1975, 1976, 1977, 1978, 1979, 1980, 1981, 1982, 1983, 1984, 1985, 1986, 1987, 1988

100 200 300 400 500

Chromium: Most of the world's chromium production is alloyed with iron and other metals to produce steels with various different properties. Combined with iron, nickel, cobalt and tungsten, chromium produces an exceptionally hard steel, resistant to heat; chrome steels are used for many household items where utility must be matched with appearance - cutlery, for example. Chromium is also used in production of refractory bricks, and its salts for tanning and dyeing leather and cloth.

Manganese: In its pure state, manganese is a hard, brittle metal. Alloyed with chrome, iron and nickel, it produces abrasion-resistant steels; manganese-aluminium alloys are light but tough. Found in batteries and inks, manganese is also used in glass production. Manganese ores are frequently found in the same location as sedimentary iron ores. Pyrolusite (MnO_2) and psilomelane are the main economically-exploitable sources.

Nickel: Combined with chrome and iron, nickel produces stainless and high-strength steels; similar alloys go to make magnets and electrical heating elements. Nickel combined with copper is widely used to make coins; cupro-nickel alloy is very resistant to corrosion. Its ores yield only modest quantities of nickel - 0.5 to 3.0% - but also contain copper, iron and small amounts of precious metals. Japan, the USA, the UK, Germany and France are the principal importers.

USSR 24.4% | China 17.2% | Brazil 15.5% | Australia 10.7% | USA 5.8% | India 5.2% | Canada 4.1% | South Africa 3.0% | Sweden 2.2%

World total production of iron ore (1989): 989,000,000 tonnes

S. Africa 33.7% | USSR 29.9% | India 7.9% | Turkey 6.7% | Albania 5.5% | Zimbabwe 4.9% | Finland 3.9%

World total (1989): 12,700,000 tonnes

USSR 36.7% | S. Africa 15.1% | China 11.3% | Gabon 9.7% | Australia 8.9% | India 5.6%

World total (1989): 24,000,000 tonnes

USSR 23.1% | Canada 22.3% | New Caledonia 10.6% | Australia 7.1% | Indonesia 6.6% | Cuba 4.9% | S. Africa 3.7%

World total (1989): 910,000 tonnes

DISTRIBUTION

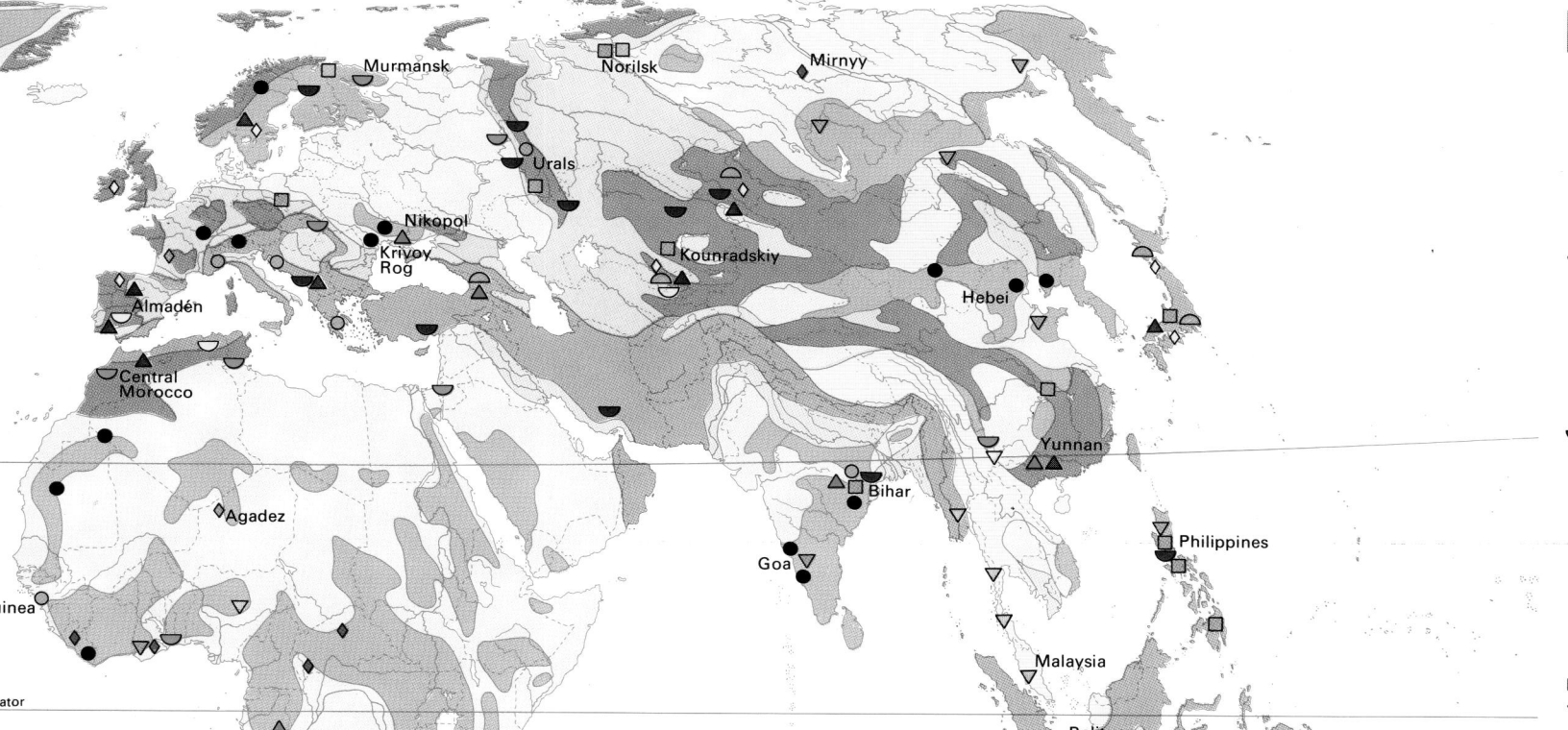

Base metals
- ▢ Copper
- ▲ Lead
- ▽ Mercury
- ▽ Tin
- ◇ Zinc

Iron and ferro-alloys
- ● Iron
- ◗ Chrome
- ▢ Nickel
- ▲ Manganese

Light metals
- ◯ Bauxite

Rare metals
- ◇ Uranium

Precious metals
- ▽ Gold
- ◠ Silver

Precious stones
- ◆ Diamonds

Mineral fertilizers
- ◗ Phosphates

Industrial minerals
- ◯ Asbestos

PRODUCTION: MANUFACTURING

16:	WATER UTILIZATION
30:	LAND USE & ECONOMY
34:	MINERAL PRODUCTION
35:	IRON & FERRO-ALLOYS
38:	TRADING NATIONS
	MAJOR EXPORTS
	TRADED PRODUCTS

In its broadest sense, manufacturing is the application of energy, labour and skill to raw materials in order to transform them into finished goods with a higher value than the various elements used in production.

Since the early days of the Industrial Revolution, manufacturing has implied the use of an organized workforce harnessed to some form of machine. The tendency has consistently been for increasingly expensive human labour to be replaced by increasingly complex machinery, which has evolved over time from water-powered looms to fully-integrated robotic plants.

Obviously, not all industries – or manufacturing countries - have reached the same level. Textiles, for example, the foundation of the early industrial revolution in the West, can be mass-produced with fairly modest technology; today, they are usually produced in developing countries, mostly in Asia, where low labour costs compensate for the large workforce the relatively simple machinery requires. Nevertheless, the trend towards high-technology production, however uneven, seems inexorable. Gains in efficiency make up.for the staggering cost of the equipment itself, and the outcome is that fewer and fewer people are employed to produce more and more goods.

One paradoxical result of the increase in industrial efficiency is a relative decline in the importance of the industrial sector of a nation's economy. The economy has already passed through one transition, generations past, when workers were drawn from the land into factories. The second transition releases labour into what is called the service sector of the economy: a diffuse but vital concept that includes not only such obvious services as transport and administration, but also finance, insurance and activities as diverse as fashion design or the writing of computer software.

The process is far advanced in the mature economies of the West, with Japan not far behind. Almost two-thirds of US wealth, for example, is now generated in the service sector, and less than half of Japanese Gross National Product comes from industry. The shrinkage, though, is only relative: between them, these two industrial giants produce almost twice as much manufactured goods as the rest of the world put together. And it is on the solid base of production that the rest of their prosperity rests.

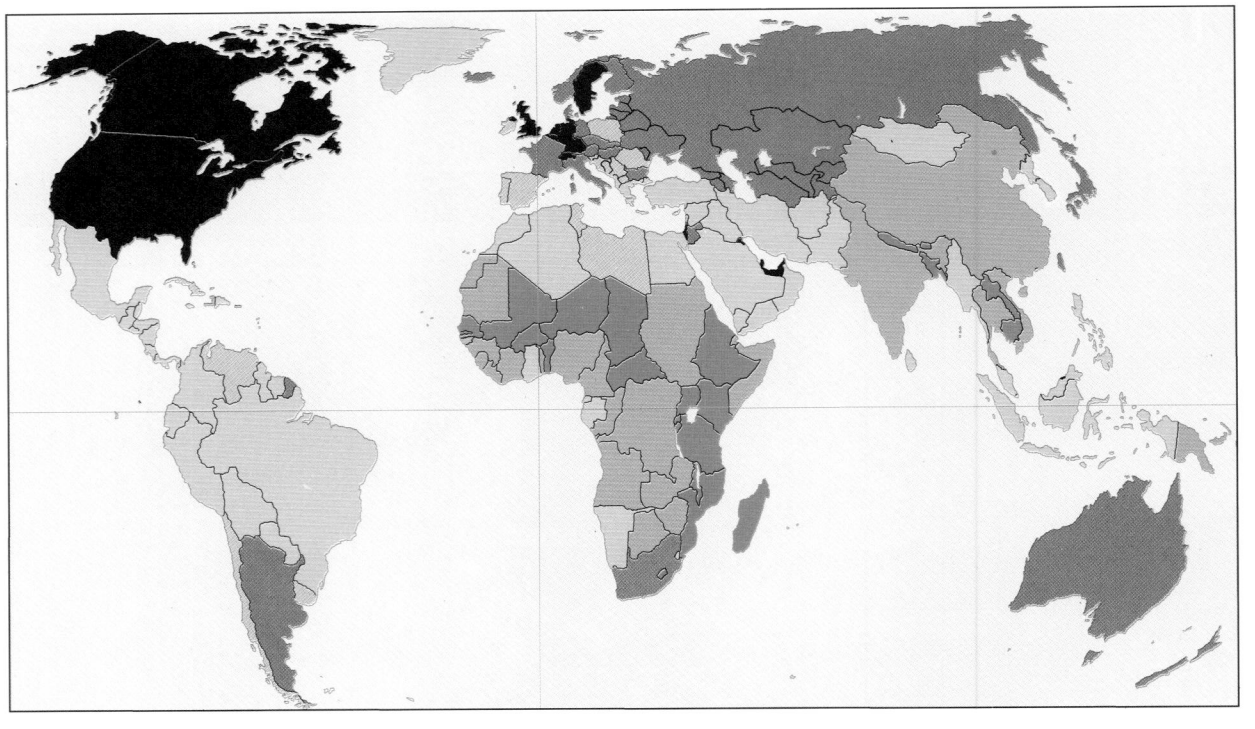

EMPLOYMENT

The number of workers employed in manufacturing for every 100 workers engaged in agriculture

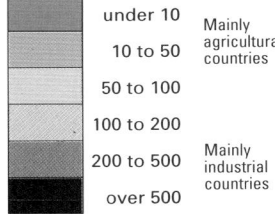

	under 10	Mainly agricultural countries
	10 to 50	
	50 to 100	
	100 to 200	Mainly industrial countries
	200 to 500	
	over 500	

Selected countries
(latest available figure, 1986-1989)

Singapore	6,166
Hong Kong	2,632
UK	912
Belgium	751
Germany (W)	749
USA	641
Sweden	615
France	331
Japan	320
Czechoslovakia	286

DIVISION OF EMPLOYMENT

Distribution of workers between agriculture, industry and services, selected countries (late 1980s)

The six countries selected illustrate the usual stages of economic development, from dependence on agriculture through industrial growth to the expansion of the services sector.

- Agriculture
- Industry
- Services

Nepal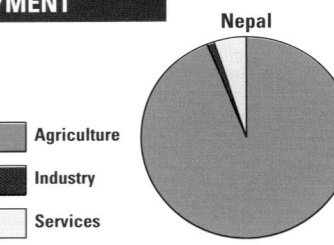

Nigeria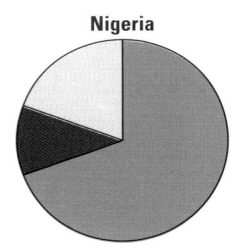

Pakistan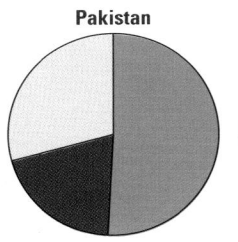

Brazil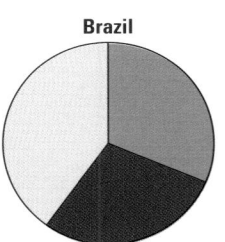

Hong Kong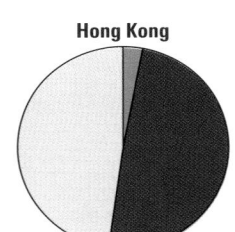

USA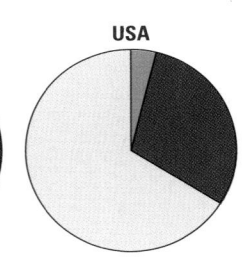

THE WORKFORCE

Percentages of men and women between 15 and 64 in employment, selected countries (late 1980s)

The figures include employees and self-employed, who in developing countries are often subsistence farmers. People in full-time education are excluded. Because of the population age structure in developing countries, the employed population has to support a far larger number of non-workers than its industrial equivalent. For example, more than 52% of Kenya's people are under 15, an age group that makes up less than a tenth of the UK population.

- Men
- Women

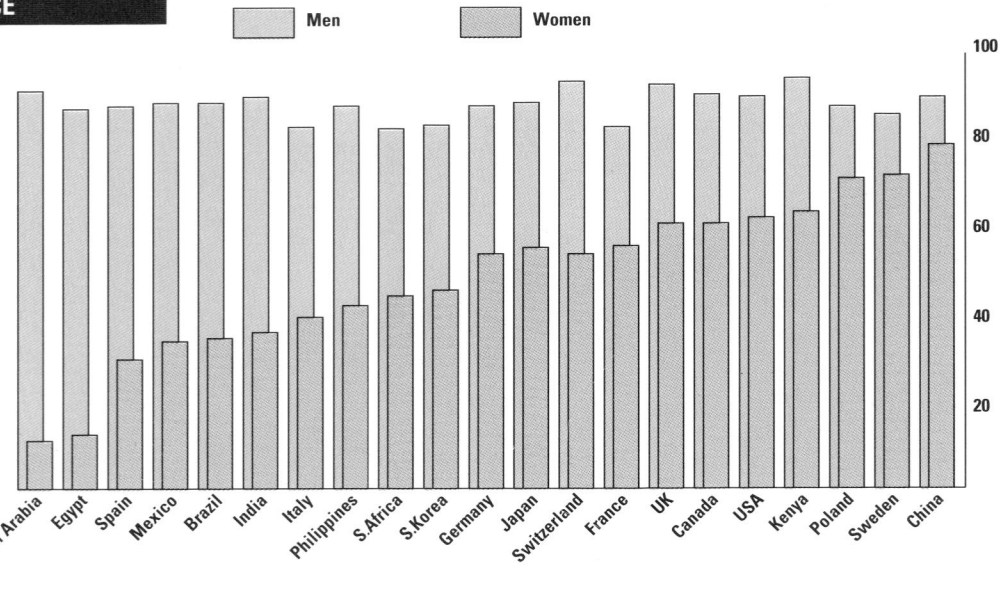

Saudi Arabia, Egypt, Spain, Mexico, Brazil, India, Italy, Philippines, S.Africa, S.Korea, Germany, Japan, Switzerland, France, UK, Canada, USA, Kenya, Poland, Sweden, China

WEALTH CREATION

The Gross National Product (GNP) of the world's largest economies, US $ billion (1989)

1.	USA	5,237,707	21.	Denmark	105,263
2.	Japan	2,920,310	22.	Norway	92,097
3.	Germany	1,272,959	23.	Saudi Arabia	89,986
4.	France	1,000,866	24.	Indonesia	87,936
5.	Italy	871,955	25.	South Africa	86,029
6.	UK	834,166	26.	Turkey	74,731
7.	Canada	500,337	27.	Argentina	68,780
8.	China	393,006	28.	Poland	66,974
9.	Brazil	375,146	29.	Thailand	64,437
10.	Spain	358,352	30.	Hong Kong	59,202
11.	India	287,383	31.	Yugoslavia	59,080
12.	Australia	242,131	32.	Greece	53,626
13.	Netherlands	237,451	33.	Algeria	53,116
14.	Switzerland	197,984	34.	Venezuela	47,164
15.	South Korea	186,467	35.	Israel	44,131
16.	Sweden	184,230	36.	Portugal	44,058
17.	Mexico	170,053	37.	Philippines	42,754
18.	Belgium	162,026	38.	Pakistan	40,134
19.	Austria	131,899	39.	New Zealand	39,437
20.	Finland	109,705	40.	Colombia	38,607

There are no accurate figures available for either the USSR or its successor nations.

PATTERNS OF PRODUCTION

Breakdown of industrial output by value, selected countries (1987)

	Food & agriculture	Textiles & clothing	Machinery & transport	Chemicals	Other
Algeria	26%	20%	11%	1%	41%
Argentina	24%	10%	16%	12%	37%
Australia	18%	7%	21%	8%	45%
Austria	17%	8%	25%	6%	43%
Belgium	19%	8%	23%	13%	36%
Brazil	15%	12%	24%	9%	40%
Burkina Faso	62%	18%	2%	1%	17%
Canada	15%	7%	25%	9%	44%
Denmark	22%	6%	23%	10%	39%
Egypt	20%	27%	13%	10%	31%
Finland	13%	6%	24%	7%	50%
France	18%	7%	33%	9%	33%
Germany	12%	5%	38%	10%	36%
Greece	20%	22%	14%	7%	38%
Hong Kong	6%	40%	20%	2%	33%
Hungary	6%	11%	37%	11%	35%
India	11%	16%	26%	15%	32%
Indonesia	23%	11%	10%	10%	47%
Iran	13%	22%	22%	7%	36%
Israel	13%	10%	28%	8%	42%
Ireland	28%	7%	20%	15%	28%
Italy	7%	13%	32%	10%	38%
Japan	10%	6%	38%	10%	37%
Kenya	35%	12%	14%	9%	29%
Malaysia	21%	5%	23%	14%	37%
Mexico	24%	12%	14%	12%	39%
Netherlands	19%	4%	28%	11%	38%
New Zealand	26%	10%	16%	6%	43%
Norway	21%	3%	26%	7%	44%
Pakistan	34%	21%	8%	12%	25%
Philippines	40%	7%	7%	10%	35%
Poland	15%	16%	30%	6%	33%
Portugal	17%	22%	16%	8%	38%
Singapore	6%	5%	46%	8%	36%
South Africa	14%	8%	17%	11%	49%
South Korea	15%	17%	24%	9%	35%
Spain	17%	9%	22%	9%	43%
Sweden	10%	2%	35%	8%	44%
Thailand	30%	17%	14%	6%	33%
Turkey	20%	14%	15%	8%	43%
UK	14%	6%	32%	11%	36%
USA	12%	5%	35%	10%	38%
Venezuela	23%	8%	9%	11%	49%
Yugoslavia	13%	17%	25%	6%	39%

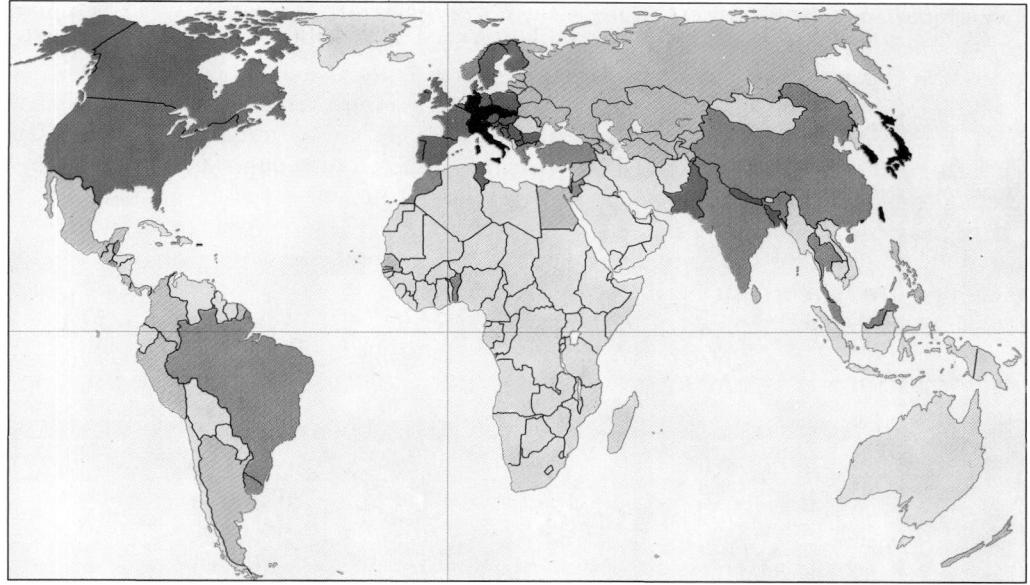

INDUSTRY & TRADE

Manufactured goods as a percentage of total exports (1989)

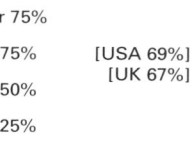

- Over 75%
- 50 - 75% [USA 69%]
- 25 - 50% [UK 67%]
- 10 - 25%
- Under 10%

The Far East & South-East Asia (Japan 99.5%, Macau 98.5%, Taiwan 96.8%, Hong Kong 96.1%, S. Korea 95.9%) is most dominant, but many countries in Europe (eg Austria 98.4%) are also heavily dependent on manufactured goods.

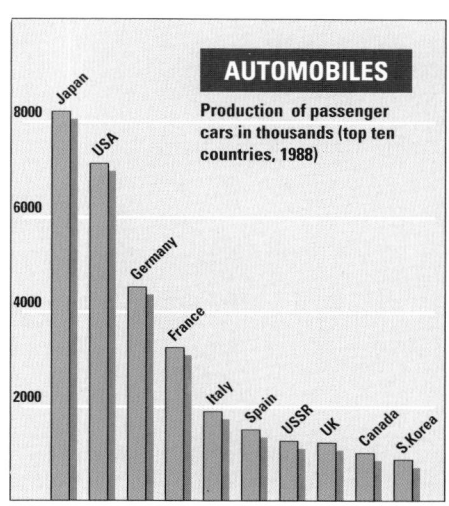

AUTOMOBILES

Production of passenger cars in thousands (top ten countries, 1988)

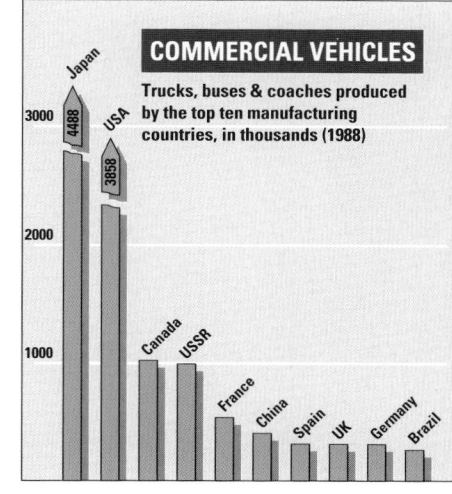

COMMERCIAL VEHICLES

Trucks, buses & coaches produced by the top ten manufacturing countries, in thousands (1988)

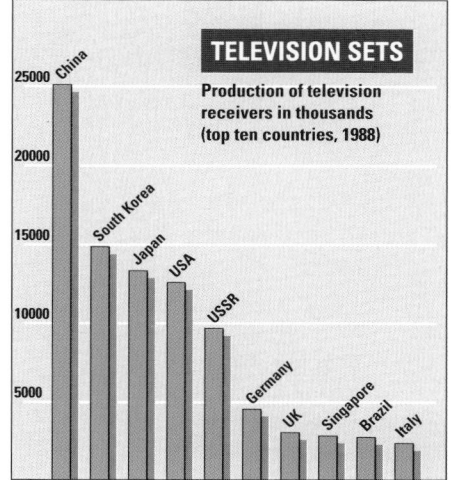

TELEVISION SETS

Production of television receivers in thousands (top ten countries, 1988)

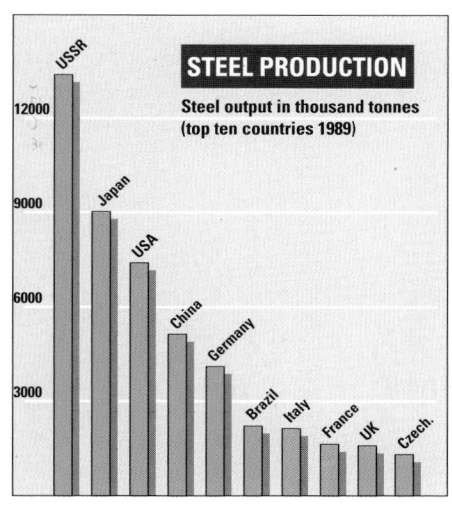

STEEL PRODUCTION

Steel output in thousand tonnes (top ten countries 1989)

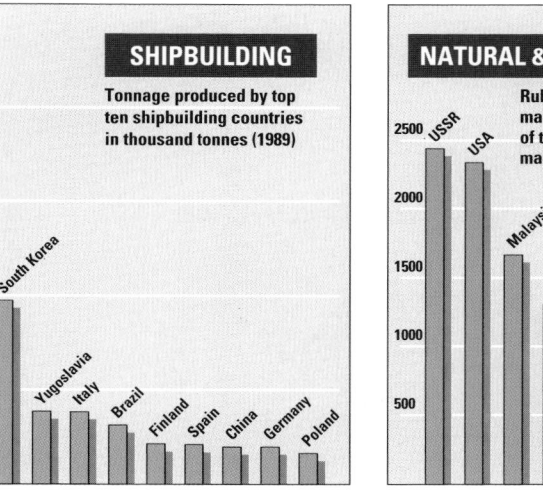

SHIPBUILDING

Tonnage produced by top ten shipbuilding countries in thousand tonnes (1989)

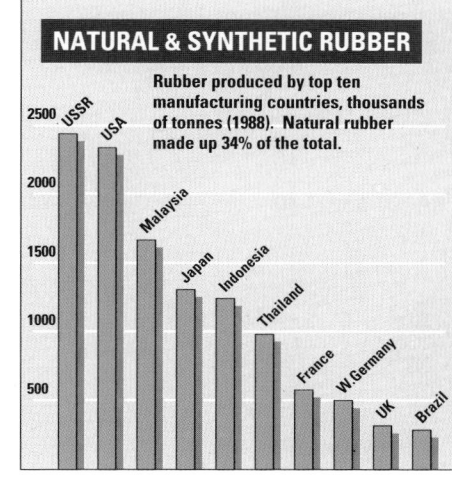

NATURAL & SYNTHETIC RUBBER

Rubber produced by top ten manufacturing countries, thousands of tonnes (1988). Natural rubber made up 34% of the total.

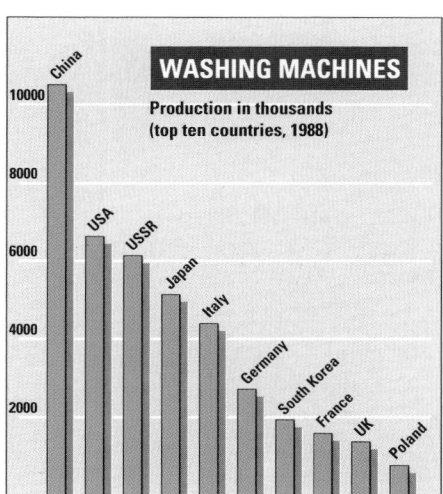

WASHING MACHINES

Production in thousands (top ten countries, 1988)

INDUSTRIAL POWER

Industrial output (mining, manufacturing, construction, energy & water production), top 40 nations, US $ billion (1988)

1. USA	1,249.54	21. Austria	50.63
2. Japan	1,155.41	22. Belgium	46.88
3. Germany	479.69	23. Poland	39.52
4. USSR	326.54	24. Finland	35.50
5. France	304.95	25. South Africa	35.46
6. UK	295.00	26. Saudi Arabia	33.36
7. Italy	286.00	27. Denmark	30.79
8. China	174.05	28. Iraq	30.27
9. Canada	171.06	29. Czechoslovakia	30.18
10. Spain	126.60	30. Yugoslavia	29.32
11. Brazil	116.13	31. Indonesia	29.03
12. Netherlands	76.48	32. Norway	28.74
13. Sweden	75.17	33. Argentina	26.27
14. South Korea	74.00	34. Turkey	26.07
15. India	72.69	35. Israel	24.15
16. Australia	72.63	36. Algeria	22.88
17. E. Germany	64.66	37. Venezuela	22.70
18. Switzerland	63.37	38. Romania	22.19
19. Mexico	61.57	39. Iran	19.90
20. Taiwan	54.81	40. Thailand	18.62

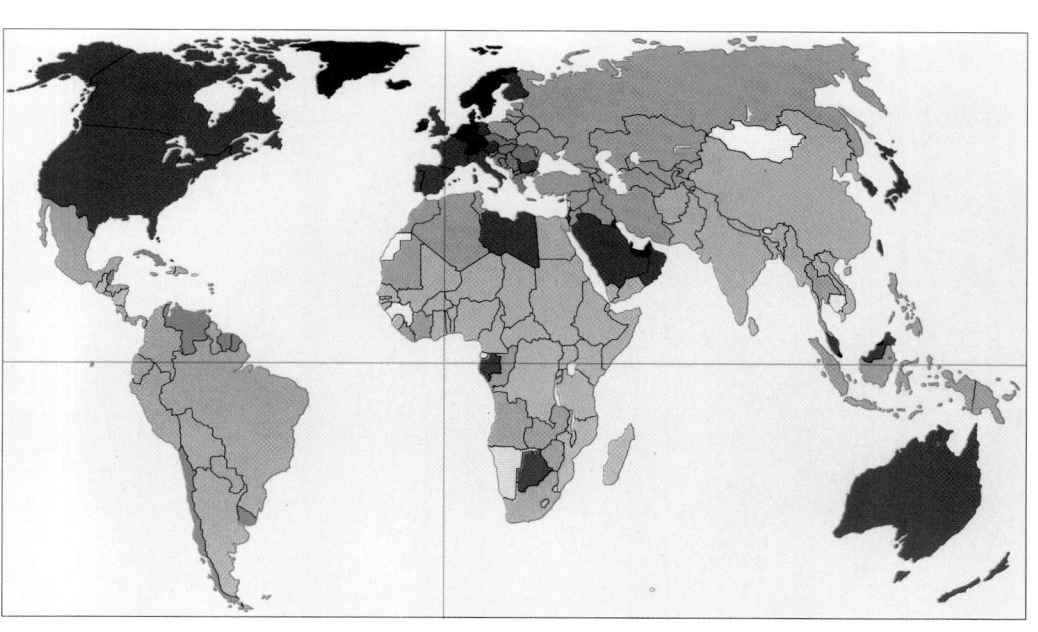

EXPORTS PER CAPITA

Value of exports in US $, divided by total population (1988)

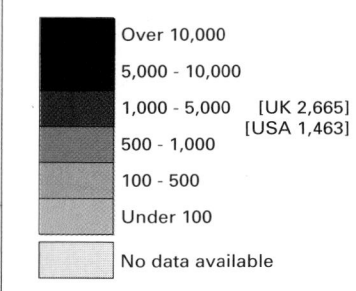

- Over 10,000
- 5,000 - 10,000
- 1,000 - 5,000 [UK 2,665]
- 500 - 1,000 [USA 1,463]
- 100 - 500
- Under 100
- No data available

Highest per capita

Singapore	16,671
Hong Kong	12,676
UAE	10,217
Belgium	10,200
Bahamas	8,580
Qatar	8,431

PRODUCTION: TRADE

29: INTERNATIONAL ORGANIZATIONS

30: SELF-SUFFICIENCY IN FOOD

33: FUEL EXPORTS MOVEMENTS OF OIL

34: MINERAL EXPORTS

37: INDUSTRY & TRADE EXPORTS PER CAPITA

43: TOURISM

Thriving international trade is the outward sign of a healthy world economy – the obvious indicator that some countries have goods to sell and others the wherewithal to buy them. Despite local fluctuations, trade throughout the 1980s grew consistently faster than output, increasing in value by almost 50% in the decade 1979-89. It remains dominated by the wealthy, industrialized countries of the Organization for Economic Development: between them, the 24 OECD members account for almost 75% of world imports and exports in most years. OECD dominance is just as marked in the trade in 'invisibles' - a column in the balance sheet that includes, among other headings, the export of services, interest payments on overseas investments, tourism and even remittances from migrant workers abroad. In the UK, 'invisibles' account for more than half all trading income.

However, the size of these great trading economies means that imports and exports usually comprise a fraction of their total wealth: in the case of the export-conscious Japanese, trade in goods and services amounts to less than 18% of GDP. In poorer countries, trade - often in a single commodity - may amount to 50% GDP or more. And there are oddities: import-export figures for the entrepôt economy of Singapore, for example, the transit point for much Asian trade, are almost double that small nation's total earnings.

WORLD TRADE

Percentage of total world exports by value (1989)

- Over 10%
- 5 - 10%
- 1 - 5%
- 0.5 - 1%
- 0.25 - 0.5%
- Under 0.25%

[USA 15.7%] [UK 6.3%]

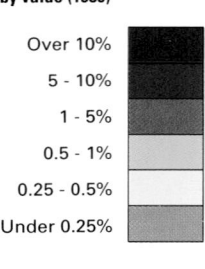

THE GREAT TRADING NATIONS

The imports and exports of the top ten trading nations as a percentage of world trade (1989). Each country's trade in manufactured goods is shown in orange.

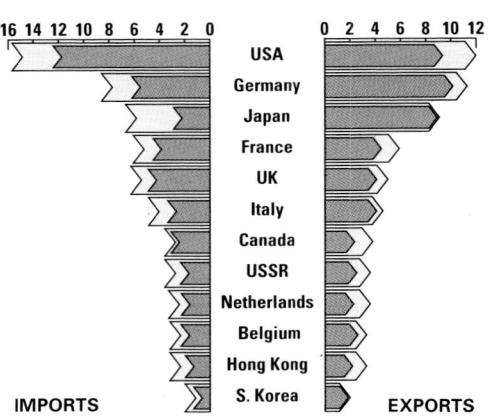

IMPORTS — EXPORTS

16 14 12 10 8 6 4 2 0 | 0 2 4 6 8 10 12

- USA
- Germany
- Japan
- France
- UK
- Italy
- Canada
- USSR
- Netherlands
- Belgium
- Hong Kong
- S. Korea

MAJOR EXPORTS

Leading manufactured items and their exporters, by percentage of world total in US dollars (late 1980s)

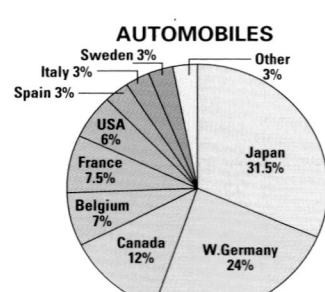

AIRCRAFT
- USA 51%
- UK 13%
- W. Germany 9%
- France 8%
- Canada 5%
- Italy 3%
- Other 11%

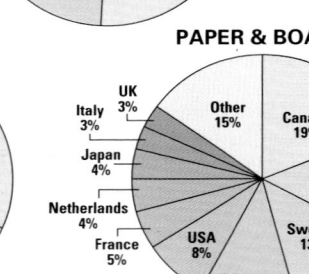

AUTOMOBILES
- Japan 31.5%
- W.Germany 24%
- Canada 12%
- Belgium 7%
- France 7.5%
- USA 6%
- Spain 3%
- Italy 3%
- Sweden 3%
- Other 3%

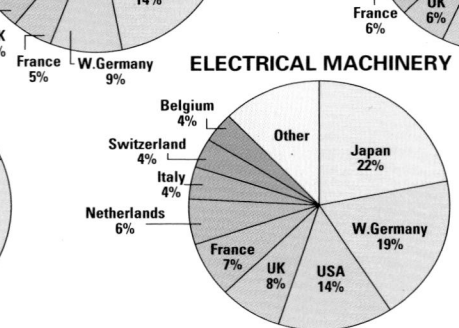

TELECOMMUNICATIONS GEAR
- Japan 33%
- USA 14%
- W.Germany 9%
- France 5%
- UK 5%
- Sweden 4%
- Hong Kong 4%
- Canada 4%
- Italy 3%
- Other 19%

PAPER & BOARD
- Canada 19%
- Finland 14%
- Sweden 13%
- W.Germany 12%
- USA 8%
- France 5%
- Netherlands 4%
- Japan 4%
- Italy 3%
- UK 3%
- Other 15%

DATA PROCESSING EQUIPMENT
- USA 24%
- Japan 22%
- W.Germany 11%
- France 6%
- UK 6%
- Ireland 5%
- Canada 4%
- Italy 4%
- Singapore 4%
- Other 14%

ELECTRICAL MACHINERY
- Japan 22%
- W.Germany 19%
- USA 14%
- UK 8%
- France 7%
- Netherlands 6%
- Italy 4%
- Switzerland 4%
- Belgium 4%
- Other

TRADED PRODUCTS

Top ten manufactures traded, by value in billions of US $ (late 1980s)

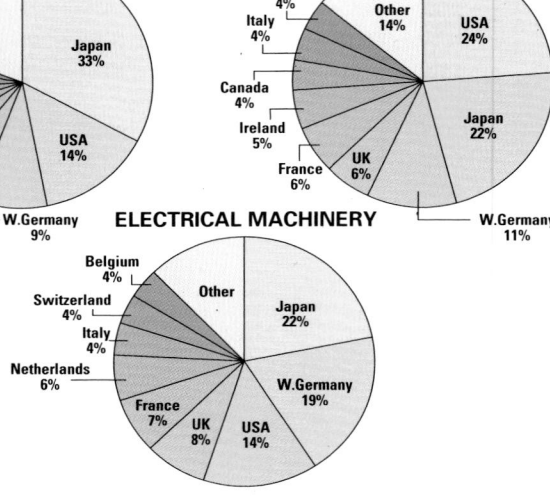

- Automobiles
- Engines & vehicle parts
- Data processing equipment
- Telecommunications
- Transistors etc
- Aircraft
- Paper & board
- Trucks
- Meas. & control instruments
- Electrical machinery

DEPENDENCE ON TRADE

Value of exports as a percentage of Gross Domestic Product (1988)

- Over 50%
- 40 - 50%
- 30 - 40%
- 20 - 30%   [UK 21%]
- 10 - 20%   [USA 6.5%]
- Under 10%

● Most dependent on industrial exports (over 75% of total exports)

● Most dependent on fuel exports (over 75% of total exports)

○ Most dependent on mineral & metal exports (over 75% of total exports)

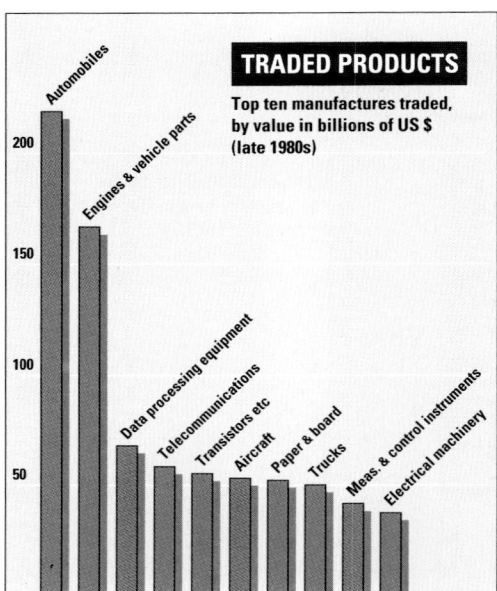

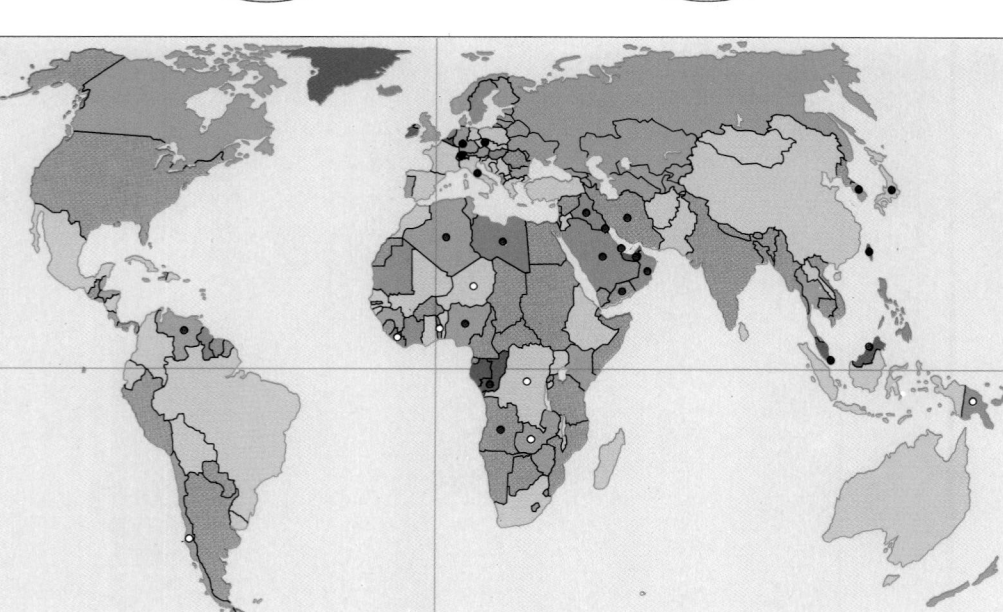
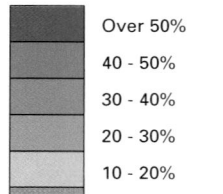

WORLD SHIPPING

While ocean passenger traffic is now relatively modest, sea transport still carries most of world trade. Oil and bulk carriers make up the majority of the world fleet, although the general cargo category was the fastest growing in 1989, a year in which total tonnage increased by 1.5%.

Almost 30% of world shipping sails under a 'flag of convenience', whereby owners take advantage of low taxes by registering their vessels in a foreign country the ships will never see, notably Panama and Liberia.

MERCHANT FLEETS

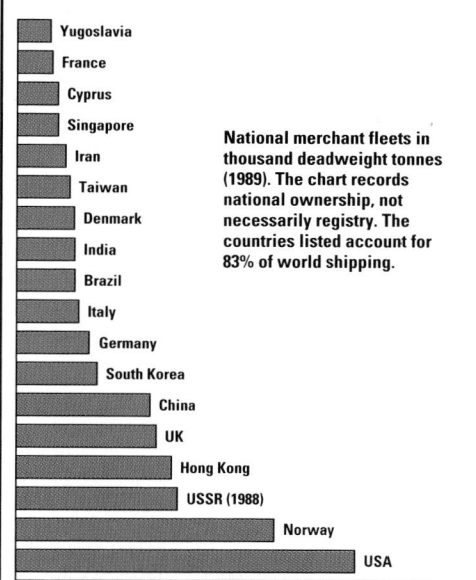

National merchant fleets in thousand deadweight tonnes (1989). The chart records national ownership, not necessarily registry. The countries listed account for 83% of world shipping.

Yugoslavia
France
Cyprus
Singapore
Iran
Taiwan
Denmark
India
Brazil
Italy
Germany
South Korea
China
UK
Hong Kong
USSR (1988)
Norway
USA
Japan
Greece

20,000   40,000   60,000   80,000

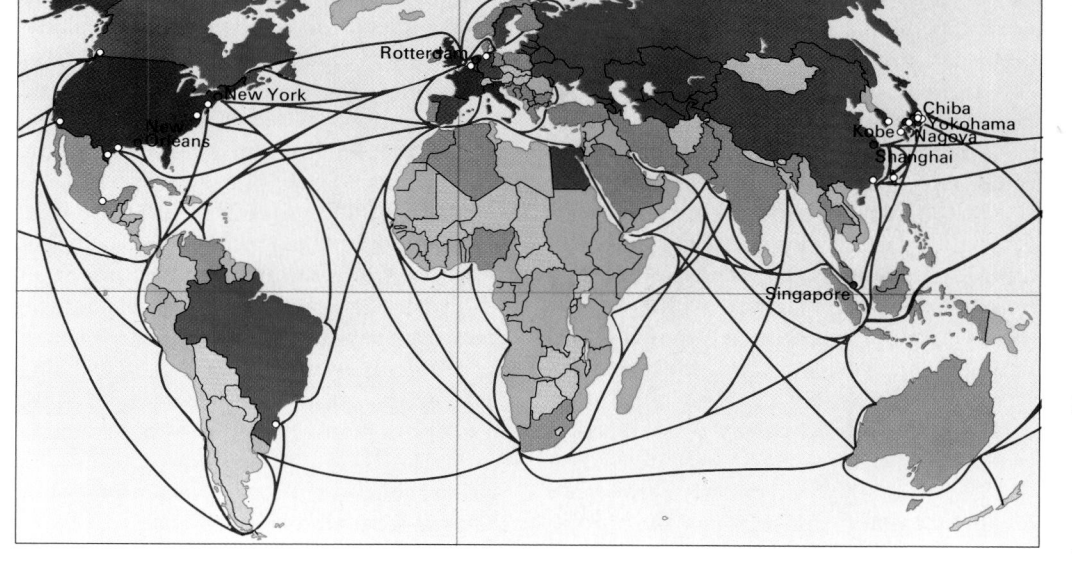

Freight unloaded in millions of tonnes (1988)

Over 100
50 - 100
10 - 50
5 - 10
Under 5
Land-locked countries

Major seaports

● Over 100 million tonnes per year
○ 50-100 million tonnes per year

Types of vessel by deadweight tonnage (1989)

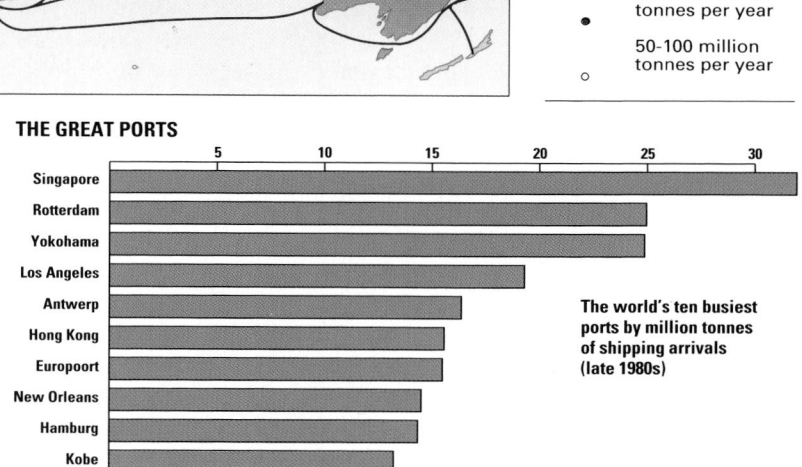

Oil tankers 38.4%
Ore & bulk carriers 29.9%
Others 9.7%
General cargo 16.1%
Ferries & passenger ships 0.5%
Liquid gas carriers 1.6%
Container ships 3.8%

THE GREAT PORTS

5   10   15   20   25   30

Singapore
Rotterdam
Yokohama
Los Angeles
Antwerp
Hong Kong
Europoort
New Orleans
Hamburg
Kobe

The world's ten busiest ports by million tonnes of shipping arrivals (late 1980s)

TRADE IN PRIMARY PRODUCTS

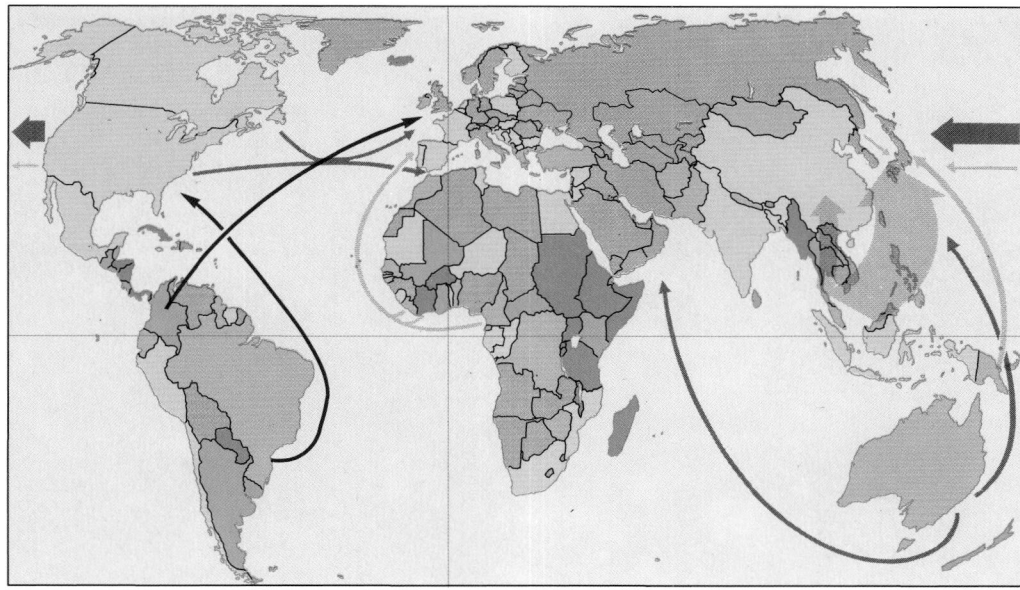

Exports in primary products (excluding fuels, minerals & metals) as a percentage of total exports (1988)

Over 75%
50 - 75%
25 - 50%
10 - 25%   [USA 17.6%]
Under 10%   [UK 9%]

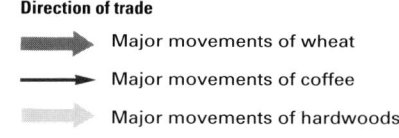

Direction of trade

➡ Major movements of wheat

➡ Major movements of coffee

➡ Major movements of hardwoods

Arrows show the major trade direction of selected primary products, & are proportional to export value

BALANCE OF TRADE

Value of exports in proportion to the value of imports (1988)

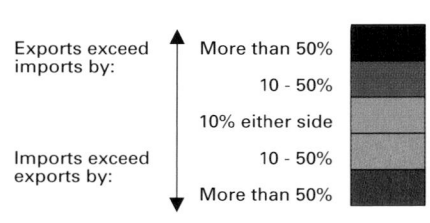

Exports exceed imports by:
More than 50%
10 - 50%
10% either side
Imports exceed exports by:
10 - 50%
More than 50%

The total world trade balance should amount to zero, since exports must equal imports on a global scale. In practice, at least $100 billions in exports go unrecorded, leaving the world with an apparent deficit and many countries in a better position than public accounting reveals. However, a favourable trade balance is not necessarily a sign of prosperity: many poorer countries must maintain a high surplus in order to service debts, and do so by restricting imports below their real requirements.

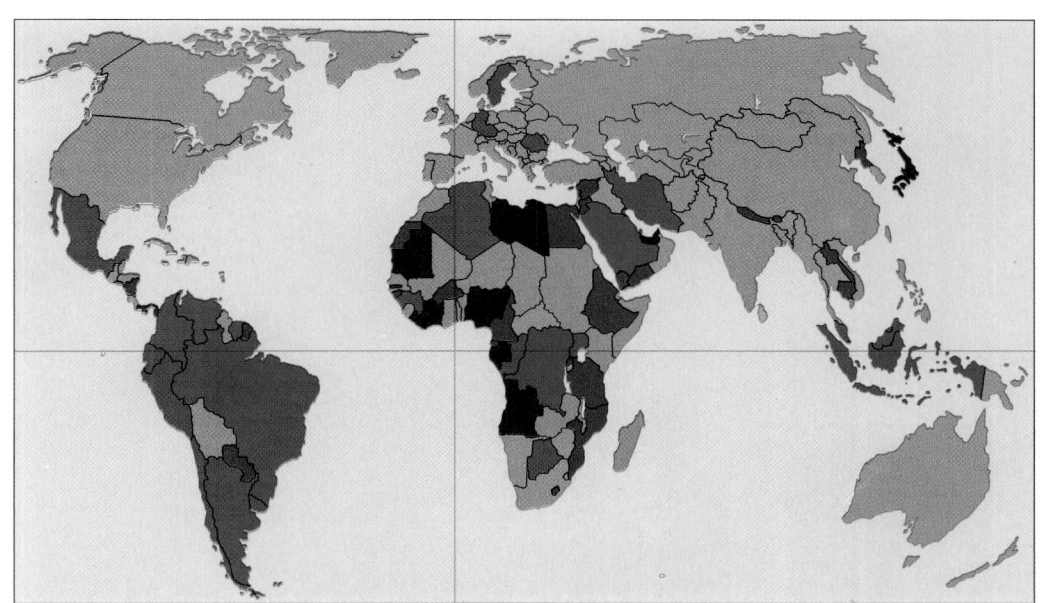

QUALITY OF LIFE: WEALTH

36:	WEALTH CREATION
37:	INDUSTRIAL POWER EXPORT PER CAPITA
38:	WORLD TRADE MAJOR EXPORTS
39:	BALANCE OF TRADE
43:	DISTRIBUTION OF SPENDING DISTRIBUTION OF INCOME

Throughout the 1980s, most of the world became at least slightly richer. There were exceptions: in Africa, the poorest of the continents, many incomes actually fell, and the upheavals in Eastern Europe in 1989 left whole populations awash with political freedom but worse off financially in economies still teetering towards capitalism.

Most of the improvements, however, came to those who were already, in world terms, extremely affluent: the gap between rich and poor grew steadily wider. And in those developing countries that showed significant statistical progress, advances were often confined to a few favoured areas while conditions in other, usually rural, districts went from bad to worse.

The pattern of world poverty varies from region to region. In most of Asia, the process of recognized development is generally under way, with production increases outpacing population growth. By 2000, less than 10% of the Chinese population should be officially rated 'poor': without the means to buy either adequate food or the basic necessities required to take a full part in everyday life. Even India's lower growth rate should be enough to reduce the burden of poverty for at least some of its people. In Latin America, average per capita production is high enough for most countries to be considered 'middle income' in world rankings. But although adequate resources exist, Latin American wealth is distributed with startling inequality. According to a 1990 World Bank report, a tax of only 2% on the richest fifth would raise enough money to pull every one of the continent's 437 million people above the poverty line.

In Africa, solutions will be harder to find. The bane of high population growth has often been aggravated by incompetent administration, a succession of natural disasters and war. Population is the crux of the problem: numbers are growing anything up to twice as fast as the economies that try to support them. Aid from the developed world is only a partial solution; although Africa receives more than any other continent, much has been wasted on over-ambitious projects or lost in webs of inexperienced or corrupt bureaucracy. Yet without aid, Africa seems doomed to permanent crisis.

The rich countries can afford to increase their spending. The 24 members of the Organization for Economic Cooperation and Development comprise only 16% of the world's population, yet between them the nations accounted for almost 80% of total world production in 1988, a share that is likely to increase as 2000 approaches.

CURRENCIES

Currency units of the world's most powerful economies

1. USA: US Dollar($,US$) = 100 cents
2. Japan: Yen (Y,¥) = 100 sen
3. Germany: Deutsche Mark (DM) = 100 Pfennige
4. France: French Franc (Fr) = 100 centimes
5. Italy: Italian Lira (L, £, Lit)
6. UK: Pound Sterling (£) = 100 pence
7. Canada: Canadian Dollar (C$, Can$) = 100 cents
8. China: Renminbi Yuan (RMBY, $, Y) = 10 jiao = 100 fen
9. Brazil: Cruzado (Cr$) = 100 centavos
10. Spain: Peseta (Pta, Pa) = 100 céntimos
11. India: Indian Rupee (Re, Rs) = 100 paisa
12. Australia: Australian Dollar ($A) = 100 cents
13. Netherlands: Guilder, Florin (Gld, f) = 100 centimes
14. Switzerland: Swiss Franc (SFr, SwF) = 100 centimes
15. South Korea: Won (W) = 100 Chon
16. Sweden: Swedish Krona (SKr) = 100 öre
17. Mexico: Mexican Pesos (Mex$) = 100 centavos
18. Belgium: Belgian Franc (BFr) = 100 centimes
19. Austria: Schilling (S, Sch) = 100 groschen
20. Finland: Markka (FMk) = 100 penni
21. Denmark: Danish Krone (DKr) = 100 öre
22. Norway: Norwegian Krone (NKr) = 100 öre
23. Saudi Arabia: Riyal (SAR, SRI$) = 100 halalah
24. Indonesia: Rupiah (Rp) = 100 sen
25. South Africa: Rand (R) = 100 cents

CONTINENTAL SHARES

Shares of population and of wealth (GNP) by continent

Generalized continental figures show the startling difference between rich and poor but mask the successes or failures of individual countries. Japan, for example, with less than 4% of Asia's population, produces almost 70% of the continent's output.

POPULATION

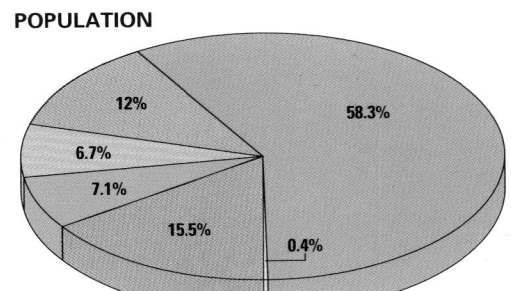

GNP

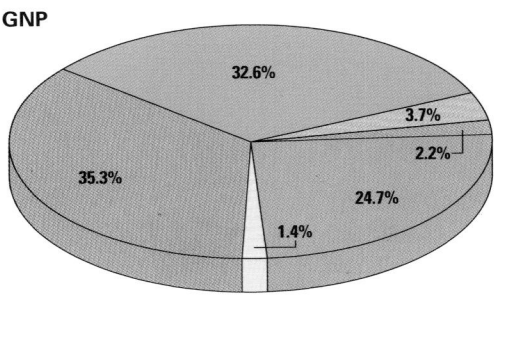

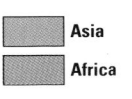

Europe   Asia   South America
Australia   Africa   North America

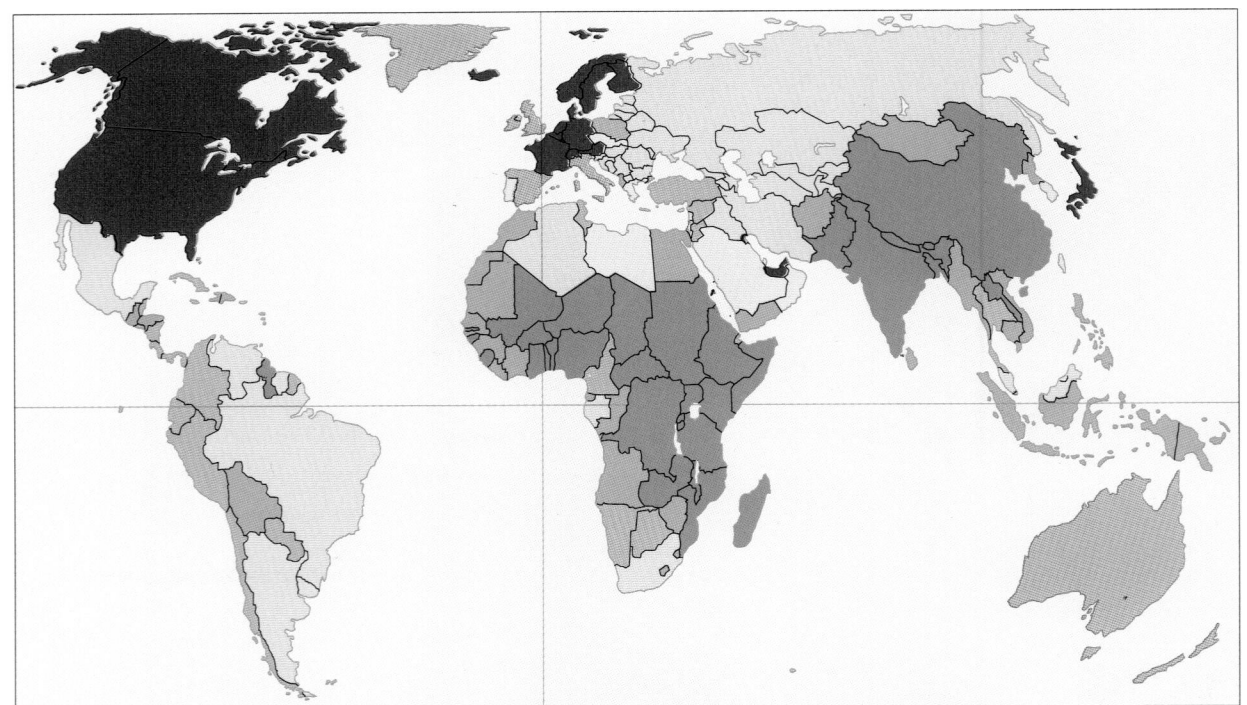

LEVELS OF INCOME

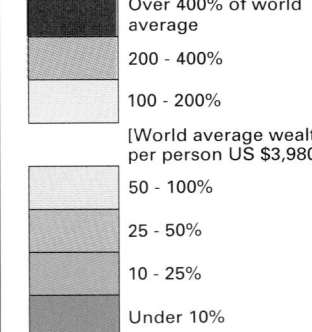

Gross National Product per capita: the value of total production divided by population (1989)

- Over 400% of world average
- 200 – 400%
- 100 – 200%

[World average wealth per person US $3,980]

- 50 – 100%
- 25 – 50%
- 10 – 25%
- Under 10%

Richest countries

Switzerland	$30,270
Luxembourg	$24,860
Japan	$23,730
Finland	$22,060

Poorest countries

Somalia	$170
Ethiopia	£120
Tanzania	$120
Mozambique	$80

INDICATORS

The gap between the world's rich and poor is now so great that it is difficult to illustrate it on a single graph. Car ownership in the USA, for example, is almost 2,000 times as common as it is in Bangladesh. Within each income group, however, comparisons have some meaning: the affluent Japanese on their overcrowded island have far fewer cars than the Americans; the Chinese, perhaps because of propaganda value, have more television sets than the Indians, whose per capita income is similar, while Nigerians prefer to spend their money on vehicles.

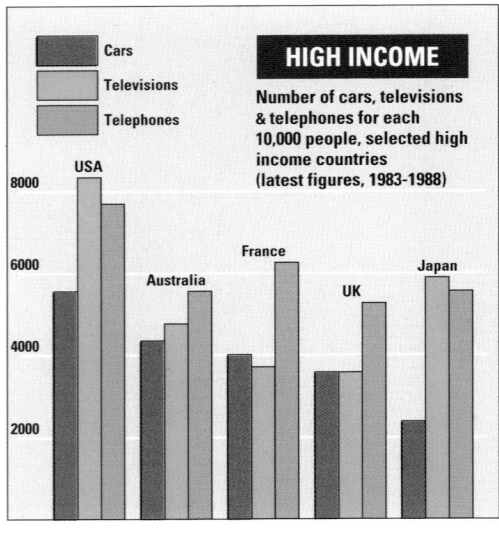

HIGH INCOME

Number of cars, televisions & telephones for each 10,000 people, selected high income countries (latest figures, 1983-1988)

Cars / Televisions / Telephones

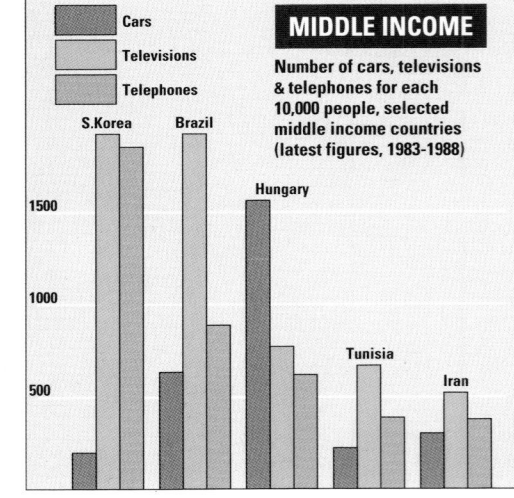

MIDDLE INCOME

Number of cars, televisions & telephones for each 10,000 people, selected middle income countries (latest figures, 1983-1988)

Cars / Televisions / Telephones

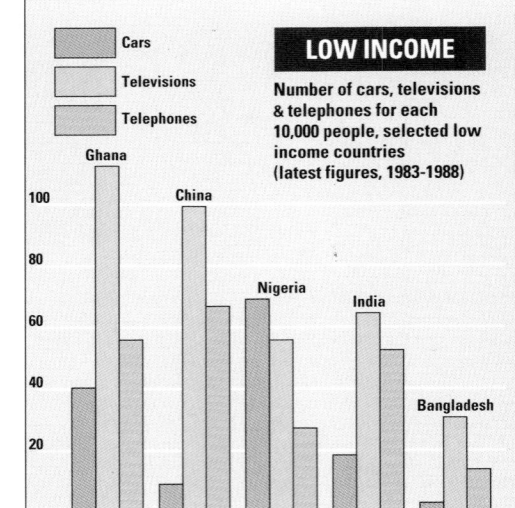

LOW INCOME

Number of cars, televisions & telephones for each 10,000 people, selected low income countries (latest figures, 1983-1988)

Cars / Televisions / Telephones

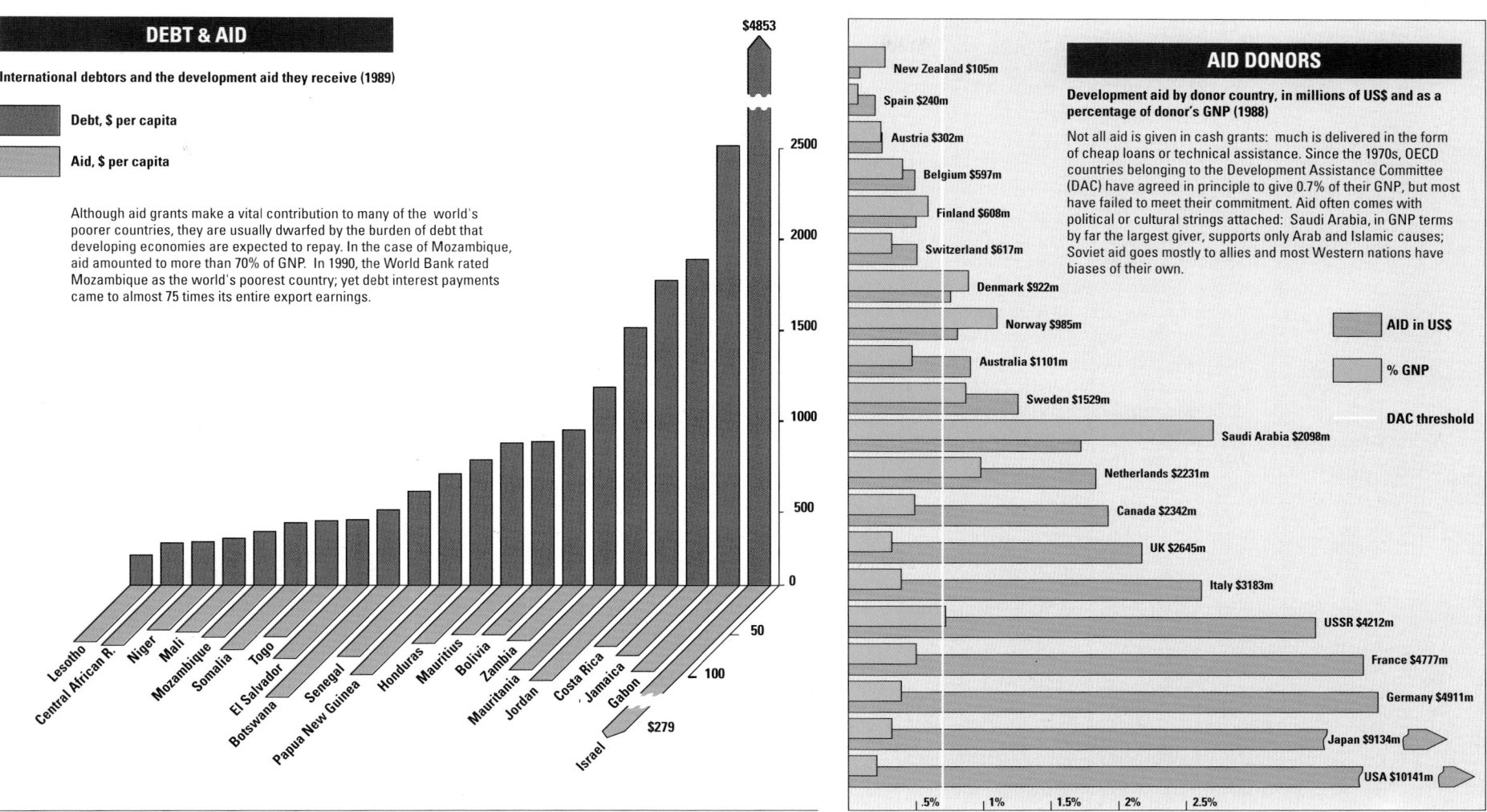

DEBT & AID

International debtors and the development aid they receive (1989)

■ Debt, $ per capita

■ Aid, $ per capita

Although aid grants make a vital contribution to many of the world's poorer countries, they are usually dwarfed by the burden of debt that developing economies are expected to repay. In the case of Mozambique, aid amounted to more than 70% of GNP. In 1990, the World Bank rated Mozambique as the world's poorest country; yet debt interest payments came to almost 75 times its entire export earnings.

$4853

Lesotho, Central African R., Niger, Mali, Mozambique, Somalia, Togo, El Salvador, Botswana, Senegal, Papua New Guinea, Honduras, Mauritius, Bolivia, Zambia, Mauritania, Jordan, Costa Rica, Jamaica, Gabon, Israel $279

AID DONORS

Development aid by donor country, in millions of US$ and as a percentage of donor's GNP (1988)

Not all aid is given in cash grants: much is delivered in the form of cheap loans or technical assistance. Since the 1970s, OECD countries belonging to the Development Assistance Committee (DAC) have agreed in principle to give 0.7% of their GNP, but most have failed to meet their commitment. Aid often comes with political or cultural strings attached: Saudi Arabia, in GNP terms by far the largest giver, supports only Arab and Islamic causes; Soviet aid goes mostly to allies and most Western nations have biases of their own.

■ AID in US$

■ % GNP

DAC threshold

New Zealand $105m, Spain $240m, Austria $302m, Belgium $597m, Finland $608m, Switzerland $617m, Denmark $922m, Norway $985m, Australia $1101m, Sweden $1529m, Saudi Arabia $2098m, Netherlands $2231m, Canada $2342m, UK $2645m, Italy $3183m, USSR $4212m, France $4777m, Germany $4911m, Japan $9134m, USA $10141m

.5% | 1% | 1.5% | 2% | 2.5%

Inflation (right) is an excellent index of a country's financial stability, and usually its prosperity or at least its prospects. Inflation rates above 20% are generally matched by slow or even negative growth; above 50%, an economy is left reeling. Most advanced countries during the 1980s had to wrestle with inflation that occasionally touched or even exceeded 10%; in Japan, the growth leader, price increases averaged only 1.8% between 1980 and 1988.

Government spending (below right) is more difficult to interpret. Obviously, very low levels indicate a weak state, and high levels a strong one; but in poor countries, the 10-20% absorbed by the government may well amount to most of the liquid cash available, whereas in rich countries most of the 35-50% typically in government hands is returned in services.

GNP per capita figures (below) should also be compared with caution. They do not reveal the vast differences in living costs between different countries: the equivalent of US $100 is worth considerably more in poorer nations than it is in the USA itself.

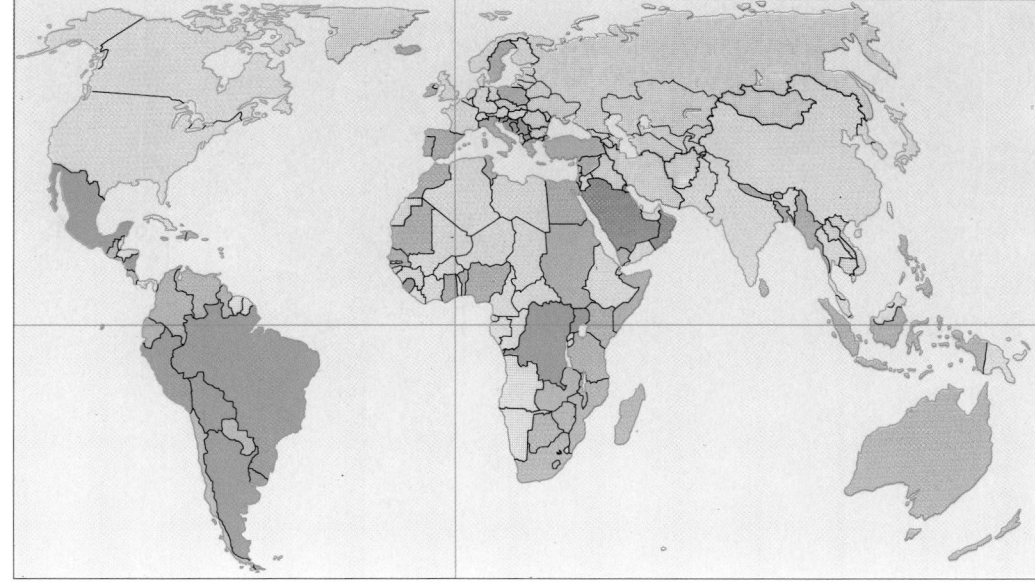

INFLATION

Average annual rate of inflation (1980-1988)

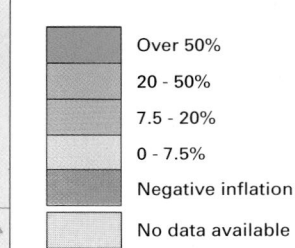

Over 50%

20 - 50%

7.5 - 20%

0 - 7.5%

Negative inflation

No data available

Highest inflation
Bolivia 483%
Argentina 291%
Brazil 189%

Lowest inflation
Oman .... -6.5%
Saudi Arabia .... -4.2%
Kuwait .... -3.9%

[UK 5.7%] [USA 4.0%]

THE WEALTH GAP

The world's richest & poorest countries, by Gross National Product per capita in US $ (1989)

1.	Liechtenstein	33,000	1. Mozambique	80
2.	Switzerland	30,270	2. Ethiopia	120
3.	Bermuda	25,000	3. Tanzania	120
4.	Luxembourg	24,860	4. Laos	170
5.	Japan	23,730	5. Nepal	170
6.	Finland	22,060	6. Somalia	170
7.	Norway	21,850	7. Bangladesh	180
8.	Sweden	21,710	8. Malawi	180
9.	Iceland	21,240	9. Bhutan	190
10.	USA	21,100	10. Chad	190
11.	Denmark	20,510	11. Sierra Leone	200
12.	Canada	19,020	12. Burundi	220
13.	UAE	18,430	13. Gambia	230
14.	France	17,830	14. Madagascar	230
15.	Austria	17,360	15. Nigeria	250
16.	Germany	16,500	16. Uganda	250
17.	Belgium	16,390	17. Mali	260
18.	Kuwait	16,380	18. Zaïre	260
19.	Netherlands	16,010	19. Niger	290
20.	Italy	15,150	20. Burkina Faso	310

GNP per capita is calculated by dividing a country's Gross National Product by its population. The UK ranks 21st, with US $14,570.

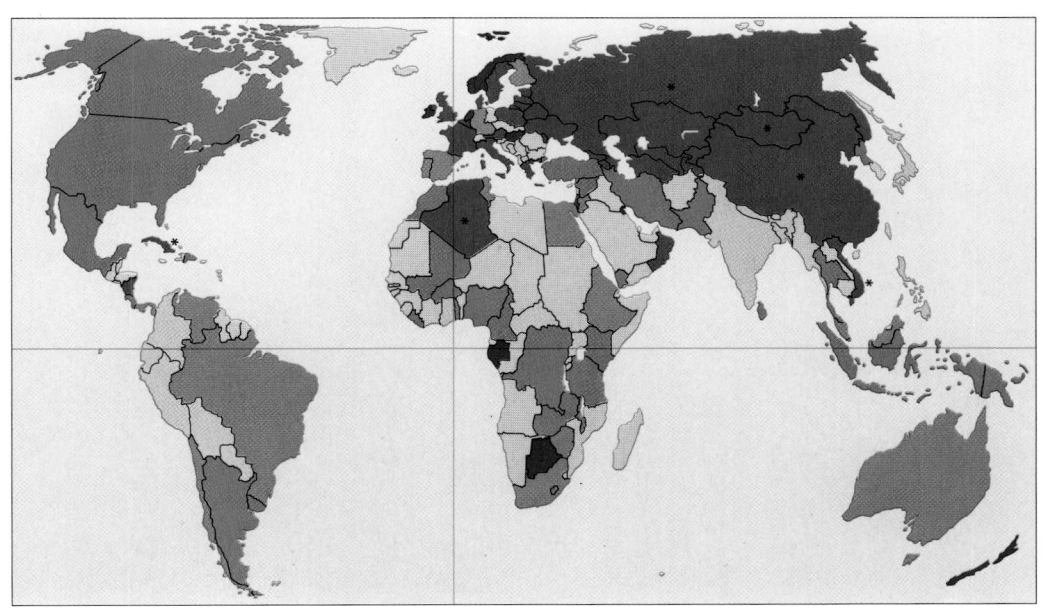

STATE REVENUE

Central government revenue as a percentage of GNP (1988) [* estimate]

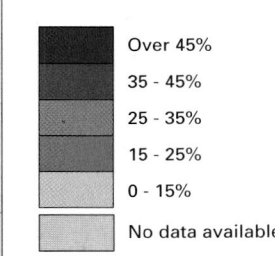

Over 45%

35 - 45%

25 - 35%

15 - 25%

0 - 15%

No data available

Highest proportion
Botswana 74%
Hungary 58%
Kuwait 52%
Netherlands 51%
Gabon 47%

[UK 36.4%] [USA 19.7%]

QUALITY OF LIFE: STANDARDS

16: WATER SUPPLY

22: POPULATION DENSITY

25: URBAN POLLUTION
INFORMAL CITIZENS
URBAN ADVANTAGES

28: WORLD'S REFUGEES
WAR SINCE 1945

36: EMPLOYMENT
THE WORK FORCE

40: THE WEALTH GAP

41: DEBT & AID

45: LIFE EXPECTANCY
INFANT MORTALITY
CRIME & PUNISHMENT

At first sight, most international contrasts are swamped by differences in wealth. The rich not only have more money, they have more of everything, including years of life. Those with only a little money are obliged to spend most of it on food and clothing, the basic maintenance costs of existence; air travel and tourism are unlikely to feature on the lists of their expenditure. However, poverty and wealth are both relative: slum-dwellers living on social security payments in an affluent industrial country have far more resources at their disposal than an average African peasant, but feel their own poverty none the less acutely. A middle-class Indian lawyer cannot command a fraction of the earnings of a counterpart in New York, London or Rome; nevertheless, he rightly sees himself as prosperous.

In 1990 the United Nations Development Programme published its first Human Development Index, an attempt to construct a comparative scale by which at least a simplified form of well-being might be measured. The index, running from 1 to 100, combined figures for life expectancy and literacy with a wealth scale that matched incomes against the official poverty lines of a group of industrialized nations. National scores ranged from a startling 98.7 for

Sweden to a miserable 11.6 for Niger, reflecting the all too familiar gap between rich and poor.

Comparisons between nations with similar incomes are more interesting, showing the effect of government policies. For example, Sri Lanka was awarded 78.9 against 43.9 for its only slightly poorer neighbour, India; Zimbabwe, at 57.6, had more than double the score of Senegal, despite no apparent disparities in average income. Some development indicators may be interpreted in two ways. There is a very clear correlation, for example, between the wealth of a nation and the level of education that its people enjoy. Education helps create wealth, of course; but are rich countries wealthy because they are educated, or well-educated because they are rich? Women's fertility rates appear to fall almost in direct proportion to the amount of secondary education they receive; but high levels of female education are associated with rich countries, where fertility is already low.

Not everything, though, is married to wealth. The countries cited on these pages have been chosen, representatively, to give a range covering different cultures as well as different economic power, revealing disparities among rich and among poor as well as between the two obvious groups.

Income distribution, for example, shows that in Brazil (following the general pattern of Latin America) most national wealth is concentrated in a few hands; Bangladesh is much poorer, but what little wealth there is, is more evenly spread.

Among the developed countries the USA, with its poorest 20% sharing less than 5% of the national cake, has a noticeably less even distribution than Japan, where despite massive industrialization traditional values act as a brake against poverty. Hungary, still enmeshed in Communism when these statistics were compiled, shows the most even distribution of all, which certainly matches with Socialist theory. However, the inequalities in Communist societies, a contributing factor in the demise of most of them in the late 1980s, are not easily measured in money terms: Communist élites are less often rewarded with cash than with power and privilege, commodities not easily expressed statistically.

There are other limits to statistical analysis. Even without taking account of such imponderables as personal satisfaction, it will always be more difficult to measure a reasonable standard of living than a nation's income or its productivity. Lack of money certainly brings misery, but its presence does not guarantee contentment.

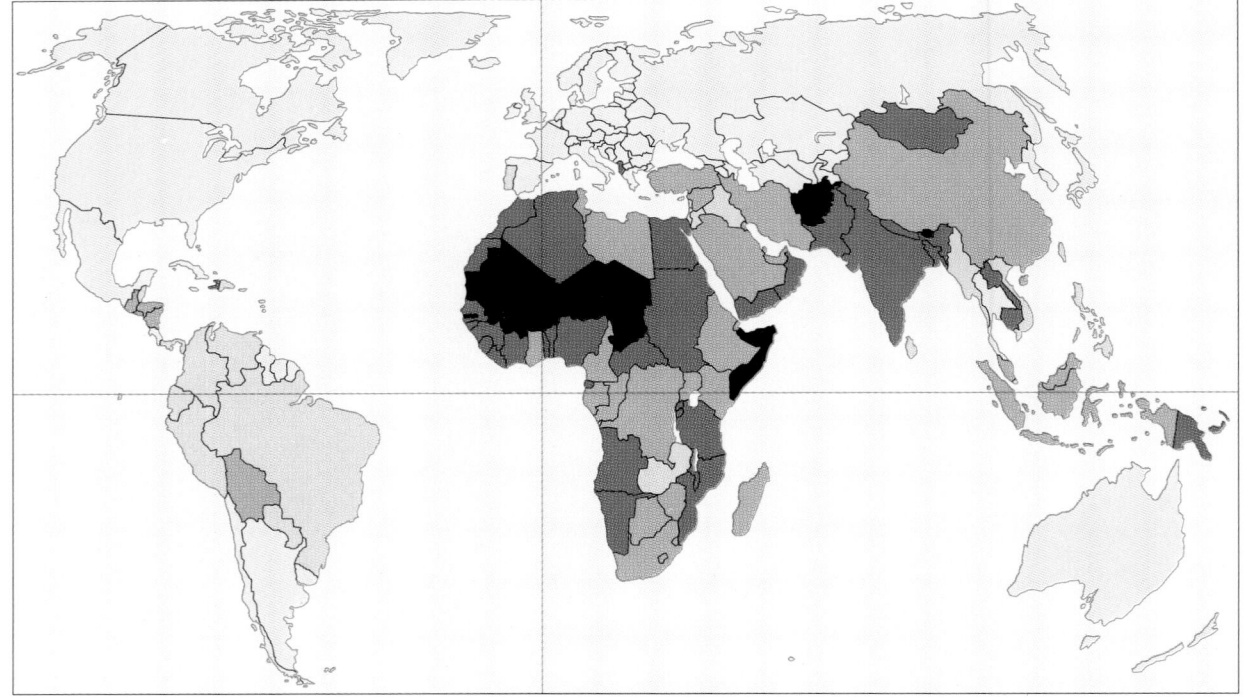

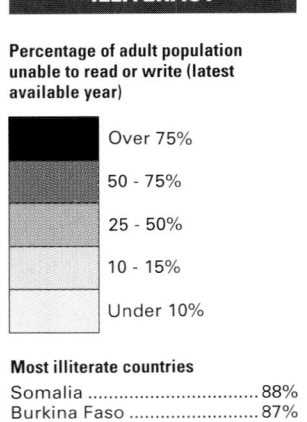

ILLITERACY

Percentage of adult population unable to read or write (latest available year)

- Over 75%
- 50 - 75%
- 25 - 50%
- 10 - 15%
- Under 10%

Most illiterate countries

Somalia	88%
Burkina Faso	87%
Niger	86%
Bhutan	85%
Mali	83%

Least illiterate countries

Canada	5%
Denmark	5%
Finland	5%
Guyana	4%
Trinidad & Tobago	4%

EDUCATION

The developing countries made great efforts in the 1970s and 1980s to bring at least a basic education to their people. Primary school enrolments rose above 60% in all but the poorest nations. Figures often include teenagers or young adults, however, and there are still an estimated 300 million children worldwide who receive no schooling at all. Secondary and higher education are expanding far more slowly, and the gap between rich and poor is probably even larger than it appears from the charts here, while the bare statistics provide no real reflection of educational quality.

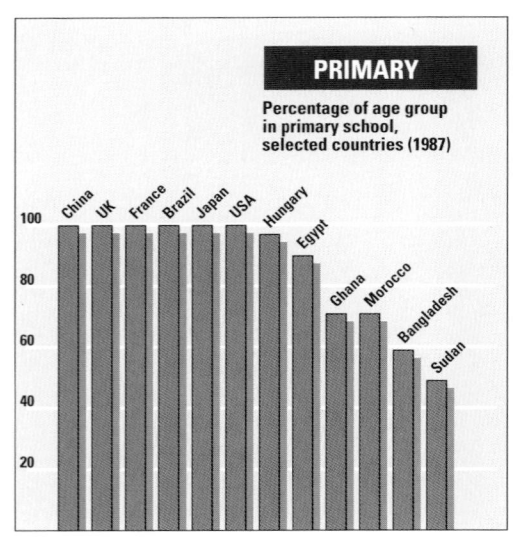

PRIMARY

Percentage of age group in primary school, selected countries (1987)

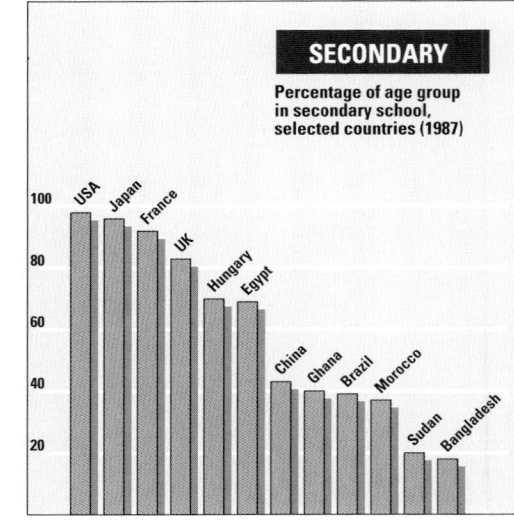

SECONDARY

Percentage of age group in secondary school, selected countries (1987)

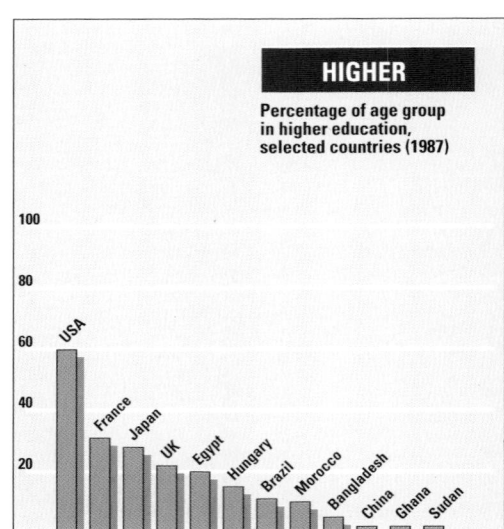

HIGHER

Percentage of age group in higher education, selected countries (1987)

DISTRIBUTION OF SPENDING

Percentage share of household spending, (1989)

- Food
- Medicine & Education
- Clothing
- Transport
- Energy & Housing
- Other

UK USA Japan Hungary Brazil Egypt Nigeria B'desh

DISTRIBUTION OF INCOME

Percentage share of household income from poorest fifth to richest fifth, selected countries (1989)

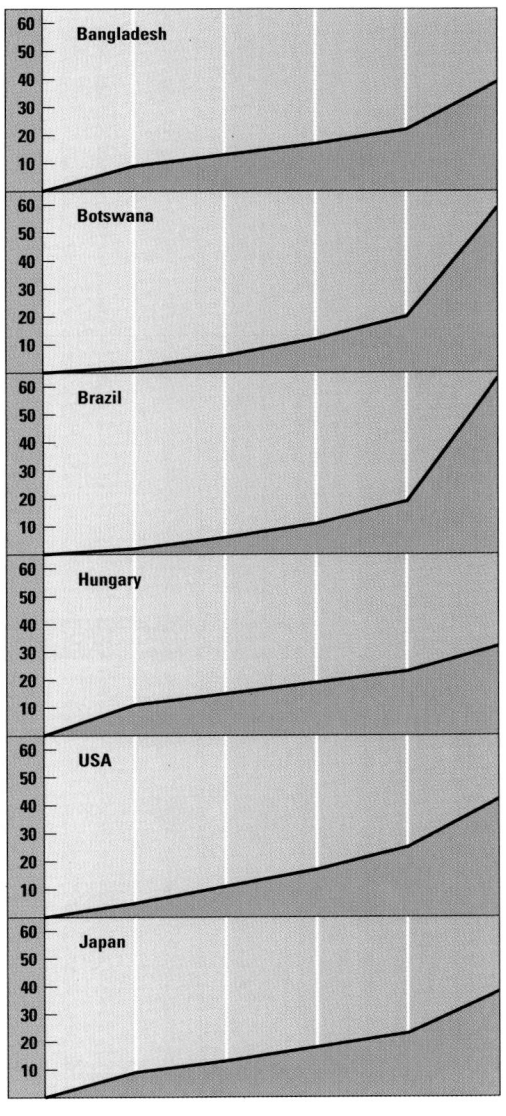

- Bangladesh
- Botswana
- Brazil
- Hungary
- USA
- Japan

FERTILITY & EDUCATION

Fertility rates compared with female education, selected countries (1988)

- Fertility rate: average number of children borne per woman
- Percentage of female age group in secondary education

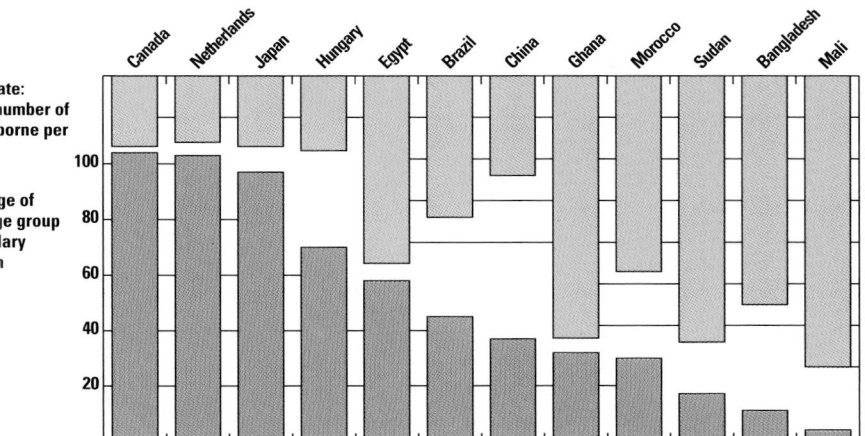

Canada Netherlands Japan Hungary Egypt Brazil China Ghana Morocco Sudan Bangladesh Mali

Since the age group for secondary schooling is usually defined as 12 to 17 years, percentages for countries with a significant number of 11- or 18-year-olds in secondary school may actually exceed 100. A high proportion of employed women may indicate either an advanced, industrial economy where female opportunities are high, or a poor country where many women's lives are dominated by agricultural toil. The lowest rates are found in Islamic nations, whose religious precepts often exclude women even from field-work.

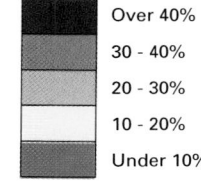

WOMEN AT WORK

Women in paid employment as a percentage of the total workforce (1989)

- Over 40%
- 30 - 40%
- 20 - 30%
- 10 - 20%
- Under 10%

Highest proportion

Burundi 53%
Ghana 51%
Mozambique 48%

Lowest proportion

UAE 6%
Saudi Arabia 7%
Bangladesh 7%

[UK 42%]   [USA 44%]

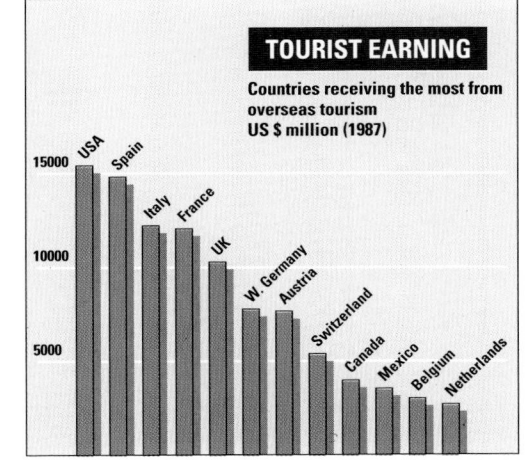

TOURIST SPENDING

Countries spending the most on overseas tourism US $ million (1987)

W. Germany US UK Japan France Netherlands Canada Italy Austria Switzerland Belgium Sweden

TOURIST EARNING

Countries receiving the most from overseas tourism US $ million (1987)

USA Spain Italy France UK W. Germany Austria Switzerland Canada Mexico Belgium Netherlands

Small economies in attractive areas are often completely dominated by tourism: in some West Indian islands, tourist spending provides over 90% of total income. In cash terms the USA is the world leader: its 1987 earnings exceeded 15 billion dollars, though that sum amounted to only 0.4% of its GDP.

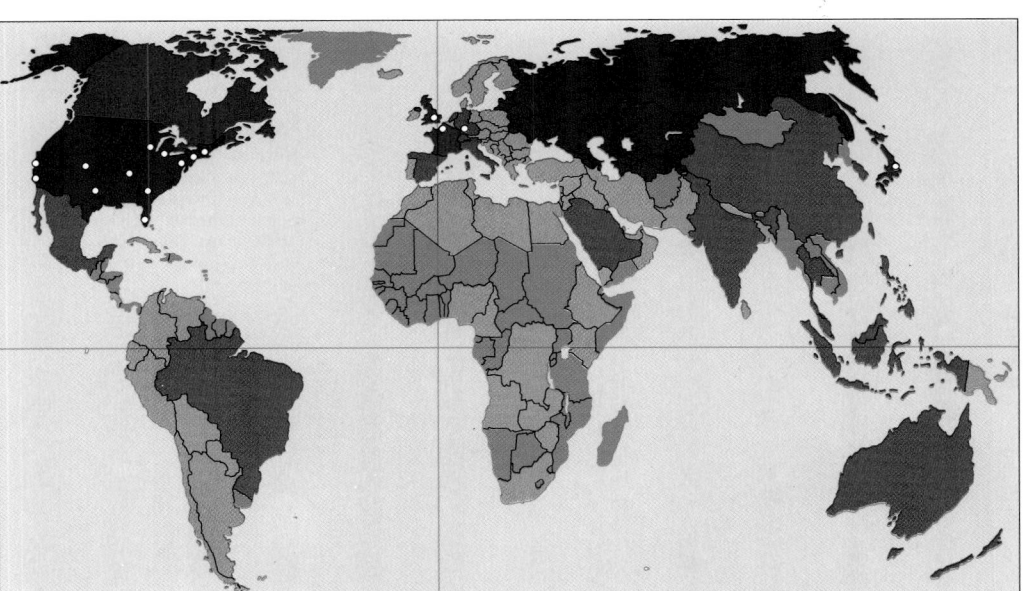

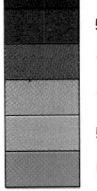

AIR TRAVEL

Millions of passenger km [number carried, international & domestic, multiplied by distance flown by each from airport of origin] (1988)

- Over 100,000
- 50,000 - 100,000
- 10,000 - 50,000
- 1,000 - 10,000
- 500 - 1,000
- Under 500

○ Major airports (over 20 million passengers a year)

The world's busiest airport in terms of total passengers is Chicago's O'Hare; the busiest international airport is Heathrow, the largest of London's airports.

QUALITY OF LIFE: HEALTH

16: WATER SUPPLY

25: URBAN POLLUTION
    INFORMAL CITIZENS
    URBAN ADVANTAGES

31: FOOD & POPULATION

43: DISTRIBUTION OF
    SPENDING

According to statistics gathered in the late 1980s and early 1990s, a third of the world's population has no access to safe drinking water: malaria is on the increase; cholera, thought vanquished, is reappearing in South America; an epidemic of the terrifying AIDS virus is gathering force in Africa; and few developing countries can stretch their health care budgets beyond US $2 per person per year.

Yet human beings, by every statistical index, have never been healthier. In the richest nations, where food is plentiful, the demands of daily work are rarely onerous and medical care is both readily available and highly advanced, the average life expectancy is often more than 75 years – approaching the perceived limits for human longevity. In middle-income nations such as Brazil and the Philippines, life expectancy usually extends at least to the mid-60s; in China, it has already reached 70. Even in poverty-stricken Ethiopia and Chad, lifespans are close to 50. Despite economic crisis, drought, famine and even war, every country in the world reported an increase between 1965 and 1990.

It was not always so, even in countries then considered rich. By comparison, in 1880 the life expectancy of an average Berliner was under 30 years and infant mortality in the United Kingdom, then the wealthiest nation, stood at 144 per thousand births – a grim toll exceeded today only by three of the poorest African countries (Mali, Sierra Leone and Guinea). Even by 1910, European death rates were almost twice as high as the world average less than 80 years later; infant mortality in Norway, Europe's healthiest country, was then higher than in present-day Indonesia. In far less than a century, human prospects have improved beyond recognition.

In global terms, the transformation is less the result of high technology medicine – still too expensive for all but a minority, even in rich countries – than of improvements in agriculture and hence nutrition, matched by the widespread diffusion of the basic concepts of disease and public health. One obvious consequence, as death rates everywhere continue to fall, is sustained population growth. Another is the rising expectation of continued improvement felt by both rich and poor nations alike.

In some ways, the task is easier for developing countries, striving with limited resources to attain health levels to which the industrialized world has only recently become accustomed. As the tables below illustrate, infectious disease is rare among the richer nations, while ailments such as cancer, which tend to kill in advanced years, do not seriously impinge on populations with shorter lifespans.

Yet infectious disease is relatively cheap to eliminate, or at least reduce, and it is likely to be easier to raise life expectancy from 60 to 70 than from 75 to 85. The ills of the developed world and its ageing population are more expensive to treat – though most poor countries would be happy to suffer from the problems of the affluent. Western nations regularly spend more money on campaigns to educate their citizens out of over-eating and other bad habits than many developing countries can devote to an entire health budget – an irony that marks the dimensions of the rich-poor divide.

Indeed, wealth itself may be the most reliable indicator of longevity. Harmful habits are usually the province of the rich; yet curiously, though the dangerous effects of tobacco have been proved beyond doubt, the affluent Japanese combine very high cigarette consumption with the longest life expectancy of all the major nations. Similarly, heavy alcohol consumption seems to have no effect on longevity: the French, world leaders in 1988 and in most previous surveys, outlive the more moderate British by a year, and the abstemious Indians by almost two decades.

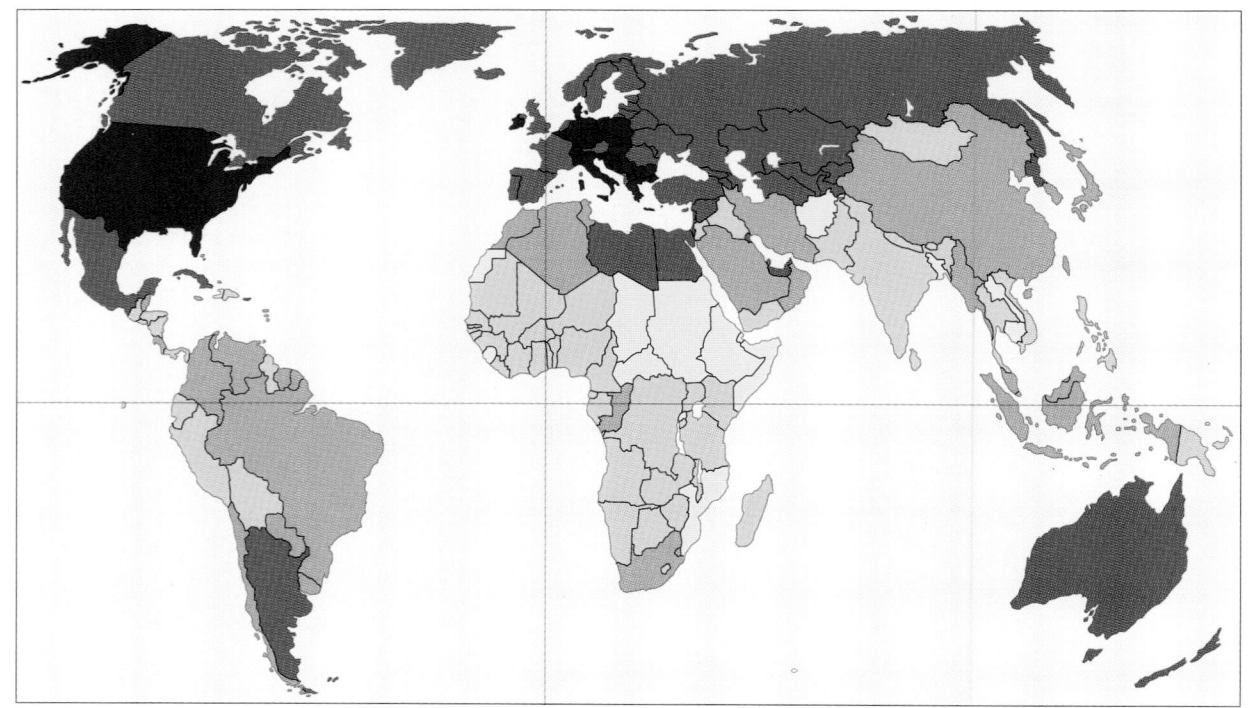

FOOD CONSUMPTION

Average daily food intake per person in calories (1986-1988)

- Over 3,500 cal.
- 3,000 - 3,500 cal.
- 2,500 - 3,000 cal.
- 2,000 - 2,500 cal.
- Under 2,000 cal.

Top 5 countries

Belgium	3,901 cal.
Greece	3,702 cal.
Ireland	3,688 cal.
Bulgaria	3,650 cal.
Germany	3,650 cal.

Bottom 5 countries

Bangladesh	1,925 cal.
Rwanda	1,817 cal.
Sierra Leone	1,813 cal.
Somalia	1,781 cal.
Mozambique	1,604 cal.

[USA 3,645] [UK 3,256]

CAUSES OF DEATH

The rich not only live longer, on average, than the poor; they also die from different causes. Infectious and parasitic diseases, all but eliminated in the developed world, remain a scourge in poorer countries. On the other hand, more than two-thirds of the populations of OECD nations eventually succumb to cancer or circulatory disease; the proportion in Latin America is only about 45%. In addition to the three major diseases shown here, respiratory infection and injury also claim more lives in developing nations, which lack the drugs and medical skills required to treat them.

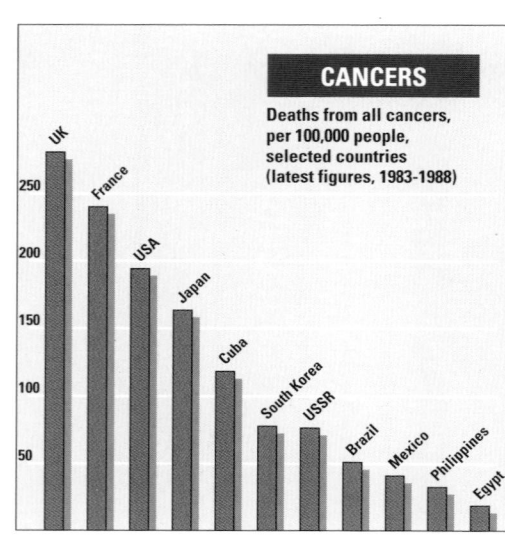

CANCERS

Deaths from all cancers, per 100,000 people, selected countries (latest figures, 1983-1988)

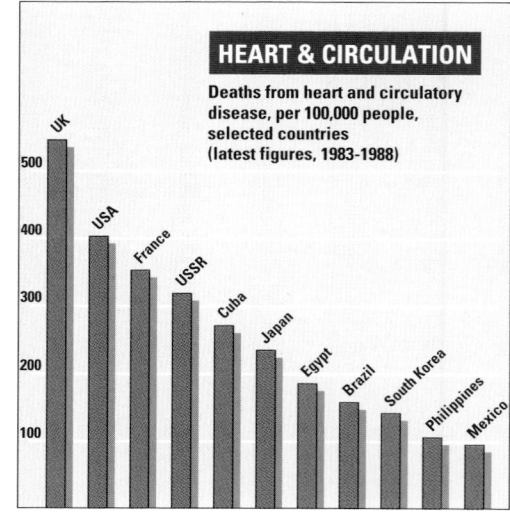

HEART & CIRCULATION

Deaths from heart and circulatory disease, per 100,000 people, selected countries (latest figures, 1983-1988)

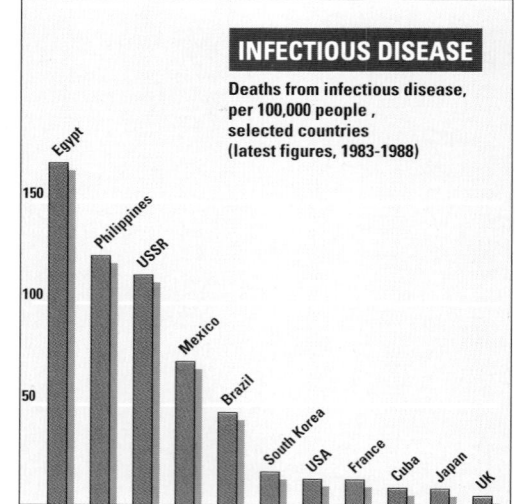

INFECTIOUS DISEASE

Deaths from infectious disease, per 100,000 people, selected countries (latest figures, 1983-1988)

LIFE EXPECTANCY

Years of life expectancy at birth, selected countries (1988-1989)

The chart shows combined data for both sexes. On average, women live longer than men worldwide, even in developing countries with high maternal mortality rates. Overall, life expectancy is steadily rising, though the difference between rich and poor nations remains dramatic.

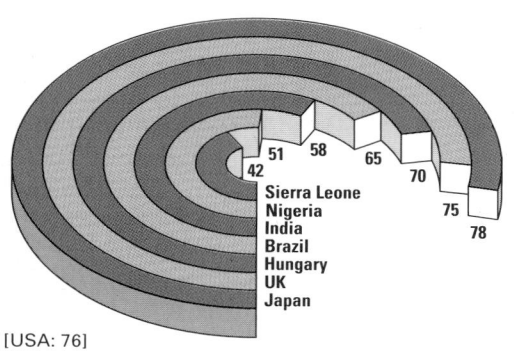

42 51 58 65 70 75 78

Sierra Leone
Nigeria
India
Brazil
Hungary
UK
Japan

[USA: 76]

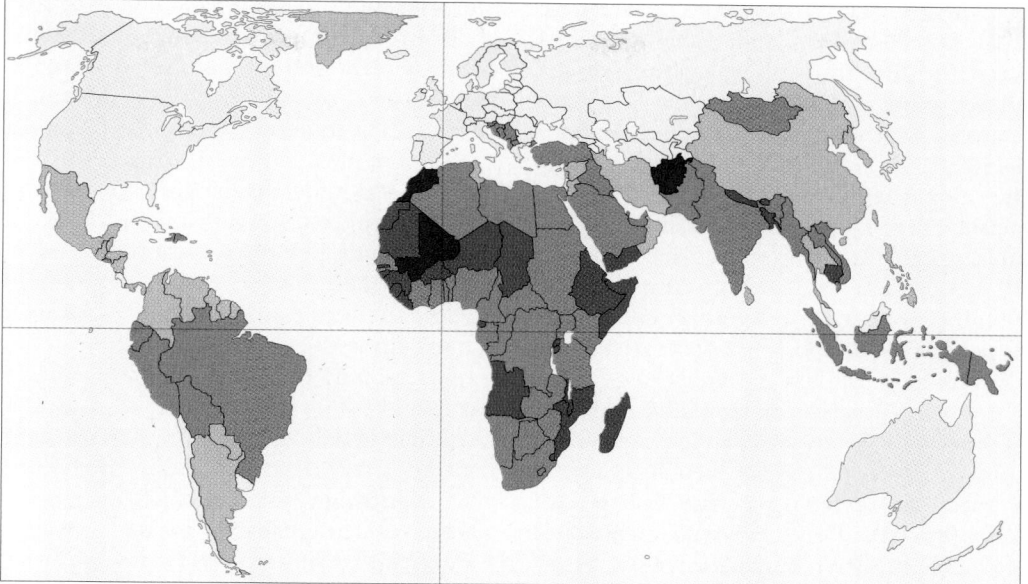
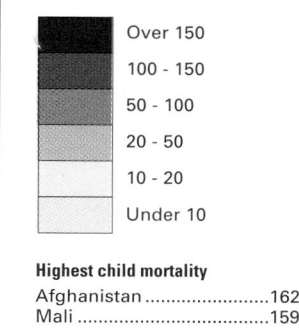

CHILD MORTALITY

Number of babies who will die before the age of one year, per 1,000 live births (average 1990-95)

- Over 150
- 100 - 150
- 50 - 100
- 20 - 50
- 10 - 20
- Under 10

Highest child mortality

Afghanistan 162
Mali 159

Lowest child mortality

Iceland 5
Finland...................................5

[USA 9]   [UK 8]

HOSPITAL CAPACITY

Hospital beds available for each 1,000 people (1983-1988)

Highest capacity		Lowest capacity	
Finland	14.9	Bangladesh	0.2
Sweden	13.2	Nepal	0.2
France	12.9	Ethiopia	0.3
USSR	12.8	Mauritania	0.4
Netherlands	12.0	Mali	0.5
North Korea	11.7	Burkina Faso	0.6
Switzerland	11.3	Pakistan	0.6
Austria	10.4	Niger	0.7
Czechoslovakia	10.1	Haiti	0.8
Hungary	9.1	Chad	0.8

[UK 8] [USA 5.9]

The availability of a bed can mean anything from a private room in a well-equipped Californian teaching hospital to a place in the overcrowded annexe of a rural African clinic. In the Third World especially, quality of treatment can vary enormously from place to place within the same country.

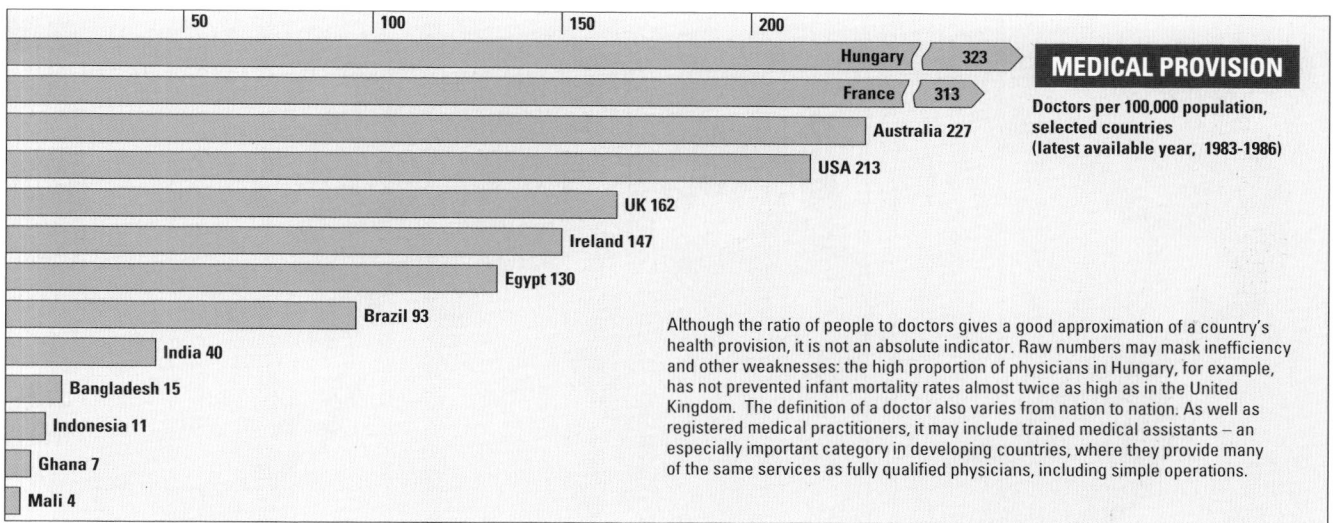

50   100   150   200

Hungary 323
France 313
Australia 227
USA 213
UK 162
Ireland 147
Egypt 130
Brazil 93
India 40
Bangladesh 15
Indonesia 11
Ghana 7
Mali 4

MEDICAL PROVISION

Doctors per 100,000 population, selected countries (latest available year, 1983-1986)

Although the ratio of people to doctors gives a good approximation of a country's health provision, it is not an absolute indicator. Raw numbers may mask inefficiency and other weaknesses: the high proportion of physicians in Hungary, for example, has not prevented infant mortality rates almost twice as high as in the United Kingdom. The definition of a doctor also varies from nation to nation. As well as registered medical practitioners, it may include trained medical assistants – an especially important category in developing countries, where they provide many of the same services as fully qualified physicians, including simple operations.

THE AIDS CRISIS

The Acquired Immune Deficiency Syndrome was first identified in 1981, when American doctors found otherwise healthy young men succumbing to rare infections. By 1984, the cause had been traced to the Human Immunodeficiency Virus (HIV), which can remain dormant for many years and perhaps indefinitely: only half of those known to carry the virus in 1981 had developed AIDS ten years later.

By 1991 the World Health Organization knew of more than 250,000 AIDS cases worldwide and suspected the true number to be at least four times as high. In Western countries in the early 1990s, most AIDS deaths were among male homosexuals or needle-sharing drug-users. However, the disease is spreading fastest among heterosexual men and women, which is its usual vector in the Third World, where most of its victims live. Africa is the most severely hit: a 1992 UN report estimated that 2 million African children will die of AIDS before the year 2000 – and some 10 million will be orphaned.

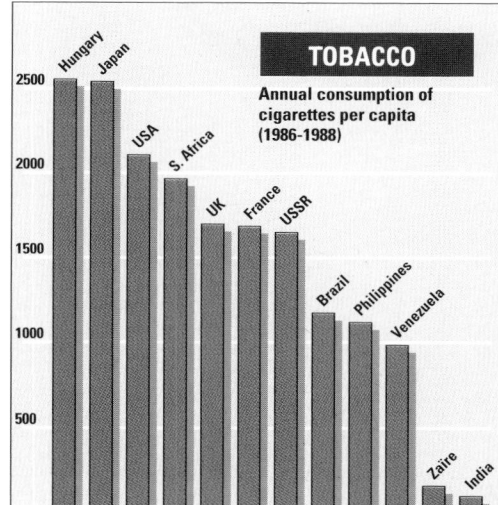

TOBACCO

Annual consumption of cigarettes per capita (1986-1988)

Hungary, Japan, USA, S. Africa, UK, France, USSR, Brazil, Philippines, Venezuela, Zaire, India

CRIME & PUNISHMENT

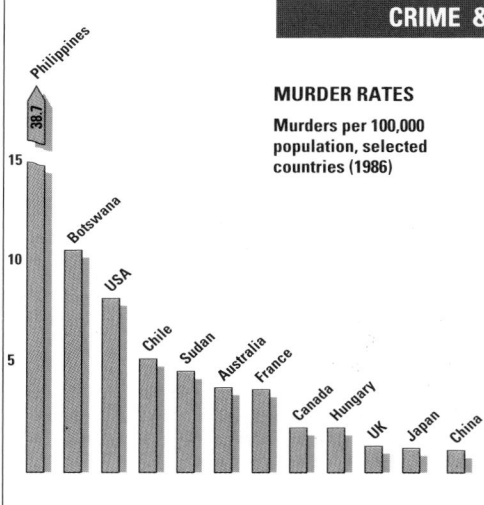

MURDER RATES

Murders per 100,000 population, selected countries (1986)

Philippines 38.7
Botswana
USA
Chile
Sudan
Australia
France
Canada
Hungary
UK
Japan
China

Crime rates are difficult to compare internationally. Standards of reporting and detection vary greatly, as do the definitions of many types of crime. Murder is probably the best detected as well as the most heinous, but different legal systems make different distinctions between murder and manslaughter or other forms of culpable homicide. By any reckoning, however, the USA's high murder rate stands out against otherwise similar Western countries, although it is dwarfed by the killings recorded in the very different culture of the Philippines.

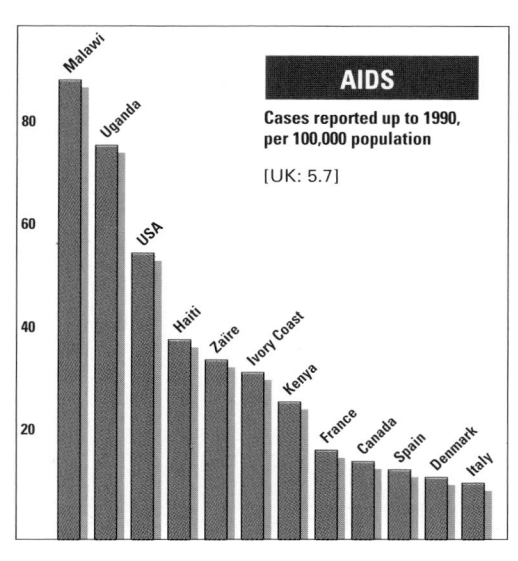

AIDS

Cases reported up to 1990, per 100,000 population

[UK: 5.7]

Malawi, Uganda, USA, Haiti, Zaire, Ivory Coast, Kenya, France, Canada, Spain, Denmark, Italy

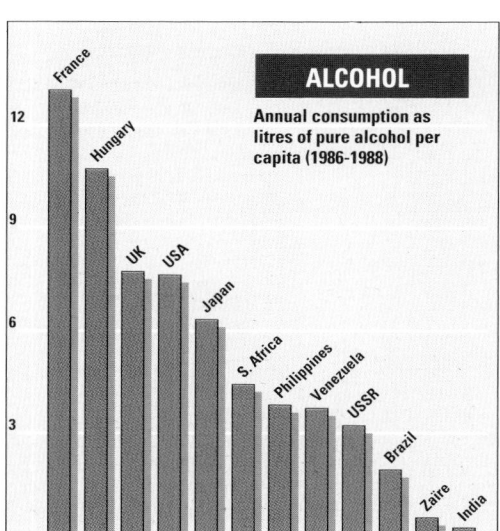

ALCOHOL

Annual consumption as litres of pure alcohol per capita (1986-1988)

France, Hungary, UK, USA, Japan, S. Africa, Philippines, Venezuela, USSR, Brazil, Zaire, India

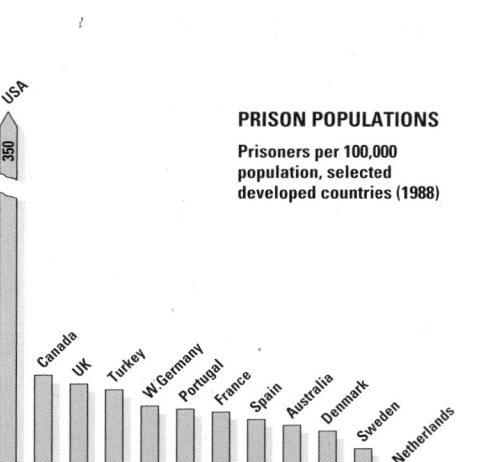

PRISON POPULATIONS

Prisoners per 100,000 population, selected developed countries (1988)

USA 350
Canada
UK
Turkey
W.Germany
Portugal
France
Spain
Australia
Denmark
Sweden
Netherlands

Differences in prison population reflect penal policies as much as the relative honesty or otherwise of different nations, and by no means all governments publish accurate figures. In more than 50 countries, people are still regularly imprisoned without trial, in 60 torture is a normal part of interrogation, and some 130 retain the death penalty, often administered for political crimes and in secret. Over 2,000 executions were recorded in 1990 by the civil rights organization Amnesty International; the real figure, as Amnesty itself maintains, was almost certainly much higher.

QUALITY OF LIFE: ENVIRONMENT

10: OCEANS

12: ATMOSPHERE

14: CLIMATE

21: GREENHOUSE EFFECT

25: URBAN POLLUTION

Humans have always had a dramatic effect on their environment, at least since the invention of agriculture almost 10,000 years ago. Generally, the Earth has accepted human interference without obvious ill effects: the complex systems that regulate the global environment have absorbed substantial damage while maintaining a stable and comfortable home for the planet's trillions of lifeforms. But advancing human technology and the rapidly expanding populations it supports are now threatening to overwhelm the Earth's ability to cope.

Industrial wastes, acid rainfall, expanding deserts and large-scale deforestation all combine to create environmental change at a rate far faster than the Earth can accommodate. Equipped with chain-saws and flame-throwers, humans can now destroy more forest in a day than their ancestors could in a century, upsetting the balance between plant and animal, carbon dioxide and oxygen, on which all life ultimately depends. The fossil fuels that power industrial civilization have pumped enough carbon dioxide and other greenhouse gases into the atmosphere to make climatic change a near-certainty. Chlorofluorocarbons (CFCs) and other man-made chemicals are rapidly eroding the ozone layer, the planet's screen against ultra-violet radiation.

As a result, the Earth's average temperature has risen by approximately 0.5°C since the beginning of this century. Further rises seem inevitable, with 1990 marked as the hottest year worldwide since records began. A warmer Earth probably means a wetter Earth, with melting icecaps raising sea levels and causing severe flooding in some of the world's most densely populated regions. Other climatic models suggest an alternative doom: rising temperatures could increase cloud cover, reflecting more solar energy back into space and causing a new ice age.

Either way, the consequences for humans could be disastrous – perhaps the Earth's own way of restoring ecological balance over the next few thousand years. Fortunately, there is a far faster mechanism available. Human ingenuity has provoked the present crisis; but human ingenuity, inspired if need be by fear, can respond to it. Production of CFCs is already almost at a standstill, and the first faltering steps towards stabilization and ultimately reduction of carbon dioxide have been taken, with Denmark pioneering the way by taxing emissions in 1991.

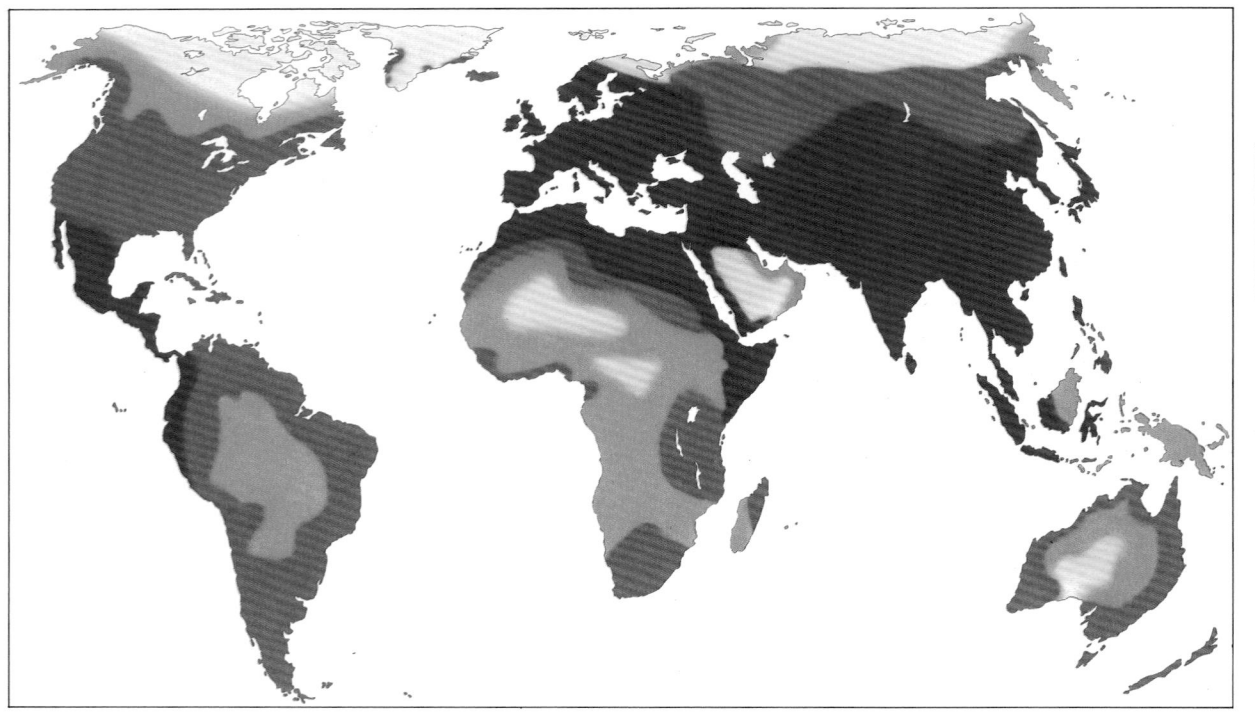

THE HISTORY OF HUMAN EXPANSION

The growth of ecological control: areas where human activity dominates the environment, from primitive times to the year 2000

By 1500 AD

By 1900 AD

By 2000 AD

Areas not dominated by human activity

THE RISE IN CARBON DIOXIDE

Emissions of carbon dioxide in millions of tonnes, 1950-1991

Atmospheric concentration of carbon dioxide, parts per million, 1750-2000. Pre-1950 data were obtained from air samples trapped in Antarctic ice.

Since the beginning of the Industrial Revolution, human activity has pumped steadily more carbon dioxide into the atmosphere. Most was quietly absorbed by the oceans, whose immense 'sink' capacity meant that 170 years were needed for levels to increase from the pre-industrial 280 parts per million to 300 (inset graph). But the vast increase in fuel-burning since 1950 (main graph) has overwhelmed even the oceanic sink. Atmospheric concentrations are now rising almost as steeply as carbon dioxide emissions themselves.

GREENHOUSE POWER

Relative contributions to the greenhouse effect by the major heat-absorbing gases in the atmosphere

The chart combines greenhouse potency and volume. Carbon dioxide has a greenhouse potential of only 1 but its concentration of 350 parts per million, makes it predominate. CFC 12 , with 25,000 times the absorption capacity of CO_2, is present only as 0.00044 ppm.

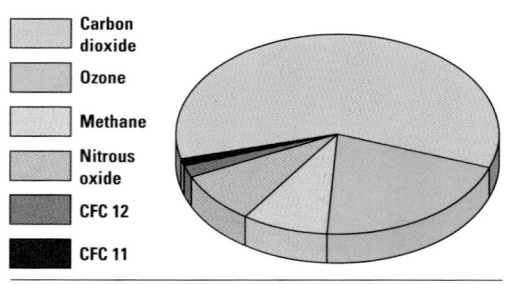

- Carbon dioxide
- Ozone
- Methane
- Nitrous oxide
- CFC 12
- CFC 11

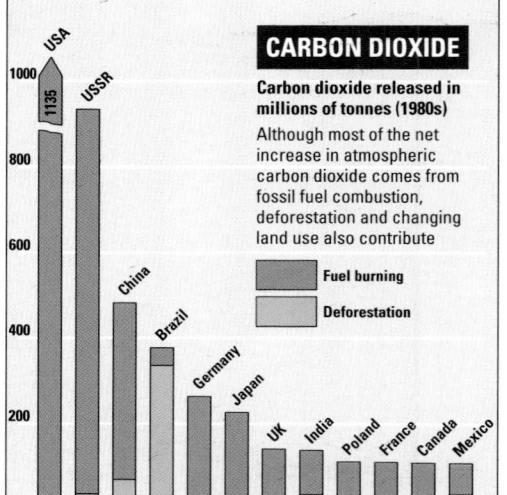

CARBON DIOXIDE

Carbon dioxide released in millions of tonnes (1980s)

Although most of the net increase in atmospheric carbon dioxide comes from fossil fuel combustion, deforestation and changing land use also contribute

- Fuel burning
- Deforestation

GLOBAL WARMING

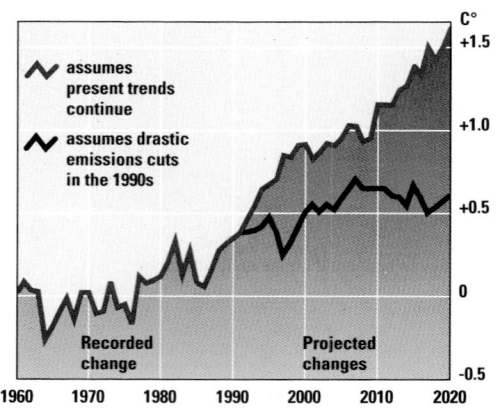

The rise in average temperatures caused by carbon dioxide and other greenhouse gases (1960-2020)

- assumes present trends continue
- assumes drastic emissions cuts in the 1990s

Recorded change

Projected changes

ACID RAIN

Acid rainfall & sources of acidic emissions (1980s)

Acid rain is caused when sulphur & nitrogen oxides in the air combine with water vapour to form sulphuric, nitric & other acids.

Regions where sulphur and nitrogen oxides are released in high concentrations, mainly from fossil fuel combustion.

• Major cities with high levels of air pollution (including nitrogen & sulphur emissions)

Areas of heavy acid deposition

pH numbers indicate acidity, decreasing from a neutral 7. Normal rain, slightly acid from dissolved carbon dioxide, never exceeds a pH of 5.6.

pH less than 4.0 (most acidic)
pH 4.0 to 4.5
pH 4.5 to 5.0

Areas where acid rain is a potential danger

THE ANTARCTIC

The vast Antarctic ice-sheet, containing some 70% of the Earth's fresh water, plays a crucial role in the circulation of atmosphere and oceans and hence in determining the planetary climate. The frozen southern continent is also the last remaining wilderness – the largest area to remain free from human colonization.

Ever since Amundsen and Scott raced for the South Pole in 1911, various countries have pressed territorial claims over sections of Antarctica, spurred in recent years by its known and suspected mineral wealth: enough iron ore to supply the world at present levels for 200 years, large oil reserves and, probably, the biggest coal deposits on Earth.

However, the 1961 Antarctic Treaty set aside the area for peaceful uses only, guaranteeing freedom of scientific investigation, banning waste disposal and nuclear testing, and suspending the issue of territorial rights. By 1990, the original 12 signatories had grown to 25, with a further 15 nations granted observer status in subsequent deliberations. However, the Treaty itself was threatened by wrangles between different countries, government agencies and international pressure groups.

Finally, in July, 1991, the belated agreement of the UK and the US assured unanimity on a new accord to ban all mineral exploration for a further 50 years. The ban can only be rescinded if all present signatories, plus a majority of any future adherents, agree. While the treaty has always lacked a formal mechanism for enforcement, it is firmly underwritten by public concern generated by the efforts of environmental pressure groups such as Greenpeace, foremost in the campaign to have Antarctica declared a 'World Park'.

It seems likely that the virtually uninhabited continent will remain untouched by tourism, nuclear-free and dedicated to peaceful scientific research.

DESERTIFICATION

Existing deserts
Areas with a high risk of desertification
Areas with a moderate risk of desertification
Former areas of rainforest
Existing rainforest

DEFORESTATION

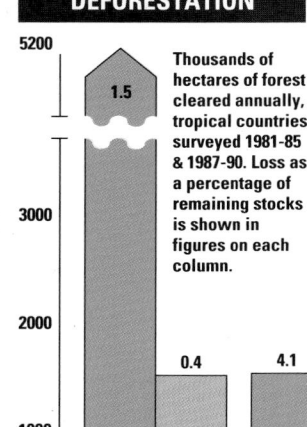

5200

1.5

Thousands of hectares of forest cleared annually, tropical countries surveyed 1981-85 & 1987-90. Loss as a percentage of remaining stocks is shown in figures on each column.

	1987-90	1981-85
Brazil	1.5	0.4
India	4.1	0.3
Indonesia	0.8	0.5
Burma	2.1	0.3
Thailand	2.5	2.4
Vietnam	2.0	0.7
Philippines	1.5	1.0
Costa Rica	7.6	4.0
Cameroon	0.6	0.4

WATER POLLUTION

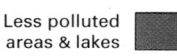
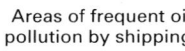
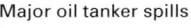

Severely polluted sea areas & lakes
Less polluted sea areas & lakes
Areas of frequent oil pollution by shipping

▶ Major oil tanker spills
▲ Major oil rig blow outs
▼ Offshore dumpsites for industrial & municipal waste

Severely polluted rivers & estuaries

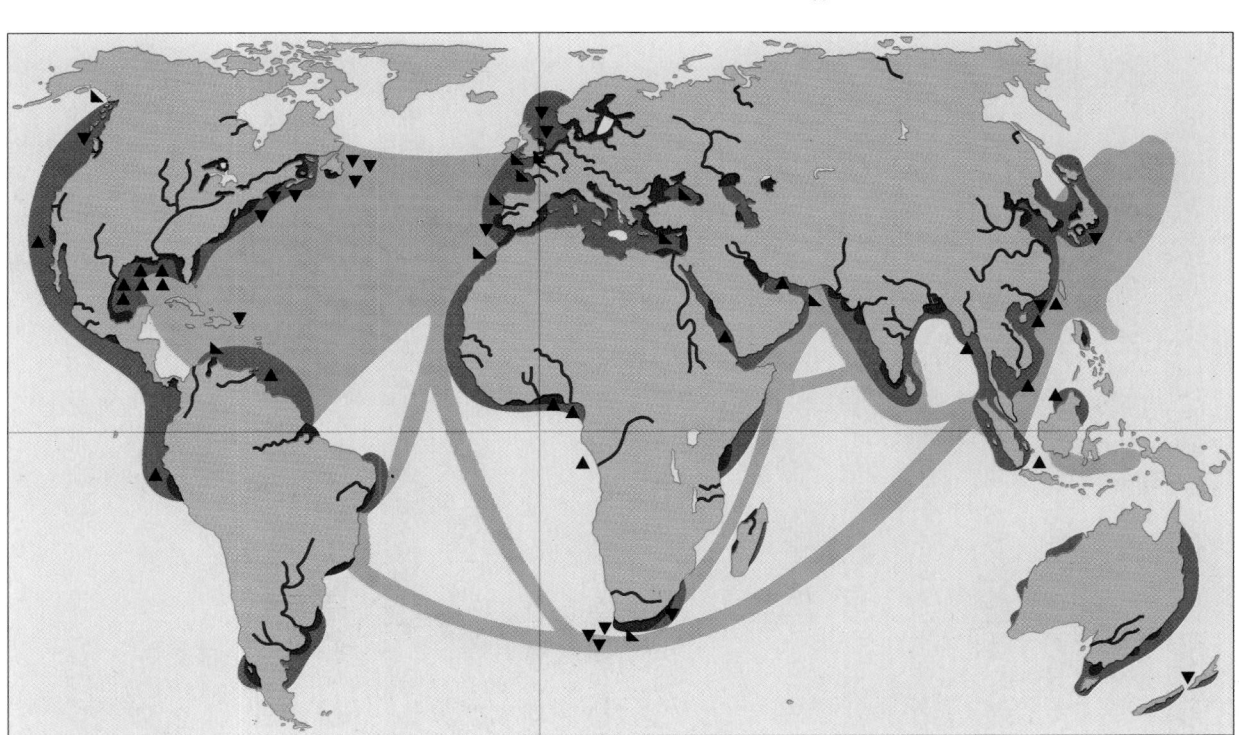

Poisoned rivers, domestic sewage and oil spillage have combined in recent years to reduce the world's oceans to a sorry state of contamination, notably near the crowded coasts of industrialized nations. Shipping routes, too, are constantly affected by tanker discharges. Oil spills of all kinds, however, declined significantly during the 1980s, from a peak of 750,000 tonnes in 1979 to under 50,000 tonnes in 1990. The most notorious tanker spill of that period – when the *Exxon Valdez* (94,999 grt) ran aground in Prince William Sound, Alaska, in March 1989 – released only 267,000 barrels, a relatively small amount compared to the results of blow-outs and war damage. 2,500,000 barrels were spilled during the Gulf War of 1991; the worst tanker accident in history occurred in July 1979, when the *Atlantic Empress* and the *Aegean Captain* collided off Trinidad, polluting the Caribbean with 1,890,000 barrels of crude oil.

WORLD MAPS

MAP SYMBOLS

SETTLEMENTS

◻ PARIS   ■ Berne   ◉ Livorno   ◉ Brugge   ◎ Algeciras   ⊙ Frèjus   ○ Oberammergau   ○ Thira

Settlement symbols and type styles vary according to the scale of each map and indicate the importance
of towns on the map rather than specific population figures

∴   Ruins or Archæological Sites   ﹀   Wells in Desert

──── ADMINISTRATION ────

———— International Boundaries

– – – International Boundaries
(Undefined or Disputed)

·····— Internal Boundaries

National Parks

Country Names

NICARAGUA

Administrative
Area Names

KENT

CALABRIA

International boundaries show the *de facto* situation where there are rival claims to territory

──── COMMUNICATIONS ────

———— Principal Roads

⌒ Other Roads

-·-·- Trails and Seasonal Roads

⋈ Passes

✿ Airfields

⌒ Principal Railways

-··- Railways
Under Construction

⌒ Other Railways

⌐--⌐ Railway Tunnels

············ Principal Canals

──── PHYSICAL FEATURES ────

⌒ Perennial Streams

········· Intermittent Streams

⬭ Perennial Lakes

⬭ Intermittent Lakes

⬭ Swamps and Marshes

▭ Permanent Ice
and Glaciers

▲ 8848   Elevations in metres

▾ 8050   Sea Depths in metres

1134   Height of Lake Surface
Above Sea Level
in metres

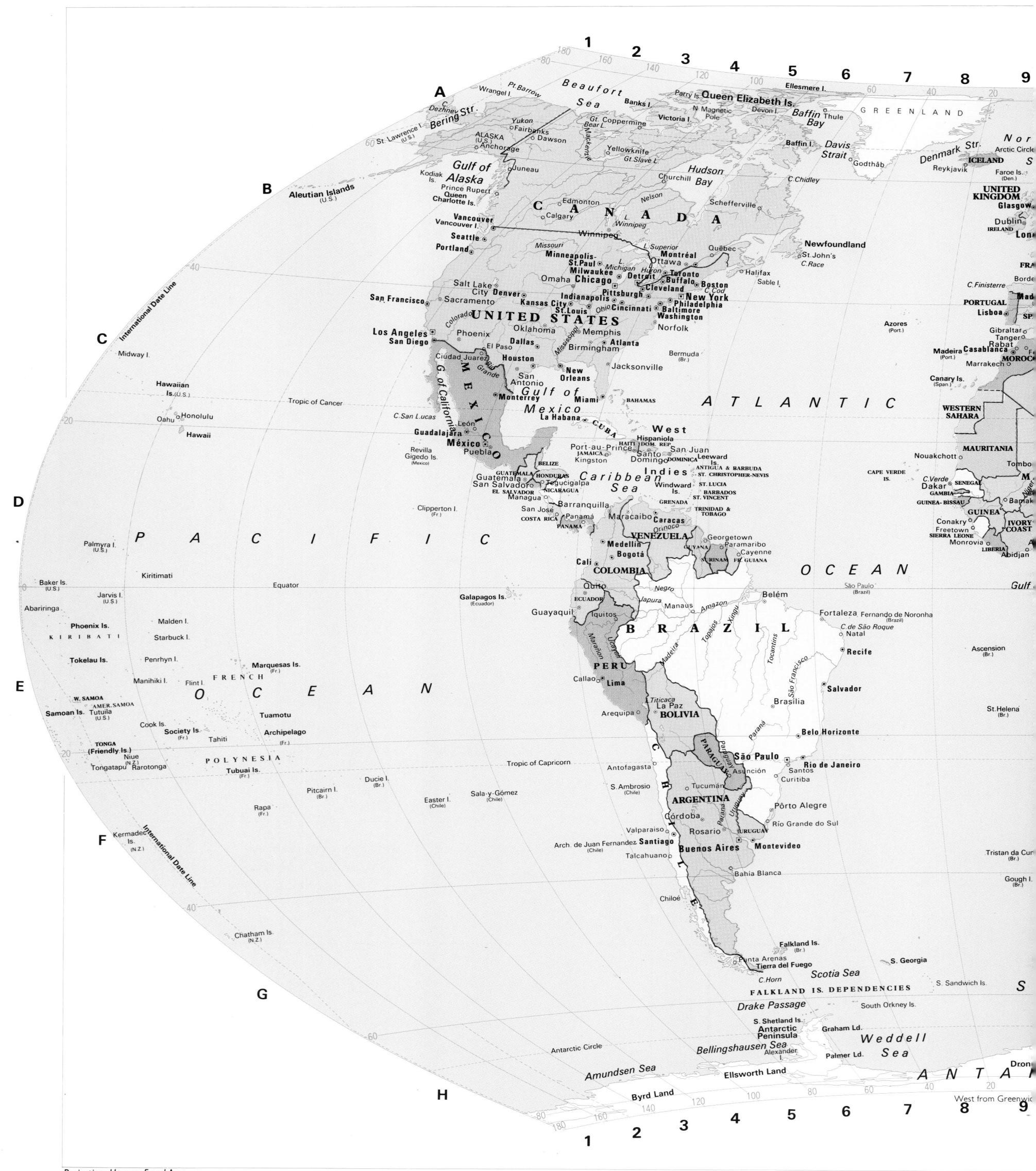

Projection: *Hammer Equal Area*

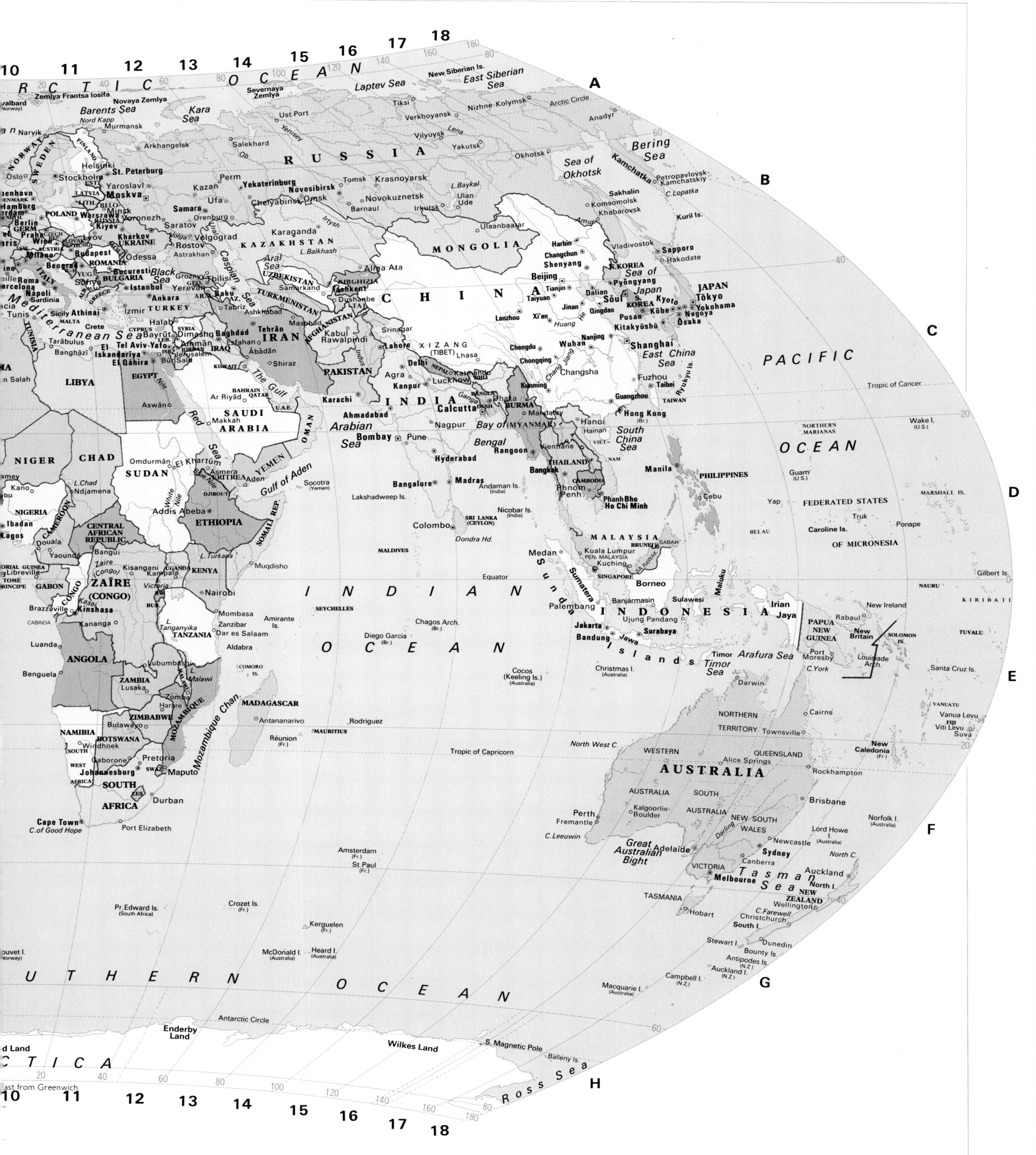

ARCTIC OCEAN

A

Laptev Sea
New Siberian Is.
East Siberian
Sea

10 11 12 13 14 15 16 17 18
20 60 80 100 120 140 160 180 80

Svalbard
(Norway)
Zemlya Frantsa Iosifa
Novaya Zemlya
Severnaya
Zemlya
Tiksi
Arctic Circle

Barents Sea
Kara
Sea
Ust Port
Verkhoyansk
Nizhne-Kolymsk
Anadyr

n
Narvik
Nord Kapp
Murmansk
Arkhangelsk
Salekhard
Yenisey
Ob
Vilyuysk
Lena
Yakutsk
Okhotsk
Bering
Sea

NORWAY
SWEDEN
FINLAND
Helsinki
St. Peterburg
RUSSIA
Tomsk
Krasnoyarsk
Sea of
Okhotsk
Kamchatka
Petropavlovsk-
Kamchatskiy
C.Lopatka
B

Oslo
Stockholm
EST.
Yaroslavl
Perm
Yekaterinburg
Novosibirsk
Novokuznetsk
Komsomolsk
Sakhalin
Khabarovsk
Kuril Is.

enhavn
Hamburg
DENMARK
LATVIA
LITH.
Moskva
Kazan
Ufa
Chelyabinsk
Omsk
Barnaul
Irkutsk
Ulan
Ude
Amur
Vladivostok
Sapporo
Hakodate

Berlin
POLAND
Warszawa
BELO-
RUSSIA
Minsk
Kiyev
Samara
Orenburg
KAZAKHSTAN
Karaganda
Ulaanbaatar
MONGOLIA
Harbin
Changchun
Shenyang
N.KOREA
Pyongyang
Sea of
Japan

aris
Praha
GERM.
Lvov
Kharkov
UKRAINE
Saratov
Volga
Rostov
Volgograd
Astrakhan
L.Balkhash
Alma Ata
Beijing
Tianjin
Dalian
Seoul
KOREA
Pusan
JAPAN
Tōkyō
Yokohama

Milano
Budapest
ROMANIA
Odessa
Aral
Sea
UZBEKISTAN
Samarkand
KIRGHIZIA
Tashkent
Taiyuan
Jinan
Qingdao
Kōbe
Nagoya
Ōsaka

Beograd
YUG.
BULGARIA
Black
Sea
Grozny
Tbilisi
TURKMENISTAN
Ashkhabad
TAJ.
Lanzhou
Xi'an
Huang
CHINA
Kitakyūshū

arcelona
Roma
ITALY
Sofiya
GREECE
Istanbul
Ankara
ARM.
Baku
AZ.
Caspian
Sea
Dushanbe
AFGHANISTAN
Srinagar
XIZANG
(TIBET)
Chengdu
Chongqing
Wuhan
Nanjing
Shanghai
East China
Sea
PACIFIC

Tunis
Sicily
Athinai
Crete
İzmir
TURKEY
Tabriz
Mashhad
Kabul
Rawalpindi
Lahore
Lhasa
Changsha
Ryukyu Is.

CYPRUS
SYRIA
Halab
Tehrān
Esfahan
Eşfahān
Kanpur
Lucknow
Kunming
Fuzhou
Taibei
TAIWAN

Medit
erranean Sea
Bayrūt
Dimashq
Baghdād
IRAN
Ābādān
Delhi
NEPAL
Kathmandu
Ganga
BANGL.
Dhaka
Guangzhou
Hong Kong
Hainan
South
China
Sea

Tel Aviv-Yafa
Al-Quds
Jerusalem
IRAQ
Ammān
Shiraz
Agra
INDIA
Calcutta
BURMA
(MYANMAR)
Hanoi
VIET-

El Qâhira
Bur Said
KUWAIT
The Gulf
BAHRAIN
QATAR
Karachi
Ahmadabad
Nagpur
Bay of
Bengal
Mandalay
Rangoon
NAM

LIBYA
EGYPT
Ar Riyād
U.A.E.
Arabian
Sea
Bombay
Pune
Hyderabad
Madras
Andaman Is.
(India)
THAILAND
Bangkok
Manila
PHILIPPINES

NIGER
CHAD
SUDAN
Aswân
Nile
SAUDI
ARABIA
OMAN
Bangalore
Lakshadweep Is.
Nicobar Is.
(India)
CAMBODIA
Phnom
Penh
Phanh Bho
Ho Chi Minh
Cebu
Guam
(U.S.)

Omdurmân
El Khartûm
Asmera
YEMEN
Aden
Gulf of Aden
Socotra
(Yemen)
Colombo
SRI LANKA
(CEYLON)
Yap
BELAU
Caroline Is.
FEDERATED STATES

NIGERIA
Ibadan
Lagos
Bangui
ERITREA
DJIBOUTI
Addis Abeba
ETHIOPIA
SOMALI
REP.
MALDIVES
Dondra Hd.
Medan
MALAYSIA
BRUNEI
SABAH
OF MICRONESIA

CENTRAL
AFRICAN
REPUBLIC
Douala
Yaoundé
L.Turkana
Muqdisho
Kuala Lumpur
PEN. MALAYSIA
SARAWAK
Truk
Ponape

EQUATORIAL GUINEA
Libreville
SÃO
TOMÉ
PRINCIPE
GABON
Kisangani
UGANDA
Kampala
KENYA
Nairobi
Equator
INDIAN
Sumatra
Kuching
SINGAPORE
Borneo
MARSHALL IS.
Gilbert Is.

CONGO
ZAÏRE
(CONGO)
Kasai
Zaïre
(Congo)
Victoria
SEYCHELLES
Palembang
Jakarta
INDONESIA
Irian
Jaya
NAURU
KIRIBATI

Brazzaville
Kinshasa
BUR.
L.
Tanganyika
TANZANIA
Mombasa
Zanzibar
Dar es Salaam
Amirante
Is.
Chagos Arch.
(Br.)
OCEAN
Bandung
Jawa
Surabaya
Ujung Pandang
Sulawesi
Maluku
PAPUA
NEW
GUINEA
New Ireland
Rabaul
New
Britain
SOLOMON
IS.
TUVALU

CABINDA
Luanda
Kananga
Aldabra
Diego Garcia
(Br.)
Islands
Timor
Port
Moresby
Louisade
Arch.
Santa Cruz Is.

ANGOLA
Lubumbashi
ZAMBIA
Lusaka
Malawi
COMORO
IS.
MADAGASCAR
Arafura Sea
Timor
Sea
C.York
E

Benguela
ZIMBABWE
Zomba
Antananarivo
Rodriguez
MAURITIUS
Darwin
VANUATU

NAMIBIA
Bulawayo
Harare
MOZAMBIQUE
Mozambique Chan.
Réunion
(Fr.)
North West C.
Tropic of Capricorn
NORTHERN
TERRITORY
Cairns
Townsville
Vanua Levu
FIJI
Viti Levu
Suva

BOTSWANA
Windhoek
Pretoria
SOUTH
Johannesburg
WESTERN
Alice Springs
QUEENSLAND
Rockhampton
New
Caledonia
(Fr.)
F

WEST
AFRICA
Gaborone
SOUTH
AFRICA
LES.
Durban
SW.
Maputo
AUSTRALIA
SOUTH
AUSTRALIA
AUSTRALIA
Brisbane

Cape Town
C.of Good Hope
Port Elizabeth
Perth
Fremantle
C.Leeuwin
Kalgoorlie-
Boulder
NEW SOUTH
WALES
Darling
Newcastle
Lord Howe I.
(Australia)
Norfolk I.
(Australia)

Amsterdam
(Fr.)
St.Paul
(Fr.)
Great
Australian
Bight
Adelaide
VICTORIA
Sydney
Canberra
North C.
Auckland
North I.

Pr.Edward Is.
(South Africa)
Crozet Is.
(Fr.)
Kerguelen
(Fr.)
TASMANIA
Melbourne
Tasman
Sea
NEW
ZEALAND
Wellington
C.Farewell
Christchurch
G

McDonald I.
(Australia)
Heard I.
(Australia)
Hobart
South I.
Stewart I.
Dunedin

SOUTHERN OCEAN
Bounty Is.
(N.Z.)
Antipodes Is.
(N.Z.)
Auckland Is.
(N.Z.)

Antarctic Circle
Enderby
Land
Wilkes Land
S. Magnetic Pole
Balleny Is.
Macquarie I.
(Australia)
Campbell I.
(N.Z.)

d Land
CTICA
East from Greenwich
Ross Sea
H

10 11 12 13 14 15 16 17 18
20 40 60 80 100 120 140 160 180 80

1 : 28 000 000

200 100 0 200 400 600 miles
200 0 400 800 1200 km

18   17   16   15

JAPAN

PACIFIC OCEAN

Aleutian Islands
Near Is.   7822
Dutch Harbor   D   Komandorskiye Ostrova
Unimak I.   Petropavlovsk-Kamchatskiy
Bristol Bay   Pribilof Is.   Vlk. Klyuchevskaya 4850
Kodiak I.   42   Bering Sea   Mys Lopatka   Kurilskiye Ostrova   La Perouse Str.   Hokkaidō
G. of Alaska   St. Matthew (U.S.A.)   Sakhalin
Seward   Mys Olyutorski   Poluostrov Kamchatka   Sea of
Pr. William Sd. Anchorage   Mys Navarin   Ostrov   Okhotsk
Cordova Mt. McKinley Nunivak   Karaginskiy   Tatarskiy Proliv
Mt. St. Elias 6194 St. Lawrence I.   Penzhina Penzhinskaya G.   Sovetskaya
5489   St Michael (U.S.A.) Anadyrskiy Gizhiginskaya Guba   Tauiskaya   Gavan
Mt. Logan   Fairbanks Nome Zaliv   Anadyr   Omolon   Guba   Amur
6050   ALASKA C. Pr. of Wales Mys Okhotsko   Okhotsk   Nikolayevsk Khabarovsk
Sitka   Kotzebue Sd. Chukotskiy Kolymskoye   Ulbanskiy
Juneau   Nizhne Kolyma   Zaliv
Pr. Rupert Copper Kuskokwim Yukon   Kolymsk Srednekolymsk Aldan   Udskaya
Skagway   Mt. Logan Noatak   Proliv Longa   Guba
Whitehorse   C. Lisburne   Russkoye Alazeya Indigirka
Rocky Mountains Lewes Pt. Hope   Ostie   Zashiversk   Stanovoy Khrebet
Dawson Peel   Chukchi   Ostrova   Verkhoyansk
Dawson Creek Stewart Porcupine Sea   Vrangelya Chaunskaya   Yana   Yakutsk
Yukon   C. Belcher   Kazache
Liard Mackenzie Herschel C. Halkett 46   Novosibirskiye Lyakhovskiye   Lena Olekma
Fort Fort McPherson Prudhoe Bay Pt. Barrow B   Ostrova Ostrova   Bulun Vilyuy
Peace Simpson Mackenzie Harrison Bay   O. Kotelnyy Tiksi Zhigansk Oleněk
Ft. Vermilion Fort Bay   Beaufort Sea   A R C T   O. Bennetta   Vilyuy
Athabasca Norman Great Bear   3767   O C E   Lena
NORTH Fort Good Hope Lake C. Bathurst Canada Mendeleyev C. Bennetta A   Laptev Anabar
Yellowknife Gt. Slave Coppermine C. Kellett Basin Ridge   Sea   Nizhnyaya Tunguska
Athabasca Lake Coppermine C. Pr. Alfred 3327   Nordvik Podkamennaya Tunguska
L. Dubawnt L. Dolphin & Union Str. Banks Abasin A   O. Petra Khatanga
AMERICA Wollaston I.   Pr. Patrick 3545 3849   Poluostrov Oz. Taymyr Plato
Pr. Albert Victoria Melville I. I.   Makarov Basin 4100 Severnaya   Taymyr   Putorana
Churchill Pen. Island V. Melville Sd. Parry Is. 4007 Lomonosov Ridge Zemlya Pyasina Kheta
King William M'Clintock Borden I. 3700 Alpha Cordillera 44484 O. Oktyabrskoy Norilsk Turukhansk
Chan. Pr. of Bathurst Ellef Ringnes I.   NORTH Fram Basin O. Revolyutsii Dudinka Kotuy
Boothia Wales I. I. Magnetic Sverdrup Is. 2104 POLE 4418 Nansen Basin   Golchikha Igarka Yenisey
Pen. Somerset Pole Axel   Nansen Str. Lomonosov O. Uedineniya   O. Vise Taz
Back I. 1990 Heiberg I. Eureka   Fram Basin O. Ushakova   Urengoy
HUDSON G. of Devon I. Ellesmere I. C. Columbia 3741 Zemlya Ostrov   Novaya
Bay Boothia Pr. Regent Inlet Jones Sd. Alert Lincoln Frantsa Graham Bell   Zemlya
Southampton I. Lancaster Str. Bylot Smith Sd. Kane Sea Iosifa Z. Vilcheka   Ostrov Belyy Poluostrov
Coats I. Melville I. Thule Basin Markham I.   Novy Port Yamal Nadym
Mansel Pen. Foxe Fury Dundas Robeson Ch. K. Morris Jesup   Ostrov Baydaratskaya
C. Foxe Basin Pr. Glacier Peary McKinley Alexandra Ld. Kara   Kolguyev Guba Surgut
Wolstenholme Channel Charles I. Rasmussen Ld. Sea Nordkapp   Vorkuta Salekhard Ob
Nettilling K. York Knud Land Independence Fj. Nordaustlandet Novaya Zemlya   Berezovo Narodnaya
2399 Baffin Kong Frederik McKinley Sea   Pechora 1894 Tobolsk
Feuilles Hudson Str. Bay VIII.s Land A 2571 Barents   Mys Kanin Ob
C. Dyer Upernavik Vestspitsbergen Longyearbyen Sea Svalbard   Nos Uralskie Gory
Prince Disko Umanak Svalbard Edgeøya (Norway)   Vorkuta Khabarova
Frobisher B. Godhavn Greenland Barents Sea Novaya   Yekaterinburg
Resolution I. Disko B. Sea Bjørnøya Zemlya   Mezen
C. Chidley (Denmark) B   Ostrov Kolguyev   Pechora Perm
Labrador Davis Godthåb Greenland Sea Vadsø Varangerfjorden Mys Kanin   Narodnaya
Str. Kong Frederik Kong Hammerfest   Kolskiy Beloye
IX.s Land Christian Nordkapp Tromsø Poluostrov   Sev. Dvina
Hamilton Inlet Frederikshåb K. Franz Joseph Fd. Murmansk Arkhangelsk   Onega Vychegda
Mont Forel Kong Lofoten   Onezhskoye
C. Charles Julianehåb Christian IX.s Land K. Oscar Fj. NORWAY   Ozero Ufa
3360 Kong 3700 Scoresbysund Bjørnøya   Ladozhskoye
Sydprøven Frederik VI.s Kyst Gunnbjørn K. Brewster Jan Mayen FINLAND Ozero   Volga
Ångmagssalik Field Iceland   St. Peterburg Samara
Breiðafjörður Plateau Norwegian Trondheim Helsinki Chudskoye   Saratov
Reykjavík ICELAND Arctic Circle Ozero Tallinn EST.   Moskva
Hekla Ørafajökull Sea   Volgograd
1491 Horn 3800 NORWAY SWEDEN Gulf of Finland LAT. Riga   Rostov
Mid-Atlantic Ridge Fontur Arctic Circle Oslo Stockholm Gulf of Bothnia LITH. Vilnius
Faroe Is.   Gotland   Kiev
Shetland Is. Bergen 60 København Nemen Baltic Sea   UKRAINE
4755 North Sea DENMARK Kaliningrad   Odessa
Rockall Skagerrak Gdańsk Wisła   Black Sea
Hebrides Orkney Is. SCOTLAND Szczecin Warszawa
ATLANTIC OCEAN BRITISH Edinburgh Hamburg POLAND
Glasgow ISLES Belfast Berlin Łódź
IRELAND Dublin Liverpool WALES ENGLAND Elbe Wrocław
Cork Amsterdam NETH. GERMANY Leipzig
C. Clear London Köln Praha

ft   m
12 000 4000
6000   2000
4500   1500
3000   1000
1200   400
600   200
0   0
500   1500
1000   3000
2000   6000
3000   9000
4000   12 000
5000   15 000
m   ft

Projection: Zenithal Equidistant   West from Greenwich   East from Greenwich   COPYRIGHT GEORGE PHILIP LTD.

Maximum extent of sea ice
Summer extent of sea ice
Ice caps and permanent ice shelf

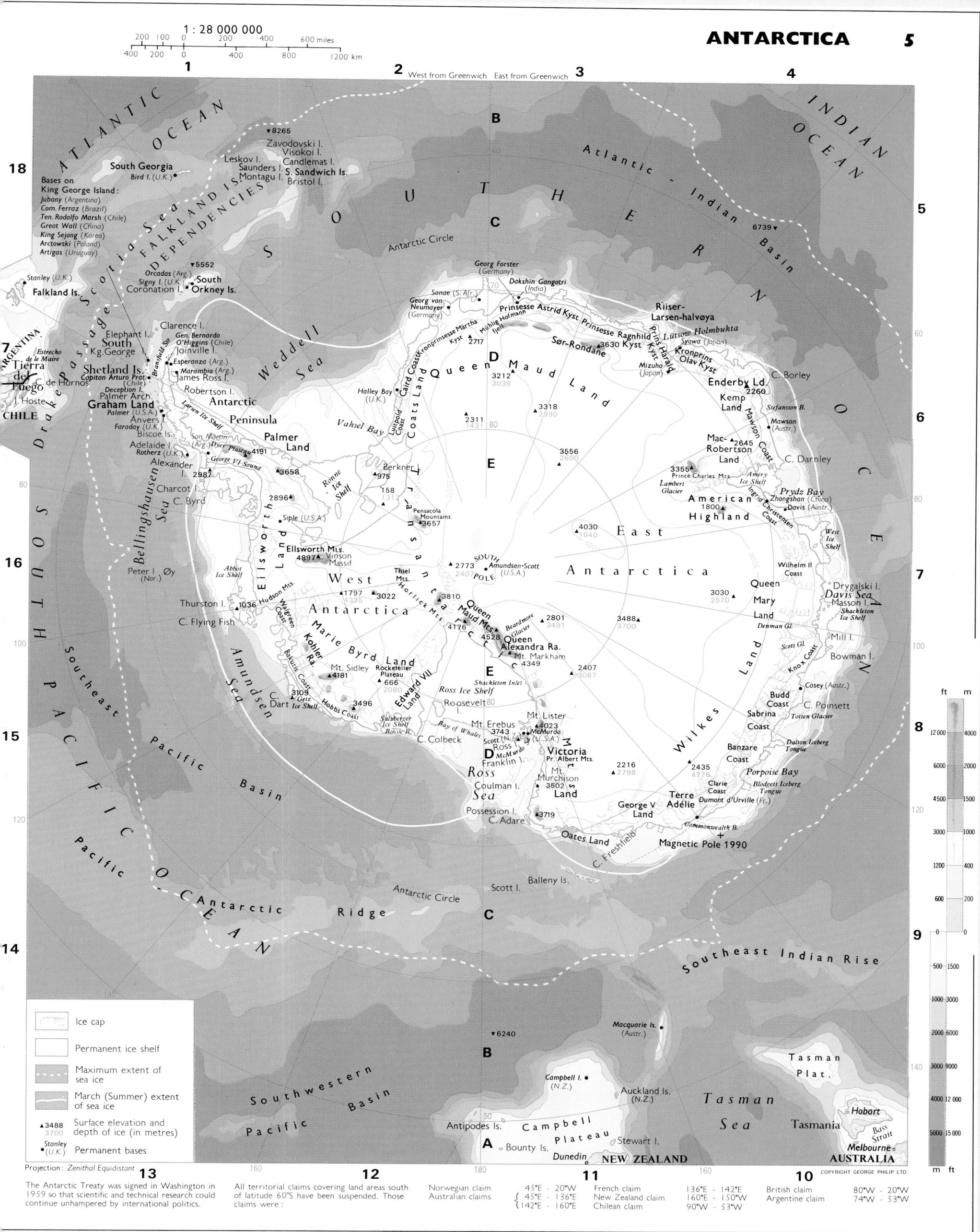

1 : 28 000 000

Projection: *Zenithal Equidistant*

The Antarctic Treaty was signed in Washington in 1959 so that scientific and technical research could continue unhampered by international politics.

All territorial claims covering land areas south of latitude 60°S have been suspended. Those claims were:

Norwegian claim	45°E - 20°W	
Australian claims	{ 45°E - 136°E	
	{ 142°E - 160°E	
French claim	136°E - 142°E	
New Zealand claim	160°E - 150°W	
Chilean claim	90°W - 53°W	
British claim	80°W - 20°W	
Argentine claim	74°W - 53°W	

COPYRIGHT GEORGE PHILIP LTD.

Legend:

- Ice cap
- Permanent ice shelf
- Maximum extent of sea ice
- March (Summer) extent of sea ice
- ▲3488 / 3700 Surface elevation and depth of ice (in metres)
- Stanley (U.K.) Permanent bases

Bases on King George Island:
Jubany (Argentina)
Com. Ferraz (Brazil)
Ten. Rodolfo Marsh (Chile)
Great Wall (China)
King Sejong (Korea)
Arctowski (Poland)
Artigas (Uruguay)

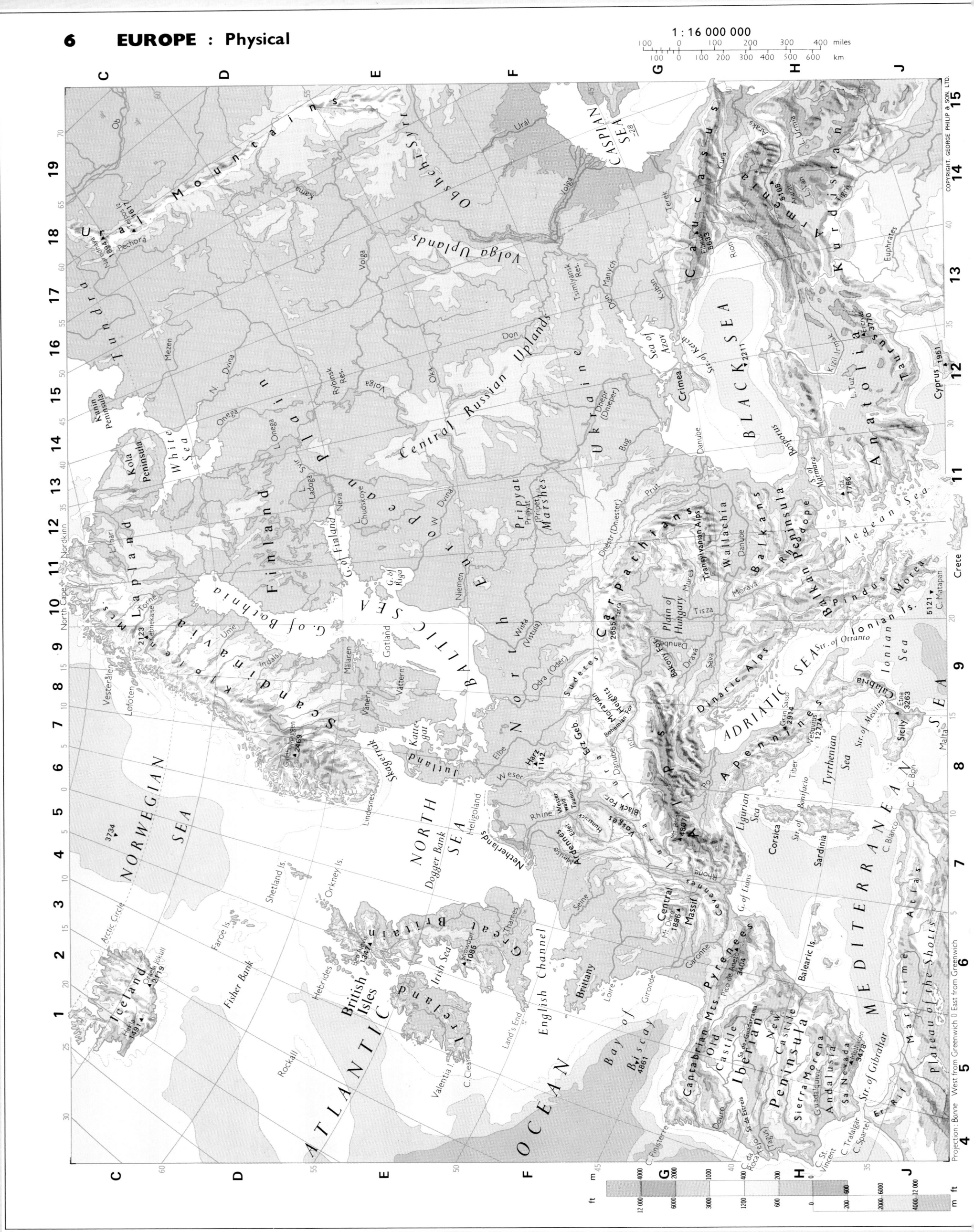

1 : 16 000 000

COPYRIGHT. GEORGE PHILIP & SON LTD.

Projection: Bonne   West from Greenwich 0 East from Greenwich

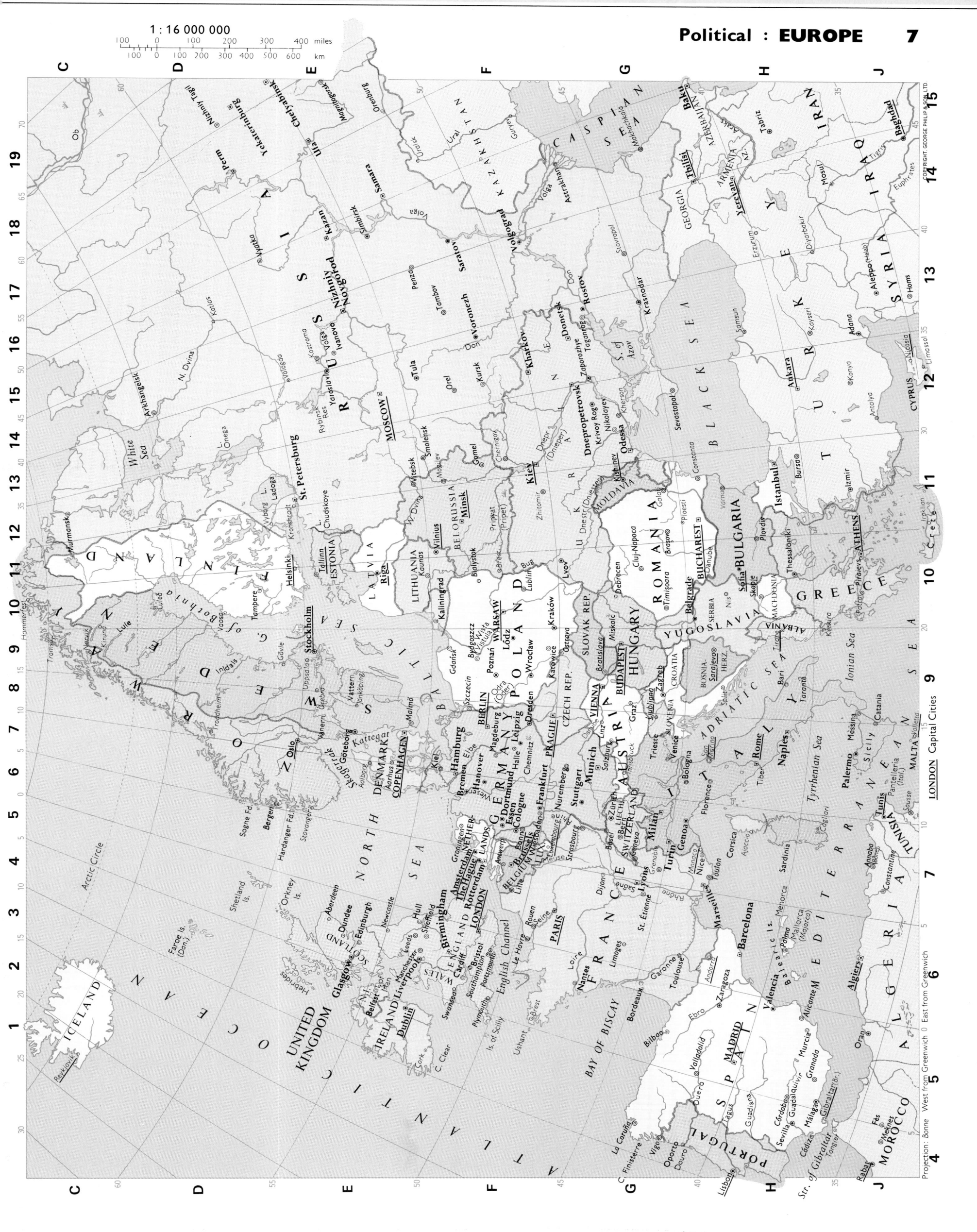

1 : 16 000 000

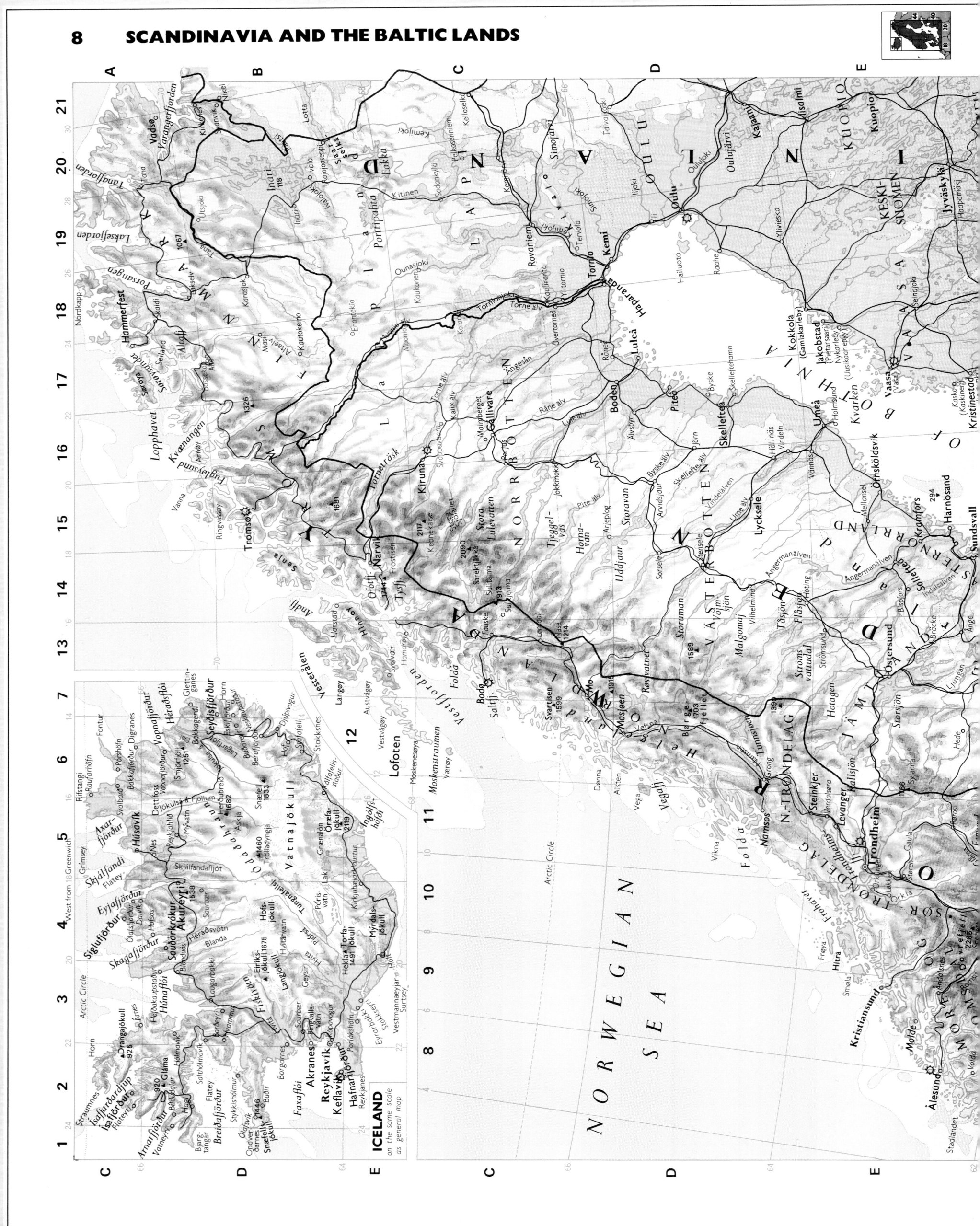

ICELAND
on the same scale
as general map

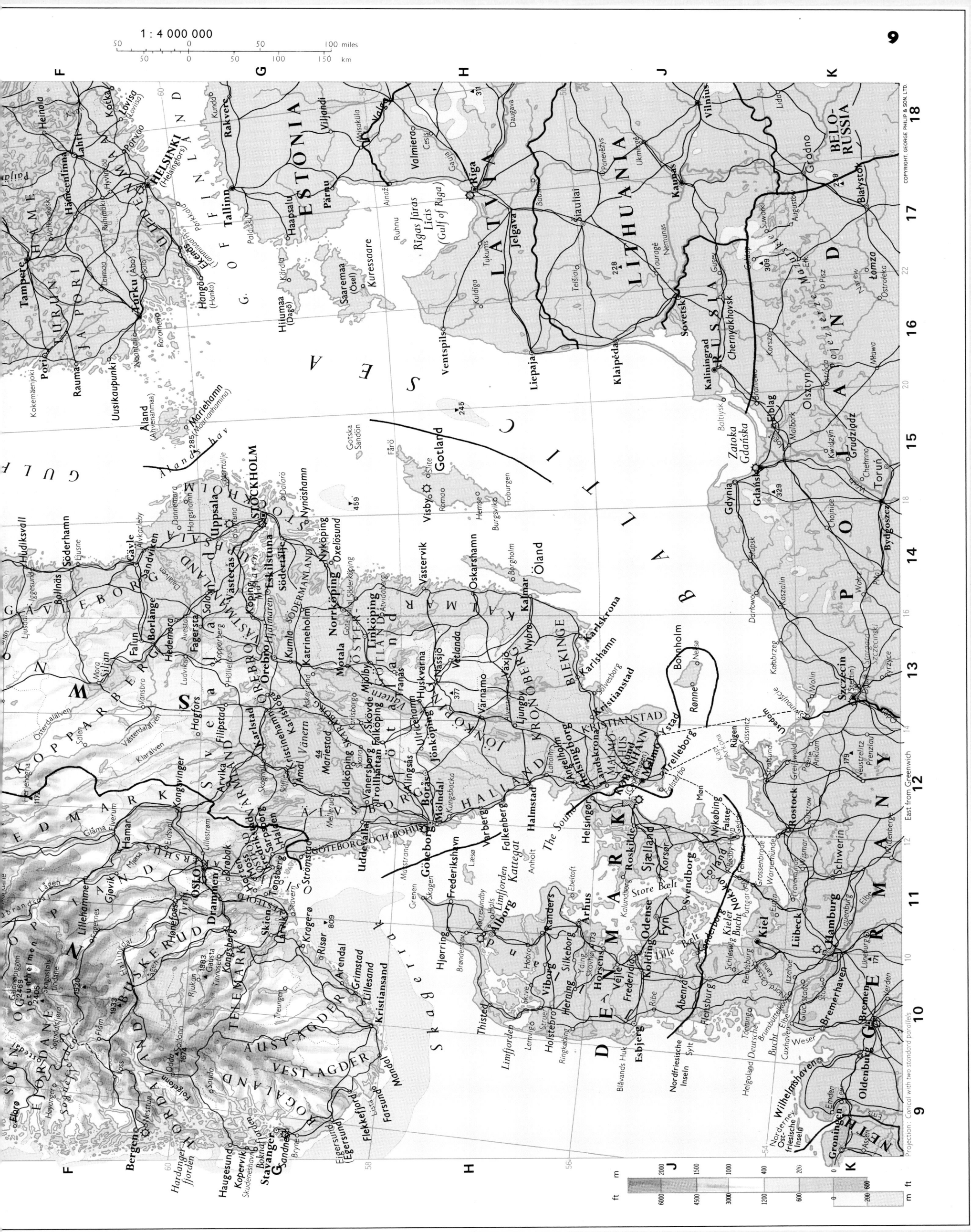

1 : 4 000 000

50   0   50   100 miles
50   0   50   100   150 km

F   G   H   J   K

18

17

16

15

14

13

12

11

10

9

BALTIC   SEA

FINLAND

ESTONIA

LATVIA

LITHUANIA

BELO-
RUSSIA

RUSSIA

POLAND

GERMANY

DENMARK

SWEDEN

NORWAY

HELSINKI
(Helsingfors)

Tampere

Tallinn

Riga

Gulf of Riga
(Rīgas Jūras Līcis)

Gotland
Visby

Öland

Kalmar

STOCKHOLM

Uppsala

OSLO

Göteborg

Kiel

Hamburg

Bremen

Lübeck

Rostock

Szczecin
(Stettin)

Gdańsk

Gdynia

Kaliningrad

Klaipėda

Vilnius

Kaunas

Helsingfors

East from Greenwich

Projection: Conical with two standard parallels

m   ft
6000
4500
3000
1500
1200
600
200
0

ft   m

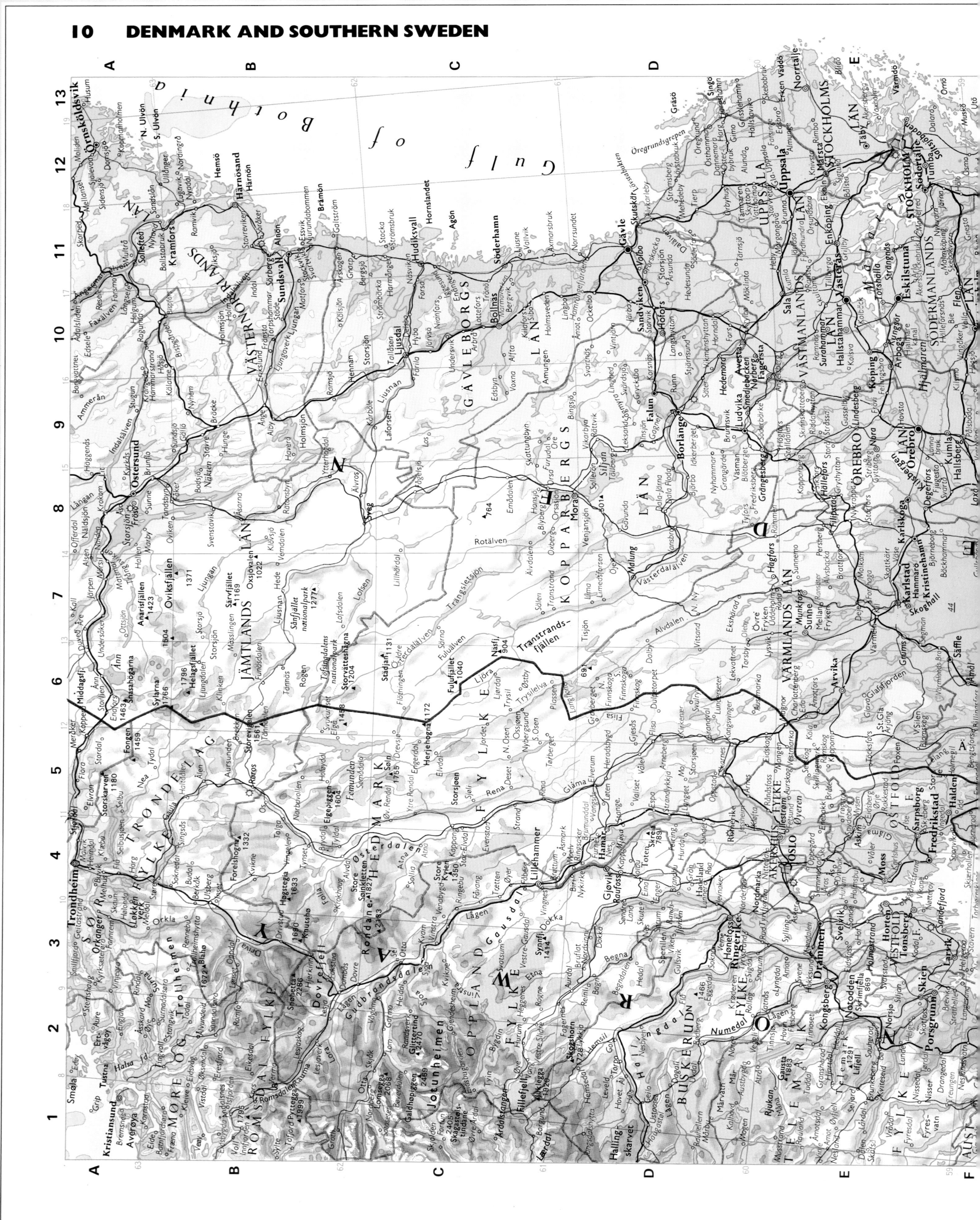

NORTH SEA

IRISH SEA

North Channel

SCOTLAND

NORTHUMBERLAND

DURHAM

CLEVELAND (Teesside)

TYNE & WEAR

NORTH YORKSHIRE

SOUTH YORKSHIRE

WEST YORKSHIRE

HUMBERSIDE

LINCOLN

NOTT

DERBY

CHESHIRE

LANCASHIRE

CUMBRIA

MERSEYSIDE

GR. MANCHESTER

STAFFORD

CLWYD

GWYNEDD

Pennine

Southern Uplands

Cheviot Hills

Cumbrian Mts.

N. York Moors

Lincoln Wolds

Galloway

Isle of Man

Anglesey

Inveraray, Crinan, Cairn, Lochgilphead, Jura, Sound of Jura, Gigha, Kintyre, Mull of Kintyre, Campbeltown, Sanda I., Ailsa Craig, Arran, Goat Fell 874, Lamlash, Brodick, Firth of Clyde, Helensburgh, Dumbarton, Clydebank, Glasgow, Paisley, Port Glasgow, Greenock, Rutherglen, Hamilton, Motherwell, Wishaw, Coatbridge, Airdrie, Falkirk, Stirling, Ochil Hills, Alloa, Kinross, L. Leven, Dunfermline, Leith, Edinburgh, Musselburgh, Haddington, North Berwick, Bass Rock, Fife Ness, Anstruther, Kirkcaldy, Firth of Forth, Saltcoats, Irvine, Kilmarnock, Ayr, Girvan, Stranraer, Portpatrick, Luce Bay, Wigtown, Newton Stewart, Merrick 843, Whithorn, Wigtown Bay, Kirkcudbright, Castle Douglas, Dalbeattie, Solway Firth, Dumfries, Annan, Nith, Sanquhar, Leadhills, Moorfoot Hills, Peebles, Galashiels, Selkirk, Hawick, Jedburgh, Kelso, Coldstream, Flodden, The Cheviot 816, Berwick-upon-Tweed, Holy I., Farne Is., Bamburgh, Alnwick, Coquet, Morpeth, Ashington, Blyth, Tynemouth, South Shields, Newcastle, Gateshead, Wallsend, Sunderland, Houghton-le-Spring, Consett, Durham, Bishop Auckland, Barnard Castle, Hartlepool, Billingham, Stockton, Middlesbrough, Redcar, Darlington, Richmond, Northallerton, Thirsk, Whitby, Scarborough, Filey, Flamborough Hd., Bridlington, Hornsea, Withernsea, Beverley, Hull, Humber, Spurn Hd., Cleethorpes, Grimsby, Immingham, Barton-upon-Humber, Gainsborough, Market Rasen, Louth, Mablethorpe, Alford, Horncastle, Skegness, Lincoln, Witham, Newark, Sleaford, Boston, Grantham, Bourne, Spalding, Cromer, North Walsham, Fakenham, Sandringham, Hunstanton, The Wash, King's Lynn, The Broads

Carlisle, Gretna Green, Silloth, Maryport, Workington, Whitehaven, St. Bees Hd., Seascale, Penrith, Cross Fell 893, Skiddaw 931, Keswick, Derwent, Helvellyn 950, Sea Fell 978, Ullswater, Windermere, Ambleside, Kendal, Millom, Barrow, Walney I., Morecambe, Fleetwood, Cleveleys, Blackpool, Lytham-St. Annes, Southport, Formby Pt., Preston, Blackburn, Burnley, Nelson, Colne, Chorley, Bolton, Bury, Rochdale, Oldham, Manchester, Salford, Stockport, Warrington, Liverpool, Bootle, Wallasey, Birkenhead, St. Helens, Wigan, Leigh, Bury, Buxton, Macclesfield, Leek, Crewe, Nantwich, Northwich, Newcastle-under-Lyme, Stoke-on-Trent, Stafford, Uttoxeter, Burton, Derby, Belper, Matlock, Chesterfield, Sheffield, Rotherham, Barnsley, Doncaster, Worksop, Mansfield, Sutton-in-Ashfield, Nottingham, Beeston, Loughborough

Leeds, Bradford, Huddersfield, Halifax, Keighley, Harrogate, Knaresborough, Ripon, Wensleydale, Swaledale, York, Selby, Goole, Pontefract, Wakefield, Dewsbury

Wrexham, Oswestry, Llangollen, Bala, L. Bala, Denbigh, Mold, Rhyl, Colwyn Bay, Llandudno, Conwy, Bangor, Beaumaris, Amlwch, Holyhead, Holy I., Caernarfon, Menai Strait, Snowdon 1085, Ffestiniog, Porthmadog, Pwllheli, Nefyn, Harlech, Barmouth, Bardsey I.

Ramsey, Douglas, Snaefell 620, Castletown, Port Erin, Peel, Calf of Man, Pt. of Ayre

Belfast, Belfast Lough, Bangor, Newtownards, Donaghadee, Strangford L., Downpatrick, Ardglass, Larne, Magee, Carrickfergus

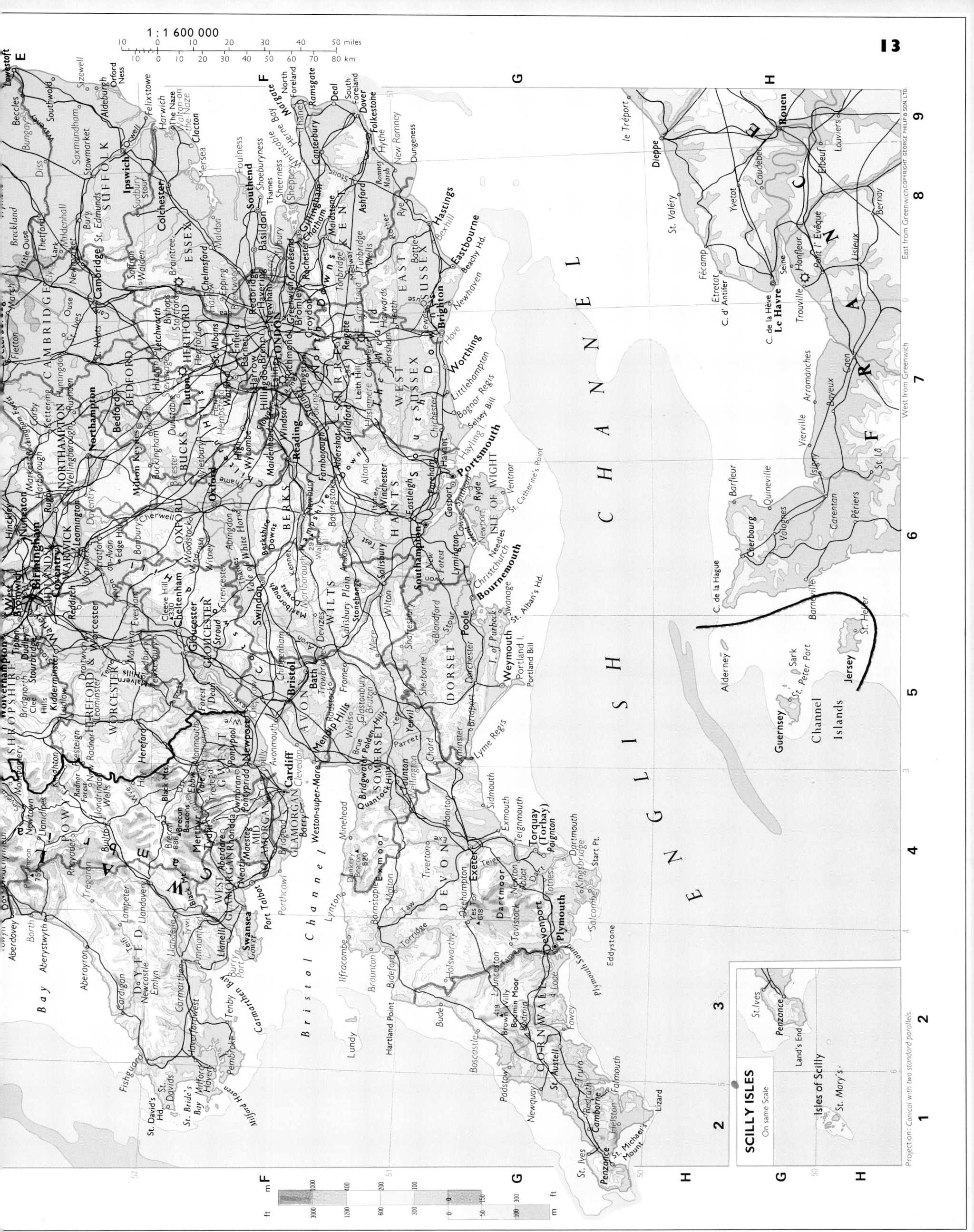

1 : 1 600 000

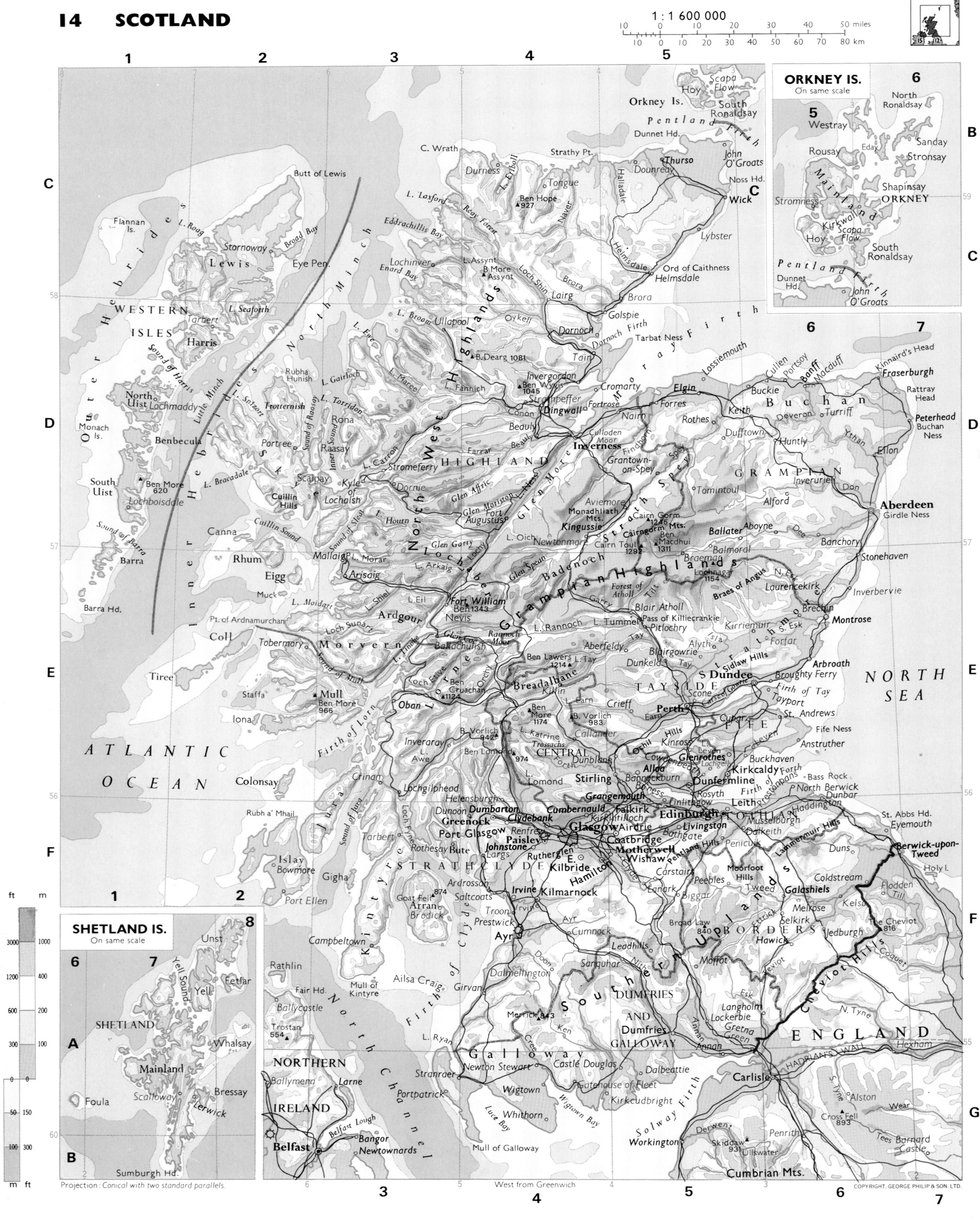

ORKNEY IS.
On same scale

SHETLAND IS.
On same scale

Projection: Conical with two standard parallels.

West from Greenwich

COPYRIGHT. GEORGE PHILIP & SON. LTD.

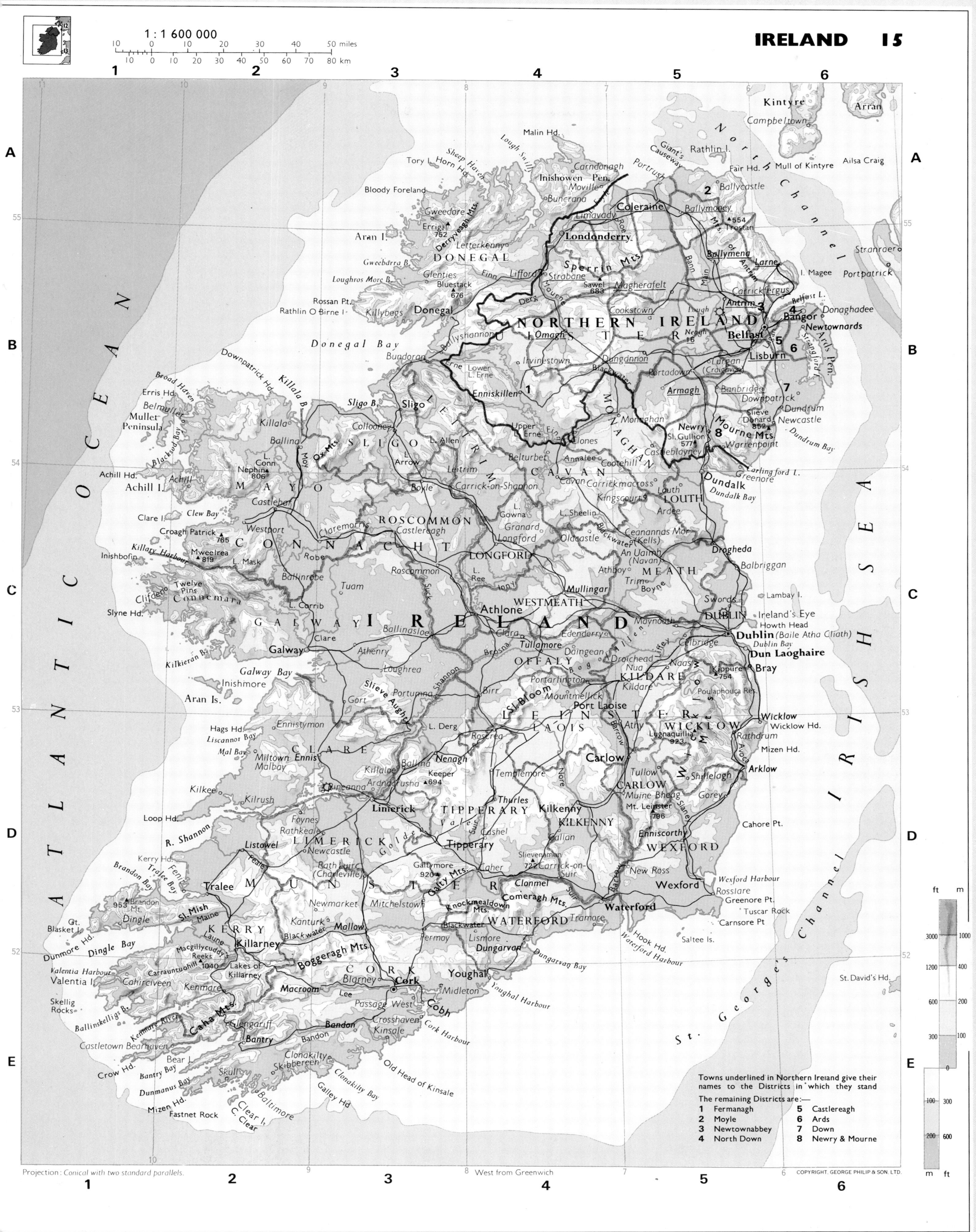

1 : 1 600 000

10   0   10   20   30   40   50 miles
10   0   10   20   30   40   50   60   70   80 km

Towns underlined in Northern Ireland give their
names to the Districts in which they stand
The remaining Districts are:—
1 Fermanagh   5 Castlereagh
2 Moyle   6 Ards
3 Newtownabbey   7 Down
4 North Down   8 Newry & Mourne

Projection : Conical with two standard parallels.

West from Greenwich

COPYRIGHT. GEORGE PHILIP & SON. LTD.

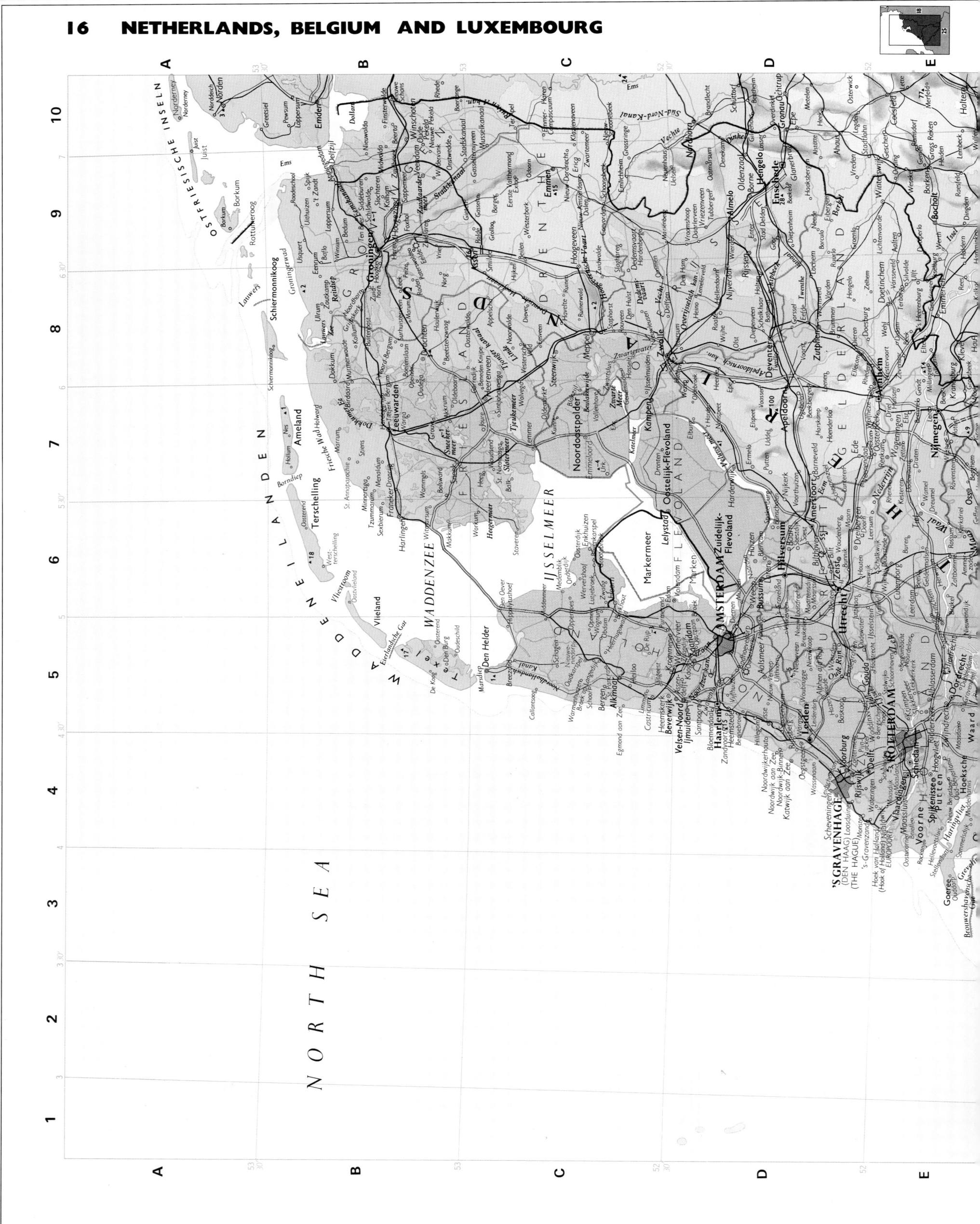

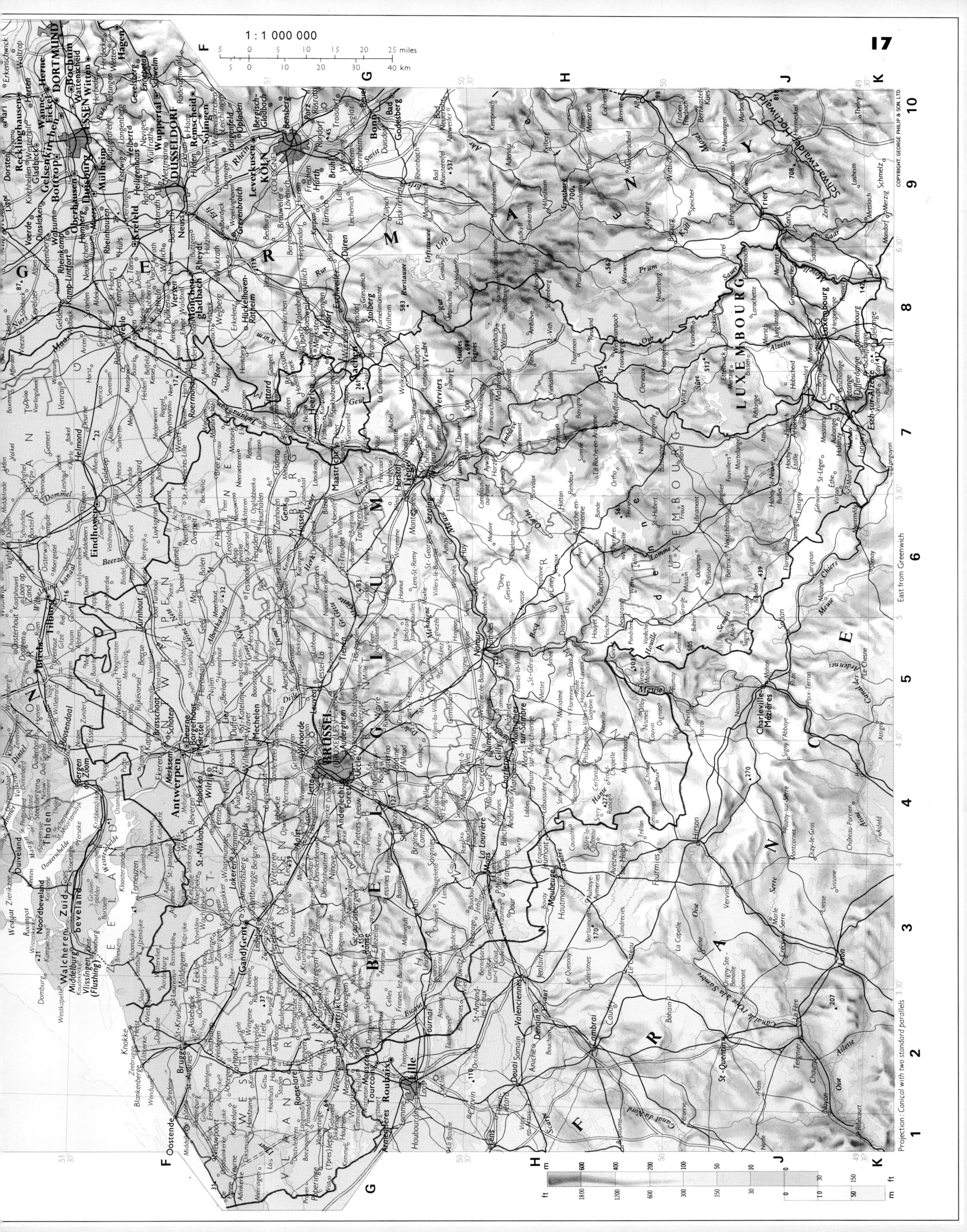

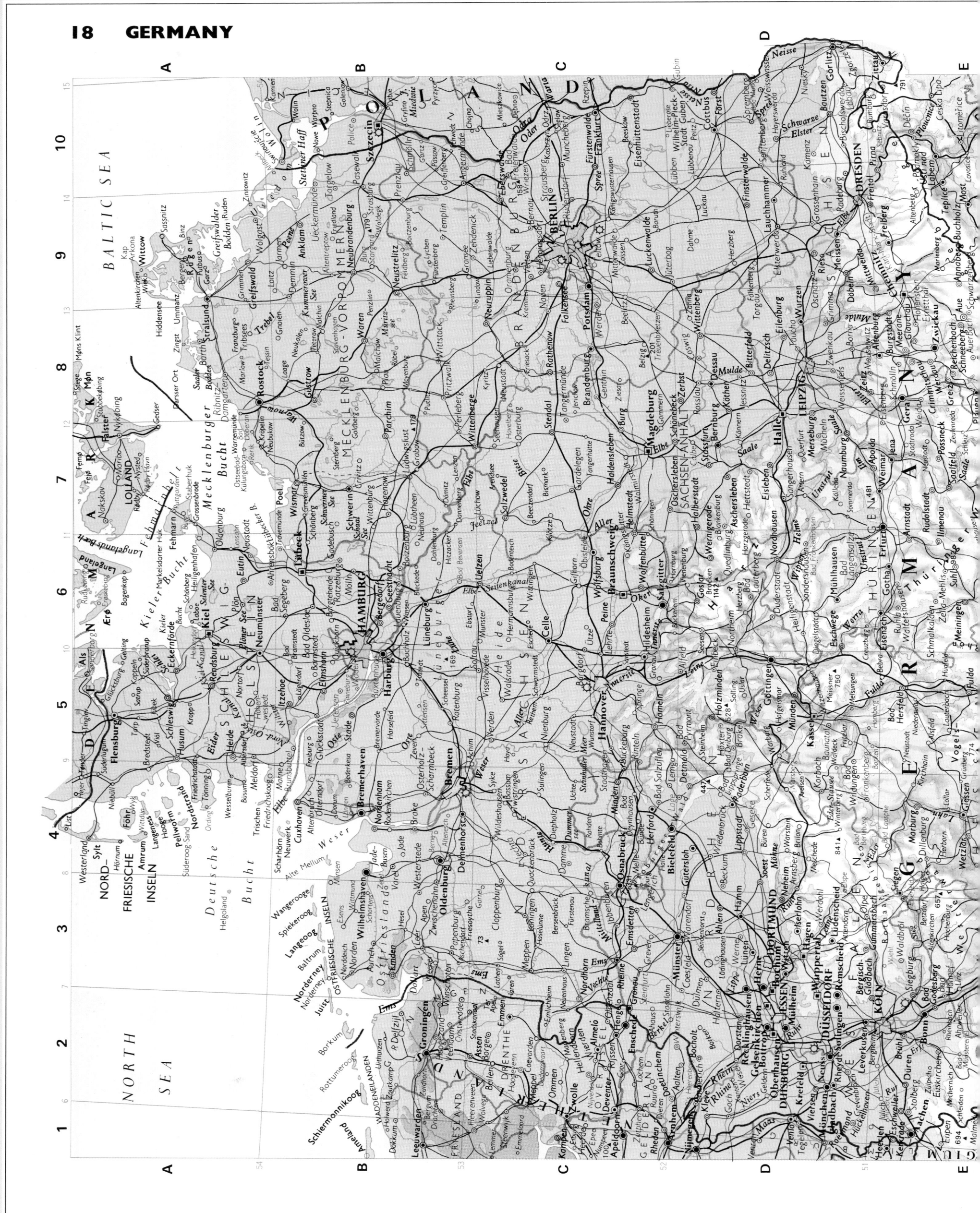

1 : 2 000 000

10   0   10   20   30   40   50 miles
10   0   10 20 30 40 50 60 70 80 km

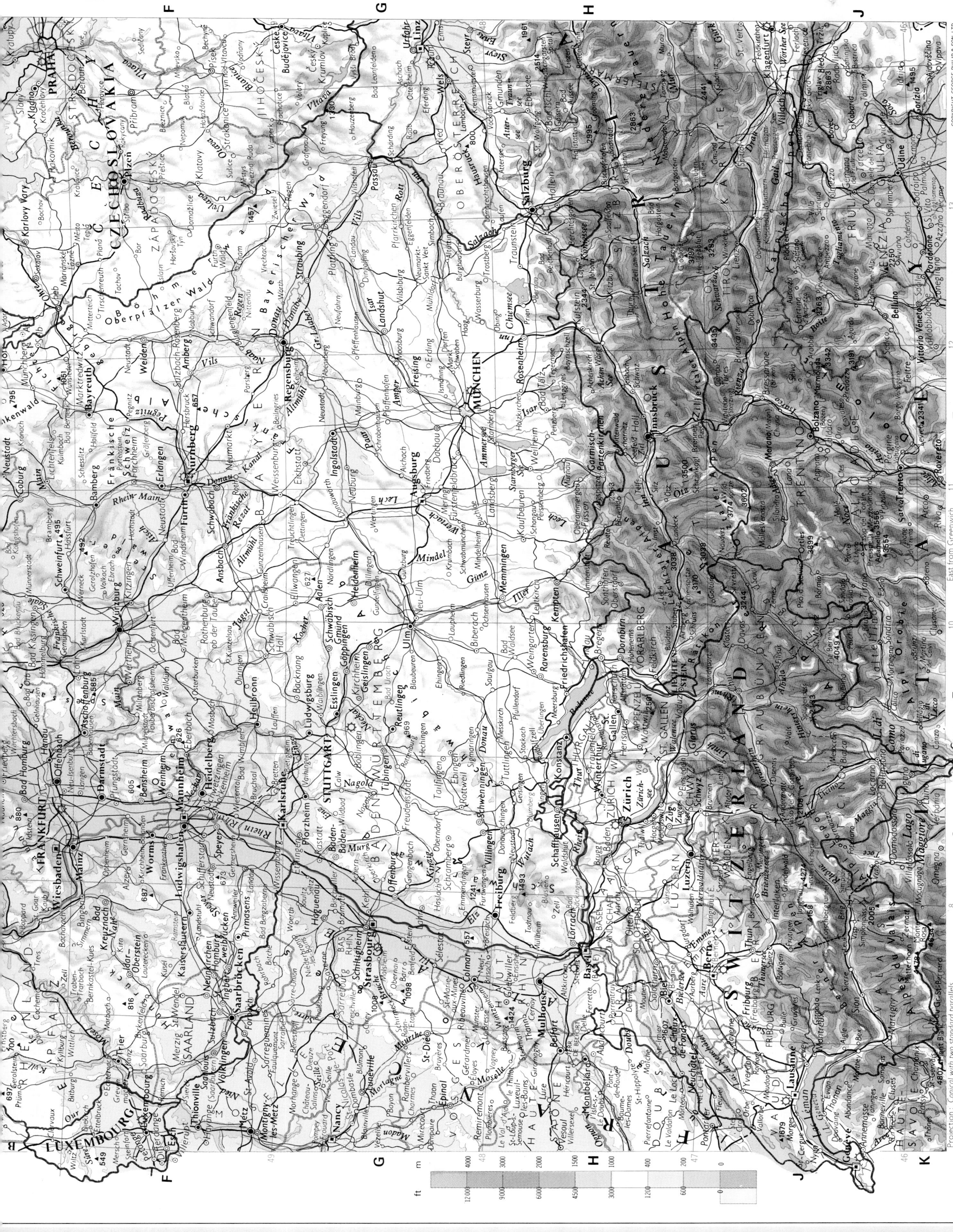

East from Greenwich

Projection: Conical with two standard parallels.

COPYRIGHT GEORGE PHILIP & SON LTD

ft   m
12000 4000
9000   3000
6000   2000
       1500
3000   1000
       600
1500   300
       200
600   0

PRAHA

Č E C H Y

Č E S K O S L O V E N S K O

Z Á P A D O Č E S K Ý

J I H O Č E S K Ý

Karlovy Vary
Plzeň
České Budějovice

L U X E M B O U R G

R H E I N L A N D - P F A L Z

S A A R L A N D

FRANKFURT
Mainz
Wiesbaden
Worms
Mannheim
Heidelberg
Karlsruhe
STUTTGART
Heilbronn
Würzburg
Bamberg
Nürnberg
Fürth
Erlangen
Bayreuth
Coburg
Schweinfurt
Offenbach
Darmstadt

B A Y E R N

B A D E N - W Ü R T T E M B E R G

Regensburg
Donau
Ingolstadt
Augsburg
MÜNCHEN
Landshut
Passau
Linz

O B E R Ö S T E R R E I C H

Salzburg

S T E I E R M A R K

K Ä R N T E N

Klagenfurt

T I R O L

Innsbruck
Garmisch
Kempten

V O R A R L B E R G

LIECHTENSTEIN

S W I T Z E R L A N D

ZÜRICH
Luzern
Bern
BASEL
St. Gallen
Winterthur
Konstanz
Schaffhausen
Friedrichshafen
Ravensburg
Memmingen
Ulm
Neu-Ulm
Reutlingen
Tübingen
Freiburg
Strasbourg
Mulhouse
Colmar
Belfort
Montbéliard

V O S G E S

H A U T E - S A V O I E

Lausanne

W A L L I S

T R E N T I N O

A L T O   A D I G E

Bolzano
Trento
Rovereto
Merano

V E N E Z I A

F R I U L I

Udine
Belluno
Vittorio Veneto
Pordenone

G R A U B Ü N D E N

Como
Lugano

Nancy
Metz
Thionville
Saarbrücken
Epinal

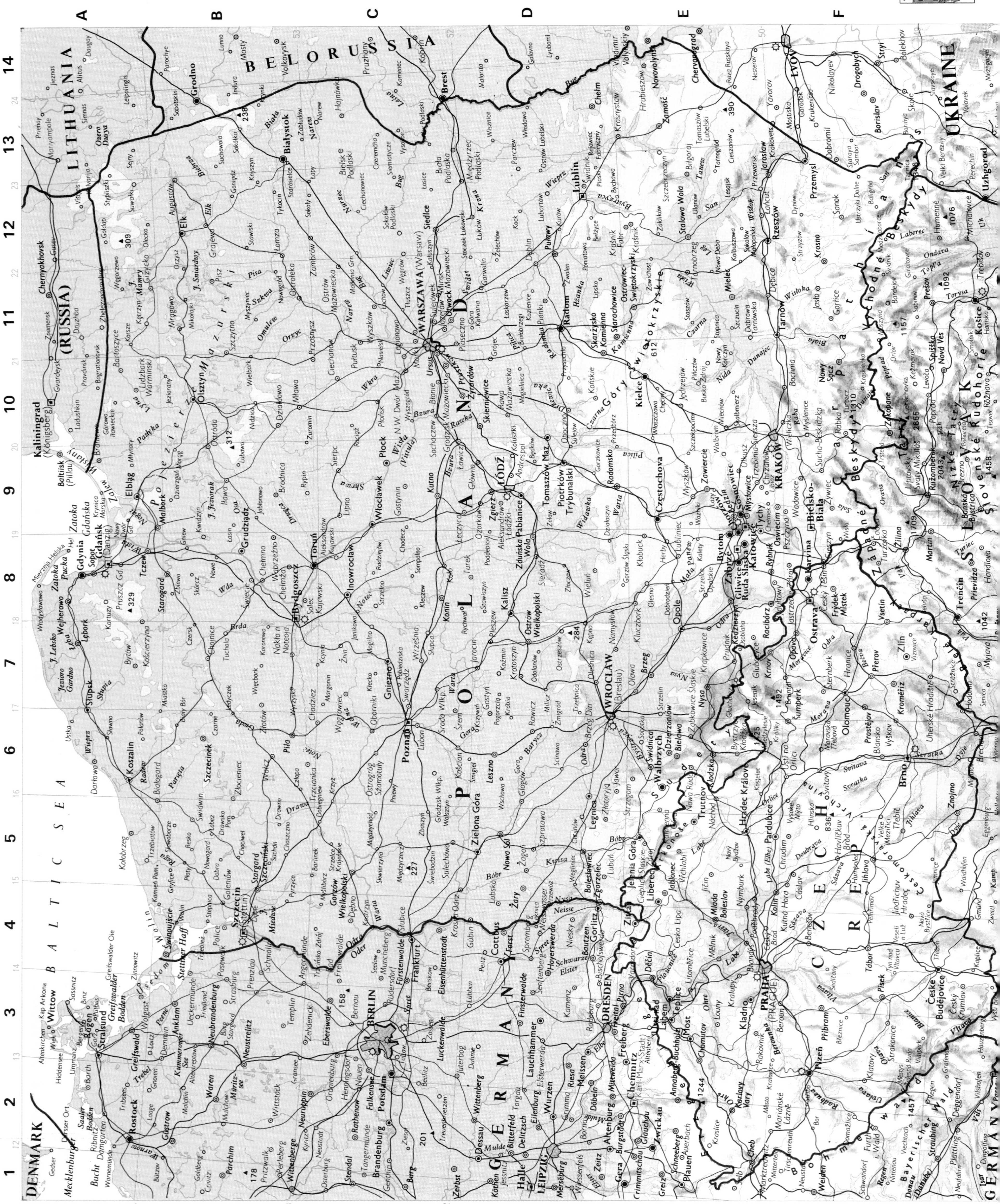

LITHUANIA

BELORUSSIA

RUSSIA
(Kaliningrad)
(Königsberg)

DENMARK

BALTIC SEA

POLAND

GERMANY

CZECH REPUBLIC

UKRAINE

Grodno
Białystok
Brest
Lublin
Chelm
Lvov
Uzhgorod
Przemyśl
Rzeszów
Kielce
Radom
WARSZAWA (Warsaw)
Łódź
Piotrków Trybunalski
Częstochowa
KRAKÓW
Katowice
Gliwice
Bytom
Zabrze
Opole
WROCŁAW (Breslau)
Wałbrzych
Legnica
Zielona Góra
POZNAŃ
Kalisz
Gniezno
Konin
Bydgoszcz
Toruń
Inowrocław
Włocławek
Grudziądz
Elbląg
Olsztyn
GDAŃSK (Danzig)
Gdynia
Sopot
Słupsk
Koszalin
Kołobrzeg
Szczecin (Stettin)
Świnoujście

BERLIN
Potsdam
Frankfurt
Cottbus
DRESDEN
LEIPZIG
Halle
Chemnitz
Zwickau
Gera
Plauen

PRAHA (PRAGUE)
Teplice
Ústí n. Labem
Most
Liberec
Hradec Králové
Pardubice
Olomouc
Ostrava
BRNO
Zlín
Trenčín
Žilina
KOŠICE
Prešov

Rostock
Stralsund
Greifswald
Neubrandenburg
Wittenberge

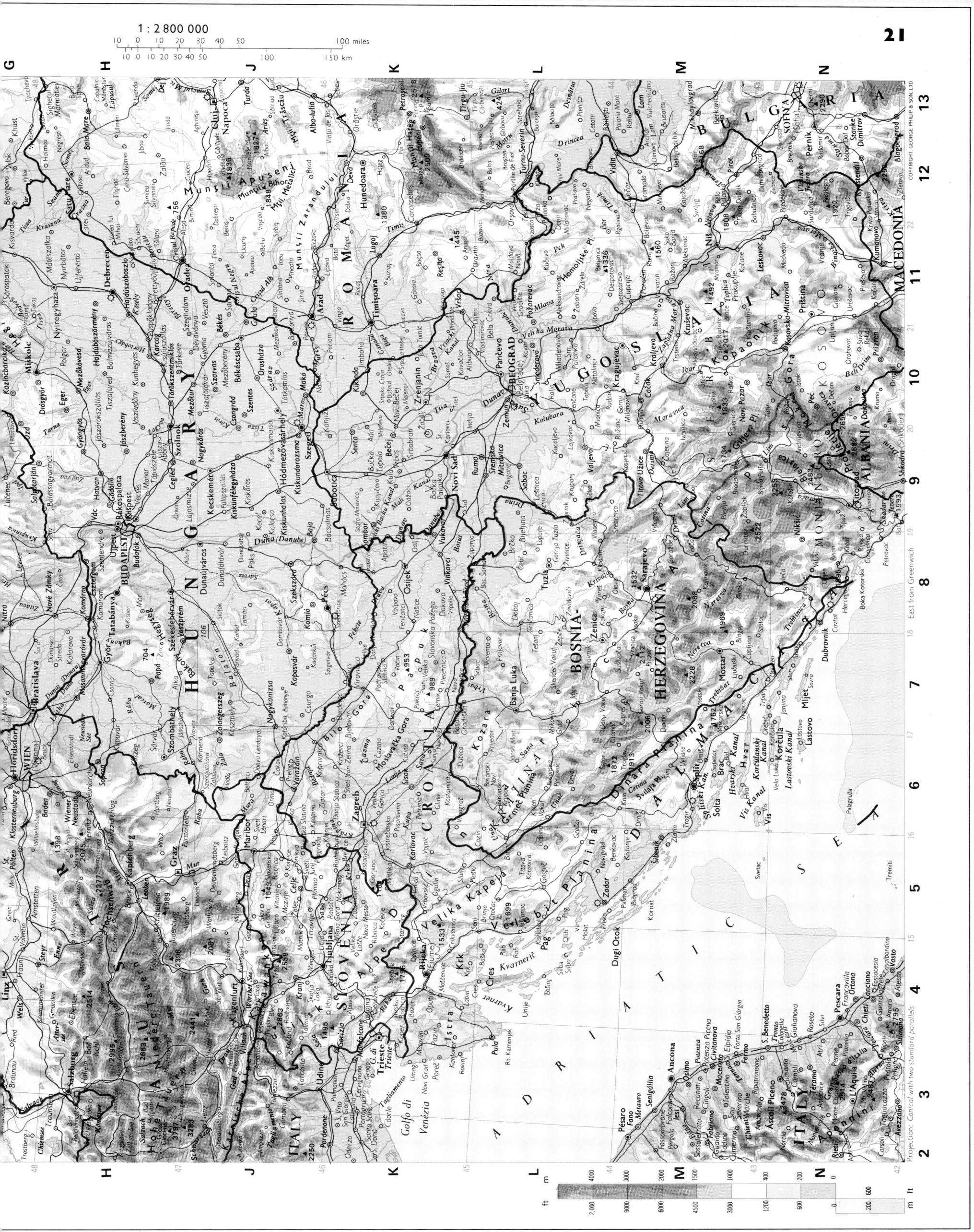

Grid columns: 1 2 3 4 5 6

Grid rows: A B C D E

Major labels:

FRANCE
HAUTE-SAÔNE
HAUT-RHIN
Sundgau
BELFORT
JURA
DOUBS
NEUCHÂTEL
BERN (BERNE)
SOLOTHURN
LANDSCHAFT
AARGAU
LUZERN
OBWALDEN
FRIBOURG (FREIBURG)
Gruyère
VAUD
VALAIS
HAUTE-SAVOIE
SAVOIE
VALLE D'AOSTA
PIEMONTE

Cities and towns:

MULHOUSE, BASEL (BASLE), Lörrach, Rheinfelden, Waldshut, Aarau, Olten, Zofingen, Sursee, Vesoul, Belfort, Montbéliard, Audincourt, Valentigney, Porrentruy, Delémont, Moutier, Grenchen, Solothurn, Biel (Bienne), Besançon, Pontarlier, La Chaux-de-Fonds, Le Locle, Neuchâtel, BERN (BERNE), Burgdorf, Langnau i. E., Thun, Steffisburg, Spiez, Interlaken, Grindelwald, Brienz, Fribourg (Freiburg), Bulle, Gruyères, Payerne, Yverdon, Ste-Croix, Grandson, Orbe, Moudon, Romont, LAUSANNE, Morges, Vevey, Montreux, Aigle, Léman (L. Geneva), Nyon, Thonon-les-Bains, Evian-les-Bains, Monthey, Martigny, Sion, Sierre, Brig, Zermatt, Saas Fee, GENÈVE (GENEVA), Annemasse, Bellegarde-s.-V., Oyonnax, St-Claude, Annecy, Lac d'Annecy, Rumilly, Aix-les-Bains, Lac du Bourget, Belley, Albertville, Ugine, Chamonix-Mont-Blanc, Mont-Blanc, Aosta, Valle d'Aosta, Monte Rosa, Matterhorn (Mte Cervino), Dufourspitze

Mountain heights (m):

4807 (Mont Blanc), 4634 (Monte Rosa), 4545 (Dom), 4505, 4478 (Matterhorn/Mte Cervino), 4274 (Finsteraarhorn), 4158, 4078, 4023 (Weisshorn), 3709, 3664 (Blümlisalphorn), 3553 (Mte Leone), 3569, 3257, 3238, 3248, 3243, 3194 (Simplonpass), 2832, 2752, 2469, 2362, 2351, 2244, 2190, 2188, 2044, 2005, 1679, 1718, 1607, 1463, 1408, 1415, 1204, 1165, 839

Other features:

Rhin / Rhine, Rhône, Doubs, Simplon tunnel, Simplonpass 2005, Lötschberg tunnel, Lac de Neuchâtel, Bielersee, Thunersee, Brienzersee, Berner Alpen, Oberland, Freiburger Alpen, Mittelland, Pennine Alps, Graie, Chablais, Faucigny, Genevois, Les Rousses

Elevation scale:
ft	m
9000	3000
6000	2000
4500	1500
3000	1000
1200	500
600	200

1 : 800 000

5   0   5   10   15   20   25 miles

5   0   10   20   30   40 km

7   8   9   10   11

EN W Ü R T T E M B E R G

Blumb'g   Stockach   Sipplingen   Baienfurt   Wolfegg   Leutkirch   Obergünzburg
Bonndorf   Heiligenberg   Weingarten   Kisslegg   Altusried   Schongau
im Schwarzwald   Singen   Radolfzell   Überlingen   Ravensburg   Wiggensbach   Wildpoldsried   Peiting
Stühlingen   Markdorf   Schussen   Isny   Kempten   St. Mang   Marktoberdorf
Thyngen   Meersburg   Meckenbeuren   1125   Buchenberg   Sulzberg   Nesselwang
SCHAFFHAUSEN   Konstanz   Friedrichshafen   Wangen i.A.   i.A. Blaichach   GERMANY
Schaffhausen   Kreuzlingen   Langenargen   1243   Immenstadt   Rettenberg   Wertach   BAYERN
Neuhausen   Steckborn   am Bodensee   Lindenberg   Hindelang   Roßhaupten   Schwangau
a.Rh.   THURGAU   (L. Constance)   i.A.   Weiler-   Sonthofen   Pfronten   Füssen

T A L Y   LOMBARDIA   BERGAMO   Lago d'Idro   Lago di Garda

East from Greenwich   COPYRIGHT. GEORGE. PHILIP & SON. LTD.

6   7   8   9   10   11

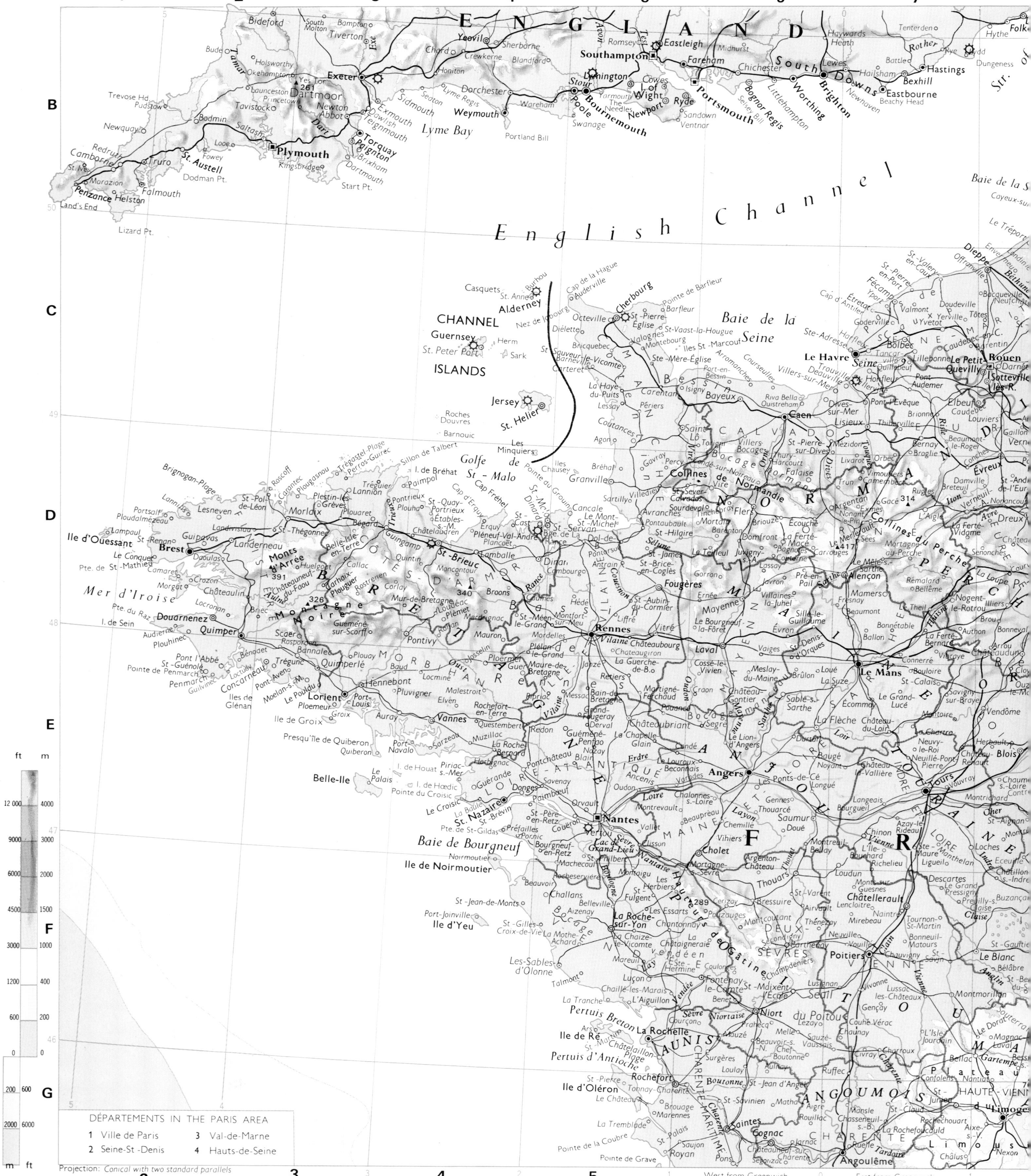

ENGLAND
English Channel
Bideford
Tiverton
Yeovil
Sherborne
Southampton
Eastleigh
Fareham
Chichester
Exeter
Dartmoor
Newton Abbot
Plymouth
Torquay
Paignton
Lyme Bay
Weymouth
Dorchester
Bournemouth
Poole
Lymington
I. of Wight
Newport
Ryde
Portsmouth
Bognor Regis
Littlehampton
Worthing
Brighton
South Downs
Lewes
Eastbourne
Hastings
Bexhill
Beachy Head
Dungeness
Penzance
Land's End
Lizard Pt.
Truro
St. Austell
Falmouth
Start Pt.
Portland Bill
CHANNEL ISLANDS
Alderney
Guernsey
St. Peter Port
Herm
Sark
Jersey
St. Helier
Cherbourg
Baie de la Seine
Le Havre
Rouen
Dieppe
Caen
Bayeux
Lisieux
Évreux
Alençon
Le Mans
Laval
Rennes
Fougères
St.-Malo
Golfe de St.-Malo
St.-Brieuc
Brest
Ile d'Ouessant
Mer d'Iroise
Quimper
Douarnenez
Lorient
Vannes
Belle-Ile
Ile de Groix
Presqu'île de Quiberon
St. Nazaire
Nantes
Baie de Bourgneuf
Ile de Noirmoutier
Ile d'Yeu
La Roche-sur-Yon
Les Sables-d'Olonne
Cholet
Angers
Saumur
Tours
Blois
Châtellerault
Poitiers
Niort
La Rochelle
Ile de Ré
Pertuis Breton
Pertuis d'Antioche
Ile d'Oléron
Rochefort
Saintes
Cognac
Angoulême
Royan
Pointe de Grave
Limoges
BRETAGNE
NORMANDIE
ANJOU
POITOU
ANGOUMOIS
AUNIS
F R
DÉPARTEMENTS IN THE PARIS AREA
1 Ville de Paris
2 Seine-St-Denis
3 Val-de-Marne
4 Hauts-de-Seine
ft m
12 000 4000
9000 3000
6000 2000
4500 1500
3000 1000
1200 400
600 200
0 0
200 600
2000 6000
m ft
West from Greenwich
East from Greenwich

Projection: *Conical with two standard parallels*

1 : 2 000 000

10   0   10   20   30   40   50 miles
10 0 10 20 30 40 50 60 70 80 km

BELGIUM

FRANCE

LUXEMBOURG

GERMANY

SWITZERLAND

ITALY

LUXEMBOURG

SAARLAND

LORRAINE

CHAMPAGNE

ARDENNES

BOURGOGNE

CÔTE D'OR

NIEVERNAIS

BOURBONNAIS

HAUTE MARNE

Calais · Dunkerque · St-Omer · Boulogne-sur-Mer · Lille · Roubaix · Tourcoing · Tournai · Arras · Douai · Valenciennes · Cambrai · Amiens · St Quentin · Abbeville · Beauvais · Compiègne · Soissons · Laon · Reims · Épernay · Châlons-sur-Marne · Troyes · Chaumont · Sens · Auxerre · Dijon · Beaune · Chalon-sur-Saône · Mâcon · Bourg-en-Bresse · Nevers · Bourges · Moulins · Vichy · Roanne · Montluçon · Clermont Ferrand · Lyon (Lyons)

BRUSSEL (Bruxelles) · Gent (Gand) · Mechelen · Aalst · Leuven · Namur · Charleroi · Mons · Liège · Verviers · Maastricht · Aachen · KÖLN · Bonn · Koblenz · FRANKFURT · Wiesbaden · Mainz · Worms · Mannheim · Ludwigshafen · Karlsruhe · Saarbrücken · Trier · Metz · Nancy · Strasbourg · Colmar · Mulhouse · Freiburg · Basel · BASEL · SWITZERLAND · Bern · Lausanne · Genève · Neuchâtel · Besançon · Belfort · Montbéliard

PARIS · Versailles · St-Germain · Fontainebleau · Melun · Montargis · Orléans · Châteauroux · Vierzon

COPYRIGHT GEORGE PHILIP & SON LTD.

SOUTHERN FRANCE map

Column references: 1 2 3 4 5 6 7

Row references: B C D E F G

ATLANTIC OCEAN

Golfe de Gascogne

FRANCE

Major places and features:

Ile de Noirmoutier, Noirmoutier, St-Philbert, Cholet, Bourges, Nevers

La Roche-sur-Yon, Les Sables-d'Olonne, Ile d'Yeu, St-Jean-de-Monts

Poitiers, VIENNE, Châtellerault, Châteauroux, Montluçon, BOURBONNAIS, Moulins, Vichy

La Rochelle, Ile de Ré, Pertuis Breton, Pertuis d'Antioche, Rochefort, Ile d'Oléron

Niort, DEUX-SÈVRES, MARCHE, CREUSE, Guéret

Cognac, Saintes, ANGOUMOIS, Angoulême, CHARENTE, HAUTE-VIENNE, Limoges, Clermont-Ferrand, PUY-DE-DÔME

Bordeaux, Bègles, Cenon, Arcachon, Bassin d'Arcachon, Cap Ferret, La Teste

Périgueux, DORDOGNE, PÉRIGORD, Brive-la-Gaillarde, Tulle, CORRÈZE, CANTAL, Aurillac

Libourne, St-Émilion, Bergerac, GIRONDE

Étang de Lacanau, Étang de Cazaux et de Sanguinet, Étang de Biscarrosse et de Parentis

LANDES, Mont-de-Marsan, LOT-ET-GARONNE, Villeneuve-sur-Lot, Agen, Marmande, Cahors, LOT, Figeac, Decazeville, Rodez, AVEYRON, Millau, Causse Méjean

GASCOGNE, ARMAGNAC, Montauban, TARN-ET-GARONNE, Castelsarrasin, Albi, TARN, Mts de Lacaune, HÉRAULT

Dax, Bayonne, Biarritz, St-Jean-de-Luz, Hendaye, PYRÉNÉES-ATLANTIQUES, BÉARN, Pau, Tarbes, HAUTES-PYRÉNÉES, Lourdes, Bagnères-de-Bigorre

Toulouse, HAUTE-GARONNE, Castres, Mazamet, Montagne Noire, Castelnaudary, Carcassonne, Canal du Midi, Béziers, AUDE, Narbonne, Sète

ARIÈGE, Foix, Pamiers, Limoux, Quillan, PYRÉNÉES-ORIENTALES, ROUSSILLON, Perpignan, Céret, Port-Vendres, Cerbère, Port-Bou

SPAIN, NAVARRA, Pamplona, Estella, Tudela, ARAGÓN, Zaragoza (Saragossa), Huesca, Jaca, Sierra de la Peña, Sierra de Guara

ANDORRA, Pic d'Estats 3141, Pica d'Estats, Pic de Montcalm 3080, Pico de Aneto 3404, Vignemale 3298, Canfranc, Mont Perdu 3375

LÉRIDA, Lérida, Balaguer, Tremp, Seo de Urgel, Sierra del Cadí, Manresa, BARCELONA, GERONA, Gerona, Figueras, Cabo Creus, Cadaqués

Spot heights: 2886, 3803, 2912, 2077, 2557, 929, 1677, 2316, 1712, 1089, 1567, 1471, 1463, 452

Elevation scale:
ft / m
12,000 / 4000
9000 / 3000
6000 / 2000
4500 / 1500
3000 / 1000
1200 / 400
600 / 200
0 / 0
200 / 600
2000 / 6000
m / ft

1 : 2 000 000

10 5 0 10 20 30 40 50 miles
10 0 10 20 30 40 50 60 70 80 km

8   9   10   11   12   13   14

SWITZERLAND

Bern Luzern Schwyz FRIBOURG VAUD GRAUBÜNDEN Davos St Moritz

Neuchâtel Lausanne Montreux Sion VALAIS Locarno Bellinzona Sòndrio

Genève Annemasse Thonon Martigny Zermatt Lugano Còmo Bergamo Brescia

LYON Bourg-en-Bresse Annecy Aosta Varese Lecco MILANO Monza

Vienne Chambéry SAVOIE Biella Novara Vercelli Pavia Crema Cremona

Grenoble Valence DAUPHINÉ TORINO PIEMONTE Asti Alessandria Tortona Piacenza Parma

Montélimar Gap HAUTES-ALPES Cúneo Savona GENOVA La Spezia Massa Carrara

Avignon Nîmes Arles HAUTE-PROVENCE Digne ALPES-MARITIMES San Remo Impéria

MARSEILLE Aix-en-Provence Toulon Hyères Cannes Nice MONACO Monte-Carlo Antibes Golfo di Génova Livorno

LIGURIAN SEA

Côte d'Azur ILES D'HYÈRES

MEDITERRANEAN SEA

CORSICA Bastia Étang de Biguglia Elba HAUTE-CORSE Corte Monte Cinto 2710 CORSE-DU-SUD Ajaccio G. de Sagone G. de Porto Bonifacio

COPYRIGHT. GEORGE PHILIP & SON. LTD.

8   9   10   11   12   13   14

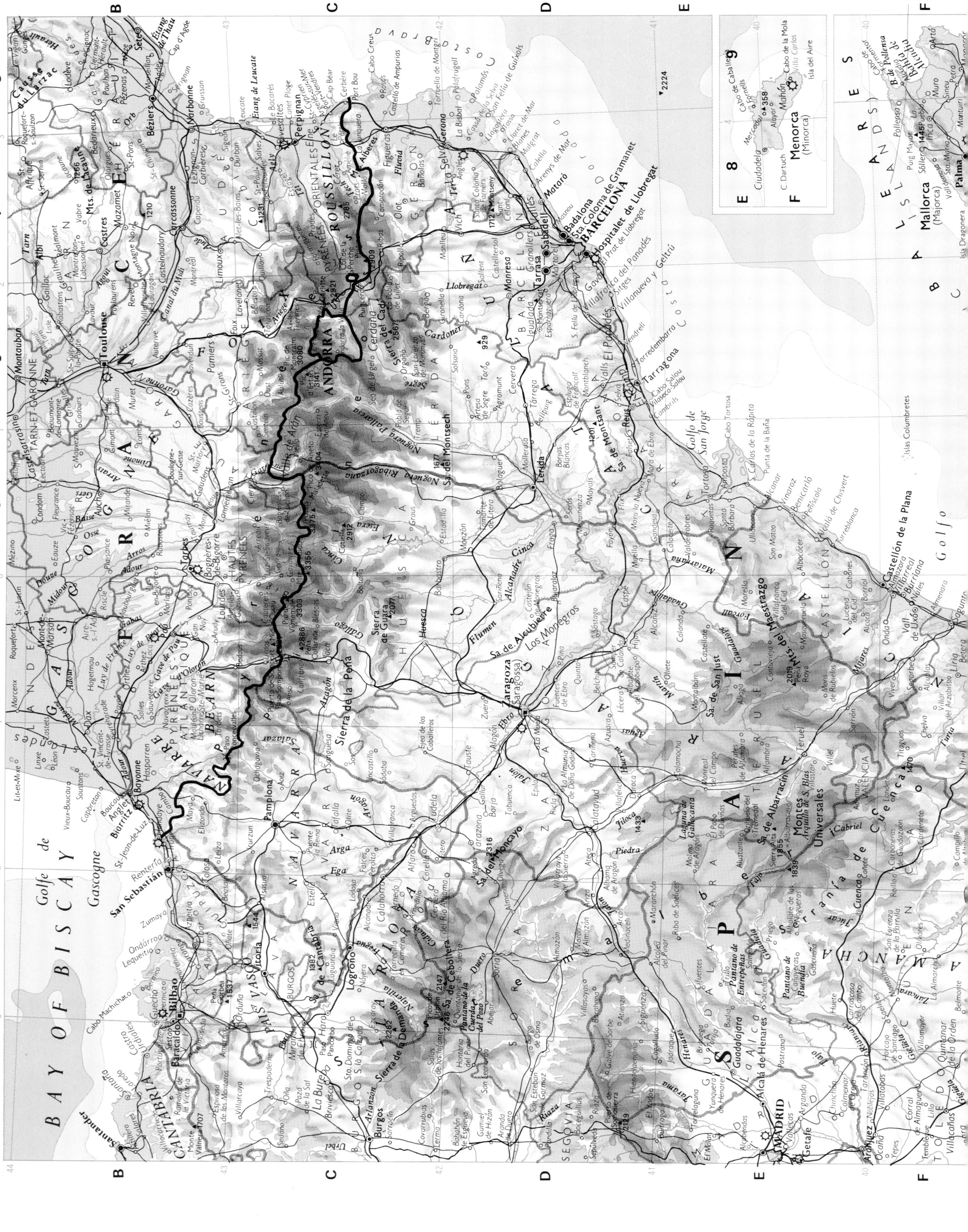

BAY OF BISCAY

Golfe de Gascogne

PYRÉNÉES

ROUSSILLON

ANDORRA

PYRÉNÉES-ORIENTALES

NAVARRA

ARAGON

CATALUÑA

LÉRIDA

GERONA

BARCELONA

TARRAGONA

CASTELLÓN

VALENCIA

CUENCA

LA MANCHA

CANTABRIA

PAÍS VASCO

LA RIOJA

SEGOVIA

Costa Brava

ISLAS BALEARES

Menorca (Minorca)

Mallorca (Majorca)

BARCELONA
Badalona
Sta Coloma de Gramanet
Hospitalet de Llobregat
Sabadell
Tarrasa

Zaragoza (Saragossa)
Huesca
Lérida
Tarragona
Reus
Castellón de la Plana
Teruel
Pamplona
Logroño
San Sebastián
Bilbao
Vitoria
Burgos
MADRID
Toulouse
Perpignan
Narbonne
Béziers
Carcassonne
Bayonne
Biarritz

1 : 2 000 000

10 0 10 20 30 40 50 miles

10 0 10 20 30 40 50 60 70 80 km

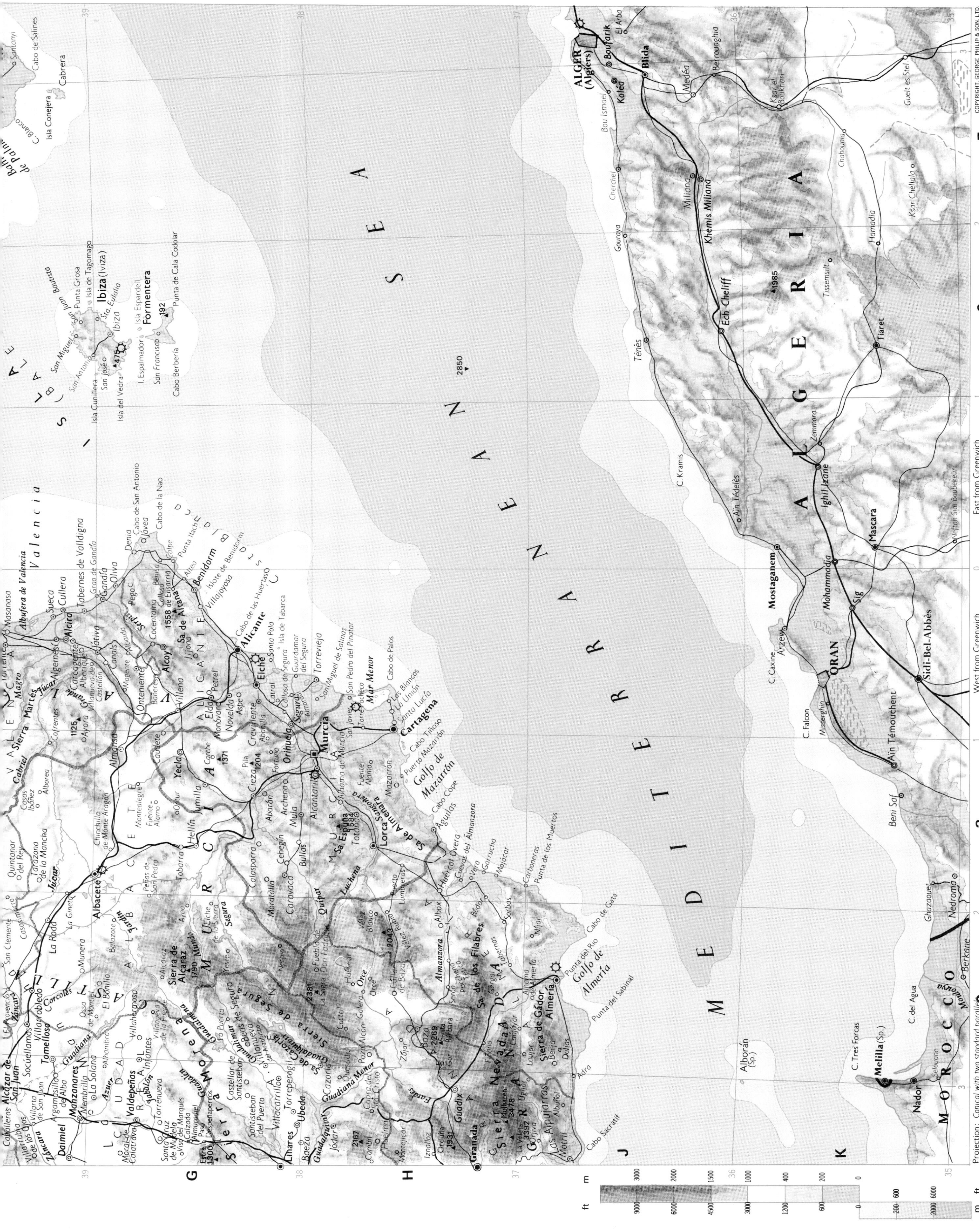

MEDITERRANEAN SEA
ALGERIA
MOROCCO
ALGER (Algiers)
Blida
Boufarik
Koléa
Médéa
Berrouaghia
Bou Ismaël
Cherchel
Gouraya
Miliana
Khemis Miliana
Ténès
Ech Cheliff
Tissemsilt
Tiaret
Zemmora
Ighil Izane
C. Kramis
Aïn Tédelès
Mostaganem
Mohammadia
Mascara
Sig
Arzew
C. Caxine
ORAN
C. Falcon
Misserghin
Aïn Témouchent
Sidi-Bel-Abbès
Beni Saf
Nedroma
Ghazaouet
Berkane
C. del Agua
Melilla (Sp.)
C. Tres Forcas
Nador
Alborán (Sp.)
Ibiza (Iviza)
Ibiza
Formentera
Isla Espalmador
Isla de Tagomago
Isla Conejera
Cabrera
Cabo de Salines
Cabo Berbería
Punta de Cala Codolar
2850
Valencia
Albufera de Valencia
Sueca
Cullera
Alcira
Gandía
Oliva
Denia
Jávea
Cabo de San Antonio
Cabo de la Nao
Benidorm
Villajoyosa
Alcoy
Alicante
Elche
Santa Pola
Torrevieja
Mar Menor
Cabo de Palos
Cartagena
Golfo de Mazarrón
Mazarrón
Águilas
Cabo Cope
Murcia
Orihuela
Lorca
Yecla
Jumilla
Hellín
Villena
Almansa
Albacete
La Roda
Tomelloso
Manzanares
Valdepeñas
Daimiel
Alcázar de San Juan
Linares
Úbeda
Baeza
Jódar
Sierra Morena
Sierra de Alcaraz
Sierra de Segura
Sierra de Cazorla
Guadiana Menor
Baza
Guadix
Granada
Sierra Nevada
Mulhacén 3478
Sierra de los Filabres
Sierra de Gádor
Almería
Golfo de Almería
Cabo de Gata
Níjar
Vera
Garrucha
Huércal Overa
Motril
Adra
Berja
Cabo Sacratif
Las Alpujarras
Punta del Sabinal
Projection: Conical with two standard parallels
East from Greenwich
West from Greenwich
COPYRIGHT, GEORGE PHILIP & SON, LTD.
m ft
3000 9000
2000 6000
1500 4500
1000 3000
400 1200
200 600
0 0
200 600
2000 6000

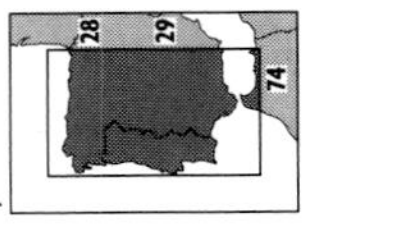

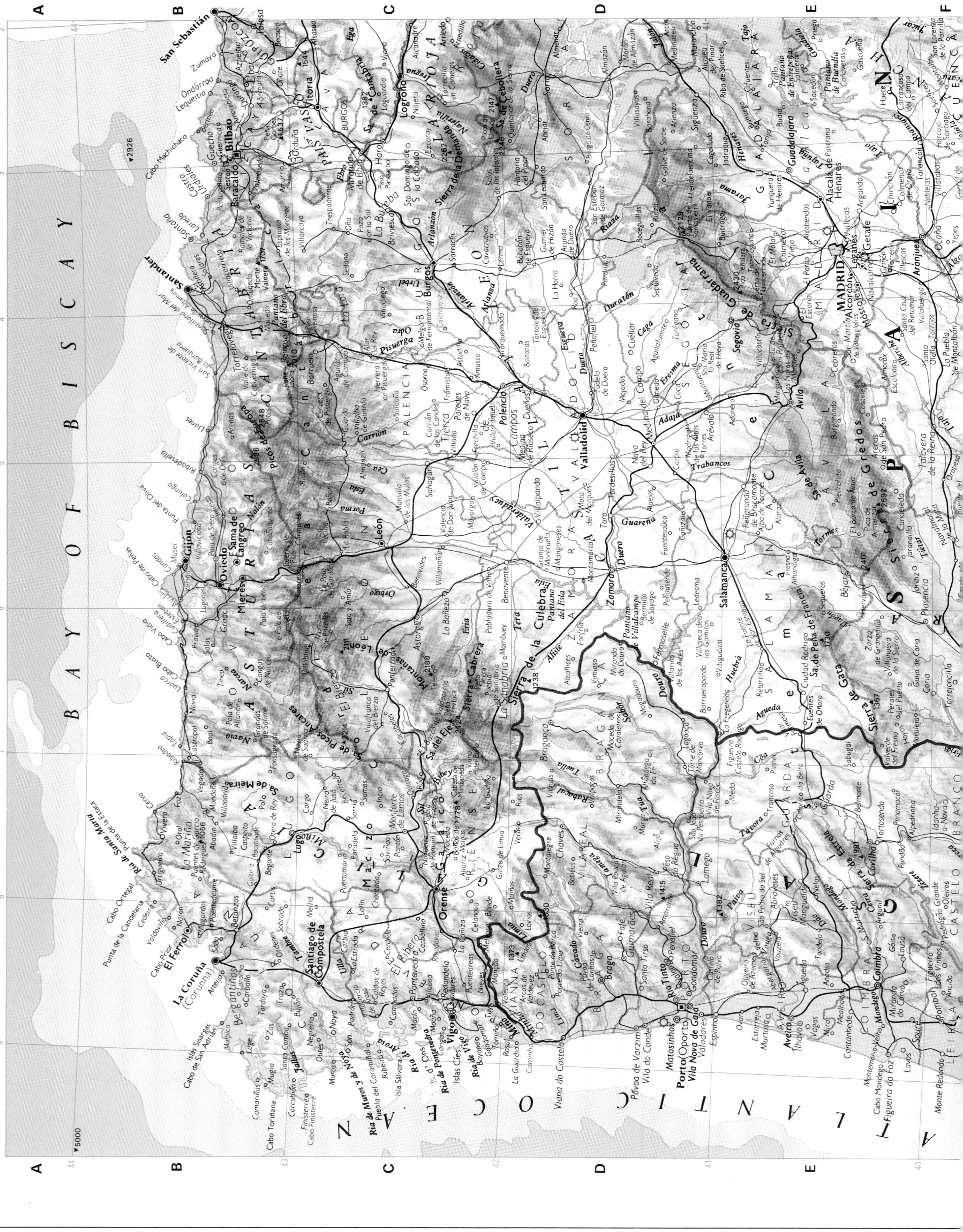

BAY OF BISCAY

ATLANTIC OCEAN

PAÍS VASCO

CANTABRIA

ASTURIAS

GALICIA

CASTILLA Y LEÓN

RIOJA

BURGOS

PALENCIA

VALLADOLID

SEGOVIA

SALAMANCA

ÁVILA

MADRID

GUADALAJARA

CUENCA

BRAGANÇA

VILA REAL

GUARDA

VISEU

COIMBRA

PORTO

BRAGA

AVEIRO

DOURO

San Sebastián · Bilbao · Baracaldo · Santander · Gijón · Oviedo · Mieres · Langreo · La Coruña (Coruña) · El Ferrol · Santiago de Compostela · Pontevedra · Vigo · Orense · Lugo · León · Palencia · Valladolid · Zamora · Salamanca · Segovia · Ávila · MADRID · Alcalá de Henares · Guadalajara · Burgos · Logroño · Vitoria · Porto (Oporto) · Vila Nova de Gaia · Matosinhos · Aveiro · Coimbra · Braga · Guimarães · Viseu · Lamego · Chaves · Bragança

1 : 2 000 000

10 0 10 20 30 40 50 miles
10 0 10 20 30 40 50 60 70 80 km

Projection: Conical with two standard parallels

West from Greenwich

MEDITERRANEAN SEA

MOROCCO

Golfo de Cádiz

Golfo de Almería

ft m
9000
6000 3000
4500 2000
3000 1500
1000
1200 600 400 200
600 200
0 0
200 — 600
2000 6000
ft m

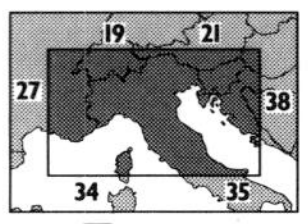

LIGURIAN SEA

Golfo di Génova

CORSE

(CORSICA)

MARSEILLE (Marseilles)

Toulon

SWITZERLAND

VORARLBERG

ST GALLEN

LUZERN

GRAUBÜNDERN

TICINO

VALAIS

Bern (Berne)

Fribourg

Lausanne

Genève (GF)

Lyon (Lyons)

Grenoble

Valence

Avignon

Aix-en-Provence

Nice

Monaco

Monte-Carlo

Cannes

San Remo

Imperia

Savona

GENOVA (Genoa)

La Spezia

Carrara

Massa

Livorno (Leghorn)

Pisa

Lucca

Pistoia

TORINO (Turin)

Asti

Alessándria

Novara

MILANO (Milan)

Monza

Bérgamo

Bréscia

Como

Varese

Pavia

Lodi

Cremona

Piacenza

Parma

Réggio

Módena

Garda

Lago Maggiore

Lago di Como

PIEMONTE

LOMBARDIA

EMILIA

PROVENCE

DAUPHINÉ

HAUTES-ALPES

ALPES-MARITIMES

BOUCHES-DU-RHÔNE

Corse

Bastia

Ajaccio

Elba

Piombino

Portoferráio

Arcipelago Toscano

Montecristo

Giglio

Pianosa

Gorgona

Capraia

CORSE-DU-SUD

HAUTE-CORSE

Toscana

Côte d'Azur

ILES D'HYÈRES

Projection: Conical with two standard parallels

East from Greenwich

1 : 2 000 000

Scale bars: 10 0 10 20 30 40 50 miles; 10 0 10 20 30 40 50 60 70 80 km

A   B   C   D   E   F

1   2   3   4   5   6

CORSE   **CORSICA**

Iles Sanguinaires
G. d'Ajaccio
Tárgoo
Petreto
Solenzara
C. di Muro
Levie
Zonza
Favone
Propriano
2136
Sartène
Porto-Vecchio
Bonifacio
I. de Cavallo
Iles Cerbicales
CORSE-DU-SUD

Bouches de Bonifacio
Santa Teresa Gallura
Maddalena
Caprera
La Maddalena

Asinara
Punta dello Scorno
Golfo dell'
Asinara
Costa
Smeralda

Coghinas
Àggius
Calangiánus
Golfo Aranci
Pto. Cervo
Arzachena
Tàvolara
Porto Tórres
Témpio Pausania
1362
Olbia
G. di Ólbia
Sorso
M. Limbara
Sássari
Sennori
Uschiri
Ósilo
Tanaunella
Fértilia
Íttiri
L. di Coghinas
Posada
Alghero
Ozieri
Pattada
Villanova
1259
Buddusò
Monteleone
Bonorva
Siniscóla
Bitti
C. Comino
Bosa
Orune
Temo
Oruné
Macomer
Nuoro
Dorgali
Ghilarza
Oliena
Golfo di
L. del Tirso
Fonni
Orosei
SARDEGNA
Sórgono
Baunei
C. di Monte Santu
C. Mannu
S A R D E G N A
Monti del
Oristano
Láconi
1834
Gennargentu
M. Arci
812
Arbatax
Arborea
Teralba
Lónusei
Golfo di
Oristano
Núrri
Jerzu
SARDINIA
Mándas
Gúspini
S. Gavino
Sanluri
Senorbì
Monreale
Muravera
Arbus
1236
Gonnosfanádiga
Villacidro
S. Vito
C. Pécora
M. Línas
Serramanna
C. Ferrato
Fluminimaggiore
Donianova
Assémini
Sinnai
1069
Iglésias
Sestu
Selárgius
Portoscuso
Siliqua
Gonnesa
Quartu Sant'Elena
Carloforte
Carbonia
Serpentara
San Pietro
1116
Cágliari
C. Carbonara
Sant'Antíoco
Santadi
Golfo di
Sant'
Cágliari
Antíoco
Porto Botte
Pula
C. Spartivento
Teulada
G. di Pálmas

T Y R R H E N I A N

S E A

3719

3589

Ústica

ROMA
(Rome)
Tívoli
Vatican City
Conca
Fregene
Subiaco
del Fúcino
Palestrina
Rocca di
Frascati
Papa
Tiber
Velletri
Valmontone
Anagni
Alatri
Véroli
Lido di Óstia
Lazio
Cori
Ferentino
Sora
(Lido di Roma)
Albano
Cisterna di Latina
Ceccano
Ceprano
Monte S. Giova
Prática
Aprilia
Ceccano
Frosinone
di Mare
Ánzio
Sezze
Priverno
Sonnino
Pontecor
Nettuno
Latina
Fondi
1533
Cássino
Pontínia
Sabáudia
Formia
Minturno
Terracina
Gaeta
Garigliano
Monte Círceo
Cariñ
541
Golfo di
Palmarola
Zannone
Mondragone
Volturno
Gaeta
283
Ponza
Casal
Ísole
Giúglia
Ponziane
Ventotene
Prc
788
Ischia
(Napl)

C. San Vito
Castellammare del Golfo
Favarotta
Terrasini
PALERMO
Levanzo
C. Gallo
Bagheria
1110
G. di Carini
Monreale
Trápani
Érice
Partinico
Mísilmeri
Términ Im
Alcamo
S. Giuseppe
Marineo
Ísole Égadi
Maréttimo
Píceco
Calatafimi
Camporeale
Favignana
Salemi
Corleone
1613
Stagnone
Gibellina
Prizzi
Lércara
Alía
Marsala
Partanna
Bisacquino
Bélice
Sambuca
di Sicília
SIC
Castelvetrano
Mazara
Menfi
Búrgio
Mussomeli
Cate
del Vallo
Campobello di Mazara
Sciacca
Caltabellotta
Castelterm.
San Catal
Ribera
Platani
Calta
Cattólica Eraclea
Racalmuto
Canic
Siculiana
Rafadali
Aragona
Naro
Porto Empédocle
Favara
Sicilian Channel
Palma di Montechiaro
Agrigento
Campobello
Lic
Palma

Iles de la
Galite

Bizerte
C. Blanc
Cani
(Binzert)
C. Serrat
Plane
Menzel–Bourguiba
Zembra
Mateur
El Kala
Golfe de Tunis
C. Bon
Tabarka
Téboursuk
Béja
TUNIS
Halq el Oued
ALGERM
Menzel–
Bou Salem
Béja
Temime
Kélibia
Medjerda
Soliman
Pantelleria
T U N I S I A
Nabeul
836
Pantelleria (It.)
Téboursouk
Hammamet
1319
Zaghouan
M E D I T E
Ma

Projection: Conical with two standard parallels
East from Greenwich

ft   m
9000   3000
6000   2000
4500   1500
3000   1000
1200   400
600   200
0   0
200   600
2000   6000
4000   12 000
m   ft

1 : 2 000 000

10 0 10 20 30 40 50 miles
10 0 10 20 30 40 50 60 70 80 km

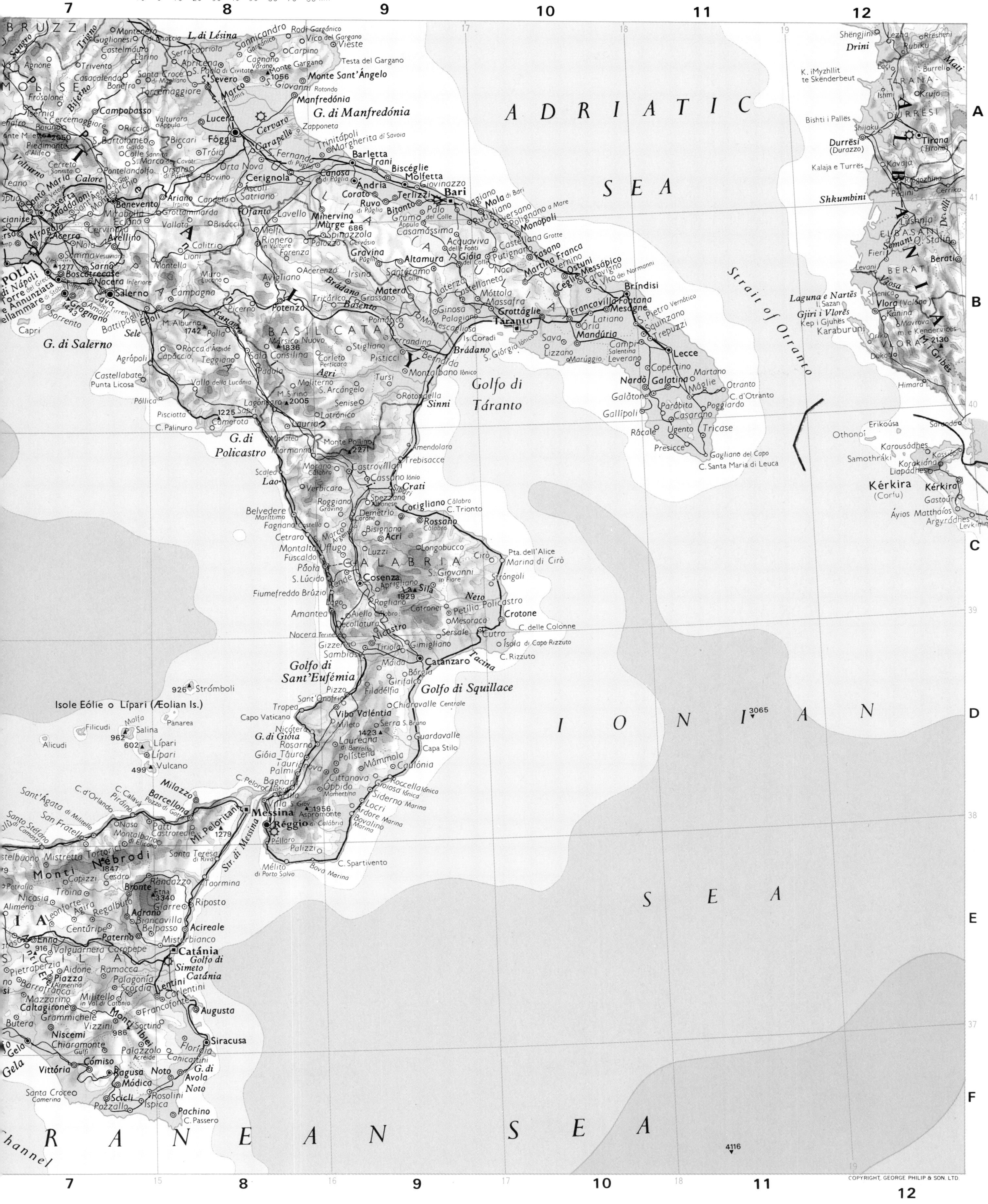

7   8   9   10   11   12

ADRIATIC

SEA

A

IONIAN

SEA

MEDITERRANEAN SEA

G. di Manfredónia

Golfo di Táranto

Golfo di Sant'Eufémia

Golfo di Squillace

Strait of Otranto

Isole Eólie o Lípari (Æolian Is.)

ABRUZZI
MOLISE
BASILICATA
CALABRIA
SICILIA
ALBANIA

Fóggia
Barletta
Trani
Bisceglie
Molfetta
Bari
Brindisi
Lecce
Táranto
Gallípoli
Otranto
Cosenza
Crotone
Catanzaro
Réggio
Messina
Catánia
Siracusa
Kérkira (Corfu)
Tiranë (Tiróna)
Durrёs (Durazzo)
Vlorё (Valóna)

Golfo di Catánia

Str. di Messina

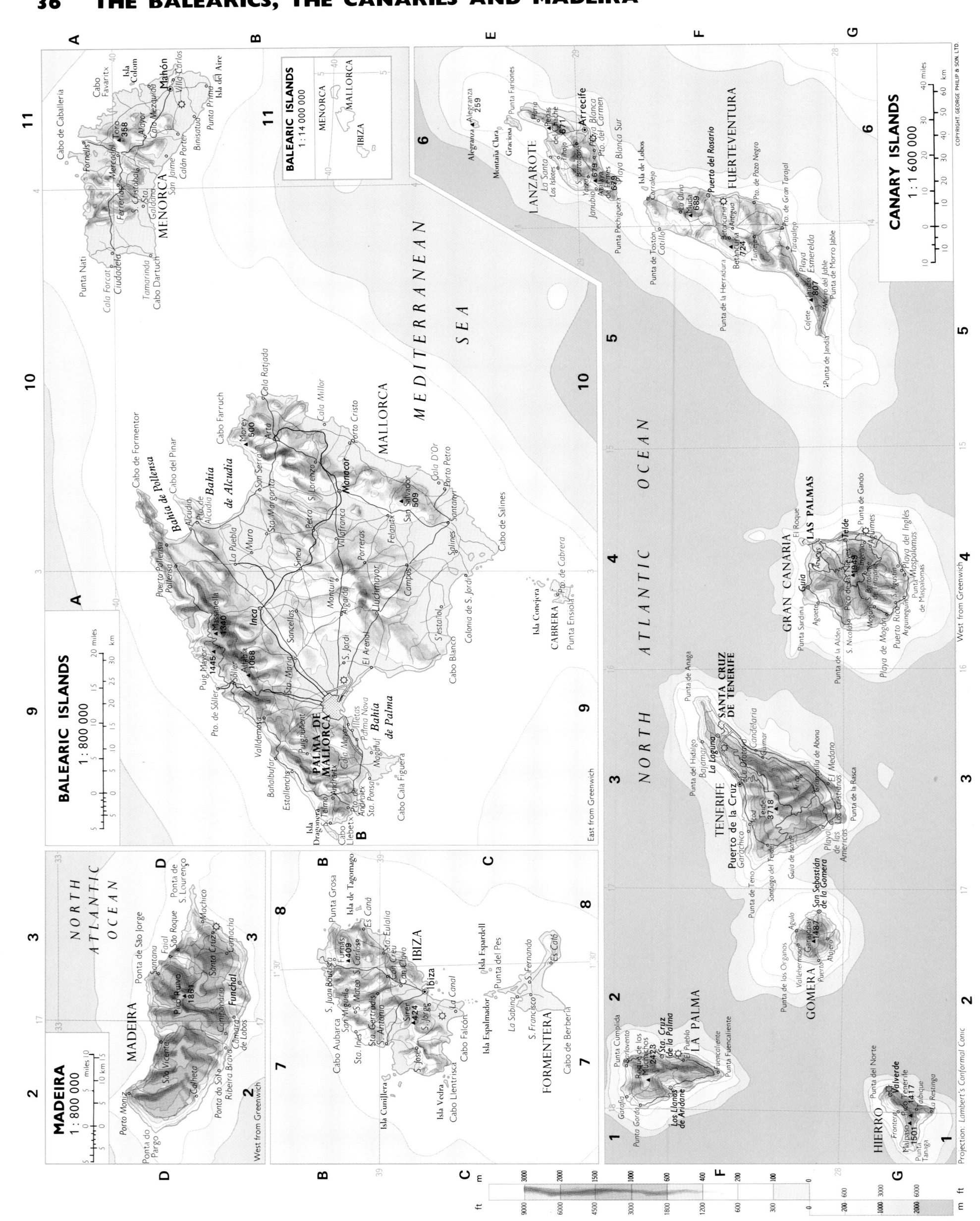

BALEARIC ISLANDS
1:14 000 000

MENORCA

MALLORCA

IBIZA

MENORCA

Cabo de Caballeria
Isla Colom
Cabo Favaritx
Mahón
Villa Carlos
Punta Prima
Isla del Aire
Cabo Mezquida
Alayor
Toro
358
Mercadal
Ferrerias
Sta.
Cristobal
San Jaime
Calan Porter
Binisalta
Galdana
Tamarinda
Cabo Dartuch
Ciudadela
Cala Forcat
Punta Nati

MALLORCA

Cabo de Formentor
Cabo del Pinar
Puerto Pollensa
Bahía de Pollensa
Pollensa
Alcudia
Pto. de Alcudia
Bahía de Alcudia
La Puebla
Muro
Sta. Margarita
Cabo Farruch
Morey
500
Arta
S. Lorenzo
Cala Ratjada
Cala Millor
Manacor
Porto Cristo
Cala D'Or
San Salvador
509
Santany
Porto Petro
Santany
Felanitx
Villafranca
Porreras
Luchmayor
Campos
Cabo de Salines
Salines
S'Estañol
Cabo Blanco
Colonia de S. Jordí
Colonia de S. Jordi

MALLORCA

Pto. de Sóller
Puig Mayor
1445
Alfabia
1068
Sóller
Sta. Maria
Inca
Sancellas
Sineu
Algaida
Montuiri
Petra
Soller
Valldemosa
Estallenchs
Banalbufar
Pollensa
Bunola
Andratx
Pto. de Andratx
Sta. Ponsa
Cabo Cala Figuera
Isla Dragonera
S. Telmo
Cabo Llebetx
PALMA DE MALLORCA
Puigpuñent
Magaluf
Palma Nova
Illetas
Cala Mayor
El Arenal
Bahía de Palma
Galilea
944

BALEARIC ISLANDS
1:800 000

MEDITERRANEAN SEA

CABRERA
Isla Conejera
Punta Ensiolá
Pto. de Cabrera
Isla Dragonera

MADEIRA
1:800 000

NORTH ATLANTIC OCEAN

MADEIRA

Porto Moniz
Ponta do Pargo
Ponta do Sol
São Vicente
Santana
Faial
São Roque
Machico
Ponta de S. Lourenço
Pico Ruivo
1861
Camacha
Santa Cruz
Funchal
Câmara de Lobos
Ribeira Brava
Calheta
Campanário
Ponta de São Jorge
Ponta do Sol
West from Greenwich

IBIZA

Punta Grosa
Isla de Tagomago
Cabo Aubarca
S. Juan Bautista
San Miguel
S. Carlos
Sta. Eulalia
Es Cand
S. Mateo
S. Lorenzo
420
Sta. Inés
Sta. Gertrudis
Conejera
Con Clavo
S. Antonio
Sines
424
IBIZA
Ibiza
S. Jorge
S. José
La Canal
Cabo Falcón
Isla Espardell
Isla Espalmador
Punta del Pes
Es Cana

FORMENTERA

La Sabina
S. Francisco
S. Fernando
La Mola
Cabo de Berbería
Isla Cunillera
Isla Vedra
Cabo Llentrisca

CANARY ISLANDS
1:1 600 000

LANZAROTE

Alegranza
259
Montaña Clara
Graciosa
Punta Fariones
Punta Farallones
Arrecife
Haria
Yaiza
Janubio
Playa Blanca
Pto. del Carmen
Pto. Blanco Sur
Los Islotes
La Santa
Tinajo

FUERTEVENTURA

Isla de Lobos
Corralejo
Puerto del Rosario
La Oliva
689
Betancuria
807
Antigua
Tuineje
Pájara
Punta de la Herradura
Punta de Jandía
Punta de Toston
Cotillo
Pozo Negro
Pto. de Gran Tarajal
Tarajalejo
Esmerelda
Playa
Cofete
Jandía
Morro Jable
Punta de Morro Jable

GRAN CANARIA

El Roque
LAS PALMAS
Guía
Telde
Arucas
Pico de las Nieves
1949
Ingenio
Agüimes
Punta Sardina
Punta de Gando
Agaete
S. Nicolás
Gáldar
Tejeda
Mogán
Maspalomas
Playa del Inglés
Punta Maspalomas
Puerto Rico
Arguineguín
Aguaete
Playa de Maspalomas
Punta de la Aldea
West from Greenwich

TENERIFE

Punta de Anaga
SANTA CRUZ DE TENERIFE
La Laguna
Bajamar
Tacoronte
La Orotava
Teide
3718
Icod
Garachico
Puerto de la Cruz
Candelaria
Güímar
Fasnia
Arico
El Medano
Punta de la Rasca
Playa de las Américas
Los Cristianos
Guía de Isora
Santiago del Teide
Punta de Teno
Punta del Hidalgo

GOMERA

San Sebastián de la Gomera
Agulo
Hermigua
Vallehermoso
1487
Chipude
Punta de los Organos

HIERRO

Valverde
Frontera
Malpaso
1501
Pico de Tenerife
1417
Sabinosa
Tamaduste
Punta del Norte
Punta de la Restinga

LA PALMA

Punta Cumplida
Sta. Cruz de la Palma
Barlovento
Roque de los Muchachos
2423
Garafía
El Pueblo
Los Llanos de Aridane
Tazacorte
Punta Gorda
Fuencaliente
Punta Fuencaliente

NORTH ATLANTIC OCEAN

Projection: Lambert's Conformal Conic

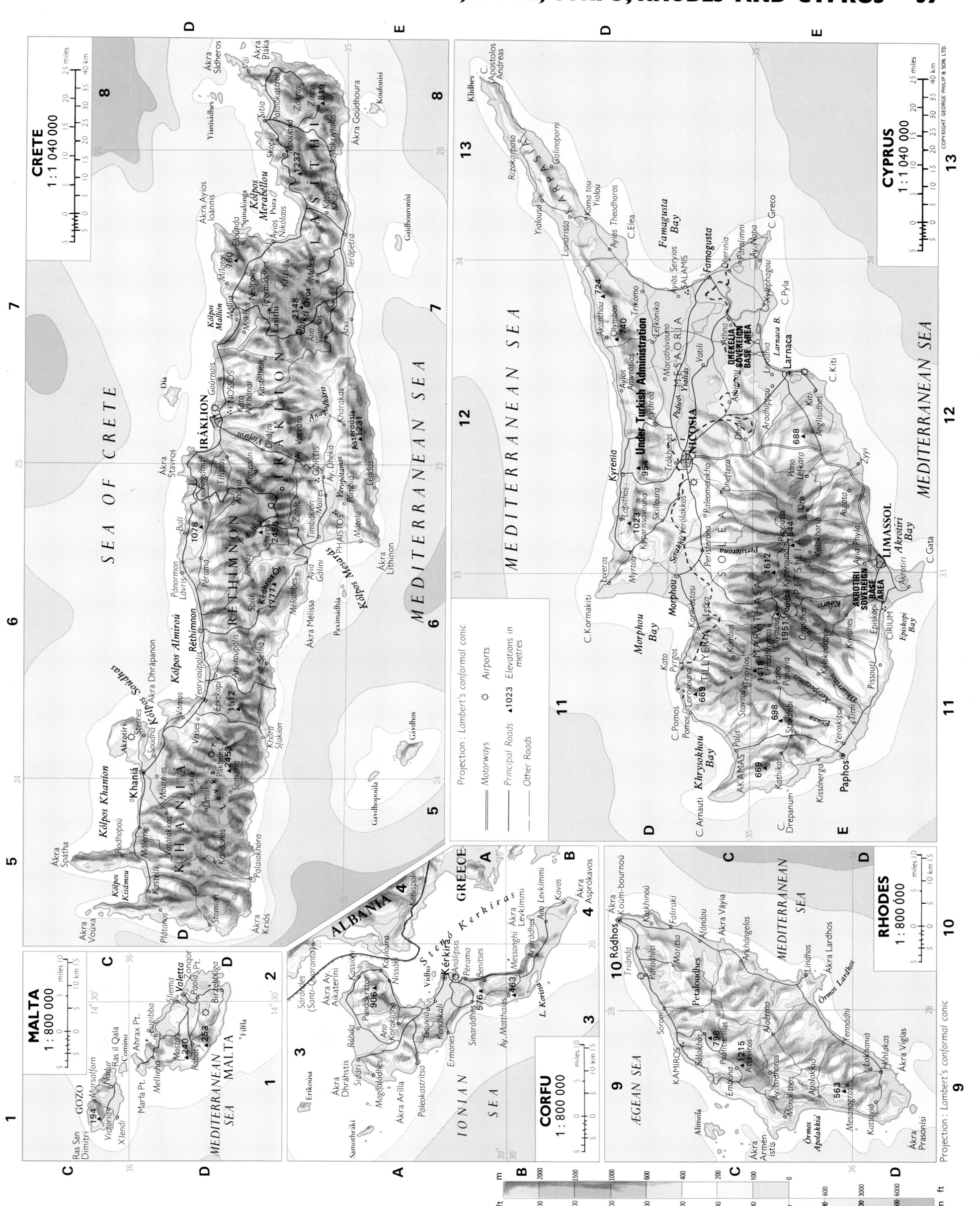

CRETE
1:1 040 000

25 miles
40 km

SEA OF CRETE

Akra Sidheros
Akra Plaka
Palaiokastron
Zakros
849
Zirós
Moulianá
Skopi
Sitía
1237
Yiannisádhes
LASÍTHI
Makriyialós
Akra Goudhoura
Koufonisi
Ierápetra
Ziros
Ayios Ioánnis
Kolpos
Merabéllou
Spinalónga
Eloúnda
Ayios Nikólaos
Kritsá
Neápolis
760
Milátos
Khanía
LASÍTHI
2148
Dhíkti Óros
Ano
Viánnos
Arví
Kolpos
Mallion
Mália
Mokhós
Nerokoúros
Tzermiádes
Gournais
IRÁKLION
Knossós
Kato
Arkhánai
Kastélli
Pezá
Kastélli
Thrapsanón
Ay. Mýrus
Anópouli
1231
IRÁKLION
Dhía
Ástérousía
Khóndros
Yiófyros
Ano
Viánnos
Akra Stavros
Arkalokhóri
Asteroúsia
Páraspori
Ay. Dhéka
Viánnos
1078
Venerato
Tílissos
GÓRTIS
Pérama
Ay. Dhéka
Pýrgos
Tympáki
Moíres
Péros
Aytá
Pómbia
Léndas
Kolpos Mésa PHAISTÓS
Akra
Lithinon
RÉTHIMNON
2456
Spíli
Amári
Timbáki
Ayía
Gálini
Melámbes
Páraspori
Paximádhia
Gaidhouronísi
Akra Ayios Ioánnis

MEDITERRANEAN   SEA

Panormon
Lávris
Pánormon
RÉTHIMNON
Kolpos
Réthimnon
Ídhi Óros
2456
Anóyioudópolis
Seliá
Ayvroupolis
Georyioúpolis
Episkopí
Vrýses
1512
Vámos
Khóra
Sfakíon
Akra Dhrápanon
Soudhá
Kolpos Khanión
Soudhías
Akrotíri
Khaniá
Stérnes
Mourniés
2454
Omalós
LEFKÁ ÓRI
Pelékanos
Kándanos
Palaiókhora
Akra Kríos
Akra
Spátha
Rodhopoú
Máleme
Stómion
Kolpos
Kíssamou
Kastélli
Plátanos
Akra Vouxa

MALTA
1:800 000

10 miles
10 km 15

GOZO
Ras San Dimitri
194
Xlendi
Marsalforn
Victoria
Nadur
Xghajra
Comino
Mellieha
Marfa Pt.
Bugibba
Ahrax Pt.
Mosta
240
Rabat
253
Filfla
Naxxar
Sliema
Valetta
St. Paul's B.
Qormi
Paola
Birzebbuga
Marsaxlokk
MALTA

MEDITERRANEAN SEA

CORFU
1:800 000

10 miles
10 km 15

GREECE

ALBANIA

Saránde
(Santi-Quaranta)

IONIAN
SEA

Stenó Kerkíras
Kérkira
Andípsis
Pérama
Benítses
Messonghi
Akra
Levkímmi
Kávos
Akra
Asprókavos

Kérkira
Kassiópi
Kalloúra
Nissáki
906
Pandokrátor
576
Sidhári
Róda
Ano
Korakianá
Gouviá
Kondokáli
Ávl. Akaterini
Sinaráddhes
Áy. Matthaíos
L. Koríssa
 Áyl. Déka

Erikoúsa
Akra
Dhráhstis
Magouládhes
Palaiokastrítsa
Pélekas
Ermónes
Akra
Arílla
Samothráki
Poleokastritsa

AEGEAN
SEA

RHODES
1:800 000

10 miles
10 km 15

Ródhos
Akra Koúm-bournoú
Tríánda
Kritiká
Kallithéa
Fáliraki
Maritsa
Paradhísi
Afándou
Akra Arkhángelos
Kámiros
798
Profítis Ilías
Arkhángelos
Soroní
1215
Atávyros
Embóna
Ápollon
Lákhania
Láerma
Lárdhos
Ormos Lárdhos
Lindhos
Akra Lárdhos
Kattaviá
563
Mesanagrós
Apolakkiá
Ormos
Apolakkiá
Akra Prasonísi
Akra Viglás
Alimniá
Akra Armenístis

MEDITERRANEAN
SEA

CYPRUS
1:1 040 000

25 miles
40 km

Kildhes
C. Apostolos
Andreas
Galinóporni
Rizokárpaso
Komatou
Yialou
KARPAS
Yialoúsa
Leonárisso
Ayios Theodhoros
C. Elea
Akanthou
724
Ayios Seryios
C. Andreas
Trikomo
SALAMIS
Famagusta
Famagusta
Bay
Under Turkish Administration
740
Olymbos
Lefkóniko
Vatili
MESAORIA
Lápithos
Kyrenia
Ayios
Amvrosios
Marathóvouno
C. Greco
Ayía Nápa
Skilloúra
NICOSIA
Paralímni
Dherinia
Dhekélia
DHEKÉLIA
SOVEREIGN
BASE AREA
1023
954
Trakhónas
Pedhiaíos
Vatili
Lýsi
Anglisídhes
Lárnaca
688
Kyrenia
Myrtoú
Kyrá
Morphou
Morphou
Bay
Skouriotissa
Peristeróna
Kythréa
Dhflios
Péra
Lefkara
C. Kiti
C. Kormakíti
Kato
Pýrgos
Sol Éa
Kakopetriá
Kalokhorió
Ora
Asgáta
Zýyi
1951
Tróodos
Prodhromos
1612
Pitsillá
LIMASSOL
Akrótiri
Bay
C. Gata
TILLYERÍA
Pólis
Khrysokhou
Bay
669
Kambós
Kykko
669
1418
Pedhoulas
Plátres
MARATHASA
Kyperounda
Pano
Panayia
Ay. Ioánnis
AKROTÍRI
SOVEREIGN
BASE AREA
CIRIUM
Episkopí
Bay
C. Pomos
Pomós
Stavrós tis
Psókas
Pissoúri
Dhiárizos
698
Strakiá
Kelokédhara
Yeroskípou
C. Arnauti
AKAMAS
Kritoú
Kathikas
Yeroskípou
Kissónerga
Páphos
C. Drepanum
Akra Prasonísi

MEDITERRANEAN   SEA

Projection: Lambert's conformal conic

Motorways
Principal Roads
▲1023 Elevations in metres
Airports ✷
Other Roads

Projection: Lambert's conformal conic

m   ft
2000   6000
1500   4500
1000   3000
600   1800
400   1200
200   600
100   300
0   0

m   ft
0   0
200   600
3000
6000

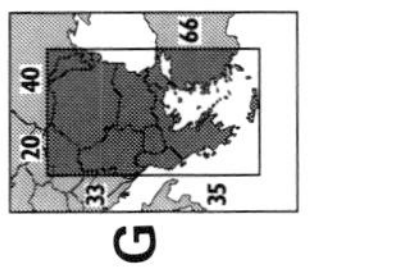

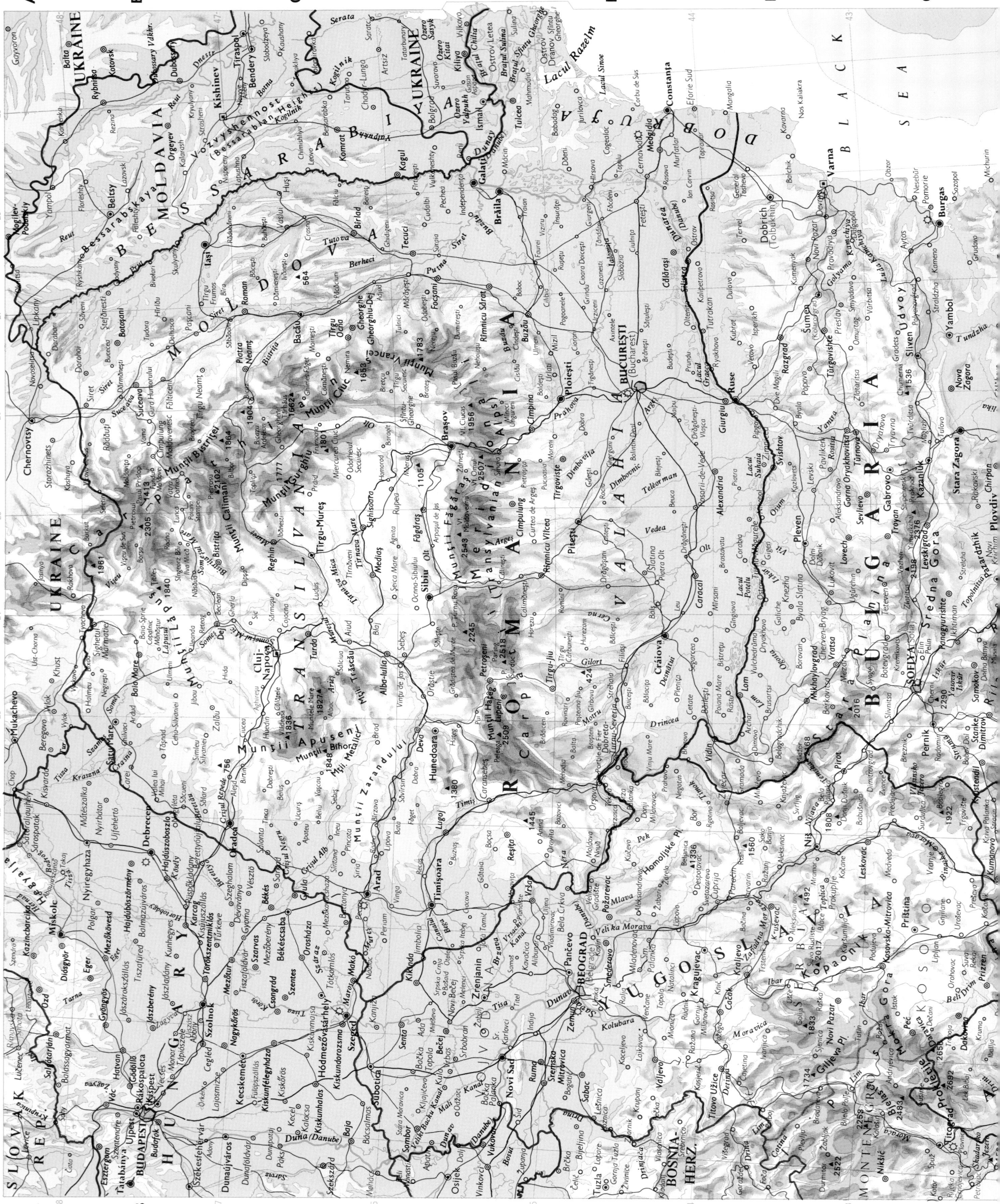

UKRAINE

MOLDAVIA

BESSARABIA

MOLDOVA

SLOVAK REP.

HUNGARY

TRANSILVANIA

CARPATII MERIDIONALI

VALAHIA

DOBRUJA

BULGARIA

YUGOSLAVIA

SRBIJA

KOSOVO

CRNA GORA

BOSNIA-HERZ.

BLACK SEA

BUCUREŞTI (Bucharest)

BUDAPEST

BEOGRAD

SOFIYA

Constanţa

Varna

Burgas

Kishinev

Iaşi

Braşov

Cluj-Napoca

Timişoara

Arad

Craiova

Ploieşti

Galaţi

Braila

Ruse

Pleven

Stara Zagora

Plovdiv

Niš

Priština

Novi Sad

Debrecen

Miskolc

Szeged

Mukachevo

Chernovtsy

Muntii Vrancei

Munţii Făgăraş 2543

Muntii Bihorului

Munţii Apuseni

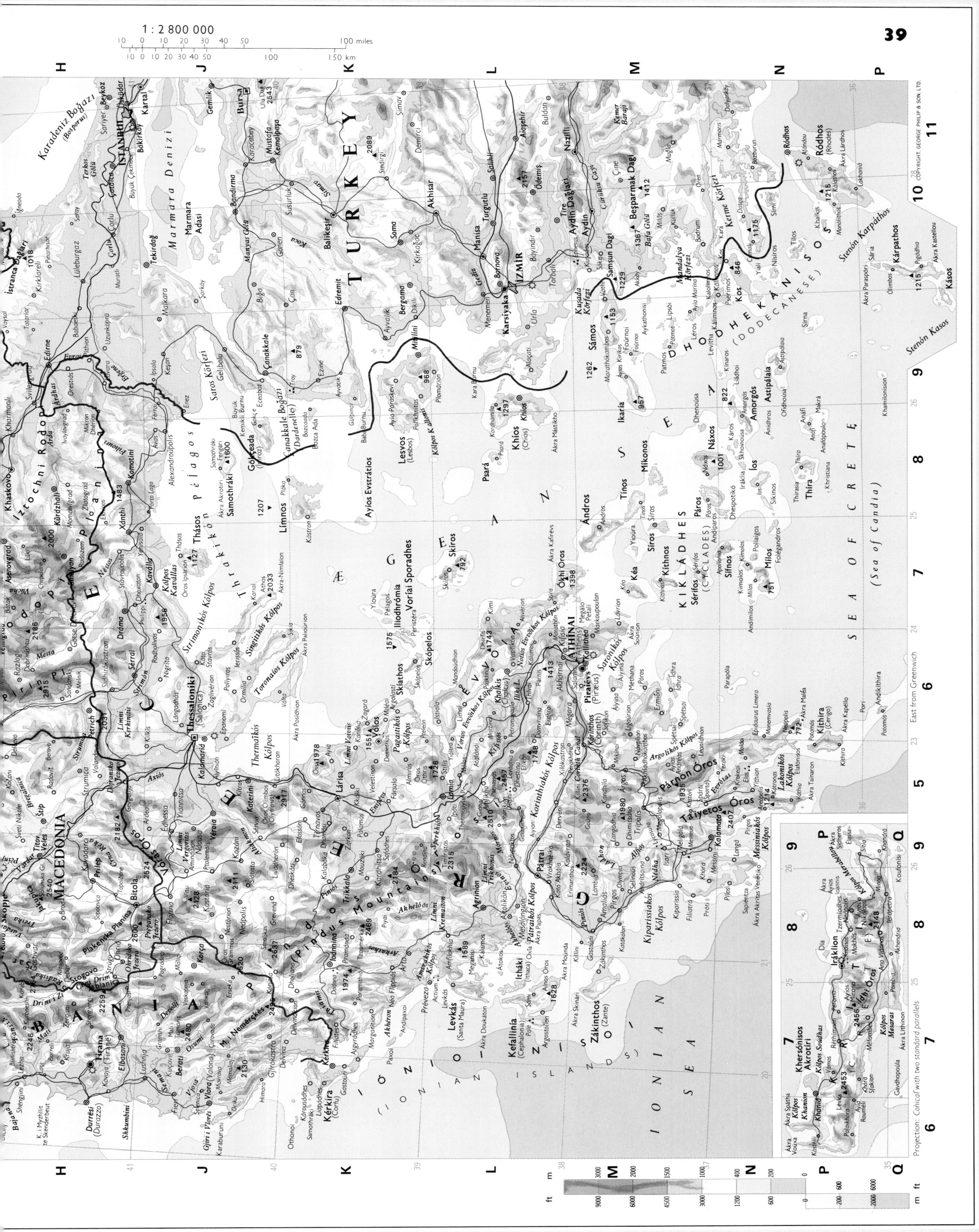

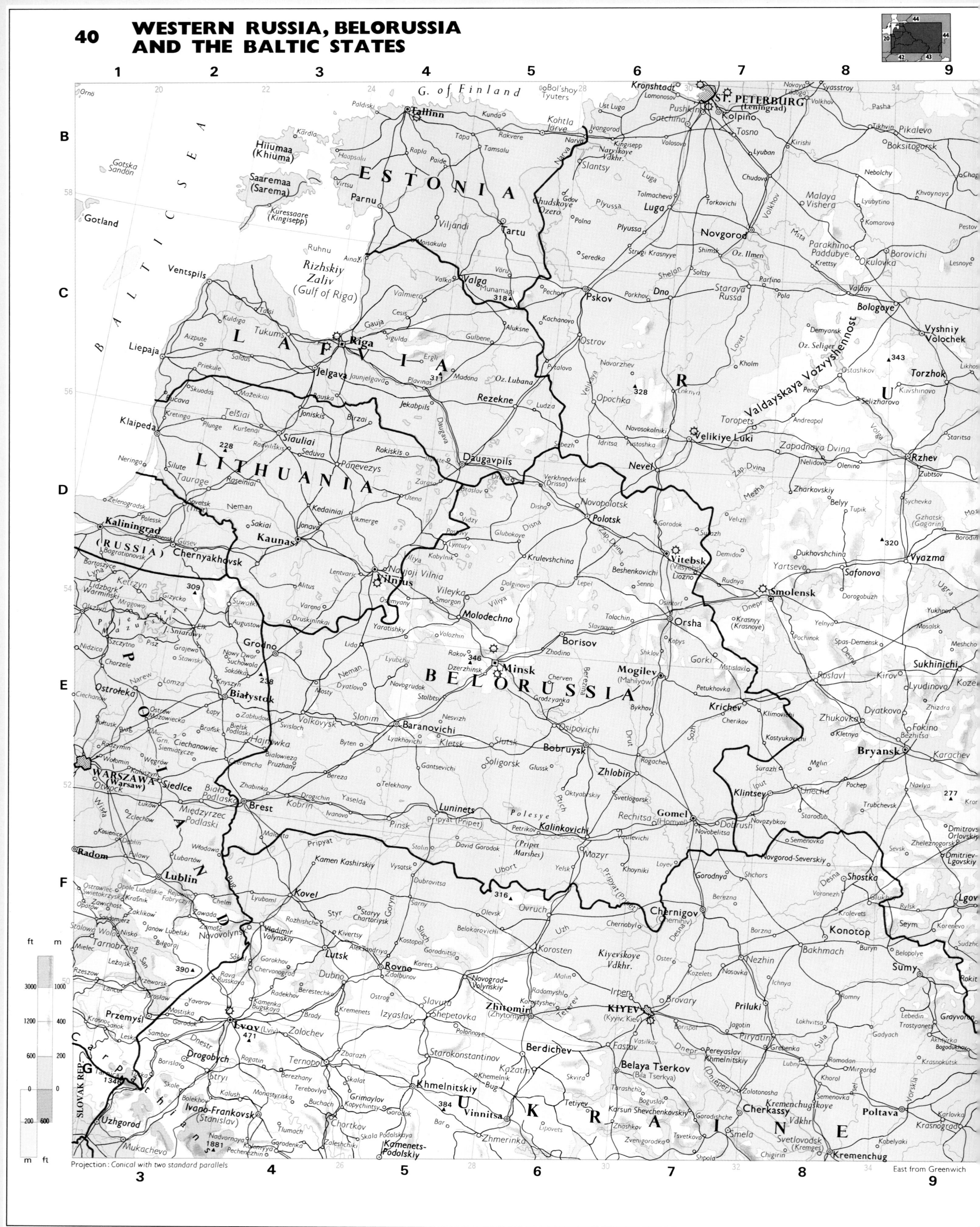

1 : 4 000 000

50   0   50   100 miles

50   0   50   100   150 km

10   11   12   13   14   15   16   17   18

B

Oz. Beloye
Belozersk
Kirillov
Uste   Dyakovskaya
Kharovsk
Totma
Nikolsk
293
Krasnoye
Murashi
Nagorsk
Vyatka
Peskovka
Zalazna
329

Cherepovets   Chebsara   **Vologda**   Sokol   Sukhona   Igoshevo   Pyshchug   Vokhma   Khalturin   **Vyatka**   Belaya Kholunitsa   Chernaya Kholunitsa   Omutninsk

58

Ustyuzhna   Ozero Kubenskoye   Shekana   Gryazovets   Soligalich   Suday   Kologriv   Vokhma   Chernovskoye   Kirovo-Chepetsk   Zuyevka   Falenki   Yar   Glazov

Vesyegonsk   Rybinskoye   Vodokhranilishche   Vokhtoga   Buy   Antropovo   Manturovo   Sharya   Leninskoye   Kotelnich   Kumeny   Novovyatsk   Uni

C
Krasnyy Kholm   Breytovo   Danilov   Lyubim   Neya   Vetluga   Shakhunya   Sovetsk   Urzhum   UDMURT REP.

Sonkovo   Volga   Kostromskoye Vdkhr.   Makaryev   Unzha   Uren   Yaransk   Arkul   Medvedok   Mozhga

Rybinsk (Andropov)   **Kostroma**   Zavolzhsk   Gorkovskoye   Vdkhr.   Krasnyye Baki   Tursha   Shurma   Malmyzh

Yaroslavl   Nerekhta   Privolzhsk   **Kineshma**   Yuryevets   Vetluzhskiy   Yoshkar Ola   Arsk   Kukmor   Vyatskiye Polyany

Uglich   Furmanov   **Vichuga**   Rodniki   Semenov   Kozmodemyansk   M   Krasnogorskiy   **56**

Kalyazin   Rostov   Gavrilov Yam   Komsomolsk   **Ivanovo**   Kokhma   **Shuya**   Chkolovsk   Gorodets   Pravdinsk   **Cheboksary**   A   **Kazan**   Nizhnekamsk

Kimry   Neri   Teykovo   Teza   Yuzha   Zavolzhye   Borisoglebskiy   **Nizhniy Novgorod (Gorkiy)**   CHUVASH   Zelenodolsk   TATAR

D
Dubna   Pereslavl Zalesskiy   Yuryev-Polskiy   Suzdal   **Kovrov**   Balakhna   Lyskovo   Yadrin   Kanash   REP.   Chistopol

Klin   Aleksandrov   Kolchugino   **Dzerzhinsk**   Volodarsk   Gorbatov   Pyana   Sergach   Shumerlya   Kuybyshev

Zelenograd   **Kaliningrad**   **Vladimir**   Pokrov   Sobinka   **Pavlovo**   Bogorodsk   Alatyr   Kuybyshevskoye Vdkhr.

MOSKVA (Moscow)   **Noginsk**   **Orekhovo-Zuyevo**   **Gus-Khrustalnyy**   **Murom**   Mukhtolovo   **Arzamas**   235   Gagino   Ardatov   Nurlat

Podolsk   **Yegoryevsk**   Melenki   Vyksa   Kulebaki   Lukoyanov   Pervomaysk   REP.

Serpukhov   Zaraysk   **Kolomna**   Spas-Klepiki   Kasimov   Yelatma   Sarova   Krasnoslobodsk   **Simbirsk**   **Dimitrovgrad**   **54**

Kaluga   Aleksin   Venev   **Ryazan**   Shilovo   Sasovo   Temnikov   Moksha   Romodanovo   Karsun   Sengiley

Tula   **Novomoskovsk**   Ryazhsk   Shatsk   Bednodemyanovsk   MORDOVIAN REP.   **Saransk**   Inza   Barysh   **Togliatti**   **SAMARA (Kuybyshev)**

E
Shchekino   Uzlovaya   Skopin   Ukholovo   Nizhniy Lomov   **Ruzayevka**   Bazarnyy Syzgan   Narodychie   Novokuybyshevsk

Orel   Novosil   Yefremov   Dankov   Chaplygin   Morshansk   Kamenka   **Penza**   **Kuznetsk**   351   **Syzran**   Chapayevsk

Yelets   Lev Tolstoy   **Michurinsk**   Kirsanov   Serdobsk   Petrovsk   Khvalynsk   **Volsk**   **Balakovo**   **52**

Lipetsk   Gryazi   **Tambov**   Kotovsk   Rtishchevo   Atkarsk   Balanda   **Saratov**   **Pokrovsk**   Pugachev

F
Semiluki   **Voronezh**   Zherdevka   Uvarovo   Arkadak   **Balashov**   Krasnoarmeysk   Volgogradskoye Vdkhr.   Krasnyy Kut

Belgorod   Gubkin   Liski (Georgiu-Dezh)   Buturlinovka   239   Uryupinsk   Novoannenskiy   358   **Kamyshin**   Nikolayevsk   Pallasovka   **50**

Novyy Oskol   Pavlovsk   Kalach   Buzuluk   Yelan   Kumylzhenskaya   Bykovo   Kaysatskoye   Aleksandrov Gay

Kharkov   Kupyansk   Kantemirovka   Boguchar   Don   Serafimovich   Frolovo   **KAZAKHSTAN**

G
Starobelsk   Millerovo   Kletskiy (Kletskaya)   Dubovka   Elton

Rubezhnoye   **Volgograd (Stalingrad)**   Krasnoslobodsk   Kapustin Yar

10   11   12   13   14   15   16

COPYRIGHT. GEORGE PHILIP & SON. LTD.

UKRAINE

ROMANIA

MOLDAVIA

BULGARIA

BLACK SEA

AZOVSKOYE MORE (Sea of Azov)

Selected place names

Lvov (Lviv), Rovno, Aleksandriya Korets, Gorodnitsa, Korosten, Nezhin, Bakhmach, Belopolye, Sudzha, Staryy Oskol, Dubno, Chervonograd, Zdolbunov, Novograd-Volynskiy, Kiyevskoye Vdkhr., Oster, Kozelets, Nosovka, Ichnya, Romny, Okhtyrka, Rokitnoye, Belgorod, Volchansk

Zolochev, Brody, Kremenets, Izyaslav, Slavuta, Shepetovka, Zhitomir (Zhytomyr), Irpen, Brovary, KIYEV (Kyyiv, Kiev), Priluki, Lokhvitsa, Gadyach, Trostyanets, Grayvoron, Kharkov (Kharkiv), Kupyansk

Ternopol, Zbarazh, Starokonstantinov, Kazatin, Berdichev, Fastov, Vasilkov, Dnepr, Pereyaslav-Khmelnitskiy, Lubny, Mirgorod, Khorol, Poltava, Karlovka, Krasnograd, Balakleya, Izyum, Rubezhnoye

Ivano-Frankovsk (Stanislav), Chortkov, Vinnitsa, Zhmerinka, Belaya Tserkov (Bila Tserkva), Tetiyev, Tarashcha, Boguslav, Korsun Shevchenkovskiy, Gorodishche, Cherkassy, Kremenchugskoye Vdkhr., Semenovka, Kobelyaki, Orel, Lozovaya, Slavyansk, Kramatorsk, Artemovsk, Lisichansk

Chernovtsy (Chernivtsi), Kamenets-Podolskiy, Mogilev-Podolskiy, Soroki, Tulchin, Gaysin, Uman, Novomirgorod, Znamenka, Smela, Chigirin, Kamenka, Aleksandrovka, Zvenigorodka, Tsvetkovo, Znamenka, Kirovograd, Dnepropetrovsk, Pavlograd, Konstantinovka, Gorlovka, Yenakiyevo, Makeyevka, Donetsk (Stalino)

BELTSY, Dubossary Vdkhr., Rybnitsa, Kotovsk, Balta, Ananyev, Pervomaysk, Bolshaya Vradyevka, Novoukrainka, Pomoshnaya, Dolinskaya, Pyatikhatki, Verchovtsevo, Dneprodzerzhinsk, Novomoskovsk, Krivoy Rog (Kryvyy Rih), Nikopol, Marganets, Orekhov, Pologi, Volnovakha, Mariupol (Zhdanov), Novoazovsk

Iasi, Tirgu-Frumos, Ungeny, Kishinev (Chişinău), Orgeyev, Dubossary, Tiraspol, Razdelnaya, Tsebrikovo, Berezovka, Voznesensk, Ingul, Novy Bug, Apostolovo, Ordzhonikidze, Kamenka-Dneprovskaya, Malaya Belozerka, Bolshoy Tokmak, Molochansk, Melitopol, Berdyansk

Bendery, Komrat, Orgeyev, Bessarabka, Dnestrovskiy, Belgorod, Odessa (Odesa), Ilyichevsk, Ovidiopol, Ochakov, Nikolayev (Mykolaiv), Zhovtnevoye (Oktyabrskoye), Snigirevka, Ingulets, Berislav, Kakhovskoye Vdkhr., Kakhovka, Novaya Kakhovka, Kherson, Golaya Pristen, Skadovsk, Akimovka, Primorskoye (Nogaysk), Priazovskoye, Taganrog, Yeysk, Primorsko-Akhtarsk

ROMANIA: Suceava, Vatra Dornei, Piatra-Neamt, Bacău, Roman, Braşov (Oraşul Stalin), Buzău, Braila, Galaţi, Focşani, Tecuci, Vaslui, Huşi, Cahul, Ismail, Kiliya, Vilkovo, Tulcea, Sulina

BUCUREŞTI (Bucharest), Ploieşti, Targovişte, Giurgiu, Ruse (Ruščuk), Calafat, Silistra, Constanţa, Mangalia, Dobrich, Balchik, Nos Kaliakra

BULGARIA: Razgrad, Popovo, Turgovishte, Shumen (Kolarovgrad), Varna, Preslav, Sliven, Chatalka, Balkan, Aitos, Karnobat, Burgas, Yambol, Elkhovo, Kirklareli, Istranca Dağları, İğneada Burnu, Demirköy, Edirne, Uzunköprü, Didhimotikhon, Babaeski, Lüleburgaz, Vize

TURKEY: İstanbul, Üsküdar, Gebze, İzmit, Yalova, İznik Gölü, Gölcük, Adapazari, Sapanca, Akyazi, Bolu, Gerede, Düzce, Çerkeş, Kızılcahamam, Çankırı, Çorum, ANKARA, Çorlu, Tekirdağ, Marmara Denizi (Sea of Marmara), Bandirma, Bursa, Balikesir, Edremit, Gelibolu (Gallipoli)

Zonguldak, Ereğli, Karabük, Kastamonu, Daday, Küre, İnebolu, Sinop, Gerze, Bafra, Samsun, Terme, Ünye, Ordu, Giresun, Amasya, Merzifon, Vezirköprü, Havza, Ladik, Zile, Turhal, Tokat

CRIMEA: Dzhankoi, Krasnogvardeysk, Nizhnegorskiy, Yevpatoriya, Saki, Simferopol, Bakhchisaray, Sevastopol, Balaklava, Yalta, Alushta, Alupka, M. Sarych, Gora Roman-Kosh 1545, Sudak, Belogorsk, Staryy Krym, Feodosiya, Lenino, Vladislavovka, Kerch, Taman, Anapa, Novorossiysk, Gelendzhik

Karkinitskiy Zaliv, Razdolnoye, Chernomorskoye, M. Tarkhankut, Krymskiy P.-ov (Crimea), Arabatskaya Strelka, Biryuchiy, Genichesk, Kerchenskiy Proliv

Spot heights: 2102, 471, 384, 429, 269, 324, 276, 2135, 2211, 2137, 1018, 1261, 2543, 2378, 2565, 2062, 1545, 14

Projection: Conical with two standard parallels

Elevation scale (ft / m)
ft	m
12,000	4000
9000	3000
6000	2000
4500	1500
3000	1000
1200	400
600	200
0	0
600	200
6000	2000

1 : 4 000 000

50 0 50 100 miles
0 50 100 150 km

8 9 10 11 12 13 14 15

KAZAKHSTAN

A

Yelan-Kolenovskiy
Bobrov Povorino Peski Orlov Gay Oz. Chalkar Chalkar
Khrenovoe Talovaya Novokhopersk Samoylovka Krasnoarmeysk Zhirnovsk Krasnyy Kut Novouzensk Dzhambeyty
otayak Liski (Georgiu-Dezh) Uryupinsk Buzuluk Kamyshin Yelan 358 Vozvyshennost Piterka Mergenevskiy Karsha
Ostrogozhsk 239 Novoannenskiy Kukvideve Yar Volgogradskoye Aleksandrov Gay Bol. Uzen Kaztalovka Chapayev
Pavlovsk Kalach Kazanskaya Panfilovo Danilovka Vdkhr. Pallasovka Bol. Uzen Furmanovo Bazartobe
stratovskiy Rossosh Boguchar Veshenskaya Serafimovich Iloulya Bykovo Dzhanybek Antonovka Mykoy
Starobelsk Melovoye Chertkovo Don (Iloulinskaya) B

ovsk Lugansk Millerovo Kletskiy Dubovka Eltan Urda Inderborskiy
adiyevka (Voroshilovgrad) (Kletskaya) Volzhskiy Leninsk Shungay Zelënyy 48
ryanka Kamensk-Shakhtinskiy Morozovsk Volgograd Krasnoslobodsk Kapustin Yar Verkhniy Baskunchak Topol
Krasnodon Sverdlovsk Lenin (Stalingrad) Volga Akhtubinsk Makhambet
orez Krasnyy Luch Belaya Kalitva Krasnoarmeysk (Petropavlovsk) (Yamankhalinka)
Snezhnoye Gukovo Surovikino Kalach na Donu Chernyshkovskiy Vladimirovka Novobogatinskoye
Novoshakhtinsk Shakhty Ust-Donetskiy **RUSSIA** Guryev C
Matveyev Kurgan Kamenolomni Tsimlyansk Kotelnikovo Kaspiyskaya Nizmennost
ganrog Tuzlov Rostov Tsimlyanskoye Volgodonsk Obilnoye Kopanovka -28 Kulyushkino
Azov Novocherkassk Vdkhr. Dubovskoye Yenotayevka Krasnyy Yar
Port Katon Bataysk Bolshaya Martynovka Zavetnoye **KALMYK** Astrakhan Kamyzyak
ashcher Zernograd Manych Konstantinovskiy Remontnoye **REP.** 46
ovskaya Yeya Veselovskoye Sinegorski Proletarskaya Priyutnoye Krasnoye Kirovskiy
Stara- Kushchevskaya Vdkhr. Yegorlykskaya Gigant Oz. Manych- Mumra
minskaya Salsk Gudilo Elista Liman Kultay
Kanevskaya Peschanokopskoye Yegorlyk Divnoye (Stepnoi) Kuma Beloye Ozero D
Pavlovskaya Belaya Krasnogvardeyskoye Leninsk Staryy Biryuzyak
Timashevsk Glina Kalaus Arzgir M. Tyub Karagan Mangyshlakskiy
Tikhoretsk Novoaleksandrovskaya Svetlograd Blagodarnoye Kulaly Zaliv
Korenovsk Izobil'nyy (Petrovskoye) Budennovsk Fort Shevchenko P-ov.
Ust-Labinsk 831 Stavropol Neftekumsk Vladimirovka Mangyshlak 44
Krasnodar Armavir Kuban Nevinnomyssk Blagodarnoye Tyuleniy Aktau
Kurganinsk Kursavka Zelenokumsk O. Chechen
Maykop (Kurgannaya) Labinsk Vorontsovo-Aleksandrovskoye Bryanskoye
Khadyzhensk Apsheronsk Urup Cherkessk Mineralnyye Vody Aleksandriyskaya
ubga Neftegorsk Dakhovskaya Georgiyevsk Lopatin
apse Yessentuki Pyatigorsk Prokhladnyy Mozdok Kizlyar C
Bol'shoy Kislovodsk Nalchik Nartkala Malgobek **CHECHENO-** Terek A
Sochi Krasnaya Polyana Karachayevsk Baksan **INGUSH** Groznyy Gudermes S
Adler Teberda Elbrus **KABARDINO-** Beslan **REP.** Kumtorkala Buynaksk Makhachkala P
Gagra **ABKHAZ** 5633 **BALKAR** Chikola Vladikavkaz Sayasan Izberbash Kaspiysk I
Gudata **REP.** Tyrnyauz **REP.** Kodori (Ordzhonikidze) Novokayakent A
Novyy Afon 5203 Sadon Khunzakh Akusha N
Sukhumi Tkvarcheli Rioni Tebulos 4151 Agvali Akhty Dagestanskiye Ogni 42
Ochamchire Gali Dzhvari 3047 Kukhib Tlyarata Derbent
Zugdidi Sachkhere Tskhinvali Dusheti Modzhalis 800
Anaklia Senaki Tsnori **GEORGIA** Telavi Kvareli Kumukh Kasumkent
Poti Kutaisi Chiatura Kaspi Kosumkent
Samtredia Zestafoni Khashuri Gori Mtskheta Lagodekhi Zakataly Kyurdamir
Kobuleti Ozurgety Borzhomi **Tbilisi** Gurdzhaani Alazan Sheki Sumgait
Batumi **ADZHAR** Akhaltsikhe Krhami Signakhi (Nukha) Gyzyl F
REP. Khulo Akhalkalaki Ckaro Belokany Kutkashen Siazan
Hopa Vale Marneuli Iori Mirzaani Mingechaurskoye Babadag
Borçka Shaumyani Rustavi Kura Vdkhr. 3629
Pazar Ardahan Çildir Alaverdi Mingechaur Agdash Geokchay Mashtaga
Gürele Akçaabat Artvin Akstafa Shamakha Surakhany
Tirebolu Trabzon Rize Kağızman Kirovabad Geokchay **AZERBAIJAN** Baku G
Sürmene Kaçkar 3192 Kumayri Karakalis **Gyandzha** (Baky) 40
3937 Kars (Kirovabad) Yevlakh Barda Kyurdamir Kozi Magomed
Bayburt Ardanuç Sevan Dashkesan Chanlar
Çakırgöl Olur Şenkaya Dilizhan Mir-Bashir Ali-Bayramly
3063 Sarıkamış Aragats Oz. Sevan **NAGORNO** Sabirabad M. Byandovan
Gümüşane Tortum Narman 4090 Kamo Adzhabedi M. Byandovan
Macka Ispir **ARMENIA** **KARABAKH** Agdam Imishly
Bayburt Oltu Kağızman Echmiadzin **Yerevan** Agdam Karachala Alyata

East from Greenwich 40 42 44 46 48 COPYRIGHT. GEORGE PHILIP & SON. LTD.

8 9 10 11 12 13 14

RUSSIA
1. Daghestan Rep.
2. Kabardino–Balkar Rep.
3. Mari Rep.
4. Mordovian Rep.
5. North Ossetian Rep.
6. Tatar Rep.
7. Udmurt Rep.
8. Chuvash Rep.
9. Checheno–Ingush Rep.
AZERBAIJAN
10. Nakhichevan Rep.
GEORGIA
11. Abkhaz Rep.
12. Adzhar Rep.

Projection: Conical Orthomorphic with two standard parallels

East from Greenwich

1 : 40 000 000

Projection: Bonne

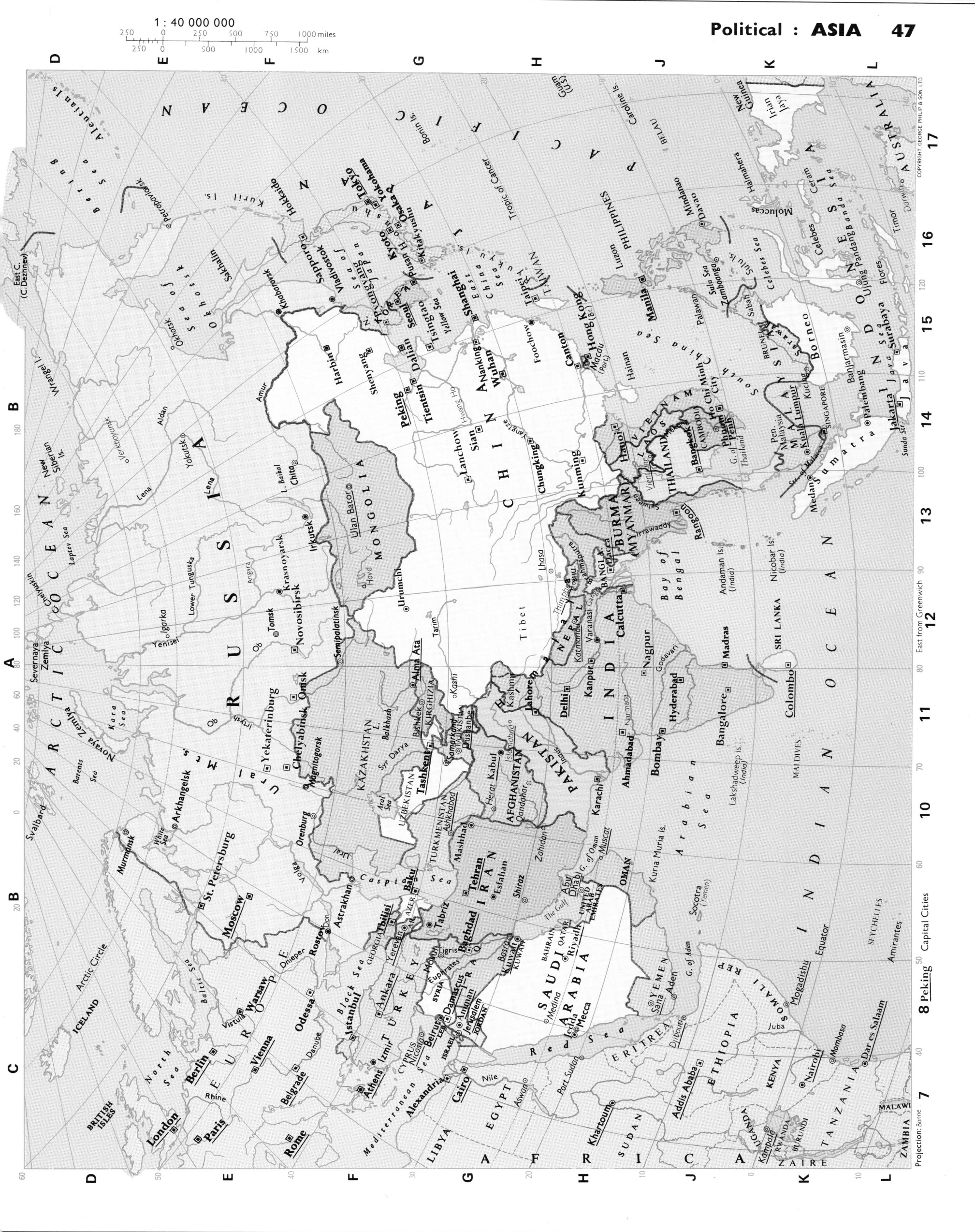

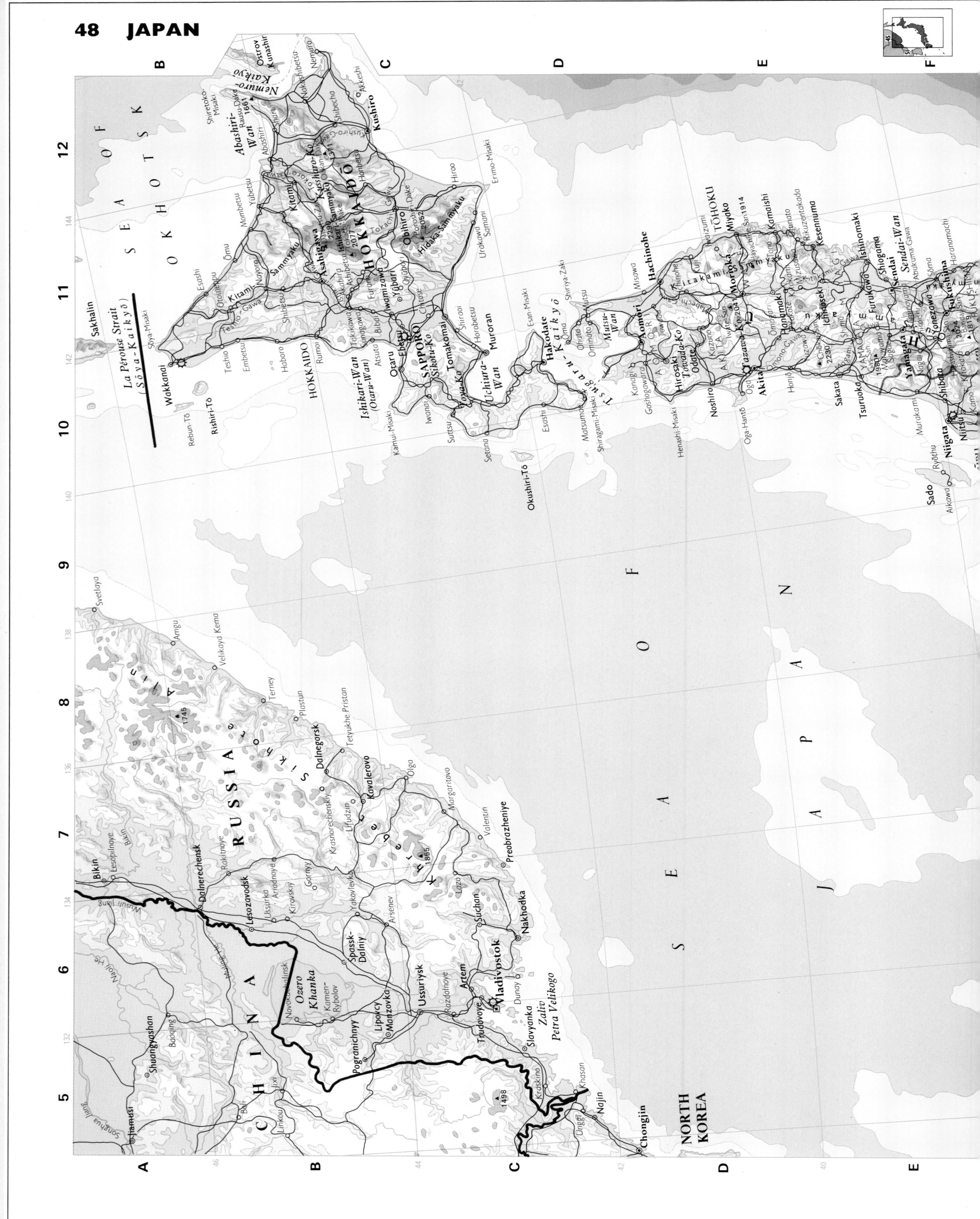

Map labels

SEA OF OKHOTSK

Sakhalin

La Pérouse Strait
(Sōya-Kaikyō)

Wakkanai
Sōya-Misaki
Rebun-Tō
Rishiri-Tō

Nemuro-Kaikyō
Ostrov Kunashir

Abashiri-Wan
Rausu-Dake 1661
Shiretoko-Misaki
Nakashibetsu
Akkeshi
Kushiro

HOKKAIDO
Tokachi-Dake 2077
Poroshiri-Dake 2052
Obihiro
Hidaka-Sammyaku
Hiroo
Erimo-Misaki

SAPPORO
Ebetsu
Otaru
Ishikari-Wan
(Otaru-Wan)

Muroran
Uchiura-Wan
Hakodate

Tsugaru-Kaikyō

Okushiri-Tō

RUSSIA

Sikhote-Alin

Svetlaya
Amgu
Velikaya Kema
Terney
Plastun
Dalnegorsk
Kavalerovo
Olga
Margaritovo
Valentin
Preobrazheniye

Bikin
Lesozavodsk
Dalnerechensk

CHINA

Shuangyashan
Baoqing
Linkou
Jixi

Spassk-Dalniy
Ussuriysk
Artem
Vladivostok
Nakhodka
Zaliv Petra Velikogo

Pogranichny
Ozero Khanka

Khasan
Najin
NORTH KOREA
Chongjin

SEA OF JAPAN

TŌHOKU
Hachinohe
Aomori
Mutsu-Wan
Hirosaki
Odate
AKITA
Morioka
Kamaishi
Kesennuma
Ishinomaki
Sendai
Sendai-Wan
Sakata
Tsuruoka
YAMA
Yonezawa
Niigata
Sado
Shibata

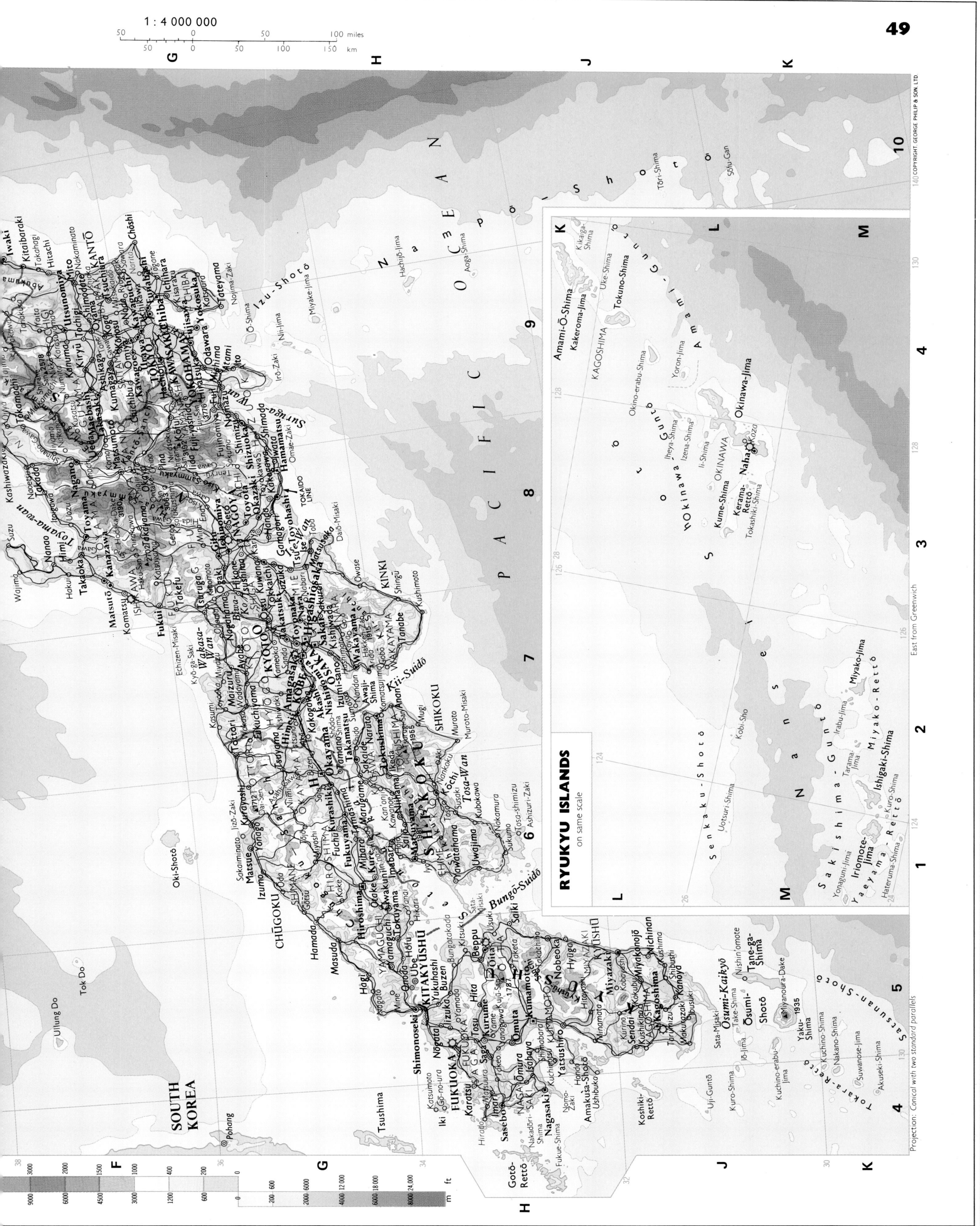

1 : 4 000 000

50   50   100 miles
50   50   100   150 km

G   H   J   K

140 COPYRIGHT GEORGE PHILIP & SON LTD

RYUKYU ISLANDS
on same scale

Projection: Conical with two standard parallels

East from Greenwich

SOUTH
KOREA

P A C I F I C   O C E A N

KANTŌ

TOKYO
KAWASAKI
YOKOHAMA

KINKI

KYOTO
ŌSAKA
KOBE

SHIKOKU

CHŪGOKU

HIROSHIMA

KITAKYŪSHŪ
FUKUOKA

KYŪSHŪ

KUMAMOTO

KAGOSHIMA

Ōsumi-Kaikyō

Amami-Ō-Shima
KAGOSHIMA

OKINAWA
Naha

Miyako-Rettō

Sakishima-Guntō

Ishigaki-Shima

ft
30000
18000
12000
6000
2000
600
200
0
200
600
1200
3000
4500
6000
9000

m
9000
6000
4500
3000
2000
1500
1000
400
200
0
200
600
2000
4000
6000
8000

ÖVÖR
CHANGAY
▲3682
Arts Bogd Uul

DUNDGOVĬ

MONGOLIA

SÜHBAATAR

Hongor
Delgerhet
Hanhongor
Sayhan-Ovoo
Mandalgovi
Har-Ayrag
Öngon
Darig

ÖMNÖGOVĬ

▲2825
Bayandalay
Dalandzadgad
Tsogttsetsiy
Manlay

DORNOGOVĬ
Sayhandulaan
Mandah
Erdene

Noyon
Hanbogd
Hövsgöl
Hatanbulag
Dzamin Üüd
Ereen

Qagan Nur
Dalai Nur

Nomgon
Bayan-Ovoo

G
O
B
I

Abagnar

Duolun

GOBI

NEI

Bayan Obo

Xianghuang Qi

Taihus

MONGGOL

Darhan Muminggan Lianheqi
Huade
Guyuan

Fengning

Lang Shan

Wuyuan
Hanggin Houqi
Linhe
Dashetai
Shiguaigou
▲2187
Urad Qianqi

Güyang
Wulanbulang
Siziwang Qi
▲2174
Qahar Youyi Zhongqi
Shangdu
Zhangbei
Chongli
Chicheng

Yabrai Shan

Dengkou

Hwang He (Hwang Ho)

Baotou
(Paot'ou)
Tumd Youqi
Bikeqi

Daqing Shan
Hohhot

Jining
Xinghe
Wangguan
Zhangjiakou (Changchiak) Kalgan

Xuanhua

Huai'an
Yanqing Miy

Jartai

Jiudengkou
▲2149
Hanggin Qi
Dongsheng
Qingshuihe

Horinger
Shahukou
Youyu

Fengzhen
Liangcheng
Tianzhen
Zhuolu

Datong

Yangyuan
▲2870
Beijing
(Peip'ing, Peking)

Alxa Zuoqi
(Bayan Hot)

Huinong
Pingluo

Mu Us Shamo
(Ordos)

Uxin Qi

Hequ
Shenchi
Shuo Xian
Hunyuan
Ying Xian
Xi Xian
Guangling

Fengtai

Minqin

Helan Shan
▲3626
3556

Taole

Shenmu
Wuzhai
Ningwu
Dai Xian
▲3058
Fanshi
Laiyuan

Zhuo Xian
Laishui
Yongding

CHINA

Yinchuan
Hengcheng

Jia Xian

Fugu
Baode
Wuzhai
Kelan
Jingle
Dingxiang
Watai
Fuping

Wan Xian
Baoding
Xiong Xian
Daicl

Yongning
Lingwu
Wuzhong

Yulin

Huang He Yellow River
Lan Xian
Fen He

Shouyang
Jingxing
Zhengding
Jin Xian
Anping

Qingtongxia Shuku
Yanchi

Hongliu He
Hengshan

Mizhi
Fangshan
▲2831
Lin Xian
TAIYUAN
(T'aiyüan)
Yangquan

Yuci

Xinhe
Ningjin
Anguo
Raoyang

Shijiazhuang

Cangzhou

Guangwu
Zhongning
Zhongwei

Baixu Shan
Dingbian

Suide
Wubu

Zichang

Wuding He
Qingjian
Zhongyang

Lishi
Wenshui

Taigu
Heshun

Neiqiu
Nangong
Ju

Xingtai
Shahe
Jize
Linqing

Dezhou

Hekou
▲4843
Jitaishan

Huang He

Haiyuan
Heichengzhen
Tongxin
Hui'anbu

Zhidan
Ansai

Yanchuan
Fenxi
Xi Xian
Yonghe
Huozhou
Jiexiu
Fenyang
Pingyao
Yushe
Zuoquan

Wu'an
Yongnian
Guantao

Handan

Jize
Liaocheng

Huang He

NINGXIA
HUIZU
ZIZHIQU
(aut. reg.)

Yanchang
Yan'an
Lin Xian

Daning
Fu Xian

Huan Jiang

Qingyang

Heshui

Ji Xian
Luochuan
Xiangning

Fenxi
Xinjiang
Hua Xian
Xiangyuan
Lucheng
Licheng

Hebei
Qinfeng

Changzhi

Cixian
Feixiang

Daming
Shen Xian
Yanggu

Lanzhou
(Lanchow)

Dingxi
Huining
▲2942
Liupanshan

Pingliang

Zhenyuan

Guyuan
Huanglong

Jishan
Hejin
Qiwo

Qinyuan
Tunliu
Qinshui

Gaoping
Jincheng

Taihang Shan

Hua Xian
Junxian
Changyuan
Dingtao

Jinxiang

Lintao
Weiyuan

Jingning
Jingchuan

Lingtai

Jing He

Yijun
Huangling

Hancheng
▲2322
Wanrong

Wenxi

Yangcheng
Hui Ji

Yuncheng
Jiaozuo
Qinyang
Wei He
Xinxiang

Changyuan
Jinxiang

Longxi

Tongwei

Qin'an

Qingshui

Lingtai
Chongwu

Bin Xian
Tongchuan
Chengcheng

Xia Xian
Yangfeng

Anyi
Wenxi

Zhongtiao Shan
Yuanqu
Mianchi

Huang He
Mengjin

Yuanyang

Chengwu

Tianshui
▲3100
Li Xian
Gangu

Qianyang

Fengxiang

Qian Xian
Jingyang

Fufeng

Qishan
Lingtong

Yongji
Anyi

Yongji

Zhongtiao
Sanmenxia
Luoyang
Xingyang
Zhengzhou
(Chengchow)
Kaifeng

Cao Xian
Shan Xian
Ningling

Shangqiu

Min Xian

Wushan

Gangu

Li Xian
Xihe
Mei Xian

Baoji
Fufeng
Xianyang
XI'AN
(Hsian, Sian)

Wei He
▲3767
Zhouzhi
Hu Xian

Lintong
Weinan
Hua Xian
Tongguan

Lingbao
Luoning
Chuankou

Yiyang
Dengfeng

Xinzheng

Yu Xian
Xuchang
Xihua

Fugou

Taikang

Zhecheng

Zhugqu
Lueyang

Qinling Shandi

Lan Xian

Huayin

Luonan
Shang Xian

Lushi
Luo He
Baisha

Linru

Pingdingshan
Wuyang

Luohe

Yu Xian

Huaiyang

Shangshui

Bo Xian

▲3002
Wen Xian

Han Shui

Liuba

Fengxian
Yang Xian
Ningshan
Zhen'an

Shanyang
Shangnan

HENAN

Song Xian

Funiu Shan
Neixiang

Xichuan

Ye Xian
Yancheng

Xiangcheng

Xiping

Shangcai

Shenqiu

Xiangyang

Guangyuan
Pingwu

Wudu

Mian Xian
Hanzhong

Chenggu
Shiquan

Xixiang
Ziyang

Hanyin

Xunyang

Ankang

Baihe

Xunyang
Yunxi

Zhenping
Zhenping

Xichuan

Xixia
Xiping

Fangcheng

Suiping

Xiangcheng

Runan

Hong He

Fuyang

Baoche
Yangpingguan

Ningqiang

Han Shui

Guangyuan

Nanyang

Biyang

Zhumadian

Projection: Conical with two standard parallels

ft	m
12,000	4000
9000	3000
6000	2000
4500	1500
3000	1000
1200	400
600	200
0	0
200	600
2000	6000

m ft

1 : 4 800 000

50 0 50 100 150 miles
50 0 50 100 150 200 km

9 10 11 12 13 14 15 16

Top row (near China–Russia–Korea):

Horqin Youyi Qianqi · Zhenlai · Nen Jiang · Bin Xian · Jixi · Turiy Rog · B

HARBIN (Haerhpin) · Acheng · Yanshou · Mishan · Hulin · RUSSIA
Ozero Khanka

Baicheng · Maoxing · Zhaoyuan · Shuangcheng · Shangzhi · Yimianpo · Mudanjiang · Maqiaohe · Pogranichnyy

Da'an · Songhua Jiang · Changchunling · Sanchaho · Wuchang · Hengdaohezi · Xiachengzi · Suifenhe

Tao'an · Anguang · Fuyu · Lalin · Shanhetun · Hailin · Muling · Suiyang · Golenki

Tuquan · Qian Gorlos · Beidaolaizhao · Jiutai · Shulan · Ning'an · Dongning · 44

Jarud Qi · Tongyu · Nong'an · Dehui · Gangyao · Zhangguangcai Ling · 690 · Suifenhe · Pokrovka

Beizhengzhen · Kooshan · 1949 · Changling · Fulongquan · Jiaohe · Emu · Dongjingcheng · Jingbo Hu · Luozigou · Ussuriysk (Voroshilov) · Razdolnoye · C

Xinkai He · Zhanwu · CHANGCHUN · JILIN (Kirin) · Chili · Songhua Hu · Xinzhan · Nanlsongdian · Chunyang · Wangqing · Daxinggou · Vladivostok

Xiliao-He · Tongliao · Huaidezhen · Maoli · Shuangyang · Jiaohe · Panshi · Huadian · Helong · Mingyuegue · Yanji · Tumen · Hunchun · Slavyanka

Shuangliao · Siping · Lishu · Liaoyuan · Dongfeng · Huifa · Huinan · Jingyu · Fusong · Antu · Musan · Hoeryong · Najin · Posyet

Bamiancheng · Xifeng · Hailong · Changbai Shan · 1677 · Puryŏng · Pugŏdong · 42

Kaiyuan · Shanchengzhen · Juhe · Paektu-san · Yupyongdong · Nanam · Chongjin

Faku · Liao He · Tieling · Qingyuan · Xinpin · Tonghua · Linjiang · Changbai · Hochon · 2541 · Kyŏngsŏng

Xinmin · FUSHUN · Tanghua · Chungsang-ni · Hyesan · Kapsan · Irhyangdong · Ondejin

SHENYANG (Mukden) · Huanren · Ji'an · Manpojin · Kuup-tong · Pungsan · Simpungdong

Liaoning / western area:

THE WALL · WILLOW · Fuxin · Xinlitun · Zhangwu · Qinghecheng · Huaijianzi · 1845 · Kasan-dong · D

Xiawa · Beipiao · Qinghemen · Heishan · Benxi · Anpng · Kuandian · Supung Sk · Chosan · Changjin-chosuji · Kimchaek (Songjin)

Chaoyang · Liaoyang · Lianshanguan · Xiuyan · Yalu Jiang · Pyŏktong · 2522 · Pujon-chosuji · Tanchon

1885 · Jinzhou · Panshan · Haicheng · Fengcheng · Gao He · Taegwan · Pukchŏng

Ningcheng · Daling He · Beizhen · Anshan · Niuzhuang · Caohekou · Ji · Dandong · Sinŭiju · Chosan · Koin-dong · Changjin · Sŏhori

Lingyuan · Jianchang · Tianzhuangtai · Xiongyuecheng · Gai Xian · Qingchengzi · Dongg · Yongampo · Sŏnchŏn · Kujang · Sinhung · Kanggye · Pukchong

Chengde · Yingkou · Yingkou · Fengcheng · Xiuyan · 131 · Gushan · Zhuanghe · Yalu Jiang · Hamhung · E

Liaodong Bandao · Fu Xian · Xinyi · Pikou · Jin Xian · Liaodong Wan · Sukchŏn · Anju · Oro · Hŭngnam · Tongjosŏn Man

Qinhuangdao · Changli · Leting · Jin Xian · Lüshun · DALIAN (Lüda) · Yŏnghŭng · Munchŏn · Wŏnsan · Anbyŏn

Tangshan · Hangu · Tanggu · Dagu · Bo Hai (Gulf of Chihli) · Korea Bay · P'YŎNGYANG · Chunghwa · Kangdong · Tongyang · Singgam · Kojo · Kosŏng

TIANJIN (Tientsin, T'ienching) · Oikou · Chinnampo · Sŏngnim · Suan · Pyŏnggang · 1638 · Hoeyang · Kansŏng · F

Huang He · Penglai · Yantai · Changyŏn · Sariwŏn · Sinmak · Nam-chŏri · Hwachon-chosuji · 1578 · Yangyang

Zhanhua · Longkou · Huang Xian · Weihai · Cho-do · Chaeryŏng · Kŭmchon · Chŏrwŏn · Kŭmhwa · Chumunjin

Huimin · Laizhou Wan · Doujindian · Fushan · Muping · 923 · Wendeng · Haeju · Kaesŏng · Panmunjŏm · Chunchŏn · Hongchŏn · Samchŏk

Shandong Bandao · Ye Xian · Qixia · Rushan · Paengnyong-do · Ongjin · Yonan · Munsan · Ŭijŏngbu · Ullung-do

Zibo · Yidu · Weifang · Changyi · Laiyang · Laixi · Nanhuang · Shidao · Cease Fire Line · SŎUL (Seoul) · Hoengsŏng

Boshan · Linqu · Anqiu · Gaomi · Jiao Xian · Changyang · Yŏngwŏl · INCH'ŎN · Ichŏn · Wŏnju · Samchŏk

1108 · Laiwu · Zhucheng · QINGDAO (Ch'ingtao) · Suwŏn · Osan · Chungju · Chechon · Ulchin

Mengyin · Wulian · Lancun · Jimo · SOUTH KOREA · Sŏsan · Chŏnan · Chŏngju · Yechŏn · Yŏngdŏk

Yishui · Rizhao · Shijiusuo · Andongwei · HUANG HAI (Yellow Sea) · Hongsŏng · Kongju · Nonsan · Sangju · Chŏngha

Kanggyŏng · Taejŏn · Iri · Kimch'ŏn · Yŏngchŏn · Pohang

Kunsan · Chŏnju · TAEGU · Kyŏngju

Linyi · Lianyungang (Hsinhailien) · Puan · Kimje · Kochang · Chinju · Masan · Ulsan

JIANGSU · Haizhou Wan · Kwangju · Hadong · Chinhae · PUSAN · G

Namwŏn · 1915 · Chinju · Samch'ŏnpo · Chungmu

Mokpo · Sunch'ŏn · Posong · Palgye-ri · Yŏsu · Korea Strait · Tsushima · Sasuna · Saka

Changhŭng · Haenam · Chindo · Izuhara · Tsushima-kaikyō · Iki

Cheju · Cheju-do · JAPAN · Karatsu

Hallim · 1950 · Onpyong-ni · Koshima · Sasebo · Ōmura · Isahaya

Mosulpo · Sŏgwi-po · Nakadóri-jima · Fukue-jima · Kuchinotsu · Nagasaki · H

9 10 11 12 13 14 15

East from Greenwich

SEA OF JAPAN

NORTH KOREA

Manchuria

Liaodong Wan

COPYRIGHT. GEORGE PHILIP & SON. LTD.

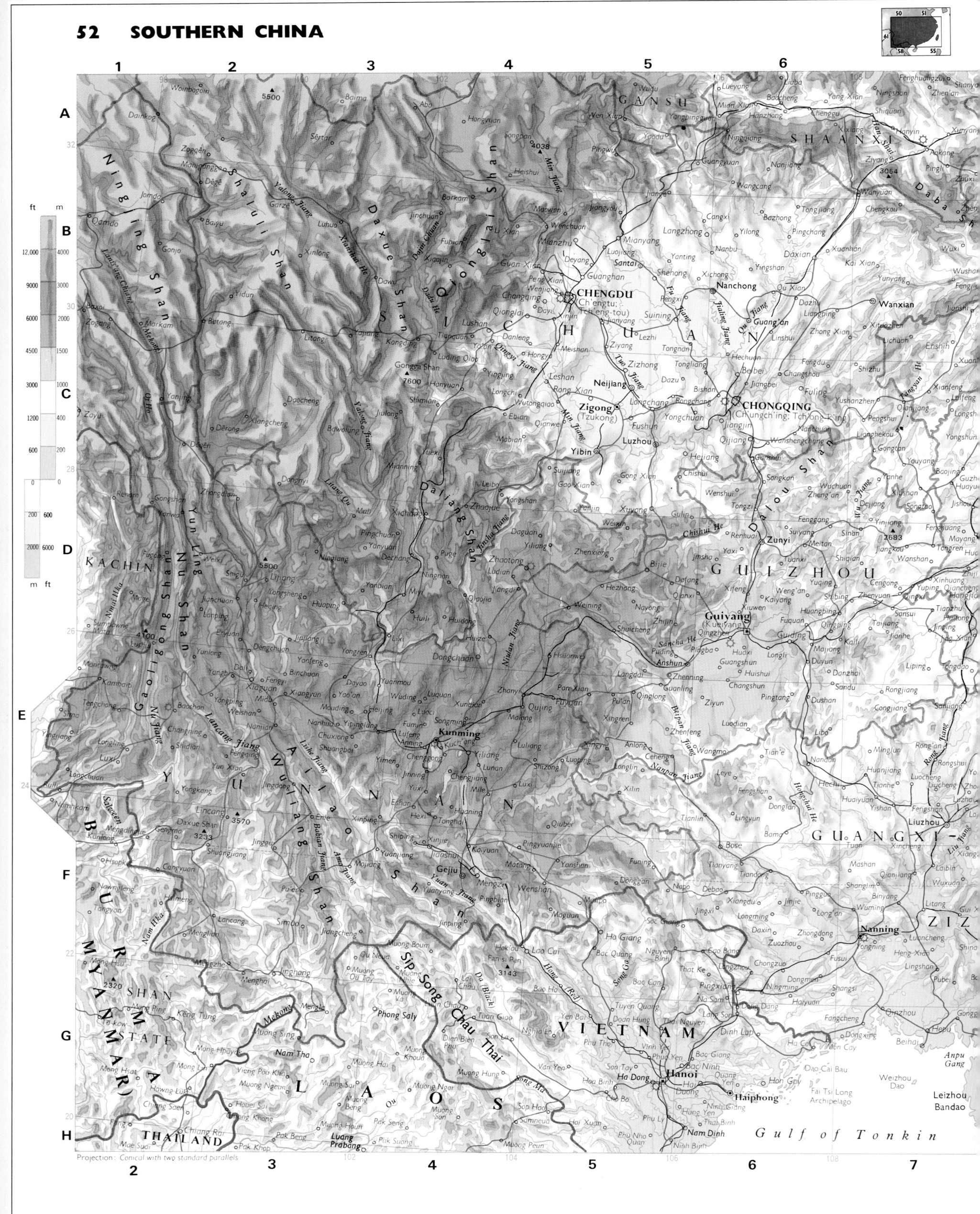

1 : 4 800 000

50 0 50 100 150 miles
50 0 50 100 150 200 km

8 9 10 11 12 13 14

HENAN
HUBEI
ANHUI
JIANGSU
ZHEJIANG
HUNAN
JIANGXI
FUJIAN
GUANGDONG
GUANGZU
TAIWAN (FORMOSA)

Shangenan Xiping Wuyang Xiangqiu Jieshou T'aiho Xifei He Guo He Mengcheng Guzhen Honqze Hu Guoyou Hu Xinghua Dongtai Hai'an
Xixia Fangchenq Shangcai Linquan Fengyang Tianchang Gaoyou Rudong
Nanyang Zhumadian Suiping Jiuxiangcheng Fuyang Yingfei He Jiashan Tianchang Yangzhou Taizhou Tai Xian Rugao
Zhenping Tanghe Hong He Yingshang Shou Xian Changfeng Chu Xian Zhenjiang Jiangyin Nantong
Xinyang Huangchuan Hefei Chao Hu Nanjing Changzhou Wuxi Changshu Shanghai

Xiangfan **Wuhan** **Hankou** **Anqing** **Nanjing** **Hangzhou** **Ningbo**
Yichang **Shashi** **Huangshi** **Jiujiang** **Jingdezhen** **Shaoxing** **Zhoushan Dao**
Changsha **Nanchang** **Shangrao** **Wenzhou**
Xiangtan **Zhuzhou** **Linchuan** **Fuzhou**
Hengyang **Ji'an** **Nanping** **Sanming**
Guilin **Ganzhou** **Quanzhou** **Xiamen** **TAIBEI**
Shaoguan **Zhangzhou** **Taizhong**
GUANGZHOU **Shantou** **Tainan**
Foshan **Jiangmen** **HONG KONG** **Kowloon** **Gaoxiong** **Pingdong**
Macau
Zhanjiang

Tropic of Cancer
Luzon Strait
SOUTH CHINA SEA
Taiwan Strait
Tungsha Tao

COPYRIGHT GEORGE PHILIP & SON LTD.

1 : 16 000 000

RUSSIA

KAZAKHSTAN

KIRGHIZIA

MONGOLIA

CHINA

INDIA

NEPAL

BHUTAN

BANGLADESH

MYANMAR (BURMA)

THAILAND

LAOS

VIETNAM

NORTH KOREA

SOUTH KOREA

JAPAN

TAIWAN (FORMOSA)

PHILIPPINES

ASSAM

XIZANG (TIBET)

XINJIANG UYGUR

QINGHAI

GANSU

SICHUAN

YUNNAN

GUIZHOU

GUANGXI

GUANGDONG

HAINAN

HUNAN

JIANGXI

FUJIAN

ZHEJIANG

JIANGSU

ANHUI

HUBEI

HENAN

SHANDONG

HEBEI

SHANXI

SHAANXI

NINGXIA

HUIZA

LIAONING

JILIN

HEILONGJIANG

BEIJING

TIANJIN

SHANGHAI

SHENYANG

HARBIN

CHANGCHUN

DALIAN

QINGDAO

NANJING

WUHAN

CHONGQING

CHENGDU

GUANGZHOU

Hong Kong

Kowloon

Macao

TAIYUAN

BAOTOU

Hohhot

Lanzhou

Xining

Yinchuan

Urumqi

Kashi

Shache

Hami

Turpan

Dunhuang

Golmud

Lhasa

Kathmandu

Dhaka

CALCUTTA

Vishakhapatnam

Cuttack

Patna

Varanasi

Lucknow

Kanpur

Allahabad

Pyongyang

SEOUL

Pusan

Taegu

Fukuoka

Nagasaki

Taibei

Gaoxiong

HANOI

Haiphong

EAST CHINA SEA

YELLOW SEA

SOUTH CHINA SEA

BAY OF BENGAL

Bo Hai

Korea Bay

Ryukyu-Retto

Tropic of Cancer

Gobi

Mu Us Shamo

Tarim Pendi

Junggar Pendi

Qaidam Pendi

Tian Shan

Altun Shan

Kunlun Shan

Qilian Shan

Tanggula Shan

Bayan Har Shan

Daxue Shan

Great Khingan Ling

Xiao Hinggan Ling

Huang He

Chang Jiang

Brahmaputra

East from Greenwich

Projection: Bonne

COPYRIGHT GEORGE PHILIP & SON, LTD.

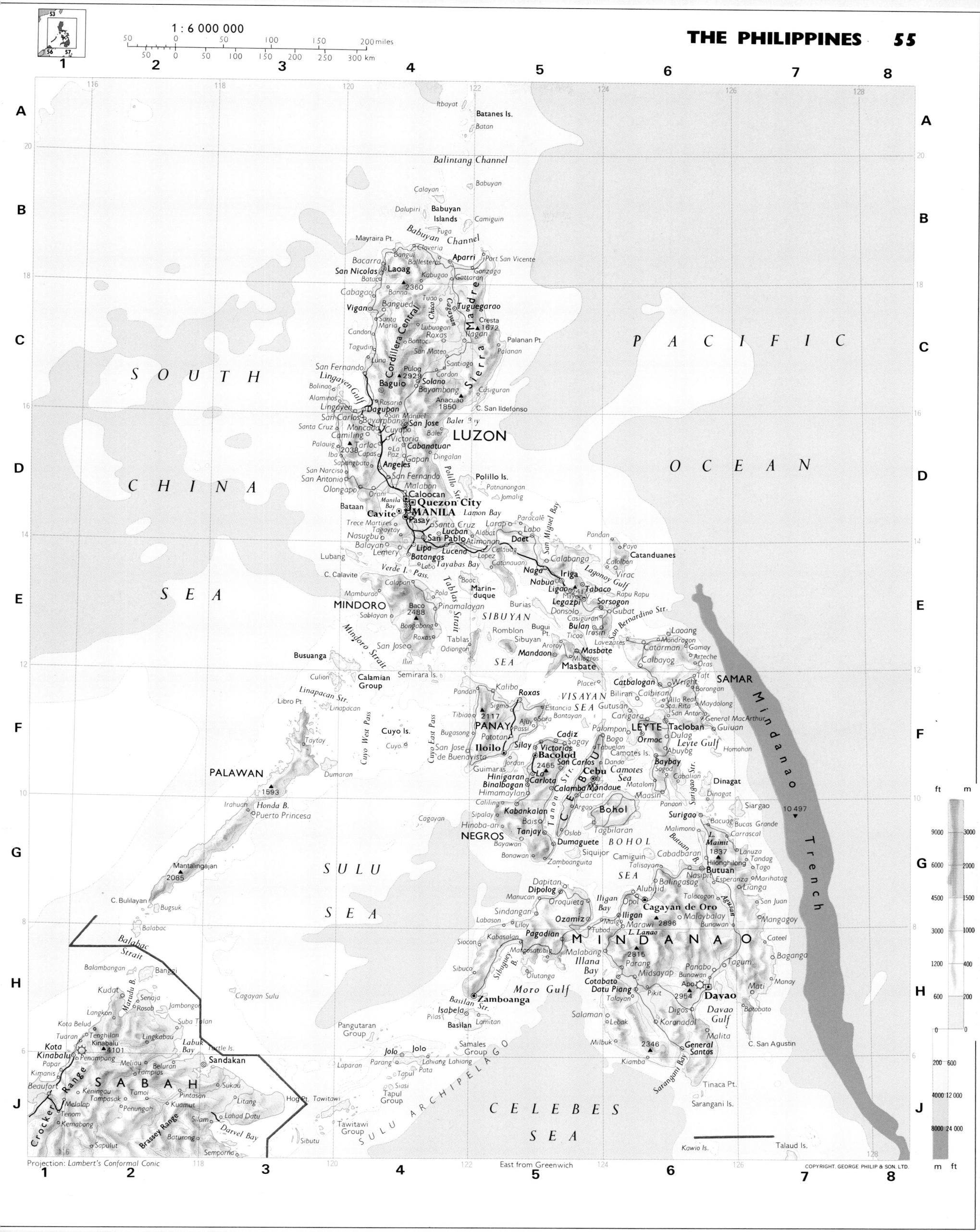

1 : 6 000 000

50   100   150   200 miles
50   0   50   100   150   200   250   300 km

A

20

Itbayat

Batanes Is.
Batan

B

Balintang Channel

Calayan   *Babuyan*

Dalupiri *Babuyan*   *Camiguin*
            Islands
Fuga
Mayraira Pt. *Babuyan Channel*

C

Bacarra *Claveria* *Ballesteros* **Aparri** *Port San Vicente*
Bangui **Laoag** *Kabugao* *Gonzaga*
San Nicolas *Batoc* ▲2360 *Tuao* *Chico* **Tuguegarao**
Banna *Tuao*
Vigan *Bangued* *Santa* *Lubuagan* *Cresta*
Maria *Roxas* ▲1672 *Nagan*
Candon *Bontoc* *Palanan Pt.*
Tagudin *Luna* *San Mateo* *Palanan*
San Fernando *Pulog* *Santiago* *Cordon* *Casiguran*
Lingayen Gulf ▲2929 **Solano** *Bayombong*
Bolinao **Baguio** *Anacuao*
Alaminos *Rosario* ▲1850 *C. San Ildefonso*
Dagupan *Bayambang* *Baler Bay*

D

16

Lingayen
San Carlos **San Manuel** **San Jose** *Baler*
Santa Cruz *Bayambang* *Cuyapo* **Cabanatuar** **LUZON**
Palauig *Moncada* *Victoria* *Dingalan*
Iba *Camiling* *La* *Gapan*
Tarlac ▲2038 *Capas* *Paz*
Sapangbato **Angeles**
San Narciso **San Fernando** *Polillo Is.*
San Antonio *Malabon* **Caloocan** *Polillo Str.* *Patnanongan*
Olongapo *Orani* **Quezon City** *Jomalig*
Bataan *Manila Bay* **MANILA**
Cavite **Pasay** *Lamon Bay*
Trece Martires *Santa Cruz* *Larap* *Paracale* *Pandan*
Tagaytay **Lucban** *Atimonan* *Labo* *Payo*
Nasugbu **San Pablo** **Daet** **Catanduanes**
Balayan **Lipa** **Lucena** *Lopez* *Calabanga* *Catolban*
Lemery **Batangas** *Tayabas Bay* *Catanauan* **Naga** *Virac*
Lubang *Labo* *Calauag* **Iriga** *Lagonoy Gulf*
C. Calavite *Verde I. Pass.* *Boac* **Nabua** *Rapu Rapu*
Mamburao *Pola* *Marinduque* **Ligao** **Tabaco**
Calapan *Pinamalayan* **Legazpi** *Mayon* *Sorsogon*
Sablayan **Baco** *Tablas* *Donsol* *Casiguran*

E

14

MINDORO ▲2488 *Strait* **SIBUYAN** *Bugui* **Bulan** *San Bernardino Str.*
Bongabong **SEA** *Irosin*
San Jose *Roxas* *Romblon* *Sibuyan* *Ticao* *Laoang*
Busuanga *Odiongan* *Tablas* **Mandaon** *Milagros* *Mondragon* *Catarman* *Gamay*
Culion *Semirara Is.* *Masbate* **Masbate** *Calbayog* *Arteche*
Calamian *Ilin* *Placer* **Catbalogan** *Oras*
Group *Pandan* *VISAYAN* *Wright* *Taft* **SAMAR**
Linapacan Str. *Kalibo* **Roxas** *Biliran* *Caibiran* *Borongan*
Libro Pt. *Sigma* *Estancia* *Gutusan* *Villa Real* *Maydolong*
Linapacan *Tibiao* ▲2117 *Ajuy* *Carigara* *Sta. Rita* *General MacArthur*
Cuyo West Pass **PANAY** *Passi* *Palompon* *Bogo* **LEYTE** **Tacloban** *Guiuan*
Taytay *Cuyo Is.* *Bugasong* *Potatan* *Sagay* *Tabuelan* *Ormoc* *Dulag*
Cuyo. *San Jose* **Iloilo** *Silay* *Cadiz* *Bogo* *Camotes Is.* *Abuyog*
de Buenavista **Bacolod** **Victorias** **San Carlos** *Dando* **Baybay** *Homonhon*
Guimaras **La** ▲2465 *Camotes* *Sogod*

F

Cagayan *Jordan* **Carlota** *Matalom* *Sea* *Cabalian* *Dinagat*
PALAWAN *Dumaran* **Hinigaran** **Calamba** **Mandaue** *Maasin*
▲1593 **Binalbagan** *Carcar* *Surigao Str.* *Dinagat*
Irahuan *Honda B.* *Himamaylan* *Siargao* ▲10 497
Puerto Princesa *Caliling* **Kabankalan** *Bohol* **Surigao** *Bucas Grande*
Sipalay *Baiso* **BOHOL** *Bacuag* *Carrascal*
NEGROS *Argao* *Malimono* *Lanuza*
Hinoba-an **Tanjay** *Tagbilaran* ▲*Mainit* *Tandag*
G *Oslob* *BOHOL* **1837** *Esperanza* *Marihatag*
Butuan *Hinonghilong* *Lianga*
Bawayan **Dumaguete** *SEA* *Cabadbaran* *San Juan*

G

10

Mantalingajan *Zamboanguita* *Camiguin* *Talisayan* *Agusan*
▲2085 *Siquijor* *Balingasag* *Mangagoy*
C. Bulilayan **Dapitan** *Opol* *Talacogon*
Bugsuk **Dipolog** *Iligan* **Cagayan de Oro** *Malaybalay* *Cateel*
Manucan *Bay* **Iligan** *Bunawan*
Oroquieta ▲2896 *Baganga*
Sindangan **Ozamiz** *Marawi* *Mangagoy*
Labason *Liloy* *Tubod* *L. Lanao*
Pagadian **MINDANAO**
Kabasalan ▲2815
Siocon *Malabang* *Parang* *Panabo*
Matasatubig *Illana* *Midsayap* *Tagum*
Sibuco *Bay* *Cotabato* *Bunawan*
H *Olutanga* **Datu Piang** *Pikit* *Apo* **Davao**
Moro Gulf *Talayan* ▲2954
Zamboanga *Pilas* *Digos* *Davao*
Basilan Str. *Salaman* *Lebak* *Koronadal* *Gulf*
Isabela *Lamitan* *Milbuk* *Malita*
Basilan ▲2346 **General** *C. San Agustin*
Pangutaran **Santos**
Group *Samales* *Sarangani Bay*
Group *Tinaca Pt.*
Jolo **Jolo** *Kiamba*
Lahiang Lahiang *Sarangani Is.*

I

SULU *Parang* *Pata*

J

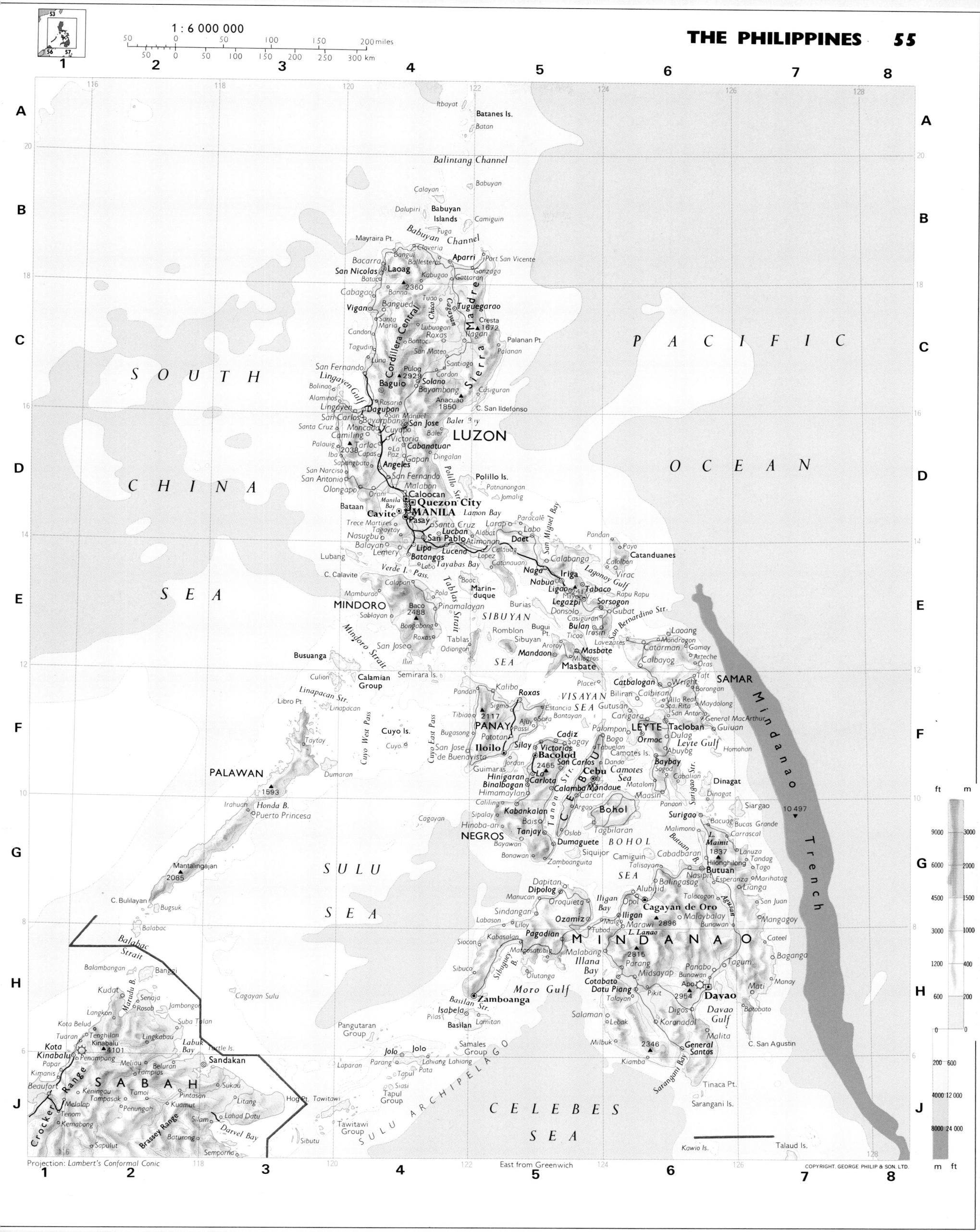

Kota Belud *Tuaran* *Meliau*
Penampang *Beluran*
Kota ▲4101 *Tampias*
Kinabalu *Papar* *Labuk*
Kimanis **Sandakan** *Bay*

SOUTH

CHINA

SEA

SULU

SEA

PACIFIC

OCEAN

Mindanao Trench

CELEBES

SEA

Kawio Is. *Talaud Is.*

ft	m
9000	3000
6000	2000
4500	1500
3000	1000
1200	400
600	200
	0
200	600
4000	12 000
8000	24 000
m	ft

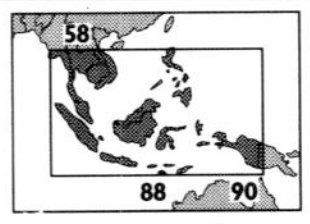

THAILAND

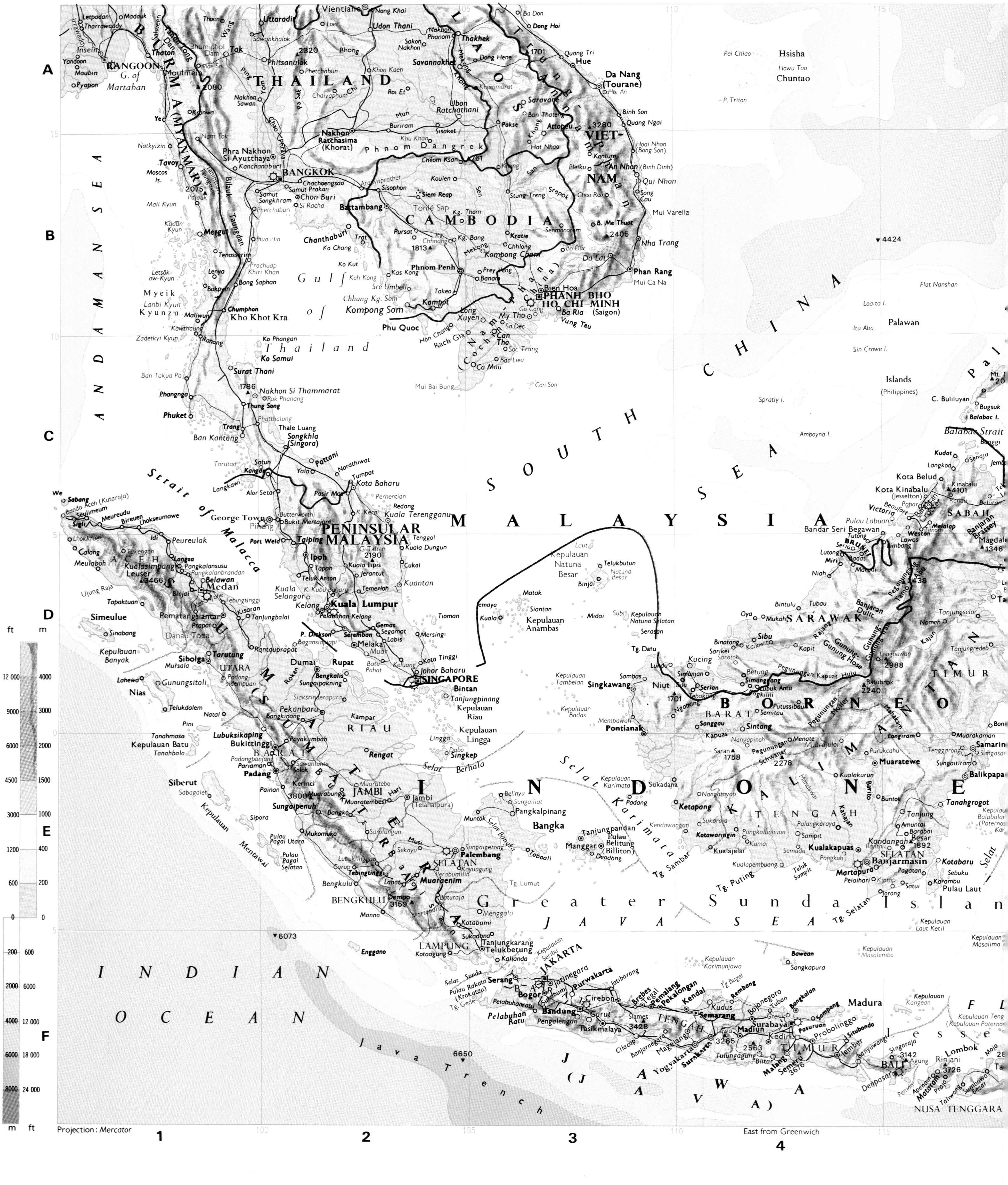

BURMA / MYANMAR

LAOS

VIET-NAM

CAMBODIA

ANDAMAN SEA

Gulf of Thailand

SOUTH CHINA SEA

MALAYSIA

PENINSULAR MALAYSIA

SABAH

SARAWAK

BRUNEI

BORNEO

KALIMANTAN

KALIMANTAN BARAT

KALIMANTAN TENGAH

KALIMANTAN SELATAN

KALIMANTAN TIMUR

SUMATERA

SUMATERA UTARA

SUMATERA SELATAN

ACEH

RIAU

JAMBI

BENGKULU

LAMPUNG

INDIAN OCEAN

Java Trench

JAVA SEA

JAWA

JAWA BARAT

JAWA TENGAH

JAWA TIMUR

BALI

MADURA

NUSA TENGGARA

Greater Sunda Islands

INDONESIA

Major cities and places:
RANGOON, Moulmein, BANGKOK, Phnom Penh, PHANH BHO HO CHI MINH (Saigon), Da Nang (Tourane), Hue, Nha Trang, Phan Rang, Vientiane, Thakhek, Savannakhet, Nakhon Ratchasima (Khorat), Phnom Penh, Battambang, Tonlé Sap, Phuket, Medan, Kuala Lumpur, SINGAPORE, Johor Baharu, Palembang, Padang, Jambi, Pekanbaru, Bengkulu, Bandung, JAKARTA, Bogor, Semarang, Surabaya, Yogyakarta, Surakarta, Denpasar, Kota Kinabalu (Jesselton), Bandar Seri Begawan, Kuching, Pontianak, Banjarmasin, Balikpapa, Samarin

Strait of Malacca

Strait of Malacca

Kepulauan Natuna Besar

Kepulauan Anambas

Kepulauan Riau

Selat Karimata

Palawan

Spratly I.

Islands (Philippines)

Hsisha

Chuntao

Projection: Mercator

East from Greenwich

ft / m (elevation scale)
12 000 / 4000
9000 / 3000
6000 / 2000
4500 / 1500
3000 / 1000
1200 / 400
600 / 200
0 / 0

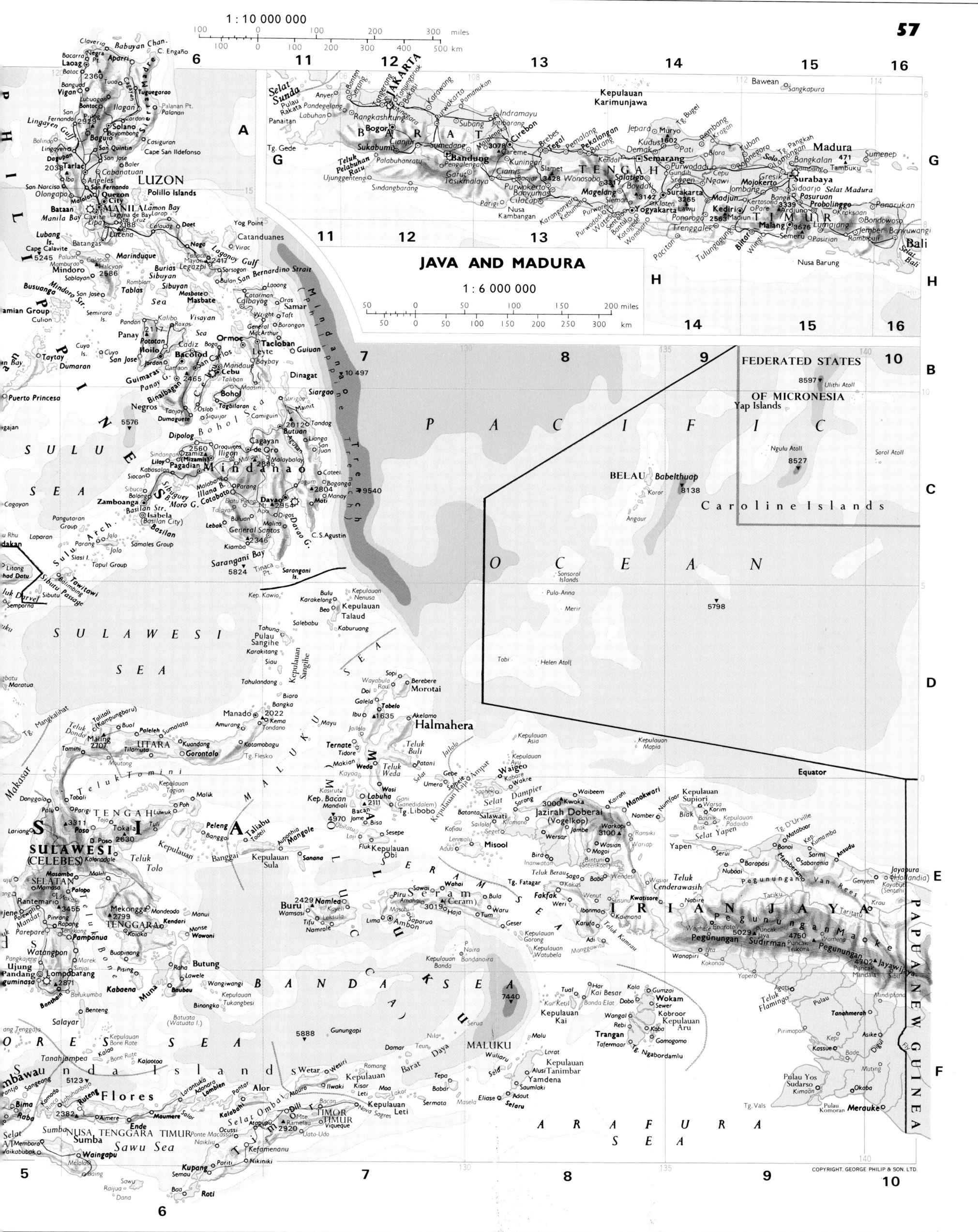

1 : 10 000 000

100   100   0   100   200   300 miles
100   0   100   200   300   400   500 km

6   11   12 JAKARTA   13   14   15   16

PHILIPPINES · LUZON

Claveria · Babuyan Chan.
Bacarra · Negros
Laoag · Batac · Pt. · Aparri
Vigan · Banguel · Tuguegarao
Bontoc · Ilagan
San Fernando · Solano
Lingayen Gulf · Bayombong
Bolinao · San Quintin
Dagupan · San Jose
Iba · Cabanatuan
Angeles · LUZON
Olongapo
Bataan · MANILA · Lamon Bay
Manila Bay · Cavite · Laguna de Bay
Lubang · Lipa · Calauag
Is. · Batangas

JAVA AND MADURA
1 : 6 000 000

50   0   50   100   150   200 miles
50   0   50   100 150 200 250 300 km

Selat Sunda · Anyer · BARAT · Bogor · Indramayu · Kepulauan Karimunjawa
Jakarta
Pulau Rakata · Labuhan · Rangkasbitung · Subang · Cirebon · Tegal · Pemalang · Pekalongan · Rembang · Kragan · Madura · Sumenep
Panaitan · Sukabumi · Bandung · TENGAH · Semarang · Kudus · Pati · Tuban · Bangkalan
Tg. Gede · Palabuhanratu · Garut · Slamet · Kendal · Demak · Cepu · Gresik · Surabaya
Teluk Pelabuhan Ratu · Ciamis · Wonosobo · Salatiga · Ngawi · Mojokerto · Selat Madura
Ujunggenteng · Tasikmalaya · Banjar · Purwokerto · Magelang · Surakarta · Madiun · Kediri · Pasuruan
Sindangbarang · Cilacap · Yogyakarta · Lawu · Ponorogo · TIMUR · Malang · Probolinggo
Nusa Kambangan · Pacitan · Tulungagung · Blitar · Semeru · Jember · Banyuwangi
Bali · Nusa Barung · Selat Bali

H

14   15   16

7   8   9   FEDERATED STATES   10   B

OF MICRONESIA
Yap Islands

8597 · Ulithi Atoll

Ngulu Atoll · 8527 · Sorol Atoll

PACIFIC

BELAU · Babelthuap
Koror · 8138
Angaur

Caroline Islands   C

OCEAN

Sonsorol Islands

Pulo-Anna
Merir · 5798

Tobi · Helen Atoll   D

PHILIPPINE SEA · Mindanao · Davao

SULU SEA · SULAWESI SEA · CELEBES SEA · Manado · Halmahera · Ternate · Tidore
Kepulauan Sangihe · Kepulauan Talaud · Morotai · Tobelo

MALUKU · Kepulauan Mapia

SULAWESI (CELEBES) · Equator

Waigeo · Manokwari · Biak · Yapen
Jazirah Doberai (Vogelkop) · Supiori

Misool · IRIAN JAYA
Buru · SERAM (Ceram) · Ambon · Fakfak · Teluk Cenderawasih · Jayapura (Hollandia)
Pegunungan Van Rees · Genyem
BANDA SEA · Pegunungan Maoke · Sudirman · Jayawijaya
Puncak Jaya 5029 · Mandala

PAPUA NEW GUINEA

Kepulauan Aru · Kepulauan Kai · Merauke
FLORES SEA · BANDA SEA
Wetar · MALUKU · Yamdena · Tanimbar
TIMOR · TIMUR
NUSA TENGGARA TIMUR · Kupang · Roti   ARAFURA SEA   F

5   6   7   8   9   10

COPYRIGHT. GEORGE PHILIP & SON. LTD.

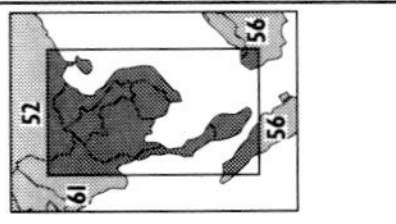

GUANGXI ZHANGZU ZIZHIQU AUTONOMOUS REGION

YUNNAN

BURMA (MYANMAR)

SHAN STATE

KAYAH

KAWTHULE

TENASSERIM

THAILAND

LAOS

CAMBODIA

ANNAM

Gulf of Tonkin

HAINAN

Red River Delta

Gulf of Martaban

Central Highlands

Phnom Dangrek

Dawna Range

Bilauk Taung

Great Tenasserim

Thiu Khao Phetchabun

Khorat

Mekong

Salween

Lancang Jiang

Chao Phraya Lowlands

BANGKOK (Krung Thep)

HANOI

Haiphong

Rangoon

Mandalay

Moulmein

Da Nang (Tourane)

Hue

Vientiane

Luang Prabang

Nanning

Zhanjiang (Tsamkong)

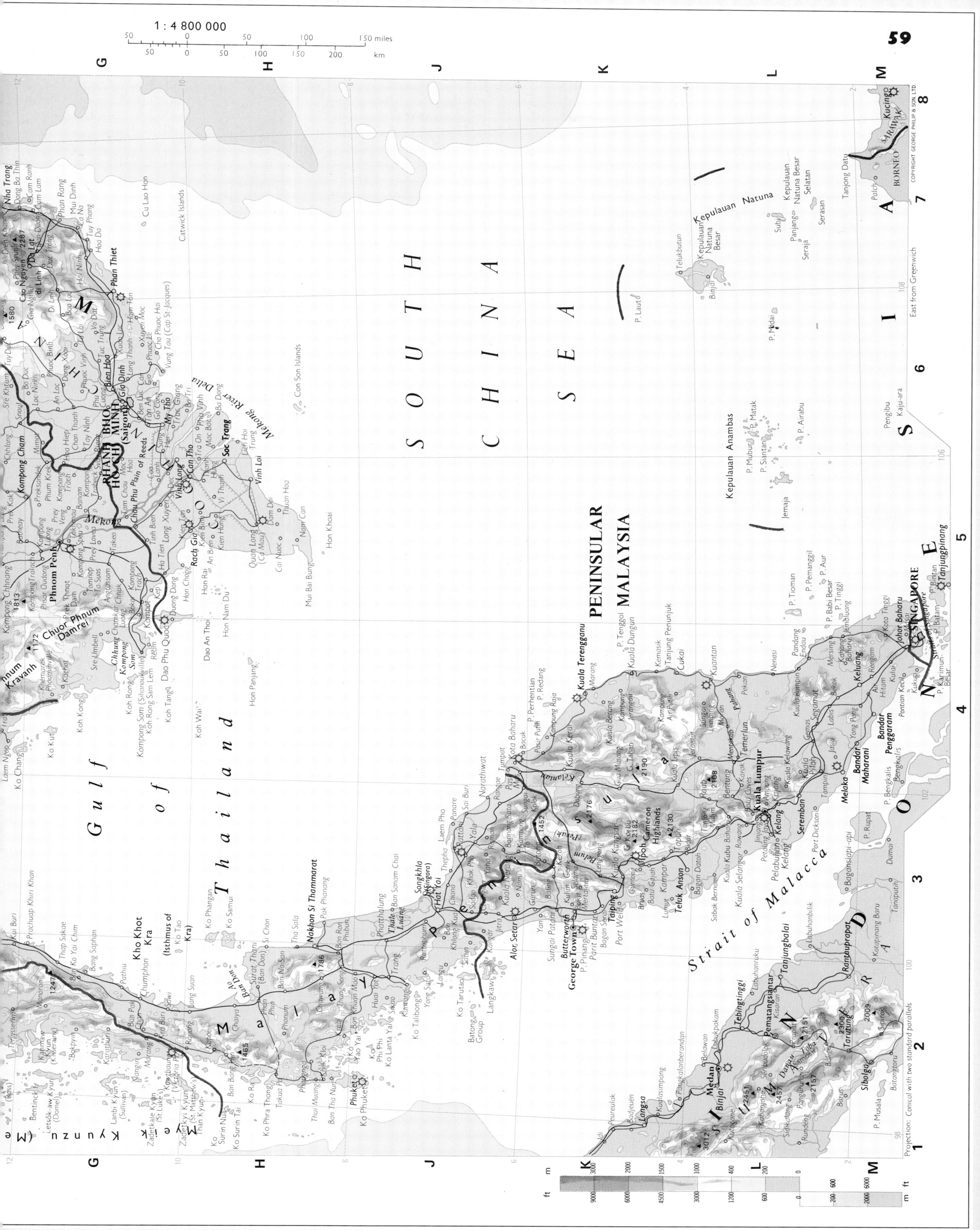

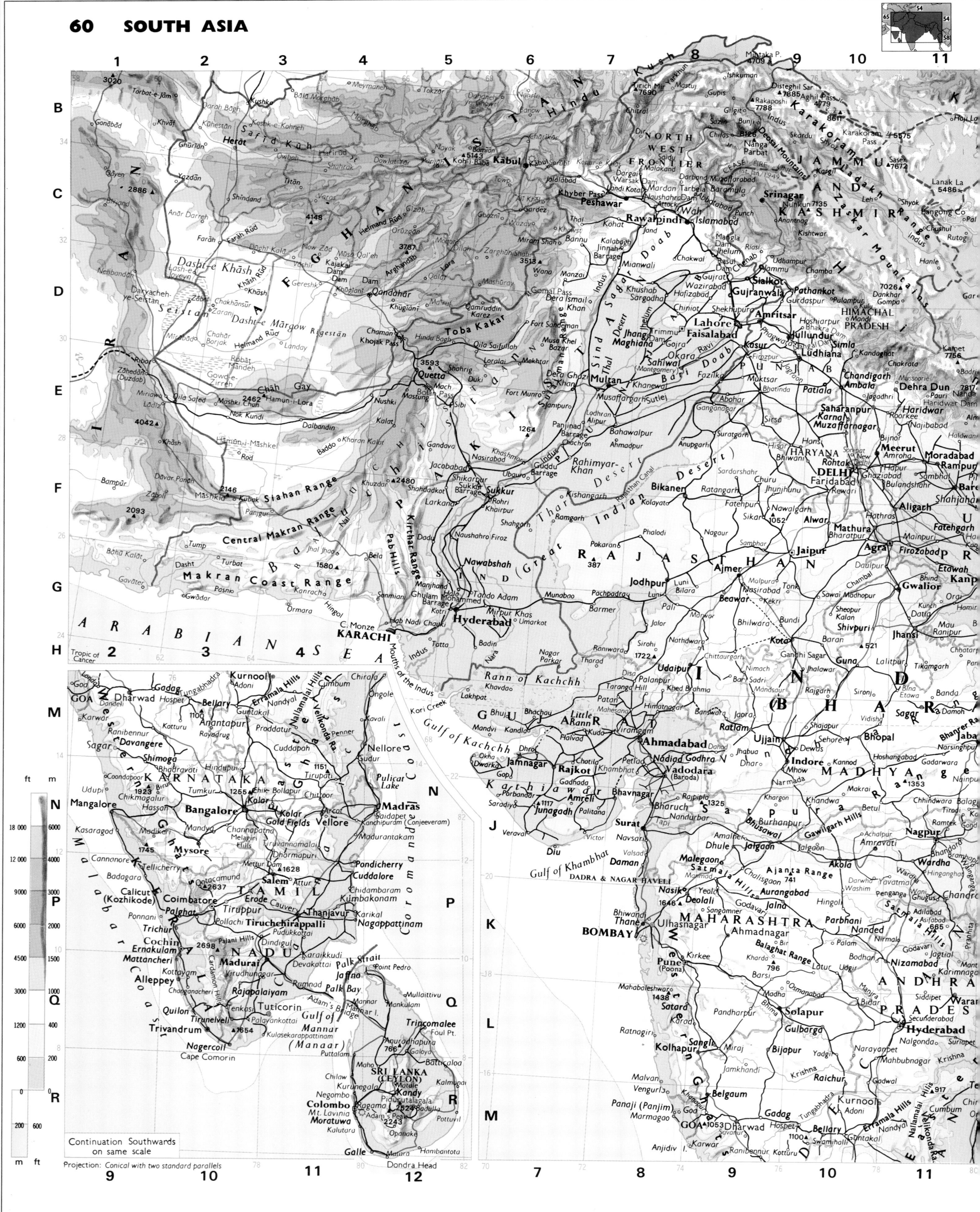

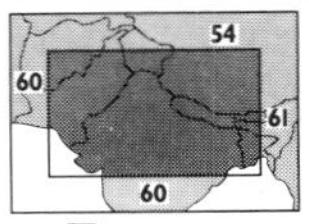

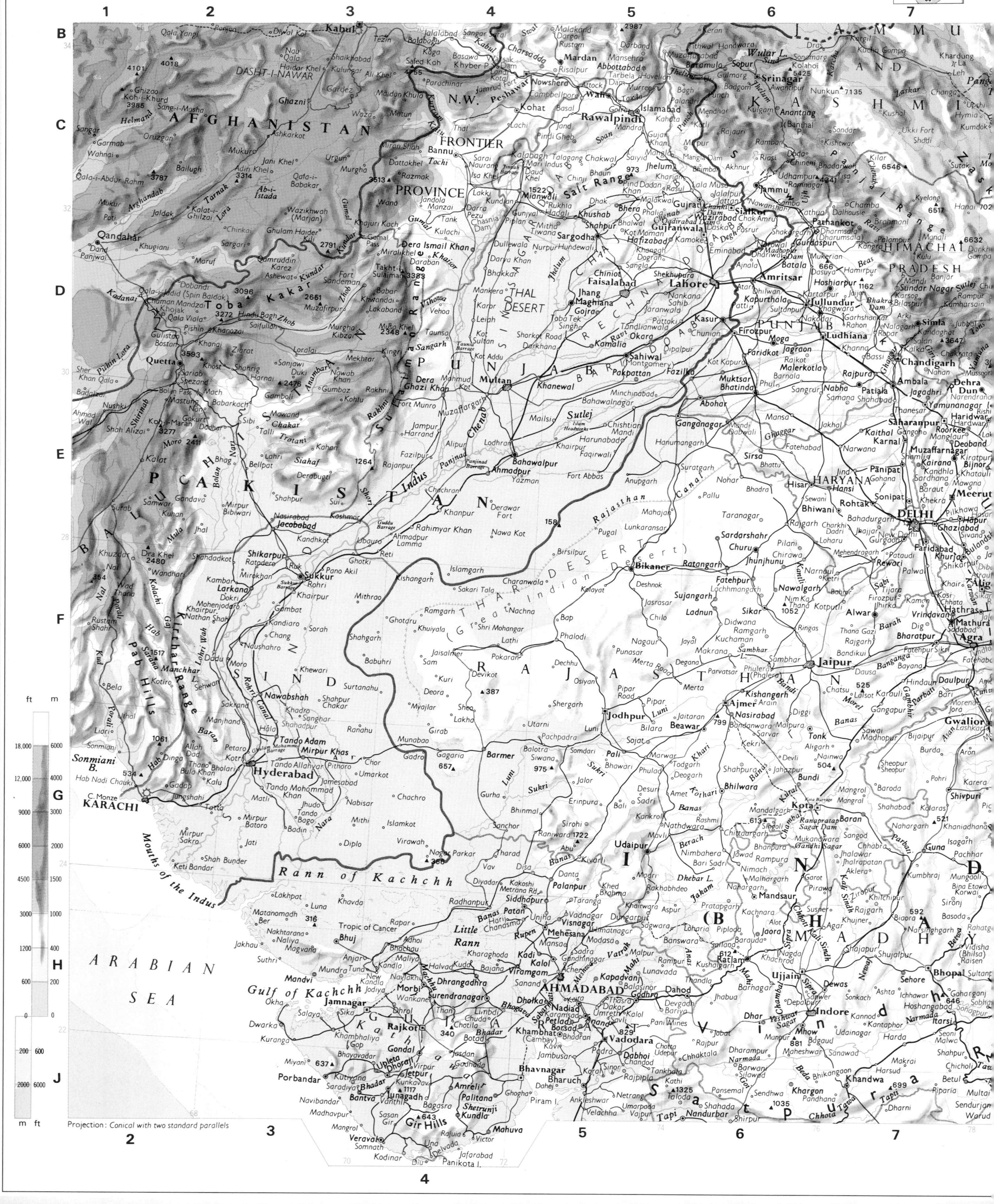

AFGHANISTAN

PAKISTAN

BALUCHISTAN

SIND

PUNJAB

N.W. FRONTIER PROVINCE

THAL DESERT

THAR DESERT

Great Indian Desert

RAJASTHAN

HARYANA

PUNJAB

HIMACHAL PRADESH

JAMMU AND KASHMIR

MADHYA PRADESH

GUJARAT

KARACHI

Kabul

DELHI

New Delhi

Srinagar

Jammu

Amritsar

Lahore

Faisalabad

Rawalpindi

Islamabad

Peshawar

Quetta

Multan

Hyderabad

AHMADABAD

Jaipur

Jodhpur

Udaipur

Vadodara

Bhopal

Indore

Gwalior

Agra

Mathura

Ludhiana

Chandigarh

Simla

Dehra Dun

Saharanpur

Meerut

Ghaziabad

ARABIAN SEA

Gulf of Kachchh

Rann of Kachchh

Little Rann

Mouths of the Indus

Tropic of Cancer

Gir Hills

Rajkot

Jamnagar

Bhavnagar

Bhuj

Porbandar

Junagadh

Projection: Conical with two standard parallels

ft m
18,000 6000
12,000 4000
9000 3000
6000 2000
4500 1500
3000 1000
1200 400
600 200
0
200 600
2000 6000
m ft

JAMMU AND KASHMIR
On same scale as Main Map

1 : 4 800 000

50   50   100 miles

50   50   100   150 km

East from Greenwich

COPYRIGHT. GEORGE PHILIP & SON, LTD.

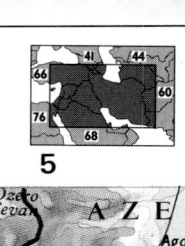

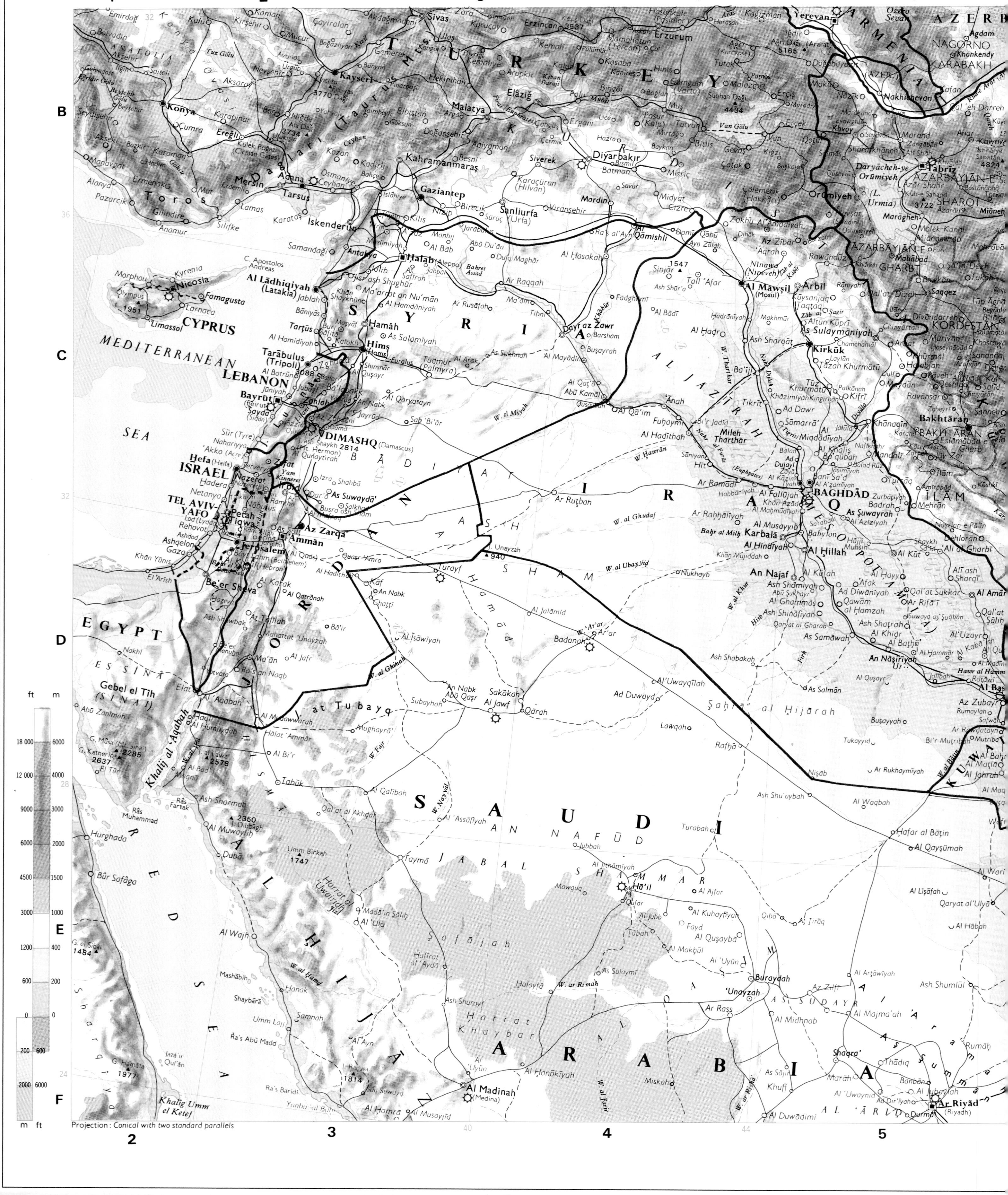

Projection: Conical with two standard parallels

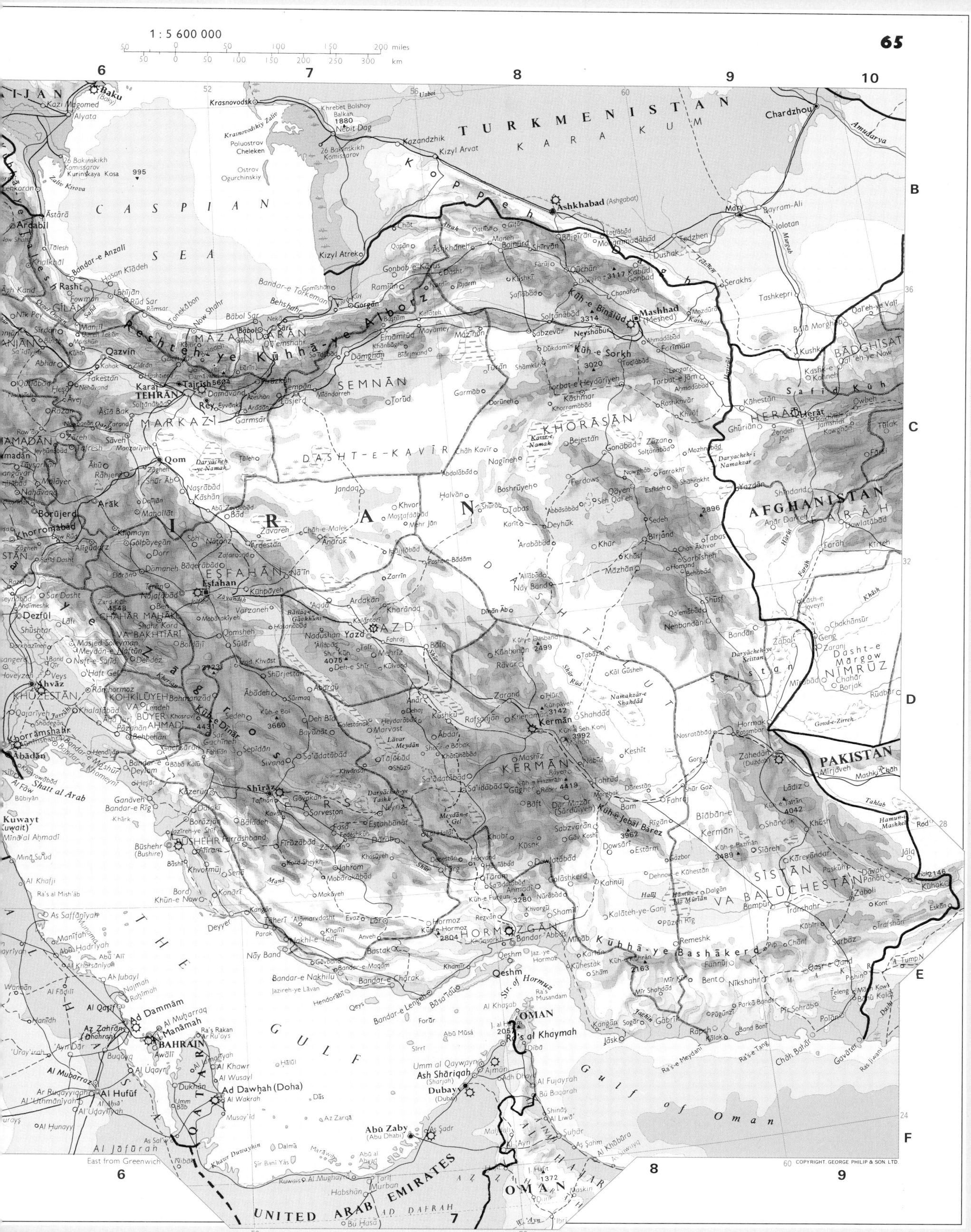

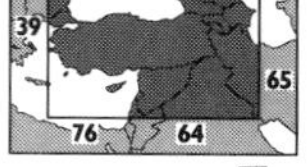

BLACK SEA

BULGARIA

GREECE

THRACE

ISTANBUL

Izmit (Kocaeli)

Adapazari (Sakarya)

Bolu

BITHYNIA

Bursa

Eskişehir

PAPHLAGONIA

Zonguldak

Karabük

Samsun

Bafra

Amasya

Çorum

Turhal

Tokat

Ankara

GALATIA

Kırıkkale

Kırşehir

CAPPADOCIA

Kayseri

Nevşehir

Aksaray

MYSIA

LYDIA

Manisa

İzmir (Smyrna)

Aydın

Nazilli

Denizli

PHRYGIA

Afyonkarahisar

Kütahya

Uşak

Anadolu (Anatolia)

CARIA

Burdur

Isparta

Konya

LYCAONIA

Karaman

Niğde

CATAONIA

Kahramanmaraş

Kozan

Adana

Tarsus

Mersin (İçel)

Ceyhan

Osmaniye

Gazian

CILICIA

PISIDIA

PAMPHYLIA

LYCIA

Antalya

Antalya Körfezi

İskenderun

İskenderun Körfezi

Antakya (Hatay)

Halab (Aleppo)

Idlib

TOROS DAĞLARI (Taurus Mountains)

Dhodhekánisos (Dodecanese)

Ródhos

Kárpathos

MEDITERRANEAN SEA

CYPRUS

Nicosia

Famagusta

Larnaca

Limassol

Troodos 1951

Paphos

Al Lādhiqiyah (Latakia)

Jablah

Bāniyās

Hamāh

Maşyāf

Tarţūs

Ḥimş (Homs)

Tarābulus (Tripoli)

LEBANON

Bayrut (Beirut)

Sayda (Sidon)

Ḍimashq (Damascus)

Nahariyya

'Akko (Acre)

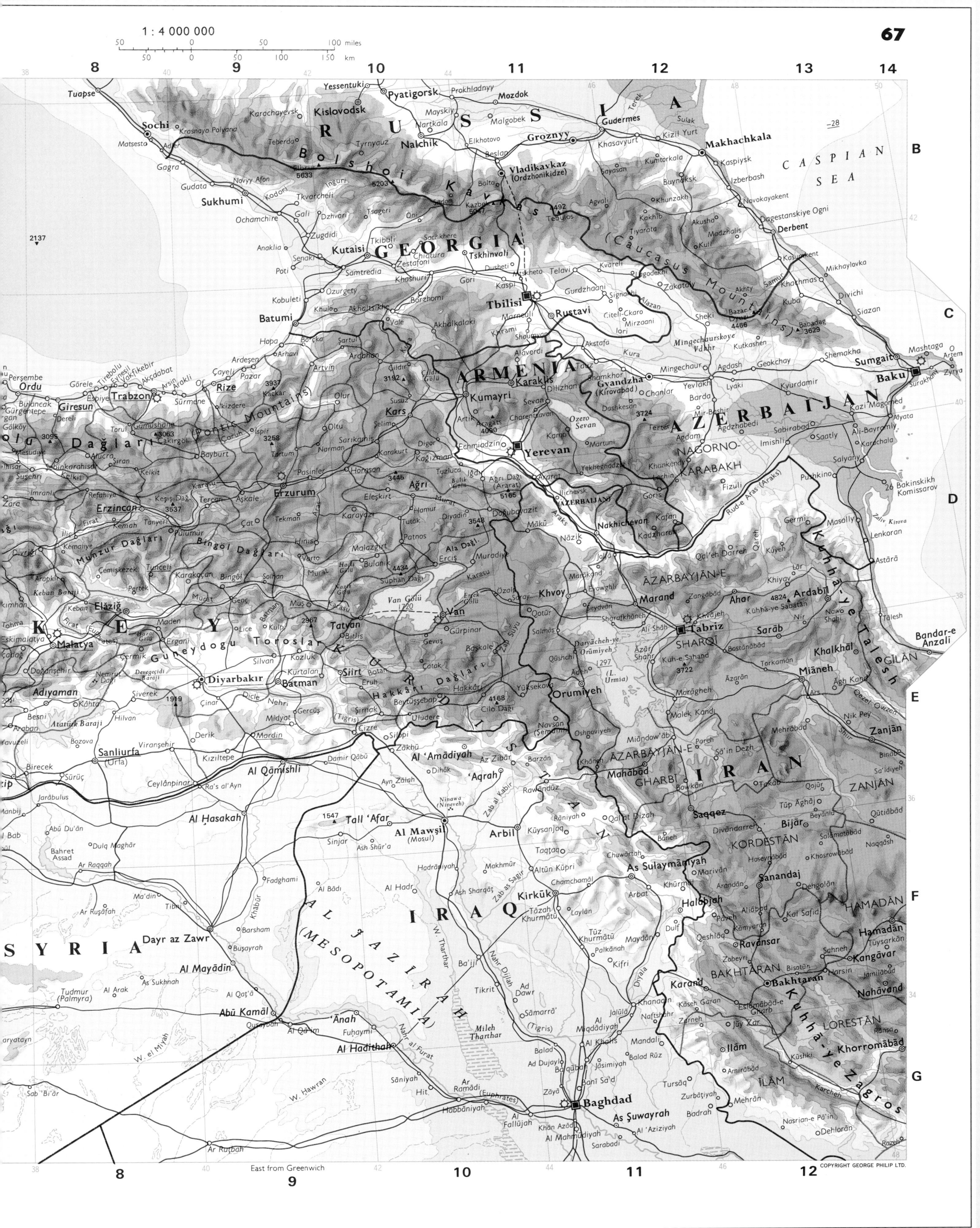

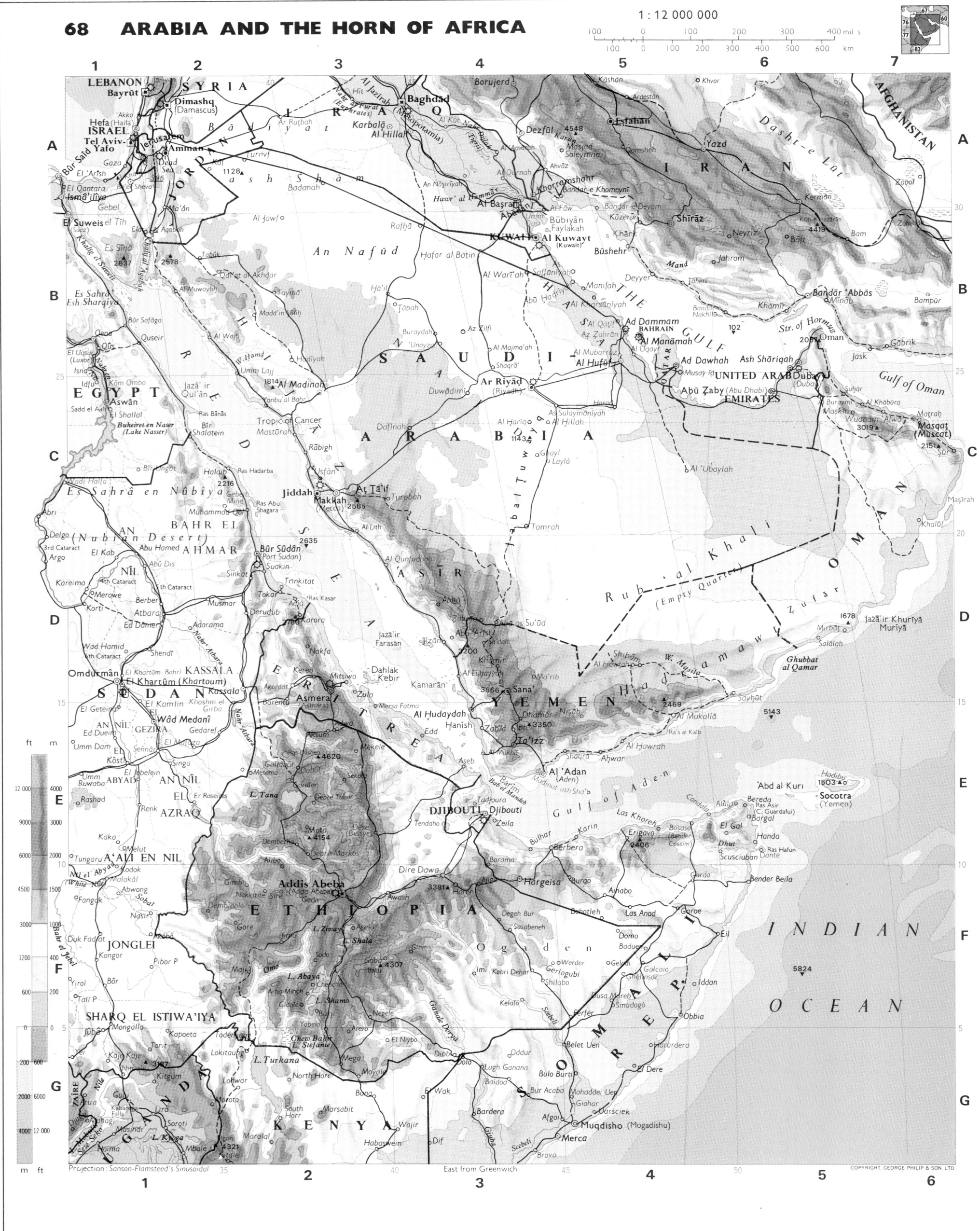

1 : 12 000 000

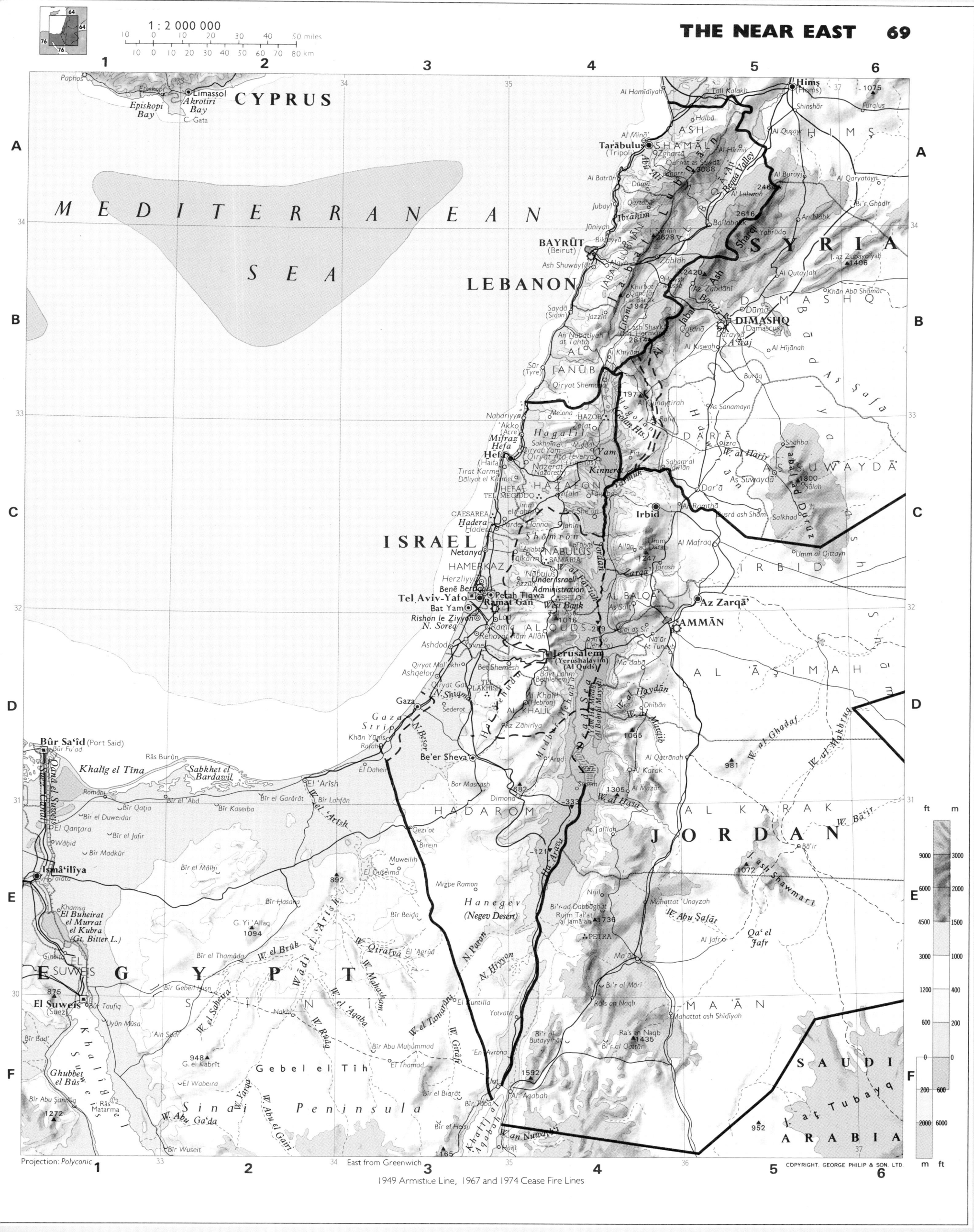

1 : 2 000 000

10   10   20   30   40   50 miles
10   0   10   20   30   40   50   60   70   80 km

CYPRUS

Paphos
Episkopi
Bay
Limassol
Akrotiri
Bay
C. Gata

M E D I T E R R A N E A N

S E A

LEBANON

Hims
(Homs)

Tall Kalakh
Al Hamidiyah
Shinshar
Furqlus
1075

ASH
Al Mina'
Tarābulus
(Tripoli)
SHAMĀLN
Halba
Al Quşayr
HIMS
Qurnat as Sawda'
3088
Al Hirmil
Al Buray
Al Qaryatayn

Al Batrūn
Dūmā
Qarţabā
2467
Bi'r Ghadir
Jubayl
Ba'labakk
An Nabk
Jūniya
Ibrahim
2616
Yabrūd
Bi'ir Ghadir
2628
Şaḥḥīn
HIMS
BAYRŪT
(Beirut)
Bikfayya
2814
SYRIA
Zaḥlah
2420
Ash
Al Qutayfah
Ash Shuwayfāt
Khirbat
al Barak
Az Zabdānī
Khān Abū Shāmat
1942
Jabal
Saydā
(Sidon)
Jazzīn
Qatanā
Al Kiswah
DIMASHQ
(Damascus)
An Nabaṭīyah
at Tahta
Jabal ash Shaykh
2814
Al Khiyām
'Arrayā
A'āj
Al Hijānah
Sūr
(Tyre)
Qiryat Shemona
1197
Burāq
Qunayţirah
As Sanamayn
Būrāq
AL
JANŪB
HAZOR
Rafīd
DAR'Ā
AS
SUWAYDA'
Shahba
Naḥariyya
Me'ona
HAZOR
Golan
1800
'Akko
(Acre)
Hagalil
Zefat
Dar'ā
Sahem
Golan
As Suwaydā'
Mifraz
Hefa
Sakhnin
Migdal
Şalāḥ
Ḥefa
(Haifa)
Qiryat Yam
Nazerat
(Nazareth)
Yam
Kinneret
Jūlān
W. al Harir
Tirat Karmel
Dāliyat el Karmel
Afula
Yarmūk
Dar'ā
Şûrâ ash Shām
Salkhad
HEFA
TEL MEGIDDO
HA'EMEQ
Umm el Fahm
Bet She'an
Irbid
Umm al Qittayn
CAESAREA
Shōmrōn
Jenin
'Ajlūn
IRBID
Hadera
Pardes Hanna
Allūn
'Ailūn
Umm
Qays
Hadera
ISRAEL
Netanya
Tulkarm
1247
Herzliyya
NĀBULUS
Zarqā'
Jarash
HAMERKAZ
SAMARIA
'Azzūn
W. al Fār'ah
Benē Beraq
Nāblus
Under Israeli
Administration
AL BALQĀ'
Petah Tiqwa
SHILO
As Salt
Az Zarqā'
Tel Aviv-Yafo
Ramat Gan
West Bank
1016
Bat Yam
Wādī aş Şīr
AMMĀN
Rishon le Ziyyon
Lod
Ram Allāh
ALQUDS
At Tunayb
N. Soreq
Ramla
Rehovot
Na'ūr
Rehovot
'En Kerem
AL 'ĀŞIMAH
Ashdod
Qiryat Mal'akhi
Bet Shemesh
Jerusalem
(Yerushalayim)
(Al Quds)
Ma'daba
Ashqelon
Bayt Laḥm
(Bethlehem)
TEL
LAKHISH
Qiryat Gat
Al Khalīl
(Hebron)
W. al Haydān
Dhibān
Gaza
N. Shiqma
Sederot
Az Zāhirīya
1065
Gaza
Strip
AL KHALĪL
W. al Mawjib
Khān Yūnis
N. Besor
Rafah
El 'Arish
Bor Mashash
Arad
981
W. al Ghadaf
Be'er Sheva
El Daheir
1305
Al Karak
W. al Hasa
Bir el Garārāt
Bir Lahfān
Dimona
At Ţafīlah
AL KARAK
W. Bā'ir
Bûr Sa'îd
(Port Said)
Bûr Fu'ad
Rās Burūn
Sabkhet el
Bardawîl
HADAROM
W. al Hasa
Al Mazār
Bir el 'Abd
Wādī al 'Arîsh
333
1072
JORDAN
Khalîg el Tîna
Romani
Bir Qaţia
El Qantara
Bir Gifgāfa
Muweilih
Birein
Nijil
Bâ'ir
Bâ'ir
Ismâ'ilîya
Wāḥid
Bir Madkûr
Qezi'ot
El Quseima
Ţash Shawmari
Khamsa
El Buheirat
el Murrat
el Kubra
(Gt. Bitter L.)
892
Bir Hasana
Mizpe Ramon
Bi'r ad Dabbāghāt
Rujm Tal'at
al Jamā'ah
1736
Mahaţţat 'Unayza
W. Abu Şafār
Al Jafr
Qā' el
Jafr
G. Yi 'Allaq
1094
E G Y P T
Hanegev
(Negev Desert)
PETRA
Ma'ān
EL SUWEIS
Bir el Thamāda
W. el Brûk
El 'Agrûd
N. Puran
N. Hiyyon
Ma'ān
MA'ĀN
Gineifa
875
El Suweis
(Suez)
Bir Gebel Hisn
W. el Sheira
W. Mahashm
El Kuntilla
Ra's on Naqb
Bir Taufiq
Nakhl
W. el 'Aqaba
Yotvata
Mahaţţat ash Shidîyah
Bir Bad'
'Ayûn Mûsa
'Ain Sudr
Bir Abu Muhammad
'En 'Avrona
Bi'r al Mārî
SAUDI
Bir Abu Şanûg
948
G. el Kabrit
Bîr al Butayyḥāt
Bi'r al Qaţţār
Lat Tubayq
Ghubbet
el Bûs
1272
El Wabeira
Gebel el Tîh
ET Thamad
1592
Ra's an Naqb
1435
ARABIA
Ras el
Matarma
Sinai
Peninsula
W. Varqa
Bir el Biarat
Al 'Aqabah
952
Bir Wuseit
W. Abu Ga'da
W. Abu Gani
Bir el Hesu
Hejl
1165

Projection: Polyconic   East from Greenwich

COPYRIGHT. GEORGE PHILIP & SON. LTD.

1949 Armistice Line, 1967 and 1974 Cease Fire Lines

ft   m
9000   3000
6000   2000
4500   1500
3000   1000
1200   400
600   200
0   0
200   600
2000   6000
m   ft

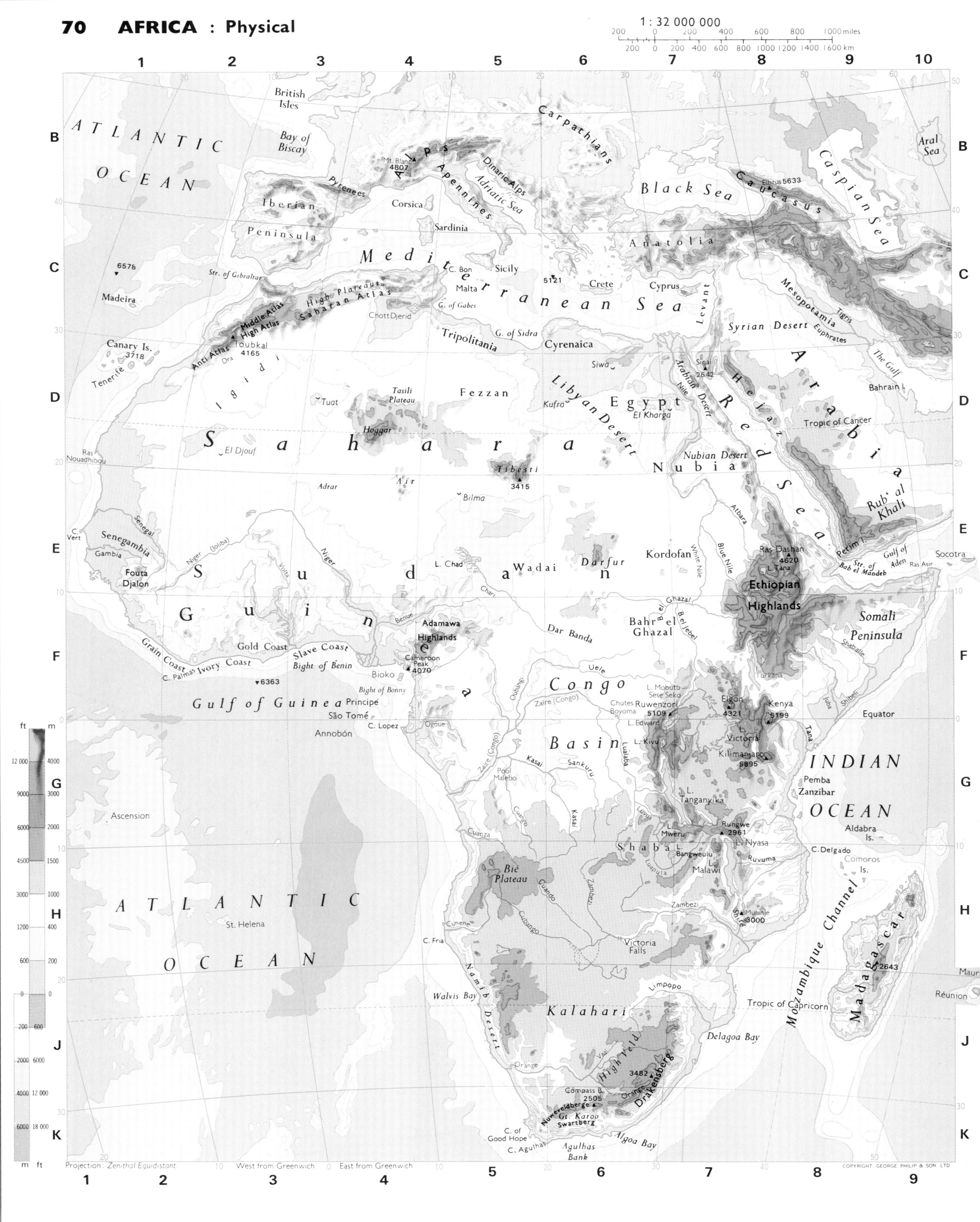

1 : 32 000 000

200   0   200   400   600   800   1000 miles
200   0   200 400 600 800 1000 1200 1400 1600 km

B ATLANTIC OCEAN

British Isles
Bay of Biscay
Alps
Mt. Blanc 4807
Pyrenees
Apennines
Dinaric Alps
Adriatic Sea
Carpathians
Black Sea
Caucasus
Elbrus 5633
Caspian Sea
Aral Sea

C Madeira
Iberian Peninsula
Corsica
Sardinia
6576
Str. of Gibraltar
High Plateaus
Saharan Atlas
Middle Atlas
High Atlas
C. Bon
Sicily
Malta
5121
Crete
Cyprus
Anatolia
Mediterranean Sea
Levant
Mesopotamia
Tigris
Euphrates
Syrian Desert
The Gulf
Bahrain I.

D Canary Is. 3718
Tenerife
Anti Atlas
Toubkal 4165
Dra
I g i d i
Tuat
Tasili Plateau
Hoggar
Chott Djerid
G. of Gabes
G. of Sidra
Tripolitania
Cyrenaica
Fezzan
Libyan Desert
Egypt
Kufra
El Kharga
Siwa
Arabian Desert
Nile
Sinai 2642
Red Sea
Hejaz
Arabia
Tropic of Cancer

E Ras Nouadhibou
S a h a r a
El Djouf
Adrar
Aïr
Bilma
Tibesti 3415
Nubia
Nubian Desert
Atbara
Ras Dashan 4620
L. Tana
Perim I.
Gulf of Aden
Bab el Mandeb
Socotra
Ras Asir
Rub' al Khali
Str. of

E C. Vert
Senegal
Senegambia
Gambia
Fouta Djalon
Niger (Joliba)
Volta
Niger
S u d a n
L. Chad
Wadai
Darfur
Kordofan
White Nile
Blue Nile
Ethiopian Highlands
Somali Peninsula
Shabeli

F Grain Coast
Ivory Coast
C. Palmas
Gold Coast
Slave Coast
Bight of Benin
Bioko
6363
Benue
Adamawa Highlands
Cameroon Peak 4070
G u i n e a
Chari
Dar Banda
Bahr el Ghazal
Bahr el Ghazal
Bahr el Jebel
Uele
Ubangi
Congo Basin
Uele
Turkana
Somali Peninsula

G Gulf of Guinea
Principe
São Tomé
Annobón
C. Lopez
Ogoue
Zaire (Congo)
Zaire (Congo)
Congo
Pool Malebo
Kasai
Sankuru
Lualaba
L. Mobutu-Sese Seko
Chutes Boyoma
Ruwenzori 5109
L. Edward
L. Kivu
L. Tanganyika
Elgon 4321
Kenya 5199
Victoria
Kilimanjaro 5895
Equator
Pemba
Zanzibar
INDIAN OCEAN
Aldabra Is.

H Ascension
St. Helena
ATLANTIC OCEAN
Cuango
Cuanza
Kasai
Congo
Cuando
Bié Plateau
Shaba
L. Mweru
Luapula
L. Bangweulu
Lugo
Rungwe 2961
L. Nyasa
L. Malawi
Ruvuma
C. Delgado
Comoros Is.
Mulanje 3000
Zambezi
Madagascar 2643
Mozambique Channel

J C. Fria
Namib Desert
Walvis Bay
Cunene
Cubango
Kalahari
Victoria Falls
Limpopo
Zambezi
Tropic of Capricorn
Delagoa Bay
Maur.
Réunion

K C. of Good Hope
Orange
Vaal
Highveld
3482
Gt. Karoo
Nieuveldberge 2505
Swartberg
Compass B. 2505
Drakensberg
Orange
C. Agulhas
Agulhas Bank
Algoa Bay

Projection : Zenithal Equidistant
West from Greenwich
East from Greenwich
COPYRIGHT GEORGE PHILIP & SON LTD

ft   m
12 000 4000
9000 3000
6000 2000
4500 1500
3000 1000
1200 400
600 200
0 0
200 600
2000 6000
4000 12 000
6000 18 000
m   ft

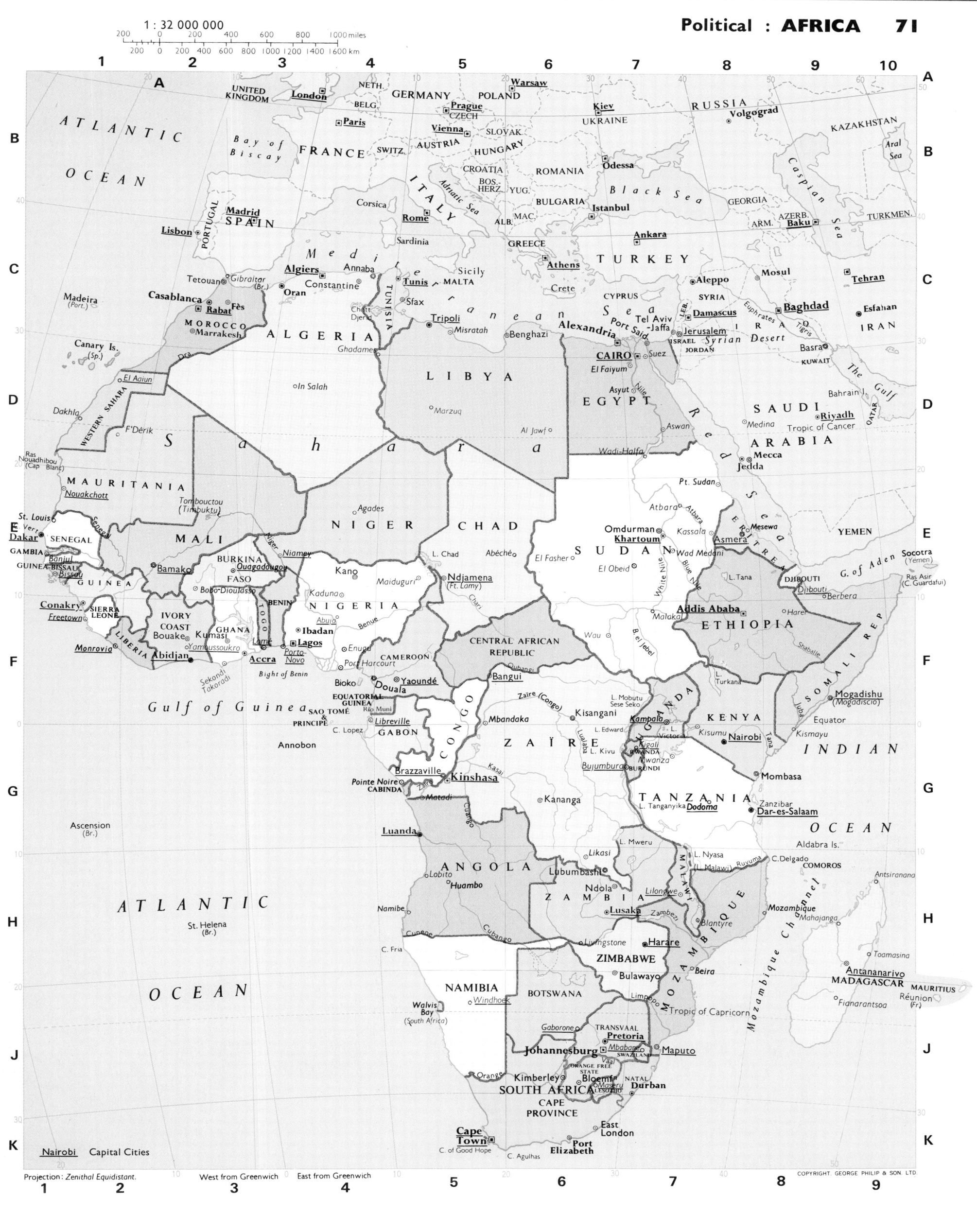

1 : 32 000 000

200   0   200   400   600   800   1000 miles
200   0   200   400 600 800 1000 1200 1400 1600 km

ATLANTIC

OCEAN

Bay of Biscay

UNITED KINGDOM   London   NETH.   GERMANY   POLAND   Warsaw

BELG.   Prague   CZECH   Kiev   RUSSIA   Volgograd

Paris   Vienna   SLOVAK.   UKRAINE   KAZAKHSTAN

FRANCE   SWITZ.   AUSTRIA   HUNGARY   Odessa   Aral Sea

CROATIA   ROMANIA   Black Sea

BOS. HERZ.   YUG.   BULGARIA   Istanbul   GEORGIA   Caspian Sea

Corsica   ITALY   MAC.   ARM.   AZERB.   Baku   TURKMEN.

Madrid   SPAIN   Rome   GREECE   Athens   TURKEY   Ankara

Lisbon   PORTUGAL   Sardinia   ALB.   CYPRUS   Aleppo   Mosul   Tehran

Tetouan   Gibraltar (Br.)   Algiers   Annaba   Sicily   MALTA   SYRIA   Damascus   Baghdad   Esfahan

Casablanca   Oran   Constantine   Tunis   Crete   Tel Aviv-Jaffa   IRAQ   Basra

Rabat   Fès   Sfax   Mediterranean Sea   Port Said   ISRAEL   Jerusalem   Tigris   IRAN

MOROCCO   Marrakesh   TUNISIA   Tripoli   Misratah   Benghazi   Alexandria   JORDAN   Syrian Desert   KUWAIT

Canary Is. (Sp.)   Ghadames   CAIRO   Suez   SAUDI   The Gulf   Bahrain I.   QATAR

Madeira (Port.)   In Salah   LIBYA   El Faiyum   EGYPT   Medina   Riyadh   ARABIA

Dakhla   WESTERN SAHARA   El Aaiun   Marzuq   Al Jawf   Aswan   Tropic of Cancer   Mecca   Jedda

F'Derik   Sahara   Wadi Halfa   Pt. Sudan   Red Sea

Ras Nouadhibou (Cap Blanc)   MAURITANIA   Nouakchott   Tombouctou (Timbuktu)   Agades   NIGER   CHAD   Atbara   Kassala   Mesewa   YEMEN

St. Louis   Senegal   Niamey   Kano   L. Chad   Abéché   Omdurman   Khartoum   Asmera   G. of Aden   Socotra (Yemen)

Dakar   SENEGAL   MALI   Bamako   BURKINA FASO   Ouagadougou   Kaduna   Maiduguri   Ndjamena (Ft. Lamy)   El Fasher   SUDAN   Wad Medani   ERITREA   DJIBOUTI   Ras Asir (C. Guardafui)

GAMBIA   Banjul   Ouagadougou   Bobo-Dioulasso   NIGERIA   Chari   El Obeid   White Nile   Blue Nile   L. Tana   Djibouti   Berbera

GUINEA-BISSAU   Bissau   GUINEA   Conakry   SIERRA LEONE   Freetown   IVORY COAST   Bouake   Kumasi   GHANA   TOGO   BENIN   Ibadan   Abuja   Benue   CENTRAL AFRICAN REPUBLIC   Wau   Malakal   Harer   ETHIOPIA   SOMALI REP.

Monrovia   LIBERIA   Yamoussoukro   Accra   Lome   Lagos   Enugu   CAMEROON   Bangui   Addis Ababa

Abidjan   Sekondi Takoradi   Porto-Novo   Port Harcourt   Bioko   Yaoundé   Oubangui   B. el Jebel   L. Turkana   Shabelle

Bight of Benin   Douala   EQUATORIAL GUINEA   Rio Muni   Zaïre (Congo)   Kisangani   UGANDA   KENYA   Juba   Mogadishu (Mogadiscio)

Gulf of Guinea   SAO TOMÉ & PRINCIPE   Libreville   GABON   CONGO   Mbandaka   L. Mobutu Sese Seko   Kampala   Kisumu   Nairobi   Equator   Kismayu

Annobon   C. Lopez   ZAÏRE   L. Edward   L. Victoria   RWANDA   Kigali   INDIAN

Brazzaville   Kinshasa   Kasai   Lualaba   L. Kivu   BURUNDI   Bujumbura   Mwanza   Mombasa

Pointe Noire   CABINDA   Matadi   Kananga   L. Tanganyika   TANZANIA   Dodoma   Zanzibar   OCEAN

Luanda   Congo   L. Mweru   Dar-es-Salaam

Ascension (Br.)   Likasi   Aldabra Is.

ATLANTIC   Lobito   ANGOLA   Lubumbashi   L. Nyasa (L. Malawi)   Ruvuma   C. Delgado   COMOROS   Antsiranana

Huambo   Ndola   ZAMBIA   MALAWI   Mozambique   Mahajanga

St. Helena (Br.)   Namibe   Lusaka   Lilongwe   Blantyre   Toamasina

Cunene   C. Fria   Livingstone   Harare   Beira   MOZAMBIQUE   Antananarivo   MADAGASCAR   MAURITIUS

OCEAN   Cubango   ZIMBABWE   Bulawayo   Mozambique Channel   Fianarantsoa   Réunion (Fr.)

NAMIBIA   Windhoek   BOTSWANA   Limpopo   Tropic of Capricorn

Walvis Bay (South Africa)   Gaborone   TRANSVAAL   Pretoria   Mbabane   Maputo

Orange   Johannesburg   Vaal   SWAZILAND

Kimberley   ORANGE FREE STATE   Bloemfontein   Maseru   NATAL   Durban   J

SOUTH AFRICA   LESOTHO

CAPE PROVINCE   East London

Cape Town   C. of Good Hope   C. Agulhas   Port Elizabeth   K

Projection: Zenithal Equidistant.   West from Greenwich   East from Greenwich

Nairobi   Capital Cities

COPYRIGHT. GEORGE PHILIP & SON. LTD.

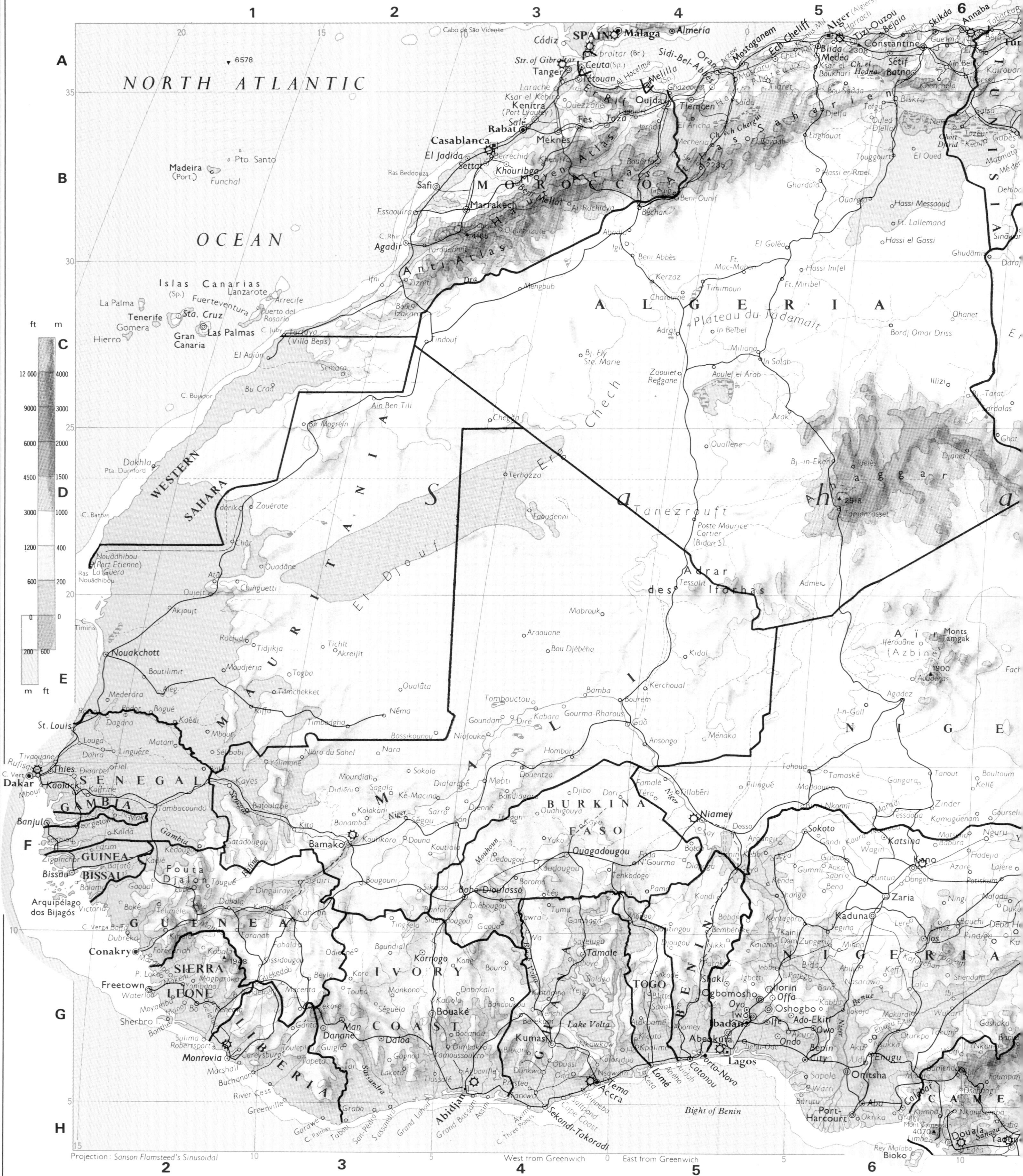

NORTH ATLANTIC

OCEAN

SPAIN

MOROCCO

WESTERN SAHARA

MAURITANIA

ALGERIA

MALI

NIGER

SENEGAL

GAMBIA

GUINEA BISSAU

GUINEA

SIERRA LEONE

LIBERIA

IVORY COAST

BURKINA FASO

GHANA

TOGO

BENIN

NIGERIA

CAMEROON

Islas Canarias (Sp.)

Madeira (Port.)

Bight of Benin

Projection: Sanson Flamsteed's Sinusoidal

West from Greenwich   East from Greenwich

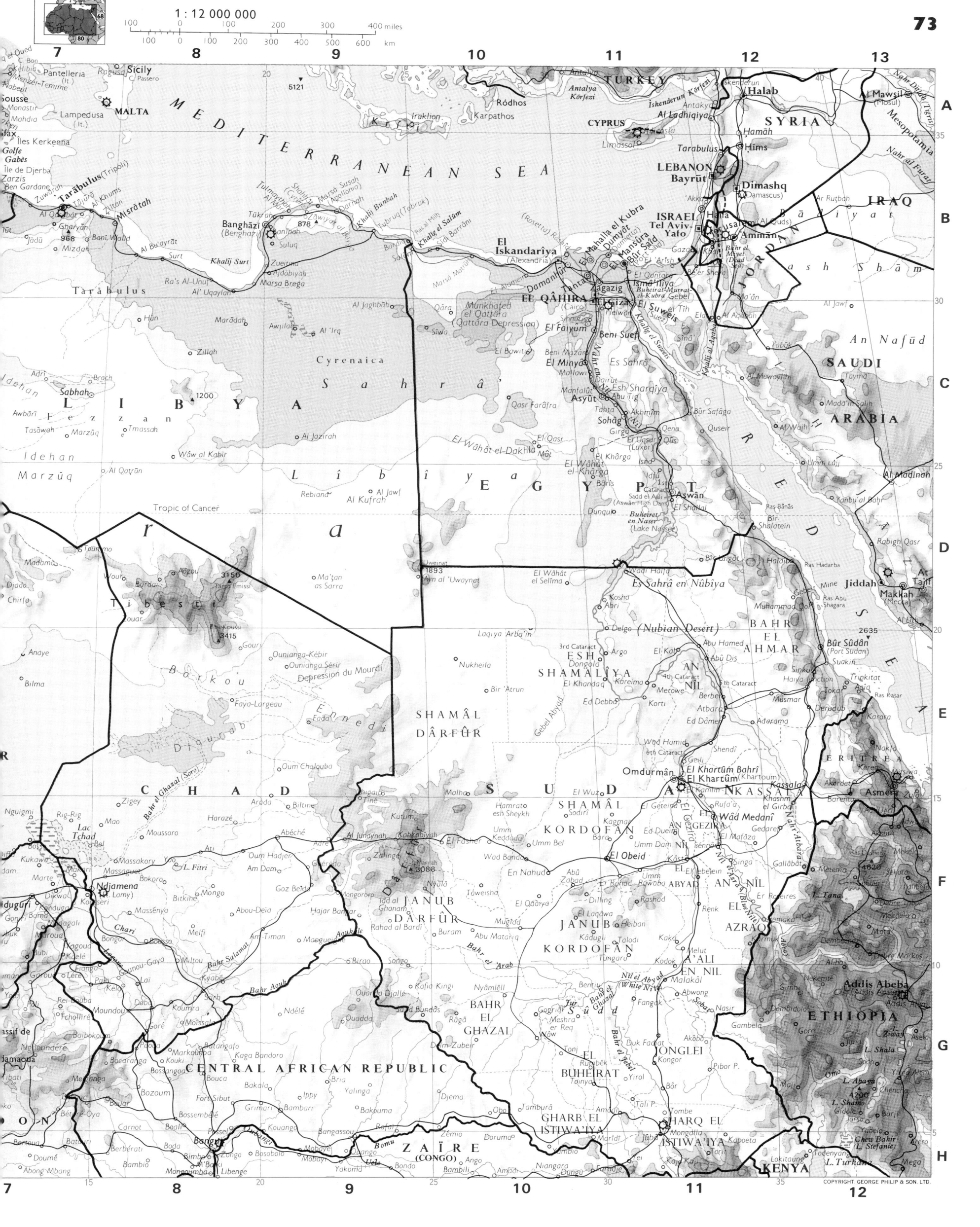

73

78 79

A

35

N O R T H   A T L A N T I C

Sanlúcar de Barrameda
SPAIN
Cádiz
Algeciras
Gibraltar
C. Trafalgar
Strait of Gibraltar
Tanger
Ceuta (Sp.)
Ras Tarf
Asilah
Martil
Tétouan
Larache
Chechaouen
Ksar el Kebir
Souk el Arba du Rharb
Ouezzane
2456
Mechra-bel-Ksiri
Allal-Tazi
Kenitra (Port Lyautey)
Sidi Slimane
Sidi Kacem
O C E A N
Salé
Volubilis
RABAT
MEKNES
Mohammedia (Fedala)
FES
CASABLANCA
Sefrou
Azemmour
Ben
Slimane
Khemisset
Azrou
El Jadida (Mazagan)
Berrechid
Benahmed
Fkih ben Salah
Khouribga
Khenifra
Settat
Oued Zem
Kasba Tadla
Ras Beddouza (C. Cantin)
Sidi Smail
Beni Mellal
Safi
Youssoufia
El Kelâa
MOROCCO
Essaouira (Mogador)
Chichaoua
MARRAKECH
4071
C. Tafelney
Tamanar
Amizmiz
4166
Toubkal
Taroudannt
Ouarzazate
Djebel Sarhro
Tinerhir
C. Rhir
Agadir
Inezgane
O. Souss
Anergane
Tizra
2359
Tinnet
Tiznit
Ifni
Foum Zguid
Zagora
O. Draa
Akka
Goulimine
Seyad
C. Draa
Oued Draa
Djebel Ouarkziz
Tindouf
Tan-tan
Tarfaya (Villa Bens)
C. Juby
Hagunia
El Masat
Messeled

B

Madeira (Port.)
I. de Porto Santo
Porto Moniz
São Vicente
Santana
Machico
Funchal
861
Ilhas Desertas

Ilhas Salvagens

La Palma
2423
Islas Canarias (Sp.)
Los Llanos de Aridane
Sta. Cruz de la Palma
Pta. Fuencaliente
Tenerife
La Laguna
Alegranza
Graciosa
Lanzarote
La Orotava
3718
Yaiza
Arrecife
Icod
Santa Cruz de Tenerife
La Oliva
I. de Lobos
S. Sebastian de la G.
Gomera
Granadilla de Abona
Guia
Puerto del Rosario
Valverde
1501
Hierro
Las Palmas
Gran Canaria
Aoreora
Pta. de la Rasca
1949
807
Pta. de Maspalomas
Fuerteventura

C

Hasi Tafrout
Daora
El Aaiún
Edchera
Saguia el Hamra
Smara
Tucat
Uad Erni
Sidi Ahmed Rguei
Munhes

WESTERN SAHARA

C. Bojador
El Hasian
Bu Craa
El Hadeb
Aridal
Tifarati
Aurist

Kreb r. Neggar
Kreb es Sefia
Kreb n-Naga
Kreb Chebiha
Gara Djebilet
O. Djebilet
Aet Legra

Ouahila
Khorb el Ethel
Tinfouchi
Hamada Tounassine
Tounassine
Rhemiles

D

12,000 4000
9000   3000
6000   2000
4500   1500
3000   1000
1200   400
600   200
0   0
200   600
2000   6000
4000   12000

Lomsid
Bu Jat
Hasi Nueifed
Zemmur
Guelta Zemmur
Amasin

Bir Moghrein (Fort Trinquet)
Agmar
Bir Bel Guerdâne
Sebkhet Iguetti

Sebkhet Oumm ed Drous Telli
Sebkhet Oumm ed Drous Guebli

Aïn Ben Tili
540

S A H A R A

El Kâghet
Yetti
Ghallamane
El Eglab

Ayoûn 'Abd el Mâlek
Mzerreb
Daya el Khadra
Tarhamanant

El Mreiti
Mdenan
Kreb en Naga
Agâraktem

Dakhla (Villa Cisneros)
Pta. Elbow
Pta. Durnford
El Aargub
B. de Rio de Oro
Bir Enzarán
Tiris
Sidi Emhamed

Sebkhet Mjill
El Aouj
Zouîrât
Hammâmi
Aguelt el Melah
M A U R I T A N I A
Agâraktem

Fdérik
Kediet Ijil
915
El Tourine
Meleizem
Bir Amrâne
Mejaouda
Terhazza
Taoudenni
En Nahrat

G. de Cintra
Pta. Negra
C. Barbas
Agailás
Aguenit
Aghreijit
Mâgteir
El Beyyed
El Ghallaouiya

Hamada Safia
Hamada el Hariche
Telig
Bir Chali

E

C. Corbeiro
Uad Tennuiur
Bir Gandús
Tichla
Zug
Char
Ahmeyim
El Mrâyer
Bir Ounane
El Ksaib Ounane
El Guettara
Dglats de Khenachiche

La Guera
Nouâdhibou (Port Etienne)
Ras Nouâdhibou
Bir el Gâreb
 Toueirma
Ouadâne
Chinguetti
Bollé
Dhar
MALI

Et Tidra
Ras Timiris
Nouâmghâr
Bennichâb
Agouifa
Amsâga
Oujeft
Oueilelen Nmâdi
Jafène
Doug
Ergg
I-n-Echai

Akjoujt

Sebkhet Te-n-Dghâmcha

Projection: Lambert's Equivalent Azimuthal

West from Greenwich

1   2   3   4

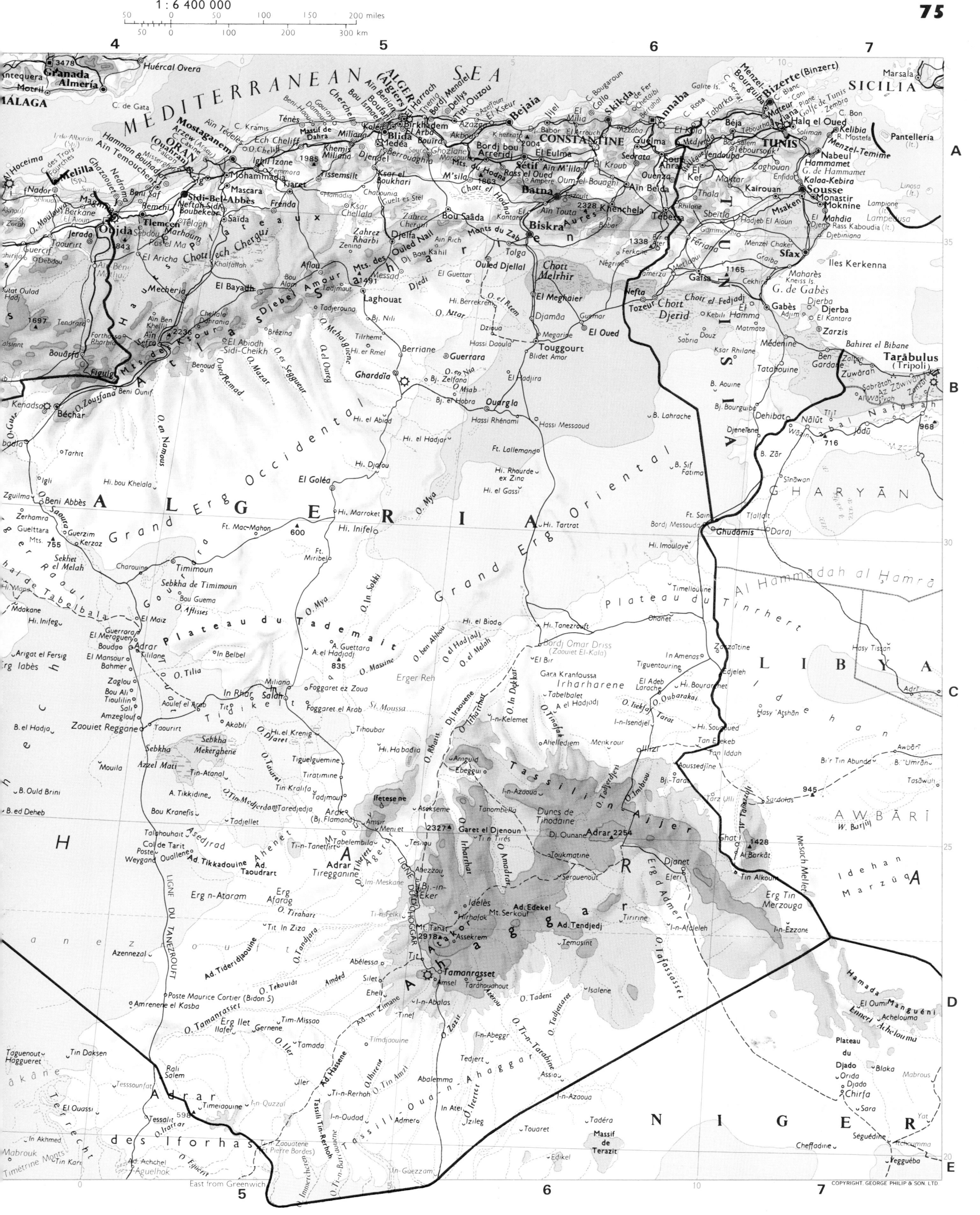

MEDITERRANEAN SEA

SICILIA

ALGERIA

TUNISIA

LIBYA

NIGER

1 : 6 400 000

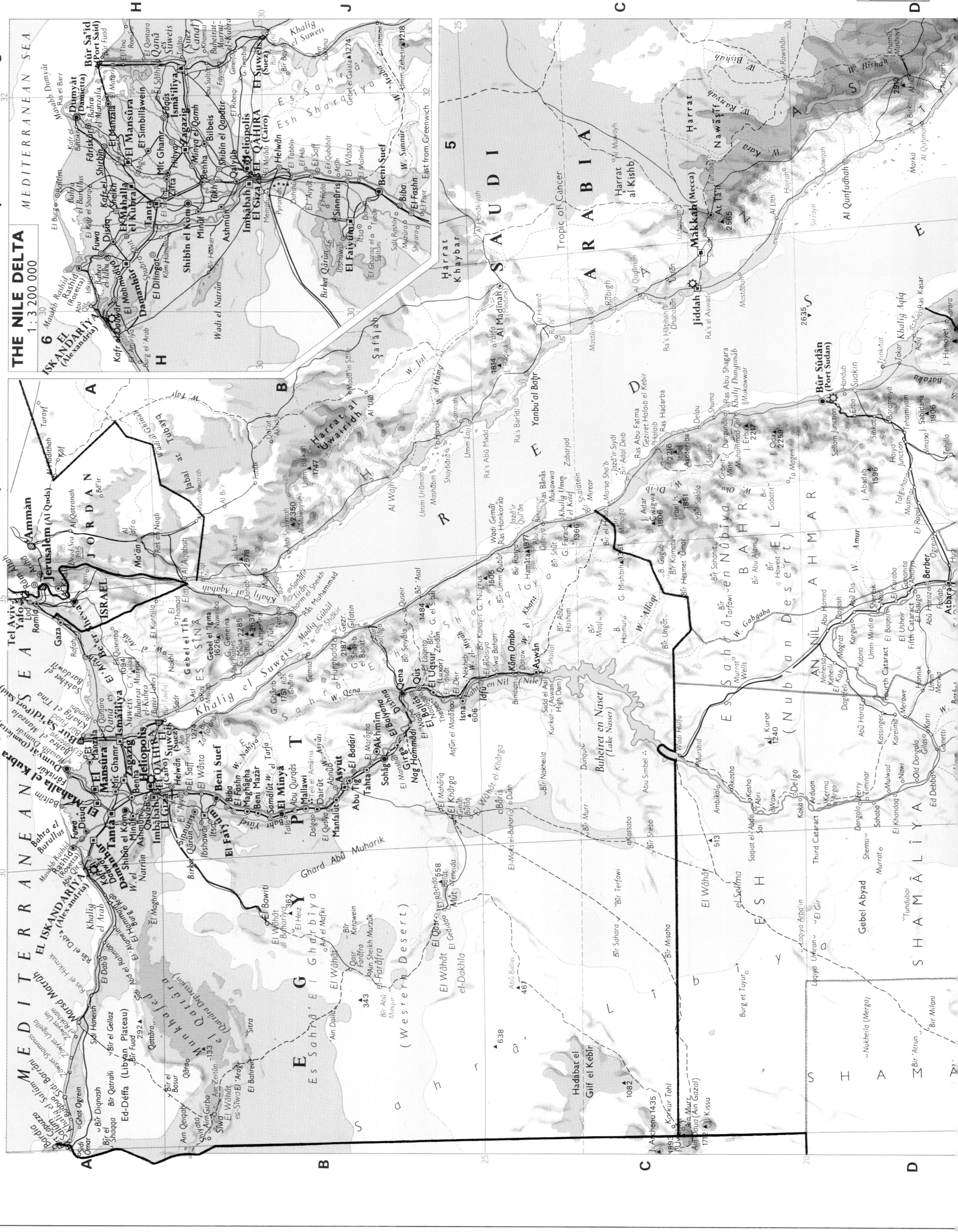

THE NILE DELTA
1 : 3 200 000

MEDITERRANEAN SEA

EGYPT

SAUDI ARABIA

JORDAN

ISRAEL

El QÂHIRA (Cairo)

El Iskandarîya (Alexandria)

Bûr Sa'îd (Port Said)

El Suweis (Suez)

Jerusalem (Al Quds)

'Ammân

Tel Aviv-Yafo

Gaza

Beni Suef

El Minyâ

Asyût

Sohâg

Nag Hammâdi

Qena

El Uqsur (Luxor)

Aswân

Kôm Ombo

Idfu

Esna

Makkah (Mecca)

Al Madînah (Medina)

Jiddah

Yanbu' al Baḥr

Bûr Sûdân (Port Sudan)

Berber

Atbara

Buheiret en Nâser (Lake Nasser)

Abu Simbel

ESH SHAMÂLÎYA

Es Saḥrâ' esh Sharqîya

Es Saḥrâ' el Gharbîya (Libyan Plateau)

(Western Desert)

(Nubian Desert)

EL BAḤR EL AḤMAR

Tropic of Cancer

East from Greenwich

Khalig el 'Aqabah

Khalig el Suweis

Sînâ'

Damietta

Dumyât

El Mansûra

Tanta

Zagazig

Ismâ'îlîya

Heliopolis

El Faiyûm

Khârga

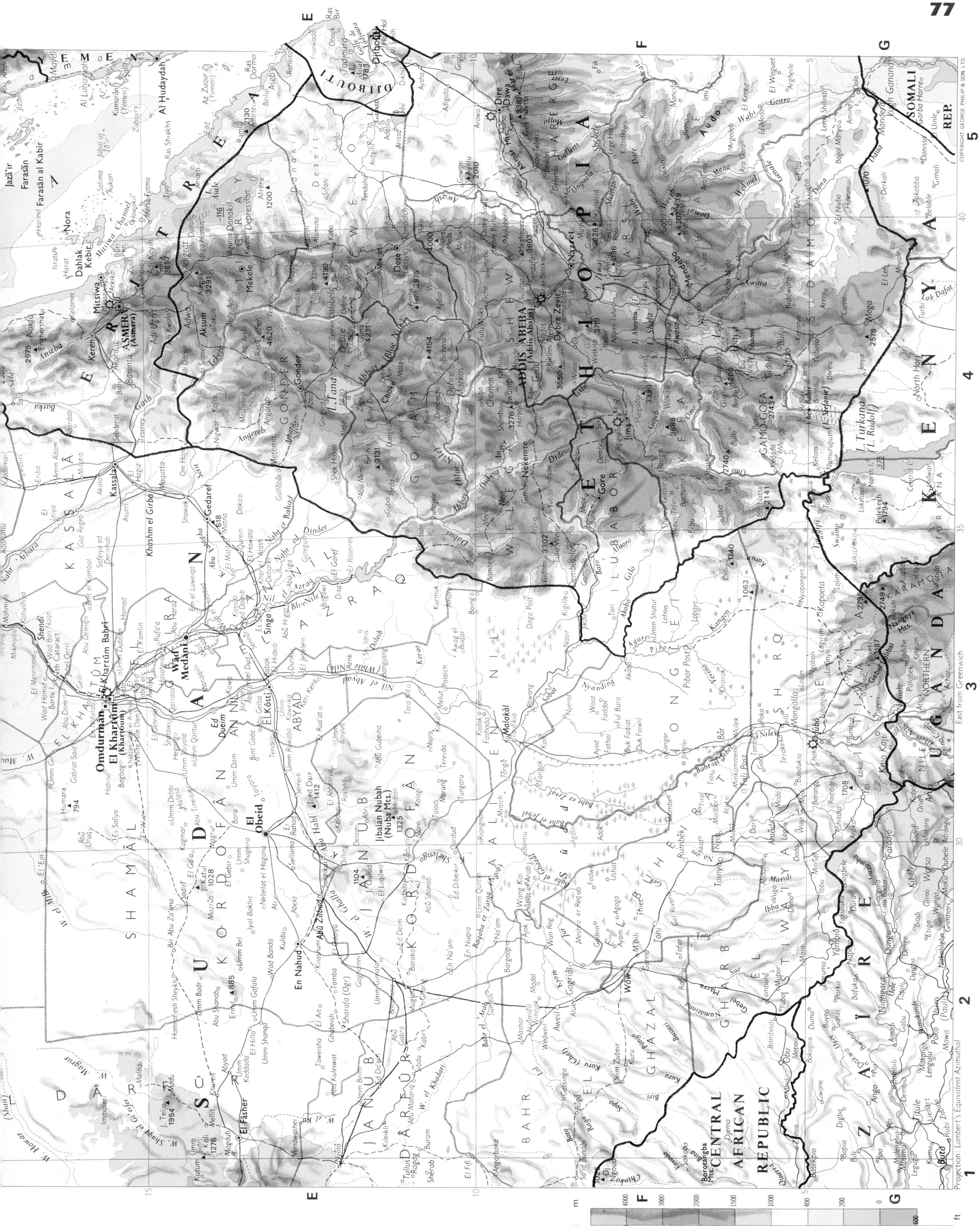

Map: Northeast Africa (Sudan, Ethiopia, Eritrea, Somalia)

Countries and major regions:

YEMEN

DJIBOUTI

ERITREA — ASMERA (Asmara), Keren, Mitsiwa, Nakfa

ETHIOPIA — ADDIS ABEBA (Addis Abeba), Gonder, Mekele, Aksum, Dese, Nazret, Debre Zeyit, Dire Dawa, Jima, Gore, Nekemte

SOMALI REP.

KENYA — L. Turkana (L. Rudolf)

UGANDA

ZAÏRE

CENTRAL AFRICAN REPUBLIC

SUDAN — El Khartûm (Khartoum), Omdurmân, El Khartûm Bahri, Wad Medani, El Obeid, El Fâsher, Kassala, Gedaref, Ed Damer, Shendi, En Nahud, El Kosti, Ed Dueim, Malakal

Regions of Sudan: KASSALA, KHARTÛM, AN NIL (White Nile), SHAMÂL DÂRFÛR, JANÛB DÂRFÛR, SHAMÂL KORDOFÂN, JANÛB KORDOFÂN, A ALI EN NIL, SHARQ EL ISTIWÂ'IYA, GHARB EL ISTIWÂ'IYA, BAHR EL GHAZAL, JUNGLEI

Water features: L. Tana, Blue Nile (Bahr el Azraq), White Nile (Bahr el Abyad), Nahr Atbara, Red Sea, Gulf of Aden, Dahlak Kebir, Farasân al Kabir

DANAKIL DESERT, Danakil Depression

Nuba Mts. (Jibalan Nubah) 1325

Selected elevations:
2854, 3291, 4190, 4620, 4231, 4154, 3603, 3375, 3550, 3276, 3131, 3302, 3319, 3560, 3381, 4307, 3386, 3300, 2578, 2743, 2740, 2141, 1063, 2749, 2130, 1200, 2010, 794, 618, 1028, 1104, 1412, 885, 1276, 1954, 1708, 1794, 375

Projection: Lambert's Equivalent Azimuthal

East from Greenwich

Scale bar (elevation):
ft: 12,000 / 9000 / 6000 / 4500 / 3000 / 1200 / 600 / 0
m: 4000 / 3000 / 2000 / 1500 / 1000 / 400 / 200 / 0 / 200–500

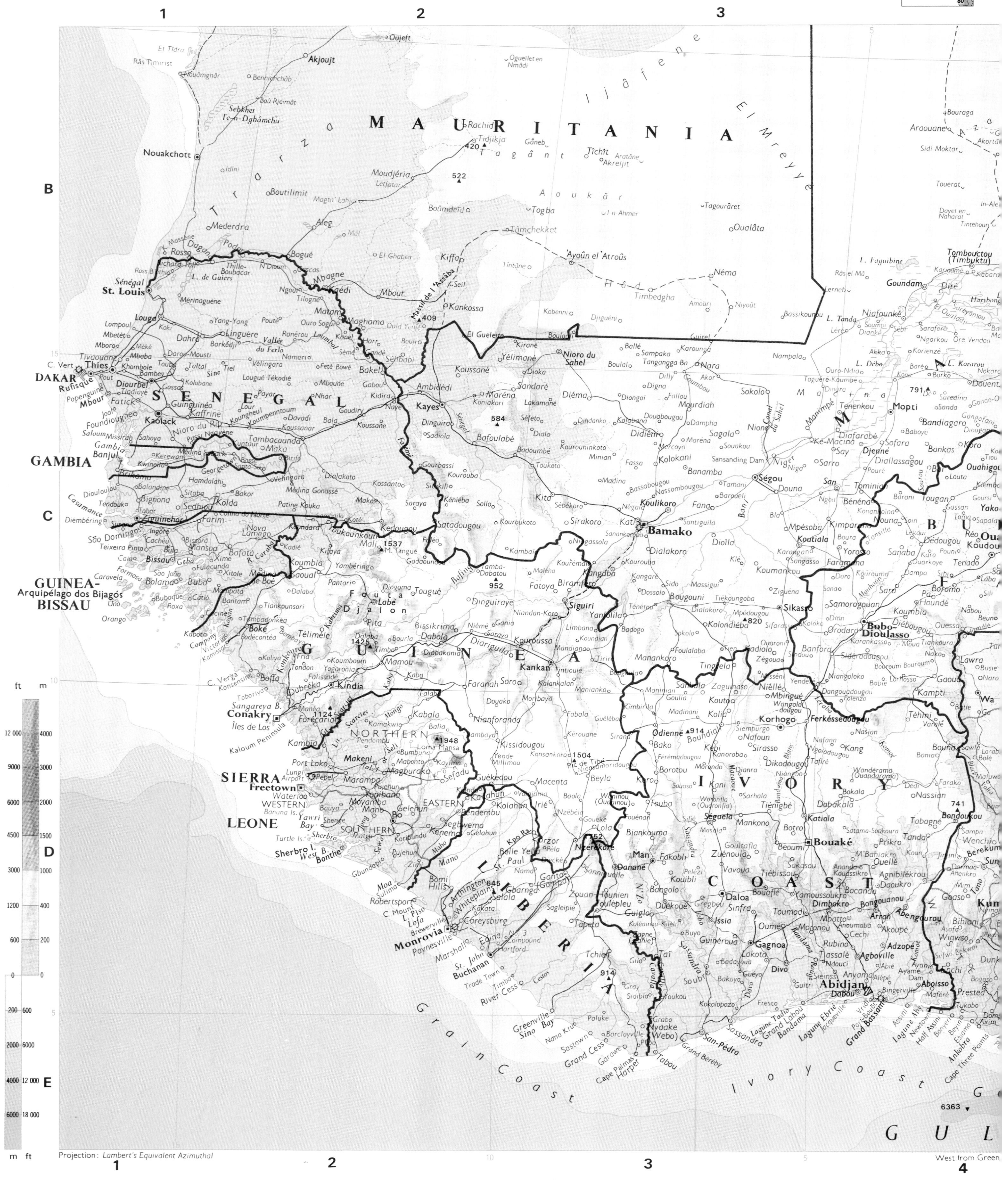

MAURITANIA

Nouakchott

SENEGAL

DAKAR · Rufisque · Thies · Diourbel · Mbour · Kaolack · Kaffrine

St. Louis · Louga · Linguère · Matam

GAMBIA · Banjul

GUINEA-BISSAU · Bissau · Arquipélago dos Bijagós

GUINEA · Conakry · Kindia · Labé · Kankan · Siguiri · Kouroussa · Mamou

SIERRA LEONE · Freetown · WESTERN · NORTHERN · EASTERN · SOUTHERN · Makeni · Port Loko · Bo

LIBERIA · Monrovia · Paynesville · Buchanan · Careysburg · Robertsport

MALI · Bamako · Kayes · Kita · Kati · Koulikoro · Ségou · Mopti · Djenné · Bafoulabé · Nioro du Sahel · Nara

IVORY COAST · Abidjan · Bouaké · Man · Daloa · Gagnoa · Divo · Korhogo · Ferkéssédougou · Bondoukou · Odienné · Séguéla · Katiola · Agboville

BURKINA · Bobo-Dioulasso · Banfora

Tombouctou (Timbuktu) · Goundam · Diré

Grain Coast · Ivory Coast

GULF

Cape Palmas · Harper · San-Pédro · Tabou

Projection: Lambert's Equivalent Azimuthal

West from Greenwich

Scale:
ft / m
12 000 / 4000
9000 / 3000
6000 / 2000
4500 / 1500
3000 / 1000
1200 / 400
600 / 200
0 / 0
200 / 600
2000 / 6000
4000 / 12 000
6000 / 18 000
m / ft

1 : 6 400 000

50   0   50   100   150   200 miles
50   0   100   200   300 km

4   5   6   7

N. E. NIGERIA
on same scale
as general map

NIGER

CHAD

ALGERIA

NIGER

NIGERIA

Adrar des Iforhas

Aïr (Azbine)

Ténéré

Massif de Terezit

BURKINA

GHANA

TOGO

BENIN

SOKOTO

KATSINA

KADUNA

KANO

BAUCHI

PLATEAU

KWARA

OYO

OGUN

ONDO

BENDEL

ANAMBRA

IMO

RIVERS

CROSS RIVER

BENUE

GONGOLA

ADAMAWA

TARABA

CAMEROON

EQUATORIAL GUINEA

BIOKO (FERNANDO POO)

Slave Coast

Bight of Benin

Niger Delta

BIGHT OF GUINEA

Bight of Bonny

LAGOS

IBADAN

Kano

Kaduna

Zaria

ACCRA

Tema

DOUALA

Yaoundé

Lac Tchad

Maiduguri

Maroua

Garoua

East from Greenwich

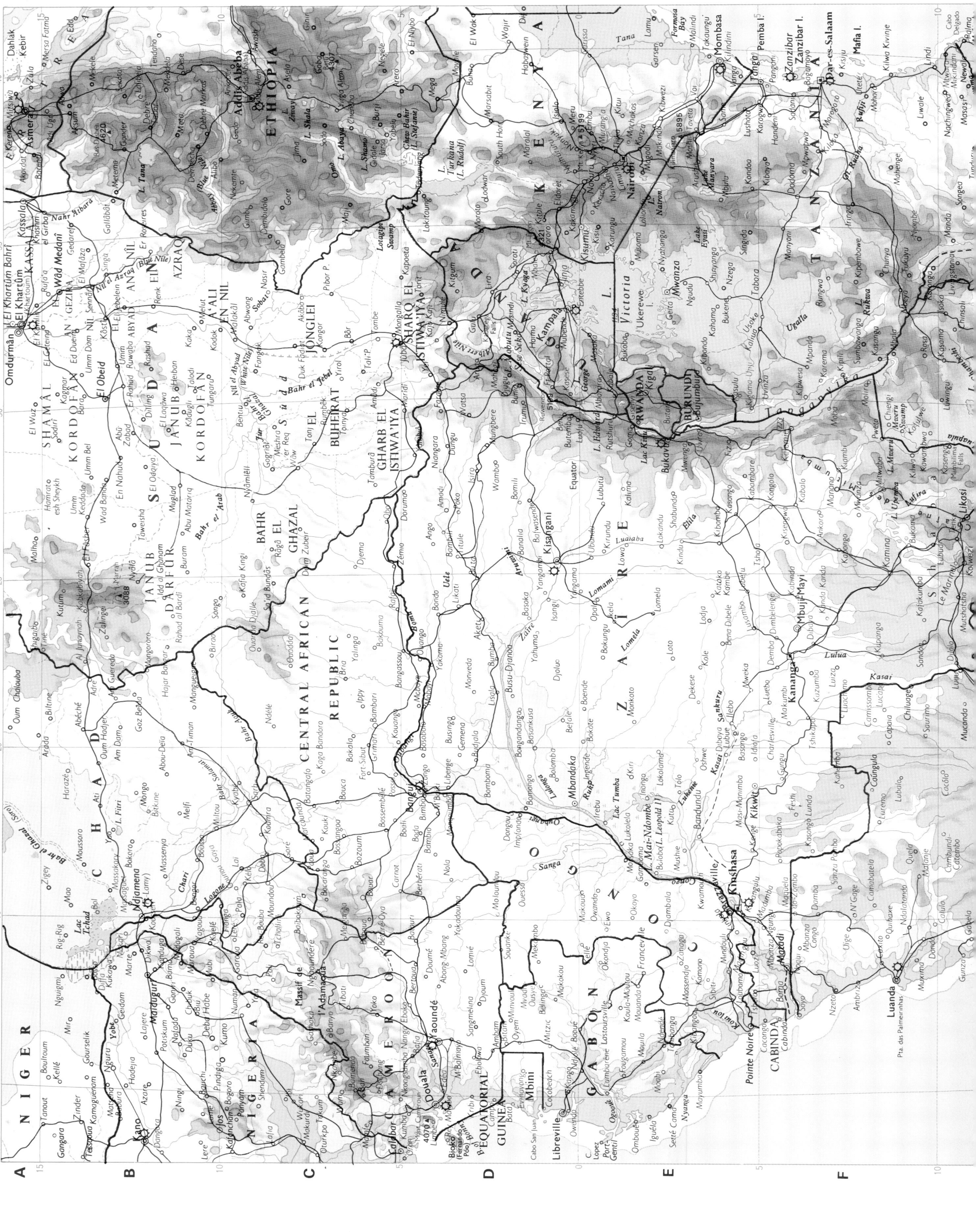

ETHIOPIA

KENYA

TANZANIA

SUDAN

CENTRAL AFRICAN REPUBLIC

ZAÏRE

CHAD

NIGER

NIGERIA

CAMEROON

GABON

CONGO

EQUATORIAL GUINEA

Mbini

CABINDA

NIGER

SHAMÂL KORDOFÂN

JANUB KORDOFÂN

JANUB DARFUR

BAHR EL GHAZAL

GHARB EL ISTIWA'IYA

SHARQ EL ISTIWA'IYA

JONGLEI

EL BUHEIRAT

A'ALI EN NIL

AZRAQ

ABYAD

GEZIRA

KASSALA

RWANDA

BURUNDI

Khartûm (El Khartûm)
Omdurmân (El Khartûm Bahrî)
Wâd Medanî
El Obeid
Addis Abeba
Asmera
L. Tana
L. Shala
L. Abaya
L. Stefanie (L. Chew Bahir)
Turkana (L. Rudolf)
Nairobi
Mombasa
Zanzibar I.
Dar-es-Salaam
Pemba I.
Mafia I.
Kampala
Entebbe
L. Victoria
Ukerewe I.
Mwanza
Tabora
Dodoma
Bukoba
Kigali
Bujumbura
Lac Kivu
L. Edward
L. George
Bangui
Kisangani
Kananga
Mbuji-Mayi
Kinshasa
Brazzaville
Matadi
Pointe Noire
Libreville
Yaoundé
Douala
Bata
N'djamena
Lac Tchad
Chari
Logone
Luanda

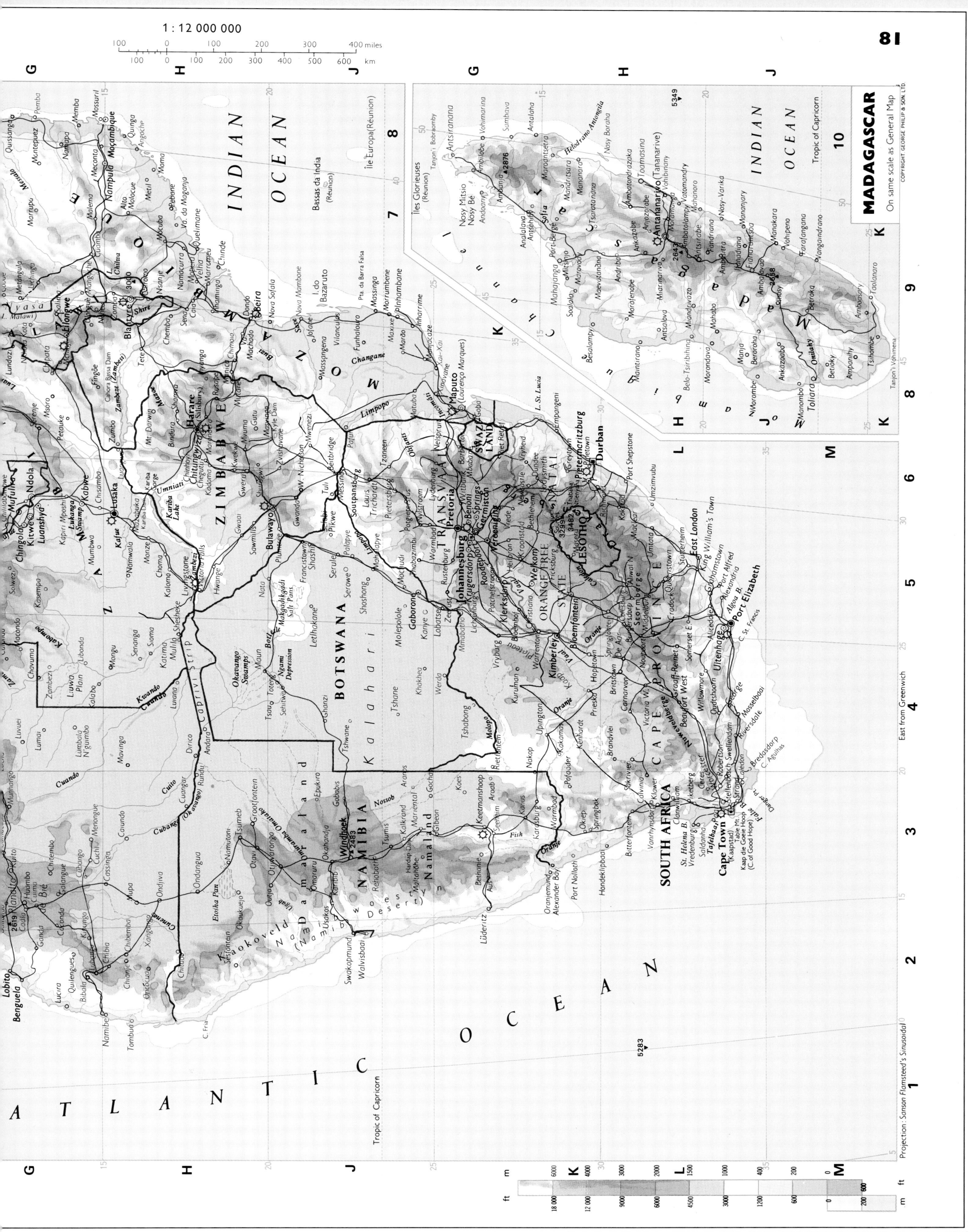

1 : 12 000 000

100   0   100   200   300   400 miles

100   0   100   200   300   400   500   600   km

MADAGASCAR
On same scale as General Map

COPYRIGHT GEORGE PHILIP & SON LTD

INDIAN OCEAN

ATLANTIC OCEAN

Tropic of Capricorn

East from Greenwich

Projection: Sanson Flamsteed's Sinusoidal

ZIMBABWE

BOTSWANA

NAMIBIA

SOUTH AFRICA

CAPE PROVINCE

TRANSVAAL

ORANGE FREE STATE

NATAL

LESOTHO

SWAZILAND

Kalahari

Namib Desert

Cape Town

Durban

Pretoria

Johannesburg

Port Elizabeth

East London

Harare

Bulawayo

Windhoek

Gaborone

Maputo

ft   m
18 000   6000
12 000   4000
9000   3000
6000   2000
4500   1500
3000   1000
1200   400
600   200
0   0   200   600

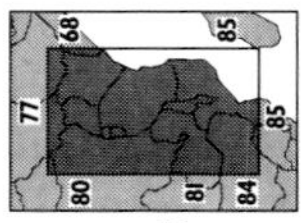

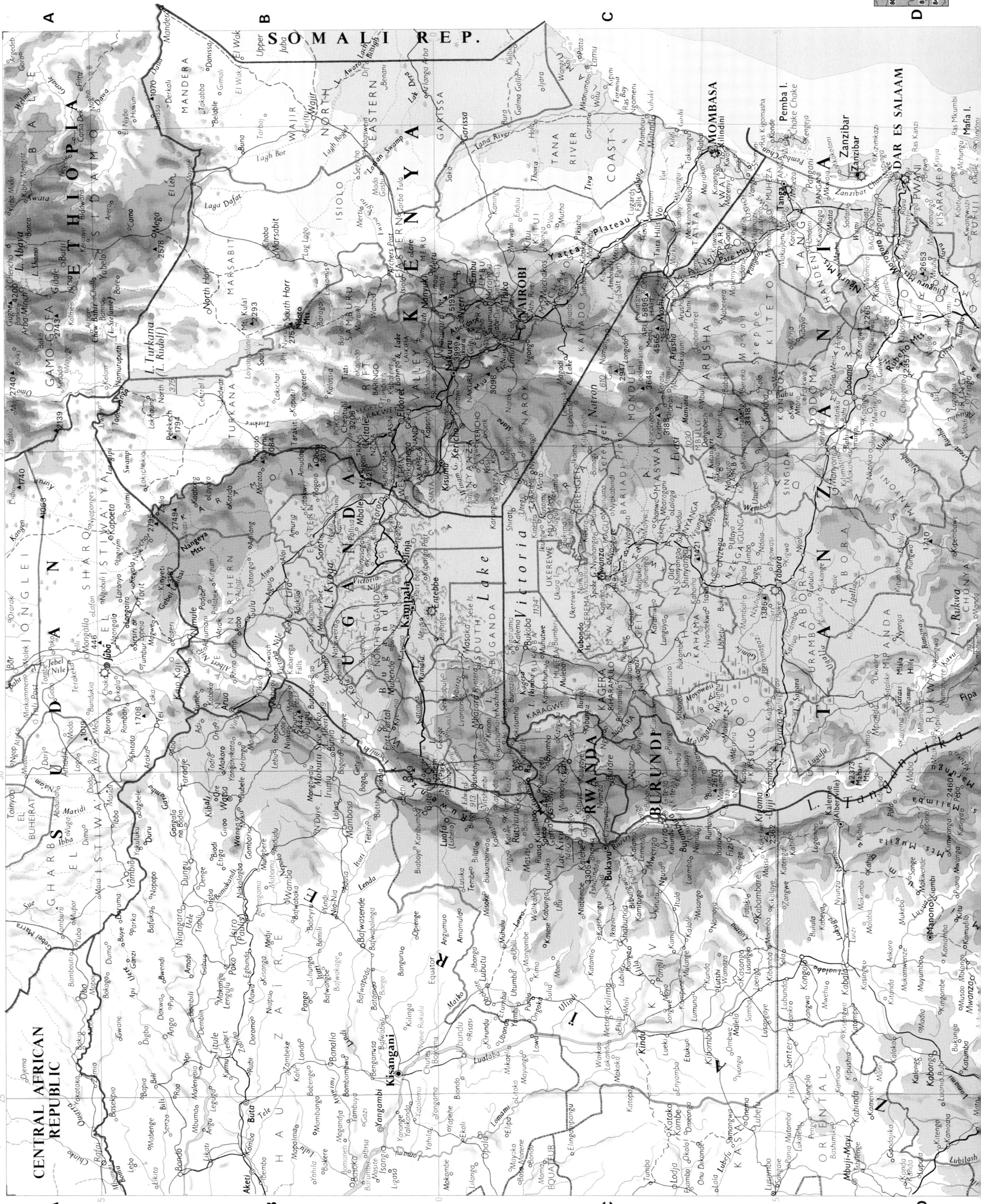

SOMALI REP.
ETHIOPIA
KENYA
UGANDA
SUDAN
ZAIRE
TANZANIA
RWANDA
BURUNDI
CENTRAL AFRICAN REPUBLIC
NAIROBI
MOMBASA
DAR ES SALAAM
Zanzibar
Pemba I.
Mafia I.
Kampala
Entebbe
Jinja
Kisumu
Kigali
Bukavu
Kisangani
Tabora
Dodoma
Arusha
Tanga
Juba
Lake Victoria
L. Turkana (L. Rudolf)
L. Tanganyika
L. Kyoga
L. Rukwa
L. Natron
L. Eyasi
L. Manyara
L. Mobutu Sese Seko
Lac Kivu
Manono
Kalemie (Albertville)
Kigoma
Ujiji
Mbale
Nakuru
Eldoret
Kericho
Garissa
Marsabit
Lamu
Malindi
Mwanza
Shinyanga
Gulu
Lira
Buta
Aketi
Kindu
Lubilash
Lualaba
Tana River
Yatta Plateau
Nangeya Mts.
Ufipa
Mbuji-Mayi
A
B
C
D
1
2
3
4
5

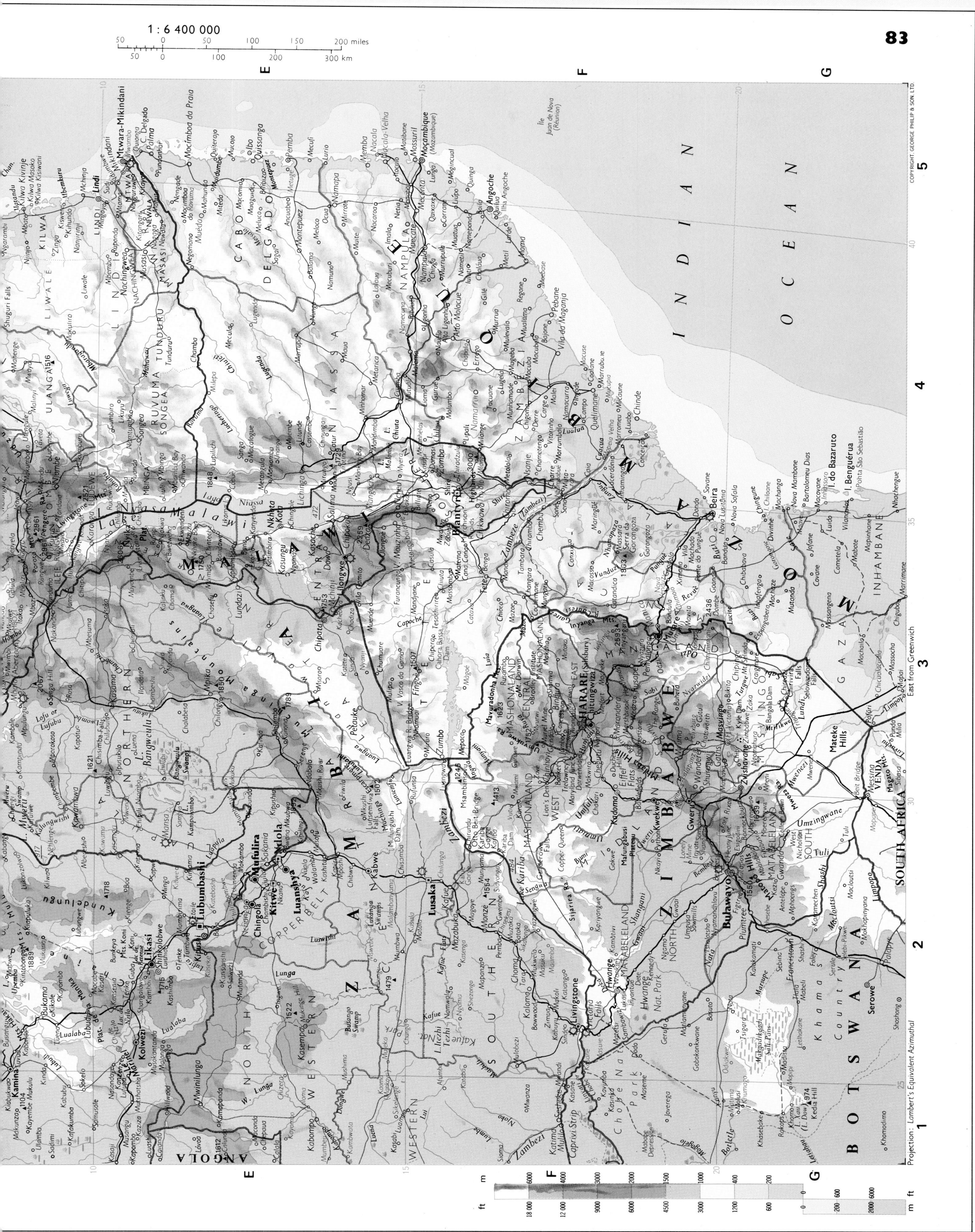

1 : 6 400 000

50   0   50   100   150   200 miles

50   0   100   200   300 km

INDIAN

OCEAN

Projection: Lambert's Equivalent Azimuthal

East from Greenwich

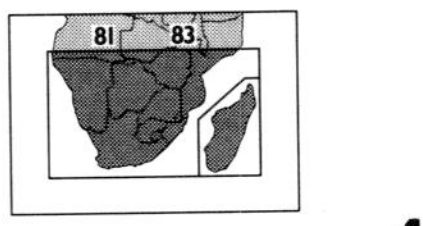

ANGOLA

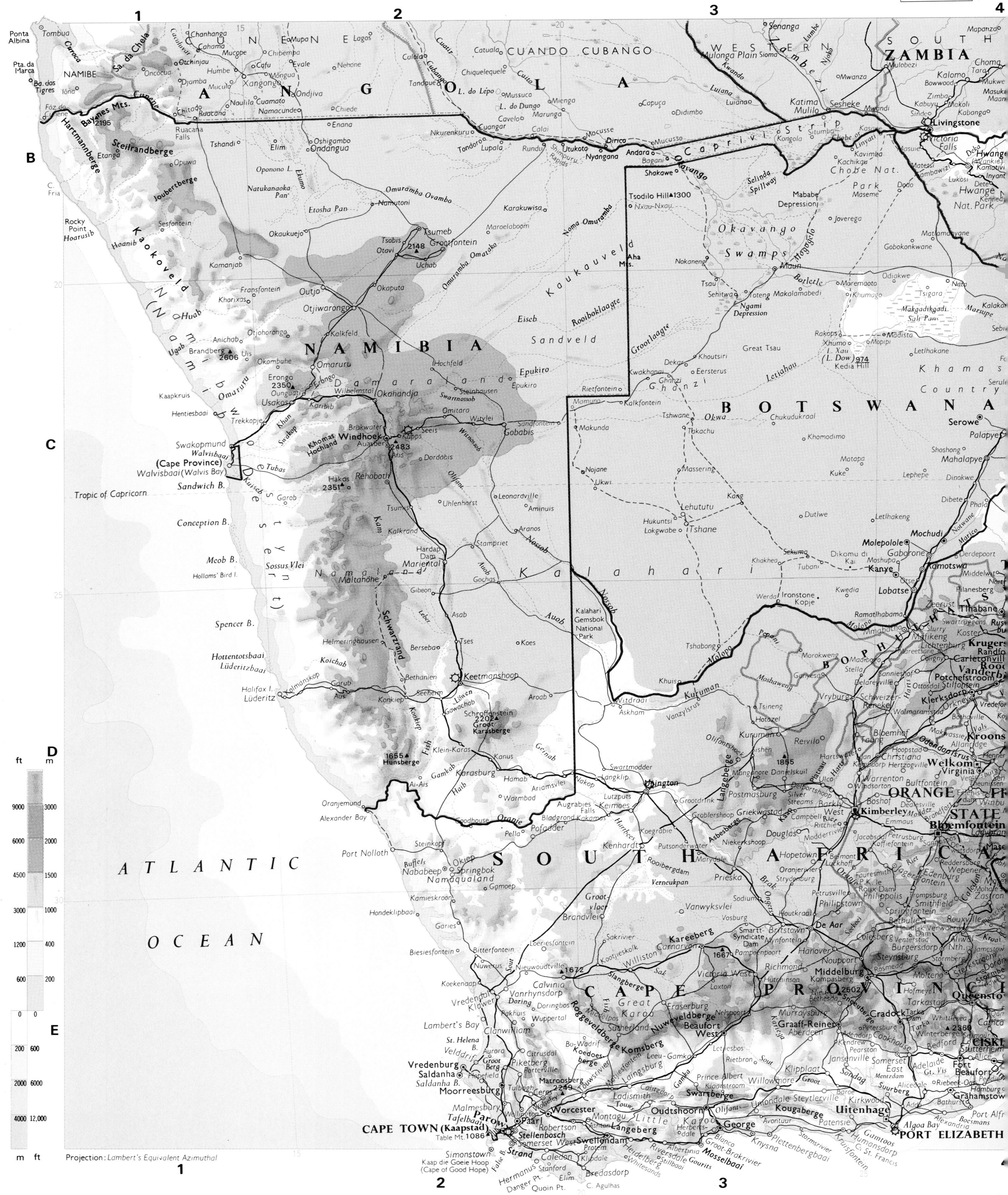

CUANDO CUBANGO

WESTERN ZAMBIA

Caprivi Strip

Livingstone

Victoria Falls

Chobe Nat. Park

Hwange Nat. Park

NAMIBIA

Etosha Pan

Okavango Swamps

Ngami Depression

Kaukauveld Mts

Sandveld

Ghanzi

BOTSWANA

Serowe
Palapye

Khamas Country

Windhoek

Swakopmund
Walvisbaai
(Cape Province)
Walvisbaai (Walvis Bay)

Tropic of Capricorn

Sandwich B.

Conception B.

Meob B.

Sossus Vlei
Hollams' Bird I.

Spencer B.

Hottentotsbaai
Lüderitzbaai
Halifax I.
Lüderitz

Kalahari

Kalahari Gemsbok National Park

Gaborone
Kanye
Lobatse

Mochudi

Molepolole

Mariental

Keetmanshoop

Groot Karasberge

Hunsberge

Karasburg

Oranjemund
Alexander Bay

ATLANTIC

OCEAN

SOUTH AFRICA

Kimberley
Bloemfontein

ORANGE FREE STATE

Welkom
Virginia

Klerksdorp

Port Nolloth

Springbok
Namaqualand

Kareeberg

De Aar

Middelburg

Cradock

CISKEI

CAPE PROVINCE

Great Karoo

Beaufort West

Graaff-Reinet

Uitenhage

Vredenburg
Saldanha
St. Helena B.
Moorreesburg

Worcester
Paarl
Stellenbosch

CAPE TOWN (Kaapstad)
Table Mt. 1086

George
Mosselbaai

PORT ELIZABETH

Kaap die Goeie Hoop
(Cape of Good Hope)
C. Agulhas

Projection: Lambert's Equivalent Azimuthal

ft   m
9000 3000
6000 2000
4500 1500
3000 1000
1200 400
600   200
0   0
200   600
2000 6000
4000 12,000
m   ft

1 : 6 400 000

50   0   50   100   150   200 miles

50   0   100   200   300 km

5   6   7

8

M O Z A M B I Q U E

C H A N N E L

MOZAMBIQUE CHANNEL

I N D I A N

O C E A N

East from Greenwich

MADAGASCAR

On same scale as General Map

COPYRIGHT. GEORGE PHILIP & SON. LTD.

5   7   8

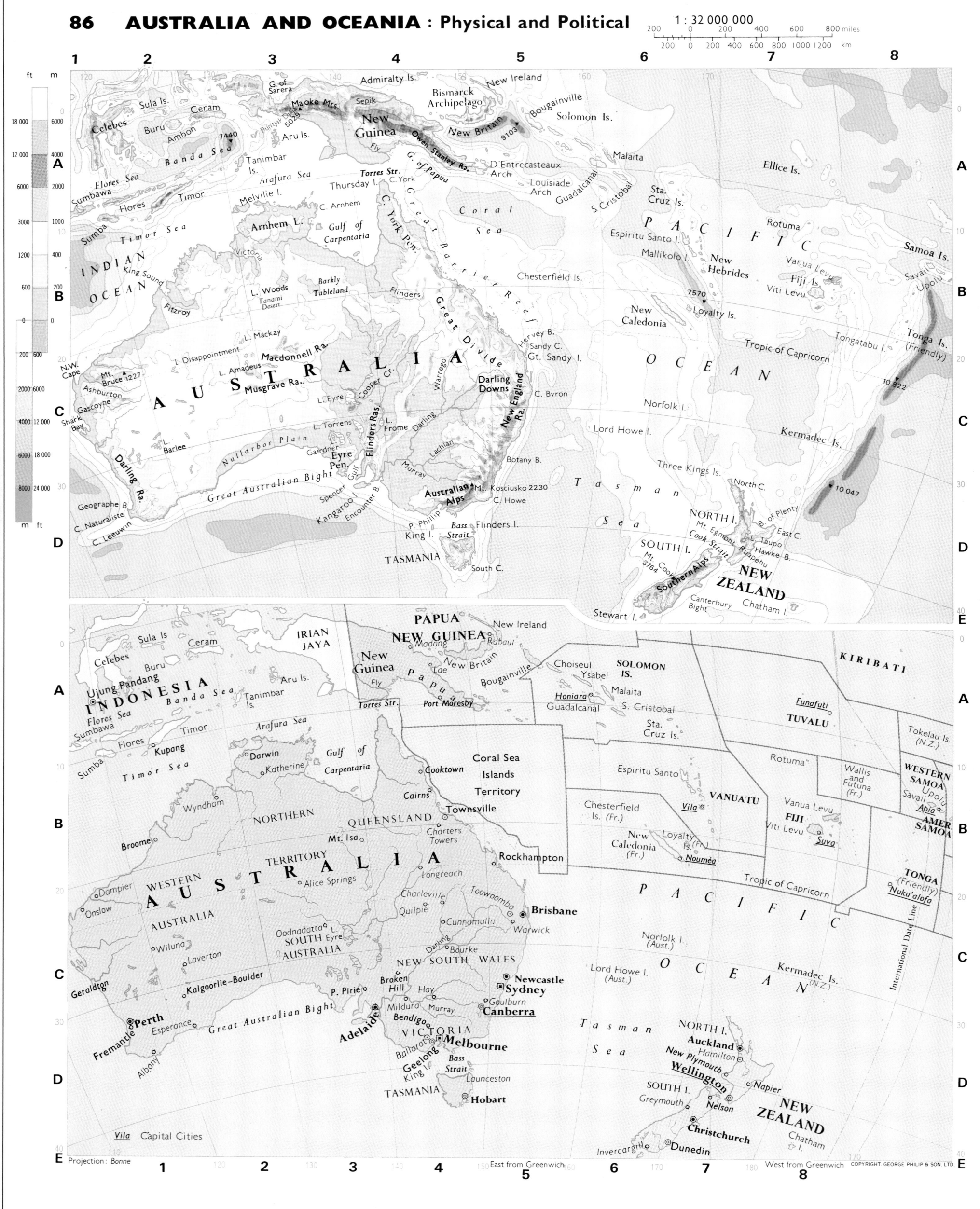

1 : 4 800 000

20 0 20 40 60 80 100 miles
20 0 40 80 120 160 km

NEW ZEALAND & S.W. PACIFIC
1 : 48 000 000

200 0 200 400 600 800 miles
200 0 400 800 1200 km

KIRIBATI

TUVALU (Ellice Is.)
Tokelau Is. (N.Z.)
Tongareva (Penrhyn) I.
WESTERN SAMOA
Pukapuka
Rakahanga
Manihiki
Nassau
Suwarrow
Northern Group
Savaii
Upolu
Tutuila
Cook Is. (N.Z.)
Îles de la Société
WALLIS & FUTUNA (Fr.)
AMER. SAMOA (U.S.)
Palmerston
Aitutaki
Atoll
Mitiaro
FIJI
Vanua Levu
Lau or Eastern Group
Rotuma
Viti Levu
TONGA (Friendly Is.)
NIUE (N.Z.)
Lower Group
Atui
Mauke
Rarotonga
Mangaia
FRENCH POLYNESIA

VAN-UATU

Tropic of Capricorn

P A C I F I C   O C E A N

Macauley
Raoul (Sunday) I.
Kermadec Is. (N.Z.)
Curtis

Three Kings Is.
Auckland
NORTH I.
Cook Strait
NEW ZEALAND
Wellington
SOUTH I.
Tasman Sea
Christchurch
Dunedin
Chatham I.
Chatham Is.
Pitt I.
Bounty Is.
Stewart I.
Snares
Antipodes Is.
Campbell I.
Macquarie I. (Austr.)

S O U T H E R N   O C E A N

SAMOA ISLANDS
1 : 9 600 000

WESTERN SAMOA
AMERICAN SAMOA
Savai'i
Apia
Upolu
Pago Pago
Tutuila
Manua Is.
Rose I.

FIJI AND TONGA ISLANDS
1 : 9 600 000

50 0 50 100 150 miles
50 0 50 100 150 200 250 km

Niuafo'ou (Tonga)
Thikombia
Vanua Levu
FIJI
Taveuni
Koro
Lambasa
Yasawa Group
Vanua Balavu
Lautoka
Nandi
Levuka
Ovalau
Koro Sea
Lakemba
Lau or Eastern Group
TONGA (Friendly Is.)
Viti Levu
Suva
Ngau
Moala
Vava'u
Moala
Kandavu
Vatoa
Tofua
Tongatapu
Nuku'alofa

COPYRIGHT. GEORGE PHILIP & SON. LTD.

Projection: Conical with two standard parallels

NORTH ISLAND
C. Reinga
C. Maria van Diemen
North C.
Houhora
Rangaunu Bay
Doubtless Bay
Ahipara B.
Mongonui
Whangaroa Bay
Kaitaia
Tauroa Pt.
Rawene
Opua
B. of Islands
C. Brett
Hokianga Harb.
Kaikohe
Hikurangi
Donnelly's Crossing
Whangarei
Whangarei Harb.
Bream Hd.
Dargaville
Waipu
Bream Bay
Lit. Barrier I.
C. Rodney
Gt. Barrier I.
Kaipara Harb.
Warkworth
C. Colville
Helensville
Hauraki Gulf
Cuvier I.
Takapuna
Devonport
Coromandel
Whitianga
Onehunga
AUCKLAND
Manukau
Papakura
Thames
Mayor I.
Pukekohe
Waihi
Waiuku
Mercer
Paeroa
Tauranga Harb.
Waikato
Te Aroha
Bay of Plenty
White I.
Runaway
Huntly
Morrinsville
Tauranga
Te Puke
Whakatane
Opotiki
East C.
Raglan
Hamilton
Cambridge
Kawerau
Raukumara Ra.
Hikurangi 1753
Kawhia Harb.
Te Awamutu
Putaruru
Rotorua
Tarawera
Waipiro
Otorohanga
Te Kuiti
Kinleith
Murupara
Tolaga Bay
North Taranaki Bight
Mokau
Mokai
Waikaremoana
Ormond
Gisborne
Waitara
Ongarue
Taupo
Poverty Bay
New Plymouth
Inglewood
Taumarunui
Turangi
Waikokopu
Mt. Egmont
Stratford
Whangamomona
Kaimanawa Mts.
Wairoa
Mahia Peninsula
C. Egmont 2518
Eltham
Raetihi
Ohakune
Ruapehu 2797
Waiguru
Bay
Hawke Bay
Opunake
Kapuni
Napier
Hawera
Taihape
Ruahine Ra.
C. Kidnappers
South Taranaki Bight
Waverley
Mangaweka
Hastings
Patea
Hunterville
Waipawa
Wanganui
Marton
Holcombe
Feilding
Waipukurau
Bulls
Foxton
Palmerston N.
Woodville
C. Turnagain
Shannon
Pahiatua
Levin
Eketahuna
Paraparaumu
Otaki
Tararua Ra.
Kapiti I.
Pelorus Sd.
Featherston
Masterton
Carterton
Up. Hutt
Greytown
Petone
Lr. Hutt
Martinborough
Eastbourne
WELLINGTON
Cook Strait

SOUTH ISLAND
C. Farewell
Collingwood
Golden Bay
D'Urville I.
Takaka
Tasman Bay
Tasman Mts.
Motueka
Karamea Bight
Nelson
Picton
Karamea
Tadmor
Richmond
Havelock
Seddonville
Wakefield
Blenheim
Granity
Lyell Ra.
Wairau
Seddon
Westport
Lyell
Inangahua Junction
Murchison
Travers 2338
Ward
Reefton
2885 Tapuaenuku
Spenser Mts.
Marlborough
Blackball
Grey
Hanmer Springs
Clarence
Runanga
Amuri P.
Kaikoura
Greymouth
Stillwater
Kumara
L. Brunner
Waiau
Hokitika
Jacksons
Culverden
Ross
Arthur's Pass
Waikari
Waipara
Abut Hd.
Waimakariri
Hurunui
Amberley
Okarito
Oxford
Rangiora
Pegasus Bay
Kaiapoi
New Brighton
Christchurch
Mt. Cook 3764
Springfield
Whitecliffs
Riccarton
Lyttelton
Jackson B.
Coleridge
Lincoln
Methven
Little River
Okuru
Southbridge
Akaroa
Banks Peninsula
Fairlie
Rakaia
L. Ellesmere
Mt. Aspiring 3027
L. Ohau
L. Pukaki
Ashburton Bight
Milford Sd.
Earnslaw 2819
Canterbury Plain
Bligh Sd.
Wanaka
Fairlie
George Sd.
L. Hawea
Burke's Pass
Timaru
Secretary I.
Queenstown
Arrowtown
Temuka
St. Andrews
Doubtful Sd.
Te Anau
Cromwell
Kurow
Waimate
Clyde
Tokarahi
Breaksea Sd.
Kingston
Alexandra
Ngapara
Maheno
Resolution I.
Mangapouri
Roxburgh
Oamaru
Dusky Sd.
Mossburn
Lumsden
Waikouaiti
Chalky Inlet
Ohai
Edievale
Palmerston
Tuatapere
Nightcaps
Lawrence
Kelso
Port Chalmers
Preservation Inlet
Orepuki
Winton
Milton
Dunedin
Mosgiel
St. Kilda
Otago Harbour
Te Waewae B.
Riverton
Gore
Balclutha
Taieri
Invercargill
Mataura
Kaitangata
Fairfield
Edendale
Wyndham
Clinton
Saunders
Gummies Bush
Owaka
Nugget Pt.
Tokanui
Tokaha
Invercargill
Bluff
Foveaux Str.
Ruapuki I.
Halfmoon Bay
Stewart I.
S.W. Cape
Port Pegasus

SOUTHERN ALPS
Westland
T A S M A N   S E A
P A C I F I C   O C E A N
Cook Strait

INDONESIA

TIMOR SEA

INDIAN OCEAN

NORTHERN TERRITORY

Tanami Desert

Great Sandy Desert

Gibson Desert

King Leopold Ranges

Hamersley Range

Lombok
Sumbawa
Sumba
Sawa
Roti
Timor
Semau
Radjua
Danu

Darwin
Melville I.
Bathurst I.
Port Darwin
Nasugadoh
Van Diemen Gulf
Cobourg Pen.
C. Croker
Croker I.
C. Don
Dundas Str.
C. Van Diemen
Gordan B.
Pt. Fawcett
C. Gambier St.
Clarence St.
C. Hotham
Peron Is.
Anson B.
Pt. Blaze
Rum Jungle
Batchelor
Adelaide River
Daly River
Mt. Greenwood 152
Katherine
Pine Creek
Oenpelly
Jabiru 480
Maranboy
Mataranka
Birdum Creek
Birdum
Larrimah
Top Springs
Montejinnie
Willeroo
Victoria River
Coolibah
Wave Hill
Victoria Downs
Humbert River
West Baines
Limbunya
Hooker Creek
Winnecke Cr.
Wyndham
Kununurra
Ord
Argyle
Yorkey Creek
Gordon Downs
Nicholson
Turner
Nelson
Lander
Willowra
Yuendumu
Mt. Leisler 901
Mt. Liebig 1524
Mt. Doreen
L. Mackay
Lake Mackay
L. White
L. Hazlett
L. Wills
Stansmore Ra.
Gregory Lake
Billiluna
Balgo
Sturt Creek
Bohemia Downs
Christmas Creek
Fitzroy Crossing
Margaret
Noonkanbah
Camballin
Derby
Fitzroy
Liveringa
Greenough's
Myroodah
Roebuck Plains
Broome
Roebuck B.
Carnot B.
Lagrange B.
Frazier Downs
Anna Plains
Wallal Downs
Eighty Mile Beach
De Grey
Port Hedland
Goldsworthy
Marble Bar
Nullagine
Hillside
Shaw
Woodstock
Roebourne
Karratha
Dampier
Dampier Archipelago
Onslow
Ashburton
Exmouth Gulf
North West C.
Barrow I.
Monte Bello Is.

Hamersley Range
Mt. Meharry 1251
Mt. Bruce 1235
Ophthalmia Ra. 1053
Newman
Chichester Ra.
Gregory Ra.
Isabella Ra.

Hibernia Reef
Ashmore Reef
Cartier I.
Scott Reef
Seringapatam Reef
Rowley Shoals
Mermaid Reef
Clerke Reef
Imperieuse Reef
Lynher Reef
Adele I.
Lacepede Is.
Legendre I.
Enderby I.

Joseph Bonaparte Gulf
Cambridge Gulf
Admiralty Gulf
Collier B.
King Sound
Buccaneer Archipelago
Bonaparte Archipelago
Yampi Sd.
Beagle Bay
Pender B.

King Leopold Ranges
Mt. Ord 1007
Mt. Hann 776
King Edward
Drysdale
Durack
Durack River
Gibb River
Hann
Tableland
Mornington
St. George Ra.
Mueller Ra.
Albert Edward Ra.
McClintock
Bedford Downs
Alice Downs
Springvale
Mount Amherst
Holls Cr.
Margaret River

Tropic of Capricorn

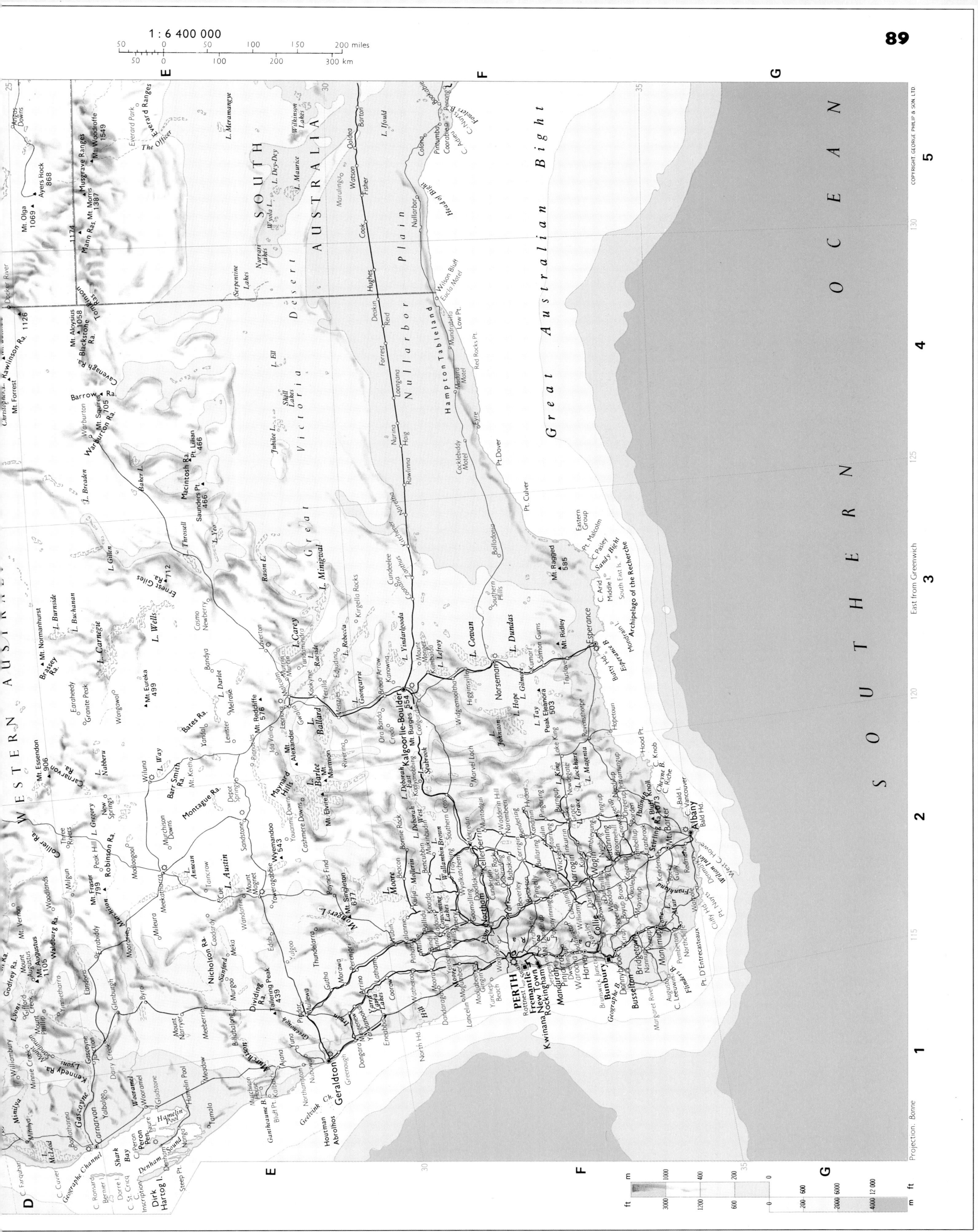

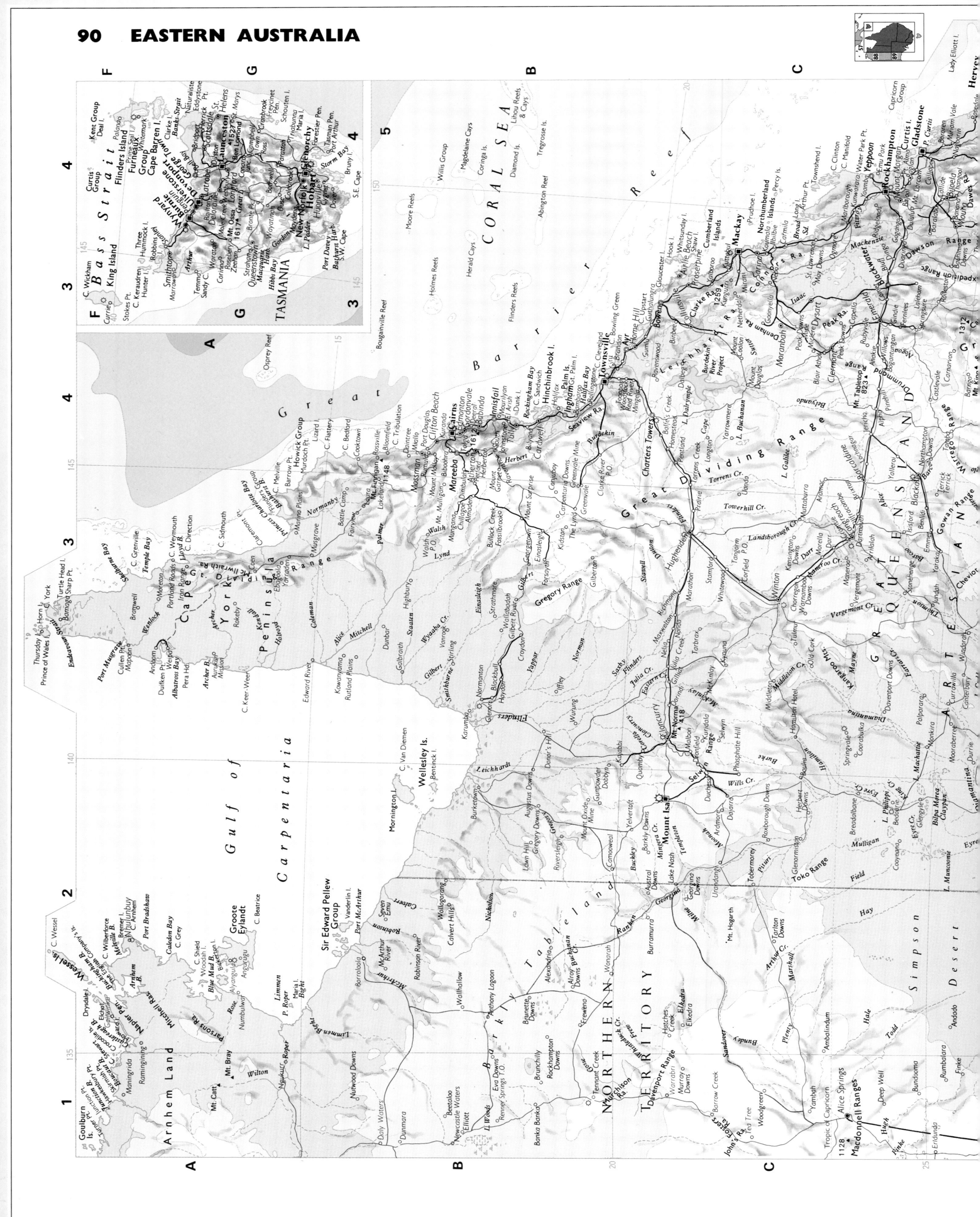

1 : 6 400 000

Projection: Bonne

COPYRIGHT: GEORGE PHILIP & SON, LTD.

East from Greenwich

TASMAN SEA

NEW SOUTH WALES

SOUTH AUSTRALIA

BRISBANE

SYDNEY

CANBERRA
COMMONWEALTH TERR.

MELBOURNE

ADELAIDE

Bass Strait

King Island

Flinders Island

Furneaux Group

Cape Barren I.

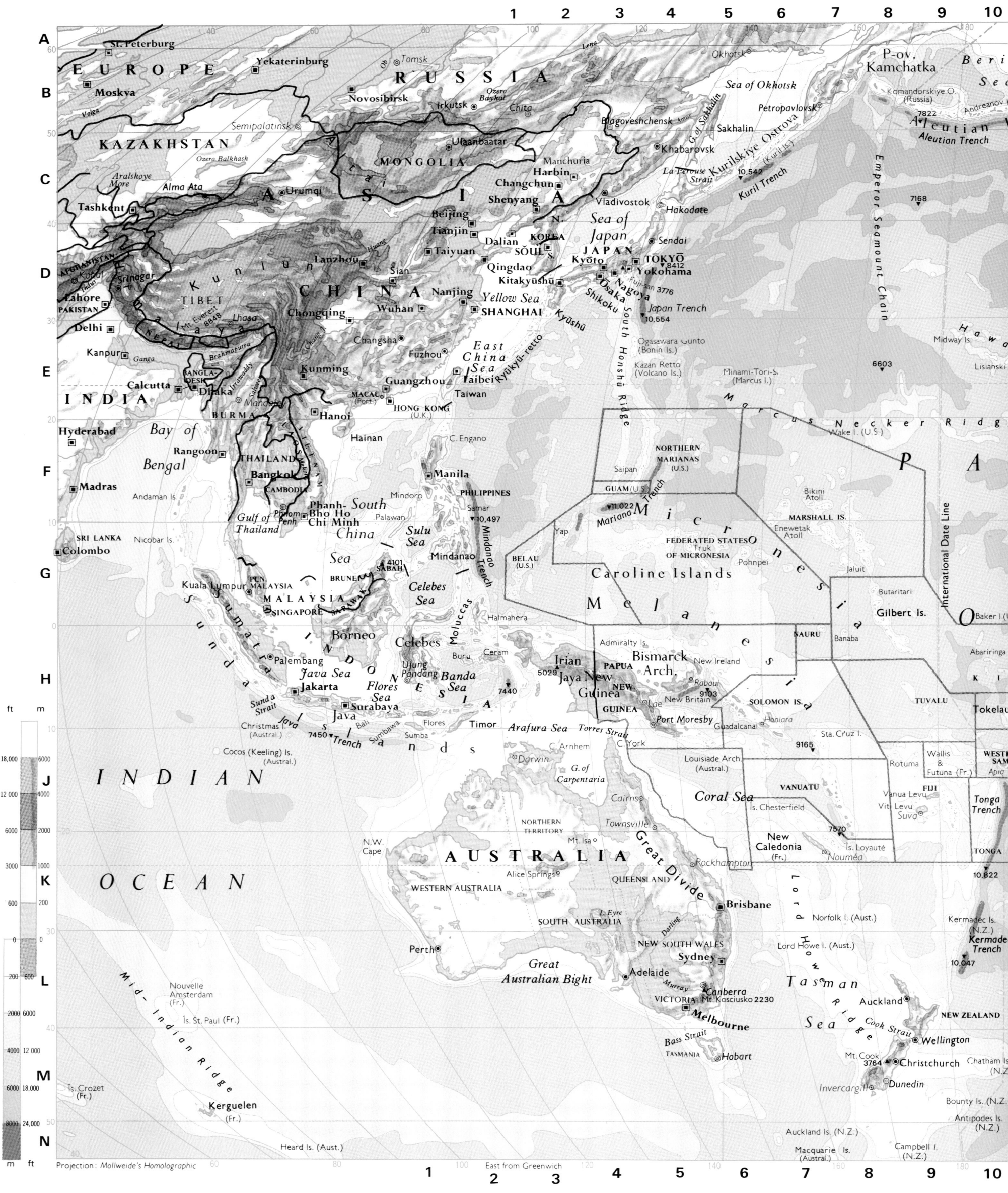

1 : 43 200 000

11　12　13　14　15　16　17　18　19　20

ALASKA (U.S.) ▲6050

Bristol Bay

Gulf of Alaska

Juneau

Prince of Wales I.

Prince Rupert
Kitimat

Queen Charlotte Is.

GREENLAND

C. Farewell

U.K.

Hudson Bay

C A N A D A

Labrador

NORTH AMERICA

NORTH

Edmonton

L. Winnipeg

Calgary
Regina
Winnipeg

Vancouver
Vancouver I.
Victoria
Seattle

Montréal
Quebec
Ottawa
Toronto
Saint John
Pr. Edward I.

Newfoundland

St. Lawrence

L. Superior

Portland

Boise
Snake

Minneapolis
Michigan
L. Huron
L. Ontario

Buffalo
Boston
C. Sable

C. Mendocino

Salt Lake City
4418

Denver
Kansas City
St. Louis

CHICAGO
Detroit
Pittsburgh
Cincinnati

NEW YORK
Philadelphia
Baltimore
Washington

ATLANTIC

▼6741

San Francisco

UNITED STATES

Oklahoma

Memphis
Atlanta

Los Angeles
San Diego

Dallas

Mississippi

C. Hatteras

OCEAN

6225 ▼

Ciudad Juárez

Houston
New Orleans

Jacksonville

Bermuda (U.K.)

Hawaiian Is. (U.S.)

Tropic of Cancer

Gulf of California

Sierra Madre

San Antonio

Gulf of Mexico

Miami

BAHAMAS

Oahu
Honolulu

Ridge

Hawaii

Is. Revilla Gigedo (Mexico)

M E X I C O

Monterrey

Florida Strait

CUBA

La Habana

West Indies

Hispaniola

7680 ▼
JAMAICA
HAITI
DOM. REP.
9200 ▼

PUERTO RICO (U.S.)

Leeward Is.

México
Guadalajara
Puebla 5700
Acapulco

Yucatan Channel
Mérida

Kingston

I F I C

Christmas Island Ridge

Palmyra Is. (U.S.)

Teraina
Tabuaeran
Kiritimati

Jarvis I. (U.S.)

Î.Clipperton (Fr.)

BELIZE
GUATEMALA 6660
Guatemala
San Salvador
EL SALVADOR

HONDURAS

NICARAGUA
Managua

Caribbean Sea

BARBADOS
Windward Is.
TRINIDAD & TOBAGO

E A N

Barranquilla
Maracaibo

Caracas
Orinoco
VENEZUELA

CENTRAL AMERICA

San José
Colón
Panama
PANAMA
Canal

Medellín
Bogota

Cali
COLOMBIA

COSTA RICA

I. del Coco (Costa Rica)

Tongareva
Penrhyn Is.

Malden I.

Caroline I.

Î. Marquises

Equator

Galápagos (Ecuador)

Quito
ECUADOR

Manihiki
Suwarrow Is.

Vostok
Flint I.

Starbuck I.

Guayaquil

Iquitos

Amazonas
Manaus

C. Pariñas

BRAZIL

SOUTH

Cook Islands (N.Z.)

Î. de la Société

Î. Tuamotu

Trujillo

East Pacific Ridge

P E R U
Lima

AMERICA

6369 ▼

Austral

Manuae

Tahiti

FRENCH POLYNESIA

Tuamotu Ridge

Cuzco

Arequipa

L. Titicaca
Illampu & Ancohuma 6550

Rarotonga

Seamount Chain

Tropic of Capricorn

Pitcairn I. (U.K.)

Peru–▼6866
Iquique
Chile

La Paz
BOLIVIA

Î. Tubuai (Îs. Australes)

Ducie I. (U.K.)

Rapa

I. de Pascua (Easter I.) (Chile)

Sala-y-Gomez (Chile)

San Félix (Chile)
San Ambrosio (Chile)

8050 ▼
Antofagasta
Trench

PARAGUAY

Asunción

Tucumán

Pto. Alegre

Arch. de Juan Fernández (Chile)

Córdoba
Rosario

URUGUAY

Pacific–Antarctic Ridge

Chile Rise

Valparaíso 6960 ▲
Santiago
Buenos Aires

Montevideo

Concepción

ARGENTINA

Río de la Plata

SOUTH

Patagonia

ATLANTIC

6212 ▼

OCEAN

Punta Arenas
Str. of Magellan
Tierra del Fuego

Falkland Is. (U.K.)

South Georgia

C. Horn

West from Greenwich

COPYRIGHT. GEORGE PHILIP & SON. LTD.

11　12　13　14　15　16　17　18　19　20

A B C D E F G H J K L M N

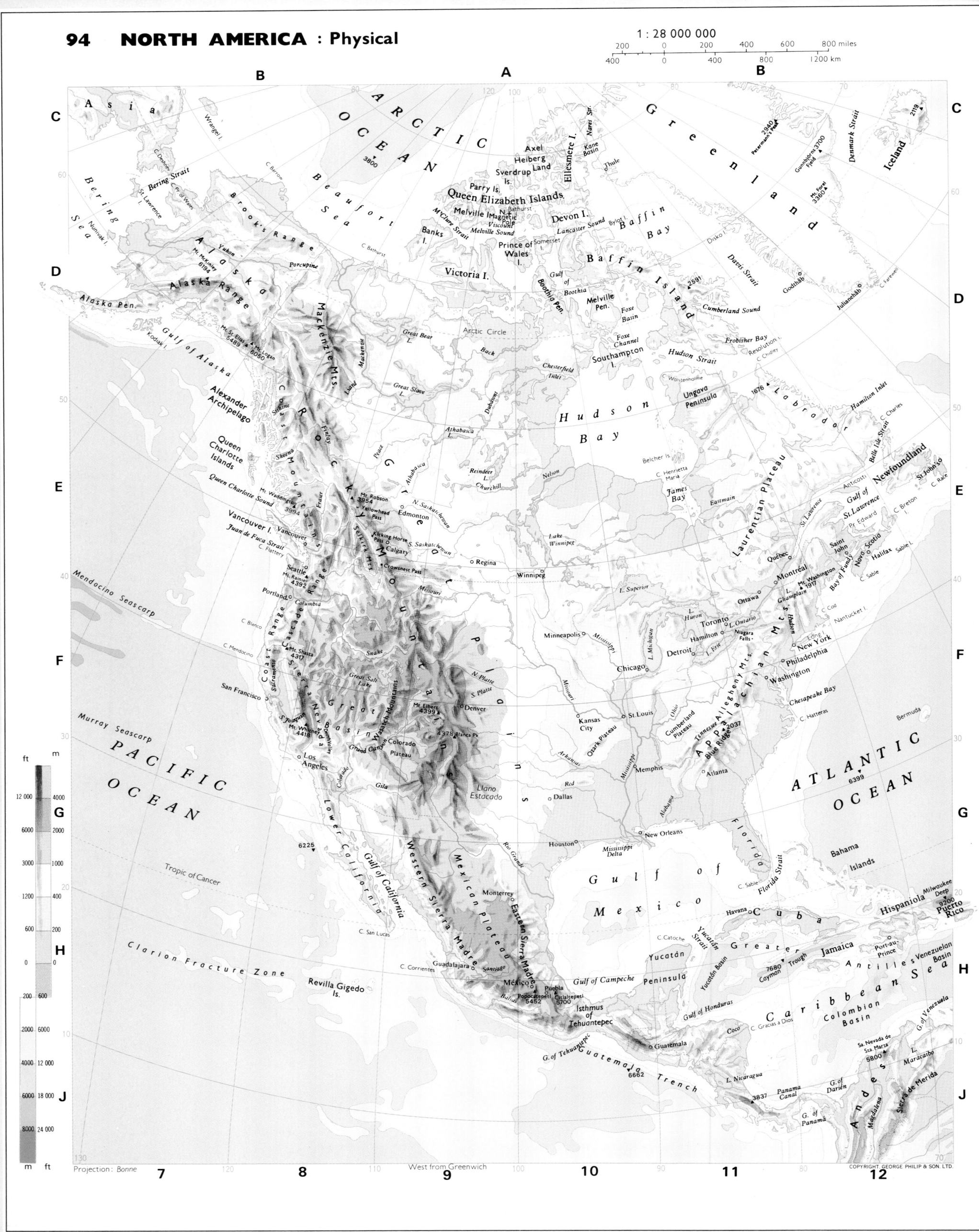

1 : 28 000 000

Projection: Bonne   West from Greenwich   COPYRIGHT. GEORGE PHILIP & SON. LTD.

1 : 28 000 000

200   0   200   400   600   800 miles
400   0   400   800   1200 km

ARCTIC OCEAN

GREENLAND (Denmark)

Denmark Strait   ICELAND   Reykjavik

Bering Strait   Bering Sea

Beaufort Sea   Queen Elizabeth Is.   Ellesmere I.

Baffin Bay

Arctic Circle   ALASKA   Yukon   Porcupine   INUVIK   Victoria I.   KITIKMEOT   BAFFIN   Baffin I.   Davis Strait   Godthaab

Fairbanks   Anchorage   YUKON TERRITORY   Great Bear L.   NORTHWEST TERRITORIES   Hudson Strait   C. Farvel

Whitehorse   FORT SMITH   Yellowknife   Buck   KEEWATIN   NEWFOUNDLAND

Gulf of Alaska   Juneau   Liard   Great Slave L.   Dubawnt   Hudson Bay

Skeena   BRITISH COLUMBIA   Finlay   Peace   Athabasca   L. Athabasca   Nelson   Churchill   Labrador

ALBERTA   Edmonton   N. Saskatchewan   SASKATCHEWAN   MANITOBA   Eastmain   QUÉBEC   St. John's   SPM

Fraser   Calgary   S. Saskatchewan   Regina   L. Winnipeg   ONTARIO   Québec   NEW BRUNS-WICK   PR. EDWARD   Charlottetown   NOVA SCOTIA   Halifax

Victoria   Vancouver   Winnipeg   L. Superior   Montréal   Fredericton   MAINE   Augusta

WASHINGTON   Seattle   MONTANA   Missouri   NORTH DAKOTA   Bismarck   MINNESOTA   Ottawa   Montpelier   N.H.   Concord

Olympia   Portland   Columbia   Salem   Helena   St. Paul   Minneapolis   WISCONSIN   Michigan   Toronto   Buffalo   NEW YORK   Albany   MASS.   Boston   Providence

OREGON   IDAHO   Boise   SOUTH DAKOTA   Pierre   Madison   MICHIGAN   Lansing   Detroit   Erie   Cleveland   PENNSYLVANIA   Harrisburg   Trenton   Philadelphia   NEW YORK

Snake   Salt Lake City   WYOMING   Cheyenne   N. Platte   NEBRASKA   Milwaukee   Chicago   ILLINOIS   INDIANA   OHIO   Columbus   Pittsburgh   Baltimore   WEST   Dover

Sacramento   Carson City   NEVADA   UTAH   Des Moines   IOWA   Toledo   Indianapolis   Cincinnati   Frankfort   Charleston   Annapolis   Washington D.C.   Richmond

San Francisco   CALIFORNIA   Lincoln   Springfield   Jefferson City   St. Louis   KENTUCKY   VIRGINIA

San Jose   Denver   COLORADO   Kansas City   MISSOURI   Nashville   Raleigh

Las Vegas   Colorado   KANSAS   Topeka   TENNESSEE   NORTH CAROLINA   Bermuda (Br.)

LOS ANGELES   Arkansas   Santa Fe   OKLAHOMA   Oklahoma City   ARKANSAS   Memphis   Columbia   SOUTH CAROLINA   ATLANTIC OCEAN

ARIZONA   Albuquerque   NEW MEXICO   Little Rock   Birmingham   GEORGIA   Atlanta

San Diego   Gila   Phoenix   Red River   Dallas   MISSISSIPPI   Alabama   Montgomery

Tucson   El Paso   TEXAS   LOUISIANA   Jackson   ALABAMA   Jacksonville

Rio Grande   Austin   Baton Rouge   Tallahassee   FLORIDA

Houston   New Orleans   Tampa   Fla.

Tropic of Cancer   Revilla Gigedo Is. (Mexico)   Monterrey   Gulf of Mexico   Miami   Nassau   BAHAMAS   Turks & Caicos (Br.)

MEXICO   Havana   CUBA   HAITI   DOMINICAN REP.   San Juan   PUERTO RICO

Guadalajara   Cayman Is. (Br.)   JAMAICA   Kingston   Port-au-Prince   Santo Domingo

MEXICO   Belmopan   BELIZE   Caribbean Sea

GUATEMALA   HONDURAS   Tegucigalpa   Maracaibo

Guatemala   San Salvador   EL SALVADOR   Managua   NICARAGUA   Barranquilla   VENEZUELA

PACIFIC OCEAN   San José   COSTA RICA   L. Nicaragua   Panamá   Medellín   COLOMBIA   Bogotá

SOUTH AMERICA

PANAMA

UNITED STATES   CANADA

Washington Capital Cities
⊙ U.S. State Capitals and Canadian Provincial Capitals

C	CONNECTICUT	N.H.	NEW HAMPSHIRE
D.	DELAWARE	N.J.	NEW JERSEY
D.C.	DISTRICT OF COLUMBIA	R.I.	RHODE ISLAND
M.	MARYLAND	VER.	VERMONT
MASS.	MASSACHUSETTS	SPM	ST. PIERRE ET MIQUELON

Projection: Bonne

West from Greenwich

COPYRIGHT GEORGE PHILIP & SON. LTD.

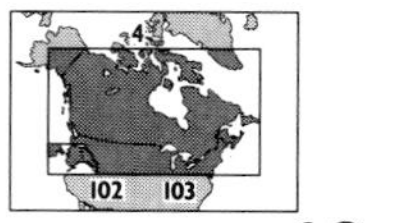

102
103

4
5
6
7
8
9
10
A
B
C
D
Fairbanks
Anchorage
ALASKA
Mt. Sanford
Wrangell Mts.
Mt. Lucania
Cordova
Mt. St. Elias
Yakutat
Mt. Fairweather
Whitehorse
YUKON TERRITORY
Dawson
Klondike
Mackenzie Mountains
Aklavik
Inuvik
INUVIK
Banks Island
Amundsen Gulf
Prince Albert Pen.
Victoria Island
Viscount Melville Sound
Prince of Wales Island
M'Clintock Channel
KITIKMEOT
Coronation Gulf
Queen Maud Gulf
Boothia Peninsula
King William I.
Gt. Bear Lake
Ft. Good Hope
Norman Wells
Coppermine
Bathurst Inlet
NORTHWEST TERRITORIES
FORT SMITH
Yellowknife
Great Slave L.
Ft. Simpson
Ft. Smith
Ft. Nelson
Churchill Pk.
Skagway
Juneau
Sitka
Ketchikan
Prince Rupert
Queen Charlotte Is.
Hecate Str.
PACIFIC OCEAN
BRITISH COLUMBIA
Rocky Mountains
Coast Mountains
Cassiar Mountains
Prince George
Cariboo Mts.
Mt. Waddington
Mt. Robson
Vancouver I.
Vancouver
Victoria
Kamloops
Kelowna
Penticton
Calgary
Edmonton
ALBERTA
Red Deer
Lethbridge
Medicine Hat
Grande Prairie
Peace R.
Fort McMurray
Lake Athabasca
Lesser Slave L.
SASKATCHEWAN
Saskatoon
Regina
Prince Albert
Moose Jaw
Reindeer Lake
MANITOBA
Churchill
Lake Winnipeg
Winnipeg
Brandon
Dauphin
Seattle
Tacoma
Spokane
WASHINGTON
MONTANA
NORTH DAKOTA
SOUTH DAKOTA
WYOMING
NEBRASKA
MINNESOTA
UNITED STATES
Minneapolis
St. Paul
Omaha
Sioux Falls
Bismarck
Projection: Bonne
ALASKA
1 : 24 000 000
100 0 100 200 300 miles
100 0 200 400 km
Barrow
Brooks Range
Nome
Fairbanks
Anchorage
Mt. McKinley
Alaska Range
Kodiak
Bering Sea
Bristol Bay
GULF OF ALASKA
Aleutian Is.
Unalaska I.
PACIFIC OCEAN
RUSSIA
West from Greenwich
ft
m
9000
3000
6000
2000
4500
1500
3000
1000
1200
400
600
200
0
0
200
600
2000
6000
m
ft

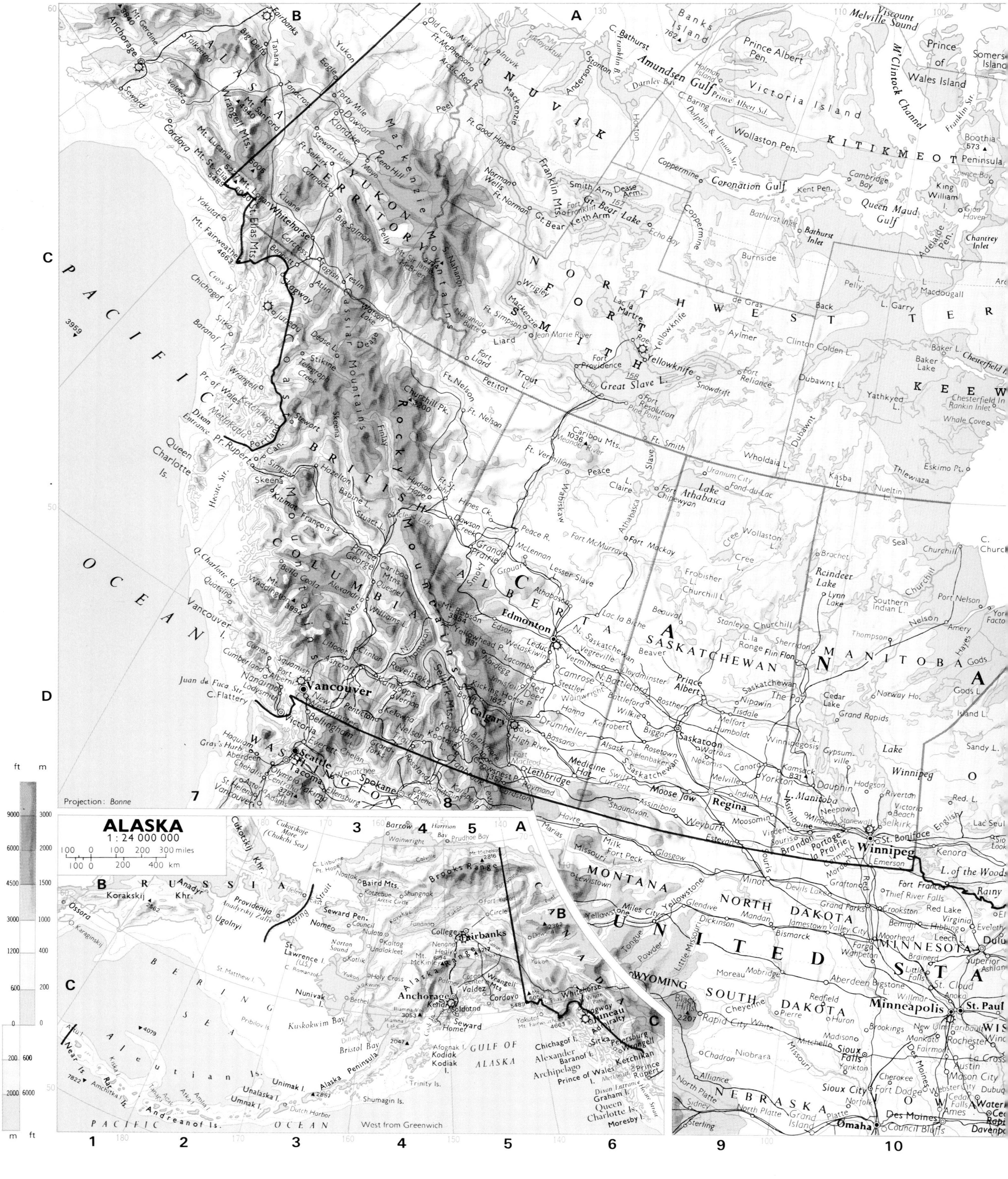

Devon Island
Lancaster Sound
Brodeur Peninsula
Arctic Bay
Bylot
Pond Inlet
Pond Inlet
Baffin Bay
Svartenhuk Halvö
2136
GREENLAND
Angmagssalik
Disko
Disko
Christianshåb
Scott I.
C. Hewett
Clyde
Home I.
Davis Strait
Holsteinsborg
Sukkertoppen
Godthåb
Frederikshåb
Ivigtut
Julianehåb
Nanortalik
Kap Farvel

ATLANTIC

Pelly Bay
Iglooik
Igloolik
Melville
Foxe Basin
Fury & Hecla Str.
Hall Lake
Prince Charles I.
Cumberland Peninsula
2591
C. Dyer
Cape Dyer
Gulf of Boothia
Committee B.
Rae Isthmus
Circle
Wager B.
Repulse Bay
Southampton I.
FOXE BASIN
Foxe Peninsula
Amadjuak L.
Amadjuak
C. Dorchester
C. Mercy
Cumberland Sd.
Pangnirtung

BAFFIN ISLAND

Jager Bay
Wager
Roes Welcome Sd.
Channel
Southampton I.
Coral Harbour
Bell Pen.
Coats I.
Digges Is.
Invuvik
Saglouc (Sugluk)
Maricourt (Wakeham)
Koartac Notre Dame de Koartac
Akpatok
Foxe Land
Iqaluit
Lake Harbour
Frobisher Bay
Resolution I.
C. Chidley

LABRADOR SEA

Hudson Strait
Ungava Bay
1676
Port Nouveau-Québec
George R.
Hebron
Nutak

Ft. Severn
Portland Promontory
Inoucdjouac (Port Harrison)
Ungava Peninsula
Payne L.
Arnaud (Bell) R.
Payne Bay
George
Nain

Winisk
257
Ottawa Isls.
Sleeper Is.
King George Is.
King George Is.
Baker's Dozen Is.
Belcher Is.
à l'Eau Claire
Lac Bienville
Petitsikapau
Schefferville
COAST OF LABRADOR
North West R.
L. Melville
Cartwright
C. Harrison
Indian Harbour
Rigolet
Hopedale
Belle Isle

HUDSON BAY

Big Trout L.
C. Henrietta Maria
Pte. Louis-XIV
Grand Baleine la-Baleine (Great Whale River)
Kanaaupscow
La Grande
Churchill Falls
Churchill
Hamilton Inlet
Bottle Hbr.
Str. of Belle Isle
Natashquan

Severn
Attawapiskat
Akimiski I.
James Bay
Ft. George
Nouveau Comptoir (Paint Hills)
Eastmain
Fort Rupert (Rupert House)
Rupert R.
L. Albanel
L. Mistassini
1128
Gagnon
Moisie
Sept Îles
Port-Cartier
Mingan
Natashquan
I. d'Anticosti
NEWFOUNDLAND
814
Grand Falls
Gander
Bonavista
Trinity B.
St. John's
Harbour Grace
Carbonear
Placentia
Plat.Blanc B.
Trepassey
C. Race

Ft. Severn
L. St. Joseph
Ft. Albany
Charlton I.
Moosonee
Albany
Nottaway
Harricana
Chibougamau
Matagami
L. Albanel
Baie-Comeau
Betsiamites
R. St. Lawrence
Matane
Gulf of St. Lawrence
Pén. de Gaspé
Gaspé
Îs. de la Madeleine
St-Augustin-Saguenay
Cabot Str.
Cape Breton I.
ST-PIERRE et MIQUELON (Fr.)
Ray
P. aux Basques
C. North
Glace Bay
Sydney
Port Hawkesbury
Mulgrave

ONTARIO

Winisk
Nipigon
L. Nipigon
Armstrong
Nakina
Kenogami
Longlac
Hearst
Cochrane
L'Abitibi
Senneterre
Rés. de Gouin
Roberval
Saguenay
Chicoutimi
Rivière-du-Loup
Edmundston
Newcastle
Chatham
Bathurst
NEW BRUNSWICK
Dalhousie
Campbellton
Northumberland Str.
PR. EDWARD I.
Summerside
Charlottetown
NOVA SCOTIA
New Glasgow
Pictou
Amherst
Moncton

Thunder Bay
Michipicoten
Heron Bay
Oba
Longlac
Franz
Timmins
Noranda
Rouyn
Kirkland Lake
Haileybury
Cobalt
L. Témiscamingue
Rés. de Cabonga
La Tuque
Shawinigan
Trois-Rivières
QUÉBEC
Lévis
Thetford Mines
Woodstock
Fredericton
Saint John
Kentville
Windsor
Truro
Dartmouth
HALIFAX
Bridgewater
Liverpool
Shelburne

Lake Superior
Calumet
Keweenaw Bay
Sault Ste. Marie
Sault Ste. Marie
Sudbury
Copper Cliff
North Bay
Parry Sound
Pembroke
Arnprior
OTTAWA
Hull
Lachine
MONTRÉAL
St. Hyacinthe
Sorel
Sherbrooke
Richmond
 St. Léonard
L. Champlain
VERMONT
Augusta
MAINE
Bangor
B. of Fundy
Digby
Yarmouth
C. Sable
Sable I. (Nova Scotia)

Ironwood
Iron Mt.
Menominee
Green Bay
Manistique
Cheboygan
Petoskey
Georgian Bay
Owen Sound
Orillia
Peterborough
Belleville
Kingston
Cornwall
Burlington
Watertown
Glens Falls
Lake Champlain
Portland
NEW HAMPSHIRE
Manchester
Concord
Lowell

Milwaukee
Racine
Kenosha
Sheboygan
Manitowoc
WISCONSIN
Appleton
Oshkosh
Fond du Lac
Lake Michigan
Ludington
Traverse City
Cadillac
Saginaw
Bay City
TORONTO
Guelph
Kitchener
Hamilton
Niagara Falls
St. Catharines
Rochester
Syracuse
Utica
Albany
Worcester
MASS.
BOSTON
C. Cod
Providence
CONN.
New Haven
Bridgeport

Madison
Rockford
Kenosha
CHICAGO
Evanston
Gary
ILLINOIS
INDIANA
South Bend
Grand Rapids
Kalamazoo
Muskegon
London
Chatham
DETROIT
Windsor
Toledo
Akron
Cleveland
Youngstown
Jamestown
Williamsport
PENNSYLVANIA
Allentown
Reading
Trenton
NEW JERSEY
NEW YORK
Newark
Jersey City
Brantford
Brampton
Elmira
Binghamton
Scranton
Wilkes-Barre
Waterbury
NEW YORK

1:12 000 000
100   0   100   200   300   400 miles
100   0   100   200   300   400   500   600 km

West from Greenwich
COPYRIGHT. GEORGE PHILIP & SON. LTD.

N. W. T E R R I T O R I E S

MANITOBA

H U D S O N   B A Y

North Belcher Is.
Baker's Dozen Is.
Kugong I.
Belcher
Tukarak I.
Flaherty I.
Innetalling I.
Islands

L. Minto
Nastapoka Is.
Laçs des Loups-Ma
L. Guillaume-Delisle
Petite Baleine
L. à l'Eau Claire
Lac D'Iberville

J A M E S   B A Y

Akimiski I.
North Twin I.
South Twin I.
Weston I.
Charlton
Tradely I.
Eastmain

O N T A R I O

Polar Bear Provincial Park
Winisk
Attawapiskat
Albany

Q U É B E C

L. Mistassini

Lake Superior
Thunder Bay
Duluth
Superior

LAKE   HURON
LAKE   MICHIGAN
LAKE   ONTARIO
LAKE   ERIE

WISCONSIN
ILLINOIS
INDIANA
OHIO
PENNSYLVANIA
NEW YORK

MILWAUKEE
CHICAGO
DETROIT
CLEVELAND
TORONTO
HAMILTON
BUFFALO
OTTAWA
Sudbury
North Bay
Timmins
Kapuskasing

ft   m
4500   1500
3000   1000
1200   400
600   200
0   0
200   600
2000   6000
4000   12 000
m   ft

Lambert's Equivalent Azimuthal

1 : 5 600 000

50   0   50   100   150   200 miles
50 0 50 100 150 200 250 300 km

COAST OF

NEWFOUNDLAND

LABRADOR

QUEBEC

Labrador City
Sept-Îles

I. d'Anticosti

GULF OF
ST. LAWRENCE

Cabot Strait

SAINT-PIERRE
ET MIQUELON
(Fr.)

NEW
BRUNSWICK

PRINCE EDWARD
ISLAND

Charlottetown

Cape Breton
Island

NOVA SCOTIA

MAINE

Halifax

Sable I.
(Nova Scotia)

ATLANTIC

BOSTON

OCEAN

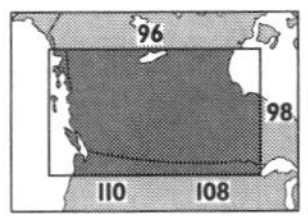

YUKON TERRITORY

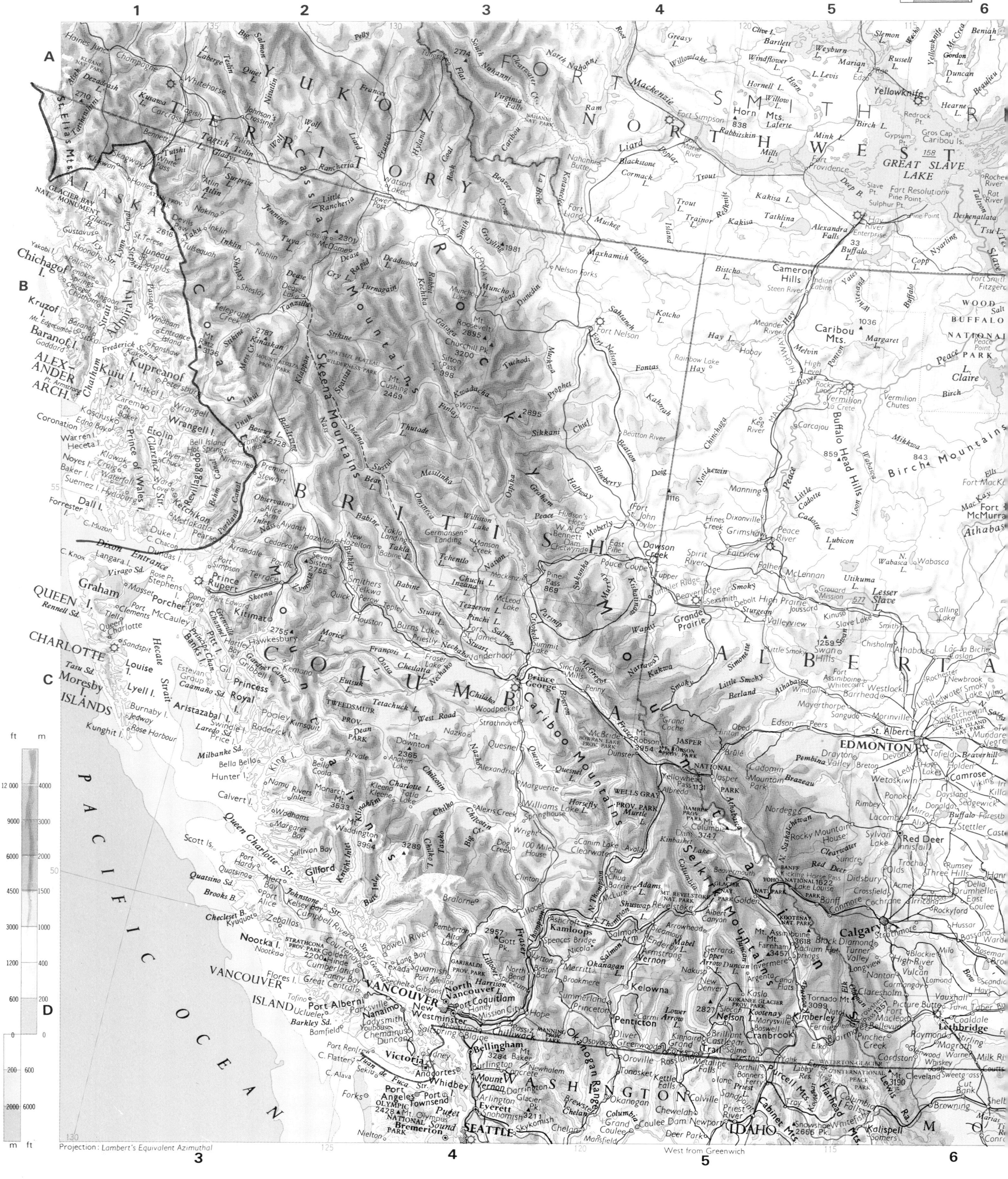

NORTHWEST

FORT SMITH

ALASKA

BRITISH COLUMBIA

ALBERTA

PACIFIC OCEAN

GREAT SLAVE LAKE

WOOD BUFFALO NATIONAL PARK

QUEEN CHARLOTTE ISLANDS

VANCOUVER ISLAND

WASHINGTON

IDAHO

EDMONTON

Calgary

Red Deer

VANCOUVER

Victoria

SEATTLE

Prince George

Prince Rupert

Kamloops

Kelowna

Dawson Creek

Fort Nelson

Whitehorse

Yellowknife

Projection: Lambert's Equivalent Azimuthal

West from Greenwich

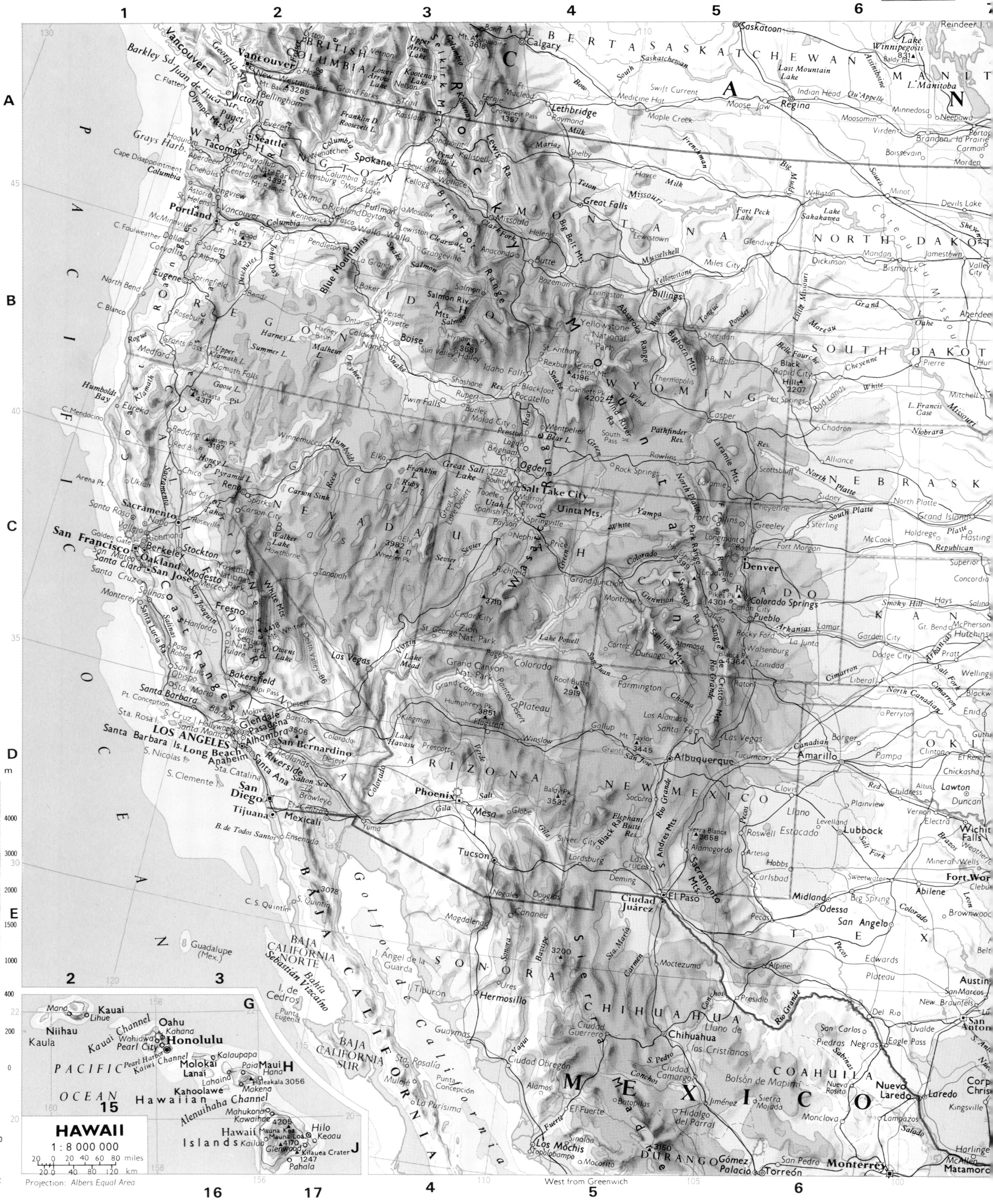

CANADA — BRITISH COLUMBIA · ALBERTA · SASKATCHEWAN · MANITOBA

Vancouver I. · Vancouver · Victoria · Seattle · Tacoma · Olympia · Portland · Salem · Eugene

WASHINGTON · OREGON · IDAHO · MONTANA · NORTH DAKOTA · SOUTH DAKOTA · NEBRASKA · KANSAS

Spokane · Missoula · Great Falls · Helena · Butte · Billings · Bismarck · Pierre

WYOMING · Yellowstone National Park · Casper · Cheyenne · Denver · Colorado Springs · Pueblo

NEVADA · UTAH · COLORADO

San Francisco · Oakland · San Jose · Sacramento · Stockton · Modesto · Fresno · Bakersfield

Reno · Las Vegas · Salt Lake City · Provo · Ogden

CALIFORNIA · ARIZONA · NEW MEXICO · OKLAHOMA · TEXAS

LOS ANGELES · Long Beach · Pasadena · San Bernardino · Riverside · Santa Barbara · San Diego

Phoenix · Mesa · Tucson · Albuquerque · Santa Fe · El Paso · Las Cruces · Roswell · Lubbock · Amarillo

PACIFIC OCEAN

BAJA CALIFORNIA NORTE · BAJA CALIFORNIA SUR · SONORA · CHIHUAHUA · COAHUILA · DURANGO

MEXICO · Tijuana · Mexicali · Ensenada · Hermosillo · Guaymas · Ciudad Juárez · Chihuahua · Monterrey · Nuevo Laredo · Torreón

Golfo de California

ft / m scale
12 000 / 4000
9000 / 3000
6000 / 2000
4500 / 1500
3000 / 1000
1200 / 400
600 / 200
0
200 / 600
2000 / 6000
m / ft

HAWAII
1 : 8 000 000
Kauai · Niihau · Oahu · Honolulu · Pearl City · Molokai · Lanai · Maui · Hawaii
Haleakala 3056 · Mauna Kea 4205 · Mauna Loa 4170 · Hilo · Kilauea Crater 1247
PACIFIC OCEAN · Hawaiian Islands
20 0 20 40 60 80 miles
20 0 40 80 120 km
Projection: Albers Equal Area

West from Greenwich

1 : 9 600 000

50   0   50   100 150 200 250 300 miles
50   0   50 100 150 200 250 300 350 400 450 km

8   9   10   11   12   13

8   9   10   11   12

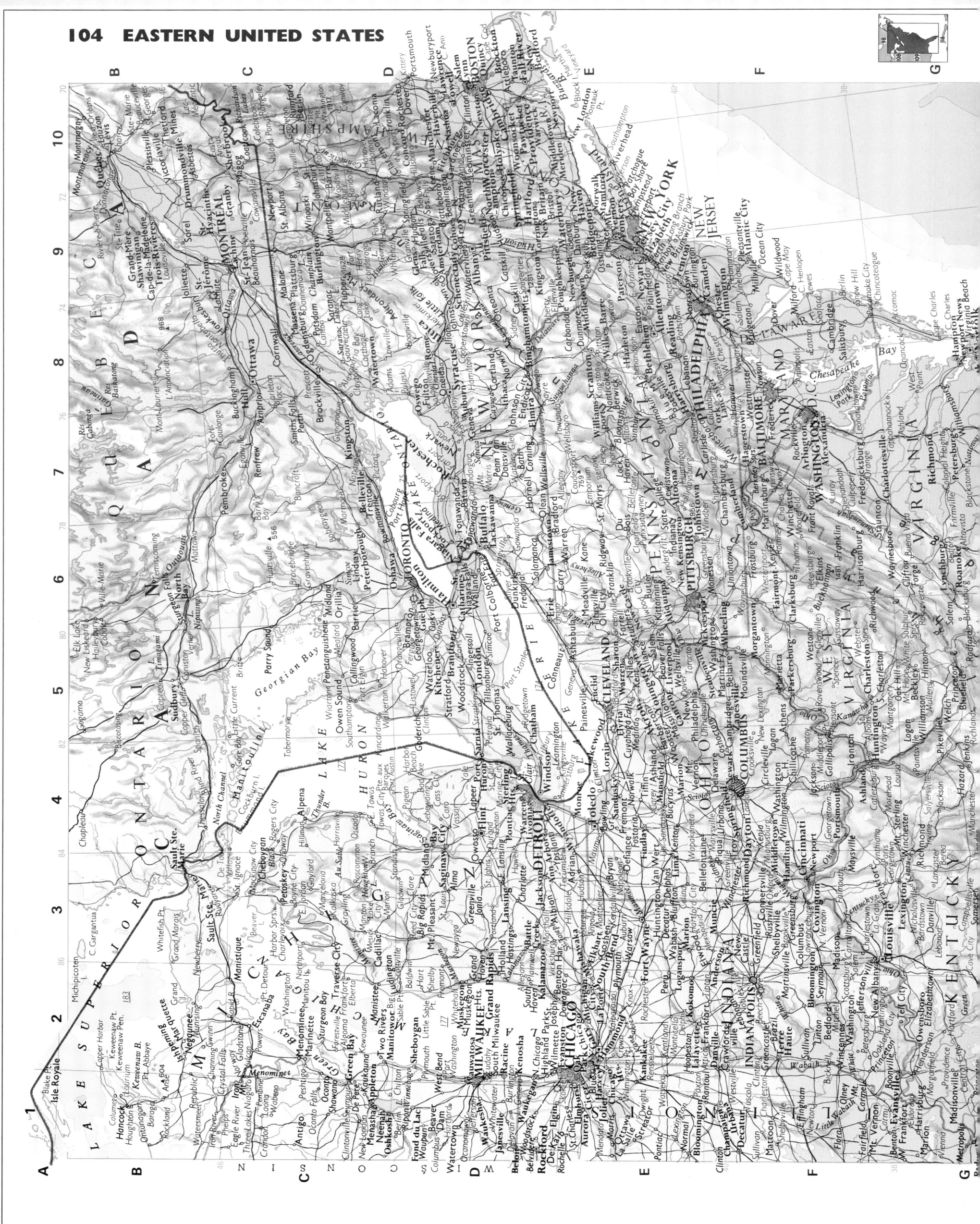

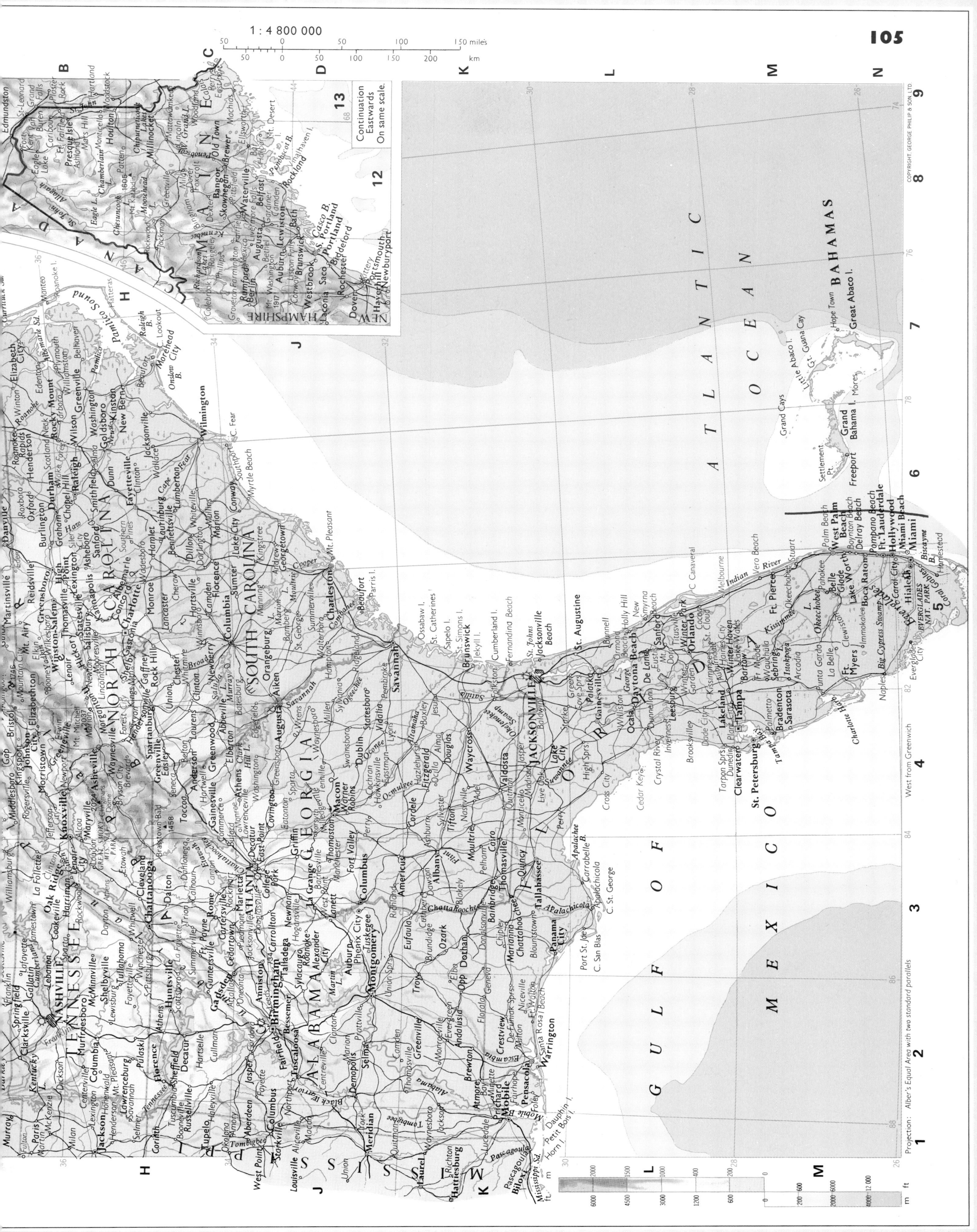

1 : 4 800 000

50   0   50   100   150 miles
50   0   50   100   150   200   km

Continuation Eastwards
On same scale.

MAINE

NEW HAMPSHIRE

CANADA

ATLANTIC

OCEAN

BAHAMAS

NORTH CAROLINA

SOUTH CAROLINA

GEORGIA

FLORIDA

ALABAMA

TENNESSEE

MISSISSIPPI

GULF OF MEXICO

Projection: Alber's Equal Area with two standard parallels

West from Greenwich

COPYRIGHT GEORGE PHILIP & SON LTD.

98
104
104 7

1 2 3 4 5 6 7

A

Georgian Bay

Fitzwilliam I.
Yeo I.
Lucas Channel
Cove I.
Tobermory
C. Hurd
Flowerpot I.
Lion's Head
C. Croker
Dyer Bay
Cabot Hd.
Shanwanaga I.
McKellar
Emsdale
Novar
Algonquin Park
Kiflaloe Sta.
Golden L.
Whitney
Madawaska
Barry's Bay
L. Clear
Combermere
Madawaska
Griffith
Nobel
Parry Sound
Waubamik
Dwight
Huntsville
Rosseau
Kawagama L.
Lake St. Peter
Denbigh
Weslemkoon L.

North Pt.
Thunder Bay
South Pt.
Blackriver
Harrisville
Greenbush

B
LAKE HURON
208
176

Penetanguishene
Midland
Port Severn
Victoria Harb.
Coldwater
Washago
L. Muskoka
Gravenhurst
Black L.
Minden
Gooderham
Coe Hill
Haliburton
Wilberforce
Bancroft
Cloyne
Apsley
Millbridge
Bannockburn
Eldorado
Arden
Kaladar

Oscoda
Au Sable
Au Sable Pt.

Nottawasaga Bay
Meaford
Thornbury
Collingwood
Stayner
Wasaga Beach
Elmvale
Orillia
Brechin
Cobocook
Fenelon Falls
Kirkfield
Bobcaygeon
Burnt River
Burleigh Falls
Stony L.
Mado
Marmora
Tweed
Tamwi

Wiarton
Hepworth
Shallow Lake
Owen Sound
Chatsworth
Tara
Chiefs Pt.
Park Head
Southampton
Port Elgin

C
ONTARIO
LAKE ONTARIO

Peterborough
Keene
Norwood
Campbellford
Stirling
Frankford
Trenton
Belleville
Consecon
Bloomfield
Picton
Wellington
Wicked Pt.

Harris
Port Austin
Pte Aux Barques
Kinde
Bad Axe
Port Hope
Harbor Beach
Ruth
Elkton

MICHIGAN
Cass
Deckerville
Sandusky
Carsonville
Croswell
Lexington
Brown City
Yale
Port Sanilac

Kincardine
Ripley
Pt. Clark
Lucknow
Teeswater
Wingham
Harriston
Arthur
Grand Valley
Orangeville
Bolton
Woodbridge
Malton
Brampton
Georgetown
Acton
Streetsville
Milton
Oakville
Port Credit
Mississauga
TORONTO
Richmond Hill
Aurora
Newmarket
Stouffville
Markham
Ajax
Whitby
Oshawa
Bowmanville
Cobourg
Port Hope
Orono

D
DETROIT
Lake St. Clair
Windsor
Chatham
LAKE ERIE

LAKE ST. CLAIR

St. Catharines
Niagara Falls
Welland
Fort Erie
BUFFALO
Lackawanna
West Seneca
Amherst
N. Tonawanda
Tonawanda
NEW YORK
Batavia
Rochester
Greece
Gates
Brighton
Irondequoit
Webster
Williamson

E
CLEVELAND
Lakewood
Euclid
Cleveland Hts.
Shaker Hts.
Parma
Sandusky
Lorain
Elyria
Oberlin
Strongsville
Brunswick
Medina

Erie
Presque I.
Lake City
North East
Westfield
Dunkirk
Fredonia
Silver Creek
Angola
Eden
N. Collins
Springville
Holland
Arcade
Warsaw
Mt. Morris
Springwater
Wayland
Keuka L.

Jamestown
Falconer
Frewsburg
Randolph
Salamanca
Olean
Allegany
Cuba
Belmont
Friendship
Andover
Wellsville
Hornell
Canisteo
Bath
Avoca
Cohocton
Dundee

F
OHIO
PENNSYLVANIA
Akron
Barberton
Wadsworth
Canton
Massillon
Alliance
Salem
Youngstown
Boardman
Struthers
Campbell
Niles
Warren
New Castle
Sharon
Farrell
Hubbard
Butler
Kittanning
Ford City
Indiana
Clearfield
Philipsburg
State College
Bellefonte
Altoona
Tyrone
Hollidaysburg

G
PITTSBURGH
McKeesport
Monroeville
Wilkinsburg
Penn Hills
Plum
New Kensington
Monessen
Washington
Weirton
Steubenville
Wheeling
W.VA.
Johnstown
Windber
Ebensburg
Greensburg
Latrobe
Jeannette
Connellsville
Uniontown
Somerset
Bedford

Newark
Zanesville
Cambridge
Coshocton
New Philadelphia
Dover

Projection: Bonne

ft m
6000 2000
4500 1500
3000 1000
1200 400
600 200
0 0
200 600
m ft

2 3 4 5 6 7

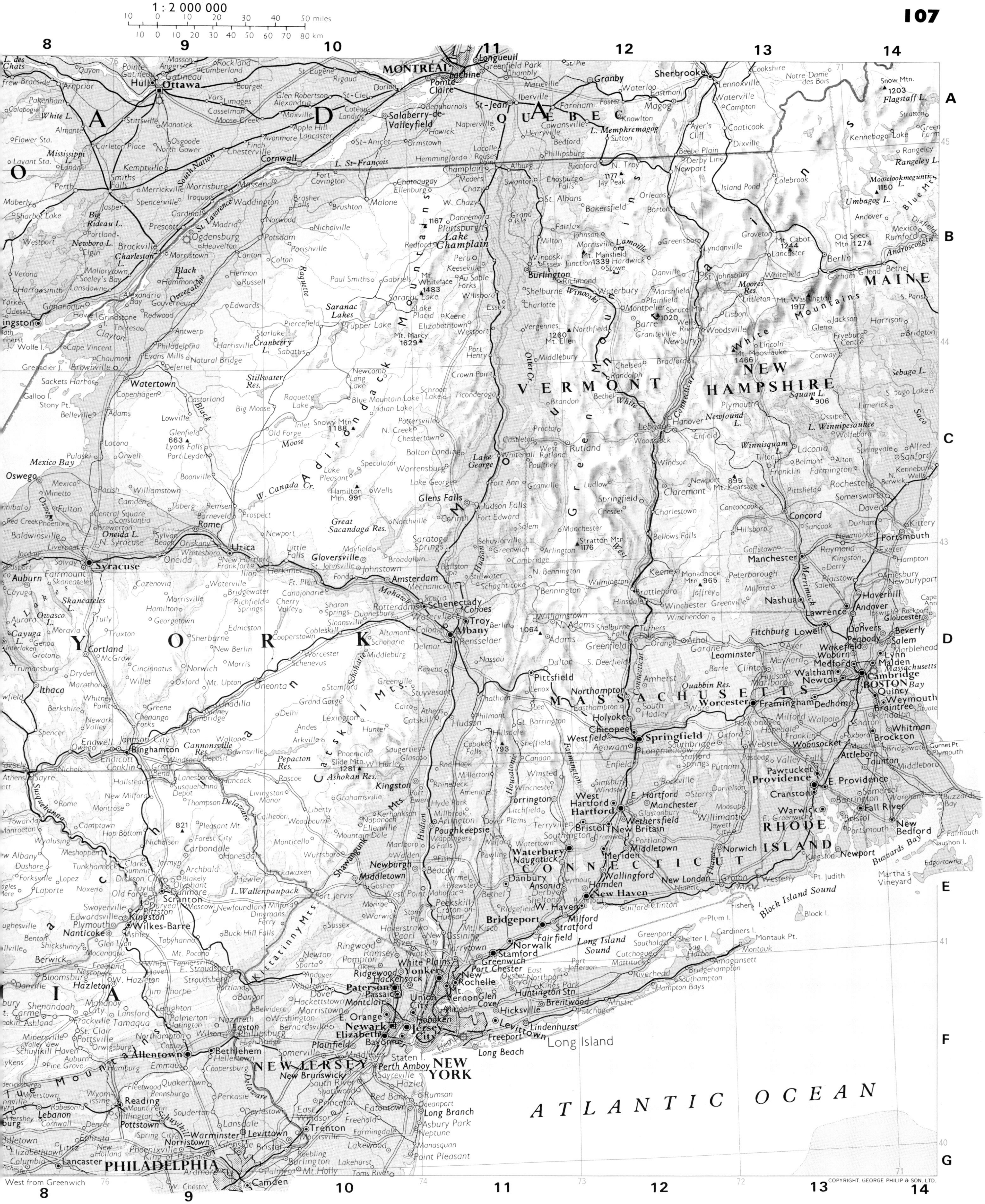

1 : 2 000 000

10   0   10   20   30   40   50 miles
10   0 10 20 30 40 50 60 70 80 km

8   9   10   11   12   13   14

MONTREAL
Longueuil
Greenfield Park

O
A
D
A

QUEBEC

VERMONT

NEW HAMPSHIRE

MAINE

Lake Champlain

Burlington

Montpelier

Mt. Washington

White Mountains

Adirondack Mountains

Mt. Marcy
1629

Lake Placid

Saranac Lakes

Ottawa
Hull

Cornwall

Ogdensburg

Watertown

Oswego

Syracuse

Utica

Rome

Schenectady

Albany

Troy

NEW YORK

Y O R K

Binghamton

Scranton

Wilkes-Barre

Kingston

Poughkeepsie

MASSACHUSETTS

Pittsfield

Springfield

Worcester

BOSTON

Cambridge

Lowell

Lawrence

Nashua

Manchester

Concord

Portsmouth

CONNECTICUT

Hartford

New Haven

Bridgeport

Waterbury

Danbury

Norwalk

Stamford

RHODE ISLAND

Providence

Pawtucket

Fall River

New Bedford

Newport

NEW JERSEY

NEW YORK

Newark
Jersey City
Elizabeth
Paterson
Passaic
Yonkers
New Rochelle
White Plains
Hackensack

Trenton

PHILADELPHIA

Camden

Reading

Allentown
Bethlehem
Easton

Long Island

Long Beach

A T L A N T I C   O C E A N

Martha's
Vineyard

Block Island Sound

Long Island Sound

Montauk Pt.

West from Greenwich

COPYRIGHT. GEORGE PHILIP & SON. LTD.

8   9   10   11   12   13   14

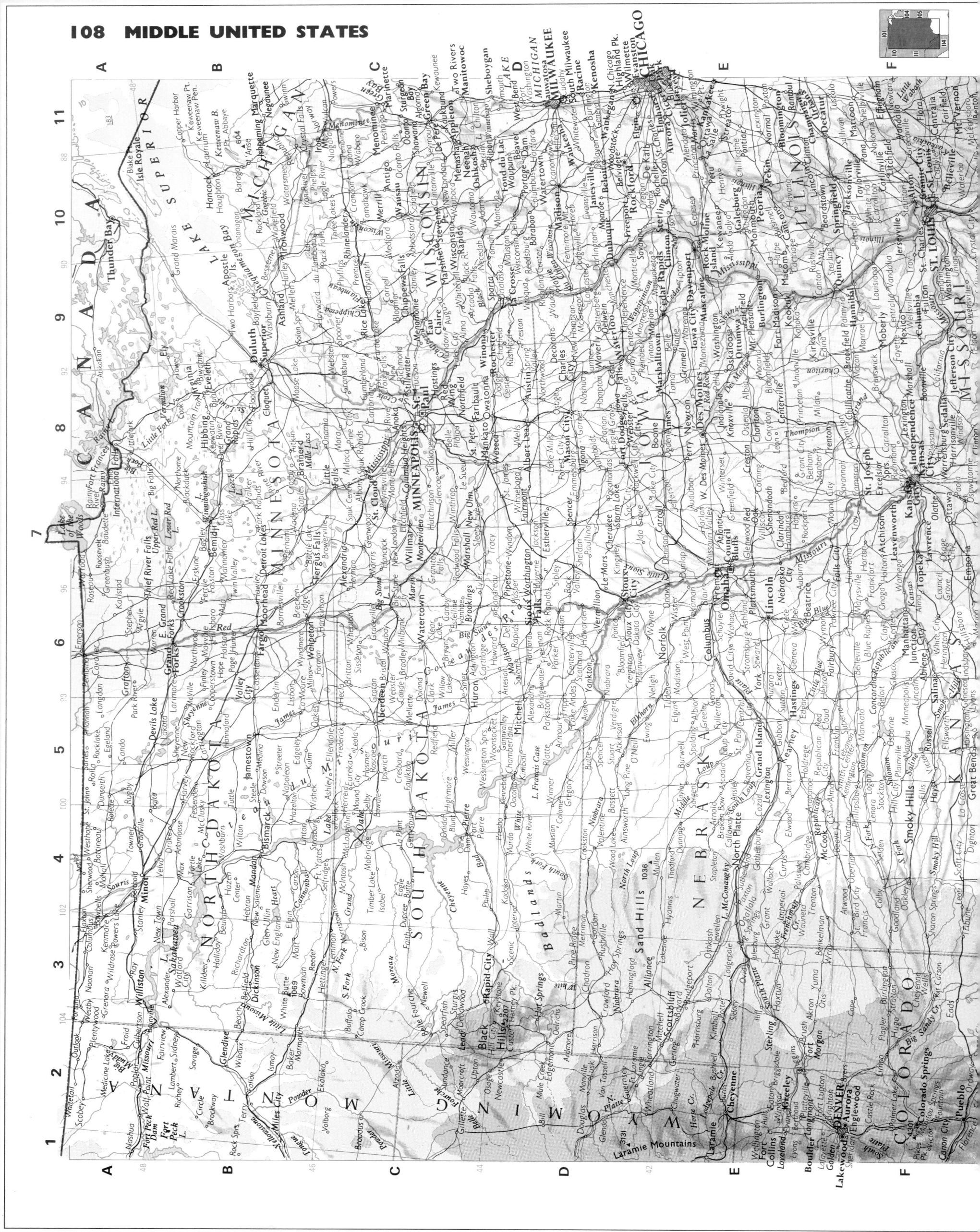

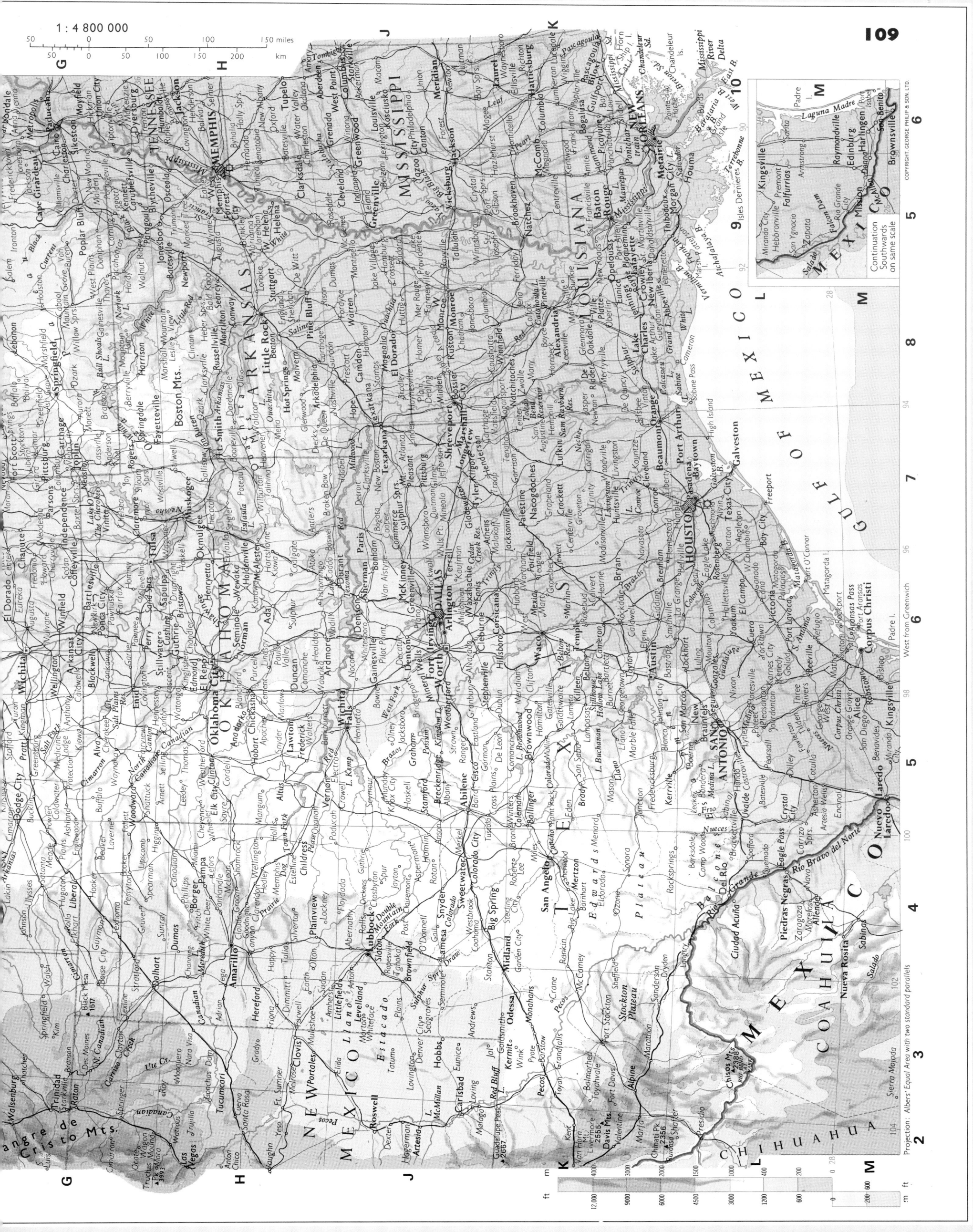

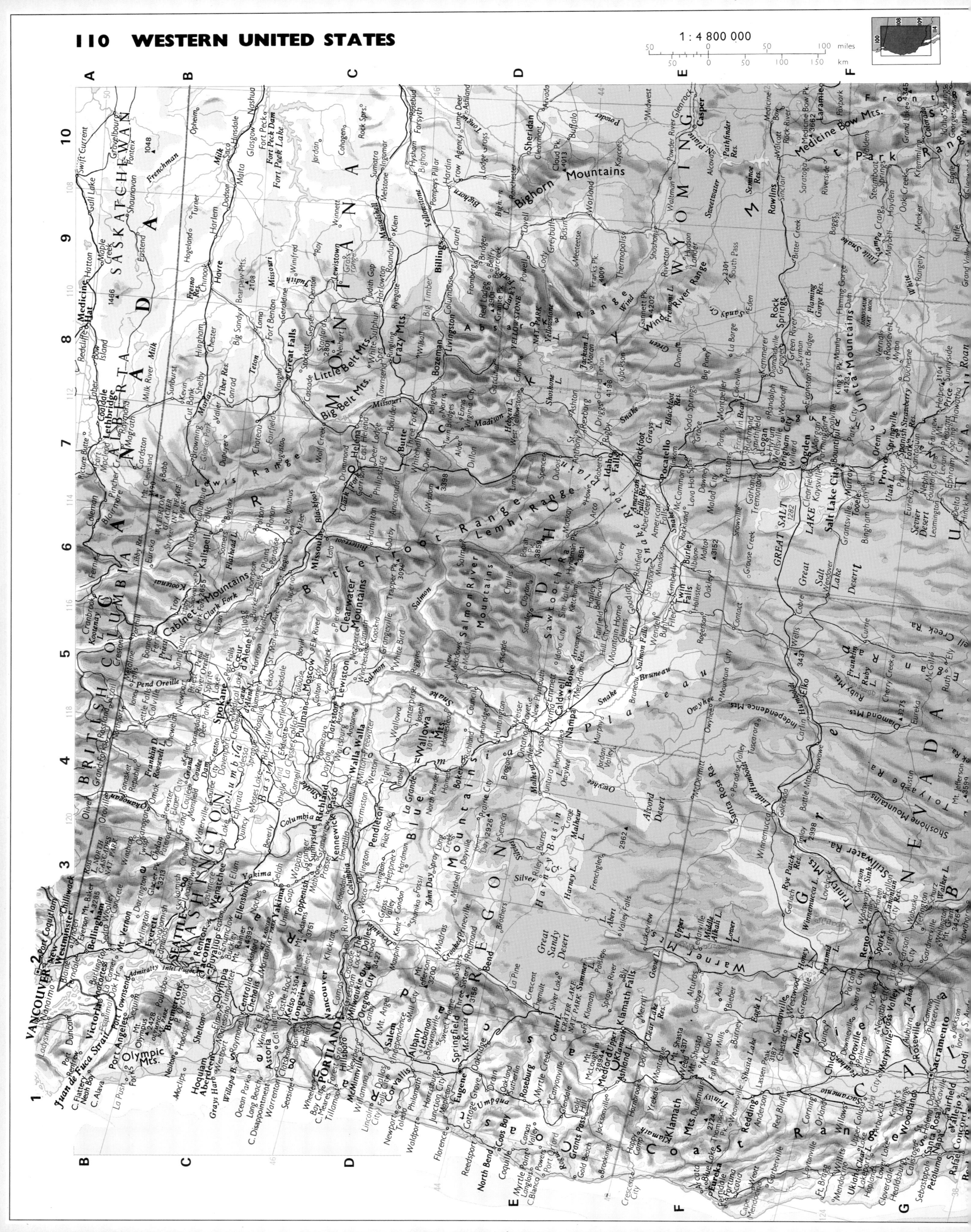

1 : 4 800 000

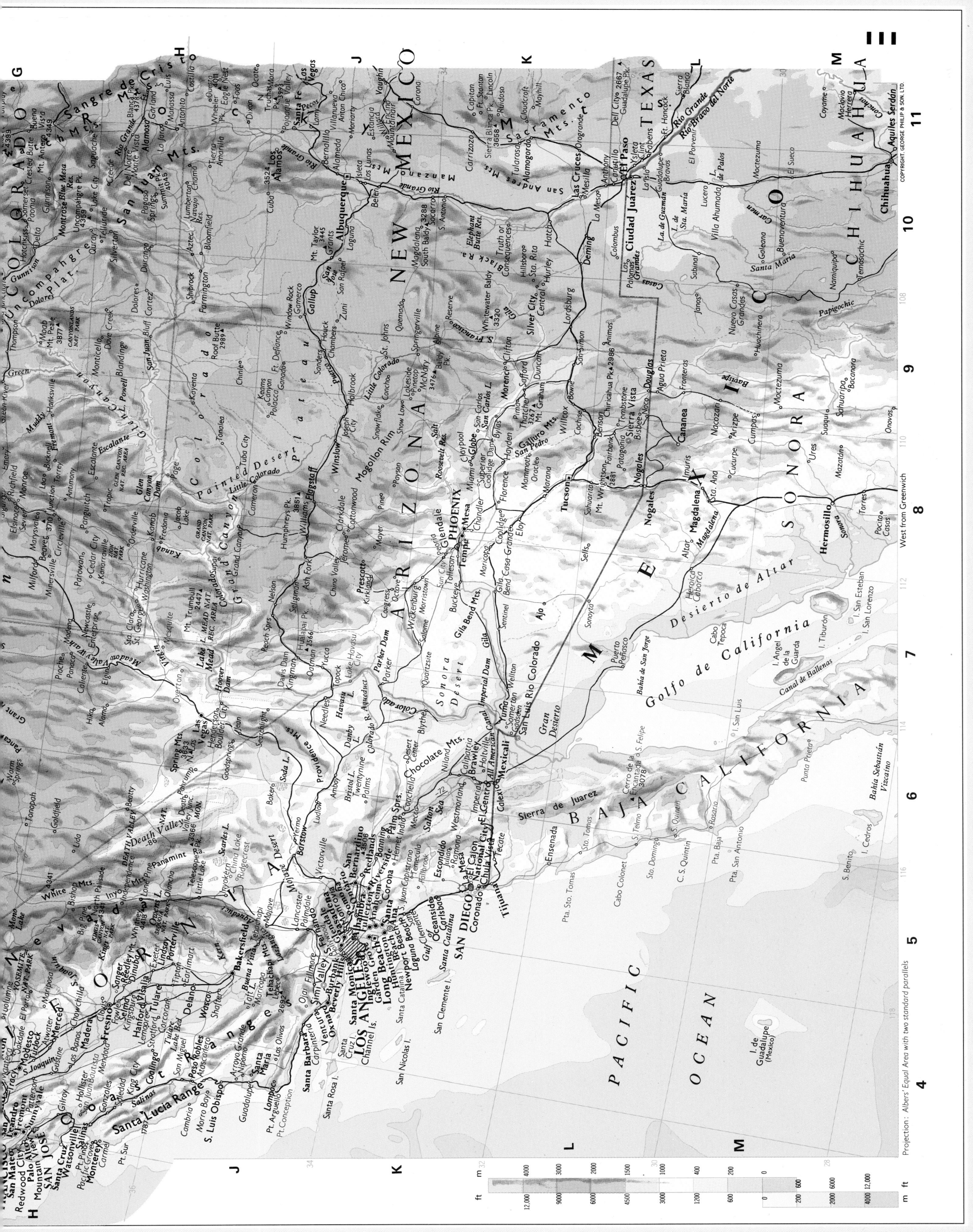

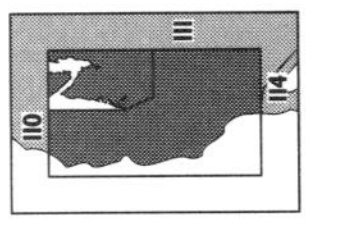

SEATTLE-PORTLAND REGION
On same scale

CANADA

WASHINGTON

OREGON

CALIFORNIA

NEVADA

Vancouver Island

Victoria

PACIFIC OCEAN

Strait of Georgia

Juan de Fuca Strait

Olympic Mountains
NATIONAL PARK

New Westminster

Vancouver

Bellingham

Everett
SEATTLE
Bellevue
Renton
Tacoma
Lakewood Center
Olympia
Bremerton
Port Angeles

Centralia
Longview
Kelso
PORTLAND
Vancouver
Oregon City

San Rafael
SAN FRANCISCO
Daly City
Oakland
Berkeley
Richmond
Vallejo
Concord
Walnut Creek
Livermore
Fremont
Hayward
San Leandro
Alameda
Palo Alto
Mountain View
Sunnyvale
Santa Clara
SAN JOSE
Campbell
Los Gatos
Saratoga
Redwood City
San Mateo
Burlingame
Pacifica
Menlo Park

Santa Rosa
Petaluma
Napa
Sonoma
St. Helena

Sacramento
Davis
Woodland
North Highlands
Carmichael
Arden
Citrus Heights
Stockton
Modesto
Antioch
Pittsburg
Fairfield
Vacaville

Chico
Oroville
Marysville
Yuba City
Grass Valley
Nevada City
Auburn
Placerville

Fresno
Clovis
Madera
Merced
Turlock
Atwater
Los Banos
Visalia
Exeter
Hanford
Tulare

Reno
Sparks
Carson City

Salinas
Monterey
Pacific Grove
Seaside
Santa Cruz
Watsonville
Gilroy
Hollister

Santa Lucia Range
Diablo Range
San Joaquin Valley
Sacramento Valley
Sierra Nevada
Inyo Mts.
White Mts.
Owens

YOSEMITE NATIONAL PARK
SEQUOIA NATIONAL PARK
KINGS CANYON NATIONAL PARK
Lake Tahoe
Mono L.
L. McClure
New Don Pedro

Clear L.
Lake Oroville
Russian River
Feather River
American River

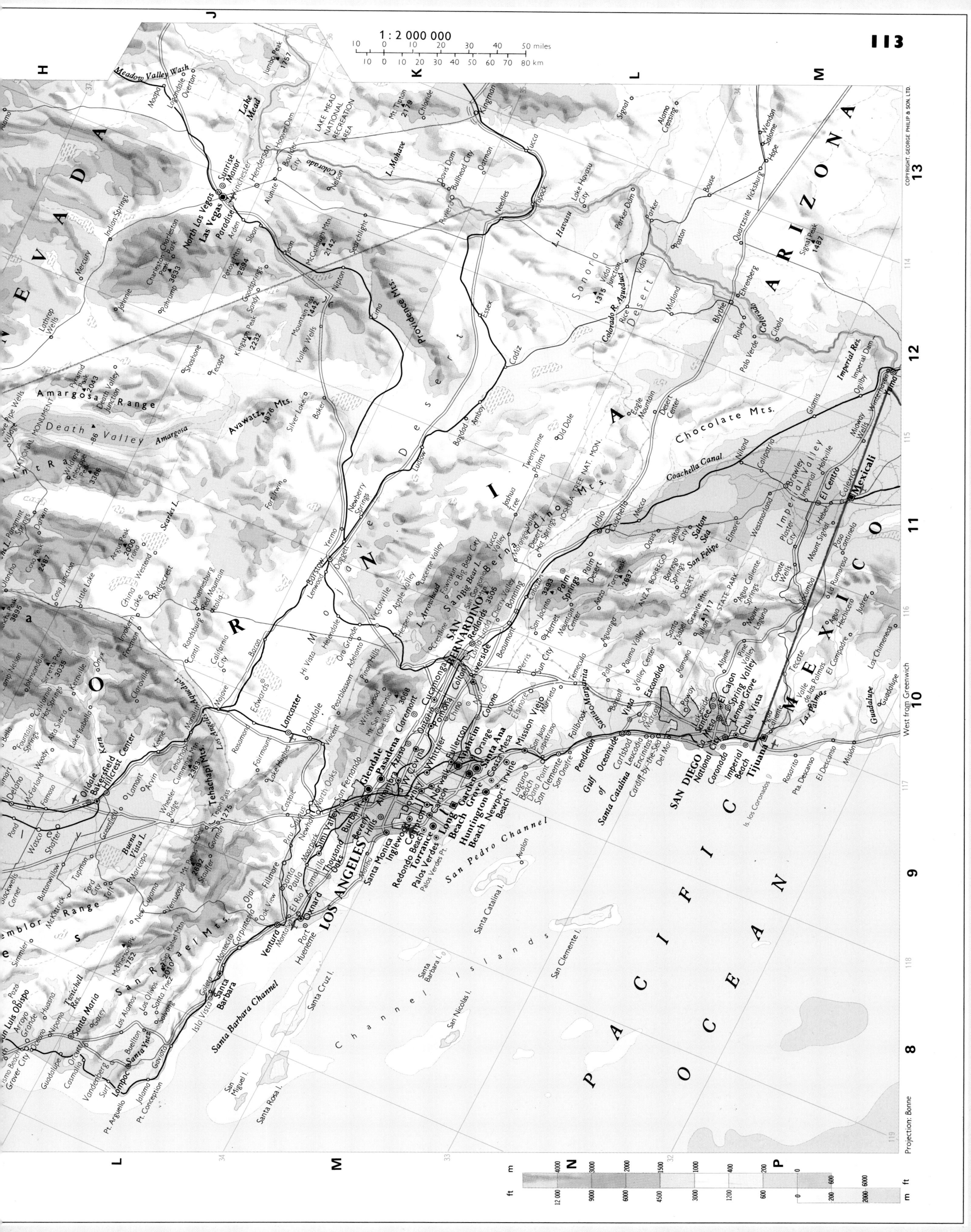

1 : 2 000 000

Projection: Bonne

102 103
116

1 2 3 4

ARIZONA

TIJUANA
MEXICALI
El Centro
Yuma
Gila
Gila Bend
San Luis Río Colorado
Globe
Miami
Christmas
Elephant Butte Res.
• Roswell
Lubbock

Ensenada
Mission
Santo Tomás
La Bomba
I. Montague
Sonoyta
S. Pedro
Gila
Lordsburg
NEW MEXICO
3658
Hobbs
Sweetwater

A

Santo Domingo
San Telmo
3078
Puerto Peñasco
TUCSON
Nogales
Bisbee
Douglas
Deming
Las Cruces
CIUDAD JUAREZ
EL PASO
UNITE
Carlsbad
Big Spring

San Quintín
Sierra de Juárez
San Felipe
El Desemboque
Nogales
Nacoci
Agua Prieta
Ascensión
La. de Guzmán
Guadalupe Bravos
Van Horn
San Angelo

30
Rosarito
San Fernando
B. de San Jorge
Concepción
Caborca
Altar
Imuris
Cananea
Fronteras
Janos
Sabinal
Lucero
El Porvenir
Río Bravo del Norte
Alpine
Sanderson

Pta. Baja
CALIFORNIA
I. San Luis
El Dátil
La Libertad
Benjamín Hill
Santa Ana
Arizpe
Cumpas
Nacozari
Villa Ahumada
Moctezuma
Presidio

BAJA
NORTE
I. Ángel de la Guarda
C. Tepoca
Magdalena
Cucurpe
Moctezuma
Bacerac
Buenaventura
El Sueco
Ojinaga
El Pueblito
Presa de la Amistad
Del Río
Acuña

Punta Prieta
El Rosarito
Canal de Ballenas
I. Tiburón
Hermosillo
Kino
Mazatán
Rayón
Huachinera
Galeana
Carmen
Conchos
Serranías del Burro
Piedras Negras
Eagle Pass

I. Cedros
I. Natividad
Pta. Falsa
Bahía Sebastián Vizcaíno
Sierra Vizcaíno
San Ignacio
I. San Lorenzo
Sonora
Torres
Ures
Suaqui
Carbó
Pocito Casas
Onavas
Ciudad Guerrero
Madera
Temosachic
Cuauhtémoc
CHIHUAHUA
Aquiles Serdán
Julimes
Boquilla del Carmen
San Carlos
Zaragoza
Nava
Allende

B

Desierto de Vizcaíno
Santa Rosalía
I. San Marcos
I. Lobos
Guaymas
Empalme
Yaqui
Movas
Yécora
Moris
Ocampo
Cusihuiriáchic
Carichíc
Satevó
S. Pedro
Presa Fco. I. Madero
Delicias
Saucillo
Ciudad Camargo
COAHUILA
Nueva Rosita
Sabinas
Progreso
Villa Juárez

Laguna San Ignacio
Pta. Abreojos
Pta. Concepción
Ciudad Obregón
Presa Mocúzari
Nuri
Torín
Bocoyna
Creel
Urique
Nonoava
Presa de la Boquilla
San Francisco del Oro
Hidalgo del Parral
Santa Bárbara
Jiménez
Bolsón de Mapimí
Sierra Mojada
Melchor Múzquiz
San Buenaventura
V. Carranza
Lampazos
Monclova
Sabinas Hidalgo

San Ignacio
La Purísima
Mulejé
Navojoa
Huatabampo
Yávaros
Álamos
Chínipas
Uruéchic
Batopilas
Verde
Morelos
Agua Caliente
Guadalupe y Calvo
Villa Ocampo
3348
Guanaceví
Conejos
Tlahualilo
Mapimi
Escalón
Cuatrociénegas
Francisco I. Madero
Reata
San Pedro de las Colonias
Sauceda
MONTERREY

25
Loreto
I. Carmen
I. Santa Catalina
Presa M. Hidalgo
Choix
Sinaloa de Leyva
Agua Caliente
El Palmito
El Salto
Gómez Palacio
Lerdo
Matamoros
Nazas
Parras
Saltillo

BAJA CALIFORNIA SUR
Santo Domingo
I. San José
Ahome
San Blas
Los Mochis
Guasave
Mocorito
Tepehuanes
Santiago Papasquiaro
Canatlán
Laguna Santiaguillo
Símón
Melchor Ocampo
Camacho
Mazapil
Concepción del Oro
Parras

Sierra de la Giganta
Llano de la Magdalena
Topolobampo
Guamúchil
Pericos
Mapimi
DURANGO
San Juan de Guadalupe
Juan Aldama
San Tiburcio
Cedral
La Escondida

C. San Lázaro
I. Santa Magdalena
B. de la Paz
I. Espíritu Santo
B. de Santa María
Navolato
Culiacán
Presa Sanalona
Tamazula
Francisco I. Madero
Victoria de Durango
Sombrerete
Río Grande
Cañitas
Matehuala
Doc

I. Santa Margarita
B. Magdalena
I. Cerralvo
Altata
Navolato
Quilá
Cosalá
Tepehuanes
Valle de Suchil
Mezquital
Chalchihuites
SAN

C

La Paz
San Pedro
Culiacán
El Dorado
San Lorenzo
La Cruz
Dimas
Concordia
Valparaiso
Jerez de García
Salinas
Fresnillo
Charcas
El Venado
Cerritos
San Luis Potosí

Tropic of Cancer
Todos Santos
San Lázaro
Mazatlán
Villa Unión
Rosario
Escuinapa
Zacatecas
Salinas
Huizá
SAN LUIS

San Lucas
San José del Cabo
C. San Lucas
Acaponeta
Tecuala
3358
Ojocaliente
Rincón de Romos
Pinos

PACIFIC
Santiago Ixcuintla
I. Isabela
San Pedro
Aguascalientes
Jalpa
Colotlán
Tepatlán
Calvillo

Tepic
NAYARIT
Huejúcar
Juan de
LEÓN
Lagos de Moreno
Guanajuato

OCEAN
Is. de Revillagigedo
San Benedicto
(México)
Roca Partida
Socorro
Chimaltitán
Los Lagos
Encarnación de Díaz
Ixtlán del Río
Etzatlán
Ameca
GUADALAJARA
Tlaquepaque
Irapuato
Celaya

B. de Banderas
Puerto Vallarta
C. Corrientes
Mascota
Ameca
Ocotlán
Zacoalco
Sahuayo
La Barca
Valle de Santiago
La Piedad
Zamora
Morolón
Acámb

20
Talpa de Allende
Autlán
L. de Chapala
Sayula
Jiquilpan
Los Reyes
Zacapu
L. de Cuitzeo
Morelia
Maravatío

Chamela
Ciudad Guzmán
4330
Nevado de Colima
Paricutín
Zitácuaro
2272

Barra de Navidad
Cihuatlán
Colima
Apatzingán
Uruapan
Ario de Rosales
Pátzcuaro
Tacámbaro
Huetamo

Manzanillo
COLIMA
Tecomán
Coalcomán
Tepalcatepec
MICHO
Cd. Altamirano

D

Coahuayana
Pómaro
Artéaga
Presa del Infiernillo
Coyuca
U. Unión
GUE

Las Truchas
Balsas
Petatlán

Zihuatanejo

REFERENCE TO NUMBERS

1	Federal District	5	México
2	Aguascalientes	6	Morelos
3	Guanajuato	7	Querétaro
4	Hidalgo	8	Tlaxcala

ft m

12 000 4000
9000   3000
6000   2000
4500   1500
3000   1000
1200   400
600   200
0   0
200   600
2000   6000
4000   12 000

m ft

Projection: Bi-polar oblique Conical Orthomorphic

West from Greenwich

110 105

2 3 4

1 : 6 400 000

50 0 50 100 150 200 miles
50 0 100 200 300 km

5 **6** **7** **8**

Wichita Falls • Denison • Paris • Texarkana • Camden • Greenville • Tuscaloosa • Opelika • Columbus • McRae • Ocmulgee
Sherman • Texarkana • ARKANSAS • El Dorado • MISSISSIPPI • Selma • Montgomery • Phenix City • Americus • Cordele • Tifton
Possum Kingdom Res. • Denton • Greenville • Monroe • Vicksburg • Meridian • ALABAMA • Troy • Albany • GEORGIA

FORT WORTH • **DALLAS** • Marshall • STATES • Jackson • Laurel • Dothan • Chattahoochee • Valdosta • Waycross **A**
Ranger • Cleburne • Longview • Tyler • Shreveport • Natchez • Hattiesburg • Jim Woodruff Res. • Tallahassee
Hillsboro • Palestine • Toledo Bend Res. • Alexandria • McComb • Bogalusa • Flomaton • FLORIDA • Lake City
Brownwood • Waco • Nacogdoches • Baton Rouge • Biloxi • Pensacola • Panama City • Apalachee Bay
Temple • Huntsville • Bryan • Lufkin • Sam Rayburn Res. • LOUISIANA • Hammond • Gulfport • MOBILE • C. San Blas • Suwannee

Austin • Beaumont • Lake Charles • Lafayette • NEW ORLEANS • Mobile Bay • Breton Sound
HOUSTON • Port Arthur • Atchafalaya Bay • Mississippi Delta • Clearwater **B**
SAN ANTONIO • Rosenberg • Galveston • Terrebonne B.
Victoria

Alice • Corpus Christi
Laredo • Kingsville
Nuevo Laredo • **G U L F   O F**
Zapata
Camargo • McAllen • Laguna Madre
M. R. Reynosa • Harlingen • Brownsville • **M E X I C O**
Matamoros • Valle Hermoso • Santa Teresa
Montemorelos • Laguna Madre
Linares • San Fernando • Tropic of Cancer • La Esperanza **C**
Ciudad Victoria • Soto la Marina • CUBA • Guane • La Fé
Isla Desterrada • Canal de Yucatán • C. San Antonio • Corrientes
Ciudad Mante • Isla Pérez
Pta. Yalkubul • Rio Lagartos • C. Catoche • Cancún
Ciudad Madero • **Tampico** • Progreso • Dzilam de Bravo • El Cuyo • Pto. Juárez
Ciudad de Valles • Motul • Temax • Tizimín • Puerto Morelos
Mérida • Izamal • Espita • Valladolid • Isla Cozumel
Laguna de Tamiahua • C. Rojo • YUCATÁN • Sotuta • Cozumel
Tuxpan • Uxmal • Ticul • Tekax • Peto • Vigía Chico • B. de la Ascensión
Poza Rica • Papantla • Tenabo • Bolonchenticul • B. del Espíritu Santo
Huauchinango • Golfo • Campeche • Felipe Carrillo Puerto
Pachuca • Tulancingo • de • Champotón • Chenkán • QUINTANA ROO • Banco Chinchorro
Teziutlán • Jalapa Enríquez • Campeche • Hopelchén • Chetumal • B. de Chetumal
MÉXICO • Veracruz • Ciudad del Carmen • Laguna de Términos • Ambergris Cay **D**
PUEBLA • Coatepec • Llave • Alvarado • Frontera • CAMPECHE • Orange Walk • Turneffe Is.
Orizaba • Córdoba • San Andrés Tuxtla • Coatzacoalcos • Paraíso • Palizada • Concepción • Hondo
Cuernavaca • Tehuacán • Cosamaloapan • Minatitlán • TABASCO • Villahermosa • Belize City • BELIZE
Iguala • Acatlán • Acayucan • Cárdenas • Belmopan • Dangriga
OAXACA • Istmo de Tehuantepec • Tenosique • Uaxactún • Tikal • San Ignacio • Benque Viejo • Maya Mts. • Golfo de Honduras • Islas de la Bahía
Chilapa • Chilpancingo • Tuxtla Gutiérrez • San Cristóbal de las Casas • CHIAPAS • L. Petén Itzá • Flores • Monkey River • Roatán • Puerto Castilla
Acapulco • Oaxaca • Ocotlán • Juchitán • Comitán • San Luis • San Antonio • Livingston • Puerto Barrios • Tela • La Ceiba
Miahuatlán • Salina Cruz • Golfo de Tehuantepec • Tonalá • GUATEMALA • Cobán • HONDURAS **E**
Tapachula • GUATEMALA • Huehuetenango • Zacapa • Chiquimula • Copán • San Pedro Sula • Tegucigalpa

5 **6** **7**

COPYRIGHT. GEORGE PHILIP & SON, LTD.

GULF OF

MEXICO

U.S.A.
Fort Myers
Naples
C. Romano
Everglades
C. Sable
Florida Bay
Dry Tortugas
Key West
West Palm Beach
Boca Raton
Fort Lauderdale
West End
Freeport
Northwest Providence Channel
Hope Town
MIAMI
Hialeah
Bimini Is.
Berry Is.
Little Abaco I.
Grand Bahama I.
Great Abaco I.
Normans Castle
Great Guana Cay
Great To
Exuma I.
Northeast Providence Channel
Dunmore To
Eleuthera
Nassau
New Providence
Andros Island
Andros Town
Nicolls Town
Governors Harbour
BAH
New
Exuma I.

Isla Desterrada
Isla Pérez

Progreso
Pta. Yalkubul
Dzilam de Bravo
Temax
Río Lagartos
C. Catoche
El Cuyo
Cancun
Pto. Juárez
Mérida
Motul
Izamal
Tizimín
Espita
Dzibilchaltún
Maxcanú
Sotuta
Mayapán
Chichén Itzá
Valladolid
Puerto Morelos
Campeche
Tenabo
Calkini
Uxmal
Tekax
Peto
Cozumel
Isla Cozumel
Champotón
Bolonchenticul
Hopelchen
Vigía Chico
Chenkan
Felipe Carrillo Puerto
B. de la Ascensión
Ciudad del Carmen
Laguna de Términos
Pital
Juárez
Pedro Antonio Santos
Bacalar
B. del Espíritu Santo
Palizada
Matamoros
Concepción
Chetumal
B. de Chetumal
Banco Chinchorro
Balancán
Orange Walk
Hondo
Tenosique
Uaxactún
Corozal
Ambergris Cay
Palenque
Ocosingo
Tikal
Belmopan
San Ignacio
Belize City
Turneffe Is.
La Independencia
L. Petén Itzá
La Libertad
Flores
Middlesex
Benque Viejo
Dangriga
BELIZE
Comitán
Sebol
Maya Mts.
San Luis
San Antonio
Monkey River
Golfo de Honduras
Islas de la Bahía

Havana (LA HABANA)
San Antonio de los Baños
MARIANAO
Guanabacoa
Santa Cruz del Norte
Straits of Florida
Matanzas
Canal Nicolás
Cay Sal Bank
Bahía Honda
La Esperanza
Cárdenas
Colón
Sagua la Grande
Santaren Channel
Pinar del Río
Güines
Batabanó
Jagüey Grande
Jovellanos
Santa Clara
Caibarién
Canal Viejo de Bahama
Guane
La Fé
Los Palacios
San Luis
Playa Larga
Cienfuegos
Placetas
Morón
Cayo Romano
Nueva Gerona
C. Corrientes
Isla de la Juventud
Trinidad
Sancti-Spíritus
Júcaro
Ciego de Ávila
Nuevitas
Archipiélago de los Canarreos
Arch. de los Jardines de la Reina
Tunas de Zaza
Florida
Camagüey
Puerto Manati
Puerto Pad
Golfo de Guacanayabo
Victoria de las Tunas
Gibar
Holgu
Bayamo
Palma
Soriano
Manzanillo
Sierra Maestra
SANTIAGO DE CUB
GREATER
CUBA
GREAT BAHAMA BANK
Jumentos Cays

Cayman Islands (Br.)
Georgetown
Cayman Brac
Little Cayman
Grand Cayman
7680
C. Cruz
2000

Swan Islands (U.S.A. & Honduras)

Montego Bay
Lucea
Falmouth
St. Ann's Bay
Annotto Bay
Port Maria
Port Antonie
Savanna la Mar
South Negril Pt.
JAMAICA
Cambric
Black River
Mandeville
May Pen
Spanish Town
KINGSTO
Pedro Cays (Jamaica)

CARIB

Puerto Barrios
Puerto Cortés
Tela
La Ceiba
Puerto Castilla
Iriona
Trujillo
C. Camarón
Pta. Patuca
Roatán
Balfate
Savá
Olanchito
C. Camáron
Brus Laguna
Laguna Caratasca
Puerto Lempira
C. Falso
Mosquitia
C. Gracias á Dios
Puerto Cabo Gracias á Dios
Bajo Nuevo (Colombia)

GUATEMALA
3993
Cuchumatanes
Huehuetenango
Cobán
Sa. de las Minas
L. de Izabal
Livingston
Quiché
Gualán
Motagua
Santa Bárbara
San Pedro Sula
El Progreso
Arenal
El Jaral
Olanchito
Catacamas
HONDURAS
San Marcos
Totonicapán
Utatlán
Zacapa
Copán
Santa Rosa de Copán
L. de Yojoa
Suaco
Juticalpa
Patuca
Coco
(Segovia)
Kisalaya
Ayutla
Sololá
Antigua
Jalapa
Chiquimula
La Esperanza
Comayagua
La Paz
Yuscarán
Danlí
Bonanza
Siuna
Cayos Miskitos (Nicaragua)
GUATEMALA
Amatitlán
Escuintla
Santa Ana
Suchitoto
Tegucigalpa
Nacaome
Choluteca
Pta. Gorda
Mazatenango
Retalhuleu
Cuyotenango
Chimaltenango
Cojutepeque
Zacatecoluca
El Jícaro
Jinotega
Somoto
Cotal
Coco
Sébaco
Estelí
Cord. Isabella
Tuma
Tungla
San Pedro del Norte
Prinzapolca
Ahuachapán
Acajutla
Sonsonate
SAN SALVADOR
San Salvador (Santa Tecla)
Nueva San Salvador
Usulután
San Miguel
La Unión
Golfo de Fonseca
Puerto Morazán
Chinandega
El Sauce
Matagalpa
Muy Muy
Río Grande
Coatepeque
EL SALVADOR
Chalteca
Corinto
León
Telica
La Paz Centro
Boaco
Siquia
Santo Domingo
Rama
Bluefields
El Bluff
NICARAGUA
MANAGUA
Masaya
Granada
Juigalpa
Cord. de Yolaina
Pta. de Perlas
Siuna
Puerto Cabezas
Diriamba
Jinotepe
Lago de Managua
L. de Managua
Rivas
Isla de Ometepe
San Carlos
Bahía de San Juan del Norte
San Juan del Sur
Nicaragua
Lago de Nicaragua
San Juan
San Juan del Norte
B. de Salinas
C. Sta. Elena
Cord. de Guanacaste
Sta. Cruz
Golfo de Papagayo
C. Velas
Liberia
Cord. Central
Guápiles
Siquirres
Limón
Santa Cruz
Nicoya
Alajuela
San José
Cartago
Pta. Mona
CARTAG
Puntarenas
Esparta
COSTA
Pen. de Nicoya
C. Blanco
RICA
3837
Chirripó Grande
Cord. de Talamanca
Almirante
Bocas del Toro
Laguna de Chiriquí
Colón
Nombre de Dios
Portobelo
Archipiélago de las Mulatas
Is. de San Bernar
Golfo de Nicoya
Bahía de Coronado
Puerto Quepos
Buenos Aires
Volcán Barú
3374
Golfo de los Mosquitos
Serranía de Tabasará
PANAMÁ
La Chorrera
Chepo
Golfo del Darién
Lori
Pen. de Osa
Golfito
Boquete
David
Remedios
Río Hato
Penonomé
Arch. de las Perlas
San Miguel
I. del Rey
Serranía de Darién
Cere
Monter
Golfo Dulce
Puerto Armuelles
Pta. Burica
Aguad
Santiago
Sona
Chitré
Golfo de Panamá
Turbo C
Mor
Pocrí
Chiman
La Palma
El Rea
I. de Coiba
I. de Cebaco
I. Jicarón
Pen. de Azuero
Las Tablas
Garachine
Jaque
Tonosí
Pta. Mala
Pta. Mariato
Golfo de Chiriquí

GREATER

CARIB

PANAMA

1 : 6 400 000

50 0 50 100 150 200 miles
50 0 100 200 300 km

5   6   7   8

ft m

12,000 4000

9000   3000

6000   2000

4500   1500

3000   1000

1500   600

0

200   600

C

2000   6000

4000   12,000

6000   18,000

8000   24,000

m ft

A T L A N T I C

O C E A N

Tropic of Cancer

Puerto Rico Trench

Milwaukee
Deep
9200

SAN JUAN

HAITI   DOMINICAN
        REP.

PORT-
AU-PRINCE San Juan
Massif de la Hotte
Les Cayes

HISPANIOLA

A N T I L L E S

SANTO DOMINGO

PUERTO
RICO
(U.S.A.)

Virgin Is.
(Br.)

Virgin Is.
(U.S.A.)

Anguilla (Br.)
St.-Martin (Guad.)
St.-Barthélemy (Fr.)

St. Maarten
(Neth.) Saba (Neth.) ST.
St. Eustatius CHRISTOPHER- ANTIGUA
(Neth.) NEVIS & BARBUDA
Basseterre St. Johns
Nevis Antigua

Redonda
Montserrat

Guadeloupe Passage

Ste-Rose Moule
GUADELOUPE Pointe-à-Pitre
Basse-Terre Marie-Galante (Fr.)
I. des Saintes Grand-Bourge
(Guad.)

Dominica Passage

Portsmouth DOMINICA
Roseau

LEEWARD ISLANDS

LESSER ANTILLES

Martinique Passage

Mt. Pelée Ste-Marie
1397 François
Fort-de-France Rivière-Pilote
St. Lucia Channel MARTINIQUE
(Fr.)
Castries ST. LUCIA
Soufrière

St. Vincent Passage
Soufrière 1234 ST. VINCENT
Kingstown Speightstown
Bridgetown
THE BARBADOS
GRENADINES

Hillsborough

St. George's GRENADA

WINDWARD ISLANDS

C A R I B B E A N   S E A

I. de Aves (Bird I.)
(Venezuela)

Aruba
(Neth.) Curaçao
Bonaire
LESSER ANTILLES

NETH.
ANTILLES

Willemstad
Punto Fijo

Is. de Aves
(Ven.)

I. Orchila
(Ven.)

Is. Los Roques
(Ven.)

I. Los Hermanos
(Ven.)

Is. Los Testigos
(Ven.)

Tobago
Scarborough
Port of
Spain

I. Blanquilla (Ven.)

I. Margarita La Asunción
NUEVA Porlamar
ESPARTA
I. La Tortuga
(Ven.)

Pen. de Paria

Galera
Pt.
TRINIDAD
Arima
Rio Claro
TRINIDAD &
TOBAGO
San Fernando
Serpent's Mouth

V E N E Z U E L A

DOMINICA

West from Greenwich

5   6   7

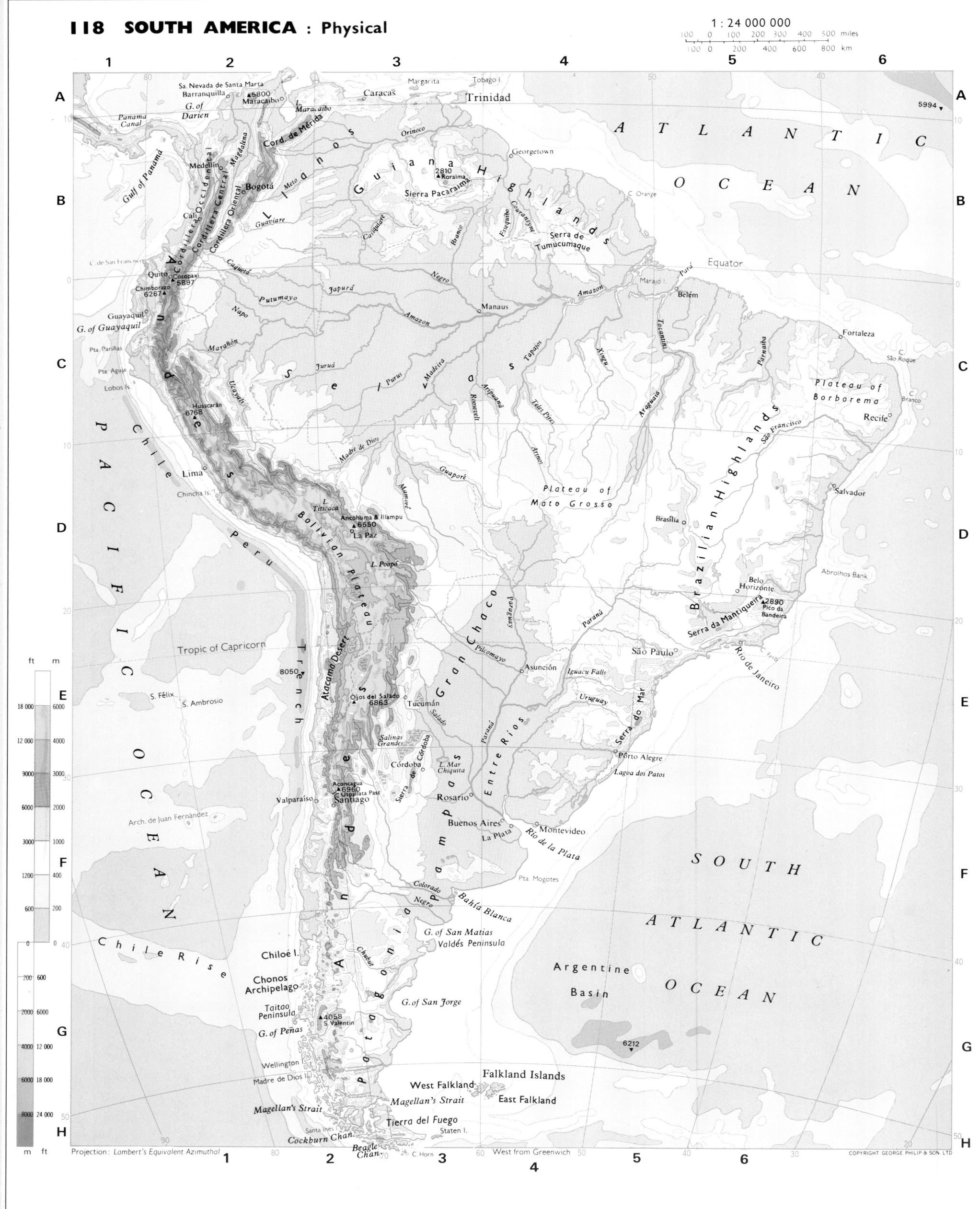

1 : 24 000 000

100 0 100 200 300 400 500 miles

100 0 200 400 600 800 km

COPYRIGHT GEORGE PHILIP & SON LTD

1 : 24 000 000

100   0   100   200   300   400   500 miles
100   0   200   400   600   800 km

1   2   3   4   5   6

A

COSTA RICA
San José
Barranquilla
Cartagena
Maracaibo
Maracaibo
Barquisimeto
Valencia
Caracas
Port of Spain
TRINIDAD AND TOBAGO
Colón
PANAMA
Panamá
Golfo de Darién
Golfo de Panamá
San Cristóbal
Cúcuta
Bucaramanga
Medellín
Bogotá
Cali
Orinoco
VENEZUELA
Ciudad Guayana
Georgetown
Paramaribo
Cayenne
GUYANA
SURINAM
FRENCH GUIANA
C. Orange

B

NORTH
ATLANTIC
OCEAN

C. de San Francisco
COLOMBIA
Meta
Orinoco
Branco
Essequibo
Corentijn
Maroni

C

Quito
ECUADOR
Guayaquil
G. de Guayaquil
Pta. Aguja
Caquetá
Putumayo
Napo
Iquitos
Japurá
Negro
Manaus
Amazonas
(Amazon)
Santarém
Ilha de Marajó
Belém
São Luís
Equator
Fortaleza (Ceara)
Teresina
C. de São Roque
Natal
João Pessoa

D

Chiclayo
Trujillo
Chimbote
Marañón
Ucayali
Juruá
Purus
Madeira
Madre de Dios
Pôrto Velho
Tapajós
Xingu
Araguaia
Tocantins
Parnaíba
São Francisco
Recife (Pernambuco)
Maceió
Aracaju

PERU
Callao
Lima
Cuzco
Titicaca
BOLIVIA
La Paz
Cochabamba
Sucre
Santa Cruz
Arequipa
B R A Z I L
Cuiabá
Brasília
Goiânia
Salvador

E

Iquique
Antofagasta
Tropic of Capricorn
Isla San Felix (Chile)
Isla San Ambrosio (Chile)
Campo Grande
PARAGUAY
Paraguay
Pilcomayo
Asunción
Salta
San Miguel de Tucumán
Resistencia
Corrientes
Paraná
Uruguay
Londrina
Ribeirão Prêto
Juiz de Fora
Campinas
São Paulo
Santos
Niterói
Vitória
Campos
RIO DE JANEIRO
Belo Horizonte
Curitiba

F

PACIFIC OCEAN
CHILE
Viña del Mar
Valparaíso
Arch de Juan Fernández (Chile)
Santiago
Talca
Concepción
Valdivia
Mendoza
San Juan
Córdoba
ARGENTINA
Santa Fe
Rosario
Paraná
Salado
BUENOS AIRES
La Plata
Río de la Plata
URUGUAY
Montevideo
Mar del Plata
Pôrto Alegre
Pelotas
Lagoa dos Patos
SOUTH
ATLANTIC
OCEAN

G

Bahía Blanca
Colorado
Negro
Viedma
Puerto Montt
Chubut
Golfo Comodoro Rivadavia
San Jorge
G. de Penas

H

FALKLAND ISLANDS
West Falkland
Stanley
(U.K.)
East Falkland
Punta Arenas
Strait of Magellan
Cape Horn
Tierra del Fuego

Projection : Lambert's Equivalent Azimuthal   West from Greenwich   COPYRIGHT. GEORGE PHILIP & SON. LTD.

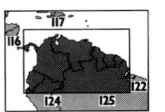

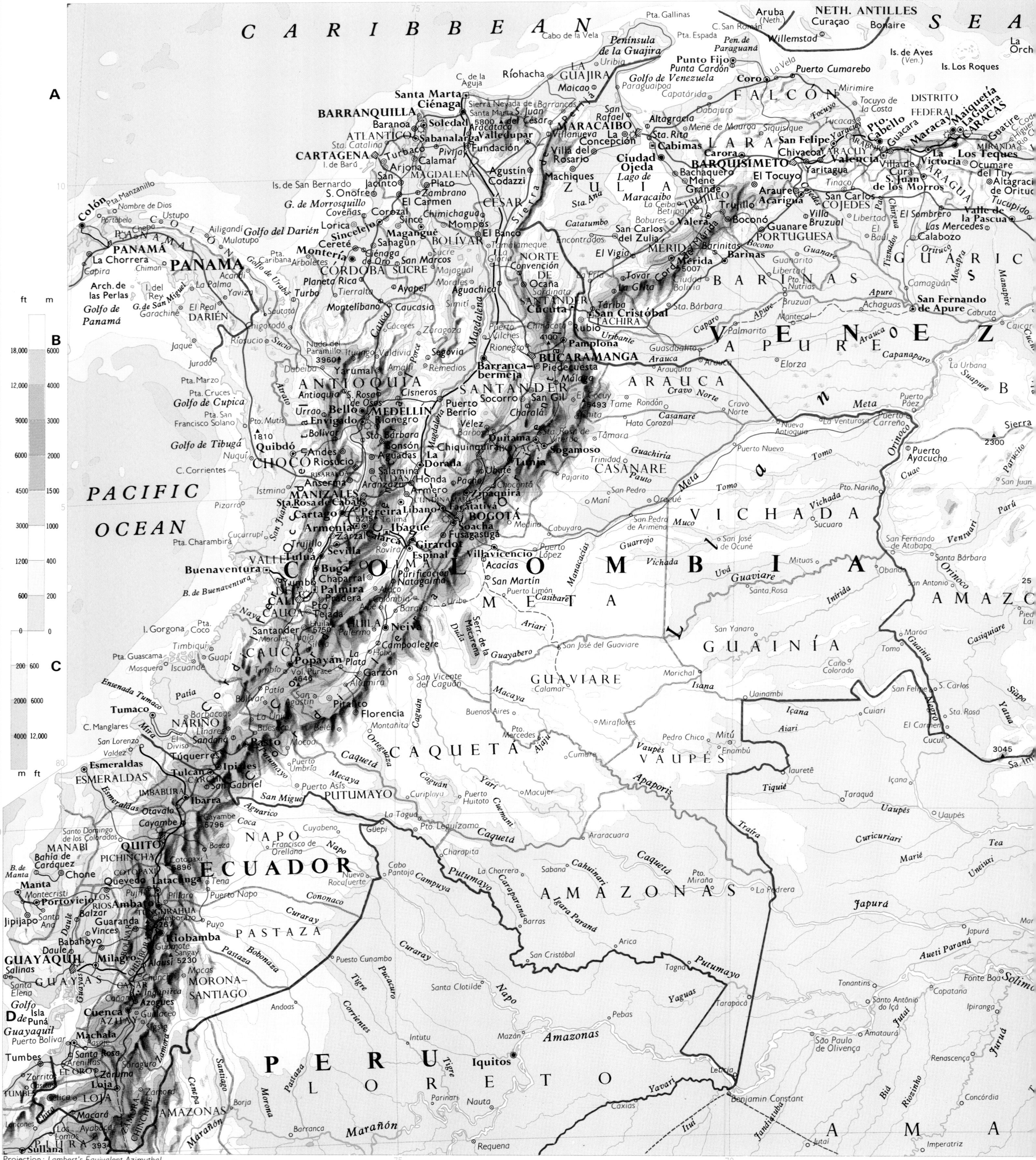

CARIBBEAN SEA

NETH. ANTILLES
Aruba (Neth.)
Curaçao
Bonaire
Willemstad
Is. de Aves (Ven.)
Is. Los Roques
La Orch

PACIFIC OCEAN

PANAMA

COLOMBIA

VENEZUELA

ECUADOR

PERU

Major cities and places:
BARRANQUILLA, CARTAGENA, Santa Marta, MARACAIBO, BARQUISIMETO, CARACAS, Valencia, MEDELLÍN, BUCARAMANGA, BOGOTÁ, CALI, MANIZALES, Pereira, Armenia, Ibagué, Neiva, Popayán, Pasto, Tumaco, QUITO, GUAYAQUIL, Cuenca, Loja, Machala, Esmeraldas, Manta, Portoviejo, Ambato, Riobamba, Iquitos, Leticia

Departments / states (Colombia, Venezuela, Ecuador):
ANTIOQUIA, SANTANDER, NORTE DE SANTANDER, CHOCÓ, CALDAS, TOLIMA, CAUCA, NARIÑO, HUILA, CAQUETÁ, PUTUMAYO, META, VICHADA, GUAINÍA, GUAVIARE, VAUPÉS, AMAZONAS, CASANARE, ARAUCA, BOLÍVAR, CÓRDOBA, SUCRE, MAGDALENA, CESAR, ATLÁNTICO, ZULIA, MÉRIDA, BARINAS, APURE, FALCÓN, LARA, PORTUGUESA, GUÁRICO, TÁCHIRA, DISTRITO FEDERAL, ARAGUA, MIRANDA, COJEDES
MANABÍ, PICHINCHA, GUAYAS, AZUAY, EL ORO, LOS RÍOS, PASTAZA, NAPO, MORONA-SANTIAGO, ZAMORA, LOJA, IMBABURA

PERU — LORETO

Projection: Lambert's Equivalent Azimuthal

1 : 6 400 000

50   50   100   150   200 miles
50   100   200   300 km

5   **6**   **7**

65   60   55

A T L A N T I C

O C E A N

La Blanquilla (Ven.)
Los Hermanos (Ven.)
St. George's **GRENADA**

NUEVA ESPARTA
Margarita
La Asunción
Is. Los Testigos (Ven.)
Tobago
Pta. Arenas
Porlamar
I. Coche
Scarborough
La Tortuga (Ven.)
Pen. de Araya
Cumaná
Carúpano
Río Caribe
Pen. de Paria
Güiria
Pta. Peñas
Port of Spain
Arima
Cariaco
El Pilar Irapa
TRINIDAD AND TOBAGO
Puerto La Cruz
Guanta
SUCRE
S. Juan
Golfo de San
San Fernando
Río Claro
Barcelona
2596
Caicara
Trinidad
Galeota Point
Aragua de Barcelona
Caripito
Awana
Serpent's Mouth
Boca de la Sierpe
Anaco
Maturín
Cantaura
MONAGAS
Guanipa
Tigre
ANZOÁTEGUI
El Tigre
Tembladar
Caño Manamo
DELTA
Santa María de Ipire
Zaraza
Pariaguán
Barrancas
Tucupita
I. Corocoro
Pao
Soledad
Pto. Ordaz
Orinoco
Grande
Boca Grande
Santa Cruz
Ciudad Guayana
AMACURO
Mapire
Morawhanna
Ciudad Bolívar
Upata
Curiapo
Mabaruma
Caparo
Guri Dam
Ciudad Piar
El Miamo
La Horqueta
Maripa
El Palmar
Barima
JELA
Serranía Turagua
BOLÍVAR
La Paragua
El Callao
Tumeremo
Matthew's Ridge
Wenamu
Charity
Anna Regina
Kokerite
Aro
Supamo
El Dorado
Cuyuni
Suddie
Georgetown
Caura
GUYANA
Parika
Buxton
Curatabaca
Peter's Mine
Bartica
Mahaicony
New Amsterdam
Angel Falls
2560
Poa
Mazaruni
Hyde Park
Rosignol
Port Mourant
Imbaimadai
Issano
Wismar
Linden (Mackenzie)
Mara
Skeldon
Luepa
Equelpa
La Gran Sabana
Mt. Roraima 2772
Kaieteur Falls
Ituni
Kwakwani
Orealla
Nieuw Nickerie
Totness
Paramaribo
Alliance
Mana
Araboro
Sta. Teresa
Mahdia
Tumatumari
Bartica
Tapoeripa
Epira
Wageningen
Groningen
Nieuw Amsterdam
Moengo
Albina
Iracoubo
Arabelo
Sierra del Zamuro
Apoteuao
Orinduik
Kurupukari
Essequibo
Nickerie
Republiek
PARA
Brokopondo
St. Laurent
Gare Tigre
Guaina
Catisimiña
Pakaraima
Irang
Wandaki
Corentyne
Corantijn
Kwakoegron
Brownsweg
Langatabbetje
Paul Isnard
Cayenne
Rémire
Motocurunya
Sa. Tepequem
Toka
Apoteri
SURINAM
Prof. Dr. Ir. W. J. Van Blommestein Meer
Grand Santi
St. Elie
Cacao
Kaw
Majari
Yupukarri
Saramacca
Posoegroene
BROKOPONDO
Benzdorp
Roura
Uraricaá
Wilhelmina Geb.
Julianatop 1280
Gran Rio
Asidonhoppo
Maripasoula
Saül
Régina
Matacuni
Urasicuera
Lethem
Rewa
Lucie
Coppename
Tapanahoni
MAROWIJNE
Eau Claire
Cabo Orange
Serra Maigualida
Boa Esperança
Wichabai
Tacutu
New River
Americankondre
Alowike
FRENCH GUIANA
Bienvenue
Vila Velha
Orinoco
Parima
Mucajaí
Boa Vista
Dadanawa
Shea
Alalaparu
Litani
Camopi
Oyapock
Clevelândia do Norte
Serra Parima
Catrimani
Serra do Apiaú
Apiaú
Isherton
Serra Acaraí
690
Serra Tumucumaque
Lourenço
Calçoene
Tepiquecá
Serra Cukupira
Serra do Mucajaí
Caracaraí
RORAIMA
Kamoa Mts.
Biloku
Essequibo
Maracá
Maripi
Paru de Oeste
Jari
Oyapoque
Araguari
AMAPÁ
I. de Maracá
734
Paru Rio
Merirumá
Sucuriju
Demini
San José de Anauá
Anauá
Maloca
Serra do Navio
Teresinha
Aporema
Tapurucuará
Serra Tabatinga
Branco
Catrimani
Trombetas
Cuminá
Amapari
Pôrto Grande
Araguari
Padauari
Janaperi
Araçá
Boiaçu
Uatumã
Mapuera
Curuapanema
Amaparí
Macapá
Preto
Tapuruquará
Negro
Jaú
Alalaú
Nhamundá
Jatapu
São Tiago
Caviana
L. Amaná
Cuiuni
Barcelos
Caurés
Carvoeiro
Moura
Unini
BRAZIL
Santa Maria
Jatapu
Faro
Óbidos
Alenquer
Prainha
Pôrto de Moz
Agua Preta
Pauini
Airão
Apuaú
Urubu
Uruçará
Nhamundá
Monte Alegre
Amazonas
Canal do Norte
I. Grande de Gurupá
Pôrto Santana
Breves
Piorini
Mucura
Arquipélago das Anavilhanas
Urucurituba
Juruti
Belterra
Santarém
Araticu
Portel
L. Amaná
L. Piorini
Caapiranga
Manacapuru
Eva
Itapiranga
Silves
Barreirinha
Brasília Legal
Almeirim
Gurupá
Ilha de Marajó
Tefé (Amazonas)
Codajás
Anamã
MANAUS
Careiro
Maués
Parintins
Aveiro
Anajás
Alvarães
Manacapuru
Itacoatiara
Ilha Tupinambaranas
Maués
Tajapuru
Rio de Tajapuru
L. Coari
Beruri
Autazes
Nova Olinda
PARÁ
Sousel
João
Coari
Nova Olinda do Norte
Itaituba
Santarém
Altamira
Itanhauá
Purus
Itaboca
Borba
Abacaxis
Mundurucus
Iriri
Pôrto Alegre
Aruma
Paricatuba
Canumã
Xingu
Carvalho
Anapu
Abufari
Preto do Igapó-Açu
Madeira
Novo Aripuana
Uruará
Bacajá
Tapajós

West from Greenwich

5   **6**   **7**

COPYRIGHT. GEORGE PHILIP & SON. LTD.

ATLANTIC OCEAN

States and Regions
PARÁ · MARANHÃO · CEARÁ · RIO GRANDE DO NORTE · PARAÍBA (Paraíba) · PERNAMBUCO · PIAUÍ · TOCANTINS · AMAPÁ · BAHIA

Major Cities
FORTALEZA (Ceará) · NATAL · JOÃO PESSOA (Paraíba) · RECIFE (Pernambuco) · MACEIÓ · BELÉM (Pará) · SÃO LUÍS (Maranhão) · Teresina · Macapá · Caruaru · Campina Grande · Olinda · Jaboatão

Place Names
I. de Maracá · Calçoene · Cabo do Norte · Sucuriju · Amapá · Pôrto Santana · M. Balique · I. Curuá · Cabo do Norte · I. Janaucu · I. Caviana · I. Mexiana · Ilha de Marajó · Chaves · Afuá · Anajás · Breves · Portel · Gurupá · Pôrto de Móz · Altamira · Xingu · Tueré · Fresco · Serra dos Carajás · Marabá · Tocantins · Araguaia · Conceição do Araguaia · Santa Isabel do Araguaia · Xambioá · Araguaína · Filadélfia · Tocantinópolis · Pôrto Franco · Carolina · Estreito · Imperatriz · Serra do Tiracambu · Gurupi · Guamá · Bragança · Capanema · Castanhal · Abaetetuba · Igarapé-Açu · Vigia · Ourém · Salinópolis · Viseu · Pinheiro · São Bento · Cururupu · Guimarães · Alcântara · Rosário · Icatu · Tutóia · Parnaíba · Luís Correia · Camocim · Granja · Sobral · Massapê · Piripiri · Campo Maior · Altos · Timon · Caxias · Codó · Coroatá · Vitorino Freire · Bacabal · Pedreiras · Pindaré-Mirim · Vargem Grande · Barra do Corda · Grajaú · Balsas · Floriano · Oeiras · Picos · Crato · Juazeiro do Norte · Iguatu · Icó · Quixadá · Quixeramobim · Senador Pompeu · Crateús · Tauá · Independência · Mombaça · Baturité · Aracati · Cascavel · Pacajus · Paracuru · Pentecoste · Canindé · Russas · Mossoró · Açu · Macau · Areia Branca · São Bento do Norte · Touros · Santa Cruz · Nova Cruz · Caicó · Currais Novos · Patos · Pombal · Sousa · Cajazeiras · Catolé do Rocha · Serra Talhada · Salgueiro · Petrolina · Juazeiro · Senhor do Bonfim · Xique-Xique · Campo Formoso · Jacobina · Penedo · Propriá · Aracaju · Estância · Vitória de S. Antão · Escada · Palmares · Garanhuns · Arcoverde · Paulo Afonso · Delmiro Gouveia · Barreiros · Goiana · Mamanguape · Guarabira · Esperança · Itabaiana · Sapé · Cabedelo · Ceará-Mirim · São José de Mipibu · Guaratetama · Bom Conselho · Palmeira dos Índios

Serra da Ibiapaba · Serra do Araripe · Chapada do Araripe · Chapada das Mangabeiras · Serra das Marrecas · Serra do Estrondo · Serra dos Gradaús · São Francisco · Parnaíba · Rio Tocantins · Rio Piauí · Baía de São Marcos · Baía de Marajó

1 : 6 400 000

ATLANTIC OCEAN

ESPÍRITO SANTO

BAHIA

MINAS GERAIS

GOIÁS

SÃO PAULO

PARANÁ

RIO DE JANEIRO

SALVADOR (Bahia)

BELO HORIZONTE

SÃO PAULO

RIO DE JANEIRO

CURITIBA

BRASÍLIA

GOIÂNIA

DISTRITO FEDERAL

Tropic of Capricorn

West from Greenwich

Projection: Lambert's Equivalent Azimuthal

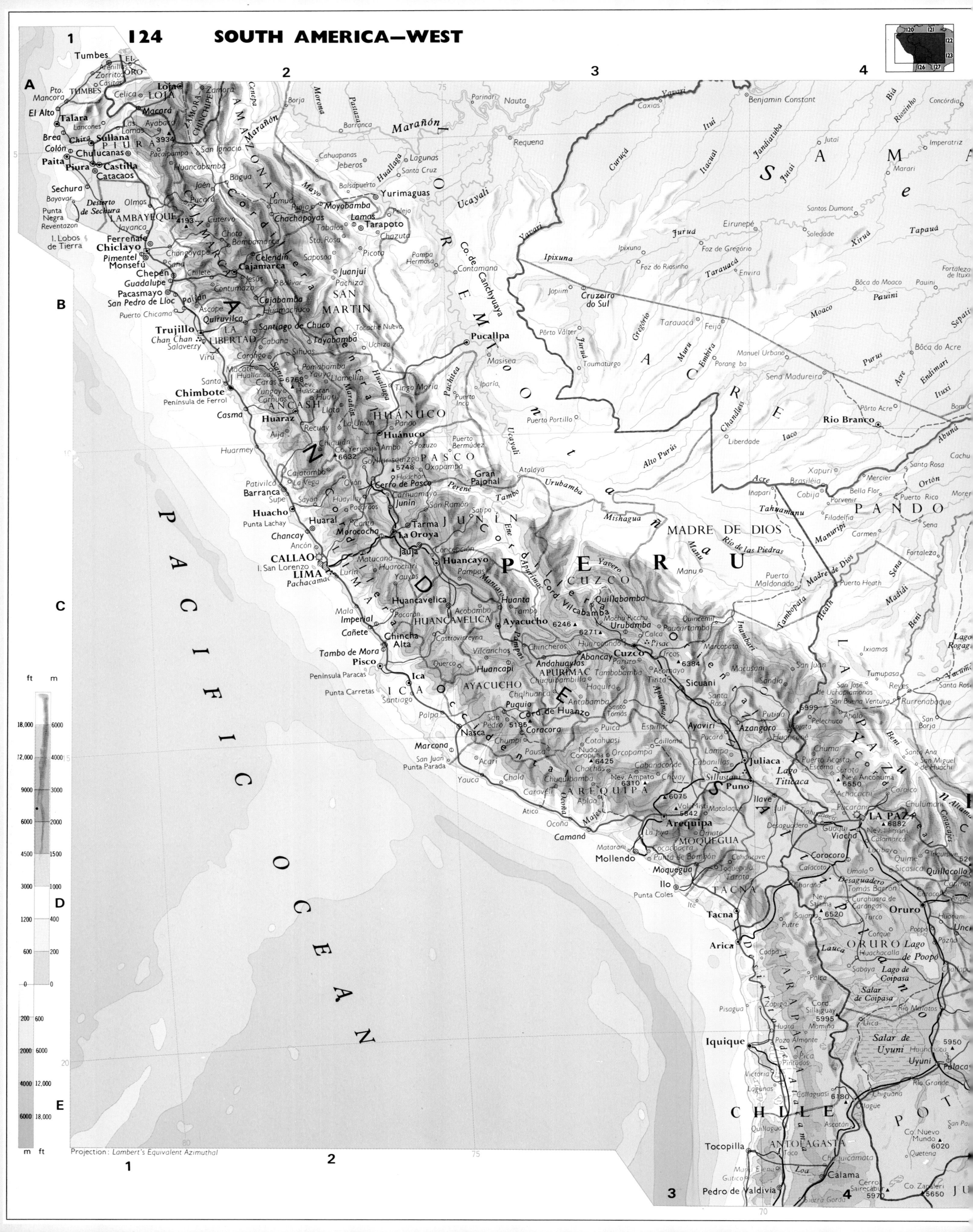

PACIFIC OCEAN

PERU

CHILE

Projection: Lambert's Equivalent Azimuthal

1 : 6 400 000

50   0   50   100   150   200 miles
50   0   100   200   300 km

5　　　　　**6**　　　　　**7**

A

B

C

D

E

Z O N A   B R A S I L
A M A Z O N A S
P A R Á

Coari   Itanhauã   Coari   L. de Coari   Paricatuba   Axinim   Itaituba   Pôrto Alegre   Bacajá
Tefé   Purus   Itaboca   Itapinima   Borba   Maués   Canumã   Entre Rios   Irriri
Tapauá   Abufari   Prêto do Igapó-Açu   Madeira   Novo Aripuanã   Abacaxis   Munducurus   Tucunaré   Nazaré   São Félix
Canutama   Itatuba   Tapauá   Santa Maria dos Marmelos   Manicoré   Miriti   Sai-Cinza   Tapajós   Xingu   Riosinho
Pinhuã   Axioma   Três Casas   Capoeira   Jamaxim   Iriri
Lábrea   Jaburu   Purus   Canumã   Prainha   Canudos   Curuá   Curuá   Alto Iriri
Majuriã   Macuim   Marmelos   Samaúma   Cururu   Teles Pires   S. Benedito   Cachimbo   Iriri Novo

M A T O   G R O S S O

Pôrto Velho   Madeira   Jamari   Calama   Barracão do Barreto   Serra do Cachimbo   Campo de Diauarum
404   Jaciparaná   Caritianas   Tabajara   Aripuanã   Serra dos Apiacás   Peixoto de Azevedo   Manitsauá-Missu   Suid Missu
Abunã   Jamari   Ariquemes   Fiparaná   Recreio   Pôrto Cajueiro   Liberdade
Guajará-Mirim   Nova Vida   Jaru   Jaru   Rondônia   Presidente Hermes   Pouso Alegre   Arraias   Roncro   Culiseu   Pôrto dos Meinacos
Sa. dos Pacaás Novos   Serra   Arinos   Xingu
R O N D Ô N I A   Pimenta Bueno   Barão de Melgaço   Serra dos Caiabis

Príncipe da Beira   663   Vilhena   Nhambiquara   Serra do Tombador   P l a n a l t o   Chavantina
Pedras Negras   Juruena   Utiariti   Arinos   Nortelândia   Diamantino   Cuiabá   do   Mortes   Aruanã
Versalles   Magdalena   Guaporé   Camararé   669   Arenápolis   Alto Paraguai   Serra Azul   Culiené
Baures   Puerto Villazón   Mato Grosso   Guaporé   Tapirapuã   Rosário Oeste   Mato   915   Grosso   Aruanã
Lago de San Luis   El Carmen   Barra do Bugres   Acorizal   Chapada dos Guimarães

B O L I V I A   Trinidad   1995   Pôrto Esperidião   Cáceres   Cuiabá   Coronel Ponce   Barro do Garças
San Javier   Perseverancia   Negro   Santa Rosa de la Roca   Aguapeí   Nossa Senhora do Livramento   Santo Antônio do Leverger   Poxoreu   Araguaiana
S A N T A   C R U Z   Concepción   San Ignacio   Santa Ana   San Matías   Poconé   Barão de Melgaço   Jaciara   Rio das Garças   Baliza   Aragarças

Villegrande   Santa Rosa del Palmar   Laguna Concepción   Santa Corazón   Lagoa Uberaba   Pôrto Jofre   Rondonópolis   Ponte Branca   Caiapó   Sa. das Divisões
Santa Cruz   Montero   Buena Vista   El Cerro   San José   La Cal   Pantanal do São Lourenço   Itiquira   Alto Garças   Santa Rita do Araguaia   Mineiros   Rio Verde
Portachuelo   Warnes   Llanos de Chiquitos   1425   Serrania de Santiago   Santa Ana   Lagoa Mandioré   Itiquira   Taquari   Baús   Jataí
El Palmar   Robore   Puerto Suárez   M A T O   G R O S S O   Araguaia

Sucre   Villa Grande   Bañados de Izozog   Corumbá   Pantanal do Rio Negro   Rio Verde de Mato Grosso   Caçu
Padilla   Grande   Ladário   Nhecolândia   D O   S U L   Cachoeira Alta
Gutiérrez   Parapeti   Albuquerque   Pôrto Esperança   Negro   Alto Sucuri   Cassilândia   Aporé
Camiri   Charagua   Fortin General Pando   Coimbra   Corguinho   Rochedo   Verde   Paranaíba

C H A C O   B O R E A L   Bahia Negra   Miranda   Aquidauana   Terenos   Ribas do Rio Pardo   Aparecida do Taboado
Fortin Ingavi   Paraguai   Corumbá   Jango   Agua Clara
N U E V A   Fortin Coronel Eugenio Garay   Fuerte Olimpo   Aquidauana   Campo Grande   Pereira Barreto
Camargo   P A R A G U A Y   Bonito   Sidrolândia   Três Lagoas   Andradina
Villa Montes   Puerto Guirini   Sa. da Bodoquena   Nioaque   Maracaju   Mirandópolis
Tarija   A S U N C I Ó N   P A R A G U A Y   Pôrto Martinho   Jardim   Guia Lopes da Laguna   Xavantina   Panorama
BOQUERÓN   La Esmeralda
Tartagal

West from Greenwich

6　　　　　**55**　　　　　**7**

COPYRIGHT GEORGE PHILIP & SON LTD.

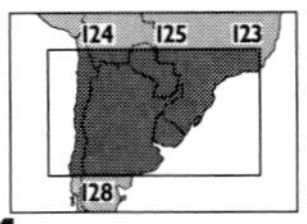

1 2 3 4

BOLIVIA
PARAGUAY
NUEVA ASUNCIÓN
ALTO PARAGUAY
BOQUERÓN
PRESIDENTE HAYES
FORMOSA
CHACO
POTOSÍ
JUJUY
SALTA
TUCUMÁN
CATAMARCA
SANTIAGO DEL ESTERO
LA RIOJA
SANTA FE
CORRIENTES
SAN JUAN
CÓRDOBA
ENTRE RÍOS
MENDOZA
SAN LUIS
BUENOS AIRES
LA PAMPA
NEUQUÉN
ARGENTINA
ANTOFAGASTA
ATACAMA
COQUIMBO
CHILE
URUGUAY
TARAPACÁ

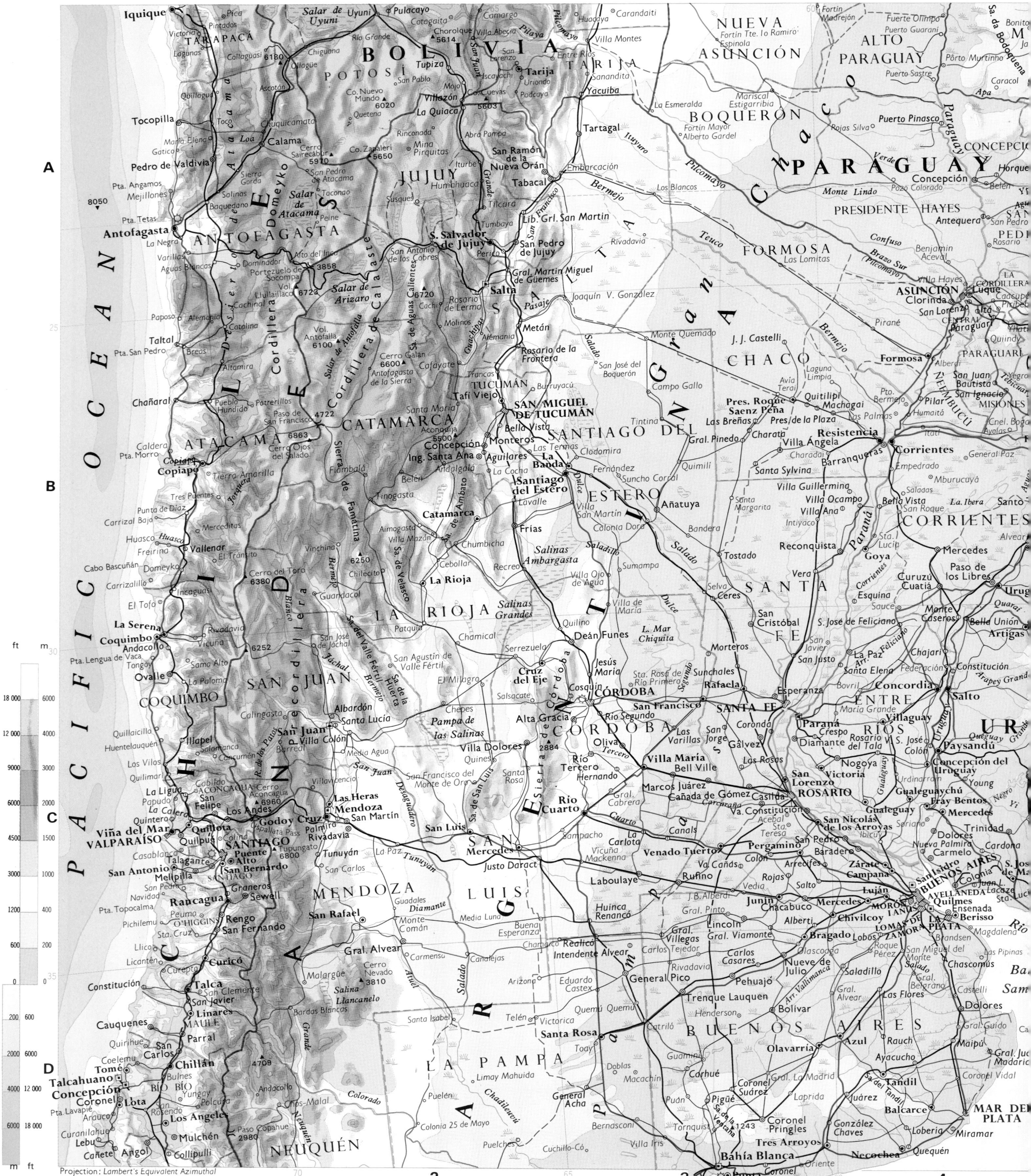

PACIFIC OCEAN

A
B
C
D

Iquique
Tocopilla
Pedro de Valdivia
Antofagasta
Taltal
Chañaral
Copiapó
Caldera
Vallenar
La Serena
Coquimbo
Ovalle
Illapel
San Antonio
VALPARAÍSO
Viña del Mar
SANTIAGO
Rancagua
San Fernando
Curicó
Talca
Constitución
Linares
Chillán
Concepción
Talcahuano
Coronel
Lota
Los Angeles
Angol

Calama
Chuquicamata
San Pedro de Atacama
La Quiaca
S. Salvador de Jujuy
Salta
San Ramón de la Nueva Orán
Tartagal
Embarcación
Metán
Rosario de la Frontera
SAN MIGUEL DE TUCUMÁN
Tafi Viejo
Concepción
Catamarca
Santiago del Estero
La Banda
Añatuya
Frías
La Rioja
Chilecito
Chamical
Deán Funes
Cruz del Eje
CÓRDOBA
San Francisco
Villa María
Río Cuarto
San Luis
Mercedes
Villa Dolores
Alta Gracia
SANTA FE
Rafaela
Esperanza
Paraná
Rosario
San Lorenzo
San Nicolás de los Arroyos
Pergamino
Junín
Chacabuco
Lincoln
General Pico
Santa Rosa
Bahía Blanca
Tres Arroyos
Necochea
MAR DEL PLATA
Tandil
Azul
Olavarría
Balcarce
Coronel Suárez
Pigüé

ASUNCIÓN
Clorinda
Formosa
Resistencia
Corrientes
Goya
Mercedes
Reconquista
Concordia
Salto
Paysandú
Concepción del Uruguay
Gualeguaychú
Gualeguay
Fray Bentos
BUENOS AIRES
AVELLANEDA
LA PLATA
Zárate
Campana
Luján
Lomas de Zamora
Quilmes

Projection: Lambert's Equivalent Azimuthal

1 : 6 400 000

50   0   50   100   150   200 miles
50   0   100   200   300 km

5   6   7

BELO
HORIZONTE
Lima
Itabirito

Três Lagoas   Andradina   Mirassol   S. Olímpia
do Rio Prêto   Bebedouro   Passos   Oliveira
Xavantina   Mirandópolis   Araçatuba   Catanduva   São Seb.   Cons.   Ouro   Ponte Nova
Panorama   Taquaritinga   Ribeirão   do Paraíso   Campo Belo   Lafaiete   Prêto
Santo Anastácio   Adamantina   Birigui   Renápolis   Novo   Prêto   Guaxupé   São João   Uba   Carangola   Muriaé
SÃO   Tietê   Lins   Jaboticabal   Mococa   Alfenas   Três   del Rei   Barbacena
Presidente   Martinópolis   PAULO   Pirajui   Araraquara   São João   Pontas   Lavras   Cataguases
Prudente   Rancharia   Marília   Garça   Bariri   da Boa Vista   Varginha   Três   Santos   Alegre
Nova   Assis   Bauru   Jaú   São   Araras   Pinhal   Pouso   Corações   Juiz de Fora   Leopoldina
Paranavaí   Esperança   Rolândia   Paraguaçu   Jacarèzinho   Carlos   Rio Claro   Limeira   Mogi-Mirim   Alegre   São   Paraíba do Sul
Umuarama   Cianorte   Londrina   Apucarana   Avaré   Piracicaba   CAMPINAS   Americana   Guaratinguetá   Mansa   Nova   Macaé

ATLANTIC

OCEAN

West from Greenwich

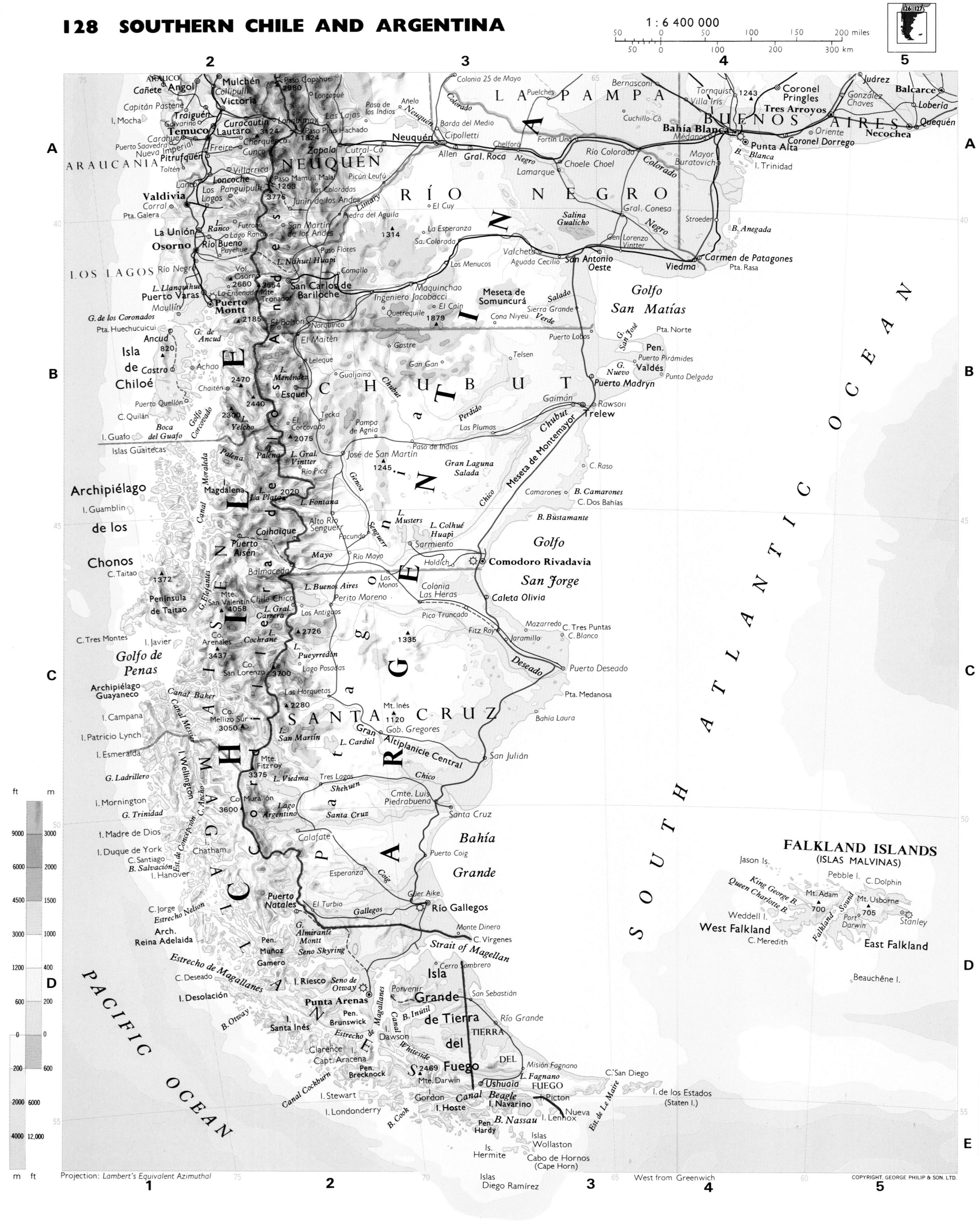

1 : 6 400 000

50   0   50   100   150   200 miles

50   0   100   200   300 km

FALKLAND ISLANDS
(ISLAS MALVINAS)

Jason Is.   Pebble I.   C. Dolphin
King George B.
Queen Charlotte B.   Mt. Adam
700   Mt. Usborne
Weddell I.   705   Port Stanley
                              Darwin
West Falkland   East Falkland

C. Meredith

Beauchêne I.

SOUTH ATLANTIC OCEAN

PACIFIC OCEAN

Projection: Lambert's Equivalent Azimuthal

West from Greenwich

COPYRIGHT. GEORGE PHILIP & SON, LTD.

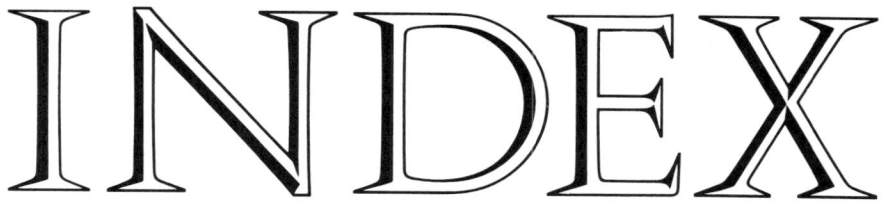

INDEX

The index contains the names of all the principal places and features shown on the World Maps. Each name is followed by an additional entry in italics giving the country or region within which it is located. The alphabetical order of names composed of two or more words is governed primarily by the first word and then by the second. This is an example of the rule:

Mīr Kūh, *Iran* **65 E8**
Mīr Shahdād, *Iran* **65 E8**
Miraj, *India* **60 L9**
Miram Shah, *Pakistan* **62 C4**
Miramar, *Mozam.* **126 D4**

Physical features composed of a proper name (Erie) and a description (Lake) are positioned alphabetically by the proper name. The description is positioned after the proper name and is usually abbreviated:

Erie, L., *N. Amer.* **106 D4**

Where a description forms part of a settlement or administrative name however, it is always written in full and put in its true alphabetic position:

Mount Morris, *U.S.A.* **106 D7**

Names beginning with M' and Mc are indexed as if they were spelt Mac. Names beginning St. are alphabetised under Saint, but Sankt, Sint, Sant', Santa and San are all spelt in full and are alphabetised accordingly. If the same place name occurs two or more times in the index and all are in the same country, each is followed by the name of the administrative subdivision in which it is located. The names are placed in the alphabetical order of the subdivisions. For example:

Jackson, *Ky., U.S.A.* **104 G4**
Jackson, *Mich., U.S.A.* **104 D3**
Jackson, *Minn., U.S.A.* **108 D7**

The number in bold type which follows each name in the index refers to the number of the map page where that feature or place will be found. This is usually the largest scale at which the place or feature appears. The letter and figure which are in bold type immediately after the page number give the grid square on the map page, within which the feature is situated. The letter represents the latitude and the figure the longitude.

In some cases the feature itself may fall within the specified square, while the name is outside. This is usually the case only with features which are larger than a grid square. Rivers are indexed to their mouths or confluences, and carry the symbol → after their names. A solid square ■ follows the name of a country while, an open square □ refers to a first order administrative area.

ABBREVIATIONS USED IN THE INDEX

A.C.T. — Australian Capital Territory
Afghan. — Afghanistan
Ala. — Alabama
Alta. — Alberta
Amer. — America(n)
Arch. — Archipelago
Ariz. — Arizona
Ark. — Arkansas
Atl. Oc. — Atlantic Ocean
B. — Baie, Bahía, Bay, Bucht, Bugt
B.C. — British Columbia
Bangla. — Bangladesh
Barr. — Barrage
Bos.-H. — Bosnia-Herzegovina
C. — Cabo, Cap, Cape, Coast
C.A.R. — Central African Republic
C. Prov. — Cape Province
Calif. — California
Cent. — Central
Chan. — Channel
Colo. — Colorado
Conn. — Connecticut
Cord. — Cordillera
Cr. — Creek
D.C. — District of Columbia
Del. — Delaware
Dep. — Dependency
Des. — Desert
Dist. — District
Dj. — Djebel
Domin. — Dominica
Dom. Rep. — Dominican Republic
E. — East
El Salv. — El Salvador
Eq. Guin. — Equatorial Guinea

Fla. — Florida
Falk. Is. — Falkland Is.
G. — Golfe, Golfo, Gulf, Guba, Gebel
Ga. — Georgia
Gt. — Great, Greater
Guinea-Biss. — Guinea-Bissau
H.K. — Hong Kong
H.P. — Himachal Pradesh
Hants. — Hampshire
Harb. — Harbor, Harbour
Hd. — Head
Hts. — Heights
I.(s). — Île, Ilha, Insel, Isla, Island, Isle
Ill. — Illinois
Ind. — Indiana
Ind. Oc. — Indian Ocean
Ivory C. — Ivory Coast
J. — Jabal, Jebel, Jazira
Junc. — Junction
K. — Kap, Kapp
Kans. — Kansas
Kep. — Kepulauan
Ky. — Kentucky
L. — Lac, Lacul, Lago, Lagoa, Lake, Limni, Loch, Lough
La. — Louisiana
Liech. — Liechtenstein
Lux. — Luxembourg
Mad. P. — Madhya Pradesh
Madag. — Madagascar
Man. — Manitoba
Mass. — Massachusetts
Md. — Maryland
Me. — Maine

Medit. S. — Mediterranean Sea
Mich. — Michigan
Minn. — Minnesota
Miss. — Mississippi
Mo. — Missouri
Mont. — Montana
Moza. — Mozambique
Mt.(e). — Mont, Monte, Monti, Montaña, Mountain
N. — Nord, Norte, North, Northern, Nouveau
N.B. — New Brunswick
N.C. — North Carolina
N. Cal. — New Caledonia
N. Dak. — North Dakota
N.H. — New Hampshire
N.I. — North Island
N.J. — New Jersey
N. Mex. — New Mexico
N.S. — Nova Scotia
N.S.W. — New South Wales
N.W.T. — North West Territory
N.Y. — New York
N.Z. — New Zealand
Nebr. — Nebraska
Neths. — Netherlands
Nev. — Nevada
Nfld. — Newfoundland
Nic. — Nicaragua
O. — Oued, Ouadi
Occ. — Occidentale
O.F.S. — Orange Free State
Okla. — Oklahoma
Ont. — Ontario
Or. — Orientale
Oreg. — Oregon

Os. — Ostrov
Oz. — Ozero
P. — Pass, Passo, Pasul, Pulau
P.E.I. — Prince Edward Island
Pa. — Pennsylvania
Pac. Oc. — Pacific Ocean
Papua N.G. — Papua New Guinea
Pass. — Passage
Pen. — Peninsula, Péninsule
Phil. — Philippines
Pk. — Park, Peak
Plat. — Plateau
P-ov. — Poluostrov
Prov. — Province, Provincial
Pt. — Point
Pta. — Ponta, Punta
Pte. — Pointe
Qué. — Québec
Queens. — Queensland
R. — Rio, River
R.I. — Rhode Island
Ra.(s). — Range(s)
Raj. — Rajasthan
Reg. — Region
Rep. — Republic
Res. — Reserve, Reservoir
S. — San, South, Sea
Si. Arabia — Saudi Arabia
S.C. — South Carolina
S. Dak. — South Dakota
S.I. — South Island
S. Leone — Sierra Leone
Sa. — Serra, Sierra
Sask. — Saskatchewan
Scot. — Scotland
Sd. — Sound

Sev. — Severnaya
Sib. — Siberia
Sprs. — Springs
St. — Saint, Sankt, Sint
Sta. — Santa, Station
Ste. — Sainte
Sto. — Santo
Str. — Strait, Stretto
Switz. — Switzerland
Tas. — Tasmania
Tenn. — Tennessee
Tex. — Texas
Tg. — Tanjung
Trin. & Tob. — Trinidad & Tobago
U.A.E. — United Arab Emirates
U.K. — United Kingdom
U.S.A. — United States of America
Ut. P. — Uttar Pradesh
Va. — Virginia
Vdkhr. — Vodokhranilishche
Vf. — Vîrful
Vic. — Victoria
Vol. — Volcano
Vt. — Vermont
W. — Wadi, West
W. Va. — West Virginia
Wash. — Washington
Wis. — Wisconsin
Wlkp. — Wielkopolski
Wyo. — Wyoming
Yorks. — Yorkshire
Yug. — Yugoslavia

A

A Coruña = La Coruña, Spain ... 30 B2
Aachen, Germany ... 18 E2
Aadorf, Switz. ... 23 B7
Aalborg = Ålborg, Denmark ... 11 G3
Aalen, Germany ... 19 G6
A'āli en Nîl □, Sudan ... 77 F3
Aalsmeer, Neths. ... 16 D5
Aalst, Belgium ... 17 G4
Aalst, Neths. ... 17 F6
Aalten, Neths. ... 16 E9
Aalter, Belgium ... 17 F2
Aarau, Switz. ... 22 B6
Aarberg, Switz. ... 22 B4
Aardenburg, Belgium ... 17 F2
Aare →, Switz. ... 22 A6
Aargau □, Switz. ... 22 B6
Aarhus = Århus, Denmark ... 11 H4
Aarle, Neths. ... 17 E7
Aarsele, Belgium ... 17 G2
Aartrijke, Belgium ... 17 F2
Aarwangen, Switz. ... 22 B5
Aba, China ... 52 A3
Aba, Nigeria ... 79 D6
Aba, Zaïre ... 82 B3
Âbâ, Jazīrat, Sudan ... 77 E3
Abacaxis →, Brazil ... 121 D6
Ābādān, Iran ... 65 D6
Abade, Ethiopia ... 77 F4
Ābādeh, Iran ... 65 D7
Abadin, Spain ... 30 B3
Abadla, Algeria ... 75 B4
Abaeté, Brazil ... 123 E2
Abaeté →, Brazil ... 123 E2
Abaetetuba, Brazil ... 122 B2
Abagnar Qi, China ... 50 C9
Abai, Paraguay ... 127 B4
Abak, Nigeria ... 79 E6
Abakaliki, Nigeria ... 79 D6
Abakan, Russia ... 45 D10
Abalemma, Niger ... 79 B6
Abana, Turkey ... 66 C6
Abancay, Peru ... 124 C3
Abanilla, Spain ... 29 G3
Abano Terme, Italy ... 33 C8
Abapó, Bolivia ... 125 D5
Abarán, Spain ... 29 G3
Abariringa, Kiribati ... 92 H10
Abarqū, Iran ... 65 D7
Abashiri, Japan ... 48 B12
Abashiri-Wan, Japan ... 48 B12
Abaújszántó, Hungary ... 21 G11
Abay, Kazakhstan ... 44 E8
Abaya, L., Ethiopia ... 77 F4
Abaza, Russia ... 44 D10
Abbadia San Salvatore, Italy ... 33 F8
'Abbāsābād, Iran ... 65 C8
Abbay = Nîl el Azraq →, Sudan ... 77 D3
Abbaye, Pt., U.S.A. ... 104 B1
Abbé, L., Ethiopia ... 77 E5
Abbeville, France ... 25 B8
Abbeville, La., U.S.A. ... 109 K8
Abbeville, S.C., U.S.A. ... 105 H4
Abbiategrasso, Italy ... 32 C5
Abbieglassie, Australia ... 91 D4
Abbot Ice Shelf, Antarctica ... 5 D16
Abbotsford, Canada ... 100 D4
Abbotsford, U.S.A. ... 108 C9
Abbottabad, Pakistan ... 62 B5
Abcoude, Neths. ... 16 D5
Abd al Kūrī, Ind. Oc. ... 68 E5
Ābdar, Iran ... 65 D7
'Abdolābād, Iran ... 65 C8
Abéché, Chad ... 73 F9
Abejar, Spain ... 28 D2
Abekr, Sudan ... 77 E2
Abélessa, Algeria ... 75 D5
Abengourou, Ivory C. ... 78 D4
Åbenrå, Denmark ... 11 J3
Abensberg, Germany ... 19 G7
Abeokuta, Nigeria ... 79 D5
Aber, Uganda ... 82 B3
Aberaeron, U.K. ... 13 E3
Aberayron = Aberaeron, U.K. ... 13 E3
Abercorn = Mbala, Zambia ... 83 D3
Abercorn, Australia ... 91 D5
Aberdare, U.K. ... 13 F4
Aberdare Ra., Kenya ... 82 C4
Aberdeen, Australia ... 91 E5
Aberdeen, Canada ... 101 C7
Aberdeen, S. Africa ... 84 E3
Aberdeen, U.K. ... 14 D6
Aberdeen, Ala., U.S.A. ... 105 J1
Aberdeen, Idaho, U.S.A. ... 110 E7
Aberdeen, S. Dak., U.S.A. ... 108 C5
Aberdeen, Wash., U.S.A. ... 112 D3
Aberdovey = Aberdyfi, U.K. ... 13 E3
Aberdyfi, U.K. ... 13 E3
Aberfeldy, U.K. ... 14 E5
Abergavenny, U.K. ... 13 F4
Abernathy, U.S.A. ... 109 J4
Abert, L., U.S.A. ... 110 E3
Aberystwyth, U.K. ... 13 E3

Abha, Si. Arabia ... 76 D5
Abhar, Iran ... 65 B6
Abhayapuri, India ... 63 F14
Abia □, Nigeria ... 79 D6
Abidiya, Sudan ... 76 D3
Abidjan, Ivory C. ... 78 D4
Abilene, Kans., U.S.A. ... 108 F6
Abilene, Tex., U.S.A. ... 109 J5
Abingdon, U.K. ... 13 F6
Abingdon, Ill., U.S.A. ... 108 E9
Abingdon, Va., U.S.A. ... 105 G5
Abington Reef, Australia ... 90 B4
Abitau →, Canada ... 101 B7
Abitau L., Canada ... 101 A7
Abitibi L., Canada ... 98 C4
Abiy Adi, Ethiopia ... 77 E4
Abkhaz Republic □, Georgia ... 43 E9
Abkit, Russia ... 45 C16
Abminga, Australia ... 91 D1
Abnûb, Egypt ... 76 B3
Abocho, Nigeria ... 79 D6
Abohar, India ... 62 D6
Aboisso, Ivory C. ... 78 D4
Abomey, Benin ... 79 D5
Abondance, France ... 27 B10
Abong-Mbang, Cameroon ... 80 D2
Abonnema, Nigeria ... 79 E6
Abony, Hungary ... 21 H10
Aboso, Ghana ... 78 D4
Abou-Deïa, Chad ... 73 F8
Aboyne, U.K. ... 14 D6
Abra Pampa, Argentina ... 126 A2
Abrantes, Portugal ... 31 F2
Abraveses, Portugal ... 30 E3
Abreojos, Pta., Mexico ... 114 B2
Abreschviller, France ... 25 D14
Abri, Esh Shamâliya, Sudan ... 76 C3
Abri, Janub Kordofân, Sudan ... 77 E3
Abrolhos, Banka, Brazil ... 123 E4
Abruzzi □, Italy ... 33 F10
Absaroka Range, U.S.A. ... 110 D9
Abū al Khaṣīb, Iraq ... 65 D6
Abū 'Alī, Si. Arabia ... 65 E6
Abū 'Alī →, Lebanon ... 69 A4
Abu 'Arīsh, Si. Arabia ... 68 D3
Abū Ballas, Egypt ... 76 C2
Abu Deleiq, Sudan ... 77 D3
Abu Dhabi = Abū Ẓāby, U.A.E. ... 65 E7
Abū Dīs, Sudan ... 76 D3
Abū Dom, Sudan ... 77 D3
Abū Du'ān, Syria ... 64 B3
Abu el Gairi, W. →, Egypt ... 69 F2
Abū Gabra, Sudan ... 77 E2
Abū Ga'da, W. →, Egypt ... 69 F1
Abū Gubeiha, Sudan ... 77 E3
Abu Habl, Khawr →, Sudan ... 77 E3
Abū Ḥadrīyah, Si. Arabia ... 65 E6
Abu Hamed, Sudan ... 76 D3
Abu Haraz, An Nîl el Azraq, Sudan ... 77 E3
Abū Haraz, Esh Shamâliya, Sudan ... 76 D3
Abū Higar, Sudan ... 77 E3
Abū Kamāl, Syria ... 64 C4
Abū Madd, Ra's, Si. Arabia ... 64 E3
Abu Matariq, Sudan ... 77 E2
Abu Qir, Egypt ... 76 H7
Abu Qireiya, Egypt ... 76 C4
Abu Qurqās, Egypt ... 76 J7
Abū Ṣafāt, W. →, Jordan ... 69 E5
Abū Simbel, Egypt ... 76 C3
Abū Ṣukhayr, Iraq ... 64 D5
Abu Tig, Egypt ... 76 B3
Abu Tiga, Sudan ... 77 E3
Abū Zabad, Sudan ... 77 E2
Abū Ẓāby, U.A.E. ... 65 E7
Abū Zeydābād, Iran ... 65 C6
Abufari, Brazil ... 125 B5
Abuja, Nigeria ... 79 D6
Abukuma-Gawa →, Japan ... 48 E10
Abukuma-Sammyaku, Japan ... 48 F10
Abunã, Brazil ... 125 B4
Abunã →, Brazil ... 125 B4
Aburo, Zaïre ... 82 B3
Abut Hd., N.Z. ... 87 K3
Abwong, Sudan ... 77 F3
Åby, Sweden ... 11 F10
Aby, Lagune, Ivory C. ... 78 D4
Acacías, Colombia ... 120 C3
Acajutla, El Salv. ... 116 D2
Açallândia, Brazil ... 122 C2
Acámbaro, Mexico ... 114 C4
Acaponeta, Mexico ... 114 C3
Acapulco, Mexico ... 115 D5
Acarai, Serra, Brazil ... 121 C6
Acaraú, Brazil ... 122 B3
Acari, Brazil ... 122 C4
Acarí, Peru ... 124 D3
Acarigua, Venezuela ... 120 B4
Acatlán, Mexico ... 115 D5
Acayucan, Mexico ... 115 D6
Accéglio, Italy ... 32 D3
Accomac, U.S.A. ... 104 G8
Accous, France ... 26 E3
Accra, Ghana ... 79 D4
Accrington, U.K. ... 12 D5
Acebal, Argentina ... 126 C3

Aceh □, Indonesia ... 56 D1
Acerenza, Italy ... 35 B8
Acerra, Italy ... 35 B7
Aceuchal, Spain ... 31 G4
Achacachi, Bolivia ... 124 D4
Achaguas, Venezuela ... 120 B4
Achalpur, India ... 60 J10
Achao, Chile ... 128 B2
Achel, Belgium ... 17 F6
Acheng, China ... 51 B14
Achenkirch, Austria ... 19 H7
Achensee, Austria ... 19 H7
Acher, India ... 62 H5
Achern, Germany ... 19 G4
Achill, Ireland ... 15 C2
Achill Hd., Ireland ... 15 C1
Achill I., Ireland ... 15 C1
Achill Sd., Ireland ... 15 C2
Achim, Germany ... 18 B5
Achinsk, Russia ... 45 D10
Achol, Sudan ... 77 F3
Acigöl, Turkey ... 66 E3
Acıgöl, Turkey ... 66 E3
Acireale, Italy ... 35 E8
Ackerman, U.S.A. ... 109 J10
Acklins I., Bahamas ... 117 B5
Acme, Canada ... 100 C6
Acobamba, Peru ... 124 C3
Acomayo, Peru ... 124 C3
Aconcagua □, Chile ... 126 C1
Aconcagua, Cerro, Argentina ... 126 C2
Aconquija, Mt. →, Argentina ... 126 B2
Acopiara, Brazil ... 122 C4
Açores, Is. dos = Azores, Atl. Oc. ... 2 C8
Acorizal, Brazil ... 125 D6
Acquapendente, Italy ... 33 F8
Acquasanta, Italy ... 33 F10
Acquaviva delle Fonti, Italy ... 35 B9
Acqui, Italy ... 32 D5
Acraman, L., Australia ... 91 E2
Acre = 'Akko, Israel ... 69 C4
Acre □, Brazil ... 124 B3
Acre →, Brazil ... 124 B4
Acri, Italy ... 35 C9
Acs, Hungary ... 21 H8
Acton, Canada ... 106 C4
Açu, Brazil ... 122 C4
Ad Dammām, Si. Arabia ... 65 E6
Ad Dawhah, Qatar ... 65 E6
Ad Dawr, Iraq ... 64 C4
Ad Dir'īyah, Si. Arabia ... 64 E5
Ad Dīwānīyah, Iraq ... 64 D5
Ad Dujayl, Iraq ... 64 C5
Ad Durūz, J., Jordan ... 69 C5
Ada, Ghana ... 79 D5
Ada, Serbia ... 21 K10
Ada, Minn., U.S.A. ... 108 B6
Ada, Okla., U.S.A. ... 109 H6
Adaja →, Spain ... 30 D6
Adalslinden, Sweden ... 10 A10
Adam, Mt., Falk. Is. ... 128 D4
Adam's Bridge, Sri Lanka ... 60 Q11
Adams, Mass., U.S.A. ... 107 D11
Adams, N.Y., U.S.A. ... 107 C8
Adams, Wis., U.S.A. ... 108 D10
Adam's Peak, Sri Lanka ... 60 R12
Adamantina, Brazil ... 123 F1
Adamaoua, Massif de l', Cameroon ... 79 D7
Adamawa □, Nigeria ... 79 D7
Adamawa Highlands = Adamaoua, Massif de l', Cameroon ... 79 D7
Adamello, Mt., Italy ... 32 B7
Adami Tulu, Ethiopia ... 77 F4
Adaminaby, Australia ... 91 F4
Adams, Mass., U.S.A. ... 107 D11
Adams, N.Y., U.S.A. ... 107 C8
Adams, Wis., U.S.A. ... 108 D10
Adam's Bridge, Sri Lanka ... 60 Q11
Adams L., Canada ... 100 C5
Adams Mt., U.S.A. ... 112 D5
Adam's Peak, Sri Lanka ... 60 R12
Adamuz, Spain ... 31 G6
Adana, Turkey ... 66 E6
Adana □, Turkey ... 66 E6
Adanero, Spain ... 30 E6
Adapazarı, Turkey ... 66 C4
Adarama, Sudan ... 77 D3
Adare, C., Antarctica ... 5 D11
Adaut, Indonesia ... 57 F8
Adavale, Australia ... 91 D3
Adda →, Italy ... 32 C6
Addis Ababa = Addis Abeba, Ethiopia ... 77 F4
Addis Abeba, Ethiopia ... 77 F4
Addis Alem, Ethiopia ... 77 F4
Addison, U.S.A. ... 106 D7
Addo, S. Africa ... 84 E4
Adebour, Niger ... 79 C7
Adeh, Iran ... 64 B5
Adel, U.S.A. ... 105 K4
Adelaide, Australia ... 91 E2
Adelaide, Bahamas ... 116 A4
Adelaide, S. Africa ... 84 E4
Adelaide I., Antarctica ... 5 C17
Adelaide Pen., Canada ... 96 B10
Adelaide River, Australia ... 88 B5
Adelanto, U.S.A. ... 113 L9
Adelboden, Switz. ... 22 D5
Adele I., Australia ... 88 C3
Adélie, Terre, Antarctica ... 5 C10
Adélie Land = Adélie, Terre, Antarctica ... 5 C10
Ademuz, Spain ... 28 E3
Aden = Al 'Adan, Yemen ... 68 E4
Aden, G. of, Asia ... 68 E4
Adendorp, S. Africa ... 84 E3
Adh Dhayd, U.A.E. ... 65 E7

Adhoi, India ... 62 H4
Adi, Indonesia ... 57 E8
Adi Daro, Ethiopia ... 77 E4
Adi Keyih, Eritrea ... 77 E4
Adi Kwala, Eritrea ... 77 E4
Adi Ugri, Eritrea ... 77 E4
Adieu, C., Australia ... 89 F5
Adieu Pt., Australia ... 88 C3
Adigala, Ethiopia ... 77 E5
Adige →, Italy ... 33 C9
Adigrat, Ethiopia ... 77 E4
Adilabad, India ... 60 K11
Adin, U.S.A. ... 110 F3
Adin Khel, Afghan. ... 60 C6
Adinkerke, Belgium ... 17 F1
Adirondack Mts., U.S.A. ... 107 C10
Adıyaman, Turkey ... 67 E8
Adıyaman □, Turkey ... 67 E8
Adjim, Tunisia ... 75 B7
Adjohon, Benin ... 79 D5
Adjud, Romania ... 38 C10
Adjumani, Uganda ... 82 B3
Adlavik Is., Canada ... 99 B8
Adler, Russia ... 43 E8
Adliswil, Switz. ... 23 B7
Admer, Algeria ... 75 D6
Admer, Erg d', Algeria ... 75 D6
Admiralty G., Australia ... 88 B4
Admiralty I., U.S.A. ... 96 C6
Admiralty Inlet, U.S.A. ... 110 C2
Admiralty Is., Papua N. G. ... 92 H6
Ado, Nigeria ... 79 D5
Ado Ekiti, Nigeria ... 79 D6
Adok, Sudan ... 77 F3
Adola, Ethiopia ... 77 F5
Adonara, Indonesia ... 57 F6
Adoni, India ... 60 M10
Adony, Hungary ... 21 H8
Adour →, France ... 26 E2
Adra, India ... 63 H12
Adra, Spain ... 29 J1
Adrano, Italy ... 35 E7
Adrar, Algeria ... 75 C4
Adré, Chad ... 73 F9
Adrī, Libya ... 75 C7
Ádria, Italy ... 33 C9
Adrian, Mich., U.S.A. ... 104 E3
Adrian, Tex., U.S.A. ... 109 H3
Adriatic Sea, Europe ... 6 G9
Adua, Indonesia ... 57 E7
Adula, Switz. ... 23 D8
Adwa, Ethiopia ... 77 E4
Adzhar Republic □, Georgia ... 43 F10
Adzopé, Ivory C. ... 78 D4
Ægean Sea, Europe ... 39 L8
Æolian Is. = Eólie, Is., Italy ... 35 D7
Aerhtai Shan, Mongolia ... 54 B4
Ærø, Denmark ... 11 K4
Ærøskøbing, Denmark ... 11 K4
Aesch, Switz. ... 22 B5
Adam, Mt., Falk. Is. ... 128 D4
'Afak, Iraq ... 64 C5
Afándou, Greece ... 37 C10
Afarag, Erg, Algeria ... 75 D5
Afars & Issas, Terr. of = Djibouti ■, Africa ... 68 E3
Affreville = Khemis Miliana, Algeria ... 75 A5
Afghanistan ■, Asia ... 60 C4
Afgoi, Somali Rep. ... 68 G3
Afikpo, Nigeria ... 79 D6
Aflou, Algeria ... 75 B5
Afogados da Ingàzeira, Brazil ... 122 C4
Afognak I., U.S.A. ... 96 C4
Afragola, Italy ... 35 B7
Afrera, Ethiopia ... 77 E5
Africa ... 70 E6
'Afrīn, Syria ... 64 B3
Afşin, Turkey ... 66 D7
Afton, U.S.A. ... 107 D9
Aftout, Algeria ... 74 C4
Afuá, Brazil ... 121 D7
Afula, Israel ... 69 C4
Afyonkarahisar, Turkey ... 66 D4
Afyonkarahisar □, Turkey ... 66 D4
Aga, Egypt ... 76 H7
Agadès = Agadez, Niger ... 79 B6
Agadez, Niger ... 79 B6
Agadir, Morocco ... 74 B3
Agaete, Canary Is. ... 36 F4
Agailás, Mauritania ... 74 D2
Agapa, Russia ... 45 B9
Agar, India ... 62 H7
Agaro, Ethiopia ... 77 F4
Agartala, India ... 61 H17
Agassiz, Canada ... 100 D4
Agats, Indonesia ... 57 F9
Agbélouvé, Togo ... 79 D5
Agboville, Ivory C. ... 78 D4
Agdam, Azerbaijan ... 43 G12
Agdash, Azerbaijan ... 43 F12
Agde, France ... 26 E7
Agde, C. d', France ... 26 E7
Agdz, Morocco ... 74 B3
Agdzhabedi, Azerbaijan ... 43 F12
Agen, France ... 26 D4
Agersø, Denmark ... 11 J5
Ageyevo, Russia ... 41 D10
Agger, Denmark ... 11 H2
Aggius, Italy ... 34 B2
Aghā Jārī, Iran ... 65 B6
Aghoueyyît, Mauritania ... 74 D1
Aginskoye, Russia ... 45 D12

Agira, Italy ... 35 E7
Ağlasun, Turkey ... 66 E4
Agly →, France ... 26 F7
Agnibilékrou, Ivory C. ... 78 D4
Agnita, Romania ... 38 D7
Agnone, Italy ... 35 A7
Agofie, Ghana ... 79 D5
Agogna →, Italy ... 32 C5
Agogo, Sudan ... 77 F2
Agon, France ... 24 C5
Ågön, Sweden ... 10 C11
Ágordo, Italy ... 33 B9
Agout →, France ... 26 E5
Agra, India ... 62 F7
Agramunt, Spain ... 28 D6
Agreda, Spain ... 28 D3
Ağri, Turkey ... 67 D10
Ağri □, Turkey ... 67 D10
Agri →, Italy ... 35 B9
Ağri Daği, Turkey ... 67 D11
Ağri Karakose, Turkey ... 67 D10
Agrigento, Italy ... 34 E6
Agrinion, Greece ... 39 L4
Agrópoli, Italy ... 35 B7
Água Branca, Brazil ... 122 C3
Agua Caliente, Baja Calif. N., Mexico ... 113 N10
Agua Caliente, Sinaloa, Mexico ... 114 B3
Agua Caliente Springs, U.S.A. ... 113 N10
Água Clara, Brazil ... 125 E7
Agua Hechicero, Mexico ... 113 N10
Agua Preta →, Brazil ... 121 D5
Agua Prieta, Mexico ... 114 A3
Aguachica, Colombia ... 120 B3
Aguada Cecilio, Argentina ... 128 B3
Aguadas, Colombia ... 120 B2
Aguadilla, Puerto Rico ... 117 C6
Aguadulce, Panama ... 116 E3
Aguanga, U.S.A. ... 113 M10
Aguanish, Canada ... 99 B7
Aguanus →, Canada ... 99 B7
Aguapeí, Brazil ... 125 D6
Aguapeí →, Brazil ... 123 E1
Aguapey →, Argentina ... 126 B4
Aguaray Guazú →, Paraguay ... 126 A4
Aguarico →, Ecuador ... 120 D2
Aguas →, Spain ... 28 D4
Aguas Blancas, Chile ... 126 A2
Aguas Calientes, Sierra de, Argentina ... 126 B2
Águas Formosas, Brazil ... 123 E3
Aguascalientes, Mexico ... 114 C4
Aguascalientes □, Mexico ... 114 C4
Agudo, Spain ... 31 G6
Águeda, Portugal ... 30 E2
Águeda →, Spain ... 30 D4
Aguié, Niger ... 79 C6
Aguilafuente, Spain ... 30 D6
Aguilar, Spain ... 31 H6
Aguilar de Campóo, Spain ... 30 C6
Aguilares, Argentina ... 126 B2
Aguilas, Spain ... 29 H3
Agüimes, Canary Is. ... 36 G4
Aguja, C. de la, Colombia ... 120 A3
Agulaa, Ethiopia ... 77 E4
Agulhas, C., S. Africa ... 84 E3
Agulo, Canary Is. ... 36 F2
Agung, Indonesia ... 56 F5
Agur, Uganda ... 82 B3
Agusan →, Phil. ... 55 G6
Agustín Codazzi, Colombia ... 120 A3
Agvali, Russia ... 43 E12
Aha Mts., Botswana ... 84 B3
Ahaggar, Algeria ... 75 D6
Ahamansu, Ghana ... 79 D5
Ahar, Iran ... 64 B5
Ahaus, Germany ... 18 C3
Ahelledjem, Algeria ... 75 C6
Ahipara B., N.Z. ... 87 F4
Ahiri, India ... 60 K12
Ahlen, Germany ... 18 D3
Ahmad Wal, Pakistan ... 62 E1
Ahmadabad, India ... 62 H5
Ahmadābād, Khorāsān, Iran ... 65 C9
Ahmadābād, Khorāsān, Iran ... 65 C8
Ahmadī, Iran ... 65 E8
Ahmadnagar, India ... 60 K9
Ahmadpur, Pakistan ... 62 E4
Ahmar, Ethiopia ... 77 F5
Ahmedabad = Ahmadabad, India ... 62 H5
Ahmednagar = Ahmadnagar, India ... 60 K9
Ahoada, Nigeria ... 79 D6
Ahome, Mexico ... 114 B3
Ahr →, Germany ... 18 E3
Ahram, Iran ... 65 D6
Ahrax Pt., Malta ... 37 D1
Ahrensbök, Germany ... 18 A6
Ahrweiler, Germany ... 18 E3
Āhū, Iran ... 65 C6
Ahuachapán, El Salv. ... 116 D2
Ahvāz, Iran ... 65 D6
Ahvenanmaa = Åland, Finland ... 9 F16
Aḥwar, Yemen ... 68 E4
Ahzar, Mali ... 79 B5
Aiari →, Brazil ... 120 C4
Aichach, Germany ... 19 G7
Aichi □, Japan ... 49 G8

Aidone, *Italy* 35 E7
Aiello Cálabro, *Italy* 35 C9
Aigle, *Switz.* 22 D3
Aignay-le-Duc, *France* .. 25 E11
Aigoual, Mt., *France* 26 D7
Aigre, *France* 26 C4
Aigua, *Uruguay* 127 C5
Aigueperse, *France* 26 B7
Aigues ─►, *France* 27 D8
Aigues-Mortes, *France* . 27 E8
Aigues-Mortes, G. d',
  France 27 E8
Aiguilles, *France* 27 D10
Aiguillon, *France* 26 D4
Aigurande, *France* 26 B5
Aihui, *China* 54 A7
Aija, *Peru* 124 B2
Aikawa, *Japan* 48 E9
Aiken, *U.S.A.* 105 J5
Ailao Shan, *China* 52 F3
Aillant-sur-Tholon, *France* 25 E10
Aillik, *Canada* 99 A8
Ailly-sur-Noye, *France* .. 25 C9
Ailsa Craig, *U.K.* 14 F3
'Ailūn, *Jordan* 69 C4
Aim, *Russia* 45 D14
Aimere, *Indonesia* 57 F6
Aimogasta, *Argentina* .. 126 B2
Aimorés, *Brazil* 123 E3
Ain □, *France* 27 B9
Ain ─►, *France* 27 C9
Aïn Beïda, *Algeria* 75 A6
Aïn Ben Khellil, *Algeria* . 75 B4
Aïn Ben Tili, *Mauritania* . 74 C3
Aïn Beni Mathar, *Morocco* 75 B4
Aïn Benian, *Algeria* 75 A5
Ain Dalla, *Egypt* 76 B2
Ain el Mafki, *Egypt* 76 B2
Ain Girba, *Egypt* 76 B2
Aïn M'lila, *Algeria* 75 A6
Ain Qeiqab, *Egypt* 76 B1
Aïn-Sefra, *Algeria* 75 B4
Ain Sheikh Murzûk, *Egypt* 76 B2
'Ain Sudr, *Egypt* 69 F2
Ain Sukhna, *Egypt* 76 J8
Aïn Tédélès, *Algeria* ... 75 A5
Aïn-Témouchent, *Algeria* . 75 A4
Aïn Touta, *Algeria* 75 A6
Ain Zeitûn, *Egypt* 76 B2
Aïn Zorah, *Morocco* 75 B4
Ainabo, *Somali Rep.* 68 F4
Ainaži, *Latvia* 40 C4
Aínos Óros, *Greece* 39 L3
Ainsworth, *U.S.A.* 108 D5
Aipe, *Colombia* 120 C2
Aiquile, *Bolivia* 125 D4
Aïr, *Niger* 79 B6
Air Hitam, *Malaysia* 59 M4
Airaines, *France* 25 C8
Airão, *Brazil* 121 D5
Airdrie, *U.K.* 14 F5
Aire ─►, *France* 25 C11
Aire ─►, *U.K.* 12 D7
Aire, I. del, *Spain* 36 B11
Aire-sur-la-Lys, *France* .. 25 B9
Aire-sur-l'Adour, *France* . 26 E3
Airlie Beach, *Australia* .. 90 C4
Airolo, *Switz.* 23 C7
Airvault, *France* 24 F6
Aisch ─►, *Germany* 19 F7
Aisen □, *Chile* 128 C2
Aisne □, *France* 25 C10
Aisne ─►, *France* 25 C9
Aitana, Sierra de, *Spain* . 29 G4
Aitkin, *U.S.A.* 108 B8
Aitolikón, *Greece* 39 L4
Aiuaba, *Brazil* 122 C3
Aiud, *Romania* 38 C6
Aix-en-Provence, *France* . 27 E9
Aix-la-Chapelle = Aachen,
  Germany 18 E2
Aix-les-Bains, *France* ... 27 C9
Aixe-sur-Vienne, *France* . 26 C5
Aiyansh, *Canada* 100 B3
Aíyina, *Greece* 39 M6
Aiyínion, *Greece* 39 J5
Aíyion, *Greece* 39 L5
Aizawl, *India* 61 H18
Aizenay, *France* 24 F5
Aizpute, *Latvia* 40 C2
Aizuwakamatsu, *Japan* ... 48 F9
Ajaccio, *France* 27 G12
Ajaccio, G. d', *France* ... 27 G12
Ajaju ─►, *Colombia* 120 C3
Ajalpan, *Mexico* 115 D5
Ajanta Ra., *India* 60 J9
Ajari Rep. = Adzhar
  Republic □, *Georgia* .. 43 F10
Ajax, *Canada* 106 C5
Ajdâbiyah, *Libya* 73 B9
Ajdovščina, *Slovenia* ... 33 C10
Ajibar, *Ethiopia* 77 E4
Ajka, *Hungary* 21 H7
'Ajmān, *U.A.E.* 65 E7
Ajmer, *India* 62 F6
Ajo, *U.S.A.* 111 K7
Ajoie, *Switz.* 22 B4
Ajok, *Sudan* 77 F2
Ajuy, *Phil.* 55 F5
Ak Dağ, *Antalya, Turkey* . 66 E4
Ak Dağ, *Sivas, Turkey* .. 66 D7
Akaba, *Togo* 79 D5
Akabira, *Japan* 48 C11
Akaki Beseka, *Ethiopia* .. 77 F4

Akala, *Sudan* 77 D4
Akamas □, *Cyprus* 37 D11
Akanthou, *Cyprus* 37 D12
Akaroa, *N.Z.* 87 K4
Akasha, *Sudan* 76 C3
Akashi, *Japan* 49 G7
Akbou, *Algeria* 75 A5
Akçaabat, *Turkey* 67 C8
Akçakoca, *Turkey* 66 C4
Akchâr, *Mauritania* 74 D2
Akdağmadeni, *Turkey* ... 66 D6
Akelamo, *Indonesia* 57 D7
Akershus fylke □, *Norway* 10 E5
Aketi, *Zaïre* 80 D4
Akhalkalaki, *Georgia* ... 43 F10
Akhaltsikhe, *Georgia* ... 43 F10
Akharnaí, *Greece* 39 L6
Akhelóös ─►, *Greece* .. 39 L4
Akhendria, *Greece* 39 Q8
Akhéron ─►, *Greece* ... 39 K3
Akhisar, *Turkey* 66 C2
Akhladhókambos, *Greece* 39 M5
Akhmîm, *Egypt* 76 B3
Akhnur, *India* 63 C6
Akhtubinsk, *Russia* 43 B12
Akhty, *Russia* 43 F12
Akhtyrka, *Ukraine* 40 F9
Aki, *Japan* 49 H6
Akimiski I., *Canada* 98 B3
Akimovka, *Ukraine* 42 C6
Akita, *Japan* 48 E10
Akita □, *Japan* 48 E10
Akjoujt, *Mauritania* 78 B2
Akka, *Morocco* 74 C3
Akkeshi, *Japan* 48 C12
'Akko, *Israel* 69 C4
Akkol, *Kazakhstan* 44 E8
Akkrum, *Neths.* 16 B7
Aklampa, *Benin* 79 D5
Aklavik, *Canada* 96 B6
Akmolinsk = Tselinograd,
  Kazakhstan 44 D8
Akmonte, *Spain* 31 H4
Aknoul, *Morocco* 75 B4
Akō, *Japan* 49 G7
Ako, *Nigeria* 79 C7
Akobo ─►, *Ethiopia* ... 77 F3
Akola, *India* 60 J10
Akonolinga, *Cameroon* .. 79 E7
Akordat, *Eritrea* 77 D4
Akosombo Dam, *Ghana* . 79 D5
Akot, *Sudan* 77 F3
Akpatok I., *Canada* 97 B13
Akranes, *Iceland* 8 D3
Akreïjit, *Mauritania* 78 B3
Akrítas Venétiko, Ákra,
  Greece 39 N4
Akron, *Colo., U.S.A.* ... 108 E3
Akron, *Ohio, U.S.A.* ... 106 E3
Akrotíri, *Cyprus* 37 E11
Akrotíri, Ákra, *Greece* .. 39 J8
Akrotiri Bay, *Cyprus* ... 37 E12
Aksai Chin, *India* 63 B8
Aksaray, *Turkey* 66 D6
Aksarka, *Russia* 44 C7
Aksay, *Kazakhstan* 44 D6
Akşehir, *Turkey* 66 D4
Akşehir Gölü, *Turkey* ... 66 D4
Aksenovo Zilovskoye,
  Russia 45 D12
Akstafa, *Azerbaijan* 43 F11
Aksu, *China* 54 B3
Aksu ─►, *Turkey* 66 E4
Aksum, *Ethiopia* 77 E4
Aktogay, *Kazakhstan* ... 44 E8
Aktyubinsk, *Kazakhstan* . 44 D6
Aku, *Nigeria* 79 D6
Akure, *Nigeria* 79 D6
Akureyri, *Iceland* 8 D4
Akuseki-Shima, *Japan* .. 49 K4
Akusha, *Russia* 43 E12
Akwa-Ibom □, *Nigeria* .. 79 E6
Akyab = Sittwe, *Burma* . 61 J18
Akyazı, *Turkey* 66 C4
Al 'Adan, *Yemen* 68 E4
Al Ahsā, *Si. Arabia* 65 E6
Al Ajfar, *Si. Arabia* 64 E4
Al Amādīyah, *Iraq* 64 B4
Al Amārah, *Iraq* 64 D5
Al 'Aqabah, *Jordan* 69 F4
Al Arak, *Syria* 64 C3
Al 'Aramah, *Si. Arabia* .. 64 E5
Al Arṭāwīyah, *Si. Arabia* . 64 E5
Al 'Āṣimah □, *Jordan* ... 69 D5
Al' Assāfīyah, *Si. Arabia* . 64 D3
Al 'Ayn, *Oman* 65 E7
Al 'Ayn, *Si. Arabia* 64 E3
Al A'zamīyah, *Iraq* 64 C5
Al 'Azīzīyah, *Iraq* 64 C5
Al 'Azīzīyah, *Libya* 75 B7
Al Bāb, *Syria* 64 B3
Al Bad', *Si. Arabia* 64 D2
Al Bādī, *Iraq* 64 C4
Al Bahrah, *Kuwait* 64 D5
Al Balqā' □, *Jordan* 69 C4
Al Barkāt, *Libya* 75 D7
Al Bārūk, J., *Lebanon* .. 69 B4
Al Başrah, *Iraq* 64 D5
Al Batḥā, *Iraq* 64 D5
Al Batrūn, *Lebanon* 69 A4
Al Bi'r, *Si. Arabia* 64 D3
Al Bu'ayrāt, *Libya* 73 B8
Al Burayj, *Syria* 69 A5
Al Fallūjah, *Iraq* 64 C4
Al Fāw, *Iraq* 65 D6
Al Fujayrah, *U.A.E.* 65 E8

Al Ghadaf, W. ─►, *Jordan* 69 D5
Al Ghammās, *Iraq* 64 D5
Al Hābah, *Si. Arabia* ... 64 E5
Al Ḥadīthah, *Iraq* 64 C4
Al Ḥadīthah, *Si. Arabia* . 64 D3
Al Hājānah, *Syria* 69 B5
Al Ḥāmad, *Si. Arabia* .. 64 D3
Al Hamdāniyah, *Syria* .. 64 C3
Al Hamīdīyah, *Syria* ... 69 A4
Al Hammādah al Ḥamrā',
  Libya 75 C7
Al Ḥammār, *Iraq* 64 D5
Al Harīr, W. ─►, *Syria* .. 69 C4
Al Ḥasā, W. ─►, *Jordan* . 69 D4
Al Hasakah, *Syria* 64 B4
Al Hawrah, *Yemen* 68 E4
Al Haydān, W. ─►, *Jordan* 69 D4
Al Hayy, *Iraq* 64 C5
Al Hijāz, *Si. Arabia* 68 B2
Al Hillah, *Iraq* 64 C5
Al Ḥillah, *Si. Arabia* 68 C4
Al Hirmil, *Lebanon* 69 A5
Al Hoceïma, *Morocco* .. 74 A4
Al Hudaydah, *Yemen* .. 68 E3
Al Hufūf, *Si. Arabia* 65 E6
Al Humaydah, Si. Arabia . 64 D2
Al Hunayy, *Si. Arabia* .. 65 E6
Al Irq, *Libya* 73 C9
Al Īsāwīyah, *Si. Arabia* .. 64 D3
Al Jafr, *Jordan* 69 E5
Al Jaghbūb, *Libya* 73 C9
Al Jahrah, *Kuwait* 64 D5
Al Jalāmīd, *Si. Arabia* .. 64 D3
Al Jamalīyah, *Qatar* 65 E6
Al Janūb □, *Lebanon* ... 69 B4
Al Jawf, *Libya* 73 D9
Al Jawf, *Si. Arabia* 64 D3
Al Jazirah, *Iraq* 64 C5
Al Jazirah, *Libya* 73 C9
Al Jithāmīyah, *Si. Arabia* . 64 E4
Al Jubayl, *Si. Arabia* ... 65 E6
Al Jubaylah, *Si. Arabia* .. 64 E5
Al Jubb, *Si. Arabia* 64 E4
Al Junaynah, *Sudan* 73 F9
Al Kabā'ish, *Iraq* 64 D5
Al Karak, *Jordan* 69 D4
Al Karak □, *Jordan* 69 D5
Al Kāzim Tyah, *Iraq* 64 C5
Al Khalīl, *Jordan* 69 D4
Al Khalīl □, *Jordan* 69 D4
Al Khawr, *Qatar* 65 E6
Al Khiḍr, *Iraq* 64 D5
Al Khiyām, *Lebanon* ... 69 B4
Al Kufrah, *Libya* 73 D9
Al Kuhayfīyah, *Si. Arabia* 64 E4
Al Kūt, *Iraq* 64 C5
Al Kuwayt, *Kuwait* 64 D5
Al Labwah, *Lebanon* ... 69 A5
Al Lādhiqīyah, *Syria* ... 64 C2
Al Līth, *Si. Arabia* 76 C5
Al Liwā', *Oman* 65 E8
Al Luḥayyah, *Yemen* ... 68 D3
Al Madīnah, *Iraq* 64 D5
Al Madīnah, *Si. Arabia* . 64 E3
Al-Mafraq, *Jordan* 69 C5
Al Maḥmūdīyah, *Iraq* ... 64 C5
Al Majma'ah, *Si. Arabia* . 64 E5
Al Makhruq, W. ─►,
  Jordan 69 D6
Al Makhūl, *Si. Arabia* ... 64 E4
Al Manāmah, *Bahrain* ... 65 E6
Al Maqwa', *Kuwait* 64 D5
Al Marj, *Libya* 73 B9
Al Maṭlā, *Kuwait* 64 D5
Al Mawjib, W. ─►, *Jordan* 69 D4
Al Mawṣil, *Iraq* 64 B4
Al Mayādin, *Syria* 64 C4
Al Mazār, *Jordan* 69 D4
Al Midhnab, *Si. Arabia* . 64 E5
Al Minā', *Lebanon* 69 A4
Al Miqdādīyah, *Iraq* 64 C5
Al Mubarraz, *Si. Arabia* . 65 E6
Al Mughayrā', *U.A.E.* ... 65 E7
Al Muḥarraq, *Bahrain* .. 65 E6
Al Mukallā, *Yemen* 68 E4
Al Mukhā, *Yemen* 68 E3
Al Musayjīd, *Si. Arabia* . 64 E3
Al Musayyib, *Iraq* 64 C5
Al Muwayliḥ, *Si. Arabia* . 64 E2
Al Owuho = Otukpa,
  Nigeria 79 D6
Al Qā'im, *Iraq* 64 C4
Al Qalībah, *Si. Arabia* .. 64 D3
Al Qaryatayn, *Syria* 69 A6
Al Qaşabát, *Libya* 73 B7
Al Qaṭ'ā, *Syria* 64 C4
Al Qaṭīf, *Si. Arabia* 65 E6
Al Qaṭrānah, *Jordan* ... 69 D5
Al Qaṭrūn, *Libya* 73 D8
Al Qayṣūmah, *Si. Arabia* 64 D5
Al Quds = Jerusalem,
  Israel 69 D4
Al Quds □, *Jordan* 69 D4
Al Qunaytirah, *Syria* ... 69 C4
Al Qunfudhah, *Si. Arabia* 76 D5
Al Qurnah, *Iraq* 64 D5
Al Quşayr, *Iraq* 64 D5
Al Quşayr, *Syria* 69 A5
Al Qutayfah, *Syria* 69 B5
Al 'Udayliyah, *Si. Arabia* 65 E6
Al 'Ulā, *Si. Arabia* 64 E3
Al Uqaylah ash Sharqîgah,
  Libya 73 B8

Al Uqayr, *Si. Arabia* 65 E6
Al 'Uwaynid, *Si. Arabia* . 64 E5
Al' 'Uwayqīlah, *Si. Arabia* 64 D4
Al 'Uyūn, *Si. Arabia* 64 E4
Al Wajh, *Si. Arabia* 64 E3
Al Wakrah, *Qatar* 65 E6
Al Wannān, *Si. Arabia* .. 65 E6
Al Waqbah, *Si. Arabia* .. 64 D5
Al Wari'ah, *Si. Arabia* .. 64 E5
Al Wāṭiyah, *Libya* 75 B7
Al Wusayl, *Qatar* 65 E6
Ala, *Italy* 32 C8
Ala Dağları, *Turkey* 67 D10
Alabama □, *U.S.A.* 105 J2
Alabama ─►, *U.S.A.* ... 105 K2
Alaca, *Turkey* 66 C6
Alaçam, *Turkey* 66 C6
Alaçam Dağları, *Turkey* . 66 D3
Alaejos, *Spain* 30 D5
Alaérma, *Greece* 37 C9
Alagna Valsésia, *Italy* .. 32 C4
Alagoa Grande, *Brazil* .. 122 C4
Alagoas □, *Brazil* 122 C4
Alagoinhas, *Brazil* 123 D4
Alagón, *Spain* 28 D3
Alagón ─►, *Spain* 31 F4
Alajero, *Canary Is.* 36 F2
Alajuela, *Costa Rica* ... 116 D3
Alakamisy, *Madag.* 85 C8
Alalapura, *Surinam* 121 C6
Alalaú ─►, *Brazil* 121 D5
Alameda, *Spain* 31 H6
Alameda, *Calif., U.S.A.* . 112 H4
Alameda, *N. Mex., U.S.A.* 111 J10
Alaminos, *Phil.* 55 C3
Alamo, *U.S.A.* 113 J11
Alamo Crossing, *U.S.A.* . 113 L13
Alamogordo, *U.S.A.* ... 111 K11
Alamos, *Mexico* 114 B3
Alamosa, *U.S.A.* 111 H11
Åland, *Finland* 9 F16
Alandroal, *Portugal* 31 G3
Ålands hav, *Sweden* ... 9 G15
Alandur, *India* 60 N12
Alange, Presa de, *Spain* . 31 G4
Alanis, *Spain* 31 G5
Alanya, *Turkey* 66 E4
Alaotra, Farihin', *Madag.* 85 B8
Alapayevsk, *Russia* 44 D7
Alar del Rey, *Spain* 30 C6
Alaraz, *Spain* 30 E5
Alaşehir, *Turkey* 66 D3
Alaska □, *U.S.A.* 96 B5
Alaska, G. of, *Pac. Oc.* . 96 C5
Alaska Highway, *Canada* 100 B3
Alaska Peninsula, *U.S.A.* 96 C4
Alaska Range, *U.S.A.* .. 96 B4
Alássio, *Italy* 32 D5
Alataw Shankou, *China* . 54 B3
Alatri, *Italy* 34 A6
Alatyr, *Russia* 41 D15
Alatyr ─►, *Russia* 41 D15
Alausi, *Ecuador* 120 D2
Álava □, *Spain* 28 C2
Alava, C., *U.S.A.* 110 B1
Alaverdi, *Armenia* 43 F11
Alawoona, *Australia* ... 91 E3
Alazan ─►, *Azerbaijan* . 43 F12
Alba, *Italy* 32 D5
Alba de Tormes, *Spain* . 30 E5
Alba Iulia, *Romania* ... 38 C6
Albac, *Romania* 38 C6
Albacete, *Spain* 29 G3
Albacete □, *Spain* 29 G3
Älbaek, *Denmark* 11 G4
Älbaek Bugt, *Denmark* .. 11 G4
Albaida, *Spain* 29 G4
Albalate de las Nogueras,
  Spain 28 E2
Albalate del Arzobispo,
  Spain 28 D4
Albania ■, *Europe* 39 J3
Albano Laziale, *Italy* ... 34 A5
Albany, *Australia* 89 G2
Albany, *Ga., U.S.A.* 105 K3
Albany, *Minn., U.S.A.* .. 108 C7
Albany, *N.Y., U.S.A.* ... 107 D11
Albany, *Oreg., U.S.A.* .. 110 D2
Albany, *Tex., U.S.A.* ... 109 J5
Albany ─►, *Canada* 98 B3
Albardón, *Argentina* ... 126 C2
Albarracín, *Spain* 28 E3
Albarracín, Sierra de, *Spain* 28 E3
Albatross B., *Australia* .. 90 A3
Albegna ─►, *Italy* 33 F8
Albemarle, *U.S.A.* 105 H5
Albemarle Sd., *U.S.A.* .. 105 H7
Albenga, *Italy* 32 D5
Alberche ─►, *Spain* ... 30 F6
Alberdi, *Paraguay* 126 B4
Alberes, Mts., *Spain* ... 28 C7
Alberique, *Spain* 29 F4
Albersdorf, *Germany* ... 18 A5
Albert, *France* 25 B9
Albert, L. = Mobutu Sese
  Seko, L., *Africa* 82 B3
Albert, L., *Australia* 91 F2
Albert Canyon, *Canada* . 100 C5
Albert Edward Ra.,
  Australia 88 C4
Albert Lea, *U.S.A.* 108 D8

Albert Nile ─►, *Uganda* . 82 B3
Albert Town, *Bahamas* .. 117 B5
Alberta □, *Canada* 100 C6
Alberti, *Argentina* 126 D3
Albertinia, *S. Africa* ... 84 E3
Albertkanaal ─►, *Belgium* 17 F4
Alberton, *Canada* 99 C7
Albertville = Kalemie,
  Zaïre 82 D2
Albertville, *France* 27 C10
Albi, *France* 26 E6
Albia, *U.S.A.* 108 E8
Albina, *Surinam* 121 B7
Albina, Ponta, *Angola* .. 84 B1
Albino, *Italy* 32 C6
Albion, *Idaho, U.S.A.* ... 110 E7
Albion, *Mich., U.S.A.* .. 104 D3
Albion, *Nebr., U.S.A.* .. 108 E5
Albion, *Pa., U.S.A.* 106 E4
Alblasserdam, *Neths.* ... 16 E5
Alborán, *Medit. S.* 31 K7
Alborea, *Spain* 29 F3
Ålborg, *Denmark* 11 G3
Ålborg Bugt, *Denmark* .. 11 H4
Alborz, Reshteh-ye Kūhhā-
  ye, *Iran* 65 C7
Albox, *Spain* 29 H2
Albreda, *Canada* 100 C5
Albufeira, *Portugal* 31 H2
Albula ─►, *Switz.* 23 C8
Albuñol, *Spain* 29 J1
Albuquerque, *Brazil* ... 125 D6
Albuquerque, *U.S.A.* ... 111 J10
Albuquerque, Cayos de,
  Caribbean 116 D3
Alburg, *U.S.A.* 107 B11
Alburno, Mte., *Italy* 35 B8
Alburquerque, *Spain* ... 31 F4
Albury, *Australia* 91 F4
Alby, *Sweden* 10 B9
Alcácer do Sal, *Portugal* . 31 G2
Alcaçovas, *Portugal* 31 G2
Alcalá de Chisvert, *Spain* . 28 E5
Alcalá de Guadaira, *Spain* 31 H5
Alcalá de Henares, *Spain* . 28 E1
Alcalá de los Gazules,
  Spain 31 J5
Alcalá la Real, *Spain* ... 31 H7
Alcamo, *Italy* 34 E5
Alcanadre, *Spain* 28 C2
Alcanadre ─►, *Spain* ... 28 D4
Alcanar, *Spain* 28 E5
Alcanede, *Portugal* 31 F2
Alcanena, *Portugal* 31 F2
Alcañices, *Spain* 30 D4
Alcañiz, *Spain* 28 D4
Alcântara, *Brazil* 122 B3
Alcántara, *Spain* 31 F4
Alcantara L., *Canada* ... 101 A7
Alcantarilla, *Spain* 29 H3
Alcaracejos, *Spain* 31 G6
Alcaraz, *Spain* 29 G2
Alcaraz, Sierra de, *Spain* . 29 G2
Alcaudete, *Spain* 31 H6
Alcázar de San Juan, *Spain* 29 F1
Alchevsk = Kommunarsk,
  Ukraine 43 B8
Alcira, *Spain* 29 F4
Alcoa, *U.S.A.* 105 H4
Alcobaça, *Portugal* 31 F2
Alcobendas, *Spain* 28 E1
Alcolea del Pinar, *Spain* . 28 D2
Alcora, *Spain* 28 E4
Alcorcón, *Spain* 30 E7
Alcoutim, *Portugal* 31 H3
Alcova, *U.S.A.* 110 E10
Alcoy, *Spain* 29 G4
Alcubierre, Sierra de, *Spain* 28 D4
Alcublas, *Spain* 28 F4
Alcudia, *Spain* 36 B10
Alcudia, B. de, *Spain* ... 36 B10
Alcudia, Sierra de la, *Spain* 31 G6
Aldabra Is., *Seychelles* . 71 G8
Aldama, *Mexico* 115 C5
Aldan, *Russia* 45 D13
Aldan ─►, *Russia* 45 C13
Aldea, Pta. de la,
  Canary Is. 36 G4
Aldeburgh, *U.K.* 13 E9
Aldeia Nova, *Portugal* .. 31 H3
Alder, *U.S.A.* 110 D7
Alder Pk., *U.S.A.* 112 K5
Alderney, *Chan. Is.* 13 H5
Aldershot, *U.K.* 13 F7
Aledo, *U.S.A.* 108 E9
Alefa, *Ethiopia* 77 E4
Aleg, *Mauritania* 78 B2
Alegranza, *Canary Is.* .. 36 E6
Alegranza, I., *Canary Is.* . 36 E6
Alegre, *Brazil* 123 F3
Alegrete, *Brazil* 127 B4
Aleisk, *Russia* 44 D9
Aleksandriya, *Ukraine* .. 41 H7
Aleksandriya, *Ukraine* .. 42 B5
Aleksandriyskaya, *Russia* 43 E12
Aleksandrov, *Russia* ... 41 C11
Aleksandrovac, *Serbia* .. 21 L11
Aleksandrovo, *Bulgaria* . 38 F7
Aleksandrovsk-
  Sakhalinskiy, *Russia* .. 45 D15
Aleksandrovskiy Zavod,
  Russia 45 D12

131

Aleksandrovskoye

Aleksandrovskoye, Russia 44 C8
Aleksandrów Kujawski, Poland 20 C8
Aleksandrów Łódźki, Poland 20 D9
Alekseyevka, Russia 41 F11
Aleksin, Russia 41 D10
Aleksinac, Serbia, Yug. 21 M11
Além Paraíba, Brazil 123 F3
Alemania, Argentina 126 B2
Alemania, Chile 126 B2
Ålen, Norway 10 B5
Alençon, France 24 D7
Alenuihaha Channel, U.S.A. 102 H17
Aleppo = Ḥalab, Syria 64 B3
Aléria, France 27 F13
Alert Bay, Canada 100 C3
Alès, France 27 D8
Aleşd, Romania 38 B5
Alessándria, Italy 32 D5
Ålestrup, Denmark 11 H3
Ålesund, Norway 8 E9
Alet-les-Bains, France 26 F6
Aletschhorn, Switz. 22 D6
Aleutian Is., Pac. Oc. 96 C2
Aleutian Trench, Pac. Oc. 92 B10
Alexander, U.S.A. 108 B3
Alexander, Mt., Australia 89 E3
Alexander Arch., U.S.A. 100 B2
Alexander B., S. Africa 84 D2
Alexander Bay, S. Africa 84 D2
Alexander City, U.S.A. 105 J3
Alexander I., Antarctica 5 C17
Alexandra, Australia 91 F4
Alexandra, N.Z. 87 L2
Alexandra Falls, Canada 100 A5
Alexandretta = İskenderun, Turkey 66 E7
Alexandria = El Iskandarîya, Egypt 76 H6
Alexandria, Australia 90 B2
Alexandria, B.C., Canada 100 C4
Alexandria, Ont., Canada 98 C5
Alexandria, Romania 38 F8
Alexandria, S. Africa 84 E4
Alexandria, Ind., U.S.A. 104 E3
Alexandria, La., U.S.A. 109 K8
Alexandria, Minn., U.S.A. 108 C7
Alexandria, S. Dak., U.S.A. 108 D6
Alexandria, Va., U.S.A. 104 F7
Alexandria Bay, U.S.A. 107 B9
Alexandrina, L., Australia 91 F2
Alexandroúpolis, Greece 39 J8
Alexis →, Canada 99 B8
Alexis Creek, Canada 100 C4
Alfabia, Spain 36 B9
Alfambra, Spain 28 E3
Alfândega da Fé, Portugal 30 D4
Alfaro, Spain 28 C3
Alfeld, Germany 18 D5
Alfenas, Brazil 127 A6
Alfiós →, Greece 39 M4
Alfonsine, Italy 33 D9
Alford, U.K. 14 D6
Alfred, Maine, U.S.A. 107 C14
Alfred, N.Y., U.S.A. 106 D7
Alfreton, U.K. 12 D6
Alga, Kazakhstan 44 E6
Algaida, Spain 36 B9
Algar, Spain 31 J5
Algarinejo, Spain 31 H6
Algarve, Portugal 31 J2
Algeciras, Spain 31 J5
Algemesí, Spain 29 F4
Alger, Algeria 75 A5
Algeria ■, Africa 75 C5
Alghero, Italy 34 B1
Algiers = Alger, Algeria 75 A5
Algoa B., S. Africa 84 E4
Algodonales, Spain 31 J5
Algodor →, Spain 30 F7
Algoma, U.S.A. 104 C2
Algona, U.S.A. 108 D7
Algonac, U.S.A. 106 D2
Alhama de Almería, Spain 29 J2
Alhama de Aragón, Spain 28 D3
Alhama de Granada, Spain 31 J7
Alhama de Murcia, Spain 29 H3
Alhambra, Spain 29 G1
Alhambra, U.S.A. 113 L8
Alhaurín el Grande, Spain 31 J6
Alhucemas = Al Hoceïma, Morocco 74 A4
'Alī al Gharbī, Iraq 64 C5
Alī ash Sharqī, Iraq 64 C5
Ali Bayramly, Azerbaijan 43 G13
'Alī Khēl, Afghan. 62 C3
Ali Sahîh, Djibouti 77 E5
Alī Shāh, Iran 64 B5
Ália, Italy 34 E6
'Alīābād, Khorāsān, Iran 65 C8
'Alīābād, Kordestān, Iran 64 C5
'Alīābād, Yazd, Iran 65 D7
Aliaga, Spain 28 E4
Aliağa, Turkey 66 D2
Aliákmon →, Greece 39 J5
Alibo, Ethiopia 77 F4
Alibunar, Serbia, Yug. 21 K10
Alicante, Spain 29 G4
Alicante □, Spain 29 G4
Alice, S. Africa 84 E4
Alice, U.S.A. 109 M5
Alice →, Queens., Australia 90 C3
Alice →, Queens., Australia 90 B3
Alice, Punta dell', Italy 35 C10
Alice Arm, Canada 100 B3
Alice Downs, Australia 88 C4
Alice Springs, Australia 90 C1
Alicedale, S. Africa 84 E4
Aliceville, U.S.A. 105 J1
Alick Cr. →, Australia 90 C3
Alicudi, I., Italy 35 D7
Alida, Canada 101 D8
Aligarh, Raj., India 62 G7
Aligarh, Ut. P., India 62 F8
Alīgūdarz, Iran 65 C6
Alijó, Portugal 30 D3
Alimena, Italy 35 E7
Alimnía, Greece 37 C9
Alingsås, Sweden 11 G6
Alipur, Pakistan 62 E4
Alipur Duar, India 61 F16
Aliquippa, U.S.A. 106 F4
Aliste →, Spain 30 D5
Alitus, Lithuania 40 D4
Alivérion, Greece 39 L7
Aliwal North, S. Africa 84 E4
Alix, Canada 100 C6
Aljezur, Portugal 31 H2
Aljustrel, Portugal 31 H2
Alkamari, Niger 79 C7
Alken, Belgium 17 G6
Alkmaar, Neths. 16 C5
All American Canal, U.S.A. 111 K6
Allada, Benin 79 D5
Allah Dad, Pakistan 62 G2
Allahabad, India 63 G9
Allakh-Yun, Russia 45 C14
Allal Tazi, Morocco 74 B3
Allan, Canada 101 C7
Allanche, France 26 C6
Allanmyo, Burma 61 K19
Allanridge, S. Africa 84 D4
Allanwater, Canada 98 B1
Allaqi, Wadi →, Egypt 76 C3
Allariz, Spain 30 C3
Allassac, France 26 C5
Alle, Belgium 17 J5
Allegan, U.S.A. 104 D3
Allegany, U.S.A. 106 D6
Allegheny →, U.S.A. 106 F5
Allegheny Plateau, U.S.A. 104 G6
Allegheny Reservoir, U.S.A. 106 E6
Allègre, France 26 C7
Allen, Argentina 128 A3
Allen, Bog of, Ireland 15 C4
Allen, L., Ireland 15 B3
Allende, Mexico 114 B4
Allentown, U.S.A. 107 F9
Alleppey, India 60 Q10
Aller →, Germany 18 C5
Alleur, Belgium 17 G7
Allevard, France 27 C10
Alliance, Surinam 121 B7
Alliance, Nebr., U.S.A. 108 D3
Alliance, Ohio, U.S.A. 106 F3
Allier □, France 26 B6
Allier →, France 25 F10
Allingåbro, Denmark 11 H4
Alliston, Canada 98 D4
Alloa, U.K. 14 E5
Allora, Australia 91 D5
Allos, France 27 D10
Alluitsup Paa = Sydprøven, Greenland 4 C5
Alma, Canada 99 C5
Alma, Ga., U.S.A. 105 K4
Alma, Kans., U.S.A. 108 F6
Alma, Mich., U.S.A. 104 D3
Alma, Nebr., U.S.A. 108 E5
Alma, Wis., U.S.A. 108 C9
Alma Ata, Kazakhstan 44 E8
Almada, Portugal 31 G1
Almaden, Australia 90 B3
Almadén, Spain 31 G6
Almagro, Spain 31 G7
Almanor, L., U.S.A. 110 F3
Almansa, Spain 29 G3
Almanza, Spain 30 C5
Almanzor, Pico de, Spain 30 E5
Almanzora →, Spain 29 H3
Almas, Brazil 123 D2
Almaty = Alma Ata, Kazakhstan 44 E8
Almazán, Spain 28 D2
Almazora, Spain 28 F4
Almeirim, Brazil 121 D7
Almeirim, Portugal 31 F2
Almelo, Neths. 16 D9
Almenar, Spain 28 D2
Almenara, Brazil 123 E3
Almenara, Spain 28 F4
Almenara, Sierra de, Spain 29 H3
Almendralejo, Spain 31 G4
Almería, Spain 29 J2
Almería □, Spain 29 H2
Almería, G. de, Spain 29 J2
Almirante, Panama 116 E3
Almirante Montt, G., Chile 128 D2
Almirós, Greece 39 K5
Almiroú, Kólpos, Greece 37 D6
Almodôvar, Portugal 31 H2
Almodóvar del Campo, Spain 31 G6
Almogia, Spain 31 J6
Almonaster la Real, Spain 31 H4
Almont, U.S.A. 106 D1
Almonte, Canada 107 A8
Almonte →, Spain 31 F4
Almora, India 63 E8
Almoradi, Spain 29 G4
Almorox, Spain 30 E6
Almoustarat, Mali 79 B5
Almuñécar, Spain 31 J7
Alnif, Morocco 74 B3
Alnwick, U.K. 12 B6
Aloi, Uganda 82 B3
Alon, Burma 61 H19
Alor, Indonesia 57 F6
Alor Setar, Malaysia 59 J3
Alora, Spain 31 J6
Alosno, Spain 31 H3
Alougoum, Morocco 74 B3
Aloysius, Mt., Australia 89 E4
Alpaugh, U.S.A. 112 K7
Alpedrinha, Portugal 30 E3
Alpena, U.S.A. 104 C4
Alpercatas →, Brazil 122 C3
Alpes-de-Haute-Provence □, France 27 D10
Alpes-Maritimes □, France 27 E11
Alpha, Australia 90 C4
Alphen, Neths. 17 F5
Alphen aan den Rijn, Neths. 16 D5
Alpiarça, Portugal 31 F2
Alpine, Ariz., U.S.A. 111 K9
Alpine, Calif., U.S.A. 113 N10
Alpine, Tex., U.S.A. 109 K3
Alpnach, Switz. 23 C6
Alps, Europe 6 F7
Alpu, Turkey 66 D4
Alrø, Denmark 11 J4
Alroy Downs, Australia 90 B2
Alsace, France 25 D14
Alsask, Canada 101 C7
Alsásua, Spain 28 C2
Alsen, Sweden 10 A7
Alsfeld, Germany 18 E5
Alsten, Norway 8 D12
Alta, Norway 8 B17
Alta, Sierra, Spain 28 E3
Alta Gracia, Argentina 126 C3
Alta Lake, Canada 100 C4
Alta Sierra, U.S.A. 113 K8
Altaelva →, Norway 8 B17
Altafjorden, Norway 8 A17
Altagracia, Venezuela 120 A3
Altagracia de Orituco, Venezuela 120 B4
Altai = Aerhtai Shan, Mongolia 54 B4
Altai = Aerhtai Shan, Mongolia 54 B4
Altamachi →, Bolivia 124 D4
Altamaha →, U.S.A. 105 K5
Altamira, Brazil 121 D7
Altamira, Chile 126 B2
Altamira, Colombia 120 C2
Altamira, Mexico 115 C5
Altamira, Cuevas de, Spain 30 B6
Altamont, U.S.A. 107 D10
Altamura, Italy 35 B9
Altanbulag, Mongolia 54 A5
Altar, Mexico 114 A2
Altata, Mexico 114 C3
Altavista, U.S.A. 104 G6
Altay, China 54 B3
Altdorf, Switz. 23 C7
Alte Mellum, Germany 18 B4
Altea, Spain 29 G4
Altenberg, Germany 18 E9
Altenbruch, Germany 18 B4
Altenburg, Germany 18 E8
Altenkirchen, Mecklenburg-Vorpommern, Germany 18 A9
Altenkirchen, Rhld-Pfz., Germany 18 E3
Altenteptow, Germany 18 B9
Alter do Chão, Portugal 31 F3
Altıntas, Turkey 66 D4
Altiplano, Bolivia 124 D4
Altkirch, France 25 E14
Altmühl →, Germany 19 G7
Alto Adige = Trentino-Alto Adige □, Italy 32 B8
Alto Araguaia, Brazil 125 D7
Alto Cuchumatanes = Cuchumatanes, Sierra de los, Guatemala 116 C1
Alto del Inca, Chile 126 A2
Alto Garças, Brazil 125 D7
Alto Iriri →, Brazil 125 B7
Alto Ligonha, Mozam. 83 F4
Alto Molocue, Mozam. 83 F4
Alto Paraguai, Brazil 125 C6
Alto Paraguay □, Paraguay 126 A4
Alto Paraná □, Paraguay 127 B5
Alto Parnaíba, Brazil 122 C2
Alto Purús →, Peru 124 B3
Alto Río Senguerr, Argentina 128 C2
Alto Santo, Brazil 122 C4
Alto Sucuriú, Brazil 125 D7
Alto Turi, Brazil 122 B2
Alton, Canada 106 C4
Alton, U.S.A. 108 F9
Alton Downs, Australia 91 D2
Altoona, U.S.A. 106 F6
Altopáscio, Italy 32 E7
Altos, Brazil 122 C3
Altötting, Germany 19 G8
Altstätten, Switz. 23 B9
Altūn Kūprī, Iraq 64 C5
Altun Shan, China 54 C3
Alturas, U.S.A. 110 F3
Altus, U.S.A. 109 H5
Alubijid, Phil. 55 G6
Alucra, Turkey 43 F8
Alūksne, Latvia 40 C5
Alūla, Somali Rep. 68 E5
Alunite, U.S.A. 113 K12
Alupka, Ukraine 42 D6
Alushta, Ukraine 42 D6
Alusi, Indonesia 57 F8
Alustante, Spain 28 E3
Al'Uzayr, Iraq 64 D5
Alva, U.S.A. 109 G5
Alvaiázere, Portugal 30 F2
Älvängen, Sweden 11 G6
Alvarado, Mexico 115 D5
Alvarado, U.S.A. 109 J6
Alvarães, Brazil 121 D5
Alvaro Obregón, Presa, Mexico 114 B3
Alvdal, Norway 10 B4
Alvear, Argentina 126 B4
Alverca, Portugal 31 G1
Alveringen, Belgium 17 F1
Alvesta, Sweden 9 H13
Alvie, Australia 91 F3
Alvin, U.S.A. 109 L7
Alvinston, Canada 106 D3
Alvito, Portugal 31 G3
Älvkarleby, Sweden 9 F14
Alvros, Sweden 10 B8
Älvsborgs län □, Sweden 11 F6
Älvsbyn, Sweden 8 D16
Älvsered, Sweden 11 G6
Alwar, India 62 F7
Alxa Zuoqi, China 50 E3
Alyaskitovyy, Russia 45 C15
Alyata, Azerbaijan 43 G13
Alyth, U.K. 14 E5
Alzada, U.S.A. 108 C2
Alzano Lombardo, Italy 32 C6
Alzette →, Lux. 17 J8
Alzey, Germany 19 F4
Am Dam, Chad 73 F9
Am-Timan, Chad 73 F9
Amacuro □, Venezuela 121 B5
Amadeus, L., Australia 89 D5
Amâdi, Sudan 77 F3
Amadi, Zaïre 82 B2
Amadjuak, Canada 97 B12
Amadjuak L., Canada 97 B12
Amadora, Portugal 31 G1
Amagasaki, Japan 49 G7
Amager, Denmark 11 J6
Amakusa-Shotō, Japan 49 H5
Amalfi, Colombia 120 B2
Amalfi, Italy 35 B7
Amaliás, Greece 39 M4
Amalner, India 60 J9
Amambaí, Brazil 127 A4
Amambaí →, Brazil 127 A5
Amambay □, Paraguay 127 A4
Amambay, Cordillera de, S. Amer. 127 A4
Amami-Guntō, Japan 49 L4
Amami-Ō-Shima, Japan 49 L4
Amana →, Venezuela 121 B5
Amaná, L., Brazil 121 D5
Amanda Park, U.S.A. 112 C3
Amándola, Italy 33 F10
Amangeldy, Kazakhstan 44 D7
Amantea, Italy 35 C9
Amapá, Brazil 121 C7
Amapá □, Brazil 121 C7
Amapari, Brazil 121 C7
Amara, Sudan 77 E3
Amarante, Brazil 122 C3
Amarante, Portugal 30 D2
Amarante do Maranhão, Brazil 122 C2
Amaranth, Canada 101 C9
Amareleja, Portugal 31 G3
Amargosa, Brazil 123 D4
Amargosa →, U.S.A. 113 J10
Amargosa Range, U.S.A. 113 J10
Amári, Greece 37 D6
Amarillo, U.S.A. 109 H4
Amaro, Mt., Italy 33 F11
Amaro Leite, Brazil 123 D2
Amarpur, India 63 G12
Amasra, Turkey 66 C5
Amassama, Nigeria 79 D6
Amasya, Turkey 66 C6
Amasya □, Turkey 66 C6
Amataurá, Brazil 120 D4
Amatikulu, S. Africa 85 D5
Amatitlán, Guatemala 116 D1
Amatrice, Italy 33 F10
Amay, Belgium 17 G6
Amazon = Amazonas →, S. Amer. 121 D7
Amazonas □, Brazil 125 B5
Amazonas □, Peru 124 B2
Amazonas □, Venezuela 120 C4
Amazonas →, S. Amer. 121 D7
Ambahakily, Madag. 85 C7
Ambala, India 62 D7
Ambalavao, Madag. 85 C8
Ambalindum, Australia 90 C2
Ambam, Cameroon 80 D2
Ambanja, Madag. 85 A8
Ambarchik, Russia 45 C17
Ambarijeby, Madag. 85 A8
Ambaro, Helodranon', Madag. 85 A8
Ambartsevo, Russia 44 D9
Ambato, Ecuador 120 D2
Ambato, Sierra de, Argentina 126 B2
Ambato Boeny, Madag. 85 B8
Ambatofinandrahana, Madag. 85 C8
Ambatolampy, Madag. 85 B8
Ambatondrazaka, Madag. 85 B8
Ambatosoratra, Madag. 85 B8
Ambenja, Madag. 85 B8
Amberg, Germany 19 F7
Ambergris Cay, Belize 115 D7
Ambérieu-en-Bugey, France 27 C9
Amberley, N.Z. 87 K4
Ambert, France 26 C7
Ambidédi, Mali 78 C2
Ambikapur, India 63 H10
Ambikol, Sudan 76 C3
Ambilobé, Madag. 85 A8
Ambinanindrano, Madag. 85 C8
Ambjörnarp, Sweden 11 G7
Ambleside, U.K. 12 C5
Amblève, Belgium 17 H8
Amblève →, Belgium 17 H7
Ambo, Ethiopia 77 E4
Ambo, Peru 124 C2
Ambodifototra, Madag. 85 B8
Ambodilazana, Madag. 85 B8
Ambohimahasoa, Madag. 85 C8
Ambohimanga, Madag. 85 C8
Ambohitra, Madag. 85 A8
Ambon, Indonesia 57 E7
Amboseli L., Kenya 82 C4
Ambositra, Madag. 85 C8
Ambovombé, Madag. 85 D8
Amboy, U.S.A. 113 L11
Amboyna I., S. China Sea 56 C4
Ambridge, U.S.A. 106 F4
Ambriz, Angola 80 F2
Amby, Australia 91 D4
Amchitka I., U.S.A. 96 C1
Amderma, Russia 44 C7
Ameca, Mexico 114 C4
Ameca →, Mexico 114 C3
Amecameca, Mexico 115 D5
Ameland, Neths. 16 B7
Amélia, Italy 33 F9
Amélie-les-Bains-Palalda, France 26 F6
Amen, Russia 45 C18
Amendolaro, Italy 35 C9
America, Neths. 17 F7
American Falls, U.S.A. 110 E7
American Falls Reservoir, U.S.A. 110 E7
American Highland, Antarctica 5 D6
American Samoa ■, Pac. Oc. 87 B13
Americana, Brazil 127 A6
Americus, U.S.A. 105 J3
Amersfoort, Neths. 16 D6
Amersfoort, S. Africa 85 D4
Amery, Australia 89 F2
Amery, Canada 101 B10
Amery Ice Shelf, Antarctica 5 C6
Ames, U.S.A. 108 E8
Amesbury, U.S.A. 107 D14
Amfíklia, Greece 39 L5
Amfilokhía, Greece 39 L4
Amga, Russia 45 C14
Amga →, Russia 45 C14
Amgu, Russia 45 E14
Amgun →, Russia 45 D14
Amherst, Burma 61 L20
Amherst, Canada 99 C7
Amherst, Mass., U.S.A. 107 D12
Amherst, N.Y., U.S.A. 106 D6
Amherst, Ohio, U.S.A. 106 E2
Amherst, Tex., U.S.A. 109 H3
Amherst I., Canada 107 B8
Amherstburg, Canada 98 D3
Amiata, Mte., Italy 33 F8
Amiens, France 25 C9
Amindaion, Greece 39 J4
Amīrābād, Iran 64 C5
Amirante Is., Seychelles 3 E12
Amisk L., Canada 101 C8
Amistad, Presa de la, Mexico 114 B4
Amite, U.S.A. 109 K9
Amizmiz, Morocco 74 B3
Åmli, Norway 11 F2
Amlwch, U.K. 12 D3
Amm Adam, Sudan 77 D4
'Ammān, Jordan 69 D4
Ammanford, U.K. 13 F3
Ammassalik = Angmagssalik, Greenland 4 C6
Ammerån, Sweden 10 A10
Ammerån →, Sweden 10 A10
Ammersee, Germany 19 G7
Ammerzoden, Neths. 16 E6
Amnat Charoen, Thailand 58 E5
Amo Jiang →, China 52 F3
Āmol, Iran 65 B7
Amorebieta, Spain 28 B2

Amorgós, Greece	39	N8	
Amory, U.S.A.	105	J1	
Amos, Canada	98	C4	
Åmot, Buskerud, Norway	10	E3	
Åmot, Telemark, Norway	10	E2	
Åmotsdal, Norway	10	E2	
Amour, Djebel, Algeria	75	B5	
Amoy = Xiamen, China	53	E12	
Ampang, Malaysia	59	L3	
Ampanihy, Madag.	85	C7	
Ampasindava, Helodranon', Madag.	85	A8	
Ampasindava, Saikanosy, Madag.	85	A8	
Ampato, Nevado, Peru	124	D3	
Ampenan, Indonesia	56	F5	
Amper, Nigeria	79	D6	
Amper →, Germany	19	G7	
Ampère, Algeria	75	A6	
Ampezzo, Italy	33	B9	
Amposta, Spain	28	E5	
Ampotaka, Madag.	85	D7	
Ampoza, Madag.	85	C7	
Amqui, Canada	99	C6	
Amravati, India	60	J10	
Amreli, India	62	J4	
Amrenene el Kasba, Algeria	75	D5	
Amriswil, Switz.	23	A8	
Amritsar, India	62	D6	
Amroha, India	63	E8	
Amrum, Germany	18	A4	
Amsel, Algeria	75	D6	
Amsterdam, Neths.	16	D5	
Amsterdam, U.S.A.	107	D10	
Amsterdam, I., Ind. Oc.	3	F13	
Amstetten, Austria	21	G4	
Amudarya →, Uzbekistan	44	E6	
Amundsen Gulf, Canada	96	A7	
Amundsen Sea, Antarctica	5	D15	
Amuntai, Indonesia	56	E5	
Amur →, Russia	45	D15	
Amurang, Indonesia	57	D6	
Amuri Pass, N.Z.	87	K4	
Amurrio, Spain	28	B1	
Amursk, Russia	45	D14	
Amurzet, Russia	45	E14	
Amusco, Spain	30	C6	
Amvrakikós Kólpos, Greece	39	L4	
Amvrosiyevka, Ukraine	43	C8	
Amyderya → Amudarya →, Uzbekistan	44	E6	
Amzeglouf, Algeria	75	C5	
An Bien, Vietnam	59	H5	
An Hoa, Vietnam	58	E7	
An Khe, Vietnam	58	F7	
An Nabatīyah at Tahta, Lebanon	69	B4	
An Nabk, Si. Arabia	64	D3	
An Nabk, Syria	69	A5	
An Nabk Abū Qaşr, Si. Arabia	64	D3	
An Nafūd, Si. Arabia	64	D4	
An Najaf, Iraq	64	C5	
An Nāşirīyah, Iraq	64	D5	
An Nhon, Vietnam	58	F7	
An Nîl □, Sudan	76	D3	
An Nîl el Abyad □, Sudan	77	E3	
An Nîl el Azraq □, Sudan	77	E3	
An Nu'ayrīyah, Si. Arabia	65	E6	
An Nuwayb'ī, W. →, Si. Arabia	69	F3	
An Thoi, Dao, Vietnam	59	H4	
An Uaimh, Ireland	15	C5	
Anabar →, Russia	45	B12	
'Anabtā, Jordan	69	C4	
Anaco, Venezuela	121	B5	
Anaconda, U.S.A.	110	C7	
Anacortes, U.S.A.	112	B4	
Anacuao, Mt., Phil.	55	C4	
Anadarko, U.S.A.	109	H5	
Anadia, Brazil	122	C4	
Anadia, Portugal	30	E2	
Anadolu, Turkey	66	D4	
Anadyr, Russia	45	C18	
Anadyr →, Russia	45	C18	
Anadyrskiy Zaliv, Russia	45	C19	
Anáfi, Greece	39	N8	
Anafópoulo, Greece	39	N8	
Anaga, Pta. de, Canary Is.	36	F3	
Anagni, Italy	34	A6	
'Ānah, Iraq	64	C4	
Anaheim, U.S.A.	113	M9	
Anahim Lake, Canada	100	C3	
Anáhuac, Mexico	114	B4	
Anajás, Brazil	122	B2	
Anajatuba, Brazil	122	B3	
Anakapalle, India	61	L13	
Anakie, Australia	90	C4	
Anaklia, Georgia	43	E9	
Analalava, Madag.	85	A8	
Análipsis, Greece	37	A3	
Anamã, Brazil	121	D5	
Anambar →, Pakistan	62	D3	
Anambas, Kepulauan, Indonesia	56	D3	
Anambas Is. = Anambas, Kepulauan, Indonesia	56	D3	
Anambra □, Nigeria	79	D6	
Anamoose, U.S.A.	108	B4	
Anamosa, U.S.A.	108	D9	
Anamur, Turkey	66	E5	
Anamur Burnu, Turkey	66	E5	
Anan, Japan	49	H7	
Anand, India	62	H5	
Anantnag, India	63	C6	
Ananyev, Ukraine	42	C3	
Anapa, Russia	42	D7	
Anapodháris →, Greece	37	E7	
Anápolis, Brazil	123	E2	
Anapu →, Brazil	121	D7	
Anār, Iran	65	D7	
Anārak, Iran	65	C7	
Anatolia = Anadolu, Turkey	66	D4	
Anatone, U.S.A.	110	C5	
Anatsogno, Madag.	85	C7	
Añatuya, Argentina	126	B3	
Anauá →, Brazil	121	C5	
Anaunethad L., Canada	101	A8	
Anavilhanas, Arquipélago das, Brazil	121	D5	
Anaye, Niger	73	E7	
Anbyŏn, N. Korea	51	E14	
Ancash □, Peru	124	B2	
Ancenis, France	24	E5	
Ancho, Canal, Chile	128	D2	
Anchor Bay, U.S.A.	112	G3	
Anchorage, U.S.A.	96	B5	
Anci, China	50	E9	
Ancohuma, Nevada, Bolivia	124	D4	
Ancón, Peru	124	C2	
Ancona, Italy	33	E10	
Ancud, Chile	128	B2	
Ancud, G. de, Chile	128	B2	
Andacollo, Argentina	126	D1	
Andacollo, Chile	126	C1	
Andado, Australia	90	D2	
Andahuaylas, Peru	124	C3	
Andalgalá, Argentina	126	B2	
Åndalsnes, Norway	10	B1	
Andalucía □, Spain	31	H6	
Andalusia, U.S.A.	105	K2	
Andalusia □ = Andalucía □, Spain	31	H6	
Andaman Is., Ind. Oc.	46	H13	
Andaman Sea, Ind. Oc.	56	B1	
Andara, Namibia	84	B3	
Andaraí, Brazil	123	D3	
Andeer, Switz.	23	C8	
Andelfingen, Switz.	23	A7	
Andelot, France	25	D12	
Andenne, Belgium	17	H6	
Anderanboukane, Mali	79	B5	
Anderlecht, Belgium	17	G4	
Anderlues, Belgium	17	H4	
Andermatt, Switz.	23	C7	
Andernach, Germany	18	E3	
Andernos-les-Bains, France	26	D2	
Anderslöv, Sweden	11	J7	
Anderson, Calif., U.S.A.	110	F2	
Anderson, Ind., U.S.A.	104	E3	
Anderson, Mo., U.S.A.	109	G2	
Anderson, S.C., U.S.A.	105	H4	
Anderson →, Canada	96	B7	
Anderson, Mt., S. Africa	85	D5	
Andes = Andes, Cord. de los, S. Amer.	124	C3	
Andes, S. Amer.	124	C2	
Andes, Cord. de los, S. Amer.	124	C3	
Andfjorden, Norway	8	B14	
Andhra Pradesh □, India	60	L11	
Andijon = Andizhan, Uzbekistan	44	E8	
Andíkíthira, Greece	39	P6	
Andīmeshk, Iran	65	C6	
Andímilos, Greece	39	N7	
Andíparos, Greece	39	N8	
Andizhan, Uzbekistan	44	E8	
Andoany, Madag.	85	A8	
Andoas, Peru	120	D2	
Andong, S. Korea	51	F15	
Andongwei, China	51	G10	
Andorra ■, Europe	28	C6	
Andorra La Vella, Andorra	28	C6	
Andover, U.K.	13	F6	
Andover, Mass., U.S.A.	107	D13	
Andover, N.Y., U.S.A.	106	D7	
Andover, Ohio, U.S.A.	106	E4	
Andradina, Brazil	123	F1	
Andrahary, Mt., Madag.	85	A8	
Andraitx, Spain	36	B9	
Andramasina, Madag.	85	B8	
Andranopasy, Madag.	85	C7	
Andreanof Is., U.S.A.	96	C2	
Andreapol, Russia	40	C8	
Andrespol, Poland	20	D9	
Andrewilla, Australia	91	D2	
Andrews, S.C., U.S.A.	105	J6	
Andrews, Tex., U.S.A.	109	J3	
Ándria, Italy	35	A9	
Andriba, Madag.	85	B8	
Andrijevica, Montenegro	21	N9	
Andrítsaina, Greece	39	M4	
Androka, Madag.	85	C7	
Andropov = Rybinsk, Russia	41	B11	
Ándros, Greece	39	M7	
Andros I., Bahamas	116	B4	
Andros Town, Bahamas	116	B4	
Andújar, Spain	31	G6	
Andulo, Angola	80	G3	
Anegada, B., Argentina	128	B4	
Anegada I., Virgin Is.	117	C7	
Anegada Passage, W. Indies	117	C7	
Aného, Togo	79	D5	
Añelo, Argentina	128	A3	
Anergane, Morocco	74	B3	
Aneto, Pico de, Spain	28	C5	
Añez, Bolivia	125	D5	
Anfu, China	53	D10	
Ang Thong, Thailand	58	E3	
Angamos, Punta, Chile	126	A1	
Ang'angxi, China	54	B7	
Angara →, Russia	45	D10	
Angarab, Ethiopia	77	E4	
Angarsk, Russia	45	D11	
Angas Downs, Australia	89	E5	
Angas Hills, Australia	88	D4	
Angaston, Australia	91	E2	
Ånge, Sweden	10	B9	
Ángel de la Guarda, I., Mexico	114	B2	
Angel Falls, Venezuela	121	B5	
Angeles, Phil.	55	D4	
Ängelholm, Sweden	11	H6	
Angellala, Australia	91	D4	
Angels Camp, U.S.A.	111	G3	
Anger →, Ethiopia	77	F4	
Angereb →, Ethiopia	77	E4	
Ångermanälven →, Sweden	10	B12	
Angermünde, Germany	18	B10	
Angers, Canada	107	A9	
Angers, France	24	E6	
Angerville, France	25	D8	
Ångesån →, Sweden	8	C17	
Anghiari, Italy	33	E9	
Angical, Brazil	123	D3	
Angikuni L., Canada	101	A9	
Angkor, Cambodia	58	F4	
Anglés, Spain	28	D7	
Anglesey, U.K.	12	D3	
Anglet, France	26	E2	
Angleton, U.S.A.	109	L7	
Angleur, Belgium	17	G7	
Anglin →, France	26	B4	
Anglisidhes, Cyprus	37	E12	
Anglure, France	25	D10	
Angmagssalik, Greenland	4	C6	
Ango, Zaïre	82	B2	
Angoche, Mozam.	83	F4	
Angoche, I., Mozam.	83	F4	
Angol, Chile	126	D1	
Angola, Ind., U.S.A.	104	E3	
Angola, N.Y., U.S.A.	106	D5	
Angola ■, Africa	81	G3	
Angoon, U.S.A.	100	B2	
Angoulême, France	26	C4	
Angoumois, France	26	C4	
Angra dos Reis, Brazil	127	A7	
Angren, Uzbekistan	44	E8	
Angtassom, Cambodia	59	G5	
Angu, Zaïre	82	B1	
Anguang, China	51	B12	
Anguilla ■, W. Indies	117	C7	
Anguo, China	50	E8	
Angurugu, Australia	90	A2	
Angus, Braes of, U.K.	14	E5	
Anhandui →, Brazil	127	A5	
Anhée, Belgium	17	H5	
Anholt, Denmark	11	H5	
Anhua, China	53	C8	
Anhui □, China	53	B11	
Anhwei □ = Anhui □, China	53	B11	
Anichab, Namibia	84	C1	
Anicuns, Brazil	123	E2	
Anidhros, Greece	39	N8	
Anie, Togo	79	D5	
Animas, U.S.A.	111	L9	
Ånimskog, Sweden	11	F6	
Anina, Romania	38	D4	
Anina, Madag.	85	B8	
Anjar, India	62	H4	
Anjidiv I., India	60	M9	
Anjou, France	24	E6	
Anjozorobe, Madag.	85	B8	
Anju, N. Korea	51	E13	
Anka, Nigeria	79	C6	
Ankaboa, Tanjona, Madag.	85	C7	
Ankang, China	50	H5	
Ankara, Turkey	66	D5	
Ankara □, Turkey	66	D5	
Ankaramena, Madag.	85	C8	
Ankazoabo, Madag.	85	C7	
Ankazobe, Madag.	85	B8	
Ankisabe, Madag.	85	B8	
Anklam, Germany	18	B9	
Ankober, Ethiopia	77	F4	
Ankoro, Zaïre	82	D2	
Anlong, China	52	E5	
Anlu, China	53	B9	
Anmyŏn-do, S. Korea	51	F14	
Ånn, Sweden	10	A6	
Ann, C., U.S.A.	107	D14	
Ann Arbor, U.S.A.	104	D4	
Anna, Russia	41	F12	
Anna, U.S.A.	109	G10	
Anna Plains, Australia	88	C3	
Anna Regina, Guyana	121	B6	
Annaba, Algeria	75	A6	
Annaberg-Buchholz, Germany	18	E8	
Annalee →, Ireland	15	B4	
Annam = Trung-Phan, Vietnam	58	E7	
Annamitique, Chaîne, Asia	58	D6	
Annan, U.K.	14	G5	
Annan →, U.K.	14	G5	
Annapolis, U.S.A.	104	F7	
Annapolis Royal, Canada	99	D6	
Annapurna, Nepal	63	E10	
Annean, L., Australia	89	E2	
Anneberg, Sweden	11	G6	
Annecy, France	27	C10	
Annecy, L. d', France	27	C10	
Annemasse, France	27	B10	
Anning, China	52	E4	
Anningie, Australia	88	D5	
Anniston, U.S.A.	105	J3	
Annobón, Atl. Oc.	71	G4	
Annonay, France	27	C8	
Annot, France	27	E10	
Annotto Bay, Jamaica	116	C4	
Annuello, Australia	91	E3	
Annville, U.S.A.	107	F8	
Annweiler, Germany	19	F3	
Áno Viánnos, Greece	37	D7	
Anoka, U.S.A.	108	C8	
Anorotsangana, Madag.	85	A8	
Anóyia, Greece	37	D6	
Anping, Hebei, China	50	E8	
Anping, Liaoning, China	51	D12	
Anpu Gang, China	52	G7	
Anqing, China	53	B11	
Anqiu, China	51	F10	
Anren, China	53	D9	
Ans, Belgium	17	G7	
Ansai, China	50	F5	
Ansbach, Germany	19	F6	
Anseba →, Eritrea	77	D4	
Anserma, Colombia	120	B2	
Anseroeul, Belgium	17	G3	
Anshan, China	54	B7	
Anshan, Liaoning, China	51	D12	
Anshun, China	52	D5	
Ansião, Portugal	30	F2	
Ansirabe, Madag.	85	B8	
Ansley, U.S.A.	108	E5	
Ansó, Spain	28	C4	
Anson, U.S.A.	109	J5	
Anson B., Australia	88	B5	
Ansongo, Mali	79	B5	
Ansonia, U.S.A.	107	E11	
Anstruther, U.K.	14	E6	
Ansudu, Indonesia	57	E9	
Antabamba, Peru	124	C3	
Antakya, Turkey	66	E7	
Antalaha, Madag.	85	A9	
Antalya, Turkey	66	E4	
Antalya □, Turkey	66	E4	
Antalya Körfezi, Turkey	66	E4	
Antananarivo, Madag.	85	B8	
Antananarivo □, Madag.	85	B8	
Antanimbaribe, Madag.	85	C7	
Antarctic Pen., Antarctica	5	C18	
Antarctica	5	E3	
Antelope, Zimbabwe	83	G2	
Antenor Navarro, Brazil	122	C4	
Antequera, Paraguay	126	A4	
Antequera, Spain	31	H6	
Antero, Mt., U.S.A.	111	G10	
Anthony, Kans., U.S.A.	109	G5	
Anthony, N. Mex., U.S.A.	111	K10	
Anthony Lagoon, Australia	90	B2	
Anti Atlas, Morocco	74	C2	
Anti-Lebanon = Ash Sharqi, Al Jabal, Lebanon	69	B5	
Antibes, France	27	E11	
Antibes, C. d', France	27	E11	
Anticosti, I. d', Canada	99	C7	
Antifer, C. d', France	24	C7	
Antigo, U.S.A.	108	C10	
Antigonish, Canada	99	C7	
Antigua, Canary Is.	36	F5	
Antigua, Guatemala	116	D1	
Antigua, W. Indies	117	C7	
Antigua & Barbuda ■, W. Indies	117	C7	
Antilla, Cuba	116	B4	
Antimony, U.S.A.	111	G8	
Antioch, U.S.A.	112	G5	
Antioche, Pertuis d', France	26	B2	
Antioquia, Colombia	120	B2	
Antioquia □, Colombia	120	B2	
Antipodes Is., Pac. Oc.	92	M9	
Antler, U.S.A.	108	A4	
Antler →, Canada	101	D8	
Antlers, U.S.A.	109	H7	
Antofagasta, Chile	126	A1	
Antofagasta □, Chile	126	A2	
Antofagasta de la Sierra, Argentina	126	B2	
Antofalla, Argentina	126	B2	
Antofalla, Salar de, Argentina	126	B2	
Antoing, Belgium	17	G2	
Anton, U.S.A.	109	J3	
Anton Chico, U.S.A.	111	J11	
Antongila, Helodrano, Madag.	85	B8	
Antonibé, Madag.	85	B8	
Antonibé, Presqu'île d', Madag.	85	A8	
Antonina, Brazil	127	B6	
Antonito, U.S.A.	111	H10	
Antonovo, Kazakhstan	43	B14	
Antrain, France	24	D5	
Antrim, U.K.	15	B5	
Antrim □, U.K.	15	B5	
Antrim, Mts. of, U.K.	15	B5	
Antrim Plateau, Australia	88	C4	
Antrodoco, Italy	33	F10	
Antropovo, Russia	41	B13	
Antsalova, Madag.	85	B7	
Antsiranana, Madag.	85	A8	
Antsohihy, Madag.	85	A8	
Antsohimbondrona Seranana, Madag.	85	A8	
Antu, China	51	C15	
Antwerp = Antwerpen, Belgium	17	F4	
Antwerp, U.S.A.	107	B9	
Antwerpen, Belgium	17	F4	
Antwerpen □, Belgium	17	F5	
Anupgarh, India	62	E5	
Anuradhapura, Sri Lanka	60	Q12	
Anveh, Iran	65	E7	
Anvers = Antwerpen, Belgium	17	F4	
Anvers I., Antarctica	5	C17	
Anxi, Fujian, China	53	E12	
Anxi, Gansu, China	54	B4	
Anxiang, China	53	C9	
Anxious B., Australia	91	E1	
Anyama, Ivory C.	78	D4	
Anyang, China	50	F8	
Anyi, Jiangxi, China	53	C10	
Anyi, Shanxi, China	50	G6	
Anyuan, China	53	E10	
Anza, U.S.A.	113	M10	
Anze, China	50	F7	
Anzhero-Sudzhensk, Russia	44	D9	
Ánzio, Italy	34	A5	
Anzoátegui □, Venezuela	121	B5	
Aoga-Shima, Japan	49	H9	
Aoiz, Spain	28	C3	
Aomori, Japan	48	D10	
Aomori □, Japan	48	D10	
Aonla, India	63	E8	
Aosta, Italy	32	C4	
Aoudéras, Niger	79	B6	
Aouinet Torkoz, Morocco	74	C3	
Aoukar, Mali	74	D4	
Aouker, Mauritania	78	B3	
Aoulef el Arab, Algeria	75	C5	
Apa →, S. Amer.	126	A4	
Apache, U.S.A.	109	H5	
Apalachee B., U.S.A.	105	L3	
Apalachicola, U.S.A.	105	L3	
Apalachicola →, U.S.A.	105	L3	
Apapa, Nigeria	79	D5	
Apaporis →, Colombia	120	D4	
Aparecida do Taboado, Brazil	123	F1	
Aparri, Phil.	55	B4	
Apazurén, Venezuela	121	B5	
Apateu, Romania	38	C4	
Apatin, Serbia	21	K8	
Apatzingán, Mexico	114	D4	
Apeldoorn, Neths.	16	D7	
Apeldoornsch Kanal →, Neths.	16	D8	
Apen, Germany	18	B3	
Apennines = Appennini, Italy	32	D7	
Apere →, Bolivia	125	C4	
Apia, W. Samoa	87	A13	
Apiacás, Serra dos, Brazil	125	B6	
Apiaú →, Brazil	121	C5	
Apiaú, Serra do, Brazil	121	C5	
Apidiá →, Brazil	125	C5	
Apinajé, Brazil	123	D2	
Apizaco, Mexico	115	D5	
Aplao, Peru	124	D3	
Apo, Mt., Phil.	57	C7	
Apodi, Brazil	122	C4	
Apolakkiá, Greece	37	C9	
Apolakkiá, Órmos, Greece	37	C9	
Apolda, Germany	18	D7	
Apollonia = Marsá Susah, Libya	73	B9	
Apollonia, Greece	39	N7	
Apolo, Bolivia	124	C4	
Apónguao →, Venezuela	121	C5	
Aporé, Brazil	125	D7	
Aporé →, Brazil	123	E1	
Apostle Is., U.S.A.	108	B9	
Apóstoles, Argentina	127	B4	
Apostolos Andreas, C., Cyprus	37	D13	
Apostolovo, Ukraine	42	C5	
Apoteri, Guyana	121	C6	
Appalachian Mts., U.S.A.	104	G6	
Appelscha, Neths.	16	C8	
Appennini, Italy	32	D7	
Appennino Ligure, Italy	32	D5	
Appenzell, Switz.	23	B8	
Appenzell-Ausser Rhoden □, Switz.	23	B8	
Appenzell-Inner Rhoden □, Switz.	23	B8	
Appiano, Italy	33	B8	
Appingedam, Neths.	16	B9	
Apple Hill, Canada	107	A10	
Apple Valley, U.S.A.	113	L9	
Appleby, U.K.	12	C5	
Appleton, U.S.A.	104	C1	
Approuague, Fr. Guiana	121	C7	
Approuague →, Fr. Guiana	121	C7	
Apricena, Italy	35	A8	
Aprigliano, Italy	35	C9	
Aprília, Italy	34	A5	
Apsheronsk, Russia	43	D8	
Apt, France	27	E9	

Apuane, Alpi, *Italy*	32	D7
Apuaú, *Brazil*	121	D5
Apucarana, *Brazil*	127	A5
Apulia = Púglia □, *Italy*	35	B9
Apure □, *Venezuela*	120	B4
Apure →, *Venezuela*	120	B4
Apurímac □, *Peru*	124	C3
Apurímac →, *Peru*	124	C3
Apuseni, Munţii, *Romania*	38	C5
Aqabah = Al 'Aqabah, *Jordan*	69	F4
'Aqabah, Khalīj al, *Red Sea*	69	D2
'Aqdā, *Iran*	65	C7
Aqīq, *Sudan*	76	D4
Aqīq, Khalīg, *Sudan*	76	D4
Aqmola = Tselinograd, *Kazakhstan*	44	D8
Aqrah, *Iraq*	64	B4
Aqtöbe = Aktyubinsk, *Kazakhstan*	44	D6
Aquidauana, *Brazil*	125	E6
Aquidauana →, *Brazil*	125	D6
Aquiles Serdán, *Mexico*	114	B3
Aquin, *Haiti*	117	C5
Ar Rachidiya, *Morocco*	74	B4
Ar Rafīd, *Syria*	69	C4
Ar Raḥḥālīyah, *Iraq*	64	C4
Ar Ramādī, *Iraq*	64	C4
Ar Ramthā, *Jordan*	69	C5
Ar Raqqah, *Syria*	64	C3
Ar Rass, *Si. Arabia*	64	E4
Ar Rifā'i, *Iraq*	64	D5
Ar Riyāḍ, *Si. Arabia*	64	E5
Ar Ru'ays, *Qatar*	65	E6
Ar Rukhaymīyah, *Iraq*	64	D5
Ar Ruqayyidah, *Si. Arabia*	65	E6
Ar Ruṣāfah, *Syria*	64	C3
Ar Ruṭbah, *Iraq*	64	C4
Ara, *India*	63	G11
'Arab, Bahr el →, *Sudan*	77	F2
Arab, Khalīg el, *Egypt*	76	H6
'Arabābād, *Iran*	65	C8
Araban, *Turkey*	67	E7
Arabatskaya Strelka, *Ukraine*	42	D6
Arabba, *Italy*	33	B8
Arabelo, *Venezuela*	121	C5
Arabia, *Asia*	68	C4
Arabian Desert = Es Sahrâ' Esh Sharqîya, *Egypt*	76	B3
Arabian Gulf = Gulf, The, *Asia*	65	E6
Arabian Sea, *Ind. Oc.*	46	H10
Araç, *Turkey*	66	C5
Aracaju, *Brazil*	122	D4
Aracataca, *Colombia*	120	A3
Aracati, *Brazil*	122	B4
Araçatuba, *Brazil*	127	A5
Aracena, *Spain*	31	H4
Aracena, Sierra de, *Spain*	31	H4
Araçuaí, *Brazil*	123	E3
Araçuaí →, *Brazil*	123	E3
'Arad, *Israel*	69	D4
Arad, *Romania*	38	C4
Arada, *Chad*	73	F9
Aradhippou, *Cyprus*	37	E12
Arafura Sea, *E. Indies*	57	F8
Aragarças, *Brazil*	125	D7
Aragats, *Armenia*	43	F11
Aragón □, *Spain*	28	D4
Aragón →, *Spain*	28	C3
Aragona, *Italy*	34	E6
Aragua □, *Venezuela*	120	B4
Aragua de Barcelona, *Venezuela*	121	B5
Araguacema, *Brazil*	122	C2
Araguaçu, *Brazil*	123	D2
Araguaia →, *Brazil*	122	C2
Araguaiana, *Brazil*	125	D7
Araguaína, *Brazil*	122	C2
Araguari, *Brazil*	123	E2
Araguari →, *Brazil*	121	C8
Araguatins, *Brazil*	122	C2
Araioses, *Brazil*	122	B3
Arak, *Algeria*	75	C5
Arāk, *Iran*	65	C6
Arakan Coast, *Burma*	61	K19
Arakan Yoma, *Burma*	61	K19
Arakli, *Turkey*	67	C9
Araks = Aras, Rūd-e →, *Iran*	64	B5
Aral Sea = Aralskoye More, *Asia*	44	E7
Aralsk, *Kazakhstan*	44	E7
Aralskoye More, *Asia*	44	E7
Aramac, *Australia*	90	C4
Arambag, *India*	63	H12
Aran I., *Ireland*	15	B3
Aran Is., *Ireland*	15	C2
Aranda de Duero, *Spain*	28	D1
Arandān, *Iran*	64	C5
Aranjuez, *Spain*	30	E7
Aranos, *Namibia*	84	C2
Aransas Pass, *U.S.A.*	109	M6
Aranzazu, *Colombia*	120	B2
Araouane, *Mali*	78	B4
Arapahoe, *U.S.A.*	108	E5
Arapari, *Brazil*	122	C2
Arapey Grande →, *Uruguay*	126	C4
Arapiraca, *Brazil*	122	C4
Arapkir, *Turkey*	67	D8
Arapongas, *Brazil*	127	A5
Ar'ar, *Si. Arabia*	64	D4

Araracuara, *Colombia*	120	D3
Araranguá, *Brazil*	127	B6
Araraquara, *Brazil*	123	F2
Araras, Serra das, *Brazil*	127	B5
Ararat, *Australia*	91	F3
Ararat, Mt. = Ağrı Dağı, *Turkey*	67	D11
Arari, *Brazil*	122	B3
Araria, *India*	63	F12
Araripe, Chapada do, *Brazil*	122	C3
Araripina, *Brazil*	122	C3
Araruama, L. de, *Brazil*	123	F3
Araruna, *Brazil*	122	C4
Aras, Rūd-e →, *Iran*	64	B5
Araticu, *Brazil*	122	B2
Arauca, *Colombia*	120	B3
Arauca □, *Colombia*	120	B3
Arauca →, *Venezuela*	120	B4
Arauco, *Chile*	126	D1
Arauco □, *Chile*	126	D1
Araújos, *Brazil*	123	E2
Arauquita, *Colombia*	120	B3
Araure, *Venezuela*	120	B4
Arawa, *Ethiopia*	77	F5
Araxá, *Brazil*	123	E2
Araya, Pen. de, *Venezuela*	121	A5
Arba Minch, *Ethiopia*	77	F4
Arbat, *Iraq*	64	C5
Arbatax, *Italy*	34	C2
Arbaza, *Russia*	45	D10
Arbedo, *Switz.*	23	D8
Arbīl, *Iraq*	64	B5
Arbois, *France*	25	F12
Arboletes, *Colombia*	120	B2
Arbon, *Switz.*	23	A8
Arbore, *Ethiopia*	77	F4
Arborea, *Italy*	34	C1
Arborfield, *Canada*	101	C8
Arborg, *Canada*	101	C9
Arbrå, *Sweden*	10	C10
Arbroath, *U.K.*	14	E6
Arbuckle, *U.S.A.*	112	F4
Arbus, *Italy*	34	C1
Arbuzinka, *Ukraine*	42	C4
Arc, *France*	25	E12
Arc →, *France*	27	C10
Arcachon, *France*	26	D2
Arcachon, Bassin d', *France*	26	D2
Arcade, *U.S.A.*	106	D6
Arcadia, *Fla., U.S.A.*	105	M5
Arcadia, *La., U.S.A.*	109	J8
Arcadia, *Nebr., U.S.A.*	108	E5
Arcadia, *Pa., U.S.A.*	106	F6
Arcadia, *Wis., U.S.A.*	108	C9
Arcata, *U.S.A.*	110	F1
Arcévia, *Italy*	33	E9
Archangel = Arkhangelsk, *Russia*	44	C5
Archar, *Bulgaria*	38	F5
Archbald, *U.S.A.*	107	E9
Archena, *Spain*	29	G3
Archer →, *Australia*	90	A3
Archer B., *Australia*	90	A3
Archers Post, *Kenya*	82	B4
Archidona, *Spain*	31	H6
Arci, Monte, *Italy*	34	C1
Arcidosso, *Italy*	33	F8
Arcila = Asilah, *Morocco*	74	A3
Arcis-sur-Aube, *France*	25	D11
Arckaringa, *Australia*	91	D1
Arckaringa Cr. →, *Australia*	91	D2
Arco, *Italy*	32	C7
Arco, *U.S.A.*	110	E7
Arcola, *Canada*	101	D8
Arcos, *Spain*	28	D2
Arcos de los Frontera, *Spain*	31	J5
Arcos de Valdevez, *Portugal*	30	D2
Arcot, *India*	60	N11
Arcoverde, *Brazil*	122	C4
Arctic Bay, *Canada*	97	A11
Arctic Ocean, *Arctic*	4	B18
Arctic Red River, *Canada*	96	B6
Arda →, *Bulgaria*	39	H9
Arda →, *Italy*	32	D6
Ardabīl, *Iran*	65	B6
Ardahan, *Turkey*	67	C10
Ardakān = Sepīdān, *Iran*	65	D7
Ardales, *Spain*	31	J6
Årdalstangen, *Norway*	10	C1
Ardatov, *Russia*	41	D15
Ardea, *Greece*	39	J5
Ardèche □, *France*	27	D8
Ardèche →, *France*	27	D8
Ardee, *Ireland*	15	C5
Arden, *Canada*	106	B8
Arden, *Denmark*	11	H3
Arden, *Calif., U.S.A.*	112	G5
Arden, *Nev., U.S.A.*	113	J11
Ardenne, *Belgium*	25	C12
Ardennes = Ardenne, *Belgium*	25	C12
Ardennes □, *France*	25	C11
Ardentes, *France*	25	F8
Ardeşen, *Turkey*	67	C9
Ardestān, *Iran*	65	C7
Árdhas →, *Greece*	39	H9
Ardila →, *Portugal*	31	G3
Ardlethan, *Australia*	91	E4
Ardmore, *Australia*	90	C2

Ardmore, *Okla., U.S.A.*	109	H6
Ardmore, *Pa., U.S.A.*	107	G9
Ardmore, *S. Dak., U.S.A.*	108	D3
Ardnacrusha, *Ireland*	15	D3
Ardnamurchan, Pt. of, *U.K.*	14	E2
Ardooie, *Belgium*	17	G2
Ardore Marina, *Italy*	35	D9
Ardres, *France*	25	B9
Ardrossan, *Australia*	91	E2
Ardrossan, *U.K.*	14	F4
Ards □, *U.K.*	15	B6
Ards Pen., *U.K.*	15	B6
Ardud, *Romania*	38	B5
Ardunac, *Turkey*	43	F10
Åre, *Sweden*	10	A7
Arecibo, *Puerto Rico*	117	C6
Areia Branca, *Brazil*	122	B4
Arena, Pt., *U.S.A.*	112	G3
Arenales, Cerro, *Chile*	128	C2
Arenápolis, *Brazil*	125	C6
Arenas, *Spain*	30	B6
Arenas de San Pedro, *Spain*	30	E5
Arendal, *Norway*	11	F2
Arendonk, *Belgium*	17	F6
Arendsee, *Germany*	18	C7
Arenillas, *Ecuador*	120	D1
Arenys de Mar, *Spain*	28	D7
Arenzano, *Italy*	32	D5
Areópolis, *Greece*	39	N5
Arequipa, *Peru*	124	D3
Arequipa □, *Peru*	124	D3
Arere, *Brazil*	121	D7
Arero, *Ethiopia*	77	G4
Arès, *France*	26	D2
Arévalo, *Spain*	30	D6
Arezzo, *Italy*	33	E8
Arga →, *Spain*	28	C3
Argalastí, *Greece*	39	K6
Argamakmur, *Indonesia*	56	E2
Argamasilla de Alba, *Spain*	29	F1
Arganda, *Spain*	28	E1
Arganil, *Portugal*	30	E2
Argelès-Gazost, *France*	26	F3
Argelès-sur-Mer, *France*	26	F7
Argens →, *France*	27	E10
Argent-sur-Sauldre, *France*	25	E9
Argenta, *Italy*	33	D8
Argentan, *France*	24	D6
Argentário, Mte., *Italy*	33	F8
Argentat, *France*	26	C5
Argentera, *Italy*	32	D3
Argentera, Monte del, *Italy*	32	D4
Argenteuil, *France*	25	D9
Argentia, *Canada*	99	C9
Argentiera, C. dell', *Italy*	34	B1
Argentière, Aiguilles d', *Switz.*	22	E4
Argentina ■, *S. Amer.*	128	B3
Argentina Is., *Antarctica*	5	C17
Argentino, L., *Argentina*	128	D2
Argenton-Château, *France*	24	F6
Argenton-sur-Creuse, *France*	26	B5
Argeş →, *Romania*	38	E9
Arghandab →, *Afghan.*	62	D1
Argo, *Sudan*	76	D3
Argolikós Kólpos, *Greece*	39	M5
Argonne, *France*	25	C12
Árgos, *Greece*	39	M5
Argostólion, *Greece*	39	L3
Arguedas, *Spain*	28	C3
Arguello, Pt., *U.S.A.*	113	L6
Arguineguín, *Canary Is.*	36	G4
Argun →, *Russia*	45	D13
Argungu, *Nigeria*	79	C5
Argus Pk., *U.S.A.*	113	K9
Argyle, *U.S.A.*	108	A6
Argyle, L., *Australia*	88	C4
Arhavi, *Turkey*	67	C9
Århus, *Denmark*	11	H4
Århus Amtskommune □, *Denmark*	11	H4
Ariadnoye, *Russia*	48	B7
Ariamsvlei, *Namibia*	84	D2
Ariana, *Tunisia*	75	A7
Ariano Irpino, *Italy*	35	A8
Ariano nel Polèsine, *Italy*	33	D9
Ariari →, *Colombia*	120	C3
Arica, *Chile*	124	D3
Arica, *Colombia*	120	D3
Arico, *Canary Is.*	36	F3
Arid, C., *Australia*	89	F3
Arida, *Japan*	49	G7
Ariège □, *France*	26	F5
Ariège →, *France*	26	E5
Arieş →, *Romania*	38	C6
Arīḥā, *Syria*	64	C3
Arīlla, Ákra, *Greece*	37	A3
Arima, *Trin. & Tob.*	117	D7
Arinos →, *Brazil*	125	C6
Ario de Rosales, *Mexico*	114	D4
Aripuanã, *Brazil*	125	B5
Aripuanã →, *Brazil*	125	B5
Ariquemes, *Brazil*	125	B5
Arisaig, *U.K.*	14	E3
Arîsh, W. el →, *Egypt*	76	H8
Arismendi, *Venezuela*	120	B4
Arissa, *Ethiopia*	77	E5
Aristazabal I., *Canada*	100	C3
Arivaca, *U.S.A.*	111	L8
Arivonimamo, *Madag.*	85	B8
Ariza, *Spain*	28	D2

Arizaro, Salar de, *Argentina*	126	A2
Arizona, *Argentina*	126	D2
Arizona □, *U.S.A.*	111	J8
Arizpe, *Mexico*	114	A2
Arjeplog, *Sweden*	8	C15
Arjona, *Colombia*	120	A2
Arjona, *Spain*	31	H6
Arjuno, *Indonesia*	57	G15
Arka, *Russia*	45	C15
Arkadak, *Russia*	41	F13
Arkadelphia, *U.S.A.*	109	H8
Arkalyk, *Kazakhstan*	44	D7
Arkansas □, *U.S.A.*	109	H8
Arkansas →, *U.S.A.*	109	J9
Arkansas City, *U.S.A.*	109	G6
Árkathos →, *Greece*	39	K4
Arkhángelos, *Greece*	37	C10
Arkhangelsk, *Russia*	44	C5
Arkhangelskoye, *Russia*	41	F12
Arkiko, *Eritrea*	77	D4
Arklow, *Ireland*	15	D5
Arkona, Kap, *Germany*	18	A9
Arkösund, *Sweden*	11	F10
Arkticheskiy, Mys, *Russia*	45	A10
Arkul, *Russia*	41	C17
Arlanc, *France*	26	C7
Arlanza →, *Spain*	30	C6
Arlanzón →, *Spain*	30	C6
Arlberg Pass, *Austria*	19	H6
Arlee, *U.S.A.*	110	C6
Arles, *France*	27	E8
Arlesheim, *Switz.*	22	B5
Arlington, *S. Africa*	85	D4
Arlington, *Oreg., U.S.A.*	110	D3
Arlington, *S. Dak., U.S.A.*	108	C6
Arlington, *Va., U.S.A.*	104	F7
Arlington, *Wash., U.S.A.*	112	B4
Arlon, *Belgium*	17	J7
Arlöv, *Sweden*	11	J7
Arly, *Burkina Faso*	79	C5
Armagh, *U.K.*	15	B5
Armagh □, *U.K.*	15	B5
Armagnac, *France*	26	E4
Armavir, *Russia*	43	D9
Armenia, *Colombia*	120	C2
Armenia ■, *Asia*	43	F11
Armenistís, Ákra, *Greece*	37	C9
Armentières, *France*	25	B9
Armidale, *Australia*	91	E5
Armour, *U.S.A.*	108	D5
Armstrong, *B.C., Canada*	100	C5
Armstrong, *Ont., Canada*	98	B2
Armstrong, *U.S.A.*	109	M6
Armstrong →, *Australia*	88	C5
Arnarfjörður, *Iceland*	8	D2
Arnaud →, *Canada*	97	B12
Arnauti, C., *Cyprus*	37	D11
Arnay-le-Duc, *France*	25	E11
Arnedillo, *Spain*	28	C2
Arnedo, *Spain*	28	C2
Arnemuiden, *Neths.*	17	F3
Árnes, *Iceland*	8	C3
Ärnes, *Norway*	10	D5
Arnett, *U.S.A.*	109	G5
Arnhem, *Neths.*	16	E7
Arnhem, C., *Australia*	90	A2
Arnhem B., *Australia*	90	A2
Arnhem Land, *Australia*	90	A1
Arno →, *Italy*	32	E7
Arno Bay, *Australia*	91	E2
Arnold, *Calif., U.S.A.*	112	G6
Arnold, *Nebr., U.S.A.*	108	E4
Arnoldstein, *Austria*	21	J3
Arnon →, *France*	25	E9
Arnot, *Canada*	101	B9
Arnøy, *Norway*	8	A16
Arnprior, *Canada*	98	C4
Arnsberg, *Germany*	18	D4
Arnstadt, *Germany*	18	E6
Aro →, *Venezuela*	121	B5
Aroab, *Namibia*	84	D2
Aroche, *Spain*	31	H4
Aroeiras, *Brazil*	122	C4
Arolla, *Switz.*	22	D4
Arolsen, *Germany*	18	D5
Aron →, *France*	26	B7
Arona, *Italy*	32	C5
Aroroy, *Phil.*	55	E5
Arosa, *Switz.*	23	C9
Arosa, Ria de, *Spain*	30	C2
Arpajon, *France*	25	D9
Arpajon-sur-Cère, *France*	26	D6
Arpino, *Italy*	34	A6
Arque, *Bolivia*	124	D4
Arrabury, *Australia*	91	D3
Arrah = Ara, *India*	63	G11
Arraias, *Brazil*	123	D2
Arraias →, *Mato Grosso, Brazil*	125	C7
Arraias →, *Pará, Brazil*	122	C2
Arraiolos, *Portugal*	31	G3
Arran, *U.K.*	14	F3
Arrandale, *Canada*	100	C3
Arras, *France*	25	B9
Arrats →, *France*	26	D4
Arreau, *France*	26	F4
Arrecife, *Canary Is.*	36	F6
Arrecifes, *Argentina*	126	C3
Arrée, Mts. d', *France*	24	D3
Arriaga, *Chiapas, Mexico*	115	D6
Arriaga, *San Luis Potosí, Mexico*	114	C4

Arrilalah P.O., *Australia*	90	C3
Arrino, *Australia*	89	E2
Arrojado →, *Brazil*	123	D3
Arromanches-les-Bains, *France*	24	C6
Arronches, *Portugal*	31	F3
Arros →, *France*	26	E3
Arrou, *France*	24	D8
Arrow, L., *Ireland*	15	B3
Arrow Rock Res., *U.S.A.*	110	E6
Arrowhead, *Canada*	100	C5
Arrowhead, L., *U.S.A.*	113	L9
Arrowtown, *N.Z.*	87	L2
Arroyo de la Luz, *Spain*	31	F4
Arroyo Grande, *U.S.A.*	113	K6
Års, *Denmark*	11	H3
Ars, *Iran*	64	B5
Ars-en-Ré, *France*	26	B2
Ars-sur-Moselle, *France*	25	C13
Arsenault L., *Canada*	101	B7
Arsenev, *Russia*	48	B6
Arsi □, *Ethiopia*	77	F4
Arsiero, *Italy*	33	C8
Arsin, *Turkey*	67	C8
Arsk, *Russia*	41	C16
Árta, *Greece*	39	K4
Artá, *Spain*	36	B10
Arteaga, *Mexico*	114	D4
Arteche, *Phil.*	55	E6
Arteijo, *Spain*	30	B2
Artem, *Russia*	48	C6
Artem, Ostrov, *Azerbaijan*	43	F14
Artemovsk, *Russia*	45	D10
Artemovsk, *Ukraine*	42	B8
Artemovski, *Russia*	43	C9
Artenay, *France*	25	D8
Artern, *Germany*	18	D7
Artesa de Segre, *Spain*	28	D6
Artesia = Mosomane, *Botswana*	84	C4
Artesia, *U.S.A.*	109	J2
Artesia Wells, *U.S.A.*	109	L5
Artesian, *U.S.A.*	108	C6
Arth, *Switz.*	23	B7
Arthez-de-Béarn, *France*	26	E3
Arthington, *Liberia*	78	D2
Arthur →, *Australia*	90	G3
Arthur Cr. →, *Australia*	90	C2
Arthur Pt., *Australia*	90	C5
Arthur's Pass, *N.Z.*	87	K3
Arthur's Town, *Bahamas*	117	B4
Artigas, *Uruguay*	126	C4
Artik, *Armenia*	43	F10
Artillery L., *Canada*	101	A7
Artois, *France*	25	B9
Artsiz, *Ukraine*	42	C3
Artvin, *Turkey*	43	F9
Artvin □, *Turkey*	67	C9
Aru, Kepulauan, *Indonesia*	57	F8
Aru Is. = Aru, Kepulauan, *Indonesia*	57	F8
Aru Meru □, *Tanzania*	82	C4
Arua, *Uganda*	82	B3
Aruanã, *Brazil*	123	D1
Aruba ■, *W. Indies*	117	D6
Arucas, *Canary Is.*	36	F4
Arudy, *France*	26	E3
Arumã, *Brazil*	121	D5
Arumpo, *Australia*	91	E3
Arun →, *Nepal*	63	F12
Arunachal Pradesh □, *India*	61	E19
Arusha, *Tanzania*	82	C4
Arusha □, *Tanzania*	82	C4
Arusha Chini, *Tanzania*	82	C4
Aruwimi →, *Zaïre*	82	B1
Arvada, *U.S.A.*	110	D10
Arvayheer, *Mongolia*	54	B10
Arve →, *France*	27	B10
Árvi, *Greece*	37	E7
Arvida, *Canada*	99	C5
Arvidsjaur, *Sweden*	8	D15
Arvika, *Sweden*	9	G12
Arvin, *U.S.A.*	113	K8
Arxan, *China*	54	B6
Aryiádhes, *Greece*	37	B3
Aryiroúpolis, *Greece*	37	D6
Arys, *Kazakhstan*	44	E7
Arzachena, *Italy*	34	A2
Arzamas, *Russia*	41	D13
Arzew, *Algeria*	75	A4
Arzgir, *Russia*	43	D11
Arzignano, *Italy*	33	C8
As, *Belgium*	17	F7
Aş Şafā, *Syria*	69	B6
'As Saffānīyah, *Si. Arabia*	65	D6
Aş Safīrah, *Syria*	64	B3
Aş Şahm, *Oman*	65	E8
As Sājir, *Si. Arabia*	64	E5
As Salamīyah, *Syria*	64	C3
As Salt, *Jordan*	69	C4
As Sal'w'a, *Qatar*	65	E6
As Samāwah, *Iraq*	64	D5
As Sanamayn, *Syria*	69	B5
As Sukhnah, *Syria*	64	C3
As Sulaymānīyah, *Iraq*	64	C5
As Sulaymī, *Si. Arabia*	64	E4
As Summān, *Si. Arabia*	64	E5
As Suwaydā, *Syria*	69	C5
As Suwaydā □, *Syria*	69	C5
As Suwayrah, *Iraq*	64	C5
Asab, *Namibia*	84	D2
Asaba, *Nigeria*	79	D6
Asafo, *Ghana*	78	D4

Name	Page	Grid
Asahi-Gawa →, Japan	49	G6
Asahigawa, Japan	48	C11
Asale, L., Ethiopia	77	E5
Asamankese, Ghana	79	D4
Asansol, India	63	H12
Åsarna, Sweden	10	B8
Asbe Teferi, Ethiopia	77	F5
Asbesberge, S. Africa	84	D3
Asbestos, Canada	99	C5
Asbury Park, U.S.A.	107	F10
Ascensión, Mexico	114	A3
Ascensión, B. de la, Mexico	115	D7
Ascension I., Atl. Oc.	2	E9
Aschaffenburg, Germany	19	F5
Aschendorf, Germany	18	B3
Aschersleben, Germany	18	D7
Asciano, Italy	33	E8
Áscoli Piceno, Italy	33	F10
Áscoli Satriano, Italy	35	A8
Ascona, Switz.	23	D7
Ascope, Peru	124	B2
Ascotán, Chile	126	A2
Aseb, Eritrea	68	E3
Asedjrad, Algeria	75	D5
Asela, Ethiopia	77	F4
Asenovgrad, Bulgaria	39	G7
Asfeld, France	25	C11
Asfûn el Matâ'na, Egypt	76	B3
Åsgårdstrand, Norway	10	E4
Asgata, Cyprus	37	E12
Ash Fork, U.S.A.	111	J7
Ash Grove, U.S.A.	109	G8
Ash Shamâl □, Lebanon	69	A5
Ash Shāmīyah, Iraq	64	D5
Ash Shāriqah, U.A.E.	65	E7
Ash Sharmah, Si. Arabia	64	D2
Ash Sharqāt, Iraq	64	C4
Ash Sharqi, Al Jabal, Lebanon	69	B5
Ash Shaṭrah, Iraq	64	D5
Ash Shawbak, Jordan	64	D2
Ash Shawmari, J., Jordan	69	E5
Ash Shaykh, J., Lebanon	69	B4
Ash Shināfīyah, Iraq	64	D5
Ash Shu'aybah, Si. Arabia	64	E5
Ash Shumlūl, Si. Arabia	64	E5
Ash Shūr'a, Iraq	64	C4
Ash Shurayf, Si. Arabia	64	E3
Ash Shuwayfāt, Lebanon	69	B4
Ashanti □, Ghana	79	D4
Ashau, Vietnam	58	D6
Ashburn, U.S.A.	105	K4
Ashburton, N.Z.	87	K3
Ashburton →, Australia	88	D1
Ashburton Downs, Australia	88	D2
Ashby de la Zouch, U.K.	12	E6
Ashcroft, Canada	100	C4
Ashdod, Israel	69	D3
Asheboro, U.S.A.	105	H6
Asherton, U.S.A.	109	L5
Asheville, U.S.A.	105	H4
Asheweig →, Canada	98	B2
Ashford, Australia	91	D5
Ashford, U.K.	13	F8
Ashford, U.S.A.	110	C2
Ashgabat = Ashkhabad, Turkmenistan	44	F6
Ashibetsu, Japan	48	C11
Ashikaga, Japan	49	F9
Ashizuri-Zaki, Japan	49	H6
Ashkarkot, Afghan.	62	C2
Ashkhabad, Turkmenistan	44	F6
Ashland, Kans., U.S.A.	109	G5
Ashland, Ky., U.S.A.	104	F4
Ashland, Maine, U.S.A.	99	B6
Ashland, Mont., U.S.A.	110	D10
Ashland, Nebr., U.S.A.	108	E6
Ashland, Ohio, U.S.A.	106	F2
Ashland, Oreg., U.S.A.	110	E2
Ashland, Pa., U.S.A.	107	F8
Ashland, Va., U.S.A.	104	G7
Ashland, Wis., U.S.A.	108	B9
Ashley, N. Dak., U.S.A.	108	B5
Ashley, Pa., U.S.A.	107	E9
Ashmont, Canada	100	C6
Ashmore Reef, Australia	88	B3
Ashmûn, Egypt	76	H7
Ashq'elon, Israel	69	D3
Ashtabula, U.S.A.	106	E4
Ashton, S. Africa	84	E3
Ashton, U.S.A.	110	D8
Ashton under Lyne, U.K.	12	D5
Ashuanipi, L., Canada	99	B6
Asia	46	E11
Asia, Kepulauan, Indonesia	57	D8
Āsīā Bak, Iran	65	C6
Asiago, Italy	33	C8
Asidonhoppo, Surinam	121	C6
Asifabad, India	60	K11
Asike, Indonesia	57	F10
Asilah, Morocco	74	A3
Asinara, Italy	34	A1
Asinara, G. dell', Italy	34	B1
Asino, Russia	44	D9
'Asīr □, Si. Arabia	68	D3
Asir, Ras, Somali Rep.	68	E5
Aşkale, Turkey	67	D9
Asker, Norway	10	E4
Askersund, Sweden	11	F8
Askham, S. Africa	84	D3
Askim, Norway	10	E5
Askja, Iceland	8	D5
Asl, Egypt	76	J8
Asmara = Asmera, Eritrea	77	D4
Asmera, Eritrea	77	D4
Asnæs, Denmark	11	J5
Asni, Morocco	74	B3
Ásola, Italy	32	C7
Asoteriba, Jebel, Sudan	76	C4
Asotin, U.S.A.	110	C5
Aspe, Spain	29	G4
Aspen, U.S.A.	111	G10
Aspendos, Turkey	66	E4
Aspermont, U.S.A.	109	J4
Aspiring, Mt., N.Z.	87	L2
Aspres-sur-Buëch, France	27	D9
Asprókavos, Ákra, Greece	37	B4
Aspromonte, Italy	35	D8
Aspur, India	62	H6
Asquith, Canada	101	C7
Assa, Morocco	74	C3
Assâba, Mauritania	78	B2
Assam □, India	61	F18
Assamakka, Niger	79	B6
Asse, Belgium	17	H4
Assebroek, Belgium	17	F2
Assekrem, Algeria	75	D6
Assémini, Italy	34	C2
Assen, Neths.	16	C9
Assendelft, Neths.	16	D5
Assenede, Belgium	17	F3
Assens, Århus, Denmark	11	H4
Assens, Fyn, Denmark	11	J3
Assesse, Belgium	17	H6
Assini, Ivory C.	78	D4
Assiniboia, Canada	101	D7
Assiniboine →, Canada	101	D9
Assis, Brazil	127	A5
Assisi, Italy	33	E9
Assynt, L., U.K.	14	C3
Astara, Azerbaijan	67	D13
Asten, Neths.	17	F7
Asterousía, Greece	37	E7
Asti, Italy	32	D5
Astipálaia, Greece	39	N9
Astorga, Spain	30	C4
Astoria, U.S.A.	112	D3
Åstorp, Sweden	11	H6
Astrakhan, Russia	43	C13
Astudillo, Spain	30	C6
Asturias □, Spain	30	B5
Asunción, Paraguay	126	B4
Asunción Nochixtlán, Mexico	115	D5
Asutri, Sudan	77	D4
Aswa →, Uganda	82	B3
Aswad, Ras al, Si. Arabia	76	C4
Aswân, Egypt	76	C3
Aswân High Dam = Sadd el Aali, Egypt	76	C3
Asyût, Egypt	76	B3
Asyûti, Wadi →, Egypt	76	B3
Aszód, Hungary	21	H9
At Ṭafilah, Jordan	69	E4
At Ṭā'if, Si. Arabia	68	C3
Aṭ Ṭirāq, Si. Arabia	64	E5
Atacama □, Chile	126	B2
Atacama, Desierto de, Chile	126	A2
Atacama, Salar de, Chile	126	A2
Ataco, Colombia	120	C2
Atakor, Algeria	75	D6
Atakpamé, Togo	79	D5
Atalándi, Greece	39	L5
Atalaya, Peru	124	C3
Atalaya de Femes, Canary Is.	36	F6
Ataléia, Brazil	123	E3
Atami, Japan	49	G9
Atapupu, Indonesia	57	F6
Atâr, Mauritania	74	D2
Atara, Russia	45	C13
Ataram, Erg n-, Algeria	75	D5
Atarfe, Spain	31	H7
Atascadero, Calif., U.S.A.	111	J3
Atascadero, Calif., U.S.A.	112	K6
Atasu, Kazakhstan	44	E8
Atauro, Indonesia	57	F7
Atbara, Sudan	76	D3
'Atbara →, Sudan	76	D3
Atbasar, Kazakhstan	44	D7
Atchafalaya B., U.S.A.	109	L9
Atchison, U.S.A.	108	F7
Atebubu, Ghana	79	D4
Ateca, Spain	28	D3
Aterno →, Italy	33	F10
Atesine, Alpi, Italy	32	B8
Atessa, Italy	33	F11
Ath, Belgium	17	G3
Athabasca, Canada	100	C6
Athabasca →, Canada	101	B6
Athabasca, L., Canada	101	B7
Athboy, Ireland	15	C5
Athenry, Ireland	15	C3
Athens = Athínai, Greece	39	M6
Athens, Ala., U.S.A.	105	H2
Athens, Ga., U.S.A.	105	J4
Athens, N.Y., U.S.A.	107	D11
Athens, Ohio, U.S.A.	104	F4
Athens, Pa., U.S.A.	107	E8
Athens, Tenn., U.S.A.	105	H3
Athens, Tex., U.S.A.	109	J7
Atherley, Canada	106	B5
Atherton, Australia	90	B4
Athíeme, Benin	79	D5
Athienou, Cyprus	37	D12
Athínai, Greece	39	M6
Athlone, Ireland	15	C4
Athna, Cyprus	37	D12
Atholl, Forest of, U.K.	14	E5
Atholville, Canada	99	C6
Áthos, Greece	39	J7
Athus, Belgium	17	J7
Athy, Ireland	15	D5
Ati, Chad	73	F8
Ati, Sudan	77	E2
Atiak, Uganda	82	B3
Atico, Peru	124	D3
Atienza, Spain	28	D2
Atikokan, Canada	98	C1
Atikonak L., Canada	99	B7
Atimonan, Phil.	55	E4
Atka, Russia	45	C16
Atkarsk, Russia	41	F14
Atkinson, U.S.A.	108	D5
Atlanta, Ga., U.S.A.	105	J3
Atlanta, Tex., U.S.A.	109	J7
Atlantic, U.S.A.	108	E7
Atlantic City, U.S.A.	104	F8
Atlantic Ocean	2	E9
Atlántico □, Colombia	120	A2
Atlas Mts. = Haut Atlas, Morocco	74	B3
Atlin, Canada	100	B2
Atlin, L., Canada	100	B2
Atmore, U.S.A.	105	K2
Atoka, U.S.A.	109	H6
Átokos, Greece	39	L3
Atolia, U.S.A.	113	K9
Atouguia, Portugal	31	F1
Atoyac →, Mexico	115	D5
Atrak →, Iran	65	B8
Åtran →, Sweden	11	G6
Atrato →, Colombia	120	B2
Atrauli, India	62	E8
Atri, Italy	33	F10
Atsbi, Ethiopia	77	E4
Atsoum, Mts., Cameroon	79	D7
Atsuta, Japan	48	C10
Attalla, U.S.A.	105	H2
Attáviros, Greece	37	C9
Attawapiskat, Canada	98	B3
Attawapiskat →, Canada	98	B3
Attawapiskat, L., Canada	98	B2
Attendorn, Germany	18	D3
Attert, Belgium	17	J7
Attica, U.S.A.	104	E2
Attichy, France	25	C10
Attigny, France	25	C11
Attikamagen L., Canada	99	A6
Attleboro, U.S.A.	107	E13
Attock, Pakistan	62	C5
Attopeu, Laos	58	E6
Attur, India	60	P11
Atuel →, Argentina	126	D2
Atvidaberg, Sweden	11	F10
Atwater, U.S.A.	111	H3
Atwood, Canada	106	C3
Atwood, U.S.A.	108	F4
Atyrau, Kazakhstan	43	C14
Au Sable →, U.S.A.	104	C4
Au Sable Pt., U.S.A.	98	C2
Aubagne, France	27	E9
Aubange, Belgium	17	J7
Aubarca, C., Spain	36	B7
Aube □, France	25	D11
Aube →, France	25	D10
Aubel, Belgium	17	G7
Aubenas, France	27	D8
Aubenton, France	25	C11
Auberry, U.S.A.	112	H7
Aubigny-sur-Nère, France	25	E9
Aubin, France	26	D6
Aubrac, Mts. d', France	26	D7
Auburn, Ala., U.S.A.	105	J3
Auburn, Calif., U.S.A.	112	G5
Auburn, Ind., U.S.A.	104	E3
Auburn, N.Y., U.S.A.	107	D8
Auburn, Nebr., U.S.A.	108	E7
Auburn, Wash., U.S.A.	112	C4
Auburn Ra., Australia	91	D5
Auburndale, U.S.A.	105	L5
Aubusson, France	26	C6
Auch, France	26	E4
Auchel, France	25	B9
Auchi, Nigeria	79	D6
Auckland, N.Z.	87	G5
Auckland Is., Pac. Oc.	92	N8
Aude □, France	26	E6
Aude →, France	26	E7
Auden, Canada	98	B2
Auderghem, Belgium	17	G4
Auderville, France	24	C5
Audierne, France	24	D2
Audincourt, France	25	E13
Audo, Ethiopia	77	F5
Audubon, U.S.A.	108	E7
Aue, Germany	18	E8
Auerbach, Germany	18	E8
Aueti Paraná →, Brazil	120	D4
Aufist, W. Sahara	74	C2
Augathella, Australia	91	D4
Augrabies Falls, S. Africa	84	D3
Augsburg, Germany	19	G6
Augusta, Italy	35	E8
Augusta, Ark., U.S.A.	109	H9
Augusta, Ga., U.S.A.	105	J5
Augusta, Kans., U.S.A.	109	G6
Augusta, Maine, U.S.A.	99	D6
Augusta, Mont., U.S.A.	110	C7
Augusta, Wis., U.S.A.	108	C9
Augustenborg, Denmark	11	K3
Augustów, Poland	20	B12
Augustus, Mt., Australia	88	D2
Augustus Downs, Australia	90	B2
Augustus I., Australia	88	C3
Aukan, Eritrea	77	D5
Aukum, U.S.A.	112	G6
Auld, L., Australia	88	D3
Aulla, Italy	32	D6
Aulnay, France	26	B3
Aulne →, France	24	D2
Aulnoye-Aymeries, France	25	B10
Ault, France	24	B8
Ault, U.S.A.	108	E2
Aulus-les-Bains, France	26	F5
Aumale, France	25	C8
Aumont-Aubrac, France	26	D7
Auna, Nigeria	79	C5
Aunis, France	26	B3
Auponhia, Indonesia	57	E7
Aups, France	27	E10
Aur, P., Malaysia	59	L5
Auraiya, India	63	F8
Aurangabad, Bihar, India	63	G11
Aurangabad, Maharashtra, India	60	K9
Auray, France	24	E4
Aurès, Algeria	75	A6
Aurich, Germany	18	B3
Aurilândia, Brazil	123	E1
Aurillac, France	26	D6
Auronza, Italy	33	B9
Aurora, Canada	106	C5
Aurora, S. Africa	84	E2
Aurora, Colo., U.S.A.	108	F2
Aurora, Ill., U.S.A.	104	E1
Aurora, Mo., U.S.A.	109	G8
Aurora, Nebr., U.S.A.	108	E6
Aurora, Ohio, U.S.A.	106	E3
Aursmoen, Norway	10	E5
Aurukun Mission, Australia	90	A3
Aus, Namibia	84	D2
Auschwitz = Oświecim, Poland	20	E9
Aust-Agder fylke □, Norway	9	G9
Austin, Minn., U.S.A.	108	D8
Austin, Nev., U.S.A.	110	G5
Austin, Pa., U.S.A.	106	E6
Austin, Tex., U.S.A.	109	K6
Austin, L., Australia	89	E2
Austral Downs, Australia	90	C2
Austral Is. = Tubuai Is., Pac. Oc.	93	K12
Austral Seamount Chain, Pac. Oc.	93	K13
Australia ■, Oceania	92	K5
Australian Alps, Australia	91	F4
Australian Capital Territory □, Australia	91	F4
Austria ■, Europe	21	H4
Austvågøy, Norway	8	B13
Autazes, Brazil	121	D6
Autelbas, Belgium	17	J7
Auterive, France	26	E5
Authie →, France	25	B8
Authon-du-Perche, France	24	D7
Autlán, Mexico	114	D4
Autun, France	25	F11
Auvelais, Belgium	17	H5
Auvergne, Australia	88	C5
Auvergne, France	26	C7
Auvergne, Mts. d', France	26	C6
Auvézère →, France	26	C4
Auxerre, France	25	E10
Auxi-le-Château, France	25	B9
Auxonne, France	25	E12
Auzances, France	26	B6
Auzat-sur-Allier, France	26	C7
Avallon, France	25	E10
Avalon, U.S.A.	113	M8
Avalon Pen., Canada	99	C9
Avanos, Turkey	66	C6
Avaré, Brazil	127	A6
Ávas, Greece	39	J8
Avawatz Mts., U.S.A.	113	K10
Aveiro, Brazil	121	D6
Aveiro, Portugal	30	E2
Aveiro □, Portugal	30	E2
Āvej, Iran	65	C6
Avelgem, Belgium	17	G2
Avellaneda, Argentina	126	C4
Avellino, Italy	35	B7
Avenal, U.S.A.	112	K6
Avenches, Switz.	22	C4
Averøya, Norway	10	A1
Aversa, Italy	35	B7
Avery, U.S.A.	110	C6
Aves, I. de, W. Indies	117	C7
Aves, Is. de, W. Indies	117	D6
Avesnes-sur-Helpe, France	25	B10
Avesta, Sweden	9	F14
Aveyron □, France	26	D6
Aveyron →, France	26	D5
Avezzano, Italy	33	F10
Aviá Terai, Argentina	126	B3
Aviano, Italy	33	B9
Avigliana, Italy	32	C4
Avigliano, Italy	35	B8
Avignon, France	27	E8
Ávila, Spain	30	E6
Ávila □, Spain	30	E6
Ávila, Sierra de, Spain	30	E5
Avila Beach, U.S.A.	113	K6
Avilés, Spain	30	B5
Avisio →, Italy	33	B8
Aviz, Portugal	31	F3
Avize, France	25	D11
Avoca, Ireland	15	D5
Avoca, U.S.A.	106	D7
Avoca →, Australia	91	F3
Avola, Canada	100	C5
Avola, Italy	35	F8
Avon, N.Y., U.S.A.	106	D7
Avon, S. Dak., U.S.A.	108	D5
Avon □, U.K.	13	F5
Avon →, Australia	89	F2
Avon →, Avon, U.K.	13	F5
Avon →, Hants., U.K.	13	G6
Avon →, Warks., U.K.	13	F5
Avondale, Zimbabwe	83	F3
Avonlea, Canada	101	D7
Avonmore, Canada	107	A10
Avonmouth, U.K.	13	F5
Avranches, France	24	D5
Avre →, France	24	D8
Awag el Baqar, Sudan	77	E3
A'waj →, Syria	69	B5
Awaji-Shima, Japan	49	G7
'Awālī, Bahrain	65	E6
Awantipur, India	63	C6
Awasa, L., Ethiopia	77	F4
Awash, Ethiopia	68	F3
Awash →, Ethiopia	77	E5
Awaso, Ghana	78	D4
Awatere →, N.Z.	87	J5
Awbārī, Libya	75	C7
Awbārī □, Libya	75	C7
Awe, L., U.K.	14	E3
Aweil, Sudan	77	F2
Awgu, Nigeria	79	D6
Awjilah, Libya	73	C9
Ax-les-Thermes, France	26	F5
Axarfjörður, Iceland	8	C5
Axel, Neths.	17	F3
Axel Heiberg I., Canada	4	B3
Axim, Ghana	78	E4
Aximim, Brazil	121	D6
Axintele, Romania	38	E9
Axioma, Brazil	125	B5
Axiós →, Greece	39	J5
Axminster, U.K.	13	G4
Axvall, Sweden	11	F7
Aÿ, France	25	C11
Ayabaca, Peru	124	A2
Ayabe, Japan	49	G7
Ayacucho, Argentina	126	D4
Ayacucho, Peru	124	C3
Ayaguz, Kazakhstan	44	E9
Ayamonte, Spain	31	H3
Ayan, Russia	45	D14
Ayancık, Turkey	42	F6
Ayapel, Colombia	120	B2
Ayas, Turkey	42	F5
Ayaviri, Peru	124	C3
Aybastı, Turkey	66	C7
Aydın, Turkey	66	E2
Aydin □, Turkey	66	E2
Aye, Belgium	17	H6
Ayenngré, Togo	79	D5
Ayer's Cliff, Canada	107	A12
Ayers Rock, Australia	89	E5
Ayiá, Greece	39	K5
Ayía Aikateríni, Ákra, Greece	37	A3
Ayía Dhéka, Greece	37	D6
Ayía Gálini, Greece	37	D6
Ayía Marína, Greece	39	M9
Ayía Napa, Cyprus	37	E13
Ayía Paraskeví, Greece	39	K9
Ayía Phyla, Cyprus	37	E12
Ayía Roúmeli, Greece	39	P6
Ayía Varvára, Greece	37	D7
Áyios Amvrósios, Cyprus	37	D12
Áyios Andréas, Greece	39	M5
Áyios Evstrátios, Greece	39	K7
Áyios Ioánnis, Ákra, Greece	37	D7
Áyios Isídhoros, Greece	37	C9
Áyios Kiríkos, Greece	39	M9
Áyios Matthaíos, Greece	37	B3
Áyios Mírones, Greece	39	P8
Áyios Nikólaos, Greece	37	D7
Áyios Seryios, Cyprus	37	D12
Áyios Theodhoros, Cyprus	37	D13
Aykathonisi, Greece	39	M9
Aylesbury, U.K.	13	F7
Aylmer, Canada	106	D4
Aylmer, L., Canada	96	B8
Ayna, Spain	29	G2
Ayolas, Paraguay	126	B4
Ayom, Sudan	77	F2
Ayon, Ostrov, Russia	45	C17
Ayora, Spain	29	F3
Ayr, Australia	90	B4
Ayr, U.K.	14	F4
Ayr →, U.K.	14	F4
Ayrancı, Turkey	66	E5
Ayre, Pt. of, U.K.	12	C3
Aysha, Ethiopia	77	E5
Aytos, Bulgaria	38	G10
Ayu, Kepulauan, Indonesia	57	D8
Ayutla, Guatemala	116	D1
Ayutla, Mexico	115	D5
Ayvacık, Turkey	66	C7
Ayvalık, Turkey	66	D2
Aywaille, Belgium	17	H7
Az Zabdānī, Syria	69	B5
Az Zāhirīyah, Jordan	69	D3
Aẓ Ẓahrān, Si. Arabia	65	E6

Az Zarqā, *Jordan* 69 C5
Az Zāwiyah, *Libya* 75 B7
Az Zībār, *Iraq* 64 B5
Az-Zilfī, *Si. Arabia* 64 E5
Az Zubayr, *Iraq* 64 D5
Azambuja, *Portugal* 31 F2
Azamgarh, *India* 63 F10
Azangaro, *Peru* 124 C3
Azaouak, Vallée de l', *Mali* 79 B5
Āzar Shahr, *Iran* 64 B5
Āzarbāyjān =
  Azerbaijan ■, *Asia* . . . 43 F12
Āzarbāyjān-e Gharbī □,
  Iran 64 B5
Āzarbāyjān-e Sharqī □,
  Iran 64 B5
Azare, *Nigeria* 79 C7
Azay-le-Rideau, *France* . . 24 E7
A'zāz, *Syria* 64 B3
Azazga, *Algeria* 75 A5
Azbine = Aïr, *Niger* 79 B6
Azefal, *Mauritania* 74 D2
Azeffoun, *Algeria* 75 A5
Azemmour, *Morocco* 74 B3
Azerbaijan ■, *Asia* 43 F12
Azerbaijchan =
  Azerbaijan ■, *Asia* . . . 43 F12
Azezo, *Ethiopia* 77 E4
Azimganj, *India* 63 G13
Aznalcóllar, *Spain* 31 H4
Azogues, *Ecuador* 120 D2
Azores, *Atl. Oc.* 2 C8
Azov, *Russia* 43 C8
Azov, Sea of = Azovskoye
  More, *Europe* 42 C7
Azovskoye More, *Europe* . 42 C7
Azovy, *Russia* 44 C7
Azpeitia, *Spain* 28 B2
Azrou, *Morocco* 74 B3
Aztec, *U.S.A.* 111 H10
Azúa, *Dom. Rep.* 117 C5
Azuaga, *Spain* 31 G5
Azuara, *Spain* 28 D4
Azuay □, *Ecuador* 120 D2
Azuer →, *Spain* 31 F7
Azuero, Pen. de, *Panama* . 116 E3
Azul, *Argentina* 126 D4
Azul, Serra, *Brazil* 125 C7
Azurduy, *Bolivia* 125 D5
Azusa, *U.S.A.* 113 L9
Azzaba, *Algeria* 75 A6
Azzano Décimo, *Italy* . . . 33 C9
'Azzūn, *Jordan* 69 C4

B

Ba Don, *Vietnam* 58 D6
Ba Dong, *Vietnam* 59 H6
Ba Ngoi = Cam Lam,
  Vietnam 59 G7
Ba Ria, *Vietnam* 59 G6
Ba Tri, *Vietnam* 59 G6
Ba Xian, *China* 50 E9
Baa, *Indonesia* 57 F6
Baamonde, *Spain* 30 B3
Baar, *Switz.* 23 B7
Baarle Nassau, *Belgium* . . 17 F5
Baarlo, *Neths.* 17 F8
Baarn, *Neths.* 16 D6
Bab el Mandeb, *Red Sea* . 68 E3
Baba Burnu, *Turkey* 66 D2
Baba dag, *Azerbaijan* . . . 43 F13
Bābā Kalū, *Iran* 65 D6
Babaçulândia, *Brazil* 122 C2
Babadag, *Romania* 38 E11
Babadayhan = Kirovsk,
  Turkmenistan 44 F7
Babaeski, *Turkey* 66 C2
Babahoyo, *Ecuador* 120 D2
Babakin, *Australia* 89 F2
Babana, *Nigeria* 79 C5
Babar, *Algeria* 75 A6
Babar, *Indonesia* 57 F7
Babar, *Pakistan* 62 D3
Babarkach, *Pakistan* 62 E3
Babayevo, *Russia* 41 B9
Babb, *U.S.A.* 110 B7
Babenhausen, *Germany* . . 19 F4
Babi Besar, P., *Malaysia* . 59 L4
Babian Jiang →, *China* . . 52 F3
Babile, *Ethiopia* 77 F5
Babinda, *Australia* 90 B4
Babine, *Canada* 100 B3
Babine →, *Canada* 100 B3
Babine L., *Canada* 100 C3
Babo, *Indonesia* 57 E8
Bābol, *Iran* 65 B7
Bābol Sar, *Iran* 65 B7
Baboua, *C.A.R.* 80 C2
Babruysk = Bobruysk,
  Belorussia 40 E6
Babura, *Nigeria* 79 C6
Babusar Pass, *Pakistan* . . 63 B5
Babušnica, *Serbia, Yug.* . 21 M12
Babuyan Chan., *Phil.* . . . 55 B4
Babuyan Is., *Phil.* 55 B4
Babylon, *Iraq* 64 C5
Bac Can, *Vietnam* 58 A5
Bac Giang, *Vietnam* 58 B6
Bac Ninh, *Vietnam* 58 B6
Bac Phan, *Vietnam* 58 B5
Bac Quang, *Vietnam* 58 A5

Bacabal, *Brazil* 122 B3
Bacajá →, *Brazil* 121 D7
Bacalar, *Mexico* 115 D7
Bacan, *Indonesia* 57 F7
Bacan, Kepulauan,
  Indonesia 57 E7
Bacan, Pulau, *Indonesia* . 57 E7
Bacarra, *Phil.* 55 B4
Bacău, *Romania* 38 C9
Baccarat, *France* 25 D13
Bacerac, *Mexico* 114 A3
Băceşti, *Romania* 38 C10
Bach Long Vi, Dao,
  Vietnam 58 B6
Bachaquero, *Venezuela* . . 120 B3
Bacharach, *Germany* 19 E3
Bachelina, *Russia* 44 D7
Bachuma, *Ethiopia* 77 F4
Bačina, *Serbia, Yug.* 21 M11
Back →, *Canada* 96 B9
Bačka Palanka,
  Serbia, Yug. 21 K9
Bačka Topola, *Serbia, Yug.* 21 K9
Bäckefors, *Sweden* 11 F6
Backnang, *Germany* 19 G5
Backstairs Passage,
  Australia 91 F2
Baco, Mt., *Phil.* 55 E4
Bacolod, *Phil.* 55 F5
Bacqueville-en-Caux,
  France 24 C8
Bácsalmás, *Hungary* 21 J9
Bacuag, *Phil.* 55 G6
Bacuk, *Malaysia* 59 J4
Bād, *Iran* 65 C7
Bad →, *U.S.A.* 108 C4
Bad Axe, *U.S.A.* 106 C2
Bad Bergzabern, *Germany* 19 F4
Bad Berleburg, *Germany* . 18 D4
Bad Bevensen, *Germany* . 18 B6
Bad Bramstedt, *Germany* . 18 B5
Bad Brückenau, *Germany* 19 E5
Bad Doberan, *Germany* . . 18 A7
Bad Driburg, *Germany* . . 18 D5
Bad Ems, *Germany* 19 E3
Bad Frankenhausen,
  Germany 18 D7
Bad Freienwalde, *Germany* 18 C10
Bad Godesberg, *Germany* 18 E3
Bad Hersfeld, *Germany* . . 18 E5
Bad Hofgastein, *Austria* . 21 H3
Bad Homburg, *Germany* . 19 E4
Bad Honnef, *Germany* . . . 18 E3
Bad Ischl, *Austria* 21 H3
Bad Kissingen, *Germany* . 19 E6
Bad Königshofen, *Germany* 19 E6
Bad Kreuznach, *Germany* 19 F3
Bad Laasphe, *Germany* . . 18 E4
Bad Lands, *U.S.A.* 108 D3
Bad Langensalza, *Germany* 18 D6
Bad Lauterberg, *Germany* 18 D6
Bad Lippspringe, *Germany* 18 D4
Bad Mergentheim,
  Germany 19 F5
Bad Münstereifel, *Germany* 18 E2
Bad Muskau, *Germany* . . 18 D10
Bad Nauheim, *Germany* . 19 E4
Bad Oeynhausen, *Germany* 18 C4
Bad Oldesloe, *Germany* . . 18 B6
Bad Orb, *Germany* 19 E5
Bad Pyrmont, *Germany* . . 18 D5
Bad Ragaz, *Switz.* 23 B9
Bad Reichenhall, *Germany* 19 H8
Bad Säckingen, *Germany* . 19 H3
Bad Salzuflen, *Germany* . 18 C4
Bad Segeberg, *Germany* . 18 B6
Bad Tölz, *Germany* 19 H7
Bad Urach, *Germany* 19 G5
Bad Waldsee, *Germany* . . 19 H5
Bad Wildungen, *Germany* 18 D5
Bad Wimpfen, *Germany* . 19 F5
Bad Windsheim, *Germany* 19 F6
Badagara, *India* 60 P9
Badagri, *Nigeria* 79 D5
Badajós, L., *Brazil* 121 D5
Badajoz, *Spain* 31 G4
Badajoz □, *Spain* 31 G4
Badalona, *Spain* 28 D7
Badalzai, *Afghan.* 62 E1
Badampahar, *India* 61 H15
Badanah, *Si. Arabia* 64 C4
Badarinath, *India* 63 D8
Badas, *Brunei* 56 D4
Badas, Kepulauan,
  Indonesia 56 D3
Baddo →, *Pakistan* 60 F4
Bade, *Indonesia* 57 F9
Baden, *Austria* 21 G6
Baden, *Switz.* 23 B6
Baden-Baden, *Germany* . . 19 G4
Baden-Württemberg □,
  Germany 19 G5
Badenoch, *U.K.* 14 E4
Badger, *Canada* 99 C8
Badger, *U.S.A.* 112 J7
Bādghīsāt □, *Afghan.* . . . 60 B3
Badgom, *India* 63 B6
Badhoevedorp, *Neths.* . . . 16 D5
Badia Polèsine, *Italy* 33 C8
Badin, *Pakistan* 62 G3
Badogo, *Mali* 78 C3
Badong, *China* 53 B8
Baduen, *Somali Rep.* 68 F4
Badulla, *Sri Lanka* 60 R12
Baena, *Spain* 31 H6

Baexem, *Neths.* 17 F7
Baeza, *Ecuador* 120 D2
Baeza, *Spain* 29 H1
Bafa Gölü, *Turkey* 66 E2
Bafang, *Cameroon* 79 D7
Bafatá, *Guinea-Biss.* 78 C2
Baffin B., *Canada* 4 B4
Baffin I., *Canada* 97 B12
Bafia, *Cameroon* 79 E7
Bafilo, *Togo* 79 D5
Bafing →, *Mali* 78 C2
Bafliyūn, *Syria* 64 B3
Baflo, *Neths.* 16 B9
Bafoulabé, *Mali* 78 C2
Bafoussam, *Cameroon* . . . 79 D7
Bāfq, *Iran* 65 D7
Bafra, *Turkey* 42 F6
Bafra Burnu, *Turkey* 42 F6
Bāft, *Iran* 65 D8
Bafut, *Cameroon* 79 D7
Bafwasende, *Zaïre* 82 B2
Bagamoyo, *Tanzania* 82 D4
Bagamoyo □, *Tanzania* . . 82 D4
Bagan Datoh, *Malaysia* . . 59 L3
Bagan Serai, *Malaysia* . . 59 K3
Baganga, *Phil.* 55 H7
Bagani, *Namibia* 84 B3
Bagansiapiapi, *Indonesia* . 56 D2
Bagasra, *India* 62 J4
Bagawi, *Nigeria* 77 E3
Bagdad, *U.S.A.* 113 L11
Bagdarin, *Russia* 45 D12
Bagé, *Brazil* 127 C5
Bagenalstown = Muine
  Bheag, *Ireland* 15 D5
Baggs, *U.S.A.* 110 F10
Bagh, *Pakistan* 63 C5
Baghdād, *Iraq* 64 C5
Bagheria, *Italy* 34 D6
Baghlān, *Afghan.* 60 A6
Bagley, *U.S.A.* 108 B7
Bagnacavallo, *Italy* 33 D8
Bagnara Cálabra, *Italy* . . 35 D8
Bagnères-de-Bigorre,
  France 26 E4
Bagnères-de-Luchon,
  France 26 F4
Bagni di Lucca, *Italy* 32 D7
Bagno di Romagna, *Italy* . 33 E8
Bagnoles-de-l'Orne, *France* 24 D6
Bagnoli di Sopra, *Italy* . . 33 C8
Bagnolo Mella, *Italy* 32 C7
Bagnols-sur-Cèze, *France* . 27 D8
Bagnorégio, *Italy* 33 F9
Bagolino, *Italy* 32 C7
Bagotville, *Canada* 99 C5
Bagua, *Peru* 124 B2
Baguio, *Phil.* 55 C4
Bahabón de Esgueva, *Spain* 28 D1
Bahadurgarh, *India* 62 E7
Bahama, Canal Viejo de,
  W. Indies 116 B4
Bahamas ■, *N. Amer.* . . . 117 B5
Baharampur, *India* 63 G13
Baharîya, El Wâhât al,
  Egypt 76 J6
Bahau, *Malaysia* 59 L4
Bahawalnagar, *Pakistan* . . 62 D5
Bahawalpur, *Pakistan* . . . 62 E4
Bahçe, *Turkey* 66 E7
Baheri, *India* 63 E8
Bahi, *Tanzania* 82 D4
Bahi Swamp, *Tanzania* . . 82 D4
Bahía = Salvador, *Brazil* . 123 D4
Bahía □, *Brazil* 123 D3
Bahía, Is. de la, *Honduras* 116 C2
Bahía Blanca, *Argentina* . 126 D3
Bahía de Caráquez,
  Ecuador 120 D1
Bahía Honda, *Cuba* 116 B3
Bahía Laura, *Argentina* . . 128 C3
Bahía Negra, *Paraguay* . . 125 E6
Bahir Dar, *Ethiopia* 77 E4
Bahmanzād, *Iran* 65 D6
Bahmer, *Algeria* 75 C4
Bahönye, *Hungary* 21 J7
Bahr el Ahmar □, *Sudan* . 76 C3
Bahr el Ghazâl □, *Sudan* . 77 F2
Bahr Salamat →, *Chad* . . 73 G8
Bahr Yûsef →, *Egypt* . . . 76 J7
Bahraich, *India* 63 F9
Bahrain ■, *Asia* 65 E6
Bahret Assad, *Syria* 64 C3
Bahror, *India* 62 F7
Bāhū Kalāt, *Iran* 65 E9
Bai, *Mali* 78 C4
Bai Bung, Mui, *Vietnam* . 59 H5
Bai Duc, *Vietnam* 58 C5
Bai Thuong, *Vietnam* . . . 58 C5
Baia Mare, *Romania* 38 B6
Baia-Sprie, *Romania* 38 B6
Baião, *Brazil* 122 B2
Baïbokoum, *Chad* 73 G8
Baicheng, *China* 51 B12
Baidoa, *Somali Rep.* 68 G3
Baie Comeau, *Canada* . . . 99 C6
Baie-St-Paul, *Canada* . . . 99 C5
Baie Trinité, *Canada* 99 C6
Baie Verte, *Canada* 99 C8
Baignes-Ste.-Radegonde,
  France 26 C3
Baigneux-les-Juifs, *France* 25 E11
Baihe, *China* 50 H6

Baihe, *Taiwan* 53 F13
Ba'ijī, *Iraq* 64 C4
Baikal, L. = Baykal, Oz.,
  Russia 45 D11
Baile Atha Cliath =
  Dublin, *Ireland* 15 C5
Bailei, *Ethiopia* 77 F5
Bailén, *Spain* 31 G7
Băileşti, *Romania* 38 E6
Baileux, *Belgium* 17 H4
Bailique, Ilha, *Brazil* 122 A2
Bailleul, *France* 25 B9
Bailundo, *Angola* 81 G3
Baima, *China* 52 A3
Bain-de-Bretagne, *France* . 24 E5
Bainbridge, Ga., *U.S.A.* . . 105 K3
Bainbridge, N.Y., *U.S.A.* . 107 D9
Baing, *Indonesia* 57 F6
Bainiu, *China* 50 H7
Bainville, *U.S.A.* 108 A2
Bā'ir, *Jordan* 69 E5
Baird, *U.S.A.* 109 J5
Baird Mts., *U.S.A.* 96 B3
Bairin Youqi, *China* 51 C10
Bairin Zuoqi, *China* 51 C10
Bairnsdale, *Australia* 91 F4
Bais, *Phil.* 55 G5
Baisha, *China* 50 G7
Baïsole →, *France* 26 E4
Baissa, *Nigeria* 79 D7
Baitadi, *Nepal* 63 E9
Baixa Grande, *Brazil* 123 D3
Baiyin, *China* 50 F3
Baiyü, *China* 52 B2
Baiyu Shan, *China* 50 F4
Baiyuda, *Sudan* 76 D3
Baj Baj, *India* 63 H13
Baja, *Hungary* 21 J8
Baja, Pta., *Mexico* 114 B1
Baja California, *Mexico* . . 114 A1
Bajamar, *Canary Is.* 36 F3
Bajana, *India* 62 H4
Bājgīrān, *Iran* 65 B8
Bajimba, Mt., *Australia* . . 91 D5
Bajo Nuevo, *Caribbean* . . 116 C4
Bajoga, *Nigeria* 79 C7
Bajool, *Australia* 90 C5
Bakala, *C.A.R.* 73 G9
Bakar, *Croatia* 33 C11
Bakchar, *Russia* 44 D9
Bakel, *Neths.* 17 E7
Bakel, *Senegal* 78 C2
Baker, Calif., *U.S.A.* 113 K10
Baker, Mont., *U.S.A.* . . . 108 B2
Baker, Oreg., *U.S.A.* 110 D5
Baker, Canal, *Chile* 128 C2
Baker, L., *Canada* 96 B10
Baker I., *Pac. Oc.* 92 G10
Baker L., *Australia* 89 E4
Baker Lake, *Canada* 96 B10
Baker Mt., *U.S.A.* 110 B3
Bakers Creek, *Australia* . . 90 C4
Baker's Dozen Is., *Canada* 98 A4
Bakersfield, Calif., *U.S.A.* 113 K7
Bakersfield, Vt., *U.S.A.* . . 107 B12
Bakhchisaray, *Ukraine* . . . 42 D5
Bakhmach, *Ukraine* 40 F8
Bākhtarān, *Iran* 64 C5
Bākhtarān □, *Iran* 64 C5
Bakhçe, *Turkey* 66 D6
Bakırdaği, *Turkey* 66 D6
Bakırköy, *Turkey* 39 H11
Bakkafjörður, *Iceland* . . . 8 C6
Bakkagerði, *Iceland* 8 D7
Bakony →, *Hungary* 21 H7
Bakony Forest = Bakony
  Hegyseg, *Hungary* . . . 21 H7
Bakony Hegyseg, *Hungary* 21 H7
Bakori, *Nigeria* 79 C6
Bakouma, *C.A.R.* 73 G9
Baku, *Azerbaijan* 43 F13
Bakutis Coast, *Antarctica* . 5 D15
Baky = Baku, *Azerbaijan* 43 F13
Bala, *Canada* 106 A5
Bâlâ, *Turkey* 66 D5
Bala, L., *U.K.* 12 E4
Balabac I., *Phil.* 55 H2
Balabac Str., *E. Indies* . . 56 C5
Balabagh, *Afghan.* 62 B4
Balabakk, *Lebanon* 69 A5
Balabalangan, Kepulauan,
  Indonesia 56 E5
Bălăciţa, *Romania* 38 E6
Balad, *Iraq* 64 C5
Balad Rūz, *Iraq* 64 C5
Bālādeh, *Fārs, Iran* 65 D6
Bālādeh, *Māzandaran, Iran* 65 B6
Balaghat, *India* 60 J12
Balaghat Ra., *India* 60 K10
Balaguer, *Spain* 28 D5
Balakhna, *Russia* 41 C13
Balaklava, *Australia* 91 E2
Balaklava, *Ukraine* 42 D5
Balakleya, *Ukraine* 42 B7
Balakovo, *Russia* 41 E15
Balancán, *Mexico* 115 D6
Balanda, *Russia* 41 F14
Balashikha, *Russia* 41 D10
Balashov, *Russia* 41 F13
Balasinor, *India* 62 H5
Balasore = Baleshwar,
  India 61 J15
Balassagyarmat, *Hungary* . 21 G9
Balât, *Egypt* 76 B2
Balaton, *Hungary* 21 J7
Balayan, *Phil.* 55 E4

Baihe, *China* 50 H6

Balazote, *Spain* 29 G2
Balboa, *Panama* 116 E4
Balbriggan, *Ireland* 15 C5
Balcarce, *Argentina* 126 D4
Balcarres, *Canada* 101 C8
Balchik, *Bulgaria* 38 F11
Balclutha, *N.Z.* 87 M2
Bald Hd., *Australia* 89 G2
Bald I., *Australia* 89 F2
Bald Knob, *U.S.A.* 109 H9
Baldock L., *Canada* 101 B9
Baldwin, *Fla., U.S.A.* . . . 105 K4
Baldwin, *Mich., U.S.A.* . . 104 D3
Baldwinsville, *U.S.A.* . . . 107 C8
Baldy Peak, *U.S.A.* 111 K9
Bale, *Croatia* 33 C10
Bale □, *Ethiopia* 77 F5
Baleares □, *Spain* 28 F7
Baleares, Is., *Spain* 36 B10
Balearic Is. = Baleares, Is.,
  Spain 36 B10
Baleia, Pta. da, *Brazil* . . . 123 E4
Balen, *Belgium* 17 F6
Baler, *Phil.* 55 D4
Baler Bay, *Phil.* 55 D4
Balerna, *Switz.* 23 E8
Baleshwar, *India* 61 J15
Balfate, *Honduras* 116 C2
Balfe's Creek, *Australia* . . 90 C4
Balfour, S. *Africa* 85 D4
Bali, *Cameroon* 79 D6
Balí, *Greece* 37 D6
Bali, *Indonesia* 56 F5
Bali □, *Indonesia* 56 F5
Bali, Selat, *Indonesia* . . . 57 H16
Baligród, *Poland* 20 F12
Balık Gölü, *Turkey* 67 D10
Balıkeşir, *Turkey* 66 D2
Balıkeşir □, *Turkey* 66 D2
Balikpapan, *Indonesia* . . . 56 E5
Balimbing, *Phil.* 57 C5
Baling, *Malaysia* 59 K3
Balintang Channel, *Phil.* . 55 B4
Balipara, *India* 61 F18
Baliza, *Brazil* 125 D7
Balk, *Neths.* 16 C7
Balkan Mts. = Stara
  Planina, *Bulgaria* . . . 38 F6
Balkan Peninsula, *Europe* . 6 G10
Balkhash, *Kazakhstan* . . . 44 E8
Balkhash, Ozero,
  Kazakhstan 44 E8
Balla, *Bangla.* 61 G17
Ballachulish, *U.K.* 14 E3
Balladonia, *Australia* 89 F3
Ballarat, *Australia* 91 F3
Ballard, L., *Australia* 89 E3
Ballater, *U.K.* 14 D5
Ballenas, Canal de, *Mexico* 114 B2
Balleny Is., *Antarctica* . . . 5 C11
Ballesteros, *Phil.* 55 B4
Ballia, *India* 63 G11
Ballidu, *Australia* 89 F2
Ballina, *Australia* 91 D5
Ballina, *Mayo, Ireland* . . . 15 B2
Ballina, *Tipp., Ireland* . . . 15 C3
Ballinasloe, *Ireland* 15 C3
Ballinger, *U.S.A.* 109 K5
Ballinrobe, *Ireland* 15 C2
Ballinskelligs B., *Ireland* . 15 E1
Ballon, *France* 24 D7
Ballycastle, *U.K.* 15 A5
Ballymena, *U.K.* 15 B5
Ballymena □, *U.K.* 15 B5
Ballymoney, *U.K.* 15 A5
Ballymoney □, *U.K.* 15 A5
Ballyshannon, *Ireland* . . . 15 B3
Balmaceda, *Chile* 128 C2
Balmazújváros, *Hungary* . 21 H11
Balmhorn, *Switz.* 22 D5
Balmoral, *Australia* 91 F3
Balmoral, *U.K.* 14 D5
Balmorhea, *U.S.A.* 109 K3
Balonne →, *Australia* . . . 91 D4
Balqash Kol = Balkhash,
  Ozero, *Kazakhstan* . . . 44 E8
Balrampur, *India* 63 F10
Balranald, *Australia* 91 E3
Balş, *Romania* 38 E7
Balsapuerto, *Peru* 124 B2
Balsas, *Mexico* 115 D5
Balsas →, *Goiás, Brazil* . . 122 C2
Balsas →, *Maranhão,
  Brazil* 122 C3
Balsas →, *Mexico* 114 D4
Bålsta, *Sweden* 10 E11
Balsthal, *Switz.* 22 B5
Balston Spa, *U.S.A.* 107 D11
Balta, *Romania* 38 E6
Balta, *Russia* 43 E11
Balta, *Ukraine* 42 B3
Balta, *U.S.A.* 108 A4
Baltanás, *Spain* 30 D6
Bălți = Beltsy, *Moldavia* . 42 C12
Baltic Sea, *Europe* 9 H15
Baltîm, *Egypt* 76 H7
Baltimore, *Ireland* 15 E2
Baltimore, *U.S.A.* 104 F7
Baltit, *Pakistan* 63 A6
Baltrum, *Germany* 18 B3
Baluchistan □, *Pakistan* . . 60 F4
Balurghat, *India* 63 G13
Balya, *Turkey* 66 D2
Balygychan, *Russia* 45 C16
Balzar, *Ecuador* 120 D2

Bam, *Iran* **65** D8
Bama, *China* **52** E6
Bama, *Nigeria* **79** C7
Bamako, *Mali* **78** C3
Bamba, *Mali* **79** B4
Bambamarca, *Peru* **124** B2
Bambari, *C.A.R.* **73** G9
Bambaroo, *Australia* **90** B4
Bamberg, *Germany* **19** F6
Bamberg, *U.S.A.* **105** J5
Bambesi, *Ethiopia* **77** F3
Bambey, *Senegal* **78** C1
Bambili, *Zaïre* **82** B2
Bambuí, *Brazil* **123** F2
Bamenda, *Cameroon* . . . **79** D7
Bamfield, *Canada* **100** D3
Bāmīān □, *Afghan.* **60** B5
Bamiancheng, *China* . . . **51** C13
Bampūr, *Iran* **65** E9
Ban Aranyaprathet,
Thailand **58** F4
Ban Ban, *Laos* **58** C4
Ban Bang Hin, *Thailand* . . **59** H2
Ban Chiang Klang,
Thailand **58** C3
Ban Chik, *Laos* **58** D4
Ban Choho, *Thailand* . . . **58** E4
Ban Dan Lan Hoi,
Thailand **58** D2
Ban Don = Surat Thani,
Thailand **59** H2
Ban Don, *Vietnam* **58** F6
Ban Don, Ao, *Thailand* . . **59** H2
Ban Dong, *Thailand* **58** C3
Ban Hong, *Thailand* **58** C2
Ban Kaeng, *Thailand* . . . **58** D3
Ban Keun, *Laos* **58** C4
Ban Khai, *Thailand* **58** F3
Ban Kheun, *Laos* **58** B3
Ban Khlong Kua, *Thailand* **59** J3
Ban Khuan Mao, *Thailand* **59** J2
Ban Khun Yuam, *Thailand* **58** C1
Ban Ko Yai Chim,
Thailand **59** G2
Ban Kok, *Thailand* **58** D4
Ban Laem, *Thailand* **58** F2
Ban Lao Ngam, *Laos* . . . **58** E6
Ban Le Kathe, *Thailand* . . **58** E2
Ban Mae Chedi, *Thailand* **58** C2
Ban Mae Laeng, *Thailand* **58** B2
Ban Mae Sariang, *Thailand* **58** C1
Ban Mê Thuôt = Buon Me
Thuot, *Vietnam* **58** F7
Ban Mi, *Thailand* **58** E3
Ban Muong Mo, *Laos* . . . **58** C4
Ban Na Mo, *Laos* **58** D5
Ban Na San, *Thailand* . . . **59** H2
Ban Na Tong, *Laos* **58** B3
Ban Nam Bac, *Laos* **58** B4
Ban Nam Ma, *Laos* **58** A3
Ban Ngang, *Laos* **58** E6
Ban Nong Bok, *Laos* **58** D5
Ban Nong Boua, *Laos* . . . **58** E6
Ban Nong Pling, *Thailand* **58** E3
Ban Pak Chan, *Thailand* . . **59** G2
Ban Phai, *Thailand* **58** D4
Ban Pong, *Thailand* **58** F2
Ban Ron Phibun, *Thailand* **59** H2
Ban Sanam Chai, *Thailand* **59** J3
Ban Sangkha, *Thailand* . . **58** E4
Ban Tak, *Thailand* **58** D2
Ban Tako, *Thailand* **58** E4
Ban Tha Dua, *Thailand* . . **58** D2
Ban Tha Li, *Thailand* **58** D3
Ban Tha Nun, *Thailand* . . **59** H2
Ban Thahine, *Laos* **58** E5
Ban Xien Kok, *Laos* **58** B3
Ban Yen Nhan, *Vietnam* . . **58** B6
Baña, Punta de la, *Spain* . **28** E5
Banaba, *Kiribati* **92** H8
Bañalbufar, *Spain* **36** B9
Banalia, *Zaïre* **82** B2
Banam, *Cambodia* **59** G5
Banamba, *Mali* **78** C3
Banana, *Australia* **90** C5
Bananal, I. do, *Brazil* . . **123** D1
Banaras = Varanasi, *India* **63** G10
Banas →, *Gujarat, India* . **62** H4
Banas →, *Mad. P., India* . **63** G9
Bânâs, Ras, *Egypt* **76** C4
Banaz, *Turkey* **66** D3
Banbān, *Si. Arabia* **64** E5
Banbridge, *U.K.* **15** B5
Banbridge □, *U.K.* **15** B5
Banbury, *U.K.* **13** E6
Banchory, *U.K.* **14** D6
Bancroft, *Canada* **98** C4
Band Bonī, *Iran* **65** E8
Band Qīr, *Iran* **65** D6
Banda, *India* **63** G9
Banda, Kepulauan,
Indonesia **57** E7
Banda Aceh, *Indonesia* . . **56** C1
Banda Banda, Mt.,
Australia **91** E5
Banda Elat, *Indonesia* . . **57** F8
Banda Is. = Banda,
Kepulauan, *Indonesia* . **57** E7
Banda Sea, *Indonesia* . . **57** F7
Bandai-San, *Japan* **48** F10
Bandama →, *Ivory C.* . . . **78** D3
Bandān, *Iran* **65** D9
Bandanaira, *Indonesia* . . **57** E7
Bandanwara, *India* **62** F6

Bandar = Machilipatnam,
India **61** L12
Bandār 'Abbās, *Iran* **65** E8
Bandar-e Anzalī, *Iran* . . . **65** B6
Bandar-e Chārak, *Iran* . . **65** E7
Bandar-e Deylam, *Iran* . . **65** D6
Bandar-e Khomeyni, *Iran* **65** D6
Bandar-e Lengeh, *Iran* . . **65** E7
Bandar-e Maqām, *Iran* . . **65** E7
Bandar-e Ma'shur, *Iran* . **65** D6
Bandar-e Nakhīlū, *Iran* . . **65** E7
Bandar-e Rīg, *Iran* **65** D6
Bandar-e Torkeman, *Iran* **65** B7
Bandar Maharani = Muar,
Malaysia **59** L4
Bandar Penggaram = Batu
Pahat, *Malaysia* **59** M4
Bandar Seri Begawan,
Brunei **56** C4
Bandawe, *Malawi* **83** E3
Bande, *Belgium* **17** H6
Bande, *Spain* **30** C3
Bandeira, Pico da, *Brazil* . **123** F3
Bandeirante, *Brazil* **123** D1
Bandera, *Argentina* **126** B3
Bandera, *U.S.A.* **109** L5
Banderas, B. de, *Mexico* . **114** C3
Bandiagara, *Mali* **78** C4
Bandırma, *Turkey* **66** C3
Bandon, *Ireland* **15** E3
Bandon →, *Ireland* **15** E3
Bandula, *Mozam.* **83** F3
Bandundu, *Zaïre* **80** E3
Bandung, *Indonesia* **57** G12
Bandya, *Australia* **89** E3
Bāneh, *Iran* **64** C5
Banes, *Cuba* **117** B4
Banff, *Canada* **100** C5
Banff, *U.K.* **14** D6
Banff Nat. Park, *Canada* . **100** C5
Banfora, *Burkina Faso* . . **78** C4
Bang Fai →, *Laos* **58** D5
Bang Hieng →, *Laos* **58** D5
Bang Krathum, *Thailand* . **58** D3
Bang Lamung, *Thailand* . . **58** F3
Bang Mun Nak, *Thailand* . **58** D3
Bang Pa In, *Thailand* . . . **58** E3
Bang Rakam, *Thailand* . . **58** D3
Bang Saphan, *Thailand* . . **59** G2
Bangala Dam, *Zimbabwe* . **83** G3
Bangalore, *India* **60** N10
Bangante, *Cameroon* . . . **79** D7
Bangaon, *India* **63** H13
Bangassou, *C.A.R.* **80** D4
Banggai, Kepulauan,
Indonesia **57** E6
Banggi, P., *Malaysia* **56** C5
Banghāzī, *Libya* **73** B9
Bangil, *Indonesia* **57** G15
Bangjang, *Sudan* **77** E3
Bangka, P., *Sulawesi,
Indonesia* **57** D7
Bangka, P., *Sumatera,
Indonesia* **56** E3
Bangka, Selat, *Indonesia* . **56** E3
Bangkalan, *Indonesia* . . . **57** G15
Bangkinang, *Indonesia* . . **56** D2
Bangko, *Indonesia* **56** E2
Bangkok, *Thailand* **58** F3
Bangladesh ■, *Asia* **61** H17
Bangolo, *Ivory C.* **78** D3
Bangong Co, *India* **63** B8
Bangor, *Down, U.K.* **15** B6
Bangor, *Gwynedd, U.K.* . . **12** D3
Bangor, *Maine, U.S.A.* . . **99** D6
Bangor, *Pa., U.S.A.* . . . **107** F9
Bangued, *Phil.* **55** C4
Bangui, *C.A.R.* **80** D3
Bangui, *Phil.* **55** B4
Banguru, *Zaïre* **82** B2
Bangweulu, L., *Zambia* . . **83** E3
Bangweulu Swamp, *Zambia* **83** E3
Bani, *Dom. Rep.* **117** C5
Bani, *Mali* **78** C4
Bani Bangou, *Niger* **79** B5
Banī Sa'd, *Iraq* **64** C5
Banī Walīd, *Libya* **73** B7
Bania, *Ivory C.* **78** D4
Banihal Pass, *India* **63** C6
Banīnah, *Libya* **73** B9
Bāniyās, *Syria* **64** C3
Banja Luka, *Bos.-H.* **21** L7
Banjar, *Indonesia* **57** G13
Banjarmasin, *Indonesia* . . **56** E4
Banjarnegara, *Indonesia* . . **57** G13
Banjul, *Gambia* **78** C1
Banka Banka, *Australia* . . **90** B1
Banket, *Zimbabwe* **83** F3
Bankilaré, *Niger* **79** C5
Bankipore, *India* **63** G11
Banks I., *B.C., Canada* . . **100** C3
Banks I., *N.W.T., Canada* . **96** A7
Banks Pen., *N.Z.* **87** K4
Banks Str., *Australia* . . . **90** G4
Bankura, *India* **63** H12
Bann →, *Down, U.K.* . . . **15** B5
Bann →, *L'derry., U.K.* . . **15** A5
Banna, *Phil.* **55** B5
Bannalec, *France* **24** E3
Banning, *U.S.A.* **113** M10
Banningville = Bandundu,
Zaïre **80** E3

Bannockburn, *Canada* . . **106** B7
Bannockburn, *U.K.* **14** E5
Bannockburn, *Zimbabwe* . **83** G2
Bannu, *Pakistan* **60** C7
Baños de la Encina, *Spain* **31** G7
Baños de Molgas, *Spain* . . **30** C3
Banská Bystrica,
Slovak Rep. **20** G9
Banská Štiavnica,
Slovak Rep. **21** G8
Banswara, *India* **62** H6
Bantayan, *Phil.* **55** F5
Banten, *Indonesia* **57** G12
Bantry, *Ireland* **15** E2
Bantry B., *Ireland* **15** E2
Bantul, *Indonesia* **57** G14
Bantva, *India* **62** J4
Banu, *Afghan.* **60** B6
Banyak, Kepulauan,
Indonesia **56** D1
Banyo, *Cameroon* **79** D7
Banyuls-sur-Mer, *France* . **26** F7
Banyumas, *Indonesia* . . . **57** G13
Banyuwangi, *Indonesia* . . **57** H16
Banzare Coast, *Antarctica* . **5** C9
Banzyville = Mobayi, *Zaïre* **80** D4
Bao Ha, *Vietnam* **58** A5
Bao Lac, *Vietnam* **58** A5
Bao Loc, *Vietnam* **59** G6
Bao'an, *China* **53** F10
Baocheng, *China* **50** H4
Baode, *China* **50** E6
Baodi, *China* **51** E9
Baoding, *China* **50** E8
Baoji, *China* **50** G4
Baojing, *China* **52** C7
Baokang, *China* **53** B8
Baoshan, *Shanghai, China* **53** B13
Baoshan, *Yunnan, China* . **52** E2
Baotou, *China* **50** D6
Baoying, *China* **51** H10
Bap, *India* **62** F5
Bapatla, *India* **61** M12
Bapaume, *France* **25** B9
Bāqerābād, *Iran* **65** C6
Ba'qūbah, *Iraq* **64** C5
Baquedano, *Chile* **126** A2
Bar, *Montenegro* **21** N9
Bar, *Ukraine* **42** B2
Bar Bigha, *India* **63** G11
Bar Harbor, *U.S.A.* **99** D6
Bar-le-Duc, *France* **25** D12
Bar-sur-Aube, *France* . . . **25** D11
Bar-sur-Seine, *France* . . . **25** D11
Barabai, *Indonesia* **56** E5
Barabinsk, *Russia* **44** D8
Baraboo, *U.S.A.* **108** D10
Baracaldo, *Spain* **28** B2
Baracoa, *Cuba* **117** B5
Baradero, *Argentina* **126** C4
Baraga, *U.S.A.* **108** B10
Barahona, *Dom. Rep.* . . **117** C5
Barahona, *Spain* **28** D2
Barail Range, *India* **61** G18
Baraka →, *Sudan* **76** D4
Barakaldo = Baracaldo,
Spain **28** B2
Barakhola, *India* **61** G18
Barakot, *India* **63** J11
Barakpur, *India* **63** H13
Barakula, *Australia* **91** D5
Baralaba, *Australia* **90** C4
Baralzon L., *Canada* . . . **101** B9
Barameiya, *Sudan* **76** D4
Baramula, *India* **63** B6
Baran, *India* **62** G7
Baranavichy =
Baranovichi, *Belorussia* **40** E5
Baranoa, *Colombia* **120** A3
Baranof I., *U.S.A.* **100** B1
Baranovichi, *Belorussia* . . **40** E5
Barão de Cocais, *Brazil* . . **123** E3
Barão de Grajaú, *Brazil* . . **122** C3
Barão de Melgaço,
Mato Grosso, Brazil . . . **125** D6
Barão de Melgaço,
Rondônia, Brazil **125** C5
Baraolt, *Romania* **38** C8
Barapasi, *Indonesia* **57** E9
Barasat, *India* **63** H13
Barat Daya, Kepulauan,
Indonesia **57** F7
Barataria B., *U.S.A.* . . . **109** L10
Baraut, *India* **62** E7
Baraya, *Colombia* **120** C2
Barbacena, *Brazil* **123** F3
Barbacoas, *Colombia* . . . **120** C2
Barbacoas, *Venezuela* . . **120** B4
Barbados ■, *W. Indies* . . **117** D8
Barbalha, *Brazil* **122** C4
Barban, *Croatia* **33** C11
Barbastro, *Spain* **28** C5
Barbate, *Spain* **31** J5
Barberino di Mugello, *Italy* **33** D8
Barberton, *S. Africa* **85** D5
Barberton, *U.S.A.* **106** E3
Barbezieux, *France* **26** C3
Barbosa, *Colombia* **120** B3
Barbourville, *U.S.A.* **105** G4
Barbuda, *W. Indies* **117** C7
Barcaldine, *Australia* . . . **90** C4
Barcarrota, *Spain* **31** G4
Barcellona Pozzo di Gotto,
Italy **35** D8
Barcelona, *Spain* **28** D7
Barcelona, *Venezuela* . . **121** A5
Barcelona □, *Spain* **28** D7

Barcelonette, *France* . . . **27** D10
Barcelos, *Brazil* **121** D5
Barcoo →, *Australia* **90** D3
Barcs, *Hungary* **21** K7
Barda, *Azerbaijan* **43** F12
Barda del Medio, *Argentina* **128** A3
Bardai, *Chad* **73** D8
Bardas Blancas, *Argentina* **126** D2
Barddhaman, *India* **63** H12
Bardejov, *Slovak Rep.* . . . **20** F11
Bardera, *Somali Rep.* . . . **68** G3
Bardi, *Italy* **32** D6
Bardolino, *Italy* **32** C7
Bardsey I., *U.K.* **12** E3
Bardstown, *U.S.A.* **104** G3
Bareilly, *India* **63** E8
Barentin, *France* **24** C7
Barenton, *France* **24** D6
Barents Sea, *Arctic* **4** B9
Barentu, *Eritrea* **77** D4
Barfleur, *France* **24** C5
Barfleur, Pte. de, *France* . **24** C5
Barga, *China* **54** C3
Barga, *Italy* **32** D7
Bargal, *Somali Rep.* **68** E5
Bargara, *Australia* **90** C5
Barge, *Italy* **32** D4
Bargnop, *Sudan* **77** F2
Bargteheide, *Germany* . . **18** B6
Barguzin, *Russia* **45** D11
Barh, *India* **63** G11
Barhaj, *India* **63** F10
Barhi, *India* **63** G11
Bari, *India* **62** F7
Bari, *Italy* **35** A9
Bari Doab, *Pakistan* **62** D5
Bariadi □, *Tanzania* **82** C3
Barīm, *Yemen* **68** E3
Barima →, *Guyana* **121** B5
Barinas, *Venezuela* **120** B3
Barinas □, *Venezuela* . . . **120** B4
Baring, C., *Canada* **96** B8
Baringo, *Kenya* **82** B4
Baringo □, *Kenya* **82** B4
Baringo, L., *Kenya* **82** B4
Barinitas, *Venezuela* . . . **120** B3
Bariri, *Brazil* **123** F2
Bârîs, *Egypt* **76** C3
Barisal, *Bangla.* **61** H17
Barisan, Bukit, *Indonesia* . **56** E2
Barito →, *Indonesia* **56** E4
Barjac, *France* **27** D8
Barjols, *France* **27** E10
Barjūj, Wadi →, *Libya* . . . **75** C7
Bark L., *Canada* **106** A7
Barka = Baraka →, *Sudan* **76** D4
Barkam, *China* **52** B4
Barker, *U.S.A.* **106** C6
Barkley Sound, *Canada* . . **100** D3
Barkly Downs, *Australia* . . **90** C2
Barkly East, *S. Africa* . . . **84** E4
Barkly Tableland, *Australia* **90** B2
Barkly West, *S. Africa* . . . **84** D3
Barkol, Wadi →, *Sudan* . . **76** D3
Barksdale, *U.S.A.* **109** L4
Barlee, L., *Australia* **89** E2
Barlee, Mt., *Australia* . . . **89** D4
Barletta, *Italy* **35** A9
Barlinek, *Poland* **20** C5
Barlovento, *Canary Is.* . . . **36** F2
Barlow L., *Canada* **101** A8
Barmedman, *Australia* . . . **91** E4
Barmer, *India* **62** G4
Barmera, *Australia* **91** E3
Barmouth, *U.K.* **12** E3
Barmstedt, *Germany* **18** B5
Barnagar, *India* **62** H6
Barnard Castle, *U.K.* . . . **12** C6
Barnato, *Australia* **91** E3
Barnaul, *Russia* **44** D9
Barnesville, *U.S.A.* **105** J3
Barnet, *U.K.* **13** F7
Barneveld, *Neths.* **16** D7
Barneveld, *U.S.A.* **107** C9
Barneville-Carteret,
France **24** C5
Barngo, *Australia* **90** D4
Barnhart, *U.S.A.* **109** K4
Barnsley, *U.K.* **12** D6
Barnstaple, *U.K.* **13** F3
Barnsville, *U.S.A.* **108** B6
Baro, *Nigeria* **79** D6
Baro →, *Ethiopia* **77** F3
Baroda = Vadodara, *India* **62** H5
Baroda, *India* **62** G7
Baroe, *S. Africa* **84** E3
Baron Ra., *Australia* **88** D4
Barpeta, *India* **61** F17
Barques, Pt. Aux, *U.S.A.* . **104** C4
Barquinha, *Portugal* **31** F2
Barquísimeto, *Venezuela* . **120** A4
Barr, *France* **25** D14
Barra, *Brazil* **122** D3
Barra, *U.K.* **14** E1
Barra, Sd. of, *U.K.* **14** D1
Barra da Estiva, *Brazil* . . **123** D3
Barra de Navidad, *Mexico* **114** D4
Barra do Corda, *Brazil* . . **122** C2
Barra do Mendes, *Brazil* . **123** D3
Barra do Piraí, *Brazil* . . . **123** F3
Barra Falsa, Pta. da,
Mozam. **85** C6
Barra Hd., *U.K.* **14** E1
Barra Mansa, *Brazil* . . . **123** F3

Barraba, *Australia* **91** E5
Barracão do Barreto, *Brazil* **125** B6
Barrackpur = Barakpur,
India **63** H13
Barrafranca, *Italy* **35** E7
Barranca, *Lima, Peru* . . . **124** C2
Barranca, *Loreto, Peru* . . **120** D2
Barrancabermeja, *Colombia* **120** B3
Barrancas, *Colombia* . . . **120** A3
Barrancas, *Venezuela* . . . **121** B5
Barrancos, *Portugal* **31** G4
Barranqueras, *Argentina* . **126** B4
Barranquilla, *Colombia* . . **120** A3
Barras, *Brazil* **122** B3
Barras, *Colombia* **120** D3
Barraute, *Canada* **98** C4
Barre, *Mass., U.S.A.* . . . **107** D12
Barre, *Vt., U.S.A.* **107** B12
Barre do Bugres, *Brazil* . . **125** C6
Barreal, *Argentina* **126** C2
Barreiras, *Brazil* **123** D3
Barreirinha, *Brazil* **121** D6
Barreirinhas, *Brazil* **122** B3
Barreiro, *Portugal* **31** G1
Barreiros, *Brazil* **122** C4
Barrême, *France* **27** E10
Barren, Nosy, *Madag.* . . . **85** B7
Barretos, *Brazil* **123** F2
Barrhead, *Canada* **100** C6
Barrie, *Canada* **98** D4
Barrier Ra., *Australia* . . . **91** E3
Barrière, *Canada* **100** C4
Barrington, *U.S.A.* **107** E13
Barrington L., *Canada* . . . **101** B8
Barrington Tops, *Australia* **91** E5
Barringun, *Australia* **91** D4
Barro do Garças, *Brazil* . . **125** D7
Barrow, *U.S.A.* **96** A4
Barrow →, *Ireland* **15** D4
Barrow, C., *U.S.A.* **94** B4
Barrow Creek, *Australia* . . **90** C1
Barrow I., *Australia* **88** D2
Barrow-in-Furness, *U.K.* . **12** C4
Barrow Pt., *Australia* . . . **90** A3
Barrow Ra., *Australia* . . . **89** E4
Barrow Str., *Canada* **4** B3
Barruecopardo, *Spain* . . . **30** D4
Barruelo, *Spain* **30** C6
Barry, *U.K.* **13** F4
Barry's Bay, *Canada* **98** C4
Barsalogho, *Burkina Faso* **79** C4
Barsat, *Pakistan* **63** A5
Barsham, *Syria* **64** C4
Barsi, *India* **60** K9
Barsø, *Denmark* **11** J3
Barsoi, *India* **61** G15
Barstow, *Calif., U.S.A.* . . **113** L9
Barstow, *Tex., U.S.A.* . . . **109** K3
Barth, *Germany* **18** A8
Barthélemy, Col, *Vietnam* **58** C5
Bartica, *Guyana* **121** B6
Bartin, *Turkey* **66** C5
Bartlesville, *U.S.A.* **109** G7
Bartlett, *Calif., U.S.A.* . . . **112** J8
Bartlett, *Tex., U.S.A.* . . . **109** K6
Bartlett, L., *Canada* **100** A5
Bartolomeu Dias, *Mozam.* **83** G4
Barton, *Australia* **89** F5
Barton upon Humber, *U.K.* **12** D7
Bartoszyce, *Poland* **20** A10
Bartow, *U.S.A.* **105** M5
Barú, I. de, *Colombia* . . . **120** A2
Barú, Volcan, *Panama* . . . **116** E3
Barumba, *Zaïre* **82** B1
Baruth, *Germany* **18** C9
Barvaux, *Belgium* **17** H6
Barvenkovo, *Ukraine* . . . **42** B7
Barwani, *India* **62** H6
Barysaw = Borisov,
Belorussia **40** D6
Barysh, *Russia* **41** E15
Barzān, *Iraq* **64** B5
Bas-Rhin □, *France* **25** D14
Bašaid, *Serbia* **21** K10
Bāsa'idū, *Iran* **65** E7
Basal, *Pakistan* **62** C5
Basankusa, *Zaïre* **80** D3
Basawa, *Afghan.* **62** B4
Bascharage, *Lux.* **17** J7
Bascuñán, C., *Chile* **126** B1
Basècles, *Belgium* **17** G3
Basel, *Switz.* **22** A5
Basel-Stadt □, *Switz.* . . . **22** A5
Baselland □, *Switz.* **22** B5
Basento →, *Italy* **35** B9
Bāshī, *Iran* **65** D6
Bashi Channel, *Phil.* **54** D7
Bashkir Republic =
Bashkortostan □, *Russia* **44** D6
Bashkortostan = Bashkir
Republic □, *Russia* . . . **44** D6
Basilan, *Phil.* **55** H5
Basilan Str., *Phil.* **55** H5
Basildon, *U.K.* **13** F8
Basilicata □, *Italy* **35** B9
Basim = Washim, *India* . . **60** J10
Basin, *U.S.A.* **110** D9
Basingstoke, *U.K.* **13** F6
Baška, *Croatia* **33** D11
Başkale, *Turkey* **67** D10
Baskatong, Rés., *Canada* . **98** C4
Basle = Basel, *Switz.* . . . **22** A5
Basoda, *India* **62** H7
Basodino, *Switz.* **23** D6
Basoka, *Zaïre* **82** B1
Basongo, *Zaïre* **80** E4

Basque, Pays, France 26 E2
Basque Provinces = País Vasco □, Spain 28 C2
Basra = Al Baṣrah, Iraq .. 64 D5
Bass Rock, U.K. 14 E6
Bass Str., Australia 90 F4
Bassano, Canada 100 C6
Bassano del Grappa, Italy 33 C8
Bassar, Togo 79 D5
Bassas da India, Ind. Oc. . 81 J7
Basse Santa-Su, Gambia . 78 C2
Basse-Terre, Guadeloupe . 117 C7
Bassecourt, Switz. 22 B4
Bassein, Burma, ... 61 L19
Basseterre, St. Christopher-Nevis . 117 C7
Bassett, Nebr., U.S.A. ... 108 D5
Bassett, Va., U.S.A. 105 G6
Bassevelde, Belgium 17 F3
Bassigny, France 25 E12
Bassikounou, Mauritania . 78 B3
Bassilly, Belgium 17 G3
Bassum, Germany 18 C4
Bassi, India 62 D7
Båstad, Sweden 11 H6
Bastak, Iran 65 E7
Bastām, Iran 65 B7
Bastar, India 61 K12
Bastelica, France 27 F13
Basti, India 63 F10
Bastia, France 27 F13
Bastia Umbra, Italy 33 E9
Bastogne, Belgium 17 H7
Bastrop, U.S.A. 109 K6
Bat Yam, Israel 69 C3
Bata, Eq. Guin. 80 D1
Bata, Romania 38 C5
Bataan, Phil. 55 D4
Batabanó, Cuba 116 B3
Batabanó, G. de, Cuba .. 116 B3
Batac, Phil. 55 B4
Batagoy, Russia 45 C14
Batak, Bulgaria 39 H7
Batalha, Portugal 31 F2
Batama, Zaïre 82 B2
Batamay, Russia 45 C13
Batan I., Phil. 55 A4
Batanes Is., Phil. 55 A4
Batang, China 52 B2
Batang, Indonesia 57 G13
Batangafo, C.A.R. 73 G8
Batangas, Phil. 55 E4
Batanta, Indonesia 57 E8
Batatais, Brazil 127 A6
Batavia, U.S.A. 106 D6
Bataysk, Russia 43 C8
Batchelor, Australia 88 B5
Bateman's B., Australia . 91 F5
Batemans Bay, Australia . 91 F5
Bates Ra., Australia 89 E3
Batesburg, U.S.A. 105 J5
Batesville, Ark., U.S.A. .. 109 H9
Batesville, Miss., U.S.A. . 109 H10
Batesville, Tex., U.S.A. .. 109 L5
Bath, U.K. 13 F5
Bath, Maine, U.S.A. 99 D6
Bath, N.Y., U.S.A. 106 D7
Batheay, Cambodia 59 G5
Bathgate, U.K. 14 F5
Bathmen, Neths. 16 D8
Bathurst = Banjul, Gambia 78 C1
Bathurst, Australia 91 E4
Bathurst, Canada 99 C6
Bathurst, S. Africa 84 E4
Bathurst, C., Canada ... 96 A7
Bathurst B., Australia ... 90 A3
Bathurst Harb., Australia . 90 G4
Bathurst I., Australia ... 88 B5
Bathurst I., Canada 4 B2
Bathurst Inlet, Canada .. 96 B9
Batie, Burkina Faso 78 D4
Batlow, Australia 91 F4
Batman, Turkey 67 E9
Batna, Algeria 75 A6
Batobato, Phil. 55 H7
Batoka, Zambia 83 F2
Baton Rouge, U.S.A. ... 109 K9
Batong, Ko, Thailand ... 59 J2
Batopilas, Mexico 114 B3
Batouri, Cameroon 80 D2
Battambang, Cambodia . 58 F4
Batticaloa, Sri Lanka ... 60 R12
Battice, Belgium 17 G7
Battipáglia, Italy 35 B7
Battle, U.K. 13 G8
Battle →, Canada 101 C7
Battle Camp, Australia .. 90 B3
Battle Creek, U.S.A. ... 104 D3
Battle Ground, U.S.A. .. 112 E4
Battle Harbour, Canada . 99 B8
Battle Lake, U.S.A. 108 B7
Battle Mountain, U.S.A. . 110 F5
Battlefields, Zimbabwe . 83 F2
Battleford, Canada 101 C7
Battonya, Hungary 21 J11
Batu, Ethiopia 68 F2
Batu, Kepulauan, Indonesia 56 E1
Batu Caves, Malaysia ... 59 L3
Batu Gajah, Malaysia .. 59 K3
Batu Is. = Batu, Kepulauan, Indonesia . 56 E1
Batu Pahat, Malaysia ... 59 M4
Batuata, Indonesia 57 F6
Batumi, Georgia 43 F9
Baturaja, Indonesia 56 E2

Baturité, Brazil 122 B4
Bau, Malaysia 56 D4
Baubau, Indonesia 57 F6
Bauchi, Nigeria 79 C6
Bauchi □, Nigeria 79 C6
Baud, France 24 E3
Baudette, U.S.A. 108 A7
Baudour, Belgium 17 H3
Bauer, C., Australia 91 E1
Baugé, France 24 E6
Bauhinia Downs, Australia 90 C4
Bauma, Switz. 23 B7
Baume-les-Dames, France 25 E13
Baunatal, Germany 18 D5
Baunei, Italy 34 B2
Baures, Bolivia 125 C5
Bauru, Brazil 127 A6
Baús, Brazil 125 D7
Bauska, Latvia 40 C4
Bautzen, Germany 18 D10
Bavānāt, Iran 65 D7
Bavaria = Bayern □, Germany 19 F7
Båven, Sweden 10 F10
Bavi Sadri, India 62 G6
Bavispe →, Mexico 114 B3
Bawdwin, Burma 61 H20
Bawean, Indonesia 56 F4
Bawku, Ghana 79 C4
Bawlake, Burma 61 K20
Bawolung, China 52 C3
Baxley, U.S.A. 105 K4
Baxoi, China 52 B1
Baxter Springs, U.S.A. .. 109 G7
Bay, L. de, Phil. 57 B6
Bay Bulls, Canada 99 C9
Bay City, Mich., U.S.A. . 104 D4
Bay City, Oreg., U.S.A. . 110 D2
Bay City, Tex., U.S.A. .. 109 L7
Bay de Verde, Canada .. 99 C9
Bay Minette, U.S.A. 105 K2
Bay St. Louis, U.S.A. ... 109 K10
Bay Springs, U.S.A. 109 K10
Bay View, N.Z. 87 H6
Baya, Zaïre 83 E2
Bayamo, Cuba 116 B4
Bayamón, Puerto Rico .. 117 C6
Bayan Har Shan, China . 54 C4
Bayan Hot = Alxa Zuoqi, China 50 E3
Bayan Obo, China 50 D5
Bayan-Ovoo, Mongolia . 50 C4
Bayana, India 62 F7
Bayanaul, Kazakhstan .. 44 D8
Bayandalay, Mongolia .. 50 C2
Bayanhongor, Mongolia . 54 B5
Bayard, U.S.A. 108 E3
Bayawan, Phil. 55 G5
Baybay, Phil. 55 F6
Bayburt, Turkey 67 C9
Bayerischer Wald, Germany 19 F8
Bayern □, Germany 19 F7
Bayeux, France 24 C6
Bayfield, Canada 106 C3
Bayfield, U.S.A. 108 B9
Bayındır, Turkey 66 D2
Baykal, Oz., Russia 45 D11
Baykit, Russia 45 C10
Baykonur, Kazakhstan .. 44 E7
Baynes Mts., Namibia .. 84 B1
Bayombong, Phil. 55 C4
Bayon, France 25 D13
Bayona, Spain 30 C2
Bayonne, France 26 E2
Bayonne, U.S.A. 107 F10
Bayovar, Peru 124 B1
Bayram-Ali, Turkmenistan 44 F7
Bayramiç, Turkey 66 D2
Bayreuth, Germany 19 F7
Bayrischzell, Germany .. 19 H8
Bayrūt, Lebanon 69 B4
Bayt Lahm, Jordan 69 D4
Baytown, U.S.A. 109 L7
Bayzo, Niger 79 C5
Baza, Spain 29 H2
Bazar Dyuzi, Russia 43 F12
Bazarny Karabulak, Russia 41 E15
Bazarnyy Syzgan, Russia . 41 E15
Bazartobe, Kazakhstan .. 43 B14
Bazaruto, I. do, Mozam. . 85 C6
Bazas, France 26 D3
Bazhong, China 52 B6
Bazmān, Kūh-e, Iran ... 65 D9
Beach, U.S.A. 108 B3
Beach City, U.S.A. 106 F3
Beachport, Australia ... 91 F2
Beachy Hd., U.K. 13 G8
Beacon, Australia 89 F2
Beacon, U.S.A. 107 E11
Beaconia, Canada 101 C9
Beagle, Canal, S. Amer. . 128 E3
Beagle Bay, Australia ... 88 C3
Bealanana, Madag. 85 A8
Beamsville, Canada 106 C5
Bear →, U.S.A. 112 G5
Béar, C., France 26 F7
Bear I., Ireland 15 E2
Bear L., B.C., Canada .. 100 B3
Bear L., Man., Canada .. 101 B9
Bear L., U.S.A. 110 E8
Bearcreek, U.S.A. 110 D9
Beardmore, Canada ... 98 C2
Beardmore Glacier, Antarctica 5 E11

Beardstown, U.S.A. 108 F9
Béarn, France 26 E3
Bearpaw Mts., U.S.A. .. 110 B9
Bearskin Lake, Canada . 98 B1
Beas de Segura, Spain .. 29 G2
Beasain, Spain 28 B2
Beata, C., Dom. Rep. ... 117 C5
Beata, I., Dom. Rep. ... 117 C5
Beatrice, U.S.A. 108 E6
Beatrice, Zimbabwe 83 F3
Beatrice, C., Australia .. 90 A2
Beatton →, Canada ... 100 B4
Beatton River, Canada .. 100 B4
Beatty, U.S.A. 111 H5
Beaucaire, France 27 E8
Beauce, Plaine de la, France 25 D8
Beauceville, Canada ... 99 C5
Beauchêne, I., Falk. Is. . 128 D5
Beaudesert, Australia .. 91 D5
Beaufort, Malaysia 56 C5
Beaufort, N.C., U.S.A. .. 105 H7
Beaufort, S.C., U.S.A. .. 105 J5
Beaufort Sea, Arctic ... 4 B1
Beaufort West, S. Africa . 84 E3
Beaugency, France 25 E8
Beauharnois, Canada .. 98 C5
Beaujeu, France 27 B8
Beaulieu →, Canada ... 100 A6
Beaulieu-sur-Dordogne, France 26 D5
Beaulieu-sur-Mer, France 27 E11
Beauly, U.K. 14 D4
Beauly →, U.K. 14 D4
Beaumaris, U.K. 12 D3
Beaumetz-lès-Loges, France 25 B9
Beaumont, Belgium ... 17 H4
Beaumont, France 26 D4
Beaumont, Calif., U.S.A. 113 M10
Beaumont, Tex., U.S.A. . 109 K7
Beaumont-de-Lomagne, France 26 E4
Beaumont-le-Roger, France 24 C7
Beaumont-sur-Oise, France 25 C9
Beaumont-sur-Sarthe, France 24 D7
Beaune, France 25 E11
Beaune-la-Rolande, France 25 D9
Beaupréau, France 24 E6
Beauraing, Belgium ... 17 H5
Beauvais, France 25 C9
Beauval, Canada 101 B7
Beauvoir-sur-Mer, France 24 F4
Beauvoir-sur-Niort, France 26 B3
Beaver, Alaska, U.S.A. .. 96 B5
Beaver, Okla., U.S.A. ... 109 G4
Beaver, Pa., U.S.A. 106 F4
Beaver, Utah, U.S.A. ... 111 G7
Beaver →, B.C., Canada 100 B4
Beaver →, Ont., Canada 98 A2
Beaver →, Sask., Canada 101 B7
Beaver City, U.S.A. 108 E5
Beaver Dam, U.S.A. ... 108 D10
Beaver Falls, U.S.A. 106 F4
Beaver Hill L., Canada .. 101 C10
Beaver I., U.S.A. 104 C3
Beaverhill L., Alta., Canada 100 C6
Beaverhill L., N.W.T., Canada 101 A8
Beaverlodge, Canada .. 100 B5
Beavermouth, Canada .. 100 C5
Beaverstone →, Canada 98 B2
Beaverton, Canada 106 B5
Beaverton, U.S.A. 112 E4
Beawar, India 62 F6
Bebedouro, Brazil 127 A6
Beboa, Madag. 85 B7
Bebra, Germany 18 E5
Beccles, U.K. 13 E9
Bečej, Serbia 21 K10
Becerreá, Spain 30 C3
Béchar, Algeria 75 B4
Beckley, U.S.A. 104 G5
Beckum, Germany 18 D4
Bečva →, Czech. 20 F7
Bédar, Spain 29 H3
Bédarieux, France 26 E7
Bédarrides, France 27 D8
Beddouza, Ras, Morocco 74 B3
Bedele, Ethiopia 77 F4
Bederkesa, Germany ... 18 B4
Bedeso, Ethiopia 77 F5
Bedford, Canada 98 C5
Bedford, S. Africa 84 E4
Bedford, U.K. 13 E7
Bedford, Ind., U.S.A. ... 104 F2
Bedford, Iowa, U.S.A. .. 108 E7
Bedford, Ohio, U.S.A. .. 106 E3
Bedford, Pa., U.S.A. ... 106 F6
Bedford, Va., U.S.A. ... 104 G6
Bedford, C., Australia .. 90 B4
Bedford Downs, Australia 88 C4
Bedfordshire □, U.K. .. 13 E7
Będków, Poland 20 D9
Bednja →, Croatia 33 B13
Bednodemyanovsk, Russia 41 E13
Bedónia, Italy 32 D6
Bedourie, Australia 90 C2
Bedretto, Switz. 23 C7
Bedum, Neths. 16 B9
Będzin, Poland 20 E9
Beech Grove, U.S.A. ... 104 F2
Beechy, Canada 101 C7

Beek, Gelderland, Neths. . 16 E8
Beek, Limburg, Neths. .. 17 G7
Beek, Noord-Brabant, Neths. 17 E7
Beekbergen, Neths. 16 D7
Beelitz, Germany 18 C8
Beenleigh, Australia ... 91 D5
Be'er Menuḥa, Israel ... 64 D2
Be'er Sheva', Israel 69 D3
Beersheba = Be'er Sheva', Israel 69 D3
Beerta, Neths. 16 B10
Beerze →, Neths. 16 E6
Beesd, Neths. 16 E6
Beeskow, Germany 18 C10
Beeston, U.K. 12 E6
Beetaloo, Australia 90 B1
Beetsterzwaag, Neths. . 16 B8
Beetzendorf, Germany .. 18 C7
Beeville, U.S.A. 109 L6
Befale, Zaïre 80 D4
Befandriana, Madag. .. 85 C7
Befotaka, Madag. 85 C8
Bega, Australia 91 F4
Bega, Canalul, Romania . 38 D3
Bégard, France 24 D3
Bègles, France 26 D3
Begna →, Norway 10 D4
Begonte, Spain 30 B3
Begusarai, India 63 G12
Behābād, Iran 65 C8
Behara, Madag. 85 C8
Behbehān, Iran 65 D6
Behshahr, Iran 65 B7
Bei Jiang →, China ... 53 F9
Bei'an, China 54 B7
Beibei, China 54 D5
Beigang, Taiwan 53 F13
Beihai, China 52 G7
Beijing, China 50 E9
Beijing □, China 50 E9
Beilen, Neths. 16 C8
Beiliu, China 53 F8
Beilngries, Germany ... 19 F7
Beilpajah, Australia ... 91 E3
Beilul, Eritrea 77 E5
Beipiao, China 51 D11
Beira, Mozam. 83 F3
Beirut = Bayrūt, Lebanon 69 B4
Beitaolaizhao, China ... 51 B13
Beitbridge, Zimbabwe .. 83 G3
Beiuș, Romania 38 C5
Beizhen, Liaoning, China . 51 D11
Beizhen, Shandong, China 51 F10
Beizhengzhen, China ... 51 B12
Beja, Portugal 31 G3
Béja, Tunisia 75 A6
Beja □, Portugal 31 H3
Bejaia, Algeria 75 A6
Béjar, Spain 30 E5
Bejestān, Iran 65 C8
Bekasi, Indonesia 57 G12
Békés, Hungary 21 J11
Békéscsaba, Hungary .. 21 J11
Bekily, Madag. 85 C8
Bekkevoort, Belgium .. 17 G5
Bekoji, Ethiopia 77 F4
Bekok, Malaysia 59 L4
Bekwai, Ghana 79 D4
Bela, India 63 G9
Bela, Pakistan 62 F2
Bela Crkva, Serbia 21 L11
Bela Palanka, Serbia ... 21 M12
Bela Vista, Brazil 126 A4
Bela Vista, Mozam. ... 85 D5
Bélâbre, France 26 B5
Belalcázar, Spain 31 G5
Belarus = Belorussia ■, Europe 40 E5
Belau ■, Pac. Oc. 92 G5
Belavenona, Madag. ... 85 C8
Belawan, Indonesia ... 56 D1
Belaya, Ethiopia 77 E4
Belaya Glina, Russia ... 43 C9
Belaya Kalitva, Russia .. 43 B9
Belaya Kholunitsa, Russia 41 B17
Belaya Tserkov, Ukraine . 40 G7
Belcher Is., Canada 97 C12
Belchite, Spain 28 D4
Belden, U.S.A. 112 E5
Belém, Brazil 122 B2
Belém de São Francisco, Brazil 122 C4
Belén, Argentina 126 B2
Belén, Colombia 120 C3
Belén, Paraguay 126 A4
Belen, U.S.A. 111 J10
Bélesta, France 26 F5
Belet Uen, Somali Rep. . 68 G4
Belev, Russia 41 E10
Belfair, U.S.A. 112 C4
Belfast, S. Africa 85 D5
Belfast, U.K. 15 B6
Belfast, Maine, U.S.A. .. 99 D6
Belfast, N.Y., U.S.A. ... 106 D6
Belfast □, U.K. 15 B6
Belfast L., U.K. 15 B6
Belfield, U.S.A. 108 B3
Belfort, France 25 E13
Belfort, Territoire de □, France 25 E13
Belfry, U.S.A. 110 D9
Belgaum, India 60 M9
Belgioioso, Italy 32 C6

Belgium ■, Europe 17 G5
Belgorod, Russia 41 F10
Belgorod-Dnestrovskiy, Ukraine 42 C4
Belgrade = Beograd, Serbia 21 L10
Belgrade, U.S.A. 110 D8
Belhaven, U.S.A. 105 H7
Beli Drim →, Europe .. 21 N10
Beli Manastir, Croatia .. 21 K8
Belice →, Italy 34 E5
Belin-Béliet, France ... 26 D3
Belinga, Gabon 80 D2
Belinskiy, Russia 41 E13
Belinyu, Indonesia 56 E3
Beliton Is. = Belitung, Indonesia 56 E3
Belitung, Indonesia 56 E3
Beliu, Romania 38 C5
Belize ■, Cent. Amer. .. 115 D7
Belize City, Belize 115 D7
Beljanica, Serbia 21 L11
Belkovskiy, Ostrov, Russia 45 B14
Bell →, Canada 98 C4
Bell Bay, Australia 90 G4
Bell I., Canada 99 B8
Bell-Irving →, Canada . 100 B3
Bell Peninsula, Canada . 97 B11
Bell Ville, Argentina ... 126 C3
Bella Bella, Canada ... 100 C3
Bella Coola, Canada ... 100 C3
Bella Flor, Bolivia 124 C4
Bella Unión, Uruguay .. 126 C4
Bella Vista, Corrientes, Argentina 126 B4
Bella Vista, Tucuman, Argentina 126 B2
Bellac, France 26 B5
Bellágio, Italy 32 C6
Bellaire, U.S.A. 106 F4
Bellary, India 60 M10
Bellata, Australia 91 D4
Belle Fourche, U.S.A. .. 108 C3
Belle Fourche →, U.S.A. 108 C3
Belle Glade, U.S.A. 105 M5
Belle-Ile, France 24 E3
Belle Isle, Canada 99 B8
Belle Isle, Str. of, Canada 99 B8
Belle-Isle-en-Terre, France 24 D3
Belle Plaine, Iowa, U.S.A. 108 E8
Belle Plaine, Minn., U.S.A. 108 C8
Belle Yella, Liberia 78 D3
Belledonne, Chaîne de, France 27 C10
Belledune, Canada 99 C6
Bellefontaine, U.S.A. .. 104 E4
Bellefonte, U.S.A. 106 F7
Bellegarde, France 25 E9
Bellegarde-en-Marche, France 26 C6
Bellegarde-sur-Valserine, France 27 B9
Bellême, France 24 D7
Belleoram, Canada 99 C8
Belleville, Canada 98 D4
Belleville, France 27 B8
Belleville, Ill., U.S.A. .. 108 F10
Belleville, Kans., U.S.A. . 108 F6
Belleville, N.Y., U.S.A. . 107 C8
Belleville-sur-Vie, France 24 F5
Bellevue, Canada 100 D6
Bellevue, Idaho, U.S.A. . 110 E6
Bellevue, Ohio, U.S.A. . 106 E2
Bellevue, Wash., U.S.A. 112 C4
Belley, France 27 C9
Bellin, Canada 97 B13
Bellingen, Australia ... 91 E5
Bellingham, U.S.A. ... 112 B4
Bellingshausen Sea, Antarctica 5 C17
Bellinzona, Switz. 23 D8
Bello, Colombia 120 B2
Bellows Falls, U.S.A. .. 107 C12
Bellpat, Pakistan 62 E3
Bellpuig, Spain 28 D6
Belluno, Italy 33 B9
Bellwood, U.S.A. 106 F6
Bélmez, Spain 31 G5
Belmont, Australia 91 E5
Belmont, Canada 106 D3
Belmont, S. Africa 84 D3
Belmont, U.S.A. 106 D6
Belmonte, Brazil 123 E11
Belmonte, Portugal ... 30 E3
Belmonte, Spain 28 F2
Belmopan, Belize 115 D7
Belmullet, Ireland 15 B2
Belo Horizonte, Brazil . 123 E10
Belo Jardim, Brazil ... 122 C4
Belo-sur-Mer, Madag. . 85 C7
Belo-Tsiribihina, Madag. 85 B7
Belogorsk, Russia 45 D13
Belogorsk, Ukraine ... 42 D6
Belogradchik, Bulgaria . 38 F5
Beloha, Madag. 85 D8
Beloit, Kans., U.S.A. .. 108 F5
Beloit, Wis., U.S.A. ... 108 D10
Belokorovichi, Ukraine . 40 F6
Belomorsk, Russia 44 C4
Belonia, India 61 H17
Belopolye, Ukraine ... 40 F9
Belorussia ■, Europe .. 40 E5
Belovo, Russia 44 D9
Beloye More, Russia ... 44 C4

Beloye Ozero, *Russia*	43	D12
Belozersk, *Russia*	41	A10
Belpasso, *Italy*	35	E7
Belsele, *Belgium*	17	F4
Belsito, *Italy*	34	E6
Beltana, *Australia*	91	E2
Belterra, *Brazil*	121	D7
Beltinci, *Slovenia*	33	B13
Belton, S.C., *U.S.A.*	105	H4
Belton, Tex., *U.S.A.*	109	K6
Belton Res., *U.S.A.*	109	K6
Beltsy, *Moldavia*	42	C3
Belturbet, *Ireland*	15	B4
Belukha, *Russia*	44	E9
Beluran, *Malaysia*	56	C5
Belvedere Maríttimo, *Italy*	35	C8
Belvès, *France*	26	D5
Belvidere, Ill., *U.S.A.*	108	D10
Belvidere, N.J., *U.S.A.*	107	F9
Belvis de la Jara, *Spain*	31	F6
Belyando →, *Australia*	90	C4
Belyy, *Russia*	40	D8
Belyy, *Russia*	44	B8
Belyy, Ostrov, *Russia*	44	B15
Belyy Yar, *Russia*	44	D9
Belzig, *Germany*	18	C8
Belzoni, *U.S.A.*	109	J9
Bemaraha, Lembalemban'i, *Madag.*	85	B7
Bemarivo, *Madag.*	85	C7
Bemarivo →, *Madag.*	85	B8
Bemavo, *Madag.*	85	C8
Bembéréke, *Benin*	79	C5
Bembesi, *Zimbabwe*	83	F2
Bembesi →, *Zimbabwe*	83	F2
Bembézar →, *Spain*	31	H5
Bemidji, *U.S.A.*	108	B7
Bemmel, *Neths.*	16	E7
Ben, *Iran*	65	C6
Ben Cruachan, *U.K.*	14	E3
Ben Dearg, *U.K.*	14	D4
Ben Gardane, *Tunisia*	75	B7
Ben Hope, *U.K.*	14	C4
Ben Lawers, *U.K.*	14	E4
Ben Lomond, N.S.W., *Australia*	91	E5
Ben Lomond, Tas., *Australia*	90	G4
Ben Lomond, *U.K.*	14	E4
Ben Luc, *Vietnam*	59	G6
Ben Macdhui, *U.K.*	14	D5
Ben Mhor, *U.K.*	14	D1
Ben More, Central, *U.K.*	14	E4
Ben More, Strath., *U.K.*	14	E2
Ben More Assynt, *U.K.*	14	C4
Ben Nevis, *U.K.*	14	E4
Ben Quang, *Vietnam*	58	D6
Ben Slimane, *Morocco*	74	B3
Ben Tre, *Vietnam*	59	G6
Ben Vorlich, *U.K.*	14	E4
Ben Wyvis, *U.K.*	14	D4
Bena, *Nigeria*	79	C6
Bena Dibele, *Zaïre*	80	E4
Benagalbón, *Spain*	31	J6
Benagerie, *Australia*	91	E3
Benahmed, *Morocco*	74	B3
Benalla, *Australia*	91	F4
Benambra, Mt., *Australia*	91	F4
Benamejí, *Spain*	31	H6
Benares = Varanasi, *India*	63	G10
Bénat, C., *France*	27	E10
Benavente, *Portugal*	31	G2
Benavente, *Spain*	30	C5
Benavides, *Spain*	30	C5
Benavides, *U.S.A.*	109	M5
Benbecula, *U.K.*	14	D1
Benbonyathe, *Australia*	91	E2
Bencubbin, *Australia*	89	F2
Bend, *U.S.A.*	110	D3
Bender Beila, *Somali Rep.*	68	F5
Bendering, *Australia*	89	F2
Bendery, *Moldavia*	42	C3
Bendigo, *Australia*	91	F3
Bendorf, *Germany*	18	E3
Beneˇ Beraq, *Israel*	69	C3
Beneden Knijpe, *Neths.*	16	C7
Benedictinos, *Brazil*	122	C3
Benedito Leite, *Brazil*	122	C3
Bénéna, *Mali*	78	C4
Benenitra, *Madag.*	85	C8
Benešov, *Czech.*	20	F4
Bénestroff, *France*	25	D13
Benet, *France*	26	B3
Benevento, *Italy*	35	A7
Benfeld, *France*	25	D14
Benga, *Mozam.*	83	F3
Bengal, Bay of, *Ind. Oc.*	61	K16
Bengbu, *China*	51	H9
Benghazi = Banghāzī, *Libya*	73	B9
Bengkalis, *Indonesia*	56	D2
Bengkulu, *Indonesia*	56	E2
Bengkulu □, *Indonesia*	56	E2
Bengough, *Canada*	101	D7
Benguela, *Angola*	81	G2
Benguerir, *Morocco*	74	B3
Benguérua, I., *Mozam.*	85	C6
Benha, *Egypt*	76	H7
Beni, *Zaïre*	82	B2
Beni □, *Bolivia*	125	C4
Beni →, *Bolivia*	125	C4
Beni Abbès, *Algeria*	75	B4
Beni-Haoua, *Algeria*	75	A5
Beni Mazâr, *Egypt*	76	J7
Beni Mellal, *Morocco*	74	B3
Beni Ounif, *Algeria*	75	B4

Beni Saf, *Algeria*	75	A4
Beni Suef, *Egypt*	76	J7
Beniah L., *Canada*	100	A6
Benicarló, *Spain*	28	E5
Benicia, *U.S.A.*	112	G4
Benidorm, *Spain*	29	G4
Benidorm, Islote de, *Spain*	29	G4
Benin ■, *Africa*	79	D5
Benin, Bight of, *W. Afr.*	79	D5
Benin City, *Nigeria*	79	D6
Benisa, *Spain*	29	G5
Benitses, *Greece*	37	A3
Benjamin Aceval, *Paraguay*	126	A4
Benjamin Constant, *Brazil*	120	D3
Benjamin Hill, *Mexico*	114	A2
Benkelman, *U.S.A.*	108	E4
Benkovac, *Croatia*	33	D12
Benlidi, *Australia*	90	C3
Bennebroek, *Neths.*	16	D5
Bennekom, *Neths.*	16	D7
Bennett, *Canada*	100	B2
Bennett, L., *Australia*	88	D5
Bennett, Ostrov, *Russia*	45	B15
Bennettsville, *U.S.A.*	105	H6
Bennington, *U.S.A.*	107	D11
Bénodet, *France*	24	E2
Benoni, S. *Africa*	85	D4
Benoud, *Algeria*	75	B5
Benque Viejo, *Belize*	115	D7
Bensheim, *Germany*	19	F4
Benson, *U.S.A.*	111	L8
Bent, *Iran*	65	E8
Benteng, *Indonesia*	57	F6
Bentinck I., *Australia*	90	B2
Bentiu, *Sudan*	77	F2
Bento Gonçalves, *Brazil*	127	B5
Benton, Ark., *U.S.A.*	109	H8
Benton, Calif., *U.S.A.*	112	H8
Benton, Ill., *U.S.A.*	108	F10
Benton Harbor, *U.S.A.*	104	D2
Bentu Liben, *Ethiopia*	77	F4
Bentung, *Malaysia*	59	L3
Benue □, *Nigeria*	79	D6
Benue →, *Nigeria*	79	D6
Benxi, *China*	51	D12
Benzdorp, *Surinam*	121	C7
Beo, *Indonesia*	57	D7
Beograd, Serbia, *Yug.*	21	L10
Beowawe, *U.S.A.*	110	F5
Bepan Jiang →, *China*	52	E6
Beppu, *Japan*	49	H5
Berati, *Albania*	39	J2
Berau, Teluk, *Indonesia*	57	E8
Berber, *Sudan*	76	D3
Berbera, *Somali Rep.*	68	E4
Berbérati, *C.A.R.*	80	D3
Berberia, C. del, *Spain*	36	C7
Berbice →, *Guyana*	121	B6
Berceto, *Italy*	32	D7
Berchtesgaden, *Germany*	19	H8
Berdichev, *Ukraine*	42	B3
Berdsk, *Russia*	44	D9
Berdyansk, *Ukraine*	42	C7
Berdychiv = Berdichev, *Ukraine*	42	B3
Berea, *U.S.A.*	104	G3
Berebere, *Indonesia*	57	D7
Bereda, *Somali Rep.*	68	E5
Berekum, *Ghana*	78	D4
Berenice, *Egypt*	76	C4
Berens →, *Canada*	101	C9
Berens I., *Canada*	101	C9
Berens River, *Canada*	101	C9
Berestechko, *Ukraine*	40	F4
Berești, *Romania*	38	C10
Beretău →, *Romania*	38	B4
Berettyo →, *Hungary*	21	J11
Berettyóújfalu, *Hungary*	21	H11
Berevo, Mahajanga, *Madag.*	85	B7
Berevo, Toliara, *Madag.*	85	B7
Bereza, *Belorussia*	40	E4
Berezhany, *Ukraine*	40	G4
Berezina →, *Belorussia*	40	E7
Berezna, *Ukraine*	40	F7
Bereznik, *Russia*	44	D6
Berezovka, *Ukraine*	42	C4
Berezovo, *Russia*	44	C7
Berga, *Spain*	28	C6
Bergama, *Turkey*	66	D2
Bergambacht, *Neths.*	16	E5
Bérgamo, *Italy*	32	C6
Bergantiños, *Spain*	30	B2
Bergara, *Spain*	28	B2
Bergedorf, *Germany*	18	B6
Bergeijk, *Neths.*	17	F6
Bergen, *Germany*	18	A9
Bergen, *Neths.*	16	C5
Bergen, *Norway*	9	F8
Bergen, *U.S.A.*	106	C7
Bergen-op-Zoom, *Neths.*	17	F4
Bergerac, *France*	26	D4
Bergheim, *Germany*	18	E2
Berghem, *Neths.*	16	E7
Bergisch-Gladbach, *Germany*	18	E3
Bergschenhoek, *Neths.*	16	E5
Bergsjö, *Sweden*	10	C11
Bergues, *France*	25	B9
Bergum, *Neths.*	16	B7
Bergville, S. *Africa*	85	D4
Berhala, Selat, *Indonesia*	56	E2
Berhampore = Baharampur, *India*	63	G13
Berhampur, *India*	61	K14

Berheci →, *Romania*	38	C10
Bering Sea, *Pac. Oc.*	96	C1
Bering Strait, *U.S.A.*	96	B3
Beringen, *Belgium*	17	F6
Beringen, *Switz.*	23	A7
Beringovskiy, *Russia*	45	C18
Berislav, *Ukraine*	42	C5
Berisso, *Argentina*	126	C4
Berja, *Spain*	29	J2
Berkane, *Morocco*	75	B4
Berkeley, *U.K.*	13	F5
Berkeley, *U.S.A.*	112	H4
Berkeley Springs, *U.S.A.*	104	F6
Berkhout, *Neths.*	16	C5
Berkner I., *Antarctica*	5	D18
Berkovitsa, *Bulgaria*	38	F6
Berkshire □, *U.K.*	13	F6
Berlaar, *Belgium*	17	F5
Berland →, *Canada*	100	C5
Berlanga, *Spain*	31	G5
Berlare, *Belgium*	17	F4
Berlenga, I., *Portugal*	31	F1
Berlin, *Germany*	18	C9
Berlin, Md., *U.S.A.*	104	F8
Berlin, N.H., *U.S.A.*	107	B13
Berlin, Wis., *U.S.A.*	104	D1
Bermejo, Sierra, *Spain*	31	J5
Bermejo →, Formosa, *Argentina*	126	B4
Bermejo →, San Juan, *Argentina*	126	C2
Bermeo, *Spain*	28	B2
Bermillo de Sayago, *Spain*	30	D4
Bermuda ■, *Atl. Oc.*	2	C6
Bern, *Switz.*	22	C4
Bern □, *Switz.*	22	C5
Bernado, *U.S.A.*	111	J10
Bernalda, *Italy*	35	B9
Bernalillo, *U.S.A.*	111	J10
Bernardo de Irigoyen, *Argentina*	127	B5
Bernardo O'Higgins □, *Chile*	126	C1
Bernasconi, *Argentina*	126	D3
Bernau, Bayern, *Germany*	19	H8
Bernau, Brandenburg, *Germany*	18	C9
Bernay, *France*	24	C7
Bernburg, *Germany*	18	D7
Berne = Bern, *Switz.*	22	C4
Berne = Bern □, *Switz.*	22	C5
Berner Alpen, *Switz.*	22	D5
Bernese Oberland = Oberland, *Switz.*	22	C5
Bernier I., *Australia*	89	D1
Bernina, Piz, *Switz.*	23	D9
Bernina, Pizzo, *Switz.*	23	D9
Bernissart, *Belgium*	17	H3
Bernkastel-Kues, *Germany*	19	F3
Beroroha, *Madag.*	85	C8
Béroubouay, *Benin*	79	C5
Beroun, *Czech.*	20	F4
Berounka →, *Czech.*	20	F4
Berovo, *Macedonia*	39	H5
Berrahal, *Algeria*	75	A6
Berre, Étang de, *France*	27	E9
Berrechid, *Morocco*	74	B3
Berri, *Australia*	91	E3
Berriane, *Algeria*	75	B5
Berrouaghia, *Algeria*	75	A5
Berry, *Australia*	91	E5
Berry, *France*	25	F8
Berry Is., *Bahamas*	116	A4
Berryessa L., *U.S.A.*	112	G4
Berryville, *U.S.A.*	109	G8
Bersenbrück, *Germany*	18	C3
Berthold, *U.S.A.*	108	A4
Berthoud, *U.S.A.*	108	E2
Bertincourt, *France*	25	B9
Bertoua, *Cameroon*	80	D2
Bertrand, *U.S.A.*	108	E5
Bertrange, *Lux.*	17	J8
Bertrix, *Belgium*	17	J6
Berufjörður, *Iceland*	8	D6
Beruri, *Brazil*	121	D5
Berwick, *U.S.A.*	107	E8
Berwick-upon-Tweed, *U.K.*	12	B5
Berwyn Mts., *U.K.*	12	E4
Berzasca, *Romania*	38	E4
Besal, *Pakistan*	63	B5
Besalampy, *Madag.*	85	B7
Besançon, *France*	25	E13
Besar, *Indonesia*	56	E5
Beshenkovichi, *Belorussia*	40	D6
Beslan, *Russia*	43	E11
Besna Kobila, *Serbia, Yug.*	21	L12?
Besni, *Turkey*	67	E7
Besor, N. →, *Egypt*	69	D3
Bessarabiya, *Moldavia*	38	B11
Bessarabka, *Moldavia*	42	C3
Bessèges, *France*	27	D8
Bessemer, Ala., *U.S.A.*	105	J2
Bessemer, Mich., *U.S.A.*	108	B9
Bessin, *France*	24	C5
Bessines-sur-Gartempe, *France*	26	B5
Best, *Neths.*	17	E6
Bet She'an, *Israel*	69	C4
Bet Shemesh, *Israel*	69	D3
Bet Tadjine, Djebel, *Algeria*	74	C4
Betafo, *Madag.*	85	B8
Betancuria, *Canary Is.*	36	F5
Betanzos, *Bolivia*	125	D4

Betanzos, *Spain*	30	B2
Bétaré Oya, *Cameroon*	80	C2
Bétera, *Spain*	28	F4
Bethal, S. *Africa*	85	D4
Bethanien, *Namibia*	84	D2
Bethany, S. *Africa*	84	D4
Bethany, *U.S.A.*	108	E7
Bethel, Alaska, *U.S.A.*	96	B3
Bethel, Vt., *U.S.A.*	107	C12
Bethel Park, *U.S.A.*	106	F4
Bethlehem = Bayt Lahm, *Jordan*	69	D4
Bethlehem, S. *Africa*	85	D4
Bethlehem, *U.S.A.*	107	F9
Bethulie, S. *Africa*	84	E4
Béthune, *France*	25	B9
Béthune →, *France*	24	C8
Betijoque, *Venezuela*	120	B3
Betim, *Brazil*	123	E3
Betioky, *Madag.*	85	C7
Beton-Bazoches, *France*	25	D10
Betong, *Thailand*	59	K3
Betoota, *Australia*	90	D3
Betroka, *Madag.*	85	C8
Betsiamites, *Canada*	99	C6
Betsiamites →, *Canada*	99	C6
Betsiboka →, *Madag.*	85	B8
Betsjoeanaland, S. *Africa*	84	D3
Bettembourg, *Lux.*	17	J8
Bettiah, *India*	63	F11
Béttola, *Italy*	32	D6
Betul, *India*	60	J10
Betung, *Malaysia*	56	D4
Betzdorf, *Germany*	18	E3
Beuca, *Romania*	38	E7
Beuil, *France*	27	D10
Beulah, *U.S.A.*	108	B4
Beuvron →, *France*	24	E8
Beveren, *Belgium*	17	F4
Beverley, *Australia*	89	F2
Beverley, *U.K.*	12	D7
Beverlo, *Belgium*	17	F6
Beverly, Mass., *U.S.A.*	107	D14
Beverly, Wash., *U.S.A.*	110	C4
Beverly Hills, *U.S.A.*	113	L8
Beverwijk, *Neths.*	16	D5
Bex, *Switz.*	22	D4
Bey Dağları, *Turkey*	66	E4
Beyānlū, *Iran*	64	C5
Beyin, *Ghana*	78	D4
Beyla, *Guinea*	78	D3
Beynat, *France*	26	C5
Beyneu, *Kazakhstan*	44	E6
Beypazarı, *Turkey*	66	C4
Beyşehir Gölü, *Turkey*	66	E4
Beytüşşebap, *Turkey*	67	E10
Bezhetsk, *Russia*	41	C10
Bezhitsa, *Russia*	40	E9
Béziers, *France*	26	E7
Bezwada = Vijayawada, *India*	61	L12
Bhachau, *India*	60	H7
Bhadarwah, *India*	63	C6
Bhadravati, *India*	60	N9
Bhagalpur, *India*	63	G12
Bhakkar, *Pakistan*	62	D4
Bhakra Dam, *India*	62	D7
Bhamo, *Burma*	61	G20
Bhandara, *India*	60	J11
Bhanrer Ra., *India*	62	H8
Bharat = India ■, *Asia*	60	K11
Bharatpur, *India*	62	F7
Bhatinda, *India*	62	D6
Bhatpara, *India*	63	H13
Bhaun, *Pakistan*	62	C5
Bhaunagar = Bhavnagar, *India*	62	J5
Bhavnagar, *India*	62	J5
Bhawanipatna, *India*	61	K12
Bhera, *Pakistan*	62	C5
Bhilsa = Vidisha, *India*	62	H7
Bhilwara, *India*	62	G6
Bhima →, *India*	60	L10
Bhimavaram, *India*	61	L12
Bhimbar, *Pakistan*	63	C6
Bhind, *India*	62	F8
Bhiwandi, *India*	60	K8
Bhiwani, *India*	62	E7
Bhola, *Bangla.*	61	H17
Bhopal, *India*	62	H7
Bhubaneshwar, *India*	61	J14
Bhuj, *India*	62	H3
Bhumiphol Dam = Phumiphon, Khuan, *Thailand*	58	D2
Bhusaval, *India*	60	J9
Bhutan ■, *Asia*	61	F17
Biá →, *Brazil*	120	D4
Biafra, B. of = Bonny, Bight of, *Africa*	79	E6
Biak, *Indonesia*	57	E9
Biała →, *Poland*	20	E10
Biała Podlaska, *Poland*	20	C13
Białogard, *Poland*	20	A5
Białystok, *Poland*	20	B13
Biancavilla, *Italy*	35	E7
Biaro, *Indonesia*	57	D7
Biarritz, *France*	26	E2
Biasca, *Switz.*	23	D7
Biba, *Egypt*	76	J7
Bibai, *Japan*	48	C10
Bibala, *Angola*	81	G2

Bibane, Bahiret el, *Tunisia*	75	B7
Bibbiena, *Italy*	33	E8
Bibby I., *Canada*	101	A10
Biberach, *Germany*	19	G5
Biberist, *Switz.*	22	B5
Bibey →, *Spain*	30	C3
Bibiani, *Ghana*	78	D4
Biboohra, *Australia*	90	B4
Bibungwa, *Zaïre*	82	C2
Bic, *Canada*	99	C6
Bicaz, *Romania*	38	C9
Biccari, *Italy*	35	A8
Bichena, *Ethiopia*	77	E4
Bickerton I., *Australia*	90	A2
Bicknell, Ind., *U.S.A.*	104	F2
Bicknell, Utah, *U.S.A.*	111	G8
Bida, *Nigeria*	79	D6
Bidar, *India*	60	L10
Biddeford, *U.S.A.*	99	D5
Biddwara, *Ethiopia*	77	F4
Bideford, *U.K.*	13	F3
Bidon 5 = Poste Maurice Cortier, *Algeria*	75	D5
Bidor, *Malaysia*	59	K3
Bié, Planalto de, *Angola*	81	G3
Bieber, *U.S.A.*	110	F3
Biel, *Switz.*	22	B4
Bielawa, *Poland*	20	E6
Bielé Karpaty, *Europe*	20	F7
Bielefeld, *Germany*	18	C4
Bielersee, *Switz.*	22	B4
Biella, *Italy*	32	C5
Bielsk Podlaski, *Poland*	20	C13
Bielsko-Biała, *Poland*	20	F9
Bien Hoa, *Vietnam*	59	G6
Bienfait, *Canada*	101	D8
Bienne = Biel, *Switz.*	22	B4
Bienvenida, *Spain*	31	G4
Bienvenue, *Fr. Guiana*	121	C7
Bienville, L., *Canada*	98	A5
Biescas, *Spain*	28	C4
Biese →, *Germany*	18	C7
Biesiesfontein, S. *Africa*	84	E2
Bietigheim, *Germany*	19	G5
Bièvre, *Belgium*	17	J6
Biferno →, *Italy*	35	A8
Big →, *Canada*	99	B8
Big B., *Canada*	99	A7
Big Bear City, *U.S.A.*	113	L10
Big Bear Lake, *U.S.A.*	113	L10
Big Beaver, *Canada*	101	D7
Big Belt Mts., *U.S.A.*	110	C8
Big Bend, *Swaziland*	85	D5
Big Bend National Park, *U.S.A.*	109	L3
Big Black →, *U.S.A.*	109	J9
Big Blue →, *U.S.A.*	108	F6
Big Cr. →, *Canada*	100	C4
Big Creek, *U.S.A.*	112	H7
Big Cypress Swamp, *U.S.A.*	105	M5
Big Falls, *U.S.A.*	108	A8
Big Fork →, *U.S.A.*	108	A8
Big Horn Mts. = Bighorn Mts., *U.S.A.*	110	D10
Big Lake, *U.S.A.*	109	K4
Big Moose, *U.S.A.*	107	C10
Big Muddy Cr. →, *U.S.A.*	108	A2
Big Pine, *U.S.A.*	111	H4
Big Piney, *U.S.A.*	110	E8
Big Quill L., *Canada*	101	C8
Big Rapids, *U.S.A.*	104	D3
Big River, *Canada*	101	C7
Big Run, *U.S.A.*	106	F6
Big Sable Pt., *U.S.A.*	104	C2
Big Sand L., *Canada*	101	B9
Big Sandy, *U.S.A.*	110	B8
Big Sandy Cr. →, *U.S.A.*	108	F3
Big Sioux →, *U.S.A.*	108	D6
Big Spring, *U.S.A.*	109	J4
Big Springs, *U.S.A.*	108	E3
Big Stone City, *U.S.A.*	108	C6
Big Stone Gap, *U.S.A.*	105	G4
Big Stone L., *U.S.A.*	108	C6
Big Sur, *U.S.A.*	112	J5
Big Timber, *U.S.A.*	110	D9
Big Trout L., *Canada*	98	B1
Biˇga, *Turkey*	66	C2
Bigadiç, *Turkey*	66	D3
Biganos, *France*	26	D3
Bigfork, *U.S.A.*	110	B6
Biggar, *Canada*	101	C7
Biggar, *U.K.*	14	F5
Bigge I., *Australia*	88	B4
Biggenden, *Australia*	91	D5
Biggs, *U.S.A.*	112	F5
Bighorn, *U.S.A.*	110	C10
Bighorn →, *U.S.A.*	110	C10
Bighorn Mts., *U.S.A.*	110	D10
Bignona, *Senegal*	78	C1
Bigorre, *France*	26	E4
Bigstone L., *Canada*	101	C9
Bigwa, *Tanzania*	82	D4
Bihać, *Bos.-H.*	33	D12
Bihar, *India*	63	G11
Bihar □, *India*	63	G11
Biharamulo, *Tanzania*	82	C3
Biharamulo □, *Tanzania*	82	C3
Bihor, Munţii, *Romania*	38	C5
Bijagós, Arquipélago dos, *Guinea-Biss.*	78	C1
Bijaipur, *India*	62	F7
Bijapur, Karnataka, *India*	60	L9
Bijapur, Mad. P., *India*	61	K12
Bīǰār, *Iran*	64	C5

Bijeljina, *Bos.-H.* 21 L9
Bijelo Polje, *Montenegro* . 21 M9
Bijie, *China* 52 D5
Bijnor, *India* 62 E8
Bikaner, *India* 62 E5
Bikapur, *India* 63 F10
Bikeqi, *China* 50 D6
Bikfayyā, *Lebanon* 69 B4
Bikin, *Russia* 45 E14
Bikin →, *Russia* 48 A7
Bikini Atoll, *Pac. Oc.* ... 92 F8
Bikoué, *Cameroon* 79 E7
Bila Tserkva = Belaya
  Tserkov, *Ukraine* 40 G7
Bilara, *India* 62 F5
Bilaspur, *Mad. P., India* . 63 H10
Bilaspur, *Punjab, India* .. 62 D7
Bilauk Taungdan, *Thailand* 58 F2
Bilbao, *Spain* 28 B2
Bilbeis, *Egypt* 76 H7
Bilbo = Bilbao, *Spain* .. 28 B2
Bilbor, *Romania* 38 B8
Bíldudalur, *Iceland* 8 D2
Bileća, *Bos.-H.* 21 N8
Bilecik, *Turkey* 66 C4
Bilecik □, *Turkey* 66 C4
Biłgoraj, *Poland* 20 E12
Bilibino, *Russia* 45 C17
Bilibiza, *Mozam.* 83 E5
Bilir, *Russia* 45 C14
Biliran, I., *Phil.* 55 F6
Bill, *U.S.A.* 108 D2
Billabalong, *Australia* ... 89 E2
Billiluna, *Australia* 88 C4
Billingham, *U.K.* 12 C6
Billings, *U.S.A.* 110 D9
Billiton Is. = Belitung,
  Indonesia 56 E3
Billom, *France* 26 C7
Bilma, *Niger* 73 E7
Bilo Gora, *Croatia* 21 K7
Biloela, *Australia* 90 C5
Biloku, *Guyana* 121 C6
Biloxi, *U.S.A.* 109 K10
Bilpa Morea Claypan,
  Australia 90 D2
Bilthoven, *Neths.* 16 D6
Biltine, *Chad* 73 F9
Bilyana, *Australia* 90 B4
Bilyarsk, *Russia* 41 D17
Bilzen, *Belgium* 17 G7
Bima, *Indonesia* 57 F5
Bimban, *Egypt* 76 C3
Bimbila, *Ghana* 79 D5
Bimbo, *C.A.R.* 80 D3
Bimini Is., *Bahamas* 116 A4
Bin Xian, *Heilongjiang,*
  China 51 B14
Bin Xian, *Shaanxi, China* . 50 G5
Bina-Etawah, *India* 62 G8
Bināb, *Iran* 65 B6
Binalbagan, *Phil.* 55 F5
Binalong, *Australia* 91 E4
Bīnālūd, Kūh-e, *Iran* ... 65 B8
Binatang, *Malaysia* 56 D4
Binbee, *Australia* 90 C4
Binche, *Belgium* 17 H4
Binchuan, *China* 52 E3
Binda, *Australia* 91 D4
Bindle, *Australia* 91 D4
Bindura, *Zimbabwe* 83 F3
Bingara, *N.S.W., Australia* 91 D5
Bingara, *Queens., Australia* 91 D3
Bingen, *Germany* 19 F3
Bingerville, *Ivory C.* 78 D4
Bingham, *U.S.A.* 99 C6
Bingham Canyon, *U.S.A.* . 110 F7
Binghamton, *U.S.A.* 107 D9
Bingöl, *Turkey* 67 D9
Bingöl □, *Turkey* 67 D9
Bingöl Dağları, *Turkey* ... 67 D9
Binh Dinh = An Nhon,
  Vietnam 58 F7
Binh Khe, *Vietnam* 58 F7
Binh Son, *Vietnam* 58 E7
Binhai, *China* 51 G10
Binisatua, *Spain* 36 B11
Binjai, *Indonesia* 56 D1
Binnaway, *Australia* 91 E4
Binongko, *Indonesia* 57 F6
Binscarth, *Canada* 101 C8
Bintan, *Indonesia* 56 D2
Bintulu, *Malaysia* 56 D4
Bintuni, *Indonesia* 57 E8
Binyang, *China* 52 F7
Binz, *Germany* 18 A9
Binzert = Bizerte, *Tunisia* 75 A6
Bío Bío □, *Chile* 126 D1
Biograd, *Croatia* 33 E12
Bioko, *Eq. Guin.* 79 E6
Biougra, *Morocco* 74 B3
Bir, *India* 60 K9
Bir, Ras, *Djibouti* 77 E5
Bîr Abu Hashim, *Egypt* . 76 C3
Bîr Abu M'nqar, *Egypt* . 76 B2
Bîr Abu Muḥammad, *Egypt* 69 F3
Bi'r ad Dabbāghāt, *Jordan* 69 E4
Bi'r al Butayyihāt, *Jordan* 69 F4
Bi'r al Mārī, *Jordan* 69 E4
Bi'r al Qaṭṭār, *Jordan* ... 69 F4
Bir Aouine, *Tunisia* 75 B6
Bîr 'Asal, *Egypt* 76 B3
Bîr Autrun, *Sudan* 76 D2

Bîr Beiḍa, *Egypt* 69 E3
Bîr Diqnash, *Egypt* 76 A2
Bir el Abbes, *Algeria* 74 C3
Bîr el 'Abd, *Egypt* 69 D2
Bîr el Ater, *Algeria* 75 B6
Bîr el Basur, *Egypt* 76 B2
Bîr el Biarât, *Egypt* 69 F3
Bîr el Duweidar, *Egypt* .. 69 E1
Bîr el Garârât, *Egypt* 69 D2
Bîr el Gellaz, *Egypt* 76 A2
Bîr el Heisi, *Egypt* 69 F3
Bîr el Jafir, *Egypt* 69 E1
Bîr el Mâlhi, *Egypt* 69 E2
Bîr el Shaqqa, *Egypt* 76 A2
Bîr el Thamâda, *Egypt* ... 69 E2
Bîr Fuad, *Egypt* 76 A2
Bîr Gebeil Ḥisn, *Egypt* .. 69 E2
Bi'r Ghaḍîr, *Syria* 69 A6
Bîr Haimur, *Egypt* 76 C3
Bîr Ḥasana, *Egypt* 69 E2
Bi'r Jadîd, *Iraq* 64 C4
Bîr Jdid, *Morocco* 74 B3
Bîr Kanayis, *Egypt* 76 C3
Bîr Kaseiba, *Egypt* 69 E2
Bîr Kerawein, *Egypt* 76 B2
Bîr Lahfân, *Egypt* 69 D2
Bir Lahrache, *Algeria* ... 75 B6
Bîr Madkûr, *Egypt* 69 E1
Bîr Maql, *Egypt* 76 C3
Bîr Misaha, *Egypt* 76 C2
Bir Mogrein, *Mauritania* . 74 C2
Bîr Murr, *Egypt* 76 C3
Bi'r Muṭribah, *Kuwait* ... 64 D5
Bîr Nakheila, *Egypt* 76 C3
Bîr Qaṭia, *Egypt* 69 E1
Bîr Qatrani, *Egypt* 76 A2
Bîr Ranga, *Egypt* 76 C4
Bîr Sahara, *Egypt* 76 C2
Bîr Seiyâla, *Egypt* 76 B3
Bir Semguine, *Morocco* .. 74 B3
Bîr Shalatein, *Egypt* 76 C4
Bîr Shebb, *Egypt* 76 C2
Bîr Shût, *Egypt* 76 C4
Bîr Terfawi, *Egypt* 76 C2
Bîr Umm Qubûr, *Egypt* .. 76 C3
Bîr Ungât, *Egypt* 76 C3
Bîr Za'farâna, *Egypt* 76 J8
Bîr Zeidûn, *Egypt* 76 B3
Bira, *Indonesia* 57 E8
Bîra, *Romania* 38 B10
Biramféro, *Guinea* 78 C3
Birao, *C.A.R.* 73 F9
Birawa, *Zaïre* 82 C2
Bîrca, *Romania* 38 F6
Birch Hills, *Canada* 101 C7
Birch I., *Canada* 101 C9
Birch L., *N.W.T., Canada* 100 A5
Birch L., *Ont., Canada* .. 98 B1
Birch L., *U.S.A.* 98 C1
Birch Mts., *Canada* 100 B6
Birch River, *Canada* 101 C8
Birchip, *Australia* 91 F3
Bird, *Canada* 101 B10
Bird City, *U.S.A.* 108 F4
Bird I. = Aves, I. de,
  W. Indies 117 C7
Bird I., *S. Africa* 84 E2
Birdaard, *Neths.* 16 B7
Birdlip, *U.K.* 13 F5
Birdsville, *Australia* 90 D2
Birdum, *Australia* 88 C5
Birein, *Israel* 69 E3
Bireuen, *Indonesia* 56 C1
Birifo, *Gambia* 78 C2
Birigui, *Brazil* 127 A5
Birkenfeld, *Germany* 19 F3
Birkenhead, *U.K.* 12 D4
Birket Qârûn, *Egypt* 76 J7
Birkhadem, *Algeria* 75 A5
Bîrlad, *Romania* 38 C10
Birmingham, *U.K.* 13 E6
Birmingham, *U.S.A.* 105 J2
Birmitrapur, *India* 61 H14
Birni Ngaouré, *Niger* ... 79 C5
Birni Nkonni, *Niger* 79 C6
Birnin Gwari, *Nigeria* ... 79 C6
Birnin Kebbi, *Nigeria* ... 79 C5
Birnin Kudu, *Nigeria* ... 79 C6
Birobidzhan, *Russia* 45 E14
Birr, *Ireland* 15 C4
Birrie →, *Australia* 91 D4
Birs →, *Switz.* 22 B5
Birsilpur, *India* 62 E5
Birsk, *Russia* 44 D6
Birtin, *Romania* 38 C5
Birtle, *Canada* 101 C8
Birur, *India* 60 N9
Biryuchiy, *Ukraine* 42 C6
Biržai, *Lithuania* 40 C4
Bîrzava, *Romania* 38 C4
Birzebbuga, *Malta* 37 D2
Bisa, *Indonesia* 57 E7
Bisáccia, *Italy* 35 A8
Bisacquino, *Italy* 34 E6
Bisalpur, *India* 63 E8
Bisbee, *U.S.A.* 111 L9
Biscarrosse et de Parentis,
  Étang de, *France* 26 D2
Biscay, B. of, *Atl. Oc.* .. 6 F5
Biscayne B., *U.S.A.* 105 N5
Biscéglie, *Italy* 35 A9
Bischofshofen, *Austria* .. 21 H3
Bischofswerda, *Germany* . 18 D10
Bischofszell, *Switz.* 23 B8
Bischwiller, *France* 25 D14

Biscoe Bay, *Antarctica* ... 5 D13
Biscoe Is., *Antarctica* 5 C17
Biscostasing, *Canada* 98 C3
Biscucuy, *Venezuela* 120 B4
Biševo, *Croatia* 33 F13
Bisha, *Eritrea* 77 D4
Bishah, W. →, *Si. Arabia* 76 C5
Bishan, *China* 52 C6
Bishkek, *Kirghizia* 44 E8
Bishnupur, *India* 63 H12
Bisho, *S. Africa* 85 E4
Bishop, *Calif., U.S.A.* .. 111 H4
Bishop, *Tex., U.S.A.* ... 109 M6
Bishop Auckland, *U.K.* .. 12 C6
Bishop's Falls, *Canada* .. 99 C8
Bishop's Stortford, *U.K.* . 13 F8
Bisignano, *Italy* 35 C9
Bisina, L., *Uganda* 82 B3
Biskra, *Algeria* 75 B6
Bislig, *Phil.* 57 C7
Bismarck, *U.S.A.* 108 B4
Bismarck Arch.,
  Papua N. G. 92 H6
Bismark, *Germany* 18 C7
Biso, *Uganda* 82 B3
Bison, *U.S.A.* 108 C3
Bīsotūn, *Iran* 64 C5
Bispfors, *Sweden* 8 E14
Bispgården, *Sweden* 10 A10
Bissagos = Bijagós,
  Arquipélago dos,
  Guinea-Biss. 78 C1
Bissau, *Guinea-Biss.* ... 78 C1
Bissett, *Canada* 101 C9
Bissikrima, *Guinea* 78 C2
Bistcho L., *Canada* 100 B5
Bistreţu, *Romania* 38 F6
Bistrica = Ilirska-Bistrica,
  Slovenia 33 C11
Bistriţa, *Romania* 38 B7
Bistriţa →, *Romania* 38 C9
Bistriţei, Munţii, *Romania* 38 B8
Biswan, *India* 63 F9
Bitam, *Gabon* 80 D2
Bitburg, *Germany* 19 F2
Bitche, *France* 25 C14
Bithynia, *Turkey* 66 C4
Bitkine, *Chad* 73 F8
Bitlis, *Turkey* 67 D10
Bitlis □, *Turkey* 67 D10
Bitola, *Macedonia* 39 H4
Bitolj = Bitola, *Macedonia* 39 H4
Bitonto, *Italy* 35 A9
Bitter Creek, *U.S.A.* ... 110 F9
Bitter L. = Buheirat-
  Murrat-el-Kubra, *Egypt* 76 H8
Bitterfeld, *Germany* 18 D8
Bitterfontein, *S. Africa* .. 84 E2
Bitterroot →, *U.S.A.* ... 110 C6
Bitterroot Range, *U.S.A.* . 110 D6
Bitterwater, *U.S.A.* 112 J6
Bitti, *Italy* 34 B2
Bittou, *Burkina Faso* ... 79 C4
Biu, *Nigeria* 79 C7
Bivolari, *Romania* 38 B10
Bivolu, *Romania* 38 B8
Biwa-Ko, *Japan* 49 G8
Biwabik, *U.S.A.* 108 B8
Bixad, *Romania* 38 B6
Biyang, *China* 50 H7
Biysk, *Russia* 44 D9
Bizana, *S. Africa* 85 E4
Bizen, *Japan* 49 G7
Bizerte, *Tunisia* 75 A6
Bjargtangar, *Iceland* 8 D1
Bjelasica, *Montenegro* .. 21 N9
Bjelovar, *Croatia* 21 K6
Bjerringbro, *Denmark* ... 11 H3
Bjørnøya, *Arctic* 4 B8
Bjuv, *Sweden* 11 H6
Blace, *Serbia* 21 M11
Black = Da →, *Vietnam* . 58 B5
Black →, *Canada* 106 B5
Black →, *Ark., U.S.A.* .. 109 H9
Black →, *N.Y., U.S.A.* .. 107 C8
Black →, *Wis., U.S.A.* .. 108 D9
Black Diamond, *Canada* . 100 C6
Black Forest =
  Schwarzwald, *Germany* . 19 H4
Black Hills, *U.S.A.* 108 C3
Black I., *Canada* 101 C9
Black L., *Canada* 101 B7
Black L., *U.S.A.* 104 C3
Black Mesa, *U.S.A.* 109 G3
Black Mt. = Mynydd Du,
  U.K. 13 F4
Black Mts., *U.K.* 13 F4
Black Range, *U.S.A.* 111 K10
Black River, *Jamaica* ... 116 C4
Black River Falls, *U.S.A.* . 108 C9
Black Sea, *Europe* 42 E6
Black Volta →, *Africa* .. 78 D4
Black Warrior →, *U.S.A.* 105 J2
Blackall, *Australia* 90 C4
Blackball, *N.Z.* 87 K3
Blackbull, *Australia* 90 B3
Blackburn, *U.K.* 12 D5
Blackduck, *U.S.A.* 108 B7
Blackfoot, *U.S.A.* 110 E7
Blackfoot →, *U.S.A.* ... 110 C7
Blackfoot River Reservoir,
  U.S.A. 110 E8
Blackie, *Canada* 100 C6
Blackpool, *U.K.* 12 D4

Blackriver, *U.S.A.* 106 B1
Blacks Harbour, *Canada* . 99 C6
Blacksburg, *U.S.A.* 104 G5
Blacksod B., *Ireland* 15 B2
Blackstone, *U.S.A.* 104 G6
Blackstone →, *Canada* .. 100 A4
Blackstone Ra., *Australia* . 89 E4
Blackville, *Canada* 99 C6
Blackwater, *Australia* ... 90 C4
Blackwater →, *Ireland* .. 15 E4
Blackwater →, *U.K.* 15 B5
Blackwater Cr. →,
  Australia 91 D3
Blackwell, *U.S.A.* 109 G6
Blackwells Corner, *U.S.A.* 113 K7
Bladel, *Neths.* 17 F6
Blaenau Ffestiniog, *U.K.* . 12 E4
Blagodarnoye, *Russia* ... 43 D10
Blagoevgrad, *Bulgaria* ... 39 G6
Blagoveshchensk, *Russia* . 45 D13
Blain, *France* 24 E5
Blaine, *U.S.A.* 112 B4
Blaine Lake, *Canada* 101 C7
Blainville-sur-l'Eau, *France* 25 D13
Blair, *U.S.A.* 108 E6
Blair Athol, *Australia* ... 90 C4
Blair Atholl, *U.K.* 14 E5
Blairgowrie, *U.K.* 14 E5
Blairsden, *U.S.A.* 112 F6
Blairsville, *U.S.A.* 106 F5
Blaj, *Romania* 38 C6
Blake Pt., *U.S.A.* 108 A10
Blakely, *U.S.A.* 105 K3
Blâmont, *France* 25 D13
Blanc, C., *Tunisia* 75 A6
Blanc, Mont, *Alps* 27 C10
Blanca, B., *Argentina* ... 128 A4
Blanca Peak, *U.S.A.* 111 H11
Blanchard, *U.S.A.* 109 H6
Blanche, C., *Australia* ... 91 E1
Blanche, L., *S. Austral.,*
  Australia 91 D2
Blanche, L., *W. Austral.,*
  Australia 88 D3
Blanco, *S. Africa* 84 E3
Blanco, *U.S.A.* 109 K5
Blanco →, *Argentina* ... 126 C2
Blanco →, *U.S.A.* 110 E1
Blanco, C., *Costa Rica* .. 116 E2
Blanco, C., *Spain* 36 B9
Blanda →, *Iceland* 8 D4
Blandford Forum, *U.K.* . 13 G5
Blanding, *U.S.A.* 111 H9
Blanes, *Spain* 28 D7
Blangy-sur-Bresle, *France* . 25 C8
Blanice →, *Czech.* 20 F4
Blankenberge, *Belgium* .. 17 F2
Blankenburg, *Germany* .. 18 D6
Blanquefort, *France* 26 D3
Blanquillo, *Uruguay* 127 C4
Blansko, *Czech.* 20 F6
Blantyre, *Malawi* 83 F4
Blarney, *Ireland* 15 E3
Blato, *Croatia* 33 F13
Blatten, *Switz.* 22 D5
Blaubeuren, *Germany* ... 19 G5
Blåvands Huk, *Denmark* . 9 J10
Blaydon, *U.K.* 12 C6
Blaye, *France* 26 C3
Blaye-les-Mines, *France* .. 26 D6
Blayney, *Australia* 91 E4
Blaze, Pt., *Australia* 88 B5
Bleckede, *Germany* 18 B6
Bled, *Slovenia* 33 B11
Blednaya, Gora, *Russia* .. 44 B7
Bléharies, *Belgium* 17 G2
Blejeşti, *Romania* 38 E8
Blekinge län □, *Sweden* . 9 H13
Blenheim, *Canada* 106 D2
Blenheim, *N.Z.* 87 J4
Bléone →, *France* 27 D10
Blerick, *Neths.* 17 F8
Bletchley, *U.K.* 13 F7
Blida, *Algeria* 75 A5
Blidet Amor, *Algeria* ... 75 B6
Blidö, *Sweden* 10 E12
Bligh Sound, *N.Z.* 87 L1
Blind River, *Canada* 98 C3
Blinnenhorn, *Switz.* 23 D7
Blitar, *Indonesia* 57 H15
Blitta, *Togo* 79 D5
Block I., *U.S.A.* 107 E13
Block Island Sd., *U.S.A.* . 107 E13
Blodgett Iceberg Tongue,
  Antarctica 5 C9
Bloemendaal, *Neths.* ... 16 D5
Bloemfontein, *S. Africa* . 84 D4
Bloemhof, *S. Africa* 84 D4
Blois, *France* 24 E8
Blokziji, *Neths.* 16 C7
Blönduós, *Iceland* 8 D3
Bloodvein →, *Canada* .. 101 C9
Bloody Foreland, *Ireland* . 15 A3
Bloomer, *U.S.A.* 108 C9
Bloomfield, *Australia* ... 90 B4
Bloomfield, *Canada* 106 C7
Bloomfield, *Iowa, U.S.A.* 108 E8
Bloomfield, *N. Mex.,*
  U.S.A. 111 H10
Bloomfield, *Nebr., U.S.A.* 108 D6
Bloomington, *Ill., U.S.A.* . 108 E10
Bloomington, *Ind., U.S.A.* 104 F2
Bloomsburg, *U.S.A.* 107 F8

Blora, *Indonesia* 57 G14
Blossburg, *U.S.A.* 106 E7
Blouberg, *S. Africa* 85 C4
Blountstown, *U.S.A.* 105 K3
Bludenz, *Austria* 19 H5
Blue Island, *U.S.A.* 104 E2
Blue Lake, *U.S.A.* 110 F2
Blue Mesa Reservoir,
  U.S.A. 111 G10
Blue Mts., *Oreg., U.S.A.* . 110 D4
Blue Mts., *Pa., U.S.A.* .. 107 F8
Blue Mud B., *Australia* .. 90 A2
Blue Nile = An Nîl el
  Azraq □, *Sudan* 77 E3
Blue Nile = Nîl el
  Azraq →, *Sudan* 77 D3
Blue Rapids, *U.S.A.* 108 F6
Blue Ridge Mts., *U.S.A.* . 105 G5
Blue Stack Mts., *Ireland* . 15 B3
Blueberry →, *Canada* ... 100 B4
Bluefield, *U.S.A.* 104 G5
Bluefields, *Nic.* 116 D3
Bluff, *Australia* 90 C4
Bluff, *N.Z.* 87 M2
Bluff, *U.S.A.* 111 H9
Bluff Knoll, *Australia* ... 89 F2
Bluff Pt., *Australia* 89 E1
Bluffton, *U.S.A.* 104 E3
Blumenau, *Brazil* 127 B6
Blümisalphorn, *Switz.* ... 22 D5
Blunt, *U.S.A.* 108 C4
Bly, *U.S.A.* 110 E3
Blyth, *Canada* 106 C3
Blyth, *U.K.* 12 B6
Blyth Bridge, *U.K.* 12 E5
Blythe, *U.S.A.* 113 M12
Bø, *Norway* 10 E3
Bo, *S. Leone* 78 D2
Bo Duc, *Vietnam* 59 G6
Bo Hai, *China* 51 E10
Bo Xian, *China* 50 H8
Boa Esperança, *Brazil* .. 121 C5
Boa Nova, *Brazil* 123 D3
Boa Viagem, *Brazil* 122 C4
Boa Vista, *Brazil* 121 C5
Boac, *Phil.* 55 E4
Boaco, *Nic.* 116 D2
Bo'ai, *China* 50 G7
Boal, *Spain* 30 B4
Boardman, *U.S.A.* 106 E4
Boatman, *Australia* 91 D4
Bobadah, *Australia* 91 E4
Bobai, *China* 52 F7
Bobbili, *India* 61 K13
Bóbbio, *Italy* 32 D6
Bobcaygeon, *Canada* ... 98 D4
Böblingen, *Germany* 19 G5
Bobo-Dioulasso,
  Burkina Faso 78 C4
Boboc, *Romania* 38 D9
Bobonaza →, *Ecuador* .. 120 D2
Bobov Dol, *Bulgaria* 38 G5
Bóbr →, *Poland* 20 C5
Bobraomby, Tanjon' i,
  Madag. 85 A8
Bobrinets, *Ukraine* 42 B5
Bobrov, *Russia* 41 F12
Bobruysk, *Belorussia* ... 40 E6
Bobures, *Venezuela* 120 B3
Boca de Drago, *Venezuela* 121 A5
Bôca do Acre, *Brazil* ... 124 B4
Bôca do Jari, *Brazil* 121 D7
Bôca do Moaco, *Brazil* .. 124 B4
Boca Grande, *Venezuela* . 121 B5
Boca Raton, *U.S.A.* 105 M5
Bocaiúva, *Brazil* 123 E3
Bocanda, *Ivory C.* 78 D4
Bocaranga, *C.A.R.* 73 G8
Bocas del Toro, *Panama* . 116 E3
Boceguillas, *Spain* 28 D1
Bochnia, *Poland* 20 F10
Bocholt, *Belgium* 17 F7
Bocholt, *Germany* 18 D2
Bochum, *Germany* 18 D3
Bockenem, *Germany* 18 C6
Bocognano, *France* 27 F13
Boconó, *Venezuela* 120 B3
Boconó →, *Venezuela* .. 120 B4
Bocoyna, *Mexico* 114 B3
Bocq →, *Belgium* 17 H5
Boda, *C.A.R.* 80 D3
Bodaybo, *Russia* 45 D12
Boddington, *Australia* ... 89 F2
Bodega Bay, *U.S.A.* 112 G3
Bodegraven, *Neths.* 16 D5
Boden, *Sweden* 8 D16
Bodensee, *Europe* 23 A8
Bodenteich, *Germany* ... 18 C6
Bodhan, *India* 60 K10
Bodinga, *Nigeria* 79 C6
Bodio, *Switz.* 23 D7
Bodmin, *U.K.* 13 G3
Bodmin Moor, *U.K.* 13 G3
Bodoquena, Serra da,
  Brazil 125 E6
Bodrog →, *Hungary* ... 21 G11
Bodrum, *Turkey* 66 C5
Boechout, *Belgium* 17 F5
Boegoebergdam, *S. Africa* 84 D3
Boekelo, *Neths.* 16 D9
Boelenslaan, *Neths.* 16 B8
Boën, *France* 27 C8
Boende, *Zaïre* 80 C4
Boerne, *U.S.A.* 109 L5
Boertange, *Neths.* 16 B10

Boezinge, *Belgium* 17 G1
Boffa, *Guinea* 78 C2
Bogalusa, *U.S.A.* 109 K10
Bogan Gate, *Australia* . . . 91 E4
Bogantungan, *Australia* . . 90 C4
Bogata, *U.S.A.* 109 J7
Bogatić, *Serbia, Yug.* 21 L9
Boğazlıyan, *Turkey* 66 D6
Bogense, *Denmark* 11 J4
Boggabilla, *Australia* 91 D5
Boggabri, *Australia* 91 E5
Boggeragh Mts., *Ireland* . . 15 D3
Bognor Regis, *U.K.* 13 G7
Bogø, *Denmark* 11 K6
Bogo, *Phil.* 55 F6
Bogodukhov, *Ukraine* 42 A6
Bogong, Mt., *Australia* . . . 91 F4
Bogor, *Indonesia* 57 G12
Bogoroditsk, *Russia* 41 E11
Bogorodsk, *Russia* 41 C13
Bogorodskoye, *Russia* . . . 45 D15
Bogoso, *Ghana* 78 D4
Bogotá, *Colombia* 120 C3
Bogotol, *Russia* 44 D9
Bogra, *Bangla.* 61 G16
Boguchany, *Russia* 45 D10
Boguchar, *Russia* 43 B9
Bogué, *Mauritania* 78 B2
Boguslav, *Ukraine* 42 B4
Bohain-en-Vermandois,
France 25 C10
Bohemia Downs, *Australia* 88 C4
Bohemian Forest =
Böhmerwald, *Germany* . 19 F8
Bohena Cr. →, *Australia* . 91 E4
Bohinjska Bistrica, *Slovenia* 33 B11
Böhmerwald, *Germany* . . 19 F8
Bohmte, *Germany* 18 C4
Bohol, *Phil.* 55 G6
Bohol Sea, *Phil.* 57 C6
Bohotleh, *Somali Rep.* . . . 68 F4
Boi, *Nigeria* 79 D6
Boi, Pta. de, *Brazil* 127 A6
Boiaçu, *Brazil* 121 D5
Boiano, *Italy* 35 A7
Boileau, C., *Australia* . . . 88 C3
Boipeba, I. de, *Brazil* . . . 123 D4
Bois →, *Brazil* 123 E1
Boischot, *Belgium* 17 F5
Boise, *U.S.A.* 110 E5
Boise City, *U.S.A.* 109 G3
Boissevain, *Canada* 101 D8
Boite →, *Italy* 33 B9
Boitzenburg, *Germany* . . . 18 B9
Boizenburg, *Germany* . . . 18 B6
Bojador C., *W. Sahara* . . . 74 C2
Bojnūrd, *Iran* 65 B8
Bojonegoro, *Indonesia* . . . 57 G14
Boju, *Nigeria* 79 D6
Boka Kotorska,
Montenegro, Yug. 21 N8
Bokala, *Ivory C.* 78 D4
Boké, *Guinea* 78 C2
Bokhara →, *Australia* . . . 91 D4
Bokkos, *Nigeria* 79 D6
Boknafjorden, *Norway* . . . 9 G8
Bokoro, *Chad* 73 F8
Bokote, *Zaïre* 80 E4
Boksitogorsk, *Russia* 40 B8
Bokungu, *Zaïre* 80 E4
Bol, *Chad* 73 F7
Bol, *Croatia* 33 E13
Bolama, *Guinea-Biss.* . . . 78 C1
Bolan Pass, *Pakistan* 60 E5
Bolaños →, *Mexico* 114 C4
Bolbec, *France* 24 C7
Boldājī, *Iran* 65 D6
Boldeşti, *Romania* 38 D9
Bole, *China* 54 B3
Bole, *Ethiopia* 77 F4
Bolekhov, *Ukraine* 40 G3
Bolesławiec, *Poland* 20 D5
Bolgatanga, *Ghana* 79 C4
Bolgrad, *Ukraine* 42 D3
Boli, *Sudan* 77 F2
Bolinao, *Phil.* 55 C3
Bolinao C., *Phil.* 57 A5
Bolívar, *Argentina* 126 D3
Bolívar, Antioquía,
Colombia 120 B2
Bolívar, Cauca, *Colombia* 120 C2
Bolívar, *Peru* 124 B2
Bolivar, Mo., *U.S.A.* 109 G8
Bolivar, Tenn., *U.S.A.* . . . 109 H10
Bolívar □, *Colombia* 120 B3
Bolívar □, *Ecuador* 120 D2
Bolívar □, *Venezuela* 121 B5
Bolivia ■, *S. Amer.* 125 D5
Bolivian Plateau, *S. Amer.* 118 D3
Bolkhov, *Russia* 41 E10
Bollène, *France* 27 D8
Bollnäs, *Sweden* 10 C10
Bollon, *Australia* 91 D4
Bollstabruk, *Sweden* 10 A11
Bollullos, *Spain* 31 H4
Bologna, *Italy* 33 D8
Bologne, *France* 25 D12
Bologoye, *Russia* 40 C9
Bolomba, *Zaïre* 80 D3
Bolonchenticul, *Mexico* . . 115 D7
Bolong, *Phil.* 57 C6
Boloven, Cao Nguyen,
Laos 58 E6
Bolpur, *India* 63 H12

Bolsena, *Italy* 33 F8
Bolsena, L. di, *Italy* 33 F8
Bolshaya Glushitsa, *Russia* 41 E17
Bolshaya Martynovka,
Russia 43 C9
Bolshaya Vradiyevka,
Ukraine 42 C4
Bolshereche, *Russia* 44 D8
Bolshevik, Ostrov, *Russia* . 45 B11
Bolshoi Kavkas, *Asia* 43 E11
Bolshoy Anyuy →, *Russia* 45 C17
Bolshoy Atlym, *Russia* . . . 44 C7
Bolshoy Begichev, Ostrov,
Russia 45 B12
Bolshoy Lyakhovskiy,
Ostrov, *Russia* 45 B15
Bolshoy Tokmak, *Ukraine* 42 C6
Bol'shoy Tyuters, *Estonia* . 40 B5
Bolsward, *Neths.* 16 B7
Boltaña, *Spain* 28 C5
Boltigen, *Switz.* 22 C4
Bolton, *Canada* 106 C5
Bolton, *U.K.* 12 D5
Bolu, *Turkey* 66 C4
Bolu □, *Turkey* 66 C4
Boluo, *China* 53 F10
Bolvadin, *Turkey* 66 D4
Bolzano, *Italy* 33 B8
Bom Comércio, *Brazil* . . 125 B4
Bom Conselho, *Brazil* . . . 122 C4
Bom Despacho, *Brazil* . . . 123 E2
Bom Jesus, *Brazil* 122 C3
Bom Jesus da Gurguéia,
Serra, *Brazil* 122 C3
Bom Jesus da Lapa, *Brazil* 123 D3
Boma, *Zaïre* 80 F2
Bomaderry, *Australia* 91 E5
Bombala, *Australia* 91 F4
Bombarral, *Portugal* 31 F1
Bombay, *India* 60 K8
Bomboma, *Zaïre* 80 D3
Bombombwa, *Zaïre* 82 B2
Bomi Hills, *Liberia* 78 D2
Bomili, *Zaïre* 82 B2
Bommel, *Neths.* 16 E4
Bomokandi →, *Zaïre* 82 B2
Bomongo, *Zaïre* 80 D3
Bomu →, *C.A.R.* 80 D4
Bon, C., *Tunisia* 75 A7
Bon Sar Pa, *Vietnam* 58 F6
Bonaduz, *Switz.* 23 C8
Bonaire, *Neth. Ant.* 117 D6
Bonang, *Australia* 91 F4
Bonanza, *Nic.* 116 D3
Bonaparte Arch., *Australia* 88 B3
Boñar, *Spain* 30 C5
Bonaventure, *Canada* 99 C6
Bonavista, *Canada* 99 C9
Bonavista, C., *Canada* . . . 99 C9
Bonawan, *Phil.* 55 G5
Bondeno, *Italy* 33 D8
Bondo, *Zaïre* 82 B1
Bondoukou, *Ivory C.* 78 D4
Bondowoso, *Indonesia* . . . 57 G15
Bonduel, *U.S.A.* 104 C1
Bondy, *France* 25 D9
Bone, Teluk, *Indonesia* . . 57 E6
Bone Rate, *Indonesia* 57 F6
Bone Rate, Kepulauan,
Indonesia 57 F6
Bonefro, *Italy* 35 A7
Bo'ness, *U.K.* 14 E5
Bong Son = Hoai Nhon,
Vietnam 58 E7
Bongabong, *Phil.* 55 E4
Bongandanga, *Zaïre* 80 D4
Bongor, *Chad* 73 F8
Bongouanou, *Ivory C.* . . . 78 D4
Bonham, *U.S.A.* 109 J6
Bonheiden, *Belgium* 17 F5
Bonifacio, *France* 27 G13
Bonifacio, Bouches de,
Medit. S. 34 A2
Bonin Is. = Ogasawara
Gunto, *Pac. Oc.* 92 E6
Bonke, *Ethiopia* 77 F4
Bonn, *Germany* 18 E3
Bonnat, *France* 26 B5
Bonne Terre, *U.S.A.* 109 G9
Bonners Ferry, *U.S.A.* . . . 110 B5
Bonnétable, *France* 24 D7
Bonneuil-Matours, *France* 24 F7
Bonneval, *France* 24 D8
Bonneville, *France* 27 B10
Bonney, L., *Australia* 91 F3
Bonnie Downs, *Australia* . 90 C3
Bonnie Rock, *Australia* . . 89 F2
Bonny, *Nigeria* 79 E6
Bonny →, *Nigeria* 79 E6
Bonny, Bight of, *Africa* . . 79 E6
Bonny-sur-Loire, *France* . . 25 E9
Bonnyville, *Canada* 101 C6
Bonoi, *Indonesia* 57 E9
Bonorva, *Italy* 34 B1
Bonsall, *U.S.A.* 113 M9
Bontang, *Indonesia* 56 D5
Bonthain, *Indonesia* 57 F5
Bonthe, *S. Leone* 78 D2
Bontoc, *Phil.* 55 C4
Bonyeri, *Ghana* 78 D4
Bonython Ra., *Australia* . . 88 D4
Bookabie, *Australia* 89 F5
Booker, *U.S.A.* 109 G4
Boolaboolka L., *Australia* . 91 E3
Booligal, *Australia* 91 E3
Boom, *Belgium* 17 F4
Boonah, *Australia* 91 D5

Boone, *Iowa, U.S.A.* 108 D8
Boone, *N.C., U.S.A.* 105 G5
Booneville, *Ark., U.S.A.* . . 109 H8
Booneville, *Miss., U.S.A.* . 105 H1
Boonville, *Calif., U.S.A.* . . 112 F3
Boonville, *Ind., U.S.A.* . . . 104 F2
Boonville, *Mo., U.S.A.* . . . 108 F8
Boonville, *N.Y., U.S.A.* . . 107 C9
Boorindal, *Australia* 91 E4
Boorowa, *Australia* 91 E4
Boothia, Gulf of, *Canada* . 97 A11
Boothia Pen., *Canada* . . . 96 A10
Bootle, *Cumb., U.K.* 12 C4
Bootle, *Mersey., U.K.* . . . 12 D4
Booué, *Gabon* 80 E2
Bophuthatswana □,
S. Africa 84 D4
Boppard, *Germany* 19 E3
Boquerón □, *Paraguay* . . 125 E5
Boquete, *Panama* 116 E3
Boquilla, Presa de la,
Mexico 114 B3
Boquillas del Carmen,
Mexico 114 B4
Bor, *Czech.* 20 F7
Bor, *Serbia, Yug.* 21 L12
Bôr, *Sudan* 77 F3
Bor, *Turkey* 66 E6
Bor Mashash, *Israel* 69 D3
Borãdã →, *Syria* 69 B5
Borah Peak, *U.S.A.* 110 D7
Borama, *Somali Rep.* 68 F3
Borang, *Sudan* 77 G3
Borås, *Sweden* 11 G6
Borãzjãn, *Iran* 65 D6
Borba, *Brazil* 121 D6
Borba, *Portugal* 31 G3
Borborema, Planalto da,
Brazil 122 C4
Borçka, *Turkey* 43 F9
Borculo, *Neths.* 16 D9
Bord Khûn-e Now, *Iran* . . 65 D6
Borda, C., *Australia* 91 F2
Bordeaux, *France* 26 D3
Borden, *Australia* 89 F2
Borden, *Canada* 99 C7
Borden I., *Canada* 4 B2
Borders □, *U.K.* 14 F6
Bordertown, *Australia* 91 F3
Borðeyri, *Iceland* 8 D3
Bordighera, *Italy* 32 E4
Bordj bou Arreridj, *Algeria* 75 A5
Bordj Bourguiba, *Tunisia* . 75 B7
Bordj el Hobra, *Algeria* . . 75 B5
Bordj Ste. Marie,
Algeria 74 C4
Bordj-in-Eker, *Algeria* . . . 75 D6
Bordj Menaiel, *Algeria* . . . 75 A5
Bordj Messouda, *Algeria* . 75 B6
Bordj Nili, *Algeria* 75 B5
Bordj Omar Driss, *Algeria* 75 C6
Bordj-Tarat, *Algeria* 75 D6
Bordj Zelfana, *Algeria* . . . 75 B5
Borensberg, *Sweden* 11 F9
Borgå, *Finland* 9 F18
Borgarnes, *Iceland* 8 D3
Børgefjellet, *Norway* 8 D12
Borger, *Neths.* 16 C9
Borger, *U.S.A.* 109 H4
Borgerhout, *Belgium* 17 F4
Borghamn, *Sweden* 11 F8
Borgholm, *Sweden* 9 H14
Bórgia, *Italy* 35 D9
Borgloon, *Belgium* 17 G6
Borgo San Dalmazzo, *Italy* 32 D4
Borgo San Lorenzo, *Italy* . 33 E8
Borgo Valsugano, *Italy* . . 33 B8
Borgomanero, *Italy* 32 C5
Borgonovo Val Tidone,
Italy 32 C6
Borgorose, *Italy* 33 F10
Borgosésia, *Italy* 32 C5
Borgvattnet, *Sweden* 10 A9
Borikhane, *Laos* 58 C4
Borislav, *Ukraine* 40 G3
Borisoglebsk, *Russia* 41 F13
Borisoglebskiy, *Russia* . . . 41 C13
Borisov, *Belorussia* 40 D6
Borispol, *Ukraine* 40 F7
Borja, *Peru* 120 D2
Borja, *Spain* 28 D3
Borjas Blancas, *Spain* . . . 28 D5
Borken, *Germany* 18 D2
Borkou, *Chad* 73 E8
Borkum, *Germany* 18 B2
Borlänge, *Sweden* 9 F13
Borley, C., *Antarctica* . . . 5 C5
Bormida →, *Italy* 32 D5
Bórmio, *Italy* 32 B7
Born, *Neths.* 17 F7
Borna, *Germany* 18 D8
Borndiep, *Neths.* 16 B7
Borne, *Neths.* 16 D9
Bornem, *Belgium* 17 F4
Borneo, *E. Indies* 56 D5
Bornholm, *Denmark* 9 J13
Borno □, *Nigeria* 79 C7
Bornos, *Spain* 31 J5
Bornu Yassa, *Nigeria* 79 C7
Borobudur, *Indonesia* . . . 57 G14
Borogontsy, *Russia* 45 C14
Boromo, *Burkina Faso* . . . 78 C4
Boron, *U.S.A.* 113 L9
Borongan, *Phil.* 55 F6

Bororen, *Australia* 90 C5
Borotangba Mts., *C.A.R.* . 77 F1
Borovan, *Bulgaria* 38 F6
Borovichi, *Russia* 40 B8
Borovsk, *Russia* 41 D10
Borrego Springs, *U.S.A.* . . 113 M10
Borriol, *Spain* 28 E4
Borroloola, *Australia* 90 B2
Borşa, *Romania* 38 B7
Borssele, *Neths.* 17 F3
Bort-les-Orgues, *France* . . 26 C6
Borth, *U.K.* 13 E3
Borujerd, *Iran* 65 C6
Borzhomi, *Georgia* 43 F10
Borzna, *Ukraine* 40 F8
Borzya, *Russia* 45 D12
Bosa, *Italy* 34 B1
Bosanska Dubica,
Bos.-H. 33 C13
Bosanska Gradiška,
Bos.-H. 21 K7
Bosanska Kostajnica,
Bos.-H. 33 C13
Bosanska Krupa,
Bos.-H. 33 D13
Bosanski Novi,
Bos.-H. 33 C13
Bosanski Šamac,
Bos.-H. 21 K8
Bosansko Grahovo,
Bos.-H. 33 D13
Bosansko Petrovac,
Bos.-H. 33 D13
Bosaso, *Somali Rep.* 68 E4
Boscastle, *U.K.* 13 G3
Boscotrecase, *Italy* 35 B7
Bose, *China* 52 F6
Boshan, *China* 51 F9
Boshoek, *S. Africa* 84 D4
Boshof, *S. Africa* 84 D4
Boshrūyeh, *Iran* 65 C8
Bosilegrad, *Serbia, Yug.* . . 21 N12
Boskoop, *Neths.* 16 D5
Bosna →, *Bos.-H.* 21 K8
Bosna i Hercegovina =
Bosnia-Herzegovina ■,
Europe 21 L7
Bosnia-Herzegovina ■,
Europe 21 L7
Bosnik, *Indonesia* 57 E9
Bosobolo, *Zaïre* 80 D3
Bosporus = Karadeniz
Boğazı, *Turkey* 66 C3
Bossangoa, *C.A.R.* 73 G8
Bossekop, *Norway* 8 B17
Bossembélé, *C.A.R.* 73 G8
Bossier City, *U.S.A.* 109 J8
Bosso, *Niger* 79 C7
Bostānābād, *Iran* 64 B5
Bosten Hu, *China* 54 B3
Boston, *U.K.* 12 E7
Boston, *U.S.A.* 107 D13
Boston Bar, *Canada* 100 D4
Bosut →, *Croatia* 21 K8
Boswell, *Canada* 100 D5
Boswell, *Okla., U.S.A.* . . . 109 H7
Boswell, *Pa., U.S.A.* 106 F5
Botad, *India* 62 H4
Botan →, *Turkey* 67 E9
Botany B., *Australia* 91 E5
Botene, *Laos* 58 D3
Botevgrad, *Bulgaria* 38 G6
Bothaville, *S. Africa* 84 D4
Bothnia, G. of, *Europe* . . . 8 E16
Bothwell, *Australia* 90 G4
Bothwell, *Canada* 106 D3
Boticas, *Portugal* 30 D3
Botletle →, *Botswana* 84 C3
Botoşani, *Romania* 38 B9
Botro, *Ivory C.* 78 D3
Botswana ■, *Africa* 84 C3
Bottineau, *U.S.A.* 108 A4
Bottrop, *Germany* 17 E9
Botucatu, *Brazil* 127 A6
Botwood, *Canada* 99 C8
Bou Alam, *Algeria* 75 B5
Bou Ali, *Algeria* 75 C4
Bou Djébéha, *Mali* 78 B4
Bou Guema, *Algeria* 75 C5
Bou Ismael, *Algeria* 75 A5
Bou Izakarn, *Morocco* . . . 74 C3
Boû Lanouâr, *Mauritania* . 74 D1
Bou Saâda, *Algeria* 75 A5
Bou Salem, *Tunisia* 75 A6
Bouaké, *Ivory C.* 78 D3
Bouar, *C.A.R.* 80 C3
Bouârfa, *Morocco* 75 B4
Bouca, *C.A.R.* 73 G8
Boucau, *France* 26 E2
Boucaut B., *Australia* 90 A1
Bouches-du-Rhône □,
France 27 E9
Bouda, *Algeria* 75 C4
Boudenib, *Morocco* 74 B4
Boudry, *Switz.* 22 C3
Boufarik, *Algeria* 75 A5
Bougainville, C., *Australia* 88 B4
Bougainville Reef,
Australia 90 B4
Bougaroun, C., *Algeria* . . . 75 A6
Bougie = Bejaia, *Algeria* . 75 A6
Bougouni, *Mali* 78 C3
Bouillon, *Belgium* 17 J6
Bouïra, *Algeria* 75 A5
Boulder, *Colo., U.S.A.* . . . 108 E2

Boulder, *Mont., U.S.A.* . . 110 C7
Boulder City, *U.S.A.* 113 K12
Boulder Creek, *U.S.A.* . . . 112 H4
Boulder Dam = Hoover
Dam, *U.S.A.* 113 K12
Bouli, *Mauritania* 78 B2
Boulia, *Australia* 90 C2
Bouligny, *France* 25 C12
Boulogne →, *France* 24 E5
Boulogne-sur-Gesse, *France* 26 E4
Boulogne-sur-Mer, *France* 25 B8
Bouloire, *France* 24 E7
Boulsa, *Burkina Faso* 79 C4
Boultoum, *Niger* 79 C7
Boumalne, *Morocco* 74 B3
Boun Neua, *Laos* 58 B3
Boun Tai, *Laos* 58 B3
Bouna, *Ivory C.* 78 D4
Boundary Peak, *U.S.A.* . . 112 H8
Boundiali, *Ivory C.* 78 D3
Bountiful, *U.S.A.* 110 F8
Bounty Is., *Pac. Oc.* 92 M9
Bourbon-Lancy, *France* . . 26 B7
Bourbon-l'Archambault,
France 26 B7
Bourbonnais, *France* 26 B7
Bourbonne-les-Bains,
France 25 E12
Bourem, *Mali* 79 B4
Bourg, *France* 26 C3
Bourg-Argental, *France* . . 27 C8
Bourg-de-Péage, *France* . . 27 C9
Bourg-en-Bresse, *France* . 27 B9
Bourg-St.-Andéol, *France* . 27 D8
Bourg-St.-Maurice, *France* 27 C10
Bourg-St.-Pierre, *Switz.* . . 22 E4
Bourganeuf, *France* 26 C5
Bourges, *France* 25 E9
Bourget, *Canada* 107 A9
Bourget, L. du, *France* . . . 27 C9
Bourgneuf, B. de, *France* . 24 E4
Bourgneuf-en-Retz, *France* 24 E5
Bourgogne, *France* 25 F11
Bourgoin-Jallieu, *France* . . 27 C9
Bourgueil, *France* 24 E7
Bourke, *Australia* 91 E4
Bournemouth, *U.K.* 13 G6
Bourriot-Bergonce, *France* 26 D3
Bouse, *U.S.A.* 113 M13
Boussac, *France* 26 B6
Boussens, *France* 26 E4
Bousso, *Chad* 73 F8
Boussu, *Belgium* 17 H3
Boutilimit, *Mauritania* . . . 78 B2
Bouvet I. = Bouvetøya,
Antarctica 3 G10
Bouvetøya, *Antarctica* . . . 3 G10
Bouznika, *Morocco* 74 B3
Bouzonville, *France* 25 C13
Bova Marina, *Italy* 35 E8
Bovalino Marina, *Italy* . . . 35 D9
Bovec, *Slovenia* 33 B10
Bovenkarspel, *Neths.* 16 C6
Bovigny, *Belgium* 17 H7
Bovill, *U.S.A.* 110 C5
Bovino, *Italy* 35 A8
Bow Island, *Canada* 100 D6
Bowbells, *U.S.A.* 108 A3
Bowdle, *U.S.A.* 108 C5
Bowelling, *Australia* 89 F2
Bowen, *Australia* 90 C4
Bowen Mts., *Australia* . . . 91 F4
Bowie, *Ariz., U.S.A.* 111 K9
Bowie, *Tex., U.S.A.* 109 J6
Bowkān, *Iran* 64 B5
Bowland, Forest of, *U.K.* . 12 D5
Bowling Green, *Ky.,
U.S.A.* 104 G2
Bowling Green, *Ohio,
U.S.A.* 104 E4
Bowling Green, C.,
Australia 90 B4
Bowman, *U.S.A.* 108 B3
Bowman I., *Antarctica* . . . 5 C8
Bowmans, *Australia* 91 E2
Bowmanville, *Canada* 98 D4
Bowmore, *U.K.* 14 F2
Bowral, *Australia* 91 E5
Bowraville, *Australia* 91 E5
Bowron →, *Canada* 100 C4
Bowser L., *Canada* 100 B3
Bowsman, *Canada* 101 C8
Bowwood, *Zambia* 83 F2
Boxholm, *Sweden* 11 F9
Boxmeer, *Neths.* 17 E7
Boxtel, *Neths.* 17 E6
Boyabat, *Turkey* 42 F6
Boyaca = Casanare □,
Colombia 120 B3
Boyce, *U.S.A.* 109 K8
Boyer →, *Canada* 100 B5
Boyle, *Ireland* 15 C3
Boyne →, *Ireland* 15 C5
Boyne City, *U.S.A.* 104 C3
Boynton Beach, *U.S.A.* . . 105 M5
Boyoma, Chutes, *Zaïre* . . 82 D5
Boyup Brook, *Australia* . . 89 F2
Boz Dağ, *Turkey* 66 E3
Boz Dağları, *Turkey* 66 C3
Bozburun, *Turkey* 66 E3
Bozdoğan, *Turkey* 66 E3
Bozeman, *U.S.A.* 110 D8
Bozen = Bolzano, *Italy* . . 33 B8
Bozkır, *Turkey* 66 E5
Bozouls, *France* 26 D6

Bozoum, C.A.R. 73 G8
Bozova, Turkey 67 E8
Bozovici, Romania 38 C5
Bozüyük, Turkey 66 D4
Bra, Italy 32 D4
Brabant □, Belgium 17 G5
Brabant L., Canada 101 B8
Brabrand, Denmark 11 H4
Brač, Croatia 33 E13
Bracadale, L., U.K. 14 D2
Bracciano, Italy 33 F9
Bracciano, L. di, Italy 33 F9
Bracebridge, Canada 98 C4
Brach, Libya 73 C7
Bracieux, France 25 E8
Bräcke, Sweden 10 B9
Brackettville, U.S.A. 109 L4
Brački Kanal, Croatia 33 E13
Brad, Romania 38 C5
Brádano →, Italy 35 B9
Bradenton, U.S.A. 105 M4
Bradford, Canada 106 B5
Bradford, U.K. 12 D6
Bradford, Pa., U.S.A. 106 E6
Bradford, Vt., U.S.A. 107 C12
Brădiceni, Romania 38 D6
Bradley, Ark., U.S.A. 109 J8
Bradley, Calif., U.S.A. 112 K6
Bradley, S. Dak., U.S.A. 108 C6
Bradley Institute, Zimbabwe 83 F3
Bradore Bay, Canada 99 B8
Bradshaw, Australia 88 C5
Brady, U.S.A. 109 K5
Brædstrup, Denmark 11 J3
Braemar, Australia 91 E2
Braeside, Canada 107 A8
Braga, Portugal 30 D2
Braga □, Portugal 30 D2
Bragado, Argentina 126 D3
Bragança, Brazil 122 B2
Bragança, Portugal 30 D4
Bragança □, Portugal 30 D4
Bragança Paulista, Brazil 127 A6
Brahmanbaria, Bangla. 61 H17
Brahmani →, India 61 J15
Brahmaputra →, India 63 G13
Braich-y-pwll, U.K. 12 E3
Braidwood, Australia 91 F4
Brăila, Romania 38 D10
Braine-l'Alleud, Belgium 17 G4
Braine-le-Comte, Belgium 17 G4
Brainerd, U.S.A. 108 B7
Braintree, U.K. 13 F8
Braintree, U.S.A. 107 D14
Brak →, S. Africa 84 D3
Brake, Niedersachsen, Germany 18 B4
Brake, Nordrhein-Westfalen, Germany 18 D5
Brakel, Neths. 16 E6
Brakwater, Namibia 84 C2
Bralorne, Canada 100 C4
Bramberg, Germany 19 E6
Bramminge, Denmark 11 J2
Brämön, Sweden 10 B11
Brampton, Canada 98 D4
Bramsche, Germany 18 C3
Bramwell, Australia 90 A3
Branco →, Brazil 121 D5
Branco, C., Brazil 122 C5
Brande, Denmark 11 J3
Brandenburg = Neubrandenburg, Germany 18 B9
Brandenburg, Germany 18 C8
Brandenburg □, Germany 18 C9
Brandfort, S. Africa 84 D4
Brandon, Canada 101 D9
Brandon, U.S.A. 107 C11
Brandon B., Ireland 15 D1
Brandon Mt., Ireland 15 D1
Brandsen, Argentina 126 D4
Brandval, Norway 10 D6
Brandvlei, S. Africa 84 E3
Brandýs, Czech. 20 E4
Branford, U.S.A. 107 E12
Braniewo, Poland 20 A9
Bransfield Str., Antarctica 5 C18
Branson, Colo., U.S.A. 109 G3
Branson, Mo., U.S.A. 109 G8
Brantford, Canada 98 D3
Brantôme, France 26 C4
Branxholme, Australia 91 F3
Branzi, Italy 32 B6
Bras d'Or, L., Canada 99 C7
Brasiléia, Brazil 124 C4
Brasília, Brazil 123 E2
Brasília Legal, Brazil 121 D6
Braslav, Belorussia 40 D5
Braslovče, Slovenia 33 B12
Braşov, Romania 38 D8
Brass, Nigeria 79 E6
Brass →, Nigeria 79 E6
Brassac-les-Mines, France 26 C7
Brasschaat, Belgium 17 F4
Brassey, Banjaran, Malaysia 56 D5
Brassey Ra., Australia 89 E3
Brasstown Bald, U.S.A. 105 H4
Bratislava, Slovakia 21 G3
Bratsk, Russia 45 D11
Brattleboro, U.S.A. 107 D12

Braunau, Austria 21 G3
Braunschweig, Germany 18 C6
Braunton, U.K. 13 F3
Brava, Somali Rep. 68 G3
Bråviken, Sweden 10 F10
Bravo del Norte →, Mexico 114 B5
Brawley, U.S.A. 113 N11
Bray, Ireland 15 C5
Bray, Mt., Australia 90 A1
Bray, Pays de, France 25 C8
Brazeau →, Canada 100 C5
Brazil, U.S.A. 104 F2
Brazil ■, S. Amer. 123 D6
Brazo Sur →, S. Amer. 126 B4
Brazos →, U.S.A. 109 L7
Brazzaville, Congo 80 E3
Brčko, Bos.-H. 21 L8
Brea, Peru 124 A1
Breadalbane, Australia 90 C2
Breadalbane, U.K. 14 E4
Breaden, L., Australia 89 E4
Breaksea Sd., N.Z. 87 L1
Bream B., N.Z. 87 F5
Bream Hd., N.Z. 87 F5
Breas, Chile 126 B1
Brebes, Indonesia 57 G13
Brechin, Canada 106 B5
Brechin, U.K. 14 E6
Brecht, Belgium 17 F5
Breckenridge, Colo., U.S.A. 110 G10
Breckenridge, Minn., U.S.A. 108 B6
Breckenridge, Tex., U.S.A. 109 J5
Breckland, U.K. 13 E8
Brecknock, Pen., Chile 128 D2
Břeclav, Czech. 20 G6
Brecon, U.K. 13 F4
Brecon Beacons, U.K. 13 F4
Breda, Neths. 17 E5
Bredasdorp, S. Africa 84 E3
Bredbo, Australia 91 F4
Bredene, Belgium 17 F1
Bredstedt, Germany 18 A4
Bree, Belgium 17 F7
Breezand, Neths. 16 C5
Bregalnica →, Macedonia 39 H5
Bregenz, Austria 19 H5
Bréhal, France 24 D5
Bréhat, I. de, France 24 D4
Breiðafjörður, Iceland 8 D2
Breil-sur-Roya, France 27 E11
Breisach, Germany 19 G3
Brejinho de Nazaré, Brazil 122 D2
Brejo, Brazil 122 B3
Bremen, Germany 18 B4
Bremen □, Germany 18 B4
Bremer I., Australia 90 A2
Bremerhaven, Germany 18 B4
Bremerton, U.S.A. 112 C4
Bremervörde, Germany 18 B5
Bremsnes, Norway 10 A1
Brenes, Spain 31 H5
Brenham, U.S.A. 109 K6
Brenner Pass, Austria 19 H7
Breno, Italy 32 C7
Brent, Canada 98 C4
Brent, U.K. 13 F7
Brenta →, Italy 33 C9
Brentwood, U.K. 13 F8
Brentwood, U.S.A. 107 F11
Bréscia, Italy 32 C7
Breskens, Neths. 17 F3
Breslau = Wrocław, Poland 20 D7
Bresle →, France 24 B8
Bresles, France 25 C9
Bressanone, Italy 33 B8
Bressay, U.K. 14 A7
Bresse, France 25 F12
Bressuire, France 24 F6
Brest, Belorussia 40 E3
Brest, France 24 D2
Brest-Litovsk = Brest, Belorussia 40 E3
Bretagne, France 24 D4
Bretçu, Romania 38 C9
Breteuil, Eure, France 24 D7
Breteuil, Oise, France 25 C9
Breton, Canada 100 C6
Breton, Pertuis, France 26 B2
Breton Sd., U.S.A. 109 L10
Brett, C., N.Z. 87 F5
Bretten, Germany 19 F4
Breukelen, Neths. 16 D6
Brevard, U.S.A. 105 H4
Breves, Brazil 122 B1
Brevik, Norway 10 E3
Brewarrina, Australia 91 D4
Brewer, U.S.A. 99 D6
Brewer, Mt., U.S.A. 112 J8
Brewster, N.Y., U.S.A. 107 E11
Brewster, Wash., U.S.A. 110 B4
Brewster, Kap, Greenland 4 B6
Brewton, U.S.A. 105 K2
Breyten, S. Africa 85 D4
Breytovo, Russia 41 B10
Brezhnev = Naberezhnyye Chelny, Russia 44 D6
Brežice, Slovenia 33 C12
Brézina, Algeria 75 B5
Březnice, Czech. 20 F3
Breznik, Bulgaria 38 G5

Brezno, Slovakia 20 G9
Bria, C.A.R. 73 G9
Briançon, France 27 D10
Briare, France 25 E9
Bribie I., Australia 91 D5
Bricquebec, France 24 C5
Bridgehampton, U.S.A. 107 F12
Bridgend, U.K. 13 F4
Bridgeport, Calif., U.S.A. 111 G4
Bridgeport, Conn., U.S.A. 107 E11
Bridgeport, Nebr., U.S.A. 108 E3
Bridgeport, Tex., U.S.A. 109 J6
Bridger, U.S.A. 110 D9
Bridgeton, U.S.A. 104 F8
Bridgetown, Australia 89 F2
Bridgetown, Barbados 117 D8
Bridgetown, Canada 99 D6
Bridgewater, Canada 99 D7
Bridgewater, Mass., U.S.A. 107 E14
Bridgewater, C., Australia 91 F3
Bridgewater, S. Dak., U.S.A. 108 D6
Bridgnorth, U.K. 13 E5
Bridgton, U.S.A. 107 B14
Bridgwater, U.K. 13 F4
Bridlington, U.K. 12 C7
Bridport, Australia 90 G4
Bridport, U.K. 13 G5
Brie, Plaine de la, France 25 D10
Brie-Comte-Robert, France 25 D9
Briec, France 24 D2
Brienne-le-Château, France 25 D11
Brienon-sur-Armançon, France 25 E10
Brienz, Switz. 22 C6
Brienzersee, Switz. 22 C5
Brig, Switz. 22 D5
Brigg, U.K. 12 D7
Briggsdale, U.S.A. 108 E2
Brigham City, U.S.A. 110 F7
Bright, Australia 91 F4
Brighton, Australia 91 F2
Brighton, Canada 98 D4
Brighton, U.K. 13 G7
Brighton, U.S.A. 108 F2
Brignogan-Plage, France 24 D2
Brignoles, France 27 E10
Brihuega, Spain 28 E2
Brikama, Gambia 78 C1
Brilliant, Canada 100 D5
Brilliant, U.S.A. 106 F4
Brilon, Germany 18 D4
Bríndisi, Italy 35 B10
Brinje, Croatia 33 D12
Brinkley, U.S.A. 109 H9
Brinkworth, Australia 91 E2
Brinnon, U.S.A. 112 C4
Brion, I., Canada 99 C7
Brionne, France 24 C7
Brionski, Croatia 33 D10
Brioude, France 26 C7
Briouze, France 24 D6
Brisbane, Australia 91 D5
Brisbane →, Australia 91 D5
Brisighella, Italy 33 D8
Bristol, U.K. 13 F5
Bristol, Conn., U.S.A. 107 E12
Bristol, Pa., U.S.A. 107 F10
Bristol, R.I., U.S.A. 107 E13
Bristol, S. Dak., U.S.A. 108 C6
Bristol, Tenn., U.S.A. 105 G4
Bristol B., U.S.A. 96 C4
Bristol Channel, U.K. 13 F3
Bristol I., Antarctica 5 B1
Bristol L., U.S.A. 111 J5
Bristow, U.S.A. 109 H6

Brockway, Mont., U.S.A. 108 B2
Brockway, Pa., U.S.A. 106 E6
Brocton, U.S.A. 106 D5
Brod, Macedonia 39 H4
Brodarevo, Serbia, Yug. 21 M9
Brodeur Pen., Canada 97 A11
Brodick, U.K. 14 F3
Brodnica, Poland 20 B9
Brody, Ukraine 40 F4
Broechem, Belgium 17 F5
Broek, Neths. 16 D6
Broek op Langedijk, Neths. 16 C5
Brogan, U.S.A. 110 D5
Broglie, France 24 C7
Broken Bow, Nebr., U.S.A. 108 E5
Broken Bow, Okla., U.S.A. 109 H7
Broken Hill = Kabwe, Zambia 83 E2
Broken Hill, Australia 91 E3
Brokind, Sweden 11 F9
Brokopondo, Surinam 121 B7
Brokopondo □, Surinam 121 C6
Bromfield, U.K. 13 E5
Bromley, U.K. 13 F8
Brønderslev, Denmark 11 G3
Brong-Ahafo □, Ghana 78 D4
Bronkhorstspruit, S. Africa 85 D4
Bronnitsy, Russia 41 D11
Bronte, Italy 35 E7
Bronte, U.S.A. 109 K4
Bronte Park, Australia 90 G4
Brook Park, U.S.A. 106 E4
Brookfield, U.S.A. 108 F8
Brookhaven, U.S.A. 109 K9
Brookings, Oreg., U.S.A. 110 E1
Brookings, S. Dak., U.S.A. 108 C6
Brooklin, Canada 106 C6
Brookmere, Canada 100 D4
Brooks, Canada 100 C6
Brooks B., Canada 100 C3
Brooks L., Canada 101 A7
Brooks Ra., U.S.A. 96 B5
Brooksville, U.S.A. 105 L4
Brookville, U.S.A. 104 F3
Brooloo, Australia 91 D5
Broom, L., U.K. 14 D3
Broome, Australia 88 C3
Broomehill, Australia 89 F2
Broons, France 24 D4
Brora, U.K. 14 C5
Brora →, U.K. 14 C5
Brosna →, Ireland 15 C4
Brothers, U.S.A. 110 E3
Brøttum, Norway 10 C4
Brou, France 24 D8
Brough, U.K. 12 C5
Broughton Island, Canada 97 B13
Broughty Ferry, U.K. 14 E6
Brouwershaven, Neths. 16 E3
Brouwershavensche Gat, Neths. 16 E3
Brovary, Ukraine 40 F7
Brovst, Denmark 11 G3
Browerville, U.S.A. 108 B7
Brown, Pt., Australia 91 E1
Brown Willy, U.K. 13 G3
Brownfield, U.S.A. 109 J3
Browning, U.S.A. 110 B7
Brownlee, Canada 101 C7
Brownsville, Oreg., U.S.A. 110 D2
Brownsville, Tenn., U.S.A. 109 H10
Brownsville, Tex., U.S.A. 109 N6
Brownsweg, Surinam 121 B6
Brownwood, U.S.A. 109 K5
Brownwood, L., U.S.A. 109 K5
Browse I., Australia 88 B3
Broye →, Switz. 22 C3
Brozas, Spain 31 F4
Bruas, Malaysia 59 K3
Bruay-en-Artois, France 25 B9
Bruce, Mt., Australia 88 D2
Bruce Pen., Canada 106 A3
Bruce Rock, Australia 89 F2
Bruche →, France 25 D14
Bruck an der Leitha, Austria 21 G6
Bruck an der Mur, Austria 21 H5
Brue →, U.K. 13 F5
Brugelette, Belgium 17 G3
Bruges = Brugge, Belgium 17 F2
Brugg, Switz. 22 B6
Brugge, Belgium 17 F2
Brühl, Germany 18 E2
Bruinisse, Neths. 17 E4
Brûlé, Canada 100 C5
Brûlon, France 24 E6
Brûly, Belgium 17 J5
Brumado, Brazil 123 D3
Brumado →, Brazil 123 D3
Brumath, France 25 D14
Brummen, Neths. 16 D8
Brumunddal, Norway 10 D4
Brunchilly, Australia 90 B1
Brundidge, U.S.A. 105 K3
Bruneau, U.S.A. 110 E6
Bruneau →, U.S.A. 110 E6
Brunei = Bandar Seri Begawan, Brunei 56 C4
Brunei ■, Asia 56 D4
Brunette Downs, Australia 90 B2

Brunflo, Sweden 10 A8
Brunico, Italy 33 B8
Brünig, P., Switz. 22 C6
Brunkeberg, Norway 10 E2
Brunna, Sweden 10 E11
Brunnen, Switz. 23 C7
Brunner, L., N.Z. 87 K3
Bruno, Canada 101 C7
Brunsbüttel, Germany 18 B5
Brunssum, Neths. 17 G7
Brunswick = Braunschweig, Germany 18 C6
Brunswick, Ga., U.S.A. 105 K5
Brunswick, Maine, U.S.A. 99 D6
Brunswick, Md., U.S.A. 104 F7
Brunswick, Mo., U.S.A. 108 F8
Brunswick, Ohio, U.S.A. 106 E3
Brunswick, Pen. de, Chile 128 D2
Brunswick B., Australia 88 C3
Brunswick Junction, Australia 89 F2
Bruntál, Czech. 20 F7
Bruny I., Australia 90 G4
Brus Laguna, Honduras 116 C3
Brusartsi, Bulgaria 38 F6
Brush, U.S.A. 108 E3
Brushton, U.S.A. 107 B10
Brusio, Switz. 23 D10
Brusque, Brazil 127 B6
Brussel, Belgium 17 G4
Brussels = Brussel, Belgium 17 G4
Brussels, Canada 106 C3
Brustem, Belgium 17 G6
Bruthen, Australia 91 F4
Bruxelles = Brussel, Belgium 17 G4
Bruyères, France 25 D13
Bryan, Ohio, U.S.A. 104 E3
Bryan, Tex., U.S.A. 109 K6
Bryan, Mt., Australia 91 E2
Bryanka, Ukraine 43 B8
Bryansk, Russia 40 E9
Bryanskoye, Russia 43 D12
Bryant, U.S.A. 108 C6
Bryne, Norway 9 G8
Bryson City, U.S.A. 105 H4
Brza Palanka, Serbia, Yug. 21 L12
Brzava →, Serbia, Yug. 21 K10
Brzeg, Poland 20 E7
Brzeg Din, Poland 20 D6
Bsharri, Lebanon 69 A5
Bū Baqarah, U.A.E. 65 E8
Bu Craa, W. Sahara 74 C2
Bū Ḥasā, U.A.E. 65 F7
Bua Yai, Thailand 58 E4
Buapinang, Indonesia 57 E6
Buayan, Phil. 57 C7
Buba, Guinea-Biss. 78 C2
Bubanza, Burundi 82 C2
Būbiyān, Kuwait 65 D6
Bucak, Turkey 66 E4
Bucaramanga, Colombia 120 B3
Bucas Grande I., Phil. 55 G6
Buccaneer Arch., Australia 88 C3
Bucchiánico, Italy 33 F11
Bucecea, Romania 38 B9
Buchach, Ukraine 40 G4
Buchan, U.K. 14 D6
Buchan Ness, U.K. 14 D7
Buchanan, Canada 101 C8
Buchanan, Liberia 78 D2
Buchanan, L., Queens., Australia 90 C4
Buchanan, L., W. Austral., Australia 89 E3
Buchanan, L., U.S.A. 109 K5
Buchanan Cr. →, Australia 90 B2
Buchans, Canada 99 C8
Bucharest = Bucureşti, Romania 38 E9
Buchholz, Germany 18 B5
Buchloe, Germany 19 G6
Buchon, Pt., U.S.A. 112 K6
Buchs, Switz. 23 B8
Bückeburg, Germany 18 C5
Buckeye, U.S.A. 111 K7
Buckhannon, U.S.A. 104 F5
Buckhaven, U.K. 14 E5
Buckie, U.K. 14 D6
Buckingham, Canada 98 C4
Buckingham, U.K. 13 F7
Buckingham B., Australia 90 A2
Buckinghamshire □, U.K. 13 F7
Buckle Hd., Australia 88 B4
Buckleboo, Australia 91 E2
Buckley, U.S.A. 110 C2
Bucklin, U.S.A. 109 G5
Bucks L., U.S.A. 112 F5
Bucquoy, France 25 B9
Buctouche, Canada 99 C7
Bucureşti, Romania 38 E9
Bucyrus, U.S.A. 104 E4
Budafok, Hungary 21 H9
Budalin, Burma 61 H19
Budapest, Hungary 21 H9
Budaun, India 63 E8
Budd Coast, Antarctica 5 C8
Buddusò, Italy 34 B2
Bude, U.K. 13 G3
Budel, Neths. 17 F7
Budennovsk, Russia 43 D11
Budeşti, Romania 38 E9

Budgewoi, Australia 91 E5
Búðareyri, Iceland 8 D6
Búðir, Iceland 8 D2
Budia, Spain 28 E2
Budjala, Zaïre 80 D3
Búðrio, Italy 33 D8
Buea, Cameroon 79 E6
Buellton, U.S.A. 113 L6
Buena Vista, Bolivia 125 D5
Buena Vista, Colo., U.S.A. 111 G10
Buena Vista, Va., U.S.A. 104 G6
Buena Vista L., U.S.A. 113 K7
Buenaventura, Colombia . 120 C2
Buenaventura, Mexico 114 B3
Buenaventura, B. de, Colombia 120 C2
Buendía, Pantano de, Spain 28 E2
Buenópolis, Brazil 123 E3
Buenos Aires, Argentina . 126 C4
Buenos Aires, Colombia . 120 C3
Buenos Aires, Costa Rica . 116 E4
Buenos Aires □, Argentina 126 D4
Buenos Aires, L., Chile . 128 C2
Buesaco, Colombia 120 C2
Buffalo, Mo., U.S.A. 109 G8
Buffalo, N.Y., U.S.A. 106 D6
Buffalo, Okla., U.S.A. 109 G5
Buffalo, S. Dak., U.S.A. . 108 C3
Buffalo, Wyo., U.S.A. 110 D10
Buffalo →, Canada 100 A5
Buffalo Head Hills, Canada 100 B5
Buffalo L., Canada 100 C6
Buffalo Narrows, Canada . 101 B7
Buffels →, S. Africa 84 D2
Buford, U.S.A. 105 H4
Bug →, Poland 20 C11
Bug →, Ukraine 42 C4
Buga, Colombia 120 C2
Buganda, Uganda 82 C3
Buganga, Uganda 82 C3
Bugasong, Phil. 55 F5
Bugeat, France 26 C5
Bugel, Tanjung, Indonesia 56 F4
Buggenhout, Belgium 17 F4
Bugibba, Malta 37 D1
Bugsuk, Phil. 55 G2
Buguma, Nigeria 79 E6
Bugun Shara, Mongolia 54 B5
Buguruslan, Russia 44 D6
Buhăeşti, Romania 38 C10
Buheirat-Murrat-el-Kubra, Egypt 76 H8
Buhl, Idaho, U.S.A. 110 E6
Buhl, Minn., U.S.A. 108 B8
Buick, U.S.A. 109 G9
Builth Wells, U.K. 13 E4
Buinsk, Russia 41 D16
Buíque, Brazil 122 C4
Buir Nur, Mongolia 54 B6
Buis-les-Baronnies, France 27 D9
Buitenpost, Neths. 16 B8
Buitrago, Spain 30 E7
Buján, Spain 30 C2
Bujaraloz, Spain 28 D4
Buje, Croatia 33 C10
Bujumbura, Burundi 82 C2
Bukachacha, Russia 45 D12
Bukama, Zaïre 83 D2
Bukavu, Zaïre 82 C2
Bukene, Tanzania 82 C3
Bukhara, Uzbekistan 44 F7
Bukhoro = Bukhara, Uzbekistan 44 F7
Bukima, Tanzania 82 C3
Bukit Mertajam, Malaysia 59 K3
Bukittinggi, Indonesia 56 E2
Bukoba, Tanzania 82 C3
Bukoba □, Tanzania 82 C3
Bukuru, Nigeria 79 D6
Bukuya, Uganda 82 B3
Bula, Guinea-Biss. 78 C1
Bula, Indonesia 57 E8
Bülach, Switz. 23 A7
Bulahdelah, Australia 91 E5
Bulan, Phil. 55 E5
Bulancak, Turkey 67 C8
Bulandshahr, India 62 E7
Bulanık, Turkey 67 D10
Bûlâq, Egypt 76 B3
Bulawayo, Zimbabwe 83 G2
Buldan, Turkey 66 D3
Bulgan, Mongolia 54 B5
Bulgaria ■, Europe 38 G8
Bulgroo, Australia 91 D3
Bulgunnia, Australia 91 E1
Bulhar, Somali Rep. 68 E3
Buli, Teluk, Indonesia 57 D7
Buliluyan, C., Phil. 55 G2
Bulki, Ethiopia 77 F4
Bulkley →, Canada 100 B3
Bull Shoals L., U.S.A. 109 G8
Bullange, Belgium 17 H8
Bullaque →, Spain 31 G6
Bullara, Australia 88 D1
Bullaring, Australia 89 F2
Bullas, Spain 29 G3
Bulle, Switz. 22 C4
Bulli, Australia 91 E5
Bullock Creek, Australia 90 B3
Bulloo →, Australia 91 D3
Bulloo Downs, Queens., Australia 91 D3
Bulloo Downs, W. Austral., Australia 88 D2

Bulloo L., Australia 91 D3
Bulls, N.Z. 87 J5
Bully-les-Mines, France 25 B9
Bulnes, Chile 126 D1
Bulo Burti, Somali Rep. 68 G4
Bulsar = Valsad, India 60 J8
Bultfontein, S. Africa 84 D4
Bulu Karakelong, Indonesia 57 D7
Bulukumba, Indonesia 57 F6
Bulun, Russia 45 B13
Bumba, Zaïre 80 D4
Bumbiri I., Tanzania 82 C3
Bumhpa Bum, Burma 61 F20
Bumi →, Zimbabwe 83 F2
Buna, Kenya 82 B4
Bunawan, Agusan del S., Phil. 55 G6
Bunawan, Davao del S., Phil. 55 H6
Bunazi, Tanzania 82 C3
Bunbah, Khalīj, Libya 73 B9
Bunbury, Australia 89 F2
Buncrana, Ireland 15 A4
Bundaberg, Australia 91 C5
Bünde, Germany 18 C4
Bundey →, Australia 90 C2
Bundi, India 62 G6
Bundooma, Australia 90 C1
Bundoran, Ireland 15 B3
Bundukia, Sudan 77 F3
Bung Kan, Thailand 58 C4
Bungatakada, Japan 49 H5
Bungil Cr. →, Australia 90 D4
Bungo-Suidō, Japan 49 H6
Bungoma, Kenya 82 B3
Bungu, Tanzania 82 D4
Bunia, Zaïre 82 B3
Bunji, Pakistan 63 B6
Bunkie, U.S.A. 109 K8
Bunnell, U.S.A. 105 L5
Bunnik, Neths. 16 D6
Buñol, Spain 29 F4
Bunsbeek, Belgium 17 G5
Bunschoten, Neths. 16 D6
Buntok, Indonesia 56 E4
Bununu, Nigeria 79 D6
Bununu Dass, Nigeria 79 C6
Bünyan, Turkey 66 D6
Bunyu, Indonesia 56 D5
Bunza, Nigeria 79 C5
Buol, Indonesia 57 D6
Buon Brieng, Vietnam 58 F7
Buon Me Thuot, Vietnam . 58 F7
Buong Long, Cambodia 58 F6
Buorkhaya, Mys, Russia 45 B14
Buqayq, Si. Arabia 65 E6
Buqbua, Egypt 76 A2
Bur Acaba, Somali Rep. 68 G3
Bûr Fuad, Egypt 76 H8
Būr Safāga, Egypt 76 B3
Būr Sa'īd, Egypt 76 H8
Būr Sūdân, Sudan 76 D4
Būr Taufiq, Egypt 76 J8
Bura, Kenya 82 C4
Burao, Somali Rep. 68 F4
Burāq, Syria 69 B5
Buras, U.S.A. 109 L10
Buraydah, Si. Arabia 64 E5
Burbank, U.S.A. 113 L8
Burcher, Australia 91 E4
Burdekin →, Australia 90 B4
Burdett, Canada 100 D6
Burdur, Turkey 66 E4
Burdur □, Turkey 66 E4
Burdur Gölü, Turkey 66 E4
Burdwan = Barddhaman, India 63 H12
Bure, Ethiopia 77 E4
Bure →, U.K. 12 E9
Büren, Germany 18 D4
Buren, Neths. 16 E6
Bureya →, Russia 45 E13
Burford, Canada 106 C4
Burg, Sachsen-Anhalt, Germany 18 C7
Burg, Schleswig-Holstein, Germany 18 A7
Burg el Arab, Egypt 76 H6
Burg et Tuyur, Sudan 76 C2
Burg Stargard, Germany 18 B9
Burgas, Bulgaria 38 G10
Burgdorf, Germany 18 C5
Burgdorf, Switz. 22 B5
Burgeo, Canada 99 C8
Burgersdorp, S. Africa 84 E4
Burges, Mt., Australia 89 F3
Burghausen, Germany 19 G8
Búrgio, Italy 34 E6
Burglengenfeld, Germany . 19 F8
Burgo de Osma, Spain 28 D1
Burgohondo, Spain 30 E6
Burgos, Spain 28 C1
Burgos □, Spain 28 C1
Burgstädt, Germany 18 E8
Burgsvik, Sweden 9 H15
Burguillos del Cerro, Spain 31 G4
Burgundy = Bourgogne, France 25 F11
Burhanpur, India 60 J10
Burhou, U.K. 24 C4
Buri Pen., Eritrea 77 D4
Burias, Phil. 55 E5
Burica, Pta., Costa Rica 116 E3
Burigi, L., Tanzania 82 C3

Burin, Canada 99 C8
Buriram, Thailand 58 E4
Buriti Alegre, Brazil 123 E2
Buriti Bravo, Brazil 122 C3
Buriti dos Lopes, Brazil 122 B3
Burj Sāfitā, Syria 64 C3
Burji, Ethiopia 77 F4
Burkburnett, U.S.A. 109 H5
Burke, U.S.A. 110 C6
Burke →, Australia 90 C2
Burketown, Australia 90 B2
Burkina Faso ■, Africa 78 C4
Burk's Falls, Canada 98 C4
Burley, U.S.A. 110 E7
Burlingame, U.S.A. 112 H4
Burlington, Canada 106 C5
Burlington, Colo., U.S.A. . 108 F3
Burlington, Iowa, U.S.A. . 108 E9
Burlington, Kans., U.S.A. . 108 F7
Burlington, N.C., U.S.A. . 105 G6
Burlington, N.J., U.S.A. 107 F10
Burlington, Vt., U.S.A. 107 B11
Burlington, Wash., U.S.A. 112 B4
Burlington, Wis., U.S.A. . 104 D1
Burlyu-Tyube, Kazakhstan 44 E8
Burma ■, Asia 61 J20
Burnaby I., Canada 100 C2
Burnet, U.S.A. 109 K5
Burney, U.S.A. 110 F3
Burngup, Australia 89 F2
Burnham, U.S.A. 106 F7
Burnie, Australia 90 G4
Burnley, U.K. 12 D5
Burns, Oreg., U.S.A. 110 E4
Burns, Wyo., U.S.A. 108 E2
Burns Lake, Canada 100 C3
Burnside →, Canada 96 B9
Burnside, L., Australia 89 E3
Burnt River, Canada 106 B6
Burntwood →, Canada 101 B9
Burntwood L., Canada 101 B8
Burqân, Kuwait 64 D5
Burqin, China 54 B3
Burra, Australia 91 E2
Burramurra, Australia 90 C2
Burreli, Albania 39 H3
Burren Junction, Australia 91 E4
Burrendong Dam, Australia 91 E4
Burriana, Spain 28 F4
Burrinjuck Res., Australia 91 F4
Burro, Serranías del, Mexico 114 B4
Burruyacú, Argentina 126 B3
Burry Port, U.K. 13 F3
Bursa, Turkey 66 C3
Bursa □, Turkey 66 C3
Burseryd, Sweden 11 G7
Burstall, Canada 101 C7
Burton L., Canada 98 B4
Burton upon Trent, U.K. . 12 E6
Burtundy, Australia 91 E3
Buru, Indonesia 57 E7
Burullus, Bahra el, Egypt . 76 H7
Burûn, Râs, Egypt 69 D2
Burundi ■, Africa 82 C3
Bururi, Burundi 82 C2
Burutu, Nigeria 79 D6
Burwell, U.S.A. 108 E5
Bury, U.K. 12 D5
Bury St. Edmunds, U.K. 13 E8
Buryat Republic □, Russia 45 D11
Buryn, Ukraine 40 F8
Busalla, Italy 32 D5
Busango Swamp, Zambia . 83 E2
Busca, Italy 32 D4
Būshehr, Iran 65 D6
Būshehr □, Iran 65 D6
Bushell, Canada 101 B7
Bushenyi, Uganda 82 C3
Bushire = Būshehr, Iran 65 D6
Bushnell, Ill., U.S.A. 108 E9
Bushnell, Nebr., U.S.A. 108 E3
Busia □, Kenya 82 B3
Busie, Ghana 78 C4
Businga, Zaïre 80 D4
Buskerud fylke □, Norway 10 D3
Busko Zdrój, Poland 20 E10
Busoga □, Uganda 82 B3
Busovača, Bos.-H. 21 L7
Busra ash Shām, Syria 69 C5
Bussang, France 25 E14
Busselton, Australia 89 F2
Busseto, Italy 32 D7
Bussigny, Switz. 22 C3
Bussum, Neths. 16 D6
Bustamante, B., Argentina 128 C3
Busto, C., Spain 30 B4
Busto Arsizio, Italy 32 C5
Busu-Djanoa, Zaïre 80 D4
Busuanga, Phil. 55 E3
Büsum, Germany 18 A4
Buta, Zaïre 82 B1
Butare, Rwanda 82 C2
Butaritari, Kiribati 92 G9
Bütgenbach, Belgium 17 H8
Butha Qi, China 54 B7
Butiaba, Uganda 82 B3
Butler, Mo., U.S.A. 108 F7

Butler, Pa., U.S.A. 106 F5
Bütschwil, Switz. 23 B8
Butte, Mont., U.S.A. 110 C7
Butte, Nebr., U.S.A. 108 D5
Butte Creek →, U.S.A. 112 F5
Butterworth = Gcuwa, S. Africa 85 E4
Butterworth, Malaysia 59 K3
Buttfield, Mt., Australia 89 D4
Button B., Canada 101 B10
Buttonwillow, U.S.A. 113 K7
Butty Hd., Australia 89 F3
Butuan, Phil. 55 G6
Butuku-Luba, Eq. Guin. 79 E6
Butung, Indonesia 57 E6
Buturlinovka, Russia 41 F12
Butzbach, Germany 18 E4
Bützow, Germany 18 B7
Buxar, India 63 G10
Buxton, Guyana 121 B6
Buxton, S. Africa 84 D3
Buxton, U.K. 12 D6
Buxy, France 25 F11
Buy, Russia 41 B12
Buyaga, Russia 45 D13
Buynaksk, Russia 43 E12
Büyük Menderes →, Turkey 66 E2
Büyükçekmece, Turkey 39 H11
Buzançais, France 24 F8
Buzău, Romania 38 D9
Buzău →, Romania 38 D10
Buzău, Pasul, Romania 38 D9
Buzen, Japan 49 H5
Buzet, Croatia 33 C10
Buzi →, Mozam. 83 F3
Buziaş, Romania 38 D4
Buzuluk, Russia 44 D6
Buzuluk →, Russia 41 F13
Bwana Mkubwe, Zaïre 83 E2
Byala, Bulgaria 38 F8
Byala Slatina, Bulgaria 38 F6
Byandovan, Mys, Azerbaijan 43 G13
Bychawa, Poland 20 D12
Bydgoszcz, Poland 20 B8
Byelarus = Belorussia ■, Europe 40 E5
Byelorussia = Belorussia ■, Europe 40 E5
Byers, U.S.A. 108 F2
Byesville, U.S.A. 106 G3
Byhalia, U.S.A. 109 H10
Bykhov, Belorussia 40 E7
Bykovo, Russia 43 B11
Bylas, U.S.A. 111 K8
Bylderup, Denmark 11 K3
Bylot I., Canada 97 A12
Byrd, C., Antarctica 5 C17
Byro, Australia 89 E2
Byrock, Australia 91 E4
Byron Bay, Australia 91 D5
Byrranga, Gory, Russia 45 B11
Byrranga Mts. = Byrranga, Gory, Russia 45 B11
Byrum, Denmark 11 G5
Byske, Sweden 8 D16
Byske älv →, Sweden 8 D16
Bystrzyca Kłodzka, Poland 20 E6
Byten, Belorussia 40 E4
Bytom, Poland 20 E8
Bytów, Poland 20 A7
Byumba, Rwanda 82 C3

C

C.I.S. = Commonwealth of Independent States ■, Eurasia 45 D11
Ca →, Vietnam 58 C5
Ca Mau = Quan Long, Vietnam 59 H5
Ca Mau, Mui = Bai Bung, Mui, Vietnam 59 H5
Ca Na, Vietnam 59 G7
Caacupé, Paraguay 126 B4
Caála, Angola 81 G3
Caamano Sd., Canada 100 C3
Caapiranga, Brazil 121 D5
Caazapá, Paraguay 126 B4
Caazapá □, Paraguay 127 B4
Cabadbaran, Phil. 55 G6
Cabalian, Phil. 55 F6
Caballeria, C. de, Spain 36 A11
Cabana, Peru 124 C2
Cabanaconde, Peru 124 D3
Cabañaquinta, Spain 30 B5
Cabanatuan, Phil. 55 D4
Cabanes, Spain 28 E5
Cabanillas, Peru 124 D3
Cabano, Canada 99 C6
Čabar, Croatia 33 C11
Cabazon, U.S.A. 113 M10
Cabedelo, Brazil 122 C5
Cabeza del Buey, Spain 31 G5
Cabildo, Chile 126 C1
Cabimas, Venezuela 120 A3
Cabinda, Angola 80 F2
Cabinda □, Angola 80 F2
Cabinet Mts., U.S.A. 110 C6
Cabo Blanco, Argentina 128 C3

Cabo Frio, Brazil 123 F3
Cabo Pantoja, Peru 120 D2
Cabo Raso, Argentina 128 B3
Cabonga, Réservoir, Canada 98 C4
Cabool, U.S.A. 109 G8
Caboolture, Australia 91 D5
Cabora Bassa Dam = Cahora Bassa Dam, Mozam. 83 F3
Caborca, Mexico 114 A2
Cabot, Mt., U.S.A. 107 B13
Cabot Str., Canada 99 C8
Cabra, Spain 31 H6
Cabra del Santo Cristo, Spain 29 H1
Cábras, Italy 34 C1
Cabrera, I., Spain 36 B9
Cabrera, Sierra, Spain 30 C4
Cabri, Canada 101 C7
Cabriel →, Spain 29 F3
Cabruta, Venezuela 120 B4
Cabugao, Phil. 55 C4
Cabuyaro, Colombia 120 C3
Cacabelos, Spain 30 C4
Čačak, Serbia 21 M10
Cacao, Fr. Guiana 121 C7
Cáceres, Brazil 125 D6
Cáceres, Colombia 120 B2
Cáceres, Spain 31 F4
Cáceres □, Spain 31 F4
Cache Bay, Canada 98 C4
Cache Cr. →, U.S.A. 112 G5
Cachepo, Portugal 31 H3
Cachéu, Guinea-Biss. 78 C1
Cachi, Argentina 126 B2
Cachimbo, Brazil 125 B7
Cachimbo, Serra do, Brazil 125 B6
Cachoeira, Brazil 123 D4
Cachoeira Alta, Brazil 123 E1
Cachoeira de Itapemirim, Brazil 123 F3
Cachoeira do Sul, Brazil . 127 C5
Cachoeiro do Arari, Brazil 122 B2
Cachopo, Portugal 31 H3
Cachuela Esperanza, Bolivia 125 C4
Cacólo, Angola 80 G3
Caconda, Angola 81 G3
Cacongo, Angola 80 F2
Caçu, Brazil 123 E1
Caculé, Brazil 123 D3
Cadarache, France 27 E9
Čadca, Slovak Rep. 20 F8
Caddo, U.S.A. 109 H6
Cadell Cr. →, Australia 90 C3
Cadenazzo, Switz. 23 D7
Cader Idris, U.K. 12 E4
Cadí, Sierra del, Spain 28 C6
Cadibarrawirracanna, L., Australia 91 D2
Cadillac, Canada 98 C4
Cadillac, France 26 D3
Cadillac, U.S.A. 104 C3
Cadiz, Phil. 55 F5
Cádiz, Spain 31 J4
Cadiz, U.S.A. 106 F4
Cádiz □, Spain 31 J5
Cádiz, G. de, Spain 31 J4
Cadney Park, Australia 91 D1
Cadomin, Canada 100 C5
Cadotte →, Canada 100 B5
Cadours, France 26 E5
Cadoux, Australia 89 F2
Caen, France 24 C6
Caernarfon, U.K. 12 D3
Caernarfon B., U.K. 12 D3
Caernarvon = Caernarfon, U.K. 12 D3
Caerphilly, U.K. 13 F4
Caesarea, Israel 69 C3
Caeté, Brazil 123 E3
Caetité, Brazil 123 D3
Cafayate, Argentina 126 B2
Cafifi, Colombia 120 B3
Cafu, Angola 84 B2
Cagayan →, Phil. 55 B4
Cagayan de Oro, Phil. 55 G6
Cagayan Is., Phil. 55 G4
Cagayan Sulu I., Phil. 55 H3
Cagli, Italy 33 E9
Cágliari, Italy 34 C2
Cágliari, G. di, Italy 34 C2
Cagnano Varano, Italy 35 A8
Cagnes-sur-Mer, France 27 E11
Caguán →, Colombia 120 D3
Caguas, Puerto Rico 117 C6
Caha Mts., Ireland 15 E2
Cahama, Angola 84 B1
Caher, Ireland 15 D4
Cahersiveen, Ireland 15 E1
Cahora Bassa Dam, Mozam. 83 F3
Cahore Pt., Ireland 15 D5
Cahors, France 26 D5
Cahuapanas, Peru 124 B2
Cahuinari →, Colombia 120 D3
Cai Bau, Dao, Vietnam 58 B6
Cai Nuoc, Vietnam 59 H5
Caia, Mozam. 83 F4
Caiabis, Serra dos, Brazil . 125 C6
Caianda, Angola 83 E1
Caiapó, Serra do, Brazil 125 D7
Caiapônia, Brazil 125 D7
Caibarién, Cuba 116 B4

Caibiran, Phil. 55 F6
Caicara, Bolívar, Venezuela 120 B4
Caicara, Monagas, Venezuela 121 B5
Caicó, Brazil 122 C4
Caicos Is., W. Indies 117 B5
Caicos Passage, W. Indies 117 B5
Cailloma, Peru 124 D3
Caine →, Bolivia 125 D4
Caird Coast, Antarctica 5 D1
Cairn Gorm, U.K. 14 D5
Cairn Toul, U.K. 14 D5
Cairngorm Mts., U.K. 14 D5
Cairns, Australia 90 B4
Cairo = El Qâhira, Egypt 76 H7
Cairo, Ga., U.S.A. 105 K3
Cairo, Ill., U.S.A. 109 G10
Cairo Montenotte, Italy 32 D5
Caithness, Ord of, U.K. 14 C5
Caiundo, Angola 81 H3
Caiza, Bolivia 125 E4
Cajabamba, Peru 124 B2
Cajamarca, Peru 124 B2
Cajamarca □, Peru 124 B2
Cajapió, Brazil 122 B3
Cajarc, France 26 D5
Cajatambo, Peru 124 C2
Cajàzeiras, Brazil 122 C4
Čajetina, Serbia, Yug. 21 M9
Çakirgol, Turkey 43 F8
Čakovec, Croatia 33 B13
Çal, Turkey 66 D3
Cala, Spain 31 H4
Cala →, Spain 31 H4
Cala Cadolar, Punta de, Spain 29 G6
Cala d'Or, Spain 36 B10
Cala Figuera, C., Spain 36 B9
Cala Forcat, Spain 36 A10
Cala Mayor, Spain 36 B9
Cala Mezquida, Spain 36 B11
Cala Millor, Spain 36 B10
Cala Ratjada, Spain 36 B10
Calabanga, Phil. 55 E5
Calabar, Nigeria 79 E6
Calabozo, Venezuela 120 B4
Calábria □, Italy 35 C9
Calaburras, Pta. de, Spain 31 J6
Calaceite, Spain 28 D5
Calacota, Bolivia 124 D4
Calafate, Argentina 128 D2
Calahorra, Spain 28 C3
Calais, France 25 B8
Calais, U.S.A. 99 C6
Calais, Pas de, France 25 B8
Calalaste, Cord. de, Argentina 126 B2
Calama, Brazil 125 B5
Calama, Chile 126 A2
Calamar, Bolívar, Colombia 120 A3
Calamar, Vaupés, Colombia 120 C3
Calamarca, Bolivia 124 D4
Calamba, Phil. 55 F5
Calamian Group, Phil. 55 F3
Calamocha, Spain 28 E3
Calán Porter, Spain 36 B11
Calañas, Spain 31 H4
Calanda, Spain 28 E4
Calang, Indonesia 56 D1
Calangiánus, Italy 34 B2
Calapan, Phil. 55 E4
Călăraşi, Romania 38 E10
Calasparra, Spain 29 G3
Calatafimi, Italy 34 E5
Calatayud, Spain 28 D3
Calato = Kálathos, Greece 39 N11
Calauag, Phil. 55 E5
Calavà, C., Italy 35 D7
Calavite, C., Phil. 55 E4
Calayan, Phil. 55 B4
Calbayog, Phil. 55 E6
Calbe, Germany 18 D7
Calca, Peru 124 C3
Calcasieu L., U.S.A. 109 L8
Calci, Italy 32 E7
Calcutta, India 63 H13
Caldaro, Italy 33 B8
Caldas □, Colombia 120 B2
Caldas da Rainha, Portugal 31 F1
Caldas de Reyes, Spain 30 C2
Caldas Novas, Brazil 123 E2
Calder →, U.K. 12 D6
Caldera, Chile 126 B1
Caldwell, Idaho, U.S.A. 110 E5
Caldwell, Kans., U.S.A. 109 G6
Caldwell, Tex., U.S.A. 109 K6
Caledon, S. Africa 84 E2
Caledon →, S. Africa 84 E4
Caledon B., Australia 90 A2
Caledonia, Canada 106 C5
Caledonia, U.S.A. 106 D7
Calella, Spain 28 D7
Calemba, Angola 84 B2
Calenzana, France 27 F12
Caleta Olivia, Argentina 128 C3
Calexico, U.S.A. 113 N11
Calf of Man, U.K. 12 C3
Calgary, Canada 100 C6
Calheta, Madeira 36 D2
Calhoun, U.S.A. 105 H3
Cali, Colombia 120 C2
Calicut, India 60 P9
Caliente, U.S.A. 111 H6
California, Mo., U.S.A. 108 F8

California, Pa., U.S.A. 106 F5
California □, U.S.A. 111 H4
California, Baja, Mexico 114 A1
California, Baja, T.N. □, Mexico 114 B2
California, Baja, T.S. □, Mexico 114 B2
California, G. de, Mexico 114 B2
California City, U.S.A. 113 K9
California Hot Springs, U.S.A. 113 K8
Călimăneşti, Romania 38 D7
Călimani, Munţii, Romania 38 B8
Călineşti, Romania 38 D7
Calingasta, Argentina 126 C2
Calipatria, U.S.A. 113 M11
Calistoga, U.S.A. 112 G4
Calitri, Italy 35 B8
Calitzdorp, S. Africa 84 E3
Callabonna, L., Australia 91 D3
Callac, France 24 D3
Callan, Ireland 15 D4
Callander, U.K. 14 E4
Callantsoog, Neths. 16 C5
Callao, Peru 124 C2
Callaway, U.S.A. 108 E5
Calles, Mexico 115 C5
Callide, Australia 90 C5
Calling Lake, Canada 100 B6
Calliope, Australia 90 C5
Callosa de Ensarriá, Spain 29 G4
Callosa de Segura, Spain 29 G4
Calola, Angola 84 B2
Calolbon, Phil. 55 E6
Caloocan, Phil. 55 D4
Calore →, Italy 35 A7
Caloundra, Australia 91 D5
Calpe, Spain 29 G5
Calpella, U.S.A. 112 F3
Calpine, U.S.A. 112 F6
Calstock, Canada 98 C3
Caltabellotta, Italy 34 E6
Caltagirone, Italy 35 E7
Caltanissetta, Italy 35 E7
Calulo, Angola 80 G2
Calumet, U.S.A. 104 B1
Calunda, Angola 81 G4
Caluso, Italy 32 C4
Calvados □, France 24 C6
Calvert, U.S.A. 109 K6
Calvert →, Australia 90 B2
Calvert Hills, Australia 90 B2
Calvert I., Canada 100 C3
Calvert Ra., Australia 88 D3
Calvi, France 27 F12
Calvillo, Mexico 114 C4
Calvinia, S. Africa 84 E2
Calw, Germany 19 G4
Calwa, U.S.A. 112 J7
Calzada Almuradiel, Spain 29 G1
Calzada de Calatrava, Spain 31 G7
Cam →, U.K. 13 E8
Cam Lam, Vietnam 59 G7
Cam Pha, Vietnam 58 B6
Cam Ranh, Vietnam 59 G7
Cam Xuyen, Vietnam 58 C6
Camabatela, Angola 80 F3
Camacã, Brazil 123 E4
Camaçari, Brazil 123 D4
Camacha, Madeira 36 D3
Camacho, Mexico 114 C4
Camacupa, Angola 81 G3
Camaguán, Venezuela 120 B4
Camagüey, Cuba 116 B4
Camaiore, Italy 32 E7
Camamu, Brazil 123 D4
Camaná, Peru 124 D3
Camanche Reservoir, U.S.A. 112 G6
Camaquã →, Brazil 127 C5
Câmara de Lobos, Madeira 36 D3
Camararé →, Brazil 125 C6
Camarat, C., France 27 E10
Camaret, France 24 D2
Camargo, Bolivia 125 E4
Camargue, France 27 E8
Camarillo, U.S.A. 113 L7
Camariñas, Spain 30 B1
Camarón, C., Honduras 116 C2
Camarones, Argentina 128 B3
Camarones, B., Argentina 128 B3
Camas, U.S.A. 112 E4
Camas Valley, U.S.A. 110 E2
Cambados, Spain 30 C2
Cambará, Brazil 127 A5
Cambay = Khambhat, India 62 H5
Cambay, G. of = Khambat, G. of, India 62 J5
Cambil, Spain 29 H1
Cambo-les-Bains, France 26 E2
Cambodia ■, Asia 58 F5
Camborne, U.K. 13 G2
Cambrai, France 25 B10
Cambria, U.S.A. 111 J3
Cambrian Mts., U.K. 13 E4
Cambridge, Canada 98 D3
Cambridge, Jamaica 116 C4
Cambridge, N.Z. 87 G5
Cambridge, U.K. 13 E8
Cambridge, Idaho, U.S.A. 110 D5
Cambridge, Mass., U.S.A. 107 D13
Cambridge, Md., U.S.A. 104 F7
Cambridge, Minn., U.S.A. 108 C8

Cambridge, N.Y., U.S.A. 107 C11
Cambridge, Nebr., U.S.A. 108 E4
Cambridge, Ohio, U.S.A. 106 F3
Cambridge Bay, Canada 96 B9
Cambridge G., Australia 88 B4
Cambridge Springs, U.S.A. 106 E4
Cambridgeshire □, U.K. 13 E8
Cambrils, Spain 28 D6
Cambuci, Brazil 123 F3
Cambundi-Catembo, Angola 80 G3
Camden, Ala., U.S.A. 105 K2
Camden, Ark., U.S.A. 109 J8
Camden, Maine, U.S.A. 99 D6
Camden, N.J., U.S.A. 107 G9
Camden, S.C., U.S.A. 105 H5
Camden Sd., Australia 88 C3
Camdenton, U.S.A. 109 F8
Cameli, Turkey 66 E3
Camembert, France 24 D7
Cámeri, Italy 32 C5
Camerino, Italy 33 E10
Cameron, Ariz., U.S.A. 111 J8
Cameron, La., U.S.A. 109 L8
Cameron, Mo., U.S.A. 108 F7
Cameron, Tex., U.S.A. 109 K6
Cameron Falls, Canada 98 C2
Cameron Highlands, Malaysia 59 K3
Cameron Hills, Canada 100 B5
Cameroon ■, Africa 73 G7
Camerota, Italy 35 B8
Cameroun →, Cameroon 79 E6
Cameroun, Mt., Cameroon 79 E6
Cametá, Brazil 122 B2
Camiguin □, Phil. 55 G6
Camiguin I., Phil. 55 B4
Camiling, Phil. 55 D4
Caminha, Portugal 30 D2
Camino, U.S.A. 112 G6
Camira Creek, Australia 91 D5
Camiranga, Brazil 122 B2
Camiri, Bolivia 125 E5
Camissombo, Angola 80 F4
Cammal, U.S.A. 106 E7
Camocim, Brazil 122 B3
Camogli, Italy 32 D6
Camooweal, Australia 90 B2
Camopi, Fr. Guiana 121 C7
Camopi →, Fr. Guiana 121 C7
Camotes Is., Phil. 55 F6
Camotes Sea, Phil. 55 F6
Camp Crook, U.S.A. 108 C3
Camp Nelson, U.S.A. 113 J8
Camp Wood, U.S.A. 109 L4
Campagna, Italy 35 B8
Campana, Argentina 126 C4
Campana, I., Chile 128 C1
Campanário, Madeira 36 D2
Campanario, Spain 31 G5
Campania □, Italy 35 B7
Campbell, S. Africa 84 D3
Campbell, Calif., U.S.A. 112 H5
Campbell, Ohio, U.S.A. 106 E4
Campbell I., Pac. Oc. 92 N8
Campbell L., Canada 101 A7
Campbell River, Canada 100 C3
Campbell Town, Australia 90 G4
Campbellford, Canada 106 B7
Campbellpur, Pakistan 62 C5
Campbellsville, U.S.A. 104 G3
Campbellton, Canada 99 C6
Campbelltown, Australia 91 E5
Campbeltown, U.K. 14 F3
Campeche, Mexico 115 D6
Campeche □, Mexico 115 D6
Campeche, B. de, Mexico 115 D6
Camperdown, Australia 91 F3
Camperville, Canada 101 C8
Campi Salentina, Italy 35 B11
Campidano, Italy 34 C1
Campíglia Maríttima, Italy 32 E7
Campillo de Altobuey, Spain 28 F3
Campillo de Llerena, Spain 31 G5
Campillos, Spain 31 H6
Campina Grande, Brazil 122 C4
Campina Verde, Brazil 123 E2
Campinas, Brazil 127 A6
Campine, Belgium 17 F6
Campli, Italy 33 F10
Campo, Cameroon 80 D1
Campo, Spain 28 C5
Campo Belo, Brazil 123 F2
Campo de Criptana, Spain 29 F1
Campo de Diauarum, Brazil 125 C7
Campo de Gibraltar, Spain 31 J5
Campo Flórido, Brazil 123 E2
Campo Formoso, Brazil 122 D3
Campo Grande, Brazil 125 E7
Campo Maíor, Brazil 122 B3
Campo Maior, Portugal 31 G3
Campo Mourão, Brazil 127 A5
Campo Tencia, Switz. 23 D7
Campo Túres, Italy 33 B8
Campoalegre, Colombia 120 C2
Campobasso, Italy 35 A7
Campobello di Licata, Italy 34 E6
Campobello di Mazara, Italy 34 E5
Campofelice, Italy 34 E6
Camporeale, Italy 34 E6
Campos, Brazil 123 F3
Campos Altos, Brazil 123 E2

Campos Belos, Brazil 123 D2
Campos del Puerto, Spain 36 B10
Campos Novos, Brazil 127 B5
Campos Sales, Brazil 122 C3
Camprodón, Spain 28 C7
Camptonville, U.S.A. 112 F5
Campuya →, Peru 120 D3
Camrose, Canada 100 C6
Camsell Portage, Canada 101 B7
Çan, Turkey 66 C2
Can Clavo, Spain 36 C7
Can Creu, Spain 36 C7
Can Gio, Vietnam 59 G6
Can Tho, Vietnam 59 G5
Canaan, U.S.A. 107 D11
Canada ■, N. Amer. 96 C10
Cañada de Gómez, Argentina 126 C3
Canadian, U.S.A. 109 H4
Canadian →, U.S.A. 109 H7
Canadian Shield, Canada 97 C10
Çanakkale, Turkey 39 J9
Çanakkale □, Turkey 66 C2
Çanakkale Boğazı, Turkey 66 C2
Canal Flats, Canada 100 C5
Canalejas, Argentina 126 D2
Canals, Argentina 126 C3
Canals, Spain 29 G4
Canandaigua, U.S.A. 106 D7
Cananea, Mexico 114 A2
Cañar, Ecuador 120 D2
Cañar □, Ecuador 120 D2
Canarias, Is., Atl. Oc. 36 F4
Canarreos, Arch. de los, Cuba 116 B3
Canary Is. = Canarias, Is., Atl. Oc. 36 F4
Canastra, Serra da, Brazil 123 F2
Canatlán, Mexico 114 C4
Canaveral, C., U.S.A. 105 L5
Cañaveras, Spain 28 E2
Canavieiras, Brazil 123 E4
Canbelego, Australia 91 E4
Canberra, Australia 91 F4
Canby, Calif., U.S.A. 110 F3
Canby, Minn., U.S.A. 108 C6
Canby, Oreg., U.S.A. 112 E4
Cancale, France 24 D5
Canche →, France 25 B8
Canchyuaya, Cordillera de, Peru 124 B3
Cancún, Mexico 115 C7
Candala, Somali Rep. 68 E4
Candarave, Peru 124 D3
Candas, Spain 30 B5
Candé, France 24 E5
Candeias →, Brazil 125 B5
Candela, Italy 35 A8
Candelaria, Argentina 127 B4
Candelaria, Canary Is. 36 F3
Candelaria, Pta. de la, Spain 30 B2
Candeleda, Spain 30 E5
Candelo, Australia 91 F4
Candia = Iráklion, Greece 37 D7
Candia, Sea of = Crete, Sea of, Greece 39 N8
Cândido de Abreu, Brazil 123 F1
Cândido Mendes, Brazil 122 B2
Candle L., Canada 101 C7
Candlemas I., Antarctica 5 B1
Cando, U.S.A. 108 A5
Candon, Phil. 55 C4
Canea = Khaniá, Greece 37 D6
Canela, Brazil 122 D2
Canelli, Italy 32 D5
Canelones, Uruguay 127 C4
Cañete, Chile 126 D1
Cañete, Peru 124 C2
Cañete, Spain 28 E3
Cañete de las Torres, Spain 31 H6
Canfranc, Spain 28 C4
Cangas, Spain 30 C2
Cangas de Narcea, Spain 30 B4
Cangas de Onís, Spain 30 B5
Canguaretama, Brazil 122 C4
Canguçu, Brazil 127 C5
Cangxi, China 52 B5
Cangyuan, China 52 F2
Cangzhou, China 50 E9
Cani, I., Tunisia 75 A7
Canicattì, Italy 34 E6
Canicattini, Italy 35 E8
Canim Lake, Canada 100 C4
Caniné, Brazil 122 B4
Caninde →, Brazil 122 C3
Canindeyu □, Paraguay 127 A4
Canipaan, Phil. 56 C5
Canisteo, U.S.A. 106 D7
Canisteo →, U.S.A. 106 D7
Cañitas, Mexico 114 C4
Cañizal, Spain 30 D5
Canjáyar, Spain 29 H2
Çankiri, Turkey 66 C5
Çankiri □, Turkey 66 C5
Cankuzo, Burundi 82 C3
Canmore, Canada 100 C5
Cann River, Australia 91 F4
Canna, U.K. 14 D2
Cannanore, India 60 P9
Cannes, France 27 E11
Canning Town = Port Canning, India 63 H13
Cannington, Canada 106 B5

Cannock, U.K. 12 E5
Cannon Ball →, U.S.A. 108 B4
Cannondale Mt., Australia 90 D4
Caño Colorado, Colombia 120 C4
Canoas, Brazil 127 B5
Canoe L., Canada 101 B7
Canon City, U.S.A. 108 F2
Canora, Canada 101 C8
Canosa di Púglia, Italy 35 A9
Canowindra, Australia 91 E4
Canso, Canada 99 C7
Canta, Peru 124 C2
Cantabria □, Spain 30 B6
Cantabria, Sierra de, Spain 28 C2
Cantabrian Mts. = Cantábrica, Cordillera, Spain 30 C5
Cantábrica, Cordillera, Spain 30 C5
Cantal □, France 26 C6
Cantal, Plomb du, France 26 C6
Cantanhede, Portugal 30 E2
Cantaura, Venezuela 121 B5
Cantavieja, Spain 28 E4
Canterbury, Australia 90 D3
Canterbury, U.K. 13 F9
Canterbury □, N.Z. 87 K3
Canterbury Bight, N.Z. 87 L3
Canterbury Plains, N.Z. 87 K3
Cantil, U.S.A. 113 K9
Cantillana, Spain 31 H5
Canto do Buriti, Brazil 122 C3
Canton = Guangzhou, Guangdong, China 53 F9
Canton = Guangzhou, Guangdong, China 53 F9
Canton, Ga., U.S.A. 105 H3
Canton, Ill., U.S.A. 108 E9
Canton, Miss., U.S.A. 109 J9
Canton, Mo., U.S.A. 108 E9
Canton, N.Y., U.S.A. 107 B9
Canton, Ohio, U.S.A. 106 F3
Canton, Okla., U.S.A. 109 G5
Canton, S. Dak., U.S.A. 108 D6
Canton L., U.S.A. 109 G5
Cantù, Italy 32 C6
Canudos, Brazil 125 B6
Canumã, Amazonas, Brazil 121 D6
Canumã, Amazonas, Brazil 125 B5
Canumã →, Brazil 125 A6
Canutama, Brazil 125 B5
Canutillo, U.S.A. 111 L10
Canyon, Tex., U.S.A. 109 H4
Canyon, Wyo., U.S.A. 110 D8
Canyonlands National Park, U.S.A. 111 G9
Canyonville, U.S.A. 110 E2
Canzo, Italy 32 C6
Cao Bang, Vietnam 58 A6
Cao He →, China 51 D13
Cao Lanh, Vietnam 59 G5
Cao Xian, China 50 G8
Cáorle, Italy 33 C9
Cap-aux-Meules, Canada 99 C7
Cap-Chat, Canada 99 C6
Cap-de-la-Madeleine, Canada 98 C5
Cap-Haïtien, Haiti 117 C5
Cap St.-Jacques = Vung Tau, Vietnam 59 G6
Capa, Vietnam 58 A4
Capa Stilo, Italy 35 D9
Capáccio, Italy 35 B8
Capanga, Angola 80 F4
Capanaparo →, Venezuela 120 B4
Capanema, Brazil 122 B2
Caparo →, Barinas, Venezuela 120 B3
Caparo →, Bolívar, Venezuela 121 B5
Capatárida, Venezuela 120 A3
Capbreton, France 26 E2
Capdenac, France 26 D6
Cape →, Australia 90 C4
Cape Barren I., Australia 90 G4
Cape Breton Highlands Nat. Park, Canada 99 C7
Cape Breton I., Canada 99 C7
Cape Charles, U.S.A. 104 G8
Cape Coast, Ghana 79 D4
Cape Dorset, Canada 97 B12
Cape Dyer, Canada 97 B13
Cape Fear →, U.S.A. 105 H6
Cape Girardeau, U.S.A. 109 G10
Cape Jervis, Australia 91 F2
Cape May, U.S.A. 104 F8
Cape May Point, U.S.A. 103 C12
Cape Palmas, Liberia 78 E3
Cape Province □, S. Africa 84 E3
Cape Tormentine, Canada 99 C7
Cape Town, S. Africa 84 E2
Cape Verde Is. ■, Atl. Oc. 2 D8
Cape Vincent, U.S.A. 107 B8
Cape York Peninsula, Australia 90 A3
Capela, Brazil 122 D4
Capela de Campo, Brazil 122 B3
Capelinha, Brazil 123 E3
Capella, Australia 90 C4
Capendu, France 26 E6
Capestang, France 26 E7
Capim, Brazil 122 B2
Capim →, Brazil 122 B2
Capinópolis, Brazil 123 E2
Capinota, Bolivia 124 D4

Capitan, *U.S.A.* 111 K11
Capitán Aracena, I., *Chile* 128 D2
Capitán Pastene, *Chile* ... 128 A2
Capitola, *U.S.A.* 112 J5
Capizzi, *Italy* 35 E7
Čapljina, *Bos.-H.* 21 M7
Capoche →, *Mozam.* 83 F3
Capoeira, *Brazil* 125 B6
Cappadocia, *Turkey* 66 D6
Capraia, *Italy* 32 E6
Caprarola, *Italy* 33 F9
Capreol, *Canada* 98 C3
Caprera, *Italy* 34 A2
Capri, *Italy* 35 B7
Capricorn Group, *Australia* 90 C5
Capricorn Ra., *Australia* . 88 D2
Caprino Veronese, *Italy* .. 32 C7
Caprivi Strip, *Namibia* .. 84 B3
Captainganj, *India* 63 F10
Captain's Flat, *Australia* . 91 F4
Captieux, *France* 26 D3
Cápua, *Italy* 35 A7
Caquetá □, *Colombia* 120 C3
Caquetá →, *Colombia* ... 120 D4
Carabobo, *Venezuela* 120 A4
Carabobo □, *Venezuela* .. 120 A4
Caracal, *Romania* 38 E7
Caracaraí, *Brazil* 121 C5
Caracas, *Venezuela* 120 A4
Caracol, *Brazil* 122 C3
Caracollo, *Bolivia* 124 D4
Caradoc, *Australia* 91 E3
Caráglio, *Italy* 32 D4
Carahue, *Chile* 128 A2
Caraí, *Brazil* 123 E3
Carajás, Serra dos, *Brazil* 122 C1
Caranapatuba, *Brazil* 125 B5
Carandaiti, *Bolivia* 125 E5
Carangola, *Brazil* 123 F3
Carani, *Australia* 89 F2
Caransebeş, *Romania* 38 D5
Carantec, *France* 24 D3
Caraparaná →, *Colombia* 120 D3
Carapelle →, *Italy* 35 A8
Caras, *Peru* 124 B2
Caratasca, L., *Honduras* . 116 C3
Caratinga, *Brazil* 123 E3
Caraúbas, *Brazil* 122 C4
Caravaca, *Spain* 29 G3
Caravággio, *Italy* 32 C6
Caravelas, *Brazil* 123 E4
Caraveli, *Peru* 124 D3
Caràzinho, *Brazil* 127 B5
Carballino, *Spain* 30 C2
Carballo, *Spain* 30 B2
Carberry, *Canada* 101 D9
Carbia, *Spain* 30 C2
Carbó, *Mexico* 114 B2
Carbon, *Canada* 100 C6
Carbonara, C., *Italy* 34 C2
Carbondale, *Colo., U.S.A.* 110 G10
Carbondale, *Ill., U.S.A.* . 109 G10
Carbondale, *Pa., U.S.A.* . 107 E9
Carbonear, *Canada* 99 C9
Carboneras, *Spain* 29 J3
Carboneras de Guadazón,
  Spain 28 F3
Carbonia, *Italy* 34 C1
Carcabuey, *Spain* 31 H6
Carcagente, *Spain* 29 F4
Carcajou, *Canada* 100 B5
Carcar, *Phil.* 55 F5
Carcasse, C., *Haiti* 117 C5
Carcassonne, *France* 26 E6
Carche, *Spain* 29 G3
Carchi □, *Ecuador* 120 C2
Carcross, *Canada* 96 B6
Cardabia, *Australia* 88 D1
Çardak, *Turkey* 66 C3
Cardamom Hills, *India* .. 60 Q10
Cárdenas, *Cuba* 116 B3
Cárdenas, *San Luis Potosí,
  Mexico* 115 C5
Cárdenas, *Tabasco, Mexico* 115 D6
Cardenete, *Spain* 28 F3
Cardiel, L., *Argentina* ... 128 C2
Cardiff, *U.K.* 13 F4
Cardiff-by-the-Sea, *U.S.A.* 113 M9
Cardigan, *U.K.* 13 E3
Cardigan B., *U.K.* 13 E3
Cardinal, *Canada* 107 B9
Cardón, Punta, *Venezuela* 120 A3
Cardona, *Spain* 28 D6
Cardona, *Uruguay* 126 C4
Cardoner →, *Spain* 28 D6
Cardross, *Canada* 101 D7
Cardston, *Canada* 100 D6
Cardwell, *Australia* 90 B4
Careen L., *Canada* 101 B7
Carei, *Romania* 38 B5
Careiro, *Brazil* 121 D6
Careme, *Indonesia* 57 G13
Carentan, *France* 24 C5
Carey, *Idaho, U.S.A.* 110 E7
Carey, *Ohio, U.S.A.* 104 E4
Carey, L., *Australia* 89 E3
Carey L., *Canada* 101 A8
Careysburg, *Liberia* 78 D2
Cargèse, *France* 27 F12
Carhaix-Plouguer, *France* . 24 D3
Carhuamayo, *Peru* 124 C2
Carhuas, *Peru* 124 B2
Carhué, *Argentina* 126 D3
Caria, *Turkey* 66 E3

Cariacica, *Brazil* 123 F3
Caribbean Sea, *W. Indies* . 117 C5
Cariboo Mts., *Canada* ... 100 C4
Caribou, *U.S.A.* 99 C6
Caribou →, *Man., Canada* 101 B10
Caribou →, *N.W.T.,
  Canada* 100 A3
Caribou I., *Canada* 98 C2
Caribou Is., *Canada* 100 A6
Caribou L., *Man., Canada* 101 B9
Caribou L., *Ont., Canada* 98 B2
Caribou Mts., *Canada* ... 100 B5
Carichic, *Mexico* 114 B3
Carigara, *Phil.* 55 F6
Carignan, *France* 25 C12
Carignano, *Italy* 32 D4
Carillo, *Mexico* 114 B4
Carinda, *Australia* 91 E4
Cariñena, *Spain* 28 D3
Carinhanha, *Brazil* 123 D3
Carinhanha →, *Brazil* ... 123 D3
Carini, *Italy* 34 D6
Carinola, *Italy* 34 A6
Caripito, *Venezuela* 121 A5
Caritianas, *Brazil* 125 B5
Carlbro = Dimitrovgrad,
  Serbia, Yug. 21 M12
Carlentini, *Italy* 35 E8
Carleton Place, *Canada* .. 98 C4
Carletonville, *S. Africa* .. 84 D4
Carlin, *U.S.A.* 110 F5
Carlingford, L., *Ireland* .. 15 B5
Carlinville, *U.S.A.* 108 F10
Carlisle, *U.K.* 12 C5
Carlisle, *U.S.A.* 106 F7
Carlit, Pic, *France* 26 F5
Carloforte, *Italy* 34 C1
Carlos Casares, *Argentina* . 126 D3
Carlos Chagas, *Brazil* ... 123 E3
Carlos Tejedor, *Argentina* 126 D3
Carlow, *Ireland* 15 D5
Carlow □, *Ireland* 15 D5
Carlsbad, *Calif., U.S.A.* .. 113 M9
Carlsbad, *N. Mex., U.S.A.* 109 J2
Carlyle, *Canada* 101 D8
Carlyle, *U.S.A.* 108 F10
Carmacks, *Canada* 96 B6
Carmagnola, *Italy* 32 D4
Carman, *Canada* 101 D9
Carmangay, *Canada* 100 C6
Carmanville, *Canada* 99 C9
Carmarthen, *U.K.* 13 F3
Carmarthen B., *U.K.* 13 F3
Carmaux, *France* 26 D6
Carmel, *U.S.A.* 107 E11
Carmel-by-the-Sea, *U.S.A.* 111 H3
Carmel Valley, *U.S.A.* ... 112 J5
Carmelo, *Uruguay* 126 C4
Carmen, *Bolivia* 124 C4
Carmen, *Colombia* 120 B2
Carmen, *Paraguay* 127 B4
Carmen →, *Mexico* 114 A3
Carmen, I., *Mexico* 114 B2
Carmen de Patagones,
  Argentina 128 B4
Cármenes, *Spain* 30 C5
Carmensa, *Argentina* 126 D2
Carmi, *U.S.A.* 104 F1
Carmichael, *U.S.A.* 112 G5
Carmila, *Australia* 90 C4
Carmona, *Spain* 31 H5
Carnarvon, *Queens.,
  Australia* 90 C4
Carnarvon, *W. Austral.,
  Australia* 89 D1
Carnarvon, *S. Africa* 84 E3
Carnarvon Ra., *Queens.,
  Australia* 90 D4
Carnarvon Ra.,
  W. Austral., Australia .. 89 E3
Carnation, *U.S.A.* 112 C5
Carnaxide, *Portugal* 31 G1
Carndonagh, *Ireland* 15 A4
Carnduff, *Canada* 101 D8
Carnegie, *U.S.A.* 106 F4
Carnegie, L., *Australia* .. 89 E3
Carnic Alps = Karnische
  Alpen, *Europe* 21 J3
Carniche Alpi = Karnische
  Alpen, *Europe* 21 J3
Carnot, *C.A.R.* 80 D3
Carnot, C., *Australia* 91 E2
Carnot B., *Australia* 88 C3
Carnsore Pt., *Ireland* 15 D5
Caro, *U.S.A.* 104 D4
Carol City, *U.S.A.* 105 N5
Carolina, *Brazil* 122 C2
Carolina, *Puerto Rico* ... 117 C6
Carolina, *S. Africa* 85 D5
Caroline I., *Kiribati* 93 H12
Caroline Is., *Pac. Oc.* 92 G6
Caron, *Canada* 101 C7
Caroni →, *Venezuela* ... 121 B5
Caroona, *Australia* 91 E5
Carora, *Venezuela* 120 A3
Carovigno, *Italy* 35 B10
Carpathians, *Europe* 20 F11
Carpaţii Meridionali,
  Romania 38 D5
Carpenédolo, *Italy* 32 C7
Carpentaria, G. of,
  Australia 90 A2
Carpentaria Downs,
  Australia 90 B3
Carpentras, *France* 27 D9

Carpi, *Italy* 32 D7
Carpina, *Brazil* 122 C4
Carpino, *Italy* 35 A8
Carpinteria, *U.S.A.* 113 L7
Carpio, *Spain* 30 D5
Carpolac = Morea,
  Australia 91 F3
Carr Boyd Ra., *Australia* . 88 C4
Carrabelle, *U.S.A.* 105 L3
Carranya, *Australia* 88 C4
Carrara, *Italy* 32 D7
Carrascal, *Phil.* 55 G6
Carrascosa del Campo,
  Spain 28 E2
Carrauntoohill, *Ireland* .. 15 E2
Carretas, Punta, *Peru* ... 124 C2
Carrick-on-Shannon,
  Ireland 15 C3
Carrick-on-Suir, *Ireland* . 15 D4
Carrickfergus, *U.K.* 15 B6
Carrickfergus □, *U.K.* ... 15 B6
Carrickmacross, *Ireland* . 15 C5
Carrieton, *Australia* 91 E2
Carrington, *U.S.A.* 108 B5
Carrión →, *Spain* 30 D6
Carrión de los Condes,
  Spain 30 C6
Carrizal Bajo, *Chile* 126 B1
Carrizalillo, *Chile* 126 B1
Carrizo Cr. →, *U.S.A.* .. 109 G3
Carrizo Springs, *U.S.A.* . 109 L5
Carrizozo, *U.S.A.* 111 K11
Carroll, *U.S.A.* 108 D7
Carrollton, *Ga., U.S.A.* .. 105 J3
Carrollton, *Ill., U.S.A.* .. 108 F9
Carrollton, *Ky., U.S.A.* .. 104 F3
Carrollton, *Mo., U.S.A.* . 108 F8
Carrollton, *Ohio, U.S.A.* 106 F3
Carron →, *U.K.* 14 D4
Carron, L., *U.K.* 14 D3
Carrot →, *Canada* 101 C8
Carrot River, *Canada* 101 C8
Carrouges, *France* 24 D6
Carruthers, *Canada* 101 C7
Çarşamba, *Turkey* 66 C7
Carse of Gowrie, *U.K.* ... 14 E5
Carsoli, *Italy* 33 F10
Carson, *Calif., U.S.A.* ... 113 M8
Carson, *N. Dak., U.S.A.* . 108 B4
Carson →, *U.S.A.* 112 F8
Carson City, *U.S.A.* 112 F7
Carson Sink, *U.S.A.* 110 G4
Carstairs, *U.K.* 14 F5
Cartagena, *Colombia* 120 A2
Cartagena, *Spain* 29 H4
Cartago, *Colombia* 120 C2
Cartago, *Costa Rica* 116 E3
Cartaxo, *Portugal* 31 F2
Cartaya, *Spain* 31 H3
Carteret, *France* 24 C5
Cartersville, *U.S.A.* 105 H3
Carterton, *N.Z.* 87 J5
Carthage, *Ark., U.S.A.* .. 109 H8
Carthage, *Ill., U.S.A.* ... 108 E9
Carthage, *Mo., U.S.A.* .. 109 G7
Carthage, *S. Dak., U.S.A.* 108 C6
Carthage, *Tex., U.S.A.* .. 109 J7
Cartier I., *Australia* 88 B3
Cartwright, *Canada* 99 B8
Caruaru, *Brazil* 122 C4
Carúpano, *Venezuela* 121 A5
Carutapera, *Brazil* 122 B2
Caruthersville, *U.S.A.* ... 109 G10
Carvin, *France* 25 B9
Carvoeiro, *Brazil* 121 D5
Carvoeiro, C., *Portugal* .. 31 F1
Casa Branca, *Brazil* 123 F2
Casa Branca, *Portugal* ... 31 G2
Casa Grande, *U.S.A.* 111 K8
Casablanca, *Chile* 126 C1
Casablanca, *Morocco* 74 B3
Casacalenda, *Italy* 35 A7
Casal di Principe, *Italy* .. 35 B7
Casalbordino, *Italy* 33 F11
Casale Monferrato, *Italy* . 32 C5
Casalmaggiore, *Italy* 32 D7
Casalpusterlengo, *Italy* .. 32 C6
Casamance →, *Senegal* .. 78 C1
Casamássima, *Italy* 35 B9
Casarano, *Italy* 35 B11
Casares, *Spain* 31 J5
Casas Grandes, *Mexico* .. 114 A3
Casas Ibáñez, *Spain* 29 F3
Casasimarro, *Spain* 29 F2
Casatejada, *Spain* 30 F5
Casavieja, *Spain* 30 E6
Cascade, *Idaho, U.S.A.* .. 110 D5
Cascade, *Mont., U.S.A.* . 110 C8
Cascade Locks, *U.S.A.* .. 112 E5
Cascade Ra., *U.S.A.* 112 D5
Cascais, *Portugal* 31 G1
Cascavel, *Brazil* 127 A5
Cáscina, *Italy* 32 E7
Caselle Torinese, *Italy* .. 32 C4
Caserta, *Italy* 35 A7
Cashel, *Ireland* 15 D4
Cashmere, *U.S.A.* 110 C3
Cashmere Downs, *Australia* 89 E2
Casibare →, *Colombia* ... 120 C3
Casiguran, *Phil.* 55 C5
Casilda, *Argentina* 126 C3

Casino, *Australia* 91 D5
Casiquiare →, *Venezuela* 120 C4
Casitas, *Peru* 124 A1
Caslan, *Canada* 100 C6
Čáslav, *Czech.* 20 F5
Casma, *Peru* 124 B2
Casmalia, *U.S.A.* 113 L6
Casola Valsenio, *Italy* ... 33 D8
Cásoli, *Italy* 33 F11
Caspe, *Spain* 28 D4
Casper, *U.S.A.* 110 E10
Caspian Sea, *Asia* 44 E6
Casquets, *Chan. Is.* 24 C4
Cass City, *U.S.A.* 104 D4
Cass Lake, *U.S.A.* 108 B7
Cassá de la Selva, *Spain* . 28 D7
Cassano Iónio, *Italy* 35 C9
Cassel, *France* 25 B9
Casselman, *Canada* 107 A9
Casselton, *U.S.A.* 108 B6
Cassiar, *Canada* 100 B3
Cassiar Mts., *Canada* 100 B2
Cassilândia, *Brazil* 125 D7
Cassino, *Italy* 34 A6
Cassis, *France* 27 E9
Cassville, *U.S.A.* 109 G8
Cástagneto Carducci, *Italy* 32 E7
Castaic, *U.S.A.* 113 L8
Castanhal, *Brazil* 122 B2
Castéggio, *Italy* 32 C6
Casteau, *Belgium* 17 G4
Castejón de Monegros,
  Spain 28 D4
Castel di Sangro, *Italy* ... 33 G11
Castel San Giovanni, *Italy* 32 C6
Castel San Pietro, *Italy* .. 33 D8
Castelbuono, *Italy* 35 E7
Casteldelfino, *Italy* 32 D4
Castelfiorentino, *Italy* ... 32 E7
Castelfranco Emília, *Italy* . 32 D8
Castelfranco Véneto, *Italy* 33 C8
Casteljaloux, *France* 26 D4
Castellabate, *Italy* 35 B7
Castellammare, G. di, *Italy* 34 D5
Castellammare del Golfo,
  Italy 34 D5
Castellammare di Stábia,
  Italy 35 B7
Castellamonte, *Italy* 32 C4
Castellana Grotte, *Italy* .. 35 B10
Castellane, *France* 27 E10
Castellaneta, *Italy* 35 B9
Castellar de Santisteban,
  Spain 29 G1
Castelleone, *Italy* 32 C6
Castelli, *Argentina* 126 D4
Castelló de Ampurias,
  Spain 28 C8
Castellón □, *Spain* 28 E4
Castellón de la Plana, *Spain* 28 F4
Castellote, *Spain* 28 E4
Castelltersol, *Spain* 28 D7
Castelmáuro, *Italy* 35 A7
Castelnau-de-Médoc,
  France 26 C3
Castelnaudary, *France* ... 26 E5
Castelnovo ne' Monti, *Italy* 32 D7
Castelnuovo di Val di
  Cécina, *Italy* 32 E7
Castelo, *Brazil* 123 F3
Castelo Branco, *Portugal* . 30 F3
Castelo Branco □, *Portugal* 30 F3
Castelo de Paiva, *Portugal* 30 D2
Castelo de Vide, *Portugal* 31 F3
Castelo do Piauí, *Brazil* . 122 C3
Castelsarrasin, *France* ... 26 D5
Casteltérmini, *Italy* 34 E6
Castelvetrano, *Italy* 34 E5
Casterton, *Australia* 91 F3
Castets, *France* 26 E2
Castiglione del Lago, *Italy* 33 E9
Castiglione della Pescáia,
  Italy 32 F7
Castiglione della Stiviere,
  Italy 32 C7
Castiglione Fiorentino, *Italy* 33 E9
Castilblanco, *Spain* 31 F5
Castilla, *Peru* 124 B1
Castilla, Playa de, *Spain* . 31 H4
Castilla La Mancha □,
  Spain 31 F7
Castilla La Nueva =
  Castilla La Mancha □,
  Spain 31 F7
Castilla La Vieja = Castilla
  y León □, *Spain* 30 D6
Castilla y León □, *Spain* . 30 D6
Castillon, Barr. de, *France* 27 E10
Castillon-en-Couserans,
  France 26 F5
Castillon-la-Bataille, *France* 26 D3
Castillonès, *France* 26 D4
Castillos, *Uruguay* 127 C5
Castle Dale, *U.S.A.* 110 G8
Castle Douglas, *U.K.* 14 G5
Castle Rock, *Colo., U.S.A.* 108 F2
Castle Rock, *Wash.,
  U.S.A.* 112 D4
Castlebar, *Ireland* 15 C2
Castleblaney, *Ireland* 15 B5
Castlegar, *Canada* 100 D5
Castlemaine, *Australia* .. 91 F3
Castlereagh, *Ireland* 15 C3
Castlereagh □, *U.K.* 15 B6

Castlereagh →, *Australia* . 91 E4
Castlereagh B., *Australia* . 90 A2
Castletown, *I. of Man* ... 12 C3
Castletown Bearhaven,
  Ireland 15 E2
Castlevale, *Australia* 90 C4
Castor, *Canada* 100 C6
Castres, *France* 26 E6
Castricum, *Neths.* 16 C5
Castries, *St. Lucia* 117 D7
Castril, *Spain* 29 H2
Castro, *Brazil* 127 A5
Castro, *Chile* 128 B2
Castro Alves, *Brazil* 123 D4
Castro del Río, *Spain* 31 H6
Castro Marim, *Portugal* .. 31 H3
Castro Urdiales, *Spain* ... 28 B1
Castro Verde, *Portugal* .. 31 H2
Castrojeriz, *Spain* 30 C6
Castropol, *Spain* 30 B3
Castroreale, *Italy* 35 D8
Castrovíllari, *Italy* 35 C9
Castroville, *Calif., U.S.A.* 112 J5
Castroville, *Tex., U.S.A.* . 109 L5
Castrovirreyna, *Peru* 124 C2
Castuera, *Spain* 31 G5
Casummit Lake, *Canada* . 98 B1
Çat, *Turkey* 67 D9
Cat Ba, Dao, *Vietnam* ... 58 B6
Cat I., *Bahamas* 117 B4
Cat I., *U.S.A.* 109 K10
Cat L., *Canada* 98 B1
Catacamas, *Honduras* ... 116 D2
Catacáos, *Peru* 124 B1
Cataguases, *Brazil* 123 F3
Catahoula L., *U.S.A.* 109 K8
Çatak, *Turkey* 67 D10
Catalão, *Brazil* 123 E2
Çatalca, *Turkey* 66 C3
Catalina, *Canada* 99 C9
Catalonia = Cataluña □,
  Spain 28 D6
Cataluña □, *Spain* 28 D6
Çatalzeytin, *Turkey* 66 C6
Catamarca, *Argentina* ... 126 B2
Catamarca □, *Argentina* . 126 B2
Catanauan, *Phil.* 55 E5
Catanduanes, *Phil.* 55 E6
Catanduva, *Brazil* 127 A6
Catánia, *Italy* 35 E8
Catánia, G. di, *Italy* 35 E8
Catanzaro, *Italy* 35 D9
Cataonia, *Turkey* 66 E6
Catarman, *Phil.* 55 E6
Catbalogan, *Phil.* 55 F6
Catende, *Brazil* 122 C4
Cathcart, *S. Africa* 84 E4
Cathlamet, *U.S.A.* 112 D3
Catio, *Guinea-Biss.* 78 C1
Catismiña, *Venezuela* 121 C5
Catita, *Brazil* 122 C3
Catlettsburg, *U.S.A.* 104 F4
Catoche, C., *Mexico* 115 C7
Catolé do Rocha, *Brazil* . 122 C4
Catral, *Spain* 29 G4
Catria, Mt., *Italy* 33 E9
Catrimani, *Brazil* 121 C5
Catrimani →, *Brazil* 121 C5
Catskill, *U.S.A.* 107 D11
Catskill Mts., *U.S.A.* 107 D10
Catt, Mt., *Australia* 90 A1
Cattaraugus, *U.S.A.* 106 D6
Cáttolica, *Italy* 33 E9
Cáttolica Eraclea, *Italy* .. 34 E6
Catu, *Brazil* 123 D4
Catuala, *Angola* 84 B2
Catur, *Mozam.* 83 E4
Catwick Is., *Vietnam* 59 G7
Cauca □, *Colombia* 120 C2
Cauca →, *Colombia* 120 B3
Caucaia, *Brazil* 122 B4
Caucasia, *Colombia* 120 B2
Caucasus = Bolshoi
  Kavkas, *Asia* 43 E11
Caudebec-en-Caux, *France* 24 C7
Caudete, *Spain* 29 G3
Caudry, *France* 25 B10
Caulnes, *France* 24 D4
Caulónia, *Italy* 35 D9
Caúngula, *Angola* 80 F3
Cauquenes, *Chile* 126 D1
Caura →, *Venezuela* 121 B5
Caurés →, *Brazil* 121 D5
Cauresi →, *Mozam.* 83 F3
Causapscal, *Canada* 99 C6
Caussade, *France* 26 D5
Causse-Méjean, *France* .. 26 D7
Cauterets, *France* 26 F3
Cautín □, *Chile* 128 A2
Cauvery →, *India* 60 P11
Caux, Pays de, *France* ... 24 C7
Cava dei Tirreni, *Italy* ... 35 B7
Cávado →, *Portugal* 30 D2
Cavaillon, *France* 27 E9
Cavalaire-sur-Mer, *France* 27 E10
Cavalcante, *Brazil* 123 D2
Cavalese, *Italy* 33 B8
Cavalier, *U.S.A.* 108 A6
Cavalla = Cavally →,
  Africa 78 E3
Cavallo, I. de, *France* 27 G13
Cavally →, *Africa* 78 E3
Cavan, *Ireland* 15 C4
Cavan □, *Ireland* 15 C4

Cavárzere, *Italy* 33 C9
Cave City, *U.S.A.* 104 G3
Cavenagh Ra., *Australia* . 89 E4
Cavendish, *Australia* 91 F3
Caviana, I., *Brazil* 121 C7
Cavite, *Phil.* 55 D4
Cavour, *Italy* 32 D4
Cavtat, *Croatia* 21 N8
Cavuşcu Gölü, *Turkey* ... 66 D4
Cawndilla L., *Australia* .. 91 E3
Cawnpore = Kanpur, *India* 63 F9
Caxias, *Brazil* 122 B3
Caxias do Sul, *Brazil* ... 127 B5
Caxine, C., *Algeria* 75 A4
Caxito, *Angola* 80 F2
Çay, *Turkey* 66 D4
Cay Sal Bank, *Bahamas* . 116 B3
Cayambe, *Ecuador* 120 C2
Cayambe, *Ecuador* 120 C2
Çaycuma, *Turkey* 66 C5
Çayeli, *Turkey* 67 C9
Cayenne, *Fr. Guiana* 121 B7
Cayenne □, *Fr. Guiana* . 121 C7
Cayeux-sur-Mer, *France* . 25 B8
Çayiralan, *Turkey* 66 D6
Caylus, *France* 26 D5
Cayman Brac, *Cayman Is.* 116 C4
Cayman Is. ■, *W. Indies* 116 C3
Cayo Romano, *Cuba* 117 B4
Cayuga, *Canada* 106 D5
Cayuga, *U.S.A.* 107 D8
Cayuga L., *U.S.A.* 107 D8
Cazalla de la Sierra, *Spain* 31 H5
Căzăneşti, *Romania* 38 E10
Cazaux et de Sanguinet,
  Étang de, *France* 26 D2
Cazères, *France* 26 E5
Cazin, *Bos.-H.* 33 D12
Čazma, *Croatia* 33 C13
Čazma →, *Croatia* 33 C13
Cazombo, *Angola* 81 G4
Cazorla, *Spain* 29 H1
Cazorla, *Venezuela* 120 B4
Cazorla, Sierra de, *Spain* . 29 G2
Cea →, *Spain* 30 C5
Ceanannus Mor, *Ireland* . . 15 C5
Ceará = Fortaleza, *Brazil* . 122 B4
Ceará □, *Brazil* 122 C4
Ceará Mirim, *Brazil* 122 C4
Cebaco, I. de, *Panama* ... 116 E3
Cebollar, *Argentina* 126 B2
Cebollera, Sierra de, *Spain* 28 D2
Cebreros, *Spain* 30 E6
Cebu, *Phil.* 55 F5
Ceccano, *Italy* 34 A6
Cechi, *Ivory C.* 78 D4
Čechy, *Czech.* 19 F9
Cecil Plains, *Australia* ... 91 D5
Cécina, *Italy* 32 E7
Cécina →, *Italy* 32 E7
Ceclavín, *Spain* 30 F4
Cedar →, *U.S.A.* 108 E9
Cedar City, *U.S.A.* 111 H7
Cedar Creek Reservoir,
  U.S.A. 109 J6
Cedar Falls, *Iowa, U.S.A.* 108 D8
Cedar Falls, *Wash., U.S.A.* 112 C5
Cedar Key, *U.S.A.* 105 L4
Cedar L., *Canada* 101 C8
Cedar Rapids, *U.S.A.* ... 108 E9
Cedartown, *U.S.A.* 105 H3
Cedarvale, *Canada* 100 B3
Cedarville, *S. Africa* 85 E4
Cedarville, *U.S.A.* 110 F3
Cedeira, *Spain* 30 B2
Cedral, *Mexico* 114 C4
Cedrino →, *Italy* 34 B2
Cedro, *Brazil* 122 C4
Cedros, I. de, *Mexico* ... 114 B1
Ceduna, *Australia* 91 E1
Cefalù, *Italy* 35 D7
Cega →, *Spain* 30 D6
Cegléd, *Hungary* 21 H9
Céglie Messápico, *Italy* .. 35 B10
Cehegín, *Spain* 29 G3
Ceheng, *China* 52 E5
Cehu-Silvaniei, *Romania* . . 38 B6
Ceira →, *Portugal* 30 E2
Cekhira, *Tunisia* 75 B7
Celano, *Italy* 33 F10
Celanova, *Spain* 30 C3
Celaya, *Mexico* 114 C4
Celbridge, *Ireland* 15 C5
Celebes = Sulawesi □,
  Indonesia 57 E6
Celebes Sea = Sulawesi
  Sea, *Indonesia* 57 D6
Celendín, *Peru* 124 B2
Čelić, *Bos.-H., Yug.* 21 L8
Celica, *Ecuador* 120 D2
Celina, *U.S.A.* 104 E3
Celje, *Slovenia* 33 B12
Celle, *Germany* 18 C6
Celles, *Belgium* 17 G2
Celorico da Beira, *Portugal* 30 E3
Cement, *U.S.A.* 109 H5
Çemişgezek, *Turkey* 67 D8
Cenepa →, *Peru* 120 D2
Cengong, *China* 52 D7
Ceno →, *Italy* 32 D7
Centallo, *Italy* 32 D4
Centenário do Sul, *Brazil* . 123 F1
Center, *N. Dak., U.S.A.* . 108 B4
Center, *Tex., U.S.A.* 109 K7
Centerfield, *U.S.A.* 111 G8

Centerville, *Calif., U.S.A.* 112 J7
Centerville, *Iowa, U.S.A.* 108 E8
Centerville, *Pa., U.S.A.* . 106 F5
Centerville, *S. Dak.,
  U.S.A.* 108 D6
Centerville, *Tenn., U.S.A.* 105 H2
Centerville, *Tex., U.S.A.* 109 K7
Cento, *Italy* 33 D8
Central, *Brazil* 122 D3
Central, *U.S.A.* 111 K9
Central □, *Kenya* 82 C4
Central □, *Malawi* 83 E3
Central □, *U.K.* 14 E4
Central □, *Zambia* 83 E2
Central, Cordillera, *Bolivia* 125 D5
Central, Cordillera,
  Colombia 120 C2
Central, Cordillera,
  Costa Rica 116 D3
Central, Cordillera,
  Dom. Rep. 117 C5
Central, Cordillera, *Peru* . 124 B2
Central, Cordillera, *Phil.* . 55 C4
Central, Sistema, *Spain* .. 30 E5
Central African Rep. ■,
  Africa 73 G9
Central City, *Ky., U.S.A.* 104 G2
Central City, *Nebr., U.S.A.* 108 E5
Central I., *Kenya* 82 B4
Central Makran Range,
  Pakistan 60 F4
Central Patricia, *Canada* . 98 B1
Central Russian Uplands,
  Europe 6 E13
Central Siberian Plateau,
  Russia 46 C14
Centralia, *Ill., U.S.A.* ... 108 F10
Centralia, *Mo., U.S.A.* .. 108 F8
Centralia, *Wash., U.S.A.* 112 D4
Centreville, *Ala., U.S.A.* . 105 J2
Centreville, *Miss., U.S.A.* 109 K9
Centúripe, *Italy* 35 E7
Cephalonia = Kefallinía,
  Greece 39 L3
Ceprano, *Italy* 34 A6
Cepu, *Indonesia* 57 G14
Ceram = Seram, *Indonesia* 57 E7
Ceram Sea = Seram Sea,
  Indonesia 57 E7
Cerbère, *France* 26 F7
Cerbicales, Is., *France* ... 27 G13
Cercal, *Portugal* 31 H2
Cercemaggiore, *Italy* 35 A7
Cerdaña, *Spain* 28 C6
Cerdedo, *Spain* 30 C2
Cère →, *France* 26 D5
Cerea, *Italy* 33 C8
Ceres, *Argentina* 126 B3
Ceres, *Brazil* 123 E2
Ceres, *Italy* 32 C4
Ceres, *S. Africa* 84 E2
Ceres, *U.S.A.* 112 H6
Céret, *France* 26 F6
Cereté, *Colombia* 120 B2
Cerfontaine, *Belgium* ... 17 H4
Cerignola, *Italy* 35 A8
Cerigo = Kíthira, *Greece* . 39 N7
Çerkeş, *Turkey* 66 C5
Çerkezköy, *Turkey* 66 C2
Cerknica, *Slovenia* 33 C11
Çermik, *Turkey* 67 D8
Cerna →, *Romania* 38 E7
Cernavodă, *Romania* 38 E11
Cernay, *France* 25 E14
Černik, *Croatia* 21 K7
Cerralvo, I., *Mexico* 114 C3
Cerreto Sannita, *Italy* ... 35 A7
Cerritos, *Mexico* 114 C4
Cerro Sombrero, *Chile* .. 128 D3
Certaldo, *Italy* 32 E8
Cervaro →, *Italy* 35 A8
Cervera, *Spain* 28 D6
Cervera de Pisuerga, *Spain* 30 C6
Cervera del Río Alhama,
  Spain 28 C3
Cérvia, *Italy* 33 D9
Cervignano del Friuli, *Italy* 33 C10
Cervinara, *Italy* 35 A7
Cervione, *France* 27 F13
Cervo, *Spain* 30 B3
César □, *Colombia* 120 B3
Cesaro, *Italy* 35 E7
Cesena, *Italy* 33 D9
Cesenático, *Italy* 33 D9
Cēsis, *Latvia* 40 C4
Česká Lípa, *Czech.* 20 E4
České Budějovice, *Czech.* 20 G4
Ceskomoravská Vrchovina,
  Czech. 20 F5
Český Brod, *Czech.* 20 E4
Český Krumlov, *Czech.* .. 20 G4
Český Těšín, *Czech.* 20 F8
Çeşme, *Turkey* 66 D2
Cessnock, *Australia* 91 E5
Cestos →, *Liberia* 78 D3
Cetin Grad, *Croatia* 33 C12
Cetina →, *Croatia* 33 E13
Cetraro, *Italy* 35 C8
Ceuta, *Morocco* 74 A3
Ceva, *Italy* 32 D5
Cévennes, *France* 26 D7
Ceyhan, *Turkey* 66 E6

Ceyhan →, *Turkey* 66 E6
Ceylânpınar, *Turkey* 67 E9
Ceylon = Sri Lanka ■,
  Asia 60 R12
Cèze →, *France* 27 D8
Cha-am, *Thailand* 58 F2
Chaam, *Neths.* 17 E5
Chabeuil, *France* 27 D9
Chablais, *France* 27 B10
Chablis, *France* 25 E10
Chabounia, *Algeria* 75 A5
Chacabuco, *Argentina* ... 126 C3
Chachapoyas, *Peru* 124 B2
Chachasp, *Peru* 124 D3
Chachoengsao, *Thailand* . 58 F3
Chachran, *Pakistan* 60 E7
Chachro, *Pakistan* 62 G4
Chaco □, *Argentina* 126 B3
Chaco □, *Paraguay* 126 B3
Chad ■, *Africa* 73 E8
Chad, L. = Tchad, L.,
  Chad 73 F7
Chadan, *Russia* 45 D10
Chadileuvú →, *Argentina* 126 D2
Chadiza, *Zambia* 83 E3
Chadron, *U.S.A.* 108 D3
Chadyr-Lunga, *Moldavia* . 42 C3
Chae Hom, *Thailand* 58 C2
Chaem →, *Thailand* 58 C2
Chaeryŏng, *N. Korea* ... 51 E13
Chagai Hills, *Afghan.* ... 60 E3
Chagda, *Russia* 45 D14
Chagny, *France* 25 F11
Chagoda, *Russia* 40 B9
Chagos Arch., *Ind. Oc.* . 46 K11
Chāh Ākhvor, *Iran* 65 C8
Chāh Bahār, *Iran* 65 E9
Chāh-e-Malek, *Iran* 65 D8
Chāh Kavīr, *Iran* 65 D7
Chahar Burjak, *Afghan.* . 60 D3
Chaibasa, *India* 61 H14
Chaillé-les-Marais, *France* 26 B2
Chainat, *Thailand* 58 E3
Chaitén, *Chile* 128 B2
Chaiya, *Thailand* 59 H2
Chaj Doab, *Pakistan* 62 C5
Chajari, *Argentina* 126 C4
Chake Chake, *Tanzania* . 82 D4
Chakhānsūr, *Afghan.* 60 D3
Chakonipau, L., *Canada* . 99 A6
Chakradharpur, *India* 63 H11
Chakwal, *Pakistan* 62 C5
Chala, *Peru* 124 D3
Chalais, *France* 26 C4
Chalchihuites, *Mexico* ... 114 C4
Chalchuanca, *Peru* 124 C3
Chalcis = Khalkís, *Greece* 39 L6
Chalfant, *U.S.A.* 112 H8
Chalhuanca, *Peru* 124 C3
Chalindrey, *France* 25 E12
Chaling, *China* 53 D9
Chalisgaon, *India* 60 J9
Chalkar, *Kazakhstan* 43 A14
Chalkar, Ozero,
  Kazakhstan 43 A14
Chalky Inlet, *N.Z.* 87 M1
Challans, *France* 24 F5
Challapata, *Bolivia* 124 D4
Challis, *U.S.A.* 110 D6
Chalna, *India* 63 H13
Chalon-sur-Saône, *France* . 25 F11
Chalonnes-sur-Loire,
  France 24 E6
Châlons-sur-Marne, *France* 25 D11
Châlus, *France* 26 C4
Chalyaphum, *Thailand* .. 58 E4
Cham, *Germany* 19 F8
Cham, *Switz.* 23 B6
Cham, Cu Lao, *Vietnam* . 58 E7
Chama, *U.S.A.* 111 H10
Chamaicó, *Argentina* ... 126 C2
Chaman, *Pakistan* 60 D5
Chamba, *India* 62 C7
Chamba, *Tanzania* 83 E4
Chambal →, *India* 63 F8
Chamberlain, *U.S.A.* 108 D5
Chamberlain →, *Australia* 88 C4
Chambers, *U.S.A.* 111 J9
Chambersburg, *U.S.A.* .. 104 F7
Chambéry, *France* 27 C9
Chambly, *Canada* 107 A11
Chambord, *Canada* 99 C5
Chamchamal, *Iraq* 64 C5
Chamela, *Mexico* 114 D3
Chamical, *Argentina* 126 C2
Chamkar Luong, *Cambodia* 59 G4
Chamonix-Mont-Blanc,
  France 27 C10
Champa, *India* 63 H10
Champagne, *Canada* 100 A1
Champagne, *France* 25 D11
Champagne, Plaine de,
  France 25 D11
Champagnole, *France* ... 25 F12
Champaign, *U.S.A.* 104 E1
Champassak, *Laos* 58 E5
Champaubert, *France* ... 25 D10
Champdeniers, *France* ... 26 B3
Champeix, *France* 26 C7
Champlain, *Canada* 104 B9
Champlain, *U.S.A.* 107 B11
Champlain, L., *U.S.A.* .. 107 B11
Champotón, *Mexico* 115 D6
Chamusca, *Portugal* 31 F2
Chan Chan, *Peru* 124 B2
Chana, *Thailand* 59 J3

Chañaral, *Chile* 126 B1
Charambirá, Punta,
  Colombia 120 C2
Charaña, *Bolivia* 124 D4
Charapita, *Colombia* 120 D3
Charata, *Argentina* 126 B3
Charcas, *Mexico* 114 C4
Charcoal L., *Canada* 101 B8
Chard, *U.K.* 13 G5
Chardara, *Kazakhstan* ... 44 E7
Chardon, *U.S.A.* 106 E3
Chardzhou, *Turkmenistan* . 44 F7
Charente □, *France* 26 C4
Charente →, *France* 26 C2
Charente-Maritime □,
  France 26 C3
Charentsavan, *Armenia* . 43 F11
Chari →, *Chad* 73 F7
Chārīkār, *Afghan.* 60 B6
Chariton →, *U.S.A.* 108 F8
Charity, *Guyana* 121 B6
Chärjew = Chardzhou,
  Turkmenistan 44 F7
Charkhari, *India* 63 G8
Charkhi Dadri, *India* 62 E7
Charleroi, *Belgium* 17 H4
Charleroi, *U.S.A.* 106 F5
Charles, C., *U.S.A.* 104 G8
Charles City, *U.S.A.* 108 D8
Charles L., *Canada* 101 B6
Charles Town, *U.S.A.* ... 104 F7
Charleston, *Ill., U.S.A.* .. 104 F1
Charleston, *Miss., U.S.A.* 109 H9
Charleston, *Mo., U.S.A.* . 109 G10
Charleston, *S.C., U.S.A.* . 105 J6
Charleston, *W. Va., U.S.A.* 104 F5
Charleston Peak, *U.S.A.* . 113 J11
Charlestown, *S. Africa* .. 85 D4
Charlestown, *U.S.A.* 104 F3
Charleville = Rath Luirc,
  Ireland 15 D3
Charleville, *Australia* 91 D4
Charleville-Mézières,
  France 25 C11
Charlevoix, *U.S.A.* 104 C3
Charlieu, *France* 27 B8
Charlotte, *Mich., U.S.A.* . 104 D3
Charlotte, *N.C., U.S.A.* . 105 H5
Charlotte Amalie,
  Virgin Is. 117 C7
Charlotte Harbor, *U.S.A.* 105 M4
Charlottesville, *U.S.A.* ... 104 F6
Charlottetown, *Canada* ... 99 C7
Charlton, *Australia* 91 F3
Charlton, *U.S.A.* 108 E8
Charlton I., *Canada* 98 B4
Charmes, *France* 25 D13
Charny, *Canada* 99 C5
Charolles, *France* 27 B8
Chârost, *France* 25 F9
Charouine, *Algeria* 75 C4
Charre, *Mozam.* 83 F4
Charsadda, *Pakistan* 62 B4
Charters Towers, *Australia* 90 C4
Chartres, *France* 24 D8
Chascomús, *Argentina* .. 126 D4
Chasefu, *Zambia* 83 E3
Chasovnya-Uchurskaya,
  Russia 45 D14
Chasseneuil-sur-Bonnieure,
  France 26 C4
Chāt, *Iran* 65 B7
Chatal Balkan = Udvoy
  Balkan, *Bulgaria* 38 G9
Château-Arnoux, *France* . 27 D10
Château-Chinon, *France* . 25 E10
Château d'Oex, *Switz.* ... 22 D4
Château-du-Loir, *France* . 24 E7
Château-Gontier, *France* . 24 E6
Château-la-Vallière, *France* 24 E7
Château-Landon, *France* . 25 D9
Château-Porcien, *France* . 25 C11
Château-Renault, *France* . 24 E7
Château-Salins, *France* .. 25 D13
Château-Thierry, *France* . 25 C10
Châteaubourg, *France* ... 24 D5
Châteaubriant, *France* ... 24 E5
Châteaudun, *France* 24 D8
Châteaugiron, *France* 24 D5
Châteaulin, *France* 24 D2
Châteaumeillant, *France* . 26 B6
Châteauneuf-du-Faou,
  France 24 D3
Châteauneuf-en-Thymerais,
  France 24 D8
Châteauneuf-sur-Charente,
  France 26 C3
Châteauneuf-sur-Cher,
  France 25 F9
Châteauneuf-sur-Loire,
  France 25 E9
Châteaurenard,
  Bouches-du-Rhône,
  France 27 E8
Châteaurenard, *Loiret*,
  France 25 E9
Châteauroux, *France* 25 F8
Châtel-St.-Denis, *Switz.* . 22 C3
Châtelaillon-Plage, *France* 26 B2
Châtelaudren, *France* 24 D4
Chatelet, *Belgium* 17 H5
Châtelguyon, *France* 26 C7
Châtellerault, *France* 24 F7
Châtelus-Malvaleix, *France* 26 B6

Chatfield, *U.S.A.* ... 108 D9
Chatham, *N.B., Canada* .. 99 C6
Chatham, *Ont., Canada* .. 98 D3
Chatham, *U.K.* ... 13 F8
Chatham, *La., U.S.A.* ... 109 J8
Chatham, *N.Y., U.S.A.* ... 107 D11
Chatham, *I., Chile* ... 128 D2
Chatham Is., *Pac. Oc.* ... 92 M10
Chatham Str., *U.S.A.* ... 100 B2
Chatillon, *Italy* ... 32 C4
Châtillon-Coligny, *France* . 25 E9
Châtillon-en-Bazois, *France* 25 E10
Châtillon-en-Diois, *France* 27 D9
Châtillon-sur-Indre, *France* 24 F8
Châtillon-sur-Loire, *France* 25 E9
Châtillon-sur-Marne,
 France ... 25 C10
Châtillon-sur-Seine, *France* 25 E11
Chatmohar, *Bangla.* ... 63 G13
Chatra, *India* ... 63 G11
Chatrapur, *India* ... 61 K14
Chats, L. des, *Canada* ... 107 A8
Chatsworth, *Canada* ... 106 B4
Chatsworth, *Zimbabwe* ... 83 F3
Chattahoochee →, *U.S.A.* 105 K3
Chattanooga, *U.S.A.* ... 105 H3
Chaturat, *Thailand* ... 58 E3
Chau Doc, *Vietnam* ... 59 G5
Chaudanne, Barr. de,
 France ... 27 E10
Chaudes-Aigues, *France* .. 26 D7
Chauffailles, *France* ... 27 B8
Chauk, *Burma* ... 61 J19
Chaukan La, *Burma* ... 61 F20
Chaulnes, *France* ... 25 C9
Chaumont, *France* ... 25 D12
Chaumont, *U.S.A.* ... 107 B8
Chaumont-en-Vexin,
 France ... 25 C8
Chaumont-sur-Loire,
 France ... 24 E8
Chaunay, *France* ... 26 B4
Chauny, *France* ... 25 C10
Chausey, Is., *France* ... 24 D5
Chaussin, *France* ... 25 F12
Chautauqua L., *U.S.A.* ... 106 D5
Chauvigny, *France* ... 24 F7
Chauvin, *Canada* ... 101 C6
Chavantina, *Brazil* ... 125 C7
Chaves, *Brazil* ... 122 B2
Chaves, *Portugal* ... 30 D3
Chavuma, *Zambia* ... 81 G4
Chawang, *Thailand* ... 59 H2
Chazelles-sur-Lyon, *France* 27 C8
Chazuta, *Peru* ... 124 B2
Chazy, *U.S.A.* ... 107 B11
Cheb, *Czech.* ... 20 E2
Cheboksary, *Russia* ... 41 C15
Cheboygan, *U.S.A.* ... 104 C3
Chebsara, *Russia* ... 41 B11
Chech, Erg, *Africa* ... 74 D4
Chechaouen, *Morocco* ... 74 A3
Chechen, Os., *Russia* ... 43 E12
Chechено-Ingush
 Republic □, *Russia* ... 43 E11
Chечon, *S. Korea* ... 51 F15
Chęciny, *Poland* ... 20 E10
Checleset B., *Canada* ... 100 C3
Checotah, *U.S.A.* ... 109 H7
Chedabucto B., *Canada* .. 99 C7
Cheduba I., *Burma* ... 61 K18
Cheepie, *Australia* ... 91 D4
Chef-Boutonne, *France* .. 26 B3
Chegdomyn, *Russia* ... 45 D14
Chegga, *Mauritania* ... 74 C3
Chegutu, *Zimbabwe* ... 83 F3
Chehalis, *U.S.A.* ... 112 D4
Cheiron, Mt., *France* ... 27 E10
Cheju Do, *S. Korea* ... 51 H14
Chekalin, *Russia* ... 41 D10
Chekiang = Zhejiang □,
 China ... 53 C13
Chel = Kuru, Bahr el →,
 Sudan ... 77 F2
Chela, Sa. da, *Angola* ... 84 B1
Chelan, *U.S.A.* ... 110 C4
Chelan, L., *U.S.A.* ... 110 C3
Cheleken, *Turkmenistan* .. 44 F6
Chelforó, *Argentina* ... 128 A3
Chéliff, O. →, *Algeria* ... 75 A5
Chelkar, *Kazakhstan* ... 44 E6
Chelkar Tengiz, Solonchak,
 Kazakhstan ... 44 E7
Chellala Dahrania, *Algeria* 75 B5
Chelles, *France* ... 25 D9
Chełm, *Poland* ... 20 D13
Chełmek, *Poland* ... 20 E9
Chełmno, *Poland* ... 20 B8
Chelmsford, *U.K.* ... 13 F8
Chelmsford Dam, *S. Africa* 85 D4
Chełmża, *Poland* ... 20 B8
Chelsea, *Okla., U.S.A.* ... 109 G7
Chelsea, *Vt., U.S.A.* ... 107 C12
Cheltenham, *U.K.* ... 13 F5
Chelva, *Spain* ... 28 F4
Chelyabinsk, *Russia* ... 44 D7
Chelyuskin, C., *Russia* ... 46 B14
Chembar = Belinskiy,
 Russia ... 41 E13
Chemillé, *France* ... 24 E6
Chemnitz, *Germany* ... 18 E8
Chemult, *U.S.A.* ... 110 E3
Chen, Gora, *Russia* ... 45 C15

Chenab →, *Pakistan* ... 62 D4
Chenachane, O. →,
 Algeria ... 74 C4
Chenango Forks, *U.S.A.* . 107 D9
Chencha, *Ethiopia* ... 77 F4
Chenchiang = Zhenjiang,
 China ... 53 A12
Chênée, *Belgium* ... 17 G7
Cheney, *U.S.A.* ... 110 C5
Cheng Xian, *China* ... 50 H3
Chengbu, *China* ... 53 D8
Chengcheng, *China* ... 50 G5
Chengchou = Zhengzhou,
 China ... 50 G7
Chengde, *China* ... 51 D9
Chengdong Hu, *China* ... 53 A11
Chengdu, *China* ... 52 B5
Chenggong, *China* ... 52 E4
Chenggu, *China* ... 50 H4
Chengjiang, *China* ... 52 E4
Chengkou, *China* ... 52 B7
Ch'engtu = Chengdu,
 China ... 52 B5
Chengwu, *China* ... 50 G8
Chengxi Hu, *China* ... 53 A11
Chengyang, *China* ... 51 F11
Chenjiagang, *China* ... 51 G10
Chenkán, *Mexico* ... 115 D6
Chenxi, *China* ... 53 C8
Cheo Reo, *Vietnam* ... 58 F7
Cheom Ksan, *Cambodia* .. 58 E5
Chepelare, *Bulgaria* ... 39 H7
Chepén, *Peru* ... 124 B2
Chepes, *Argentina* ... 126 C2
Chepo, *Panama* ... 116 E4
Cheptsa →, *Russia* ... 41 B17
Chequamegon B., *U.S.A.* 108 B9
Cher □, *France* ... 25 E9
Cher →, *France* ... 24 E7
Cherasco, *Italy* ... 32 D4
Cheratte, *Belgium* ... 17 G7
Cheraw, *U.S.A.* ... 105 H6
Cherbourg, *France* ... 24 C5
Cherchell, *Algeria* ... 75 A5
Cherdakly, *Russia* ... 41 D16
Cherdyn, *Russia* ... 44 C6
Cheremkhovo, *Russia* ... 45 D11
Cherepanovo, *Russia* ... 44 D9
Cherepovets, *Russia* ... 41 B10
Chergui, Chott ech, *Algeria* 75 B5
Cherikov, *Belorussia* ... 40 E7
Cherkassy, *Ukraine* ... 42 B5
Cherkasy = Cherkassy,
 Ukraine ... 42 B5
Cherkessk, *Russia* ... 43 D10
Cherlak, *Russia* ... 44 D8
Chernaya Kholunitsa,
 Russia ... 41 B17
Cherni, *Bulgaria* ... 38 G6
Chernigov, *Ukraine* ... 40 F7
Chernihiv = Chernigov,
 Ukraine ... 40 F7
Chernivtsi = Chernovtsy,
 Ukraine ... 42 B1
Chernobyl, *Ukraine* ... 40 F7
Chernogorsk, *Russia* ... 45 D10
Chernomorskoye, *Ukraine* 42 D5
Chernovskoye, *Russia* ... 41 B15
Chernovtsy, *Ukraine* ... 42 B1
Chernoye, *Russia* ... 45 B9
Chernyakhovsk, *Russia* .. 40 D2
Chernyshkovskiy, *Russia* .. 43 B10
Chernyshovskiy, *Russia* .. 45 C12
Cherokee, *Iowa, U.S.A.* . 108 D7
Cherokee, *Okla., U.S.A.* . 109 G5
Cherokees, Lake O' The,
 U.S.A. ... 109 G7
Cherquenco, *Chile* ... 128 A2
Cherrapunji, *India* ... 61 G17
Cherry Creek, *U.S.A.* ... 110 G6
Cherry Valley, *U.S.A.* ... 113 M10
Cherryvale, *U.S.A.* ... 109 G7
Cherskiy, *Russia* ... 45 C17
Cherskogo Khrebet, *Russia* 45 C15
Chertkovo, *Russia* ... 43 B9
Cherven, *Belorussia* ... 40 E6
Cherven-Bryag, *Bulgaria* . 38 F7
Chervonograd, *Ukraine* .. 40 F4
Cherwell →, *U.K.* ... 13 F6
Chesapeake, *U.S.A.* ... 104 G7
Chesapeake B., *U.S.A.* ... 104 F7
Cheshire □, *U.K.* ... 12 D5
Cheshskaya Guba, *Russia* .. 44 C5
Cheslatta L., *Canada* ... 100 C3
Chesley, *Canada* ... 106 B3
Cheste, *Spain* ... 29 F4
Chester, *U.K.* ... 12 D5
Chester, *Calif., U.S.A.* ... 110 F3
Chester, *Ill., U.S.A.* ... 109 G10
Chester, *Mont., U.S.A.* ... 110 B8
Chester, *Pa., U.S.A.* ... 104 F8
Chester, *S.C., U.S.A.* ... 105 H5
Chesterfield, *U.S.A.* ... 104 F5
Chesterfield, Is., *N. Cal.* . 92 J7
Chesterfield Inlet, *Canada* 96 B10
Chesterton Ra., *Australia* . 91 D4
Chesterville, *Canada* ... 107 A9
Chesuncook L., *U.S.A.* ... 99 C6
Chetaibi, *Algeria* ... 75 A6
Chéticamp, *Canada* ... 99 C7
Chetumal, *Mexico* ... 115 D7
Chetumal, B. de, *Mexico* . 115 D7
Chetwynd, *Canada* ... 100 B4
Chevanceaux, *France* ... 26 C3
Cheviot, The, *U.K.* ... 12 B5

Cheviot Hills, *U.K.* ... 12 B5
Cheviot Ra., *Australia* ... 90 D3
Chew Bahir, *Ethiopia* ... 77 G4
Chewelah, *U.S.A.* ... 110 B5
Cheyenne, *Okla., U.S.A.* 109 H5
Cheyenne, *Wyo., U.S.A.* 108 E2
Cheyenne →, *U.S.A.* ... 108 C4
Cheyenne Wells, *U.S.A.* .. 108 F3
Cheyne B., *Australia* ... 89 F2
Chhabra, *India* ... 62 G7
Chhapra, *India* ... 63 G11
Chhata, *India* ... 62 F7
Chhatarpur, *India* ... 63 G8
Chhep, *Cambodia* ... 58 F5
Chhindwara, *India* ... 63 H8
Chhlong, *Cambodia* ... 59 F5
Chhuk, *Cambodia* ... 59 G5
Chi →, *Thailand* ... 58 E5
Chiamis, *Indonesia* ... 57 G13
Chiamussu = Jiamusi,
 China ... 54 B8
Chiang Dao, *Thailand* ... 58 C2
Chiang Kham, *Thailand* .. 58 C3
Chiang Khan, *Thailand* ... 58 D3
Chiang Khong, *Thailand* .. 58 B3
Chiang Mai, *Thailand* ... 58 C2
Chiang Saen, *Thailand* ... 58 B3
Chiange, *Angola* ... 81 H2
Chiapa →, *Mexico* ... 115 D6
Chiapa de Corzo, *Mexico* . 115 D6
Chiapas □, *Mexico* ... 115 D6
Chiaramonte Gulfi, *Italy* .. 35 E7
Chiaravalle, *Italy* ... 33 E10
Chiaravalle Centrale, *Italy* 35 D9
Chiari, *Italy* ... 32 C6
Chiasso, *Switz.* ... 23 E8
Chiatura, *Georgia* ... 43 E10
Chiautla, *Mexico* ... 115 D5
Chiávari, *Italy* ... 32 D6
Chiavenna, *Italy* ... 32 B6
Chiba, *Japan* ... 49 G10
Chiba □, *Japan* ... 49 G10
Chibabava, *Mozam.* ... 85 C5
Chibatu, *Indonesia* ... 57 G12
Chibemba, *Cunene, Angola* 81 H2
Chibemba, *Huila, Angola* . 84 B2
Chibia, *Angola* ... 81 H2
Chibougamau, *Canada* ... 98 C5
Chibougamau L., *Canada* . 98 C5
Chibuk, *Nigeria* ... 79 C7
Chic-Chocs, Mts., *Canada* . 99 C6
Chicacole = Srikakulam,
 India ... 61 K13
Chicago, *U.S.A.* ... 104 E2
Chicago Heights, *U.S.A.* .. 104 E2
Chichagof I., *U.S.A.* ... 100 B1
Chichaoua, *Morocco* ... 74 B3
Chicheng, *China* ... 50 D8
Chichester, *U.K.* ... 13 G7
Chichibu, *Japan* ... 49 F9
Ch'ich'ihaerh = Qiqihar,
 China ... 45 E13
Chickasha, *U.S.A.* ... 109 H5
Chiclana de la Frontera,
 Spain ... 31 J4
Chiclayo, *Peru* ... 124 B2
Chico, *U.S.A.* ... 112 F5
Chico →, *Chubut,*
 Argentina ... 128 B3
Chico →, *Santa Cruz,*
 Argentina ... 128 C3
Chicomo, *Mozam.* ... 85 C5
Chicontepec, *Mexico* ... 115 C5
Chicopee, *U.S.A.* ... 107 D12
Chicoutimi, *Canada* ... 99 C5
Chicualacuala, *Mozam.* ... 85 C5
Chidambaram, *India* ... 60 P11
Chidenguele, *Mozam.* ... 85 C5
Chidley, C., *Canada* ... 97 B13
Chiede, *Angola* ... 84 B2
Chiefs Pt., *Canada* ... 106 B3
Chiem Hoa, *Vietnam* ... 58 A5
Chiemsee, *Germany* ... 19 H8
Chiengi, *Zambia* ... 83 D2
Chiengmai = Chiang Mai,
 Thailand ... 58 C2
Chienti →, *Italy* ... 33 E10
Chieri, *Italy* ... 32 D4
Chiers →, *France* ... 25 C11
Chiese →, *Italy* ... 32 C7
Chieti, *Italy* ... 33 F11
Chièvres, *Belgium* ... 17 G3
Chifeng, *China* ... 51 C10
Chigirin, *Ukraine* ... 42 B5
Chignecto B., *Canada* ... 99 C7
Chigorodó, *Colombia* ... 120 B2
Chiguana, *Bolivia* ... 126 A2
Chiha-ri, *N. Korea* ... 51 E14
Chihli, G. of = Bo Hai,
 China ... 51 E10
Chihuahua, *Mexico* ... 114 B3
Chihuahua □, *Mexico* ... 114 B3
Chiili, *Kazakhstan* ... 44 E7
Chik Bollapur, *India* ... 60 N10
Chikmagalur, *India* ... 60 N9
Chilac, *Mexico* ... 115 D5
Chilako →, *Canada* ... 100 C4
Chilam Chavki, *Pakistan* . 63 B6
Chilanga, *Zambia* ... 83 F2
Chilapa, *Mexico* ... 115 D5
Chilas, *Pakistan* ... 63 B6
Chilaw, *Sri Lanka* ... 60 R11
Chilcotin →, *Canada* ... 100 C4
Childers, *Australia* ... 91 D5
Childress, *U.S.A.* ... 109 H4

Chile ■, *S. Amer.* ... 128 B2
Chile Chico, *Chile* ... 128 C2
Chile Rise, *Pac. Oc.* ... 93 L18
Chilecito, *Argentina* ... 126 B2
Chilete, *Peru* ... 124 B2
Chilia, Brațul →, *Romania* 38 D12
Chililabombwe, *Zambia* .. 83 E2
Chilin = Jilin, *China* ... 51 C14
Chilka L., *India* ... 61 K14
Chilko →, *Canada* ... 100 C4
Chilko, L., *Canada* ... 100 C4
Chillagoe, *Australia* ... 90 B3
Chillán, *Chile* ... 126 D1
Chillicothe, *Ill., U.S.A.* ... 108 E10
Chillicothe, *Mo., U.S.A.* .. 108 F8
Chillicothe, *Ohio, U.S.A.* . 104 F4
Chilliwack, *Canada* ... 100 D4
Chilo, *India* ... 62 F5
Chiloane, I., *Mozam.* ... 85 C5
Chiloé □, *Chile* ... 128 B2
Chiloé, I. de, *Chile* ... 128 B2
Chilpancingo, *Mexico* ... 115 D5
Chiltern Hills, *U.K.* ... 13 F7
Chilton, *U.S.A.* ... 104 C1
Chiluage, *Angola* ... 80 F4
Chilubi, *Zambia* ... 83 E3
Chilubula, *Zambia* ... 83 E3
Chilumba, *Malawi* ... 83 E3
Chilwa, L., *Malawi* ... 83 F4
Chimaltitán, *Mexico* ... 114 C4
Chimán, *Panama* ... 116 E4
Chimay, *Belgium* ... 17 H4
Chimbay, *Uzbekistan* ... 44 E6
Chimborazo, *Ecuador* ... 120 D2
Chimborazo □, *Ecuador* .. 120 D2
Chimbote, *Peru* ... 124 B2
Chimkent, *Kazakhstan* ... 44 E7
Chimoio, *Mozam.* ... 83 F3
Chimpembe, *Zambia* ... 83 D2
Chin □, *Burma* ... 61 J18
Chin Ling Shan = Qinling
 Shandi, *China* ... 50 H5
China, *Mexico* ... 115 B5
China ■, *Asia* ... 50 E3
China Lake, *U.S.A.* ... 113 K9
Chinacota, *Colombia* ... 120 B3
Chinan = Jinan, *China* ... 50 F9
Chinandega, *Nic.* ... 116 D2
Chinati Peak, *U.S.A.* ... 109 K2
Chincha Alta, *Peru* ... 124 C2
Chinchilla, *Australia* ... 91 D5
Chinchilla de Monte
 Aragón, *Spain* ... 29 G3
Chinchón, *Spain* ... 28 E1
Chinchorro, Banco, *Mexico* 115 D7
Chinchou = Jinzhou, *China* 51 D11
Chincoteague, *U.S.A.* ... 104 G8
Chinde, *Mozam.* ... 83 F4
Chindo, *S. Korea* ... 51 G14
Chindwin →, *Burma* ... 61 J19
Chineni, *India* ... 63 C6
Chinga, *Mozam.* ... 83 F4
Chingola, *Zambia* ... 83 E2
Chingole, *Malawi* ... 83 E3
Ch'ingtao = Qingdao,
 China ... 51 F11
Chinguetti, *Mauritania* ... 74 D2
Chingune, *Mozam.* ... 85 C5
Chinhae, *S. Korea* ... 51 G15
Chinhanguanine, *Mozam.* . 85 D5
Chinhoyi, *Zimbabwe* ... 83 F3
Chiniot, *Pakistan* ... 62 D5
Chínipas, *Mexico* ... 114 B3
Chinju, *S. Korea* ... 51 G15
Chinle, *U.S.A.* ... 111 H9
Chinnampo, *N. Korea* ... 51 E13
Chino, *Japan* ... 49 G9
Chino, *U.S.A.* ... 113 L9
Chino Valley, *U.S.A.* ... 111 J7
Chinon, *France* ... 24 E7
Chinook, *Canada* ... 101 C6
Chinook, *U.S.A.* ... 110 B9
Chinsali, *Zambia* ... 83 E3
Chióggia, *Italy* ... 33 C9
Chíos = Khíos, *Greece* ... 39 L9
Chipata, *Zambia* ... 83 E3
Chipewyan L., *Canada* ... 101 B9
Chipinge, *Zimbabwe* ... 83 G3
Chipiona, *Spain* ... 31 J4
Chipley, *U.S.A.* ... 105 K3
Chipman, *Canada* ... 99 C6
Chipoka, *Malawi* ... 83 E3
Chippenham, *U.K.* ... 13 F5
Chippewa →, *U.S.A.* ... 108 C8
Chippewa Falls, *U.S.A.* ... 108 C9
Chiquián, *Peru* ... 124 C2
Chiquimula, *Guatemala* .. 116 D2
Chiquinquira, *Colombia* .. 120 B3
Chiquitos, Llanos de,
 Bolivia ... 125 D5
Chir →, *Russia* ... 43 B10
Chirala, *India* ... 60 M12
Chiramba, *Mozam.* ... 83 F3
Chirawa, *India* ... 62 E6
Chirchik, *Uzbekistan* ... 44 E7
Chirgua →, *Venezuela* ... 120 B4
Chiricahua Peak, *U.S.A.* .. 111 L9
Chiriquí, G. de, *Panama* . 116 E3
Chiriquí, L. de, *Panama* .. 116 E3
Chirivira Falls, *Zimbabwe* 83 G3
Chirmiri, *India* ... 61 H13
Chiromo, *Malawi* ... 81 H7
Chirpan, *Bulgaria* ... 38 G8
Chirripó Grande, Cerro,
 Costa Rica ... 116 E3

Chisamba, *Zambia* ... 83 E2
Chisapani Garhi, *Nepal* ... 61 F14
Chisholm, *Canada* ... 100 C6
Chishtian Mandi, *Pakistan* 62 E5
Chishui, *China* ... 52 C5
Chishui He →, *China* ... 52 C5
Chisimba Falls, *Zambia* ... 83 E3
Chişinău = Kishinev,
 Moldavia ... 42 C3
Chisone →, *Italy* ... 32 D4
Chisos Mts., *U.S.A.* ... 109 L3
Chistopol, *Russia* ... 41 D17
Chita, *Colombia* ... 120 B3
Chita, *Russia* ... 45 D12
Chitado, *Angola* ... 81 H2
Chitembo, *Angola* ... 81 G3
Chitipa, *Malawi* ... 83 D3
Chitose, *Japan* ... 48 C10
Chitral, *Pakistan* ... 60 B7
Chitré, *Panama* ... 116 E3
Chittagong, *Bangla.* ... 61 H17
Chittagong □, *Bangla.* ... 61 G17
Chittaurgarh, *India* ... 62 G6
Chittoor, *India* ... 60 N11
Chitungwiza, *Zimbabwe* .. 83 F3
Chiusa, *Italy* ... 33 B8
Chiusi, *Italy* ... 33 E8
Chiva, *Spain* ... 29 F4
Chivacoa, *Venezuela* ... 120 A4
Chivasso, *Italy* ... 32 C4
Chivay, *Peru* ... 124 D3
Chivhu, *Zimbabwe* ... 83 F3
Chivilcoy, *Argentina* ... 126 C4
Chiwanda, *Tanzania* ... 83 E3
Chixi, *China* ... 53 G9
Chizera, *Zambia* ... 83 E1
Chkalov = Orenburg,
 Russia ... 44 D6
Chkolovsk, *Russia* ... 41 C13
Chloride, *U.S.A.* ... 113 K12
Cho Bo, *Vietnam* ... 58 B5
Cho-do, *N. Korea* ... 51 E13
Cho Phuoc Hai, *Vietnam* . 59 G6
Choba, *Kenya* ... 82 B4
Chobe National Park,
 Botswana ... 84 B3
Chochiwŏn, *S. Korea* ... 51 F14
Chociwel, *Poland* ... 20 B5
Chocó □, *Colombia* ... 120 B2
Chocontá, *Colombia* ... 120 B3
Choctawhatchee B., *U.S.A.* 103 D9
Chodecz, *Poland* ... 20 C9
Chodziez, *Poland* ... 20 C6
Choele Choel, *Argentina* .. 128 A3
Choisy-le-Roi, *France* ... 25 D9
Choix, *Mexico* ... 114 B3
Chojnice, *Poland* ... 20 B7
Chojnów, *Poland* ... 20 D5
Chōkai-San, *Japan* ... 48 E10
Choke, *Ethiopia* ... 77 E4
Chokurdakh, *Russia* ... 45 B15
Cholame, *U.S.A.* ... 112 K6
Cholet, *France* ... 24 E6
Choluteca, *Honduras* ... 116 D2
Choluteca →, *Honduras* .. 116 D2
Chom Bung, *Thailand* ... 58 F2
Chom Thong, *Thailand* ... 58 C2
Choma, *Zambia* ... 83 F2
Chomen Swamp, *Ethiopia* 77 F4
Chomun, *India* ... 62 F6
Chomutov, *Czech.* ... 20 E3
Chon Buri, *Thailand* ... 58 F3
Chon Thanh, *Vietnam* ... 59 G6
Chonan, *S. Korea* ... 51 F14
Chone, *Ecuador* ... 120 D2
Chong Kai, *Cambodia* ... 58 F4
Chong Mek, *Thailand* ... 58 E5
Chong'an, *China* ... 53 D12
Chongde, *China* ... 53 B13
Chŏngdo, *S. Korea* ... 51 G15
Chŏngha, *S. Korea* ... 51 F15
Chongjin, *N. Korea* ... 51 D15
Chŏngju, *N. Korea* ... 51 E13
Chŏngju, *S. Korea* ... 51 F14
Chongli, *China* ... 50 D8
Chongming, *China* ... 53 B13
Chongming Dao, *China* ... 53 B13
Chongoyape, *Peru* ... 124 B2
Chongqing, *Sichuan, China* 52 C6
Chongqing, *Sichuan, China* 52 B4
Chongren, *China* ... 53 D11
Chŏngŭp, *S. Korea* ... 51 G14
Chongzuo, *China* ... 52 F6
Chŏnju, *S. Korea* ... 51 G14
Chonos, Arch. de los, *Chile* 128 C2
Chopim →, *Brazil* ... 127 B5
Chorbat La, *India* ... 63 B7
Chorley, *U.K.* ... 12 D5
Chornobyl = Chernobyl,
 Ukraine ... 40 F7
Chorolque, Cerro, *Bolivia* 126 A2
Chorregon, *Australia* ... 90 C3
Chortkov, *Ukraine* ... 40 G4
Chŏrwŏn, *S. Korea* ... 51 E14
Chorzów, *Poland* ... 20 E8
Chos-Malal, *Argentina* ... 126 D1
Chosan, *N. Korea* ... 51 D13
Choszczno, *Poland* ... 20 B5
Chota, *Peru* ... 124 B2
Choteau, *U.S.A.* ... 110 C7
Chotila, *India* ... 62 H4
Chowchilla, *U.S.A.* ... 111 H3
Choybalsan, *Mongolia* ... 54 B6
Christchurch, *N.Z.* ... 87 K4
Christchurch, *U.K.* ... 13 G6

Christian I., *Canada* 106 B4
Christiana, *S. Africa* 84 D4
Christiansfeld, *Denmark* .. 11 J3
Christiansted, *Virgin Is.* .. 117 C7
Christie B., *Canada* 101 A6
Christina →, *Canada* 101 B6
Christmas Cr. →, *Australia* 88 C4
Christmas Creek, *Australia* 88 C4
Christmas I. = Kiritimati,
  Kiribati 93 G12
Christmas I., *Ind. Oc.* 92 J2
Christopher L., *Australia* . 89 D4
Chrudim, *Czech.* 20 F5
Chrzanów, *Poland* 20 E9
Chtimba, *Malawi* 83 E3
Chu, *Kazakhstan* 44 E8
Chu →, *Vietnam* 58 C5
Chu Chua, *Canada* 100 C4
Chu Lai, *Vietnam* 58 E7
Chu Xian, *China* 53 A12
Ch'uanchou = Quanzhou,
  China 53 E12
Chuankou, *China* 50 G6
Chūbu □, *Japan* 49 F8
Chubut □, *Argentina* 128 B3
Chubut →, *Argentina* 128 B3
Chuchi L., *Canada* 100 B4
Chudovo, *Russia* 40 B7
Chudskoye, Oz., *Estonia* . 40 B5
Chūgoku □, *Japan* 49 G6
Chūgoku-Sanchi, *Japan* .. 49 G6
Chuguyev, *Ukraine* 42 B7
Chugwater, *U.S.A.* 108 E2
Chukhloma, *Russia* 41 B13
Chukotskiy Khrebet, *Russia* 45 C18
Chukotskoye More, *Russia* 45 C19
Chula Vista, *U.S.A.* 113 N9
Chulman, *Russia* 45 D13
Chulucanas, *Peru* 124 B1
Chulumani, *Bolivia* 124 D4
Chulym →, *Russia* 44 D9
Chum Phae, *Thailand* 58 D4
Chum Saeng, *Thailand* ... 58 E3
Chuma, *Bolivia* 124 D4
Chumar, *India* 63 C8
Chumbicha, *Argentina* ... 126 B2
Chumerna, *Bulgaria* 38 G8
Chumikan, *Russia* 45 D14
Chumphon, *Thailand* 59 G2
Chumpi, *Peru* 124 D3
Chumuare, *Mozam.* 83 E3
Chumunjin, *S. Korea* 51 F15
Chuna →, *Russia* 45 D10
Chun'an, *China* 53 C12
Chunchón, *S. Korea* 51 F14
Chunchura, *India* 63 H13
Chunga, *Zambia* 83 F2
Chunggang-ŭp, *N. Korea* . 51 D14
Chunghwa, *N. Korea* 51 E13
Chungju, *S. Korea* 51 F14
Chungking = Chongqing,
  China 52 C6
Chungmu, *S. Korea* 51 G15
Chungt'iaoshan =
  Zhongtiao Shan, *China* . 50 G6
Chunian, *Pakistan* 62 D6
Chunya, *Tanzania* 83 D3
Chunya →, *Tanzania* 82 D3
Chunyang, *China* 51 C15
Chuquibamba, *Peru* 124 D3
Chuquibambilla, *Peru* 124 C3
Chuquicamata, *Chile* 126 A2
Chuquisaca □, *Bolivia* ... 125 E5
Chur, *Switz.* 23 C9
Churachandpur, *India* 61 G18
Churchill, *Canada* 101 B10
Churchill →, *Man.*,
  Canada 101 B10
Churchill →, *Nfld.*,
  Canada 99 B7
Churchill, C., *Canada* 101 B10
Churchill Falls, *Canada* .. 99 B7
Churchill L., *Canada* 101 B7
Churchill Pk., *Canada* 100 B3
Churfisten, *Switz.* 23 B8
Churu, *India* 62 E6
Churwalden, *Switz.* 23 C9
Chushal, *India* 63 C8
Chusovoy, *Russia* 44 D6
Chuuronjang, *N. Korea* .. 51 D15
Chuvash Republic □,
  Russia 41 D15
Chuwārtah, *Iraq* 64 C5
Chuxiong, *China* 52 E3
Ci Xian, *China* 50 F8
Ciacova, *Romania* 38 D4
Cianjur, *Indonesia* 57 G12
Cibadok, *Indonesia* 57 G12
Cibatu, *Indonesia* 57 G12
Cibola, *U.S.A.* 113 M12
Cicero, *U.S.A.* 104 E2
Cícero Dantas, *Brazil* 122 D4
Cidacos →, *Spain* 28 C3
Cide, *Turkey* 42 F5
Ciechanów, *Poland* 20 C10
Ciego de Avila, *Cuba* 116 B4
Ciénaga, *Colombia* 120 A3
Ciénaga de Oro, *Colombia* 120 B2
Cienfuegos, *Cuba* 116 B3
Cieplice Śląskie Zdrój,
  Poland 20 E5
Cierp, *France* 26 F4
Cíes, Is., *Spain* 30 C2
Cieszyn, *Poland* 20 F8
Cieza, *Spain* 29 G3

Çifteler, *Turkey* 66 D4
Cifuentes, *Spain* 28 E2
Cihanbeyli, *Turkey* 66 D5
Cihuatlán, *Mexico* 114 D4
Cijara, Pantano de, *Spain* . 31 F6
Cijulang, *Indonesia* 57 G13
Cikajang, *Indonesia* 57 G12
Cikampek, *Indonesia* 57 G12
Cilacap, *Indonesia* 57 G13
Çıldır, *Turkey* 43 F10
Çıldır Gölü, *Turkey* 67 C10
Cili, *China* 53 C8
Cilicia, *Turkey* 66 E5
Cilo Dağı, *Turkey* 67 E10
Cima, *U.S.A.* 113 K11
Cimahi, *Indonesia* 57 G12
Cimarron, *Kans.*, *U.S.A.* . 109 G4
Cimarron, *N. Mex.*, *U.S.A.* 109 G2
Cimarron →, *U.S.A.* 109 G6
Cimone, Mte., *Italy* 32 D7
Cîmpina, *Romania* 38 D8
Cîmpulung, *Argeş*,
  Romania 38 D8
Cîmpulung, *Suceava*,
  Romania 38 B8
Çınar, *Turkey* 67 E9
Cinca →, *Spain* 28 D5
Cincinnati, *U.S.A.* 104 F3
Çindeşti, *Romania* 38 D9
Çine, *Turkey* 66 E3
Ciney, *Belgium* 17 H6
Cíngoli, *Italy* 33 E10
Cinigiano, *Italy* 33 F8
Cinto, Mte., *France* 27 F12
Ciorani, *Romania* 38 E9
Čiovo, *Croatia* 33 E13
Cipó, *Brazil* 122 D4
Circeo, Monte, *Italy* 34 A6
Çirçir, *Turkey* 66 C7
Circle, *Alaska, U.S.A.* 96 B5
Circle, *Mont.*, *U.S.A.* ... 108 B2
Circleville, *Ohio*, *U.S.A.* 104 F4
Circleville, *Utah*, *U.S.A.* 111 G7
Cirebon, *Indonesia* 57 G13
Cirencester, *U.K.* 13 F6
Cirey-sur-Vezouze, *France* 25 D13
Ciriè, *Italy* 32 C4
Cirium, *Cyprus* 37 E11
Cirò, *Italy* 35 C10
Ciron →, *France* 26 D3
Cisco, *U.S.A.* 109 J5
Ciskei □, *S. Africa* 85 E4
Cislău, *Romania* 38 D9
Cisneros, *Colombia* 120 B2
Cisterna di Latina, *Italy* .. 34 A5
Cisternino, *Italy* 35 B10
Citaré →, *Brazil* 121 C7
Citeli-Ckaro, *Georgia* 43 F12
Citlaltépetl, *Mexico* 115 D5
Citrus Heights, *U.S.A.* ... 112 G5
Città della Pieve, *Italy* ... 33 F9
Città di Castello, *Italy* ... 33 E9
Città Sant' Angelo, *Italy* . 33 F11
Cittadella, *Italy* 33 C8
Cittaducale, *Italy* 33 F9
Cittanova, *Italy* 35 D9
Ciucaş, *Romania* 38 D8
Ciudad Altamirano, *Mexico* 114 D4
Ciudad Bolívar, *Venezuela* 121 B5
Ciudad Camargo, *Mexico* . 114 B3
Ciudad Chetumal, *Mexico* 115 D7
Ciudad de Valles, *Mexico* . 115 C5
Ciudad del Carmen, *Mexico* 115 D6
Ciudad Delicias = Delicias,
  Mexico 114 B3
Ciudad Guayana,
  Venezuela 121 B5
Ciudad Guerrero, *Mexico* . 114 B3
Ciudad Guzmán, *Mexico* . 114 D4
Ciudad Juárez, *Mexico* ... 114 A3
Ciudad Madero, *Mexico* .. 115 C5
Ciudad Mante, *Mexico* ... 115 C5
Ciudad Obregón, *Mexico* . 114 B3
Ciudad Ojeda, *Venezuela* . 120 A3
Ciudad Real, *Spain* 31 G7
Ciudad Real □, *Spain* 31 G7
Ciudad Rodrigo, *Spain* ... 30 E4
Ciudad Trujillo = Santo
  Domingo, *Dom. Rep.* .. 117 C6
Ciudad Victoria, *Mexico* . 115 C5
Ciudadela, *Spain* 36 B10
Ciulniţa, *Romania* 38 E10
Civa Burnu, *Turkey* 66 C7
Cividale del Friuli, *Italy* .. 33 B10
Cívita Castellana, *Italy* ... 33 F9
Civitanova Marche, *Italy* . 33 E10
Civitavécchia, *Italy* 33 F8
Civitella del Tronto, *Italy* . 33 F10
Civray, *France* 26 B4
Çivril, *Turkey* 66 D3
Cixerri →, *Italy* 34 C1
Cizre, *Turkey* 67 E10
Clacton-on-Sea, *U.K.* 13 F9
Clain →, *France* 24 F7
Claire, L., *Canada* 100 B6
Clairemont, *U.S.A.* 109 J4
Clairton, *U.S.A.* 106 F5
Clairvaux-les-Lacs, *France* 27 B9
Clallam Bay, *U.S.A.* 112 B2
Clamecy, *France* 25 E10
Clanton, *U.S.A.* 105 J2
Clanwilliam, *S. Africa* ... 84 E2
Clara, *Ireland* 15 C4
Clara →, *Australia* 90 B3

Claraville, *U.S.A.* 113 K8
Clare, *Australia* 91 E2
Clare, *U.S.A.* 104 D3
Clare □, *Ireland* 15 D3
Clare →, *Ireland* 15 C2
Clare I., *Ireland* 15 C2
Claremont, *Calif.*, *U.S.A.* 113 L9
Claremont, *N.H.*, *U.S.A.* 107 C12
Claremont Pt., *Australia* .. 90 A3
Claremore, *U.S.A.* 109 G7
Claremorris, *Ireland* 15 C3
Clarence →, *Australia* ... 91 D5
Clarence →, *N.Z.* 87 K4
Clarence, I., *Chile* 128 D2
Clarence I., *Antarctica* ... 5 C18
Clarence Str., *Australia* ... 88 B5
Clarence Town, *Bahamas* . 117 B5
Clarendon, *Ark.*, *U.S.A.* . 109 H9
Clarendon, *Tex.*, *U.S.A.* . 109 H4
Clarenville, *Canada* 99 C9
Claresholm, *Canada* 100 C6
Clarie Coast, *Antarctica* .. 5 C9
Clarinda, *U.S.A.* 108 E7
Clarion, *Iowa*, *U.S.A.* ... 108 D8
Clarion, *Pa.*, *U.S.A.* 106 E5
Clarion →, *U.S.A.* 106 E5
Clark, *U.S.A.* 108 C6
Clark, Pt., *Canada* 106 B3
Clark Fork, *U.S.A.* 110 B5
Clark Fork →, *U.S.A.* ... 110 B5
Clark Hill Res., *U.S.A.* ... 105 J4
Clarkdale, *U.S.A.* 111 J7
Clarke City, *Canada* 99 B6
Clarke I., *Australia* 90 G4
Clarke L., *Canada* 101 C7
Clarke Ra., *Australia* 90 C4
Clark's Fork →, *U.S.A.* .. 110 D9
Clark's Harbour, *Canada* . 99 D6
Clarks Summit, *U.S.A.* ... 107 E9
Clarksburg, *U.S.A.* 104 F5
Clarksdale, *U.S.A.* 109 H9
Clarkston, *U.S.A.* 110 C5
Clarksville, *Ark.*, *U.S.A.* 109 H8
Clarksville, *Tenn.*, *U.S.A.* 105 G2
Clarksville, *Tex.*, *U.S.A.* 109 J7
Claro →, *Brazil* 123 E1
Clatskanie, *U.S.A.* 112 D3
Claude, *U.S.A.* 109 H4
Claveria, *Phil.* 55 B4
Clay, *U.S.A.* 112 G5
Clay Center, *U.S.A.* 108 F6
Claypool, *U.S.A.* 111 K8
Claysville, *U.S.A.* 106 F4
Clayton, *Idaho*, *U.S.A.* . 110 D6
Clayton, *N. Mex.*, *U.S.A.* 109 G3
Cle Elum, *U.S.A.* 110 C3
Clear, C., *Ireland* 15 E2
Clear I., *Ireland* 15 E2
Clear L., *U.S.A.* 112 F4
Clear Lake, *S. Dak.*,
  U.S.A. 108 C6
Clear Lake, *Wash.*, *U.S.A.* 110 B2
Clear Lake Reservoir,
  U.S.A. 110 F3
Clearfield, *Pa.*, *U.S.A.* .. 104 E6
Clearfield, *Utah*, *U.S.A.* 110 F7
Clearlake Highlands,
  U.S.A. 112 G4
Clearmont, *U.S.A.* 110 D10
Clearwater, *Canada* 100 C4
Clearwater, *U.S.A.* 105 M4
Clearwater →, *Alta.*,
  Canada 100 C6
Clearwater →, *Alta.*,
  Canada 101 B6
Clearwater Cr. →, *Canada* 100 A3
Clearwater Mts., *U.S.A.* .. 110 C6
Clearwater Prov. Park,
  Canada 101 C8
Cleburne, *U.S.A.* 109 J6
Cleethorpes, *U.K.* 12 D7
Cleeve Hill, *U.K.* 13 F6
Clelles, *France* 27 D9
Clemency, *Lux.* 17 J7
Clerke Reef, *Australia* 88 C2
Clermont, *Australia* 90 C4
Clermont, *France* 25 C9
Clermont-en-Argonne,
  France 25 C12
Clermont-Ferrand, *France* 26 C7
Clermont-l'Hérault, *France* 26 E7
Clerval, *France* 25 E13
Clervaux, *Lux.* 17 H8
Cléry-St.-André, *France* .. 25 E8
Cles, *Italy* 32 B8
Cleveland, *Miss.*, *U.S.A.* 109 J9
Cleveland, *Ohio*, *U.S.A.* 106 E3
Cleveland, *Okla.*, *U.S.A.* 109 G6
Cleveland, *Tenn.*, *U.S.A.* 105 H3
Cleveland, *Tex.*, *U.S.A.* . 109 K7
Cleveland □, *U.K.* 12 C6
Cleveland, C., *Australia* .. 90 B4
Cleveland Heights, *U.S.A.* 106 E3
Clevelândia, *Brazil* 127 B5
Clevelândia do Norte,
  Brazil 121 C7
Clew B., *Ireland* 15 C2
Clewiston, *U.S.A.* 105 M5
Clifden, *Ireland* 15 C1
Clifden, *N.Z.* 87 M1
Cliffdell, *U.S.A.* 112 D5
Clifton, *Australia* 91 D5
Clifton, *Ariz.*, *U.S.A.* ... 111 K9

Clifton, *Tex.*, *U.S.A.* ... 109 K6
Clifton Beach, *Australia* .. 90 B4
Clifton Forge, *U.S.A.* 104 G6
Clifton Hills, *Australia* ... 91 D2
Climax, *Canada* 101 D7
Clinch →, *U.S.A.* 105 H3
Clingmans Dome, *U.S.A.* . 105 H4
Clint, *U.S.A.* 111 L10
Clinton, *B.C.*, *Canada* .. 100 C4
Clinton, *Ont.*, *Canada* .. 98 D3
Clinton, *N.Z.* 87 M2
Clinton, *Ark.*, *U.S.A.* ... 109 H8
Clinton, *Ill.*, *U.S.A.* 108 E10
Clinton, *Ind.*, *U.S.A.* ... 104 F2
Clinton, *Iowa*, *U.S.A.* ... 108 E9
Clinton, *Mass.*, *U.S.A.* . 107 D13
Clinton, *Mo.*, *U.S.A.* ... 108 F8
Clinton, *N.C.*, *U.S.A.* ... 105 H6
Clinton, *Okla.*, *U.S.A.* .. 109 H5
Clinton, *S.C.*, *U.S.A.* ... 105 H5
Clinton, *Tenn.*, *U.S.A.* .. 105 G3
Clinton, *Wash.*, *U.S.A.* . 112 C4
Clinton C., *Australia* 90 C5
Clinton Colden L., *Canada* 96 B9
Clintonville, *U.S.A.* 108 C10
Clipperton, I., *Pac. Oc.* .. 93 F17
Clisson, *France* 24 E5
Clive L., *Canada* 100 A5
Cliza, *Bolivia* 125 D4
Cloates, Pt., *Australia* 88 D1
Clocolan, *S. Africa* 85 D4
Clodomira, *Argentina* 126 B3
Clonakilty, *Ireland* 15 E3
Clonakilty B., *Ireland* 15 E3
Cloncurry, *Australia* 90 C3
Cloncurry →, *Australia* .. 90 B3
Clones, *Ireland* 15 B4
Clonmel, *Ireland* 15 D4
Cloppenburg, *Germany* .. 18 C4
Cloquet, *U.S.A.* 108 B8
Cloud Peak, *U.S.A.* 110 D10
Cloudcroft, *U.S.A.* 111 K11
Cloverdale, *U.S.A.* 112 G4
Clovis, *Calif.*, *U.S.A.* ... 111 H4
Clovis, *N. Mex.*, *U.S.A.* . 109 H3
Cloyes-sur-le-Loir, *France* 24 E8
Cluj-Napoca, *Romania* ... 38 C6
Clunes, *Australia* 91 F3
Cluny, *France* 27 B8
Cluses, *France* 27 B10
Clusone, *Italy* 32 C6
Clutha →, *N.Z.* 87 M2
Clwyd □, *U.K.* 12 D4
Clwyd →, *U.K.* 12 D4
Clyde, *N.Z.* 87 L2
Clyde, *U.S.A.* 106 C8
Clyde →, *U.K.* 14 F4
Clyde, Firth of, *U.K.* 14 F3
Clyde River, *Canada* 97 A13
Clydebank, *U.K.* 14 F4
Clymer, *U.S.A.* 106 D5
Côa →, *Portugal* 30 D3
Coachella, *U.S.A.* 113 M10
Coachella Canal, *U.S.A.* . 113 N12
Coahoma, *U.S.A.* 109 J4
Coahuayana →, *Mexico* . 114 D4
Coahuayutla, *Mexico* 114 D4
Coahuila □, *Mexico* 114 B4
Coal →, *Canada* 100 B3
Coalane, *Mozam.* 83 F4
Coalcomán, *Mexico* 114 D4
Coaldale, *Canada* 100 D6
Coalgate, *U.S.A.* 109 H6
Coalinga, *U.S.A.* 111 H3
Coalville, *U.K.* 12 E6
Coalville, *U.S.A.* 110 F8
Coaraci, *Brazil* 123 D4
Coari, *Brazil* 121 D5
Coari →, *Brazil* 121 D5
Coari, L. de, *Brazil* 121 D5
Coast □, *Kenya* 82 C4
Coast Mts., *Canada* 100 C3
Coast Ranges, *U.S.A.* 112 E4
Coatbridge, *U.K.* 14 F4
Coatepec, *Mexico* 115 D5
Coatepeque, *Guatemala* .. 116 D1
Coatesville, *U.S.A.* 104 F8
Coaticook, *Canada* 99 C5
Coats I., *Canada* 97 B11
Coats Land, *Antarctica* ... 5 D1
Coatzacoalcos, *Mexico* ... 115 D6
Cobalt, *Canada* 98 C4
Cobán, *Guatemala* 116 C1
Cobar, *Australia* 91 E4
Cobbora, *Australia* 91 E4
Cobh, *Ireland* 15 E3
Cobham, *Australia* 91 E3
Cobija, *Bolivia* 124 C4
Cobleskill, *U.S.A.* 107 D10
Coboconk, *Canada* 106 B6
Cobourg, *Canada* 98 D4
Cobourg Pen., *Australia* . 88 B5
Cobram, *Australia* 91 F4
Cobre, *U.S.A.* 110 F6
Cóbué, *Mozam.* 83 E3
Coca →, *Ecuador* 120 D2
Cocachacra, *Peru* 124 D3
Cocal, *Brazil* 122 B3
Cochabamba, *Bolivia* 125 D4
Coche, I., *Venezuela* 121 A5

Cochem, *Germany* 19 E3
Cochemane, *Mozam.* 83 F3
Cochin, *India* 60 Q10
Cochin China = Nam-
  Phan, *Vietnam* 59 G6
Cochise, *U.S.A.* 111 K9
Cochran, *U.S.A.* 105 J4
Cochrane, *Alta.*, *Canada* . 100 C6
Cochrane, *Ont.*, *Canada* . 98 C3
Cochrane →, *Canada* 101 B8
Cochrane, L., *Chile* 128 C2
Cockburn, *Australia* 91 E3
Cockburn, Canal, *Chile* .. 128 D2
Cockburn I., *Canada* 98 C3
Cockburn Ra., *Australia* . 88 C4
Cocklebiddy Motel,
  Australia 89 F4
Coco →, *Cent. Amer.* ... 116 D3
Coco, Pta., *Colombia* 120 C2
Cocoa, *U.S.A.* 105 L5
Cocobeach, *Gabon* 80 D1
Côcos, *Brazil* 123 D3
Côcos →, *Brazil* 123 D3
Cocos Is., *Ind. Oc.* 92 J1
Cod, C., *U.S.A.* 103 B13
Codajás, *Brazil* 121 D5
Codera, C., *Venezuela* ... 120 A4
Coderre, *Canada* 101 C7
Codigoro, *Italy* 33 D9
Codó, *Brazil* 122 B3
Codogno, *Italy* 32 C6
Codpa, *Chile* 124 D4
Codróipo, *Italy* 33 C10
Cody, *U.S.A.* 110 D9
Coe Hill, *Canada* 98 D4
Coelemu, *Chile* 126 D1
Coelho Neto, *Brazil* 122 B3
Coen, *Australia* 90 A3
Coeroeni →, *Surinam* ... 121 C6
Coesfeld, *Germany* 18 D3
Cœur d'Alene, *U.S.A.* ... 110 C5
Cœur d'Alene L., *U.S.A.* . 110 C5
Coevorden, *Neths.* 16 C9
Cofete, *Canary Is.* 36 F5
Coffeyville, *U.S.A.* 109 G7
Coffin B., *Australia* 91 E2
Coffin Bay Peninsula,
  Australia 91 E2
Coffs Harbour, *Australia* . 91 E5
Cofrentes, *Spain* 29 F3
Cogealac, *Romania* 38 E11
Coghinas →, *Italy* 34 B1
Coghinas, L. di, *Italy* 34 B2
Cognac, *France* 26 C3
Cogne, *Italy* 32 C4
Cogolludo, *Spain* 28 E1
Cohagen, *U.S.A.* 110 C10
Cohoes, *U.S.A.* 107 D11
Cohuna, *Australia* 91 F3
Coiba, I., *Panama* 116 E3
Coig →, *Argentina* 128 D3
Coihaique, *Chile* 128 C2
Coimbatore, *India* 60 P10
Coimbra, *Brazil* 125 D6
Coimbra, *Portugal* 30 E2
Coimbra □, *Portugal* 30 E2
Coín, *Spain* 31 J6
Coipasa, L. de, *Bolivia* ... 124 D4
Coipasa, Salar de, *Bolivia* 124 D4
Cojata, *Peru* 124 D4
Cojedes □, *Venezuela* ... 120 B4
Cojedes →, *Venezuela* .. 120 B4
Cojimies, *Ecuador* 120 C1
Cojocna, *Romania* 38 C6
Cojutepeque, *El Salv.* 116 D2
Cokeville, *U.S.A.* 110 E8
Colac, *Australia* 91 F3
Colares, *Portugal* 31 G1
Colatina, *Brazil* 123 E3
Colbeck, C., *Antarctica* ... 5 D13
Colbinabbin, *Australia* ... 91 F3
Colborne, *Canada* 106 B7
Colby, *U.S.A.* 108 F4
Colchagua □, *Chile* 126 C1
Colchester, *U.K.* 13 F8
Coldstream, *U.K.* 14 F6
Coldwater, *Canada* 106 B5
Coldwater, *U.S.A.* 109 G5
Colebrook, *Australia* 90 G4
Colebrook, *U.S.A.* 107 B13
Coleman, *Canada* 100 D6
Coleman, *U.S.A.* 109 K5
Coleman →, *Australia* ... 90 B3
Colenso, *S. Africa* 85 D4
Coleraine, *Australia* 91 F3
Coleraine, *U.K.* 15 A5
Coleraine □, *U.K.* 15 A5
Coleridge, L., *N.Z.* 87 K3
Colesberg, *S. Africa* 84 E4
Coleville, *U.S.A.* 112 G7
Colfax, *Calif.*, *U.S.A.* ... 112 F6
Colfax, *La.*, *U.S.A.* 109 K8
Colfax, *Wash.*, *U.S.A.* .. 110 C5
Colhué Huapi, L.,
  Argentina 128 C3
Cólico, *Italy* 32 B6
Coligny, *France* 27 B9
Coligny, *S. Africa* 85 D4
Colima, *Mexico* 114 D4
Colima □, *Mexico* 114 D4
Colima, Nevado de, *Mexico* 114 D4
Colina, *Chile* 126 C1
Colina do Norte,
  Guinea-Biss. 78 C2

Coso Junction

Colinas, *Goiás, Brazil* 123 D2
Colinas, *Maranhão, Brazil* 122 C3
Coll, *U.K.* 14 E2
Collaguasi, *Chile* 126 A2
Collarada, Peña, *Spain* 28 C4
Collarenebri, *Australia* 91 D4
Collbran, *U.S.A.* 111 G10
Colle di Val d'Elsa, *Italy* 33 E8
Colle Salvetti, *Italy* 32 E7
Colle Sannita, *Italy* 35 A7
Collécchio, *Italy* 32 D7
Colleen Bawn, *Zimbabwe* 83 G2
College Park, *U.S.A.* 105 J3
Collette, *Canada* 99 C6
Collie, *Australia* 89 F2
Collier B., *Australia* 88 C3
Collier Ra., *Australia* 88 D2
Colline Metallifere, *Italy* 32 E7
Collingwood, *Canada* 98 D3
Collingwood, *N.Z.* 87 J4
Collins, *Canada* 98 B2
Collinsville, *Australia* 90 C4
Collipulli, *Chile* 126 D1
Collo, *Algeria* 75 A6
Collonges, *France* 27 B9
Collooney, *Ireland* 15 B3
Colmar, *France* 25 D14
Colmars, *France* 27 D10
Colmenar, *Spain* 31 J6
Colmenar de Oreja, *Spain* 28 E1
Colmenar Viejo, *Spain* 30 E7
Colne, *U.K.* 12 D5
Colo →, *Australia* 91 E5
Cologna Véneta, *Italy* 33 C8
Cologne = Köln, *Germany* 18 E2
Colom, I., *Spain* 36 B11
Coloma, *U.S.A.* 112 G6
Colomb-Béchar = Béchar, *Algeria* 75 B4
Colombey-les-Belles, *France* 25 D12
Colombey-les-Deux-Églises, *France* 25 D11
Colômbia, *Brazil* 123 F2
Colombia ■, *S. Amer.* 120 C3
Colombier, *Switz.* 22 C3
Colombo, *Sri Lanka* 60 R11
Colome, *U.S.A.* 108 D5
Colón, *Argentina* 126 C4
Colón, *Cuba* 116 B3
Colón, *Panama* 116 E4
Colón, *Peru* 124 A1
Colona, *Australia* 89 F5
Colonella, *Italy* 33 F10
Colonia, *Uruguay* 126 C4
Colonia de San Jordi, *Spain* 36 B9
Colonia Dora, *Argentina* 126 B3
Colonial Heights, *U.S.A.* 104 G7
Colonne, C. delle, *Italy* 35 C10
Colonsay, *Canada* 101 C7
Colonsay, *U.K.* 14 E2
Colorado □, *U.S.A.* 111
Colorado →, *Argentina* 128 A4
Colorado →, *N. Amer.* 111 L6
Colorado →, *U.S.A.* 109 L7
Colorado City, *U.S.A.* 109 J4
Colorado Desert, *U.S.A.* 102 D3
Colorado Plateau, *U.S.A.* 111 H8
Colorado River Aqueduct, *U.S.A.* 113 L12
Colorado Springs, *U.S.A.* 108 F2
Colorno, *Italy* 32 D7
Colotlán, *Mexico* 114 C4
Colquechaca, *Bolivia* 125 D4
Colton, *Calif., U.S.A.* 113 L9
Colton, *N.Y., U.S.A.* 107 B10
Colton, *Wash., U.S.A.* 110 C5
Columbia, *La., U.S.A.* 109 J8
Columbia, *Miss., U.S.A.* 109 K10
Columbia, *Mo., U.S.A.* 108 F8
Columbia, *Pa., U.S.A.* 107 F8
Columbia, *S.C., U.S.A.* 105 H5
Columbia, *Tenn., U.S.A.* 105 H2
Columbia →, *U.S.A.* 110 C1
Columbia, C., *Canada* 4 A4
Columbia, District of □, *U.S.A.* 104 F7
Columbia, Mt., *Canada* 100 C5
Columbia Basin, *U.S.A.* 110 C4
Columbia Falls, *U.S.A.* 110 B6
Columbia Heights, *U.S.A.* 108 C8
Columbiana, *U.S.A.* 106 F4
Columbretes, Is., *Spain* 28 F5
Columbus, *Ga., U.S.A.* 105 J3
Columbus, *Ind., U.S.A.* 104 F3
Columbus, *Kans., U.S.A.* 109 G7
Columbus, *Miss., U.S.A.* 105 J1
Columbus, *Mont., U.S.A.* 110 D9
Columbus, *N. Dak., U.S.A.* 108 A3
Columbus, *N. Mex., U.S.A.* 111 L10
Columbus, *Nebr., U.S.A.* 108 E6
Columbus, *Ohio, U.S.A.* 104 F4
Columbus, *Tex., U.S.A.* 109 L6
Columbus, *Wis., U.S.A.* 108 D10
Colunga, *Spain* 30 B5
Colusa, *U.S.A.* 112 F4
Colville, *U.S.A.* 110 B5
Colville →, *U.S.A.* 96 A4
Colville, C., *N.Z.* 87 G5
Colwyn Bay, *U.K.* 12 D4
Coma, *Ethiopia* 77 F4
Comácchio, *Italy* 33 D9
Comalcalco, *Mexico* 115 D6
Comallo, *Argentina* 128 B2
Comanche, *Okla., U.S.A.* 109 H6
Comanche, *Tex., U.S.A.* 109 K5
Comandante Luis Piedrabuena, *Argentina* 128 C3
Comăneşti, *Romania* 38 C9
Comarapa, *Bolivia* 125 D5
Comayagua, *Honduras* 116 D2
Combahee →, *U.S.A.* 105 J5
Combeaufontaine, *France* 25 E12
Comber, *Canada* 106 D2
Comblain-au-Pont, *Belgium* 17 H7
Combles, *France* 25 B9
Combourg, *France* 24 D5
Combronde, *France* 26 C7
Comeragh Mts., *Ireland* 15 D4
Comet, *Australia* 90 C4
Comilla, *Bangla.* 61 H17
Comines, *Belgium* 17 G1
Comino, *Malta* 37 C1
Comino, C., *Italy* 34 B2
Cómiso, *Italy* 35 F7
Comitán, *Mexico* 115 D6
Commentry, *France* 26 B6
Commerce, *Ga., U.S.A.* 105 H4
Commerce, *Tex., U.S.A.* 109 J7
Commercy, *France* 25 D12
Commewijne □, *Surinam* 121 B7
Committee B., *Canada* 97 B11
Commonwealth B., *Antarctica* 5 C10
Commonwealth of Independent States ■, *Eurasia* 45 D11
Commoron Cr. →, *Australia* 91 D5
Communism Pk. = Kommunizma, Pik, *Tajikistan* 44 F8
Como, *Italy* 32 C6
Como, L. di, *Italy* 32 B6
Comodoro Rivadavia, *Argentina* 128 C3
Comorin, C., *India* 60 Q10
Comoro Is. = Comoros ■, *Ind. Oc.* 71 H8
Comoros ■, *Ind. Oc.* 71 H8
Comox, *Canada* 100 D4
Compiègne, *France* 25 C9
Comporta, *Portugal* 31 G2
Compostela, *Mexico* 114 C4
Comprida, I., *Brazil* 127 A6
Compton, *U.S.A.* 113 M8
Compton Downs, *Australia* 91 E4
Con Cuong, *Vietnam* 58 C5
Con Son, Is., *Vietnam* 59 H6
Cona Niyeu, *Argentina* 128 B3
Conakry, *Guinea* 78 D2
Conara Junction, *Australia* 90 G4
Concarneau, *France* 24 E3
Conceição, *Brazil* 122 C4
Conceição, *Mozam.* 83 F4
Conceição da Barra, *Brazil* 123 E4
Conceição do Araguaia, *Brazil* 122 C2
Conceição do Canindé, *Brazil* 122 C3
Concepción, *Argentina* 126 B2
Concepción, *Bolivia* 125 D5
Concepción, *Chile* 126 D1
Concepción, *Mexico* 115 D6
Concepción, *Paraguay* 126 A4
Concepción, *Peru* 124 C2
Concepción □, *Chile* 126 D1
Concepción →, *Mexico* 114 A2
Concepción, Est. de, *Chile* 128 D2
Concepción, L., *Bolivia* 125 D5
Concepción, Punta, *Mexico* 114 B2
Concepción del Oro, *Mexico* 114 C4
Concepción del Uruguay, *Argentina* 126 C4
Conception, Pt., *U.S.A.* 113 L6
Conception B., *Namibia* 84 C1
Conception I., *Bahamas* 117 B4
Concession, *Zimbabwe* 83 F3
Conchas Dam, *U.S.A.* 109 H2
Conche, *Canada* 99 B8
Concho, *U.S.A.* 111 J9
Concho →, *U.S.A.* 109 K5
Conchos →, *Chihuahua, Mexico* 114 B4
Conchos →, *Tamaulipas, Mexico* 115 B5
Concord, *Calif., U.S.A.* 112 H4
Concord, *N.C., U.S.A.* 105 H5
Concord, *N.H., U.S.A.* 107 C13
Concordia, *Argentina* 126 C4
Concórdia, *Brazil* 120 D4
Concordia, *Mexico* 114 C3
Concordia, *U.S.A.* 108 F6
Concots, *France* 26 D5
Concrete, *U.S.A.* 110 B3
Condamine, *Australia* 91 D5
Condat, *France* 26 C6
Conde, *Brazil* 123 D4
Conde, *U.S.A.* 108 C5
Condé-sur-l'Escaut, *France* 25 B10
Condé-sur-Noireau, *France* 24 D6
Condeúba, *Brazil* 123 D3
Condobolin, *Australia* 91 E4
Condom, *France* 26 E4
Condon, *U.S.A.* 110 D3
Condove, *Italy* 32 C4
Conegliano, *Italy* 33 C9
Conejera, I., *Spain* 36 B9
Conejos, *Mexico* 114 B4
Conflans-en-Jarnisy, *France* 25 C12
Confolens, *France* 26 B4
Confuso →, *Paraguay* 126 B4
Congjiang, *China* 52 E7
Congleton, *U.K.* 12 D5
Congo = Zaïre →, *Africa* 80 F2
Congo, *Brazil* 122 C4
Congo (Kinshasa) = Zaïre ■, *Africa* 80 E4
Congo ■, *Africa* 80 E3
Congo Basin, *Africa* 70 G6
Congonhas, *Brazil* 123 F3
Congress, *U.S.A.* 111 J7
Conil, *Spain* 31 J4
Coniston, *Canada* 98 C3
Conjeeveram = Kanchipuram, *India* 60 N11
Conjuboy, *Australia* 90 B3
Conklin, *Canada* 101 B6
Conlea, *Australia* 91 E3
Conn, L., *Ireland* 15 B2
Connacht, *Ireland* 15 C3
Conneaut, *U.S.A.* 106 E4
Connecticut □, *U.S.A.* 107 E12
Connecticut →, *U.S.A.* 107 E12
Connell, *U.S.A.* 110 C4
Connellsville, *U.S.A.* 106 F5
Connemara, *Ireland* 15 C2
Connemaugh →, *U.S.A.* 106 F5
Connerré, *France* 24 D7
Connersville, *U.S.A.* 104 F3
Connors Ra., *Australia* 90 C4
Conoble, *Australia* 91 E3
Cononaco →, *Ecuador* 120 D2
Cononbridge, *U.K.* 14 D4
Conquest, *Canada* 101 C7
Conrad, *U.S.A.* 110 B8
Conran, C., *Australia* 91 F4
Conroe, *U.S.A.* 109 K7
Conselheiro Lafaiete, *Brazil* 123 F3
Conselheiro Pena, *Brazil* 123 E3
Consort, *Canada* 101 C6
Constance = Konstanz, *Germany* 19 H5
Constance, L. = Bodensee, *Europe* 23 A8
Constanţa, *Romania* 38 E11
Constantina, *Spain* 31 H5
Constantine, *Algeria* 75 A6
Constitución, *Chile* 126 D1
Constitución, *Uruguay* 126 C4
Consuegra, *Spain* 31 F7
Consul, *Canada* 101 D7
Contact, *U.S.A.* 110 F6
Contai, *India* 63 J12
Contamana, *Peru* 124 B3
Contarina, *Italy* 33 C9
Contas →, *Brazil* 123 D4
Contes, *France* 27 E11
Conthey, *Switz.* 22 D4
Contoocook, *U.S.A.* 107 C13
Contra Costa, *Mozam.* 85 D5
Contres, *France* 24 E8
Contrexéville, *France* 25 D12
Contumaza, *Peru* 124 B2
Convención, *Colombia* 120 B3
Conversano, *Italy* 35 B10
Conway = Conwy, *U.K.* 12 D4
Conway = Conwy →, *U.K.* 12 D4
Conway, *Ark., U.S.A.* 109 H8
Conway, *N.H., U.S.A.* 107 C13
Conway, *S.C., U.S.A.* 105 J6
Conway, L., *Australia* 91 D2
Conwy, *U.K.* 12 D4
Conwy →, *U.K.* 12 D4
Coober Pedy, *Australia* 91 D1
Cooch Behar = Koch Bihar, *India* 61 F16
Coodardy, *Australia* 89 E2
Cook, *Australia* 89 F5
Cook, *U.S.A.* 108 B8
Cook, B., *Chile* 128 E2
Cook, Mt., *N.Z.* 87 K3
Cook Inlet, *U.S.A.* 96 C4
Cook Is., *Pac. Oc.* 93 J11
Cook Strait, *N.Z.* 87 J5
Cookeville, *U.S.A.* 105 G3
Cookhouse, *S. Africa* 84 E4
Cookshire, *Canada* 107 A13
Cookstown, *U.K.* 15 B5
Cookstown □, *U.K.* 15 B5
Cooksville, *Canada* 106 C5
Cooktown, *Australia* 90 B4
Coolabah, *Australia* 91 E4
Cooladdi, *Australia* 91 D4
Coolah, *Australia* 91 E4
Coolamon, *Australia* 91 E4
Coolangatta, *Australia* 91 D5
Coolgardie, *Australia* 89 F3
Coolibah, *Australia* 88 C5
Coolidge, *U.S.A.* 111 K8
Coolidge Dam, *U.S.A.* 111 K8
Cooma, *Australia* 91 F4
Coonabarabran, *Australia* 91 E4
Coonamble, *Australia* 91 E4
Coonana, *Australia* 89 F3
Coondapoor, *India* 60 N9
Coongie, *Australia* 91 D3
Coongoola, *Australia* 91 D4
Cooninie, L., *Australia* 91 D2
Cooper, *U.S.A.* 109 J7
Cooper →, *U.S.A.* 105 J6
Cooper Cr. →, *Australia* 91 D2
Cooperstown, *N. Dak., U.S.A.* 108 B5
Cooperstown, *N.Y., U.S.A.* 107 D10
Coorabie, *Australia* 89 F5
Coorabulka, *Australia* 90 C3
Coorow, *Australia* 89 E2
Cooroy, *Australia* 91 D5
Coos Bay, *U.S.A.* 110 E1
Cootamundra, *Australia* 91 E4
Cootehill, *Ireland* 15 B4
Cooyar, *Australia* 91 D5
Cooyeana, *Australia* 90 C2
Copahue Paso, *Argentina* 126 D1
Copainalá, *Mexico* 115 D6
Copán, *Honduras* 116 D2
Copatana, *Brazil* 120 D4
Cope, *U.S.A.* 108 F3
Cope, C., *Spain* 29 H3
Copenhagen = København, *Denmark* 11 J6
Copertino, *Italy* 35 B11
Copiapó, *Chile* 126 B1
Copiapó →, *Chile* 126 B1
Copley, *Australia* 91 E2
Copp L., *Canada* 100 A6
Copparo, *Italy* 33 D8
Coppename →, *Surinam* 121 B6
Copper Center, *U.S.A.* 96 B5
Copper Cliff, *Canada* 98 C3
Copper Harbor, *U.S.A.* 104 B2
Copper Queen, *Zimbabwe* 83 F2
Copperbelt □, *Zambia* 83 E2
Coppermine, *Canada* 96 B8
Coppermine →, *Canada* 96 B8
Copperopolis, *U.S.A.* 112 H6
Coquet →, *U.K.* 12 B6
Coquilhatville = Mbandaka, *Zaïre* 80 D3
Coquille, *U.S.A.* 110 E1
Coquimbo, *Chile* 126 B1
Coquimbo □, *Chile* 126 C1
Corabia, *Romania* 38 F7
Coração de Jesus, *Brazil* 123 E3
Coracora, *Peru* 124 D3
Coradi, Is., *Italy* 35 B10
Coral Gables, *U.S.A.* 105 N5
Coral Harbour, *Canada* 97 B11
Coral Sea, *Pac. Oc.* 92 J7
Corantijn →, *Surinam* 121 B6
Coraopolis, *U.S.A.* 106 F4
Corato, *Italy* 35 A9
Corbeil-Essonnes, *France* 25 D9
Corbie, *France* 25 C9
Corbières, *France* 26 F6
Corbigny, *France* 25 E10
Corbin, *U.S.A.* 104 G3
Corbion, *Belgium* 17 J6
Corbones →, *Spain* 31 H5
Corby, *U.K.* 13 E7
Corby Glen, *U.K.* 13 E7
Corcoles →, *Spain* 29 F1
Corcoran, *U.S.A.* 111 H4
Corcubión, *Spain* 30 C1
Cordele, *U.S.A.* 105 K4
Cordell, *U.S.A.* 109 H5
Cordenons, *Italy* 33 C9
Cordes, *France* 26 D5
Cordisburgo, *Brazil* 123 E3
Córdoba, *Argentina* 126 C3
Córdoba, *Mexico* 115 D5
Córdoba, *Spain* 31 H6
Córdoba □, *Argentina* 126 C3
Córdoba □, *Colombia* 120 B2
Córdoba □, *Spain* 31 G6
Córdoba, Sierra de, *Argentina* 126 C3
Cordon, *Phil.* 55 C4
Cordova, *Ala., U.S.A.* 105 J2
Cordova, *Alaska, U.S.A.* 96 B5
Corella, *Spain* 28 C3
Corella →, *Australia* 90 B3
Coremas, *Brazil* 122 C4
Corentyne →, *Guyana* 121 B6
Corfield, *Australia* 90 C3
Corfu = Kérkira, *Greece* 37 A3
Corfu, Str of, *Greece* 37 A4
Corgo, *Spain* 30 C3
Corguinho, *Brazil* 125 D7
Cori, *Italy* 34 A5
Coria, *Spain* 30 F4
Corigliano Cálabro, *Italy* 35 C9
Coringa Is., *Australia* 90 B4
Corinna, *Australia* 90 G4
Corinth = Kórinthos, *Greece* 39 M5
Corinth, *Miss., U.S.A.* 105 H1
Corinth, *N.Y., U.S.A.* 107 C11
Corinth, G. of = Korinthiakós Kólpos, *Greece* 39 L5
Corinth Canal, *Greece* 39 M6
Corinto, *Brazil* 123 E3
Corinto, *Nic.* 116 D2
Cork, *Ireland* 15 E3
Cork □, *Ireland* 15 E3
Cork Harbour, *Ireland* 15 E3
Corlay, *France* 24 D3
Corleone, *Italy* 34 E6
Corleto Perticara, *Italy* 35 B9
Çorlu, *Turkey* 39 H10
Cormack L., *Canada* 100 A4
Cormóns, *Italy* 33 C10
Cormorant, *Canada* 101 C8
Cormorant L., *Canada* 101 C8
Corn Is. = Maiz, Is. del, *Nic.* 116 D3
Cornélio Procópio, *Brazil* 127 A5
Cornell, *U.S.A.* 108 C9
Corner Brook, *Canada* 99 C8
Corníglio, *Italy* 32 D7
Corning, *Ark., U.S.A.* 109 G9
Corning, *Calif., U.S.A.* 110 G2
Corning, *Iowa, U.S.A.* 108 E7
Corning, *N.Y., U.S.A.* 106 D7
Corno, Monte, *Italy* 33 F10
Cornwall, *Canada* 98 C5
Cornwall □, *U.K.* 13 G3
Corny Pt., *Australia* 91 E2
Coro, *Venezuela* 120 A4
Coroaci, *Brazil* 123 E3
Coroatá, *Brazil* 122 B3
Corocoro, *Bolivia* 124 D4
Corocoro, I., *Venezuela* 121 B5
Coroico, *Bolivia* 124 D4
Coromandel, *Brazil* 123 E2
Coromandel, *N.Z.* 87 G5
Coromandel Coast, *India* 60 N12
Corona, *Australia* 91 E3
Corona, *Calif., U.S.A.* 113 M9
Corona, *N. Mex., U.S.A.* 111 J11
Coronado, *U.S.A.* 113 N9
Coronado, B. de, *Costa Rica* 116 E3
Coronados, G. de los, *Chile* 128 B2
Coronados, Is. los, *U.S.A.* 113 N9
Coronation, *Canada* 100 C6
Coronation Gulf, *Canada* 96 B8
Coronation I., *Antarctica* 5 C18
Coronation I., *U.S.A.* 100 B2
Coronation Is., *Australia* 88 B3
Coronda, *Argentina* 126 C3
Coronel, *Chile* 126 D1
Coronel Bogado, *Paraguay* 126 B4
Coronel Dorrego, *Argentina* 126 D3
Coronel Fabriciano, *Brazil* 123 E3
Coronel Murta, *Brazil* 123 E3
Coronel Oviedo, *Paraguay* 126 B4
Coronel Ponce, *Brazil* 125 D6
Coronel Pringles, *Argentina* 126 D3
Coronel Suárez, *Argentina* 126 D3
Coronel Vidal, *Argentina* 126 D4
Corongo, *Peru* 124 B2
Coronie □, *Surinam* 121 B6
Coropuna, Nevado, *Peru* 124 D3
Çorovoda, *Albania* 39 J3
Corowa, *Australia* 91 F4
Corozal, *Belize* 115 D7
Corozal, *Colombia* 120 B2
Corps, *France* 27 D9
Corpus, *Argentina* 127 B4
Corpus Christi, *U.S.A.* 109 M6
Corpus Christi, L., *U.S.A.* 109 L6
Corque, *Bolivia* 124 D4
Corral, *Chile* 128 A2
Corral de Almaguer, *Spain* 28 F1
Corralejo, *Canary Is.* 36 F6
Corréggio, *Italy* 32 D7
Corrente, *Brazil* 122 D2
Corrente →, *Brazil* 123 D3
Correntes →, *Brazil* 125 D6
Correntes, C. das, *Mozam.* 85 C6
Correntina, *Brazil* 123 D3
Corrèze □, *France* 26 C5
Corrèze →, *France* 26 C5
Corrib, L., *Ireland* 15 C2
Corrientes, *Argentina* 126 B4
Corrientes □, *Argentina* 126 B4
Corrientes →, *Argentina* 126 C4
Corrientes →, *Peru* 120 D3
Corrientes, C., *Colombia* 120 B2
Corrientes, C., *Cuba* 116 B3
Corrientes, C., *Mexico* 114 C3
Corrigan, *U.S.A.* 109 K7
Corrigin, *Australia* 89 F2
Corry, *U.S.A.* 106 E5
Corse, *France* 27 F13
Corse, C., *France* 27 E13
Corse-du-Sud □, *France* 27 G13
Corsica = Corse, *France* 27 F13
Corsicana, *U.S.A.* 109 J6
Corte, *France* 27 F13
Corte do Pinto, *Portugal* 31 H3
Cortegana, *Spain* 31 H4
Cortez, *U.S.A.* 111 H9
Cortina d'Ampezzo, *Italy* 33 B9
Cortland, *U.S.A.* 107 D8
Cortona, *Italy* 33 E8
Coruche, *Portugal* 31 G2
Çoruh →, *Turkey* 67 C9
Çorum, *Turkey* 66 C6
Çorum □, *Turkey* 66 C6
Corumbá, *Brazil* 125 D6
Corumbá →, *Brazil* 123 E2
Corumbá de Goiás, *Brazil* 123 E2
Corumbaíba, *Brazil* 123 E2
Corunna = La Coruña, *Spain* 30 B2
Corvallis, *U.S.A.* 110 D2
Corvette, L. de la, *Canada* 98 B5
Corydon, *U.S.A.* 108 E8
Cosalá, *Mexico* 114 C3
Cosamaloapan, *Mexico* 115 D5
Cosenza, *Italy* 35 C9
Coshocton, *U.S.A.* 106 F3
Cosmo Newberry, *Australia* 89 E3
Cosne-sur-Loire, *France* 25 E9
Coso Junction, *U.S.A.* 113 J9

Coso Pk., *U.S.A.* 113 J9
Cospeito, *Spain* 30 B3
Cosquín, *Argentina* 126 C3
Cossato, *Italy* 32 C5
Cossé-le-Vivien, *France* 24 E6
Cosson →, *France* 24 E8
Costa Blanca, *Spain* 29 G4
Costa Brava, *Spain* 28 D8
Costa del Sol, *Spain* 31 J6
Costa Dorada, *Spain* 28 E6
Costa Mesa, *U.S.A.* 113 M9
Costa Rica ■, *Cent. Amer.* 116 D3
Costa Smeralda, *Italy* 34 A2
Costigliole d'Asti, *Italy* 32 D5
Costilla, *U.S.A.* 111 H11
Cosumnes →, *U.S.A.* 112 G5
Coswig, *Germany* 18 D8
Cotabato, *Phil.* 55 H6
Cotacajes →, *Bolivia* 124 D4
Cotagaita, *Bolivia* 126 A2
Cotahuasi, *Peru* 124 D3
Côte d'Azur, *France* 27 E11
Côte-d'Ivoire ■ = Ivory
  Coast ■, *Africa* 78 D3
Côte d'Or, *France* 25 E11
Côte-d'Or □, *France* 25 E11
Coteau des Prairies, *U.S.A.* 108 C6
Coteau du Missouri, *U.S.A.* 108 B4
Coteau Landing, *Canada* 107 A10
Cotegipe, *Brazil* 123 D3
Cotentin, *France* 24 C5
Côtes-d'Armor □, *France* 24 D4
Côtes de Meuse, *France* 25 C12
Côtes-du-Nord = Côtes-
  d'Armor □, *France* 24 D4
Cotiella, *Spain* 28 C5
Cotillo, *Canary Is.* 36 F5
Cotina →, *Bos.-H.* 21 M8
Cotoca, *Bolivia* 125 D5
Cotonou, *Benin* 79 D5
Cotopaxi, *Ecuador* 120 D2
Cotopaxi □, *Ecuador* 120 D2
Cotronei, *Italy* 35 C9
Cotswold Hills, *U.K.* 13 F5
Cottage Grove, *U.S.A.* 110 E2
Cottbus, *Germany* 18 D10
Cottingham, *U.K.* 12 C5
Cottonwood, *U.S.A.* 111 J7
Cotulla, *U.S.A.* 109 L5
Coubre, Pte. de la, *France* 26 C2
Couches, *France* 25 F11
Couço, *Portugal* 31 G2
Coudersport, *U.S.A.* 106 E6
Couedic, C. du, *Australia* 91 F2
Couëron, *France* 24 E5
Couesnon →, *France* 24 D5
Couhé, *France* 26 B4
Coulanges-sur-Yonne,
  France 25 E10
Coulee City, *U.S.A.* 110 C4
Coulman I., *Antarctica* 5 D11
Coulommiers, *France* 25 D10
Coulonge →, *Canada* 98 C4
Coulonges-sur-l'Autize,
  France 26 B3
Coulterville, *U.S.A.* 112 H6
Council, *Alaska, U.S.A.* 96 B3
Council, *Idaho, U.S.A.* 110 D5
Council Bluffs, *U.S.A.* 108 E7
Council Grove, *U.S.A.* 108 F6
Coupeville, *U.S.A.* 112 B4
Courantyne →, *S. Amer.* 121 B6
Courcelles, *Belgium* 17 H4
Courçon, *France* 26 B3
Couronne, C., *France* 27 E9
Cours-la-Ville, *France* 27 B8
Coursan, *France* 26 E7
Courseulles-sur-Mer,
  France 24 C6
Court-St.-Etienne, *Belgium* 17 G5
Courtenay, *Canada* 100 D3
Courtland, *U.S.A.* 112 G5
Courtrai = Kortrijk,
  Belgium 17 G2
Courtright, *Canada* 106 D2
Courville-sur-Eure, *France* 24 D8
Coushatta, *U.S.A.* 109 J8
Coutances, *France* 24 C5
Couterne, *France* 24 D6
Coutras, *France* 26 C3
Coutts, *Canada* 100 D6
Couvet, *Switz.* 22 C3
Couvin, *Belgium* 17 H4
Covarrubias, *Spain* 28 C1
Coveñas, *Colombia* 120 B2
Coventry, *U.K.* 13 E6
Coventry L., *Canada* 101 A7
Covilhã, *Portugal* 30 E3
Covington, *Ga., U.S.A.* 105 J4
Covington, *Ky., U.S.A.* 104 F3
Covington, *Okla., U.S.A.* 109 G6
Covington, *Tenn., U.S.A.* 109 H10
Cowal, L., *Australia* 91 E4
Cowan, *Canada* 101 C8
Cowan, L., *Australia* 89 F3
Cowan L., *Canada* 101 C7
Cowangie, *Australia* 91 F3
Cowansville, *Canada* 107 A12
Cowarie, *Australia* 91 D2
Cowcowing Lakes,
  Australia 89 F2
Cowdenbeath, *U.K.* 14 E5
Cowell, *Australia* 91 E2
Cowes, *U.K.* 13 G6
Cowlitz →, *U.S.A.* 112 D4

Cowra, *Australia* 91 E4
Coxilha Grande, *Brazil* 127 B5
Coxim, *Brazil* 125 D7
Coxim →, *Brazil* 125 D7
Cox's Bazar, *Bangla.* 61 J17
Cox's Cove, *Canada* 99 C8
Coyame, *Mexico* 114 B3
Coyote Wells, *U.S.A.* 113 N11
Coyuca de Benítez, *Mexico* 115 D4
Coyuca de Catalan, *Mexico* 114 D4
Cozad, *U.S.A.* 108 E5
Cozumel, *Mexico* 115 C7
Cozumel, I. de, *Mexico* 115 C7
Craboon, *Australia* 91 E4
Cracow = Kraków, *Poland* 20 E9
Cracow, *Australia* 91 D5
Cradock, *S. Africa* 84 E4
Craig, *Alaska, U.S.A.* 100 B2
Craig, *Colo., U.S.A.* 110 F10
Craigavon = Lurgan, *U.K.* 15 B5
Craigmore, *Zimbabwe* 83 G3
Crailsheim, *Germany* 19 F6
Craiova, *Romania* 38 E6
Cramsie, *Australia* 90 C3
Cranberry Portage, *Canada* 101 C8
Cranbrook, *Tas., Australia* 90 G4
Cranbrook, *W. Austral.,*
  Australia 89 F2
Cranbrook, *Canada* 100 D5
Crandon, *U.S.A.* 108 C10
Crane, *Oreg., U.S.A.* 110 E4
Crane, *Tex., U.S.A.* 109 K3
Cranston, *U.S.A.* 107 E13
Craon, *France* 24 E6
Craonne, *France* 25 C10
Craponne-sur-Arzon,
  France 26 C7
Crasna, *Romania* 38 C10
Crater L., *U.S.A.* 110 E2
Crateús, *Brazil* 122 C3
Crati →, *Italy* 35 C9
Crato, *Brazil* 122 C4
Crato, *Portugal* 31 F3
Cravo Norte, *Colombia* 120 B3
Cravo Norte →, *Colombia* 120 B3
Crawford, *U.S.A.* 108 D3
Crawfordsville, *U.S.A.* 104 E2
Crawley, *U.K.* 13 F7
Crazy Mts., *U.S.A.* 110 C8
Crean L., *Canada* 101 C7
Crécy-en-Brie, *France* 25 D9
Crécy-en-Ponthieu, *France* 25 B8
Crediton, *Canada* 106 C3
Credo, *Australia* 89 F3
Cree →, *Canada* 101 B7
Cree →, *U.K.* 14 G4
Cree L., *Canada* 101 B7
Creede, *U.S.A.* 111 H10
Creel, *Mexico* 114 B3
Creighton, *U.S.A.* 108 D6
Creil, *France* 25 C9
Crema, *Italy* 32 C6
Cremona, *Italy* 32 C7
Crepori →, *Brazil* 125 B6
Crépy, *France* 25 C10
Crépy-en-Valois, *France* 25 C9
Cres, *Croatia* 33 D11
Cresbard, *U.S.A.* 108 C5
Crescent, *Okla., U.S.A.* 109 H6
Crescent, *Oreg., U.S.A.* 110 E3
Crescent City, *U.S.A.* 110 F1
Crescentino, *Italy* 32 C5
Crespino, *Italy* 33 D8
Crespo, *Argentina* 126 C3
Cressy, *Australia* 91 F3
Crest, *France* 27 D9
Cresta, Mt., *Phil.* 55 C5
Crested Butte, *U.S.A.* 111 G10
Crestline, *Calif., U.S.A.* 113 L9
Crestline, *Ohio, U.S.A.* 106 F2
Creston, *Canada* 100 D5
Creston, *Calif., U.S.A.* 112 K6
Creston, *Iowa, U.S.A.* 108 E7
Creston, *Wash., U.S.A.* 110 C4
Crestview, *Calif., U.S.A.* 112 H8
Crestview, *Fla., U.S.A.* 105 K2
Crete = Kríti, *Greece* 37 D7
Crete, *U.S.A.* 108 E6
Crete, Sea of, *Greece* 39 N8
Creus, C., *Spain* 28 C8
Creuse □, *France* 26 B6
Creuse →, *France* 26 B4
Creuzburg, *Germany* 18 D6
Crevalcore, *Italy* 33 D8
Crèvecœur-le-Grand,
  France 25 C9
Crevillente, *Spain* 29 G4
Criciúma, *Brazil* 127 B6
Crieff, *U.K.* 14 E5
Crikvenica, *Croatia* 33 C11
Crimea = Krymskiy
  Poluostrov, *Ukraine* 42 D5
Crimmitschau, *Germany* 18 E8
Cristalândia, *Brazil* 122 D2
Cristino Castro, *Brazil* 122 C3
Crişul Alb →, *Romania* 38 C4
Crişul Negru →, *Romania* 38 C4
Crişul Repede →,
  Romania 38 C3
Crivitz, *Germany* 18 B7
Crixás, *Brazil* 123 D2
Crna Gora =
  Montenegro □,
  Montenegro, Yug. 21 N9

Crni Drim →,
  Macedonia 39 H3
Črnomelj, *Slovenia* 33 C12
Croaghpatrick, *Ireland* 15 C2
Croatia ■, *Europe* 33 C13
Crocker, Banjaran,
  Malaysia 56 C5
Crockett, *U.S.A.* 109 K7
Crocodile = Krokodil →,
  Mozam. 85 D5
Crocodile Is., *Australia* 90 A1
Crocq, *France* 26 C6
Croisette, C., *France* 27 E9
Croisic, Pte. du, *France* 24 E4
Croix, L. La, *Canada* 98 C1
Croker, *Australia* 88 B5
Croker I., *Australia* 88 B5
Cromarty, *Canada* 101 B10
Cromarty, *U.K.* 14 D4
Cromer, *U.K.* 12 E9
Cromwell, *N.Z.* 87 L2
Cronat, *France* 25 F10
Cronulla, *Australia* 91 E5
Crooked →, *Canada* 100 C4
Crooked →, *U.S.A.* 110 D3
Crooked I., *Bahamas* 117 B5
Crooked Island Passage,
  Bahamas 117 B5
Crookston, *Minn., U.S.A.* 108 B6
Crookston, *Nebr., U.S.A.* 108 D4
Crooksville, *U.S.A.* 104 F4
Crookwell, *Australia* 91 E4
Crosby, *Minn., U.S.A.* 108 B8
Crosby, *N. Dak., U.S.A.* 101 D8
Crosby, *Pa., U.S.A.* 106 E6
Crosbyton, *U.S.A.* 109 J4
Cross →, *Nigeria* 79 E6
Cross City, *U.S.A.* 105 L4
Cross Fell, *U.K.* 12 C5
Cross L., *Canada* 101 C9
Cross Plains, *U.S.A.* 109 J5
Cross River □, *Nigeria* 79 D6
Cross Sound, *U.S.A.* 96 C6
Crossett, *U.S.A.* 109 J9
Crossfield, *Canada* 100 C6
Crosshaven, *Ireland* 15 E3
Croton-on-Hudson, *U.S.A.* 107 E11
Crotone, *Italy* 35 C10
Crow →, *Canada* 100 B4
Crow Agency, *U.S.A.* 110 D10
Crow Hd., *Ireland* 15 E1
Crowell, *U.S.A.* 109 J5
Crowley, *U.S.A.* 109 K8
Crowley, L., *U.S.A.* 112 H8
Crown Point, *U.S.A.* 104 E2
Crows Landing, *U.S.A.* 112 H5
Crows Nest, *Australia* 91 D5
Crowsnest Pass, *Canada* 100 D6
Croydon, *Australia* 90 B3
Croydon, *U.K.* 13 F7
Crozet Is., *Ind. Oc.* 3 G12
Crozon, *France* 24 D2
Cruz, C., *Cuba* 116 C4
Cruz Alta, *Brazil* 127 B5
Cruz das Almas, *Brazil* 123 D4
Cruz de Malta, *Brazil* 122 C3
Cruz del Eje, *Argentina* 126 C3
Cruzeiro, *Brazil* 123 F2
Cruzeiro do Oeste, *Brazil* 127 A5
Cruzeiro do Sul, *Brazil* 124 B3
Cry L., *Canada* 100 B3
Crystal Bay, *U.S.A.* 112 F7
Crystal Brook, *Australia* 91 E2
Crystal City, *Mo., U.S.A.* 108 F9
Crystal City, *Tex., U.S.A.* 109 L5
Crystal Falls, *U.S.A.* 104 B1
Crystal River, *U.S.A.* 105 L4
Crystal Springs, *U.S.A.* 109 K9
Csongrád, *Hungary* 21 J10
Csorna, *Hungary* 21 H7
Csurgo, *Hungary* 21 J7
Cu Lao Hon, *Vietnam* 59 G7
Cua Rao, *Vietnam* 58 C5
Cuácua →, *Mozam.* 83 F4
Cuamato, *Angola* 84 B2
Cuamba, *Mozam.* 83 E4
Cuando →, *Angola* 81 H4
Cuando Cubango □,
  Angola 84 B3
Cuangar, *Angola* 84 B2
Cuanza →, *Angola* 70 G5
Cuarto →, *Argentina* 126 C3
Cuatrociénegas, *Mexico* 114 B4
Cuauhtémoc, *Mexico* 114 B3
Cuba, *Portugal* 31 G3
Cuba, *N. Mex., U.S.A.* 111 J10
Cuba, *N.Y., U.S.A.* 106 D6
Cuba ■, *W. Indies* 116 B4
Cuballing, *Australia* 89 F2
Cubango →, *Africa* 84 B3
Çubuk, *Turkey* 66 C5
Cucamonga, *U.S.A.* 113 L9
Cuchi, *Angola* 81 G3
Cuchillo-Có, *Argentina* 128 A4
Cuchivero →, *Venezuela* 120 B5
Cuchumatanes, Sierra de
  los, *Guatemala* 116 C1
Cucuí, *Brazil* 120 C4
Cucurpe, *Mexico* 114 A2
Cucurrupí, *Colombia* 120 C2
Cúcuta, *Colombia* 120 B3
Cudahy, *U.S.A.* 104 D2
Cudalbi, *Romania* 38 D10
Cuddalore, *India* 60 P11
Cuddapah, *India* 60 M11

Cuddapan, L., *Australia* 90 D3
Cudgewa, *Australia* 91 F4
Cudillero, *Spain* 30 B4
Cue, *Australia* 89 E2
Cuéllar, *Spain* 30 D6
Cuenca, *Ecuador* 120 D2
Cuenca, *Spain* 28 E2
Cuenca □, *Spain* 28 F2
Cuenca, Serranía de 28 F3
Cuerdo del Pozo, Pantano
  de la, *Spain* 28 D2
Cuernavaca, *Mexico* 115 D5
Cuero, *U.S.A.* 109 L6
Cuers, *France* 27 E10
Cuervo, *U.S.A.* 109 H2
Cuesmes, *Belgium* 17 H3
Cuevas, Cerro, *Bolivia* 125 E4
Cuevas del Almanzora,
  Spain 29 H3
Cuevo, *Bolivia* 125 E5
Cuiabá, *Brazil* 125 D6
Cuiabá →, *Brazil* 125 D6
Cuilco, *Guatemala* 116 C1
Cuillin Hills, *U.K.* 14 D2
Cuillin Sd., *U.K.* 14 D2
Cuima, *Angola* 81 G3
Cuiseaux, *France* 27 B9
Cuité, *Brazil* 122 C4
Cuito →, *Angola* 84 B3
Cuiuni →, *Brazil* 121 D5
Cukai, *Malaysia* 59 K4
Culan, *France* 26 B6
Culbertson, *U.S.A.* 108 A2
Culcairn, *Australia* 91 F4
Culebra, Sierra de la, *Spain* 30 D4
Culemborg, *Neths.* 16 E6
Culgoa →, *Australia* 91 D4
Culiacán, *Mexico* 114 C3
Culiacán →, *Mexico* 114 C3
Culion, *Phil.* 55 F4
Cullarin Ra., *Australia* 91 E4
Cullen, *U.K.* 14 D6
Cullen Pt., *Australia* 90 A3
Cullera, *Spain* 29 F4
Cúllar de Baza, *Spain* 29 H2
Cullman, *U.S.A.* 105 H2
Culloden Moor, *U.K.* 14 D4
Culoz, *France* 27 C9
Culpeper, *U.S.A.* 104 F7
Culuene →, *Brazil* 125 C7
Culver, Pt., *Australia* 89 F3
Culverden, *N.Z.* 87 K4
Cumaná, *Venezuela* 121 A5
Cumare, *Colombia* 120 C3
Cumari, *Brazil* 123 E2
Cumberland, *Canada* 100 D3
Cumberland, *Md., U.S.A.* 104 F6
Cumberland, *Wis., U.S.A.* 108 C8
Cumberland →, *U.S.A.* 105 G2
Cumberland I., *U.S.A.* 105 K5
Cumberland Is., *Australia* 90 C4
Cumberland L., *Canada* 101 C8
Cumberland Pen., *Canada* 97 B13
Cumberland Plateau,
  U.S.A. 105 H3
Cumberland Sd., *Canada* 97 B13
Cumborah, *Australia* 91 D4
Cumbres Mayores, *Spain* 31 G4
Cumbria □, *U.K.* 12 C5
Cumbrian Mts., *U.K.* 12 C4
Cumbum, *India* 60 M11
Cuminá →, *Brazil* 121 D6
Cuminapanema →, *Brazil* 121 D7
Cummings Mt., *U.S.A.* 113 K8
Cummins, *Australia* 91 E2
Cumnock, *Australia* 91 E4
Cumnock, *U.K.* 14 F4
Cumpas, *Mexico* 114 A3
Cumplida, Pta., *Canary Is.* 36 F2
Çumra, *Turkey* 66 E5
Cuncumén, *Chile* 126 C1
Cundeelee, *Australia* 89 F3
Cunderdin, *Australia* 89 F2
Cundinamarca □, *Colombia* 120 C3
Cunene →, *Angola* 84 B1
Cúneo, *Italy* 32 D4
Cunillera, I., *Spain* 36 C7
Cunlhat, *France* 26 C7
Cunnamulla, *Australia* 91 D4
Cuorgnè, *Italy* 32 C4
Cupar, *Canada* 101 C8
Cupar, *U.K.* 14 E5
Cupica, G. de, *Colombia* 120 B2
Čuprija, *Serbia, Yug.* 21 M11
Curaçá, *Brazil* 122 C4
Curaçao, *Neth. Ant.* 117 D6
Curacautín, *Chile* 128 A2
Curahuara de Carangas,
  Bolivia 124 D4
Curanilahue, *Chile* 126 D1
Curaray →, *Peru* 120 D3
Curatabaca, *Venezuela* 121 B5
Cure →, *France* 25 E10
Curepto, *Chile* 126 D1
Curiapo, *Venezuela* 121 B5
Curicó, *Chile* 126 C1
Curicó □, *Chile* 126 C1
Curicuriari →, *Brazil* 120 D4
Curimatá, *Brazil* 122 D3
Curiplaya, *Colombia* 120 C3
Curitiba, *Brazil* 127 B6
Currabubula, *Australia* 91 E5
Currais Novos, *Brazil* 122 C4

Curralinho, *Brazil* 122 B2
Currant, *U.S.A.* 110 G6
Curraweena, *Australia* 91 E4
Currawilla, *Australia* 90 D3
Current →, *U.S.A.* 109 G9
Currie, *Australia* 90 F3
Currie, *U.S.A.* 110 F6
Currie, Mt., *S. Africa* 85 E4
Currituck Sd., *U.S.A.* 105 G8
Curtea de Argeş, *Romania* 38 D7
Curtis, *Spain* 30 B2
Curtis, *U.S.A.* 108 E4
Curtis Group, *Australia* 90 F4
Curtis I., *Australia* 90 C5
Curuá →, *Pará, Brazil* 121 D7
Curuá →, *Pará, Brazil* 125 B7
Curuá, I., *Brazil* 122 A1
Curuáes →, *Brazil* 125 B7
Curuápanema →, *Brazil* 121 D6
Curuçá, *Brazil* 122 B2
Curuguaty, *Paraguay* 127 A4
Curup, *Indonesia* 56 E2
Curupira, Serra, *S. Amer.* 121 C5
Cururu →, *Brazil* 125 B6
Cururupu, *Brazil* 122 B3
Curuzú Cuatiá, *Argentina* 126 B4
Curvelo, *Brazil* 123 E3
Cushing, *U.S.A.* 109 H6
Cushing, Mt., *Canada* 100 B3
Cusihuiriáchic, *Mexico* 114 B3
Cusna, Monte, *Italy* 32 D7
Cusset, *France* 26 B7
Custer, *U.S.A.* 108 D3
Cut Bank, *U.S.A.* 110 B7
Cutervo, *Peru* 124 B2
Cuthbert, *U.S.A.* 105 K3
Cutler, *U.S.A.* 112 J7
Cutral-Có, *Argentina* 128 A3
Cutro, *Italy* 35 C9
Cuttaburra →, *Australia* 91 D3
Cuttack, *India* 61 J14
Cuvier, C., *Australia* 89 D1
Cuvier I., *N.Z.* 87 G5
Cuxhaven, *Germany* 18 B4
Cuyabeno, *Ecuador* 120 D2
Cuyahoga Falls, *U.S.A.* 106 E3
Cuyapo, *Phil.* 55 D4
Cuyo, *Phil.* 55 F4
Cuyo East Pass, *Phil.* 55 F4
Cuyo West Pass, *Phil.* 55 F4
Cuyuni →, *Guyana* 121 B6
Cuzco, *Bolivia* 124 E4
Cuzco, *Peru* 124 C3
Cuzco □, *Peru* 124 C3
Cwmbran, *U.K.* 13 F4
Cyangugu, *Rwanda* 82 C2
Cyclades = Kikládhes,
  Greece 39 M7
Cygnet, *Australia* 90 G4
Cynthiana, *U.S.A.* 104 F3
Cypress Hills, *Canada* 101 D7
Cyprus ■, *Asia* 37 E12
Cyrenaica, *Libya* 70 C6
Cyrene = Shaḥḥāt, *Libya* 73 B9
Czar, *Canada* 101 C6
Czarne, *Poland* 20 B6
Czech Rep. ■, *Europe* 20 F4
Czersk, *Poland* 20 B6
Częstochowa, *Poland* 20 E9

D

Da →, *Vietnam* 58 B5
Da Hinggan Ling, *China* 54 B7
Da Lat, *Vietnam* 59 G7
Da Nang, *Vietnam* 58 D7
Da Qaidam, *China* 54 C4
Da Yunhe →, *China* 51 G11
Da'an, *China* 51 B13
Daarlerveen, *Neths.* 16 D9
Dab'a, Râs el, *Egypt* 76 H6
Daba Shan, *China* 52 B7
Dabai, *Nigeria* 79 C6
Dabajuro, *Venezuela* 120 A3
Dabakala, *Ivory C.* 78 D4
Dabeiba, *Colombia* 120 B2
Dabhoi, *India* 62 H5
Dąbie, *Poland* 20 B4
Dabie Shan, *China* 53 B10
Dabo, *Indonesia* 56 E2
Dabola, *Guinea* 78 C2
Dabou, *Ivory C.* 78 D4
Daboya, *Ghana* 79 D4
Dabrowa Tarnówska,
  Poland 20 E10
Dabu, *China* 53 E11
Dabung, *Malaysia* 59 K4
Dabus →, *Ethiopia* 77 E4
Dacato →, *Ethiopia* 77 F5
Dacca = Dhaka, *Bangla.* 63 H14
Dacca = Dhaka □, *Bangla.* 63 G14
Dachau, *Germany* 19 G7
Dadanawa, *Guyana* 121 C6
Daday, *Turkey* 42 F5
Dade City, *U.S.A.* 105 L4
Dades →, *Morocco* 74 B3
Dadiya, *Nigeria* 79 D7
Dadra and Nagar Haveli □,
  India 60 J8
Dadri = Charkhi Dadri,
  India 62 E7
Dadu, *Pakistan* 62 F2

Dadu He →, China 52 C4
Dăeni, Romania 38 E11
Daet, Phil. 55 D5
Dafang, China 52 D5
Dagana, Senegal 78 B1
Dagash, Sudan 76 D3
Dagestanskiye Ogni, Russia 43 E13
Daggett, U.S.A. 113 L10
Daghestan Republic □, Russia 43 E12
Daghfeli, Sudan 76 D3
Dagö = Hiiumaa, Estonia 40 B3
Dagu, China 51 E9
Daguan, China 52 D4
Dagupan, Phil. 55 C4
Dahab, Egypt 76 B3
Dahlak Kebir, Eritrea 68 D3
Dahlenburg, Germany 18 B6
Dahlonega, U.S.A. 105 H4
Dahme, Germany 18 D9
Dahod, India 62 H6
Dahomey = Benin ■, Africa 79 D5
Dahong Shan, China 53 B9
Dahra, Senegal 78 B1
Dahra, Massif de, Algeria 75 A5
Dai Hao, Vietnam 58 C6
Dai-Sen, Japan 49 G6
Dai Shan, China 53 B14
Dai Xian, China 50 E7
Daicheng, China 50 E9
Daimiel, Spain 29 F1
Daingean, Ireland 15 C4
Dainkog, China 52 A1
Daintree, Australia 90 B4
Daiō-Misaki, Japan 49 G8
Dairût, Egypt 76 B3
Daisetsu-Zan, Japan 48 C11
Dajarra, Australia 90 C2
Dajia, Taiwan 53 E13
Dajin Chuan →, China 52 B3
Dak Dam, Cambodia 58 F6
Dak Nhe, Vietnam 58 E6
Dak Pek, Vietnam 58 E6
Dak Song, Vietnam 59 F6
Dak Sui, Vietnam 58 E6
Dakar, Senegal 78 C1
Dakhla, W. Sahara 74 D1
Dakhla, El Wâhât el-, Egypt 76 B2
Dakhovskaya, Russia 43 D9
Dakingari, Nigeria 79 C5
Dakor, India 62 H5
Dakoro, Niger 79 C6
Dakota City, U.S.A. 108 D6
Đakovica, Serbia 21 N10
Đakovo, Croatia 21 K8
Dalaba, Guinea 78 C2
Dalachi, China 50 F3
Dalai Nur, China 50 C9
Dālakī, Iran 65 D6
Dalälven, Sweden 9 F14
Dalaman, Turkey 66 E3
Dalaman →, Turkey 66 E3
Dalandzadgad, Mongolia 50 C3
Dalarö, Sweden 9 G15
Dālbandīn, Pakistan 60 E4
Dalbeattie, U.K. 14 G5
Dalbosjön, Sweden 11 F6
Dalby, Australia 91 D5
Dalby, Sweden 11 J7
Dalen, Neths. 16 C9
Dalen, Norway 10 E2
Dalfsen, Neths. 16 C8
Dalga, Egypt 76 B3
Dalgān, Iran 65 E8
Dalhart, U.S.A. 109 G3
Dalhousie, Canada 99 C6
Dalhousie, India 62 C6
Dali, Shaanxi, China 50 G5
Dali, Yunnan, China 52 E3
Dalian, China 51 E11
Daliang Shan, China 52 D4
Dalias, Spain 29 J2
Daling He →, China 51 D11
Dāliyat el Karmel, Israel 69 C4
Dalkeith, U.K. 14 F5
Dall I., U.S.A. 100 C2
Dallarnil, Australia 91 D5
Dallas, Oreg., U.S.A. 110 D2
Dallas, Tex., U.S.A. 109 J6
Dallol, Ethiopia 77 E5
Dalmacija = Dalmatia □, Croatia 21 M7
Dalmatia □, Croatia 21 M7
Dalmellington, U.K. 14 F4
Dalnegorsk, Russia 45 E14
Dalnerechensk, Russia 45 E14
Daloa, Ivory C. 78 D3
Dalou Shan, China 52 C6
Dalsjöfors, Sweden 11 G7
Dalskog, Sweden 11 F6
Daltenganj, India 63 G11
Dalton, Canada 98 C3
Dalton, Ga., U.S.A. 105 H3
Dalton, Mass., U.S.A. 107 D11
Dalton, Nebr., U.S.A. 108 E3
Dalton Iceberg Tongue, Antarctica 5 C9
Dalupiri I., Phil. 55 B4
Dalvík, Iceland 8 D4
Daly →, Australia 88 B5
Daly City, U.S.A. 112 H4
Daly L., Canada 101 B7
Daly Waters, Australia 90 B1

Dam Doi, Vietnam 59 H5
Dam Ha, Vietnam 58 B6
Daman, India 60 J8
Dămaneh, Iran 65 C6
Damanhûr, Egypt 76 H7
Damanzhuang, China 50 E9
Damar, Indonesia 57 F7
Damaraland, Namibia 84 C2
Damascus = Dimashq, Syria 69 B5
Damaturu, Nigeria 79 C7
Damāvand, Iran 65 C7
Damāvand, Qolleh-ye, Iran 65 C7
Damba, Angola 80 F3
Dame Marie, Haiti 117 C5
Dāmghān, Iran 65 B7
Dămienesti, Romania 38 C10
Damietta = Dumyât, Egypt 76 H7
Daming, China 50 F8
Damīr Qābū, Syria 64 B4
Dammam = Ad Dammām, Si. Arabia 65 E6
Dammarie, France 24 D8
Dammartin-en-Goële, France 25 C9
Dammastock, Switz. 23 C6
Damme, Germany 18 C4
Damodar →, India 63 H12
Damoh, India 63 H8
Damous, Algeria 75 A5
Dampier, Australia 88 D2
Dampier, Selat, Indonesia 57 E8
Dampier Arch., Australia 88 D2
Damrei, Chuor Phnum, Cambodia 59 G4
Damville, France 24 D8
Damvillers, France 25 C12
Dan-Gulbi, Nigeria 79 C6
Dana, Indonesia 57 F6
Dana, L., Canada 98 B4
Dana, Mt., U.S.A. 112 H7
Danakil Depression, Ethiopia 77 E5
Danao, Phil. 55 F6
Danbury, U.S.A. 107 E11
Danby L., U.S.A. 111 J6
Dand, Afghan. 62 D1
Dandaragan, Australia 89 F2
Dandeldhura, Nepal 63 E9
Dandeli, India 60 M9
Dandenong, Australia 91 F4
Dandong, China 51 D13
Danfeng, China 50 H6
Danforth, U.S.A. 99 C6
Dangan Liedao, China 53 F10
Danger Is. = Pukapuka, Cook Is. 93 J11
Danger Pt., S. Africa 84 E2
Dangla, Ethiopia 77 E4
Dangora, Nigeria 79 C6
Dangrek, Phnom, Thailand 58 E5
Dangriga, Belize 115 D7
Dangshan, China 50 G9
Dangtu, China 53 B12
Dangyang, China 53 B8
Daniel, U.S.A. 110 E8
Daniel's Harbour, Canada 99 B8
Danielskuil, S. Africa 84 D3
Danielson, U.S.A. 107 E13
Danilov, Russia 41 B12
Danilovka, Russia 41 F14
Daning, China 50 F6
Danissa, Kenya 82 B5
Danja, Nigeria 79 C6
Dankalwa, Nigeria 79 C7
Dankama, Nigeria 79 C6
Dankhar Gompa, India 60 C11
Dankov, Russia 41 E11
Danleng, China 52 B4
Danlí, Honduras 116 D2
Dannemora, Sweden 9 F14
Dannemora, U.S.A. 107 B11
Dannenberg, Germany 18 B7
Dannevirke, N.Z. 87 J6
Dannhauser, S. Africa 85 D5
Dansville, U.S.A. 106 D7
Dantan, India 63 J12
Dante, Somali Rep. 68 E5
Danvers, U.S.A. 107 D14
Danville, Ill., U.S.A. 104 E2
Danville, Ky., U.S.A. 104 G3
Danville, Va., U.S.A. 105 G6
Danyang, China 53 B12
Danzhai, China 52 D6
Danzig = Gdańsk, Poland 20 A8
Dao, Phil. 55 B6
Dão →, Portugal 30 E2
Dao Xian, China 53 E8
Daocheng, China 52 C3
Daora, W. Sahara 74 C2
Daoud = Aïn Beïda, Algeria 75 A6
Daoulas, France 24 D2
Dapitan, Phil. 55 G5
Dapong, Togo 79 C5
Daqing Shan, China 50 D6
Daqu Shan, China 53 B14
Dar es Salaam, Tanzania 82 D4
Dar Mazār, Iran 65 D8
Dar'ā, Syria 69 C5
Dar'ā □, Syria 69 C5
Dārāb, Iran 65 D7
Daraj, Libya 75 B7
Dārān, Iran 65 C6

Daravica, Serbia 21 N10
Daraw, Egypt 76 C3
Dārayyā, Syria 69 B5
Darazo, Nigeria 79 C7
Darband, Pakistan 62 B5
Darband, Kūh-e, Iran 65 D8
Darbhanga, India 63 F11
Darby, U.S.A. 110 C6
Dardanelle, Ark., U.S.A. 109 H8
Dardanelle, Calif., U.S.A. 112 G7
Dardanelles = Çanakkale Boğazı, Turkey 66 C2
Darende, Turkey 66 D7
Dārestān, Iran 65 D8
Darfo, Italy 32 C7
Dârfûr, Sudan 70 E6
Dargai, Pakistan 62 B4
Dargan Ata, Uzbekistan 44 E7
Dargaville, N.Z. 87 F4
Darhan Muminggan Lianheqi, China 50 D6
Dari, Sudan 77 F3
Darién, G. del, Colombia 120 B2
Darién, Serranía del, Colombia 120 B2
Dariganga, Mongolia 50 B7
Darjeeling = Darjiling, India 63 F13
Darjiling, India 63 F13
Dark Cove, Canada 99 C9
Darkan, Australia 89 F2
Darkhazīneh, Iran 65 D6
Darkot Pass, Pakistan 63 A5
Darling →, Australia 91 E3
Darling Downs, Australia 91 D5
Darling Ra., Australia 89 F2
Darlington, U.K. 12 C6
Darlington, S.C., U.S.A. 105 H6
Darlington, Wis., U.S.A. 108 D9
Darlot, L., Australia 89 E3
Darlowo, Poland 20 A6
Darmstadt, Germany 19 F4
Darnah, Libya 73 B9
Darnall, S. Africa 85 D5
Darnétal, France 24 C8
Darney, France 25 D13
Darnley, C., Antarctica 5 C6
Darnley B., Canada 96 B7
Daroca, Spain 28 D3
Darr, Australia 90 C3
Darr →, Australia 90 C3
Darrington, U.S.A. 110 B3
Darsser Ort, Germany 18 A8
Dart →, U.K. 13 G4
Dart, C., Antarctica 5 D14
Dartmoor, U.K. 13 G4
Dartmouth, Australia 90 C3
Dartmouth, Canada 99 D7
Dartmouth, U.K. 13 G4
Dartmouth, L., Australia 91 D4
Dartuch, C., Spain 36 B10
Darvaza, Turkmenistan 44 E6
Darvel, Teluk, Malaysia 57 D5
Darwha, India 60 J10
Darwin, Australia 88 B5
Darwin, U.S.A. 113 J9
Darwin, Mt., Chile 128 D3
Darwin River, Australia 88 B5
Daryoi Amu = Amudarya →, Uzbekistan 44 E6
Dās, U.A.E. 65 E7
Dashetai, China 50 D5
Dashkesan, Azerbaijan 43 F12
Dasht, Iran 65 B8
Dasht →, Pakistan 60 G2
Dasht-e Mārgow, Afghan. 60 D3
Dasht-i-Nawar, Afghan. 62 C3
Daska, Pakistan 62 C6
Dassa-Zoume, Benin 79 D5
Dasseneiland, S. Africa 84 E2
Datça, Turkey 66 E2
Datia, India 63 G8
Datian, China 53 E11
Datong, Anhui, China 53 B11
Datong, Shanxi, China 50 D7
Datu, Tanjung, Indonesia 56 D3
Datu Piang, Phil. 55 H6
Daugava →, Latvia 40 C4
Daugavpils, Latvia 40 D5
Daulpur, India 62 F7
Daun, Germany 19 E2
Dauphin, Canada 101 C8
Dauphin I., U.S.A. 105 K1
Dauphin L., Canada 101 C9
Dauphiné, France 27 C9
Daura, Borno, Nigeria 79 C7
Daura, Kaduna, Nigeria 79 C6
Dausa, India 62 F7
Davangere, India 60 M9
Davao, Phil. 55 H6
Davao, G. of, Phil. 55 H6
Dāvar Panāh, Iran 65 E9
Davenport, Calif., U.S.A. 112 H4
Davenport, Iowa, U.S.A. 108 E9
Davenport, Wash., U.S.A. 110 C4
Davenport Downs, Australia 90 C3
Davenport Ra., Australia 90 C1
David, Panama 116 E3
David City, U.S.A. 108 E6
David Gorodok, Belorussia 40 E5
Davidson, Canada 101 C7

Davis, U.S.A. 112 G5
Davis Dam, U.S.A. 113 K12
Davis Inlet, Canada 99 A7
Davis Mts., U.S.A. 109 K2
Davis Sea, Antarctica 5 C7
Davis Str., N. Amer. 97 B14
Davos, Switz. 23 C9
Davy L., Canada 101 B7
Dawa →, Ethiopia 77 G5
Dawaki, Bauchi, Nigeria 79 D6
Dawaki, Kano, Nigeria 79 C6
Dawes Ra., Australia 90 C5
Dawson, Canada 96 B6
Dawson, Ga., U.S.A. 105 K3
Dawson, N. Dak., U.S.A. 108 B5
Dawson, I., Chile 128 D2
Dawson Creek, Canada 100 B4
Dawson Inlet, Canada 101 A10
Dawson Ra., Australia 90 C4
Dawu, China 52 B3
Dax, France 26 E2
Daxian, China 52 B6
Daxin, China 52 F6
Daxindian, China 51 F11
Daxinggou, China 51 C15
Daxue Shan, Sichuan, China 52 B3
Daxue Shan, Yunnan, China 52 F3
Daye, China 53 B10
Dayi, China 52 B4
Daylesford, Australia 91 F3
Dayong, China 53 C8
Dayr az Zawr, Syria 64 C4
Daysland, Canada 100 C6
Dayton, Nev., U.S.A. 112 F7
Dayton, Ohio, U.S.A. 104 F3
Dayton, Pa., U.S.A. 106 F5
Dayton, Tenn., U.S.A. 105 H3
Dayton, Wash., U.S.A. 110 C4
Daytona Beach, U.S.A. 105 L5
Dayu, China 53 E10
Dayville, U.S.A. 110 D4
Dazhu, China 52 B6
Dazu, China 52 C5
De Aar, S. Africa 84 E3
De Bilt, Neths. 16 D6
De Funiak Springs, U.S.A. 105 K2
De Grey, Australia 88 D2
De Grey →, Australia 88 D2
De Kalb, U.S.A. 108 E10
De Koog, Neths. 16 B5
De Land, U.S.A. 105 L5
De Leon, U.S.A. 109 J5
De Panne, Belgium 17 F1
De Pere, U.S.A. 104 C1
De Queen, U.S.A. 109 H7
De Quincy, U.S.A. 109 K8
De Ridder, U.S.A. 109 K8
De Rijp, Neths. 16 C5
De Smet, U.S.A. 108 C6
De Soto, U.S.A. 108 F9
De Tour Village, U.S.A. 104 C4
De Witt, U.S.A. 109 H9
Dead Sea, Asia 69 D4
Deadwood, U.S.A. 108 C3
Deadwood L., Canada 100 B3
Deakin, Australia 89 F4
Deal, U.K. 13 F9
Deal I., Australia 90 F4
Dealesville, S. Africa 84 D4
Dean, Forest of, U.K. 13 F5
Deán Funes, Argentina 126 C3
Dearborn, U.S.A. 98 D3
Dease →, Canada 100 B3
Dease L., Canada 100 B2
Dease Lake, Canada 100 B2
Death Valley, U.S.A. 113 J10
Death Valley Junction, U.S.A. 113 J10
Death Valley National Monument, U.S.A. 113 J10
Deauville, France 24 C7
Deba Habe, Nigeria 79 C7
Debao, China 52 F6
Debar, Macedonia 39 H3
Debden, Canada 101 C7
Debdou, Morocco 75 B4
Dębica, Poland 20 E11
Dęblin, Poland 20 D11
Débo, L., Mali 78 B4
Debolt, Canada 100 B5
Deborah East, L., Australia 89 F2
Deborah West, L., Australia 89 F2
Debre Birhan, Ethiopia 77 F4
Debre Markos, Ethiopia 77 E4
Debre May, Ethiopia 77 E4
Debre Sina, Ethiopia 77 F4
Debre Tabor, Ethiopia 77 E4
Debre Zebit, Ethiopia 77 E4
Debrecen, Hungary 21 H11
Dečani, Serbia 21 N10
Decatur, Ala., U.S.A. 105 H2
Decatur, Ga., U.S.A. 105 J3
Decatur, Ill., U.S.A. 108 F10
Decatur, Ind., U.S.A. 104 E3
Decatur, Tex., U.S.A. 109 J6
Decazeville, France 26 D6
Deccan, India 60 M10
Deception L., Canada 101 B8

Dechang, China 52 D4
Děčín, Czech. 20 E4
Decize, France 25 F10
Deckerville, U.S.A. 106 C2
Decollatura, Italy 35 C9
Decorah, U.S.A. 108 D9
Dedéagach = Alexandroúpolis, Greece 39 J8
Dedegöl Dağları, Turkey 66 E4
Dedemsvaart, Neths. 16 C8
Dedham, U.S.A. 107 D13
Dedilovo, Russia 41 E10
Dédougou, Burkina Faso 78 C4
Dedza, Malawi 83 E3
Dee →, Clwyd, U.K. 12 D4
Dee →, Gramp., U.K. 14 D6
Deep B., Canada 100 A5
Deep Well, Australia 90 C1
Deepwater, Australia 91 D5
Deer →, Canada 101 B10
Deer Lake, Nfld., Canada 99 C8
Deer Lake, Ont., Canada 101 C10
Deer Lodge, U.S.A. 110 C7
Deer Park, U.S.A. 110 C5
Deer River, U.S.A. 108 B8
Deeral, Australia 90 B4
Deerdepoort, S. Africa 84 C4
Deerlijk, Belgium 17 G2
Deferiet, U.S.A. 107 B9
Defiance, U.S.A. 104 E3
Dêgê, China 52 B2
Degebe →, Portugal 31 G3
Degeh Bur, Ethiopia 68 F3
Degema, Nigeria 79 E6
Degersheim, Switz. 23 B8
Deggendorf, Germany 19 G8
Deh Bīd, Iran 65 D7
Deh-e Shīr, Iran 65 D7
Dehaj, Iran 65 D7
Dehdez, Iran 65 D6
Dehestān, Iran 65 D7
Dehgolān, Iran 64 C5
Dehi Titan, Afghan. 60 C3
Dehibat, Tunisia 75 B7
Dehlorān, Iran 64 C5
Dehnow-e Kūhestān, Iran 65 E8
Dehra Dun, India 62 D8
Dehri, India 63 G11
Dehua, China 53 E12
Dehui, China 51 B13
Deinze, Belgium 17 G3
Dej, Romania 38 B6
Dejiang, China 52 C7
Dekemhare, Eritrea 77 D4
Dekese, Zaïre 80 E4
Del Mar, U.S.A. 113 N9
Del Norte, U.S.A. 111 H10
Del Rio, U.S.A. 109 L4
Delai, Sudan 76 D4
Delano, U.S.A. 113 K7
Delareyville, S. Africa 84 D4
Delavan, U.S.A. 108 D10
Delaware, U.S.A. 104 E4
Delaware □, U.S.A. 104 F8
Delaware →, U.S.A. 104 F8
Delaware B., U.S.A. 103 C12
Delegate, Australia 91 F4
Delémont, Switz. 22 B4
Delft, Neths. 16 D4
Delfzijl, Neths. 16 B9
Delgado, C., Mozam. 83 E5
Delgerhet, Mongolia 50 B6
Delgo, Sudan 76 C3
Delhi, Canada 106 D4
Delhi, India 62 E7
Delhi, U.S.A. 107 D10
Delia, Canada 100 C6
Delice, Turkey 66 D6
Delice →, Turkey 66 D6
Delicias, Mexico 114 B3
Delījān, Iran 65 C6
Delitzsch, Germany 18 D8
Dell City, U.S.A. 111 L11
Dell Rapids, U.S.A. 108 D6
Delle, France 25 E14
Dellys, Algeria 75 A5
Delmar, U.S.A. 107 D11
Delmenhorst, Germany 18 B4
Delmiro Gouveia, Brazil 122 C4
Delnice, Croatia 33 C11
Delong, Ostrova, Russia 45 B15
Deloraine, Australia 90 G4
Deloraine, Canada 101 D8
Delphi, U.S.A. 104 E2
Delphos, U.S.A. 104 E3
Delportshoop, S. Africa 84 D3
Delray Beach, U.S.A. 105 M5
Delsbo, Sweden 10 C10
Delta, Colo., U.S.A. 111 G9
Delta, Utah, U.S.A. 110 G7
Delta □, Nigeria 79 D6
Delta Amacuro □, Venezuela 121 B5
Delungra, Australia 91 D5
Delvina, Albania 39 K3
Delvinákion, Greece 39 K3
Demanda, Sierra de la, Spain 28 C1
Demavand = Damāvand, Iran 65 C7
Demba, Zaïre 80 F4
Dembecha, Ethiopia 77 E4
Dembi, Ethiopia 77 F4
Dembia, Zaïre 82 B2
Dembidolo, Ethiopia 77 F3

Demer →, *Belgium* 17 G5
Demidov, *Russia* 40 D7
Deming, *N. Mex., U.S.A.* 111 K10
Deming, *Wash., U.S.A.* .. 112 B4
Demini →, *Brazil* 121 D5
Demirci, *Turkey* 66 D3
Demirköy, *Turkey* 66 C2
Demmin, *Germany* 18 B9
Demnate, *Morocco* 74 B3
Demonte, *Italy* 32 D4
Demopolis, *U.S.A.* 105 J2
Dempo, *Indonesia* 56 E2
Demyansk, *Russia* 40 C8
Den Burg, *Neths.* 16 B5
Den Chai, *Thailand* 58 D3
Den Dungen, *Neths.* 17 E6
Den Haag = 's-
 Gravenhage, *Neths.* .. 16 D4
Den Ham, *Neths.* 16 D8
Den Helder, *Neths.* 16 C5
Den Hulst, *Neths.* 16 C8
Den Oever, *Neths.* 16 C6
Denain, *France* 25 B10
Denair, *U.S.A.* 112 H6
Denau, *Uzbekistan* 44 F7
Denbigh, *U.K.* 12 D4
Dendang, *Indonesia* 56 E3
Dender →, *Belgium* 17 F4
Denderhoutem, *Belgium* .. 17 G4
Denderleeuw, *Belgium* .. 17 G4
Dendermonde, *Belgium* .. 17 F4
Deneba, *Ethiopia* 77 F4
Denekamp, *Neths.* 16 D10
Deng Xian, *China* 53 A9
Dengchuan, *China* 52 E3
Denge, *Nigeria* 79 C6
Dengfeng, *China* 50 G7
Dengi, *Nigeria* 79 D6
Dengkou, *China* 50 D5
Denham, *Australia* 89 E1
Denham Ra., *Australia* .. 90 C4
Denham Sd., *Australia* .. 89 E1
Denia, *Spain* 29 G5
Denial B., *Australia* 91 E1
Deniliquin, *Australia* .. 91 F3
Denison, *Iowa, U.S.A.* .. 108 D7
Denison, *Tex., U.S.A.* .. 109 J6
Denison Plains, *Australia* 88 C4
Denizli, *Turkey* 66 E3
Denizli □, *Turkey* 66 E3
Denman Glacier, *Antarctica* 5 C7
Denmark, *Australia* 89 F2
Denmark ■, *Europe* 11 J3
Denmark Str., *Atl. Oc.* ... 4 C6
Dennison, *U.S.A.* 106 F3
Denny, *U.K.* 14 E5
Denpasar, *Indonesia* 56 F5
Denton, *Mont., U.S.A.* .. 110 C9
Denton, *Tex., U.S.A.* .. 109 J6
D'Entrecasteaux, Pt.,
 Australia 89 F2
Dents du Midi, *Switz.* 22 D3
Denu, *Ghana* 79 D5
Denver, *U.S.A.* 108 F2
Denver City, *U.S.A.* 109 J3
Deoband, *India* 62 E7
Deoghar, *India* 63 G12
Deolali, *India* 60 K8
Deoli = Devli, *India* 62 G6
Deoria, *India* 63 F10
Deosai Mts., *Pakistan* .. 63 B6
Deping, *China* 51 F9
Deposit, *U.S.A.* 107 D9
Depot Springs, *Australia* 89 E3
Deputatskiy, *Russia* 45 C14
Dêqên, *China* 52 C2
Deqing, *China* 53 F8
Dera Ghazi Khan, *Pakistan* 62 D4
Dera Ismail Khan, *Pakistan* 62 D4
Derbent, *Russia* 43 E13
Derby, *Australia* 88 C3
Derby, *U.K.* 12 E6
Derby, *Conn., U.S.A.* .. 107 E11
Derby, *N.Y., U.S.A.* .. 106 D6
Derbyshire □, *U.K.* 12 E6
Dereli, *Turkey* 67 C8
Derg →, *U.K.* 15 B4
Derg, L., *Ireland* 15 D3
Dergachi, *Ukraine* 42 A7
Dergaon, *India* 61 F19
Derik, *Turkey* 67 E9
Derinkuyu, *Turkey* 66 D6
Dernieres, Isles, *U.S.A.* . 109 L9
Dêrong, *China* 52 C2
Derry = Londonderry,
 U.K. 15 B4
Derryveagh Mts., *Ireland* . 15 B3
Derudub, *Sudan* 76 D4
Derval, *France* 24 E5
Dervéni, *Greece* 39 L5
Derwent, *Canada* 101 C6
Derwent →, *Derby, U.K.* 12 E6
Derwent →, *N. Yorks.,
 U.K.* 12 D7
Derwent Water, *U.K.* 12 C4
Des Moines, *Iowa, U.S.A.* 108 E8
Des Moines, *N. Mex.,
 U.S.A.* 109 G3
Des Moines →, *U.S.A.* .. 108 E9
Desaguadero →, *Argentina* 126 C2
Desaguadero →, *Bolivia* . 124 D4
Descanso, Pta., *Mexico* .. 113 N9
Descartes, *France* 26 B4
Deschaillons, *Canada* .. 99 C5
Descharme →, *Canada* .. 101 B7
Deschutes →, *U.S.A.* .. 110 D3

Dese, *Ethiopia* 68 E2
Deseado, C., *Chile* 128 D2
Desenzano del Gardo, *Italy* 32 C7
Desert Center, *U.S.A.* .. 113 M11
Desert Hot Springs, *U.S.A.* 113 M10
Désirade, I., *Guadeloupe* 117 C7
Deskenatlata L., *Canada* 100 A6
Desna →, *Ukraine* 40 F7
Desnățui →, *Romania* .. 38 E6
Desolación, I., *Chile* .. 128 D2
Despeñaperros, Paso, *Spain* 29 G1
Despotovac, *Serbia, Yug.* 21 L11
Dessau, *Germany* 18 D8
Dessel, *Belgium* 17 F6
Dessye = Dese, *Ethiopia* 68 E2
D'Estrees B., *Australia* .. 91 F2
Desuri, *India* 62 G5
Desvres, *France* 25 B8
Det Udom, *Thailand* 58 E5
Dete, *Zimbabwe* 83 F2
Detinja →, *Serbia, Yug.* 21 M9
Detmold, *Germany* 18 D4
Detour, Pt., *U.S.A.* 104 C2
Detroit, *Mich., U.S.A.* .. 98 D3
Detroit, *Tex., U.S.A.* .. 109 J7
Detroit Lakes, *U.S.A.* .. 108 B7
Deurne, *Belgium* 17 F4
Deurne, *Neths.* 17 F7
Deutsche Bucht, *Germany* 18 A4
Deutschlandsberg, *Austria* 21 J5
Deux-Sèvres □, *France* .. 24 F6
Deva, *Romania* 38 D5
Devakottai, *India* 60 Q11
Devaprayag, *India* 63 D8
Dévaványa, *Hungary* .. 21 H10
Deveci Dağı, *Turkey* 42 F7
Deveci Dağları, *Turkey* .. 66 C6
Develi, *Turkey* 66 D6
Deventer, *Neths.* 16 D8
Deveron →, *U.K.* 14 D6
Devgadh Bariya, *India* .. 62 H5
Devils Den, *U.S.A.* 112 K7
Devils Lake, *U.S.A.* 108 A5
Devils Paw, *Canada* 100 B2
Devizes, *U.K.* 13 F6
Devli, *India* 62 G6
Devnya, *Bulgaria* 38 F10
Devolii →, *Albania* 39 J3
Devon, *Canada* 100 C6
Devon □, *U.K.* 13 G4
Devon I., *Canada* 4 B3
Devonport, *Australia* .. 90 G4
Devonport, *N.Z.* 87 G5
Devonport, *U.K.* 13 G3
Devrek, *Turkey* 66 C4
Devrekâni, *Turkey* 66 C5
Devrez →, *Turkey* 66 C6
Dewas, *India* 62 H7
Dewetsdorp, *S. Africa* .. 84 D4
Dewsbury, *U.K.* 12 D6
Dexing, *China* 53 C11
Dexter, *Mo., U.S.A.* .. 109 G9
Dexter, *N. Mex., U.S.A.* 109 J2
Dey-Dey, L., *Australia* .. 89 E5
Deyang, *China* 52 B5
Deyhūk, *Iran* 65 C8
Deyyer, *Iran* 65 E6
Dezadeash L., *Canada* .. 100 A1
Dezfūl, *Iran* 65 C6
Dezhneva, Mys, *Russia* .. 45 C19
Dezhou, *China* 50 F9
Dháfni, *Greece* 37 D7
Dhahaban, *Si. Arabia* .. 76 C4
Dhahiriya = Aẓ Ẓāhīrīyah,
 Jordan 69 D3
Dhahran = Aẓ Ẓahrān,
 Si. Arabia 65 E6
Dhaka, *Bangla.* 63 H14
Dhaka □, *Bangla.* 63 G14
Dhali, *Cyprus* 37 D12
Dhamar, *Yemen* 68 E3
Dhamási, *Greece* 39 K5
Dhampur, *India* 63 E8
Dhamtari, *India* 61 J12
Dhanbad, *India* 63 H12
Dhangarhi, *Nepal* 61 E12
Dhankuta, *Nepal* 63 F12
Dhar, *India* 62 H6
Dharampur, *India* 62 H6
Dharamsala = Dharmsala,
 India 62 C7
Dharmapuri, *India* 60 N11
Dharmsala, *India* 62 C7
Dharwad, *India* 60 M9
Dharwar, *India* 60 M9
Dhaulagiri, *Nepal* 63 E10
Dhebar, L., *India* 62 G6
Dheftera, *Cyprus* 37 D12
Dhenkanal, *India* 61 J14
Dhenoúsa, *Greece* 39 M8
Dherinia, *Cyprus* 37 D12
Dheskáti, *Greece* 39 K4
Dhespotikó, *Greece* 39 N7
Dhestina, *Greece* 39 L5
Dhiarrizos →, *Cyprus* .. 37 E11
Dhíbān, *Jordan* 69 D4
Dhíkti Óros, *Greece* 37 D7
Dhimitsána, *Greece* 39 M5
Dhírfis, *Greece* 39 L6
Dhodhekánisos, *Greece* .. 39 N10
Dholiana, *Greece* 39 K3
Dholka, *India* 62 H5
Dhoraji, *India* 62 J4
Dhoxáton, *Greece* 39 H7
Dhráhstis, Ákra, *Greece* .. 37 A3

Dhrangadhra, *India* 62 H4
Dhrápanon, Ákra, *Greece* 37 D6
Dhrol, *India* 62 H4
Dhubri, *India* 61 F16
Dhule, *India* 60 J9
Dhut →, *Somali Rep.* 68 E5
Di Linh, *Vietnam* 59 G7
Di Linh, Cao Nguyen,
 Vietnam 59 G7
Día, *Greece* 37 D7
Diablo, Mt., *U.S.A.* 112 H5
Diablo Range, *U.S.A.* .. 112 J5
Diafarabé, *Mali* 78 C4
Diamante, *Argentina* .. 126 C3
Diamante →, *Argentina* . 126 C2
Diamantina, *Brazil* 123 E3
Diamantina →, *Australia* 91 D2
Diamantino, *Brazil* 125 C6
Diamond Harbour, *India* 63 H13
Diamond Is., *Australia* .. 90 B5
Diamond Mts., *U.S.A.* .. 110 G6
Diamond Springs, *U.S.A.* 112 G6
Diamondville, *U.S.A.* .. 110 F8
Dianbai, *China* 53 G8
Diancheng, *China* 53 G8
Diano Marina, *Italy* 32 E5
Dianópolis, *Brazil* 123 D2
Dianra, *Ivory C.* 78 D3
Diapaga, *Burkina Faso* .. 79 C5
Diapangou, *Burkina Faso* 79 C5
Diariguila, *Guinea* 78 C2
Dībā, *Oman* 65 E8
Dibaya, *Zaïre* 80 F4
Dibaya-Lubue, *Zaïre* 80 E3
Dibbi, *Ethiopia* 68 G3
Dibete, *Botswana* 84 C4
Dibrugarh, *India* 61 F19
Dickinson, *U.S.A.* 108 B3
Dickson, *U.S.A.* 105 G2
Dickson City, *U.S.A.* .. 107 E9
Dicomano, *Italy* 33 E8
Didam, *Neths.* 16 E8
Didesa, W. →, *Ethiopia* . 77 F4
Didiéni, *Mali* 78 C3
Didsbury, *Canada* 100 C6
Didwana, *India* 62 F6
Die, *France* 27 D9
Diébougou, *Burkina Faso* 78 C4
Diefenbaker L., *Canada* . 101 C7
Diego Garcia, *Ind. Oc.* .. 3 E13
Diekirch, *Lux.* 17 J8
Diélette, *France* 24 C5
Diéma, *Mali* 78 C3
Diémbéring, *Senegal* 78 C1
Diemen, *Neths.* 16 D5
Dien Ban, *Vietnam* 58 E7
Dien Bien, *Vietnam* 58 B4
Dien Khanh, *Vietnam* .. 59 F7
Diepenbeek, *Belgium* .. 17 G6
Diepenheim, *Neths.* 16 D9
Diepenveen, *Neths.* 16 D8
Diepholz, *Germany* 18 C4
Diepoldsau, *Switz.* 23 B9
Dieppe, *France* 24 C8
Dieren, *Neths.* 16 D8
Dierks, *U.S.A.* 109 H7
Diessen, *Neths.* 17 F6
Diessenhofen, *Switz.* .. 23 A7
Diest, *Belgium* 17 G6
Dietikon, *Switz.* 23 B6
Dieulefit, *France* 27 D9
Dieuze, *France* 25 D13
Diever, *Neths.* 16 C8
Differdange, *Lux.* 17 J7
Dig, *India* 62 F7
Digba, *Zaïre* 82 B2
Digby, *Canada* 99 D6
Digges, *Canada* 101 B10
Digges Is., *Canada* 97 B12
Dighinala, *Bangla.* 61 H18
Dighton, *U.S.A.* 108 F4
Digne, *France* 27 D10
Digoin, *France* 26 B7
Digor, *Turkey* 67 C10
Digos, *Phil.* 55 H6
Digranes, *Iceland* 8 C6
Digul →, *Indonesia* 57 F9
Dihang →, *India* 61 F19
Dihōk, *Iraq* 64 B3
Dijlah, Nahr →, *Asia* .. 64 D5
Dijle →, *Belgium* 17 G5
Dijon, *France* 25 E12
Dikala, *Sudan* 77 G3
Dikili, *Turkey* 66 C2
Dikkil, *Djibouti* 77 E5
Dikomu di Kai, *Botswana* 84 C3
Diksmuide, *Belgium* 17 F1
Dikson, *Russia* 44 B9
Dikwa, *Nigeria* 79 C7
Dila, *Ethiopia* 77 F4
Dilbeek, *Belgium* 17 G4
Dili, *Indonesia* 57 F7
Dilijan, *Armenia* 43 F11
Dillenburg, *Germany* .. 18 E4
Dilley, *U.S.A.* 109 L5
Dilling, *Sudan* 77 E2
Dillingen, *Germany* 19 G6
Dillingham, *U.S.A.* 96 C4
Dillon, *Canada* 101 B7
Dillon, *Mont., U.S.A.* .. 110 D7
Dillon, *S.C., U.S.A.* .. 105 H6
Dillon →, *Canada* 101 B7

Dilsen, *Belgium* 17 F7
Dilston, *Australia* 90 G4
Dimas, *Mexico* 114 C3
Dimashq, *Syria* 69 B5
Dimashq □, *Syria* 69 B5
Dimbaza, *S. Africa* 85 E4
Dimbokro, *Ivory C.* 78 D4
Dimboola, *Australia* 91 F3
Dîmbovița →, *Romania* .. 38 E9
Dîmbovnic →, *Romania* .. 38 E8
Dimbulah, *Australia* 90 B4
Dimitrovgrad, *Bulgaria* . 39 G8
Dimitrovgrad, *Russia* .. 41 D16
Dimitrovgrad, *Serbia, Yug.* 21 M12
Dimitrovo = Pernik,
 Bulgaria 38 G6
Dimmitt, *U.S.A.* 109 H3
Dimo, *Sudan* 77 F2
Dimona, *Israel* 69 D4
Dimovo, *Bulgaria* 38 F5
Dinagat, *Phil.* 55 F6
Dinajpur, *Bangla.* 61 G16
Dinan, *France* 24 D4
Dinant, *Belgium* 17 H5
Dinapur, *India* 63 G11
Dinar, *Turkey* 66 D4
Dinara Planina, *Croatia* 33 E13
Dinard, *France* 24 D4
Dinaric Alps = Dinara
 Planina, *Croatia* 33 E13
Dinder, Nahr ed →, *Sudan* 77 E3
Dindigul, *India* 60 P11
Ding Xian, *China* 50 E8
Dingalan, *Phil.* 55 D4
Dingbian, *China* 50 F4
Dingelstädt, *Germany* .. 18 D6
Dinghai, *China* 53 B14
Dingle, *Ireland* 15 D1
Dingle B., *Ireland* 15 D1
Dingmans Ferry, *U.S.A.* 107 E10
Dingnan, *China* 53 E10
Dingo, *Australia* 90 C4
Dingolfing, *Germany* .. 19 G8
Dingtao, *China* 50 G8
Dinguiraye, *Guinea* 78 C2
Dingwall, *U.K.* 14 D4
Dingxi, *China* 50 G3
Dingxiang, *China* 50 E7
Dingyuan, *China* 53 A11
Dinh, Mui, *Vietnam* 59 G7
Dinh Lap, *Vietnam* 58 B6
Dinkel →, *Neths.* 16 D9
Dinokwe, *Botswana* 84 C4
Dinosaur National
 Monument, *U.S.A.* .. 110 F9
Dinslaken, *Germany* 17 E9
Dintel →, *Neths.* 17 E4
Dinteloord, *Neths.* 17 E4
Dinuba, *U.S.A.* 111 H4
Dinxperlo, *Neths.* 16 E9
Diósgyőr, *Hungary* 21 G10
Diourbel, *Senegal* 78 C1
Diplo, *Pakistan* 62 G3
Dipolog, *Phil.* 55 G5
Dipşa, *Romania* 38 C7
Dir, *Pakistan* 62 B7
Diré, *Mali* 78 B4
Dire Dawa, *Ethiopia* .. 68 F3
Diriamba, *Nic.* 116 D2
Dirico, *Angola* 81 H4
Dirk Hartog I., *Australia* 89 E1
Dirranbandi, *Australia* . 91 D4
Disa, *India* 62 G5
Disa, *Sudan* 77 E3
Disappointment, C.,
 U.S.A. 110 C1
Disappointment, L.,
 Australia 88 D3
Disaster B., *Australia* .. 91 F4
Discovery B., *Australia* . 91 F3
Disentis, *Switz.* 23 C7
Dishna, *Egypt* 76 B3
Disina, *Nigeria* 79 C6
Disko, *Greenland* 4 C5
Disko Bugt, *Greenland* .. 4 C5
Disna →, *Belorussia* 40 D6
Dison, *Belgium* 17 G7
Disteghil Sar, *Pakistan* .. 63 A6
Distrito Federal □, *Brazil* 123 E2
Distrito Federal □,
 Venezuela 120 A4
Disûq, *Egypt* 76 H7
Diu, *India* 62 J4
Dīvāndarreh, *Iran* 64 C5
Dives →, *France* 24 C6
Dives-sur-Mer, *France* .. 24 C6
Divichi, *Azerbaijan* 43 F13
Divide, *U.S.A.* 110 D7
Dividing Ra., *Australia* . 89 E2
Divinópolis, *Brazil* 123 F3
Divisões, Serra dos, *Brazil* 123 E1
Divnoye, *Russia* 43 D10
Divo, *Ivory C.* 78 D3
Divriği, *Turkey* 67 D8
Dīwāl Kol, *Afghan.* 62 B2
Dixie Mt., *U.S.A.* 112 F6
Dixon, *Calif., U.S.A.* .. 112 G5
Dixon, *Ill., U.S.A.* 108 E10
Dixon, *Mont., U.S.A.* .. 110 C6
Dixon, *N. Mex., U.S.A.* 111 H11
Dixon Entrance, *U.S.A.* 100 C2
Dixonville, *Canada* 100 B5

Diyarbakir □, *Turkey* .. 67 E9
Djado, *Niger* 73 D7
Djakarta = Jakarta,
 Indonesia 57 G12
Djamâa, *Algeria* 75 B6
Djamba, *Angola* 84 B1
Djambala, *Congo* 80 E2
Djanet, *Algeria* 75 D6
Djawa = Jawa, *Indonesia* 57 G14
Djebiniana, *Tunisia* 75 A7
Djelfa, *Algeria* 75 B5
Djema, *C.A.R.* 82 A2
Djendel, *Algeria* 75 A5
Djeneïene, *Tunisia* 75 B7
Djenné, *Mali* 78 C4
Djenoun, Garet el, *Algeria* 75 C6
Djerba, *Tunisia* 75 B7
Djerba, I. de, *Tunisia* .. 73 B7
Djerid, Chott, *Tunisia* .. 75 B6
Djibo, *Burkina Faso* 79 C4
Djibouti, *Djibouti* 68 E3
Djibouti ■, *Africa* 68 E3
Djolu, *Zaïre* 80 D4
Djougou, *Benin* 79 D5
Djoum, *Cameroon* 80 D2
Djourab, *Chad* 73 E8
Djugu, *Zaïre* 82 B3
Djúpivogur, *Iceland* 8 D6
Djursholm, *Sweden* 10 E12
Djursland, *Denmark* 11 H4
Dmitriev-Lgovskiy, *Russia* 40 E9
Dmitriya Lapteva, Proliv,
 Russia 45 B15
Dmitrov, *Russia* 41 C10
Dmitrovsk-Orlovskiy,
 Russia 40 E9
Dnepr →, *Ukraine* 42 C5
Dneprodzerzhinsk, *Ukraine* 42 B6
Dneprodzerzhinskoye
 Vdkhr., *Ukraine* 42 B6
Dnepropetrovsk, *Ukraine* . 42 B6
Dneprorudnoye, *Ukraine* . 42 C6
Dnestr →, *Europe* 42 C4
Dnestrovski = Belgorod,
 Russia 41 F10
Dnieper = Dnepr →,
 Ukraine 42 C5
Dniester = Dnestr →,
 Europe 42 C4
Dnipro = Dnepr →,
 Ukraine 42 C5
Dniprodzerzhynsk =
 Dneprodzerzhinsk,
 Ukraine 42 B6
Dnipropetrovsk =
 Dnepropetrovsk, *Ukraine* 42 B6
Dno, *Russia* 40 C6
Dnyapro = Dnepr →,
 Ukraine 42 C5
Doan Hung, *Vietnam* .. 58 B5
Doba, *Chad* 73 G8
Dobbiaco, *Italy* 33 B9
Dobbyn, *Australia* 90 B2
Döbeln, *Germany* 18 D9
Doberai, Jazirah, *Indonesia* 57 E8
Dobiegniew, *Poland* 20 C5
Doblas, *Argentina* 126 D3
Dobo, *Indonesia* 57 F8
Doboj, *Bos.-H.* 21 L8
Dobra, Dîmbovita,
 Romania 38 E8
Dobra, Hunedoara,
 Romania 38 D5
Dobreta-Turnu-Severin,
 Romania 38 E5
Dobrinishta, *Bulgaria* .. 39 H6
Dobrodzień, *Poland* 20 E8
Dobropole, *Ukraine* 42 B7
Dobruja, *Romania* 38 E11
Dobrush, *Belorussia* 40 E7
Dobtong, *Sudan* 77 F3
Doc, Mui, *Vietnam* 58 D6
Doce →, *Brazil* 123 E4
Doda, *India* 63 C6
Dodecanese =
 Dhodhekánisos, *Greece* . 39 N10
Dodewaard, *Neths.* 16 E7
Dodge Center, *U.S.A.* .. 108 C8
Dodge City, *U.S.A.* 109 G5
Dodge L., *Canada* 101 B7
Dodgeville, *U.S.A.* 108 D9
Dodo, *Sudan* 77 F2
Dodola, *Ethiopia* 77 F4
Dodoma, *Tanzania* 82 D4
Dodoma □, *Tanzania* .. 82 D4
Dodsland, *Canada* 101 C7
Dodson, *U.S.A.* 110 B9
Doesburg, *Neths.* 16 D8
Doetinchem, *Neths.* 16 E8
Dog Creek, *Canada* 100 C4
Dog L., *Man., Canada* .. 101 C9
Dog L., *Ont., Canada* .. 98 C2
Doğanşehir, *Turkey* 67 D8
Dogger Bank, *N. Sea* 6 E6
Dogi, *Afghan.* 60 C3
Dogliani, *Italy* 32 D4
Dogondoutchi, *Niger* .. 79 C5
Dogran, *Pakistan* 62 D5
Doğubayazıt, *Turkey* .. 67 D11
Doguéraoua, *Niger* 79 C6
Doha = Ad Dawhah, *Qatar* 65 E6
Dohazari, *Bangla.* 61 H18
Doi, *Indonesia* 57 D7
Doi Luang, *Thailand* .. 58 C3
Doi Saket, *Thailand* 58 C2

Doig →, Canada 100 B4
Dois Irmãos, Sa., Brazil . 122 C3
Dokka, Norway 9 F11
Dokka, Norway 10 D4
Dokkum, Neths. 16 B7
Dokkumer Ee →, Neths. . 16 B7
Dokri, Pakistan 62 F3
Dol-de-Bretagne, France . 24 D5
Doland, U.S.A. 108 C5
Dolbeau, Canada 99 C5
Dole, France 25 E12
Doleib, Wadi →, Sudan . 77 E3
Dolgellau, U.K. 12 E4
Dolgelley = Dolgellau,
  U.K. 12 E4
Dolginovo, Belorussia ... 40 D5
Dolianova, Italy 34 C2
Dolinskaya, Ukraine 42 B5
Dollart, Neths. 16 B10
Dolna Banya, Bulgaria .. 38 G6
Dolni Důbnik, Bulgaria . 38 F7
Dolo, Ethiopia 77 G5
Dolo, Italy 33 C9
Dolomites = Dolomiti,
  Italy 33 B8
Dolomiti, Italy 33 B8
Dolores, Argentina 126 D4
Dolores, Uruguay 126 C4
Dolores, U.S.A. 111 H9
Dolores →, U.S.A. 111 G9
Dolphin, C., Falk. Is. ... 128 D5
Dolphin and Union Str.,
  Canada 96 B8
Dom, Switz. 22 D5
Dom Joaquim, Brazil ... 123 E3
Dom Pedrito, Brazil ... 127 C5
Dom Pedro, Brazil 122 B3
Doma, Nigeria 79 D6
Domaniç, Turkey 66 D3
Domasi, Malawi 83 F4
Domat Ems, Switz. 23 C8
Domazlice, Czech. 20 F2
Dombarovskiy, Russia ... 44 D6
Dombås, Norway 9 E10
Dombasle-sur-Meurthe,
  France 25 D13
Dombes, France 27 B8
Dombóvár, Hungary 21 J8
Domburg, Neths. 17 E3
Domérat, France 26 B6
Domeyko, Chile 126 B1
Domeyko, Cordillera, Chile 126 A2
Domfront, France 24 D6
Dominador, Chile 126 A2
Dominica ■, W. Indies . 117 C7
Dominica Passage,
  W. Indies 117 C7
Dominican Rep. ■,
  W. Indies 117 C5
Dömitz, Germany 18 B7
Domme, France 26 D5
Dommel →, Neths. 17 E6
Domo, Ethiopia 68 F4
Domodóssola, Italy 32 B5
Dompaire, France 25 D13
Dompierre-sur-Besbre,
  France 26 B7
Dompim, Ghana 78 D4
Domrémy-la-Pucelle,
  France 25 D12
Domsjö, Sweden 10 A12
Domville, Mt., Australia . 91 D5
Domvraína, Greece 39 L5
Domžale, Slovenia 33 B11
Don →, Russia 43 C8
Don →, Gramp., U.K. .. 14 D6
Don →, S. Yorks., U.K. . 12 D7
Don, C., Australia 88 B5
Don Benito, Spain 31 G5
Don Duong, Vietnam ... 59 G7
Don Martín, Presa de,
  Mexico 114 B4
Dona Ana = Nhamaubé,
  Mozam. 83 F4
Donaghadee, U.K. 15 B6
Donald, Australia 91 F3
Donalda, Canada 100 C6
Donaldsonville, U.S.A. . 109 K9
Donalsonville, U.S.A. .. 105 K3
Donau →, Austria 21 G7
Donaueschingen, Germany 19 H4
Donauwörth, Germany .. 19 G6
Doncaster, U.K. 12 D6
Dondo, Angola 80 F2
Dondo, Mozam. 83 F3
Dondo, Teluk, Indonesia . 57 D6
Dondra Head, Sri Lanka . 60 S12
Donegal, Ireland 15 B3
Donegal □, Ireland 15 B4
Donegal B., Ireland 15 B3
Donets →, Russia 43 C9
Donetsk, Ukraine 42 C7
Dong Ba Thin, Vietnam . 59 F7
Dong Dang, Vietnam ... 58 B6
Dong Giam, Vietnam ... 58 C5
Dong Ha, Vietnam 58 D6
Dong Hene, Laos 58 D5
Dong Hoi, Vietnam 58 D6
Dong Jiang →, China .. 53 F10
Dong Khe, Vietnam 58 A6
Dong Ujimqin Qi, China . 50 B9
Dong Van, Vietnam 58 A5
Dong Xoai, Vietnam ... 59 G6
Donga, Nigeria 79 D7
Dong'an, China 53 D8
Dongara, Australia 89 E1

Dongbei, China 51 D13
Dongchuan, China 52 D4
Dongen, Neths. 17 E5
Donges, France 24 E4
Dongfang, China 58 C7
Dongfeng, China 51 C13
Donggala, Indonesia ... 57 E5
Donggan, China 52 F5
Donggou, China 51 E13
Dongguan, China 53 F9
Dongguang, China 50 F9
Donghai Dao, China ... 53 G8
Dongjingcheng, China .. 51 B15
Donglan, China 52 E6
Dongliu, China 53 B11
Dongmen, China 52 F6
Dongning, China 51 B16
Dongnyi, China 52 C3
Dongola, Sudan 76 D3
Dongou, Congo 80 D3
Dongping, China 50 G9
Dongshan, China 53 F11
Dongsheng, China 50 E6
Dongshi, Taiwan 53 E13
Dongtai, China 51 H11
Dongting Hu, China ... 53 C9
Dongxiang, China 53 C11
Dongxing, China 52 G7
Dongyang, China 53 C13
Dongzhi, China 53 B11
Donington, C., Australia . 91 E2
Doniphan, U.S.A. 109 G9
Donja Stubica, Croatia . 33 C13
Donji Dušnik, Serbia .. 21 M12
Donji Miholjac, Croatia . 21 K8
Donji Milanovac, Serbia . 21 L12
Donji Vakuf, Bos.-H. ... 21 L7
Dønna, Norway 8 C12
Donna, U.S.A. 109 M5
Donnaconna, Canada ... 99 C5
Donnelly's Crossing, N.Z. 87 F4
Donnybrook, Australia . 89 F2
Donnybrook, S. Africa . 85 D4
Donora, U.S.A. 106 F5
Donor's Hill, Australia .. 90 B3
Donostia = San Sebastián,
  Spain 28 B3
Donskoy, Russia 41 E11
Donsol, Phil. 55 E5
Donya Lendava, Slovenia . 33 B13
Donzère, France 27 D8
Donzère-Mondragon, Barr.
  de, France 27 D8
Donzy, France 25 E10
Doon →, U.K. 14 F4
Doorn, Neths. 16 D6
Dora, L., Australia 88 D3
Dora Báltea →, Italy ... 32 C5
Dora Riparia →, Italy .. 32 C4
Doran L., Canada 101 A7
Dorchester, U.K. 13 G5
Dorchester, C., Canada . 97 B12
Dordogne □, France ... 26 C4
Dordogne →, France ... 26 C3
Dordrecht, Neths. 16 E5
Dordrecht, S. Africa ... 84 E4
Dore →, France 26 C7
Dore, Mts., France 26 C6
Doré L., Canada 101 C7
Doré Lake, Canada 101 C7
Dorfen, Germany 19 G8
Dorgali, Italy 34 B2
Dori, Burkina Faso 79 C4
Doring →, S. Africa ... 84 E2
Doringbos, S. Africa ... 84 E2
Dorion, Canada 98 C5
Dormaa-Ahenkro, Ghana . 78 D4
Dormo, Ras, Eritrea ... 77 E5
Dormo, Slovenia 33 C10
Dornbirn, Austria 19 H5
Dornes, France 25 F10
Dornoch, U.K. 14 D4
Dornoch Firth, U.K. ... 14 D4
Dornogovĭ □, Mongolia . 50 B6
Doro, Mali 79 B4
Dorogobuzh, Russia ... 40 D8
Dorohoi, Romania 38 B9
Dörööö Nuur, Mongolia . 54 B4
Dorr, Iran 65 C6
Dorre I., Australia 89 E1
Dorrigo, Australia 91 E5
Dorris, U.S.A. 110 F3
Dorset, Canada 106 A6
Dorset, U.S.A. 106 E4
Dorset □, U.K. 13 G5
Dorsten, Germany 18 D2
Dortmund, Germany ... 18 D3
Dörtyol, Turkey 66 E7
Dorum, Germany 18 B4
Doruma, Zaïre 82 B2
Dorūneh, Iran 65 C8
Dos Bahías, C., Argentina 128 B3
Dos Hermanas, Spain .. 31 H5
Dos Palos, U.S.A. 112 J6
Dosso, Niger 79 C5
Dothan, U.S.A. 105 K3
Dottignies, Belgium ... 17 G2
Douai, France 25 B10
Douala, Cameroon 79 E6
Douarnenez, France ... 24 D2
Double Island Pt., Australia 91 D5
Doubrava →, Czech. 20 F5

Doubs □, France 25 E13
Doubs →, France 25 F12
Doubtful Sd., N.Z. 87 L1
Doubtless B., N.Z. 87 F4
Doudeville, France 24 C7
Doué-la-Fontaine, France . 24 E6
Douentza, Mali 78 C4
Douglas, S. Africa 84 D3
Douglas, U.K. 12 C3
Douglas, Alaska, U.S.A. . 100 B2
Douglas, Ariz., U.S.A. .. 111 L9
Douglas, Ga., U.S.A. ... 105 K4
Douglas, Wyo., U.S.A. .. 108 D2
Douglastown, Canada .. 99 C7
Douglasville, U.S.A. ... 105 J3
Douirat, Morocco 74 B4
Doukkala, Greece 39 L3
Doulevant-le-Château,
  France 25 D11
Doullens, France 25 B9
Doumé, Cameroon 80 D2
Douna, Mali 78 C4
Dounan, Taiwan 53 F13
Dounreay, U.K. 14 C5
Dour, Belgium 17 H3
Dourada, Serra, Brazil . 123 D2
Dourados, Brazil 127 A5
Dourados →, Brazil ... 127 A5
Dourdan, France 25 D9
Douro →, Europe 30 D2
Douvaine, France 27 B10
Douz, Tunisia 75 B6
Douze →, France 26 E3
Douzy, France 25 C11
Dove →, U.K. 12 E6
Dove Creek, U.S.A. ... 111 H9
Dover, Australia 90 G4
Dover, U.K. 13 F9
Dover, Del., U.S.A. 104 F8
Dover, N.H., U.S.A. ... 107 C14
Dover, N.J., U.S.A. 107 F10
Dover, Ohio, U.S.A. ... 106 F3
Dover, Pt., Australia ... 89 F4
Dover, Str. of, Europe .. 24 B8
Dover-Foxcroft, U.S.A. . 99 C6
Dover Plains, U.S.A. ... 107 E11
Dovey = Dyfi →, U.K. . 13 E4
Dovrefjell, Norway 10 B3
Dow Rūd, Iran 65 C6
Dowa, Malawi 83 E3
Dowagiac, U.S.A. 104 E2
Dowgha'i, Iran 65 B8
Dowlatābād, Iran 65 D8
Down □, U.K. 15 B6
Downey, Calif., U.S.A. . 113 M8
Downey, Idaho, U.S.A. . 110 E7
Downham Market, U.K. . 13 E8
Downieville, U.S.A. ... 112 F6
Downpatrick, U.K. 15 B6
Downpatrick Hd., Ireland 15 B2
Dowsārī, Iran 65 D8
Doyle, U.S.A. 112 E6
Doylestown, U.S.A. ... 107 F9
Draa, C., Morocco 74 C2
Draa, Oued →, Morocco 74 C2
Drac →, France 27 C9
Drachten, Neths. 16 B8
Drăgănești, Romania .. 38 E7
Drăgănești-Viaşca,
  Romania 38 E8
Dragaš, Serbia 21 N10
Drăgăsani, Romania ... 38 E7
Dragonera, I., Spain ... 36 B9
Draguignan, France ... 27 E10
Drain, U.S.A. 110 E2
Drake, Australia 91 D5
Drake, U.S.A. 108 B4
Drake Passage, S. Ocean . 5 B17
Drakensberg, S. Africa .. 85 E4
Dráma, Greece 39 H7
Drammen, Norway 10 E4
Drangajökull, Iceland .. 8 C2
Drangedal, Norway 10 E3
Dranov, Ostrov, Romania 38 E12
Drau = Drava →, Croatia 21 K8
Drava →, Croatia 21 K8
Draveil, France 25 D9
Dravograd, Slovenia ... 33 B12
Drawa →, Poland 20 C5
Drawno, Poland 20 B5
Drayton Valley, Canada . 100 C6
Dreibergen, Neths. 16 D6
Drenthe □, Neths. 16 C9
Drentsche Hoofdvaart,
  Neths. 16 C8
Drepanum, C., Cyprus . 37 E11
Dresden, Canada 106 D2
Dresden, Germany 18 D9
Dreux, France 24 D8
Driel, Neths. 16 E7
Driffield = Great Driffield,
  U.K. 12 C7
Driftwood, U.S.A. 106 E6
Driggs, U.S.A. 110 E8
Drin i zi →, Albania ... 39 H3
Drina →, Bos.-H. 21 L9
Drincea →, Romania .. 38 E5
Drini →, Albania 38 G3
Drinjača →, Bos.-H. ... 21 L9
Drissa = Verkhnedvinsk,
  Belorussia 40 D5
Drivstua, Norway 10 B3
Drniš, Croatia 33 E13
Drøbak, Norway 10 E4
Drogheda, Ireland 15 C5
Drogichin, Belorussia .. 40 E4

Drogobych, Ukraine 40 G3
Drohobych = Drogobych,
  Ukraine 40 G3
Droichead Nua, Ireland . 15 C5
Droitwich, U.K. 13 E5
Drôme □, France 27 D9
Drôme →, France 27 D8
Dromedary, C., Australia 91 F5
Dronero, Italy 32 D4
Dronfield, Australia ... 90 C3
Dronne →, France 26 C3
Dronning Maud Land,
  Denmark 11 G4
Dronrijp, Neths. 16 B7
Dropt →, France 26 D3
Drumbo, Canada 106 C4
Drumheller, Canada ... 100 C6
Drummond, U.S.A. ... 110 C7
Drummond I., U.S.A. .. 98 C4
Drummond Pt., Australia 91 E2
Drummond Ra., Australia 90 C4
Drummondville, Canada . 98 C5
Drumright, U.S.A. 109 H6
Drunen, Neths. 17 E6
Druskininkai, Lithuania . 40 D3
Drut →, Belorussia ... 40 E7
Druten, Neths. 16 E7
Druya, Latvia 40 D5
Druzhina, Russia 45 C15
Drvar, Bos.-H. 33 D13
Drvenik, Croatia 33 E13
Dry Tortugas, U.S.A. .. 116 B3
Dryanovo, Bulgaria ... 38 G8
Dryden, Canada 101 D10
Dryden, U.S.A. 109 K3
Drygalski I., Antarctica . 5 C7
Drysdale →, Australia . 88 B4
Drysdale I., Australia .. 90 A2
Dschang, Cameroon ... 79 D7
Du Bois, U.S.A. 106 E6
Du Quoin, U.S.A. 108 G10
Duanesburg, U.S.A. ... 107 D10
Duaringa, Australia ... 90 C4
Ďubã, Si. Arabia 64 E2
Dubai = Dubayy, U.A.E. 65 E7
Dubawnt →, Canada .. 101 A8
Dubawnt, L., Canada .. 101 A8
Dubayy, U.A.E. 65 E7
Dubbeldam, Neths. 16 E5
Dubbo, Australia 91 E4
Dubele, Zaïre 82 B2
Dübendorf, Switz. 23 B7
Dubica, Croatia 33 C13
Dublin, Ireland 15 C5
Dublin, Ga., U.S.A. ... 105 J4
Dublin, Tex., U.S.A. ... 109 J5
Dublin □, Ireland 15 C5
Dublin B., Ireland 15 C5
Dubna, Russia 41 C10
Dubna, Russia 41 D10
Dubno, Ukraine 40 F4
Dubois, U.S.A. 110 D7
Dubossary, Moldavia .. 42 C3
Dubossary Vdkhr.,
  Moldavia 42 C3
Dubovka, Russia 43 B11
Dubovskoye, Russia ... 43 C10
Dubrajpur, India 63 H12
Dubréka, Guinea 78 D2
Dubrovitsa, Ukraine ... 40 F5
Dubrovnik, Croatia ... 21 N8
Dubrovskoye, Russia .. 45 D12
Dubuque, U.S.A. 108 D9
Duchang, China 53 C11
Duchesne, U.S.A. 110 F8
Duchess, Australia 90 C2
Ducie I., Pac. Oc. 93 K15
Duck Cr. →, Australia . 88 D2
Duck Lake, Canada ... 101 C7
Duck Mountain Prov. Park,
  Canada 101 C8
Duckwall, Mt., U.S.A. . 112 H6
Düdelange, Lux. 17 K8
Duderstadt, Germany .. 18 D6
Dudhi, India 61 G13
Dudinka, Russia 45 C9
Dudley, U.K. 13 E5
Dueñas, Spain 30 D6
Dueré, Brazil 123 D2
Duero = Douro →,
  Europe 30 D2
Duffel, Belgium 17 F5
Dufftown, U.K. 14 D5
Dufourspitz, Switz. ... 22 E5
Dugi Otok, Croatia ... 33 E12
Dugo Selo, Croatia ... 33 C13
Duifken Pt., Australia .. 90 A3
Duisburg, Germany ... 18 D2
Duitama, Colombia ... 120 B3
Duiveland, Neths. 17 E4
Duiwelskloof, S. Africa . 85 C5
Dükdamīn, Iran 65 C8
Duke I., U.S.A. 100 C2
Dukelský Průsmyk,
  Slovak Rep. 20 F11
Dukhān, Qatar 65 E6
Dukhovshchina, Russia . 40 D8
Duki, Pakistan 60 D6
Duku, Bauchi, Nigeria . 79 C7
Duku, Sokoto, Nigeria . 79 C5
Dulag, Phil. 55 F6
Dulce →, Argentina ... 126 C3
Dulce, G., Costa Rica .. 116 E3
Dulf, Iraq 64 C5
Dŭlgopol, Bulgaria 38 F10
Dulit, Banjaran, Malaysia 56 D4
Duliu, China 50 E9
Dullewala, Pakistan ... 62 D4

Dülmen, Germany 18 D3
Dulovo, Bulgaria 38 F10
Dulq Maghār, Syria ... 64 B3
Dululu, Australia 90 C5
Duluth, U.S.A. 108 B8
Dum Dum, India 63 H13
Dum Duma, India 61 F19
Dum Hadjer, Chad 73 F8
Dūmā, Lebanon 69 A4
Dūmā, Syria 69 B5
Dumaguete, Phil. 55 G5
Dumai, Indonesia 56 D2
Dumaran, Phil. 55 F3
Dumas, Ark., U.S.A. .. 109 J9
Dumas, Tex., U.S.A. .. 109 H4
Dumbarton, U.K. 14 F4
Dumbleyung, Australia . 89 F2
Dumfries, U.K. 14 F5
Dumfries & Galloway □,
  U.K. 14 F5
Dumka, India 63 G12
Dümmersee, Germany .. 18 C4
Dumoine →, Canada .. 98 C4
Dumoine L., Canada .. 98 C4
Dumraon, India 63 G11
Dumyât, Egypt 76 H7
Dumyât, Masabb, Egypt . 76 H7
Dun Laoghaire, Ireland . 15 C5
Dun-le-Palestel, France . 26 B5
Dun-sur-Auron, France . 25 F9
Duna →, Hungary 21 K8
Dunaföldvár, Hungary . 21 J8
Dunaj →, Slovak Rep. . 21 H8
Dunajec →, Poland ... 20 E10
Dunajska Streda,
  Slovak Rep. 21 H7
Dunapatai, Hungary ... 21 J9
Dunărea →, Romania .. 38 D12
Dunaújváros, Hungary . 21 J8
Dunav →, Serbia 21 L11
Dunay, Russia 48 C6
Dunback, N.Z. 87 L3
Dunbar, Australia 90 B3
Dunbar, U.K. 14 E6
Dunblane, U.K. 14 E5
Duncan, Canada 100 D4
Duncan, Ariz., U.S.A. . 111 K9
Duncan, Okla., U.S.A. . 109 H6
Duncan, L., Canada ... 98 B4
Duncan L., Canada ... 100 A6
Duncan Town, Bahamas 116 B4
Duncannon, U.S.A. ... 106 F7
Dundalk, Canada 106 B4
Dundalk, Ireland 15 B5
Dundalk Bay, Ireland .. 15 C5
Dundas, Canada 98 D4
Dundas, L., Australia .. 89 F3
Dundas I., Canada 100 C2
Dundas Str., Australia . 88 B5
Dundee, S. Africa 85 D5
Dundee, U.K. 14 E6
Dundgovĭ □, Mongolia . 50 B4
Dundoo, Australia 91 D3
Dundrum, U.K. 15 B6
Dundrum B., U.K. 15 B6
Dundwara, India 63 F8
Dunedin, N.Z. 87 L3
Dunedin, U.S.A. 105 L4
Dunedin →, Canada .. 100 B4
Dunfermline, U.K. 14 E5
Dungannon, Canada .. 106 C3
Dungannon, U.K. 15 B5
Dungannon □, U.K. ... 15 B5
Dungarpur, India 62 H5
Dungarvan, Ireland ... 15 D4
Dungarvan Bay, Ireland . 15 D4
Dungeness, U.K. 13 G8
Dungo, L. do, Angola .. 84 B2
Dungog, Australia 91 E5
Dungu, Zaïre 82 B2
Dungunâb, Sudan 76 C4
Dungunâb, Khalij, Sudan 76 C4
Dunhua, China 51 C15
Dunhuang, China 54 B4
Dunières, France 27 C8
Dunk I., Australia 90 B4
Dunkeld, U.K. 14 E5
Dunkerque, France ... 25 A9
Dunkery Beacon, U.K. . 13 F4
Dunkirk = Dunkerque,
  France 25 A9
Dunkirk, U.S.A. 106 D5
Dunkuj, Sudan 77 E3
Dunkwa, Central, Ghana . 78 D4
Dunkwa, Central, Ghana . 79 D4
Dunlap, U.S.A. 108 E7
Dúnleary = Dun
  Laoghaire, Ireland ... 15 C5
Dunmanus B., Ireland .. 15 E2
Dunmara, Australia ... 90 B1
Dunmore, U.S.A. 107 E9
Dunmore Hd., Ireland . 15 D1
Dunmore Town, Bahamas 116 A4
Dunn, U.S.A. 105 H6
Dunnellon, U.S.A. 105 L4
Dunnet Hd., U.K. 14 C5
Dunning, U.S.A. 108 E4
Dunnville, Canada 106 D5
Dunolly, Australia 91 F3
Dunoon, U.K. 14 F4
Dunqul, Egypt 76 C3
Duns, U.K. 14 F6
Dunseith, U.S.A. 108 A4
Dunsmuir, U.S.A. 110 F2
Dunstable, U.K. 13 F7
Dunstan Mts., N.Z. ... 87 L2
Dunster, Canada 100 C5

Dunvegan L., Canada 101 A7
Duolun, China 50 C9
Duong Dong, Vietnam 59 G4
Dupree, U.S.A. 108 C4
Dupuyer, U.S.A. 110 B7
Duque de Caxias, Brazil . 123 F3
Duque de York, I., Chile . 128 D1
Durack →, Australia 88 C4
Durack Ra., Australia ... 88 C4
Durağan, Turkey 66 C6
Durance →, France 27 E8
Durand, U.S.A. 104 D4
Durango = Victoria de Durango, Mexico 114 C4
Durango, Spain 28 B2
Durango, U.S.A. 111 H10
Durango □, Mexico 114 C4
Duranillin, Australia 89 F2
Durant, U.S.A. 109 J6
Duratón →, Spain 30 D6
Durazno, Uruguay 126 C4
Durazzo = Durrësi, Albania 39 H2
Durban, France 26 F6
Durban, S. Africa 85 D5
Dúrcal, Spain 31 J7
Düren, Germany 18 E2
Durg, India 61 J12
Durgapur, India 63 H12
Durham, Canada 98 D3
Durham, U.K. 12 C6
Durham, Calif., U.S.A. .. 112 F5
Durham, N.C., U.S.A. ... 105 G6
Durham □, U.K. 12 C6
Durham Downs, Australia 91 D4
Durmitor, Montenegro ... 21 M9
Durness, U.K. 14 C4
Durrësi, Albania 39 H2
Durrie, Australia 90 D3
Dursunbey, Turkey 66 D3
Durtal, France 24 E6
Duru, Zaïre 82 B2
D'Urville, Tanjung, Indonesia 57 E9
D'Urville I., N.Z. 87 J4
Duryea, U.S.A. 107 E9
Dusa Mareb, Somali Rep. 68 F4
Dûsh, Egypt 76 C3
Dushak, Turkmenistan ... 44 F7
Dushan, China 52 E6
Dushanbe, Tajikistan ... 44 F7
Dusheti, Georgia 43 E11
Dusky Sd., N.Z. 87 L1
Dussejour, C., Australia . 88 B4
Düsseldorf, Germany 18 D2
Dussen, Neths. 16 E5
Dutch Harbor, U.S.A. ... 96 C3
Dutlwe, Botswana 84 C3
Dutsan Wai, Nigeria 79 C6
Dutton, Canada 106 D3
Dutton →, Australia 90 C3
Duved, Sweden 10 A6
Duvno, Bos.-H. 21 M7
Duyun, China 52 D6
Düzce, Turkey 66 C4
Duzdab = Zāhedān, Iran 65 D9
Dvina, Sev. →, Russia ... 44 C5
Dvinsk = Daugavpils, Latvia 40 D5
Dvor, Croatia 33 C13
Dwarka, India 62 H3
Dwellingup, Australia ... 89 F2
Dwight, Canada 106 A5
Dwight, U.S.A. 104 E1
Dyakovskoya, Russia 41 A12
Dyatkovo, Russia 40 E9
Dyatlovo, Belorussia ... 40 E4
Dyer, C., Canada 97 B13
Dyer Plateau, Antarctica . 5 D17
Dyersburg, U.S.A. 109 G10
Dyersville, U.S.A. 108 D9
Dyfed □, U.K. 13 E3
Dyfi →, U.K. 13 E4
Dyje →, Czech. 20 G6
Dyle →, Belgium 17 G5
Dynevor Downs, Australia 91 D3
Dynów, Poland 20 F12
Dysart, Canada 101 C8
Dzamin Üüd, Mongolia .. 50 C6
Dzerzhinsk, Belorussia .. 40 E5
Dzerzhinsk, Russia 41 C13
Dzhalinda, Russia 45 D13
Dzhambeyty, Kazakhstan 43 A15
Dzhambul, Kazakhstan .. 44 E8
Dzhankoi, Ukraine 42 D6
Dzhanybek, Kazakhstan . 43 B12
Dzhardzhan, Russia 45 C13
Dzhelinde, Russia 45 C12
Dzhetygara, Kazakhstan . 44 D7
Dzhezkazgan, Kazakhstan 44 E7
Dzhikimde, Russia 45 D13
Dzhizak, Uzbekistan 44 E7
Dzhugdzur, Khrebet, Russia 45 D14
Dzhvari, Georgia 43 E10
Działdowo, Poland 20 B10
Działoszyn, Poland 20 D8
Dzierżgoń, Poland 20 B9
Dzierzoniów, Poland 20 E6
Dzilam de Bravo, Mexico . 115 C7
Dzioua, Algeria 75 B6
Dzungaria = Junggar Pendi, China 54 B3
Dzungarian Gate = Alataw Shankou, China 54 B3
Dzuunmod, Mongolia ... 54 B5

E

Eabamet, L., Canada 98 B2
Eads, U.S.A. 108 F3
Eagle, U.S.A. 110 G10
Eagle →, Canada 99 B8
Eagle Butte, U.S.A. 108 C4
Eagle Grove, U.S.A. 108 D8
Eagle L., Calif., U.S.A. .. 110 F3
Eagle L., Maine, U.S.A. . 99 C6
Eagle Lake, U.S.A. 109 L6
Eagle Mountain, U.S.A. . 113 M11
Eagle Nest, U.S.A. 111 H11
Eagle Pass, U.S.A. 109 L4
Eagle Pk., U.S.A. 112 G7
Eagle Pt., Australia 88 C3
Eagle River, U.S.A. 108 C10
Ealing, U.K. 13 F7
Earaheedy, Australia ... 89 E3
Earl Grey, Canada 101 C8
Earle, U.S.A. 109 H9
Earlimart, U.S.A. 113 K7
Earn →, U.K. 14 E5
Earn, L., U.K. 14 E4
Earnslaw, Mt., N.Z. 87 L2
Earth, U.S.A. 109 H3
Easley, U.S.A. 105 H4
East Angus, Canada 99 C5
East Aurora, U.S.A. 106 D6
East B., U.S.A. 109 L10
East Bengal, Bangla. ... 61 G17
East Beskids = Východné Beskydy, Europe 20 F11
East Brady, U.S.A. 106 F5
East C., N.Z. 87 G7
East Chicago, U.S.A. ... 104 E2
East China Sea, Asia ... 54 C7
East Coulee, Canada ... 100 C6
East Falkland, Falk. Is. . 128 D5
East Grand Forks, U.S.A. 108 B6
East Greenwich, U.S.A. . 107 E13
East Hartford, U.S.A. ... 107 E12
East Helena, U.S.A. 110 C8
East Indies, Asia 57 E6
East Jordan, U.S.A. 104 C3
East Lansing, U.S.A. ... 104 D3
East Liverpool, U.S.A. .. 106 F4
East London, S. Africa .. 85 E4
East Main = Eastmain, Canada 98 B4
East Orange, U.S.A. 107 F10
East Pacific Ridge, Pac. Oc. 93 J17
East Pakistan = Bangladesh ■, Asia .. 61 H17
East Palestine, U.S.A. ... 106 F4
East Pine, Canada 100 B4
East Pt., Canada 99 C7
East Point, U.S.A. 105 J3
East Providence, U.S.A. . 107 E13
East Retford, U.K. 12 D7
East St. Louis, U.S.A. ... 108 F9
East Schelde → = Oosterschelde, Neths. . 17 E4
East Siberian Sea, Russia . 45 B17
East Stroudsburg, U.S.A. . 107 E9
East Sussex □, U.K. 13 G8
East Tawas, U.S.A. 104 C4
East Toorale, Australia .. 91 E4
East Walker →, U.S.A. .. 112 G7
Eastbourne, N.Z. 87 J5
Eastbourne, U.K. 13 G8
Eastend, Canada 101 D7
Easter Dal = Österdalälven →, Sweden 9 F12
Easter Islands = Pascua, I. de, Pac. Oc. 93 K17
Eastern □, Kenya 82 B4
Eastern □, Uganda 82 B3
Eastern Cr. →, Australia . 90 C3
Eastern Ghats, India ... 60 N11
Eastern Group = Lau Group, Fiji 87 C9
Eastern Group, Australia . 89 F3
Eastern Province □, S. Leone 78 D2
Easterville, Canada 101 C9
Easthampton, U.S.A. ... 107 D12
Eastland, U.S.A. 109 J5
Eastleigh, U.K. 13 G6
Eastmain, Canada 98 B4
Eastmain →, Canada ... 98 B4
Eastman, Canada 107 A12
Eastman, U.S.A. 105 J4
Easton, Md., U.S.A. 104 F7
Easton, Pa., U.S.A. 107 F9
Easton, Wash., U.S.A. .. 112 C5
Eastport, U.S.A. 99 D6
Eastsound, U.S.A. 112 B4
Eaton, U.S.A. 108 E2
Eatonia, Canada 101 C7
Eatonton, U.S.A. 105 J4
Eatontown, U.S.A. 107 F10
Eatonville, U.S.A. 112 D4
Eau Claire, Fr. Guiana .. 121 C7
Eauze, France 26 E4
Ebagoola, Australia 90 A3
Eban, Nigeria 79 D5
Ebbw Vale, U.K. 13 F4
Ebeggui, Algeria 75 C6
Ebeltoft, Denmark 9 H11
Ebensburg, U.S.A. 106 F6

Ebensee, Austria 21 H3
Eber Gölü, Turkey 66 D4
Eberbach, Germany 19 F4
Eberswalde, Germany .. 18 C9
Ebetsu, Japan 48 C10
Ebian, China 52 C4
Ebikon, Switz. 23 B6
Ebingen, Germany 19 G5
Ebnat-Kappel, Switz. ... 23 B8
Eboli, Italy 35 B8
Ebolowa, Cameroon 79 E7
Ebrach, Germany 19 F6
Ébrié, Lagune, Ivory C. . 78 D4
Ebro →, Spain 28 E5
Ebro, Pantano del, Spain . 30 B7
Ebstorf, Germany 18 B6
Ecaussines-d' Enghien, Belgium 17 G4
Eceabat, Turkey 66 C2
Ech Cheliff, Algeria 75 A5
Echallens, Switz. 22 C3
Echeng, China 53 B10
Echigo-Sammyaku, Japan 49 F9
Echizen-Misaki, Japan .. 49 G7
Echmiadzin, Armenia ... 43 F11
Echo Bay, N.W.T., Canada 96 B8
Echo Bay, Ont., Canada . 98 C3
Echoing →, Canada 101 B10
Echt, Neths. 17 F7
Echternach, Lux. 17 J8
Echuca, Australia 91 F3
Ecija, Spain 31 H5
Eckernförde, Germany .. 18 A5
Eclipse Is., Australia ... 88 B4
Écommoy, France 24 E7
Ecoporanga, Brazil 123 E3
Écos, France 25 C8
Écouché, France 24 D6
Ecuador ■, S. Amer. ... 120 D2
Écueillé, France 24 E8
Ed, Sweden 11 F5
Ed Dabbura, Sudan 76 D3
Ed Dâmer, Sudan 76 D3
Ed Debba, Sudan 76 D3
Ed-Déffa, Egypt 76 A2
Ed Deim, Sudan 77 E2
Ed Dueim, Sudan 77 E3
Edah, Australia 89 E2
Edam, Canada 101 C7
Edam, Neths. 16 C6
Eday, U.K. 14 B6
Edd, Eritrea 68 E3
Eddrachillis B., U.K. ... 14 C3
Eddystone, U.K. 13 G3
Eddystone Pt., Australia . 90 G4
Ede, Neths. 16 D7
Ede, Nigeria 79 D5
Édea, Cameroon 79 E7
Edegem, Belgium 17 F4
Edehon L., Canada 101 A9
Edekel, Adrar, Algeria .. 75 D6
Eden, Australia 91 F4
Eden, N.C., U.S.A. 105 G6
Eden, N.Y., U.S.A. 106 D6
Eden, Tex., U.S.A. 109 K5
Eden, Wyo., U.S.A. 110 E9
Eden →, U.K. 12 C4
Eden L., Canada 101 B8
Edenburg, S. Africa ... 84 D4
Edendale, S. Africa 85 D5
Edenderry, Ireland 15 C4
Edenton, U.S.A. 105 G7
Edenville, S. Africa 85 D4
Eder →, Germany 18 D5
Ederstausee, Germany . 18 D4
Edgar, U.S.A. 108 E5
Edgartown, U.S.A. 107 E14
Edge Hill, U.K. 13 E6
Edgefield, U.S.A. 105 J5
Edgeley, U.S.A. 108 B5
Edgemont, U.S.A. 108 D3
Edgeøya, Svalbard 4 B9
Edhessa, Greece 39 J5
Edievale, N.Z. 87 L2
Edina, Liberia 78 D2
Edina, U.S.A. 108 E8
Edinburg, U.S.A. 109 M5
Edinburgh, U.K. 14 F5
Edirne, Turkey 39 H9
Edirne □, Turkey 66 C2
Edison, U.S.A. 112 B4
Edithburgh, Australia .. 91 F2
Edjeleh, Algeria 75 C6
Edjudina, Australia 89 E3
Edmeston, U.S.A. 107 D9
Edmond, U.S.A. 109 H6
Edmonds, U.S.A. 112 C4
Edmonton, Australia ... 90 B4
Edmonton, Canada 100 C6
Edmund L., Canada ... 101 C10
Edmundston, Canada .. 99 C6
Edna, U.S.A. 109 L6
Edna Bay, U.S.A. 100 B2
Edo □, Nigeria 79 D6
Edolo, Italy 32 B7
Edremit, Turkey 66 D2
Edremit Körfezi, Turkey . 66 D2
Edsbyn, Sweden 10 C9
Edsele, Sweden 10 A10
Edson, Canada 100 C5
Eduardo Castex, Argentina 126 D3
Edward →, Australia ... 91 F3
Edward, L., Africa 82 C2
Edward I., Canada 98 C2
Edward River, Australia . 90 A3

Edward VII Land, Antarctica 5 E13
Edwards, U.S.A. 113 L9
Edwards Plateau, U.S.A. 109 K4
Edwardsville, U.S.A. ... 107 E9
Edzo, Canada 100 A5
Eefde, Neths. 16 D8
Eekloo, Belgium 17 F3
Eelde, Neths. 16 B9
Eem →, Neths. 16 D6
Eems →, Neths. 16 B9
Eems Kanaal, Neths. ... 16 C9
Eenrum, Neths. 16 B8
Eernegem, Belgium 17 F2
Eerste Valthermond, Neths. 16 C9
Eferi, Algeria 75 D6
Effingham, U.S.A. 104 F1
Effretikon, Switz. 23 B7
Eforie Sud, Romania ... 38 E11
Ega →, Spain 28 C3
Égadi, Ísole, Italy 34 E5
Eganville, Canada 98 C4
Egeland, U.S.A. 108 A5
Egenolf L., Canada 101 B9
Eger = Cheb, Czech. ... 20 E2
Eger, Hungary 21 H10
Eger →, Hungary 21 H10
Egersund, Norway 9 G9
Egg L., Canada 101 B7
Eggenburg, Austria 20 G5
Eggenfelden, Germany . 19 G8
Eggiwil, Switz. 22 C5
Éghezée, Belgium 17 G5
Égletons, France 26 C6
Eglisau, Switz. 23 A7
Egmond-aan-Zee, Neths. 16 C5
Egmont, C., N.Z. 87 H4
Egmont, Mt., N.Z. 87 H5
Eğridir, Turkey 66 E4
Eğridir Gölü, Turkey ... 66 E4
Egtved, Denmark 11 J3
Éguas →, Brazil 123 D3
Egume, Nigeria 79 D6
Éguzon, France 26 B5
Egvekinot, Russia 45 C19
Egypt ■, Africa 76 J7
Eha Amufu, Nigeria 79 D6
Ehime □, Japan 49 H6
Ehingen, Germany 19 G5
Ehrenberg, U.S.A. 113 M12
Ehrwald, Austria 19 H6
Eibar, Spain 28 B2
Eibergen, Neths. 16 D9
Eichstatt, Germany 19 G7
Eider →, Germany 18 A4
Eidsvold, Australia 91 D5
Eidsvoll, Norway 9 F11
Eifel, Germany 19 E2
Eiffel Flats, Zimbabwe .. 83 F3
Eigg, U.K. 14 E2
Eighty Mile Beach, Australia 88 C3
Eil, Somali Rep. 68 F4
Eil, L., U.K. 14 E3
Eildon, L., Australia ... 91 F4
Eileen L., Canada 101 A7
Eilenburg, Germany ... 18 D8
Ein el Luweiqa, Sudan . 77 E3
Einasleigh, Australia ... 90 B3
Einasleigh →, Australia . 90 B3
Einbeck, Germany 18 D5
Eindhoven, Neths. 17 F6
Einsiedeln, Switz. 23 B7
Eire = Ireland ■, Europe 15 D4
Eiríksjökull, Iceland ... 8 D3
Eirlandsche Gat, Neths. . 16 B5
Eirunepé, Brazil 124 B4
Eisden, Belgium 17 G7
Eisenach, Germany 18 E6
Eisenberg, Germany ... 18 E7
Eisenerz, Austria 21 H4
Eisenhüttenstadt, Germany 18 C10
Eisenstadt, Austria 21 H6
Eiserfeld, Germany 18 E3
Eisfeld, Germany 18 E6
Eisleben, Germany 18 D7
Eivissa = Ibiza, Spain .. 36 C7
Ejby, Denmark 11 J3
Eje, Sierra del, Spain ... 30 C4
Ejea de los Caballeros, Spain 28 C3
Ejutla, Mexico 115 D5
Ekalaka, U.S.A. 108 C2
Ekeren, Belgium 17 F4
Eket, Nigeria 79 E6
Eketahuna, N.Z. 87 J5
Ekhínos, Greece 39 H8
Ekibastuz, Kazakhstan . 44 D8
Ekimchan, Russia 45 D14
Ekoli, Zaïre 82 C1
Ekwan →, Canada 98 B3
Ekwan Pt., Canada 98 B3
El Aaiún, W. Sahara ... 74 C2
El Aargub, Mauritania .. 74 D1
El Abiodh-Sidi-Cheikh, Algeria 75 B5
El Aïoun, Morocco 75 B4
El 'Aiyat, Egypt 76 J7
El Alamein, Egypt 76 H6
El Alto, Peru 124 A1
El 'Aqaba, W. →, Egypt . 69 E2

El 'Arag, Egypt 76 B2
El Arahal, Spain 31 H5
El Arenal, Spain 36 B9
El Aricha, Algeria 75 B4
El Arīhā, Jordan 69 D4
El Arish, Australia 90 B4
El 'Arîsh, Egypt 69 D2
El 'Arîsh, W. →, Egypt . 69 D2
El Arrouch, Algeria 75 A6
El Asnam = Ech Cheliff, Algeria 75 A5
El Astillero, Spain 30 B7
El Badâri, Egypt 76 B3
El Bahrein, Egypt 76 B2
El Ballâs, Egypt 76 B3
El Balyana, Egypt 76 B3
El Banco, Colombia ... 120 B3
El Baqeir, Sudan 76 D3
El Barco de Ávila, Spain 30 E5
El Barco de Valdeorras, Spain 30 C4
El Bauga, Sudan 76 D3
El Baúl, Venezuela 120 B4
El Bawiti, Egypt 76 J6
El Bayadh, Algeria 75 B5
El Bierzo, Spain 30 C4
El Bluff, Nic. 116 D3
El Bolsón, Argentina ... 128 B2
El Bonillo, Spain 29 G2
El Brûk, W. →, Egypt .. 69 E2
El Buheirat □, Sudan .. 77 F2
El Caín, Argentina 128 B3
El Cajon, U.S.A. 113 N10
El Callao, Venezuela ... 121 B5
El Camp, Spain 28 D6
El Campo, U.S.A. 109 L6
El Carmen, Bolivia 125 C5
El Carmen, Venezuela .. 120 C4
El Castillo, Spain 31 H4
El Centro, U.S.A. 113 N11
El Cerro, Bolivia 125 D5
El Cerro, Spain 31 H4
El Cocuy, Colombia ... 120 B3
El Compadre, Mexico ... 113 N10
El Corcovado, Argentina 128 B2
El Coronil, Spain 31 H5
El Cuy, Argentina 128 A3
El Cuyo, Mexico 115 C7
El Dab'a, Egypt 76 H6
El Daheir, Egypt 69 D3
El Deir, Egypt 76 B3
El Dere, Somali Rep. ... 68 G4
El Descanso, Mexico ... 113 N10
El Desemboque, Mexico . 114 A2
El Dilingat, Egypt 76 H7
El Diviso, Colombia ... 120 C2
El Djem, Tunisia 75 A7
El Djouf, Mauritania ... 70 D3
El Dorado, Ark., U.S.A. . 109 J8
El Dorado, Kans., U.S.A. 109 G6
El Dorado, Venezuela .. 121 B5
El Eglab, Algeria 74 C4
El Escorial, Spain 30 E6
El Eulma, Algeria 75 A6
El Faiyûm, Egypt 76 J7
El Fâsher, Sudan 77 E2
El Fashn, Egypt 76 J7
El Ferrol, Spain 30 B2
El Fifi, Sudan 77 E1
El Fuerte, Mexico 114 B3
El Gal, Somali Rep. 68 E5
El Gebir, Sudan 77 E2
El Gedida, Egypt 76 B2
El Geteina, Sudan 77 E3
El Gezira □, Sudan 77 E3
El Gîza, Egypt 76 H7
El Goléa, Algeria 75 B5
El Guettar, Algeria 75 B6
El Hadeb, W. Sahara ... 74 C2
El Hadjira, Algeria 75 B6
El Hagiz, Sudan 77 D4
El Hajeb, Morocco 74 B3
El Hammam, Egypt 76 H6
El Hammâmi, Mauritania 74 D2
El Hank, Mauritania ... 74 D3
El Harrach, Algeria 75 A5
El Hasian, W. Sahara .. 74 C2
El Hawata, Sudan 77 E3
El Heiz, Egypt 76 B2
El 'Idisât, Egypt 76 B3
El Iskandarîya, Egypt .. 76 H6
El Jadida, Morocco 74 B3
El Jebelein, Sudan 77 E3
El Kab, Sudan 76 D3
El Kabrît, G., Egypt ... 69 F2
El Kala, Algeria 75 A6
El Kalâa, Morocco 74 B3
El Kamlin, Sudan 77 D3
El Kantara, Algeria 75 A6
El Kantara, Tunisia 75 B7
El Karaba, Sudan 76 D3
El Kef, Tunisia 75 A6
El Khandaq, Sudan 76 D3
El Khârga, Egypt 76 B3
El Khartûm, Sudan 77 D3
El Khartûm □, Sudan .. 77 D3
El Khartûm Bahrî, Sudan 77 D3
El Khroub, Algeria 75 A6
El Kseur, Algeria 75 A6
El Ksiba, Morocco 74 B3
El Kuntilla, Egypt 69 E3
El Laqâwa, Sudan 77 E2
El Laqeita, Egypt 76 B3
El Leiya, Sudan 77 D4
El Mafâza, Sudan 77 E3

El Mahalla el Kubra, Egypt 76 H7
El Maḥârîq, Egypt 76 B3
El Mahmûdîya, Egypt 76 H7
El Maitén, Argentina .. 128 B2
El Maiz, Algeria 75 C4
El-Maks el-Bahari, Egypt . 76 C3
El Manshâh, Egypt 76 B3
El Mansour, Algeria 75 C4
El Mansûra, Egypt 76 H7
El Mantico, Venezuela ... 121 B5
El Manzala, Egypt 76 H7
El Marâgha, Egypt 76 B3
El Masid, Sudan 77 D3
El Matariya, Egypt 76 H8
El Medano, Canary Is. ... 36 F3
El Meghaier, Algeria 75 B6
El Meraguen, Algeria 75 C4
El Metemma, Sudan 77 D3
El Miamo, Venezuela ... 121 B5
El Milagro, Argentina ... 126 C2
El Milia, Algeria 75 A6
El Minyâ, Egypt 76 J7
El Molar, Spain 28 E1
El Mreyye, Mauritania ... 78 B3
El Obeid, Sudan 77 E3
El Odaiya, Sudan 77 E2
El Oro, Mexico 115 D4
El Oro □, Ecuador 120 D2
El Oued, Algeria 75 B6
El Palmar, Bolivia 125 D5
El Palmar, Venezuela ... 121 B5
El Palmito, Presa, Mexico 114 B3
El Panadés, Spain 28 D6
El Pardo, Spain 30 E7
El Paso, U.S.A. 111 L10
El Paso Robles, U.S.A. .. 112 K6
El Pedernoso, Spain 29 F2
El Pedroso, Spain 31 H5
El Pobo de Dueñas, Spain 28 E3
El Portal, U.S.A. 111 H4
El Porvenir, Mexico 114 A3
El Prat de Llobregat, Spain 28 D7
El Progreso, Honduras ... 116 C2
El Provencío, Spain 29 F2
El Pueblito, Mexico 114 B3
El Pueblo, Canary Is. ... 36 F2
El Qâhira, Egypt 76 H7
El Qantara, Egypt 69 E1
El Qasr, Egypt 76 B2
El Quseima, Egypt 69 E3
El Qusîya, Egypt 76 B3
El Râshda, Egypt 76 B2
El Reno, U.S.A. 109 H6
El Ribero, Spain 30 C2
El Rîdisiya, Egypt 76 C3
El Rio, U.S.A. 113 L7
El Ronquillo, Spain 31 H4
El Roque, Pta., Canary Is. 36 F4
El Rosarito, Mexico 114 B4
El Rubio, Spain 31 H5
El Saff, Egypt 76 J7
El Saheira, W. →, Egypt . 69 E2
El Salto, Mexico 114 C3
El Salvador ■, Cent. Amer. 116 D2
El Sancejo, Spain 31 H5
El Sauce, Nic. 116 D2
El Shallal, Egypt 76 C3
El Simbillawein, Egypt ... 76 H7
El Sombrero, Venezuela . 120 B4
El Suweis, Egypt 76 J8
El Tamarâni, W. →, Egypt 69 E3
El Thamad, Egypt 69 F3
El Tigre, Venezuela ... 121 B5
El Tîh, Egypt 69 F2
El Tîna, Khalîg, Egypt ... 69 D1
El Tocuyo, Venezuela ... 120 B4
El Tofo, Chile 126 B1
El Tránsito, Chile 126 B1
El Tûr, Egypt 76 J8
El Turbio, Argentina ... 128 D2
El Uqsur, Egypt 76 B3
El Vado, Spain 28 D1
El Vallés, Spain 28 D7
El Venado, Mexico 114 C4
El Vigía, Venezuela ... 120 B3
El Wabeira, Egypt 69 F2
El Wak, Kenya 82 B5
El Waqf, Egypt 76 B3
El Wâsta, Egypt 76 J7
El Weguet, Ethiopia 77 F5
El Wuz, Sudan 77 D3
Elafónisos, Greece 39 N5
Elandsvlei, S. Africa 84 E2
Élassa, Greece 39 P9
Elassón, Greece 39 K5
Elat, Israel 69 F3
Elâzığ, Turkey 67 D8
Elâzığ □, Turkey 67 D8
Elba, Italy 32 F7
Elba, U.S.A. 105 K2
Elbasani, Albania 39 H3
Elbe →, Europe 18 B4
Elbe-Seiten Kanal,
  Germany 18 C6
Elbert, Mt., U.S.A. 111 G10
Elberta, U.S.A. 104 C2
Elberton, U.S.A. 105 H4
Elbeuf, France 24 C8
Elbing = Elbląg, Poland . 20 A9
Elbistan, Turkey 66 D7
Elbląg, Poland 20 A9
Elbow, Canada 101 C7
Elbrus, Asia 43 E10
Elburg, Neths. 16 D7

Elburz Mts. = Alborz,
  Reshteh-ye Kühhâ-ye,
  Iran 65 C7
Elche, Spain 29 G4
Elche de la Sierra, Spain . 29 G2
Elcho I., Australia 90 A2
Elda, Spain 29 G4
Eldon, Mo., U.S.A. 108 F8
Eldon, Wash., U.S.A. .. 112 C3
Eldora, U.S.A. 108 D8
Eldorado, Argentina ... 127 B5
Eldorado, Canada 101 B7
Eldorado, Mexico 114 C3
Eldorado, Ill., U.S.A. .. 104 G1
Eldorado, Tex., U.S.A. . 109 K4
Eldorado Springs, U.S.A. 109 G8
Eldoret, Kenya 82 B4
Eldred, U.S.A. 106 E6
Elea, C., Cyprus 37 D13
Electra, U.S.A. 109 H5
Elefantes →, Mozam. ... 85 C5
Elefantes, G., Chile 128 C2
Elektrogorsk, Russia ... 41 D11
Elektrostal, Russia ... 41 D11
Elele, Nigeria 79 D6
Elephant Butte Reservoir,
  U.S.A. 111 K10
Elephant I., Antarctica ... 5 C18
Elesbão Veloso, Brazil .. 122 C3
Eleşkirt, Turkey 67 D10
Eleuthera, Bahamas .. 116 A4
Elgepiggen, Norway 10 B5
Elgeyo-Marakwet □, Kenya 82 B4
Elgg, Switz. 23 B7
Elgin, N.B., Canada 99 C6
Elgin, Ont., Canada 107 B8
Elgin, U.K. 14 D5
Elgin, Ill., U.S.A. 104 D1
Elgin, N. Dak., U.S.A. .. 108 B4
Elgin, Nebr., U.S.A. 108 E5
Elgin, Nev., U.S.A. 111 H6
Elgin, Oreg., U.S.A. 110 D5
Elgin, Tex., U.S.A. 109 K6
Elgon, Mt., Africa 82 B3
Eliase, Indonesia 57 F8
Elida, U.S.A. 109 J3
Elikón, Greece 39 L5
Elim, S. Africa 84 E2
Elisabethville =
  Lubumbashi, Zaïre 83 E2
Eliseu Martins, Brazil .. 122 C3
Elista, Russia 43 C11
Elizabeth, Australia 91 E2
Elizabeth, U.S.A. 107 F10
Elizabeth City, U.S.A. .. 105 G7
Elizabethton, U.S.A. .. 105 G4
Elizabethtown, Ky., U.S.A. 104 G3
Elizabethtown, N.Y.,
  U.S.A. 107 B11
Elizabethtown, Pa., U.S.A. 107 F8
Elizondo, Spain 28 B3
Elk, Poland 20 B12
Elk City, U.S.A. 109 H5
Elk Creek, U.S.A. 112 F4
Elk Grove, U.S.A. 112 G5
Elk Island Nat. Park,
  Canada 100 C6
Elk Lake, Canada 98 C3
Elk Point, Canada 101 C6
Elk River, Idaho, U.S.A. 110 C5
Elk River, Minn., U.S.A. 108 C8
Elkedra, Australia 90 C2
Elkedra →, Australia 90 C2
Elkhart, Ind., U.S.A. .. 104 E3
Elkhart, Kans., U.S.A. .. 109 G4
Elkhorn, Canada 101 D8
Elkhorn →, U.S.A. 108 E6
Elkhotovo, Russia 43 E11
Elkhovo, Bulgaria 38 G9
Elkin, U.S.A. 105 G5
Elkins, U.S.A. 104 F6
Elko, Canada 100 D5
Elko, U.S.A. 110 F6
Ell, L., Australia 89 E4
Ellecom, Neths. 16 D8
Ellef Ringnes I., Canada . 4 B2
Ellen, Mt., U.S.A. 111 G8
Ellendale, Australia 88 C3
Ellendale, U.S.A. 108 B5
Ellensburg, U.S.A. 110 C3
Ellenville, U.S.A. 107 E10
Ellery, Mt., Australia .. 91 F4
Ellesmere, L., N.Z. 87 M4
Ellesmere I., Canada ... 4 B4
Ellesmere Port, U.K. ... 12 D5
Ellezelles, Belgium 17 G3
Ellice Is. = Tuvalu ■,
  Pac. Oc. 92 H9
Ellinwood, U.S.A. 108 F5
Elliot, Australia 90 B1
Elliot, S. Africa 85 E4
Elliot Lake, Canada 98 C3
Elliotdale = Xhora,
  S. Africa 85 E4
Ellis, U.S.A. 108 F5
Elliston, Australia 91 E1
Ellisville, U.S.A. 109 K10
Ellon, U.K. 14 D6
Ellore = Eluru, India ... 61 L12
Ells →, Canada 100 B6
Ellsworth, U.S.A. 108 F5
Ellsworth Land, Antarctica 5 D16
Ellsworth Mts., Antarctica 5 D16
Ellwangen, Germany ... 19 G6
Ellwood City, U.S.A. .. 106 F4
Elm, Switz. 23 C8

Elma, Canada 101 D9
Elma, U.S.A. 112 D3
Elmadağ, Turkey 66 D5
Elmalı, Turkey 66 E3
Elmhurst, U.S.A. 104 E2
Elmina, Ghana 79 D4
Elmira, Canada 106 C4
Elmira, U.S.A. 106 D8
Elmore, Australia 91 F3
Elmore, U.S.A. 101 C8
Elmshorn, Germany ... 18 B5
Elmvale, Canada 106 B5
Elne, France 26 F6
Elora, Canada 106 C4
Elorza, Venezuela 120 B4
Eloúnda, Greece 37 D7
Eloy, U.S.A. 111 K8
Éloyes, France 25 D13
Elrose, Canada 101 C7
Elsas, Canada 98 C3
Elsie, U.S.A. 112 E3
Elsinore = Helsingør,
  Denmark 11 H6
Elsinore, U.S.A. 111 G7
Elspe, Germany 18 D4
Elspeet, Neths. 16 D7
Elst, Neths. 16 E7
Elster →, Germany 18 D7
Elsterwerda, Germany ... 18 D9
Elten, Neths. 16 E8
Eltham, N.Z. 87 H5
Elton, Russia 43 B12
Eluanbi, Taiwan 53 G13
Eluru, India 61 L12
Elvas, Portugal 31 G3
Elven, France 24 E4
Elverum, Norway 10 D5
Elvire →, Australia 88 C4
Elvo →, Italy 32 C5
Elvran, Norway 10 A5
Elwood, Ind., U.S.A. .. 104 E3
Elwood, Nebr., U.S.A. . 108 E5
Elx = Elche, Spain 29 G4
Ely, U.K. 13 E8
Ely, Minn., U.S.A. 108 B9
Ely, Nev., U.S.A. 110 G6
Elyria, U.S.A. 106 E2
Elz →, Germany 19 G3
Emāmrūd, Iran 65 B7
Emba, Kazakhstan 44 E6
Emba →, Kazakhstan .. 44 E6
Embarcación, Argentina . 126 A3
Embarras Portage, Canada 101 B6
Embetsu, Japan 48 B10
Embira →, Brazil 124 B3
Embóna, Greece 37 C9
Embrach, Switz. 23 A7
Embrun, France 27 D10
Embu, Kenya 82 C4
Embu □, Kenya 82 C4
Emden, Germany 18 B3
Emerald, Australia 90 C4
Emerson, Canada 101 D9
Emery, U.S.A. 111 G8
Emet, Turkey 66 D3
Emi Koussi, Chad 73 E8
Emilia-Romagna □, Italy . 32 D7
Emilius, Mte., Italy 32 C4
Eminabad, Pakistan 62 C6
Emirdağ, Turkey 66 D4
Emlenton, U.S.A. 106 E5
Emlichheim, Germany ... 18 C2
Emme →, Switz. 22 B5
Emmeloord, Neths. 16 C7
Emmen, Neths. 16 C9
Emmendingen, Germany . 19 G3
Emmental, Switz. 22 C4
Emmer-Compascuum,
  Neths. 16 C10
Emmerich, Germany ... 18 D2
Emmet, Australia 90 C3
Emmetsburg, U.S.A. .. 108 D7
Emmett, U.S.A. 110 E5
Empalme, Mexico 114 B2
Empangeni, S. Africa .. 85 D5
Empedrado, Argentina . 126 B4
Emperor Seamount Chain,
  Pac. Oc. 92 D9
Empoli, Italy 32 E7
Emporia, Kans., U.S.A. . 108 F6
Emporia, Va., U.S.A. .. 105 G7
Emporium, U.S.A. 106 E6
Empress, Canada 101 C6
Emptinne, Belgium ... 17 H6
Empty Quarter = Rub' al
  Khali, Si. Arabia 68 D4
Ems →, Germany 18 B3
Emsdale, Canada 106 A5
Emsdetten, Germany ... 18 C3
Emu, China 51 C15
Emu Park, Australia 90 C5
'En 'Avrona, Israel 69 F3
En Nahud, Sudan 77 E2
Ena, Japan 49 G8
Enafors, Sweden 10 A6
Enambú, Colombia 120 C3
Enana, Namibia 84 B2
Enaratoli, Indonesia 57 E9
Enard B., U.K. 14 C3
Enare = Inarijärvi, Finland 8 B19
Encantadas, Serra, Brazil 127 C5
Encanto, C., Phil. 57 A6
Encarnación, Paraguay . 127 B4
Encarnación de Díaz,
  Mexico 114 C4

Enchi, Ghana 78 D4
Encinal, U.S.A. 109 L5
Encinitas, U.S.A. 113 M9
Encino, U.S.A. 111 J11
Encontrados, Venezuela . 120 B3
Encounter B., Australia .. 91 F2
Encruzilhada, Brazil ... 123 E3
Ende, Indonesia 57 F6
Endeavour, Canada 101 C8
Endeavour Str., Australia . 90 A3
Endelave, Denmark 11 J4
Enderbury I., Kiribati .. 92 H10
Enderby, Canada 100 C5
Enderby, Australia 88 D2
Enderby Land, Antarctica . 5 C5
Enderlin, U.S.A. 108 B6
Endicott, N.Y., U.S.A. .. 107 D8
Endicott, Wash., U.S.A. . 110 C5
Endyalgout I., Australia . 88 B5
Ene →, Peru 124 C3
Enewetak Atoll, Pac. Oc. 92 F8
Enez, Turkey 66 C2
Enfida, Tunisia 75 A7
Enfield, U.K. 13 F7
Engadin, Switz. 19 J6
Engaño, C., Dom. Rep. . 117 C6
Engaño, C., Phil. 57 A6
Engcobo, S. Africa 85 E4
Engelberg, Switz. 23 C6
Engels = Pokrovsk, Russia 41 F15
Engemann L., Canada .. 101 B7
Enger, Norway 10 D4
Enggano, Indonesia 56 F2
Enghien, Belgium 17 G4
Engil, Morocco 74 B4
Engkilili, Malaysia 56 D4
England, U.S.A. 109 H9
England □, U.K. 7 E5
Englee, Canada 99 B8
Englehart, Canada 98 C4
Engler L., Canada 101 B7
Englewood, Colo., U.S.A. 108 F2
Englewood, Kans., U.S.A. 109 G5
English →, Canada 101 C10
English Bazar = Ingraj
  Bazar, India 63 G13
English Channel, Europe . 13 G6
English River, Canada .. 98 C1
Enid, U.S.A. 109 G6
Enipévs →, Greece 39 K5
Enkhuizen, Neths. 16 C6
Enköping, Sweden 10 E11
Enle, China 52 E3
Enna, Italy 35 E7
Ennadai, Canada 101 A8
Ennadai L., Canada 101 A8
Ennedi, Chad 73 E9
Enngonia, Australia 91 D4
Ennis, Ireland 15 D3
Ennis, Mont., U.S.A. .. 110 D8
Ennis, Tex., U.S.A. 109 J6
Enniscorthy, Ireland ... 15 D5
Enniskillen, U.K. 15 B4
Ennistimon, Ireland 15 D2
Enns →, Austria 21 G4
Enontekiö, Finland 8 B17
Enping, China 53 F9
Enriquillo, L., Dom. Rep. 117 C5
Ens, Neths. 16 C7
Enschede, Neths. 16 D9
Ensenada, Argentina ... 126 C4
Ensenada, Mexico 114 A1
Enshi, China 52 B7
Ensiola, Pta., Spain 36 B9
Ensisheim, France 25 E14
Entebbe, Uganda 82 B3
Enter, Neths. 16 D9
Enterprise, Canada 100 A5
Enterprise, Oreg., U.S.A. 110 D5
Enterprise, Utah, U.S.A. . 111 H7
Entlebuch, Switz. 22 C6
Entre Ríos, Bolivia 126 A3
Entre Rios, Bahia, Brazil . 123 D4
Entre Rios, Pará, Brazil . 125 B7
Entre Ríos □, Argentina . 126 C4
Entrepeñas, Pantano de,
  Spain 28 E2
Enugu, Nigeria 79 D6
Enugu □, Nigeria 79 D6
Enugu Ezike, Nigeria .. 79 D6
Enumclaw, U.S.A. 112 C5
Envermeu, France 24 C8
Envigado, Colombia 120 B2
Envira, Brazil 124 B3
Enz →, Germany 19 F5
Enza →, Italy 32 D7
Eólie, Is., Italy 35 D7
Epanomí, Greece 39 J5
Epe, Neths. 16 D7
Epe, Nigeria 79 D5
Épernay, France 25 C10
Epernon, France 25 D8
Ephesus, Turkey 66 E2
Ephraim, U.S.A. 110 G8
Ephrata, U.S.A. 110 C4
Epila, Spain 28 D3
Épinac-les-Mines, France 25 F11
Épinal, France 25 D13
Epira, Guyana 121 B6
Episkopi, Cyprus 37 E11
Episkopi, Greece 37 D6
Episkopi Bay, Cyprus .. 37 E11
Epping, U.K. 13 F8

Equatorial Guinea ■,
  Africa 80 D1
Equeipa, Venezuela 121 B5
Er Rahad, Sudan 77 E3
Er Rif, Morocco 75 A4
Er Roseires, Sudan 77 E3
Erāwadī Myit =
  Irrawaddy →, Burma . 61 M19
Erba, Italy 32 C6
Erba, Sudan 76 D4
Erbaa, Turkey 66 C7
Erbil = Arbīl, Iraq 64 B5
Erçek Gölü, Turkey 67 D10
Ercha, Russia 45 C15
Erçiş, Turkey 67 D10
Erciyaş Dağı, Turkey ... 66 D6
Erdao Jiang →, China . 51 C14
Erdek, Turkey 66 C2
Erdemli, Turkey 66 E6
Erdene, Mongolia 50 B6
Erding, Germany 19 G7
Erdre →, France 24 E5
Erebato →, Venezuela . 121 B5
Erebus, Mt., Antarctica . 5 D11
Erechim, Brazil 127 B5
Ereğli, Konya, Turkey ... 66 E6
Ereğli, Zonguldak, Turkey 66 C4
Erei, Monti, Italy 35 E7
Erembodegem, Belgium . 17 G4
Erenhot, China 50 C7
Eresma →, Spain 30 D6
Erewadī Myitwanya, Burma 61 M19
Erfenisdam, S. Africa .. 84 D4
Erfoud, Morocco 74 B4
Erft →, Germany 18 D2
Erfurt, Germany 18 E7
Ergani, Turkey 67 D8
Ergeni Vozvyshennost,
  Russia 43 C11
Ērgli, Latvia 40 C4
Eria →, Spain 30 C5
Eriba, Sudan 77 D4
Eribol, L., U.K. 14 C4
Erica, Neths. 16 C9
Érice, Italy 34 D5
Erie, U.S.A. 106 D4
Erie, L., N. Amer. 106 D3
Erie Canal, U.S.A. 106 C6
Erieau, Canada 106 D3
Erigavo, Somali Rep. .. 68 E4
Erikoúsa, Greece 37 A3
Eriksdale, Canada 101 C9
Erikslund, Sweden 10 B9
Erímanthos, Greece 39 M4
Erimo-misaki, Japan .. 48 D11
Eriswil, Switz. 22 B5
Erithraí, Greece 39 L6
Eritrea ■, Africa 77 E4
Erjas →, Portugal 31 F3
Erlangen, Germany ... 19 F7
Erldunda, Australia 90 D1
Erlin, Taiwan 53 F13
Ermelo, Neths. 16 D7
Ermelo, S. Africa 85 D4
Ermenak, Turkey 66 E5
Ermióni, Greece 39 M6
Ermones, Greece 37 A3
Ermoúpolis = Síros, Greece 39 M7
Ernakulam = Cochin, India 60 Q10
Erne →, Ireland 15 B3
Erne, Lower L., U.K. .. 15 B4
Erne, Upper L., U.K. .. 15 B4
Ernée, France 24 D6
Ernest Giles Ra., Australia 89 E3
Ernstberg, Germany ... 19 E2
Erode, India 60 P10
Eromanga, Australia ... 91 D3
Erongo, Namibia 84 C2
Erp, Neths. 17 E7
Erquelinnes, Belgium .. 17 H4
Erquy, France 24 D4
Erquy, C. d', France .. 24 D4
Err, Piz d', Switz. 23 C9
Errabiddy, Australia 89 E2
Erramala Hills, India .. 60 M11
Errer →, Ethiopia 77 F5
Errigal, Ireland 15 A3
Erris Hd., Ireland 15 B1
Erseka, Albania 39 J3
Erskine, U.S.A. 108 B7
Erstein, France 25 D14
Erstfeld, Switz. 23 C7
Ertil, Russia 41 F12
Ertis = Irtysh →, Russia . 44 C7
Ertvelde, Belgium 17 F3
Eruh, Turkey 67 E10
Eruwa, Nigeria 79 D5
Ervy-le-Châtel, France . 25 D10
Erwin, U.S.A. 105 G4
Eryuan, China 52 D2
Erzgebirge, Germany ... 18 E9
Erzin, Russia 45 D10
Erzincan, Turkey 67 D8
Erzincan □, Turkey 67 D8
Erzurum, Turkey 67 D9
Erzurum □, Turkey 67 D9
Es Caló, Spain 36 C8
Es Caná, Spain 36 B8
Es Sahrâ' Esh Sharqîya,
  Egypt 76 B3
Es Sînâ', Egypt 76 J8
Es Sûkî, Sudan 77 E3
Esambo, Zaïre 82 C1
Esan-Misaki, Japan 48 D10
Esashi, Hokkaidō, Japan . 48 B11

Esashi, *Hokkaidō, Japan* . 48 D10
Esbjerg, *Denmark* 11 J2
Escada, *Brazil* 122 C4
Escalante, *U.S.A.* 111 H8
Escalante →, *U.S.A.* 111 H8
Escalón, *Mexico* 114 B4
Escalona, *Spain* 30 E6
Escambia →, *U.S.A.* 105 K2
Escanaba, *U.S.A.* 104 C2
Escaut →, *Belgium* 17 F3
Esch-sur-Alzette, *Lux.* ... 17 J7
Eschede, *Germany* 18 C6
Escholzmatt, *Switz.* 22 C5
Eschwege, *Germany* 18 D6
Eschweiler, *Germany* 18 E2
Escoma, *Bolivia* 124 D4
Escondido, *U.S.A.* 113 M9
Escuinapa, *Mexico* 114 C3
Escuintla, *Guatemala* ... 116 D1
Eséka, *Cameroon* 79 E7
Esens, *Germany* 18 B3
Esera →, *Spain* 28 C5
Eşfahān, *Iran* 65 C6
Esfīdeh, *Iran* 65 C8
Esgueva →, *Spain* 30 D6
Esh Sham = Dimashq, *Syria* 69 B5
Esh Shamâlîya □, *Sudan* . 76 D2
Eshan, *China* 52 E4
Eshowe, *S. Africa* 85 D5
Esiama, *Ghana* 78 E4
Esil = Ishim →, *Russia* .. 44 D8
Esino →, *Italy* 33 E10
Esk →, *Dumf. & Gall., U.K.* 14 G5
Esk →, *N. Yorks., U.K.* . 12 C7
Eskifjörður, *Iceland* 8 D7
Eskilstuna, *Sweden* 10 E10
Eskimalatya, *Turkey* 67 D8
Eskimo Pt., *Canada* 101 A10
Eskişehir, *Turkey* 66 D4
Eskişehir □, *Turkey* 66 D4
Esla →, *Spain* 30 D4
Esla, Pantano del, *Spain* . 30 D4
Eslāmābād-e Gharb, *Iran* . 64 C5
Eslöv, *Sweden* 11 J7
Eşme, *Turkey* 66 D3
Esmeralda, I., *Chile* 128 C1
Esmeraldas, *Ecuador* ... 120 C2
Esmeraldas □, *Ecuador* . 120 C2
Esmeraldas →, *Ecuador* . 120 C2
Esneux, *Belgium* 17 G7
Espada, Pta., *Colombia* . 120 A3
Espalion, *France* 26 D6
Espalmador, I., *Spain* ... 36 C7
Espardell, I. del, *Spain* .. 36 C7
Esparraguera, *Spain* 28 D6
Esparta, *Costa Rica* 116 E3
Espejo, *Spain* 31 H6
Esperança, *Brazil* 122 C4
Esperance, *Australia* 89 F3
Esperance B., *Australia* .. 89 F3
Esperantinópolis, *Brazil* . 122 B3
Esperanza, *Santa Cruz, Argentina* 128 D2
Esperanza, *Santa Fe, Argentina* 126 C3
Esperanza, *Phil.* 55 G6
Espéraza, *France* 26 F6
Espichel, C., *Portugal* ... 31 G1
Espiel, *Spain* 31 G5
Espigão, Serra do, *Brazil* . 127 B5
Espinal, *Colombia* 120 C3
Espinar, *Peru* 124 C3
Espinazo, Sierra del = Espinhaço, Serra do, *Brazil* 123 E3
Espinhaço, Serra do, *Brazil* 123 E3
Espinho, *Portugal* 30 D2
Espinilho, Serra do, *Brazil* 127 B5
Espino, *Venezuela* 120 B4
Espinosa de los Monteros, *Spain* 30 B7
Espírito Santo □, *Brazil* . 123 F3
Espíritu Santo, B. del, *Mexico* 115 D7
Espíritu Santo, I., *Mexico* 114 C2
Espita, *Mexico* 115 C7
Espiye, *Turkey* 67 C8
Esplanada, *Brazil* 123 D4
Espluga de Francolí, *Spain* 28 D6
Espuña, Sierra, *Spain* ... 29 H3
Espungabera, *Mozam.* ... 85 C5
Esquel, *Argentina* 128 E2
Esquina, *Argentina* 126 B4
Essaouira, *Morocco* 74 B3
Essebie, *Zaïre* 82 B3
Essen, *Belgium* 17 F4
Essen, *Germany* 18 D2
Essendon, Mt., *Australia* . 89 E3
Essequibo →, *Guyana* ... 121 B6
Essex, *Canada* 106 D2
Essex, *Calif., U.S.A.* 113 L11
Essex, *N.Y., U.S.A.* 107 B11
Essex □, *U.K.* 13 F8
Esslingen, *Germany* 19 G5
Essonne □, *France* 25 D9
Essvik, *Sweden* 10 B11
Estaca, Pta. del, *Spain* .: 30 B3
Estadilla, *Spain* 28 C5
Estados, I. de Los, *Argentina* 128 D4
Estagel, *France* 26 F6
Eştahbānāt, *Iran* 65 D7

Estallenchs, *Spain* 36 B9
Estância, *Brazil* 122 D4
Estancia, *U.S.A.* 111 J10
Estārm, *Iran* 65 D8
Estarreja, *Portugal* 30 E2
Estats, Pic d', *Spain* 28 C6
Estavayer-le-Lac, *Switz.* .. 22 C3
Estcourt, *S. Africa* 85 D4
Este, *Italy* 33 C8
Esteban, *Spain* 30 B4
Estelí, *Nic.* 116 D2
Estella, *Spain* 28 C2
Estelline, *S. Dak., U.S.A.* . 108 C6
Estelline, *Tex., U.S.A.* ... 109 H4
Estena →, *Spain* 31 F6
Estepa, *Spain* 31 H6
Estepona, *Spain* 31 J5
Esterhazy, *Canada* 101 C8
Esternay, *France* 25 D10
Esterri de Aneu, *Spain* .. 28 C6
Estevan, *Canada* 101 D8
Estevan Group, *Canada* . 100 C3
Estherville, *U.S.A.* 108 D7
Estissac, *France* 25 D10
Eston, *Canada* 101 C7
Estonia ■, *Europe* 40 B4
Estoril, *Portugal* 31 G1
Estouk, *Mali* 79 B5
Estrêla, Serra da, *Portugal* 30 E3
Estrella, *Spain* 29 G1
Estremoz, *Portugal* 31 G3
Esztergom, *Hungary* 21 H8
Et Tidra, *Mauritania* 78 B1
Étables-sur-Mer, *France* . 24 D4
Etadunna, *Australia* 91 D2
Etah, *India* 63 F8
Étain, *France* 25 C12
Etalle, *Belgium* 17 J7
Etamamu, *Canada* 99 B8
Étampes, *France* 25 D9
Étang-sur-Arroux, *France* . 27 B8
Etanga, *Namibia* 84 B1
Étaples, *France* 25 B8
Etawah, *India* 63 F8
Etawah →, *U.S.A.* 105 H3
Etawney L., *Canada* 101 B9
Ete, *Nigeria* 79 D6
Éthe, *Belgium* 17 J7
Ethel, *U.S.A.* 112 D4
Ethel, Oued el →, *Algeria* 74 C4
Ethel Creek, *Australia* .. 88 D3
Ethelbert, *Canada* 101 C8
Ethiopia ■, *Africa* 68 F3
Ethiopian Highlands, *Ethiopia* 70 E7
Etive, L., *U.K.* 14 E3
Etna, *Italy* 35 E8
Etoile, *Zaïre* 83 E2
Etolin I., *U.S.A.* 100 B2
Etosha Pan, *Namibia* ... 84 B2
Etowah, *U.S.A.* 105 H3
Étrépagny, *France* 25 C8
Étretat, *France* 24 C7
Ettelbruck, *Lux.* 17 J8
Etten, *Neths.* 17 E5
Ettlingen, *Germany* 19 G4
Ettrick Water →, *U.K.* .. 14 F6
Etuku, *Zaïre* 82 C2
Etzatlán, *Mexico* 114 C4
Eu, *France* 24 B8
Euboea = Évvoia, *Greece* 39 L7
Eucla Motel, *Australia* .. 89 F4
Euclid, *U.S.A.* 106 E3
Euclides da Cunha, *Brazil* 122 D4
Eucumbene, L., *Australia* . 91 F4
Eudora, *U.S.A.* 109 J9
Eufaula, *Ala., U.S.A.* ... 105 K3
Eufaula, *Okla., U.S.A.* .. 109 H7
Eufaula L., *U.S.A.* 109 H7
Eugene, *U.S.A.* 110 E2
Eugowra, *Australia* 91 E4
Eulo, *Australia* 91 D4
Eunice, *La., U.S.A.* 109 K8
Eunice, *N. Mex., U.S.A.* . 109 J3
Eupen, *Belgium* 17 G8
Euphrates = Furāt, Nahr al →, *Asia* 64 D5
Eure □, *France* 24 C8
Eure →, *France* 24 C8
Eure-et-Loir □, *France* .. 24 D8
Eureka, *Canada* 4 B3
Eureka, *Calif., U.S.A.* ... 110 F1
Eureka, *Kans., U.S.A.* .. 109 G6
Eureka, *Mont., U.S.A.* .. 110 B6
Eureka, *Nev., U.S.A.* ... 110 G5
Eureka, *S. Dak., U.S.A.* . 108 C5
Eureka, *Utah, U.S.A.* ... 110 G7
Eureka, Mt., *Australia* .. 89 E3
Euroa, *Australia* 91 F4
Europa, I., *Ind. Oc.* 81 J8
Europa, Picos de, *Spain* . 30 B6
Europa, Pta. de, *Gib.* ... 31 J5
Europa Pt. = Europa, Pta. de, *Gib.* 31 J5
Europe 6 F10
Europoort, *Neths.* 16 E4
Euskirchen, *Germany* ... 18 E2
Eustis, *U.S.A.* 105 L5
Eutin, *Germany* 18 A6
Eutsuk L., *Canada* 100 C3
Eva, *Brazil* 121 D6
Eva Downs, *Australia* ... 90 B1
Evale, *Angola* 84 B2
Evans, *U.S.A.* 108 E2

Evans Head, *Australia* ... 91 D5
Evans L., *Canada* 98 B4
Evans Mills, *U.S.A.* 107 B9
Evanston, *Ill., U.S.A.* ... 104 D2
Evanston, *Wyo., U.S.A.* . 110 F8
Evansville, *Ind., U.S.A.* .. 104 F2
Evansville, *Wis., U.S.A.* . 108 D10
Évaux-les-Bains, *France* . 26 B6
Evaz, *Iran* 65 E7
Eveleth, *U.S.A.* 108 B8
Evensk, *Russia* 45 C16
Evenstad, *Norway* 10 C5
Everard, L., *Australia* ... 91 E1
Everard Park, *Australia* . 89 E5
Everard Ras., *Australia* .. 89 E5
Evere, *Belgium* 17 G4
Everest, Mt., *Nepal* 63 E12
Everett, *Pa., U.S.A.* 106 F6
Everett, *Wash., U.S.A.* .. 112 C4
Evergem, *Belgium* 17 F3
Everglades, The, *U.S.A.* . 105 N5
Everglades City, *U.S.A.* . 105 N5
Everglades National Park, *U.S.A.* 105 N5
Evergreen, *U.S.A.* 105 K2
Everson, *U.S.A.* 110 B2
Evesham, *U.K.* 13 E6
Évian-les-Bains, *France* .. 27 B10
Evinayong, *Eq. Guin.* ... 80 D2
Évinos →, *Greece* 39 L4
Évisa, *France* 27 F12
Évora, *Portugal* 31 G3
Évora □, *Portugal* 31 G3
Évreux, *France* 24 C8
Évron, *France* 24 D6
Evrótas →, *Greece* 39 N5
Évvoia, *Greece* 39 L7
Évvoia □, *Greece* 39 L6
Ewe, L., *U.K.* 14 D3
Ewing, *U.S.A.* 108 D5
Ewo, *Congo* 80 E2
Exaltación, *Bolivia* 125 C4
Excelsior Springs, *U.S.A.* . 108 F7
Excideuil, *France* 26 C5
Exe →, *U.K.* 13 G4
Exeter, *Canada* 106 C3
Exeter, *U.K.* 13 G4
Exeter, *Calif., U.S.A.* ... 111 H4
Exeter, *N.H., U.S.A.* ... 107 D14
Exeter, *Nebr., U.S.A.* ... 108 E6
Exloo, *Neths.* 16 C9
Exmes, *France* 24 D7
Exmoor, *U.K.* 13 F4
Exmouth, *Australia* 88 D1
Exmouth, *U.K.* 13 G4
Exmouth G., *Australia* .. 88 D1
Expedition Ra., *Australia* . 90 C4
Extremadura □, *Spain* .. 31 F4
Exuma Sound, *Bahamas* . 116 B4
Eyasi, L., *Tanzania* 82 C4
Eyeberry L., *Canada* ... 101 A8
Eyemouth, *U.K.* 14 F6
Eygurande, *France* 26 C6
Eyjafjörður, *Iceland* 8 C4
Eymet, *France* 26 D4
Eymoutiers, *France* 26 C5
Eynesil, *Turkey* 67 C8
Eyrarbakki, *Iceland* 8 E3
Eyre, *Australia* 89 F4
Eyre (North), L., *Australia* 91 D2
Eyre (South), L., *Australia* 91 D2
Eyre Cr. →, *Australia* .. 91 D2
Eyre Mts., *N.Z.* 87 L2
Eyre Pen., *Australia* 91 E2
Eyvānkī, *Iran* 65 C6
Ez Zidab, *Sudan* 76 D3
Ezcaray, *Spain* 28 C2
Ezine, *Turkey* 66 D2
Ezmul, *Mauritania* 74 D1
Ezouza →, *Cyprus* 37 E11

F

Fabens, *U.S.A.* 111 L10
Fåborg, *Denmark* 11 J4
Fabriano, *Italy* 33 E9
Făcăeni, *Romania* 38 E10
Facatativá, *Colombia* ... 120 C3
Fachi, *Niger* 72 E7
Facture, *France* 26 D3
Fada, *Chad* 73 E9
Fada-n-Gourma, *Burkina Faso* 79 C5
Faddeyevskiy, Ostrov, *Russia* 45 B15
Fadghāmī, *Syria* 64 C4
Fadlab, *Sudan* 76 D3
Faenza, *Italy* 33 D8
Fafa, *Mali* 79 B5
Fafe, *Portugal* 30 D2
Fagam, *Nigeria* 79 C7
Făgăras, *Romania* 38 D7
Făgăras, Munţii, *Romania* 38 D7
Fågelsjö, *Sweden* 10 C8
Fagernes, *Norway* 9 F9
Fagersta, *Sweden* 9 F13
Făget, *Romania* 38 D5
Fagnano, L., *Argentina* . 128 D3
Fagnano Castello, *Italy* . 35 C9
Fagnières, *France* 25 D11
Fahlīān, *Iran* 65 D6

Fahraj, *Kermān, Iran* ... 65 D8
Fahraj, *Yazd, Iran* 65 D7
Faial, *Madeira* 36 D3
Faido, *Switz.* 23 D7
Fair Hd., *U.K.* 15 A5
Fair Oaks, *U.S.A.* 112 G5
Fairbank, *U.S.A.* 111 L8
Fairbanks, *U.S.A.* 96 B5
Fairbury, *U.S.A.* 108 E6
Fairfax, *U.S.A.* 109 G6
Fairfield, *Ala., U.S.A.* ... 105 J2
Fairfield, *Calif., U.S.A.* .. 112 G4
Fairfield, *Conn., U.S.A.* . 107 E11
Fairfield, *Idaho, U.S.A.* . 110 E6
Fairfield, *Ill., U.S.A.* ... 104 F1
Fairfield, *Iowa, U.S.A.* .. 108 E9
Fairfield, *Mont., U.S.A.* . 110 C8
Fairfield, *Tex., U.S.A.* .. 109 K7
Fairford, *Canada* 101 C9
Fairhope, *U.S.A.* 105 K2
Fairlie, *N.Z.* 87 L3
Fairmead, *U.S.A.* 112 H6
Fairmont, *Minn., U.S.A.* . 108 D7
Fairmont, *W. Va., U.S.A.* 104 F5
Fairmount, *U.S.A.* 113 L8
Fairplay, *U.S.A.* 111 G11
Fairport, *U.S.A.* 106 C7
Fairport Harbor, *U.S.A.* . 106 E3
Fairview, *Australia* 90 B3
Fairview, *Canada* 100 B5
Fairview, *Mont., U.S.A.* . 108 B2
Fairview, *Okla., U.S.A.* . 109 G5
Fairview, *Utah, U.S.A.* .. 110 G8
Fairweather, Mt., *U.S.A.* . 96 C6
Faisalabad, *Pakistan* ... 62 D5
Faith, *U.S.A.* 108 C3
Faizabad, *India* 63 F10
Fajardo, *Puerto Rico* ... 117 C6
Fakfak, *Indonesia* 57 E8
Fakobli, *Ivory C.* 78 D3
Fakse, *Denmark* 11 J6
Fakse B., *Denmark* 11 J6
Fakse Ladeplads, *Denmark* 11 J6
Faku, *China* 51 C12
Falaise, *France* 24 D6
Falaise, Mui, *Vietnam* .. 58 C5
Falam, *Burma* 61 H18
Falces, *Spain* 28 C3
Fălciu, *Romania* 38 C11
Falcón □, *Venezuela* ... 120 A4
Falcón, C., *Spain* 36 C7
Falcon, C., *Algeria* 75 A4
Falcon Dam, *U.S.A.* ... 109 M5
Falconara Marittima, *Italy* 33 E10
Falconer, *U.S.A.* 106 D5
Faléa, *Mali* 78 C2
Falenki, *Russia* 41 B17
Faleshty, *Moldova* 42 C2
Falfurrias, *U.S.A.* 109 M5
Falher, *Canada* 100 B5
Falirakí, *Greece* 37 C10
Falkenberg, *Germany* .. 18 D9
Falkenberg, *Sweden* ... 11 H6
Falkensee, *Germany* ... 18 C9
Falkenstein, *Germany* .. 18 E8
Falkirk, *U.K.* 14 F5
Falkland, East, I., *Falk. Is.* 128 D5
Falkland, West, I., *Falk. Is.* 128 D4
Falkland Is. ■, *Atl. Oc.* .. 128 D5
Falkland Is. Dependency □, *Atl. Oc.* 5 B1
Falkland Sd., *Falk. Is.* ... 128 D5
Falköping, *Sweden* 11 F7
Fall River, *U.S.A.* 107 E13
Fall River Mills, *U.S.A.* . 110 F3
Fallbrook, *U.S.A.* 111 K5
Fallbrook, *Calif., U.S.A.* . 113 M9
Fallon, *Mont., U.S.A.* .. 108 B2
Fallon, *Nev., U.S.A.* ... 110 G4
Falls City, *Nebr., U.S.A.* . 108 E7
Falls City, *Oreg., U.S.A.* . 110 D2
Falls Creek, *U.S.A.* 106 E6
Falmouth, *Jamaica* 116 C4
Falmouth, *U.K.* 13 G2
Falmouth, *U.S.A.* 104 F3
False B., *S. Africa* 84 E2
Falset, *Spain* 28 D5
Falso, C., *Honduras* ... 116 C3
Falster, *Denmark* 11 K5
Falsterbo, *Sweden* 11 J6
Fălticeni, *Romania* 38 B9
Falun, *Sweden* 9 F13
Famagusta, *Cyprus* 37 D12
Famagusta Bay, *Cyprus* . 37 D13
Famatina, Sierra de, *Argentina* 126 B2
Family L., *Canada* 101 C9
Famoso, *U.S.A.* 113 K7
Fan Xian, *China* 50 G8
Fana, *Mali* 78 C3
Fandriana, *Madag.* 85 C8
Fang, *Thailand* 58 C2
Fang Xian, *China* 53 A8
Fangcheng, *China* 53 B12
Fangcheng, *Guangxi Zhuangzu, China* 52 G7
Fangcheng, *Henan, China* 50 H7
Fangliao, *Taiwan* 53 F13
Fangshan, *China* 50 E6
Fangzi, *China* 51 F10
Fani i Madh →, *Albania* . 39 H3
Fanjiatun, *China* 51 C13
Fannich, L., *U.K.* 14 D4
Fannūj, *Iran* 65 E8

Fanny Bay, *Canada* 100 D4
Fanø, *Denmark* 11 J2
Fano, *Italy* 33 E10
Fanshaw, *U.S.A.* 100 B2
Fanshi, *China* 50 E7
Fao = Al Fāw, *Iraq* 65 D6
Faqirwali, *Pakistan* 62 E5
Fara in Sabina, *Italy* ... 33 F9
Faradje, *Zaïre* 82 B2
Farafangana, *Madag.* ... 85 C8
Farāfra, El Wâhât el-, *Egypt* 76 B2
Farāh, *Afghan.* 60 C3
Farāh □, *Afghan.* 60 C3
Farahalana, *Madag.* 85 A9
Faraid, Gebel, *Egypt* ... 76 C4
Faramana, *Burkina Faso* . 78 C4
Faranah, *Guinea* 78 C2
Farasān, Jazā'ir, *Si. Arabia* 68 D3
Farasan Is. = Farasān, Jazā'ir, *Si. Arabia* ... 68 D3
Faratsiho, *Madag.* 85 B8
Fardes →, *Spain* 29 H1
Fareham, *U.K.* 13 G6
Farewell, C., *N.Z.* 87 J4
Farewell C. = Farvel, Kap, *Greenland* 4 D5
Farghona = Fergana, *Uzbekistan* 44 E8
Fargo, *U.S.A.* 108 B6
Fari'a →, *Jordan* 69 C4
Faribault, *U.S.A.* 108 C8
Faridkot, *India* 62 D6
Faridpur, *Bangla.* 63 H13
Färila, *Sweden* 10 C9
Farim, *Guinea-Biss.* 78 C1
Farīmān, *Iran* 65 C8
Farina, *Australia* 91 E2
Farinha →, *Brazil* 122 C2
Fariones, Pta., *Canary Is.* 36 E6
Fâriskûr, *Egypt* 76 H7
Farmerville, *U.S.A.* 109 J8
Farmington, *Calif., U.S.A.* 112 H6
Farmington, *N.H., U.S.A.* 107 C13
Farmington, *N. Mex., U.S.A.* 111 H9
Farmington, *Utah, U.S.A.* 110 F8
Farmington →, *U.S.A.* . 107 E12
Farmville, *U.S.A.* 104 G6
Farnborough, *U.K.* 13 F7
Farne Is., *U.K.* 12 B6
Farnham, *Canada* 107 A12
Faro, *Brazil* 121 D6
Faro, *Portugal* 31 H3
Fårö, *Sweden* 9 H15
Faro □, *Portugal* 31 H2
Faroe Is. = Føroyar, *Atl. Oc.* 7 C4
Farquhar, C., *Australia* . 89 D1
Farrars Cr. →, *Australia* . 90 D3
Farrāshband, *Iran* 65 D7
Farrell, *U.S.A.* 106 E4
Farrell Flat, *Australia* .. 91 E2
Farrokhī, *Iran* 65 C8
Farruch, C., *Spain* 36 B10
Farrukhabad-cum-Fatehgarh, *India* 63 F8
Fārs □, *Iran* 65 D7
Fársala, *Greece* 39 K5
Farsø, *Denmark* 11 H3
Farsund, *Norway* 9 G9
Fartak, Râs, *Si. Arabia* .. 64 D2
Fartura, Serra da, *Brazil* . 127 B5
Farū, *Nigeria* 79 C6
Fārūj, *Iran* 65 B8
Farum, *Denmark* 11 J6
Farvel, Kap, *Greenland* . 4 D5
Farwell, *U.S.A.* 109 H3
Fasā, *Iran* 65 D7
Fasano, *Italy* 35 B10
Fashoda, *Sudan* 77 F3
Fastnet Rock, *Ireland* .. 15 E2
Fastov, *Ukraine* 40 F6
Fatagar, Tanjung, *Indonesia* 57 E8
Fatehgarh, *India* 63 F8
Fatehpur, *Raj., India* ... 62 F6
Fatehpur, *Ut. P., India* .. 63 G9
Fatesh, *Russia* 41 E9
Fatick, *Senegal* 78 C1
Fatima, *Canada* 99 C7
Fátima, *Portugal* 31 F2
Fatoya, *Guinea* 78 C3
Faucille, Col de la, *France* 27 B10
Faulkton, *U.S.A.* 108 C5
Faulquemont, *France* .. 25 C13
Fauquembergues, *France* 25 B9
Faure I., *Australia* 89 E1
Făureni, *Romania* 38 D10
Fauresmith, *S. Africa* .. 84 D4
Fauske, *Norway* 8 C13
Fauvillers, *Belgium* 17 J7
Favara, *Italy* 34 E6
Favaritx, C., *Spain* 36 A11
Favignana, *Italy* 34 E5
Favignana, I., *Italy* 34 E5
Favourable Lake, *Canada* 98 B1
Fawn →, *Canada* 98 A2
Fawnskin, *U.S.A.* 113 L10
Faxaflói, *Iceland* 8 D2
Faya-Largeau, *Chad* ... 73 E8
Fayd, *Si. Arabia* 64 E4
Fayence, *France* 27 E10
Fayette, *Ala., U.S.A.* ... 105 J2
Fayette, *Mo., U.S.A.* ... 108 F8
Fayetteville, *Ark., U.S.A.* 109 G7

Fayetteville, *N.C., U.S.A.*	**105**	H6	
Fayetteville, *Tenn., U.S.A.*	**105**	H2	
Fayón, *Spain*	**28**	D5	
Fazenda Nova, *Brazil*	**123**	E1	
Fazilka, *India*	**62**	D6	
Fazilpur, *Pakistan*	**62**	E4	
Fdérik, *Mauritania*	**74**	D2	
Feale →, *Ireland*	**15**	D2	
Fear, C., *U.S.A.*	**105**	J7	
Feather →, *U.S.A.*	**110**	G3	
Feather Falls, *U.S.A.*	**112**	F5	
Featherston, *N.Z.*	**87**	J5	
Featherstone, *Zimbabwe*	**83**	F3	
Fécamp, *France*	**24**	C7	
Fedala = Mohammedia, *Morocco*	**74**	B3	
Federación, *Argentina*	**126**	C4	
Fedeshküh, *Iran*	**65**	D7	
Fedjadj, Chott el, *Tunisia*	**75**	B6	
Fehmarn, *Germany*	**18**	A7	
Fehmarn Bælt, *Denmark*	**18**	A7	
Fei Xian, *China*	**51**	G9	
Feijó, *Brazil*	**124**	B3	
Feilding, *N.Z.*	**87**	J5	
Feira de Santana, *Brazil*	**123**	D4	
Feixiang, *China*	**50**	F8	
Fejø, *Denmark*	**11**	K5	
Feke, *Turkey*	**66**	E6	
Felanitx, *Spain*	**36**	B10	
Feldberg, *Baden-W., Germany*	**19**	H3	
Feldberg, *Mecklenburg-Vorpommern, Germany*	**18**	B9	
Feldkirch, *Austria*	**19**	H5	
Felipe Carrillo Puerto, *Mexico*	**115**	D7	
Felixlândia, *Brazil*	**123**	E3	
Felixstowe, *U.K.*	**13**	F9	
Felletin, *France*	**26**	C6	
Felton, *U.K.*	**12**	B6	
Felton, *U.S.A.*	**112**	H4	
Feltre, *Italy*	**33**	B8	
Femø, *Denmark*	**11**	K5	
Femunden, *Norway*	**10**	B5	
Fen He →, *China*	**50**	G6	
Fenelon Falls, *Canada*	**106**	B6	
Feneroa, *Ethiopia*	**77**	E4	
Feng Xian, *Jiangsu, China*	**50**	G9	
Feng Xian, *Shaanxi, China*	**50**	H4	
Fengári, *Greece*	**39**	J8	
Fengcheng, *Jiangsu, China*	**53**	C10	
Fengcheng, *Liaoning, China*	**51**	D10	
Fengdu, *China*	**52**	C6	
Fengfeng, *China*	**50**	F8	
Fenggang, *China*	**52**	D6	
Fenghua, *China*	**53**	C13	
Fenghuang, *China*	**52**	D7	
Fenghuangzui, *China*	**52**	A7	
Fengjie, *China*	**52**	B7	
Fengkai, *China*	**53**	F8	
Fengle, *China*	**53**	B9	
Fengning, *China*	**50**	D9	
Fengqing, *China*	**52**	E2	
Fengqiu, *China*	**50**	G8	
Fengrun, *China*	**51**	E10	
Fengshan, *Guangxi Zhuangzu, China*	**52**	E7	
Fengshan, *Guangxi Zhuangzu, China*	**52**	E6	
Fengtai, *Anhui, China*	**53**	A11	
Fengtai, *Beijing, China*	**50**	E9	
Fengxian, *China*	**53**	B13	
Fengxiang, *China*	**50**	G4	
Fengxin, *China*	**53**	C10	
Fengyang, *China*	**51**	H9	
Fengyi, *China*	**52**	E3	
Fengzhen, *China*	**50**	D7	
Fenit, *Ireland*	**15**	D2	
Fennimore, *U.S.A.*	**108**	D9	
Feno, C. de, *France*	**27**	G12	
Fenoarivo Afovoany, *Madag.*	**85**	B8	
Fenoarivo Atsinanana, *Madag.*	**85**	B8	
Fens, The, *U.K.*	**12**	E8	
Fenton, *U.S.A.*	**104**	D4	
Fenxi, *China*	**50**	F6	
Fenyang, *China*	**54**	C6	
Fenyang, *Shanxi, China*	**50**	F6	
Fenyi, *China*	**53**	D10	
Feodosiya, *Ukraine*	**42**	D6	
Ferdows, *Iran*	**65**	C8	
Fère-Champenoise, *France*	**25**	D10	
Fère-en-Tardenois, *France*	**25**	C10	
Ferentino, *Italy*	**34**	A6	
Ferfer, *Somali Rep.*	**68**	F4	
Fergana, *Uzbekistan*	**44**	E8	
Fergus, *Canada*	**98**	D3	
Fergus Falls, *U.S.A.*	**108**	B6	
Fériana, *Tunisia*	**75**	B6	
Feričanci, *Croatia*	**21**	K8	
Ferkane, *Algeria*	**75**	B6	
Ferkéssédougou, *Ivory C.*	**78**	D3	
Ferlach, *Austria*	**21**	J4	
Ferland, *Canada*	**98**	B2	
Ferlo, Vallée du, *Senegal*	**78**	B2	
Fermanagh □, *U.K.*	**15**	B4	
Fermo, *Italy*	**33**	E10	
Fermoselle, *Spain*	**30**	D4	
Fermoy, *Ireland*	**15**	D3	
Fernán Nuñéz, *Spain*	**31**	H6	
Fernández, *Argentina*	**126**	B3	
Fernandina Beach, *U.S.A.*	**105**	K5	
Fernando de Noronha, *Brazil*	**122**	B5	
Fernando Póo = Bioko, *Eq. Guin.*	**79**	E6	
Fernandópolis, *Brazil*	**123**	F1	
Ferndale, *Calif., U.S.A.*	**110**	F1	
Ferndale, *Wash., U.S.A.*	**112**	B4	
Fernie, *Canada*	**100**	D5	
Fernlees, *Australia*	**90**	C4	
Fernley, *U.S.A.*	**110**	G4	
Ferozepore = Firozpur, *India*	**62**	D6	
Férrai, *Greece*	**39**	J9	
Ferrandina, *Italy*	**35**	B9	
Ferrara, *Italy*	**33**	D8	
Ferrato, C., *Italy*	**34**	C2	
Ferreira do Alentejo, *Portugal*	**31**	G2	
Ferreñafe, *Peru*	**124**	B2	
Ferrerías, *Spain*	**36**	B11	
Ferret, C., *France*	**26**	D2	
Ferrette, *France*	**25**	E14	
Ferriday, *U.S.A.*	**109**	K9	
Ferrières, *France*	**25**	D9	
Ferriete, *Italy*	**32**	D6	
Ferrol = El Ferrol, *Spain*	**30**	B2	
Ferrol, Pen. de, *Peru*	**124**	B2	
Ferron, *U.S.A.*	**111**	G8	
Ferros, *Brazil*	**123**	E3	
Ferryland, *Canada*	**99**	C9	
Fertile, *U.S.A.*	**108**	B6	
Fertília, *Italy*	**34**	B1	
Fès, *Morocco*	**74**	B4	
Feschaux, *Belgium*	**17**	H5	
Fessenden, *U.S.A.*	**108**	B5	
Fetești, *Romania*	**38**	E10	
Fethiye, *Turkey*	**66**	E3	
Fetlar, *U.K.*	**14**	A8	
Feuerthalen, *Switz.*	**23**	A7	
Feuilles →, *Canada*	**97**	C12	
Feurs, *France*	**27**	C8	
Fezzan, *Libya*	**70**	D5	
Festiniog, *U.K.*	**12**	E4	
Fiambalá, *Argentina*	**126**	B2	
Fianarantsoa, *Madag.*	**85**	C8	
Fianarantsoa □, *Madag.*	**85**	B8	
Fianga, *Cameroon*	**73**	G8	
Fichtelgebirge, *Germany*	**19**	E7	
Ficksburg, *S. Africa*	**85**	D4	
Fidenza, *Italy*	**32**	D7	
Fiditi, *Nigeria*	**79**	D5	
Field, *Canada*	**98**	C3	
Field →, *Australia*	**90**	C2	
Field I., *Australia*	**88**	B5	
Fieri, *Albania*	**39**	J2	
Fiesch, *Switz.*	**22**	D6	
Fife □, *U.K.*	**14**	E5	
Fife Ness, *U.K.*	**14**	E6	
Fifth Cataract, *Sudan*	**76**	D3	
Figeac, *France*	**26**	D6	
Figline Valdarno, *Italy*	**33**	E8	
Figtree, *Zimbabwe*	**83**	G2	
Figueira Castelo Rodrigo, *Portugal*	**30**	E4	
Figueira da Foz, *Portugal*	**30**	E2	
Figueiró dos Vinhos, *Portugal*	**30**	F2	
Figueras, *Spain*	**28**	C7	
Figuig, *Morocco*	**75**	B4	
Fihaonana, *Madag.*	**85**	B8	
Fiherenana, *Madag.*	**85**	B8	
Fiherenana →, *Madag.*	**85**	C7	
Fiji ■, *Pac. Oc.*	**87**	C8	
Fika, *Nigeria*	**79**	C7	
Filabres, Sierra de los, *Spain*	**29**	H2	
Filadelfia, *Bolivia*	**124**	C4	
Filadelfia, *Brazil*	**122**	C2	
Filadélfia, *Italy*	**35**	D9	
Filer, *U.S.A.*	**110**	E6	
Filey, *U.K.*	**12**	C7	
Filfla, *Malta*	**37**	D1	
Filiași, *Romania*	**38**	E6	
Filiátes, *Greece*	**39**	K3	
Filiatrá, *Greece*	**39**	M4	
Filicudi, *Italy*	**35**	D7	
Filiourí →, *Greece*	**39**	H8	
Filipstad, *Sweden*	**9**	G13	
Filisur, *Switz.*	**23**	C9	
Fillmore, *Canada*	**101**	D8	
Fillmore, *Calif., U.S.A.*	**113**	L8	
Fillmore, *Utah, U.S.A.*	**111**	G7	
Filottrano, *Italy*	**33**	E10	
Filyos, *Turkey*	**42**	F5	
Finale Ligure, *Italy*	**32**	D5	
Finale nell' Emília, *Italy*	**33**	D8	
Fiñana, *Spain*	**29**	H2	
Finch, *Canada*	**107**	A9	
Findhorn →, *U.K.*	**14**	D5	
Findlay, *U.S.A.*	**104**	E4	
Finger L., *Canada*	**101**	C10	
Fíngõe, *Mozam.*	**83**	E3	
Finike, *Turkey*	**66**	E4	
Finistère □, *France*	**24**	D2	
Finisterre, *Spain*	**30**	C1	
Finisterre, C., *Spain*	**30**	C1	
Finke, *Australia*	**90**	D1	
Finke →, *Australia*	**91**	D2	
Finland ■, *Europe*	**9**	E19	
Finland, G. of, *Europe*	**9**	G19	
Finlay →, *Canada*	**100**	B3	
Finley, *Australia*	**91**	F4	
Finley, *U.S.A.*	**108**	B6	
Finn →, *Ireland*	**15**	B4	
Finnigan, Mt., *Australia*	**90**	B4	
Finniss, C., *Australia*	**91**	E1	
Finnmark fylke □, *Norway*	**8**	B18	
Finsteraarhorn, *Switz.*	**22**	C6	
Finsterwalde, *Germany*	**18**	D9	
Finsterwolde, *Neths.*	**16**	B10	
Fiora →, *Italy*	**33**	F8	
Fiorenzuola d'Arda, *Italy*	**32**	D6	
Fīq, *Syria*	**69**	C4	
Firat = Furāt, Nahr al →, *Asia*	**64**	D5	
Fire River, *Canada*	**98**	C3	
Firebag →, *Canada*	**101**	B6	
Firebaugh, *U.S.A.*	**112**	J6	
Firedrake L., *Canada*	**101**	A8	
Firenze, *Italy*	**33**	E8	
Firk →, *Iraq*	**64**	D5	
Firmi, *France*	**26**	D6	
Firminy, *France*	**27**	C8	
Firozabad, *India*	**63**	F8	
Firozpur, *India*	**62**	D6	
Fīrūzābād, *Iran*	**65**	D7	
Fīrūzkūh, *Iran*	**65**	C7	
Firvale, *Canada*	**100**	C3	
Fish →, *Namibia*	**84**	D2	
Fish →, *S. Africa*	**84**	E3	
Fisher, *Australia*	**89**	F5	
Fisher B., *Canada*	**101**	C9	
Fishguard, *U.K.*	**13**	F3	
Fishing L., *Canada*	**101**	C9	
Fismes, *France*	**25**	C10	
Fitchburg, *U.S.A.*	**107**	D13	
Fitero, *Spain*	**28**	C3	
Fitri, L., *Chad*	**73**	F8	
Fitz Roy, *Argentina*	**128**	C3	
Fitzgerald, *Canada*	**100**	B6	
Fitzgerald, *U.S.A.*	**105**	K4	
Fitzmaurice →, *Australia*	**88**	B5	
Fitzroy →, *Queens., Australia*	**90**	C5	
Fitzroy →, *W. Austral., Australia*	**88**	C3	
Fitzroy Crossing, *Australia*	**88**	C4	
Fitzwilliam I., *Canada*	**106**	A3	
Fiume = Rijeka, *Croatia*	**33**	C11	
Fiumefreddo Brúzio, *Italy*	**35**	C9	
Five Points, *U.S.A.*	**112**	J6	
Fivizzano, *Italy*	**32**	D7	
Fizi, *Zaïre*	**82**	C2	
Fjellerup, *Denmark*	**11**	H4	
Fjerritslev, *Denmark*	**11**	G3	
Fkih ben Salah, *Morocco*	**74**	B3	
Flå, *Norway*	**10**	A4	
Flagler, *U.S.A.*	**108**	F3	
Flagstaff, *U.S.A.*	**111**	J8	
Flaherty I., *Canada*	**98**	A4	
Flåm, *Norway*	**9**	F9	
Flambeau →, *U.S.A.*	**108**	C9	
Flamborough Hd., *U.K.*	**12**	C7	
Flaming Gorge Dam, *U.S.A.*	**110**	F9	
Flaming Gorge Reservoir, *U.S.A.*	**110**	F9	
Flamingo, Teluk, *Indonesia*	**57**	F9	
Flanders = West-Vlaanderen □, *Belgium*	**17**	G2	
Flanders = West-Vlaanderen □, *Belgium*	**17**	G2	
Flandre Occidentale = West-Vlaanderen □, *Belgium*	**17**	G2	
Flandre Orientale = Oost-Vlaanderen □, *Belgium*	**17**	F3	
Flandreau, *U.S.A.*	**108**	C6	
Flanigan, *U.S.A.*	**112**	E7	
Flannan Is., *U.K.*	**14**	C1	
Flåsjön, *Sweden*	**8**	D13	
Flat →, *Canada*	**100**	A3	
Flat River, *U.S.A.*	**109**	G9	
Flatey, *Barðastrandarsýsla, Iceland*	**8**	C5	
Flatey, *Suður-þingeyjarsýsla, Iceland*	**8**	D2	
Flathead L., *U.S.A.*	**110**	C6	
Flattery, C., *U.S.A.*	**112**	B2	
Flattery, C., *Australia*	**90**	A4	
Flavy-le-Martel, *France*	**25**	C10	
Flaxton, *U.S.A.*	**108**	A3	
Flekkefjord, *Norway*	**9**	G9	
Flémalle, *Belgium*	**17**	G6	
Flemington, *U.S.A.*	**106**	E7	
Flensborg Fjord, *Germany*	**11**	K3	
Flensburg, *Germany*	**18**	A5	
Flers, *France*	**24**	D6	
Flesherton, *Canada*	**106**	B4	
Flesko, Tanjung, *Indonesia*	**57**	D6	
Fleurance, *France*	**26**	E4	
Fleurier, *Switz.*	**22**	C3	
Fleurus, *Belgium*	**17**	H5	
Flevoland □, *Neths.*	**16**	C7	
Flin Flon, *Canada*	**101**	C8	
Flinders →, *Australia*	**90**	B3	
Flinders B., *Australia*	**89**	F2	
Flinders Group, *Australia*	**90**	A3	
Flinders I., *Australia*	**90**	F4	
Flinders Ras., *Australia*	**91**	E2	
Flinders Reefs, *Australia*	**90**	B4	
Flint, *U.K.*	**12**	D4	
Flint, *U.S.A.*	**104**	D4	
Flint →, *U.S.A.*	**105**	K3	
Flint I., *Kiribati*	**93**	J12	
Flinton, *Australia*	**91**	D4	
Flix, *Spain*	**28**	D5	
Flixecourt, *France*	**25**	B9	
Flobecq, *Belgium*	**17**	G3	
Flodden, *U.K.*	**12**	B5	
Floodwood, *U.S.A.*	**108**	B8	
Flora, *Norway*	**10**	A5	
Flora, *U.S.A.*	**104**	F1	
Florac, *France*	**26**	D7	
Florala, *U.S.A.*	**105**	K2	
Florânia, *Brazil*	**122**	C4	
Floreffe, *Belgium*	**17**	H5	
Florence = Firenze, *Italy*	**33**	E8	
Florence, *Ala., U.S.A.*	**105**	H2	
Florence, *Ariz., U.S.A.*	**111**	K8	
Florence, *Colo., U.S.A.*	**108**	F2	
Florence, *Oreg., U.S.A.*	**110**	E1	
Florence, *S.C., U.S.A.*	**105**	H6	
Florence, L., *Australia*	**91**	D2	
Florennes, *Belgium*	**17**	H5	
Florensac, *France*	**26**	E7	
Florenville, *Belgium*	**17**	J6	
Flores, *Brazil*	**122**	C4	
Flores, *Guatemala*	**116**	C2	
Flores, *Indonesia*	**57**	F6	
Flores I., *Canada*	**100**	D3	
Flores Sea, *Indonesia*	**57**	F6	
Floresta, *Brazil*	**122**	C4	
Floresville, *U.S.A.*	**109**	L5	
Floriano, *Brazil*	**122**	C3	
Florianópolis, *Brazil*	**127**	B6	
Florida, *Cuba*	**116**	B4	
Florida, *Uruguay*	**127**	C4	
Florida □, *U.S.A.*	**105**	L5	
Florida, Straits of, *U.S.A.*	**116**	B3	
Florida B., *U.S.A.*	**116**	A3	
Florida Keys, *U.S.A.*	**103**	F10	
Florída, *Italy*	**35**	E8	
Floridsdorf, *Austria*	**21**	G6	
Flórina, *Greece*	**39**	J4	
Florø, *Norway*	**9**	F8	
Flower Station, *Canada*	**107**	A8	
Flower's Cove, *Canada*	**99**	B8	
Floydada, *U.S.A.*	**109**	J4	
Fluk, *Indonesia*	**57**	E7	
Flumen →, *Spain*	**28**	D4	
Flumendosa →, *Italy*	**34**	C2	
Fluminimaggiore, *Italy*	**34**	C1	
Flushing = Vlissingen, *Neths.*	**17**	F3	
Fluviá →, *Spain*	**28**	C8	
Flying Fish, C., *Antarctica*	**5**	D15	
Foam Lake, *Canada*	**101**	C8	
Foča, *Bos.-H.*	**21**	M8	
Foça, *Turkey*	**66**	D2	
Focșani, *Romania*	**38**	D10	
Fogang, *China*	**53**	F9	
Foggaret el Arab, *Algeria*	**75**	C5	
Foggaret ez Zoua, *Algeria*	**75**	C5	
Fóggia, *Italy*	**35**	A8	
Foglia →, *Italy*	**33**	E9	
Foggo, *Nigeria*	**79**	C6	
Fogo, *Canada*	**99**	C9	
Fogo I., *Canada*	**99**	C9	
Fohnsdorf, *Austria*	**21**	H4	
Föhr, *Germany*	**18**	A4	
Foia, *Portugal*	**31**	H2	
Foix, *France*	**26**	F5	
Fokino, *Russia*	**40**	E9	
Folda, *Nord-Trøndelag, Norway*	**8**	D11	
Folda, *Nordland, Norway*	**8**	C13	
Foleyet, *Canada*	**98**	C3	
Folgefonn, *Norway*	**9**	F9	
Foligno, *Italy*	**33**	F9	
Folkestone, *U.K.*	**13**	F9	
Folkston, *U.S.A.*	**105**	K5	
Follett, *U.S.A.*	**109**	G4	
Follónica, *Italy*	**32**	F7	
Follónica, G. di, *Italy*	**32**	F7	
Folsom Res., *U.S.A.*	**112**	G5	
Fond-du-Lac, *Canada*	**101**	B7	
Fond du Lac, *U.S.A.*	**108**	D10	
Fond-du-Lac →, *Canada*	**101**	B7	
Fonda, *U.S.A.*	**107**	D10	
Fondi, *Italy*	**34**	A6	
Fonfría, *Spain*	**30**	D4	
Fongen, *Norway*	**10**	A5	
Fonni, *Italy*	**34**	B2	
Fonsagrada, *Spain*	**30**	B3	
Fonseca, G. de, *Cent. Amer.*	**116**	D2	
Fontaine-Française, *France*	**25**	E12	
Fontainebleau, *France*	**25**	D9	
Fontana, L., *Argentina*	**128**	C2	
Fontas →, *Canada*	**100**	B4	
Fonte Boa, *Brazil*	**120**	D4	
Fontem, *Cameroon*	**79**	D6	
Fontenay-le-Comte, *France*	**26**	B3	
Fontur, *Iceland*	**8**	C6	
Fonyód, *Hungary*	**21**	J7	
Foochow = Fuzhou, *China*	**53**	D12	
Foping, *China*	**50**	H4	
Foppiano, *Italy*	**32**	B5	
Forbach, *France*	**25**	C13	
Forbes, *Australia*	**91**	E4	
Forbesganj, *India*	**63**	F12	
Forcados, *Nigeria*	**79**	D6	
Forcados →, *Nigeria*	**79**	D6	
Forcall →, *Spain*	**28**	E4	
Forcalquier, *France*	**27**	E9	
Forchheim, *Germany*	**19**	F7	
Forclaz, Col de la, *Switz.*	**22**	D4	
Ford City, *Calif., U.S.A.*	**113**	K7	
Ford City, *Pa., U.S.A.*	**106**	F5	
Ford's Bridge, *Australia*	**91**	D4	
Fordyce, *U.S.A.*	**109**	J8	
Forécariah, *Guinea*	**78**	D2	
Forel, Mt., *Greenland*	**4**	C6	
Foremost, *Canada*	**100**	D6	
Forenza, *Italy*	**35**	B8	
Forest, *Belgium*	**17**	G4	
Forest, *Canada*	**106**	C3	
Forest, *U.S.A.*	**109**	J10	
Forest City, *Iowa, U.S.A.*	**108**	D8	
Forest City, *N.C., U.S.A.*	**105**	H5	
Forest City, *Pa., U.S.A.*	**107**	E9	
Forest Grove, *U.S.A.*	**112**	E3	
Forestburg, *Canada*	**100**	C6	
Foresthill, *U.S.A.*	**112**	F6	
Forestier Pen., *Australia*	**90**	G4	
Forestville, *Canada*	**99**	C6	
Forestville, *Calif., U.S.A.*	**112**	G4	
Forestville, *Wis., U.S.A.*	**104**	C2	
Forez, Mts. du, *France*	**26**	C7	
Forfar, *U.K.*	**14**	E6	
Forges-les-Eaux, *France*	**25**	C8	
Forks, *U.S.A.*	**112**	C2	
Forlì, *Italy*	**33**	D9	
Forman, *U.S.A.*	**108**	B6	
Formazza, *Italy*	**32**	B5	
Formby Pt., *U.K.*	**12**	D4	
Formentera, *Spain*	**36**	C7	
Formentor, C. de, *Spain*	**36**	B10	
Fórmia, *Italy*	**34**	A6	
Formiga, *Brazil*	**123**	F2	
Formigine, *Italy*	**32**	D7	
Formiguères, *France*	**26**	F6	
Formosa = Taiwan ■, *Asia*	**53**	F13	
Formosa, *Argentina*	**126**	B4	
Formosa, *Brazil*	**123**	E2	
Formosa □, *Argentina*	**126**	B3	
Formosa, Serra, *Brazil*	**125**	C6	
Formosa Bay, *Kenya*	**82**	C5	
Formosa Strait, *Asia*	**53**		
Formoso →, *Brazil*	**123**	D2	
Fornells, *Spain*	**36**	A11	
Fornos de Algodres, *Portugal*	**30**	E3	
Fornovo di Taro, *Italy*	**32**	D7	
Føroyar, *Atl. Oc.*	**7**	C4	
Forres, *U.K.*	**14**	D5	
Forrest, *Vic., Australia*	**91**	F3	
Forrest, *W. Austral., Australia*	**89**	F4	
Forrest, Mt., *Australia*	**89**	D4	
Forrest City, *U.S.A.*	**109**	H9	
Forrières, *Belgium*	**17**	H6	
Forsa, *Sweden*	**10**	C10	
Forsayth, *Australia*	**90**	B3	
Forsmo, *Sweden*	**10**	A11	
Forst, *Germany*	**18**	D10	
Forster, *Australia*	**91**	E5	
Forsyth, *Ga., U.S.A.*	**105**	J4	
Forsyth, *Mont., U.S.A.*	**110**	C10	
Fort Albany, *Canada*	**98**	B3	
Fort Apache, *U.S.A.*	**111**	K9	
Fort Assiniboine, *Canada*	**100**	C6	
Fort Augustus, *U.K.*	**14**	D4	
Fort Beaufort, *S. Africa*	**84**	E4	
Fort Benton, *U.S.A.*	**110**	C8	
Fort Bragg, *U.S.A.*	**110**	G2	
Fort Bridger, *U.S.A.*	**110**	F8	
Fort Chipewyan, *Canada*	**101**	B6	
Fort Collins, *U.S.A.*	**108**	E2	
Fort-Coulonge, *Canada*	**98**	C4	
Fort Davis, *U.S.A.*	**109**	K3	
Fort-de-France, *Martinique*	**117**	D7	
Fort de Possel = Possel, *C.A.R.*	**80**	C3	
Fort Defiance, *U.S.A.*	**111**	J9	
Fort Dodge, *U.S.A.*	**108**	D7	
Fort Edward, *U.S.A.*	**107**	C11	
Fort Frances, *Canada*	**101**	D10	
Fort Franklin, *Canada*	**96**	B7	
Fort Garland, *U.S.A.*	**111**	H11	
Fort George, *Canada*	**98**	B4	
Fort Good-Hope, *Canada*	**96**	B7	
Fort Hancock, *U.S.A.*	**111**	L11	
Fort Hertz = Putao, *Burma*	**61**	F20	
Fort Hope, *Canada*	**98**	B2	
Fort Irwin, *U.S.A.*	**113**	K10	
Fort Jameson = Chipata, *Zambia*	**83**	E3	
Fort Kent, *U.S.A.*	**99**	C6	
Fort Klamath, *U.S.A.*	**110**	E3	
Fort Lallemand, *Algeria*	**75**	B6	
Fort-Lamy = Ndjamena, *Chad*	**73**	F7	
Fort Laramie, *U.S.A.*	**108**	D2	
Fort Lauderdale, *U.S.A.*	**105**	M5	
Fort Liard, *Canada*	**100**	A4	
Fort Liberté, *Haiti*	**117**	C5	
Fort Lupton, *U.S.A.*	**108**	E2	
Fort Mackay, *Canada*	**100**	B6	
Fort McKenzie, *Canada*	**99**	A6	
Fort Macleod, *Canada*	**100**	D6	
Fort MacMahon, *Algeria*	**75**	C5	
Fort McMurray, *Canada*	**100**	B6	
Fort McPherson, *Canada*	**96**	B6	
Fort Madison, *U.S.A.*	**108**	E9	
Fort Meade, *U.S.A.*	**105**	M5	
Fort Miribel, *Algeria*	**75**	C5	
Fort Morgan, *U.S.A.*	**108**	E3	
Fort Myers, *U.S.A.*	**105**	M5	
Fort Nelson, *Canada*	**100**	B4	
Fort Nelson →, *Canada*	**100**	B4	

Fort Norman, *Canada* 96 B7
Fort Payne, *U.S.A.* 105 H3
Fort Peck, *U.S.A.* 110 B10
Fort Peck Dam, *U.S.A.* ... 110 C10
Fort Peck L., *U.S.A.* 110 C10
Fort Pierce, *U.S.A.* 105 M5
Fort Pierre, *U.S.A.* 108 C4
Fort Pierre Bordes = Ti-n-
  Zaouatène, *Algeria* ... 75 E5
Fort Plain, *U.S.A.* 107 D10
Fort Portal, *Uganda* 82 B3
Fort Providence, *Canada* . 100 A5
Fort Qu'Appelle, *Canada* . 101 C8
Fort Resolution, *Canada* . 100 A6
Fort Rixon, *Zimbabwe* ... 83 G2
Fort Rosebery = Mansa,
  Zambia 83 E2
Fort Ross, *U.S.A.* 112 G3
Fort Rupert, *Canada* 98 B4
Fort Saint, *Tunisia* 75 B6
Fort St. James, *Canada* .. 100 C4
Fort St. John, *Canada* ... 100 B4
Fort Sandeman, *Pakistan* . 62 D3
Fort Saskatchewan, *Canada* 100 C6
Fort Scott, *U.S.A.* 109 G7
Fort Severn, *Canada* 98 A2
Fort Shevchenko,
  Kazakhstan 43 E14
Fort-Sibut, *C.A.R.* 73 G8
Fort Simpson, *Canada* ... 100 A4
Fort Smith, *Canada* 100 B6
Fort Smith, *U.S.A.* 109 H7
Fort Stanton, *U.S.A.* 111 K11
Fort Stockton, *U.S.A.* ... 109 K3
Fort Sumner, *U.S.A.* 109 H2
Fort Trinquet = Bir
  Mogrein, *Mauritania* .. 74 C2
Fort Valley, *U.S.A.* 105 J4
Fort Vermilion, *Canada* .. 100 B5
Fort Walton Beach, *U.S.A.* 105 K2
Fort Wayne, *U.S.A.* 104 E3
Fort William, *U.K.* 14 E3
Fort Worth, *U.S.A.* 109 J6
Fort Yates, *U.S.A.* 108 B4
Fort Yukon, *U.S.A.* 96 B5
Fortaleza, *Bolivia* 124 C4
Fortaleza, *Brazil* 122 B4
Forteau, *Canada* 99 B8
Forth, →, *U.K.* 14 E5
Forth, Firth of, *U.K.* 14 E6
Forthassa Rharbia, *Algeria* 75 B4
Fortín Coronel Eugenio
  Garay, *Paraguay* 125 E5
Fortín Garrapatal,
  Paraguay 125 E5
Fortín General Pando,
  Paraguay 125 D6
Fortín Madrejón, *Paraguay* 125 E6
Fortín Uno, *Argentina* ... 128 A4
Fortore →, *Italy* 33 G12
Fortrose, *U.K.* 14 D4
Fortuna, *Spain* 29 G3
Fortuna, *Calif., U.S.A.* .. 110 F1
Fortuna, *N. Dak., U.S.A.* 108 A3
Fortune B., *Canada* 99 C8
Foshan, *China* 53 F9
Fossacesia, *Italy* 33 F11
Fossano, *Italy* 32 D4
Fosses-la-Ville, *Belgium* . 17 H5
Fossil, *U.S.A.* 110 D3
Fossilbrook, *Australia* ... 90 B3
Fossombrone, *Italy* 33 E9
Fosston, *U.S.A.* 108 B7
Foster, *Canada* 107 A12
Foster →, *Canada* 101 B7
Fosters Ra., *Australia* ... 90 C1
Fostoria, *U.S.A.* 104 E4
Fougamou, *Gabon* 80 E2
Fougères, *France* 24 D5
Foul Pt., *Sri Lanka* 60 Q12
Foula, *U.K.* 14 A6
Foulness I., *U.K.* 13 F8
Foulpointe, *Madag.* 85 B8
Foum Assaka, *Morocco* . 74 C2
Foum Zguid, *Morocco* ... 74 B3
Foumban, *Cameroon* 79 D7
Foundiougne, *Senegal* ... 78 C1
Fountain, *Colo., U.S.A.* . 108 F2
Fountain, *Utah, U.S.A.* .. 110 G8
Fountain Springs, *U.S.A.* . 113 K8
Fourchambault, *France* .. 25 E10
Fourchu, *Canada* 99 C7
Fouriesburg, *S. Africa* ... 84 D4
Fourmies, *France* 25 B11
Fours, *France* 25 F10
Fouta Djalon, *Guinea* ... 78 C2
Foux, Cap-à-, *Haiti* 117 C5
Foveaux Str., *N.Z.* 87 M2
Fowey, *U.K.* 13 G3
Fowler, *Calif., U.S.A.* ... 111 H4
Fowler, *Colo., U.S.A.* ... 108 F2
Fowler, *Kans., U.S.A.* ... 109 G4
Fowlers B., *Australia* 89 F5
Fowlerton, *U.S.A.* 109 L5
Fox →, *Canada* 101 B10
Fox Valley, *Canada* 101 C7
Foxe Basin, *Canada* 97 B12
Foxe Chan., *Canada* 97 B11
Foxe Pen., *Canada* 97 B12
Foxhol, *Neths.* 16 B9
Foxpark, *U.S.A.* 110 F10
Foxton, *N.Z.* 87 J5
Foyle, Lough, *U.K.* 15 A4

Foynes, *Ireland* 15 D2
Foz, *Spain* 30 B3
Fóz do Cunene, *Angola* . 84 B1
Foz do Gregório, *Brazil* . 124 B3
Foz do Iguaçu, *Brazil* ... 127 B5
Foz do Riosinho, *Brazil* . 124 B3
Frackville, *U.S.A.* 107 F8
Fraga, *Spain* 28 D5
Fraire, *Belgium* 17 H5
Frameries, *Belgium* 17 H3
Framingham, *U.S.A.* 107 D13
Franca, *Brazil* 123 F2
Francavilla al Mare, *Italy* . 33 F11
Francavilla Fontana, *Italy* . 35 B10
France ■, *Europe* 7 F6
Frances, *Australia* 91 F3
Frances →, *Canada* 100 A3
Frances L., *Canada* 100 A3
Francés Viejo, C.,
  Dom. Rep. 117 C6
Franceville, *Gabon* 80 E2
Franche-Comté, *France* . 25 F12
Franches Montagnes, *Switz.* 22 B4
Francisco de Orellana,
  Ecuador 120 D2
Francisco I. Madero,
  Coahuila, Mexico 114 B4
Francisco I. Madero,
  Durango, Mexico 114 C4
Francisco Sá, *Brazil* 123 E3
Francistown, *Botswana* .. 85 C4
Francofonte, *Italy* 35 E7
François, *Canada* 99 C8
François L., *Canada* 100 C3
Francorchamps, *Belgium* . 17 H7
Franeker, *Neths.* 16 B7
Frankado, *Djibouti* 77 E5
Frankenberg, *Germany* .. 18 D4
Frankenthal, *Germany* ... 19 F4
Frankenwald, *Germany* .. 19 E7
Frankfort, *S. Africa* 85 D4
Frankfort, *Ind., U.S.A.* .. 104 E2
Frankfort, *Kans., U.S.A.* . 108 F6
Frankfort, *Ky., U.S.A.* ... 104 F3
Frankfort, *Mich., U.S.A.* . 104 C2
Frankfurt am Main,
  Germany 19 E4
Frankfurt an der Oder,
  Germany 18 C10
Fränkische Alb, *Germany* . 19 F7
Fränkische Rezal →,
  Germany 19 F7
Fränkische Saale →,
  Germany 19 E5
Fränkische Schweiz,
  Germany 19 F7
Frankland →, *Australia* .. 89 G2
Franklin, *Ky., U.S.A.* 105 G2
Franklin, *La., U.S.A.* 109 L9
Franklin, *Mass., U.S.A.* . 107 D13
Franklin, *N.H., U.S.A.* .. 107 C13
Franklin, *Nebr., U.S.A.* .. 108 E5
Franklin, *Pa., U.S.A.* 106 E5
Franklin, *Tenn., U.S.A.* . 105 H2
Franklin, *Va., U.S.A.* 105 G7
Franklin, *W. Va., U.S.A.* . 104 F6
Franklin B., *Canada* 96 B7
Franklin D. Roosevelt L.,
  U.S.A. 110 B4
Franklin I., *Antarctica* ... 5 D11
Franklin L., *U.S.A.* 110 F6
Franklin Mts., *Canada* .. 96 B7
Franklin Str., *Canada* ... 96 A10
Franklinton, *U.S.A.* 109 K9
Franklinville, *U.S.A.* 106 D6
Franks Pk., *U.S.A.* 110 E9
Frankston, *Australia* 91 F4
Fränsta, *Sweden* 10 B10
Frantsa Iosifa, Zemlya,
  Russia 44 A6
Franz, *Canada* 98 C3
Franz Josef Land = Frantsa
  Iosifa, Zemlya, *Russia* . 44 A6
Franzburg, *Germany* 18 A8
Frascati, *Italy* 34 A5
Fraser →, *B.C., Canada* . 100 D4
Fraser →, *Nfld., Canada* . 99 A7
Fraser, Mt., *Australia* ... 89 E2
Fraser I., *Australia* 91 D5
Fraser Lake, *Canada* 100 C4
Fraserburg, *S. Africa* 84 E3
Fraserburgh, *U.K.* 14 D6
Fraserdale, *Canada* 98 C3
Frasne, *France* 25 F13
Frauenfeld, *Switz.* 23 A7
Fray Bentos, *Uruguay* ... 126 C4
Frazier Downs, *Australia* . 88 C3
Frechilla, *Spain* 30 C6
Fredericia, *Denmark* 11 J3
Frederick, *Md., U.S.A.* .. 104 F7
Frederick, *Okla., U.S.A.* . 109 H5
Frederick, *S. Dak., U.S.A.* 108 C5
Frederick Sd., *U.S.A.* ... 100 B2
Fredericksburg, *Tex.,
  U.S.A.* 109 K5
Fredericksburg, *Va.,
  U.S.A.* 104 F7
Fredericktown, *U.S.A.* .. 109 G9
Frederico I. Madero, Presa,
  Mexico 114 B3
Fredericton, *Canada* 99 C6
Fredericton Junc., *Canada* 99 C6
Frederikshåb, *Greenland* . 4 C5
Frederikshavn, *Denmark* . 11 G4
Frederikssund, *Denmark* . 11 J6

Frederiksted, *Virgin Is.* ... 117 C7
Fredonia, *Ariz., U.S.A.* .. 111 H7
Fredonia, *Kans., U.S.A.* . 109 G7
Fredonia, *N.Y., U.S.A.* .. 106 D5
Fredrikstad, *Norway* 10 E4
Freehold, *U.S.A.* 107 F10
Freel Peak, *U.S.A.* 112 G7
Freeland, *U.S.A.* 107 E9
Freels, C., *Canada* 99 C9
Freeman, *Calif., U.S.A.* . 113 K9
Freeman, *S. Dak., U.S.A.* 108 D6
Freeport, *Bahamas* 116 A4
Freeport, *Canada* 99 D6
Freeport, *Ill., U.S.A.* 108 D10
Freeport, *N.Y., U.S.A.* .. 107 F11
Freeport, *Tex., U.S.A.* .. 109 L7
Freetown, *S. Leone* 78 D2
Frégate, L., *Canada* 98 B5
Fregenal de la Sierra, *Spain* 31 G4
Fregene, *Italy* 34 A5
Fréhel, C., *France* 24 D4
Freiberg, *Germany* 18 E9
Freibourg = Fribourg,
  Switz. 22 C4
Freiburg, *Baden-W.,
  Germany* 19 H3
Freiburg, *Niedersachsen,
  Germany* 18 B5
Freiburger Alpen, *Switz.* . 22 C4
Freire, *Chile* 128 A2
Freirina, *Chile* 126 B1
Freising, *Germany* 19 G7
Freistadt, *Austria* 20 G4
Freital, *Germany* 18 E9
Fréjus, *France* 27 E10
Fremantle, *Australia* 89 F2
Fremont, *Calif., U.S.A.* .. 111 H2
Fremont, *Mich., U.S.A.* . 104 D3
Fremont, *Nebr., U.S.A.* . 108 E6
Fremont, *Ohio, U.S.A.* .. 104 E4
Fremont →, *U.S.A.* 111 G8
Fremont L., *U.S.A.* 110 E9
French Camp, *U.S.A.* ... 112 H5
French Creek, *U.S.A.* ... 106 E5
French Guiana ■, *S. Amer.* 121 C7
French Pass, *N.Z.* 87 J4
French Polynesia ■,
  Pac. Oc. 93 J13
French Terr. of Afars &
  Issas = Djibouti ■,
  Africa 68 E3
Frenchglen, *U.S.A.* 110 E4
Frenchman Butte, *Canada* 101 C7
Frenchman Cr. →, *Mont.,
  U.S.A.* 110 B10
Frenchman Cr. →, *Nebr.,
  U.S.A.* 108 E4
Frenda, *Algeria* 75 A5
Fresco, *Brazil* 125 B7
Freshfield, C., *Antarctica* . 5 C10
Fresnay-sur-Sarthe, *France* 24 D7
Fresnillo, *Mexico* 114 C4
Fresno, *U.S.A.* 111 H4
Fresno Alhandiga, *Spain* . 30 E5
Fresno Reservoir, *U.S.A.* . 110 B9
Freudenstadt, *Germany* .. 19 G4
Freux, *Belgium* 17 J6
Frévent, *France* 25 B9
Frew →, *Australia* 90 C2
Frewena, *Australia* 90 B2
Freycinet Pen., *Australia* . 90 G4
Freyming-Merlebach,
  France 25 C13
Freyung, *Germany* 19 G9
Fria, *Guinea* 78 C2
Fria, C., *Namibia* 84 B1
Friant, *U.S.A.* 112 J7
Frías, *Argentina* 126 B2
Fribourg, *Switz.* 22 C4
Fribourg □, *Switz.* 22 C4
Frick, *Switz.* 22 A6
Friday Harbor, *U.S.A.* ... 112 B3
Friedberg, *Bayern,
  Germany* 19 G6
Friedberg, *Hessen,
  Germany* 19 E4
Friedland, *Germany* 18 B9
Friedrichshafen, *Germany* 19 H5
Friedrichskoog, *Germany* . 18 A4
Friedrichstadt, *Germany* . 18 A5
Friendly Is. = Tonga ■,
  Pac. Oc. 87 D11
Friesack, *Germany* 18 C8
Friesche Wad, *Neths.* ... 16 B7
Friesland □, *Neths.* 16 B7
Friesoythe, *Germany* 18 B3
Frillesås, *Sweden* 11 G6
Frío →, *U.S.A.* 109 L5
Friona, *U.S.A.* 109 H3
Frisian Is., *Europe* 18 B2
Fristad, *Sweden* 11 G6
Fritch, *U.S.A.* 109 H4
Fritsla, *Sweden* 11 G6
Fritzlar, *Germany* 18 D5
Friuli-Venezia Giulia □,
  Italy 33 B10
Frobisher B., *Canada* 97 B13
Frobisher Bay = Iqaluit,
  Canada 97 B13
Frobisher L., *Canada* 101 B7
Frohavet, *Norway* 8 E10
Froid, *U.S.A.* 108 A2
Froid-Chapelle, *Belgium* . 17 H4
Frolovo, *Russia* 43 B10
Fromberg, *U.S.A.* 110 D9

Frome, *U.K.* 13 F5
Frome, L., *Australia* 91 E2
Frome Downs, *Australia* . 91 E2
Frómista, *Spain* 30 C6
Front Range, *U.S.A.* 110 G11
Front Royal, *U.S.A.* 104 F6
Fronteira, *Portugal* 31 F3
Fronteiras, *Brazil* 122 C3
Frontera, *Canary Is.* 36 G2
Frontera, *Mexico* 115 D6
Frontignan, *France* 26 E7
Frosinone, *Italy* 34 A6
Frosolone, *Italy* 35 A7
Frostburg, *U.S.A.* 104 F6
Frostisen, *Norway* 8 B14
Frouard, *France* 25 D13
Frøya, *Norway* 8 E10
Fruges, *France* 25 B9
Frumoasa, *Romania* 38 C6
Frunze = Bishkek,
  Kirghizia 44 E8
Frutal, *Brazil* 123 F2
Frutigen, *Switz.* 22 C5
Frýdek-Místek, *Czech.* .. 20 F8
Frýdlant, *Czech.* 20 E5
Fu Jiang →, *China* 52 C6
Fu Xian, *Liaoning, China* . 51 E11
Fu Xian, *Shaanxi, China* . 50 F5
Fu'an, *China* 53 D12
Fubian, *China* 52 B4
Fucécchio, *Italy* 32 E7
Fucheng, *China* 50 F9
Fuchou = Fuzhou, *China* . 53 D12
Fuchū, *Japan* 49 G6
Fuchuan, *China* 53 E8
Fuchun Jiang →, *China* .. 53 B13
Fúcino, Conca del, *Italy* . 33 F10
Fuding, *China* 53 D13
Fuencaliente, *Canary Is.* . 36 F2
Fuencaliente, *Spain* 31 G6
Fuencaliente, Pta.,
  Canary Is. 36 F2
Fuengirola, *Spain* 31 J6
Fuente Alamo, *Albacete,
  Spain* 29 G3
Fuente Álamo, *Murcia,
  Spain* 29 H3
Fuente de Cantos, *Spain* . 31 G4
Fuente del Maestre, *Spain* 31 G4
Fuente el Fresno, *Spain* . 31 F7
Fuente Ovejuna, *Spain* .. 31 G5
Fuentes de Andalucía,
  Spain 31 H5
Fuentes de Ebro, *Spain* .. 28 D4
Fuentes de León, *Spain* . 31 G4
Fuentes de Oñoro, *Spain* . 30 E4
Fuentesaúco, *Spain* 30 D5
Fuerte →, *Mexico* 114 B3
Fuerte Olimpo, *Paraguay* . 126 A4
Fuerteventura, *Canary Is.* . 36 F6
Fufeng, *China* 50 G4
Fuga I., *Phil.* 55 B4
Fugløysund, *Norway* 8 A16
Fugong, *China* 52 D2
Fugou, *China* 50 G8
Fugu, *China* 50 E6
Fuhai, *China* 54 B3
Fuḥaymī, *Iraq* 64 C4
Fuji, *Japan* 49 G9
Fuji-San, *Japan* 49 G9
Fuji-yoshida, *Japan* 49 G9
Fujian □, *China* 53 E12
Fujinomiya, *Japan* 49 G9
Fujisawa, *Japan* 49 G9
Fukien = Fujian □, *China* . 53 E12
Fukuchiyama, *Japan* 49 G7
Fukue-Shima, *Japan* 49 H4
Fukui, *Japan* 49 F8
Fukui □, *Japan* 49 G8
Fukuoka, *Japan* 49 H5
Fukuoka □, *Japan* 49 H5
Fukushima, *Japan* 48 F10
Fukushima □, *Japan* 48 F10
Fukuyama, *Japan* 49 G6
Fulda, *Germany* 18 E5
Fulda →, *Germany* 18 D5
Fuling, *China* 52 C6
Fullerton, *Calif., U.S.A.* . 113 M9
Fullerton, *Nebr., U.S.A.* . 108 E5
Fulongquan, *China* 51 B13
Fulton, *Mo., U.S.A.* 108 F9
Fulton, *N.Y., U.S.A.* 107 C8
Fulton, *Tenn., U.S.A.* ... 105 G1
Fumay, *France* 25 C11
Fumel, *France* 26 D4
Fumin, *China* 52 E4
Funabashi, *Japan* 49 G10
Funchal, *Madeira* 36 D3
Fundación, *Colombia* ... 120 A3
Fundão, *Brazil* 123 E3
Fundão, *Portugal* 30 E3
Fundy, B. of, *Canada* ... 99 D6
Funing, *Hebei, China* ... 51 E10
Funing, *Jiangsu, China* .. 51 H10
Funing, *Yunnan, China* .. 52 F5
Funiu Shan, *China* 50 H7
Funtua, *Nigeria* 79 C6
Fuping, *Hebei, China* ... 50 E8
Fuping, *Shaanxi, China* .. 50 G5
Fuqing, *China* 53 E12
Fuquan, *China* 52 D6
Fur, *Denmark* 11 H3

Furano, *Japan* 48 C11
Furāt, Nahr al →, *Asia* .. 64 D5
Furg, *Iran* 65 D7
Furkapass, *Switz.* 23 C7
Furmanov, *Russia* 41 C12
Furmanovo, *Kazakhstan* . 43 B13
Furnás, *Spain* 36 B8
Furnas, Reprêsa de, *Brazil* 123 F2
Furneaux Group, *Australia* 90 G4
Furness, *U.K.* 12 C4
Furqlus, *Syria* 69 A6
Fürstenau, *Germany* 18 C3
Fürstenberg, *Germany* ... 18 B9
Fürstenfeld, *Austria* 21 H6
Fürstenfeldbruck, *Germany* 19 G7
Fürstenwalde, *Germany* . 18 C10
Fürth, *Germany* 19 F6
Furth im Wald, *Germany* . 19 F8
Furtwangen, *Germany* ... 19 G4
Furukawa, *Japan* 48 E10
Furusund, *Sweden* 10 E12
Fury and Hecla Str.,
  Canada 97 B11
Fusagasuga, *Colombia* .. 120 C3
Fuscaldo, *Italy* 35 C9
Fushan, *Shandong, China* 51 F11
Fushan, *Shanxi, China* .. 50 G6
Fushun, *Liaoning, China* . 51 D12
Fushun, *Sichuan, China* . 52 C5
Fusio, *Switz.* 23 D7
Fusong, *China* 51 C14
Füssen, *Germany* 19 H6
Fusui, *China* 52 F6
Futrono, *Chile* 128 B2
Futuna, *Wall. & F. Is.* ... 87 B8
Fuwa, *Egypt* 76 H7
Fuxin, *China* 51 C11
Fuyang, *Anhui, China* ... 50 H8
Fuyang, *Zhejiang, China* . 53 B12
Fuyang He →, *China* 50 E9
Fuying Dao, *China* 53 D13
Fuyu, *China* 51 B13
Fuyuan, *Heilongjiang,
  China* 54 B8
Fuyuan, *Yunnan, China* . 52 E5
Fuzhou, *China* 53 D12
Fylde, *U.K.* 12 D5
Fyn, *Denmark* 11 J4
Fyne, L., *U.K.* 14 F3
Fyns Amtskommune □,
  Denmark 11 J4
Fyresvatn, *Norway* 10 E2

G

Gaanda, *Nigeria* 79 C7
Gabarin, *Nigeria* 79 C7
Gabas →, *France* 26 E3
Gabela, *Angola* 80 G2
Gabès, *Tunisia* 75 B7
Gabès, G. de, *Tunisia* ... 75 B7
Gabgaba, W. →, *Egypt* .. 76 C3
Gabon ■, *Africa* 80 E2
Gaborone, *Botswana* ... 84 C4
Gabriels, *U.S.A.* 107 B10
Gābrīk, *Iran* 65 E8
Gabrovo, *Bulgaria* 38 G8
Gacé, *France* 24 D7
Gāch Sār, *Iran* 65 B6
Gachsārān, *Iran* 65 D6
Gacko, *Bos.-H.* 21 M8
Gadag, *India* 60 M9
Gadamai, *Sudan* 77 D4
Gadap, *Pakistan* 62 G2
Gadarwara, *India* 63 H8
Gadebusch, *Germany* ... 18 B7
Gadein, *Sudan* 77 F2
Gadhada, *India* 62 J4
Gadmen, *Switz.* 23 C6
Gádor, Sierra de, *Spain* . 29 J2
Gadsden, *Ala., U.S.A.* .. 105 H2
Gadsden, *Ariz., U.S.A.* . 111 K6
Gadwal, *India* 60 L10
Gadyach, *Ukraine* 40 F8
Găeşti, *Romania* 38 E8
Gaeta, *Italy* 34 A6
Gaeta, G. di, *Italy* 34 A6
Gaffney, *U.S.A.* 105 H5
Gafsa, *Tunisia* 75 B6
Gagarin = Gzhatsk, *Russia* 40 D9
Gagetown, *Canada* 99 C6
Gagino, *Russia* 41 D14
Gagliano del Capo, *Italy* . 35 C11
Gagnoa, *Ivory C.* 78 D3
Gagnon, *Canada* 99 B6
Gagnon, L., *Canada* 101 A6
Gagra, *Georgia* 43 E9
Gahini, *Rwanda* 82 C3
Gahmar, *India* 63 G10
Gai Xian, *China* 51 D12
Gaïdhouronísi, *Greece* .. 37 E7
Gail →, *Austria* 21 J3
Gaillac, *France* 26 E5
Gaillon, *France* 24 C8
Gaimán, *Argentina* 128 B3
Gaines, *U.S.A.* 106 E7
Gainesville, *Fla., U.S.A.* . 105 L4
Gainesville, *Ga., U.S.A.* . 105 H4
Gainesville, *Mo., U.S.A.* . 109 G8
Gainesville, *Tex., U.S.A.* . 109 J6
Gainsborough, *U.K.* 12 D7

Gairdner, L., *Australia* 91 E2
Gairloch, L., *U.K.* 14 D3
Gais, *Switz.* 23 B8
Gakuch, *Pakistan* 63 A5
Galán, Cerro, *Argentina* . 126 B2
Galana, *Kenya* 82 C5
Galangue, *Angola* 81 G3
Galápagos, *Pac. Oc.* .. 93 H18
Galashiels, *U.K.* 14 F6
Galaţi, *Romania* 38 D11
Galatia, *Turkey* 66 D5
Galatina, *Italy* 35 B11
Galátone, *Italy* 35 B11
Galax, *U.S.A.* 105 G5
Galaxídhion, *Greece* ... 39 L5
Galbraith, *Australia* 90 B3
Galcaio, *Somali Rep.* ... 68 F4
Galdhøpiggen, *Norway* . 10 C2
Galeana, *Mexico* 114 C4
Galela, *Indonesia* 57 D7
Galera, *Spain* 29 H2
Galera, Pta., *Chile* ... 128 A2
Galera Point, *Trin. & Tob.* 117 D7
Galesburg, *U.S.A.* 108 E9
Galeton, *U.S.A.* 106 E7
Galheirão →, *Brazil* .. 123 D2
Galheiros, *Brazil* 123 D2
Gali, *Georgia* 43 E9
Galich, *Russia* 41 B13
Galiche, *Bulgaria* 38 F6
Galicia □, *Spain* 30 C3
Galilee = Hagalil, *Israel* . 69 C4
Galilee, L., *Australia* ... 90 C4
Galilee, Sea of = Yam
  Kinneret, *Israel* 69 C4
Galinoporni, *Cyprus* ... 37 D13
Galion, *U.S.A.* 106 F2
Galite, Is. de la, *Tunisia* . 75 A6
Galiuro Mts., *U.S.A.* . 111 K8
Gallabat, *Sudan* 77 E4
Gallardon, *France* 25 D8
Gallarte, *Italy* 32 C5
Gallatin, *U.S.A.* 105 G2
Galle, *Sri Lanka* 60 R12
Gállego →, *Spain* 28 D4
Gallegos →, *Argentina* . 128 D3
Galley Hd., *Ireland* 15 E3
Galliate, *Italy* 32 C5
Gallinas, Pta., *Colombia* 120 A3
Gallipoli = Gelibolu,
  Turkey 39 J9
Gallípoli, *Italy* 35 B11
Gallipolis, *U.S.A.* ... 104 F4
Gällivare, *Sweden* 8 C16
Gallo, C., *Italy* 34 D6
Gallocanta, L. de, *Spain* . 28 E3
Galloway, *U.K.* 14 G4
Galloway, Mull of, *U.K.* . 14 G4
Gallup, *U.S.A.* 111 J9
Gallur, *Spain* 28 D3
Galong, *Australia* 91 E4
Galoya, *Sri Lanka* 60 Q12
Galt, *U.S.A.* 112 G5
Galtström, *Sweden* ... 10 B11
Galtür, *Austria* 19 J6
Galty Mts., *Ireland* 15 D3
Galtymore, *Ireland* ... 15 D3
Galva, *U.S.A.* 108 E9
Galvarino, *Chile* 128 A2
Galve de Sorbe, *Spain* . 28 D1
Galveston, *U.S.A.* ... 109 L7
Galveston B., *U.S.A.* . 109 L7
Gálvez, *Argentina* 126 C3
Gálvez, *Spain* 31 F6
Galway, *Ireland* 15 C2
Galway □, *Ireland* 15 C2
Galway B., *Ireland* 15 C2
Gam →, *Vietnam* 58 B5
Gamagori, *Japan* 49 G8
Gamari, L., *Ethiopia* ... 77 E5
Gamawa, *Nigeria* 79 C7
Gamay, *Phil.* 55 E6
Gambaga, *Ghana* 79 C4
Gambat, *Pakistan* 62 F3
Gambela, *Ethiopia* 77 F3
Gambia ■, *W. Afr.* ... 78 C1
Gambia →, *W. Afr.* ... 78 C1
Gambier, C., *Australia* . 88 B5
Gambier Is., *Australia* . 91 F2
Gamboli, *Pakistan* 62 E3
Gamboma, *Congo* 80 E3
Gamerco, *U.S.A.* 111 J9
Gamlakarleby = Kokkola,
  Finland 8 E17
Gammon →, *Canada* .. 101 C9
Gammouda, *Tunisia* ... 75 A6
Gamu-Gofa □, *Ethiopia* 77 F4
Gan, *France* 26 E3
Gan Gan, *Argentina* .. 128 B3
Gan Goriama, Mts.,
  Cameroon 79 D7
Gan Jiang →, *China* .. 53 C10
Ganado, *Ariz., U.S.A.* . 111 J9
Ganado, *Tex., U.S.A.* . 109 L6
Gananoque, *Canada* ... 98 D4
Ganaveh, *Iran* 65 D6
Gäncä = Gyandzha,
  Azerbaijan 43 F12
Gand = Gent, *Belgium* . 17 F3
Ganda, *Angola* 81 G2
Gandak →, *India* 63 G11
Gandava, *Pakistan* 62 E2
Gander, *Canada* 99 C9
Gander L., *Canada* 99 C9
Ganderowe Falls,
  Zimbabwe 83 F2

Gandesa, *Spain* 28 D5
Gandhi Sagar, *India* ... 62 G6
Gandi, *Nigeria* 79 C6
Gandía, *Spain* 29 G4
Gandino, *Italy* 32 C6
Gando, Pta., *Canary Is.* . 36 G4
Gandole, *Nigeria* 79 D7
Gandu, *Brazil* 123 D4
Ganedidalem = Gani,
  Indonesia 57 E7
Ganetti, *Sudan* 76 D3
Ganga →, *India* 63 H14
Ganga, Mouths of the,
  India 63 J14
Ganganagar, *India* 62 E5
Gangapur, *India* 62 F7
Gangara, *Niger* 79 C6
Gangaw, *Burma* 61 H19
Gangdisê Shan, *China* . 61 D12
Ganges = Ganga →, *India* 63 H14
Ganges, *France* 26 E7
Gangoh, *India* 62 E7
Gangtok, *India* 61 F16
Gangu, *China* 50 G3
Gangyao, *China* 51 B14
Gani, *Indonesia* 57 E7
Ganj, *India* 63 F8
Gannat, *France* 26 B7
Gannett Peak, *U.S.A.* . 110 E9
Gannvalley, *U.S.A.* .. 108 C5
Ganquan, *China* 50 F5
Gänserdorf, *Austria* ... 21 G6
Ganshui, *China* 52 C6
Gansu □, *China* 50 G3
Ganta, *Liberia* 78 D3
Gantheaume, C., *Australia* 91 F2
Gantheaume B., *Australia* 89 E1
Gantsevichi, *Belorussia* . 40 E5
Ganyem, *Indonesia* ... 57 E10
Ganyu, *China* 51 G10
Ganyushkino, *Kazakhstan* 43 C13
Ganzhou, *China* 53 E10
Gao, *Mali* 79 B5
Gao Xian, *China* 52 C5
Gao'an, *China* 53 C10
Gaohe, *China* 53 F9
Gaohebu, *China* 53 B11
Gaokeng, *China* 53 D9
Gaolan Dao, *China* ... 53 G9
Gaoligong Shan, *China* . 52 E2
Gaomi, *China* 51 F10
Gaoping, *China* 50 G7
Gaotang, *China* 50 F9
Gaoua, *Burkina Faso* .. 78 C4
Gaoual, *Guinea* 78 C2
Gaoxiong, *Taiwan* 53 F13
Gaoyang, *China* 50 E8
Gaoyou, *China* 53 A12
Gaoyou Hu, *China* ... 51 H10
Gaoyuan, *China* 51 F9
Gaozhou, *China* 53 G8
Gap, *France* 27 D10
Gapan, *Phil.* 55 D4
Gar, *China* 54 C2
Garabogazkol Aylagy =
  Kara Bogaz Gol, Zaliv,
  Turkmenistan 44 E6
Garachico, *Canary Is.* . 36 F3
Garachiné, *Panama* ... 116 E4
Garafia, *Canary Is.* ... 36 F2
Garajonay, *Canary Is.* . 36 F2
Garanhuns, *Brazil* 122 C4
Garawe, *Liberia* 78 E3
Garba Tula, *Kenya* ... 82 B4
Garber, *U.S.A.* 109 G6
Garberville, *U.S.A.* ... 110 F2
Garça, *Brazil* 123 F2
Garças →, *Mato Grosso,
  Brazil* 125 D7
Garças →, *Pernambuco,
  Brazil* 122 C4
Garcias, *Brazil* 125 E7
Gard □, *France* 27 D8
Gard →, *France* 27 E8
Garda, L. di, *Italy* ... 32 C7
Gardanne, *France* 27 E9
Garde L., *Canada* 101 A7
Gardelegen, *Germany* . 18 C7
Garden City, *Kans., U.S.A.* 109 G4
Garden City, *Tex., U.S.A.* 109 K4
Garden Grove, *U.S.A.* . 113 M9
Gardêz, *Afghan.* 62 C3
Gardiner, *U.S.A.* 110 D8
Gardiners I., *U.S.A.* .. 107 E12
Gardner, *U.S.A.* 107 D13
Gardner Canal, *Canada* 100 C3
Gardnerville, *U.S.A.* .. 112 G7
Gare Tigre, *Fr. Guiana* 121 C7
Garéssio, *Italy* 32 D5
Garey, *U.S.A.* 113 L6
Garfield, *U.S.A.* 110 C5
Gargan, Mt., *France* .. 26 C5
Gargano, Mte., *Italy* .. 35 A8
Gargouna, *Mali* 79 B5
Garhshankar, *India* ... 62 D7
Garibaldi Prov. Park,
  Canada 100 D4
Garies, *S. Africa* 84 E2
Garigliano →, *Italy* ... 34 A6
Garissa, *Kenya* 82 C4
Garissa □, *Kenya* 82 C5
Garkida, *Nigeria* 79 C7
Garko, *Nigeria* 79 C6
Garland, *U.S.A.* 110 F7

Garlasco, *Italy* 32 C5
Garm, *Tajikistan* 44 F8
Garmāb, *Iran* 65 C8
Garmisch-Partenkirchen,
  Germany 19 H7
Garmsār, *Iran* 65 C7
Garner, *U.S.A.* 108 D8
Garnett, *U.S.A.* 108 F7
Garo Hills, *India* 63 G14
Garoe, *Somali Rep.* ... 68 F4
Garonne →, *France* .. 26 C3
Garonne, Canal Latéral à
  la →, *France* 26 D4
Garoua, *Cameroon* ... 79 D7
Garrel, *Germany* 18 C3
Garrigue, *France* 26 E7
Garrison, *Mont., U.S.A.* 110 C7
Garrison, *N. Dak., U.S.A.* 108 B4
Garrison, *Tex., U.S.A.* 109 K7
Garrison Res. =
  Sakakawea, L., *U.S.A.* . 108 B3
Garrovillas, *Spain* 31 F4
Garrucha, *Spain* 29 H3
Garry →, *U.K.* 14 E5
Garry, L., *Canada* 96 B9
Garsen, *Kenya* 82 C5
Garson →, *Canada* ... 101 B7
Gartempe →, *France* . 26 B4
Gartz, *Germany* 18 B10
Garu, *Ghana* 79 C4
Garub, *Namibia* 84 D2
Garut, *Indonesia* 57 G12
Garvão, *Portugal* 31 H2
Garvie Mts., *N.Z.* ... 87 L2
Garwa = Garoua,
  Cameroon 79 D7
Garwa, *India* 63 G10
Garwolin, *Poland* 20 D11
Gary, *U.S.A.* 104 E2
Garz, *Germany* 18 A9
Garzê, *China* 52 B3
Garzón, *Colombia* ... 120 C2
Gas-San, *Japan* 48 E10
Gasan Kuli, *Turkmenistan* 44 F6
Gascogne, *France* 26 E4
Gascogne, G. de, *Europe* . 28 B2
Gascony = Gascogne,
  France 26 E4
Gascoyne →, *Australia* . 89 D1
Gascoyne Junc. T.O.,
  Australia 89 E2
Gascueña, *Spain* 28 E2
Gash, Wadi →, *Ethiopia* 77 D4
Gashaka, *Nigeria* 79 D7
Gasherbrum, *Pakistan* . 63 B7
Gashua, *Nigeria* 79 C7
Gaspé, *Canada* 99 C7
Gaspé, C. de, *Canada* . 99 C7
Gaspé, Pén. de, *Canada* 99 C6
Gaspésie, Parc Prov. de la,
  Canada 99 C6
Gassaway, *U.S.A.* ... 104 F5
Gasselte, *Neths.* 16 C9
Gasselternijveen, *Neths.* . 16 C9
Gassol, *Nigeria* 79 D7
Gasteiz = Vitoria, *Spain* . 28 C2
Gastonia, *U.S.A.* 105 H5
Gastoúni, *Greece* 39 M4
Gastoúri, *Greece* 39 K2
Gastre, *Argentina* 128 B3
Gata, C., *Cyprus* 37 E12
Gata, C. de, *Spain* ... 29 J2
Gata, Sierra de, *Spain* . 30 E4
Gataga →, *Canada* ... 100 B3
Gătaia, *Romania* 38 D4
Gatchina, *Russia* 40 B7
Gates, *U.S.A.* 106 C7
Gateshead, *U.K.* 12 C6
Gatesville, *U.S.A.* ... 109 K6
Gaths, *Zimbabwe* 83 G3
Gatico, *Chile* 126 A1
Gâtinais, *France* 25 D9
Gâtine, Hauteurs de,
  France 26 B3
Gatineau →, *Canada* . 98 C4
Gatineau, Parc de la,
  Canada 98 C4
Gattaran, *Phil.* 55 B4
Gattinara, *Italy* 32 C5
Gatun, L., *Panama* ... 116 E4
Gatyana, *S. Africa* 85 E4
Gau, *Fiji* 87 D8
Gaucín, *Spain* 31 J5
Gauer L., *Canada* 101 B9
Gauhati, *India* 63 F14
Gauja →, *Latvia* 40 C4
Gaula →, *Norway* 8 E11
Gaurain-Ramecroix,
  Belgium 17 G3
Gausta, *Norway* 10 E2
Gāv Koshī, *Iran* 65 D8
Gavá, *Spain* 28 D6
Gāvakān, *Iran* 65 D7
Gavarnie, *France* 26 F3
Gavāter, *Iran* 65 E9
Gāvbandī, *Iran* 65 E7
Gavdhopoúla, *Greece* . 37 E6
Gávdhos, *Greece* 37 E6
Gavere, *Belgium* 17 G3
Gavião, *Portugal* 31 F3
Gaviota, *U.S.A.* 113 L6
Gavleborgs län □, *Sweden* 10 C10
Gavorrano, *Italy* 32 F7
Gavray, *France* 24 D5

Gavrilov Yam, *Russia* 41 C11
Gawachab, *Namibia* ... 84 D2
Gawilgarh Hills, *India* .. 60 J10
Gawler, *Australia* 91 E2
Gaxun Nur, *China* 54 B5
Gaya, *India* 63 G11
Gaya, *Niger* 79 C5
Gaya, *Nigeria* 79 C6
Gaylord, *U.S.A.* 104 C3
Gayndah, *Australia* ... 91 D5
Gaysin, *Ukraine* 42 B3
Gayvoron, *Ukraine* ... 42 B3
Gaza, *Egypt* 69 D3
Gaza □, *Mozam.* 85 C5
Gaza Strip, *Egypt* 69 D3
Gazaoua, *Niger* 79 C6
Gāzbor, *Iran* 65 D8
Gazi, *Zaïre* 82 B1
Gaziantep, *Turkey* 66 E7
Gaziantep □, *Turkey* . 66 E7
Gazipaşa, *Turkey* 66 E5
Gazli, *Uzbekistan* 44 E7
Gbarnga, *Liberia* 78 D3
Gbekebo, *Nigeria* 79 D5
Gboko, *Nigeria* 79 D6
Gbongan, *Nigeria* 79 D5
Gdańsk, *Poland* 20 A8
Gdańska, Zatoka, *Poland* . 20 A9
Gdov, *Russia* 40 B5
Gdynia, *Poland* 20 A8
Gebe, *Indonesia* 57 D7
Gebeit Mine, *Sudan* ... 76 C4
Gebel Mûsa, *Egypt* ... 76 J8
Gebze, *Turkey* 66 C3
Gecha, *Ethiopia* 77 F4
Gedaref, *Sudan* 77 E4
Gede, Tanjung, *Indonesia* 56 F3
Gedinne, *Belgium* 17 J5
Gediz, *Turkey* 66 D3
Gediz →, *Turkey* 66 D2
Gedo, *Ethiopia* 77 F4
Gèdre, *France* 26 F4
Gedser, *Denmark* 11 K5
Gedser Odde, *Denmark* . 11 K5
Geegully Cr. →, *Australia* 88 C3
Geel, *Belgium* 17 F5
Geelong, *Australia* 91 F3
Geelvink Chan., *Australia* 89 E1
Geer →, *Belgium* 17 G7
Geesthacht, *Germany* . 18 B6
Geffen, *Neths.* 16 E6
Geidam, *Nigeria* 79 C7
Geikie →, *Canada* ... 101 B8
Geili, *Sudan* 77 D3
Geilo, *Norway* 10 D2
Geisingen, *Germany* .. 19 H4
Geislingen, *Germany* .. 19 G5
Geita, *Tanzania* 82 C3
Geita □, *Tanzania* 82 C3
Gejiu, *China* 52 F4
Gel →, *Sudan* 77 F2
Gel River, *Sudan* 77 F2
Gela, *Italy* 35 E7
Gela, G. di, *Italy* 35 F7
Geladi, *Ethiopia* 68 F4
Gelderland □, *Neths.* . 16 D8
Geldermalsen, *Neths.* . 16 E6
Geldern, *Germany* 18 D2
Geldrop, *Neths.* 17 F7
Geleen, *Neths.* 17 G7
Gelehun, S. *Leone* 78 D2
Gelendost, *Turkey* 66 D4
Gelendzhik, *Russia* ... 42 D8
Gelibolu, *Turkey* 39 J9
Gelidonya Burnu, *Turkey* . 66 E4
Gelnhausen, *Germany* . 19 E5
Gelsenkirchen, *Germany* . 18 D3
Gelting, *Germany* 18 A5
Gemas, *Malaysia* 59 L4
Gembloux, *Belgium* ... 17 G5
Gemena, *Zaïre* 80 D3
Gemerek, *Turkey* 66 D7
Gemert, *Neths.* 17 E7
Gemlik, *Turkey* 66 C3
Gemona del Friuli, *Italy* . 33 B10
Gemsa, *Egypt* 76 B3
Gemünden, *Germany* . 19 E5
Genale, *Ethiopia* 77 F4
Genappe, *Belgium* 17 G4
Genç, *Turkey* 67 D9
Gençay, *France* 26 B4
Gendringen, *Neths.* ... 16 E8
Gendt, *Neths.* 16 E7
Geneina, Gebel, *Egypt* . 76 J8
General Acha, *Argentina* . 126 D3
General Alvear,
  Buenos Aires, Argentina 126 D3
General Alvear, *Mendoza,
  Argentina* 126 D2
General Artigas, *Paraguay* 126 B4
General Belgrano,
  Argentina 126 D4
General Cabrera, *Argentina* 126 C3
General Carrera, L., *Chile* 128 C2
General Cepeda, *Mexico* . 114 B4
General Conesa, *Argentina* 128 B4
General Guido, *Argentina* 126 D4
General Juan Madariaga,
  Argentina 126 D4
General La Madrid,
  Argentina 126 D3
General Lorenzo Vintter,
  Argentina 128 B4

General MacArthur, *Phil.* 55 F6
General Martin Miguel de
  Güemes, *Argentina* .. 126 A3
General Paz, *Argentina* . 126 B4
General Pico, *Argentina* . 126 D3
General Pinedo, *Argentina* 126 B3
General Pinto, *Argentina* . 126 C3
General Sampaio, *Brazil* 122 B4
General Santos, *Phil.* ... 55 H6
General Toshevo, *Bulgaria* 38 F11
General Trevino, *Mexico* . 115 B5
General Trías, *Mexico* .. 114 B3
General Viamonte,
  Argentina 126 D3
General Villegas, *Argentina* 126 D3
General Vintter, L.,
  Argentina 128 B2
Generoso, Mte., *Switz.* . 23 E8
Genesee, *Idaho, U.S.A.* . 110 C5
Genesee, *Pa., U.S.A.* .. 106 E7
Genesee →, *U.S.A.* .. 106 C7
Geneseo, *Ill., U.S.A.* .. 108 E9
Geneseo, *Kans., U.S.A.* 108 F5
Geneseo, *N.Y., U.S.A.* . 106 D7
Geneva = Genève, *Switz.* 22 D2
Geneva, *Ala., U.S.A.* .. 105 K3
Geneva, *N.Y., U.S.A.* . 106 D7
Geneva, *Nebr., U.S.A.* . 108 E6
Geneva, *Ohio, U.S.A.* . 106 E4
Geneva, L. = Léman, Lac,
  Switz. 22 D3
Geneva, L., *U.S.A.* ... 104 D1
Genève, *Switz.* 22 D2
Genève □, *Switz.* 22 D2
Gengenbach, *Germany* . 19 G4
Gengma, *China* 52 F2
Genichesk, *Ukraine* ... 42 C6
Genil →, *Spain* 31 H5
Génissiat, Barr. de, *France* 27 B9
Genk, *Belgium* 17 G7
Genlis, *France* 25 E12
Gennargentu, Mti. del,
  Italy 34 C2
Gennep, *Neths.* 17 E7
Gennes, *France* 24 E6
Genoa = Génova, *Italy* . 32 D5
Genoa, *Australia* 91 F4
Genoa, *N.Y., U.S.A.* .. 107 D8
Genoa, *Nebr., U.S.A.* . 108 E6
Genoa, *Nev., U.S.A.* .. 112 F7
Genoa →, *Argentina* . 128 B2
Génova, *Italy* 32 D5
Génova, G. di, *Italy* .. 32 E6
Gent, *Belgium* 17 F3
Gentbrugge, *Belgium* .. 17 F3
Genthin, *Germany* 18 C8
Gentio do Ouro, *Brazil* . 122 D2
Geographe B., *Australia* . 89 F2
Geographe Chan., *Australia* 89 D1
Geokchay, *Azerbaijan* . 43 F12
Georga, Zemlya, *Russia* . 44 A5
George, S. *Africa* 84 E3
George →, *Canada* ... 99 A6
George, L., *N.S.W.,
  Australia* 91 F4
George, L., *S. Austral.,
  Australia* 91 F3
George, L., *W. Austral.,
  Australia* 88 D3
George, L., *Uganda* ... 82 B3
George, L., *Fla., U.S.A.* . 105 L5
George, L., *N.Y., U.S.A.* 107 C11
George Gill Ra., *Australia* 88 D5
George River = Port
  Nouveau-Québec,
  Canada 97 C13
George Sound, *N.Z.* .. 87 L1
George Town, *Bahamas* 116 B4
George Town, *Malaysia* . 59 K3
George V Land, *Antarctica* 5 C10
George VI Sound,
  Antarctica 5 D17
George West, *U.S.A.* . 109 L5
Georgetown, *Australia* . 90 B3
Georgetown, *Ont., Canada* 98 D4
Georgetown, *P.E.I.,
  Canada* 99 C7
Georgetown, *Cayman Is.* 116 C3
Georgetown, *Gambia* .. 78 C2
Georgetown, *Guyana* .. 121 B6
Georgetown, *Calif., U.S.A.* 112 G6
Georgetown, *Colo., U.S.A.* 110 G11
Georgetown, *Ky., U.S.A.* 104 F3
Georgetown, *S.C., U.S.A.* 105 J6
Georgetown, *Tex., U.S.A.* 109 K6
Georgia □, *U.S.A.* ... 105 J4
Georgia ■, *Asia* 43 E10
Georgia, Str. of, *Canada* 100 D4
Georgian B., *Canada* .. 98 C3
Georgievsk, *Russia* ... 43 D10
Georgina →, *Australia* . 90 C2
Georgina Downs, *Australia* 90 C2
Georgiu-Dezh = Liski,
  Russia 41 F11
Gera, *Germany* 18 E8
Geraardsbergen, *Belgium* . 17 G3
Geral, Serra, *Bahia, Brazil* 123 D3
Geral, Serra, *Goiás, Brazil* 122 D2
Geral, Serra, *Sta. Catarina,
  Brazil* 127 B6
Geral de Goiás, Serra,
  Brazil 123 D2
Geral do Paraná Serra,
  Brazil 123 E2
Geraldine, *U.S.A.* 110 C8

Geraldton, *Australia* 89 E1
Geraldton, *Canada* 98 C2
Gérardmer, *France* 25 D13
Gerçüş, *Turkey* 67 E9
Gerede, *Turkey* 42 F5
Gereshk, *Afghan.* 60 D4
Gérgal, *Spain* 29 H2
Gerik, *Malaysia* 59 K3
Gering, *U.S.A.* 108 E3
Gerlach, *U.S.A.* 110 F4
Gerlachovka, *Slovakia* 20 F10
Gerlogubi, *Ethiopia* 68 F4
Germansen Landing, *Canada* 100 B4
Germany ■, *Europe* 18 E6
Germersheim, *Germany* 19 F4
Germiston, *S. Africa* 85 D4
Gernsheim, *Germany* 19 F4
Gero, *Japan* 49 G8
Gerolstein, *Germany* 19 E2
Gerolzhofen, *Germany* 19 F6
Gerona, *Spain* 28 D7
Gerona □, *Spain* 28 C7
Gérouville, *Belgium* 17 J6
Gerrard, *Canada* 100 C5
Gers □, *France* 26 E4
Gers →, *France* 26 D4
Gersfeld, *Germany* 18 E5
Gerze, *Turkey* 66 C6
Geseke, *Germany* 18 D4
Geser, *Indonesia* 57 E8
Gesso →, *Italy* 32 D4
Gestro, Wabi →, *Ethiopia* 77 G5
Gesves, *Belgium* 17 H6
Getafe, *Spain* 30 E7
Gethsémani, *Canada* 99 B7
Gettysburg, Pa., *U.S.A.* 104 F7
Gettysburg, S. Dak., *U.S.A.* 108 C5
Getz Ice Shelf, *Antarctica* 5 D14
Geul →, *Neths.* 17 G7
Gevaş, *Turkey* 67 D10
Gévaudan, *France* 26 D7
Gevgelija, *Macedonia* 39 H5
Gévora →, *Spain* 31 G4
Gex, *France* 27 B10
Geyser, *U.S.A.* 110 C8
Geyserville, *U.S.A.* 112 G4
Geysir, *Iceland* 8 D3
Geyve, *Turkey* 66 C4
Ghâbat el Arab = Wang Kai, *Sudan* 77 F2
Ghaghara →, *India* 63 G11
Ghalla, Wadi el →, *Sudan* 77 E2
Ghallamane, *Mauritania* 74 D3
Ghana ■, *W. Afr.* 79 D4
Ghansor, *India* 63 H9
Ghanzi, *Botswana* 84 C3
Ghanzi □, *Botswana* 84 C3
Gharb el Istiwa'iya □, *Sudan* 77 F2
Gharbîya, Es Sahrâ el, *Egypt* 76 B2
Ghard Abû Muharik, *Egypt* 76 B2
Ghardaïa, *Algeria* 75 B5
Ghârib, G., *Egypt* 76 J8
Ghârib, Râs, *Egypt* 76 J8
Gharyân, *Libya* 75 B7
Gharyân □, *Libya* 75 B7
Ghat, *Libya* 75 D7
Ghatal, *India* 63 H12
Ghatampur, *India* 63 F9
Ghaţţī, *Si. Arabia* 64 D3
Ghawdex = Gozo, *Malta* 37 C1
Ghazal, Bahr el →, *Chad* 73 F8
Ghazâl, Bahr el →, *Sudan* 77 F3
Ghazaouet, *Algeria* 75 A4
Ghaziabad, *India* 62 E7
Ghazipur, *India* 63 G10
Ghaznī, *Afghan.* 62 C3
Ghaznī □, *Afghan.* 60 C6
Ghedi, *Italy* 32 C7
Ghèlinsor, *Somali Rep.* 68 F4
Ghent = Gent, *Belgium* 17 F3
Gheorghe Gheorghiu-Dej, *Romania* 38 C9
Gheorgheni, *Romania* 38 C8
Ghergani, *Romania* 38 E8
Gherla, *Romania* 38 B6
Ghilarza, *Italy* 34 B1
Ghisonaccia, *France* 27 F13
Ghisoni, *France* 27 F13
Ghizao, *Afghan.* 62 C1
Ghizar →, *Pakistan* 63 A5
Ghogha, *India* 62 J5
Ghot Ogrein, *Egypt* 76 A2
Ghotaru, *India* 62 F4
Ghotki, *Pakistan* 62 E3
Ghowr □, *Afghan.* 60 C4
Ghudaf, W. al →, *Iraq* 64 C4
Ghudāmis, *Libya* 75 B6
Ghughri, *India* 63 H9
Ghugus, *India* 60 K11
Ghulam Mohammad Barrage, *Pakistan* 62 G3
Ghūrīān, *Afghan.* 60 B2
Gia Dinh, *Vietnam* 59 G6
Gia Lai = Pleiku, *Vietnam* 58 F7
Gia Nghia, *Vietnam* 59 G6
Gia Ngoc, *Vietnam* 58 E7
Gia Vuc, *Vietnam* 58 E7
Gian, *Phil.* 57 C7
Giannutri, *Italy* 32 F8
Giant Forest, *U.S.A.* 112 J8
Giant Mts. = Krkonoše, *Czech.* 20 E5

Giants Causeway, *U.K.* 15 A5
Giarabub = Al Jaghbūb, *Libya* 73 C9
Giarre, *Italy* 35 E8
Giaveno, *Italy* 32 C4
Gibara, *Cuba* 116 B4
Gibb River, *Australia* 88 C4
Gibbon, *U.S.A.* 108 E5
Gibe →, *Ethiopia* 77 F4
Gibellina, *Italy* 34 E6
Gibraléon, *Spain* 31 H4
Gibraltar ■, *Europe* 31 J5
Gibraltar, Str. of, *Medit. S.* 31 K5
Gibson Desert, *Australia* 88 D4
Gibsons, *Canada* 100 D4
Gibsonville, *U.S.A.* 112 F6
Giddings, *U.S.A.* 109 K6
Gidole, *Ethiopia* 77 F4
Gien, *France* 25 E9
Giessen, *Germany* 18 E4
Gieten, *Neths.* 16 B9
Gīfān, *Iran* 65 B8
Gifatin, Geziret, *Egypt* 76 B3
Gifford Creek, *Australia* 88 D2
Gifhorn, *Germany* 18 C6
Gifu, *Japan* 49 G8
Gifu □, *Japan* 49 G8
Gigant, *Russia* 43 C9
Giganta, Sa. de la, *Mexico* 114 B2
Gigen, *Bulgaria* 38 F7
Gigha, *U.K.* 14 F3
Giglio, *Italy* 32 F7
Gignac, *France* 26 E7
Giguela →, *Spain* 29 F1
Gijón, *Spain* 30 B5
Gil I., *Canada* 100 C3
Gila →, *U.S.A.* 111 K6
Gila Bend, *U.S.A.* 111 K7
Gila Bend Mts., *U.S.A.* 111 K7
Gīlān □, *Iran* 65 B6
Gilbert →, *Australia* 90 B3
Gilbert Is., *Kiribati* 92 G9
Gilbert Plains, *Canada* 101 C8
Gilbert River, *Australia* 90 B3
Gilberton, *Australia* 90 B3
Gilbués, *Brazil* 122 C2
Gilf el Kebîr, Hadabat el, *Egypt* 76 C2
Gilford I., *Canada* 100 C3
Gilgandra, *Australia* 91 E4
Gilgil, *Kenya* 82 C4
Gilgit, *India* 63 B6
Gilgit →, *Pakistan* 63 B6
Giljeva Planina, *Serbia, Yug.* 21 M10
Gillam, *Canada* 101 B10
Gilleleje, *Denmark* 11 H6
Gillen, L., *Australia* 89 E3
Gilles, L., *Australia* 91 E2
Gillette, *U.S.A.* 108 C2
Gilliat, *Australia* 90 C3
Gillingham, *U.K.* 13 F8
Gilly, *Belgium* 17 H4
Gilmer, *U.S.A.* 109 J7
Gilmore, *Australia* 91 F4
Gilmore, L., *Australia* 89 F3
Gilmour, *Canada* 98 D4
Gilo →, *Ethiopia* 77 F3
Gilort →, *Romania* 38 E6
Gilroy, *U.S.A.* 111 H3
Gilze, *Neths.* 17 E5
Gimbi, *Ethiopia* 77 F4
Gimigliano, *Italy* 35 D9
Gimli, *Canada* 101 C9
Gimone →, *France* 26 E5
Gimont, *France* 26 E4
Gin Gin, *Australia* 91 D5
Ginâh, *Egypt* 76 B3
Gindie, *Australia* 90 C4
Gingin, *Australia* 89 F2
Gîngiova, *Romania* 38 F6
Ginir, *Ethiopia* 68 F3
Ginosa, *Italy* 35 B9
Ginzo de Limia, *Spain* 30 C3
Giohar, *Somali Rep.* 68 G4
Gióia, G. di, *Italy* 35 D8
Gióia del Colle, *Italy* 35 B9
Gióia Táuro, *Italy* 35 D8
Gioiosa Iónica, *Italy* 35 D9
Gióna, Óros, *Greece* 39 L5
Giovi, Passo dei, *Italy* 32 D5
Giovinazzo, *Italy* 35 A9
Gir Hills, *India* 62 J4
Girab, *India* 62 F4
Girâfi, W. →, *Egypt* 69 F3
Giraltovce, *Slovakia* 20 F11
Girard, Kans., *U.S.A.* 109 G7
Girard, Ohio, *U.S.A.* 106 E4
Girard, Pa., *U.S.A.* 106 D4
Girardot, *Colombia* 120 C3
Girdle Ness, *U.K.* 14 D6
Giresun, *Turkey* 67 C8
Giresun □, *Turkey* 67 C8
Girga, *Egypt* 76 B3
Giridih, *India* 63 G12
Girifalco, *Italy* 35 D9
Girilambone, *Australia* 91 E4
Giro, *Nigeria* 79 C5
Giromagny, *France* 25 E13
Girona = Gerona, *Spain* 28 D7
Gironde □, *France* 26 D3
Gironde →, *France* 26 C2
Gironella, *Spain* 28 C6
Giru, *Australia* 90 B4
Girvan, *U.K.* 14 F4

Gisborne, *N.Z.* 87 H7
Gisenyi, *Rwanda* 82 C2
Gisors, *France* 25 C8
Gistel, *Belgium* 17 F1
Giswil, *Switz.* 22 C6
Gitega, *Burundi* 82 C2
Gits, *Belgium* 17 F2
Giuba →, *Somali Rep.* 68 G3
Giugliano in Campania, *Italy* 35 B7
Giuliánova, *Italy* 33 F10
Giurgeni, *Romania* 38 E10
Giurgiu, *Romania* 38 F8
Give, *Denmark* 11 J3
Givet, *France* 25 B11
Givors, *France* 27 C8
Givry, *Belgium* 17 H4
Givry, *France* 25 F11
Giyon, *Ethiopia* 77 F4
Giza = El Giza, *Egypt* 76 H7
Gizhiga, *Russia* 45 C17
Gizhiginskaya Guba, *Russia* 45 C16
Giżycko, *Poland* 20 A11
Gizzeria, *Italy* 35 D9
Gjegjan, *Albania* 39 H3
Gjerstad, *Norway* 10 F3
Gjirokastra, *Albania* 39 J3
Gjoa Haven, *Canada* 96 B10
Gjøl, *Denmark* 11 G3
Gjøvik, *Norway* 10 D4
Glace Bay, *Canada* 99 C8
Glacier Bay, *U.S.A.* 100 B1
Glacier Nat. Park, *Canada* 100 C5
Glacier Park, *U.S.A.* 110 B7
Glacier Peak, *U.S.A.* 110 B3
Gladewater, *U.S.A.* 109 J7
Gladstone, Queens., *Australia* 90 C5
Gladstone, S. Austral., *Australia* 91 E2
Gladstone, W. Austral., *Australia* 89 E1
Gladstone, *Canada* 101 C9
Gladstone, *U.S.A.* 104 C2
Gladwin, *U.S.A.* 104 D3
Gladys L., *Canada* 100 B2
Gláma, *Iceland* 8 D2
Gláma →, *Norway* 10 E5
Glamis, *U.S.A.* 113 N11
Glamoč, *Bos.-H.* 33 D13
Glan, *Sweden* 11 F10
Glanerbrug, *Neths.* 16 D9
Glarner Alpen, *Switz.* 23 C8
Glärnisch, *Switz.* 23 C7
Glarus, *Switz.* 23 B8
Glarus □, *Switz.* 23 C8
Glasco, Kans., *U.S.A.* 108 F6
Glasco, N.Y., *U.S.A.* 107 D11
Glasgow, *U.K.* 14 F4
Glasgow, Ky., *U.S.A.* 104 G3
Glasgow, Mont., *U.S.A.* 110 B10
Glastonbury, *U.K.* 13 F5
Glastonbury, *U.S.A.* 107 E12
Glatt →, *Switz.* 23 B7
Glattfelden, *Switz.* 23 A7
Glauchau, *Germany* 18 E8
Glazov, *Russia* 41 B18
Gleiwitz = Gliwice, *Poland* 20 E8
Glen, *U.S.A.* 107 B13
Glen Affric, *U.K.* 14 D4
Glen Canyon Dam, *U.S.A.* 111 H8
Glen Canyon National Recreation Area, *U.S.A.* 111 H8
Glen Coe, *U.K.* 14 E4
Glen Cove, *U.S.A.* 107 F11
Glen Garry, *U.K.* 14 D3
Glen Innes, *Australia* 91 D5
Glen Lyon, *U.S.A.* 107 E8
Glen Mor, *U.K.* 14 D4
Glen Moriston, *U.K.* 14 D4
Glen Orchy, *U.K.* 14 E4
Glen Spean, *U.K.* 14 E4
Glen Ullin, *U.S.A.* 108 B4
Glénan, Is. de, *France* 24 E2
Glenburgh, *Australia* 89 E2
Glencoe, *Canada* 106 D3
Glencoe, *S. Africa* 85 D5
Glencoe, *U.S.A.* 108 C7
Glendale, Ariz., *U.S.A.* 111 K7
Glendale, Calif., *U.S.A.* 113 L8
Glendale, Oreg., *U.S.A.* 110 E2
Glendale, *Zimbabwe* 83 F3
Glendive, *U.S.A.* 108 B2
Glendo, *U.S.A.* 108 D2
Glenelg, *Australia* 91 E2
Glenelg →, *Australia* 91 F3
Glenflorrie, *Australia* 88 D2
Glengarriff, *Ireland* 15 E2
Glengyle, *Australia* 90 C2
Glenmora, *U.S.A.* 109 K8
Glenmorgan, *Australia* 91 D4
Glenn, *U.S.A.* 112 F4
Glenns Ferry, *U.S.A.* 110 E6
Glenorchy, *Australia* 90 G4
Glenore, *Australia* 90 B3
Glenormiston, *Australia* 90 C2
Glenreagh, *Australia* 91 E5
Glenrock, *U.S.A.* 110 E11
Glenrothes, *U.K.* 14 E5
Glens Falls, *U.S.A.* 107 C11
Glenties, *Ireland* 15 B3
Glenville, *U.S.A.* 104 F5
Glenwood, Alta., *Canada* 100 D6
Glenwood, Nfld., *Canada* 99 C9

Glenwood, Ark., *U.S.A.* 109 H8
Glenwood, Hawaii, *U.S.A.* 102 J17
Glenwood, Iowa, *U.S.A.* 108 E7
Glenwood, Minn., *U.S.A.* 108 C7
Glenwood, Wash., *U.S.A.* 112 D5
Glenwood Springs, *U.S.A.* 110 G10
Gletsch, *Switz.* 23 C6
Glina, *Croatia* 33 C13
Glittertind, *Norway* 10 C2
Gliwice, *Poland* 20 E8
Glödnitz, *Austria* 21 J4
Głogów, *Poland* 20 D6
Glorieuses, Is., *Ind. Oc.* 85 A8
Glossop, *U.K.* 12 D6
Gloucester, *Australia* 91 E5
Gloucester, *U.K.* 13 F5
Gloucester, *U.S.A.* 107 D14
Gloucester I., *Australia* 90 B4
Gloucestershire □, *U.K.* 13 F5
Gloversville, *U.S.A.* 107 C10
Glovertown, *Canada* 99 C9
Główno, *Poland* 20 D9
Głubczyce, *Poland* 20 E7
Glubokiy, *Russia* 43 B9
Glubokoye, *Belorussia* 40 D5
Głuchołazy, *Poland* 20 E7
Glücksburg, *Germany* 18 A5
Glückstadt, *Germany* 18 B5
Glukhov, *Ukraine* 40 F8
Glussk, *Belorussia* 40 E6
Glyngøre, *Denmark* 11 H2
Gmünd, Kärnten, *Austria* 21 J3
Gmünd, Niederösterreich, *Austria* 20 G5
Gnarp, *Sweden* 10 B11
Gnesta, *Sweden* 10 E11
Gniew, *Poland* 20 B8
Gniezno, *Poland* 20 C7
Gnoien, *Germany* 18 B8
Gnowangerup, *Australia* 89 F2
Go Cong, *Vietnam* 59 G6
Gō-no-ura, *Japan* 49 H4
Go Quao, *Vietnam* 59 H5
Goa, *India* 60 M8
Goa □, *India* 60 M8
Goalen Hd., *Australia* 91 F5
Goalpara, *India* 61 F17
Goalundo Ghat, *Bangla.* 63 H13
Goaso, *Ghana* 78 D4
Goat Fell, *U.K.* 14 F3
Goba, *Ethiopia* 68 F2
Goba, *Mozam.* 85 D5
Gobabis, *Namibia* 84 C2
Gobernador Gregores, *Argentina* 128 C2
Gobi, *Asia* 50 C5
Gobō, *Japan* 49 H7
Gobo, *Sudan* 77 F3
Goch, *Germany* 18 D2
Gochas, *Namibia* 84 C2
Godavari →, *India* 61 L13
Godavari Point, *India* 61 L13
Godbout, *Canada* 99 C6
Godda, *India* 63 G12
Godegård, *Sweden* 11 F9
Goderich, *Canada* 98 D3
Goderville, *France* 24 C7
Godhavn, *Greenland* 4 C5
Godhra, *India* 62 H5
Gödöllő, *Hungary* 21 H9
Godoy Cruz, *Argentina* 126 C2
Gods →, *Canada* 101 B10
Gods L., *Canada* 101 C10
Godthåb, *Greenland* 97 B14
Godwin Austen = K2, Mt., *Pakistan* 63 B7
Goeie Hoop, Kaap die = Good Hope, C. of, *S. Africa* 84 E2
Goéland, L. au, *Canada* 98 C4
Goeree, *Neths.* 16 E4
Goes, *Neths.* 17 F3
Gogama, *Canada* 98 C3
Gogango, *Australia* 90 C5
Gogebic, L., *U.S.A.* 108 B10
Gogra = Ghaghara →, *India* 63 G11
Gogrial, *Sudan* 77 F2
Goiana, *Brazil* 122 C5
Goianésia, *Brazil* 123 E2
Goiânia, *Brazil* 123 E2
Goiás, *Brazil* 123 E1
Goiás □, *Brazil* 122 D2
Goiatuba, *Brazil* 123 E2
Goio-Ere, *Brazil* 127 A5
Goirle, *Neths.* 17 E6
Góis, *Portugal* 30 E2
Gojam □, *Ethiopia* 77 E4
Gojeb, Wabi →, *Ethiopia* 77 F4
Gojō, *Japan* 49 G7
Gojra, *Pakistan* 62 D5
Gokarannath, *India* 63 F9
Gökçeada, *Turkey* 39 J8
Gökirmak →, *Turkey* 66 C6
Göksu →, *Turkey* 66 E6
Göksun, *Turkey* 66 D7
Gokteik, *Burma* 61 H20
Gokurt, *Pakistan* 62 E2
Gola, *India* 63 E9
Golakganj, *India* 63 F13
Golan Heights = Hagolan, *Syria* 69 B4
Golāshkerd, *Iran* 65 E8
Golaya Pristen, *Ukraine* 42 C5

Gölbaşı, Adiyaman, *Turkey* 67 E7
Gölbaşı, Ankara, *Turkey* 66 D5
Golchikha, *Russia* 4 B12
Golconda, *U.S.A.* 110 F5
Gölcük, Kocaeli, *Turkey* 66 C3
Gölcük, Niğde, *Turkey* 66 D6
Gold Beach, *U.S.A.* 110 E1
Gold Coast, *Australia* 91 D5
Gold Coast, *W. Afr.* 70 F3
Gold Hill, *U.S.A.* 110 E2
Goldach, *Switz.* 23 B8
Goldau, *Switz.* 23 B7
Goldberg, *Germany* 18 B8
Golden, *Canada* 100 C5
Golden, *U.S.A.* 108 F2
Golden B., *N.Z.* 87 J4
Golden Gate, *U.S.A.* 110 H2
Golden Hinde, *Canada* 100 D3
Golden Lake, *Canada* 106 A7
Golden Prairie, *Canada* 101 C7
Golden Vale, *Ireland* 15 D3
Goldendale, *U.S.A.* 110 D3
Goldfield, *U.S.A.* 111 H5
Goldfields, *Canada* 101 B7
Goldsand L., *Canada* 101 B8
Goldsboro, *U.S.A.* 105 H7
Goldsmith, *U.S.A.* 109 K3
Goldsworthy, *Australia* 88 D2
Goldthwaite, *U.S.A.* 109 K5
Golegã, *Portugal* 31 F2
Goleniów, *Poland* 20 B4
Goleta, *U.S.A.* 113 L7
Golfito, *Costa Rica* 116 E3
Golfo Aranci, *Italy* 34 B2
Gölgeli Dağları, *Turkey* 66 E3
Goliad, *U.S.A.* 109 L6
Golija, *Serbia, Yug.* 21 M10
Gölköy, *Turkey* 67 C7
Golo →, *France* 27 F13
Golovanevsk, *Ukraine* 42 B4
Golpāyegān, *Iran* 65 C6
Gölpazarı, *Turkey* 66 C4
Golra, *Pakistan* 62 C5
Golspie, *U.K.* 14 D5
Golyama Kamchiya →, *Bulgaria* 38 F10
Goma, *Rwanda* 82 C2
Goma, *Zaïre* 82 C2
Gomati →, *India* 63 G10
Gombari, *Zaïre* 82 B2
Gombe, *Nigeria* 79 C7
Gombe →, *Tanzania* 82 C3
Gombi, *Nigeria* 79 C7
Gomel, *Belorussia* 40 E7
Gomera, *Canary Is.* 36 F2
Gómez Palacio, *Mexico* 114 B4
Gomīshān, *Iran* 65 B7
Gommern, *Germany* 18 C7
Gomogomo, *Indonesia* 57 F8
Gomoh, *India* 63 H15
Gompa = Ganta, *Liberia* 78 D3
Goms, *Switz.* 22 D6
Gonābād, *Iran* 65 C8
Gonaïves, *Haiti* 117 C5
Gonâve, G. de la, *Haiti* 117 C5
Gonâve, I. de la, *Haiti* 117 C5
Gonbab-e Kāvūs, *Iran* 65 B7
Gonda, *India* 63 F9
Gondal, *India* 62 J4
Gonder, *Ethiopia* 77 E4
Gonder □, *Ethiopia* 77 E4
Gondia, *India* 60 J12
Gondola, *Mozam.* 83 F3
Gondomar, *Portugal* 30 D2
Gondomar, *Spain* 30 C2
Gondrecourt-le-Château, *France* 25 D12
Gönen, *Turkey* 66 C2
Gong Xian, *China* 52 C5
Gong'an, *China* 53 B9
Gongcheng, *China* 53 E8
Gongga Shan, *China* 52 C3
Gongguan, *China* 52 G7
Gonghe, *China* 54 C5
Gongola →, *Nigeria* 79 D7
Gongolgon, *Australia* 91 E4
Gongshan, *China* 52 D2
Gongtan, *China* 52 C7
Goniadz, *Poland* 20 B12
Goniri, *Nigeria* 79 C7
Gonjo, *China* 52 B2
Gonnesa, *Italy* 34 C1
Gónnos, *Greece* 39 K5
Gonnosfanadiga, *Italy* 34 C1
Gonzaga, *Phil.* 55 B5
Gonzales, Calif., *U.S.A.* 111 J5
Gonzales, Tex., *U.S.A.* 109 L6
González Chaves, *Argentina* 126 D3
Good Hope, C. of, *S. Africa* 84 E2
Gooderham, *Canada* 98 D4
Goodeve, *Canada* 101 C8
Gooding, *U.S.A.* 110 E6
Goodland, *U.S.A.* 108 F4
Goodnight, *U.S.A.* 109 H4
Goodooga, *Australia* 91 D4
Goodsoil, *Canada* 101 C7
Goodsprings, *U.S.A.* 111 J6
Goole, *U.K.* 12 D7
Goolgowi, *Australia* 91 E4
Goomalling, *Australia* 89 F2
Goombalie, *Australia* 91 D4
Goonda, *Mozam.* 83 F3

Goondiwindi, *Australia*	91	D5
Goongarrie, L., *Australia*	89	F3
Goonyella, *Australia*	90	C4
Goor, *Neths.*	16	D9
Gooray, *Australia*	91	D5
Goose →, *Canada*	99	B7
Goose L., *U.S.A.*	110	F3
Gop, *India*	60	H6
Gopalganj, *India*	63	F11
Goppenstein, *Switz.*	22	D5
Göppingen, *Germany*	19	G5
Gor, *Spain*	29	H2
Góra, *Poland*	20	D6
Gorakhpur, *India*	63	F10
Gorbatov, *Russia*	41	C13
Gorbea, Peña, *Spain*	28	B2
Gorda, *U.S.A.*	112	K5
Gorda, Pta., *Nic.*	116	D3
Gorda, Pta., *Canary Is.*	36	F2
Gordan B., *Australia*	88	B5
Gordon, *U.S.A.*	108	D3
Gordon →, *Australia*	90	G4
Gordon, I., *Chile*	128	D3
Gordon Downs, *Australia*	88	C4
Gordon, Alta., *Canada*	101	B6
Gordon L., N.W.T., *Canada*	100	A6
Gordonia, *S. Africa*	84	D3
Gordonvale, *Australia*	90	B4
Gore, *Australia*	91	D5
Goré, *Chad*	73	G8
Gore, *Ethiopia*	77	F4
Gore, *N.Z.*	87	M2
Gore Bay, *Canada*	98	C3
Görele, *Turkey*	67	C8
Gorey, *Ireland*	15	D5
Gorg, *Iran*	65	D8
Gorgān, *Iran*	65	B7
Gorgona, *Italy*	32	E6
Gorgora, *Ethiopia*	77	E4
Gorham, *U.S.A.*	107	B13
Gori, *Georgia*	43	E11
Gorinchem, *Neths.*	16	E5
Gorinhatã, *Brazil*	123	E2
Goritsy, *Russia*	41	C10
Gorízia, *Italy*	33	C10
Gorki = Nizhniy Novgorod, *Russia*	41	C14
Gorki, *Belorussia*	40	D7
Gorkiy = Nizhniy Novgorod, *Russia*	41	C14
Gorkovskoye Vdkhr., *Russia*	41	C13
Gørlev, *Denmark*	11	J5
Gorlice, *Poland*	20	F11
Görlitz, *Germany*	18	D10
Gorlovka, *Ukraine*	42	B8
Gorman, Calif., *U.S.A.*	113	L8
Gorman, Tex., *U.S.A.*	109	J5
Gorna Dzhumayo = Blagoevgrad, *Bulgaria*	39	G6
Gorna Oryakhovitsa, *Bulgaria*	38	F8
Gornja Radgona, *Slovenia*	33	B13
Gornja Tuzla, *Bos.-H.*	21	L8
Gornji Grad, *Slovenia*	33	B11
Gornji Milanovac, *Serbia, Yug.*	21	M10
Gornji Vakuf. *Bos.-H.*	21	M7
Gorno-Altaysk, *Russia*	44	D9
Gorno Slinkino, *Russia*	44	C8
Gornyi, *Russia*	48	B6
Gornyy, *Russia*	41	F16
Gorodenka, *Ukraine*	42	B1
Gorodets, *Russia*	41	C13
Gorodishche, *Russia*	41	E14
Gorodishche, *Ukraine*	42	B4
Gorodnitsa, *Ukraine*	40	F5
Gorodnya, *Ukraine*	40	F7
Gorodok, *Belorussia*	40	D7
Gorodok, *Ukraine*	40	G3
Gorokhov, *Ukraine*	40	F4
Gorokhovets, *Russia*	41	C13
Gorom Gorom, *Burkina Faso*	79	C4
Goromonzi, *Zimbabwe*	83	F3
Gorongose →, *Mozam.*	85	C5
Gorongoza, *Mozam.*	83	F3
Gorongoza, Sa. da, *Mozam.*	83	F3
Gorontalo, *Indonesia*	57	D6
Goronyo, *Nigeria*	79	C6
Gorredijk, *Neths.*	16	C8
Gorron, *France*	24	D6
Gorssel, *Neths.*	16	D8
Gort, *Ireland*	15	C3
Gortis, *Greece*	37	D6
Gorzkowice, *Poland*	20	D9
Gorzów Śląski, *Poland*	20	D8
Gorzów Wielkopolski, *Poland*	20	C5
Göschenen, *Switz.*	23	C7
Gosford, *Australia*	91	E5
Goshen, Calif., *U.S.A.*	112	J7
Goshen, Ind., *U.S.A.*	104	E3
Goshen, N.Y., *U.S.A.*	107	E10
Goshogawara, *Japan*	48	D10
Goslar, *Germany*	18	D6
Gospič, *Croatia*	33	D12
Gosport, *U.K.*	13	G6
Gossau, *Switz.*	23	B8
Gosse →, *Australia*	90	B1
Gostivar, *Macedonia, Yug.*	39	H3
Gostyń, *Poland*	20	D7
Gostynin, *Poland*	20	C9
Göta älv →, *Sweden*	11	G5
Göta kanal, *Sweden*	9	G12
Göteborg, *Sweden*	11	G5
Göteborgs och Bohus län □, *Sweden*	9	G11
Götene, *Sweden*	11	F7
Gotha, *Germany*	18	E6
Gothenburg, *U.S.A.*	108	E4
Gotland, *Sweden*	9	H15
Gotse Delchev, *Bulgaria*	39	H6
Gotska Sandön, *Sweden*	9	G15
Gōtsu, *Japan*	49	G6
Göttingen, *Germany*	18	D5
Gottwald = Zmiyev, *Ukraine*	42	B7
Gottwaldov = Zlin, *Czech.*	20	F7
Goubangzi, *China*	51	D11
Gouda, *Neths.*	16	D5
Goúdhoura, Ákra, *Greece*	37	E8
Goudiry, *Senegal*	78	C2
Gough I., *Atl. Oc.*	2	G9
Gouin, Rés., *Canada*	98	C5
Gouitafla, *Ivory C.*	78	D3
Goulburn, *Australia*	91	E4
Goulburn Is., *Australia*	90	A1
Goulia, *Ivory C.*	78	C3
Goulimime, *Morocco*	74	C3
Goulmima, *Morocco*	74	B4
Gounou-Gaya, *Chad*	73	G8
Goúra, *Greece*	39	M5
Gouraya, *Algeria*	75	A5
Gourdon, *France*	26	D5
Gouré, *Niger*	79	C7
Gouri, *Chad*	73	E8
Gourits →, *S. Africa*	84	E3
Gourma Rharous, *Mali*	79	B4
Goúrnais, *Greece*	37	D7
Gournay-en-Bray, *France*	25	C8
Gourock Ra., *Australia*	91	F4
Goursi, *Burkina Faso*	78	C4
Gouvêa, *Brazil*	123	E3
Gouverneur, *U.S.A.*	107	B9
Gouviá, *Greece*	37	A3
Gouzon, *France*	26	B6
Govan, *Canada*	101	C8
Governador Valadares, *Brazil*	123	E3
Governor's Harbour, *Bahamas*	116	A4
Gowan Ra., *Australia*	90	C4
Gowanda, *U.S.A.*	106	D6
Gowd-e Zirreh, *Afghan.*	60	E3
Gower, *U.K.*	13	F3
Gowna, L., *Ireland*	15	C4
Goya, *Argentina*	126	B4
Goyder Lagoon, *Australia*	91	D2
Goyllarisquisga, *Peru*	124	C2
Göynük, *Turkey*	66	C4
Goz Beïda, *Chad*	73	F9
Goz Regeb, *Sudan*	77	D4
Gozo, *Malta*	37	C1
Graaff-Reinet, *S. Africa*	84	E3
Grabow, *Germany*	18	B7
Grabs, *Switz.*	23	B8
Gračac, *Croatia*	33	D12
Gračanica, *Bos.-H.*	21	L8
Graçay, *France*	25	E8
Grace, *U.S.A.*	110	E8
Graceville, *U.S.A.*	108	C6
Gracias a Dios, C., *Honduras*	116	C3
Graciosa, I., *Canary Is.*	36	E6
Gradaús, *Brazil*	122	C1
Gradaús, Serra dos, *Brazil*	122	C1
Gradets, *Bulgaria*	38	G9
Grado, *Italy*	33	C10
Grado, *Spain*	30	B4
Gradule, *Australia*	91	D4
Grady, *U.S.A.*	109	H3
Graeca, Lacul, *Romania*	38	E9
Graénalón, L., *Iceland*	8	D5
Grafenau, *Germany*	19	G9
Gräfenberg, *Germany*	19	F7
Grafton, *Australia*	91	D5
Grafton, *U.S.A.*	108	A6
Gragnano, *Italy*	35	B7
Graham, *Canada*	98	C1
Graham, N.C., *U.S.A.*	105	G6
Graham, Tex., *U.S.A.*	109	J5
Graham, Mt., *U.S.A.*	111	K9
Graham →, *Canada*	100	B4
Graham Bell, Os., *Russia*	44	A7
Graham I., *Canada*	100	C2
Graham Land, *Antarctica*	5	C17
Grahamdale, *Canada*	101	C9
Grahamstown, *S. Africa*	84	E4
Graïba, *Tunisia*	75	B7
Graide, *Belgium*	17	J6
Graie, Alpi, *Europe*	32	C4
Grain Coast, *W. Afr.*	70	F2
Grajaú, *Brazil*	122	C2
Grajaú →, *Brazil*	122	B3
Grajewo, *Poland*	20	B12
Gramada, *Bulgaria*	38	F5
Gramat, *France*	26	D5
Grammichele, *Italy*	35	E7
Grampian □, *U.K.*	14	D6
Grampian Highlands = Grampian Mts., *U.K.*	14	E5
Grampian Mts., *U.K.*	14	E5
Gran →, *Surinam*	121	C6
Gran Altiplanicie Central, *Argentina*	128	C3
Gran Canaria, *Canary Is.*	36	F4
Gran Chaco, *S. Amer.*	126	B3
Gran Paradiso, *Italy*	32	C4
Gran Sasso d'Italia, *Italy*	33	F10
Granada, *Nic.*	116	D2
Granada, *Spain*	29	H1
Granada, *U.S.A.*	109	F3
Granada □, *Spain*	31	H7
Granadilla de Abona, *Canary Is.*	36	F3
Granard, *Ireland*	15	C4
Granbury, *U.S.A.*	109	J6
Granby, *Canada*	98	C5
Grand →, Mo., *U.S.A.*	108	F8
Grand →, S. Dak., *U.S.A.*	108	C4
Grand Bahama, *Bahamas*	116	A4
Grand Bank, *Canada*	99	C8
Grand Bassam, *Ivory C.*	78	D4
Grand Béréby, *Ivory C.*	78	E3
Grand-Bourg, *Guadeloupe*	117	C7
Grand Canal = Yun Ho →, *China*	51	E9
Grand Canyon, *U.S.A.*	111	H7
Grand Canyon National Park, *U.S.A.*	111	H7
Grand Cayman, *Cayman Is.*	116	C3
Grand Cess, *Liberia*	78	E3
Grand Coulee, *U.S.A.*	110	C4
Grand Coulee Dam, *U.S.A.*	110	C4
Grand Erg Occidental, *Algeria*	75	B5
Grand Erg Oriental, *Algeria*	75	C6
Grand Falls, *Canada*	99	C8
Grand Forks, *Canada*	100	D5
Grand Forks, *U.S.A.*	108	B6
Grand-Fougeray, *France*	24	E5
Grand Haven, *U.S.A.*	104	D2
Grand I., *U.S.A.*	104	B2
Grand Island, *U.S.A.*	108	E5
Grand Isle, *U.S.A.*	109	L10
Grand Junction, *U.S.A.*	111	G9
Grand L., *U.S.A.*	109	L8
Grand Lac Victoria, *Canada*	98	C4
Grand Lahou, *Ivory C.*	78	D3
Grand L., N.B., *Canada*	99	C6
Grand L., Nfld., *Canada*	99	C8
Grand L., Nfld., *Canada*	99	B7
Grand Lake, *U.S.A.*	110	F11
Grand-Leez, *Belgium*	17	G5
Grand-Lieu, L. de, *France*	24	E5
Grand Manan I., *Canada*	99	D6
Grand Marais, *Canada*	108	B9
Grand Marais, *U.S.A.*	104	B3
Grand-Mère, *Canada*	98	C5
Grand Popo, *Benin*	79	D5
Grand Portage, *U.S.A.*	98	C2
Grand Rapids, *Canada*	101	C9
Grand Rapids, Mich., *U.S.A.*	104	D2
Grand Rapids, Minn., *U.S.A.*	108	B8
Grand St-Bernard, Col du, *Switz.*	22	E4
Grand Santi, *Fr. Guiana*	121	C7
Grand Teton, *U.S.A.*	110	E8
Grand Valley, *U.S.A.*	110	G9
Grand View, *Canada*	101	C8
Grandas de Salime, *Spain*	30	B4
Grande →, Jujuy, *Argentina*	126	A2
Grande →, Mendoza, *Argentina*	126	D2
Grande →, *Bolivia*	125	D5
Grande →, Bahia, *Brazil*	122	D3
Grande →, Minas Gerais, *Brazil*	123	F1
Grande →, *Spain*	29	F4
Grande →, *Venezuela*	121	B5
Grande, B., *Argentina*	128	D3
Grande, I., *Brazil*	123	F3
Grande, Rio →, *U.S.A.*	109	N6
Grande, Serra, Goiás, *Brazil*	122	D2
Grande, Serra, Piauí, *Brazil*	122	C2
Grande Baie, *Canada*	99	C5
Grande Baleine, R. de la →, *Canada*	98	A4
Grande Cache, *Canada*	100	C5
Grande de Santiago →, *Mexico*	114	C3
Grande Dixence, Barr. de la, *Switz.*	22	D4
Grande-Entrée, *Canada*	99	C7
Grande Prairie, *Canada*	100	B5
Grande-Rivière, *Canada*	99	C7
Grande Sauldre →, *France*	25	E9
Grande-Vallée, *Canada*	99	C6
Grandes-Bergeronnes, *Canada*	99	C6
Grandfalls, *U.S.A.*	109	K3
Grandoe Mines, *Canada*	100	B3
Grândola, *Portugal*	31	G2
Grandpré, *France*	25	C11
Grandson, *Switz.*	22	C3
Grandview, *U.S.A.*	110	C4
Grandvilliers, *France*	25	C8
Graneros, *Chile*	126	C1
Grangemouth, *U.K.*	14	E5
Granger, Wash., *U.S.A.*	110	C3
Granger, Wyo., *U.S.A.*	110	F9
Grangeville, *U.S.A.*	110	D5
Granite City, *U.S.A.*	108	F9
Granite Falls, *U.S.A.*	108	C7
Granite Mt., *U.S.A.*	113	M10
Granite Peak, *Australia*	89	E3
Granite Peak, *U.S.A.*	110	D9
Granity, *N.Z.*	87	J3
Granja, *Brazil*	122	B3
Granja de Moreruela, *Spain*	30	D5
Granja de Torrehermosa, *Spain*	31	G5
Granollers, *Spain*	28	D7
Gransee, *Germany*	18	B9
Grant, *U.S.A.*	108	E4
Grant, Mt., *U.S.A.*	110	G4
Grant City, *U.S.A.*	108	E7
Grant I., *Australia*	88	B5
Grant Range, *U.S.A.*	111	G6
Grantham, *U.K.*	12	E7
Grantown-on-Spey, *U.K.*	14	D5
Grants, *U.S.A.*	111	J10
Grants Pass, *U.S.A.*	110	E2
Grantsburg, *U.S.A.*	108	C8
Grantsville, *U.S.A.*	110	F7
Granville, *France*	24	D5
Granville, N. Dak., *U.S.A.*	108	A4
Granville, N.Y., *U.S.A.*	107	C11
Granville L., *Canada*	101	B8
Grao de Gandía, *Spain*	29	F4
Grapeland, *U.S.A.*	109	K7
Gras, L. de, *Canada*	96	B8
Graskop, *S. Africa*	85	C5
Grass →, *Canada*	101	B9
Grass Range, *U.S.A.*	110	C9
Grass River Prov. Park, *Canada*	101	C8
Grass Valley, Calif., *U.S.A.*	112	F6
Grass Valley, Oreg., *U.S.A.*	110	D3
Grassano, *Italy*	35	B9
Grasse, *France*	27	E10
Grassmere, *Australia*	91	E3
Graulhet, *France*	26	E5
Graus, *Spain*	28	C5
Gravatá, *Brazil*	122	C4
Grave, *Neths.*	16	E7
Grave, Pte. de, *France*	26	C2
's-Graveland, *Neths.*	16	D6
Gravelbourg, *Canada*	101	D7
Gravelines, *France*	25	B9
's-Gravendeel, *Neths.*	16	E5
's-Gravenhage, *Neths.*	16	D4
Gravenhurst, *Canada*	106	B5
's-Gravenpolder, *Neths.*	17	F3
Gravesend, *Australia*	91	D5
Gravesend, *U.K.*	13	F8
Gravina di Púglia, *Italy*	35	B9
Gravois, Pointe-à-, *Haiti*	117	C5
Gravone →, *France*	27	G12
Gray, *France*	25	E12
Grayling, *U.S.A.*	104	C3
Grayling →, *Canada*	100	B3
Grays Harbor, *U.S.A.*	110	C1
Grays L., *U.S.A.*	110	E8
Grays River, *U.S.A.*	112	D3
Grayson, *Canada*	101	C8
Graz, *Austria*	21	H5
Grazalema, *Spain*	31	J5
Greasy L., *Canada*	100	A4
Great Abaco I., *Bahamas*	116	A4
Great Artesian Basin, *Australia*	90	C3
Great Australian Bight, *Australia*	89	F5
Great Bahama Bank, *Bahamas*	116	B4
Great Barrier I., *N.Z.*	87	G5
Great Barrier Reef, *Australia*	90	B4
Great Barrington, *U.S.A.*	107	D11
Great Basin, *U.S.A.*	110	G5
Great Bear →, *Canada*	96	B7
Great Bear L., *Canada*	96	B7
Great Belt = Store Bælt, *Denmark*	11	J5
Great Bend, Kans., *U.S.A.*	108	F5
Great Bend, Pa., *U.S.A.*	107	E9
Great Blasket I., *Ireland*	15	D1
Great Britain, *Europe*	6	E5
Great Central, *Canada*	100	D3
Great Dividing Ra., *Australia*	90	C4
Great Driffield, *U.K.*	12	C7
Great Exuma I., *Bahamas*	116	B4
Great Falls, *Canada*	101	C9
Great Falls, *U.S.A.*	110	C8
Great Fish = Groot Vis →, *S. Africa*	84	E4
Great Guana Cay, *Bahamas*	116	B4
Great Harbour Deep, *Canada*	99	B8
Great Inagua I., *Bahamas*	117	B5
Great Indian Desert = Thar Desert, *India*	62	F4
Great I., *Canada*	101	B9
Great Karoo, *S. Africa*	84	E3
Great Lake, *Australia*	90	G4
Great Ormes Head, *U.K.*	12	D4
Great Ouse →, *U.K.*	12	E8
Great Palm I., *Australia*	90	B4
Great Plains, *N. Amer.*	102	A6
Great Ruaha →, *Tanzania*	82	D4
Great Saint Bernard P. = Grand St-Bernard, Col du, *Switz.*	22	E4
Great Salt L., *U.S.A.*	110	F7
Great Salt Lake Desert, *U.S.A.*	110	F7
Great Salt Plains L., *U.S.A.*	109	G5
Great Sandy Desert, *Australia*	88	D3
Great Sangi = Sangihe, P., *Indonesia*	57	D7
Great Scarcies →, *S. Leone*	78	D2
Great Slave L., *Canada*	100	A5
Great Smoky Mts. Nat. Pk., *U.S.A.*	105	H4
Great Stour = Stour →, *U.K.*	13	F9
Great Victoria Desert, *Australia*	89	E4
Great Wall, *China*	50	E5
Great Whernside, *U.K.*	12	C6
Great Yarmouth, *U.K.*	12	E9
Greater Antilles, *W. Indies*	117	C5
Greater London □, *U.K.*	13	F7
Greater Manchester □, *U.K.*	12	D5
Greater Sunda Is., *Indonesia*	56	F4
Grebbestad, *Sweden*	11	F5
Grebenka, *Ukraine*	40	F8
Greco, C., *Cyprus*	37	E13
Greco, Mte., *Italy*	34	A6
Gredos, Sierra de, *Spain*	30	E5
Greece ■, *Europe*	39	K6
Greeley, Colo., *U.S.A.*	108	E2
Greeley, Nebr., *U.S.A.*	108	E5
Green →, Ky., *U.S.A.*	104	G2
Green →, Utah, *U.S.A.*	111	G9
Green B., *U.S.A.*	104	C2
Green Bay, *U.S.A.*	104	C2
Green C., *Australia*	91	F5
Green Cove Springs, *U.S.A.*	105	L5
Green River, *U.S.A.*	111	G8
Greenbank, *U.S.A.*	112	B4
Greenbush, Mich., *U.S.A.*	106	B1
Greenbush, Minn., *U.S.A.*	108	A6
Greencastle, *U.S.A.*	104	F2
Greene, *U.S.A.*	107	D9
Greenfield, Calif., *U.S.A.*	112	J5
Greenfield, Calif., *U.S.A.*	113	K8
Greenfield, Ind., *U.S.A.*	104	F3
Greenfield, Iowa, *U.S.A.*	108	E7
Greenfield, Mass., *U.S.A.*	107	D12
Greenfield, Mo., *U.S.A.*	109	G8
Greenfield Park, *Canada*	107	A11
Greenland ■, *N. Amer.*	4	C5
Greenland Sea, *Arctic*	4	B7
Greenock, *U.K.*	14	F4
Greenore, *Ireland*	15	B5
Greenore Pt., *Ireland*	15	D5
Greenough →, *Australia*	89	E1
Greenport, *U.S.A.*	107	E12
Greensboro, Ga., *U.S.A.*	105	J4
Greensboro, N.C., *U.S.A.*	105	G6
Greensburg, Ind., *U.S.A.*	104	F3
Greensburg, Kans., *U.S.A.*	109	G5
Greensburg, Pa., *U.S.A.*	106	F5
Greenville, *Liberia*	78	D3
Greenville, Ala., *U.S.A.*	105	K2
Greenville, Calif., *U.S.A.*	112	E6
Greenville, Ill., *U.S.A.*	108	F10
Greenville, Maine, *U.S.A.*	99	C6
Greenville, Mich., *U.S.A.*	104	D3
Greenville, Miss., *U.S.A.*	109	J9
Greenville, N.C., *U.S.A.*	105	H7
Greenville, Ohio, *U.S.A.*	104	E3
Greenville, Pa., *U.S.A.*	106	E4
Greenville, S.C., *U.S.A.*	105	H4
Greenville, Tenn., *U.S.A.*	105	G4
Greenville, Tex., *U.S.A.*	109	J6
Greenwater Lake Prov. Park, *Canada*	101	C8
Greenwich, *U.K.*	13	F8
Greenwich, Conn., *U.S.A.*	107	E11
Greenwich, N.Y., *U.S.A.*	107	C11
Greenwich, Ohio, *U.S.A.*	106	E2
Greenwood, *Canada*	100	D5
Greenwood, Miss., *U.S.A.*	109	J9
Greenwood, S.C., *U.S.A.*	105	H4
Greenwood, Mt., *Australia*	88	B5
Gregório →, *Brazil*	124	B3
Gregory, *U.S.A.*	108	D5
Gregory →, *Australia*	90	B2
Gregory, L., S. Austral., *Australia*	91	D2
Gregory, L., W. Austral., *Australia*	89	E2
Gregory Downs, *Australia*	90	B2
Gregory L., *Australia*	88	D4
Gregory Ra., Queens., *Australia*	90	B3
Gregory Ra., W. Austral., *Australia*	88	D3
Greiffenberg, *Germany*	18	B9
Greifswald, *Germany*	18	A9
Greifswalder Bodden, *Germany*	18	A9
Grein, *Austria*	21	G4
Greiz, *Germany*	18	E8
Gremikha, *Russia*	44	C4
Grenå, *Denmark*	11	H4

Grenada, *U.S.A.* 109 J10
Grenada ■, *W. Indies* 117 D7
Grenade, *France* 26 E5
Grenadines, *W. Indies* 117 D7
Grenchen, *Switz.* 22 B4
Grenen, *Denmark* 11 G4
Grenfell, *Australia* 91 E4
Grenfell, *Canada* 101 C8
Grenoble, *France* 27 C9
Grenora, *U.S.A.* 108 A3
Grenville, C., *Australia* 90 A3
Grenville Chan., *Canada* . . 100 C3
Gréoux-les-Bains, *France* . . 27 E9
Gresham, *U.S.A.* 112 E4
Gresik, *Indonesia* 57 G15
Grëssoney St. Jean, *Italy* . . 32 C4
Gretna Green, *U.K.* 14 F5
Grevelingen Krammer,
  Neths. 16 E4
Greven, *Germany* 18 C3
Grevená, *Greece* 39 J4
Grevenbroich, *Germany* . . 18 D2
Grevenmacher, *Lux.* 17 J8
Grevesmühlen, *Germany* . . 18 B7
Grevie, *Sweden* 11 H6
Grey →, *N.Z.* 87 K3
Grey, C., *Australia* 90 A2
Grey Ra., *Australia* 91 D3
Grey Res., *Canada* 99 C8
Greybull, *U.S.A.* 110 D9
Greymouth, *N.Z.* 87 K3
Greytown, *N.Z.* 87 J5
Greytown, *S. Africa* 85 D5
Gribanovskiy, *Russia* 41 F12
Gribbell I., *Canada* 100 C3
Gridley, *U.S.A.* 112 F5
Griekwastad, *S. Africa* . . . 84 D3
Griffin, *U.S.A.* 105 J3
Griffith, *Australia* 91 E4
Grijpskerk, *Neths.* 16 B8
Grillby, *Sweden* 10 E11
Grimari, *C.A.R.* 73 G9
Grimaylov, *Ukraine* 40 G5
Grimbergen, *Belgium* 17 G4
Grimes, *U.S.A.* 112 F5
Grimma, *Germany* 18 D8
Grimmen, *Germany* 18 A9
Grimsby, *Canada* 106 C5
Grimsby, *U.K.* 12 D7
Grimselpass, *Switz.* 23 C6
Grímsey, *Iceland* 8 C5
Grimshaw, *Canada* 100 B5
Grimstad, *Norway* 11 F2
Grindelwald, *Switz.* 22 C6
Grindsted, *Denmark* 11 J2
Grindu, *Romania* 38 E9
Grinnell, *U.S.A.* 108 E8
Griñón, *Spain* 30 E7
Grintavec, *Slovenia* 33 B11
Grip, *Norway* 10 A1
Gris-Nez, C., *France* 25 B8
Grisolles, *France* 26 E5
Grisons = Graubünden □,
  Switz. 23 C9
Grivegnée, *Belgium* 17 G7
Grmeč Planina,
  Bos.-H. 33 D13
Groais I., *Canada* 99 B8
Groblersdal, *S. Africa* . . . 85 D4
Grobming, *Austria* 21 H3
Grodno, *Belorussia* 40 E3
Grodzisk Mazowiecki,
  Poland 20 C10
Grodzisk Wielkopolski,
  Poland 20 C6
Grodzyanka, *Belorussia* . . 40 E6
Groenlo, *Neths.* 16 D9
Groesbeck, *U.S.A.* 109 K6
Groesbeek, *Neths.* 16 E7
Groix, *France* 24 E3
Groix, I. de, *France* 24 E3
Grójec, *Poland* 20 D10
Grolloo, *Neths.* 16 C9
Gronau, *Niedersachsen,*
  Germany 18 C5
Gronau,
  Nordrhein-Westfalen,
  Germany 18 C3
Grong, *Norway* 8 D12
Groningen, *Neths.* 16 B9
Groningen, *Surinam* 121 B6
Groningen □, *Neths.* 16 B9
Groninger Wad, *Neths.* . . 16 B9
Gronsveld, *Neths.* 17 G7
Groom, *U.S.A.* 109 H4
Groot →, *S. Africa* 84 E3
Groot Berg →, *S. Africa* . . 84 E2
Groot-Brakrivier, *S. Africa* 84 E3
Groot-Kei →, *S. Africa* . . . 85 E4
Groot Vis →, *S. Africa* . . . 84 E4
Groote Eylandt, *Australia* . 90 A2
Grootebroek, *Neths.* 16 C6
Grootfontein, *Namibia* . . . 84 B2
Grootlaagte →, *Africa* 84 C3
Grootvloer, *S. Africa* 84 E3
Gros C., *Canada* 100 A6
Grosa, Pta., *Spain* 36 B8
Grósio, *Italy* 32 B7
Grosne →, *France* 27 B8
Gross Glockner, *Austria* . . 21 H2
Grossenbrode, *Germany* . . 18 A7
Grossenhain, *Germany* . . . 18 D9
Grosseto, *Italy* 32 F8
Groswater B., *Canada* . . . 99 B8
Grote Gette →, *Neths.* . . 17 G6

Grote Nete →, *Belgium* . . 17 F5
Groton, *Conn., U.S.A.* . . . 107 E12
Groton, *S. Dak., U.S.A.* . . 108 C5
Grottáglie, *Italy* 35 B10
Grottaminarda, *Italy* 35 A8
Grottammare, *Italy* 33 F10
Grouard Mission, *Canada* . 100 B5
Grouin, Pte. du, *France* . . 24 D5
Groundhog →, *Canada* . . . 98 C3
Grouse Creek, *U.S.A.* . . . 110 F7
Grouw, *Neths.* 16 B7
Grove City, *U.S.A.* 106 E4
Groveland, *U.S.A.* 112 H6
Grover City, *U.S.A.* 113 K6
Groveton, *N.H., U.S.A.* . . 107 B13
Groveton, *Tex., U.S.A.* . . 109 K7
Grožnjan, *Croatia* 33 C10
Groznyy, *Russia* 43 E11
Grubbenvorst, *Neths.* . . . 17 F8
Grudziądz, *Poland* 20 B8
Gruissan, *France* 26 E7
Grumo Áppula, *Italy* 35 A9
Grünberg, *Germany* 18 E4
Grundy Center, *U.S.A.* . . 108 D8
Gruver, *U.S.A.* 109 G4
Gruyéres, *Switz.* 22 C4
Gryazi, *Russia* 41 E11
Gryazovets, *Russia* 41 B12
Gstaad, *Switz.* 22 D4
Gua, *India* 61 H14
Gua Musang, *Malaysia* . . . 59 K4
Guacanayabo, G. de, *Cuba* 116 B4
Guacara, *Venezuela* 120 A4
Guachípas →, *Argentina* . 126 B2
Guachiría →, *Colombia* . . 120 B3
Guadajoz →, *Spain* 31 H6
Guadalajara, *Mexico* 114 C4
Guadalajara, *Spain* 28 E1
Guadalajara □, *Spain* 28 E2
Guadalcanal, *Solomon Is.* . 92 H8
Guadalcanal, *Spain* 31 G5
Guadalén →, *Spain* 31 G7
Guadales, *Argentina* 126 C2
Guadalete →, *Spain* 31 J4
Guadalhorce →, *Spain* . . . 31 J6
Guadalimar →, *Spain* 29 G1
Guadalmena →, *Spain* . . . 29 G2
Guadalmez →, *Spain* 31 G5
Guadalope →, *Spain* 28 D4
Guadalquivir →, *Spain* . . . 31 J4
Guadalupe =
  Guadeloupe ■, *W. Indies* 117 C7
Guadalupe, *Brazil* 122 C3
Guadalupe, *Mexico* 113 N10
Guadalupe, *Spain* 31 F5
Guadalupe, *U.S.A.* 113 L6
Guadalupe →, *Mexico* . . 113 N10
Guadalupe →, *U.S.A.* . . . 109 L6
Guadalupe, Sierra de,
  Spain 31 F5
Guadalupe Bravos, *Mexico* 114 A3
Guadalupe Peak, *U.S.A.* . 111 L11
Guadalupe y Calvo, *Mexico* 114 B3
Guadarrama, Sierra de,
  Spain 30 E6
Guadeloupe ■, *W. Indies* . 117 C7
Guadeloupe Passage,
  W. Indies 117 C7
Guadiamar →, *Spain* 31 J4
Guadiana →, *Portugal* . . . 31 H3
Guadiana Menor →, *Spain* 29 H1
Guadiaro →, *Spain* 31 J5
Guadiato →, *Spain* 31 H5
Guadiela →, *Spain* 28 E2
Guadix, *Spain* 29 H1
Guafo, Boca del, *Chile* . . 128 B2
Guafo, I., *Chile* 128 B2
Guainía □, *Colombia* 120 C4
Guainía →, *Colombia* 120 C4
Guaíra, *Brazil* 127 A5
Guaitecas, Is., *Chile* 128 B2
Guajará-Mirim, *Brazil* . . . 125 C4
Guajira □, *Colombia* 120 A3
Guajira, Pen. de la,
  Colombia 120 A3
Gualaceo, *Ecuador* 120 D2
Gualán, *Guatemala* 116 C2
Gualdo Tadino, *Italy* 33 E9
Gualeguay, *Argentina* . . . 126 C4
Gualeguaychú, *Argentina* . 126 C4
Gualicho, Salina, *Argentina* 128 B3
Gualjaina, *Argentina* 128 B2
Guam ■, *Pac. Oc.* 92 F6
Guamá, *Brazil* 122 B2
Guamá →, *Brazil* 122 B2
Guamblin, I., *Chile* 128 B1
Guamini, *Argentina* 126 D3
Guamote, *Ecuador* 120 D2
Guampí, Sierra de,
  Venezuela 121 B4
Guamúchil, *Mexico* 114 B3
Guan Xian, *China* 52 B4
Guanabacoa, *Cuba* 116 B3
Guanacaste, Cordillera del,
  Costa Rica 116 D2
Guanaceví, *Mexico* 114 B3
Guanahani = San Salvador,
  Bahamas 117 B5
Guanajay, *Cuba* 116 B3
Guanajuato, *Mexico* 114 C4
Guanajuato □, *Mexico* . . 114 C4
Guanambi, *Brazil* 123 D3
Guanare, *Venezuela* 120 B4
Guanare →, *Venezuela* . . 120 B4
Guandacol, *Argentina* . . . 126 B2

Guane, *Cuba* 116 B3
Guang'an, *China* 52 B6
Guangchang, *China* 53 D11
Guangde, *China* 53 B12
Guangdong □, *China* 53 F9
Guangfeng, *China* 53 C12
Guanghan, *China* 52 B5
Guanghua, *China* 53 A8
Guangji, *China* 53 C10
Guangling, *China* 50 E8
Guangning, *China* 53 F9
Guangrao, *China* 51 F10
Guangshun, *China* 52 D6
Guangwu, *China* 50 F3
Guangxi Zhuangzu
  Zizhiqu □, *China* 52 E7
Guangyuan, *China* 52 A5
Guangze, *China* 53 D11
Guangzhou, *China* 53 F9
Guanhães, *Brazil* 123 E3
Guanipa →, *Venezuela* . . 121 B5
Guanling, *China* 52 E5
Guannan, *China* 51 G10
Guanta, *Venezuela* 121 A5
Guantánamo, *Cuba* 117 B4
Guantao, *China* 50 F8
Guanyang, *China* 53 E8
Guanyun, *China* 51 G10
Guapí, *Colombia* 120 C2
Guápiles, *Costa Rica* 116 D3
Guaporé →, *Brazil* 125 C4
Guaqui, *Bolivia* 124 D4
Guara, Sierra de, *Spain* . . 28 C4
Guarabira, *Brazil* 122 C4
Guaranda, *Ecuador* 120 D2
Guarapari, *Brazil* 123 F3
Guarapuava, *Brazil* 123 G1
Guaratinguetá, *Brazil* . . . 127 A6
Guaratuba, *Brazil* 127 B6
Guarda, *Portugal* 30 E3
Guarda □, *Portugal* 30 E3
Guardafui, C. = Asir, Ras,
  Somali Rep. 68 E5
Guardamar del Segura,
  Spain 29 G4
Guardavalle, *Italy* 35 D9
Guardiagrele, *Italy* 33 F11
Guardo, *Spain* 30 C6
Guareña, *Spain* 31 G4
Guareña →, *Spain* 30 D5
Guaria □, *Paraguay* 126 B4
Guárico □, *Venezuela* . . . 120 B4
Guarrojo →, *Colombia* . . 120 C3
Guarujá, *Brazil* 127 A6
Guarus, *Brazil* 123 F3
Guasave, *Mexico* 114 B3
Guascama, Pta., *Colombia* 120 C2
Guasdualito, *Venezuela* . . 120 B3
Guasipati, *Venezuela* . . . 121 B5
Guastalla, *Italy* 32 D7
Guatemala, *Guatemala* . . 116 D1
Guatemala ■, *Cent. Amer.* 116 C1
Guatire, *Venezuela* 120 A4
Guaviare □, *Colombia* . . . 120 C3
Guaviare →, *Colombia* . . 120 C4
Guaxupé, *Brazil* 127 A6
Guayabero →, *Colombia* . 120 C3
Guayama, *Puerto Rico* . . 117 C6
Guayaneco, Arch., *Chile* . 128 C1
Guayaquil, *Ecuador* 120 D2
Guayaquil, G. de, *Ecuador* 120 D1
Guayaramerín, *Bolivia* . . 125 C4
Guayas →, *Ecuador* 120 D2
Guaymas, *Mexico* 114 B2
Guazhou, *China* 53 A12
Guba, *Zaïre* 83 E2
Gûbâl, Madîq, *Egypt* 76 B3
Gubat, *Phil.* 55 E6
Gúbbio, *Italy* 33 E9
Gubio, *Nigeria* 79 C7
Gubkin, *Russia* 41 F10
Gudata, *Georgia* 43 E9
Gudbrandsdalen, *Norway* . 9 F10
Gudená, *Denmark* 11 H3
Gudermes, *Russia* 43 E12
Gudivada, *India* 61 L12
Gudur, *India* 60 M11
Guebwiller, *France* 25 E14
Guecho, *Spain* 28 B2
Guékédou, *Guinea* 78 D2
Guelma, *Algeria* 75 A6
Guelph, *Canada* 98 D3
Guelt es Stel, *Algeria* . . . 75 A5
Guelttara, *Algeria* 75 C4
Guémené-Penfao, *France* . 24 E5
Guémené-sur-Scorff, *France* 24 D3
Guéné, *Benin* 79 C5
Güepi, *Peru* 120 D2
Guer, *France* 24 E4
Güer Aike, *Argentina* . . . 128 D3
Guérande, *France* 24 E4
Guercif, *Morocco* 75 B4
Guéréda, *Chad* 73 F9
Guéret, *France* 26 B5
Guérigny, *France* 25 E10
Guerneville, *U.S.A.* 112 G4
Guernica, *Spain* 28 B2
Guernsey, *U.K.* 13 H5
Guernsey, *U.S.A.* 108 D2
Guerrara, Oasis, *Algeria* . 75 B5
Guerrara, Saoura, *Algeria* 75 C4
Guerrero □, *Mexico* 115 D5
Guerzim, *Algeria* 75 C4

Gueugnon, *France* 27 B8
Gueydan, *U.S.A.* 109 K8
Gügher, *Iran* 65 D8
Guglionesi, *Italy* 35 A7
Gui Jiang →, *China* 53 F8
Gui Xian, *China* 52 F7
Guia, *Canary Is.* 36 F4
Guia de Isora, *Canary Is.* . 36 F3
Guia Lopes da Laguna,
  Brazil 127 A4
Guichi, *China* 53 B11
Guider, *Cameroon* 79 D7
Guidimouni, *Niger* 79 C6
Guiding, *China* 52 D6
Guidong, *China* 53 D9
Guiglo, *Ivory C.* 78 D3
Guijá, *Mozam.* 85 C5
Guijo de Coria, *Spain* . . . 30 E4
Guildford, *U.K.* 13 F7
Guilford, *U.S.A.* 99 C6
Guilin, *China* 53 E8
Guillaumes, *France* 27 D10
Guillestre, *France* 27 D10
Guilvinec, *France* 24 E2
Güimar, *Canary Is.* 36 F3
Guimarães, *Brazil* 122 B3
Guimarães, *Portugal* 30 D2
Guimaras, *Phil.* 55 F5
Guinda, *U.S.A.* 112 G4
Guinea ■, *W. Afr.* 78 C2
Guinea, Gulf of, *Atl. Oc.* . 70 F3
Guinea-Bissau ■, *Africa* . . 78 C2
Güines, *Cuba* 116 B3
Guingamp, *France* 24 D3
Guipavas, *France* 24 D2
Guiping, *China* 53 F8
Guipúzcoa □, *Spain* 28 B2
Guir, O. →, *Algeria* 75 B4
Guiratinga, *Brazil* 125 D7
Güiria, *Venezuela* 121 A5
Guiscard, *France* 25 C10
Guise, *France* 25 C10
Guitiriz, *Spain* 30 B3
Guiuan, *Phil.* 55 F6
Guixi, *China* 53 C11
Guiyang, *Guizhou, China* . 52 D6
Guiyang, *Hunan, China* . . 53 E9
Guizhou □, *China* 52 D6
Gujan-Mestras, *France* . . 26 D2
Gujar □, *India* 62 H4
Gujiang, *China* 53 D10
Gujranwala, *Pakistan* 62 C6
Gujrat, *Pakistan* 62 C6
Gukovo, *Russia* 43 B8
Gulbarga, *India* 60 L10
Gulbene, *Latvia* 40 C5
Gulf, The, *Asia* 65 E6
Gulfport, *U.S.A.* 109 K10
Gulgong, *Australia* 91 E4
Gulin, *China* 52 C5
Gulistan, *Pakistan* 62 D2
Gull Lake, *Canada* 101 C7
Gullegem, *Belgium* 17 G2
Güllük, *Turkey* 66 E2
Gulma, *Nigeria* 79 C5
Gulmarg, *India* 63 B6
Gulnar, *Turkey* 66 E5
Gulpen, *Neths.* 17 G7
Gülşehir, *Turkey* 66 D6
Gulshad, *Kazakhstan* 44 E8
Gulsvik, *Norway* 10 D3
Gulu, *Uganda* 82 B3
Gulwe, *Tanzania* 82 D4
Gulyaypole, *Ukraine* 42 C7
Gum Lake, *Australia* 91 E3
Gumal →, *Pakistan* 62 D4
Gumbaz, *Pakistan* 62 D3
Gumel, *Nigeria* 79 C6
Gumiel de Hizán, *Spain* . . 28 D1
Gumlu, *Australia* 90 B4
Gumma □, *Japan* 49 F9
Gummersbach, *Germany* . 18 D3
Gummi, *Nigeria* 79 C6
Gümüshacıköy, *Turkey* . . 42 F6
Gümüshane, *Turkey* 67 C8
Gümüşhane □, *Turkey* . . . 67 C8
Gumzai, *Indonesia* 57 F8
Guna, *Ethiopia* 77 E4
Guna, *India* 62 G7
Gundagai, *Australia* 91 F4
Gundelfingen, *Germany* . . 19 G6
Gundih, *Indonesia* 57 G14
Guneydogu Toroslar,
  Turkey 67 D9
Gungu, *Zaïre* 80 F3
Gunisao →, *Canada* 101 C9
Gunisao L., *Canada* 101 C9
Gunnbjørn Fjeld,
  Greenland 4 C6
Gunnedah, *Australia* 91 E5
Gunningbar Cr. →,
  Australia 91 E4
Gunnison, *Colo., U.S.A.* . 111 G10
Gunnison, *Utah, U.S.A.* . 110 G8
Gunnison →, *U.S.A.* 111 G9
Gunpowder, *Australia* . . . 90 B2
Guntakal, *India* 60 M10
Guntersville, *U.S.A.* 105 H2
Guntong, *Malaysia* 59 K3
Guntur, *India* 61 L12
Gunungapi, *Indonesia* . . . 57 F7
Gunungsitoli, *Indonesia* . 56 D1
Gunza, *Angola* 80 G2
Günzburg, *Germany* 19 G6

Gunzenhausen, *Germany* . 19 F6
Guo He →, *China* 51 H9
Guoyang, *China* 50 H9
Gupis, *Pakistan* 63 A5
Gura Humorului, *Romania* 38 B8
Gurag, *Ethiopia* 77 F4
Gurdaspur, *India* 62 C6
Gurdon, *U.S.A.* 109 J8
Gurdzhaani, *Georgia* 43 F11
Gurgaon, *India* 62 E7
Gúrgei, *India* 62 G4
Gurguéia →, *Brazil* 122 C3
Gurha, *India* 62 G4
Guri, Embalse de,
  Venezuela 121 B5
Gurk →, *Austria* 21 J4
Gurkha, *Nepal* 63 E11
Gurley, *Australia* 91 D4
Gurné, *Mozam.* 83 F4
Gurun, *Malaysia* 59 K3
Gürün, *Turkey* 66 D7
Gurupá, *Brazil* 121 D7
Gurupá, I. Grande de,
  Brazil 121 D7
Gurupi, *Brazil* 123 D2
Gurupi →, *Brazil* 122 B2
Gurupi, Serra do, *Brazil* . 122 C2
Guryev = Atyrau,
  Kazakhstan 43 C14
Gus-Khrustalnyy, *Russia* . 41 D12
Gusau, *Nigeria* 79 C6
Gusev, *Russia* 40 D3
Gushan, *China* 51 E12
Gushi, *China* 53 A10
Gushiago, *Ghana* 79 D4
Gusinje, *Montenegro, Yug.* 21 N9
Gusinoozersk, *Russia* . . . 45 D11
Gúspini, *Italy* 34 C1
Gustanj, *Slovenia* 33 B11
Gustine, *U.S.A.* 111 H3
Güstrow, *Germany* 18 B8
Gusum, *Sweden* 11 F10
Guta = Kalárovo, *Slovakia* 21 H7
Gütersloh, *Germany* 18 D4
Gutha, *Australia* 89 E2
Guthalongra, *Australia* . . 90 B4
Guthrie, *U.S.A.* 109 H6
Gutian, *China* 53 D12
Gutiérrez, *Bolivia* 125 D5
Guttannen, *Switz.* 23 C6
Guttenberg, *U.S.A.* 108 D9
Guyana ■, *S. Amer.* 121 B6
Guyane française ■ =
  French Guiana ■,
  S. Amer. 121 C7
Guyang, *China* 50 D6
Guyenne, *France* 26 D4
Guymon, *U.S.A.* 109 G4
Guyra, *Australia* 91 E5
Guyuan, *Hebei, China* . . . 50 D8
Guyuan, *Ningxia Huizu,*
  China 50 F4
Guzhang, *China* 52 C7
Guzhen, *China* 51 H9
Guzmán, L. de, *Mexico* . . 114 A3
Gwa, *Burma* 61 L19
Gwaai, *Zimbabwe* 83 F2
Gwabegar, *Australia* 91 E4
Gwadabawa, *Nigeria* 79 C6
Gwādar, *Pakistan* 60 G3
Gwagwada, *Nigeria* 79 C6
Gwalia, *Australia* 89 E3
Gwalior, *India* 62 F8
Gwanda, *Zimbabwe* 83 G2
Gwandu, *Nigeria* 79 C5
Gwane, *Zaïre* 82 B2
Gwaram, *Nigeria* 79 C7
Gwarzo, *Nigeria* 79 C6
Gweebarra B., *Ireland* . . . 15 B3
Gweedore, *Ireland* 15 A3
Gwent □, *U.K.* 13 F5
Gweru, *Zimbabwe* 83 F2
Gwi, *Nigeria* 79 D6
Gwinn, *U.S.A.* 104 B2
Gwio Kura, *Nigeria* 79 C7
Gwol, *Ghana* 78 C4
Gwoza, *Nigeria* 79 C7
Gwydir →, *Australia* 91 D4
Gwynedd □, *U.K.* 12 E4
Gyandzha, *Azerbaijan* . . . 43 F12
Gyaring Hu, *China* 54 C4
Gydanskiy P-ov., *Russia* . 44 C8
Gympie, *Australia* 91 D5
Gyoma, *Hungary* 21 J10
Gyöngyös, *Hungary* 21 H9
Györ, *Hungary* 21 H7
Gypsum Pt., *Canada* 100 A6
Gypsumville, *Canada* . . . 101 C9
Gyula, *Hungary* 21 J11
Gyumri = Kumayri,
  Armenia 43 F10
Gzhatsk, *Russia* 40 D9

H

Ha 'Arava →, *Israel* 69 E4
Ha Coi, *Vietnam* 58 B6
Ha Dong, *Vietnam* 58 B5
Ha Giang, *Vietnam* 58 A5
Ha Tien, *Vietnam* 59 G5
Ha Tinh, *Vietnam* 58 C5
Ha Trung, *Vietnam* 58 C5

Haacht, *Belgium* 17 G5
Haag, *Germany* 19 G8
Haaksbergen, *Neths.* 16 D9
Haaltert, *Belgium* 17 G4
Haamstede, *Neths.* 17 E3
Haapamäki, *Finland* 8 E18
Haapsalu, *Estonia* 40 B3
Haarlem, *Neths.* 16 D5
Haast →, *N.Z.* 87 K2
Haast Bluff, *Australia* .. 88 D5
Haastrecht, *Neths.* 16 E5
Hab Nadi Chauki, *Pakistan* 62 G2
Habaswein, *Kenya* 82 B4
Habay, *Canada* 100 B5
Habay-la-Neuve, *Belgium* . 17 J7
Habbānīyah, *Iraq* 64 C4
Haboro, *Japan* 48 B10
Haccourt, *Belgium* 17 G7
Hachenburg, *Germany* 18 E3
Hachijō-Jima, *Japan* 49 H9
Hachinohe, *Japan* 48 D10
Hachiōji, *Japan* 49 G9
Hachŏn, *N. Korea* 51 D15
Hachy, *Belgium* 17 J7
Hacıbektaş, *Turkey* 66 D6
Hacılar, *Turkey* 66 D6
Hackensack, *U.S.A.* 107 F10
Haçlı Gölü, *Turkey* 67 D10
Hadali, *Pakistan* 62 C5
Hadarba, Ras, *Sudan* 76 C4
Hadarom □, *Israel* 69 E3
Haddington, *U.K.* 14 F6
Hadejia, *Nigeria* 79 C7
Hadejia →, *Nigeria* 79 C7
Haden, *Australia* 91 D5
Hadera, *Israel* 69 C3
Hadera, N. →, *Israel* 69 C3
Haderslev, *Denmark* 11 J3
Hadhramaut =
  Ḥaḍramawt, *Yemen* .. 68 D4
Hadım, *Turkey* 66 E5
Hadjeb El Aïoun, *Tunisia* 75 A6
Hadong, *S. Korea* 51 G14
Ḥaḍramawt, *Yemen* 68 D4
Ḥadrānīyah, *Iraq* 64 C4
Hadrian's Wall, *U.K.* 12 C5
Hadsten, *Denmark* 11 H4
Hadsund, *Denmark* 11 H4
Haeju, *N. Korea* 51 E13
Haenam, *S. Korea* 51 G14
Haerhpin = Harbin, *China* 51 B14
Hafar al Bāṭin, *Si. Arabia* 64 D5
Hafik, *Turkey* 66 D7
Ḥafirat al 'Aydā, *Si. Arabia* 64 E3
Hafizabad, *Pakistan* 62 C5
Haflong, *India* 61 G18
Hafnarfjörður, *Iceland* ... 8 D3
Hafun, Ras, *Somali Rep.* . 68 E5
Hagalil, *Israel* 69 C4
Hagen, *Germany* 18 D3
Hagenow, *Germany* 18 B7
Hagerman, *U.S.A.* 109 J2
Hagerstown, *U.S.A.* 104 F7
Hagetmau, *France* 26 E3
Hagfors, *Sweden* 9 F12
Häggenäs, *Sweden* 10 A8
Hagi, *Iceland* 8 D2
Hagi, *Japan* 49 G5
Hagolan, *Syria* 69 B4
Hagondange-Briey, *France* 25 C13
Hags Hd., *Ireland* 15 D2
Hague, C. de la, *France* .. 24 C5
Hague, The = 's-
  Gravenhage, *Neths.* 16 D4
Haguenau, *France* 25 D14
Hai □, *Tanzania* 82 C4
Hai Duong, *Vietnam* 58 B6
Hai'an, *Guangdong, China* 53 G8
Hai'an, *Jiangsu, China* .. 53 A13
Haicheng, *Fujian, China* . 53 E11
Haicheng, *Liaoning, China* 51 D12
Haidar Khel, *Afghan.* 62 C3
Haifa = Ḥefa, *Israel* 69 C3
Haifeng, *China* 53 F10
Haig, *Australia* 89 F4
Haiger, *Germany* 18 E4
Haikang, *China* 53 G8
Haikou, *China* 54 D6
Ḥā'il, *Si. Arabia* 64 E4
Hailar, *China* 54 B6
Hailey, *U.S.A.* 110 E6
Haileybury, *Canada* 98 C4
Hailin, *China* 51 B15
Hailing Dao, *China* 53 G8
Hailong, *China* 51 C13
Hailun, *China* 54 B7
Hailuoto, *Finland* 8 D18
Haimen, *Guangdong,
  China* 53 F11
Haimen, *Jiangsu, China* . 53 B13
Haimen, *Zhejiang, China* . 53 C13
Hainan □, *China* 54 E5
Hainaut □, *Belgium* 17 H4
Haines, *U.S.A.* 110 D5
Haines City, *U.S.A.* 105 L5
Haines Junction, *Canada* . 100 A1
Haining, *China* 53 B13
Haiphong, *Vietnam* 54 D5
Haiti ■, *W. Indies* 117 C5
Haiya Junction, *Sudan* .. 76 D4
Haiyan, *China* 53 B13
Haiyang, *China* 51 F11
Haiyuan,
  *Guangxi Zhuangzu,
  China* 52 F6

Haiyuan, *Ningxia Huizu,
  China* 50 F3
Haizhou, *China* 51 G10
Haizhou Wan, *China* 51 G10
Haja, *Indonesia* 57 E7
Hajar Bangar, *Sudan* 73 F9
Hajdúböszörmény, *Hungary* 21 H11
Hajdúszoboszló, *Hungary* . 21 H11
Hajipur, *India* 63 G11
Ḥājjī Muḥsin, *Iraq* 64 C5
Ḥājjīābād, *Eṣfahan, Iran* . 65 C7
Ḥājjīābād, *Hormozgān,
  Iran* 65 D7
Hakansson, Mts., *Zaïre* .. 83 D2
Håkantorp, *Sweden* 11 F6
Hakkâri, *Turkey* 67 E10
Hakkâri □, *Turkey* 67 E10
Hakkâri Dağları, *Turkey* . 67 E10
Hakken-Zan, *Japan* 49 G7
Hakodate, *Japan* 48 D10
Haku-San, *Japan* 49 F8
Hakui, *Japan* 49 F8
Hala, *Pakistan* 60 G6
Ḥalab, *Syria* 64 B3
Ḥalabjah, *Iraq* 64 C5
Halaib, *Sudan* 76 C4
Halanzy, *Belgium* 17 J7
Ḥalat' Ammār, *Si. Arabia* 64 D3
Halbā, *Lebanon* 69 A5
Halberstadt, *Germany* .. 18 D7
Halcombe, *N.Z.* 87 J5
Halcon, Mt., *Phil.* 57 B6
Halden, *Norway* 10 E5
Haldensleben, *Germany* . 18 C7
Haldia, *India* 61 H16
Haldwani, *India* 63 E8
Hale →, *Australia* 90 C2
Haleakala Crater, *U.S.A.* . 102 H16
Halen, *Belgium* 17 G6
Haleyville, *U.S.A.* 105 H2
Half Assini, *Ghana* 78 D4
Halfway →, *Canada* 100 B4
Haliburton, *Canada* 98 C4
Halifax, *Australia* 90 B4
Halifax, *Canada* 99 D7
Halifax, *U.K.* 12 D6
Halifax B., *Australia* 90 B4
Halifax I., *Namibia* 84 D2
Ḥalīl →, *Iran* 65 E8
Hall, *Austria* 19 H7
Hall Beach, *Canada* 97 B11
Hall Pt., *Australia* 88 C3
Hallands län □, *Sweden* . 11 H6
Hallands Väderö, *Sweden* . 11 H6
Hallandsås, *Sweden* 11 H7
Halle, *Belgium* 17 G4
Halle, *Nordrhein-Westfalen,
  Germany* 18 C4
Halle, *Sachsen-Anhalt,
  Germany* 18 D7
Hällefors, *Sweden* 9 G13
Hallein, *Austria* 21 H3
Hällekis, *Sweden* 11 F7
Hallett, *Australia* 91 E2
Hallettsville, *U.S.A.* 109 L6
Halliday, *U.S.A.* 108 B3
Halliday L., *Canada* 101 A7
Hallim, *S. Korea* 51 H14
Hallingdal →, *Norway* .. 9 F10
Hällnäs, *Sweden* 8 D15
Hallock, *U.S.A.* 101 D9
Halls Creek, *Australia* .. 88 C4
Hallstahammar, *Sweden* . 10 E10
Hallstead, *U.S.A.* 107 E9
Halmahera, *Indonesia* .. 57 D7
Halmeu, *Romania* 38 B6
Halmstad, *Sweden* 11 H6
Halq el Oued, *Tunisia* .. 75 A7
Hals, *Denmark* 11 H4
Halsafjorden, *Norway* ... 10 A2
Hälsingborg = Helsingborg,
  Sweden 11 H6
Halstad, *U.S.A.* 108 B6
Haltdalen, *Norway* 10 B5
Haltern, *Germany* 18 D3
Halul, *Qatar* 65 E7
Ḥalvān, *Iran* 65 C8
Ham, *France* 25 C10
Ham Tan, *Vietnam* 59 G6
Ham Yen, *Vietnam* 58 A5
Hamab, *Namibia* 84 D2
Hamad, *Sudan* 77 D3
Hamada, *Japan* 49 G6
Hamadān, *Iran* 65 C6
Hamadān □, *Iran* 65 C6
Hamadia, *Algeria* 75 A5
Hamāh, *Syria* 64 C3
Hamamatsu, *Japan* 49 G8
Hamar, *Norway* 10 D5
Hamarøy, *Norway* 8 B13
Hamâta, Gebel, *Egypt* .. 76 C3
Hambantota, *Sri Lanka* . 60 R12
Hamber Prov. Park,
  Canada 100 C5
Hamburg, *Germany* 18 B5
Hamburg, *Ark., U.S.A.* .. 109 J9
Hamburg, *Iowa, U.S.A.* . 108 E7
Hamburg, *N.Y., U.S.A.* . 106 D6
Hamburg, *Pa., U.S.A.* .. 107 F9
Hamburg □, *Germany* .. 18 B6
Ḥamḍ, W. al →,
  Si. Arabia 64 E3
Hamden, *U.S.A.* 107 E12
Hame □ = Hämeen
  lääni □, *Finland* 9 F18

Hämeen lääni □, *Finland* . 9 F18
Hämeenlinna, *Finland* 9 F18
Hamélé, *Ghana* 78 C4
Hamelin Pool, *Australia* . 89 E1
Hameln, *Germany* 18 C5
Hamer Koke, *Ethiopia* .. 77 F4
Hamerkaz □, *Israel* 69 C3
Hamersley Ra., *Australia* . 88 D2
Hamhung, *N. Korea* 51 E14
Hami, *China* 54 B4
Hamilton, *Australia* 91 F3
Hamilton, *Canada* 98 D4
Hamilton, *N.Z.* 87 G5
Hamilton, *U.K.* 14 F4
Hamilton, *Mo., U.S.A.* .. 108 F8
Hamilton, *Mont., U.S.A.* . 110 C6
Hamilton, *N.Y., U.S.A.* . 107 D9
Hamilton, *Ohio, U.S.A.* . 104 F3
Hamilton, *Tex., U.S.A.* .. 109 K5
Hamilton →, *Australia* .. 90 C2
Hamilton City, *U.S.A.* .. 112 F4
Hamilton Hotel, *Australia* 90 C3
Hamilton Inlet, *Canada* .. 99 B8
Hamiota, *Canada* 101 C8
Hamlet, *U.S.A.* 105 H6
Hamley Bridge, *Australia* . 91 E2
Hamlin = Hameln,
  Germany 18 C5
Hamlin, *N.Y., U.S.A.* .. 106 C7
Hamlin, *Tex., U.S.A.* .. 109 J4
Hamm, *Germany* 18 D3
Hammam Bouhadjar,
  Algeria 75 A4
Hammamet, *Tunisia* 75 A7
Hammamet, G. de, *Tunisia* 75 A7
Hammarstrand, *Sweden* . 10 A10
Hamme, *Belgium* 17 F4
Hamme-Mille, *Belgium* .. 17 G5
Hammel, *Denmark* 11 H3
Hammelburg, *Germany* .. 19 E5
Hammerfest, *Norway* 8 A17
Hammond, *Ind., U.S.A.* . 104 E2
Hammond, *La., U.S.A.* .. 109 K9
Hammonton, *U.S.A.* 104 F8
Hamoir, *Belgium* 17 H7
Hamont, *Belgium* 17 F7
Hamoyet, Jebel, *Sudan* .. 76 D4
Hampden, *N.Z.* 87 L3
Hampshire □, *U.K.* 13 F6
Hampshire Downs, *U.K.* . 13 F6
Hampton, *Ark., U.S.A.* .. 109 J8
Hampton, *Iowa, U.S.A.* . 108 D8
Hampton, *N.H., U.S.A.* . 107 D14
Hampton, *S.C., U.S.A.* .. 105 J5
Hampton, *Va., U.S.A.* .. 104 G7
Hampton Tableland,
  Australia 89 F4
Hamrat esh Sheykh, *Sudan* 77 E2
Hamur, *Turkey* 67 D10
Hamyang, *S. Korea* 51 G14
Han Jiang →, *China* 53 F11
Han Shui →, *China* 53 B10
Hana, *U.S.A.* 102 H17
Hanak, *Si. Arabia* 64 E3
Hanamaki, *Japan* 48 E10
Hanang, *Tanzania* 82 C4
Hanau, *Germany* 19 E4
Hanbogd, *Mongolia* 50 C4
Hancheng, *China* 50 G6
Hanchuan, *China* 53 B9
Hancock, *Mich., U.S.A.* . 108 B10
Hancock, *Minn., U.S.A.* . 108 C7
Hancock, *N.Y., U.S.A.* . 107 E9
Handa, *Japan* 49 G8
Handa, *Somali Rep.* 68 E5
Handan, *China* 50 F8
Handen, *Sweden* 10 E12
Handeni, *Tanzania* 82 D4
Handeni □, *Tanzania* .. 82 D4
Handub, *Sudan* 76 D4
Handwara, *India* 63 B6
Handzame, *Belgium* 17 F2
Hanegev, *Israel* 69 E3
Haney, *Canada* 100 D4
Hanford, *U.S.A.* 111 H4
Hang Chat, *Thailand* .. 58 C2
Hang Dong, *Thailand* .. 58 C2
Hangang →, *S. Korea* .. 51 F14
Hangayn Nuruu, *Mongolia* 54 B4
Hangchou = Hangzhou,
  China 53 B13
Hanggin Houqi, *China* .. 50 D4
Hanggin Qi, *China* 50 E5
Hangö, *Finland* 9 G17
Hangu, *China* 51 E9
Hangzhou, *China* 53 B13
Hangzhou Wan, *China* .. 53 B13
Hanhongor, *Mongolia* .. 50 C3
Ḥanīdh, *Si. Arabia* 65 E6
Hanish, *Yemen* 68 E3
Hanjiang, *China* 53 E12
Hankinson, *U.S.A.* 108 B6
Hanko = Hangö, *Finland* . 9 G17
Hanko, *Finland* 9 G17
Hankou, *China* 53 B10
Hanksville, *U.S.A.* 111 G8
Hanle, *India* 63 C8
Hanmer Springs, *N.Z.* .. 87 K4
Hann →, *Australia* 88 C4
Hann, Mt., *Australia* 88 C4
Hanna, *Canada* 100 C6
Hannaford, *U.S.A.* 108 B5
Hannah, *U.S.A.* 108 A5
Hannah B., *Canada* 98 B4
Hannibal, *U.S.A.* 108 F9

Hannik, *Sudan* 76 D3
Hannover, *Germany* 18 C5
Hannut, *Belgium* 17 G6
Hanoi, *Vietnam* 54 D5
Hanover = Hannover,
  Germany 18 C5
Hanover, *Canada* 106 B3
Hanover, *S. Africa* 84 E3
Hanover, *N.H., U.S.A.* . 107 C12
Hanover, *Ohio, U.S.A.* . 106 F2
Hanover, *Pa., U.S.A.* .. 104 F7
Hanover, I., *Chile* 128 D2
Hanshou, *China* 53 C8
Hansi, *India* 62 E6
Hanson, L., *Australia* .. 91 E2
Hanyang, *China* 53 B10
Hanyin, *China* 52 A7
Hanyuan, *China* 52 C4
Hanzhong, *China* 50 H4
Hanzhuang, *China* 51 G9
Haora, *India* 63 H13
Haparanda, *Sweden* 8 D18
Hapert, *Neths.* 17 F6
Happy, *U.S.A.* 109 H4
Happy Camp, *U.S.A.* .. 110 F2
Happy Valley-Goose Bay,
  Canada 99 B7
Hapsu, *N. Korea* 51 D15
Hapur, *India* 62 E7
Haql, *Si. Arabia* 69 F3
Haquira, *Peru* 124 C3
Har, *Indonesia* 57 F8
Har-Ayrag, *Mongolia* .. 50 B5
Har Hu, *China* 54 C4
Har Us Nuur, *Mongolia* . 54 B4
Har Yehuda, *Israel* 69 D3
Ḥaraḍ, *Si. Arabia* 68 C4
Haranomachi, *Japan* 48 F10
Harardera, *Somali Rep.* .. 68 G4
Harare, *Zimbabwe* 83 F3
Harat, *Eritrea* 77 D4
Harazé, *Chad* 73 F8
Harbin, *China* 51 B14
Harbiye, *Turkey* 66 E7
Harboør, *Denmark* 11 H2
Harbor Beach, *U.S.A.* .. 104 C4
Harbor Springs, *U.S.A.* . 104 C3
Harbour Breton, *Canada* . 99 C8
Harbour Grace, *Canada* . 99 C9
Harburg, *Germany* 18 B5
Harda, *India* 62 H7
Hardangerfjorden, *Norway* 9 F8
Hardap Dam, *Namibia* .. 84 C2
Hardegarijp, *Neths.* 16 B7
Hardenberg, *Neths.* 16 C9
Harderwijk, *Neths.* 16 D7
Hardey →, *Australia* 88 D2
Hardin, *U.S.A.* 110 D10
Harding, *S. Africa* 85 E4
Harding Ra., *Australia* .. 88 C3
Hardisty, *Canada* 100 C6
Hardman, *U.S.A.* 110 D4
Hardoi, *India* 63 F9
Hardware = Haridwar, *India* 62 E8
Hardwick, *U.S.A.* 107 B12
Hardy, *U.S.A.* 109 G9
Hardy, Pen., *Chile* 128 E3
Hare B., *Canada* 99 B8
Harelbeke, *Belgium* 17 G2
Haren, *Germany* 18 C3
Haren, *Neths.* 16 B9
Harer, *Ethiopia* 68 F3
Harerge □, *Ethiopia* 77 F5
Hareto, *Ethiopia* 77 F4
Harfleur, *France* 24 C7
Hargeisa, *Somali Rep.* .. 68 F3
Hargshamn, *Sweden* 9 F15
Hari →, *Indonesia* 56 E2
Haria, *Canary Is.* 36 E6
Haricha, Hamada el, *Mali* 74 D4
Haridwar, *India* 62 E8
Haringhata →, *Bangla.* .. 61 J16
Haringvliet, *Neths.* 16 E4
Harīrūd →, *Asia* 60 A2
Harlan, *Iowa, U.S.A.* .. 108 E7
Harlan, *Ky., U.S.A.* 105 G4
Harlech, *U.K.* 12 E3
Harlem, *U.S.A.* 110 B9
Harlingen, *Neths.* 16 B6
Harlingen, *U.S.A.* 109 M6
Harlowton, *U.S.A.* 110 C9
Harmånger, *Sweden* 10 C11
Harmil, *Eritrea* 77 D5
Harney Basin, *U.S.A.* .. 110 E4
Harney L., *U.S.A.* 110 E4
Harney Peak, *U.S.A.* .. 108 D3
Härnön, *Sweden* 10 B12
Härnösand, *Sweden* 10 B11
Haro, *Spain* 28 C2
Harp L., *Canada* 99 A7
Harper, *Liberia* 78 E3
Harplinge, *Sweden* 11 H6
Harrand, *Pakistan* 62 E4
Harriman, *U.S.A.* 105 H3
Harrington Harbour,
  Canada 99 B8
Harris, *U.K.* 14 D2
Harris, Sd. of, *U.K.* 14 D1
Harris L., *Australia* 91 E2
Harrisburg, *Ill., U.S.A.* . 109 G10
Harrisburg, *Nebr., U.S.A.* 108 E3
Harrisburg, *Oreg., U.S.A.* 110 D2
Harrisburg, *Pa., U.S.A.* . 106 F8

Harrismith, *S. Africa* 85 D4
Harrison, *Ark., U.S.A.* .. 109 G8
Harrison, *Idaho, U.S.A.* . 110 C5
Harrison, *Nebr., U.S.A.* . 108 D3
Harrison, C., *Canada* 99 B8
Harrison Bay, *U.S.A.* 96 A4
Harrison L., *Canada* 100 D4
Harrisonburg, *U.S.A.* .. 104 F6
Harrisonville, *U.S.A.* .. 108 F7
Harriston, *Canada* 98 D3
Harrisville, *U.S.A.* 106 B1
Harrogate, *U.K.* 12 D6
Harrow, *U.K.* 13 F7
Harsefeld, *Germany* 18 B5
Harskamp, *Neths.* 16 D7
Harstad, *Norway* 8 B14
Hart, *U.S.A.* 104 D2
Hart, L., *Australia* 91 E2
Hartbees →, *S. Africa* .. 84 D3
Hartberg, *Austria* 21 H5
Hartford, *Conn., U.S.A.* . 107 E12
Hartford, *Ky., U.S.A.* .. 104 G2
Hartford, *S. Dak., U.S.A.* 108 D6
Hartford, *Wis., U.S.A.* . 108 D10
Hartford City, *U.S.A.* .. 104 E3
Hartland, *Canada* 99 C6
Hartland Pt., *U.K.* 13 F3
Hartlepool, *U.K.* 12 C6
Hartley Bay, *Canada* 100 C3
Hartmannberge, *Namibia* 84 B1
Hartney, *Canada* 101 D8
Harts →, *S. Africa* 84 D3
Hartselle, *U.S.A.* 105 H2
Hartshorne, *U.S.A.* 109 H7
Hartsville, *U.S.A.* 105 H5
Hartwell, *U.S.A.* 105 H4
Harunabad, *Pakistan* .. 62 E5
Harvand, *Iran* 65 D7
Harvey, *Australia* 89 F2
Harvey, *Ill., U.S.A.* 104 E2
Harvey, *N. Dak., U.S.A.* 108 B5
Harwich, *U.K.* 13 F9
Haryana □, *India* 62 E7
Harz, *Germany* 18 D6
Harzé, *Belgium* 17 H7
Harzgerode, *Germany* .. 18 D7
Hasaheisa, *Sudan* 77 E3
Hasan Kīādeh, *Iran* 65 B6
Ḥasanābād, *Iran* 65 C7
Hasanpur, *India* 62 E8
Haselünne, *Germany* .. 18 C3
Hashimoto, *Japan* 49 G7
Hashtjerd, *Iran* 65 C6
Håsjö, *Sweden* 10 A10
Haskell, *Okla., U.S.A.* .. 109 H7
Haskell, *Tex., U.S.A.* .. 109 J5
Haslach, *Germany* 19 G4
Haslev, *Denmark* 11 J5
Hasparren, *France* 26 E2
Hassa, *Turkey* 66 E7
Hasselt, *Belgium* 17 G6
Hasselt, *Neths.* 16 C8
Hassene, Adrar, *Algeria* . 75 D5
Hassfurt, *Germany* 19 E6
Hassi Berrekrem, *Algeria* . 75 B6
Hassi bou Khelala, *Algeria* 75 B4
Hassi Daoula, *Algeria* .. 75 B6
Hassi Djafou, *Algeria* .. 75 B5
Hassi el Abiod, *Algeria* . 75 C5
Hassi el Biod, *Algeria* .. 75 C6
Hassi el Gassi, *Algeria* .. 75 B6
Hassi el Hadjar, *Algeria* . 75 B5
Hassi er Rmel, *Algeria* .. 75 B5
Hassi Imoukraze, *Algeria* 75 C6
Hassi Inifel, *Algeria* 75 C5
Hassi Messaoud, *Algeria* . 75 B6
Hassi Rhénami, *Algeria* . 75 B6
Hassi Tartrat, *Algeria* .. 75 B6
Hassi Zerzour, *Morocco* . 74 B4
Hastière-Lavaux, *Belgium* 17 H5
Hastings, *N.Z.* 87 H6
Hastings, *U.K.* 13 G8
Hastings, *Mich., U.S.A.* . 104 D3
Hastings, *Minn., U.S.A.* . 108 C8
Hastings, *Nebr., U.S.A.* . 108 E5
Hastings Ra., *Australia* .. 91 E5
Hat Yai, *Thailand* 59 J3
Hatanbulag, *Mongolia* .. 50 C5
Hatay = Antalya, *Turkey* . 66 E4
Hatay □, *Turkey* 66 E7
Hatch, *U.S.A.* 111 K10
Hatches Creek, *Australia* . 90 C2
Hatchet L., *Canada* 101 B8
Haţeg, *Romania* 38 D5
Haţeg, Mţii., *Romania* .. 38 D6
Hatert, *Neths.* 16 E7
Hateruma-Shima, *Japan* . 49 M1
Hatfield P.O., *Australia* .. 91 E3
Hatgal, *Mongolia* 54 A5
Hathras, *India* 62 F8
Hatia, *Bangla.* 61 H17
Hato de Corozal, *Colombia* 120 B3
Hato Mayor, *Dom. Rep.* . 117 C6
Hattah, *Australia* 91 E3
Hattem, *Neths.* 16 D8
Hatteras, C., *U.S.A.* 105 H8
Hattiesburg, *U.S.A.* 109 K10
Hatvan, *Hungary* 21 H9
Hau Bon = Cheo Reo,
  Vietnam 58 F7
Hau Duc, *Vietnam* 58 E7
Haug, *Norway* 10 D4
Haugastøl, *Norway* 10 D1
Haugesund, *Norway* 9 G8

Haulerwijk, *Neths.*	16	B8
Haultain →, *Canada*	101	B7
Hauraki G., *N.Z.*	87	G5
Haut Atlas, *Morocco*	74	B3
Haut-Rhin □, *France*	25	E14
Haut Zaïre □, *Zaïre*	82	B2
Haute-Corse □, *France*	27	F13
Haute-Garonne □, *France*	26	E5
Haute-Loire □, *France*	26	C7
Haute-Marne □, *France*	25	D12
Haute-Saône □, *France*	25	E13
Haute-Savoie □, *France*	27	C10
Haute-Vienne □, *France*	26	C5
Hauterive, *Canada*	99	C6
Hautes-Alpes □, *France*	27	D10
Hautes Fagnes = Hohe Venn, *Belgium*	17	H8
Hautes Fagnes, *Belgium*	17	G8
Hautes-Pyrénées □, *France*	26	F4
Hauteville-Lompnès, *France*	27	C9
Hautmont, *France*	25	B10
Hautrage, *Belgium*	17	H3
Hauts-de-Seine □, *France*	25	D9
Hauts Plateaux, *Algeria*	75	B4
Hauzenberg, *Germany*	19	G9
Havana = La Habana, *Cuba*	116	B3
Havana, *U.S.A.*	108	E9
Havant, *U.K.*	13	G7
Havasu, L., *U.S.A.*	113	L12
Havel →, *Germany*	18	C8
Havelange, *Belgium*	17	H6
Havelian, *Pakistan*	62	B5
Havelock, *N.B., Canada*	99	C6
Havelock, *Ont., Canada*	98	D4
Havelock, *N.Z.*	87	J4
Havelte, *Neths.*	16	C8
Haverfordwest, *U.K.*	13	F3
Haverhill, *U.S.A.*	107	D13
Havering, *U.K.*	13	F8
Haverstraw, *U.S.A.*	107	E11
Håverud, *Sweden*	11	F6
Havlíčkův Brod, *Czech.*	20	F5
Havneby, *Denmark*	11	J2
Havre, *U.S.A.*	110	B9
Havre-Aubert, *Canada*	99	C7
Havre-St.-Pierre, *Canada*	99	B7
Havza, *Turkey*	66	C6
Haw →, *U.S.A.*	105	H6
Hawaii □, *U.S.A.*	102	H16
Hawaii I., *Pac. Oc.*	102	J17
Hawaiian Is., *Pac. Oc.*	102	H17
Hawaiian Ridge, *Pac. Oc.*	93	E11
Hawarden, *Canada*	101	C7
Hawarden, *U.S.A.*	108	D6
Hawea, L., *N.Z.*	87	L2
Hawera, *N.Z.*	87	H5
Hawick, *U.K.*	14	F6
Hawk Junction, *Canada*	98	C3
Hawke B., *N.Z.*	87	H6
Hawker, *Australia*	91	E2
Hawkesbury, *Canada*	98	C5
Hawkesbury I., *Canada*	100	C3
Hawkesbury Pt., *Australia*	90	A1
Hawkinsville, *U.S.A.*	105	J4
Hawkwood, *Australia*	91	D5
Hawley, *U.S.A.*	108	B6
Hawrān, *Syria*	69	C5
Hawsh Mūssá, *Lebanon*	69	B4
Hawthorne, *U.S.A.*	110	G4
Hawzen, *Ethiopia*	77	E4
Haxtun, *U.S.A.*	108	E3
Hay, *Australia*	91	E3
Hay →, *Australia*	90	C2
Hay →, *Canada*	100	A5
Hay, C., *Australia*	88	B4
Hay L., *Canada*	100	B5
Hay Lakes, *Canada*	100	C6
Hay-on-Wye, *U.K.*	13	E4
Hay River, *Canada*	100	A5
Hay Springs, *U.S.A.*	108	D3
Hayachine-San, *Japan*	48	E10
Hayange, *France*	25	C13
Hayden, *Ariz., U.S.A.*	111	K8
Hayden, *Colo., U.S.A.*	110	F10
Haydon, *Australia*	90	B3
Hayes, *U.S.A.*	108	C4
Hayes →, *Canada*	101	B10
Haymana, *Turkey*	66	D5
Haynesville, *U.S.A.*	109	J8
Hayrabolu, *Turkey*	66	C2
Hays, *Canada*	100	C6
Hays, *U.S.A.*	108	F5
Hayward, *Calif., U.S.A.*	112	H4
Hayward, *Wis., U.S.A.*	108	B9
Haywards Heath, *U.K.*	13	F7
Hazafon □, *Israel*	69	C4
Hazar Gölü, *Turkey*	67	D8
Hazārām, Kūh-e, *Iran*	65	D8
Hazard, *U.S.A.*	104	G4
Hazaribag, *India*	63	H11
Hazaribag Road, *India*	63	G11
Hazebrouck, *France*	25	B9
Hazelton, *Canada*	100	B3
Hazelton, *U.S.A.*	108	B4
Hazen, *N. Dak., U.S.A.*	108	B4
Hazen, *Nev., U.S.A.*	110	G4
Hazerswoude, *Neths.*	16	D5
Hazlehurst, *Ga., U.S.A.*	105	K4
Hazlehurst, *Miss., U.S.A.*	109	K9
Hazleton, *U.S.A.*	107	F9
Hazlett, L., *Australia*	88	D4
Hazor, *Israel*	69	B4
He Xian, *Anhui, China*	53	B12
He Xian, *Guangxi Zhuangzu, China*	53	E8
Head of Bight, *Australia*	89	F5
Headlands, *Zimbabwe*	83	F3
Healdsburg, *U.S.A.*	112	G4
Healdton, *U.S.A.*	109	H6
Healesville, *Australia*	91	F4
Heanor, *U.K.*	12	D6
Heard I., *Ind. Oc.*	3	G13
Hearne, *U.S.A.*	109	K6
Hearne B., *Canada*	101	A9
Hearne L., *Canada*	100	A6
Hearst, *Canada*	98	C3
Heart →, *U.S.A.*	108	B4
Heart's Content, *Canada*	99	C9
Heath →, *Bolivia*	124	C4
Heath Pt., *Canada*	99	C7
Heath Steele, *Canada*	99	C6
Heavener, *U.S.A.*	109	H7
Hebbronville, *U.S.A.*	109	M5
Hebei □, *China*	50	E9
Hebel, *Australia*	91	D4
Heber, *U.S.A.*	113	N11
Heber Springs, *U.S.A.*	109	H9
Hebert, *Canada*	101	C7
Hebgen L., *U.S.A.*	110	D8
Hebi, *China*	50	G8
Hebrides, *U.K.*	14	D1
Hebron = Al Khalīl, *Jordan*	69	D4
Hebron, *Canada*	97	C13
Hebron, *N. Dak., U.S.A.*	108	B3
Hebron, *Nebr., U.S.A.*	108	E6
Hecate Str., *Canada*	100	C2
Hechi, *China*	52	E7
Hechingen, *Germany*	19	G4
Hechtel, *Belgium*	17	F6
Hechuan, *China*	52	B6
Hecla, *U.S.A.*	108	C5
Hecla I., *Canada*	101	C9
Heddal, *Norway*	10	E3
Hédé, *France*	24	D5
Hede, *Sweden*	10	B7
Hedemora, *Sweden*	9	F13
Hedley, *U.S.A.*	109	H4
Hedmark fylke □, *Norway*	10	C5
Hedrum, *Norway*	10	E4
Heeg, *Neths.*	16	C7
Heegermeer, *Neths.*	16	C7
Heemskerk, *Neths.*	16	C5
Heemstede, *Neths.*	16	D5
Heer, *Neths.*	17	G7
Heerde, *Neths.*	16	D8
's Heerenburg, *Neths.*	16	E8
Heerenveen, *Neths.*	16	C7
Heerhugowaard, *Neths.*	16	C5
Heerlen, *Neths.*	17	G7
Heers, *Belgium*	17	G6
Heesch, *Neths.*	16	E7
Heestert, *Belgium*	17	G2
Heeze, *Neths.*	17	F7
Hefa, *Israel*	69	C3
Hefa □, *Israel*	69	C4
Hefei, *China*	53	B11
Hegang, *China*	54	B8
Hegyalja, *Hungary*	21	G11
Heichengzhen, *China*	50	F4
Heide, *Germany*	18	A5
Heidelberg, *Germany*	19	F4
Heidelberg, *S. Africa*	84	E3
Heidelberg, *C. Prov., S. Africa*	84	E3
Heidelberg, *Trans., S. Africa*	85	D4
Heidenheim, *Germany*	19	G6
Heijing, *China*	52	E3
Heilbron, *S. Africa*	85	D4
Heilbronn, *Germany*	19	F5
Heiligenblut, *Austria*	21	H2
Heiligenhafen, *Germany*	18	A6
Heiligenstadt, *Germany*	18	D6
Heilongjiang □, *China*	51	B14
Heilunkiang = Heilongjiang □, *China*	51	B14
Heino, *Neths.*	16	D8
Heinola, *Finland*	9	F19
Heinsch, *Belgium*	17	J7
Heinze Is., *Burma*	61	M20
Heishan, *China*	51	D12
Heishui, *Liaoning, China*	51	C10
Heishui, *Sichuan, China*	52	A4
Heist, *Belgium*	17	F2
Heist-op-den-Berg, *Belgium*	17	F5
Hejaz = Al Ḥijāz, *Si. Arabia*	68	B2
Hejian, *China*	50	E9
Hejiang, *China*	52	C5
Hejin, *China*	50	G6
Hekelgem, *Belgium*	17	G4
Hekimhan, *Turkey*	67	D7
Hekla, *Iceland*	8	E4
Hekou, *Gansu, China*	50	F2
Hekou, *Guangdong, China*	53	F9
Hekou, *Yunnan, China*	54	D5
Helagsfjället, *Sweden*	10	B6
Helan Shan, *China*	50	E3
Helchteren, *Belgium*	17	F6
Helechosa, *Spain*	31	F6
Helena, *Ark., U.S.A.*	109	H9
Helena, *Mont., U.S.A.*	110	C7
Helendale, *U.S.A.*	113	L9
Helensburgh, *U.K.*	14	E4
Helensville, *N.Z.*	87	G5
Helgeroa, *Norway*	10	F3
Helgoland, *Germany*	18	A3
Heligoland = Helgoland, *Germany*	18	A3
Heligoland B. = Deutsche Bucht, *Germany*	18	A4
Heliopolis, *Egypt*	76	H7
Hellebæk, *Denmark*	11	H6
Hellendoorn, *Neths.*	16	D8
Hellevoetsluis, *Neths.*	16	E4
Hellín, *Spain*	29	G3
Helmand □, *Afghan.*	60	D4
Helmand →, *Afghan.*	60	D2
Helme →, *Germany*	18	D7
Helmond, *Neths.*	17	F7
Helmsdale, *U.K.*	14	C5
Helmstedt, *Germany*	18	C7
Helnæs, *Denmark*	11	J4
Helong, *China*	51	C15
Helper, *U.S.A.*	110	G8
Helsingborg, *Sweden*	11	H6
Helsinge, *Denmark*	11	H6
Helsingfors, *Finland*	9	F18
Helsingør, *Denmark*	11	H6
Helsinki, *Finland*	9	F18
Helston, *U.K.*	13	G2
Helvellyn, *U.K.*	12	C4
Helvoirt, *Neths.*	17	E6
Helwân, *Egypt*	76	J7
Hemet, *U.S.A.*	113	M10
Hemingford, *U.S.A.*	108	D3
Hemphill, *U.S.A.*	109	K8
Hempstead, *U.S.A.*	109	K6
Hemse, *Sweden*	9	H15
Hemsö, *Sweden*	10	B12
Henan □, *China*	50	G8
Henares →, *Spain*	28	E1
Henashi-Misaki, *Japan*	48	D9
Hendaye, *France*	26	E2
Hendek, *Turkey*	66	C4
Henderson, *Argentina*	126	D3
Henderson, *Ky., U.S.A.*	104	G2
Henderson, *N.C., U.S.A.*	105	G6
Henderson, *Nev., U.S.A.*	113	J12
Henderson, *Tenn., U.S.A.*	105	H1
Henderson, *Tex., U.S.A.*	109	J7
Hendersonville, *U.S.A.*	105	H4
Hendījān, *Iran*	65	D6
Hendon, *Australia*	91	D5
Heng Xian, *China*	52	F7
Hengcheng, *China*	50	E4
Hengdaohezi, *China*	51	B15
Hengelo, *Gelderland, Neths.*	16	D8
Hengelo, *Overijssel, Neths.*	16	D9
Hengfeng, *China*	53	C10
Hengshan, *Hunan, China*	53	D9
Hengshan, *Shaanxi, China*	50	F5
Hengshui, *China*	50	F8
Hengyang, *Hunan, China*	53	D9
Hengyang, *Hunan, China*	53	D9
Hénin-Beaumont, *France*	25	B9
Henlopen, C., *U.S.A.*	104	F8
Hennan, *Sweden*	10	B9
Hennebont, *France*	24	E3
Hennenman, *S. Africa*	84	D4
Hennessey, *U.S.A.*	109	G6
Hennigsdorf, *Germany*	18	C9
Henrichemont, *France*	25	E9
Henrietta, *U.S.A.*	109	J5
Henrietta, Ostrov, *Russia*	45	B16
Henrietta Maria C., *Canada*	98	A3
Henry, *U.S.A.*	108	E10
Henryetta, *U.S.A.*	109	H6
Hensall, *Canada*	106	C3
Hentiyn Nuruu, *Mongolia*	54	B5
Henty, *Australia*	91	F4
Henzada, *Burma*	61	L19
Heping, *China*	53	E10
Heppner, *U.S.A.*	110	D4
Hepu, *China*	52	G7
Hepworth, *Canada*	106	B3
Heqing, *China*	52	D3
Hequ, *China*	50	E6
Heradhsflói, *Iceland*	8	D6
Heradhsvötn →, *Iceland*	8	D4
Herald Cays, *Australia*	90	B4
Herāt, *Afghan.*	60	B3
Herāt □, *Afghan.*	60	B3
Hérault □, *France*	26	E7
Hérault →, *France*	26	E7
Herbault, *France*	24	E8
Herbert →, *Australia*	90	B4
Herbert Downs, *Australia*	90	C2
Herberton, *Australia*	90	B4
Herbignac, *France*	24	E4
Herborn, *Germany*	18	E4
Herby, *Poland*	20	E8
Hercegnovi, *Montenegro, Yug.*	21	N8
Herdhubreidh, *Iceland*	8	D5
Hereford, *U.K.*	13	E5
Hereford, *U.S.A.*	109	H3
Hereford and Worcester □, *U.K.*	13	E5
Herefoss, *Norway*	11	F2
Herent, *Belgium*	17	G5
Herentals, *Belgium*	17	F5
Herenthout, *Belgium*	17	F5
Herfølge, *Denmark*	11	J6
Herford, *Germany*	18	C4
Héricourt, *France*	25	E13
Herington, *U.S.A.*	108	F6
Herisau, *Switz.*	23	B8
Hérisson, *France*	26	B6
Herjehogna, *Norway*	9	F12
Herk →, *Belgium*	17	G6
Herkenbosch, *Neths.*	17	F8
Herkimer, *U.S.A.*	107	D10
Herlong, *U.S.A.*	112	E6
Herm, *Chan. Is.*	24	C4
Hermagor-Presseger See, *Austria*	21	J3
Herman, *U.S.A.*	108	C6
Hermann, *U.S.A.*	108	F9
Hermannsburg, *Germany*	18	C6
Hermannsburg Mission, *Australia*	88	D5
Hermanus, *S. Africa*	84	E2
Herment, *France*	26	C6
Hermidale, *Australia*	91	E4
Hermiston, *U.S.A.*	110	D4
Hermitage, *N.Z.*	87	K3
Hermite, I., *Chile*	128	E3
Hermon, Mt. = Ash Shaykh, J., *Lebanon*	69	B4
Hermosillo, *Mexico*	114	B2
Hernád →, *Hungary*	21	H11
Hernandarias, *Paraguay*	127	B5
Hernandez, *U.S.A.*	112	J6
Hernando, *Argentina*	126	C3
Hernando, *U.S.A.*	109	H10
Herne, *Belgium*	17	G4
Herne, *Germany*	17	E10
Herne Bay, *U.K.*	13	F9
Herning, *Denmark*	11	H2
Heroica = Caborca, *Mexico*	114	A2
Heroica Nogales = Nogales, *Mexico*	114	A2
Herradura, Pta. de la, *Canary Is.*	36	F5
Herreid, *U.S.A.*	108	C4
Herrera, *Spain*	31	H6
Herrera de Alcántar, *Spain*	31	F3
Herrera de Pisuerga, *Spain*	30	C6
Herrera del Duque, *Spain*	31	F5
Herrick, *Australia*	90	G4
Herrin, *U.S.A.*	109	G10
Herrljunga, *Sweden*	11	F7
Hersbruck, *Germany*	19	F7
Herseaux, *Belgium*	17	G2
Herselt, *Belgium*	17	F5
Hersonissos, *Greece*	37	D7
Herstal, *Belgium*	17	G7
Hertford, *U.K.*	13	F7
Hertfordshire □, *U.K.*	13	F7
's-Hertogenbosch, *Neths.*	17	E6
Hertzogville, *S. Africa*	84	D4
Hervás, *Spain*	30	E5
Herve, *Belgium*	17	G7
Herwijnen, *Neths.*	16	E6
Herzberg, *Brandenburg, Germany*	18	D9
Herzberg, *Niedersachsen, Germany*	18	D6
Herzele, *Belgium*	17	G3
Herzliyya, *Israel*	69	C3
Herzogenbuchsee, *Switz.*	22	B5
Heşar, *Fārs, Iran*	65	D6
Heşār, *Markazī, Iran*	65	C6
Hesdin, *France*	25	B9
Hesel, *Germany*	18	B3
Heshui, *China*	50	G5
Heshun, *China*	50	F7
Hesperange, *Lux.*	17	J8
Hesperia, *U.S.A.*	113	L9
Hesse = Hessen □, *Germany*	18	E5
Hessen □, *Germany*	18	E5
Hetch Hetchy Aqueduct, *U.S.A.*	112	H5
Hettinger, *U.S.A.*	108	C3
Hettstedt, *Germany*	18	D7
Heugem, *Neths.*	17	G7
Heule, *Belgium*	17	G2
Heusden, *Belgium*	17	F6
Heusden, *Neths.*	16	E6
Hève, C. de la, *France*	24	C7
Heverlee, *Belgium*	17	G5
Hewett, C., *Canada*	97	A13
Hexham, *U.K.*	12	C5
Hexi, *Yunnan, China*	52	E4
Hexi, *Zhejiang, China*	53	D12
Hexigten Qi, *China*	51	C9
Hexrivier, *S. Africa*	84	E2
Heydarābād, *Iran*	65	D7
Heyfield, *Australia*	91	F4
Heysham, *U.K.*	12	C5
Heythuysen, *Neths.*	17	F7
Heyuan, *China*	53	F10
Heywood, *Australia*	91	F3
Heze, *China*	50	G8
Hezhang, *China*	52	D5
Hi Vista, *U.S.A.*	113	L9
Hialeah, *U.S.A.*	105	N5
Hiawatha, *Kans., U.S.A.*	108	F7
Hiawatha, *Utah, U.S.A.*	110	G8
Hibbing, *U.S.A.*	108	B8
Hibbs B., *Australia*	90	G4
Hibernia Reef, *Australia*	88	B3
Hickory, *U.S.A.*	105	H5
Hicks, Pt., *Australia*	91	F4
Hicksville, *U.S.A.*	107	F11
Hida, *Romania*	38	B6
Hida-Gawa →, *Japan*	49	G8
Hida-Sammyaku, *Japan*	49	F8
Hidaka-Sammyaku, *Japan*	48	C11
Hidalgo, *Mexico*	115	C5
Hidalgo □, *Mexico*	115	C5
Hidalgo, Presa M., *Mexico*	114	B3
Hidalgo, Pta. del, *Canary Is.*	36	F3
Hidalgo del Parral, *Mexico*	114	B3
Hiddensee, *Germany*	18	A9
Hidrolândia, *Brazil*	123	E2
Hieflau, *Austria*	21	H4
Hiendelaencina, *Spain*	28	D1
Hierapolis, *Turkey*	66	E3
Hierro, *Canary Is.*	36	G1
Higashiajima-San, *Japan*	48	F10
Higashiōsaka, *Japan*	49	G7
Higgins, *U.S.A.*	109	G4
Higgins Corner, *U.S.A.*	112	F5
Higginsville, *Australia*	89	F3
High Atlas = Haut Atlas, *Morocco*	74	B3
High I., *Canada*	99	A7
High Island, *U.S.A.*	109	L7
High Level, *Canada*	100	B5
High Point, *U.S.A.*	105	H6
High Prairie, *Canada*	100	B5
High River, *Canada*	100	C6
High Springs, *U.S.A.*	105	L4
High Tatra = Tatry, *Slovakia*	20	F9
High Wycombe, *U.K.*	13	F7
Highbury, *Australia*	90	B3
Highland □, *U.K.*	14	D4
Highland Park, *U.S.A.*	104	D2
Highmore, *U.S.A.*	108	C5
Highrock L., *Canada*	101	B7
Higüay, *Dom. Rep.*	117	C6
Hihya, *Egypt*	76	H7
Hiiumaa, *Estonia*	40	B3
Híjar, *Spain*	28	D4
Ḥijāz □, *Si. Arabia*	68	C2
Hijken, *Neths.*	16	C8
Hijo = Tagum, *Phil.*	55	H6
Hikari, *Japan*	49	H5
Hiko, *U.S.A.*	111	H6
Hikone, *Japan*	49	G8
Hikurangi, *N.Z.*	87	F5
Hikurangi, Mt., *N.Z.*	87	H6
Hildburghausen, *Germany*	19	E6
Hildesheim, *Germany*	18	C5
Hill →, *Australia*	89	F2
Hill City, *Idaho, U.S.A.*	110	E6
Hill City, *Kans., U.S.A.*	108	F5
Hill City, *Minn., U.S.A.*	108	B8
Hill City, *S. Dak., U.S.A.*	108	D3
Hill Island L., *Canada*	101	A7
Hillared, *Sweden*	11	G7
Hillcrest Center, *U.S.A.*	113	K8
Hillegom, *Neths.*	16	D5
Hillerød, *Denmark*	11	J6
Hillingdon, *U.K.*	13	F7
Hillman, *U.S.A.*	104	C4
Hillmond, *Canada*	101	C7
Hillsboro, *Kans., U.S.A.*	108	F6
Hillsboro, *N. Dak., U.S.A.*	108	B6
Hillsboro, *N.H., U.S.A.*	107	C13
Hillsboro, *N. Mex., U.S.A.*	111	K10
Hillsboro, *Oreg., U.S.A.*	112	E4
Hillsboro, *Tex., U.S.A.*	109	J6
Hillsborough, *Grenada*	117	D7
Hillsdale, *Mich., U.S.A.*	104	E3
Hillsdale, *N.Y., U.S.A.*	107	D11
Hillside, *Australia*	88	D2
Hillsport, *Canada*	98	C2
Hillston, *Australia*	91	E4
Hilo, *U.S.A.*	102	J17
Hilton, *U.S.A.*	106	C7
Hilvan, *Turkey*	67	E8
Hilvarenbeek, *Neths.*	17	F6
Hilversum, *Neths.*	16	D6
Himachal Pradesh □, *India*	62	D7
Himalaya, *Asia*	63	E11
Himamaylan, *Phil.*	55	F5
Himara, *Albania*	39	J2
Himatnagar, *India*	60	H8
Himeji, *Japan*	49	G7
Himi, *Japan*	49	F8
Himmerland, *Denmark*	11	H3
Ḥimş, *Syria*	69	A5
Ḥimş □, *Syria*	69	A5
Hinche, *Haiti*	117	C5
Hinchinbrook I., *Australia*	90	B4
Hinckley, *U.K.*	13	E6
Hinckley, *U.S.A.*	110	G7
Hindås, *Sweden*	11	G6
Hindaun, *India*	62	F7
Hindmarsh, L., *Australia*	91	F3
Hindsholm, *Denmark*	11	J4
Hindu Bagh, *Pakistan*	62	D2
Hindu Kush, *Asia*	60	B7
Hindubagh, *Pakistan*	60	D5
Hindupur, *India*	60	N10
Hines Creek, *Canada*	100	B5
Hinganghat, *India*	60	J11
Hingeon, *Belgium*	17	G5
Hingham, *U.S.A.*	110	B8
Hingoli, *India*	60	K10
Hinigaran, *Phil.*	55	F5
Hinis, *Turkey*	67	D9
Hinna = Imi, *Ethiopia*	68	F3
Hinna, *Nigeria*	79	C7
Hinojosa del Duque, *Spain*	31	G5
Hinsdale, *U.S.A.*	110	B10
Hinterrhein →, *Switz.*	23	C8
Hinton, *Canada*	100	C5
Hinton, *U.S.A.*	104	G5
Hinwil, *Switz.*	23	B7
Hınzır Burnu, *Turkey*	66	E6
Hippolytushoef, *Neths.*	16	C5
Hirado, *Japan*	49	H4
Hirakud Dam, *India*	61	J13

Hiratsuka, *Japan* 49 G9
Hirfanlı Baraji, *Turkey* 66 D5
Hirhafok, *Algeria* 75 D6
Hîrlău, *Romania* 38 B9
Hiroo, *Japan* 48 C11
Hirosaki, *Japan* 48 D10
Hiroshima, *Japan* 49 G6
Hiroshima □, *Japan* 49 G6
Hirsholmene, *Denmark* 11 G4
Hirson, *France* 25 C11
Hîrşova, *Romania* 38 E10
Hirtshals, *Denmark* 11 G3
Hisar, *India* 62 E6
Hisb →, *Iraq* 64 D5
Ḥismá, *Si. Arabia* 64 D3
Hispaniola, *W. Indies* 117 C5
Hīt, *Iraq* 64 C4
Hita, *Japan* 49 H5
Hitachi, *Japan* 49 F10
Hitchin, *U.K.* 13 F7
Hitoyoshi, *Japan* 49 H5
Hitra, *Norway* 8 E10
Hitzacker, *Germany* 18 B7
Ḥiyyon, N. →, *Israel* 69 E4
Hjalmar L., *Canada* 101 A7
Hjälmar kanal, *Sweden* 10 E9
Hjälmaren, *Sweden* 10 E9
Hjartdal, *Norway* 10 E2
Hjerkinn, *Norway* 10 B3
Hjørring, *Denmark* 11 G3
Hjortkvarn, *Sweden* 11 F9
Hlinsko, *Czech.* 20 F5
Hluhluwe, *S. Africa* 85 D5
Ho, *Ghana* 79 D5
Ho Chi Minh City = Phanh Bho Ho Chi Minh, *Vietnam* 59 G6
Ho Thuong, *Vietnam* 58 C5
Hoa Binh, *Vietnam* 58 B5
Hoa Da, *Vietnam* 59 G7
Hoa Hiep, *Vietnam* 59 G5
Hoai Nhon, *Vietnam* 58 E7
Hoare B., *Canada* 97 B13
Hobart, *Australia* 90 G4
Hobart, *U.S.A.* 109 H5
Hobbs, *U.S.A.* 109 J3
Hobbs Coast, *Antarctica* 5 D14
Hobo, *Colombia* 120 C2
Hoboken, *Belgium* 17 F4
Hoboken, *U.S.A.* 107 F10
Hobro, *Denmark* 11 H3
Hobscheid, *Lux.* 17 J7
Hoburgen, *Sweden* 9 H15
Hochdorf, *Switz.* 23 B6
Hochschwab, *Austria* 21 H5
Höchstadt, *Germany* 19 F6
Hockenheim, *Germany* 19 F4
Hodaka-Dake, *Japan* 49 F8
Hodgson, *Canada* 101 C9
Hódmezóvásárhely, *Hungary* 21 J10
Hodna, Chott el, *Algeria* 75 A5
Hodna, Monts du, *Algeria* 75 A5
Hodonín, *Czech.* 20 G7
Hoeamdong, *N. Korea* 51 C16
Hœdic, I. de, *France* 24 E4
Hoegaarden, *Belgium* 17 G5
Hoek van Holland, *Neths.* 16 E4
Hoeksche Waard, *Neths.* 16 D7
Hoengsŏng, *S. Korea* 51 F14
Hoensbroek, *Neths.* 17 G7
Hoeryong, *N. Korea* 51 C15
Hoeselt, *Belgium* 17 G6
Hoeven, *Neths.* 17 E5
Hoeyang, *N. Korea* 51 E14
Hof, *Germany* 19 E7
Hof, *Iceland* 8 D6
Höfðakaupstaður, *Iceland* 8 D3
Hofgeismar, *Germany* 18 D5
Hofmeyr, *S. Africa* 84 E4
Hofsjökull, *Iceland* 8 D4
Hofsós, *Iceland* 8 D4
Hōfu, *Japan* 49 G5
Hogan Group, *Australia* 90 F4
Hogansville, *U.S.A.* 105 J3
Hogeland, *U.S.A.* 110 B9
Hoggar = Ahaggar, *Algeria* 75 D6
Högsäter, *Sweden* 11 F6
Hogsty Reef, *Bahamas* 117 B5
Hoh →, *U.S.A.* 112 C2
Hoh Xil Shan, *China* 54 C3
Hohe Rhön, *Germany* 19 E5
Hohe Tauern, *Austria* 21 H2
Hohe Venn, *Belgium* 17 H8
Hohenau, *Austria* 20 G6
Hohenems, *Austria* 19 H5
Hohenstein-Ernstthal, *Germany* 18 E8
Hohenwald, *U.S.A.* 105 H2
Hohenwestedt, *Germany* 18 A5
Hohhot, *China* 50 D6
Hóhlakas, *Greece* 37 D9
Hohoe, *Ghana* 79 D5
Hoi An, *Vietnam* 58 E7
Hoi Xuan, *Vietnam* 58 B5
Hoisington, *U.S.A.* 108 F5
Hōjō, *Japan* 49 H6
Hökerum, *Sweden* 11 G7
Hokianga Harbour, *N.Z.* 87 F4
Hokitika, *N.Z.* 87 K3
Hokkaidō □, *Japan* 48 C11
Hokksund, *Norway* 10 E3
Hol-Hol, *Djibouti* 77 E5
Holbæk, *Denmark* 11 J5

Holbrook, *Australia* 91 F4
Holbrook, *U.S.A.* 111 J8
Holden, *Canada* 100 C6
Holden, *U.S.A.* 110 G7
Holdenville, *U.S.A.* 109 H6
Holderness, *U.K.* 12 D7
Holdfast, *Canada* 101 C7
Holdich, *Argentina* 128 C3
Holdrege, *U.S.A.* 108 E5
Holguín, *Cuba* 116 B4
Hollabrunn, *Austria* 20 G6
Hollams Bird I., *Namibia* 84 C1
Holland = Jayapura, *Indonesia* 104 D2
Hollandia = Jayapura, *Indonesia* 57 E10
Hollandsch Diep, *Neths.* 17 E5
Hollandsch IJssel →, *Neths.* 16 E5
Hollfeld, *Germany* 19 F7
Hollidaysburg, *U.S.A.* 106 F6
Hollis, *U.S.A.* 109 H5
Hollister, *Calif., U.S.A.* 111 H3
Hollister, *Idaho, U.S.A.* 110 E6
Hollum, *Neths.* 16 B7
Holly, *U.S.A.* 108 F3
Holly Hill, *U.S.A.* 105 L5
Holly Springs, *U.S.A.* 109 H10
Hollywood, *Calif., U.S.A.* 111 J4
Hollywood, *Fla., U.S.A.* 105 N5
Holm, *Sweden* 10 B10
Holman Island, *Canada* 96 A8
Hólmavík, *Iceland* 8 D3
Holmes Reefs, *Australia* 90 B4
Holmestrand, *Norway* 10 E4
Holmsbu, *Norway* 10 E4
Holmsjön, *Sweden* 10 B9
Holmsland Klit, *Denmark* 11 J2
Holmsund, *Sweden* 8 E16
Holroyd →, *Australia* 90 A3
Holstebro, *Denmark* 11 H2
Holsworthy, *U.K.* 13 G3
Holt, *Iceland* 8 E4
Holte, *Denmark* 11 J6
Holten, *Neths.* 16 D8
Holton, *Canada* 99 B8
Holton, *U.S.A.* 108 F7
Holtville, *U.S.A.* 113 N11
Holwerd, *Neths.* 16 B7
Holy Cross, *U.S.A.* 96 B4
Holy I., *Gwynedd, U.K.* 12 D3
Holy I., *Northumb., U.K.* 12 B6
Holyhead, *U.K.* 12 D3
Holyoke, *Colo., U.S.A.* 108 E3
Holyoke, *Mass., U.S.A.* 107 D12
Holyrood, *Canada* 99 C9
Holzkirchen, *Germany* 19 H7
Holzminden, *Germany* 18 D5
Homa Bay, *Kenya* 82 C3
Homa Bay □, *Kenya* 82 C3
Homalin, *Burma* 61 G19
Homand, *Iran* 65 C8
Homberg, *Germany* 18 D5
Hombori, *Mali* 79 B4
Homburg, *Germany* 19 F3
Home B., *Canada* 97 B13
Home Hill, *Australia* 90 B4
Homedale, *U.S.A.* 110 E5
Homer, *Alaska, U.S.A.* 96 C4
Homer, *La., U.S.A.* 109 J8
Homestead, *Australia* 90 C4
Homestead, *Fla., U.S.A.* 105 N5
Homestead, *Oreg., U.S.A.* 110 D5
Homewood, *U.S.A.* 112 F6
Hominy, *U.S.A.* 109 G6
Homoine, *Mozam.* 85 C6
Homoljske Planina, *Serbia* 21 L11
Homorod, *Romania* 38 C8
Homs = Ḥimṣ, *Syria* 69 A5
Homyel = Gomel, *Belorussia* 40 E7
Hon Chong, *Vietnam* 59 G5
Hon Me, *Vietnam* 58 C5
Hon Quan, *Vietnam* 59 G6
Honan = Henan □, *China* 50 G8
Honbetsu, *Japan* 48 C11
Honcut, *U.S.A.* 112 F5
Honda, *Colombia* 120 B3
Honda Bay, *Phil.* 55 G3
Hondeklipbaai, *S. Africa* 84 E2
Hondo, *Japan* 49 H5
Hondo, *U.S.A.* 109 L5
Hondo →, *Belize* 115 D7
Honduras ■, *Cent. Amer.* 116 D2
Honduras, G. de, *Caribbean* 116 C2
Hønefoss, *Norway* 9 F11
Honesdale, *U.S.A.* 107 E9
Honey L., *U.S.A.* 112 E6
Honfleur, *France* 24 C7
Hong Gai, *Vietnam* 58 B6
Hong He →, *China* 50 H8
Hong Kong ■, *Asia* 53 F10
Hong'an, *China* 53 B10
Hongch'ŏn, *S. Korea* 51 F14
Honghai Wan, *China* 53 F10
Honghu, *China* 53 C9
Hongjiang, *China* 52 D7
Hongliu He →, *China* 50 F5
Hongor, *Mongolia* 50 B7
Hongsa, *Laos* 58 C3
Hongshui He →, *China* 52 F7
Hongsŏng, *S. Korea* 51 F14
Hongtong, *China* 50 F6
Honguedo, Détroit d', *Canada* 99 C7

Hongwon, *N. Korea* 51 E14
Hongya, *China* 52 C4
Hongyuan, *China* 52 A4
Hongze Hu, *China* 51 H10
Honiara, *Solomon Is.* 92 H7
Honiton, *U.K.* 13 G4
Honjō, *Japan* 48 E10
Honkorâb, Ras, *Egypt* 76 C4
Honolulu, *U.S.A.* 102 H16
Honshū, *Japan* 49 G9
Hontoria del Pinar, *Spain* 28 D1
Hood, Mt., *U.S.A.* 110 D3
Hood, Pt., *Australia* 89 F2
Hood River, *U.S.A.* 110 D3
Hoodsport, *U.S.A.* 112 C3
Hooge, *Germany* 18 A4
Hoogerheide, *Neths.* 17 F4
Hoogeveen, *Neths.* 16 C8
Hoogeveensche Vaart, *Neths.* 16 C8
Hoogezand, *Neths.* 16 B9
Hooghly →= Hughli →, *India* 63 J13
Hooghly-Chinsura = Chunchura, *India* 63 H13
Hoogkerk, *Neths.* 16 B9
Hooglede, *Belgium* 17 G2
Hoogstraten, *Belgium* 17 F5
Hoogvliet, *Neths.* 16 E4
Hook Hd., *Ireland* 15 D5
Hook I., *Australia* 90 C4
Hook of Holland = Hoek van Holland, *Neths.* 16 E4
Hooker, *U.S.A.* 109 G4
Hooker Creek, *Australia* 88 C5
Hoopeston, *U.S.A.* 104 E2
Hoopstad, *S. Africa* 84 D4
Hoorn, *Neths.* 16 C6
Hoover Dam, *U.S.A.* 113 K12
Hooversville, *U.S.A.* 106 F6
Hop Bottom, *U.S.A.* 107 E9
Hopa, *Turkey* 43 F9
Hope, *Canada* 100 D4
Hope, *Ariz., U.S.A.* 113 M13
Hope, *Ark., U.S.A.* 109 J8
Hope, *N. Dak., U.S.A.* 108 B6
Hope, L., *Australia* 91 D2
Hope, Pt., *U.S.A.* 96 B3
Hope Town, *Bahamas* 116 A4
Hopedale, *Canada* 99 A7
Hopefield, *S. Africa* 84 E2
Hopei = Hebei □, *China* 50 E9
Hopelchén, *Mexico* 115 D7
Hopetoun, *Vic., Australia* 91 F3
Hopetoun, *W. Austral., Australia* 89 F3
Hopetown, *S. Africa* 84 D3
Hopkins, *U.S.A.* 108 E7
Hopkins, L., *Australia* 88 D4
Hopkinsville, *U.S.A.* 105 G2
Hopland, *U.S.A.* 112 G3
Hoptrup, *Denmark* 11 J3
Hoquiam, *U.S.A.* 112 D3
Horasan, *Turkey* 67 C10
Horcajo de Santiago, *Spain* 28 F1
Hordaland fylke □, *Norway* 9 F9
Horden Hills, *Australia* 88 D5
Horezu, *Romania* 38 D6
Horgen, *Switz.* 23 B7
Horinger, *China* 50 D6
Horlick Mts., *Antarctica* 5 E15
Horlivka = Gorlovka, *Ukraine* 42 B8
Hormoz, *Iran* 65 E7
Hormoz, Jaz. ye, *Iran* 65 E8
Hormuz Str. of, *The Gulf* 65 E8
Horn, *Ísafjarðarsýsla, Iceland* 8 C2
Horn, *Suður-Múlasýsla, Iceland* 8 D7
Horn, *Neths.* 17 F7
Horn →, *Canada* 100 A5
Horn, Cape = Hornos, C. de, *Chile* 128 E3
Horn Head, *Ireland* 15 A3
Horn I., *Australia* 90 A3
Horn I., *U.S.A.* 105 K1
Horn Mts., *Canada* 100 A5
Hornachuelos, *Spain* 31 H5
Hornavan, *Sweden* 8 C14
Hornbæk, *Denmark* 11 H6
Hornbeck, *U.S.A.* 109 K8
Hornbrook, *U.S.A.* 110 F2
Hornburg, *Germany* 18 C6
Horncastle, *U.K.* 12 D7
Hornell, *U.S.A.* 106 D7
Hornell L., *Canada* 100 A5
Hornepayne, *Canada* 98 C3
Hornitos, *U.S.A.* 112 H6
Hornos, C. de, *Chile* 128 E3
Hornoy, *France* 25 C8
Hornsby, *Australia* 91 E5
Hornsea, *U.K.* 12 D7
Hornslandet, *Sweden* 10 C11
Hornslet, *Denmark* 11 H4
Hornu, *Belgium* 17 H4
Hörnum, *Germany* 18 A4
Horobetsu, *Japan* 48 C10
Horqin Youyi Qianqi, *China* 51 A12
Horqueta, *Paraguay* 126 A4
Horred, *Sweden* 11 G6
Horse Creek, *U.S.A.* 108 E3
Horse Is., *Canada* 99 B8
Horsefly L., *Canada* 100 C4
Horsens, *Denmark* 11 J3

Horsens Fjord, *Denmark* 11 J4
Horsham, *Australia* 91 F3
Horsham, *U.K.* 13 F7
Horst, *Neths.* 17 F8
Horten, *Norway* 10 E4
Hortobágy →, *Hungary* 21 H11
Horton, *U.S.A.* 108 F7
Horton →, *Canada* 96 B7
Horw, *Switz.* 23 B6
Horwood, L., *Canada* 98 C3
Hose, Gunung-Gunung, *Malaysia* 56 D4
Ḥoseynābād, *Khuzestān, Iran* 65 C6
Ḥoseynābād, *Kordestān, Iran* 64 C5
Hoshangabad, *India* 62 H7
Hoshiarpur, *India* 62 D6
Hosingen, *Lux.* 17 H8
Hosmer, *U.S.A.* 108 C5
Hospental, *Switz.* 23 C7
Hospet, *India* 60 M10
Hospitalet de Llobregat, *Spain* 28 D7
Hoste, I., *Chile* 128 E3
Hostens, *France* 26 D3
Hot, *Thailand* 58 C2
Hot Creek Range, *U.S.A.* 110 G5
Hot Springs, *Ark., U.S.A.* 109 H8
Hot Springs, *S. Dak., U.S.A.* 108 D3
Hotagen, *Sweden* 8 E13
Hotan, *China* 54 C2
Hotazel, *S. Africa* 84 D3
Hotchkiss, *U.S.A.* 111 G10
Hotham, C., *Australia* 88 B5
Hoting, *Sweden* 8 D14
Hotte, Massif de la, *Haiti* 117 C5
Hottentotsbaai, *Namibia* 84 D1
Hotton, *Belgium* 17 H6
Houat, I. de, *France* 24 E4
Houck, *U.S.A.* 111 J9
Houdan, *France* 25 D8
Houdeng-Goegnies, *Belgium* 17 H4
Houei Sai, *Laos* 58 B3
Houffalize, *Belgium* 17 H7
Houghton, *U.S.A.* 108 B10
Houghton L., *U.S.A.* 104 C3
Houghton-le-Spring, *U.K.* 12 C6
Houhora Heads, *N.Z.* 87 F4
Houille →, *Belgium* 17 H5
Houlton, *U.S.A.* 99 C6
Houma, *U.S.A.* 109 L9
Houndé, *Burkina Faso* 78 C4
Hourtin, *France* 26 C2
Hourtin-Carcans, Étang d', *France* 26 C2
Houston, *Canada* 100 C3
Houston, *Mo., U.S.A.* 109 G9
Houston, *Tex., U.S.A.* 109 L7
Houten, *Neths.* 16 D6
Houthalen, *Belgium* 17 F6
Houthem, *Belgium* 17 G1
Houthulst, *Belgium* 17 G2
Houtman Abrolhos, *Australia* 89 E1
Houyet, *Belgium* 17 H6
Hov, *Denmark* 11 J4
Hova, *Sweden* 11 F8
Høvåg, *Norway* 11 F2
Hovd, *Mongolia* 54 B4
Hove, *U.K.* 13 G7
Hoveyzeh, *Iran* 65 D6
Hövsgöl, *Mongolia* 50 C5
Hövsgöl Nuur, *Mongolia* 54 A5
Howakil, *Eritrea* 77 D5
Howar, Wadi →, *Sudan* 77 D2
Howard, *Australia* 91 D5
Howard, *Kans., U.S.A.* 109 G6
Howard, *Pa., U.S.A.* 106 E7
Howard, *S. Dak., U.S.A.* 108 C6
Howard I., *Australia* 90 A2
Howard L., *Canada* 101 A7
Howe, *U.S.A.* 110 E7
Howe, C., *Australia* 91 F5
Howell, *U.S.A.* 104 D4
Howick, *Canada* 107 A11
Howick, *S. Africa* 85 D5
Howick Group, *Australia* 90 A4
Howitt, L., *Australia* 91 D2
Howley, *Canada* 99 C8
Howrah = Haora, *India* 63 H13
Howth Hd., *Ireland* 15 C5
Höxter, *Germany* 18 D5
Hoy, *U.K.* 14 C5
Hoya, *Germany* 18 C5
Høyanger, *Norway* 9 F9
Hoyerswerda, *Germany* 18 D10
Hoyos, *Spain* 30 E4
Hpungan Pass, *Burma* 61 F20
Hradec Králové, *Czech.* 20 E5
Hranice, *Czech.* 20 F7
Hrodna = Grodno, *Belorussia* 40 E3
Hron →, *Slovak Rep.* 21 H8
Hrubieszów, *Poland* 20 E13
Hrvatska = Croatia ■, *Europe* 33 C13
Hsenwi, *Burma* 61 H20
Hsiamen = Xiamen, *China* 53 E12
Hsian = Xi'an, *China* 50 G5
Hsinhailien = Lianyungang, *China* 51 G10
Hsisha Chuntao, *Pac. Oc.* 56 A4

Hsüchou = Xuzhou, *China* 51 G9
Hu Xian, *China* 50 G5
Hua Hin, *Thailand* 58 F2
Hua Xian, *Henan, China* 50 G8
Hua Xian, *Shaanxi, China* 50 G5
Hua'an, *China* 53 E11
Huacaya, *Bolivia* 125 E5
Huacheng, *China* 53 E10
Huachinera, *Mexico* 114 A3
Huacho, *Peru* 124 C2
Huachón, *Peru* 124 C2
Huade, *China* 50 D7
Huadian, *China* 51 C14
Huai He →, *China* 53 A12
Huai Yot, *Thailand* 59 J2
Huai'an, *Hebei, China* 50 D8
Huai'an, *Jiangsu, China* 51 H10
Huaide, *China* 51 C13
Huaidezhen, *China* 51 C13
Huaihua, *China* 52 D7
Huaiji, *China* 53 F9
Huainan, *China* 53 A11
Huaining, *China* 53 B11
Huairen, *China* 50 E7
Huairou, *China* 50 D9
Huaiyang, *China* 50 H8
Huaiyuan, *Anhui, China* 51 H9
Huaiyuan, *Guangxi Zhuangzu, China* 52 E7
Huajianzi, *China* 51 D13
Huajuapan de Leon, *Mexico* 115 D5
Hualapai Peak, *U.S.A.* 111 J7
Hualian, *Taiwan* 53 F13
Huallaga →, *Peru* 124 B2
Huallanca, *Peru* 124 B2
Huamachuco, *Peru* 124 B2
Huambo, *Angola* 81 G3
Huan Jiang →, *China* 50 G5
Huan Xian, *China* 50 F4
Huancabamba, *Peru* 124 B2
Huancane, *Peru* 124 D4
Huancapi, *Peru* 124 C3
Huancavelica, *Peru* 124 C3
Huancavelica □, *Peru* 124 C3
Huancayo, *Peru* 124 C2
Huanchaca, *Bolivia* 124 E4
Huanchaca, Serranía de, *Bolivia* 125 C5
Huang Hai = Yellow Sea, *China* 51 G12
Huang He →, *China* 51 F10
Huang Xian, *China* 51 F11
Huangchuan, *China* 53 A10
Huanggang, *China* 53 B10
Huangling, *China* 50 G5
Huangliu, *China* 54 E5
Huanglong, *China* 50 G5
Huanglongtan, *China* 53 A8
Huangmei, *China* 53 B10
Huangpi, *China* 53 B10
Huangping, *China* 52 D6
Huangshi, *China* 53 B10
Huangsongdian, *China* 51 C14
Huangyan, *China* 53 C13
Huangyangsi, *China* 53 D8
Huaning, *China* 52 E4
Huanjiang, *China* 52 E7
Huanta, *Peru* 124 C3
Huantai, *China* 51 F9
Huánuco, *Peru* 124 B2
Huánuco □, *Peru* 124 B2
Huanuni, *Bolivia* 124 D4
Huanzo, Cordillera de, *Peru* 124 C3
Huaping, *China* 52 D3
Huaral, *Peru* 124 C2
Huaraz, *Peru* 124 B2
Huari, *Peru* 124 B2
Huarmey, *Peru* 124 C2
Huarochiri, *Peru* 124 C2
Huarocondo, *Peru* 124 C3
Huarong, *China* 53 C9
Huascarán, *Peru* 124 B2
Huascarán, Nevado, *Peru* 124 B2
Huasco, *Chile* 126 B1
Huasco →, *Chile* 126 B1
Huasna, *U.S.A.* 113 K6
Huatabampo, *Mexico* 114 B3
Huauchinango, *Mexico* 115 C5
Huautla de Jiménez, *Mexico* 115 D5
Huaxi, *China* 52 D6
Huay Namota, *Mexico* 114 C4
Huayin, *China* 50 G6
Huayllay, *Peru* 124 C2
Huayuan, *China* 52 C7
Huazhou, *China* 53 F8
Hubbard, *U.S.A.* 109 K6
Hubbart Pt., *Canada* 101 B10
Hubei □, *China* 53 B9
Hubli-Dharwad = Dharwad, *India* 60 M9
Huchang, *N. Korea* 51 D14
Hückelhoven, *Germany* 18 D2
Hudi, *Sudan* 76 D3
Hudiksvall, *Sweden* 10 C11
Hudson, *Canada* 101 C10
Hudson, *Mass., U.S.A.* 107 D13
Hudson, *Mich., U.S.A.* 104 E3
Hudson, *N.Y., U.S.A.* 107 D11
Hudson, *Wis., U.S.A.* 108 C8
Hudson, *Wyo., U.S.A.* 110 E9
Hudson →, *U.S.A.* 107 F10

Hudson Bay, N.W.T., Canada 97 C11
Hudson Bay, Sask., Canada 101 C8
Hudson Falls, U.S.A. 107 C11
Hudson Mts., Antarctica .. 5 D16
Hudson Str., Canada 97 B13
Hudson's Hope, Canada .. 100 B4
Hue, Vietnam 58 D6
Huebra →, Spain 30 D4
Huechucuicui, Pta., Chile . 128 B2
Huedin, Romania 38 C6
Huehuetenango, Guatemala 116 C1
Huejúcar, Mexico 114 C4
Huelgoat, France 24 D3
Huelma, Spain 29 H1
Huelva, Spain 31 H4
Huelva □, Spain 31 H4
Huelva →, Spain 31 H5
Huentelauquén, Chile 126 C1
Huércal Overa, Spain 29 H3
Huerta, Sa. de la,
  Argentina 126 C2
Huertas, C. de las, Spain . 29 G4
Huerva →, Spain 28 D4
Huesca, Spain 28 C4
Huesca □, Spain 28 C5
Huéscar, Spain 29 H2
Huetamo, Mexico 114 D4
Huete, Spain 28 E2
Hugh →, Australia 90 D1
Hughenden, Australia 90 C3
Hughes, Australia 89 F4
Hughli →, India 63 J13
Hugo, U.S.A. 108 F3
Hugoton, U.S.A. 109 G4
Hui Xian, Gansu, China .. 50 H4
Hui Xian, Henan, China .. 50 G7
Hui'an, China 53 E12
Hui'anbu, China 50 F4
Huichang, China 53 E10
Huidong, China 52 D4
Huichapán, Mexico 115 C5
Huifa He →, China 51 C14
Huila □, Colombia 120 C2
Huila, Nevado del,
  Colombia 120 C2
Huilai, China 53 F11
Huili, China 52 D4
Huimin, China 51 F9
Huinan, China 51 C14
Huinca Renancó, Argentina 126 C3
Huining, China 50 G3
Huinong, China 50 E4
Huise, Belgium 17 G3
Huishui, China 52 D6
Huisne →, France 24 E7
Huissen, Neths. 16 E7
Huiting, China 50 G9
Huitong, China 52 D7
Huixtla, Mexico 115 D6
Huize, China 52 D4
Huizen, Neths. 16 D6
Huizhou, China 53 F10
Hukawng Valley, Burma .. 61 F20
Hukou, China 53 C11
Hukuntsi, Botswana 84 C3
Hula, Ethiopia 77 F4
Hulan, China 54 B7
Ḥulayfā', Si. Arabia 64 E4
Huld, Mongolia 50 B3
Hulin He →, China 51 B12
Hull = Kingston upon
  Hull, U.K. 12 D7
Hull, Canada 98 C4
Hull →, U.K. 12 D7
Hulst, Neths. 17 F4
Hulun Nur, China 54 B6
Humahuaca, Argentina ... 126 A2
Humaitá, Brazil 125 B5
Humaitá, Paraguay 126 B4
Humansdorp, S. Africa ... 84 E3
Humbe, Angola 84 B1
Humber →, U.K. 12 D7
Humberside □, U.K. 12 D7
Humbert River, Australia . 88 C5
Humble, U.S.A. 109 L8
Humboldt, Canada 101 C7
Humboldt, Iowa, U.S.A. .. 108 D7
Humboldt, Tenn., U.S.A. . 109 H10
Humboldt →, U.S.A. 110 F4
Humboldt Gletscher,
  Greenland 4 B4
Hume, U.S.A. 112 J8
Hume, L., Australia 91 F4
Humenné, Slovakia 20 G11
Humphreys, Mt., U.S.A. .. 112 H8
Humphreys Peak, U.S.A. . 111 J8
Humpolec, Czech. 20 F5
Humptulips, U.S.A. 112 C3
Ḥūn, Libya 73 C8
Hun Jiang →, China 51 D13
Húnaflói, Iceland 8 D3
Hunan □, China 53 D9
Hunchun, China 51 C16
Hundested, Denmark 11 J5
Hundred Mile House,
  Canada 100 C4
Hunedoara, Romania 38 D5
Hünfeld, Germany 18 E5
Hung Yen, Vietnam 58 B6
Hungary ■, Europe 21 H9
Hungary, Plain of, Europe . 6 F9
Hungerford, Australia 91 D3
Hŭngnam, N. Korea 51 E14
Huni Valley, Ghana 78 D4
Hunsberge, Namibia 84 D2

Hunsrück, Germany 19 F3
Hunstanton, U.K. 12 E8
Hunte →, Germany 18 C4
Hunter, N. Dak., U.S.A. .. 108 B6
Hunter, N.Y., U.S.A. 107 D10
Hunter I., Australia 90 G3
Hunter I., Canada 100 C3
Hunter Ra., Australia 91 E5
Hunters Road, Zimbabwe . 83 F2
Hunterville, N.Z. 87 H5
Huntingburg, U.S.A. 104 F2
Huntingdon, Canada 98 C5
Huntingdon, U.K. 13 E7
Huntingdon, U.S.A. 106 F6
Huntington, Ind., U.S.A. .. 104 E3
Huntington, N.Y., U.S.A. . 107 F11
Huntington, Oreg., U.S.A. . 110 D5
Huntington, Utah, U.S.A. . 110 G8
Huntington, W. Va.,
  U.S.A. 104 F4
Huntington Beach, U.S.A. 113 M8
Huntington Park, U.S.A. . 111 K4
Huntly, N.Z. 87 G5
Huntly, U.K. 14 D6
Huntsville, Canada 98 C4
Huntsville, Ala., U.S.A. .. 105 H2
Huntsville, Tex., U.S.A. .. 109 K7
Hunyani →, Zimbabwe .. 83 F3
Hunyuan, China 50 E7
Huo Xian, China 50 F6
Huong Hoa, Vietnam 58 D6
Huong Khe, Vietnam 58 C5
Huonville, Australia 90 G4
Huoqiu, China 53 H10
Huoshan, Anhui, China .. 53 A12
Huoshan, Anhui, China .. 53 B11
Huoshao Dao, Taiwan ... 53 F13
Hupeh = Hubei □, China 53 B9
Ḥūr, Iran 65 D8
Hure Qi, China 51 C11
Hurezani, Romania 38 E6
Hurghada, Egypt 76 B3
Hurley, N. Mex., U.S.A. . 111 K9
Hurley, Wis., U.S.A. 108 B9
Huron, Calif., U.S.A. 112 J6
Huron, Ohio, U.S.A. 106 E2
Huron, S. Dak., U.S.A. .. 108 C5
Huron, L., U.S.A. 106 B2
Hurricane, U.S.A. 111 H7
Hurso, Ethiopia 77 F5
Hurum, Norway 10 C2
Hurunui →, N.Z. 87 K4
Hurup, Denmark 11 H2
Húsavík, Iceland 8 C5
Huşi, Romania 38 C11
Huskvarna, Sweden 9 H13
Hussar, Canada 100 C6
Husum, Germany 18 A5
Husum, Sweden 10 A13
Hutchinson, Kans., U.S.A. 109 F6
Hutchinson, Minn., U.S.A. 108 C7
Huttig, U.S.A. 109 J8
Hutton, Mt., Australia ... 91 D4
Huttwil, Switz. 22 B5
Huwun, Ethiopia 77 G5
Huy, Belgium 17 G6
Hvammur, Iceland 8 D3
Hvar, Croatia 33 E13
Hvarski Kanal, Croatia ... 33 E13
Hvítá, Iceland 8 D3
Hvítá, Iceland 8 D3
Hvítárvatn, Iceland 8 D4
Hwachon-chosuji, S. Korea 51 E14
Hwang Ho = Huang
  He →, China 51 F10
Hwange, Zimbabwe 83 F2
Hwange Nat. Park,
  Zimbabwe 84 B4
Hyannis, U.S.A. 108 E4
Hyargas Nuur, Mongolia . 54 B4
Hybo, Sweden 10 C10
Hyde Park, Guyana 121 B6
Hyden, Australia 89 F2
Hyderabad, India 60 L11
Hyderabad, Pakistan 62 G3
Hyères, France 27 E10
Hyères, Is. d', France 27 F10
Hyesan, N. Korea 51 D15
Hyland →, Canada 100 B3
Hyltebruk, Sweden 11 H7
Hymia, India 63 C8
Hyndman Peak, U.S.A. .. 110 E6
Hyōgo □, Japan 49 G7
Hyrum, U.S.A. 110 F8
Hysham, U.S.A. 110 C10
Hythe, U.K. 13 F9
Hyūga, Japan 49 H5
Hyvinge = Hyvinkää,
  Finland 9 F18
Hyvinkää, Finland 9 F18

I

I-n-Échaï, Mali 74 D4
I-n-Gall, Niger 79 B6
Iabès, Erg, Algeria 75 C4
Iaco →, Brazil 124 B4
Iaçu, Brazil 123 D3
Iakora, Madag. 85 C8
Iaşi, Romania 38 B10
Iauaretê, Colombia 120 C4

Iba, Phil. 55 D3
Ibadan, Nigeria 79 D5
Ibagué, Colombia 120 C2
Ibaiti, Brazil 123 F1
Iballja, Albania 38 G3
Ibănești, Romania 38 C7
Ibar →, Serbia, Yug. 21 M10
Ibaraki □, Japan 49 F10
Ibarra, Ecuador 120 C2
Ibba, Sudan 77 G2
Ibba, Bahr el →, Sudan .. 77 F2
Ibbenbüren, Germany 18 C3
Ibembo, Zaïre 82 B1
Ibera, L., Argentina 126 B4
Iberian Peninsula, Europe . 6 H5
Iberico, Sistema, Spain ... 28 E2
Iberville, Canada 98 C5
Iberville, Lac d', Canada . 98 A5
Ibi, Nigeria 79 D6
Ibiá, Brazil 123 E2
Ibicaraí, Brazil 123 D4
Ibicuí, Brazil 123 D4
Ibicuy, Argentina 126 C4
Ibioapaba, Sa. da, Brazil . 122 B3
Ibipetuba, Brazil 122 D3
Ibitiara, Brazil 123 D3
Ibiza, Spain 36 C7
Íblei, Monti, Italy 35 E7
Ibo, Mozam. 83 E5
Ibonma, Indonesia 57 E8
Ibotirama, Brazil 123 D3
Ibrāhīm →, Lebanon 69 A4
Ibshawâi, Egypt 76 J7
Iburg, Germany 18 C4
Ibusuki, Japan 49 J5
Icá, Peru 124 C2
Ica □, Peru 124 C2
Iça →, Brazil 124 A4
Icabarú, Venezuela 121 C5
Icabarú →, Venezuela ... 121 C5
Içana, Brazil 120 C4
Içana →, Brazil 120 C4
Icatu, Brazil 122 B3
İçel = Mersin, Turkey ... 66 E6
İçel □, Turkey 66 E6
Iceland ■, Europe 8 D4
Icha, Russia 45 D16
Ich'ang = Yichang, China 53 B8
Ichchapuram, India 61 K14
Ichihara, Japan 49 G10
Ichikawa, Japan 49 G9
Ichilo →, Bolivia 125 D5
Ichinohe, Japan 48 D10
Ichinomiya, Japan 49 G8
Ichinoseki, Japan 48 E10
Ichnya, Ukraine 40 F8
Ichŏn, S. Korea 51 F14
Icht, Morocco 74 C3
Ichtegem, Belgium 17 F2
Icó, Brazil 122 C4
Icod, Canary Is. 36 F3
Icoracci, Brazil 122 B2
Icy Str., U.S.A. 100 B1
Ida Grove, U.S.A. 108 D7
Ida Valley, Australia 89 E3
Idabel, U.S.A. 109 J7
Idaga Hamus, Ethiopia .. 77 E4
Idah, Nigeria 79 D6
Idaho □, U.S.A. 110 D6
Idaho City, U.S.A. 110 E6
Idaho Falls, U.S.A. 110 E7
Idaho Springs, U.S.A. ... 110 G11
Idanha-a-Nova, Portugal . 30 F3
Idar-Oberstein, Germany . 19 F3
Idd el Ghanam, Sudan ... 73 F9
Iddan, Somali Rep. 68 F4
Idehan, Libya 75 C7
Idehan Marzūq, Libya ... 73 D7
Idelès, Algeria 75 D6
Idfû, Egypt 76 C3
Ídhi Óros, Greece 37 D6
Ídhra, Greece 39 M6
Idi, Indonesia 56 C1
Idiofa, Zaïre 80 E3
Idku, Bahra el, Egypt ... 76 H7
Idlib, Syria 64 C3
Idria, U.S.A. 112 J6
Idrija, Slovenia 33 B11
Idritsa, Russia 40 C6
Idstein, Germany 19 E4
Idutywa, S. Africa 85 E4
Ieper, Belgium 17 G1
Ierápetra, Greece 37 E7
Ierissós, Greece 39 J6
Ierzu, Italy 34 C2
Iesi, Italy 33 E10
Ifach, Punta, Spain 29 G5
'Ifāl, W. al →, Si. Arabia 64 D2
Ifanadiana, Madag. 85 C8
Ife, Nigeria 79 D5
Iférouâne, Niger 79 B6
Iffley, Australia 90 B3
Ifni, Morocco 74 C2
Ifon, Nigeria 79 D6
Iforas, Adrar des, Mali .. 79 B5
Ifould, L., Australia 89 F5
Iframo, Morocco 74 B3
Iganga, Uganda 82 B3
Igara Paraná →, Colombia 120 D3
Igarapava, Brazil 123 F2
Igarapé Açu, Brazil 122 B2
Igarapé-Mirim, Brazil ... 122 B2
Igarka, Russia 44 C9
Igatimi, Paraguay 127 A4

Igbetti, Nigeria 79 D5
Igbo-Ora, Nigeria 79 D5
Igboho, Nigeria 79 D5
Iğdır, Turkey 67 D11
Iggesund, Sweden 10 C11
Ighil Izane, Algeria 75 A5
Iglésias, Italy 34 C1
Igli, Algeria 75 B4
Igloolik, Canada 97 B11
Igma, Gebel el, Egypt ... 76 J8
Ignace, Canada 98 C1
İğneada Burnu, Turkey .. 66 C3
Igoshevo, Russia 41 B13
Iguaçu →, Brazil 127 B5
Iguaçu, Cat. del, Brazil .. 127 B5
Iguaçu Falls = Iguaçu, Cat.
  del, Brazil 127 B5
Iguala, Mexico 115 D5
Igualada, Spain 28 D6
Iguape, Brazil 123 F2
Iguassu = Iguaçu →,
  Brazil 127 B5
Iguatu, Brazil 122 C4
Iguéla, Gabon 80 E1
Iguna →, Tanzania 82 C3
Iheya-Shima, Japan 49 L3
Ihiala, Nigeria 79 D6
Ihosy, Madag. 85 C8
Ihotry, L., Madag. 85 C7
Ii, Finland 8 D18
Ii-Shima, Japan 49 L3
Iijoki →, Finland 8 D18
Iisalmi, Finland 8 E19
Iiyama, Japan 49 F9
Iizuka, Japan 49 H5
Ijâfene, Mauritania 74 D3
Ijebu-Igbo, Nigeria 79 D5
Ijebu-Ode, Nigeria 79 D5
IJmuiden, Neths. 16 D5
IJssel →, Neths. 16 C7
IJsselmeer, Neths. 16 C6
IJsselmuiden, Neths. 16 C7
IJsselstein, Neths. 16 D6
Ijuí →, Brazil 127 B4
IJzendijke, Neths. 17 F3
IJzer →, Belgium 17 F1
Ikale, Nigeria 79 D6
Ikare, Nigeria 79 D6
Ikaría, Greece 39 M9
Ikast, Denmark 11 H3
Ikeda, Japan 49 G6
Ikeja, Nigeria 79 D5
Ikela, Zaïre 80 E4
Ikerre-Ekiti, Nigeria 79 D6
Ikhtiman, Bulgaria 38 G6
Iki, Japan 49 H4
Ikimba L., Tanzania 82 C3
Ikire, Nigeria 79 D5
Ikizdere, Turkey 67 C9
Ikom, Nigeria 79 D6
Ikopa →, Madag. 85 B8
Ikot Ekpene, Nigeria 79 D6
Ikungu, Tanzania 82 C3
Ikurun, Nigeria 79 D5
Ila, Nigeria 79 D5
Ilagan, Phil. 55 C4
Īlām, Iran 64 C5
Ilam, Nepal 63 F12
Ilanskiy, Russia 45 D10
Ilanz, Switz. 23 C8
Ilaro, Nigeria 79 D5
Iława, Poland 20 B9
Ilbilbie, Australia 90 C4
Île-à-la-Crosse, Canada .. 101 B7
Île-à-la-Crosse, Lac,
  Canada 101 B7
Île-de-France, France 25 D9
Ilebo, Zaïre 80 E4
Ileje □, Tanzania 83 D3
Ilek, Russia 44 D6
Ilek →, Russia 44 D6
Ilero, Nigeria 79 D5
Ilesha, Kwara, Nigeria ... 79 D5
Ilesha, Oyo, Nigeria 79 D5
Ilford, Canada 101 B9
Ilfracombe, Australia 90 C3
Ilfracombe, U.K. 13 F3
Ilgaz, Turkey 66 C5
Ilgaz Dağları, Turkey ... 66 C5
Ilgın, Turkey 66 D4
Ilha Grande, Brazil 124 D4
Ilha Grande, B. da, Brazil 123 F3
Ílhavo, Portugal 30 E2
Ilhéus, Brazil 123 D4
Ili →, Kazakhstan 44 E8
Iliç, Turkey 67 D8
Ilıça, Kazakhstan 44 E7
Iliff, U.S.A. 108 E3
Iligan, Phil. 55 G6
Iligan Bay, Phil. 55 G6
Ilíkí, L., Greece 39 L6
Ilin I., Phil. 55 E4
Iliodhrómia, Greece 39 K6
Ilion, U.S.A. 107 D9
Ilirska-Bistrica, Slovenia . 33 C11
Ilkeston, U.K. 12 E6
Illampu = Ancohuma,
  Nevada, Bolivia 124 D4
Illana B., Phil. 55 H5
Illapel, Chile 126 C1
Ille-et-Vilaine □, France . 24 D5
Ille-sur-Têt, France 26 F6
Iller →, Germany 19 G5
Illescas, Spain 30 E7

Illetas, Spain 36 B9
Illiers-Combray, France .. 24 D8
Illimani, Bolivia 124 D4
Illinois □, U.S.A. 103 C9
Illinois →, U.S.A. 103 C8
Illium = Troy, Turkey ... 66 D2
Illizi, Algeria 75 C6
Illora, Spain 31 H7
Ilm →, Germany 18 D7
Ilmen, Oz., Russia 40 B7
Ilmenau, Germany 18 E6
Ilo, Peru 124 D3
Ilobu, Nigeria 79 D5
Iloilo, Phil. 55 F5
Ilora, Nigeria 79 D5
Ilorin, Nigeria 79 D5
Iloulya, Russia 43 B11
Ilovatka, Russia 41 F14
Ilovlya, Russia 43 B10
Ilubabor □, Ethiopia 77 F3
Ilūkste, Latvia 40 D5
Ilva Mică, Romania 38 B7
Ilwaco, U.S.A. 112 D2
Ilwaki, Indonesia 57 F7
Ilyichevsk, Ukraine 42 C4
Imabari, Japan 49 G6
Imaloto →, Madag. 85 C8
İmamoğlu, Turkey 66 E6
Imandra, Oz., Russia 44 C4
Imari, Japan 49 H4
Imasa, Sudan 76 D4
Imbâbah, Egypt 76 H7
Imbabura □, Ecuador 120 C2
Imbler, U.S.A. 110 D5
Imdahane, Morocco 74 B3
imeni 26 Bakinskikh
  Komissarov, Azerbaijan 67 D13
Imeni Poliny Osipenko,
  Russia 45 D14
Imeri, Serra, Brazil 120 C4
Imerimandroso, Madag. .. 85 B8
Imesan, Mauritania 74 D1
Imi, Ethiopia 68 F3
Imishly, Azerbaijan 43 G13
Imitek, Morocco 74 C3
Imlay, U.S.A. 110 F4
Imlay City, U.S.A. 106 C1
Immenstadt, Germany ... 19 H6
Immingham, U.K. 12 D7
Immokalee, U.S.A. 105 M5
Imo □, Nigeria 79 D6
Imola, Italy 33 D8
Imotski, Croatia 21 M7
Imperatriz, Amazonas,
  Brazil 124 B4
Imperatriz, Maranhão,
  Brazil 122 C2
Impéria, Italy 32 E5
Imperial, Canada 101 C7
Imperial, Peru 124 C2
Imperial, Calif., U.S.A. . 113 N11
Imperial, Nebr., U.S.A. .. 108 E4
Imperial Beach, U.S.A. .. 113 N9
Imperial Dam, U.S.A. ... 113 N12
Imperial Reservoir, U.S.A. 113 N12
Imperial Valley, U.S.A. .. 113 N11
Imperieuse Reef, Australia 88 C2
Impfondo, Congo 80 D3
Imphal, India 61 G18
Imphy, France 26 B7
Imralı, Turkey 66 C3
Imranlı, Turkey 67 D8
Imroz = Gökçeada, Turkey 39 J8
Imst, Austria 19 H6
Imuruan B., Phil. 55 B5
In Belbel, Algeria 75 C5
In Delimane, Mali 79 B5
In Rhar, Algeria 75 C5
In Salah, Algeria 75 C5
In Tallak, Mali 79 B5
Ina, Japan 49 G8
Inajá, Brazil 122 C4
Inangahua Junction, N.Z. . 87 J3
Inanwatan, Indonesia 57 E8
Iñapari, Peru 124 C4
Inari, Finland 8 B19
Inarijärvi, Finland 8 B19
Inawashiro-Ko, Japan ... 48 F10
Inca, Spain 36 B9
Incaguasi, Chile 126 B1
İnce-Burnu, Turkey 42 E6
İncekum Burnu, Turkey . 66 E5
Inchon, S. Korea 51 F14
Incio, Spain 30 C3
Incirliova, Turkey 66 E2
Incomáti →, Mozam. 85 D5
Inda Silase, Ethiopia 77 E4
Indalsälven →, Sweden .. 10 B11
Indaw, Burma 61 G20
Indbir, Ethiopia 77 F4
Independence, Calif.,
  U.S.A. 111 H4
Independence, Iowa,
  U.S.A. 108 D9
Independence, Kans.,
  U.S.A. 109 G7
Independence, Mo., U.S.A. 108 F7
Independence, Oreg.,
  U.S.A. 110 D2
Independence Fjord,
  Greenland 4 A6
Independence Mts., U.S.A. 110 F5
Independência, Brazil ... 122 C4
Independenţa, Romania .. 38 D10

Inderborskiy, *Kazakhstan* . 43 B14
Index, *U.S.A.* 112 C5
India ■, *Asia* 60 K11
Indian →, *U.S.A.* 105 M5
Indian Cabins, *Canada* . . . 100 B5
Indian Harbour, *Canada* . . 99 B8
Indian Head, *Canada* 101 C8
Indian Ocean 46 K11
Indian Springs, *U.S.A.* . . 113 J11
Indiana □, *U.S.A.* 106 F5
Indiana □, *U.S.A.* 104 E3
Indianapolis, *U.S.A.* 104 F2
Indianola, *Iowa, U.S.A.* . . 108 E8
Indianola, *Miss., U.S.A.* . 109 J9
Indiapora, *Brazil* 123 E1
Indiga, *Russia* 44 C5
Indigirka →, *Russia* 45 B15
Indija, *Serbia, Yug.* 21 K10
Indio, *U.S.A.* 113 M10
Indonesia ■, *Asia* 56 F5
Indore, *India* 62 H6
Indramayu, *Indonesia* . . . 57 G13
Indravati →, *India* 61 K12
Indre □, *France* 25 F8
Indre →, *France* 24 E7
Indre-et-Loire □, *France* . 24 E7
Indus →, *Pakistan* 62 G2
Indus, Mouth of the,
  Pakistan 62 H2
İnebolu, *Turkey* 66 C5
İnegöl, *Turkey* 66 C3
Inés, Mt., *Argentina* 128 C3
Ineu, *Romania* 38 C4
Inezgane, *Morocco* 74 B3
Infantes, *Spain* 29 G1
Infiernillo, Presa del,
  Mexico 114 D4
Infiesto, *Spain* 30 B5
Ingapirca, *Ecuador* 120 D2
Ingelmunster, *Belgium* . . . 17 G2
Ingende, *Zaïre* 80 E3
Ingeniero Jacobacci,
  Argentina 128 B3
Ingenio, *Canary Is.* 36 G4
Ingenio Santa Ana,
  Argentina 126 B2
Ingersoll, *Canada* 106 C4
Ingham, *Australia* 90 B4
Ingleborough, *U.K.* 12 C5
Inglewood, *Queens.,*
  Australia 91 D5
Inglewood, *Vic., Australia* 91 F3
Inglewood, *N.Z.* 87 H5
Inglewood, *U.S.A.* 113 M8
Ingólfshöfði, *Iceland* 8 E5
Ingolstadt, *Germany* 19 G7
Ingomar, *U.S.A.* 110 C10
Ingonish, *Canada* 99 C7
Ingore, *Guinea-Biss.* 78 C1
Ingraj Bazar, *India* 63 G13
Ingrid Christensen Coast,
  Antarctica 5 C6
Ingul →, *Ukraine* 42 C5
Ingulec, *Ukraine* 42 C5
Ingulets →, *Ukraine* 42 C5
Inguri →, *Georgia* 43 E9
Ingwavuma, *S. Africa* . . . 85 D5
Inhaca, I., *Mozam.* 85 D5
Inhafenga, *Mozam.* 85 C5
Inhambane, *Mozam.* 85 C6
Inhambane □, *Mozam.* . . . 85 C6
Inhambupe, *Brazil* 123 D4
Inhaminga, *Mozam.* 83 F4
Inharrime, *Mozam.* 85 C6
Inharrime →, *Mozam.* . . . 85 C6
Inhuma, *Brazil* 122 C3
Inhumas, *Brazil* 123 E2
Iniesta, *Spain* 29 F3
Ining = Yining, *China* . . . 44 E9
Inini □, *Fr. Guiana* 121 C7
Inírida →, *Colombia* 120 C4
Inishbofin, *Ireland* 15 C1
Inishmore, *Ireland* 15 C2
Inishowen, *Ireland* 15 A4
Injune, *Australia* 91 D4
Inklin, *Canada* 100 B2
Inklin →, *Canada* 100 B2
Inkom, *U.S.A.* 110 E7
Inle L., *Burma* 61 J20
Inn →, *Austria* 19 G9
Innamincka, *Australia* . . . 91 D3
Inner Hebrides, *U.K.* 14 D2
Inner Mongolia = Nei
  Monggol Zizhiqu □,
  China 50 C6
Inner Sound, *U.K.* 14 D3
Innerkip, *Canada* 106 C4
Innerkirchen, *Switz.* 22 C6
Innerste →, *Germany* 18 C5
Innetalling I., *Canada* . . . 98 A4
Innisfail, *Australia* 90 B4
Innisfail, *Canada* 100 C6
In'no-shima, *Japan* 49 G6
Innsbruck, *Austria* 19 H7
Inny →, *Ireland* 15 C4
Inocência, *Brazil* 123 E1
Inongo, *Zaïre* 80 E3
Inoucdjouac, *Canada* 97 C12
Inowrocław, *Poland* 20 C8
Inpundong, *N. Korea* 51 D14
Inquisivi, *Bolivia* 124 D4
Ins, *Switz.* 22 B4
Inscription, C., *Australia* . 89 E1
Insein, *Burma* 61 L20
Însurăţei, *Romania* 38 E10

Intendente Alvear,
  Argentina 126 D3
Interior, *U.S.A.* 108 D4
Interlaken, *Switz.* 25 F14
International Falls, *U.S.A.* 108 A8
Intiyaco, *Argentina* 126 B3
Intragna, *Switz.* 23 D7
Intutu, *Peru* 120 D3
Inútil, B., *Chile* 128 D2
Inuvik, *Canada* 96 B6
Inveraray, *U.K.* 14 E3
Inverbervie, *U.K.* 14 E6
Invercargill, *N.Z.* 87 M2
Inverell, *Australia* 91 D5
Invergordon, *U.K.* 14 D4
Invermere, *Canada* 100 C5
Inverness, *Canada* 99 C7
Inverness, *U.K.* 14 D4
Inverness, *U.S.A.* 105 L4
Inverurie, *U.K.* 14 D6
Inverway, *Australia* 88 C4
Investigator Group,
  Australia 91 E1
Investigator Str., *Australia* 91 F2
Inya, *Russia* 44 D9
Inyanga, *Zimbabwe* 83 F3
Inyangani, *Zimbabwe* 83 F3
Inyantue, *Zimbabwe* 83 F2
Inyo Mts., *U.S.A.* 111 H5
Inyokern, *U.S.A.* 113 K9
Inza, *Russia* 41 E15
Inzhavino, *Russia* 41 E13
Iō-Jima, *Japan* 49 J5
Ioánnina, *Greece* 39 K3
Iola, *U.S.A.* 109 G7
Ion Corvin, *Romania* 38 E10
Iona, *U.K.* 14 E2
Ione, *Calif., U.S.A.* 112 G6
Ione, *Wash., U.S.A.* 110 B5
Ionia, *U.S.A.* 104 D3
Ionian Is. = Iónioi Nísoi,
  Greece 39 L3
Ionian Sea, *Europe* 6 H9
Iónioi Nísoi, *Greece* 39 L3
Iori →, *Azerbaijan* 43 F12
Íos, *Greece* 39 N8
Iowa □, *U.S.A.* 108 D8
Iowa City, *U.S.A.* 108 E9
Iowa Falls, *U.S.A.* 108 D8
Ipala, *Tanzania* 82 C3
Ipameri, *Brazil* 123 E2
Iparía, *Peru* 124 B3
Ipáti, *Greece* 39 L5
Ipatinga, *Brazil* 123 E3
Ipatovo, *Russia* 43 D10
Ipel →, *Europe* 21 G9
Ipiales, *Colombia* 120 C2
Ipiaú, *Brazil* 123 D4
Ipin = Yibin, *China* 52 C5
Ipirá, *Brazil* 123 D4
Ipiranga, *Brazil* 120 D4
Ipixuna, *Brazil* 124 B3
Ipixuna →, *Amazonas,*
  Brazil 124 B3
Ipixuna →, *Amazonas,*
  Brazil 125 B5
Ipoh, *Malaysia* 59 K3
Iporá, *Brazil* 123 D1
Ippy, *C.A.R.* 73 G9
Ipsala, *Turkey* 66 C2
Ipsárion Óros, *Greece* . . . 39 J7
Ipswich, *Australia* 91 D5
Ipswich, *U.K.* 13 E9
Ipswich, *Mass., U.S.A.* . . 107 D14
Ipswich, *S. Dak., U.S.A.* . 108 C5
Ipu, *Brazil* 122 B3
Ipueiras, *Brazil* 122 B3
Ipupiara, *Brazil* 123 D3
Iput →, *Belorussia* 40 E7
Iqaluit, *Canada* 97 B13
Iquique, *Chile* 124 E3
Iquitos, *Peru* 120 D3
Irabu-Jima, *Japan* 49 M2
Iracoubo, *Fr. Guiana* . . . 121 B7
Irafshān, *Iran* 65 E9
Irahuan, *Phil.* 55 G3
Iráklia, *Greece* 39 N8
Iráklion, *Greece* 37 D7
Iráklion □, *Greece* 37 D7
Irala, *Paraguay* 127 B5
Iramba □, *Tanzania* 82 C3
Iran ■, *Asia* 65 C7
Iran, Gunung-Gunung,
  Malaysia 56 D4
Iran Ra. = Iran, Gunung-
  Gunung, *Malaysia* 56 D4
Īrānshahr, *Iran* 65 E9
Irapa, *Venezuela* 121 A5
Irapuato, *Mexico* 114 C4
Iraq ■, *Asia* 64 C5
Irarrar, O. →, *Mali* 75 D5
Irati, *Brazil* 127 B5
Irbid, *Jordan* 69 C4
Irbid □, *Jordan* 69 C5
Irebu, *Zaïre* 80 E3
Irecê, *Brazil* 122 D3
Iregua →, *Spain* 28 C7
Ireland ■, *Europe* 15 D4
Ireland's Eye, *Ireland* . . . 15 C5
Irele, *Nigeria* 79 D6
Ireng →, *Brazil* 121 C6
Iret, *Russia* 45 C16
Irgiz, Bolshaya →, *Russia* 41 E16
Irharharene, *Algeria* 75 C6
Irharrhar, O. →, *Algeria* . 75 C6
Irherm, *Morocco* 74 B3

Irhil Mgoun, *Morocco* . . . 74 B3
Irhyangdong, *N. Korea* . . 51 D15
Iri, *S. Korea* 51 G14
Irian Jaya □, *Indonesia* . . 57 E9
Irié, *Guinea* 78 D3
Iriga, *Phil.* 55 E5
Iringa, *Tanzania* 82 D4
Iringa □, *Tanzania* 82 D4
Iriomote-Jima, *Japan* 49 M1
Iriona, *Honduras* 116 C2
Iriri →, *Brazil* 121 D7
Iriri Novo →, *Brazil* 125 B7
Irish Republic ■, *Europe* . 15 D4
Irish Sea, *Europe* 12 D3
Irkineyeva, *Russia* 45 D10
Irkutsk, *Russia* 45 D11
Irma, *Canada* 101 C6
Irō-Zaki, *Japan* 49 G9
Iroise, Mer d', *France* . . . 24 D2
Iron Baron, *Australia* 91 E2
Iron Gate = Portile de
  Fier, *Europe* 38 E5
Iron Knob, *Australia* 91 E2
Iron Mountain, *U.S.A.* . . 104 C1
Iron Ra., *Australia* 90 A3
Iron River, *U.S.A.* 108 B10
Irondequoit, *U.S.A.* 106 C7
Ironton, *Mo., U.S.A.* 109 G9
Ironton, *Ohio, U.S.A.* . . . 104 F4
Ironwood, *U.S.A.* 108 B9
Iroquois Falls, *Canada* . . . 98 C3
Irosin, *Phil.* 55 E6
Irpen, *Ukraine* 40 F7
Irrara Cr. →, *Australia* . . 91 D4
Irrawaddy □, *Burma* 61 L19
Irrawaddy →, *Burma* 61 M19
Irsina, *Italy* 35 B9
Irtysh →, *Russia* 44 C7
Irumu, *Zaïre* 82 B2
Irún, *Spain* 28 B3
Irunea = Pamplona, *Spain* 28 C3
Irurzun, *Spain* 28 C3
Irvine, *Canada* 101 D6
Irvine, *U.K.* 14 F4
Irvine, *Calif., U.S.A.* . . . 113 M9
Irvine, *Ky., U.S.A.* 104 G4
Irvinestown, *U.K.* 15 B4
Irving, *U.S.A.* 109
Irvona, *U.S.A.* 106 F6
Irwin →, *Australia* 89 E1
Irymple, *Australia* 91 E3
Is-sur-Tille, *France* 25 E12
Isa, *Nigeria* 79 C6
Isaac →, *Australia* 90 C4
Isabel, *U.S.A.* 108 C4
Isabela, I., *Mexico* 114 C3
Isabela, *Phil.* 55 H5
Isabela, Cord., *Nic.* 116 D2
Isabella Ra., *Australia* . . . 88 D3
Ísafjarðardjúp, *Iceland* . . 8 C2
Ísafjörður, *Iceland* 8 C2
Isagarh, *India* 62 G7
Isahaya, *Japan* 49 H5
Isaka, *Tanzania* 82 C3
Isana = Içana →, *Brazil* . 120 C4
Isangi, *Zaïre* 80 D4
Isar →, *Germany* 19 G8
Isarco →, *Italy* 33 B8
Ísari, *Greece* 39 M5
Isbergues, *France* 25 B9
Iscayachi, *Bolivia* 125 E4
Íschia, *Italy* 34 B6
Iscuandé, *Colombia* 120 C2
Isdell →, *Australia* 88 C3
Ise, *Japan* 49 G8
Ise-Wan, *Japan* 49 G8
Isefjord, *Denmark* 11 J5
Iseltwald, *Switz.* 22 C5
Isenthal, *Switz.* 23 C7
Iseo, *Italy* 32 C7
Iseo, L. d', *Italy* 32 C7
Isère □, *France* 27 C9
Isère →, *France* 27 D8
Iserlohn, *Germany* 18 D3
Isérnia, *Italy* 35 A7
Iseyin, *Nigeria* 79 D5
Isherton, *Guyana* 121 C6
Ishigaki-Shima, *Japan* . . . 49 M2
Ishikari-Gawa →, *Japan* . 48 C10
Ishikari-Sammyaku, *Japan* 48 C11
Ishikari-Wan, *Japan* 48 C10
Ishikawa □, *Japan* 49 F8
Ishim, *Russia* 44 D7
Ishim →, *Russia* 44 D8
Ishinomaki, *Japan* 48 E10
Ishioka, *Japan* 49 F10
Ishkuman, *Pakistan* 63 A5
Ishpeming, *U.S.A.* 104 B2
Isigny-sur-Mer, *France* . . 24 C5
Isil Kul, *Russia* 44 D8
Isiolo, *Kenya* 82 B4
Isiolo □, *Kenya* 82 B4
Isipingo Beach, *S. Africa* . 85 E5
Isiro, *Zaïre* 82 B2
Isisford, *Australia* 90 C3
İskederun, *Turkey* 66 E7
İskenderun, *Turkey* 66 E7
İskenderun Körfezi, *Turkey* 66 E6
İskilip, *Turkey* 42 F6
İskŭr →, *Bulgaria* 38 F7
Iskut →, *Canada* 100 B2
Isla →, *U.K.* 14 E5
Isla Cristina, *Spain* 31 H3

Isla Vista, *U.S.A.* 113 L7
İslâhiye, *Turkey* 66 E7
Islamabad, *Pakistan* 62 C5
Islamkot, *Pakistan* 62 G4
Island →, *Canada* 100 A4
Island Falls, *Canada* 98 C3
Island Falls, *U.S.A.* 99 C6
Island L., *Canada* 101 C10
Island Lagoon, *Australia* . 91 E2
Island Pond, *U.S.A.* 107 B13
Islands, B. of, *Canada* . . . 99 C8
Islay, *U.K.* 14 F2
Isle →, *France* 26 D3
Isle aux Morts, *Canada* . . 99 C8
Isle of Wight □, *U.K.* . . . 13 G6
Isle Royale, *U.S.A.* 108 A10
Isleta, *U.S.A.* 111 J10
Isleton, *U.S.A.* 112 G5
Ismail, *Ukraine* 42 D3
Ismâ'îlîya, *Egypt* 76 H8
Ismaning, *Germany* 19 G7
Ismay, *U.S.A.* 108 B2
Isna, *Egypt* 76 B3
Isogstalo, *India* 63 B8
Isola del Gran Sasso
  d'Italia, *Italy* 33 F10
Ísola del Liri, *Italy* 34 A6
Ísola della Scala, *Italy* . . . 32 C8
Ísola di Capo Rizzuto, *Italy* 35 D10
Ísparta, *Turkey* 66 E4
Ísparta □, *Turkey* 66 E4
Isperikh, *Bulgaria* 38 F9
Íspica, *Italy* 35 F7
Íspir, *Turkey* 43 F9
Israel ■, *Asia* 69 D3
Issano, *Guyana* 121 B6
Issia, *Ivory C.* 78 D3
Issoire, *France* 26 C7
Issoudun, *France* 25 F8
Issyk-Kul, Ozero, *Kirghizia* 44 E8
Ist, *Croatia* 33 D11
Istaihah, *U.A.E.* 65 F7
İstanbul, *Turkey* 66 C3
İstanbul □, *Turkey* 66 C3
Istmina, *Colombia* 120 B2
Istok, *Serbia, Yug.* 21 N10
Istokpoga, L., *U.S.A.* . . . 105 M5
Istra, *Croatia* 33 C11
Istra, *Russia* 41 D10
İstranca Dağları, *Turkey* . 39 H10
Istres, *France* 27 E8
Istria = Istra, *Croatia* . . . 33 C11
Itá, *Paraguay* 126 B4
Itabaiana, *Paraíba, Brazil* . 122 C4
Itabaiana, *Sergipe, Brazil* . 122 D4
Itabaianinha, *Brazil* 122 D4
Itaberaba, *Brazil* 123 D3
Itaberaí, *Brazil* 123 E2
Itabira, *Brazil* 123 E3
Itabirito, *Brazil* 123 F3
Itaboca, *Brazil* 121 D5
Itabuna, *Brazil* 123 D4
Itacajá, *Brazil* 122 C2
Itacaunas →, *Brazil* 122 C2
Itacoatiara, *Brazil* 121 D6
Itacuaí →, *Brazil* 124 A3
Itaguaçu, *Brazil* 123 E3
Itaguari →, *Brazil* 123 D3
Itaguatins, *Brazil* 122 C2
Itaim →, *Brazil* 122 C3
Itainópolis, *Brazil* 122 C3
Itaipu Dam, *Brazil* 127 B5
Itaituba, *Brazil* 121 D6
Itajaí, *Brazil* 127 B6
Itajubá, *Brazil* 123 F2
Itajuípe, *Brazil* 123 D4
Itaka, *Tanzania* 83 D3
Italy ■, *Europe* 7 G8
Itamataré, *Brazil* 122 B2
Itambacuri, *Brazil* 123 E3
Itambé, *Brazil* 123 E3
Itampolo, *Madag.* 85 C7
Itanhauã →, *Brazil* 121 D5
Itanhém, *Brazil* 123 E3
Itapaci, *Brazil* 123 D2
Itapagé, *Brazil* 122 B4
Itaparica, I. de, *Brazil* . . . 123 D4
Itapebi, *Brazil* 123 E4
Itapecuru-Mirim, *Brazil* . . 122 B3
Itaperuna, *Brazil* 123 F3
Itapetinga, *Brazil* 123 E3
Itapetininga, *Brazil* 127 A6
Itapeva, *Brazil* 127 A6
Itapicuru →, *Bahia, Brazil* 122 D4
Itapicuru →, *Maranhão,*
  Brazil 122 B3
Itapinima, *Brazil* 125 B5
Itapipoca, *Brazil* 122 B4
Itapiranga, *Brazil* 121 D6
Itapiúna, *Brazil* 122 B4
Itaporanga, *Brazil* 122 C4
Itapuá □, *Paraguay* 127 B4
Itapuranga, *Brazil* 123 D2
Itaquari, *Brazil* 123 F3
Itaquatiara, *Brazil* 121 D6
Itaquí, *Brazil* 126 B4
Itararé, *Brazil* 127 A6
Itarsi, *India* 62 H7
Itatí, *Argentina* 126 B4
Itatira, *Brazil* 122 B4
Itatuba, *Brazil* 125 B5
Itatupa, *Brazil* 121 D7
Itaueira, *Brazil* 122 C3
Itaueira →, *Brazil* 122 C3
Itaúna, *Brazil* 123 F3

Itbayat, *Phil.* 55 A4
Itchen →, *U.K.* 13 G6
Ite, *Peru* 124 D3
Itezhi Tezhi, L., *Zambia* . 83 F2
Ithaca = Itháki, *Greece* . . 39 L3
Ithaca, *U.S.A.* 107 D8
Itháki, *Greece* 39 L3
Itinga, *Brazil* 123 E3
Itiquira, *Brazil* 125 D7
Itiquira →, *Brazil* 125 D6
Itiruçu, *Brazil* 123 D3
Itiúba, *Brazil* 122 D4
Ito, *Japan* 49 G9
Itoigawa, *Japan* 49 F8
Iton →, *France* 24 C8
Itonamas →, *Bolivia* 125 C5
Itsa, *Egypt* 76 J7
İttiri, *Italy* 34 B1
Ittoqqortoormiit =
  Scoresbysund, *Greenland* 4 B6
Itu, *Brazil* 127 A6
Itu, *Nigeria* 79 D6
Ituaçu, *Brazil* 123 D3
Ituango, *Colombia* 120 B2
Ituiutaba, *Brazil* 123 E2
Itumbiara, *Brazil* 123 E2
Ituna, *Canada* 101 C8
Itunge Port, *Tanzania* . . . 83 D3
Ituni, *Guyana* 121 B6
Itupiranga, *Brazil* 122 C2
Iturama, *Brazil* 123 E1
Iturbe, *Argentina* 126 A2
Ituri →, *Zaïre* 82 B2
Iturup, Ostrov, *Russia* . . . 45 E15
Ituverava, *Brazil* 123 F2
Ituxi →, *Brazil* 125 B5
Ituyuro →, *Argentina* . . . 126 A3
Itzehoe, *Germany* 18 B5
Ivaí →, *Brazil* 127 A5
Ivalo, *Finland* 8 B19
Ivalojoki →, *Finland* 8 B19
Ivangorod, *Russia* 40 B6
Ivanhoe, *N.S.W., Australia* 91 E3
Ivanhoe, *W. Austral.,*
  Australia 88 C4
Ivanhoe, *U.S.A.* 112 J7
Ivanhoe L., *Canada* 101 A7
Ivanić Grad, *Croatia* 33 C13
Ivanjica, *Serbia, Yug.* . . . 21 M10
Ivanjščice, *Croatia* 33 B13
Ivankoyskoye Vdkhr.,
  Russia 41 C10
Ivano-Frankivsk = Ivano-
  Frankovsk, *Ukraine* . . . 40 G4
Ivano-Frankovsk, *Ukraine* 40 G4
Ivanovo, *Belorussia* 40 E4
Ivanovo, *Russia* 41 C12
Ivato, *Madag.* 85 C8
Ivaylovgrad, *Bulgaria* . . . 39 H9
Ivinheima →, *Brazil* 127 A5
Ivohibe, *Madag.* 85 C8
Ivolândia, *Brazil* 123 E1
Ivory Coast ■, *Africa* . . . 78 D3
Ivrea, *Italy* 32 C4
Ivugivik, *Canada* 97 B12
Iwahig, *Phil.* 56 C5
Iwaizumi, *Japan* 48 E10
Iwaki, *Japan* 49 F10
Iwakuni, *Japan* 49 G6
Iwamizawa, *Japan* 48 C10
Iwanai, *Japan* 48 C10
Iwata, *Japan* 49 G8
Iwate □, *Japan* 48 E10
Iwate-San, *Japan* 48 E10
Iwo, *Nigeria* 79 D5
Ixiamas, *Bolivia* 124 C4
Ixopo, *S. Africa* 85 E5
Ixtepec, *Mexico* 115 D5
Ixtlán del Río, *Mexico* . . 114 C4
Iyo, *Japan* 49 H6
Izabal, L. de, *Guatemala* . 116 C2
Izamal, *Mexico* 115 C7
Izberbash, *Russia* 43 E12
Izegem, *Belgium* 17 G2
Izena-Shima, *Japan* 49 L3
Izhevsk, *Russia* 44 D6
Izmayil = Ismail, *Ukraine* 42 D3
İzmir, *Turkey* 66 D2
İzmir □, *Turkey* 66 D2
İzmit, *Turkey* 66 C3
Iznajar, *Spain* 31 H6
Iznalloz, *Spain* 29 H1
İznik Gölü, *Turkey* 66 C3
Izobil'nyy, *Russia* 43 D9
Izola, *Slovenia* 33 C10
Izozog, Bañados de, *Bolivia* 125 D5
Izra, *Syria* 69 C5
Iztochni Rodopi, *Bulgaria* 39 H8
Izu-Shotō, *Japan* 49 G10
Izumi-sano, *Japan* 49 G7
Izumo, *Japan* 49 G6
Izyaslav, *Ukraine* 40 F5
Izyum, *Ukraine* 42 B7

J

J.F. Rodrigues, *Brazil* . . . 122 B1
Jaba, *Ethiopia* 77 F4
Jabal el Awlîya, *Sudan* . . 77 D3
Jabal Lubnān, *Lebanon* . . 69 B4
Jabalón →, *Spain* 31 G6
Jabalpur, *India* 63 H8

Jabbūl, *Syria* 64 B3
Jablah, *Syria* 64 C3
Jablanac, *Croatia* 33 D11
Jablonec, *Czech.* 20 E5
Jabłonowo, *Poland* 20 B9
Jaboatão, *Brazil* 122 C4
Jaboticabal, *Brazil* 127 A6
Jaburu, *Brazil* 125 B5
Jaca, *Spain* 28 C4
Jacaré →, *Brazil* 122 D3
Jacareí, *Brazil* 127 A6
Jacarèzinho, *Brazil* 127 A6
Jaciara, *Brazil* 125 D7
Jacinto, *Brazil* 123 E3
Jaciparaná, *Brazil* 125 B5
Jackman, *U.S.A.* 99 C5
Jacksboro, *U.S.A.* 109 J5
Jackson, *Australia* 91 D4
Jackson, *Ala., U.S.A.* 105 K2
Jackson, *Calif., U.S.A.* .. 112 G6
Jackson, *Ky., U.S.A.* 104 G4
Jackson, *Mich., U.S.A.* ... 104 D3
Jackson, *Minn., U.S.A.* .. 108 D7
Jackson, *Miss., U.S.A.* .. 109 J9
Jackson, *Mo., U.S.A.* 109 G10
Jackson, *Ohio, U.S.A.* ... 104 F4
Jackson, *Tenn., U.S.A.* .. 105 H1
Jackson, *Wyo., U.S.A.* ... 110 E8
Jackson B., *N.Z.* 87 K2
Jackson L., *U.S.A.* 110 E8
Jacksons, *N.Z.* 87 K3
Jacksonville, *Ala., U.S.A.* 105 J3
Jacksonville, *Calif., U.S.A.* 112 H6
Jacksonville, *Fla., U.S.A.* . 105 K5
Jacksonville, *Ill., U.S.A.* .. 108 F9
Jacksonville, *N.C., U.S.A.* 105 H7
Jacksonville, *Oreg., U.S.A.* 110 E2
Jacksonville, *Tex., U.S.A.* 109 K7
Jacksonville Beach, *U.S.A.* 105 K5
Jacmel, *Haiti* 117 C5
Jacob Lake, *U.S.A.* 111 H7
Jacobabad, *Pakistan* 62 E3
Jacobina, *Brazil* 122 D3
Jacques-Cartier, Mt.,
  Canada 99 C6
Jacqueville, *Ivory C.* 78 D4
Jacuí →, *Brazil* 127 C5
Jacumba, *U.S.A.* 113 N10
Jacundá →, *Brazil* 122 B1
Jade, *Germany* 18 B4
Jadebusen, *Germany* 18 B4
Jadoigne, *Belgium* 17 G5
Jadotville = Likasi, *Zaïre* 83 E2
Jadraque, *Spain* 28 E2
Jādū, *Libya* 75 B7
Jaén, *Peru* 124 B2
Jaén, *Spain* 31 H7
Jaén □, *Spain* 31 H7
Jafène, *Africa* 74 D3
Jaffa = Tel Aviv-Yafo,
  Israel 69 C3
Jaffa, C., *Australia* 91 F2
Jaffna, *Sri Lanka* 60 Q12
Jagadhri, *India* 62 D7
Jagadishpur, *India* 63 G11
Jagdalpur, *India* 61 K12
Jagersfontein, *S. Africa* .. 84 D4
Jagraon, *India* 60 D9
Jagst →, *Germany* 19 F5
Jagtial, *India* 60 K11
Jaguaquara, *Brazil* 123 D4
Jaguariaíva, *Brazil* 127 A6
Jaguaribe, *Brazil* 122 C4
Jaguaribe →, *Brazil* 122 B4
Jaguaruana, *Brazil* 122 B4
Jagüey Grande, *Cuba* 116 B3
Jahangirabad, *India* 62 E8
Jahrom, *Iran* 65 D7
Jaicós, *Brazil* 122 C3
Jailolo, *Indonesia* 57 D7
Jailolo, Selat, *Indonesia* . 57 D7
Jaipur, *India* 62 F6
Jājarm, *Iran* 65 B8
Jajce, *Bos.-H.* 21 L7
Jakarta, *Indonesia* 57 G12
Jakobstad, *Finland* 8 E17
Jakupica, *Macedonia* 39 H4
Jal, *U.S.A.* 109 J3
Jalalabad, *Afghan.* 62 B4
Jalalabad, *India* 63 F8
Jalalpur Jattan, *Pakistan* . 62 C6
Jalama, *U.S.A.* 113 L6
Jalapa, *Guatemala* 116 D2
Jalapa Enríquez, *Mexico* . 115 D5
Jalaun, *India* 63 F8
Jales, *Brazil* 123 F1
Jaleswar, *Nepal* 63 F11
Jalgaon, *Maharashtra, India* 60 J10
Jalgaon, *Maharashtra, India* 60 J9
Jalhay, *Belgium* 17 G7
Jalībah, *Iraq* 64 D5
Jalingo, *Nigeria* 79 D7
Jalisco □, *Mexico* 114 C4
Jalkot, *Pakistan* 63 B5
Jallas →, *Spain* 30 C1
Jalna, *India* 60 K9
Jalón →, *Spain* 28 D3
Jalpa, *Mexico* 114 C4
Jalpaiguri, *India* 61 F16
Jalūlā, *Iraq* 64 C5
Jamaari, *Nigeria* 79 C6
Jamaica ■, *W. Indies* 116 C4
Jamalpur, *Bangla.* 61 G16
Jamalpur, *India* 63 G12

Jamalpurganj, *India* 63 H13
Jamanxim →, *Brazil* 125 A6
Jamari, *Brazil* 125 B5
Jamari →, *Brazil* 125 B5
Jambe, *Indonesia* 57 E8
Jambes, *Belgium* 17 H5
Jambi, *Indonesia* 56 E2
Jambi □, *Indonesia* 56 E2
Jambusar, *India* 62 H5
James →, *U.S.A.* 108 D6
James B., *Canada* 97 C11
James Ras., *Australia* ... 88 D5
James Ross I., *Antarctica* . 5 C18
Jamestown, *Australia* ... 91 E2
Jamestown, *S. Africa* ... 84 E4
Jamestown, *Ky., U.S.A.* . 104 G3
Jamestown, *N. Dak.,*
  U.S.A. 108 B5
Jamestown, *N.Y., U.S.A.* . 106 D5
Jamestown, *Pa., U.S.A.* . 106 E4
Jamestown, *Tenn., U.S.A.* 105 G3
Jamīlābād, *Iran* 65 C6
Jamiltepec, *Mexico* 115 D5
Jamkhandi, *India* 60 L9
Jammerbugt, *Denmark* ... 11 G3
Jammu, *India* 62 C6
Jammu & Kashmir □, *India* 63 B7
Jamnagar, *India* 62 H4
Jamner, *India* 60 J9
Jampur, *Pakistan* 62 E4
Jamrud, *Pakistan* 62 C4
Jamshedpur, *India* 63 H12
Jamtara, *India* 63 H12
Jämtlands län □, *Sweden* . 10 B7
Jan Kempdorp, *S. Africa* . 84 D3
Jan L., *Canada* 101 C8
Jan Mayen, *Arctic* 4 B7
Janaúba, *Brazil* 123 E3
Janaucu, I., *Brazil* 122 A1
Jand, *Pakistan* 62 C5
Janda, L. de la, *Spain* ... 31 J5
Jandaia, *Brazil* 123 E1
Jandaq, *Iran* 65 C7
Jandia, *Canary Is.* 36 F5
Jandia, Pta. de, *Canary Is.* 36 F5
Jandiatuba →, *Brazil* ... 120 D4
Jandola, *Pakistan* 62 C4
Jandowae, *Australia* 91 D5
Jandrain-Jandrenouilles,
  Belgium 17 G5
Jándula →, *Spain* 31 G6
Janesville, *U.S.A.* 108 D10
Janga, *Ghana* 79 C4
Jango, *Brazil* 125 E6
Janīn, *Jordan* 69 C4
Janjina, *Croatia* 21 N7
Janos, *Mexico* 114 A3
Jánosháza, *Hungary* 21 H7
Jánów Podlaski, *Poland* .. 20 C13
Januária, *Brazil* 123 E3
Janub Dârfûr □, *Sudan* . 77 E2
Janub Kordofân □, *Sudan* 77 E3
Janubio, *Canary Is.* 36 F6
Janville, *France* 25 D8
Janzé, *France* 24 E5
Jaora, *India* 62 H6
Japan ■, *Asia* 49 G8
Japan, Sea of, *Asia* 48 E7
Japan Trench, *Pac. Oc.* . 92 D6
Japen = Yapen, *Indonesia* 57 E9
Japurá →, *Brazil* 120 D4
Jaque, *Panama* 120 B2
Jarābulus, *Syria* 64 B3
Jaraguá, *Brazil* 123 E2
Jaraguari, *Brazil* 125 E7
Jaraicejo, *Spain* 31 F5
Jaraiz, *Spain* 30 E5
Jarama →, *Spain* 28 E1
Jaramillo, *Argentina* 128 C3
Jarandilla, *Spain* 30 E5
Jaranwala, *Pakistan* 62 D5
Jarash, *Jordan* 69 C4
Jarauçu →, *Brazil* 121 D7
Jardim, *Brazil* 126 A4
Jardín →, *Spain* 29 G2
Jardines de la Reina, Is.,
  Cuba 116 B4
Jargalang, *China* 51 C12
Jargalant = Hovd,
  Mongolia 54 B4
Jargeau, *France* 25 E9
Jari →, *Brazil* 121 D7
Jarīr, W. al →, *Si. Arabia* 64 E4
Jarmen, *Germany* 18 B9
Jarnac, *France* 26 C3
Jarny, *France* 25 C12
Jarocin, *Poland* 20 D7
Jarosław, *Poland* 20 E12
Järpås, *Sweden* 11 F6
Järpen, *Sweden* 10 A7
Jarrahdale, *Australia* ... 89 F2
Jarres, Plaine des, *Laos* . 58 C4
Jarso, *Ethiopia* 77 F4
Jartai, *China* 50 E3
Jaru, *Brazil* 125 C5
Jaru →, *Brazil* 125 C5
Jarud Qi, *China* 51 B11
Jarvis, *Canada* 106 D4
Jarvis I., *Pac. Oc.* 93 H12
Jarwa, *India* 63 F10
Jaša Tomić, *Serbia, Yug.* 21 K10
Jāsimīyah, *Iraq* 64 C5
Jasin, *Malaysia* 59 L4
Jāsk, *Iran* 65 E8
Jasło, *Poland* 20 F11

Jason, Is., *Falk. Is.* 128 D4
Jasper, *Alta., Canada* ... 100 C5
Jasper, *Ont., Canada* ... 107 B9
Jasper, *Ala., U.S.A.* 105 J2
Jasper, *Fla., U.S.A.* 105 K4
Jasper, *Minn., U.S.A.* ... 108 D6
Jasper, *Tex., U.S.A.* 109 K8
Jasper Nat. Park, *Canada* 100 C5
Jassy = Iaşi, *Romania* ... 38 B10
Jastrebarsko, *Croatia* ... 33 C12
Jastrzębie Zdrój, *Poland* . 20 F8
Jászárokszállás, *Hungary* . 21 H10
Jászberény, *Hungary* 21 H9
Jászladány, *Hungary* 21 H10
Jataí, *Brazil* 123 E1
Jatapu →, *Brazil* 121 D6
Jati, *Pakistan* 62 G3
Jatibarang, *Indonesia* ... 57 G13
Jatinegara, *Indonesia* ... 57 G12
Játiva, *Spain* 29 G4
Jatobal, *Brazil* 122 B2
Jaú, *Brazil* 127 A6
Jaú →, *Brazil* 121 D5
Jauaperí →, *Brazil* 121 D5
Jauche, *Belgium* 17 G5
Jauja, *Peru* 124 C2
Jaunjelgava, *Latvia* 40 C4
Jaunpur, *India* 63 G10
Jauru →, *Brazil* 125 D6
Java = Jawa, *Indonesia* . 57 G14
Java Sea, *Indonesia* 56 E3
Java Trench, *Ind. Oc.* ... 92 H2
Jávea, *Spain* 29 G5
Javhlant = Ulyasutay,
  Mongolia 54 B4
Javier, I., *Chile* 128 C2
Javron, *France* 24 D6
Jawa, *Indonesia* 57 G14
Jawor, *Poland* 20 D6
Jaworzno, *Poland* 20 E9
Jay, *U.S.A.* 109 G7
Jaya, Puncak, *Indonesia* . 57 E9
Jayanca, *Peru* 124 B2
Jayanti, *India* 61 F16
Jayapura, *Indonesia* 57 E10
Jayawijaya, Pegunungan,
  Indonesia 57 E9
Jaynagar, *India* 61 F15
Jayrūd, *Syria* 64 C3
Jayton, *U.S.A.* 109 J4
Jazīreh-ye Shīf, *Iran* 65 D6
Jazminal, *Mexico* 114 C4
Jazzīn, *Lebanon* 69 B4
Jean, *U.S.A.* 113 K11
Jean Marie River, *Canada* 100 A4
Jean Rabel, *Haiti* 117 C5
Jeanerette, *U.S.A.* 109 L9
Jeannette, *Ostrov, Russia* 45 B16
Jeannette, *U.S.A.* 106 F5
Jebba, *Morocco* 74 A4
Jebba, *Nigeria* 79 D5
Jebel, Bahr el →, *Sudan* . 77 F3
Jebel Qerri, *Sudan* 77 D3
Jeberos, *Peru* 124 B2
Jedburgh, *U.K.* 14 F6
Jedda = Jiddah, *Si. Arabia* 68 C2
Jędrzejów, *Poland* 20 E10
Jedway, *Canada* 100 C2
Jeetzel →, *Germany* 18 B7
Jefferson, *Iowa, U.S.A.* .. 108 D7
Jefferson, *Ohio, U.S.A.* . 106 E4
Jefferson, *Tex., U.S.A.* .. 109 J7
Jefferson, *Wis., U.S.A.* .. 108 D10
Jefferson, Mt., *Nev.,*
  U.S.A. 110 G5
Jefferson, Mt., *Oreg.,*
  U.S.A. 110 D3
Jefferson City, *Mo., U.S.A.* 108 F8
Jefferson City, *Tenn.,*
  U.S.A. 105 G4
Jeffersonville, *U.S.A.* ... 104 F3
Jega, *Nigeria* 79 C5
Jēkabpils, *Latvia* 40 C4
Jelenia Góra, *Poland* 20 E5
Jelgava, *Latvia* 9 H17
Jelli, *Sudan* 77 F3
Jellicoe, *Canada* 98 C2
Jemaja, *Indonesia* 56 D3
Jemaluang, *Malaysia* 59 L4
Jemappes, *Belgium* 17 H3
Jember, *Indonesia* 57 H15
Jembongan, *Malaysia* ... 56 C5
Jemeppe, *Belgium* 17 G7
Jemnice, *Czech.* 20 F5
Jena, *Germany* 18 E7
Jena, *U.S.A.* 109 K8
Jendouba, *Tunisia* 75 A6
Jenkins, *U.S.A.* 104 G4
Jenner, *U.S.A.* 112 G3
Jennings, *U.S.A.* 109 K8
Jennings →, *Canada* 100 B2
Jeparit, *Australia* 91 F3
Jequié, *Brazil* 123 D3
Jequitaí →, *Brazil* 123 E3
Jequitinhonha, *Brazil* ... 123 E3
Jequitinhonha →, *Brazil* . 123 E4
Jerada, *Morocco* 75 B4
Jerantut, *Malaysia* 59 L4
Jérémie, *Haiti* 117 C5
Jeremoabo, *Brazil* 122 D4
Jerez, Punta, *Mexico* 115 C5
Jerez de García Salinas,
  Mexico 114 C4
Jerez de la Frontera, *Spain* 31 J4
Jerez de los Caballeros,
  Spain 31 G4

Jericho = Arīḥā, *Syria* ... 64 C3
Jericho = El Arīḥā, *Jordan* 69 D4
Jericho, *Australia* 90 C4
Jerilderie, *Australia* 91 F4
Jermyn, *U.S.A.* 107 E9
Jerome, *U.S.A.* 111 J8
Jersey, *Chan. Is.* 13 H5
Jersey City, *U.S.A.* 107 F10
Jersey Shore, *U.S.A.* ... 106 E7
Jerseyville, *U.S.A.* 108 F9
Jerusalem, *Israel* 69 D4
Jervis B., *Australia* 91 F5
Jesenice, *Slovenia* 33 B11
Jesenké, *Slovakia* 21 G10
Jesselton = Kota Kinabalu,
  Malaysia 56 C5
Jessnitz, *Germany* 18 D8
Jessore, *Bangla.* 61 H16
Jesup, *U.S.A.* 105 K5
Jesús, *Peru* 124 B2
Jesús Carranza, *Mexico* . 115 D5
Jesús María, *Argentina* .. 126 C3
Jetmore, *U.S.A.* 109 F5
Jetpur, *India* 62 J4
Jette, *Belgium* 17 G4
Jevnaker, *Norway* 10 D4
Jewett, *Ohio, U.S.A.* 106 F3
Jewett, *Tex., U.S.A.* 109 K6
Jewett City, *U.S.A.* 107 E13
Jeyḥūnābād, *Iran* 65 C6
Jeypore, *India* 61 K13
Jhajjar, *India* 62 E7
Jhal Jhao, *Pakistan* 60 F4
Jhalawar, *India* 62 G7
Jhang Maghiana, *Pakistan* 62 D5
Jhansi, *India* 63 G8
Jharia, *India* 63 H12
Jharsaguda, *India* 61 J14
Jhelum, *Pakistan* 62 C5
Jhelum →, *Pakistan* 62 D5
Jhunjhunu, *India* 62 E6
Ji Xian, *Hebei, China* 50 F8
Ji Xian, *Henan, China* ... 50 G8
Ji Xian, *Shanxi, China* ... 50 F6
Jia Xian, *Henan, China* .. 50 H7
Jia Xian, *Shaanxi, China* . 50 F6
Jiading, *China* 53 B13
Jiahe, *China* 53 E9
Jiali, *Taiwan* 53 F13
Jialing Jiang →, *China* ... 52 C6
Jiamusi, *China* 54 B8
Ji'an, *Jiangxi, China* 53 D10
Ji'an, *Jilin, China* 51 D14
Jianchang, *China* 51 D11
Jianchangying, *China* ... 51 D10
Jianchuan, *China* 52 D2
Jiande, *China* 53 C12
Jiangbei, *China* 52 C6
Jiangcheng, *China* 52 F3
Jiangdi, *China* 52 D4
Jiange, *China* 52 A5
Jiangjin, *China* 52 C6
Jiangkou, *China* 52 D7
Jiangle, *China* 53 D11
Jiangling, *China* 53 B9
Jiangmen, *China* 53 F9
Jiangshan, *China* 53 C12
Jiangsu □, *China* 51 H10
Jiangxi □, *China* 53 D10
Jiangyin, *China* 53 B13
Jiangyong, *China* 53 E8
Jiangyou, *China* 52 B5
Jianhe, *China* 52 D7
Jianli, *China* 53 C9
Jianning, *China* 53 D11
Jian'ou, *China* 53 D12
Jianshi, *China* 52 B7
Jianshui, *China* 52 F4
Jianyang, *Fujian, China* . 53 D12
Jianyang, *Sichuan, China* 52 B5
Jiao Xian, *China* 51 F11
Jiaohe, *Hebei, China* 50 E9
Jiaohe, *Jilin, China* 51 C14
Jiaoling, *China* 53 E11
Jiaozhou Wan, *China* ... 51 F11
Jiaozuo, *China* 50 G7
Jiashan, *China* 53 A11
Jiawang, *China* 51 G9
Jiaxiang, *China* 50 G9
Jiaxing, *China* 53 B13
Jiayi, *Taiwan* 53 F13
Jiayu, *China* 53 C9
Jibão, Serra do, *Brazil* .. 123 D3
Jibiya, *Nigeria* 79 C6
Jibou, *Romania* 38 B6
Jibuti = Djibouti ■, *Africa* 68 E3
Jicarón, I., *Panama* 116 E3
Jičín, *Czech.* 20 E5
Jiddah, *Si. Arabia* 68 C2
Jido, *India* 61 E19
Jieshou, *China* 50 H8
Jiexiu, *China* 50 F6
Jieyang, *China* 53 F11
Jigawa □, *Nigeria* 79 C6
Jiggalong, *Australia* 88 D3
Jihlava, *Czech.* 20 F5
Jijiga, *Ethiopia* 68 F3
Jijona, *Spain* 29 G4
Jikamshi, *Nigeria* 79 C6
Jilin, *China* 51 C14
Jilin □, *China* 51 C13
Jiloca →, *Spain* 28 D3
Jilong, *Taiwan* 53 E13

Jima, *Ethiopia* 77 F4
Jimbolia, *Romania* 38 D3
Jimena de la Frontera,
  Spain 31 J5
Jiménez, *Mexico* 114 B4
Jimo, *China* 51 F11
Jin Jiang →, *China* 53 C10
Jin Xian, *China* 50 E8
Jin Xian, *Liaoning, China* 51 E11
Jinan, *China* 50 F9
Jincheng, *China* 50 G7
Jinchuan, *China* 52 B4
Jind, *India* 62 E7
Jindabyne, *Australia* 91 F4
Jindrichuv Hradeç, *Czech.* 20 F5
Jing He →, *China* 50 G5
Jing Shan, *China* 53 B8
Jing Xian, *Anhui, China* . 53 B12
Jing Xian, *Hunan, China* 52 D7
Jing'an, *China* 53 C10
Jingbian, *China* 50 F5
Jingchuan, *China* 50 G4
Jingde, *China* 53 B12
Jingdezhen, *China* 53 C11
Jingdong, *China* 52 E3
Jinggu, *China* 52 F3
Jinghai, *China* 50 E9
Jinghong, *China* 52 F3
Jingjiang, *China* 53 A13
Jingle, *China* 50 E6
Jingmen, *China* 53 B9
Jingning, *China* 50 G3
Jingpo Hu, *China* 51 C15
Jingshan, *China* 53 B9
Jingtai, *China* 50 F3
Jingxi, *China* 52 F6
Jingxing, *China* 50 E8
Jingyang, *China* 50 G5
Jingyu, *China* 51 C14
Jingyuan, *China* 50 F3
Jingziguan, *China* 50 H6
Jining,
  Nei Mongol Zizhiqu,
  China 50 D7
Jining, *Shandong, China* . 50 G9
Jinja, *Uganda* 82 B3
Jinjang, *Malaysia* 59 L3
Jinji, *China* 50 F4
Jinjiang, *Fujian, China* .. 53 E12
Jinjiang, *Yunnan, China* . 52 D3
Jinjie, *China* 52 F6
Jinjini, *Ghana* 78 D4
Jinkou, *China* 53 B10
Jinmen Dao, *China* 53 E12
Jinning, *China* 52 E4
Jinotega, *Nic.* 116 D2
Jinotepe, *Nic.* 116 D2
Jinping, *Guizhou, China* . 52 D7
Jinping, *Yunnan, China* . 52 F4
Jinsha, *China* 52 D6
Jinsha Jiang →, *China* .. 52 D5
Jinshan, *China* 53 B13
Jinshi, *China* 53 C8
Jintan, *China* 53 B12
Jinxi, *Jiangxi, China* 53 D11
Jinxi, *Liaoning, China* ... 51 D11
Jinxian, *China* 53 C11
Jinxiang, *China* 50 G9
Jinyun, *China* 53 C13
Jinzhai, *China* 53 B10
Jinzhou, *China* 51 D11
Jiparaná →, *Brazil* 125 B5
Jipijapa, *Ecuador* 120 D1
Jiquilpan, *Mexico* 114 D4
Jishan, *China* 50 G6
Jishou, *China* 52 C7
Jishui, *China* 53 D10
Jisr ash Shughūr, *Syria* . 64 C3
Jitarning, *Australia* 89 F2
Jitra, *Malaysia* 59 J3
Jiu →, *Romania* 38 F6
Jiudengkou, *China* 50 E4
Jiujiang, *Guangdong, China* 53 F9
Jiujiang, *Jiangxi, China* .. 53 C10
Jiuling Shan, *China* 53 C10
Jiulong, *China* 52 C3
Jiuquan, *China* 54 C4
Jiutai, *China* 51 B13
Jiuxiangcheng, *China* ... 50 H8
Jiuxincheng, *China* 50 E8
Jiuyuhang, *China* 53 B12
Jixi, *Anhui, China* 53 B12
Jixi, *Heilongjiang, China* . 51 B16
Jiyang, *China* 51 F9
Jīzān, *Si. Arabia* 68 D3
Jize, *China* 50 F8
Jizera →, *Czech.* 20 E4
Jizō-Zaki, *Japan* 49 G6
Joaçaba, *Brazil* 127 B5
Joaíma, *Brazil* 123 E3
João, *Brazil* 122 B1
João Amaro, *Brazil* 123 D3
João Câmara, *Brazil* 122 C4
João Pessoa, *Brazil* 122 C5
João Pinheiro, *Brazil* ... 123 E2
Joaquim Távora, *Brazil* . 123 F2
Joaquín V. González,
  Argentina 126 B3
Jobourg, Nez de, *France* . 24 C5
Jódar, *Spain* 29 H1
Jodhpur, *India* 62 F5
Jœuf, *France* 25 C13
Jofane, *Mozam.* 85 C5
Joggins, *Canada* 99 C7

Jogjakarta = Yogyakarta, Indonesia 57 G14
Johannesburg, S. Africa 85 D4
Johannesburg, U.S.A. 113 K9
John Day, U.S.A. 110 D4
John Day →, U.S.A. 110 D3
John H. Kerr Reservoir, U.S.A. 105 G6
John o' Groats, U.K. 14 C5
Johnnie, U.S.A. 113 J10
John's Ra., Australia 90 C1
Johnson, U.S.A. 109 G4
Johnson City, N.Y., U.S.A. 107 D9
Johnson City, Tenn., U.S.A. 105 G4
Johnson City, Tex., U.S.A. 109 K5
Johnsonburg, U.S.A. 106 E6
Johnsondale, U.S.A. 113 K8
Johnson's Crossing, Canada 100 A2
Johnston, L., Australia 89 F3
Johnston Falls = Mambilima Falls, Zambia 83 E2
Johnston I., Pac. Oc. 93 F11
Johnstone Str., Canada 100 C3
Johnstown, N.Y., U.S.A. 107 D10
Johnstown, Pa., U.S.A. 106 F6
Johor Baharu, Malaysia 59 M4
Joigny, France 25 E10
Joinvile, Brazil 127 B6
Joinville, France 25 D12
Joinville I., Antarctica 5 C18
Jojutla, Mexico 115 D5
Jokkmokk, Sweden 8 C15
Jökulsá á Bru →, Iceland 8 D6
Jökulsá á Fjöllum →, Iceland 8 C5
Jolfā, Āzarbājān-e Sharqī, Iran 64 B5
Jolfā, Eṣfahan, Iran 65 C6
Joliet, U.S.A. 104 E1
Joliette, Canada 98 C5
Jolo, Phil. 55 J4
Jolon, U.S.A. 112 K5
Jomalig, Phil. 55 D5
Jombang, Indonesia 57 G15
Jomda, China 52 B2
Jome, Indonesia 57 E7
Jomfruland, Norway 11 F3
Jönåker, Sweden 11 F10
Jonava, Lithuania 40 D4
Jones Sound, Canada 4 B3
Jonesboro, Ark., U.S.A. 109 H9
Jonesboro, Ill., U.S.A. 109 G10
Jonesboro, La., U.S.A. 109 J8
Jonesport, U.S.A. 99 D6
Jonglei, Sudan 77 F3
Jonglei □, Sudan 77 F3
Joniškis, Lithuania 40 C3
Jönköping, Sweden 9 H13
Jönköpings län □, Sweden 9 H13
Jonquière, Canada 99 C5
Jonsberg, Sweden 11 F10
Jonsered, Sweden 11 G6
Jonzac, France 26 C3
Joplin, U.S.A. 109 G7
Jordan ■, Asia 69 E5
Jordan →, Asia 69 D4
Jordan Valley, U.S.A. 110 E5
Jordânia, Brazil 123 E3
Jorge, C., Chile 128 D1
Jorhat, India 61 F19
Jörn, Sweden 8 D16
Jorong, Indonesia 56 E4
Jorquera →, Chile 126 B2
Jos, Nigeria 79 D6
José Batlle y Ordóñez, Uruguay 127 C4
José de San Martín, Argentina 128 B2
Joseph, U.S.A. 110 D5
Joseph, L., Nfld., Canada 99 B6
Joseph, L., Ont., Canada 106 A5
Joseph Bonaparte G., Australia 88 B4
Joseph City, U.S.A. 111 J8
Joshua Tree, U.S.A. 113 L10
Joshua Tree National Monument, U.S.A. 113 M10
Josselin, France 24 E4
Jostedal, Norway 9 F9
Jotunheimen, Norway 10 C2
Jourdanton, U.S.A. 109 L5
Joure, Neths. 16 C7
Joussard, Canada 100 B5
Jovellanos, Cuba 116 B3
Joyeuse, France 27 D8
Józefów, Poland 20 C11
Ju Xian, China 51 F10
Juan Aldama, Mexico 114 C4
Juan Bautista Alberdi, Argentina 126 C3
Juan de Fuca Str., Canada 112 B2
Juan de Nova, Ind. Oc. 85 B7
Juan Fernández, Arch. de, Pac. Oc. 93 L20
Juan José Castelli, Argentina 126 B3
Juan L. Lacaze, Uruguay 126 C4
Juan José, Peru 124 B2
Juàrez, Argentina 126 D4
Juárez, Mexico 113 N11
Juárez, Sierra de, Mexico 114 A1
Juatinga, Ponta de, Brazil 123 F3
Juàzeiro, Brazil 122 C3
Juàzeiro do Norte, Brazil 122 C4

Jubayl, Lebanon 69 A4
Jubbah, Si. Arabia 64 D4
Jubbulpore = Jabalpur, India 63 H8
Jübek, Germany 18 A5
Jubga, Russia 43 D8
Jubilee L., Australia 89 E4
Juby, C., Morocco 72 C2
Júcar →, Spain 29 F4
Júcaro, Cuba 116 B4
Juchitán, Mexico 115 D5
Judaea = Har Yehuda, Israel 69 D3
Judenburg, Austria 21 H4
Judith →, U.S.A. 110 C9
Judith, Pt., U.S.A. 107 E13
Judith Gap, U.S.A. 110 C9
Jufari →, Brazil 121 D5
Jugoslavia = Yugoslavia ■, Europe 21 M10
Juigalpa, Nic. 116 D2
Juillac, France 26 C5
Juist, Germany 18 B2
Juiz de Fora, Brazil 123 F3
Jujuy, Argentina 126 A2
Jujuy □, Argentina 126 A2
Juli, Peru 124 D4
Julesburg, U.S.A. 108 E3
Julia Cr. →, Australia 90 C3
Julia Creek, Australia 90 C3
Juliaca, Peru 124 D3
Julian, U.S.A. 113 M10
Julian Alps = Julijske Alpe, Slovenia 33 B11
Julianakanaal, Neths. 17 F7
Julianatop, Surinam 121 C6
Julianehåb, Greenland 4 C5
Jülich, Germany 18 E2
Julierpass, Switz. 23 D9
Julijske Alpe, Slovenia 33 B11
Julimes, Mexico 114 B3
Jullundur, India 62 D6
Julu, China 50 F8
Jumbo, Zimbabwe 83 F3
Jumbo Pk., U.S.A. 113 J12
Jumentos Cays, Bahamas 117 B4
Jumet, Belgium 17 H4
Jumilla, Spain 29 G3
Jumla, Nepal 63 E10
Jumna = Yamuna →, India 63 G9
Junagadh, India 62 J4
Junction, Tex., U.S.A. 109 K5
Junction, Utah, U.S.A. 111 G7
Junction B., Australia 90 A1
Junction City, Kans., U.S.A. 108 F6
Junction City, Oreg., U.S.A. 110 D2
Junction Pt., Australia 90 A1
Jundah, Australia 90 C3
Jundiaí, Brazil 127 A6
Juneau, U.S.A. 96 C6
Junee, Australia 91 E4
Jungfrau, Switz. 22 C5
Junggar Pendi, China 54 B3
Junglinster, Lux. 17 J8
Jungshahi, Pakistan 62 G2
Juniata →, U.S.A. 106 F7
Junín, Argentina 126 C3
Junín, Peru 124 C2
Junín □, Peru 124 C3
Junín de los Andes, Argentina 128 A2
Jūniyah, Lebanon 69 B4
Juntura, U.S.A. 110 E4
Juparaná, L., Brazil 123 E3
Jupiter →, Canada 99 C7
Juquiá, Brazil 123 F2
Jur, Nahr el →, Sudan 77 F2
Jura = Jura, Mts. du, Europe 27 B10
Jura = Schwäbische Alb, Germany 19 G5
Jura, Europe 25 F13
Jura, U.K. 14 F3
Jura →, France 25 F12
Jura, Mts. du, Europe 27 B10
Jura, Sd. of, U.K. 14 F3
Jura Suisse, Switz. 22 B3
Jurado, Colombia 120 B2
Jurilovca, Romania 38 E11
Jurong, China 53 B12
Juruá →, Brazil 120 D4
Juruena, Brazil 125 C6
Juruena →, Brazil 125 B6
Juruti, Brazil 121 D6
Jussey, France 25 E12
Justo Daract, Argentina 126 C2
Jutaí, Brazil 124 B4
Jutaí →, Brazil 120 D4
Jüterbog, Germany 18 D9
Juticalpa, Honduras 116 D2
Jutland = Jylland, Denmark 11 H3
Jutphaas, Neths. 16 D6
Juventud, I. de la, Cuba 116 B3
Juvigny-sous-Andaine, France 24 D6
Juvisy-sur-Orge, France 25 D9
Juwain, Afghan. 60 D2
Jūy Zar, Iran 64 C5
Juye, China 50 G9
Juzennecourt, France 25 D11
Jylland, Denmark 11 H3
Jyväskylä, Finland 8 E18

K

K2, Mt., Pakistan 63 B7
Kaap Plateau, S. Africa 84 D3
Kaapkruis, Namibia 84 C1
Kaapstad = Cape Town, S. Africa 84 E2
Kaatsheuvel, Neths. 17 E6
Kabaena, Indonesia 57 F6
Kabala, S. Leone 78 D2
Kabale, Uganda 82 C3
Kabalo, Zaïre 82 D2
Kabambare, Zaïre 82 C2
Kabango, Zaïre 83 D2
Kabanjahe, Indonesia 56 D1
Kabankalan, Phil. 55 G5
Kabara, Mali 78 B4
Kabardinka, Russia 42 D7
Kabardino-Balkar Republic □, Russia 43 E10
Kabare, Indonesia 57 E8
Kabarega Falls, Uganda 82 B3
Kabasalan, Phil. 55 H5
Kabba, Nigeria 79 D6
Kabin Buri, Thailand 58 F3
Kabinakagami L., Canada 98 C3
Kabīr, Zab al →, Iraq 64 C4
Kabkabīyah, Sudan 73 F9
Kabna, Sudan 76 D3
Kabompo, Zambia 83 E1
Kabompo →, Zambia 81 G4
Kabondo, Zaïre 83 D2
Kabongo, Zaïre 82 D2
Kabou, Togo 79 D5
Kaboudia, Rass, Tunisia 75 A7
Kabra, Australia 90 C5
Kabūd Gonbad, Iran 65 B8
Kabugao, Phil. 55 B4
Kabul, Afghan. 62 B3
Kābul □, Afghan. 60 B6
Kabul →, Pakistan 62 C5
Kabunga, Zaïre 82 C2
Kaburuang, Indonesia 57 D7
Kabushiya, Sudan 77 D3
Kabwe, Zambia 83 E2
Kačanik, Serbia, Yug. 21 N11
Kachanovo, Russia 40 C5
Kachchh, Gulf of, India 62 H3
Kachchh, Rann of, India 62 G4
Kachebera, Zambia 83 E3
Kachin □, Burma 61 F20
Kachira, L., Uganda 82 C3
Kachiry, Kazakhstan 44 D8
Kachisi, Ethiopia 77 F4
Kachot, Cambodia 59 G4
Kackar, Turkey 43 F9
Kadan Kyun, Burma 56 B1
Kadanai →, Afghan. 62 D1
Kadarkút, Hungary 21 J7
Kade, Ghana 79 D4
Kadi, India 62 H5
Kadina, Australia 91 E2
Kadınhanı, Turkey 66 D5
Kadirli, Turkey 66 E7
Kadiyevka, Ukraine 43 B8
Kadoka, U.S.A. 108 D4
Kadom, Russia 41 D13
Kadoma, Zimbabwe 83 F2
Kaduna, Nigeria 79 C6
Kaduna □, Nigeria 79 C6
Kaédi, Mauritania 78 B2
Kaélé, Cameroon 79 C7
Kaeng Khoï, Thailand 58 E3
Kaesŏng, N. Korea 51 F14
Kāf, Si. Arabia 64 D3
Kafakumba, Zaïre 80 F4
Kafan, Armenia 67 D12
Kafanchan, Nigeria 79 D6
Kafareti, Nigeria 79 C7
Kaffa Kingi, Sudan 73 G9
Kafinda, Zambia 83 E3
Kafir el Dauwâr, Egypt 76 H7
Kafr el Sheikh, Egypt 76 H7
Kafue, Zambia 83 F2
Kafue →, Zambia 81 H5
Kafue Flats, Zambia 83 F2
Kafue Nat. Park, Zambia 83 F2
Kafulwe, Zambia 83 D2
Kaga, Afghan. 62 B4
Kaga Bandoro, C.A.R. 73 G8
Kagan, Uzbekistan 44 F7
Kagawa □, Japan 49 G6
Kagera □, Tanzania 82 C3
Kagera →, Uganda 82 C3
Kağizman, Turkey 67 C10
Kagoshima, Japan 49 J5
Kagoshima □, Japan 49 J5
Kagul, Moldavia 42 D3
Kahak, Iran 65 B6
Kahama, Tanzania 82 C3
Kahama □, Tanzania 82 C3
Kahang, Malaysia 59 L4
Kahayan →, Indonesia 56 E4
Kahe, Tanzania 82 C4
Kahemba, Zaïre 80 F3
Kahil, Djebel bou, Algeria 75 B5
Kahniah →, Canada 100 B4
Kahnūj, Iran 65 E8
Kahoka, U.S.A. 108 E9
Kahoolawe, U.S.A. 102 H16
Kahramanmaraş, Turkey 66 E7

Kahramanmaraş □, Turkey 66 E7
Kâhta, Turkey 67 E8
Kai, Kepulauan, Indonesia 57 F8
Kai Besar, Indonesia 57 F8
Kai Is. = Kai, Kepulauan, Indonesia 57 F8
Kai-Ketil, Indonesia 57 F8
Kai Xian, China 52 B7
Kaiama, Nigeria 79 D5
Kaiapoi, N.Z. 87 K4
Kaieteur Falls, Guyana 121 B6
Kaifeng, China 50 G8
Kaihua, China 53 C12
Kaikohe, N.Z. 87 F4
Kaikoura, N.Z. 87 K4
Kaikoura Ra., N.Z. 87 J4
Kailahun, S. Leone 78 D2
Kaili, China 52 D6
Kailu, China 51 C11
Kailua Kona, U.S.A. 102 J17
Kaimana, Indonesia 57 E8
Kaimanawa Mts., N.Z. 87 H5
Kaimganj, India 63 F8
Kaimur Hills, India 63 G9
Kaingaroa Forest, N.Z. 87 H6
Kainji Res., Nigeria 79 C5
Kaipara Harbour, N.Z. 87 G5
Kaiping, China 53 F9
Kaipokok B., Canada 99 B8
Kairana, India 62 E7
Kairi, Indonesia 57 E8
Kairouan, Tunisia 75 A7
Kaiserslautern, Germany 19 F3
Kaitaia, N.Z. 87 F4
Kaitangata, N.Z. 87 M2
Kaithal, India 62 E7
Kaitu →, Pakistan 62 C4
Kaiwi Channel, U.S.A. 102 H16
Kaiyang, China 52 D6
Kaiyuan, Liaoning, China 51 C13
Kaiyuan, Yunnan, China 52 F4
Kajaani, Finland 8 D19
Kajabbi, Australia 90 B3
Kajana = Kajaani, Finland 8 D19
Kajang, Malaysia 59 L3
Kajiado, Kenya 82 C4
Kajiado □, Kenya 82 C4
Kajo Kaji, Sudan 77 G3
Kaka, Sudan 77 E3
Kakabeka Falls, Canada 98 C2
Kakamas, S. Africa 84 D3
Kakamega, Kenya 82 B3
Kakamega □, Kenya 82 B3
Kakanj, Bos.-H. 21 L8
Kakanui Mts., N.Z. 87 L3
Kake, Japan 49 G6
Kakegawa, Japan 49 G9
Kakeroma-Jima, Japan 49 K4
Kakhib, Russia 43 E12
Kakhovka, Ukraine 42 C5
Kakhovskoye Vdkhr., Ukraine 42 C6
Kakinada, India 61 L13
Kakisa →, Canada 100 A5
Kakisa L., Canada 100 A5
Kakogawa, Japan 49 G7
Kakwa →, Canada 100 C5
Kāl Gūsheh, Iran 65 D8
Kala, Nigeria 79 C7
Kalaa-Kebira, Tunisia 75 A7
Kalabagh, Pakistan 62 C4
Kalabahi, Indonesia 57 F6
Kalábaka, Greece 39 K4
Kalabo, Zambia 81 G4
Kalach, Russia 41 F12
Kalach na Donu, Russia 43 B10
Kaladan →, Burma 61 J18
Kaladar, Canada 106 B7
Kalahari, Africa 84 C3
Kalahari Gemsbok Nat. Park, S. Africa 84 D3
Kālak, Iran 65 E9
Kalakamati, Botswana 85 C4
Kalakan, Russia 45 D12
Kalakh, Syria 64 C3
K'alak'unlun Shank'ou, Pakistan 63 B7
Kalam, Pakistan 63 B5
Kalama, U.S.A. 112 E4
Kalama, Zaïre 82 C2
Kalamariá, Greece 39 J5
Kalamata, Greece 39 M5
Kalamazoo, U.S.A. 104 D3
Kalamazoo →, U.S.A. 104 D2
Kalambo Falls, Tanzania 83 D3
Kálamos, Greece 39 L3
Kalannie, Australia 89 F2
Kalāntarī, Iran 65 C7
Kalao, Indonesia 57 F6
Kalaotoa, Indonesia 57 F6
Kälarne, Sweden 10 B10
Kalárovo, Slovakia 21 H7
Kalasin, Thailand 58 D4
Kalat, Pakistan 60 E5
Kalāteh, Iran 65 B7
Kalāteh-ye-Ganj, Iran 65 E8
Kalathos, Greece 39 N11
Kalávrita, Greece 39 L5
Kalbarri, Australia 89 E1
Kale, Turkey 66 E3
Kalecik, Turkey 42 F5
Kalegauk Kyun, Burma 61 M20

Kalehe, Zaïre 82 C2
Kalema, Tanzania 82 C3
Kalemie, Zaïre 82 D2
Kalety, Poland 20 E8
Kalewa, Burma 61 H19
Kálfafellsstaður, Iceland 8 D6
Kalgan = Zhangjiakou, China 50 D8
Kalgoorlie-Boulder, Australia 89 F3
Kaliakra, Nos, Bulgaria 38 F11
Kalianda, Indonesia 56 F3
Kalibo, Phil. 55 F5
Kaliganj, Bangla. 63 H13
Kalima, Zaïre 82 C2
Kalimantan, Indonesia 56 E4
Kalimantan Barat □, Indonesia 56 E4
Kalimantan Selatan □, Indonesia 56 E5
Kalimantan Tengah □, Indonesia 56 E4
Kalimantan Timur □, Indonesia 56 D5
Kálimnos, Greece 39 N10
Kalimpong, India 63 F13
Kalinin = Tver, Russia 41 C9
Kaliningrad, Russia 40 D2
Kalinkavichy = Kalinkovichi, Belorussia 40 E6
Kalinkovichi, Belorussia 40 E6
Kalinovik, Bos.-H. 21 M8
Kalipetrovo, Bulgaria 38 E10
Kaliro, Uganda 82 B3
Kalispell, U.S.A. 110 B6
Kalisz, Poland 20 D8
Kaliua, Tanzania 82 D3
Kalix →, Sweden 8 D17
Kalka, India 62 D7
Kalkan, Turkey 66 E3
Kalkaska, U.S.A. 104 C3
Kalkfeld, Namibia 84 C2
Kalkfontein, Botswana 84 C3
Kalkrand, Namibia 84 C2
Källandsö, Sweden 11 F7
Kallithéa, Greece 39 M6
Kallonís, Kólpos, Greece 39 K9
Kallsjön, Sweden 8 E12
Kalmalo, Nigeria 79 C6
Kalmar, Sweden 9 H14
Kalmthout, Belgium 17 F4
Kalmyk Republic □, Russia 43 C12
Kalmykovo, Kazakhstan 43 B14
Kalna, India 63 H13
Kalocsa, Hungary 21 J9
Kalokhorio, Cyprus 37 E12
Kaloko, Zaïre 82 D2
Kalol, Gujarat, India 62 H5
Kalol, Gujarat, India 62 H5
Kalolímnos, Greece 39 M10
Kalomo, Zambia 83 F2
Kalpi, India 63 F8
Kaltbrunn, Switz. 23 B8
Kaltungo, Nigeria 79 D7
Kalu, Pakistan 62 G2
Kaluga, Russia 41 D10
Kalulushi, Zambia 83 E2
Kalundborg, Denmark 11 J5
Kalush, Ukraine 40 G4
Kałuszyn, Poland 20 C11
Kalutara, Sri Lanka 60 R11
Kalyazin, Russia 41 C10
Kama, Zaïre 82 C2
Kama →, Russia 44 D6
Kamachumu, Tanzania 82 C3
Kamaishi, Japan 48 E10
Kamalia, Pakistan 62 D5
Kamapanda, Zambia 83 E1
Kamaran, Yemen 68 D3
Kamativi, Zimbabwe 83 F2
Kamba, Nigeria 79 C5
Kambalda, Australia 89 F3
Kambar, Pakistan 62 F3
Kambia, S. Leone 78 D2
Kambolé, Zambia 83 D3
Kambos, Cyprus 37 D11
Kambove, Zaïre 83 E2
Kamchatka, P-ov., Russia 45 D16
Kamchatka Pen. = Kamchatka, P-ov., Russia 45 D16
Kamen, Russia 44 D9
Kamen Kashirskiy, Ukraine 40 F4
Kamen-Rybolov, Russia 48 B6
Kamenets-Podolskiy, Ukraine 42 B2
Kamenjak, Rt., Croatia 33 D10
Kamenka, Russia 41 E14
Kamenka, Russia 41 F11
Kamenka, Russia 42 B5
Kamenka Bugskaya, Ukraine 40 F4
Kamenka Dneprovskaya, Ukraine 42 C6
Kamenolomni, Russia 43 C9
Kamensk-Shakhtinskiy, Russia 43 B9
Kamensk Uralskiy, Russia 44 D7
Kamenskiy, Russia 41 F14
Kamenskiy, Russia 43 B9
Kamenskoye, Russia 45 C17
Kamenyak, Bulgaria 38 F9
Kamenz, Germany 18 D10
Kameoka, Japan 49 G7
Kamiah, U.S.A. 110 C5
Kamień Pomorski, Poland 20 B4

Kamieskroon, S. Africa ... 84 E2
Kamilukuak, L., Canada . 101 A8
Kamina, Zaïre 83 D1
Kaminak L., Canada 101 A9
Kaminoyama, Japan 48 E10
Kamiros, Greece 37 C9
Kamituga, Zaïre 82 C2
Kamloops, Canada 100 C4
Kamnik, Slovenia 33 B11
Kamo, Armenia 43 F11
Kamo, Japan 48 F9
Kamoa Mts., Guyana .. 121 C6
Kamoke, Pakistan 62 C6
Kamp →, Austria 21 G5
Kampala, Uganda 82 B3
Kampar, Malaysia 59 K3
Kampar →, Indonesia .. 56 D2
Kampen, Neths. 16 C7
Kamperland, Neths. 17 E3
Kamphaeng Phet, Thailand 58 D2
Kampolombo, L., Zambia 83 E2
Kampong To, Thailand . 59 J3
Kampot, Cambodia 59 G5
Kampti, Burkina Faso ... 78 C4
Kampuchea =
  Cambodia ■, Asia ... 58 F5
Kampung →, Indonesia .. 57 F9
Kampung Air Putih,
  Malaysia 59 K4
Kampung Jerangau,
  Malaysia 59 K4
Kampung Raja, Malaysia . 59 K4
Kampungbaru = Tolitoli,
  Indonesia 57 D6
Kamrau, Teluk, Indonesia 57 E8
Kamsack, Canada 101 C8
Kamskoye Ustye, Russia . 41 D16
Kamuchawie L., Canada . 101 B8
Kamui-Misaki, Japan ... 48 C10
Kamyanets-Podilskyy =
  Kamenets-Podolskiy,
  Ukraine 42 B2
Kāmyārān, Iran 64 C5
Kamyshin, Russia 41 F14
Kamyzyak, Russia 43 C13
Kanaaupscow, Canada .. 98 B4
Kanab, U.S.A. 111 H7
Kanab →, U.S.A. 111 H7
Kanagi, Japan 48 D10
Kanairiktok →, Canada .. 99 A7
Kanália, Greece 39 K5
Kananga, Zaïre 80 F4
Kanarraville, U.S.A. ... 111 H7
Kanash, Russia 41 D15
Kanaskat, U.S.A. 112 C5
Kanawha →, U.S.A. ... 104 F4
Kanazawa, Japan 49 F8
Kanchanaburi, Thailand . 58 E4
Kanchenjunga, Nepal .. 63 F13
Kanchipuram, India ... 60 N11
Kanda Kanda, Zaïre ... 80 F4
Kandahar = Qandahār,
  Afghan. 60 D4
Kandalaksha, Russia ... 44 C4
Kandalu, Afghan. 60 E3
Kandangan, Indonesia .. 56 E5
Kandanos, Greece 37 D5
Kander →, Switz. 22 C5
Kandersteg, Switz. 22 D5
Kandhíla, Greece 39 M5
Kandhkot, Pakistan ... 62 E3
Kandhla, India 62 E7
Kandi, Benin 79 C5
Kandi, India 63 H13
Kandira, Turkey 66 C4
Kandla, India 62 H4
Kandos, Australia 91 E4
Kandy, Sri Lanka 60 R12
Kane, U.S.A. 106 E6
Kane Basin, Greenland .. 4 B4
Kanevskaya, Russia ... 43 C8
Kanfanar, Croatia 33 C10
Kangaba, Mali 78 C3
Kangal, Turkey 66 D7
Kangān, Fārs, Iran 65 E7
Kangān, Hormozgān, Iran 65 E8
Kangar, Malaysia 59 J3
Kangaroo I., Australia .. 91 F2
Kangavar, Iran 65 C6
Kangding, China 52 B3
Kǎngdong, N. Korea ... 51 E14
Kangean, Kepulauan,
  Indonesia 56 F5
Kangean Is. = Kangean,
  Kepulauan, Indonesia .. 56 F5
Kanggye, N. Korea 51 D14
Kanggyǒng, S. Korea .. 51 F14
Kanghwa, S. Korea ... 51 F14
Kangnǔng, S. Korea ... 51 F15
Kango, Gabon 80 D2
Kangping, China 51 C12
Kangto, India 61 F18
Kani, Ivory C. 78 D3
Kaniama, Zaïre 82 D1
Kaniapiskau →, Canada . 99 A6
Kaniapiskau L., Canada . 99 B6
Kanin, P-ov., Russia ... 44 C5
Kanin Nos, Mys, Russia . 44 C5
Kanin Pen. = Kanin, P-ov.,
  Russia 44 C5
Kaniva, Australia 91 F3
Kanjiža, Serbia, Yug. .. 21 J10
Kanjut Sar, Pakistan .. 63 A6
Kankakee, U.S.A. 104 E2
Kankakee →, U.S.A. ... 104 E1

Kankan, Guinea 78 C3
Kanker, India 61 J12
Kankunskiy, Russia 45 D13
Kannapolis, U.S.A. 105 H5
Kannauj, India 63 F8
Kannod, India 60 H10
Kano, Nigeria 79 C6
Kano □, Nigeria 79 C6
Kan'onji, Japan 49 G6
Kanoroba, Ivory C. 78 D3
Kanowit, Malaysia 56 D4
Kanowna, Australia ... 89 F3
Kanoya, Japan 49 J5
Kanpetlet, Burma 61 J18
Kanpur, India 63 F9
Kansas □, U.S.A. 108 F6
Kansas →, U.S.A. 108 F7
Kansas City, Kans., U.S.A. 108 F7
Kansas City, Mo., U.S.A. 108 F7
Kansenia, Zaïre 83 E2
Kansk, Russia 45 D10
Kansŏng, S. Korea 51 E15
Kansu = Gansu □, China 50 G3
Kantang, Thailand 59 J2
Kantché, Niger 79 C6
Kanté, Togo 79 D5
Kantemirovka, Russia .. 43 B8
Kantharalak, Thailand .. 58 E5
Kantō □, Japan 49 F9
Kantō-Sanchi, Japan ... 49 G9
Kanturk, Ireland 15 D3
Kanuma, Japan 49 F9
Kanus, Namibia 84 D2
Kanye, Botswana 84 C4
Kanzenze, Zaïre 83 E2
Kanzi, Ras, Tanzania .. 82 D4
Kaohsiung = Gaoxiong,
  Taiwan 53 F13
Kaokoveld, Namibia ... 84 B1
Kaolack, Senegal 78 C1
Kaoshan, China 51 B13
Kapadvanj, India 62 H5
Kapanga, Zaïre 80 F4
Kapchagai, Kazakhstan . 44 E8
Kapellen, Belgium 17 F4
Kapéllo, Ákra, Greece .. 39 N6
Kapema, Zaïre 83 E2
Kapfenberg, Austria ... 21 H5
Kapiri Mposhi, Zambia . 83 E2
Kapiskau →, Canada ... 98 B3
Kapit, Malaysia 56 D4
Kapiti I., N.Z. 87 J5
Kaplice, Czech. 20 G4
Kapoe, Thailand 59 H2
Kapoeta, Sudan 77 G3
Kapos →, Hungary 21 J8
Kaposvár, Hungary ... 21 J7
Kapowsin, U.S.A. 112 D4
Kappeln, Germany 18 A5
Kaprije, Croatia 33 E12
Kaprijke, Belgium 17 F3
Kapsan, N. Korea 51 D15
Kapsukas = Mariyampol,
  Lithuania 40 D3
Kapuas →, Indonesia .. 56 E3
Kapuas Hulu, Pegunungan,
  Malaysia 56 D4
Kapuas Hulu Ra. =
  Kapuas Hulu,
  Pegunungan, Malaysia .. 56 D4
Kapulo, Zaïre 83 D2
Kapunda, Australia ... 91 E2
Kapuni, N.Z. 87 H5
Kapurthala, India 62 D6
Kapuskasing, Canada .. 98 C3
Kapuskasing →, Canada . 98 C3
Kapustin Yar, Russia .. 43 B11
Kaputar, Australia 91 E5
Kaputir, Kenya 82 B4
Kapuvár, Hungary ... 21 H7
Kara, Russia 44 C7
Kara Bogaz Gol, Zaliv,
  Turkmenistan 44 E6
Kara Kalpak Republic □,
  Uzbekistan 44 E6
Kara Kum = Karakum,
  Peski, Turkmenistan ... 44 F6
Kara Sea, Russia 44 B7
Karabük, Turkey 42 F5
Karaburun, Turkey 66 D2
Karaburuni, Albania ... 39 J2
Karabutak, Kazakhstan . 44 E7
Karacabey, Turkey 66 C3
Karacasu, Turkey 66 E3
Karachala, Azerbaijan .. 43 G13
Karachayevsk, Russia .. 43 E9
Karachev, Russia 40 E9
Karachi, Pakistan 62 G2
Karad, India 60 L9
Karadeniz Boğazı, Turkey 66 C3
Karaga, Ghana 79 D4
Karaganda, Kazakhstan . 44 E8
Karagayly, Kazakhstan . 44 E8
Karaginskiy, Ostrov, Russia 45 D17
Karagüney Dağları, Turkey 66 C6
Karagwe □, Tanzania .. 82 C3
Karaikal, India 60 P11
Karaikkudi, India 60 P11
Karaisali, Turkey 66 E6
Karaj, Iran 65 C6
Karak, Malaysia 59 L4
Karakas, Kazakhstan .. 44 E9
Karakitang, Indonesia .. 57 D7
Karaklis, Armenia 43 F11

Karakoçan, Turkey 67 D9
Karakoram Pass, Pakistan 63 B7
Karakoram Ra., Pakistan . 63 B7
Karakum, Peski,
  Turkmenistan 44 F6
Karakurt, Turkey 67 C10
Karalon, Russia 45 D12
Karaman, Turkey 66 E5
Karamay, China 54 B3
Karambu, Indonesia ... 56 E5
Karamea Bight, N.Z. ... 87 J3
Karamoja □, Uganda .. 82 B3
Karamsad, India 62 H5
Karand, Iran 64 C5
Karanganyar, Indonesia . 57 G13
Karapinar, Turkey 66 E5
Karasburg, Namibia ... 84 D2
Karasino, Russia 44 C9
Karasu, Turkey 66 C4
Karasu →, Turkey 67 D8
Karasuk, Russia 44 D8
Karasuyama, Japan ... 49 F10
Karataş Burnu, Turkey . 66 E6
Karatau, Kazakhstan .. 44 E8
Karatau, Khrebet,
  Kazakhstan 44 E7
Karatepe, Turkey 66 E7
Karauli, India 62 F7
Karavostasi, Cyprus ... 37 D11
Karawang, Indonesia .. 57 G12
Karawanken, Europe .. 21 J4
Karayazar, Turkey 67 D10
Karazhal, Kazakhstan .. 44 E8
Karbalā, Iraq 64 C5
Kårböle, Sweden 10 C9
Karcag, Hungary 21 H10
Karcha →, Pakistan ... 63 B7
Karda, Russia 45 D11
Kardhámila, Greece ... 39 L9
Kardhítsa, Greece 39 K4
Kärdla, Estonia 40 B3
Kareeberge, S. Africa .. 84 E3
Kareima, Sudan 76 D3
Karelian Republic □,
  Russia 44 C4
Kārevāndar, Iran 65 E9
Kargasok, Russia 44 D9
Kargat, Russia 44 D9
Kargı, Turkey 42 F6
Kargil, India 63 B7
Karguéri, Niger 79 C7
Karia ba Mohammed,
  Morocco 74 B3
Kariān, Iran 65 E8
Kariba, Zimbabwe 83 F2
Kariba, L., Zimbabwe .. 83 F2
Kariba Dam, Zimbabwe . 83 F2
Kariba Gorge, Zambia . 83 F2
Karibib, Namibia 84 C2
Karimata, Kepulauan,
  Indonesia 56 E3
Karimata, Selat, Indonesia 56 E3
Karimata Is. = Karimata,
  Kepulauan, Indonesia .. 56 E3
Karimnagar, India 60 K11
Karimunjawa, Kepulauan,
  Indonesia 56 F4
Karin, Somali Rep. 68 E4
Karīt, Iran 65 C8
Kariya, Japan 49 G8
Karkaralinsk, Kazakhstan 44 E8
Karkinitskiy Zaliv, Ukraine 42 D5
Karkur Tohl, Egypt ... 76 C2
Karl Libknecht, Russia . 40 F9
Karl-Marx-Stadt =
  Chemnitz, Germany 18 E8
Karla, L. = Voïviïs Límni,
  Greece 39 K5
Karlobag, Croatia 33 D12
Karlovac, Croatia 33 C12
Karlovka, Ukraine 42 B6
Karlovy Vary, Czech. .. 20 E2
Karlsbad = Karlovy Vary,
  Czech. 20 E2
Karlsborg, Sweden 11 F8
Karlshamn, Sweden ... 9 H13
Karlskoga, Sweden ... 9 G13
Karlskrona, Sweden ... 9 H13
Karlsruhe, Germany ... 19 F4
Karlstad, Sweden 9 G12
Karlstad, U.S.A. 108 A6
Karlstadt, Germany ... 19 F5
Karnal, India 62 E7
Karnali →, Nepal 63 E9
Karnaphuli Res., Bangla. . 61 H18
Karnataka □, India ... 60 N10
Karnes City, U.S.A. ... 109 L6
Karnische Alpen, Europe . 21 J3
Karo, Mali 78 C4
Karoi, Zimbabwe 83 F2
Karonga, Malawi 83 D3
Karoonda, Australia .. 91 F2
Karora, Sudan 76 D4
Káros, Greece 39 N8
Karousádhes, Greece .. 39 K2
Karpasia □, Cyprus ... 37 D13
Kárpathos, Greece 39 P10
Kárpathos, Stenón, Greece 39 P10
Karrebæk, Denmark ... 11 J5
Kars, Turkey 43 F10
Kars □, Turkey 67 C10
Karsakpay, Kazakhstan . 44 E7
Karsha, Russia 43 B14
Karshi, Uzbekistan ... 44 F7

Karsiyang, India 63 F13
Karst, Croatia 33 C11
Karsun, Russia 41 D15
Kartaly, Russia 44 D7
Kartapur, India 62 D6
Karthaus, U.S.A. 106 E6
Kartuzy, Poland 20 A8
Karufa, Indonesia 57 E8
Karumba, Australia ... 90 B3
Karumo, Tanzania 82 C3
Karumwa, Tanzania ... 82 C3
Karungu, Kenya 82 C3
Karup, Denmark 11 H3
Karviná, Czech. 20 F8
Karwar, India 60 M9
Karwi, India 63 G9
Kaş, Turkey 66 E3
Kasache, Malawi 83 E3
Kasai →, Zaïre 80 E3
Kasai Oriental □, Zaïre . 82 C1
Kasaji, Zaïre 83 E1
Kasama, Zambia 83 E3
Kasan-dong, N. Korea . 51 D14
Kasane, Namibia 84 B3
Kasanga, Tanzania ... 83 D3
Kasangulu, Zaïre 80 E3
Kasaragod, India 60 N9
Kasba L., Canada 101 A8
Kasba Tadla, Morocco . 74 B3
Kāseh Garān, Iran 64 C5
Kasempa, Zambia 83 E2
Kasenga, Zaïre 83 E2
Kasese, Uganda 82 B3
Kasewa, Zambia 83 E2
Kasganj, India 63 F8
Kashabowie, Canada .. 98 C1
Kāshān, Iran 65 C6
Kashi, China 54 C2
Kashimbo, Zaïre 83 E2
Kashin, Russia 41 C10
Kashipur, India 63 E8
Kashira, Russia 41 D11
Kashiwazaki, Japan ... 49 F9
Kashk-e Kohneh, Afghan. 60 B3
Kāshmar, Iran 65 C8
Kashmir, Asia 63 C7
Kashmor, Pakistan ... 62 E3
Kashpirovka, Russia .. 41 E16
Kashun Noerh = Gaxun
  Nur, China 54 B5
Kasimov, Russia 41 D12
Kasinge, Zaïre 82 D2
Kasiruta, Indonesia ... 57 E7
Kaskaskia →, U.S.A. .. 108 G10
Kaskattama →, Canada . 101 B10
Kaskinen, Finland 8 E16
Kaskö, Finland 8 E16
Kaslo, Canada 100 D5
Kasmere L., Canada .. 101 B8
Kasongo, Zaïre 82 C2
Kasongo Lunda, Zaïre . 80 F3
Kásos, Greece 39 P9
Kásos, Stenón, Greece . 39 P9
Kaspi, Georgia 43 F11
Kaspiysk, Russia 43 E12
Kaspiyskiy, Russia ... 43 D12
Kassab ed Doleib, Sudan 77 E3
Kassaba, Egypt 76 C2
Kassalâ, Sudan 77 D4
Kassalâ □, Sudan 77 D4
Kassel, Germany 18 D5
Kassinger, Sudan 76 D3
Kassiópi, Greece 37 A3
Kassue, Indonesia 57 F9
Kastamonu, Turkey ... 66 C5
Kastamonu □, Turkey . 66 C5
Kastav, Croatia 33 C11
Kastélli, Greece 37 D5
Kastéllion, Greece 37 D7
Kastellou, Ákra, Greece . 39 P10
Kasterlee, Belgium ... 17 F5
Kastóri, Greece 39 M5
Kastoría, Greece 39 J4
Kastornoye, Russia ... 41 F11
Kástron, Greece 39 K8
Kasulu, Tanzania 82 C3
Kasulu □, Tanzania ... 82 C3
Kasumi, Japan 49 G7
Kasumkent, Azerbaijan . 43 F13
Kasungu, Malawi 83 E3
Kasur, Pakistan 62 D6
Kata, Russia 45 D11
Kataba, Zambia 83 F2
Katako Kombe, Zaïre .. 82 C1
Katale, Tanzania 82 C3
Katamatite, Australia . 91 F4
Katanda, Kivu, Zaïre .. 82 C2
Katanda, Shaba, Zaïre . 82 D1
Katangi, India 60 J11
Katangli, Russia 45 D15
Katanning, Australia .. 89 F2
Katastári, Greece 39 M3
Katavi Swamp, Tanzania 82 D3
Katerína, Gebel, Egypt . 76 J8
Katherine, Australia .. 88 B5
Kathiawar, India 62 H4
Kathikas, Cyprus 37 E11
Kati, Mali 78 C3
Katihar, India 63 G12
Katima Mulilo, Zambia . 84 B3
Katimbira, Malawi ... 83 E3
Katingan = Mendawai →,
  Indonesia 56 E4
Katiola, Ivory C. 78 D3

Katmandu, Nepal 63 F11
Kato Akhaïa, Greece .. 39 L4
Káto Arkhánai, Greece . 37 D7
Káto Khorió, Greece .. 37 D7
Káto Pyrgos, Cyprus .. 37 D11
Káto Stavros, Greece .. 39 J6
Katompe, Zaïre 82 D2
Katonga →, Uganda .. 82 B3
Katoomba, Australia .. 91 E5
Katowice, Poland 20 E9
Katrine, L., U.K. 14 E4
Katrineholm, Sweden . 10 E10
Katsepe, Madag. 85 B8
Katsina, Nigeria 79 C6
Katsina □, Nigeria ... 79 C6
Katsina Ala →, Nigeria . 79 D6
Katsumoto, Japan 49 H4
Katsuura, Japan 49 G10
Katsuyama, Japan 49 F8
Kattaviá, Greece 37 D9
Kattegat, Denmark ... 11 H5
Katumba, Zaïre 82 D2
Katungu, Kenya 82 C5
Katwa, India 63 H13
Katwijk-aan-Zee, Neths. . 16 D4
Kauai, U.S.A. 102 H15
Kauai Channel, U.S.A. . 102 H15
Kaub, Germany 19 E3
Kaufbeuren, Germany . 19 H6
Kaufman, U.S.A. 109 J6
Kaukauna, U.S.A. ... 104 C1
Kaukauveld, Namibia .. 84 C3
Kaukonen, Finland ... 8 C18
Kauliranta, Finland ... 8 C17
Kaunas, Lithuania ... 40 D3
Kaura Namoda, Nigeria . 79 C6
Kautokeino, Norway .. 8 B17
Kavacha, Russia 45 C17
Kavadarci,
  Macedonia 39 H5
Kavaja, Albania 39 H2
Kavak, Turkey 66 C7
Kavalerovo, Russia ... 48 B7
Kavali, India 60 M12
Kaválla, Greece 39 J7
Kavār, Iran 65 D7
Kavarna, Bulgaria 38 F11
Kavos, Greece 37 B4
Kaw, Fr. Guiana 121 C7
Kawa, Sudan 77 E3
Kawagama L., Canada . 106 A6
Kawagoe, Japan 49 G9
Kawaguchi, Japan ... 49 G9
Kawaihae, U.S.A. 102 H17
Kawambwa, Zambia .. 83 D2
Kawanoe, Japan 49 G6
Kawardha, India 63 J9
Kawasaki, Japan 49 G9
Kawene, Canada 98 C1
Kawerau, N.Z. 87 H6
Kawhia Harbour, N.Z. . 87 H5
Kawio, Kepulauan,
  Indonesia 57 D7
Kawnro, Burma 61 H21
Kawthoolei = Kawthule □,
  Burma 61 L20
Kawthule □, Burma ... 61 L20
Kaya, Burkina Faso ... 79 C4
Kayah □, Burma 61 K20
Kayan →, Indonesia .. 56 D5
Kaycee, U.S.A. 110 E10
Kayeli, Indonesia 57 E7
Kayenta, U.S.A. 111 H8
Kayes, Mali 78 C2
Kayima, S. Leone 78 D2
Kayl, Lux. 17 K8
Kayoa, Indonesia 57 D7
Kayomba, Zambia 83 E1
Kayoro, Ghana 79 C4
Kayrunnera, Australia . 91 E3
Kaysatskoye, Russia .. 43 B12
Kayseri, Turkey 66 D6
Kayseri □, Turkey 66 D6
Kaysville, U.S.A. 110 F8
Kayuagung, Indonesia . 56 E2
Kazachinskoye, Russia . 45 D11
Kazachye, Russia 45 B14
Kazakhstan ■, Asia ... 44 E7
Kazan, Russia 41 D16
Kazan-Rettō, Pac. Oc. . 92 E6
Kazanlúk, Bulgaria ... 38 G8
Kazanskaya, Russia .. 43 B9
Kazatin, Ukraine 42 B3
Kazbek, Georgia 43 E11
Kāzerūn, Iran 65 D6
Kazi Magomed, Azerbaijan 43 F13
Kazincbarcika, Hungary . 21 G10
Kaztalovka, Kazakhstan . 43 B13
Kazumba, Zaïre 80 F4
Kazuno, Japan 48 D10
Kazym →, Russia 44 C7
Kcynia, Poland 20 C7
Ké-Macina, Mali 78 C3
Kéa, Greece 39 M7
Keams Canyon, U.S.A. . 111 J8
Kearney, U.S.A. 108 E5
Keban, Turkey 67 D8
Keban Baraji, Turkey .. 67 D8
Kebbje, Nigeria 79 C6
Kébi, Ivory C. 78 D3
Kebili, Tunisia 75 B6
Kebnekaise, Sweden .. 8 C15
Kebri Dehar, Ethiopia . 68 F3
Kebumen, Indonesia .. 57 G13
Kecel, Hungary 21 J9

Kechika →, Canada 100 B3
Kecskemét, Hungary 21 J9
Kedada, Ethiopia 77 F4
Kedgwick, Canada 99 C6
Kédhros Óros, Greece ... 37 D6
Kedia Hill, Botswana 84 C3
Kediniai, Lithuania 40 D4
Kediri, Indonesia 57 G15
Kédougou, Senegal 78 C2
Kedzierzyn, Poland 20 E8
Keeler, U.S.A. 112 J9
Keeley L., Canada 101 C7
Keeling Is. = Cocos Is.,
    Ind. Oc. 92 J1
Keene, Calif., U.S.A. ... 113 K8
Keene, N.H., U.S.A. 107 D12
Keeper Hill, Ireland 15 D3
Keer-Weer, C., Australia . 90 A3
Keerbergen, Belgium ... 17 F5
Keeseville, U.S.A. 107 B11
Keeten Mastgat, Neths. ... 17 E4
Keetmanshoop, Namibia .. 84 D2
Keewatin, U.S.A. 108 B8
Keewatin □, Canada 101 A9
Keewatin →, Canada 101 B8
Kefa □, Ethiopia 77 F4
Kefallinía, Greece 39 L3
Kefamenanu, Indonesia .. 57 F6
Keffi, Nigeria 79 D6
Kefken, Turkey 66 C4
Keflavík, Iceland 8 D2
Keg River, Canada 100 B5
Kegaska, Canada 99 B7
Kehl, Germany 19 G3
Keighley, U.K. 12 D6
Keimoes, S. Africa 84 D3
Keita, Niger 79 C6
Keith, Australia 91 F3
Keith, U.K. 14 D6
Keith Arm, Canada 96 B7
Kejser Franz Joseph
    Fjord = Kong Franz
    Joseph Fd., Greenland . 4 B6
Kekri, India 62 G6
Këл, Russia 45 C13
Kelamet, Eritrea 77 D4
Kelan, China 50 E6
Kelang, Malaysia 59 L3
Kelantan →, Malaysia ... 59 J4
Kelheim, Germany 19 G7
Kelibia, Tunisia 75 A7
Kelkit, Turkey 67 C8
Kelkit →, Turkey 66 C7
Kellé, Congo 80 E2
Keller, U.S.A. 110 B4
Kellerberrin, Australia ... 89 F2
Kellett, C., Canada 4 B1
Kelleys I., U.S.A. 106 E2
Kellogg, U.S.A. 110 C5
Kelloselkä, Finland 8 C20
Kells = Ceanannus Mor,
    Ireland 15 C5
Kélo, Chad 73 G8
Kelokedhara, Cyprus 37 E11
Kelowna, Canada 100 D5
Kelsey Bay, Canada 100 C3
Kelseyville, U.S.A. 112 G4
Kelso, N.Z. 87 L2
Kelso, U.K. 14 F6
Kelso, U.S.A. 112 D4
Keluang, Malaysia 59 L4
Kelvington, Canada 101 C8
Kem, Russia 44 C4
Kem-Kem, Morocco 74 B4
Kema, Indonesia 57 D7
Kemah, Turkey 67 D8
Kemaliye, Turkey 67 D8
Kemano, Canada 100 C3
Kemasik, Malaysia 59 K4
Kembolcha, Ethiopia 77 E4
Kemer, Turkey 66 E4
Kemerovo, Russia 44 D9
Kemi, Finland 8 D18
Kemi älv = Kemijoki →,
    Finland 8 D18
Kemijärvi, Finland 8 C19
Kemijoki →, Finland ... 8 D18
Kemmel, Belgium 17 G1
Kemmerer, U.S.A. 110 F8
Kemmuna = Comino,
    Malta 37 C1
Kemp, U.S.A. 109 J5
Kemp Land, Antarctica .. 5 C5
Kempsey, Australia 91 E5
Kempt, L., Canada 98 C5
Kempten, Germany 19 H6
Kemptville, Canada 98 C4
Kenadsa, Algeria 75 B4
Kendal, Indonesia 56 F4
Kendal, U.K. 12 C5
Kendall, Australia 91 E5
Kendall →, Australia ... 90 A3
Kendallville, U.S.A. 104 E3
Kendari, Indonesia 57 E6
Kendawangan, Indonesia .. 56 E4
Kende, Nigeria 79 C5
Kendenup, Australia 89 F2
Kendrapara, India 61 J15
Kendrew, S. Africa 84 E3
Kendrick, U.S.A. 110 C5
Kene Thao, Laos 58 D3
Kenedy, U.S.A. 109 L6
Kenema, S. Leone 78 D2
Keng Kok, Laos 58 D5
Keng Tawng, Burma 61 J21

Keng Tung, Burma 61 J21
Kenge, Zaïre 80 E3
Kengeja, Tanzania 82 D4
Kenhardt, S. Africa 84 D3
Kenitra, Morocco 74 B3
Kenli, China 51 F10
Kenmare, Ireland 15 E2
Kenmare, U.S.A. 108 A3
Kenmare →, Ireland 15 E2
Kennebec, U.S.A. 108 D5
Kennedy, Zimbabwe 83 F2
Kennedy Ra., Australia .. 89 D2
Kennedy Taungdeik,
    Burma 61 H18
Kennet →, U.K. 13 F7
Kenneth Ra., Australia ... 88 D2
Kennett, U.S.A. 109 G9
Kennewick, U.S.A. 110 C4
Kénogami, Canada 99 C5
Kenogami →, Canada .. 98 B3
Kenora, Canada 101 D10
Kenosha, U.S.A. 104 D2
Kensington, Canada 99 C7
Kensington, U.S.A. 108 F5
Kensington Downs,
    Australia 90 C3
Kent, Ohio, U.S.A. 106 E3
Kent, Oreg., U.S.A. 110 D3
Kent, Tex., U.S.A. 109 K2
Kent, Wash., U.S.A. 112 C4
Kent □, U.K. 13 F8
Kent Group, Australia ... 90 F4
Kent Pen., Canada 96 B9
Kentau, Kazakhstan 44 E7
Kentland, U.S.A. 104 E2
Kenton, U.S.A. 104 E4
Kentucky □, U.S.A. 104 G3
Kentucky →, U.S.A. ... 104 F3
Kentucky L., U.S.A. ... 105 G2
Kentville, Canada 99 C7
Kentwood, La., U.S.A. .. 109 K9
Kentwood, La., U.S.A. .. 109 K9
Kenya ■, Africa 82 B4
Kenya, Mt., Kenya 82 C4
Keo Neua, Deo, Vietnam . 58 C5
Keokuk, U.S.A. 108 E9
Kep, Cambodia 59 G5
Kep, Vietnam 58 B6
Kepi, Indonesia 57 F9
Kępno, Poland 20 D7
Kepsut, Turkey 66 D3
Kerala □, India 60 P10
Kerama-Rettō, Japan ... 49 L3
Keran, Pakistan 63 B5
Kerang, Australia 91 F3
Keraudren, C., Australia . 88 C2
Kerch, Ukraine 42 D7
Kerchenskiy Proliv,
    Black Sea 42 D7
Kerchoual, Mali 79 B5
Kerempe Burnu, Turkey .. 66 B5
Keren, Eritrea 77 D4
Kerewan, Gambia 78 C1
Kerguelen, Ind. Oc. ... 3 G13
Keri Kera, Sudan 77 E3
Kericho, Kenya 82 C4
Kericho □, Kenya 82 C4
Kerinci, Indonesia 56 E2
Kerkdriel, Neths. 16 E6
Kerkenna, Is., Tunisia ... 75 B7
Kerki, Turkmenistan ... 44 F7
Kérkira, Greece 37 A3
Kerkrade, Neths. 17 G8
Kerma, Sudan 76 D3
Kermadec Is., Pac. Oc. .. 92 K10
Kermadec Trench, Pac. Oc. 92 L10
Kermān, Iran 65 D8
Kerman, U.S.A. 112 J6
Kermān □, Iran 65 D8
Kermānshāh = Bākhtarān,
    Iran 64 C5
Kerme Körfezi, Turkey .. 66 E2
Kermit, U.S.A. 109 K3
Kern →, U.S.A. 113 K7
Kerns, Switz. 23 C6
Kernville, U.S.A. 113 K8
Keroh, Malaysia 59 K3
Kerrobert, Canada 101 C7
Kerrville, U.S.A. 109 K5
Kerry □, Ireland 15 D2
Kerry Hd., Ireland 15 D2
Kersa, Ethiopia 77 F5
Kerteminde, Denmark .. 11 J4
Kertosono, Indonesia .. 57 G15
Kerulen →, Asia 54 B6
Kerzaz, Algeria 75 C4
Kerzers, Switz. 22 C4
Kesagami →, Canada .. 98 B4
Kesagami L., Canada ... 98 B3
Keşan, Turkey 66 C2
Kesch, Piz, Switz. 23 C9
Kesennuma, Japan 48 E10
Keshit, Iran 65 D8
Keşiş Dağ, Turkey 67 D8
Keski-Suomen lääni □,
    Finland 8 E18
Keskin, Turkey 66 D5
Kessel, Belgium 17 F6
Kessel, Neths. 17 F8
Kessel-Lo, Belgium ... 17 G5
Kestell, S. Africa 85 D4
Kestenga, Russia 44 C4
Keszthely, Hungary ... 21 J7

Ket →, Russia 44 D9
Keta, Ghana 79 D5
Ketapang, Indonesia ... 56 E4
Ketchikan, U.S.A. 96 C6
Ketchum, U.S.A. 110 E6
Kete Krachi, Ghana ... 79 D4
Ketef, Khalig Umm el,
    Egypt 76 C4
Ketelmeer, Neths. 16 C7
Keti Bandar, Pakistan .. 62 G2
Ketri, India 62 E6
Kętrzyn, Poland 20 A11
Kettering, U.K. 13 E7
Kettle →, Canada 101 B11
Kettle Falls, U.S.A. ... 110 B4
Kettleman City, U.S.A. . 112 J7
Kevin, U.S.A. 110 B8
Kewanee, U.S.A. 108 E10
Kewaunee, U.S.A. 104 C2
Keweenaw B., U.S.A. ... 104 B1
Keweenaw Pen., U.S.A. . 104 B2
Keweenaw Pt., U.S.A. .. 104 B2
Key Harbour, Canada .. 98 C3
Key West, U.S.A. 103 F10
Keyser, U.S.A. 104 F6
Keystone, U.S.A. 108 D3
Kezhma, Russia 45 D11
Kežmarok, Slovak Rep. .. 20 F10
Khabarovo, Russia 44 C7
Khabarovsk, Russia ... 45 E14
Khabr, Iran 65 D8
Khābūr →, Syria 64 C4
Khachmas, Azerbaijan .. 43 F13
Khachrod, India 62 H6
Khadari, W. el →, Sudan 77 E2
Khadro, Pakistan 62 F3
Khadyzhensk, Russia .. 43 D8
Khadzhilyangar, India .. 63 B8
Khagaria, India 63 G12
Khaipur, Bahawalpur,
    Pakistan 62 E5
Khaipur, Hyderabad,
    Pakistan 62 F3
Khair, India 62 F7
Khairabad, India 63 F9
Khairagarh, India 63 J9
Khairpur, Pakistan ... 60 F6
Khakhea, Botswana ... 84 C3
Khalafābād, Iran 65 D6
Khalafallah, Algeria ... 75 B5
Khalilabad, India 63 F10
Khalili, Iran 65 E7
Khalkhāl, Iran 65 B6
Khálki, Greece 39 K5
Khalkís, Greece 39 L6
Khalmer-Sede = Tazovskiy,
    Russia 44 C8
Khalmer Yu, Russia ... 44 C7
Khalturin, Russia 41 B16
Khalūf, Oman 68 C6
Kham Keut, Laos 58 C5
Khamas Country, Botswana 84 C4
Khambat, G. of, India .. 62 J5
Khambhaliya, India ... 62 H3
Khambhat, India 62 H5
Khamilonísion, Greece .. 39 P9
Khamīr, Iran 65 E7
Khamir, Yemen 68 D3
Khamsa, Egypt 69 E1
Khān Abū Shāmat, Syria 69 B5
Khān Azād, Iraq 64 C5
Khān Mujiddah, Iraq .. 64 C4
Khān Shaykhūn, Syria .. 64 C3
Khān Yūnis, Egypt 69 D3
Khānaqīn, Iraq 64 C5
Khānbāghī, Iran 65 B7
Khandrá, Greece 39 P9
Khandwa, India 60 J10
Khandyga, Russia 45 C14
Khāneh, Iran 64 B5
Khanewal, Pakistan ... 62 D4
Khanh Duong, Vietnam . 58 F7
Khaniá, Greece 37 D6
Khaniá □, Greece 37 D6
Khanión, Kólpos, Greece . 37 D5
Khanka, Ozero, Asia ... 45 E14
Khankendy, Azerbaijan .. 67 C12
Khanna, India 62 D7
Khanpur, Pakistan ... 62 E4
Khanty-Mansiysk, Russia . 44 C7
Khapalu, Pakistan ... 63 B7
Khapcheranga, Russia .. 45 E12
Kharagpur, India 63 H12
Kharan Kalat, Pakistan . 60 E4
Kharānaq, Iran 65 C7
Kharda, India 60 K9
Khardung La, India ... 63 B7
Khārga, El Wâhât el, Egypt 76 B3
Khargon, India 60 J9
Kharit, Wadi el →, Egypt 76 C3
Khārk, Jazireh, Iran ... 65 D6
Kharkiv = Kharkov,
    Ukraine 42 B7
Kharkov, Ukraine 42 B7
Kharmanli, Bulgaria .. 39 H8
Kharovsk, Russia 41 B12
Khartoum = El Khartûm,
    Sudan 77 D3
Khasan, Russia 48 C5
Khasavyurt, Russia ... 43 E12
Khāsh, Iran 60 E2
Khashm el Girba, Sudan . 77 E4
Khashuri, Georgia ... 43 F10
Khaskovo, Bulgaria ... 39 H8

Khatanga, Russia 45 B11
Khatanga →, Russia ... 45 B11
Khatauli, India 62 E7
Khātūnābād, Iran 65 C6
Khatyrka, Russia 45 C18
Khaybar, Harrat,
    Si. Arabia 64 E4
Khāzimiyah, Iraq 64 C4
Khazzān Jabal el Awliyâ,
    Sudan 77 D3
Khe Bo, Vietnam 58 C5
Khe Long, Vietnam .. 58 B5
Khed Brahma, India .. 60 G8
Khekra, India 62 E7
Khemarak Phouminville,
    Cambodia 59 G4
Khemelnik, Ukraine .. 42 B2
Khemis Miliana, Algeria .. 75 A5
Khemissèt, Morocco ... 74 B3
Khemmarat, Thailand .. 58 D5
Khenāmān, Iran 65 D8
Khenchela, Algeria ... 75 A6
Khenifra, Morocco ... 74 B3
Kherrata, Algeria 75 A6
Kherson, Ukraine 42 C5
Khersónisos Akrotíri,
    Greece 37 D6
Kheta →, Russia 45 B11
Khilok, Russia 45 D12
Khimki, Russia 41 D10
Khíos, Greece 39 L9
Khirbat Qanāfar, Lebanon 69 B4
Khiuma = Hiiumaa,
    Estonia 40 B3
Khiva, Uzbekistan ... 44 E7
Khīyāv, Iran 64 B5
Khlong Khlung, Thailand . 58 D2
Khmelnitskiy, Ukraine .. 40 G5
Khmelnytskyy =
    Khmelnitskiy, Ukraine .. 40 G5
Khmer Rep. =
    Cambodia ■, Asia 58 F5
Khoai, Hon, Vietnam .. 59 H5
Khodzent, Tajikistan .. 44 E7
Khojak P., Afghan. 60 D5
Khok Kloi, Thailand .. 59 H2
Khok Pho, Thailand .. 59 J3
Khokholskiy, Russia .. 41 F11
Kholm, Russia 40 C7
Kholmsk, Russia 45 E15
Khomas Hochland,
    Namibia 84 C2
Khomayn, Iran 65 C6
Khon Kaen, Thailand .. 58 D4
Khong, Laos 58 E5
Khong Sedone, Laos .. 58 E5
Khonu, Russia 45 C15
Khoper →, Russia ... 41 G13
Khor 'Atash, Sudan .. 77 E3
Khóra, Greece 39 M4
Khóra Sfakíon, Greece .. 37 D6
Khorāsān □, Iran 65 C8
Khorat = Nakhon
    Ratchasima, Thailand .. 58 E4
Khorat, Cao Nguyen,
    Thailand 58 E4
Khorb el Ethel, Algeria .. 74 C3
Khorixas, Namibia 84 C1
Khorog, Tajikistan ... 44 F8
Khorol, Ukraine 42 B5
Khorramābād, Khorāsān,
    Iran 65 C8
Khorramābād, Lorestān,
    Iran 65 C6
Khorrāmshahr, Iran ... 65 D6
Khosravī, Iran 65 D6
Khosrowābād, Khuzestān,
    Iran 65 D6
Khosrowābād, Kordestān,
    Iran 64 C5
Khosūyeh, Iran 65 D7
Khotin, Ukraine 42 B2
Khouribga, Morocco .. 74 B3
Khowai, Bangla. 61 G17
Khoyniki, Belorussia .. 40 F6
Khrami →, Azerbaijan .. 43 F11
Khrenovoye, Russia ... 41 F12
Khristianá, Greece ... 39 N8
Khrysokhou B., Cyprus .. 37 D11
Khu Khan, Thailand .. 58 E5
Khuff, Si. Arabia 64 E5
Khūgīānī, Afghan. 62 D1
Khulna, Bangla. 61 H16
Khulna □, Bangla. ... 61 H16
Khulo, Georgia 43 F10
Khumago, Botswana .. 84 C3
Khūnsorkh, Iran 65 E8
Khunzakh, Russia 43 E12
Khūr, Iran 65 C8
Khurai, India 62 G8
Khurayş, Si. Arabia .. 65 E6
Khūrīyā Mūrīyā, Jazā 'ir,
    Oman 68 D6
Khurja, India 62 E7
Khush, Afghan. 60 C3
Khushab, Pakistan ... 62 C5
Khuzdar, Pakistan ... 62 F2
Khūzestān □, Iran ... 65 D6
Khvānsār, Iran 65 D7
Khvatovka, Russia ... 41 E15
Khvor, Iran 65 C7
Khvorgū, Iran 65 E8

Khvormūj, Iran 65 D6
Khvoy, Iran 64 B5
Khvoynaya, Russia 40 B9
Khyber Pass, Afghan. .. 62 B4
Kiabukwa, Zaïre 83 D1
Kiama, Australia 91 E5
Kiamba, Phil. 55 H6
Kiambi, Zaïre 82 D2
Kiambu, Kenya 82 C4
Kiangsi = Jiangxi □, China 53 D10
Kiangsu = Jiangsu □,
    China 51 H10
Kibæk, Denmark 11 H2
Kibanga Port, Uganda .. 82 B3
Kibangou, Congo 80 E2
Kibara, Tanzania 82 C3
Kibare, Mts., Zaïre ... 82 D2
Kibombo, Zaïre 82 C2
Kibondo, Tanzania ... 82 C3
Kibondo □, Tanzania .. 82 C3
Kibumbu, Burundi ... 82 C2
Kibungu, Rwanda 82 C3
Kibuye, Burundi 82 C2
Kibuye, Rwanda 82 C2
Kibwesa, Tanzania ... 82 D2
Kibwezi, Kenya 82 C4
Kichiga, Russia 45 D17
Kicking Horse Pass,
    Canada 100 C5
Kidal, Mali 79 B5
Kidderminster, U.K. .. 13 E5
Kidete, Tanzania 82 D4
Kidira, Senegal 78 C2
Kidnappers, C., N.Z. .. 87 H6
Kidston, Australia ... 90 B3
Kidugallo, Tanzania .. 82 D4
Kiel, Germany 18 A6
Kiel Kanal = Nord-Ostsee
    Kanal, Germany 18 A5
Kielce, Poland 20 E10
Kielder Bucht, Germany ... 18 A6
Kien Binh, Vietnam .. 59 H5
Kien Tan, Vietnam .. 59 G5
Kienge, Zaïre 83 E2
Kiessé, Niger 79 C5
Kiev = Kiyev, Ukraine .. 40 F7
Kiffa, Mauritania ... 78 B2
Kifisiá, Greece 39 L6
Kifissós →, Greece ... 39 L6
Kifrī, Iraq 64 C5
Kigali, Rwanda 82 C3
Kigarama, Tanzania .. 82 C3
Kigoma □, Tanzania .. 82 D2
Kigoma-Ujiji, Tanzania .. 82 C2
Kigomasha, Ras, Tanzania 82 C4
Kihee, Australia 91 D3
Kii-Sanchi, Japan ... 49 G7
Kii-Suidō, Japan 49 H7
Kikaiga-Shima, Japan .. 49 K4
Kikinda, Serbia 21 K10
Kikládhes, Greece ... 39 M7
Kikwit, Zaïre 80 E3
Kílalki, Greece 39 N10
Kilauea Crater, U.S.A. .. 102 J17
Kilchberg, Switz. 23 B7
Kilcoy, Australia 91 D5
Kildare, Ireland 15 C5
Kildare □, Ireland ... 15 C5
Kilgore, U.S.A. 109 J7
Kilifi, Kenya 82 C4
Kilifi □, Kenya 82 C4
Kilimanjaro, Tanzania .. 82 C4
Kilimanjaro □, Tanzania .. 82 C4
Kilindini, Kenya 82 C4
Kilis, Turkey 66 E7
Kiliya, Ukraine 42 D3
Kilju, N. Korea 51 D15
Kilkee, Ireland 15 D2
Kilkenny, Ireland ... 15 D4
Kilkenny □, Ireland .. 15 D4
Kilkieran B., Ireland .. 15 C2
Kilkís, Greece 39 J5
Killala, Ireland 15 B2
Killala B., Ireland ... 15 B2
Killaloe, Ireland 15 D3
Killaloe Sta., Canada .. 106 A7
Killam, Canada 100 C6
Killarney, Australia .. 91 D5
Killarney, Canada ... 98 C3
Killarney, Ireland ... 15 D2
Killarney, Lakes of, Ireland 15 E2
Killary Harbour, Ireland .. 15 C2
Killdeer, Canada 101 D7
Killdeer, U.S.A. 108 B3
Killeen, U.S.A. 109 K6
Killiecrankie, Pass of, U.K. 14 E5
Killin, U.K. 14 E4
Killíni, Ilía, Greece .. 39 M4
Killíni, Korinthía, Greece . 39 M5
Killybegs, Ireland ... 15 B3
Kilmarnock, U.K. ... 14 F4
Kilmez, Russia 41 C17
Kilmez →, Russia ... 41 C17
Kilmore, Australia .. 91 F3
Kilondo, Tanzania .. 83 D3
Kilosa, Tanzania ... 82 D4
Kilosa □, Tanzania .. 82 D4
Kilrush, Ireland 15 D2
Kilwa □, Tanzania .. 83 D4
Kilwa Kisiwani, Tanzania . 83 D4
Kilwa Kivinje, Tanzania .. 83 D4
Kilwa Masoko, Tanzania .. 83 D4
Kim, U.S.A. 109 G3
Kimaam, Indonesia 57 F9

Kimamba, Tanzania 82 D4
Kimba, Australia 91 E2
Kimball, Nebr., U.S.A. 108 E3
Kimball, S. Dak., U.S.A. . . 108 D5
Kimberley, Canada 100 D5
Kimberley, S. Africa 84 D3
Kimberley Downs,
 Australia 88 C3
Kimberly, U.S.A. 110 E6
Kimchaek, N. Korea 51 D15
Kimchŏn, S. Korea 51 F15
Kími, Greece 39 L7
Kimje, S. Korea 51 G14
Kímolos, Greece 39 N7
Kimovsk, Russia 41 D11
Kimparana, Mali 78 C4
Kimry, Russia 41 C10
Kimsquit, Canada 100 C3
Kimstad, Sweden 11 F9
Kinabalu, Gunong,
 Malaysia 56 C5
Kínaros, Greece 39 N9
Kinaskan L., Canada 100 B2
Kinbasket L., Canada 100 C5
Kincaid, Canada 101 D7
Kincardine, Canada 98 D3
Kinda, Zaïre 83 D2
Kinder Scout, U.K. 12 D6
Kindersley, Canada 101 C7
Kindia, Guinea 78 C2
Kindu, Zaïre 82 C2
Kinel, Russia 41 E17
Kineshma, Russia 41 C13
Kinesi, Tanzania 82 C3
King, L., Australia 89 F2
King, Mt., Australia 90 D4
King City, U.S.A. 111 H3
King Cr. →, Australia 90 C2
King Edward →, Australia . . 88 B4
King Frederick VI Land =
 Kong Frederik VI.s Kyst,
 Greenland 4 C5
King George B., Falk. Is. . 128 D4
King George I., Antarctica . 5 C18
King George Is., Canada . 97 C11
King I. = Kadan Kyun,
 Burma 56 B1
King I., Australia 90 F3
King I., Canada 100 C3
King Leopold Ras.,
 Australia 88 C4
King Sd., Australia 88 C3
King William I., Canada . . 96 B10
King William's Town,
 S. Africa 84 E4
Kingaroy, Australia 91 D5
Kingfisher, U.S.A. 109 H6
Kingirbān, Iraq 64 C5
Kingisepp = Kuressaare,
 Estonia 40 B3
Kingisepp, Russia 40 B6
Kingman, Ariz., U.S.A. . . . 113 K12
Kingman, Kans., U.S.A. . . . 109 G5
Kingoonya, Australia 91 E2
Kings →, U.S.A. 111 H4
Kings Canyon National
 Park, U.S.A. 111 H4
King's Lynn, U.K. 12 E8
Kings Mountain, U.S.A. . . . 105 H5
King's Peak, U.S.A. 110 F8
Kingsbridge, U.K. 13 G4
Kingsburg, U.S.A. 111 H4
Kingscote, Australia 91 F2
Kingscourt, Ireland 15 C5
Kingsley, U.S.A. 108 D7
Kingsport, U.S.A. 105 G4
Kingston, Canada 98 D4
Kingston, Jamaica 116 C4
Kingston, N.Z. 87 L2
Kingston, N.Y., U.S.A. . . 107 E10
Kingston, Pa., U.S.A. . . . 107 E9
Kingston, R.I., U.S.A. . . 107 E13
Kingston Pk., U.S.A. 113 K11
Kingston South East,
 Australia 91 F2
Kingston upon Hull, U.K. . . 12 D7
Kingston-upon-Thames,
 U.K. 13 F7
Kingstown, St. Vincent . . . 117 D7
Kingstree, U.S.A. 105 J6
Kingsville, Canada 98 D3
Kingsville, U.S.A. 109 M6
Kingussie, U.K. 14 D4
Kinistino, Canada 101 C7
Kinkala, Congo 80 E2
Kinki □, Japan 49 H8
Kinleith, N.Z. 87 H5
Kinmount, Canada 106 B6
Kinna, Sweden 11 G6
Kinnaird, Canada 100 D5
Kinnairds Hd., U.K. 14 D7
Kinnared, Sweden 11 G7
Kinnarodden, Norway 6 A11
Kino, Mexico 114 B2
Kinoje →, Canada 98 B3
Kinomoto, Japan 49 G8
Kinoni, Uganda 82 C3
Kinrooi, Belgium 17 F7
Kinross, U.K. 14 E5
Kinsale, Ireland 15 E3
Kinsale, Old Hd. of,
 Ireland 15 E3
Kinsha = Chang Jiang →,
 China 53 B13
Kinshasa, Zaïre 80 E3

Kinsley, U.S.A. 109 G5
Kinston, U.S.A. 105 H7
Kintampo, Ghana 79 D4
Kintap, Indonesia 56 E5
Kintore Ra., Australia 88 D4
Kintyre, U.K. 14 F3
Kintyre, Mull of, U.K. 14 F3
Kinushseo →, Canada 98 A3
Kinuso, Canada 100 B5
Kinyangiri, Tanzania 82 C3
Kinzig →, Germany 19 G3
Kinzua, U.S.A. 106 E6
Kinzua Dam, U.S.A. 106 E5
Kiosk, Canada 98 C4
Kiowa, Kans., U.S.A. 109 G5
Kiowa, Okla., U.S.A. 109 H7
Kipahigan L., Canada 101 B8
Kipanga, Tanzania 82 D4
Kiparissía, Greece 39 M4
Kiparissiakós Kólpos,
 Greece 39 M4
Kipembawe, Tanzania 82 D3
Kipengere Ra., Tanzania . . . 83 D3
Kipili, Tanzania 82 D3
Kipini, Kenya 82 C5
Kipling, Canada 101 C8
Kippure, Ireland 15 C5
Kipushi, Zaïre 83 E2
Kiratpur, India 62 E8
Kirchberg, Switz. 22 B5
Kirchhain, Germany 18 E4
Kirchheim, Germany 19 G5
Kirchheim-Bolanden,
 Germany 19 F4
Kirensk, Russia 45 D11
Kirgella Rocks, Australia . . 89 F3
Kirghizia ■, Asia 44 E8
Kirghizstan = Kirghizia ■,
 Asia 44 E8
Kirgizia = Kirghizia ■,
 Asia 44 E8
Kiri, Zaïre 80 E3
Kiribati ■, Pac. Oc. 92 H10
Kırıkhan, Turkey 66 E7
Kırıkkale, Turkey 66 D5
Kirillov, Russia 41 B11
Kirin = Jilin, China 51 C14
Kirin = Jilin □, China . . . 51 C13
Kirishi, Russia 40 B7
Kiritimati, Kiribati 93 G12
Kirka, Turkey 66 D4
Kirkcaldy, U.K. 14 E5
Kirkcudbright, U.K. 14 G4
Kirkee, India 60 K8
Kirkenær, Norway 10 D6
Kirkenes, Norway 8 B21
Kirkintilloch, U.K. 14 F4
Kirkjubæjarklaustur,
 Iceland 8 E4
Kirkland, U.S.A. 111 J7
Kirkland Lake, Canada 98 C3
Kırklareli, Turkey 39 H10
Kırklareli □, Turkey 66 C2
Kirksville, U.S.A. 108 E8
Kirkūk, Iraq 64 C5
Kirkwall, U.K. 14 C6
Kirkwood, S. Africa 84 E4
Kirn, Germany 19 F3
Kirov = Vyatka, Russia . . . 41 B16
Kirov, Russia 40 D9
Kirovabad = Gyandzha,
 Azerbaijan 43 F12
Kirovakan = Karaklis,
 Armenia 43 F11
Kirovo-Chepetsk, Russia . . 41 B17
Kirovograd, Ukraine 42 B5
Kirovohrad = Kirovograd,
 Ukraine 42 B5
Kirovsk, Russia 44 C4
Kirovsk, Turkmenistan 44 F7
Kirovsk, Ukraine 43 B8
Kirovski, Russia 43 D13
Kirovskiy, Russia 45 D16
Kirovskiy, Russia 48 B6
Kirriemuir, U.K. 14 E6
Kirsanov, Russia 41 E13
Kırşehir, Turkey 66 D6
Kırşehir □, Turkey 66 D6
Kirstonia, S. Africa 84 D3
Kirtachi, Niger 79 C5
Kirthar Range, Pakistan . . . 62 F2
Kirundu, Zaïre 82 C2
Kirup, Australia 89 F2
Kirya, Russia 41 D15
Kiryū, Japan 49 F9
Kisaga, Tanzania 82 C3
Kisalaya, Nic. 116 D3
Kisámou, Kólpos, Greece . . 37 D5
Kisanga, Zaïre 82 B2
Kisangani, Zaïre 82 B2
Kisar, Indonesia 57 F7
Kisaran, Indonesia 56 D1
Kisarawe, Tanzania 82 D4
Kisarawe □, Tanzania 82 D4
Kisarazu, Japan 49 G9
Kisbér, Hungary 21 H8
Kiselevsk, Russia 44 D9
Kishanganga →, Pakistan . . 63 B5
Kishanganj, India 63 F13
Kishangarh, India 62 F7
Kishi, Nigeria 79 D5
Kishinev, Moldavia 42 C3
Kishiwada, Japan 49 G7
Kishtwar, India 63 C6

Kisii, Kenya 82 C3
Kisii □, Kenya 82 C3
Kisiju, Tanzania 82 D4
Kısır Dağ, Turkey 43 F10
Kisizi, Uganda 82 C2
Kiska I., U.S.A. 96 C1
Kiskatinaw →, Canada . . . 100 B4
Kiskittogisu L., Canada . . 101 C9
Kiskörös, Hungary 21 J10
Kiskundorozsma, Hungary . 21 J10
Kiskunfélegyháza, Hungary . 21 J9
Kiskunhalas, Hungary 21 J9
Kiskunmajsa, Hungary 21 J9
Kislovodsk, Russia 43 E10
Kiso-Gawa →, Japan 49 G8
Kiso-Sammyaku, Japan . . . 49 G8
Kisofukushima, Japan 49 G8
Kisoro, Uganda 82 C2
Kispest, Hungary 21 H9
Kissidougou, Guinea 78 D2
Kissimmee, U.S.A. 105 L5
Kissimmee →, U.S.A. 105 M5
Kississing L., Canada 101 B8
Kissónerga, Cyprus 37 E11
Kistanje, Croatia 33 E12
Kisújszállás, Hungary 21 H10
Kisumu, Kenya 82 C3
Kisvárda, Hungary 21 G12
Kiswani, Tanzania 82 C4
Kiswere, Tanzania 83 D4
Kit Carson, U.S.A. 108 F3
Kita, Mali 78 C3
Kitab, Uzbekistan 44 F7
Kitaibaraki, Japan 49 F10
Kitakami, Japan 48 E10
Kitakami-Gawa →, Japan . . 48 E10
Kitakami-Sammyaku, Japan . 48 E10
Kitakata, Japan 48 F9
Kitakyūshū, Japan 49 H5
Kitale, Kenya 82 B4
Kitami, Japan 48 C11
Kitami-Sammyaku, Japan . . 48 B11
Kitangiri, L., Tanzania 82 C3
Kitaya, Tanzania 83 E5
Kitchener, Australia 89 F3
Kitchener, Canada 98 D3
Kitega = Gitega, Burundi . . 82 C2
Kitengo, Zaïre 82 D1
Kiteto □, Tanzania 82 C4
Kitgum, Uganda 82 B3
Kíthira, Greece 39 N7
Kíthnos, Greece 39 M7
Kiti, Cyprus 37 E12
Kiti, C., Cyprus 37 E12
Kitikmeot □, Canada 96 A9
Kitimat, Canada 100 C3
Kitinen →, Finland 8 C19
Kitiyab, Sudan 77 D3
Kitros, Greece 39 J5
Kitsuki, Japan 49 H5
Kittakittaooloo, L.,
 Australia 91 D2
Kittanning, U.S.A. 106 F5
Kittatinny Mts., U.S.A. . . . 107 E10
Kittery, U.S.A. 105 D10
Kitui, Kenya 82 C4
Kitui □, Kenya 82 C4
Kitwe, Zambia 83 E2
Kitzbühel, Austria 19 H8
Kitzingen, Germany 19 F6
Kivalo, Finland 8 C19
Kivarli, India 62 G5
Kividhes, Cyprus 37 E11
Kivu □, Zaïre 82 C2
Kivu, L., Zaïre 82 C2
Kiyev, Ukraine 40 F7
Kiyevskoye Vdkhr.,
 Ukraine 40 F7
Kiziguru, Rwanda 82 C3
Kızıl Irmak →, Turkey . . . 42 F6
Kizil Jilga, India 63 B8
Kizil Yurt, Russia 43 E12
Kızılcahamam, Turkey 42 F5
Kızılhisar, Turkey 66 E3
Kızılırmak, Turkey 66 C5
Kızıltepe, Turkey 67 E9
Kizimkazi, Tanzania 82 D4
Kizlyar, Russia 43 E12
Kizyl-Arvat, Turkmenistan . 44 F6
Kjellerup, Denmark 11 H3
Kladanj, Bos.-H. 21 L8
Kladno, Czech. 20 E4
Kladovo, Serbia, Yug. 21 L12
Klaeng, Thailand 58 F3
Klagenfurt, Austria 21 J4
Klagshamn, Sweden 11 J6
Klagstorp, Sweden 11 J7
Klaipėda, Lithuania 40 D2
Klamath →, U.S.A. 110 F1
Klamath Falls, U.S.A. 110 E3
Klamath Mts., U.S.A. 110 F2
Klanjec, Croatia 33 B12
Klappan →, Canada 100 B3
Klarälven →, Sweden 9 G12
Klaten, Indonesia 57 G14
Klatovy, Czech. 20 F3
Klawer, S. Africa 84 E2
Klawock, U.S.A. 100 B2
Klazienaveen, Neths. 16 C10
Kleczew, Poland 20 C8
Kleena Kleene, Canada . . . 100 C4
Klein, U.S.A. 110 C9
Klein-Karas, Namibia 84 D2
Kleine Gette →, Belgium . . 17 G6
Kleine Nete →, Belgium . . 17 F5

Klekovača, Bos.-H. 33 D13
Klenovec, Macedonia 39 H3
Klenovec, Slovakia 20 G9
Klerksdorp, S. Africa 84 D4
Kletnya, Russia 40 E8
Kletsk, Belorussia 40 E5
Kletskiy, Russia 43 B10
Kleve, Germany 18 D2
Klickitat, U.S.A. 110 D3
Klickitat →, U.S.A. 112 D5
Klidhes, Cyprus 37 D13
Klimovichi, Belorussia . . . 40 E8
Klin, Russia 41 C10
Klinaklini →, Canada 100 C3
Klintsy, Russia 40 E8
Klipdale, S. Africa 84 E2
Klipplaat, S. Africa 84 E3
Klitmøller, Denmark 11 G2
Kljajićevo, Serbia, Yug. . . . 21 K9
Ključ, Bos.-H. 33 D13
Kłobuck, Poland 20 E8
Kłodzko, Poland 20 E6
Kloetinge, Neths. 17 F3
Kloosterzande, Neths. 17 F4
Klondike, Canada 96 B6
Klosterneuburg, Austria . . . 21 G6
Klosters, Switz. 23 C9
Kloten, Switz. 23 B7
Klötze, Germany 18 C7
Klouto, Togo 79 D5
Kluane L., Canada 96 B6
Kluczbork, Poland 20 E8
Klundert, Neths. 17 E5
Klyuchevskaya, Gora,
 Russia 45 D17
Knaresborough, U.K. 12 C6
Knee L., Man., Canada . . 101 B10
Knee L., Sask., Canada . . 101 B7
Kneïss, Is., Tunisia 75 B7
Knesselare, Belgium 17 F2
Knezha, Bulgaria 38 F7
Knić, Serbia, Yug. 21 M10
Knight Inlet, Canada 100 C3
Knighton, U.K. 13 E4
Knights Ferry, U.S.A. 112 H6
Knights Landing, U.S.A. . . 112 G5
Knin, Croatia 33 D13
Knittelfeld, Austria 21 H4
Knjaževac, Serbia, Yug. . . 21 M12
Knob, C., Australia 89 F2
Knockmealdown Mts.,
 Ireland 15 D4
Knokke, Belgium 17 F2
Knossós, Greece 37 D7
Knox, U.S.A. 104 E2
Knox, C., Canada 100 C2
Knox City, U.S.A. 109 J5
Knox Coast, Antarctica . . . 5 C8
Knoxville, Iowa, U.S.A. . . 108 E8
Knoxville, Tenn., U.S.A. . . 105 H4
Knutshø, Norway 10 B3
Knysna, S. Africa 84 E3
Ko Kha, Thailand 58 C2
Ko Tao, Thailand 59 G2
Koartac, Canada 97 B13
Koba, Aru, Indonesia 57 F8
Koba, Bangka, Indonesia . . 56 E3
Kobarid, Slovenia 33 B10
Kobayashi, Japan 49 J5
Kobdo = Hovd, Mongolia . . 54 B4
Kōbe, Japan 49 G7
Kobelyaki, Ukraine 42 B6
København, Denmark 11 J6
Kōbi-Sho, Japan 49 M1
Koblenz, Germany 19 E3
Koblenz, Switz. 22 A6
Kobo, Ethiopia 77 E4
Kobroor, Kepulauan,
 Indonesia 57 F8
Kobrin, Belorussia 40 E4
Kobuleti, Georgia 43 F9
Kobyłka, Poland 20 C11
Kobylkino, Russia 41 D13
Kobylnik, Belorussia 40 D5
Kocaeli = İzmit, Turkey . . 66 C3
Kocaeli □, Turkey 66 C3
Kočani, Macedonia 39 H5
Koceljevo, Serbia, Yug. . . . 21 L9
Kočevje, Slovenia 33 C11
Koch Bihar, India 61 F16
Kochang, S. Korea 51 G14
Kochas, India 63 G10
Kocher →, Germany 19 F5
Kocheya, Russia 45 D13
Kōchi, Japan 49 H6
Kōchi □, Japan 49 H6
Kochiu = Gejiu, China . . . 52 F4
Kodiak, U.S.A. 96 C4
Kodiak I., U.S.A. 96 C4
Kodinar, India 62 J4
Kodori →, Georgia 43 E9
Koekelare, Belgium 17 F1
Koersel, Belgium 17 F6
Koes, Namibia 84 D2
Koffiefontein, S. Africa . . . 84 D4
Kofiau, Indonesia 57 E7
Koforidua, Ghana 79 D4
Kōfu, Japan 49 G9
Kogaluk →, Canada 99 A7
Kogan, Australia 91 D5
Kogi □, Nigeria 79 D6
Kogin Baba, Nigeria 79 D7
Koh-i-Bābā, Afghan. 60 B5

Koh-i-Khurd, Afghan. 62 C1
Kohat, Pakistan 62 C4
Kohima, India 61 G19
Kohkīlūyeh va Būyer
 Aḥmadi □, Iran 65 D6
Kohler Ra., Antarctica 5 D15
Kohtla-Järve, Estonia 40 B5
Koin-dong, N. Korea 51 D14
Kojŏ, N. Korea 51 E14
Kojonup, Australia 89 F2
Kojūr, Iran 65 B6
Koka, Sudan 76 C3
Kokand, Uzbekistan 44 E8
Kokanee Glacier Prov.
 Park, Canada 100 D5
Kokas, Indonesia 57 E8
Kokchetav, Kazakhstan . . . 44 D7
Kokemäenjoki, Finland . . . 9 F16
Kokerite, Guyana 121 B6
Kokhma, Russia 41 C12
Kokkola, Finland 8 E17
Koko, Nigeria 79 C5
Koko Kyunzu, Burma 61 M18
Kokolopozo, Ivory C. 78 D3
Kokomo, U.S.A. 104 E2
Kokonau, Indonesia 57 E9
Kokoro, Niger 79 C5
Koksan, N. Korea 51 E14
Koksoak →, Canada 97 C13
Kokstad, S. Africa 85 E4
Kokubu, Japan 49 J5
Kokuora, Russia 45 B15
Kola, Indonesia 57 F8
Kola, Russia 44 C4
Kola Pen. = Kolskiy
 Poluostrov, Russia 44 C4
Kolahoi, India 63 B6
Kolahun, Liberia 78 D2
Kolaka, Indonesia 57 E6
Kolar, India 60 N11
Kolar Gold Fields, India . . 60 N11
Kolari, Finland 8 C17
Kolayat, India 62 F5
Kolby Kås, Denmark 11 J4
Kolchugino = Leninsk-
 Kuznetskiy, Russia 44 D9
Kolchugino, Russia 41 C11
Kolda, Senegal 78 C2
Kolding, Denmark 11 J3
Kole, Zaïre 80 E4
Koléa, Algeria 75 A5
Kolepom = Yos Sudarso,
 Pulau, Indonesia 57 F9
Kolguyev, Ostrov, Russia . . 44 C5
Kolham, Neths. 16 B9
Kolhapur, India 60 L9
Kolia, Ivory C. 78 D3
Kolín, Czech. 20 E5
Kolind, Denmark 11 H4
Kölleda, Germany 18 D7
Kollum, Neths. 16 B8
Kolmanskop, Namibia 84 D2
Köln, Germany 18 E2
Koło, Poland 20 C8
Kołobrzeg, Poland 20 A5
Kologriv, Russia 41 B14
Kolokani, Mali 78 C3
Kolomna, Russia 41 D11
Kolomyya, Ukraine 42 B1
Kolondiéba, Mali 78 C3
Kolonodale, Indonesia 57 E6
Kolosib, India 61 G18
Kolpashevo, Russia 44 D9
Kolpino, Russia 40 B7
Kolpny, Russia 41 E10
Kolskiy Poluostrov, Russia . 44 C4
Kolubara →, Serbia, Yug. . 21 L10
Koluszki, Poland 20 D9
Kolwezi, Zaïre 83 E2
Kolyberovo, Russia 41 D11
Kolyma →, Russia 45 C17
Kolymskoye, Okhotsko,
 Russia 45 C16
Kôm Ombo, Egypt 76 C3
Komandorskiye Is. =
 Komandorskiye Ostrova,
 Russia 45 D17
Komandorskiye Ostrova,
 Russia 45 D17
Komárno, Slovakia 21 H8
Komárom, Hungary 21 H8
Komarovo, Russia 40 B8
Komatipoort, S. Africa . . . 85 D5
Komatou Yialou, Cyprus . . 37 D13
Komatsu, Japan 49 F8
Komatsujima, Japan 49 H7
Kombissiri, Burkina Faso . . 79 C4
Kombori, Burkina Faso . . . 78 C4
Komen, Slovenia 33 C10
Komenda, Ghana 79 D4
Komi Republic □, Russia . . 44 B10
Komiža, Croatia 33 E13
Komló, Hungary 21 J8
Kommunarsk, Ukraine 43 B8
Kommunizma, Pik,
 Tajikistan 44 F8
Komodo, Indonesia 57 F5
Komoé, Ivory C. 78 D4
Komono, Congo 80 E2
Komoran, Pulau, Indonesia . 57 F9
Komoro, Japan 49 F9
Komotini, Greece 39 H8
Kompasberg, S. Africa . . . 84 E3
Kompong Bang, Cambodia . 59 F5
Kompong Cham, Cambodia . 59 F5

Kompong Chhnang, Cambodia 59 F5
Kompong Chikreng, Cambodia 58 F5
Kompong Kleang, Cambodia 58 F5
Kompong Luong, Cambodia 59 G5
Kompong Pranak, Cambodia 58 F5
Kompong Som, Cambodia 59 G4
Kompong Som, Chhung, Cambodia 59 G4
Kompong Speu, Cambodia 59 G5
Kompong Sralao, Cambodia 58 E5
Kompong Thom, Cambodia 58 F5
Kompong Trabeck, Cambodia 58 F5
Kompong Trabeck, Cambodia 59 G5
Kompong Trach, Cambodia 59 G5
Kompong Tralach, Cambodia 59 G5
Komrat, Moldavia 42 C3
Komsberg, S. Africa 84 E3
Komsomolets, Ostrov, Russia 45 A10
Komsomolsk, Russia 41 C12
Komsomolsk, Russia 45 D14
Komsomolskiy, Russia ... 41 E16
Konakovo, Russia 41 C10
Konarhá □, Afghan. 60 B7
Konāri, Iran 65 D6
Konawa, U.S.A. 109 H6
Konch, India 63 G8
Kondakovo, Russia 45 C16
Konde, Tanzania 82 C4
Kondinin, Australia 89 F2
Kondoa, Tanzania 82 C4
Kondoa □, Tanzania 82 D4
Kondókali, Greece 37 A3
Kondratyevo, Russia ... 45 D10
Konduga, Nigeria 79 C7
Kong, Ivory C. 78 D4
Kong →, Cambodia 58 F5
Kong, Koh, Cambodia ... 59 G4
Kong Christian IX.s Land, Greenland 4 C6
Kong Christian X.s Land, Greenland 4 B6
Kong Franz Joseph Fd., Greenland 4 B6
Kong Frederik IX.s Land, Greenland 4 C5
Kong Frederik VI.s Kyst, Greenland 4 C5
Kong Frederik VIII.s Land, Greenland 4 B6
Kong Oscar Fjord, Greenland 4 B6
Kongeå →, Denmark 11 J3
Kongju, S. Korea 51 F14
Konglu, Burma 61 F20
Kongolo, Kasai Or., Zaïre 82 D1
Kongolo, Shaba, Zaïre .. 82 D2
Kongor, Sudan 77 F3
Kongoussi, Burkina Faso 79 C4
Kongsberg, Norway 10 E3
Kongsvinger, Norway ... 10 D6
Kongwa, Tanzania 82 D4
Koni, Zaïre 83 E2
Koni, Mts., Zaïre 83 E2
Königsberg = Kaliningrad, Russia 40 D2
Königslutter, Germany ... 18 C6
Königswusterhausen, Germany 18 C9
Konin, Poland 20 C8
Kónitsa, Greece 39 J3
Köniz, Switz. 22 C4
Konjice, Slovenia 33 B12
Konkiep, Namibia 84 D2
Konkouré →, Guinea ... 78 D2
Könnern, Germany 18 D7
Kono, S. Leone 78 D2
Konolfingen, Switz. 22 C5
Konongo, Ghana 79 D4
Konosha, Russia 44 C5
Kōnosu, Japan 49 F9
Konotop, Ukraine 40 F8
Konqi He →, China ... 54 B4
Końskie, Poland 20 D10
Konstantinovka, Ukraine 42 B7
Konstantinovski, Russia . 43 C9
Konstanz, Germany 19 H5
Kont, Iran 65 E9
Kontagora, Nigeria 79 C6
Kontich, Belgium 17 F4
Kontum, Vietnam 58 E7
Kontum, Plateau du, Vietnam 58 E7
Konya, Turkey 66 E5
Konya □, Turkey 66 E5
Konya Ovasi, Turkey ... 66 D5
Konz, Germany 19 F2
Konza, Kenya 82 C4
Kookynie, Australia ... 89 E3
Kooline, Australia 88 D2
Kooloonong, Australia .. 91 E3
Koolyanobbing, Australia 89 F2
Koondrook, Australia .. 91 F3
Koonibba, Australia ... 91 E1
Koorawatha, Australia .. 91 E4
Koorda, Australia 89 F2

Kooskia, U.S.A. 110 C6
Kootenai →, Canada ... 110 B5
Kootenay L., Canada ... 100 D5
Kootenay Nat. Park, Canada 100 C5
Kootjieskolk, S. Africa .. 84 E3
Kopanovka, Russia ... 43 C12
Kopaonik, Serbia, Yug. . 21 M11
Kópavogur, Iceland 8 D3
Koper, Slovenia 33 C10
Kopervik, Norway 9 G8
Kopeysk, Russia 44 D7
Kopi, Australia 91 E2
Köping, Sweden 10 E10
Kopiste, Croatia 33 F13
Köpmanholmen, Sweden . 10 A12
Koppang, Norway 10 C5
Kopparberg, Sweden ... 9 G13
Kopparbergs län □, Sweden 9 F13
Kopperå, Norway 10 A5
Koppies, S. Africa 85 D4
Koprivnica, Croatia ... 33 B13
Kopychintsy, Ukraine ... 40 G4
Kopys, Belorussia 40 D7
Korab, Macedonia ... 39 H3
Korakiána, Greece 37 A3
Korba, India 63 H10
Korbach, Germany 18 D4
Korbu, G., Malaysia ... 59 K3
Korça, Albania 39 J3
Korce = Korça, Albania . 39 J3
Korčula, Croatia 33 F14
Korčulanski Kanal, Croatia 33 E13
Kord Kūy, Iran 65 B7
Kord Sheykh, Iran 65 D7
Kordestān □, Iran 64 C5
Korea, North ■, Asia ... 51 E14
Korea, South ■, Asia ... 51 F15
Korea Bay, Korea 51 E13
Korea Strait, Asia 51 G15
Korenevo, Russia 40 F9
Korenovsk, Russia 43 D8
Korets, Ukraine 40 F5
Korgan, Turkey 67 C7
Korgus, Sudan 76 D3
Korhogo, Ivory C. 78 D3
Koribundu, S. Leone ... 78 D2
Korim, Indonesia 57 E9
Korinthiakós Kólpos, Greece 39 L5
Kórinthos, Greece 39 M5
Korioumé, Mali 78 B4
Koríssa, Límni, Greece . 37 B3
Kōriyama, Japan 48 F10
Korkuteli, Turkey 66 E4
Kormakiti, C., Cyprus .. 37 D11
Körmend, Hungary ... 21 H6
Kornat, Croatia 33 E12
Korneshty, Moldavia ... 42 C3
Kornsjø, Norway 10 F5
Kornstad, Norway 10 B1
Koro, Fiji 87 C8
Koro, Ivory C. 78 D3
Koro, Mali 78 C4
Koro Sea, Fiji 87 C9
Korocha, Russia 41 F10
Köroğlu Dağları, Turkey . 66 C4
Korogwe, Tanzania ... 82 D4
Korogwe □, Tanzania .. 82 D4
Koroit, Australia 91 F3
Koronadal, Phil. 55 H6
Koronowo, Poland ... 20 B7
Koror, Pac. Oc. 57 C8
Körös →, Hungary ... 21 J10
Korosten, Ukraine 40 F6
Korotoyak, Russia 41 F11
Korraraika, Helodranon' i, Madag. 85 B7
Korsakov, Russia 45 E15
Korshunovo, Russia ... 45 D12
Korsør, Denmark 9 J11
Korsun Shevchenkovskiy, Ukraine 42 B4
Korsze, Poland 20 A11
Kortemark, Belgium ... 17 F2
Kortessem, Belgium ... 17 G6
Korti, Sudan 76 D3
Kortrijk, Belgium 17 G2
Korwai, India 62 G8
Koryakskiy Khrebet, Russia 45 C18
Koryŏng, S. Korea ... 51 G15
Kos, Greece 39 N10
Kosa, Ethiopia 77 F4
Kosaya Gora, Russia .. 41 D10
Koschagyl = Kochechyl, Kazakhstan 44 D7
Kościan, Poland 20 C6
Kościerzyna, Poland ... 20 A7
Kosciusko, U.S.A. ... 109 J10
Kosciusko, Mt., Australia 91 F4
Kosciusko I., U.S.A. ... 100 B2
Kösély →, Hungary ... 21 H11
Kosha, Sudan 76 C3
Koshiki-Rettō, Japan .. 49 J4
Kosi, India 62 F7
Kosi-meer, S. Africa ... 85 D5
Košice, Slovakia 20 G11
Kosjerić, Serbia, Yug. .. 21 M9
Koskhinoú, Greece ... 37 C10
Kosŏng, N. Korea ... 51 E15
Kosovska-Mitrovica, Serbia, Yug. 21 N10
Kostajnica, Croatia ... 33 C13
Kostanjevica, Slovenia . 33 C12

Kostelec, Czech. 20 E6
Koster, S. Africa 84 D4
Köstī, Sudan 77 E3
Kostopol, Ukraine 40 F5
Kostroma, Russia 41 C12
Kostromskoye Vdkhr., Russia 41 C12
Kostyantynivka = Konstantinovka, Ukraine 42 B7
Kostyukovichi, Belorussia 40 E8
Koszalin, Poland 20 A6
Kőszeg, Hungary 21 H6
Kot Addu, Pakistan ... 62 D4
Kot Moman, Pakistan .. 62 C5
Kota, India 62 G6
Kota Baharu, Malaysia . 59 J4
Kota Belud, Malaysia .. 56 C5
Kota Kinabalu, Malaysia 56 C5
Kota Tinggi, Malaysia .. 59 M4
Kotaagung, Indonesia .. 56 F2
Kotabaru, Indonesia .. 56 E5
Kotabumi, Indonesia .. 56 E2
Kotagede, Indonesia .. 57 G14
Kotamobagu, Indonesia 57 D6
Kotaneelee →, Canada . 100 A4
Kotawaringin, Indonesia 56 E4
Kotcho L., Canada 100 B4
Kotelnich, Russia 41 B16
Kotelnikovo, Russia .. 43 C10
Kotelnyy, Ostrov, Russia . 45 B14
Kothi, India 63 G9
Kotiro, Pakistan 62 F2
Kotka, Finland 9 F19
Kotlas, Russia 44 C5
Kotli, Pakistan 62 C5
Kotmul, Pakistan 63 B6
Kotonkoro, Nigeria ... 79 C6
Kotor, Montenegro, Yug. 21 N8
Kotoriba, Croatia 33 B13
Kotovo, Russia 41 F14
Kotovsk, Ukraine 42 C3
Kotputli, India 62 F7
Kotri, Pakistan 62 G3
Kótronas, Greece 39 N5
Kottayam, India 60 Q10
Kotturu, India 60 M10
Kotuy →, Russia 45 B11
Kotzebue, U.S.A. ... 96 B3
Kouango, C.A.R. 80 C4
Koudekerke, Neths. ... 17 F3
Koudougou, Burkina Faso 78 C4
Koufonísi, Greece 37 E8
Kougaberge, S. Africa ... 84 E3
Kouibli, Ivory C. 78 D3
Kouilou →, Congo ... 80 E2
Kouki, C.A.R. 80 C3
Koula Moutou, Gabon . 80 E2
Koulen, Cambodia ... 58 F5
Koulikoro, Mali 78 C3
Kouloúra, Greece 37 A3
Koúm-bournoú, Ákra, Greece 37 C10
Koumala, Australia ... 90 C4
Koumankou, Mali 78 C3
Koumbia, Burkina Faso 78 C4
Koumbia, Guinea 78 C2
Koumboum, Guinea ... 78 C2
Koumpenntoum, Senegal 78 C2
Koumra, Chad 73 G9
Koundara, Guinea 78 C2
Kounradskiy, Kazakhstan 44 E8
Kountze, U.S.A. ... 109 K7
Koupéla, Burkina Faso . 79 C4
Kouris →, Cyprus 37 E11
Kourou, Fr. Guiana ... 121 B7
Kouroussa, Guinea ... 78 C3
Koussané, Mali 78 C2
Kousseri, Cameroon .. 73 F7
Koutiala, Mali 78 C3
Kouto, Ivory C. 78 D3
Kouvé, Togo 79 D5
Kovačica, Serbia, Yug. . 21 K10
Kovel, Ukraine 40 F4
Kovin, Serbia, Yug. ... 21 L10
Kovrov, Russia 41 C12
Kowanyama, Australia . 90 B3
Kowkash, Canada 98 B2
Kowloon, H.K. 53 F10
Kowŏn, N. Korea 51 E14
Koyabuti, Indonesia ... 57 E10
Köyceğiz, Turkey 66 E3
Koyuk, U.S.A. 96 B3
Koyukuk →, U.S.A. .. 96 B4
Koyulhisar, Turkey ... 42 F7
Koza, Japan 49 L3
Kozan, Turkey 66 E6
Kozáni, Greece 39 J4
Kozara, Bos.-H. 33 D14
Kozarac, Bos.-H. 33 D13
Kozelsk, Russia 40 D9
Kozhikode = Calicut, India 60 P9
Kozje, Slovenia 33 B12
Kozlovets, Bulgaria ... 38 F8
Kozlu, Turkey 66 C4
Kozluk, Turkey 67 D9
Kożmin, Poland 20 D7
Kozmodemyansk, Russia 41 C15
Kpabia, Ghana 79 D4
Kpalimé, Togo 79 D5
Kpandae, Ghana 79 D4
Kpessi, Togo 79 D5
Kra, Isthmus of = Kra, Kho Khot, Thailand ... 59 G2
Kra, Kho Khot, Thailand . 59 G2

Kra Buri, Thailand 59 G2
Krabbendijke, Neths. ... 17 F4
Krabi, Thailand 59 H2
Kragan, Indonesia ... 57 G14
Kragerø, Norway 9 G9
Kragujevac, Serbia, Yug. . 21 L10
Krajina, Bos.-H. 33 D13
Krakatau = Rakata, Pulau, Indonesia 56 F3
Krakor, Cambodia ... 58 F5
Kraków, Poland 20 E9
Kraksaan, Indonesia .. 57 G15
Kralanh, Cambodia ... 58 F4
Kraljevo, Serbia, Yug. . 21 M10
Kralovice, Czech. 20 F3
Kralupy, Czech. 20 E4
Kramatorsk, Ukraine .. 42 B7
Kramfors, Sweden ... 10 B11
Kramis, C., Algeria ... 75 A5
Krångede, Sweden ... 10 A10
Kranj, Slovenia 33 B11
Kranjska Gora, Slovenia . 33 B10
Krankskop, S. Africa .. 85 D5
Krapina, Croatia 33 B12
Krapina →, Croatia ... 33 C12
Krapivna, Russia 41 E10
Krapkowice, Poland .. 20 E7
Kraskino, Russia 45 E14
Kraslice, Czech. 20 E2
Krasnaya Gorbatka, Russia 41 D12
Krasnik, Poland 20 E12
Krasnik Fabryczny, Poland 20 E12
Krasnoarmeisk, Ukraine 42 B7
Krasnoarmeysk, Russia . 41 F14
Krasnoarmeysk, Russia . 43 B11
Krasnodar, Russia ... 43 D8
Krasnodon, Ukraine .. 43 B8
Krasnodonetskaya, Russia 43 B9
Krasnogorskiy, Russia .. 41 C16
Krasnograd, Ukraine .. 42 B6
Krasnogvardeyskoye, Russia 43 D9
Krasnogvardeysk, Ukraine 42 D6
Krasnokutsk, Ukraine .. 42 F9
Krasnoperekopsk, Ukraine 42 D5
Krasnorechenskiy, Russia . 48 B7
Krasnoselkupsk, Russia . 44 C9
Krasnoslobodsk, Russia . 41 D13
Krasnoslobodsk, Russia . 43 B11
Krasnoturinsk, Russia .. 44 C11
Krasnoufimsk, Russia .. 44 C6
Krasnouralsk, Russia .. 44 C7
Krasnovodsk, Turkmenistan 44 E6
Krasnoyarsk, Russia ... 45 D10
Krasnoye = Krasnyy, Russia 40 D7
Krasnoye, Russia 41 B15
Krasnoye, Russia 43 C11
Krasnozavodsk, Russia . 41 C11
Krasny Liman, Ukraine . 42 B7
Krasny Sulin, Russia ... 43 C9
Krasnystaw, Poland .. 20 E13
Krasnyy, Russia 40 D7
Krasnyy Kholm, Russia . 41 B10
Krasnyy Kut, Russia .. 41 F15
Krasnyy Luch, Ukraine . 43 B8
Krasnyy Profintern, Russia 41 C12
Krasnyy Yar, Russia .. 41 E17
Krasnyy Yar, Russia .. 41 F14
Krasnyy Yar, Russia .. 43 C13
Krasnyye Baki, Russia . 41 C14
Krasnyyoskolskoye Vdkhr., Ukraine 42 B7
Kraszna →, Hungary .. 21 G12
Kratie, Cambodia ... 58 F6
Krau, Indonesia 57 E10
Kravanh, Chuor Phnum, Cambodia 59 G4
Krefeld, Germany 18 D2
Kremaston, Límni, Greece 39 L4
Kremenchug, Ukraine ... 42 B5
Kremenchugskoye Vdkhr., Ukraine 42 B5
Kremenchuk = Kremenchug, Ukraine . 42 B5
Kremenets, Ukraine ... 42 A1
Kremennaya, Ukraine .. 42 B8
Kremges = Svetlovodsk, Ukraine 40 G8
Kremikovtsi, Bulgaria .. 38 G6
Kremmen, Germany .. 18 C9
Kremmling, U.S.A. ... 110 F10
Krems, Austria 21 G5
Kremsmünster, Austria . 21 G4
Kretinga, Lithuania ... 40 D2
Krettamia, Algeria ... 74 C4
Krettsy, Russia 40 B8
Krim, Slovenia 33 C11
Krimpen, Neths. 16 E5
Kriós, Ákra, Greece ... 37 D5
Krishna →, India 61 M12
Krishnanagar, India ... 63 H13
Kristiansand, Norway .. 9 G10
Kristianstad, Sweden .. 9 H13
Kristianstads län □, Sweden 9 H13
Kristiansund, Norway .. 10 A1
Kristiinankaupunki, Finland 8 E16

Kristinehamn, Sweden 9 G13
Kristinestad, Finland ... 8 E16
Kríti, Greece 37 D7
Kritsá, Greece 37 D7
Kriva →, Macedonia .. 38 G4
Kriva Palanka, Macedonia 38 G5
Krivaja →, Bos.-H. ... 21 L8
Krivoy Rog, Ukraine ... 42 C5
Križevci, Croatia 33 B13
Krk, Croatia 33 C11
Krka →, Croatia 33 C12
Krkonoše, Czech. 20 E5
Krnov, Czech. 20 E7
Krobia, Poland 20 D6
Krokeaí, Greece 39 N5
Krokodil →, Mozam. .. 85 D5
Krokom, Sweden 10 A8
Krolevets, Ukraine ... 40 F8
Kroměříž, Czech. 20 F7
Krommenie, Neths. ... 16 D5
Kromy, Russia 40 E9
Kronach, Germany .. 19 E7
Kronobergs län □, Sweden 9 H13
Kronprins Olav Kyst, Antarctica 5 C5
Kronshtadt, Russia ... 40 A6
Kroonstad, S. Africa .. 84 D4
Kröpelin, Germany .. 18 A7
Kropotkin, Russia ... 43 D9
Kropotkin, Russia ... 45 D12
Kropp, Germany 18 A5
Krościenko, Poland .. 20 F10
Krosno, Poland 20 F11
Krosno Odrzańskie, Poland 20 C5
Krotoszyn, Poland .. 20 D7
Kroussón, Greece 37 D6
Krško, Slovenia 33 C12
Kruger Nat. Park, S. Africa 85 C5
Krugersdorp, S. Africa . 85 D4
Kruiningen, Neths. ... 17 F4
Kruisfontein, S. Africa . 84 E3
Kruishoutem, Belgium . 17 G3
Kruisland, Neths. 17 E4
Kruja, Albania 39 H2
Krulevshchina, Belorussia 40 D5
Kruma, Albania 38 G3
Krumbach, Germany .. 19 G6
Krung Thep = Bangkok, Thailand 58 F3
Krupanj, Serbia, Yug. ... 21 L9
Krupinica →, Slovakia .. 21 G8
Kruševac, Serbia, Yug. . 21 M11
Kruzof I., U.S.A. 100 B1
Krychaw = Krichev, Belorussia 40 E7
Krymsk Abinsk, Russia .. 42 D8
Krymskiy Poluostrov, Ukraine 42 D5
Krynica Morska, Poland . 20 A9
Krynki, Poland 20 B13
Kryvy Rih = Krivoy Rog, Ukraine 42 C5
Krzywiń, Poland 20 D6
Krzyż, Poland 20 C6
Ksabi, Morocco 74 B4
Ksar Chellala, Algeria .. 75 A5
Ksar el Boukhari, Algeria . 75 A5
Ksar el Kebir, Morocco .. 74 B3
Ksar es Souk = Ar Rachidiya, Morocco 74 B4
Ksar Rhilane, Tunisia .. 75 B6
Ksour, Mts. des, Algeria . 75 B4
Kstovo, Russia 41 C14
Kuala, Indonesia 56 D3
Kuala Berang, Malaysia . 59 K4
Kuala Dungun, Malaysia . 59 K4
Kuala Kangsar, Malaysia 59 K3
Kuala Kelawang, Malaysia 59 L4
Kuala Kerai, Malaysia .. 59 K4
Kuala Kubu Baharu, Malaysia 59 L3
Kuala Lipis, Malaysia .. 59 K4
Kuala Lumpur, Malaysia 59 L3
Kuala Nerang, Malaysia 59 J3
Kuala Pilah, Malaysia .. 59 L4
Kuala Rompin, Malaysia 59 L4
Kuala Selangor, Malaysia . 59 L3
Kuala Terengganu, Malaysia 59 K4
Kualajelai, Indonesia .. 56 E4
Kualakapuas, Indonesia 56 E4
Kualakurun, Indonesia . 56 E4
Kualapembuang, Indonesia 56 E4
Kualasimpang, Indonesia . 56 D1
Kuancheng, China ... 51 D10
Kuandang, Indonesia .. 57 D6
Kuandian, China 51 D13
Kuangchou = Guangzhou, China 53 F9
Kuantan, Malaysia ... 59 L4
Kuba, Azerbaijan 43 F13
Kuban →, Russia 42 D7
Kubenskoye, Oz., Russia . 41 B11
Kuberle, Russia 43 C10
Kubokawa, Japan .. 49 H6
Kubrat, Bulgaria 38 F9
Kučevo, Serbia, Yug. .. 21 L11
Kucha Gompa, India .. 63 B7
Kuchaman, India 62 F6
Kuchino-eruba-Jima, Japan 49 J5
Kuchino-Shima, Japan . 49 K4
Kuchinotsu, Japan ... 49 H5
Kucing, Malaysia ... 56 D4
Kuçove = Qytet Stalin, Albania 39 J2

Kud →, *Pakistan* 62 F2
Kuda, *India* 60 H7
Kudat, *Malaysia* 56 C5
Kudus, *Indonesia* 57 G14
Kudymkar, *Russia* 44 D6
Kueiyang = Guiyang, *China* 52 D6
Kufstein, *Austria* 19 H8
Kugong I., *Canada* 98 A4
Kūh-e Dīnār, *Iran* 65 D6
Kūh-e Hazārām, *Iran* 65 D8
Kūhak, *Iran* 60 F3
Kūhbonān, *Iran* 65 D8
Kūhestak, *Iran* 65 E8
Kūhīn, *Iran* 65 C6
Kūhīrī, *Iran* 65 E9
Kuhnsdorf, *Austria* 21 J4
Kūhpāyeh, *Eşfahan, Iran* . 65 C7
Kūhpāyeh, *Kermān, Iran* . 65 D8
Kui Buri, *Thailand* 59 F2
Kuinre, *Neths.* 16 C7
Kuito, *Angola* 81 G3
Kujang, *N. Korea* 51 E14
Kuji, *Japan* 48 D10
Kujū-San, *Japan* 49 H5
Kukawa, *Nigeria* 79 C7
Kukerin, *Australia* 89 F2
Kukmor, *Russia* 41 C17
Kukup, *Malaysia* 59 M4
Kukvidze, *Russia* 41 F13
Kula, *Serbia, Yug.* 21 K9
Kulai, *Malaysia* 59 M4
Kulal, Mt., *Kenya* 82 B4
Kulaly, Os., *Kazakhstan* .. 43 D14
Kulasekarappattinam, *India* 60 Q11
Kuldiga, *Latvia* 40 C2
Kuldja = Yining, *China* .. 44 E9
Kuldu, *Sudan* 77 E2
Kulebaki, *Russia* 41 D13
Kulen Vakuf, *Bos.-H.* 33 D13
Kulgam, *India* 63 C6
Kuli, *Russia* 43 E12
Kulim, *Malaysia* 59 K3
Kulin, *Australia* 89 F2
Kulja, *Australia* 89 F2
Kulm, *U.S.A.* 108 B5
Kulmbach, *Germany* 19 E7
Kulp, *Turkey* 67 D9
Kulsary, *Kazakhstan* 44 E6
Kultay, *Kazakhstan* 43 D14
Kulti, *India* 63 H12
Kulu, *Turkey* 66 D5
Kulumbura, *Australia* 88 B4
Kulunda, *Russia* 44 D8
Kulungar, *Afghan.* 62 C3
Kūlvand, *Iran* 65 D7
Kulwin, *Australia* 91 F3
Kulyab, *Tajikistan* 44 F7
Kum Tekei, *Kazakhstan* .. 44 E8
Kuma →, *Russia* 43 D12
Kumaganum, *Nigeria* 79 C7
Kumagaya, *Japan* 49 F9
Kumai, *Indonesia* 56 E4
Kumamba, Kepulauan, *Indonesia* 57 E9
Kumamoto, *Japan* 49 H5
Kumamoto □, *Japan* 49 H5
Kumanovo, *Macedonia* 38 G4
Kumara, *N.Z.* 87 K3
Kumarl, *Australia* 89 F3
Kumasi, *Ghana* 78 D4
Kumayri, *Armenia* 43 F10
Kumba, *Cameroon* 79 E6
Kumbakonam, *India* 60 P11
Kumbarilla, *Australia* 91 D5
Kumbo, *Cameroon* 79 D7
Kŭmchŏn, *N. Korea* 51 E14
Kumdok, *India* 63 C8
Kume-Shima, *Japan* 49 L3
Kumeny, *Russia* 41 B16
Kŭmhwa, *S. Korea* 51 E14
Kumi, *Uganda* 82 B3
Kumla, *Sweden* 9 G13
Kumluca, *Turkey* 66 E4
Kummerower See, *Germany* 18 B8
Kumo, *Nigeria* 79 C7
Kumon Bum, *Burma* 61 F20
Kumortkala, *Russia* 43 E12
Kumylzhenskaya, *Russia* .. 43 B10
Kunama, *Australia* 91 F4
Kunashir, Ostrov, *Russia* .. 45 E15
Kunda, *Estonia* 40 B5
Kundla, *India* 62 J4
Kungala, *Australia* 91 D5
Kungälv, *Sweden* 11 G5
Kunghit I., *Canada* 100 C2
Kungrad, *Uzbekistan* 44 E6
Kungsbacka, *Sweden* 11 G6
Kungur, *Russia* 44 D6
Kungurri, *Australia* 90 C4
Kunhar →, *Pakistan* 63 B5
Kunhegyes, *Hungary* 21 H10
Kuningan, *Indonesia* 57 G13
Kunlong, *Burma* 61 H21
Kunlun Shan, *Asia* 54 C3
Kunming, *China* 52 E4
Kunrade, *Neths.* 17 G7
Kunsan, *S. Korea* 51 G14
Kunshan, *China* 53 B13
Kununurra, *Australia* 88 C4
Kunwarara, *Australia* 90 C5
Kunya-Urgench, *Turkmenistan* 44 E6

Künzelsau, *Germany* 19 F5
Kuopio, *Finland* 8 E19
Kuopion lääni □, *Finland* . 8 E19
Kupa →, *Croatia* 33 C13
Kupang, *Indonesia* 57 F6
Kupyansk, *Ukraine* 42 B7
Kupyansk-Uzlovoi, *Ukraine* 42 B7
Kuqa, *China* 54 B3
Kuranda, *Australia* 90 B4
Kurashiki, *Japan* 49 G6
Kurayoshi, *Japan* 49 G6
Kurdistan, *Asia* 67 E10
Kūrdzhali, *Bulgaria* 39 H8
Kure, *Japan* 49 G6
Küre, *Turkey* 66 C5
Küre Dağları, *Turkey* 66 C6
Kuressaare, *Estonia* 40 B3
Kurgaldzhino, *Kazakhstan* . 44 D8
Kurgan, *Russia* 44 D7
Kurganinsk, *Russia* 43 D9
Kurgannaya = Kurganinsk, *Russia* 43 D9
Kuria Maria Is. = Khūrīyā Mūrīyā, Jazā 'ir, *Oman* . 68 D6
Kuridala, *Australia* 90 C3
Kurigram, *Bangla.* 61 G16
Kuril Is. = Kurilskiye Ostrova, *Russia* 45 E15
Kuril Trench, *Pac. Oc.* ... 92 C7
Kurilsk, *Russia* 45 E15
Kurilskiye Ostrova, *Russia* 45 E15
Kuringen, *Belgium* 17 G6
Kurino, *Japan* 49 J5
Kurkur, *Egypt* 76 C3
Kurlovskiy, *Russia* 41 D12
Kurmuk, *Sudan* 77 E3
Kurnool, *India* 60 M10
Kuro-Shima, *Kagoshima, Japan* 49 J4
Kuro-Shima, *Okinawa, Japan* 49 M2
Kurovskoye, *Russia* 41 D11
Kurow, *N.Z.* 87 L3
Kurrajong, *Australia* 91 E5
Kurram →, *Pakistan* 62 C4
Kurri Kurri, *Australia* 91 E5
Kursavka, *Russia* 43 D10
Kuršėnai, *Lithuania* 40 C3
Kursk, *Russia* 41 F10
Kuršumlija, *Serbia, Yug.* . 21 M11
Kurşunlu, *Turkey* 66 C5
Kurtalan, *Turkey* 67 E9
Kuru, Bahr el →, *Sudan* .. 77 F2
Kurucaşile, *Turkey* 66 C5
Kuruktag, *China* 54 B3
Kuruman, *S. Africa* 84 D3
Kuruman →, *S. Africa* ... 84 D3
Kurume, *Japan* 49 H5
Kurunegala, *Sri Lanka* ... 60 R12
Kurupukari, *Guyana* 121 C6
Kurya, *Russia* 45 C11
Kus Gölü, *Turkey* 66 C2
Kuşadası, *Turkey* 66 E2
Kusatsu, *Japan* 49 F9
Kusawa L., *Canada* 100 A1
Kusel, *Germany* 19 F3
Kushchevskaya, *Russia* ... 43 C8
Kushikino, *Japan* 49 J5
Kushima, *Japan* 49 J5
Kushimoto, *Japan* 49 H7
Kushiro, *Japan* 48 C12
Kushiro →, *Japan* 48 C12
Kūshk, *Iran* 65 D8
Kushka, *Turkmenistan* ... 44 F7
Kūshkī, *Īlām, Iran* 64 C5
Kūshkī, *Khorāsān, Iran* .. 65 B8
Kushkū, *Iran* 65 E7
Kushol, *India* 63 C7
Kushtia, *Bangla.* 61 H16
Kushum →, *Kazakhstan* .. 43 B14
Kuskokwim →, *U.S.A.* .. 96 B3
Kuskokwim B., *U.S.A.* ... 96 C3
Küsnacht, *Switz.* 23 B7
Kussharo-Ko, *Japan* 48 C12
Küssnacht, *Switz.* 23 B6
Kustanay, *Kazakhstan* ... 44 D7
Kut, Ko, *Thailand* 59 G4
Kutahya, *Turkey* 66 D4
Kütahya □, *Turkey* 66 D4
Kutaisi, *Georgia* 43 E10
Kutaraja = Banda Aceh, *Indonesia* 56 C1
Kutch, Gulf of = Kachchh, Gulf of →, *India* 62 H3
Kutch, Rann of = Kachchh, Rann of →, *India* 62 G4
Kutina, *Croatia* 33 C13
Kutiyana, *India* 62 J4
Kutkashen, *Azerbaijan* ... 43 F12
Kutná Hora, *Czech.* 20 F5
Kutno, *Poland* 20 C9
Kuttabul, *Australia* 90 C4
Kutu, *Zaïre* 80 E3
Kutum, *Sudan* 77 E1
Kuujjuaq, *Canada* 97 C13
Kuŭp-tong, *N. Korea* 51 D14
Kuurne, *Belgium* 17 G2
Kuvshinovo, *Russia* 40 C9
Kuwait = Al Kuwayt, *Kuwait* 64 D5
Kuwait ■, *Asia* 64 D5
Kuwana, *Japan* 49 G8
Kuybyshev = Samara, *Russia* 41 E17

Kuybyshev, *Russia* 44 D8
Kuybyshevo, *Ukraine* 42 C7
Kuybyshevskoye Vdkhr., *Russia* 41 D16
Kuye He →, *China* 50 E6
Kūyeh, *Iran* 64 B5
Kūysanjaq, *Iraq* 64 B5
Kuyumba, *Russia* 45 C10
Kuzey Anadolu Dağları, *Turkey* 66 C6
Kuznetsk, *Russia* 41 E15
Kvænangen, *Norway* 8 A16
Kvam, *Norway* 10 C3
Kvareli, *Georgia* 43 F11
Kvarner, *Croatia* 33 D11
Kvarnerič, *Croatia* 33 D11
Kviteseid, *Norway* 10 E2
Kwabhaca, *S. Africa* 85 E4
Kwadacha →, *Canada* .. 100 B3
Kwakhanai, *Botswana* ... 84 C3
Kwakoegron, *Surinam* ... 121 B6
Kwale, *Kenya* 82 C4
Kwale, *Nigeria* 79 D6
Kwale □, *Kenya* 82 C4
KwaMashu, *S. Africa* 85 D5
Kwamouth, *Zaïre* 80 E3
Kwando →, *Africa* 84 B3
Kwangdaeri, *N. Korea* ... 51 D14
Kwangju, *S. Korea* 51 G14
Kwangsi-Chuang = Guangxi Zhuangzu Zizhiqu □, *China* ... 52 E7
Kwangtung = Guangdong □, *China* . 53 F9
Kwara □, *Nigeria* 79 D5
Kwataboahegan →, *Canada* 98 B3
Kwatisore, *Indonesia* 57 E8
Kweichow = Guizhou □, *China* 52 D6
Kwekwe, *Zimbabwe* 83 F2
Kwimba □, *Tanzania* 82 C3
Kwinana New Town, *Australia* 89 F2
Kwoka, *Indonesia* 57 E8
Kyabé, *Chad* 73 G8
Kyabra Cr. →, *Australia* . 91 D3
Kyabram, *Australia* 91 F4
Kyaikto, *Burma* 58 D1
Kyakhta, *Russia* 45 D11
Kyancutta, *Australia* 91 E2
Kyangin, *Burma* 61 K19
Kyaukpadaung, *Burma* ... 61 J19
Kyaukpyu, *Burma* 61 K18
Kyaukse, *Burma* 61 J20
Kyburz, *U.S.A.* 112 G6
Kycen, *Russia* 45 D11
Kyenjojo, *Uganda* 82 B3
Kyle Dam, *Zimbabwe* ... 83 G3
Kyle of Lochalsh, *U.K.* .. 14 D3
Kyll →, *Germany* 19 F2
Kyllburg, *Germany* 19 E2
Kyneton, *Australia* 91 F3
Kynuna, *Australia* 90 C3
Kyō-ga-Saki, *Japan* 49 G7
Kyogle, *Australia* 91 D5
Kyoga, L., *Uganda* 82 B3
Kyongju, *S. Korea* 51 G15
Kyongpyaw, *Burma* 61 L19
Kyŏngsŏng, *N. Korea* ... 51 D15
Kyōto, *Japan* 49 G7
Kyōto □, *Japan* 49 G7
Kyparissovouno, *Cyprus* . 37 D12
Kyperounda, *Cyprus* 37 E11
Kyrenia, *Cyprus* 37 D12
Kyrgystan = Kirghizia ■, *Asia* 44 E8
Kyritz, *Germany* 18 C8
Kystatyam, *Russia* 45 C13
Kytal Ktakh, *Russia* 45 C13
Kythréa, *Cyprus* 37 D12
Kyulyunken, *Russia* 45 C14
Kyunhla, *Burma* 61 H19
Kyuquot, *Canada* 100 C3
Kyurdamir, *Azerbaijan* ... 43 F13
Kyūshū, *Japan* 49 H5
Kyūshū □, *Japan* 49 H5
Kyūshū-Sanchi, *Japan* ... 49 H5
Kyustendil, *Bulgaria* 38 G5
Kyusyur, *Russia* 45 B13
Kywong, *Australia* 91 E4
Kyyiv = Kiyev, *Ukraine* .. 40 F7
Kyzyl, *Russia* 45 D10
Kyzyl-Kiya, *Kirghizia* 44 E8
Kyzylkum, Peski, *Uzbekistan* 44 E7
Kzyl-Orda, *Kazakhstan* ... 44 E7

L

La Albuera, *Spain* 31 G4
La Alcarria, *Spain* 28 E2
La Algaba, *Spain* 31 H4
La Almarcha, *Spain* 28 F2
La Almunia de Doña Godina, *Spain* 28 D3
La Asunción, *Venezuela* .. 121 A5
La Banda, *Argentina* 126 B3
La Bañeza, *Spain* 30 C5
La Barca, *Mexico* 114 C4
La Barge, *U.S.A.* 110 E8
La Bassée, *France* 25 B9

La Bastide-Puylaurent, *France* 26 D7
La Baule, *France* 24 E4
La Belle, *U.S.A.* 105 M5
La Biche →, *Canada* 100 B4
La Bisbal, *Spain* 28 D8
La Blanquilla, *Venezuela* . 121 A5
La Bomba, *Mexico* 114 A1
La Bresse, *France* 25 D13
La Bureba, *Spain* 28 C1
La Cal →, *Bolivia* 125 D6
La Calera, *Chile* 126 C1
La Campiña, *Spain* 31 H6
La Canal, *Spain* 36 C7
La Cañiza, *Spain* 30 C2
La Capelle, *France* 25 C10
La Carlota, *Argentina* ... 126 C3
La Carlota, *Phil.* 55 F5
La Carolina, *Spain* 31 G7
La Cavalerie, *France* 26 D7
La Ceiba, *Honduras* 116 C2
La Chaise-Dieu, *France* .. 26 C7
La Chaize-le-Vicomte, *France* 24 F5
La Chapelle d'Angillon, *France* 25 E9
La Chapelle-Glain, *France* 24 E5
La Charité-sur-Loire, *France* 25 E10
La Chartre-sur-le-Loir, *France* 24 E7
La Châtaigneraie, *France* . 26 B3
La Châtre, *France* 26 B5
La Chaux de Fonds, *Switz.* 22 B3
La Chorrera, *Colombia* .. 120 D3
La Ciotat, *France* 27 E9
La Clayette, *France* 27 B8
La Cocha, *Argentina* 126 B2
La Concepción = Ri-Aba, *Eq. Guin.* 79 E6
La Concepción, *Venezuela* 120 A3
La Concordia, *Mexico* ... 115 D6
La Conner, *U.S.A.* 110 B2
La Coruña, *Spain* 30 B2
La Coruña □, *Spain* 30 B2
La Côte, *Switz.* 22 D2
La Côte-St.-André, *France* 27 C9
La Courtine-le-Trucq, *France* 26 C6
La Crau, *France* 27 E8
La Crete, *Canada* 100 B5
La Crosse, *Kans., U.S.A.* . 108 F5
La Crosse, *Wis., U.S.A.* .. 108 D9
La Cruz, *Costa Rica* 116 D2
La Cruz, *Mexico* 114 C3
La Dorada, *Colombia* ... 120 B3
La Ensenada, *Chile* 128 B2
La Escondida, *Mexico* ... 114 C5
La Esmeralda, *Paraguay* .. 126 A3
La Esperanza, *Argentina* . 128 B3
La Esperanza, *Cuba* 116 B3
La Esperanza, *Honduras* . 116 D2
La Estrada, *Spain* 30 C2
La Fayette, *U.S.A.* 105 H3
La Fé, *Cuba* 116 B3
La Fère, *France* 25 C10
La Ferté-Bernard, *France* . 24 D7
La Ferté-Macé, *France* ... 24 D6
La Ferté-St.-Aubin, *France* 25 E8
La Ferté-sous-Jouarre, *France* 25 D10
La Ferté-Vidame, *France* . 24 D7
La Flèche, *France* 24 E6
La Follette, *U.S.A.* 105 G3
La Fregeneda, *Spain* 30 E4
La Fría, *Venezuela* 120 B3
La Fuente de San Esteban, *Spain* 30 E4
La Gineta, *Spain* 29 F2
La Gloria, *Colombia* 120 B3
La Gran Sabana, *Venezuela* 121 B5
La Grand-Combe, *France* . 27 D8
La Grande, *U.S.A.* 110 D4
La Grange, *Ga., U.S.A.* .. 105 J3
La Grange, *Ky., U.S.A.* .. 104 F3
La Grange, *Tex., U.S.A.* . 109 L6
La Grita, *Venezuela* 120 B3
La Guaira, *Venezuela* 120 A4
La Guardia, *Spain* 30 D2
La Gudiña, *Spain* 30 C3
La Güera, *Mauritania* ... 74 D1
La Guerche-de-Bretagne, *France* 24 E5
La Guerche-sur-l'Aubois, *France* 25 F9
La Habana, *Cuba* 116 B3
La Harpe, *U.S.A.* 108 E9
La Haye-du-Puits, *France* . 24 C5
La Horqueta, *Venezuela* .. 121 B5
La Horra, *Spain* 30 D7
La Independencia, *Mexico* 115 D6
La Isabela, *Dom. Rep.* ... 117 C5
La Joya, *Peru* 124 D3
La Junquera, *Spain* 28 C7
La Junta, *U.S.A.* 109 F3
La Laguna, *Canary Is.* ... 36 F3
La Libertad, *Guatemala* .. 116 C1
La Libertad, *Mexico* 114 B2
La Libertad □, *Peru* 124 B2
La Ligua, *Chile* 126 C1
La Línea de la Concepción, *Spain* 31 J5

La Loche, *Canada* 101 B7
La Londe-les-Maures, *France* 27 E10
La Lora, *Spain* 30 C7
La Loupe, *France* 24 D8
La Louvière, *Belgium* 17 H4
La Machine, *France* 25 F10
La Maddalena, *Italy* 34 A2
La Malbaie, *Canada* 99 C5
La Mancha, *Spain* 29 F3
La Mariña, *Spain* 30 B3
La Mesa, *Calif., U.S.A.* .. 113 N9
La Mesa, *N. Mex., U.S.A.* 111 K10
La Misión, *Mexico* 114 A1
La Mothe-Achard, *France* . 24 F5
La Motte, *France* 27 D10
La Motte-Chalançon, *France* 27 D9
La Moure, *U.S.A.* 108 B5
La Muela, *Spain* 28 D3
La Mure, *France* 27 D9
La Negra, *Chile* 126 A1
La Neuveville, *Switz.* 22 B4
La Oliva, *Canary Is.* 36 F6
La Oraya, *Peru* 124 C2
La Orotava, *Canary Is.* ... 36 F3
La Pacaudière, *France* ... 26 B7
La Palma, *Canary Is.* 36 F2
La Palma, *Panama* 116 E4
La Palma, *Spain* 31 H4
La Paloma, *Chile* 126 C1
La Pampa □, *Argentina* .. 126 D2
La Paragua, *Venezuela* ... 121 B5
La Paz, *Entre Ríos, Argentina* 126 C4
La Paz, *San Luis, Argentina* 126 C2
La Paz, *Bolivia* 124 D4
La Paz, *Honduras* 116 D2
La Paz, *Mexico* 114 C2
La Paz, *Phil.* 55 D4
La Paz □, *Bolivia* 124 D4
La Paz Centro, *Nic.* 116 D2
La Pedrera, *Colombia* ... 120 D4
La Perouse Str., *Asia* ... 48 B11
La Pesca, *Mexico* 115 C5
La Piedad, *Mexico* 114 C4
La Pine, *U.S.A.* 110 E3
La Plant, *U.S.A.* 108 C4
La Plata, *Argentina* 126 D4
La Plata, *Colombia* 120 C2
La Plata, L., *Argentina* .. 128 B2
La Pobla de Lillet, *Spain* . 28 C6
La Pola de Gordón, *Spain* 30 C5
La Porte, *U.S.A.* 104 E2
La Puebla, *Spain* 28 F8
La Puebla de Cazalla, *Spain* 31 H5
La Puebla de los Infantes, *Spain* 31 H5
La Puebla de Montalbán, *Spain* 30 F6
La Puerta, *Spain* 29 G2
La Punt, *Switz.* 23 C9
La Purísima, *Mexico* 114 B2
La Push, *U.S.A.* 112 C2
La Quiaca, *Argentina* ... 126 A2
La Rambla, *Spain* 31 H6
La Reine, *Canada* 98 C4
La Réole, *France* 26 D3
La Restinga, *Canary Is.* .. 36 G2
La Rioja, *Argentina* 126 B2
La Rioja □, *Argentina* ... 126 B2
La Rioja □, *Spain* 28 C2
La Robla, *Spain* 30 C5
La Roche, *Switz.* 22 C4
La Roche-Bernard, *France* 24 E4
La Roche-Canillac, *France* 26 C5
La Roche-en-Ardenne, *Belgium* 17 H7
La Roche-sur-Yon, *France* . 24 F5
La Rochefoucauld, *France* . 26 C4
La Rochelle, *France* 26 B2
La Roda, *Albacete, Spain* . 29 F2
La Roda, *Sevilla, Spain* ... 31 H6
La Romana, *Dom. Rep.* .. 117 C6
La Ronge, *Canada* 101 B7
La Rumorosa, *Mexico* ... 113 N10
La Sabina, *Spain* 36 C7
La Sagra, *Spain* 29 H2
La Salle, *U.S.A.* 108 E10
La Sanabria, *Spain* 30 C4
La Santa, *Canary Is.* 36 E6
La Sarraz, *Switz.* 22 C3
La Sarre, *Canada* 98 C4
La Scie, *Canada* 99 C8
La Selva, *Spain* 28 D7
La Selva Beach, *U.S.A.* .. 112 J5
La Serena, *Chile* 126 B1
La Serena, *Spain* 31 G5
La Seyne, *France* 27 E9
La Sila, *Italy* 35 C9
La Solana, *Spain* 29 G1
La Souterraine, *France* ... 26 B5
La Spézia, *Italy* 32 D6
La Suze-sur-Sarthe, *France* 24 E7
La Tagua, *Colombia* 120 C3
La Teste, *France* 26 D2
La Tortuga, *Venezuela* ... 117 D6
La Tour-du-Pin, *France* ... 27 C9
La Tranche-sur-Mer, *France* 24 F5
La Tremblade, *France* 26 C2
La Tuque, *Canada* 98 C5
La Unión, *Chile* 128 B2

La Unión, Colombia 120 C2
La Unión, El Salv. 116 D2
La Unión, Mexico 114 D4
La Unión, Peru 124 B2
La Unión, Spain 29 H4
La Urbana, Venezuela ... 120 B4
La Vecilla, Spain 30 C5
La Vega, Dom. Rep. 117 C5
La Vega, Peru 124 C2
La Vela, Venezuela 120 A4
La Veleta, Spain 31 H7
La Venta, Mexico 115 D6
La Ventura, Mexico 114 C4
La Victoria, Venezuela .. 120 A4
La Voulte-sur-Rhône,
  France 27 D8
La Zarza, Spain 31 H4
Laaber →, Germany 19 G8
Laage, Germany 18 B8
Laba →, Russia 43 D8
Labason, Phil. 55 G5
Labastide-Murat, France . 26 D5
Labastide-Rouairoux,
  France 26 E6
Labbézenga, Mali 79 B5
Labe = Elbe →, Europe . 18 B4
Labé, Guinea 78 C2
Laberec →, Slovakia 20 G11
Laberge, L., Canada 100 A1
Labin, Croatia 33 C11
Labinsk, Russia 43 D9
Labis, Malaysia 59 L4
Labo, Phil. 55 D5
Laboe, Germany 18 A6
Labouheyre, France 26 D3
Laboulaye, Argentina ... 126 C3
Labra, Peña, Spain 30 B6
Labrador, Coast of □,
  Canada 99 B7
Labrador City, Canada .. 99 B6
Lábrea, Brazil 125 B5
Labrède, France 26 D3
Labuan, Pulau, Malaysia . 56 C5
Labuha, Indonesia 57 E7
Labuhan, Indonesia 57 G11
Labuhanbajo, Indonesia . 57 F6
Labuissière, Belgium ... 17 H4
Labuk, Telok, Malaysia . 56 C5
Labyrinth, L., Australia . 91 E2
Labytnangi, Russia 44 C7
Lac Allard, Canada 99 B7
Lac Bouchette, Canada .. 99 C5
Lac du Flambeau, U.S.A. 108 B10
Lac Édouard, Canada ... 98 C5
Lac La Biche, Canada ... 100 C6
Lac la Martre, Canada ... 96 B8
Lac-Mégantic, Canada ... 99 C5
Lac Seul, Res., Canada .. 98 B1
Lac Thien, Vietnam 58 F7
Lacanau, France 26 D2
Lacanau, Étang de, France 26 D2
Lacantúm →, Mexico ... 115 D6
Lacara →, Spain 31 G4
Lacaune, France 26 E6
Lacaune, Mts. de, France . 26 E6
Laccadive Is. =
  Lakshadweep Is.,
  Ind. Oc. 46 J11
Lacepede B., Australia .. 91 F2
Lacepede Is., Australia .. 88 C3
Lacerdónia, Mozam. ... 83 F4
Lacey, U.S.A. 112 C4
Lachay, Pta., Peru 124 C2
Lachen, Switz. 23 B7
Lachhmangarh, India ... 62 F6
Lachi, Pakistan 62 C4
Lachine, Canada 98 C5
Lachlan →, Australia ... 91 E3
Lachute, Canada 98 C5
Lackawanna, U.S.A. ... 106 D6
Lacolle, Canada 107 A11
Lacombe, Canada 100 C6
Lacona, U.S.A. 107 C8
Láconi, Italy 34 C2
Laconia, U.S.A. 107 C13
Lacq, France 26 E3
Lacrosse, U.S.A. 110 C5
Ladakh Ra., India 63 B8
Ladário, Brazil 125 D6
Ládhon →, Greece 39 M4
Lâdik, Turkey 42 F6
Ladismith, S. Africa ... 84 E3
Lādīz, Iran 65 D9
Ladnun, India 62 F6
Ladoga, L. = Ladozhskoye
  Ozero, Russia 44 C4
Ladon, France 25 D9
Ladozhskoye Ozero, Russia 44 C4
Ladrillero, G., Chile ... 128 C1
Lady Grey, S. Africa ... 84 E4
Ladybrand, S. Africa ... 84 D4
Ladysmith, Canada 100 D4
Ladysmith, S. Africa ... 85 D4
Ladysmith, U.S.A. 108 C9
Lae, Papua N. G. 92 H6
Laem Ngop, Thailand .. 59 F4
Laem Pho, Thailand ... 59 J3
Læsø, Denmark 11 G4
Læsø Rende, Denmark .. 11 G4
Lafayette, Colo., U.S.A. . 108 F2
Lafayette, Ind., U.S.A. .. 104 E2
Lafayette, La., U.S.A. ... 109 K9
Lafayette, Tenn., U.S.A. . 105 G3
Laferte →, Canada 100 A5

Lafia, Nigeria 79 D6
Lafiagi, Nigeria 79 D6
Lafleche, Canada 101 D7
Lafon, Sudan 77 F3
Laforsen, Sweden 10 C9
Lagan →, Sweden 11 H7
Lagan →, U.K. 15 B6
Lagarfljót →, Iceland .. 8 D6
Lagarto, Brazil 122 D4
Lage, Germany 18 D4
Lage, Spain 30 B2
Lage-Mierde, Neths. ... 17 F6
Lågen →, Norway 9 F11
Lägerdorf, Germany ... 18 B5
Laghouat, Algeria 75 B5
Lagnieu, France 27 C9
Lagny, France 25 D9
Lago, Italy 35 C9
Lago Posadas, Argentina . 128 C2
Lago Ranco, Chile 128 B2
Lagôa, Portugal 31 H2
Lagoaça, Portugal 30 D4
Lagodekhi, Georgia 43 F12
Lagónegro, Italy 35 B8
Lagonoy Gulf, Phil. ... 55 E6
Lagos, Nigeria 79 D5
Lagos, Portugal 31 H2
Lagos de Moreno, Mexico 114 C4
Lagrange, Australia 88 C3
Lagrange B., Australia .. 88 C3
Laguardia, Spain 28 C2
Laguépie, France 26 D5
Laguna, Brazil 127 B6
Laguna, U.S.A. 111 J10
Laguna Beach, U.S.A. .. 113 M9
Laguna de la Janda, Spain 31 J5
Laguna Limpia, Argentina 126 B4
Laguna Madre, U.S.A. .. 115 B5
Lagunas, Chile 126 A2
Lagunas, Peru 124 B2
Lagunillas, Bolivia 125 D5
Lahad Datu, Malaysia .. 57 C5
Lahan Sai, Thailand ... 58 E4
Lahanam, Laos 58 D5
Laharpur, India 63 F9
Lahat, Indonesia 56 E2
Lahewa, Indonesia 56 D1
Lahiang Lahiang, Phil. .. 55 H4
Lahijan, Iran 65 B6
Lahn →, Germany 19 E3
Laholm, Sweden 11 H7
Laholmsbukten, Sweden . 11 H6
Lahontan Reservoir,
  U.S.A. 110 G4
Lahore, Pakistan 62 D6
Lahr, Germany 19 G3
Lahti, Finland 9 F18
Lahtis = Lahti, Finland .. 9 F18
Laï, Chad 73 G8
Lai Chau, Vietnam 58 A4
Lai'an, China 53 A12
Laibin, China 52 F7
Laidley, Australia 91 D5
Laifeng, China 52 C7
L'Aigle, France 24 D7
Laignes, France 25 E11
L'Aiguillon-sur-Mer, France 26 B2
Laikipia □, Kenya 82 B4
Laingsburg, S. Africa ... 84 E3
Lairg, U.K. 14 C4
Laishui, China 50 E8
Laiwu, China 51 F9
Laixi, China 51 F11
Laiyang, China 51 F11
Laiyuan, China 50 E8
Laizhou Wan, China ... 51 F10
Laja →, Mexico 114 C4
Lajere, Nigeria 79 C7
Lajes, Rio Grande do N.,
  Brazil 122 C4
Lajes, Sta. Catarina, Brazil 127 B5
Lajinha, Brazil 123 F3
Lajkovac, Serbia, Yug. .. 21 L10
Lajosmizse, Hungary ... 21 H9
Lak Sao, Laos 58 C5
Lakaband, Pakistan 62 D3
Lakar, Indonesia 57 F7
Lake Alpine, U.S.A. ... 112 G7
Lake Andes, U.S.A. 108 D5
Lake Anse, U.S.A. 104 B1
Lake Arthur, U.S.A. ... 109 K8
Lake Cargelligo, Australia 91 E4
Lake Charles, U.S.A. ... 109 K8
Lake City, Colo., U.S.A. 111 G10
Lake City, Fla., U.S.A. .. 105 K4
Lake City, Iowa, U.S.A. . 108 D7
Lake City, Mich., U.S.A. 104 C3
Lake City, Minn., U.S.A. 108 C8
Lake City, Pa., U.S.A. .. 106 D4
Lake City, S.C., U.S.A. . 105 J6
Lake George, U.S.A. ... 107 C11
Lake Grace, Australia .. 89 F2
Lake Harbour, Canada . 97 B13
Lake Havasu City, U.S.A. 113 L12
Lake Hughes, U.S.A. ... 113 L8
Lake Isabella, U.S.A. .. 113 K8
Lake King, Australia ... 89 F2
Lake Lenore, Canada ... 101 C8
Lake Louise, Canada ... 100 C5
Lake Mead National
  Recreation Area, U.S.A. 113 K12
Lake Mills, U.S.A. 108 D8
Lake Nash, Australia ... 90 C2
Lake Providence, U.S.A. 109 J9
Lake River, Canada 98 B3

Lake Superior Prov. Park,
  Canada 98 C3
Lake Village, U.S.A. ... 109 J9
Lake Wales, U.S.A. 105 M5
Lake Worth, U.S.A. 105 M5
Lakefield, Canada 98 D4
Lakeland, Australia 90 B3
Lakeland, U.S.A. 105 L5
Lakemba, Fiji 87 D9
Lakeport, U.S.A. 112 F4
Lakes Entrance, Australia 91 F4
Lakeside, Ariz., U.S.A. . 111 J9
Lakeside, Calif., U.S.A. . 113 N10
Lakeside, Nebr., U.S.A. . 108 D3
Lakeview, U.S.A. 110 E3
Lakewood, Colo., U.S.A. 108 F2
Lakewood, N.J., U.S.A. . 107 F10
Lakewood, Ohio, U.S.A. 106 E3
Lakewood Center, U.S.A. 112 C4
Lakhaniá, Greece 37 D9
Lakhonpheng, Laos 58 E5
Lakhpat, India 62 H3
Laki, Iceland 8 D4
Lakin, U.S.A. 109 G4
Lakitusaki →, Canada .. 98 B3
Lákkoi, Greece 37 D5
Lakonikós Kólpos, Greece 39 N5
Lakota, Ivory C. 78 D3
Lakota, U.S.A. 108 A5
Laksefjorden, Norway .. 8 A19
Lakselv, Norway 8 A18
Lakshadweep Is., Ind. Oc. 46 J11
Lakshmikantapur, India . 63 H13
Lala Ghat, India 61 G18
Lala Musa, Pakistan ... 62 C5
Lalago, Tanzania 82 C3
Lalapanzi, Zimbabwe .. 83 F3
Lalganj, India 63 G11
Lalibela, Ethiopia 77 E4
Lalin, China 51 B14
Lalín, Spain 30 C2
Lalin He →, China 51 B13
Lalinde, France 26 D4
Lalitapur = Patan, Nepal . 61 F14
Lalitpur, India 63 G8
Lam, Vietnam 58 B6
Lam Pao Res., Thailand . 58 D4
Lama Kara, Togo 79 D5
Lamaing, Burma 61 M20
Lamar, Colo., U.S.A. .. 108 F3
Lamar, Mo., U.S.A. ... 109 G7
Lamarque, Argentina ... 128 A3
Lamas, Peru 124 B2
Lamastre, France 27 D8
Lamballe, France 24 D4
Lambaréné, Gabon 80 E2
Lambasa, Fiji 87 C8
Lambay I., Ireland 15 C5
Lambayeque □, Peru ... 124 B2
Lambert, U.S.A. 108 B2
Lambert Glacier, Antarctica 5 D6
Lamberts Bay, S. Africa . 84 E2
Lambesc, France 27 E9
Lámbia, Greece 39 M4
Lambro →, Italy 32 C6
Lame, Nigeria 79 C6
Lame Deer, U.S.A. 110 D10
Lamego, Portugal 30 D3
Lamèque, Canada 99 C7
Lameroo, Australia 91 F3
Lamesa, U.S.A. 109 J4
Lamía, Greece 39 L5
Lamitan, Phil. 55 H5
Lammermuir Hills, U.K. . 14 F6
Lamon Bay, Phil. 55 D5
Lamont, Canada 100 C6
Lamont, U.S.A. 113 K8
Lampa, Peru 124 D3
Lampang, Thailand 58 C2
Lampasas, U.S.A. 109 K5
Lampaul, France 24 D1
Lampazos de Naranjo,
  Mexico 114 B4
Lampedusa, Medit. S. .. 75 A7
Lampeter, U.K. 13 E3
Lampione, Medit. S. ... 75 A7
Lampman, Canada 101 D8
Lampung □, Indonesia . 56 F2
Lamprey, Canada 101 B10
Lamu, Kenya 82 C5
Lamu □, Kenya 82 C5
Lamud, Peru 124 B2
Lamy, U.S.A. 111 J11
Lan Xian, China 50 E6
Lan Yu, Taiwan 53 F13
Lanai I., U.S.A. 102 H16
Lanak La, India 63 B8
Lanak'o Shank'ou = Lanak
  La, India 63 B8
Lanao, L., Phil. 55 H6
Lanark, Canada 107 A8
Lanark, U.K. 14 F5
Lancang, China 52 F2
Lancang Jiang →, China 52 G3
Lancashire □, U.K. 12 D5
Lancaster, Canada 107 A10
Lancaster, U.K. 12 C5
Lancaster, Calif., U.S.A. 113 L8
Lancaster, Ky., U.S.A. . 104 G3
Lancaster, N.H., U.S.A. 107 B13
Lancaster, N.Y., U.S.A. 106 D6
Lancaster, Pa., U.S.A. . 107 F8
Lancaster, S.C., U.S.A. . 105 H5
Lancaster, Wis., U.S.A. 108 D9
Lancaster Sd., Canada .. 97 A11

Lancer, Canada 101 C7
Lanchow = Lanzhou,
  China 50 F2
Lanciano, Italy 33 F11
Lanco, Chile 128 A2
Lancones, Peru 124 A1
Lancun, China 51 F11
Lancy, Switz. 22 D2
Landau, Bayern, Germany 19 G8
Landau, Rhld-Pfz.,
  Germany 19 F4
Landeck, Austria 19 H6
Landen, Belgium 17 G6
Lander, U.S.A. 110 E9
Lander →, Australia ... 88 D5
Landerneau, France ... 24 D2
Landeryd, Sweden 11 G7
Landes, France 26 D3
Landes □, France 26 E3
Landete, Spain 28 F3
Landi Kotal, Pakistan .. 62 B4
Landivisiau, France ... 24 D2
Landor, Australia 89 E2
Landquart, Switz. 23 C9
Landquart →, Switz. .. 23 C9
Landrecies, France 25 B10
Land's End, U.K. 13 G2
Landsberg, Germany ... 19 G6
Landsborough Cr. →,
  Australia 90 C3
Landshut, Germany ... 19 G8
Landskrona, Sweden .. 11 J6
Landstuhl, Germany ... 19 F3
Landvetter, Sweden ... 11 G6
Laneffe, Belgium 17 H5
Lanesboro, U.S.A. 107 E9
Lanett, U.S.A. 105 J3
Lang Bay, Canada 100 D4
Lang Qua, Vietnam ... 58 A5
Lang Shan, China 50 D4
Lang Son, Vietnam ... 58 B6
Lang Suan, Thailand .. 59 H2
La'nga Co, China 61 D12
Lángadhás, Greece 39 J6
Langádhia, Greece 39 M5
Långan →, Sweden ... 10 A8
Langar, Iran 65 C9
Langara I., Canada 100 C2
Langatabbetje, Surinam . 121 C7
Langdai, China 52 D5
Langdon, U.S.A. 108 A5
Langdorp, Belgium ... 17 G5
Langeac, France 26 C7
Langeais, France 24 E7
Langeb Baraka →, Sudan 76 D4
Langeberg, S. Africa ... 84 E3
Langeberge, S. Africa .. 84 D3
Langeland, Denmark .. 11 K4
Langemark, Belgium .. 17 G1
Langen, Germany 19 F4
Langenburg, Canada ... 101 C8
Langeness, Germany .. 18 A4
Langenthal, Switz. 22 B5
Langeoog, Germany ... 18 B3
Langeskov, Denmark .. 11 J4
Langesund, Norway ... 10 F3
Länghem, Sweden 11 G7
Langhirano, Italy 32 D7
Langholm, U.K. 14 F6
Langhus, Norway 10 E4
Langjökull, Iceland ... 8 D3
Langkawi, P., Malaysia . 59 J2
Langklip, S. Africa 84 D3
Langkon, Malaysia 56 C5
Langlade, St- P. & M. .. 99 C8
Langlois, U.S.A. 110 E1
Langnau, Switz. 22 C5
Langogne, France 26 D7
Langon, France 26 D3
Langøya, Norway 8 B13
Langres, France 25 E12
Langres, Plateau de, France 25 E12
Langsa, Indonesia 56 D1
Långsele, Sweden 10 A11
Langtry, U.S.A. 109 L4
Langu, Thailand 59 J2
Languedoc, France 26 E7
Langwies, Switz. 23 C9
Langxi, China 53 B12
Langxiangzhen, China . 50 E9
Langzhong, China 52 B5
Lanigan, Canada 101 C7
Lankao, China 50 G8
Lannemezan, France .. 26 E4
Lannilis, France 24 D2
Lannion, France 24 D3
L'Annonciation, Canada . 98 C5
Lanouaille, France 26 C5
Lanping, China 52 D2
Lansdale, U.S.A. 107 F9
Lansdowne, Australia .. 91 E5
Lansdowne, Canada ... 107 B8
Lansdowne House, Canada 98 B2
L'Anse, U.S.A. 98 C2
L'Anse au Loup, Canada 99 B8
Lansford, U.S.A. 107 F9
Lanshan, China 53 E9
Lansing, U.S.A. 104 D3
Lanslebourg-Mont-Cenis,
  France 27 C10
Lanta Yai, Ko, Thailand . 59 J2
Lantian, China 50 G5
Lanus, Argentina 126 C4
Lanusei, Italy 34 C2

Lanuza, Phil. 55 G7
Lanxi, China 53 C12
Lanzarote, Canary Is. .. 36 E6
Lanzhou, China 50 F2
Lanzo Torinese, Italy ... 32 C4
Lao →, Italy 35 C8
Lao Bao, Laos 58 D6
Lao Cai, Vietnam 58 A4
Laoag, Phil. 55 B4
Laoang, Phil. 55 E6
Laoha He →, China ... 51 C11
Laois □, Ireland 15 D4
Laon, France 25 C10
Laona, U.S.A. 104 C1
Laos ■, Asia 58 D5
Lapa, Brazil 127 B6
Lapalisse, France 26 B7
Laparan, Phil. 57 C6
Lapeer, U.S.A. 104 D4
Lapi □ = Lapin lääni □,
  Finland 8 C19
Lapin lääni □, Finland ... 8 C19
Lapithos, Cyprus 37 D12
Lapland = Lappland,
  Europe 8 B18
Laporte, U.S.A. 107 E8
Lapovo, Serbia, Yug. ... 21 L11
Lappland, Europe 8 B18
Laprida, Argentina 126 D3
Laptev Sea, Russia 45 B13
Lăpuşul →, Romania .. 38 B6
L'Aquila, Italy 33 F10
Lār, Āzarbājān-e Sharqī,
  Iran 64 B5
Lār, Fārs, Iran 65 E7
Lara □, Venezuela 120 A4
Larabanga, Ghana 78 D4
Laracha, Spain 30 B2
Larache, Morocco 74 A3
Laragne-Montéglin, France 27 D9
Laramie, U.S.A. 108 E2
Laramie Mts., U.S.A. .. 108 E2
Laranjeiras, Brazil 122 D4
Laranjeiras do Sul, Brazil 127 B5
Larantuka, Indonesia .. 57 F6
Larap, Phil. 55 D5
Larat, Indonesia 57 F8
L'Arbresle, France 27 C8
Larde, Mozam. 83 F4
Larder Lake, Canada ... 98 C4
Lardhos, Ákra, Greece . 37 C10
Lardhos, Órmos, Greece 37 C10
Laredo, Spain 28 B1
Laredo, U.S.A. 109 M5
Laredo Sd., Canada ... 100 C3
Laren, Neths. 16 D6
Largentière, France ... 27 D8
L'Argentière-la-Bessée,
  France 27 D10
Largs, U.K. 14 F4
Lari, Italy 32 E7
Lariang, Indonesia 57 E5
Larimore, U.S.A. 108 B6
Lārīn, Iran 65 C7
Larino, Italy 35 A7
Lárisa, Greece 39 K5
Larkana, Pakistan 62 F3
Larnaca, Cyprus 37 E12
Larnaca Bay, Cyprus .. 37 E12
Larne, U.K. 15 B6
Larned, U.S.A. 108 F5
Larochette, Belgium ... 17 J8
Laroquebrou, France .. 26 D6
Larrimah, Australia ... 88 C5
Larsen Ice Shelf, Antarctica 5 C17
Larvik, Norway 10 E4
Laryak, Russia 44 C8
Larzac, Causse du, France 26 E7
Las Alpujarras, Spain .. 29 J1
Las Animas, U.S.A. ... 108 F3
Las Anod, Somali Rep. . 68 F4
Las Blancos, Spain 29 H4
Las Brenãs, Argentina .. 126 B3
Las Cabezas de San Juan,
  Spain 31 J5
Las Chimeneas, Mexico 113 N10
Las Coloradas, Argentina 128 A2
Las Cruces, U.S.A. 111 K10
Las Flores, Argentina .. 126 D4
Las Heras, Argentina .. 126 C2
Las Horquetas, Argentina 128 C2
Las Khoreh, Somali Rep. 68 E4
Las Lajas, Argentina ... 128 A2
Las Lomas, Peru 124 A1
Las Lomitas, Argentina . 126 A3
Las Marismas, Spain ... 31 H4
Las Mercedes, Venezuela 120 B4
Las Navas de la
  Concepción, Spain ... 31 H5
Las Navas de Tolosa, Spain 31 G7
Las Navas del Marqués,
  Spain 30 E6
Las Palmas, Argentina .. 126 B4
Las Palmas, Canary Is. . 36 F4
Las Palmas →, Mexico 113 N10
Las Piedras, Uruguay .. 127 C4
Las Pipinas, Argentina . 126 D4
Las Plumas, Argentina . 128 B3
Las Rosas, Argentina .. 126 C3
Las Tablas, Panama ... 116 E3
Las Termas, Argentina . 126 B3
Las Truchas, Mexico .. 114 D4
Las Varillas, Argentina . 126 C3
Las Vegas, N. Mex.,
  U.S.A. 111 J11

175

Las Vegas, *Nev., U.S.A.* . 113 J11
Lascano, *Uruguay* 127 C5
Lashburn, *Canada* 101 C7
Lashio, *Burma* 61 H20
Lashkar, *India* 62 F8
Łasin, *Poland* 20 B9
Lasíthi, *Greece* 37 D7
Lasíthi □, *Greece* 37 D7
Laško, *Slovenia* 33 B12
Lassance, *Brazil* 123 E3
Lassay, *France* 24 D6
Lassen Pk., *U.S.A.* 110 F3
Last Mountain L., *Canada* 101 C7
Lastchance Cr. →, *U.S.A.* 112 E5
Lastoursville, *Gabon* ... 80 E2
Lastovo, *Croatia* 33 F13
Lastovski Kanal, *Croatia* . 33 F13
Lat Yao, *Thailand* 58 E2
Latacunga, *Ecuador* 120 D2
Latakia = Al Lādhiqīyah,
  Syria 64 C2
Latchford, *Canada* 98 C4
Laterza, *Italy* 35 B9
Latham, *Australia* 89 E2
Lathen, *Germany* 18 C3
Lathrop Wells, *U.S.A.* ... 113 J10
Latiano, *Italy* 35 B10
Latina, *Italy* 34 A5
Latisana, *Italy* 33 C10
Latium = Lazio □, *Italy* . 33 F9
Laton, *U.S.A.* 112 J7
Latorica →, *Slovakia* ... 21 G11
Latouche Treville, C.,
  Australia 88 C3
Latrobe, *Australia* 90 G4
Latrobe, *U.S.A.* 106 F5
Latrónico, *Italy* 35 B9
Latvia ■, *Europe* 40 C3
Lau Group, *Fiji* 87 C9
Lauca →, *Bolivia* 124 D4
Lauchhammer, *Germany* .. 18 D9
Lauenburg, *Germany* ... 18 B6
Läufelfingen, *Switz.* ... 22 B5
Laufen, *Switz.* 22 B5
Lauffen, *Germany* 19 F5
Laugarbakki, *Iceland* ... 8 D3
Launceston, *Australia* .. 90 G4
Launceston, *U.K.* 13 G3
Laune →, *Ireland* 15 D2
Laupheim, *Germany* ... 19 G5
Laura, *Australia* 90 B3
Laureana di Borrello, *Italy* 35 D9
Laurel, *Miss., U.S.A.* ... 109 K10
Laurel, *Mont., U.S.A.* ... 110 D9
Laurencekirk, *U.K.* 14 E6
Laurens, *U.S.A.* 105 H4
Laurentian Plateau, *Canada* 99 B6
Laurentides, Parc Prov.
  des, *Canada* 99 C5
Lauria, *Italy* 35 B8
Laurie L., *Canada* 101 B8
Laurinburg, *U.S.A.* 105 H6
Laurium, *U.S.A.* 104 B1
Lausanne, *Switz.* 22 C3
Laut, *Indonesia* 56 D3
Laut Ketil, Kepulauan,
  Indonesia 56 E5
Lautaro, *Chile* 128 A2
Lauterbach, *Germany* ... 18 E5
Lauterbrunnen, *Switz.* .. 22 C5
Lauterecken, *Germany* .. 19 F3
Lautoka, *Fiji* 87 C7
Lauwe, *Belgium* 17 G2
Lauwers, *Neths.* 16 A8
Lauwers Zee, *Neths.* ... 16 B8
Lauzon, *Canada* 99 C5
Lava Hot Springs, *U.S.A.* 110 E7
Lavadores, *Spain* 30 C2
Lavagna, *Italy* 32 D6
Laval, *France* 24 D6
Lavalle, *Argentina* ... 126 B2
Lávara, *Greece* 39 H9
Lavardac, *France* 26 D4
Lavaur, *France* 26 E5
Lavaux, *Switz.* 22 D3
Lavelanet, *France* 26 F5
Lavello, *Italy* 35 A8
Laverne, *U.S.A.* 109 G5
Laverton, *Australia* ... 89 E3
Lavos, *Portugal* 30 E2
Lavras, *Brazil* 123 F3
Lavre, *Portugal* 31 G2
Lavrentiya, *Russia* ... 45 C19
Lávrion, *Greece* 39 M7
Lávris, *Greece* 37 D6
Lavumisa, *Swaziland* .. 85 D5
Lawas, *Malaysia* 56 D5
Lawele, *Indonesia* 57 F6
Lawn Hill, *Australia* .. 90 B2
Lawng Pit, *Burma* 61 G20
Lawqar, *Si. Arabia* ... 64 D4
Lawra, *Ghana* 78 C4
Lawrence, *N.Z.* 87 L2
Lawrence, *Kans., U.S.A.* . 108 F7
Lawrence, *Mass., U.S.A.* . 107 D13
Lawrenceburg, *Ind.,*
  U.S.A. 104 F3
Lawrenceburg, *Tenn.,*
  U.S.A. 105 H2
Lawrenceville, *U.S.A.* .. 105 J4
Laws, *U.S.A.* 112 H8
Lawton, *U.S.A.* 109 H5
Ławy, *Indonesia* 57 G14
Laxford, L., *U.K.* 14 C3

Laylān, *Iraq* 64 C5
Layon →, *France* 24 E6
Laysan I., *Pac. Oc.* ... 93 E11
Laytonville, *U.S.A.* ... 110 G2
Lazio □, *Italy* 33 F9
Lazo, *Russia* 48 C6
Le Barcarès, *France* .. 26 F7
Le Beausset, *France* .. 27 E9
Le Blanc, *France* 26 B5
Le Bleymard, *France* .. 26 D7
Le Bourgneuf-la-Fôret,
  France 24 D6
Le Bouscat, *France* ... 26 D3
Le Brassus, *Switz.* ... 22 C2
Le Bugue, *France* 26 D4
Le Canourgue, *France* . 26 D7
Le Cateau, *France* ... 25 B10
Le Chambon-Feugerolles,
  France 27 C8
Le Château-d'Oléron,
  France 26 C2
Le Châtelard, *Switz.* .. 22 D3
Le Châtelet, *France* .. 26 B6
Le Châtelet-en-Brie, *France* 25 D9
Le Chesne, *France* ... 25 C11
Le Cheylard, *France* .. 27 D8
Le Conquet, *France* .. 24 D2
Le Creusot, *France* .. 25 F11
Le Croisic, *France* ... 24 E4
Le Donjon, *France* ... 26 B7
Le Dorat, *France* 26 B5
Le François, *Martinique* . 117 D7
Le Grand-Lucé, *France* . 24 E7
Le Grand-Pressigny, *France* 24 F7
Le Havre, *France* 24 C7
Le Lavandou, *France* .. 27 E10
Le Lion-d'Angers, *France* 24 E6
Le Luc, *France* 27 E10
Le Madonie, *Italy* ... 34 E6
Le Maire, Est. de,
  Argentina 128 D4
Le Mans, *France* 24 E7
Le Marinel, *Zaïre* ... 83 E2
Le Mars, *U.S.A.* 108 D6
Le Mêle-sur-Sarthe, *France* 24 D7
Le Merlerault, *France* . 24 D7
Le Monastier-sur-Gazeille,
  France 26 D7
Le Monêtier-les-Bains,
  France 27 D10
Le Mont d'Or, *France* . 25 F13
Le Mont-Dore, *France* . 26 C6
Le Mont-St.-Michel, *France* 24 D5
Le Moule, *Guadeloupe* . 117 C7
Le Muy, *France* 27 E10
Le Palais, *France* 24 E3
Le Perthus, *France* .. 26 F6
Le Pont, *Switz.* 22 C2
Le Pouldu, *France* ... 24 E3
Le Puy, *France* 26 C7
Le Quesnoy, *France* .. 25 B10
Le Roy, *U.S.A.* 109 F7
Le Sentier, *Switz.* ... 22 C2
Le Sueur, *U.S.A.* 108 C8
Le Teil, *France* 27 D8
Le Teilleul, *France* .. 24 D6
Le Theil, *France* 24 D7
Le Thillot, *France* ... 25 E13
Le Thuy, *Vietnam* ... 58 D6
Le Touquet-Paris-Plage,
  France 25 B8
Le Tréport, *France* ... 24 B8
Le Val-d'Ajol, *France* . 25 E13
Le Verdon-sur-Mer, *France* 26 C2
Le Vigan, *France* 26 E7
Lea →, *U.K.* 13 F7
Leach, *Cambodia* 59 F4
Lead, *U.S.A.* 108 C3
Leader, *Canada* 101 C7
Leadhills, *U.K.* 14 F5
Leadville, *U.S.A.* 111 G10
Leaf →, *U.S.A.* 109 K10
Leakey, *U.S.A.* 109 L5
Leamington, *Canada* .. 98 D3
Leamington, *U.S.A.* .. 110 G7
Leamington Spa = Royal
  Leamington Spa, *U.K.* . 13 E6
Le'an, *China* 53 D10
Leandro Norte Alem,
  Argentina 127 B4
Learmonth, *Australia* . 88 D1
Leask, *Canada* 101 C7
Leavenworth, *Kans.,*
  U.S.A. 108 F7
Leavenworth, *Wash.,*
  U.S.A. 110 C3
Łeba, *Poland* 20 A7
Lebak, *Phil.* 55 H6
Lebam, *U.S.A.* 112 D3
Lebanon, *Ind., U.S.A.* . 104 E2
Lebanon, *Kans., U.S.A.* . 108 F5
Lebanon, *Ky., U.S.A.* .. 104 G3
Lebanon, *Mo., U.S.A.* . 109 G8
Lebanon, *Oreg., U.S.A.* . 110 D2
Lebanon, *Pa., U.S.A.* .. 107 F8
Lebanon, *Tenn., U.S.A.* . 105 G2
Lebanon ■, *Asia* 69 B4
Lebbeke, *Belgium* ... 17 G4
Lebec, *U.S.A.* 113 L8
Lebedin, *Ukraine* ... 40 F9
Lebedyan, *Russia* ... 41 E11
Lebomboberge, *S. Africa* . 85 C5

Lębork, *Poland* 20 A7
Lebrija, *Spain* 31 J4
Lebu, *Chile* 126 D1
Lecce, *Italy* 35 B11
Lecco, *Italy* 32 C6
Lecco, L. di, *Italy* ... 32 C6
Lécera, *Spain* 28 D4
Lech, *Austria* 19 H6
Lech →, *Germany* ... 19 G6
Lechang, *China* 53 E9
Lechtaler Alpen, *Austria* . 19 H6
Lectoure, *France* 26 E4
Łęczyca, *Poland* 20 C9
Ledbury, *U.K.* 13 E5
Lede, *Belgium* 17 G3
Ledeberg, *Belgium* ... 17 F3
Ledesma, *Spain* 30 D5
Ledong, *China* 58 C7
Leduc, *Canada* 100 C6
Ledyczek, *Poland* ... 20 B6
Lee, *U.S.A.* 107 D11
Lee →, *Ireland* 15 E3
Lee Vining, *U.S.A.* ... 112 H7
Leech L., *U.S.A.* 108 B7
Leedey, *U.S.A.* 109 H5
Leeds, *U.K.* 12 D6
Leeds, *U.S.A.* 105 J2
Leek, *Neths.* 16 B8
Leek, *U.K.* 12 D5
Leende, *Neths.* 17 F7
Leer, *Germany* 18 B3
Leerdam, *Neths.* 16 E6
Leersum, *Neths.* 16 E6
Leesburg, *U.S.A.* 105 L5
Leesville, *U.S.A.* 109 K8
Leeton, *Australia* ... 91 E4
Leetonia, *U.S.A.* 106 F4
Leeu Gamka, *S. Africa* . 84 E3
Leeuwarden, *Neths.* .. 16 B7
Leeuwin, C., *Australia* . 89 F2
Leeward Is., *Atl. Oc.* . 117 C7
Lefka, *Cyprus* 37 D11
Lefkoniko, *Cyprus* ... 37 D12
Lefors, *U.S.A.* 109 H4
Lefroy, L., *Australia* .. 89 F3
Legal, *Canada* 100 C6
Leganés, *Spain* 30 E7
Legazpi, *Phil.* 55 E5
Legendre I., *Australia* . 88 D2
Leghorn = Livorno, *Italy* . 32 E7
Legionowo, *Poland* ... 20 C10
Léglise, *Belgium* 17 J7
Legnago, *Italy* 33 C8
Legnano, *Italy* 32 C5
Legnica, *Poland* 20 D6
Legrad, *Croatia* 33 B13
Legume, *Australia* ... 91 D5
Leh, *India* 63 B7
Lehi, *U.S.A.* 110 F8
Lehighton, *U.S.A.* ... 107 F9
Lehrte, *Germany* ... 18 C5
Lehututu, *Botswana* .. 84 C3
Lei Shui →, *China* .. 53 D9
Leiah, *Pakistan* 62 D4
Leibnitz, *Austria* ... 21 J5
Leibo, *China* 52 C4
Leicester, *U.K.* 13 E6
Leicestershire □, *U.K.* . 13 E6
Leichhardt →, *Australia* 90 B2
Leichhardt Ra., *Australia* . 90 C4
Leiden, *Neths.* 16 D5
Leiderdorp, *Neths.* .. 16 D5
Leidschendam, *Neths.* . 16 D4
Leie →, *Belgium* ... 25 A10
Leignon, *Belgium* ... 17 H6
Leine →, *Germany* .. 18 C5
Leinster, *Australia* .. 89 E3
Leinster □, *Ireland* .. 15 C4
Leinster, Mt., *Ireland* . 15 D5
Leipzig, *Germany* ... 18 D8
Leiria, *Portugal* 31 F2
Leiria □, *Portugal* ... 31 F2
Leisler, Mt., *Australia* . 88 D4
Leith, *U.K.* 14 F5
Leith Hill, *U.K.* 13 F7
Leitha →, *Europe* ... 21 H7
Leitrim, *Ireland* 15 B3
Leitrim □, *Ireland* ... 15 B3
Leiyang, *China* 53 D9
Leiza, *Spain* 28 B3
Leizhou Bandao, *China* . 54 D6
Leizhou Wan, *China* .. 53 G8
Lek →, *Neths.* 16 E5
Leke, *Belgium* 17 F1
Lekkerkerk, *Neths.* .. 16 E5
Leksula, *Indonesia* .. 57 E7
Leland, *U.S.A.* 109 J9
Leland Lakes, *Canada* . 101 A6
Leleque, *Argentina* .. 128 E3
Lelystad, *Neths.* 16 D6
Lema, *Nigeria* 79 C5
Léman, Lac, *Switz.* .. 22 D3
Lemelerveld, *Neths.* .. 16 D8
Lemera, *Zaïre* 82 C2
Lemery, *Phil.* 55 E4
Lemgo, *Germany* ... 18 C4
Lemhi Ra., *U.S.A.* ... 110 D7
Lemmer, *Neths.* 16 C7
Lemmon, *U.S.A.* 108 C3
Lemon Grove, *U.S.A.* . 113 N9
Lemoore, *U.S.A.* 111 H4
Lempdes, *France* 26 C7
Lemsid, *W. Sahara* .. 74 C2
Lemvig, *Denmark* ... 11 H2
Lena →, *Russia* 45 B13

Lencloître, *France* 24 F7
Lençóis, *Brazil* 123 D3
Léndas, *Greece* 37 E6
Lendeh, *Iran* 65 D6
Lendelede, *Belgium* ... 17 G2
Lendinara, *Italy* 33 C8
Lengerich, *Germany* .. 18 C3
Lenggong, *Malaysia* .. 59 K3
Lenggries, *Germany* .. 19 H7
Lengua de Vaca, Pta.,
  Chile 126 C1
Lenin, *Russia* 43 B9
Leninabad = Khodzent,
  Tajikistan 44 E7
Leninakan = Kumayri,
  Armenia 43 F10
Leningrad = Sankt-
  Peterburg, *Russia* ... 40 B7
Lenino, *Ukraine* 42 D6
Leninogorsk = Ridder,
  Kazakhstan 44 D9
Leninsk, *Russia* 43 B11
Leninsk, *Russia* 43 C10
Leninsk-Kuznetskiy, *Russia* 44 D9
Leninskaya Sloboda, *Russia* 41 C14
Leninskoye, *Russia* ... 41 B15
Leninskoye, *Russia* ... 45 E14
Lenk, *Switz.* 22 D4
Lenkoran, *Azerbaijan* . 67 D13
Lenmalu, *Indonesia* .. 57 E8
Lenne →, *Germany* .. 18 D3
Lennox, I., *Chile* 128 E3
Lennoxville, *Canada* .. 107 A13
Leno, *Italy* 32 C7
Lenoir, *U.S.A.* 105 H5
Lenoir City, *U.S.A.* ... 105 H3
Lenora, *U.S.A.* 108 F4
Lenore L., *Canada* ... 101 C8
Lenox, *U.S.A.* 107 D11
Lens, *Belgium* 17 G3
Lens, *France* 25 B9
Lens St. Remy, *Belgium* . 17 G6
Lensk, *Russia* 45 C12
Lenskoye, *Ukraine* ... 42 D6
Lent, *Neths.* 16 E7
Lentini, *Italy* 35 E8
Lentvaric, *Lithuania* .. 40 D4
Lenwood, *U.S.A.* 113 L9
Lenzburg, *Switz.* 22 B6
Lenzen, *Germany* ... 18 B7
Lenzerheide, *Switz.* .. 23 C9
Léo, *Burkina Faso* ... 78 C4
Leoben, *Austria* 21 H5
Leola, *U.S.A.* 108 C5
Leominster, *U.K.* 13 E5
Leominster, *U.S.A.* ... 107 D13
Léon, *France* 26 E2
León, *Mexico* 114 C4
León, *Nic.* 116 D2
León, *Spain* 30 C5
León □, *Spain* 30 C5
León, Montañas de, *Spain* 30 C4
Leonardtown, *U.S.A.* . 104 F7
Leone, Mte., *Switz.* .. 22 D6
Leonforte, *Italy* 35 E7
Leongatha, *Australia* . 91 F4
Leonídhion, *Greece* .. 39 M5
Leonora, *Australia* .. 89 E3
Léopold II, Lac = Mai-
  Ndombe, L., *Zaïre* .. 80 E3
Leopoldina, *Brazil* ... 123 F3
Leopoldo Bulhões, *Brazil* . 123 E2
Leopoldsburg, *Belgium* . 17 F6
Léopoldville = Kinshasa,
  Zaïre 80 E3
Leoti, *U.S.A.* 108 F4
Leoville, *Canada* 101 C7
Lépa, L. do, *Angola* .. 84 B2
Lepe, *Spain* 31 H3
Lepel, *Belorussia* ... 40 D6
Lepikha, *Russia* 45 C13
Leping, *China* 53 C11
Lepontine, Alpi, *Italy* . 23 D6
Lequeitio, *Spain* 28 B2
Lercara Friddi, *Italy* .. 34 E6
Lerdo, *Mexico* 114 B4
Léré, *Chad* 73 G7
Lere, *Nigeria* 79 D6
Leribe, *Lesotho* 85 D4
Lérici, *Italy* 32 D6
Lérida, *Spain* 28 D5
Lérida □, *Spain* 28 C6
Lérins, Is. de, *France* . 27 E11
Lerma, *Spain* 30 C7
Léros, *Greece* 39 M9
Lérouville, *France* .. 25 D12
Lerwick, *U.K.* 14 A7
Les Abrets, *France* .. 27 C9
Les Andelys, *France* . 24 C8
Les Arcs, *France* ... 27 E10
Les Baux-de-Provence,
  France 27 E8
Les Bois, *Switz.* 22 B3
Les Cayes, *Haiti* 117 C5
Les Diablerets, *Switz.* . 22 D4
Les Échelles, *France* .. 27 C9
Les Essarts, *France* .. 24 F5
Les Étroits, *Canada* .. 99 C6
Les Eyzies-de-Tayac-
  Sireuil, *France* 26 D5
Les Herbiers, *France* . 24 F5
Les Minquiers, *Chan. Is.* . 24 D4
Les Ponts-de-Cé, *France* . 24 E6
Les Riceys, *France* ... 25 E11

Les Sables-d'Olonne,
  France 26 B2
Les Vans, *France* 27 D8
Les Verrières, *Switz.* .. 22 C2
Lesbos = Lésvos, *Greece* . 39 K9
Leshan, *China* 52 C4
Lésina, L. di, *Italy* ... 33 G12
Lesja, *Norway* 10 B2
Leskov I., *Antarctica* . 5 B1
Leskovac, *Serbia, Yug.* . 21 M11
Leslie, *U.S.A.* 109 H8
Lesneven, *France* ... 24 D2
Lešnica, *Serbia, Yug.* . 21 L9
Lesnoye, *Russia* 40 B9
Lesopilnoye, *Russia* .. 48 A7
Lesotho ■, *Africa* ... 85 D4
Lesozavodsk, *Russia* .. 45 E14
Lesparre-Médoc, *France* . 26 C3
Lessay, *France* 24 C5
Lesse →, *Belgium* ... 17 H5
Lesser Antilles, *W. Indies* . 117 C7
Lesser Slave L., *Canada* . 100 B5
Lesser Sunda Is., *Indonesia* 57 F6
Lessines, *Belgium* ... 17 G3
Lester, *U.S.A.* 112 C5
Lestock, *Canada* 101 C8
Lesuer I., *Australia* .. 88 B3
Lésvos, *Greece* 39 K9
Leszno, *Poland* 20 D6
Letchworth, *U.K.* 13 F7
Letea, Ostrov, *Romania* . 38 D12
Lethbridge, *Canada* .. 100 D6
Lethem, *Guyana* 121 C6
Leti, Kepulauan, *Indonesia* 57 F7
Leti Is. = Leti, Kepulauan,
  Indonesia 57 F7
Letiahau →, *Botswana* . 84 C3
Leticia, *Colombia* ... 120 D4
Leting, *China* 51 E10
Letjiesbos, *S. Africa* .. 84 E3
Letlhakeng, *Botswana* . 84 C3
Letpadan, *Burma* ... 61 L19
Letpan, *Burma* 61 K19
Letterkenny, *Ireland* . 15 B4
Leu, *Romania* 38 E7
Leucadia, *U.S.A.* 113 M9
Leucate, *France* 26 F7
Leucate, Étang de, *France* 26 F7
Leuk, *Switz.* 22 D5
Leukerbad, *Switz.* ... 22 D5
Leupegem, *Belgium* .. 17 G3
Leuser, G., *Indonesia* . 56 D1
Leutkirch, *Germany* .. 19 H6
Leuven, *Belgium* ... 17 G5
Leuze, *Hainaut, Belgium* 17 G3
Leuze, *Namur, Belgium* . 17 G5
Lev Tolstoy, *Russia* .. 41 E11
Levádhia, *Greece* ... 39 L5
Levan, *U.S.A.* 110 G8
Levanger, *Norway* ... 8 E11
Levant, I. du, *France* . 27 E10
Lévanto, *Italy* 32 D6
Levanzo, *Italy* 34 E5
Levelland, *U.S.A.* ... 109 J3
Leven, *U.K.* 14 E6
Leven, L., *U.K.* 14 E5
Leven, Toraka, *Madag.* . 85 A8
Levens, *France* 27 E11
Leveque C., *Australia* . 88 C3
Leverano, *Italy* 35 B10
Leverkusen, *Germany* . 18 D2
Levet, *France* 25 F9
Levice, *Slovakia* 21 G8
Levico, *Italy* 33 C8
Levie, *France* 27 G13
Levier, *France* 25 F13
Levin, *N.Z.* 87 J5
Lévis, *Canada* 99 C5
Levis, L., *Canada* ... 100 A5
Levítha, *Greece* 39 M9
Levittown, *N.Y., U.S.A.* . 107 F11
Levittown, *Pa., U.S.A.* . 107 F10
Lévka Óri, *Greece* ... 37 D6
Levkás, *Greece* 39 L3
Levkímmi, *Greece* ... 37 B4
Levkímmi, Ákra, *Greece* . 37 B4
Levkôsia = Nicosia, *Cyprus* 37 D12
Levoča, *Slovakia* 20 F10
Levroux, *France* 25 F8
Levski, *Bulgaria* 38 F8
Levskigrad, *Bulgaria* . 38 G7
Lewellen, *U.S.A.* 108 E3
Lewes, *U.K.* 13 G8
Lewes, *U.S.A.* 104 F8
Lewis, *U.K.* 14 C2
Lewis →, *U.S.A.* 112 E4
Lewis, Butt of, *U.K.* . 14 C2
Lewis Ra., *Australia* .. 88 D4
Lewis Range, *U.S.A.* . 110 C7
Lewisburg, *Pa., U.S.A.* . 106 F8
Lewisburg, *Tenn., U.S.A.* 105 H2
Lewisporte, *Canada* .. 99 C8
Lewiston, *Idaho, U.S.A.* . 110 C5
Lewiston, *Maine, U.S.A.* . 105 C11
Lewistown, *Mont., U.S.A.* 110 C9
Lewistown, *Pa., U.S.A.* . 106 F7
Lexington, *Ill., U.S.A.* . 108 E10
Lexington, *Ky., U.S.A.* . 104 F3
Lexington, *Miss., U.S.A.* . 109 J9
Lexington, *Mo., U.S.A.* . 108 F8
Lexington, *N.C., U.S.A.* . 105 H5
Lexington, *Nebr., U.S.A.* . 108 E5
Lexington, *Ohio, U.S.A.* . 106 F2
Lexington, *Oreg., U.S.A.* . 110 D4

Lexington, Tenn., U.S.A. . 105 H1
Lexington Park, U.S.A. . . 104 F7
Leye, China 52 E6
Leyre →, France 26 D2
Leysin, Switz. 22 D4
Leyte, Phil. 55 F6
Leyte Gulf, Phil. 55 F6
Lezay, France 26 B4
Lezha, Albania 39 H2
Lezhi, China 52 B5
Lézignan-Corbières, France 26 E6
Lezoux, France 26 C7
Lgov, Russia 40 F9
Lhasa, China 54 D4
Lhazê, China 54 D3
Lhokkruet, Indonesia ... 56 C1
Lhokseumawe, Indonesia . 56 C1
Lhuntsi Dzong, India ... 61 F17
Li, Thailand 58 D2
Li Shui →, China 53 C9
Li Xian, Gansu, China .. 50 G3
Li Xian, Hebei, China .. 50 E8
Li Xian, Hunan, China ... 53 C8
Li Xian, Sichuan, China . 52 B4
Liádhoi, Greece 39 N9
Lian Xian, China 53 E9
Liancheng, China 53 E11
Lianga, Phil. 55 G7
Liangcheng,
  Nei Mongol Zizhiqu,
  China 50 D7
Liangcheng, Shandong,
  China 51 G10
Liangdang, China 50 H4
Lianghekou, China 52 C7
Liangping, China 52 B6
Lianhua, China 53 D9
Lianjiang, Fujian, China . 53 D12
Lianjiang, Guangdong,
  China 53 G8
Lianping, China 53 E10
Lianshan, China 53 E9
Lianshanguan, China ... 51 D12
Lianshui, China 51 H10
Lianyuan, China 53 D8
Lianyungang, China ... 51 G10
Liao He →, China 51 D11
Liaocheng, China 50 F8
Liaodong Bandao, China . 51 E12
Liaodong Wan, China .. 51 D11
Liaoning □, China 54 B7
Liaoning □, Liaoning,
  China 51 D12
Liaoyang, China 51 D12
Liaoyuan, China 51 C13
Liaozhong, China 51 D12
Liapádhes, Greece 39 K2
Liard →, Canada 100 A4
Liari, Pakistan 62 G2
Líbano, Colombia 120 C2
Libau = Liepāja, Latvia . 40 C2
Libby, U.S.A. 110 A6
Libenge, Zaïre 80 D3
Liberal, Kans., U.S.A. . 109 G4
Liberal, Mo., U.S.A. .. 109 G7
Liberec, Czech. 20 E5
Liberia, Costa Rica ... 116 D2
Liberia ■, W. Afr. 78 D3
Libertad, Venezuela ... 120 B4
Liberty, Mo., U.S.A. .. 108 F7
Liberty, Tex., U.S.A. .. 109 K7
Libin, Belgium 17 J6
Lîbîya, Sahrâ', Africa .. 73 C9
Libo, China 52 E6
Libobo, Tanjung, Indonesia 57 E7
Libode, S. Africa 85 E4
Libonda, Zambia 81 G4
Libourne, France 26 D3
Libramont, Belgium ... 17 J6
Libreville, Gabon 80 D1
Libya ■, N. Afr. 73 C8
Libyan Desert = Lîbîya,
  Sahrâ', Africa 73 C9
Libyan Plateau = Ed-
  Déffa, Egypt 76 A2
Licantén, Chile 126 D1
Licata, Italy 34 E6
Lice, Turkey 67 D9
Licheng, China 50 F7
Lichfield, U.K. 12 E6
Lichinga, Mozam. 83 E4
Lichtaart, Belgium ... 17 F5
Lichtenburg, S. Africa .. 84 D4
Lichtenfels, Germany .. 19 E7
Lichtenvoorde, Neths. .. 16 E9
Lichtervelde, Belgium .. 17 F2
Lichuan, Hubei, China . 52 B7
Lichuan, Jiangxi, China . 53 D11
Licosa, Punta, Italy 35 B7
Lida, Belorussia 40 E4
Lida, U.S.A. 111 H5
Lidingö, Sweden 10 E12
Lidköping, Sweden 11 F7
Lido, Italy 33 C9
Lido, Niger 79 C5
Lido di Roma = Óstia,
  Lido di, Italy 34 A5
Lidzbark Warminski,
  Poland 20 A10
Liebenwalde, Germany . 18 C9
Lieberose, Germany ... 18 D10
Liebig, Mt., Australia .. 88 D5
Liechtenstein ■, Europe . 23 B9

Liederkerke, Belgium ... 17 G4
Liège, Belgium 17 G7
Liège □, Belgium 17 G7
Liegnitz = Legnica, Poland 20 D6
Liempde, Neths. 17 E6
Lienart, Zaïre 82 B2
Lienyünchiangshih =
  Lianyungang, China ... 51 G10
Lienz, Austria 21 J2
Liepāja, Latvia 40 C2
Lier, Belgium 17 F5
Lierneux, Belgium 17 H7
Lieshout, Neths. 17 E7
Liestal, Switz. 22 B5
Liévin, France 25 B9
Lièvre →, Canada 98 C4
Liezen, Austria 21 H4
Liffey →, Ireland 15 C5
Lifford, Ireland 15 B4
Liffré, France 24 D5
Lifjell, Norway 10 E2
Lifudzin, Russia 48 B7
Ligao, Phil. 55 E5
Lightning Ridge, Australia 91 D4
Lignano, Italy 33 C10
Ligny-en-Barrois, France . 25 D12
Ligny-le-Châtel, France .. 25 E10
Ligoúrion, Greece 39 M6
Ligueil, France 24 E7
Liguria □, Italy 32 D6
Ligurian Sea, Italy 32 E5
Lihou Reefs and Cays,
  Australia 90 B5
Lihue, U.S.A. 102 H15
Lijiang, China 52 D3
Likasi, Zaïre 83 E2
Likati, Zaïre 80 D4
Likhoslavl, Russia 40 C9
Likhovski, Russia 43 B9
Likoma I., Malawi 83 E3
Likumburu, Tanzania .. 83 D4
L'Île-Bouchard, France . 24 E7
L'Île-Rousse, France ... 27 F12
Liling, China 53 D9
Lille, Belgium 17 F5
Lille, France 25 B10
Lille Bælt, Denmark ... 11 J3
Lillebonne, France 24 C7
Lillehammer, Norway .. 10 C4
Lillers, France 25 B9
Lillesand, Norway 11 F2
Lilleshall, U.K. 13 E5
Lillestrøm, Norway ... 10 E5
Lillian Point, Mt., Australia 89 E4
Lillo, Spain 28 F1
Lillooet →, Canada ... 100 D4
Lilongwe, Malawi 83 E3
Liloy, Phil. 57 C6
Lim →, Bos.-H. 21 M9
Lima, Indonesia 57 E7
Lima, Peru 124 C2
Lima, Mont., U.S.A. .. 110 D7
Lima, Ohio, U.S.A. ... 104 E3
Lima □, Peru 124 C2
Lima →, Portugal 30 D2
Limages, Canada 107 A9
Liman, Russia 43 D12
Limassol, Cyprus 37 E12
Limavady, U.K. 15 A5
Limavady □, U.K. ... 15 B5
Limay →, Argentina .. 128 A3
Limay Mahuida, Argentina 126 D2
Limbang, Brunei 56 D5
Limbara, Monti, Italy .. 34 B2
Limbdi, India 62 H4
Limbe, Cameroon 79 E6
Limbourg, Belgium ... 17 G7
Limbri, Australia 91 E5
Limbunya, Australia .. 88 C4
Limburg, Germany ... 19 E4
Limburg □, Belgium .. 17 F6
Limburg □, Neths. ... 17 F7
Limeira, Brazil 127 A6
Limerick, Ireland 15 D3
Limerick □, Ireland .. 15 D3
Limestone, U.S.A. 106 D6
Limestone →, Canada . 101 B10
Limfjorden, Denmark .. 11 H3
Limia = Lima →, Portugal 30 D2
Limmared, Sweden ... 11 G7
Limmat →, Switz. 23 B6
Limmen, Neths. 16 C5
Limmen Bight, Australia 90 A2
Limmen Bight →,
  Australia 90 B2
Límni, Greece 39 L6
Límnos, Greece 39 K8
Limoeiro, Brazil 122 C4
Limoeiro do Norte, Brazil 122 C4
Limoges, France 26 C5
Limón, Costa Rica 116 D3
Limon, U.S.A. 108 F3
Limone Piemonte, Italy . 32 D4
Limousin, France 26 C5
Limousin, Plateaux du,
  France 26 C5
Limoux, France 26 E6
Limpopo →, Africa ... 85 D5
Limuru, Kenya 82 C4
Lin Xian, China 50 F6
Lin'an, China 53 B12
Linapacan I., Phil. ... 55 F3
Linapacan Str., Phil. .. 55 F3
Linares, Chile 126 D1
Linares, Colombia 120 C2

Linares, Mexico 115 C5
Linares, Spain 29 G1
Linares □, Chile 126 D1
Línas Mte., Italy 34 C1
Lincang, China 52 F3
Lincheng, China 50 F8
Linchuan, China 53 D11
Lincoln, Argentina ... 126 C3
Lincoln, N.Z. 87 K4
Lincoln, U.K. 12 D7
Lincoln, Calif., U.S.A. . 112 G5
Lincoln, Ill., U.S.A. .. 108 E10
Lincoln, Kans., U.S.A. . 108 F5
Lincoln, Maine, U.S.A. . 99 C6
Lincoln, N.H., U.S.A. . 107 B13
Lincoln, N. Mex., U.S.A. 111 K11
Lincoln, Nebr., U.S.A. . 108 E6
Lincoln Hav = Lincoln
  Sea, Arctic 4 A5
Lincoln Sea, Arctic ... 4 A5
Lincoln Wolds, U.K. .. 12 D7
Lincolnshire □, U.K. .. 12 D7
Lincolnton, U.S.A. ... 105 H5
L'Incudine, France ... 27 G13
Lind, U.S.A. 110 C4
Linda, U.S.A. 112 F5
Lindau, Germany 19 H5
Linde →, Neths. 16 C7
Linden, Guyana 121 B6
Linden, Calif., U.S.A. . 112 G5
Linden, Tex., U.S.A. .. 109 J7
Lindenheuvel, Neths. .. 17 G7
Lindenhurst, U.S.A. .. 107 F11
Linderöd, Sweden 11 J7
Linderödsåsen, Sweden . 11 J7
Lindesnes, Norway ... 6 D7
Líndhos, Greece 37 C10
Lindi, Tanzania 83 D4
Lindi □, Tanzania 83 D4
Lindi →, Zaïre 82 B2
Lindoso, Portugal 30 D2
Lindow, Germany 18 C8
Lindsay, Canada 98 D4
Lindsay, Calif., U.S.A. . 111 H4
Lindsay, Okla., U.S.A. . 109 H6
Lindsborg, U.S.A. ... 108 F6
Linfen, China 50 F6
Ling Xian, Hunan, China . 53 D9
Ling Xian, Shandong,
  China 50 F9
Lingao, China 58 C7
Lingayen, Phil. 55 C4
Lingayen G., Phil. ... 55 C4
Lingbi, China 51 H9
Lingchuan,
  Guangxi Zhuangzu,
  China 53 E8
Lingchuan, Shanxi, China . 50 G7
Lingen, Germany 18 C3
Lingga, Indonesia 56 E2
Lingga, Kepulauan,
  Indonesia 56 E2
Lingga Arch. = Lingga,
  Kepulauan, Indonesia . 56 E2
Lingle, U.S.A. 108 D2
Lingling, China 53 D8
Lingqiu, China 50 E8
Lingshan, China 52 F7
Lingshi, China 50 F6
Lingshou, China 50 E8
Lingshui, China 58 C8
Lingtai, China 50 G4
Linguère, Senegal 78 B1
Lingwu, China 50 E4
Lingyuan, China 51 D10
Lingyun, China 52 E6
Linh Cam, Vietnam ... 58 C5
Linhai, China 53 C13
Linhares, Brazil 123 E3
Linhe, China 50 D4
Linjiang, China 51 D14
Linköping, Sweden ... 11 F9
Linkou, China 51 B16
Linli, China 53 C8
Linlithgow, U.K. 14 F5
Linnhe, L., U.K. 14 E3
Linosa, I., Medit. S. ... 75 A7
Linqi, China 50 G7
Linqing, China 50 F8
Linqu, China 51 F10
Linru, China 50 G7
Lins, Brazil 127 A6
Linshui, China 52 B6
Lintao, China 50 G2
Linth →, Switz. 19 H5
Linthal, Switz. 23 C8
Lintlaw, Canada 101 C8
Linton, Canada 99 C5
Linton, Ind., U.S.A. .. 104 F2
Linton, N. Dak., U.S.A. 108 B4
Lintong, China 50 G5
Linville, Australia ... 91 D5
Linwood, Canada 106 C4
Linwu, China 53 E9
Linxi, China 51 C10
Linxia, China 54 C5
Linxiang, China 53 C9
Linyanti →, Africa ... 84 B4
Linyi, China 51 G10

Lioni, Italy 35 B8
Lions, G. of = Lion, G.
  du, France 27 E8
Lion's Den, Zimbabwe . 83 F3
Lion's Head, Canada .. 98 D3
Liozno, Belorussia ... 40 D7
Lipa, Phil. 55 E4
Lipali, Mozam. 83 F4
Lípari, Italy 35 D7
Lípari, Is., Italy 35 D7
Lipetsk, Russia 41 E11
Liping, China 52 D7
Lipkany, Moldavia ... 42 B2
Lipljan, Serbia, Yug. .. 21 N11
Lipno, Poland 20 C9
Lipova, Romania 38 C4
Lipovcy Manzovka, Russia 48 B5
Lipovets, Ukraine 42 B3
Lippe →, Germany ... 18 D2
Lippstadt, Germany .. 18 D4
Lipscomb, U.S.A. 109 G4
Lipsko, Poland 20 D11
Lipsói, Greece 39 M9
Liptovsky Svaty Milkuláš,
  Slovakia 20 F9
Liptrap C., Australia .. 91 F4
Lipu, China 53 E8
Lira, Uganda 82 B3
Liri →, Italy 34 A6
Liria, Spain 28 F4
Lisala, Zaïre 80 D4
Lisboa, Portugal 31 G1
Lisboa □, Portugal ... 31 G1
Lisbon = Lisboa, Portugal 31 G1
Lisbon, N. Dak., U.S.A. 108 B6
Lisbon, N.H., U.S.A. . 107 B13
Lisbon, Ohio, U.S.A. .. 106 F4
Lisburn, U.K. 15 B5
Lisburne, C., U.S.A. .. 96 B3
Liscannor, B., Ireland . 15 D2
Liscia →, Italy 34 A2
Lishe Jiang →, China . 52 E3
Lishi, China 50 F6
Lishu, China 51 C13
Lishui, Jiangsu, China . 53 B12
Lishui, Zhejiang, China . 53 C12
Lisianski I., Pac. Oc. .. 92 E10
Lisichansk, Ukraine ... 42 B8
Lisieux, France 24 C7
Liski, Russia 41 F11
L'Isle-Adam, France .. 25 C9
L'Isle-Jourdain, Gers,
  France 26 E5
L'Isle-Jourdain, Vienne,
  France 26 B4
L'Isle-sur-le-Doubs, France 25 E13
Lisle-sur-Tarn, France . 26 E5
Lismore, Australia ... 91 D5
Lismore, Ireland 15 D4
Lisse, Neths. 16 D5
List, Germany 18 A4
Lista, Norway 9 G9
Lista, Sweden 9 G14
Lister, Mt., Antarctica . 5 D11
Liston, Australia 91 D5
Listowel, Canada 98 D3
Listowel, Ireland 15 D2
Lit-et-Mixe, France ... 26 D2
Litang, Guangxi Zhuangzu,
  China 52 F7
Litang, Sichuan, China . 52 B3
Litang, Malaysia 57 C5
Litang Qu →, China .. 52 C3
Litani →, Lebanon ... 69 B4
Litchfield, Calif., U.S.A. 112 E6
Litchfield, Conn., U.S.A. 107 E11
Litchfield, Ill., U.S.A. . 108 F10
Litchfield, Minn., U.S.A. 108 C7
Lithgow, Australia ... 91 E5
Líthinon, Ákra, Greece . 37 E6
Lithuania ■, Europe .. 40 D3
Litija, Slovenia 33 B11
Litókhoron, Greece ... 39 J5
Litoměřice, Czech. ... 20 E4
Little Abaco I., Bahamas 116 A4
Little Barrier I., N.Z. .. 87 G5
Little Belt Mts., U.S.A. . 110 C8
Little Blue →, U.S.A. . 108 F6
Little Bushman Land,
  S. Africa 84 D2
Little Cadotte →, Canada 100 B5
Little Cayman, I.,
  Cayman Is. 116 C3
Little Churchill →, Canada 101 B9
Little Colorado →, U.S.A. 111 H8
Little Current, Canada . 98 C3
Little Current →, Canada 98 B3
Little Falls, Minn., U.S.A. 108 C7
Little Falls, N.Y., U.S.A. 107 C10
Little Fork →, U.S.A. . 108 A8
Little Grand Rapids,
  Canada 101 C9
Little Humboldt →,
  U.S.A. 110 F5
Little Inagua I., Bahamas 117 B5
Little Karoo, S. Africa . 84 E3
Little Lake, U.S.A. ... 113 K9
Little Laut Is. = Laut
  Ketil, Kepulauan,
  Indonesia 56 E5
Little Minch, U.K. ... 14 D2
Little Missouri →, U.S.A. 108 B3
Little Namaqualand,
  S. Africa 84 D2
Little Ouse →, U.K. .. 13 E8

Little Rann, India 62 H4
Little Red →, U.S.A. . 109 H9
Little River, N.Z. 87 K4
Little Rock, U.S.A. ... 109 H8
Little Ruaha →, Tanzania 82 D4
Little Sable Pt., U.S.A. . 104 D2
Little Sioux →, U.S.A. . 108 E6
Little Smoky →, Canada 100 C5
Little Snake →, U.S.A. . 110 F9
Little Valley, U.S.A. .. 106 D6
Little Wabash →, U.S.A. 104 G1
Littlefield, U.S.A. 109 J3
Littlefork, U.S.A. 108 A8
Littlehampton, U.K. .. 13 G7
Littleton, U.S.A. 107 B13
Liu He →, China 51 D11
Liu Jiang →, China .. 52 F7
Liuba, China 50 H4
Liucheng, China 52 E7
Liugou, China 51 D10
Liuhe, China 51 C13
Liuheng Dao, China .. 53 C14
Liukang Tenggaja,
  Indonesia 57 F5
Liuli, Tanzania 83 E3
Liuwa Plain, Zambia .. 81 G4
Liuyang, China 53 C9
Liuyuan, China 54 B4
Liuzhou, China 52 E7
Liuzhuang, China 51 H11
Livadherón, Greece ... 39 J4
Livadhia, Cyprus 37 E12
Livarot, France 24 D7
Live Oak, Calif., U.S.A. 112 F5
Live Oak, Fla., U.S.A. . 105 K4
Liveras, Cyprus 37 D11
Liveringa, Australia .. 88 C3
Livermore, U.S.A. ... 112 H5
Livermore, Mt., U.S.A. 109 K2
Liverpool, Australia .. 91 E5
Liverpool, Canada ... 99 D7
Liverpool, U.K. 12 D5
Liverpool Plains, Australia 91 E5
Liverpool Ra., Australia 91 E5
Livingston, Guatemala . 116 C2
Livingston, Calif., U.S.A. 112 H6
Livingston, Mont., U.S.A. 110 D8
Livingston, Tex., U.S.A. 109 K7
Livingstone, Zambia .. 83 F2
Livingstone Mts., Tanzania 83 D3
Livingstonia, Malawi .. 83 E3
Livny, Russia 41 E10
Livonia, U.S.A. 104 D4
Livorno, Italy 32 E7
Livramento, Brazil ... 127 C4
Livramento do Brumado,
  Brazil 123 D3
Livron-sur-Drôme, France 27 D8
Liwale, Tanzania 83 D4
Liwale □, Tanzania ... 83 D4
Lixi, China 52 D3
Liyang, China 53 B12
Lizard I., Australia ... 90 A4
Lizard Pt., U.K. 13 H2
Lizarda, Brazil 122 C2
Lizzano, Italy 35 B10
Ljubija, Bos.-H. 33 D13
Ljubljana, Slovenia ... 33 B11
Ljubno, Slovenia 33 B11
Ljubuški, Bos.-H. 21 M7
Ljung, Sweden 11 F7
Ljungaverk, Sweden .. 10 B10
Ljungby, Sweden 9 H12
Ljusdal, Sweden 10 C10
Ljusnan = Ljungan →,
  Sweden 10 B11
Ljusne, Sweden 9 F14
Ljutomer, Slovenia ... 33 B13
Llagostera, Spain 28 D7
Llamellín, Peru 124 B2
Llancanelo, Salina,
  Argentina 126 D2
Llandeilo, U.K. 13 F3
Llandovery, U.K. 13 F4
Llandrindod Wells, U.K. 13 E4
Llandudno, U.K. 12 D4
Llanelli, U.K. 13 F3
Llanes, Spain 30 B6
Llangollen, U.K. 12 E4
Llanidloes, U.K. 13 E4
Llano, U.S.A. 109 K5
Llano →, U.S.A. 109 K5
Llano Estacado, U.S.A. . 109 J3
Llanos, S. Amer. 118 C3
Llanquihue □, Chile .. 128 B2
Llanquihue, L., Chile .. 128 B1
Llebetx, C., Spain 36 B9
Lleida = Lérida, Spain . 28 D5
Llentrisca, C., Spain .. 36 C7
Llera, Mexico 115 C5
Llerena, Spain 31 G4
Llica, Bolivia 124 D4
Llico, Chile 126 C1
Llobregat →, Spain ... 28 D7
Lloret de Mar, Spain .. 28 D7
Lloyd B., Australia ... 90 A3
Lloyd L., Canada 101 B7
Lloydminster, Canada . 101 C6
Llullaillaco, Volcán,
  S. Amer. 126 A2
Lo, Belgium 17 G2
Lo →, Vietnam 58 B5
Loa, U.S.A. 111 G8

Loa →, Chile 126 A1
Loano, Italy 32 D5
Lobatse, Botswana 84 D4
Löbau, Germany 18 D10
Lobbes, Belgium 17 H4
Lobenstein, Germany 18 E7
Lobería, Argentina 126 D4
Lobito, Angola 81 G2
Lobón, Canal de, Spain 31 G4
Lobos, Argentina 126 D4
Lobos, I., Mexico 114 B2
Lobos, Is., Peru 118 C1
Lobos, I. de, Canary Is. 36 F6
Lobos de Tierra, I., Peru 124 B1
Loc Binh, Vietnam 58 B6
Loc Ninh, Vietnam 59 G6
Locarno, Switz. 23 D7
Lochaber, U.K. 14 E4
Lochcarron, U.K. 14 D3
Lochem, Neths. 16 D8
Loches, France 24 E8
Lochgelly, U.K. 14 E5
Lochgilphead, U.K. 14 E3
Lochinver, U.K. 14 C3
Lochnagar, Australia 90 C4
Lochnagar, U.K. 14 E5
Łochów, Poland 20 C11
Lochy →, U.K. 14 E3
Lock, Australia 91 E2
Lock Haven, U.S.A. 106 E7
Lockeford, U.S.A. 112 G5
Lockeport, Canada 99 D6
Lockerbie, U.K. 14 F5
Lockhart, U.S.A. 109 L6
Lockhart, L., Australia 89 F2
Lockney, U.S.A. 109 H4
Lockport, U.S.A. 106 C6
Locminé, France 24 E4
Locri, Italy 35 D9
Locronan, France 24 D2
Loctudy, France 24 E2
Lod, Israel 69 D3
Lodève, France 26 E7
Lodge Grass, U.S.A. 110 D10
Lodgepole, U.S.A. 108 E3
Lodgepole Cr. →, U.S.A. 108 E2
Lodhran, Pakistan 62 E4
Lodi, Italy 32 C6
Lodi, U.S.A. 112 G5
Lodja, Zaïre 82 C1
Lodosa, Spain 28 C2
Lödöse, Sweden 11 F6
Lodwar, Kenya 82 B4
Łódź, Poland 20 D9
Loei, Thailand 58 D3
Loenen, Neths. 16 D8
Loengo, Zaïre 82 C2
Loeriesfontein, S. Africa 84 E2
Lofoten, Norway 8 B13
Lofsdalen, Sweden 10 B7
Lofsen →, Sweden 10 B7
Logan, Kans., U.S.A. 108 F5
Logan, Ohio, U.S.A. 104 F4
Logan, Utah, U.S.A. 110 F8
Logan, W. Va., U.S.A. 104 G5
Logan, Mt., Canada 96 B5
Logan Pass, U.S.A. 100 D6
Logandale, U.S.A. 113 J12
Logansport, Ind., U.S.A. 104 E2
Logansport, La., U.S.A. 109 K8
Logo, Sudan 77 F3
Logone →, Chad 73 F8
Logroño, Spain 28 C2
Logrosán, Spain 31 F5
Løgstør, Denmark 11 H3
Lohardaga, India 63 H11
Lohr, Germany 19 F5
Loi-kaw, Burma 61 K20
Loimaa, Finland 9 F17
Loir →, France 24 E6
Loir-et-Cher □, France 24 E8
Loire □, France 27 C8
Loire →, France 24 E4
Loire-Atlantique □, France 24 E4
Loiret □, France 25 E9
Loitz, Germany 18 B9
Loja, Ecuador 124 A2
Loja, Spain 31 H6
Loja □, Ecuador 120 D2
Loji, Indonesia 57 E7
Loka, Sudan 77 G3
Lokandu, Zaïre 82 C2
Løken, Norway 10 E5
Lokeren, Belgium 17 F3
Lokhvitsa, Ukraine 40 F8
Lokichokio, Kenya 82 B3
Lokitaung, Kenya 82 B4
Lokka, Finland 8 C19
Løkken, Denmark 11 G3
Løkken Verk, Norway 10 A3
Loknya, Russia 40 C7
Lokoja, Nigeria 79 D6
Lokolama, Zaïre 80 E3
Lol →, Sudan 77 F2
Lola, Guinea 78 D3
Lola, Mt., U.S.A. 112 F6
Lolibai, Gebel, Sudan 77 G3
Lolimi, Sudan 77 G3
Loliondo, Tanzania 82 C4
Lolland, Denmark 11 K5
Lollar, Germany 18 E4
Lolo, U.S.A. 110 C6
Lolodorf, Cameroon 79 E7
Lom, Bulgaria 38 F6
Lom →, Bulgaria 38 F6

Lom Kao, Thailand 58 D3
Lom Sak, Thailand 58 D3
Loma, U.S.A. 110 C8
Loma Linda, U.S.A. 113 L9
Lomami →, Zaïre 82 B1
Lomas de Zamóra, Argentina 126 C4
Lombadina, Australia 88 C3
Lombardia □, Italy 32 C6
Lombardy = Lombardia □, Italy 32 C6
Lombez, France 26 E4
Lomblen, Indonesia 57 F6
Lombok, Indonesia 56 F5
Lomé, Togo 79 D5
Lomela, Zaïre 80 E4
Lomela →, Zaïre 80 E4
Lomello, Italy 32 C5
Lometa, U.S.A. 109 K5
Lomié, Cameroon 80 D2
Lomma, Sweden 11 J7
Lomme →, Belgium 17 H6
Lommel, Belgium 17 F6
Lomond, Canada 100 C6
Lomond, L., U.K. 14 E4
Lomonosov, Russia 40 B6
Lomphat, Cambodia 58 F6
Lompobatang, Indonesia 57 F5
Lompoc, U.S.A. 113 L6
Lomsegga, Norway 10 C2
Łomża, Poland 20 B12
Loncoche, Chile 128 A2
Loncopuè, Argentina 128 A2
Londa, India 60 M9
Londerzeel, Belgium 17 G4
Londiani, Kenya 82 C4
Londinières, France 24 C8
London, Canada 98 D3
London, U.K. 13 F7
London, Ky., U.S.A. 104 G3
London, Ohio, U.S.A. 104 F4
London, Greater □, U.K. 13 F7
Londonderry, U.K. 15 B4
Londonderry □, U.K. 15 B4
Londonderry, C., Australia 88 B4
Londonderry, I., Chile 128 E2
Londrina, Brazil 127 A5
Lone Pine, U.S.A. 111 H4
Long Beach, Calif., U.S.A. 113 M8
Long Beach, N.Y., U.S.A. 107 F11
Long Beach, Wash., U.S.A. 112 D2
Long Branch, U.S.A. 107 F11
Long Creek, U.S.A. 110 D4
Long Eaton, U.K. 12 E6
Long I., Australia 90 C4
Long I., Bahamas 117 B4
Long I., U.S.A. 107 F11
Long Island Sd., U.S.A. 107 E12
Long L., Canada 98 C2
Long Lake, U.S.A. 107 C10
Long Pine, U.S.A. 108 D5
Long Pt., Nfld., Canada 99 C8
Long Pt., Ont., Canada 106 D4
Long Point B., Canada 106 D4
Long Range Mts., Canada 99 C8
Long Reef, Australia 88 B4
Long Str. = Longa, Proliv, Russia 4 C16
Long Thanh, Vietnam 59 G6
Long Xian, China 50 G4
Long Xuyen, Vietnam 59 G5
Longá, Greece 39 N4
Longa, Proliv, Russia 4 C16
Long'an, China 52 F6
Longarone, Italy 33 B9
Longchang, China 52 C5
Longchi, China 52 C4
Longchuan, Guangdong, China 53 E10
Longchuan, Yunnan, China 52 E1
Longde, China 50 G4
Longeau, France 25 E12
Longford, Australia 90 G4
Longford, Ireland 15 C4
Longford □, Ireland 15 C4
Longguan, China 50 D8
Longhua, China 51 D9
Longhui, China 53 D8
Longido, Tanzania 82 C4
Longiram, Indonesia 56 E5
Longkou, Jiangxi, China 53 D10
Longkou, Shandong, China 51 F11
Longlac, Canada 98 C2
Longli, China 52 D6
Longlier, Belgium 17 J6
Longlin, China 52 E5
Longling, China 52 E2
Longmen, China 53 F10
Longming, China 52 F6
Longmont, U.S.A. 108 E2
Longnan, China 53 E10
Longnawan, Indonesia 56 D4
Longobucco, Italy 35 C9
Longquan, China 53 C12
Longreach, Australia 90 C3
Longshan, China 52 C7
Longsheng, China 53 E8
Longton, Australia 90 C4
Longtown, U.K. 13 F5
Longué-Jumelles, France 24 E6
Longueau, France 25 C9
Longueuil, Canada 107 A11
Longuyon, France 25 C12
Longview, Canada 100 C6
Longview, Tex., U.S.A. 109 J7

Longview, Wash., U.S.A. 112 D4
Longvilly, Belgium 17 H7
Longwy, France 25 C12
Longxi, China 50 G3
Longyou, China 53 C12
Longzhou, China 52 F6
Lonigo, Italy 33 C8
Lonja →, Croatia 33 C13
Lonoke, U.S.A. 109 H9
Lonquimay, Chile 128 A2
Lons-le-Saunier, France 25 F12
Lønstrup, Denmark 11 G3
Lookout, C., U.S.A. 105 H7
Lookout, C., Canada 98 A3
Loolmalasin, Tanzania 82 C4
Loon →, Alta., Canada 100 B5
Loon →, Man., Canada 101 B8
Loon Lake, Canada 101 C7
Loon-op-Zand, Neths. 17 E6
Loongana, Australia 89 F4
Loop Hd., Ireland 15 D2
Loosduinen, Neths. 16 D4
Lop Buri, Thailand 58 E3
Lop Nor = Lop Nur, China 54 B4
Lop Nur, China 54 B4
Lopare, Bos.-H. 21 L8
Lopatin, Russia 43 E12
Lopatina, G., Russia 45 D15
Lopaye, Sudan 77 F3
Lopera, Spain 31 H6
Lopez, Phil. 55 E5
Lopez, C., Gabon 80 E1
Loppersum, Neths. 16 B9
Lopphavet, Norway 8 A16
Lora →, Afghan. 60 D4
Lora, Hamun-i-, Pakistan 60 E4
Lora Cr. →, Australia 91 D2
Lora del Río, Spain 31 H5
Lorain, U.S.A. 106 E2
Loralai, Pakistan 62 D3
Lorca, Spain 29 H3
Lord Howe I., Pac. Oc. 92 L7
Lord Howe Ridge, Pac. Oc. 92 L8
Lordsburg, U.S.A. 111 K9
Loreto, Bolivia 125 D5
Loreto, Brazil 122 C2
Loreto, Italy 33 E10
Loreto, Mexico 114 B2
Loreto □, Peru 120 D3
Loreto Aprutina, Italy 33 F10
Lorgues, France 27 E10
Lorient, France 24 E3
Lorn, U.K. 14 E3
Lorn, Firth of, U.K. 14 E3
Lorne, Australia 91 F3
Lorovouno, Cyprus 37 D11
Lörrach, Germany 19 H3
Lorraine, France 25 D12
Lorrainville, Canada 98 C4
Los, Îles de, Guinea 78 D2
Los Alamos, Calif., U.S.A. 113 L6
Los Alamos, N. Mex., U.S.A. 111 J10
Los Altos, U.S.A. 112 H4
Los Andes, Chile 126 C1
Los Angeles, Chile 126 D1
Los Angeles, U.S.A. 113 L8
Los Angeles Aqueduct, U.S.A. 113 K9
Los Antiguos, Argentina 128 C2
Los Banos, U.S.A. 111 H3
Los Barrios, Spain 31 J5
Los Blancos, Argentina 126 A3
Los Cristianos, Canary Is. 36 F3
Los Gatos, U.S.A. 112 H5
Los Hermanos, Venezuela 117 D7
Los Islotes, Canary Is. 36 E6
Los Lagos, Chile 128 A2
Los Llanos de Aridane, Canary Is. 36 F2
Los Lomas, Peru 124 A1
Los Lunas, U.S.A. 111 J10
Los Menucos, Argentina 128 B3
Los Mochis, Mexico 114 B3
Los Monegros, Spain 28 D4
Los Monos, Argentina 128 C3
Los Olivos, U.S.A. 113 L6
Los Palacios, Cuba 116 B3
Los Palacios y Villafranca, Spain 31 H5
Los Reyes, Mexico 114 D4
Los Ríos □, Ecuador 120 D2
Los Roques, Venezuela 120 A4
Los Santos de Maimona, Spain 31 G4
Los Teques, Venezuela 120 A4
Los Testigos, Venezuela 121 A5
Los Vilos, Chile 126 C1
Los Yébenes, Spain 31 F7
Losada →, Colombia 120 C3
Loshkalakh, Russia 45 C15
Lošinj, Croatia 33 D11
Losser, Neths. 16 D10
Lossiemouth, U.K. 14 D5
Lot □, France 26 D5
Lot →, France 26 D4
Lot-et-Garonne □, France 26 D4
Lota, Chile 126 D1
Løten, Norway 10 D5
Lothair, S. Africa 85 D5
Lothian □, U.K. 14 F5

Lothiers, France 25 F8
Lötschbergtunnel, Switz. 22 D5
Lottefors, Sweden 10 C10
Lotzwil, Switz. 22 B5
Loubomo, Congo 80 E2
Loudéac, France 24 D4
Loudi, China 53 D8
Loudon, U.S.A. 105 H3
Loudonville, U.S.A. 106 F2
Loudun, France 24 E7
Loué, France 24 E6
Loue →, France 25 E12
Louga, Senegal 78 B1
Loughborough, U.K. 12 E6
Loughrea, Ireland 15 C3
Loughros More B., Ireland 15 B3
Louhans, France 27 B9
Louis Trichardt, S. Africa 85 C4
Louis XIV, Pte., Canada 98 B4
Louisa, U.S.A. 104 F4
Louisbourg, Canada 99 C8
Louise I., Canada 100 C2
Louiseville, Canada 98 C5
Louisiade Arch., Papua N. G. 92 J7
Louisiana, U.S.A. 108 F9
Louisiana □, U.S.A. 109 K9
Louisville, Ky., U.S.A. 104 F3
Louisville, Miss., U.S.A. 109 J10
Loulay, France 26 B3
Loulé, Portugal 31 H2
Louny, Czech. 20 E3
Loup City, U.S.A. 108 E5
Lourdes, France 26 E3
Lourdes-du-Blanc-Sablon, Canada 99 B8
Lourenço, Brazil 121 C7
Lourenço-Marques = Maputo, Mozam. 85 D5
Loures, Portugal 31 G1
Lourinhã, Portugal 31 F1
Lousã, Portugal 30 E2
Louth, Australia 91 E4
Louth, Ireland 15 C5
Louth, U.K. 12 D7
Louth □, Ireland 15 C5
Louvain = Leuven, Belgium 17 G5
Louveigné, Belgium 17 G7
Louviers, France 24 C8
Louwsburg, S. Africa 85 D5
Lovat →, Russia 40 B7
Lovech, Bulgaria 38 F7
Loveland, U.S.A. 108 E2
Lovell, U.S.A. 110 D9
Lovelock, U.S.A. 110 F4
Lóvere, Italy 32 C7
Loviisa = Lovisa, Finland 9 F19
Lovington, U.S.A. 109 J3
Lovios, Spain 30 D2
Lovisa, Finland 9 F19
Lovran, Croatia 33 C11
Low Pt., Australia 89 F4
Low Tatra = Nízké Tatry, Slovakia 20 G9
Lowa, Zaïre 82 C2
Lowa →, Zaïre 82 C2
Lowell, U.S.A. 107 D13
Lower Arrow L., Canada 100 D5
Lower California = Baja California, Mexico 114 A1
Lower California = California, Baja, Mexico 114 A1
Lower Hutt, N.Z. 87 J5
Lower L., U.S.A. 110 F3
Lower Lake, U.S.A. 112 G4
Lower Post, Canada 100 B3
Lower Red L., U.S.A. 108 B7
Lower Saxony = Niedersachsen □, Germany 18 C5
Lower Tunguska = Tunguska, Nizhnyaya →, Russia 45 C9
Lowestoft, U.K. 13 E9
Łowicz, Poland 20 C9
Lowville, U.S.A. 107 C9
Loxton, Australia 91 E3
Loxton, S. Africa 84 E3
Loyalton, U.S.A. 112 F6
Loyalty Is. = Loyauté, Is., N. Cal. 92 K8
Loyang = Luoyang, China 50 G7
Loyauté, Is., N. Cal. 92 K8
Loyev, Belorussia 40 F7
Loyoro, Uganda 82 B3
Lož, Slovenia 33 C11
Lozère □, France 26 D7
Loznica, Serbia, Yug. 21 L9
Lozova, Ukraine 42 B7
Luachimo, Angola 80 F4
Luacono, Angola 80 G4
Lualaba →, Zaïre 82 B5
Luampa, Zambia 83 F1
Lu'an, China 53 B11
Luan Chau, Vietnam 58 B4
Luan He →, China 51 E10
Luan Xian, China 51 E10
Luancheng, Guangxi Zhuangzu, China 52 F7
Luancheng, Hebei, China 50 F8
Luanda, Angola 80 F2

Luang Prabang, Laos 58 C4
Luang Thale, Thailand 59 J3
Luangwa, Zambia 83 F3
Luangwa →, Zambia 83 E3
Luangwa Valley, Zambia 83 E3
Luanne, China 51 D9
Luanping, China 51 D9
Luanshya, Zambia 83 E2
Luapula □, Zambia 83 E2
Luapula →, Africa 83 D2
Luarca, Spain 30 B4
Luashi, Zaïre 83 E1
Luau, Angola 80 G4
Lubalo, Angola 80 F3
Lubań, Poland 20 D5
Lubana, Ozero, Latvia 40 C5
Lubang, Phil. 55 E4
Lubang Is., Phil. 57 B6
Lubartów, Poland 20 D12
Lubawa, Poland 20 B9
Lubbeek, Belgium 17 G5
Lübben, Germany 18 D9
Lübbenau, Germany 18 D9
Lubbock, U.S.A. 109 J4
Lübeck, Germany 18 B6
Lübecker Bucht, Germany 18 A7
Lubefu, Zaïre 82 C1
Lubefu →, Zaïre 82 C1
Lubero = Luofu, Zaïre 82 C2
Lubicon L., Canada 100 B5
Lublin, Poland 20 D12
Lubliniec, Poland 20 E8
Lubnán, J., Lebanon 69 B4
Lubny, Ukraine 40 F8
Lubon, Poland 20 C6
Lubongola, Zaïre 82 C2
Lubsko, Poland 20 D4
Lübtheen, Germany 18 B7
Lubuagan, Phil. 55 C4
Lubudi →, Zaïre 83 D2
Lubuk Antu, Malaysia 56 D4
Lubuklinggau, Indonesia 56 E2
Lubuksikaping, Indonesia 56 D2
Lubumbashi, Zaïre 83 E2
Lubunda, Zaïre 82 D2
Lubungu, Zambia 83 E2
Lubutu, Zaïre 82 C2
Luc An Chau, Vietnam 58 A5
Luc-en-Diois, France 27 D9
Lucan, Canada 106 C3
Lucban, Phil. 55 D4
Lucca, Italy 32 E7
Luce Bay, U.K. 14 G4
Lucea, Jamaica 116 C4
Lucedale, U.S.A. 105 K1
Lucena, Phil. 55 E4
Lucena, Spain 31 H6
Lucena del Cid, Spain 28 E4
Lučenec, Slovakia 21 G9
Lucens, Switz. 22 C3
Lucera, Italy 35 A8
Lucerne = Luzern, Switz. 23 B6
Lucerne, U.S.A. 112 F4
Lucerne Valley, U.S.A. 113 L10
Lucero, Mexico 114 A3
Luchena →, Spain 29 H3
Lucheng, China 50 F7
Lucheringo →, Mozam. 83 E4
Lüchow, Germany 18 C7
Luchuan, China 53 F8
Lucie →, Surinam 121 C6
Lucira, Angola 81 G2
Luckau, Germany 18 D9
Luckenwalde, Germany 18 C9
Lucknow, India 63 F9
Luçon, France 26 B2
Lüda = Dalian, China 51 E11
Luda Kamchiya →, Bulgaria 38 F10
Ludbreg, Croatia 33 B13
Lüdenscheid, Germany 18 D3
Lüderitz, Namibia 84 D2
Ludewe □, Tanzania 83 D3
Ludhiana, India 62 D6
Ludian, China 52 D4
Luding Qiao, China 52 C4
Lüdinghausen, Germany 18 D3
Ludington, U.S.A. 104 D2
Ludlow, U.K. 13 E5
Ludlow, Calif., U.S.A. 113 L10
Ludlow, Vt., U.S.A. 107 C12
Ludus, Romania 38 C7
Ludvika, Sweden 9 F13
Ludwigsburg, Germany 19 G5
Ludwigshafen, Germany 19 F4
Ludwigslust, Germany 18 B7
Ludza, Latvia 40 C5
Luebo, Zaïre 80 F4
Lueki, Zaïre 82 C2
Luena, Zaïre 83 D2
Luena, Zambia 83 E3
Luepa, Venezuela 121 B5
Lüeyang, China 50 H4
Lufeng, Guangdong, China 53 F10
Lufeng, Yunnan, China 52 E4
Lufira →, Zaïre 83 D2
Lufkin, U.S.A. 109 K7
Lufupa, Zaïre 83 E1
Luga, Russia 40 B6
Luga →, Russia 40 B6
Lugang, Taiwan 53 E13
Lugano, Switz. 23 D7
Lugano, L. di, Switz. 23 D8
Lugansk, Ukraine 43 B8
Lugard's Falls, Kenya 82 C4

Lugela, Mozam. 83 F4
Lugenda →, Mozam. 83 E4
Lugh Ganana, Somali Rep. 68 G3
Lugnaquilla, Ireland ... 15 D5
Lugnvik, Sweden ... 10 B11
Lugo, Italy ... 33 D8
Lugo, Spain ... 30 B3
Lugo □, Spain ... 30 C3
Lugoj, Romania ... 38 D4
Lugones, Spain ... 30 B5
Lugovoye, Kazakhstan ... 44 E8
Luhansk = Lugansk, Ukraine ... 43 B8
Luhe, China ... 53 A12
Luhe →, Germany ... 18 B6
Luhuo, China ... 52 B3
Luiana, Angola ... 84 B3
Luino, Italy ... 32 C5
Luís Correia, Brazil ... 122 B3
Luís Gonçalves, Brazil ... 122 C1
Luitpold Coast, Antarctica 5 D1
Luiza, Zaïre ... 80 F4
Luizi, Zaïre ... 82 D2
Luján, Argentina ... 126 C4
Lujiang, China ... 53 B11
Lukanga Swamp, Zambia 83 E2
Lukenie →, Zaïre ... 80 E3
Lukhisaral, India ... 63 G12
Lüki, Bulgaria ... 39 H7
Lukolela, Equateur, Zaïre 80 D1
Lukolela, Kasai Or., Zaïre 82 D1
Lukosi, Zimbabwe ... 83 F2
Lukovit, Bulgaria ... 38 F7
Łuków, Poland ... 20 D12
Lukoyanov, Russia ... 41 D14
Lule älv →, Sweden ... 8 D17
Luleå, Sweden ... 8 D17
Lüleburgaz, Turkey ... 39 H10
Luliang, China ... 52 E4
Luling, U.S.A. ... 109 L6
Lulong, China ... 51 E10
Lulonga →, Zaïre ... 80 D3
Lulua →, Zaïre ... 80 E4
Luluabourg = Kananga, Zaïre ... 80 F4
Lumai, Angola ... 81 G4
Lumajang, Indonesia ... 57 H15
Lumbala N'guimbo, Angola 81 G4
Lumberton, Miss., U.S.A. 109 K10
Lumberton, N.C., U.S.A. 105 H6
Lumberton, N. Mex., U.S.A. ... 111 H10
Lumbres, France ... 25 B9
Lumbwa, Kenya ... 82 C4
Lummen, Belgium ... 17 G6
Lumsden, N.Z. ... 87 L2
Lumut, Malaysia ... 59 K3
Lumut, Tg., Indonesia ... 56 E3
Luna, Phil. ... 55 C4
Lunan, China ... 52 E4
Lunavada, India ... 62 H5
Lunca, Romania ... 38 B8
Lund, Sweden ... 11 J7
Lund, U.S.A. ... 110 G6
Lundazi, Zambia ... 83 E3
Lunde, Norway ... 10 E3
Lundi →, Zimbabwe ... 83 G3
Lundu, Malaysia ... 56 D3
Lundy, U.K. ... 13 F3
Lune →, U.K. ... 12 C5
Lüneburg, Germany ... 18 B6
Lüneburg Heath = Lüneburger Heide, Germany ... 18 C6
Lüneburger Heide, Germany ... 18 C6
Lunel, France ... 27 E8
Lünen, Germany ... 18 D3
Lunenburg, Canada ... 99 D7
Lunéville, France ... 25 D13
Lunga →, Zambia ... 83 E2
Lungern, Switz. ... 22 C6
Lungi Airport, S. Leone ... 78 D2
Lunglei, India ... 61 H18
Luni, India ... 62 F5
Luni →, India ... 62 G4
Luninets, Belorussia ... 40 E5
Luning, U.S.A. ... 110 G4
Lunino, Russia ... 41 E14
Luninyets = Luninets, Belorussia ... 40 E5
Lunner, Norway ... 10 D4
Lunsemfwa →, Zambia ... 83 E3
Lunsemfwa Falls, Zambia 83 E2
Lunteren, Neths. ... 16 D7
Luo He →, China ... 50 G6
Luocheng, China ... 52 E7
Luochuan, China ... 50 G5
Luoci, China ... 52 E4
Luodian, China ... 52 E6
Luoding, China ... 53 F8
Luodong, Taiwan ... 53 E13
Luofu, Zaïre ... 82 C2
Luohe, China ... 50 H8
Luojiang, China ... 52 B5
Luonan, China ... 50 G6
Luoning, China ... 50 G6
Luoshan, China ... 53 A10
Luotian, China ... 53 B10
Luoyang, China ... 50 G7
Luoyuan, China ... 53 D12
Luozi, Zaïre ... 80 E2
Luozigou, China ... 51 C16
Lupeni, Romania ... 38 D6

Lupilichi, Mozam. ... 83 E4
Lupoing, China ... 52 E5
Luquan, China ... 52 E4
Luque, Paraguay ... 126 B4
Luque, Spain ... 31 H6
Luray, U.S.A. ... 104 F6
Lure, France ... 25 E13
Luremo, Angola ... 80 F3
Lurgan, U.K. ... 15 B5
Luribay, Bolivia ... 124 D4
Lurin, Peru ... 124 C2
Lusaka, Zambia ... 83 F2
Lusambo, Zaïre ... 82 C1
Lusangaye, Zaïre ... 82 C2
Luseland, Canada ... 101 C7
Lushan, Henan, China ... 50 H7
Lushan, Sichuan, China ... 52 B4
Lushi, China ... 50 G6
Lushnja, Albania ... 39 J2
Lushoto, Tanzania ... 82 C4
Lushoto □, Tanzania ... 82 C4
Lushui, China ... 52 E2
Lüshun, China ... 51 E11
Lusignan, France ... 26 B4
Lusigny-sur-Barse, France 25 D11
Lusk, U.S.A. ... 108 D2
Lussac-les-Châteaux, France ... 26 B4
Lussanvira, Brazil ... 123 F1
Luta = Dalian, China ... 51 E11
Luton, U.K. ... 13 F7
Lutong, Malaysia ... 56 D4
Lutry, Switz. ... 22 C3
Lutsk, Ukraine ... 40 F4
Lützputs, S. Africa ... 84 D3
Lützow Holmbukta, Antarctica ... 5 C4
Lutzputs, S. Africa ... 84 D3
Luverne, U.S.A. ... 108 D6
Luvua, Zaïre ... 83 D2
Luvua →, Zaïre ... 82 D2
Luwegu →, Tanzania ... 83 D4
Luwuk, Indonesia ... 57 E6
Luxembourg, Lux. ... 17 J8
Luxembourg □, Belgium ... 17 J7
Luxembourg ■, Europe ... 17 J8
Luxeuil-les-Bains, France 25 E13
Luxi, Hunan, China ... 53 C8
Luxi, Yunnan, China ... 52 E4
Luxi, Yunnan, China ... 52 E4
Luxor = El Uqsur, Egypt 76 B3
Luy →, France ... 26 E2
Luy-de-Béarn →, France 26 E3
Luy-de-France →, France 26 E3
Luyi, China ... 50 H8
Luyksgestel, Neths. ... 17 F6
Luz-St.-Sauveur, France 26 F4
Luzern, Switz. ... 23 B6
Luzern □, Switz. ... 22 B5
Luzhai, China ... 52 E7
Luzhou, China ... 52 C5
Luziânia, Brazil ... 123 E2
Luzilândia, Brazil ... 122 B3
Luzon, Phil. ... 55 D4
Luzy, France ... 25 F10
Luzzi, Italy ... 35 C9
Lviv = Lvov, Ukraine ... 40 G4
Lvov, Ukraine ... 40 G4
Lyakhovichi, Belorussia ... 40 E5
Lyakhovskiye, Ostrova, Russia ... 45 B15
Lyaki, Azerbaijan ... 43 F12
Lyallpur = Faisalabad, Pakistan ... 62 D5
Lycaonia, Turkey ... 66 D5
Lychen, Germany ... 18 B9
Lycia, Turkey ... 66 E3
Lycksele, Sweden ... 8 D15
Lydda = Lod, Israel ... 69 D3
Lydenburg, S. Africa ... 85 D5
Lydia, Turkey ... 66 D3
Lyell, N.Z. ... 87 J4
Lyell I., Canada ... 100 C2
Lygnern, Sweden ... 11 G6
Lyman, U.S.A. ... 110 F8
Lyme Regis, U.K. ... 13 G5
Lymington, U.K. ... 13 G6
Lynchburg, U.S.A. ... 104 G6
Lynd →, Australia ... 90 B3
Lynd Ra., Australia ... 91 D4
Lynden, Canada ... 106 C4
Lynden, U.S.A. ... 112 B4
Lyndhurst, Queens., Australia ... 90 B3
Lyndhurst, S. Austral., Australia ... 91 E2
Lyndon →, Australia ... 89 D1
Lyndonville, N.Y., U.S.A. 106 C6
Lyndonville, Vt., U.S.A. 107 B12
Lyngdal, Norway ... 10 E3
Lynher Reef, Australia ... 88 C3
Lynn, U.S.A. ... 107 D14
Lynn Canal, U.S.A. ... 100 B1
Lynn Lake, Canada ... 101 B8
Lynnwood, U.S.A. ... 112 C4
Lynton, U.K. ... 13 F4
Lyntupy, Belorussia ... 40 D5
Lynx L., Canada ... 101 A7
Lyø, Denmark ... 11 J4
Lyon, France ... 27 C8
Lyonnais, France ... 27 C8
Lyons = Lyon, France ... 27 C8
Lyons, Colo., U.S.A. ... 108 E2
Lyons, Ga., U.S.A. ... 105 J4
Lyons, Kans., U.S.A. ... 108 F5
Lyons, N.Y., U.S.A. ... 106 C8

Lyrestad, Sweden ... 11 F8
Lys = Leie →, Belgium 25 A10
Lysekil, Sweden ... 11 F5
Lyskovo, Russia ... 41 D14
Lyss, Switz. ... 22 B4
Lytle, U.S.A. ... 109 L5
Lyttelton, N.Z. ... 87 K4
Lytton, Canada ... 100 C4
Lyuban, Russia ... 40 B7
Lyubcha, Belorussia ... 40 E5
Lyubertsy, Russia ... 41 D10
Lyubim, Russia ... 41 B12
Lyuboml, Ukraine ... 40 F4
Lyubotin, Ukraine ... 42 B3
Lyubytino, Russia ... 40 B8
Lyudinovo, Russia ... 40 E9

M

Ma →, Vietnam ... 58 C5
Ma'adaba, Jordan ... 69 E4
Maamba, Zambia ... 84 B4
Ma'ān, Jordan ... 69 E4
Ma'ān □, Jordan ... 69 F5
Ma'anshan, China ... 53 B12
Maarheeze, Neths. ... 17 F7
Maarianhamina, Finland 9 F15
Maarn, Neths. ... 16 D6
Ma'arrat an Nu'mān, Syria 64 C3
Maarssen, Neths. ... 16 D6
Maartensdijk, Neths. ... 16 D6
Maas →, Neths. ... 16 E5
Maasbracht, Belgium ... 17 F7
Maasbree, Neths. ... 17 F8
Maasdam, Neths. ... 16 E5
Maasdijk, Neths. ... 16 E4
Maaseik, Belgium ... 17 F7
Maasland, Neths. ... 16 E4
Maasniel, Neths. ... 17 F8
Maassluis, Neths. ... 16 E4
Maastricht, Neths. ... 17 G7
Maave, Mozam. ... 85 C5
Mabaruma, Guyana ... 121 B6
Mabel L., Canada ... 100 C5
Mabenge, Zaïre ... 82 B1
Mabian, China ... 52 C4
Mablethorpe, U.K. ... 12 D8
Maboma, Zaïre ... 82 B2
Mabrouk, Mali ... 79 B4
Mabton, U.S.A. ... 110 C3
Mac Bac, Vietnam ... 59 H6
Macachín, Argentina ... 126 D3
Macaé, Brazil ... 123 F3
Macaíba, Brazil ... 122 C4
Macajuba, Brazil ... 123 D3
McAlester, U.S.A. ... 109 H7
McAllen, U.S.A. ... 109 M5
Macamic, Canada ... 98 C4
Macao = Macau ■, China 53 F9
Macão, Portugal ... 31 F3
Macapá, Brazil ... 121 C7
Macará, Ecuador ... 120 D2
Macarani, Brazil ... 123 E3
Macarena, Serranía de la, Colombia ... 120 C3
McArthur →, Australia ... 90 B2
McArthur, Port, Australia 90 B2
McArthur River, Australia 90 B2
Macas, Ecuador ... 120 D2
Macate, Peru ... 124 B2
Macau, Brazil ... 122 C4
Macau ■, China ... 53 F9
Macaúbas, Brazil ... 123 D3
Macaya →, Colombia ... 120 C3
McBride, Canada ... 100 C4
McCall, U.S.A. ... 110 D5
McCamey, U.S.A. ... 109 K3
McCammon, U.S.A. ... 110 E7
McCauley I., Canada ... 100 C2
McCleary, U.S.A. ... 112 C3
Macclesfield, U.K. ... 12 D5
McClintock, Canada ... 101 B10
McClintock Ra., Australia 88 C4
McCloud, U.S.A. ... 110 F2
McCluer I., Australia ... 88 B5
McClure, U.S.A. ... 106 F7
McClure, L., U.S.A. ... 112 H6
M'Clure Str., Canada ... 4 B2
McClusky, U.S.A. ... 108 B4
McComb, U.S.A. ... 109 K9
McConaughy, L., U.S.A. 108 E4
McCook, U.S.A. ... 108 E4
McCullough Mt., U.S.A. 113 K11
McCusker →, Canada ... 101 B7
McDame, Canada ... 100 B3
McDermitt, U.S.A. ... 110 F5
Macdonald, L., Australia 88 D4
Macdonnell Ras., Australia 88 D5
McDouall Peak, Australia 91 D1
Macdougall L., Canada 96 B10
MacDowell L., Canada 98 B1
Macduff, U.K. ... 14 D6
Maceda, Spain ... 30 C3
Macedonia ■, Europe ... 39 H4
Maceió, Brazil ... 122 C4
Macenta, Guinea ... 78 D3
Macerata, Italy ... 33 E10
McFarland, U.S.A. ... 113 K7
McFarlane →, Canada ... 101 B7
Macfarlane, L., Australia 91 E2

McGehee, U.S.A. ... 109 J9
McGill, U.S.A. ... 110 G6
Macgillycuddy's Reeks, Ireland ... 15 D2
MacGregor, Canada ... 101 D9
McGregor, U.S.A. ... 108 D9
McGregor →, Canada ... 100 B4
McGregor Ra., Australia 91 D3
Mach, Pakistan ... 60 E5
Māch Kowr, Iran ... 65 E9
Machacalis, Brazil ... 123 E3
Machado = Jiparaná →, Brazil ... 125 B5
Machagai, Argentina ... 126 B3
Machakos, Kenya ... 82 C4
Machakos □, Kenya ... 82 C4
Machala, Ecuador ... 120 D2
Machanga, Mozam. ... 85 C6
Machattie, L., Australia 90 C2
Machava, Mozam. ... 85 D5
Machece, Mozam. ... 83 F4
Machecoul, France ... 24 F5
Machelen, Belgium ... 17 G4
Macheng, China ... 53 B10
Machevna, Russia ... 45 C18
Machezo, Spain ... 31 F6
Machias, U.S.A. ... 99 D6
Machichaco, C., Spain ... 28 B2
Machichi →, Canada ... 101 B10
Machico, Madeira ... 36 D3
Machilipatnam, India ... 61 L12
Machiques, Venezuela ... 120 A3
Machupicchu, Peru ... 124 C3
Machynlleth, U.K. ... 13 E4
McIlwraith Ra., Australia 90 A3
Măcin, Romania ... 38 D11
Macina, Mali ... 78 C4
McIntosh, U.S.A. ... 108 C4
McIntosh L., Canada ... 101 B8
Macintyre →, Australia 91 D5
Macizo Galaico, Spain ... 30 C3
Mackay, Australia ... 90 C4
Mackay, U.S.A. ... 110 E7
MacKay →, Canada ... 100 B6
Mackay, L., Australia ... 88 D4
McKay Ra., Australia ... 88 D3
McKeesport, U.S.A. ... 106 F5
McKenna, U.S.A. ... 112 D4
Mackenzie, Canada ... 100 B4
Mackenzie, Guyana ... 121 B6
McKenzie, U.S.A. ... 105 G1
Mackenzie →, Australia 90 C4
Mackenzie →, Canada ... 96 B6
McKenzie →, U.S.A. ... 110 D2
Mackenzie Bay, Canada 4 B1
Mackenzie City = Linden, Guyana ... 121 B6
Mackenzie Highway, Canada ... 100 B5
Mackinaw City, U.S.A. 104 C3
McKinlay, Australia ... 90 C3
McKinlay →, Australia 90 C3
McKinley, Mt., U.S.A. ... 96 B4
McKinley Sea, Arctic ... 4 A7
McKinney, U.S.A. ... 109 J6
Mackinnon Road, Kenya 82 C4
Macksville, Australia ... 91 E5
McLaughlin, U.S.A. ... 108 C4
Maclean, Australia ... 91 D5
McLean, U.S.A. ... 109 H4
McLeansboro, U.S.A. ... 108 F10
MacLeod, B., Canada ... 101 A7
McLeod, L., Australia ... 89 D1
MacLeod Lake, Canada 100 C4
M'Clintock Chan., Canada 96 A9
McLoughlin, Mt., U.S.A. 110 E2
McLure, Canada ... 100 C4
McMechen, U.S.A. ... 106 G4
McMillan, L., U.S.A. ... 109 J2
McMinnville, Oreg., U.S.A. 110 D2
McMinnville, Tenn., U.S.A. ... 105 H3
McMorran, Canada ... 101 C7
McMurdo Sd., Antarctica 5 D11
McMurray = Fort McMurray, Canada ... 100 B6
McMurray, U.S.A. ... 112 B4
McNary, U.S.A. ... 111 J9
MacNutt, Canada ... 101 C8
Macodoene, Mozam. ... 85 C6
Macomb, U.S.A. ... 108 E9
Macomer, Italy ... 34 B1
Mâcon, France ... 27 B8
Macon, Ga., U.S.A. ... 105 J4
Macon, Miss., U.S.A. ... 105 J1
Macon, Mo., U.S.A. ... 108 F8
Macondo, Angola ... 81 G4
Macossa, Mozam. ... 83 F3
Macoun L., Canada ... 101 B8
Macovane, Mozam. ... 85 C6
Macquarie Harbour, Australia ... 90 G4
Macquarie Is., Pac. Oc. 92 N7
MacRobertson Land, Antarctica ... 5 D6
Macroom, Ireland ... 15 E3
Macroy, Australia ... 88 D2

MacTier, Canada ... 106 A5
Macubela, Mozam. ... 83 F4
Macugnaga, Italy ... 32 C4
Macuiza, Mozam. ... 83 F3
Macujer, Colombia ... 120 C3
Macusani, Peru ... 124 C3
Macuse, Mozam. ... 83 F4
Macuspana, Mexico ... 115 D6
Macusse, Angola ... 84 B3
McVille, U.S.A. ... 108 B5
Madadeni, S. Africa ... 85 D5
Madagali, Nigeria ... 79 C7
Madagascar ■, Africa ... 85 C8
Madā'in Sālih, Si. Arabia 64 E3
Madama, Niger ... 73 D7
Madame I., Canada ... 99 C7
Madaoua, Niger ... 79 C6
Madara, Nigeria ... 79 C7
Madaripur, Bangla. ... 61 H17
Madauk, Burma ... 61 L20
Madawaska, Canada ... 106 A7
Madawaska →, Canada 98 C4
Madaya, Burma ... 61 H20
Madbar, Sudan ... 77 F3
Maddaloni, Italy ... 35 A7
Made, Neths. ... 17 E5
Madeira, Atl. Oc. ... 36 D3
Madeira →, Brazil ... 121 D6
Madeleine, Îs. de la, Canada ... 99 C7
Maden, Turkey ... 67 D8
Madera, U.S.A. ... 111 H3
Madha, India ... 60 L9
Madhubani, India ... 63 F12
Madhya Pradesh □, India 62 J7
Madian, China ... 53 A11
Madidi →, Bolivia ... 124 C4
Madikeri, India ... 60 N9
Madimba, Zaïre ... 80 E3
Ma'din, Syria ... 64 C3
Madīnat ash Sha'b, Yemen 68 E3
Madingou, Congo ... 80 E2
Madirovalo, Madag. ... 85 B8
Madison, Calif., U.S.A. 112 G5
Madison, Fla., U.S.A. ... 105 K4
Madison, Ind., U.S.A. ... 104 F3
Madison, Nebr., U.S.A. 108 E6
Madison, Ohio, U.S.A. ... 106 E3
Madison, S. Dak., U.S.A. 108 D6
Madison, Wis., U.S.A. ... 108 D10
Madison →, U.S.A. ... 110 D8
Madisonville, Ky., U.S.A. 104 G2
Madisonville, Tex., U.S.A. 109 K7
Madista, Botswana ... 84 C4
Madiun, Indonesia ... 57 G14
Madley, U.K. ... 13 E5
Madol, Sudan ... 77 F2
Madona, Latvia ... 40 C5
Madras = Tamil Nadu □, India ... 60 P10
Madras, India ... 60 N12
Madras, U.S.A. ... 110 D3
Madre, L., Mexico ... 115 B5
Madre, Laguna, U.S.A. 109 M6
Madre, Sierra, Phil. ... 55 C5
Madre de Dios □, Peru 124 C3
Madre de Dios →, Bolivia 124 C4
Madre de Dios, I., Chile 128 D1
Madre del Sur, Sierra, Mexico ... 115 D5
Madre Occidental, Sierra, Mexico ... 114 B3
Madre Oriental, Sierra, Mexico ... 114 C4
Madri, India ... 62 G5
Madrid, Spain ... 30 E7
Madrid □, Spain ... 30 E7
Madridejos, Spain ... 31 F7
Madrigal de las Altas Torres, Spain ... 30 D6
Madrona, Sierra, Spain 31 G6
Madroñera, Spain ... 31 F5
Madu, Sudan ... 77 E2
Madura, Selat, Indonesia 57 G15
Madura Motel, Australia 89 F4
Madurai, India ... 60 Q11
Madurantakam, India ... 60 N11
Madzhalis, Russia ... 43 E12
Mae Chan, Thailand ... 58 B2
Mae Hong Son, Thailand 58 C2
Mae Khlong →, Thailand 58 F3
Mae Phrik, Thailand ... 58 D2
Mae Ramat, Thailand ... 58 D2
Mae Rim, Thailand ... 58 C2
Mae Sot, Thailand ... 58 D2
Mae Suai, Thailand ... 58 C2
Mae Tha, Thailand ... 58 C2
Maebashi, Japan ... 49 F9
Maella, Spain ... 28 D5
Măeruş, Romania ... 38 D8
Maesteg, U.K. ... 13 F4
Maestra, Sierra, Cuba ... 116 B4
Maestrazgo, Mts. del, Spain 28 E4
Maevatanana, Madag. ... 85 B8
Mafeking = Mafikeng, S. Africa ... 84 D4
Mafeking, Canada ... 101 C8
Maféré, Ivory C. ... 78 D4
Mafeteng, Lesotho ... 84 D4
Maffe, Belgium ... 17 H6
Maffra, Australia ... 91 F4
Mafia I., Tanzania ... 82 D4
Mafikeng, S. Africa ... 84 D4

Mafra, *Brazil* 127 B6
Mafra, *Portugal* 31 G1
Mafungabusi Plateau,
  Zimbabwe 83 F2
Magadan, *Russia* 45 D16
Magadi, *Kenya* 82 C4
Magadi, L., *Kenya* 82 C4
Magaliesburg, *S. Africa* . 85 D4
Magallanes □, *Chile* 128 D2
Magallanes, Estrecho de,
  Chile 128 D2
Magangué, *Colombia* 120 B3
Magaria, *Niger* 79 C6
Magburaka, *S. Leone* 78 D2
Magdalen Is. = Madeleine,
  Is. de la, *Canada* 99 C7
Magdalena, *Argentina* ... 126 D4
Magdalena, *Bolivia* 125 C5
Magdalena, *Malaysia* 56 D5
Magdalena, *Mexico* 114 A2
Magdalena, *U.S.A.* 111 J10
Magdalena □, *Colombia* . 120 A3
Magdalena →, *Colombia* . 120 A3
Magdalena →, *Mexico* ... 114 A2
Magdalena, B., *Mexico* .. 114 C2
Magdalena, I., *Chile* 128 B2
Magdalena, Llano de la,
  Mexico 114 C2
Magdeburg, *Germany* 18 C7
Magdelaine Cays, *Australia* 90 B5
Magdub, *Sudan* 77 E2
Magee, *U.S.A.* 109 K10
Magee, I., *U.K.* 15 B6
Magelang, *Indonesia* 57 G14
Magellan's Str. =
  Magallanes, Estrecho de,
  Chile 128 D2
Magenta, *Italy* 32 C5
Magenta, L., *Australia* .. 89 F2
Maggia, *Switz.* 23 D7
Maggia →, *Switz.* 23 D7
Maggiorasca, Mte., *Italy* . 32 D6
Maggiore, L., *Italy* 32 C5
Maghama, *Mauritania* ... 78 B2
Magherafelt, *U.K.* 15 B5
Maghnia, *Algeria* 75 B4
Magione, *Italy* 33 E9
Magliano in Toscana, *Italy* 33 F8
Máglie, *Italy* 35 B11
Magnac-Laval, *France* ... 26 B5
Magnetic Pole (North) =
  North Magnetic Pole,
  Canada 4 B2
Magnetic Pole (South) =
  South Magnetic Pole,
  Antarctica 5 C9
Magnitogorsk, *Russia* ... 44 D6
Magnolia, *Ark., U.S.A.* . 109 J8
Magnolia, *Miss., U.S.A.* . 109 K9
Magnor, *Norway* 10 E6
Magny-en-Vexin, *France* . 25 C8
Magog, *Canada* 99 C5
Magoro, *Uganda* 82 B3
Magosa = Famagusta,
  Cyprus 37 D12
Magouládhes, *Greece* 37 A3
Magoye, *Zambia* 83 F2
Magpie L., *Canada* 99 B7
Magrath, *Canada* 100 D6
Magro →, *Spain* 29 F4
Magrur, Wadi →, *Sudan* . 77 D2
Magu □, *Tanzania* 82 C3
Maguan, *China* 52 F5
Maguarinho, C., *Brazil* .. 122 B2
Maguse L., *Canada* 101 A9
Maguse Pt., *Canada* 101 A10
Magwe, *Burma* 61 J19
Maha Sarakham, *Thailand* 58 D4
Mahābād, *Iran* 64 B5
Mahabharat Lekh, *Nepal* . 63 E9
Mahabo, *Madag.* 85 C7
Mahadeo Hills, *India* 62 H8
Mahagi, *Zaïre* 82 B3
Mahaicony, *Guyana* 121 B6
Mahajamba →, *Madag.* .. 85 B8
Mahajamba, Helodranon' i,
  Madag. 85 B8
Mahajan, *India* 62 E5
Mahajanga, *Madag.* 85 B8
Mahajanga □, *Madag.* ... 85 B8
Mahajilo →, *Madag.* 85 B8
Mahakam →, *Indonesia* .. 56 E5
Mahalapye, *Botswana* ... 84 C4
Mahallāt, *Iran* 65 C6
Maḥallāt, *Iran* 65 C6
Māhān, *Iran* 65 D8
Mahanadi →, *India* 61 J15
Mahanoro, *Madag.* 85 B8
Mahanoy City, *U.S.A.* ... 107 F8
Maharashtra □, *India* 60 J9
Maharès, *Tunisia* 75 B7
Mahari Mts., *Tanzania* .. 82 D2
Mahasham, W. →, *Egypt* . 69 E3
Mahasolo, *Madag.* 85 B8
Mahattat ash Shīdīyah,
  Jordan 69 F4
Mahattat 'Unayzah, *Jordan* 69 E4
Mahaxay, *Laos* 58 D5
Mahbes, W. *Sahara* 74 C3
Mahbubnagar, *India* 60 L10
Maḥḍah, *Oman* 65 E7
Mahdia, *Guyana* 121 B6
Mahdia, *Tunisia* 75 A4
Mahe, *India* 63 C8
Mahenge, *Tanzania* 83 D4
Maheno, *N.Z.* 87 L3

Mahesana, *India* 62 H5
Mahia Pen., *N.Z.* 87 H6
Mahilyow = Mogilev,
  Belorussia 40 D7
Mahirija, *Morocco* 75 B4
Mahmiya, *Sudan* 77 D3
Mahmud Kot, *Pakistan* .. 62 D4
Mahmudia, *Romania* 38 D12
Mahnomen, *U.S.A.* 108 B7
Mahoba, *India* 63 G8
Mahón, *Spain* 36 B11
Mahone Bay, *Canada* 99 D7
Mahuta, *Nigeria* 79 C5
Mai-Ndombe, L., *Zaïre* .. 80 E3
Mai-Sai, *Thailand* 58 B2
Maicao, *Colombia* 120 A3
Maîche, *France* 25 E13
Maici →, *Brazil* 125 B5
Maicurú →, *Brazil* 121 D7
Máida, *Italy* 35 D9
Maidan Khula, *Afghan.* .. 62 C3
Maidenhead, *U.K.* 13 F7
Maidi, *Yemen* 77 D5
Maidstone, *Canada* 101 C7
Maidstone, *U.K.* 13 F8
Maiduguri, *Nigeria* 79 C7
Maignelay, *France* 25 C9
Maigo, *Phil.* 55 G5
Maigualida, Sierra,
  Venezuela 121 B4
Maigudo, *Ethiopia* 77 F4
Maijdi, *Bangla.* 61 H17
Maikala Ra., *India* 61 J12
Mailly-le-Camp, *France* .. 25 D11
Mailsi, *Pakistan* 62 E5
Main →, *Germany* 19 F4
Main →, *U.K.* 15 B5
Main Centre, *Canada* 101 C7
Mainburg, *Germany* 19 G7
Maine, *France* 24 E6
Maine □, *U.S.A.* 99 C6
Maine →, *Ireland* 15 D2
Maine-et-Loire □, *France* . 24 E6
Maïne-Soroa, *Niger* 79 C7
Maingkwan, *Burma* 61 F20
Mainit, L., *Phil.* 55 G6
Mainland, *Orkney, U.K.* . 14 C5
Mainland, *Shet., U.K.* ... 14 A7
Mainpuri, *India* 63 F8
Maintenon, *France* 25 D8
Maintirano, *Madag.* 85 B7
Mainvault, *Belgium* 17 G3
Mainz, *Germany* 19 F4
Maipú, *Argentina* 126 D4
Maiquetía, *Venezuela* ... 120 A4
Maira →, *Italy* 32 D4
Mairabari, *India* 61 F18
Mairipotaba, *Brazil* 123 E2
Maisí, *Cuba* 117 B5
Maisi, Pta. de, *Cuba* 117 B5
Maisse, *France* 25 D9
Maissin, *Belgium* 17 J6
Maitland, *N.S.W., Australia* 91 E5
Maitland,
  S. Austral.,
  Australia 91 E2
Maitland →, *Canada* 106 C3
Maiyema, *Nigeria* 79 C5
Maiyuan, *China* 53 E11
Maiz, Is. del, *Nic.* 116 D3
Maizuru, *Japan* 49 G7
Majagual, *Colombia* 120 B3
Majalengka, *Indonesia* ... 57 G13
Majari →, *Brazil* 121 C5
Majene, *Indonesia* 57 E5
Majes →, *Peru* 124 D3
Maji, *Ethiopia* 77 F4
Majiang, *China* 52 D6
Major, *Canada* 101 C7
Majorca = Mallorca, *Spain* 36 B10
Majuriã, *Brazil* 125 B5
Maka, *Senegal* 78 C2
Makak, *Cameroon* 79 E7
Makale, *Indonesia* 57 E5
Makamba, *Burundi* 82 C2
Makari, *Cameroon* 80 C7
Makarikari =
  Makgadikgadi Salt Pans,
  Botswana 84 C4
Makarovo, *Russia* 45 D11
Makarska, *Croatia* 21 M7
Makaryev, *Russia* 41 C13
Makasar = Ujung Pandang,
  Indonesia 57 F5
Makasar, Selat, *Indonesia* . 57 E5
Makasar, Str. of =
  Makasar, Selat, *Indonesia* 57 E5
Makat, *Kazakhstan* 44 E6
Makedonija =
  Macedonia ■, *Europe* .. 39 H4
Makena, *U.S.A.* 102 H16
Makeni, *S. Leone* 78 D2
Makeyevka, *Ukraine* 42 B7
Makgadikgadi Salt Pans,
  Botswana 84 C4
Makhachkala, *Russia* 43 E12
Makhambet, *Kazakhstan* . 43 C14
Makharadze = Ozurgety,
  Georgia 43 F10
Makhmūr, *Iraq* 64 C4
Makian, *Indonesia* 57 D7
Makindu, *Kenya* 82 C4
Makinsk, *Kazakhstan* 44 D8
Makiyivka = Makeyevka,
  Ukraine 42 B7
Makkah, *Si. Arabia* 68 C2

Makkovik, *Canada* 99 A8
Makkum, *Neths.* 16 B6
Makó, *Hungary* 21 J10
Makokou, *Gabon* 80 D2
Makongo, *Zaïre* 82 B2
Makoro, *Zaïre* 82 B2
Makoua, *Congo* 80 E3
Makrá, *Greece* 39 N8
Makrai, *India* 60 H10
Makran Coast Range,
  Pakistan 60 G4
Makrana, *India* 62 F6
Makriyialos, *Greece* 37 D7
Maksimkin Yar, *Russia* .. 44 D9
Maktar, *Tunisia* 75 A6
Mākū, *Iran* 64 B5
Makumbi, *Zaïre* 80 F4
Makunda, *Botswana* 84 C3
Makurazaki, *Japan* 49 J5
Makurdi, *Nigeria* 79 D6
Makūyeh, *Iran* 65 D7
Makwassie, *S. Africa* 84 D4
Mal B., *Ireland* 15 D2
Mal i Nemërçkës, *Albania* 39 J3
Mal i Tomorit, *Albania* ... 39 J3
Mala, *Peru* 124 C2
Mala, Pta., *Panama* 116 E3
Mala Kapela, *Croatia* 33 D12
Malabang, *Phil.* 55 H6
Malabar Coast, *India* 60 P9
Malabo = Rey Malabo,
  Eq. Guin. 79 E6
Malabon, *Phil.* 55 D4
Malacca, Str. of, *Indonesia* 59 L3
Malacky, *Slovakia* 21 G7
Malad City, *U.S.A.* 110 E7
Maladzyechna =
  Molodechno, *Belorussia* 40 D5
Málaga, *Colombia* 120 B3
Málaga, *Spain* 31 J6
Malaga, *U.S.A.* 109 J2
Málaga □, *Spain* 31 J6
Malagarasi, *Tanzania* 82 D3
Malagarasi →, *Tanzania* . 82 D2
Malagón, *Spain* 31 F7
Malagón →, *Spain* 31 H3
Malaimbandy, *Madag.* ... 85 C8
Malakâl, *Sudan* 77 F3
Malakand, *Pakistan* 62 B4
Malakoff, *U.S.A.* 109 J7
Malamyzh, *Russia* 45 E14
Malang, *Indonesia* 57 G15
Malanje, *Angola* 80 F3
Mälaren, *Sweden* 10 E11
Malargüe, *Argentina* 126 D2
Malartic, *Canada* 98 C4
Malatya, *Turkey* 67 D8
Malatya □, *Turkey* 67 D8
Malawi ■, *Africa* 83 E3
Malawi, L., *Africa* 83 E3
Malay Pen., *Asia* 59 J3
Malaya Belozërka, *Ukraine* 42 C6
Malaya Vishera, *Russia* .. 40 B8
Malaya Viska, *Ukraine* ... 42 B4
Malaybalay, *Phil.* 55 G6
Malāyer, *Iran* 65 C6
Malaysia ■, *Asia* 56 D4
Malazgirt, *Turkey* 67 C10
Malbon, *Australia* 90 C3
Malbooma, *Australia* 91 E1
Malbork, *Poland* 20 A9
Malcésine, *Italy* 32 C7
Malchin, *Germany* 18 B8
Malchow, *Germany* 18 B8
Malcolm, *Australia* 89 E3
Malcolm, Pt., *Australia* .. 89 F3
Maldegem, *Belgium* 17 F2
Malden, *Mass., U.S.A.* .. 107 D13
Malden, *Mo., U.S.A.* 109 G10
Malden I., *Kiribati* 93 H12
Maldives ■, *Ind. Oc.* 47 J11
Maldonado, *Uruguay* 127 C5
Maldonado, Punta, *Mexico* 115 D5
Malè, *Italy* 32 B7
Maléa, Ákra, *Greece* 39 N6
Malebo, Pool, *Africa* 70 G5
Malegaon, *India* 60 J9
Malei, *Mozam.* 83 F4
Malek Kandī, *Iran* 64 B5
Malela, *Zaïre* 82 C2
Malema, *Mozam.* 83 E4
Máleme, *Greece* 37 D5
Malerkotla, *India* 62 D6
Máles, *Greece* 37 D7
Malesherbes, *France* 25 D9
Malestroit, *France* 24 E4
Malfa, *Italy* 35 D7
Malgobek, *Russia* 43 E11
Malgomaj, *Sweden* 8 D14
Malgrat, *Spain* 28 D7
Malha, *Sudan* 77 D2
Malheur →, *U.S.A.* 110 D5
Malheur L., *U.S.A.* 110 E4
Mali, *Guinea* 78 C2
Mali ■, *Africa* 78 B4
Mali →, *Burma* 61 G20
Mali Kanal, *Serbia, Yug.* . 21 K9
Malibu, *U.S.A.* 113 L8
Malik, *Indonesia* 57 E6
Malili, *Indonesia* 57 E6
Malimba, Mts., *Zaïre* 82 D2
Malin, *Ukraine* 40 F6
Malin Hd., *Ireland* 15 A4
Malindi, *Kenya* 82 C5
Malines = Mechelen,
  Belgium 17 F4

Maling, *Indonesia* 57 D6
Malinyi, *Tanzania* 83 D4
Malipo, *China* 52 F5
Maliqi, *Albania* 39 J3
Malita, *Phil.* 57 C7
Malkara, *Turkey* 66 C2
Małkinia Górna, *Poland* .. 20 C12
Malko Tŭrnovo, *Bulgaria* . 39 H10
Mallacoota, *Australia* 91 F4
Mallacoota Inlet, *Australia* 91 F4
Mallaig, *U.K.* 14 E3
Mallawan, *India* 63 F9
Mallawi, *Egypt* 76 B3
Malleco □, *Chile* 128 A2
Mallemort, *France* 27 E9
Málles Venosta, *Italy* 32 B7
Mállia, *Greece* 37 D7
Mallión, Kólpos, *Greece* . 37 D7
Mallorca, *Spain* 36 B10
Mallorytown, *Canada* 107 B9
Mallow, *Ireland* 15 D3
Malmberget, *Sweden* 8 C16
Malmédy, *Belgium* 17 H8
Malmesbury, *S. Africa* ... 84 E2
Malmö, *Sweden* 11 J6
Malmöhus län □, *Sweden* . 11 J7
Malmslätt, *Sweden* 11 F9
Malmyzh, *Russia* 41 C17
Maloarkhangelsk, *Russia* . 41 E10
Maloca, *Brazil* 121 C6
Maloja, *Switz.* 23 D9
Maloja, P., *Switz.* 23 D9
Malolos, *Phil.* 57 B6
Malombe L., *Malawi* 83 E4
Malone, *U.S.A.* 107 B10
Malong, *China* 52 E4
Malorita, *Belorussia* 40 F4
Maloyaroslavets, *Russia* .. 41 D10
Malpartida, *Spain* 31 F4
Malpaso, *Canary Is.* 36 G1
Malpica, *Spain* 30 B2
Malta, *Brazil* 122 C4
Malta, *Idaho, U.S.A.* ... 110 E7
Malta, *Mont., U.S.A.* ... 110 B10
Malta ■, *Europe* 37 D1
Malta Channel, *Medit. S.* . 34 F6
Maltahöhe, *Namibia* 84 C2
Malters, *Switz.* 22 B6
Malton, *Canada* 106 C5
Malton, *U.K.* 12 C7
Maluku, *Indonesia* 57 E7
Maluku □, *Indonesia* 57 E7
Maluku Sea, *Indonesia* ... 57 E6
Malumfashi, *Nigeria* 79 C6
Malvan, *India* 60 L8
Malvern, *U.S.A.* 109 H8
Malvern Hills, *U.K.* 13 E5
Malvik, *Norway* 10 A4
Malvinas, Is. = Falkland
  Is. ■, *Atl. Oc.* 128 D5
Malya, *Tanzania* 82 C3
Malyy Lyakhovskiy,
  Ostrov, *Russia* 45 B15
Mama, *Russia* 45 D12
Mamadysh, *Russia* 41 D17
Mamanguape, *Brazil* 122 C4
Mamasa, *Indonesia* 57 E5
Mambasa, *Zaïre* 82 B2
Mamberamo →, *Indonesia* 57 E9
Mambilima Falls, *Zambia* . 83 E2
Mambirima, *Zaïre* 83 E2
Mambo, *Tanzania* 82 C4
Mambrui, *Kenya* 82 C5
Mamburao, *Phil.* 55 E4
Mameigwess L., *Canada* . 98 B2
Mamer, *Lux.* 17 J8
Mamers, *France* 24 D7
Mamfe, *Cameroon* 79 D6
Mamiña, *Chile* 124 E4
Mámmola, *Italy* 35 D9
Mammoth, *U.S.A.* 111 K8
Mamoré →, *Bolivia* 125 C4
Mamou, *Guinea* 78 C2
Mampatá, *Guinea-Biss.* .. 78 C2
Mampong, *Ghana* 79 D4
Mamuil Malal, Paso,
  S. Amer. 128 A2
Mamuju, *Indonesia* 57 E5
Man, *Ivory C.* 78 D3
Man, I. of, *U.K.* 12 C3
Man Na, *Burma* 61 H20
Mana, *Fr. Guiana* 121 B7
Mana →, *Fr. Guiana* 121 B7
Måna →, *Norway* 10 E2
Manaar, G. of = Mannar,
  G. of, *Asia* 60 Q11
Manabí □, *Ecuador* 120 D1
Manacacías →, *Colombia* 120 C3
Manacapuru, *Brazil* 121 D5
Manacapuru →, *Brazil* ... 121 D5
Manacor, *Spain* 36 B10
Manado, *Indonesia* 57 D6
Manage, *Belgium* 17 G4
Managua, *Nic.* 116 D2
Managua, L., *Nic.* 116 D2
Manakara, *Madag.* 85 C8
Manama = Al Manāmah,
  Bahrain 65 E6
Manambao →, *Madag.* ... 85 B7
Manambato, *Madag.* 85 A8
Manambolo →, *Madag.* .. 85 B7
Manambolosy, *Madag.* ... 85 B8
Mananara, *Madag.* 85 B8
Mananara →, *Madag.* 85 C8
Mananjary, *Madag.* 85 C8

Manantenina, *Madag.* 85 C8
Manaos = Manaus, *Brazil* 121 D6
Manapire →, *Venezuela* .. 120 B4
Manapouri, *N.Z.* 87 L1
Manapouri, L., *N.Z.* 87 L1
Manas, *China* 54 B3
Manas →, *India* 61 F17
Manaslu, *Nepal* 63 E11
Manasquan, *U.S.A.* 107 F10
Manassa, *U.S.A.* 111 H11
Manaung, *Burma* 61 K18
Manaus, *Brazil* 121 D6
Manavgat, *Turkey* 66 E4
Manawan L., *Canada* 101 B8
Manay, *Phil.* 55 H7
Manbij, *Syria* 64 B3
Mancelona, *U.S.A.* 104 C3
Mancha Real, *Spain* 31 H7
Manche □, *France* 24 C5
Manchester, *U.K.* 12 D5
Manchester, *Calif., U.S.A.* 112 G3
Manchester, *Conn., U.S.A.* 107 E12
Manchester, *Ga., U.S.A.* . 105 J3
Manchester, *Iowa, U.S.A.* 108 D9
Manchester, *Ky., U.S.A.* . 104 G4
Manchester, *N.H., U.S.A.* 107 D13
Manchester, *N.Y., U.S.A.* 106 D7
Manchester, *Vt., U.S.A.* . 107 C11
Manchester L., *Canada* ... 101 A7
Manchuria = Dongbei,
  China 51 D13
Manciano, *Italy* 33 F8
Mancifa, *Ethiopia* 77 F5
Mancora, Pta., *Peru* 124 A1
Mand →, *Iran* 65 D7
Manda, Chunya, *Tanzania* 82 D3
Manda, Ludewe, *Tanzania* 83 E3
Mandabé, *Madag.* 85 C7
Mandaguari, *Brazil* 127 A5
Mandah, *Mongolia* 50 B5
Mandal, *Norway* 9 G9
Mandalay, *Burma* 61 J20
Mandale = Mandalay,
  Burma 61 J20
Mandalgovi, *Mongolia* ... 50 B4
Mandalī, *Iraq* 64 C5
Mandan, *U.S.A.* 108 B4
Mandaon, *Phil.* 55 E5
Mandar, Teluk, *Indonesia* . 57 E5
Mandas, *Italy* 34 C2
Mandasor = Mandsaur,
  India 62 G6
Mandaue, *Phil.* 55 F5
Mandelieu-la-Napoule,
  France 27 E10
Mandera, *Kenya* 82 B5
Mandera □, *Kenya* 82 B5
Manderfeld, *Belgium* 17 H8
Mandi, *India* 62 D7
Mandimba, *Mozam.* 83 E4
Mandioli, *Indonesia* 57 E7
Mandioré, L., *S. Amer.* .. 125 D6
Mandla, *India* 63 H9
Mandø, *Denmark* 11 J2
Mandoto, *Madag.* 85 B8
Mandoúdhion, *Greece* ... 39 L6
Mandra, *Pakistan* 62 C5
Mandrare →, *Madag.* 85 D8
Mandritsara, *Madag.* 85 B8
Mandsaur, *India* 62 G6
Mandurah, *Australia* 89 F2
Mandúria, *Italy* 35 B10
Mandvi, *India* 62 H3
Mandya, *India* 60 N10
Mandzai, *Pakistan* 62 D2
Mané, *Burkina Faso* 79 C4
Maneh, *Iran* 65 B8
Manengouba, Mts.,
  Cameroon 79 D6
Maneroo, *Australia* 90 C3
Maneroo Cr. →, *Australia* 90 C3
Manfalût, *Egypt* 76 B3
Manfred, *Australia* 91 E3
Manfredónia, *Italy* 35 A8
Manfredónia, G. di, *Italy* . 35 A9
Manga, *Brazil* 123 D3
Manga, *Burkina Faso* 79 C4
Manga, *Niger* 79 C7
Mangabeiras, Chapada das,
  Brazil 122 D2
Mangalia, *Romania* 38 F11
Mangalore, *India* 60 N9
Manganeses, *Spain* 30 D5
Mangaweka, *N.Z.* 87 H5
Manggar, *Indonesia* 56 E3
Manggawitu, *Indonesia* .. 57 E8
Mangkalihat, Tanjung,
  Indonesia 57 D5
Mangla Dam, *Pakistan* ... 63 C5
Manglares, C., *Colombia* . 120 C2
Manglaur, *India* 62 E7
Mangnai, *China* 54 C4
Mango, *Togo* 79 C5
Mangoche, *Malawi* 83 E4
Mangoky →, *Madag.* 85 C7
Mangole, *Indonesia* 57 E7
Mangombe, *Zaïre* 82 C2
Mangonui, *N.Z.* 87 F4
Mangualde, *Portugal* 30 E3
Mangueigne, *Chad* 73 F9
Mangueira, L. da, *Brazil* . 127 C5
Manguéni, Hamada, *Niger* 75 D7
Mangum, *U.S.A.* 109 H5
Mangyshlak Poluostrov,
  Kazakhstan 43 D15

Mangyshlakskiy Zaliv, Kazakhstan 43 D14
Manhattan, U.S.A. 108 F6
Manhiça, Mozam. 85 D5
Manhuaçu, Brazil 123 F3
Manhumirim, Brazil 123 F3
Maní, Colombia 120 C3
Mania →, Madag. 85 B8
Maniago, Italy 33 B9
Manica, Mozam. 85 B5
Manica e Sofala □, Mozam. 85 B5
Manicaland □, Zimbabwe 83 F3
Manicoré, Brazil 125 B5
Manicoré →, Brazil 125 B5
Manicouagan →, Canada . 99 C6
Manīfah, Si. Arabia 65 E6
Manifold, Australia 90 C5
Manifold, C., Australia .. 90 C5
Maniganggo, China 52 B2
Manigotagan, Canada ... 101 C9
Manihiki, Cook Is. 93 J11
Manika, Plateau de la, Zaïre 83 E2
Manila, Phil. 55 D4
Manila, U.S.A. 110 F9
Manila B., Phil. 55 D4
Manilla, Australia 91 E5
Manimpé, Mali 78 C3
Maningrida, Australia ... 90 A1
Manipur □, India 61 G18
Manipur →, Burma 61 H19
Manisa, Turkey 66 C2
Manisa □, Turkey 66 D2
Manistee, U.S.A. 104 C2
Manistee →, U.S.A. 104 C2
Manistique, U.S.A. 104 C2
Manito L., Canada 101 C7
Manitoba □, Canada 101 B9
Manitoba, L., Canada ... 101 C9
Manitou, Canada 101 D9
Manitou I., U.S.A. 98 C2
Manitou Is., U.S.A. 104 C2
Manitou L., Canada 99 B6
Manitou Springs, U.S.A. 108 F2
Manitoulin I., Canada ... 98 C3
Manitowaning, Canada .. 98 C3
Manitowoc, U.S.A. 104 C2
Manitsauá-Missu →, Brazil 125 C7
Manizales, Colombia 120 B2
Manja, Madag. 85 C7
Manjacaze, Mozam. 85 C5
Manjakandriana, Madag. . 85 B8
Manjhand, Pakistan 62 G3
Manjil, Iran 65 B6
Manjimup, Australia 89 F2
Manjra →, India 60 K10
Mankato, Kans., U.S.A. . 108 F5
Mankato, Minn., U.S.A. . 108 C8
Mankayane, Swaziland .. 85 D5
Mankono, Ivory C. 78 D3
Mankota, Canada 101 D7
Manlay, Mongolia 50 B4
Manlleu, Spain 28 C7
Manly, Australia 91 E5
Manmad, India 60 J9
Mann Ras., Australia ... 89 E5
Manna, Indonesia 56 E2
Mannahill, Australia 91 E3
Mannar, Sri Lanka 60 Q11
Mannar, G. of, Asia 60 Q11
Mannar I., Sri Lanka ... 60 Q11
Männedorf, Switz. 23 B7
Mannheim, Germany 19 F4
Manning, Canada 100 B5
Manning, Oreg., U.S.A. . 112 E3
Manning, S.C., U.S.A. .. 105 J5
Manning Prov. Park, Canada 100 D4
Mannington, U.S.A. 104 F5
Mannu →, Italy 34 C2
Mannu, C., Italy 34 B1
Mannum, Australia 91 E2
Mano, S. Leone 78 D2
Manoa, Bolivia 125 B4
Manokwari, Indonesia ... 57 E8
Manombo, Madag. 85 C7
Manono, Zaïre 82 D2
Manosque, France 27 E9
Manouane, L., Canada .. 99 B5
Manpojin, N. Korea 51 D14
Manresa, Spain 28 D6
Mansa, Gujarat, India .. 62 H5
Mansa, Punjab, India ... 62 E6
Mansa, Zambia 83 E2
Mansehra, Pakistan 62 B5
Mansel I., Canada 97 B11
Mansfield, Australia 91 F4
Mansfield, U.K. 12 D6
Mansfield, La., U.S.A. .. 109 J8
Mansfield, Mass., U.S.A. 107 D13
Mansfield, Ohio, U.S.A. . 106 F2
Mansfield, Pa., U.S.A. .. 106 E7
Mansfield, Wash., U.S.A. 110 C4
Mansidão, Brazil 122 D3
Mansilla de las Mulas, Spain 30 C5
Mansle, France 26 C4
Manso →, Brazil 123 D2
Mansoa, Guinea-Biss. ... 78 C1
Manson Creek, Canada .. 100 B4
Mansoura, Algeria 75 A5
Manta, Ecuador 120 D1
Manta, B. de, Ecuador .. 120 D1
Mantalingajan, Mt., Phil. 55 G2

Mantare, Tanzania 82 C3
Manteca, U.S.A. 111 H3
Mantecal, Venezuela 120 B4
Mantena, Brazil 123 E3
Manteo, U.S.A. 105 H8
Mantes-la-Jolie, France . 25 D8
Manthani, India 60 K11
Manthelan, France 24 E7
Manti, U.S.A. 110 G8
Mantiqueira, Serra da, Brazil 123 F3
Manton, U.S.A. 104 C3
Mantorp, Sweden 11 F9
Mántova, Italy 32 C7
Mantua = Mántova, Italy . 32 C7
Manturovo, Russia 41 B14
Manu, Peru 124 C3
Manu →, Peru 124 C3
Manua Is., Amer. Samoa . 87 B14
Manuae, Cook Is. 93 J12
Manuel Alves →, Brazil . 123 D2
Manuel Alves Grande →, Brazil 122 C2
Manuel Urbano, Brazil .. 124 B4
Manui, Indonesia 57 E6
Manuripi →, Bolivia 124 C4
Manville, U.S.A. 108 D2
Many, U.S.A. 109 K8
Manyara, L., Tanzania .. 82 C4
Manych →, Russia 43 C8
Manych-Gudilo, Oz., Russia 43 C10
Manyonga →, Tanzania . 82 C3
Manyoni, Tanzania 82 D3
Manyoni □, Tanzania ... 82 D3
Manzai, Pakistan 62 C4
Manzala, Bahra el, Egypt 76 H7
Manzanares, Spain 29 F1
Manzaneda, Cabeza de, Spain 30 C3
Manzanillo, Cuba 116 B4
Manzanillo, Mexico 114 D4
Manzanillo, Pta., Panama 116 E4
Manzano Mts., U.S.A. .. 111 J10
Manzarīyeh, Iran 65 C6
Manzhouli, China 54 B6
Manzini, Swaziland 85 D5
Mao, Chad 73 F8
Maoke, Pegunungan, Indonesia 57 E9
Maolin, China 51 C12
Maoming, China 53 G8
Maowen, China 52 B4
Maoxing, China 51 B13
Mapam Yumco, China .. 54 C3
Mapastepec, Mexico 115 D6
Mapia, Kepulauan, Indonesia 57 D8
Mapimí, Mexico 114 B4
Mapimí, Bolsón de, Mexico 114 B4
Maping, China 53 B9
Mapinga, Tanzania 82 D4
Mapinhane, Mozam. 85 C6
Mapire, Venezuela 121 B5
Maple Creek, Canada ... 101 D7
Maple Valley, U.S.A. ... 112 C4
Mapleton, U.S.A. 110 D2
Mapuera →, Brazil 121 D6
Maputo, Mozam. 85 D5
Maputo, B. de, Mozam. . 85 D5
Maqiaohe, China 51 B16
Maqnā, Si. Arabia 64 D2
Maqteïr, Mauritania 74 D2
Maquela do Zombo, Angola 80 F3
Maquinchao, Argentina . 128 B3
Maquoketa, U.S.A. 108 D9
Mar, Serra do, Brazil ... 127 B6
Mar Chiquita, L., Argentina 126 C3
Mar del Plata, Argentina 126 D4
Mar Menor, L., Spain ... 29 H4
Mara, Guyana 121 B6
Mara, Tanzania 82 C3
Mara □, Tanzania 82 C3
Maraã, Brazil 120 D4
Marabá, Brazil 122 C2
Maracá, I. de, Brazil ... 121 C7
Maracaibo, Venezuela ... 120 A3
Maracaibo, L. de, Venezuela 120 B3
Maracaju, Brazil 127 A4
Maracajú, Serra de, Brazil 125 E6
Maracanã, Brazil 122 B2
Maracás, Brazil 123 D3
Maracay, Venezuela 120 A4
Marādah, Libya 73 C8
Maradi, Niger 79 C6
Maradun, Nigeria 79 C6
Marāgheh, Iran 64 B5
Maragogipe, Brazil 123 D4
Marāh, Si. Arabia 64 E5
Marajó, B. de, Brazil ... 122 B2
Marajó, I. de, Brazil ... 122 B2
Marākand, Iran 64 B5
Maralal, Kenya 82 B4
Maralinga, Australia 89 F5
Marama, Australia 91 F3
Marampa, S. Leone 78 D2
Maran, Malaysia 59 L4
Marana, U.S.A. 111 K8
Maranboy, Australia 88 B5
Maranchón, Spain 28 D2
Marand, Iran 64 B5

Marang, Malaysia 59 K4
Maranguape, Brazil 122 B4
Maranhão = São Luís, Brazil 122 B3
Maranhão □, Brazil 122 B2
Marano, L. di, Italy 33 C10
Maranoa →, Australia .. 91 D4
Marañón →, Peru 124 A3
Marão, Mozam. 85 C5
Marapi →, Brazil 121 C6
Marari, Brazil 124 B4
Maraş = Kahramanmaraş, Turkey 66 E7
Mărăşeşti, Romania 38 D10
Maratea, Italy 35 C8
Marateca, Portugal 31 G2
Marathasa □, Cyprus ... 37 E11
Marathókambos, Greece . 39 M9
Marathon, Australia 90 C3
Marathon, Canada 98 C2
Marathón, Greece 39 L6
Marathon, N.Y., U.S.A. . 107 D8
Marathon, Tex., U.S.A. . 109 K3
Marathóvouno, Cyprus .. 37 D12
Maratua, Indonesia 57 D5
Maraú, Brazil 123 D4
Marāwih, U.A.E. 65 E7
Marawi City, Phil. 55 G6
Marbella, Spain 31 J6
Marble Bar, Australia ... 88 D2
Marble Falls, U.S.A. ... 109 K5
Marblehead, U.S.A. 107 D14
Marburg, Germany 18 E4
Marby, Sweden 10 A8
Marcal →, Hungary 21 H7
Marcapata, Peru 124 C3
Marcaria, Italy 32 C7
March, U.K. 13 E8
Marchand = Rommani, Morocco 74 B3
Marche, France 26 B5
Marche □, Italy 33 E10
Marche-en-Famenne, Belgium 17 H6
Marchena, Spain 31 H5
Marches = Marche □, Italy 33 E10
Marciana Marina, Italy .. 32 F7
Marcianise, Italy 35 A7
Marcigny, France 27 B8
Marcillat-en-Combraille, France 26 B6
Marcinelle, Belgium 17 H4
Marck, France 25 B8
Marckolsheim, France .. 25 D14
Marcona, Peru 124 D2
Marcos Juárez, Argentina 126 C3
Marcus I. = Minami-Tori-Shima, Pac. Oc. 92 E7
Marcus Necker Ridge, Pac. Oc. 92 F9
Marcy, Mt., U.S.A. 107 B11
Mardan, Pakistan 62 B5
Mardie, Australia 88 D2
Mardin, Turkey 67 E9
Marechal Deodoro, Brazil 122 C4
Maree L., U.K. 14 D3
Mareeba, Australia 90 B4
Marek = Stanke Dimitrov, Bulgaria 38 G6
Marek, Indonesia 57 E6
Maremma, Italy 32 F8
Maréna, Mali 78 C3
Marenberg, Slovenia ... 33 B12
Marengo, U.S.A. 108 E8
Marennes, France 26 C2
Marenyi, Kenya 82 C4
Marerano, Madag. 85 C7
Maréttimo, Italy 34 E5
Mareuil-sur-Lay, France . 26 B2
Marfa, U.S.A. 109 K2
Marfa Pt., Malta 37 D1
Marganets, Ukraine 42 C6
Margaret →, Australia .. 88 C4
Margaret Bay, Canada .. 100 C3
Margaret L., Canada ... 100 B5
Margaret River, Australia 88 C4
Margarita, I. de, Venezuela 121 A5
Margarítion, Greece 39 K3
Margaritovo, Russia 48 C7
Margate, S. Africa 85 E5
Margate, U.K. 13 F9
Margelan, Uzbekistan ... 44 E8
Margeride, Mts. de la, France 26 D7
Margherita di Savola, Italy 35 A9
Margosatubig, Phil. 55 H5
Marguerite, Canada 100 C4
Marhoum, Algeria 75 B4
Mari Republic □, Russia . 41 C16
María Elena, Chile 126 A2
María Grande, Argentina 126 C4
Maria I., N. Terr., Australia 90 A2
Maria I., Tas., Australia . 90 G4
Maria van Diemen, C., N.Z. 87 F4
Mariager, Denmark 11 H4
Mariager Fjord, Denmark 11 H4
Mariakani, Kenya 82 C4
Marian L., Canada 100 A5
Mariana Trench, Pac. Oc. 92 F6
Marianao, Cuba 116 B3
Marianna, Ark., U.S.A. . 109 H9
Marianna, Fla., U.S.A. . 105 K3

Mariánské Lázně, Czech. . 20 F2
Marias →, U.S.A. 110 C8
Mariato, Punta, Panama 116 E3
Mariazell, Austria 21 H5
Ma'rib, Yemen 68 D4
Maribo, Denmark 11 K5
Maribor, Slovenia 33 B12
Marico →, Africa 84 C4
Maricopa, Ariz., U.S.A. . 111 K7
Maricopa, Calif., U.S.A. 113 K7
Maricourt, Canada 97 C12
Marīdī, Sudan 77 G2
Maridi, Wadi →, Sudan . 77 F2
Marié →, Brazil 120 D4
Marie Byrd Land, Antarctica 5 D14
Marie-Galante, Guadeloupe 117 C7
Mariecourt, Canada 97 B12
Mariefred, Sweden 10 E11
Mariehamn, Finland ... 9 F15
Marienbad = Mariánské Lázně, Czech. 20 F2
Marienberg, Germany .. 18 E9
Marienberg, Neths. 16 D9
Marienbourg, Belgium .. 17 H5
Mariental, Namibia 84 C2
Marienville, U.S.A. 106 E5
Mariestad, Sweden 11 F7
Marietta, Ga., U.S.A. .. 105 J3
Marietta, Ohio, U.S.A. . 104 F5
Marieville, Canada 107 A11
Marignane, France 27 E9
Marihatag, Phil. 55 G7
Mariinsk, Russia 44 D9
Mariinskiy Posad, Russia 41 C15
Marília, Brazil 127 A5
Marillana, Australia 88 D2
Marín, Spain 30 C2
Marina, U.S.A. 112 J5
Marina di Cirò, Italy ... 35 C10
Marina Plains, Australia . 90 A3
Marinduque, Phil. 55 E5
Marine City, U.S.A. 104 D4
Marineo, Italy 34 E6
Marinette, U.S.A. 104 C2
Maringá, Brazil 127 A5
Marinha Grande, Portugal 31 F2
Marion, Ala., U.S.A. ... 105 J2
Marion, Ill., U.S.A. 109 G10
Marion, Ind., U.S.A. ... 104 E3
Marion, Iowa, U.S.A. .. 108 D9
Marion, Kans., U.S.A. .. 108 F6
Marion, Mich., U.S.A. .. 104 C3
Marion, N.C., U.S.A. ... 105 H4
Marion, Ohio, U.S.A. ... 104 E4
Marion, S.C., U.S.A. ... 105 H6
Marion, Va., U.S.A. 105 G5
Marion, L., U.S.A. 105 J5
Maripa, Venezuela 121 B4
Maripasoula, Fr. Guiana 121 C7
Mariposa, U.S.A. 111 H4
Mariscal Estigarribia, Paraguay 126 A3
Maritime Alps = Maritimes, Alpes, Europe 27 D11
Maritimes, Alpes, Europe 27 D11
Maritsa, Greece 37 C10
Mariupol, Ukraine 42 C7
Marīvān, Iran 64 C5
Mariyampol, Lithuania .. 40 D3
Markam, China 52 C2
Markazī □, Iran 65 C6
Markdale, Canada 106 B4
Marke, Belgium 17 G2
Marked Tree, U.S.A. ... 109 H9
Markelsdorfer Huk, Germany 18 A6
Marken, Neths. 16 D6
Markermeer, Neths. 16 C6
Market Drayton, U.K. .. 12 E5
Market Harborough, U.K. 13 E7
Markham, Canada 106 C5
Markham, Mt., Antarctica 5 E11
Markham L., Canada ... 101 A8
Marki, Poland 20 C11
Markleeville, U.S.A. 112 G7
Markoupoulon, Greece .. 39 M6
Markovo, Russia 45 C17
Markoye, Burkina Faso . 79 C5
Marks, Russia 41 F15
Marksville, U.S.A. 109 K8
Markt Schwaben, Germany 19 G7
Marktredwitz, Germany . 19 E8
Marla, Australia 91 D1
Marlboro, U.S.A. 107 D13
Marlborough, Australia . 90 C4
Marlborough Downs, U.K. 13 F6
Marle, France 25 C10
Marlin, U.S.A. 109 K6
Marlow, Germany 18 A8
Marlow, U.S.A. 109 H6
Marly-le-Grand, Switz. . 22 C4
Marmagao, India 60 M8
Marmande, France 26 D4
Marmara, Turkey 42 F2
Marmara, Sea of = Marmara Denizi, Turkey 66 C3
Marmara Denizi, Turkey . 66 C3
Marmara Gölü, Turkey .. 66 D3
Marmaris, Turkey 66 D3
Marmarth, U.S.A. 108 B3
Marmelos →, Brazil 125 B5
Marmion, Mt., Australia . 89 E2
Marmion L., Canada ... 98 C1

Marmolada, Mte., Italy . 33 B8
Marmolejo, Spain 31 G6
Marmora, Canada 98 D4
Marnay, France 25 E12
Marne □, Germany 18 B5
Marne □, France 25 D11
Marne →, France 25 D9
Marneuli, Georgia 43 F11
Maroa, Venezuela 120 C4
Maroala, Madag. 85 B8
Maroantsetra, Madag. .. 85 B8
Maromandia, Madag. ... 85 A8
Marondera, Zimbabwe .. 83 F3
Maroni →, Fr. Guiana .. 121 B7
Maronne →, France ... 26 C5
Maroochydore, Australia 91 D5
Maroona, Australia 91 F3
Maros →, Hungary 21 J10
Marosakoa, Madag. ... 85 B8
Marostica, Italy 33 C8
Maroua, Cameroon 79 C7
Marovoay, Madag. 85 B8
Marowijne □, Surinam .. 121 C7
Marowijne →, Surinam . 121 B7
Marquard, S. Africa 84 D4
Marqueira, Portugal ... 31 G1
Marquesas Is. = Marquises, Is., Pac. Oc. 93 H14
Marquette, U.S.A. 104 B2
Marquise, France 25 B8
Marquises, Is., Pac. Oc. . 93 H14
Marra, Gebel, Sudan ... 77 F2
Marracuene, Mozam. ... 85 D5
Marradi, Italy 33 D8
Marrakech, Morocco ... 74 B3
Marrawah, Australia ... 90 G3
Marrecas, Serra das, Brazil 122 C3
Marree, Australia 91 D2
Marrilla, Australia 88 D1
Marrimane, Mozam. ... 85 C5
Marromeu, Mozam. 85 B6
Marroquí, Punta, Spain . 31 K5
Marrowie Cr. →, Australia 91 E4
Marrubane, Mozam. 83 F4
Marrum, Neths. 16 B7
Marrupa, Mozam. 83 E4
Marsá Matrûh, Egypt ... 76 A2
Marsá Susah, Libya 73 B9
Marsabit, Kenya 82 B4
Marsabit □, Kenya 82 B4
Marsala, Italy 34 E5
Marsalforn, Malta 37 C1
Marsberg, Germany 18 D4
Marsciano, Italy 33 F9
Marsden, Australia 91 E4
Marsdiep, Neths. 16 C5
Marseillan, France 26 E7
Marseille, France 27 E9
Marseilles = Marseille, France 27 E9
Marsh I., U.S.A. 109 L9
Marsh L., U.S.A. 108 C6
Marshall, Liberia 78 D2
Marshall, Ark., U.S.A. .. 109 H8
Marshall, Mich., U.S.A. . 104 D3
Marshall, Minn., U.S.A. 108 C7
Marshall, Mo., U.S.A. .. 108 F8
Marshall, Tex., U.S.A. .. 109 J7
Marshall →, Australia .. 90 C2
Marshall Is. ■, Pac. Oc. 92 G9
Marshalltown, U.S.A. .. 108 D8
Marshfield, Mo., U.S.A. 109 G8
Marshfield, Wis., U.S.A. 108 C9
Marshūn, Iran 65 B6
Mársico Nuovo, Italy ... 35 B8
Märsta, Sweden 10 E11
Marstal, Denmark 11 K4
Marstrand, Sweden 11 G5
Mart, U.S.A. 109 K6
Marta →, Italy 33 F8
Martaban, Burma 61 L20
Martaban, G. of, Burma 61 L20
Martano, Italy 35 B11
Martapura, Kalimantan, Indonesia 56 E4
Martapura, Sumatera, Indonesia 56 E2
Marte, Nigeria 79 C7
Martel, France 26 D5
Martelange, Belgium ... 17 J7
Martés, Sierra, Spain ... 29 F4
Martha's Vineyard, U.S.A. 107 E14
Martigné-Ferchaud, France 24 E5
Martigny, Switz. 22 D4
Martigues, France 27 E9
Martil, Morocco 74 A3
Martin, Slovakia 20 F8
Martin, S. Dak., U.S.A. . 108 D4
Martin, Tenn., U.S.A. .. 109 G10
Martín →, Spain 28 D4
Martin L., U.S.A. 105 J3
Martina, Switz. 23 C10
Martina Franca, Italy ... 35 B10
Martinborough, N.Z. ... 87 J5
Martinez, U.S.A. 112 G4
Martinho Campos, Brazil 123 E2
Martinique ■, W. Indies 117 D7
Martinique Passage, W. Indies 117 C7
Martínon, Greece 39 L6
Martinópolis, Brazil 127 A5
Martins Ferry, U.S.A. .. 106 F4
Martinsburg, Pa., U.S.A. 106 F6
Martinsburg, W. Va., U.S.A. 104 F7

Martinsville, *Ind., U.S.A.*	104	F2
Martinsville, *Va., U.S.A.*	105	G6
Marton, *N.Z.*	87	J5
Martorell, *Spain*	28	D6
Martos, *Spain*	31	H7
Martuni, *Armenia*	43	F11
Maru, *Nigeria*	79	C6
Marudi, *Malaysia*	56	D4
Ma'ruf, *Afghan.*	60	D5
Marugame, *Japan*	49	G6
Maruim, *Brazil*	122	D4
Marulan, *Australia*	91	E5
Marum, *Neths.*	16	B8
Marunga, *Angola*	84	B3
Marungu, Mts., *Zaïre*	82	D2
Marvast, *Iran*	65	D7
Marvejols, *France*	26	D7
Marwar, *India*	62	G5
Mary, *Turkmenistan*	44	F7
Mary Frances L., *Canada*	101	A7
Mary Kathleen, *Australia*	90	C2
Maryborough = Port Laoise, *Ireland*	15	C4
Maryborough, *Queens., Australia*	91	D5
Maryborough, *Vic., Australia*	91	F3
Maryfield, *Canada*	101	D8
Maryland □, *U.S.A.*	104	F7
Maryland Junction, *Zimbabwe*	83	F3
Maryport, *U.K.*	12	C4
Mary's Harbour, *Canada*	99	B8
Marystown, *Canada*	99	C8
Marysvale, *U.S.A.*	111	G7
Marysville, *Canada*	100	D5
Marysville, *Calif., U.S.A.*	112	F5
Marysville, *Kans., U.S.A.*	108	F6
Marysville, *Mich., U.S.A.*	106	D2
Marysville, *Ohio, U.S.A.*	104	E4
Marysville, *Wash., U.S.A.*	112	B4
Maryvale, *Australia*	91	D5
Maryville, *U.S.A.*	105	H4
Marzo, Punta, *Colombia*	120	B2
Marzūq, *Libya*	73	C7
Masahunga, *Tanzania*	82	C3
Masai, *Malaysia*	59	M4
Masai Steppe, *Tanzania*	82	C4
Masaka, *Uganda*	82	C3
Masalembo, Kepulauan, *Indonesia*	56	F4
Masalima, Kepulauan, *Indonesia*	56	F5
Masamba, *Indonesia*	57	E6
Masan, *S. Korea*	51	G15
Masanasa, *Spain*	29	F4
Masasi, *Tanzania*	83	E4
Masasi □, *Tanzania*	83	E4
Masaya, *Nic.*	116	D2
Masba, *Nigeria*	79	C7
Masbate, *Phil.*	55	E5
Mascara, *Algeria*	75	A5
Mascota, *Mexico*	114	C4
Masela, *Indonesia*	57	F7
Maseru, *Lesotho*	84	D4
Mashaba, *Zimbabwe*	83	G3
Mashābih, *Si. Arabia*	64	E3
Mashan, *China*	52	F7
Masherbrum, *Pakistan*	63	B7
Mashhad, *Iran*	65	B8
Mashi, *Nigeria*	79	C6
Mashīz, *Iran*	65	D8
Mashkel, Hamun-i-, *Pakistan*	60	E3
Mashki Chāh, *Pakistan*	60	E3
Mashonaland Central □, *Zimbabwe*	85	B5
Mashonaland East □, *Zimbabwe*	85	B5
Mashonaland West □, *Zimbabwe*	85	B4
Mashtaga, *Azerbaijan*	43	F13
Masi, *Norway*	8	B17
Masi Manimba, *Zaïre*	80	E3
Masindi, *Uganda*	82	B3
Masindi Port, *Uganda*	82	B3
Masisea, *Peru*	124	B3
Masisi, *Zaïre*	82	C2
Masjed Soleyman, *Iran*	65	D6
Mask, L., *Ireland*	15	C2
Maslinica, *Croatia*	33	E13
Masnou, *Spain*	28	D7
Masoala, Tanjon' i, *Madag.*	85	B9
Masoarivo, *Madag.*	85	B7
Masohi, *Indonesia*	57	E7
Masomeloka, *Madag.*	85	C8
Mason, *Nev., U.S.A.*	112	G7
Mason, *Tex., U.S.A.*	109	K5
Mason City, *U.S.A.*	108	D8
Maspalomas, *Canary Is.*	36	G4
Maspalomas, Pta., *Canary Is.*	36	G4
Masqat, *Oman*	68	C6
Massa, *Italy*	32	D7
Massa, O. →, *Morocco*	74	B3
Massa Maríttima, *Italy*	32	E7
Massachusetts □, *U.S.A.*	107	D12
Massachusetts B., *U.S.A.*	107	D14
Massafra, *Italy*	35	B10
Massaguet, *Chad*	73	F8
Massakory, *Chad*	73	F8
Massanella, *Spain*	36	B9
Massangena, *Mozam.*	85	C5
Massapê, *Brazil*	122	B3
Massarosa, *Italy*	32	E7
Massat, *France*	26	F5
Massawa = Mitsiwa, *Eritrea*	77	D4
Massena, *U.S.A.*	107	B10
Massénya, *Chad*	73	F8
Masset, *Canada*	100	C2
Massiac, *France*	26	C7
Massif Central, *France*	26	D7
Massillon, *U.S.A.*	106	F3
Massinga, *Mozam.*	85	C6
Masson, *Canada*	107	A9
Masson I., *Antarctica*	5	C7
Mastanli = Momchilgrad, *Bulgaria*	39	H8
Masterton, *N.Z.*	87	J5
Mástikho, Ákra, *Greece*	39	L9
Mastuj, *Pakistan*	63	A5
Mastung, *Pakistan*	60	E5
Mastūrah, *Si. Arabia*	76	C4
Masuda, *Japan*	49	G5
Masvingo, *Zimbabwe*	83	G3
Masvingo □, *Zimbabwe*	83	G3
Maswa □, *Tanzania*	82	C3
Maşyāf, *Syria*	64	C3
Mata de São João, *Brazil*	123	D4
Matabeleland North □, *Zimbabwe*	83	F2
Matabeleland South □, *Zimbabwe*	83	G2
Mataboor, *Indonesia*	57	E9
Matachel →, *Spain*	31	G4
Matachewan, *Canada*	98	C3
Matacuni →, *Venezuela*	121	C4
Matad, *Mongolia*	54	B6
Matadi, *Zaïre*	80	F2
Matagalpa, *Nic.*	116	D2
Matagami, *Canada*	98	C4
Matagami, L., *Canada*	98	C4
Matagorda, *U.S.A.*	109	L7
Matagorda B., *U.S.A.*	109	L6
Matagorda I., *U.S.A.*	109	L6
Matak, P., *Indonesia*	59	L6
Matakana, *Australia*	91	E4
Mátala, *Greece*	37	E6
Matalaque, *Peru*	124	D3
Matam, *Senegal*	78	B2
Matameye, *Niger*	79	C6
Matamoros, *Campeche, Mexico*	115	D6
Matamoros, *Coahuila, Mexico*	114	B4
Matamoros, *Puebla, Mexico*	115	D5
Matamoros, *Tamaulipas, Mexico*	115	B5
Ma'ṭan as Sarra, *Libya*	73	D9
Matandu →, *Tanzania*	83	D3
Matane, *Canada*	99	C6
Matang, *China*	52	F5
Matankari, *Niger*	79	C5
Matanzas, *Cuba*	116	B3
Matapan, C. = Taínaron, Ákra, *Greece*	39	N5
Matapédia, *Canada*	99	C6
Matara, *Sri Lanka*	60	S12
Mataram, *Indonesia*	56	F5
Matarani, *Peru*	124	D3
Mataranka, *Australia*	88	B5
Matarma, Râs, *Egypt*	69	E1
Mataró, *Spain*	28	D7
Matarraña →, *Spain*	28	D5
Matatiele, *S. Africa*	85	E4
Mataura, *N.Z.*	87	M2
Mategua, *Bolivia*	125	C5
Matehuala, *Mexico*	114	C4
Mateira, *Brazil*	123	E1
Mateke Hills, *Zimbabwe*	83	G3
Matélica, *Italy*	33	E10
Matera, *Italy*	35	B9
Mátészalka, *Hungary*	21	H12
Matetsi, *Zimbabwe*	83	F2
Mateur, *Tunisia*	75	A6
Matfors, *Sweden*	10	B11
Matha, *France*	26	C3
Matheson Island, *Canada*	101	C9
Mathis, *U.S.A.*	109	L6
Mathura, *India*	62	F7
Mati, *Phil.*	55	H7
Mati →, *Albania*	39	H2
Matías Romero, *Mexico*	115	D5
Matibane, *Mozam.*	83	E5
Matima, *Botswana*	84	C3
Matiri Ra., *N.Z.*	87	J4
Matlock, *U.K.*	12	D6
Matmata, *Tunisia*	75	B6
Matna, *Sudan*	77	E4
Mato, Serrania de, *Venezuela*	120	B4
Mato Grosso □, *Brazil*	125	C6
Mato Grosso, Planalto do, *Brazil*	125	C7
Mato Grosso do Sul □, *Brazil*	125	D7
Matochkin Shar, *Russia*	44	B6
Matopo Hills, *Zimbabwe*	83	G2
Matopos, *Zimbabwe*	83	G2
Matosinhos, *Portugal*	30	D2
Matour, *France*	27	B8
Matsena, *Nigeria*	79	C7
Matsesta, *Russia*	43	E8
Matsue, *Japan*	49	G6
Matsumae, *Japan*	48	D10
Matsumoto, *Japan*	49	F9
Matsusaka, *Japan*	49	G8
Matsuura, *Japan*	49	H4
Matsuyama, *Japan*	49	H6
Mattagami →, *Canada*	98	B3
Mattancheri, *India*	60	Q10
Mattawa, *Canada*	98	C4
Mattawamkeag, *U.S.A.*	99	C6
Matterhorn, *Switz.*	22	E5
Matthew Town, *Bahamas*	117	B5
Matthew's Ridge, *Guyana*	121	B5
Mattice, *Canada*	98	C3
Mattituck, *U.S.A.*	107	F12
Mattmar, *Sweden*	10	A7
Matuba, *Mozam.*	85	C5
Matucana, *Peru*	124	C2
Matun, *Afghan.*	62	C3
Maturín, *Venezuela*	121	B5
Matveyev Kurgan, *Russia*	43	C8
Mau, *India*	63	G10
Mau Escarpment, *Kenya*	82	C4
Mau Ranipur, *India*	63	G8
Maubeuge, *France*	25	B10
Maubourguet, *France*	26	E4
Maud, Pt., *Australia*	88	D1
Maude, *Australia*	91	E3
Maudin Sun, *Burma*	61	M19
Maués, *Brazil*	121	D6
Mauganj, *India*	61	G12
Maui, *U.S.A.*	102	H16
Maulamyaing = Moulmein, *Burma*	61	L20
Maule □, *Chile*	126	D1
Mauléon-Licharre, *France*	26	E3
Maullín, *Chile*	128	B2
Maumee, *U.S.A.*	104	E4
Maumee →, *U.S.A.*	104	E4
Maumere, *Indonesia*	57	F6
Maun, *Botswana*	84	C3
Mauna Kea, *U.S.A.*	102	J17
Mauna Loa, *U.S.A.*	102	J17
Maungmagan Kyunzu, *Burma*	61	M20
Maupin, *U.S.A.*	110	D3
Maure-de-Bretagne, *France*	24	E5
Maurepas, L., *U.S.A.*	109	K9
Maures, *France*	27	E10
Mauriac, *France*	26	C6
Maurice, L., *Australia*	89	E5
Mauritania ■, *Africa*	74	D3
Mauritius ■, *Ind. Oc.*	71	J9
Mauron, *France*	24	D4
Maurs, *France*	26	D6
Mauston, *U.S.A.*	108	D9
Mauterndorf, *Austria*	21	H3
Mauvezin, *France*	26	E4
Mauzé-sur-le-Mignon, *France*	26	B3
Mavaca →, *Venezuela*	121	C4
Mavinga, *Angola*	81	H4
Mavli, *India*	62	G5
Mavrova, *Albania*	39	J2
Mavuradonha Mts., *Zimbabwe*	83	F3
Mawa, *Zaïre*	82	B2
Mawana, *India*	62	E7
Mawand, *Pakistan*	62	E3
Mawk Mai, *Burma*	61	J20
Mawlaik, *Burma*	61	H19
Mawquq, *Si. Arabia*	64	E4
Mawson Coast, *Antarctica*	5	C6
Max, *U.S.A.*	108	B4
Maxcanú, *Mexico*	115	C6
Maxesibeni, *S. Africa*	85	E4
Maxhamish L., *Canada*	100	B4
Maxixe, *Mozam.*	85	C6
Maxville, *Canada*	107	A10
Maxwell, *U.S.A.*	112	F4
Maxwelton, *Australia*	90	C3
May Downs, *Australia*	90	C4
May Pen, *Jamaica*	116	C4
Maya, *Spain*	28	B3
Maya →, *Russia*	45	D14
Maya Mts., *Belize*	115	D7
Mayaguana, *Bahamas*	117	B5
Mayagüez, *Puerto Rico*	117	C6
Mayahi, *Niger*	79	C6
Mayals, *Spain*	28	D5
Mayāmey, *Iran*	65	B7
Mayang, *China*	52	D7
Mayarí, *Cuba*	117	B4
Maybell, *U.S.A.*	110	F9
Maychew, *Ethiopia*	77	E4
Maydān, *Iraq*	64	C5
Maydena, *Australia*	90	G4
Mayen, *Germany*	19	E3
Mayenne, *France*	24	D6
Mayenne □, *France*	24	D6
Mayenne →, *France*	24	E6
Mayer, *U.S.A.*	111	J7
Mayerthorpe, *Canada*	100	C5
Mayfield, *U.S.A.*	105	G1
Mayhill, *U.S.A.*	111	K11
Maykop, *Russia*	43	D9
Maymyo, *Burma*	58	A1
Maynard, *U.S.A.*	112	C4
Maynard Hills, *Australia*	89	E2
Mayne →, *Australia*	90	C3
Maynooth, *Ireland*	15	C5
Mayo, *Canada*	96	B6
Mayo □, *Ireland*	15	C2
Mayo →, *Argentina*	128	C3
Mayo →, *Peru*	124	B2
Mayo L., *Canada*	96	B6
Mayon Volcano, *Phil.*	55	E5
Mayor I., *N.Z.*	87	G6
Mayorga, *Spain*	30	C5
Mayraira Pt., *Phil.*	55	B4
Mayskiy, *Russia*	43	E11
Mayson L., *Canada*	101	B7
Maysville, *U.S.A.*	104	F4
Mayu, *Indonesia*	57	D7
Mayville, *N. Dak., U.S.A.*	108	B6
Mayville, *N.Y., U.S.A.*	106	D5
Mayya, *Russia*	45	C14
Mazabuka, *Zambia*	83	F2
Mazagán = El Jadida, *Morocco*	74	B3
Mazagão, *Brazil*	121	D7
Mazamet, *France*	26	E6
Mazán, *Peru*	120	D3
Māzandarān □, *Iran*	65	B7
Mazapil, *Mexico*	114	C4
Mazar, O. →, *Algeria*	75	B5
Mazara del Vallo, *Italy*	34	E5
Mazarredo, *Argentina*	128	C3
Mazarrón, *Spain*	29	H3
Mazarrón, G. de, *Spain*	29	H3
Mazaruni →, *Guyana*	121	B6
Mazatán, *Mexico*	114	B2
Mazatenango, *Guatemala*	116	D1
Mazatlán, *Mexico*	114	C3
Mažeikiai, *Lithuania*	40	C3
Māzhān, *Iran*	65	C8
Mazīnān, *Iran*	65	B8
Mazoe, *Mozam.*	83	F3
Mazoe →, *Mozam.*	83	F3
Mazowe, *Zimbabwe*	83	F3
Mazrūb, *Sudan*	77	E2
Mazu Dao, *China*	53	D12
Mazurian Lakes = Mazurski, Pojezierze, *Poland*	20	B10
Mazurski, Pojezierze, *Poland*	20	B10
Mazzarino, *Italy*	35	E7
Mbaba, *Senegal*	78	C1
Mbabane, *Swaziland*	85	D5
Mbagne, *Mauritania*	78	B2
M'bahiakro, *Ivory C.*	78	D4
Mbaïki, *C.A.R.*	80	D3
Mbala, *Zambia*	83	D3
Mbale, *Uganda*	82	B3
Mbalmayo, *Cameroon*	79	E7
Mbamba Bay, *Tanzania*	83	E3
Mbandaka, *Zaïre*	80	D3
Mbanga, *Cameroon*	79	E6
Mbanza Congo, *Angola*	80	F2
Mbanza Ngungu, *Zaïre*	80	F2
Mbarara, *Uganda*	82	C3
Mbashe →, *S. Africa*	85	E4
Mbatto, *Ivory C.*	78	D4
Mbenkuru →, *Tanzania*	83	D4
Mberengwa, *Zimbabwe*	83	G2
Mberengwa, Mt., *Zimbabwe*	83	G2
Mberubu, *Nigeria*	79	D6
Mbesuma, *Zambia*	83	D3
Mbeya, *Tanzania*	83	D3
Mbeya □, *Tanzania*	82	D3
Mbinga, *Tanzania*	83	E4
Mbinga □, *Tanzania*	83	E3
Mbini □, *Eq. Guin.*	80	D2
Mboki, *C.A.R.*	77	F2
Mboro, *Senegal*	78	B1
Mboune, *Senegal*	78	C2
Mbour, *Senegal*	78	C1
Mbout, *Mauritania*	78	B2
Mbozi □, *Tanzania*	83	D3
Mbuji-Mayi, *Zaïre*	82	D1
Mbulu, *Tanzania*	82	C4
Mbulu □, *Tanzania*	82	C4
Mburucuyá, *Argentina*	126	B4
Mcherrah, *Algeria*	74	C4
Mchinja, *Tanzania*	83	D4
Mchinji, *Malawi*	83	E3
Mdennah, *Mauritania*	74	D3
Mead, L., *U.S.A.*	113	J12
Meade, *U.S.A.*	109	G4
Meadow, *Australia*	89	E1
Meadow Lake, *Canada*	101	C7
Meadow Lake Prov. Park, *Canada*	101	C7
Meadow Valley Wash →, *U.S.A.*	113	J12
Meadville, *U.S.A.*	106	E4
Meaford, *Canada*	98	D3
Mealhada, *Portugal*	30	E2
Mealy Mts., *Canada*	99	B8
Meander River, *Canada*	100	B5
Meares, C., *U.S.A.*	110	D2
Mearim →, *Brazil*	122	B3
Meath □, *Ireland*	15	C5
Meath Park, *Canada*	101	C7
Meaulne, *France*	26	B6
Meaux, *France*	25	D9
Mebechi-Gawa →, *Japan*	48	D10
Mecanhelas, *Mozam.*	83	F4
Mecaya →, *Colombia*	120	C2
Mecca = Makkah, *Si. Arabia*	68	C2
Mecca, *U.S.A.*	113	M10
Mechanicsburg, *U.S.A.*	106	F8
Mechanicville, *U.S.A.*	107	D11
Mechara, *Ethiopia*	77	F5
Mechelen, *Antwerpen, Belgium*	17	F4
Mechelen, *Limburg, Belgium*	17	G7
Mecheria, *Algeria*	75	B4
Mechernich, *Germany*	18	E2
Mechetinskaya, *Russia*	43	C9
Mechra Benâbbou, *Morocco*	74	B3
Mecitözü, *Turkey*	42	F6
Mecklenburg-Vorpommern □, *Germany*	18	B8
Mecklenburger Bucht, *Germany*	18	A7
Meconta, *Mozam.*	83	E4
Meda, *Australia*	88	C3
Meda, *Portugal*	30	E3
Medan, *Indonesia*	56	D1
Médanos, *Argentina*	128	A4
Medanosa, Pta., *Argentina*	128	C3
Médéa, *Algeria*	75	A5
Medeiros Neto, *Brazil*	123	E3
Medel, Pic, *Switz.*	23	C7
Medellín, *Colombia*	120	B2
Medemblik, *Neths.*	16	C6
Médenine, *Tunisia*	75	B7
Mederdra, *Mauritania*	78	B1
Medford, *Mass., U.S.A.*	107	D13
Medford, *Oreg., U.S.A.*	110	E2
Medford, *Wis., U.S.A.*	108	C9
Medgidia, *Romania*	38	E11
Medi, *Sudan*	77	F3
Media Agua, *Argentina*	126	C2
Media Luna, *Argentina*	126	C2
Mediaş, *Romania*	38	C7
Medical Lake, *U.S.A.*	110	C5
Medicina, *Italy*	33	D8
Medicine Bow, *U.S.A.*	110	F10
Medicine Bow Pk., *U.S.A.*	110	F10
Medicine Bow Ra., *U.S.A.*	110	F10
Medicine Hat, *Canada*	101	D6
Medicine Lake, *U.S.A.*	108	A2
Medicine Lodge, *U.S.A.*	109	G5
Medina = Al Madīnah, *Si. Arabia*	64	E3
Medina, *Brazil*	123	E3
Medina, *Colombia*	120	C3
Medina, *N. Dak., U.S.A.*	108	B5
Medina, *N.Y., U.S.A.*	106	C6
Medina, *Ohio, U.S.A.*	106	E3
Medina →, *U.S.A.*	109	L5
Medina de Ríoseco, *Spain*	30	D5
Medina del Campo, *Spain*	30	D6
Medina L., *U.S.A.*	109	L5
Medina-Sidonia, *Spain*	31	J5
Medinaceli, *Spain*	28	D2
Medinipur, *India*	63	H12
Mediterranean Sea, *Europe*	70	C5
Medjerda, O. →, *Tunisia*	75	A6
Medley, *Canada*	101	C6
Médoc, *France*	26	C3
Medstead, *Canada*	101	C7
Medulin, *Croatia*	33	D10
Medveda, *Serbia*	21	N11
Medveditsa →, *Russia*	41	G13
Medveditsa →, *Russia*	41	C10
Medvedok, *Russia*	41	C17
Medvezhi, Ostrava, *Russia*	45	B17
Medvezhyegorsk, *Russia*	44	C4
Medway →, *U.K.*	13	F8
Medyn, *Russia*	41	D10
Medzilaborce, *Slovak Rep.*	20	F11
Meeberrie, *Australia*	89	E2
Meekatharra, *Australia*	89	E2
Meeker, *U.S.A.*	110	F10
Meer, *Belgium*	17	F5
Meerane, *Germany*	18	E8
Meerbeke, *Belgium*	17	G4
Meerhout, *Belgium*	17	F6
Meerle, *Belgium*	17	F5
Meersburg, *Germany*	19	H5
Meerssen, *Neths.*	17	G7
Meerut, *India*	62	E7
Meeteetse, *U.S.A.*	110	D9
Meeuwen, *Belgium*	17	F7
Mega, *Ethiopia*	77	G4
Megalo Petali, *Greece*	39	M7
Megalópolis, *Greece*	39	M5
Meganísi, *Greece*	39	L3
Mégara, *Greece*	39	M6
Megarine, *Algeria*	75	B6
Megève, *France*	27	C10
Meghalaya □, *India*	61	G17
Meghezez, *Ethiopia*	77	F4
Mégiscane, L., *Canada*	98	C4
Mehadia, *Romania*	38	E5
Mehaigne →, *Belgium*	17	G6
Mehaïguene, O. →, *Algeria*	75	B5
Meheisa, *Sudan*	76	D3
Mehndawal, *India*	63	F10
Mehr Jān, *Iran*	65	C7
Mehrābād, *Iran*	64	B5
Mehrān, *Iran*	64	C5
Mehrīz, *Iran*	65	D7
Mehun-sur-Yèvre, *France*	25	E9
Mei Jiang →, *China*	53	E11
Mei Xian, *Guangdong, China*	53	E11
Mei Xian, *Shaanxi, China*	50	G4
Meia Ponte →, *Brazil*	123	E2
Meicheng, *China*	53	C12
Meichengzhen, *China*	53	C8
Meichuan, *China*	53	B10
Meiganga, *Cameroon*	80	C2
Meijel, *Neths.*	17	F7
Meiktila, *Burma*	61	J19
Meilen, *Switz.*	23	B7
Meiningen, *Germany*	18	E6
Meio →, *Brazil*	123	D3
Meira, Sierra de, *Spain*	30	B3

Meiringen, *Switz.* 22 C6
Meishan, *China* 52 B4
Meissen, *Germany* 18 D9
Meissner, *Germany* 18 D5
Meitan, *China* 52 D6
Mejillones, *Chile* 126 A1
Meka, *Australia* 89 E2
Mékambo, *Gabon* 80 D2
Mekdela, *Ethiopia* 77 E4
Mekele, *Ethiopia* 77 E4
Mekhtar, *Pakistan* 60 D6
Meknès, *Morocco* 74 B3
Meko, *Nigeria* 79 D5
Mekong →, *Asia* 59 H6
Mekongga, *Indonesia* 57 E6
Melagiri Hills, *India* 60 N10
Melah, Sebkhet el, *Algeria* 75 C4
Melaka, *Malaysia* 59 L4
Melalap, *Malaysia* 56 C5
Mélambes, *Greece* 37 D6
Melanesia, *Pac. Oc.* 92 H7
Melbourne, *Australia* 91 F3
Melbourne, *U.S.A.* 105 L5
Melchor Múzquiz, *Mexico* 114 B4
Melchor Ocampo, *Mexico* 114 C4
Méldola, *Italy* 33 D9
Meldorf, *Germany* 18 A5
Melegnano, *Italy* 32 C6
Melenci, *Serbia* 21 K10
Melenki, *Russia* 41 D12
Mélèzes →, *Canada* 97 C12
Melfi, *Chad* 73 F8
Melfi, *Italy* 35 B8
Melfort, *Canada* 101 C8
Melfort, *Zimbabwe* 83 F3
Melgaço, *Madeira* 30 C2
Melgar de Fernamental, *Spain* 30 C6
Melhus, *Norway* 10 A4
Melick, *Neths.* 17 F8
Melide, *Switz.* 23 E7
Meligalá, *Greece* 39 M4
Melilla, *Morocco* 75 A4
Melipilla, *Chile* 126 C1
Mélissa, Ákra, *Greece* 37 D6
Melita, *Canada* 101 D8
Mélito di Porto Salvo, *Italy* 35 E8
Melitopol, *Ukraine* 42 C6
Melk, *Austria* 21 G5
Mellansel, *Sweden* 8 E15
Melle, *Belgium* 17 G3
Melle, *France* 26 B3
Melle, *Germany* 18 C4
Mellégue, O. →, *Tunisia* 75 A6
Mellen, *U.S.A.* 108 B9
Mellerud, *Sweden* 11 F6
Mellette, *U.S.A.* 108 C5
Mellid, *Spain* 30 C2
Mellieha, *Malta* 37 D1
Mellit, *Sudan* 77 E2
Mellizo Sur, Cerro, *Chile* 128 C2
Mellrichstadt, *Germany* 19 E6
Melnik, *Bulgaria* 39 H6
Mělník, *Czech.* 20 E4
Melo, *Uruguay* 127 C5
Melolo, *Indonesia* 57 F6
Melouprey, *Cambodia* 58 F5
Melovoye, *Ukraine* 43 B9
Melrhir, Chott, *Algeria* 75 B6
Melrose, *N.S.W., Australia* 91 E4
Melrose, *W. Austral., Australia* 89 E3
Melrose, *U.K.* 14 F6
Melrose, *U.S.A.* 109 H3
Mels, *Switz.* 23 B8
Melsele, *Belgium* 17 F4
Melstone, *U.S.A.* 110 C10
Melsungen, *Germany* 18 D5
Melton Mowbray, *U.K.* 12 E7
Melun, *France* 25 D9
Melut, *Sudan* 77 E3
Melville, *Canada* 101 C8
Melville, C., *Australia* 90 A3
Melville, L., *Canada* 99 B8
Melville B., *Australia* 90 A2
Melville I., *Australia* 88 B5
Melville I., *Canada* 4 B2
Melville Pen., *Canada* 97 B11
Melvin →, *Canada* 100 B5
Memaliaj, *Albania* 39 J2
Memba, *Mozam.* 83 E5
Memboro, *Indonesia* 57 F5
Membrilla, *Spain* 29 G1
Memel = Klaìpéda, *Lithuania* 40 D2
Memel, *S. Africa* 85 D4
Memmingen, *Germany* 19 H6
Mempawah, *Indonesia* 56 D3
Memphis, *Tenn., U.S.A.* 109 H10
Memphis, *Tex., U.S.A.* 109 H4
Mena, *U.S.A.* 109 H7
Mena →, *Ethiopia* 77 F5
Menai Strait, *U.K.* 12 D3
Ménaka, *Mali* 79 B5
Menaldum, *Neths.* 16 B7
Menan = Chao Phraya →, *Thailand* 58 F3
Menarandra →, *Madag.* 85 D7
Menard, *U.S.A.* 109 K5
Menasha, *U.S.A.* 104 C1
Menate, *Indonesia* 56 E4
Mendawai →, *Indonesia* 56 E4
Mende, *France* 26 D7
Mendebo, *Ethiopia* 77 F4
Mendez, *Mexico* 115 B5
Mendhar, *India* 63 C6
Mendi, *Ethiopia* 77 F4
Mendip Hills, *U.K.* 13 F5
Mendocino, *U.S.A.* 110 G2
Mendocino, C., *U.S.A.* 110 F1
Mendota, *Calif., U.S.A.* 111 H3
Mendota, *Ill., U.S.A.* 108 E10
Mendoza, *Argentina* 126 C2
Mendoza □, *Argentina* 126 C2
Mendrisio, *Switz.* 23 E7
Mene Grande, *Venezuela* 120 B3
Menemen, *Turkey* 66 D2
Menen, *Belgium* 17 G2
Menéndez, L., *Argentina* 128 B2
Menfi, *Italy* 34 E5
Mengcheng, *China* 53 A11
Mengdingjie, *China* 52 F2
Mengeš, *Slovenia* 33 B11
Menggala, *Indonesia* 56 E3
Menghai, *China* 52 G3
Mengíbar, *Spain* 31 H7
Mengjin, *China* 50 G7
Mengla, *China* 52 G3
Menglian, *China* 52 F2
Mengoub, *Algeria* 74 C3
Mengshan, *China* 53 E8
Mengyin, *China* 51 G9
Mengzhe, *China* 52 F3
Mengzi, *China* 52 F4
Menihek L., *Canada* 99 B6
Menin = Menen, *Belgium* 17 G2
Menindee, *Australia* 91 E3
Menindee L., *Australia* 91 E3
Meningie, *Australia* 91 F2
Menlo Park, *U.S.A.* 112 H4
Menominee, *U.S.A.* 104 C2
Menominee →, *U.S.A.* 104 C2
Menomonie, *U.S.A.* 108 C9
Menongue, *Angola* 81 G3
Menorca, *Spain* 36 B11
Mentakab, *Malaysia* 59 L4
Mentawai, Kepulauan, *Indonesia* 56 E1
Menton, *France* 27 E11
Mentor, *U.S.A.* 106 E3
Mentz Dam, *S. Africa* 84 E4
Menzel-Bourguiba, *Tunisia* 75 A6
Menzel Chaker, *Tunisia* 75 B7
Menzel-Temime, *Tunisia* 75 A7
Menzies, *Australia* 89 E3
Me'ona, *Israel* 69 B4
Meoqui, *Mexico* 114 B3
Mepaco, *Mozam.* 83 F3
Meppel, *Neths.* 16 C8
Meppen, *Germany* 18 C3
Mequinenza, *Spain* 28 D5
Mer Rouge, *U.S.A.* 109 J9
Merabéllou, Kólpos, *Greece* 37 D7
Meramangye, L., *Australia* 89 E5
Meran = Merano, *Italy* 33 B8
Merano, *Italy* 33 B8
Merate, *Italy* 32 C6
Merauke, *Indonesia* 57 F10
Merbabu, *Indonesia* 57 G14
Merbein, *Australia* 91 E3
Merca, *Somali Rep.* 68 G3
Mercadal, *Spain* 36 B11
Mercato Saraceno, *Italy* 33 E9
Merced, *U.S.A.* 111 H3
Merced Pk., *U.S.A.* 112 H7
Mercedes, *Buenos Aires, Argentina* 126 C4
Mercedes, *Corrientes, Argentina* 126 B4
Mercedes, *San Luis, Argentina* 126 C2
Mercedes, *Uruguay* 126 C4
Merceditas, *Chile* 126 B1
Mercer, *N.Z.* 87 G5
Mercer, *U.S.A.* 106 E4
Merchtem, *Belgium* 17 G4
Mercier, *Bolivia* 124 C4
Mercury, *U.S.A.* 113 J11
Mercy C., *Canada* 97 B13
Merdrignac, *France* 24 D4
Mere, *Belgium* 17 G3
Meredith, C., *Falk. Is.* 128 D4
Meredith, L., *U.S.A.* 109 H4
Merelbeke, *Belgium* 17 G3
Méréville, *France* 25 D9
Merga = Nukheila, *Sudan* 76 D2
Mergenevsky, *Kazakhstan* 43 B14
Mergui Arch. = Myeik Kyunzu, *Burma* 59 G1
Mérida, *Mexico* 115 C7
Mérida, *Spain* 31 G4
Mérida, *Venezuela* 120 B3
Mérida □, *Venezuela* 120 B3
Mérida, Cord. de, *Venezuela* 118 B2
Meriden, *U.S.A.* 107 E12
Meridian, *Calif., U.S.A.* 112 F5
Meridian, *Idaho, U.S.A.* 110 E5
Meridian, *Miss., U.S.A.* 105 J1
Meridian, *Tex., U.S.A.* 109 K6
Mering, *Germany* 19 G7
Meriruma, *Brazil* 121 C7
Merkel, *U.S.A.* 109 J4
Merksem, *Belgium* 17 F4
Merksplas, *Belgium* 17 F5
Mermaid Reef, *Australia* 88 C2
Mern, *Denmark* 11 J6
Merowe, *Sudan* 76 D3
Merredin, *Australia* 89 F2
Merrick, *U.K.* 14 F4
Merrickville, *Canada* 107 B9
Merrill, *Oreg., U.S.A.* 110 E3
Merrill, *Wis., U.S.A.* 108 C10
Merriman, *U.S.A.* 108 D4
Merritt, *Canada* 100 C4
Merriwa, *Australia* 91 E5
Merriwagga, *Australia* 91 E4
Merry I., *Canada* 98 A4
Merrygoen, *Australia* 91 E4
Merryville, *U.S.A.* 109 K8
Mersa Fatma, *Eritrea* 68 E3
Mersch, *Lux.* 17 J8
Merseburg, *Germany* 18 D7
Mersey →, *U.K.* 12 D5
Merseyside □, *U.K.* 12 D5
Mersin, *Turkey* 66 E6
Mersing, *Malaysia* 59 L4
Merta, *India* 62 F6
Mertert, *Lux.* 17 J8
Merthyr Tydfil, *U.K.* 13 F4
Mértola, *Portugal* 31 H3
Mertzig, *Lux.* 17 J8
Mertzon, *U.S.A.* 109 K4
Méru, *France* 25 C9
Meru, *Kenya* 82 B4
Meru, *Tanzania* 82 C4
Meru □, *Kenya* 82 B4
Merville, *France* 25 B9
Méry-sur-Seine, *France* 25 D10
Merzifon, *Turkey* 42 F6
Merzig, *Germany* 19 F2
Merzouga, Erg Tin, *Algeria* 75 D7
Mesa, *U.S.A.* 111 K8
Mesach Mellet, *Libya* 75 D7
Mesagne, *Italy* 35 B10
Mesanagrós, *Greece* 37 C9
Mesaoría □, *Cyprus* 37 D12
Mesarás, Kólpos, *Greece* 37 D6
Meschede, *Germany* 18 D4
Mesfinto, *Ethiopia* 77 E4
Mesgouez, L., *Canada* 98 B4
Meshchovsk, *Russia* 40 D9
Meshed = Mashhad, *Iran* 65 B8
Meshoppen, *U.S.A.* 107 E8
Meshra er Req, *Sudan* 77 F2
Mesick, *U.S.A.* 104 C3
Mesilinka →, *Canada* 100 B4
Mesilla, *U.S.A.* 111 K10
Meslay-du-Maine, *France* 24 E6
Mesocco, *Switz.* 23 D8
Mesolóngion, *Greece* 39 L4
Mesopotamia = Al Jazirah, *Iraq* 64 C5
Mesoraca, *Italy* 35 C9
Mesquite, *U.S.A.* 111 H6
Mess Cr. →, *Canada* 100 B2
Messac, *France* 24 E5
Messad, *Algeria* 75 B5
Messalo →, *Mozam.* 83 E4
Méssaména, *Cameroon* 79 E7
Messancy, *Belgium* 17 J7
Messier, Canal, *Chile* 128 C2
Messina, *Italy* 35 D8
Messina, *S. Africa* 85 C5
Messina, Str. di, *Italy* 35 D8
Messíni, *Greece* 39 M5
Messiniakós Kólpos, *Greece* 39 N5
Messkirch, *Germany* 19 H5
Messonghi, *Greece* 37 B3
Mesta →, *Bulgaria* 39 H7
Mestanza, *Spain* 31 G6
Mestre, *Italy* 33 C9
Mestre, Espigão, *Brazil* 123 D2
Městys Zelezná Ruda, *Czech.* 20 F3
Meta □, *Colombia* 120 C3
Meta →, *S. Amer.* 120 B4
Metairie, *U.S.A.* 109 L9
Metaline Falls, *U.S.A.* 110 B5
Metán, *Argentina* 126 B3
Metangula, *Mozam.* 83 E3
Metauro →, *Italy* 33 E10
Metema, *Ethiopia* 77 E4
Metengobalame, *Mozam.* 83 E3
Méthana, *Greece* 39 M6
Methven, *N.Z.* 87 K3
Methy L., *Canada* 101 B7
Metil, *Mozam.* 83 F4
Metlakatla, *U.S.A.* 100 B2
Metlaoui, *Tunisia* 75 B6
Metlika, *Slovenia* 33 C12
Metropolis, *U.S.A.* 109 G10
Mettet, *Belgium* 17 H5
Mettur Dam, *India* 60 P10
Metz, *France* 25 C13
Meulaboh, *Indonesia* 56 D1
Meulan, *France* 25 C8
Meung-sur-Loire, *France* 25 E8
Meureudu, *Indonesia* 56 C1
Meurthe →, *France* 25 D13
Meurthe-et-Moselle □, *France* 25 D13
Meuse □, *France* 25 C12
Meuse →, *Europe* 17 G7
Meuselwitz, *Germany* 18 D8
Mexborough, *U.K.* 12 D6
Mexia, *U.S.A.* 109 K6
Mexiana, I., *Brazil* 122 A2
Mexicali, *Mexico* 114 A1
México, *Mexico* 115 D5
Mexico, *Maine, U.S.A.* 107 B14
Mexico, *Mo., U.S.A.* 108 F9
México □, *Mexico* 114 D5
Mexico ■, *Cent. Amer.* 114 C4
Mexico, G. of, *Cent. Amer.* 115 C7
Meyenburg, *Germany* 18 B8
Meymac, *France* 26 C6
Meymaneh, *Afghan.* 60 B4
Meyrargues, *France* 27 E9
Meyrueis, *France* 26 D7
Meyssac, *France* 26 C5
Mezdra, *Bulgaria* 38 F6
Mèze, *France* 26 E7
Mezen, *Russia* 44 C5
Mezen →, *Russia* 44 C5
Mézenc, Mt., *France* 27 D8
Mezha →, *Russia* 40 D7
Mézidon, *France* 24 C6
Mézilhac, *France* 27 D8
Mézin, *France* 26 D4
Mezőberény, *Hungary* 21 J11
Mezőkövácsháza, *Hungary* 21 J10
Mezőkövesd, *Hungary* 21 H10
Mézos, *France* 26 D2
Mezőtúr, *Hungary* 21 J10
Mezquital, *Mexico* 114 C4
Mezzolombardo, *Italy* 32 B8
Mgeta, *Tanzania* 83 D4
Mglin, *Russia* 40 E8
Mhlaba Hills, *Zimbabwe* 83 F3
Mhow, *India* 62 H6
Miahuatlán, *Mexico* 115 D5
Miajadas, *Spain* 31 F5
Miallo, *Australia* 90 B4
Miami, *Ariz., U.S.A.* 111 K8
Miami, *Fla., U.S.A.* 105 N5
Miami, *Tex., U.S.A.* 109 H4
Miami →, *U.S.A.* 104 F3
Miami Beach, *U.S.A.* 105 N5
Miamisburg, *U.S.A.* 104 F3
Mian Xian, *China* 50 H4
Mianchi, *China* 50 G6
Mīāndowāb, *Iran* 64 B5
Miandrivazo, *Madag.* 85 B8
Mīāneh, *Iran* 64 B5
Mianning, *China* 52 C4
Mianwali, *Pakistan* 62 C4
Mianyang, *Hubei, China* 53 B9
Mianyang, *Sichuan, China* 52 B5
Mianzhu, *China* 52 B5
Miaoli, *Taiwan* 53 E13
Miarinarivo, *Madag.* 85 B8
Miass, *Russia* 44 D7
Miastko, *Poland* 20 A6
Michelstadt, *Germany* 19 F5
Michigan □, *U.S.A.* 104 C3
Michigan, L., *U.S.A.* 104 C2
Michigan City, *U.S.A.* 104 E2
Michikamau L., *Canada* 99 B7
Michipicoten, *Canada* 98 C3
Michipicoten I., *Canada* 98 C2
Michoacan □, *Mexico* 114 D4
Michurin, *Bulgaria* 38 G10
Michurinsk, *Russia* 41 E12
Miclere, *Australia* 90 C4
Mico, Pta., *Nic.* 116 D3
Micronesia, Federated States of ■, *Pac. Oc.* 92 G7
Mid Glamorgan □, *U.K.* 13 F4
Midai, P., *Indonesia* 59 L6
Midale, *Canada* 101 D8
Middagsfjället, *Sweden* 10 A6
Middelbeers, *Neths.* 17 F6
Middelburg, *Neths.* 17 F3
Middelburg, *C. Prov., S. Africa* 84 E3
Middelburg, *Trans., S. Africa* 85 D4
Middelfart, *Denmark* 11 J3
Middelharnis, *Neths.* 16 E4
Middelkerke, *Belgium* 17 F1
Middelrode, *Neths.* 17 E6
Middelwit, *S. Africa* 84 C4
Middle Alkali L., *U.S.A.* 110 F3
Middle Fork Feather →, *U.S.A.* 112 F5
Middle I., *Australia* 89 F3
Middle Loup →, *U.S.A.* 108 E5
Middleboro, *U.S.A.* 107 E14
Middleburg, *N.Y., U.S.A.* 107 D10
Middleburg, *Pa., U.S.A.* 106 F7
Middlebury, *U.S.A.* 107 B11
Middleport, *U.S.A.* 104 F4
Middlesboro, *Ky., U.S.A.* 103 C10
Middlesboro, *Ky., U.S.A.* 105 G4
Middlesbrough, *U.K.* 12 C6
Middlesex, *Belize* 116 C2
Middlesex, *U.S.A.* 107 F10
Middleton, *Australia* 90 C3
Middleton, *Canada* 99 D6
Middletown, *Calif., U.S.A.* 112 G4
Middletown, *Conn., U.S.A.* 107 E12
Middletown, *N.Y., U.S.A.* 107 E10
Middletown, *Ohio, U.S.A.* 104 F3
Middletown, *Pa., U.S.A.* 107 F8
Midelt, *Morocco* 74 B4
Midi, Canal du →, *France* 26 E5
Midi d'Ossau, Pic du, *France* 26 F3
Midland, *Canada* 98 D4
Midland, *Calif., U.S.A.* 113 M12
Midland, *Mich., U.S.A.* 104 D3
Midland, *Pa., U.S.A.* 106 F4
Midland, *Tex., U.S.A.* 109 K3
Midlands □, *Zimbabwe* 83 F2
Midleton, *Ireland* 15 E3
Midlothian, *U.S.A.* 109 J6
Midongy, Tangorombohitr' i, *Madag.* 85 C8
Midongy Atsimo, *Madag.* 85 C8
Midou →, *France* 26 E3
Midouze →, *France* 26 E3
Midsayap, *Phil.* 55 H6
Midu, *China* 52 E3
Midway Is., *Pac. Oc.* 92 E10
Midway Wells, *U.S.A.* 113 N11
Midwest, *U.S.A.* 103 B9
Midwest, *Wyo., U.S.A.* 110 E10
Midwolda, *Neths.* 16 B9
Midyat, *Turkey* 67 E9
Mie □, *Japan* 49 G8
Miechów, *Poland* 20 E10
Międzychód, *Poland* 20 C5
Międzyrzec Podlaski, *Poland* 20 D12
Międzyrzecz, *Poland* 20 C5
Miélan, *France* 26 E4
Mielec, *Poland* 20 E11
Mienga, *Angola* 84 B2
Miercurea Ciuc, *Romania* 38 C8
Mieres, *Spain* 30 B5
Mierlo, *Neths.* 17 F7
Mieso, *Ethiopia* 77 F5
Mifflintown, *U.S.A.* 106 F7
Mifraz Ḥefa, *Israel* 69 C4
Migdāl, *Israel* 69 C4
Migennes, *France* 25 E10
Migliarino, *Italy* 33 D8
Miguel Alemán, Presa, *Mexico* 115 D5
Miguel Alves, *Brazil* 122 B3
Miguel Calmon, *Brazil* 122 D3
Mihaliççık, *Turkey* 66 D4
Mihara, *Japan* 49 G6
Mijares →, *Spain* 28 F4
Mijas, *Spain* 31 J6
Mikese, *Tanzania* 82 D4
Mikha-Tskhakaya = Senaki, *Georgia* 43 E10
Mikhailovka, *Ukraine* 42 C6
Mikhaylovgrad, *Bulgaria* 38 F6
Mikhaylovka, *Azerbaijan* 43 F13
Mikhaylovka, *Russia* 41 D11
Mikhaylovka, *Russia* 41 F13
Mikhnevo, *Russia* 41 D10
Mikínai, *Greece* 39 M5
Mikkeli, *Finland* 9 F19
Mikkeli □ = Mikkelin lääni □, *Finland* 8 F20
Mikkelin lääni □, *Finland* 8 F20
Mikkwa →, *Canada* 100 B6
Mikniya, *Sudan* 77 D3
Mikołajki, *Poland* 20 B11
Míkonos, *Greece* 39 M8
Mikrón Dhérion, *Greece* 39 H9
Mikulov, *Czech.* 20 G6
Mikumi, *Tanzania* 82 D4
Milaca, *U.S.A.* 108 C8
Milagro, *Ecuador* 120 D2
Milagros, *Phil.* 55 E5
Milan = Milano, *Italy* 32 C6
Milan, *Mo., U.S.A.* 108 E8
Milan, *Tenn., U.S.A.* 105 H1
Milang, *Australia* 91 E2
Milange, *Mozam.* 83 F4
Milano, *Italy* 32 C6
Milâs, *Turkey* 66 E2
Milatos, *Greece* 37 D7
Milazzo, *Italy* 35 D8
Milbank, *U.S.A.* 108 C6
Milden, *Canada* 101 C7
Mildmay, *Canada* 106 B3
Mildura, *Australia* 91 E3
Mile, *China* 52 E4
Miléai, *Greece* 39 K6
Mileh Tharthār, *Iraq* 64 C4
Miles, *Australia* 91 D5
Miles, *U.S.A.* 109 K4
Miles City, *U.S.A.* 108 B2
Milestone, *Canada* 101 D8
Mileto, *Italy* 35 D9
Miletto, Mte., *Italy* 35 A7
Miletus, *Turkey* 66 E2
Mileura, *Australia* 89 E2
Milford, *Calif., U.S.A.* 112 E6
Milford, *Conn., U.S.A.* 107 E11
Milford, *Del., U.S.A.* 104 F8
Milford, *Mass., U.S.A.* 107 D13
Milford, *Pa., U.S.A.* 107 E10
Milford, *Utah, U.S.A.* 111 G7
Milford Haven, *U.K.* 13 F2
Milford Sd., *N.Z.* 87 L1
Milgun, *Australia* 89 D2
Milḥ, Baḥr al, *Iraq* 64 C4
Miliana, *Aïn Salah, Algeria* 75 C5
Miliana, *Médéa, Algeria* 75 A5
Miling, *Australia* 89 F2
Militello in Val di Catánia, *Italy* 35 E7
Milk →, *U.S.A.* 110 B10
Milk, Wadi el →, *Sudan* 76 D3
Milk River, *Canada* 100 D6
Mill, *Neths.* 17 E7
Mill City, *U.S.A.* 110 D2
Mill I., *Antarctica* 5 C8
Mill Valley, *U.S.A.* 112 H4
Millau, *France* 26 D7
Millbridge, *Canada* 106 B7
Millbrook, *Canada* 106 B6
Mille Lacs, L. des, *Canada* 98 C1
Mille Lacs L., *U.S.A.* 108 B8
Milledgeville, *U.S.A.* 105 J4
Millen, *U.S.A.* 105 J5
Miller, *U.S.A.* 108 C5
Millerovo, *Russia* 43 B9

Millersburg, *Ohio, U.S.A.* . 106 F3
Millersburg, *Pa., U.S.A.* . . 106 F8
Millerton, *U.S.A.* 107 E11
Millerton L., *U.S.A.* 112 J7
Millevaches, Plateau de,
France 26 C6
Millicent, *Australia* 91 F3
Millingen, *Neths.* 16 E8
Millinocket, *U.S.A.* 99 C6
Mills L., *Canada* 100 A5
Millsboro, *U.S.A.* 106 G4
Milltown Malbay, *Ireland* . 15 D2
Millville, *U.S.A.* 104 F8
Millwood L., *U.S.A.* 109 J8
Milly-la-Forêt, *France* 25 D9
Milna, *Croatia* 33 E13
Milne →, *Australia* 90 C2
Milne Inlet, *Canada* 97 A11
Milnor, *U.S.A.* 108 B6
Milo, *Canada* 100 C6
Mílos, *Greece* 39 N7
Miloševo, *Serbia* 21 K10
Milparinka P.O., *Australia* . 91 D3
Miltenberg, *Germany* 19 F5
Milton, *Canada* 106 C5
Milton, *N.Z.* 87 M2
Milton, *U.K.* 14 D4
Milton, *Calif., U.S.A.* 112 G6
Milton, *Fla., U.S.A.* 105 K2
Milton, *Pa., U.S.A.* 106 F8
Milton-Freewater, *U.S.A.* . 110 D4
Milton Keynes, *U.K.* 13 E7
Miltou, *Chad* 73 F8
Milverton, *Canada* 106 C4
Milwaukee, *U.S.A.* 104 D2
Milwaukee Deep, *Atl. Oc.* . 117 C6
Milwaukie, *U.S.A.* 112 E4
Mim, *Ghana* 78 D4
Mimizan, *France* 26 D2
Mimoso, *Brazil* 123 E2
Min Chiang →, *China* 53 E12
Min Jiang →, *China* 52 C5
Min Xian, *China* 50 G3
Mina, *U.S.A.* 111 G4
Mina Pirquitas, *Argentina* . 126 A2
Mīnā Su'ud, *Si. Arabia* . . . 65 D6
Mīnā'al Aḥmadī, *Kuwait* . . 65 D6
Mīnāb, *Iran* 65 E8
Minago →, *Canada* 101 C9
Minaki, *Canada* 101 D10
Minamata, *Japan* 49 H5
Minami-Tori-Shima,
Pac. Oc. 92 E7
Minas, *Uruguay* 127 C4
Minas, Sierra de las,
Guatemala 116 C2
Minas Basin, *Canada* 99 C7
Minas de Rio Tinto, *Spain* . 31 H4
Minas de San Quintín,
Spain 31 G6
Minas Gerais □, *Brazil* . . . 123 E2
Minas Novas, *Brazil* 123 E3
Minatitlán, *Mexico* 115 D6
Minbu, *Burma* 61 J19
Mincio →, *Italy* 32 C7
Mindanao, *Phil.* 55 H6
Mindanao Sea = Bohol
Sea, *Phil.* 57 C6
Mindanao Trench, *Pac. Oc.* 55 F7
Mindel →, *Germany* 19 G6
Mindelheim, *Germany* 19 G6
Minden, *Canada* 106 B6
Minden, *Germany* 18 C4
Minden, *La., U.S.A.* 109 J8
Minden, *Nev., U.S.A.* 112 G7
Mindiptana, *Indonesia* . . . 57 F10
Mindoro, *Phil.* 55 E4
Mindoro Str., *Phil.* 55 E4
Mindouli, *Congo* 80 E2
Mine, *Japan* 49 G5
Minehead, *U.K.* 13 F4
Mineiros, *Brazil* 125 D7
Mineola, *U.S.A.* 109 J7
Mineral King, *U.S.A.* 112 J8
Mineral Wells, *U.S.A.* 109 J5
Mineralnyye Vody, *Russia* . 43 D10
Minersville, *Pa., U.S.A.* . . . 107 F8
Minersville, *Utah, U.S.A.* . 111 G7
Minerva, *U.S.A.* 106 F3
Minervino Murge, *Italy* . . . 35 A9
Minetto, *U.S.A.* 107 C8
Mingan, *Canada* 99 B7
Mingechaur, *Azerbaijan* . . 43 F12
Mingechaurskoye Vdkhr.,
Azerbaijan 43 F12
Mingela, *Australia* 90 B4
Mingenew, *Australia* 89 E2
Mingera Cr. →, *Australia* . 90 C2
Minggang, *China* 53 A10
Mingin, *Burma* 61 H19
Minglanilla, *Spain* 28 F3
Mingkun, *China* 53 E8
Mingorria, *Spain* 30 E6
Mingt'iehkaitafan =
Mintaka Pass, *Pakistan* . 63 A6
Mingxi, *China* 53 D11
Mingyuegue, *China* 51 C15
Minhou, *China* 53 E12
Minićevo, *Serbia* 21 M12
Minidoka, *U.S.A.* 110 E7
Minigwal, L., *Australia* . . . 89 E3
Minilya, *Australia* 89 D1
Minilya →, *Australia* 89 D1
Minipi, L., *Canada* 99 B7

Mink L., *Canada* 100 A5
Minna, *Nigeria* 79 D6
Minneapolis, *Kans., U.S.A.* 108 F6
Minneapolis, *Minn., U.S.A.* 108 C8
Minnedosa, *Canada* 101 C9
Minnesota □, *U.S.A.* 108 B7
Minnesund, *Norway* 10 D5
Minnie Creek, *Australia* . . 89 D2
Minnipa, *Australia* 91 E2
Minnitaki L., *Canada* 98 C1
Mino, *Japan* 49 G8
Miño →, *Spain* 30 D2
Minorca = Menorca, *Spain* 36 B11
Minore, *Australia* 91 E4
Minot, *U.S.A.* 108 A4
Minqin, *China* 50 E2
Minqing, *China* 53 D12
Minsen, *Germany* 18 B3
Minsk, *Belorussia* 40 E5
Mińsk Mazowiecki, *Poland* 20 C11
Mintaka Pass, *Pakistan* . . . 63 A6
Minto, *U.S.A.* 96 B5
Minton, *Canada* 101 D8
Minturn, *U.S.A.* 110 G10
Minturno, *Italy* 34 A6
Minûf, *Egypt* 76 H7
Minusinsk, *Russia* 45 D10
Minutang, *India* 61 E20
Minvoul, *Gabon* 80 D2
Minya el Qamh, *Egypt* . . . 76 H7
Mionica, *Serbia* 21 L10
Mir, *Niger* 79 C7
Mir-Bashir, *Azerbaijan* . . . 43 F12
Mīr Kūh, *Iran* 65 E8
Mīr Shahdād, *Iran* 65 E8
Mira, *Italy* 33 C9
Mira, *Portugal* 30 E2
Mira →, *Colombia* 120 C2
Mira →, *Portugal* 31 H2
Mira por vos Cay, *Bahamas* 117 B5
Mirabella Eclano, *Italy* . . . 35 A7
Miracema do Norte, *Brazil* 122 C2
Mirador, *Brazil* 122 C3
Miraflores, *Colombia* 120 C3
Miraj, *India* 60 L9
Miram Shah, *Pakistan* 62 C4
Miramar, *Argentina* 126 D4
Miramar, *Mozam.* 85 C6
Miramas, *France* 27 E8
Mirambeau, *France* 26 C3
Miramichi B., *Canada* 99 C7
Miramont-de-Guyenne,
France 26 D4
Miranda, *Brazil* 125 E6
Miranda □, *Venezuela* 120 A4
Miranda →, *Brazil* 125 D6
Miranda de Ebro, *Spain* . . 28 C2
Miranda do Corvo, *Spain* . 30 E2
Miranda do Douro,
Portugal 30 D4
Mirande, *France* 26 E4
Mirandela, *Portugal* 30 D3
Mirando City, *U.S.A.* 109 M5
Mirandola, *Italy* 32 D8
Mirandópolis, *Brazil* 127 A5
Mirango, *Malawi* 83 E3
Mirani, *Australia* 90 C4
Mirano, *Italy* 33 C9
Mirassol, *Brazil* 127 A6
Mirbāṭ, *Oman* 68 D5
Mirear, *Egypt* 76 C4
Mirebeau, *Côte-d'Or,
France* 25 E12
Mirebeau, *Vienne, France* . 24 F7
Mirecourt, *France* 25 D13
Mirgorod, *Ukraine* 40 G8
Miri, *Malaysia* 56 D4
Miriam Vale, *Australia* . . . 90 C5
Mirim, L., *S. Amer.* 127 C5
Mirimire, *Venezuela* 120 A4
Miriti, *Brazil* 125 B6
Mirnyy, *Russia* 45 C12
Mirond L., *Canada* 101 B8
Mirpur, *Pakistan* 63 C5
Mirpur Bibiwari, *Pakistan* . 62 E2
Mirpur Khas, *Pakistan* . . . 62 G3
Mirpur Sakro, *Pakistan* . . . 62 G2
Mirria, *Niger* 79 C6
Mirror, *Canada* 100 C6
Mîrşani, *Romania* 38 E6
Miryang, *S. Korea* 51 G15
Mirzaani, *Georgia* 43 F12
Mirzapur, *India* 63 G10
Mirzapur-cum-
Vindhyachal = Mirzapur,
India 63 G10
Misantla, *Mexico* 115 D5
Misawa, *Japan* 48 D10
Miscou I., *Canada* 99 C7
Mish'āb, Ra's al,
Si. Arabia 65 D6
Mishagua →, *Peru* 124 C3
Mishan, *China* 54 B8
Mishawaka, *U.S.A.* 104 E2
Mishbih, Gebel, *Egypt* . . . 76 C3
Mishima, *Japan* 49 G9
Misilmeri, *Italy* 34 D6
Misión, *Mexico* 113 N10
Misión Fagnano, *Argentina* 128 D3
Misiones □, *Argentina* . . . 127 B5
Misiones □, *Paraguay* 126 B4
Miskah, *Si. Arabia* 64 E4
Miskitos, Cayos, *Nic.* 116 D3
Miskolc, *Hungary* 21 G10
Misoke, *Zaïre* 82 C2

Misool, *Indonesia* 57 E8
Miṣrātah, *Libya* 73 B8
Missanabie, *Canada* 98 C3
Missão Velha, *Brazil* 122 C4
Missinaibi →, *Canada* 98 B3
Missinaibi L., *Canada* 98 C3
Mission, *S. Dak., U.S.A.* . . 108 D4
Mission, *Tex., U.S.A.* 109 M5
Mission City, *Canada* 100 D4
Mission Viejo, *U.S.A.* 113 M9
Missisa L., *Canada* 98 B2
Mississagi →, *Canada* 98 C3
Mississippi □, *U.S.A.* 109 J10
Mississippi →, *U.S.A.* 109 L10
Mississippi L., *Canada* . . . 107 A8
Mississippi River Delta,
U.S.A. 109 L9
Mississippi Sd., *U.S.A.* . . . 109 K10
Missoula, *U.S.A.* 110 C6
Missour, *Morocco* 74 B4
Missouri □, *U.S.A.* 108 F8
Missouri →, *U.S.A.* 108 F9
Missouri Valley, *U.S.A.* . . . 108 E7
Mist, *U.S.A.* 112 E3
Mistake B., *Canada* 101 A10
Mistassini →, *Canada* 99 C5
Mistassini L., *Canada* 98 B5
Mistastin L., *Canada* 99 A7
Mistelbach, *Austria* 20 G6
Misterbianco, *Italy* 35 E8
Mistretta, *Italy* 35 E7
Misty L., *Canada* 101 B8
Misurata = Miṣrātah, *Libya* 73 B8
Mît Ghamr, *Egypt* 76 H7
Mitatib, *Sudan* 77 D4
Mitchell, *Australia* 91 D4
Mitchell, *Canada* 106 C3
Mitchell, *Ind., U.S.A.* 104 F2
Mitchell, *Nebr., U.S.A.* . . . 108 E3
Mitchell, *Oreg., U.S.A.* . . . 110 D4
Mitchell, *S. Dak., U.S.A.* . 108 D5
Mitchell →, *Australia* 90 B3
Mitchell Ras., *Australia* . . . 90 A2
Mitchelstown, *Ireland* 15 D3
Mitha Tiwana, *Pakistan* . . 62 C5
Mitilíni, *Greece* 39 K9
Mito, *Japan* 49 F10
Mitsinjo, *Madag.* 85 B8
Mitsiwa, *Eritrea* 77 D4
Mitsiwa Channel, *Eritrea* . 77 D5
Mitsukaidō, *Japan* 49 F9
Mittagong, *Australia* 91 E5
Mittelland, *Switz.* 22 C4
Mittelland Kanal, *Germany* 18 C3
Mittenwalde, *Germany* . . . 18 C9
Mitterteich, *Germany* 19 F8
Mittweida, *Germany* 18 E8
Mitú, *Colombia* 120 C3
Mituas, *Colombia* 120 C4
Mitumba, *Tanzania* 82 D3
Mitumba, Chaîne des,
Zaïre 82 D2
Mitumba Mts. = Mitumba,
Chaîne des, *Zaïre* 82 D2
Mitwaba, *Zaïre* 83 D2
Mityana, *Uganda* 82 B3
Mitzic, *Gabon* 80 D2
Mixteco →, *Mexico* 115 D5
Miyagi □, *Japan* 48 E10
Miyāh, W. el →, *Egypt* . . . 76 B3
Miyah, W. el →, *Syria* 64 C3
Miyake-Jima, *Japan* 49 G9
Miyako, *Japan* 48 E10
Miyako-Jima, *Japan* 49 M2
Miyako-Rettō, *Japan* 49 M2
Miyakonojō, *Japan* 49 J5
Miyanoura-Dake, *Japan* . . 49 J5
Miyazaki, *Japan* 49 J5
Miyazaki □, *Japan* 49 H5
Miyazu, *Japan* 49 G7
Miyet, Bahr el = Dead
Sea, *Asia* 69 D4
Miyi, *China* 52 D4
Miyoshi, *Japan* 49 G6
Miyun, *China* 50 D9
Miyun Shuiku, *China* 51 D9
Mizamis = Ozamiz, *Phil.* . . 55 G5
Mizdah, *Libya* 75 B7
Mizen Hd., *Cork, Ireland* . 15 E2
Mizen Hd., *Wick., Ireland* . 15 D5
Mizhi, *China* 50 F6
Mizil, *Romania* 38 E9
Mizoram □, *India* 61 H18
Mizpe Ramon, *Israel* 69 E3
Mizusawa, *Japan* 48 E10
Mjöbäck, *Sweden* 11 G6
Mjölby, *Sweden* 11 F9
Mjörn, *Sweden* 11 G6
Mjøsa, *Norway* 10 D5
Mkata, *Tanzania* 82 D4
Mkokotoni, *Tanzania* 82 D4
Mkomazi, *Tanzania* 82 C4
Mkomazi →, *S. Africa* 85 E5
Mkulwe, *Tanzania* 83 D3
Mkumbi, Ras, *Tanzania* . . . 82 D4
Mkushi, *Zambia* 83 E2
Mkushi River, *Zambia* 83 E2
Mkuze, *S. Africa* 85 D5
Mkuze →, *S. Africa* 85 D5
Mladá Boleslav, *Czech.* . . 20 E4
Mladenovac, *Serbia* 21 L10
Mlala Hills, *Tanzania* 82 D3
Mlange, *Malawi* 83 F4

Mlava →, *Serbia* 21 L11
Mława, *Poland* 20 B10
Mljet, *Croatia* 21 N7
Mlinište, *Bos.-H.* 33 D13
Mlynary, *Poland* 20 A9
Mmabatho, *S. Africa* 84 D4
Mme, *Cameroon* 79 D7
Mo i Rana, *Norway* 8 C17
Moa, *Indonesia* 57 F7
Moa →, *S. Leone* 78 D2
Moab, *U.S.A.* 111 G9
Moabi, *Gabon* 80 E2
Moala, *Fiji* 87 D8
Moalie Park, *Australia* 91 D3
Moaña, *Spain* 30 C2
Moba, *Zaïre* 82 D2
Mobārakābād, *Iran* 65 D7
Mobārakīyeh, *Iran* 65 C6
Mobaye, *C.A.R.* 80 D4
Mobayi, *Zaïre* 80 D4
Moberly, *U.S.A.* 108 F8
Moberly →, *Canada* 100 B4
Mobile, *U.S.A.* 105 K1
Mobile B., *U.S.A.* 105 K2
Mobridge, *U.S.A.* 108 C4
Mobutu Sese Seko, L.,
Africa 82 B3
Moc Chau, *Vietnam* 58 B5
Moc Hoa, *Vietnam* 59 G5
Mocabe Kasari, *Zaïre* 83 D2
Mocajuba, *Brazil* 122 B2
Moçambique, *Mozam.* . . . 83 F5
Moçâmedes = Namibe,
Angola 81 H2
Mocapra →, *Venezuela* . . . 120 B4
Mocha, I., *Chile* 128 A2
Mochudi, *Botswana* 84 C4
Mocimboa da Praia,
Mozam. 83 E5
Moclips, *U.S.A.* 112 C2
Mocoa, *Colombia* 120 C2
Mococa, *Brazil* 127 A6
Mocorito, *Mexico* 114 B3
Moctezuma, *Mexico* 114 B3
Moctezuma →, *Mexico* . . . 115 C5
Mocuba, *Mozam.* 83 F4
Mocúzari, Presa, *Mexico* . . 114 B3
Modane, *France* 27 C10
Modasa, *India* 62 H5
Modave, *Belgium* 17 H6
Modder →, *S. Africa* 84 D3
Modderrivier, *S. Africa* . . . 84 D3
Módena, *Italy* 32 D7
Modena, *U.S.A.* 111 H7
Modesto, *U.S.A.* 111 H3
Módica, *Italy* 35 F7
Modigliana, *Italy* 33 D8
Modo, *Sudan* 77 F3
Modra, *Slovak Rep.* 21 G7
Moe, *Australia* 91 F4
Moebase, *Mozam.* 83 F4
Moëlan-sur-Mer, *France* . . 24 E3
Moengo, *Surinam* 121 B7
Moergestel, *Neths.* 17 E6
Moers, *Germany* 17 F9
Moësa →, *Switz.* 23 D8
Moffat, *U.K.* 14 F5
Moga, *India* 62 D6
Mogadishu = Muqdisho,
Somali Rep. 68 G4
Mogador = Essaouira,
Morocco 74 B3
Mogadouro, *Portugal* 30 D4
Mogalakwena →, *S. Africa* 85 C4
Mogami →, *Japan* 48 E10
Mogán, *Canary Is.* 36 G4
Mogaung, *Burma* 61 G20
Møgeltønder, *Denmark* . . . 11 K2
Mogente, *Spain* 29 G4
Mogho, *Ethiopia* 77 G5
Mogi das Cruzes, *Brazil* . . 127 A6
Mogi-Guaçu →, *Brazil* . . . 127 A6
Mogi-Mirim, *Brazil* 127 A6
Mogielnica, *Poland* 20 D10
Mogilev, *Belorussia* 40 E7
Mogilev-Podolskiy,
Moldavia 42 B2
Mogilno, *Poland* 20 C7
Mogincual, *Mozam.* 83 F5
Mogliano Véneto, *Italy* . . . 33 C9
Mogocha, *Russia* 45 D12
Mogoi, *Indonesia* 57 E8
Mogok, *Burma* 61 H20
Moguer, *Spain* 31 H4
Mogumber, *Australia* 89 F2
Mohács, *Hungary* 21 K8
Mohales Hoek, *Lesotho* . . 84 E4
Mohall, *U.S.A.* 108 A4
Moḥammadābād, *Iran* . . . 65 B8
Mohammadia, *Algeria* 75 A5
Mohammedia, *Morocco* . . 74 B3
Mohave, L., *U.S.A.* 113 K12
Mohawk →, *U.S.A.* 107 D11
Möhne →, *Germany* 18 D3
Moholm, *Sweden* 11 F8
Mohoro, *Tanzania* 82 D4
Moia, *Sudan* 77 F2
Moidart, L., *U.K.* 14 E3
Moineşti, *Romania* 38 C9
Mointy, *Kazakhstan* 44 E8
Moirans, *France* 27 C9
Moirans-en-Montagne,
France 27 B9
Moíres, *Greece* 37 D6

Moisaküla, *Estonia* 40 B4
Moisie, *Canada* 99 B6
Moisie →, *Canada* 99 B6
Moissac, *France* 26 D5
Moïssala, *Chad* 73 G8
Moita, *Portugal* 31 G2
Mojácar, *Spain* 29 H3
Mojados, *Spain* 30 D6
Mojave, *U.S.A.* 113 K8
Mojave Desert, *U.S.A.* . . . 113 L10
Mojiang, *China* 52 F3
Mojo, *Bolivia* 126 A2
Mojo, *Ethiopia* 77 F4
Mojokerto, *Indonesia* 57 G15
Mojos, Llanos de, *Bolivia* . 125 D5
Moju →, *Brazil* 122 B2
Mokai, *N.Z.* 87 H5
Mokambo, *Zaïre* 83 E2
Mokameh, *India* 63 G11
Mokelumne →, *U.S.A.* . . . 112 G5
Mokelumne Hill, *U.S.A.* . . . 112 G6
Mokhós, *Greece* 37 D7
Mokhotlong, *Lesotho* 85 D4
Moknine, *Tunisia* 75 A7
Mokokchung, *India* 61 F19
Mokra Gora, *Serbia* 21 N10
Mokronog, *Slovenia* 33 C12
Moksha →, *Russia* 41 D12
Mokshan, *Russia* 41 E14
Mol, *Belgium* 17 F6
Mola, C. de la, *Spain* 28 F9
Mola di Bari, *Italy* 35 A10
Moláoi, *Greece* 39 N5
Molat, *Croatia* 33 D11
Molchanovo, *Russia* 44 D9
Mold, *U.K.* 12 D4
Moldavia = Moldova,
Romania 38 C10
Moldavia ■, *Europe* 42 C3
Molde, *Norway* 8 E9
Moldova, *Romania* 38 C10
Moldova ■ = Moldavia ■,
Europe 42 C3
Moldova Nouă, *Romania* . 38 E4
Moldoveanu, *Romania* . . . 38 D7
Molepolole, *Botswana* . . . 84 C4
Moléson, *Switz.* 22 C4
Molfetta, *Italy* 35 A9
Molina de Aragón, *Spain* . 28 E3
Moline, *U.S.A.* 108 E9
Molinella, *Italy* 33 D8
Molinos, *Argentina* 126 B2
Moliro, *Zaïre* 82 D3
Molise □, *Italy* 33 G11
Moliterno, *Italy* 35 B8
Mollahat, *Bangla.* 63 H13
Mölle, *Sweden* 11 H6
Molledo, *Spain* 30 B6
Mollendo, *Peru* 124 D3
Mollerin, L., *Australia* 89 F2
Mollerusa, *Spain* 28 D5
Mollina, *Spain* 31 H6
Mölln, *Germany* 18 B6
Mölltorp, *Sweden* 11 F8
Mölndal, *Sweden* 11 G6
Molochansk, *Ukraine* 42 C6
Molochnaya →, *Ukraine* . . 42 C6
Molodechno, *Belorussia* . . 40 D5
Molokai, *U.S.A.* 102 H16
Moloma →, *Russia* 41 B16
Molong, *Australia* 91 E4
Molopo →, *Africa* 84 D3
Mólos, *Greece* 39 L5
Molotov = Perm, *Russia* . . 44 D6
Moloundou, *Cameroon* . . . 80 D3
Molsheim, *France* 25 D14
Molson L., *Canada* 101 C9
Molteno, *S. Africa* 84 E4
Molu, *Indonesia* 57 F8
Molucca Sea = Maluku
Sea, *Indonesia* 57 E6
Moluccas = Maluku,
Indonesia 57 E7
Moma, *Mozam.* 83 F4
Moma, *Zaïre* 82 C1
Mombaça, *Brazil* 122 C4
Mombasa, *Kenya* 82 C4
Mombetsu, *Japan* 48 B11
Mombuey, *Spain* 30 C4
Momchilgrad, *Bulgaria* . . . 39 H8
Momi, *Zaïre* 82 C2
Momignies, *Belgium* 17 H4
Mompós, *Colombia* 120 B3
Møn, *Denmark* 11 K6
Mon →, *Burma* 61 J19
Mona, Canal de la,
W. Indies 117 C6
Mona, Isla, *Puerto Rico* . . 117 C6
Mona, Pta., *Costa Rica* . . . 116 E3
Mona, Pta., *Spain* 31 J7
Monach Is., *U.K.* 14 D1
Monaco ■, *Europe* 27 E11
Monadhliath Mts., *U.K.* . . 14 D4
Monagas □, *Venezuela* . . . 121 B5
Monaghan, *Ireland* 15 B5
Monaghan □, *Ireland* 15 B5
Monahans, *U.S.A.* 109 K3
Monapo, *Mozam.* 83 E5
Monarch Mt., *Canada* 100 C3
Monastir = Bitola,
Macedonia 39 H4
Monastir, *Tunisia* 75 A7
Monastyriska, *Ukraine* . . . 40 G4
Moncada, *Phil.* 55 D4
Moncada, *Spain* 28 F4

Moncalieri, *Italy* 32 D4
Moncalvo, *Italy* 32 C5
Moncão, *Portugal* 30 C2
Moncarapacho, *Portugal* . . 31 H3
Moncayo, Sierra del, *Spain* 28 D3
Mönchengladbach,
  Germany 18 D2
Monchique, *Portugal* 31 H2
Monclova, *Mexico* 114 B4
Moncontour, *France* 24 D4
Moncoutant, *France* 26 B3
Moncton, *Canada* 99 C7
Mondego →, *Portugal* . . . 30 E2
Mondego, C., *Portugal* . . . 30 E2
Mondeodo, *Indonesia* . . . 57 E6
Mondolfo, *Italy* 33 E10
Mondoñedo, *Spain* 30 B3
Mondoví, *Italy* 32 D4
Mondovi, *U.S.A.* 108 C9
Mondragon, *France* 27 D8
Mondragon, *Phil.* 55 E6
Mondragone, *Italy* 34 A6
Mondrain I., *Australia* . . . 89 F3
Monduli □, *Tanzania* 82 C4
Monemvasía, *Greece* 39 N6
Monessen, *U.S.A.* 106 F5
Monesterio, *Spain* 31 G4
Monestier-de-Clermont,
  France 27 D9
Monett, *U.S.A.* 109 G8
Monfalcone, *Italy* 33 C10
Monflanquin, *France* 26 D4
Monforte, *Portugal* 31 F3
Monforte de Lemos, *Spain* 30 C3
Mong Hsu, *Burma* 61 J21
Mong Kung, *Burma* 61 J20
Mong Nai, *Burma* 61 J20
Mong Pawk, *Burma* 61 H21
Mong Ton, *Burma* 61 J21
Mong Wa, *Burma* 61 J22
Mong Yai, *Burma* 61 H21
Mongalla, *Sudan* 77 F3
Mongers, L., *Australia* . . . 89 E2
Monghyr = Munger, *India* 63 G12
Mongo, *Chad* 73 F8
Mongolia ■, *Asia* 45 E10
Mongonu, *Nigeria* 79 C7
Mongororo, *Chad* 73 F9
Mongu, *Zambia* 81 H4
Môngua, *Angola* 84 B2
Monistrol-d'Allier, *France* 26 D7
Monistrol-sur-Loire, *France* 27 C8
Monkey Bay, *Malawi* 83 E4
Monkey River, *Belize* . . . 115 D7
Monkira, *Australia* 90 C3
Monkoto, *Zaïre* 80 E4
Monmouth, *U.K.* 13 F5
Monmouth, *U.S.A.* 108 E9
Mono L., *U.S.A.* 111 H4
Monolith, *U.S.A.* 113 K8
Monólithos, *Greece* 37 C9
Monongahela, *U.S.A.* . . . 106 F5
Monópoli, *Italy* 35 B10
Monor, *Hungary* 21 H9
Mónovar, *Spain* 29 G4
Monqoumba, *C.A.R.* 80 D3
Monreal del Campo, *Spain* 28 E3
Monreale, *Italy* 34 D6
Monroe, *Ga., U.S.A.* 105 J4
Monroe, *La., U.S.A.* 109 J8
Monroe, *Mich., U.S.A.* . . 104 E4
Monroe, *N.C., U.S.A.* . . . 105 H5
Monroe, *N.Y., U.S.A.* . . . 107 E10
Monroe, *Utah, U.S.A.* . . . 111 G7
Monroe, *Wash., U.S.A.* . . 112 C5
Monroe, *Wis., U.S.A.* . . . 108 D10
Monroe City, *U.S.A.* 108 F9
Monroeville, *Ala., U.S.A.* 105 K2
Monroeville, *Pa., U.S.A.* . 106 F5
Monrovia, *Liberia* 78 D2
Monrovia, *U.S.A.* 111 J4
Mons, *Belgium* 17 H3
Monsaraz, *Portugal* 31 G3
Monse, *Indonesia* 57 E6
Monsefú, *Peru* 124 B2
Monségur, *France* 26 D4
Monselice, *Italy* 33 C8
Monster, *Neths.* 16 D4
Mont Cenis, Col du, *France* 27 C10
Mont-de-Marsan, *France* . 26 E3
Mont-Joli, *Canada* 99 C6
Mont-Laurier, *Canada* . . . 98 C4
Mont-St.-Michel, Le = Le
  Mont-St.-Michel, *France* 24 D5
Mont-sous-Vaudrey, *France* 25 F12
Mont-sur-Marchienne,
  Belgium 17 H4
Mont Tremblant Prov.
  Park, *Canada* 98 C5
Montabaur, *Germany* 18 E3
Montagnac, *France* 26 E7
Montagnana, *Italy* 33 C8
Montagu, *S. Africa* 84 E3
Montagu I., *Antarctica* . . . 5 B1
Montague, *Canada* 99 C7
Montague, *U.S.A.* 110 F2
Montague, I., *Mexico* . . . 114 A2
Montague Ra., *Australia* . . 89 E2
Montague Sd., *Australia* . . 88 B4
Montaigu, *France* 24 F5
Montalbán, *Spain* 28 E4
Montalbano di Elicona,
  Italy 35 D8
Montalbano Iónico, *Italy* . 35 B9
Montalbo, *Spain* 28 F2

Montalcino, *Italy* 33 E8
Montalegre, *Portugal* 30 D3
Montalto di Castro, *Italy* . 33 F8
Montalto Uffugo, *Italy* . . 35 C9
Montalvo, *U.S.A.* 113 L7
Montamarta, *Spain* 30 D5
Montaña, *Peru* 124 B3
Montana, *Switz.* 22 D4
Montana □, *U.S.A.* 110
Montaña Clara, I.,
  Canary Is. 36 E6
Montánchez, *Spain* 31 F4
Montañita, *Colombia* . . . 120 C2
Montargis, *France* 25 E9
Montauban, *France* 26 D5
Montauk, *U.S.A.* 107 E13
Montauk Pt., *U.S.A.* 107 E13
Montbard, *France* 25 E11
Montbéliard, *France* 25 E13
Montblanch, *Spain* 28 D6
Montbrison, *France* 27 C8
Montcalm, Pic de, *France* . 26 F5
Montceau-les-Mines, *France* 25 F11
Montchanin, *France* 27 B8
Montclair, *U.S.A.* 107 F10
Montcornet, *France* 25 C11
Montcuq, *France* 26 D5
Montdidier, *France* 25 C9
Monte Albán, *Mexico* . . . 115 D5
Monte Alegre, *Brazil* . . . 121 D7
Monte Alegre de Goiás,
  Brazil 123 D2
Monte Alegre de Minas,
  Brazil 123 E2
Monte Azul, *Brazil* 123 E3
Monte Bello Is., *Australia* 88 D2
Monte-Carlo, *Monaco* . . . 27 E11
Monte Carmelo, *Brazil* . . 123 E2
Monte Caseros, *Argentina* 126 C4
Monte Comán, *Argentina* . 126 C2
Monte Cristi, *Dom. Rep.* . 117 C5
Monte Dinero, *Argentina* . 128 D3
Monte Lindo →, *Paraguay* 126 A4
Monte Quemado, *Argentina* 126 B3
Monte Redondo, *Portugal* . 30 F2
Monte Rio, *U.S.A.* 112 G4
Monte San Giovanni, *Italy* 34 A6
Monte San Savino, *Italy* . . 33 E8
Monte Sant' Ángelo, *Italy* 35 A8
Monte Santu, C. di, *Italy* . 34 B2
Monte Vista, *U.S.A.* 111 H10
Monteagudo, *Argentina* . . 127 B5
Monteagudo, *Bolivia* 125 D5
Montealegre, *Spain* 29 G3
Montebello, *Canada* 98 C5
Montebelluna, *Italy* 33 C9
Montebourg, *France* 24 C5
Montecastrilli, *Italy* 33 F9
Montecatini Terme, *Italy* . 32 E7
Montecito, *U.S.A.* 113 L7
Montecristi, *Ecuador* . . . 120 D1
Montecristo, *Italy* 32 F7
Montefalco, *Italy* 33 F9
Montefiascone, *Italy* 33 F9
Montefrío, *Spain* 31 H6
Montegnée, *Belgium* 17 G7
Montego Bay, *Jamaica* . . 116 C4
Montegranaro, *Italy* 33 E10
Monteiro, *Brazil* 122 C4
Montejicar, *Spain* 29 H1
Montejinnie, *Australia* . . . 88 C5
Montelíbano, *Colombia* . . 120 B2
Montélimar, *France* 27 D8
Montella, *Italy* 35 B8
Montellano, *Spain* 31 J5
Montello, *U.S.A.* 108 D10
Montelupo Fiorentino, *Italy* 32 E8
Montemor-o-Novo,
  Portugal 31 G2
Montemor-o-Velho,
  Portugal 30 E2
Montemorelos, *Mexico* . . 115 B5
Montendre, *France* 26 C3
Montenegro, *Brazil* 127 B5
Montenegro □,
  Montenegro, Yug. 21 N9
Montenero di Bisaccia,
  Italy 33 G11
Montepuez, *Mozam.* 83 E4
Montepuez →, *Mozam.* . . 83 E5
Montepulciano, *Italy* 33 E8
Montereale, *Italy* 33 F10
Montereau-Fault-Yonne,
  France 25 D9
Monterey, *U.S.A.* 111 H3
Monterey B., *U.S.A.* 112 J5
Montería, *Colombia* 120 B2
Montero, *Bolivia* 125 D5
Monteros, *Argentina* 126 B2
Monterotondo, *Italy* 33 F9
Monterrey, *Mexico* 114 B4
Montes Altos, *Brazil* 122 C2
Montes Claros, *Brazil* . . . 123 E3
Montesano, *U.S.A.* 112 D3
Montesárchio, *Italy* 35 A7
Montescaglioso, *Italy* . . . 35 B9
Montesilvano, *Italy* 33 F11
Montevarchi, *Italy* 33 E8
Montevideo, *Uruguay* . . . 127 C4
Montevideo, *U.S.A.* 108 C7
Montezuma, *U.S.A.* 108 E8
Montfaucon, *France* 25 C12
Montfaucon-en-Velay,
  France 27 C8
Montfort, *France* 24 D5

Montfort, *Neths.* 17 F7
Montfort-l'Amaury, *France* 25 D8
Montgenèvre, *France* 27 D10
Montgomery = Sahiwal,
  Pakistan 62 D5
Montgomery, *U.K.* 13 E4
Montgomery, *Ala., U.S.A.* 105 J2
Montgomery, *W. Va.,
  U.S.A.* 104 F5
Montguyon, *France* 26 C3
Monticelli d'Ongina, *Italy* . 32 C6
Monticello, *Ark., U.S.A.* . 109 J9
Monticello, *Fla., U.S.A.* . 105 K4
Monticello, *Ind., U.S.A.* . 104 E2
Monticello, *Iowa, U.S.A.* . 108 D9
Monticello, *Ky., U.S.A.* . 105 G3
Monticello, *Minn., U.S.A.* 108 C8
Monticello, *Miss., U.S.A.* 109 K9
Monticello, *N.Y., U.S.A.* . 107 E10
Monticello, *Utah, U.S.A.* . 111 H9
Montichiari, *Italy* 32 C7
Montier-en-Der, *France* . . 25 D11
Montignac, *France* 26 C5
Montignies-sur-Sambre,
  Belgium 17 H4
Montigny, *France* 25 C13
Montigny-sur-Aube, *France* 25 E11
Montijo, *Spain* 31 G4
Montijo, Presa de, *Spain* . 31 G4
Montilla, *Spain* 31 H6
Montlhéry, *France* 25 D9
Montluçon, *France* 26 B6
Montmagny, *Canada* 99 C5
Montmarault, *France* 26 B6
Montmartre, *Canada* 101 C8
Montmédy, *France* 25 C12
Montmélian, *France* 27 C10
Montmirail, *France* 25 D10
Montmoreau-St.-Cybard,
  France 26 C4
Montmorency, *Canada* . . . 99 C5
Montmorillon, *France* . . . 26 B4
Montmort, *France* 25 D10
Monto, *Australia* 90 C5
Montoir-sur-le-Loir, *France* 24 E7
Montório al Vomano, *Italy* 33 F10
Montoro, *Spain* 31 G6
Montour Falls, *U.S.A.* . . . 106 D8
Montpelier, *Idaho, U.S.A.* 110 E8
Montpelier, *Ohio, U.S.A.* . 104 E3
Montpelier, *Vt., U.S.A.* . . 107 B12
Montpellier, *France* 26 E7
Montpezat-de-Quercy,
  France 26 D5
Montpon-Ménestérol,
  France 26 D4
Montréal, *Canada* 98 C5
Montréal, *France* 26 E6
Montreal L., *Canada* 101 C7
Montreal Lake, *Canada* . . 101 C7
Montredon-Labessonnié,
  France 26 E6
Montréjeau, *France* 26 E4
Montrésor, *France* 24 E8
Montreuil, *France* 25 B8
Montreuil-Bellay, *France* . 24 E6
Montreux, *Switz.* 22 D3
Montrevault, *France* 24 E5
Montrevel-en-Bresse,
  France 27 B9
Montrichard, *France* 24 E8
Montrose, *U.K.* 14 E6
Montrose, *Colo., U.S.A.* . 111 G10
Montrose, *Pa., U.S.A.* . . . 107 E9
Monts, Pte. des, *Canada* . . 99 C6
Monts-sur-Guesnes, *France* 24 F7
Montsalvy, *France* 26 D6
Montsant, Sierra de, *Spain* 28 D5
Montsauche, *France* 25 E11
Montsech, Sierra del, *Spain* 28 C5
Montseny, *Spain* 28 D2
Montserrat ■, *W. Indies* . . 117 C7
Montserrat, *Spain* 28 D6
Montuenga, *Spain* 30 D6
Montuiri, *Spain* 36 B9
Monveda, *Zaïre* 80 D4
Monywa, *Burma* 61 H19
Monza, *Italy* 32 C6
Monze, *Zambia* 83 F2
Monze, C., *Pakistan* 62 G2
Monzón, *Spain* 28 D5
Mooi River, *S. Africa* . . . 85 D4
Mook, *Neths.* 16 E7
Moolawatana, *Australia* . . 91 D2
Mooliabeenee, *Australia* . . 89 F2
Mooloogool, *Australia* . . . 89 E2
Moomin Cr. →, *Australia* . 91 D4
Moonah →, *Australia* 90 C2
Moonbeam, *Canada* 98 C3
Moonda, L., *Australia* . . . 90 D3
Moonie, *Australia* 91 D5
Moonie →, *Australia* 91 D4
Moonta, *Australia* 91 E2
Moora, *Australia* 89 F2
Moore, L., *Australia* 89 E2
Moore Reefs, *Australia* . . 90 B4
Moorefield, *U.S.A.* 104 F6
Moores Res., *U.S.A.* 107 B13
Mooresville, *U.S.A.* 105 H5
Moorfoot Hills, *U.K.* 14 F5

Moorhead, *U.S.A.* 108 B6
Mooroopna, *Australia* . . . 91 F4
Moorpark, *U.S.A.* 113 L8
Moorreesburg, *S. Africa* . . 84 E2
Moorslede, *Belgium* 17 G2
Moosburg, *Germany* 19 G7
Moose →, *Canada* 98 B3
Moose Factory, *Canada* . . 98 B3
Moose I., *Canada* 101 C9
Moose Jaw, *Canada* 101 C7
Moose Jaw →, *Canada* . . 101 C7
Moose Lake, *Canada* 101 C8
Moose Lake, *U.S.A.* 108 B8
Moose Mountain Cr. →,
  Canada 101 D8
Moose Mountain Prov.
  Park, *Canada* 101 D8
Moose River, *U.S.A.* 98 B3
Moosehead L., *U.S.A.* . . . 99 C6
Moosomin, *Canada* 101 C8
Moosonee, *Canada* 98 B3
Moosup, *U.S.A.* 107 E13
Mopeia Velha, *Mozam.* . . 83 F4
Mopipi, *Botswana* 84 C3
Mopoi, *C.A.R.* 82 A2
Mopti, *Mali* 78 C4
Moqatta, *Sudan* 77 E4
Moquegua, *Peru* 124 D3
Moquegua □, *Peru* 124 D3
Mór, *Hungary* 21 H8
Móra, *Portugal* 31 G2
Mora, *Sweden* 9 F13
Mora, *Minn., U.S.A.* 108 C8
Mora, *N. Mex., U.S.A.* . . 111 J11
Mora de Ebro, *Spain* 28 D5
Mora de Rubielos, *Spain* . 28 E4
Mora la Nueva, *Spain* . . . 28 D5
Morača →,
  Montenegro, Yug. 21 N9
Morada Nova, *Brazil* 122 C4
Morada Nova de Minas,
  Brazil 123 E2
Moradabad, *India* 63 E8
Morafenobe, *Madag.* 85 B7
Morag, *Poland* 20 B9
Moral de Calatrava, *Spain* 29 G1
Moraleja, *Spain* 30 E4
Morales, *Colombia* 120 C2
Moramanga, *Madag.* 85 B8
Moran, *Kans., U.S.A.* . . . 109 G7
Moran, *Wyo., U.S.A.* . . . 110 E8
Moranbah, *Australia* 90 C4
Morano Cálabro, *Italy* . . . 35 C9
Morant Cays, *Jamaica* . . 116 C4
Morant Pt., *Jamaica* 116 C4
Morar, L., *U.K.* 14 E3
Moratalla, *Spain* 29 G3
Moratuwa, *Sri Lanka* 60 R11
Morava →, *Europe* 20 G6
Morava →, *Serbia, Yug.* . 21 M10
Moravice →, *Czech.* 20 F7
Moraviţa, *Romania* 21 K11
Moravská Třebová, *Czech.* 20 F6
Morawa, *Australia* 89 E2
Morawhanna, *Guyana* . . . 121 B6
Moray Firth, *U.K.* 14 D5
Morbach, *Germany* 19 F3
Morbegno, *Italy* 32 B6
Morbi, *India* 62 H4
Morbihan □, *France* 24 E4
Morcenx, *France* 26 D3
Mordelles, *France* 24 D5
Morden, *Canada* 101 D9
Mordovian Republic □,
  Russia 41 D14
Mordovo, *Russia* 41 E12
Mordvinia = Mordovian
  Republic □, *Russia* 41 D14
Møre og Romsdal fylke □,
  Norway 10 B2
Morea, *Australia* 91 F3
Morea, *Greece* 6 H10
Moreau →, *U.S.A.* 108 C4
Morecambe, *U.K.* 12 C5
Morecambe B., *U.K.* 12 C5
Moree, *Australia* 91 D4
Morehead, *U.S.A.* 104 F4
Morehead City, *U.S.A.* . . 105 H7
Morelia, *Mexico* 114 D4
Morella, *Australia* 90 C3
Morella, *Spain* 28 E4
Morelos, *Mexico* 114 B3
Morelos □, *Mexico* 115 D5
Morena, Sierra, *Spain* . . . 31 G7
Morenci, *U.S.A.* 111 K9
Moreni, *Romania* 38 E8
Morero, *Bolivia* 125 C5
Moreru →, *Brazil* 125 C6
Moresby I., *Canada* 100 C2
Morestel, *France* 27 C9
Moret-sur-Loing, *France* . 25 D9
Moreton, *Australia* 90 A3
Moreton I., *Australia* 91 D5
Moreuil, *France* 25 C9
Morey, *Spain* 36 B10
Morez, *France* 27 B10
Morgan, *Australia* 91 E2
Morgan, *U.S.A.* 110 F8
Morgan City, *U.S.A.* 109 L9
Morgan Hill, *U.S.A.* 112 H5
Morganfield, *U.S.A.* 104 G2

Morganton, *U.S.A.* 105 H5
Morgantown, *U.S.A.* 104 F6
Morgat, *France* 24 D2
Morgenzon, *S. Africa* . . . 85 D4
Morges, *Switz.* 22 C2
Morghak, *Iran* 65 D8
Mori, *Italy* 32 C7
Morialmée, *Belgium* 17 H5
Morice L., *Canada* 100 C3
Morichal, *Colombia* 120 C3
Morichal Largo →,
  Venezuela 121 B5
Moriki, *Nigeria* 79 C6
Morinville, *Canada* 100 C6
Morioka, *Japan* 48 E10
Moris, *Mexico* 114 B3
Morlaàs, *France* 26 E3
Morlaix, *France* 24 D3
Morlanwelz, *Belgium* . . . 17 H4
Mormanno, *Italy* 35 C8
Mormant, *France* 25 D9
Mornington, *Vic., Australia* 91 F4
Mornington, W. Austral.,
  Australia 88 C4
Mornington, *Chile* 128 C1
Mornington I., *Australia* . . 90 B2
Mórnos →, *Greece* 39 L4
Moro, *Sudan* 77 E3
Moro G., *Phil.* 55 H5
Morocco ■, *N. Afr.* 74 B3
Morocamba, *Peru* 124 C2
Morogoro, *Tanzania* 82 D4
Morogoro □, *Tanzania* . . . 82 D4
Moroleón, *Mexico* 114 C4
Morombe, *Madag.* 85 C7
Moron, *Argentina* 126 C4
Morón, *Cuba* 116 B4
Mörön, *Mongolia* 54 B6
Morón de Almazán, *Spain* 28 D2
Morón de la Frontera,
  Spain 31 H5
Morona →, *Peru* 120 D2
Morona-Santiago □,
  Ecuador 120 D2
Morondava, *Madag.* 85 C7
Morondo, *Ivory C.* 78 D3
Morongo Valley, *U.S.A.* . . 113 L10
Moronou, *Ivory C.* 78 D4
Morotai, *Indonesia* 57 D7
Moroto, *Uganda* 82 B3
Moroto Summit, *Kenya* . . 82 B3
Morozovsk, *Russia* 43 B9
Morpeth, *U.K.* 12 B6
Morphou, *Cyprus* 37 D11
Morphou Bay, *Cyprus* . . . 37 D11
Morrilton, *U.S.A.* 109 H8
Morrinhos, *Ceara, Brazil* . 122 B3
Morrinhos, *Minas Gerais,
  Brazil* 123 E2
Morrinsville, *N.Z.* 87 G5
Morris, *Canada* 101 D9
Morris, *Ill., U.S.A.* 104 E1
Morris, *Minn., U.S.A.* . . . 108 C7
Morris, Mt., *Australia* . . . 89 E5
Morrisburg, *Canada* 98 D4
Morrison, *U.S.A.* 108 E10
Morristown, *Ariz., U.S.A.* 111 K7
Morristown, *N.J., U.S.A.* . 107 F10
Morristown, S. Dak.,
  U.S.A. 108 C4
Morristown, *Tenn., U.S.A.* 105 G4
Morro, Pta., *Chile* 126 B1
Morro Bay, *U.S.A.* 111 J3
Morro del Jable, *Canary Is.* 36 F5
Morro do Chapéu, *Brazil* . 123 D3
Morro Jable, Pta. de,
  Canary Is. 36 F5
Morros, *Brazil* 122 B3
Morrosquillo, G. de,
  Colombia 116 E4
Morrumbene, *Mozam.* . . . 85 C6
Mors, *Denmark* 11 H2
Morshansk, *Russia* 41 E12
Mörsil, *Sweden* 10 A7
Mortagne →, *France* 25 D13
Mortagne-au-Perche,
  France 24 D7
Mortagne-sur-Gironde,
  France 26 C3
Mortagne-sur-Sèvre, *France* 24 F6
Mortain, *France* 24 D6
Mortara, *Italy* 32 C5
Morteau, *France* 25 E13
Morteros, *Argentina* 126 C3
Mortes, R. das →, *Brazil* . 123 D1
Mortlake, *Australia* 91 F3
Morton, *Tex., U.S.A.* 109 J3
Morton, *Wash., U.S.A.* . . 112 D4
Mortsel, *Belgium* 17 F4
Morundah, *Australia* 91 E4
Moruya, *Australia* 91 F5
Morvan, *France* 25 E11
Morven, *Australia* 91 D4
Morwell, *Australia* 91 F4
Morvern, *U.K.* 14 E3
Mosalsk, *Russia* 40 D9
Mosbach, *Germany* 19 F5
Mošćenice, *Croatia* 33 C11
Mosciano Sant' Ángelo,
  Italy 33 F10
Moscos Is., *Burma* 58 E1
Moscow = Moskva, *Russia* 41 D10
Moscow, *U.S.A.* 110 C5
Mosel →, *Europe* 19 E3

Moselle = Mosel →,
  Europe 19 E3
Moselle □, France 25 D13
Moses Lake, U.S.A. 110 C4
Mosgiel, N.Z. 87 L3
Moshi, Tanzania 82 C4
Moshi □, Tanzania 82 C4
Moshupa, Botswana 84 C4
Mosjøen, Norway 8 D12
Moskenesøya, Norway ... 8 C12
Moskenstraumen, Norway 8 C12
Moskva, Russia 41 D10
Moskva →, Russia 41 D11
Moslavačka Gora, Croatia 33 C13
Mosomane, Botswana 84 C4
Mosonmagyaróvár,
  Hungary 21 H7
Mospino, Ukraine 42 C7
Mosquera, Colombia 120 C2
Mosquero, U.S.A. 109 H3
Mosqueruela, Spain 28 E4
Mosquitia, Honduras 116 C3
Mosquitos, G. de los,
  Panama 116 E3
Moss, Norway 10 E4
Moss Vale, Australia 91 E5
Mossaka, Congo 80 E3
Mossâmedes, Brazil 123 E1
Mossbank, Canada 101 D7
Mossburn, N.Z. 87 L2
Mosselbaai, S. Africa ... 84 E3
Mossendjo, Congo 80 E2
Mosses, Col des, Switz. .. 22 D4
Mossgiel, Australia 91 E3
Mossman, Australia 90 B4
Mossoró, Brazil 122 C4
Mossuril, Mozam. 83 E5
Mossy →, Canada 101 C8
Most, Czech. 20 E3
Mosta, Malta 37 D1
Mostafáábád, Iran 65 C7
Mostaganem, Algeria ... 75 A5
Mostar, Bos.-H. 21 M7
Mostardas, Brazil 127 C5
Mostefa, Rass, Tunisia .. 75 A7
Mostiska, Ukraine 40 G3
Móstoles, Spain 30 E7
Mosty, Belorussia 40 E4
Mosul = Al Mawşil, Iraq 64 B4
Mosulpo, S. Korea 51 H14
Mota del Cuervo, Spain . 28 F2
Mota del Marqués, Spain . 30 D5
Motagua →, Guatemala . . 116 C2
Motala, Sweden 11 F9
Motherwell, U.K. 14 F5
Motihari, India 63 F11
Motilla del Palancar, Spain 28 F3
Motnik, Slovenia 33 B11
Motocurunya, Venezuela . 121 C5
Motovun, Croatia 33 C10
Motozintla de Mendoza,
  Mexico 115 D6
Motril, Spain 29 J1
Motru →, Romania 38 E6
Mott, U.S.A. 108 B3
Móttola, Italy 35 B10
Motueka, N.Z. 87 J4
Motueka →, N.Z. 87 J4
Motul, Mexico 115 C7
Mouanda, Gabon 80 E2
Mouchalagane →, Canada 99 B6
Mouding, China 52 E3
Moudjeria, Mauritania .. 78 B2
Moudon, Switz. 22 C3
Mouila, Gabon 80 E2
Moulamein, Australia .. 91 F3
Mouliana, Greece 37 D7
Moulins, France 26 B7
Moulmein, Burma 61 L20
Moulouya, O. →, Morocco 75 A4
Moulton, U.S.A. 109 L6
Moultrie, U.S.A. 105 K4
Moultrie, L., U.S.A. 105 J5
Mound City, Mo., U.S.A. 108 E7
Mound City, S. Dak.,
  U.S.A. 108 C4
Moúnda, Ákra, Greece ... 39 L3
Moundou, Chad 73 G8
Moundsville, U.S.A. ... 106 G4
Moung, Cambodia 58 F4
Mount Airy, U.S.A. 105 G5
Mount Albert, Canada .. 106 B5
Mount Amherst, Australia 88 C4
Mount Angel, U.S.A. ... 110 D2
Mount Augustus, Australia 88 D2
Mount Barker, S. Austral.,
  Australia 91 F2
Mount Barker, W. Austral.,
  Australia 89 F2
Mount Carmel, U.S.A. ... 104 F2
Mount Clemens, U.S.A. .. 98 D4
Mount Coolon, Australia . 90 C4
Mount Darwin, Zimbabwe 83 F3
Mount Desert I., U.S.A. .. 99 D6
Mount Dora, U.S.A. 105 L5
Mount Douglas, Australia . 90 C4
Mount Eba, Australia ... 91 E2
Mount Edgecumbe, U.S.A. 100 B1
Mount Elizabeth, Australia 88 C4
Mount Fletcher, S. Africa . 85 E4
Mount Forest, Canada ... 98 D3
Mount Gambier, Australia 91 F3
Mount Garnet, Australia . 90 B4
Mount Hope, N.S.W.,
  Australia 91 E4

Mount Hope, S. Austral.,
  Australia 91 E2
Mount Hope, U.S.A. 104 G5
Mount Horeb, U.S.A. ... 108 D10
Mount Howitt, Australia . 91 D3
Mount Isa, Australia 90 C2
Mount Keith, Australia .. 89 E3
Mount Laguna, U.S.A. . . 113 N10
Mount Larcom, Australia . 90 C5
Mount Lofty Ra., Australia 91 E2
Mount McKinley National
  Park, U.S.A. 96 B5
Mount Magnet, Australia . 89 E2
Mount Margaret, Australia 91 D3
Mount Maunganui, N.Z. . 87 G6
Mount Molloy, Australia . 90 B4
Mount Monger, Australia . 89 F3
Mount Morgan, Australia . 90 C5
Mount Morris, U.S.A. ... 106 D7
Mount Mulligan, Australia 90 B3
Mount Narryer, Australia . 89 E2
Mount Olympus = Uludağ,
  Turkey 66 C3
Mount Oxide Mine,
  Australia 90 B2
Mount Pearl, Canada ... 99 C9
Mount Perry, Australia .. 91 D5
Mount Phillips, Australia . 88 D2
Mount Pleasant, Iowa,
  U.S.A. 108 E9
Mount Pleasant, Mich.,
  U.S.A. 104 D3
Mount Pleasant, Pa.,
  U.S.A. 106 F5
Mount Pleasant, S.C.,
  U.S.A. 105 J6
Mount Pleasant, Tenn.,
  U.S.A. 105 H2
Mount Pleasant, Tex.,
  U.S.A. 109 J7
Mount Pleasant, Utah,
  U.S.A. 110 G8
Mount Pocono, U.S.A. ... 107 E9
Mount Rainier National
  Park, U.S.A. 112 D5
Mount Revelstoke Nat.
  Park, Canada 100 C5
Mount Robson Prov. Park,
  Canada 100 C5
Mount Sandiman, Australia 89 D2
Mount Shasta, U.S.A. ... 110 F2
Mount Signal, U.S.A. . . . 113 N11
Mount Sterling, Ill., U.S.A. 108 F9
Mount Sterling, Ky.,
  U.S.A. 104 F4
Mount Surprise, Australia . 90 B3
Mount Union, U.S.A. ... 106 F7
Mount Vernon, Australia . 88 D2
Mount Vernon, Ind.,
  U.S.A. 108 F10
Mount Vernon, N.Y.,
  U.S.A. 107 F11
Mount Vernon, Ohio,
  U.S.A. 106 F2
Mount Vernon, Wash.,
  U.S.A. 112 B4
Mountain Center, U.S.A. . 113 M10
Mountain City, Nev.,
  U.S.A. 110 F6
Mountain City, Tenn.,
  U.S.A. 105 G5
Mountain Grove, U.S.A. . 109 G8
Mountain Home, Ark.,
  U.S.A. 109 G8
Mountain Home, Idaho,
  U.S.A. 110 E6
Mountain Iron, U.S.A. .. 108 B8
Mountain Park, Canada .. 100 C5
Mountain Pass, U.S.A. . . 113 K11
Mountain View, Ark.,
  U.S.A. 109 H8
Mountain View, Calif.,
  U.S.A. 111 H2
Mountainair, U.S.A. 111 J10
Mountmellick, Ireland ... 15 C4
Moura, Australia 90 C4
Moura, Brazil 121 D5
Moura, Portugal 31 G3
Mourão, Portugal 31 G3
Mourdi, Dépression du,
  Chad 73 E9
Mourdiah, Mali 78 C3
Mourenx-Ville-Nouvelle,
  France 26 E3
Mouri, Ghana 79 D4
Mourilyan, Australia ... 90 B4
Mourmelon-le-Grand,
  France 25 C11
Mourne →, U.K. 15 B4
Mourne Mts., U.K. 15 B5
Mournies, Greece 37 D6
Mouscron, Belgium 17 G2
Moussoro, Chad 73 F8
Mouthe, France 25 F13
Moutier, Switz. 22 B4
Moûtiers, France 27 C10
Moutohara, N.Z. 87 H6
Moutong, Indonesia ... 57 D6
Mouy, France 25 C9
Mouzáki, Greece 39 K4
Movas, Mexico 114 B3
Moville, Ireland 15 A4
Moxhe, Belgium 17 G6
Moxotó →, Brazil 122 C4
Moy →, Ireland 15 B3

Moyale, Kenya 68 G2
Moyamba, S. Leone 78 D2
Moyen Atlas, Morocco .. 74 B3
Moyle □, U.K. 15 A5
Moyo, Indonesia 56 F5
Moyobamba, Peru 124 B2
Moyyero →, Russia ... 45 C11
Mozambique =
  Moçambique, Mozam. . 83 F5
Mozambique ■, Africa .. 83 F4
Mozambique Chan., Africa 85 B7
Mozdok, Russia 43 E11
Mozdūrān, Iran 65 B9
Mozhaysk, Russia 41 D10
Mozhga, Russia 41 C18
Mozhnābād, Iran 65 C9
Mozirje, Slovenia 33 B11
Mozyr, Belorussia 40 E6
Mpanda, Tanzania 82 D3
Mpanda □, Tanzania ... 82 D3
Mpésoba, Mali 78 C3
Mpika, Zambia 83 E3
Mpulungu, Zambia 83 D3
Mpumalanga, S. Africa . 85 D5
Mpwapwa, Tanzania ... 82 D4
Mpwapwa □, Tanzania . 82 D4
Mrągowo, Poland 20 B11
Mramor, Serbia, Yug. .. 21 M11
Mrimina, Morocco 74 C3
Mrkonjić Grad,
  Bos.-H. 21 L7
Mrkopalj, Croatia 33 C11
Msab, Oued en →, Algeria 75 B6
Msaken, Tunisia 75 A7
Msambansovu, Zimbabwe 83 F3
M'sila, Algeria 75 A5
Msoro, Zambia 83 E3
Msta →, Russia 40 B7
Mstislavl, Belorussia ... 40 E7
Mtama, Tanzania 83 E4
Mtilikwe →, Zimbabwe . 83 G3
Mtsensk, Russia 41 E10
Mtskheta, Georgia 43 F11
Mtubatuba, S. Africa ... 85 D5
Mtwara-Mikindani,
  Tanzania 83 E5
Mu Gia, Deo, Vietnam ... 58 D5
Mu Us Shamo, China ... 50 E5
Muaná, Brazil 122 B2
Muang Chiang Rai,
  Thailand 58 C2
Muang Lamphun, Thailand 58 C2
Muang Pak Beng, Laos .. 58 C3
Muar, Malaysia 59 L4
Muarabungo, Indonesia .. 56 E2
Muaraenim, Indonesia .. 56 E2
Muarajuloi, Indonesia .. 56 E4
Muarakaman, Indonesia . 56 E5
Muaratebo, Indonesia .. 56 E2
Muaratembesi, Indonesia . 56 E2
Muaratewe, Indonesia .. 56 E4
Mubarakpur, India 63 F10
Mubarraz = Al Mubarraz,
  Si. Arabia 65 E6
Mubende, Uganda 82 B3
Mubi, Nigeria 79 C7
Mubur, P., Indonesia ... 59 L6
Mucajaí →, Brazil 121 C5
Mucajaí, Serra do, Brazil . 121 C5
Muchachos, Roque de los,
  Canary Is. 36 F2
Mücheln, Germany 18 D7
Muchinga Mts., Zambia . 83 E3
Muchkapskiy, Russia ... 41 F13
Muck, U.K. 14 E2
Muckadilla, Australia ... 91 D4
Muco →, Colombia ... 120 C3
Muconda, Angola 80 G4
Mucuim →, Brazil 125 B5
Mucur, Turkey 66 D6
Mucura, Brazil 121 D5
Mucuri, Brazil 123 E4
Mucurici, Brazil 123 E3
Mucusso, Angola 84 B3
Muda, Canary Is. 36 F6
Mudan Jiang →, China . 51 A15
Mudanjiang, China 51 B15
Mudanya, Turkey 42 F3
Muddy Cr. →, U.S.A. . 111 H8
Mudgee, Australia 91 E4
Mudjatik →, Canada .. 101 B7
Mudurnu, Turkey 66 C5
Muecate, Mozam. 83 E4
Mueda, Mozam. 83 E4
Mueller Ra., Australia .. 88 C4
Muende, Mozam. 83 E3
Muerto, Mar, Mexico .. 115 D6
Muertos, Punta de los,
  Spain 29 J3
Mufindi □, Tanzania ... 83 D4
Mufu Shan, China 53 C10
Mufulira, Zambia 83 E2
Mufumbiro Range, Africa 82 C2
Mugardos, Spain 30 B2
Muge, Portugal 31 F2
Muge →, Portugal ... 31 F2
Múggia, Italy 33 C10
Mughayrā', Si. Arabia .. 64 D3
Mugi, Japan 49 H7
Mugia, Spain 30 B1
Mugila, Mts., Zaïre ... 82 D2
Muğla, Turkey 66 E3
Muğla □, Turkey 66 E3
Muğlizh, Bulgaria 38 G8
Mugu, Nepal 63 E10

Muhammad, Râs, Egypt .. 76 B3
Muhammad Qol, Sudan .. 76 C4
Muhammadabad, India .. 63 F10
Muhesi →, Tanzania ... 82 D4
Muheza □, Tanzania ... 82 C4
Mühldorf, Germany ... 19 G8
Mühlhausen, Germany .. 18 D6
Mühlig Hofmann fjella,
  Antarctica 5 D3
Muhutwe, Tanzania ... 82 C3
Muiden, Neths. 16 D6
Muikamachi, Japan 49 F9
Muine Bheag, Ireland .. 15 D5
Muiños, Spain 30 D3
Muir, L., Australia 89 F2
Mukachevo, Ukraine ... 40 G3
Mukah, Malaysia 56 D4
Mukawwa, Geziret, Egypt 76 C4
Mukdahan, Thailand ... 58 D5
Mukden = Shenyang,
  China 51 D12
Mukhtolovo, Russia ... 41 D13
Mukhtuya = Lensk, Russia 45 C12
Mukinbudin, Australia ... 89 F2
Mukishi, Zaïre 83 D1
Mukomuko, Indonesia .. 56 E2
Mukomwenze, Zaïre ... 82 D2
Mukwela, Zambia 83 F2
Mula, Spain 29 G3
Mulange, Zaïre 82 C2
Mulchén, Chile 126 D1
Mulde →, Germany ... 18 D8
Mule Creek, U.S.A. ... 108 D2
Muleba, Tanzania 82 C3
Muleba □, Tanzania ... 82 C3
Mulegns, Switz. 23 C9
Muleshoe, U.S.A. 109 H3
Mulgathing, Australia .. 91 E1
Mulgrave, Canada 99 C7
Mulhacén, Spain 29 H1
Mülheim, Germany ... 18 D2
Mulhouse, France 25 E14
Muli, China 52 D3
Muling, China 51 B16
Mull, U.K. 14 E3
Mullaittvu, Sri Lanka .. 60 Q12
Mullen, U.S.A. 108 D4
Mullengudgery, Australia 91 E4
Mullens, U.S.A. 104 G5
Muller, Pegunungan,
  Indonesia 56 D4
Mullet Pen., Ireland ... 15 B1
Mullewa, Australia ... 89 E2
Müllheim, Germany ... 19 H3
Mulligan →, Australia . 90 C2
Mullin, U.S.A. 109 K5
Mullingar, Ireland 15 C4
Mullins, U.S.A. 105 H6
Mullumbimby, Australia . 91 D5
Mulobezi, Zambia 83 F2
Multan, Pakistan 62 D4
Multrå, Sweden 10 A11
Mulumbe, Mts., Zaïre .. 83 D2
Mulungushi Dam, Zambia 83 E2
Mulvane, U.S.A. 109 G6
Mulwad, Sudan 76 D3
Mulwala, Australia ... 91 F4
Mumbwa, Zambia 83 E2
Mumra, Russia 43 D12
Mun →, Thailand 58 E5
Muna, Indonesia 57 F6
Munamagi, Estonia ... 40 C5
Münchberg, Germany .. 19 E7
Müncheberg, Germany .. 18 C10
München, Germany ... 19 G7
Munchen-Gladbach =
  Mönchengladbach,
  Germany 18 D2
Muncho Lake, Canada .. 100 B3
Munchŏn, N. Korea ... 51 E14
Müncho Lake, Canada .. 100 B3
Münchwilen, Switz. ... 23 B7
Muncie, U.S.A. 104 E3
Muncoonie, L., Australia 90 D2
Mundala, Indonesia ... 57 E10
Mundare, Canada 100 C6
Munday, U.S.A. 109 J5
Münden, Germany 18 D5
Mundiwindi, Australia .. 88 D3
Mundo →, Spain 29 G2
Mundo Novo, Brazil ... 123 D3
Mundra, India 62 H3
Mundrabilla, Australia .. 89 F4
Munducurus, Brazil ... 121 D6
Munera, Spain 29 F2
Mungallala, Australia .. 91 D4
Mungallala Cr. →,
  Australia 91 D4
Mungana, Australia ... 90 B3
Mungaoli, India 62 G8
Mungari, Mozam. 83 F3
Mungbere, Zaïre 82 B2
Munger, India 63 G12
Mungindi, Australia ... 91 D4
Munhango, Angola ... 81 G3
Munich = München,
  Germany 19 G7
Munising, U.S.A. 104 B2
Munka-Ljungby, Sweden 11 H6
Munkedal, Sweden ... 11 F5
Munku-Sardyk, Russia .. 45 D11
Münnerstadt, Germany . 19 E6
Muñoz Gamero, Pen.,
  Chile 128 D2

Munroe L., Canada 101 B9
Munsan, S. Korea 51 F14
Münsingen, Switz. 22 C5
Munster, France 25 D14
Munster, Niedersachsen,
  Germany 18 C6
Münster,
  Nordrhein-Westfalen,
  Germany 18 D3
Münster □, Ireland ... 23 D6
Munster □, Ireland ... 15 D3
Muntadgin, Australia .. 89 F2
Muntele Mare, Romania . 38 C6
Muntok, Indonesia ... 56 E3
Munyak, Uzbekistan ... 44 E6
Munyama, Zambia 83 F2
Muong Beng, Laos ... 58 B3
Muong Boum, Vietnam . 58 A4
Muong Et, Laos 58 B5
Muong Hai, Laos 58 B3
Muong Hiem, Laos ... 58 B4
Muong Houn, Laos ... 58 B3
Muong Hung, Vietnam . 58 B4
Muong Kau, Laos 58 E5
Muong Khao, Laos ... 58 C4
Muong Khoua, Laos .. 58 B4
Muong Liep, Laos 58 C3
Muong May, Laos 58 E6
Muong Ngeun, Laos .. 58 B3
Muong Ngoi, Laos ... 58 B4
Muong Nhie, Vietnam . 58 A4
Muong Nong, Laos ... 58 D6
Muong Ou Tay, Laos .. 58 A3
Muong Oua, Laos 58 C3
Muong Peun, Laos ... 58 B4
Muong Phalane, Laos .. 58 D5
Muong Phieng, Laos .. 58 C3
Muong Phine, Laos ... 58 D6
Muong Sai, Laos 58 B3
Muong Saiapoun, Laos . 58 C3
Muong Sen, Vietnam .. 58 C5
Muong Sing, Laos 58 B3
Muong Son, Laos 58 B4
Muong Soui, Laos 58 C4
Muong Va, Laos 58 B4
Muong Xia, Vietnam .. 58 B5
Muonio, Finland 8 C17
Muotathal, Switz. 23 C7
Mupa, Angola 81 H3
Muping, China 51 F11
Muqaddam, Wadi →,
  Sudan 76 D3
Muqdisho, Somali Rep. . 68 G4
Mur-de-Bretagne, France . 24 D4
Mura →, Slovenia 33 B13
Muradiye, Turkey 67 D10
Murakami, Japan 48 E9
Murallón, Cuerro, Chile . 128 C2
Muralto, Switz. 23 D7
Muranda, Rwanda 82 C2
Murang'a, Kenya 82 C4
Murashi, Russia 41 B16
Murat, France 26 C6
Murat →, Turkey 67 D8
Muratlı, Turkey 66 C2
Muravera, Italy 34 C2
Murayama, Japan 48 E10
Murban, U.A.E. 65 F7
Murchison →, Australia . 89 E1
Murchison, Mt., Antarctica 5 D11
Murchison Falls =
  Kabarega Falls, Uganda 82 B3
Murchison House, Australia 89 E1
Murchison Ra., Australia . 90 C1
Murchison Rapids, Malawi 83 F3
Murcia, Spain 29 G3
Murcia □, Spain 29 H3
Murdo, U.S.A. 108 D4
Murdoch Pt., Australia .. 90 A3
Mureş →, Romania ... 38 C3
Mureşul = Mureş →,
  Romania 38 C3
Muret, France 26 E5
Murfatlar, Romania ... 38 E11
Murfreesboro, U.S.A. .. 105 H2
Murg, Switz. 23 B8
Murg →, Germany ... 19 G4
Murgab, Tajikistan 44 F8
Murgenthal, Switz. ... 22 B5
Murgon, Australia ... 91 D5
Murgoo, Australia ... 89 E2
Muri, Switz. 23 B6
Muria, Indonesia 57 G14
Muriaé, Brazil 123 F3
Murias de Paredes, Spain . 30 C4
Murici, Brazil 122 C4
Muriel Mine, Zimbabwe . 83 F3
Müritz See, Germany .. 18 B8
Murka, Kenya 82 C4
Murmansk, Russia 44 C4
Murmerwoude, Neths. . 16 B8
Murnau, Germany ... 19 H7
Muro, France 27 F12
Muro, Spain 36 B10
Muro, C. de, France .. 27 G12
Muro Lucano, Italy ... 35 B8
Murom, Russia 41 D13
Muroran, Japan 48 C10
Muros, Spain 30 C1
Muros y de Noya, Ría de,
  Spain 30 C2
Muroto, Japan 49 H7
Muroto-Misaki, Japan .. 49 H7
Murphy, U.S.A. 110 E5

Murphys, *U.S.A.* 112 G6
Murphysboro, *U.S.A.* 109 G10
Murrat, *Sudan* 76 D2
Murray, *Ky., U.S.A.* 105 G1
Murray, *Utah, U.S.A.* 110 F8
Murray →, *Australia* 91 F2
Murray →, *Canada* 100 B4
Murray, L., *U.S.A.* 105 H5
Murray Bridge, *Australia* . 91 F2
Murray Downs, *Australia* . 90 C1
Murray Harbour, *Canada* . 99 C7
Murraysburg, *S. Africa* .. 84 E3
Murree, *Pakistan* 62 C5
Murrieta, *U.S.A.* 113 M9
Murrin Murrin, *Australia* . 89 E3
Murrumbidgee →,
  Australia 91 E3
Murrumburrah, *Australia* . 91 E4
Murrurundi, *Australia* ... 91 E5
Mursala, *Indonesia* 56 D1
Murshid, *Sudan* 76 C3
Murshidabad, *India* 63 G13
Murska Sobota, *Slovenia* . 33 B13
Murten, *Switz.* 22 C4
Murtensee, *Switz.* 22 C4
Murtle L., *Canada* 100 C5
Murtoa, *Australia* 91 F3
Murtosa, *Portugal* 30 E2
Muru →, *Brazil* 124 B3
Murungu, *Tanzania* 82 C3
Murwara, *India* 63 H9
Murwillumbah, *Australia* . 91 D5
Mürz →, *Austria* 21 H5
Mürzzuschlag, *Austria* ... 21 H5
Muş, *Turkey* 67 D9
Muş □, *Turkey* 67 D9
Mûsa, G., *Egypt* 76 J8
Musa Khel, *Pakistan* 62 D3
Mūsá Qal'eh, *Afghan.* ... 60 C4
Musaffargarh, *Pakistan* .. 60 D7
Musala, *Bulgaria* 38 G6
Musan, *N. Korea* 51 C15
Musangu, *Zaïre* 83 E1
Musasa, *Tanzania* 82 C3
Musay'īd, *Qatar* 65 E6
Muscat = Masqat, *Oman* . 68 C6
Muscat & Oman =
  Oman ■, *Asia* 68 C6
Muscatine, *U.S.A.* 108 E9
Musel, *Spain* 30 B5
Musgrave, *Australia* 90 A3
Musgrave Ras., *Australia* . 89 E5
Mushie, *Zaïre* 80 E3
Mushin, *Nigeria* 79 D5
Musi →, *Indonesia* 56 E2
Muskeg →, *Canada* 100 A4
Muskegon, *U.S.A.* 104 D2
Muskegon →, *U.S.A.* 104 D2
Muskegon Heights, *U.S.A.* 104 D2
Muskogee, *U.S.A.* 109 H7
Muskwa →, *Canada* 100 B4
Muslīmiyah, *Syria* 64 B3
Musmar, *Sudan* 76 D4
Musofu, *Zambia* 83 E2
Musoma, *Tanzania* 82 C3
Musoma □, *Tanzania* 82 C3
Musquaro, L., *Canada* ... 99 B7
Musquodoboit Harbour,
  Canada 99 D7
Musselburgh, *U.K.* 14 F5
Musselkanaal, *Neths.* 16 C10
Musselshell →, *U.S.A.* ... 110 C10
Mussidan, *France* 26 C4
Mussomeli, *Italy* 34 E6
Musson, *Belgium* 17 J7
Mussoorie, *India* 62 D8
Mussuco, *Angola* 84 B2
Mustafakemalpaşa, *Turkey* 66 C3
Mustang, *Nepal* 63 E10
Musters, L., *Argentina* ... 128 C3
Musudan, *N. Korea* 51 D15
Muswellbrook, *Australia* . 91 E5
Mût, *Egypt* 76 B2
Mut, *Turkey* 66 E5
Mutanda, *Mozam.* 85 C5
Mutanda, *Zambia* 83 E2
Mutaray, *Russia* 45 C11
Mutare, *Zimbabwe* 83 F3
Muting, *Indonesia* 57 F10
Mutshatsha, *Zaïre* 83 E1
Mutsu, *Japan* 48 D10
Mutsu-Wan, *Japan* 48 D10
Muttaburra, *Australia* ... 90 C3
Mutuáli, *Mozam.* 83 E4
Mutunópolis, *Brazil* 123 D2
Muweilih, *Egypt* 69 E3
Muxima, *Angola* 80 F2
Muy Muy, *Nic.* 116 D2
Muya, *Russia* 45 D12
Muyinga, *Burundi* 82 C3
Muzaffarabad, *Pakistan* .. 63 B5
Muzaffargarh, *Pakistan* .. 62 D4
Muzaffarnagar, *India* 62 E7
Muzaffarpur, *India* 63 F11
Muzhi, *Russia* 44 C7
Muzillac, *France* 24 E4
Muzon, C., *U.S.A.* 100 C2
Muztag, *China* 54 C3
Mvôlô, *Sudan* 77 F2
Mvuma, *Zimbabwe* 83 F3
Mvurwi, *Zimbabwe* 83 F3
Mwadui, *Tanzania* 82 C3
Mwambo, *Tanzania* 83 E5
Mwandi, *Zambia* 83 F1
Mwanza, *Tanzania* 82 C3

Mwanza, *Zaïre* 82 D2
Mwanza, *Zambia* 83 F1
Mwanza □, *Tanzania* 82 C3
Mwaya, *Tanzania* 83 D3
Mweelrea, *Ireland* 15 C2
Mweka, *Zaïre* 80 E4
Mwenezi, *Zimbabwe* 83 G3
Mwenezi →, *Mozam.* ... 83 G3
Mwenga, *Zaïre* 82 C2
Mweru, L., *Zambia* 83 D2
Mweza Range, *Zimbabwe* 83 G3
Mwilambwe, *Zaïre* 82 D5
Mwimbi, *Tanzania* 83 D3
Mwinilunga, *Zambia* 83 E1
My Tho, *Vietnam* 59 G6
Mya, O. →, *Algeria* 75 B5
Myajlar, *India* 62 F4
Myanaung, *Burma* 61 K19
Myanmar = Burma ■, *Asia* 61 J20
Myaungmya, *Burma* 61 L19
Mycenae = Mikínai, *Greece* 39 M5
Myeik Kyunzu, *Burma* ... 59 G1
Myerstown, *U.S.A.* 107 F8
Myingyan, *Burma* 61 J19
Myitkyina, *Burma* 61 G20
Myjava, *Slovak Rep.* 20 G7
Mykolayiv = Nikolayev,
  Ukraine 42 C4
Mymensingh, *Bangla.* ... 61 G17
Mynydd Du, *U.K.* 13 F4
Mýrdalsjökull, *Iceland* ... 8 E4
Myroodah, *Australia* 88 C3
Myrtle Beach, *U.S.A.* 105 J6
Myrtle Creek, *U.S.A.* 110 E2
Myrtle Point, *U.S.A.* 110 E1
Myrtou, *Cyprus* 37 D12
Mysen, *Norway* 10 E5
Mysia, *Turkey* 66 D2
Myslenice, *Poland* 20 F9
Myślibórz, *Poland* 20 C4
Mysłowice, *Poland* 20 E9
Mysore = Karnataka □,
  India 60 N10
Mysore, *India* 60 N10
Mystic, *U.S.A.* 107 E13
Myszków, *Poland* 20 E9
Mythen, *Switz.* 23 B7
Mytishchi, *Russia* 41 D10
Myton, *U.S.A.* 110 F8
Mývatn, *Iceland* 8 D5
Mzimba, *Malawi* 83 E3
Mzimkulu →, *S. Africa* .. 85 E5
Mzimvubu →, *S. Africa* . 85 E4
Mzuzu, *Malawi* 83 E3

N

N' Dioum, *Senegal* 78 B2
Na Noi, *Thailand* 58 C3
Na Phao, *Laos* 58 D5
Na Sam, *Vietnam* 58 A6
Na San, *Vietnam* 58 B5
Naab →, *Germany* 19 F8
Naaldwijk, *Neths.* 16 E4
Na'am, *Sudan* 77 F2
Naantali, *Finland* 9 F17
Naarden, *Neths.* 16 D6
Naas, *Ireland* 15 C5
Nababiep, *S. Africa* 84 D2
Nabadwip = Navadwip,
  India 63 H13
Nabari, *Japan* 49 G8
Nabawa, *Australia* 89 E1
Nabberu, L., *Australia* ... 89 E3
Nabburg, *Germany* 19 F8
Naberezhnyye Chelny,
  Russia 44 D6
Nabeul, *Tunisia* 75 A7
Nabha, *India* 62 D7
Nabīd, *Iran* 65 D8
Nabire, *Indonesia* 57 E9
Nabisar, *Pakistan* 62 G3
Nabisipi →, *Canada* 99 B7
Nabiswera, *Uganda* 82 B3
Nablus = Nābulus, *Jordan* 69 C4
Naboomspruit, *S. Africa* . 85 C4
Nabua, *Phil.* 55 E5
Nābulus, *Jordan* 69 C4
Nābulus □, *Jordan* 69 C4
Nacala, *Mozam.* 83 E5
Nacala-Velha, *Mozam.* .. 83 E5
Nacaome, *Honduras* 116 D2
Nacaroa, *Mozam.* 83 E4
Naches, *U.S.A.* 110 C3
Naches →, *U.S.A.* 112 D6
Nachingwea, *Tanzania* .. 83 E4
Nachingwea □, *Tanzania* . 83 E4
Nachna, *India* 62 F4
Náchod, *Czech.* 20 E6
Nacimiento Reservoir,
  U.S.A. 112 K6
Nacka, *Sweden* 10 E12
Nackara, *Australia* 91 E2
Naco, *Mexico* 114 A3
Naco, *U.S.A.* 111 L9
Nacogdoches, *U.S.A.* ... 109 K7
Nácori Chico, *Mexico* ... 114 B3
Nacozari, *Mexico* 114 A3
Nadi, *Sudan* 76 D3
Nadiad, *India* 62 H5
Nădlac, *Romania* 38 C3
Nador, *Morocco* 75 A4

Nadur, *Malta* 37 C1
Nadūshan, *Iran* 65 C7
Nadvornaya, *Ukraine* ... 42 B1
Nadym, *Russia* 44 C8
Nadym →, *Russia* 44 C8
Næstved, *Denmark* 11 J5
Nafada, *Nigeria* 79 C7
Näfels, *Switz.* 23 B8
Naftshahr, *Iran* 64 C5
Nafud Desert = An Nafūd,
  Si. Arabia 64 D4
Nafūsah, Jabal, *Libya* ... 75 B7
Nag Hammâdi, *Egypt* ... 76 B3
Naga, *Phil.* 55 E5
Naga, Kreb en, *Africa* ... 74 D3
Nagagami →, *Canada* ... 98 C3
Nagahama, *Japan* 49 G8
Nagai, *Japan* 48 E10
Nagaland □, *India* 61 F19
Nagano, *Japan* 49 F9
Nagano □, *Japan* 49 F9
Nagaoka, *Japan* 49 F9
Nagappattinam, *India* ... 60 P11
Nagar Parkar, *Pakistan* . 62 G4
Nagasaki, *Japan* 49 H4
Nagasaki □, *Japan* 49 H4
Nagato, *Japan* 49 G5
Nagaur, *India* 62 F5
Nagercoil, *India* 60 Q10
Nagina, *India* 63 E8
Nagīneh, *Iran* 65 C8
Nagir, *Pakistan* 63 A6
Nagold, *Germany* 19 G4
Nagold →, *Germany* ... 19 G4
Nagoorin, *Australia* 90 C5
Nagornyy, *Russia* 45 D13
Nagorsk, *Russia* 41 B17
Nagoya, *Japan* 49 G8
Nagpur, *India* 60 J11
Nagua, *Dom. Rep.* 117 C6
Nagykanizsa, *Hungary* .. 21 J7
Nagykőrös, *Hungary* ... 21 H9
Nagyléta, *Hungary* 21 H11
Naha, *Japan* 49 L3
Nahanni Butte, *Canada* .. 100 A4
Nahanni Nat. Park, *Canada* 100 A3
Nahariyya, *Israel* 64 C2
Nahāvand, *Iran* 65 C6
Nahe →, *Germany* 19 F3
Nahîya, Wadi →, *Egypt* . 76 J7
Nahlin, *Canada* 100 B2
Nahuel Huapi, L.,
  Argentina 128 B2
Naicá, *Mexico* 114 B3
Naicam, *Canada* 101 C8
Naila, *Germany* 19 E7
Nain, *Canada* 99 A7
Nā'īn, *Iran* 65 C7
Naini Tal, *India* 63 E8
Nainpur, *India* 60 H12
Naintré, *France* 24 F7
Naipu, *Romania* 38 E8
Naira, *Indonesia* 57 E7
Nairn, *U.K.* 14 D5
Nairobi, *Kenya* 82 C4
Naivasha, *Kenya* 82 C4
Naivasha, L., *Kenya* 82 C4
Najac, *France* 26 D5
Najafābād, *Iran* 65 C6
Nájera, *Spain* 28 C2
Najerilla →, *Spain* 28 C2
Najibabad, *India* 62 E8
Najin, *N. Korea* 51 C16
Najmah, *Si. Arabia* 65 E6
Naju, *S. Korea* 51 G14
Nakadōri-Shima, *Japan* . 49 H4
Nakalagba, *Zaïre* 82 B2
Nakaminato, *Japan* 49 F10
Nakamura, *Japan* 49 H6
Nakano, *Japan* 49 F9
Nakano-Shima, *Japan* ... 49 K4
Nakashibetsu, *Japan* 48 C12
Nakfa, *Eritrea* 77 D4
Nakhichevan, *Azerbaijan* 67 D11
Nakhichevan Republic □,
  Azerbaijan 44 F5
Nakhl, *Egypt* 69 F2
Nakhl-e Taqī, *Iran* 65 E7
Nakhodka, *Russia* 45 E14
Nakhon Nayok, *Thailand* 58 E3
Nakhon Pathom, *Thailand* 58 F3
Nakhon Phanom, *Thailand* 58 D5
Nakhon Ratchasima,
  Thailand 58 E4
Nakhon Sawan, *Thailand* 58 E3
Nakhon Si Thammarat,
  Thailand 59 H3
Nakhon Thai, *Thailand* .. 58 D3
Nakina, B.C., *Canada* ... 100 B2
Nakina, Ont., *Canada* ... 98 B2
Nakło nad Notecią, *Poland* 20 B7
Nakodar, *India* 62 D6
Naksksov, *Denmark* 11 K5
Näkten, *Sweden* 10 B8
Naktong →, *S. Korea* ... 51 G15
Naku'alofa, *Tonga* 87
Nakuru, *Kenya* 82 C4
Nakuru, L., *Kenya* 82 C4
Nakusp, *Canada* 100 C5
Nal →, *Pakistan* 62 G1
Nalchik, *Russia* 43 E11
Nälden, *Sweden* 10 A8
Näldsjön, *Sweden* 10 A8

Nalerigu, *Ghana* 79 C4
Nalgonda, *India* 60 L11
Nalhati, *India* 63 G12
Nallamalai Hills, *India* .. 60 M11
Nallıhan, *Turkey* 66 C4
Nalón →, *Spain* 30 B4
Nālūt, *Libya* 75 B7
Nam Can, *Vietnam* 59 H5
Nam Co, *China* 54 C4
Nam Dinh, *Vietnam* 58 B6
Nam Du, Hon, *Vietnam* . 59 H5
Nam Ngum Dam, *Laos* .. 58 C4
Nam-Phan, *Vietnam* 59 G6
Nam Phong, *Thailand* ... 58 D4
Nam Tha, *Laos* 58 B3
Nam Tok, *Thailand* 58 E2
Namacunde, *Angola* 84 B2
Namacurra, *Mozam.* 85 B6
Namak, Daryācheh-ye, *Iran* 65 C7
Namak, Kavir-e, *Iran* ... 65 C8
Namaland, *Namibia* 84 C2
Namangan, *Uzbekistan* . 44 E8
Namapa, *Mozam.* 83 E4
Namaqualand, *S. Africa* . 84 D2
Namasagali, *Uganda* 82 B3
Namber, *Indonesia* 57 E8
Nambour, *Australia* 91 D5
Nambucca Heads, *Australia* 91 E5
Namche Bazar, *Nepal* ... 63 F12
Namchonjŏm, *N. Korea* . 51 E14
Nameche, *Belgium* 17 H6
Namecunda, *Mozam.* ... 83 E4
Nameh, *Indonesia* 56 D5
Nameponda, *Mozam.* ... 83 F4
Nametil, *Mozam.* 83 F4
Namew L., *Canada* 101 C8
Namib Desert =
  Namibwoestyn, *Namibia* 84 C2
Namibe, *Angola* 81 H2
Namibe □, *Angola* 84 B1
Namibia ■, *Africa* 84 C2
Namibwoestyn, *Namibia* . 84 C2
Namlea, *Indonesia* 57 E7
Namoi →, *Australia* 91 E4
Namous, O. en →, *Algeria* 75 B4
Nampa, *U.S.A.* 110 E5
Nampō-Shotō, *Japan* ... 49 J10
Nampula, *Mozam.* 83 F4
Namrole, *Indonesia* 57 E7
Namse Shankou, *China* .. 61 E13
Namsen →, *Norway* ... 8 D11
Namsos, *Norway* 8 D11
Namtay, *Russia* 45 C13
Namtu, *Burma* 61 H20
Namtumbo, *Tanzania* ... 83 E4
Namu, *Canada* 100 C3
Namur, *Belgium* 17 H5
Namur □, *Belgium* 17 H6
Namutoni, *Namibia* 84 B2
Namwala, *Zambia* 83 F2
Namwŏn, *S. Korea* 51 G14
Namysłów, *Poland* 20 D7
Nan, *Thailand* 58 C3
Nan →, *Thailand* 58 E3
Nan Xian, *China* 53 C9
Nanaimo, *Canada* 100 D4
Nanam, *N. Korea* 51 D15
Nanan, *China* 53 E12
Nanango, *Australia* 91 D5
Nan'ao, *China* 53 F11
Nanao, *Japan* 49 F8
Nanbu, *China* 52 B6
Nanchang, *China* 53 C10
Nancheng, *China* 53 D11
Nanchong, *China* 52 B6
Nanchuan, *China* 52 C6
Nancy, *France* 25 D13
Nanda Devi, *India* 63 D8
Nandan, *China* 52 E6
Nandan, *Japan* 49 G7
Nanded, *India* 60 K10
Nandewar Ra., *Australia* 91 E5
Nandi, *Fiji* 87 C7
Nandi □, *Kenya* 82 B4
Nandurbar, *India* 60 J9
Nandyal, *India* 60 M11
Nanfeng, Guangdong,
  China 53 F8
Nanfeng, Jiangxi, *China* . 53 D11
Nanga, *Australia* 89 E1
Nanga-Eboko, *Cameroon* 79 E7
Nanga Parbat, *Pakistan* . 63 B6
Nangade, *Mozam.* 83 E4
Nangapinoh, *Indonesia* .. 56 E4
Nangarhár □, *Afghan.* .. 60 B7
Nangatayap, *Indonesia* .. 56 E4
Nangeya Mts., *Uganda* .. 82 B3
Nangis, *France* 25 D10
Nangong, *China* 50 F8
Nanhua, *China* 52 E3
Nanhuang, *China* 51 F11
Nanhui, *China* 53 B13
Nanjeko, *Zambia* 83 F1
Nanji Shan, *China* 53 D13
Nanjiang, *China* 52 A6
Nanjing, Fujian, *China* .. 53 E11
Nanjing, Jiangsu, *China* . 53 A12
Nankana Sahib, *Pakistan* 62 D5
Nankang, *China* 53 E10
Nanking = Nanjing, *China* 53 A12

Nankoku, *Japan* 49 H6
Nanling, *China* 53 B12
Nanning, *China* 52 F7
Nannup, *Australia* 89 F2
Nanpan Jiang →, *China* . 52 E6
Nanpara, *India* 63 F9
Nanpi, *China* 50 E9
Nanping, Fujian, *China* .. 53 D12
Nanping, Henan, *China* . 53 C9
Nanri Dao, *China* 53 E12
Nanripe, *Mozam.* 83 E4
Nansei-Shotō = Ryūkyū-
  rettō, *Japan* 49 M2
Nansen Sd., *Canada* 4 A3
Nansio, *Tanzania* 82 C3
Nant, *France* 26 D7
Nantes, *France* 24 E5
Nanteuil-le-Haudouin,
  France 25 C9
Nantiat, *France* 26 B5
Nanticoke, *U.S.A.* 107 E8
Nanton, *Canada* 100 C6
Nantong, *China* 53 A13
Nantua, *France* 27 B9
Nantucket I., *U.S.A.* 94 E12
Nanuque, *Brazil* 123 E3
Nanutarra, *Australia* 88 D2
Nanxiong, *China* 53 E10
Nanyang, *China* 50 H7
Nanyi Hu, *China* 53 B12
Nanyuan, *China* 50 E9
Nanyuki, *Kenya* 82 B4
Nanzhang, *China* 53 B8
Náo, C. de la, *Spain* 29 G5
Naococane L., *Canada* .. 99 B5
Naoetsu, *Japan* 49 F9
Náousa, *Greece* 39 J5
Naozhou Dao, *China* ... 53 G8
Napa, *U.S.A.* 112 G4
Napa →, *U.S.A.* 112 G4
Napanee, *Canada* 98 D4
Napanoch, *U.S.A.* 107 E10
Nape, *Laos* 58 C5
Nape Pass = Keo Neua,
  Deo, *Vietnam* 58 C5
Napf, *Switz.* 22 B5
Napier, *N.Z.* 87 H6
Napier Broome B.,
  Australia 88 B4
Napier Downs, *Australia* . 88 C3
Napier Pen., *Australia* ... 90 A2
Naples = Nápoli, *Italy* ... 35 B7
Naples, *U.S.A.* 105 M5
Napo, *China* 52 F5
Napo □, *Ecuador* 120 D2
Napo →, *Peru* 120 D3
Napoleon, N. Dak., *U.S.A.* 108 B5
Napoleon, Ohio, *U.S.A.* . 104 E3
Nápoli, *Italy* 35 B7
Nápoli, G. di, *Italy* 35 B7
Napopo, *Zaïre* 82 B2
Nappa Merrie, *Australia* . 91 D3
Naqâda, *Egypt* 76 B3
Naqqāsh, *Iran* 65 C6
Nara, *Japan* 49 G7
Nara, *Mali* 78 B3
Nara □, *Japan* 49 G8
Nara Canal, *Pakistan* ... 62 G3
Nara Visa, *U.S.A.* 109 H3
Naracoorte, *Australia* ... 91 F3
Naradhan, *Australia* 91 E4
Narasapur, *India* 61 L12
Narathiwat, *Thailand* ... 59 J3
Narayanganj, *Bangla.* ... 61 H17
Narayanpet, *India* 60 L10
Narbonne, *France* 26 E7
Narcea →, *Spain* 30 B4
Nardīn, *Iran* 65 B7
Nardò, *Italy* 35 B11
Narembeen, *Australia* ... 89 F2
Nares Str., *Arctic* 94 B13
Naretha, *Australia* 89 F3
Narew →, *Poland* 20 C10
Nari →, *Pakistan* 62 E2
Narin, *Afghan.* 60 A6
Narindra, Helodranon' i,
  Madag. 85 A8
Narino □, *Colombia* 120 C2
Narmada →, *India* 62 J5
Narman, *Turkey* 67 C9
Narnaul, *India* 62 E7
Narni, *Italy* 33 F9
Naro, *Ghana* 78 C4
Naro, *Italy* 34 E6
Naro Fominsk, *Russia* ... 41 D10
Narodnaya, *Russia* 6 B17
Narok, *Kenya* 82 C4
Narok □, *Kenya* 82 C4
Narón, *Spain* 30 B2
Narooma, *Australia* 91 F5
Narowal, *Pakistan* 62 C6
Narrabri, *Australia* 91 E4
Narran →, *Australia* ... 91 D4
Narrandera, *Australia* ... 91 E4
Narraway →, *Canada* .. 100 B5
Narrogin, *Australia* 89 F2
Narromine, *Australia* ... 91 E4
Narsimhapur, *India* 63 H8
Nartkala, *Russia* 43 E10
Naruto, *Japan* 49 G7
Narva, *Estonia* 40 B6
Narva →, *Russia* 40 B6
Narvik, *Norway* 8 B14
Narvskoye Vdkhr., *Russia* 40 B6

Narwana

Narwana, *India* 62 E7
Naryan-Mar, *Russia* 44 C6
Naryilco, *Australia* 91 D3
Narym, *Russia* 44 D9
Narymskoye, *Kazakhstan* 44 E9
Naryn, *Kirghizia* 44 E8
Nasa, *Norway* 8 C13
Nasarawa, *Nigeria* 79 D6
Năsăud, *Romania* 38 B7
Naseby, *N.Z.* 87 L3
Naselle, *U.S.A.* 112 D3
Naser, Buheirat en, *Egypt* 76 C3
Nashua, *Iowa, U.S.A.* 108 D8
Nashua, *Mont., U.S.A.* 110 B10
Nashua, *N.H., U.S.A.* 107 D13
Nashville, *Ark., U.S.A.* 109 J8
Nashville, *Ga., U.S.A.* 105 K4
Nashville, *Tenn., U.S.A.* 105 G2
Našice, *Croatia* 21 K8
Nasielsk, *Poland* 20 C10
Nasik, *India* 60 K8
Nasipit, *Phil.* 55 G6
Nasirabad, *India* 62 F6
Naskaupi →, *Canada* 99 B7
Naso, *Italy* 35 D7
Naṣriān-e Pā'īn, *Iran* 64 C5
Nass →, *Canada* 100 B3
Nassau, *Bahamas* 116 A4
Nassau, *U.S.A.* 107 D11
Nassau, B., *Chile* 128 E3
Nasser, L. = Naser, Buheirat en, *Egypt* 76 C3
Nasser City = Kôm Ombo, *Egypt* 76 C3
Nassian, *Ivory C.* 78 D4
Nässjö, *Sweden* 9 H13
Nasugbu, *Phil.* 55 D4
Näsviken, *Sweden* 10 C10
Nat Kyizin, *Burma* 61 M20
Nata, *Botswana* 84 C4
Natagaima, *Colombia* 120 C2
Natal, *Brazil* 122 C4
Natal, *Canada* 100 D6
Natal, *Indonesia* 56 D1
Natal □, *S. Africa* 85 D5
Natalinci, *Serbia, Yug.* 21 L10
Naṭanz, *Iran* 65 C6
Natashquan, *Canada* 99 B7
Natashquan →, *Canada* 99 B7
Natchez, *U.S.A.* 109 K9
Natchitoches, *U.S.A.* 109 K8
Naters, *Switz.* 22 D5
Nathalia, *Australia* 91 F4
Nathdwara, *India* 62 G5
Nati, Pta., *Spain* 36 A10
Natimuk, *Australia* 91 F3
Nation →, *Canada* 100 B4
National City, *U.S.A.* 113 N9
Natitingou, *Benin* 79 C5
Natividad, I., *Mexico* 114 B1
Natoma, *U.S.A.* 108 F5
Natron, L., *Tanzania* 82 C4
Natrona Heights, *U.S.A.* 106 F5
Natrûn, W. el →, *Egypt* 76 H7
Natuna Besar, Kepulauan, *Indonesia* 59 L7
Natuna Is. = Natuna Besar, Kepulauan, *Indonesia* 59 L7
Natuna Selatan, Kepulauan, *Indonesia* 59 L7
Natural Bridge, *U.S.A.* 107 B9
Naturaliste, C., *Australia* 90 G4
Nau Qala, *Afghan.* 62 B3
Naubinway, *U.S.A.* 98 C2
Naucelle, *France* 26 D6
Nauders, *Austria* 19 J6
Nauen, *Germany* 18 C8
Naugatuck, *U.S.A.* 107 E11
Naujoji Vilnia, *Lithuania* 40 D4
Naumburg, *Germany* 18 D7
Nā'ūr at Tunayb, *Jordan* 69 D4
Nauru ■, *Pac. Oc.* 92 H8
Naushahra = Nowshera, *Pakistan* 60 B8
Nauta, *Peru* 120 D3
Nautanwa, *India* 61 F13
Nautla, *Mexico* 115 C5
Nava, *Mexico* 114 B4
Nava del Rey, *Spain* 30 D5
Navacerrada, Puerto de, *Spain* 30 E7
Navadwip, *India* 63 H13
Navahermosa, *Spain* 31 F6
Navajo Reservoir, *U.S.A.* 111 H10
Navalcarnero, *Spain* 30 E6
Navalmoral de la Mata, *Spain* 30 F5
Navalvillar de Pela, *Spain* 31 F5
Navan = An Uaimh, *Ireland* 15 C5
Navarino, I., *Chile* 128 E3
Navarra □, *Spain* 28 C3
Navarre, *U.S.A.* 106 F3
Navarrenx, *France* 26 E3
Navarro →, *U.S.A.* 112 F3
Navasota, *U.S.A.* 109 K6
Navassa, *W. Indies* 117 C4
Nave, *Italy* 32 C7
Naver →, *U.K.* 14 C4
Navia, *Spain* 30 B4
Navia →, *Spain* 30 B4
Navia de Suarna, *Spain* 30 C4
Navidad, *Chile* 126 C1
Navlya, *Russia* 40 E9
Navoi, *Uzbekistan* 44 E7
Navojoa, *Mexico* 114 B3
Navolato, *Mexico* 114 C3
Návpaktos, *Greece* 39 L4
Návplion, *Greece* 39 M5
Navrongo, *Ghana* 79 C4
Navsari, *India* 60 J8
Nawa Kot, *Pakistan* 62 E4
Nawabganj, *Ut. P., India* 63 F9
Nawabganj, *Ut. P., India* 63 E8
Nawabshah, *Pakistan* 62 F3
Nawada, *India* 63 G11
Nawakot, *Nepal* 63 F11
Nawalgarh, *India* 62 F6
Nawanshahr, *India* 63 C6
Nawi, *Sudan* 76 D3
Náxos, *Greece* 39 M8
Nay, *France* 26 E3
Nāy Band, *Iran* 65 E7
Naya →, *Colombia* 120 C2
Nayakhan, *Russia* 45 C16
Nayarit □, *Mexico* 114 C4
Nayé, *Senegal* 78 C2
Nayong, *China* 52 D5
Nayoro, *Japan* 48 B11
Nayyāl, W. →, *Si. Arabia* 64 D3
Nazaré, *Bahia, Brazil* 123 D4
Nazaré, *Goiás, Brazil* 122 C2
Nazaré, *Pará, Brazil* 125 B7
Nazaré, *Portugal* 31 F1
Nazareth = Nazerat, *Israel* 69 C4
Nazas, *Mexico* 114 B4
Nazas →, *Mexico* 114 B4
Naze, The, *U.K.* 13 F9
Nazerat, *Israel* 69 C4
Nāzīk, *Iran* 64 B5
Nazik Gölü, *Turkey* 67 D10
Nazilli, *Turkey* 66 E3
Nazir Hat, *Bangla.* 61 H17
Nazko, *Canada* 100 C4
Nazko →, *Canada* 100 C4
Nazret, *Ethiopia* 77 F4
Nchanga, *Zambia* 83 E2
Ncheu, *Malawi* 83 E3
Ndala, *Tanzania* 82 C3
Ndalatando, *Angola* 80 F2
Ndali, *Benin* 79 D5
Ndareda, *Tanzania* 82 C4
Ndélé, *C.A.R.* 73 G9
Ndendé, *Gabon* 80 E2
Ndjamena, *Chad* 73 F7
Ndjolé, *Gabon* 80 E2
Ndola, *Zambia* 83 E2
Ndoto Mts., *Kenya* 82 B4
Nduguti, *Tanzania* 82 C3
Nëa →, *Norway* 10 A5
Néa Flippiás, *Greece* 39 K3
Neagh, Lough, *U.K.* 15 B5
Neah Bay, *U.S.A.* 112 B2
Neale, L., *Australia* 88 D5
Neápolis, *Kozan, Greece* 39 J4
Neápolis, *Kríti, Greece* 37 D7
Neápolis, *Lakonia, Greece* 39 N6
Near Is., *U.S.A.* 96 C1
Neath, *U.K.* 13 F4
Nebbou, *Burkina Faso* 79 C4
Nebine Cr. →, *Australia* 91 D4
Nebit Dag, *Turkmenistan* 44 F6
Nebolchy, *Russia* 40 B8
Nebraska □, *U.S.A.* 108 E5
Nebraska City, *U.S.A.* 108 E7
Nébrodi, Monti, *Italy* 35 E7
Necedah, *U.S.A.* 108 C9
Nechako →, *Canada* 100 C4
Neches →, *U.S.A.* 109 L8
Neckar →, *Germany* 19 F4
Necochea, *Argentina* 126 D4
Nedelišće, *Croatia* 33 B13
Neder Rijn →, *Neths.* 16 E8
Nederbrakel, *Belgium* 17 G3
Nederweert, *Neths.* 17 F7
Nédha →, *Greece* 39 M4
Nedroma, *Algeria* 75 A4
Neede, *Neths.* 16 D9
Needles, *U.S.A.* 113 L12
Needles, The, *U.K.* 13 G6
Ñeembucú □, *Paraguay* 126 B4
Neemuch = Nimach, *India* 62 G6
Neenah, *U.S.A.* 104 C1
Neepawa, *Canada* 101 C9
Neer, *Neths.* 17 F7
Neerpelt, *Belgium* 17 F6
Neft-chala = imeni 26 Bakinskikh Komissarov, *Azerbaijan* 67 D13
Nefta, *Tunisia* 75 B6
Neftah Sidi Boubekeur, *Algeria* 75 A5
Neftegorsk, *Russia* 43 D8
Neftekumsk, *Russia* 43 D11
Neftenbach, *Switz.* 23 A7
Negapatam = Nagappattinam, *India* 60 P11
Negaunee, *U.S.A.* 104 B2
Negele, *Ethiopia* 68 F2
Negev Desert = Hanegev, *Israel* 69 E3
Negombo, *Sri Lanka* 60 R11
Negotin, *Serbia, Yug.* 21 L12
Negra, Peña, *Spain* 30 C4
Negra, Pta., *Mauritania* 74 D1
Negra, Pta., *Peru* 124 B1
Negra Pt., *Phil.* 57 A6
Negrais, C. = Maudin Sun, *Burma* 61 M19
Negreira, *Spain* 30 C2
Négrine, *Algeria* 75 B6
Negro →, *Argentina* 128 B4
Negro →, *Bolivia* 125 C5
Negro →, *Brazil* 121 D6
Negro →, *Uruguay* 127 C4
Negros, *Phil.* 55 G5
Nehalem →, *U.S.A.* 112 E3
Nehāvand, *Iran* 65 C6
Nehbandān, *Iran* 65 D9
Neheim, *Germany* 18 D3
Nehoiașu, *Romania* 38 D9
Nei Monggol Zizhiqu □, *China* 50 C6
Neidpath, *Canada* 101 C7
Neihart, *U.S.A.* 110 C8
Neijiang, *China* 52 C5
Neilton, *U.S.A.* 110 C2
Neiqiu, *China* 50 F8
Neira de Jusá, *Spain* 30 C3
Neiva, *Colombia* 120 C2
Neixiang, *China* 50 H6
Nejanilini L., *Canada* 101 B9
Nejo, *Ethiopia* 77 F4
Nekā, *Iran* 65 B7
Nekemte, *Ethiopia* 77 F4
Nêkheb, *Egypt* 76 B3
Neksø, *Denmark* 9 J13
Nelas, *Portugal* 30 E3
Nelia, *Australia* 90 C3
Nelidovo, *Russia* 40 C8
Neligh, *U.S.A.* 108 D5
Nelkan, *Russia* 45 D14
Nellore, *India* 60 M11
Nelma, *Russia* 45 E14
Nelson, *Canada* 100 D5
Nelson, *N.Z.* 87 J4
Nelson, *U.K.* 12 D5
Nelson, *U.S.A.* 111 J7
Nelson →, *Canada* 101 C9
Nelson, C., *Australia* 91 F3
Nelson, Estrecho, *Chile* 128 D2
Nelson Forks, *Canada* 100 B4
Nelson House, *Canada* 101 B9
Nelson L., *Canada* 101 B8
Nelspoort, *S. Africa* 84 E3
Nelspruit, *S. Africa* 85 D5
Néma, *Mauritania* 78 B3
Neman →, *Lithuania* 40 D2
Nemeiben L., *Canada* 101 B7
Nemira, *Romania* 38 C9
Nemours, *France* 25 D9
Nemunas = Neman →, *Lithuania* 40 D2
Nemuro, *Japan* 48 C12
Nemuro-Kaikyō, *Japan* 48 C12
Nemuy, *Russia* 45 D14
Nen Jiang →, *China* 51 B13
Nenagh, *Ireland* 15 D3
Nenana, *U.S.A.* 96 B5
Nenasi, *Malaysia* 59 L4
Nene →, *U.K.* 12 E8
Nenjiang, *China* 54 B7
Neno, *Malawi* 83 F3
Nenusa, Kepulauan, *Indonesia* 57 D7
Neodesha, *U.S.A.* 109 G7
Neópolis, *Brazil* 122 D4
Neosho, *U.S.A.* 109 G7
Neosho →, *U.S.A.* 109 H7
Nepal ■, *Asia* 63 F11
Nepalganj, *Nepal* 63 E9
Nephi, *U.S.A.* 110 G8
Nephin, *Ireland* 15 B2
Neptune, *U.S.A.* 107 F10
Néra →, *Romania* 38 E4
Nérac, *France* 26 D4
Nerchinsk, *Russia* 45 D12
Nerchinskiy Zavod, *Russia* 45 D12
Nereju, *Romania* 38 D9
Nerekhta, *Russia* 41 C12
Néret L., *Canada* 99 B5
Neringa, *Lithuania* 40 D2
Nerja, *Spain* 31 J7
Nerl →, *Russia* 41 C12
Nerpio, *Spain* 29 G2
Nerva, *Spain* 31 H4
Nes, *Iceland* 8 D5
Nes, *Neths.* 16 B7
Nesbyen, *Norway* 10 D3
Nesebŭr, *Bulgaria* 38 G10
Neskaupstaður, *Iceland* 8 D7
Nesland, *Norway* 10 E1
Neslandsvatn, *Norway* 10 F3
Nesle, *France* 25 C9
Nesodden, *Norway* 10 E4
Nesque →, *France* 27 E8
Ness, L., *U.K.* 14 D4
Nesslau, *Switz.* 23 B8
Néstos →, *Greece* 39 H7
Nesttun, *Norway* 9 F8
Nesvizh, *Belorussia* 40 E5
Netanya, *Israel* 69 C3
Nète →, *Belgium* 17 F4
Netherdale, *Australia* 90 C4
Netherlands ■, *Europe* 16 E6
Netherlands Antilles ■, *W. Indies* 120 A4
Neto →, *Italy* 35 C10
Nettancourt, *France* 25 D11
Nettilling L., *Canada* 97 B12
Nettuno, *Italy* 34 A5
Netzahualcoyotl, Presa, *Mexico* 115 D6
Neu-Isenburg, *Germany* 19 E4
Neu-Ulm, *Germany* 19 G6
Neubrandenburg, *Germany* 18 B9
Neubukow, *Germany* 18 A7
Neuburg, *Germany* 19 G7
Neuchâtel, *Switz.* 22 C3
Neuchâtel □, *Switz.* 22 C3
Neuchâtel, Lac de, *Switz.* 22 C3
Neudau, *Austria* 21 H6
Neuenegg, *Switz.* 22 C4
Neuenhaus, *Germany* 18 C2
Neuf-Brisach, *France* 25 D14
Neufahrn, *Germany* 19 G8
Neufchâteau, *Belgium* 17 J6
Neufchâteau, *France* 25 D12
Neufchâtel-en-Bray, *France* 24 C8
Neufchâtel-sur-Aisne, *France* 25 C11
Neuhaus, *Germany* 18 B6
Neuhausen, *Switz.* 23 A7
Neuillé-Pont-Pierre, *France* 24 E7
Neuilly-St.-Front, *France* 25 C10
Neukalen, *Germany* 18 B8
Neumarkt, *Germany* 19 F7
Neumarkt-Sankt Veit, *Germany* 19 G8
Neumünster, *Germany* 18 A5
Neung-sur-Beuvron, *France* 25 E8
Neunkirchen, *Austria* 21 H6
Neunkirchen, *Germany* 19 F3
Neuquén, *Argentina* 128 A3
Neuquén □, *Argentina* 126 D2
Neuquén →, *Argentina* 128 A3
Neuruppin, *Germany* 18 C8
Neuse →, *U.S.A.* 105 H7
Neusiedler See, *Austria* 21 H6
Neuss, *Germany* 17 F9
Neussargues-Moissac, *France* 26 C7
Neustadt, *Baden-W., Germany* 19 H4
Neustadt, *Bayern, Germany* 19 F8
Neustadt, *Bayern, Germany* 19 G7
Neustadt, *Bayern, Germany* 19 F6
Neustadt, *Bayern, Germany* 19 E7
Neustadt, *Brandenburg, Germany* 18 C8
Neustadt, *Hessen, Germany* 18 E5
Neustadt, *Niedersachsen, Germany* 18 C5
Neustadt, *Rhld-Pfz., Germany* 19 F4
Neustadt, *Schleswig-Holstein, Germany* 18 A6
Neustadt, *Thüringen, Germany* 18 E7
Neustrelitz, *Germany* 18 B9
Neuvic, *France* 26 C6
Neuville, *Belgium* 17 H5
Neuville-aux-Bois, *France* 25 D9
Neuville-de-Poitou, *France* 26 B4
Neuville-sur-Saône, *France* 27 C8
Neuvy-le-Roi, *France* 24 E7
Neuvy-St.-Sépulchre, *France* 26 B5
Neuvy-sur-Barangeon, *France* 25 E9
Neuwerk, *Germany* 18 B4
Neuwied, *Germany* 18 E3
Neva →, *Russia* 6 D12
Nevada, *U.S.A.* 109 G7
Nevada □, *U.S.A.* 110 G5
Nevada, Sierra, *Spain* 29 H1
Nevada, Sierra, *U.S.A.* 110 G3
Nevada City, *U.S.A.* 112 F6
Nevado, Cerro, *Argentina* 126 D2
Nevanka, *Russia* 45 D10
Nevel, *Russia* 40 D6
Nevele, *Belgium* 17 F3
Nevers, *France* 25 F10
Nevertire, *Australia* 91 E4
Neville, *Canada* 101 D7
Nevinnomyssk, *Russia* 43 D9
Nevis, *W. Indies* 117 C7
Nevrokop = Gotse Delchev, *Bulgaria* 39 H6
Nevşehir, *Turkey* 66 D6
Nevşehir □, *Turkey* 66 D6
New →, *Guyana* 121 C6
New Albany, *Ind., U.S.A.* 104 F3
New Albany, *Miss., U.S.A.* 109 H10
New Albany, *Pa., U.S.A.* 107 E8
New Amsterdam, *Guyana* 121 B6
New Angledool, *Australia* 91 D4
New Bedford, *U.S.A.* 107 E14
New Bern, *U.S.A.* 105 H7
New Bethlehem, *U.S.A.* 106 E5
New Bloomfield, *U.S.A.* 106 F7
New Boston, *U.S.A.* 109 J7
New Braunfels, *U.S.A.* 109 L5
New Brighton, *N.Z.* 87 K4
New Brighton, *U.S.A.* 106 F4
New Britain, *Papua N. G.* 92 H7
New Britain, *U.S.A.* 107 E12
New Brunswick, *U.S.A.* 107 F10
New Brunswick □, *Canada* 99 C6
New Bussa, *Nigeria* 79 D5
New Caledonia, *Pac. Oc.* 92 K8
New Castile = Castilla La Mancha □, *Spain* 31 F7
New Castle, *Ind., U.S.A.* 104 F3
New Castle, *Pa., U.S.A.* 106 E4
New City, *U.S.A.* 107 E11
New Cumberland, *U.S.A.* 106 F4
New Cuyama, *U.S.A.* 113 L7
New Delhi, *India* 62 E7
New Denver, *Canada* 100 D5
New Don Pedro Reservoir, *U.S.A.* 112 H6
New England, *U.S.A.* 108 B3
New England Ra., *Australia* 91 E5
New Forest, *U.K.* 13 G6
New Glasgow, *Canada* 99 C7
New Guinea, *Oceania* 92 H5
New Hamburg, *Canada* 106 C4
New Hampshire □, *U.S.A.* 107 C13
New Hampton, *U.S.A.* 108 D8
New Hanover, *S. Africa* 85 D5
New Haven, *Conn., U.S.A.* 107 E12
New Haven, *Mich., U.S.A.* 106 D2
New Hazelton, *Canada* 100 B3
New Hebrides = Vanuatu ■, *Pac. Oc.* 92 J8
New Iberia, *U.S.A.* 109 K9
New Ireland, *Papua N. G.* 92 H7
New Jersey □, *U.S.A.* 107 F10
New Kensington, *U.S.A.* 106 F5
New Lexington, *U.S.A.* 104 F4
New Liskeard, *Canada* 98 C4
New London, *Conn., U.S.A.* 107 E12
New London, *Minn., U.S.A.* 108 C7
New London, *Ohio, U.S.A.* 106 E2
New London, *Wis., U.S.A.* 108 C10
New Madrid, *U.S.A.* 109 G10
New Meadows, *U.S.A.* 110 D5
New Melones L., *U.S.A.* 112 H6
New Mexico □, *U.S.A.* 111
New Milford, *Conn., U.S.A.* 107 E11
New Milford, *Pa., U.S.A.* 107 E9
New Norcia, *Australia* 89 F2
New Norfolk, *Australia* 90 G4
New Orleans, *U.S.A.* 109 K9
New Philadelphia, *U.S.A.* 106 F3
New Plymouth, *N.Z.* 87 H5
New Plymouth, *U.S.A.* 110 E5
New Providence, *Bahamas* 116 A4
New Radnor, *U.K.* 13 E4
New Richmond, *U.S.A.* 108 C8
New Roads, *U.S.A.* 109 K9
New Rochelle, *U.S.A.* 107 F11
New Rockford, *U.S.A.* 108 B5
New Ross, *Ireland* 15 D5
New Salem, *U.S.A.* 108 B4
New Scone, *U.K.* 14 E5
New Siberian Is. = Novaya Sibir, Ostrov, *Russia* 45 B16
New Siberian Is. = Novosibirskiye Ostrova, *Russia* 45 B15
New Smyrna Beach, *U.S.A.* 105 L5
New South Wales □, *Australia* 91 E4
New Springs, *Australia* 89 E3
New Town, *U.S.A.* 108 A3
New Ulm, *U.S.A.* 108 C7
New Waterford, *Canada* 99 C7
New Westminster, *Canada* 100 D4
New York □, *U.S.A.* 107 D9
New York City, *U.S.A.* 107 F11
New Zealand ■, *Oceania* 87 J5
Newala, *Tanzania* 83 E4
Newala □, *Tanzania* 83 E4
Newark, *Del., U.S.A.* 104 F8
Newark, *N.J., U.S.A.* 107 F10
Newark, *N.Y., U.S.A.* 106 C7
Newark, *Ohio, U.S.A.* 106 F2
Newark-on-Trent, *U.K.* 12 D7
Newaygo, *U.S.A.* 104 D3
Newberg, *U.S.A.* 110 D2
Newberry, *Mich., U.S.A.* 104 B3
Newberry, *S.C., U.S.A.* 105 H5
Newberry Springs, *U.S.A.* 113 L10
Newbrook, *Canada* 100 C6
Newburgh, *U.S.A.* 107 E10
Newbury, *U.K.* 13 F6
Newbury, *U.S.A.* 107 B12
Newburyport, *U.S.A.* 107 D14
Newcastle, *Australia* 91 E5
Newcastle, *Canada* 99 C6
Newcastle, *S. Africa* 85 D4
Newcastle, *U.K.* 15 B6
Newcastle, *Calif., U.S.A.* 112 G5
Newcastle, *Wyo., U.S.A.* 108 D2
Newcastle Emlyn, *U.K.* 13 E3
Newcastle Ra., *Australia* 88 C5
Newcastle-under-Lyme, *U.K.* 12 D5
Newcastle-upon-Tyne, *U.K.* 12 C6
Newcastle Waters, *Australia* 90 B1
Newdegate, *Australia* 89 F2
Newell, *U.S.A.* 108 C3
Newfoundland □, *Canada* 99 B8
Newhalem, *U.S.A.* 100 D4
Newhall, *U.S.A.* 113 L8
Newham, *U.K.* 13 F8
Newhaven, *U.K.* 13 G8
Newkirk, *U.S.A.* 109 G6
Newman, *Australia* 88 D2
Newman, *U.S.A.* 112 H5
Newmarket, *Canada* 106 B5
Newmarket, *Ireland* 15 D3
Newmarket, *U.K.* 13 E8
Newmarket, *U.S.A.* 107 C14
Newnan, *U.S.A.* 105 J3
Newport, *Gwent, U.K.* 13 F5
Newport, *I. of W., U.K.* 13 G6

North Frisian Is.

Newport, *Shrops., U.K.* 13 E5
Newport, *Ark., U.S.A.* 109 H9
Newport, *Ky., U.S.A.* 104 F3
Newport, *N.H., U.S.A.* 107 C12
Newport, *Oreg., U.S.A.* 110 D1
Newport, *Pa., U.S.A.* 106 F7
Newport, *R.I., U.S.A.* 107 E13
Newport, *Tenn., U.S.A.* 105 H4
Newport, *Vt., U.S.A.* 107 B12
Newport, *Wash., U.S.A.* 110 B5
Newport Beach, *U.S.A.* 113 M9
Newport News, *U.S.A.* 104 G7
Newquay, *U.K.* 13 G2
Newry, *U.K.* 15 B5
Newry & Mourne □, *U.K.* 15 B5
Newton, *Iowa, U.S.A.* 108 E8
Newton, *Mass., U.S.A.* 107 D13
Newton, *Miss., U.S.A.* 109 J10
Newton, *N.C., U.S.A.* 105 H5
Newton, *N.J., U.S.A.* 107 E10
Newton, *Tex., U.S.A.* 109 K8
Newton Abbot, *U.K.* 13 G4
Newton Boyd, *Australia* 91 D5
Newton Stewart, *U.K.* 14 G4
Newtonmore, *U.K.* 14 D4
Newtown, *U.K.* 13 E4
Newtownabbey □, *U.K.* 15 B6
Newtownards, *U.K.* 15 B6
Newville, *U.S.A.* 106 F7
Nexon, *France* 26 C5
Neya, *Russia* 41 B13
Neyrīz, *Iran* 65 D7
Neyshābūr, *Iran* 65 B8
Nezhin, *Ukraine* 40 F7
Nezperce, *U.S.A.* 110 C5
Ngabang, *Indonesia* 56 D3
Ngabordamlu, Tanjung, *Indonesia* 57 F8
Ngambé, *Cameroon* 79 D7
Ngami Depression, *Botswana* 84 C3
Ngamo, *Zimbabwe* 83 F2
Nganglong Kangri, *China* 61 C12
Nganjuk, *Indonesia* 57 G14
Ngao, *Thailand* 58 C2
Ngaoundéré, *Cameroon* 80 C2
Ngapara, *N.Z.* 87 L3
Ngara, *Tanzania* 82 C3
Ngara □, *Tanzania* 82 C3
Ngawi, *Indonesia* 57 G14
Nghia Lo, *Vietnam* 58 B5
Ngoma, *Malawi* 83 E3
Ngomahura, *Zimbabwe* 83 G3
Ngomba, *Tanzania* 83 D3
Ngop, *Sudan* 77 F3
Ngoring Hu, *China* 54 C4
Ngorkou, *Mali* 78 B4
Ngorongoro, *Tanzania* 82 C4
Ngozi, *Burundi* 82 C2
Ngudu, *Tanzania* 82 C3
Nguigmi, *Niger* 73 F7
Ngukurr, *Australia* 90 A1
Ngunga, *Tanzania* 82 C3
Nguru, *Nigeria* 79 C7
Nguru Mts., *Tanzania* 82 D4
Nguyen Binh, *Vietnam* 58 A5
Nha Trang, *Vietnam* 59 F7
Nhacoongo, *Mozam.* 85 C6
Nhamaabué, *Mozam.* 83 F4
Nhambiquara, *Brazil* 125 C6
Nhamundá, *Brazil* 121 D6
Nhamundá →, *Brazil* 121 D6
Nhangutazi, L., *Mozam.* 85 C5
Nhecolândia, *Brazil* 125 D6
Nhill, *Australia* 91 F3
Nho Quan, *Vietnam* 58 B5
Nhulunbuy, *Australia* 90 A2
Nia-nia, *Zaïre* 82 B2
Niafounké, *Mali* 78 B4
Niagara, *U.S.A.* 104 C1
Niagara Falls, *Canada* 98 D4
Niagara Falls, *U.S.A.* 106 C6
Niagara-on-the-Lake, *Canada* 106 C5
Niah, *Malaysia* 56 D4
Niamey, *Niger* 79 C5
Nianforando, *Guinea* 78 D2
Nianfors, *Sweden* 10 C10
Niangara, *Zaïre* 82 B2
Nias, *Indonesia* 56 D1
Niassa □, *Mozam.* 83 E4
Nibbiano, *Italy* 32 D6
Nibe, *Denmark* 11 H3
Nicaragua ■, *Cent. Amer.* 116 D2
Nicaragua, L. de, *Nic.* 116 D2
Nicastro, *Italy* 35 D9
Nice, *France* 27 E11
Niceville, *U.S.A.* 105 K2
Nichinan, *Japan* 49 J5
Nicholás, Canal, *W. Indies* 116 B3
Nicholasville, *U.S.A.* 104 G3
Nichols, *U.S.A.* 107 D8
Nicholson, *Australia* 88 C4
Nicholson, *U.S.A.* 107 E9
Nicholson →, *Australia* 90 B2
Nicholson Ra., *Australia* 89 E2
Nickerie □, *Surinam* 121 C6
Nickerie →, *Surinam* 121 B6
Nicobar Is., *Ind. Oc.* 46 J13
Nicoclí, *Colombia* 120 B2
Nicola, *Canada* 100 C4
Nicolet, *Canada* 98 C5
Nicolls Town, *Bahamas* 116 A4
Nicosia, *Cyprus* 37 D12
Nicosia, *Italy* 35 E7
Nicótera, *Italy* 35 D8
Nicoya, *Costa Rica* 116 D2
Nicoya, G. de, *Costa Rica* 116 E3
Nicoya, Pen. de, *Costa Rica* 116 E2
Nidau, *Switz.* 22 B4
Nidd →, *U.K.* 12 C6
Nidda, *Germany* 18 E5
Nidda →, *Germany* 19 E4
Nidwalden □, *Switz.* 23 C6
Nidzica, *Poland* 20 B10
Niebüll, *Germany* 18 A4
Nied →, *Germany* 25 C13
Niederaula, *Germany* 18 E5
Niederbipp, *Switz.* 22 B5
Niederbronn-les-Bains, *France* 25 D14
Niedere Tauern, *Austria* 21 H4
Niedersachsen □, *Germany* 18 C5
Niekerkshoop, *S. Africa* 84 D3
Niel, *Belgium* 17 F4
Niellé, *Ivory C.* 78 C3
Niemba, *Zaïre* 82 D2
Niemen = Neman →, *Lithuania* 40 D2
Nienburg, *Germany* 18 C5
Niers →, *Germany* 18 D2
Niesen, *Switz.* 22 C5
Niesky, *Germany* 18 D10
Nieu Bethesda, *S. Africa* 84 E3
Nieuw-Amsterdam, *Neths.* 16 C9
Nieuw Amsterdam, *Surinam* 121 B6
Nieuw Beijerland, *Neths.* 16 E4
Nieuw-Dordrecht, *Neths.* 16 C9
Nieuw Loosdrecht, *Neths.* 16 D6
Nieuw Nickerie, *Surinam* 121 B6
Nieuw-Schoonebeek, *Neths.* 16 C10
Nieuw-Vennep, *Neths.* 16 D5
Nieuw-Vossemeer, *Neths.* 17 E4
Nieuwe-Niedorp, *Neths.* 16 C5
Nieuwe-Pekela, *Neths.* 16 B9
Nieuwe-Schans, *Neths.* 16 B10
Nieuwendijk, *Neths.* 16 E5
Nieuwerkerken, *Belgium* 17 G6
Nieuwkoop, *Neths.* 16 D5
Nieuwleusen, *Neths.* 16 C8
Nieuwnamen, *Neths.* 17 F4
Nieuwolda, *Neths.* 16 B9
Nieuwoudtville, *S. Africa* 84 E2
Nieuwpoort, *Belgium* 17 F1
Nieuwveen, *Neths.* 16 D5
Nieves, *Spain* 30 C2
Nieves, Pico de las, *Canary Is.* 36 G4
Nièvre □, *France* 25 E10
Niğde, *Turkey* 66 E6
Niğde □, *Turkey* 66 E6
Nigel, *S. Africa* 85 D4
Niger □, *Nigeria* 79 C6
Niger ■, *W. Afr.* 79 B6
Niger →, *W. Afr.* 79 D6
Nigeria ■, *W. Afr.* 79 D6
Nightcaps, *N.Z.* 87 L2
Nigríta, *Greece* 39 J6
Nihtaur, *India* 63 E8
Nii-Jima, *Japan* 49 G9
Niigata, *Japan* 48 F9
Niigata □, *Japan* 49 F9
Niihama, *Japan* 49 H6
Niihau, *U.S.A.* 102 H14
Niimi, *Japan* 49 G6
Niitsu, *Japan* 48 F9
Níjar, *Spain* 29 J2
Nijil, *Jordan* 69 E4
Nijkerk, *Neths.* 16 D7
Nijlen, *Belgium* 17 F5
Nijmegen, *Neths.* 16 E7
Nijverdal, *Neths.* 16 D8
Nīk Pey, *Iran* 65 B6
Nike, *Nigeria* 79 D6
Nikel, *Russia* 8 B21
Nikiniki, *Indonesia* 57 F6
Nikki, *Benin* 79 D5
Nikkō, *Japan* 49 F9
Nikolayev, *Ukraine* 42 C4
Nikolayevsk, *Russia* 41 G14
Nikolayevsk-na-Amur, *Russia* 45 D15
Nikolsk, *Russia* 41 B14
Nikolskoye, *Russia* 45 D17
Nikopol, *Bulgaria* 38 F7
Nikopol, *Ukraine* 42 C6
Niksar, *Turkey* 42 F7
Nīkshahr, *Iran* 65 E9
Nikšić, *Montenegro* 21 N8
Nîl, Nahr en →, *Africa* 76 H7
Nîl el Abyad →, *Sudan* 77 D3
Nîl el Azraq →, *Sudan* 77 D3
Niland, *U.S.A.* 113 M11
Nile = Nîl, Nahr en →, *Africa* 76 H7
Nile □, *Uganda* 82 B3
Nile Delta, *Egypt* 76 H7
Niles, *U.S.A.* 106 E4
Nilo Peçanha, *Brazil* 123 D4
Nimach, *India* 62 G6
Nimbahera, *India* 62 G6
Nîmes, *France* 27 E8
Nimfaíon, Ákra-, *Greece* 39 J7
Nimmitabel, *Australia* 91 F4
Nimneryskiy, *Russia* 45 D13
Nimule, *Sudan* 77 G3
Nin, *Croatia* 33 D12
Nīnawá, *Iraq* 64 B4
Nindigully, *Australia* 91 D4
Ninemile, *U.S.A.* 100 B2
Nineveh = Nīnawá, *Iraq* 64 B4
Ning Xian, *China* 50 G4
Ningaloo, *Australia* 88 D1
Ning'an, *China* 51 B15
Ningbo, *China* 53 C13
Ningcheng, *China* 51 D10
Ningde, *China* 53 D12
Ningdu, *China* 53 D10
Ninggang, *China* 53 D9
Ningguo, *China* 53 B12
Ninghai, *China* 53 C13
Ninghua, *China* 53 D11
Ningjin, *China* 50 F8
Ningjing Shan, *China* 52 B2
Ninglang, *China* 52 D3
Ningling, *China* 50 G8
Ningming, *China* 52 F6
Ningnan, *China* 52 D4
Ningpo = Ningbo, *China* 53 C13
Ningqiang, *China* 50 H4
Ningshan, *China* 50 H5
Ningsia Hui A.R. = Ningxia Huizu Zizhiqu □, *China* 50 E3
Ningwu, *China* 50 E7
Ningxia Huizu Zizhiqu □, *China* 50 E3
Ningxiang, *China* 53 C9
Ningyang, *China* 50 G9
Ningyuan, *China* 53 E8
Ninh Binh, *Vietnam* 58 B5
Ninh Giang, *Vietnam* 58 B6
Ninh Hoa, *Vietnam* 58 F7
Ninh Ma, *Vietnam* 58 F7
Ninove, *Belgium* 17 G4
Nioaque, *Brazil* 127 A4
Niobrara, *U.S.A.* 108 D6
Niobrara →, *U.S.A.* 108 D6
Niono, *Mali* 78 C3
Nioro du Rip, *Senegal* 78 C1
Nioro du Sahel, *Mali* 78 B3
Niort, *France* 26 B3
Nipawin, *Canada* 101 C8
Nipawin Prov. Park, *Canada* 101 C8
Nipigon, *Canada* 98 C2
Nipigon, L., *Canada* 98 C2
Nipin →, *Canada* 101 B7
Nipishish L., *Canada* 99 B7
Nipissing L., *Canada* 98 C4
Nipomo, *U.S.A.* 113 K6
Nipton, *U.S.A.* 113 K11
Niquelândia, *Brazil* 123 D2
Nīr, *Iran* 64 B5
Nirasaki, *Japan* 49 G9
Nirmal, *India* 60 K11
Nirmali, *India* 63 F12
Niš, *Serbia* 21 M11
Nisa, *Portugal* 31 F3
Nişāb, *Yemen* 68 E4
Nišava →, *Serbia* 21 M11
Niscemi, *Italy* 35 E7
Nishinomiya, *Japan* 49 G7
Nishin'omote, *Japan* 49 J5
Nishiwaki, *Japan* 49 G7
Nísíros, *Greece* 39 N10
Niskibi →, *Canada* 98 A2
Nispen, *Neths.* 17 F4
Nisqually →, *U.S.A.* 112 C4
Nissáki, *Greece* 37 A3
Nissan →, *Sweden* 11 H6
Nissedal, *Norway* 10 E2
Nisser, *Norway* 10 E2
Nissum Fjord, *Denmark* 11 H2
Nistelrode, *Neths.* 17 E7
Nisutlin →, *Canada* 100 A2
Nitchequon, *Canada* 99 B5
Niterói, *Brazil* 123 F3
Nith →, *U.K.* 14 F5
Nitra, *Slovak Rep.* 21 G8
Nittedal, *Norway* 10 D4
Nittendau, *Germany* 19 F8
Niuafo'ou, *Tonga* 87 B11
Niue, *Cook Is.* 93 J11
Niulan Jiang →, *China* 52 D4
Niut, *Indonesia* 56 D4
Niutou Shan, *China* 53 C13
Niuzhuang, *China* 51 D12
Nivelles, *Belgium* 17 G4
Nivernais, *France* 25 E10
Nixon, *U.S.A.* 109 L6
Nizamabad, *India* 60 K11
Nizamghat, *India* 61 E19
Nizhne Kolymsk, *Russia* 45 C17
Nizhne-Vartovsk, *Russia* 44 C8
Nizhneangarsk, *Russia* 45 D11
Nizhnegorskiy, *Ukraine* 42 D6
Nizhnekamsk, *Russia* 41 D17
Nizhneudinsk, *Russia* 45 D10
Nizhneyansk, *Russia* 45 B14
Nizhniy Lomov, *Russia* 41 E13
Nizhniy Novgorod, *Russia* 41 C14
Nizhniy Tagil, *Russia* 44 D6
Nizip, *Turkey* 67 E7
Nizké Tatry, *Slovak Rep.* 20 G9
Nizza Monferrato, *Italy* 32 D5
Njakwa, *Malawi* 83 E3
Njanji, *Zambia* 83 E3
Njinjo, *Tanzania* 83 D4
Njombe, *Tanzania* 83 D3
Njombe □, *Tanzania* 83 D3
Njombe →, *Tanzania* 82 D4
Nkambe, *Cameroon* 79 D7
Nkana, *Zambia* 83 E2
Nkawkaw, *Ghana* 79 D4
Nkayi, *Zimbabwe* 83 F2
Nkhata Bay, *Malawi* 80 G6
Nkhota Kota, *Malawi* 83 E3
Nkongsamba, *Cameroon* 79 E6
Nkurenkuru, *Namibia* 84 B2
Nkwanta, *Ghana* 78 D4
Nmai →, *Burma* 61 G20
Noakhali = Maijdi, *Bangla.* 61 H17
Noatak, *U.S.A.* 96 B3
Nobel, *Canada* 106 A4
Nobeoka, *Japan* 49 H5
Noblejas, *Spain* 28 F1
Noblesville, *U.S.A.* 104 E3
Noce →, *Italy* 32 B8
Nocera Inferiore, *Italy* 35 B7
Nocera Terinese, *Italy* 35 C9
Nocera Umbra, *Italy* 33 E9
Noci, *Italy* 35 B10
Nockatunga, *Australia* 91 D3
Nocona, *U.S.A.* 109 J6
Noda, *Japan* 49 G9
Noel, *U.S.A.* 109 G7
Nogales, *Mexico* 114 A2
Nogales, *U.S.A.* 111 L8
Nōgata, *Japan* 49 H5
Nogent-en-Bassigny, *France* 25 D12
Nogent-le-Rotrou, *France* 24 D7
Nogent-sur-Seine, *France* 25 D10
Noggerup, *Australia* 89 F2
Noginsk, *Russia* 41 D11
Noginsk, *Sib., Russia* 45 C10
Nogoa →, *Australia* 90 C4
Nogoyá, *Argentina* 126 C4
Nogueira de Ramuin, *Spain* 30 C3
Noguera Pallaresa →, *Spain* 28 D5
Noguera Ribagorzana →, *Spain* 28 D5
Nohar, *India* 62 E6
Noire, Mt., *France* 24 D3
Noirétable, *France* 26 C7
Noirmoutier, I. de, *France* 24 F4
Noirmoutier-en-l'Ile, *France* 24 F4
Nojane, *Botswana* 84 C3
Nojima-Zaki, *Japan* 49 G9
Nok Kundi, *Pakistan* 60 E3
Nokaneng, *Botswana* 84 B3
Nokhtuysk, *Russia* 45 C12
Nokomis, *Canada* 101 C8
Nokomis L., *Canada* 101 B8
Nol, *Sweden* 11 G6
Nola, *C.A.R.* 80 D3
Nola, *Italy* 35 B7
Nolay, *France* 25 F11
Noli, C. di, *Italy* 32 D5
Nolinsk, *Russia* 41 C16
Noma Omuramba →, *Namibia* 84 B3
Noman L., *Canada* 101 A7
Nombre de Dios, *Panama* 116 E4
Nome, *U.S.A.* 96 B3
Nomo-Zaki, *Japan* 49 H4
Nonacho L., *Canada* 101 A7
Nonancourt, *France* 24 D8
Nonant-le-Pin, *France* 24 D7
Nonda, *Australia* 90 C3
Nong Chang, *Thailand* 58 E2
Nong Het, *Laos* 58 C4
Nong Khai, *Thailand* 58 D4
Nong'an, *China* 51 B13
Nongoma, *S. Africa* 85 D5
Nonoava, *Mexico* 114 B3
Nonthaburi, *Thailand* 58 F3
Nontron, *France* 26 C4
Nonza, *France* 27 F13
Noonamah, *Australia* 88 B5
Noonan, *U.S.A.* 108 A3
Noondoo, *Australia* 91 D4
Noonkanbah, *Australia* 88 C3
Noord-Bergum, *Neths.* 16 B8
Noord Brabant □, *Neths.* 17 E6
Noord Holland □, *Neths.* 16 D5
Noordbeveland, *Neths.* 17 E3
Noordeloos, *Neths.* 16 E5
Noordhollandsch Kanaal, *Neths.* 16 C5
Noordhorn, *Neths.* 16 B8
Noordoostpolder, *Neths.* 16 C7
Noordwijk aan Zee, *Neths.* 16 D4
Noordwijk-Binnen, *Neths.* 16 D4
Noordwijkerhout, *Neths.* 16 D5
Noordzee Kanaal, *Neths.* 16 D5
Noorwolde, *Neths.* 16 C8
Nootka, *Canada* 100 D3
Nootka I., *Canada* 100 D3
Nóqui, *Angola* 80 F2
Nora, *Eritrea* 77 D5
Noranda, *Canada* 98 C4
Nórcia, *Italy* 33 F10
Norco, *U.S.A.* 113 M9
Nord □, *France* 25 B10
Nord-Ostsee Kanal, *Germany* 18 A5
Nord-Trøndelag fylke □, *Norway* 8 D12
Nordagutu, *Norway* 10 E3
Nordaustlandet, *Svalbard* 4 B9
Nordborg, *Denmark* 11 J3
Nordby, *Århus, Denmark* 11 J4
Nordby, *Ribe, Denmark* 11 J2
Norddeich, *Germany* 18 B3
Nordegg, *Canada* 100 C5
Norden, *Germany* 18 B3
Nordenham, *Germany* 18 B4
Norderhov, *Norway* 10 D4
Norderney, *Germany* 18 B3
Nordfriesische Inseln, *Germany* 18 A4
Nordhausen, *Germany* 18 D6
Nordhorn, *Germany* 18 C3
Nordjyllands Amtskommune □, *Denmark* 11 H4
Nordkapp, *Norway* 8 A18
Nordkapp, *Svalbard* 4 A9
Nordkinn = Kinnarodden, *Norway* 6 A11
Nordland fylke □, *Norway* 8 D12
Nördlingen, *Germany* 19 G6
Nordrhein-Westfalen □, *Germany* 18 D3
Nordstrand, *Germany* 18 A4
Nordvik, *Russia* 45 B12
Nore, *Norway* 10 D3
Norefjell, *Norway* 10 D3
Norembega, *Canada* 98 C3
Noresund, *Norway* 10 D3
Norfolk, *Nebr., U.S.A.* 108 D6
Norfolk, *Va., U.S.A.* 104 G7
Norfolk □, *U.K.* 12 E9
Norfolk Broads, *U.K.* 12 E9
Norfolk I., *Pac. Oc.* 92 K8
Norfork Res., *U.S.A.* 109 G8
Norg, *Neths.* 16 B8
Norilsk, *Russia* 45 C9
Norley, *Australia* 91 D3
Norma, Mt., *Australia* 90 C3
Normal, *U.S.A.* 108 E10
Norman, *U.S.A.* 109 H6
Norman →, *Australia* 90 B3
Norman Wells, *Canada* 96 B7
Normanby →, *Australia* 90 A3
Normandie, *France* 24 D7
Normandie, Collines de, *France* 24 D6
Normandin, *Canada* 98 C5
Normandy = Normandie, *France* 24 D7
Normanhurst, Mt., *Australia* 89 E3
Normanton, *Australia* 90 B3
Norquay, *Canada* 101 C8
Norquinco, *Argentina* 128 B2
Norrbotten □, *Sweden* 8 C17
Norrby, *Sweden* 8 D15
Nørre Åby, *Denmark* 11 J3
Nørre Nebel, *Denmark* 11 J2
Nørresundby, *Denmark* 11 G3
Norris, *U.S.A.* 110 D8
Norristown, *U.S.A.* 107 F9
Norrköping, *Sweden* 11 F10
Norrland, *Sweden* 8 E13
Norrtälje, *Sweden* 10 E12
Norseman, *Australia* 89 F3
Norsholm, *Sweden* 11 F9
Norsk, *Russia* 45 D14
Norte, Pta., *Argentina* 128 B4
Norte, Pta. del, *Canary Is.* 36 G2
Norte de Santander □, *Colombia* 120 B3
Nortelândia, *Brazil* 125 C6
North Adams, *U.S.A.* 107 D11
North America 94 F10
North Battleford, *Canada* 101 C7
North Bay, *Canada* 98 C4
North Belcher Is., *Canada* 98 A4
North Bend, *Canada* 100 D4
North Bend, *Oreg., U.S.A.* 110 E1
North Bend, *Pa., U.S.A.* 106 E7
North Bend, *Wash., U.S.A.* 112 C5
North Berwick, *U.K.* 14 E6
North Berwick, *U.S.A.* 107 C14
North Buganda □, *Uganda* 82 B3
North Canadian →, *U.S.A.* 109 H7
North Cape = Nordkapp, *Norway* 8 A18
North Cape = Nordkapp, *Svalbard* 4 A9
North C., *Canada* 99 C7
North C., *N.Z.* 87 F4
North Caribou L., *Canada* 98 B1
North Carolina □, *U.S.A.* 105 H5
North Channel, *Canada* 98 C3
North Channel, *U.K.* 14 G3
North Chicago, *U.S.A.* 104 D2
North Dakota □, *U.S.A.* 108 B5
North Dandalup, *Australia* 89 F2
North Down □, *U.K.* 15 B6
North Downs, *U.K.* 13 F8
North East, *U.S.A.* 106 D5
North East Frontier Agency = Arunachal Pradesh □, *India* 61 E19
North East Providence Chan., *W. Indies* 116 A4
North Eastern □, *Kenya* 82 B5
North Esk →, *U.K.* 14 E6
North European Plain, *Europe* 6 D11
North Foreland, *U.K.* 13 F9
North Fork, *U.S.A.* 112 H7
North Fork American →, *U.S.A.* 112 G5
North Fork Feather →, *U.S.A.* 112 F5
North Frisian Is. = Nordfriesische Inseln, *Germany* 18 A4

North Henik L., *Canada* . . 101 A9
North Highlands, *U.S.A.* . . 112 G5
North Horr, *Kenya* 82 B4
North I., *Kenya* 82 B4
North I., *N.Z.* 87 H5
North Kingsville, *U.S.A.* . . 106 E4
North Knife →, *Canada* . . 101 B10
North Koel →, *India* 63 G10
North Korea ■, *Asia* 51 E14
North Lakhimpur, *India* . . 61 F19
North Las Vegas, *U.S.A.* . . 113 J11
North Loup →, *U.S.A.* . . . 108 E5
North Magnetic Pole,
 Canada 4 B2
North Minch, *U.K.* 14 C3
North Nahanni →, *Canada* 100 A4
North Olmsted, *U.S.A.* . . . 106 E3
North Ossetian Republic □,
 Russia 43 E11
North Pagai, I. = Pagai
 Utara, *Indonesia* 56 E2
North Palisade, *U.S.A.* . . . 111 H4
North Platte, *U.S.A.* 108 E4
North Platte →, *U.S.A.* . . . 108 E4
North Pt., *Canada* 99 C7
North Pole, *Arctic* . . . . . . 4 A
North Portal, *Canada* 101 D8
North Powder, *U.S.A.* 110 D5
North Rhine
 Westphalia □ =
 Nordrhein-Westfalen □,
 Germany 18 D3
North Ronaldsay, *U.K.* . . . 14 B6
North Saskatchewan →,
 Canada 101 C7
North Sea, *Europe* 6 D6
North Sporades = Voríai
 Sporádhes, *Greece* 39 K6
North Sydney, *Canada* . . . 99 C7
North Taranaki Bight, *N.Z.* 87 H5
North Thompson →,
 Canada 100 C4
North Tonawanda, *U.S.A.* . 106 C6
North Troy, *U.S.A.* 107 B12
North Truchas Pk., *U.S.A.* 111 J11
North Twin I., *Canada* . . . 98 B3
North Tyne →, *U.K.* 12 C5
North Uist, *U.K.* 14 D1
North Vancouver, *Canada* 100 D4
North Vernon, *U.S.A.* 104 F3
North Wabasca L., *Canada* 100 B6
North Walsham, *U.K.* 12 E9
North West C., *Australia* . . 88 D1
North West Christmas I.
 Ridge, *Pac. Oc.* 93 G11
North West Frontier □,
 Pakistan 62 C4
North West Highlands,
 U.K. 14 D3
North West Providence
 Channel, *W. Indies* 116 A4
North West River, *Canada* 99 B7
North West Territories □,
 Canada 96 B9
North Western □, *Zambia* 83 E2
North York Moors, *U.K.* . . 12 C7
North Yorkshire □, *U.K.* . . 12 C6
Northallerton, *U.K.* 12 C6
Northam, *S. Africa* 84 C4
Northam, *Australia* 89 E1
Northampton, *Australia* . . 89 E1
Northampton, *U.K.* 13 E7
Northampton, *Mass.,*
 U.S.A. 107 D12
Northampton, *Pa., U.S.A.* 107 F9
Northampton Downs,
 Australia 90 C4
Northamptonshire □, *U.K.* 13 E7
Northbridge, *U.S.A.* 107 D13
Northcliffe, *Australia* 89 F2
Northeim, *Germany* 18 D6
Northern □, *Malawi* 83 E3
Northern □, *Uganda* 82 B3
Northern □, *Zambia* 83 E3
Northern Circars, *India* . . 61 L13
Northern Indian L.,
 Canada 101 B9
Northern Ireland □, *U.K.* . 15 B5
Northern Light, L., *Canada* 98 C1
Northern Marianas ■,
 Pac. Oc. 92 F6
Northern Province □,
 S. Leone 78 D2
Northern Territory □,
 Australia 88 D5
Northfield, *U.S.A.* 108 C8
Northland □, *N.Z.* 87 F4
Northome, *U.S.A.* 108 B7
Northport, *Ala., U.S.A.* . . 105 J2
Northport, *Mich., U.S.A.* . 104 C3
Northport, *Wash., U.S.A.* 110 B5
Northumberland □, *U.K.* . 12 B5
Northumberland, C.,
 Australia 91 F3
Northumberland Is.,
 Australia 90 C4
Northumberland Str.,
 Canada 99 C7
Northwich, *U.K.* 12 D5
Northwood, *Iowa, U.S.A.* . 108 D8
Northwood, *N. Dak.,*
 U.S.A. 108 B6
Norton, *U.S.A.* 108 F5
Norton, *Zimbabwe* 83 F3
Norton Sd., *U.S.A.* 96 B3
Nortorf, *Germany* 18 A5

Norwalk, *Calif., U.S.A.* . . 113 M8
Norwalk, *Conn., U.S.A.* . . 107 E11
Norwalk, *Ohio, U.S.A.* . . . 106 E2
Norway, *U.S.A.* 104 C2
Norway ■, *Europe* 8 E11
Norway House, *Canada* . . 101 C9
Norwegian Sea, *Atl. Oc.* . 4 C8
Norwich, *Canada* 106 D4
Norwich, *U.K.* 12 E9
Norwich, *Conn., U.S.A.* . . 107 E12
Norwich, *N.Y., U.S.A.* . . . 107 D9
Norwood, *Canada* 106 B7
Noshiro, *Japan* 48 D10
Nosok, *Russia* 44 B9
Nosovka, *Ukraine* 40 F7
Noss Hd., *U.K.* 14 C5
Nossa Senhora da Glória,
 Brazil 122 D4
Nossa Senhora das Dores,
 Brazil 122 D4
Nossa Senhora do
 Livramento, *Brazil* . . . 125 D6
Nossebro, *Sweden* 11 F6
Nossob →, *S. Africa* 84 D3
Nosy Bé, *Madag.* 81 G9
Nosy Boraha, *Madag.* . . . 85 B8
Nosy Mitsio, *Madag.* 81 G9
Nosy Varika, *Madag.* 85 C8
Noteć →, *Poland* 20 C5
Notigi Dam, *Canada* 101 B9
Notikewin →, *Canada* . . . 100 B5
Notios Evvoïkos Kólpos,
 Greece 39 L7
Noto, *Italy* 35 F8
Noto, G. di, *Italy* 35 F8
Notodden, *Norway* 10 E3
Notre-Dame, *Canada* 99 C7
Notre Dame B., *Canada* . . 99 C8
Notre Dame de Koartac =
 Koartac, *Canada* 97 B13
Notre Dame d'Ivugivic =
 Ivugivik, *Canada* 97 B12
Notsé, *Togo* 79 D5
Nottaway →, *Canada* 98 B4
Nøtterøy, *Norway* 10 E4
Nottingham, *U.K.* 12 E6
Nottinghamshire □, *U.K.* . 12 D7
Nottoway →, *U.S.A.* 104 G7
Notwane →, *Botswana* . . . 84 C4
Nouâdhibou, *Mauritania* . 74 D1
Nouâdhibou, Ras,
 Mauritania 74 D1
Nouakchott, *Mauritania* . 78 B1
Nouméa, *N. Cal.* 92 K8
Noupoort, *S. Africa* 84 E3
Nouveau Comptoir, *Canada* 98 B4
Nouvelle-Calédonie = New
 Caledonia, *Pac. Oc.* . . . 92 K8
Nouzonville, *France* 25 C11
Nová Baña, *Slovakia* 21 G8
Nová Bystřice, *Czech.* . . . 20 F5
Nova Casa Nova, *Brazil* . . 122 C3
Nova Cruz, *Brazil* 122 C4
Nova Era, *Brazil* 123 E3
Nova Esperança, *Brazil* . . 127 A5
Nova Friburgo, *Brazil* . . . 123 F3
Nova Gaia = Cambundi-
 Catembo, *Angola* 80 G3
Nova Gradiška, *Croatia* . . 21 K7
Nova Granada, *Brazil* . . . 123 F2
Nova Iguaçu, *Brazil* 123 F3
Nova Iorque, *Brazil* 122 C3
Nova Lamego, *Guinea-Biss.* 78 C2
Nova Lima, *Brazil* 127 A7
Nova Lisboa = Huambo,
 Angola 81 G3
Nova Lusitânia, *Mozam.* . 83 F3
Nova Mambone, *Mozam.* . 85 C6
Nova Mesto, *Slovenia* . . . 33 C12
Nova Ponte, *Brazil* 123 E2
Nova Scotia □, *Canada* . . 99 C7
Nova Sofala, *Mozam.* . . . 85 C5
Nova Venécia, *Brazil* 123 E3
Nova Vida, *Brazil* 125 C5
Nova Zagora, *Bulgaria* . . 38 G8
Novaleksandrovskaya,
 Russia 43 D9
Novannenskiy, *Russia* . . . 41 F13
Novara, *Italy* 32 C5
Novato, *U.S.A.* 112 G4
Novaya Kakhovka, *Ukraine* 42 C5
Novaya Lyalya, *Russia* . . . 44 D7
Novaya Sibir, Ostrov,
 Russia 45 B16
Novaya Zemlya, *Russia* . . 44 B6
Novelda, *Spain* 29 G4
Novellara, *Italy* 32 D7
Noventa Vicentina, *Italy* . 33 C8
Novgorod, *Russia* 40 B7
Novgorod-Severskiy,
 Ukraine 40 E8
Novi Bečej, *Serbia, Yug.* . 21 K10
Novi Grad, *Croatia* 33 C10
Novi Krichim, *Bulgaria* . . 38 G7
Novi Lígure, *Italy* 32 D5
Novi Pazar, *Bulgaria* 38 F10
Novi Pazar, *Serbia, Yug.* . 21 M10
Novi Sad, *Serbia, Yug.* . . 21 K9
Novi Vinodolski, *Croatia* . 33 C11
Novigrad, *Croatia* 33 D12
Noville, *Belgium* 17 H7
Novo Acôrdo, *Brazil* 122 D2
Novo Aripuanã, *Brazil* . . . 121 E5
Nôvo Cruzeiro, *Brazil* . . . 123 E3
Nôvo Hamburgo, *Brazil* . . 127 B5

Novo Horizonte, *Brazil* . . 123 F2
Novo Remanso, *Brazil* . . . 122 C3
Novo-Zavidovskiy, *Russia* 41 C10
Novoakrainka, *Ukraine* . . 42 B4
Novoataysk, *Russia* 44 D9
Novoazovsk, *Ukraine* 42 C8
Novobelitsa, *Belorussia* . . 40 E7
Novobogatinskoye,
 Kazakhstan 43 C14
Novocherkassk, *Russia* . . 43 C9
Novodevichye, *Russia* . . . 41 E16
Novograd-Volynskiy,
 Ukraine 40 F5
Novogrudok, *Belorussia* . . 40 E4
Novokachalinsk, *Russia* . . 48 B6
Novokayakent, *Russia* . . . 43 E12
Novokazalinsk, *Kazakhstan* 44 E7
Novokhoperск, *Russia* . . . 41 F12
Novokuybyshevsk, *Russia* 41 E16
Novokuznetsk, *Russia* . . . 44 D9
Novomirgorod, *Ukraine* . . 42 B4
Novomoskovsk, *Russia* . . 41 D11
Novomoskovsk, *Ukraine* . 42 B6
Novopolotsk, *Belorussia* . . 40 D6
Novorossiysk, *Russia* 42 D7
Novorybnoye, *Russia* 45 B11
Novorzhev, *Russia* 40 C6
Novoselitsa, *Ukraine* 42 B2
Novoshakhtinsk, *Russia* . . 43 C8
Novosibirsk, *Russia* 44 D9
Novosibirskiye Ostrova,
 Russia 45 B15
Novosil, *Russia* 41 E10
Novosokolniki, *Russia* . . . 40 C7
Novotroitsk, *Russia* 44 D6
Novotulskiy, *Russia* 41 D10
Novouzensk, *Russia* 41 F16
Novovolynsk, *Ukraine* . . . 40 F4
Novovyatsk, *Russia* 41 B16
Novozybkov, *Russia* 40 E8
Novska, *Croatia* 21 K6
Novvy Port, *Russia* 44 C8
Novy Bug, *Ukraine* 42 C5
Nový Bydžov, *Czech.* 20 E5
Novy Dwór Mazowiecki,
 Poland 20 C10
Novyy Afon, *Georgia* 43 E9
Novyy Oskol, *Russia* 41 F10
Now Shahr, *Iran* 65 B6
Nowa Deba, *Poland* 20 E11
Nowa Ruda, *Poland* 20 E6
Nowa Sól, *Poland* 20 D5
Nowbaran, *Iran* 65 C6
Nowe, *Poland* 20 B8
Nowghāb, *Iran* 65 C8
Nowgong, *India* 61 F18
Nowogard, *Poland* 20 B5
Nowogród, *Poland* 20 B11
Nowra, *Australia* 91 E5
Nowshera, *Pakistan* 60 B8
Nowy Korczyn, *Poland* . . . 20 E10
Nowy Sącz, *Poland* 20 F10
Noxen, *U.S.A.* 107 E8
Noxon, *U.S.A.* 110 C6
Noya, *Spain* 30 C2
Noyant, *France* 24 E7
Noyers, *France* 25 E10
Noyes I., *U.S.A.* 100 B2
Noyon, *France* 25 C9
Noyon, *Mongolia* 50 C2
Nozay, *France* 24 E5
Nsa, O. en →, *Algeria* . . . 75 B6
Nsanje, *Malawi* 83 F4
Nsawam, *Ghana* 79 D4
Nsomba, *Zambia* 83 E2
Nsukka, *Nigeria* 79 D6
Nu Jiang →, *China* 52 C1
Nu Shan, *China* 52 D2
Nuba Mts. = Nubah,
 Jibalal, *Sudan* 77 E3
Nubah, Jibalal, *Sudan* . . . 77 E3
Nubian Desert = Nûbîya,
 Es Sahrâ En, *Sudan* . . . 76 C3
Nûbîya, Es Sahrâ En,
 Sudan 76 C3
Ñuble □, *Chile* 126 D1
Nuboai, *Indonesia* 57 E9
Nubra →, *India* 63 B7
Nueces →, *U.S.A.* 109 M6
Nueltin L., *Canada* 101 A9
Nuenen, *Neths.* 17 F7
Nueva, I., *Chile* 128 E3
Nueva Antioquia,
 Colombia 120 B4
Nueva Asunción □,
 Paraguay 126 A3
Nueva Esparta □,
 Venezuela 121 A5
Nueva Gerona, *Cuba* 116 B3
Nueva Imperial, *Chile* . . . 128 A2
Nueva Palmira, *Uruguay* . 126 C4
Nueva Rosita, *Mexico* . . . 114 B4
Nueva San Salvador,
 El Salv. 116 D2
Nuéve de Julio, *Argentina* 126 D3
Nuevitas, *Cuba* 116 B4
Nuevo, G., *Argentina* 128 B4
Nuevo Guerrero, *Mexico* . 115 B5
Nuevo Laredo, *Mexico* . . 115 B5
Nuevo León □, *Mexico* . . 114 C4
Nuevo Mundo, Cerro,
 Bolivia 124 E4
Nuevo Rocafuerte, *Ecuador* 120 D2
Nugget Pt., *N.Z.* 87 M2
Nugrus, Gebel, *Egypt* . . . 76 C3

Nuhaka, *N.Z.* 87 H6
Nuits-St.-Georges, *France* . 25 E11
Nukey Bluff, *Australia* . . . 91 E2
Nukheila, *Sudan* 76 D2
Nuku'alofa, *Tonga* 87 E11
Nukus, *Uzbekistan* 44 E6
Nuland, *Neths.* 16 E6
Nulato, *U.S.A.* 96 B4
Nules, *Spain* 28 F4
Nullagine →, *Australia* . . . 88 D3
Nullarbor, *Australia* 89 F5
Nullarbor Plain, *Australia* . 89 F4
Numalla, L., *Australia* . . . 91 D3
Numan, *Nigeria* 79 D7
Numansdorp, *Neths.* 16 E4
Numata, *Japan* 49 F9
Numatinna →, *Sudan* 77 F2
Numazu, *Japan* 49 G9
Numbulwar, *Australia* . . . 90 A2
Numfoor, *Indonesia* 57 E8
Numurkah, *Australia* 91 F4
Nunaksaluk I., *Canada* . . . 99 A7
Nuneaton, *U.K.* 13 E6
Nungo, *Mozam.* 83 E4
Nungwe, *Tanzania* 82 C3
Nunivak I., *U.S.A.* 96 B3
Nunkun, *India* 63 C7
Nunspeet, *Neths.* 16 D7
Nuoro, *Italy* 34 B2
Nuquí, *Colombia* 120 B2
Nūrābād, *Iran* 65 E8
Nure →, *Italy* 32 C6
Nuremburg = Nürnberg,
 Germany 19 F7
Nuri, *Mexico* 114 B3
Nurina, *Australia* 89 F4
Nuriootpa, *Australia* 91 E2
Nurlat, *Russia* 41 D17
Nürnberg, *Germany* 19 F7
Nurran, L. = Terewah, L.,
 Australia 91 D4
Nurrari Lakes, *Australia* . . 89 E5
Nurri, *Italy* 34 C2
Nusa Barung, *Indonesia* . . 57 H15
Nusa Kambangan,
 Indonesia 57 G13
Nusa Tenggara Barat □,
 Indonesia 56 F5
Nusa Tenggara Timur □,
 Indonesia 57 F6
Nushki, *Pakistan* 62 E2
Nutak, *Canada* 97 C13
Nuth, *Neths.* 17 G7
Nutwood Downs, *Australia* 90 B1
Nuuk = Godthåb,
 Greenland 97 B14
Nuwakot, *Nepal* 63 E10
Nuweiba', *Egypt* 76 B3
Nuweveldberge, *S. Africa* . 84 E3
Nuyts, C., *Australia* 89 F5
Nuyts Arch., *Australia* . . . 91 E1
Nxau-Nxau, *Botswana* . . . 84 B3
Nyaake, *Liberia* 78 E3
Nyack, *U.S.A.* 107 E11
Nyadal, *Sweden* 10 B11
Nyah West, *Australia* 91 F3
Nyahanga, *Tanzania* 82 C3
Nyahua, *Tanzania* 82 D3
Nyahururu, *Kenya* 82 B4
Nyaingentanglha Shan,
 China 54 C4
Nyakanazi, *Tanzania* 82 C3
Nyakrom, *Ghana* 79 D4
Nyamandhlovu, *Zimbabwe* 83 F2
Nyambiti, *Tanzania* 82 C3
Nyamwaga, *Tanzania* 82 C3
Nyandekwa, *Tanzania* . . . 82 C3
Nyanding →, *Sudan* 77 F3
Nyangana, *Namibia* 84 B3
Nyanguge, *Tanzania* 82 C3
Nyankpala, *Ghana* 79 D4
Nyanza, *Burundi* 82 C2
Nyanza, *Rwanda* 82 C2
Nyanza □, *Kenya* 82 C3
Nyarling →, *Canada* 100 A6
Nyasa, L. = Malawi, L.,
 Africa 83 E3
Nyazura, *Zimbabwe* 83 F3
Nyazwidzi →, *Zimbabwe* . 83 F3
Nyborg, *Denmark* 11 J4
Nybro, *Sweden* 9 H13
Nyda, *Russia* 44 C8
Nyeri, *Kenya* 82 C4
Nyerol, *Sudan* 77 F3
Nyhem, *Sweden* 10 B9
Nyiel, *Sudan* 77 F3
Nyinahin, *Ghana* 78 D4
Nyirbátor, *Hungary* 21 H12
Nyíregyháza, *Hungary* . . . 21 H11
Nykarleby, *Finland* 8 E17
Nykøbing, Sjælland,
 Denmark 11 J5
Nykøbing, Storstrøm,
 Denmark 11 K5
Nykøbing, Viborg,
 Denmark 11 H2
Nyköping, *Sweden* 11 F11
Nykvarn, *Sweden* 10 E11
Nyland, *Sweden* 10 A11
Nylstroom, *S. Africa* 85 C4
Nymagee, *Australia* 91 E4
Nymburk, *Czech.* 20 E5
Nynäshamn, *Sweden* 10 F11
Nyngan, *Australia* 91 E4

Nyon, *Switz.* 22 D2
Nyong →, *Cameroon* 79 E6
Nyons, *France* 27 D9
Nyord, *Denmark* 11 J6
Nyou, *Burkina Faso* 79 C4
Nysa, *Poland* 20 E7
Nysa →, *Europe* 18 C10
Nyssa, *U.S.A.* 110 E5
Nysted, *Denmark* 11 K5
Nyunzu, *Zaïre* 82 D2
Nyurba, *Russia* 45 C12
Nzega, *Tanzania* 82 C3
Nzega □, *Tanzania* 82 C3
N'Zérékoré, *Guinea* 78 D3
Nzeto, *Angola* 80 F2
Nzilo, Chutes de, *Zaïre* . . 83 E2
Nzubuka, *Tanzania* 82 C3

O

Õ-Shima, *Nagasaki, Japan* 49 G4
Õ-Shima, *Shizuoka, Japan* 49 G9
Oacoma, *U.S.A.* 108 D5
Oahe, L., *U.S.A.* 108 C4
Oahe Dam, *U.S.A.* 108 C4
Oahu, *U.S.A.* 102 H16
Oak Creek, *U.S.A.* 110 F10
Oak Harbor, *U.S.A.* 112 B4
Oak Hill, *U.S.A.* 104 G5
Oak Park, *U.S.A.* 104 E2
Oak Ridge, *U.S.A.* 105 G3
Oak View, *U.S.A.* 113 L7
Oakan-Dake, *Japan* 48 C12
Oakbank, *Australia* 91 E3
Oakdale, *Calif., U.S.A.* . . 111 H3
Oakdale, *La., U.S.A.* 109 K8
Oakengates, *U.K.* 12 E5
Oakes, *U.S.A.* 108 B5
Oakesdale, *U.S.A.* 110 C5
Oakey, *Australia* 91 D5
Oakham, *U.K.* 12 E7
Oakhurst, *U.S.A.* 112 H7
Oakland, *Calif., U.S.A.* . . 111 H2
Oakland, *Oreg., U.S.A.* . . 110 E2
Oakland City, *U.S.A.* 104 F2
Oakley, *Idaho, U.S.A.* . . . 110 E7
Oakley, *Kans., U.S.A.* . . . 108 F4
Oakover →, *Australia* 88 D3
Oakridge, *U.S.A.* 110 E2
Oakville, *U.S.A.* 112 D3
Oamaru, *N.Z.* 87 L3
Oasis, *Calif., U.S.A.* 113 M10
Oasis, *Nev., U.S.A.* 112 H9
Oates Land, *Antarctica* . . . 5 C11
Oatman, *U.S.A.* 113 K12
Oaxaca, *Mexico* 115 D5
Oaxaca □, *Mexico* 115 D5
Ob →, *Russia* 44 C7
Oba, *Canada* 98 C3
Obala, *Cameroon* 79 E7
Obama, *Japan* 49 G7
Oban, *U.K.* 14 E3
Obbia, *Somali Rep.* 68 F4
Obdam, *Neths.* 16 C5
Obed, *Canada* 100 C5
Ober-Aagau, *Switz.* 22 B5
Obera, *Argentina* 127 B4
Oberalppass, *Switz.* 23 C7
Oberalpstock, *Switz.* 23 C7
Oberammergau, *Germany* . 19 H7
Oberdrauburg, *Austria* . . . 21 J2
Oberengadin, *Switz.* 23 C9
Oberentfelden, *Switz.* . . . 22 B5
Oberhausen, *Germany* . . . 18 D2
Oberkirch, *Germany* 19 G4
Oberland, *Switz.* 22 C5
Oberlin, *Kans., U.S.A.* . . . 108 F4
Oberlin, *La., U.S.A.* 109 K8
Oberlin, *Ohio, U.S.A.* . . . 106 E2
Obernai, *France* 25 D14
Oberndorf, *Germany* 19 G4
Oberon, *Australia* 91 E4
Oberpfälzer Wald,
 Germany 19 F8
Obersiggenthal, *Switz.* . . . 23 B6
Oberstdorf, *Germany* 19 H6
Oberwil, *Switz.* 22 A5
Obi, Kepulauan, *Indonesia* 57 E7
Obi Is. = Obi, Kepulauan,
 Indonesia 57 E7
Obiaruku, *Nigeria* 79 D6
Óbidos, *Brazil* 121 D6
Óbidos, *Portugal* 31 F1
Obihiro, *Japan* 48 C11
Obilatu, *Indonesia* 57 E7
Obilnoye, *Russia* 43 C11
Obing, *Germany* 19 H8
Obisfelde, *Germany* 18 C6
Objat, *France* 26 C5
Obluchye, *Russia* 45 E14
Obninsk, *Russia* 41 D10
Obo, *C.A.R.* 82 A2
Obo, *Ethiopia* 77 F4
Oboa, Mt., *Uganda* 82 B3
Obock, *Djibouti* 77 E5
Oborniki, *Poland* 20 C6
Oboyan, *Russia* 41 F10
Obozerskaya, *Russia* 44 C5
Obrovac, *Croatia* 33 D12
Obruk, *Turkey* 66 D5
Observatory Inlet, *Canada* 100 B3
Obshchi Syrt, *Kazakhstan* . 6 E16

Obskaya Guba, *Russia* . . . 44 C8
Obuasi, *Ghana* 79 D4
Obubra, *Nigeria* 79 D6
Obwalden □, *Switz.* 22 C6
Obzor, *Bulgaria* 38 G10
Ocala, *U.S.A.* 105 L4
Ocamo →, *Venezuela* 121 C4
Ocampo, *Mexico* 114 B3
Ocaña, *Colombia* 120 B3
Ocaña, *Spain* 28 F1
Ocanomowoc, *U.S.A.* 108 D10
Ocate, *U.S.A.* 109 G2
Occidental, Cordillera,
Colombia 120 C3
Occidental, Cordillera,
Peru 124 C3
Ocean City, *N.J., U.S.A.* . . 104 F8
Ocean City, *Wash., U.S.A.* 112 C2
Ocean I. = Banaba,
Kiribati 92 H8
Ocean Park, *U.S.A.* 112 D2
Oceano, *U.S.A.* 113 K6
Oceanport, *U.S.A.* 107 F10
Oceanside, *U.S.A.* 113 M9
Ochagavia, *Spain* 28 C3
Ochamchire, *Georgia* 43 E9
Ochamps, *Belgium* 17 J6
Ochil Hills, *U.K.* 14 E5
Ochre River, *Canada* 101 C9
Ochsenfurt, *Germany* 19 F6
Ochsenhausen, *Germany* . 19 G5
Ocilla, *U.S.A.* 105 K4
Ocmulgee →, *U.S.A.* 105 K4
Ocna Sibiului, *Romania* . . 38 D7
Ocoña, *Peru* 124 D3
Ocoña →, *Peru* 124 D3
Oconee →, *U.S.A.* 105 K4
Oconto, *U.S.A.* 104 C2
Oconto Falls, *U.S.A.* 104 C1
Ocosingo, *Mexico* 115 D6
Ocotal, *Nic.* 116 D2
Ocotlán, *Mexico* 114 C4
Ocquier, *Belgium* 17 H6
Ocreza →, *Portugal* 31 F3
Octave, *U.S.A.* 111 J7
Octeville, *France* 24 C5
Ocumare del Tuy,
Venezuela 120 A4
Ocuri, *Bolivia* 125 D4
Oda, *Ghana* 79 D4
Ōda, *Japan* 49 G6
Oda, J., *Sudan* 76 C4
Ódáðahraun, *Iceland* 8 D5
Ödåkra, *Sweden* 11 H6
Odate, *Japan* 48 D10
Odawara, *Japan* 49 G9
Odda, *Norway* 9 F9
Odder, *Denmark* 11 J4
Oddur, *Somali Rep.* 68 G3
Ödeborg, *Sweden* 11 F5
Odei →, *Canada* 101 B9
Odemira, *Portugal* 31 H2
Ödemiş, *Turkey* 66 D3
Odendaalsrus, *S. Africa* . . 84 D4
Odense, *Denmark* 11 J4
Odenwald, *Germany* 19 F5
Oder →, *Germany* 18 B10
Oderzo, *Italy* 33 C9
Odesa = Odessa, *Ukraine* 42 C4
Odessa, *Canada* 107 B8
Odessa, *Ukraine* 42 C4
Odessa, *Tex., U.S.A.* 109 K3
Odessa, *Wash., U.S.A.* . . . 110 C4
Odiakwe, *Botswana* 84 C4
Odiel →, *Spain* 31 H4
Odienné, *Ivory C.* 78 D3
Odintsovo, *Russia* 41 D10
Odiongan, *Phil.* 55 E4
Odobeşti, *Romania* 38 D10
O'Donnell, *U.S.A.* 109 J4
Odoorn, *Neths.* 16 C9
Odorheiu Secuiesc,
Romania 38 C8
Odoyevo, *Russia* 41 E10
Odra →, *Poland* 20 B4
Odra →, *Spain* 30 C6
Odžaci, *Serbia* 21 K9
Odzi, *Zimbabwe* 85 B5
Oedelem, *Belgium* 17 F2
Oegstgeest, *Neths.* 16 D4
Oeiras, *Brazil* 122 C3
Oeiras, *Portugal* 31 G1
Oelrichs, *U.S.A.* 108 D3
Oelsnitz, *Germany* 18 E8
Oelwein, *U.S.A.* 108 D9
Oenpelli, *Australia* 88 B5
Of, *Turkey* 67 C9
Ofanto →, *Italy* 35 A9
Offa, *Nigeria* 79 D5
Offaly □, *Ireland* 15 C4
Offenbach, *Germany* 19 E4
Offenburg, *Germany* 19 G3
Offerdal, *Sweden* 10 A8
Offida, *Italy* 33 F10
Offranville, *France* 24 C8
Ofidhousa, *Greece* 39 N9
Ofotfjorden, *Norway* 8 B14
Ōfunato, *Japan* 48 E10
Oga, *Japan* 48 E9
Oga-Hantō, *Japan* 48 E9
Ogahalla, *Canada* 98 B2
Ōgaki, *Japan* 49 G8
Ogallala, *U.S.A.* 108 E4
Ogasawara Gunto,
Pac. Oc. 92 E6
Ogbomosho, *Nigeria* 79 D5
Ogden, *Iowa, U.S.A.* 108 D8
Ogden, *Utah, U.S.A.* 110 F7
Ogdensburg, *U.S.A.* 107 B9
Ogeechee →, *U.S.A.* 105 K5
Ogilby, *U.S.A.* 113 N12
Oglio →, *Italy* 32 C7
Ogmore, *Australia* 90 C4
Ognon →, *France* 25 E12
Ogoja, *Nigeria* 79 D6
Ogoki →, *Canada* 98 B2
Ogoki L., *Canada* 98 B2
Ogoki Res., *Canada* 98 B2
Ogooué →, *Gabon* 80 E1
Ogosta →, *Bulgaria* 38 F6
Ogowe = Ogooué →,
Gabon 80 E1
Ogr = Sharafa, *Sudan* 77 E2
Ogrein, *Sudan* 76 D3
Ogulin, *Croatia* 33 C12
Ogun □, *Nigeria* 79 D5
Oguta, *Nigeria* 79 D6
Ogwashi-Uku, *Nigeria* 79 D6
Ogwe, *Nigeria* 79 E6
Ohai, *N.Z.* 87 L2
Ohakune, *N.Z.* 87 H5
Ohanet, *Algeria* 75 C6
Ohata, *Japan* 48 D10
Ohau, L., *N.Z.* 87 L2
Ohey, *Belgium* 17 H6
Ohio □, *U.S.A.* 104 E3
Ohio →, *U.S.A.* 104 G1
Ohře →, *Czech.* 20 E4
Ohre →, *Germany* 18 C7
Ohrid, *Macedonia* 39 H3
Ohridsko, Jezero,
Macedonia 39 H3
Ohrigstad, *S. Africa* 85 C5
Öhringen, *Germany* 19 F5
Oiapoque →, *Brazil* 121 C7
Oikou, *China* 51 E9
Oil City, *U.S.A.* 106 E5
Oildale, *U.S.A.* 113 K7
Oirschot, *Neths.* 17 E6
Oise □, *France* 25 C9
Oise →, *France* 25 D9
Oisterwijk, *Neths.* 17 E6
Ōita, *Japan* 49 H5
Ōita □, *Japan* 49 H5
Oiticica, *Brazil* 122 C3
Ojai, *U.S.A.* 113 L7
Ojinaga, *Mexico* 114 B4
Ojiya, *Japan* 49 F9
Ojos del Salado, Cerro,
Argentina 126 B2
Oka →, *Russia* 41 C13
Okaba, *Indonesia* 57 F9
Okahandja, *Namibia* 84 C2
Okahukura, *N.Z.* 87 H5
Okanagan L., *Canada* 100 C5
Okandja, *Gabon* 80 E2
Okanogan, *U.S.A.* 110 B4
Okanogan →, *U.S.A.* 110 B4
Okaputa, *Namibia* 84 C2
Okara, *Pakistan* 62 D5
Okarito, *N.Z.* 87 K3
Okaukuejo, *Namibia* 84 B2
Okavango Swamps,
Botswana 84 B3
Okaya, *Japan* 49 F9
Okayama, *Japan* 49 G6
Okayama □, *Japan* 49 G6
Okazaki, *Japan* 49 G8
Oke-Iho, *Nigeria* 79 D5
Okeechobee, *U.S.A.* 105 M5
Okeechobee, L., *U.S.A.* . . 105 M5
Okefenokee Swamp,
U.S.A. 105 K4
Okehampton, *U.K.* 13 G3
Okene, *Nigeria* 79 D6
Oker →, *Germany* 18 C6
Okha, *Russia* 45 D15
Ókhi Óros, *Greece* 39 L7
Okhotsk, *Russia* 45 D15
Okhotsk, Sea of, *Asia* 45 D15
Okhotskiy Perevoz, *Russia* 45 C14
Okhotsko Kolymskoye,
Russia 45 C16
Oki-Shotō, *Japan* 49 F6
Okiep, *S. Africa* 84 D2
Okigwi, *Nigeria* 79 D6
Okija, *Nigeria* 79 D6
Okinawa □, *Japan* 49 L3
Okinawa-Guntō, *Japan* . . . 49 L3
Okinawa-Jima, *Japan* 49 L4
Okino-erabu-Shima, *Japan* 49 L4
Okitipupa, *Nigeria* 79 D5
Oklahoma □, *U.S.A.* 109 H6
Oklahoma City, *U.S.A.* . . 109 H6
Okmulgee, *U.S.A.* 109 H7
Oknitsa, *Ukraine* 42 B2
Okolo, *Uganda* 82 B3
Okolona, *U.S.A.* 109 H10
Okrika, *Nigeria* 79 E6
Oktabrsk, *Kazakhstan* 44 E6
Oktyabrsk, *Russia* 41 E16
Oktyabrskiy, *Belorussia* . . 40 E6
Oktyabrskoy Revolyutsii,
Os., *Russia* 45 B10
Oktyabrskoye =
Zhovtnevoye, *Ukraine* . . 42 C5
Oktyabrskoye, *Russia* 44 C7
Okulovka, *Russia* 40 B8
Okuru, *N.Z.* 87 K2
Okushiri-Tō, *Japan* 48 C9
Okuta, *Nigeria* 79 D5
Okwa →, *Botswana* 84 C3
Ola, *U.S.A.* 109 H8
Ólafsfjörður, *Iceland* 8 C4
Ólafsvík, *Iceland* 8 D2
Olancha, *U.S.A.* 113 J8
Olancha Pk., *U.S.A.* 113 J8
Olanchito, *Honduras* 116 C2
Öland, *Sweden* 9 H14
Olargues, *France* 26 E6
Olary, *Australia* 91 E3
Olascoaga, *Argentina* 126 D3
Olathe, *U.S.A.* 108 F7
Olavarría, *Argentina* 126 D3
Oława, *Poland* 20 E7
Ólbia, *Italy* 34 B2
Ólbia, G. di, *Italy* 34 B2
Old Bahama Chan. =
Bahama, Canal Viejo de,
W. Indies 116 B4
Old Baldy Pk. = San
Antonio, Mt., *U.S.A.* . . 113 L9
Old Castile = Castilla y
Leon □, *Spain* 30 D6
Old Castle, *Ireland* 15 C4
Old Cork, *Australia* 90 C3
Old Crow, *Canada* 96 B6
Old Dale, *U.S.A.* 113 L11
Old Dongola, *Sudan* 76 D3
Old Fletton, *U.K.* 13 E7
Old Forge, *N.Y., U.S.A.* . 107 C10
Old Forge, *Pa., U.S.A.* . . . 107 E9
Old Fort →, *Canada* 101 B6
Old Shinyanga, *Tanzania* . 82 C3
Old Speck Mt., *U.S.A.* . . . 107 B14
Old Town, *U.S.A.* 99 D6
Old Wives L., *Canada* 101 C7
Oldbury, *U.K.* 13 F5
Oldeani, *Tanzania* 82 C4
Oldenburg, *Niedersachsen,*
Germany 18 B4
Oldenburg,
Schleswig-Holstein,
Germany 18 A6
Oldenzaal, *Neths.* 16 D9
Oldham, *U.K.* 12 D5
Oldman →, *Canada* 100 D6
Olds, *Canada* 100 C6
Olean, *U.S.A.* 106 D6
Oléggio, *Italy* 32 C5
Oleiros, *Portugal* 30 F3
Olekma →, *Russia* 45 C13
Olekminsk, *Russia* 45 C13
Olema, *U.S.A.* 112 G4
Olen, *Belgium* 17 F5
Olenek, *Russia* 45 C12
Olenek →, *Russia* 45 B13
Olenino, *Russia* 40 C8
Oléron, I. d', *France* 26 C2
Oleśnica, *Poland* 20 D7
Olesno, *Poland* 20 E8
Olevsk, *Ukraine* 40 F5
Olga, *Russia* 45 E14
Olga, L., *Canada* 98 C4
Olga, Mt., *Australia* 89 E5
Ølgod, *Denmark* 11 J2
Olhão, *Portugal* 31 H3
Olib, *Croatia* 33 D11
Oliena, *Italy* 34 B2
Oliete, *Spain* 28 D4
Olifants →, *Africa* 85 C5
Olifantshoek, *S. Africa* . . . 84 D3
Ólimbos, *Greece* 39 P10
Ólimbos, Óros, *Greece* . . . 39 J5
Olímpia, *Brazil* 127 A6
Olinda, *Brazil* 122 C5
Olindiná, *Brazil* 122 D4
Olite, *Spain* 28 C3
Oliva, *Argentina* 126 C3
Oliva, *Spain* 29 G4
Oliva, Punta del, *Spain* . . . 30 B5
Oliva de la Frontera, *Spain* 31 G4
Olivares, *Spain* 28 F2
Olivehurst, *U.S.A.* 112 F5
Oliveira, *Brazil* 123 F3
Oliveira de Azemeis,
Portugal 30 E2
Oliveira dos Brejinhos,
Brazil 123 D3
Olivenza, *Spain* 31 G3
Oliver, *Canada* 100 D5
Oliver L., *Canada* 101 B8
Olivone, *Switz.* 23 C7
Olkhovka, *Russia* 43 B11
Olkusz, *Poland* 20 E9
Ollagüe, *Chile* 126 A2
Olloy, *Belgium* 17 H5
Olmedo, *Spain* 30 D6
Olmos, *Peru* 124 B2
Olney, *Ill., U.S.A.* 104 F1
Olney, *Tex., U.S.A.* 109 J5
Oloma, *Cameroon* 79 E7
Olomane →, *Canada* 99 B7
Olomouc, *Czech.* 20 F7
Olongapo, *Phil.* 55 D4
Oloron, Gave d' →,
France 26 E2
Oloron-Ste.-Marie, *France* 26 E3
Olot, *Spain* 28 C7
Olovo, *Bos.-H.* 21 L8
Olovyannaya, *Russia* 45 D12
Oloy →, *Russia* 45 C16
Olpe, *Germany* 18 D3
Olshanka, *Ukraine* 42 B4
Olshany, *Ukraine* 42 A6
Olst, *Neths.* 16 D8
Olsztyn, *Poland* 20 B10
Olt →, *Romania* 38 F7
Olten, *Switz.* 22 B5
Olteniţa, *Romania* 38 E9
Olton, *U.S.A.* 109 H3
Oltu, *Turkey* 67 C9
Olur, *Turkey* 67 C10
Olutanga, *Phil.* 55 H5
Olvega, *Spain* 28 D3
Olvera, *Spain* 31 J5
Olymbos, *Cyprus* 37 D12
Olympia, *Greece* 39 M4
Olympia, *U.S.A.* 112 D4
Olympic Mts., *U.S.A.* 112 C3
Olympic Nat. Park, *U.S.A.* 112 C3
Olympus, *Cyprus* 37 E11
Olympus, Mt. = Ólimbos,
Óros, *Greece* 39 J5
Olympus, Mt., *U.S.A.* 112 C3
Olyphant, *U.S.A.* 107 E9
Om →, *Russia* 44 D8
Om Hajer, *Eritrea* 77 E4
Om Koi, *Thailand* 58 D2
Ōma, *Japan* 48 D10
Ōmachi, *Japan* 49 F8
Omae-Zaki, *Japan* 49 G9
Ōmagari, *Japan* 48 E10
Omagh, *U.K.* 15 B4
Omagh □, *U.K.* 15 B4
Omaha, *U.S.A.* 108 E7
Omak, *U.S.A.* 110 B4
Omalos, *Greece* 37 D5
Oman ■, *Asia* 68 C6
Oman, G. of, *Asia* 65 E8
Omaruru, *Namibia* 84 C2
Omaruru →, *Namibia* 84 C1
Omate, *Peru* 124 D3
Ombai, Selat, *Indonesia* . . 57 F6
Omboué, *Gabon* 80 E1
Ombrone →, *Italy* 32 F8
Omdurmân, *Sudan* 77 D3
Omegna, *Italy* 32 C5
Omeonga, *Zaïre* 82 C1
Ometepe, I. de, *Nic.* 116 D2
Ometepec, *Mexico* 115 D5
Ominato, *Japan* 48 D10
Omineca →, *Canada* 100 B4
Omiš, *Croatia* 33 E13
Omišalj, *Croatia* 33 C11
Omitara, *Namibia* 84 C2
Ōmiya, *Japan* 49 G9
Omme Å →, *Denmark* . . . 11 J2
Ommen, *Neths.* 16 C8
Ömnögovĭ □, *Mongolia* . . 50 C3
Omo →, *Ethiopia* 77 F4
Omodhos, *Cyprus* 37 E11
Omolon →, *Russia* 45 C16
Omono-Gawa →, *Japan* . 48 E10
Omsk, *Russia* 44 D8
Omsukchan, *Russia* 45 C16
Ōmu, *Japan* 48 B11
Omul, Vf., *Romania* 38 D8
Ōmura, *Japan* 49 H4
Omuramba Omatako →,
Namibia 81 H4
Omurtag, *Bulgaria* 38 F9
Ōmuta, *Japan* 49 H5
Omutninsk, *Russia* 41 B18
On, *Belgium* 17 H6
Oña, *Spain* 28 C1
Onaga, *U.S.A.* 108 F6
Onalaska, *U.S.A.* 108 D9
Onamia, *U.S.A.* 108 B8
Onancock, *U.S.A.* 104 G8
Onang, *Indonesia* 57 E5
Onaping L., *Canada* 98 C3
Oñate, *Spain* 28 B2
Onavas, *Mexico* 114 B3
Onawa, *U.S.A.* 108 D6
Onaway, *U.S.A.* 104 C3
Oncócua, *Angola* 84 B1
Onda, *Spain* 28 F4
Ondaejin, *N. Korea* 51 D15
Ondangua, *Namibia* 84 B2
Ondárroa, *Spain* 28 B2
Ondas →, *Brazil* 123 D3
Ondava →, *Slovak Rep.* . 20 G11
Onderdijk, *Neths.* 16 C6
Ondjiva, *Angola* 84 B2
Ondo, *Nigeria* 79 D5
Ondo □, *Nigeria* 79 D6
Öndörhaan, *Mongolia* 54 B6
Öndörshil, *Mongolia* 50 B5
Öndverðarnes, *Iceland* 8 D1
Onega, *Russia* 44 C4
Onega →, *Russia* 6 C13
Onega, G. of =
Onezhskaya Guba,
Russia 44 C4
Onega, L. = Onezhskoye
Ozero, *Russia* 44 C4
Onehunga, *N.Z.* 87 G5
Oneida, *U.S.A.* 107 C9
Oneida L., *U.S.A.* 107 C9
O'Neill, *U.S.A.* 108 D5
Onekotan, Ostrov, *Russia* 45 E16
Onema, *Zaïre* 82 C1
Oneonta, *Ala., U.S.A.* 105 J2
Oneonta, *N.Y., U.S.A.* . . . 107 D9
Onezhskaya Guba, *Russia* 44 C4
Onezhskoye Ozero, *Russia* 44 C4
Ongarue, *N.Z.* 87 H5
Ongerup, *Australia* 89 F2
Ongjin, *N. Korea* 51 F13
Ongkharak, *Thailand* 58 E3
Ongniud Qi, *China* 51 C10
Ongoka, *Zaïre* 82 C2
Ongole, *India* 60 M12
Ongon, *Mongolia* 50 B7
Onguren, *Russia* 45 D11
Onhaye, *Belgium* 17 H5
Oni, *Georgia* 43 E10
Onida, *U.S.A.* 108 C4
Onilahy →, *Madag.* 85 C7
Onitsha, *Nigeria* 79 D6
Onoda, *Japan* 49 G5
Onpyŏng-ni, *S. Korea* 51 H14
Ons, Is. d', *Spain* 30 C2
Onsala, *Sweden* 11 G6
Onslow, *Australia* 88 D2
Onslow B., *U.S.A.* 105 H7
Onstwedde, *Neths.* 16 B10
Ontake-San, *Japan* 49 G8
Ontaneda, *Spain* 30 B7
Ontario, *Calif., U.S.A.* . . . 113 L9
Ontario, *Oreg., U.S.A.* . . . 110 D5
Ontario □, *Canada* 98 B2
Ontario, L., *U.S.A.* 98 D4
Onteniente, *Spain* 29 G4
Ontonagon, *U.S.A.* 108 B10
Ontur, *Spain* 29 G3
Onyx, *U.S.A.* 113 K8
Oodnadatta, *Australia* 91 D2
Ooldea, *Australia* 89 F5
Ooltgensplaat, *Neths.* 17 E4
Oombulgurri, *Australia* . . . 88 C4
Oona River, *Canada* 100 C2
Oordegem, *Belgium* 17 G3
Oorindi, *Australia* 90 C3
Oost-Vlaanderen □,
Belgium 17 F3
Oost-Vlieland, *Neths.* 16 B6
Oostakker, *Belgium* 17 F3
Oostburg, *Neths.* 17 F3
Oostduinkerke, *Belgium* . . 17 F1
Oostelijk-Flevoland, *Neths.* 16 C7
Oostende, *Belgium* 17 F1
Oosterbeek, *Neths.* 16 E7
Oosterdijk, *Neths.* 16 C6
Oosterend, *Friesland,*
Neths. 16 B6
Oosterend, *Noord-Holland,*
Neths. 16 B5
Oosterhout,
Noord-Brabant, Neths. . 17 E7
Oosterhout,
Noord-Brabant, Neths. . 17 E5
Oosterschelde, *Neths.* 17 E4
Oosterwolde, *Neths.* 16 B8
Oosterzele, *Belgium* 17 G3
Oostkamp, *Belgium* 17 F2
Oostmalle, *Belgium* 17 F5
Oostrozebekke, *Belgium* . . 17 G2
Oostvleteven, *Belgium* . . . 17 G1
Oostvoorne, *Neths.* 16 E4
Oostzaan, *Neths.* 16 D5
Ootacamund, *India* 60 P10
Ootmarsum, *Neths.* 16 D9
Ootsa L., *Canada* 100 C3
Opala, *Russia* 45 D16
Opala, *Zaïre* 82 C1
Opanake, *Sri Lanka* 60 R12
Opasatika, *Canada* 98 C3
Opasquia, *Canada* 101 C10
Opatija, *Croatia* 33 C11
Opava, *Czech.* 20 F7
Opeinde, *Neths.* 16 B8
Opelousas, *U.S.A.* 109 K8
Opémisca, L., *Canada* 98 C5
Opglabbeek, *Belgium* 17 F7
Opheim, *U.S.A.* 110 B10
Ophthalmia Ra., *Australia* 88 D2
Opi, *Nigeria* 79 D6
Opinaca →, *Canada* 98 B4
Opinaca L., *Canada* 98 B4
Opiskotish, L., *Canada* . . . 99 B6
Oploo, *Neths.* 17 E7
Opmeer, *Neths.* 16 C5
Opobo, *Nigeria* 79 E6
Opochka, *Russia* 40 C6
Opoczno, *Poland* 20 D10
Opol, *Phil.* 55 G6
Opole, *Poland* 20 E7
Oporto = Porto, *Portugal* 30 D2
Opotiki, *N.Z.* 87 H6
Opp, *U.S.A.* 105 K2
Oppenheim, *Germany* 19 F4
Opperdoes, *Neths.* 16 C6
Óppido Mamertina, *Italy* . 35 D8
Oppland fylke □, *Norway* 10 C3
Oppstad, *Norway* 10 D5
Oprtalj, *Croatia* 33 C10
Opua, *N.Z.* 87 F5
Opunake, *N.Z.* 87 H4
Opuzen, *Croatia* 21 M7
Ora, *Cyprus* 37 E12
Ora, *Italy* 33 B8
Ora Banda, *Australia* 89 F3
Oracle, *U.S.A.* 111 K8
Oradea, *Romania* 38 B4
Öræfajökull, *Iceland* 8 D5
Orahovac, *Serbia* 21 N10
Orai, *India* 63 G8
Oraison, *France* 27 E9
Oral = Ural →,
Kazakhstan 43 C14
Oral = Uralsk, *Kazakhstan* 44 D6
Oran, *Algeria* 75 A4
Oran, *Argentina* 126 A3

Orange = Oranje →, S. Africa 84 D2
Orange, Australia 91 E4
Orange, France 27 D8
Orange, Calif., U.S.A. 113 M9
Orange, Mass., U.S.A. 107 D12
Orange, Tex., U.S.A. 109 K8
Orange, Va., U.S.A. 104 F6
Orange, C., Brazil 121 C7
Orange Cove, U.S.A. 112 J7
Orange Free State □, S. Africa 84 D4
Orange Grove, U.S.A. 109 M6
Orange Walk, Belize 115 D7
Orangeburg, U.S.A. 105 J5
Orangeville, Canada 98 D3
Orani, Phil. 55 D4
Oranienburg, Germany 18 C9
Oranje →, S. Africa 84 D2
Oranje Vrystaat = Orange Free State □, S. Africa 84 D4
Oranjemund, Namibia 84 D2
Oranjerivier, S. Africa 84 D3
Oras, Phil. 55 E6
Orăştie, Romania 38 D6
Oraşul Stalin = Braşov, Romania 38 D8
Orava →, Slovakia 20 F9
Oravita, Romania 38 D4
Orb →, France 26 E7
Orba →, Italy 32 D5
Ørbæk, Denmark 11 J4
Orbe, Switz. 22 C3
Orbec, France 24 C7
Orbetello, Italy 33 F8
Órbigo →, Spain 30 C5
Orbost, Australia 91 F4
Orce, Spain 29 H2
Orce →, Spain 29 H2
Orchies, France 25 B10
Orchila, I., Venezuela 120 A4
Orco →, Italy 32 C4
Orcopampa, Peru 124 D3
Orcutt, U.S.A. 113 L6
Ord →, Australia 88 C4
Ord, Mt., Australia 88 C4
Ordenes, Spain 30 B2
Orderville, U.S.A. 111 H7
Ording, Germany 18 A4
Ordos = Mu Us Shamo, Nei Mongol Zizhiqu, China 50 E5
Ordos = Mu Us Shamo, Nei Mongol Zizhiqu, China 50 E5
Ordu, Turkey 67 C7
Ordu □, Turkey 67 C7
Orduña, Álava, Spain 28 C7
Orduña, Granada, Spain 29 H1
Ordway, U.S.A. 108 F3
Ordzhonikidze = Vladikavkaz, Russia 43 E11
Ordzhonikidze, Ukraine 42 C6
Ore, Zaïre 82 B2
Ore Mts. = Erzgebirge, Germany 18 E9
Orealla, Guyana 121 B6
Orebić, Croatia 21 M7
Örebro, Sweden 9 G13
Örebro län □, Sweden 9 G13
Oregon, U.S.A. 108 D10
Oregon □, U.S.A. 110 E4
Oregon City, U.S.A. 112 E4
Orekhov, Ukraine 42 C6
Orekhovo-Zuyevo, Russia 41 D11
Orel, Russia 41 E10
Orel →, Ukraine 42 B6
Orellana, Canal de, Spain 31 F5
Orellana, Pantano de, Spain 31 F5
Orellana la Vieja, Spain 31 F5
Orem, U.S.A. 110 F8
Ören, Turkey 66 E2
Orenburg, Russia 44 D6
Orense, Spain 30 C3
Orense □, Spain 30 C3
Orepuki, N.Z. 87 M1
Orestiás, Greece 39 H9
Øresund, Europe 11 J6
Orford Ness, U.K. 13 E9
Orgañá, Spain 28 C6
Organos, Pta. de los, Canary Is. 36 F2
Orgaz, Spain 31 F7
Orgeyev, Moldavia 42 C3
Orgon, France 27 E9
Orhaneli, Turkey 66 D3
Orhangazi, Turkey 66 C13
Orhon Gol →, Mongolia 54 A5
Ória, Italy 35 B10
Oriku, Albania 39 J2
Orinduik, Guyana 121 C5
Orinoco →, Venezuela 121 B5
Orissa □, India 61 K14
Oristano, Italy 34 C1

Oristano, G. di, Italy 34 C1
Orituco →, Venezuela 120 B5
Orizaba, Mexico 115 D5
Orizona, Brazil 123 E2
Orjen, Bos.-H. 21 N8
Orjiva, Spain 29 J1
Orkanger, Norway 10 A3
Örkelljunga, Sweden 11 H7
Örkény, Hungary 21 H9
Orkla →, Norway 10 A3
Orkney, S. Africa 84 D4
Orkney, U.K. 14 C6
Orkney Is., U.K. 14 C6
Orland, U.S.A. 112 F4
Orlando, U.S.A. 105 L5
Orlando, C. d', Italy 35 D7
Orléanais, France 25 E9
Orléans, France 25 E8
Orleans, U.S.A. 107 B12
Orléans, I. d', Canada 99 C5
Orlice →, Czech. 20 E6
Orlov, Slovakia 20 F10
Orlov Gay, Russia 41 F16
Ormara, Pakistan 60 G4
Ormea, Italy 32 D4
Ormília, Greece 39 J6
Ormoc, Phil. 55 F6
Ormond, N.Z. 87 H6
Ormond Beach, U.S.A. 105 L5
Ormož, Slovenia 33 B13
Ormstown, Canada 107 A11
Ornans, France 25 E13
Orne □, France 24 D7
Orne →, France 24 C6
Ørnhøj, Denmark 11 H2
Ørnö, Sweden 10 E12
Örnsköldsvik, Sweden 10 A12
Oro, N. Korea 51 D14
Oro →, Mexico 114 B3
Oro Grande, U.S.A. 113 L9
Orobie, Alpi, Italy 32 B6
Orocué, Colombia 120 C3
Orodo, Nigeria 79 D6
Orogrande, U.S.A. 111 K10
Orol, Spain 30 B3
Oromocto, Canada 99 C6
Oron, Nigeria 79 E6
Oron, Switz. 22 C3
Orono, Canada 106 C6
Oropesa, Spain 30 F5
Oroquieta, Phil. 55 G5
Orós, Brazil 122 C4
Orosei, G. di, Italy 34 B2
Orosháza, Hungary 21 J10
Qrotukan, Russia 45 C16
Oroville, Calif., U.S.A. 112 F5
Oroville, Wash., U.S.A. 110 B4
Oroville, L., U.S.A. 112 F5
Orroroo, Australia 91 E2
Orrville, U.S.A. 106 F3
Orsara di Púglia, Italy 35 A8
Orsha, Belorussia 40 D7
Orsières, Switz. 22 D4
Orsk, Russia 44 D6
Ørslev, Denmark 11 J5
Orsogna, Italy 33 F11
Orşova, Romania 38 E5
Ørsted, Denmark 11 H4
Orta, L. d', Italy 32 C5
Orta Nova, Italy 35 A8
Ortaca, Turkey 66 E3
Ortaköy, Çorum, Turkey 66 C6
Ortaköy, Niğde, Turkey 66 D6
Orte, Italy 33 F9
Ortegal, C., Spain 30 B3
Orteguaza →, Colombia 120 C2
Orthez, France 26 E3
Ortho, Belgium 17 H7
Ortigueira, Spain 30 B3
Orting, U.S.A. 112 C4
Ortles, Italy 32 B7
Ortón →, Bolivia 124 C4
Ortona, Italy 33 F11
Orūmīyeh, Iran 64 B5
Orūmīyeh, Daryācheh-ye, Iran 64 B5
Orune, Italy 34 B2
Oruro, Bolivia 124 D4
Oruro □, Bolivia 124 D4
Orust, Sweden 11 F5
Oruzgān □, Afghan. 60 C5
Orvault, France 24 E5
Orvieto, Italy 33 F9
Orwell, U.S.A. 106 E4
Orwell →, U.K. 13 E9
Oryakhovo, Bulgaria 38 F6
Orzinuovi, Italy 32 C6
Orzysz, Poland 20 B11
Osa, Pen. de, Costa Rica 116 E3
Osage, Iowa, U.S.A. 108 D8
Osage, Wyo., U.S.A. 108 D2
Osage →, U.S.A. 108 F9
Osage City, U.S.A. 108 F7
Ōsaka, Japan 49 G7
Osan, S. Korea 51 F14
Osawatomie, U.S.A. 108 F7
Osborne, U.S.A. 108 F5
Osceola, Ark., U.S.A. 109 H10
Osceola, Iowa, U.S.A. 108 E8
Oschatz, Germany 18 D9
Oschersleben, Germany 18 C7
Óschiri, Italy 34 B2
Oscoda, U.S.A. 106 B1
Ösel = Saaremaa, Estonia 40 B3
Osěry, Russia 41 D11

Osh, Kirghizia 44 E8
Oshawa, Canada 98 D4
Oshkosh, Nebr., U.S.A. 108 E3
Oshkosh, Wis., U.S.A. 108 C10
Oshmyany, Belorussia 40 D4
Oshnovīyeh, Iran 64 B5
Oshogbo, Nigeria 79 D5
Oshtorīnān, Iran 65 C6
Oshwe, Zaïre 80 E3
Osijek, Croatia 21 K8
Ósilo, Italy 34 B1
Osimo, Italy 33 E10
Osintorf, Belorussia 40 D7
Osipenko = Berdyansk, Ukraine 42 C7
Osipovichi, Belorussia 40 E6
Osizweni, S. Africa 85 D5
Oskaloosa, U.S.A. 108 E8
Oskarshamn, Sweden 9 H14
Oskélanéo, Canada 98 C4
Öskemen = Ust-Kamenogorsk, Kazakhstan 44 E9
Oskol →, Ukraine 41 G10
Oslo, Norway 10 E4
Oslob, Phil. 55 G5
Oslofjorden, Norway 10 E4
Osmanabad, India 60 K10
Osmancık, Turkey 42 F6
Osmaniye, Turkey 66 E7
Ösmo, Sweden 10 F11
Osnabrück, Germany 18 C4
Osor, Italy 33 D11
Osório, Brazil 127 B5
Osorno, Chile 128 B2
Osorno, Spain 30 C6
Osorno □, Chile 128 B2
Osorno, Vol., Chile 128 B2
Osoyoos, Canada 100 D5
Ospika →, Canada 100 B4
Osprey Reef, Australia 90 A4
Oss, Neths. 16 E7
Ossa, Mt., Australia 90 G4
Óssa, Oros, Greece 39 K5
Ossa de Montiel, Spain 29 G2
Ossabaw I., U.S.A. 105 K5
Osse →, France 26 D4
Ossendrecht, Neths. 17 F4
Ossining, U.S.A. 107 E11
Ossipee, U.S.A. 107 C13
Ossokmanuan L., Canada 99 B7
Ossora, Russia 45 D17
Ostashkov, Russia 40 C8
Oste →, Germany 18 B5
Ostend = Oostende, Belgium 17 F1
Oster, Ukraine 40 F7
Osterburg, Germany 18 C7
Osterburken, Germany 19 F5
Österdalälven →, Sweden 9 F12
Östergötlands län □, Sweden 11 F9
Osterholz-Scharmbeck, Germany 18 B4
Østerild, Denmark 11 G2
Ostermundigen, Switz. 22 C4
Östersund, Sweden 10 A8
Østfold fylke □, Norway 10 E5
Ostfriesische Inseln, Germany 18 B3
Ostfriesland, Germany 18 B3
Óstia, Lido di, Italy 34 A5
Ostíglia, Italy 33 C8
Ostra, Italy 33 E10
Ostrava, Czech. 20 F8
Ostróda, Poland 20 B9
Ostróg, Ukraine 40 F5
Ostrogozhsk, Russia 41 F11
Ostrołęka, Poland 20 B11
Ostrov, Bulgaria 38 F7
Ostrov, Romania 38 E10
Ostrov, Russia 40 C6
Ostrów Mazowiecka, Poland 20 C11
Ostrów Wielkopolski, Poland 20 D7
Ostrowiec-Świętokrzyski, Poland 20 E11
Ostrzeszów, Poland 20 D7
Ostseebad-Kühlungsborn, Germany 18 A7
Osttirol □, Austria 19 J8
Ostuni, Italy 35 B10
Osum →, Bulgaria 38 F7
Osumi →, Albania 39 J3
Ōsumi-Kaikyō, Japan 49 J5
Ōsumi-Shotō, Japan 49 J5
Osun □, Nigeria 79 D5
Osuna, Spain 31 H5
Oswego, U.S.A. 107 C8
Oswestry, U.K. 12 E4
Oświęcim, Poland 20 E9
Otago □, N.Z. 87 L2
Otago Harbour, N.Z. 87 L3
Ōtake, Japan 49 G6
Otaru, Japan 48 C10
Otaru-Wan = Ishikari-Wan, Japan 48 C10
Otava →, Czech. 20 F4
Otavalo, Ecuador 120 C2
Otavi, Namibia 84 B2
Otchinjau, Angola 84 B1

Otelec, Romania 38 D3
Otero de Rey, Spain 30 B3
Othello, U.S.A. 110 C4
Othonoí, Greece 39 K2
Óthris, Óros, Greece 39 K5
Otira Gorge, N.Z. 87 K3
Otis, U.S.A. 108 E3
Otjiwarongo, Namibia 84 C2
Otočac, Croatia 33 D12
Otoineppu, Japan 48 B11
Otorohanga, N.Z. 87 H5
Otoskwin →, Canada 98 B2
Otosquen, Canada 101 C8
Otranto, Italy 35 B11
Otranto, C. d', Italy 35 B11
Otranto, Str. of, Italy 35 B11
Otse, S. Africa 84 D4
Ōtsu, Japan 49 G7
Ōtsuki, Japan 49 G9
Ottawa = Outaouais →, Canada 98 C5
Ottawa, Canada 98 C4
Ottawa, Ill., U.S.A. 108 E10
Ottawa, Kans., U.S.A. 108 F7
Ottawa Is., Canada 97 C11
Ottélé, Cameroon 79 E7
Otter L., Canada 101 B8
Otter Rapids, Ont., Canada 98 B3
Otter Rapids, Sask., Canada 101 B8
Otterndorf, Germany 18 B4
Otterup, Denmark 11 J4
Otterville, Canada 106 D4
Ottignies, Belgium 17 G5
Otto Beit Bridge, Zimbabwe 83 F2
Ottosdal, S. Africa 84 D4
Ottoshoop, S. Africa 84 D4
Ottsjön, Sweden 10 A7
Ottumwa, U.S.A. 108 E8
Otu, Nigeria 79 D5
Otukpa, Nigeria 79 D6
Oturkpo, Nigeria 79 D6
Otway, B., Chile 128 D2
Otway, C., Australia 91 F3
Otwock, Poland 20 C11
Ötz, Austria 19 H6
Ötz →, Austria 19 H6
Ötztaler Alpen, Austria 19 J7
Ou →, Laos 58 B4
Ou Neua, Laos 58 A3
Ou-Sammyaku, Japan 48 E10
Ouachita →, U.S.A. 109 K9
Ouachita, L., U.S.A. 109 H8
Ouachita Mts., U.S.A. 109 H7
Ouadâne, Mauritania 74 D2
Ouadda, C.A.R. 73 G9
Ouagadougou, Burkina Faso 79 C4
Ouahigouya, Burkina Faso 78 C4
Ouahila, Algeria 74 C3
Ouahran = Oran, Algeria 75 A4
Oualâta, Mauritania 78 B3
Ouallene, Algeria 75 D5
Ouanda Djallé, C.A.R. 73 G9
Ouango, C.A.R. 80 D4
Ouarâne, Mauritania 74 D2
Ouargla, Algeria 75 B6
Ouarkziz, Djebel, Algeria 74 C3
Ouarzazate, Morocco 74 B3
Ouatagouna, Mali 79 B5
Oubangi →, Zaïre 80 E3
Oubarakai, O. →, Algeria 75 C6
Ouche →, France 25 E12
Oud-Beijerland, Neths. 16 E4
Oud-Gastel, Neths. 17 E4
Oud Turnhout, Belgium 17 F6
Ouddorp, Neths. 16 E3
Oude-Pekela, Neths. 16 B10
Oude Rijn →, Neths. 16 D5
Oudega, Neths. 16 B8
Oudenaarde, Belgium 17 G3
Oudenbosch, Neths. 17 E4
Oudenburg, Belgium 17 F2
Ouderkerk, Utrecht, Neths. 16 D5
Ouderkerk, Zuid-Holland, Neths. 16 E5
Oudeschild, Neths. 16 B5
Oudewater, Neths. 16 D5
Oudkarspel, Neths. 16 C5
Oudon, France 24 E5
Oudtshoorn, S. Africa 84 E3
Oued Zem, Morocco 74 B3
Ouellé, Ivory C. 78 D4
Ouenza, Algeria 75 A6
Ouessa, Burkina Faso 78 C4
Ouessant, Î. d', France 24 D1
Ouesso, Congo 80 D3
Ouest, Pte., Canada 99 C7
Ouezzane, Morocco 74 B3
Ouffet, Belgium 17 H6
Ouidah, Benin 79 D5
Ouistreham, France 24 C6
Oujda, Morocco 75 B4
Oujeft, Mauritania 74 D2
Ould Yenjé, Mauritania 78 B2
Ouled Djellal, Algeria 75 B6
Ouled Naïl, Mts. des, Algeria 75 B5
Oulmès, Morocco 74 B3
Oulu, Finland 8 D18
Oulu = Oulun lääni □, Finland 8 D19
Oulujärvi, Finland 8 D19
Oulujoki →, Finland 8 D18

Oulujoki →, Finland 8 D18
Oulun lääni □, Finland 8 D19
Oulx, Italy 32 C3
Oum Chalouba, Chad 73 E9
Oum-el-Bouaghi, Algeria 75 A6
Oum el Ksi, Algeria 74 C3
Oum-er-Rbia, O. →, Morocco 74 B3
Oumè, Ivory C. 78 D3
Ounane, Dj., Algeria 75 C6
Ounguati, Namibia 84 C2
Ounianga-Kébir, Chad 73 E9
Ounianga Sérir, Chad 73 E9
Our →, Lux. 17 J8
Ouray, U.S.A. 111 G10
Ourcq →, France 25 C10
Oureg, Oued el →, Algeria 75 B5
Ourém, Brazil 122 B2
Ouricuri, Brazil 122 C3
Ourinhos, Brazil 127 A6
Ourique, Portugal 31 H2
Ouro Fino, Brazil 127 A6
Ouro Prêto, Brazil 123 F3
Ouro Sogui, Senegal 78 B2
Oursi, Burkina Faso 79 C4
Ourthe →, Belgium 17 H7
Ouse, Australia 90 G4
Ouse →, E. Susx., U.K. 13 G8
Ouse →, N. Yorks., U.K. 12 C8
Oust, France 26 F5
Oust →, France 24 E4
Outaouais →, Canada 98 C5
Outardes →, Canada 99 C6
Outat Oulad el Haj, Morocco 75 B4
Outer Hebrides, U.K. 14 D1
Outer I., Canada 99 B8
Outes, Spain 30 C2
Outjo, Namibia 84 C2
Outlook, Canada 101 C7
Outlook, U.S.A. 108 A2
Outreau, France 25 B8
Ouvèze →, France 27 E8
Ouyen, Australia 91 F3
Ouzouer-le-Marché, France 25 E8
Ovada, Italy 32 D5
Ovalau, Fiji 87 C8
Ovalle, Chile 126 C1
Ovar, Portugal 30 E2
Ovejas, Colombia 120 B2
Overdinkel, Neths. 16 D10
Overflakkee, Neths. 16 E4
Overijse, Belgium 17 G5
Overijssel □, Neths. 16 D9
Overijsselsch Kanaal →, Neths. 16 C8
Overpelt, Belgium 17 F6
Overton, U.S.A. 113 J12
Övertorneå, Sweden 8 C17
Ovid, U.S.A. 108 E3
Ovidiopol, Ukraine 42 C4
Oviedo, Spain 30 B5
Oviedo □, Spain 30 B5
Oviken, Sweden 10 A8
Oviksfjällen, Sweden 10 B7
Övör Hangay □, Mongolia 50 B2
Ovoro, Nigeria 79 D6
Ovruch, Ukraine 40 F6
Owaka, N.Z. 87 M2
Owase, Japan 49 G8
Owatonna, U.S.A. 108 C8
Owbeh, Afghan. 60 B3
Owego, U.S.A. 107 D8
Owen Falls, Uganda 82 B3
Owen Sound, Canada 98 D3
Owendo, Gabon 80 D1
Owens →, U.S.A. 112 J9
Owens L., U.S.A. 113 J9
Owensboro, U.S.A. 104 G2
Owensville, U.S.A. 108 F9
Owerri, Nigeria 79 D6
Owl →, Canada 101 B10
Owo, Nigeria 79 D6
Owosso, U.S.A. 104 D3
Owyhee, U.S.A. 110 F5
Owyhee →, U.S.A. 110 E5
Owyhee, L., U.S.A. 110 E5
Ox Mts., Ireland 15 B3
Oxapampa, Peru 124 C2
Oxelösund, Sweden 11 F11
Oxford, N.Z. 87 K4
Oxford, U.K. 13 F6
Oxford, Miss., U.S.A. 109 H10
Oxford, N.C., U.S.A. 105 G6
Oxford, Ohio, U.S.A. 104 F3
Oxford L., Canada 101 C9
Oxfordshire □, U.K. 13 F6
Oxley, Australia 91 E3
Oxnard, U.S.A. 113 L7
Oxus = Amudarya →, Uzbekistan 44 E6
Oya, Malaysia 56 D4
Oyama, Japan 49 F9
Oyapock →, Fr. Guiana 121 C7
Oyem, Gabon 80 D2
Oyen, Canada 101 C6
Øyeren, Norway 10 E5
Oykel →, U.K. 14 D4
Oymyakon, Russia 45 C15
Oyo, Nigeria 79 D5
Oyo □, Nigeria 79 D5
Oyón, Peru 124 C2
Oyonnax, France 27 B9
Oyster Bay, U.S.A. 107 F11

Parkersburg

Ōyūbari, *Japan* 48 C11
Özalp, *Turkey* 67 D10
Ozamiz, *Phil.* 55 G5
Ozark, *Ala., U.S.A.* 105 K3
Ozark, *Ark., U.S.A.* 109 H8
Ozark, *Mo., U.S.A.* 109 G8
Ozark Plateau, *U.S.A.* 109 G9
Ozarks, L. of the, *U.S.A.* 108 F8
Ózd, *Hungary* 21 G10
Ozette L., *U.S.A.* 112 B2
Ozieri, *Italy* 34 B2
Ozona, *U.S.A.* 109 K4
Ozorków, *Poland* 20 D9
Ozuluama, *Mexico* 115 C5
Ozurgety, *Georgia* 43 F10

P

P.K. le Roux Dam, *S. Africa* 84 E3
Pa, *Burkina Faso* 78 C4
Pa-an, *Burma* 61 L20
Pa Mong Dam, *Thailand* 58 D4
Paal, *Belgium* 17 F6
Paamiut = Frederikshåb, *Greenland* 4 C5
Paar →, *Germany* 19 G6
Paarl, *S. Africa* 84 E2
Paatsi →, *Russia* 8 B20
Paauilo, *U.S.A.* 102 H17
Pab Hills, *Pakistan* 62 F2
Pabianice, *Poland* 20 D9
Pabna, *Bangla.* 61 G16
Pabo, *Uganda* 82 B3
Pacaás Novos, Serra dos, *Brazil* 125 C5
Pacaipampa, *Peru* 124 B2
Pacaja →, *Brazil* 122 B1
Pacajus, *Brazil* 122 B4
Pacaraima, Sierra, *Venezuela* 121 C5
Pacarán, *Peru* 124 C2
Pacaraos, *Peru* 124 C2
Pacasmayo, *Peru* 124 B2
Paceco, *Italy* 34 E5
Pachacamac, *Peru* 124 C2
Pachhar, *India* 62 G7
Pachino, *Italy* 35 F8
Pachitea →, *Peru* 124 B3
Pachiza, *Peru* 124 B2
Pacho, *Colombia* 120 B3
Pachpadra, *India* 60 G8
Pachuca, *Mexico* 115 C5
Pacific, *Canada* 100 C3
Pacific-Antarctic Ridge, *Pac. Oc.* 93 M16
Pacific Grove, *U.S.A.* 111 H3
Pacific Ocean, *Pac. Oc.* 93 G14
Pacifica, *U.S.A.* 112 H4
Pacitan, *Indonesia* 57 H14
Packwood, *U.S.A.* 112 D5
Pacuí →, *Brazil* 123 E2
Padaido, Kepulauan, *Indonesia* 57 E9
Padang, *Indonesia* 56 E2
Padangpanjang, *Indonesia* 56 E2
Padangsidempuan, *Indonesia* 56 D1
Padauari →, *Brazil* 121 D5
Padborg, *Denmark* 11 K3
Padcaya, *Bolivia* 125 E5
Paddockwood, *Canada* 101 C7
Paderborn, *Germany* 18 D4
Padilla, *Bolivia* 125 D5
Padloping Island, *Canada* 97 B13
Pádova, *Italy* 33 C8
Padra, *India* 62 H5
Padrauna, *India* 63 F10
Padre I., *U.S.A.* 109 M6
Padro, Mte., *France* 27 F12
Padrón, *Spain* 30 C2
Padstow, *U.K.* 13 G3
Padua = Pádova, *Italy* 33 C8
Paducah, *Ky., U.S.A.* 104 G1
Paducah, *Tex., U.S.A.* 109 H4
Padul, *Spain* 31 H7
Padula, *Italy* 35 B8
Paengnyong-do, *S. Korea* 51 F13
Paeroa, *N.Z.* 87 G5
Paesana, *Italy* 32 D4
Pafúri, *Mozam.* 85 C5
Pag, *Croatia* 33 D11
Paga, *Ghana* 79 C4
Pagadian, *Phil.* 55 H5
Pagai Selatan, P., *Indonesia* 56 E2
Pagai Utara, *Indonesia* 56 E2
Pagalu = Annobón, *Atl. Oc.* 71 G4
Pagastikós Kólpos, *Greece* 39 K6
Pagatan, *Indonesia* 56 E5
Page, *Ariz., U.S.A.* 111 H8
Page, *N. Dak., U.S.A.* 108 B6
Paglieta, *Italy* 33 F11
Pagny-sur-Moselle, *France* 25 D13
Pago Pago, *Amer. Samoa* 87 B13
Pagosa Springs, *U.S.A.* 111 H10
Pagwa River, *Canada* 98 B2
Pahala, *U.S.A.* 102 J17
Pahang →, *Malaysia* 59 L4
Pahiatua, *N.Z.* 87 J5
Pahokee, *U.S.A.* 105 M5
Pahrump, *U.S.A.* 113 J11
Pahute Mesa, *U.S.A.* 112 H10
Pai, *Thailand* 58 C2
Paia, *U.S.A.* 102 H16
Paicines, *U.S.A.* 112 J5
Paide, *Estonia* 40 B4
Paignton, *U.K.* 13 G4
Paiján, *Peru* 124 B2
Päijänne, *Finland* 9 F18
Paimbœuf, *France* 24 E4
Paimpol, *France* 24 D3
Painan, *Indonesia* 56 E2
Painesville, *U.S.A.* 106 E3
Paint Hills = Nouveau Comptoir, *Canada* 98 B4
Paint L., *Canada* 101 B9
Paint Rock, *U.S.A.* 109 K5
Painted Desert, *U.S.A.* 111 J8
Paintsville, *U.S.A.* 104 G4
País Vasco □, *Spain* 28 C2
Paisley, *Canada* 106 B3
Paisley, *U.K.* 14 F4
Paisley, *U.S.A.* 110 E3
Paita, *Peru* 124 B1
Paiva →, *Portugal* 30 D2
Paizhou, *China* 53 B9
Pajares, *Spain* 30 B5
Pajares, Puerto de, *Spain* 30 C5
Pak Lay, *Laos* 58 C3
Pak Phanang, *Thailand* 59 H3
Pak Sane, *Laos* 58 C4
Pak Song, *Laos* 58 E6
Pak Suong, *Laos* 58 C4
Pakaraima Mts., *Guyana* 121 B5
Pákhnes, *Greece* 37 D6
Pakistan ■, *Asia* 62 E3
Pakistan, East = Bangladesh ■, *Asia* 61 H17
Pakkading, *Laos* 58 C4
Pakokku, *Burma* 61 J19
Pakpattan, *Pakistan* 62 D5
Pakrac, *Croatia* 21 K7
Paks, *Hungary* 21 J8
Pakse, *Laos* 58 E5
Paktīā □, *Afghan.* 60 C6
Pakwach, *Uganda* 82 B3
Pala, *Chad* 73 G8
Pala, *U.S.A.* 113 M9
Pala, *Zaïre* 82 D2
Palabek, *Uganda* 82 B3
Palacios, *U.S.A.* 109 L6
Palafrugell, *Spain* 28 D8
Palagiano, *Italy* 35 B10
Palagonía, *Italy* 35 E7
Palagruža, *Croatia* 33 F13
Palaiókastron, *Greece* 37 D8
Palaiokhóra, *Greece* 37 D5
Palam, *India* 60 K10
Palamás, *Greece* 39 K5
Palamós, *Spain* 28 D8
Palampur, *India* 62 C7
Palana, *Australia* 90 F4
Palana, *Russia* 45 D16
Palanan, *Phil.* 55 C5
Palanan Pt., *Phil.* 55 C5
Palandri, *Pakistan* 63 C5
Palangkaraya, *Indonesia* 56 E4
Palani Hills, *India* 60 P10
Palanpur, *India* 62 G5
Palapye, *Botswana* 84 C4
Palas, *Pakistan* 63 B5
Palatka, *Russia* 45 C16
Palatka, *U.S.A.* 105 L5
Palau = Belau ■, *Pac. Oc.* 92 G5
Palawan, *Phil.* 55 G3
Palayankottai, *India* 60 Q10
Palazzo, Pte., *France* 27 F12
Palazzo San Gervásio, *Italy* 35 B8
Palazzolo Acreide, *Italy* 35 E7
Palca, *Chile* 124 D4
Paldiski, *Estonia* 40 B4
Paleleh, *Indonesia* 57 D6
Palembang, *Indonesia* 56 E2
Palena →, *Chile* 128 B2
Palena, L., *Chile* 128 B2
Palencia, *Spain* 30 C6
Palencia □, *Spain* 30 C6
Paleokastrítsa, *Greece* 37 A3
Paleometokho, *Cyprus* 37 D12
Palermo, *Colombia* 120 C2
Palermo, *Italy* 34 D6
Palermo, *U.S.A.* 110 G3
Palestine, *Asia* 69 D4
Palestine, *U.S.A.* 109 K7
Palestrina, *Italy* 34 A5
Paletwa, *Burma* 61 J18
Palghat, *India* 60 P10
Palgrave, Mt., *Australia* 88 D2
Pali, *India* 62 G5
Palinuro, C., *Italy* 35 B8
Palisade, *U.S.A.* 108 E4
Paliseul, *Belgium* 17 J6
Palitana, *India* 62 J4
Palizada, *Mexico* 115 D6
Palizzi, *Italy* 35 E8
Palk Bay, *Asia* 60 Q11
Palk Strait, *Asia* 60 Q11
Palkānah, *Iraq* 64 C5
Palla Road = Dinokwe, *Botswana* 84 C4
Pallanza = Verbánia, *Italy* 32 C5
Pallasovka, *Russia* 41 F15
Pallisa, *Uganda* 82 B3
Pallu, *India* 62 E6
Palm Beach, *U.S.A.* 105 M6
Palm Desert, *U.S.A.* 113 M10
Palm Is., *Australia* 90 B4
Palm Springs, *U.S.A.* 113 M10
Palma, *Mozam.* 83 E5
Palma →, *Brazil* 123 D2
Palma, B. de, *Spain* 36 B9
Palma de Mallorca, *Spain* 36 B9
Palma del Río, *Spain* 31 H5
Palma di Montechiaro, *Italy* 34 E6
Palma Soriano, *Cuba* 116 B4
Palmanova, *Italy* 33 C10
Palmares, *Brazil* 122 C4
Palmarito, *Venezuela* 120 B3
Palmarola, *Italy* 34 B5
Palmas, *Brazil* 127 B5
Palmas, C., *Liberia* 78 E3
Pálmas, G. di, *Italy* 34 C1
Palmas de Monte Alto, *Brazil* 123 D3
Palmdale, *U.S.A.* 113 L8
Palmeira, *Brazil* 123 G2
Palmeira dos Índios, *Brazil* 122 C4
Palmeirais, *Brazil* 122 C3
Palmeiras →, *Brazil* 123 D2
Palmeirinhas, Pta. das, *Angola* 80 F2
Palmela, *Portugal* 31 G2
Palmelo, *Brazil* 123 E2
Palmer, *U.S.A.* 96 B5
Palmer →, *Australia* 90 B3
Palmer Arch., *Antarctica* 5 C17
Palmer Lake, *U.S.A.* 108 F2
Palmer Land, *Antarctica* 5 D18
Palmerston, *Canada* 106 C4
Palmerston, *N.Z.* 87 L3
Palmerston North, *N.Z.* 87 J5
Palmerton, *U.S.A.* 107 F9
Palmetto, *U.S.A.* 105 M4
Palmi, *Italy* 35 D8
Palmira, *Argentina* 126 C2
Palmira, *Colombia* 120 C2
Palmyra = Tudmur, *Syria* 64 C3
Palmyra, *Mo., U.S.A.* 108 F9
Palmyra, *N.Y., U.S.A.* 106 C7
Palmyra Is., *Pac. Oc.* 93 G11
Palo Alto, *U.S.A.* 111 H2
Palo del Colle, *Italy* 35 A9
Palo Verde, *U.S.A.* 113 M12
Palombara Sabina, *Italy* 33 F9
Palompon, *Phil.* 55 F6
Palopo, *Indonesia* 57 E6
Palos, C. de, *Spain* 29 H4
Palos Verdes, *U.S.A.* 113 M8
Palos Verdes, Pt., *U.S.A.* 113 M8
Palouse, *U.S.A.* 110 C5
Palpa, *Peru* 124 C2
Palparara, *Australia* 90 C3
Pålsboda, *Sweden* 10 E9
Palu, *Indonesia* 57 E5
Paluan, *Phil.* 57 B6
Palwal, *India* 62 E7
Pama, *Burkina Faso* 79 C5
Pamanukan, *Indonesia* 57 G12
Pamekasan, *Indonesia* 57 G15
Pamiers, *France* 26 E5
Pamirs, *Tajikistan* 44 F8
Pamlico →, *U.S.A.* 105 H7
Pamlico Sd., *U.S.A.* 105 H8
Pampa, *U.S.A.* 109 H4
Pampa de Agma, *Argentina* 128 B3
Pampa de las Salinas, *Argentina* 126 C2
Pampa Grande, *Bolivia* 125 D5
Pampa Hermosa, *Peru* 124 B2
Pampanua, *Indonesia* 57 E6
Pamparato, *Italy* 32 D4
Pampas, *Argentina* 126 D3
Pampas, *Peru* 124 C3
Pampas →, *Peru* 124 C3
Pamphylia, *Turkey* 66 E4
Pamplona, *Colombia* 120 B3
Pamplona, *Spain* 28 C3
Pampoenpoort, *S. Africa* 84 E3
Pamukkale, *Turkey* 66 E3
Pan Xian, *China* 52 E5
Pana, *U.S.A.* 108 F10
Panabo, *Phil.* 55 H6
Panaca, *U.S.A.* 111 H6
Panagyurishte, *Bulgaria* 38 G7
Panaitan, *Indonesia* 57 G11
Panaji, *India* 60 M8
Panamá, *Panama* 116 E4
Panama ■, *Cent. Amer.* 116 E4
Panamá, G. de, *Panama* 116 E4
Panama Canal, *Panama* 116 E4
Panama City, *U.S.A.* 105 K3
Panamint Range, *U.S.A.* 113 J9
Panamint Springs, *U.S.A.* 113 J9
Panão, *Peru* 124 B2
Panaon I., *Phil.* 55 F6
Panare, *Thailand* 59 J3
Panarea, *Italy* 35 D8
Panaro →, *Italy* 32 D8
Panarukan, *Indonesia* 57 G15
Panay, *Phil.* 55 F5
Panay, G., *Phil.* 57 B6
Pancake Range, *U.S.A.* 111 G6
Pančevo, *Serbia, Yug.* 21 L10
Pancorbo, Paso, *Spain* 28 C1
Pandan, *Antique, Phil.* 55 F5
Pandan, *Catanduanes, Phil.* 55 D6
Pandegelang, *Indonesia* 57 G12
Pandharpur, *India* 60 L9
Pandilla, *Spain* 28 D1
Pando, *Uruguay* 127 C4
Pando □, *Bolivia* 124 C4
Pando, L. = Hope, L., *Australia* 91 D2
Pandokrátor, *Greece* 37 A3
Pandora, *Costa Rica* 116 E3
Panevėžys, *Lithuania* 40 D4
Panfilov, *Kazakhstan* 44 E8
Panfilovo, *Russia* 41 F13
Pang-Long, *Burma* 61 H21
Pang-Yang, *Burma* 61 H21
Panga, *Zaïre* 82 B2
Pangalanes, Canal des, *Madag.* 85 C8
Pangani, *Tanzania* 82 D4
Pangani □, *Tanzania* 82 D4
Pangani →, *Tanzania* 82 D4
Pangfou = Bengbu, *China* 51 H9
Pangil, *Zaïre* 82 C2
Pangkah, Tanjung, *Indonesia* 57 G15
Pangkajene, *Indonesia* 57 E5
Pangkalanbrandan, *Indonesia* 56 D1
Pangkalanbuun, *Indonesia* 56 E4
Pangkalansusu, *Indonesia* 56 D1
Pangkalpinang, *Indonesia* 56 E3
Pangkoh, *Indonesia* 56 E4
Pangnirtung, *Canada* 97 B13
Pangrango, *Indonesia* 57 G12
Panguipulli, *Chile* 128 A2
Panguitch, *U.S.A.* 111 H7
Pangutaran Group, *Phil.* 55 H4
Panhandle, *U.S.A.* 109 H4
Pani Mines, *India* 62 H5
Pania-Mutombo, *Zaïre* 82 D1
Panipat, *India* 62 E7
Panjal Range, *India* 62 C7
Panjgur, *Pakistan* 60 F4
Panjim = Panaji, *India* 60 M8
Panjinad Barrage, *Pakistan* 60 E7
Panjwai, *Afghan.* 62 D1
Pankshin, *Nigeria* 79 D6
Panmunjŏm, *N. Korea* 51 F14
Panna, *India* 63 G9
Panna Hills, *India* 63 G9
Pano Lefkara, *Cyprus* 37 E12
Pano Panayia, *Cyprus* 37 E11
Panorama, *Brazil* 127 A5
Pánormon, *Greece* 37 D6
Panshan, *China* 51 D12
Panshi, *China* 51 C14
Pantar, *Indonesia* 57 F6
Pante Macassar, *Indonesia* 57 F6
Pantelleria, *Italy* 34 F5
Pantón, *Spain* 30 C3
Pánuco, *Mexico* 115 C5
Panyam, *Nigeria* 79 D6
Panyu, *China* 53 F9
Pao →, *Anzoátegui, Venezuela* 121 B5
Pao →, *Apure, Venezuela* 120 B4
Páola, *Italy* 35 C9
Paola, *Malta* 37 D2
Paola, *U.S.A.* 108 F7
Paonia, *U.S.A.* 111 G10
Paoting = Baoding, *China* 50 E8
Paot'ou = Baotou, *China* 50 D6
Paoua, *C.A.R.* 73 G8
Pápa, *Hungary* 21 H7
Papagayo →, *Mexico* 115 D5
Papagayo, G. de, *Costa Rica* 116 D2
Papakura, *N.Z.* 87 G5
Papantla, *Mexico* 115 C5
Papar, *Malaysia* 56 C5
Pápas, Ákra, *Greece* 39 L4
Papenburg, *Germany* 18 B3
Paphlagonia, *Turkey* 66 C5
Paphos, *Cyprus* 37 E11
Papien Chiang = Da →, *Vietnam* 58 B5
Papigochic →, *Mexico* 114 B3
Paposo, *Chile* 126 B1
Papoutsa, *Cyprus* 37 E12
Papua New Guinea ■, *Oceania* 92 H6
Papuča, *Croatia* 33 D12
Papudo, *Chile* 126 C1
Papuk, *Croatia* 21 K7
Papun, *Burma* 61 K20
Papunya, *Australia* 88 D5
Pará = Belém, *Brazil* 122 B2
Pará □, *Brazil* 125 A7
Pará □, *Surinam* 121 B6
Parábita, *Italy* 35 B11
Paraburdoo, *Australia* 88 D2
Paracale, *Phil.* 55 D5
Paracas, Pen., *Peru* 124 C2
Paracatu, *Brazil* 123 E2
Paracatu →, *Brazil* 123 E2
Paracel Is. = Hsisha Chuntao, *Pac. Oc.* 56 A4
Parachilna, *Australia* 91 E2
Parachinar, *Pakistan* 62 C4
Paraćin, *Serbia, Yug.* 21 M11
Paracuru, *Brazil* 122 B4
Parada, Punta, *Peru* 124 D2
Paradas, *Spain* 31 H5
Paradela, *Spain* 30 C3
Paradhísi, *Greece* 37 C10
Paradip, *India* 61 J15
Paradise, *Calif., U.S.A.* 112 F5
Paradise, *Mont., U.S.A.* 110 C6
Paradise, *Nev., U.S.A.* 113 J11
Paradise →, *Canada* 99 B8
Paradise Valley, *U.S.A.* 110 F5
Parado, *Indonesia* 57 F5
Paragould, *U.S.A.* 109 G9
Paraguá →, *Bolivia* 125 C5
Paragua →, *Venezuela* 121 B5
Paraguaçu →, *Brazil* 123 D4
Paraguaçu Paulista, *Brazil* 127 A5
Paraguaipoa, *Venezuela* 120 A3
Paraguaná, Pen. de, *Venezuela* 120 A3
Paraguarí, *Paraguay* 126 B4
Paraguarí □, *Paraguay* 126 B4
Paraguay ■, *S. Amer.* 126 A4
Paraguay →, *Paraguay* 126 B4
Paraíba = João Pessoa, *Brazil* 122 C5
Paraíba □, *Brazil* 122 C4
Paraíba do Sul →, *Brazil* 123 F3
Parainen, *Finland* 9 F17
Paraiso, *Mexico* 115 D6
Parak, *Iran* 65 E7
Parakhino Paddubye, *Russia* 40 B8
Parakou, *Benin* 79 D5
Paralimni, *Cyprus* 37 D12
Paramaribo, *Surinam* 121 B6
Parambu, *Brazil* 122 C3
Paramillo, Nudo del, *Colombia* 120 B2
Paramirim, *Brazil* 123 D3
Paramirim →, *Brazil* 123 D3
Paramithiá, *Greece* 39 K3
Paramushir, Ostrov, *Russia* 45 D16
Paran →, *Israel* 69 E4
Paraná, *Argentina* 126 C3
Paranã, *Brazil* 123 D2
Paraná □, *Brazil* 127 A5
Paraná →, *Argentina* 126 C4
Paranaguá, *Brazil* 127 B6
Paranaíba →, *Brazil* 123 F1
Paranapanema →, *Brazil* 127 A5
Paranapiacaba, Serra do, *Brazil* 127 A6
Paranavaí, *Brazil* 127 A5
Parang, *Jolo, Phil.* 55 J4
Parang, *Mindanao, Phil.* 57 C6
Parangaba, *Brazil* 122 B4
Parapóla, *Greece* 39 N6
Paraspóri, Ákra, *Greece* 39 P10
Paratinga, *Brazil* 123 D3
Paratoo, *Australia* 91 E2
Parattah, *Australia* 90 G4
Paraúna, *Brazil* 123 E1
Paray-le-Monial, *France* 27 B8
Parbati →, *India* 62 G7
Parbhani, *India* 60 K10
Parchim, *Germany* 18 B7
Parczew, *Poland* 20 D12
Pardes Hanna, *Israel* 69 C3
Pardilla, *Spain* 30 D7
Pardo →, *Bahia, Brazil* 123 E4
Pardo →, *Mato Grosso, Brazil* 127 A5
Pardo →, *Minas Gerais, Brazil* 123 E3
Pardo →, *São Paulo, Brazil* 123 F2
Pardubice, *Czech.* 20 E5
Pare, *Indonesia* 57 G15
Pare □, *Tanzania* 82 C4
Pare Mts., *Tanzania* 82 C4
Parecis, Serra dos, *Brazil* 125 C6
Paredes de Nava, *Spain* 30 C6
Pareh, *Iran* 64 B5
Parelhas, *Brazil* 122 C4
Paren, *Russia* 45 C17
Parent, *Canada* 98 C5
Parent, L., *Canada* 98 C4
Parentis-en-Born, *France* 26 D2
Parepare, *Indonesia* 57 E5
Parfino, *Russia* 40 C7
Pargo, Pta. do, *Madeira* 36 D2
Paria, G. de, *Venezuela* 121 A5
Paria, Pen. de, *Venezuela* 121 A5
Pariaguán, *Venezuela* 121 B5
Pariaman, *Indonesia* 56 E2
Paricatuba, *Brazil* 121 D5
Paricutín, Cerro, *Mexico* 114 D4
Parigi, *Java, Indonesia* 57 G13
Parigi, *Sulawesi, Indonesia* 57 E6
Parika, *Guyana* 121 B6
Parima, Serra, *Brazil* 121 C5
Parinari, *Peru* 124 A3
Parîng, *Romania* 38 D6
Parintins, *Brazil* 121 D6
Pariparit Kyun, *Burma* 61 M18
Paris, *Canada* 98 D3
Paris, *France* 25 D9
Paris, *Idaho, U.S.A.* 110 E8
Paris, *Ky., U.S.A.* 104 F3
Paris, *Tenn., U.S.A.* 105 G1
Paris, *Tex., U.S.A.* 109 J7
Paris, Ville de □, *France* 25 D9
Parish, *U.S.A.* 107 C8
Pariti, *Indonesia* 57 F6
Park, *U.S.A.* 112 B4
Park City, *U.S.A.* 110 F8
Park Falls, *U.S.A.* 108 C9
Park Range, *U.S.A.* 110 G10
Park Rapids, *U.S.A.* 108 B7
Park River, *U.S.A.* 108 A6
Park Rynie, *S. Africa* 85 E5
Parkā Bandar, *Iran* 65 E8
Parker, *Ariz., U.S.A.* 113 L12
Parker, *S. Dak., U.S.A.* 108 D6
Parker Dam, *U.S.A.* 113 L12
Parkersburg, *U.S.A.* 104 F5

Parkerview, Canada 101 C8
Parkes, Australia 91 E4
Parkfield, U.S.A. 112 K6
Parkland, U.S.A. 112 C4
Parkside, Canada 101 C7
Parkston, U.S.A. 108 D5
Parksville, Canada 100 D4
Parma, Italy 32 D7
Parma, Idaho, U.S.A. 110 E5
Parma, Ohio, U.S.A. 106 E3
Parma →, Italy 32 D7
Parnaguá, Brazil 122 D3
Parnaíba, Piauí, Brazil .. 122 B3
Parnaíba, São Paulo, Brazil 125 D7
Parnaíba →, Brazil 122 B3
Parnamirim, Brazil 122 C4
Parnarama, Brazil 122 C3
Parnassós, Greece 39 L5
Párnis, Greece 39 L6
Párnon Óros, Greece 39 M5
Pärnu, Estonia 40 B4
Paroo →, Australia 91 E3
Páros, Greece 39 M8
Parowan, U.S.A. 111 H7
Parpaillon, France 27 D10
Parral, Chile 126 D1
Parramatta, Australia ... 91 E5
Parras, Mexico 114 B4
Parrett →, U.K. 13 F5
Parris I., U.S.A. 105 J5
Parrsboro, Canada 99 C7
Parry Is., Canada 4 B2
Parry Sound, Canada 98 C3
Parsberg, Germany 19 F7
Parshall, U.S.A. 108 B3
Parsnip →, Canada 100 B4
Parsons, U.S.A. 109 G7
Parsons Ra., Australia .. 90 A2
Partanna, Italy 34 E5
Parthenay, France 24 F6
Partinico, Italy 34 D6
Paru →, Brazil 121 D7
Parú →, Venezuela 120 C4
Paru de Oeste →, Brazil . 121 C6
Parucito →, Venezuela ... 120 B4
Paruro, Peru 124 C3
Parván □, Afghan. 60 B6
Parvatipuram, India 61 K13
Parys, S. Africa 84 D4
Pas-de-Calais □, France . 25 B9
Pasadena, Calif., U.S.A. . 113 L8
Pasadena, Tex., U.S.A. .. 109 L7
Pasaje, Ecuador 120 D2
Pasaje →, Argentina 126 B3
Pasay, Phil. 55 D4
Pascagoula, U.S.A. 109 K10
Pascagoula →, U.S.A. 109 K10
Paşcani, Romania 38 B9
Pasco, U.S.A. 110 C4
Pasco □, Peru 124 C2
Pasco, Cerro de, Peru ... 124 C2
Pascua, I. de la, Pac. Oc. 93 K17
Pasewalk, Germany 18 B10
Pasfield L., Canada 101 B7
Pasha →, Russia 40 B8
Pashiwari, Pakistan 63 B6
Pashmakli = Smolyan,
  Bulgaria 39 H7
Pasinler, Turkey 67 D9
Pasirian, Indonesia 57 H15
Paskūh, Iran 65 E9
Pasley, C., Australia ... 89 F3
Pašman, Croatia 33 E12
Pasni, Pakistan 60 G3
Paso Cantinela, Mexico .. 113 N11
Paso de Indios, Argentina . 128 B3
Paso de los Libres,
  Argentina 126 B4
Paso de los Toros, Uruguay 126 C4
Paso Flores, Argentina .. 128 B2
Paso Robles, U.S.A. 111 J3
Pasorapa, Bolivia 125 D5
Paspébiac, Canada 99 C6
Pasrur, Pakistan 62 C6
Passage West, Ireland ... 15 E3
Passaic, U.S.A. 107 F10
Passau, Germany 19 G9
Passendale, Belgium 17 G2
Passero, C., Italy 35 F8
Passo Fundo, Brazil 127 B5
Passos, Brazil 123 F2
Passow, Germany 18 B10
Passwang, Switz. 22 B5
Passy, France 27 C10
Pastaza □, Ecuador 120 D2
Pastaza →, Peru 120 D2
Pastęk, Poland 20 A9
Pasto, Colombia 120 C2
Pastos Bons, Brazil 122 C3
Pastrana, Spain 28 E2
Pasuruan, Indonesia 57 G15
Patagonia, Argentina 128 C2
Patagonia, U.S.A. 111 L8
Patambar, Iran 65 D9
Patan, India 60 H8
Patan, Maharashtra, India 62 H5
Patan, Nepal 61 F14
Patani, Indonesia 57 D7
Pataudi, India 62 E7
Patay, France 25 D8
Patchewollock, Australia . 91 F3
Patchogue, U.S.A. 107 F11
Patea, N.Z. 87 H5
Pategi, Nigeria 79 D6
Patensie, S. Africa 84 E3
Paternò, Italy 35 E7

Pateros, U.S.A. 110 B4
Paterson, U.S.A. 107 F10
Paterson Ra., Australia . 88 D3
Paterswolde, Neths. 16 B9
Pathankot, India 62 C6
Pathfinder Reservoir,
  U.S.A. 110 E10
Pathiu, Thailand 59 G2
Pathum Thani, Thailand .. 58 E3
Pati, Indonesia 57 G14
Patía, Colombia 120 C2
Patía →, Colombia 120 C2
Patiala, India 62 D7
Patine Kouka, Senegal ... 78 C2
Pativilca, Peru 124 C2
Patkai Bum, India 61 F19
Pátmos, Greece 39 M9
Patna, India 63 G11
Patnos, Turkey 67 D10
Patonga, Uganda 82 B3
Patos, Brazil 122 C4
Patos, L. dos, Brazil ... 127 C5
Patos de Minas, Brazil .. 123 E2
Patquía, Argentina 126 C2
Pátrai, Greece 39 L4
Pátraikós Kólpos, Greece . 39 L4
Patricio Lynch, I., Chile . 128 C1
Patrocínio, Brazil 123 E2
Patta, Kenya 82 C5
Pattada, Italy 34 B2
Pattani, Thailand 59 J3
Patten, U.S.A. 99 C6
Patterson, Calif., U.S.A. . 111 H3
Patterson, La., U.S.A. .. 109 L9
Patterson, Mt., U.S.A. .. 112 G7
Patti, India 62 D6
Patti, Italy 35 D7
Pattoki, Pakistan 62 D5
Patton, U.S.A. 106 F6
Patu, Brazil 122 C4
Patuakhali, Bangla. 61 H17
Patuca →, Honduras 116 C3
Patuca, Punta, Honduras . 116 C3
Pâturages, Belgium 17 H3
Pátzcuaro, Mexico 114 D4
Pau, France 26 E3
Pau, Gave de →, France .. 26 E2
Pau d' Arco, Brazil 122 C2
Pau dos Ferros, Brazil .. 122 C4
Paucartambo, Peru 124 C3
Pauillac, France 26 C3
Pauini, Brazil 124 B4
Pauini →, Brazil 121 D5
Pauk, Burma 61 J19
Paul I., Canada 99 A7
Paul Isnard, Fr. Guiana . 121 C7
Paulhan, France 26 E7
Paulis = Isiro, Zaïre ... 82 B2
Paulista, Brazil 122 C5
Paulistana, Brazil 122 C3
Paullina, U.S.A. 108 D7
Paulo Afonso, Brazil 122 C4
Paulo de Faria, Brazil .. 123 F2
Paulpietersburg, S. Africa 85 D5
Pauls Valley, U.S.A. 109 H6
Pauma Valley, U.S.A. 113 M10
Pausa, Peru 124 D3
Pauto →, Colombia 120 B3
Päveh, Iran 64 C5
Pavelets, Russia 41 E11
Pavia, Italy 32 C6
Pavlikeni, Bulgaria 38 F8
Pavlodar, Kazakhstan 44 D8
Pavlograd, Ukraine 47 H8
Pavlovo, Russia 41 D13
Pavlovo, Russia 45 C12
Pavlovsk, Russia 41 F12
Pavlovskaya, Russia 43 C8
Pavlovskiy-Posad, Russia . 41 D11
Pavullo nel Frignano, Italy 32 D7
Pawhuska, U.S.A. 109 G6
Pawling, U.S.A. 107 E11
Pawnee, U.S.A. 109 G6
Pawnee City, U.S.A. 108 E6
Pawtucket, U.S.A. 107 E13
Paxói, Greece 39 K3
Paxton, Ill., U.S.A. 104 E1
Paxton, Nebr., U.S.A. ... 108 E4
Payakumbuh, Indonesia ... 56 E2
Payerne, Switz. 22 C3
Payette, U.S.A. 110 D5
Paymogo, Spain 31 H3
Payne Bay = Bellin,
  Canada 97 B13
Payne L., Canada 97 C12
Paynes Find, Australia .. 89 E2
Paynesville, Liberia 78 D2
Paynesville, U.S.A. 108 C7
Paysandú, Uruguay 126 C4
Payson, Ariz., U.S.A. ... 111 J8
Payson, Utah, U.S.A. 110 F8
Paz →, Guatemala 116 D1
Paz, B. la, Mexico 114 C2
Pazanān, Iran 65 D6
Pazar, Turkey 67 C9
Pazarcık, Turkey 66 E7
Pazardzhik, Bulgaria 38 G7
Pazin, Croatia 33 C10
Pazña, Bolivia 124 D4
Pčinja →,
  Macedonia 39 H4
Pe Ell, U.S.A. 112 D3
Peabody, U.S.A. 107 D14
Peace →, Canada 100 B6
Peace Point, Canada 100 B6

Peace River, Canada 100 B5
Peach Springs, U.S.A. ... 111 J7
Peak, The = Kinder Scout,
  U.K. 12 D6
Peak Downs, Australia ... 90 C4
Peak Downs Mine,
  Australia 90 C4
Peak Hill, N.S.W.,
  Australia 91 E4
Peak Hill, W. Austral.,
  Australia 89 E2
Peak Ra., Australia 90 C4
Peake, Australia 91 F2
Peake Cr. →, Australia .. 91 D2
Peale, Mt., U.S.A. 111 G9
Pearblossom, U.S.A. 113 L9
Pearl →, U.S.A. 109 K10
Pearl City, U.S.A. 102 H16
Pearsall, U.S.A. 109 L5
Pearse I., Canada 100 C2
Peary Land, Greenland ... 4 A6
Pease →, U.S.A. 109 H5
Pebane, Mozam. 83 F4
Pebas, Peru 120 D3
Pebble, I., Falk. Is. ... 128 D5
Pebble Beach, U.S.A. 112 J5
Peč, Serbia, Yug. 21 N10
Peçanha, Brazil 123 E3
Péccioli, Italy 32 E7
Pechea, Romania 38 D10
Pechenezhin, Ukraine 42 B1
Pechenga, Russia 44 C4
Pechiguera, Pta.,
  Canary Is. 36 F6
Pechnezhskoye Vdkhr.,
  Ukraine 42 A7
Pechora, Russia 44 C6
Pechora →, Russia 44 C6
Pechorskaya Guba, Russia 44 C6
Pecica, Romania 38 C4
Pečka, Serbia, Yug. 21 L9
Pecos, U.S.A. 109 K3
Pecos →, U.S.A. 109 L3
Pécs, Hungary 21 J8
Pedder, L., Australia ... 90 G4
Peddie, S. Africa 85 E4
Pédernales, Dom. Rep. ... 117 C5
Pedieos →, Cyprus 37 D12
Pedirka, Australia 91 D2
Pedra Azul, Brazil 123 E3
Pedra Grande, Recifes de,
  Brazil 123 E4
Pedras Negras, Brazil ... 125 C5
Pedreiras, Brazil 122 B3
Pedro Afonso, Brazil 122 C2
Pedro Cays, Jamaica 116 C4
Pedro Chico, Colombia ... 120 C3
Pedro de Valdivia, Chile . 126 A2
Pedro Juan Caballero,
  Paraguay 127 A4
Pedro Muñoz, Spain 29 F2
Pedrógão Grande, Portugal 30 F2
Peebinga, Australia 91 E3
Peebles, U.K. 14 F5
Peekskill, U.S.A. 107 E11
Peel, U.K. 12 C3
Peel →, Australia 91 E5
Peel →, Canada 96 B6
Peene →, Germany 18 A9
Peera Peera Poolanna L.,
  Australia 91 D2
Peers, Canada 100 C5
Pegasus Bay, N.Z. 87 K4
Pegnitz, Germany 19 F7
Pegnitz →, Germany 19 F6
Pego, Spain 29 G4
Pegu, Burma 61 L20
Pegu Yoma, Burma 61 K19
Pehuajó, Argentina 126 D3
Pei Xian, China 50 G9
Peine, Chile 126 A2
Peine, Germany 18 C6
Peip'ing = Beijing, China 50 E9
Peissenberg, Germany 19 H7
Peitz, Germany 18 D10
Peixe, Brazil 123 D2
Peixe →, Brazil 123 F1
Peixoto de Azeredo →,
  Brazil 125 C6
Peize, Neths. 16 B8
Pek →, Serbia, Yug. 21 L11
Pekalongan, Indonesia ... 57 G13
Pekan, Malaysia 59 L4
Pekanbaru, Indonesia 56 D2
Pekin, U.S.A. 108 E10
Peking = Beijing, Beijing,
  China 50 E9
Peking = Beijing, Beijing,
  China 50 E9
Pelabuhan Kelang,
  Malaysia 59 L3
Pelabuhan Ratu, Teluk,
  Indonesia 57 G12
Pelabuhanratu, Indonesia . 57 G12
Pélagos, Greece 39 K7
Pelaihari, Indonesia 56 E4
Pelat, Mt., France 27 D10
Peleaga, Romania 38 D6
Pelechuco, Bolivia 124 C4
Pelée, Mt., Martinique .. 117 D7
Pelee, Pt., Canada 98 D3
Pelee I., Canada 98 D3
Pelejo, Peru 124 B2
Pelekech, Kenya 82 B4
Peleng, Indonesia 57 E6

Pelham, U.S.A. 105 K3
Pelhřimov, Czech. 20 F5
Pelican L., Canada 101 C8
Pelican Narrows, Canada . 101 B8
Pelican Rapids, Canada .. 101 C8
Pelkosenniemi, Finland .. 8 C19
Pella, S. Africa 84 D2
Pella, U.S.A. 108 E8
Péllaro, Italy 35 D8
Pellworm, Germany 18 A4
Pelly →, Canada 96 B6
Pelly Bay, Canada 97 B11
Pelly L., Canada 96 B9
Peloponnese =
  Pelopónnisos □, Greece . 39 M5
Pelopónnisos □, Greece .. 39 M5
Peloritani, Monti, Italy . 35 D8
Peloro, C., Italy 35 D8
Pelorus Sd., N.Z. 87 J4
Pelotas, Brazil 127 C5
Pelvoux, Massif de, France 27 D10
Pemalang, Indonesia 57 G13
Pematangsiantar, Indonesia 56 D1
Pemba, Mozam. 83 E5
Pemba, Zambia 83 F2
Pemba Channel, Tanzania . 82 D4
Pemba I., Tanzania 82 D4
Pemberton, Australia 89 F2
Pemberton, Canada 100 C4
Pembina, U.S.A. 101 D9
Pembina →, U.S.A. 101 D9
Pembine, U.S.A. 104 C2
Pembino, U.S.A. 108 A6
Pembroke, Canada 98 C4
Pembroke, U.K. 13 F3
Pembroke, U.S.A. 105 J5
Pen-y-Ghent, U.K. 12 C5
Peña, Sierra de la, Spain . 28 C4
Peña de Francia, Sierra de,
  Spain 30 E4
Penafiel, Portugal 30 D2
Peñafiel, Spain 30 D6
Peñaflor, Spain 31 H5
Peñalara, Pico, Spain ... 30 E7
Penalva, Brazil 122 B2
Penamacôr, Portugal 30 E3
Penang = Pinang, Malaysia 59 K3
Penápolis, Brazil 127 A6
Peñaranda de Bracamonte,
  Spain 30 E5
Peñarroya-Pueblonuevo,
  Spain 31 G5
Peñas, C. de, Spain 30 B5
Penas, G. de, Chile 128 C2
Peñas, Pta., Venezuela .. 121 A5
Peñas de San Pedro, Spain 29 G2
Peñas del Chache,
  Canary Is. 36 E6
Peñausende, Spain 30 D5
Pench'i = Benxi, China .. 51 D12
Pend Oreille →, U.S.A. .. 110 B5
Pend Oreille L., U.S.A. . 110 C5
Pendembu, S. Leone 78 D2
Pendleton, Calif., U.S.A. 113 M9
Pendleton, Oreg., U.S.A. . 110 D4
Penedo, Brazil 122 D4
Penetanguishene, Canada . 98 D4
Peng Xian, China 52 B4
Pengalengan, Indonesia .. 57 G12
Penge, Kasai Or., Zaïre . 82 D1
Penge, Kivu, Zaïre 82 C2
Penglai, China 51 F11
Penguin, Australia 90 G4
Pengxi, China 52 B5
Pengze, China 53 C11
Penhalonga, Zimbabwe 83 F3
Peniche, Portugal 31 F1
Penicuik, U.K. 14 F5
Penida, Indonesia 56 F5
Peninsular Malaysia □,
  Malaysia 59 L4
Peñíscola, Spain 28 E5
Penitente, Serra dos, Brazil 122 C2
Penmarch, France 24 E2
Penmarch, Pte. de, France 24 E2
Penn Hills, U.S.A. 106 F5
Penn Yan, U.S.A. 106 D7
Pennabilli, Italy 33 E9
Pennant, Canada 101 C7
Penne, Italy 33 F10
Penner →, India 60 M12
Pennine, Alpi, Alps 32 B4
Pennines, U.K. 12 C5
Pennington, U.S.A. 112 F5
Pennino, Mte., Italy 33 E9
Pennsylvania □, U.S.A. .. 104 E6
Penny, Canada 100 C4
Peno, Russia 40 C8
Penola, Australia 91 F3
Penong, Australia 89 F5
Penonomé, Panama 116 E3
Penrith, Australia 91 E5
Penrith, U.K. 12 C5
Pensacola, U.S.A. 105 K2
Pensacola Mts., Antarctica 5 E1
Pense, Canada 101 C8
Penshurst, Australia 91 F3
Pentecoste, Brazil 122 B4
Penticton, Canada 100 D5
Pentland, Australia 90 C4
Pentland Firth, U.K. 14 C5
Pentland Hills, U.K. 14 F5
Penylan L., Canada 101 A7

Penza, Russia 41 E14
Penzance, U.K. 13 G2
Penzberg, Germany 19 H7
Penzhino, Russia 45 C17
Penzhinskaya Guba, Russia 45 C17
Penzlin, Germany 18 B9
Peoria, Ariz., U.S.A. ... 111 K7
Peoria, Ill., U.S.A. 108 E10
Pepingen, Belgium 17 G4
Pepinster, Belgium 17 G7
Pera Hd., Australia 90 A3
Perabumilih, Indonesia .. 56 E2
Perakhóra, Greece 39 L5
Perales de Alfambra, Spain 28 E3
Perales del Puerto, Spain 30 E4
Peralta, Spain 28 C3
Pérama, Kérkira, Greece . 37 A3
Pérama, Kríti, Greece ... 37 D6
Percé, Canada 99 C7
Perche, France 24 D8
Perche, Collines du, France 24 D7
Percival Lakes, Australia 88 D4
Percy, France 24 D5
Percy Is., Australia 90 C5
Perdido →, Argentina 128 B3
Perdido, Mte., Spain 26 F4
Perdu, Mt. = Perdido,
  Mte., Spain 26 F4
Pereira, Colombia 120 C2
Pereira Barreto, Brazil . 123 F1
Perekerten, Australia ... 91 E3
Perené →, Peru 124 C3
Perenjori, Australia 89 E2
Pereslavl-Zalesskiy, Russia 41 C11
Pereyaslav Khmelnitskiy,
  Ukraine 40 F7
Pérez, I., Mexico 115 C7
Pergamino, Argentina 126 C3
Pérgine Valsugano, Italy . 33 B8
Pérgola, Italy 33 E9
Perham, U.S.A. 108 B7
Perhentian, Kepulauan,
  Malaysia 59 K4
Periam, Romania 38 C3
Péribonca →, Canada 99 C5
Péribonca, L., Canada ... 99 B5
Perico, Argentina 126 A2
Pericos, Mexico 114 B3
Périers, France 24 C5
Périgord, France 26 D4
Périgueux, France 26 C4
Perijá, Sierra de, Colombia 120 B3
Peristéra, Greece 39 K6
Peristerona →, Cyprus ... 37 D12
Perito Moreno, Argentina . 128 C2
Peritoró, Brazil 122 B3
Perković, Croatia 33 E13
Perlas, Arch. de las,
  Panama 116 E4
Perlas, Punta de, Nic. .. 116 D3
Perleberg, Germany 18 B7
Perlevka, Russia 41 F11
Perm, Russia 44 D6
Pernambuco = Recife,
  Brazil 122 C5
Pernambuco □, Brazil 122 C4
Pernatty Lagoon, Australia 91 E2
Pernik, Bulgaria 38 G6
Peron, C., Australia 89 E1
Peron Is., Australia 88 B5
Peron Pen., Australia ... 89 E1
Péronne, France 25 C9
Pérosa Argentina, Italy . 32 D4
Perow, Canada 100 C3
Perpendicular Pt., Australia 91 E5
Perpignan, France 26 F6
Perris, U.S.A. 113 M9
Perros-Guirec, France ... 24 D3
Perry, Fla., U.S.A. 105 K4
Perry, Ga., U.S.A. 105 J4
Perry, Iowa, U.S.A. 108 E7
Perry, Maine, U.S.A. 105 C12
Perry, Okla., U.S.A. 109 G6
Perryville, U.S.A. 109 G10
Perryton, U.S.A. 109 G4
Perşembe, Turkey 67 C7
Persia = Iran ■, Asia ... 65 C7
Persian Gulf = Gulf, The,
  Asia 65 E6
Perstorp, Sweden 11 H7
Pertek, Turkey 67 D8
Perth, Australia 89 F2
Perth, Canada 98 D4
Perth, U.K. 14 E5
Perth Amboy, U.S.A. 107 F10
Pertuis, France 27 E9
Peru, Ill., U.S.A. 108 E10
Peru, Ind., U.S.A. 104 E2
Peru ■, S. Amer. 120 D2
Peru-Chile Trench,
  Pac. Oc. 93 K20
Perúgia, Italy 33 E9
Perušić, Croatia 33 D12
Péruwelz, Belgium 17 G3
Pervomaysk, Russia 41 D13
Pervomaysk, Ukraine 42 B4
Pervouralsk, Russia 44 D6
Perwez, Belgium 17 G5
Pes, Pta. del, Spain 36 C7
Pésaro, Italy 33 E9
Pescara, Italy 33 F11
Pescara →, Italy 33 F11
Péscia, Italy 32 E7

Pescina, *Italy*	33 G10	Phangnga, *Thailand*	59 H2

Pescina, *Italy* 33 G10
Peseux, *Switz.* 22 C3
Peshawar, *Pakistan* 62 B4
Peshtigo, *U.S.A.* 104 C2
Peski, *Russia* 41 F13
Peskovka, *Russia* 41 B18
Pêso da Régua, *Portugal* . 30 D3
Pesqueira, *Brazil* 122 C4
Pessac, *France* 26 D3
Pessoux, *Belgium* 17 H6
Pestovo, *Russia* 40 B9
Pestravka, *Russia* 41 E16
Petah Tiqwa, *Israel* 69 C3
Petaling Jaya, *Malaysia* . 59 L3
Petaloudhes, *Greece* 37 C10
Petaluma, *U.S.A.* 112 G4
Petange, *Lux.* 17 J7
Petatlán, *Mexico* 114 D4
Petauke, *Zambia* 83 E3
Petawawa, *Canada* 98 C4
Petén Itzá, L., *Guatemala* 116 C2
Peter I.s Øy, *Antarctica* . 5 C16
Peter Pond L., *Canada* .. 101 B7
Peterbell, *Canada* 98 C3
Peterborough, *Australia* . 91 E2
Peterborough, *Canada* ... 97 D12
Peterborough, *U.K.* 13 E7
Peterborough, *U.S.A.* ... 107 D13
Peterhead, *U.K.* 14 D7
Petermann Bjerg,
  Greenland 94 B17
Peter's Mine, *Guyana* ... 121 B6
Petersburg, *Alaska, U.S.A.* 100 B2
Petersburg, *Ind., U.S.A.* . 104 F2
Petersburg, *Va., U.S.A.* . 104 G7
Petersburg, *W. Va., U.S.A.* 104 F5
Petford, *Australia* 90 B3
Petília Policastro, *Italy* . 35 C9
Petit Bois I., *U.S.A.* ... 105 K1
Petit-Cap, *Canada* 99 C7
Petit Goâve, *Haiti* 117 C5
Petit Lac Manicouagan,
  Canada 99 B6
Petit Saint Bernard, Col
  du, *Italy* 32 C3
Petitcodiac, *Canada* 99 C6
Petite Baleine →, *Canada* . 98 A4
Petite Saguenay, *Canada* . 99 C5
Petitsikapau, L., *Canada* . 99 B6
Petlad, *India* 62 H5
Peto, *Mexico* 115 C7
Petone, *N.Z.* 87 J5
Petoskey, *U.S.A.* 104 C3
Petra, *Jordan* 69 E4
Petra, *Spain* 36 B10
Petra, Ostrova, *Russia* . 4 B13
Petra Velikogo, Zaliv,
  Russia 48 C5
Petralia, *Italy* 35 E7
Petrel, *Spain* 29 G4
Petreto-Bicchisano, *France* 27 G12
Petrich, *Bulgaria* 39 H6
Petrijanec, *Croatia* 33 B13
Petrikov, *Belorussia* ... 40 E6
Petrinja, *Croatia* 33 C13
Petrograd = Sankt-
  Peterburg, *Russia* 40 B7
Petrolândia, *Brazil* 122 C4
Petrolia, *Canada* 98 D3
Petrolina, *Brazil* 122 C3
Petropavlovsk, *Kazakhstan* 44 D7
Petropavlovsk-
  Kamchatskiy, *Russia* . 45 D16
Petropavlovskiy =
  Akhtubinsk, *Russia* ... 43 B12
Petrópolis, *Brazil* 123 F3
Petroşeni, *Romania* 38 D6
Petrova Gora, *Croatia* .. 33 C12
Petrovac, *Montenegro, Yug.* 21 N8
Petrovsk, *Russia* 41 E14
Petrovsk-Zabaykalskiy,
  Russia 45 D11
Petrovskoye = Svetlograd,
  Russia 43 D10
Petrozavodsk, *Russia* ... 44 C4
Petrus Steyn, *S. Africa* . 85 D4
Petrusburg, *S. Africa* .. 84 D4
Petukhovka, *Belorussia* . 40 E7
Peumo, *Chile* 126 C1
Peureulak, *Indonesia* ... 56 D1
Pevek, *Russia* 45 C18
Peveragno, *Italy* 32 D4
Peyrehorade, *France* 26 E2
Peyruis, *France* 27 D9
Pézenas, *France* 26 E7
Pfaffenhofen, *Germany* .. 19 G7
Pfäffikon, *Switz.* 23 B7
Pfarrkirchen, *Germany* .. 19 G8
Pfeffenhausen, *Germany* . 19 G7
Pforzheim, *Germany* 19 G4
Pfullendorf, *Germany* ... 19 H5
Pfungstadt, *Germany* 19 F4
Phagwara, *India* 60 D9
Phaistós, *Greece* 37 D6
Phala, *Botswana* 84 C4
Phalera = Phulera, *India* 62 F6
Phalodi, *India* 62 F5
Phalsbourg, *France* 25 D14
Phan, *Thailand* 58 C2
Phan Rang, *Vietnam* 59 G7
Phan Ri = Hoa Da,
  Vietnam 59 G7
Phan Thiet, *Vietnam* 59 G7
Phanat Nikhom, *Thailand* . 58 F3
Phangan, Ko, *Thailand* ... 59 H3

Phangnga, *Thailand* 59 H2
Phanh Bho Ho Chi Minh,
  Vietnam 59 G6
Phanom Sarakham,
  Thailand 58 F3
Pharenda, *India* 63 F10
Phatthalung, *Thailand* .. 59 J3
Phayao, *Thailand* 58 C2
Phelps, *N.Y., U.S.A.* ... 106 D7
Phelps, *Wis., U.S.A.* ... 108 B10
Phelps L., *Canada* 101 B8
Phenix City, *U.S.A.* 105 J3
Phet Buri, *Thailand* 58 F2
Phetchabun, *Thailand* ... 58 D3
Phetchabun, Thiu Khao,
  Thailand 58 E3
Phetchaburi = Phet Buri,
  Thailand 58 F2
Phi Phi, Ko, *Thailand* .. 59 J2
Phiafay, *Laos* 58 E6
Phibun Mangsahan,
  Thailand 58 E5
Phichai, *Thailand* 58 D3
Phichit, *Thailand* 58 D3
Philadelphia, *Miss., U.S.A.* 109 J10
Philadelphia, *N.Y., U.S.A.* 107 B9
Philadelphia, *Pa., U.S.A.* 107 F9
Philip, *U.S.A.* 108 C4
Philippeville, *Belgium* . 17 H5
Philippi L., *Australia* . 90 C2
Philippines ■, *Asia* 55 F5
Philippolis, *S. Africa* . 84 E4
Philippopolis = Plovdiv,
  Bulgaria 38 G7
Philipsburg, *Mont., U.S.A.* 110 C7
Philipsburg, *Pa., U.S.A.* . 106 F6
Philipstown, *S. Africa* . 84 E3
Phillip I., *Australia* .. 91 F4
Phillips, *Tex., U.S.A.* . 109 H4
Phillips, *Wis., U.S.A.* . 108 C9
Phillipsburg, *Kans., U.S.A.* 108 F5
Phillipsburg, *N.J., U.S.A.* 107 F9
Phillott, *Australia* 91 D4
Philmont, *U.S.A.* 107 D11
Philomath, *U.S.A.* 110 D2
Phimai, *Thailand* 58 E4
Phitsanulok, *Thailand* .. 58 D3
Phnom Dangrek, *Thailand* . 58 E5
Phnom Penh, *Cambodia* ... 59 G5
Phoenix, *Ariz., U.S.A.* . 111 K7
Phoenix, *N.Y., U.S.A.* .. 107 C8
Phoenix Is., *Kiribati* .. 92 H10
Phoenixville, *U.S.A.* ... 107 F9
Phon, *Thailand* 58 E4
Phon Tiou, *Laos* 58 D5
Phong →, *Thailand* 58 D4
Phong Saly, *Laos* 58 B4
Phong Tho, *Vietnam* 58 A4
Phonhong, *Laos* 58 C4
Phonum, *Thailand* 59 H2
Phosphate Hill, *Australia* . 90 C2
Photharam, *Thailand* 58 F2
Phra Chedi Sam Ong,
  Thailand 58 E2
Phra Nakhon Si Ayutthaya,
  Thailand 58 E3
Phra Thong, Ko, *Thailand* 59 H2
Phrae, *Thailand* 58 C3
Phrom Phiram, *Thailand* . 58 D3
Phrygia, *Turkey* 66 D3
Phu Dien, *Vietnam* 58 C5
Phu Loi, *Laos* 58 B4
Phu Ly, *Vietnam* 58 B5
Phu Tho, *Vietnam* 58 B5
Phuc Yen, *Vietnam* 58 B5
Phuket, *Thailand* 59 J2
Phuket, Ko, *Thailand* ... 59 J2
Phulera, *India* 62 F6
Phumiphon, Khuan,
  Thailand 58 D2
Phun Phin, *Thailand* 59 H2
Piacá, *Brazil* 122 C2
Piacenza, *Italy* 32 C6
Piaçabuçu, *Brazil* 122 D4
Piádena, *Italy* 32 C7
Pialba, *Australia* 91 D5
Pian Cr. →, *Australia* .. 91 E4
Piana, *France* 27 F12
Pianella, *Italy* 33 F11
Pianoro, *Italy* 33 D8
Pianosa, *Puglia, Italy* . 33 F12
Pianosa, *Toscana, Italy* 32 F7
Piapot, *Canada* 101 D7
Piare →, *Italy* 33 C9
Pias, *Portugal* 31 G3
Piaseczno, *Poland* 20 C11
Piatã, *Brazil* 123 D3
Piatra, *Romania* 38 F8
Piatra Neamţ, *Romania* .. 38 C9
Piauí □, *Brazil* 122 C3
Piauí →, *Brazil* 122 C3
Piave →, *Italy* 33 C9
Piazza Ármerina, *Italy* . 35 E7
Pibor →, *Sudan* 77 F3
Pibor Post, *Sudan* 77 F3
Pica, *Chile* 124 E4
Picardie, *France* 25 C9
Picardie, Plaine de, *France* 25 C9
Picardy = Picardie, *France* 25 C9
Picayune, *U.S.A.* 109 K10
Picerno, *Italy* 35 B8
Pichilemu, *Chile* 126 C1
Pichincha, □, *Ecuador* .. 120 D2
Pickerel L., *Canada* 98 C1
Pickle Lake, *Canada* 98 B1
Pico Truncado, *Argentina* . 128 C3

Picos, *Brazil* 122 C3
Picos Ancares, Sierra de,
  Spain 30 C4
Picota, *Peru* 124 B2
Picquigny, *France* 25 C9
Picton, *Australia* 91 E5
Picton, *Canada* 98 D4
Picton, *N.Z.* 87 J5
Picton, I., *Chile* 128 E3
Pictou, *Canada* 99 C7
Picture Butte, *Canada* .. 100 D6
Picuí, *Brazil* 122 C4
Picún Leufú, *Argentina* . 128 A3
Pidurutalagala, *Sri Lanka* 60 R12
Piedecuesta, *Colombia* .. 120 B3
Piedicavallo, *Italy* 32 C4
Piedmont = Piemonte □,
  Italy 32 D4
Piedmont, *U.S.A.* 105 J3
Piedmont Plateau, *U.S.A.* 105 J5
Piedmonte d'Alife, *Italy* 35 A7
Piedra →, *Spain* 28 D3
Piedra del Anguila,
  Argentina 128 B3
Piedra Lais, *Venezuela* . 120 C4
Piedrabuena, *Spain* 31 F6
Piedrahita, *Spain* 30 E5
Piedras, R. de las →, *Peru* 124 C4
Piedras Negras, *Mexico* . 114 B4
Piemonte □, *Italy* 32 D4
Pierce, *U.S.A.* 110 C6
Piercefield, *U.S.A.* 107 B10
Pierre, *U.S.A.* 108 C4
Pierre Bénite, Barrage de
  la, *France* 27 C8
Pierre-de-Bresse, *France* 27 B9
Pierrefeu-du-Var, *France* 27 E10
Pierrefonds, *France* 25 C9
Pierrefontaine-les-Varans,
  France 25 E13
Pierrefort, *France* 26 D6
Pierrelatte, *France* 27 D8
Pieštany, *Slovakia* 20 G7
Piesting →, *Austria* 21 G6
Piet Retief, *S. Africa* . 85 D5
Pietarsaari = Jakobstad,
  Finland 8 E17
Pietermaritzburg, *S. Africa* 85 D5
Pietersburg, *S. Africa* . 85 C4
Pietraperzia, *Italy* 35 E7
Pietrasanta, *Italy* 32 E7
Pietrosu, *Romania* 38 B8
Pietrosul, *Romania* 38 B7
Pieve di Cadore, *Italy* . 33 B9
Pieve di Teco, *Italy* ... 32 D4
Pievepélago, *Italy* 32 D7
Pigádhia, *Greece* 39 P10
Pigeon, *U.S.A.* 104 D4
Piggott, *U.S.A.* 109 G9
Pigna, *Italy* 32 E4
Pigüe, *Argentina* 126 D3
Pihani, *India* 63 F9
Pijnacker, *Neths.* 16 D4
Pikalevo, *Russia* 40 B9
Pikes Peak, *U.S.A.* 108 F2
Piketberg, *S. Africa* ... 84 E2
Pikeville, *U.S.A.* 104 G4
Pikou, *China* 51 E12
Pikwitonei, *Canada* 101 B9
Piła, *Poland* 20 B6
Pila, *Spain* 29 G3
Pilani, *India* 62 E6
Pilar, *Brazil* 122 C4
Pilar, *Paraguay* 126 B4
Pilas Group, *Phil.* 57 C6
Pilaya →, *Bolivia* 125 E5
Pilcomayo →, *Paraguay* .. 126 B4
Pilibhit, *India* 63 E8
Pilica →, *Poland* 20 D10
Pilkhawa, *India* 62 E7
Pillaro, *Ecuador* 120 D2
Pílos, *Greece* 39 N4
Pilot Mound, *Canada* 101 D9
Pilot Point, *U.S.A.* 109 J6
Pilot Rock, *U.S.A.* 110 D4
Pilsen = Plzeň, *Czech.* . 20 F3
Pilštanj, *Slovenia* 33 B12
Pima, *U.S.A.* 111 K9
Pimba, *Australia* 91 E2
Pimenta Bueno, *Brazil* .. 125 C5
Pimentel, *Peru* 124 B2
Pina, *Spain* 28 D4
Pinamalayan, *Phil.* 55 E4
Pinang, *China* 59 K3
Pinar, C. del, *Spain* ... 36 B10
Pinar del Río, *Cuba* 116 B3
Pinarbaşi, *Turkey* 66 D7
Pincher Creek, *Canada* .. 100 D6
Pinchi L., *Canada* 100 C4
Pinckneyville, *U.S.A.* .. 108 F10
Pińczów, *Poland* 20 E10
Pindar, *Australia* 89 E2
Pindaré →, *Brazil* 122 B3
Pindaré Mirim, *Brazil* .. 122 B3
Pindi Gheb, *Pakistan* ... 62 C5
Pindiga, *Nigeria* 79 D7
Pindobal, *Brazil* 122 B2
Pindos Óros, *Greece* 39 K4
Pindus Mts. = Pindos
  Óros, *Greece* 39 K4
Pine, *U.S.A.* 111 J8
Pine →, *Canada* 101 B7
Pine, C., *Canada* 99 C9
Pine Bluff, *U.S.A.* 109 H8

Pine City, *U.S.A.* 108 C8
Pine Falls, *Canada* 101 C9
Pine Flat L., *U.S.A.* ... 112 J7
Pine Pass, *Canada* 100 B4
Pine Point, *Canada* 100 A6
Pine Ridge, *U.S.A.* 108 D3
Pine River, *Canada* 101 C8
Pine River, *U.S.A.* 108 B7
Pine Valley, *U.S.A.* 113 N10
Pinecrest, *U.S.A.* 112 G6
Pinedale, *U.S.A.* 112 J7
Pinega →, *Russia* 44 C5
Pinehill, *Australia* 90 C4
Pinerolo, *Italy* 32 D4
Pinetop, *U.S.A.* 111 J9
Pinetown, *S. Africa* 85 D5
Pinetree, *U.S.A.* 110 E11
Pineville, *Ky., U.S.A.* . 105 G4
Pineville, *La., U.S.A.* . 109 K8
Piney, *France* 25 D11
Ping →, *Thailand* 58 E3
Pingaring, *Australia* ... 89 F2
Pingba, *China* 52 D6
Pingchuan, *China* 52 D3
Pingding, *China* 50 F7
Pingdingshan, *China* 50 H7
Pingdong, *Taiwan* 53 F13
Pingdu, *China* 51 F10
Pingelly, *Australia* 89 F2
Pingguo, *China* 52 F6
Pinghe, *China* 53 E11
Pinghu, *China* 53 B13
Pingjiang, *China* 53 C9
Pingle, *China* 53 E8
Pingli, *China* 52 A7
Pingliang, *China* 50 G4
Pinglu, *China* 50 E7
Pingluo, *China* 50 E4
Pingnan, *Fujian, China* . 53 D12
Pingnan,
  Guangxi Zhuangzu,
  China 53 F8
Pingquan, *China* 51 D10
Pingrup, *Australia* 89 F2
Pingtan, *China* 53 E12
Pingtang, *China* 52 E6
Pingwu, *China* 50 H3
Pingxiang,
  Guangxi Zhuangzu,
  China 52 F6
Pingxiang, *Jiangxi, China* 53 D9
Pingyao, *China* 50 F7
Pingyi, *China* 51 G9
Pingyin, *China* 50 F9
Pingyuan, *Guangdong,*
  China 53 E10
Pingyuan, *Shandong, China* 50 F9
Pingyuanjie, *China* 52 F5
Pinhal, *Brazil* 127 A6
Pinheiro, *Brazil* 122 B2
Pinhel, *Portugal* 30 E3
Pinhuá →, *Brazil* 125 B4
Pini, *Indonesia* 56 D1
Piniós →, *Ilía, Greece* . 39 M4
Piniós →, *Trikkala, Greece* 39 K5
Pinjarra, *Australia* 89 F2
Pink →, *Canada* 101 B8
Pinnacles, *Australia* ... 89 E3
Pinnacles, *U.S.A.* 112 J5
Pinnaroo, *Australia* 91 F3
Pinneberg, *Germany* 18 B5
Pino Hachado, Paso,
  S. Amer. 128 A2
Pinon Hills, *U.S.A.* 113 L9
Pinos, *Mexico* 114 C4
Pinos, Mt., *U.S.A.* 113 L7
Pinos Pt., *U.S.A.* 111 H3
Pinos Puente, *Spain* 31 H7
Pinotepa Nacional, *Mexico* 115 D5
Pinrang, *Indonesia* 57 E5
Pins, Pte. aux, *Canada* . 98 D3
Pinsk, *Belorussia* 40 E5
Pintados, *Chile* 124 E4
Pintumba, *Australia* 89 F5
Pinyang, *China* 53 D13
Pinyug, *Russia* 44 C5
Pinzolo, *Italy* 32 B7
Pio XII, *Brazil* 122 B2
Pioche, *U.S.A.* 111 H6
Piombino, *Italy* 32 F7
Piombino, Canale di, *Italy* 32 F7
Pioner, Os., *Russia* 45 B10
Pionki, *Poland* 20 D11
Piorini →, *Brazil* 121 D5
Piorini, L., *Brazil* 121 D5
Piotrków Trybunalski,
  Poland 20 D9
Piove di Sacco, *Italy* .. 33 C9
Pip, *Iran* 65 E9
Pipar, *India* 62 F5
Pipariá, *India* 62 H8
Pipestone, *U.S.A.* 108 D6
Pipestone →, *Canada* 98 B2
Pipestone Cr. →, *Canada* 101 D8
Pipmuacan, Rés., *Canada* 99 C5
Pippingarra, *Australia* . 88 D2
Pipriac, *France* 24 E5
Piqua, *U.S.A.* 104 E3
Piquet Carneiro, *Brazil* 122 C4
Piquiri →, *Brazil* 127 A5
Pir Sohrāb, *Iran* 65 E9
Piracanjuba, *Brazil* 123 E2
Piracicaba, *Brazil* 127 A6
Piracuruca, *Brazil* 122 B3
Piræus = Piraiévs, *Greece* 39 M6
Piraiévs, *Greece* 39 M6

Piráino, *Italy* 35 D7
Pirajuí, *Brazil* 127 A6
Piran, *Slovenia* 33 C10
Pirané, *Argentina* 126 B4
Piranhas, *Brazil* 122 C4
Pirano = Piran, *Slovenia* 33 C10
Pirapemas, *Brazil* 122 B3
Pirapora, *Brazil* 123 E3
Piray →, *Bolivia* 125 D5
Pires do Rio, *Brazil* ... 123 E2
Pírgos, *Ilía, Greece* ... 39 M4
Pírgos, *Messinía, Greece* 39 N5
Pirgovo, *Bulgaria* 38 F8
Piriac-sur-Mer, *France* . 24 E4
Piribebuy, *Paraguay* 126 B4
Pirin Planina, *Bulgaria* 39 H6
Pirineos, *Spain* 28 C6
Piripiri, *Brazil* 122 B3
Piritu, *Venezuela* 120 B4
Pirmasens, *Germany* 19 F3
Pirna, *Germany* 18 E9
Pirot, *Serbia, Yug.* 21 M12
Piru, *Indonesia* 57 E7
Piru, *U.S.A.* 113 L8
Piryatin, *Ukraine* 40 F8
Pisa, *Italy* 32 E7
Pisac, *Peru* 124 C3
Pisagua, *Chile* 124 D3
Pisarovina, *Croatia* 33 C12
Pisciotta, *Italy* 35 B8
Pisco, *Peru* 124 C2
Písek, *Czech.* 20 F4
Pishan, *China* 54 C2
Pishin Lora →, *Pakistan* 62 E1
Pisidia, *Turkey* 66 E4
Pising, *Indonesia* 57 F6
Pismo Beach, *U.S.A.* 113 K6
Pissos, *France* 26 D3
Pissouri, *Cyprus* 37 E11
Pisticci, *Italy* 35 B9
Pistóia, *Italy* 32 E7
Pistol B., *Canada* 101 A10
Pisuerga →, *Spain* 30 D6
Pisz, *Poland* 20 B11
Pitanga, *Brazil* 123 F1
Pitangui, *Brazil* 123 E3
Pitarpunga, L., *Australia* 91 E3
Pitcairn I., *Pac. Oc.* .. 93 K14
Pite älv →, *Sweden* 8 D16
Piteå, *Sweden* 8 D16
Piterka, *Russia* 41 F15
Piteşti, *Romania* 38 E7
Pithapuram, *India* 61 L13
Pithara, *Australia* 89 F2
Píthion, *Greece* 39 H9
Pithiviers, *France* 25 D9
Pitigliano, *Italy* 33 F8
Pitlochry, *U.K.* 14 E5
Pitrufquén, *Chile* 128 A2
Pitsilia □, *Cyprus* 37 E12
Pitt I., *Canada* 100 C3
Pittem, *Belgium* 17 F2
Pittsburg, *Kans., U.S.A.* 109 G7
Pittsburg, *Tex., U.S.A.* 109 J7
Pittsburgh, *U.S.A.* 106 F5
Pittsfield, *Ill., U.S.A.* 108 F9
Pittsfield, *Mass., U.S.A.* 107 D11
Pittsfield, *N.H., U.S.A.* 107 C13
Pittston, *U.S.A.* 107 E9
Pittsworth, *Australia* .. 91 D5
Pituri →, *Australia* 90 C2
Piuí, *Brazil* 123 F2
Pium, *Brazil* 122 D2
Piura, *Peru* 124 B1
Piura □, *Peru* 124 A2
Pivijay, *Colombia* 120 A3
Pixley, *U.S.A.* 112 K7
Piyai, *Greece* 39 K4
Pizarro, *Colombia* 120 C2
Pizol, *Switz.* 23 C8
Pizzo, *Italy* 35 D9
Placentia, *Canada* 99 C9
Placentia B., *Canada* ... 99 C9
Placer, *Phil.* 55 F5
Placerville, *U.S.A.* 112 G6
Placetas, *Cuba* 116 B4
Plaffeien, *Switz.* 22 C4
Plain Dealing, *U.S.A.* .. 109 J8
Plainfield, *U.S.A.* 107 F10
Plains, *Kans., U.S.A.* .. 109 G4
Plains, *Mont., U.S.A.* .. 110 C6
Plains, *Tex., U.S.A.* ... 109 J3
Plainview, *Nebr., U.S.A.* 108 D6
Plainview, *Tex., U.S.A.* 109 H4
Plainville, *U.S.A.* 108 F5
Plainwell, *U.S.A.* 104 D3
Plaisance, *France* 26 E4
Pláka, *Greece* 39 J8
Pláka, Ákra, *Greece* 37 D8
Plakhino, *Russia* 44 C9
Plana Cays, *Bahamas* 117 B5
Planada, *U.S.A.* 112 H6
Plancoët, *France* 24 D4
Planeta Rica, *Colombia* . 120 B2
Planina, *Slovenia* 33 B12
Planina, *Slovenia* 33 C11
Plankinton, *U.S.A.* 108 D5
Plano, *U.S.A.* 109 J6
Plant City, *U.S.A.* 105 L4
Plaquemine, *U.S.A.* 109 K9
Plasencia, *Spain* 30 E4
Plaški, *Croatia* 33 C12
Plaster City, *U.S.A.* ... 113 N11
Plaster Rock, *Canada* ... 99 C6

Plastun, *Russia* 48 B8
Plata, Río de la, *S. Amer.* 126 C4
Platani →, *Italy* 34 E6
Plátanos, *Greece* 37 D5
Plateau □, *Nigeria* 79 D6
Plateau du Coteau du
  Missouri, *U.S.A.* 108 B4
Plato, *Colombia* 120 B3
Platta, Piz, *Switz.* 23 D9
Platte, *U.S.A.* 108 D5
Platte →, *U.S.A.* 108 F7
Platteville, *U.S.A.* 108 E2
Plattling, *Germany* 19 G8
Plattsburgh, *U.S.A.* 107 B11
Plattsmouth, *U.S.A.* 108 E7
Plau, *Germany* 18 B8
Plauen, *Germany* 18 E8
Plavinas, *Latvia* 40 C4
Plavnica, *Montenegro, Yug.* 21 N9
Plavsk, *Russia* 41 E10
Playa Blanca, *Canary Is.* 36 F6
Playa Blanca Sur,
  Canary Is. 36 F6
Playa de las Americas,
  Canary Is. 36 F3
Playa de Mogán, *Canary Is.* 36 G4
Playa del Inglés, *Canary Is.* 36 G4
Playa Esmeralda,
  Canary Is. 36 F5
Playgreen L., *Canada* ... 101 C9
Pleasant Bay, *Canada* .. 99 C7
Pleasant Hill, *Calif.,*
  U.S.A. 112 H4
Pleasant Hill, *Mo., U.S.A.* 108 F7
Pleasanton, *U.S.A.* 109 L5
Pleasantville, *U.S.A.* ... 104 F8
Pléaux, *France* 26 C6
Pleiku, *Vietnam* 58 F7
Plélan-le-Grand, *France* .. 24 D4
Plémet-la-Pierre, *France* . 24 D4
Pléneuf-Val-André, *France* 24 D4
Plenița, *Romania* 38 E6
Plenty →, *Australia* 90 C2
Plenty, B. of, *N.Z.* 87 G6
Plentywood, *U.S.A.* 108 A2
Plessisville, *Canada* 99 C5
Plestin-les-Grèves, *France* . 24 D3
Pleszew, *Poland* 20 D7
Pleternica, *Croatia* 21 K7
Pletipi L., *Canada* 99 B5
Pleven, *Bulgaria* 38 F7
Plevlja, *Montenegro, Yug.* 21 M9
Płock, *Poland* 20 C9
Plöcken Passo, *Italy* 33 B9
Ploegsteert, *Belgium* ... 17 G1
Ploemeur, *France* 24 E3
Ploërmel, *France* 24 E4
Ploiești, *Romania* 38 E9
Plombières-les-Bains,
  France 25 E13
Plomin, *Croatia* 33 C11
Plön, *Germany* 18 A6
Plöner See, *Germany* ... 18 A6
Plonge, Lac la, *Canada* .. 101 B7
Płońsk, *Poland* 20 C10
Plouaret, *France* 24 D3
Plouay, *France* 24 E3
Ploudalmézeau, *France* .. 24 D2
Plougasnou, *France* 24 D3
Plouha, *France* 24 D4
Plouhinec, *France* 24 E2
Plovdiv, *Bulgaria* 38 G7
Plum, *U.S.A.* 106 F5
Plum I., *U.S.A.* 107 E12
Plummer, *U.S.A.* 110 C5
Plumtree, *Zimbabwe* ... 83 G2
Plunge, *Lithuania* 40 D2
Pluvigner, *France* 24 E3
Plymouth, *U.K.* 13 G3
Plymouth, *Calif., U.S.A.* . 112 G6
Plymouth, *Ind., U.S.A.* .. 104 E2
Plymouth, *Mass., U.S.A.* 107 E14
Plymouth, *N.C., U.S.A.* . 105 H7
Plymouth, *N.H., U.S.A.* . 107 C13
Plymouth, *Pa., U.S.A.* .. 107 E9
Plymouth, *Wis., U.S.A.* . 104 D2
Plynlimon = Pumlumon
  Fawr, *U.K.* 13 E4
Plyussa, *Russia* 40 B6
Plyussa →, *Russia* 40 B6
Plzeň, *Czech.* 20 F3
Pniewy, *Poland* 20 C6
Pô, *Burkina Faso* 79 C4
Po →, *Italy* 33 D9
Po, Foci del, *Italy* 33 D9
Po Hai = Bo Hai, *China* . 51 E10
Pobé, *Benin* 79 D5
Pobeda, *Russia* 45 C15
Pobedino, *Russia* 45 E15
Pobedy Pik, *Kirghizia* .. 44 E8
Pobiedziska, *Poland* 20 C7
Pobla de Segur, *Spain* .. 28 C5
Pobladura de Valle, *Spain* 30 C5
Pocahontas, *Ark., U.S.A.* 109 G9
Pocahontas, *Iowa, U.S.A.* 108 D7
Pocatello, *U.S.A.* 110 E7
Pochep, *Russia* 40 E8
Pochinki, *Russia* 41 D14
Pochinok, *Russia* 40 D8
Pochutla, *Mexico* 115 D5
Poci, *Venezuela* 121 B5
Pocinhos, *Brazil* 122 C4
Pocito Casas, *Mexico* .. 114 B2
Poções, *Brazil* 123 D3

Pocomoke City, *U.S.A.* .. 104 F8
Poconé, *Brazil* 125 D6
Poços de Caldas, *Brazil* . 127 A6
Poddebice, *Poland* 20 D8
Poděbrady, *Czech.* 20 E5
Podensac, *France* 26 D3
Podgorica,
  Montenegro, Yug. ... 21 N9
Podkamennaya
  Tunguska →, *Russia* ... 45 C10
Podlapac, *Croatia* 33 D12
Podolsk, *Russia* 41 D10
Podor, *Senegal* 78 B1
Podravska Slatina, *Croatia* 21 K7
Podujevo, *Serbia, Yug.* .. 21 N11
Poel, *Germany* 18 B7
Pofadder, *S. Africa* 84 D2
Pogamasing, *Canada* ... 98 C3
Poggiardo, *Italy* 35 B11
Poggibonsi, *Italy* 33 E8
Pogoanele, *Romania* ... 38 E9
Pogradeci, *Albania* 39 J3
Pogranitšnyi, *Russia* ... 48 B5
Poh, *Indonesia* 57 E6
Pohang, *S. Korea* 51 F15
Pohnpei, *Pac. Oc.* 92 G7
Pohorelá, *Slovakia* 20 G10
Pohorje, *Slovenia* 33 B12
Poiana Mare, *Romania* .. 38 F6
Poindimié, C., *Antarctica* 5 C11
Point Edward, *Canada* .. 98 D3
Point Pedro, *Sri Lanka* .. 60 Q12
Point Pleasant, *N.J.,*
  U.S.A. 107 F10
Point Pleasant, *W. Va.,*
  U.S.A. 104 F4
Pointe-à-la Hache, *U.S.A.* 109 L10
Pointe-à-Pitre, *Guadeloupe* 117 C7
Pointe Noire, *Congo* ... 80 E2
Poirino, *Italy* 32 D4
Poisonbush Ra., *Australia* 88 D3
Poissy, *France* 25 D9
Poitiers, *France* 24 F7
Poitou, *France* 26 B3
Poitou, Seuil du, *France* . 26 B4
Poix de Picardie, *France* . 25 C8
Poix-Terron, *France* ... 25 C11
Pojoaque Valley, *U.S.A.* . 111 J11
Pokaran, *India* 60 F7
Pokataroo, *Australia* ... 91 D4
Poko, *Sudan* 77 F3
Poko, *Zaïre* 82 B2
Pokrov, *Russia* 41 D11
Pokrovsk, *Russia* 41 F15
Pokrovsk, *Russia* 45 C13
Pol, *Spain* 30 B3
Pola = Pula, *Croatia* ... 33 D10
Pola de Allande, *Spain* .. 30 B4
Pola de Lena, *Spain* ... 30 B5
Pola de Siero, *Spain* ... 30 B5
Pola de Somiedo, *Spain* . 30 B4
Polacca, *U.S.A.* 111 J8
Polan, *Iran* 65 E9
Poland ■, *Europe* 20 C9
Polanów, *Poland* 20 A6
Polatsk = Polotsk,
  Belorussia 40 D6
Polcura, *Chile* 126 D1
Polden Hills, *U.K.* 13 F5
Polessk, *Russia* 40 D2
Polesye, *Belorussia* 40 E6
Polewali, *Indonesia* ... 57 E5
Polgar, *Hungary* 21 H11
Pólgyo-ri, *S. Korea* 51 G14
Poli, *Cameroon* 80 C2
Políaigos, *Greece* 39 N7
Policastro, G. di, *Italy* .. 35 C8
Police, *Poland* 20 B4
Polignano a Mare, *Italy* . 35 B10
Poligny, *France* 25 F12
Polkhnitsa, *Greece* 39 K9
Polillo Is., *Phil.* 55 D4
Polillo Strait, *Phil.* 55 D4
Polis, *Cyprus* 37 D11
Polístena, *Italy* 35 D9
Políyiros, *Greece* 39 J6
Polk, *U.S.A.* 106 E5
Polla, *Italy* 35 B8
Pollachi, *India* 60 P10
Pollensa, *Spain* 36 B10
Pollensa, B. de, *Spain* .. 36 B10
Póllica, *Italy* 35 B8
Pollino, Mte., *Italy* 35 C9
Pollock, *U.S.A.* 108 C4
Polna, *Russia* 40 B6
Polnovat, *Russia* 44 C7
Polo, *U.S.A.* 108 E10
Pologi, *Ukraine* 42 C7
Polonnoye, *Ukraine* ... 40 F5
Polotsk, *Belorussia* ... 40 D6
Polson, *U.S.A.* 110 C6
Poltava, *Ukraine* 42 B6
Polunochnoye, *Russia* .. 44 C7
Polynesia, *Pac. Oc.* 93 H11
Polynésie française □ =
  French Polynesia ■,
  Pac. Oc. 93 J13
Pomarance, *Italy* 32 E7
Pomarico, *Italy* 35 B9
Pomaro, *Mexico* 114 D4
Pombal, *Brazil* 122 C4
Pombal, *Portugal* 30 F2
Pómbia, *Greece* 37 D6
Pomeroy, *Ohio, U.S.A.* . 104 F4
Pomeroy, *Wash., U.S.A.* 110 C5
Pomona, *U.S.A.* 113 L9

Pomorie, *Bulgaria* 38 G10
Pomos, *Cyprus* 37 D11
Pomos, C., *Cyprus* 37 D11
Pomoshnaya, *Ukraine* .. 42 B4
Pompano Beach, *U.S.A.* . 105 M5
Pompei, *Italy* 35 B7
Pompey, *France* 25 D13
Pompeys Pillar, *U.S.A.* . 110 D10
Ponape = Pohnpei,
  Pac. Oc. 92 G7
Ponask, L., *Canada* ... 98 B1
Ponass L., *Canada* 101 C8
Ponca, *U.S.A.* 108 D6
Ponca City, *U.S.A.* 109 G6
Ponce, *Puerto Rico* 117 C6
Ponchatoula, *U.S.A.* ... 109 K9
Poncheville, L., *Canada* . 98 B4
Poncin, *France* 27 B9
Pond, *U.S.A.* 113 K7
Pond Inlet, *Canada* 97 A12
Pondicherry, *India* 60 P11
Pondrôme, *Belgium* ... 17 H6
Ponds, I. of, *Canada* ... 99 B8
Ponferrada, *Spain* 30 C4
Pongo, Wadi →, *Sudan* . 77 F2
Poniatowa, *Poland* 20 D12
Ponikva, *Slovenia* 33 B12
Ponnani, *India* 60 P9
Ponnyadaung, *Burma* .. 61 J19
Ponoi, *Russia* 44 C5
Ponoi →, *Russia* 44 C5
Ponoka, *Canada* 100 C6
Ponorogo, *Indonesia* .. 57 G14
Pons, *France* 26 C3
Pons, *Spain* 28 D6
Ponsul →, *Portugal* ... 31 F3
Pont-à-Celles, *Belgium* . 17 G4
Pont-à-Mousson, *France* 25 D13
Pont-Audemer, *France* . 24 C7
Pont-Aven, *France* 24 E3
Pont Canavese, *Italy* ... 32 C4
Pont-de-Roide, *France* .. 25 E13
Pont-de-Salars, *France* .. 26 D6
Pont-de-Vaux, *France* .. 25 F11
Pont-de-Veyle, *France* .. 27 B8
Pont-l'Abbé, *France* ... 24 E2
Pont-l'Évêque, *France* .. 24 C7
Pont-St.-Esprit, *France* . 27 D8
Pont-sur-Yonne, *France* 25 D10
Ponta de Pedras, *Brazil* . 122 B2
Ponta do Sol, *Madeira* .. 36 D2
Ponta Grossa, *Brazil* ... 127 B5
Ponta Pora, *Brazil* 127 A4
Pontacq, *France* 26 E3
Pontailler-sur-Saône,
  France 25 E12
Pontal →, *Brazil* 122 C3
Pontalina, *Brazil* 123 E2
Pontarlier, *France* 25 F13
Pontassieve, *Italy* 33 E8
Pontaubault, *France* ... 24 D5
Pontaumur, *France* ... 26 C6
Pontcharra, *France* ... 27 C10
Pontchartrain L., *U.S.A.* 109 K9
Pontchâteau, *France* .. 24 E4
Ponte Alta, Serra do,
  Brazil 123 E2
Ponte Alta do Norte, *Brazil* 122 D2
Ponte Branca, *Brazil* ... 125 D7
Ponte da Barca, *Portugal* 30 D2
Ponte de Sor, *Portugal* . 31 F3
Ponte dell 'Olio, *Italy* ... 32 D6
Ponte di Legno, *Italy* ... 32 B7
Ponte do Lima, *Portugal* 30 D2
Ponte do Pungué, *Mozam.* 83 F3
Ponte-Leccia, *France* ... 27 F13
Ponte nell' Alpi, *Italy* ... 33 B9
Ponte Nova, *Brazil* 123 F3
Ponte San Martino, *Italy* 32 C4
Ponte San Pietro, *Italy* . 32 C6
Pontebba, *Italy* 33 B10
Pontecorvo, *Italy* 34 A6
Pontedera, *Italy* 32 E7
Pontefract, *U.K.* 12 D6
Ponteix, *Canada* 101 D7
Pontelandolfo, *Italy* ... 35 A7
Pontevedra, *Spain* 30 C2
Pontevedra □, *Spain* ... 30 C2
Pontevedra, R. de →,
  Spain 30 C2
Pontevico, *Italy* 32 C7
Pontiac, *Ill., U.S.A.* 108 E10
Pontiac, *Mich., U.S.A.* . 104 D4
Pontian Kecil, *Malaysia* . 59 M4
Pontianak, *Indonesia* .. 56 E3
Pontic Mts. = Kuzey
  Anadolu Dağları, *Turkey* 66 C6
Pontine Is. = Ponziane,
  Isole, *Italy* 34 B5
Pontine Mts. = Kuzey
  Anadolu Dağları, *Turkey* 66 C6
Pontínia, *Italy* 34 A6
Pontivy, *France* 24 D4
Pontoise, *France* 25 C9
Ponton →, *Canada* 100 B5
Pontorson, *France* 24 D5
Pontrémoli, *Italy* 32 D6
Pontresina, *Switz.* 23 D9
Pontrieux, *France* 24 D3
Pontypool, *U.K.* 13 F4
Pontypridd, *U.K.* 13 F4
Ponza, *Italy* 34 B5
Ponziane, Isole, *Italy* ... 34 B5
Poochera, *Australia* ... 91 E1
Poole, *U.K.* 13 G6
Pooley I., *Canada* 100 C3

Poona = Pune, *India* ... 60 K8
Pooncarie, *Australia* ... 91 E3
Poopelloe L., *Australia* . 91 E3
Poopó, *Bolivia* 124 D4
Poopó, L. de, *Bolivia* .. 124 D4
Popanyinning, *Australia* 89 F2
Popayán, *Colombia* ... 120 C2
Poperinge, *Belgium* ... 17 G1
Popigay, *Russia* 45 B12
Popilta, L., *Australia* ... 91 E3
Popio L., *Australia* 91 E3
Poplar, *U.S.A.* 108 A2
Poplar →, *Man., Canada* 101 C9
Poplar →, *N.W.T.,*
  Canada 100 A4
Poplar Bluff, *U.S.A.* ... 109 G9
Poplarville, *U.S.A.* 109 K10
Popocatepetl, *Mexico* .. 115 D5
Popokabaka, *Zaïre* 80 F3
Pópoli, *Italy* 33 F10
Popovača, *Croatia* 33 C13
Popovo, *Bulgaria* 38 F9
Poppel, *Belgium* 17 F6
Poprád, *Slovakia* 20 F10
Poprád →, *Slovakia* ... 20 F10
Porali →, *Pakistan* 62 G2
Porangaba, *Brazil* 124 B3
Porangatu, *Brazil* 123 D2
Porbandar, *India* 62 J3
Porce →, *Colombia* 120 B3
Porcher I., *Canada* 100 C2
Porco, *Bolivia* 124 D4
Porcos →, *Brazil* 123 D2
Porcuna, *Spain* 31 H6
Porcupine →, *Canada* . 101 B8
Porcupine →, *U.S.A.* .. 96 B5
Pordenone, *Italy* 33 C9
Poreč, *Croatia* 33 C10
Porecatu, *Brazil* 123 F1
Poretskoye, *Russia* ... 41 D15
Pori, *Finland* 9 F16
Porjus, *Sweden* 8 C15
Porkhov, *Russia* 40 C6
Porkkala, *Finland* 9 G18
Porlamar, *Venezuela* .. 121 A5
Porlezza, *Italy* 32 B6
Porma →, *Spain* 30 C5
Pornic, *France* 24 E4
Poronaysk, *Russia* 45 E15
Póros, *Greece* 39 M6
Poroshiri-Dake, *Japan* .. 48 C11
Poroto Mts., *Tanzania* . 83 D3
Porpoise B., *Antarctica* . 5 C9
Porquerolles, I. de, *France* 27 F10
Porrentruy, *Switz.* 22 B4
Porreras, *Spain* 36 B10
Porretta, Passo di, *Italy* . 32 D7
Porsangen, *Norway* ... 8 A18
Porsgrunn, *Norway* ... 10 E3
Port Adelaide, *Australia* 91 E2
Port Alberni, *Canada* .. 100 D4
Port Alfred, *Canada* ... 99 C5
Port Alfred, *S. Africa* .. 84 E4
Port Alice, *Canada* 100 C3
Port Allegany, *U.S.A.* .. 106 E6
Port Allen, *U.S.A.* 109 K9
Port Alma, *Australia* ... 90 C5
Port Angeles, *U.S.A.* .. 112 B3
Port Antonio, *Jamaica* . 116 C4
Port Aransas, *U.S.A.* .. 109 M6
Port Arthur = Lüshun,
  China 51 E11
Port Arthur, *Australia* . 90 G4
Port Arthur, *U.S.A.* ... 109 L8
Port au Port B., *Canada* 99 C8
Port-au-Prince, *Haiti* .. 117 C5
Port Augusta, *Australia* . 91 E2
Port Augusta West,
  Australia 91 E2
Port Austin, *U.S.A.* ... 98 D3
Port Bell, *Uganda* 82 B3
Port Bergé Vaovao,
  Madag. 85 B8
Port Blandford, *Canada* 99 C9
Port Bou, *Spain* 28 C8
Port Bouët, *Ivory C.* ... 78 D4
Port Bradshaw, *Australia* 90 A2
Port Broughton, *Australia* 91 E2
Port Burwell, *Canada* .. 98 D3
Port Canning, *India* ... 63 H13
Port-Cartier, *Canada* .. 99 B6
Port Chalmers, *N.Z.* ... 87 L3
Port Chester, *U.S.A.* .. 107 F11
Port Clements, *Canada* . 100 C2
Port Clinton, *U.S.A.* .. 104 E4
Port Colborne, *Canada* . 98 D4
Port Coquitlam, *Canada* 100 D4
Port Credit, *Canada* ... 106 C5
Port Curtis, *Australia* .. 90 C5
Port Dalhousie, *Canada* 106 C5
Port Darwin, *Australia* . 88 B5
Port Darwin, *Falk. Is.* . 128 D5
Port Davey, *Australia* .. 90 G4
Port-de-Bouc, *France* .. 27 E8
Port-de-Paix, *Haiti* ... 117 C5
Port Dickson, *Malaysia* . 59 L3
Port Douglas, *Australia* 90 B4
Port Dover, *Canada* ... 106 D4
Port Edward, *Canada* .. 100 C2
Port Elgin, *Canada* 98 D3
Port Elizabeth, *S. Africa* 84 E4
Port Ellen, *U.K.* 14 F2
Port-en-Bessin, *France* . 24 C6
Port Erin, *I. of Man* ... 12 C3
Port Essington, *Australia* 88 B5

Port Etienne =
  Nouâdhibou, *Mauritania* 74 D1
Port Fairy, *Australia* ... 91 F3
Port Fouâd = Bûr Fuad,
  Egypt 76 H8
Port Gamble, *U.S.A.* ... 112 C4
Port-Gentil, *Gabon* 80 E1
Port Gibson, *U.S.A.* ... 109 K9
Port Glasgow, *U.K.* ... 14 F4
Port Harcourt, *Nigeria* . 79 E6
Port Hardy, *Canada* ... 100 C3
Port Harrison =
  Inoucdjouac, *Canada* .. 97 C12
Port Hawkesbury, *Canada* 99 C7
Port Hedland, *Australia* . 88 D2
Port Henry, *U.S.A.* 107 B11
Port Hood, *Canada* 99 C7
Port Hope, *Canada* 98 D4
Port Hueneme, *U.S.A.* . 113 L7
Port Huron, *U.S.A.* ... 104 D4
Port Isabel, *U.S.A.* 109 M6
Port Jefferson, *U.S.A.* . 107 F11
Port Jervis, *U.S.A.* 107 E10
Port-Joinville, *France* .. 24 F4
Port Katon, *Russia* 43 C8
Port Kelang = Pelabuhan
  Kelang, *Malaysia* ... 59 L3
Port Kembla, *Australia* . 91 E5
Port Kenny, *Australia* .. 91 E1
Port-la-Nouvelle, *France* 26 E7
Port Laoise, *Ireland* ... 15 C4
Port Lavaca, *U.S.A.* ... 109 L6
Port-Leucate, *France* .. 26 F7
Port Lincoln, *Australia* . 91 E2
Port Loko, *S. Leone* ... 78 D2
Port Louis, *France* 24 E3
Port Lyautey = Kenitra,
  Morocco 74 B3
Port MacDonnell, *Australia* 91 F3
Port Macquarie, *Australia* 91 E5
Port Maria, *Jamaica* ... 116 C4
Port Mellon, *Canada* ... 100 D4
Port-Menier, *Canada* .. 99 C7
Port Morant, *Jamaica* .. 116 C4
Port Moresby, *Papua N. G.* 92 H6
Port Mourant, *Guyana* . 121 B6
Port Mouton, *Canada* .. 99 D7
Port Musgrave, *Australia* 90 A3
Port-Navalo, *France* ... 24 E3
Port Nelson, *Canada* ... 101 B10
Port Nolloth, *S. Africa* . 84 D2
Port Nouveau-Québec,
  Canada 97 C13
Port O'Connor, *U.S.A.* . 109 L6
Port of Spain, *Trin. & Tob.* 117 D7
Port Orchard, *U.S.A.* .. 112 C4
Port Orford, *U.S.A.* ... 110 E1
Port Pegasus, *N.Z.* 87 M1
Port Perry, *Canada* 98 D4
Port Phillip B., *Australia* 91 F3
Port Pirie, *Australia* ... 91 E2
Port Radium = Echo Bay,
  Canada 96 B8
Port Renfrew, *Canada* .. 100 D4
Port Roper, *Australia* .. 90 A2
Port Rowan, *Canada* ... 98 D3
Port Safaga = Bûr Safâga,
  Egypt 76 B3
Port Said = Bûr Sa'îd,
  Egypt 76 H8
Port St. Joe, *U.S.A.* ... 105 L3
Port St. Johns, *S. Africa* 85 E4
Port-St.-Louis-du-Rhône,
  France 27 E8
Port San Vicente, *Phil.* . 55 B5
Port Sanilac, *U.S.A.* ... 98 D3
Port Saunders, *Canada* . 99 B8
Port Severn, *Canada* ... 106 B5
Port Shepstone, *S. Africa* 85 E5
Port Simpson, *Canada* . 100 C2
Port Stanley = Stanley,
  Falk. Is. 128 D5
Port Stanley, *Canada* .. 98 D3
Port Sudan = Bûr Sûdân,
  Sudan 76 D4
Port-sur-Saône, *France* . 25 E13
Port Talbot, *U.K.* 13 F4
Port Taufiq = Bûr Taufiq,
  Egypt 76 J8
Port Townsend, *U.S.A.* . 112 B4
Port-Vendres, *France* .. 26 F7
Port Wakefield, *Australia* 91 E2
Port Washington, *U.S.A.* 104 D2
Port Weld, *Malaysia* ... 59 K3
Portachuelo, *Bolivia* ... 125 D5
Portadown, *U.K.* 15 B5
Portage, *U.S.A.* 108 D10
Portage La Prairie, *Canada* 101 D9
Portageville, *U.S.A.* ... 109 G10
Portalegre, *Portugal* ... 31 F3
Portalegre □, *Portugal* . 31 F3
Portales, *U.S.A.* 109 H3
Portarlington, *Ireland* .. 15 C4
Porteirinha, *Brazil* 123 E3
Portel, *Brazil* 122 B1
Portel, *Portugal* 31 G3
Porter L., *N.W.T., Canada* 101 A7
Porter L., *Sask., Canada* 101 B7
Porterville, *S. Africa* ... 84 E2
Porterville, *U.S.A.* 111 H4
Porthcawl, *U.K.* 13 F4
Porthill, *U.S.A.* 110 B5
Portile de Fier, *Europe* . 38 E5
Portimão, *Portugal* ... 31 H2
Portland, *N.S.W., Australia* 91 E4
Portland, *Vic., Australia* . 91 F3

Portland, *Canada* 107 B8
Portland, *Conn., U.S.A.* .. 107 E12
Portland, *Maine, U.S.A.* . 99 D5
Portland, *Mich., U.S.A.* .. 104 D3
Portland, *Oreg., U.S.A.* .. 112 E4
Portland, I. of, *U.K.* 13 G5
Portland B., *Australia* ... 91 F3
Portland Bill, *U.K.* 13 G5
Portland Prom., *Canada* .. 97 C12
Portlands Roads, *Australia* 90 A3
Portneuf, *Canada* 99 C5
Pôrto, *Brazil* 122 B3
Porto, *France* 27 F12
Porto, *Portugal* 30 D2
Porto □, *Portugal* 30 D2
Pôrto Acre, *Brazil* 124 B4
Pôrto Alegre, *Pará, Brazil* 121 D7
Pôrto Alegre,
  Rio Grande do S., Brazil 127 C5
Porto Amboim = Gunza,
  Angola 80 G2
Porto Argentera, *Italy* ... 32 D4
Porto Azzurro, *Italy* 32 F7
Pôrto Botte, *Italy* 34 C1
Pôrto Cajueiro, *Brazil* .. 125 C6
Porto Civitanova, *Italy* .. 33 E10
Porto Cristo, *Spain* 36 B10
Pôrto da Fôlha, *Brazil* .. 122 C4
Pôrto de Móz, *Brazil* 121 D7
Pôrto de Pedras, *Brazil* .. 122 C4
Pôrto des Meinacos, *Brazil* 125 C7
Porto Empédocle, *Italy* .. 34 E6
Pôrto Esperança, *Brazil* .. 125 D6
Pôrto Esperidão, *Brazil* .. 125 D6
Pôrto Franco, *Brazil* 122 C2
Pôrto Garibaldi, *Italy* ... 33 D9
Pôrto Grande, *Brazil* 121 C7
Pôrto Jofre, *Brazil* 125 D6
Pórto Lágo, *Greece* 39 J8
Porto Mendes, *Brazil* 127 A5
Pôrto Moniz, *Madeira* ... 36 D2
Porto Murtinho, *Brazil* .. 125 E6
Pôrto Nacional, *Brazil* ... 122 D2
Porto Novo, *Benin* 79 D5
Porto Petro, *Spain* 36 B10
Porto Recanati, *Italy* 33 E10
Porto San Giórgio, *Italy* . 33 E10
Pôrto Santana, *Brazil* ... 121 D7
Porto Santo, *Madeira* ... 72 B1
Pôrto Santo Stefano, *Italy* 32 F8
Pôrto São José, *Brazil* ... 127 A5
Pôrto Seguro, *Brazil* 123 E4
Porto Tolle, *Italy* 33 D9
Pórto Tórres, *Italy* 34 B1
Pôrto União, *Brazil* 127 B5
Pôrto Válter, *Brazil* 124 B3
Porto-Vecchio, *France* ... 27 G13
Pôrto Velho, *Brazil* 125 B5
Portobelo, *Panama* 116 E4
Portoferráio, *Italy* 32 F7
Portogruaro, *Italy* 33 C9
Portola, *U.S.A.* 112 F6
Portomaggiore, *Italy* 33 D8
Portoscuso, *Italy* 34 C1
Portovénere, *Italy* 32 D6
Portoviejo, *Ecuador* 120 D1
Portpatrick, *U.K.* 14 G3
Portree, *U.K.* 14 D2
Portrush, *U.K.* 15 A5
Portsall, *France* 24 D2
Portsmouth, *Domin.* 117 C7
Portsmouth, *U.K.* 13 G6
Portsmouth, *N.H., U.S.A.* 107 C14
Portsmouth, *Ohio, U.S.A.* 104 F4
Portsmouth, *R.I., U.S.A.* 107 E13
Portsmouth, *Va., U.S.A.* 104 G7
Portsoy, *U.K.* 14 D6
Porttipahta, *Finland* 8 B19
Portugal ■, *Europe* 30 F3
Portugalete, *Spain* 28 B1
Portuguesa □, *Venezuela* . 120 B4
Portuguese-Guinea =
  Guinea-Bissau ■, *Africa* 78 C2
Portumna, *Ireland* 15 C3
Portville, *U.S.A.* 106 D6
Porvenir, *Bolivia* 124 C4
Porvenir, *Chile* 128 D2
Porvoo = Borgå, *Finland* . 9 F18
Porzuna, *Spain* 31 F6
Posada →, *Italy* 34 B2
Posadas, *Argentina* 127 B4
Posadas, *Spain* 31 H5
Poschiavo, *Switz.* 23 D10
Posets, *Spain* 28 C5
Poshan = Boshan, *China* . 51 F9
Posht-e-Badam, *Iran* 65 C7
Posídhion, Ákra, *Greece* . 39 K6
Poso, *Indonesia* 57 E6
Posoegroenoe, *Surinam* . 121 C6
Posong, *S. Korea* 51 G14
Posse, *Brazil* 123 D2
Possel, *C.A.R.* 80 C3
Possession I., *Antarctica* . 5 D11
Pössneck, *Germany* 18 E7
Post, *U.S.A.* 109 J4
Post Falls, *U.S.A.* 110 C5
Postavy, *Belorussia* 40 D5
Poste Maurice Cortier,
  Algeria 75 D5
Postmasburg, *S. Africa* .. 84 D3
Postojna, *Slovenia* 33 C11
Poston, *U.S.A.* 113 M12
Potchefstroom, *S. Africa* . 84 D4
Poté, *Brazil* 123 E3
Poteau, *U.S.A.* 109 H7

Poteet, *U.S.A.* 109 L5
Potelu, Lacul, *Romania* .. 38 F7
Potenza, *Italy* 35 B8
Potenza →, *Italy* 33 E10
Potenza Picena, *Italy* ... 33 E10
Poteriteri, L., *N.Z.* 87 M1
Potes, *Spain* 30 B6
Potgietersrus, *S. Africa* .. 85 C4
Poti, *Georgia* 43 E9
Potiraguá, *Brazil* 123 E4
Potiskum, *Nigeria* 79 C7
Potomac →, *U.S.A.* 104 F7
Potosí, *Bolivia* 125 D4
Potosí □, *Bolivia* 124 E4
Potosi Mt., *U.S.A.* 113 K11
Pototan, *Phil.* 55 F5
Potrerillos, *Chile* 126 B2
Potsdam, *Germany* 18 C9
Potsdam, *U.S.A.* 107 B10
Pottenstein, *Germany* ... 19 F7
Potter, *U.S.A.* 108 E3
Pottery Hill = Abû Ballas,
  Egypt 76 C2
Pottstown, *U.S.A.* 107 F9
Pottsville, *U.S.A.* 107 F8
Pottuvil, *Sri Lanka* 60 R12
Pouancé, *France* 24 E5
Pouce Coupé, *Canada* ... 100 B4
Poughkeepsie, *U.S.A.* ... 107 E11
Pouilly-sur-Loire, *France* . 25 E9
Poulaphouca Res., *Ireland* 15 C5
Poulsbo, *U.S.A.* 112 C4
Pourri, Mt., *France* 27 C10
Pouso Alegre,
  Mato Grosso, Brazil .. 125 C6
Pouso Alegre,
  Minas Gerais, Brazil .. 127 A6
Pouzauges, *France* 24 F6
Povenets, *Russia* 44 C4
Poverty B., *N.Z.* 87 H7
Póvoa de Lanhosa,
  Portugal 30 D2
Póvoa de Varzim, *Portugal* 30 D2
Povorino, *Russia* 41 F13
Powassan, *Canada* 98 C4
Powder →, *U.S.A.* 108 B2
Powder River, *U.S.A.* ... 110 E10
Powell, *U.S.A.* 110 D9
Powell L., *U.S.A.* 111 H8
Powell River, *Canada* ... 100 D4
Powers, *Mich., U.S.A.* .. 104 C2
Powers, *Oreg., U.S.A.* .. 110 E1
Powers Lake, *U.S.A.* ... 108 A3
Powys □, *U.K.* 13 E4
Poxoreu, *Brazil* 125 D7
Poyang Hu, *China* 53 C11
Poyarkovo, *Russia* 45 E13
Poza de la Sal, *Spain* ... 28 C1
Poza Rica, *Mexico* 115 C5
Pozanti, *Turkey* 66 E6
Požarevac, *Serbia, Yug.* . 21 L11
Pozi, *Taiwan* 53 F13
Pozo, *U.S.A.* 113 K6
Pozo Alcón, *Spain* 29 H2
Pozo Almonte, *Chile* 124 E4
Pozo Colorado, *Paraguay* 126 A4
Pozo del Dátil, *Mexico* .. 114 B2
Pozoblanco, *Spain* 31 G6
Pozuzo, *Peru* 124 C2
Pozzallo, *Italy* 35 F7
Pozzuoli, *Italy* 35 B7
Pra →, *Ghana* 79 D4
Prachin Buri, *Thailand* .. 58 E3
Prachuap Khiri Khan,
  Thailand 59 G2
Pradelles, *France* 26 D7
Pradera, *Colombia* 120 C2
Prades, *France* 26 F6
Prado, *Brazil* 123 E4
Prado del Rey, *Spain* ... 31 J5
Præstø, *Denmark* 11 J6
Pragersko, *Slovenia* 33 B12
Prague = Praha, *Czech.* . 20 E4
Praha, *Czech.* 20 E4
Prahecq, *France* 26 B3
Prahova →, *Romania* ... 38 E8
Prahovo, *Serbia, Yug.* .. 21 L12
Praid, *Romania* 38 C8
Prainha, *Amazonas, Brazil* 125 B5
Prainha, *Pará, Brazil* ... 121 D7
Prairie, *Australia* 90 C3
Prairie →, *U.S.A.* 109 H5
Prairie City, *U.S.A.* 110 D4
Prairie du Chien, *U.S.A.* 108 D9
Prairies, *Canada* 96 C9
Pramánda, *Greece* 39 K4
Pran Buri, *Thailand* 58 F2
Prang, *Ghana* 79 D4
Prapat, *Indonesia* 56 D1
Prasonísi, Ákra, *Greece* . 37 D9
Prata, *Brazil* 123 E2
Pratapgarh, *India* 62 G6
Prática di Mare, *Italy* ... 34 A5
Prätigau, *Switz.* 23 C9
Prato, *Italy* 32 E8
Prátola Peligna, *Italy* ... 33 F10
Pratovécchio, *Italy* 33 E8
Prats-de-Mollo-la-Preste,
  France 26 F6
Pratt, *U.S.A.* 109 G5
Prattein, *Switz.* 22 A5
Prattville, *U.S.A.* 105 J2
Pravdinsk, *Russia* 41 C13
Pravia, *Spain* 30 B4

Praya, *Indonesia* 56 F5
Pré-en-Pail, *France* 24 D6
Pré St. Didier, *France* ... 32 C4
Precordillera, *Argentina* . 126 C2
Predáppio, *Italy* 33 D8
Predazzo, *Italy* 33 B8
Predejane, *Serbia, Yug.* . 21 N12
Preeceville, *Canada* 101 C8
Préfailles, *France* 24 E4
Pregonero, *Venezuela* ... 120 B3
Pregrada, *Croatia* 33 B12
Preko, *Croatia* 33 D12
Prelate, *Canada* 101 C7
Prelog, *Croatia* 33 B13
Premier, *Canada* 100 B3
Premont, *U.S.A.* 109 M5
Premuda, *Croatia* 33 D11
Prenjasi, *Albania* 39 H3
Prentice, *U.S.A.* 108 C9
Prenzlau, *Germany* 18 B9
Preobrazheniye, *Russia* . 48 C6
Prepansko Jezero,
  Macedonia 39 J4
Preparis North Channel,
  Ind. Oc. 61 M18
Preparis South Channel,
  Ind. Oc. 61 M18
Přerov, *Czech.* 20 F7
Presanella, *Italy* 32 B7
Prescott, *Canada* 98 D4
Prescott, *Ariz., U.S.A.* .. 111 J7
Prescott, *Ark., U.S.A.* .. 109 J8
Preservation Inlet, *N.Z.* . 87 M1
Preševo, *Serbia, Yug.* ... 21 N11
Presho, *U.S.A.* 108 D4
Presicce, *Italy* 35 C11
Presidencia de la Plaza,
  Argentina 126 B4
Presidencia Roque Saenz
  Peña, *Argentina* 126 B3
Presidente Epitácio, *Brazil* 123 F1
Presidente Hayes □,
  Paraguay 126 A4
Presidente Hermes, *Brazil* 125 C5
Presidente Prudente, *Brazil* 127 A5
Presidio, *Mexico* 114 B4
Presidio, *U.S.A.* 109 L2
Preslav, *Bulgaria* 38 F9
Prespa, L. = Prespansko
  Jezero, *Macedonia* ... 39 J4
Presque Isle, *U.S.A.* 99 C6
Prestbury, *U.K.* 13 F5
Prestea, *Ghana* 78 D4
Presteigne, *U.K.* 13 E5
Presto, *Bolivia* 125 D5
Preston, *Canada* 106 C4
Preston, *U.K.* 12 D5
Preston, *Idaho, U.S.A.* .. 110 E8
Preston, *Minn., U.S.A.* .. 108 D8
Preston, *Nev., U.S.A.* ... 110 G6
Preston, C., *Australia* ... 88 C3
Prestonpans, *U.K.* 14 F6
Prestwick, *U.K.* 14 F4
Prêto →, *Amazonas,
  Brazil* 121 D5
Prêto →, *Bahia, Brazil* .. 122 D3
Prêto do Igapó-Açu →,
  Brazil 121 D6
Pretoria, *S. Africa* 85 D4
Preuilly-sur-Claise, *France* 24 F7
Préveza, *Greece* 39 L3
Priazovskoye, *Ukraine* .. 42 C6
Pribilof Is., *Bering S.* ... 4 D17
Priboj, *Serbia, Yug.* 21 M9
Příbram, *Czech.* 20 F4
Price, *U.S.A.* 110 G8
Price I., *Canada* 100 C3
Prichalnaya, *Russia* 43 B11
Prichard, *U.S.A.* 105 K1
Priego, *Spain* 28 E2
Priego de Córdoba, *Spain* 31 H6
Priekule, *Latvia* 40 C7
Priek_le, *Latvia* 40 C7
Prien, *Germany* 19 H8
Prieska, *S. Africa* 84 D3
Priest →, *U.S.A.* 110 B5
Priest L., *U.S.A.* 110 B5
Priest Valley, *U.S.A.* ... 112 J6
Priestly, *Canada* 100 B3
Prievidza, *Slovakia* 20 G8
Prijedor, *Bos.-H.* 33 D13
Prikaspiyskaya Nizmennost,
  Asia 43 C13
Prilep, *Macedonia* 39 H4
Priluki, *Ukraine* 40 F8
Prime Seal I., *Australia* .. 90 G4
Primeira Cruz, *Brazil* ... 122 B3
Primorsko-Akhtarsk, *Russia* 42 C8
Primorskoye, *Ukraine* .. 42 C7
Primrose L., *Canada* 101 C7
Prince Albert, *Canada* ... 101 C7
Prince Albert, *S. Africa* .. 84 E3
Prince Albert Mts.,
  Antarctica 5 D11
Prince Albert Nat. Park,
  Canada 101 C7
Prince Albert Pen., *Canada* 96 A8
Prince Albert Sd., *Canada* 96 A8
Prince Alfred, C., *Canada* 4 B1
Prince Charles I., *Canada* 97 B12
Prince Charles Mts.,
  Antarctica 5 D6
Prince Edward I. □,
  Canada 99 C7
Prince Edward Is., *Ind. Oc.* 3 G11

Prince of Wales, C., *U.S.A.* 94 C3
Prince of Wales I.,
  Australia 90 A3
Prince of Wales I., *Canada* 96 A10
Prince of Wales I., *U.S.A.* 100 B2
Prince Patrick I., *Canada* . 4 B2
Prince Regent Inlet,
  Canada 4 B3
Prince Rupert, *Canada* .. 100 C2
Princenhage, *Neths.* 17 F5
Princesa Isabel, *Brazil* .. 122 C4
Princess Charlotte B.,
  Australia 90 A3
Princess May Ras.,
  Australia 88 C4
Princess Royal I., *Canada* 100 C3
Princeton, *Canada* 100 D4
Princeton, *Calif., U.S.A.* 112 F4
Princeton, *Ill., U.S.A.* .. 108 E10
Princeton, *Ind., U.S.A.* . 104 F2
Princeton, *Ky., U.S.A.* .. 104 G2
Princeton, *Mo., U.S.A.* . 108 E8
Princeton, *N.J., U.S.A.* . 107 F10
Princeton, *W. Va., U.S.A.* 104 G5
Principe, I. de, *Atl. Oc.* . 70 F4
Principe Chan., *Canada* . 100 C2
Principe da Beira, *Brazil* . 125 C5
Prineville, *U.S.A.* 110 D3
Prins Harald Kyst,
  Antarctica 5 D4
Prinsesse Astrid Kyst,
  Antarctica 5 D3
Prinsesse Ragnhild Kyst,
  Antarctica 5 D4
Prinzapolca, *Nic.* 116 D3
Prior, C., *Spain* 30 B2
Pripet = Pripyat →,
  Europe 40 F7
Pripet Marshes = Polesye,
  Belorussia 40 E6
Pripyat →, *Europe* 40 F7
Pripyat Marshes = Polesye,
  Belorussia 40 E6
Prislop, Pasul, *Romania* . 38 B8
Pristen, *Russia* 41 F10
Priština, *Serbia, Yug.* ... 21 N11
Pritzwalk, *Germany* 18 B8
Privas, *France* 27 D8
Priverno, *Italy* 34 A6
Privolzhsk, *Russia* 41 C12
Privolzhskaya
  Vozvyshennost, *Russia* . 41 F15
Privolzhskiy, *Russia* 41 F15
Privolzhye, *Russia* 41 E16
Priyutnoye, *Russia* 43 C10
Prizren, *Serbia, Yug.* ... 21 N10
Prizzi, *Italy* 34 E6
Prnjavor, *Bos.-H.* 21 L7
Probolinggo, *Indonesia* . 57 G15
Procida, *Italy* 35 B7
Proddatur, *India* 60 M11
Prodhromos, *Cyprus* ... 37 E11
Proença-a-Nova, *Portugal* . 31 F3
Prof. Van Blommestein
  Meer, *Surinam* 121 C6
Profítis Ilías, *Greece* 37 C9
Profondeville, *Belgium* .. 17 H5
Progreso, *Mexico* 115 C7
Prokhladnyy, *Russia* 43 E11
Prokletije, *Albania* 38 G2
Prokopyevsk, *Russia* 44 D9
Prokuplje, *Serbia, Yug.* . 21 M11
Proletarskaya, *Russia* ... 43 C9
Prome = Pyè, *Burma* ... 61 K19
Prophet →, *Canada* 100 B4
Propriá, *Brazil* 122 D4
Propriano, *France* 27 G12
Proserpine, *Australia* ... 90 C4
Prosser, *U.S.A.* 110 C4
Prostějov, *Czech.* 20 F7
Proston, *Australia* 91 D5
Protection, *U.S.A.* 109 G5
Próti, *Greece* 39 M4
Provadiya, *Bulgaria* 38 F10
Proven, *Belgium* 17 G1
Provence, *France* 27 E9
Providence, *Ky., U.S.A.* . 104 G2
Providence, *R.I., U.S.A.* 107 E13
Providence Bay, *Canada* . 98 C3
Providence Mts., *U.S.A.* 111 J6
Providencia, *Ecuador* ... 120 D2
Providencia, I. de,
  Colombia 116 D3
Provideniya, *Russia* 45 C19
Provins, *France* 25 D10
Provo, *U.S.A.* 110 F8
Provost, *Canada* 101 C6
Prozor, *Bos.-H.* 21 M7
Prudentópolis, *Brazil* ... 123 G1
Prud'homme, *Canada* ... 101 C7
Prudnik, *Poland* 20 E7
Prüm, *Germany* 19 E2
Pruszcz Gdański, *Poland* . 20 A8
Pruszków, *Poland* 20 C10
Prut →, *Romania* 38 D11
Pruzhany, *Belorussia* ... 40 E4
Prvič, *Croatia* 33 D11
Prydz B., *Antarctica* 5 C6
Pryluky = Priluki, *Ukraine* 40 F8
Pryor, *U.S.A.* 109 G7
Przasnysz, *Poland* 20 B10
Przedbórz, *Poland* 20 D9
Przemyśl, *Poland* 20 F12
Przeworsk, *Poland* 20 E12
Przewóz, *Poland* 20 D4
Przhevalsk, *Kirghizia* ... 44 E8

Przysuchla, *Poland* 20 D10
Psakhná, *Greece* 39 L6
Psará, *Greece* 39 L8
Psel →, *Ukraine* 42 B5
Pserimos, *Greece* 39 N10
Psíra, *Greece* 37 D7
Pskov, *Russia* 40 C6
Psunj, *Croatia* 21 K7
Pszczyna, *Poland* 20 F8
Ptich →, *Belorussia* 40 E6
Ptolemaís, *Greece* 39 J4
Ptuj, *Slovenia* 33 B12
Ptujska Gora, *Slovenia* .. 33 B12
Pu Xian, *China* 50 F6
Pua, *Thailand* 58 C3
Púan, *Argentina* 126 D3
Pu'an, *China* 52 E5
Puan, *S. Korea* 51 G14
Pubei, *China* 52 F7
Pucacuro →, *Peru* 120 D3
Pucallpa, *Peru* 124 B3
Pucará, *Bolivia* 125 D5
Pucará, *Peru* 124 D3
Pucarani, *Bolivia* 124 D4
Pucheng, *China* 53 D12
Puchheim, *Germany* .... 50 F6 (?)
Pučišće, *Croatia* 33 E13
Pucka, Zatoka, *Poland* .. 20 A8
Puding, *China* 52 D5
Pudukkottai, *India* 60 P11
Puebla, *Mexico* 115 D5
Puebla □, *Mexico* 115 D5
Puebla de Alcocer, *Spain* 31 G5
Puebla de Don Fadrique,
  Spain 29 H2
Puebla de Don Rodrigo,
  Spain 31 F6
Puebla de Guzmán, *Spain* 31 H3
Puebla de Sanabria, *Spain* 30 C4
Puebla de Trives, *Spain* . 30 C3
Puebla del Caramiñal,
  Spain 30 C2
Pueblo, *U.S.A.* 108 F2
Pueblo Hundido, *Chile* .. 126 B1
Pueblo Nuevo, *Venezuela* 120 B3
Puelches, *Argentina* 126 D2
Puelén, *Argentina* 126 D2
Puente Alto, *Chile* 126 C1
Puente del Arzobispo,
  Spain 30 F5
Puente-Genil, *Spain* 31 H6
Puente la Reina, *Spain* .. 28 C3
Puenteareas, *Spain* 30 C2
Puentedeume, *Spain* ... 30 B2
Puentes de Garcia
  Rodriguez, *Spain* 30 B3
Pu'er, *China* 52 F3
Puerco →, *U.S.A.* 111 J10
Puerto, *Canary Is.* 36 F2
Puerto Acosta, *Bolivia* .. 124 D4
Puerto Aisén, *Chile* 128 C2
Puerto Ángel, *Mexico* ... 115 D5
Puerto Arista, *Mexico* .. 115 D6
Puerto Armuelles, *Panama* 116 E3
Puerto Ayacucho,
  Venezuela 120 B4
Puerto Barrios, *Guatemala* 116 C2
Puerto Bermejo, *Argentina* 126 B4
Puerto Bermúdez, *Peru* . 124 C3
Puerto Bolívar, *Ecuador* . 120 D2
Puerto Cabello, *Venezuela* 120 A4
Puerto Cabezas, *Nic.* ... 116 D3
Puerto Cabo Gracias á
  Dios, *Nic.* 116 D3
Puerto Capaz = Jebha,
  Morocco 74 A4
Puerto Carreño, *Colombia* 120 B4
Puerto Castilla, *Honduras* 116 C2
Puerto Chicama, *Peru* .. 124 B2
Puerto Coig, *Argentina* .. 128 D3
Puerto Cortes, *Costa Rica* 116 E3
Puerto Cortés, *Honduras* 116 C2
Puerto Cumarebo,
  Venezuela 120 A4
Puerto de Alcudia, *Spain* 36 B10
Puerto de Andraitx, *Spain* 36 B9
Puerto de Cabrera, *Spain* . 36 B9
Puerto de Gran Tarajal,
  Canary Is. 36 F5
Puerto de la Cruz,
  Canary Is. 36 F3
Puerto de Pozo Negro,
  Canary Is. 36 F6
Puerto de Santa María,
  Spain 31 J4
Puerto de Sóller, *Spain* .. 36 B9
Pto. del Carmen,
  Canary Is. 36 F6
Puerto del Rosario,
  Canary Is. 36 F6
Puerto Deseado, *Argentina* 128 C3
Puerto Guaraní, *Paraguay* 125 E6
Puerto Heath, *Bolivia* ... 124 C4
Puerto Huitoto, *Colombia* 120 C3
Puerto Inca, *Peru* 124 B3
Puerto Juárez, *Mexico* .. 115 C7
Puerto La Cruz, *Venezuela* 121 A5
Puerto Leguízamo,
  Colombia 120 D3
Puerto Limón, *Colombia* 120 C3
Puerto Lobos, *Argentina* 128 B3
Puerto López, *Colombia* . 120 C3
Puerto Lumbreras, *Spain* . 29 H3
Puerto Madryn, *Argentina* 128 B3
Puerto Maldonado, *Peru* 124 C4
Puerto Manotí, *Cuba* ... 116 B4

Puerto Mazarrón, *Spain* . . 29 H3
Puerto Mercedes, *Colombia* 120 C3
Puerto Miraña, *Colombia* . 120 D3
Puerto Montt, *Chile* 128 B2
Puerto Morelos, *Mexico* . . 115 C7
Puerto Nariño, *Colombia* . 120 C4
Puerto Natales, *Chile* 128 D2
Puerto Nuevo, *Colombia* . 120 B4
Puerto Nutrias, *Venezuela* 120 B4
Puerto Ordaz, *Venezuela* . 121 B5
Puerto Padre, *Cuba* 116 B4
Puerto Páez, *Venezuela* . . 120 B4
Puerto Peñasco, *Mexico* . . 114 A2
Puerto Pinasco, *Paraguay* . 126 A4
Puerto Pirámides,
  Argentina 128 B4
Puerto Plata, *Dom. Rep.* . 117 C5
Puerto Pollensa, *Spain* . . 36 B10
Puerto Portillo, *Peru* 124 B3
Puerto Princesa, *Phil.* . . . 55 G3
Puerto Quellón, *Chile* . . . 128 B2
Puerto Quepos, *Costa Rica* 116 E3
Puerto Real, *Spain* 31 J4
Puerto Rico, *Bolivia* 124 C4
Puerto Rico, *Canary Is.* . . 36 G4
Puerto Rico ■, *W. Indies* . 117 C6
Puerto Rico Trench,
  Atl. Oc. 117 C6
Puerto Saavedra, *Chile* . . . 128 A2
Puerto Sastre, *Paraguay* . . 126 A4
Puerto Siles, *Bolivia* 125 C4
Puerto Suárez, *Bolivia* . . . 125 D6
Puerto Tejada, *Colombia* . 120 C2
Puerto Umbría, *Colombia* . 120 C2
Puerto Vallarta, *Mexico* . . 114 C3
Puerto Varas, *Chile* 128 B2
Puerto Villazón, *Bolivia* . . 125 C5
Puerto Wilches, *Colombia* . 120 B3
Puertollano, *Spain* 31 G6
Puertomarín, *Spain* 30 C3
Puesto Cunambo, *Peru* . . 120 D2
Pueyrredón, L., *Argentina* 128 C2
Pugachev, *Kazakhstan* . . . 41 F16
Puge, *China* 52 D4
Puge, *China* 82 C3
Puget Sound, *U.S.A.* 110 C2
Puget-Théniers, *France* . . 27 E10
Púglia □, *Italy* 35 B9
Pugŏdong, *N. Korea* 51 C16
Pugu, *Tanzania* 82 D4
Pūgūnzī, *Iran* 65 E8
Pui, *Romania* 38 D6
Puica, *Peru* 124 C3
Puig Mayor, *Spain* 36 B9
Puigcerdà, *Spain* 28 C6
Puigmal, *Spain* 28 C7
Puigpuñent, *Spain* 36 B9
Puisaye, Collines de la,
  France 25 E10
Puiseaux, *France* 25 D9
Pujilí, *Ecuador* 120 D2
Pujon-chosuji, *N. Korea* . . 51 D14
Puka, *Albania* 38 G2
Pukaki L., *N.Z.* 87 L3
Pukapuka, *Cook Is.* 93 J11
Pukatawagan, *Canada* . . . 101 B8
Pukchin, *N. Korea* 51 D13
Pukch'ŏng, *N. Korea* 51 D15
Pukekohe, *N.Z.* 87 G5
Pukou, *China* 53 A12
Pula, *Croatia* 33 D10
Pula, *Italy* 34 D2
Pulacayo, *Bolivia* 124 E4
Pulaski, *N.Y., U.S.A.* . . . 107 C8
Pulaski, *Tenn., U.S.A.* . . 105 H2
Pulaski, *Va., U.S.A.* 104 G5
Puławy, *Poland* 20 D11
Pulga, *U.S.A.* 112 F5
Pulicat, L., *India* 60 N12
Pullman, *U.S.A.* 110 C5
Pulog, *Phil.* 55 C4
Pułtusk, *Poland* 20 C11
Pülümür, *Turkey* 67 D8
Pumlumon Fawr, *U.K.* . . 13 E4
Puna, *Bolivia* 125 D4
Puná, I., *Ecuador* 120 D1
Punakha, *Bhutan* 61 F16
Punasar, *India* 62 F5
Punata, *Bolivia* 125 D4
Punch, *India* 63 C6
Pune, *India* 60 K8
Pungsan, *N. Korea* 51 D15
Pungue, Ponte de, *Mozam.* 83 F3
Puning, *China* 53 F11
Punjab □, *India* 62 D6
Punjab □, *Pakistan* 62 E6
Puno, *Peru* 124 D3
Punta Alta, *Argentina* . . . 128 A4
Punta Arenas, *Chile* 128 D2
Punta Cardón, *Venezuela* . 120 A3
Punta Coles, *Peru* 124 D3
Punta de Bombón, *Peru* . . 124 D3
Punta de Díaz, *Chile* 126 B1
Punta Delgada, *Argentina* . 128 B4
Punta Gorda, *Belize* 115 D7
Punta Gorda, *U.S.A.* 105 M5
Punta Prieta, *Mexico* 114 B2
Punta Prima, *Spain* 36 B11
Puntabie, *Australia* 91 E1
Puntarenas, *Costa Rica* . . 116 E3
Punto Fijo, *Venezuela* . . . 120 A3
Punxsutawney, *U.S.A.* . . . 106 F5
Puqi, *China* 53 C9
Puquio, *Peru* 124 C3
Pur →, *Russia* 44 C8
Puraco, Vol., *Colombia* . . 120 C2

Puralia = Puruliya, *India* . 63 H12
Purbeck, Isle of, *U.K.* . . . 13 G5
Purcell, *U.S.A.* 109 H6
Purchena Tetica, *Spain* . . 29 H2
Puri, *India* 61 K14
Purificación, *Colombia* . . 120 C3
Purmerend, *Neths.* 16 C5
Purnia, *India* 63 G12
Purukcahu, *Indonesia* . . . 56 E4
Puruliya, *India* 63 H12
Purus →, *Brazil* 121 D5
Pŭrvomay, *Bulgaria* 38 G8
Purwakarta, *Indonesia* . . 57 G12
Purwodadi, *Jawa, Indonesia* 57 G14
Purwodadi, *Jawa, Indonesia* 57 G13
Purwokerto, *Indonesia* . . 57 G13
Purworejo, *Indonesia* . . . 57 G14
Puryŏng, *N. Korea* 51 C15
Pusan, *S. Korea* 51 G15
Pushchino, *Russia* 45 D16
Pushkin, *Russia* 40 B7
Pushkino, *Russia* 41 F13
Pushkino, *Russia* 41 C10
Püspökladány, *Hungary* . . 21 H11
Pustoshka, *Russia* 40 C6
Putahow L., *Canada* 101 B8
Putao, *Burma* 61 F20
Putaruru, *N.Z.* 87 H5
Putbus, *Germany* 18 A9
Puthein Myit →, *Burma* . . 61 M19
Putian, *China* 53 E12
Putignano, *Italy* 35 B10
Putina, *Peru* 124 C4
Puting, Tanjung, *Indonesia* 56 E4
Putlitz, *Germany* 18 B8
Putna →, *Romania* 38 D10
Putnam, *U.S.A.* 107 E13
Putorana, Gory, *Russia* . . 45 C10
Putre, *Chile* 124 D4
Puttalam, *Sri Lanka* 60 Q11
Putte, *Neths.* 17 F4
Putten, *Neths.* 16 D7
Puttgarden, *Germany* . . . 18 A7
Putumayo →, *S. Amer.* . . 120 D4
Putuo, *China* 53 C14
Putussibau, *Indonesia* . . . 56 D4
Puurs, *Belgium* 17 F4
Puy-de-Dôme, *France* . . . 26 C6
Puy-de-Dôme □, *France* . 26 C7
Puy-Guillaume, *France* . . 26 C7
Puy-l'Évêque, *France* . . . 26 D5
Puyallup, *U.S.A.* 112 C4
Puyang, *China* 50 G8
Puyehue, *Chile* 128 B2
Puylaurens, *France* 26 E6
Puyo, *Ecuador* 120 D2
Pūzeh Rīg, *Iran* 65 E8
Pwani □, *Tanzania* 82 D4
Pweto, *Zaïre* 83 D2
Pwllheli, *U.K.* 12 E3
Pyana →, *Russia* 41 D15
Pyapon, *Burma* 61 L19
Pyasina →, *Russia* 45 B9
Pyatigorsk, *Russia* 43 D10
Pyatikhatki, *Ukraine* 42 B5
Pyè, *Burma* 61 K19
Pyinmana, *Burma* 61 K20
Pyla, C., *Cyprus* 37 E12
Pyŏktong, *N. Korea* 51 D13
Pyŏnggang, *N. Korea* . . . 51 E14
Pyŏngtaek, *S. Korea* 51 F14
P'yŏngyang, *N. Korea* . . . 51 E13
Pyote, *U.S.A.* 109 K3
Pyramid L., *U.S.A.* 110 G4
Pyramid Pk., *U.S.A.* 113 J10
Pyramids, *Egypt* 76 J7
Pyrénées, *Europe* 26 F4
Pyrénées-Atlantiques □,
  France 26 E3
Pyrénées-Orientales □,
  France 26 F6
Pyrzyce, *Poland* 20 B4
Pyshchug, *Russia* 41 B14
Pytalovo, *Russia* 40 C5
Pyttegga, *Norway* 10 B1
Pyu, *Burma* 61 K20

Q

Qaanaaq = Thule,
  Greenland 4 B4
Qachasnek, *S. Africa* 85 E4
Qādib, *Yemen* 68 E5
Qa'el Jafr, *Jordan* 69 E5
Qa'emābād, *Iran* 65 D9
Qā'emshahr, *Iran* 65 B7
Qagan Nur, *China* 50 C8
Qahar Youyi Zhongqi,
  China 50 D7
Qahremānshahr =
  Bākhtarān, *Iran* 64 C5
Qaidam Pendi, *China* . . . 54 C4
Qajarīyeh, *Iran* 65 D6
Qala, Ras il, *Malta* 37 C1
Qala-i-Jadid, *Afghan.* . . . 62 D2
Qala Yangi, *Afghan.* 62 B2
Qal'at al Akhḍar,
  Si. Arabia 64 E3
Qal'at Sukkar, *Iraq* 64 D5
Qal'eh Darreh, *Iran* 64 B5
Qal'eh Shaharak, *Afghan.* . 60 B4
Qalyûb, *Egypt* 76 H7

Qamar, Ghubbat al, *Yemen* 68 D5

Qamdo, *China* 52 B1
Qamruddin Karez, *Pakistan* 62 D3
Qandahār, *Afghan.* 60 D4
Qandahār □, *Afghan.* . . . 60 D4
Qapān, *Iran* 65 B7
Qaqortoq = Julianehåb,
  Greenland 4 C5
Qâra, *Egypt* 76 B2
Qara Qash →, *India* 63 B8
Qaraghandy = Karaganda,
  Kazakhstan 44 E8
Qārah, *Si. Arabia* 64 D4
Qardud, *Sudan* 77 E2
Qareh →, *Iran* 64 B5
Qareh Tekān, *Iran* 65 B6
Qarqan, *China* 54 C3
Qarqan He →, *China* . . . 54 C3
Qarrasa, *Sudan* 77 E3
Qarshi = Karshi,
  Uzbekistan 44 F7
Qartabā, *Lebanon* 69 A4
Qaryat al Gharab, *Iraq* . . 64 D5
Qaryat al 'Ulyā, *Si. Arabia* 64 E5
Qasr 'Amra, *Jordan* 64 D3
Qaşr-e Qand, *Iran* 65 E9
Qasr Farâfra, *Egypt* 76 B2
Qatanā, *Syria* 69 B5
Qatar ■, *Asia* 65 E6
Qatlîsh, *Iran* 65 B8
Qattâra, *Egypt* 76 A2
Qattâra, Munkhafed el,
  Egypt 76 B2
Qattâra Depression =
  Qattâra, Munkhafed el,
  Egypt 76 B2
Qawām al Ḥamzah, *Iraq* . 64 D5
Qāyen, *Iran* 65 C8
Qazaqstan =
  Kazakhstan ■, *Asia* . . 44 E7
Qazvin, *Iran* 65 B6
Qena, *Egypt* 76 B3
Qena, Wadi →, *Egypt* . . . 76 B3
Qeqertarsuaq = Disko,
  Greenland 4 C5
Qeqertarsuaq = Godhavn,
  Greenland 4 C5
Qeshlāq, *Iran* 64 C5
Qeshm, *Iran* 65 E8
Qezi'ot, *Israel* 69 E3
Qi Xian, *China* 50 G8
Qian Gorlos, *China* 51 B13
Qian Xian, *China* 50 G5
Qiancheng, *China* 52 D7
Qianjiang,
  Guangxi Zhuangzu,
  China 52 F7
Qianjiang, *Hubei, China* . 53 B9
Qianjiang, *Sichuan, China* 52 C7
Qianshan, *China* 53 B11
Qianwei, *China* 52 C4
Qianxi, *China* 52 D6
Qianyang, *Hunan, China* . 53 D8
Qianyang, *Shaanxi, China* 50 G4
Qianyang, *Zhejiang, China* 53 B12
Qiaojia, *China* 52 D4
Qichun, *China* 53 B10
Qidong, *Hunan, China* . . 53 D9
Qidong, *Jiangsu, China* . . 53 B13
Qijiang, *China* 52 C6
Qila Safed, *Pakistan* 60 E2
Qila Saifullāh, *Pakistan* . . 62 D3
Qilian Shan, *China* 54 C4
Qimen, *China* 53 C11
Qin He →, *China* 50 G7
Qin Jiang →, *China* 53 D10
Qin Ling = Qinling Shandi,
  China 50 H5
Qin'an, *China* 50 G3
Qing Xian, *China* 50 E9
Qingcheng, *China* 51 F9
Qingdao, *China* 51 F11
Qingfeng, *China* 50 G8
Qinghai □, *China* 54 C4
Qinghai Hu, *China* 54 C5
Qinghecheng, *China* 51 D13
Qinghemen, *China* 51 D11
Qingjian, *China* 50 F6
Qingjiang, *Jiangsu, China* . 51 H10
Qingjiang, *Jiangxi, China* . 53 C10
Qingliu, *China* 53 D11
Qinglong, *China* 52 E5
Qingping, *China* 52 D6
Qingpu, *China* 53 B13
Qingshui, *China* 50 G4
Qingshuihe, *China* 50 E6
Qingtian, *China* 53 C13
Qingtongxia Shuiku, *China* 50 F3
Qingxi, *China* 52 D7
Qingxu, *China* 50 F7
Qingyang, *Anhui, China* . 53 B11
Qingyang, *Gansu, China* . 50 F4
Qingyi Jiang →, *China* . . 52 C4
Qingyuan, *Guangdong,*
  China 53 F9
Qingyuan, *Liaoning, China* 51 C13
Qingyuan, *Zhejiang, China* 53 D12
Qingyun, *China* 51 F9
Qingzhen, *China* 52 D6
Qinhuangdao, *China* 51 E10
Qinling Shandi, *China* . . . 50 H5
Qinshui, *China* 50 G7
Qinyang, *China* 50 G7
Qinyuan, *China* 50 F7
Qinzhou, *China* 52 G7
Qionghai, *China* 58 C8

Qionglai, *China* 52 B4
Qiongshan, *China* 58 C8
Qiongzhou Haixia, *China* . 58 B8
Qiqihar, *China* 45 E13
Qiraîya, W. →, *Egypt* . . . 69 E3
Qiryat Ata, *Israel* 69 C4
Qiryat Gat, *Israel* 69 D3
Qiryat Mal'akhi, *Israel* . . 69 D3
Qiryat Shemona, *Israel* . . 69 B4
Qiryat Yam, *Israel* 69 C4
Qishan, *China* 50 G4
Qishan, *Taiwan* 53 F13
Qitai, *China* 54 B3
Qiubei, *China* 52 E5
Qixia, *China* 51 F11
Qiyang, *China* 53 D8
Qojūr, *Iran* 64 B5
Qom, *Iran* 65 C6
Qomsheh, *Iran* 65 D6
Qostanay = Kustanay,
  Kazakhstan 44 D7
Qu Jiang →, *China* 52 B6
Qu Xian, *Sichuan, China* . 52 B6
Qu Xian, *Zhejiang, China* 53 C12
Quackenbrück, *Germany* . 18 C3
Quairading, *Australia* . . . 89 F2
Quakertown, *U.S.A.* 107 F9
Qualeup, *Australia* 89 F2
Quambatook, *Australia* . . 91 F3
Quambone, *Australia* . . . 91 E4
Quamby, *Australia* 90 C3
Quan Long, *Vietnam* . . . 59 H5
Quanah, *U.S.A.* 109 H5
Quandialla, *Australia* . . . 91 E4
Quang Ngai, *Vietnam* . . . 58 E7
Quang Yen, *Vietnam* . . . 58 B6
Quannan, *China* 53 E10
Quantock Hills, *U.K.* . . . 13 F4
Quanzhou, *Fujian, China* . 53 E12
Quanzhou,
  Guangxi Zhuangzu,
  China 53 E8
Quaraí, *Brazil* 126 C4
Quarré-les-Tombes, *France* 25 E10
Quartu Sant' Elena, *Italy* . 34 C2
Quartzsite, *U.S.A.* 113 M12
Quatsino, *Canada* 100 C3
Quatsino Sd., *Canada* . . . 100 C3
Qūchān, *Iran* 65 B8
Queanbeyan, *Australia* . . 91 F4
Québec, *Canada* 99 C5
Québec □, *Canada* 99 B6
Quedlinburg, *Germany* . . 18 D7
Queen Alexandra Ra.,
  Antarctica 5 E11
Queen Charlotte, *Canada* . 100 C2
Queen Charlotte Bay,
  Falk. Is. 128 D4
Queen Charlotte Is.,
  Canada 100 C2
Queen Charlotte Str.,
  Canada 100 C3
Queen Elizabeth Is.,
  Canada 94 B10
Queen Elizabeth Nat. Park,
  Uganda 82 C3
Queen Mary Land,
  Antarctica 5 D7
Queen Maud G., *Canada* . 96 B9
Queen Maud Land,
  Antarctica 5 D3
Queen Maud Mts.,
  Antarctica 5 E13
Queens Chan., *Australia* . 88 C4
Queenscliff, *Australia* . . . 91 F3
Queensland □, *Australia* . 90 C3
Queenstown, *Australia* . . 90 G4
Queenstown, *N.Z.* 87 L2
Queenstown, *S. Africa* . . 84 E4
Queets, *U.S.A.* 112 C2
Queguay Grande →,
  Uruguay 126 C4
Queimadas, *Brazil* 122 D4
Quela, *Angola* 80 F3
Quelimane, *Mozam.* 83 F4
Quelpart = Cheju Do,
  S. Korea 51 H14
Quemado, *N. Mex., U.S.A.* 111 J9
Quemado, *Tex., U.S.A.* . . 109 L4
Quemú-Quemú, *Argentina* 126 D3
Quequén, *Argentina* 126 D4
Querco, *Peru* 124 C3
Querétaro, *Mexico* 114 C4
Querétaro □, *Mexico* . . . 114 C5
Querfurt, *Germany* 18 D7
Quesada, *Spain* 29 H1
Queshan, *China* 50 H8
Quesnel, *Canada* 100 C4
Quesnel →, *Canada* 100 C4
Quesnel L., *Canada* 100 C4
Questa, *U.S.A.* 111 H11
Questembert, *France* . . . 24 E4
Quetena, *Bolivia* 124 E4
Quetico Prov. Park,
  Canada 98 C1
Quetrequile, *Argentina* . . 128 B3
Quetta, *Pakistan* 62 D2
Quevedo, *Ecuador* 120 D2
Quezaltenango, *Guatemala* 116 D1
Quezon City, *Phil.* 55 D4
Qufār, *Si. Arabia* 64 E4
Qui Nhon, *Vietnam* 58 F7
Quibaxe, *Angola* 80 F2
Quibdo, *Colombia* 120 B2
Quiberon, *France* 24 E3

Quíbor, *Venezuela* 120 B4
Quick, *Canada* 100 C3
Quickborn, *Germany* . . . 18 B5
Quiet L., *Canada* 100 A2
Quiévrain, *Belgium* 17 H3
Quiindy, *Paraguay* 126 B4
Quila, *Mexico* 114 C3
Quilán, C., *Chile* 128 B2
Quilcene, *U.S.A.* 112 C4
Quilengues, *Angola* 81 G2
Quilimarí, *Chile* 126 C1
Quilino, *Argentina* 126 C3
Quillabamba, *Peru* 124 C3
Quillacollo, *Bolivia* 124 D4
Quillagua, *Chile* 126 A2
Quillaicillo, *Chile* 126 C1
Quillan, *France* 26 F6
Quillebeuf-sur-Seine,
  France 24 C7
Quillota, *Chile* 126 C1
Quilmes, *Argentina* 126 C4
Quilon, *India* 60 Q10
Quilpie, *Australia* 91 D3
Quilpué, *Chile* 126 C1
Quilua, *Mozam.* 83 F4
Quime, *Bolivia* 124 D4
Quimilí, *Argentina* 126 B3
Quimper, *France* 24 D2
Quimperlé, *France* 24 E3
Quinault →, *U.S.A.* 112 C2
Quincemil, *Peru* 124 C3
Quincy, *Calif., U.S.A.* . . . 112 F6
Quincy, *Fla., U.S.A.* 105 K3
Quincy, *Ill., U.S.A.* 108 F9
Quincy, *Mass., U.S.A.* . . 107 D14
Quincy, *Wash., U.S.A.* . . 110 C4
Quines, *Argentina* 126 C2
Quinga, *Mozam.* 83 F5
Quingey, *France* 25 E12
Quintana de la Serena,
  Spain 31 G5
Quintana Roo □, *Mexico* . 115 D7
Quintanar de la Orden,
  Spain 28 F1
Quintanar de la Sierra,
  Spain 28 D2
Quintanar del Rey, *Spain* . 29 F3
Quintero, *Chile* 126 C1
Quintin, *France* 24 D4
Quinto, *Spain* 28 D4
Quinyambie, *Australia* . . 91 E3
Quípar →, *Spain* 29 G3
Quipungo, *Angola* 81 G2
Quirihue, *Chile* 126 D1
Quirindi, *Australia* 91 E5
Quiroga, *Spain* 30 C3
Quiruvilca, *Peru* 124 B2
Quissac, *France* 27 E8
Quissanga, *Mozam.* 83 E5
Quitilipi, *Argentina* 126 B3
Quitman, *Ga., U.S.A.* . . . 105 K4
Quitman, *Miss., U.S.A.* . . 105 J1
Quitman, *Tex., U.S.A.* . . 109 J7
Quito, *Ecuador* 120 D2
Quixadá, *Brazil* 122 B4
Quixaxe, *Mozam.* 83 F5
Quixeramobim, *Brazil* . . . 122 C4
Qujing, *China* 52 E4
Qul'ān, Jazā'ir, *Egypt* . . . 76 B3
Qumbu, *S. Africa* 85 E4
Quneitra, *Syria* 69 B4
Quoin I., *Australia* 88 B4
Quoin Pt., *S. Africa* 84 E2
Quondong, *Australia* . . . 91 E3
Quorn, *Australia* 91 E2
Quqon = Kokand,
  Uzbekistan 44 E8
Qurein, *Sudan* 77 E3
Qurnat as Sawdâ', *Lebanon* 69 A5
Qûs, *Egypt* 76 B3
Qusaybah, *Iraq* 64 C4
Quseir, *Egypt* 76 B3
Qüshchī, *Iran* 64 B5
Quthing, *Lesotho* 85 E4
Qūṭīābād, *Iran* 65 C6
Quwo, *China* 50 G6
Quyang, *China* 50 E8
Quynh Nhai, *Vietnam* . . . 58 B4
Quzi, *China* 50 F4
Qytet Stalin, *Albania* 39 J2
Qyzylorda = Kzyl-Orda,
  Kazakhstan 44 E7

R

Ra, Ko, *Thailand* 59 H2
Råå, *Sweden* 11 J6
Raahe, *Finland* 8 D18
Raalte, *Neths.* 16 D8
Raamsdonksveer, *Neths.* . 17 E5
Raasay, *U.K.* 14 D2
Raasay, Sd. of, *U.K.* 14 D2
Rab, *Croatia* 33 D11
Raba, *Indonesia* 57 F5
Rába →, *Hungary* 21 H7
Rabaçal →, *Portugal* . . . 30 D3
Rabah, *Nigeria* 79 C6
Rabai, *Kenya* 82 C4
Rabastens, *France* 26 E5
Rabastens-de-Bigorre,
  France 26 E4
Rabat, *Malta* 37 D1
Rabat, *Morocco* 74 B3

Rabaul, *Papua N. G.* 92 H7
Rabbit →, *Canada* 100 B3
Rabbit Lake, *Canada* 101 C7
Rabbitskin →, *Canada* ... 100 A4
Rabka, *Poland* 20 F9
Rābor, *Iran* 65 D8
Rácale, *Italy* 35 C11
Racalmuto, *Italy* 34 E6
Racconigi, *Italy* 32 D4
Race, C., *Canada* 99 C9
Rach Gia, *Vietnam* 59 G5
Raciąż, *Poland* 20 C10
Racibórz, *Poland* 20 E8
Racine, *U.S.A.* 104 D2
Rackerby, *U.S.A.* 112 F5
Radama, Nosy, *Madag.* .. 85 A8
Radama, Saikanosy,
   Madag. 85 A8
Rădăuţi, *Romania* 38 B8
Radbuza →, *Czech.* 20 F3
Radeburg, *Germany* 18 D9
Radeče, *Slovenia* 33 B12
Radekhov, *Ukraine* 40 F4
Radford, *U.S.A.* 104 G5
Radhanpur, *India* 62 H4
Radisson, *Canada* 101 C7
Radium Hot Springs,
   Canada 100 C5
Radna, *Romania* 38 C4
Radnor Forest, *U.K.* 13 E4
Radolfzell, *Germany* 19 H4
Radom, *Poland* 20 D11
Radomir, *Bulgaria* 38 G6
Radomsko, *Poland* 20 D9
Radomyshl, *Ukraine* 40 F6
Radoviš, *Macedonia* 39 H5
Radovljica, *Slovenia* 33 B11
Radstock, *U.K.* 13 F5
Radstock, C., *Australia* .. 91 E1
Răducăneni, *Romania* 38 C10
Radviliškis, *Lithuania* 40 D3
Radville, *Canada* 101 D8
Rae, *Canada* 100 A5
Rae Bareli, *India* 63 F9
Rae Isthmus, *Canada* 97 B11
Raeren, *Belgium* 17 G8
Raeside, L., *Australia* 89 E3
Raetihi, *N.Z.* 87 H5
Rafaela, *Argentina* 126 C3
Rafah, *Egypt* 69 D3
Rafai, *C.A.R.* 82 B1
Raffadali, *Italy* 34 E6
Rafḥā, *Si. Arabia* 64 D4
Rafsanjān, *Iran* 65 D8
Raft Pt., *Australia* 88 C3
Ragag, *Sudan* 77 E1
Ragama, *Sri Lanka* 60 R11
Ragged, Mt., *Australia* ... 89 F3
Raglan, *Australia* 90 C5
Raglan, *N.Z.* 87 G5
Ragunda, *Sweden* 10 A10
Ragusa, *Italy* 35 F7
Raha, *Indonesia* 57 E6
Rahad →, *Sudan* 77 E3
Rahad al Bardī, *Sudan* ... 73 F9
Rahaeng = Tak, *Thailand* . 58 D2
Rahden, *Germany* 18 C4
Raheita, *Eritrea* 77 E5
Raḥīmah, *Si. Arabia* 65 E6
Rahimyar Khan, *Pakistan* . 62 E4
Rāhjerd, *Iran* 65 C6
Raichur, *India* 60 L10
Raiganj, *India* 63 G13
Raigarh, *India* 61 J13
Raijua, *Indonesia* 57 F6
Railton, *Australia* 90 G4
Rainbow Lake, *Canada* ... 100 B5
Rainier, *U.S.A.* 112 D4
Rainier, Mt., *U.S.A.* 112 D4
Rainy L., *Canada* 101 D10
Rainy River, *Canada* 101 D10
Raipur, *India* 61 J12
Raj Nandgaon, *India* 61 J12
Raja, Ujung, *Indonesia* ... 56 D1
Raja Ampat, Kepulauan,
   Indonesia 57 E7
Rajahmundry, *India* 61 L12
Rajapalaiyam, *India* 60 Q10
Rajasthan □, *India* 62 F5
Rajasthan Canal, *India* ... 62 E5
Rajauri, *India* 63 C6
Rajgarh, Mad. P., *India* .. 62 G7
Rajgarh, Raj., *India* 62 E6
Rajhenburg, *Slovenia* 33 B12
Rajkot, *India* 62 H4
Rajmahal Hills, *India* 63 G12
Rajpipla, *India* 60 J8
Rajpura, *India* 62 D7
Rajshahi, *Bangla.* 61 G16
Rajshahi □, *Bangla.* 63 G13
Rakaia, *N.Z.* 87 K4
Rakaia →, *N.Z.* 87 K4
Rakan, Ra's, *Qatar* 65 E6
Rakata, Pulau, *Indonesia* . 56 F3
Rakhni, *Pakistan* 62 D3
Rakitnoye, *Russia* 48 B7
Rakops, *Botswana* 84 C3
Rákospalota, *Hungary* 21 H9
Rakov, *Belorussia* 40 E5
Rakovica, *Croatia* 33 D12

Rakovník, *Czech.* 20 E3
Rakovski, *Bulgaria* 38 G7
Rakvere, *Estonia* 40 B5
Raleigh, *U.S.A.* 105 H6
Raleigh B., *U.S.A.* 105 H7
Ralja, *Serbia* 21 L10
Ralls, *U.S.A.* 109 J4
Ram →, *Canada* 100 A4
Rām Allāh, *Jordan* 69 D4
Ram Hd., *Australia* 91 F4
Rama, *Nic.* 116 D3
Ramacca, *Italy* 35 E7
Ramales de la Victoria,
   Spain 28 B1
Ramalho, Serra do, *Brazil* 123 D3
Raman, *Thailand* 59 J3
Ramanathapuram, *India* .. 60 Q11
Ramanetaka, B. de,
   Madag. 85 A8
Ramat Gan, *Israel* 69 C3
Ramatlhabama, *S. Africa* . 84 D4
Ramban, *India* 63 C6
Rambervillers, *France* 25 D13
Rambipuji, *Indonesia* 57 H15
Rambouillet, *France* 25 D8
Ramea, *Canada* 99 C8
Ramechhap, *Nepal* 63 F12
Ramelau, *Indonesia* 57 F7
Ramenskoye, *Russia* 41 D11
Ramgarh, Bihar, *India* ... 63 H11
Ramgarh, Raj., *India* 62 F6
Ramgarh, Raj., *India* 62 F4
Rāmhormoz, *Iran* 65 D6
Ramīān, *Iran* 65 B7
Ramingining, *Australia* ... 90 A2
Ramla, *Israel* 69 D3
Ramlu, *Eritrea* 77 E5
Ramme, *Denmark* 11 H2
Ramnad =
   Ramanathapuram, *India* 60 Q11
Ramnagar, *India* 63 C6
Ramnäs, *Sweden* 10 E10
Ramon, *Russia* 41 F11
Ramona, *U.S.A.* 113 M10
Ramore, *Canada* 98 C3
Ramotswa, *Botswana* 84 C4
Rampur, H.P., *India* 62 D7
Rampur, Mad. P., *India* .. 62 H5
Rampur, Ut. P., *India* 63 E8
Rampur Hat, *India* 63 G12
Rampura, *India* 62 G6
Ramree I. = Ramree
   Kyun, *Burma* 61 K18
Ramree Kyun, *Burma* ... 61 K18
Rāmsar, *Iran* 65 B6
Ramsel, *Belgium* 17 F5
Ramsey, *Canada* 98 C3
Ramsey, *U.K.* 12 C3
Ramsgate, *U.K.* 13 F9
Ramsjö, *Sweden* 10 B9
Ramtek, *India* 60 J11
Ramvik, *Sweden* 10 B11
Ranaghat, *India* 63 H13
Ranahu, *Pakistan* 62 G3
Ranau, *Malaysia* 56 C5
Rancagua, *Chile* 126 C1
Rance, *Belgium* 17 H4
Rance →, *France* 24 D5
Rance, Barrage de la,
   France 24 D4
Rancharia, *Brazil* 123 F1
Rancheria →, *Canada* ... 100 A3
Ranchester, *U.S.A.* 110 D10
Ranchi, *India* 63 H11
Ranco, L., *Chile* 128 B2
Randan, *France* 26 B7
Randazzo, *Italy* 35 E7
Randle, *U.S.A.* 112 D5
Randolph, Mass., *U.S.A.* . 107 D13
Randolph, N.Y., *U.S.A.* .. 106 D6
Randolph, Utah, *U.S.A.* .. 110 F8
Randolph, Vt., *U.S.A.* ... 107 C12
Randsfjord, *Norway* 10 D4
Råne älv →, *Sweden* 8 D17
Rangae, *Thailand* 59 J3
Rangaunu B., *N.Z.* 87 F4
Rångedala, *Sweden* 11 G7
Rangeley, *U.S.A.* 107 B14
Rangely, *U.S.A.* 110 F9
Ranger, *U.S.A.* 109 J5
Rangia, *India* 61 F17
Rangiora, *N.Z.* 87 K4
Rangitaiki →, *N.Z.* 87 G6
Rangitata →, *N.Z.* 87 K3
Rangkasbitung, *Indonesia* 57 G12
Rangon →, *Burma* 61 L20
Rangoon, *Burma* 61 L20
Rangpur, *Bangla.* 61 G16
Rangsit, *Thailand* 58 F3
Ranibennur, *India* 60 M9
Raniganj, *India* 63 H12
Raniwara, *India* 60 G8
Rānīyah, *Iraq* 64 B5
Ranken →, *Australia* 90 C2
Rankin, *U.S.A.* 109 K4
Rankin Inlet, *Canada* 96 B10
Rankins Springs, *Australia* 91 E4
Rannoch, L., *U.K.* 14 E4
Rannoch Moor, *U.K.* 14 E4
Ranobe, Helodranon' i,
   Madag. 85 C7
Ranohira, *Madag.* 85 C8

Ranomafana, *Toamasina,
   Madag.* 85 B8
Ranomafana, *Toliara,
   Madag.* 85 C8
Ranong, *Thailand* 59 H2
Ransiki, *Indonesia* 57 E8
Rantau, *Indonesia* 56 E5
Rantauprapat, *Indonesia* . 56 D1
Rantekombola, *Indonesia* . 57 E5
Rantoul, *U.S.A.* 104 E1
Ranum, *Denmark* 11 H3
Raon l'Étape, *France* 25 D13
Raoui, Erg er, *Algeria* ... 75 C4
Raoyang, *China* 50 E8
Rapa, *Pac. Oc.* 93 K13
Rapallo, *Italy* 32 D6
Rāpch, *Iran* 65 E8
Rapid →, *Canada* 100 B3
Rapid City, *U.S.A.* 108 D3
Rapid River, *U.S.A.* 104 C2
Rapides des Joachims,
   Canada 98 C4
Rapla, *Estonia* 40 B4
Rapperswil, *Switz.* 23 B7
Rapu Rapu I., *Phil.* 55 E6
Rarotonga, *Cook Is.* 93 K12
Ra's al' Ayn, *Syria* 64 B4
Ra's al-Khaymah, *U.A.E.* . 65 E8
Ra's al-Unuf, *Libya* 73 B8
Ra's an Naqb, *Jordan* 69 F4
Ras Bânâs, *Egypt* 76 C4
Ras Dashen, *Ethiopia* 77 E4
Ras el Ma, *Algeria* 75 B4
Ras Mallap, *Egypt* 76 J8
Rās Timirist, *Mauritania* . 78 B1
Rasa, Punta, *Argentina* .. 128 B4
Rasca, Pta. de la,
   Canary Is. 36 G3
Raseiniai, *Lithuania* 40 D3
Rashad, *Sudan* 77 E3
Rashīd, *Egypt* 76 H7
Rashīd, Masabb, *Egypt* .. 76 H7
Rasht, *Iran* 65 B6
Rasi Salai, *Thailand* 58 E5
Raška, *Serbia* 21 M10
Rason L., *Australia* 89 E3
Raşova, *Romania* 38 E10
Rasra, *India* 63 G10
Rass el Oued, *Algeria* 75 A6
Rasskazovo, *Russia* 41 E12
Rastatt, *Germany* 19 G4
Rat Buri, *Thailand* 58 F2
Rat Islands, *U.S.A.* 96 C1
Rat River, *Canada* 100 A6
Ratangarh, *India* 62 E6
Raṭāwī, *Iraq* 64 D5
Rath, *India* 63 G8
Rath Luirc, *Ireland* 15 D3
Rathdrum, *Ireland* 15 D5
Rathenow, *Germany* 18 C8
Rathkeale, *Ireland* 15 D3
Rathlin, *U.K.* 15 A5
Rathlin O'Birne I., *Ireland* 15 B3
Ratibor = Racibórz,
   Poland 20 E8
Ratlam, *India* 62 H6
Ratnagiri, *India* 60 L8
Raton, *U.S.A.* 109 G2
Rattaphum, *Thailand* 59 J3
Rattray Hd., *U.K.* 14 D7
Ratz, Mt., *Canada* 100 B2
Ratzeburg, *Germany* 18 B6
Raub, *Malaysia* 59 L3
Rauch, *Argentina* 126 D4
Raufarhöfn, *Iceland* 8 C6
Raufoss, *Norway* 10 D4
Raukumara Ra., *N.Z.* 87 H6
Rauland, *Norway* 10 E2
Rauma, *Finland* 9 F16
Rauma →, *Norway* 10 B1
Raurkela, *India* 63 H11
Rausu-Dake, *Japan* 48 B12
Rava Russkaya, *Ukraine* . 40 F3
Ravānsar, *Iran* 64 C5
Ravar, *Iran* 65 D8
Ravels, *Belgium* 17 F6
Ravena, *U.S.A.* 107 D11
Ravenna, *Italy* 33 D9
Ravenna, Nebr., *U.S.A.* .. 108 E5
Ravenna, Ohio, *U.S.A.* .. 106 E3
Ravensburg, *Germany* ... 19 H5
Ravenshoe, *Australia* 90 B4
Ravenstein, *Neths.* 16 E7
Ravensthorpe, *Australia* .. 89 F3
Ravenswood, *Australia* ... 90 C4
Ravenswood, *U.S.A.* 104 F5
Ravi →, *Pakistan* 62 D4
Ravna Gora, *Croatia* 33 C11
Rawa Mazowiecka, *Poland* 20 D10
Rawalpindi, *Pakistan* 62 C5
Rawāndūz, *Iraq* 64 B5
Rawang, *Malaysia* 59 L3
Rawdon, *Canada* 98 C5
Rawene, *N.Z.* 87 F4
Rawicz, *Poland* 20 D6
Rawlinna, *Australia* 89 F4
Rawlins, *U.S.A.* 110 F10
Rawlinson Ra., *Australia* . 89 D4
Rawson, *Argentina* 128 B3
Ray, *U.S.A.* 108 A3
Ray, C., *Canada* 99 C8
Rayadurg, *India* 60 M10
Rayagada, *India* 61 K13

Raychikhinsk, *Russia* 45 E13
Rāyen, *Iran* 65 D8
Raymond, *Canada* 100 D6
Raymond, Calif., *U.S.A.* . 112 H7
Raymond, Wash., *U.S.A.* . 112 D3
Raymondville, *U.S.A.* 109 M6
Raymore, *Canada* 101 C8
Rayne, *U.S.A.* 109 K8
Rayón, *Mexico* 114 B2
Rayong, *Thailand* 58 F3
Rayville, *U.S.A.* 109 J9
Raz, Pte. du, *France* 24 D2
Razan, *Iran* 65 C6
Ražana, *Serbia* 21 L9
Ražanj, *Serbia* 21 M11
Razdel'naya, *Ukraine* 42 C4
Razdolnoye, *Russia* 48 C5
Razdolnoye, *Ukraine* 42 D5
Razeh, *Iran* 65 C6
Razelm, Lacul, *Romania* . 38 E12
Razgrad, *Bulgaria* 38 F9
Razmak, *Pakistan* 62 C3
Ré, I. de, *France* 26 B2
Reading, *U.K.* 13 F7
Reading, *U.S.A.* 107 F9
Real, Cordillera, *Bolivia* .. 124 D4
Realicó, *Argentina* 126 D3
Réalmont, *France* 26 E6
Reata, *Mexico* 114 B4
Rebais, *France* 25 D10
Rebecca, L., *Australia* ... 89 F3
Rebi, *Indonesia* 57 F8
Rebiana, *Libya* 73 D9
Rebun-Tō, *Japan* 48 B10
Recanati, *Italy* 33 E10
Recaş, *Romania* 38 D4
Recherche, Arch. of the,
   Australia 89 F3
Rechitsa, *Belorussia* 40 E7
Recht, *Belgium* 17 H8
Recife, *Brazil* 122 C5
Recklinghausen, *Germany* 17 D10
Reconquista, *Argentina* .. 126 B4
Recreio, *Brazil* 125 B6
Recreo, *Argentina* 126 B2
Recuay, *Peru* 124 B2
Red →, La., *U.S.A.* 109 K9
Red →, N. Dak., *U.S.A.* . 108 A6
Red Bank, *U.S.A.* 107 F10
Red Bay, *Canada* 99 B8
Red Bluff, *U.S.A.* 110 F2
Red Bluff L., *U.S.A.* 109 K3
Red Cliffs, *Australia* 91 E3
Red Cloud, *U.S.A.* 108 E5
Red Deer, *Canada* 100 C6
Red Deer →, Alta.,
   Canada 101 C6
Red Deer →, Man.,
   Canada 101 C8
Red Deer L., *Canada* 101 C8
Red Indian L., *Canada* ... 99 C8
Red Lake, *Canada* 101 C10
Red Lake Falls, *U.S.A.* ... 108 B6
Red Lodge, *U.S.A.* 110 D9
Red Mountain, *U.S.A.* ... 113 K9
Red Oak, *U.S.A.* 108 E7
Red Rock, *Canada* 98 C2
Red Rock, L., *U.S.A.* 108 E8
Red Rocks Pt., *Australia* . 89 F4
Red Sea, *Asia* 68 C2
Red Slate Mt., *U.S.A.* ... 112 H8
Red Sucker L., *Canada* .. 101 C10
Red Tower Pass = Turnu
   Roşu Pasul, *Romania* . 38 D7
Red Wing, *U.S.A.* 108 C8
Rédange, *Lux.* 17 J7
Redbridge, *U.K.* 13 F8
Redcar, *U.K.* 12 C6
Redcliff, *Canada* 101 C6
Redcliffe, *Australia* 91 D5
Redcliffe, Mt., *Australia* .. 89 E3
Reddersburg, *S. Africa* ... 84 D4
Redding, *U.S.A.* 110 F2
Redditch, *U.K.* 13 E6
Redenção, *Brazil* 122 B4
Redfield, *U.S.A.* 108 C5
Redknife →, *Canada* 100 A5
Redlands, *U.S.A.* 113 M9
Redmond, *Australia* 89 F2
Redmond, Oreg., *U.S.A.* . 110 D3
Redmond, Wash., *U.S.A.* 112 C4
Redon, *France* 24 E4
Redonda, *Antigua* 117 C7
Redondela, *Spain* 30 C2
Redondo, *Portugal* 31 G3
Redondo Beach, *U.S.A.* . 113 M8
Redrock Pt., *Canada* 100 A5
Redruth, *U.K.* 13 G2
Redvers, *Canada* 101 D8
Redwater, *Canada* 100 C6
Redwood, *U.S.A.* 107 B9
Redwood City, *U.S.A.* ... 111 H2
Redwood Falls, *U.S.A.* ... 108 C7
Ree, L., *Ireland* 15 C4
Reed, L., *Canada* 101 C8
Reed City, *U.S.A.* 104 D3
Reeder, *U.S.A.* 108 B3
Reedley, *U.S.A.* 111 H4
Reedsburg, *U.S.A.* 108 D9
Reedsport, *U.S.A.* 110 E1
Reefton, *N.Z.* 87 K3
Refahiye, *Turkey* 67 D8
Refugio, *U.S.A.* 109 L6
Rega →, *Poland* 20 A5
Regalbuto, *Italy* 35 E7
Regen, *Germany* 19 G9

Regen →, *Germany* 19 F8
Regeneração, *Brazil* 122 C3
Regensburg, *Germany* ... 19 F8
Regensdorf, *Switz.* 23 B6
Réggio di Calábria, *Italy* . 35 D8
Réggio nell' Emilia, *Italy* . 32 D7
Regina, *Canada* 101 C8
Régina, *Fr. Guiana* 121 C7
Registro, *Brazil* 127 A6
Reguengos de Monsaraz,
   Portugal 31 G3
Rehar →, *India* 63 H10
Rehoboth, *Namibia* 84 C2
Rehovot, *Israel* 69 D3
Rei-Bouba, *Cameroon* ... 73 G7
Reichenbach, *Germany* .. 18 E8
Reichenbach, *Switz.* 22 C5
Reid, *Australia* 89 F4
Reid River, *Australia* 90 B4
Reiden, *Switz.* 22 B5
Reidsville, *U.S.A.* 105 G6
Reigate, *U.K.* 13 F7
Reillo, *Spain* 28 F3
Reims, *France* 25 C11
Reina Adelaida, Arch.,
   Chile 128 D2
Reinach, Aargau, *Switz.* . 22 B6
Reinach, Basel, *Switz.* ... 22 B5
Reinbeck, *U.S.A.* 108 D8
Reindeer →, *Canada* 101 B8
Reindeer I., *Canada* 101 C9
Reindeer L., *Canada* 101 B8
Reinga, C., *N.Z.* 87 F4
Reinosa, *Spain* 30 B6
Reinosa, Paso, *Spain* 30 C6
Reitdiep, *Neths.* 16 B8
Reitz, *S. Africa* 85 D4
Reivilo, *S. Africa* 84 D3
Rejmyre, *Sweden* 11 F9
Reka →, *Slovenia* 33 C11
Rekinniki, *Russia* 45 C17
Reliance, *Canada* 101 A7
Remad, Oued →, *Algeria* 75 B4
Rémalard, *France* 24 D7
Remarkable, Mt., *Australia* 91 E2
Rembang, *Indonesia* 57 G14
Remchi, *Algeria* 75 A4
Remedios, *Colombia* 120 B3
Remedios, *Panama* 116 E3
Remeshk, *Iran* 65 E8
Remich, *Lux.* 17 J8
Rémire, *Fr. Guiana* 121 C7
Remiremont, *France* 25 D13
Remo, *Ethiopia* 77 F5
Remontnoye, *Russia* 43 C10
Remoulins, *France* 27 E8
Remscheid, *Germany* 18 D3
Ren Xian, *China* 50 F8
Renascença, *Brazil* 120 D4
Rende, *Italy* 35 C9
Rendeux, *Belgium* 17 H7
Rendína, *Greece* 39 K4
Rendsburg, *Germany* 18 A5
Rene, *Russia* 45 C19
Renfrew, *Canada* 98 C4
Renfrew, *U.K.* 14 F4
Rengat, *Indonesia* 56 E2
Rengo, *Chile* 126 C1
Renhua, *China* 53 E9
Renhuai, *China* 52 D6
Reni, *Moldavia* 42 D3
Renk, *Sudan* 77 E3
Renkum, *Neths.* 16 E7
Renmark, *Australia* 91 E3
Rennell Sd., *Canada* 100 C2
Renner Springs T.O.,
   Australia 90 B1
Rennes, *France* 24 D5
Rennes, Bassin de, *France* 24 E5
Reno, *U.S.A.* 112 F7
Reno →, *Italy* 33 D9
Renovo, *U.S.A.* 106 E7
Renqiu, *China* 50 E9
Rensselaer, Ind., *U.S.A.* . 104 E2
Rensselaer, N.Y., *U.S.A.* . 107 D11
Rentería, *Spain* 28 B3
Renton, *U.S.A.* 112 C4
Réo, *Burkina Faso* 78 C4
Reotipur, *India* 63 G10
Republic, Mich., *U.S.A.* .. 104 B2
Republic, Wash., *U.S.A.* . 110 B4
Republican →, *U.S.A.* ... 108 F6
Republican City, *U.S.A.* .. 108 E5
Republiek, *Surinam* 121 B6
Repulse Bay, *Canada* 97 B11
Requena, *Peru* 124 B3
Requena, *Spain* 29 F3
Resadiye = Datça, *Turkey* 66 E2
Reşadiye, *Turkey* 66 C7
Resele, *Sweden* 10 A11
Reserve, *Canada* 101 C8
Reserve, *U.S.A.* 111 K9
Resht = Rasht, *Iran* 65 B6
Resistencia, *Argentina* ... 126 B4
Resita, *Romania* 38 D4
Resolution I., *Canada* 97 B13
Resolution I., *N.Z.* 87 L1
Resplandes, *Brazil* 122 C2
Resplendor, *Brazil* 123 E3
Ressano Garcia, *Mozam.* . 85 D5
Reston, *Canada* 101 C8
Retalhuleu, *Guatemala* ... 116 D1
Reteag, *Romania* 38 B7
Retenue, L. de, *Zaïre* 83 E2
Rethel, *France* 25 C11
Rethem, *Germany* 18 C5

Réthímnon

Réthímnon, *Greece* 37 D6
Réthímnon □, *Greece* 37 D6
Retiche, Alpi, *Switz.* 23 D10
Retie, *Belgium* 17 F6
Retiers, *France* 24 E5
Retortillo, *Spain* 30 E4
Reuland, *Belgium* 17 H8
Réunion ■, *Ind. Oc.* 71 J9
Reus, *Spain* 28 D6
Reusel, *Neths.* 17 F6
Reuss →, *Switz.* 23 B6
Reutlingen, *Germany* 19 G5
Reutte, *Austria* 19 H6
Reuver, *Neths.* 17 F8
Reval = Tallinn, *Estonia* 40 B4
Revel, *France* 26 E6
Revelganj, *India* 63 G11
Revelstoke, *Canada* 100 C5
Reventazón, *Peru* 124 B1
Revigny-sur-Ornain, *France* 25 D11
Revilla Gigedo, Is., *Pac. Oc.* 93 F16
Revillagigedo I., *U.S.A.* 100 B2
Revin, *France* 25 C11
Revuè →, *Mozam.* 83 F3
Rewa, *India* 63 G9
Rewa →, *Guyana* 121 C6
Rewari, *India* 62 E7
Rexburg, *U.S.A.* 110 E8
Rey, *Iran* 65 C6
Rey, Rio del →, *Nigeria* 79 E6
Rey Malabo, *Eq. Guin.* 79 E6
Reyes, *Bolivia* 124 C4
Reyes, Pt., *U.S.A.* 112 H3
Reykjahlið, *Iceland* 8 D5
Reykjanes, *Iceland* 8 E2
Reykjavík, *Iceland* 8 D3
Reynolds, *Canada* 101 D9
Reynolds Ra., *Australia* 88 D5
Reynoldsville, *U.S.A.* 106 E6
Reynosa, *Mexico* 115 B5
Rēzekne, *Latvia* 40 C5
Rezvān, *Iran* 65 E8
Rharis, O. →, *Algeria* 75 C6
Rhayader, *U.K.* 13 E4
Rheden, *Neths.* 16 D8
Rhein, *Canada* 101 C8
Rhein →, *Europe* 16 E8
Rhein-Main-Donau-Kanal, *Germany* 19 F7
Rheinbach, *Germany* 18 E2
Rheine, *Germany* 18 C3
Rheineck, *Switz.* 23 B9
Rheinfelden, *Switz.* 22 A5
Rheinland-Pfalz □, *Germany* 19 E2
Rheinsberg, *Germany* 18 B8
Rheinwaldhorn, *Switz.* 23 D8
Rhenen, *Neths.* 16 E7
Rheriss, Oued →, *Morocco* 74 B4
Rheydt, *Germany* 18 D2
Rhin = Rhein →, *Europe* 16 E8
Rhinau, *France* 25 D14
Rhine = Rhein →, *Europe* 16 E8
Rhineland-Palatinate □ = Rheinland-Pfalz □, *Germany* 19 E2
Rhinelander, *U.S.A.* 108 C10
Rhino Camp, *Uganda* 82 B3
Rhir, Cap, *Morocco* 74 B3
Rhisnes, *Belgium* 17 G5
Rho, *Italy* 32 C6
Rhode Island □, *U.S.A.* 107 E13
Rhodes = Ródhos, *Greece* 37 C10
Rhodesia = Zimbabwe ■, *Africa* 83 F2
Rhodope Mts. = Rhodopi Planina, *Bulgaria* 39 H7
Rhodopi Planina, *Bulgaria* 39 H7
Rhön = Hohe Rhön, *Germany* 19 E5
Rhondda, *U.K.* 13 F4
Rhône □, *France* 27 C8
Rhône →, *France* 27 E8
Rhum, *U.K.* 14 E2
Rhyl, *U.K.* 12 D4
Rhymney, *U.K.* 13 F4
Ri-Aba, *Eq. Guin.* 79 E6
Riachão, *Brazil* 122 C2
Riacho de Santana, *Brazil* 123 D3
Rialma, *Brazil* 123 E2
Riaño, *Spain* 30 C5
Rians, *France* 27 E9
Riansares →, *Spain* 28 F1
Riasi, *India* 63 C6
Riau □, *Indonesia* 56 D2
Riau, Kepulauan, *Indonesia* 56 D2
Riau Arch. = Riau, Kepulauan, *Indonesia* 56 D2
Riaza, *Spain* 28 D1
Riaza →, *Spain* 28 D1
Riba de Saelices, *Spain* 28 E2
Ribadavia, *Spain* 30 C2
Ribadeo, *Spain* 30 B3
Ribadesella, *Spain* 30 B5
Ribamar, *Brazil* 122 B3
Ribas, *Spain* 28 C7
Ribas do Rio Pardo, *Brazil* 125 E7
Ribble →, *U.K.* 12 C5
Ribe, *Denmark* 11 J2
Ribeauvillé, *France* 25 D14
Ribécourt, *France* 25 C9
Ribeira, *Spain* 30 C2
Ribeira Brava, *Madeira* 36 D2
Ribeira do Pombal, *Brazil* 122 D4
Ribeirão Prêto, *Brazil* 127 A6
Ribeiro Gonçalves, *Brazil* 122 C2
Ribemont, *France* 25 C10
Ribera, *Italy* 34 E6
Ribérac, *France* 26 C4
Riberalta, *Bolivia* 125 C4
Ribnica, *Slovenia* 33 C11
Ribnitz-Damgarten, *Germany* 18 A8
Riccarton, *N.Z.* 87 K4
Riccia, *Italy* 35 A7
Riccione, *Italy* 33 D9
Rice, *U.S.A.* 113 L12
Rice L., *Canada* 106 B6
Rice Lake, *U.S.A.* 108 C9
Rich, *Morocco* 74 B4
Rich Hill, *U.S.A.* 109 F7
Richards Bay, *S. Africa* 85 D5
Richards L., *Canada* 101 B7
Richardson →, *Canada* 101 B6
Richardson Springs, *U.S.A.* 112 F5
Richardton, *U.S.A.* 108 B3
Riche, C., *Australia* 89 F2
Richelieu, *France* 24 E7
Richey, *U.S.A.* 108 B2
Richfield, *Idaho, U.S.A.* 110 E6
Richfield, *Utah, U.S.A.* 111 G8
Richford, *U.S.A.* 107 B12
Richibucto, *Canada* 99 C7
Richland, *Ga., U.S.A.* 105 J3
Richland, *Oreg., U.S.A.* 110 D5
Richland, *Wash., U.S.A.* 110 C4
Richland Center, *U.S.A.* 108 D9
Richlands, *U.S.A.* 104 G5
Richmond, *N.S.W., Australia* 91 E5
Richmond, *Queens., Australia* 90 C3
Richmond, *N.Z.* 87 J4
Richmond, *S. Africa* 85 D5
Richmond, *U.K.* 12 C6
Richmond, *Calif., U.S.A.* 112 H4
Richmond, *Ind., U.S.A.* 104 F3
Richmond, *Ky., U.S.A.* 104 G3
Richmond, *Mich., U.S.A.* 106 D2
Richmond, *Mo., U.S.A.* 108 F8
Richmond, *Tex., U.S.A.* 109 L7
Richmond, *Utah, U.S.A.* 110 F8
Richmond, *Va., U.S.A.* 104 G7
Richmond Ra., *Australia* 91 D5
Richmond-upon-Thames, *U.K.* 13 F7
Richterswil, *Switz.* 23 B7
Richton, *U.S.A.* 105 K1
Richwood, *U.S.A.* 104 F5
Ricla, *Spain* 28 D3
Ridder, *Kazakhstan* 44 D9
Ridderkerk, *Neths.* 16 E5
Riddes, *Switz.* 22 D4
Ridgecrest, *U.S.A.* 113 K9
Ridgedale, *Canada* 101 C8
Ridgefield, *U.S.A.* 112 E4
Ridgeland, *U.S.A.* 105 J5
Ridgelands, *Australia* 90 C5
Ridgetown, *Canada* 98 D3
Ridgewood, *U.S.A.* 107 F10
Ridgway, *U.S.A.* 106 E6
Riding Mountain Nat. Park, *Canada* 101 C8
Ridley, Mt., *Australia* 89 F3
Ried, *Austria* 21 G3
Riedlingen, *Germany* 19 G5
Riel, *Neths.* 17 E6
Rienza →, *Italy* 33 B8
Riesa, *Germany* 18 D9
Riesco, I., *Chile* 128 D2
Riesi, *Italy* 35 E7
Riet →, *S. Africa* 84 D3
Rieti, *Italy* 33 F9
Rieupeyroux, *France* 26 D6
Riez, *France* 27 E10
Riffe L., *U.S.A.* 112 D4
Rifle, *U.S.A.* 110 G10
Rifstangi, *Iceland* 8 C5
Rift Valley □, *Kenya* 82 B4
Rig Rig, *Chad* 73 F7
Riga, *Latvia* 40 C4
Riga, G. of = Rīgas Jūras Līcis, *Latvia* 40 C3
Rīgān, *Iran* 65 D8
Rīgas Jūras Līcis, *Latvia* 40 C3
Rigaud, *Canada* 107 A10
Rigby, *U.S.A.* 110 E8
Rīgestān □, *Afghan.* 60 D4
Riggins, *U.S.A.* 110 D5
Rignac, *France* 26 D6
Rigolet, *Canada* 99 B8
Riihimäki, *Finland* 9 F18
Riiser-Larsen-halvøya, *Antarctica* 5 C4
Rijau, *Nigeria* 79 C6
Rijeka, *Croatia* 33 C11
Rijen, *Neths.* 17 E5
Rijkevorsel, *Belgium* 17 F5
Rijn →, *Neths.* 16 D4
Rijnsberg, *Neths.* 16 D4
Rijsbergen, *Neths.* 17 E5
Rijssen, *Neths.* 16 D9
Rijswijk, *Neths.* 16 D4
Rike, *Ethiopia* 77 E4
Rikuzentakada, *Japan* 48 E10
Rila Planina, *Bulgaria* 38 G6
Riley, *U.S.A.* 110 E4
Rima →, *Nigeria* 79 C6
Rimah, Wadi ar →, *Si. Arabia* 64 E4
Rimavská Sobota, *Slovakia* 21 G10
Rimbey, *Canada* 100 C6
Rimbo, *Sweden* 10 E12
Rimi, *Nigeria* 79 C6
Rímini, *Italy* 33 D9
Rîmnicu Sărat, *Romania* 38 D10
Rîmnicu Vîlcea, *Romania* 38 D7
Rimouski, *Canada* 99 C6
Rimrock, *U.S.A.* 112 D5
Rinca, *Indonesia* 57 F5
Rincón de Romos, *Mexico* 114 C4
Rinconada, *Argentina* 126 A2
Ringarum, *Sweden* 11 F10
Ringe, *Denmark* 11 J4
Ringim, *Nigeria* 79 C6
Ringkøbing, *Denmark* 11 H2
Ringling, *U.S.A.* 110 C8
Ringsaker, *Norway* 10 D4
Ringsted, *Denmark* 11 J5
Ringvassøy, *Norway* 8 B15
Rinjani, *Indonesia* 56 F5
Rinteln, *Germany* 18 C5
Río, Punta del, *Spain* 29 J2
Rio Branco, *Brazil* 124 B4
Río Branco, *Uruguay* 127 C5
Rio Brilhante, *Brazil* 127 A5
Río Bueno, *Chile* 128 B2
Río Chico, *Venezuela* 120 A4
Rio Claro, *Brazil* 127 A6
Rio Claro, *Trin. & Tob.* 117 D7
Río Colorado, *Argentina* 128 A4
Río Cuarto, *Argentina* 126 C3
Rio das Pedras, *Mozam.* 85 C6
Rio de Contas, *Brazil* 123 D3
Rio de Janeiro, *Brazil* 123 F3
Rio de Janeiro □, *Brazil* 123 F3
Rio do Prado, *Brazil* 123 E3
Rio do Sul, *Brazil* 127 B6
Río Gallegos, *Argentina* 128 D3
Río Grande, *Argentina* 128 D3
Río Grande, *Bolivia* 124 E4
Rio Grande, *Brazil* 127 C5
Río Grande, *Mexico* 114 C4
Río Grande, *Nic.* 116 D3
Rio Grande →, *U.S.A.* 109 N6
Rio Grande City, *U.S.A.* 109 M5
Río Grande del Norte →, *N. Amer.* 103 E7
Rio Grande do Norte □, *Brazil* 122 C4
Rio Grande do Sul □, *Brazil* 127 C5
Río Hato, *Panama* 116 E3
Río Lagartos, *Mexico* 115 C7
Rio Largo, *Brazil* 122 C4
Rio Maior, *Portugal* 31 F2
Rio Marina, *Italy* 32 F7
Río Mayo, *Argentina* 128 C2
Río Mulatos, *Bolivia* 124 D4
Río Muni = Mbini □, *Eq. Guin.* 80 D2
Rio Negro, *Brazil* 127 B6
Río Negro, *Chile* 128 B2
Rio Negro, Pantanal do, *Brazil* 125 D6
Rio Pardo, *Brazil* 127 C5
Río Pico, *Argentina* 128 B2
Rio Real, *Brazil* 123 D4
Río Segundo, *Argentina* 126 C3
Río Tercero, *Argentina* 126 C3
Rio Tinto, *Brazil* 122 C4
Rio Tinto, *Portugal* 30 D2
Rio Verde, *Brazil* 123 E1
Río Verde, *Mexico* 115 C5
Rio Verde de Mato Grosso, *Brazil* 125 D7
Rio Vista, *U.S.A.* 112 G5
Ríobamba, *Ecuador* 120 D2
Ríohacha, *Colombia* 120 A3
Rioja, *Peru* 124 B2
Riom, *France* 26 C7
Riom-ès-Montagnes, *France* 26 C6
Rion-des-Landes, *France* 26 E3
Rionero in Vúlture, *Italy* 35 B8
Rioni →, *Georgia* 43 E9
Rios, *Spain* 30 D3
Riosucio, *Caldas, Colombia* 120 B2
Riosucio, *Choco, Colombia* 120 B2
Riou L., *Canada* 101 B7
Rioz, *France* 25 E13
Riozinho →, *Brazil* 120 D4
Riparia, Dora →, *Italy* 32 C4
Ripatransone, *Italy* 33 F10
Ripley, *Canada* 106 B3
Ripley, *Calif., U.S.A.* 113 M12
Ripley, *N.Y., U.S.A.* 106 D5
Ripley, *Tenn., U.S.A.* 109 H10
Ripoll, *Spain* 28 C7
Ripon, *U.K.* 12 C6
Ripon, *Calif., U.S.A.* 112 H5
Ripon, *Wis., U.S.A.* 104 D1
Riposto, *Italy* 35 E8
Risalpur, *Pakistan* 62 B4
Risan, *Montenegro, Yug.* 21 N8
Risaralda □, *Colombia* 120 B2
Riscle, *France* 26 E3
Rishā', W. ar →, *Si. Arabia* 64 E5
Rishiri-Tō, *Japan* 48 B10
Rishon le Ẕiyyon, *Israel* 69 D3
Risle →, *France* 24 C7
Rison, *U.S.A.* 109 J8
Risør, *Norway* 11 F3
Rissani, *Morocco* 74 B4
Riti, *Nigeria* 79 D6
Rittman, *U.S.A.* 106 F3
Ritzville, *U.S.A.* 110 C4
Riva Bella, *France* 24 C6
Riva del Garda, *Italy* 32 C7
Rivadavia, *Buenos Aires, Argentina* 126 D3
Rivadavia, *Mendoza, Argentina* 126 C2
Rivadavia, *Salta, Argentina* 126 A3
Rivadavia, *Chile* 126 B1
Rivarolo Canavese, *Italy* 32 C4
Rivas, *Nic.* 116 D2
Rive-de-Gier, *France* 27 C8
River Cess, *Liberia* 78 D3
Rivera, *Uruguay* 127 C4
Riverdale, *U.S.A.* 112 J7
Riverhead, *U.S.A.* 107 F12
Riverhurst, *Canada* 101 C7
Riverina, *Australia* 89 E3
Rivers, *Canada* 101 C8
Rivers □, *Nigeria* 79 E6
Rivers, L. of the, *Canada* 101 D7
Rivers Inlet, *Canada* 100 C3
Riversdale, *S. Africa* 84 E3
Riverside, *Calif., U.S.A.* 113 M9
Riverside, *Wyo., U.S.A.* 110 F10
Riversleigh, *Australia* 90 B2
Riverton, *Australia* 91 E2
Riverton, *Canada* 101 C9
Riverton, *N.Z.* 87 M1
Riverton, *U.S.A.* 110 E9
Riverton Heights, *U.S.A.* 112 C4
Rives, *France* 27 C9
Rivesaltes, *France* 26 F6
Riviera, *Europe* 32 E5
Rivière-à-Pierre, *Canada* 99 C5
Rivière-au-Renard, *Canada* 99 C7
Rivière-du-Loup, *Canada* 99 C6
Rivière-Pentecôte, *Canada* 99 C6
Rivière-Pilote, *Martinique* 117 D7
Rivne = Rovno, *Ukraine* 40 F5
Rívoli, *Italy* 32 C4
Rivoli B., *Australia* 91 F3
Rixensart, *Belgium* 17 G5
Riyadh = Ar Riyāḑ, *Si. Arabia* 64 E5
Rize, *Turkey* 67 C9
Rize □, *Turkey* 67 C9
Rizhao, *China* 51 G10
Rizokarpaso, *Cyprus* 37 D13
Rizzuto, C., *Italy* 35 D10
Rjukan, *Norway* 10 E2
Roa, *Norway* 10 D4
Roa, *Spain* 30 D7
Road Town, *Virgin Is.* 117 C7
Roag, L., *U.K.* 14 C2
Roanne, *France* 27 B8
Roanoke, *Ala., U.S.A.* 105 J3
Roanoke, *Va., U.S.A.* 104 G6
Roanoke →, *U.S.A.* 105 H7
Roanoke I., *U.S.A.* 105 H8
Roanoke Rapids, *U.S.A.* 105 G7
Roatán, *Honduras* 116 C2
Robbins I., *Australia* 90 G4
Robe →, *Australia* 88 D2
Robe →, *Ireland* 15 C2
Röbel, *Germany* 18 B8
Robert Lee, *U.S.A.* 109 K4
Roberts, *U.S.A.* 110 E7
Robertsganj, *India* 63 G10
Robertson, *S. Africa* 84 E2
Robertson I., *Antarctica* 5 C18
Robertson Ra., *Australia* 88 D3
Robertsport, *Liberia* 78 D2
Robertstown, *Australia* 91 E2
Roberval, *Canada* 99 C5
Robeson Chan., *Greenland* 4 A4
Robinson →, *Australia* 90 B2
Robinson Ra., *Australia* 89 E2
Robinson River, *Australia* 90 B2
Robinvale, *Australia* 91 E3
Roblin, *Canada* 101 C8
Roboré, *Bolivia* 125 D6
Robson, Mt., *Canada* 100 C5
Robstown, *U.S.A.* 109 M6
Roca, C. da, *Portugal* 6 H4
Roca Partida, I., *Mexico* 114 D2
Rocas, I., *Brazil* 122 B5
Rocca d'Aspidé, *Italy* 35 B8
Rocca San Casciano, *Italy* 33 D8
Roccalbegna, *Italy* 33 F8
Roccastrada, *Italy* 33 F8
Roccella Iónica, *Italy* 35 D9
Rocha, *Uruguay* 127 C5
Rochdale, *U.K.* 12 D5
Rochechouart, *France* 26 C4
Rochedo, *Brazil* 125 D7
Rochefort, *Belgium* 17 H6
Rochefort, *France* 26 C3
Rochefort-en-Terre, *France* 24 E4
Rochelle, *U.S.A.* 108 E10
Rocher River, *Canada* 100 A6
Rocherath, *Belgium* 17 H8
Rocheservière, *France* 24 F5
Rochester, *Canada* 100 C6
Rochester, *U.K.* 13 F8
Rochester, *Ind., U.S.A.* 104 E2
Rochester, *Minn., U.S.A.* 108 C8
Rochester, *N.H., U.S.A.* 107 C14
Rochester, *N.Y., U.S.A.* 106 C7
Rociana, *Spain* 31 H4
Rociu, *Romania* 38 E8
Rock →, *Canada* 100 A3
Rock Hill, *U.S.A.* 105 H5
Rock Island, *U.S.A.* 108 E9
Rock Rapids, *U.S.A.* 108 D6
Rock River, *U.S.A.* 110 F11
Rock Sound, *Bahamas* 116 B4
Rock Springs, *Mont., U.S.A.* 110 C10
Rock Springs, *Wyo., U.S.A.* 110 F9
Rock Valley, *U.S.A.* 108 D6
Rockall, *Atl. Oc.* 6 D3
Rockanje, *Neths.* 16 E4
Rockdale, *Tex., U.S.A.* 109 K6
Rockdale, *Wash., U.S.A.* 112 C5
Rockefeller Plateau, *Antarctica* 5 E14
Rockford, *U.S.A.* 108 D10
Rockglen, *Canada* 101 D7
Rockhampton, *Australia* 90 C5
Rockhampton Downs, *Australia* 90 B2
Rockingham, *Australia* 89 F2
Rockingham B., *Australia* 90 B4
Rockingham Forest, *U.K.* 13 E7
Rocklake, *U.S.A.* 108 A5
Rockland, *Canada* 107 A9
Rockland, *Idaho, U.S.A.* 110 E7
Rockland, *Maine, U.S.A.* 99 D6
Rockland, *Mich., U.S.A.* 108 B10
Rocklin, *U.S.A.* 112 G5
Rockmart, *U.S.A.* 105 H3
Rockport, *Mo., U.S.A.* 108 E7
Rockport, *Tex., U.S.A.* 109 L6
Rocksprings, *U.S.A.* 109 K4
Rockville, *Conn., U.S.A.* 107 E12
Rockville, *Md., U.S.A.* 104 F7
Rockwall, *U.S.A.* 109 J6
Rockwell City, *U.S.A.* 108 D7
Rockwood, *U.S.A.* 105 H3
Rocky Ford, *U.S.A.* 108 F3
Rocky Gully, *Australia* 89 F2
Rocky Lane, *Canada* 100 B5
Rocky Mount, *U.S.A.* 105 H7
Rocky Mountain House, *Canada* 100 C6
Rocky Mts., *N. Amer.* 100 C4
Rockyford, *Canada* 100 C6
Rocroi, *France* 25 C11
Rod, *Pakistan* 60 E3
Rødberg, *Norway* 10 D2
Rødby, *Denmark* 11 K5
Rødbyhavn, *Denmark* 11 K5
Roddickton, *Canada* 99 B8
Rødding, *Denmark* 11 J3
Rødekro, *Denmark* 11 J3
Roden, *Neths.* 16 B8
Rødenes, *Norway* 10 E5
Rodenkirchen, *Germany* 18 B4
Roderick I., *Canada* 100 C3
Rodez, *France* 26 D6
Rodholívas, *Greece* 39 J6
Rodhopoú, *Greece* 37 D5
Ródhos, *Greece* 37 C10
Rodi Garganico, *Italy* 35 A8
Rodna, *Romania* 38 B7
Rodney, *Canada* 106 D3
Rodney, C., *N.Z.* 87 G5
Rodniki, *Russia* 41 C12
Rodriguez, *Ind. Oc.* 3 E13
Roe →, *U.K.* 15 A5
Roebling, *U.S.A.* 107 F10
Roebourne, *Australia* 88 D2
Roebuck B., *Australia* 88 C3
Roebuck Plains, *Australia* 88 C3
Roer →, *Neths.* 17 F7
Roermond, *Neths.* 17 F7
Roes Welcome Sd., *Canada* 97 B11
Roeselare, *Belgium* 17 G2
Rœulx, *Belgium* 17 G4
Rogachev, *Belorussia* 40 E7
Rogagua, L., *Bolivia* 124 C4
Rogaland fylke □, *Norway* 9 G9
Rogaška Slatina, *Slovenia* 33 B12
Rogatec, *Slovenia* 33 B12
Rogatin, *Ukraine* 40 G4
Rogdhia, *Greece* 37 D7
Rogers, *U.S.A.* 109 G7
Rogers City, *U.S.A.* 104 C4
Rogerson, *U.S.A.* 110 E6
Rogersville, *U.S.A.* 105 G4
Roggan River, *Canada* 98 B4
Roggel, *Neths.* 17 F7
Roggeveldberge, *S. Africa* 84 E3
Roggiano Gravina, *Italy* 35 C9
Rogliano, *France* 27 F13
Rogliano, *Italy* 35 C9
Rogoaguado, L., *Bolivia* 125 C4
Rogue →, *U.S.A.* 110 E1
Rohan, *France* 24 D4
Róhda, *Greece* 37 A3
Rohnert Park, *U.S.A.* 112 G4
Rohrbach-lès-Bitche, *France* 25 C14
Rohri, *Pakistan* 62 F3
Rohri Canal, *Pakistan* 62 F3
Rohtak, *India* 62 E7
Roi Et, *Thailand* 58 D4
Roisel, *France* 25 C10
Rojas, *Argentina* 126 C3
Rojo, C., *Mexico* 115 C5
Rokan →, *Indonesia* 56 D2
Rokeby, *Australia* 90 A3
Rokiškis, *Lithuania* 40 D4
Rokitno, *Russia* 40 F9
Rolândia, *Brazil* 127 A5
Rolde, *Neths.* 16 C9
Rolette, *U.S.A.* 108 A5
Rolla, *Kans., U.S.A.* 109 G4
Rolla, *Mo., U.S.A.* 109 G9

Rolla, *N. Dak., U.S.A.* ... 108 A5
Rollag, *Norway* ... 10 D3
Rolle, *Switz.* ... 22 D2
Rolleston, *Australia* ... 90 C4
Rollingstone, *Australia* ... 90 B4
Rom, *Sudan* ... 77 F3
Roma, *Australia* ... 91 D4
Roma, *Italy* ... 34 A5
Roma, *Sweden* ... 9 H15
Roman, *Romania* ... 38 C9
Roman, *Russia* ... 45 C12
Roman-Kosh, Gora, *Ukraine* ... 42 D6
Romanche →, *France* ... 27 C9
Romang, *Indonesia* ... 57 F7
Români, *Egypt* ... 69 E1
Romania ■, *Europe* ... 38 D8
Romano, Cayo, *Cuba* ... 116 B4
Romano di Lombardía, *Italy* ... 32 C6
Romanovka = Bessarabka, *Moldavia* ... 42 C3
Romans-sur-Isère, *France* ... 27 C9
Romanshorn, *Switz.* ... 23 A8
Romblon, *Phil.* ... 55 E5
Rombo □, *Tanzania* ... 82 C4
Rome = Roma, *Italy* ... 34 A5
Rome, *Ga., U.S.A.* ... 105 H3
Rome, *N.Y., U.S.A.* ... 107 C9
Romeleåsen, *Sweden* ... 11 J7
Romenay, *France* ... 27 B9
Romerike, *Norway* ... 10 D5
Romilly-sur-Seine, *France* ... 25 D10
Romîni, *Romania* ... 38 E7
Rommani, *Morocco* ... 74 B3
Romney, *U.S.A.* ... 104 F6
Romney Marsh, *U.K.* ... 13 F8
Romny, *Ukraine* ... 40 F8
Rømø, *Denmark* ... 11 J2
Romodan, *Ukraine* ... 40 G8
Romodanovo, *Russia* ... 41 D14
Romont, *Switz.* ... 22 C3
Romorantin-Lanthenay, *France* ... 25 E8
Romsdalen, *Norway* ... 10 B2
Ron, *Vietnam* ... 58 D6
Rona, *U.K.* ... 14 D3
Ronan, *U.S.A.* ... 110 C6
Roncador, Cayos, *Caribbean* ... 116 D3
Roncador, Serra do, *Brazil* ... 123 D1
Roncesvalles, Paso, *Spain* ... 28 B3
Ronceverte, *U.S.A.* ... 104 G5
Ronciglione, *Italy* ... 33 F9
Ronco →, *Italy* ... 33 D9
Ronda, *Spain* ... 31 J5
Ronda, Serranía de, *Spain* ... 31 J5
Rondane, *Norway* ... 10 C3
Rondón, *Colombia* ... 120 B3
Rondônia, *Brazil* ... 125 C5
Rondônia □, *Brazil* ... 125 C5
Rondonópolis, *Brazil* ... 125 D7
Rong Jiang →, *China* ... 52 E7
Rong Xian, *Guangxi Zhuangzu, China* ... 53 F8
Rong Xian, *Sichuan, China* ... 52 C5
Rong'an, *China* ... 52 E7
Rongchang, *China* ... 52 C5
Ronge, L. la, *Canada* ... 101 B7
Rongjiang, *China* ... 52 E7
Rongshui, *China* ... 52 E7
Ronne Ice Shelf, *Antarctica* ... 5 D18
Ronsard, C., *Australia* ... 89 D1
Ronse, *Belgium* ... 17 G3
Ronuro →, *Brazil* ... 125 C7
Roodepoort, *S. Africa* ... 85 D4
Roodeschool, *Neths.* ... 16 B9
Roof Butte, *U.S.A.* ... 111 H9
Roompot, *Neths.* ... 17 E4
Roorkee, *India* ... 62 E7
Roosendaal, *Neths.* ... 17 E4
Roosevelt, *Minn., U.S.A.* ... 108 A7
Roosevelt, *Utah, U.S.A.* ... 110 F8
Roosevelt →, *Brazil* ... 125 B5
Roosevelt, Mt., *Canada* ... 100 B3
Roosevelt I., *Antarctica* ... 5 D12
Roosevelt Res., *U.S.A.* ... 111 K8
Roper →, *Australia* ... 90 A2
Ropesville, *U.S.A.* ... 109 J3
Roque Pérez, *Argentina* ... 126 D4
Roquefort, *France* ... 26 D3
Roquemaure, *France* ... 27 D8
Roquetas, *Spain* ... 28 E5
Roquevaire, *France* ... 27 E9
Roraima □, *Brazil* ... 121 C5
Roraima, Mt., *Venezuela* ... 121 B5
Rorketon, *Canada* ... 101 C8
Røros, *Norway* ... 10 B5
Rorschach, *Switz.* ... 23 B8
Rosa, *Zambia* ... 83 D3
Rosa, C., *Algeria* ... 75 A6
Rosa, Monte, *Europe* ... 22 E5
Rosal, *Spain* ... 30 D2
Rosal de la Frontera, *Spain* ... 31 H3
Rosalia, *U.S.A.* ... 110 C5
Rosamond, *U.S.A.* ... 113 L8
Rosans, *France* ... 27 D9
Rosário, *Argentina* ... 126 C3
Rosário, *Brazil* ... 122 B3
Rosario, *Baja Calif. N., Mexico* ... 114 A1
Rosario, *Sinaloa, Mexico* ... 114 C3
Rosario, *Paraguay* ... 126 A4
Rosario, Villa del, *Venezuela* ... 120 A3

Rosario de la Frontera, *Argentina* ... 126 B3
Rosario de Lerma, *Argentina* ... 126 A2
Rosario del Tala, *Argentina* ... 126 C4
Rosário do Sul, *Brazil* ... 127 C5
Rosário Oeste, *Brazil* ... 125 C6
Rosarito, *U.S.A.* ... 113 N9
Rosas, *Spain* ... 28 C8
Roscoe, *U.S.A.* ... 108 C5
Roscoff, *France* ... 24 D3
Roscommon, *Ireland* ... 15 C3
Roscommon, *U.S.A.* ... 104 C3
Roscommon □, *Ireland* ... 15 C3
Roscrea, *Ireland* ... 15 D4
Rose →, *Australia* ... 90 A2
Rose Blanche, *Canada* ... 99 C8
Rose Harbour, *Canada* ... 100 C2
Rose Pt., *Canada* ... 100 C2
Rose Valley, *Canada* ... 101 C8
Roseau, *Domin.* ... 117 C7
Roseau, *U.S.A.* ... 108 A7
Rosebery, *Australia* ... 90 G4
Rosebud, *U.S.A.* ... 109 K6
Roseburg, *U.S.A.* ... 110 E2
Rosedale, *Australia* ... 90 C5
Rosedale, *U.S.A.* ... 109 J9
Rosée, *Belgium* ... 17 H5
Roseland, *U.S.A.* ... 112 G4
Rosemary, *Canada* ... 100 C6
Rosenberg, *U.S.A.* ... 109 L7
Rosendaël, *France* ... 25 A9
Rosenheim, *Germany* ... 19 H8
Roseto degli Abruzzi, *Italy* ... 33 F11
Rosetown, *Canada* ... 101 C7
Rosetta = Rashîd, *Egypt* ... 76 H7
Roseville, *U.S.A.* ... 112 G5
Rosewood, *N. Terr., Australia* ... 88 C4
Rosewood, *Queens., Australia* ... 91 D5
Roshkhvār, *Iran* ... 65 C8
Rosières-en-Santerre, *France* ... 25 C9
Rosignano Marittimo, *Italy* ... 32 E7
Rosignol, *Guyana* ... 121 B6
Roşiori de Vede, *Romania* ... 38 E8
Rositsa, *Bulgaria* ... 38 F10
Rositsa →, *Bulgaria* ... 38 F8
Roskilde, *Denmark* ... 11 J6
Roskilde Amtskommune □, *Denmark* ... 11 J6
Roskilde Fjord, *Denmark* ... 11 J6
Roslavl, *Russia* ... 40 E8
Roslyn, *Australia* ... 91 E4
Rosmaninhal, *Portugal* ... 31 F3
Rosmead, *S. Africa* ... 84 E4
Røsnæs, *Denmark* ... 11 J4
Rosolini, *Italy* ... 35 F7
Rosporden, *France* ... 24 E3
Ross, *Australia* ... 90 G4
Ross, *N.Z.* ... 87 K3
Ross I., *Antarctica* ... 5 D11
Ross Ice Shelf, *Antarctica* ... 5 E12
Ross L., *U.S.A.* ... 110 B3
Ross-on-Wye, *U.K.* ... 13 F5
Ross Sea, *Antarctica* ... 5 D11
Rossa, *Switz.* ... 23 D8
Rossan Pt., *Ireland* ... 15 B3
Rossano Cálabro, *Italy* ... 35 C9
Rossburn, *Canada* ... 101 C8
Rosseau, *Canada* ... 106 A5
Rossignol, L., *Canada* ... 98 B5
Rossignol Res., *Canada* ... 99 D6
Rossland, *Canada* ... 100 D5
Rosslare, *Ireland* ... 15 D5
Rosslau, *Germany* ... 18 D8
Rosso, *Mauritania* ... 78 B1
Rossosh, *Russia* ... 43 A8
Rossport, *Canada* ... 98 C2
Rossum, *Neths.* ... 16 E6
Røssvatnet, *Norway* ... 8 D13
Rossville, *Australia* ... 90 B4
Rosthern, *Canada* ... 101 C7
Rostock, *Germany* ... 18 A8
Rostov, *Russia* ... 41 C11
Rostov, *Russia* ... 43 C8
Rostrenen, *France* ... 24 D3
Roswell, *U.S.A.* ... 109 J2
Rosyth, *U.K.* ... 14 E5
Rota, *Spain* ... 31 J4
Rotälven →, *Sweden* ... 10 C8
Rotan, *U.S.A.* ... 109 J4
Rotem, *Belgium* ... 17 F7
Rotenburg, *Germany* ... 18 B5
Roth, *Germany* ... 19 F7
Rothaargebirge, *Germany* ... 18 E4
Rothenburg, *Switz.* ... 23 B6
Rothenburg ob der Tauber, *Germany* ... 19 F6
Rother →, *U.K.* ... 13 G8
Rotherham, *U.K.* ... 12 D6
Rothes, *U.K.* ... 14 D5
Rothesay, *Canada* ... 99 C6
Rothesay, *U.K.* ... 14 F3
Rothrist, *Switz.* ... 22 B5
Roti, *Indonesia* ... 57 F6
Roto, *Australia* ... 91 E4
Rotondella, *Italy* ... 35 B9
Rotoroa, L., *N.Z.* ... 87 J4
Rotorua, *N.Z.* ... 87 H6
Rotorua, L., *N.Z.* ... 87 H6
Rotselaar, *Belgium* ... 17 G5
Rott →, *Germany* ... 19 G9
Rotten →, *Switz.* ... 22 D5

Rottenburg, *Germany* ... 19 G4
Rotterdam, *Neths.* ... 16 E5
Rottnest I., *Australia* ... 89 F2
Rottumeroog, *Neths.* ... 16 A9
Rottweil, *Germany* ... 19 G4
Rotuma, *Fiji* ... 92 J9
Roubaix, *France* ... 25 B10
Rouen, *France* ... 24 C8
Rouillac, *France* ... 26 C3
Rouleau, *Canada* ... 101 C8
Round Mt., *Australia* ... 91 E5
Round Mountain, *U.S.A.* ... 110 G5
Roundup, *U.S.A.* ... 110 C9
Roura, *Fr. Guiana* ... 121 C7
Rousay, *U.K.* ... 14 B5
Rouses Point, *U.S.A.* ... 107 B11
Roussillon, *Isère, France* ... 27 C8
Roussillon, *Pyrénées-Or., France* ... 26 F6
Rouveen, *Neths.* ... 16 C8
Rouxville, *S. Africa* ... 84 E4
Rouyn, *Canada* ... 98 C4
Rovaniemi, *Finland* ... 8 C18
Rovato, *Italy* ... 32 C7
Rovenki, *Ukraine* ... 43 B8
Rovereto, *Italy* ... 32 C8
Rovigo, *Italy* ... 33 C8
Rovinari, *Romania* ... 38 E6
Rovinj, *Croatia* ... 33 C10
Rovira, *Colombia* ... 120 C2
Rovno, *Ukraine* ... 40 F5
Rovnoye, *Russia* ... 41 F15
Rovuma →, *Tanzania* ... 83 E5
Row'ān, *Iran* ... 65 C6
Rowena, *Australia* ... 91 D4
Rowley Shoals, *Australia* ... 88 C2
Roxa, *Guinea-Biss.* ... 78 C1
Roxas, *Capiz, Phil.* ... 55 F5
Roxas, *Isabela, Phil.* ... 55 C4
Roxas, *Mindoro, Phil.* ... 55 E4
Roxboro, *U.S.A.* ... 105 G6
Roxborough Downs, *Australia* ... 90 C2
Roxburgh, *N.Z.* ... 87 L2
Roxen, *Sweden* ... 11 F9
Roy, *Mont., U.S.A.* ... 110 C9
Roy, *N. Mex., U.S.A.* ... 109 H2
Roy Hill, *Australia* ... 88 D2
Roya, Peña, *Spain* ... 28 E4
Royal Leamington Spa, *U.K.* ... 13 E6
Royan, *France* ... 26 C2
Roye, *France* ... 25 C9
Røyken, *Norway* ... 10 E4
Rozay-en-Brie, *France* ... 25 D9
Rožaj, *Montenegro, Yug.* ... 21 N10
Rozhishche, *Ukraine* ... 40 F4
Rozoy-sur-Serre, *France* ... 25 C11
Rtishchevo, *Russia* ... 41 D13
Rúa, *Spain* ... 30 C3
Ruacaná, *Angola* ... 84 B1
Ruahine Ra., *N.Z.* ... 87 H6
Ruapehu, *N.Z.* ... 87 H5
Ruapuke I., *N.Z.* ... 87 M2
Ruâq, W. →, *Egypt* ... 69 F2
Rub' al Khali, *Si. Arabia* ... 68 D4
Rubeho Mts., *Tanzania* ... 82 D4
Rubezhnoye, *Ukraine* ... 42 B8
Rubh a' Mhail, *U.K.* ... 14 F2
Rubha Hunish, *U.K.* ... 14 D2
Rubiataba, *Brazil* ... 123 E2
Rubicon →, *U.S.A.* ... 112 G5
Rubicone →, *Italy* ... 33 D9
Rubinéia, *Brazil* ... 123 F1
Rubino, *Ivory C.* ... 78 D4
Rubio, *Venezuela* ... 120 B3
Rubizhne = Rubezhnoye, *Ukraine* ... 42 B8
Rubtsovsk, *Russia* ... 44 D9
Ruby L., *U.S.A.* ... 110 F6
Ruby Mts., *U.S.A.* ... 110 F6
Rucava, *Latvia* ... 40 C2
Rucheng, *China* ... 53 E9
Rud, *Norway* ... 10 D4
Rūd Sar, *Iran* ... 65 B6
Ruda Śląska, *Poland* ... 20 E8
Rudall, *Australia* ... 91 E2
Rudall →, *Australia* ... 88 D3
Ruden, *Germany* ... 18 A9
Rüdersdorf, *Germany* ... 18 C9
Rudewa, *Tanzania* ... 83 E3
Rudkøbing, *Denmark* ... 11 K4
Rudnik, *Serbia, Yug.* ... 21 L10
Rudnogorsk, *Russia* ... 45 D11
Rudnya, *Russia* ... 40 D7
Rudnyy, *Kazakhstan* ... 44 D7
Rudolf, Ostrov, *Russia* ... 44 A6
Rudolstadt, *Germany* ... 18 E7
Rudong, *China* ... 53 A13
Rudozem, *Bulgaria* ... 39 H7
Rudyard, *U.S.A.* ... 104 B3
Rue, *France* ... 25 B8
Ruelle, *France* ... 26 C4
Rufa'a, *Sudan* ... 77 E3
Ruffec, *France* ... 26 B4
Rufiji □, *Tanzania* ... 82 D4
Rufiji →, *Tanzania* ... 82 D4
Rufino, *Argentina* ... 126 C3
Rufisque, *Senegal* ... 78 C1
Rufunsa, *Zambia* ... 83 F2
Rugao, *China* ... 53 A13
Rugby, *U.K.* ... 13 E6
Rugby, *U.S.A.* ... 108 A5
Rügen, *Germany* ... 18 A9
Rugles, *France* ... 24 D7

Ruhengeri, *Rwanda* ... 82 C2
Ruhla, *Germany* ... 18 E6
Ruhland, *Germany* ... 18 D9
Ruhr →, *Germany* ... 18 D2
Ruhuhu →, *Tanzania* ... 83 E3
Rui'an, *China* ... 53 D13
Ruichang, *China* ... 53 C10
Ruidosa, *U.S.A.* ... 109 L2
Ruidoso, *U.S.A.* ... 111 K11
Ruili, *China* ... 52 E1
Ruinen, *Neths.* ... 16 C8
Ruinerwold, *Neths.* ... 16 C8
Ruiten A Kanaal →, *Neths.* ... 16 C10
Ruivo, Pico, *Madeira* ... 36 D3
Rujm Tal'at al Jamā'ah, *Jordan* ... 69 E4
Ruk, *Pakistan* ... 62 F3
Rukwa □, *Tanzania* ... 82 D3
Rukwa L., *Tanzania* ... 82 D3
Rulhieres, C., *Australia* ... 88 B4
Rulles, *Belgium* ... 17 J7
Rum Cay, *Bahamas* ... 117 B5
Rum Jungle, *Australia* ... 88 B5
Ruma, *Serbia, Yug.* ... 21 K9
Rumāḥ, *Si. Arabia* ... 64 E5
Rumania = Romania ■, *Europe* ... 38 D8
Rumaylah, *Iraq* ... 64 D5
Rumbalara, *Australia* ... 90 D1
Rumbêk, *Sudan* ... 77 F2
Rumbeke, *Belgium* ... 17 G2
Rumelange, *Lux.* ... 17 K8
Rumford, *U.S.A.* ... 107 B14
Rumilly, *France* ... 27 C9
Rumoi, *Japan* ... 48 C10
Rumonge, *Burundi* ... 82 C2
Rumsey, *Canada* ... 100 C6
Rumula, *Australia* ... 90 B4
Rumuruti, *Kenya* ... 82 B4
Runan, *China* ... 50 H8
Runanga, *N.Z.* ... 87 K3
Runaway, C., *N.Z.* ... 87 G6
Runcorn, *U.K.* ... 12 D5
Rungwa, *Tanzania* ... 82 D3
Rungwa →, *Tanzania* ... 82 D3
Rungwe, *Tanzania* ... 83 D3
Rungwe □, *Tanzania* ... 83 D3
Runka, *Nigeria* ... 79 C6
Runton Ra., *Australia* ... 88 D3
Ruoqiang, *China* ... 54 C3
Rupa, *India* ... 61 F18
Rupar, *India* ... 62 D7
Rupat, *Indonesia* ... 56 D2
Rupert →, *Canada* ... 98 B4
Rupert House = Fort Rupert, *Canada* ... 98 B4
Rupununi →, *Guyana* ... 121 C6
Rur →, *Germany* ... 18 E2
Rurrenabaque, *Bolivia* ... 124 C4
Rus →, *Spain* ... 29 C2
Rusambo, *Zimbabwe* ... 83 F3
Rusape, *Zimbabwe* ... 83 F3
Ruschuk = Ruse, *Bulgaria* ... 38 F8
Ruse, *Bulgaria* ... 38 F8
Rushan, *China* ... 51 F11
Rushden, *U.K.* ... 13 E7
Rushford, *U.S.A.* ... 108 D9
Rushville, *Ill., U.S.A.* ... 108 E9
Rushville, *Ind., U.S.A.* ... 104 F3
Rushville, *Nebr., U.S.A.* ... 108 D3
Rushworth, *Australia* ... 91 F4
Russas, *Brazil* ... 122 B4
Russell, *Canada* ... 101 C8
Russell, *U.S.A.* ... 108 F5
Russell L., *Man., Canada* ... 101 B8
Russell L., *N.W.T., Canada* ... 100 A5
Russellkonda, *India* ... 61 K14
Russellville, *Ala., U.S.A.* ... 105 H2
Russellville, *Ark., U.S.A.* ... 109 H8
Russellville, *Ky., U.S.A.* ... 105 G2
Russi, *Italy* ... 33 D9
Russia ■, *Eurasia* ... 45 C11
Russian →, *U.S.A.* ... 112 G3
Russkaya Polyana, *Kazakhstan* ... 44 D8
Russkoye Ustie, *Russia* ... 4 B15
Rustam, *Pakistan* ... 62 B5
Rustam Shahr, *Pakistan* ... 62 F2
Rustavi, *Georgia* ... 43 F11
Rustenburg, *S. Africa* ... 84 D4
Ruston, *U.S.A.* ... 109 J8
Rutana, *Burundi* ... 82 C2
Rute, *Spain* ... 31 H6
Ruteng, *Indonesia* ... 57 F6
Ruth, *Mich., U.S.A.* ... 106 C2
Ruth, *Nev., U.S.A.* ... 110 G6
Rutherford, *U.S.A.* ... 112 G4
Rutherglen, *U.K.* ... 14 F4
Rüti, *Switz.* ... 23 B7
Rutigliano, *Italy* ... 35 A10
Rutland Plains, *Australia* ... 90 B3
Rutledge →, *Canada* ... 101 A6
Rutledge L., *Canada* ... 101 A6
Rutshuru, *Zaïre* ... 82 C2
Rutul, *Russia* ... 43 E12
Ruurlo, *Neths.* ... 16 D8
Ruvo di Púglia, *Italy* ... 35 A9
Ruvu, *Tanzania* ... 82 D4
Ruvu →, *Tanzania* ... 82 D4
Ruvuma □, *Tanzania* ... 83 E4
Ruwais, *U.A.E.* ... 65 E7
Ruwenzori, *Africa* ... 82 B2

Ruyigi, *Burundi* ... 82 C3
Ruyuan, *China* ... 53 E9
Ruzayevka, *Russia* ... 41 D14
Ružomberok, *Slovakia* ... 20 F9
Rwanda ■, *Africa* ... 82 C3
Ry, *Denmark* ... 11 H3
Ryakhovo, *Bulgaria* ... 38 F9
Ryan, L., *U.K.* ... 14 G3
Ryazan, *Russia* ... 41 D11
Ryazhsk, *Russia* ... 41 E12
Rybache, *Kazakhstan* ... 44 E9
Rybachye, *Russia* ... 44 B11
Rybinsk, *Russia* ... 41 B11
Rybinskoye Vdkhr., *Russia* ... 41 B11
Rybnik, *Poland* ... 20 E8
Rybnitsa, *Moldavia* ... 42 C3
Rybnoye, *Russia* ... 41 D11
Rychwał, *Poland* ... 20 C8
Ryde, *U.K.* ... 13 G6
Ryderwood, *U.S.A.* ... 112 D3
Rydöbruk, *Sweden* ... 11 H7
Rydułtowy, *Poland* ... 20 E8
Rye, *U.K.* ... 13 G8
Rye →, *U.K.* ... 12 C7
Rye Patch Reservoir, *U.S.A.* ... 110 F4
Ryegate, *U.S.A.* ... 110 C9
Rylsk, *Russia* ... 40 F9
Rylstone, *Australia* ... 91 E4
Ryōthu, *Japan* ... 48 E9
Rypin, *Poland* ... 20 B9
Ryūgasaki, *Japan* ... 49 G10
Ryūkyū Is. = Ryūkyū-rettō, *Japan* ... 49 M2
Ryūkyū-rettō, *Japan* ... 49 M2
Rzeszów, *Poland* ... 20 E11
Rzhev, *Russia* ... 40 C9

S

Sa, *Thailand* ... 58 C3
Sa Dec, *Vietnam* ... 59 G5
Sa'ādatābād, *Fārs, Iran* ... 65 D7
Sa'ādatābād, *Kermān, Iran* ... 65 D7
Saale →, *Germany* ... 18 D7
Saaler Bodden, *Germany* ... 18 A8
Saalfeld, *Germany* ... 18 E7
Saane →, *Switz.* ... 22 B4
Saar →, *Europe* ... 25 C13
Saarbrücken, *Germany* ... 19 F2
Saarburg, *Germany* ... 19 F2
Saaremaa, *Estonia* ... 40 B3
Saariselkä, *Finland* ... 8 B20
Saarland □, *Germany* ... 25 C13
Saarlouis, *Germany* ... 19 F2
Saas Fee, *Switz.* ... 22 D5
Sab 'Bi'ār, *Syria* ... 64 C3
Saba, *W. Indies* ... 117 C7
Šabac, *Serbia, Yug.* ... 21 L9
Sabadell, *Spain* ... 28 D7
Sabah □, *Malaysia* ... 56 C5
Sabak Bernam, *Malaysia* ... 59 L3
Sábana de la Mar, *Dom. Rep.* ... 117 C6
Sábanalarga, *Colombia* ... 120 A3
Sabang, *Indonesia* ... 56 C1
Sabará, *Brazil* ... 123 E3
Sabarania, *Indonesia* ... 57 E9
Sabattis, *U.S.A.* ... 107 B10
Sabáudia, *Italy* ... 34 A6
Sabaya, *Bolivia* ... 124 D4
Sabhah, *Libya* ... 73 C7
Sabie, *S. Africa* ... 85 D5
Sabinal, *Mexico* ... 114 A3
Sabinal, *U.S.A.* ... 109 L5
Sabinal, Punta del, *Spain* ... 29 J2
Sabinas, *Mexico* ... 114 B4
Sabinas →, *Mexico* ... 114 B4
Sabinas Hidalgo, *Mexico* ... 114 B4
Sabine →, *U.S.A.* ... 109 L8
Sabine L., *U.S.A.* ... 109 L8
Sabine Pass, *U.S.A.* ... 109 L8
Sabinópolis, *Brazil* ... 123 E3
Sabinov, *Slovakia* ... 20 F11
Sabirabad, *Azerbaijan* ... 43 F13
Sabkhet el Bardawîl, *Egypt* ... 69 D2
Sablayan, *Phil.* ... 55 E4
Sable, C., *Canada* ... 99 D6
Sable, C., *U.S.A.* ... 103 E10
Sable I., *Canada* ... 99 D8
Sablé-sur-Sarthe, *France* ... 24 E6
Saboeiro, *Brazil* ... 122 C4
Sabolev, *Russia* ... 45 D16
Sabor →, *Portugal* ... 30 D3
Sabou, *Burkina Faso* ... 78 C4
Sabrātah, *Libya* ... 75 B7
Sabria, *Tunisia* ... 75 B6
Sabrina Coast, *Antarctica* ... 5 C9
Sabugal, *Portugal* ... 30 E3
Sabulubek, *Indonesia* ... 56 E1
Sabzevār, *Iran* ... 65 B8
Sabzvārān, *Iran* ... 65 D8
Sac City, *U.S.A.* ... 108 D7
Sacedón, *Spain* ... 28 E2
Sachigo →, *Canada* ... 98 A2
Sachigo, L., *Canada* ... 98 B1
Sachkhere, *Georgia* ... 43 E10
Sachseln, *Switz.* ... 23 C6
Sachsen □, *Germany* ... 18 E9
Sachsen-Anhalt □, *Germany* ... 18 D8
Sacile, *Italy* ... 33 C9
Sackets Harbor, *U.S.A.* ... 107 C8
Saco, *Maine, U.S.A.* ... 105 D10

Saco, *Mont., U.S.A.* 110 B10
Sacramento, *Brazil* 123 E2
Sacramento, *U.S.A.* 112 G5
Sacramento →, *U.S.A.* ... 112 G5
Sacramento Mts., *U.S.A.* . 111 K11
Sacramento Valley, *U.S.A.* 112 G5
Sacratif, C., *Spain* 29 J1
Săcueni, *Romania* 38 B5
Sada, *Spain* 30 B2
Sádaba, *Spain* 28 C3
Sadani, *Tanzania* 82 D4
Sadao, *Thailand* 59 J3
Sadd el Aali, *Egypt* 76 C3
Saddle Mt., *U.S.A.* 112 E3
Sade, *Nigeria* 79 C7
Sadimi, *Zaïre* 83 D1
Sado, *Japan* 48 E9
Sado →, *Portugal* 31 G2
Sadon, *Burma* 61 G20
Sadon, *Russia* 43 E10
Sæby, *Denmark* 11 G4
Saegerstown, *U.S.A.* . 106 E4
Saelices, *Spain* 28 F2
Safaga, *Egypt* 76 B3
Şafājah, *Si. Arabia* .. 64 E3
Säffle, *Sweden* 9 G12
Safford, *U.S.A.* 111 K9
Saffron Walden, *U.K.* . 13 E8
Safi, *Morocco* 74 B3
Safīd Dasht, *Iran* ... 65 C6
Safīd Kūh, *Afghan.* .. 60 B3
Safonovo, *Russia* ... 40 D8
Safranbolu, *Turkey* .. 42 F5
Safwān, *Iraq* 64 D5
Sag Harbor, *U.S.A.* .. 107 F12
Saga, *Indonesia* 57 E8
Saga, *Japan* 49 H5
Saga □, *Japan* 49 H5
Sagae, *Japan* 48 E10
Sagala, *Mali* 78 C3
Sagar, *India* 60 M9
Sagara, *Tanzania* ... 82 D3
Sagay, *Phil.* 55 F5
Sagil, *Mongolia* 54 A4
Saginaw, *U.S.A.* ... 104 D4
Saginaw B., *U.S.A.* . 104 D4
Sagīr, Zab as →, *Iraq* 64 C4
Sagleipie, *Liberia* .. 78 D3
Saglouc, *Canada* ... 97 B12
Sagŏ-ri, *S. Korea* .. 51 G14
Sagone, *France* 27 F12
Sagone, G. de, *France* 27 F12
Sagres, *Portugal* ... 31 J2
Sagua la Grande, *Cuba* 116 B3
Saguache, *U.S.A.* .. 111 G10
Saguenay →, *Canada* 99 C5
Sagunto, *Spain* 28 F4
Sahaba, *Sudan* 76 D3
Sahagún, *Colombia* . 120 B2
Sahagún, *Spain* 30 C5
Saham al Jawlān, *Syria* 69 C4
Sahand, Kūh-e, *Iran* . 64 B5
Sahara, *Africa* 70 D4
Saharan Atlas = Saharien, Atlas, *Algeria* ... 75 B5
Saharanpur, *India* .. 62 E7
Saharien, Atlas, *Algeria* 75 B5
Sahasinaka, *Madag.* . 85 C8
Sahaswan, *India* ... 63 E8
Sahel, Canal du, *Mali* 78 C3
Sahibganj, *India* ... 63 G12
Sahiwal, *Pakistan* .. 62 D5
Şaḥneh, *Iran* 64 C5
Sahtaneh →, *Canada* 100 B4
Sahuaripa, *Mexico* . 114 B3
Sahuarita, *U.S.A.* .. 111 L8
Sahuayo, *Mexico* ... 114 C4
Sahy, *Slovakia* 21 G8
Sai Buri, *Thailand* .. 59 J3
Sai-Cinza, *Brazil* ... 125 B6
Sa'id Bundas, *Sudan* 73 G9
Saïda, *Algeria* 75 B5
Saïdābād, *Kermān, Iran* 65 D7
Sa'īdābād, *Semnān, Iran* 65 B7
Saïdia, *Morocco* ... 75 A4
Sa'idiyeh, *Iran* 65 B6
Saidpur, *Bangla.* ... 61 G16
Saidu, *Pakistan* ... 63 B5
Saignelégier, *Switz.* . 22 B3
Saignes, *France* ... 26 C6
Saigon = Phanh Bho Ho Chi Minh, *Vietnam* . 59 G6
Saijō, *Japan* 49 H6
Saikhoa Ghat, *India* . 61 F19
Saiki, *Japan* 49 H5
Saillans, *France* ... 27 D9
Sailolof, *Indonesia* . 57 E8
Saimbeyli, *Turkey* . 66 E7
Şa'in Dezh, *Iran* ... 64 B5
St. Abb's Head, *U.K.* 14 F6
St. Aegyd, *Austria* .. 21 H5
St.-Affrique, *France* . 26 E6
St.-Agrève, *France* . 27 C8
St.-Aignan, *France* . 24 E8
St. Alban's, *Canada* . 99 C8
St. Albans, *U.K.* ... 13 F7
St. Albans, *Vt., U.S.A.* 107 B11
St. Albans, *W. Va., U.S.A.* 104 F5
St. Alban's Head, *U.K.* 13 G5
St. Albert, *Canada* .. 100 C6
St.-Amand-en-Puisaye, *France* 25 E10
St.-Amand-les-Eaux, - *France* 25 B10

St.-Amand-Mont-Rond, *France* 26 B6
St.-Amarin, *France* .. 25 E14
St.-Amour, *France* .. 27 B9
St.-André-de-Cubzac, *France* 26 D3
St.-André-de-l'Eure, *France* 24 D8
St.-André-les-Alpes, *France* 27 E10
St. Andrew's, *Canada* 99 C8
St. Andrews, *U.K.* .. 14 E6
St-Anicet, *Canada* .. 107 A10
St. Ann B., *Canada* . 99 C7
St. Anne, *U.K.* 24 C4
St. Ann's Bay, *Jamaica* 116 C4
St. Anthony, *Canada* 99 B8
St. Anthony, *U.S.A.* . 110 E8
St.-Antonin-Noble-Val, *France* 26 D5
St. Arnaud, *Australia* 91 F3
St. Arthur, *Canada* . 99 C6
St. Asaph, *U.K.* ... 12 D4
St.-Astier, *France* .. 26 C4
St.-Aubin, *Switz.* ... 22 C3
St.-Aubin-du-Cormier, *France* 24 D5
St.-Augustin-Saguenay, *Canada* 99 B8
St. Augustine, *U.S.A.* 105 L5
St. Austell, *U.K.* ... 13 G3
St.-Avold, *France* .. 25 C13
St.-Barthélemy, I., *W. Indies* 117 C7
St. Bee's Hd., *U.K.* . 12 C4
St.-Benoît-du-Sault, *France* 26 B5
St.-Bernard, Col du Grand, *Europe* 22 E4
St.-Bernard, Col du Petit, *France* 27 C10
St.-Blaise, *Switz.* ... 22 B3
St. Boniface, *Canada* 101 D9
St.-Bonnet, *France* . 27 D10
St.-Brévin-les-Pins, *France* 24 E4
St.-Brice-en-Coglès, *France* 24 D5
St. Bride's, *Canada* . 99 C9
St. Brides B., *U.K.* . 13 F2
St.-Brieuc, *France* .. 24 D4
St.-Calais, *France* .. 24 E7
St.-Cast-le-Guildo, *France* 24 D4
St. Catharines, *Canada* 98 D4
St. Catherines I., *U.S.A.* 105 K5
St. Catherine's Pt., *U.K.* 13 G6
St.-Céré, *France* ... 26 D5
St.-Cergue, *Switz.* .. 22 D2
St.-Cernin, *France* .. 26 C6
St.-Chamond, *France* 27 C8
St. Charles, *Ill., U.S.A.* 104 E1
St. Charles, *Mo., U.S.A.* 108 F9
St.-Chély-d'Apcher, *France* 26 D7
St.-Chinian, *France* . 26 E6
St. Christopher = St. Kitts, *W. Indies* 117 C7
St. Christopher-Nevis ■, *W. Indies* 117 C7
St.-Ciers-sur-Gironde, *France* 26 C3
St. Clair, *Mich., U.S.A.* . 106 D2
St. Clair, *Pa., U.S.A.* 107 F8
St. Clair, L., *Canada* 98 D3
St. Clairsville, *U.S.A.* 106 F4
St.-Claud, *France* .. 26 C4
St. Claude, *Canada* . 101 D9
St.-Claude, *France* . 27 B9
St. Cloud, *Fla., U.S.A.* 105 L5
St. Cloud, *Minn., U.S.A.* 108 C7
St-Coeur de Marie, *Canada* 99 C5
St. Cricq, C., *Australia* 89 E1
St. Croix, *Virgin Is.* . 117 C7
St. Croix →, *U.S.A.* 108 C8
St. Croix Falls, *U.S.A.* 108 C8
St.-Cyr-sur-Mer, *France* 27 E9
St. David's, *Canada* . 99 C8
St. David's, *U.K.* ... 13 F2
St. David's Head, *U.K.* 13 F2
St.-Denis, *France* .. 25 D9
St.-Denis-d'Orques, *France* 24 D6
St.-Dié, *France* 25 D13
St.-Dizier, *France* .. 25 D11
St.-Égrève, *France* . 27 C9
St. Elias, Mt., *U.S.A.* 96 B5
St. Elias Mts., *Canada* 100 A1
St.-Élie, *Fr. Guiana* . 121 C7
St.-Éloy-les-Mines, *France* 26 B6
St.-Émilion, *France* . 26 D3
St.-Étienne, *France* . 27 C8
St.-Étienne-de-Tinée, *France* 27 D10
St. Eugène, *Canada* . 107 A10
St. Eustatius, *W. Indies* 117 C7
St.-Félicien, *Canada* 98 C5
St.-Florent, *France* . 27 F13
St.-Florent-sur-Cher, *France* 25 F9
St.-Florentin, *France* 25 D10
St.-Flour, *France* .. 26 C7
St.-Fons, *France* ... 27 C8
St. Francis, *U.S.A.* . 108 F4
St. Francis →, *U.S.A.* 109 H9
St. Francis, C., *S. Africa* 84 E3
St-Francisville, *U.S.A.* 109 K9
St-François, L., *Canada* 107 A10
St.-Fulgent, *France* . 24 F5
St-Gabriel-de-Brandon, *Canada* 98 C5
St. Gallen = Sankt Gallen, *Switz.* 23 B8
St.-Gaudens, *France* 26 E4

St.-Gengoux-le-National, *France* 27 B8
St.-Geniez-d'Olt, *France* 26 D6
St. George, *Australia* 91 D4
St. George, *Canada* . 99 C6
St. George, *S.C., U.S.A.* 105 J5
St. George, *Utah, U.S.A.* 111 H7
St. George, C., *Canada* 99 C8
St. George, C., *U.S.A.* 105 L3
St. George Ra., *Australia* 88 C4
St.-Georges, *Belgium* 17 G6
St. George's, *Canada* 99 C8
St.-Georges, *Canada* 99 C5
St.-Georges, *Fr. Guiana* 121 C7
St. George's, *Grenada* 117 D7
St. George's B., *Canada* 99 C8
St. Georges Basin, *Australia* 88 C4
St. George's Channel, *U.K.* 15 E6
St.-Georges-de-Didonne, *France* 26 C3
St. Georges Hd., *Australia* 91 F5
St.-Gérard, *Belgium* 17 H5
St.-Germain-de-Calberte, *France* 26 D7
St.-Germain-des-Fossés, *France* 26 B7
St.-Germain-du-Plain, *France* 25 F11
St.-Germain-en-Laye, *France* 25 D9
St.-Germain-Laval, *France* 27 C8
St.-Germain-Lembron, *France* 26 C7
St.-Gervais-d'Auvergne, *France* 26 B6
St.-Gervais-les-Bains, *France* 27 C10
St.-Gildas, Pte. de, *France* 24 E4
St.-Gilles, *France* .. 27 E8
St.-Gilles-Croix-de-Vie, *France* 24 E4
St.-Gingolph, *Switz.* 22 D3
St.-Girons, *France* . 26 F5
St. Gotthard P. = San Gottardo, Paso del, *Switz.* 23 C7
St.-Gualtier, *France* 24 F8
St.-Guénolé, *France* 24 E2
St. Helena, *U.S.A.* . 110 G2
St. Helena ■, *Atl. Oc.* 2 E9
St. Helena, Mt., *U.S.A.* 112 G4
St. Helena B., *S. Africa* 84 E2
St. Helens, *Australia* 90 G4
St. Helens, *U.K.* ... 12 D5
St. Helens, *U.S.A.* . 112 E4
St. Helens, Mt., *U.S.A.* 112 D4
St. Helier, *U.K.* ... 13 H5
St.-Hilaire-du-Harcouët, *France* 24 D5
St.-Hippolyte, *France* 25 E13
St.-Hippolyte-du-Fort, *France* 26 E7
St.-Honoré-les-Bains, *France* 25 F10
St-Hubert, *Belgium* . 17 H6
St.-Hyacinthe, *Canada* 98 C5
St. Ignace, *U.S.A.* . 104 C3
St. Ignace I., *Canada* 98 C2
St. Ignatius, *U.S.A.* 110 C6
St.-Imier, *Switz.* ... 22 B3
St. Ives, *Cambs., U.K.* 13 E7
St. Ives, *Corn., U.K.* 13 G2
St. James, *France* .. 24 D5
St. James, *U.S.A.* . 108 D7
St-Jean, *Canada* ... 98 C5
St-Jean →, *Canada* . 99 B7
St-Jean, L., *Canada* 99 C5
St. Jean Baptiste, *Canada* 101 D9
St.-Jean-d'Angély, *France* 26 C3
St.-Jean-de-Bournay, *France* 27 C9
St.-Jean-de-Luz, *France* . 26 E2
St.-Jean-de-Maurienne, *France* 27 C10
St.-Jean-de-Monts, *France* 24 F4
St.-Jean-du-Gard, *France* 26 D7
St.-Jean-en-Royans, *France* 27 C9
St-Jean-Port-Joli, *Canada* 99 C5
St-Jérôme, *Qué., Canada* 98 C5
St-Jérôme, *Qué., Canada* 99 C5
St. John, *Canada* ... 99 C6
St. John, *Kans., U.S.A.* 109 G5
St. John, *N. Dak., U.S.A.* 108 A5
St. John →, *U.S.A.* 99 C6
St. John, C., *Canada* 99 B8
St. John's, *Antigua* 117 C7
St. John's, *Canada* 99 C9
St. Johns, *Ariz., U.S.A.* 111 J9
St. Johns, *Mich., U.S.A.* 104 D3
St. Johns →, *U.S.A.* 105 K5
St. Johnsbury, *U.S.A.* 107 B12
St. Johnsville, *U.S.A.* 107 C10
St. Joseph, *La., U.S.A.* 109 K9
St. Joseph, *Mich., U.S.A.* 104 D2
St. Joseph, *Mo., U.S.A.* 108 F7
St. Joseph →, *U.S.A.* 104 D2
St. Joseph, I., *Canada* 98 C3
St. Joseph, L., *Canada* 98 B1
St-Jovite, *Canada* .. 98 C5
St.-Juéry, *France* .. 26 E6
St.-Julien-Chapteuil, *France* 27 C8
St.-Julien-du-Sault, *France* 25 D10
St.-Julien-en-Genevois, *France* 27 B10
St.-Junien, *France* . 26 C4

St.-Just-en-Chaussée, *France* 25 C9
St.-Just-en-Chevalet, *France* 26 E3
St.-Justin, *France* .. 26 E3
St. Kilda, *N.Z.* 87 L3
St. Kitts, *W. Indies* 117 C7
St. Kitts-Nevis = St. Christopher-Nevis ■, *W. Indies* 117 C7
St. Laurent, *Canada* 101 C9
St.-Laurent, *Fr. Guiana* 121 B7
St.-Laurent-du-Pont, *France* 27 C9
St.-Laurent-en-Grandvaux, *France* 27 B9
St. Lawrence, *Australia* 90 C4
St. Lawrence, *Canada* 99 C8
St. Lawrence →, *Canada* . 99 C6
St. Lawrence, Gulf of, *Canada* 99 C7
St. Lawrence I., *U.S.A.* 96 B3
St.-Léger, *Belgium* 17 J7
St. Leonard, *Canada* 99 C6
St.-Léonard-de-Noblat, *France* 26 C5
St. Lewis →, *Canada* 99 B8
St.-Lô, *France* 24 C5
St-Louis, *Senegal* .. 78 B1
St. Louis, *Mich., U.S.A.* 104 D3
St. Louis, *Mo., U.S.A.* 108 F9
St. Louis →, *U.S.A.* 108 B8
St.-Loup-sur-Semouse, *France* 25 E13
St. Lucia ■, *W. Indies* 117 D7
St. Lucia, L., *S. Africa* 85 D5
St. Lucia Channel, *W. Indies* 117 D7
St. Lunaire-Griquet, *Canada* 99 B8
St. Maarten, *W. Indies* 117 C7
St.-Maixent-l'École, *France* 26 B3
St.-Malo, *France* ... 24 D4
St.-Malo, G. de, *France* 24 D4
St.-Mandrier-sur-Mer, *France* 27 E9
St-Marc, *Haiti* 117 C5
St.-Marcellin, *France* 27 C9
St.-Marcouf, Is., *France* 24 C5
St. Maries, *U.S.A.* . 110 C5
St-Martin, *W. Indies* 117 C7
St. Martin, L., *Canada* 101 C9
St.-Martin-de-Ré, *France* 26 B2
St.-Martin-Vésubie, *France* 27 D11
St. Martins, *Canada* 99 C6
St. Martinville, *U.S.A.* 109 K9
St.-Martory, *France* 26 E4
St. Mary Pk., *Australia* 91 E2
St. Marys, *Australia* 90 G4
St. Marys, *Canada* . 106 C3
St. Mary's, *U.K.* ... 13 H1
St. Marys, *U.S.A.* . 106 E6
St. Mary's, C., *Canada* 99 C9
St. Mary's B., *Canada* 99 C9
St. Marys Bay, *Canada* 99 D6
St.-Mathieu, Pte., *France* . 24 D2
St. Matthews, I. = Zadetkyi Kyun, *Burma* 59 H2
St.-Maur-des-Fossés, *France* 25 D9
St. Maurice, *Switz.* . 22 D4
St-Maurice →, *Canada* 98 C5
St.-Médard-de-Guizières, *France* 26 C3
St.-Méen-le-Grand, *France* 24 D4
St. Michael's Mount, *U.K.* 13 G2
St.-Michel-de-Maurienne, *France* 27 C10
St.-Mihiel, *France* . 25 D12
St.-Nazaire, *France* 24 E4
St. Neots, *U.K.* ... 13 E7
St.-Nicolas-de-Port, *France* 25 D13
St. Niklass = Sint Niklaas, *Belgium* 17 F4
St. Niklaus, *Switz.* . 22 D5
St.-Omer, *France* .. 25 B9
St-Pacome, *Canada* 99 C6
St.-Palais-sur-Mer, *France* 26 C2
St-Pamphile, *Canada* 99 C6
St.-Pardoux-la-Rivière, *France* 26 C4
St. Pascal, *Canada* . 99 C6
St. Paul, *Canada* .. 100 C6
St. Paul, *Minn., U.S.A.* 108 C8
St. Paul, *Nebr., U.S.A.* 108 E5
St. Paul, I., *Ind. Oc.* 3 F13
St. Paul I., *Canada* . 99 C7
St.-Paul-de-Fenouillet, *France* 26 F6
St.-Paul-lès-Dax, *France* 26 E2
St.-Péray, *France* .. 27 D8
St.-Père-en-Retz, *France* 24 E4
St. Peter, *U.S.A.* .. 108 C8
St. Peter Port, *Chan. Is.* 13 H5
St. Peters, *N.S., Canada* 99 C7
St. Peters, *P.E.I., Canada* 99 C7
St. Petersburg = Sankt-Peterburg, *Russia* 40 B7
St. Petersburg, *U.S.A.* 105 M4
St.-Philbert-de-Grand-Lieu, *France* 24 E5
St.-Pierre, *St-P. & M.* 99 C8
St-Pierre, L., *Canada* 98 C5
St.-Pierre-d'Oléron, *France* 26 C2
St.-Pierre-Église, *France* 24 C5
St.-Pierre-en-Port, *France* 24 C7
St.-Pierre et Miquelon □, *St-P. & M.* 99 C8

St.-Pierre-le-Moûtier, *France* 25 F10
St.-Pierre-sur-Dives, *France* 24 C6
St.-Pieters Leew, *Belgium* 17 G4
St.-Pol-de-Léon, *France* 24 D3
St.-Pol-sur-Mer, *France* ... 25 A9
St.-Pol-sur-Ternoise, *France* 25 B9
St.-Pons, *France* ... 26 E6
St.-Pourçain-sur-Sioule, *France* 26 B7
St.-Quay-Portrieux, *France* 24 D4
St.-Quentin, *France* 25 C10
St.-Rambert-d'Albon, *France* 27 C8
St.-Raphaël, *France* 27 E10
St. Regis, *U.S.A.* .. 110 C6
St.-Rémy-de-Provence, *France* 27 E8
St.-Renan, *France* . 24 D2
St.-Saëns, *France* .. 24 C8
St.-Sauveur-en-Puisaye, *France* 25 E10
St.-Sauveur-le-Vicomte, *France* 24 C5
St.-Savin, *France* .. 26 B4
St.-Savinien, *France* 26 C3
St. Sebastien, Tanjon' i, *Madag.* 85 A8
St.-Seine-l'Abbaye, *France* 25 E11
St.-Sernin-sur-Rance, *France* 26 E6
St.-Servan-sur-Mer, *France* 24 D4
St.-Sever, *France* .. 26 E3
St.-Sever-Calvados, *France* 24 D5
St.-Siméon, *Canada* 99 C6
St. Stephen, *Canada* 99 C6
St.-Sulpice, *France* 26 E5
St.-Sulpice-Laurière, *France* 26 B5
St.-Syprien, *France* 26 F7
St.-Thégonnec, *France* 24 D3
St. Thomas, *Canada* 98 D3
St. Thomas I., *Virgin Is.* 117 C7
St-Tite, *Canada* ... 98 C5
St.-Tropez, *France* 27 E10
St. Troud = Sint Truiden, *Belgium* 17 G6
St.-Vaast-la-Hougue, *France* 24 C5
St.-Valéry-en-Caux, *France* 24 C7
St.-Valéry-sur-Somme, *France* 25 B8
St.-Vallier, *France* . 27 C8
St.-Vallier-de-Thiey, *France* 27 E10
St.-Varent, *France* 24 F6
St. Vincent, *W. Indies* 117 D7
St. Vincent, G., *Australia* 91 F2
St. Vincent & the Grenadines ■, *W. Indies* 117 D7
St.-Vincent-de-Tyrosse, *France* 26 E2
St. Vincent Passage, *W. Indies* 117 D7
St-Vith, *Belgium* ... 17 H8
St.-Yrieix-la-Perche, *France* 26 C5
Ste.-Adresse, *France* 24 C7
Ste-Agathe-des-Monts, *Canada* 98 C5
Ste-Anne de Beaupré, *Canada* 99 C5
Ste-Anne-des-Monts, *Canada* 99 C6
Ste-Croix, *Switz.* .. 22 C3
Ste.-Enimie, *France* 26 D7
Ste.-Foy-la-Grande, *France* 26 D4
Ste. Genevieve, *U.S.A.* 108 G9
Ste.-Hermine, *France* 26 B2
Ste.-Livrade-sur-Lot, *France* 26 D4
Ste-Marguerite →, *Canada* 99 B6
Ste.-Marie, *Martinique* 117 D7
Ste.-Marie-aux-Mines, *France* 25 D14
Ste-Marie de la Madeleine, *Canada* 99 C5
Ste.-Maure-de-Touraine, *France* 24 E7
Ste.-Maxime, *France* 27 E10
Ste.-Menehould, *France* 25 C11
Ste.-Mère-Église, *France* 24 C5
Ste.-Rose, *Guadeloupe* 117 C7
Ste. Rose du Lac, *Canada* 101 C9
Saintes, *France* ... 26 C3
Saintes, I. des, *Guadeloupe* 117 C7
Stes.-Maries-de-la-Mer, *France* 27 E8
Saintonge, *France* . 26 C3
Saipan, *Pac. Oc.* .. 92 F6
Sairang, *India* 61 H18
Sairecábur, Cerro, *Bolivia* 126 A2
Saitama □, *Japan* .. 49 F9
Sajama, *Bolivia* ... 124 D4
Sajum, *India* 63 C8
Sak →, *S. Africa* .. 84 E3
Sakai, *Japan* 49 G7
Sakaide, *Japan* ... 49 G6
Sakaiminato, *Japan* . 49 G6
Sakākah, *Si. Arabia* 64 D4
Sakakawea, L., *U.S.A.* 108 B3
Sakami, *Canada* ... 98 B4
Sâkâne, 'Erg i-n, *Mali* 74 D4
Sakania, *Zaïre* 83 E2
Sakarya = Adapazarı, *Turkey* 66 C4
Sakarya, *Turkey* ... 66 C4
Sakarya →, *Turkey* 42 F4
Sakashima-Guntō, *Japan* 49 M2

Sakata, Japan 48 E9
Sakchu, N. Korea 51 D13
Sakeny →, Madag. 85 C8
Sakété, Benin 79 D5
Sakha = Yakut
  Republic □, Russia .. 45 C13
Sakhalin, Russia 45 D15
Sakhalinskiy Zaliv, Russia 45 D15
Saki, Ukraine 42 D5
Šakiai, Lithuania 40 D3
Sakon Nakhon, Thailand . 58 D5
Sakrand, Pakistan 62 F3
Sakrivier, S. Africa 84 E3
Sakskøbing, Denmark .. 11 K5
Sakuma, Japan 49 G8
Sakurai, Japan 49 G7
Sal →, Russia 43 C9
Sala, Sweden 9 G14
Sala Consilina, Italy ... 35 B8
Sala-y-Gómez, Pac. Oc. . 93 K17
Salaberry-de-Valleyfield,
  Canada 98 C5
Saladas, Argentina 126 B4
Saladillo, Argentina ... 126 D4
Salado →, Buenos Aires,
  Argentina 126 D4
Salado →, La Pampa,
  Argentina 128 A3
Salado →, Río Negro,
  Argentina 128 B3
Salado →, Santa Fe,
  Argentina 126 C3
Salado →, Mexico 114 B5
Salaga, Ghana 79 D4
Sālah, Syria 69 C5
Sálakhos, Greece 37 C9
Salala, Liberia 78 D2
Salala, Sudan 76 C4
Salālah, Oman 68 D5
Salamanca, Chile 126 C1
Salamanca, Spain 30 E5
Salamanca, U.S.A. 106 D6
Salamanca □, Spain ... 30 E5
Salāmatābād, Iran 64 C5
Salamina, Colombia ... 120 B2
Salamis, Cyprus 37 D12
Salamis, Greece 39 M6
Salar de Atacama, Chile . 126 C1
Salar de Uyuni, Bolivia . 124 E4
Sălard, Romania 38 B5
Salas, Spain 30 B4
Salas de los Infantes, Spain 28 C1
Salatiga, Indonesia 57 G14
Salaverry, Peru 124 B2
Salawati, Indonesia ... 57 E8
Salayar, Indonesia 57 F6
Salazar →, Spain 28 C3
Salbris, France 25 E9
Salcombe, U.K. 13 G4
Saldaña, Spain 30 C6
Saldanha, S. Africa ... 84 E2
Saldanha B., S. Africa .. 84 E2
Saldus, Latvia 40 C3
Sale, Australia 91 F4
Salé, Morocco 74 B3
Sale, U.K. 12 D5
Salekhard, Russia 44 C7
Salem, India 60 P11
Salem, Ind., U.S.A. ... 104 F2
Salem, Mass., U.S.A. .. 107 D14
Salem, Mo., U.S.A. ... 109 G9
Salem, N.J., U.S.A. ... 104 F8
Salem, Ohio, U.S.A. ... 106 F4
Salem, Oreg., U.S.A. .. 110 D2
Salem, S. Dak., U.S.A. . 108 D6
Salem, Va., U.S.A. 104 G5
Salemi, Italy 34 E5
Salernes, France 27 E10
Salerno, Italy 35 B7
Salerno, G. di, Italy ... 35 B7
Salford, U.K. 12 D5
Salgir →, Ukraine 42 D6
Salgótarján, Hungary .. 21 G9
Salgueiro, Brazil 122 C4
Salida, U.S.A. 102 C5
Salies-de-Béarn, France . 26 E3
Salihli, Turkey 66 D3
Salima, Malawi 81 G6
Salina, Italy 35 D7
Salina, U.S.A. 108 F6
Salina Cruz, Mexico ... 115 D5
Salinas, Brazil 123 E3
Salinas, Chile 126 A2
Salinas, Ecuador 120 D1
Salinas, U.S.A. 111 H3
Salinas →, Guatemala . 115 D6
Salinas →, U.S.A. 111 H3
Salinas, B. de, Nic. 116 D2
Salinas, C. de, Spain ... 36 B10
Salinas, Pampa de las,
  Argentina 126 C2
Salinas Ambargasta,
  Argentina 126 B3
Salinas de Hidalgo, Mexico 114 C4
Salinas Grandes, Argentina 126 B2
Saline →, Ark., U.S.A. . 109 J8
Saline →, Kans., U.S.A. 108 F6
Salines, Spain 36 B10
Salinópolis, Brazil 122 B2
Salins-les-Bains, France 25 F12
Salir, Portugal 31 H2
Salisbury = Harare,
  Zimbabwe 83 F3
Salisbury, Australia ... 91 E2
Salisbury, U.K. 13 F6

Salisbury, Md., U.S.A. ... 104 F8
Salisbury, N.C., U.S.A. .. 105 H5
Salisbury Plain, U.K. 13 F6
Săliște, Romania 38 D6
Salitre →, Brazil 122 C3
Salka, Nigeria 79 C5
Salkhad, Jordan 69 C5
Sallent, Spain 28 D6
Salles-Curan, France 26 D6
Salling, Denmark 11 H2
Sallisaw, U.S.A. 109 H7
Sallom Junction, Sudan .. 76 D4
Salmās, Iran 64 B5
Salmerón, Spain 28 E2
Salmo, Canada 100 D5
Salmon, U.S.A. 110 D7
Salmon →, Canada 100 C4
Salmon →, U.S.A. 110 D5
Salmon Arm, Canada ... 100 C5
Salmon Falls, U.S.A. ... 110 E6
Salmon Gums, Australia . 89 F3
Salmon Res., Canada ... 99 C8
Salmon River Mts., U.S.A. 110 D6
Salo, Finland 9 F17
Salò, Italy 32 C7
Salobreña, Spain 31 J7
Salome, U.S.A. 113 M13
Salon-de-Provence, France 27 E9
Salonica = Thessaloníki,
  Greece 39 J5
Salonta, Romania 38 C4
Salor →, Spain 31 F3
Salou, C., Spain 28 D6
Salsacate, Argentina ... 126 C2
Salses, France 26 F6
Salsk, Russia 43 C9
Salso →, Italy 34 E6
Salsomaggiore, Italy ... 32 D6
Salt →, Canada 100 B6
Salt →, U.S.A. 111 K7
Salt Creek, Australia .. 91 F2
Salt Fork Arkansas →,
  U.S.A. 109 G6
Salt Lake City, U.S.A. .. 110 F8
Salt Range, Pakistan ... 62 C5
Salta, Argentina 126 A2
Salta □, Argentina 126 A2
Saltcoats, U.K. 14 F4
Saltee Is., Ireland 15 D5
Saltfjorden, Norway ... 8 C13
Saltholm, Denmark 11 J6
Salthólmavík, Iceland .. 8 D3
Saltillo, Mexico 114 B4
Salto, Argentina 126 C3
Salto, Uruguay 126 C4
Salto da Divisa, Brazil . 123 E4
Salton City, U.S.A. 113 M11
Salton Sea, U.S.A. 113 M11
Saltpond, Ghana 79 D4
Saltsjöbaden, Sweden .. 10 E12
Saltville, U.S.A. 104 G5
Saluda →, U.S.A. 105 H5
Salûm, Egypt 76 A2
Salûm, Khâlig el, Egypt . 76 A2
Salur, India 61 K13
Salut, Is. du, Fr. Guiana 121 B7
Saluzzo, Italy 32 D4
Salvación, B., Chile ... 128 D1
Salvador, Brazil 123 D4
Salvador, Canada 101 C7
Salvador, L., U.S.A. ... 109 L9
Salvaterra, Brazil 122 B2
Salvaterra de Magos,
  Portugal 31 F2
Sálvora, I., Spain 30 C2
Salween →, Burma ... 61 L20
Salyany, Azerbaijan ... 67 D13
Salyersville, U.S.A. ... 104 G4
Salza →, Austria 21 H4
Salzach →, Austria ... 21 G2
Salzburg, Austria 21 H3
Salzgitter, Germany ... 18 C6
Salzwedel, Germany ... 18 C7
Sam Neua, Laos 58 B5
Sam Ngao, Thailand ... 58 D2
Sam Rayburn Reservoir,
  U.S.A. 109 K7
Sam Son, Vietnam 58 C5
Sam Teu, Laos 58 C5
Sama, Russia 44 C7
Sama de Langreo, Spain . 30 B5
Samagaltai, Russia 45 D10
Samales Group, Phil. ... 55 J4
Samâlût, Egypt 76 J7
Samana, India 62 D7
Samana Cay, Bahamas . 117 B5
Samanga, Tanzania 83 D4
Samangwa, Zaïre 82 C1
Samani, Japan 48 C11
Samar, Phil. 55 F6
Samara, Russia 41 E17
Samaria = Shōmrōn,
  Jordan 69 C4
Samariá, Greece 37 D5
Samarinda, Indonesia .. 56 E5
Samarkand, Uzbekistan . 44 F7
Samarqand = Samarkand,
  Uzbekistan 44 F7
Sāmarrā, Iraq 64 C4
Samastipur, India 63 G11
Samatan, France 26 E4
Samaúma, Brazil 125 B5
Samba, India 63 C6
Samba, Zaïre 82 C2

Sambaíba, Brazil 122 C2
Sambalpur, India 61 J14
Sambar, Tanjung, Indonesia 56 E4
Sambas, Indonesia 56 D3
Sambava, Madag. 85 A9
Sambawizi, Zimbabwe . 83 F2
Sambhal, India 63 E8
Sambhar, India 62 F6
Sambiase, Italy 35 D9
Sambonifacio, Italy ... 32 C8
Sambor, Cambodia 58 F6
Sambor, Ukraine 40 G3
Sambre →, Europe ... 17 H5
Sambuca di Sicilia, Italy . 34 E6
Samburu □, Kenya 82 B4
Samchŏk, S. Korea 51 F15
Samchonpo, S. Korea .. 51 G15
Same, Tanzania 82 C4
Samedan, Switz. 23 C9
Samer, France 25 B8
Samfya, Zambia 83 E2
Sámi, Greece 39 L3
Samnah, Si. Arabia ... 64 E3
Samnaun, Switz. 23 C10
Samo Alto, Chile 126 C1
Samobor, Croatia 33 C12
Samoëns, France 27 B10
Samokov, Bulgaria ... 38 G6
Samoorombón, B.,
  Argentina 126 D4
Samorogouan,
  Burkina Faso 78 C4
Sámos, Greece 39 M9
Samoš, Serbia, Yug. ... 21 K10
Samos, Spain 30 C3
Samothráki, Évros, Greece 39 J8
Samothráki, Kérkira,
  Greece 37 A3
Samoylovka, Russia ... 41 F13
Sampa, Ghana 78 D4
Sampacho, Argentina .. 126 C3
Sampang, Indonesia ... 57 G15
Samper de Calanda, Spain 28 D4
Sampit, Indonesia 56 E4
Sampit, Teluk, Indonesia 56 E4
Samrée, Belgium 17 H7
Samrong, Cambodia .. 58 E4
Samrong, Thailand ... 58 E3
Samsø, Denmark 11 J4
Samsø Bælt, Denmark . 11 J4
Samsun, Turkey 66 C7
Samtredia, Georgia ... 43 E10
Samui, Ko, Thailand .. 59 H3
Samun □, Turkey 66 C7
Samur →, Azerbaijan . 43 F13
Samusole, Zaïre 83 E1
Samut Prakan, Thailand 58 F3
Samut Sakhon, Thailand 58 F3
Samut Songkhram →,
  Thailand 58 F3
Samwari, Pakistan 62 E2
San, Mali 78 C4
San →, Cambodia 58 F5
San →, Poland 20 E11
San Adrián, C. de, Spain . 30 B2
San Agustín, Colombia . 120 C2
San Agustín, C., Phil. .. 55 H7
San Agustín de Valle Fértil,
  Argentina 126 C2
San Ambrosio, Pac. Oc. . 93 K20
San Andreas, U.S.A. ... 112 G6
San Andrés, I. de,
  Caribbean 116 D3
San Andres Mts., U.S.A. 111 K10
San Andrés Tuxtla, Mexico 115 D5
San Angelo, U.S.A. 109 K4
San Anselmo, U.S.A. .. 112 H4
San Antonio, Belize ... 115 D7
San Antonio, Chile 126 C1
San Antonio, N. Mex.,
  U.S.A. 111 K10
San Antonio, Tex., U.S.A. 109 L5
San Antonio, Venezuela 120 C4
San Antonio →, U.S.A. 109 L6
San Antonio, C., Argentina 126 D4
San Antonio, C., Cuba . 116 B3
San Antonio, C. de, Spain 29 G5
San Antonio, Mt., U.S.A. 113 L9
San Antonio Abad, Spain 36 C7
San Antonio de los Baños,
  Cuba 116 B3
San Antonio de los Cobres,
  Argentina 126 A2
San Antonio Oeste,
  Argentina 128 B4
San Arcángelo, Italy ... 35 B9
San Ardo, U.S.A. 112 J6
San Augustín, Canary Is. 36 G4
San Augustine, U.S.A. . 109 K7
San Bartolomé, Canary Is. 36 F6
San Bartolomé de Tirajana,
  Canary Is. 36 G4
San Bartolomeo in Galdo,
  Italy 35 A8
San Benedetto, Italy ... 32 C7
San Benedetto del Tronto,
  Italy 33 F10
San Benedicto, I., Mexico 114 D2
San Benito, U.S.A. 109 M6
San Benito →, U.S.A. . 112 J5
San Benito Mt., U.S.A. . 112 J6
San Bernardino, U.S.A. . 113 L9
San Bernardino, Paso del,
  Switz. 23 D8

San Bernardino Mts.,
  U.S.A. 113 L10
San Bernardino Str., Phil. 55 E6
San Bernardo, Chile ... 126 C1
San Bernardo, I. de,
  Colombia 120 B2
San Blas, Mexico 114 B3
San Blas, Arch. de,
  Panama 116 E4
San Blas, C., U.S.A. ... 105 L3
San Borja, Bolivia 124 C4
San Buenaventura, Bolivia 124 C4
San Buenaventura, Mexico 114 B4
San Carlos = Butuku-Luba,
  Eq. Guin. 79 E6
San Carlos, Argentina .. 126 C2
San Carlos, Bolivia ... 125 D5
San Carlos, Chile 126 D1
San Carlos, Mexico ... 114 B4
San Carlos, Nic. 116 D3
San Carlos, Negros, Phil. 55 F5
San Carlos, Pangasinan,
  Phil. 55 D4
San Carlos, Spain 36 B8
San Carlos, Uruguay .. 127 C5
San Carlos, U.S.A. 111 K8
San Carlos, Amazonas,
  Venezuela 120 C4
San Carlos, Cojedes,
  Venezuela 120 B4
San Carlos de Bariloche,
  Argentina 128 B2
San Carlos de la Rápita,
  Spain 28 E5
San Carlos del Zulia,
  Venezuela 120 B3
San Carlos L., U.S.A. .. 111 K8
San Cataldo, Italy 34 E6
San Celoni, Spain 28 D7
San Clemente, Chile ... 126 D1
San Clemente, Spain .. 29 F2
San Clemente, U.S.A. .. 113 M9
San Clemente I., U.S.A. 113 N8
San Constanzo, Italy .. 33 E10
San Cristóbal, Argentina 126 C3
San Cristóbal, Colombia 120 D3
San Cristóbal, Dom. Rep. 117 C5
San Cristóbal, Mexico . 115 D6
San Cristóbal, Spain .. 36 B11
San Cristóbal, Venezuela 120 B3
San Damiano d'Asti, Italy 32 D5
San Daniele del Friuli, Italy 33 B10
San Demétrio Corone, Italy 35 C9
San Diego, Calif., U.S.A. 113 N9
San Diego, Tex., U.S.A. . 109 M5
San Diego, C., Argentina 128 D3
San Diego de la Unión,
  Mexico 114 C4
San Dimitri, Ras, Malta . 37 C1
San Donà di Piave, Italy 33 C9
San Elpídio a Mare, Italy 33 E10
San Estanislao, Paraguay 126 A4
San Esteban de Gormaz,
  Spain 28 D1
San Felice sul Panaro, Italy 32 D8
San Felipe, Chile 126 C1
San Felipe, Colombia .. 120 C4
San Felipe, Mexico 114 A2
San Felipe, Venezuela . 120 A4
San Felipe →, U.S.A. . 113 M11
San Felíu de Guíxols, Spain 28 D8
San Felíu de Llobregat,
  Spain 28 D7
San Félix, Pac. Oc. 93 K20
San Fernando, Chile ... 126 C1
San Fernando, Mexico . 114 B1
San Fernando, La Union,
  Phil. 55 C4
San Fernando, Pampanga,
  Phil. 55 D4
San Fernando, Baleares,
  Spain 36 C7
San Fernando, Cádiz, Spain 31 J4
San Fernando,
  Trin. & Tob. 117 D7
San Fernando, U.S.A. .. 113 L8
San Fernando →, Mexico 114 C5
San Fernando de Apure,
  Venezuela 120 B4
San Fernando de Atabapo,
  Venezuela 120 C4
San Fernando di Púglia,
  Italy 35 A9
San Francisco, Argentina 126 C3
San Francisco, Bolivia . 125 D5
San Francisco, U.S.A. .. 111 H2
San Francisco →, U.S.A. 111 K9
San Francisco, Paso de,
  S. Amer. 126 B2
San Francisco de Macorís,
  Dom. Rep. 117 C5
San Francisco del Monte de
  Oro, Argentina 126 C2
San Francisco del Oro,
  Mexico 114 B3
San Francisco Javier, Spain 36 C7
San Francisco Solano, Pta.,
  Colombia 120 B2
San Fratello, Italy 35 D7
San Gabriel, Ecuador .. 120 C3
San Gavino Monreale, Italy 34 C1
San Gil, Colombia 120 B3
San Gimignano, Italy .. 32 E8
San Giórgio di Nogaro,
  Italy 33 C10
San Giórgio Iónico, Italy 35 B10

San Giovanni Bianco, Italy 32 C6
San Giovanni in Fiore, Italy 35 C9
San Giovanni in Persieceto,
  Italy 33 D8
San Giovanni Rotondo,
  Italy 35 A8
San Giovanni Valdarno,
  Italy 33 E8
San Giuliano Terme, Italy 32 E7
San Gorgonio Mt., U.S.A. 113 L10
San Gottardo, Paso del,
  Switz. 23 C7
San Gregorio, Uruguay . 127 C4
San Gregorio, U.S.A. .. 112 H4
San Guiseppe Iato, Italy . 34 E6
San Ignacio, Belize 115 D7
San Ignacio, Bolivia ... 125 D5
San Ignacio, Mexico ... 114 B2
San Ignacio, Paraguay . 126 B4
San Ignacio, L., Mexico . 114 B2
San Ildefonso, C., Phil. . 55 C5
San Isidro, Argentina .. 126 C4
San Jacinto, Colombia . 120 B2
San Jacinto, U.S.A. 113 M10
San Jaime, Spain 36 B11
San Javier, Misiones,
  Argentina 127 B4
San Javier, Santa Fe,
  Argentina 126 C4
San Javier, Beni, Bolivia . 125 C5
San Javier, Santa Cruz,
  Bolivia 125 D5
San Javier, Chile 126 D1
San Javier, Spain 29 H4
San Jerónimo, Sa. de,
  Colombia 120 B2
San Jeronimo Taviche,
  Mexico 115 D5
San Joaquín, Bolivia ... 125 C5
San Joaquin, U.S.A. ... 112 J6
San Joaquín, Venezuela 120 A4
San Joaquín →, Bolivia 125 C5
San Joaquin →, U.S.A. 111 G3
San Joaquin Valley, U.S.A. 112 J6
San Jordi, Spain 36 B9
San Jorge, Argentina .. 126 C3
San Jorge, Spain 36 C7
San Jorge, B. de, Mexico 114 A2
San Jorge, G. de, Argentina 128 C3
San Jorge, G. de, Spain . 28 E4
San José, Bolivia 125 D5
San José, Costa Rica ... 116 E3
San José, Guatemala .. 116 D1
San José, Mexico 114 C2
San Jose, Phil. 55 D4
San José, Spain 36 C7
San Jose, U.S.A. 111 H3
San Jose →, U.S.A. ... 111 J10
San Jose de Buenovista,
  Phil. 55 E4
San José de Feliciano,
  Argentina 126 C4
San José de Jáchal,
  Argentina 126 C2
San José de Mayo, Uruguay 126 C4
San José de Ocune,
  Colombia 120 C3
San José de Uchapiamonas,
  Bolivia 124 C4
San José del Cabo, Mexico 114 C3
San José del Guaviare,
  Colombia 120 C3
San José do Anauá, Brazil 121 C5
San Juan, Argentina ... 126 C2
San Juan, Colombia ... 120 B2
San Juan, Mexico 114 C4
San Juan, Ica, Peru ... 124 D2
San Juan, Puno, Peru .. 124 D2
San Juan, Phil. 55 G7
San Juan, Puerto Rico . 117 C6
San Juan □, Argentina . 126 C2
San Juan →, Argentina 126 C2
San Juan →, Bolivia .. 125 E4
San Juan →, Colombia 120 C2
San Juan →, Nic. 116 D3
San Juan →, U.S.A. .. 111 H8
San Juan →, Venezuela 121 A5
San Juan, C., Eq. Guin. . 80 D1
San Juan Bautista,
  Paraguay 126 B4
San Juan Bautista, Spain 36 B8
San Juan Bautista, U.S.A. 111 H3
San Juan Bautista Valle
  Nacional, Mexico 115 D5
San Juan Capistrano,
  U.S.A. 113 M9
San Juan Cr. →, U.S.A. 112 J5
San Juan de Guadalupe,
  Mexico 114 C4
San Juan de los Morros,
  Venezuela 120 B4
San Juan del César,
  Colombia 120 A3
San Juan del Norte, Nic. 116 D3
San Juan del Norte, B. de,
  Nic. 116 D3
San Juan del Puerto, Spain 31 H4
San Juan del Río, Mexico 115 C5
San Juan del Sur, Nic. .. 116 D2
San Juan I., U.S.A. 112 B3
San Juan Mts., U.S.A. . 111 H10
San Julián, Argentina .. 128 C3
San Just, Sierra de, Spain 28 E4
San Justo, Argentina .. 126 C3
San Kamphaeng, Thailand 58 C2
San Lázaro, C., Mexico . 114 C2

San Lázaro, Sa., *Mexico* .. 114 C3
San Leandro, *U.S.A.* 111 H2
San Leonardo, *Spain* 28 D1
San Lorenzo, *Argentina* .. 126 C3
San Lorenzo, *Beni, Bolivia* 125 D4
San Lorenzo, *Tarija,*
  Bolivia 125 E5
San Lorenzo, *Ecuador* 120 C2
San Lorenzo, *Paraguay* ... 126 B4
San Lorenzo, *Spain* 36 B10
San Lorenzo, *Venezuela* .. 120 B3
San Lorenzo →, *Mexico* . 114 C3
San Lorenzo, I., *Mexico* .. 114 B2
San Lorenzo, I., *Peru* 124 C2
San Lorenzo, Mt.,
  Argentina 128 C2
San Lorenzo de la Parrilla,
  Spain 28 F2
San Lorenzo de Morunys,
  Spain 28 C6
San Lucas, *Bolivia* 125 E4
San Lucas, *Baja Calif. S.,*
  Mexico 114 C3
San Lucas, *Baja Calif. S.,*
  Mexico 114 B2
San Lucas, *U.S.A.* 112 J5
San Lucas, C., *Mexico* .. 114 C3
San Lúcido, *Italy* 35 C9
San Luis, *Argentina* 126 C2
San Luis, *Cuba* 116 B3
San Luis, *Guatemala* 116 C2
San Luis, *U.S.A.* 111 H11
San Luis □, *Argentina* ... 126 C2
San Luis, I., *Mexico* 114 B2
San Luis, L. de, *Bolivia* .. 125 C5
San Luis, Sierra de,
  Argentina 126 C2
San Luis de la Paz, *Mexico* 114 C4
San Luis Obispo, *U.S.A.* .. 113 K6
San Luis Potosí, *Mexico* .. 114 C4
San Luis Potosí □, *Mexico* 114 C4
San Luis Reservoir, *U.S.A.* 112 H5
San Luis Río Colorado,
  Mexico 114 A2
San Marco Argentano, *Italy* 35 C9
San Marco dei Cavoti, *Italy* 35 A7
San Marco in Lámis, *Italy* 35 A8
San Marcos, *Colombia* ... 120 B2
San Marcos, *Guatemala* .. 116 D1
San Marcos, *Mexico* 114 B2
San Marcos, *U.S.A.* 109 L6
San Marino ■, *Europe* ... 33 E9
San Martín, *Argentina* ... 126 C2
San Martín, *Colombia* ... 120 C3
San Martín →, *Bolivia* ... 125 C5
San Martín, L., *Argentina* 128 C2
San Martin de los Andes,
  Argentina 128 B2
San Martín de
  Valdeiglesias, *Spain* 30 E6
San Martino di Calvi, *Italy* 32 C6
San Mateo, *Phil.* 55 C4
San Mateo, *Baleares, Spain* 36 B7
San Mateo, *Valencia, Spain* 28 E5
San Mateo, *U.S.A.* 111 H2
San Matías, *Bolivia* 125 D6
San Matías, G., *Argentina* 128 B4
San Miguel, *El Salv.* 116 D2
San Miguel, *Panama* 116 E4
San Miguel, *Spain* 36 B7
San Miguel, *U.S.A.* 111 J3
San Miguel, *Venezuela* .. 120 B4
San Miguel →, *Bolivia* .. 125 C5
San Miguel →, *S. Amer.* . 120 C2
San Miguel de Huachi,
  Bolivia 124 D4
San Miguel de Salinas,
  Spain 29 H4
San Miguel de Tucumán,
  Argentina 126 B2
San Miguel del Monte,
  Argentina 126 D4
San Miguel I., *U.S.A.* 113 L6
San Miniato, *Italy* 32 E7
San Narciso, *Phil.* 55 D4
San Nicolás, *Canary Is.* .. 36 G4
San Nicolas, *Phil.* 55 B4
San Nicolás de los Arroyas,
  Argentina 126 C3
San Nicolas I., *U.S.A.* ... 113 M7
San Onofre, *Colombia* ... 120 B2
San Onofre, *U.S.A.* 113 M9
San Pablo, *Bolivia* 126 A2
San Pablo, *Phil.* 55 D4
San Paolo di Civitate, *Italy* 35 A8
San Pedro, *Buenos Aires,*
  Argentina 127 B5
San Pedro, *Jujuy, Argentina* 126 A3
San Pedro, *Colombia* 120 C3
San-Pédro, *Ivory C.* 78 E4
San Pedro, *Mexico* 114 C2
San Pedro, *Peru* 124 C3
San Pedro □, *Paraguay* .. 126 A4
San Pedro, *Chihuahua,*
  Mexico 114 B3
San Pedro →, *Michoacan,*
  Mexico 114 D4
San Pedro →, *Nayarit,*
  Mexico 114 C3
San Pedro →, *U.S.A.* 111 K8
San Pedro, Pta., *Chile* ... 126 B1
San Pedro, Sierra de, *Spain* 31 F4
San Pedro Channel, *U.S.A.* 113 M8
San Pedro de Arimena,
  Colombia 120 C3

San Pedro de Atacama,
  Chile 126 A2
San Pedro de Jujuy,
  Argentina 126 A3
San Pedro de las Colonias,
  Mexico 114 B4
San Pedro de Lloc, *Peru* . 124 B2
San Pedro de Macorís,
  Dom. Rep. 117 C6
San Pedro del Norte, *Nic.* 116 D3
San Pedro del Paraná,
  Paraguay 126 B4
San Pedro del Pinatar,
  Spain 29 H4
San Pedro Mártir, Sierra,
  Mexico 114 A1
San Pedro Mixtepec,
  Mexico 115 D5
San Pedro Ocampo =
  Melchor Ocampo,
  Mexico 114 C4
San Pedro Sula, *Honduras* 116 C2
San Pietro, I., *Italy* 34 C1
San Pietro Vernótico, *Italy* 35 B11
San Quintín, *Mexico* 114 A1
San Rafael, *Argentina* ... 126 C2
San Rafael, *Calif., U.S.A.* 112 H4
San Rafael, *N. Mex.,*
  U.S.A. 111 J10
San Rafael, *Venezuela* ... 120 A3
San Rafael Mt., *U.S.A.* ... 113 L7
San Rafael Mts., *U.S.A.* .. 113 L7
San Ramón, *Bolivia* 125 C5
San Ramón, *Peru* 124 C2
San Ramón de la Nueva
  Orán, *Argentina* 126 A3
San Remo, *Italy* 32 E4
San Román, C., *Venezuela* 120 A3
San Roque, *Argentina* ... 126 B4
San Roque, *Spain* 31 J5
San Rosendo, *Chile* 126 D1
San Saba, *U.S.A.* 109 K5
San Salvador, *Bahamas* .. 117 B5
San Salvador, *El Salv.* ... 116 D2
San Salvador, *Spain* 36 B10
San Salvador de Jujuy,
  Argentina 126 A3
San Salvador I., *Bahamas* . 117 B5
San Sebastián, *Argentina* . 128 D3
San Sebastián, *Spain* 28 B3
San Sebastián, *Venezuela* . 120 B4
San Sebastian de la
  Gomera, *Canary Is.* 36 F2
San Serra, *Spain* 36 B10
San Serverino Marche, *Italy* 33 E10
San Simeon, *U.S.A.* 112 K5
San Simon, *U.S.A.* 111 K9
San Stéfano di Cadore,
  Italy 33 B9
San Telmo, *Mexico* 114 A1
San Telmo, *Spain* 36 B9
San Tiburcio, *Mexico* 114 C4
San Valentin, Mte., *Chile* . 128 C2
San Vicente de Alcántara,
  Spain 31 F3
San Vicente de la
  Barquera, *Spain* 30 B6
San Vicente del Caguán,
  Colombia 120 C3
San Vincenzo, *Italy* 32 E7
San Vito, *Italy* 34 C2
San Vito, C., *Italy* 34 D5
San Vito al Tagliamento,
  Italy 33 C9
San Vito Chietino, *Italy* .. 33 F11
San Vito dei Normanni,
  Italy 35 B10
San Yanaro, *Colombia* ... 120 C4
San Ygnacio, *U.S.A.* 109 M5
Saña, *Peru* 124 B2
Sana', *Yemen* 68 D3
Sana →, *Bos.-H.* 33 C13
Sanaba, *Burkina Faso* ... 78 C4
Şanâfir, *Si. Arabia* 76 B3
Sanaga →, *Cameroon* ... 79 E6
Sanaloa, Presa, *Mexico* .. 114 C3
Sanana, *Indonesia* 57 E7
Sanand, *India* 62 H5
Sanandaj, *Iran* 64 C5
Sanandita, *Bolivia* 126 A3
Sanary-sur-Mer, *France* .. 27 E9
Sanawad, *India* 62 H7
Sancellas, *Spain* 36 B9
Sancergues, *France* 25 E9
Sancerre, *France* 25 E9
Sancerrois, Collines du,
  France 25 E9
Sancha He →, *China* 52 D6
Sanchahe, *China* 51 B14
Sánchez, *Dom. Rep.* 117 C6
Sanchor, *India* 62 G4
Sanco Pt., *Phil.* 57 C7
Sancoins, *France* 25 F9
Sancti-Spíritus, *Cuba* 116 B4
Sancy, Puy de, *France* ... 26 C6
Sand →, *S. Africa* 85 C5
Sand Springs, *U.S.A.* 109 G6
Sanda, *Japan* 49 G7
Sandakan, *Malaysia* 56 C5
Sandan = Sambor,
  Cambodia 58 F6
Sandanski, *Bulgaria* 39 H6
Sandaré, *Mali* 78 C2
Sanday, *U.K.* 14 B6
Sandefjord, *Norway* 10 E4
Sanders, *U.S.A.* 111 J9

Sanderson, *U.S.A.* 109 K3
Sandfly L., *Canada* 101 B7
Sandgate, *Australia* 91 D5
Sandía, *Peru* 124 C4
Sandıklı, *Turkey* 66 D4
Sandnes, *Norway* 9 G8
Sandness, *U.K.* 14 A7
Sandoa, *Zaïre* 80 F4
Sandona, *Colombia* 120 C2
Sandover →, *Australia* .. 90 C2
Sandoway, *Burma* 61 K19
Sandpoint, *U.S.A.* 110 B5
Sandringham, *U.K.* 12 E8
Sandslån, *Sweden* 10 A11
Sandspit, *Canada* 100 C2
Sandstone, *Australia* 89 E2
Sandu, *China* 52 E6
Sandusky, *Mich., U.S.A.* . 98 D3
Sandusky, *Ohio, U.S.A.* . 106 E2
Sandvig, *Sweden* 11 J8
Sandviken, *Sweden* 9 F14
Sandwich, C., *Australia* .. 90 B4
Sandwich B., *Canada* 99 B8
Sandwich B., *Namibia* ... 84 C1
Sandwip Chan., *Bangla.* .. 61 H17
Sandy, *Nev., U.S.A.* 113 K11
Sandy, *Oreg., U.S.A.* 112 E4
Sandy Bight, *Australia* ... 89 F3
Sandy C., *Queens.,*
  Australia 90 C5
Sandy C., *Tas., Australia* . 90 G3
Sandy Cay, *Bahamas* 117 B4
Sandy Cr. →, *U.S.A.* 110 F9
Sandy L., *Canada* 98 B1
Sandy Lake, *Canada* 98 B1
Sandy Narrows, *Canada* . 101 B8
Sanford, *Fla., U.S.A.* 105 L5
Sanford, *Maine, U.S.A.* .. 107 C14
Sanford, *N.C., U.S.A.* ... 105 H6
Sanford →, *Australia* 89 E2
Sanford, Mt., *U.S.A.* 96 B5
Sang-i-Masha, *Afghan.* ... 62 C2
Sanga, *Mozam.* 83 E4
Sanga →, *Congo* 80 E3
Sanga-Tolon, *Russia* 45 C15
Sangamner, *India* 60 K9
Sangar, *Afghan.* 62 C1
Sangar, *Russia* 45 C13
Sangar Sarai, *Afghan.* ... 62 B4
Sangasangadalam,
  Indonesia 56 E5
Sangay, *Ecuador* 120 D2
Sange, *Zaïre* 82 D2
Sangeang, *Indonesia* 57 F5
Sangerhausen, *Germany* . 18 D7
Sanggan He →, *China* ... 50 E9
Sanggau, *Indonesia* 56 D4
Sangihe, Kepulauan,
  Indonesia 57 D7
Sangihe, P., *Indonesia* ... 57 D7
Sangju, *S. Korea* 51 F15
Sangkapura, *Indonesia* ... 56 F4
Sangkhla, *Thailand* 58 E2
Sangli, *India* 60 L9
Sangmélima, *Cameroon* .. 79 E7
Sangonera →, *Spain* 29 H3
Sangre de Cristo Mts.,
  U.S.A. 109 G2
Sangro →, *Italy* 33 F11
Sangudo, *Canada* 100 C6
Sangue →, *Brazil* 125 C6
Sangüesa, *Spain* 28 C3
Sanguinaires, Is., *France* . 27 G12
Sangzhi, *China* 53 C8
Sanhala, *Ivory C.* 78 C3
Sãniyah, *Iraq* 64 C4
Sanje, *Uganda* 82 C3
Sanjiang, *China* 52 E7
Sanjo, *Japan* 48 F9
Sankt Antönien, *Switz.* ... 23 C9
Sankt Blasien, *Germany* . 19 H4
Sankt Gallen, *Switz.* 23 B8
Sankt Gallen □, *Switz.* .. 23 B8
Sankt Goar, *Germany* ... 19 E3
Sankt Ingbert, *Germany* . 19 F3
Sankt Margrethen, *Switz.* 23 B9
Sankt Moritz, *Switz.* 23 D9
Sankt-Peterburg, *Russia* .. 40 B7
Sankt Pölten, *Austria* 21 G5
Sankt Valentin, *Austria* .. 21 G4
Sankt Veit, *Austria* 21 J4
Sankt Wendel, *Germany* . 19 F3
Sankuru →, *Zaïre* 80 E4
Sanlúcar de Barrameda,
  Spain 31 J4
Sanlúcar la Mayor, *Spain* . 31 H4
Sanluri, *Italy* 34 C1
Sanmenxia, *China* 50 G6
Sanming, *China* 53 D11
Sannaspos, *S. Africa* 84 D4
Sannicandro Gargánico,
  Italy 35 A8
Sannidal, *Norway* 10 F3
Sannieshof, *S. Africa* 84 D4
Sannīn, J., *Lebanon* 69 B4
Sanok, *Poland* 20 F12
Sanquhar, *U.K.* 14 F5
Sansanding Dam, *Mali* ... 78 C3
Sansepolcro, *Italy* 33 E9
Sansha, *China* 53 D13
Sanshui, *China* 53 F9
Sanski Most, *Bos.-H.* 33 D13
Sansui, *China* 52 D7
Santa, *Peru* 124 B2
Sant' Ágata de Goti, *Italy* 35 A7

Sant' Ágata di Militello,
  Italy 35 D7
Santa Ana, *Beni, Bolivia* . 125 C4
Santa Ana, *Santa Cruz,*
  Bolivia 125 D6
Santa Ana, *Santa Cruz,*
  Bolivia 125 D5
Santa Ana, *Ecuador* 120 D1
Santa Ana, *El Salv.* 116 D2
Santa Ana, *Mexico* 114 A2
Santa Ana, *U.S.A.* 113 M9
Santa Ana →, *Venezuela* . 120 B3
Sant' Ángelo Lodigiano,
  Italy 32 C6
Sant' Antíoco, *Italy* 34 C1
Santa Bárbara, *Colombia* . 120 B2
Santa Barbara, *Honduras* . 116 D2
Santa Bárbara, *Mexico* .. 114 B3
Santa Bárbara, *Spain* 28 E5
Santa Bárbara, *U.S.A.* ... 113 L7
Santa Bárbara, *Venezuela* 120 B3
Santa Bárbara, Mt., *Spain* 29 H2
Santa Barbara Channel,
  U.S.A. 113 L7
Santa Barbara I., *U.S.A.* .. 113 M7
Santa Catalina, *Colombia* . 120 A2
Santa Catalina, *Mexico* .. 114 B2
Santa Catalina, Gulf of,
  U.S.A. 113 N9
Santa Catalina I., *U.S.A.* . 113 M8
Santa Catarina □, *Brazil* . 127 B6
Santa Catarina, I. de,
  Brazil 127 B6
Santa Caterina Villarmosa,
  Italy 35 E7
Santa Cecília, *Brazil* 127 B5
Santa Clara, *Cuba* 116 B4
Santa Clara, *Calif., U.S.A.* 111 H3
Santa Clara, *Utah, U.S.A.* 111 H7
Santa Clara de Olimar,
  Uruguay 127 C5
Santa Clotilde, *Peru* 120 D3
Santa Coloma de Farners,
  Spain 28 D7
Santa Coloma de
  Gramanet, *Spain* 28 D7
Santa Comba, *Spain* 30 B2
Santa Croce Camerina,
  Italy 35 F7
Santa Croce di Magliano,
  Italy 35 A7
Santa Cruz, *Argentina* ... 128 D3
Santa Cruz, *Bolivia* 125 D5
Santa Cruz, *Brazil* 122 C4
Santa Cruz, *Chile* 126 C1
Santa Cruz, *Costa Rica* .. 116 D2
Santa Cruz, *Madeira* 36 D3
Santa Cruz, *Peru* 124 B2
Santa Cruz, *Phil.* 55 D4
Santa Cruz, *U.S.A.* 111 H2
Santa Cruz, *Venezuela* ... 121 B5
Santa Cruz □, *Argentina* . 128 C3
Santa Cruz □, *Bolivia* ... 125 D5
Santa Cruz →, *Argentina* . 128 D3
Santa Cruz Cabrália, *Brazil* 123 E4
Santa Cruz de la Palma,
  Canary Is. 36 F2
Santa Cruz de Mudela,
  Spain 29 G1
Santa Cruz de Tenerife,
  Canary Is. 36 F3
Santa Cruz del Norte, *Cuba* 116 B3
Santa Cruz del Retamar,
  Spain 30 E6
Santa Cruz del Sur, *Cuba* . 116 B4
Santa Cruz do Rio Pardo,
  Brazil 127 A6
Santa Cruz do Sul, *Brazil* . 127 B5
Santa Cruz I., *Solomon Is.* 92 J8
Santa Cruz I., *U.S.A.* 113 M7
Santa Domingo, Cay,
  Bahamas 116 B4
Santa Elena, *Argentina* .. 126 C4
Santa Elena, *Ecuador* ... 120 D1
Santa Elena, C., *Costa Rica* 116 D2
Sant' Eufémia, G. di, *Italy* 35 D9
Santa Eugenia, Pta.,
  Mexico 114 B1
Santa Eulalia, *Spain* 36 C8
Santa Fe, *Argentina* 126 C3
Santa Fe, *Spain* 31 H7
Santa Fe, *U.S.A.* 111 J11
Santa Fé □, *Argentina* ... 126 C3
Santa Filomena, *Brazil* ... 122 C2
Santa Galdana, *Spain* ... 36 B10
Santa Gertrudis, *Spain* ... 36 B7
Santa Helena, *Brazil* 122 B2
Santa Helena de Goiás,
  Brazil 123 E1
Santa Inés, *Brazil* 123 D4
Santa Inés, *Baleares, Spain* 36 B7
Santa Inés, *Extremadura,*
  Spain 31 G5
Santa Inés, I., *Chile* 128 D2
Santa Isabel = Rey
  Malabo, *Eq. Guin.* 79 E6
Santa Isabel, *Argentina* .. 126 D2
Santa Isabel, *Brazil* 123 D1
Santa Isabel, Pico,
  Eq. Guin. 79 E6
Santa Isabel do Araguaia,
  Brazil 122 C2
Santa Isabel do Morro,
  Brazil 123 D1

Santa Lucía, *Corrientes,*
  Argentina 126 B4
Santa Lucía, *San Juan,*
  Argentina 126 C2
Santa Lucia, *Spain* 29 H4
Santa Lucía, *Uruguay* ... 126 C4
Santa Lucia Range, *U.S.A.* 111 J3
Santa Magdalena, I.,
  Mexico 114 C2
Santa Margarita, *Argentina* 126 D3
Santa Margarita, *Mexico* . 114 C2
Santa Margarita, *Spain* .. 36 B10
Santa Margarita, *U.S.A.* .. 112 K6
Santa Margarita →,
  U.S.A. 113 M9
Santa Margherita, *Italy* ... 32 D6
Santa María, *Argentina* .. 126 B2
Santa Maria, *Brazil* 127 B5
Santa Maria, *Phil.* 55 C4
Santa Maria, *Spain* 36 B9
Santa Maria, *Switz.* 23 C10
Santa Maria, *U.S.A.* 113 L6
Santa María →, *Mexico* .. 114 A3
Santa María, B. de, *Mexico* 114 B3
Santa María, C. de,
  Portugal 31 J3
Santa Maria Capua Vetere,
  Italy 35 A7
Santa María da Vitória,
  Brazil 123 D3
Santa María de Ipire,
  Venezuela 121 B4
Santa Maria di Leuca, C.,
  Italy 35 C11
Santa Maria do Suaçuí,
  Brazil 123 E3
Santa Maria dos Marmelos,
  Brazil 125 B5
Santa María la Real de
  Nieva, *Spain* 30 D6
Santa Marta, *Colombia* .. 120 A3
Santa Marta, *Spain* 31 G4
Santa Marta, Ría de, *Spain* 30 B3
Santa Marta, Sierra Nevada
  de, *Colombia* 120 A3
Santa Marta Grande, C.,
  Brazil 127 B6
Santa Maura = Levkás,
  Greece 39 L3
Santa Monica, *U.S.A.* ... 113 M8
Santa Olalla, *Huelva, Spain* 31 H4
Santa Olalla, *Toledo, Spain* 30 E6
Sant' Onofrio, *Italy* 35 D9
Santa Pola, *Spain* 29 G4
Santa Ponsa, *Spain* 36 B9
Santa Quitéria, *Brazil* ... 122 B3
Santa Rita, *U.S.A.* 111 K10
Santa Rita, *Guarico,*
  Venezuela 120 B4
Santa Rita, *Zulia,*
  Venezuela 120 A3
Santa Rita do Araguaia,
  Brazil 125 D7
Santa Rosa, *La Pampa,*
  Argentina 126 D3
Santa Rosa, *San Luis,*
  Argentina 126 C2
Santa Rosa, *Bolivia* 124 C4
Santa Rosa, *Brazil* 127 B5
Santa Rosa, *Colombia* ... 120 C4
Santa Rosa, *Ecuador* 120 D2
Santa Rosa, *Peru* 124 C3
Santa Rosa, *Calif., U.S.A.* 112 G4
Santa Rosa, *N. Mex.,*
  U.S.A. 109 H2
Santa Rosa, *Venezuela* ... 120 C4
Santa Rosa de Cabal,
  Colombia 120 C2
Santa Rosa de Copán,
  Honduras 116 D2
Santa Rosa de Osos,
  Colombia 120 B2
Santa Rosa de Río
  Primero, *Argentina* ... 126 C3
Santa Rosa de Viterbo,
  Colombia 120 B3
Santa Rosa del Palmar,
  Bolivia 125 D5
Santa Rosa I., *Calif.,*
  U.S.A. 113 M6
Santa Rosa I., *Fla., U.S.A.* 105 K2
Santa Rosa Range, *U.S.A.* 110 F5
Santa Rosalía, *Mexico* ... 114 B2
Santa Sofia, *Italy* 33 E8
Santa Sylvina, *Argentina* . 126 B3
Santa Tecla = Nueva San
  Salvador, *El Salv.* 116 D2
Santa Teresa, *Argentina* . 126 C3
Santa Teresa, *Brazil* 123 E3
Santa Teresa, *Mexico* 115 B5
Santa Teresa, *Venezuela* . 121 C5
Santa Teresa di Riva, *Italy* 35 E8
Santa Teresa Gallura, *Italy* 34 A2
Santa Vitória, *Brazil* 123 E1
Santa Vitória do Palmar,
  Brazil 127 C5
Santa Ynez →, *U.S.A.* ... 113 L6
Santa Ynez Mts., *U.S.A.* . 113 L6
Santa Ysabel, *U.S.A.* 113 M10
Santadi, *Italy* 34 C1
Santai, *China* 52 B5
Santaluz, *Brazil* 122 D4
Santana, *Brazil* 123 D3
Santana, *Madeira* 36 D3
Santana, Coxilha de, *Brazil* 127 C4
Santana do Ipanema, *Brazil* 122 C4

Santana do Livramento, Brazil 127 C4
Santanayi, Spain 36 B10
Santander, Colombia 120 C2
Santander, Spain 30 B7
Santander Jiménez, Mexico 115 C5
Santaquin, U.S.A. 110 G8
Santarém, Brazil 121 D7
Santarém, Portugal 31 F2
Santarém □, Portugal 31 F2
Santaren Channel, W. Indies 116 B4
Santee, U.S.A. 113 N10
Santéramo in Colle, Italy 35 B9
Santerno →, Italy 33 D8
Santhia, Italy 32 C5
Santiago, Bolivia 125 D6
Santiago, Brazil 127 B5
Santiago, Chile 126 C1
Santiago, Panama 116 E3
Santiago, Peru 124 C2
Santiago, Phil. 55 C4
Santiago □, Chile 126 C1
Santiago →, Peru 120 D2
Santiago, C., Chile 128 D1
Santiago, Punta de, Eq. Guin. 79 E6
Santiago, Serranía de, Bolivia 125 D6
Santiago de Chuco, Peru 124 B2
Santiago de Compostela, Spain 30 C2
Santiago de Cuba, Cuba 116 C4
Santiago de los Cabelleros, Dom. Rep. 117 C5
Santiago del Estero, Argentina 126 B3
Santiago del Estero □, Argentina 126 B3
Santiago del Teide, Canary Is. 36 F3
Santiago do Cacém, Portugal 31 G2
Santiago Ixcuintla, Mexico 114 C3
Santiago Papasquiaro, Mexico 114 B3
Santiaguillo, L. de, Mexico 114 C4
Santillana del Mar, Spain 30 B6
Säntis, Switz. 23 B8
Santisteban del Puerto, Spain 29 G1
Santo →, Peru 124 B2
Santo Amaro, Brazil 123 D4
Santo Anastácio, Brazil 127 A5
Santo André, Brazil 127 A6
Santo Ângelo, Brazil 127 B5
Santo Antonio, Brazil 125 D6
Santo Antônio de Jesus, Brazil 123 D4
Santo Antônio do Içá, Brazil 120 D4
Santo Antônio do Leverger, Brazil 125 D6
Santo Corazón, Bolivia 125 D6
Santo Domingo, Dom. Rep. 117 C6
Santo Domingo, Baja Calif. N., Mexico 114 A1
Santo Domingo, Baja Calif. S., Mexico 114 B2
Santo Domingo, Nic. 116 D3
Santo Domingo de la Calzada, Spain 28 C2
Santo Domingo de los Colorados, Ecuador 120 D2
Santo Stéfano di Camastro, Italy 35 D7
Santo Stino di Livenza, Italy 33 C9
Santo Tirso, Portugal 30 D2
Santo Tomás, Mexico 114 A1
Santo Tomás, Peru 124 C3
Santo Tomé, Argentina 127 B4
Santo Tomé de Guayana = Ciudad Guayana, Venezuela 121 B5
Santoña, Spain 30 B7
Santos, Brazil 127 A6
Santos, Sierra de los, Spain 31 G5
Santos Dumont, Brazil 123 F3
Santpoort, Neths. 16 D5
Sanvignes-les-Mines, France 25 F11
Sanyuan, China 50 G5
Sanza Pombo, Angola 80 F3
São Anastácio, Brazil 127 A5
São Bartolomeu de Messines, Portugal 31 H2
São Benedito, Brazil 122 B3
São Bento, Brazil 122 B3
São Bento do Norte, Brazil 122 C4
São Bernado de Campo, Brazil 123 F2
São Borja, Brazil 127 B4
São Bras d'Alportel, Portugal 31 H3
São Caitano, Brazil 122 C4
São Carlos, Brazil 127 A6
São Cristóvão, Brazil 122 D4
São Domingos, Brazil 123 D2
São Domingos do Maranhão, Brazil 122 C3
São Félix, Brazil 123 D1
São Francisco, Brazil 123 E3
São Francisco →, Brazil 122 D4
São Francisco do Maranhão, Brazil 122 C3

São Francisco do Sul, Brazil 127 B6
São Gabriel, Brazil 127 C5
São Gabriel da Palha, Brazil 123 E3
São Gonçalo, Brazil 123 F3
São Gotardo, Brazil 123 E2
Sao Hill, Tanzania 83 D4
São João da Boa Vista, Brazil 127 A6
São João da Pesqueira, Portugal 30 D3
São João da Ponte, Brazil 123 E3
São João del Rei, Brazil 123 F3
São João do Araguaia, Brazil 122 C2
São João do Paraíso, Brazil 123 E3
São João do Piauí, Brazil 122 C3
São João dos Patos, Brazil 122 C3
São Joaquim da Barra, Brazil 123 F2
São José, Pta. de, Madeira 36 D3
São José, B. de, Brazil 122 B3
São José da Laje, Brazil 122 C4
São José de Mipibu, Brazil 122 C4
São José do Peixe, Brazil 122 C3
São José do Rio Prêto, Brazil 127 A6
São José dos Campos, Brazil 127 A6
São Leopoldo, Brazil 127 B5
São Lourenço, Brazil 123 F2
São Lourenço →, Brazil 125 D6
São Lourenço, Pantanal do, Brazil 125 D6
São Lourenço, Pta. de, Madeira 36 D3
São Luís, Brazil 122 B3
São Luís do Curu, Brazil 122 B4
São Luís Gonzaga, Brazil 127 B5
São Marcos →, Brazil 123 E2
São Marcos, B. de, Brazil 122 B3
São Martinho, Portugal 30 E2
São Mateus, Brazil 123 E4
São Mateus →, Brazil 123 E4
São Miguel do Araguaia, Brazil 123 D1
São Miguel dos Campos, Brazil 122 C4
São Nicolau →, Brazil 122 C3
São Paulo, Brazil 127 A6
São Paulo □, Brazil 127 A6
São Paulo, I., Atl. Oc. 2 D8
São Paulo de Olivença, Brazil 120 D4
São Pedro do Sul, Portugal 30 E2
São Rafael, Brazil 122 C4
São Raimundo das Mangabeiras, Brazil 122 C2
São Raimundo Nonato, Brazil 122 C3
São Romão, Brazil 123 E2
São Roque, Madeira 36 D3
São Roque, C. de, Brazil 122 C4
São Sebastião, I. de, Brazil 127 A6
São Sebastião do Paraíso, Brazil 127 A6
São Simão, Brazil 123 E1
São Teotónio, Portugal 31 H2
São Tomé, Atl. Oc. 70 F4
São Tomé, Brazil 122 C4
São Tomé, C. de, Brazil 123 F3
São Tomé & Principe ■, Africa 71 F4
São Vicente, Brazil 127 A6
São Vicente, Madeira 36 D2
São Vicente, C. de, Portugal 31 H2
Saona, I., Dom. Rep. 117 C6
Saône →, France 27 C8
Saône-et-Loire □, France 25 F11
Saonek, Indonesia 57 E8
Saoura, O. →, Algeria 75 C4
Sapanca, Turkey 66 C4
Sapão →, Brazil 122 D2
Saparua, Indonesia 57 E7
Sapé, Brazil 122 C4
Sapele, Nigeria 79 D6
Sapelo I., U.S.A. 105 K5
Sapiéntza, Greece 39 N4
Sapone, Burkina Faso 79 C4
Saposoa, Peru 124 B2
Sapozhok, Russia 41 E12
Sappemeer, Neths. 16 B9
Sappho, U.S.A. 112 B2
Sapporo, Japan 48 C10
Sapri, Italy 35 B8
Sapudi, Indonesia 57 G16
Sapulpa, U.S.A. 109 G7
Saqqez, Iran 64 B5
Sar Dasht, Iran 65 C6
Sar Gachīneh, Iran 65 D6
Sar Planina, Macedonia 38 G4
Sara, Burkina Faso 78 C4
Sara, Phil. 55 F5
Sara Buri, Thailand 58 E3
Sarāb, Iran 64 B5
Sarabadi, Iraq 64 C5
Sarada →, India 61 F12
Saragossa = Zaragoza, Spain 28 D4
Saraguro, Ecuador 120 D2
Sarajevo, Bos.-H. 21 M8
Saramacca □, Surinam 121 C6
Saramacca →, Surinam 121 B6

Saran, G., Indonesia 56 E4
Saranac Lake, U.S.A. 107 B10
Saranda, Tanzania 82 D3
Sarandí del Yi, Uruguay 127 C4
Sarandí Grande, Uruguay 126 C4
Sarangani B., Phil. 55 J6
Sarangani Is., Phil. 55 J6
Sarangarh, India 61 J13
Saransk, Russia 41 D14
Sarapul, Russia 44 D6
Sarasota, U.S.A. 105 M4
Saratoga, Calif., U.S.A. 112 H4
Saratoga, Wyo., U.S.A. 110 F10
Saratoga Springs, U.S.A. 107 C11
Saratov, Russia 41 F15
Saravane, Laos 58 E6
Sarawak □, Malaysia 56 D4
Saray, Turkey 67 D11
Saraya, Senegal 78 C2
Sarayköy, Turkey 66 E3
Sarayönü, Turkey 66 D5
Sarbāz, Iran 65 E9
Sarbīsheh, Iran 65 C8
Sarca →, Italy 32 C7
Sarda → = Sarada →, India 61 F12
Sardalas, Libya 75 C7
Sardarshahr, India 62 E6
Sardegna □, Italy 34 B2
Sardhana, India 62 E7
Sardina, Pta., Canary Is. 36 F4
Sardinata, Colombia 120 B3
Sardinia = Sardegna, Italy 34 B2
Sardis, Turkey 66 C2
Sardūīyeh = Dar Mazār, Iran 65 D8
Saréyamou, Mali 78 B4
Sargent, U.S.A. 108 E5
Sargodha, Pakistan 62 C5
Sarh, Chad 73 G8
Sārī, Iran 65 B7
Sária, Greece 39 P10
Sarigöl, Turkey 66 D3
Sarikamiş, Turkey 67 C10
Sarikaya, Turkey 66 D6
Sarikei, Malaysia 56 D4
Sarina, Australia 90 C4
Sariñena, Spain 28 D4
Sarita, U.S.A. 109 M6
Sariwŏn, N. Korea 51 E13
Sark, Chan. Is. 13 H5
Sarkad, Hungary 21 J11
Şarkişla, Turkey 66 D7
Şarköy, Turkey 66 C2
Sarlat-la-Canéda, France 26 D5
Sarles, U.S.A. 108 A5
Sărmaşu, Romania 38 C7
Sarmi, Indonesia 57 E9
Sarmiento, Argentina 128 C3
Särna, Sweden 10 C7
Sarnano, Italy 33 E10
Sarnen, Switz. 22 C6
Sarnia, Canada 98 D3
Sarno, Italy 35 B7
Sarny, Ukraine 40 F5
Särö, Sweden 11 G5
Sarolangun, Indonesia 56 E2
Saronikós Kólpos, Greece 39 M6
Saronno, Italy 32 C6
Saros Körfezi, Turkey 66 C2
Sárospatak, Hungary 21 G11
Sarova, Russia 41 D13
Sarpsborg, Norway 10 E5
Sarracín, Spain 28 C1
Sarralbe, France 25 D14
Sarre = Saar →, Europe 25 C13
Sarre-Union, France 25 D14
Sarrebourg, France 25 D14
Sarreguemines, France 25 C14
Sarriá, Spain 30 C3
Sarrión, Spain 28 E4
Sarro, Mali 78 C3
Sarstedt, Germany 18 C5
Sartène, France 27 G12
Sarthe □, France 24 E7
Sarthe →, France 24 E6
Sartilly, France 24 D5
Sartynya, Russia 44 C7
Sárvár, Hungary 21 H6
Sarvestān, Iran 65 D7
Sárviz →, Hungary 21 J8
Saryagach, Kazakhstan 44 E7
Sary-Tash, Kirghizia 44 F8
Sarych, Mys, Ukraine 42 D5
Saryshagan, Kazakhstan 44 E8
Sarzana, Italy 32 D6
Sarzeau, France 24 E4
Sas van Gent, Neths. 17 F3
Sasabeneh, Ethiopia 68 F3
Sasaram, India 63 G11
Sasebo, Japan 49 H4
Saser, India 63 B7
Saskatchewan □, Canada 101 C7
Saskatchewan →, Canada 101 C8
Saskatoon, Canada 101 C7
Saskylakh, Russia 45 B12
Sasnovka, Russia 41 C17
Sasolburg, S. Africa 85 D4
Sasovo, Russia 41 D12
Sassandra, Ivory C. 78 E3
Sassandra →, Ivory C. 78 E3
Sássari, Italy 34 B1
Sassenheim, Neths. 16 D5
Sassnitz, Germany 18 A9
Sasso Marconi, Italy 33 D8

Sassocorvaro, Italy 33 E9
Sassoferrato, Italy 33 E9
Sassuolo, Italy 32 D7
Sástago, Spain 28 D4
Sastown, Liberia 78 E3
Sasumua Dam, Kenya 82 C4
Sasyk, Ozero, Ukraine 42 C8
Sata-Misaki, Japan 49 J5
Satadougou, Mali 78 C2
Satanta, U.S.A. 109 G4
Satara, India 60 L8
Satilla →, U.S.A. 105 K5
Satipo, Peru 124 C3
Satmala Hills, India 60 J9
Satna, India 63 G9
Sátor, Bos.-H. 33 D13
Sátoraljaújhely, Hungary 21 G11
Satpura Ra., India 62 J7
Satrup, Germany 18 A5
Satsuna-Shotō, Japan 49 K5
Sattahip, Thailand 58 F3
Satui, Indonesia 56 E5
Satun, Thailand 59 J3
Saturnina →, Brazil 125 C6
Sauce, Argentina 126 C4
Sauceda, Mexico 114 B4
Saucillo, Mexico 114 B3
Sauda, Norway 9 G9
Sauðarkrókur, Iceland 8 D4
Saudi Arabia ■, Asia 68 B3
Sauer →, Germany 17 J9
Saugeen →, Canada 106 B3
Saugerties, U.S.A. 107 D11
Saugues, France 26 D7
Saujon, France 26 C3
Sauk Centre, U.S.A. 108 C7
Sauk Rapids, U.S.A. 108 C7
Saül, Fr. Guiana 121 C7
Saulgau, Germany 19 G5
Saulieu, France 25 E11
Sault, France 27 D9
Sault Ste. Marie, Canada 98 C3
Sault Ste. Marie, U.S.A. 104 B3
Saumlaki, Indonesia 57 F8
Saumur, France 24 E6
Saunders C., N.Z. 87 L3
Saunders I., Antarctica 5 B1
Saunders Point, Australia 89 E4
Saurbær, Borgarfjarðarsýsla, Iceland 8 D3
Saurbær, Eyjafjarðarsýsla, Iceland 8 D4
Sauri, Nigeria 79 C6
Saurimo, Angola 80 F4
Sausalito, U.S.A. 112 H4
Sautatá, Colombia 120 B2
Sauveterre-de-Béarn, France 26 E3
Sauzé-Vaussais, France 26 B4
Savá, Honduras 116 C2
Sava, Serbia, Yug. 21 L10
Sava →, Serbia, Yug. 21 L10
Savage, U.S.A. 108 B2
Savage I. = Niue, Cook Is. 93 J11
Savai'i, W. Samoa 87 A12
Savalou, Benin 79 D5
Savane, Mozam. 83 F4
Savanna, U.S.A. 108 D9
Savanna la Mar, Jamaica 116 C4
Savannah, Ga., U.S.A. 105 J5
Savannah, Mo., U.S.A. 108 F7
Savannah, Tenn., U.S.A. 105 H1
Savannah →, U.S.A. 105 J5
Savannakhet, Laos 58 D5
Savant L., Canada 98 B1
Savant Lake, Canada 98 B1
Savanur, India 60 M9
Savé, Benin 79 D5
Save →, France 26 E5
Save →, Mozam. 85 C5
Sāveh, Iran 65 C6
Savelugu, Ghana 79 D4
Savenay, France 24 E5
Saverdun, France 26 E5
Saverne, France 25 D14
Savièse, Switz. 22 D4
Savigliano, Italy 32 D4
Savigny-sur-Braye, France 24 E7
Saviñao, Spain 30 C3
Savio →, Italy 33 D9
Savognin, Switz. 23 C9
Savoie □, France 27 C10
Savona, Italy 32 D5
Savonlinna, Finland 44 C4
Sawahlunto, Indonesia 56 E2
Sawai, Indonesia 57 E7
Sawai Madhopur, India 62 F7
Sawang Daen Din, Thailand 58 D4
Sawankhalok, Thailand 58 D2
Sawara, Japan 49 G10
Sawatch Mts., U.S.A. 111 G10
Sawel, U.K. 15 B4
Sawi, Thailand 59 G2
Sawmills, Zimbabwe 83 F2
Sawu, Indonesia 57 F6
Sawu Sea, Indonesia 57 F6
Saxby →, Australia 90 B3
Saxon, Switz. 22 D4
Saxony, Lower = Niedersachsen □, Germany 18 C5
Saxton, U.S.A. 106 F6
Say, Niger 79 C5
Saya, Nigeria 79 D5

Sayabec, Canada 99 C6
Sayaboury, Laos 58 C3
Sayán, Peru 124 C2
Sayan, Vostochnyy, Russia 45 D10
Sayan, Zapadnyy, Russia 45 D10
Sayasan, Russia 43 E12
Saydā, Lebanon 69 B4
Sayhan-Ovoo, Mongolia 50 B2
Sayhandulaan, Mongolia 50 B5
Sayḥut, Yemen 68 D5
Saynshand, Mongolia 50 B6
Sayre, Okla., U.S.A. 109 H5
Sayre, Pa., U.S.A. 107 E8
Sayula, Mexico 114 D4
Sazin, Pakistan 63 B5
Sazlika →, Bulgaria 39 H8
Sbeïtla, Tunisia 75 A6
Scaër, France 24 D3
Scafell Pikes, U.K. 12 C4
Scalea, Italy 35 C8
Scalpay, U.K. 14 D2
Scandia, Canada 100 C6
Scandiano, Italy 32 D7
Scandinavia, Europe 8 E12
Scansano, Italy 33 F8
Scapa Flow, U.K. 14 C5
Scappoose, U.S.A. 112 E4
Scarborough, Trin. & Tob. 117 D7
Scarborough, U.K. 12 C7
Scebeli, Wabi →, Somali Rep. 68 G3
Šćedro, Croatia 33 E13
Scenic, U.S.A. 108 D3
Schaal See, Germany 18 B6
Schaan, Liech. 23 B9
Schaesberg, Neths. 17 G8
Schaffen, Belgium 17 G6
Schaffhausen, Switz. 23 A7
Schaffhausen □, Switz. 23 A7
Schagen, Neths. 16 C5
Schaijk, Neths. 16 E7
Schalkhaar, Neths. 16 D8
Schalkwijk, Neths. 16 E6
Schangnau, Switz. 22 C5
Schänis, Switz. 23 B8
Schärding, Austria 20 G3
Scharhörn, Germany 18 B4
Scharnitz, Austria 19 H7
Scheessel, Germany 18 B5
Schefferville, Canada 99 B6
Schelde →, Belgium 17 F4
Schell Creek Ra., U.S.A. 110 G6
Schenectady, U.S.A. 107 D11
Scherfede, Germany 18 D5
Scherpenheuvel, Belgium 17 G5
Scherpenisse, Neths. 17 E4
Scherpenzeel, Neths. 16 D7
Schesaplana, Switz. 23 B9
Schesslitz, Germany 19 F7
Scheveningen, Neths. 16 D4
Schiedam, Neths. 16 E4
Schiermonnikoog, Neths. 16 B8
Schiers, Switz. 23 C9
Schifferstadt, Germany 19 F4
Schifflange, Lux. 17 K8
Schijndel, Neths. 17 E6
Schiltigheim, France 25 D14
Schio, Italy 33 C8
Schipbeek, Neths. 16 D8
Schipluiden, Neths. 16 E4
Schirmeck, France 25 D14
Schlei →, Germany 18 A5
Schleiden, Germany 18 E2
Schleiz, Germany 18 E8
Schleswig, Germany 18 A5
Schleswig-Holstein □, Germany 18 A5
Schlieren, Switz. 23 B6
Schlüchtern, Germany 19 E5
Schmalkalden, Germany 18 E6
Schmölln, Brandenburg, Germany 18 B10
Schmölln, Thüringen, Germany 18 E8
Schneeberg, Austria 21 H5
Schneeberg, Germany 18 E8
Schoenberg, Germany 17 H8
Schofield, U.S.A. 108 C10
Scholls, U.S.A. 112 E4
Schönberg, Mecklenburg-Vorpommern, Germany 18 B6
Schönberg, Schleswig-Holstein, Germany 18 A6
Schönebeck, Germany 18 C7
Schönenwerd, Switz. 22 B5
Schongau, Germany 19 H6
Schöningen, Germany 18 C6
Schoondijke, Neths. 17 F3
Schoonebeek, Neths. 16 C9
Schoonhoven, Neths. 16 E5
Schoorl, Neths. 16 C5
Schortens, Germany 18 B3
Schoten, Belgium 17 F5
Schouten I., Australia 90 G4
Schouten Is. = Supriori, Kepulauan, Indonesia 57 E9
Schouwen, Neths. 17 E3
Schramberg, Germany 19 G4
Schrankogl, Austria 19 H7
Schreckhorn, Switz. 22 C6
Schreiber, Canada 98 C2
Schrobenhausen, Germany 19 G7
Schruns, Austria 19 H5
Schuler, Canada 101 C6

Schuls, *Switz.* 23 C10
Schumacher, *Canada* 98 C3
Schüpfen, *Switz.* 22 B4
Schüpfheim, *Switz.* 22 C6
Schurz, *U.S.A.* 110 G4
Schuyler, *U.S.A.* 108 E6
Schuylkill Haven, *U.S.A.* . . 107 F8
Schwabach, *Germany* 19 F7
Schwäbisch Gmünd,
  Germany 19 G5
Schwäbisch Hall, *Germany* . 19 F5
Schwäbische Alb, *Germany* . 19 G5
Schwabmünchen, *Germany* . 19 G6
Schwanden, *Switz.* 23 C8
Schwandorf, *Germany* 19 F8
Schwaner, Pegunungan,
  Indonesia 56 E4
Schwarmstedt, *Germany* . . 18 C5
Schwärze, *Germany* 18 C9
Schwarze Elster →,
  Germany 18 D8
Schwarzenberg, *Germany* . 18 E8
Schwarzenburg, *Switz.* . . . 22 C4
Schwarzwald, *Germany* . . . 19 H4
Schwaz, *Austria* 19 H7
Schwedt, *Germany* 18 B10
Schweinfurt, *Germany* . . . 19 E6
Schweizer Mittelland,
  Switz. 22 C4
Schweizer-Reneke,
  S. Africa 84 D4
Schwenningen, *Germany* . . 19 G4
Schwerin, *Germany* 18 B7
Schweriner See, *Germany* . 18 B7
Schwetzingen, *Germany* . . 19 F4
Schwyz, *Switz.* 23 B7
Schwyz □, *Switz.* 23 B7
Sciacca, *Italy* 34 E6
Scicli, *Italy* 35 F7
Scilla, *Italy* 35 D8
Scilly, Isles of, *U.K.* 13 H1
Ścinawa, *Poland* 20 D6
Scioto →, *U.S.A.* 104 F4
Scobey, *U.S.A.* 108 A2
Scone, *Australia* 91 E5
Scordia, *Italy* 35 E7
Scoresbysund, *Greenland* . . 4 B6
Scorno, Punta dello, *Italy* . 34 A1
Scotia, *Calif., U.S.A.* 110 F1
Scotia, *N.Y., U.S.A.* 107 D11
Scotia Sea, *Antarctica* 5 B18
Scotland, *U.S.A.* 108 D6
Scotland □, *U.K.* 14 E5
Scotland Neck, *U.S.A.* . . . 105 G7
Scott, C., *Australia* 88 B4
Scott Glacier, *Antarctica* . . 5 C8
Scott I., *Antarctica* 5 C11
Scott Inlet, *Canada* 97 A12
Scott Is., *Canada* 100 C3
Scott L., *Canada* 101 B7
Scott Reef, *Australia* 88 B3
Scottburgh, *S. Africa* 85 E5
Scottdale, *U.S.A.* 106 F5
Scottsbluff, *U.S.A.* 108 E3
Scottsboro, *U.S.A.* 105 H2
Scottsburg, *U.S.A.* 104 F3
Scottsdale, *Australia* 90 G4
Scottsville, *Ky., U.S.A.* . . . 105 G2
Scottsville, *N.Y., U.S.A.* . . 106 C7
Scottville, *U.S.A.* 104 D2
Scranton, *U.S.A.* 107 E9
Scugog, L., *Canada* 106 B6
Scunthorpe, *U.K.* 12 D7
Scuol, *Switz.* 23 C10
Scusciuban, *Somali Rep.* . . 68 E5
Scutari = Üsküdar, *Turkey* . 39 H11
Seabra, *Brazil* 123 D3
Seabrook, L., *Australia* . . . 89 F2
Seaford, *U.S.A.* 104 F8
Seaforth, *Canada* 98 D3
Seagraves, *U.S.A.* 109 J3
Seal →, *Canada* 101 B10
Seal Cove, *Canada* 99 C8
Seal L., *Canada* 99 B7
Sealy, *U.S.A.* 109 L6
Searchlight, *U.S.A.* 113 K12
Searcy, *U.S.A.* 109 H9
Searles, *U.S.A.* 113 K9
Seaside, *Calif., U.S.A.* . . . 112 J5
Seaside, *Oreg., U.S.A.* . . . 112 E3
Seaspray, *Australia* 91 F4
Seattle, *U.S.A.* 112 C4
Seaview Ra., *Australia* . . . 90 B4
Sebastián Vizcaíno, B.,
  Mexico 114 B2
Sebastopol = Sevastopol,
  Ukraine 42 D5
Sebastopol, *U.S.A.* 112 G4
Sebderat, *Eritrea* 77 D4
Sebdou, *Algeria* 75 B4
Seben, *Turkey* 66 C4
Sebewaing, *U.S.A.* 104 D4
Sebezh, *Russia* 40 C6
Sebha = Sabhah, *Libya* . . . 73 C7
Sébi, *Mali* 78 B4
Şebinkarahisar, *Turkey* . . . 42 F8
Sebiş, *Romania* 38 C5
Sebkhet Te-n-Dghâmcha,
  Mauritania 78 B1
Sebkra Azzel Mati, *Algeria* . 75 C5
Sebkra Mekerghene,
  Algeria 75 C5
Sebnitz, *Germany* 18 E10
Sebou, Oued →, *Morocco* . 74 B3
Sebring, *Fla., U.S.A.* 105 M5

Sebring, *Ohio, U.S.A.* 106 F3
Sebringville, *Canada* 106 C3
Sebta = Ceuta, *Morocco* . . 74 A3
Sebuku, *Indonesia* 56 E5
Sebuku, Teluk, *Malaysia* . . 56 D5
Secchia →, *Italy* 32 C8
Sechelt, *Canada* 100 D4
Sechura, *Peru* 124 B1
Sechura, Desierto de, *Peru* 124 B1
Seclin, *France* 25 B4
Secondigny, *France* 24 F6
Secretary I., *N.Z.* 87 L1
Secunderabad, *India* 60 L11
Sécure →, *Bolivia* 125 D5
Sedalia, *U.S.A.* 108 F8
Sedan, *Australia* 91 E2
Sedan, *France* 25 C11
Sedan, *U.S.A.* 109 G6
Sedano, *Spain* 28 C1
Seddon, *N.Z.* 87 J5
Seddonville, *N.Z.* 87 J4
Sedeh, *Fārs, Iran* 65 D7
Sedeh, *Khorāsān, Iran* . . . 65 C8
Séderon, *Israel* 69 D3
Sedgewick, *Canada* 100 C6
Sedhiou, *Senegal* 78 C1
Sedičany, *Czech.* 20 F4
Sedico, *Italy* 33 B9
Sedley, *Canada* 101 C8
Sedova, Pik, *Russia* 44 B6
Sedrata, *Algeria* 75 A6
Sedro-Woolley, *U.S.A.* . . . 112 B4
Sedrun, *Switz.* 23 C7
Šeduva, *Lithuania* 40 D3
Seebad Ahlbeck, *Germany* . 18 B10
Seehausen, *Germany* 18 C7
Seeheim, *Namibia* 84 D2
Seekoei →, *S. Africa* 84 E4
Seelaw, *Germany* 18 C10
Sées, *France* 24 D7
Seesen, *Germany* 18 D6
Sefadu, *S. Leone* 78 D2
Seferihisar, *Turkey* 66 D2
Séfeto, *Mali* 78 C3
Sefrou, *Morocco* 74 B4
Sefwi Bekwai, *Ghana* 78 D4
Segamat, *Malaysia* 59 L4
Segarcea, *Romania* 38 E6
Segbwema, *S. Leone* 78 D2
Seget, *Indonesia* 57 E8
Segezha, *Russia* 44 C4
Seggueur, O. →, *Algeria* . . 75 B5
Segonzac, *France* 26 C3
Segorbe, *Spain* 28 F4
Ségou, *Mali* 78 C3
Segovia = Coco →,
  Cent. Amer. 116 D3
Segovia, *Colombia* 120 B3
Segovia, *Spain* 30 E6
Segovia □, *Spain* 30 E6
Segré, *France* 24 E6
Segre →, *Spain* 28 D5
Séguéla, *Ivory C.* 78 D3
Seguin, *U.S.A.* 109 L6
Segundo →, *Argentina* . . . 126 C3
Segura →, *Spain* 29 G4
Segura, Sierra de, *Spain* . . 29 G2
Seh Qal'eh, *Iran* 65 C8
Sehitwa, *Botswana* 84 C3
Sehore, *India* 62 H7
Sehwan, *Pakistan* 62 F2
Şeica Mare, *Romania* 38 C7
Seiland, *Norway* 8 A17
Seiling, *U.S.A.* 109 G5
Seille →, *France* 27 B8
Seilles, *Belgium* 17 G6
Sein, I. de, *France* 24 D2
Seinäjoki →, *Finland* 8 E17
Seine →, *France* 24 C7
Seine, B. de la, *France* . . . 24 C6
Seine-et-Marne □, *France* . 25 D9
Seine-Maritime □, *France* . 24 C7
Seine-St-Denis □, *France* . 25 D9
Seistan, *Iran* 65 D9
Sejerø, *Denmark* 11 J5
Sejerø Bugt, *Denmark* . . . 11 J5
Seka, *Ethiopia* 77 F4
Sekayu, *Indonesia* 56 E2
Seke, *Tanzania* 82 C3
Sekenke, *Tanzania* 82 C3
Sekken Veøy, *Norway* 10 B1
Sekondi-Takoradi, *Ghana* . 78 E4
Sekuma, *Botswana* 84 C3
Selah, *U.S.A.* 110 C3
Selama, *Malaysia* 59 K3
Selárgius, *Italy* 34 C2
Selaru, *Indonesia* 57 F8
Selb, *Germany* 19 E8
Selby, *U.K.* 12 D6
Selby, *U.S.A.* 108 C4
Selca, *Croatia* 33 E13
Selçuk, *Turkey* 66 E2
Selden, *U.S.A.* 108 F4
Sele →, *Italy* 35 B7
Selenga = Selenge
  Mörön →, *Asia* 54 A5
Selenge Mörön →, *Asia* . . . 54 A5
Selenica, *Albania* 39 J2
Selenter See, *Germany* . . . 18 A6
Sélestat, *France* 25 D14
Seletan, Tg., *Indonesia* . . . 56 E4
Seletin, *Romania* 38 B8
Selfridge, *U.S.A.* 108 B4
Sélibabi, *Mauritania* 78 B2
Seliger, Oz., *Russia* 40 C8
Seligman, *U.S.A.* 111 J7

Şelim, *Turkey* 43 F10
Selîma, El Wâhât el, *Sudan* 76 C2
Selinda Spillway, *Botswana* 84 B3
Selinoús, *Greece* 39 M4
Selizharovo, *Russia* 40 C2
Seljord, *Norway* 10 E2
Selkirk, *Canada* 101 C9
Selkirk, *U.K.* 14 F6
Selkirk I., *Canada* 101 C9
Selkirk Mts., *Canada* 100 C5
Selles-sur-Cher, *France* . . 25 E8
Selliá, *Greece* 37 D6
Sellières, *France* 25 F12
Sells, *U.S.A.* 111 L8
Sellye, *Hungary* 21 K7
Selma, *Ala., U.S.A.* 105 J2
Selma, *Calif., U.S.A.* 111 H4
Selma, *N.C., U.S.A.* 105 H6
Selmer, *U.S.A.* 105 H1
Selongey, *France* 25 E12
Selowandoma Falls,
  Zimbabwe 83 G3
Selpele, *Indonesia* 57 E8
Selsey Bill, *U.K.* 13 G7
Seltz, *France* 25 D15
Selu, *Indonesia* 57 F8
Sélune →, *France* 24 D5
Selva, *Argentina* 126 B3
Selva, *Italy* 33 B8
Selva, *Spain* 28 D6
Selvas, *Brazil* 124 B4
Selwyn, *Australia* 90 C3
Selwyn L., *Canada* 101 A8
Selwyn Ra., *Australia* 90 C3
Seman →, *Albania* 39 J2
Semara, *W. Sahara* 74 C2
Semarang, *Indonesia* 57 G14
Semau, *Indonesia* 57 F6
Sembabule, *Uganda* 82 C3
Sémé, *Senegal* 78 B2
Semeih, *Sudan* 77 E3
Semenov, *Russia* 41 C14
Semenovka, *Ukraine* 40 E8
Semenovka, *Ukraine* 42 B5
Semeru, *Indonesia* 57 H15
Semey = Semipalatinsk,
  Kazakhstan 44 D9
Semiluki, *Russia* 41 F11
Seminoe Reservoir, *U.S.A.* 110 E10
Seminole, *Okla., U.S.A.* . . 109 H6
Seminole, *Tex., U.S.A.* . . . 109 J3
Semiozernoye, *Kazakhstan* 44 D7
Semipalatinsk, *Kazakhstan* 44 D9
Semirara Is., *Phil.* 55 F4
Semisopochnoi I., *U.S.A.* . 96 C2
Semitau, *Indonesia* 56 D4
Semiyarskoye, *Kazakhstan* 44 D8
Semmering Pass, *Austria* . 21 H5
Semnān, *Iran* 65 C7
Semnān □, *Iran* 65 C7
Semois →, *Europe* 17 J5
Semporna, *Malaysia* 57 D5
Semuda, *Indonesia* 56 E4
Semur-en-Auxois, *France* . 25 E11
Sena, *Bolivia* 124 C4
Senā, *Iran* 65 D6
Sena, *Mozam.* 83 F3
Sena →, *Bolivia* 124 C4
Sena Madureira, *Brazil* . . . 124 B4
Senador Pompeu, *Brazil* . . 122 C4
Senaja, *Malaysia* 56 C5
Senaki, *Georgia* 43 E10
Senanga, *Zambia* 84 B3
Senatobia, *U.S.A.* 109 H10
Sendafa, *Ethiopia* 77 F4
Sendai, *Kagoshima, Japan* 49 J5
Sendai, *Miyagi, Japan* . . . 48 E10
Sendai-Wan, *Japan* 48 E10
Sendenhorst, *Germany* . . . 18 D3
Seneca, *Oreg., U.S.A.* 110 D4
Seneca, *S.C., U.S.A.* 105 H4
Seneca Falls, *U.S.A.* 107 D8
Seneca L., *U.S.A.* 106 D8
Seneffe, *Belgium* 17 G4
Senegal ■, *W. Afr.* 78 C2
Senegal →, *W. Afr.* 78 B1
Senegambia, *Africa* 70 E2
Senekal, *S. Africa* 85 D4
Senftenberg, *Germany* . . . 18 D10
Senga Hill, *Zambia* 83 D3
Senge Khambab =
  Indus →, *Pakistan* 62 G2
Sengerema □, *Tanzania* . . 82 C3
Sengiley, *Russia* 41 E16
Sengkang, *Indonesia* 57 E6
Sengua →, *Zimbabwe* 83 F2
Senguerr →, *Argentina* . . . 128 C3
Senhor-do-Bonfim, *Brazil* . 122 D4
Senica, *Slovak Rep.* 20 G7
Senigállia, *Italy* 33 E10
Senio →, *Italy* 33 D9
Senirkent, *Turkey* 66 D4
Senise, *Italy* 35 B9
Senj, *Croatia* 33 D11
Senja, *Norway* 8 B14
Senlis, *France* 25 C9
Senmonorom, *Cambodia* . 58 F6
Sennâr, *Sudan* 77 E3
Senne →, *Belgium* 17 G4
Senneterre, *Canada* 98 C4
Senniquelle, *Liberia* 78 D3
Senno, *Belorussia* 40 D6
Sennori, *Italy* 34 B1
Seno, *Laos* 58 D5
Senonches, *France* 24 D8
Senorbì, *Italy* 34 C2

Senožeče, *Slovenia* 33 C11
Sens, *France* 25 D10
Senta, *Serbia* 21 K10
Sentery, *Zaïre* 82 D2
Sentinel, *U.S.A.* 111 K7
Sentolo, *Indonesia* 57 G14
Senya Beraku, *Ghana* 79 D4
Seo de Urgel, *Spain* 28 C6
Seohara, *India* 63 E8
Seoni, *India* 63 H8
Seoul = Sŏul, *S. Korea* . . . 51 F14
Separation Point, *Canada* . 99 B8
Sepīdān, *Iran* 65 D7
Sepo-ri, *N. Korea* 51 E14
Sepone, *Laos* 58 D6
Sept-Îles, *Canada* 99 B6
Sepúlveda, *Spain* 30 D7
Sequeros, *Spain* 30 E4
Sequim, *U.S.A.* 112 B3
Sequoia National Park,
  U.S.A. 111 H4
Serafimovich, *Russia* 43 B10
Seraing, *Belgium* 17 G7
Seraja, *Indonesia* 59 L7
Serakhis →, *Cyprus* 37 D11
Seram, *Indonesia* 57 E7
Seram Laut, Kepulauan,
  Indonesia 57 E8
Seram Sea, *Indonesia* 57 E7
Serang, *Indonesia* 57 G12
Serasan, *Indonesia* 59 L7
Seravezza, *Italy* 32 E7
Serbia □, *Yugoslavia* 21 M11
Serdo, *Ethiopia* 77 E5
Serdobsk, *Russia* 41 E14
Serëdka, *Russia* 40 B6
Şereflikoçhisar, *Turkey* . . . 66 D5
Seregno, *Italy* 32 C6
Seremban, *Malaysia* 59 L3
Serengeti □, *Tanzania* 82 C3
Serengeti Plain, *Tanzania* . 82 C3
Serenje, *Zambia* 83 E3
Sereth = Siret →,
  Romania 38 D11
Sergach, *Russia* 41 D14
Serge →, *Spain* 28 D5
Sergino, *Russia* 44 C7
Sergipe □, *Brazil* 122 D4
Sergiyev Posad, *Russia* . . 41 C11
Seria, *Brunei* 56 D4
Serian, *Malaysia* 56 D4
Seriate, *Italy* 32 C6
Seribu, Kepulauan,
  Indonesia 56 F3
Sérifontaine, *France* 25 C8
Sérifos, *Greece* 39 M7
Sérignan, *France* 26 E7
Serik, *Turkey* 66 E4
Seringapatam Reef,
  Australia 88 B3
Sermaize-les-Bains, *France* 25 D11
Sermata, *Indonesia* 57 F7
Sérmide, *Italy* 33 C8
Sernovodsk, *Russia* 41 E17
Serny Zavod, *Turkmenistan* 44 F6
Serón, *Spain* 29 H2
Serós, *Spain* 28 D5
Serov, *Russia* 44 D7
Serowe, *Botswana* 84 C4
Serpa, *Portugal* 31 H3
Serpeddi, Punta, *Italy* . . . 34 C2
Serpentara, *Italy* 34 C2
Serpentine, *Australia* 89 F2
Serpentine Lakes, *Australia* 89 E4
Serpis →, *Spain* 29 G4
Serpukhov, *Russia* 41 D10
Serra do Navio, *Brazil* . . . 121 C7
Serra San Bruno, *Italy* . . . 35 D9
Serra Talhada, *Brazil* 122 C4
Serracapriola, *Italy* 35 A8
Serradilla, *Spain* 30 F4
Sérrai, *Greece* 39 H6
Serramanna, *Italy* 34 C1
Serrat, C., *Tunisia* 75 A6
Serre-Ponçon, L. de,
  France 27 D10
Serres, *France* 27 D9
Serrezuela, *Argentina* 126 C2
Serrinha, *Brazil* 123 D4
Serrita, *Brazil* 122 C4
Sersale, *Italy* 35 C9
Sertã, *Portugal* 30 F2
Sertânia, *Brazil* 122 C4
Sertanópolis, *Brazil* 127 A5
Sêrtar, *China* 52 A3
Sertig, *Switz.* 23 C9
Serua, *Indonesia* 57 F8
Serui, *Indonesia* 57 E9
Serule, *Botswana* 84 C4
Sérvia, *Greece* 39 J4
Sese Is., *Uganda* 82 C3
Sesepe, *Indonesia* 57 E7
Sesfontein, *Namibia* 84 B1
Sesheke, *Zambia* 84 B3
Sesia →, *Italy* 32 C5
Sesimbra, *Portugal* 31 G1
Sessa Aurunca, *Italy* 34 A6
S'estanol, *Spain* 36 B9
Sesto San Giovanni, *Italy* . 32 C6
Sestri Levante, *Italy* 32 D6
Sestrières, *Italy* 32 D3
Sestrunj, *Croatia* 33 D12
Sestu, *Italy* 34 C2
Sesvenna, *Switz.* 23 C10
Setana, *Japan* 48 C9

Sète, *France* 26 E7
Sete Lagôas, *Brazil* 123 E3
Sétif, *Algeria* 75 A6
Seto, *Japan* 49 G8
Setonaikai, *Japan* 49 G6
Settat, *Morocco* 74 B3
Setté-Cama, *Gabon* 80 E1
Séttimo Tor., *Italy* 32 C4
Setting L., *Canada* 101 B9
Settle, *U.K.* 12 C5
Settlement Pt., *Bahamas* . . 105 M6
Setto Calende, *Italy* 32 C5
Setúbal, *Portugal* 31 G2
Setúbal □, *Portugal* 31 G2
Setúbal, B. de, *Portugal* . . 31 G2
Seugne →, *France* 26 C3
Seulimeum, *Indonesia* . . . 56 C1
Seuzach, *Switz.* 23 A7
Sevan, *Armenia* 43 F11
Sevan, Ozero, *Armenia* . . . 43 F11
Sevastopol, *Ukraine* 42 D5
Sevelen, *Switz.* 23 B8
Seven Emu, *Australia* 90 B2
Seven Sisters, *Canada* . . . 100 C3
Sevenum, *Neths.* 17 F8
Sever →, *Spain* 31 F3
Sévérac-le-Château, *France* 26 D7
Severn →, *Canada* 98 A2
Severn →, *U.K.* 13 F5
Severn L., *Canada* 98 B1
Severnaya Zemlya, *Russia* . 45 B10
Severo-Kurilsk, *Russia* . . . 45 D16
Severo-Yeniseyskiy, *Russia* 45 C10
Serbia □, *Yugoslavia* 43 B8
Severodonetsk, *Ukraine* . . 43 B8
Severodvinsk, *Russia* 44 C4
Sevier, *U.S.A.* 111 G7
Sevier →, *U.S.A.* 111 G7
Sevier L., *U.S.A.* 110 G7
Sevilla, *Colombia* 120 C2
Sevilla, *Spain* 31 H5
Sevilla □, *Spain* 31 H5
Seville = Sevilla, *Spain* . . . 31 H5
Sevnica, *Slovenia* 33 B12
Sèvre-Nantaise →, *France* . 24 E5
Sèvre-Niortaise →, *France* . 26 B3
Sevsk, *Russia* 40 E9
Seward, *Alaska, U.S.A.* . . . 96 B5
Seward, *Nebr., U.S.A.* 108 E6
Seward Pen., *U.S.A.* 96 B3
Sewell, *Chile* 126 C1
Sewer, *Indonesia* 57 F8
Sewickley, *U.S.A.* 106 F4
Sexbierum, *Neths.* 16 B6
Sexsmith, *Canada* 100 B5
Seychelles ■, *Ind. Oc.* . . . 47 K9
Seyðisfjörður, *Iceland* 8 D7
Seydvān, *Iran* 64 B5
Seyfe Gölü, *Turkey* 66 D6
Seyhan Barajı, *Turkey* . . . 66 E6
Seyhan →, *Turkey* 66 E6
Seyitgazi, *Turkey* 66 D4
Seym →, *Ukraine* 40 F8
Seymchan, *Russia* 45 C16
Seymour, *Australia* 91 F4
Seymour, *S. Africa* 85 E4
Seymour, *Conn., U.S.A.* . . 107 E11
Seymour, *Ind., U.S.A.* 104 F3
Seymour, *Tex., U.S.A.* . . . 109 J5
Seymour, *Wis., U.S.A.* . . . 104 C1
Seyne, *France* 27 D10
Seyssel, *France* 27 C9
Sežana, *Slovenia* 33 C10
Sézanne, *France* 25 D10
Sezze, *Italy* 34 A6
Sfax, *Tunisia* 75 B7
Sfântu Gheorghe, *Romania* 38 D8
Sfântu Gheorghe,
  Brațul →, *Romania* 38 E12
Sha Xi →, *China* 53 D12
Sha Xian, *China* 53 D11
Shaanxi □, *China* 50 G5
Shaba □, *Zaïre* 82 D2
Shabunda, *Zaïre* 82 C2
Shache, *China* 54 C2
Shackleton Ice Shelf,
  Antarctica 5 C8
Shackleton Inlet, *Antarctica* 5 E11
Shādegān, *Iran* 65 D6
Shadi, *China* 53 D10
Shadi, *India* 63 C7
Shadrinsk, *Russia* 44 D7
Shaffa, *Nigeria* 79 C7
Shafter, *Calif., U.S.A.* 113 K7
Shafter, *Tex., U.S.A.* 109 L2
Shaftesbury, *U.K.* 13 F5
Shagamu, *Nigeria* 79 D5
Shagram, *Pakistan* 63 A5
Shah Bunder, *Pakistan* . . . 62 G2
Shahabad, *Punjab, India* . . 62 D7
Shahabad, *Raj., India* 62 G7
Shahabad, *Ut. P., India* . . 63 F8
Shahadpur, *Pakistan* 62 G3
Shahba, *Syria* 69 C5
Shahdād, *Iran* 65 D8
Shahdadkot, *Pakistan* . . . 62 F2
Shahe, *China* 50 F8
Shahganj, *India* 63 F10
Shahgarh, *India* 60 F6
Shaḥḥāt, *Libya* 73 B9
Shahjahanpur, *India* 63 F8
Shahpur, *India* 62 H7
Shahpur, *Pakistan* 62 E3
Shahpura, *India* 63 G9
Shahr Kord, *Iran* 65 C6
Shāhrakht, *Iran* 65 C9
Shahrig, *Pakistan* 62 D2
Shahukou, *China* 50 D7

Shaikhabad, *Afghan.* 62 B3
Shajapur, *India* 62 H7
Shakargarh, *Pakistan* 62 C6
Shakawe, *Botswana* 84 B3
Shaker Heights, *U.S.A.* .. 106 E3
Shakhty, *Russia* 43 C9
Shakhunya, *Russia* 41 C15
Shaki, *Nigeria* 79 D5
Shakopee, *U.S.A.* 108 C8
Shala, L., *Ethiopia* 77 F4
Shallow Lake, *Canada* ... 106 B3
Shaluli Shan, *China* 52 B2
Shām, *Iran* 65 E8
Shamâl Dârfûr □, *Sudan* . 77 D2
Shamâl Kordofân □, *Sudan* 77 D2
Shamattawa, *Canada* 101 B10
Shamattawa →, *Canada* .. 98 A2
Shambe, *Sudan* 77 F3
Shambu, *Ethiopia* 77 F4
Shamîl, *Iran* 65 E8
Shamkhor, *Azerbaijan* ... 43 F12
Shāmkūh, *Iran* 65 C8
Shamli, *India* 62 E7
Shamo = Gobi, *Asia* 50 C5
Shamo, L., *Ethiopia* 77 F4
Shamokin, *U.S.A.* 107 F8
Shamrock, *U.S.A.* 109 H4
Shamva, *Zimbabwe* 83 F3
Shan □, *Burma* 61 J21
Shan Xian, *China* 50 G9
Shanan →, *Ethiopia* 77 F5
Shanchengzhen, *China* ... 51 C13
Shāndak, *Iran* 65 D9
Shandon, *U.S.A.* 112 K6
Shandong □, *China* 51 F10
Shandong Bandao, *China* . 51 F11
Shang Xian, *China* 50 H5
Shangalowe, *Zaïre* 83 E2
Shangani →, *Zimbabwe* .. 83 F2
Shangbancheng, *China* ... 51 D10
Shangcai, *China* 53 A10
Shangcheng, *China* 53 B10
Shangchuan Dao, *China* .. 53 G9
Shangdu, *China* 50 D7
Shanggao, *China* 53 C10
Shanghai, *China* 53 B13
Shanghang, *China* 53 E11
Shanghe, *China* 51 F9
Shangjin, *China* 53 A8
Shanglin, *China* 52 F7
Shangnan, *China* 50 H6
Shangqiu, *China* 50 G8
Shangrao, *China* 53 C11
Shangshui, *China* 50 H8
Shangsi, *China* 52 F6
Shangyou, *China* 53 E10
Shangzhi, *China* 51 B14
Shanhetun, *China* 51 B14
Shani, *Nigeria* 79 C7
Shaniko, *U.S.A.* 110 D3
Shannon, *Greenland* 4 B17
Shannon, *N.Z.* 87 J5
Shannon →, *Ireland* 15 D2
Shansi = Shanxi □, *China* 50 F7
Shantar, Ostrov Bolshoy,
Russia 45 D14
Shantipur, *India* 63 H13
Shantou, *China* 53 F11
Shantung = Shandong □,
China 51 F10
Shanxi □, *China* 50 F7
Shanyang, *China* 50 H5
Shanyin, *China* 50 E7
Shaoguan, *China* 53 E9
Shaowu, *China* 53 D11
Shaoxing, *China* 53 C13
Shaoyang, *Hunan, China* . 53 D8
Shaoyang, *Hunan, China* . 53 D8
Shapinsay, *U.K.* 14 B6
Shaqra', *Si. Arabia* 64 E5
Shaqrā', *Yemen* 68 E4
Sharafa, *Sudan* 77 E2
Sharbot Lake, *Canada* ... 107 B8
Shari, *Japan* 48 C12
Sharjah = Ash Shāriqah,
U.A.E. 65 E7
Shark B., *Australia* 89 E1
Sharm el Sheikh, *Egypt* .. 76 B3
Sharon, *Mass., U.S.A.* .. 107 D13
Sharon, *Pa., U.S.A.* 106 E4
Sharon Springs, *U.S.A.* .. 108 F4
Sharp Pt., *Australia* 90 A3
Sharpe L., *Canada* 101 C10
Sharpsville, *U.S.A.* 106 E4
Sharq el Istiwa'iya □,
Sudan 77 F3
Sharya, *Russia* 41 B14
Shasha, *Ethiopia* 77 F4
Shashemene, *Ethiopia* ... 77 F4
Shashi, *Botswana* 85 C4
Shashi, *China* 53 B9
Shashi →, *Africa* 83 G2
Shasta, Mt., *U.S.A.* 110 F2
Shasta L., *U.S.A.* 110 F2
Shatsk, *Russia* 41 D12
Shatt al'Arab →, *Iraq* ... 65 D6
Shattuck, *U.S.A.* 109 G5
Shatura, *Russia* 41 D11
Shaumyani, *Georgia* 43 F11
Shaunavon, *Canada* 101 D7
Shaver L., *U.S.A.* 112 H7
Shaw →, *Australia* 88 D2
Shaw I., *Australia* 90 C4
Shawan, *China* 54 B3
Shawanaga, *Canada* 106 A4
Shawano, *U.S.A.* 104 C1

Shawinigan, *Canada* 98 C5
Shawnee, *U.S.A.* 109 H6
Shaybārā, *Si. Arabia* 64 E3
Shayib el Banat, Gebel,
Egypt 76 B3
Shaykh Sa'īd, *Iraq* 64 C5
Shchekino, *Russia* 41 D10
Shcherbakov = Rybinsk,
Russia 41 B11
Shchigri, *Russia* 41 F10
Shchors, *Ukraine* 40 F7
Shchuchiosk, *Kazakhstan* . 44 D8
She Xian, *Anhui, China* .. 53 C12
She Xian, *Hebei, China* .. 50 F7
Shea, *Guyana* 121 C6
Shebekino, *Russia* 41 F10
Shebele = Scebeli,
Wabi →, *Somali Rep.* .. 68 G3
Sheboygan, *U.S.A.* 104 D2
Shediac, *Canada* 99 C7
Sheelin, L., *Ireland* 15 C4
Sheep Haven, *Ireland* ... 15 A4
Sheerness, *U.K.* 13 F8
Sheet Harbour, *Canada* .. 99 D7
Sheffield, *U.K.* 12 D6
Sheffield, *Ala., U.S.A.* .. 105 H2
Sheffield, *Mass., U.S.A.* 107 D11
Sheffield, *Pa., U.S.A.* ... 106 E5
Sheffield, *Tex., U.S.A.* .. 109 K4
Sheho, *Canada* 101 C8
Shehojele, *Ethiopia* 77 E4
Shehong, *China* 52 B5
Shehuen →, *Argentina* .. 128 C3
Sheikhpura, *India* 63 G11
Shek Hasan, *Ethiopia* ... 77 E4
Shekhupura, *Pakistan* ... 62 D5
Sheki, *Azerbaijan* 43 F12
Sheksna →, *Russia* 41 B11
Shelburne, *N.S., Canada* . 99 D6
Shelburne, *Ont., Canada* . 98 D3
Shelburne, *U.S.A.* 107 B11
Shelburne B., *Australia* .. 90 A3
Shelburne Falls, *U.S.A.* . 107 D12
Shelby, *Mich., U.S.A.* ... 104 D2
Shelby, *Mont., U.S.A.* ... 110 B8
Shelby, *N.C., U.S.A.* 105 H5
Shelby, *Ohio, U.S.A.* 106 F2
Shelbyville, *Ill., U.S.A.* . 108 F10
Shelbyville, *Ind., U.S.A.* 104 F3
Shelbyville, *Tenn., U.S.A.* 105 H2
Sheldon, *U.S.A.* 108 D7
Sheldrake, *Canada* 99 B7
Shelikhova, Zaliv, *Russia* . 45 D16
Shell Lake, *Canada* 101 C7
Shell Lakes, *Australia* ... 89 E4
Shellbrook, *Canada* 101 C7
Shellharbour, *Australia* .. 91 E5
Shelling Rocks, *Ireland* .. 15 E1
Shelon →, *Russia* 40 B7
Shelton, *Conn., U.S.A.* .. 107 E11
Shelton, *Wash., U.S.A.* .. 112 C3
Shemakha, *Azerbaijan* ... 43 F13
Shen Xian, *China* 50 F8
Shenandoah, *Iowa, U.S.A.* 108 E7
Shenandoah, *Pa., U.S.A.* 107 F8
Shenandoah, *Va., U.S.A.* 104 F7
Shenandoah →, *U.S.A.* .. 104 F7
Shenchi, *China* 50 E7
Shendam, *Nigeria* 79 D6
Shendî, *Sudan* 77 D3
Sheng Xian, *China* 53 C13
Shengfang, *China* 50 E9
Shëngjergji, *Albania* 39 H3
Shëngjini, *Albania* 39 H2
Shenjingzi, *China* 51 B13
Shenmu, *China* 50 E6
Shennongjia, *China* 53 B8
Shenqiu, *China* 50 H8
Shenqiucheng, *China* 50 H8
Shensi = Shaanxi □, *China* 50 G5
Shenyang, *China* 51 D12
Sheopur Kalan, *India* 60 G10
Shepetovka, *Ukraine* 40 F5
Shepparton, *Australia* ... 91 F4
Sheqi, *China* 50 H7
Sher Qila, *Pakistan* 63 A6
Sherborne, *U.K.* 13 G5
Sherbro I., *S. Leone* 78 D2
Sherbrooke, *Canada* 99 C5
Shereik, *Sudan* 76 D3
Sheridan, *Ark., U.S.A.* .. 109 H8
Sheridan, *Wyo., U.S.A.* . 110 D10
Sherkot, *India* 63 E8
Sherman, *U.S.A.* 109 J6
Sherridon, *Canada* 101 B8
Sherwood, *N. Dak., U.S.A.* 108 A4
Sherwood, *Tex., U.S.A.* . 109 K4
Sherwood Forest, *U.K.* .. 12 D6
Sheslay, *Canada* 100 B2
Sheslay →, *Canada* 100 B2
Shethanei L., *Canada* ... 101 B9
Shetland □, *U.K.* 14 A7
Shetland Is., *U.K.* 14 A7
Shewa □, *Ethiopia* 77 F4
Shewa Gimira, *Ethiopia* . 77 F4
Sheyenne, *U.S.A.* 108 B5
Sheyenne →, *U.S.A.* 108 B6
Shibām, *Yemen* 68 D4
Shibata, *Japan* 48 F9
Shibecha, *Japan* 48 C12
Shibetsu, *Japan* 48 B11
Shibīn el Kôm, *Egypt* ... 76 H7
Shibīn el Qanâtir, *Egypt* . 76 H7
Shibing, *China* 52 D7
Shibogama L., *Canada* ... 98 B2
Shibushi, *Japan* 49 J5

Shicheng, *China* 53 D11
Shickshock Mts. = Chic-
Chocs, Mts., *Canada* ... 99 C6
Shidao, *China* 51 F12
Shidian, *China* 52 E2
Shido, *Japan* 49 G7
Shiel, L., *U.K.* 14 E3
Shield, C., *Australia* 90 A2
Shiga □, *Japan* 49 G8
Shigaib, *Sudan* 73 E9
Shigu, *China* 52 D2
Shiguaigou, *China* 50 D6
Shihchiachuangi =
Shijiazhuang, *China* 50 E8
Shijiazhuang, *China* 50 E8
Shijiu Hu, *China* 53 B12
Shikarpur, *India* 62 E8
Shikarpur, *Pakistan* 62 F3
Shikoku □, *Japan* 49 H6
Shikoku-Sanchi, *Japan* ... 49 H6
Shilabo, *Ethiopia* 68 F3
Shiliguri, *India* 61 F16
Shilka, *Russia* 45 D12
Shilka →, *Russia* 45 D13
Shillelagh, *Ireland* 15 D5
Shillong, *India* 61 G17
Shilo, *Jordan* 69 C4
Shilong, *China* 53 F9
Shilou, *China* 50 F6
Shilovo, *Russia* 41 D12
Shimabara, *Japan* 49 H5
Shimada, *Japan* 49 G9
Shimane □, *Japan* 49 G6
Shimanovsk, *Russia* 45 D13
Shimen, *China* 53 C8
Shimenjie, *China* 53 C11
Shimian, *China* 52 C4
Shimizu, *Japan* 49 G9
Shimodate, *Japan* 49 F9
Shimoga, *India* 60 N9
Shimoni, *Kenya* 82 C4
Shimonoseki, *Japan* 49 H5
Shimpuru Rapids, *Angola* . 84 B2
Shimsk, *Russia* 40 B7
Shin, L., *U.K.* 14 C4
Shin-Tone →, *Japan* 49 G10
Shinan, *China* 52 F7
Shinano →, *Japan* 49 F9
Shindand, *Afghan.* 60 C3
Shingleton, *U.S.A.* 98 C2
Shingū, *Japan* 49 H7
Shinjō, *Japan* 48 E10
Shinkafe, *Nigeria* 79 C6
Shinshār, *Syria* 69 A5
Shinyanga, *Tanzania* 82 C3
Shinyanga □, *Tanzania* .. 82 C3
Shiogama, *Japan* 48 E10
Shiojiri, *Japan* 49 F8
Ship I., *U.S.A.* 109 K10
Shipehenski Prokhod,
Bulgaria 38 G8
Shiping, *China* 52 F4
Shipki La, *India* 60 D11
Shippegan, *Canada* 99 C7
Shippensburg, *U.S.A.* 106 F7
Shiprock, *U.S.A.* 111 H9
Shiqian, *China* 52 D7
Shiqma, N. →, *Israel* 69 D3
Shiquan, *China* 50 H5
Shīr Kūh, *Iran* 65 D7
Shiragami-Misaki, *Japan* . 48 D10
Shirakawa, *Fukushima,
Japan* 49 F10
Shirakawa, *Gifu, Japan* .. 49 F8
Shirane-San, *Gumma,
Japan* 49 F9
Shirane-San, *Yamanashi,
Japan* 49 G9
Shiraoi, *Japan* 48 C10
Shīrāz, *Iran* 65 D7
Shirbin, *Egypt* 76 H7
Shire →, *Africa* 83 F4
Shiretoko-Misaki, *Japan* . 48 B12
Shirinab →, *Pakistan* 62 D2
Shiringushi, *Russia* 41 E13
Shiriya-Zaki, *Japan* 48 D10
Shiroishi, *Japan* 48 E10
Shīrvān, *Iran* 65 B8
Shirwa, L. = Chilwa, L.,
Malawi 83 F4
Shishou, *China* 53 C9
Shitai, *China* 53 B11
Shivpuri, *India* 62 G7
Shixian, *China* 51 C15
Shixing, *China* 53 E10
Shiyan, *China* 53 A8
Shiyata, *Egypt* 76 B2
Shizhu, *China* 52 C7
Shizong, *China* 52 E5
Shizuishan, *China* 50 E4
Shizuoka, *Japan* 49 G9
Shizuoka □, *Japan* 49 G9
Shklov, *Belorussia* 40 D7
Shkoder = Shkodra,
Albania 38 G2
Shkodra, *Albania* 38 G2
Shkumbini →, *Albania* ... 39 H2
Shmidta, O., *Russia* 45 A10
Shō-Gawa →, *Japan* 49 F8
Shoal Lake, *Canada* 101 C8
Shōdo-Shima, *Japan* 49 G7
Shoeburyness, *U.K.* 13 F8
Sholapur = Solapur, *India* 60 L9
Shologontsy, *Russia* 45 C12
Shōmrōn, *Jordan* 69 C4
Shoshone, *Calif., U.S.A.* 113 K10

Shoshone, *Idaho, U.S.A.* . 110 E6
Shoshone, L., *U.S.A.* 110 D8
Shoshone Mts., *U.S.A.* ... 110 G5
Shoshong, *Botswana* 84 C4
Shoshoni, *U.S.A.* 110 E9
Shostka, *Ukraine* 40 F8
Shou Xian, *China* 53 A11
Shouchang, *China* 53 C12
Shouguang, *China* 51 F10
Shouning, *China* 53 D12
Shouyang, *China* 50 F7
Show Low, *U.S.A.* 111 J9
Shpola, *Ukraine* 42 B4
Shreveport, *U.S.A.* 109 J8
Shrewsbury, *U.K.* 12 E5
Shrirampur, *India* 63 H13
Shropshire □, *U.K.* 13 E5
Shuangbai, *China* 52 E3
Shuangcheng, *China* 51 B14
Shuangfeng, *China* 53 D9
Shuanggou, *China* 51 G9
Shuangjiang, *China* 52 F2
Shuangliao, *China* 51 C12
Shuangshanzi, *China* 51 D10
Shuangyang, *China* 51 C13
Shuangyashan, *China* 54 B8
Shucheng, *China* 53 B11
Shuguri Falls, *Tanzania* .. 83 D4
Shuicheng, *China* 52 D5
Shuiji, *China* 53 D12
Shuiye, *China* 50 F8
Shujalpur, *India* 62 H7
Shukpa Kunzang, *India* ... 63 B8
Shulan, *China* 51 B14
Shule, *China* 54 C2
Shumagin Is., *U.S.A.* 96 C4
Shumerlya, *Russia* 41 D15
Shumikha, *Russia* 44 D7
Shunchang, *China* 53 D11
Shunde, *China* 53 F9
Shungay, *Kazakhstan* 43 B12
Shungnak, *U.S.A.* 96 B4
Shuo Xian, *China* 50 E7
Shūr →, *Iran* 65 D7
Shūr Āb, *Iran* 65 C6
Shūr Gaz, *Iran* 65 D8
Shūrāb, *Iran* 65 C8
Shūrjestān, *Iran* 65 D7
Shurma, *Russia* 41 C17
Shurugwi, *Zimbabwe* 83 F3
Shūsf, *Iran* 65 D9
Shūshtar, *Iran* 65 D6
Shuswap L., *Canada* 100 C5
Shuya, *Russia* 41 C12
Shuyang, *China* 51 G10
Shūzū, *Iran* 65 D7
Shwebo, *Burma* 61 H19
Shwegu, *Burma* 61 G20
Shweli →, *Burma* 61 H20
Shymkent = Chimkent,
Kazakhstan 44 E7
Shyok, *India* 63 B8
Shyok →, *Pakistan* 63 B6
Si Chon, *Thailand* 59 H2
Si Kiang = Xi Jiang →,
China 53 F9
Si-ngan = Xi'an, *China* .. 50 G5
Si Prachan, *Thailand* 58 E3
Si Racha, *Thailand* 58 F3
Si Xian, *China* 51 H9
Siahan Range, *Pakistan* .. 60 F4
Siaksrindrapura, *Indonesia* 56 D2
Sialkot, *Pakistan* 62 C6
Siam = Thailand ■, *Asia* . 58 E4
Siantan, P., *Indonesia* ... 59 L6
Siàpo →, *Venezuela* 120 C4
Siāreh, *Iran* 65 D9
Siargao, *Phil.* 55 G7
Siari, *Pakistan* 63 B7
Siasi, *Phil.* 57 C6
Siasi I., *Phil.* 55 J4
Siátista, *Greece* 39 J4
Siau, *Indonesia* 57 D7
Šiauliai, *Lithuania* 40 D3
Siaya □, *Kenya* 82 B3
Siazan, *Azerbaijan* 43 F13
Sibâi, Gebel el, *Egypt* ... 76 B3
Sibari, *Italy* 35 C9
Sibasa, *S. Africa* 85 C5
Sibayi, L., *S. Africa* 85 D5
Šibenik, *Croatia* 33 E12
Siberia, *Russia* 4 D13
Siberut, *Indonesia* 56 E1
Sibi, *Pakistan* 62 E2
Sibil, *Indonesia* 57 E10
Sibiti, *Congo* 80 E2
Sibiu, *Romania* 38 D7
Sibley, *Iowa, U.S.A.* 108 D7
Sibley, *La., U.S.A.* 109 J8
Sibolga, *Indonesia* 56 D1
Sibret, *Belgium* 17 J7
Sibsagar, *India* 61 F19
Sibu, *Malaysia* 56 D4
Sibuco, *Phil.* 55 H5
Sibuguey B., *Phil.* 55 H5
Sibutu, *Phil.* 57 D5
Sibutu Group, *Phil.* 55 J3
Sibutu Passage, *E. Indies* . 57 D5
Sibuyan, *Phil.* 55 E5
Sibuyan Sea, *Phil.* 55 E5
Sicamous, *Canada* 100 C5
Sichuan □, *China* 52 B5
Sicilia, *Italy* 35 E7
Sicilia □, *Italy* 35 E7
Sicilia, Canale di, *Italy* ... 34 E5

Sicilian Channel = Sicilia,
Canale di, *Italy* 34 E5
Sicily = Sicilia, *Italy* 35 E7
Sicuani, *Peru* 124 C3
Siculiana, *Italy* 34 E6
Sidamo □, *Ethiopia* 77 G4
Sidaouet, *Niger* 79 B6
Sidári, *Greece* 37 A3
Siddeburen, *Neths.* 16 B9
Siddhapur, *India* 62 H5
Siddipet, *India* 60 K11
Side, *Turkey* 66 E4
Sidéradougou,
Burkina Faso 78 C4
Siderno Marina, *Italy* 35 D9
Sídheros, Ákra, *Greece* .. 37 D8
Sidhirókastron, *Greece* ... 39 H6
Sîdi Abd el Rahmân, *Egypt* 76 H6
Sîdi Barrâni, *Egypt* 76 A2
Sidi-bel-Abbès, *Algeria* .. 75 A4
Sidi Bennour, *Morocco* .. 74 B3
Sidi Haneish, *Egypt* 76 A2
Sidi Kacem, *Morocco* 74 B3
Sidi Omar, *Egypt* 76 A1
Sidi Slimane, *Morocco* ... 74 B3
Sidi Smaïl, *Morocco* 74 B3
Sidlaw Hills, *U.K.* 14 E5
Sidley, Mt., *Antarctica* ... 5 D14
Sidmouth, *U.K.* 13 G4
Sidmouth, C., *Australia* .. 90 A3
Sidney, *Canada* 100 D4
Sidney, *Mont., U.S.A.* .. 108 B2
Sidney, *N.Y., U.S.A.* ... 107 D9
Sidney, *Nebr., U.S.A.* .. 108 E3
Sidney, *Ohio, U.S.A.* ... 104 E3
Sidoarjo, *Indonesia* 57 G15
Sidon = Saydā, *Lebanon* . 69 B4
Sidra, G. of = Surt, Khalîj,
Libya 73 B8
Siedlce, *Poland* 20 C12
Sieg →, *Germany* 18 E3
Siegburg, *Germany* 18 E3
Siegen, *Germany* 18 E4
Siem Pang, *Cambodia* ... 58 E6
Siem Reap, *Cambodia* ... 58 F4
Siena, *Italy* 33 E8
Sieradz, *Poland* 20 D8
Sierck-les-Bains, *France* .. 25 C13
Sierpc, *Poland* 20 C9
Sierpe, Bocas de la,
Venezuela 121 B5
Sierra Blanca, *U.S.A.* ... 111 L11
Sierra Blanca Peak, *U.S.A.* 111 K11
Sierra City, *U.S.A.* 112 F6
Sierra Colorada, *Argentina* 128 B3
Sierra de Yeguas, *Spain* . 31 H6
Sierra Gorda, *Chile* 126 A2
Sierra Grande, *Argentina* . 128 B3
Sierra Leone ■, *W. Afr.* .. 78 D2
Sierra Madre, *Mexico* ... 115 D6
Sierra Mojada, *Mexico* .. 114 B4
Sierraville, *U.S.A.* 112 F6
Sierre, *Switz.* 22 D5
Sif Fatima, *Algeria* 75 B6
Sífnos, *Greece* 39 N7
Sifton, *Canada* 101 C8
Sifton Pass, *Canada* 100 B3
Sig, *Algeria* 75 A4
Sigdal, *Norway* 10 D3
Sigean, *France* 26 E6
Sighetu-Marmatiei,
Romania 38 B6
Sighişoara, *Romania* 38 C7
Sigli, *Indonesia* 56 C1
Siglufjörður, *Iceland* 8 C4
Sigmaringen, *Germany* ... 19 G5
Signakhi, *Georgia* 43 F11
Signal, *U.S.A.* 113 L13
Signal Pk., *U.S.A.* 113 M12
Signau, *Switz.* 22 C5
Signy-l'Abbaye, *France* .. 25 C11
Sigsig, *Ecuador* 120 D2
Sigtuna, *Sweden* 10 E11
Sigüenza, *Spain* 28 D2
Siguiri, *Guinea* 78 C3
Sigulda, *Latvia* 40 C4
Sigurd, *U.S.A.* 111 G8
Sihanoukville = Kompong
Som, *Cambodia* 59 G4
Sihaus, *Peru* 124 B2
Sihui, *China* 53 F9
Siirt, *Turkey* 67 E9
Siirt □, *Turkey* 67 E9
Sijarira Ra., *Zimbabwe* .. 83 F2
Sikao, *Thailand* 59 J2
Sikar, *India* 62 F6
Sikasso, *Mali* 78 C3
Sikeston, *U.S.A.* 109 G10
Sikhote Alin, Khrebet,
Russia 45 E14
Sikhote Alin Ra. = Sikhote
Alin, Khrebet, *Russia* ... 45 E14
Sikiá., *Greece* 39 J6
Síkinos, *Greece* 39 N8
Sikkani Chief →, *Canada* . 100 B4
Sikkim □, *India* 61 F16
Sikotu-Ko, *Japan* 48 C10
Sil →, *Spain* 30 C3
Silacayoapan, *Mexico* ... 115 D5
Silandro, *Italy* 32 B7
Silay, *Phil.* 55 F5
Silba, *Croatia* 33 D11
Silchar, *India* 61 G18
Silcox, *Canada* 101 B10
Şile, *Turkey* 66 C3
Silenrieux, *Belgium* 17 H4

Siler City, *U.S.A.* 105 H6
Silesia = Śląsk, *Poland* .. 20 E6
Silet, *Algeria* 75 D5
Silgarhi Doti, *Nepal* 63 E9
Silghat, *India* 61 F18
Silifke, *Turkey* 66 E5
Siliguri = Shiliguri, *India* 61 F16
Siling Co, *China* 54 C3
Silíqua, *Italy* 34 C1
Silistra, *Bulgaria* 38 E10
Silivri, *Turkey* 66 C3
Siljan, *Sweden* 9 F13
Silkeborg, *Denmark* 11 H3
Sillajhuay, Cordillera, *Chile* 124 D4
Sillé-le-Guillaume, *France* 24 D6
Sillustani, *Peru* 124 D3
Siloam Springs, *U.S.A.* 109 G7
Silopi, *Turkey* 67 E10
Silsbee, *U.S.A.* 109 K7
Silute, *Lithuania* 40 D2
Silva Porto = Kuito, *Angola* 81 G3
Silvan, *Turkey* 67 D9
Silvaplana, *Switz.* 23 D9
Silver City, *N. Mex.,* *U.S.A.* 111 K9
Silver City, *Nev., U.S.A.* 110 G4
Silver Cr. →, *U.S.A.* .. 110 E4
Silver Creek, *U.S.A.* ... 106 D5
Silver L., *Calif., U.S.A.* 112 G6
Silver L., *Calif., U.S.A.* 113 K10
Silver Lake, *U.S.A.* 110 E3
Silver Streams, *S. Africa* 84 D3
Silverton, *Colo., U.S.A.* 111 H10
Silverton, *Tex., U.S.A.* 109 H4
Silves, *Portugal* 31 H2
Silvi, *Italy* 33 F11
Silvia, *Colombia* 120 C2
Silvies →, *U.S.A.* 110 E4
Silvolde, *Neths.* 16 E8
Silvretta-Gruppe, *Switz.* 23 C10
Silwa Bahari, *Egypt* ... 76 C3
Silz, *Austria* 19 H6
Sim, C., *Morocco* 74 B3
Simanggang, *Malaysia* .. 56 D4
Simao, *China* 52 F3
Simão Dias, *Brazil* 122 D4
Simard, L., *Canada* 98 C4
Simav, *Turkey* 66 D3
Simba, *Tanzania* 82 C4
Simbach, *Germany* 19 G9
Simbirsk, *Russia* 41 D16
Simbo, *Tanzania* 82 C2
Simcoe, *Canada* 98 D3
Simcoe, L., *Canada* 98 D4
Simenga, *Russia* 45 C11
Simeto →, *Italy* 35 E8
Simeulue, *Indonesia* ... 56 D1
Simferopol, *Ukraine* ... 42 D6
Sími, *Greece* 39 N10
Simi Valley, *U.S.A.* ... 113 L8
Simikot, *Nepal* 63 E9
Simití, *Colombia* 120 B3
Simla, *India* 62 D7
Şimleu-Silvaniei, *Romania* 38 B5
Simme →, *Switz.* 22 C4
Simmern, *Germany* 19 F3
Simmie, *Canada* 101 D7
Simmler, *U.S.A.* 113 K7
Simões, *Brazil* 122 C3
Simojärvi, *Finland* ... 8 C19
Simojoki →, *Finland* . 8 D18
Simojovel, *Mexico* 115 D6
Simonette →, *Canada* 100 B5
Simonstown, *S. Africa* . 84 E2
Simplício Mendes, *Brazil* 122 C3
Simplon, *Switz.* 22 D6
Simplon Pass = Simplonpass, *Switz.* .. 22 D6
Simplon Tunnel, *Switz.* .. 22 D6
Simplonpass, *Switz.* ... 22 D6
Simpson Desert, *Australia* 90 D2
Simpungdong, *N. Korea* .. 51 D15
Simunjan, *Malaysia* 56 D4
Simushir, Ostrov, *Russia* . 45 E16
Sinabang, *Indonesia* ... 56 D1
Sinadogo, *Somali Rep.* .. 68 F4
Sinai = Es Sînâ', *Egypt* ... 76 J8
Sinai, Mt. = Mûsa, G., *Egypt* 76 J8
Sinai Peninsula, *Egypt* .. 69 F2
Sinaia, *Romania* 38 D8
Sinaloa □, *Mexico* 114 C3
Sinaloa de Levya, *Mexico* . 114 B3
Sinalunga, *Italy* 33 E8
Sinan, *China* 52 D7
Sinarádhes, *Greece* ... 37 A3
Sînâwan, *Libya* 75 B7
Sincé, *Colombia* 120 B2
Sincelejo, *Colombia* ... 120 B2
Sinchang, *N. Korea* ... 51 D15
Sinchang-ni, *N. Korea* . 51 E14
Sinclair, *U.S.A.* 110 F10
Sinclair Mills, *Canada* .. 100 C4
Sincorá, Serra do, *Brazil* 123 D3
Sind, *Pakistan* 62 G3
Sind □, *Pakistan* 62 F3
Sind →, *India* 63 B6
Sind Sagar Doab, *Pakistan* 62 D4
Sindal, *Denmark* 11 G4
Sindangan, *Phil.* 55 G5
Sindangbarang, *Indonesia* 57 G12
Sinde, *Zambia* 83 F2
Sinegorski, *Russia* 43 C9
Sinelnikovo, *Ukraine* .. 42 B6
Sines, *Portugal* 31 H2

Sines, C. de, *Portugal* 31 H2
Sineu, *Spain* 36 B10
Sinfra, *Ivory C.* 78 D3
Sing Buri, *Thailand* 58 E3
Singa, *Sudan* 77 E3
Singapore ■, *Asia* 59 M4
Singapore, Straits of, *Asia* 59 M5
Singaraja, *Indonesia* ... 56 F5
Singen, *Germany* 19 H4
Singida, *Tanzania* 82 C3
Singida □, *Tanzania* ... 82 D3
Singitikós Kólpos, *Greece* 39 J6
Singkaling Hkamti, *Burma* 61 G19
Singkawang, *Indonesia* . 56 D3
Singleton, *Australia* ... 91 E5
Singleton, Mt., *N. Terr.,* *Australia* 88 D5
Singleton, Mt., *W. Austral.,* *Australia* 89 E2
Singoli, *India* 62 G6
Singora = Songkhla, *Thailand* 59 J3
Singosan, *N. Korea* 51 E14
Sinhung, *N. Korea* 51 D14
Siniscóla, *Italy* 34 B2
Sinj, *Croatia* 33 E13
Sinjai, *Indonesia* 57 F6
Sinjār, *Iraq* 64 B4
Sinkat, *Sudan* 76 D4
Sinkiang Uighur = Xinjiang Uygur Zizhiqu □, *China* 54 B3
Sinmak, *N. Korea* 51 E14
Sínnai, *Italy* 34 C2
Sinni →, *Italy* 35 B9
Sinnuris, *Egypt* 76 J7
Sinoe, L., *Romania* ... 38 E11
Sinop, *Turkey* 42 E6
Sinop □, *Turkey* 66 C6
Sinpo, *N. Korea* 51 E15
Sins, *Switz.* 23 B6
Sinskoye, *Russia* 45 C13
Sint-Amandsberg, *Belgium* 17 F3
Sint Annaland, *Neths.* . 17 E4
Sint Annaparoch, *Neths.* 16 B7
Sint-Denijs, *Belgium* .. 17 G2
Sint Eustatius, I., *Neth. Ant.* 117 C7
Sint-Genesius-Rode, *Belgium* 17 G4
Sint-Gillis-Waas, *Belgium* . 17 F4
Sint-Huibrechts-Lille, *Belgium* 17 F6
Sint-Katelijne-Waver, *Belgium* 17 F5
Sint-Kruis, *Belgium* ... 17 F2
Sint-Laureins, *Belgium* . 17 F3
Sint Maarten, I., *W. Indies* 117 C7
Sint-Michiels, *Belgium* . 17 F2
Sint Nicolaasga, *Neths.* 16 C7
Sint Niklaas, *Belgium* . 17 F4
Sint Oedenrode, *Neths.* 17 E6
Sint Pancras, *Neths.* .. 16 C5
Sint Philipsland, *Neths.* 17 E4
Sint Truiden, *Belgium* . 17 G6
Sint Willebrord, *Neths.* 17 E5
Sîntana, *Romania* 38 C4
Sintang, *Indonesia* 56 D4
Sintjohannesga, *Neths.* 16 C7
Sinton, *U.S.A.* 109 L6
Sintra, *Portugal* 31 G1
Sinŭiju, *N. Korea* 51 D13
Sinyukha →, *Ukraine* . 42 B4
Siocon, *Phil.* 55 H5
Siófok, *Hungary* 21 J8
Sioma, *Zambia* 84 B3
Sion, *Switz.* 22 D4
Sioux City, *U.S.A.* 108 D6
Sioux Falls, *U.S.A.* ... 108 D6
Sioux Lookout, *Canada* 98 B1
Sip Song Chau Thai, *Vietnam* 58 B4
Sipalay, *Phil.* 55 G5
Siping, *China* 51 C13
Sipiwesk L., *Canada* .. 101 B9
Sipora, *Indonesia* 56 E1
Siquia →, *Nic.* 116 D3
Siquijor, *Phil.* 55 G5
Siquirres, *Costa Rica* . 116 D3
Siquisique, *Venezuela* . 120 A4
Sir Edward Pellew Group, *Australia* 90 B2
Sir Graham Moore Is., *Australia* 88 B4
Siracusa, *Italy* 35 E8
Sirajganj, *Bangla.* 63 G13
Sirakoro, *Mali* 78 C3
Şiran, *Turkey* 67 C8
Sirasso, *Ivory C.* 78 D3
Sīrdān, *Iran* 65 B6
Sirer, *Spain* 36 C7
Siret, *Romania* 38 B9
Siret →, *Romania* ... 38 D11
Şiria, *Romania* 38 C4
Sirino, Monte, *Italy* .. 35 B8
Sírna, *Greece* 39 N9
Sírnach, *Switz.* 23 B7
Şirnak, *Turkey* 67 E10
Sirohi, *India* 62 G5
Sironj, *India* 62 G7
Síros, *Greece* 39 M7
Sirretta Pk., *U.S.A.* .. 113 K8
Sirsa, *India* 62 E6
Siruela, *Spain* 31 G5
Sisak, *Croatia* 33 C13
Sisaket, *Thailand* 58 E5

Sisante, *Spain* 29 F2
Sisargas, Is., *Spain* 30 B2
Sishen, *S. Africa* 84 D3
Sishui, *Henan, China* .. 50 G7
Sishui, *Shandong, China* 51 G9
Sisipuk L., *Canada* 101 B8
Sisophon, *Cambodia* ... 58 F4
Sissach, *Switz.* 22 B5
Sisseton, *U.S.A.* 108 C6
Sissonne, *France* 25 C10
Sīstān va Balūchestān □, *Iran* 65 E9
Sisteron, *France* 27 D9
Sisters, *U.S.A.* 110 D3
Sitamarhi, *India* 63 F11
Sitapur, *India* 63 F9
Siteki, *Swaziland* 85 D5
Sitges, *Spain* 28 D6
Sitía, *Greece* 37 D8
Sítio da Abadia, *Brazil* 123 D2
Sitka, *U.S.A.* 96 C6
Sitoti, *Botswana* 84 C3
Sitra, *Egypt* 76 B2
Sittang Myit →, *Burma* 61 L20
Sittard, *Neths.* 17 G7
Sittensen, *Germany* ... 18 B5
Sittona, *Eritrea* 77 E4
Sittwe, *Burma* 61 J18
Siuna, *Nic.* 116 D3
Siuri, *India* 63 H12
Sivana, *India* 62 E8
Sīvand, *Iran* 65 D7
Sivas, *Turkey* 66 D7
Sivas □, *Turkey* 66 D7
Siverek, *Turkey* 67 E8
Sivrihisar, *Turkey* ... 66 D4
Sivry, *Belgium* 17 H4
Sîwa, *Egypt* 76 B2
Sîwa, El Wâhât es, *Egypt* . 76 B2
Siwalik Range, *Nepal* . 63 F10
Siwan, *India* 63 F11
Siyâl, Jazâ'ir, *Egypt* .. 76 C4
Sizewell, *U.K.* 13 E9
Siziwang Qi, *China* ... 50 D6
Sjælland, *Denmark* ... 11 J5
Sjællands Odde, *Denmark* 11 J5
Själevad, *Sweden* 10 A12
Sjenica, *Serbia* 21 M10
Sjoa, *Norway* 10 C3
Sjöbo, *Sweden* 11 J7
Sjösa, *Sweden* 11 F11
Sjumen = Šumen, *Bulgaria* 38 F9
Skadovsk, *Ukraine* ... 42 C5
Skagafjörður, *Iceland* .. 8 D4
Skagastølstindane, *Norway* 9 F9
Skagen, *Denmark* 11 G4
Skagerrak, *Denmark* .. 11 G3
Skagit →, *U.S.A.* ... 112 B4
Skagway, *U.S.A.* 100 B1
Skaidi, *Norway* 8 A18
Skala Podolskaya, *Ukraine* 42 B2
Skalat, *Ukraine* 40 G4
Skalni Dol = Kamenyak, *Bulgaria* 38 F9
Skals, *Denmark* 11 H3
Skanderborg, *Denmark* 11 H3
Skänör, *Sweden* 11 J6
Skara, *Sweden* 9 G12
Skaraborgs län □, *Sweden* 9 G12
Skardu, *Pakistan* ... 63 B6
Skarrild, *Denmark* .. 11 J2
Skarzysko Kamienna, *Poland* 20 D10
Skebokvarn, *Sweden* . 10 E10
Skeena →, *Canada* .. 100 C2
Skeena Mts., *Canada* . 100 B3
Skegness, *U.K.* 12 D8
Skeldon, *Guyana* 121 B6
Skellefte älv →, *Sweden* . 8 D16
Skellefteå, *Sweden* .. 8 D16
Skelleftehamn, *Sweden* 8 D16
Skender Vakuf, *Bos.-H.* 21 L7
Skene, *Sweden* 11 G6
Skerries, The, *U.K.* .. 12 D3
Skhoinoúsa, *Greece* .. 39 N8
Ski, *Norway* 10 E4
Skíathos, *Greece* 39 K6
Skibbereen, *Ireland* .. 15 E2
Skiddaw, *U.K.* 12 C4
Skien, *Norway* 10 E3
Skierniewice, *Poland* . 20 D10
Skikda, *Algeria* 75 A6
Skilloura, *Cyprus* ... 37 D12
Skinári, Ákra, *Greece* . 39 M3
Skipton, *Australia* ... 91 F3
Skipton, *U.K.* 12 D5
Skirmish Pt., *Australia* 90 A1
Skíros, *Greece* 39 L7
Skivarp, *Sweden* ... 11 J7
Skive, *Denmark* 11 H3
Skjálfandafljót →, *Iceland* 8 D5
Skjálfandi, *Iceland* .. 8 C5
Skjeberg, *Norway* ... 10 E5
Skjern, *Denmark* ... 11 J2
Škofja Loka, *Slovenia* 33 B11
Skoghall, *Sweden* ... 9 G12
Skole, *Ukraine* 40 G3
Skópelos, *Greece* ... 39 K6
Skopí, *Greece* 37 D8
Skopje, *Macedonia* .. 39 G4
Skórcz, *Poland* 20 B8
Skövde, *Sweden* ... 9 G12
Skovorodino, *Russia* . 45 D13
Skowhegan, *U.S.A.* . 99 D6

Skownan, *Canada* 101 C9
Skradin, *Croatia* 33 E12
Skreanäs, *Sweden* 11 H6
Skudeneshavn, *Norway* . 9 G8
Skull, *Ireland* 15 E2
Skultorp, *Sweden* 11 F7
Skunk →, *U.S.A.* 108 E9
Skuodas, *Lithuania* 40 C2
Skurup, *Sweden* 11 J7
Skutskär, *Sweden* 10 D11
Skvira, *Ukraine* 42 B3
Skye, *U.K.* 14 D2
Skykomish, *U.S.A.* ... 110 C3
Skyros = Skíros, *Greece* 39 L7
Slagelse, *Denmark* ... 11 J5
Slagharen, *Neths.* ... 16 C9
Slamet, *Indonesia* ... 56 F3
Slaney →, *Ireland* .. 15 D5
Slangerup, *Denmark* . 11 J6
Slano, *Croatia* 21 N7
Slantsy, *Russia* 40 B6
Śląsk, *Poland* 20 E6
Slate Is., *Canada* ... 98 C2
Slatina, *Romania* ... 38 E7
Slaton, *U.S.A.* 109 J4
Slave →, *Canada* .. 100 A6
Slave Coast, *W. Afr.* . 70 F4
Slave Lake, *Canada* . 100 B6
Slave Pt., *Canada* .. 100 A5
Slavgorod, *Russia* .. 44 D8
Slavnoye, *Belorussia* . 40 D5
Slavonska Požega, *Croatia* 21 K7
Slavonski Brod, *Croatia* 21 K8
Slavuta, *Ukraine* ... 40 F5
Slavyanka, *Russia* .. 48 C5
Slavyansk, *Ukraine* . 42 B7
Slavyansk-na-Kubani, *Russia* 42 D8
Sławno, *Poland* 20 A6
Sławoborze, *Poland* . 20 B5
Sleaford, *U.K.* 12 E7
Sleaford B., *Australia* 91 E2
Sleat, Sd. of, *U.K.* . 14 D3
Sleeper Is., *Canada* . 97 C11
Sleepy Eye, *U.S.A.* . 108 C7
Sleidinge, *Belgium* . 17 F3
Sleman, *Indonesia* . 57 G14
Slemon L., *Canada* . 100 A5
Slidell, *U.S.A.* 109 K10
Sliedrecht, *Neths.* . 16 E5
Sliema, *Malta* 37 D2
Slieve Aughty, *Ireland* 15 C3
Slieve Bloom, *Ireland* 15 C4
Slieve Donard, *U.K.* . 15 B6
Slieve Gullion, *U.K.* . 15 B5
Slieve Mish, *Ireland* . 15 D2
Slievenamon, *Ireland* 15 D4
Sligo, *Ireland* 15 B3
Sligo □, *Ireland* ... 15 B3
Sligo B., *Ireland* ... 15 B3
Slijpe, *Belgium* 17 F1
Slikkerveer, *Neths.* . 16 E5
Slite, *Sweden* 9 H15
Sliven, *Bulgaria* ... 38 G9
Slivnitsa, *Bulgaria* . 38 G6
Sljeme, *Croatia* ... 33 C12
Sloan, *U.S.A.* 113 K11
Sloansville, *U.S.A.* . 107 D10
Slobodskoy, *Russia* . 41 B17
Slobozia, *Romania* . 38 E10
Slocan, *Canada* 100 D5
Slochteren, *Neths.* . 16 B9
Slöinge, *Sweden* ... 11 H6
Slonim, *Belorussia* . 40 E4
Slotermeer, *Neths.* . 16 C7
Slough, *U.K.* 13 F7
Sloughhouse, *U.S.A.* 112 G5
Slovak Rep. ■, *Europe* 20 G9
Slovakia = Slovak Rep. ■, *Europe* 20 G9
Slovakian Ore Mts. = Slovenské Rudohorie, *Slovak Rep.* 20 G9
Slovenia ■, *Europe* .. 33 C11
Slovenija = Slovenia ■, *Europe* 33 C11
Slovenj Gradec, *Slovenia* 33 B12
Slovenska Bistrica, *Slovenia* 33 B12
Slovenská Republika = Slovak Rep. ■, *Europe* 20 G9
Slovenské Rudohorie, *Slovak Rep.* 20 G9
Slovyansk = Slavyansk, *Ukraine* 42 B7
Słubice, *Poland* 20 C4
Sluch →, *Ukraine* . 40 F5
Sluis, *Neths.* 17 F2
Slunj, *Croatia* 33 C12
Słupca, *Poland* 20 C7
Słupsk, *Poland* 20 A7
Slurry, *S. Africa* ... 84 D4
Slutsk, *Belorussia* . 40 E5
Slyne Hd., *Ireland* . 15 C1
Slyudyanka, *Russia* . 45 D11
Smålandsfarvandet, *Denmark* 11 J5
Smålandsstenar, *Sweden* 11 G7
Smalltree L., *Canada* 101 A7
Smara, *Morocco* ... 72 B3
Smarje, *Slovenia* ... 33 B12
Smartt Syndicate Dam, *S. Africa* 84 E3
Smartville, *U.S.A.* .. 112 F5
Smeaton, *Canada* ... 101 C8
Smederevo, *Serbia* . 21 L10

Smederevska Palanka, *Serbia* 21 L10
Smela, *Ukraine* 42 B4
Smethport, *U.S.A.* ... 106 E6
Smidovich, *Russia* ... 45 E14
Smilde, *Neths.* 16 C8
Smiley, *Canada* 101 C7
Smith, *Canada* 100 B6
Smith →, *Canada* ... 100 B3
Smith Arm, *Canada* .. 96 B7
Smith Center, *U.S.A.* . 108 F5
Smith Sund, *Greenland* . 4 B4
Smithburne →, *Australia* . 90 B3
Smithers, *Canada* ... 100 C3
Smithfield, *S. Africa* . 85 E4
Smithfield, *N.C., U.S.A.* 105 H6
Smithfield, *Utah, U.S.A.* 110 F8
Smiths Falls, *Canada* . 98 D4
Smithton, *Australia* .. 90 G4
Smithtown, *Australia* . 91 E5
Smithville, *Canada* ... 106 C5
Smithville, *U.S.A.* ... 109 K6
Smoky →, *Canada* .. 100 B5
Smoky Bay, *Australia* . 91 E1
Smoky Falls, *Canada* . 98 B3
Smoky Hill →, *U.S.A.* 108 F6
Smoky Lake, *Canada* . 100 C6
Smøla, *Norway* 10 A2
Smolensk, *Russia* ... 40 D8
Smolikas, Óros, *Greece* 39 J3
Smolník, *Slovak Rep.* . 20 G10
Smolyan, *Bulgaria* .. 39 H7
Smooth Rock Falls, *Canada* 98 C3
Smoothstone L., *Canada* 101 C7
Smorgon, *Belorussia* . 40 D5
Smyadovo, *Bulgaria* . 38 F10
Smyrna = İzmir, *Turkey* 66 D2
Snaefell, *U.K.* 12 C3
Snæfellsjökull, *Iceland* 8 D2
Snake →, *U.S.A.* ... 110 C4
Snake I., *Australia* .. 91 F4
Snake L., *Canada* ... 101 B7
Snake Range, *U.S.A.* . 110 G6
Snake River Plain, *U.S.A.* 110 E7
Snarum, *Norway* ... 10 D3
Snedsted, *Denmark* . 11 H2
Sneek, *Neths.* 16 B7
Sneeker-meer, *Neths.* 16 B7
Sneeuberge, *S. Africa* 84 E3
Snejbjerg, *Denmark* . 11 H2
Snelling, *U.S.A.* ... 112 H6
Snezhnoye, *Ukraine* . 43 C8
Snežnik, *Slovenia* .. 33 C11
Snigirevka, *Ukraine* . 42 C5
Snizort, L., *U.K.* ... 14 D2
Snohomish, *U.S.A.* . 112 C4
Snoul, *Cambodia* ... 59 F6
Snow Hill, *U.S.A.* .. 104 F8
Snow Lake, *Canada* . 101 C8
Snow Mt., *U.S.A.* .. 112 F4
Snowbird L., *Canada* 101 A8
Snowdon, *U.K.* 12 D3
Snowdrift, *Canada* .. 101 A6
Snowdrift →, *Canada* 101 A6
Snowflake, *U.S.A.* .. 111 J8
Snowshoe Pk., *U.S.A.* 110 B6
Snowtown, *Australia* 91 E2
Snowville, *U.S.A.* .. 110 F7
Snowy →, *Australia* 91 F4
Snowy Mts., *Australia* 91 F4
Snug Corner, *Bahamas* 117 B5
Snyatyn, *Ukraine* .. 42 B1
Snyder, *Okla., U.S.A.* 109 H5
Snyder, *Tex., U.S.A.* 109 J4
Soacha, *Colombia* .. 120 C3
Soahanina, *Madag.* . 85 B7
Soalala, *Madag.* ... 85 B8
Soan →, *Pakistan* . 62 C4
Soanierana-Ivongo, *Madag.* 85 B8
Soap Lake, *U.S.A.* . 110 C4
Sobat, Nahr →, *Sudan* 77 F3
Sobhapur, *India* ... 62 H8
Sobinka, *Russia* ... 41 D12
Sobótka, *Poland* ... 20 E6
Sobrado, *Spain* ... 30 B2
Sobral, *Brazil* 122 B3
Sobreira Formosa, *Portugal* 31 F3
Soc Giang, *Vietnam* . 58 A6
Soc Trang, *Vietnam* . 59 H5
Soča →, *Europe* ... 33 B10
Sochaczew, *Poland* . 20 C10
Soch'e = Shache, *China* 54 C2
Sochi, *Russia* 43 E8
Société, Is. de la, *Pac. Oc.* 93 J12
Society Is. = Société, Is. de la, *Pac. Oc.* ... 93 J12
Socompa, Portezuelo de, *Chile* 126 A2
Socorro, *Colombia* .. 120 B3
Socorro, *U.S.A.* ... 111 J10
Socorro, I., *Mexico* . 114 D2
Socotra, *Ind. Oc.* .. 68 E5
Socuéllmos, *Spain* .. 29 F2
Soda L., *U.S.A.* ... 111 J5
Soda Plains, *India* .. 63 B8
Soda Springs, *U.S.A.* 110 E8
Söderhamn, *Sweden* . 9 F14
Söderköping, *Sweden* 9 G14
Södermanlands län □, *Sweden* 10 E11
Södertälje, *Sweden* . 10 E11
Sodiri, *Sudan* 77 E2
Sodo, *Ethiopia* 77 F4
Sodražica, *Slovenia* . 33 C11
Sodus, *U.S.A.* 106 C7

Squillace, G. di

Soekmekaar, *S. Africa* ... 85 C4
Soest, *Germany* ... 18 D4
Soest, *Neths.* ... 16 D6
Soestdijk, *Neths.* ... 16 D6
Sofádhes, *Greece* ... 39 K5
Sofara, *Mali* ... 78 C4
Sofia = Sofiya, *Bulgaria* .. 38 G6
Sofia →, *Madag.* ... 85 B8
Sofievka, *Ukraine* ... 42 B5
Sofiiski, *Russia* ... 45 D14
Sofikón, *Greece* ... 39 M6
Sofiya, *Bulgaria* ... 38 G6
Sōfu-Gan, *Japan* ... 49 K10
Sogakofe, *Ghana* ... 79 D5
Sogamoso, *Colombia* ... 120 B3
Sogār, *Iran* ... 65 E8
Sögel, *Germany* ... 18 C3
Sogn og Fjordane fylke □, *Norway* ... 9 F9
Sogndalsfjøra, *Norway* ... 9 F9
Sognefjorden, *Norway* ... 9 F8
Söğüt, *Turkey* ... 66 C4
Söğüt Gölü, *Turkey* ... 66 E3
Sŏgwi-po, *S. Korea* ... 51 H14
Soh, *Iran* ... 65 C6
Sohâg, *Egypt* ... 76 B3
Sŏhori, *N. Korea* ... 51 D15
Soignies, *Belgium* ... 17 G4
Soira, *Eritrea* ... 77 E4
Soissons, *France* ... 25 C10
Sōja, *Japan* ... 49 G6
Sojat, *India* ... 62 G5
Sok →, *Russia* ... 41 E17
Sokal, *Ukraine* ... 40 F4
Söke, *Turkey* ... 66 E2
Sokelo, *Zaïre* ... 83 D1
Sokhumi = Sukhumi, *Georgia* ... 43 E9
Sokki, Oued In →, *Algeria* 75 C5
Sokna, *Norway* ... 10 D3
Soknedal, *Norway* ... 10 B4
Soko Banja, *Serbia* ... 21 M11
Sokodé, *Togo* ... 79 D5
Sokol, *Russia* ... 41 B12
Sokółka, *Poland* ... 20 B13
Sokolo, *Mali* ... 78 C3
Sokołów Małpolski, *Poland* 20 E12
Sokołów Podlaski, *Poland* 20 C12
Sokoto, *Nigeria* ... 79 C6
Sokoto □, *Nigeria* ... 79 C6
Sokoto →, *Nigeria* ... 79 C5
Sol Iletsk, *Russia* ... 44 D6
Solai, *Kenya* ... 82 B4
Solano, *Phil.* ... 55 C4
Solapur, *India* ... 60 L9
Solares, *Spain* ... 30 B7
Soléa □, *Cyprus* ... 37 D12
Solec Kujawski, *Poland* ... 20 B8
Soledad, *Colombia* ... 120 A3
Soledad, *U.S.A.* ... 111 H3
Soledad, *Venezuela* ... 121 B5
Solent, The, *U.K.* ... 13 G6
Solenzara, *France* ... 27 G13
Solesmes, *France* ... 25 B10
Solfonn, *Norway* ... 9 F9
Solhan, *Turkey* ... 67 D9
Soligalich, *Russia* ... 41 B13
Soligorsk, *Belorussia* ... 40 E5
Solikamsk, *Russia* ... 44 D6
Solila, *Madag.* ... 85 C8
Solimões = Amazonas →, *S. Amer.* ... 121 D7
Solingen, *Germany* ... 17 F10
Sollebrunn, *Sweden* ... 11 F6
Sollefteå, *Sweden* ... 10 A11
Sollentuna, *Sweden* ... 10 E11
Sóller, *Spain* ... 36 B9
Solling, *Germany* ... 18 D5
Solna, *Sweden* ... 10 E12
Solnechnogorsk, *Russia* ... 41 C10
Sologne, *France* ... 25 E8
Solok, *Indonesia* ... 56 E2
Sololá, *Guatemala* ... 116 D1
Solomon, N. Fork →, *U.S.A.* ... 108 F5
Solomon, S. Fork →, *U.S.A.* ... 108 F5
Solomon Is. ■, *Pac. Oc.* .. 92 H7
Solon, *China* ... 54 B7
Solon Springs, *U.S.A.* ... 108 B9
Solonópole, *Brazil* ... 122 C4
Solor, *Indonesia* ... 57 F6
Solotcha, *Russia* ... 41 D11
Solothurn, *Switz.* ... 22 B5
Solothurn □, *Switz.* ... 22 B5
Solsona, *Spain* ... 28 D6
Solta, *Croatia* ... 33 E13
Solṭānābād, *Khorāsān, Iran* 65 C8
Solṭānābād, *Khorāsān, Iran* 65 B8
Solṭānābād, *Markazī, Iran* 65 C6
Soltau, *Germany* ... 18 C5
Soltsy, *Russia* ... 40 B7
Solunska Glava, *Macedonia* 39 H4
Solvang, *U.S.A.* ... 113 L6
Solvay, *U.S.A.* ... 107 C8
Solway Firth, *U.K.* ... 12 C4
Solwezi, *Zambia* ... 83 E2
Sōma, *Japan* ... 48 F10
Soma, *Turkey* ... 66 D2
Somali Rep. ■, *Africa* ... 68 F4
Somalia ■ = Somali Rep. ■, *Africa* ... 68 F4
Sombernon, *France* ... 25 E11
Sombor, *Serbia* ... 21 K9
Sombra, *Canada* ... 106 D2
Sombrerete, *Mexico* ... 114 C4
Sombrero, *Anguilla* ... 117 C7
Someren, *Neths.* ... 17 F7
Somers, *U.S.A.* ... 110 B6
Somerset, *Canada* ... 101 D9
Somerset, *Colo., U.S.A.* .. 111 G10
Somerset, *Ky., U.S.A.* ... 104 G3
Somerset, *Mass., U.S.A.* .. 107 E13
Somerset, *Pa., U.S.A.* ... 106 F5
Somerset □, *U.K.* ... 13 F5
Somerset East, *S. Africa* .. 84 E4
Somerset I., *Canada* ... 96 A10
Somerset West, *S. Africa* . 84 E2
Somerton, *U.S.A.* ... 111 K6
Somerville, *U.S.A.* ... 107 F10
Someş →, *Romania* ... 38 B5
Someşul Mare →, *Romania* ... 38 B7
Somma Lombardo, *Italy* .. 32 C5
Somma Vesuviana, *Italy* .. 35 B7
Sommariva, *Australia* ... 91 D4
Sommatino, *Italy* ... 34 E6
Somme □, *France* ... 25 C9
Somme →, *France* ... 25 B8
Somme, B. de la, *France* . 24 B8
Sommelsdijk, *Neths.* ... 16 E4
Sommepy-Tahure, *France* . 25 C11
Sömmerda, *Germany* ... 18 D7
Sommesous, *France* ... 25 D11
Sommières, *France* ... 27 E8
Somoto, *Nic.* ... 116 D2
Sompolno, *Poland* ... 20 C8
Somport, Paso, *Spain* ... 28 C4
Somport, Puerto de, *Spain* 28 C4
Somuncurá, Meseta de, *Argentina* ... 128 B3
Son, *Neths.* ... 17 E6
Son, *Norway* ... 10 E4
Son, *Spain* ... 30 C2
Son Ha, *Vietnam* ... 58 E7
Son Hoa, *Vietnam* ... 58 F7
Son La, *Vietnam* ... 58 B4
Son Tay, *Vietnam* ... 58 B5
Soná, *Panama* ... 116 E3
Sonamarg, *India* ... 63 B6
Sonamukhi, *India* ... 63 H12
Sŏnchŏn, *N. Korea* ... 51 E13
Soncino, *Italy* ... 32 C6
Sondags →, *S. Africa* ... 84 E4
Sóndalo, *Italy* ... 32 B7
Sondar, *India* ... 63 C6
Sønder Omme, *Denmark* .. 11 J2
Sønder Tornby, *Denmark* . 11 G3
Sønderborg, *Denmark* ... 11 K3
Sønderjyllands Amtskommune □, *Denmark* ... 11 J3
Sondershausen, *Germany* . 18 D6
Søndre Strømfjord, *Greenland* ... 97 B14
Sóndrio, *Italy* ... 32 B6
Sone, *Mozam.* ... 83 F3
Sonepur, *India* ... 61 J13
Song, *Thailand* ... 58 C3
Song Cau, *Vietnam* ... 58 F7
Song Xian, *China* ... 50 G7
Songchŏn, *N. Korea* ... 51 E14
Songea, *Tanzania* ... 83 E4
Songea □, *Tanzania* ... 83 E4
Songeons, *France* ... 25 C8
Songhua Hu, *China* ... 51 C14
Songhua Jiang →, *China* . 54 B8
Songjiang, *China* ... 53 B13
Songjin, *N. Korea* ... 51 D15
Songjŏng-ni, *S. Korea* ... 51 G14
Songkan, *China* ... 52 C6
Songkhla, *Thailand* ... 59 J3
Songming, *China* ... 52 E4
Songnim, *N. Korea* ... 51 E13
Songpan, *China* ... 52 A4
Songtao, *China* ... 52 C7
Songwe, *Zaïre* ... 82 C2
Songwe →, *Africa* ... 83 D3
Songxi, *China* ... 53 D12
Songzi, *China* ... 53 B8
Sonid Youqi, *China* ... 50 C7
Sonipat, *India* ... 62 E7
Sonkovo, *Russia* ... 41 C10
Sonmiani, *Pakistan* ... 62 G2
Sonnino, *Italy* ... 34 A6
Sono →, *Goiás, Brazil* ... 122 C2
Sono →, *Minas Gerais, Brazil* ... 123 E2
Sonogno, *Switz.* ... 23 D7
Sonora, *Calif., U.S.A.* ... 111 H3
Sonora, *Tex., U.S.A.* ... 109 K4
Sonora □, *Mexico* ... 114 B2
Sonora →, *Mexico* ... 114 B2
Sonora Desert, *U.S.A.* ... 113 M12
Sonoyta, *Mexico* ... 114 A2
Sŏnsan, *S. Korea* ... 51 F15
Sonsonate, *El Salv.* ... 116 D2
Sonthofen, *Germany* ... 19 H6
Soochow = Suzhou, *China* 53 B13
Sop Hao, *Laos* ... 58 B5
Sop Prap, *Thailand* ... 58 D2
Sopachuy, *Bolivia* ... 125 D5
Sopi, *Indonesia* ... 57 D7
Sopo, Nahr →, *Sudan* ... 77 F2
Sopot, *Poland* ... 20 A8
Sopotnica, *Macedonia* ... 39 H4
Sopron, *Hungary* ... 21 H6
Sop's Arm, *Canada* ... 99 C8
Sopur, *India* ... 63 B6
Sør-Rondane, *Antarctica* .. 5 D4
Sør-Trøndelag fylke □, *Norway* ... 10 B3
Sora, *Italy* ... 34 A6
Sorah, *Pakistan* ... 62 F3
Söråker, *Sweden* ... 10 B11
Sorano, *Italy* ... 33 F8
Sorata, *Bolivia* ... 124 D4
Sorbas, *Spain* ... 29 H2
Sorel, *Canada* ... 98 C5
Sörenberg, *Switz.* ... 22 C6
Soreq, N. →, *Israel* ... 69 D3
Soresina, *Italy* ... 32 C6
Sorgono, *Italy* ... 34 B2
Sorgues, *France* ... 27 D8
Sorgun, *Turkey* ... 66 D6
Soria, *Spain* ... 28 D2
Soria □, *Spain* ... 28 D2
Soriano, *Uruguay* ... 126 C4
Soriano nel Cimino, *Italy* . 33 F9
Sorkh, Kuh-e, *Iran* ... 65 C8
Sorø, *Denmark* ... 11 J5
Soro, *Guinea* ... 78 C3
Sorocaba, *Brazil* ... 127 A6
Soroki, *Moldavia* ... 42 B3
Soron, *India* ... 63 F8
Sorong, *Indonesia* ... 57 E8
Soroní, *Greece* ... 37 C10
Soroti, *Uganda* ... 82 B3
Sørøya, *Norway* ... 8 A17
Sørøysundet, *Norway* ... 8 A17
Sorraia →, *Portugal* ... 31 G2
Sorrento, *Australia* ... 91 F3
Sorrento, *Italy* ... 35 B7
Sorsele, *Sweden* ... 8 D14
Sorso, *Italy* ... 34 B1
Sorsogon, *Phil.* ... 55 E6
Sortino, *Italy* ... 35 E8
Sorvizhi, *Russia* ... 41 C16
Sos, *Spain* ... 28 C3
Sŏsan, *S. Korea* ... 51 F14
Soscumica, L., *Canada* ... 98 B4
Sosna →, *Russia* ... 41 E11
Sosnovka, *Russia* ... 41 E12
Sosnovka, *Russia* ... 45 D11
Sosnowiec, *Poland* ... 20 E9
Sospel, *France* ... 27 E11
Sostanj, *Slovenia* ... 33 B12
Sŏsura, *N. Korea* ... 51 C16
Soto la Marina →, *Mexico* 115 C5
Soto y Amío, *Spain* ... 30 C5
Sotteville-lès-Rouen, *France* 24 C8
Sotuta, *Mexico* ... 115 C7
Souanké, *Congo* ... 80 D2
Soúdha, *Greece* ... 37 D6
Soúdhas, Kólpos, *Greece* . 37 D6
Sougne-Remouchamps, *Belgium* ... 17 H7
Souillac, *France* ... 26 D5
Souk-Ahras, *Algeria* ... 75 A6
Souk el Arba du Rharb, *Morocco* ... 74 B3
Soukhouma, *Laos* ... 58 E5
Sŏul, *S. Korea* ... 51 F14
Soulac-sur-Mer, *France* .. 26 C2
Soultz-sous-Forêts, *France* 25 D14
Soumagne, *Belgium* ... 17 G7
Sound, The = Øresund, *Europe* ... 11 J6
Sound, The, *U.K.* ... 13 G3
Soúnion, Ákra, *Greece* ... 39 M7
Sour el Ghozlane, *Algeria* 75 A5
Sources, Mt. aux, *Lesotho* 85 D4
Sourdeval, *France* ... 24 D6
Soure, *Brazil* ... 122 B2
Soure, *Portugal* ... 30 E2
Souris, *Man., Canada* ... 101 D8
Souris, *P.E.I., Canada* ... 99 C7
Souris →, *Canada* ... 108 A5
Sousa, *Brazil* ... 122 C4
Sousel, *Brazil* ... 122 B1
Sousel, *Portugal* ... 31 G3
Souss, O. →, *Morocco* ... 74 B3
Sousse, *Tunisia* ... 75 A7
Soustons, *France* ... 26 E2
South Africa ■, *Africa* ... 84 E3
South Aulatsivik I., *Canada* 99 A7
South Australia □, *Australia* ... 91 E2
South Baldy, *U.S.A.* ... 111 J10
South Bend, *Ind., U.S.A.* . 104 E2
South Bend, *Wash., U.S.A.* 112 D3
South Boston, *U.S.A.* ... 105 G6
South Branch, *Canada* ... 99 C8
South Brook, *Canada* ... 99 C8
South Buganda □, *Uganda* 82 C3
South Carolina □, *U.S.A.* 105 J5
South Charleston, *U.S.A.* . 104 F5
South China Sea, *Asia* ... 56 C4
South Dakota □, *U.S.A.* . 108 C5
South Downs, *U.K.* ... 13 G7
South East C., *Australia* .. 90 G4
South East Is., *Australia* .. 89 F3
South Esk →, *U.K.* ... 14 E5
South Foreland, *U.K.* ... 13 F9
South Fork →, *U.S.A.* ... 110 C7
South Fork, American →, *U.S.A.* ... 112 G5
South Fork, Feather →, *U.S.A.* ... 112 F5
South Georgia, *Antarctica* 5 B1
South Glamorgan □, *U.K.* 13 F4
South Haven, *U.S.A.* ... 104 D2
South Henik, L., *Canada* . 101 A9
South Honshu Ridge, *Pac. Oc.* ... 92 E6
South Horr, *Kenya* ... 82 B4
South I., *Kenya* ... 82 B4
South I., *N.Z.* ... 87 L3
South Invercargill, *N.Z.* .. 87 M2
South Knife →, *Canada* .. 101 B10
South Korea ■, *Asia* ... 51 F15
South Lake Tahoe, *U.S.A.* 112 G6
South Loup →, *U.S.A.* .. 108 E5
South Magnetic Pole, *Antarctica* ... 5 C9
South Milwaukee, *U.S.A.* . 104 D2
South Molton, *U.K.* ... 13 F4
South Nahanni →, *Canada* 100 A4
South Natuna Is. = Natuna Selatan, Kepulauan, *Indonesia* ... 59 L7
South Negril Pt., *Jamaica* . 116 C4
South Orkney Is., *Antarctica* ... 5 C18
South Pagai, I. = Pagai Selatan, P., *Indonesia* .. 56 E2
South Pass, *U.S.A.* ... 110 E9
South Pittsburg, *U.S.A.* ... 105 H3
South Platte →, *U.S.A.* .. 108 E4
South Pole, *Antarctica* ... 5 E
South Porcupine, *Canada* . 98 C3
South River, *Canada* ... 98 C4
South River, *U.S.A.* ... 107 F10
South Ronaldsay, *U.K.* ... 14 C6
South Sandwich Is., *Antarctica* ... 5 B1
South Saskatchewan →, *Canada* ... 101 C7
South Seal →, *Canada* ... 101 B9
South Shetland Is., *Antarctica* ... 5 C18
South Shields, *U.K.* ... 12 C6
South Sioux City, *U.S.A.* . 108 D6
South Taranaki Bight, *N.Z.* 87 H5
South Thompson →, *Canada* ... 100 C4
South Twin I., *Canada* ... 98 B4
South Tyne →, *U.K.* ... 12 C5
South Uist, *U.K.* ... 14 D1
South West Africa = Namibia ■, *Africa* ... 84 C2
South West C., *Australia* . 90 G4
South Yorkshire □, *U.K.* . 12 D6
Southampton, *Canada* ... 98 D3
Southampton, *U.K.* ... 13 G6
Southampton, *U.S.A.* ... 107 F12
Southampton I., *Canada* .. 97 B11
Southbridge, *N.Z.* ... 87 K4
Southbridge, *U.S.A.* ... 107 D12
Southend, *Canada* ... 101 B8
Southend-on-Sea, *U.K.* ... 13 F8
Southern □, *Malawi* ... 83 F4
Southern □, *S. Leone* ... 78 D2
Southern □, *Zambia* ... 83 F2
Southern Alps, *N.Z.* ... 87 K3
Southern Cross, *Australia* . 89 F2
Southern Hills, *Australia* .. 89 F3
Southern Indian L., *Canada* 101 B9
Southern Ocean, *Antarctica* 5 C6
Southern Pines, *U.S.A.* ... 105 H6
Southern Uplands, *U.K.* .. 14 F5
Southington, *U.S.A.* ... 107 E12
Southold, *U.S.A.* ... 107 E12
Southport, *Australia* ... 91 D5
Southport, *U.K.* ... 12 D4
Southport, *U.S.A.* ... 105 J6
Southwest C., *N.Z.* ... 87 M1
Southwold, *U.K.* ... 13 E9
Soutpansberg, *S. Africa* ... 85 C4
Souvigny, *France* ... 26 B7
Sovetsk, *Russia* ... 40 D2
Sovetsk, *Russia* ... 41 C16
Sovetskaya Gavan, *Russia* 45 E15
Sovicille, *Italy* ... 33 E8
Soviet Union = Commonwealth of Independent States ■, *Eurasia* ... 45 D11
Sovra, *Croatia* ... 21 N7
Soweto, *S. Africa* ... 85 D4
Sōya-Kaikyō = La Perouse Str., *Asia* ... 48 B11
Sōya-Misaki, *Japan* ... 48 B10
Soyo, *Angola* ... 80 F2
Sozh →, *Belorussia* ... 40 F7
Sozopol, *Bulgaria* ... 38 G10
Spa, *Belgium* ... 17 H7
Spain ■, *Europe* ... 7 H5
Spakenburg, *Neths.* ... 16 D6
Spalding, *Australia* ... 91 E2
Spalding, *U.K.* ... 12 E7
Spalding, *U.S.A.* ... 108 E5
Spangler, *U.S.A.* ... 106 F6
Spaniard's Bay, *Canada* ... 99 C9
Spanish, *Canada* ... 98 C3
Spanish Fork, *U.S.A.* ... 110 F8
Spanish Town, *Jamaica* ... 116 C4
Sparks, *U.S.A.* ... 112 F7
Sparta = Spárti, *Greece* ... 39 M5
Sparta, *Ga., U.S.A.* ... 105 J4
Sparta, *Wis., U.S.A.* ... 108 D9
Spartanburg, *U.S.A.* ... 105 H4
Spartansburg, *U.S.A.* ... 106 E5
Spartel, C., *Morocco* ... 74 A3
Spárti, *Greece* ... 39 M5
Spartivento, C., *Calabria, Italy* ... 35 E9
Spartivento, C., *Sard., Italy* 34 D1
Spas-Demensk, *Russia* ... 40 D8
Spas-Klepiki, *Russia* ... 41 D12
Spassk-Dalniy, *Russia* ... 45 E14
Spassk-Ryazanskiy, *Russia* 41 D12
Spátha, Ákra, *Greece* ... 37 D5
Spatsizi →, *Canada* ... 100 B3
Spearfish, *U.S.A.* ... 108 C3
Spearman, *U.S.A.* ... 109 G4
Speer, *Switz.* ... 23 B8
Speers, *Canada* ... 101 C7
Speightstown, *Barbados* .. 117 D8
Speke Gulf, *Tanzania* ... 82 C3
Spekholzerheide, *Neths.* ... 17 G8
Spence Bay, *Canada* ... 96 B10
Spencer, *Idaho, U.S.A.* ... 110 D7
Spencer, *Iowa, U.S.A.* ... 108 D7
Spencer, *N.Y., U.S.A.* ... 107 D8
Spencer, *Nebr., U.S.A.* ... 108 D5
Spencer, *W. Va., U.S.A.* . 104 F5
Spencer, C., *Australia* ... 91 F2
Spencer B., *Namibia* ... 84 D1
Spencer G., *Australia* ... 91 E2
Spencerville, *Canada* ... 107 B9
Spences Bridge, *Canada* .. 100 C4
Spenser Mts., *N.Z.* ... 87 K4
Sperkhiós →, *Greece* ... 39 L5
Sperrin Mts., *U.K.* ... 15 B5
Spessart, *Germany* ... 19 E5
Spétsai, *Greece* ... 39 M6
Spey →, *U.K.* ... 14 D5
Speyer, *Germany* ... 19 F4
Speyer →, *Germany* ... 19 F4
Spezzano Albanese, *Italy* . 35 C9
Spiekeroog, *Germany* ... 18 B3
Spielfeld, *Austria* ... 33 B12
Spiez, *Switz.* ... 22 C5
Spijk, *Neths.* ... 16 B9
Spijkenisse, *Neths.* ... 16 E4
Spíli, *Greece* ... 37 D6
Spilimbergo, *Italy* ... 33 B9
Spin Baldak = Qala-i-Jadid, *Afghan.* ... 62 D2
Spinalónga, *Greece* ... 37 D7
Spinazzola, *Italy* ... 35 B9
Spirit Lake, *Idaho, U.S.A.* 110 C5
Spirit Lake, *Wash., U.S.A.* 112 D4
Spirit River, *Canada* ... 100 B5
Spiritwood, *Canada* ... 101 C7
Spišská Nová Ves, *Slovak Rep.* ... 20 G10
Spithead, *U.K.* ... 13 G6
Spittal, *Austria* ... 21 J3
Spitzbergen = Svalbard, *Arctic* ... 4 B8
Split, *Croatia* ... 33 E13
Split L., *Canada* ... 101 B9
Splitski Kanal, *Croatia* ... 33 E13
Splügen, *Switz.* ... 23 C8
Splügenpass, *Switz.* ... 23 C8
Spofford, *U.S.A.* ... 109 L4
Spokane, *U.S.A.* ... 110 C5
Spoleto, *Italy* ... 33 F9
Spooner, *U.S.A.* ... 108 C9
Sporyy Navolok, Mys, *Russia* ... 44 B7
Spragge, *Canada* ... 98 C3
Sprague, *U.S.A.* ... 110 C5
Sprague River, *U.S.A.* ... 110 E3
Spratly I., *S. China Sea* ... 56 C4
Spray, *U.S.A.* ... 110 D4
Spree →, *Germany* ... 18 C9
Spremberg, *Germany* ... 18 D10
Sprimont, *Belgium* ... 17 G7
Spring City, *U.S.A.* ... 110 G8
Spring Garden, *U.S.A.* ... 112 F6
Spring Mts., *U.S.A.* ... 111 H6
Spring Valley, *Calif., U.S.A.* ... 113 N10
Spring Valley, *Minn., U.S.A.* ... 108 D8
Springbok, *S. Africa* ... 84 D2
Springdale, *Canada* ... 99 C8
Springdale, *Ark., U.S.A.* . 109 G7
Springdale, *Wash., U.S.A.* 110 B5
Springe, *Germany* ... 18 C5
Springer, *U.S.A.* ... 109 G2
Springerville, *U.S.A.* ... 111 J9
Springfield, *Canada* ... 106 D4
Springfield, *N.Z.* ... 87 K3
Springfield, *Colo., U.S.A.* . 109 G3
Springfield, *Ill., U.S.A.* ... 108 F10
Springfield, *Mass., U.S.A.* 107 D12
Springfield, *Mo., U.S.A.* . 109 G8
Springfield, *Ohio, U.S.A.* . 104 F4
Springfield, *Oreg., U.S.A.* 110 D2
Springfield, *Tenn., U.S.A.* 105 G2
Springfield, *Vt., U.S.A.* .. 107 C12
Springfontein, *S. Africa* .. 84 E4
Springhill, *Canada* ... 99 C7
Springhouse, *Canada* ... 100 C4
Springhurst, *Australia* ... 91 F4
Springs, *S. Africa* ... 85 D4
Springsure, *Australia* ... 90 C4
Springvale, *Queens., Australia* ... 90 C3
Springvale, *W. Austral., Australia* ... 88 C4
Springvale, *U.S.A.* ... 107 C14
Springville, *Calif., U.S.A.* 112 J8
Springville, *N.Y., U.S.A.* . 106 D6
Springville, *Utah, U.S.A.* . 110 F8
Springwater, *Canada* ... 101 C7
Spruce-Creek, *U.S.A.* ... 106 F6
Spur, *U.S.A.* ... 109 J4
Spurn Hd., *U.K.* ... 12 D8
Spuž, *Montenegro* ... 21 N9
Spuzzum, *Canada* ... 100 D4
Squam L., *U.S.A.* ... 107 C13
Squamish, *Canada* ... 100 D4
Square Islands, *Canada* ... 99 B8
Squillace, G. di, *Italy* ... 35 D9

Squinzano

Squinzano, Italy 35 B11
Squires, Mt., Australia 89 E4
Sragen, Indonesia 57 G14
Srbac, Bos.-H 21 K7
Srbija = Serbia □, Yugoslavia 21 M11
Srbobran, Serbia, Yug. 21 K9
Sre Khtum, Cambodia 59 F6
Sre Umbell, Cambodia 59 G4
Srebrnica, Bos.-H. 21 L9
Sredinny Ra. = Sredinnyy Khrebet, Russia 45 D16
Sredinnyy Khrebet, Russia 45 D16
Središče, Slovenia 33 B13
Sredna Gora, Bulgaria 38 G7
Sredne Tambovskoye, Russia 45 D14
Srednekolymsk, Russia 45 C16
Srednevilyuysk, Russia 45 C13
Śrem, Poland 20 C7
Sremska Mitrovica, Serbia, Yug. 21 L9
Srepok →, Cambodia 58 F6
Sretensk, Russia 45 D12
Sri Lanka ■, Asia 60 R12
Srikakulam, India 61 K13
Srinagar, India 63 B6
Środa Wielkopolski, Poland 20 C7
Srpska Itabej, Serbia, Yug. 21 K10
Staaten →, Australia 90 B3
Staberhuk, Germany 18 A7
Stabroek, Belgium 17 F4
Stad Delden, Neths. 16 D9
Stade, Germany 18 B5
Staden, Belgium 17 G2
Staðarhólskirkja, Iceland 8 D3
Städjan, Sweden 10 C6
Stadlandet, Norway 8 E8
Stadskanaal, Neths. 16 B9
Stadthagen, Germany 18 C5
Stadtlohn, Germany 18 D2
Stadtroda, Germany 18 E7
Stäfa, Switz. 23 B7
Stafafell, Iceland 8 D6
Staffa, U.K. 14 E2
Stafford, U.K. 12 E5
Stafford, U.S.A. 109 G5
Stafford Springs, U.S.A. 107 E12
Staffordshire □, U.K. 12 E5
Stagnone, Italy 34 E5
Staines, U.K. 13 F7
Stakhanov = Kadiyevka, Ukraine 43 B8
Stalden, Switz. 22 D5
Stalingrad = Volgograd, Russia 43 B11
Staliniri = Tskhinvali, Georgia 43 E11
Stalino = Donetsk, Ukraine 42 C7
Stalinogorsk = Novomoskovsk, Russia 41 D11
Stalís, Greece 37 D7
Stalowa Wola, Poland 20 E12
Stalybridge, U.K. 12 D5
Stamford, Australia 90 C3
Stamford, U.K. 13 E7
Stamford, Conn., U.S.A. 107 E11
Stamford, Tex., U.S.A. 109 J5
Stamps, U.S.A. 109 J8
Stanberry, U.S.A. 108 E7
Stančevo = Kalipetrovo, Bulgaria 38 E10
Standerton, S. Africa 85 D4
Standish, U.S.A. 104 D4
Stanford, U.S.A. 110 C8
Stange, Norway 10 D5
Stanger, S. Africa 85 D5
Stanislaus →, U.S.A. 112 H5
Stanislav = Ivano-Frankovsk, Ukraine 40 G4
Stanke Dimitrov, Bulgaria 38 G6
Stanley, Australia 90 G4
Stanley, N.B., Canada 99 C6
Stanley, Sask., Canada 101 B8
Stanley, Falk. Is. 128 D5
Stanley, Idaho, U.S.A. 110 D6
Stanley, N. Dak., U.S.A. 108 A3
Stanley, N.Y., U.S.A. 106 D7
Stanley, Wis., U.S.A. 108 C9
Stanovoy Khrebet, Russia 45 D13
Stanovoy Ra. = Stanovoy Khrebet, Russia 45 D13
Stans, Switz. 23 C6
Stansmore Ra., Australia 88 D4
Stanthorpe, Australia 91 D5
Stanton, U.S.A. 109 J4
Stanwood, U.S.A. 112 B4
Staphorst, Neths. 16 C8
Staples, U.S.A. 108 B7
Stapleton, U.S.A. 108 E4
Star City, Canada 101 C8
Stara-minskaya, Russia 43 C8
Stara Moravica, Serbia, Yug. 21 K9
Stara Planina, Bulgaria 38 F6
Stara Zagora, Bulgaria 38 G8
Starachowice, Poland 20 D11
Starashcherbinovskaya, Russia 43 C8
Staraya Russa, Russia 40 C7
Starbuck I., Kiribati 93 H12
Stargard Szczeciński, Poland 20 B5
Stari Trg, Slovenia 33 C12
Staritsa, Russia 40 C9
Starke, U.S.A. 105 K4
Starkville, Colo., U.S.A. 109 G2
Starkville, Miss., U.S.A. 105 J1
Starnberg, Germany 19 G7
Starnberger See, Germany 19 H7
Starobelsk, Ukraine 43 B8
Starodub, Russia 40 E8
Starogard, Poland 20 B8
Starokonstantinov, Ukraine 42 B2
Start Pt., U.K. 13 G4
Staryy Biryuzyak, Russia 43 D12
Staryy Chartoriysk, Ukraine 40 F4
Staryy Kheydzhan, Russia 45 C15
Staryy Krym, Ukraine 42 D6
Staryy Oskol, Russia 41 F10
Stassfurt, Germany 18 D7
State College, U.S.A. 106 F7
Stateline, U.S.A. 112 G7
Staten, I. = Estados, I. de Los, Argentina 128 D4
Staten I., U.S.A. 107 F10
Statesboro, U.S.A. 105 J5
Statesville, U.S.A. 105 H5
Stauffer, U.S.A. 113 L7
Staunton, Ill., U.S.A. 108 F10
Staunton, Va., U.S.A. 104 F6
Stavanger, Norway 9 G8
Staveley, N.Z. 87 K3
Stavelot, Belgium 17 H7
Stavenhagen, Germany 18 B8
Stavenisse, Neths. 17 E4
Staveren, Neths. 16 C6
Stavern, Norway 10 F4
Stavre, Sweden 10 B9
Stavropol, Russia 43 D10
Stavros, Cyprus 37 D11
Stavrós, Greece 37 D6
Stavrós, Ákra, Greece 37 D6
Stavroúpolis, Greece 39 H7
Stawell, Australia 91 F3
Stawell →, Australia 90 C3
Stawiszyn, Poland 20 D8
Stayner, Canada 106 B4
Steamboat Springs, U.S.A. 110 F10
Steckborn, Switz. 23 A7
Steele, U.S.A. 108 B5
Steelton, U.S.A. 106 F8
Steelville, U.S.A. 109 G9
Steen River, Canada 100 B5
Steenbergen, Neths. 17 E4
Steenkool = Bintuni, Indonesia 57 E8
Steenvoorde, France 25 B9
Steenwijk, Neths. 16 C8
Steep Pt., Australia 89 E1
Steep Rock, Canada 101 C9
Ştefăneşti, Romania 38 B10
Stefanie L. = Chew Bahir, Ethiopia 77 G4
Stefansson Bay, Antarctica 5 C5
Steffisburg, Switz. 22 C5
Stege, Denmark 11 K6
Steiermark □, Austria 21 H5
Steigerwald, Germany 19 F6
Steilacoom, U.S.A. 112 C4
Stein, Neths. 17 G7
Steinbach, Canada 101 D9
Steinfort, Lux. 17 J7
Steinfurt, Germany 18 C3
Steinheim, Germany 18 D5
Steinhuder Meer, Germany 18 C5
Steinkjer, Norway 8 E11
Steinkopf, S. Africa 84 D2
Stekene, Belgium 17 F4
Stellarton, Canada 99 C7
Stellenbosch, S. Africa 84 E2
Stellendam, Neths. 16 E4
Stelvio, Paso dello, Italy 23 C10
Stemshaug, Norway 10 A2
Stendal, Germany 18 C7
Stene, Belgium 17 F1
Stensele, Sweden 8 D14
Stenstorp, Sweden 11 F7
Stepanakert = Khankendy, Azerbaijan 67 D12
Stephen, U.S.A. 108 A6
Stephens Creek, Australia 91 E3
Stephens I., Canada 100 C2
Stephenville, Canada 99 C8
Stephenville, U.S.A. 109 J5
Stepnica, Poland 20 B4
Stepnoi = Elista, Russia 43 C11
Stepnyak, Kazakhstan 44 D8
Steppe, Asia 46 E9
Sterkstroom, S. Africa 84 E4
Sterling, Colo., U.S.A. 108 E3
Sterling, Ill., U.S.A. 108 E10
Sterling, Kans., U.S.A. 108 F5
Sterling City, U.S.A. 109 K4
Sterling Run, U.S.A. 106 E6
Sterlitamak, Russia 44 D6
Sternberg, Germany 18 B7
Šternberk, Czech. 20 F7
Stérnes, Greece 37 D6
Stettin = Szczecin, Poland 20 B4
Stettiner Haff, Germany 18 B10
Stettler, Canada 100 C6
Steubenville, U.S.A. 106 F4
Stevens Point, U.S.A. 108 C10
Stevenson, U.S.A. 112 E5
Stevenson L., Canada 101 C9
Stevns Klint, Denmark 11 J6
Stewart, B.C., Canada 100 B3
Stewart, N.W.T., Canada 96 B6
Stewart, U.S.A. 112 F7
Stewart, C., Australia 90 A1
Stewart, I., Chile 128 D2
Stewart I., N.Z. 87 M1
Stewarts Point, U.S.A. 112 G3
Stewiacke, Canada 99 C7
Steynsburg, S. Africa 84 E4
Steyr, Austria 21 G4
Steytlerville, S. Africa 84 E3
Stia, Italy 33 E8
Stiens, Neths. 16 B7
Stigler, U.S.A. 109 H7
Stigliano, Italy 35 B9
Stigsnæs, Denmark 11 J5
Stigtomta, Sweden 11 F10
Stikine →, Canada 100 B2
Stilfontein, S. Africa 84 D4
Stilís, Greece 39 L5
Stillwater, N.Z. 87 K3
Stillwater, Minn., U.S.A. 108 C8
Stillwater, N.Y., U.S.A. 107 D11
Stillwater, Okla., U.S.A. 109 G6
Stillwater Range, U.S.A. 110 G4
Stilwell, U.S.A. 109 H7
Štip, Macedonia 39 H5
Stíra, Greece 39 L7
Stirling, Australia 90 B3
Stirling, Canada 100 D6
Stirling, U.K. 14 E5
Stirling Ra., Australia 89 F2
Stittsville, Canada 107 A9
Stockach, Germany 19 H5
Stockerau, Austria 21 G6
Stockett, U.S.A. 110 C8
Stockholm, Sweden 10 E12
Stockholms län □, Sweden 10 E12
Stockhorn, Switz. 22 C5
Stockport, U.K. 12 D5
Stockton, Calif., U.S.A. 111 H3
Stockton, Kans., U.S.A. 108 F5
Stockton, Mo., U.S.A. 109 G8
Stockton-on-Tees, U.K. 12 C6
Stockvik, Sweden 10 B11
Stöde, Sweden 10 B10
Stogovo, Macedonia 39 H3
Stoke on Trent, U.K. 12 D5
Stokes Bay, Canada 98 C3
Stokes Pt., Australia 90 G3
Stokes Ra., Australia 88 C5
Stokkseyri, Iceland 8 E3
Stokksnes, Iceland 8 D6
Stolac, Bos.-H. 21 M7
Stolberg, Germany 18 E2
Stolbovaya, Russia 41 D10
Stolbovaya, Russia 45 C16
Stolbovoy, Ostrov, Russia 45 D17
Stolbtsy, Belorussia 40 E5
Stolin, Belorussia 40 F5
Stolwijk, Neths. 16 E5
Stomíon, Greece 37 D5
Ston, Croatia 21 N7
Stonehaven, U.K. 14 E6
Stonehenge, Australia 90 C3
Stonewall, Canada 101 C9
Stony L., Man., Canada 101 B9
Stony L., Ont., Canada 106 B6
Stony Rapids, Canada 101 B7
Stony Tunguska = Podkamennaya Tunguska →, Russia 45 C10
Stonyford, U.S.A. 112 F4
Stopnica, Poland 20 E10
Stora Lulevatten, Sweden 8 C15
Stora Sjöfallet, Sweden 8 C15
Storavan, Sweden 8 D15
Store Bælt, Denmark 11 J5
Store Creek, Australia 91 E4
Store Heddinge, Denmark 11 J6
Støren, Norway 10 A4
Storlulea = Stora Lulevatten, Sweden 8 C15
Storm B., Australia 90 G4
Storm Lake, U.S.A. 108 D7
Stormberge, S. Africa 84 E4
Stormsrivier, S. Africa 84 E3
Stornoway, U.K. 14 C2
Storozhinets, Ukraine 42 B1
Storsjö, Sweden 10 B7
Storsjøen, Hedmark, Norway 10 D5
Storsjøen, Hedmark, Norway 10 C5
Storsjön, Sweden 10 B7
Storstrøms Amt. □, Denmark 11 K5
Storuman, Sweden 8 D14
Stoughton, Canada 101 D8
Stour →, Dorset, U.K. 13 G5
Stour →, Here. & Worcs., U.K. 13 E5
Stour →, Kent, U.K. 13 F9
Stour →, Suffolk, U.K. 13 F9
Stourbridge, U.K. 13 E5
Stout, L., Canada 101 C10
Stove Pipe Wells Village, U.S.A. 113 J9
Stowmarket, U.K. 13 E9
Strabane, U.K. 15 B4
Strabane □, U.K. 15 B4
Stracin, Macedonia 38 G5
Stradella, Italy 32 C6
Strahan, Australia 90 G4
Strakonice, Czech. 20 F3
Straldzha, Bulgaria 38 G9
Stralsund, Germany 18 A9
Strand, S. Africa 84 E2
Strangford L., U.K. 15 B6
Strängnäs, Sweden 10 E11
Strangsville, U.S.A. 106 E3
Stranraer, U.K. 14 G3
Strasbourg, Canada 101 C8
Strasbourg, France 25 D14
Strasburg, Germany 18 B9
Strasburg, U.S.A. 108 B4
Strassen, Lux. 17 J8
Stratford, Canada 98 D3
Stratford, N.Z. 87 H5
Stratford, Calif., U.S.A. 111 H4
Stratford, Conn., U.S.A. 107 E11
Stratford, Tex., U.S.A. 109 G3
Stratford-upon-Avon, U.K. 13 E6
Strath Spey, U.K. 14 D5
Strathalbyn, Australia 91 F2
Strathclyde □, U.K. 14 F4
Strathcona Prov. Park, Canada 100 D3
Strathmore, Australia 90 B3
Strathmore, Canada 100 C6
Strathmore, U.K. 14 E5
Strathmore, U.S.A. 112 J7
Strathnaver, Canada 100 C4
Strathpeffer, U.K. 14 D4
Strathroy, Canada 98 D3
Strathy Pt., U.K. 14 C4
Stratton, U.S.A. 108 F3
Straubing, Germany 19 G8
Straumnes, Iceland 8 C2
Strausberg, Germany 18 C9
Strawberry Reservoir, U.S.A. 110 F8
Strawn, U.S.A. 109 J5
Strážnice, Czech. 20 G7
Streaky B., Australia 91 E1
Streaky Bay, Australia 91 E1
Streator, U.S.A. 108 E10
Streé, Belgium 17 H4
Streeter, U.S.A. 108 B5
Streetsville, Canada 106 C5
Strehaia, Romania 38 E6
Strelcha, Bulgaria 38 G7
Strelka, Russia 45 D10
Streng →, Cambodia 58 F4
Strésa, Italy 32 C5
Strezhevoy, Russia 44 C8
Stříbro, Czech. 20 F3
Strijen, Neths. 16 E5
Strimón →, Greece 39 J6
Strimonikós Kólpos, Greece 39 J6
Stroeder, Argentina 128 B4
Strofádhes, Greece 39 M4
Strömbacka, Sweden 10 C10
Strómboli, Italy 35 D8
Stromeferry, U.K. 14 D3
Stromness, U.K. 14 C5
Ströms vattudal, Sweden 8 D13
Strömstad, Sweden 9 G11
Strömsund, Sweden 8 E13
Stróngoli, Italy 35 C10
Stronsay, U.K. 14 B6
Stronsburg, U.S.A. 108 E6
Stroud, U.K. 13 F5
Stroud Road, Australia 91 E5
Stroudsburg, U.S.A. 107 F9
Stroumbi, Cyprus 37 E11
Struer, Denmark 11 H2
Struga, Macedonia 39 H3
Strugi Krasnyye, Russia 40 B6
Strumica, Macedonia 39 H5
Strumica →, Europe 39 H6
Struthers, Canada 98 C2
Struthers, U.S.A. 106 E4
Stryi, Ukraine 40 G3
Stryker, U.S.A. 110 B6
Strzegom, Poland 20 E6
Strzelce Krajeńskie, Poland 20 C5
Strzelecki Cr. →, Australia 91 D2
Strzelin, Poland 20 E7
Strzelno, Poland 20 C8
Strzyzów, Poland 20 F11
Stuart, Fla., U.S.A. 105 M5
Stuart, Nebr., U.S.A. 108 D5
Stuart →, Canada 100 C4
Stuart Bluff Ra., Australia 88 D5
Stuart L., Canada 100 C4
Stuart Ra., Australia 91 D1
Stubbekøbing, Denmark 11 K6
Stugun, Sweden 10 A9
Stull, L., Canada 98 B1
Stung Treng, Cambodia 58 F5
Stupart →, Canada 101 B10
Stupino, Russia 41 D11
Sturgeon B., Canada 101 C9
Sturgeon Bay, U.S.A. 104 C2
Sturgeon Falls, Canada 98 C4
Sturgeon L., Alta., Canada 100 B5
Sturgeon L., Ont., Canada 106 B6
Sturgeon L., Ont., Canada 98 B1
Sturgis, Mich., U.S.A. 104 E3
Sturgis, S. Dak., U.S.A. 108 C3
Sturt Cr. →, Australia 88 C4
Sturt Creek, Australia 88 C4
Stutterheim, S. Africa 84 E4
Stuttgart, Germany 19 G5
Stuttgart, U.S.A. 109 H9
Stuyvesant, U.S.A. 107 D11
Stykkishólmur, Iceland 8 D2
Styr →, Belorussia 40 E5
Styria = Steiermark □, Austria 21 H5
Su Xian, China 50 H9
Suakin, Sudan 76 D4
Suan, N. Korea 51 E14
Suapure →, Venezuela 120 B4
Suaqui, Mexico 114 B3
Suatá →, Venezuela 121 B4
Subang, Indonesia 57 G12
Subansiri →, India 61 F18
Subayhah, Si. Arabia 64 D3
Subi, Indonesia 59 L7
Subiaco, Italy 33 G10
Subotica, Serbia, Yug. 21 J9
Success, Canada 101 C7
Suceava, Romania 38 B9
Suceava →, Romania 38 B9
Sucha-Beskidzka, Poland 20 F9
Suchan, Poland 20 B5
Suchan, Russia 48 C6
Suchitoto, El Salv. 116 D2
Suchou = Suzhou, China 53 B13
Süchow = Xuzhou, China 51 G9
Suchowola, Poland 20 B13
Sucio →, Colombia 120 B2
Suck →, Ireland 15 C3
Sucre, Bolivia 125 D4
Sucre, Colombia 120 B3
Sucre □, Colombia 120 B2
Sucre □, Venezuela 121 A5
Sucuaro, Colombia 120 C4
Sućuraj, Croatia 33 E14
Sucuriju, Brazil 122 A2
Sucuriú →, Brazil 125 E7
Sud, Pte., Canada 99 C7
Sud-Ouest, Pte. du, Canada 99 C7
Suda →, Russia 41 B10
Sudak, Ukraine 42 D6
Sudan, U.S.A. 109 H3
Sudan ■, Africa 77 E3
Suday, Russia 41 B13
Sudbury, Canada 98 C3
Sudbury, U.K. 13 E8
Sûdd, Sudan 77 F2
Suddie, Guyana 121 B6
Süderbrarup, Germany 18 A5
Süderlügum, Germany 18 A4
Süderoog-Sand, Germany 18 A4
Sudeten Mts. = Sudety, Europe 20 E6
Sudety, Europe 20 E6
Sudi, Tanzania 83 E4
Sudirman, Pegunungan, Indonesia 57 E9
Sudogda, Russia 41 D12
Sudr, Egypt 76 J8
Sudzha, Russia 40 F9
Sueca, Spain 29 F4
Suedala, Sweden 11 J7
Suez = El Suweis, Egypt 76 J8
Suez, G. of = Suweis, Khalîg el, Egypt 76 J8
Suez Canal = Suweis, Qanâl es, Egypt 76 H8
Suffield, Canada 101 C6
Suffolk, U.S.A. 104 G7
Suffolk □, U.K. 13 E9
Sugar City, U.S.A. 108 F3
Suğla Gölü, Turkey 66 E5
Sugluk = Saglouc, Canada 97 B12
Sugny, Belgium 17 J5
Suhaia, L., Romania 38 F8
Suhār, Oman 65 E8
Suhbaatar, Mongolia 54 A5
Sühbaatar □, Mongolia 50 B8
Suhl, Germany 18 E6
Suhr, Switz. 22 B6
Şuhut, Turkey 66 D4
Sui Xian, Henan, China 50 G8
Sui Xian, Henan, China 53 B9
Suiá Missu →, Brazil 125 C7
Suichang, China 53 C12
Suichuan, China 53 D10
Suide, China 50 F6
Suifenhe, China 51 B16
Suihua, China 54 B7
Suijiang, China 52 C4
Suining, Hunan, China 53 D8
Suining, Jiangsu, China 51 H9
Suining, Sichuan, China 52 B5
Suiping, China 50 H7
Suippes, France 25 C11
Suir →, Ireland 15 D4
Suixi, China 53 G8
Suiyang, Guizhou, China 52 D6
Suiyang, Heilongjiang, China 51 B16
Suizhong, China 51 D11
Sujangarh, India 62 F6
Sukabumi, Indonesia 57 G12
Sukadana, Kalimantan, Indonesia 56 E3
Sukadana, Sumatera, Indonesia 56 F3
Sukagawa, Japan 49 F10
Sukaraja, Indonesia 56 E4
Sukarnapura = Jayapura, Indonesia 57 E10
Sukchŏn, N. Korea 51 E13
Sukhinichi, Russia 40 D9
Sukhona →, Russia 44 D4
Sukhothai, Thailand 58 D2
Sukhumi, Georgia 43 E9
Sukkur, Pakistan 62 F3
Sukkur Barrage, Pakistan 62 F3
Sukumo, Japan 49 H6
Sukunka →, Canada 100 B4
Sul, Canal do, Brazil 122 B2
Sula →, Ukraine 40 G8
Sula, Kepulauan, Indonesia 57 E7
Sulaco →, Honduras 116 C2
Sulaiman Range, Pakistan 62 D3
Sulak →, Russia 43 E12
Sūlār, Iran 65 D6

Sulawesi □, *Indonesia* 57 E6
Sulawesi Sea, *Indonesia* ... 57 D6
Sulechów, *Poland* 20 C5
Sulejów, *Poland* 20 D9
Sulgen, *Switz.* 23 A8
Sulima, *S. Leone* 78 D2
Sulina, *Romania* 38 D12
Sulina, Braţul →, *Romania* . 38 D12
Sulingen, *Germany* 18 C4
Sulitälma, *Sweden* 8 C14
Sulitjelma, *Norway* 8 C14
Sullana, *Peru* 124 A1
Sullivan, *Ill., U.S.A.* 108 F10
Sullivan, *Ind., U.S.A.* 104 F2
Sullivan, *Mo., U.S.A.* 108 F9
Sullivan Bay, *Canada* 100 C3
Sully-sur-Loire, *France* ... 25 E9
Sulmona, *Italy* 33 F10
Sulphur, *La., U.S.A.* 109 K8
Sulphur, *Okla., U.S.A.* 109 H6
Sulphur Pt., *Canada* 100 A6
Sulphur Springs, *U.S.A.* ... 109 J7
Sulphur Springs Draw →,
  U.S.A. 109 J4
Sultan, *Canada* 98 C3
Sultan, *U.S.A.* 112 C5
Sultanpur, *India* 63 F10
Sulu Arch., *Phil.* 55 J4
Sulu Sea, *E. Indies* 55 G4
Sülüklü, *Turkey* 66 D5
Suluova, *Turkey* 66 C6
Suluq, *Libya* 73 B9
Sulzbach, *Germany* 19 F3
Sulzbach-Rosenberg,
  Germany 19 F7
Sulzberger Ice Shelf,
  Antarctica 5 D10
Sumalata, *Indonesia* 57 D6
Sumampa, *Argentina* 126 B3
Sumatera □, *Indonesia* 56 D2
Sumatra = Sumatera □,
  Indonesia 56 D2
Sumatra, *U.S.A.* 110 C10
Sumba, *Indonesia* 57 F5
Sumba, Selat, *Indonesia* ... 57 F5
Sumbawa, *Indonesia* 56 F5
Sumbawa Besar, *Indonesia* .. 56 F5
Sumbawanga □, *Tanzania* 82 D3
Sumbe, *Angola* 80 G2
Sumburgh Hd., *U.K.* 14 B7
Sumdo, *India* 63 B8
Sumé, *Brazil* 122 C4
Sumedang, *Indonesia* 57 G12
Šumen, *Bulgaria* 38 F9
Sumenep, *Indonesia* 57 G15
Sumgait, *Azerbaijan* 43 F13
Sumiswald, *Switz.* 22 B5
Summer L., *U.S.A.* 110 E4
Summerland, *Canada* 100 D5
Summerside, *Canada* 99 C7
Summerville, *Ga., U.S.A.* .. 105 H3
Summerville, *S.C., U.S.A.* . 105 J5
Summit Lake, *Canada* 100 C4
Summit Peak, *U.S.A.* 111 H10
Sumner, *Iowa, U.S.A.* 108 D8
Sumner, *Wash., U.S.A.* 112 C4
Sumoto, *Japan* 49 G7
Sumqayıt = Sumgait,
  Azerbaijan 43 F13
Sumter, *U.S.A.* 105 J5
Sumy, *Ukraine* 40 F9
Sun City, *Ariz., U.S.A.* ... 111 K7
Sun City, *Calif., U.S.A.* .. 113 M9
Sunagawa, *Japan* 48 C10
Sunan, *N. Korea* 51 E13
Sunart, L., *U.K.* 14 E3
Sunburst, *U.S.A.* 110 B8
Sunbury, *Australia* 91 F3
Sunbury, *U.S.A.* 107 F8
Sunchales, *Argentina* 126 C3
Suncho Corral, *Argentina* .. 126 B3
Sunchon, *S. Korea* 51 G14
Suncook, *U.S.A.* 107 C13
Sunda, Selat, *Indonesia* ... 56 F3
Sunda Is., *Indonesia* 46 K14
Sunda Str. = Sunda, Selat,
  Indonesia 56 F3
Sundance, *U.S.A.* 108 C2
Sundarbans, The, *Asia* 61 J16
Sundargarh, *India* 61 H14
Sundays = Sondags →,
  S. Africa 84 E4
Sundbyberg, *Sweden* 10 E11
Sunderland, *Canada* 106 B5
Sunderland, *U.K.* 12 C6
Sundre, *Canada* 100 C6
Sundridge, *Canada* 98 C4
Sunds, *Denmark* 11 H3
Sundsjö, *Sweden* 10 B9
Sundsvall, *Sweden* 10 B11
Sung Hei, *Vietnam* 59 G6
Sungai Kolok, *Thailand* 59 J3
Sungai Lembing, *Malaysia* .. 59 L4
Sungai Patani, *Malaysia* ... 59 K3
Sungaigerong, *Indonesia* ... 56 E2
Sungailiat, *Indonesia* 56 E3
Sungaipakning, *Indonesia* .. 56 D2
Sungaipenuh, *Indonesia* 56 E2
Sungaitiram, *Indonesia* 56 E5
Sungari = Songhua
  Jiang →, *China* 54 B8
Sungguminasa, *Indonesia* ... 57 F5
Sunghua Chiang = Songhua
  Jiang →, *China* 54 B8
Sungikai, *Sudan* 77 E2

Sungurlu, *Turkey* 42 F6
Sunja, *Croatia* 33 C13
Sunnyside, *Utah, U.S.A.* ... 110 G8
Sunnyside, *Wash., U.S.A.* .. 110 C3
Sunnyvale, *U.S.A.* 111 H2
Sunray, *U.S.A.* 109 G4
Suntar, *Russia* 45 C12
Sunyani, *Ghana* 78 D4
Supai, *U.S.A.* 111 H7
Supamo →, *Venezuela* 121 B5
Supaul, *India* 63 F12
Supe, *Peru* 124 C2
Superior, *Ariz., U.S.A.* ... 111 K8
Superior, *Mont., U.S.A.* ... 110 C6
Superior, *Nebr., U.S.A.* ... 108 E5
Superior, *Wis., U.S.A.* 108 B8
Superior, L., *U.S.A.* 98 C2
Supetar, *Croatia* 33 E13
Suphan Buri, *Thailand* 58 E3
Suphan Dağı, *Turkey* 67 D10
Supiori, Kepulauan,
  Indonesia 57 E9
Supung Sk., *China* 51 D13
Sūq Suwayq, *Si. Arabia* 64 E3
Suqian, *China* 51 H10
Şūr, *Lebanon* 69 B4
Sur, Pt., *U.S.A.* 111 H3
Sura →, *Russia* 41 C15
Surab, *Pakistan* 62 E2
Surabaja = Surabaya,
  Indonesia 57 G15
Surabaya, *Indonesia* 57 G15
Suraia, *Romania* 38 D10
Surakarta, *Indonesia* 57 G14
Surakhany, *Azerbaijan* 43 F14
Surat, *Australia* 91 D4
Surat, *India* 60 J8
Surat Thani, *Thailand* 59 H2
Suratgarh, *India* 62 E5
Surazh, *Belorussia* 40 D7
Surazh, *Russia* 40 E8
Surduc Pasul, *Romania* 38 D6
Surdulica, *Serbia, Yug.* ... 21 N12
Sûre = Sauer →, *Germany* ... 17 J9
Surendranagar, *India* 62 H4
Surf, *U.S.A.* 113 L6
Surgères, *France* 26 B3
Surgut, *Russia* 44 C8
Surhuisterveen, *Neths.* 16 B8
Suriapet, *India* 60 L11
Surigao, *Phil.* 55 G6
Surigao Strait, *Phil.* 55 F6
Surin, *Thailand* 58 E4
Surin Nua, Ko, *Thailand* ... 59 H1
Surinam ■, *S. Amer.* 121 C6
Suriname □, *Surinam* 121 B6
Suriname ■ = Surinam ■,
  S. Amer. 121 C6
Suriname →, *Surinam* 121 B6
Sürmaq, *Iran* 65 D7
Sürmene, *Turkey* 43 F9
Surovikino, *Russia* 43 B10
Surprise L., *Canada* 100 B2
Surrey □, *U.K.* 13 F7
Sursee, *Switz.* 22 B6
Sursk, *Russia* 41 E14
Surt, *Libya* 73 B8
Surt, Khalīj, *Libya* 73 B8
Surtsey, *Iceland* 8 E3
Surubim, *Brazil* 122 C4
Sürüç, *Turkey* 67 E8
Suruga-Wan, *Japan* 49 G9
Surumu →, *Brazil* 121 C5
Susa, *Italy* 32 C4
Susã →, *Denmark* 11 J5
Sušac, *Croatia* 33 F13
Susak, *Croatia* 33 D11
Susaki, *Japan* 49 H6
Süsangerd, *Iran* 65 D6
Susanino, *Russia* 45 D15
Susanville, *U.S.A.* 110 F3
Susch, *Switz.* 23 C10
Susehri, *Turkey* 67 C8
Susong, *China* 53 B11
Susquehanna →, *U.S.A.* 107 G8
Susquehanna Depot,
  U.S.A. 107 E9
Susques, *Argentina* 126 A2
Sussex, *Canada* 99 C6
Sussex, *U.S.A.* 107 E10
Sussex, E. □, *U.K.* 13 G8
Sussex, W. □, *U.K.* 13 G7
Susteren, *Neths.* 17 F7
Sustut →, *Canada* 100 B3
Susuman, *Russia* 45 C15
Susunu, *Indonesia* 57 E8
Susurluk, *Turkey* 66 D3
Susuz, *Turkey* 67 C10
Sütçüler, *Turkey* 66 E4
Sutherland, *S. Africa* 84 E3
Sutherland, *U.S.A.* 108 E4
Sutherland Falls, *N.Z.* 87 L1
Sutherlin, *U.S.A.* 110 E2
Sutivan, *Croatia* 33 E13
Sutlej →, *Pakistan* 62 E4
Sutter, *U.S.A.* 112 F5
Sutter Creek, *U.S.A.* 112 G6
Sutton, *Canada* 107 A12
Sutton, *U.S.A.* 108 E6
Sutton →, *Canada* 98 A3
Sutton, *Australia* 90 C4
Sutton in Ashfield, *U.K.* .. 12 D6
Suttor →, *Australia* 90 C4
Suttsu, *Japan* 48 C10
Suva, *Fiji* 87 D8
Suva Reka, *Serbia, Yug.* ... 21 N10
Suvo Rudište, *Serbia, Yug.* 21 M10

Suvorov, *Russia* 41 D10
Suvorov Is. = Suwarrow
  Is., *Cook Is.* 93 J11
Suwałki, *Poland* 20 A12
Suwannaphum, *Thailand* 58 E4
Suwannee →, *U.S.A.* 105 L4
Suwanose-Jima, *Japan* 49 K4
Suwarrow Is., *Cook Is.* 93 J11
Suwayq aş Şuqban, *Iraq* 64 D5
Suweis, Khalîg el, *Egypt* .. 76 J8
Suweis, Qanâl es, *Egypt* ... 76 H8
Suwŏn, *S. Korea* 51 F14
Suzdal, *Russia* 41 C12
Suzhou, *China* 53 B13
Suzu, *Japan* 49 F8
Suzu-Misaki, *Japan* 49 F8
Suzuka, *Japan* 49 G8
Suzzara, *Italy* 32 C7
Svalbard, *Arctic* 4 B8
Svalbarð, *Iceland* 8 C6
Svalöv, *Sweden* 11 J7
Svanvik, *Norway* 8 B21
Svappavaara, *Sweden* 8 C16
Svarstad, *Norway* 10 E3
Svartisen, *Norway* 8 C12
Svartvik, *Sweden* 10 B11
Svatovo, *Ukraine* 42 B8
Svay Chek, *Cambodia* 58 F4
Svay Rieng, *Cambodia* 59 G5
Svealand □, *Sweden* 9 G13
Sveg, *Sweden* 9 E13
Svendborg, *Denmark* 11 J4
Svene, *Norway* 10 E3
Svenljunga, *Sweden* 11 G7
Svenstrup, *Denmark* 11 H3
Sverdlovsk =
  Yekaterinburg, *Russia* ... 44 D7
Sverdlovsk, *Ukraine* 43 B8
Sverdrup Is., *Canada* 4 B3
Svetac, *Croatia* 33 E12
Sveti Ivan Zelina, *Croatia* 33 C13
Sveti Jurij, *Slovenia* 33 B12
Sveti Lenart, *Slovenia* 33 B12
Sveti Nikole,
  Macedonia 39 H4
Sveti Trojica, *Slovenia* ... 33 B12
Svetlaya, *Russia* 48 A9
Svetlogorsk, *Belorussia* ... 40 E6
Svetlograd, *Russia* 43 D10
Svetlovodsk, *Ukraine* 40 G8
Svetozarevo, *Serbia, Yug.* . 21 L11
Svidník, *Slovakia* 20 F11
Svilaja Planina, *Croatia* .. 33 E13
Svilengrad, *Bulgaria* 39 H9
Svir →, *Russia* 6 C12
Svishtov, *Bulgaria* 38 F8
Svisloch, *Belorussia* 40 E4
Svitava →, *Czech.* 20 F6
Svitavy, *Czech.* 20 F6
Svobodnyy, *Russia* 45 D13
Svolvær, *Norway* 8 B13
Svratka →, *Czech.* 20 F6
Svrljig, *Serbia, Yug.* 21 M12

Syke, *Germany* 18 C4
Syktyvkar, *Russia* 44 C6
Sylacauga, *U.S.A.* 105 J2
Sylarna, *Sweden* 8 E12
Sylhet, *Bangla.* 61 G17
Sylt, *Germany* 18 A4
Sylvan Lake, *Canada* 100 C6
Sylvania, *U.S.A.* 105 J5
Sylvester, *U.S.A.* 105 K4
Sym, *Russia* 44 C9
Symón, *Mexico* 114 C4
Synnott Ra., *Australia* 88 C4
Syracuse, *Kans., U.S.A.* ... 109 F4
Syracuse, *N.Y., U.S.A.* 107 C8
Syrdarya →, *Kazakhstan* 44 E7
Syria ■, *Asia* 64 C3
Syul'dzhyukyor, *Russia* 45 C12
Syzran, *Russia* 41 E16
Szaraz →, *Hungary* 21 J10
Szarvas, *Hungary* 21 J10
Szczebrzeszyn, *Poland* 20 E12
Szczecin, *Poland* 20 B4
Szczecinek, *Poland* 20 B6
Szczekociny, *Poland* 20 E9
Szczytno, *Poland* 20 B11
Szechwan = Sichuan □,
  China 52 B5
Szeged, *Hungary* 21 J10
Szeghalom, *Hungary* 21 H11
Székesfehérvár, *Hungary* ... 21 H8
Szekszárd, *Hungary* 21 J8
Szendrö, *Hungary* 21 G10
Szentendre, *Hungary* 21 H9
Szentes, *Hungary* 21 J10
Szentgotthárd, *Hungary* 21 J6
Szentlörinc, *Hungary* 21 J7
Szigetvár, *Hungary* 21 J7
Szolnok, *Hungary* 21 H10
Szombathely, *Hungary* 21 H6
Szprotawa, *Poland* 20 D5
Szydłowiec, *Poland* 20 D10
Szypliszki, *Poland* 20 A13

T

't Harde, *Neths.* 16 D7
't Zandt, *Neths.* 16 B9
Ta Khli Khok, *Thailand* 58 E3
Ta Lai, *Vietnam* 59 G6
Tabacal, *Argentina* 126 A3
Tabaco, *Phil.* 55 E5
Tabagné, *Ivory C.* 78 D4
Ţabah, *Si. Arabia* 64 E4
Tabajara, *Brazil* 125 B5
Tabalos, *Peru* 124 B2
Tabarca, I. de, *Spain* 29 G4
Tabarka, *Tunisia* 75 A6
Ţabas, *Khorāsān, Iran* 65 C9
Ţabas, *Khorāsān, Iran* 65 C8
Tabasará, Serranía de,
  Panama 116 E3
Tabasco □, *Mexico* 115 D6
Tabatinga, Serra da, *Brazil* 122 D3
Tabāzīn, *Iran* 65 D8
Tabelbala, Kahal de,
  Algeria 75 C4
Taber, *Canada* 100 D6
Tabernas, *Spain* 29 H2
Tabernes de Valldigna,
  Spain 29 F4
Tabira, *Brazil* 122 C4
Tablas, *Phil.* 55 E5
Tablas Strait, *Phil.* 55 E4
Table B. = Tafelbaai,
  S. Africa 84 E2
Table B., *Canada* 99 B8
Table Mt., *S. Africa* 84 E2
Tableland, *Australia* 88 C4
Tabletop, Mt., *Australia* .. 90 C4
Tábor, *Czech.* 20 F4
Tabora, *Tanzania* 82 D3
Tabora □, *Tanzania* 82 D3
Tabou, *Ivory C.* 78 E3
Tabrīz, *Iran* 64 B5
Tabuaeran, *Pac. Oc.* 93 G12
Tabuelan, *Phil.* 55 F5
Tabuenca, *Spain* 28 D3
Tabūk, *Si. Arabia* 64 D3
Tacámbaro de Codallos,
  Mexico 114 D4
Tacheng, *China* 54 B3
Tach'ing Shan = Daqing
  Shan, *China* 50 D6
Táchira □, *Venezuela* 120 B3
Tácina →, *Italy* 35 D9
Tacloban, *Phil.* 55 F6
Tacna, *Peru* 124 D3
Tacna □, *Peru* 124 D3
Tacoma, *U.S.A.* 112 C4
Tacuarembó, *Uruguay* 127 C4
Tacutu →, *Brazil* 121 C5
Tademaït, Plateau du,
  Algeria 75 C5
Tadent, O. →, *Algeria* 75 D6
Tadjerdjeri, O. →, *Algeria* 75 C6
Tadjerouna, *Algeria* 75 B5
Tadjettaret, O. →, *Algeria* 75 D6
Tadjmout, *Oasis, Algeria* .. 75 B5
Tadjmout, *Saoura, Algeria* . 75 C5
Tadjoura, *Djibouti* 68 E3

Tadjoura, Golfe de,
  Djibouti 77 E5
Tadmor, *N.Z.* 87 J4
Tadoule, L., *Canada* 101 B9
Tadoussac, *Canada* 99 C6
Tadzhikistan =
  Tajikistan ■, *Asia* 44 F8
Taechŏn-ni, *S. Korea* 51 F14
Taegu, *S. Korea* 51 G15
Taegwan, *N. Korea* 51 D13
Taejŏn, *S. Korea* 51 F14
Tafalla, *Spain* 28 C3
Tafar, *Sudan* 77 F2
Tafassasset, O. →, *Algeria* 75 D6
Tafelbaai, *S. Africa* 84 E2
Tafelney, C., *Morocco* 74 B3
Tafermaar, *Indonesia* 57 F8
Taffermit, *Morocco* 74 C3
Tafí Viejo, *Argentina* 126 B2
Tafīhān, *Iran* 65 D7
Tafiré, *Ivory C.* 78 D3
Tafnidilt, *Morocco* 74 C2
Tafraoute, *Morocco* 74 C3
Taft, *Iran* 65 D7
Taft, *Phil.* 55 F6
Taft, *Calif., U.S.A.* 113 K7
Taft, *Tex., U.S.A.* 109 M6
Taga Dzong, *Bhutan* 61 F16
Taganrog, *Russia* 43 C8
Taganrogskiy Zaliv, *Russia* 42 C8
Tagânt, *Mauritania* 78 B2
Tagatay, *Phil.* 55 D4
Tagbilaran, *Phil.* 55 G5
Tággia, *Italy* 32 E4
Taghzout, *Morocco* 74 B4
Tagish, *Canada* 100 A2
Tagish L., *Canada* 100 A2
Tagliacozzo, *Italy* 33 F10
Tagliamento →, *Italy* 33 C10
Táglio di Po, *Italy* 33 C9
Tagna, *Colombia* 120 D3
Tago, *Phil.* 55 G7
Tagomago, I. de, *Spain* 36 B8
Taguatinga, *Brazil* 123 D3
Tagudin, *Phil.* 55 C4
Tagum, *Phil.* 55 H6
Tagus = Tejo →, *Europe* 31 G1
Tahakopa, *N.Z.* 87 M2
Tahala, *Morocco* 74 B4
Tahan, Gunong, *Malaysia* ... 59 K4
Tahat, *Algeria* 75 D6
Tāherī, *Iran* 65 E7
Tahiti, *Pac. Oc.* 93 J13
Tahoe, L., *U.S.A.* 112 G6
Tahoe City, *U.S.A.* 112 F6
Taholah, *U.S.A.* 112 C2
Tahoua, *Niger* 79 C6
Tahta, *Egypt* 76 B3
Tahtali Dağları, *Turkey* ... 66 D6
Tahuamanu →, *Bolivia* 124 C4
Tahulandang, *Indonesia* 57 D7
Tahuna, *Indonesia* 57 D7
Taï, *Ivory C.* 78 D3
Tai Hu, *China* 54 C7
Tai Shan, *China* 51 F9
Tai Xian, *China* 53 A13
Tai'an, *China* 51 F9
Taibei, *Taiwan* 53 E13
Taibique, *Canary Is.* 36 G2
Taibus Qi, *China* 50 D8
T'aichung = Taizhong,
  Taiwan 53 E13
Taidong, *Taiwan* 53 F13
Taieri →, *N.Z.* 87 M3
Taigu, *China* 50 F7
Taihang Shan, *China* 50 G7
Taihape, *N.Z.* 87 H5
Taihe, *Anhui, China* 50 H8
Taihe, *Jiangxi, China* 53 D10
Taihu, *China* 53 B11
Taijiang, *China* 52 D7
Taikang, *China* 50 G8
Tailem Bend, *Australia* 91 F2
Tailfingen, *Germany* 19 G5
Taimyr Peninsula =
  Taymyr, Poluostrov,
  Russia 45 B11
Tain, *U.K.* 14 D4
Taínaron, Ákra, *Greece* 39 N5
Taining, *China* 53 D11
Taintignies, *Belgium* 17 G2
Taiobeiras, *Brazil* 123 E3
T'aipei = Taibei, *Taiwan* .. 53 E13
Taiping, *China* 53 B12
Taiping, *Malaysia* 59 K3
Taipingzhen, *China* 50 H6
Taipu, *Brazil* 122 C4
Taishan, *China* 53 F9
Taishun, *China* 53 D12
Taita □, *Kenya* 82 C4
Taita Hills, *Kenya* 82 C4
Taitao, C., *Chile* 128 C1
Taitao, Pen. de, *Chile* 128 C2
Taivalkoski, *Finland* 8 D20
Taiwan ■, *Asia* 53 F13
Taiwan Shan, *Taiwan* 53 F13
Taixing, *China* 53 A13
Taiyetos Óros, *Greece* 39 N5
Taiyiba, *Israel* 69 C4
Taiyuan, *China* 50 F7
Taizhong, *Taiwan* 53 E13
Taizhou, *China* 53 A12
Taizhou Liedao, *China* 53 C13
Ta'izz, *Yemen* 68 E3
Tājābād, *Iran* 65 D7

Tajapuru, Furo do, Brazil 122 B1
Tajikistan ■, Asia 44 F8
Tajima, Japan 49 F9
Tajo = Tejo →, Europe 31 G1
Tajrīsh, Iran 65 C6
Tājūrā, Libya 73 B7
Tak, Thailand 58 D2
Takāb, Iran 64 B5
Takachiho, Japan 49 H5
Takada, Japan 49 F9
Takahagi, Japan 49 F10
Takaka, N.Z. 87 J4
Takamatsu, Japan 49 G7
Takaoka, Japan 49 F8
Takapuna, N.Z. 87 G5
Takasaki, Japan 49 F9
Takatsuki, Japan 49 G7
Takaungu, Kenya 82 C4
Takayama, Japan 49 F8
Take-Shima, Japan 49 J5
Takefu, Japan 49 G8
Takengon, Indonesia 56 D1
Takeo, Cambodia 59 G5
Takeo, Japan 49 H5
Tåkern, Sweden 11 F8
Tākestān, Iran 65 C6
Taketa, Japan 49 H5
Takh, India 63 C7
Takhman, Cambodia 59 G5
Takikawa, Japan 48 C10
Takla L., Canada 100 B3
Takla Landing, Canada 100 B3
Takla Makan = Taklamakan Shamo, China 54 C3
Taklamakan Shamo, China 54 C3
Taku →, Canada 100 B2
Takum, Nigeria 79 D6
Takutu →, Guyana 121 C5
Tal Halāl, Iran 65 D7
Tala, Uruguay 127 C4
Talacogan, Phil. 55 G6
Talagante, Chile 126 C1
Talaïnt, Morocco 74 C3
Talak, Niger 79 B6
Talamanca, Cordillera de, Cent. Amer. 116 D3
Talara, Peru 124 A1
Talas, Kirghizia 44 E8
Talas, Turkey 66 D6
Talâta, Egypt 69 E1
Talata Mafara, Nigeria 79 C6
Talaud, Kepulauan, Indonesia 57 D7
Talaud Is. = Talaud, Kepulauan, Indonesia 57 D7
Talavera de la Reina, Spain 30 F6
Talawana, Australia 88 D3
Talayan, Phil. 55 H6
Talbert, Sillon de, France 24 D3
Talbot, C., Australia 88 B4
Talbragar →, Australia 91 E4
Talca, Chile 126 D1
Talca □, Chile 126 D1
Talcahuano, Chile 126 D1
Talcher, India 61 J14
Talcho, Niger 79 C5
Taldy Kurgan, Kazakhstan 44 E8
Taldyqorghan = Taldy Kurgan, Kazakhstan 44 E8
Talesh, Iran 65 B6
Talesh, Kūhhā-ye, Iran 65 B6
Talguharai, Sudan 76 D4
Tali Post, Sudan 77 F3
Taliabu, Indonesia 57 E6
Talibon, Phil. 57 B6
Talibong, Ko, Thailand 59 J2
Talihina, U.S.A. 109 H7
Talisayan, Phil. 55 G6
Taliwang, Indonesia 56 F5
Tall 'Asūr, Jordan 69 D4
Tall Kalakh, Syria 69 A5
Talla, Egypt 76 J7
Talladega, U.S.A. 105 J2
Tallahassee, U.S.A. 105 K3
Tallangatta, Australia 91 F4
Tallarook, Australia 91 F4
Tallering Pk., Australia 89 E2
Tallinn, Estonia 40 B4
Tallulah, U.S.A. 109 J9
Talmest, Morocco 74 B3
Talmont, France 26 B2
Talnoye, Ukraine 42 B4
Talodi, Sudan 77 E3
Talovaya, Russia 41 F12
Talpa de Allende, Mexico 114 C4
Talsi, Latvia 40 C3
Talsinnt, Morocco 75 B4
Taltal, Chile 126 B1
Taltson →, Canada 100 A6
Talwood, Australia 91 D4
Talyawalka Cr. →, Australia 91 E3
Tam Chau, Vietnam 59 G5
Tam Ky, Vietnam 58 E7
Tam Quan, Vietnam 58 E7
Tama, U.S.A. 108 E8
Tamala, Australia 89 E1
Tamalameque, Colombia 120 B3
Tamale, Ghana 79 D4
Taman, Russia 42 D7
Tamanar, Morocco 74 B3
Tamano, Japan 49 G6
Tamanrasset, Algeria 75 D6
Tamanrasset, O. →, Algeria 75 D5

Tamaqua, U.S.A. 107 F9
Tamar →, U.K. 13 G3
Támara, Colombia 120 B3
Tamarang, Australia 91 E5
Tamarinda, Spain 36 B10
Tamarite de Litera, Spain 28 D5
Tamashima, Japan 49 G6
Tamaské, Niger 79 C6
Tamaulipas □, Mexico 115 C5
Tamaulipas, Sierra de, Mexico 115 C5
Tamazula, Mexico 114 C4
Tamazunchale, Mexico 115 C5
Tamba-Dabatou, Guinea 78 C2
Tambacounda, Senegal 78 C2
Tambelan, Kepulauan, Indonesia 56 D3
Tambellup, Australia 89 F2
Tambo, Australia 90 C4
Tambo, Peru 124 C3
Tambo →, Peru 124 C3
Tambo de Mora, Peru 124 C2
Tambobamba, Peru 124 C3
Tambohorano, Madag. 85 B7
Tambopata →, Peru 124 C4
Tambora, Indonesia 56 F5
Tambov, Russia 41 E12
Tambre →, Spain 30 C2
Tambuku, Indonesia 57 G15
Tamburà, Sudan 77 F2
Tâmchekket, Mauritania 78 B2
Tame, Colombia 120 B3
Tamega →, Portugal 30 D2
Tamelelt, Morocco 74 B3
Tamenglong, India 61 G18
Tamerza, Tunisia 75 B6
Tamgak, Mts., Niger 72 E6
Tamiahua, L. de, Mexico 115 C5
Tamil Nadu □, India 60 P10
Tamines, Belgium 17 H5
Tamis →, Serbia, Yug. 38 E3
Tamluk, India 63 H12
Tammerfors = Tampere, Finland 9 F17
Tammisaari = Tampere, Finland 9 F17
Tamo Abu, Pegunungan, Malaysia 56 D5
Tampa, U.S.A. 105 M4
Tampa B., U.S.A. 105 M4
Tampere, Finland 9 F17
Tampico, Mexico 115 C5
Tampin, Malaysia 59 L4
Tamri, Morocco 74 B3
Tamrida = Qādib, Yemen 68 E5
Tamsagbulag, Mongolia 54 B6
Tamsalu, Estonia 40 B5
Tamu, Burma 61 G19
Tamuja →, Spain 31 F4
Tamworth, Australia 91 E5
Tamworth, U.K. 13 E6
Tamyang, S. Korea 51 G14
Tan An, Vietnam 59 G6
Tan-tan, Morocco 74 C2
Tana, Norway 8 A20
Tana →, Kenya 82 C5
Tana →, Norway 8 A20
Tana, L., Ethiopia 77 E4
Tana River, Kenya 82 C4
Tanabe, Japan 49 H7
Tanabi, Brazil 123 F2
Tanafjorden, Norway 8 A20
Tanaga, Pta., Canary Is. 36 G1
Tanagro →, Italy 35 B8
Tanahbala, Indonesia 56 E1
Tanahgrogot, Indonesia 56 E5
Tanahjampea, Indonesia 57 F6
Tanahmasa, Indonesia 56 E1
Tanahmerah, Indonesia 57 F10
Tanakura, Japan 49 F10
Tanami, Australia 88 C4
Tanami Desert, Australia 88 C4
Tanana, U.S.A. 96 B4
Tanana →, U.S.A. 96 B4
Tananarive = Antananarivo, Madag. 85 B8
Tanannt, Morocco 74 B3
Tánaro →, Italy 32 C5
Tanaunella, Italy 34 B2
Tanbar, Australia 90 D3
Tancarville, France 24 C7
Tancheng, China 51 G10
Tanchŏn, N. Korea 51 D15
Tanda, Ut. P., India 63 F10
Tanda, Ut. P., India 63 E8
Tanda, Ivory C. 78 D4
Tandag, Phil. 55 G7
Tandaia, Tanzania 83 D3
Tăndărei, Romania 38 E10
Tandaué, Angola 84 B2
Tandil, Argentina 126 D4
Tandil, Sa. del, Argentina 126 D4
Tandlianwala, Pakistan 62 D5
Tando Adam, Pakistan 62 G3
Tandou L., Australia 91 E3
Tandsbyn, Sweden 10 A8
Tane-ga-Shima, Japan 49 J5
Taneatua, N.Z. 87 H6
Tanen Tong Dan, Burma 58 D2
Tanezrouft, Algeria 75 D5
Tang, Koh, Cambodia 59 G4
Tang Krasang, Cambodia 58 F5
Tanga, Tanzania 82 D4
Tanga □, Tanzania 82 D4
Tanganyika, L., Africa 82 D2
Tanger, Morocco 74 A3
Tangerang, Indonesia 57 G12

Tangerhütte, Germany 18 C7
Tangermünde, Germany 18 C7
Tanggu, China 51 E9
Tanggula Shan, China 54 C4
Tanghe, China 50 H7
Tangier = Tanger, Morocco 74 A3
Tangorin P.O., Australia 90 C3
Tangshan, China 51 E10
Tangtou, China 51 G10
Tanguiéta, Benin 79 C5
Tangxi, China 53 C12
Tangyan He →, China 52 C7
Tanimbar, Kepulauan, Indonesia 57 F8
Tanimbar Is. = Tanimbar, Kepulauan, Indonesia 57 F8
Taninges, France 27 B10
Tanjay, Phil. 55 G5
Tanjong Malim, Malaysia 59 L3
Tanjore = Thanjavur, India 60 P11
Tanjung, Indonesia 56 E5
Tanjungbalai, Indonesia 56 D1
Tanjungbatu, Indonesia 56 D5
Tanjungkarang Telukbetung, Indonesia 56 F3
Tanjungpandan, Indonesia 56 E3
Tanjungpinang, Indonesia 56 D2
Tanjungpriok, Indonesia 57 G12
Tanjungredeb, Indonesia 56 D5
Tanjungselor, Indonesia 56 D5
Tank, Pakistan 62 C4
Tänndalen, Sweden 10 B6
Tannis Bugt, Denmark 11 G4
Tannu-Ola, Russia 45 D10
Tano →, Ghana 78 D4
Tanon Str., Phil. 55 F5
Tanout, Niger 79 C6
Tanquinho, Brazil 123 D4
Tanta, Egypt 76 H7
Tantoyuca, Mexico 115 C5
Tantung = Dandong, China 51 D13
Tanumshede, Sweden 11 F5
Tanunda, Australia 91 E2
Tanus, France 26 D6
Tanyeri, Turkey 67 D8
Tanzania ■, Africa 82 D3
Tanzilla →, Canada 100 B2
Tao Ko, Thailand 59 G2
Tao'an, China 51 B12
Tao'er He →, China 51 B13
Taohua Dao, China 53 C14
Taolanaro, Madag. 85 D8
Taole, China 50 E4
Taormina, Italy 35 E8
Taos, U.S.A. 111 H11
Taoudenni, Mali 74 D4
Taoudrart, Adrar, Algeria 75 D5
Taounate, Morocco 74 B4
Taourirt, Algeria 75 C5
Taourirt, Morocco 75 B4
Taouz, Morocco 74 B4
Taoyuan, China 53 C8
Taoyuan, Taiwan 53 E13
Tapa, Estonia 40 B4
Tapa Shan = Daba Shan, China 52 B7
Tapachula, Mexico 115 E6
Tapah, Malaysia 59 K3
Tapajós →, Brazil 121 D7
Tapaktuan, Indonesia 56 D1
Tapanahoni →, Surinam 121 C7
Tapanui, N.Z. 87 L2
Tapauá, Brazil 125 B5
Tapauá →, Brazil 125 B5
Tapeta, Liberia 78 D3
Taphan Hin, Thailand 58 D3
Tapi →, India 60 J8
Tapia, Spain 30 B4
Tápiószele, Hungary 21 H9
Tapirai, Brazil 123 E2
Tapiraí →, Brazil 122 D1
Tapirapecó, Serra, Venezuela 121 C5
Tapirapuã, Brazil 125 C6
Tapoeripa, Surinam 121 B6
Tapolca, Hungary 21 J7
Tappahannock, U.S.A. 104 G7
Tapuaenuku, Mt., N.Z. 87 J4
Tapul Group, Phil. 55 J4
Tapurucuará, Brazil 121 D4
Taqīābād, Iran 65 C8
Taquara, Brazil 127 B5
Taquari →, Brazil 125 D6
Taquaritinga, Brazil 123 F2
Tara, Australia 91 D5
Tara, Canada 106 B3
Tara, Russia 44 D8
Tara, Zambia 83 F2
Tara →, Russia 44 D8
Taraba →, Nigeria 79 D7
Tarabagatay, Khrebet, Kazakhstan 44 E9
Tarabuco, Bolivia 125 D5
Tarābulus, Lebanon 69 A4
Tarābulus, Libya 75 B7
Tarahouahout, Algeria 75 D6
Tarajalejo, Canary Is. 36 F5
Tarakan, Indonesia 56 D5
Tarakit, Mt., Kenya 82 B4
Taralga, Australia 91 E4
Tarama-Jima, Japan 49 M2
Taranagar, India 62 E6
Taranaki □, N.Z. 87 H5
Tarancón, Spain 28 E1

Taranga, India 62 H5
Taranga Hill, India 62 H5
Táranto, Italy 35 B10
Táranto, G. di, Italy 35 B10
Tarapacá, Colombia 120 D4
Tarapacá □, Chile 126 A2
Tarapoto, Peru 124 B2
Taraquá, Brazil 120 C4
Tarare, France 27 C8
Tararua Ra., N.Z. 87 J5
Tarascon, France 27 E8
Tarascon-sur-Ariège, France 26 F5
Tarashcha, Ukraine 42 B4
Tarata, Peru 124 D3
Tarauacá, Brazil 124 B3
Tarauacá →, Brazil 124 B3
Tarawera, N.Z. 87 H6
Tarawera L., N.Z. 87 H6
Tarazona, Spain 28 D3
Tarazona de la Mancha, Spain 29 F3
Tarbat Ness, U.K. 14 D5
Tarbela Dam, Pakistan 62 B5
Tarbert, Strath., U.K. 14 F3
Tarbert, W. Isles, U.K. 14 D2
Tarbes, France 26 E4
Tarboro, U.S.A. 105 H7
Tarbrax, Australia 90 C3
Tarcento, Italy 33 B10
Tarcoola, Australia 91 E1
Tarcoon, Australia 91 E4
Tardets-Sorholus, France 26 E3
Tardoire →, France 26 C4
Taree, Australia 91 E5
Tarentaise, France 27 C10
Tarf, Ras, Morocco 74 A3
Tarfa, Wadi el →, Egypt 76 J7
Tarfaya, Morocco 74 C2
Targon, France 26 D3
Targuist, Morocco 74 B4
Tarhbalt, Morocco 74 B3
Tarhit, Algeria 75 B4
Tarhūna, Libya 73 B7
Tariana, Venezuela 120 B3
Tarifa, Spain 31 J5
Tarija, Bolivia 126 A3
Tarija □, Bolivia 126 A3
Tariku →, Indonesia 57 E9
Tarim Basin = Tarim Pendi, China 54 C3
Tarim He →, China 54 C3
Tarim Pendi, China 54 C3
Taritatu →, Indonesia 57 E9
Tarka →, S. Africa 84 E4
Tarkastad, S. Africa 84 E4
Tarkhankut, Mys, Ukraine 42 D5
Tarko Sale, Russia 44 C8
Tarkwa, Ghana 78 D4
Tarlac, Phil. 55 D4
Tarlton Downs, Australia 90 C2
Tarm, Denmark 11 J2
Tarma, Peru 124 C2
Tarn □, France 26 E6
Tarn →, France 26 D5
Tarn-et-Garonne □, France 26 D5
Tarna →, Hungary 21 H9
Tårnby, Denmark 11 J6
Tarnobrzeg, Poland 20 E11
Tarnów, Poland 20 F11
Táro →, Italy 32 D7
Taroom, Australia 91 D4
Taroudannt, Morocco 74 B3
Tarp, Germany 18 A5
Tarpon Springs, U.S.A. 105 L4
Tarquínia, Italy 33 F8
Tarragona, Spain 28 D6
Tarragona □, Spain 28 D6
Tarrasa, Spain 28 D7
Tárrega, Spain 28 D6
Tarrytown, U.S.A. 107 E11
Tarshiha = Me'ona, Israel 69 B4
Tarso Emissi, Chad 73 D8
Tarsus, Turkey 66 E6
Tartagal, Argentina 126 A3
Tartas, France 26 E3
Tartu, Estonia 40 B5
Tarțūs, Syria 64 C2
Tarumirim, Brazil 123 E3
Tarumizu, Japan 49 J5
Tarussa, Russia 41 D10
Tarutao, Ko, Thailand 59 J2
Tarutung, Indonesia 56 D1
Tarvisio, Italy 33 B10
Tarz Ulli, Libya 75 C7
Tasāwah, Libya 73 C7
Taschereau, Canada 98 C4
Taseko →, Canada 100 C4
Tash-Kumyr, Kirghizia 44 E8
Tashauz, Turkmenistan 44 E6
Tashi Chho Dzong = Thimphu, Bhutan 61 F16
Tashkent, Uzbekistan 44 E7
Tashtagol, Russia 44 D9
Tasikmalaya, Indonesia 57 G13
Tåsjön, Sweden 8 D13
Taskan, Russia 45 C16
Taşköprü, Turkey 42 F6
Tasman B., N.Z. 87 J4
Tasman Mts., N.Z. 87 J4
Tasman Pen., Australia 90 G4
Tasman Sea, Pac. Oc. 92 L8
Tasmania □, Australia 90 G4
Taşnad, Romania 38 B5
Tassil Tin-Rerhoh, Algeria 75 D5

Tassili n-Ajjer, Algeria 75 C6
Tassili-Oua-n-Ahaggar, Algeria 75 D6
Tasu Sd., Canada 100 C2
Tata, Morocco 74 C3
Tatabánya, Hungary 21 H8
Tatahouine, Tunisia 75 B7
Tatar Republic □, Russia 44 D6
Tatarbunary, Ukraine 42 D3
Tatarsk, Russia 44 D8
Tateyama, Japan 49 G9
Tathlina L., Canada 100 A5
Tathra, Australia 91 F4
Tatinnai L., Canada 101 A9
Tatnam, C., Canada 101 B10
Tatra = Tatry, Slovakia 20 F9
Tatry, Slovakia 20 F9
Tatsuno, Japan 49 G7
Tatta, Pakistan 62 G2
Tatuí, Brazil 127 A6
Tatum, U.S.A. 109 J3
Tat'ung = Datong, China 50 D7
Tatvan, Turkey 67 D10
Tauá, Brazil 122 C3
Taubaté, Brazil 127 A6
Tauberbischofsheim, Germany 19 F5
Taucha, Germany 18 D8
Taufikia, Sudan 77 F3
Taumarunui, N.Z. 87 H5
Taumaturgo, Brazil 124 B3
Taung, S. Africa 84 D3
Taungdwingyi, Burma 61 J19
Taunggyi, Burma 61 J20
Taungup, Burma 61 K19
Taungup Pass, Burma 61 K19
Taungup Taunggya, Burma 61 K18
Taunsa Barrage, Pakistan 62 D4
Taunton, U.K. 13 F4
Taunton, U.S.A. 107 E13
Taunus, Germany 19 E4
Taupo, N.Z. 87 H6
Taupo, L., N.Z. 87 H5
Taurage, Lithuania 40 D3
Tauranga, N.Z. 87 G6
Tauranga Harb., N.Z. 87 G6
Taurianova, Italy 35 D9
Taurus Mts. = Toros Dağları, Turkey 66 E5
Tauste, Spain 28 D3
Tauz, Azerbaijan 43 F11
Tavannes, Switz. 22 B4
Tavda, Russia 44 D7
Tavda →, Russia 44 D7
Taverny, France 25 C9
Taveta, Tanzania 82 C4
Taveuni, Fiji 87 C9
Tavignano →, France 27 F13
Tavira, Portugal 31 H3
Tavistock, Canada 106 C4
Tavistock, U.K. 13 G3
Tavolara, Italy 34 B2
Távora →, Portugal 30 D3
Tavoy, Burma 58 E2
Tavşanlı, Turkey 66 D3
Taw →, U.K. 13 F3
Tawas City, U.S.A. 104 C4
Tawau, Malaysia 56 D5
Tawitawi, Phil. 55 J4
Taxila, Pakistan 62 C5
Tay →, U.K. 14 E5
Tay, Firth of, U.K. 14 E5
Tay, L., Australia 89 F3
Tay, L., U.K. 14 E4
Tay Ninh, Vietnam 59 G6
Tayabamba, Peru 124 B2
Tayabas Bay, Phil. 55 E4
Taylakovy, Russia 44 D8
Taylor, Canada 100 B4
Taylor, Nebr., U.S.A. 108 E5
Taylor, Pa., U.S.A. 107 E9
Taylor, Tex., U.S.A. 109 K6
Taylor, Mt., U.S.A. 111 J10
Taylorville, U.S.A. 108 F10
Taymā, Si. Arabia 64 E3
Taymyr, Oz., Russia 45 B11
Taymyr, Poluostrov, Russia 45 B11
Tayport, U.K. 14 E6
Tayshet, Russia 45 D10
Tayside □, U.K. 14 E5
Taytay, Phil. 55 F3
Taz →, Russia 44 C8
Taza, Morocco 74 B4
Tāzah Khurmātū, Iraq 64 C5
Tazawa-Ko, Japan 48 E10
Tazenakht, Morocco 74 B3
Tazin L., Canada 101 B7
Tazoult, Algeria 75 A6
Tazovskiy, Russia 44 C8
Tbilisi, Georgia 43 F11
Tchad = Chad ■, Africa 73 E8
Tchad, L. = Chad, L., Chad 73 F7
Tchaourou, Benin 79 D5
Tch'eng-tou = Chengdu, China 52 B5
Tchentlo L., Canada 100 B4
Tchibanga, Gabon 80 E2
Tchien, Liberia 78 D3
Tchin Tabaraden, Niger 79 B6
Tch'ong-k'ing = Chongqing, China 52 C6
Tczew, Poland 20 A8
Te Anau, L., N.Z. 87 L1
Te Aroha, N.Z. 87 G5
Te Awamutu, N.Z. 87 H5
Te Kuiti, N.Z. 87 H5

Thurles

Te Puke, *N.Z.* 87 G6
Te Waewae B., *N.Z.* 87 M1
Tea →, *Brazil* 120 D4
Tea Tree, *Australia* 90 C1
Teague, *U.S.A.* 109 K6
Teano, *Italy* 35 A7
Teapa, *Mexico* 115 D6
Teba, *Spain* 31 J6
Tebakang, *Malaysia* 56 D4
Teberda, *Russia* 43 E9
Tébessa, *Algeria* 75 A6
Tebicuary →, *Paraguay* 126 B4
Tebingtinggi, *Indonesia* 56 D1
Tébourba, *Tunisia* 75 A6
Téboursouk, *Tunisia* 75 A6
Tebulos, *Russia* 43 E11
Tecate, *Mexico* 113 N10
Tecer Dağı, *Turkey* 66 D7
Tech →, *France* 26 F7
Techiman, *Ghana* 78 D4
Tecka, *Argentina* 128 B2
Tecomán, *Mexico* 114 D4
Tecopa, *U.S.A.* 113 K10
Tecoripa, *Mexico* 114 B3
Tecuala, *Mexico* 114 C3
Tecuci, *Romania* 38 D10
Tecumseh, *U.S.A.* 104 D4
Tedzhen, *Turkmenistan* 44 F7
Tees →, *U.K.* 12 C6
Teesside, *U.K.* 12 C6
Teeswater, *Canada* 106 C3
Tefé, *Brazil* 121 D5
Tefé →, *Brazil* 121 D5
Tefenni, *Turkey* 66 E3
Tegal, *Indonesia* 57 G13
Tegelen, *Neths.* 17 F8
Tegernsee, *Germany* 19 H7
Teggiano, *Italy* 35 B8
Teghra, *India* 63 G11
Tegid, L. = Bala, L., *U.K.* 12 E4
Tegina, *Nigeria* 79 C6
Tegucigalpa, *Honduras* 116 D2
Tehachapi, *U.S.A.* 113 K8
Tehachapi Mts., *U.S.A.* 113 L8
Tehamiyam, *Sudan* 76 D4
Tehilla, *Sudan* 76 D4
Téhini, *Ivory C.* 78 D4
Tehrān, *Iran* 65 C6
Tehuacán, *Mexico* 115 D5
Tehuantepec, *Mexico* 115 D5
Tehuantepec, G. de, *Mexico* 115 D5
Tehuantepec, Istmo de, *Mexico* 115 D6
Teide, *Canary Is.* 36 F3
Teifi →, *U.K.* 13 E3
Teign →, *U.K.* 13 G4
Teignmouth, *U.K.* 13 G4
Teixeira, *Brazil* 122 C4
Teixeira Pinto, *Guinea-Biss.* 78 C1
Tejo →, *Europe* 31 G1
Tejon Pass, *U.S.A.* 113 L8
Tekamah, *U.S.A.* 108 E6
Tekapo, L., *N.Z.* 87 K3
Tekax, *Mexico* 115 C7
Tekeli, *Kazakhstan* 44 E8
Tekeze →, *Ethiopia* 77 E4
Tekija, *Serbia* 21 L12
Tekirdağ, *Turkey* 66 C2
Tekirdağ □, *Turkey* 66 C2
Tekkali, *India* 61 K14
Tekke, *Turkey* 66 C7
Tekman, *Turkey* 67 D9
Tekoa, *U.S.A.* 110 C5
Tekouiât, O. →, *Algeria* 75 D5
Tel Aviv-Yafo, *Israel* 69 C3
Tel Lakhish, *Israel* 69 D3
Tel Megiddo, *Israel* 69 C4
Tela, *Honduras* 116 C2
Télagh, *Algeria* 75 B4
Telanaipura = Jambi, *Indonesia* 56 E2
Telavi, *Georgia* 43 F11
Telde, *Canary Is.* 36 G4
Telegraph Creek, *Canada* 100 B2
Telekhany, *Belorussia* 40 E4
Telemark fylke □, *Norway* 10 E2
Telén, *Argentina* 126 D2
Teleng, *Iran* 65 E9
Teleño, *Spain* 30 C4
Teleorman →, *Romania* 38 E8
Teles Pires →, *Brazil* 125 B6
Telescope Pk., *U.S.A.* 113 J9
Teletaye, *Mali* 79 B5
Telford, *U.K.* 12 E5
Telfs, *Austria* 19 H7
Télimélé, *Guinea* 78 C2
Telkwa, *Canada* 100 C3
Tell City, *U.S.A.* 104 G2
Tellicherry, *India* 60 P9
Tellin, *Belgium* 17 H6
Telluride, *U.S.A.* 111 H10
Teloloapán, *Mexico* 115 D5
Telpos Iz, *Russia* 6 C17
Telsen, *Argentina* 128 B3
Telšiai, *Lithuania* 40 D3
Teltow, *Germany* 18 C9
Teluk Anson, *Malaysia* 59 K3
Teluk Betung = Tanjungkarang Telukbetung, *Indonesia* 56 F3
Teluk Intan = Teluk Anson, *Malaysia* 59 K3
Telukbutun, *Indonesia* 59 K7
Telukdalem, *Indonesia* 56 D1
Tema, *Ghana* 79 D5
Temanggung, *Indonesia* 57 G14
Temapache, *Mexico* 115 C5
Temax, *Mexico* 115 C7
Temba, *S. Africa* 85 D4
Tembe, *Zaïre* 82 C2
Temblador, *Venezuela* 121 B5
Tembleque, *Spain* 28 F1
Temblor Range, *U.S.A.* 113 K7
Teme →, *U.K.* 13 E5
Temecula, *U.S.A.* 113 M9
Temerloh, *Malaysia* 59 L4
Temir, *Kazakhstan* 44 E6
Temirtau, *Kazakhstan* 44 D8
Temirtau, *Russia* 44 D9
Témiscaming, *Canada* 98 C4
Temma, *Australia* 90 G3
Temnikov, *Russia* 41 D13
Temo →, *Italy* 34 B1
Temora, *Australia* 91 E4
Temosachic, *Mexico* 114 B3
Tempe, *U.S.A.* 111 K8
Tempe Downs, *Australia* 88 D5
Témpio Pausania, *Italy* 34 B2
Tempiute, *U.S.A.* 112 H11
Temple, *U.S.A.* 109 K6
Temple B., *Australia* 90 A3
Templemore, *Ireland* 15 D4
Templeton, *U.S.A.* 112 K6
Templeton →, *Australia* 90 C2
Templeuve, *Belgium* 17 G2
Templin, *Germany* 18 B9
Tempoal, *Mexico* 115 C5
Temryuk, *Russia* 42 D7
Temse, *Belgium* 17 F4
Temska →, *Serbia* 21 M12
Temuco, *Chile* 128 A2
Temuka, *N.Z.* 87 L3
Ten Boer, *Neths.* 16 B9
Tena, *Ecuador* 120 D2
Tenabo, *Mexico* 115 C6
Tenaha, *U.S.A.* 109 K7
Tenali, *India* 60 L12
Tenancingo, *Mexico* 115 D5
Tenango, *Mexico* 115 D5
Tenasserim, *Burma* 59 F2
Tenasserim □, *Burma* 58 F2
Tenay, *France* 27 C9
Tenby, *U.K.* 13 F3
Tenda, Col di, *France* 27 D11
Tendaho, *Ethiopia* 68 E3
Tende, *France* 27 D11
Tendelti, *Sudan* 77 E3
Tendjedi, Adrar, *Algeria* 75 D6
Tendrara, *Morocco* 75 B4
Tendre, Mt., *Switz.* 22 C2
Teneida, *Egypt* 76 B2
Tenente Marques →, *Brazil* 125 C6
Ténéré, *Niger* 79 B7
Tenerife, *Canary Is.* 36 F3
Tenerife, Pico, *Canary Is.* 36 G1
Ténès, *Algeria* 75 A5
Teng Xian, *Guangxi Zhuangzu, China* 53 F8
Teng Xian, *Shandong, China* 51 G9
Tengah □, *Indonesia* 57 E6
Tengah Kepulauan, *Indonesia* 56 F5
Tengchong, *China* 52 E2
Tengchowfu = Penglai, *China* 51 F11
Tenggara □, *Indonesia* 57 E6
Tenggarong, *Indonesia* 56 E5
Tenggol, P., *Malaysia* 59 K4
Tengiz, Ozero, *Kazakhstan* 44 D7
Tenigerbad, *Switz.* 23 C7
Tenino, *U.S.A.* 112 D4
Tenkasi, *India* 60 Q10
Tenke, *Shaba, Zaïre* 83 E2
Tenke, *Shaba, Zaïre* 83 E2
Tenkodogo, *Burkina Faso* 79 C4
Tenna →, *Italy* 33 E10
Tennant Creek, *Australia* 90 B1
Tennessee □, *U.S.A.* 105 H2
Tennessee →, *U.S.A.* 104 G1
Tenneville, *Belgium* 17 H7
Tennille, *U.S.A.* 105 J4
Tennsift, Oued →, *Morocco* 74 B3
Teno, Pta. de, *Canary Is.* 36 F3
Tenom, *Malaysia* 56 C5
Tenosique, *Mexico* 115 D6
Tenryū-Gawa →, *Japan* 49 G8
Tent L., *Canada* 101 A7
Tenterfield, *Australia* 91 D5
Teófilo Otoni, *Brazil* 123 E3
Teotihuacán, *Mexico* 115 D5
Tepa, *Indonesia* 57 F7
Tepalcatepec →, *Mexico* 114 D4
Tepehuanes, *Mexico* 114 B3
Tepequem, Serra, *Brazil* 121 C5
Tepetongo, *Mexico* 114 C4
Tepic, *Mexico* 114 C4
Tepoca, C., *Mexico* 114 A2
Tequila, *Mexico* 114 C4
Ter →, *Spain* 28 C8
Ter Apel, *Neths.* 16 C10
Téra, *Niger* 79 C5
Tera →, *Spain* 30 D5
Teraina, *Kiribati* 93 G11
Téramo, *Italy* 33 F10
Terang, *Australia* 91 F3
Terborg, *Neths.* 16 E8
Tercan, *Turkey* 67 D9
Tercero →, *Argentina* 126 C3
Terebovlya, *Ukraine* 40 G4
Terek →, *Russia* 43 E12
Terenos, *Brazil* 125 E7
Tereshka →, *Russia* 41 F15
Teresina, *Brazil* 122 C3
Teresinha, *Brazil* 121 C7
Terewah, L., *Australia* 91 D4
Terges →, *Portugal* 31 H3
Tergnier, *France* 25 C10
Terhazza, *Mali* 74 D3
Terheijden, *Neths.* 17 E5
Teridgerie Cr. →, *Australia* 91 E4
Terlizzi, *Italy* 35 A9
Terme, *Turkey* 42 F7
Termez, *Uzbekistan* 44 F7
Términi Imerese, *Italy* 34 E6
Términos, L. de, *Mexico* 115 D6
Térmoli, *Italy* 33 F12
Ternate, *Indonesia* 57 D7
Terneuzen, *Neths.* 17 F3
Terney, *Russia* 45 E14
Terni, *Italy* 33 F9
Ternitz, *Austria* 21 H6
Ternopol, *Ukraine* 42 B1
Terowie, *N.S.W., Australia* 91 E4
Terowie, *S. Austral., Australia* 91 E2
Terra Bella, *U.S.A.* 113 K7
Terrace, *Canada* 100 C3
Terrace Bay, *Canada* 98 C2
Terracina, *Italy* 34 A6
Terralba, *Italy* 34 C1
Terranova = Ólbia, *Italy* 34 B2
Terranuova Bracciolini, *Italy* 33 E8
Terrasini Favarotta, *Italy* 34 D6
Terrassa = Tarrasa, *Spain* 28 D7
Terrasson-la-Villedieu, *France* 26 C5
Terre Haute, *U.S.A.* 104 F2
Terrebonne B., *U.S.A.* 109 L9
Terrecht, *Mali* 75 D4
Terrell, *U.S.A.* 109 J6
Terrenceville, *Canada* 99 C9
Terrick Terrick, *Australia* 90 C4
Terry, *U.S.A.* 108 B2
Terschelling, *Neths.* 16 B6
Terter →, *Azerbaijan* 43 F12
Teruel, *Spain* 28 E3
Teruel □, *Spain* 28 E4
Tervel, *Bulgaria* 38 F10
Tervola, *Finland* 8 C18
Teryaweyna L., *Australia* 91 E3
Tešanj, *Bos.-H.* 21 L7
Teseney, *Eritrea* 77 D4
Tesha →, *Russia* 41 D13
Teshio, *Japan* 48 B10
Teshio-Gawa →, *Japan* 48 B10
Tesiyn Gol →, *Mongolia* 54 A4
Teslin, *Canada* 100 A2
Teslin →, *Canada* 100 A2
Teslin L., *Canada* 100 A2
Tesouro, *Brazil* 125 D7
Tessalit, *Mali* 79 A5
Tessaoua, *Niger* 79 C6
Tessenderlo, *Belgium* 17 F6
Tessin, *Germany* 18 A8
Tessit, *Mali* 79 B5
Test →, *U.K.* 13 F6
Testa del Gargano, *Italy* 35 A9
Têt →, *France* 26 F7
Tetachuck L., *Canada* 100 C3
Tetas, Pta., *Chile* 126 A1
Tete, *Mozam.* 83 F3
Tete □, *Mozam.* 83 F3
Teterev →, *Ukraine* 40 F7
Teteringen, *Neths.* 17 E5
Teterow, *Germany* 18 B8
Teteven, *Bulgaria* 38 G7
Tethul →, *Canada* 100 A6
Tetiyev, *Ukraine* 42 B3
Teton →, *U.S.A.* 110 C8
Tétouan, *Morocco* 74 A3
Tetovo, *Macedonia* 38 G4
Tetuán = Tétouan, *Morocco* 74 A3
Tetyukhe Pristan, *Russia* 48 B7
Tetyushi, *Russia* 41 D16
Teuco →, *Argentina* 126 B3
Teufen, *Switz.* 23 B8
Teulada, *Italy* 34 D1
Teulon, *Canada* 101 C9
Teun, *Indonesia* 57 F7
Teutoburger Wald, *Germany* 18 C4
Tevere →, *Italy* 33 G9
Teverya, *Israel* 69 C4
Teviot →, *U.K.* 14 F6
Tewantin, *Australia* 91 D5
Tewkesbury, *U.K.* 13 F5
Texada I., *Canada* 100 D4
Texarkana, *Ark., U.S.A.* 109 J8
Texarkana, *Tex., U.S.A.* 109 J7
Texas, *Australia* 91 D5
Texas □, *U.S.A.* 109 K5
Texas City, *U.S.A.* 109 L7
Texel, *Neths.* 16 B5
Texhoma, *U.S.A.* 109 G4
Texline, *U.S.A.* 109 G3
Texoma, L., *U.S.A.* 109 J6
Teykovo, *Russia* 41 C12
Teza →, *Russia* 41 C12
Tezin, *Afghan.* 62 B3
Teziutlán, *Mexico* 115 D5
Tezpur, *India* 61 F18
Tezzeron L., *Canada* 100 C4
Tha-anne →, *Canada* 101 A10
Tha Deua, *Laos* 58 D4
Tha Deua, *Laos* 58 C3
Tha Pla, *Thailand* 58 D3
Tha Rua, *Thailand* 58 E3
Tha Sala, *Thailand* 59 H2
Tha Song Yang, *Thailand* 58 D1
Thaba Nchu, *S. Africa* 84 D4
Thaba Putsoa, *Lesotho* 85 D4
Thabana Ntlenyana, *Lesotho* 85 D4
Thabazimbi, *S. Africa* 85 C4
Thai Binh, *Vietnam* 58 B6
Thai Hoa, *Vietnam* 58 C5
Thai Muang, *Thailand* 59 H2
Thai Nguyen, *Vietnam* 58 B5
Thailand ■, *Asia* 58 E4
Thailand, G. of, *Asia* 59 G3
Thakhek, *Laos* 58 D5
Thal, *Pakistan* 62 C4
Thal Desert, *Pakistan* 62 D4
Thala, *Tunisia* 75 A6
Thala La, *Burma* 61 E20
Thalabarivat, *Cambodia* 58 F5
Thalkirch, *Switz.* 23 C8
Thallon, *Australia* 91 D4
Thalwil, *Switz.* 23 B7
Thame →, *U.K.* 13 F6
Thames, *N.Z.* 87 G5
Thames →, *Canada* 98 D3
Thames →, *U.K.* 13 F8
Thames →, *U.S.A.* 107 E12
Thamesford, *Canada* 106 C3
Thamesville, *Canada* 106 D3
Than Uyen, *Vietnam* 58 B4
Thane, *India* 60 K8
Thanesar, *India* 62 D7
Thanet, I. of, *U.K.* 13 F9
Thangoo, *Australia* 88 C3
Thangool, *Australia* 90 C5
Thanh Hoa, *Vietnam* 58 C5
Thanh Hung, *Vietnam* 59 H5
Thanh Pho Ho Chi Minh = Phanh Bho Ho Chi Minh, *Vietnam* 59 G6
Thanh Thuy, *Vietnam* 58 A5
Thanjavur, *India* 60 P11
Thann, *France* 25 E14
Thaon-les-Vosges, *France* 25 D13
Thap Sakae, *Thailand* 59 G2
Thap Than, *Thailand* 58 E2
Thar Desert, *India* 62 F4
Tharad, *India* 62 G4
Thargomindah, *Australia* 91 D3
Tharrawaddy, *Burma* 61 L19
Tharthar, W. →, *Iraq* 64 C4
Thásos, *Greece* 39 J7
That Khe, *Vietnam* 58 A6
Thatcher, *Ariz., U.S.A.* 111 K9
Thatcher, *Colo., U.S.A.* 109 G2
Thaton, *Burma* 61 L20
Thau, Bassin de, *France* 26 E7
Thaungdut, *Burma* 61 G19
Thayer, *U.S.A.* 109 G9
Thayetmyo, *Burma* 61 K19
Thayngen, *Switz.* 23 A7
Thazi, *Burma* 61 J20
The Alberga →, *Australia* 91 D2
The Bight, *Bahamas* 117 B4
The Coorong, *Australia* 91 F2
The Dalles, *U.S.A.* 110 D3
The English Company's Is., *Australia* 90 A2
The Frome →, *Australia* 91 D2
The Grampians, *Australia* 91 F3
The Great Divide = Great Dividing Ra., *Australia* 90 C4
The Hague = 's-Gravenhage, *Neths.* 16 D4
The Hamilton →, *Australia* 91 D2
The Macumba →, *Australia* 91 D2
The Neales →, *Australia* 91 D2
The Officer →, *Australia* 89 E5
The Pas, *Canada* 101 C8
The Range, *Zimbabwe* 83 F3
The Rock, *Australia* 91 F4
The Salt L., *Australia* 91 E3
The Stevenson →, *Australia* 91 D2
The Warburton →, *Australia* 91 D2
Thebes = Thívai, *Greece* 39 L6
Thebes, *Egypt* 76 B3
Thedford, *Canada* 106 C3
Thedford, *U.S.A.* 108 E4
Theebine, *Australia* 91 D5
Thekulthili L., *Canada* 101 A7
Thelon →, *Canada* 101 A8
Thénezay, *France* 24 F6
Thenia, *Algeria* 75 A5
Thenon, *France* 26 C5
Theodore, *Australia* 90 C5
Thepha, *Thailand* 59 J3
Thérain →, *France* 25 C9
Theresa, *U.S.A.* 107 B9
Thermaïkos Kólpos, *Greece* 39 J5
Thermopolis, *U.S.A.* 110 E9
Thermopylae P., *Greece* 39 L5
Thessalía □, *Greece* 39 L4
Thessalon, *Canada* 98 C3
Thessaloníki, *Greece* 39 J5
Thessaloniki, Gulf of = Thermaïkos Kólpos, *Greece* 39 J5
Thessaly = Thessalía □, *Greece* 39 L4
Thetford, *U.K.* 13 E8
Thetford Mines, *Canada* 99 C5
Theun →, *Laos* 58 C5
Theunissen, *S. Africa* 84 D4
Theux, *Belgium* 17 G7
Thevenard, *Australia* 91 E1
Thiámis →, *Greece* 39 K3
Thiberville, *France* 24 C7
Thibodaux, *U.S.A.* 109 L9
Thicket Portage, *Canada* 101 B9
Thief River Falls, *U.S.A.* 108 A6
Thiel Mts., *Antarctica* 5 E16
Thiene, *Italy* 33 C8
Thiérache, *France* 25 C10
Thiers, *France* 26 C7
Thies, *Senegal* 78 C1
Thiet, *Sudan* 77 F2
Thika, *Kenya* 82 C4
Thikombia, *Fiji* 87 B9
Thille-Boubacar, *Senegal* 78 B1
Thimphu, *Bhutan* 61 F16
þingvallavatn, *Iceland* 8 D3
Thionville, *France* 25 C13
Thíra, *Greece* 39 N8
Thirasía, *Greece* 39 N8
Thirsk, *U.K.* 12 C6
Thisted, *Denmark* 9 H10
Thistle I., *Australia* 91 F2
Thívai, *Greece* 39 L6
Thiviers, *France* 26 C4
Thizy, *France* 27 B8
þjórsá →, *Iceland* 8 E3
Thlewiaza →, *Man., Canada* 101 B8
Thlewiaza →, *N.W.T., Canada* 101 A10
Thmar Puok, *Cambodia* 58 F4
Tho Vinh, *Vietnam* 58 C5
Thoa →, *Canada* 101 A7
Thoen, *Thailand* 58 D2
Thoeng, *Thailand* 58 C3
Thoissey, *France* 27 B8
Tholdi, *Pakistan* 63 B7
Tholen, *Neths.* 17 E4
Thomas, *Okla., U.S.A.* 109 H5
Thomas, *W. Va., U.S.A.* 104 F6
Thomas, L., *Australia* 91 D2
Thomaston, *U.S.A.* 105 J3
Thomasville, *Ala., U.S.A.* 105 K2
Thomasville, *Ga., U.S.A.* 105 K3
Thomasville, *N.C., U.S.A.* 105 H5
Thommen, *Belgium* 17 H8
Thompson, *Canada* 101 B9
Thompson, *U.S.A.* 111 G9
Thompson →, *Canada* 100 C4
Thompson →, *U.S.A.* 108 F8
Thompson Falls, *U.S.A.* 110 C6
Thompson Landing, *Canada* 101 A6
Thompson Pk., *U.S.A.* 110 F2
Thomson's Falls = Nyahururu, *Kenya* 82 B4
Thon Buri, *Thailand* 59 F3
Thônes, *France* 27 C10
Thonon-les-Bains, *France* 27 B10
Thorez, *Ukraine* 43 B8
þórisvatn, *Iceland* 8 D4
þorlákshöfn, *Iceland* 8 E3
Thornaby on Tees, *U.K.* 12 C6
Thornbury, *Canada* 106 B4
Thorold, *Canada* 106 C5
þórshöfn, *Iceland* 8 C6
Thouarcé, *France* 24 E6
Thouars, *France* 24 F6
Thouin, C., *Australia* 88 D2
Thousand Oaks, *U.S.A.* 113 L8
Thrace, *Turkey* 66 C2
Thrakikón Pélagos, *Greece* 39 J8
Three Forks, *U.S.A.* 110 D8
Three Hills, *Canada* 100 C6
Three Hummock I., *Australia* 90 G3
Three Lakes, *U.S.A.* 108 C10
Three Points, C., *Ghana* 78 E4
Three Rivers, *Australia* 89 E2
Three Rivers, *Calif., U.S.A.* 112 J8
Three Rivers, *Tex., U.S.A.* 109 L5
Three Sisters, *U.S.A.* 110 D3
Throssell, L., *Australia* 89 E3
Throssell Ra., *Australia* 88 D3
Thuan Hoa, *Vietnam* 59 H5
Thubun Lakes, *Canada* 101 A6
Thueyts, *France* 27 D8
Thuillies, *Belgium* 17 H4
Thuin, *Belgium* 17 H4
Thuir, *France* 26 F6
Thule, *Greenland* 4 B4
Thun, *Switz.* 22 C5
Thundelarra, *Australia* 89 E2
Thunder B., *U.S.A.* 106 B1
Thunder Bay, *Canada* 98 C2
Thunersee, *Switz.* 22 C5
Thung Song, *Thailand* 59 H2
Thunkar, *Bhutan* 61 F17
Thuong Tra, *Vietnam* 58 D6
Thur →, *Switz.* 23 A8
Thurgau □, *Switz.* 23 A8
Thüringen □, *Germany* 18 E7
Thüringer Wald, *Germany* 18 E7
Thurles, *Ireland* 15 D4

Thurloo Downs

Thurloo Downs, *Australia* 91 D3
Thurn P., *Austria* 19 H8
Thursday I., *Australia* 90 A3
Thurso, *Canada* 98 C4
Thurso, *U.K.* 14 C5
Thurston I., *Antarctica* 5 D16
Thury-Harcourt, *France* 24 D6
Thusis, *Switz.* 23 C8
Thutade L., *Canada* 100 B3
Thyborøn, *Denmark* 11 H2
Thylungra, *Australia* 91 D3
Thyolo, *Malawi* 83 F4
Thysville = Mbanza
　Ngungu, *Zaïre* 80 F2
Ti-n-Barraouene, O. →,
　Africa 79 B5
Ti-n-Medjerdam, O. →,
　Algeria 75 C5
Ti-n-Tarabine, O. →,
　Algeria 75 D6
Ti-n-Zaouatène, *Algeria* 75 E5
Tia, *Australia* 91 E5
Tiahuanacu, *Bolivia* 124 D4
Tian Shan, *China* 54 B3
Tianchang, *China* 53 A12
Tiandong, *China* 52 F6
Tian'e, *China* 52 E6
Tianguá, *Brazil* 122 B3
Tianhe, *China* 52 E7
Tianjin, *China* 51 E9
Tiankoura, *Burkina Faso* 78 C4
Tianlin, *China* 52 E6
Tianmen, *China* 53 B9
Tianquan, *China* 52 B4
Tianshui, *China* 50 G3
Tianyang, *China* 52 F6
Tianzhen, *China* 50 D8
Tianzhu, *China* 52 D7
Tianzhuangtai, *China* 51 D12
Tiaret, *Algeria* 75 A5
Tiassalé, *Ivory C.* 78 D4
Tibagi, *Brazil* 127 A5
Tibagi →, *Brazil* 127 A5
Tibati, *Cameroon* 79 D7
Tiber = Tevere →, *Italy* 33 G9
Tiber Reservoir, *U.S.A.* 110 B8
Tiberias = Teverya, *Israel* 69 C4
Tiberias, L. = Yam
　Kinneret, *Israel* 69 C4
Tibesti, *Chad* 73 D8
Tibet = Xizang □, *China* 54 C3
Tibiao, *Phil.* 55 F5
Tibiri, *Niger* 79 C6
Tîbleş, *Romania* 38 B7
Tibnī, *Syria* 64 C3
Tibooburra, *Australia* 91 D3
Tibro, *Sweden* 11 F8
Tibugá, G. de, *Colombia* 120 B2
Tiburón, *Mexico* 114 B2
Ticao I., *Phil.* 55 E5
Tîchît, *Mauritania* 78 B3
Tichla, *Mauritania* 74 D2
Ticho, *Ethiopia* 77 F4
Ticino □, *Switz.* 23 D7
Ticino →, *Italy* 32 C6
Ticonderoga, *U.S.A.* 107 C11
Ticul, *Mexico* 115 C7
Tidaholm, *Sweden* 11 F7
Tiddim, *Burma* 61 H18
Tideridjaouine, Adrar,
　Algeria 75 D5
Tidikelt, *Algeria* 75 C5
Tidjikja, *Mauritania* 78 B2
Tidore, *Indonesia* 57 D7
Tiébissou, *Ivory C.* 78 D3
Tiefencastel, *Switz.* 23 C9
Tiel, *Neths.* 16 E6
Tiel, *Senegal* 78 C1
Tieling, *China* 51 C12
Tielt, *Belgium* 17 F2
Tien Shan, *Asia* 46 E11
Tien-tsin = Tianjin, *China* 51 E9
Tien Yen, *Vietnam* 58 B6
T'ienching = Tianjin, *China* 51 E9
Tienen, *Belgium* 17 G5
Tiénigbé, *Ivory C.* 78 D3
Tientsin = Tianjin, *China* 51 E9
Tierra Amarilla, *Chile* 126 B1
Tierra Amarilla, *U.S.A.* 111 H10
Tierra Colorada, *Mexico* 115 D5
Tierra de Barros, *Spain* 31 G4
Tierra de Campos, *Spain* 30 C6
Tierra del Fuego □,
　Argentina 128 D3
Tierra del Fuego, I. Gr. de,
　Argentina 128 D3
Tierralta, *Colombia* 120 B2
Tiétar →, *Spain* 30 F4
Tietê →, *Brazil* 127 A5
Tieyon, *Australia* 91 D1
Tifarati, *W. Sahara* 74 C3
Tiffin, *U.S.A.* 104 E4
Tiflèt, *Morocco* 74 B3
Tiflis = Tbilisi, *Georgia* 43 F11
Tifton, *U.S.A.* 105 K4
Tifu, *Indonesia* 57 E7
Tigil, *Russia* 45 D16
Tignish, *Canada* 99 C7
Tigray □, *Ethiopia* 77 E4
Tigre →, *Peru* 120 D3
Tigre →, *Venezuela* 121 B5
Tigris = Dijlah, Nahr →,
　Asia 64 D5
Tiguentourine, *Algeria* 75 C6
Tigyaing, *Burma* 61 H20

Tigzerte, O. →, *Morocco* 74 C3
Tîh, Gebel el, *Egypt* 76 J8
Tihodaine, Dunes de,
　Algeria 75 C6
Tijesno, *Croatia* 33 E12
Tijī, *Libya* 75 B7
Tijuana, *Mexico* 113 N9
Tikal, *Guatemala* 116 C2
Tikamgarh, *India* 63 G8
Tikhoretsk, *Russia* 43 D9
Tikhvin, *Russia* 40 B8
Tikkadouine, Adrar,
　Algeria 75 D5
Tiko, *Cameroon* 79 E6
Tikrît, *Iraq* 64 C4
Tiksi, *Russia* 45 B13
Tilamuta, *Indonesia* 57 D6
Tilburg, *Neths.* 17 E6
Tilbury, *Canada* 98 D3
Tilbury, *U.K.* 13 F8
Tilcara, *Argentina* 126 A2
Tilden, *Nebr., U.S.A.* 108 D6
Tilden, *Tex., U.S.A.* 109 L5
Tilemses, *Niger* 79 B5
Tilemsi, Vallée du, *Mali* 79 B5
Tilhar, *India* 63 F8
Tilia, O. →, *Algeria* 75 C5
Tilichiki, *Russia* 45 C17
Tiligul →, *Ukraine* 42 C4
Tililane, *Algeria* 75 C4
Tílissos, *Greece* 37 D7
Till →, *U.K.* 12 B5
Tillabéri, *Niger* 79 C5
Tillamook, *U.S.A.* 110 D2
Tillberga, *Sweden* 10 E10
Tillia, *Niger* 79 B5
Tillsonburg, *Canada* 98 D3
Tillyeria □, *Cyprus* 37 D11
Tílos, *Greece* 39 N10
Tilpa, *Australia* 91 E3
Tilrhemt, *Algeria* 75 B5
Tilsit = Sovetsk, *Russia* 40 D2
Tilt →, *U.K.* 14 E5
Tilton, *U.S.A.* 107 C13
Timagami L., *Canada* 98 C3
Timaru, *N.Z.* 87 L3
Timashevsk, *Russia* 43 D8
Timau, *Italy* 33 B10
Timau, *Kenya* 82 B4
Timbákion, *Greece* 37 D6
Timbaúba, *Brazil* 122 C4
Timbedgha, *Mauritania* 78 B3
Timber Lake, *U.S.A.* 108 C4
Timber Mt., *U.S.A.* 112 H10
Timbío, *Colombia* 120 C2
Timbiqui, *Colombia* 120 C2
Timboon, *Australia* 91 F3
Timbuktu = Tombouctou,
　Mali 78 B4
Timellouline, *Algeria* 75 C6
Timétrine Montagnes, *Mali* 79 B4
Timfristós, Óros, *Greece* 39 L4
Timhadit, *Morocco* 74 B3
Timi, *Cyprus* 37 E11
Timia, *Niger* 79 B6
Timimoun, *Algeria* 75 C5
Timiş = Tamiş →, *Serbia* 38 E3
Timişoara, *Romania* 38 D4
Timmins, *Canada* 98 C3
Timok →, *Serbia* 21 L12
Timon, *Brazil* 122 C3
Timor, *Indonesia* 57 F7
Timor □, *Indonesia* 57 F7
Timor Sea, *Ind. Oc.* 88 B4
Tin Alkoum, *Algeria* 75 D7
Tin Gornai, *Mali* 79 B4
Tin Mt., *U.S.A.* 112 J9
Tina, Khalîg el, *Egypt* 76 H8
Tinaca Pt., *Phil.* 55 J6
Tinaco, *Venezuela* 120 B4
Tinafak, O. →, *Algeria* 75 C6
Tinajo, *Canary Is.* 36 E6
Tinaquillo, *Venezuela* 120 B4
Tinca, *Romania* 38 C4
Tinchebray, *France* 24 D6
Tindouf, *Algeria* 74 C3
Tinée →, *France* 27 E11
Tineo, *Spain* 30 B4
Tinerhir, *Morocco* 74 B3
Tinfouchi, *Algeria* 74 C3
Ting Jiang →, *China* 53 E11
Tinggi, Pulau, *Malaysia* 59 L5
Tinglev, *Denmark* 11 K3
Tingo Maria, *Peru* 124 B2
Tinh Bien, *Vietnam* 59 G5
Tinharé, I. de, *Brazil* 123 D4
Tinjoub, *Algeria* 72 C3
Tinkurrin, *Australia* 89 F2
Tinnevelly = Tirunelveli,
　India 60 Q10
Tinnoset, *Norway* 10 E3
Tinnsjø, *Norway* 10 E2
Tinogasta, *Argentina* 126 B2
Tínos, *Greece* 39 M8
Tiñoso, C., *Spain* 29 H3
Tinta, *Peru* 124 C3
Tintigny, *Belgium* 17 J7
Tintina, *Argentina* 126 B3
Tintinara, *Australia* 91 F3
Tinto →, *Spain* 31 H4
Tioga, *U.S.A.* 106 E7
Tioman, Pulau, *Malaysia* 59 L5
Tione di Trento, *Italy* 32 B7
Tionesta, *U.S.A.* 106 E5
Tior, *Sudan* 77 F3

Tioulilin, *Algeria* 75 C4
Tipongpani, *India* 61 F19
Tipperary, *Ireland* 15 D3
Tipperary □, *Ireland* 15 D4
Tipton, *U.K.* 13 E5
Tipton, *Calif., U.S.A.* 111 H4
Tipton, *Ind., U.S.A.* 104 E2
Tipton, *Iowa, U.S.A.* 108 E9
Tipton Mt., *U.S.A.* 113 K12
Tiptonville, *U.S.A.* 109 G10
Tiquié →, *Brazil* 120 C4
Tiracambu, Serra do, *Brazil* 122 B2
Tīrān, *Iran* 65 C6
Tîrân, *Si. Arabia* 76 B3
Tirana, *Albania* 39 H2
Tiranë = Tirana, *Albania* 39 H2
Tirano, *Italy* 32 B7
Tiraspol, *Moldavia* 42 C3
Tirat Karmel, *Israel* 69 C3
Tiratimine, *Algeria* 75 C5
Tirdout, *Mali* 79 B4
Tire, *Turkey* 66 D2
Tirebolu, *Turkey* 67 C8
Tiree, *U.K.* 14 E2
Tîrgovişte, *Romania* 38 E8
Tîrgu Frumos, *Romania* 38 B10
Tîrgu-Jiu, *Romania* 38 D6
Tîrgu Mureş, *Romania* 38 C7
Tîrgu Neamţ, *Romania* 38 B9
Tîrgu Ocna, *Romania* 38 C9
Tîrgu Secuiesc, *Romania* 38 D9
Tirich Mir, *Pakistan* 60 A7
Tiriola, *Italy* 35 D9
Tiririca, Serra da, *Brazil* 123 E2
Tiris, *W. Sahara* 74 D2
Tîrnava Mare →, *Romania* 38 C7
Tîrnava Mică →, *Romania* 38 C7
Tîrnăveni, *Romania* 38 C7
Tírnavos, *Greece* 39 K5
Tirodi, *India* 60 J11
Tiros, *Brazil* 123 E2
Tirschenreuth, *Germany* 19 F8
Tirso →, *Italy* 34 C1
Tirso, L. del, *Italy* 34 B1
Tiruchchirappalli, *India* 60 P11
Tirunelveli, *India* 60 Q10
Tirupati, *India* 60 N11
Tiruppur, *India* 60 P10
Tiruvannamalai, *India* 60 N11
Tisa →, *Hungary* 21 J10
Tisa →, *Serbia* 21 K10
Tisdale, *Canada* 101 C8
Tishomingo, *U.S.A.* 109 H6
Tisnaren, *Sweden* 10 F9
Tisovec, *Slovak Rep.* 20 G9
Tissemsilt, *Algeria* 75 A5
Tissint, *Morocco* 74 C3
Tissø, *Denmark* 11 J5
Tisza = Tisa →, *Hungary* 21 J10
Tiszafüred, *Hungary* 21 H10
Tiszavasvári, *Hungary* 21 H11
Tit, *Ahaggar, Algeria* 75 D6
Tit, *Tademait, Algeria* 75 C5
Tit-Ary, *Russia* 45 B13
Titaguas, *Spain* 28 F3
Titel, *Serbia* 21 K10
Tithwal, *Pakistan* 63 B5
Titicaca, L., *S. Amer.* 124 D4
Titiwa, *Nigeria* 79 C7
Titlis, *Switz.* 23 C6
Titograd = Podgorica,
　Montenegro 21 N9
Titov Veles, *Macedonia* 39 H4
Titova Korenica, *Croatia* 33 D12
Titovo Užice, *Serbia* 21 M9
Titule, *Zaïre* 82 B2
Titumate, *Colombia* 120 B2
Titusville, *Fla., U.S.A.* 105 L5
Titusville, *Pa., U.S.A.* 106 E5
Tivaouane, *Senegal* 78 C1
Tiveden, *Sweden* 11 F8
Tiverton, *U.K.* 13 G4
Tívoli, *Italy* 33 G9
Tiyo, *Eritrea* 77 E5
Tizga, *Morocco* 74 B3
Ti'zi N'Isli, *Morocco* 74 B3
Tizi-Ouzou, *Algeria* 75 A5
Tizimín, *Mexico* 115 C7
Tiznados →, *Venezuela* 120 B4
Tiznit, *Morocco* 74 C3
Tjeggelvas, *Sweden* 8 C14
Tjirebon = Cirebon,
　Indonesia 57 G13
Tjøme, *Norway* 10 E4
Tjonger Kanaal, *Neths.* 16 C7
Tjörn, *Sweden* 11 G5
Tkibuli, *Georgia* 43 E10
Tkvarcheli, *Georgia* 43 E9
Tlacotalpan, *Mexico* 115 D5
Tlahualilo, *Mexico* 114 B4
Tlaquepaque, *Mexico* 114 C4
Tlaxcala, *Mexico* 115 D5
Tlaxcala □, *Mexico* 115 D5
Tlaxiaco, *Mexico* 115 D5
Tlell, *Canada* 100 C2
Tlemcen, *Algeria* 75 B4
Tleta Sidi Bouguedra,
　Morocco 74 B3
Tlumach, *Ukraine* 42 B1
Tlyarata, *Russia* 43 E12
Tmassah, *Libya* 73 C8
Tnine d'Anglou, *Morocco* 74 C3
To Bong, *Vietnam* 58 F7
Toad →, *Canada* 100 B4
Toamasina, *Madag.* 85 B8

Toamasina □, *Madag.* 85 B8
Toay, *Argentina* 126 D3
Toba, *Japan* 49 G8
Toba Kakar, *Pakistan* 62 D3
Toba Tek Singh, *Pakistan* 62 D5
Tobago, *W. Indies* 117 D7
Tobarra, *Spain* 29 G3
Tobelo, *Indonesia* 57 D7
Tobermorey, *Australia* 90 C2
Tobermory, *Canada* 98 C3
Tobermory, *U.K.* 14 E2
Tobin, *U.S.A.* 112 F5
Tobin, L., *Australia* 88 D4
Tobin L., *Canada* 101 C8
Toboali, *Indonesia* 56 E3
Tobol, *Kazakhstan* 44 D7
Tobol →, *Russia* 44 D7
Toboli, *Indonesia* 57 E6
Tobolsk, *Russia* 44 D7
Tobruk = Tubruq, *Libya* 73 B9
Tobyhanna, *U.S.A.* 107 E9
Tocache Nuevo, *Peru* 124 B2
Tocantínia, *Brazil* 122 C2
Tocantinópolis, *Brazil* 122 C2
Tocantins □, *Brazil* 122 B2
Toccoa, *U.S.A.* 105 H4
Toce →, *Italy* 32 C5
Tochigi, *Japan* 49 F9
Tochigi □, *Japan* 49 F9
Tocina, *Spain* 31 H5
Tocopilla, *Chile* 126 A1
Tocumwal, *Australia* 91 F4
Tocuyo →, *Venezuela* 120 A4
Tocuyo de la Costa,
　Venezuela 120 A4
Todd →, *Australia* 90 C2
Todeli, *Indonesia* 57 E6
Todenyang, *Kenya* 82 B4
Todi, *Italy* 33 F9
Tödi, *Switz.* 23 C7
Todos os Santos, B. de,
　Brazil 123 D4
Todos Santos, *Mexico* 114 C2
Todtnau, *Germany* 19 H3
Toecé, *Burkina Faso* 79 C4
Tofield, *Canada* 100 C6
Tofino, *Canada* 100 D3
Töfsingdalens nationalpark,
　Sweden 10 B6
Toftlund, *Denmark* 11 J3
Tofua, *Tonga* 87 D11
Tōgane, *Japan* 49 G10
Togba, *Mauritania* 78 B2
Toggenburg, *Switz.* 23 B8
Togian, Kepulauan,
　Indonesia 57 E6
Togliatti, *Russia* 41 E16
Togo ■, *W. Afr.* 79 D5
Togtoh, *China* 50 D6
Tohma →, *Turkey* 67 D8
Toinya, *Sudan* 77 F2
Tojikiston = Tajikistan ■,
　Asia 44 F8
Tojo, *Indonesia* 57 E6
Tōjō, *Japan* 49 G6
Toka, *Guyana* 121 C6
Tokachi-Dake, *Japan* 48 C11
Tokachi-Gawa →, *Japan* 48 C11
Tokaj, *Hungary* 21 G11
Tokala, *Indonesia* 57 E6
Tōkamachi, *Japan* 49 F9
Tokanui, *N.Z.* 87 M2
Tokar, *Sudan* 76 D4
Tokara-Rettō, *Japan* 49 K4
Tokarahi, *N.Z.* 87 L3
Tokashiki-Shima, *Japan* 49 L3
Tokat, *Turkey* 66 C7
Tokat □, *Turkey* 66 C7
Tŏkchŏn, *N. Korea* 51 E14
Tokeland, *U.S.A.* 112 D3
Tokelau Is., *Pac. Oc.* 92 H10
Tokmak, *Kirghizia* 44 E8
Toko Ra., *Australia* 90 C2
Tokoro-Gawa →, *Japan* 48 B12
Tokuno-Shima, *Japan* 49 L4
Tokushima, *Japan* 49 G7
Tokushima □, *Japan* 49 H7
Tokuyama, *Japan* 49 G5
Tōkyō, *Japan* 49 G9
Tolaga Bay, *N.Z.* 87 H7
Tolbukhin, *Bulgaria* 38 F10
Toledo, *Spain* 30 F6
Toledo, *Ohio, U.S.A.* 104 E4
Toledo, *Oreg., U.S.A.* 110 D2
Toledo, *Wash., U.S.A.* 110 C3
Toledo, Montes de, *Spain* 31 F6
Tolentino, *Italy* 33 E10
Tolga, *Algeria* 75 B6
Tolga, *Norway* 10 B5
Toliara, *Madag.* 85 C7
Toliara □, *Madag.* 85 C8
Tolima, *Colombia* 120 C2
Tolima □, *Colombia* 120 C2
Tolitoli, *Indonesia* 57 D6
Tolkamer, *Neths.* 16 E8
Tolleson, *U.S.A.* 111 K7
Tollhouse, *U.S.A.* 112 H7
Tolmachevo, *Russia* 40 B6
Tolmezzo, *Italy* 33 B10
Tolmin, *Slovenia* 33 B10
Tolo, *Zaïre* 80 E3
Tolo, Teluk, *Indonesia* 57 E6
Tolochin, *Belorussia* 40 D6
Tolosa, *Spain* 28 B2

Tolox, *Spain* 31 J6
Toltén, *Chile* 128 A2
Toluca, *Mexico* 115 D5
Tom Burke, *S. Africa* 85 C4
Tom Price, *Australia* 88 D2
Tomah, *U.S.A.* 108 D9
Tomahawk, *U.S.A.* 108 C10
Tomakomai, *Japan* 48 C10
Tomales, *U.S.A.* 112 G4
Tomales B., *U.S.A.* 112 G3
Tomar, *Portugal* 31 F2
Tomarza, *Turkey* 66 D6
Tomás Barrón, *Bolivia* 124 D4
Tomaszów Mazowiecki,
　Poland 20 D9
Tomatlán, *Mexico* 114 D3
Tombador, Serra do, *Brazil* 125 C6
Tombé, *Sudan* 77 F3
Tombigbee →, *U.S.A.* 105 K2
Tombouctou, *Mali* 78 B4
Tombstone, *U.S.A.* 111 L8
Tombua, *Angola* 84 B1
Tomé, *Chile* 126 D1
Tomé-Açu, *Brazil* 122 B2
Tomelilla, *Sweden* 11 J7
Tomelloso, *Spain* 29 F1
Tomingley, *Australia* 91 E4
Tomini, *Indonesia* 57 D6
Tomini, Teluk, *Indonesia* 57 E6
Tominian, *Mali* 78 C4
Tomiño, *Spain* 30 D2
Tomkinson Ras., *Australia* 89 E4
Tommot, *Russia* 45 D13
Tomnavoulin, *U.K.* 14 D5
Tomnop Ta Suos,
　Cambodia 59 G5
Tomo, *Colombia* 120 C4
Tomo →, *Colombia* 120 B4
Toms Place, *U.S.A.* 112 H8
Toms River, *U.S.A.* 107 G10
Tomsk, *Russia* 44 D9
Tonalá, *Mexico* 115 D6
Tonale, Passo del, *Italy* 32 B7
Tonalea, *U.S.A.* 111 H8
Tonantins, *Brazil* 120 D5
Tonasket, *U.S.A.* 110 B4
Tonate, Fr. Guiana* 121 C7
Tonawanda, *U.S.A.* 106 D6
Tonbridge, *U.K.* 13 F8
Tondano, *Indonesia* 57 D6
Tondela, *Portugal* 30 E2
Tønder, *Denmark* 11 K2
Tondi Kiwindi, *Niger* 79 C5
Tondibi, *Mali* 79 B4
Tonekābon, *Iran* 65 B6
Tong Xian, *China* 50 E9
Tonga ■, *Pac. Oc.* 87 D11
Tonga Trench, *Pac. Oc.* 92 J10
Tongaat, *S. Africa* 85 D5
Tong'an, *China* 53 E12
Tongareva, *Cook Is.* 93 H12
Tongatapu, *Tonga* 87 E11
Tongbai, *China* 53 A9
Tongcheng, *Anhui, China* 53 B11
Tongcheng, *Hubei, China* 53 C9
Tongchŏn-ni, *N. Korea* 51 E14
Tongchuan, *China* 50 G5
Tongdao, *China* 52 D7
Tongeren, *Belgium* 17 G6
Tonggu, *China* 53 C10
Tongguan, *China* 50 G6
Tonghai, *China* 52 E4
Tonghua, *China* 51 D13
Tongjiang, *Heilongjiang,
　China* 54 B8
Tongjiang, *Sichuan, China* 52 B6
Tongjosŏn Man, *N. Korea* 51 E14
Tongking, G. of = Tonkin,
　G. of, *Asia* 58 B7
Tongliang, *China* 52 C6
Tongliao, *China* 51 C12
Tongling, *China* 53 B11
Tonglu, *China* 53 C12
Tongnae, *S. Korea* 51 G15
Tongnan, *China* 52 B5
Tongobory, *Madag.* 85 C7
Tongoy, *Chile* 126 C1
Tongren, *China* 52 D7
Tongres = Tongeren,
　Belgium 17 G6
Tongsa Dzong, *Bhutan* 61 F17
Tongue, *U.K.* 14 C4
Tongue →, *U.S.A.* 108 B2
Tongwei, *China* 50 G3
Tongxin, *China* 50 F3
Tongyang, *N. Korea* 51 E14
Tongyu, *China* 51 B12
Tongzi, *China* 52 C6
Tonj, *Sudan* 77 F2
Tonk, *India* 62 F6
Tonkawa, *U.S.A.* 109 G6
Tonkin = Bac Phan,
　Vietnam 58 B5
Tonkin, G. of, *Asia* 58 B7
Tonlé Sap, *Cambodia* 58 F4
Tonnay-Charente, *France* 26 C3
Tonneins, *France* 26 D4
Tonnerre, *France* 25 E10
Tönning, *Germany* 18 A4
Tono, *Japan* 48 E10
Tonopah, *U.S.A.* 111 G5
Tonosí, *Panama* 116 E3
Tønsberg, *Norway* 10 E4
Tooele, *U.S.A.* 110 F7
Toompine, *Australia* 91 D3
Toonpan, *Australia* 90 B4

Toora, *Australia* 91 F4
Toora-Khem, *Russia* 45 D10
Toowoomba, *Australia* .. 91 D5
Topalu, *Romania* 38 E11
Topaz, *U.S.A.* 112 G7
Topeka, *U.S.A.* 108 F7
Topki, *Russia* 44 D9
Topl'a →, *Slovakia* 20 G11
Topley, *Canada* 100 C3
Toplica →, *Serbia, Yug.* . 21 M11
Topliţa, *Romania* 38 C8
Topocalma, Pta., *Chile* . 126 C1
Topock, *U.S.A.* 113 L12
Topola, *Serbia, Yug.* ... 21 L10
Topolčany, *Slovakia* ... 20 G8
Topoli, *Kazakhstan* 43 C14
Topolnitsa →, *Bulgaria* . 38 G7
Topolobampo, *Mexico* .. 114 B3
Topolovgrad, *Bulgaria* .. 38 G9
Toppenish, *U.S.A.* 110 C3
Topusko, *Croatia* 33 C12
Toquepala, *Peru* 124 D3
Torá, *Spain* 28 D6
Tora Kit, *Sudan* 77 E3
Toraka Vestale, *Madag.* . 85 B7
Torata, *Peru* 124 D3
Torbalı, *Turkey* 66 D2
Torbat, *Turkey* 66 D2
Torbay, *Canada* 99 C9
Torbay, *U.K.* 13 G4
Tørdal, *Norway* 10 E2
Tordesillas, *Spain* 30 D6
Tordoya, *Spain* 30 B2
Töreboda, *Sweden* 11 F8
Torfajökull, *Iceland* 8 E4
Torgau, *Germany* 18 D8
Torgelow, *Germany* 18 B9
Torhout, *Belgium* 17 F2
Tori, *Ethiopia* 77 F3
Tori-Shima, *Japan* 49 J10
Torigni-sur-Vire, *France* . 24 C6
Torija, *Spain* 28 E1
Torin, *Mexico* 114 B2
Toriñana, C., *Spain* 30 B1
Torino, *Italy* 32 C4
Torit, *Sudan* 77 G3
Torkovichi, *Russia* 40 B7
Tormes →, *Spain* 30 D4
Tornado Mt., *Canada* .. 100 D6
Torne älv →, *Sweden* ... 8 D18
Torneå = Tornio, *Finland* 8 D18
Torneträsk, *Sweden* ... 8 B15
Tornio, *Finland* 8 D18
Tornionjoki →, *Finland* . 8 D18
Tornquist, *Argentina* ... 126 D3
Toro, *Baleares, Spain* .. 36 B11
Toro, *Zamora, Spain* ... 30 D5
Torö, *Sweden* 11 F11
Toro, Cerro del, *Chile* .. 126 B2
Toro Pk., *U.S.A.* 113 M10
Törökszentmiklós, *Hungary* 21 H10
Toronío Kólpos, *Greece* . 39 J6
Toronto, *Australia* 91 E5
Toronto, *Canada* 98 D4
Toronto, *U.S.A.* 106 F4
Toropets, *Russia* 40 C7
Tororo, *Uganda* 82 B3
Toros Dağları, *Turkey* .. 66 E5
Torotoro, *Bolivia* 125 D4
Torpshammar, *Sweden* . 10 B10
Torquay, *Canada* 101 D8
Torquay, *U.K.* 13 G4
Torquemada, *Spain* 30 C6
Torralba de Calatrava,
   Spain 31 F7
Torrance, *U.S.A.* 113 M8
Torrão, *Portugal* 31 G2
Tôrre de Moncorvo,
   Portugal 30 D3
Torre del Greco, *Italy* .. 35 B7
Torre del Mar, *Spain* ... 31 J6
Torre-Pacheco, *Spain* .. 29 H4
Torre Pellice, *Italy* 32 D4
Torreblanca, *Spain* 28 E5
Torrecampo, *Spain* 31 G6
Torrecilla en Cameros,
   Spain 28 C2
Torredembarra, *Spain* ... 28 D6
Torredonjimeno, *Spain* .. 31 H7
Torrejoncillo, *Spain* 30 F4
Torrelaguna, *Spain* 28 E1
Torrelavega, *Spain* 30 B6
Torremaggiore, *Italy* 35 A8
Torremolinos, *Spain* 31 J6
Torrens, L., *Australia* ... 91 E2
Torrens Cr. →, *Australia* . 90 C4
Torrens Creek, *Australia* . 90 C4
Torrente, *Spain* 29 F4
Torrenueva, *Spain* 29 G1
Torréon, *Mexico* 114 B4
Torreperogil, *Spain* 29 G1
Torres, *Mexico* 114 B2
Torres Novas, *Portugal* . 31 F2
Torres Strait, *Australia* .. 92 H6
Torres Vedras, *Portugal* . 31 F1
Torrevieja, *Spain* 29 H4
Torrey, *U.S.A.* 111 G8
Torridge →, *U.K.* 13 G3
Torridon, L., *U.K.* 14 D3
Torrijos, *Spain* 30 F6
Torrington, Conn., *U.S.A.* 107 E11
Torrington, Wyo., *U.S.A.* 108 D2
Torroella de Montgrí, *Spain* 28 C8
Torrox, *Spain* 31 J7
Torsö, *Sweden* 11 F7
Tortola, *Virgin Is.* 117 C7

Tórtoles de Esgueva, *Spain* 30 D6
Tortona, *Italy* 32 D5
Tortoreto, *Italy* 33 F10
Tortorici, *Italy* 35 D7
Tortosa, *Spain* 28 E5
Tortosa, C., *Spain* 28 E5
Tortosendo, *Portugal* ... 30 E3
Tortue, I. de la, *Haiti* .. 117 B5
Tortum, *Turkey* 67 C9
Ţorūd, *Iran* 65 C7
Torul, *Turkey* 67 C8
Toruń, *Poland* 20 B8
Torup, *Denmark* 11 G3
Torup, *Sweden* 11 H7
Tory I., *Ireland* 15 A3
Torysa →, *Slovakia* 20 G11
Torzhok, *Russia* 40 C9
Tosa, *Japan* 49 H6
Tosa-Shimizu, *Japan* ... 49 H6
Tosa-Wan, *Japan* 49 H6
Toscana, *Italy* 32 E8
Toscano, Arcipelago, *Italy* 32 F7
Toshkent = Tashkent,
   Uzbekistan 44 E7
Tosno, *Russia* 40 B7
Tossa, *Spain* 28 D7
Tostado, *Argentina* 126 B3
Tostedt, *Germany* 18 B5
Tostón, Pta. de, *Canary Is.* 36 F5
Tosu, *Japan* 49 H5
Tosya, *Turkey* 66 C6
Totana, *Spain* 29 H3
Toten, *Norway* 10 D4
Toteng, *Botswana* 84 C3
Tôtes, *France* 24 C8
Tótkomlós, *Hungary* ... 21 J10
Totma, *Russia* 41 B13
Totnes, *U.K.* 13 G4
Totness, *Surinam* 121 B6
Totonicapán, *Guatemala* . 116 D1
Totora, *Bolivia* 125 D4
Totten Glacier, *Antarctica* 5 C8
Tottenham, *Australia* ... 91 E4
Tottenham, *Canada* 106 B5
Tottori, *Japan* 49 G7
Tottori □, *Japan* 49 G7
Touat, *Algeria* 75 C5
Touba, *Ivory C.* 78 D3
Toubkal, Djebel, *Morocco* 74 B3
Toucy, *France* 25 E10
Tougan, *Burkina Faso* .. 78 C4
Touggourt, *Algeria* 75 B6
Tougué, *Guinea* 78 C2
Toukmatine, *Algeria* ... 75 D6
Toul, *France* 25 D12
Toulepleu, *Ivory C.* 78 D3
Toulon, *France* 27 E9
Toulouse, *France* 26 E5
Toummo, *Niger* 73 D7
Toumodi, *Ivory C.* 78 D3
Tounassine, Hamada,
   Algeria 74 C3
Toungoo, *Burma* 61 K20
Touques →, *France* 24 C7
Touraine, *France* 24 C7
Tourane = Da Nang,
   Vietnam 58 D7
Tourcoing, *France* 25 B10
Tourine, *Mauritania* 74 D2
Tournai, *Belgium* 17 G2
Tournan-en-Brie, *France* . 25 D9
Tournay, *France* 26 E4
Tournon, *France* 27 C8
Tournon-St.-Martin, *France* 24 F7
Tournus, *France* 27 B8
Touros, *Brazil* 122 C4
Tours, *France* 24 E7
Touwsrivier, *S. Africa* ... 84 E3
Tovar, *Venezuela* 120 B3
Tovarkovskiy, *Russia* ... 41 E11
Tovdal, *Norway* 11 F2
Tovdalselva →, *Norway* . 11 F2
Towada, *Japan* 48 D10
Towada-Ko, *Japan* 48 D10
Towamba, *Australia* 91 F4
Towanda, *U.S.A.* 107 E8
Towang, *India* 61 F17
Tower, *U.S.A.* 108 B8
Towerhill Cr. →, *Australia* 90 C3
Towner, *U.S.A.* 108 A4
Townsend, *U.S.A.* 110 C8
Townshend I., *Australia* . 90 C5
Townsville, *Australia* ... 90 B4
Towson, *U.S.A.* 104 F7
Toya-Ko, *Japan* 48 C10
Toyah, *U.S.A.* 109 K3
Toyahvale, *U.S.A.* 109 K3
Toyama, *Japan* 49 F8
Toyama □, *Japan* 49 F8
Toyama-Wan, *Japan* ... 49 F8
Toyohashi, *Japan* 49 G8
Toyokawa, *Japan* 49 G8
Toyonaka, *Japan* 49 G7
Toyooka, *Japan* 49 G7
Toyota, *Japan* 49 G8
Tozeur, *Tunisia* 75 B6
Tra On, *Vietnam* 59 H5
Trabancos →, *Spain* ... 30 D5
Traben Trarbach, *Germany* 19 F3
Trabzon, *Turkey* 42 F8
Trabzon □, *Turkey* 67 C8
Tracadie, *Canada* 99 C7
Tracy, Calif., *U.S.A.* 111 H3
Tracy, Minn., *U.S.A.* ... 108 C7
Tradate, *Italy* 32 C5
Tradovoye, *Russia* 48 C6

Trafalgar, C., *Spain* 31 J4
Traiguén, *Chile* 128 A2
Trail, *Canada* 100 D5
Trainor L., *Canada* 100 A4
Traíra →, *Brazil* 120 D4
Trákhonas, *Cyprus* 37 D12
Tralee, *Ireland* 15 D2
Tralee B., *Ireland* 15 D2
Tramelan, *Switz.* 22 B4
Tramore, *Ireland* 15 D4
Tran Ninh, Cao Nguyen,
   Laos 58 C4
Tranås, *Sweden* 9 G13
Trancas, *Argentina* 126 B2
Trancoso, *Portugal* 30 E3
Tranebjerg, *Denmark* ... 11 J4
Tranemo, *Sweden* 11 G7
Trang, *Thailand* 59 J2
Trangahy, *Madag.* 85 B7
Trangan, *Indonesia* 57 F8
Trangie, *Australia* 91 E4
Trångsviken, *Sweden* ... 10 A8
Trani, *Italy* 35 A9
Tranoroa, *Madag.* 85 C8
Tranqueras, *Uruguay* ... 127 C4
Trans Nzoia □, *Kenya* ... 82 B3
Transantarctic Mts.,
   Antarctica 5 E12
Transcaucasia =
   Zakavkazye, *Asia* 43 F11
Transcona, *Canada* 101 D9
Transilvania, *Romania* .. 38 D8
Transkei □, *S. Africa* ... 85 E4
Transvaal □, *S. Africa* ... 84 D4
Transylvania =
   Transilvania, *Romania* .. 38 D8
Transylvanian Alps,
   Romania 6 F10
Trápani, *Italy* 34 D5
Trapper Pk., *U.S.A.* 110 D6
Traralgon, *Australia* 91 F4
Trarza, *Mauritania* 78 B2
Trasacco, *Italy* 33 G10
Trasimeno, L., *Italy* 33 E9
Trat, *Thailand* 59 F4
Traun, *Austria* 21 G4
Traunstein, *Germany* ... 19 H8
Travers, Mt., *N.Z.* 87 K4
Traverse City, *U.S.A.* ... 104 C3
Tråvad, *Sweden* 11 F7
Traveller's L., *Australia* .. 91 E3
Travemünde, *Germany* .. 18 B6
Travnik, *Bos.-H.* 21 L7
Trayning, *Australia* 89 F2
Trazo, *Spain* 30 B2
Trébbia →, *Italy* 32 C6
Trebel →, *Germany* 18 B9
Trebinje, *Bos.-H., Yug.* .. 21 N8
Trebisacce, *Italy* 35 C9
Trebišnjica →,
   Bos.-H. 21 N8
Trebišov, *Slovakia* 20 G11
Trebižat →, *Bos.-H.* 21 M7
Trebnje, *Slovenia* 33 C12
Třeboň, *Czech.* 20 G4
Trebujena, *Spain* 31 J4
Trecate, *Italy* 32 C5
Trece Martires, *Phil.* 55 D4
Tredegar, *U.K.* 13 F4
Tregaron, *U.K.* 13 E4
Trégastel-Plage, *France* . 24 D3
Tregnago, *Italy* 33 C8
Tregrosse Is., *Australia* . 90 B5
Tréguier, *France* 24 D3
Trégunc, *France* 24 E3
Treherne, *Canada* 101 D9
Tréia, *Italy* 33 E10
Treignac, *France* 26 C5
Treinta y Tres, *Uruguay* . 127 C5
Treis, *Germany* 19 E3
Trekveld, *S. Africa* 84 E2
Trelde Næs, *Denmark* ... 11 J3
Trelew, *Argentina* 128 B3
Trélissac, *France* 26 C4
Trelleborg, *Sweden* 11 J7
Trélon, *France* 25 B11
Tremiti, *Italy* 33 F12
Tremonton, *U.S.A.* 110 F7
Tremp, *Spain* 28 C5
Trenche →, *Canada* 98 C5
Trenčín, *Slovakia* 20 G8
Trenggalek, *Indonesia* .. 57 H14
Trenque Lauquen,
   Argentina 126 D3
Trent →, *U.K.* 12 D7
Trentino-Alto Adige □,
   Italy 32 B8
Trento, *Italy* 32 B8
Trenton, *Canada* 98 D4
Trenton, Mo., *U.S.A.* ... 108 E8
Trenton, N.J., *U.S.A.* ... 107 F10
Trenton, Nebr., *U.S.A.* .. 108 E4
Trenton, Tenn., *U.S.A.* .. 109 H10
Trepassey, *Canada* 99 C9
Trepuzzi, *Italy* 35 B11
Tres Arroyos, *Argentina* . 126 D3
Três Corações, *Brazil* ... 123 F2
Três Lagôas, *Brazil* 123 F1
Tres Lagos →, *Argentina* . 128 C2
Três Marias, Reprêsa,
   Brazil 123 E2
Tres Montes, C., *Chile* .. 128 C1
Tres Pinos, *U.S.A.* 112 J5

Três Pontas, *Brazil* 123 F2
Tres Puentes, *Chile* 126 B1
Tres Puntas, C., *Argentina* 128 C3
Três Rios, *Brazil* 123 F3
Tres Valles, *Mexico* 115 D5
Treska →,
   Macedonia 39 H4
Trespaderne, *Spain* 28 C1
Trets, *France* 27 E9
Treuchtlingen, *Germany* . 19 G6
Treuenbrietzen, *Germany* . 18 C8
Treungen, *Norway* 9 G10
Trevíglio, *Italy* 32 C6
Trevínca, Peña, *Spain* ... 30 C4
Treviso, *Italy* 33 C9
Trévoux, *France* 27 C8
Treysa, *Germany* 18 E5
Trgovište, *Serbia, Yug.* . 21 N12
Triabunna, *Australia* 90 G4
Triánda, *Greece* 37 C10
Triang, *Malaysia* 59 L4
Triaucourt-en-Argonne,
   France 25 D12
Tribsees, *Germany* 18 A8
Tribulation, C., *Australia* . 90 B4
Tribune, *U.S.A.* 108 F4
Tricárico, *Italy* 35 B9
Tricase, *Italy* 35 C11
Trichinopoly =
   Tiruchchirappalli, *India* . 60 P11
Trichur, *India* 60 P10
Trida, *Australia* 91 E4
Trier, *Germany* 19 F2
Trieste, *Italy* 33 C10
Trieste, G. di, *Italy* 33 C10
Trieux →, *France* 24 D3
Triggiano, *Italy* 35 A9
Triglav, *Slovenia* 33 B10
Trigno →, *Italy* 33 F11
Trigueros, *Spain* 31 H4
Trikhonis, Límni, *Greece* . 39 L4
Tríkkala, *Greece* 39 K4
Trikomo, *Cyprus* 37 D12
Trikora, Puncak, *Indonesia* 57 E9
Trilj, *Croatia* 33 E13
Trillo, *Spain* 28 E2
Trim, *Ireland* 15 C5
Trincomalee, *Sri Lanka* . 60 Q12
Trindade, *Brazil* 123 E2
Trindade, I., *Atl. Oc.* 2 F8
Trinidad, *Bolivia* 125 C5
Trinidad, *Colombia* 120 B3
Trinidad, *Cuba* 116 B3
Trinidad, *Uruguay* 126 C4
Trinidad, *U.S.A.* 109 G2
Trinidad, *W. Indies* 117 D7
Trinidad →, *Mexico* 115 D5
Trinidad, G., *Chile* 128 C1
Trinidad, I., *Argentina* .. 128 A4
Trinidad & Tobago ■,
   W. Indies 117 D7
Trinitápoli, *Italy* 35 A9
Trinity, *Canada* 99 C9
Trinity, *U.S.A.* 109 K7
Trinity →, Calif., *U.S.A.* . 110 F2
Trinity →, Tex., *U.S.A.* .. 109 L7
Trinity B., *Canada* 99 C9
Trinity Range, *U.S.A.* ... 110 F4
Trinkitat, *Sudan* 76 D4
Trino, *Italy* 32 C5
Trion, *U.S.A.* 105 H3
Trionto, C., *Italy* 35 C9
Triora, *Italy* 32 E4
Tripoli = Tarābulus,
   Lebanon 69 A4
Tripoli = Tarābulus, *Libya* 75 B7
Tripp, *U.S.A.* 108 D6
Tripura □, *India* 61 H17
Tripylos, *Cyprus* 37 E11
Trischen, *Germany* 18 A4
Tristan da Cunha, *Atl. Oc.* 2 F9
Trivandrum, *India* 60 Q10
Trivento, *Italy* 35 A7
Trnava, *Slovakia* 21 G7
Trochu, *Canada* 100 C6
Trodely I., *Canada* 98 B4
Trogir, *Croatia* 33 E13
Troglav, *Croatia* 33 E13
Trøgstad, *Norway* 10 E5
Tróia, *Italy* 35 A8
Troilus, L., *Canada* 98 B5
Troina, *Italy* 35 E7
Trois Fourches, Cap des,
   Morocco 75 A4
Trois-Pistoles, *Canada* .. 99 C6
Trois-Rivières, *Canada* .. 98 C5
Troisvierges, *Belgium* ... 17 H8
Troitsk, *Russia* 44 D7
Troitsko Pechorsk, *Russia* 44 B10
Trölladyngja, *Iceland* ... 8 D5
Trollhättan, *Sweden* 11 F6
Trollheimen, *Norway* ... 10 B3
Trombetas →, *Brazil* ... 121 D6
Troms fylke □, *Norway* .. 8 B15
Tromsø, *Norway* 8 B15
Trona, *U.S.A.* 113 K9
Tronador, *Argentina* 128 B2
Trondheim, *Norway* 10 A4
Trondheimsfjorden,
   Norway 8 E11
Trönninge, *Sweden* 11 H6
Trönö, *Sweden* 10 C10
Tronto →, *Italy* 33 F10
Troodos, *Cyprus* 37 E11
Troon, *U.K.* 14 F4
Tropea, *Italy* 35 D8

Tropic, *U.S.A.* 111 H7
Tropoja, *Albania* 38 G3
Trossachs, The, *U.K.* ... 14 E4
Trostan, *U.K.* 15 A5
Trostberg, *Germany* 19 G8
Trostyanets, *Ukraine* ... 40 F9
Trotternish, *U.K.* 14 D2
Troup, *U.S.A.* 109 J7
Trout →, *Canada* 100 A5
Trout L., *N.W.T., Canada* 100 A4
Trout L., *Ont., Canada* .. 101 C10
Trout Lake, *Mich., U.S.A.* 98 C2
Trout Lake, *Wash., U.S.A.* 112 E5
Trout River, *Canada* 99 C8
Trouville-sur-Mer, *France* . 24 C7
Trowbridge, *U.K.* 13 F5
Troy, *Turkey* 66 D2
Troy, Ala., *U.S.A.* 105 K3
Troy, Idaho, *U.S.A.* 110 C5
Troy, Kans., *U.S.A.* 108 F7
Troy, Mo., *U.S.A.* 108 F9
Troy, Mont., *U.S.A.* 110 B6
Troy, N.Y., *U.S.A.* 107 D11
Troy, Ohio, *U.S.A.* 104 E3
Troyan, *Bulgaria* 38 G7
Troyes, *France* 25 D11
Trpanj, *Croatia* 21 M7
Trstena, *Slovakia* 20 F9
Trstenik, *Serbia, Yug.* .. 21 M10
Trubchevsk, *Russia* 40 E8
Trucial States = United
   Arab Emirates ■, *Asia* . 65 F7
Truckee, *U.S.A.* 112 F6
Trujillo, *Colombia* 120 C2
Trujillo, *Honduras* 116 C2
Trujillo, *Peru* 124 B2
Trujillo, *Spain* 31 F5
Trujillo, *U.S.A.* 109 H2
Trujillo, *Venezuela* 120 B3
Trujillo □, *Venezuela* ... 120 B3
Truk, *Pac. Oc.* 92 G7
Trumann, *U.S.A.* 109 H9
Trumbull, Mt., *U.S.A.* .. 111 H7
Trun, *France* 24 D7
Trun, *Switz.* 23 C7
Trundle, *Australia* 91 E4
Trung-Phan, *Vietnam* ... 58 E7
Truro, *Canada* 99 C7
Truro, *U.K.* 13 G2
Truslove, *Australia* 89 F3
Trustrup, *Denmark* 11 H4
Truth or Consequences,
   U.S.A. 111 K10
Trutnov, *Czech.* 20 E5
Truyère →, *France* 26 D6
Tryavna, *Bulgaria* 38 G8
Tryon, *U.S.A.* 105 H4
Tryonville, *U.S.A.* 106 E5
Trzcianka, *Poland* 20 B6
Trzebiatów, *Poland* 20 A5
Trzebiez, *Poland* 20 B4
Trzebinia-Siersza, *Poland* . 20 E9
Trzebnica, *Poland* 20 D7
Tržič, *Slovenia* 33 B11
Tsageri, *Georgia* 43 E10
Tsau, *Botswana* 84 C3
Tsebrikovo, *Ukraine* 42 C4
Tselinograd, *Kazakhstan* . 44 D8
Tsetserleg, *Mongolia* ... 54 B5
Tshabong, *Botswana* ... 84 D3
Tshane, *Botswana* 84 C3
Tshela, *Zaïre* 80 E2
Tshesebe, *Botswana* ... 85 C4
Tshibeke, *Zaïre* 82 C2
Tshibinda, *Zaïre* 82 C2
Tshikapa, *Zaïre* 80 F4
Tshilenge, *Zaïre* 82 D1
Tshinsenda, *Zaïre* 83 E2
Tshofa, *Zaïre* 82 D2
Tshwane, *Botswana* 84 C3
Tsigara, *Botswana* 84 C4
Tsihombe, *Madag.* 85 D8
Tsimlyansk, *Russia* 43 C10
Tsimlyansk Res. =
   Tsimlyanskoye Vdkhr.,
   Russia 43 B10
Tsimlyanskoye Vdkhr.,
   Russia 43 B10
Tsinan = Jinan, *China* .. 50 F9
Tsineng, *S. Africa* 84 D3
Tsinghai = Qinghai □,
   China 54 C4
Tsingtao = Qingdao, *China* 51 F11
Tsinjomitondraka, *Madag.* 85 B8
Tsiroanomandidy, *Madag.* 85 B8
Tsivilsk, *Russia* 41 D15
Tsivory, *Madag.* 85 C8
Tskhinvali, *Georgia* 43 E11
Tsna →, *Russia* 41 D12
Tso Moriri, L., *India* 63 C8
Tsodilo Hill, *Botswana* .. 84 B3
Tsogttsetsiy, *Mongolia* .. 50 C3
Tsolo, *S. Africa* 85 E4
Tsomo, *S. Africa* 85 E4
Tsu, *Japan* 49 G8
Tsu L., *Canada* 100 A6
Tsuchiura, *Japan* 49 F10
Tsugaru-Kaikyō, *Japan* .. 48 D10
Tsumeb, *Namibia* 84 B2
Tsumis, *Namibia* 84 C2

Tsuruga, *Japan* 49 G8
Tsurugi-San, *Japan* 49 H7
Tsuruoka, *Japan* 48 E9
Tsushima, *Gifu, Japan* ... 49 G8
Tsushima, *Nagasaki, Japan* 49 G4
Tsvetkovo, *Ukraine* 42 B4
Tua →, *Portugal* 30 D3
Tual, *Indonesia* 57 F8
Tuam, *Ireland* 15 C3
Tuamotu Arch. = Tuamotu
  Is., *Pac. Oc.* 93 J13
Tuamotu Is., *Pac. Oc.* ... 93 J13
Tuamotu Ridge, *Pac. Oc.* . 93 K14
Tuanfeng, *China* 53 B10
Tuanxi, *China* 52 D6
Tuao, *Phil.* 55 C4
Tuapse, *Russia* 43 D8
Tuatapere, *N.Z.* 87 M1
Tuba City, *U.S.A.* 111 H8
Tuban, *Indonesia* 57 G15
Tubarão, *Brazil* 127 B6
Tūbās, *Jordan* 69 C4
Tubau, *Malaysia* 56 D4
Tubbergen, *Neths.* 16 D9
Tübingen, *Germany* 19 G5
Tubize, *Belgium* 17 G4
Tubruq, *Libya* 73 B9
Tubuai Is., *Pac. Oc.* 93 K12
Tuc Trung, *Vietnam* 59 G6
Tucacas, *Venezuela* 120 A4
Tucano, *Brazil* 122 D4
Tuchang, *Taiwan* 53 E13
Tuchodi →, *Canada* 100 B4
Tuchola, *Poland* 20 B7
Tucson, *U.S.A.* 111 K8
Tucumán □, *Argentina* ... 126 B2
Tucumcari, *U.S.A.* 109 H3
Tucunaré, *Brazil* 125 B6
Tucupido, *Venezuela* 120 B4
Tucupita, *Venezuela* 121 B5
Tucuruí, *Brazil* 122 B2
Tudela, *Spain* 28 C3
Tudela de Duero, *Spain* .. 30 D6
Tudmur, *Syria* 64 C3
Tudor, L., *Canada* 99 A6
Tudora, *Romania* 38 B9
Tuella →, *Portugal* 30 D3
Tuen, *Australia* 91 D4
Tueré →, *Brazil* 122 B1
Tugela →, *S. Africa* 85 D5
Tuguegarao, *Phil.* 55 C4
Tugur, *Russia* 45 D14
Tuineje, *Canary Is.* 36 F5
Tukangbesi, Kepulauan,
  Indonesia 57 F6
Tukarak I., *Canada* 98 A4
Tukayyid, *Iraq* 64 D5
Tûkh, *Egypt* 76 H7
Tukobo, *Ghana* 78 D4
Tūkrah, *Libya* 73 B9
Tuktoyaktuk, *Canada* 96 B6
Tukums, *Latvia* 40 C3
Tukuyu, *Tanzania* 83 D3
Tula, *Hidalgo, Mexico* ... 115 C5
Tula, *Tamaulipas, Mexico* 115 C5
Tula, *Nigeria* 79 D7
Tula, *Russia* 41 D10
Tulancingo, *Mexico* 115 C5
Tulare, *U.S.A.* 111 H4
Tulare Lake Bed, *U.S.A.* . 111 J4
Tularosa, *U.S.A.* 111 K10
Tulbagh, *S. Africa* 84 E2
Tulcán, *Ecuador* 120 C2
Tulcea, *Romania* 38 D11
Tulchin, *Ukraine* 42 B3
Tūleh, *Iran* 65 C7
Tulemalu L., *Canada* 101 A9
Tuli, *Indonesia* 57 E6
Tuli, *Zimbabwe* 83 G2
Tulia, *U.S.A.* 109 H4
Ṭülkarm, *Jordan* 69 C4
Tullahoma, *U.S.A.* 105 H2
Tullamore, *Australia* 91 E4
Tullamore, *Ireland* 15 C4
Tulle, *France* 26 C5
Tullibigeal, *Australia* ... 91 E4
Tullins, *France* 27 C9
Tulln, *Austria* 21 G6
Tullow, *Ireland* 15 D4
Tullus, *Sudan* 77 E1
Tully, *Australia* 90 B4
Ṭulmaythah, *Libya* 73 B9
Tulmur, *Australia* 90 C3
Tulnici, *Romania* 38 D9
Tulovo, *Bulgaria* 38 G8
Tulsa, *U.S.A.* 109 G7
Tulsequah, *Canada* 100 B2
Tulu Milki, *Ethiopia* 77 F4
Tulu Welel, *Ethiopia* 77 F3
Tulua, *Colombia* 120 C2
Tulun, *Russia* 45 D11
Tuma →, *Nic.* 116 D3
Tumaco, *Colombia* 120 C2
Tumaco, Ensenada,
  Colombia 120 C2
Tumatumari, *Guyana* 121 B6
Tumba, *Sweden* 10 E11
Tumba, L., *Zaïre* 80 E3
Tumbarumba, *Australia* .. 91 F4
Tùmbes, *Peru* 124 A1
Tumbes □, *Peru* 124 A1
Tumbwe, *Zaïre* 83 E2

Tumby Bay, *Australia* 91 E2
Tumd Youqi, *China* 50 D6
Tumen, *China* 51 C15
Tumen Jiang →, *China* ... 51 C16
Tumeremo, *Venezuela* 121 B5
Tumiritinga, *Brazil* 123 E3
Tumkur, *India* 60 N10
Tummel, L., *U.K.* 14 E5
Tump, *Pakistan* 60 F3
Tumpat, *Malaysia* 59 J4
Tumu, *Ghana* 78 C4
Tumucumaque, Serra,
  Brazil 121 C7
Tumupasa, *Bolivia* 124 C4
Tumut, *Australia* 91 F4
Tumwater, *U.S.A.* 110 C2
Tunas de Zaza, *Cuba* 116 B4
Tunbridge Wells, *U.K.* ... 13 F8
Tunceli, *Turkey* 67 D8
Tunceli □, *Turkey* 67 D8
Tuncurry, *Australia* 91 E5
Tunduru, *Tanzania* 83 E4
Tunduru □, *Tanzania* 83 E4
Tundzha →, *Bulgaria* 39 H9
Tunga Pass, *India* 61 E19
Tungabhadra →, *India* ... 60 M11
Tungaru, *Sudan* 77 E3
Tungla, *Nic.* 116 D3
Tungnafellsjökull, *Iceland* 8 D5
Tungsten, *Canada* 100 A3
Tungurahua □, *Ecuador* .. 120 D2
Tunguska, Nizhnyaya →,
  Russia 45 C9
Tunia, *Colombia* 120 C2
Tunica, *U.S.A.* 109 H9
Tunis, *Tunisia* 75 A7
Tunis, Golfe de, *Tunisia* . 75 A7
Tunisia ■, *Africa* 75 B6
Tunja, *Colombia* 120 B3
Tunkhannock, *U.S.A.* ... 107 E9
Tunliu, *China* 50 F7
Tunnsjøen, *Norway* 8 D12
Tunungayualok I., *Canada* 99 A7
Tunuyán, *Argentina* 126 C2
Tunuyán →, *Argentina* .. 126 C2
Tunxi, *China* 53 C12
Tuo Jiang →, *China* 52 C5
Tuolumne, *U.S.A.* 111 H3
Tuolumne →, *U.S.A.* 112 H5
Tuoy-Khaya, *Russia* 45 C12
Tūpā, *Brazil* 127 A5
Tupaciguara, *Brazil* 123 E2
Tupelo, *U.S.A.* 105 H1
Tupik, *Russia* 40 D8
Tupik, *Russia* 45 D12
Tupinambaranas, *Brazil* .. 121 D6
Tupirama, *Brazil* 122 C2
Tupiratins, *Brazil* 122 C2
Tupiza, *Bolivia* 126 A2
Tupman, *U.S.A.* 113 K7
Tupper, *Canada* 100 B4
Tupper Lake, *U.S.A.* 107 B10
Tupungato, Cerro,
  S. Amer. 126 C2
Tuquan, *China* 51 B11
Túquerres, *Colombia* 120 C2
Tura, *Russia* 45 C11
Turabah, *Si. Arabia* 64 D4
Turagua, Serranía,
  Venezuela 121 B5
Tūrān, *Iran* 65 C8
Turan, *Russia* 45 D10
Turayf, *Si. Arabia* 64 D3
Turbenthal, *Switz.* 23 B7
Turégano, *Spain* 30 D6
Turek, *Poland* 20 C8
Turen, *Venezuela* 120 B4
Turfan = Turpan, *China* . 54 B3
Turfan Depression =
  Turpan Hami, *China* ... 54 B3
Tŭrgovishte, *Bulgaria* ... 38 F9
Turgutlu, *Turkey* 66 D2
Turhal, *Turkey* 42 F7
Turia →, *Spain* 29 F4
Turiaçu, *Brazil* 122 B2
Turiaçu →, *Brazil* 122 B2
Turin = Torino, *Italy* ... 32 C4
Turin, *Canada* 100 D6
Turka, *Ukraine* 40 G3
Turkana □, *Kenya* 82 B4
Turkana, L., *Africa* 82 B4
Turkestan, *Kazakhstan* ... 44 E7
Túrkeve, *Hungary* 21 H13
Turkey ■, *Eurasia* 66 D7
Turkey Creek, *Australia* . 88 C4
Turki, *Russia* 41 F13
Turkmenistan ■, *Asia* ... 44 F6
Türkoğlu, *Turkey* 66 E7
Turks & Caicos Is. ■,
  W. Indies 117 B5
Turks Island Passage,
  W. Indies 117 B5
Turku, *Finland* 9 F17
Turkwe →, *Kenya* 82 B4
Turlock, *U.S.A.* 111 H3
Turnagain →, *Canada* ... 100 B3
Turnagain, C., *N.Z.* 87 J6
Turneffe Is., *Belize* 115 D7
Turner, *Australia* 88 C4
Turner, *U.S.A.* 110 B9
Turner Pt., *Australia* 90 A1
Turner Valley, *Canada* ... 100 C6
Turners Falls, *U.S.A.* ... 107 D12
Turnhout, *Belgium* 17 F5
Turnor L., *Canada* 101 B7

Tŭrnovo, *Bulgaria* 38 F8
Turnu Măgurele, *Romania* 38 F7
Turnu Rosu Pasul,
  Romania 38 D7
Turon, *U.S.A.* 109 G5
Turpan, *China* 54 B3
Turpan Hami, *China* 54 B3
Turriff, *U.K.* 14 D6
Tursāq, *Iraq* 64 C5
Tursha, *Russia* 41 C15
Tursi, *Italy* 35 B9
Turtle Head I., *Australia* . 90 A3
Turtle L., *Canada* 101 C7
Turtle Lake, *N. Dak.,*
  U.S.A. 108 B4
Turtle Lake, *Wis., U.S.A.* 108 C8
Turtleford, *Canada* 101 C7
Turukhansk, *Russia* 45 C9
Turun ja Porin lääni □,
  Finland 9 F17
Turzovka, *Slovakia* 20 F8
Tuscaloosa, *U.S.A.* 105 J2
Tuscánia, *Italy* 33 F8
Tuscany = Toscana, *Italy* . 32 E8
Tuscola, *Ill., U.S.A.* 104 F1
Tuscola, *Tex., U.S.A.* ... 109 J5
Tuscumbia, *U.S.A.* 105 H2
Tuskar Rock, *Ireland* 15 D5
Tuskegee, *U.S.A.* 105 J3
Tustna, *Norway* 10 A2
Tutak, *Turkey* 67 D10
Tutayev, *Russia* 41 C11
Tuticorin, *India* 60 Q11
Tutin, *Serbia, Yug.* 21 N10
Tutóia, *Brazil* 122 B3
Tutong, *Brunei* 56 D4
Tutova →, *Romania* 38 C10
Tutrakan, *Bulgaria* 38 E9
Tutshi L., *Canada* 100 B2
Tuttle, *U.S.A.* 108 B5
Tuttlingen, *Germany* 19 H4
Tutuala, *Indonesia* 57 F7
Tutuila, *Amer. Samoa* ... 87 B13
Tututepec, *Mexico* 115 D5
Tuva Republic □, *Russia* . 45 D10
Tuvalu ■, *Pac. Oc.* 92 H9
Tuxpan, *Mexico* 115 C5
Tuxtla Gutiérrez, *Mexico* . 115 D6
Tuy, *Spain* 30 C2
Tuy An, *Vietnam* 58 F7
Tuy Duc, *Vietnam* 59 F6
Tuy Hoa, *Vietnam* 58 F7
Tuy Phong, *Vietnam* 59 G7
Tuya L., *Canada* 100 B2
Tuyen Hoa, *Vietnam* 58 D6
Tuyen Quang, *Vietnam* .. 58 B5
Tüysarkān, *Iran* 65 C6
Tuz Gölü, *Turkey* 66 D5
Ţūz Khurmātū, *Iraq* 64 C5
Tuzla, *Bos.-H.* 21 L8
Tuzla Gölü, *Turkey* 66 D6
Tuzlov →, *Russia* 43 C8
Tvååker, *Sweden* 11 G6
Tvedestrand, *Norway* ... 11 F2
Tver, *Russia* 41 C9
Tvŭrditsa, *Bulgaria* 38 G8
Twain, *U.S.A.* 112 E5
Twain Harte, *U.S.A.* 112 H6
Tweed, *Canada* 106 B7
Tweed →, *U.K.* 14 F7
Tweed Heads, *Australia* . 91 D5
Tweedsmuir Prov. Park,
  Canada 100 C3
Twello, *Neths.* 16 D8
Twentynine Palms, *U.S.A.* 113 L10
Twillingate, *Canada* 99 C9
Twin Bridges, *U.S.A.* ... 110 D7
Twin Falls, *U.S.A.* 110 E6
Twin Valley, *U.S.A.* 108 B6
Twisp, *U.S.A.* 110 B3
Twistringen, *Germany* ... 18 C4
Two Harbors, *U.S.A.* 108 B9
Two Hills, *Canada* 100 C6
Two Rivers, *U.S.A.* 104 C2
Twofold B., *Australia* 91 F4
Tychy, *Poland* 20 E8
Tykocin, *Poland* 20 B12
Tyldal, *Norway* 10 B4
Tyler, *U.S.A.* 103 D7
Tyler, *Minn., U.S.A.* 108 C6
Tyler, *Tex., U.S.A.* 109 J7
Týn nad Vltavou, *Czech.* . 20 F4
Tynda, *Russia* 45 D13
Tyne →, *U.K.* 12 C6
Tyne & Wear □, *U.K.* ... 12 C6
Tynemouth, *U.K.* 12 B6
Tynset, *Norway* 10 B4
Tyre = Sūr, *Lebanon* 69 B4
Tyrifjorden, *Norway* 10 D4
Tyringe, *Sweden* 11 H7
Tyristrand, *Norway* 10 D4
Tyrnyauz, *Russia* 43 E10
Tyrone, *U.S.A.* 106 F6
Tyrrell →, *Australia* 91 F3
Tyrrell, L., *Australia* 91 F3
Tyrrell Arm, *Canada* 101 A9
Tyrrell L., *Canada* 101 A7
Tyrrhenian Sea, *Europe* . 34 B5
Tysfjorden, *Norway* 8 B14
Tystberga, *Sweden* 11 F11
Tyub Karagan, Mys,
  Kazakhstan 43 D14
Tyulenly, *Russia* 43 D12
Tyumen, *Russia* 44 D7
Tywi →, *U.K.* 13 F3
Tywyn, *U.K.* 13 E3

Tzaneen, *S. Africa* 85 C5
Tzermiádhes, *Greece* 37 D7
Tzermíadhes Neápolis,
  Greece 39 P8
Tzoumérka, Óros, *Greece* . 39 K4
Tzukong = Zigong, *China* . 52 C5
Tzummarum, *Neths.* 16 B7

U

U Taphao, *Thailand* 58 F3
U.S.A. = United States of
  America ■, *N. Amer.* .. 102 C7
Uachadi, Sierra, *Venezuela* 121 C4
Uainambi, *Colombia* 120 C4
Uanda, *Australia* 90 C3
Uarsciek, *Somali Rep.* ... 68 G4
Uasin □, *Kenya* 82 B4
Uato-Udo, *Indonesia* 57 F7
Uatumã →, *Brazil* 121 D6
Uauá, *Brazil* 122 C4
Uaupés, *Brazil* 120 D4
Uaupés →, *Brazil* 120 C4
Uaxactún, *Guatemala* 116 C2
Ubá, *Brazil* 123 F3
Ubaitaba, *Brazil* 123 D4
Ubangi = Oubangi →,
  Zaïre 80 E3
Ubaté, *Colombia* 120 B3
Ubauro, *Pakistan* 62 E3
Ubaye →, *France* 27 D10
Ube, *Japan* 49 H5
Ubeda, *Spain* 29 G1
Uberaba, *Brazil* 123 E2
Uberaba, L., *Brazil* 125 D6
Uberlândia, *Brazil* 123 E2
Überlingen, *Germany* 19 H5
Ubiaja, *Nigeria* 79 D6
Ubolratna Res., *Thailand* . 58 D4
Ubombo, *S. Africa* 85 D5
Ubon Ratchathani,
  Thailand 58 E5
Ubondo, *Zaïre* 82 C2
Ubort →, *Belorussia* 40 E6
Ubrique, *Spain* 31 J5
Ubundu, *Zaïre* 82 C2
Ucayali →, *Peru* 124 A3
Uccle, *Belgium* 17 G4
Uchi Lake, *Canada* 101 C10
Uchiura-Wan, *Japan* 48 C10
Uchiza, *Peru* 124 B2
Uchte, *Germany* 18 C4
Uchur →, *Russia* 45 D14
Uclulelet, *Canada* 100 D3
Ucuriş, *Romania* 38 C4
Uda →, *Russia* 45 D14
Udaipur, *India* 62 G5
Udaipur Garhi, *Nepal* ... 63 F12
Uddel, *Neths.* 16 D7
Uddevalla, *Sweden* 11 F5
Uddjaur, *Sweden* 8 D16
Uden, *Neths.* 17 E7
Udgir, *India* 60 K10
Udhampur, *India* 63 C6
Udi, *Nigeria* 79 D6
Udine, *Italy* 33 B10
Udmurt Republic □, *Russia* 44 D6
Udon Thani, *Thailand* ... 58 D4
Udupi, *India* 60 N9
Udvoy Balkan, *Bulgaria* .. 38 G9
Udzungwa Range,
  Tanzania 83 D4
Ueckermünde, *Germany* . 18 B10
Ueda, *Japan* 49 F9
Uedineniya, Os., *Russia* . 4 B12
Uele →, *Zaïre* 80 D4
Uelen, *Russia* 45 C19
Uelzen, *Germany* 18 C6
Uetendorf, *Switz.* 22 C5
Ufa, *Russia* 44 D6
Uffenheim, *Germany* 19 F6
Ugab →, *Namibia* 84 C1
Ugalla →, *Tanzania* 82 D3
Uganda ■, *Africa* 82 B3
Ugchelen, *Neths.* 16 D7
Ugento, *Italy* 35 C11
Ugep, *Nigeria* 79 D6
Ugie, *S. Africa* 85 E4
Ugijar, *Spain* 29 J1
Ugine, *France* 27 C10
Uglegorsk, *Russia* 45 E15
Uglich, *Russia* 41 C11
Ugljane, *Croatia* 33 E13
Ugolyak, *Russia* 45 C13
Ugra →, *Russia* 41 D10
Uğûn Mûsa, *Egypt* 69 F1
Ugûrchin, *Bulgaria* 38 F7
Uh →, *Slovakia* 21 G11
Uherske Hradiště, *Czech.* . 20 F7
Uhrichsville, *U.S.A.* 106 F3
Uíge, *Angola* 80 F2
Uijŏngbu, *S. Korea* 51 F14
Úiju, *N. Korea* 51 D13
Uinta Mts., *U.S.A.* 110 F8
Uitenhage, *S. Africa* 84 E4
Uitgeest, *Neths.* 16 C5
Uithoorn, *Neths.* 16 D5
Uithuizen, *Neths.* 16 B9
Uitkerke, *Belgium* 17 F2
Újfehértó, *Hungary* 21 H11
Ujhani, *India* 63 F8
Uji-guntō, *Japan* 49 J4

Ujjain, *India* 62 H6
Újpest, *Hungary* 21 H9
Újszász, *Hungary* 21 H10
Ujung Pandang, *Indonesia* 57 F5
Uka, *Russia* 45 D17
Ukara I., *Tanzania* 82 C3
Uke-Shima, *Japan* 49 K4
Ukerewe □, *Tanzania* 82 C3
Ukerewe I., *Tanzania* 82 C3
Ukholovo, *Russia* 41 E12
Ukhrul, *India* 61 G19
Ukhta, *Russia* 44 C6
Ukiah, *U.S.A.* 112 F3
Ukki Fort, *India* 63 C7
Ukmerge, *Lithuania* 40 D4
Ukraine ■, *Europe* 42 B4
Ukwi, *Botswana* 84 C3
Ulaanbaatar, *Mongolia* .. 45 E11
Ulaangom, *Mongolia* 54 A4
Ulamba, *Zaïre* 83 D1
Ulan Bator = Ulaanbaatar,
  Mongolia 45 E11
Ulan Ude, *Russia* 45 D11
Ulanga □, *Tanzania* 83 D4
Ulanów, *Poland* 20 E12
Ulaş, *Turkey* 66 D7
Ulaya, *Morogoro, Tanzania* 82 D4
Ulaya, *Tabora, Tanzania* . 82 C3
Ulcinj, *Montenegro, Yug.* . 39 H2
Ulco, *S. Africa* 84 D3
Ulfborg, *Denmark* 11 H2
Ulft, *Neths.* 16 E8
Ulhasnagar, *India* 60 K8
Uljma, *Serbia, Yug.* 21 K11
Ulla →, *Spain* 30 C2
Ulladulla, *Australia* 91 F5
Ullånger, *Sweden* 10 B12
Ullapool, *U.K.* 14 D3
Ullared, *Sweden* 11 G6
Ulldecona, *Spain* 28 E5
Ullung-do, *S. Korea* 51 F16
Ulm, *Germany* 19 G5
Ulmarra, *Australia* 91 D5
Ulmeni, *Romania* 38 D9
Ulonguè, *Mozam.* 83 E3
Ulricehamn, *Sweden* 9 H12
Ulrum, *Neths.* 16 B8
Ulsan, *S. Korea* 51 G15
Ulsberg, *Norway* 10 B3
Ulster □, *U.K.* 15 B5
Ulubaria, *India* 63 H13
Ulubat Gölü, *Turkey* 66 C3
Ulubey, *Turkey* 66 D3
Uluborlu, *Turkey* 66 D4
Uludağ, *Turkey* 66 C3
Uludere, *Turkey* 67 E10
Uluguru Mts., *Tanzania* .. 82 D4
Ulukışla, *Turkey* 66 E6
Ulungur He →, *China* ... 54 B3
Ulutau, *Kazakhstan* 44 E7
Ulvenhout, *Neths.* 17 E5
Ulverston, *U.K.* 12 C4
Ulverstone, *Australia* 90 G4
Ulya, *Russia* 45 D15
Ulyanovsk = Simbirsk,
  Russia 41 D16
Ulyasutay, *Mongolia* 54 B4
Ulysses, *U.S.A.* 109 G4
Umag, *Croatia* 33 C10
Umala, *Bolivia* 124 D4
Uman, *Ukraine* 42 B4
Umaria, *India* 61 H12
Umarkot, *Pakistan* 60 G6
Umatilla, *U.S.A.* 110 D4
Umba, *Russia* 44 C4
Umbertide, *Italy* 33 E9
Umbrella Mts., *N.Z.* 87 L2
Umbria □, *Italy* 33 F9
Ume älv →, *Sweden* 8 E16
Umeå, *Sweden* 8 E16
Umera, *Indonesia* 57 E7
Umfuli →, *Zimbabwe* ... 83 F2
Umgusa, *Zimbabwe* 83 F2
Umka, *Serbia, Yug.* 21 L10
Umkomaas, *S. Africa* 85 E5
Umm ad Daraj, J., *Jordan* 69 C4
Umm al Qaywayn, *U.A.E.* 65 E7
Umm al Qittayn, *Jordan* .. 69 C5
Umm Arda, *Sudan* 77 D3
Umm Bāb, *Qatar* 65 E6
Umm Bel, *Sudan* 77 E2
Umm Dubban, *Sudan* 77 D3
Umm el Fahm, *Israel* 69 C4
Umm Koweika, *Sudan* ... 77 E3
Umm Lajj, *Si. Arabia* 64 E3
Umm Merwa, *Sudan* 76 D3
Umm Ruwaba, *Sudan* ... 77 E3
Umm Sidr, *Sudan* 77 E2
Ummanz, *Germany* 18 A9
Umnak I., *U.S.A.* 96 C3
Umniati →, *Zimbabwe* .. 83 F2
Umpqua →, *U.S.A.* 110 E1
Umreth, *India* 62 H5
Umtata, *S. Africa* 85 E4
Umuahia, *Nigeria* 79 D6
Umuarama, *Brazil* 127 A5
Umvukwe Ra., *Zimbabwe* 83 F3
Umzimvubu = Port St.
  Johns, *S. Africa* 85 E4
Umzingwane →,
  Zimbabwe 83 G2
Umzinto, *S. Africa* 85 E5
Una, *India* 62 J4
Una →, *Bos.-H.* 33 C13
Unac →, *Bos.-H.* 33 D13

Unadilla, U.S.A. 107 D9
Unalaska, U.S.A. 96 C3
Uncastillo, Spain 28 C3
Uncía, Bolivia 124 D4
Uncompahgre Peak, U.S.A. 111 G10
Unden, Sweden 11 F8
Underberg, S. Africa 85 D4
Underbool, Australia 91 F3
Undersaker, Sweden 10 A7
Undersvik, Sweden 10 C10
Unecha, Russia 40 E8
Uneiuxi →, Brazil 120 D4
Ungarie, Australia 91 E4
Ungarra, Australia 91 E2
Ungava B., Canada 97 C13
Ungava Pen., Canada ... 97 C12
Ungeny, Moldavia 42 C2
Unggi, N. Korea 51 C16
Ungwatiri, Sudan 77 D4
Uni, Russia 41 C17
União da Vitória, Brazil .. 127 B5
União dos Palmares, Brazil 122 C4
Unije, Croatia 33 D11
Unimak I., U.S.A. 96 C3
Unini →, Brazil 121 D5
Union, Miss., U.S.A. ... 109 J10
Union, Mo., U.S.A. 108 F9
Union, S.C., U.S.A. 105 H5
Union, Mt., U.S.A. 111 J7
Union City, Calif., U.S.A. 112 H4
Union City, N.J., U.S.A. 107 F10
Union City, Pa., U.S.A. 106 E5
Union City, Tenn., U.S.A. 109 G10
Union Gap, U.S.A. 110 C3
Union of Soviet Socialist
  Republics =
  Commonwealth of
  Independent States ■,
  Eurasia 45 D11
Union Springs, U.S.A. .. 105 J3
Uniondale, S. Africa ... 84 E3
Uniontown, U.S.A. 104 F6
Unionville, U.S.A. 108 E8
United Arab Emirates ■,
  Asia 65 F7
United Kingdom ■, Europe 7 E5
United States of
  America ■, N. Amer. .. 102 C7
Unity, Canada 101 C7
Universales, Mtes., Spain 28 E3
Unjha, India 62 H5
Unnao, India 63 F9
Uno, Ilha, Guinea-Biss. .. 78 C1
Unst, U.K. 14 A8
Unstrut →, Germany ... 18 D7
Unter-engadin, Switz. .. 23 C10
Unterägeri, Switz. 23 B7
Unterkulm, Switz. 22 B6
Unterseen, Switz. 22 C5
Unterwaldner Alpen, Switz. 23 C6
Unuk →, Canada 100 B2
Ünye, Turkey 42 F7
Unzha, Russia 41 B14
Unzha →, Russia 41 C13
Uors, Switz. 23 C8
Uozu, Japan 49 F8
Upa →, Czech. 20 E6
Upata, Venezuela 121 B5
Upemba, L., Zaïre 83 D2
Upernavik, Greenland ... 4 B5
Upington, S. Africa 84 D3
Upleta, India 62 J4
Upolu, W. Samoa 87 A13
Upper Alkali Lake, U.S.A. 110 F3
Upper Arrow L., Canada . 100 C5
Upper Foster L., Canada . 101 B7
Upper Hutt, N.Z. 87 J5
Upper Klamath L., U.S.A. 110 E3
Upper Lake, U.S.A. ... 112 F4
Upper Musquodoboit,
  Canada 99 C7
Upper Red L., U.S.A. .. 108 A7
Upper Sandusky, U.S.A. . 104 E4
Upper Volta = Burkina
  Faso ■, Africa 78 C4
Upphärad, Sweden 11 F6
Uppsala, Sweden 10 E11
Uppsala län □, Sweden . 9 G14
Upshi, India 63 C7
Upstart, C., Australia ... 90 B4
Upton, U.S.A. 108 C2
Ur, Iraq 64 D5
Urabá, G. de, Colombia . 120 B2
Uracara, Brazil 121 D6
Urad Qianqi, China 50 D5
Urakawa, Japan 48 C11
Ural, Australia 91 E4
Ural →, Kazakhstan ... 43 C14
Ural Mts. = Uralskie Gory,
  Russia 44 D6
Uralla, Australia 91 E5
Uralsk, Kazakhstan 44 D6
Uralskie Gory, Russia ... 44 D6
Urambo, Tanzania 82 D3
Urambo □, Tanzania ... 82 D3
Urandangi, Australia ... 90 C2
Uranium City, Canada .. 101 B7
Uranquinty, Australia ... 91 F4
Uraricaá →, Brazil ... 121 D6
Uraricuera →, Brazil .. 121 C5
Urawa, Japan 49 G9
Uray, Russia 44 C7
'Uray'irah, Si. Arabia .. 65 E6
Urbana, Ill., U.S.A. ... 104 E1
Urbana, Ohio, U.S.A. .. 104 E4

Urbánia, Italy 33 E9
Urbano Santos, Brazil ... 122 B3
Urbel →, Spain 28 C1
Urbino, Italy 33 E9
Urbión, Picos de, Spain . 28 C2
Urcos, Peru 124 C3
Urda, Kazakhstan 43 B12
Urda, Spain 31 F7
Urdinarrain, Argentina .. 126 C4
Urdos, France 26 F3
Urdzhar, Kazakhstan ... 44 E9
Ure →, U.K. 12 C6
Uren, Russia 41 C14
Ures, Mexico 114 B2
Urfa, Turkey 67 E8
Urfa □, Turkey 67 E8
Urfahr, Austria 21 G4
Urganch = Urgench,
  Uzbekistan 44 E7
Urgench, Uzbekistan ... 44 E7
Uri, India 63 B6
Uri □, Switz. 23 C7
Uribante →, Venezuela . 120 B3
Uribe, Colombia 120 C3
Uribia, Colombia 120 A3
Uriondo, Bolivia 126 A3
Urique, Mexico 114 B3
Urique →, Mexico 114 B3
Urirotstock, Switz. 23 C7
Urk, Neths. 16 C7
Urla, Turkey 66 D2
Urlati, Romania 38 E9
Urmia = Orūmīyeh, Iran 64 B5
Urmia, L. = Orūmīyeh,
  Daryācheh-ye, Iran .. 64 B5
Urner Alpen, Switz. 23 C7
Uroševac, Serbia, Yug. .. 21 N11
Urrao, Colombia 120 B2
Ursus, Poland 20 C10
Uruaçu, Brazil 123 D2
Uruana, Brazil 123 E2
Uruapan, Mexico 114 D4
Uruará, Brazil 121 D7
Urubamba, Peru 124 C3
Urubamba →, Peru ... 124 C3
Urubaxi →, Brazil 121 D5
Urubu →, Brazil 121 D6
Uruçara, Brazil 121 D6
Uruçuí, Brazil 122 C3
Uruçuí, Serra do, Brazil . 122 C3
Uruçuí Prêto →, Brazil . 122 C3
Urucuia →, Brazil 123 E2
Urucurituba, Brazil 121 D6
Uruguai →, Brazil 127 B5
Uruguaiana, Brazil 126 B4
Uruguay ■, S. Amer. ... 126 C4
Uruguay →, S. Amer. .. 126 C4
Urumchi = Ürümqi, China 44 E9
Ürümqi, China 44 E9
Urup →, Russia 43 D9
Urup, Os., Russia 45 E16
Urutaí, Brazil 123 E2
Uryung-Khaya, Russia .. 45 B12
Uryupinsk, Russia 41 F12
Urzhum, Russia 41 C16
Urziceni, Romania 38 E9
Uşak, Turkey 66 D3
Uşak □, Turkey 66 D3
Usakos, Namibia 84 C2
Usborne, Mt., Falk. Is. .. 128 D5
Ušče, Serbia, Yug. 21 M10
Usedom, Germany 18 B9
'Usfān, Si. Arabia 76 C4
Ush-Tobe, Kazakhstan .. 44 E8
Ushakova, Os., Russia .. 4 A12
Ushant = Ouessant, I. d',
  France 24 D1
Ushashi, Tanzania 82 C3
Ushat, Sudan 77 F2
Ushibuka, Japan 49 H5
Ushuaia, Argentina 128 D3
Ushumun, Russia 45 D13
Usk →, U.K. 13 F5
Usk, U.K. 13 F5
Üsküdar, Turkey 39 H11
Uslar, Germany 18 D5
Usman, Russia 41 E11
Usoke, Tanzania 82 D3
Usolye Sibirskoye, Russia . 45 D11
Usoro, Nigeria 79 D6
Uspallata, P. de, Argentina 126 C2
Uspenskiy, Kazakhstan . 44 E8
Usquert, Neths. 16 B9
Ussel, France 26 C6
Ussuri →, Asia 48 A7
Ussuriysk, Russia 45 E14
Ussurka, Russia 48 B6
Ust-Aldan = Batamay,
  Russia 45 C13
Ust Amginskoye =
  Khandyga, Russia .. 45 C14
Ust-Bolsheretsk, Russia . 45 D16
Ust Buzulukskaya, Russia 41 F13
Ust Chaun, Russia 45 C18
Ust-Donetskiy, Russia .. 43 C9
Ust'-Ilga, Russia 45 D11
Ust Ilimpeya = Yukti,
  Russia 45 C11
Ust-Ilimsk, Russia 45 D11
Ust Ishim, Russia 44 D8
Ust-Kamchatsk, Russia . 45 D17
Ust-Kamenogorsk,
  Kazakhstan 44 E9
Ust-Karenga, Russia ... 45 D12
Ust Khayryuzova, Russia . 45 D16
Ust-Kut, Russia 45 D11

Ust Kuyga, Russia 45 B14
Ust-Labinsk, Russia 43 D8
Ust Luga, Russia 40 B3
Ust Maya, Russia 45 C14
Ust-Mil, Russia 45 D14
Ust-Nera, Russia 45 C15
Ust-Nyukzha, Russia 45 D13
Ust Olenek, Russia 45 B12
Ust-Omchug, Russia 45 C15
Ust Port, Russia 44 C9
Ust Tsilma, Russia 44 C6
Ust-Tungir, Russia 45 D13
Ust Urt = Ustyurt, Plato,
  Kazakhstan 44 E6
Ust Vorkuta, Russia 44 C7
Ustaoset, Norway 10 D2
Ustaritz, France 26 E2
Uste, Russia 41 B11
Uster, Switz. 23 B7
Ústí nad Labem, Czech. . 20 E4
Ústí nad Orlicí, Czech. .. 20 F6
Ustica, Italy 34 D6
Ustinov = Izhevsk, Russia 44 D6
Ustka, Poland 20 A6
Ustrzyki Dolne, Poland . 20 F12
Ustye, Russia 45 D10
Ustyurt, Plato, Kazakhstan 44 E6
Ustyuzhna, Russia 41 B10
Usu, China 54 B3
Usuki, Japan 49 H5
Usulután, El Salv. 116 D2
Usumacinta →, Mexico . 115 D6
Usumbura = Bujumbura,
  Burundi 82 C2
Usure, Tanzania 82 C3
Uta, Indonesia 57 E9
Utah □, U.S.A. 110 G8
Utah, L., U.S.A. 110 F8
Ute Creek →, U.S.A. .. 109 H3
Utena, Lithuania 40 D4
Útersen, Germany 18 B5
Utete, Tanzania 82 D4
Uthai Thani, Thailand .. 58 E3
Uthal, Pakistan 62 G2
Utiariti, Brazil 125 C6
Utica, N.Y., U.S.A. 107 C9
Utica, Ohio, U.S.A. 106 F2
Utiel, Spain 28 F3
Utik L., Canada 101 B9
Utikuma L., Canada ... 100 B5
Utinga, Brazil 123 D3
Utrecht, Neths. 16 D6
Utrecht, S. Africa 85 D5
Utrecht □, Neths. 16 D6
Utrera, Spain 31 H5
Utsjoki, Finland 8 B19
Utsunomiya, Japan 49 F9
Uttar Pradesh □, India . 63 F9
Uttaradit, Thailand 58 D3
Uttoxeter, U.K. 12 E6
Utze, Germany 18 C6
Uudenmaan lääni □,
  Finland 9 F18
Uusikaarlepyy, Finland . 8 E17
Uusikaupunki, Finland .. 9 F16
Uva, Russia 41 C18
Uvá →, Colombia 120 C3
Uvalde, U.S.A. 109 L5
Uvarovo, Russia 41 F13
Uvat, Russia 44 D7
Uvinza, Tanzania 82 D3
Uvira, Zaïre 82 C2
Uvs Nuur, Mongolia ... 54 A4
Uwajima, Japan 49 H6
Uweinat, Jebel, Sudan .. 76 C1
Uxbridge, Canada 106 B5
Uxin Qi, China 50 E5
Uxmal, Mexico 115 C7
Uyandi, Russia 45 C15
Uyo, Nigeria 79 D6
Uyuni, Bolivia 124 E4
Uzbekistan ■, Asia 44 E7
Uzen, Bol. →, Kazakhstan 41 G16
Uzen, Mal. →, Kazakhstan 41 G16
Uzerche, France 26 C5
Uzès, France 27 D8
Uzh →, Ukraine 40 F7
Uzhgorod, Ukraine 40 G3
Uzlovaya, Russia 41 E11
Uzunköprü, Turkey 39 H9
Uzwil, Switz. 23 B8

V

Vaal →, S. Africa 84 D3
Vaal Dam, S. Africa ... 85 D4
Vaals, Neths. 17 G8
Vaalwater, S. Africa ... 85 C4
Vaasa, Finland 8 E16
Vaasan lääni □, Finland . 8 E17
Vaassen, Neths. 16 D7
Vabre, France 26 E6
Vác, Hungary 21 H9
Vacaria, Brazil 127 B5
Vacaville, U.S.A. 112 G5
Vaccarès, Étang de, France 27 E8
Vach →, Russia 44 C8
Vache, I. à-, Haiti 117 C5
Vadnagar, India 62 H5
Vado Lígure, Italy 32 D5
Vadodara, India 62 H5
Vadsø, Norway 8 A20

Vadstena, Sweden 11 F8
Vaduz, Liech. 23 B9
Værøy, Norway 8 C12
Vagnhärad, Sweden 10 F11
Vagos, Portugal 30 E2
Váh →, Slovakia 21 H8
Vahsel B., Antarctica ... 5 D1
Vái, Greece 37 D8
Vaigach, Russia 44 B6
Vaiges, France 24 D6
Vaihingen, Germany ... 19 G4
Vailly-sur-Aisne, France . 25 C10
Vaison-la-Romaine, France 27 D9
Vakfıkebir, Turkey 67 C8
Val-de-Marne □, France . 25 D9
Val-d'Oise □, France ... 25 C9
Val d'Or, Canada 98 C4
Val Marie, Canada 101 D7
Valadares, Portugal 30 D2
Valahia, Romania 38 E8
Valais □, Switz. 22 D5
Valais, Alpes du, Switz. . 22 D5
Valandovo,
  Macedonia 39 H5
Valcheta, Argentina 128 B3
Valdagno, Italy 33 C8
Valday, Russia 40 C8
Valdayskaya
  Vozvyshennost, Russia . 40 C8
Valdeazogues →, Spain . 31 G6
Valdemarsvik, Sweden . 11 F10
Valdepeñas, Ciudad Real,
  Spain 31 G7
Valdepeñas, Jaén, Spain . 31 H7
Valderaduey →, Spain . 30 D5
Valderrobres, Spain 28 E5
Valdés, Pen., Argentina . 128 B4
Valdez, Ecuador 120 C2
Valdez, U.S.A. 96 B5
Valdivia, Chile 128 A2
Valdivia, Colombia 120 B2
Valdivia □, Chile 128 B2
Valdobbiádene, Italy ... 33 C9
Valdosta, U.S.A. 105 K4
Valdoviño, Spain 30 B2
Valdres, Norway 10 D3
Vale, Georgia 43 F10
Vale, U.S.A. 110 E5
Valea lui Mihai, Romania 38 B5
Valença, Brazil 123 D4
Valença, Portugal 30 C2
Valença do Piauí, Brazil . 122 C3
Valençay, France 25 E8
Valence, Drôme, France . 27 D8
Valence, Tarn-et-Garonne,
  France 26 D4
Valencia, Spain 29 F4
Valencia, Venezuela ... 120 A4
Valencia □, Spain 29 F4
Valencia, Albufera de,
  Spain 29 F4
Valencia, G. de, Spain . 29 F5
Valencia de Alcántara,
  Spain 31 F3
Valencia de Don Juan,
  Spain 30 C5
Valencia del Ventoso,
  Spain 31 G4
Valenciennes, France .. 25 B10
Valensole, France 27 E9
Valentia Harbour, Ireland 15 E1
Valentia I., Ireland 15 E1
Valentim, Sa. do, Brazil . 122 C3
Valentin, Russia 48 C7
Valentine, Nebr., U.S.A. . 108 D4
Valentine, Tex., U.S.A. . 109 K2
Valenza, Italy 32 C5
Valera, Venezuela 120 B3
Valguarnera Caropepe,
  Italy 35 E7
Valier, U.S.A. 110 B7
Valinco, G. de, France . 27 G12
Valjevo, Serbia, Yug. .. 21 L9
Valka, Estonia 40 C5
Valkeakoski, Finland ... 9 F18
Valkenburg, Neths. ... 17 G7
Valkenswaard, Neths. .. 17 F6
Vall de Uxó, Spain 28 F4
Valla, Sweden 10 E10
Valladolid, Mexico 115 C7
Valladolid, Spain 30 D6
Valladolid □, Spain ... 30 D6
Vallata, Italy 35 A8
Valldemosa, Spain 36 B9
Valle d'Aosta □, Italy .. 32 C4
Valle de Arán, Spain .. 28 C5
Valle de Cabuérniga, Spain 30 B6
Valle de la Pascua,
  Venezuela 120 B4
Valle de las Palmas, Mexico 113 N10
Valle de Santiago, Mexico 114 C4
Valle de Suchil, Mexico . 114 C4
Valle de Zaragoza, Mexico 114 B3
Valle del Cauca □,
  Colombia 120 C2
Valle Fértil, Sierra del,
  Argentina 126 C2
Valle Hermoso, Mexico . 115 B5
Vallecas, Spain 30 E7
Valledupar, Colombia .. 120 A3
Vallehermoso, Canary Is. 36 F2
Vallejo, U.S.A. 112 G4
Vallenar, Chile 126 B1
Valleraugue, France ... 26 D7
Vallet, France 24 E5

Valletta, Malta 37 D2
Valley Center, U.S.A. ... 113 M9
Valley City, U.S.A. 108 B6
Valley Falls, U.S.A. 110 E3
Valley Springs, U.S.A. . 112 G6
Valley Wells, U.S.A. ... 113 K11
Valleyview, Canada 100 B5
Valli di Comácchio, Italy . 33 D9
Vallimanca, Arroyo,
  Argentina 126 D4
Vallo della Lucánia, Italy . 35 B8
Vallon-Pont-d'Arc, France 27 D8
Vallorbe, Switz. 22 C2
Valls, Spain 28 D6
Vallsta, Sweden 10 C10
Valmaseda, Spain 28 B1
Valmiera, Latvia 40 C4
Valmont, France 24 C7
Valmontone, Italy 34 A5
Valmy, France 25 C11
Valnera, Mte., Spain .. 28 B1
Valognes, France 24 C5
Valona = Vlóra, Albania . 39 J2
Valongo, Portugal 30 D2
Valpaços, Portugal 30 D3
Valparaíso, Chile 126 C1
Valparaíso, Mexico 114 C4
Valparaíso, U.S.A. 104 E2
Valparaíso □, Chile 126 C1
Valpovo, Croatia 21 K8
Valréas, France 27 D8
Vals, Switz. 23 C8
Vals →, S. Africa 84 D4
Vals, Tanjung, Indonesia . 57 F9
Vals-les-Bains, France . 27 D8
Valsad, India 60 J8
Valskog, Sweden 10 E9
Válta, Greece 39 J6
Valtellina, Italy 32 B6
Valuyki, Russia 41 F11
Valverde, Canary Is. .. 36 G2
Valverde del Camino,
  Spain 31 H4
Valverde del Fresno, Spain 30 E4
Vama, Romania 38 B8
Vámos, Greece 37 D6
Van, Turkey 67 D10
Van □, Turkey 67 D10
Van, L. = Van Gölü,
  Turkey 67 D10
Van Alstyne, U.S.A. ... 109 J6
Van Bruyssel, Canada . 99 C5
Van Buren, Canada ... 99 C6
Van Buren, Ark., U.S.A. . 109 H7
Van Buren, Maine, U.S.A. 105 B11
Van Buren, Mo., U.S.A. 109 G9
Van Canh, Vietnam ... 58 F7
Van Diemen, C., N. Terr.,
  Australia 88 B5
Van Diemen, C., Queens.,
  Australia 90 B2
Van Diemen G., Australia 88 B5
Van Gölü, Turkey 67 D10
Van Horn, U.S.A. 109 K2
Van Ninh, Vietnam ... 58 F7
Van Reenen P., S. Africa . 85 D4
Van Rees, Pegunungan,
  Indonesia 57 E9
Van Tassell, U.S.A. ... 108 D2
Van Wert, U.S.A. 104 E3
Van Yen, Vietnam 58 B5
Vanavara, Russia 45 C11
Vancouver, Canada ... 100 D4
Vancouver, U.S.A. ... 112 E4
Vancouver, C., Australia . 89 G2
Vancouver I., Canada .. 100 D3
Vandalia, Ill., U.S.A. .. 108 F10
Vandalia, Mo., U.S.A. . 108 F9
Vandenburg, U.S.A. ... 113 L6
Vanderbijlpark, S. Africa . 85 D4
Vandergrift, U.S.A. ... 106 F5
Vanderhoof, Canada .. 100 C4
Vanderlin I., Australia .. 90 B2
Vandyke, Australia ... 90 C4
Vänern, Sweden 11 F7
Vänersborg, Sweden .. 11 F6
Vang Vieng, Laos 58 C4
Vanga, Kenya 82 C4
Vangaindrano, Madag. . 85 C8
Vanguard, Canada ... 101 D7
Vanier, Canada 98 C4
Vankarem, Russia 45 C18
Vankleek Hill, Canada . 98 C5
Vanna, Norway 8 A15
Vännäs, Sweden 8 E15
Vannes, France 24 E4
Vanoise, Massif de la,
  France 27 C10
Vanrhynsdorp, S. Africa . 84 E2
Vanrook, Australia ... 90 B3
Vansbro, Sweden 9 F13
Vansittart B., Australia .. 88 B4
Vanthli, India 62 J4
Vanua Levu, Fiji 87 C8
Vanua Mbalavu, Fiji .. 87 C9
Vanuatu ■, Pac. Oc. .. 92 J8
Vanwyksvlei, S. Africa . 84 E3
Vanzylsrus, S. Africa .. 84 D3
Vapnyarka, Ukraine .. 42 B3
Var □, France 27 E10
Var →, France 27 E11
Vara, Sweden 11 F6
Varades, France 24 E5
Varaita →, Italy 32 D4
Varallo, Italy 32 C5

Varanasi, *India* 63 G10
Varangerfjorden, *Norway* . 8 A20
Varaždin, *Croatia* 33 B13
Varazze, *Italy* 32 D5
Varberg, *Sweden* 11 G6
Vardar = Axiós →, *Greece* 39 J5
Varde, *Denmark* 11 J2
Varde Å →, *Denmark* 11 J2
Varel, *Germany* 18 B4
Varella, Mui, *Vietnam* .. 58 F7
Varena, *Lithuania* 40 D4
Varennes-sur-Allier, *France* 26 B7
Vareš, *Bos.-H.* 21 L8
Varese, *Italy* 32 C5
Varese Lígure, *Italy* 32 D6
Vårgårda, *Sweden* 11 F6
Vargem Bonita, *Brazil* ... 123 F2
Vargem Grande, *Brazil* .. 122 B3
Varginha, *Brazil* 127 A6
Vargön, *Sweden* 11 F6
Variadero, *U.S.A.* 109 H2
Varillas, *Chile* 126 A1
Väring, *Sweden* 11 F8
Värmlands län □, *Sweden* 9 G12
Varna, *Bulgaria* 38 F10
Värnamo, *Sweden* 9 H13
Varön, *Sweden* 11 G6
Vars, *Canada* 107 A9
Varsseveld, *Neths.* 16 E8
Varto, *Turkey* 67 D9
Varvarin, *Serbia, Yug.* .. 21 M11
Varzaneh, *Iran* 65 C7
Várzea Alegre, *Brazil* ... 122 C4
Várzea da Palma, *Brazil* . 123 E3
Várzea Grande, *Brazil* .. 125 D6
Varzi, *Italy* 32 D6
Varzo, *Italy* 32 B5
Varzy, *France* 25 E10
Vasa, *Finland* 8 E16
Vasa Barris →, *Brazil* .. 122 D4
Vascão →, *Portugal* 31 H3
Vașcău, *Romania* 38 C5
Vascongadas = País
   Vasco □, *Spain* 28 C2
Vasht = Khâsh, *Iran* ... 60 E2
Vasilevichi, *Belorussia* .. 40 E6
Vasilikón, *Greece* 39 L6
Vasilkov, *Ukraine* 40 F7
Vaslui, *Romania* 38 C10
Vassar, *Canada* 101 D9
Vassar, *U.S.A.* 104 D4
Västerås, *Sweden* 10 E10
Västerbottens län □,
   Sweden 8 D14
Västernorrlands län □,
   Sweden 10 A11
Västervik, *Sweden* 9 H14
Västmanlands län □,
   Sweden 9 G14
Vasto, *Italy* 33 F11
Vasvár, *Hungary* 21 H6
Vatan, *France* 25 E8
Vathí, *Greece* 39 M10
Váthia, *Greece* 39 N5
Vatican City ■, *Europe* . 33 G9
Vaticano, C., *Italy* 35 D8
Vatili, *Cyprus* 37 D12
Vatnajökull, *Iceland* 8 D5
Vatnås, *Norway* 10 E3
Vatneyri, *Iceland* 8 D2
Vatoa, *Fiji* 87 D9
Vatólakkos, *Greece* 37 D5
Vatoloha, *Madag.* 85 B8
Vatomandry, *Madag.* 85 B8
Vatra-Dornei, *Romania* .. 38 B8
Vättern, *Sweden* 11 F8
Vättis, *Switz.* 23 C8
Vaucluse □, *France* 27 E9
Vaucouleurs, *France* 25 D12
Vaud □, *Switz.* 22 C2
Vaughn, *Mont., U.S.A.* .. 110 C8
Vaughn, *N. Mex., U.S.A.* 111 J11
Vaulruz, *Switz.* 22 C3
Vaupés = Uaupés →,
   Brazil 120 C4
Vaupes □, *Colombia* ... 120 C3
Vauvert, *France* 27 E8
Vauxhall, *Canada* 100 C6
Vava'u, *Tonga* 87 D11
Vaxholm, *Sweden* 10 E12
Vaygach, Ostrov, *Russia* . 44 C6
Váyia, Ákra, *Greece* 37 C10
Veadeiros, *Brazil* 123 D2
Vechta, *Germany* 18 C4
Vechte →, *Neths.* 16 C8
Vecsés, *Hungary* 21 H9
Veddige, *Sweden* 11 G6
Vedea →, *Romania* 38 F8
Vedia, *Argentina* 126 C3
Vedra, I. del, *Spain* 36 C7
Vedrin, *Belgium* 17 G5
Veendam, *Neths.* 16 B9
Veenendaal, *Neths.* 16 D7
Veerle, *Belgium* 17 F5
Vefsna →, *Norway* 8 D12
Vega, *Norway* 8 D11
Vega, *U.S.A.* 109 H3
Vegadeo, *Spain* 30 B3
Vegafjorden, *Norway* ... 8 D12
Veghel, *Neths.* 17 E7
Vegorritis, Límni, *Greece* 39 J4
Vegreville, *Canada* 100 C6
Vegusdal, *Norway* 11 F2

Veii, *Italy* 33 F9
Vejen, *Denmark* 11 J3
Vejer de la Frontera, *Spain* 31 J5
Vejle, *Denmark* 11 J3
Vejle Fjord, *Denmark* ... 11 J3
Vela Luka, *Croatia* 33 F13
Velas, C., *Costa Rica* ... 116 D2
Velasco, Sierra de,
   Argentina 126 B2
Velay, Mts. du, *France* .. 26 D7
Velddrif, *S. Africa* 84 E2
Veldegem, *Belgium* 17 F2
Velden, *Neths.* 17 F8
Veldhoven, *Neths.* 17 F6
Velebit Planina, *Croatia* . 33 D12
Velebitski Kanal, *Croatia* 33 D11
Veleka →, *Bulgaria* 38 G10
Velenje, *Slovenia* 33 B12
Velestínon, *Greece* 39 K5
Vélez, *Colombia* 120 B3
Vélez Blanco, *Spain* 29 H2
Vélez Málaga, *Spain* 31 J6
Vélez Rubio, *Spain* 29 H2
Velhas →, *Brazil* 123 E3
Velika, *Croatia* 21 K7
Velika Gorica, *Croatia* .. 33 C13
Velika Kapela, *Croatia* .. 33 C12
Velika Kladuša,
   Bos.-H. 33 C12
Velika Morava →,
   Serbia, Yug. 21 L11
Velikaya →, *Russia* 40 C6
Velikaya Kema, *Russia* .. 48 B8
Velikaya Lepetikha,
   Ukraine 42 C5
Velike Lašče, *Slovenia* .. 33 C11
Velikiye Luki, *Russia* ... 40 C7
Velikonda Range, *India* . 60 M11
Velikoye, Oz., *Russia* ... 41 D12
Velingrad, *Bulgaria* 39 G6
Velino, Mte., *Italy* 33 F10
Velizh, *Russia* 40 D7
Velke Mezířici, *Czech.* .. 20 F6
Velletri, *Italy* 34 A5
Vellinge, *Sweden* 11 J7
Vellore, *India* 60 N11
Velp, *Neths.* 16 D7
Velsen-Noord, *Neths.* ... 16 D5
Velten, *Germany* 18 C9
Veluwe Meer, *Neths.* ... 16 D7
Velva, *U.S.A.* 108 A4
Veme, *Norway* 10 D4
Ven, *Sweden* 11 J6
Venaco, *France* 27 F13
Venado Tuerto, *Argentina* 126 C3
Venafro, *Italy* 35 A7
Venarey-les-Laumes,
   France 25 E11
Venaria, *Italy* 32 C4
Vence, *France* 27 E11
Venda □, *S. Africa* 85 C5
Vendas Novas, *Portugal* . 31 G2
Vendée □, *France* 24 F5
Vendée →, *France* 24 F5
Vendéen, Bocage, *France* 26 B2
Vendeuvre-sur-Barse,
   France 25 D11
Vendôme, *France* 24 E8
Vendrell, *Spain* 28 D6
Vendsyssel, *Denmark* ... 11 G4
Véneta, L., *Italy* 33 C9
Véneto □, *Italy* 33 C9
Venev, *Russia* 41 D11
Venézia, *Italy* 33 C9
Venézia, G. di, *Italy* 33 C10
Venezuela ■, *S. Amer.* . 120 B4
Venezuela, G. de,
   Venezuela 120 A3
Vengurla, *India* 60 M8
Venice = Venézia, *Italy* . 33 C9
Venkatapuram, *India* ... 61 K12
Venlo, *Neths.* 17 F8
Venraij, *Neths.* 17 E7
Venta de Cárdena, *Spain* 31 G6
Venta de San Rafael, *Spain* 30 E6
Ventana, Punta de la,
   Mexico 114 C3
Ventana, Sa. de la,
   Argentina 126 D3
Ventersburg, *S. Africa* .. 84 D4
Venterstad, *S. Africa* ... 84 E4
Ventimíglia, *Italy* 32 E4
Ventnor, *U.K.* 13 G6
Ventotene, *Italy* 34 B6
Ventoux, Mt., *France* ... 27 D9
Ventspils, *Latvia* 9 H16
Ventuarí →, *Venezuela* . 120 C4
Ventucopa, *U.S.A.* 113 L7
Ventura, *U.S.A.* 113 L7
Venus B., *Australia* 91 F4
Vera, *Argentina* 126 B3
Vera, *Spain* 29 H3
Veracruz, *Mexico* 115 D5
Veracruz □, *Mexico* 115 D5
Veraval, *India* 62 J4
Verbánia, *Italy* 32 C5
Verbicaro, *Italy* 35 C8
Verbier, *Switz.* 22 D4
Vercelli, *Italy* 32 C5
Verchovchevo, *Ukraine* . 42 B6
Verdalsøra, *Norway* 8 E11
Verde →, *Goiás, Brazil* . 123 E1
Verde →, *Goiás, Brazil* . 123 E1

Verde →, *Mato Grosso,
   Brazil* 125 E7
Verde →, *Mato Grosso,
   Brazil* 125 C6
Verde →, *Chihuahua,
   Mexico* 114 B3
Verde →, *Oaxaca, Mexico* 115 D5
Verde →, *Veracruz,
   Mexico* 114 C4
Verde →, *Paraguay* 126 A4
Verde, Cay, *Bahamas* ... 116 B4
Verde Grande →, *Brazil* 123 E3
Verde Island Pass, *Phil.* . 55 E4
Verde Pequeno →, *Brazil* 123 D3
Verden, *Germany* 18 C5
Verdi, *U.S.A.* 112 F7
Verdigre, *U.S.A.* 108 D5
Verdon →, *France* 27 E9
Verdun, *France* 25 C12
Verdun-sur-le-Doubs,
   France 25 F12
Vereeniging, *S. Africa* ... 85 D4
Vérendrye, Parc Prov. de
   la, *Canada* 98 C4
Verga, C., *Guinea* 78 C2
Vergato, *Italy* 32 D8
Vergemont, *Australia* ... 90 C3
Vergemont Cr. →,
   Australia 90 C3
Vergennes, *U.S.A.* 107 B11
Vergt, *France* 26 C4
Verín, *Spain* 30 D3
Veriña, *Spain* 30 B5
Verkhnedvinsk, *Belorussia* 40 D5
Verkhnevilyuysk, *Russia* . 45 C13
Verkhneye Kalinino, *Russia* 45 D11
Verkhniy Baskunchak,
   Russia 43 B12
Verkhovye, *Russia* 41 E10
Verkhoyansk, *Russia* 45 C14
Verkhoyansk Ra. =
   Verkhoyanskiy Khrebet,
   Russia 45 C13
Verkhoyanskiy Khrebet,
   Russia 45 C13
Verlo, *Canada* 101 C7
Verma, *Norway* 10 B2
Vermenton, *France* 25 E10
Vermilion, *Canada* 101 C6
Vermilion →, *Alta.,
   Canada* 101 C6
Vermilion →, *Qué.,
   Canada* 98 C5
Vermilion, B., *U.S.A.* ... 109 L9
Vermilion Bay, *Canada* . 101 D10
Vermilion Chutes, *Canada* 100 B6
Vermilion L., *U.S.A.* 108 B8
Vermillion, *U.S.A.* 108 D6
Vermont □, *U.S.A.* 107 C12
Vernal, *U.S.A.* 110 F9
Vernalis, *U.S.A.* 112 H5
Verner, *Canada* 98 C3
Verneuil-sur-Avre, *France* 24 D7
Verneukpan, *S. Africa* .. 84 D3
Vernier, *Switz.* 22 D2
Vernon, *Canada* 100 C5
Vernon, *France* 24 C8
Vernon, *U.S.A.* 109 H5
Vernonia, *U.S.A.* 112 E3
Vero Beach, *U.S.A.* 105 M5
Véroia, *Greece* 39 J5
Verolanuova, *Italy* 32 C7
Véroli, *Italy* 34 A6
Verona, *Italy* 32 C8
Veropol, *Russia* 45 C17
Versailles, *France* 25 D9
Versalles, *Bolivia* 125 C5
Versoix, *Switz.* 22 D2
Vert, C., *Senegal* 78 C1
Vertou, *France* 24 E5
Vertus, *France* 25 D11
Verulam, *S. Africa* 85 D5
Verviers, *Belgium* 17 G7
Vervins, *France* 25 C10
Verwood, *Canada* 101 D7
Verzej, *Slovenia* 33 B13
Vescavato, *France* 27 F13
Vesdre →, *Belgium* 17 G7
Veselí nad Lužnicí, *Czech.* 20 F4
Veselovskoye Vdkhr.,
   Russia 43 C9
Veshenskaya, *Russia* 43 B9
Vesle →, *France* 25 C10
Vesoul, *France* 25 E13
Vessigebro, *Sweden* 11 H6
Vest-Agder fylke □,
   Norway 9 G9
Vesterålen, *Norway* 8 B13
Vestersche Veld, *Neths.* . 16 C8
Vestfjorden, *Norway* ... 8 C13
Vestfold fylke □, *Norway* 9 G11
Vestmannaeyjar, *Iceland* . 8 E3
Vestmarka, *Norway* 10 E5
Vestone, *Italy* 32 C7
Vestsjællands
   Amtskommune □,
   Denmark 11 J5
Vestspitsbergen, *Svalbard* 4 B8
Vestvågøy, *Norway* 8 B12
Vesuvio, Mt., *Laos* 58 B3
Vesuvius, Mt. = Vesuvio,
   Italy 35 B7
Vesyegonsk, *Russia* 41 B10
Veszprém, *Hungary* 21 H7
Vésztő, *Hungary* 21 J11

Vetlanda, *Sweden* 9 H13
Vetluga, *Russia* 41 C14
Vetlugu →, *Russia* 41 C15
Vetluzhskiy, *Russia* 41 C14
Vetovo, *Bulgaria* 38 F9
Vetralia, *Italy* 33 F9
Vettore, Monte, *Italy* ... 33 F10
Veurne, *Belgium* 17 F1
Vevey, *Switz.* 22 D3
Veynes, *France* 27 D9
Vézelise, *France* 25 D13
Vézère →, *France* 26 D4
Vezirköprü, *Turkey* 66 C6
Vi Thanh, *Vietnam* 59 H5
Viacha, *Bolivia* 124 D4
Viadana, *Italy* 32 D7
Viamão, *Brazil* 127 C5
Viana, *Brazil* 122 B3
Viana, *Spain* 28 C2
Viana del Bollo, *Spain* .. 30 C3
Viana do Alentejo,
   Portugal 31 G3
Viana do Castelo, *Portugal* 30 D2
Vianna do Castelo □,
   Portugal 30 D2
Vianden, *Belgium* 17 J8
Vianen, *Neths.* 16 E6
Vianópolis, *Brazil* 123 E2
Viar →, *Spain* 31 H5
Viaréggio, *Italy* 32 E7
Viaur →, *France* 26 D5
Vibank, *Canada* 101 C8
Vibo Valéntia, *Italy* 35 D9
Viborg, *Denmark* 11 H3
Vibraye, *France* 24 D7
Vic-en-Bigorre, *France* .. 26 E4
Vic-Fézensac, *France* ... 26 E4
Vic-sur-Cère, *France* ... 26 D6
Vicenza, *Italy* 33 C8
Vich, *Spain* 28 D7
Vichada □, *Colombia* ... 120 C4
Vichada →, *Colombia* .. 120 C4
Vichuga, *Russia* 41 C12
Vichy, *France* 26 B7
Vicksburg, *Ariz., U.S.A.* 113 M13
Vicksburg, *Mich., U.S.A.* 104 D3
Vicksburg, *Miss., U.S.A.* 109 J9
Vico, L. di, *Italy* 33 F9
Vico del Gargaro, *Italy* . 35 A8
Viçosa, *Brazil* 122 C4
Viçosa do Ceará, *Brazil* . 122 B3
Vicosoprano, *Switz.* 23 D9
Victor, *India* 62 J4
Victor, *Colo., U.S.A.* ... 108 F2
Victor, *N.Y., U.S.A.* 106 D7
Victor Harbor, *Australia* . 91 F2
Victoria, *Argentina* 126 C3
Victoria, *Canada* 100 D4
Victoria, *Chile* 128 A2
Victoria, *Guinea* 78 C2
Victoria, *Malaysia* 56 C5
Victoria, *Malta* 37 C1
Victoria, *Phil.* 55 D4
Victoria, *Kans., U.S.A.* . 108 F5
Victoria, *Tex., U.S.A.* ... 109 L6
Victoria □, *Australia* 91 F3
Victoria →, *Australia* ... 88 C4
Victoria, Grand L., *Canada* 98 C4
Victoria, L., *Africa* 82 C3
Victoria, L., *Australia* ... 91 E3
Victoria Beach, *Canada* . 101 C9
Victoria de Durango,
   Mexico 114 C4
Victoria de las Tunas, *Cuba* 116 B4
Victoria Falls, *Zimbabwe* 83 F2
Victoria Harbour, *Canada* 98 D4
Victoria I., *Canada* 96 A8
Victoria Ld., *Antarctica* . 5 D11
Victoria Nile →, *Uganda* 82 B3
Victoria Res., *Canada* ... 99 C8
Victoria River Downs,
   Australia 88 C5
Victoria Taungdeik, *Burma* 61 J18
Victoria West, *S. Africa* . 84 E3
Victorias, *Phil.* 55 F5
Victoriaville, *Canada* 99 C5
Victorica, *Argentina* 126 D2
Victorville, *U.S.A.* 113 L9
Vicuña, *Chile* 126 C1
Vicuña Mackenna,
   Argentina 126 C3
Vidal, *U.S.A.* 113 L12
Vidal Junction, *U.S.A.* .. 113 L12
Vidalia, *U.S.A.* 105 J4
Vidauban, *France* 27 E10
Vídho, *Greece* 37 A3
Vidigueira, *Portugal* 31 G3
Vidin, *Bulgaria* 38 F5
Vidio, C., *Spain* 30 B4
Vidisha, *India* 62 H7
Vidzy, *Belorussia* 40 D5
Viechtach, *Germany* 19 F8
Viedma, *Argentina* 128 B4
Viedma, L., *Argentina* .. 128 C2
Vieira, *Portugal* 30 D2
Viella, *Spain* 28 C5
Vielsalm, *Belgium* 17 H7
Vienenburg, *Germany* ... 18 D6
Vieng Pou Kha, *Laos* ... 58 B3
Vienna = Wien, *Austria* . 21 G6
Vienna, *U.S.A.* 109 G10
Vienne, *France* 27 C8
Vienne □, *France* 26 B4
Vienne →, *France* 24 E7

Vientiane, *Laos* 58 D4
Vientos, Paso de los,
   Caribbean 117 C5
Vierlingsbeek, *Neths.* ... 17 E8
Viersen, *Germany* 18 D2
Vierwaldstättersee, *Switz.* 23 C7
Vierzon, *France* 25 E9
Vieste, *Italy* 35 A9
Vietnam ■, *Asia* 58 C5
Vieux-Boucau-les-Bains,
   France 26 E2
Vif, *France* 27 C9
Vigan, *Phil.* 55 C4
Vigévano, *Italy* 32 C5
Vigia, *Brazil* 122 B2
Vigía Chico, *Mexico* 115 D7
Víglas, Ákra, *Greece* ... 37 D9
Vignemale, Pic du, *France* 26 F3
Vigneulles-lès-Hattonchâtel,
   France 25 D12
Vignola, *Italy* 32 D8
Vigo, *Spain* 30 C2
Vigo, Ría de, *Spain* 30 C2
Vihiers, *France* 24 E6
Vijayawada, *India* 61 L12
Vijfhuizen, *Neths.* 16 D5
Viken, *Sweden* 11 F8
Viking, *Canada* 100 C6
Vikna, *Norway* 8 D11
Viksjö, *Sweden* 10 B11
Vikulovo, *Russia* 44 D8
Vila de Maganja, *Mozam.* 83 F4
Vila de João Belo = Xai-
   Xai, *Mozam.* 85 D5
Vila de Rei, *Portugal* ... 31 F2
Vila do Bispo, *Portugal* . 31 H2
Vila do Chibuto, *Mozam.* 85 C5
Vila do Conde, *Portugal* . 30 D2
Vila Franca de Xira,
   Portugal 31 G2
Vila Gamito, *Mozam.* ... 83 E3
Vila Gomes da Costa,
   Mozam. 85 C5
Vila Machado, *Mozam.* . 83 F3
Vila Mouzinho, *Mozam.* . 83 E3
Vila Nova de Foscôa,
   Portugal 30 D3
Vila Nova de Ourém,
   Portugal 31 F2
Vila Novo de Gaia,
   Portugal 30 D2
Vila Pouca de Aguiar,
   Portugal 30 D3
Vila Real, *Portugal* 30 D3
Vila Real de Santo
   António, *Portugal* .. 31 H3
Vila Vasco da Gama,
   Mozam. 83 E3
Vila Velha, *Amapá, Brazil* 121 C7
Vila Velha, *Espírito Santo,
   Brazil* 123 F3
Vila Viçosa, *Portugal* ... 31 G3
Vilaboa, *Spain* 30 C2
Vilaine →, *France* 24 E4
Vilanandro, Tanjona,
   Madag. 85 B7
Vilanculos, *Mozam.* 85 C6
Vilar Formoso, *Portugal* . 30 E4
Vilareal □, *Portugal* 30 D3
Vilaseca-Salou, *Spain* ... 28 D6
Vilcabamba, Cordillera,
   Peru 124 C3
Vilcanchos, *Peru* 124 C3
Vileyka, *Belorussia* 40 D5
Vilhelmina, *Sweden* 8 D14
Vilhena, *Brazil* 125 C5
Viliga, *Russia* 45 C16
Viliya →, *Lithuania* 40 D4
Viljandi, *Estonia* 40 B4
Vilkovo, *Ukraine* 42 D3
Villa Abecia, *Bolivia* 126 A2
Villa Ahumada, *Mexico* . 114 A3
Villa Ana, *Argentina* 126 B4
Villa Ángela, *Argentina* . 126 B3
Villa Bella, *Bolivia* 125 C4
Villa Bens = Tarfaya,
   Morocco 74 C2
Villa Cañas, *Argentina* .. 126 C3
Villa Carlos, *Spain* 36 B11
Villa Cisneros = Dakhla,
   W. Sahara 74 D1
Villa Colón, *Argentina* .. 126 C2
Villa Constitución,
   Argentina 126 C3
Villa de Cura, *Venezuela* 120 A4
Villa de María, *Argentina* 126 B3
Villa del Rosario,
   Venezuela 120 A3
Villa Dolores, *Argentina* . 126 C2
Villa Frontera, *Mexico* .. 114 B4
Villa Guillermina,
   Argentina 126 B4
Villa Hayes, *Paraguay* .. 126 B4
Villa Iris, *Argentina* 126 D3
Villa Juárez, *Mexico* 114 B4
Villa María, *Argentina* .. 126 C3
Villa Mazán, *Argentina* . 126 B2
Villa Minozzo, *Italy* 32 D7
Villa Montes, *Bolivia* ... 126 A3
Villa Ocampo, *Argentina* 126 B4
Villa Ocampo, *Mexico* .. 114 B3
Villa Ojo de Agua,
   Argentina 126 B3
Villa San Giovanni, *Italy* . 35 D8
Villa San José, *Argentina* . 126 C4

Villa San Martín, *Argentina*	126	B3
Villa Santina, *Italy*	33	B9
Villa Unión, *Mexico*	114	C3
Villablino, *Spain*	30	C4
Villacañas, *Spain*	28	F1
Villacarriedo, *Spain*	28	B1
Villacarrillo, *Spain*	29	G1
Villacastín, *Spain*	30	E6
Villach, *Austria*	21	J3
Villaciado, *Italy*	34	C1
Villada, *Spain*	30	C6
Villadiego, *Spain*	30	C6
Villadóssola, *Italy*	32	B5
Villafeliche, *Spain*	28	D3
Villafranca, *Spain*	28	C3
Villafranca de los Barros, *Spain*	31	G4
Villafranca de los Caballeros, *Spain*	29	F1
Villafranca de los Caballeros, *Spain*	36	B10
Villafranca del Bierzo, *Spain*	30	C4
Villafranca del Cid, *Spain*	28	E4
Villafranca del Panadés, *Spain*	28	D6
Villafranca di Verona, *Italy*	32	C7
Villagarcía de Arosa, *Spain*	30	C2
Villagrán, *Mexico*	115	C5
Villaguay, *Argentina*	126	C4
Villaharta, *Spain*	31	G6
Villahermosa, *Mexico*	115	D6
Villahermosa, *Spain*	29	G2
Villaines-la-Juhel, *France*	24	D6
Villajoyosa, *Spain*	29	G4
Villalba, *Spain*	30	B3
Villalba de Guardo, *Spain*	30	C6
Villalcampo, Pantano de, *Spain*	30	D4
Villalón de Campos, *Spain*	30	C5
Villalpando, *Spain*	30	D5
Villaluenga, *Spain*	30	E7
Villamañán, *Spain*	30	C5
Villamartín, *Spain*	31	J5
Villamayor, *Spain*	28	F2
Villamblard, *France*	26	C4
Villanova Monteleone, *Italy*	34	B1
Villanueva, *Colombia*	120	A3
Villanueva, *U.S.A.*	111	J11
Villanueva de Castellón, *Spain*	29	F4
Villanueva de Córdoba, *Spain*	31	G6
Villanueva de la Fuente, *Spain*	29	G2
Villanueva de la Serena, *Spain*	31	G5
Villanueva de la Sierra, *Spain*	30	E4
Villanueva de los Castillejos, *Spain*	31	H3
Villanueva del Arzobispo, *Spain*	29	G1
Villanueva del Duque, *Spain*	31	G5
Villanueva del Fresno, *Spain*	31	G3
Villanueva y Geltrú, *Spain*	28	D6
Villaodrid, *Spain*	30	B3
Villaputzu, *Italy*	34	C2
Villar del Arzobispo, *Spain*	28	F4
Villar del Rey, *Spain*	31	F4
Villarcayo, *Spain*	28	C1
Villard-Bonnot, *France*	27	C9
Villard-de-Lans, *France*	27	C9
Villarino de los Aires, *Spain*	30	D4
Villarosa, *Italy*	35	E7
Villarramiel, *Spain*	30	C6
Villarreal, *Spain*	28	F4
Villarrica, *Chile*	128	A2
Villarrica, *Paraguay*	126	B4
Villarrobledo, *Spain*	29	F2
Villarroya de la Sierra, *Spain*	28	D3
Villarrubia de los Ojos, *Spain*	29	F1
Villars-les-Dombes, *France*	27	B9
Villarta de San Juan, *Spain*	29	F1
Villasayas, *Spain*	28	D2
Villaseca de los Gamitos, *Spain*	30	D4
Villastar, *Spain*	28	E3
Villatobas, *Spain*	28	F1
Villavicencio, *Argentina*	126	C2
Villavicencio, *Colombia*	120	C3
Villaviciosa, *Spain*	30	B5
Villazón, *Bolivia*	126	A2
Ville-Marie, *Canada*	98	C4
Ville Platte, *U.S.A.*	109	K8
Villedieu-les-Poêlles, *France*	24	D5
Villefort, *France*	26	D7
Villefranche-de-Lauragais, *France*	26	E5
Villefranche-de-Rouergue, *France*	26	D6
Villefranche-du-Périgord, *France*	26	D5
Villefranche-sur-Cher, *France*	25	E8
Villefranche-sur-Saône, *France*	27	C8
Villegrande, *Bolivia*	125	D5
Villel, *Spain*	28	E3
Villemaur-sur-Vanne, *France*	25	D10
Villemur-sur-Tarn, *France*	26	E5
Villena, *Spain*	29	G4
Villenauxe-la-Grande, *France*	25	D10
Villeneuve-d'Ornon, *France*	26	D3
Villeneuve, *Italy*	32	C4
Villeneuve, *Switz.*	22	D3
Villeneuve-l'Archevêque, *France*	25	D10
Villeneuve-lès-Avignon, *France*	27	E8
Villeneuve-St.-Georges, *France*	25	D9
Villeneuve-sur-Allier, *France*	26	B7
Villeneuve-sur-Lot, *France*	26	D4
Villeréal, *France*	26	D4
Villers-Bocage, *France*	24	C6
Villers-Bretonneux, *France*	25	C9
Villers-Cotterêts, *France*	25	C10
Villers-le-Bouillet, *Belgium*	17	G6
Villers-le-Gambon, *Belgium*	17	H5
Villers-sur-Mer, *France*	24	C6
Villersexel, *France*	25	E13
Villerupt, *France*	25	C12
Villerville, *France*	24	C7
Villiers, *S. Africa*	85	D4
Villingen, *Germany*	19	G4
Villisca, *U.S.A.*	108	E7
Vilna, *Canada*	100	C6
Vilnius, *Lithuania*	40	D4
Vils →, *Germany*	19	G9
Vilsbiburg, *Germany*	19	G8
Vilshofen, *Germany*	19	G9
Vilskutskogo, Proliv, *Russia*	45	B11
Vilusi, *Montenegro, Yug.*	21	N8
Vilvoorde, *Belgium*	17	G4
Vilyuy →, *Russia*	45	C13
Vilyuysk, *Russia*	45	C13
Vimercate, *Italy*	32	C6
Vimioso, *Portugal*	30	D4
Vimoutiers, *France*	24	D7
Vimperk, *Czech.*	20	F3
Viña del Mar, *Chile*	126	C1
Vinaroz, *Spain*	28	E5
Vincennes, *U.S.A.*	104	F2
Vincent, *U.S.A.*	113	L8
Vinces, *Ecuador*	120	D2
Vinchina, *Argentina*	126	B2
Vindel älven →, *Sweden*	8	E15
Vindeln, *Sweden*	8	D15
Vinderup, *Denmark*	11	H2
Vindhya Ra., *India*	62	H7
Vineland, *U.S.A.*	104	F8
Vinga, *Romania*	38	D4
Vingnes, *Norway*	10	C4
Vinh, *Vietnam*	58	C5
Vinh Linh, *Vietnam*	58	D6
Vinh Long, *Vietnam*	59	G5
Vinh Yen, *Vietnam*	58	B5
Vinhais, *Portugal*	30	D3
Vinica, *Croatia*	33	B13
Vinica, *Slovenia*	33	C12
Vinita, *U.S.A.*	109	G7
Vinkeveen, *Neths.*	16	D5
Vinkovci, *Croatia*	21	K8
Vinnitsa, *Ukraine*	42	B3
Vinnytsya = Vinnitsa, *Ukraine*	42	B3
Vinstra, *Norway*	10	C3
Vinton, *Calif., U.S.A.*	112	F6
Vinton, *Iowa, U.S.A.*	108	D8
Vinton, *La., U.S.A.*	109	K8
Vințu de Jos, *Romania*	38	D6
Viöl, *Germany*	18	A5
Vipava, *Slovenia*	33	C10
Vipiteno, *Italy*	33	B8
Viqueque, *Indonesia*	57	F7
Vir, *Croatia*	33	D12
Virac, *Phil.*	55	E6
Virachei, *Cambodia*	58	F6
Virago Sd., *Canada*	100	C2
Viramgam, *India*	62	H5
Viranşehir, *Turkey*	67	E8
Virden, *Canada*	101	D8
Vire, *France*	24	D6
Vire →, *France*	24	C5
Virgem da Lapa, *Brazil*	123	E3
Vírgenes, C., *Argentina*	128	D3
Virgin →, *Canada*	101	B7
Virgin →, *U.S.A.*	111	H6
Virgin Gorda, *Virgin Is.*	117	C7
Virgin Is. (British) ■, *W. Indies*	117	C7
Virgin Is. (U.S.) ■, *W. Indies*	117	C7
Virginia, *S. Africa*	84	D4
Virginia, *U.S.A.*	108	B8
Virginia □, *U.S.A.*	104	G7
Virginia Beach, *U.S.A.*	104	G8
Virginia City, *Mont., U.S.A.*	110	D8
Virginia City, *Nev., U.S.A.*	112	F7
Virginia Falls, *Canada*	100	A3
Virginiatown, *Canada*	98	C4
Virieu-le-Grand, *France*	27	C9
Viroqua, *U.S.A.*	108	D9
Virovitica, *Croatia*	21	K7
Virton, *Belgium*	17	J7
Virtsu, *Estonia*	40	B3
Virú, *Peru*	124	B2
Virudunagar, *India*	60	Q10
Vis, *Croatia*	33	E13
Vis Kanal, *Croatia*	33	E13
Visalia, *U.S.A.*	111	H4
Visayan Sea, *Phil.*	55	F5
Visby, *Sweden*	9	H15
Viscount Melville Sd., *Canada*	4	B2
Visé, *Belgium*	17	G7
Višegrad, *Bos.-H.*	21	M9
Viseu, *Brazil*	122	B2
Viseu, *Portugal*	30	E3
Viseu □, *Portugal*	30	E3
Vişeu de Sus, *Romania*	38	B7
Vishakhapatnam, *India*	61	L13
Viskafors, *Sweden*	11	G6
Visnagar, *India*	62	H5
Višnja Gora, *Slovenia*	33	C11
Viso, Mte., *Italy*	32	D4
Viso del Marqués, *Spain*	29	G1
Visoko, *Bos.-H.*	21	M8
Visokoi I., *Antarctica*	5	B1
Visp, *Switz.*	22	D5
Vispa →, *Switz.*	22	D5
Visselhövede, *Germany*	18	C5
Vissoie, *Switz.*	22	D5
Vista, *U.S.A.*	113	M9
Vistula = Wisła →, *Poland*	20	A8
Vit →, *Bulgaria*	38	F7
Vitanje, *Slovenia*	33	B12
Vitebsk, *Belorussia*	40	D7
Viterbo, *Italy*	33	F9
Viti Levu, *Fiji*	87	C7
Vitigudino, *Spain*	30	D4
Vitim, *Russia*	45	D12
Vitim →, *Russia*	45	D12
Vitória, *Brazil*	123	F3
Vitoria, *Spain*	28	C2
Vitória da Conquista, *Brazil*	123	D3
Vitória de São Antão, *Brazil*	122	C4
Vitorino Friere, *Brazil*	122	B2
Vitré, *France*	24	D5
Vitry-le-François, *France*	25	D11
Vitsi, Óros, *Greece*	39	J4
Vitsyebsk = Vitebsk, *Belorussia*	40	D7
Vitteaux, *France*	25	E11
Vittel, *France*	25	D12
Vittória, *Italy*	35	F7
Vittório Véneto, *Italy*	33	C9
Vivario, *France*	27	F13
Vivegnis, *Belgium*	17	G7
Viver, *Spain*	28	F4
Vivero, *Spain*	30	B3
Viviers, *France*	27	D8
Vivonne, *France*	26	B4
Vizcaíno, Desierto de, *Mexico*	114	B2
Vizcaíno, Sierra, *Mexico*	114	B2
Vizcaya □, *Spain*	28	B2
Vize, *Turkey*	66	C2
Vizianagaram, *India*	61	K13
Vizille, *France*	27	C9
Viziñada, *Croatia*	33	C10
Viziru, *Romania*	38	E10
Vizovice, *Czech.*	20	F7
Vizzini, *Italy*	35	E7
Vlaardingen, *Neths.*	16	E4
Vlădeasa, *Romania*	38	C5
Vladikavkaz, *Russia*	43	E11
Vladimir, *Russia*	41	C12
Vladimir Volynskiy, *Ukraine*	40	F4
Vladimirovac, *Serbia, Yug.*	21	K10
Vladimirovka, *Russia*	43	B12
Vladimirovka, *Russia*	43	D11
Vladislavovka, *Ukraine*	42	D6
Vladivostok, *Russia*	45	E14
Vlamertinge, *Belgium*	17	G1
Vlasenica, *Bos.-H., Yug.*	21	L8
Vlasinsko Jezero, *Serbia, Yug.*	21	N12
Vleuten, *Neths.*	16	D6
Vlieland, *Neths.*	16	B5
Vliestroom, *Neths.*	16	B6
Vlijmen, *Neths.*	17	E6
Vlissingen, *Neths.*	17	F3
Vlóra, *Albania*	39	J2
Vlorës, Gjiri i, *Albania*	39	J2
Vltava →, *Czech.*	20	E4
Vo Dat, *Vietnam*	59	G6
Vobarno, *Italy*	32	C7
Voćin, *Croatia*	21	K7
Vodice, *Croatia*	33	E12
Vodnjan, *Croatia*	33	D10
Vogelkop = Doberai, Jazirah, *Indonesia*	57	E8
Vogelsberg, *Germany*	18	E5
Voghera, *Italy*	32	D6
Vohibinany, *Madag.*	85	B8
Vohimarina, *Madag.*	85	A9
Vohimena, Tanjon' i, *Madag.*	85	D8
Vohipeno, *Madag.*	85	C8
Voi, *Kenya*	82	C4
Void, *France*	25	D12
Voiron, *France*	27	C9
Voisey B., *Canada*	99	A7
Voitsberg, *Austria*	21	H5
Voiviís Límni, *Greece*	39	K5
Vojens, *Denmark*	11	J3
Vojmsjön, *Sweden*	8	D14
Vojnić, *Croatia*	33	C12
Vojnik, *Italy*	33	B11
Vokhma, *Russia*	41	B15
Vokhma →, *Russia*	41	C15
Vokhtoga, *Russia*	41	B12
Volborg, *U.S.A.*	108	C2
Volcano Is. = Kazan-Rettõ, *Pac. Oc.*	92	E6
Volchansk, *Ukraine*	42	A7
Volchayevka, *Russia*	45	E14
Volchya →, *Ukraine*	42	C7
Volda, *Norway*	8	E9
Volendam, *Neths.*	16	D6
Volga, *Russia*	41	C11
Volga →, *Russia*	43	C13
Volga Hts. = Privolzhskaya Vozvyshennost, *Russia*	41	F15
Volgodonsk, *Russia*	43	C10
Volgograd, *Russia*	43	B11
Volgogradskoye Vdkhr., *Russia*	41	F14
Volgorechensk, *Russia*	41	C12
Volkach, *Germany*	19	F6
Volkerak, *Neths.*	17	E4
Volkhov, *Russia*	40	B8
Volkhov →, *Russia*	40	A8
Völklingen, *Germany*	19	F2
Volkovysk, *Belorussia*	40	E4
Volksrust, *S. Africa*	85	D4
Vollenhove, *Neths.*	16	C7
Vol'n'ansk, *Ukraine*	42	C6
Volnovakha, *Ukraine*	42	C7
Volochanka, *Russia*	45	B10
Volodarsk, *Russia*	41	C13
Vologda, *Russia*	41	B11
Volokolamsk, *Russia*	41	C9
Volokonovka, *Russia*	41	F10
Vólos, *Greece*	39	K5
Volosovo, *Russia*	40	B6
Volozhin, *Belorussia*	40	D5
Volsk, *Russia*	41	E15
Volta →, *Ghana*	70	F4
Volta, L., *Ghana*	79	D5
Volta Blanche = White Volta →, *Ghana*	79	D4
Volta Redonda, *Brazil*	123	F3
Voltaire, C., *Australia*	88	B4
Volterra, *Italy*	32	E7
Voltri, *Italy*	32	D5
Volturara Áppula, *Italy*	35	A8
Volturno →, *Italy*	34	A6
Volubilis, *Morocco*	74	B3
Volvo, *Australia*	91	E3
Volzhsk, *Russia*	41	D16
Volzhskiy, *Russia*	43	B11
Voorburg, *Neths.*	16	D4
Voorne Putten, *Neths.*	16	E4
Voorst, *Neths.*	16	D8
Voorthuizen, *Neths.*	16	D7
Vopnafjörður, *Iceland*	8	D6
Vóras Óros, *Greece*	39	J4
Vorbasse, *Denmark*	11	J3
Vorden, *Neths.*	16	D8
Vorderrhein →, *Switz.*	23	C8
Vordingborg, *Denmark*	11	K5
Voreppe, *France*	27	C9
Voríai Sporádhes, *Greece*	39	K6
Vórios Evvoïkos Kólpos, *Greece*	39	L6
Vorkuta, *Russia*	44	C7
Vorma →, *Norway*	10	D5
Vorona →, *Russia*	41	F13
Voronezh, *Russia*	41	F11
Voronezh, *Ukraine*	40	F8
Voronezh →, *Russia*	41	F10
Vorontsovo-Aleksandrovskoye = Zelenokumsk, *Russia*	43	D10
Voroshilovgrad = Lugansk, *Ukraine*	43	B8
Voroshilovsk = Kommunarsk, *Ukraine*	43	B8
Vorovskoye, *Russia*	45	D16
Vorselaar, *Belgium*	17	F5
Vorskla →, *Ukraine*	42	B6
Võru, *Estonia*	40	C5
Vorupør, *Denmark*	11	H2
Vosges, *France*	25	D14
Vosges □, *France*	25	D13
Voskopoja, *Albania*	39	J3
Voskresensk, *Russia*	41	D11
Voskresenskoye, *Russia*	41	C14
Voss, *Norway*	9	F9
Vosselaar, *Belgium*	17	F5
Vostok I., *Kiribati*	93	J12
Votkinsk, *Russia*	44	C4
Votkinskoye Vdkhr., *Russia*	44	C5
Votsuri-Shima, *Japan*	49	M1
Vouga →, *Portugal*	30	E2
Vouillé, *France*	24	F7
Vouvray, *France*	24	E7
Vouvry, *Switz.*	22	D3
Vouzela, *Portugal*	30	E2
Vouziers, *France*	25	C11
Voves, *France*	25	D8
Voxna, *Sweden*	10	C9
Vozhgaly, *Russia*	41	B17
Voznesenka, *Russia*	45	D10
Voznesensk, *Ukraine*	42	C4
Voznesenye, *Russia*	44	C4
Vrådal, *Norway*	10	E2
Vrakhneíka, *Greece*	39	L4
Vrancea, Munţii, *Romania*	38	D9
Vranica, *Bos.-H.*	21	M7
Vrangelya, Ostrov, *Russia*	45	B19
Vranje, *Serbia, Yug.*	21	N11
Vransko, *Slovenia*	33	B11
Vratsa, *Bulgaria*	38	F6
Vrbas, *Serbia, Yug.*	21	K9
Vrbas →, *Bos.-H.*	21	K7
Vrbnik, *Croatia*	33	C11
Vrbovec, *Croatia*	33	C13
Vrbovsko, *Croatia*	33	C12
Vrchlabí, *Czech.*	20	E5
Vrede, *S. Africa*	85	D4
Vredefort, *S. Africa*	84	D4
Vredenburg, *S. Africa*	84	E2
Vredendal, *S. Africa*	84	E2
Vreeswijk, *Neths.*	16	D6
Vrena, *Sweden*	11	F10
Vrgorac, *Croatia*	21	M7
Vrhnika, *Slovenia*	33	C11
Vríði, *Ivory C.*	78	D4
Vries, *Neths.*	16	B9
Vriezenveen, *Neths.*	16	D9
Vrindavan, *India*	62	F7
Vríses, *Greece*	37	D6
Vrnograč, *Bos.-H.*	33	C12
Vroomshoop, *Neths.*	16	D9
Vršac, *Serbia, Yug.*	21	K11
Vrsacki Kanal, *Serbia, Yug.*	21	K11
Vryburg, *S. Africa*	84	D3
Vryheid, *S. Africa*	85	D5
Vsetín, *Czech.*	20	F8
Vu Liet, *Vietnam*	58	C5
Vucha →, *Bulgaria*	39	G7
Vught, *Neths.*	17	E6
Vukovar, *Croatia*	21	K8
Vulcan, *Canada*	100	C6
Vulcan, *U.S.A.*	104	C2
Vulcano, *Italy*	35	D7
Vǔlchedruma, *Bulgaria*	38	F6
Vulci, *Italy*	33	F8
Vulkaneshty, *Moldavia*	42	D3
Vunduzi →, *Mozam.*	83	F3
Vung Tau, *Vietnam*	59	G6
Vǔrbitsa, *Bulgaria*	38	G9
Vyasniki, *Russia*	41	C13
Vyatka, *Russia*	41	B16
Vyatka →, *Russia*	41	C17
Vyatskiye Polyany, *Russia*	41	C17
Vyazemskiy, *Russia*	45	E14
Vyazma, *Russia*	40	D9
Vyborg, *Russia*	44	C3
Vychegda →, *Russia*	44	C5
Vychodné Beskydy, *Europe*	20	F11
Vyksa, *Russia*	41	D13
Vyrnwy, L., *U.K.*	12	E4
Vyshniy Volochek, *Russia*	40	C9
Vyškov, *Czech.*	20	F6
Vysoké Mýto, *Czech.*	20	F6
Vysokovsk, *Russia*	41	C10
Vysotsk, *Ukraine*	40	F5

W

W.A.C. Bennett Dam, *Canada*	100	B4
Wa, *Ghana*	78	C4
Waal →, *Neths.*	16	E6
Waalwijk, *Neths.*	17	E6
Waarschoot, *Belgium*	17	F3
Waasmunster, *Belgium*	17	F4
Wabakimi L., *Canada*	98	B2
Wabana, *Canada*	99	C9
Wabasca, *Canada*	100	B6
Wabash, *U.S.A.*	104	E3
Wabash →, *U.S.A.*	104	G1
Wabeno, *U.S.A.*	104	C1
Wabi →, *Ethiopia*	77	F5
Wabigoon L., *Canada*	101	D10
Wabowden, *Canada*	101	C9
Wąbrzeźno, *Poland*	20	B8
Wabu Hu, *China*	53	A11
Wabuk Pt., *Canada*	98	A2
Wabush, *Canada*	99	B6
Wabuska, *U.S.A.*	110	G4
Wachtebeke, *Belgium*	17	F3
Wächtersbach, *Germany*	19	E5
Waco, *U.S.A.*	109	K6
Waconichi, L., *Canada*	98	B5
Wad Ban Naqa, *Sudan*	77	D3
Wad Banda, *Sudan*	77	E2
Wad el Haddad, *Sudan*	77	E3
Wad en Nau, *Sudan*	77	E3
Wad Hamid, *Sudan*	77	D3
Wâd Medanî, *Sudan*	77	E3
Wad Thana, *Pakistan*	62	F2
Wadayama, *Japan*	49	G7
Waddeneilanden, *Neths.*	16	B6
Waddenzee, *Neths.*	16	B6
Wadderin Hill, *Australia*	89	F2
Waddington, *U.S.A.*	107	B9
Waddington, Mt., *Canada*	100	C3
Waddinxveen, *Neths.*	16	D5
Waddy Pt., *Australia*	91	C5
Wadena, *Canada*	101	C8
Wadena, *U.S.A.*	108	B7
Wädenswil, *Switz.*	23	B7
Wadesboro, *U.S.A.*	105	H5
Wadhams, *Canada*	100	C3
Wādī as Sīr, *Jordan*	69	D4
Wadi Gemâl, *Egypt*	76	C4
Wadi Halfa, *Sudan*	76	C3
Wadian, *China*	53	A9
Wadowice, *Poland*	20	F9
Wadsworth, *U.S.A.*	110	G4
Waegwan, *S. Korea*	51	G15
Wafrah, *Si. Arabia*	64	D5
Wagenberg, *Neths.*	17	E5
Wageningen, *Neths.*	16	E7

Wageningen, *Surinam* 121 B6
Wager B., *Canada* 97 B11
Wager Bay, *Canada* 97 B10
Wagga Wagga, *Australia* .. 91 F4
Waghete, *Indonesia* 57 E9
Wagin, *Australia* 89 F2
Wagon Mound, *U.S.A.* ... 109 G2
Wagoner, *U.S.A.* 109 G7
Wagrowiec, *Poland* 20 C7
Wah, *Pakistan* 62 C5
Wahai, *Indonesia* 57 E7
Wahiawa, *U.S.A.* 102 H15
Wâḥid, *Egypt* 69 E1
Wahnai, *Afghan.* 62 C1
Wahoo, *U.S.A.* 108 E6
Wahpeton, *U.S.A.* 108 B6
Wai, Koh, *Cambodia* 59 H4
Waiau →, *N.Z.* 87 K4
Waibeem, *Indonesia* 57 E8
Waiblingen, *Germany* 19 G5
Waidhofen,
  Niederösterreich, Austria 20 G5
Waidhofen,
  Niederösterreich, Austria 21 H4
Waigeo, *Indonesia* 57 E8
Waihi, *N.Z.* 87 G5
Waihou →, *N.Z.* 87 G5
Waika, *Zaïre* 82 C2
Waikabubak, *Indonesia* ... 57 F5
Waikari, *N.Z.* 87 K4
Waikato →, *N.Z.* 87 G5
Waikerie, *Australia* 91 E2
Waikokopu, *N.Z.* 87 H6
Waikouaiti, *N.Z.* 87 L3
Waimakariri →, *N.Z.* 87 K4
Waimate, *N.Z.* 87 L3
Waimes, *Belgium* 17 H8
Wainganga →, *India* 60 K11
Waingapu, *Indonesia* 57 F6
Waini →, *Guyana* 121 B6
Wainwright, *Canada* 101 C6
Wainwright, *U.S.A.* 96 A3
Waiouru, *N.Z.* 87 H5
Waipara, *N.Z.* 87 K4
Waipawa, *N.Z.* 87 H6
Waipiro, *N.Z.* 87 H7
Waipu, *N.Z.* 87 F5
Waipukurau, *N.Z.* 87 J6
Wairakei, *N.Z.* 87 H6
Wairarapa, L., *N.Z.* 87 J5
Wairoa, *N.Z.* 87 H6
Waitaki →, *N.Z.* 87 L3
Waitara, *N.Z.* 87 H5
Waitsburg, *U.S.A.* 110 C5
Waiuku, *N.Z.* 87 G5
Wajima, *Japan* 49 F8
Wajir, *Kenya* 82 B5
Wajir □, *Kenya* 82 B5
Wakasa, *Japan* 49 G7
Wakasa-Wan, *Japan* 49 G7
Wakatipu, L., *N.Z.* 87 L2
Wakaw, *Canada* 101 C7
Wakayama, *Japan* 49 G7
Wakayama-ken □, *Japan* . 49 H7
Wake Forest, *U.S.A.* 105 H6
Wake I., *Pac. Oc.* 92 F8
Wakefield, *N.Z.* 87 J4
Wakefield, *U.K.* 12 D6
Wakefield, *Mass., U.S.A.* . 107 D13
Wakefield, *Mich., U.S.A.* . 108 B10
Wakeham Bay =
  Maricourt, *Canada* 97 C12
Wakema, *Burma* 61 L19
Wakkanai, *Japan* 48 B10
Wakkerstroom, *S. Africa* . 85 D5
Wakool, *Australia* 91 F3
Wakool →, *Australia* 91 F3
Wakre, *Indonesia* 57 E8
Wakuach L., *Canada* 99 A6
Walamba, *Zambia* 83 E2
Wałbrzych, *Poland* 20 E6
Walbury Hill, *U.K.* 13 F6
Walcha, *Australia* 91 E5
Walcheren, *Neths.* 17 E3
Walcott, *U.S.A.* 110 F10
Wałcz, *Poland* 20 B6
Wald, *Switz.* 23 B7
Waldbröl, *Germany* 18 E3
Waldburg Ra., *Australia* . 88 D2
Waldeck, *Germany* 18 D5
Walden, *Colo., U.S.A.* .. 110 F10
Walden, *N.Y., U.S.A.* ... 107 E10
Waldenburg, *Switz.* 22 B5
Waldport, *U.S.A.* 110 D1
Waldron, *U.S.A.* 109 H7
Waldshut, *Germany* 19 H4
Walembele, *Ghana* 78 C4
Walensee, *Switz.* 23 B8
Walenstadt, *Switz.* 23 B8
Wales □, *U.K.* 13 E4
Walewale, *Ghana* 79 C4
Walgett, *Australia* 91 E4
Walgreen Coast, *Antarctica* 5 D15
Walhalla, *Australia* 91 F4
Walhalla, *U.S.A.* 101 D9
Walker, *U.S.A.* 108 B7
Walker L., *Man., Canada* 101 C9
Walker L., *Qué., Canada* . 99 B6
Walker L., *U.S.A.* 110 G4
Walkerston, *Australia* ... 90 C4
Walkerton, *Canada* 106 B3
Wall, *U.S.A.* 108 C3
Walla Walla, *U.S.A.* 110 C4
Wallabadah, *Australia* ... 90 B3
Wallace, *Idaho, U.S.A.* .. 110 C6

Wallace, *N.C., U.S.A.* ... 105 H7
Wallace, *Nebr., U.S.A.* ... 108 E4
Wallaceburg, *Canada* 98 D3
Wallachia = Valahia,
  Romania 38 E8
Wallal, *Australia* 91 D4
Wallal Downs, *Australia* .. 88 C3
Wallambin, L., *Australia* . 89 F2
Wallaroo, *Australia* 91 E2
Wallasey, *U.K.* 12 D4
Walldürn, *Germany* 19 F5
Wallerawang, *Australia* ... 91 E5
Wallhallow, *Australia* ... 90 B2
Wallingford, *U.S.A.* 107 E12
Wallis & Futuna, Is.,
  Pac. Oc. 92 J10
Wallisellen, *Switz.* 23 B7
Wallowa, *U.S.A.* 110 D5
Wallowa Mts., *U.S.A.* ... 110 D5
Wallsend, *Australia* 91 E5
Wallsend, *U.K.* 12 C6
Wallula, *U.S.A.* 110 C4
Wallumbilla, *Australia* ... 91 D4
Walmsley, L., *Canada* ... 101 A7
Walney, I. of, *U.K.* 12 C4
Walnut Creek, *U.S.A.* ... 112 H4
Walnut Ridge, *U.S.A.* ... 109 G9
Walsall, *U.K.* 13 E6
Walsenburg, *U.S.A.* 109 G2
Walsh, *U.S.A.* 109 G3
Walsh →, *Australia* 90 B3
Walsh P.O., *Australia* ... 90 B3
Walshoutem, *Belgium* ... 17 G6
Walsrode, *Germany* 18 C5
Walterboro, *U.S.A.* 105 J5
Walters, *U.S.A.* 109 H5
Waltershausen, *Germany* . 18 E6
Waltham, *U.S.A.* 107 D13
Waltham Station, *Canada* . 98 C4
Waltman, *U.S.A.* 110 E10
Walton, *U.S.A.* 107 D9
Walvisbaai, *S. Africa* 84 C1
Wamba, *Kenya* 82 B4
Wamba, *Zaïre* 82 B2
Wamego, *U.S.A.* 108 F6
Wamena, *Indonesia* 57 E9
Wamsasi, *Indonesia* 57 E7
Wan Xian, *China* 50 E8
Wana, *Pakistan* 62 C3
Wanaaring, *Australia* ... 91 D3
Wanaka, *N.Z.* 87 L2
Wanaka L., *N.Z.* 87 L2
Wan'an, *China* 53 D10
Wanapiri, *Indonesia* 57 E9
Wanapitei L., *Canada* ... 98 C3
Wanbi, *Australia* 91 E3
Wandaik, *Guyana* 121 C6
Wandarrie, *Australia* 89 E2
Wanderer, *Zimbabwe* ... 83 F3
Wandoan, *Australia* 91 D4
Wandre, *Belgium* 17 G7
Wanfercée-Baulet, *Belgium* 17 H5
Wanfu, *China* 51 D12
Wang →, *Thailand* 58 D2
Wang Kai, *Sudan* 77 F2
Wang Noi, *Thailand* 58 E3
Wang Saphung, *Thailand* . 58 D3
Wang Thong, *Thailand* .. 58 D3
Wanga, *Zaïre* 82 B2
Wangal, *Indonesia* 57 F8
Wanganella, *Australia* ... 91 F3
Wanganui, *N.Z.* 87 H5
Wangaratta, *Australia* ... 91 F4
Wangary, *Australia* 91 E2
Wangcang, *China* 52 A4
Wangdu, *China* 50 E8
Wangerooge, *Germany* .. 18 B3
Wangi, *Kenya* 82 C5
Wangiwangi, *Indonesia* .. 57 F6
Wangjiang, *China* 53 B11
Wangmo, *China* 52 E6
Wangqing, *China* 51 C15
Wankaner, *India* 62 H4
Wanless, *Canada* 101 C8
Wannian, *China* 53 C11
Wanon Niwat, *Thailand* . 58 D4
Wanquan, *China* 50 D8
Wanrong, *China* 50 G6
Wanshan, *China* 52 D7
Wanshengchang, *China* .. 52 C6
Wanssum, *Neths.* 17 E8
Wanxian, *China* 52 B7
Wanyuan, *China* 52 A7
Wanzai, *China* 53 C10
Wanze, *Belgium* 17 G6
Wapakoneta, *U.S.A.* 104 E3
Wapato, *U.S.A.* 110 C3
Wapawekka L., *Canada* . 101 C8
Wapikopa L., *Canada* ... 98 B2
Wappingers Falls, *U.S.A.* . 107 E11
Wapsipinicon →, *U.S.A.* . 108 E9
Warangal, *India* 60 L11
Waratah, *Australia* 90 G4
Waratah B., *Australia* ... 91 F4
Warburg, *Germany* 18 D5
Warburton, *Vic., Australia* 91 F4
Warburton, *W. Austral.,*
  Australia 89 E4
Warburton Ra., *Australia* . 89 E4
Ward, *N.Z.* 87 J5
Ward →, *Australia* 91 D4
Ward Cove, *U.S.A.* 100 B2
Ward Mt., *U.S.A.* 112 H8
Warden, *S. Africa* 85 D4
Wardha, *India* 60 J11

Wardha →, *India* 60 K11
Wardlow, *Canada* 100 C6
Ware, *Canada* 100 B3
Ware, *U.S.A.* 107 D12
Waregem, *Belgium* 17 G2
Wareham, *U.S.A.* 107 E14
Waremme, *Belgium* 17 G6
Waren, *Germany* 18 B8
Warendorf, *Germany* ... 18 D3
Warialda, *Australia* 91 D5
Wariap, *Indonesia* 57 E8
Warin Chamrap, *Thailand* 58 E5
Warkopi, *Indonesia* 57 E8
Warley, *U.K.* 13 E6
Warm Springs, *U.S.A.* .. 111 G5
Warman, *Canada* 101 C7
Warmbad, *Namibia* 84 D2
Warmbad, *S. Africa* 85 C4
Warmenhuizen, *Neths.* .. 16 C5
Warmeriville, *France* 25 C11
Warmond, *Neths.* 16 D5
Warnambool Downs,
  Australia 90 C3
Warnemünde, *Germany* . 18 A8
Warner, *Canada* 100 D6
Warner Mts., *U.S.A.* 110 F3
Warner Robins, *U.S.A.* .. 105 J4
Warnes, *Bolivia* 125 D5
Warneton, *Belgium* 17 G1
Warnow →, *Germany* ... 18 A8
Warnsveld, *Neths.* 16 D8
Waroona, *Australia* 89 F2
Warracknabeal, *Australia* . 91 F3
Warragul, *Australia* 91 F4
Warrawagine, *Australia* .. 88 D3
Warrego →, *Australia* ... 91 E4
Warrego Ra., *Australia* .. 90 C4
Warren, *Australia* 91 E4
Warren, *Ark., U.S.A.* ... 109 J8
Warren, *Mich., U.S.A.* .. 104 D4
Warren, *Minn., U.S.A.* .. 108 A6
Warren, *Ohio, U.S.A.* ... 106 E4
Warren, *Pa., U.S.A.* 106 E5
Warrenpoint, *U.K.* 15 B5
Warrensburg, *U.S.A.* ... 108 F8
Warrenton, *S. Africa* 84 D3
Warrenton, *U.S.A.* 112 D3
Warrenville, *Australia* ... 91 D4
Warri, *Nigeria* 79 D6
Warrina, *Australia* 91 D2
Warrington, *U.K.* 12 D5
Warrington, *U.S.A.* 105 K2
Warrnambool, *Australia* . 91 F3
Warroad, *U.S.A.* 108 A7
Warsa, *Indonesia* 57 E9
Warsaw = Warszawa,
  Poland 20 C11
Warsaw, *Ind., U.S.A.* ... 104 E3
Warsaw, *N.Y., U.S.A.* ... 106 D6
Warsaw, *Ohio, U.S.A.* .. 106 F2
Warstein, *Germany* 18 D4
Warszawa, *Poland* 20 C11
Warta →, *Poland* 20 C4
Warthe = Warta →,
  Poland 20 C4
Waru, *Indonesia* 57 E8
Warwick, *Australia* 91 D5
Warwick, *U.K.* 13 E6
Warwick, *U.S.A.* 107 E13
Warwickshire □, *U.K.* .. 13 E6
Wasaga Beach, *Canada* .. 106 B4
Wasatch Ra., *U.S.A.* 110 F8
Wasbank, *S. Africa* 85 D5
Wasco, *Calif., U.S.A.* ... 113 K7
Wasco, *Oreg., U.S.A.* ... 110 D3
Waseca, *U.S.A.* 108 C8
Wasekamio L., *Canada* .. 101 B7
Wash, The, *U.K.* 12 E8
Washago, *Canada* 106 B5
Washburn, *N. Dak.,*
  U.S.A. 108 B4
Washburn, *Wis., U.S.A.* . 108 B9
Washim, *India* 60 J10
Washington, *D.C., U.S.A.* 104 F7
Washington, *Ga., U.S.A.* . 105 J4
Washington, *Ind., U.S.A.* 104 F2
Washington, *Iowa, U.S.A.* 108 E9
Washington, *Mo., U.S.A.* 108 F9
Washington, *N.C., U.S.A.* 105 H7
Washington, *N.J., U.S.A.* 107 F10
Washington, *Pa., U.S.A.* . 106 F4
Washington, *Utah, U.S.A.* 111 H7
Washington □, *U.S.A.* .. 110 C3
Washington, Mt., *U.S.A.* 107 B13
Washington I., *U.S.A.* .. 104 C2
Washougal, *U.S.A.* 112 E4
Wasian, *Indonesia* 57 E8
Wasior, *Indonesia* 57 E8
Waskaiowaka, L., *Canada* 101 B9
Waskesiu Lake, *Canada* . 101 C7
Wasmes, *Belgium* 17 H3
Waspik, *Neths.* 17 E5
Wassen, *Switz.* 23 C7
Wassenaar, *Neths.* 16 D4
Wasserburg, *Germany* .. 19 G8
Wasserkuppe, *Germany* . 18 E5
Wassy, *France* 25 D11
Watangpone, *Indonesia* .. 57 E6
Water Park Pt., *Australia* . 90 C5
Water Valley, *U.S.A.* ... 109 H10
Waterberge, *S. Africa* ... 85 C4
Waterbury, *Conn., U.S.A.* 107 E11
Waterbury, *Vt., U.S.A.* . 107 B12

Waterbury L., *Canada* .. 101 B8
Waterdown, *Canada* 106 C5
Waterford, *Canada* 106 D4
Waterford, *Ireland* 15 D4
Waterford, *U.S.A.* 112 H6
Waterford □, *Ireland* ... 15 D4
Waterford Harbour, *Ireland* 15 D5
Waterhen L., *Man.,*
  Canada 101 C9
Waterhen L., *Sask.,*
  Canada 101 C7
Wateringen, *Neths.* 16 D4
Waterloo, *Belgium* 17 G4
Waterloo, *Ont., Canada* . 98 D3
Waterloo, *Qué., Canada* . 107 A12
Waterloo, *S. Leone* 78 D2
Waterloo, *Ill., U.S.A.* ... 108 F9
Waterloo, *Iowa, U.S.A.* . 108 D8
Waterloo, *N.Y., U.S.A.* . 106 D8
Watermeal-Boitsford,
  Belgium 17 G4
Watersmeet, *U.S.A.* 108 B10
Waterton-Glacier
  International Peace Park,
  U.S.A. 110 B7
Watertown, *Conn., U.S.A.* 107 E11
Watertown, *N.Y., U.S.A.* 107 C9
Watertown, *S. Dak.,*
  U.S.A. 108 C6
Watertown, *Wis., U.S.A.* 108 D10
Waterval-Boven, *S. Africa* 85 D5
Waterville, *Canada* 107 A13
Waterville, *Maine, U.S.A.* 99 D6
Waterville, *N.Y., U.S.A.* 107 D9
Waterville, *Pa., U.S.A.* . 106 E7
Waterville, *Wash., U.S.A.* 110 C3
Watervliet, *Belgium* 17 F3
Watervliet, *U.S.A.* 107 D11
Wates, *Indonesia* 57 G14
Watford, *Canada* 106 D3
Watford, *U.K.* 13 F7
Watford City, *U.S.A.* ... 108 B3
Wathaman →, *Canada* .. 101 B8
Watheroo, *Australia* 89 F2
Wating, *China* 50 G4
Watkins Glen, *U.S.A.* .. 106 D8
Watling I. = San Salvador,
  Bahamas 117 B5
Watonga, *U.S.A.* 109 H5
Watou, *Belgium* 17 G1
Watrous, *Canada* 101 C7
Watrous, *U.S.A.* 109 H2
Watsa, *Zaïre* 82 B2
Watseka, *U.S.A.* 104 E2
Watson, *Australia* 89 F5
Watson, *Canada* 101 C8
Watson Lake, *Canada* ... 100 A3
Watsonville, *U.S.A.* 111 H3
Wattenwil, *Switz.* 22 C5
Wattiwarriganna Cr. →,
  Australia 91 D2
Wattwil, *Switz.* 23 B8
Watubela Is. = Watubela,
  Kepulauan, *Indonesia* .. 57 E8
Watubela, Kepulauan,
  Indonesia 57 E8
Waubach, *Neths.* 17 G8
Waubamik, *Canada* 106 A4
Waubay, *U.S.A.* 108 C6
Waubra, *Australia* 91 F3
Wauchope, *Australia* ... 91 E5
Wauchula, *U.S.A.* 105 M5
Waugh, *Canada* 101 D9
Waukarlycarly, L.,
  Australia 88 D3
Waukegan, *U.S.A.* 104 D2
Waukesha, *U.S.A.* 104 D1
Waukon, *U.S.A.* 108 D9
Wauneta, *U.S.A.* 108 E4
Waupaca, *U.S.A.* 108 C10
Waupun, *U.S.A.* 108 D10
Waurika, *U.S.A.* 109 H6
Wausau, *U.S.A.* 108 C10
Wautoma, *U.S.A.* 108 C10
Wauwatosa, *U.S.A.* 104 D2
Wave Hill, *Australia* 88 C5
Waveney →, *U.K.* 13 E9
Waverley, *N.Z.* 87 H5
Waverly, *Iowa, U.S.A.* .. 108 D8
Waverly, *N.Y., U.S.A.* .. 107 D8
Wavre, *Belgium* 17 G5
Wavreille, *Belgium* 17 H6
Wâw, *Sudan* 77 F2
Wāw al Kabīr, *Libya* ... 73 C8
Wawa, *Canada* 98 C3
Wawa, *Nigeria* 79 D5
Wawa, *Sudan* 76 C3
Wawanesa, *Canada* 101 D9
Wawona, *U.S.A.* 112 H7
Waxahachie, *U.S.A.* 109 J6
Way, L., *Australia* 89 E3
Wayabula Rau, *Indonesia* 57 D7
Wayatinah, *Australia* ... 90 G4
Waycross, *U.S.A.* 105 K4
Wayi, *Sudan* 77 F3
Wayne, *Nebr., U.S.A.* .. 108 D6
Wayne, *W. Va., U.S.A.* . 104 F4
Waynesboro, *Ga., U.S.A.* 105 J4
Waynesboro, *Miss., U.S.A.* 105 K1
Waynesboro, *Pa., U.S.A.* 104 F7
Waynesboro, *Va., U.S.A.* 104 F6
Waynesburg, *U.S.A.* 104 F5
Waynesville, *U.S.A.* 105 H4

Waynoka, *U.S.A.* 109 G5
Wazin, *Libya* 75 B7
Wazirabad, *Pakistan* 62 C6
We, *Indonesia* 56 C1
Weald, The, *U.K.* 13 F8
Wear →, *U.K.* 12 C6
Weatherford, *Okla.,*
  U.S.A. 109 H5
Weatherford, *Tex., U.S.A.* 109 J6
Weaverville, *U.S.A.* 110 F2
Webb City, *U.S.A.* 109 G7
Webo = Nyaake, *Liberia* . 78 E3
Webster, *Mass., U.S.A.* . 107 D13
Webster, *N.Y., U.S.A.* .. 106 C7
Webster, *S. Dak., U.S.A.* 108 C6
Webster, *Wis., U.S.A.* .. 108 C8
Webster City, *U.S.A.* ... 108 D8
Webster Green, *U.S.A.* . 108 F9
Webster Springs, *U.S.A.* 104 F5
Weda, *Indonesia* 57 D7
Weda, Teluk, *Indonesia* . 57 D7
Weddell I., *Falk. Is.* 128 D1
Weddell Sea, *Antarctica* . 5 D1
Wedderburn, *Australia* .. 91 F3
Wedgeport, *Canada* 99 D6
Wedza, *Zimbabwe* 83 F3
Wee Waa, *Australia* 91 E4
Weed, *U.S.A.* 110 F2
Weed Heights, *U.S.A.* .. 112 G7
Weedsport, *U.S.A.* 107 C8
Weedville, *U.S.A.* 106 E6
Weemelah, *Australia* ... 91 D4
Weenen, *S. Africa* 85 D5
Weener, *Germany* 18 B3
Weert, *Neths.* 17 F7
Weesp, *Neths.* 16 D6
Weggis, *Switz.* 23 B6
Wegliniec, *Poland* 20 D5
Węgorzewo, *Poland* 20 A11
Węgrów, *Poland* 20 C12
Wehl, *Neths.* 16 E8
Wei He →, *Hebei, China* 50 F8
Wei He →, *Shaanxi, China* 50 G6
Weichang, *China* 51 D9
Weichuan, *China* 50 G7
Weida, *Germany* 18 E8
Weiden, *Germany* 19 F8
Weifang, *China* 54 C6
Weifang, *Shandong, China* 51 F10
Weihai, *China* 51 F12
Weilburg, *Germany* 18 E4
Weilheim, *Germany* 19 H7
Weimar, *Germany* 18 E7
Weinan, *China* 50 G5
Weinfelden, *Switz.* 23 A8
Weingarten, *Germany* .. 19 H5
Weinheim, *Germany* ... 19 F4
Weining, *China* 52 D5
Weipa, *Australia* 90 A3
Weir →, *Australia* 91 D4
Weir →, *Canada* 101 B10
Weir River, *Canada* 101 B10
Weirton, *U.S.A.* 106 F4
Weisen, *Switz.* 23 C9
Weiser, *U.S.A.* 110 D5
Weishan, *Shandong, China* 51 G9
Weishan, *Yunnan, China* . 52 E3
Weissenburg, *Germany* . 19 F6
Weissenfels, *Germany* .. 18 D8
Weisshorn, *Switz.* 22 D5
Weissmies, *Switz.* 22 D6
Weisstannen, *Switz.* 23 C8
Weisswasser, *Germany* . 18 D10
Weiswampach, *Belgium* . 17 H8
Weixi, *China* 52 D2
Weixin, *China* 52 D5
Weiyuan, *China* 50 G3
Weiz, *Austria* 21 H5
Weizhou Dao, *China* ... 52 G7
Wejherowo, *Poland* 20 A8
Wekusko L., *Canada* ... 101 C9
Welbourn Hill, *Australia* . 91 D1
Welch, *U.S.A.* 104 G5
Weldya, *Ethiopia* 77 E4
Welega □, *Ethiopia* 77 F3
Welkenraedt, *Belgium* .. 17 G7
Welkite, *Ethiopia* 77 F4
Welkom, *S. Africa* 84 D4
Welland, *Canada* 98 D4
Welland →, *U.K.* 12 E7
Wellen, *Belgium* 17 G6
Wellesley Is., *Australia* .. 90 B2
Wellin, *Belgium* 17 H6
Wellingborough, *U.K.* .. 13 E7
Wellington, *Australia* ... 91 E4
Wellington, *Canada* 98 D4
Wellington, *N.Z.* 87 J5
Wellington, *S. Africa* ... 84 E2
Wellington, *Shrops., U.K.* 12 E5
Wellington, *Somst., U.K.* 13 G4
Wellington, *Colo., U.S.A.* 108 E2
Wellington, *Kans., U.S.A.* 109 G6
Wellington, *Nev., U.S.A.* 112 G7
Wellington, *Ohio, U.S.A.* 106 E2
Wellington, *Tex., U.S.A.* 109 H4
Wellington, I., *Chile* 128 C2
Wellington, L., *Australia* 91 F4
Wells, *Norfolk, U.K.* ... 12 E8
Wells, *Somst., U.K.* 13 F5
Wells, *Maine, U.S.A.* ... 107 C14
Wells, *Minn., U.S.A.* ... 108 D8
Wells, *Nev., U.S.A.* 110 F6
Wells, L., *Australia* 89 E3
Wells Gray Prov. Park,
  Canada 100 C4

Winsen

Wells River, *U.S.A.* 107 B12
Wellsboro, *U.S.A.* 106 E7
Wellsburg, *U.S.A.* 106 F4
Wellsville, *Mo., U.S.A.* 108 F9
Wellsville, *N.Y., U.S.A.* 106 D7
Wellsville, *Ohio, U.S.A.* 106 F4
Wellsville, *Utah, U.S.A.* 110 F8
Wellton, *U.S.A.* 111 K6
Welmel, Wabi →, *Ethiopia* 77 F5
Welo □, *Ethiopia* 77 E4
Wels, *Austria* 21 G4
Welshpool, *U.K.* 13 E4
Wem, *U.K.* 12 E5
Wembere →, *Tanzania* 82 C3
Wemmel, *Belgium* 17 G4
Wen Xian, *Gansu, China* 50 H3
Wen Xian, *Henan, China* 50 G7
Wenatchee, *U.S.A.* 110 C3
Wenchang, *China* 58 C8
Wencheng, *China* 53 D13
Wenchi, *Ghana* 78 D4
Wenchow = Wenzhou, *China* 53 C13
Wenchuan, *China* 52 B4
Wendell, *U.S.A.* 110 E6
Wenden, *U.S.A.* 113 M13
Wendeng, *China* 51 F12
Wendesi, *Indonesia* 57 E8
Wendo, *Ethiopia* 77 F4
Wendover, *U.S.A.* 110 F6
Wenduine, *Belgium* 17 F2
Weng'an, *China* 52 D6
Wengcheng, *China* 53 E9
Wengen, *Switz.* 22 C5
Wengyuan, *China* 53 E10
Wenjiang, *China* 52 B4
Wenling, *China* 53 C13
Wenlock →, *Australia* 90 A3
Wenshan, *China* 52 F5
Wenshang, *China* 50 G9
Wenshui, *Guizhou, China* 52 C6
Wenshui, *Shanxi, China* 50 F7
Wensu, *China* 54 B3
Wentworth, *Australia* 91 E3
Wenut, *Indonesia* 57 E8
Wenxi, *China* 50 G6
Wenzhou, *China* 53 C13
Weott, *U.S.A.* 110 F2
Wepener, *S. Africa* 84 D4
Werbomont, *Belgium* 17 H7
Werda, *Botswana* 84 D3
Werdau, *Germany* 18 E8
Werder, *Ethiopia* 68 F4
Werder, *Germany* 18 C8
Werdohl, *Germany* 18 D3
Wereilu, *Ethiopia* 77 E4
Weri, *Indonesia* 57 E8
Werkendam, *Neths.* 16 E5
Werne, *Germany* 18 D3
Werneck, *Germany* 19 F6
Wernigerode, *Germany* 18 D6
Werra →, *Germany* 18 D5
Werribee, *Australia* 91 F3
Werrimull, *Australia* 91 E3
Werris Creek, *Australia* 91 E5
Wersar, *Indonesia* 57 E8
Wertach →, *Germany* 19 G6
Wertheim, *Germany* 19 F5
Wertingen, *Germany* 19 G6
Wervershoof, *Neths.* 16 C6
Wervik, *Belgium* 17 G2
Wesel, *Germany* 18 D2
Weser →, *Germany* 18 B4
Wesiri, *Indonesia* 57 F7
Wesley Vale, *U.S.A.* 111 J10
Wesleyville, *Canada* 99 C9
Wesleyville, *U.S.A.* 106 D4
Wessel, C., *Australia* 90 A2
Wessel Is., *Australia* 90 A2
Wesselburen, *Germany* 18 A4
Wessem, *Neths.* 17 F7
Wessington, *U.S.A.* 108 C5
Wessington Springs, *U.S.A.* 108 C5
West, *U.S.A.* 109 K6
West B., *U.S.A.* 109 L10
West Baines →, *Australia* 88 C4
West Bend, *U.S.A.* 104 D1
West Bengal □, *India* 63 H12
West Beskids = Západné Beskydy, *Europe* 20 F9
West Branch, *U.S.A.* 104 C3
West Bromwich, *U.K.* 13 E5
West Cape Howe, *Australia* 89 G2
West Chazy, *U.S.A.* 107 B11
West Chester, *U.S.A.* 104 F8
West Columbia, *U.S.A.* 109 L7
West Covina, *U.S.A.* 113 L9
West Des Moines, *U.S.A.* 108 E8
West End, *Bahamas* 116 A4
West Falkland, *Falk. Is.* 128 D4
West Fjord = Vestfjorden, *Norway* 8 C13
West Frankfort, *U.S.A.* 108 G10
West Glamorgan □, *U.K.* 13 F4
West Hartford, *U.S.A.* 107 E12
West Haven, *U.S.A.* 107 E12
West Helena, *U.S.A.* 109 H9
West Ice Shelf, *Antarctica* 5 C7
West Indies, *Cent. Amer.* 117 C7
West Lorne, *Canada* 106 D3
West Lunga →, *Zambia* 83 E1
West Memphis, *U.S.A.* 109 H9
West Midlands □, *U.K.* 13 E6
West Mifflin, *U.S.A.* 106 F5
West Monroe, *U.S.A.* 109 J8
West Newton, *U.S.A.* 106 F5
West Nicholson, *Zimbabwe* 83 G2
West Palm Beach, *U.S.A.* 105 M5
West Plains, *U.S.A.* 109 G9
West Pt. = Ouest, Pte., *Canada* 99 C7
West Pt., *Australia* 91 F2
West Point, *Ga., U.S.A.* 105 J3
West Point, *Miss., U.S.A.* 105 J1
West Point, *Nebr., U.S.A.* 108 E6
West Point, *Va., U.S.A.* 104 G7
West Pokot □, *Kenya* 82 B4
West Road →, *Canada* 100 C4
West Rutland, *U.S.A.* 107 C11
West Schelde = Westerschelde →, *Neths.* 17 F2
West Seneca, *U.S.A.* 106 D6
West Siberian Plain, *Russia* 46 C11
West Sussex □, *U.K.* 13 G7
West-Terschelling, *Neths.* 16 B6
West Virginia □, *U.S.A.* 104 F5
West-Vlaanderen □, *Belgium* 17 G2
West Walker →, *U.S.A.* 112 G7
West Wyalong, *Australia* 91 E4
West Yellowstone, *U.S.A.* 110 D8
West Yorkshire □, *U.K.* 12 D6
Westall Pt., *Australia* 91 E1
Westbrook, *Maine, U.S.A.* 105 D10
Westbrook, *Tex., U.S.A.* 109 J4
Westbury, *Australia* 90 G4
Westby, *U.S.A.* 108 A2
Westend, *U.S.A.* 113 K9
Westerbork, *Neths.* 16 C9
Westerland, *Germany* 18 A4
Western □, *Kenya* 82 B3
Western □, *Uganda* 82 B3
Western □, *Zambia* 83 F1
Western Australia □, *Australia* 89 E2
Western Ghats, *India* 60 N9
Western Isles □, *U.K.* 14 D1
Western Sahara ■, *Africa* 74 D2
Western Samoa ■, *Pac. Oc.* 87 A13
Westernport, *U.S.A.* 104 F6
Westerschelde →, *Neths.* 17 F2
Westerstede, *Germany* 18 B3
Westervoort, *Neths.* 16 E7
Westerwald, *Germany* 18 E4
Westfield, *Mass., U.S.A.* 107 D12
Westfield, *N.Y., U.S.A.* 106 D5
Westfield, *Pa., U.S.A.* 106 E7
Westgat, *Neths.* 17 E3
Westhope, *U.S.A.* 108 A4
Westkapelle, *Belgium* 17 F2
Westkapelle, *Neths.* 17 E2
Westland Bight, *N.Z.* 87 K3
Westlock, *Canada* 100 C6
Westmalle, *Belgium* 17 F5
Westmeath □, *Ireland* 15 C4
Westminster, *U.S.A.* 104 F7
Westmorland, *U.S.A.* 111 K6
Weston, *Malaysia* 56 C5
Weston, *Oreg., U.S.A.* 110 D4
Weston, *W. Va., U.S.A.* 104 F5
Weston I., *Canada* 98 B4
Weston-super-Mare, *U.K.* 13 F5
Westport, *Canada* 107 B8
Westport, *Ireland* 15 C2
Westport, *N.Z.* 87 J3
Westport, *Oreg., U.S.A.* 112 D3
Westport, *Wash., U.S.A.* 110 C1
Westray, *Canada* 101 C8
Westray, *U.K.* 14 B6
Westree, *Canada* 98 C3
Westville, *Calif., U.S.A.* 112 F6
Westville, *Ill., U.S.A.* 104 E2
Westville, *Okla., U.S.A.* 109 G7
Westwood, *U.S.A.* 110 F3
Wetar, *Indonesia* 57 F7
Wetaskiwin, *Canada* 100 C6
Wethersfield, *U.S.A.* 107 E12
Wetteren, *Belgium* 17 G3
Wettingen, *Switz.* 23 B6
Wetzikon, *Switz.* 23 B7
Wetzlar, *Germany* 18 E4
Wevelgem, *Belgium* 17 G2
Wewoka, *U.S.A.* 109 H6
Wexford, *Ireland* 15 D5
Wexford □, *Ireland* 15 D5
Wexford Harbour, *Ireland* 15 D5
Weyburn, *Canada* 101 D8
Weyburn L., *Canada* 100 A5
Weyer, *Austria* 21 H4
Weyib →, *Ethiopia* 77 F5
Weymouth, *Canada* 99 D6
Weymouth, *U.K.* 13 G5
Weymouth, *U.S.A.* 107 D14
Weymouth, C., *Australia* 90 A3
Wezemaal, *Belgium* 17 G5
Wezep, *Neths.* 16 D7
Whakatane, *N.Z.* 87 G6
Whale →, *Canada* 99 A6
Whale Cove, *Canada* 101 A10
Whales, B. of, *Antarctica* 5 D12
Whalsay, *U.K.* 14 A7
Whangamomona, *N.Z.* 87 H5
Whangarei, *N.Z.* 87 F5
Whangarei Harb., *N.Z.* 87 F5
Wharfe →, *U.K.* 12 D6
Wharfedale, *U.K.* 12 C5
Wharton, *N.J., U.S.A.* 107 F10
Wharton, *Pa., U.S.A.* 106 E6
Wharton, *Tex., U.S.A.* 109 L6
Wheatland, *Calif., U.S.A.* 112 F5
Wheatland, *Wyo., U.S.A.* 108 D2
Wheatley, *Canada* 106 D2
Wheaton, *U.S.A.* 108 C6
Wheelbarrow Pk., *U.S.A.* 112 H10
Wheeler, *Oreg., U.S.A.* 110 D2
Wheeler, *Tex., U.S.A.* 109 H4
Wheeler →, *Canada* 101 B7
Wheeler Pk., *N. Mex., U.S.A.* 111 H11
Wheeler Pk., *Nev., U.S.A.* 111 G6
Wheeler Ridge, *U.S.A.* 113 L8
Wheeling, *U.S.A.* 106 F4
Whernside, *U.K.* 12 C5
Whidbey I., *U.S.A.* 100 D4
Whiskey Gap, *Canada* 100 D6
Whiskey Jack L., *Canada* 101 B8
Whistleduck Cr. →, *Australia* 90 C2
Whitby, *Canada* 106 C6
Whitby, *U.K.* 12 C7
White →, *Ark., U.S.A.* 109 J9
White →, *Ind., U.S.A.* 104 F2
White →, *S. Dak., U.S.A.* 108 D5
White →, *Utah, U.S.A.* 110 F9
White →, *Wash., U.S.A.* 112 C4
White, L., *Australia* 88 D4
White B., *Canada* 99 B8
White Bear Res., *Canada* 99 C8
White Bird, *U.S.A.* 110 D5
White Butte, *U.S.A.* 108 B3
White City, *U.S.A.* 108 F6
White Cliffs, *Australia* 91 E3
White Deer, *U.S.A.* 109 H4
White Hall, *U.S.A.* 108 F9
White Haven, *U.S.A.* 107 E9
White I., *N.Z.* 87 G6
White L., *Canada* 107 A8
White L., *U.S.A.* 109 L8
White Mts., *Calif., U.S.A.* 111 H4
White Mts., *N.H., U.S.A.* 107 B13
White Nile = Nîl el Abyad →, *Sudan* 77 D3
White Nile Dam = Khazzân Jabal el Awliyâ, *Sudan* 77 D3
White Otter L., *Canada* 98 C1
White Pass, *Canada* 100 B1
White Pass, *U.S.A.* 112 D5
White Plains, *U.S.A.* 107 E11
White River, *Canada* 98 C2
White River, *S. Africa* 85 D5
White River, *U.S.A.* 108 D4
White Russia = Belorussia ■, *Europe* 40 E5
White Sea = Beloye More, *Russia* 44 C4
White Sulphur Springs, *Mont., U.S.A.* 110 C8
White Sulphur Springs, *W. Va., U.S.A.* 104 G5
White Swan, *U.S.A.* 112 D6
White Volta →, *Ghana* 79 D4
Whitecliffs, *N.Z.* 87 K3
Whitecourt, *Canada* 100 C5
Whiteface, *U.S.A.* 109 J3
Whitefield, *U.S.A.* 107 B13
Whitefish, *U.S.A.* 110 B6
Whitefish L., *Canada* 101 A7
Whitefish Point, *U.S.A.* 104 B3
Whitegull, L., *Canada* 99 A7
Whitehall, *Mich., U.S.A.* 104 D2
Whitehall, *Mont., U.S.A.* 110 D7
Whitehall, *N.Y., U.S.A.* 107 C11
Whitehall, *Wis., U.S.A.* 108 C9
Whitehaven, *U.K.* 12 C4
Whitehorse, *Canada* 100 A1
Whitehorse, Vale of, *U.K.* 13 F6
Whitemark, *Australia* 90 G4
Whitemouth, *Canada* 101 D9
Whiteplains, *Liberia* 78 D2
Whitesboro, *N.Y., U.S.A.* 107 C9
Whitesboro, *Tex., U.S.A.* 109 J6
Whiteshell Prov. Park, *Canada* 101 C9
Whiteside, Canal, *Chile* 128 D2
Whitetail, *U.S.A.* 108 A2
Whiteville, *U.S.A.* 105 H6
Whitewater, *U.S.A.* 104 D1
Whitewater Baldy, *U.S.A.* 111 K9
Whitewater L., *Canada* 98 B2
Whitewood, *Australia* 90 C3
Whitewood, *Canada* 101 C8
Whitfield, *Australia* 91 F4
Whithorn, *U.K.* 14 G4
Whitianga, *N.Z.* 87 G5
Whitman, *U.S.A.* 107 D14
Whitmire, *U.S.A.* 105 H5
Whitney, *Canada* 98 C4
Whitney, Mt., *U.S.A.* 111 H4
Whitney Point, *U.S.A.* 107 D9
Whitstable, *U.K.* 13 F9
Whitsunday I., *Australia* 90 C4
Whittier, *U.S.A.* 113 M8
Whittlesea, *Australia* 91 F4
Whitwell, *U.S.A.* 105 H3
Wholdaia L., *Canada* 101 A8
Whyalla, *Australia* 91 E2
Whyjonta, *Australia* 91 D3
Wiarton, *Canada* 98 D3
Wiawso, *Ghana* 78 D4
Wibaux, *U.S.A.* 108 B2
Wichabai, *Guyana* 121 C6
Wichian Buri, *Thailand* 58 E3
Wichita, *U.S.A.* 109 G6
Wichita Falls, *U.S.A.* 109 J5
Wick, *U.K.* 14 C5
Wickenburg, *U.S.A.* 111 K7
Wickepin, *Australia* 89 F2
Wickham, C., *Australia* 90 F3
Wickliffe, *U.S.A.* 106 E3
Wicklow, *Ireland* 15 D5
Wicklow □, *Ireland* 15 D5
Wicklow Hd., *Ireland* 15 D5
Widgiemooltha, *Australia* 89 F3
Widnes, *U.K.* 12 D5
Wiedenbrück, *Germany* 18 D4
Wiek, *Germany* 18 A9
Wielbark, *Poland* 20 B10
Wieliczka, *Poland* 20 F10
Wieluń, *Poland* 20 D8
Wien, *Austria* 21 G6
Wiener Neustadt, *Austria* 21 H6
Wieprz →, *Koszalin, Poland* 20 A6
Wieprz →, *Lublin, Poland* 20 D11
Wierden, *Neths.* 16 D9
Wiers, *Belgium* 17 H3
Wiesbaden, *Germany* 19 E4
Wiesental, *Germany* 19 F4
Wigan, *U.K.* 12 D5
Wiggins, *Colo., U.S.A.* 108 E2
Wiggins, *Miss., U.S.A.* 109 K10
Wight, I. of □, *U.K.* 13 G6
Wigtown, *U.K.* 14 G4
Wigtown B., *U.K.* 14 G4
Wijchen, *Neths.* 16 E7
Wijhe, *Neths.* 16 D8
Wijk bij Duurstede, *Neths.* 16 E6
Wil, *Switz.* 23 B8
Wilber, *U.S.A.* 108 E6
Wilberforce, *Canada* 106 A6
Wilberforce, C., *Australia* 90 A2
Wilburton, *U.S.A.* 109 H7
Wilcannia, *Australia* 91 E3
Wilcox, *U.S.A.* 106 E6
Wildbad, *Germany* 19 G4
Wildervank, *Neths.* 16 B9
Wildeshausen, *Germany* 18 C4
Wildhorn, *Switz.* 22 D4
Wildrose, *Calif., U.S.A.* 113 J9
Wildrose, *N. Dak., U.S.A.* 108 A3
Wildspitze, *Austria* 19 J6
Wildstrubel, *Switz.* 22 D5
Wildwood, *U.S.A.* 104 F8
Wilge →, *S. Africa* 85 D4
Wilhelm II Coast, *Antarctica* 5 C7
Wilhelm-Pieck-Stadt Guben, *Germany* 18 D10
Wilhelmina, Geb., *Surinam* 121 C6
Wilhelmina Kanaal, *Neths.* 17 E6
Wilhelmsburg, *Austria* 21 G5
Wilhelmshaven, *Germany* 18 B4
Wilhelmstal, *Namibia* 84 C2
Wilkes-Barre, *U.S.A.* 107 E9
Wilkesboro, *U.S.A.* 105 G5
Wilkie, *Canada* 101 C7
Wilkinsburg, *U.S.A.* 106 F5
Wilkinson Lakes, *Australia* 89 E5
Willamina, *U.S.A.* 110 D2
Willandra Billabong Creek →, *Australia* 91 E4
Willapa B., *U.S.A.* 110 C2
Willapa Hills, *U.S.A.* 112 D3
Willard, *N. Mex., U.S.A.* 111 J10
Willard, *Utah, U.S.A.* 110 F7
Willcox, *U.S.A.* 111 K9
Willebroek, *Belgium* 17 F4
Willemstad, *Neth. Ant.* 117 D6
Willeroo, *Australia* 88 C5
William →, *Canada* 101 B7
William Creek, *Australia* 91 D2
Williambury, *Australia* 89 D2
Williams, *Australia* 89 F2
Williams, *Ariz., U.S.A.* 111 J7
Williams, *Calif., U.S.A.* 112 F4
Williams Lake, *Canada* 100 C4
Williamsburg, *Ky., U.S.A.* 105 G3
Williamsburg, *Pa., U.S.A.* 106 F6
Williamsburg, *Va., U.S.A.* 104 G7
Williamson, *N.Y., U.S.A.* 106 C7
Williamson, *W. Va., U.S.A.* 104 G4
Williamsport, *U.S.A.* 106 E7
Williamston, *U.S.A.* 105 H7
Williamstown, *Australia* 91 F3
Williamstown, *Mass., U.S.A.* 107 D11
Williamstown, *N.Y., U.S.A.* 107 C9
Williamsville, *U.S.A.* 109 G9
Willimantic, *U.S.A.* 107 E12
Willis Group, *Australia* 90 B5
Willisau, *Switz.* 22 B6
Williston, *S. Africa* 84 E3
Williston, *Fla., U.S.A.* 105 L4
Williston, *N. Dak., U.S.A.* 108 A3
Williston L., *Canada* 100 B4
Willits, *U.S.A.* 110 G2
Willmar, *U.S.A.* 108 C7
Willoughby, *U.S.A.* 106 E3
Willow Bunch, *Canada* 101 D7
Willow L., *Canada* 100 A5
Willow Lake, *U.S.A.* 108 C6
Willow Springs, *U.S.A.* 109 G8
Willow Wall, The, *China* 51 C12
Willowlake →, *Canada* 100 A4
Willowmore, *S. Africa* 84 E3
Willows, *Australia* 90 C4
Willows, *U.S.A.* 112 F4
Willowvale = Gatyana, *S. Africa* 85 E4
Wills, L., *Australia* 88 D4
Wills Cr. →, *Australia* 90 C3
Wills Point, *U.S.A.* 109 J7
Willunga, *Australia* 91 F2
Wilmette, *U.S.A.* 104 D2
Wilmington, *Australia* 91 E2
Wilmington, *Del., U.S.A.* 104 F8
Wilmington, *Ill., U.S.A.* 104 E1
Wilmington, *N.C., U.S.A.* 105 H7
Wilmington, *Ohio, U.S.A.* 104 F4
Wilpena Cr. →, *Australia* 91 E2
Wilrijk, *Belgium* 17 F4
Wilsall, *U.S.A.* 110 D8
Wilson, *U.S.A.* 105 H7
Wilson →, *Queens., Australia* 91 D3
Wilson →, *W. Austral., Australia* 88 C4
Wilson Bluff, *Australia* 89 F4
Wilsons Promontory, *Australia* 91 F4
Wilster, *Germany* 18 B5
Wilton, *U.K.* 13 F6
Wilton, *U.S.A.* 108 B4
Wilton →, *Australia* 90 A1
Wiltshire □, *U.K.* 13 F6
Wiltz, *Lux.* 17 J7
Wiluna, *Australia* 89 E3
Wimereux, *France* 25 B8
Wimmera →, *Australia* 91 F3
Winam G., *Kenya* 82 C3
Winburg, *S. Africa* 84 D4
Winchendon, *U.S.A.* 107 D12
Winchester, *U.K.* 13 F6
Winchester, *Conn., U.S.A.* 107 E11
Winchester, *Idaho, U.S.A.* 110 C5
Winchester, *Ind., U.S.A.* 104 E3
Winchester, *Ky., U.S.A.* 104 G3
Winchester, *N.H., U.S.A.* 107 D12
Winchester, *Nev., U.S.A.* 113 J11
Winchester, *Tenn., U.S.A.* 105 H2
Winchester, *Va., U.S.A.* 104 F6
Wind →, *U.S.A.* 110 E9
Wind River Range, *U.S.A.* 110 E9
Windau = Ventspils, *Latvia* 9 H16
Windber, *U.S.A.* 106 F6
Windermere, L., *U.K.* 12 C5
Windfall, *Canada* 100 C5
Windflower L., *Canada* 100 A5
Windhoek, *Namibia* 84 C2
Windom, *U.S.A.* 108 D7
Windorah, *Australia* 90 D3
Window Rock, *U.S.A.* 111 J9
Windrush →, *U.K.* 13 F6
Windsor, *Australia* 91 E5
Windsor, *N.S., Canada* 99 D7
Windsor, *Nfld., Canada* 99 C8
Windsor, *Ont., Canada* 98 D3
Windsor, *U.K.* 13 F7
Windsor, *Colo., U.S.A.* 108 E2
Windsor, *Conn., U.S.A.* 107 E12
Windsor, *Mo., U.S.A.* 108 F8
Windsor, *N.Y., U.S.A.* 107 D9
Windsor, *Vt., U.S.A.* 107 C12
Windsorton, *S. Africa* 84 D3
Windward Is., *W. Indies* 117 D7
Windward Passage = Vientos, Paso de los, *Caribbean* 117 C5
Windy L., *Canada* 101 A8
Winefred L., *Canada* 101 B6
Winejok, *Sudan* 77 F2
Winfield, *U.S.A.* 109 G6
Wingate Mts., *Australia* 88 B5
Wingen, *Australia* 91 E5
Wingene, *Belgium* 17 F2
Wingham, *Australia* 91 E5
Wingham, *Canada* 98 D3
Winifred, *U.S.A.* 110 C9
Winisk, *Canada* 98 A2
Winisk →, *Canada* 98 A2
Winisk L., *Canada* 98 B2
Wink, *U.S.A.* 109 K3
Winkler, *Canada* 101 D9
Winlock, *U.S.A.* 112 D4
Winneba, *Ghana* 79 D4
Winnebago, *U.S.A.* 108 D7
Winnebago, L., *U.S.A.* 104 D1
Winnecke Cr. →, *Australia* 88 C5
Winnemucca, *U.S.A.* 110 F5
Winnemucca L., *U.S.A.* 110 F4
Winner, *U.S.A.* 108 D5
Winnett, *U.S.A.* 110 C9
Winnfield, *U.S.A.* 109 K8
Winnibigoshish, L., *U.S.A.* 108 B7
Winning, *Australia* 88 D1
Winnipeg, *Canada* 101 D9
Winnipeg →, *Canada* 101 C9
Winnipeg, L., *Canada* 101 C9
Winnipeg Beach, *Canada* 101 C9
Winnipegosis, *Canada* 101 C9
Winnipegosis L., *Canada* 101 C9
Winnipesaukee, L., *U.S.A.* 107 C13
Winnsboro, *La., U.S.A.* 109 J9
Winnsboro, *S.C., U.S.A.* 105 H5
Winnsboro, *Tex., U.S.A.* 109 J7
Winokapau, L., *Canada* 99 B7
Winona, *Minn., U.S.A.* 108 C9
Winona, *Miss., U.S.A.* 109 J10
Winooski, *U.S.A.* 107 B11
Winschoten, *Neths.* 16 B10
Winsen, *Germany* 18 B6

Winslow, *Ariz., U.S.A.* ... 111 J8
Winslow, *Wash., U.S.A.* ... 112 C4
Winsted, *U.S.A.* 107 E11
Winston-Salem, *U.S.A.* ... 105 G5
Winsum, *Neths.* 16 B9
Winter Garden, *U.S.A.* ... 105 L5
Winter Haven, *U.S.A.* ... 105 M5
Winter Park, *U.S.A.* 105 L5
Winterberg, *Germany* 18 D4
Winterhaven, *U.S.A.* 113 N12
Winters, *Calif., U.S.A.* .. 112 G5
Winters, *Tex., U.S.A.* ... 109 K5
Winterset, *U.S.A.* 108 E7
Wintersville, *U.S.A.* 106 F4
Winterswijk, *Neths.* 16 E9
Winterthur, *Switz.* 23 B7
Winthrop, *Minn., U.S.A.* . 108 C7
Winthrop, *Wash., U.S.A.* . 110 B3
Winton, *Australia* 90 C3
Winton, *N.Z.* 87 M2
Winton, *U.S.A.* 105 G7
Wintzenheim, *France* 25 D14
Wipper →, *Germany* 18 D7
Wirral, *U.K.* 12 D4
Wirrulla, *Australia* 91 E1
Wisbech, *U.K.* 12 E8
Wisconsin □, *U.S.A.* 108 C10
Wisconsin →, *U.S.A.* 108 D9
Wisconsin Dells, *U.S.A.* . 108 D10
Wisconsin Rapids, *U.S.A.* 108 C10
Wisdom, *U.S.A.* 110 D7
Wishaw, *U.K.* 14 F5
Wishek, *U.S.A.* 108 B5
Wisła, *Poland* 20 F8
Wisła →, *Poland* 20 A8
Wisłok →, *Poland* 20 E12
Wisłoka →, *Poland* 20 E11
Wismar, *Germany* 18 B7
Wismar, *Guyana* 121 B6
Wisner, *U.S.A.* 108 E6
Wissant, *France* 25 B8
Wissembourg, *France* ... 25 C14
Wissenkerke, *Neths.* 17 E3
Witbank, *S. Africa* 85 D4
Witdraai, *S. Africa* 84 D3
Witham, →, *U.K.* 12 D7
Withernsea, *U.K.* 12 D8
Witmarsum, *Neths.* 16 B6
Witney, *U.K.* 13 F6
Witnossob →, *Namibia* .. 84 D3
Wittdün, *Germany* 18 A4
Witten, *Germany* 17 F10
Wittenberg, *Germany* ... 18 D8
Wittenberge, *Germany* .. 18 B7
Wittenburg, *Germany* ... 18 B7
Wittenoom, *Australia* ... 88 D2
Wittingen, *Germany* 18 C6
Wittlich, *Germany* 19 F2
Wittmund, *Germany* 18 B3
Wittow, *Germany* 18 A9
Wittstock, *Germany* 18 B8
Witzenhausen, *Germany* . 18 D5
Wlingi, *Indonesia* 57 H15
Włocławek, *Poland* 20 C9
Włodawa, *Poland* 20 D13
Włoszczowa, *Poland* 20 E9
Woburn, *U.S.A.* 107 D13
Wodian, *China* 50 H7
Wodonga, *Australia* 91 F4
Woerden, *Neths.* 16 D5
Woerth, *France* 25 D14
Woëvre, *France* 25 C12
Wognum, *Neths.* 16 C6
Wohlen, *Switz.* 23 B6
Woinbogoin, *China* 52 A2
Wokam, *Indonesia* 57 F8
Wolbrom, *Poland* 20 E9
Woldegk, *Germany* 18 B9
Wolf →, *Canada* 100 A2
Wolf Creek, *U.S.A.* 110 C7
Wolf L., *Canada* 100 A2
Wolf Point, *U.S.A.* 108 A2
Wolfe I., *Canada* 98 D4
Wolfenbüttel, *Germany* .. 18 C6
Wolfheze, *Neths.* 16 D7
Wolfsberg, *Austria* 21 J4
Wolfsburg, *Germany* 18 C6
Wolgast, *Germany* 18 A9
Wolhusen, *Switz.* 22 B6
Wolin, *Poland* 20 B4
Wollaston, Is., *Chile* 128 E3
Wollaston L., *Canada* ... 101 B8
Wollaston Pen., *Canada* . 96 B8
Wollogorang, *Australia* .. 90 B2
Wollongong, *Australia* ... 91 E5
Wolmaransstad, *S. Africa* 84 D4
Wolmirstedt, *Germany* .. 18 C7
Wolseley, *Australia* 91 F3
Wolseley, *Canada* 101 C8
Wolseley, *S. Africa* 84 E2
Wolstenholme, C., *Canada* 94 C12
Wolsztyn, *Poland* 20 C6
Wolvega, *Neths.* 16 C7
Wolverhampton, *U.K.* ... 13 E5
Wommels, *Neths.* 16 B7
Wonarah, *Australia* 90 B2
Wonck, *Belgium* 17 G7
Wondai, *Australia* 91 D5
Wondelgem, *Belgium* 17 F3
Wongalarroo L., *Australia* 91 E3
Wongan Hills, *Australia* . 89 F2
Wongawol, *Australia* 89 E3
Wŏnju, *S. Korea* 51 F14
Wonosari, *Indonesia* 57 G14
Wŏnsan, *N. Korea* 51 E14

Wonthaggi, *Australia* 91 F4
Woocalla, *Australia* 91 E2
Wood Buffalo Nat. Park,
  Canada 100 B6
Wood Is., *Australia* 88 C3
Wood L., *Canada* 101 B8
Wood Lake, *U.S.A.* 108 D4
Woodah I., *Australia* 90 A2
Woodanilling, *Australia* . 89 F2
Woodbridge, *Canada* 106 C5
Woodburn, *Australia* 91 D5
Woodend, *Australia* 91 F3
Woodfords, *U.S.A.* 112 G7
Woodgreen, *Australia* ... 90 C1
Woodlake, *U.S.A.* 112 J7
Woodland, *U.S.A.* 112 G5
Woodlands, *Australia* ... 88 D2
Woodpecker, *Canada* 100 C4
Woodridge, *Canada* 101 D9
Woodroffe, Mt., *Australia* 89 E5
Woodruff, *Ariz., U.S.A.* . 111 J8
Woodruff, *Utah, U.S.A.* . 110 F8
Woods, L., *Australia* 90 B1
Woods, L., *Canada* 99 B6
Woods, L. of the, *Canada* 101 D10
Woodstock, *Queens.,
  Australia* 90 B4
Woodstock, *W. Austral.,
  Australia* 88 D2
Woodstock, *N.B., Canada* 99 C6
Woodstock, *Ont., Canada* 98 D3
Woodstock, *U.K.* 13 F6
Woodstock, *Ill., U.S.A.* .. 108 D10
Woodstock, *Vt., U.S.A.* . 107 C12
Woodsville, *U.S.A.* 107 B13
Woodville, *N.Z.* 87 J5
Woodville, *U.S.A.* 109 K7
Woodward, *U.S.A.* 109 G5
Woody, *U.S.A.* 113 K8
Woolamai, C., *Australia* . 91 F4
Woolgoolga, *Australia* ... 91 E5
Woombye, *Australia* 91 D5
Woomera, *Australia* 91 E2
Woonsocket, *R.I., U.S.A.* 107 D13
Woonsocket, *S. Dak.,
  U.S.A.* 108 C5
Wooramel, *Australia* 89 E1
Wooramel →, *Australia* . 89 E1
W
Wooroloo, *Australia* 89 F2
Wooster, *U.S.A.* 106 F3
Worb, *Switz.* 22 C5
Worcester, *S. Africa* 84 E2
Worcester, *U.K.* 13 E5
Worcester, *Mass., U.S.A.* 107 D13
Worcester, *N.Y., U.S.A.* . 107 D10
Wörgl, *Austria* 19 H8
Workington, *U.K.* 12 C4
Worksop, *U.K.* 12 D6
Workum, *Neths.* 16 C6
Worland, *U.S.A.* 110 D10
Wormerveer, *Neths.* 16 D5
Wormhoudt, *France* 25 B9
Worms, *Germany* 19 F4
Wörth, *Germany* 19 F9
Wortham, *U.S.A.* 109 K6
Wörther See, *Austria* 21 J4
Worthing, *U.K.* 13 G7
Worthington, *U.S.A.* 108 D7
Wosi, *Indonesia* 57 E7
Wou-han = Wuhan, *China* 53 B10
Woubrugge, *Neths.* 16 D5
Woudenberg, *Neths.* 16 D6
Woudsend, *Neths.* 16 C7
Wour, *Chad* 73 D8
Wousi = Wuxi, *China* 53 B13
Wouw, *Neths.* 17 E4
Wowoni, *Indonesia* 57 E6
Woy Woy, *Australia* 91 E5
Wrangel I. = Vrangelya,
  Ostrov, *Russia* 45 B19
Wrangell, *U.S.A.* 96 C6
Wrangell I., *U.S.A.* 100 B2
Wrangell Mts., *U.S.A.* ... 96 B5
Wrath, C., *U.K.* 14 C3
Wray, *U.S.A.* 108 E3
Wrekin, The, *U.K.* 12 E5
Wrens, *U.S.A.* 105 J4
Wrexham, *U.K.* 12 D4
Wriezen, *Germany* 18 C10
Wright, *Canada* 100 C4
Wright, *Phil.* 55 F6
Wrightson Mt., *U.S.A.* .. 111 L8
Wrightwood, *U.S.A.* 113 L9
Wrigley, *Canada* 96 B7
Wrocław, *Poland* 20 D7
Września, *Poland* 20 C7
Wschowa, *Poland* 20 D6
Wu Jiang →, *China* 52 C6
Wu'an, *China* 50 F8
Wubin, *Australia* 89 F2
Wubu, *China* 50 F6
Wuchang, *China* 51 B14
Wucheng, *China* 50 F9
Wuchuan, *Guangdong,
  China* 53 G8
Wuchuan, *Guizhou, China* 52 C7
Wuchuan,
  *Nei Mongol Zizhiqu,
  China* 50 D6
Wudi, *China* 51 F9
Wuding, *China* 52 E4
Wuding He →, *China* 50 F6
Wudu, *China* 50 H3
Wufeng, *China* 53 B8

Wugang, *China* 53 D8
Wugong Shan, *China* 53 D9
Wuhan, *China* 53 B10
Wuhe, *China* 51 H9
Wuhsi = Wuxi, *China* ... 53 B13
Wuhu, *China* 53 B12
Wujiang, *China* 53 B13
Wukari, *Nigeria* 79 D6
Wulajie, *China* 51 B14
Wulanbulang, *China* 50 D6
Wulehe, *Ghana* 79 D5
Wulian, *China* 51 G10
Wuliang Shan, *China* 52 E3
Wuliaru, *Indonesia* 57 F8
Wulumuchi = Ürümqi,
  China 44 E9
Wum, *Cameroon* 79 D7
Wuming, *China* 52 F7
Wuning, *China* 53 C10
Wunnummin L., *Canada* . 98 B2
Wunsiedel, *Germany* 19 E8
Wunstorf, *Germany* 18 C5
Wuntho, *Burma* 61 H19
Wuping, *China* 53 E11
Wuppertal, *Germany* 18 D3
Wuppertal, *S. Africa* 84 E2
Wuqing, *China* 51 E9
Würenlingen, *Switz.* 23 A6
Wurung, *Australia* 90 B3
Würzburg, *Germany* 19 F5
Wurzen, *Germany* 18 D8
Wushan, *Gansu, China* .. 50 G3
Wushan, *Sichuan, China* . 52 B7
Wusuli Jiang = Ussuri →,
  Asia 48 A7
Wutach →, *Germany* 19 H4
Wutai, *China* 50 E7
Wuting = Huimin, *China* . 51 F9
Wutong, *China* 53 E8
Wutonghaolai, *China* 51 C11
Wutongqiao, *China* 52 C4
Wuustwezel, *Belgium* ... 17 F5
Wuwei, *Anhui, China* 53 B11
Wuwei, *Gansu, China* ... 54 C5
Wuxi, *Jiangsu, China* 53 B13
Wuxi, *Sichuan, China* ... 52 B7
Wuxiang, *China* 50 F7
Wuxing, *China* 53 B13
Wuxuan, *China* 52 F7
Wuyang, *China* 50 H7
Wuyi, *Hebei, China* 50 F8
Wuyi, *Zhejiang, China* .. 53 C12
Wuyi Shan, *China* 53 D11
Wuyo, *Nigeria* 79 C7
Wuyuan, *Jiangxi, China* . 53 C11
Wuyuan,
  *Nei Mongol Zizhiqu,
  China* 50 D5
Wuzhai, *China* 50 E6
Wuzhi Shan, *China* 54 E5
Wuzhong, *China* 50 E4
Wuzhou, *China* 53 F8
Wyaaba Cr. →, *Australia* 90 B3
Wyalkatchem, *Australia* . 89 F2
Wyalusing, *U.S.A.* 107 E8
Wyandotte, *U.S.A.* 104 D4
Wyandra, *Australia* 91 D4
Wyangala Res., *Australia* 91 E4
Wyara, L., *Australia* 91 D3
Wycheproof, *Australia* .. 91 F3
Wye →, *U.K.* 13 F5
Wyemandoo, *Australia* .. 89 E2
Wymondham, *U.K.* 13 E7
Wymore, *U.S.A.* 108 E6
Wynbring, *Australia* 91 E1
Wyndham, *Australia* 88 C4
Wyndham, *N.Z.* 87 M2
Wyndmere, *U.S.A.* 108 B6
Wynne, *U.S.A.* 109 H9
Wynnum, *Australia* 91 D5
Wynyard, *Australia* 90 G4
Wynyard, *Canada* 101 C8
Wyola, L., *Australia* 89 E5
Wyoming □, *U.S.A.* 110
Wyong, *Australia* 91 E5
Wyszków, *Poland* 20 C11
Wyszogród, *Poland* 20 C10
Wytheville, *U.S.A.* 104 G5

X

Xai-Xai, *Mozam.* 85 D5
Xainza, *China* 54 C3
Xambioá, *Brazil* 122 C2
Xangongo, *Angola* 84 B2
Xanten, *Germany* 18 D2
Xánthi, *Greece* 39 H7
Xanthos, *Turkey* 66 E3
Xapuri, *Brazil* 124 C4
Xar Moron He →, *China* . 51 C11
Xau, L., *Botswana* 84 C3
Xavantina, *Brazil* 127 A5
Xenia, *U.S.A.* 104 F4
Xeropòtamos →, *Cyprus* . 37 E11
Xhora, *S. Africa* 85 E4
Xhumo, *Botswana* 84 C3
Xi Jiang →, *China* 53 F9
Xi Xian, *Henan, China* .. 53 A10
Xi Xian, *Shanxi, China* .. 50 F6
Xia Xian, *China* 50 G6
Xiachengzi, *China* 51 B16

Xiachuan Dao, *China* ... 53 G9
Xiaguan, *China* 52 E3
Xiajiang, *China* 53 D10
Xiajin, *China* 50 F8
Xiamen, *China* 53 E12
Xi'an, *China* 50 G5
Xian Xian, *China* 50 E9
Xianfeng, *China* 52 C7
Xiang Jiang →, *China* ... 53 C9
Xiangcheng, *Henan, China* 50 H8
Xiangcheng, *Henan, China* 50 H7
Xiangcheng, *Sichuan,
  China* 52 C2
Xiangdu, *China* 52 F6
Xiangfan, *China* 53 A9
Xianghuang Qi, *China* ... 50 C7
Xiangning, *China* 50 G6
Xiangquan, *China* 50 F7
Xiangshan, *China* 53 C13
Xiangshui, *China* 51 G10
Xiangtan, *China* 53 D9
Xiangxiang, *China* 53 D9
Xiangyin, *China* 53 C9
Xiangyun, *China* 52 E3
Xiangzhou, *China* 52 F7
Xianju, *China* 53 C13
Xianning, *China* 53 C10
Xianshui He →, *China* ... 52 B3
Xianyang, *China* 50 G5
Xianyou, *China* 53 E12
Xiao Hinggan Ling, *China* 54 B7
Xiao Xian, *China* 50 G9
Xiaofeng, *China* 53 B12
Xiaogan, *China* 53 B9
Xiaojin, *China* 52 B4
Xiaolan, *China* 53 F9
Xiaoshan, *China* 53 B13
Xiaoyi, *China* 50 F6
Xiapu, *China* 53 D12
Xiawa, *China* 51 C11
Xiayi, *China* 50 G9
Xichang, *China* 52 D4
Xichong, *China* 52 B5
Xichuan, *China* 50 H6
Xiemahe, *China* 53 B8
Xieng Khouang, *Laos* ... 58 C4
Xifei He →, *China* 50 H9
Xifeng, *Guizhou, China* . 52 D6
Xifeng, *Liaoning, China* . 51 C13
Xifengzhen, *China* 50 G4
Xigazê, *China* 54 D3
Xihe, *China* 50 G3
Xihua, *China* 50 H8
Xiliao He →, *China* 51 C12
Xilin, *China* 52 E5
Xilókastron, *Greece* 39 L5
Xin Jiang →, *China* 53 C11
Xin Xian, *China* 50 E7
Xinavane, *Mozam.* 85 D5
Xinbin, *China* 51 D13
Xincai, *China* 53 A10
Xinchang, *China* 53 C13
Xincheng,
  *Guangxi Zhuangzu,
  China* 52 E7
Xincheng, *Jiangxi, China* 53 D10
Xinfeng, *Guangdong,
  China* 53 E10
Xinfeng, *Jiangxi, China* . 53 D11
Xinfeng, *Jiangxi, China* . 53 E10
Xing Xian, *China* 50 E6
Xing'an,
  *Guangxi Zhuangzu,
  China* 53 E8
Xingan, *Jiangxi, China* .. 53 D10
Xingcheng, *China* 51 D11
Xingguo, *China* 53 D10
Xinghe, *China* 50 D7
Xinghua, *China* 51 H10
Xinghua Wan, *China* 53 E12
Xinglong, *China* 51 D9
Xingning, *China* 53 E10
Xingping, *China* 50 G5
Xingren, *China* 52 E5
Xingshan, *China* 53 B8
Xingtai, *China* 50 F8
Xingu →, *Brazil* 121 D7
Xingyang, *China* 50 G7
Xinhe, *China* 50 F8
Xinhua, *China* 53 D8
Xinhuang, *China* 52 D7
Xinhui, *China* 53 F9
Xining, *China* 54 C5
Xinjiang, *China* 50 G6
Xinjiang Uygur Zizhiqu □,
  China 54 B3
Xinjie, *China* 52 D3
Xinjin, *Liaoning, China* . 51 E11
Xinjin, *Sichuan, China* .. 52 B4
Xinkai He →, *China* 51 C12
Xinle, *China* 50 E8
Xinlitun, *China* 51 D12
Xinlong, *China* 52 B3
Xinmin, *China* 51 D12
Xinning, *China* 53 D8
Xinping, *China* 52 E3
Xinshao, *China* 53 D8
Xintai, *China* 51 G9
Xintian, *China* 53 E9
Xinxiang, *China* 50 G7
Xinxing, *China* 53 F9
Xinyang, *China* 53 A10
Xinye, *China* 53 A9
Xinyi, *China* 53 F8
Xinyi, *China* 53 D10

Xinzhan, *China* 51 C14
Xinzheng, *China* 50 G7
Xinzhou, *China* 53 B10
Xinzhu, *Taiwan* 53 E13
Xiong Xian, *China* 50 E9
Xiongyuecheng, *China* .. 51 D12
Xiping, *Henan, China* ... 50 H8
Xiping, *Henan, China* ... 50 H6
Xiping, *Zhejiang, China* . 53 C12
Xique-Xique, *Brazil* 122 D3
Xiruá →, *Brazil* 124 B4
Xisha Qundao = Hsisha
  Chuntao, *Pac. Oc.* ... 56 A4
Xishui, *China* 53 B10
Xituozhen, *China* 52 B7
Xiuning, *China* 53 C12
Xiuren, *China* 53 E8
Xiushan, *China* 52 C7
Xiushui, *China* 53 C10
Xiuwen, *China* 52 D6
Xiuyan, *China* 51 D12
Xixabangma Feng, *China* 61 E14
Xixia, *China* 50 H6
Xixiang, *China* 50 H4
Xiyang, *China* 50 F7
Xizang □, *China* 54 C3
Xlendi, *Malta* 37 C1
Xu Jiang →, *China* 53 D11
Xuan Loc, *Vietnam* 59 G6
Xuancheng, *China* 53 B12
Xuan'en, *China* 52 C7
Xuanhan, *China* 52 B6
Xuanhua, *China* 50 D8
Xuchang, *China* 50 G7
Xuefeng Shan, *China* 53 D8
Xuejiaping, *China* 53 B8
Xun Jiang →, *China* 53 F8
Xun Xian, *China* 50 G8
Xundian, *China* 52 E4
Xunwu, *China* 53 E10
Xunyang, *China* 50 H5
Xunyi, *China* 50 G5
Xupu, *China* 53 D8
Xushui, *China* 50 E8
Xuwen, *China* 53 G8
Xuyen Moc, *Vietnam* 59 G6
Xuyong, *China* 52 C5
Xuzhou, *China* 51 G9
Xylophagou, *Cyprus* 37 E12

Y

Ya Xian, *China* 58 C7
Yaamba, *Australia* 90 C5
Ya'an, *China* 52 C4
Yaapeet, *Australia* 91 F3
Yabassi, *Cameroon* 79 E6
Yabelo, *Ethiopia* 77 G4
Yablonovy Khrebet, *Russia* 45 D12
Yablonovy Ra. =
  Yablonovy Khrebet,
  Russia 45 D12
Yabrai Shan, *China* 50 E2
Yabrūd, *Syria* 69 B5
Yacuiba, *Bolivia* 126 A3
Yacuma →, *Bolivia* 125 C4
Yadgir, *India* 60 L10
Yadkin →, *U.S.A.* 105 H5
Yadrin, *Russia* 41 D15
Yagaba, *Ghana* 79 C4
Yagodnoye, *Russia* 45 C15
Yagoua, *Cameroon* 80 B3
Yaguas →, *Peru* 120 D3
Yaha, *Thailand* 59 J3
Yahila, *Zaïre* 82 B1
Yahk, *Canada* 100 D5
Yahuma, *Zaïre* 80 D4
Yahyalı, *Turkey* 66 D6
Yaita, *Japan* 49 F9
Yaiza, *Canary Is.* 36 F6
Yajiang, *China* 52 B3
Yajua, *Nigeria* 79 C7
Yakima, *U.S.A.* 110 C3
Yakima →, *U.S.A.* 110 C3
Yako, *Burkina Faso* 78 C4
Yakoruda, *Bulgaria* 39 G6
Yakovlevka, *Russia* 48 B6
Yaku-Shima, *Japan* 49 J5
Yakut Republic □, *Russia* 45 C13
Yakutat, *U.S.A.* 96 C6
Yakutsk, *Russia* 45 C13
Yala, *Thailand* 59 J3
Yalbalgo, *Australia* 89 E1
Yalboroo, *Australia* 90 C4
Yale, *U.S.A.* 106 C2
Yalgoo, *Australia* 89 E2
Yalinga, *C.A.R.* 73 G9
Yalkubul, Punta, *Mexico* . 115 C7
Yalleroi, *Australia* 90 C4
Yalobusha →, *U.S.A.* ... 109 J9
Yalong Jiang →, *China* .. 52 D3
Yalova, *Turkey* 66 C3
Yalpukh, Oz., *Ukraine* .. 38 D11
Yalta, *Ukraine* 42 D6
Yalu Jiang →, *China* 51 E13
Yalutorovsk, *Russia* 44 D7
Yalvaç, *Turkey* 66 D4
Yam Ha Melah = Dead
  Sea, *Asia* 69 D4
Yam Kinneret, *Israel* ... 69 C4
Yamada, *Japan* 49 H5
Yamagata, *Japan* 48 E10

Yushu

Yamagata □, Japan 48 E10
Yamaguchi, Japan 49 G5
Yamaguchi □, Japan 49 G5
Yamal, Poluostrov, Russia 44 B8
Yamal Pen. = Yamal, Poluostrov, Russia 44 B8
Yamanashi □, Japan 49 G9
Yamantau, Gora, Russia 44 D6
Yamba, N.S.W., Australia 91 D5
Yamba, S. Austral., Australia 91 E3
Yambah, Australia 90 C1
Yambarran Ra., Australia 88 C5
Yâmbiô, Sudan 77 G2
Yambol, Bulgaria 38 G9
Yamdena, Indonesia 57 F8
Yame, Japan 49 H5
Yamethin, Burma 61 J20
Yamil, Nigeria 79 C6
Yamma-Yamma, L., Australia 91 D3
Yamoussoukro, Ivory C. 78 D3
Yampa →, U.S.A. 110 F9
Yampi Sd., Australia 88 C3
Yampol, Ukraine 42 B3
Yamrat, Nigeria 79 C6
Yamrukchal, Bulgaria 38 G7
Yamuna →, India 63 G9
Yamzho Yumco, China 54 D4
Yan, Nigeria 79 C7
Yana →, Russia 45 B14
Yanac, Australia 91 F3
Yanagawa, Japan 49 H5
Yanai, Japan 49 H6
Yan'an, China 50 F5
Yanbian, China 52 D3
Yanbu 'al Baḩr, Si. Arabia 64 F3
Yancannia, Australia 91 E3
Yanchang, China 50 F6
Yancheng, Henan, China 50 H7
Yancheng, Jiangsu, China 51 H11
Yanchi, China 50 F4
Yanchuan, China 50 F6
Yanco Cr. →, Australia 91 F4
Yandal, Australia 89 E3
Yandanooka, Australia 89 E2
Yandaran, Australia 90 C5
Yandoon, Burma 61 L19
Yanfeng, China 52 E3
Yanfolila, Mali 78 C3
Yang Xian, China 50 H4
Yangambi, Zaïre 82 B1
Yangbi, China 52 E2
Yangcheng, China 50 G7
Yangch'ü = Taiyuan, China 50 F7
Yangchun, China 53 F8
Yanggao, China 50 D7
Yanggu, China 50 F8
Yangi-Yer, Kazakhstan 44 E7
Yangjiang, China 53 G8
Yangliuqing, China 51 E9
Yangon = Rangoon, Burma 61 L20
Yangping, China 53 B8
Yangpingguan, China 50 H4
Yangquan, China 50 F7
Yangshan, China 53 E9
Yangshuo, China 53 E8
Yangtze Kiang = Chang Jiang →, China 53 B13
Yangxin, China 53 C10
Yangyang, S. Korea 51 E15
Yangyuan, China 50 D8
Yangzhou, China 53 A12
Yanhe, China 52 C7
Yanji, China 51 C15
Yanjin, China 52 C5
Yanjing, China 52 C2
Yankton, U.S.A. 108 D6
Yanna, Australia 91 D4
Yanonge, Zaïre 82 B1
Yanqi, China 54 B3
Yanqing, China 50 D8
Yanshan, Hebei, China 51 E9
Yanshan, Jiangxi, China 53 C11
Yanshan, Yunnan, China 52 F5
Yanshou, China 51 B15
Yantabulla, Australia 91 D4
Yantai, China 51 F11
Yanting, China 52 B5
Yantra →, Bulgaria 38 F8
Yanwa, China 52 D2
Yanyuan, China 52 D3
Yanzhou, China 50 G9
Yao, Chad 73 F8
Yao Xian, China 50 G5
Yao Yai, Ko, Thailand 59 J2
Yao'an, China 52 E3
Yaodu, China 52 A5
Yaoundé, Cameroon 79 E7
Yaowan, China 51 G10
Yap I., Pac. Oc. 92 G5
Yapen, Indonesia 57 E9
Yapen, Selat, Indonesia 57 E9
Yappar →, Australia 90 B3
Yaqui →, Mexico 114 B2
Yar, Russia 41 B18
Yar-Sale, Russia 44 C8
Yaracuy □, Venezuela 120 A4
Yaracuy →, Venezuela 120 A4
Yaraka, Australia 90 C3
Yarangüme, Turkey 66 E3
Yaransk, Russia 41 C15
Yaratishky, Belorussia 40 D4
Yardea P.O., Australia 91 E2
Yare →, U.K. 13 E9
Yarensk, Russia 44 C5
Yarí →, Colombia 120 D3
Yaritagua, Venezuela 120 A4
Yarkand = Shache, China 54 C2
Yarker, Canada 107 B8
Yarkhun →, Pakistan 63 A5
Yarmouth, Canada 99 D6
Yarmūk →, Syria 69 C4
Yaroslavl, Russia 41 C11
Yarqa, W. →, Egypt 69 F2
Yarra Yarra Lakes, Australia 89 E2
Yarraden, Australia 90 A3
Yarraloola, Australia 88 D2
Yarram, Australia 91 F4
Yarraman, Australia 91 D5
Yarranvale, Australia 91 D4
Yarras, Australia 91 E5
Yarrowmere, Australia 90 C4
Yartsevo, Russia 40 D8
Yartsevo, Russia 45 C10
Yarumal, Colombia 120 B2
Yasawa Group, Fiji 87 C7
Yaselda →, Belorussia 40 E5
Yashi, Nigeria 79 C6
Yasin, Pakistan 63 A5
Yasinovataya, Ukraine 42 B7
Yasinski, L., Canada 98 B4
Yasothon, Thailand 58 E5
Yass, Australia 91 E4
Yata →, Bolivia 125 C4
Yatağan, Turkey 66 E3
Yates Center, U.S.A. 109 G7
Yathkyed L., Canada 101 A9
Yatsushiro, Japan 49 H5
Yatta Plateau, Kenya 82 C4
Yauca, Peru 124 D3
Yauya, Peru 124 B2
Yauyos, Peru 124 C2
Yavari →, Peru 124 A3
Yavatmal, India 60 J11
Yavne, Israel 69 D3
Yavorov, Ukraine 40 G3
Yavuzeli, Turkey 67 E7
Yawatahama, Japan 49 H6
Yawri B., S. Leone 78 D2
Yaxi, China 52 D6
Yayama-Rettō, Japan 49 M1
Yazd, Iran 65 D7
Yazd □, Iran 65 D7
Yazoo →, U.S.A. 109 J9
Yazoo City, U.S.A. 109 J9
Yding Skovhøj, Denmark 9 J10
Ye Xian, Henan, China 50 H7
Ye Xian, Shandong, China 51 F10
Yealering, Australia 89 F2
Yebyu, Burma 61 M21
Yechŏn, S. Korea 51 F15
Yecla, Spain 29 G3
Yécora, Mexico 114 B3
Yedintsy, Moldavia 42 B2
Yeeda, Australia 88 C3
Yeelanna, Australia 91 E2
Yefremov, Russia 41 E11
Yegorlyk →, Russia 43 C9
Yegorlykskaya, Russia 43 C9
Yegoryevsk, Russia 41 D11
Yegros, Paraguay 126 B4
Yehuda, Midbar, Israel 69 D4
Yei, Sudan 77 G3
Yei, Nahr →, Sudan 77 F3
Yekaterinburg, Russia 44 D7
Yekaterinodar = Krasnodar, Russia 43 D8
Yelan, Russia 41 F13
Yelan-Kolenovskiy, Russia 41 F12
Yelanskoye, Russia 45 C13
Yelarbon, Australia 91 D5
Yelatma, Russia 41 D12
Yelcho, L., Chile 128 B2
Yelets, Russia 41 E11
Yélimané, Mali 78 B2
Yelizavetgrad = Kirovograd, Ukraine 42 B5
Yell, U.K. 14 A7
Yell Sd., U.K. 14 A7
Yellow Sea, China 51 G12
Yellowhead Pass, Canada 100 C5
Yellowknife, Canada 100 A6
Yellowknife →, Canada 100 A6
Yellowstone →, U.S.A. 108 B3
Yellowstone L., U.S.A. 110 D8
Yellowstone National Park, U.S.A. 110 D8
Yellowtail Res., U.S.A. 110 D9
Yelnya, Russia 40 D8
Yelsk, Belorussia 40 F6
Yelvertoft, Australia 90 C2
Yelwa, Nigeria 79 C5
Yemen ■, Asia 68 E3
Yen Bai, Vietnam 58 B5
Yenakiyevo, Ukraine 42 B8
Yenangyaung, Burma 61 J19
Yenbo = Yanbu 'al Baḩr, Si. Arabia 64 F3
Yenda, Australia 91 E4
Yendéré, Ivory C. 78 C4
Yendi, Ghana 79 D4
Yenice, Turkey 66 D2
Yenice →, Turkey 66 E6
Yenisaía, Greece 39 H7
Yenişehir, Turkey 66 C3
Yenisey →, Russia 44 B9
Yeniseysk, Russia 45 D10
Yeniseyskiy Zaliv, Russia 44 B9
Yennádhi, Greece 37 C9
Yenne, France 27 C9
Yenotayevka, Russia 43 C12
Yenyuka, Russia 45 D13
Yeo, L., Australia 89 E3
Yeola, India 60 J9
Yeoryioúpolis, Greece 37 D6
Yeovil, U.K. 13 G5
Yepes, Spain 28 F1
Yeppoon, Australia 90 C5
Yeráki, Greece 39 N4
Yerbent, Turkmenistan 44 F6
Yerbogachen, Russia 45 C11
Yerevan, Armenia 43 F11
Yerilla, Australia 89 E3
Yerköy, Turkey 66 D6
Yermak, Kazakhstan 44 D8
Yermakovo, Russia 45 D13
Yermo, U.S.A. 113 L10
Yerofey Pavlovich, Russia 45 D13
Yerólakkos, Cyprus 37 D12
Yeropótamos →, Greece 37 D6
Yeroskipos, Cyprus 37 E11
Yerseke, Neths. 17 F4
Yershov, Russia 41 F16
Yerunaja, Cerro, Peru 124 C2
Yerushalayim = Jerusalem, Israel 69 D4
Yerville, France 24 C7
Yes Tor, U.K. 13 G4
Yesan, S. Korea 51 F14
Yeşilhisar, Turkey 66 D6
Yeşilırmak →, Turkey 66 C7
Yesilkent, Turkey 66 E7
Yesnogorsk, Russia 41 D10
Yeso, U.S.A. 109 H2
Yessentuki, Russia 43 D10
Yessey, Russia 45 C11
Yeste, Spain 29 G2
Yeu, I. d', France 24 F4
Yevlakh, Azerbaijan 43 F12
Yevpatoriya, Ukraine 42 D5
Yevstratovskiy, Russia 41 F11
Yeya →, Russia 43 C8
Yeysk, Russia 42 C8
Yezd = Yazd, Iran 65 D7
Yhati, Paraguay 126 B4
Yhú, Paraguay 127 B4
Yi →, Uruguay 126 C4
Yi 'Allaq, G., Egypt 69 E2
Yi He →, China 51 G10
Yi Xian, Anhui, China 53 C11
Yi Xian, Hebei, China 50 E8
Yi Xian, Liaoning, China 51 D11
Yialí, Greece 39 N10
Yialiás →, Cyprus 37 D12
Yi'allaq, G., Egypt 76 H8
Yialousa, Cyprus 37 D13
Yiáltra, Greece 39 L5
Yianisádhes, Greece 37 D8
Yiannitsa, Greece 39 J5
Yibin, China 52 C5
Yichang, China 53 B8
Yicheng, Henan, China 53 B9
Yicheng, Shanxi, China 50 G6
Yichuan, China 50 F6
Yichun, Heilongjiang, China 54 B7
Yichun, Jiangxi, China 53 D10
Yidu, Hubei, China 53 B8
Yidu, Shandong, China 51 F10
Yidun, China 52 B2
Yihuang, China 53 D11
Yijun, China 50 G5
Yilan, Taiwan 53 E13
Yıldızeli, Turkey 66 D7
Yiliang, Yunnan, China 52 D5
Yiliang, Yunnan, China 52 E4
Yilong, China 52 B6
Yimen, China 52 E4
Yimianpo, China 51 B15
Yinchuan, China 50 E4
Yindarlgooda, L., Australia 89 F3
Ying He →, China 50 H9
Ying Xian, China 50 E7
Yingcheng, China 53 B9
Yingde, China 53 E9
Yingjiang, China 52 E1
Yingjing, China 52 C4
Yingkou, China 51 D12
Yingshan, Henan, China 53 B9
Yingshan, Hubei, China 53 B10
Yingshan, Sichuan, China 52 B6
Yingshang, China 53 A11
Yingtan, China 54 D6
Yining, China 44 E9
Yinjiang, China 52 C7
Yinmabin, Burma 61 H19
Yinnietharra, Australia 88 D2
Yiofiros →, Greece 37 D7
Yioúra, Greece 39 K7
Yipinglang, China 52 E3
Yirga Alem, Ethiopia 77 F4
Yishan, China 52 E7
Yishui, China 51 G10
Yíthion, Greece 39 N5
Yitiaoshan, China 50 F3
Yitong, China 51 C13
Yiwu, China 53 C13
Yixing, China 53 B12
Yiyang, Henan, China 50 G7
Yiyang, Hunan, China 53 C9
Yiyang, Jiangxi, China 53 C11
Yizhang, China 53 E9
Yizheng, China 53 A12
Ylitornio, Finland 8 C17
Ylivieska, Finland 8 D18
Yngaren, Sweden 11 F10
Ynykchanskiy, Russia 45 C14
Yoakum, U.S.A. 109 L6
Yobe □, Nigeria 79 C7
Yog Pt., Phil. 57 B6
Yogan, Togo 79 D5
Yogyakarta, Indonesia 57 G14
Yoho Nat. Park, Canada 100 C5
Yojoa, L. de, Honduras 116 D2
Yŏju, S. Korea 51 F14
Yokadouma, Cameroon 80 D2
Yokkaichi, Japan 49 G8
Yoko, Cameroon 79 D7
Yokohama, Japan 49 G9
Yokosuka, Japan 49 G9
Yokote, Japan 48 E10
Yola, Nigeria 79 D7
Yolaina, Cordillera de, Nic. 116 D3
Yonago, Japan 49 G6
Yonaguni-Jima, Japan 49 M1
Yŏnan, N. Korea 51 F14
Yonezawa, Japan 48 F10
Yong Peng, Malaysia 59 L4
Yong Sata, Thailand 59 J2
Yongampo, N. Korea 51 E13
Yong'an, China 53 E11
Yongcheng, China 50 H9
Yŏngchŏn, S. Korea 51 G15
Yongchuan, China 52 C5
Yongchun, China 53 E12
Yongdeng, China 50 F2
Yongding, China 53 E11
Yŏngdŏk, S. Korea 51 F15
Yŏngdŭngpo, S. Korea 51 F14
Yongfeng, China 53 D10
Yongfu, China 52 E7
Yonghe, China 50 F6
Yŏnghŭng, N. Korea 51 E14
Yongji, China 50 G6
Yŏngju, S. Korea 51 F15
Yongkang, Yunnan, China 52 E2
Yongkang, Zhejiang, China 53 C13
Yongnian, China 50 F8
Yongning, Guangxi Zhuangzu, China 52 F7
Yongning, Ningxia Huizu, China 50 E4
Yongping, China 52 E2
Yongqing, China 50 E9
Yongren, China 52 D3
Yongshan, China 52 C4
Yongsheng, China 52 D3
Yongshun, China 52 C7
Yongtai, China 53 E12
Yŏngwŏl, S. Korea 51 F15
Yongxin, China 53 D10
Yongxing, China 53 D9
Yongxiu, China 53 C10
Yonibana, S. Leone 78 D2
Yonkers, U.S.A. 107 F11
Yonne □, France 25 E10
Yonne →, France 25 D9
York, Australia 89 F2
York, U.K. 12 D6
York, Ala., U.S.A. 105 J1
York, Nebr., U.S.A. 108 E6
York, Pa., U.S.A. 104 F7
York, C., Australia 90 A3
York, Kap, Greenland 4 B4
York Sd., Australia 88 B4
Yorke Pen., Australia 91 E2
Yorkshire Wolds, U.K. 12 D7
Yorkton, Canada 101 C8
Yorktown, U.S.A. 109 L6
Yorkville, U.S.A. 112 G3
Yornup, Australia 89 F2
Yoro, Honduras 116 C2
Yoron-Jima, Japan 49 L4
Yos Sudarso, Pulau, Indonesia 57 F9
Yosemite National Park, U.S.A. 111 H4
Yosemite Village, U.S.A. 112 H7
Yoshkar Ola, Russia 41 C15
Yŏsu, S. Korea 51 G14
Yotala, Bolivia 125 D4
Yotvata, Israel 69 F4
You Xian, China 53 D9
Youbou, Canada 100 D4
Youghal, Ireland 15 E4
Youghal B., Ireland 15 E4
Youkounkoun, Guinea 78 C2
Young, Australia 91 E4
Young, Canada 101 C7
Young, Uruguay 126 C4
Younghusband, L., Australia 91 E2
Younghusband Pen., Australia 91 F2
Youngstown, Canada 101 C6
Youngstown, N.Y., U.S.A. 106 C5
Youngstown, Ohio, U.S.A. 106 E4
Youngsville, U.S.A. 106 E5
Youssoufia, Morocco 74 B3
Youxi, China 53 D12
Youyang, China 52 C7
Youyu, China 50 D7
Yoweragabbie, Australia 89 E2
Yozgat, Turkey 66 D6
Yozgat □, Turkey 66 D6
Ypané →, Paraguay 126 A4
Yport, France 24 C7
Ypres = Ieper, Belgium 17 G1
Ypsilanti, U.S.A. 104 D4
Yreka, U.S.A. 110 F2
Ysleta, U.S.A. 111 L10
Yssingeaux, France 27 C8
Ystad, Sweden 11 J7
Ysyk-Köl = Issyk-Kul, Ozero, Kirghizia 44 E8
Ythan →, U.K. 14 D7
Ytterhogdal, Sweden 10 B8
Ytyk-Kel, Russia 45 C14
Yu Jiang →, China 54 D6
Yu Shan, Taiwan 53 F13
Yu Xian, Hebei, China 50 E8
Yu Xian, Henan, China 50 G7
Yu Xian, Shanxi, China 50 E7
Yuan Jiang →, Hunan, China 53 C8
Yuan Jiang →, Yunnan, China 52 F4
Yuan'an, China 53 B8
Yuanjiang, Hunan, China 53 C9
Yuanjiang, Yunnan, China 52 F4
Yuanli, Taiwan 53 E13
Yuanlin, Taiwan 53 F13
Yuanling, China 53 C8
Yuanmou, China 52 E3
Yuanqu, China 50 G6
Yuanyang, Henan, China 50 G7
Yuanyang, Yunnan, China 52 F4
Yuba →, U.S.A. 112 F5
Yuba City, U.S.A. 112 F5
Yūbari, Japan 48 C10
Yūbetsu, Japan 48 B11
Yucatán □, Mexico 115 C7
Yucatán, Canal de, Caribbean 116 B2
Yucatan Str. = Yucatán, Canal de, Caribbean 116 B2
Yucca, U.S.A. 113 L12
Yucca Valley, U.S.A. 113 L10
Yucheng, China 50 F9
Yuci, China 50 F7
Yudino, Russia 41 D16
Yudino, Russia 44 D7
Yudu, China 53 E10
Yuendumu, Australia 88 D5
Yueqing, China 53 C13
Yueqing Wan, China 53 C13
Yuexi, Anhui, China 53 B11
Yuexi, Sichuan, China 52 C4
Yueyang, China 53 C9
Yugan, China 53 C11
Yugoslavia ■, Europe 21 M10
Yuhuan, China 53 C13
Yujiang, China 53 C11
Yukhnov, Russia 40 D9
Yukon →, U.S.A. 96 B3
Yukon Territory □, Canada 96 B6
Yüksekova, Turkey 67 E11
Yukti, Russia 45 C11
Yukuhashi, Japan 49 H5
Yule →, Australia 88 D2
Yuli, Nigeria 79 D7
Yulin, Guangxi Zhuangzu, China 53 F8
Yulin, Shaanxi, China 50 E5
Yuma, Ariz., U.S.A. 113 N12
Yuma, Colo., U.S.A. 108 E3
Yuma, B. de, Dom. Rep. 117 C6
Yumbe, Uganda 82 B3
Yumbi, Zaïre 82 C2
Yumbo, Colombia 120 C2
Yumen, China 54 C4
Yumurtalık, Turkey 66 E6
Yun Ho →, China 51 E9
Yun Xian, Hubei, China 53 A8
Yun Xian, Yunnan, China 52 E3
Yunak, Turkey 66 D4
Yunan, China 53 F8
Yuncheng, Henan, China 50 G8
Yuncheng, Shanxi, China 50 G6
Yundamindra, Australia 89 E3
Yunfu, China 53 F9
Yungas, Bolivia 125 D4
Yungay, Chile 126 D1
Yungay, Peru 124 B2
Yunhe, China 53 C12
Yunlin, Taiwan 53 F13
Yunling, China 52 D2
Yunlong, China 52 E2
Yunmeng, China 53 B9
Yunnan □, China 52 E4
Yunquera de Henares, Spain 28 E1
Yunta, Australia 91 E2
Yunxi, China 50 H6
Yunxiao, China 53 F11
Yunyang, China 52 B7
Yuping, China 52 D7
Yupukarri, Guyana 121 C6
Yupyongdong, N. Korea 51 D15
Yuqing, China 52 D6
Yur, Russia 45 D14
Yurgao, Russia 44 D9
Yuribei, Russia 44 B8
Yurimaguas, Peru 124 B2
Yurya, Russia 41 B16
Yuryev-Polskiy, Russia 41 C11
Yuryevets, Russia 41 C13
Yuscarán, Honduras 116 D2
Yushanzhen, China 52 C7
Yushe, China 50 F7
Yushu, Jilin, China 51 B14

Yushu

Yushu, Qinghai, China 54 C4
Yutai, China 50 G9
Yutian, China 51 E9
Yuxi, China 52 E4
Yuyao, China 53 B13
Yuzawa, Japan 48 E10
Yuzha, Russia 41 C13
Yuzhno-Sakhalinsk, Russia 45 E15
Yvelines □, France 25 D8
Yverdon, Switz. 22 C3
Yvetot, France 24 C7
Yvonand, Switz. 22 C3

Z

Zaamslag, Neths. 17 F3
Zaan →, Neths. 16 D5
Zaandam, Neths. 16 D5
Zab, Monts du, Algeria 75 B6
Žabalj, Serbia 21 K10
Žabari, Serbia 21 L11
Zabarjad, Egypt 76 C4
Zabaykalskiy, Russia 45 E12
Zabid, Yemen 68 E3
Ząbkowice Śląskie, Poland 20 E6
Zabłudów, Poland 20 B13
Zābol, Iran 65 D9
Zābolī, Iran 65 E9
Zabré, Burkina Faso 79 C4
Zabrze, Poland 20 E8
Zacapa, Guatemala 116 D2
Zacapu, Mexico 114 D4
Zacatecas, Mexico 114 C4
Zacatecas □, Mexico 114 C4
Zacatecoluca, El Salv. 116 D2
Zacoalco, Mexico 114 C4
Zacualtipán, Mexico 115 C5
Zadar, Croatia 33 D12
Zadawa, Nigeria 79 C7
Zadetkyi Kyun, Burma 59 H2
Zadonsk, Russia 41 E11
Zafarqand, Iran 65 C7
Zafra, Spain 31 G4
Żagań, Poland 20 D5
Zagazig, Egypt 76 H7
Zāgheh, Iran 65 C6
Zaghouan, Tunisia 75 A7
Zaglivérion, Greece 39 J6
Zaglou, Algeria 75 C4
Zagnanado, Benin 79 D5
Zagorá, Greece 39 K6
Zagora, Morocco 74 B3
Zagorsk = Sergiyev Posad, Russia 41 C11
Zagreb, Croatia 33 C12
Zāgros, Kuhhā-ye, Iran 65 C6
Zagros Mts. = Zāgros, Kuhhā-ye, Iran 65 C6
Zaguinaso, Ivory C. 78 C3
Zāhedān, Fārs, Iran 65 D7
Zāhedān, Sīstān va Balūchestān, Iran 65 D9
Zahlah, Lebanon 69 B4
Zahna, Germany 18 D8
Zahrez Chergui, Algeria 75 A5
Zahrez Rharbi, Algeria 75 B5
Zaïre ■, Africa 80 E4
Zaïre →, Africa 80 F2
Zaječar, Serbia 21 M12
Zakamensk, Russia 45 D11
Zakataly, Azerbaijan 43 F12
Zakavkazye, Asia 43 F11
Zākhū, Iraq 64 B4
Zákinthos, Greece 39 M3
Zakopane, Poland 20 F9
Zákros, Greece 37 D8
Zala →, Hungary 21 J7
Zalaegerszeg, Hungary 21 J6
Zalalövő, Hungary 21 J6
Zalamea de la Serena, Spain 31 G5
Zalamea la Real, Spain 31 H4
Zalazna, Russia 41 B18
Žalec, Slovenia 33 B12
Zaleshchiki, Ukraine 42 B1
Zalingei, Sudan 73 F9
Zaltbommel, Neths. 16 E6
Zambeke, Zaïre 82 B2
Zambeze →, Africa 83 F4
Zambezi = Zambeze →, Africa 83 F4
Zambezi, Zambia 81 G4
Zambezia □, Mozam. 83 F4
Zambia ■, Africa 83 E2
Zamboanga, Phil. 55 H5
Zamboanguita, Phil. 55 G5
Zambrano, Colombia 120 B3
Zambrów, Poland 20 C12
Zametchino, Russia 41 E13
Zamora, Ecuador 120 D2
Zamora, Mexico 114 C4
Zamora, Spain 30 D5
Zamora □, Spain 30 D5
Zamora-Chinchipe □, Ecuador 120 D2
Zamość, Poland 20 E13
Zamuro, Sierra del, Venezuela 121 C5
Zan, Ghana 79 D4
Zanaga, Congo 80 E2
Záncara →, Spain 29 F1
Zandijk, Neths. 16 D5
Zandvoort, Neths. 16 D5
Zanesville, U.S.A. 106 G2
Zangābād, Iran 64 B5
Zangue →, Mozam. 83 F4
Zanjan, Iran 65 B6
Zanjān □, Iran 65 B6
Zannone, Italy 34 B6
Zante = Zákinthos, Greece 39 M3
Zanthus, Australia 89 F3
Zanzibar, Tanzania 82 D4
Zanzūr, Libya 75 B7
Zaouiet El-Kala = Bordj Omar Driss, Algeria 75 C6
Zaouiet Reggane, Algeria 75 C5
Zaoyang, China 53 A9
Zaozhuang, China 51 G9
Zapadna Morava →, Serbia 21 M11
Zapadnaya Dvina, Russia 40 C8
Zapadnaya Dvina →, Belorussia 40 C4
Západné Beskydy, Europe 20 F9
Zapala, Argentina 128 A2
Zapaleri, Cerro, Bolivia 126 A2
Zapata, U.S.A. 109 M5
Zapatón →, Spain 31 G4
Zapiga, Chile 124 D4
Zaporizhzhya = Zaporozhye, Ukraine 42 C6
Zaporozhye, Ukraine 42 C6
Zapponeta, Italy 35 A8
Zara, Turkey 67 D7
Zaragoza, Colombia 120 B3
Zaragoza, Coahuila, Mexico 114 B4
Zaragoza, Nuevo León, Mexico 115 C5
Zaragoza, Spain 28 D4
Zaragoza □, Spain 28 D4
Zarand, Kermān, Iran 65 D8
Zarand, Markazī, Iran 65 C6
Zărandului, Munţii, Romania 38 C5
Zaranj, Afghan. 60 D2
Zarasai, Lithuania 40 D5
Zarate, Argentina 126 C4
Zaraysk, Russia 41 D11
Zaraza, Venezuela 121 B4
Zāreh, Iran 65 C6
Zarembo I., U.S.A. 100 B2
Zaria, Nigeria 79 C6
Zarneh, Iran 64 C5
Zarós, Greece 37 D6
Zarqā' →, Jordan 69 C4
Zarrīn, Iran 65 C7
Zaruma, Ecuador 120 D2
Żary, Poland 20 D5
Zarza de Alange, Spain 31 G4
Zarza de Granadilla, Spain 30 E4
Zarzaïtine, Algeria 75 C6
Zarzal, Colombia 120 C2
Zarzis, Tunisia 75 B7
Zas, Spain 30 B2
Zashiversk, Russia 45 C15
Zaskar →, India 63 B7
Zaskar Mts., India 63 C7
Zastron, S. Africa 84 E4
Zavāreh, Iran 65 C7
Zaventem, Belgium 17 G4
Zavetnoye, Russia 43 C10
Zavidovići, Bos.-H. 21 L8
Zavitinsk, Russia 45 D13
Zavodovski, I., Antarctica 5 B1
Zavolzhsk, Russia 41 C13
Zavolzhye, Russia 41 C13
Zawiercie, Poland 20 E9
Zāwiyat al Bayḑā, Libya 73 B9
Zâwyet Shammâs, Egypt 76 A2
Zâwyet Um el Rakham, Egypt 76 A2
Zâwyet Ungeîla, Egypt 76 A2
Zāyā, Iraq 64 C5
Zayarsk, Russia 45 D11
Zaysan, Kazakhstan 44 E9
Zaysan, Oz., Kazakhstan 44 E9
Zayü, China 52 C1
Zazir, O. →, Algeria 75 D6
Zbarazh, Ukraine 40 G4
Zbąszyń, Poland 20 C5
Zblewo, Poland 20 B8
Zdolbunov, Ukraine 40 F5
Ždrelo, Serbia 21 L11
Zduńska Wola, Poland 20 D8
Zeballos, Canada 100 D3
Zebediela, S. Africa 85 C4
Zedelgem, Belgium 17 F2
Zeebrugge, Belgium 17 F2
Zeehan, Australia 90 G4
Zeeland, Neths. 17 E7
Zeeland □, Neths. 17 F3
Zeelst, Neths. 17 F6
Zeerust, S. Africa 84 D4
Zefat, Israel 69 C4
Zegdou, Algeria 74 C4
Zege, Ethiopia 77 E4
Zegelsem, Belgium 17 G3
Zégoua, Mali 78 C3
Zehdenick, Germany 18 C9
Zeil, Mt., Australia 88 D5
Zeila, Somali Rep. 68 E3
Zeist, Neths. 16 D6
Zeitz, Germany 18 D8
Zele, Belgium 17 F4
Zelenodolsk, Russia 41 D16
Zelenograd, Russia 41 C10
Zelenogradsk, Russia 40 D2
Zelenokumsk, Russia 43 D10
Zelënyy, Kazakhstan 43 B14
Zelhem, Neths. 16 D8
Zell, Baden-W., Germany 19 H3
Zell, Rhld-Pfz., Germany 19 E3
Zell am See, Austria 21 H2
Zella Mehlis, Germany 18 E6
Zelzate, Belgium 17 F3
Zembra, I., Tunisia 75 A7
Zémio, C.A.R. 82 A2
Zemmora, Algeria 75 A5
Zemmur, W. Sahara 74 C2
Zemoul, O. →, Algeria 74 C3
Zemst, Belgium 17 G4
Zemun, Serbia 21 L10
Zengbe, Cameroon 79 D7
Zengcheng, China 53 F9
Zenica, Bos.-H. 21 L7
Zenina, Algeria 75 B5
Žepče, Bos.-H. 21 L8
Zeraf, Bahr ez →, Sudan 77 F3
Zerbst, Germany 18 D8
Zermatt, Switz. 22 D5
Zernez, Switz. 23 C10
Zernograd, Russia 43 C9
Zerqani, Albania 39 H3
Zestafoni, Georgia 43 E10
Zetel, Germany 18 B3
Zetten, Neths. 16 E7
Zeulenroda, Germany 18 E7
Zeven, Germany 18 B5
Zevenaar, Neths. 16 E8
Zevenbergen, Neths. 17 E5
Zévio, Italy 32 C8
Zeya, Russia 45 D13
Zeya →, Russia 45 D13
Zêzere →, Portugal 31 F2
Zghartā, Lebanon 69 A4
Zgierz, Poland 20 D9
Zgorzelec, Poland 20 D5
Zhabinka, Belorussia 40 E4
Zhailma, Kazakhstan 44 D7
Zhambyl = Dzhambul, Kazakhstan 44 E8
Zhangbei, China 50 D8
Zhangguangcai Ling, China 51 B15
Zhanghua, Taiwan 53 E13
Zhangjiakou, China 50 D8
Zhangping, China 53 E11
Zhangpu, China 53 E11
Zhangwu, China 51 C12
Zhangye, China 54 C5
Zhangzhou, China 53 E11
Zhanhua, China 51 F10
Zhanjiang, China 53 G8
Zhanyi, China 52 E4
Zhanyu, China 51 B12
Zhao Xian, China 50 F8
Zhao'an, China 53 F11
Zhaocheng, China 50 F6
Zhaojue, China 52 C4
Zhaoping, China 53 E8
Zhaoqing, China 53 F9
Zhaotong, China 52 D4
Zhaoyuan, Heilongjiang, China 51 B13
Zhaoyuan, Shandong, China 51 F11
Zharkovskiy, Russia 40 D8
Zhashkov, Ukraine 42 B4
Zhashui, China 50 H5
Zhayyq = Ural →, Kazakhstan 43 C14
Zhdanov = Mariupol, Ukraine 42 C7
Zhecheng, China 50 G8
Zhegao, China 53 B11
Zhejiang □, China 53 C13
Zheleznogorsk, Russia 40 E9
Zheleznogorsk-Ilimskiy, Russia 45 D11
Zheltyye Vody, Ukraine 42 B5
Zhen'an, China 50 H5
Zhenfeng, China 52 E5
Zheng'an, China 52 C6
Zhengding, China 50 E8
Zhenghe, China 53 D12
Zhengyang, China 53 A10
Zhengyangguan, China 53 A11
Zhengzhou, China 50 G7
Zhenhai, China 53 C13
Zhenjiang, China 53 A12
Zhenlai, China 51 B12
Zhenning, China 52 D5
Zhenping, Henan, China 50 H7
Zhenping, Shaanxi, China 52 B7
Zhenxiong, China 52 D5
Zhenyuan, Gansu, China 50 G4
Zhenyuan, Guizhou, China 52 D7
Zherdevka, Russia 41 F12
Zherong, China 53 D12
Zhidan, China 50 F5
Zhigansk, Russia 45 C13
Zhigulevsk, Russia 41 E16
Zhijiang, Hubei, China 53 B8
Zhijiang, Hunan, China 52 D7
Zhijin, China 52 D5
Zhirnovsk, Russia 41 F14
Zhitomir, Ukraine 40 F6
Zhizdra, Russia 40 E9
Zhlobin, Belorussia 40 E6
Zhmerinka, Ukraine 42 B3
Zhodino, Belorussia 40 D6
Zhokhova, Ostrov, Russia 45 B16
Zhong Xian, China 52 B7
Zhongdian, China 52 D2
Zhongdong, China 52 F6
Zhongdu, China 52 E7
Zhongning, China 50 F3
Zhongshan, Guangdong, China 53 F9
Zhongshan, Guangxi Zhuangzu, China 53 E8
Zhongtiao Shan, China 50 G6
Zhongwei, China 50 F3
Zhongxiang, China 53 B9
Zhongyang, China 50 F6
Zhoucun, China 51 F9
Zhouning, China 53 D12
Zhoushan Dao, China 53 C14
Zhouzhi, China 50 G5
Zhovtnevoye, Ukraine 42 C5
Zhuanghe, China 51 E12
Zhucheng, China 51 G10
Zhugqu, China 50 H3
Zhuhai, China 53 F9
Zhuji, China 53 C13
Zhukovka, Russia 40 E8
Zhumadian, China 50 H8
Zhuo Xian, China 50 E8
Zhuolu, China 50 D8
Zhuozi, China 50 D7
Zhupanovo, Russia 45 D16
Zhushan, China 53 A8
Zhuxi, China 52 A7
Zhuzhou, China 53 D9
Zhytomyr = Zhitomir, Ukraine 40 F6
Zi Shui →, China 53 C9
Zīārān, Iran 65 B6
Ziarat, Pakistan 62 D2
Zibo, China 51 F10
Zichang, China 50 F5
Zichem, Belgium 17 F5
Zielona Góra, Poland 20 D5
Zierikzee, Neths. 17 E3
Ziesar, Germany 18 C8
Zifta, Egypt 76 H7
Zigey, Chad 73 F8
Zigong, China 52 C5
Zigui, China 53 B8
Ziguinchor, Senegal 78 C1
Zihuatanejo, Mexico 114 D4
Zijin, China 53 F10
Zile, Turkey 66 C6
Žilina, Slovak Rep. 20 F8
Zillah, Libya 73 C8
Zillertaler Alpen, Austria 19 H7
Zima, Russia 45 D11
Zimane, Adrar in, Algeria 75 D5
Zimapán, Mexico 115 C5
Zimba, Zambia 83 F2
Zimbabwe, Zimbabwe 83 G3
Zimbabwe ■, Africa 83 F2
Zimovniki, Russia 43 C10
Zinal, Switz. 22 D5
Zinder, Niger 79 C6
Zinga, Tanzania 83 D4
Zingem, Belgium 17 G3
Zingst, Germany 18 A8
Ziniaré, Burkina Faso 79 C4
Zinkgruvan, Sweden 11 F9
Zinnowitz, Germany 18 A9
Zion National Park, U.S.A. 111 H7
Zipaquirá, Colombia 120 C3
Zirc, Hungary 21 H7
Žiri, Slovenia 33 B11
Žirje, Croatia 33 E12
Zirl, Austria 19 H7
Ziros, Greece 37 D8
Zitácuaro, Mexico 114 D4
Zitava →, Slovak Rep. 21 G8
Zittau, Germany 18 E10
Zitundo, Mozam. 85 D5
Živinice, Bos.-H. 21 L8
Ziway, L., Ethiopia 77 F4
Zixi, China 53 D11
Zixing, China 53 E9
Ziyang, Shaanxi, China 50 H5
Ziyang, Sichuan, China 52 B5
Ziyun, China 52 E6
Ziz, Oued →, Morocco 74 B4
Zizhixian, China 53 E8
Zizhong, China 52 C5
Zlarin, Croatia 33 E12
Zlatar, Croatia 33 B13
Zlataritsa, Bulgaria 38 F8
Zlatitsa, Bulgaria 38 G7
Zlatograd, Bulgaria 39 H8
Zlatoust, Russia 44 D6
Zletovo, Macedonia 39 H5
Zlin, Czech. 20 F7
Zlītan, Libya 73 B7
Złocieniec, Poland 20 B6
Złoczew, Poland 20 D8
Złotoryja, Poland 20 D5
Złotów, Poland 20 B7
Zmeinogorsk, Kazakhstan 44 D9
Żmigród, Poland 20 D6
Zmiyev, Ukraine 42 B7
Znamenka, Ukraine 42 B5
Znamensk, Russia 40 D2
Żnin, Poland 20 C7
Znojmo, Czech. 20 G6
Zoar, S. Africa 84 E3
Zobeyrī, Iran 64 C5
Zobia, Zaïre 82 B2
Zoetermeer, Neths. 16 D5
Zofingen, Switz. 22 B5
Zogang, China 52 C1
Zogno, Italy 32 C6
Zogqên, China 52 A2
Zolder, Belgium 17 F6
Zollikofen, Switz. 22 C4
Zollikon, Switz. 23 B7
Zolochev, Ukraine 40 G4
Zolotonosha, Ukraine 42 B5
Zomba, Malawi 83 F4
Zomergem, Belgium 17 F3
Zongo, Zaïre 80 D3
Zonguldak, Turkey 42 F4
Zonguldak □, Turkey 66 C4
Zonhoven, Belgium 17 G6
Zonqor Pt., Malta 37 D2
Zonza, France 27 G13
Zorgo, Burkina Faso 79 C4
Zorita, Spain 31 F5
Zorritos, Peru 124 A1
Zorzor, Liberia 78 D3
Zossen, Germany 18 C9
Zottegem, Belgium 17 G3
Zou Xiang, China 50 G9
Zouar, Chad 73 D8
Zouérate, Mauritania 74 D2
Zousfana, O. →, Algeria 75 B4
Zoushan Dao, China 53 B14
Zoutkamp, Neths. 16 B8
Zrenjanin, Serbia 21 K10
Zuarungu, Ghana 79 C4
Zuba, Nigeria 79 D6
Zubayr, Yemen 77 D5
Zubia, Spain 31 H7
Zubtsov, Russia 40 C9
Zudáñez, Bolivia 125 D5
Zuénoula, Ivory C. 78 D3
Zuera, Spain 28 D4
Zuetina, Libya 73 B9
Zufar, Oman 68 D5
Zug, Switz. 23 B7
Zug □, Switz. 23 B7
Zugdidi, Georgia 43 E9
Zugersee, Switz. 23 B7
Zugspitze, Germany 19 H6
Zuid-Holland □, Neths. 16 E5
Zuidbeveland, Neths. 17 F3
Zuidbroek, Neths. 16 B9
Zuidelijk-Flevoland, Neths. 16 D6
Zuidhorn, Neths. 16 B8
Zuidlaarder meer, Neths. 16 B9
Zuidlaren, Neths. 16 B9
Zuidwolde, Neths. 16 C8
Zújar, Spain 29 H2
Zújar →, Spain 31 F5
Zújar, Pantano del, Spain 31 G5
Zula, Eritrea 77 D4
Zulia □, Venezuela 120 B3
Zulpich, Germany 18 E2
Zumaya, Spain 28 B2
Zumbo, Mozam. 83 F3
Zummo, Nigeria 79 D7
Zumpango, Mexico 115 D5
Zundert, Neths. 17 F5
Zungeru, Nigeria 79 D6
Zunhua, China 51 D9
Zuni, U.S.A. 111 J9
Zunyi, China 52 D6
Zuoquan, China 50 F7
Zuozhou, China 52 F6
Županja, Croatia 21 K8
Zurbātīyah, Iraq 64 C5
Zürich, Switz. 23 B7
Zürich □, Switz. 23 B7
Zürichsee, Switz. 23 B7
Zuromin, Poland 20 B9
Zuru, Nigeria 79 C6
Zurzach, Switz. 23 A6
Žut, Croatia 33 E12
Zutendaal, Belgium 17 G7
Zutphen, Neths. 16 D8
Zuwārah, Libya 75 B7
Zuyevka, Russia 41 B17
Zūzan, Iran 65 C8
Žužemberk, Slovenia 33 C11
Zvenigorodka, Ukraine 42 B4
Zverinogolovskoye, Russia 44 D7
Zvezdets, Bulgaria 38 G10
Zvishavane, Zimbabwe 83 G3
Zvolen, Slovak Rep. 20 G9
Zvonce, Serbia 21 N12
Zvornik, Bos.-H. 21 L9
Zwaag, Neths. 16 C6
Zwanenburg, Neths. 16 D5
Zwarte Meer, Neths. 16 C7
Zwarte Waler, Neths. 16 C8
Zwartemeer, Neths. 16 C10
Zwartsluis, Neths. 16 C8
Zwedru = Tchien, Liberia 78 D3
Zweibrücken, Germany 19 F3
Zwenkau, Germany 18 D8
Zwevegem, Belgium 17 G2
Zwickau, Germany 18 E8
Zwiesel, Germany 19 F9
Zwijnaarde, Belgium 17 F3
Zwijndrecht, Belgium 17 F4
Zwijndrecht, Neths. 16 E5
Zwischenahn, Germany 18 B4
Zwolle, Neths. 16 C8
Zwolle, U.S.A. 109 K8
Zymoetz →, Canada 100 C3
Żyrardów, Poland 20 C10
Zyrya, Azerbaijan 43 F14
Zyryanka, Russia 45 C16
Zyryanovsk, Kazakhstan 44 E9
Zyyi, Cyprus 37 E12

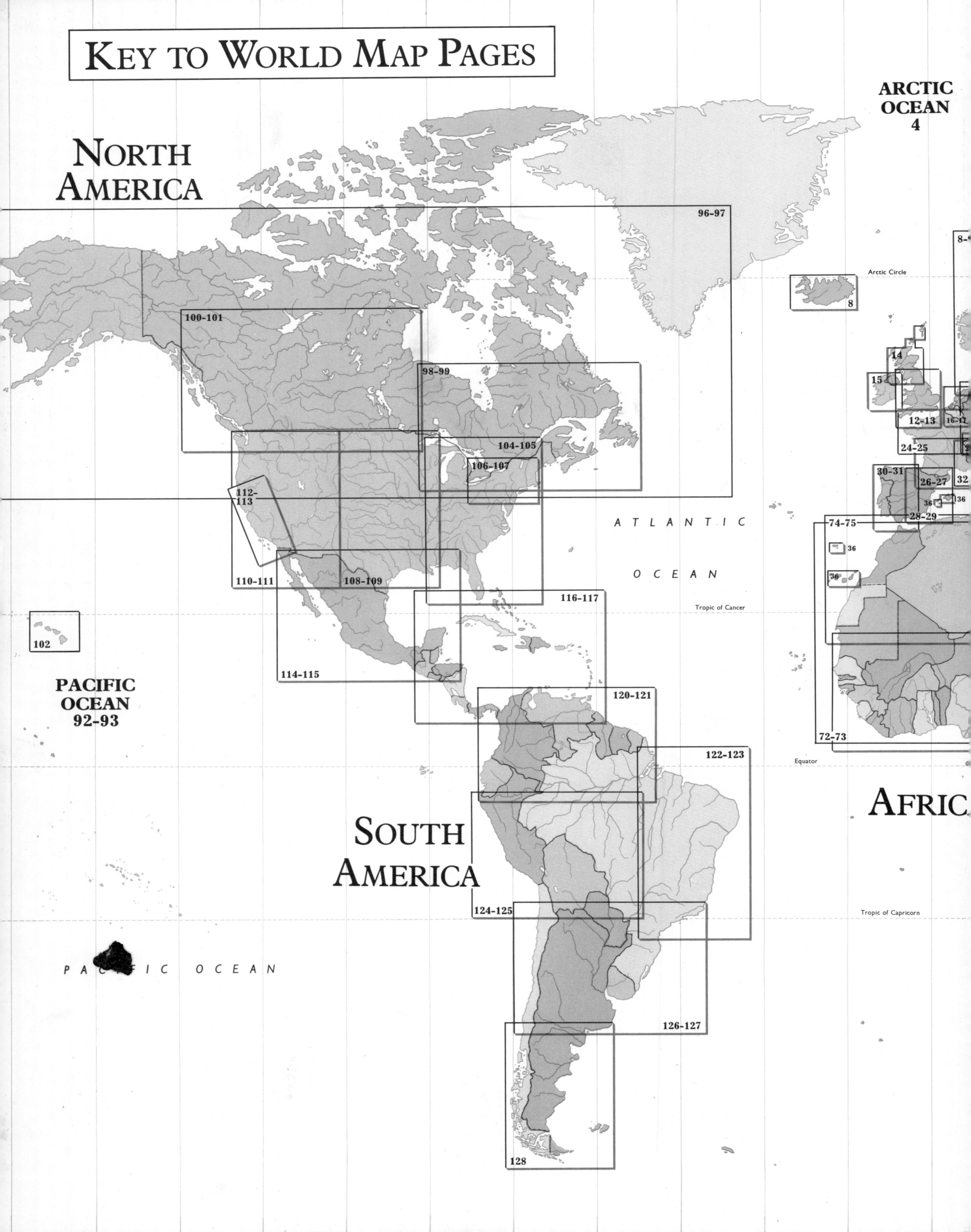

KEY TO WORLD MAP PAGES

NORTH AMERICA

ARCTIC OCEAN
4

Arctic Circle

96-97

8-

8

14

15

100-101

98-99

12-13

16-1

104-105

24-25

106-107

30-31

26-27

32

ATLANTIC

36

36

28-29

74-75

112-113

36

OCEAN

36

110-111

108-109

116-117

Tropic of Cancer

72-73

102

114-115

120-121

**PACIFIC
OCEAN
92-93**

122-123

Equator

AFRIC

**SOUTH
AMERICA**

Tropic of Capricorn

124-125

PACIFIC OCEAN

126-127

128